PROPHECY AND PEOPLE IN RENAISSANCE ITALY

PROPHECY AND PEOPLE IN RENAISSANCE ITALY

Ottavia Niccoli

translated by

Lydia G. Cochrane

PRINCETON UNIVERSITY PRESS

PRINCETON, NEW JERSEY

TRANSLATED FROM *PROFETI E POPOLO NELL'ITALIA DEL RINASCIMENTO*
© 1987 GIUS. LATERZA & FIGLI SPA, ROMA-BARI
PUBLISHED BY PRINCETON UNIVERSITY PRESS, 41 WILLIAM STREET,
PRINCETON, NEW JERSEY 08540

LIBRARY OF CONGRESS CATALOGING-IN-PUBLICATION DATA

NICCOLI, OTTAVIA.
[PROFETI E POPOLO NELL'ITALIA DEL RINASCIMENTO. ENGLISH]
PROPHECY AND PEOPLE IN RENAISSANCE ITALY / OTTAVIA NICCOLI ;
TRANSLATED BY LYDIA G. COCHRANE.
P. CM.
TRANSLATION OF: PROFETI E POPOLO NELL'ITALIA DEL RINASCIMENTO.
INCLUDES BIBLIOGRAPHICAL REFERENCES.
ISBN 0-691-05568-8 (ALK. PAPER) — ISBN 0-691-00835-3
(PBK. : ALK. PAPER)
1. PROPHECIES (OCCULTISM)—ITALY—HISTORY—16TH CENTURY.
2. OCCULTISM—ITALY—HISTORY—16TH CENTURY. 3. ITALY—
HISTORY—1492–1559. I. TITLE.
BF1812.I88N53213 1990 133.3'0945'09031—DC20 90-31111

WE ARE GRATEFUL TO THE ITALIAN MINISTRY OF FOREIGN AFFAIRS FOR ITS SUPPORT
PUBLICATION OF THIS BOOK HAS BEEN AIDED BY A GRANT FROM THE PAUL MELLON FUND OF PRINCETON UNIVERSITY PRESS

THIS BOOK HAS BEEN COMPOSED IN LINOTRON GALLIARD

PRINCETON UNIVERSITY PRESS BOOKS ARE PRINTED ON ACID-FREE PAPER, AND MEET THE GUIDELINES FOR PERMANENCE AND DURABILITY OF THE COMMITTEE ON PRODUCTION GUIDELINES FOR BOOK LONGEVITY OF THE COUNCIL ON LIBRARY RESOURCES

PRINTED IN THE UNITED STATES OF AMERICA BY PRINCETON UNIVERSITY PRESS, PRINCETON, NEW JERSEY

1 3 5 7 9 10 8 6 4 2

1 3 5 7 9 10 8 6 4 2
(PBK)

CONTENTS

EPILOGUE

ILLUSTRATIONS

INTRODUCTION

THIS STUDY was conceived many years ago, the offspring of a headlong reading of an extraordinary volume, the British Museum Library catalog of sixteenth-century Italian books. Reading this volume was not only fascinating ("je ne sais pas de lecture plus facile, plus attrayante, plus douce, que celle d'un catalogue," as Sylvestre Bonnard said) but fruitful. Although my scrutiny was guided by no preordained criteria, it produced (among many other things) a good many prophetic print pieces of a "popular" sort (popular according to the criteria established by Francesco Novati, to be treated in chapter 1 of this book) published between the end of the fifteenth century and about 1530. Since I was fortunate enough to be in London where I could immediately get my hands on the texts whose titles had piqued my curiosity and peruse them, scrutiny of the catalog gave rise to more methodical study as I attempted to comprehend both the vast success of this publishing genre and the nature of its public. At the same time, going through the stacks of the Warburg Institute library, I occasionally came across traces—marginalia in books, extracts, *plaquettes*—of studies that the institute's creator had begun but never completed that also led me back to the theme of the dissemination of prophecy and divination and their significance in the early modern era. In short, from an awareness that materials existed grew a realization of the full-blown phenomenon that lay behind them: the extraordinary dissemination of prophetic tensions among vast but socially and culturally varied milieus in Italy during the *guerre horrende* from the invasion of Charles VIII to that of Charles V. The dates are significant and suggest at least a partial interpretation of the phenomenon, which clearly appears to be linked to the political instability of those years. Prophecy during the Renaissance and, even more, during the Middle Ages, is well known and has been widely studied. The picture that emerges here, however, is at least partially new: A generalized culture that had profound ties to the political and religious events of the period was disseminated very broadly through many different channels. In other words, it was a different aspect of the Renaissance.

In their first phase, my labors took the form of a study of early sixteenth-century popular prophecy as it was transmitted orally from high culture and as a divinatory science autonomous from high culture that even reached the illiterate through itinerant preachers and tale singers, or *cantastorie*. As my research broadened, my perspective to some extent shifted. I shall attempt to describe that change in perspective in these introductory remarks, leaving full discussion to the chapters that follow.

First, the adjective "popular" (an ambiguous term laden with echoes of diatribes that I do not intend to go into here) will, I hope, acquire greater precision by reference to a precise category: the "people" of cities and towns. I have preferred the terms "folk" or "folklore" when the oral transmission of residual pre-Christian elements or elements extraneous to official culture were involved.[1] The prophetic phenomena studied here seem, in fact, to be genuinely urban. Prophecy was a living experience communicated from a portable platform to listeners in the town square, from the pulpit to the nave, in the workshops and the markets, where print pieces and broadsheets were displayed, sold, and discussed. It was an important part of townspeople's practical knowledge. Machiavelli and Guicciardini, Leo X and the Venetian ambassadors will also be heard from in these pages, but only from time to time, when they came into contact with that knowledge. Otherwise the elites of the courts and the universities are excluded from the picture. Nonetheless, the cultural domain that I have attempted to analyze appears extraordinarily varied and composite. It includes "donazole e poltronaglia" (silly womenfolk and common good-for-nothings), as one Milanese chronicler wrote, but also artisans, merchants, and notaries. One should also keep in mind the infinite gradations between illiteracy and fluent reading and writing ability in the period. I have done my best to respect the irreducible individuality of each case while seeking out the characteristics that unify them.

Willem Frijhoff, speaking about the ambiguity of the adjective "popular" (also in a prophetic context), offers this advice: "It is better to attempt first to determine with as much precision as possible . . . the lines of transmission and the circulation groups for texts [and] to examine the nature of the changes that occurred during this process."[2]

This is precisely what can be done for the aspects of sixteenth-century prophecy that will be examined here. In point of fact, it has gradually become clear that the most outstanding characteristic of that phenomenon is not its location within a specific cultural and social milieu but rather an exceptionally open circulation and exchange of its content through different social and cultural strata. Such transfers did not occur only from high to low; quite the contrary. Fragments of a system of prophetic signs that clearly pertained to popular culture appeared, taken out of context, within a higher culture, finally to be used even for political ends—as can be seen repeatedly in Rome under Leo X. More generally speaking, we might say

[1] I concur here with the anthropological viewpoint of Jean-Claude Schmitt, *The Holy Greyhound: Guinefort, Healer of Children since the Thirteenth Century*, tr. Martin Thom (Cambridge and New York: Cambridge University Press, 1983), p. 7.

[2] Willem Frijhoff, "Prophétie et société dans les Provinces Unies au XVIIe et XVIIIe siècles," in Marie-Sylvie Dupont-Bouchat, Willem Frijhoff, and Robert Muchembled, *Prophètes et sorciers dans les Pays Bas. XVIe–XVIIIe siècle* (Paris: Hachette, 1978), p. 360.

that until about 1530 ecclesiastical high culture accepted and freely manipulated materials from folklore. Peter Burke, borrowing the term from Claude Lévi-Strauss, speaks of a *bricolage* in which low culture reassembled and reorganized elements from high culture;[3] the present work will furnish full testimony to the fact that in the time span studied here, that phenomenon operated in the opposite direction as well. Moreover, these transfers of cultural content through various strata of society were usually accompanied by a change in their social and political function. This is an observation that Jean-Claude Schmitt makes concerning medieval culture,[4] but it is certainly valid for the beginning of the modern era as well. The present work exemplifies this hypothesis.

The picture can become even more complicated, however. At times one has an impression of parallel traditions, analogous in content but on different cultural levels; not truly independent of one another but with points of coincidence and reciprocal encroachment. This is the case of the *monstra*—a term that designated the abnormal and the monstrous, but also the marvelous, the prodigious, or the portentous—to which the present work gives particular attention. In the early sixteenth century a fascination with portents doubtlessly reflected the renewed interest in classical culture (in particular, in Cicero's *De divinatione*); at the same time, however, strange occurrences were part of the system of signs of the culture that came to be called *divinatio popularis*. The humanists' interests were not limited to classical texts but ranged from antiquity to their own day, creating a system of interconnected references. As Machiavelli said in a well-known passage of his *Discourses*:

> How it comes about I know not, but it is clear both from ancient and modern cases that no serious misfortune ever befalls a city or a province that has not been predicted either by divination or revelation or by prodigies or by other heavenly signs.[5]

Guicciardini also declared it believable "that now is like the past [and] that great things have been signified ahead of time by great prodigies."[6]

[3] Peter Burke, *Popular Culture in Early Modern Europe* (New York: New York University Press, 1978), p. 123.

[4] Jean-Claude Schmitt, "Les Traditions folkloriques dans la culture médiévale. Quelques réflexions de méthode," *Archives de sciences sociales des religions* 52, no. 1 (1981): 5–20. See also a somewhat analogous point of view in Manuel Martín Serrano, *Sociología del milagro. Las caras de Bélmez* (Barcelona: Barral Editores, 1972), p. 13.

[5] Niccolò Machiavelli, *Discorsi sopra la prima deca di Tito Livio*, ed. Corrado Vivanti (Turin: G. Einaudi, 1972), I, 56, pp. 194–95; quoted here from *The Discourses*, tr. Leslie J. Walker, revised by Brian Richardson; ed. Bernard Crick (Harmondsworth: Penguin Books, 1970), p. 249.

[6] Francesco Guicciardini to Goro Gheri, 19 January 1518, in Guicciardini, *Carteggi*, ed. Roberto Palmarocchi, 17 vols. (Bologna: Nicola Zanichelli, 1938–1955), vol. 2, p. 240.

"Both ancient and modern cases"; "now is like the past": For men of the Renaissance, the classical world was not closed tight, nor was it an object of mere archaeological investigation. It became more comprehensible with the aid of signs manifested even in latter times that repeated their ancient predecessors. Thus the monsters represented both an element from classical tradition and a part of folklore. Nor did these two different aspects necessarily signify independent and separate levels of culture, particularly since even in the ancient world interest in prodigies was considered part of popular superstition.[7]

All these considerations enter into my reasons for emphasizing the channels of transmission for prophecy and the people who served to spread its message. As a contribution to the history of communication, the present work will speak at length of broadsheets, drawings, and letters, of preachers and of *cantastorie*, the professional tale tellers. It will also touch on the more general problems of the transmission of information and of what defined culture in Italy in the period under discussion. Indeed, if the distinctive sign of the culture that I have sought to reconstruct was exchange; if it lay at the intersection of different cultural and social strata and was imbued with motivations and meanings that varied underneath a certain number of consistent and stereotyped formulas (and all the materials presented here may at times seem even monotonous), then studying the means, the techniques, and the go-betweens that assured those transfers is indispensable. This explains the type of sources used. They tend to be printed rather than manuscript because print pieces are more likely to provide a good grasp of the problems involved in the distribution of a text, of its public, and of the uses to which it was put. They are iconographic because images had a great importance within a culture that was in great part oral. Finally, they are city chronicles which, because they offer an extremely rich variety of information on all aspects of urban life, in particular on those that concern us, bear the direct imprint of urban culture. I have used (and cited on almost every page) one chronicle that stands out from all the rest, the journals of Marin Sanudo.[8] In my opinion, this extraordinarily valuable source has not yet been utilized as much as it deserves. More than a chronicle, Sanudo's *Diarii* are a true archive in book form, and at times in more than book form, given their compiler's singular talent for gathering, sifting through, and transcribing materials of every sort. It would be extremely useful, even from the bibliographical point of view, to draw up a catalog of the pamphlets, broadsheets, drawings, and other materials that Sanudo inserted into the original manuscript of his chronicle. It gives sin-

[7] Raymond Bloch, *Prodigi e divinazione nel mondo antico* (Rome: Newton Compton, 1981), pp. 36–40.

[8] Marino Sanuto, *Diarii*, 58 vols. (Venice: R. Deputazione Veneta di storia patria, 1879–1903).

gular testimony to its compiler's omnivorous appetite for news. Not only does it furnish a mass of all manner of information on the greatest imaginable range of social, religious, cultural, and, of course, political topics in contemporary life over a thirty-year period; it also provides a view, albeit through a privileged observer, of the dynamics of the circulation of information within Italy and between Italy and Europe (as Pierre Sardella realized forty years ago).[9] The *Diarii* have, of course, been heavily used and much cited, especially in studies of ecclesiastical history in the Veneto, but close scrutiny shows that they contain a wealth of still largely unexplored material.

One of the ways to study prophecy is to examine it as an instrument of propaganda. There have been a number of studies (largely but not exclusively regarding England) that emphasize the relationships between prophecy and political propaganda, such, for example, as the works of G. R. Elton, Katharine Firth, B. S. Capp, Jean Céard, and Elisabeth Labrousse.[10] Investigation of this sort usually proves fruitful, in the sense that prophecy in the early modern era was an undeniable part of the arsenal of power (as festivities were another), and the propagandistic use of prophecies will arise often in these pages. In my opinion, however, too exclusive an emphasis on propaganda is in some measure insufficient. First, the very variability in the function of prophetic material makes it evident that propaganda was not its only purpose. But that is not all. Thomas A. Kselman's study of miracles, prophecies, and visions in nineteenth-century France has shown that a purely political approach to these problems, analyzing them in terms of instruments for and symptoms of the conflicts between church and state, is deceiving and reductive, just as any study of "mentality" that neglects the political, institutional, and intellectual context represents a distorted reflection of reality.[11] Like other phenomena that served to bind together or patch up connections between the popular world and ecclesiastical and, on occasion, political institutions, prophecy was a unified and complex entity requiring evaluation both for its specificity and for the re-

[9] Pierre Sardella, *Nouvelles et spéculations à Venise au début du XVIe siècle* (Paris: Armand Colin: [1948]).

[10] B. S. Capp, *The Fifth Monarchy Men: A Study in Seventeenth-Century English Millenarianism* (London and Totawa, N.J.: Rowman and Littlefield, 1972); Jean Céard, "P. A. de Chavigny: le premier commentateur de Nostradamus," in *Scienze, credenze occulte, livelli di cultura: Convegno internazionale di studi (Firenze, 26–30 giugno 1980)* (Florence: L. S. Olschki, 1982), pp. 427–42; G. R. Elton, *Policy and Police: The Enforcement of Reformation in the Age of Thomas Cromwell* (Cambridge: Cambridge University Press, 1972); Katharine R. Firth, *The Apocalyptic Tradition in Reformation Britain, 1530–1645* (Oxford and New York: Oxford University Press, 1979); Elisabeth Labrousse, *L'Entrée de Saturne au lion. L'éclipse de soleil du 12 août 1654* (The Hague: Martinus Nijhoff, 1974).

[11] Thomas A. Kselman, *Miracles and Prophecies in Nineteenth-Century France* (New Brunswick, N.J.: Rutgers University Press, 1983), pp. 5–7.

lational networks that it created. In point of fact, during the years in question, prophecy seems to have constituted a unifying sign connecting nature to religion and religion to politics and coordinating all the scattered shreds of a culture that in the end turned out to be an integral way of knowing embracing observation of nature, political analysis, and religious reflection. If God is the lord of history and of the cosmos, to seek in the *orribeli segnali* of nature and in the voices of the prophets signs of his judgment of human history becomes at once a scientific, political, and religious process. Tzvetan Todorov gives an analogous interpretation of Aztec culture, in which, as he observes, the most urgent problem seems not to have been communication between one person and another, but communication between the person and the world, or, as he puts it,

> between the person and his social group, the person and the natural world, the person and the religious universe. And it is this second type of communication that plays a predominant part in the life of Aztec man, who *interprets the divine, the natural, and the social through indices and omens.*[12]

Todorov was probably suggesting too rigid a contrast between Western culture and Aztec culture in this domain. I might in fact note, without any desire to propose superfluous comparisons, that an attitude analogous to the one that Todorov describes was doubtless true of many of Montezuma's Italian contemporaries. It was a *mens* that did not last long in Italy, however. By about 1530, tacit acceptance of prophecy on the part of large sectors of the ecclesiastical world came to an end, and even the urban population seems to have acquiesced without protest. Even in the present study, the years immediately following the sack of Rome emerge as a fundamental turning point in both the religious and the political history of Italy. The spread in Italy of Reformed preaching—hence of militant opposition to it—doubtlessly played an important part in this shift. As the Counter-Reformation progressed, the unity of prophetic knowledge was destroyed and divinatory science was degraded into a negative body of knowledge possessed by the negative—the female—part of society. Thus the end of prophecy was connected with the revival of misogyny that swept through Europe between the latter half of the sixteenth century and the seventeenth century.

This book will thus seek to pass in review the paraphernalia of a culture—visions, signs, monstrous events, prophecies, and prognostications—viewed not in the abstract but in their concrete operation. It will consider their expression in print works and pictures, in the songs of tale singers, and in ephemeral works, personal colloquies, and sermons in an

[12] Tzvetan Todorov, *The Conquest of America: The Question of the Other*, tr. Richard Howard (New York: Harper and Row, 1983), p. 69 (emphasis mine).

attempt, often arduous and certainly not always successful, to reach down to their specific users. This study makes no claims to be exhaustive; in fact it is highly selective (some will find it arbitrarily so) in that for the most part I have chosen to discuss the cases and specific events that seemed to me the most significant. Following this method has meant that some of my research has already been published, albeit in partial form.[13] Working out those essays and writing them down gradually opened my eyes to their common grounding in the Italy of the *guerre horrende* and of the first stirrings of the Reformation, much as if the events I had been following with my magnifying glass were caterpillars or beetles in a total ecosystem.

It may be useful to add a word on the method I have used to reconstruct those events. In a research field in which many fragments of the culture one seeks to reconstruct have been lost, either because they were transmitted orally or because they had been entrusted to ephemeral media (and popular print pieces are eminently perishable), any attempt to recuperate them has to be based, first, on a reading as thorough and as scrupulous as possible—an intensive reading—of apparently irrelevant sources containing indirect information; and, second, it has to be based on a wide use of the category of the plausible. Alessandro Manzoni wrote, with surprising modernity (and we Italians may have to admit that Manzoni is our Michelet), that historians must do their best to cultivate an "art of unhesitatingly seizing upon the most important revelations, [which have] escaped the writer who was not thinking of giving information, and of extending a few positive cognitive acquisitions by means of well-founded deductions."[14] Elsewhere, in a passage also cited by Carlo Ginzburg, Manzoni appeals to verisimilitude:

> It will not be inappropriate to observe that history can even, on occasion, make use of verisimilitude, and without impropriety, because it does so in the right manner; that is, exposing it in its own guise and thus distinguishing it from the real. . . . It is part of man's miserable lot to know only some of what has been, even in his small world; and it is a part of his nobility and his strength

[13] Ottavia Niccoli, "Profezie in piazza. Note sul profetismo popolare nell'Italia del primo Cinquecento," *Quaderni storici* 41 (1979): 500–539; Niccoli, "Il diluvio del 1524 fra panico collettivo e irrisione carnevalesca," in *Scienze, credenze occulte, livelli di cultura*, pp. 369–92; Niccoli, "I re dei morti sul campo di Agnadello," *Quaderni storici* 51 (1982): 929–58; Niccoli, "Il mostro di Sassonia. Conoscenza e non conoscenza di Lutero in Italia nel Cinquecento (1520–1530 ca.)," in *Lutero in Italia. Studi storici nel V centenario della nascita* (Casale Monferrato, 1983), pp. 3–25; Niccoli, "Il mostro di Ravenna: teratologia e propaganda nei fogli volanti del primo Cinquecento," in Dante Bolognesi, ed., *Ravenna in età veneziana* (Ravenna: Longo, 1986), pp. 245–77. Editorial requirements have necessitated limiting the bibliographical apparatus in the present volume; bibliography on all questions considered here can be found in these essays.

[14] Alessandro Manzoni, *Saggi storici e politici*, ed. F. Ghisalberti (Milan: Mondadori, 1963), p. 39.

to conjecture beyond what he can know. History, when it has recourse to the likely, simply seconds or excites such a tendency. . . . Conjecturing, like narrating, always aims at the real: that is where its unity lies.[15]

Elsewhere, to tell the truth, Manzoni was moved to call the term "verisimilitude" "a terrible word." He did so in his best-known work of history, the *Storia della colonna infame*, a book in which the word *verosimile* returns time and again with an ambiguous and sinister meaning, since for the judges in a trial involving alleged plague spreaders, verisimilitude was a quite different matter than it is (or should be) for historians. When I have spoken of plausible hypotheses (as indeed I have on many occasions), however, I am speaking of a supposition that seems to me not only likely but also the most likely, the most convincing, and the best adapted to the data we possess, even if it is not ascertainable, certain, or positively provable. In short, I have acted like an archaeologist restoring an artifact: It is not indispensable to have all its fragments in order to reconstruct a vase or a statue. The ones we possess can, after attentive examination, be placed into the form held to be most acceptable for them, and the voids filled with clearly distinguishable neutral material. This is what I have sought to do in another discipline. Of course, one runs the risk of imitating the Renaissance restorers of the Laocoön, who erroneously extended an arm that has now once again been returned to its correct bent position. Perhaps it is better to have a statue with a wrongly placed arm than a pile of fragments waiting to be swept away by some impatient historian intent on tidying up.

Many friends have generously discussed all or part of this work with me, helping me to improve it by their criticisms, remarks, and suggestions. I thank them all, and in particular Pier Cesare Bori, Massimo Firpo, Carlo Ginzburg, Alessandro Pastore, Adriano Prosperi, and Roberto Rusconi. I also owe much to my long epistolary friendship with William Christian.

A large part of the research for the present work was aided by a grant from the Ministry of Public Instruction for "Aspetti della comunicazione dei contenuti culturali nell'Italia del primo Cinquecento."

O.N.

[15] Alessandro Manzoni, *Scritti di teoria letteraria*, ed. A. Sozzi Casanova (Milan: Rizzoli, 1981), pp. 213–14; cited in Carlo Ginzburg, "Prove e possibilità," in Natalie Zemon Davis, *Il ritorno di Martin Guerre. Un caso di doppia identità nella Francia del Cinquecento* (Turin: G. Einaudi, 1984), pp. 146–47, the Italian edition of her *The Return of Martin Guerre* (London and Cambridge, Mass.: Harvard University Press, 1983).

PROPHECY AND PEOPLE IN RENAISSANCE ITALY

PROPHECIES AND THE ITALIAN WARS

Prophecy and History

WHEN CHARLES VIII invaded Italy in 1494 the Tuscans found him short and extremely ugly; it was even said that he was more a monster than a man. Surprise soon gave way to acknowledgement of a reality that must in some way have been predicted, for, as Francesco Matarazzo of Perugia wrote in his chronicle, "he was found so by prophecies and signs." There followed a frantic search for other instruments for reading and interpreting the current "novelties," if not future events. Matarazzo continues: "And in these times prophecies without end were found and published anew, as you might think, all of Italy having been peaceful up to this time, because in these times new things began to happen all over Italy."[1]

The "prophecies without end" that became popular toward the end of the forty-year period of peace that followed the Treaty of Lodi would continue to be published, circulated, and used to take the pulse of political and religious trauma for yet another forty years. On 19 May 1527, a few days after the sack of Rome, the Modenese notary Tommasino Lancellotti noted in his journal that he had been shown "a prophecy of St. Bridget that speaks of the deaths in Rome, so that at present it is said that they happen to the pope."[2] There are a number of texts that might fit this description. This prophecy may indeed have been an edition of the *Revelationes* of St. Bridget of Sweden; it may have been the *Pronosticatio* of the German monk and astrologer Johannes Lichtenberger, which was published in many different editions and contained several predictions credited to St. Bridget that could have been interpreted in Lancellotti's sense; it might have been a manuscript transcription of all or part of one of these

[1] Francesco Matarazzo (called Maturanzio), *Cronaca della città di Perugia dal 1492 al 1503*, ed. Ariodante Fabretti, *Archivio storico italiano* 16, pt. 2 (1851): 1–243; p. 16. See Carlo De Frede, " 'Più simile a mostro che a uomo.' La bruttezza e l'incultura di Carlo VIII nella rappresentazione degli italiani del Rinascimento," *Bibliothèque d'humanisme et renaissance* 44 (1982): 545–85.

[2] Tommasino Lancellotti, *Cronaca modenese*, ed. Carlo Borghi, 12 vols. (Parma: F. Fiaccadori, 1863), vol. 2, p. 224. On prophecy in Modena, see Susanna Peyronel Rambaldi, *Speranze e crisi nel Cinquecento modenese. Tensioni religiose e vita cittadina ai tempi di Giovanni Morone* (Milan: Franco Angeli, 1979), pp. 51–59.

texts. The similarity in their titles, however, suggests instead a small book entitled *Prophetia de santa Brigida con alcune altre Prophetie*, published in Venice by Francesco Bindoni only two years earlier. In reality, we know of two different verse compositions published under the approximate title of *Profezie di santa Brigida*, one from the end of the fourteenth century, the other from the early fifteenth century, that went through a dozen editions, nearly all of them printed between 1478 and about 1525.[3] Comparison of the two texts is of little help because both are a jumbled, confused mass in which a modern reader has difficulty finding allusions to the sack of Rome. It is clear, however, that a severely distorted, partial reading was possible for the "book consumer" of the sixteenth century. The discrepancy between books someone read and the interpretation of those same books could be great; furthermore, the recent invention of printing, which threw on the market a mass of texts composed in very different epochs, had suddenly torn texts out of their cultural and historical contexts.[4] For the reader who did not belong within high culture, the book was simply what it was declared to be at that time. That is, readers lacked the instinctive ability of their modern counterparts to mentally locate works of the past, according to their age, on the various shelves of an imaginary bookcase. Furthermore, the literary genre of "prophecy," at least in its specific manifestation under discussion here, was for the most part deciphered under the pressure of present events. Present concerns invaded a text (that was usually deliberately ambiguous), overwhelmed it, and constrained the reader to a noticeably distorted reading of what it contained. Thus Tommasino Lancellotti read St. Bridget uniquely in order to find the sack that in those very days was devastating Rome, not for some echo of far-off events or any admonitions applicable to a distant future. Thus also the Florentines examined and reprinted prophecies in order to grasp the meaning of the arrival of short, ugly King Charles VIII. Such texts, then, cannot be read or understood historically apart from the medium that diffused them, the milieus in which they circulated, and the political context in which they were used.

Popular Print Prophecies

The literary genre of vernacular verse prophecy seems to have met with great favor at the end of the fifteenth century and in the first decades of the

[3] See Ottavia Niccoli, "Profezie in piazza. Note sul profetismo popolare nell'Italia del primo Cinquecento," *Quaderni storici* 41 (1979): 500–539, "Appendice," pp. 535–36 (hereafter cited as "Appendice").

[4] Carlo Ginzburg, *The Cheese and the Worms: The Cosmos of a Sixteenth-Century Miller*, tr. John and Anne Tedeschi (Baltimore: Johns Hopkins University Press, 1980; New York: Penguin Books, 1982), p. 32; Ginzburg, "Folklore, magia, religione," in *Storia d'Italia*, 6 vols. (Turin: G. Einaudi, 1972–1977), vol. 1, pp. 636–37.

sixteenth century.[5] The list of print pieces concerning prophecy that I have attempted to draw up elsewhere, and which is certainly not complete, includes more than fifty items pertaining to twenty or so texts printed and reprinted in a fifty-year period ranging from 1480 to about 1530, with a handful of editions published later than that date.[6] The number of editions, in itself already high, becomes truly extraordinary when the physical specifications of these publications are taken into account. They were small in format (octavo- or, at the most, quarto-sized volumes), of few leaves (two or four, less often eight, at the most twelve), poorly printed with no indication of place, date, or printer, often printed in two columns with antiquated and worn type, using poor-quality ink that has bled into the porous paper. In all cases, they fit into what scholars from Francesco Novati to today have agreed to call "popular literature."[7] These texts were not only "popular" in the sense of aiming at a wide audience; they also enjoyed a large distribution thanks to their low price and their low technical demands. They were subject to rapid deterioration, however, so that they are now quite rare. Entire editions must certainly have disappeared, and the better part of those of which some trace remains exist in at most one copy or extremely few copies.

These limitations explain why the ascertainable existence of more than fifty different works of vernacular prophecies classifiable as "popular" according to the criteria stated above, nearly all in verse, and published within a fifty-year period can be considered a homogeneous and consistent

[5] See Angelo Messini, *Profetismo e profezie ritmiche italiane d'ispirazione gioachimito-francescana nei secoli XIII, XIV e XV* (Rome, 1939), pp. 54–56, 91; Giuseppe Mazzatinti, "Una profezia attribuita al b. Tomassuccio da Foligno," *Miscellanea francescana* 2, no. 1 (1887): 1–7; Enrico Filippini, *La "Prophetia fratris Mucii de Perusio" estratta da un cod. napoletano del sec. XV* (Fabriano, 1892); Francesco Novati, "I codici Trivulzio-Trotti," *Giornale storico della letteratura italiana* 9 (1887): 137–85; p. 182; Alfons Hilka, "Randglossen zu mittelalterliche Handschriften," *Beiträge zur Forschung: Studien und mitteilungen aus dem antiquariat Jacques Rosenthal, München* (Munich: J. Rosenthal, 1915–), 1st ser., no. 6 (1915): 171–75; Hilka, "Über einige italienischen Prophezeiungen des XIV. und XV. Jahrhunderts, vornehmlich über einem deutschen Friedenkaiser," *Schlesische Gesellschaft fur Vaterlandische Cultur* 66 (1917): 11–12; Roberto Rusconi, *L'attesa della fine. Crisi della società, profezia e Apocalisse in Italia al tempo del grande scisma d'Occidente (1378–1417)* (Rome: Istituto storico italiano per il Medio Evo, 1979), pp. 111–20, 158–63. All these studies concern manuscripts on prophecy, not print pieces.

[6] See Niccoli, "Appendice."

[7] Francesco Novati, *La storia e la stampa nella produzione popolare italiana* . . . (Bergamo: n.p., 1907); Arnaldo Segarizzi, *Bibliografia delle stampe popolari italiane della R. Biblioteca nazionale di S. Marco di Venezia* (Bergamo: Istituto italiano d'arti grafiche, 1913–), vol. 1; Carlo Angeleri, *Bibliografia delle stampe popolari a carattere profano dei secoli XVI e XVII conservate nella Biblioteca Nazionale di Firenze* (Florence: Sansoni, 1953); Caterina Santoro, ed., *Mostra di libri di profezie, astrologia, chiromanzia, alchimia* (Milan: Edizioni dell'ente Manifestazioni Milanesi, 1953); Armando Petrucci, "Introduzione," *Libri, editori e pubblico nell'Europa moderna. Guida storica e critica* (Rome and Bari: Laterza, 1977), pp. ix–xxix.

literary current. The real dimensions of this current must have been a great deal larger than the materials presented here, and their distribution was surely much wider, as they were addressed to a public much less select and cultivated than was the case with more refined publications. In short, although up to now they have been little studied, they represent an important aspect, both qualitatively and quantitatively, of the broader phenomenon of prophecy in the sixteenth century.[8]

To return for a moment to the problem of the sort of reading that these texts solicited from less sophisticated readers, I might note that so-called popular publications were addressed to a completely new public that had never before had relations with the written word and was just then making its entry into the "Gutenberg galaxy." The impact of these texts was thus all the more intense. Naturally, their potential and actual purchasers did not belong exclusively to the underclasses. The case of a refined bibliophile like Fernando Colombo, who acquired and catalogued many publications of this sort during his voyages in Italy, among them a good number of books of prophecies now conserved in the Biblioteca Capitular y Colombina of Seville, is sufficient proof of this.[9] It is undeniable, however, that the artisan or the worker who came into contact with the written word did so through this type of publication.

Most of these print pieces omitted information judged irrelevant for the readers targeted but necessary in other instances, such as the printer's name and the place and date of publication. This was true of our prophetic pieces as well. They were almost always presented anonymously or with false attributions to give them greater prestige and authority. Aside from the two often reprinted works known by the name of St. Bridget that have already been mentioned, the names of the thirteenth-century physician and astrologer Pietro d'Abano of Padua and St. Anselmus (probably Anselmus, bishop of Marisco Nuovo, credited with the amplification of the *Vaticinia pontificum*, also falsely attributed to Joachim of Fiore) were attached to two other frequently reprinted texts.[10] Another prophecy was published under the name of St. Angelus of Jerusalem, but in reality, as we shall see, it was an anonymous and interpolated biography of that figure.[11] Very few texts

[8] As a minimum, see Marjorie Reeves, *The Influence of Prophecy in the Late Middle Ages. A Study in Joachimism* (Oxford: Clarendon Press, 1969); "Ricerche sull'influenza della profezia nel basso medioevo," *Bullettino dell'Istituto storico italiano per il Medioevo* 82 (1970) [1974]: 1–158; Rusconi, *L'attesa della fine*.

[9] See Niccoli, "Appendice," nos. 28, 29, 36, 43, 44.

[10] *Questa è la vera prophetia prophetizata dal glorioso santo Anselmo* (n.p., n.d.); *Questa sie la profetia composta per el reverendissimo negromante Piero dabano* (n.p., n.d.). For other editions, see Niccoli, "Appendice," p. 536.

[11] *Vita de santo Angelo carmelitano martyre con la prophetia data a lui per el nostro signor Jesu Christo de tutto quello che e advenuto e advegnira alla christianitade per infedeli et della setta et leze falsa luterina* (n.p., n.d.).

bear the name of their true authors. There is the *Del diluvio di Roma del MCCCCLXXXXV* of Giuliano Dati, a canon from Florence who lived in Rome; there are the *Proffetia de Nocturno* and the *Iuditio sopra tutta la Italia* of the prolific *cantastorie* Notturno Napolitano;[12] there are three publications that bear the name of Tommasuccio da Foligno, the authorship of which is impossible to confirm.[13]

In a literary genre in which anonymity was generally the rule, the formulation of a work's title took on particular importance. Among other things, we know that itinerant vendors customarily hawked their wares. Furthermore, because these publications represented an advantageous commercial operation for the printer, who on occasion could use them to finance more refined works,[14] we can suppose that their titles were contrived with a view to stimulating the public's curiosity and to placing the merchandise that was being offered in a category known to be popular. As is obvious, the word *profezia* recurs in most of the titles, but it is also interesting to note the frequent use of the terms *pronostico*, *pronosticatione*, and *iuditio*, references to the more "official" level of astrology that seem to underscore a desire to give a scientific cast to the predictions contained in the text.[15] In short, there seems to be an intent to lend nobility to these little works by suggesting references to aspects of a higher culture. Another way to lend prestige to titles was by referring to epigraphs and monuments of classical and Oriental antiquity. Thus there is a *Prophetia trovata in Roma intagliata in marmoro in versi latini tratta in vulghar sentimento*; there is the *Iuditio sopra tutta la Italia quale è stato trovato nella città di Roma in una pirramida* already referred to (and which, in another edition, becomes *Profetia over Pronosticatione trovata in Roma in una piramide in versi latini tradotti in vulgare*). There is, finally, a *Profetia nuovamente trovata sotto la torre di Nembrot, dove s'intende tutta la renovatione del mondo*. Reference to the antiquity of the texts must have been thought to guarantee their authenticity (another publication bears the title *Profetie antiche*).[16] At the same time, however, references to epigraphs, pyramids, and towers return us to Renaissance Italy's lively taste for archaeology and antiquarianism sensed and represented in these modest compositions with the evident aim of giving

[12] Giuliano Dati, *Del diluvio di Roma del MCCCCLXXXXV adi iiii di dicembre et daltre cose di gran meraviglia* (n.p., n.d.); Notturno Napolitano, *Proffetia de Nocturno* in his *Opera nova amorosa* (n.p., n.d.); *Iuditio sopra tutta la Italia quale e stato trovato nella citta di Roma* (n.p., n.d.).

[13] Published in Vicenza, 1510; Fano, n.d.; Foligno, 1566.

[14] See Rosanna Alhaique Pettinelli, "Elementi culturali e fattori socio-economici della produzione libraria a Roma nel '400," in Walter Binni et al., eds, *Letteratura e critica. Studi in onore di Natalino Sapegno*, 5 vols. (Rome: Bulzoni, 1976), vol. 3, pp. 101–43.

[15] See Niccoli, "Appendice."

[16] Ibid., nos. 18, 34, 35, 37, 46, 47, 51.

them luster, just as other prophecies gained prestige by being attributed to famous persons.

The vast circulation of these prophetic publications and their success among the public for whom they were designed are attested in many ways. The genre must have been one of the first to be exploited by printers, if we remember that the presses of San Iacopo a Ripoli, one of the first print shops to operate in Tuscany, had already published two different works of prophecy by 1479. One was a *Profezia di santa Brigida*, listed in the print shop's register, under the date of 25 January 1479, as sold to one Giovanni Michele, presumably at the price of one *soldo*; the second was another *Profezie* not further identified, printed before 28 June 1479 together with other works (the *Confessioni di santa Maria Maddalena*, *Le sette allegrezze*, and *Il lamento di Giuliano*) for Giovanni di Nato, stationer at the Porto al Prato.[17] Stationers (*cartolari*), together with tale singers (*cantambanchi*), were frequent customers of the Ripoli print shop, from which they ordered the texts that they thought they could sell most easily. Until the end of the fifteenth century, Florence was undoubtedly the most important center for the distribution of popular print publications on prophecy, with at least six works published there before 1500.[18] Tuscany during the years when Savonarola was preaching and veneration of St. Bridget was well entrenched must have provided a particularly receptive market for this sort of publication.[19]

The Circulation of Prophecy in Manuscript

These first printed works on prophecy, Florentine for the most part and dated or datable between the late fifteenth century and the first years of the sixteenth century, showed several consistent characteristics. They offered one, but more often two, three, or even four compositions not written for the occasion but already known in manuscript form at least since the beginning of the fifteenth century; works laden with Joachimite echoes and that often had been written originally to fulfill various tasks of political propaganda.[20] Thus we find in them the two prophecies of St. Bridget that have already been mentioned, a satirical poem entitled *El se movera un gato*, the *Prophetia de uno sancto homo*, the *Prophetia de Santo Severo* (later repub-

[17] Emilia Nesi, *Il diario della stamperia di Ripoli* (Florence: B. Seeber, 1903), pp. 20, 41–42, 115.

[18] Niccoli, "Appendice," nos 1, 2, 4, 17, 19.

[19] See Roberto Rusconi, "Note sulla predicazione di Manfredi da Vercelli O.P. e il movimento penitenziale dei terziari manfredini," *Archivum fratrum praedicatorum* 48 (1978): 99.

[20] See Rusconi, *L'attesa della fine*.

lished in the works of Galatino and Postel),[21] the so-called "Prophecy of the second Charlemagne," written around 1380 to apply to Charles VI of France and subsequently adapted to fit Charles VIII and Charles V,[22] and others.

These publications were the direct heirs of the many manuscript anthologies of prophecies in circulation in the fourteenth and the fifteenth centuries.[23] In more general terms, they represent the final outcome of an intense circulation of this sort of material in manuscript—a phenomenon not difficult to explain when we recall that after the invention of print, works composed in every epoch, presented as current, suddenly appeared on the market. Before we can compare the audience for these publications with the users of printed prophecies, we need to reach a better understanding (and in some cases this is possible) of the social group to which the transcribers of prophecies belonged and of the use they made of them.

Transcribers were often jurists, like Tibaldo Civeri of Lombardy (possibly of Piedmont), who copied prophecies indefatigably for nearly fifty years (at least from 1327 to 1481) until he had a volume of some two hundred fifty leaves. He copied "ex quodam antiquo libelleto, et satis vetusto scriptura" that belonged to a schoolmaster who lived in Vercelli, or from a *scriptura* owned by a goldsmith in Asti, or from pages lent to him by another jurist.[24] It was another jurist—in fact, a "doctor *in utroque*

[21] See Niccoli, "Appendice," nos. 7–11, 14, 15, 18, 22. See also Guillaume Postel, *Le Thresor des prophéties de l'univers*, ed. François Secret (The Hague: Martinus Nijhoff, 1969), pp. 165–66; Arduinus Kleinhans, "De vita et operibus Petri Galatini O.F.M. scientiarum biblicarum cultoris (c. 1460–1540)," *Antonianum* 1 (1926): 154–79.

[22] Niccoli, "Appendice," nos. 20, 21, 22. No. 22 clearly refers to Charles V. On the fortunes and origins of this text, see Reeves, *The Influence of Prophecy*, pp. 328–29 and 359; Maurice Chaume, "Une prophétie relative à Charles VI," *Revue du Moyen Age latin* 3 (1947): 27–42. On prophecies concerning Charles VIII, see also Donald Weinstein, *Savonarola and Florence: Prophecy and Patriotism in the Renaissance* (Princeton: Princeton University Press, 1970), p. 242.

[23] See Reeves, *The Influence of Prophecy*, pp. 534–40.

[24] See Gustavo Vinay, "Riflessi culturali sconosciuti del minoritismo subalpino," *Bollettino storico bibliografico subalpino* 37 (1935): 136–49, which examines the MS K^2.IV.13 of the Biblioteca Nazionale di Torino. Information on the source of the prophecies can be found on pp. 139–40 and 146. Vinay does not seem to have remarked, however, that he might also have considered MS K^2.V.8 of the same library, which is quite evidently part of the same manuscript, restored and erroneously bound separately after a disastrous fire in the library in 1904. Both manuscripts, in fact, begin with a folio that belongs to the same series of the *Vaticinia Pontificum*. They contain, respectively, 185 and 58 folios, and they belonged to a manuscript of 244 folios. In fact 185 plus 58 equals 243, plus one extra, probably the back flyleaf, which would make 244, the number written on the back flyleaf in an eighteenth-century hand. Because the two remaining folios of the *Vaticinia Pontificum* contain only sixteen pictures of popes, it is presumable that two others have been lost and were already missing in the eighteenth century, when the existing folios were counted and the sum written on the back flyleaf. For his help with these problems, I am indebted to Dr. Angelo Giaccaria.

iure"—Marco Amaseo of Udine, whose nephew Gregorio found among his papers, after his death, two prophecies "written on parchment in handsome letters" (from what I can gather, the *Prophetia de Santo Severo* and the prophecy of the second Charlemagne) "to which then in my hand [Gregorio is speaking] I added others given me from time to time by diverse [persons]."[25] Another transcriber was a notary, thus someone of a lower social and cultural level, Marco Antonio Gatti from Piacenza. Between 1473 and 1501, following a custom common in his profession, he inserted a number of historical notations and moralistic and political poems into the pages of his notarial records, among them an extract of the prophecy of St. Cataldo. For Gatti, then, this prophecy was as noteworthy as a poetic dialogue of Antonio Cammelli, known as Il Pistoia, "with the Turk's brother . . . asking him about the powers of Italy" that he also noted down, or as historical notations and verse compositions about Charles VIII's arrival in Italy and his death.[26] Another notary, Gaspare Marri of Cesena, transcribed a prediction of the cataclysmic end of the world on the back of an act that he drew up on 25 September 1472;[27] while in 1536 we find among the acts of yet another notary, Antonio Belloni of Udine, a copy of the well-known Latin prophecy *Gallorum levitas*.[28]

On other occasions it was chroniclers who acquired prophecies and recopied them into their journals. To take just one example, the verses of the prophecy known by its incipit, *Gallorum levitas*, mentioned above (never printed in the works under consideration here, however), were inserted in a number of chronicles in Bologna as early as the mid-fourteenth century. They appear in 1461 in the *Notabilia temporum* of Angelo Tummulilli; in 1495 in the *Annali* of Domenico Malipiero; in 1509 in the journal of Canon Tommaso di Silvestro of Orvieto; in 1527 (probably, as we shall see) in the papers of Leonello Beliardi of Modena; and again in 1552 in the chronicle of another Modenese, Tommasino Lancellotti, who states that he had found them in another compilation of forty years earlier.[29]

[25] Leonardo and Gregorio Amaseo and Gio. Antonio Azio, *Diarii udinesi, dall'anno 1508 al 1541*, Monumenti Storici ser. 3, vol. 1, (Venice: R. Deputazione di storia patria per le Venezie, 1884), p. 388.

[26] A. G. Tononi, "Note storiche e rime politiche e morali tra gli atti di un notaio piacentino del secolo XV," *Strenna piacentina* 18 (1892): 28–44, esp. p. 37. On the prophecy of St. Cataldo, see Giampaolo Tognetti, "Le fortune della pretesa profezia di san Cataldo," *Bullettino dell'Istituto storico italiano per il Medioevo* 80 (1968): 273–317.

[27] Carlo Grigioni, "Una tradizione del finimondo nel 1472," *Arte e storia* 27 (1908): 154–55.

[28] Antonio Medin, "La battaglia di Pavia. Profeti e poeti italiani," *Archivio storico lombardo* 52 (1925): 252–90; p. 255.

[29] Rusconi, *L'attesa della fine*, p. 143; Angelo de Tummulillis, *Notabilia temporum*, ed. Costantino Corvisieri (Livorno: Tip. F. Vigo, 1890), p. 112; Domenico Malipiero, *Annali veneti dall'anno 1457 al 1500*, *Archivio storico italiano* 7 (1843–44): 5–586; p. 372; Tommaso di

Even before they appeared in urban chronicles, however, these texts were copied for personal use, lent, and read aloud in public within a given social group until the paper was worn to shreds, as with the *Gallorum levitas* in verse, which was transcribed in 1495 by ser Tommaso di Silvestro and later, in 1509, copied into his journal. Tommaso tells us that he "kept them tacked up in the bedroom. They broke into pieces because I wanted everyone to read them."[30] This literature was a true consumer product, then, and the object of impassioned and voracious circulation.

Some of these collections or transcriptions give texts in Latin or in a mixture of Latin and the vernacular; others contain only texts in the vernacular, giving us a glimpse of the continuity that must have existed in certain cases (allowing for some disparity in the readers' social level, however) between the manuscript anthologies of prophecies and the printed versions of the same. One example of apparent continuity emerges in an unassuming small paper codex of twenty-four leaves—a true fifteenth-century *libro da bisaccia*.[31] It contains four prophecies in vernacular, three of which are in verse and at least two of which—the so-called prophecy of St. Bridget and the one known by its incipit, *El se movera un gato*—were among those most often republished. In any event, manuscript compilations of this sort were made for political purposes with the aim of comparing predictions with events in course and preparing oneself to face the future that they foretold. Leone Cobelli, a painter from Forlì, had a "little book of prophecies" provided him by a Third Order Franciscan friar in 1480. From that time on, Cobelli compared the tumultuous political scene in Forlì with his book of prophecies and transcribed long passages from them into his chronicles. In particular, after April 1488, when Count Girolamo Riario, lord of the city, lost his life in an attempted coup (which was, however, soon foiled by the widowed Caterina Sforza), Cobelli's citations become continuous, accompanied by such admiring comments as

Silvestro, *Diario*, ed. Luigi Fumi, in *Rerum italicarum scriptores* (hereafter cited as RIS) 15, pt. 5 (Bologna: Nicola Zanichelli, 1923), vol. 2, p. 410; Lancellotti, *Cronaca modenese*, vol. 11, p. 156; Leonello Beliardi, *Cronaca della città di Modena (1512–1518)*, ed. Alberto Biondi and Michele Oppi (Modena: Panini, 1981), p. 150.

[30] Tommaso di Silvestro, *Diario*, p. 410. It is probable that his first transcription of the prophecy in 1495 was prompted by the battle of Fornovo.

[31] See Novati, "I codici Trivulzio-Trotti"; Hilka, "Randglossen"; Hilka, "Über einige italienischen Prophezeiungen." My description of the codex is based on information given by Novati and Hilka. The location of the manuscript is unknown; it is reported to have been sold in the United States, but it does not appear in Seymour De Ricci and W. J. Wilson, eds, *Census of Medieval and Renaissance Manuscripts in the United States and Canada*, 4 vols. (New York: H. W. Wilson Co., 1935–1962). In 1916 it belonged to an antique dealer in Monaco. The expression *libro da bisaccia*, "saddlebag book or haversack book," has been borrowed from Armando Petrucci, "Alle origini del libro moderno: libri da banco, libri da bisaccia, libretti da mano," in his *Libri, scrittura e pubblico nel Rinascimento: Guida storica e critica* (Rome and Bari: Laterza, 1979), pp. 139–56.

"note, reader, [how] perfectly"; "here again it follows the prophecy"; "now note, reader, whether this prophecy seems true or not to you."[32] What strikes the modern reader is the contrast between Cobelli's passion as he identifies events with predictions and the extreme obscurity of the prophetic book, a work in tercets full of reminiscences of Dante that must have been extremely long, given that the chronicler quotes over two hundred lines of verse and the last page he cites is page 136. Cobelli's notations provide us with a useful example because they allow us to grasp directly, step by step, the strength of the tension that urged readers of prophecies to consider them realized in events that bore only a vague resemblance to them.

Cobelli's case is paradigmatic but it is by no means unique. Periodically, in moments of political tension, Gregorio Amaseo went back to the collection of prophecies that he and his uncle had compiled. He comments on one work of prophecy (the prognostications of Antonio Arquato) that "there having occurred things that vary marvelously little from that time to this, we can presume that the rest will follow, since they were true for all the past."[33] The chronicler Leonello Beliardi also collected a handful of prophecies, Latin and vernacular (probably immediately after the sack of Rome, hence they range from 1519 to 1528), which he quite obviously regarded as a description of Emperor Charles V and a tribute to his sacred and redemptory role.[34]

In comparison to the large number of manuscripts that circulated, however, the brief print pieces that interest us here represent merely a selection. Except in a few isolated cases, the texts chosen for publication were all in the vernacular. Furthermore, their low price and small size guaranteed that they would be accessible to a broader public than those—for the most part jurists, as we have seen—who collected such texts and copied them by hand.

The Role of the *Cantastorie*

At the same time, however, starting at the very end of the fifteenth century, new prophecies were composed and published, more often in Venice or other cities of north-central Italy like Ferrara and Bologna. These were sim-

[32] Leone Cobelli, *Cronache forlivesi dalla fondazione della città all'anno 1498*, ed. Giosuè Carducci and Enrico Frati (Bologna: Regia tipografia, 1874), pp. 282, 302, 326, and elsewhere (information on the book of prophecies, p. 458). See also Andrea Bernardi (called Novacula), *Cronache forlivesi . . . dal 1476 al 1517*, ed. Giuseppe Mazzatinti, 2 vols. (Bologna: R. Deputazione di storia patria, 1895–1897), vol. 1, pt. 1, p. 272; pt. 2, p. 105.

[33] Amaseo, Amaseo, and Azio, *Diarii udinesi*, p. 412.

[34] Beliardi, *Cronaca della città di Modena*, pp. 144–55 and 166–68. See below, pp. 177–81, however.

ple texts with a schematic syntax, an elementary vocabulary, and none of the complicated symbolism of the older publications. The rhyming lines punctuated with facile refrains used sure signs sent by God to predict suffering and pain, famine, pestilence, and marauding armies, but they also foretold final victory over the infidels, their conversion, and an eventual age of universal peace under an *imperator iocondo*. One of the earliest, perhaps the very first, of these new prophecies is the short poem entitled *Del diluvio di Roma del MCCCCLXXXXV adi iii di dicembre et daltre cose di gran meraviglia*, unusual in that it was published under the name of its actual author, the canon Giuliano Dati. Dati had also written a number of short verse works on subjects ranging from the recent discovery of America to Prester John and the Holy House of Loreto. I shall return to Dati's cultural function.[35] The title, *Del diluvio di Roma*, might not seem appropriate for a prophetic text (although we shall return in chapter 6 to a particular and quite popular verse genre on floods that usually included both prophetic and meteorological elements). The colophon describes the work's contents a good deal better. It reads:

> End of the treatise on celestial signs and on modern tribulations and on the recent waters that inundated the ancient and holy city of Rome in our iron and last age collected and put in verse by messer Iuliano de Dati in praise of the celestial Court. M. CCCC. LXXXXV. Finis.

The Roman Deluge (that is, the flooding of the Tiber in December 1495) was, Dati tells us, simply the most recent of many signs that God had sent to Italy:

> voltata tutta in ira e furore
> certo mi pare la divina clementia,
> per tanti segni grandi e smisurati
> che sono a nostri die e de' passati.
>
> (divine clemency seems to me completely turned to anger and fury, [made] clear by many great signs beyond measure that are in our day and in days past.)

Among these "segni grandi e smisurati" the canon poet placed all the political and military disasters on the Italian peninsula, from Turkish forays

[35] On Dati, see Achille Neri, "La gran magnificenza del Prete Janni. Poemetto di Giuliano Dati e quattro lettere inedite di Carlo Roberto Dati," *Il Propugnatore* 9 (1876): 138–72; Leonardo Olschki, "I 'Cantàri dell'India' di Giuliano Dati," *La bibliofilia* 40 (1938): 289–316; Renato Lefevre, "Fiorentini a Roma nel '400. I Dati," *Studi romani* 20 (1972): 187–97; Antonio M. Adorisio, "Cultura in lingua volgare a Roma fra Quattro e Cinquecento," in Giorgio De Gregori, Maria Valenti, and Giovanna Merola, eds., *Studi di biblioteconomia e storia del libro in onore di Francesco Barberi* (Rome: Associazione italiana biblioteche, 1976), pp. 20–24.

to the invasions of "men from beyond the mountains [the Alps] who have turned all Italy upside down." Italy, however, had refused to believe in either signs or prophets sent by God; thus God had sent a last warning, the great flood that in this "nostra ferrea et ultima etade" (the eschatological allusion is noteworthy) was to lead men to penitence, to righteous acts, and to life eternal:

> là ci conduca l'alto Iddio di gloria,
> al cui onor fo fine alla mia storia.
>
> (that is where the highest God of glory is leading us, to whose honor I put an end to my story.)

Thus this was a *story*, and a story to be *sung* ("perhaps I have bored you, O hearer, by making my singing so prolix"), and to be sung to an audience accustomed to listening sitting down:

> bench'io voglia il mio dire abreviare,
> perché non sia la storia a 'lcun noiosa;
> so che chi si diletta d'ascoltare
> non si cura star rito o se si posa,
> ma pur lo star posato al auditore
> fa molte volte grate el parlatore.
>
> (although I want to shorten my tale so that it will not bore anyone, I know that whoever loves to listen does not care whether he is standing or seated, but still, by allowing him to sit the speaker often pleases the listener.)[36]

We can easily imagine the stage, the singer, and the public. We are in a square, and the person declaiming the poem and talking so familiarly with his *auditore* is certainly the *cantastorie*, or professional tale singer. The allusion to the possibility for the listener to be "posato," seated, contains an indirect request that he or she pay for that comfort, and in fact the *cantastorie*, between the fifteenth and the sixteenth centuries, owned and brought along with them both the platform on which they stood to declaim their repertory and benches for the audience.[37] The singer interrupted the reci-

[36] *Del diluvio di Roma*, fols. a vi*v*, a i*v*, a iii*v*, a vi*v*, a iii*r*, a iv*r*.

[37] See Guido Fusinato, "Un cantastorie chioggiotto," *Giornale di filologia romanza* 4 (1880): 170–83; Francesco Flamini, *La lirica toscana del Rinascimento anteriore ai tempi del Magnifico* (Pisa: Tip. T. Nistri, 1891), p. 152; Francesco Novati, "La poesia sulla natura delle frutta e i canterini del comune di Firenze," in his *Attraverso il Medio Evo: Studi e ricerche* (Bari: G. Laterza e figli, 1905), pp. 327–65; Benedetto Soldati, "Improvvisatori, canterini e buffoni in un dialogo del Pontano," in Arnaldo della Torre and Pier Liberale Rambaldi, eds., *Miscellanea di studi critici, pubblicati in onore di Guido Mazzoni*, 2 vols. (Florence: Successori B. Seeber, 1907), vol. 1, pp. 321–42, esp. p. 328; Ezio Levi, *I cantari leggendari del popolo italiano nei secoli XIV–XV* (Turin: Loescher, 1914), pp. 5–19. On professional entertainers in

tation from time to time to pass the hat among the seated listeners, and in fact the verses I have cited represent a transitional moment in the poem that could easily have been followed by such a pause. With *Del diluvio*, then, prophecy entered into the repertory of the bench singers, the *cantambanchi*, hence into the patrimony of urban oral culture. It was to remain there.

That Giuliano Dati, the polygraph to whom we owe this "treatise on celestial signs and on modern tribulations," wrote for the professional tale singers was established by Leonardo Olschki, who deduced from a study of the texts themselves that the singers used to illustrate the verse tales written by the canon of Santa Maria Maggiore with schematic drawings or pictures,[38] following a custom that professional street singers were to continue up to modern times. Moreover, it is known that the tale singers enjoyed a preferential relationship with printers, in particular the printers who specialized in "prognostications, histories, songs, letters, and other similar things," as the Council of Ten in Venice expressed it in a decree of 10 February 1542.[39] The category of *historiari* was defined in similar terms more than a century later in the statutes of the printers' trade association of Rome, the "Venerabile Compagnia et Università de' Librai di Roma," as those who printed and sold "short histories, prayer books, almanacs, and other small books usually paper bound or center-sewn, not frame-sewn on their spines, provided they not exceed 10 sheets each."[40] The tale singers placed orders with these printer-booksellers, even with printers who published both popular texts and more demanding works.

The registers of the Ripoli print shop, which published two different works of prophecy, offer an interesting example of this special relationship. Fra Domenico, the manager of the print shop, wrote in his account book, "Bernardino who sings on a bench took, on the 16th day of November 1482, one hundred of the *Bellezze di Firenze*; we agreed that he must give venti *soldi* for them. And he left me a tablecloth as a gage. He paid on the 18th day and took back the said tablecloth."[41]

Bernardino the *cantambanco* continued to buy from the Ripoli print shop. On eleven occasions between 1483 and 1485 he took a total of 495 copies of *Sale di Malagigi* and fifty copies of *Pistole della domenica*, each time

general, see also Peter Burke, *Popular Culture in Early Modern Europe* (New York: New York University Press, 1978), pp. 92–102.

[38] Olschki, "I 'Cantàri dell'India,' " p. 292.

[39] Giuliano Pesenti, "Libri censurati a Venezia nei secoli XVI–XVII," *La bibliofilia* 58 (1956): 15–30; p. 16.

[40] Francesco Lumachi, *Nella repubblica del libro . . . Bibliomani celebri, librai d'altri tempi, spigolature e curiosità bibliografiche* (Florence: F. Lumachi, 1907), p. 97.

[41] Nesi, *Il diario della stamperia di Ripoli*, p. 80.

paying after a few days.[42] Other names of "cerretani e ciurmatori" (sharpers and pitchmen) appear in Fra Domenico's journal, but the name of "Bernardino who sings on a bench" is the most significant example of the singular economic exchange that Fra Domenico describes: The tale singer commissions a text from the printer, takes delivery without payment, at least for the first few times, but leaves a personal possession as a gage (one Florentine named Giovanni sent in his young son with "a small sheet [as] security"),[43] then recites and sells the printed verses in the town square and, with the profits, pays off the printer. The introduction of printing had thus helped the tale singers to keep up and broaden their repertories and to raise their revenues by selling printed works. In only a few years, Bernardino the *cantambanco* had the Ripoli press print more than six hundred copies of these slim works, a figure that obviously implies a higher number of listeners. We find another proof of the wide diffusion of this practice in a Lombard chronicle that reports "many laments" in the vernacular on the destruction of Otranto by the Turks in 1480, "sung everywhere in the squares before people and offered for sale."[44]

Before the advent of print, a manuscript copy of the work recited was probably posted to make it available to anyone who wanted to copy it, as the final lines of a song on a historical topic from Genoa, dated 1467, seem to indicate:

> Chi me leze me lassa stare
> aziò che possa essere exemplata.
>
> (May he who reads me let me be so that I can be copied.)[45]

When already reproduced texts could be distributed, this custom was no longer needed and disappeared. This worked to the economic advantage of the tale singers, some of whom used printing as a base for new and

[42] Ibid., pp. 97–113. Bernardino of Florence was the author of a short poem in Italian in ten cantos or chapters of tercets, *De laudibus clarissime familie Vendramine ad Magnificum et generosum D. Lodovicum Vendraminum Tarvisii potestatem et capitanum benemeritum* (Biblioteca Marciana di Venezia, MS Marc. it. IX.370 [=6762]), composed for the triumphal entry into Treviso in 1481 of the *podestà* Luigi Vendramin (about which, see Giovanni Bonifaccio, *Historia Trivigiana* [Treviso: D. Amici, 1591], pp. 647–48, available in reproduction of the Venice 1744 edition as *Istoria di Trivigi* [Bologna: Forni, 1968]); as well as the *Bellezze e casati di Firenze*, just mentioned (on which, see Carlo Dionisotti, *Machiavellerie. Storia e fortuna di Machiavelli* [Turin: G. Einaudi, 1980], p. 20).

[43] Nesi, *Il diario della stamperia di Ripoli*, p. 86.

[44] "Multae lamentationes . . . ubique per plateas cantatur coram populum et vendunter": *Cronica gestorum in partibus Lombardie et reliquis Italie (aa. 1476–1482)*, ed. Giuliano Bonazzi, RIS, new ed., vol. 22, pt. 3 (Città di Castello: S. Lapi, 1904), p. 84.

[45] Cornelio Desimoni, "Tre cantari dei secoli XV e XVI concernenti fatti di storia genovese," *Atti della società ligure di storia patria* 10 (1876): 610–82; p. 643.

broader activities. Paolo Danza, born in Florence but active in Venice, was both a printer and a seller of poems of his own composition, which he probably also sang. We owe to him at least one prophetic publication (the *Prophetia de uno imperatore*) and possibly another work that uses the same text but with a different title and showing a few variants (*Profecia de santo Anselmo*)—a shrewd commercial operation aimed at selling the same merchandise twice to a public seemingly eager to purchase such merchandise.[46] Often the process was more complex, involving at least the tale singer and the printer. At times, as in the case of Giuliano Dati, a third person was involved—the "poet," who composed the verse tales and poems that were declaimed and offered for sale. (He probably worked on commission too.) We should thus link Dati's name with those of Giovan Battista Verini and Eustachio Celebrino, whose roles as "cultural operators" and "professionals, albeit humble and part-time, of the pen" merits further investigation, as has been suggested.[47]

We can postulate that in many cases prophecies were composed with recitation, even declamation, in mind. Particularly in their introductory and final passages, they frequently refer to listening rather than reading:

> Ascoltati, mortali,
> li orribeli segnali
> che annuntiano gran mali
> alla età nostra
>
> Vo' far fine al mio cantare
> excellente auditore,
> . . .
> questa nobil prophetia
> è finita al vostro onore
>
> O auditor iocondo
> qui fo fine al mio trattato.

[46] An earlier edition bore the title *La vera prophetia prophetizata dal glorioso Santo Anselmo la quale declara la venuta de uno imperatore: el qual mettera pace fra li christiani e conquistara infideli trovata in Roma*, "stampata in Collicuti per Maestro Francesco da Udine." On this printer and his activities as a publisher of prophecies, see Giovanni Comelli, "Francesco da Udine tipografo a Roma nel primo Cinquecento," in *Studi forogiuliesi in onore di Carlo Guido Mor* (Udine: Deputazione di storia patria per il Friuli, 1984), pp. 163–69. The two editions to which I refer appeared around 1520; the one entitled *Profecia de santo Anselmo* lacked the refrain ("Vegnirà uno imperatore") and the opening stanza ("Vegnirà uno imperatore / tutto il mondo meterà in pace / mai fu homo sì verace / poi che nacque el Salvatore"). Carlo Dionisotti has used the edition entitled *Prophetia de uno imperatore* in "La guerra d'Oriente nella letteratura veneziana del Cinquecento," in his *Geografia e storia della letteratura italiana* (2nd ed.; Turin: G. Einaudi, 1971), p. 210.

[47] Petrucci, "Introduzione," in his *Libri, editori e pubblico*, pp. xxv–xxvii.

(Listen, mortals, to the horrible signs that announce great trials to our age; I wish to bring an end to my song, excellent listener, . . . this noble prophecy is ended, to your honor; O merry listener, here I make an end to my discourse.)[48]

These allusions to the relationship between recitation and listening rather than to the one between writing and reading signify that not only were these texts recited but they had been composed expressly to be recited. Interestingly enough, the compositions that contain these passages had all gone through several printings (at least three or four each) in editions that often consistently reproduced the same variants and additions. We might deduce that the compositions were part of the repertory of a number of tale singers, each one of whom introduced additions or what he felt to be improvements.

One specific testimony that prophecies were recited and spoken rather than merely put into books can be drawn from a notation in the journal of ser Tommaso di Silvestro. He wrote, early in 1504:

Jaco de Colavabbo, a man of seventy-five years of age, a jocular man, died today, which was Monday, first day of January of the year 1504. He was at home after dinner by the fireside; he was singing to himself the prophecy of St. Bridget with great festivity and joy. He felt a sudden pain and suffered a stroke and he died of it.[49]

Neither of the two prophecies of St. Bridget known to us seems to lend itself to being sung merrily of an evening by the fireside, and certainly it was important to our chronicler to emphasize Jaco di Colavabbo's serenity before his sudden death. The fact remains, however, that Jaco was reciting or singing the text, not reading it, so that the text was considered in some way separable from the written or printed word.

At this point, then, we can state that in the early sixteenth century manifestations of prophecy connected with the expectation of catastrophe and with a subsequent regeneration were not restricted to narrow or esoteric groups,[50] but existed and circulated even among the underclasses and

[48] *Memoria delli novi segni et spaventevoli prodigii comparsi in piu loci de Italia et in varie parte del mondo lanno mille cinquecento undese* (n.p., n.d.), fol. 1*r*; *Questa è la vera Profecia de santo Anselmo*, fol. 2*v*; *Prophetia trovata in Roma / Intagliata in marmoro in versi latini / Tratta in vulghar sentimento*, "Stampata in Roma per Maestro Francesco da Udine" (n.d.), fol. 2*v*.

[49] Tommaso di Silvestro, *Diario*, p. 241.

[50] Maria Pia Billanovich, "Una miniera di epigrafi e di antichità. Il Chiostro Maggiore di S. Giustina a Padova," *Italia medioevale e umanistica* 12 (1969): 197–293; Billanovich, "Bernardino da Parenzo pittore e Bernardino (Lorenzo) da Parenzo eremita," *Italia medioevale e umanistica* 24 (1981): 385–404; Maria Teresa Binaghi, "L'immagine sacra in Luini e il Circolo di Santa Marta," in *Sacro e profano nella pittura di Bernardino Luini* (Milan: Silvana,

among people who could not read (let alone write, an ability that reflects a higher degree of instruction than minimal reading literacy). There was, in short, a notable qualitative change from the milieus of notaries, priests, schoolmasters, and jurists among whom, as we have seen, manuscript prophecies circulated. The "Gutenberg effect" applies even to this literary and publishing genre.

Italian Wars from the Descent of Charles VIII to Agnadello in Popular Prophecy

Printed prophecies circulated widely and in large numbers, as we have seen, until about 1530, after which the phenomenon seems to have died out suddenly. This rise and fall probably has a complex explanation, but a first hypothesis would certainly connect prophecy, in the manifestations that concern us here, with the political and religious disintegration that occurred during the first decades of the sixteenth century—with the *guerre horrende de Italia* and the continual passage of troops that brought with it the scourges of pestilence, famine, and devastation that gave credibility to the catastrophes predicted by the preachers and the tale singers. After 1530, however, that period seemed to be coming to an end, and Italy enjoyed a phase of greater tranquillity, which caused prophecies to lose their interest and topicality and to disappear from circulation.

In point of fact, the connection between prophecy and the political disintegration of the peninsula was clear in the minds of contemporaries. Both Francesco Matarazzo in Perugia and Andrea Bernardi, the barber-surgeon from Forlì, acknowledge this relationship explicitly.[51] It is also clearly perceptible in our publications, even when they contain texts that had been written more than a century earlier. Prophecy, as we have seen, was read with immediate reference to current events, whatever they might be. Thus even the prophecy of St. Bridget into which Tommasino Lancellotti read a prediction of the sack of Rome came to be considered an account of the Italian wars in one piece published at the end of the fifteenth

1975), pp. 49–76; Bernard McGinn, "Circoli gioachimiti veneziani (1450–1530)," *Cristianesimo nella storia* 7 (1986): 19–39; Anna Morisi, *Apocalypsis nova. Ricerche sull'origine e la formazione del testo dello pseudo-Amadeo* (Rome: Istituto storico italiano per il Medio Evo, 1970); Giampaolo Tognetti, "Note sul profetismo nel Rinascimento e la letteratura relativa," *Bullettino dell'Istituto storico italiano per il Medioevo* 82 (1970) [1974]: 129–57; Cesare Vasoli, *Profezia e ragione. Studi sulla cultura del Cinquecento e del Seicento* (Naples: Morano, 1974); Vasoli, *I miti e gli astri* (Naples: Guida, 1977); Vasoli, *La cultura delle corti* (Bologna: Cappelli, 1980), esp. pp. 129–218.

[51] Matarazzo, *Cronaca*, p. 16; Bernardi, *Cronache forlivesi*, vol. 1, pt. 2, p. 72.

century.[52] The versatility of these texts rendered them capable of illustrating whatever political trauma came along, with no need for modifications, which allows us to make reasonable inductions concerning the sort of reading that could be made of them in other cases as well. Thus when in 1495 the printer Angelo Ugoletti published separately the prophecy *El se movera un gato*, a text that had first appeared early in the century and that two years before had been printed in an appendix to the *Libro de Santo Iusto paladino de Franza*,[53] it is not difficult to suppose that this republication was prompted by an updated reading, in particular of the final lines:

> O Italia piange, disse
> —ube ube ube bis bis Italia—
> che li stranieri e stracie
> guarderà el vostro paese;
> e queste seran l'imprese
> che ferà di voi li vostri signori.
> E picoli e mazori
> se graterà la rogna
> più che non bisogna
> e con gran sangue.

> (O Italy, weep, he said—sob, sob, sob, gasp, gasp; Italy!—for your land will see foreigners and disasters, and these will be enterprises that your lords will involve you in. And great and small will be troubled out of measure and with great bloodshed.)[54]

In a few cases (actually, very few), reprinting led to modifications in the text in the interest of adapting it better to a specific situation. One example of this is the prophecy of the second Charlemagne that was written for Charles VI of France and printed in Italy at the end of the fifteenth century on the occasion of the French invasion. When it was later attributed to Emperor Charles V, he was no longer called "fiol de Caroli" (Charles' son) but "Philippi filius" to recall his descent from Philip the Handsome. In other cases, the texts were expressly written to fit a specific context. Certain titles indicate this clearly, such as the *Imminente flagello de Italia*, or *Queste sono quattro prophetie novamente cavate le qual narra le grandissime guerre che ha da occorrere in la Italia et fora d'Italia*, or, again, *Pronostico e profecia de le cose debeno succedere generalmente maxime dele guere comenziate per magni*

[52] *Queste sono quattro prophetie novamente cavate le qual narra le grandissime guerre che a da occorrere in la Italia et fora ditalia* (n.p., n.d.).

[53] Published in Parma, 1493.

[54] *El se movera un gato*, fol. 2*v*.

potentati contra venetiani.[55] The texts themselves present allusions to current happenings, in particular to wars and battles. Giuliano Dati had already referred directly to the invasion of Charles VIII, presenting it as a sign of divine wrath and a portent of further afflictions to come;[56] later, even the battle of Agnadello and the events of the War of the League of Cambrai would find strong echoes in verse prophecies to testify to prophecy's role as a sounding board for political events.

In reality, the battle of Agnadello, in which the Venetian troops under Bartolomeo Alviano were routed by the French cavalry and the Swiss infantry, making the collapse of the power of the Serenissima in north-central Italy inevitable, almost immediately gave rise to a prophetic myth that long remained as alive among the Venetian patriciate as it was in folklore and that was clearly symptomatic of the political importance of that event. Some days before the battle a strange old man clothed in a bearskin had appeared before Alviano and, showing him "a long pike with a bent point," warned him that, like that weapon, the Venetians would have to bend in order not to break. He was later reported to have come back to scatter flaming embers and give out "writings of various predictions."[57] He was Francesco da Bergamo, Luigi da Porto tells us, a former mason "who, no longer exercising his craft, gave himself over exclusively to divination and philosophy, for which everyone thought him mad." The picture Da Porto presents of him has indeed something ludicrous about it, recalling a well-known theatrical tradition. This *om salvadegh* (wild man) who spoke only Bergamo dialect seems to us today more like a Carnival Zanni (the "mask" or stock character of a peasant from the mountains of Bergamo) than like St. John the Baptist, the prototype and model of the prophet in Italy of that period.[58] Within a few days, however, Venice lent a more attentive ear to prognostications. "Prodigious happenings and signs" had multiplied, Luigi da Porto tells us: "Already many people are afflicted. Even the comets seen these past days and the birth of several small monsters, and the entrance of wolves into many cities have disturbed many people."[59]

After the battle of Agnadello, prophetic tension seems to have increased further, becoming more contradictory, however. Since the catastrophe had

[55] The three publications bear no indication of place or date.

[56] *Del diluvio di Roma*, fol. a iii*v*.

[57] Luigi da Porto, *Lettere storiche di Luigi da Porto vicentino dall'anno 1509 al 1528*, ed. Bartolommeo Bressan (Florence: Felice Le Monnier, 1857), pp. 38–40. See also Innocenzo Cervelli, *Machiavelli e la crisi dello stato veneziano* (Naples: Guida, 1974), pp. 150–57, 215–16.

[58] See Domenico Merlini, *Saggio di ricerche sulla satira contro il villano* (Turin: E. Loescher, 1894), pp. 120–48; Lucia Lazzerini, "Preistoria degli zanni: mito e spettacolo nella coscienza populare," in *Scienze, credenze occulte, livelli di cultura. Convegno internazionale di studi (Firenze, 26–30 giugno 1980)*, 445–76, esp. pp. 465–74.

[59] Da Porto, *Lettere storiche*, p. 52. For monstrous births, see chap. 2 of this book.

now occurred, prediction of its immediate consequences was mingled with more consoling forecasts. In the weeks following Agnadello, Marin Sanudo included in his journals notes on astrological prognostications and celestial signs and even a report of a supernatural vision: On 19 June a woman dressed in white—the Virgin—had appeared to a widowed wool spinner and charged her to demand processions "so that this land may have victory against its enemies." As early as the end of May, however, Sanudo tells us that "*la brigà* [the throng] at present expects much from prophecies." He himself had been to the island of San Clemente to consult an old friar, Don Piero Nani, "a gentleman of our own, of ninety years of age, who says many things, such as drawing prophecies . . . of which he has a great store." Thus Don Piero was another collector of prophecies (in manuscript, we may suppose), a noble, consulted by other nobles ("he has a great following of patricians"). Nani stated that Venice would lose all its mainland empire, but would win back its territories at a later date; that the emperor would go to Rome, where he would cut the pope's head off; that later he would be chased out of Rome and replaced by another monarch, whom Nani "thinks is Duke Charles of Burgundy, who is rumored to be alive and in a hermitage," and who would assure the election of "a good pope." Finally, the Turk would be converted to Christianity.[60]

Identifying the various predictions on which Nani founded his meditations is an impossible task. Certainly in 1509 many prophecies circulated on the fall (definitive or temporary) of Venice and its state, as is clear even from a contemporary French source, the *Legende des Venitiens* of Jean Lemaire de Belges.[61] There was also a *Prophetia beati fratris Bartholomaei de Vincentia ordinis predicatorum*, conserved in a codex in the Biblioteca Marciana in Venice, which predicted a great war in 1509 "in quo Veneti in terra et in mari quicquid habent perdent, Venetiis exceptis."[62] The most interesting aspects of Sanudo's remarks lie elsewhere, however. First, he points to a clear social distinction in the circulation of the prophecies that centered on Nani: Nobles had recourse to the hidden wisdom of another noble to receive the same sort of comfort that other milieus and cultural and social levels would obtain, only a few weeks later, through the direct mediation of a visionary experience (or at least a visual experience, as we

[60] Sanuto, *Diarii*, vol. 8, cols. 419, 326.

[61] Jean Lemaire de Belges, *Le traicté nommé la legende des Venitiens, ou leur Chronique abregée*, in his *Oeuvres*, ed. J. Stecher, 4 vols. (Louvain: Imp. de J. Le Fever, 1882–1891), vol. 3 (1885), pp. 361–63, 409. On Lemaire, see Jennifer Britnell, "Jean Lemaire de Belges and prophecy," *Journal of the Warburg and Courtauld Institutes* 42 (1979): 144–66, esp. pp. 144–46; the article, however, does not mention the *Legende des Venitiens*.

[62] Biblioteca Marciana di Venezia, MS Marc, it. XI. 66 (=6730), fol. 119*v*. See also a *Prophetia abbatis Joachim Astrologi summi (re vera prophetia de civitate Venetiarum)*, Biblioteca Apostolica Vaticana, Vat. lat. 6085, fols. 195*r*.–196*v*.

shall see). Also, Nani proposes that the emperor of peace who was to create an angelic pope was Charles the Bold, duke of Burgundy, "who is reputed to be alive and living in a hermitage." This choice can be explained by the hypothesis, first, that Nani owned a copy of the prophecy of the second Charlemagne (perhaps in the version that began with the words, "Carolus Philippi filius," since Charles the Bold was in fact the son of Philip the Good) predicting the advent of a monarch named Charles who would bring peace, and second, that he interpreted it in the sense of the rumors that had spread after the death of Charles the Bold in the battle of Nancy in 1477. As Luca Landucci wrote, "It was never known what became of the duke's body, and it was never found; so that some were of opinion that he was not dead, but had been carried off, and would one day appear again."[63]

What we have here is one more example of the full operation of the mechanisms of prophecy. We have many texts (in this case, probably manuscript), a moment of political crisis, the selection of an appropriate text, the application to it of a rumor spread by word of mouth (there is no evidence that news of the survival of Charles the Bold was transmitted in writing),[64] and, finally, re-elaboration by an exegete for the purpose of comforting members of his own social group.

"Prophecies in Mosaics" in the Basilica of San Marco

Opposed to the *patricij* who consulted Piero Nani stood a broader and less clearly defined category: *la brigà*, the throng. "It is known [that] the throng at present expects much from prophecies, and goes to the church of San Marco seeing prophecies in mosaics, such as the abbot Joachim had made."

Just what were these *prophetie di musaicho* that all could see (rather than being shut up in a monk's cell) we learn from Jean Lemaire de Belges and, later, from Giovanni Stringa, writing at the beginning of the seventeenth century. They were figures that actually existed in the mosaic pavement of the basilica.[65] One was a cock (interpreted as the king of France) who was

[63] Luca Landucci, *Diario fiorentino dal 1450 al 1516*, ed. Iodaco del Badia (Florence: G. C. Sansoni, 1883), p. 15 (quoted from *A Florentine Diary from 1450 to 1516*, tr. Alice de Rosen Jervis [London: J. M. Dent; New York, E. P. Dutton, 1927], p. 13).

[64] In particular, nothing of the sort appears in Reeves, *The Influence of Prophecy*.

[65] See the reproductions in Giuseppe Marino Urbani de Gheltof, "Il pavimento," in Camillo Boito, *La Basilica di San Marco in Venezia illustrata nella storia e nell'arte da scrittori veneziani*, 18 vols. (Venice, F. Ongania, 1878–1893), vol. 15, pt. 3, table 42, fig. 3, and table 43, fig. 12. See also Giovanni Stringa, *La chiesa di S. Marco* (Venice: F. Rampezetto, 1610), fols. 20*r*–*v*.

pecking out the eyes of a fox (Venice); another showed two lions, one fat and sturdy, swimming through the waves, the other, thin and emaciated, on dry land. According to Lemaire, repeating an interpretation he had heard in Venice, the portrayal of the two lions had been ordered by Joachim of Fiore and were to be understood as the Republic, opulent and peaceful so long as Venetians remained lords of the sea, but which would lose power and wealth should it "begin to usurp on the mainland."[66] What Lemaire reports as prognostication was in reality a clearly defined political opinion that sought to acquire a broader hearing and borrow greater authority from prophecy. It was even a broadly held opinion, shared, for example, and expressed well by the anonymous author of a sonnet printed a few months later, which contrasts the noble activity of seafaring with the latest mania of the Venetians for agrarian expansion on the *terraferma* and cultivating fields and crops.

> et mai finisse questa rural fame.
> Uscite di tal trame,
> ché chi si vol far ricco vadi in mare,
> e lassi i buo' al villan per seminare.

> (and this rural hunger never ended. Get free of those trammels, and anyone who wants to get rich can go to sea; leave oxen to peasants for sowing.)[67]

To return to the "prophecies in mosaics," their fame was established all the more easily because it was based on a tradition that had arisen in Franciscan circles in the latter half of the fourteenth century, well accepted by the sixteenth century, that not only scattered details of the pavement but the entire plan for the mosaics of San Marco had been drawn up by Joachim of Fiore.[68] Thus the basilica was a precious coffer filled with prophecies to be conserved and investigated, and as late as 1566 its supervisors

[66] Lemaire de Belges, *Le Traicté nommé la legende des Venitiens*, p. 363.

[67] These are the final lines of a sonnet entitled "Ad illustres Venetos dominos ut mare pernavigent," the "inspired opening" of which ("Andate in mar, signori venetiani / che sete i primi marinar del mondo" [Go to sea, Venetian lords, who are the first sailors of the world]) Dionisotti records in his *Geografia e storia*, p. 208. The sonnet appears in the anonymous collection *Laus Venetorum* (Venice, 1509), fol. 3*r*.

[68] On this topic (to which I intend to return on another occasion), see Otto Demus, *The Mosaics of San Marco in Venice*, 2 vols. (Chicago and London: University of Chicago Press, 1984), vol. 1, pp. 256–59. The tradition of prophetic reading of the mosaics of San Marco throws new light on the behavior of the armorer Benedetto, who, around 1560, expounded to a group of followers on his *Espositione nell'Apocalipse*, which he had written (in manuscript form) with the help of the mosaics on that theme, newly mounted on the west face of the west dome by the Zuccato brothers (see Adriano Prosperi, "Intorno a un catechismo figurato del tardo '500," in *Von der Macht der Bilder* (Leipzig: E. A. Seeman; Karl-Marx-Universität, 1983), p. 111.

gave firm orders not to do away with any inscription or mosaic without taking due note of it, "so that those same works and prophecies, which it is said were ordered by St. Joachim, can be worked on and returned."[69] That these prophecies concerned the fortunes of the Serenissima was suggested by the utterly political tone, well attuned to political functions and demands, of all religious practice in the basilica and in Venice.[70] These images, publicly displayed inside the principal temple of the Republic, were thus open to exegesis by the *brigà*, who enjoyed much greater freedom of interpretation than Friar Piero Nani. They even solicited interpretation by the evocation of the glorious name of Abbot Joachim, and they gave efficacious expression to a hard political truth—the collapse of Venetian power—and to proposals for emerging from a difficult situation by abandoning the mainland empire and returning to sea power. The role of such prophecies far surpassed simple consolation: They were an instrument for political analysis and the proposal of political programs—a rough-hewn tool, perhaps, but one with an important impact on public opinion.

The War of Cambrai in Prophetic Publications

The same complex role can be seen in vernacular prophetic print pieces published during the same period. One example of these emerges out of a burlesque anti-Venetian text, the *Iudicio del frate Bechierante da Cervia commissario e studiante*,[71] probably printed in the early months of 1510. This piece is a bizarre mixture of Latin and vernacular, of rhythmic prose and nonsense verse, of anticlerical attitudes and homage to Pope Julius II. It is structured like the traditional prognostications, with an introduction, a dedication, then various chapters: "De Iulio II," "De rege Francorum," "De infirmitate," "De le guerre," "Del ricolto," and so forth. References to political events are frequent. With a good bit of irony and pointed satire, interspersed with street players' gags and macaronic doggerel, Julius II and the other members of the League of Cambrai are promised victory over Venice and, at a later time, over the Turks. Another edition of this strange text bears a more explicit title (already cited): *Pronostico e profecia de le cose debeno succedere maxime dele guere comenziate per magni potentati contra venetiani. Adi XX de zenaro M.V.X.*[72] It was illustrated with a woodcut that

[69] *Documenti per la storia dell'augusta ducale Basilica di San Marco in Venezia dal nono secolo sino alla fine del decimo ottavo* (Venice: Ferdinand Ongania, 1886), p. 80.

[70] Edward Muir, *Civic Ritual in Renaissance Venice* (Princeton: Princeton University Press, 1981).

[71] N.p., n.d.

[72] N.p., n.d.

Fig. 1. Frontispiece to *Pronostico e profecia de le cose debeno succedere* . . . (n.p., 1510).

referred to events concerning the League of Cambrai (see Figure 1). The four principal allies (the pope, the emperor, the kings of France and of Spain), each recognizable by an emblematic element, are seated around a playing field on which there are bowling pins, for the most part knocked down, to symbolize the cities that they threatened to take or had already taken from Venice early in 1510. To one side there is a pin with a joker's head, labeled *Mato*, and a sort of wheel—the *zurlo*—which obviously serves as a bowling ball. A two-line caption explains the rules of the game and warns the allies not to be too sure of their luck:

> Guardate il zurlo non abati il Mato,
> perché, abatendo, nula fia sto tracto.
>
> (Take care that the zurlo does not strike down the Mato because if it does the match is off.)[73]

[73] *Pronostico e profecia de la cose debeno succedere*, fol. 1*r*.

That is, if the ball strikes down the Fool, the turn is invalid and the other pins already knocked down will not count. In nonmetaphorical terms, imponderables can take from the leaders of the League what they think they hold securely. The joking tone of the prophecy is contradicted by this prudent warning.

The dedication of the piece to Julius II is dated, in the author's bizarre style, "de l'anno cinquecento e nove, de dicembre a XX che sempre piove" (in the year five hundred and nine, December 20, and still raining). At precisely the same time (the immediately preceding entry concerns Christmas night, 1509), ser Tommaso di Silvestro in Orvieto transcribed in his journal a "Pater Noster made in tercets signifying what is to be, according to the prophecies."[74] This prayer was a parody of the "Our Father," a literary genre well known and particularly widely practiced in the sixteenth century.[75] Following a *topos* of biblical origin, it predicts "plagues, wars, and famines . . . until the coming of a Christian Lord" who is to defeat and convert the Turks. Wars and tribulations would then continue until the year 1509; then, under the aegis of "a Roman shepherd . . . all the world will be pacified." This was to be the new Golden Age:

> et in tal tempo non varrà né carlino né ducato
> . . .
> multi superbi seranno in basso stato;
> qualunche serrà humile, esaltato,
> non se extimarà né seta, né imbroccato.

> (and in that time neither the *carlino* nor the *ducato* will be worth anything. . . . Many of the proud will be in low estate; some of the humble [will be] exalted, neither silk nor brocade will be esteemed.)[76]

To offer a prophecy at the end of 1509, when the war of the League of Cambrai was raging, explicitly dating the defeat of the Venetians in that year and predicting the conversion of the Turks after many wars, to be followed by universal peace and social palingenesis under a "Roman shepherd," was equivalent to implicit support of the current political aims of Julius II. We should keep in mind, among other things, that one of the official reasons for taking up arms against Venice lay in its attitude toward the Turks, which was judged unpropitious to an anti-Ottoman crusade. One logical deduction was that war against Venice was a necessary precon-

[74] Tommaso di Silvestro, *Diario*, pp. 415–17.

[75] See Francesco Novati, "Una poesia politica del Cinquecento: il Pater Noster dei Lombardi," *Giornale di filologia romanza* 2 (1879): 121–52; Novati, "La parodia sacra nelle letterature moderne," in his *Studi critici e letterari* (Turin, Florence, and Rome: E. Loescher, 1889), pp. 177–310.

[76] Tommaso di Silvestro, *Diario*, p. 416.

dition to a crusade against the Turks, hence itself a crusade.[77] Furthermore, the prophecy could very well have been drawn up in Roman circles: Certain grammatical forms (*speramo*, *magnaranno*, *imbroccato*) support this, and we can reasonably hypothesize that Tommaso di Silvestro's usual sources of information were Roman.

These were not the only instances of the appearance, direct or indirect, of the War of Cambrai in prophecies. In 1511 a very short work of only two leaves was put out, probably by Giovanni Antonio Benedetti, a printer in Bologna, containing a narrative ballad entitled *Memoria delli novi segni et spaventevoli prodigii comparsi in piu loci de Italia et in varie parti del mondo lanno mille cinquecento undese*. This is a singular text, fascinating for its lack of polish, to which we shall have frequent occasion to return. It continued to be reprinted, with additions, corrections, and adaptations, past the mid-century. We have already encountered the incipit: "Ascoltati mortali / li orribeli segnali" (Listen, mortals, to the horrible signs). As the title and the opening words tell us, this was a collection of omens, portents, and extraordinary occurrences that foretold of divine wrath directed at the world in general and at Italy in particular. The signs described in greatest detail were "an impious and fierce serpent" sighted in the air on 5 May between Brescia and Cremona, ghostly fires that appeared "where the conflict with the Venetians had been," sounds of mysterious battles between specters in the same area on 7 May (the identity of the ghostly combatants will be revealed in chapter 3), finally, two angels who appeared for three hours with drawn swords "over the territory of Padua."[78] All these prodigies concerned the area involved in the Cambrai War in 1509–1510, which culminated in the battle of Agnadello ("where the conflict with the Venetians had been") and the imperial assault on Padua. In fact, the poet deliberately and erroneously transfers the angels with drawn swords from a bell tower in Udine, where a good number of other contemporary accounts place this apparition, to the skies over Padua.[79] A good fifteen quatrains are devoted to these phenomena, whereas the *cantastorie* used only eight to describe the signs that had appeared in Venice, Rome, and Florence, and seven for those that had occurred in Turkey. Although this disproportionate concentration on prodigies in the war zone cannot be coincidental, here we are not dealing with propagandistic and celebrative demands as in the two texts examined earlier. The *Memoria delli novi segni* is better considered as an echo of the devastation and suffering that the War of the League of Cambrai had brought to the populations of the Veneto and Lombardy. To use places that were, as Ruzante put it, "se no cielo e uossi de morti"

[77] Dionisotti, *Geografia e storia*, pp. 207–208; Cervelli, *Machiavelli*, pp. 160–63.

[78] *Memoria delli novi segni*, fol. 1*r*–*v*.

[79] Ottavia Niccoli, "Visioni e racconti di visioni nell'Italia del primo Cinquecento," *Società e storia* 28 (1985): 253–73; pp. 262, 264.

("nothing but sky and dead men's bones")[80] as a background for portents and prodigies was to draw upon them for presages of affliction that deeply involved the listeners' emotions. The tale singers' verse shows an unconscious but clear connection between war, political disintegration, and prophecy.

[80] Angelo Beolco, called Ruzante, *Parlamento de Ruzante che iera vegnù dal campo* in his *Teatro*, ed. Ludovico Zorzi (Turin: G. Einaudi, 1967), p. 529.

2

MONSTERS, DIVINATION, AND PROPAGANDA IN BROADSHEETS

Signs and Popular Divination

IN HIS *Del diluvio di Roma del MCCCCLXXXXV* Giuliano Dati declared to his *auditori*, through the voice of a tale singer, that divine castigation was imminent. The announcement was presumably based on incontrovertible indications, on "signs great and immeasurable" clearly of religious origin and pertinence, on which Dati expounded for thirty-five eight-line stanzas:

> Par che 'l Signor tal cosa lui ci mandi
> quel che su nella croce fu defunto;
> per farci più acciepti in ne' sua regni
> ci manda gl'infrascripti e detti segni.
> . . .
> Questi segni ci manda l'alto Idio
> che no' ci prepariamo, al parer mio.
>
> (It seems that the Lord, who died upon the Cross, sends us such a thing; in order that we be made more acceptable in his kingdom he sends us the said signs, written below. . . . These signs almighty God sends us so we will prepare ourselves, it seems to me.)[1]

What exactly did he mean by "infrascripti e detti segni" or by "segni grandi e smisurati"? Precisely what were these signs? In this context, the word obviously has biblical origins, its most explicit utilization being in the Gospel according to St. Luke:

> And there shall be signs in the sun, and in the moon, and in the stars: and upon the earth distress of nations, by reason of the confusion of the roaring of the sea and of the waves. Men withering away for fear, and expectation of what shall come upon the whole world. . . . But when these things begin to come

[1] Giuliano Dati, *Del diluvio di Roma del MCCCCLXXXXV adi iiii di dicembre et daltre cose di gran meraviglia* (n.p., n.d.), fol. a ii*r*.

to pass, look up and lift up your heads: because your redemption is at hand. *(Luke 21:25–28)*

Thus the signs in question were alterations in the stars (and in nature in general) observed attentively and interpreted as portents of imminent and terrible events. The word *segno* or its equivalent occurs with overwhelming frequency in this sense and with these connotations. Signs were not simply extraordinary events, however; taken as a whole, they served as something like an elementary set of orally transmitted techniques common to both the learned and the unlettered and instrumental for predicting the future on the basis of changes in what was considered the natural course of things. As Leone Cobelli, a painter from Forlì, said in 1497, "signs never come without some matter."[2] With the focus on classical divination in humanistic culture and philosophical study of the occult following Pomponazzi (in the *De incantationibus*, for example), an interest in portents and in what came to be defined as *divinatio popularis* even reached learned circles.[3] Still, as we shall see, this relationship worked both ways; if anything, it was a case of reciprocal influence.

Signs and portents could be a generic indication of the wrath of God, as in the verse of Giuliano Dati, or they could have a more carefully worked out political reading, as in a lively passage in Marin Sanudo's journals. Sanudo saw Italy's imminent liberation from the barbarians at the hands of the Republic of Venice in the disastrous effects of the earthquake that struck the city in March 1511:

> First, there fell four marble kings that before had stood over the façade of the church of St. Mark. . . . There fell a woman in marble who represented Prudence, even though she was standing amid other virtues. . . . The upper portion of the decorations over the great balcony of the Great Hall of the Major Council, which was high, fell, [along] with a Justice that was there, but a marble St. Mark held firm and did not fall. . . . A marble merlon decorated with a plaster seal bearing a lily blossom fell, and many held this to be a good sign, because the lily, which is the crest of France, will fall and come to ruin, which is what God wants for the good of Italy, sorely tried by barbarians. . . . And I saw the holy Mark, who remained intact on top of the palace. . . . Thus this city will be the savior of Italy and of the faith of Christ by chasing the barbarians from Italy.[4]

[2] Leone Cobelli, *Cronache forlivesi dalla fondazione della città all'anno 1498*, ed. Giosuè Carducci and Enrico Frati (Bologna: Regia tipografia, 1874), p. 412.

[3] For a definition of *divinatio popularis*, see p. 187.

[4] Marino Sanuto, *Diarii*, 58 vols. (Venice: R. Deputazione veneta di storia patria, 1879–1903), vol. 11, cols. 79–80.

Not only were imposing phenomena such as earthquakes, eclipses of the sun, and comets carefully noted; so were much less clamorous events such as the five meteorites that fell near Forlì on 26 January 1496, the unusual rainbow that appeared in Orvieto on 25 May 1507, and the myriad of red butterflies that invaded Brescia on Friday, 23 May 1522.[5] Monstrous creatures like the strange pig and the four-legged hen recorded in the *Diluvio di Roma* came in for particular attention:

> E una troia un porco partorì
> col capo tutto d'homo, e poi morì.
> Con quattro piedi nacque una gallina,
> e sequitò dipoi una gran peste;
> d'animal e di gente fu rovina,
> e le gente rimasen tutte meste.
>
> (And a sow gave birth to a pig with a man's head, and then died. A hen was born with four feet, and a great pestilence followed; it was the ruination of animals and people, and people were greatly distressed by it.)[6]

On the Meaning of Monsters

Within this system of divination by signs, increasing attention was paid to the birth of malformed infants in the waning Middle Ages and the first decades of the early modern age.[7] It was a phenomenon that differed radically from both the preceding century's interest in fantastic monstrosities and the passion for classification that was to explode after 1550 and provide a precedent and encouragement for the new science. The "monsters" born as the fifteenth moved into the sixteenth century were actual births, and although descriptions of them tended to include some fantastic elements they had little in common with the Oriental monsters that the Indies so generously furnished in the Middle Ages. They often had a purely human fate. First and most obviously, they died, and not only from natural

[5] Cobelli, *Cronache forlivesi*, pp. 398–99; Tommaso di Silvestro, *Diario*, ed. Luigi Fumi, RIS 25, pt. 5 (Bologna: Nicola Zanichelli, 1923), vol. 2, pp. 1–512; p. 340; Paolo Guerrini, ed., *Le cronache bresciane inedite dei secoli XV–XIX*, 5 vols. (Brescia: Editrice Brixia Sacra, 1922–1932), vol. 2, p. 50.

[6] *Del diluvio di Roma*, fol. a iir.

[7] Aby Warburg, *La rinascita del paganesimo antico*, tr. Emma Cantimori Mezzomonti (Florence: La Nuova Italia, 1966), pp. 348–54 (also available in his *Ausgewählte Schriften und Würdigungen*, ed. Dieter Wuttke [Baden-Baden: Verlag Valentin Koerner, 1980]); Jean Céard, *La Nature et les prodiges. L'insolite au XVIe siècle en France* (Geneva: Droz, 1977). In classical antiquity, the word *tératon* originally signified "terrifying prodigy," so by antomasia the monstrous creatures were terrible and prodigious events.

causes, but also from the deliberate withdrawal of care and nourishment. This is what happened in the case of a misbirth in Florence in 1506, who "by order of the Signoria was not fed and died," and to another malformed infant abandoned to the Hospital of the Pietà in Venice in 1513, who "was let die" in like manner.[8] These were patterns of behavior for which there is long-standing testimony and which continued into the eighteenth century and probably longer, as did the custom of displaying malformed babies for money, also well attested in these decades. Such was the case of the female Siamese twins born in 1475 outside Verona, who, as Conrad Wollfhart (Conrad Lycosthenes) recalls, "parentes multum diuque per Italiae urbes quaestus causa circumtulere,"[9] or of the other female misbirth in Ficarolo in the Polesine on 31 December 1531, of whom Tommasino Lancellotti says that she "has a permit from the vicar of the bishop of Ferrara, and whoever wants to see her pays."[10]

The display of abnormal infants hid another, deeper divinatory function. The monstrous creature, alive or embalmed, was shown not only because it was a "cosa spaventevole," a "cossa stupenda," or a "prodigio" but also because it was taken as a portent. As the physician Francesco Bonafede wrote to his father-in-law, Alessandro Pesaro, in March 1514 concerning various monstrous creatures of which he had had recent news, prognostications of the "tumult of wars, killing, [and] destruction" could be drawn from such events. Bonafede did not agree with this divinatory analysis, however, and he offered his father-in-law a detailed naturalistic explanation of abnormalities based on Aristotle. He had his own divinatory system, however, and his letter went on to describe "the revolution of the present year made by the most enlightened astrologer messer Pelegrin di Presciani [Pellegrino Prisciani]."[11] The contrast he sets up between astrology and the analysis of omens thus appears to imply a substantial difference in levels of culture.

The predictions that Bonafede noted were fairly generic, albeit catastrophic in content: *guerre, occisione, stragie*. Similarly, as early as 1489, Luca Landucci, after transcribing in his journal a letter containing a description of monsters that had been sent from Venice to Tanai de' Nerli's bank, concludes that "such signs signify great trouble in the city where they

[8] Sanuto, *Diarii*, vol. 6, col. 390; vol. 17, col. 347.

[9] Conrad Lycosthenes [Conrad Wollfhart], *Prodigiorum ac ostentorum chronicon* (Basel, 1557), p. 490.

[10] Tommasino Lancellotti, *Cronaca modenese*, ed. Carlo Borghi, 12 vols. (Parma: P. Fiaccadori, 1863), vol. 4, p. 23.

[11] Sanuto, *Diarii*, vol. 18, col. 33. On Bonafede, see Valerio Giacomini, "Bonafede, Francesco," in *Dizionario Biografico degli Italiani* (Rome: Istituto della Enciclopedia Italiana, 1960–), hereafter cited as DBI, vol. 11, pp. 491–92.

take place."[12] Aside from this generic prophetic function, however, misbirths had another, more specific function. From the late fifteenth century to 1530, a true literary genre emerged in Germany and Italy in the brief ephemeral works, pamphlets, and broadsheets that, in many cases, strove not only to give a global and cataclysmic prophetic sense to the monstrous creature but also a political-prophetic interpretation, arrived at through analysis of its various deformities.[13] This was what happened in the cases of misbirths in Rome in 1495, in Ravenna in 1512, in Bologna in 1514, in Freiberg in Saxony in 1522, in Castelbaldo in the Polesine in 1525, and so forth. Analysis of the monstrous bodies of these beings seems linked to the specific historical moment. Indeed, interpreters presented their expertise as political knowledge, explicitly contrasting it to that of "these modern sages with their tricks and their con games who advise princes, 'non timentes Deum, sed in sua versutia confisi,' " as one anonymous author wrote concerning the monster born in Bologna in January 1514, or, as another anonymous author said, commenting on a creature born with three legs in the Polesine in 1525, to the "secret cogitation of rulers."[14] Thus what was needed was a different sort of knowledge—a political analysis of the monstrous creatures aimed more at tracing the signs of divine wrath than investigating the maneuvers of men but tied to elements and events also considered by the *savieti* of the anonymous author of 1514, in substance, to use his words, the sorry condition of "misera Italia."

[12] Luca Landucci, *Diario fiorentino dal 1450 al 1516*, ed. Iodaco del Badia (Florence: G. C. Sansoni, 1883), p. 57; quoted from *A Florentine Diary from 1450 to 1516*, tr. Alice de Rosen Jervis (London: J. M. Dent; New York: E. P. Dutton, 1927), p. 47. The same event, reported in a different manner, can be found in Domenico Malipiero, "Annali veneti dall'anno 1457 al 1500," *Archivio storico italiano* 7 (1843–44): 5–586; p. 309, which connects the births to the attempted coup in which Girolamo Riario was killed.

[13] A model for the political interpretation of monstrous births emerged out of humanistic milieus surrounding the emperor Maximilian: See *Varia Sebastiani Brant Carmina* (Basel: [Johan Bergmann de] Olpe, 1498). See also Dieter Wuttke, "Sebastian Brant und Maximilian I. Eine Studie zu Brants Donnerstein-Flugblatt des Jahres 1492," in Otto Herding and Robert Stupperich, eds., *Die Humanisten in ihrer politischen und sozialen Umwelt* (Boppard: Harald Boldt, 1976), pp. 141–76; Wuttke, "Wunderdeutung und Politik. Zu den Auslegung der sogenannten Wormser Zwillinge des Jahres 1495," in Kaspar Elm, Eberhard Gönner, and Engen Hillenbrand, eds., *Landesgeschichte und Geistesgeschichte. Festschrift für Otto Herding zum 65. Geburtstag* (Stuttgart: W. Kohlhammer, 1977), pp. 217–44; Wuttke, "Sebastian Brants Verhältnis zu Wunderdeutung und Astrologie," in *Studien zur deutschen Literatur und Sprache des Mittelalters. Festschrift für Hugo Moser zum 65. Geburtstag* (Berlin: Erich Schmidt, 1974), pp. 272–86. On the Roman monster of 1496, see Konrad von Lange, *Der Papstesel; Ein Beitrage zur Kultur- und Kunstgeschichte des Reformationszeitsalters* (Göttingen: Vandenhoeck and Ruprecht, 1891) and Antonio Rotondò, "Pellegrino Prisciani," *Rinascimento* 11 (1960): 69–110; pp. 106–107. For the monster of Ravenna, see also Rudolf Schenda, "Das Monstrum von Ravenna. Eine Studie zur Prodigienliteratur," in *Zeitschrift für Volkskunde* 56 (1960): 209–225.

[14] Sanuto, *Diarii*, vol. 17, col. 516; vol. 40, col. 652.

The wealth and the polyvalence of prophetic language emerges with particular clarity from the pamphlets, broadsheets (often illustrated), and other written or pictorial descriptions of the monsters. We have already encountered some of these pieces, and others will be taken up, at least in some of their aspects, in a later chapter. Here I shall focus on two such monsters, the creature born in Ravenna in March 1512, best known for foreshadowing the battle of 11 April of that year, in which the French forces inflicted a bloody defeat on the pontifical army,[15] and another, less famous monster born in Bologna in January 1514.

The Monster of Ravenna: How the News Got Around

Information on the monster of Ravenna is plentiful and of various sorts, but deeper understanding of its meaning requires careful analysis. We need first to reconstruct the origin and the circulation of pamphlets and broadsheets, then to pass on to the figures that illustrated these pieces and to investigate their origin, and finally, we need to turn to the texts themselves and to the significance and global function of these materials.

The earliest testimony available to us is that of the Roman chronicler Sebastiano di Branca Tedallini:

> The 8th day of March. How in Ravenna there was born to a nun and a friar an infant such as I shall write to you. It had a big head, with a horn on its forehead and a large mouth; on its chest, three letters, as you see here: YXV, with three [tufts of] hairs on its chest; one leg hairy with a devil's hoof, the other a man's leg with an eye in the middle of the leg; never in memory of man has there been anything like this. The governor of the land sent [information] of it on paper to Pope Julius II.[16]

The news thus arrived in Rome on 8 March: "Lo governatore de la tera [Marco Coccapane] mandàne nella carta a papa Iulio 2o."[17] The phrase suggests fairly swift communication (as we shall see, another source tells us that the monster was born 6 March), according to Tedallini transmitted "nella carta," an expression that probably indicates that a drawing picturing the monster was sent along with the news itself and a description.

[15] On the Battle of Ravenna, see Giancarlo Schizzerotto, *Otto poemetti volgari sulla battaglia di Ravenna del 1512* (Ravenna: Edizioni del Girasole, 1968), and the bibliography given in that work.

[16] Sebastiano di Branca Tedallini, *Diario romano dal 3 maggio 1485 al 6 giugno 1524*, ed. Paolo Piccolomini, RIS 23, pt. 3, pp. 287–445; p. 327.

[17] Silvio Bernicoli, *Governi di Ravenna e di Romagna dalla fine del secolo XII alla fine del secolo XIX. Tavole di cronologia* (Ravenna: tip. Ravegnana, 1898), p. 57. This work is available in reproduction (Bologna: Forni, 1968).

Our next piece of information comes from Luca Landucci in Florence: "11th March. We heard that a monster had been born at Ravenna, of which a drawing was sent here." Landucci continues, after a description much like Branca Tedallini's, "I saw it painted, and anyone who wishes could see this painting in Florence."[18] Landucci was thus aware of a drawing, not a written description: The monster, he says, "venne qui [that is, notice of it arrived in Florence] disegnato" or "dipinto." It must have been a colored drawing, probably with a caption, perhaps reproduced in many copies, and certainly posted in public, as indicated by the notation that "chi lo volle vedere" could do so. There is an ample fund of information on the public posting of pictures, *scartabelli* (pamphlets), and manuscript texts of various sorts, a topic that would repay further reflection. Even infamatory depiction—the judicial penalty of displaying a picture of a condemned criminal in a public place—is attested in Bologna and Venice as late as the end of the 1530s in the modest form of broadsheets and paintings rather than the more usual wall paintings.[19]

But "revenons à nos monstres." With the drawing cited by Landucci we are apparently still in the phase of the circulation of manuscript texts and illustrations, and a brief word on the continuing importance of these two channels of communication in the early sixteenth century might not be amiss. The piece that arrived in Spain and that Pietro Martire d'Anghiera described in a letter to Marchese Pietro Fajardo dated 20 March (however, Anghiera's letters are often misdated) may also have been a captioned drawing or perhaps a broadsheet.[20] Anghiera's description concurs in substance with that of the Spanish historian Andrés Bernáldez, who mentioned the matter a few months later in his *Historia de los reyes católicos* (in particular, both insist on the leonine aspect of the creature's face and hair). Anghiera concludes, "cuius imaginem ab Urbe allatam vidimus"; Bernáldez tells us that the monster "fué llevado al Papa, el cual lo vidó y mandó dibujarle de la manera y forma que era" (was shown to the Pope, who saw

[18] Quoted from Landucci, *A Florentine Diary*, pp. 249–50.

[19] For infamatory paintings, see Gherardo Ortalli, *". . . Pingatur in palatio. . .": La pittura infamante nei secoli XIII–XVI* (Rome: Jouvence 1979). See also cases mentioned in Giuliano Fantaguzzi, *Caos. Cronache cesenati del sec. XV*, ed. Dino Bazzocchi (Cesena: Tip. Arturo Bettini, 1915), pp. 117, 134–35 (for the years 1495 and 1500); Sanuto, *Diarii*, vol. 47, cols. 100, 495–97, 514 (for the year 1528); Jacopo Rainieri, *Diario bolognese*, ed. Olindo Guerrini and Corrado Ricci (Bologna: Deputazione di storia patria per le provincie di Romagna, 1888), pp. 35 and 38 (for the year 1538); Girolamo Bonoli, *Storia di Lugo ed annessi* (Faenza: nella stampa dell'Archi impressor camerale e del S. Ufizio, 1732), p. 495 (for the year 1646).

[20] *Opus epistolarum Petri Martyris Anglerii* (Amsterdam: typis Elzevirianis, 1670), p. 256. On the dating of Anghiera's letters, see L. Gazzero Righi, "L'Opus epistolarum' di Pietro Martire d'Anghiera visto alla luce della critica tedesca della fine del XIX secolo," in *Pietro Martire d'Anghiera nella storia e nella cultura* (Genoa, 1980), pp. 261–85.

it and sent to ask of the manner and form that it was).[21] Both Anghiera and Bernáldez thus stress that the image and the description of the malformed creature originated in Rome and circulated at the pope's initiative. It was also in Rome that versions of the image shifted from largely figurative, hand-done pieces to a greater emphasis on writing and to print. On 22 March 1512 Marin Sanudo notes in his *Diarii*, "Item: There was sent me from Rome a monster born in Ravenna in this year; a horrendous thing, which was put into print there in Rome."[22]

The "monster"—that is, the pamphlet or the broadsheet that depicted and described it, on the identity of which I shall offer a hypothesis below—was enclosed in a letter of 18 March from the Venetian ambassador in Rome, Francesco Foscari. Thus very little time separated the misbirth from its being "butado a stampa": First circulated in largely illustrative manuscript pieces, the news appeared in print within ten days or so. Such dispatch was not unusual, however, nor was the stir that this sort of news created in court circles in Rome, as evidenced by the interest aroused by the so-called pope-ass, by the monster found on the banks of the Tiber after the flood in December 1495 ("sung" by Giuliano Dati), by another Roman monster born in 1513,[23] and by the Bolognese monster of 1514.

The news reached Venice from Ravenna, but via Rome. This is a sign, it seems to me, of Ravenna's passage from Venetian to Roman domination. In early Cinquecento Italy, the circulation of news (important news, at least) inevitably followed the paths of political power.

A Genealogy of Images

From Rome news of the monstrous birth was spread throughout Europe. We have already seen that it arrived in Spain; in France as well, broadsheets were printed on the topic. We have one such piece, or, more accurately, we have it transposed and inserted into a longer text that appeared in Valence on 18 September 1513 entitled *Les Avertissemens es trois estatz du monde selon la signification de ung monstre ne lan mille. v. cens et xij*.[24] The author,

[21] Andrés Bernáldez, *Historia de los reyes católicos, Don Fernando y Doña Isabel*, 2 vols. (Seville: J. M. Geofrin, 1870), vol. 2, p. 373 (available in a modern edition edited by Luciano de la Calzada; Madrid: Aguilar, 1959).

[22] Sanuto, *Diarii*, vol. 14, col. 200.

[23] On which, see a brief publication of four leaves, Ioannis Baptiste Ruberti Pegasei, *Monstrum apud Urbem natum* (n.p., n.d. [Rome, after 11 March 1513]). A broadsheet on the same topic bearing an engraving analogous to the one in this work and a verse caption in German is reproduced in Eugen Holländer, *Wunder, Wundergeburt und Wundergestalt in Einblattdrucken des funfzehnten bis achtzehnten Jahrhunderts* (Stuttgart: F. Enke, 1921), p. 312.

[24] The title continues: *Par lequelz on pourra prendre avis a soy regir a tousioursmais* (Valence: Iehan Belon, 1513).

one François Inoy or Yvoy, succeeded in blending together in this singular work a broadsheet describing the Ravenna monster, a prophetic text that had been immensely popular for more than a quarter century, the *Pronosticatio* of the German astrologer Johannes Lichtenberger (Inoy's principal source),[25] and his own typically medieval erudition. Inoy's *auctoritates* are, first, the Bible, then Albertus Magnus, Albumazar, the glosses of Nicolas de Lyra, Aristotle, the patristic texts, Aratus, Varro, Lucan, and the medieval encyclopedia *Lueur de Philosophie*, written in the early fourteenth century by one Jehan Bonnet and here cited under the better-known title of *Placides et Tymeo*.[26] The print that gave Inoy his point of departure was inserted into the text, and under an engraving portraying the monstrous creature (Figure 2) was a description very similar to the ones we have already seen, in all probability a caption to the broadsheet that Inoy had in hand.[27] It is here, among other places, that we find 6 March given as the monster's date of birth.

The picture illustrating this learned Frenchman's pamphlet seems closely related to one that appeared on a German broadsheet, also printed in 1512 (see Figure 3), referring, however, to another monstrous birth that supposedly occurred in Florence on 27 February (a place and date that will require explanation later).[28] Both presumably derived from a common source, now lost. Another Italian broadsheet, also now lost, was the source of another group of images: the first illustrating a short, four-folio work containing a poem in Latin by Giano Vitale of Palermo entitled *De monstro nato*, published in at least two editions in 1512;[29] the second a German broadsheet of a slightly later date, since it mentions a battle that occurred

[25] On Lichtenberger, see Warburg, *La rinascita del paganesimo antico*, pp. 340–48; Dietrich Kurze, *Johannes Lichtenberger (d. 1503). Eine studie zur Geschichte der Prophetie und Astrologie* (Lübeck and Hamburg: Hattiesen, 1960); Kurze, "Popular Astrology and Prophecy in the fifteenth and sixteenth Centuries: Johannes Lichtenberger," in Paola Zambelli, ed., *"Astrologi hallucinati": Stars and the End of the World in Luther's Time* (Berlin and New York: W. de Gruyter, 1986), pp. 177–93; Marjorie Reeves, *The Influence of Prophecy in the Late Middle Ages: A Study in Joachimism* (Oxford: Clarendon Press, 1969), pp. 347ff.

[26] *Sen suit le Lueur de Philosophie contenant plusieurs demandes et questions proposées par le sage Placides au Philosophe Tymeo et les responses contenues in icelluy*, à Paris par Denis Janot, n.d.

[27] *Les Avertissemens en trois estatz du monde*, fol. 6*v*. The passage in question corresponds to the first chapter of that pamphlet, "De la forme que a le monstre."

[28] See Holländer, *Wunder*, p. 318; Gisela Ecker, *Einblattdrucke von dem Anfänge bis 1555* (Göppingen, 1981), no. 192.

[29] Ioannes Franciscus Vitalis Panormitanus, *De monstro nato* (n.p., n.d.). Another edition, nearly identical to this one except for a few lines of Latin verse, "Ad lectorem," on fol. 4*v*, not present in the preceding copy, appeared in Erfurt in July of that year with the imprint: "Impressum Erfordiae per Mattheum Pictorium Anno novi seculi xij Mensis Iulio." On Vitale, see, above all, Girolamo Tumminello, "Giano Vitale umanista del secolo XVI," *Archivio storico siciliano*, n.s. 8 (1883): 1–94; Fernanda Ascarelli, *Annali tipografici di Giacomo Mazzocchi* (Florence: Sansoni antiquariato, 1961), pp. 68–69.

Fig. 2. The Monster of Ravenna. From François Inoy, *Les Avertissemens es trois estatz du monde* . . . (Valence, 1513).

on 11 April, now preserved in Nuremberg, the only piece extant on the monster of Ravenna.[30] The two illustrations contain a number of features such as the "leonine" face of the creature and a leg terminating in a webbed frog foot rather than birdlike claws. These were also mentioned by Bernáldez, who thus must have seen an image of this group and used it as the basis of his description. Finally, an analogous figure accompanied by a verse description ("cum interpretatione carmine expressa") must have come into the hands of Conrad Wollfhart (Lycosthenes), who used it in his *Prodigiorum ac ostentorum chronicon*, published in Basel in 1557.[31] Ly-

[30] Ecker, *Einblattdrucke*, no. 67.

[31] Lycosthenes, *Prodigiorum ac ostentorum chronicon*, p. 517.

Fig. 3. The Florentine Monster of 1512. German broadsheet, Bayerische Staatsbibliothek, Munich.

costhenes also furnished another and quite different version of the monster, pictured with only one leg with a clawed foot and with bird's wings instead of bat's wings (Figure 4). In his description and explanation of this second image, Lycosthenes made use of additions that Johannes Multivallis of Tournai had made to the *Chronicon* of Eusebius of Caesarea.[32] Thus we have at least two different iconographic models and perhaps three, because in his poem in Latin on the Battle of Ravenna, published in Rome

[32] Eusebii Caesariensis Episcopi, *Chronicon . . . ad quem . . . et Ioannes Multivallis complura quae ad haec usque tempora subsecuta sunt adiecere* (Paris: H. Etienne and J. Bade, 13 June 1512).

Fig. 4. Two versions of the Monster of Ravenna from Conrad Wollfhart, *Prodigiorum ac ostentorum chronicon* (Basel, 1557).

in October 1513, Marcello Palonio, a Roman, describes the monster in a lateral gloss to his verse as having two heads ("gemino capite").[33]

Such details do more than satisfy erudite curiosity, since we can trace the iconographic and other origins of each of these models, thus increasing our understanding of the many and interwoven cultural threads in the network of broadsheets that, as we have seen, extended throughout most of Europe. In fact, although we cannot exclude the possibility that a gravely malformed infant was indeed born in Ravenna on the date indicated, it is nonetheless certain that the various depictions were constructed almost totally from preexisting figurative materials. This is particularly clear in the largest group of images showing the misshapen creature with only one head and two legs, which follow, nearly trait for trait, images of the other monster (mentioned above) that the explanatory caption says was born in July 1506 in Florence. This explains, in particular, the German sheets that, as late as 1512, still place the monstrous birth in Florence, an event that might be deemed the incestuous fruit of a liaison between two already related news items and images. News of this Florentine monster of 1506 also passed beyond the Alps, where it was circulated in various forms. The remaining evidence includes a colored drawing that Marin Sanudo pasted into the manuscript of his *Diarii* in August 1506[34] and a nearly identical German broadsheet,[35] which must thus have been taken from a drawing

[33] Marcello Palonio, *Clades ravennas* (Rome, 1513), fol. F iii*r*.

[34] Biblioteca Marciana di Venezia, MS Marc. it. VII.234 (=9221), fol. 179*v*. In the printed edition, the description of the monster is in Sanuto, *Diarii*, vol. 6, col. 390.

[35] Ecker, *Einblattdrucke*, no. 189.

Fig. 5. The Florentine Monster of 1506. Colored drawing, Biblioteca Marciana, Venice.

analogous to the one Sanudo had procured or, more probably, from an Italian broadsheet based on that same drawing (Figures 5 and 6).

The group of images and descriptions representing the monster with only one leg and an avian, clawed foot had a less immediate origin. One likely common source—perhaps not the only source, however—lies in images, fairly common in late medieval German lands, in particular, in the area bounded by Alsace, Switzerland, and Bohemia, which personified the sinful world as Frau Welt.[36] Dame World was portrayed as a woman with

[36] On this iconographical theme, see Wolfgang Stammler, *Frau Welt. Eine mittelalterliche Allegorie* (Fribourg [Switzerland]: Universitätsverlag, 1959); Fritz Saxl, "A Spiritual Ency-

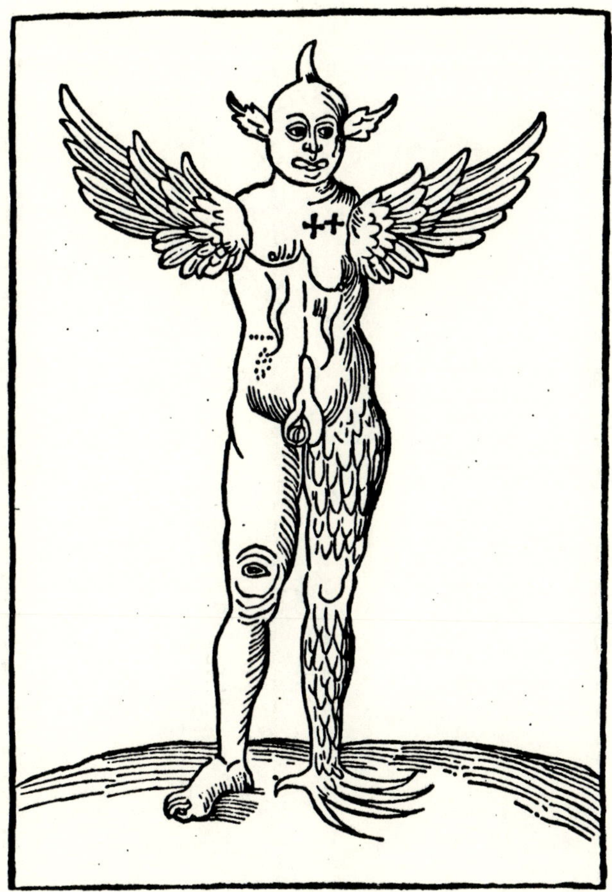

Fig. 6. The Florentine Monster of 1506. German broadside, Bayerische Staatsbibliothek, Munich.

bat's wings, tufts of hair or feathers on her head, standing on her one raptor's leg; the various parts of her body symbolized the seven capital sins. We have a number of depictions of Frau Welt in illuminations or drawings in manuscript encyclopedic miscellanies of a symbolic and spiritual nature. Above all and most appropriate to our interests, we have several engravings of the late fifteenth century from Switzerland and Alsace. One of these (Figure 7), now preserved in the British Library, recalls particularly closely the one-legged version of the monster of Ravenna.[37]

clopedia of the later Middle Ages," *Journal of the Warburg and Courtauld Institutes* 5 (1942): 82–142, esp. 126–28 and figs. 31a, b, c, d.

[37] Saxl, "A Spiritual Encyclopedia." Among the manuscripts Saxl cites, the one owned by the Casanatense Library of Rome has recently been illustrated in Fabio Troncarelli, ed., *La*

Fig. 7. Frau Welt. Alsacian or Swiss engraving (late fifteenth century), British Library, London. Reproduced by Courtesy of the Trustees of the British Museum.

The next problem is whether this was a simple figurative association reemerging from a common mind-set or a true iconographic source. We should ask first if it is plausible to suppose that a print of this type circulated in early sixteenth-century Italy, in particular, in Ravenna or in Rome, the two possible cultural birthplaces of the monster. The answer for both cities is yes, thanks to relations maintained, for differing reasons, with Ven-

città dei segreti. Magia, astrologia e cultura esoterica a Roma (XV–XVIII secolo), Convegno Roma ermetica (1983: Rome, Italy) (Milan: Franco Angeli, 1985). For the print in the British Museum, see Campbell Dodgson, *Woodcuts of the XV Century in the Department of Prints and Drawings, British Museum*, 2 vols. (London: British Museum, 1935), vol. 2, pp. 20–21, n. 240, table 102.

ice—Rome through a long-standing political and cultural tradition,[38] and Ravenna because until 1509 it was part of the Venetian domain. Venice in the latter half of the Quattrocento and the beginning of the Cinquecento was, in fact, an important center of diffusion for "figure stampide depente," as one contemporary put it, works either engraved in Venice by both local talent and German craftsmen or directly imported from the north.[39] Toward the end of the fifteenth century, a notary from Parma, Jacopo Rubieri, collected a number of print pieces and pasted them into his records as decorations. Several of these were of German origin, and certainly came to him by way of Venice, the great commercial center.[40] The engravings that Rubieri collected nearly all had sacred subject matter, but we know that prints on profane subjects also penetrated into Italy from the north, albeit in lesser numbers, and that their echo is perceptible in Italian images.[41] Thus we cannot exclude the circulation in the Venetian states (hence in Ravenna) during the first decade of the Cinquecento of prints analogous to those conserved in the British Museum, and certainly the iconography of the monster of Ravenna in its monoped version would seem to confirm this. A further sign that prints like those portraying Frau Welt circulated in Venice can be inferred from the iconography of one of the five paintings of the so-called Restello Catena, now in the galleries of the Accademia in Venice, the *Summa Virtus*, formerly attributed to Giovanni Bellini and now to Andrea Previtali, which shows the four cardinal and the three theological virtues represented symbolically concentrated in one figure.[42] In both instances we see a winged female figure with a high headdress or feathers on her head, a cup or goblet in her hand, and her clawed feet or foot affixed onto a globe. Naturally, Previtali's inspiration (or his client's) might be sought elsewhere—for example, in the classical iconography of the Harpies—but it seems to me that we cannot exclude the possibility of contact with the north European print, also because of the close parallel between the theme of the seven sins and that of the seven virtues.

As we have seen, the monster was described in a third fashion (not given pictorial form, however) in Marcello Palonio's poem, where it had two heads ("gemino capite"). When he translated part of the *Historiae* of Gi-

[38] Pierre Sardella, *Nouvelles et spéculations à Venise au début du XVIe siècle* (Paris: Armand Colin, [1948]), esp. pp. 56–57.

[39] Giancarlo Schizzerotto, *Le incisioni quattrocentesche della Classense* (Ravenna: Zaccarini, 1971), pp. 107–8.

[40] Ibid. For biographical information on Rubieri, see pp. 37–69.

[41] See, for example, the well-known Florentine engraving showing twelve women fighting over a pair of trousers, used by Warburg (*La rinascita del paganesimo antico*, pp. 173–75) precisely to illustrate the influence of northern graphics on Italian artistic milieus.

[42] See Gustav Ludwig, "Restello. Spiegel und Toilettenutensilien in Venedig zur Zeit der Renaissance," *Italienischen Forschungen vom Kunsthistorischen Institut in Florenz* 1 (1906): 185–368.

rolamo Rossi in 1826, Jacopo Landoni added a note to a passage in Rossi based on Palonio's poem, offering this explanation:

> Marcello Palonio poetically gave a body and a soul to a marble [statue] in this guise that he had seen fixed to a wall in Ravenna, sculpted in later [Roman] days. Since no written trace of this strange figure in marble had ever existed, that was enough for the fantasy of the people, who loved marvels, to conform to the fantasy of the poet, and, heedless of the signs of antiquity of that marble, to consider the original a copy, and the copy the original.[43]

Attempts at a plausible identification of the late classical marble statue to which Landoni refers have come to naught, but in reality, the solution to the enigma probably lies elsewhere, as we shall see. If there were any truth to it, the notion would be interesting, however, precisely because it would help us to understand the multiple cultural influences—classical forms and medieval symbolic systems, popular prints and learned elaborations—that went into the formation of symbolic figures during that period.

Political Uses of the Monster

Finally, we need to examine the social function and political uses of the monsters. The first broadsheets of which we have a record appear to limit their text to a brief description that usually serves simply as a caption for a preeminent image. The earliest recorded notice, that of the chronicler Sebastiano di Branca Tedallini, contains one detail that deserves to be remarked, however: The deformed creature was born "of a nun and a friar." Moreover, one of his two legs, which in later descriptions was presented as scaly or feathered, like a frog's leg or that of a bird of prey, is called a *zampa di diavolo*, seeming to imply that the corruption of the clergy led ineluctably to demoniacal results. We can perhaps see a trace of this connection between the monster, ecclesiastical corruption, and divine chastisement in an oration given several weeks later (3 May) by Egidio Canisio of Viterbo, general of the Augustinian order, to open the Fifth Lateran Council. After painting a catastrophic picture of the moral decadence of the Church, Canisio exclaims:

> When have there ever appeared so frequently and with such horrible aspect monsters, portents, [and] prodigies, signs of celestial threats and of terror on the earth? When will there ever be a bloodier disaster or battle than that of

[43] Girolamo Rossi, *Ravenna dall'anno 1500 sino all'anno 1513, volgarizzamento dalla latina storia da Jacopo Landoni* (Ravenna: A. Roveri e figli, 1826), p. 112. Landoni was basing his version on the edition with additions published in Venice in 1589.

Brescia or that of Ravenna? . . . This year the earth has been drenched with more blood than rain.[44]

Among the monsters to which Canisio refers, the one born in Ravenna, the city of divine castigation, was certainly the most recent and perhaps to his eyes the most indicative. The connection between the monster and the immorality of the clergy is quite explicit in the brief French work mentioned earlier, the *Avertissemens es trois estatz du monde*, which accompanies its analysis of the various parts of the deformed creature's body with repeated and insistent references to the greed, immorality, and abuses of the clergy, citing the widely known proverb: "Rome is the glory of cardinals and the paradise of whores."[45]

It is interesting that the detail of the nun and friar as parents soon disappears, at least in the texts that we know. We find it again only in the *Historia* of Bernáldez (who speaks only of a *monja*, however) and, in its full form, in the broadsheet that circulated in Germany and is conserved in Nuremberg. Otherwise, reference to a sacrilegious conception for the creature was not only omitted but in some cases even replaced by counterindications, which leads us to suppose a deliberate attempt to annul the anticlerical note. Thus Landucci says simply, "era nato d'una donna un mostro."[46] Pietro Martire d'Anghiera presents the creature's parentage more specifically, informing his correspondent, Marchese Fajardo, that he had received from Rome ("ab urbe allatam") the picture of a monster born in Ravenna to a married woman ("Ravennae ortum ex coniugata").[47] Here there is little doubt that a specific decision must have been made at the source of the news—Rome—to eliminate a clearly anticlerical element from the general picture.

On the whole, then, the moral and religious analysis of the monster sketched out in pamphlets and broadsheets had an anti-Roman cast to it, confutation of which went through the same channels. We also find traces of a more strictly political analysis, however. Almost as soon as news of the

[44] *Oratio Prima Synodi Lateranensis habita per Egidium Viterbiensem Augustiniani Ordinis Generalem* (n.p., n.d. [Rome: Johannes Beplin, 1512]), unnumbered fols 9*v*–10*r*. There is a recent critical edition in Clare O'Reilly, " 'Without Councils we cannot be saved . . .' Giles of Viterbo addresses the Fifth Lateran Council," *Augustiniana* 27 (1977): 166–204; passage cited, pp. 202–3.

[45] "Lon dit par ung proverbe commun a Rome de Rome, que cest la gloire des cardinaulx et le paradis des putains": *Les Avertissemens es trois estatz du monde*, fol. D i*v*. There is a more ample version of the same proverb reported in Francisco Delicado, *Retrato de la loçana andaluza* (1524): "So it is said: Observe Rome, the glory of men of power, a paradise for whores, a purgatory for the young, a fraud for the poor, a drudgery for the beast of burden, a market-place for swindlers and a hell for all": *Portrait of Lozana: The Lusty Andalusian Woman*, tr. Bruno M. Damiani (Potomac Md.: Scripta Humanistica, 1987), p. 63.

[46] Landucci, *Diario fiorentino*, p. 314.

[47] *Opus epistolarum Petri Martyris Anglerii*, p. 256.

monstrous birth reached Rome, Giovan Francesco Vitale of Palermo, a Latin poet connected with the papal court, produced an interpretation of it in Latin verse. The brief work (mentioned earlier) must have been composed rapidly, because in the two printed editions extant it is preceded by a letter from Carlo Pontelli dated 16 March 1512 addressed to Vitale and praising him for the "attentive scrutiny the poet has given to that most deformed monster." Under its burden of incongruous mythological erudition, Vitale's verse offers some interesting insights that appear to be closely related to the contingent political situation, in particular, the crisis opposing Louis XII and Julius II. Lands where the French set their feet, the poet says, bear monsters:

> Gallica monstriferis ornataque terra figuris;
> . . .
> heu pia relligio, monstrum te cernimus atrum!
> nam solum corpus bina cervice retectum
> dicitur.

The French, that is, had reduced the Church itself to a horrible monster, a body with two heads. The lines allude to the pro-French cardinals who had met in schismatic council in Pisa and were at that moment meeting in Milan. But Jove, Vitale continues, will strike the Giants (the French) with his lightning bolts as they attempt to scale Olympus (that is, to defeat the papacy with military and spiritual arms). Why these hopes were well founded becomes clear in the final tercet: Amid fertile fields, shady groves, and fruit orchards lay the city of Ravenna, "sub ingentis pedibus ditissima Iuli"—wondrously wealthy so long as it was under the feet of the great Julius. But in that land, on which the French now marched, a monster had been born:

> Haec pius Omnipotens misit portenta petenti.
> Non te, Roma, suis vexant pia sidera monstris,
> nec vereare: petunt non tua funera Parcae.

To paraphrase: The Omnipotent sends such prodigies to those who invite them. It is not you, Rome, whom the pious stars torment with their monsters; nor should you fear that it is your end that the Fates are seeking. May the stars be favorable to the court of Rome, Vitale goes on to say, and may they proclaim the excellence of the divine Julius even to the new Thule (the Americas).[48]

Thus the monster was useful in encouraging and supporting the policy of Rome against the French and their allies at a moment of serious division in the Roman See in the early months of 1512. Giano Vitale's short poem

[48] Vitalis, *De monstro nato*, fols. 1*v*, 2*r*, 4*r*.

enjoyed a limited circulation and he was sufficiently well known that some of his works fell into the hands of Erasmus.[49] He had important connections in Rome, including the Latin poets attached to the academy of Giovanni Goritz (of which Vitale does not seem to have been a member, although he contributed to their collection *Coryciana*), Giovanni Pierio Valeriano, and above all Egidio da Viterbo, who, as we have seen, was much interested in the *monstra* and their interpretation, took part in the assemblies at the houses of Goritz and Angelo Colocci, and received Vitale as a house guest in 1521.[50] *De monstro nato* had at least two editions, one without indication of place or date, but probably printed in Italy soon after the event, the other printed in Erfurt in July 1512.

The haste with which the brief work was composed and perhaps printed makes it likely that *De monstro nato* was the piece referred to as the *monstro* that ambassador Francesco Foscari sent to Sanudo from Rome. The timing is tight, but in substance the dates mesh (the dedication is dated 16 March). It also seems probable that Vitale's poem was the pamphlet *cum interpretatione carmine expressa* received by Lycosthenes, as we can see by comparing the pictures. Finally, it is possible that Vitale's poem and not a marble statue from Ravenna was the source of Marcello Palonio's verse. Vitale and Palonio frequented the same circles, and ten years later they both contributed to a collection of *Lachrime in M. Antonium Columnam*, for which Palonio wrote a dedicatory letter and Giano Vitale some verse.[51] It would not be surprising that one knew the other's work. This hypothesis would permit us to explain the strange detail of the "gemino capite" attrib-

[49] Fritz Husner, "Die Bibliotek des Erasmus," in *Gedenkschrift zum 400. Todestage des Erasmus von Rotterdam* (Basel: Braus-Riggenback, 1936), p. 239, n. 95. At the death of Erasmus, Vitale composed a somewhat pungent epitaph for him: "Lubrica si tibi mens fuit, et spinosior aequo, / ingenium certe nobile Erasme fuit." See Silvana Seidel Menchi, "Alcuni atteggiamenti della cultura italiana di fronte ad Erasmo (1520–1536)," in *Eresia e Riforma nell'Italia del Cinquecento: Miscellanea I* (Florence: G. C. Sansoni; Chicago: The Newberry Library, 1974), pp. 67–128; p. 109.

[50] Vitale's connections with the Latin poets attached to Goritz and Colocci are demonstrated by his participation in several collective enterprises of this group, such as the collections *In Celsi Archelai Mellini funere amicorum lacrimae* (Rome, 1519), *Lachrime in M. Antonium Columnam* (Rome, 1522), and *Coryciana* (Rome, 1524). Verse of Giovanni Pierio Valeriano, Giovan Battista Sanga, Francesco Maria Grapaldo, and others in praise of Vitale can be found in Iani Vitalis Panormitani, *Teratorizion* (Rome: Mazzocchi, 1514). That Vitale did not take part in the meetings at the homes of Goritz and Colocci is clear from lists of the participants, which do, however, include the name of Egidio da Viterbo. See Federigo Ubaldini, *Vita di Mons. Angelo Colocci. Edizione del testo originale italiano (Barb. Lat. 4882)*, ed. Vittorio Fanelli (Vatican City: Biblioteca apostolica vaticana, 1969), pp. 111, 114–15. On Vitale's visit with Egidio da Viterbo, see Tumminello, "Giano Vitale," p. 43.

[51] See Carlo Dionisotti, "Appunti su Leone Ebreo," *Italia medioevale e umanistica* 2 (1959): 409–28; esp. 425–26; information on Marcello Palonio, p. 426. See also Domenico Gnoli, *La Roma di Leon X* (Milan: Ulrico Hoepli, 1938), pp. 180–84, 300–304. Palonio was still alive in 1541: *Trattato dell'entrar in Milano di Carlo V* (Milan: Andrea Calvo, 1541), fol. 2*r*.

uted to the monster in the lateral gloss to Palonio's verse, since the two heads could result from a hasty reading of the Vitale passage already cited: ". . . monstrum . . . cernimus atrum! / nam solum corpus bina cervice retectum / dicitur."

As we have seen, though, Vitale is referring here not to the monster of Ravenna but to the two Councils of 1511–1512, the schismatic council convoked in Pisa and the Lateran Council in Rome. It is an interesting example of how an error can slip into literary and figurative descriptions.

After the battle of 11 April and the sack of Ravenna that occurred immediately after, a propapal, anti-French interpretation of the monster made little sense, so it acquired the more generic significance of a forewarning of great ills about to fall upon Ravenna and Italy. Egidio da Viterbo's homily is exemplary in this sense, as is Landucci's comment on hearing news of the sack, which seems to express a commonly shared thought, almost an accepted aphorism:

> It was evident what evil the monster had meant for them! It seems as if some great misfortune always befalls the city where such things are born; the same thing happened at Volterra, which was sacked a short time after a similar monster had been born there.[52]

Landucci proposes here the globally prophetic and catastrophic interpretation of the *monstra* discussed above and that he himself had offered twenty-five years earlier when he copied the letter from Venice at Tanai de' Nerli's bank. The German broadsheet follows the same tendency, but extends the threat of divine punishment to all Italy: "Alia denique per Italiam mala plurima et multifaria portenduntur." It is clear from the fact that this sheet addressed a quite different social and cultural public that this type of letter had an extremely broad audience: The text is given in both Latin and German, and the space devoted to the illustration made it at least partly available to the illiterate.[53]

Finally, we need to keep in mind the interpretation of Johannes Multivallis in his continuation of the *Chronicon* of Eusebius of Caesarea to 13 June 1512. In the final page of this work, Multivallis speaks of the Italian

[52] Landucci, *A Florentine Diary*, tr. Jervis, p. 250.

[53] For problems connected with the multiple possible uses of broadsheets, see Ecker, *Einblattdrücke*; Roger Chartier, "L'ancien régime typographique: réflexions sur quelques travaux récents," *Annales E.S.C.* 36 (1981): 191–209, esp. p. 206; Hans-Joachim Köhler, ed., *Flugschriften als Massenmedium der Reformationzeit, Beiträge zum Tübinger Symposium* (Stuttgart: Klett-Cotta, 1981). Köhler has taken up the question of broadsheets elsewhere: "Die Flugschriften. Versuch der Präzisierung eines geläufigen Begriff," in Hansgeorg Molitor and Hans-Christoph Rublack, eds., *Festgabe Ernst Walter Zeeden zum 60. Geburtstag am 14 Mai 1976* (Münster in Westfalen: Aschendorff, 1976), pp. 36–61; "The Flugschriften and their Importance in Religious Debate: A Quantitative Approach," in Zambelli, ed., "*Astrologi hallucinati*," pp. 153–75.

wars. He notes Julius II's preparations for war, describes the sack of Brescia and the taking of Ravenna, and concludes, precisely, with a description of the monster, which in the treatise thus becomes a worthy seal put by God to the history that humankind constructs with its own hands and by its evil deeds. The passage runs thus:

> Ravannae paulo ante natum fuerat monstrum cornu in capite; allas habebat; brachia nulla; pedem unum ut avis rapax; occulum in genu; sexum utrumque; in medio pectore ypsilon et crucis effigiem. Aliqui interpretati sunt: cornu superbiam; allas brevitatem mentis et incostantiam; carentiam brachiorum defectum bonorum operum; pedem rapacem rapinam, usuram et omnimodam avaritiam; oculum in genu solum ad res terrenas mentis deflectionem; utrunque sexum sodomiam. Et propter haec vicia Italiam sic bellicis contritionibus quati; regem autem Franciae non sua virtute id facere, sed solum esse Dei flagellum. Ypsilon vero et + signa esse salutis; nam ypsilon figura est virtutis. Ideo, si ad virtutem recurrant ed ad Christi crucem, ab his pressuris et tribulationibus conveniat respirationem et pacem, conquassationibus desiderabiliorem, quam dare dignetur Christus in omnia saecula benedictus. Amen.[54]

It is difficult to say who are the "aliqui" whose interpretations Multivallis reports here—perhaps a pamphlet or a broadsheet that has not survived. The analysis somewhat resembles that of the *Avertissemens es trois estatz du monde* of Inoy, which appeared the following year, however, and presents several differences of detail. It also recalls the prints of Frau Welt, and in that connection I might add that this text signals the beginning of the model of the monster with a single leg of a bird of prey, which became prevalent in teratological treatises of the latter sixteenth century (Figure 8). One might hypothesize that Multivallis's source made available a print of the Frau Welt sort and made use of it for its interpretation of the monster. What is more interesting to note is the national coloration of the text, which contrasts the Italians, whose sins have brought on the destruction of Brescia and Ravenna, and the king of France, who carried out that destruction not as a political decision but acting as a simple instrument of divine wrath: "regem autem Franciae non sua virtute id facere, sed solum esse Dei flagellum."

The Monster of Bologna: A Different Political Science

The monster and its various body parts thus served as a flexible instrument for a political and religious reading of the War of the Holy League, just as the verse prophecies and interpretation of mosaics had done at the time of

[54] Eusebii Caesariensis, *Chronicon*, fols. 175*r*–*v*.

Fig. 8. The Monster of Ravenna. From Pierre Boaistuau, *Histoires prodigieuses* (Paris, 1560).

Charles VIII's invasion of Italy and the War of Cambrai. Another sort of analysis arose, however, that lent itself particularly well to criticism of ecclesiastical life-styles. Both interpretive formulas seem to have been applied to another deformed infant born near Bologna in January 1514. This time—and the case is exceptional—it was not a semifantastic being but a real human child for whom it is impossible not to feel sympathy. She was the daughter of a man named Domenico Malatendi, who raised vegetables in Marano, not far from the gates of Bologna.[55] The child had two faces

[55] The case is reported in Giovan Francesco Negri, *Annali della patria*, VII, fol. 145*r* (Biblioteca Universitaria di Bologna, hereafter cited as BUB, MS 1107); *Cronica di Friano degli Ubaldini*, fol. 32*v* (BUB, MS 430); *Cronaca della città di Bologna di Nicolò Seccadinari* [Fileno delle Tuate], III, unnumbered (BUB, MS 437); *Cronica Bianchetti*, II, p. 366 (Biblioteca dell'Archiginnasio di Bologna, MS Malvezzi 60).

("as Prudence is figured," one chronicler notes), two mouths, three eyes, and no nose. On the top of her head she had an excrescence defined as "like a red cockscomb" or "a vulva."[56] She was brought to Bologna to be baptized in the cathedral of San Pietro on Sunday, 9 January, probably the day she was born. The bishop himself, Cardinal Achille Grassi, administered the sacrament of baptism, showing by this act the significance he attributed to the person of the infant, whom he named Maria.[57] Maria lived only four days, but her brief life caused a considerable stir, though nothing approaching that caused by the other monstrous creatures. This was particularly because it coincided with other prodigious events: a terrible fire that gutted the quarter of the Rialto in Venice on the night of 10 January and three suns, three moons, and a mysterious light seen in the sky at various times on 11 January.[58] These were "things that gave material to ingenious minds curious to prognosticate."[59] Indeed, as Leonello Beliardi of Modena said concerning the birth of little Maria, "the Bolognese astrologers made a prognostication about this, which was a sign of great pestilence and war."[60] That publication, *Pronostico de Thomaso Philologo Gianotho da Ravenna sopra la significatione del Monstro nato a Bologna: e nel Iudicio suo del presente anno da lui pronosticato*, was a broadsheet printed in Gothic letters in two versions, vernacular and Latin (the version examined here).[61] Tommaso Giannotti, the author, was a figure we shall encounter again. In later years he attempted to increase his repute by adding to his name that of his patron, Guido Rangoni, commander of the pontifical states' military installation in Modena (or, more accurately, by replacing his own name with Rangoni's). Early in 1514, Giannotti seems to have taken steps toward obtaining the patronage of Cardinal Achille Grassi, to whom his prediction is dedicated. It is dated from Bologna, 15 January 1514, and in its Latin version speaks of "strages malignas . . . gravissimam pestem . . . lue . . . terremotus . . . bella," basing these predictions less on the body of the de-

[56] Negri, *Annali*; Leonello Beliardi, *Cronaca della città di Modena (1512–1518)*, ed. Albano Biondi and Michele Oppi (Modena: Panini, 1981), p. 92; Sanuto, *Diarii*, vol. 17, col. 515.

[57] Negri, *Annali*; *Cronaca della città di Bologna*; *Cronica Bianchetti*.

[58] See Sanuto, *Diarii*, vol. 17, cols. 458–61, 506, 530. The connection between Maria's birth and these signs appears also in Negri, *Annali*.

[59] Negri, *Annali*.

[60] Beliardi, *Cronaca della città di Modena*, p. 92.

[61] There is mention of the vernacular edition in Alberto Serra-Zanetti, *L'arte della stampa in Bologna nel primo ventennio del Cinquecento* (Biblioteca de "l'Archiginnasio," n.s. 1; Bologna: Archiginnasio, 1959), pp. 258–59, who cites the *Catalogue de la Bibliothèque de feu le Duc Mario Massimo de Rignano* (Rome, 1909), p. 13, n. 55, and in Carlo Piancastelli, *Pronostici ed Almanacchi. Studio di bibliografia romagnola* (Rome: D. Ripamonti, 1913), pp. 27–28. The Latin edition, which was also printed in Gothic type, is not otherwise noted. Sig. Luciano Borrelli of Trent owns a copy, and I wish to thank him warmly for informing me of it and allowing me to examine it.

formed child than on a conjunction of Saturn and Jupiter that had occurred the previous 29 December, of which Maria was merely the first horrible result. It is interesting to note, in fact, that Beliardi's chronicle fails to place the abnormal birth within the schemes of astrological science. The same sort of hasty interpretation (that is, one that simply establishes a relationship between the monster and the catastrophe, eliminating reference to the conjunction of planets) can probably be seen in the letter of Francesco Bonafede mentioned above, who only a few weeks later deplored that recent "monstrous" births had been misused to predict "tumulti di guerre, occisioni, stragie."[62] As an astrologer, Giannotti had attempted to rely more on the stars than on the monsters, but for much of the public the operation failed, and the tradition of interpretation of *orribeli segnali* had the better of the science of major planetary conjunctions.

The broadsheet concludes with a warm invitation to the pope and the emperor to renew their vigilance against the threat of the Turks and foreigners, "ne Italia reliqueve Christianorum urbes dilapidentur," and with an odd puzzle in Latin verse:

> Fixa manet summo si nunc clementia celo,
> *u* vertant in *o*, *p* ac gemino vel *a* sidera iungant,
> ut sacro una horum is fungi diademate possit:
> aurea tunc aetas; in pace et cuncta regentur.

In that the text speaks, among other things, of *lue*, it is not too farfetched to suppose that the solution to this *Tetrasticon sub enigmate* is *Leo papa*, the pope under whom the star-studded tiara was to ensure the world a new Golden Age. Giannotti's vocation for flattery was to continue to flourish in the years to come, and, as is evident, seems already more than mature here. The myth of a Golden Age under a Medici pope had gained one more proselyte.

A letter on the matter sent from Rome on 25 January to the pontifical ambassador in Venice, Pietro Dovizi of Bibbiena,[63] offers more details. It analyzes little Maria's body in symbolic and political terms, even proposing a specifically political model that differed markedly from the others (which, I might add, enjoyed greater fame and fortune). The writer, whose name is not given in the copy extant, states, "You have seen the figure of the monster of Bologna, with two faces and three eyes, and on its head a woman's open vulva." This means that prints or drawings were in circulation (Giannotti's prognostication was not illustrated). After noting that the news had reached Rome through the governor of Bologna (presumably,

[62] Sanuto, *Diarii*, vol. 18, col. 34.
[63] Ibid., vol. 17, cols. 515–16.

Lorenzo Fieschi),[64] the writer continues, "of which portent, along with the fire that followed in Venice, one could give a wondrous and profound interpretation, two parts of which I will leave out quia non omnia sunt litteris committenda." There follows a brief summary of the two parts left out. The first was

> that of the little church untouched in the middle of much fire, in its ancient foundation and its primitive state; the second part I shall say nothing about, but I think that I apply well that double forehead with three eyes, why two of them are entirely closed, and [why] one cannot discern of the third, which is in the middle, how much sight it has or what it sees, even though it is open.

The second part of this is obscure, only hinting at ambiguity and blindness, but the meaning of the first part is singularly clear and relevant. The little church of San Giacometto in Rialto, which Marin Sanudo tells us, following a widespread tradition,[65] was the first church built in Venice, serves as the symbol and the silent, physical embodiment of the myth of the primitive church.

But "non omnia sunt litteris committenda," and our anonymous Roman prefers not to expatiate on this point. Instead, he continues with a full interpretation of the body of the Bologna monster that merits quotation in full for its stylistic intensity and the interest of its contents:

> I turn to the third figure of the vulva with tears in my eyes: I saw that Italy has become this monster with closed eyes and two faces looking in two different directions because of its divisions; one part looking west to follow its affections and its own convenience; the other [looking] north according to its passions; and thus divided and blinded, O miserable wretch! it has become a monster. The open vulva on its head is that land and province that has so long conserved and defended the beauty, the virginity, and the modesty of calamity-stricken Italy; now, so prostrated and lying with open vulva that many outsiders, whom we have seen before us, have come to luxuriate and run wild. Even in this hour it invites still others even more foreign to us. And note well, that this monster born in the Bolognese has two faces, and by its two mouths—as the governor of that city writes—it takes milk and nourishment, which descends through the same channel to the stomach, because the two faces respond to only one neck, and the rest of the body is made as a female, like poor Italy, of which every man takes his pleasure as of a female and a prostitute. With all my heart I pray to almighty God, and I invite all religious persons and

[64] See Maria Ferretti, "Legati, vicelegati e governatori di Bologna nel sec. XVI," tesi di laurea discussa presso l'Università di Bologna a. a. 1967–1968, relatore Paolo Prodi, pp. 103–105.

[65] Ferdinando Forlati, *La basilica di San Marco attraverso i suoi restauri* (Trieste: Lint, 1975), pp. 53 and 69, n. 13.

true Christians in Italy to pray that he turn the eyes of his mercy upon us, quod solus habet spiritus et ministros et ignem urentem; ipse enim est Dominus exercituum, qui facit mirabilia magna solus; et non respiciat pecata nostra sed fidem et misterium Ecclasiae suae. I am certain that these modern sages with their tricks and their con games who advise princes, non timentes Deum, sed in sua versutia confisi, would laugh at my discourse. And I laugh at theirs, knowing that I communicate and write to a man Catholic and well-mannered, grave, experienced, old, and prudent, and removed from all passion and avarice, as I find myself to be, by divina gratia. Romae 25 Januari 1514.[66]

In explaining this letter we need to keep in mind the political situation in Italy during the winter of 1513–1514. The letter was sent, as we have seen, to the pontifical ambassador, Pietro Dovizi, called Il Bibbiena from his birthplace, as was his better-known younger brother Bernardo. Pietro had received his charge from the new pope, Leo X, on 21 March 1513.[67] The two Bibbienas were close to Leo and the Medici family, but Pietro had for many years lived in Venice, where he had taken a wife and had many close friends (Sanudo calls him "very much my friend").[68] Thus he had particularly high qualifications for his office. In reality, it gave him nothing but trouble, of which, according to his friend Sanudo, he died on 8 February, only a few days after receiving the letter in question.[69] In point of fact, the pope, after an initial show of friendship to the Venetians, had become more ambiguous and hesitant in his attitude toward them. In particular, after the Venetians had been roundly defeated by the Spanish army under Raymond de Cardona near Creazzo, in the territory of Vicenza, Leo X leaned toward the imperial side, partly because of the influence of Cardinal Matthäus Lang, the bishop of Gurk, and encouraged the Venetians to break their alliance with France and move in the direction of an alliance with the emperor.[70] This strategy was by no means clearly defined, however, and in January 1514 the pope spoke with the Venetian ambassador, Pietro Lando, and showed every sign of being open to an agreement with Venice and with France.[71] This situation continued for some time (as much as a year later Niccolò Machiavelli was called upon to give his opinion on

[66] Sanuto, *Diarii*, vol. 17, cols. 515–16.

[67] Ibid., vol. 16, col. 54.

[68] Ibid., vol. 17, col. 533. Information on Bibbiena's stay in Venice can also be found in col. 542.

[69] Sanuto, *Diarii*, vol. 17, cols. 533 and 542.

[70] Vittorio Cian, "A proposito di un'ambascieria di M. Pietro Bembo (dicembre 1514)," *Archivio Veneto* 30 (1885): 355–407, and 31 (1886): 71–128; Franco Gaeta, "Il Bibbiena diplomatico," *Rinascimento* 9 (1969): 69–94. See also Sanuto, *Diarii*, vol. 17, cols. 341–42, 364, 372, and so forth.

[71] Sanuto, *Diarii*, vol. 17, col. 511.

the pope's dilemma),[72] and it prompted discontent even in Roman circles. At the end of November 1513, Marin Sanudo noted that "Romans are complaining that the pope gives his men to Germans and Spaniards, saying that if this were not so, the Spanish would be torn to pieces by our men, and Italy freed from the hands of barbarians."[73]

The letter on the Bologna monster may easily have come from the same Roman circles. The writer identified the monstrous body of Maria Malatendi as Italy, an Italy blinded and divided, turning alternately to the west and the north, toward France or the Holy Roman Empire. Her chief deformity was on her head, where an "open vulva" stood for "quella patria et provintia" that in the past had protected and defended the integrity of Italian soil but that now, prostrate and open to every sort of violence, left free passage to so many foreigners and indeed called others to come from even more distant places. As we now know, the allusion to the monster's two faces referred to the two possible choices in international policy facing the pope (which was the bone of contention between Venice and Rome), while the second part clearly referred to Venice itself. Venice was traditionally considered the "outer bulwark of Italy," but now its territories had been devastated by Spanish and imperial troops and, above all, alarming rumors were circulating that Venice was thinking of calling the Turks into Italy for their aid and support. These rumors, which circulated above all in Rome toward the end of December 1513, were far from unfounded. Early in February 1514 an ambassador from Selim, the Ottoman ruler, came to Venice and was received with the greatest honors. On that occasion a peace treaty between Venice and the Ottoman Turks signed 17 October was made public and several Venetian noblemen of ancient family—a Grimani, a Tron, an Emo—went so far as to state "that there is no other redemption for our affairs than leaguing ourselves with Turks and bringing them into Italy."[74]

[72] Niccolò Machiavelli to Francesco Vettori, Florence, 10 December 1514, in Machiavelli, *Lettere*, ed. Franco Gaeta (Milan: Feltrinelli, 1961), pp. 351–61.

[73] Sanuto, *Diarii*, vol. 17, col. 342.

[74] Ibid., cols. 423–24, 426, 529, 535, 539–40. The mixed expectation and fear deriving from a Venetian appeal to the Turks was already widespread immediately after the battle of Agnadello, as is clear from a verse lament of that period: "Si non vedo pace o tregua / chiamarò in mare in terra / il gran Turcho con sua guerra / como gente disperata" (If I see no peace or truce, I will call, on sea and on land, the Great Turk with his army, as desperate men): [Simone Litta], *Lamento de venetiani novamente composto. Per domino Simeone el quale se contene el paexe che ano perse in Italia he fora de Italia* (Mondovi: Berruero, n. d. [1509]), fol. 4*v*. The same possibility is also clear from an oration of Egidio da Viterbo delivered in the presence of the doge in the Collegio dei Savi on 9 June 1519, referred to by Marin Sanudo thus: "All Christendom was sworn to our ruin . . . in these persecutions [Venice] never agreed to call for aid from infidels, but strove to persevere in the faith of Christ; nevertheless, many expected [that] in order not to perish this state must demand help from those enemies of the

The alarm prompted by a notion of the sort is easy to imagine. The letter cited above is imbued with it, and with a sense of malaise over the slow and painful contacts between Rome and Venice. Who might have written it? Bibbiena clearly was acting with discretion in giving Sanudo a copy lacking the salutation, final greeting, and signature. Although we cannot identify the writer by name, we can nonetheless reconstruct a fairly clear portrait of him. He must have been a person Bibbiena knew directly, as indicated by the last lines of the letter, which presuppose personal acquaintance; he must have been connected with the papal court and with Medici circles, as Bibbiena was; he shows full awareness of the latest political maneuvers, but he was also interested in ecclesiastical reform (as we can gather from his mention of the primitive church). He was, in short, a person of a certain stature.[75]

After displaying his own erudition and invoking divine aid, the writer sets up his ideal opponents; they are "questi savieti moderni, with their tricks and their con games who advise princes, non timentes Deum, sed in sua versutia confisi." This reference can (and perhaps should) be understood in a generic sense. The "savieti" then would be all those involved in politics who rely on their skill alone and pay little attention to the signs that the hand of God places in history to admonish humankind. It is tempting, though, to give a name to at least one of these "savieti," who only recently had finished a work in which, precisely, he proposed to advise princes—or rather, *a* prince—with his "versuzie" (wiles, cunning tricks) while bitterly lamenting the fate of poor Italy, "beaten, despoiled, torn apart, overrun." Is it possible, though, that our anonymous Roman could have had a copy of Machiavelli's *Prince* in his hands and that his quarrel was with that work? Certainly, in the preceding weeks, the treatise had been sent by Machiavelli to Rome, where, as is known, Francesco Vettori had read it, although perhaps not from start to finish.[76] We also know that a few months later Vettori showed to the pope, to Cardinal de' Medici (the future Clement VII), and to Cardinal Bibbiena (the younger brother of

---

Christian faith, which thing God had frowned on" (Sanuto, *Diarii*, vol. 27, col. 367). See also Paolo Preto, *Venezia e i Turchi* (Florence: G. C. Sansoni, 1975), pp. 37–38.

[75] It could not have been Vincenzo Quirini, who otherwise would fulfill all the requirements, because his vernacular letters never show the continual Latin inserts present in this text. Furthermore, it is not certain that Quirini had yet returned to Rome in January 1514, although he was surely there in April of that year. On this period of his life, see Cian, "A proposito di un'ambascieria," and Hubert Jedin, "Vincenzo Quirini und Pietro Bembo," in *Miscellanea Giovanni Mercati*, 6 vols. (Vatican City: Biblioteca Apostolica Vaticana, 1946; 2nd ed., 1973), vol. 4, pp. 407–424 (Jedin, *Kirche des Glaubens, Kirche der Gesehichte: aus gewählte Aufsätze und Vorträge* [Frieberg: Herder, 1966]), also available in Italian translation as *Chiesa della fede, Chiesa della storia* (Brescia: Morcelliana, 1972).

[76] Francesco Vettori to Niccolò Machiavelli, Rome, 18 January 1514, in Machiavelli, *Lettere*, p. 319.

Pietro, who had died by that time) two letters of Machiavelli in which he gave his opinion on pontifical policies, in substance blaming the pope for his indecision.[77] It is not inconceivable that Vettori had shown *The Prince* (which was to be dedicated to the pope's brother), in whole or in part, to some Medici functionaries in Rome, among them the anonymous personage who then wrote to Pietro Bibbiena.

The Roman Career of the *monstra* and the Reasons Thereof

In brief, the prophetic language of signs and, especially, of those signs such as monsters that permitted a more fully developed interpretation could be used not only to express a generic concern for a traumatic situation—as we have seen, in particular, for prophecies connected with the invasion of Charles VIII and the widespread destruction caused by the War of Cambrai—but also, especially on a higher social and cultural level, to formulate a quite specific political analysis or to organize a line of propaganda. The phenomenon of the *monstra* had pan-European dimensions, at least in an area embracing France, Germany, Spain, and central and northern Italy, and it was publicized through an unusually varied set of channels ranging from personal letters to prints and multicopy drawings. The success of these print pieces was also based on the variety of readings that it was possible to give them and on their position at the point of contact between different levels of culture. They thus became a significant element in political debate and in the formation of public opinion, particularly in periods of crisis, and their use was quite consciously contrasted (as we have seen in the anonymous letter from Rome) with other modes of furthering political ends. They had particular success in Rome, and it was in fact in Rome that the "political" description of monsters seems to have evoked the most lively interest, as we have seen for the monster of Ravenna, that of Bologna, and the one born in Rome itself early in March 1513, "sung of" by Giovan Battista Ruberti.[78] It was to Rome that news of misbirths was sent in official communications through the governors of the cities in which the monstrous creatures were born. I might add that teratological subjects had a ready success among Latin poets in Roman circles,[79] a success also to be

[77] Niccolò Machiavelli to Francesco Vettori, Florence, 10 December 1514, in *Lettere*, pp. 351–61; Machiavelli to Vettori, Florence, 20 December 1514, pp. 363–67; Francesco Vettori to Niccolò Machiavelli, Rome, 30 December 1514, p. 369.

[78] See Ruberti, *Monstrum apud Urbem natum*, and Holländer, *Wunder, Wundergeburt und Wundergestalt*, p. 312.

[79] See the works already cited plus Vitalis, *Teratorizion*. The same characteristics of court poetry and antiquarianism (well described in Rotondò, "Pellegrino Prisciani," p. 106) are found in a work that appeared in a quite different context: *Ad illustrissimum ac Excellentissi-*

attributed to the profound influence of the memory of classical divination in such circles. The success and the use of courtly and antiquarian poetry are, in the last analysis, political, but they also arose out of a new interest in the monsters as signs that was present among all levels of the urban population.

Not only the deformed creatures but also other prodigious events (which, as prodigious events, were signs of God's will or divine warnings) elaborated and first circulated in the domain of folklore would be used for precise political purposes by the court of Leo X in the years immediately following. This is what we shall examine next.

---

mum Principem Divum Herculem Estensem Francisci Rococioli Mutinensis Libellus de Monstro in Tyberi reperto anno D.ni MCCCCLXXXXVI (n.p., n.d. [Modena: Domenico Rocociolo]), 4 fols. I refer to the copy in the Biblioteca Estense, Modena.

3

APPARITIONS AS SIGNS: THE KINGS OF THE DEAD ON THE BATTLEGROUND OF AGNADELLO

Ghostly Combatants in the Bergamo Countryside

A PRINTED pamphlet circulated in Cesena in January 1518, the chronicler Giuliano Fantaguzzi tells us, that told "about the visions and combats of spirits taking place in the Bergamasco."[1] About the same time, word that near Bergamo "were seen visions and prodigies of great quantities of armed men on foot and on horseback [fighting] against one another" was reported in the journal of an anonymous French cleric who had long lived in Rome,[2] Marin Sanudo gathered a number of letters concerning the incident, and it was even noted in the *Journal d'un Bourgeois de Paris*. The printed pamphlets mentioned by the Cesena chronicler circulated in Italy in at least two different versions, and they were also translated into French and German. One version from Rome reached Valladolid, where a copy came into the hands of Pietro Martire d'Anghiera, who mentions it in a letter dated 23 February 1518.[3]

Obviously, the incident had repercussions far and wide. On 12 January, Gian Giacomo Caroldo, secretary to the doge of Venice attached to Viscount de Lautrec, governor of Milan, gave a disparaging explanation of it, however. Caroldo wrote to his brother: "There is no truth to what has appeared in the Bergamasco. Some simple people saw the fumes above

[1] *Occhurrentie et nove notate per me Juliano Fantaguzzo Cesenate*, in Claudio Riva, "La vita in Cesena agli inizi del '500. Dal 'Caos' di Giuliano Fantaguzzi," tesi di laurea discussa presso l'università di Bologna, a.a. 1969/70, relatore Paolo Prodi, which transcribes parts of Fantaguzzi's chronicle not included in the earlier edition edited by Dino Bazzocchi: *Caos. Cronache cesanati del sec. XV* (Cesena: Tip. Arturo Bettini, 1915), pp. 158–59.

[2] Biblioteca Apostolica Vaticana, MS Barb. Lat. 3552, fol. 32*v*. See Louis Madelin, "Le Journal d'un habitant français de Rome au XVIe siècle (1509–1540). (Etude sur le Manuscrit XLIII–98 de la Bibliothèque Barberini)," *Mélanges d'archéologie et d'histoire. Ecole française de Rome* 22 (1902): 251–300.

[3] *Opus epistolarum Petri Martyris Anglerii* (Amsterdam: typis Elzevirianis, 1670), p. 337. Anghiera connected the apparitions at Verdello with the Ravenna monster: "De ravennate monstro ex Urbe ad nos misso, priusquam Gallorum saevitiae Ravenna succumberet, vidistis suo tempore. Nunc accipite quae nuper prelis formata chalcographorum et sparsa per universum emerserunt. . . . Est in bergomensi agro in Insubria, quae vulgo Lombardia dicitur, nobile vicina sylva oppidulum, nomine Verdelum. . . ."

some manure piles, and in their great fearfulness they thought they were armed men. . . . So you should not lend credence to such things."[4] Nonetheless, this does not explain why some "simplice persone" should have seen hosts of specters fighting in the vapors released in the winter from dung heaps. We also need to place this incident within the broader question of how traditions circulated through nonhomogeneous cultural strata, how they were transformed by such shifts, and by what means (means that often were related to their function within a specific social context) they were transmitted. In this instance, we shall see that an item of ascertainable folk origin was connected, on a second level, to a prophetic system of signs, only to be picked up again on a different and higher cultural and social level and ultimately used for political purposes by Pope Leo X himself.

Supernatural Visions and Visions of Battles

Portentous visions were not unheard of in the early years of the modern era.[5] They were singular experiences, but not totally out of the ordinary scheme of things. We have already seen examples from the times of the War of Cambrai. In general, they represented one aspect of the complex set of manifestations and warnings of the divine presence discussed earlier. Supernatural apparitions—both religious and nonreligious—are an extremely interesting field of investigation, because visions (and, in many cases, dreams)[6] provide us with an external (hence definable) projection of an inherited set of mental images. By that token, they offer a valuable opportunity for learning about that heritage. Italian chronicles of the early

[4] Marino Sanuto, *Diarii*, 58 vols. (Venice: R. Deputazione Veneta di Storia Patria, 1879–1903), vol. 25, col. 209. On Caroldo, see Antonio Carile, "Caroldo, Gian Giacomo," in DBI, vol. 20, pp. 514–17.

[5] See William A. Christian, Jr., *Apparitions in Late Medieval and Renaissance Spain* (Princeton: Princeton University Press, 1981); Ottavia Niccoli, "Visioni e racconti di visioni nell'Italia del primo Cinquecento," *Società e storia* 28 (1985): 253–79. On apparitions in the Paleo-Christian age and the early Middle Ages, see Johannes Lindblom, *Geschichte und Offenbarungen. Vorstellungen von göttlichen Weisungen und übernatüralichen Erscheinungen in ältesten Christentum* (Lund: Gleerup, 1968); Michel Aubrun, "Caractères et portée religieuse et sociale des 'Visiones' en Occident du VIe au XIe siècle," *Cahiers de civilisation médiévale Xe–XIIe siècles* 23, no. 2 (1980): 109–30; Vito Fumagalli, "Il paesaggio dei morti. Luoghi d'incontro fra i morti e i vivi sulla terra nel medioevo," *Quaderni storici* 59 (1982): 411–25; Paolo Siniscalco, "Pagani e cristiani antichi di fronte all'esperienza di sogni e visioni," in Vittore Branca, Carlo Ossola, and Salomon Resnik, eds., *I linguaggi del sogno* (Florence: Sansoni, 1984), pp. 143–62.

[6] For a historical reading of dreams, see Peter Burke, "L'histoire sociale des rêves," *Annales E.S.C.* 28 (1973): 329–42, and Jacques Le Goff, "Dreams in the Culture and Collective Psychology in the Medieval West," in his *Time, Work and Culture in the Middle Ages*, tr. Arthur Goldhammer (Chicago: University of Chicago Press, 1980), pp. 201–4.

modern period include a wealth of materials of this sort. For instance, only a few months before the apparitions that concern us here, the shipwrecked sailors of the galley *Magna*, which went down off Cyprus, declared, when they arrived in Famagusta after many adventures that "they had seen a number of saints . . . in the sky with lighted candles."[7] The phenomenon did not cease with the spread of the Reformation, nor was it limited exclusively to Catholic confessional circles, as we might suspect from this tale, which calls to mind well-known passages in Erasmus and Rabelais on devotion to the saints on the part of mariners caught in storms. Apparitions and dreams appear often in the pages of Melanchthon,[8] and one need only pick up the *De spectris, lemuribus . . . variisque praesagitationibus* of the Protestant physician Ludwig Lavater, published in Zurich in 1570, to find an impressive and varied picture of supernatural visions. Among the variety of phenomena he discusses, Lavater devotes particular attention to spectral combats, which, he states, are to be understood as bad omens. Such were swords, lances, and a large number of other objects seen in the air; clashing armies or fleeing troops seen or heard in the air or on the ground; the horrible sound of shouting voices and the clangor of clashing arms.[9]

There are vast numbers of examples of the specific typology of visions of clashing armies outside Lavater's pages, beginning with a passage in Pausanias concerning the battlefield of Marathon.[10] A phantom army accompanied Attila to the battle of the Catalaunian Plains, in premonition of his defeat.[11] In the tenth century, when the Persian voyager Ibn Fadlans was making his way from Baghdad to the Volga, he saw on the night of 11 to 12 May 922 two fire-red armies clashing in the air with a muted roar.[12] Analogous examples are plentiful for the late Middle Ages,[13] and in the sixteenth century aerial battles had become so common that on several occasions they were predicted by preachers.[14] In France the topic appears to have been a favorite of the broadsheets on current occurrences known as

[7] Sanuto, *Diarii*, vol. 24, col. 25.

[8] In particular in Philipp Melanchthon, *Historiae quaedam recitatae inter publicas lectiones*, *Corpus Reformatorum* (Brunswick: Schwetschke et filium), vol. 20 (1854), cols. 519–608.

[9] Ludwig Lavater, *De spectris, lemuribus et magnis, atque insolitis fragoribus, variisque praesagitationibus* . . . , 4th ed. (Leiden: J. Luchtmans, 1687), pp. 112–13.

[10] Pausanias, *Descriptio Graeciae* 1.32.4.

[11] Leo Weber, "Die katalaunische Geisterschlact," *Archiv für Religionswissenschaft* 33 (1936): 162–66.

[12] Otto Weinreich, in a note added to Weber, "Die Katalaunische Geisterschlact," p. 166.

[13] There is an ample list in Knut Martin Stjerna, "Mossfunden och Walhallastrom," *Från filologiska föringen i. Lund, Språkliga uppsatser* (1906): 148ff., which I was unable to consult but which is cited in Otto Höfler, *Kultische Geheimbünde der Germanen* (Frankfurt am Main: M. Diesterweg, 1934–), p. 242.

[14] Sanuto, *Diarii*, vol. 10, cols. 48–49; Tommaso di Silvestro, *Diario*, ed. Luigi Fumi, in RIS 15, pt. 5 (Bologna: Nicola Zanichelli, 1923), vol. 2, p. 482. The two mentions refer, respectively, to the years 1510 and 1513.

canards.[15] On 28 January 1664, during an eclipse of the sun observed in the territory around Ljubljana, a Capuchin friar from Friuli, Cristoforo da Cividale, saw in succession in the sun, "with the interval of about one *Miserere*" between them:

> 1. Four men seen in the sun.
> 2. Two men on horseback.
> 3. Four men on horseback.
> 4. A company of cavalry.
> 5. An army of cavalry.
> 6. A church.
> 7. A giant on horseback.
> 8. A squadron of infantry.
> 9. A great body of cavalry.
> 10. A very large army of cavalry . . . and for a good length of time fierce and doleful combats were seen.[16]

These prodigies were signs of wars to come, and the pamphlet narrating them concludes with the hope of "weakening the pride of the haughty Ottoman and giving glorious victory to the Christian armies."

[15] Jean-Pierre Seguin, "Notes sur des feuilles d'information relatant des combats apparus dans le ciel (1575–1656)," *Arts et traditions populaires* 7 (1959): 51–62, 256–70. Aerial battles are included in all treatises on *mirabilia* of the age: Freidrich Nausea, *Libri mirabilium septem* (Cologne: P. Quentell, 1532), fols. 37*r*–38*r*; Conrad Lycosthenes (Conrad Wollfhart), *Prodigiorum ac ostentorum chronicon* (Basel, 1557), pp. 556, 608, and so forth; Ambroise Paré, *Des monstres et prodiges*, ed. Jean Céard (Geneva: Droz, 1971), pp. 146–47 [*On Monsters and Marvels*, tr. Janis L. Pallister (Chicago: University of Chicago Press, 1982), pp. 156–57]; Pietro Pomponazzi, *De naturalium effectuum admirandorum causis seu de incantationibus liber* . . . (Basel: ex officina Henricpetrina, 1567), p. 130; Ulisse Aldrovandi, *Monstrorum historia* (Bologna: Marco Antonio Bernia, 1642), pp. 143, 717. As late as 1650 a Spanish pamphlet appeared describing the passage of a "fantastic army . . . formed of many infantrymen and cavalry" (*Copia de una carta embiada a esta corte, en que se da cuenta de las notables visiones que en diversas vezes se ha visto entre Rosell y Traiguera, y otras partes, en el Reino de Valencia, de exercitos formados de infanteria y cavalleria y que se vieron pelear unos con otros* [Madrid: Alonso de Paredes, 1650]). Even the English almanac, *Nuncius coelistis or The Starry Messenger*, compiled in 1682 by Henry Coley, described an aerial battle between ships and armies in its 1682 edition, for which see Bernard Capp, *English Almanacs 1500–1800: Astrology and the Popular Press* (Ithaca, N.Y.: Cornell University Press, 1979), p. 24. Naturalistic interpretations have seen in the phenomenon a fantastic description of the aurora borealis or the effect of sunspots: Frantisek Link, "On the History of the Aurora Borealis," *Vistas in Astronomy* 9 (1967): 297–306; D. Justin Schove, *Sunspot Cycles* (Stroudsburg, Pa.: Hutchinson Ross Pub. Co., 1983).

[16] Cristoforo da Cividale, *Prodigii portentosi osservati in vari luoghi da molte persone degne di fede. E da PP. Cappuccini con ogni fedeltà osservati e posti in scritto* (Parma, Milan, and Genoa: per Gio. Ambrosio de Vincenti, n.d. [c.1665]), fols. 2*v*–4*r*. The same events were reported in a letter from Gorizia dated 2 February 1664, conserved in the Archivio di Stato di Bologna, Senato, Diari, 1656–1671, fols. 45*v*–46*r*. I owe the last item to the courtesy of Giovanna Ferrari.

It is of course difficult to give a single explanation for materials that, although repetitive, are culturally so heterogeneous. Still, the battles of spirits that were observed in the territory of Bergamo toward the end of 1517 seem to have a greater specificity, and it is perhaps possible to situate them within a more precise scheme in folklore and to show their specific but multiple political reverberations. What makes them even more relevant is that it is possible, given the various accounts of these events available to us, to suggest a historical reading of them and to grasp the gradual and ongoing construction of that scheme and its subsequent rapid disintegration.

"Littera de le maravigliose battaglie"

The fullest description of an apparition and the one with the most details comes from an octavo-sized pamphlet of four leaves with no imprint entitled *Littera de le maravigliose battaglie apparse novamente in Bergamasca.*[17] The pamphlet is in the form of a letter sent by "Bartholomeo de Villachiara al suo charissimo misser Onofrio Bonnuncio veronese" and is dated from the castle of Villachiara 23 December 1517. The text plunges right into its topic: Three or four times daily for eight days in Verdello, in the territory of Bergamo, formidable battalions of infantry, cavalry, and artillery were seen advancing in battle array "with the greatest organization and in perfect order." Before them rode three or four kingly figures, led by another sovereign who appeared to be the greatest among them. They advanced to parley with another king standing before his own troops and who awaited them, surrounded by his barons, halfway between the two armies.

> And there, after much negotiation, one sees one armed king, with most ferocious aspect and little patience, take the glove (which is of iron [mail]) from his hand and toss it in the air, and at once at once [*sic*] with a troubled expression he shakes his head, and immediately turns toward his men in battle array. And in that instant there are heard so many sounds of trumpets, drums, and rattles, and the most terrible racket of artillery (no less, I believe, is made by the infernal forge; in fact, truly one cannot believe that they come from anywhere but there). And then one sees no small array of banners and standards come into the fray, and with the greatest fierceness and force assault one another, and in most cruel battle all are cut to bits. . . . Half an hour later everything is still and nothing else is seen. And anyone who has the courage to draw

[17] The *Index Aureliensis* hypothesizes the following publication data: Rome: Gabriele da Bologna, 1517. As we shall see, the place of printing seems to be confirmed by the documentation, but the date is more probably 14 or 15 January 1518.

near to that place [sees] an infinite number of pigs, which stay a short while and then enter into the said wood.[18]

The writer adds that he wanted to verify these events in person, so he went there with other gentlemen. They confirmed that at the end of the apparitions, "nothing is found in that very place but marks of horses' hoofprints and men's footprints, cart tracks and burned spots, and many trees torn to bits." The letter concludes with expressions of marvel and terror ("truly the thing is so terrible that I cannot compare it to anything but one's own death"), and the writer states that he would have added other news, but refrains from doing so because "this is so great that the others would be naught."

The Furious Horde of the Dead of Agnadello

The components of this account seem to be: first, the place and date of the apparitions; next, four (or five?) kings, one of whom has command, at the head of an endless army on the march; a sole, terrible king leading another army; his terrifying aspect and fierceness as he throws his mail gauntlet into the air; the battle between the two forces; the tremendous noise that accompanies the battle; the tracks remaining on the ground; the pigs that at the end of the apparition are seen returning to the wood; finally, the author of the letter. We shall return to him later. For the moment, let it suffice to say that he was a historical person, Count Bartolomeo III Martinengo da Villachiara, who belonged to one branch of the Martinengo family, some of whom opted for the Reformation in later generations and had to emigrate to the Graubünden and to Geneva.

The apparitions took place in an open space before a wood, from which the armed specters emerged. In one account, this space is described as "spacious fields covered with snow, and in them two heaps of stable litter, and not far from there is a wood."[19] The village of Verdello is a few kilometers from the confluence of the Adda and the Brembo; Agnadello is not far away, and the battle left such a mark on the entire district that the first accounts Sanudo gathers of the apparitions in Verdello (29 December) speak, with characteristic imprecision, of "a certain thing that occurred around Treviglio or Cassan [now Cassano d'Adda], where the encounter with the French and the Swiss took place."

As for the date, the *Littera de le maravigliose battaglie* was dated 23 December, as we have seen, but it stated that the apparitions had begun eight

[18] *Littera de le maravigliose battaglie*, fols. A ii*v*–A iii*v*.

[19] Antonio Verdello to Paolo of the late Marco Morosini, Brescia, 4 January 1518, in Sanuto, *Diarii*, vol. 25, cols. 187–88.

days earlier, thus pushing the date back to 16 December, which in 1517 was the first of the winter Ember Days. As it happens, the four series of Ember Days, the winter ones above all, were the times of the year when phantom armies were most apt to appear. This was a myth of Germanic origin, tied to the origins of witchcraft,[20] which until now has been supposed to have had little influence in Italy, but which seems without doubt to apply in this instance.

The saga of the furious horde existed in a good part of Europe, branching off into Scandinavian and Slavic lands, but it seems certain that it originated in the Germanic world. As has rightly been remarked,[21] a fairly ancient trace of this myth can be seen in a passage from the *Germania* of Tacitus in which he records that the Harii were the most ferocious of the Germanic warriors, fighting at night with black shields and their bodies dyed black: "feralis exercitus . . . nullo hostium sustinente novum et infernum aspectum" (The sudden and funereal gloom of such a band of sable warriors are sure to strike a panic through the adverse army).[22] Thus they appeared as an army of the dead, like ghosts risen from the tomb, defeating all enemies by striking terror in their hearts. This tradition was doubtless based, on the one hand, on the custom, documented among the Germans, of using disguises to terrorize their adversaries;[23] on the other, on beliefs concerning the dead and their night wanderings that were widespread in the Germanic world. As early as the time of Tacitus, the army of the dead was thought to be led by Wotan, whom Tacitus equates with Mercury, thus emphasizing his role as a psychopomp god. Warriors who had died in battle followed this spectral guide, but with the Christianization of the myth, all those who had died before their time (suicides and unbaptized infants, for instance) were added to their number. The myth found a ready

[20] This is the hypothesis offered in Carlo Ginzburg, *I benandanti. Stregoneria e culti agrari fra Cinquecento e Seicento*, 2nd ed. (Turin, G. Einaudi, 1971), esp. pp. 61–103 [*The Night Battles*, tr. John and Anne Tedeschi (Baltimore: Johns Hopkins University Press, 1983), pp. 33–68]; Ginzburg, "Charivari, associazioni giovanili, caccia selvaggia," *Quaderni storici* 49 (1982): 164–77; Ginzburg, "Présomptions sur le Sabbat," *Annales E.S.C.* 39 (1984): 341–54; and now Ginzburg, *Storia notturna. Una decifrazione del Sabba* (Turin: G. Einaudi, 1989), esp. pp. 65–98. For further bibliographical information on the myth of the furious horde, see these studies and the comments of Vittore Branca in his edition of Giovanni Boccaccio, *Decameron*, 2nd ed.; 2 vols., (Florence: Le Monnier, 1960), vol. 2, p. 83.

[21] By Ludwig Weniger, "Feralis exercitus," *Archiv für Religionswissenschaft* 9 (1906): 201–47, and 10 (1907): 61–81, 229–56.

[22] Tacitus, *The History, Germania and Agricola*, tr. Arthur Murphy, Loeb's Classical Library (London and Toronto: J. M. Dent; New York, E. P. Dutton, 1926), p. 339.

[23] Gunter Müller, "Zum Namen *Wolfhetan* und seinen Verwandten," *Frühmittelalterliche studien* 1 (1967): 200–212; Müller, "Germanische Tiersymbolik und Namengebung," *Frümittelalterliche studien* 2 (1968): 202–217; Claude Lecouteux, "Les Cynocéphales. Etude d'une tradition tératologique de l'Antiquité au XIIe siècle," *Cahiers de civilisation médiévale Xe–XIIe* 24 (1981): 117–28, esp. p. 27. I owe these citations to the courtesy of Vito Fumagalli.

reception in learned circles as well, since it coincided at least partially with traditions in Roman religion according to which the souls of the dead periodically rose from the infernal regions to the earth's surface through certain crevasses in the earth, notably through the *mundus*, the pit dug at the center of every Latin city at its founding to establish yearly contact between the upper and the lower earth.[24] In Roman religion, what is more, the spirits of those who had suffered premature or violent death, warriors killed in battle in particular, were destined to wander in the air. Such spirits could be formidable and were often invoked by necromancers.

Parallels between the Germanic myth and the Roman myth probably favored the spread of this notion over ever larger and more varied cultural and territorial areas. It appears well-rooted in France in the thirteenth century, where a number of literary texts—the *Tournoiement Antechrist*, the *Roman de Fauvel*, *Le Jeu de la feuillée*, and others—contain rhetorical comparisons between some unusually noisy event and the racket made by the Mesnie Hellequin, as the furious horde appears to have been called in France (Hellequin or Herlechinus—from which the stock figure of Harlequin was derived—was the demon who took over from Wotan the task of leading the troops of the dead).[25] Soon after 1250, Etienne de Bourbon gave fixed form to the myth, by that time totally Christianized and demonic, in one of his sermons: "Aliquando [diaboli] ludificant transmutando se . . . in similitudinem militum venacium vel ludencium, qui dicunt de familia Allequini vel Arturi."[26]

A text dated 1278 explicitly and for the first time places the army of the dead on the battlefield of their last combat,[27] which was to remain an intrinsic part of the myth. It lends significance to the fact that the apparitions of 1517 took place not far from Agnadello, or at least that the battle was referred to in order to locate the site of the apparitions. In the sixteenth century the temporal placement of the phantom army during the Ember Days, particularly the winter Ember Days, seems definitive, as is clear from a passage in a sermon of Johannes Geiler von Kaisersberg, a Strasbourg

[24] Franz Cumont, *Lux perpetua* (1949; reprint ed., New York: Garland, 1987), pp. 58, 82–89, 105, 332; Ernesto De Martino, *La fine del mondo. Contributo all'analisi delle apocalissi culturali* (Turin: Einaudi, 1977), pp. 212–15.

[25] Otto Driesen, *Der Ursprung des Harlekin. Ein kulturgeshichtliches Problem* (Berlin: A. Duncker, 1904), pp. 34–35, 41, 106. See also John Colin Dunlop, *John Dunlop's Geschichte der Prosadictungen oder Geschichte der Romane, Novellen, Märchen, u. s. w.*, tr. and ed. Felix Liebrecht (Berlin: G.W.F. Müller, 1851), p. 474, n. 170 and p. 546, n. 541a [*The History of Prose Fiction*, ed. Henry Wilson, 2 vols. (London: George Bell and Sons, 1888), vol. 1, pp. 229–30, n. 2].

[26] Albert Lecoy de La Marche, *Anecdotes historiques, légendes et apologues tirés du receuil inédit d'Etienne de Bourbon, Dominicain du XIIIe siècle* (Paris: Librairie Renouard, H. Loones, successeur, 1877), pp. 321–22.

[27] Lavater, *De spectris*, pp. 116–17.

preacher, given in 1508 but printed in 1516 and again in 1517, the same year as the apparition at Verdello ("die lauffen aller meisten in der fronfasten, und vorausz in den fronfasten vor Weinnachten; das ist die heiligest Zeit").[28]

Nonetheless, the place and the date of the visions—the fact that they involved armies that clashed during the winter Ember Days on or near a former battleground—are not the only reasons to define them as manifestations of the furious horde. According to all the eyewitnesses, the appearances were always accompanied by a fearful racket.[29] We have even seen that in thirteenth-century France this noise had become such a cliché that it could be applied to any unusual amount of noise, even to a charivari, as in an interpolated incident in the *Roman de Fauvel*. We also know of an unusual manifestation of Herlechinus's troops in a somewhat earlier period (mid-thirteenth century) in which the horde appears to be composed of craftsmen who fill the skies with the clanging of the tools of their trades. The armies at Verdello clashed amid a "terribilissimo strepito" judged not inferior to the racket that "si faccia all'infernal fucina, che veramente altro non è da credere se non che de lì eschino." Even the terrible aspect and ferocity of the king who throws his mail gauntlet into the air, the traditional gesture to set off a battle,[30] has a parallel in the terrible countenance always attributed to the leader of the troops of the dead,[31] whether he was Herlechinus or the "man of the four Ember Days," as he was called (Kwaternik, Quatembermann) in the northern and eastern border areas of Italy (Trentino, Carniola, Carinthia, Slovenia, Switzerland).[32]

One last important element of the account remains to be clarified: the

[28] Johannes Geiler von Kaisersberg, *Zur Geschichte des Volks-Aberglaubens im Anfange des XVI. Jahrhunderts. Aus der Joh. Geilers von Kaisersberg Emeis*, ed. August Stöber (Basel: Schweighauser, 1856), p. 21.

[29] Felix Liebrecht, *Des Gervasius von Tilbury Otia Imperialia. In einer Auswahl neu herausgegeben* . . . (Hannover: C. Rümpler, 1856), app. 2, "La Mesnie furieuse ou la chasse sauvage," pp. 181–82; Driesen, *Der Ursprung des Harlekin*; Höfler, *Kultische Geheimbünde*, pp. 8–9, 108–10, 300; Lucia Lazzerini, "Preistoria degli zanni: mito e spettacolo nella coscienza populare," in *Scienze, credenze occulte, livelli di cultura. Convegno internazionale di studi (Firenze, 26–30 giugno 1980)* (Florence: L. S. Olschki, 1982), pp. 445–76; p. 459. On two examples given later, see Ginzburg, "Charivari."

[30] According to Luigi da Porto, before the battle of Agnadello the king of France, Louis XII, sent a herald to Venice who "in sign of challenge . . . threw at the feet of the doge the bloody glove"; before the battle of Ravenna in 1512 "monsignor Foix sent to Don Raimondo di Cardona the bloody glove of the battle." See *Lettere storiche di Luigi da Porto vicentino dall'anno 1509 al 1528*, ed. Bartolommeo Bressan (Florence: Felice Le Monnier, 1857), pp. 35, 302.

[31] Liebrecht, "La Mesnie furieuse," p. 177.

[32] Waldemar Liungman, *Traditionswanderungen, Euphrat-Rhein. Studien zur Geschichte des Volksbräuche*, 2 vols. (Helsinki: Suomalainen tiedeakamia, Academia scientiarum fennica, 1937–1938), vol. 2, pp. 640–41.

four kings (though this number can vary) who head the second army. The oft-cited passages from Guillaume d'Auvergne concerning the phantom army contain a few additional details. When Guillaume speaks of night armies at the end of the 1230s ("quos alii hellequin vocant, alii exercitum antiquum") and of the troops led by Abundia or Satia, he also speaks of four kings who, when the necromancers call on them (thus making them kings of the dead), "a quatuor mundi partibus cum exercitibus innumerabilibus suis convenire dicuntur."[33] In a later passage, still in connection with the phantom army, Guillaume returns to the topic: The four kings who spring out of the earth followed by their armies at the call of the necromancers receive their names from the parts of the world from which they come: "ita ut primus vocatus sit Oriens, secundus Occidens, tertius rex Austri, quartus rex Septentrionis."[34] Chief among them is the king of the East. Guillaume goes on to argue that the four kings can only be kings of the demons and are themselves demons, thus attempting to reduce to Christian coordinates a myth that appears to precede Christianity and to be extraneous to it. Other traces of this myth can be found in a well-known passage of the *Historia ecclesiastica* of Ordericus Vitalis, which relates the encounter of a priest, Gauchelin, with the nocturnal army on 1 January 1091 near Saint Aubain de Bonneval: Among the dead there stood out "quatuor horrendi equites . . . terribiliter vociferantes," who intervene when Gauchelin attempts to catch a riderless horse that belongs to the horde.[35]

This part of the myth of the furious horde—that the army of the dead was led by four kings and that it was possible to call them up by means of the necromantic arts—was not completely spent in the sixteenth century. In 1544 some students wandering about the countryside of Swabia boasted of being able to call up the furious horde on nights of the sabbath during the four Ember Days and the three Thursdays of Advent.[36] They experimented with necromantic techniques to discover hidden treasure and used a circle traced on the ground, salt and holy water, magic herbs,

[33] Guillaume d'Auvergne, *Opera omnia*, 2 vols. (Paris: Edmundus Couterot, 1674), vol. 2, p. 948. In medieval culture the number four was of course the number of the cosmos: "the *fabrica mundi* developed in a vast *ordo quadratus* that remained permanent within temporal flux" (Henri de Lubac, *Exégèse médiévale. Les quatre sens de l'Ecriture*, 4 vols. [Paris: Aubier, 1959–1964], vol. 2, p. 27).

[34] Guillaume d'Auvergne, *Opera omnia*, vol. 2, p. 1037.

[35] Ordericus Vitalis, *Historiae ecclesiasticae libri treaecim*, ed. Augustus Le Prevost, 5 vols. (Paris: apud J. Renouard et socios, 1838–1855), vol. 3, p. 372. The work is available in English as *The Ecclesiastical History*, ed. and tr. Marjorie Chibnall, 6 vols. (Oxford: Clarendon Press, 1969–), where the citation is in vol. 3, p. 245.

[36] Martin Crusius, *Annalium Svevicorum dodecas tertia* (Frankfurt: ex officina typographica Nicolai Bassai, 1596), pp. 653–54.

lighted candles, and glowing embers as part of a scheme to befuddle and cheat a peasant from Chomburg. The Swabian students thus emulated Wotan, the god who called up the dead and knew the places in which treasure was buried. Their science may have had other sources besides folk tradition, for example (and this is a hypothesis), the *De occulta philosophia* of Heinrich Cornelius Agrippa, published eleven years earlier in Cologne.[37] Agrippa discusses techniques for finding buried treasure and the necromantic arts most easily exercised on the "sepultura carentium vagabundas umbras, manesque Acheronte remissos et hospites inferum, quos immatura mors in Tartara astraxit." Both the classical tradition and the Germanic and folk tradition seem evident in these lines. Contaminations of this sort must have been frequent, as Agrippa's own work shows. Elsewhere he speaks of the four kings of the subterranean world, giving them names that derive from rabbinic wisdom:

> In malis spiritibus praesunt . . . quatuor reges potentissimi iuxta quatuor partes mundi, quorum nomina appellantur Urieus, rex Orientis, Amaymon, rex Meridiei, Paymon, rex Occidentis, Egyn, rex Septentrionis; quos Ebreorum doctores forte rectius vocant Samael, Azazel, Azael, Mahazael; sub quibus plures alii dominantur principes legionum et presides.

Thus the myth of the four kings of the world who led the army of the dead and whom the power of the necromantic arts could raise out of the earth was certainly alive in sixteenth-century Germany, even if it had classical and Oriental admixtures. Furthermore, fragments of the same mythology persisted in the Po valley as well. A formula for invoking the four kings of the world by the names Agrippa had attributed to them appears in an Inquisitional document from Modena that bears no date but is probably from approximately the same period as the apparitions in Verdello.[38] Fragments of these beliefs are also discernible in the *Littera de le maravigliose battaglie*, which seems to evoke a combat between several armed groups, some led by the king of the four seasonal Ember Days, the others by the four kings of the world under the leadership of the king of the East.

[37] Heinrich Cornelius Agrippa von Nettesheim, *De occulta philosophia libri tres* (n.p. [Cologne: Johann Soter], 1533). The two quotations that follow are on pp. cccv and cclvi. The reference to Wotan's functions is taken from Georges Dumézil, *Gods of the Ancient Northmen*, ed. Einar Haugen (Berkeley: University of California Press, 1973), pp. 40–42.

[38] This document is a loose page conserved in the Archivio di Stato di Modena in a file containing love spells and marked Inquisizione, envelope 1. It has been studied in Albano Biondi, "La signora delle erbe e la magia della vegetazione," in *Medicina, erbe e magia* (Bologna: Federazione delle Casse di Risparmio e delle Banche del Monte dell'Emilia Romagna, 1981), pp. 190, 192.

The Construction of a Myth

The *canard* described above seems to present a fairly fully developed version of the events. Although the myth of the spectral army is not mentioned explicitly, it is suggested with great exactitude and a wealth of detail. At the opposite extreme is the stripped-down version of the events in the skeptical letter written by the doge's secretary in Milan, Gian Giacomo Caroldo ("some simple people saw the fumes above some manure piles"). More relevant to our purposes, however, we can grasp the intermediate phases or, more accurately, the raw materials that were subsequently sifted, re-elaborated, and modified to create a mythical event. The first traces of this process go back even some years before the event, though they seem not to have had any direct result. In the anonymous minstrel's *frottola* (popular poem) published in 1511 under the title *Memoria delli novi segni*, already examined for the large number of signs it describes in connection with the War of Cambrai, we read the following lines:

Là dove fu il conflitto
delli Venitiani
de molti segni strani
son comparsi:

fochi per l'aere sparsi
de nocte visti sonno
da quei che guardar vonno
spesse volte;

rumor de squadre folte
e soni di trombette
di maggio a giorni sette
furno auditi.

(Where there was the conflict of the Venetians many strange signs have appeared: lights dispersed in the air have often been seen at night by those who care to look; the din of close-ranked squadrons and sounds of trumpets were heard on 7 May.)[39]

Thus as early as 7 May 1511 the nucleus of what later was to be seen as a clear manifestation of the furious horde was recorded in the sighting of will-o'-the-wisps (the souls of the fallen?) on the site of the battle of Agna-

[39] *Memoria delli novi segni et spaventevoli prodigii comparsi in piu loci de Italia et in varie parte del mondo lanno mille cinquecento undese* (n.p., n.d.), fol. 1*v* (unnumbered).

dello (by antonomasia, "il conflitto delli Venitiani").[40] Above all, the din of a large army was heard, accompanied by the shrill squeals of trumpets. No vision is recorded, however, and the date is not relevant, since in that year 7 May was the Wednesday following the second Sunday after Easter, known in Italy at the time as *Misericordia Domini* Sunday. What is more, the events of 1517 were by no means immediately placed within the winter Ember Days (which, as we have seen, lent them further significance). A letter dated 4 January 1518,[41] to which I shall return, declares that the visions began "about twenty days ago," thus around 10 December, whereas the *Littera de le maravigliose battaglie*, dated 23 December, refers to the week just past, thus placing the events within the feast days of the winter Ember Days.

The progressive construction of the myth, or rather the adaptation of materials that came from eyewitness reports to the myth is even clearer from a direct examination of the reports themselves. The most singular among these is the long letter just mentioned, sent by Antonio Verdello of Brescia on 4 January 1518 to Paolo Morosini. Verdello tells his correspondent that he had interrogated a number of people about the visions and, in particular, that he had discussed them at length with three trustworthy eyewitnesses. He gives an extremely precise description of the place and offers no fewer than six different accounts of the apparitions, all introduced by formulas such as "some say," "others say," and "another man says," which allow us an extraordinarily immediate grasp of both the subjectivity of the interpretations and the innate fluidity of this sort of phenomena (a quality that facilitates accommodation to the schemata of a preexistent mental image). The inherent interest of this multiple testimony is intensified by the fact that there is no indication that any of the informants had access to printed texts that may already have been in circulation or that they had based their reports on such texts, as is the case with other accounts. Here we see a culture still in an exclusively oral phase.

The first version reported seems already quite complex, however. As with the later printed text, it includes foot soldiers, horsemen, artillery, and supply wagons all racing full tilt across the snow-covered fields between a wood and a small church dedicated to St. George. The images are unclear, however, as if shrouded in clouds of dust ("per tal corere levarsi gran polvere a l'aiere"), and they soon dissolve into nothing ("poco andati inanti,

[40] Phosphorescent lights appearing on battlefields were a recurrent commonplace, to the point that in the mid-eighteenth century Lenglet Dufresnoy felt it necessary to state that they "are only gross exhalations that rise naturally from cadavers and that easily take fire." See Nicolas Lenglet Dufresnoy, *Recueil des dissertations anciennes et nouvelles sur les apparitions, les visions, et les songes*, 2 vols. (Avignon and Paris: J. N. Leloup, 1751), vol. 2, pt. 1, p. 247.

[41] Antonio Verdello to Paolo of the late Marco Morosini, Brescia, 4 January 1518, in Sanuto, *Diarii*, vol. 25, cols. 187–88.

disparere et perdersi totalmente"). Furthermore, here the furious horde leaves no trace of its presence on the snow ("non si vedeva ne la neve un minimo vestigio"), whereas the *Littera de le maravigliose battaglie* devoted a good deal of space to describing the footprints of the infantry and the hoofprints of the cavalry left to bear witness to the prodigy.

The next account is more subdued, speaking only of "shades like men with no heads" ("umbre a modo de homeni senza capo") that seemed to move about and group together in ever shifting number ("pareano se movessero et hora se unissero insieme, hora fusseno pur assai et hora pochissimi"). Still, those unstable shades, now many, now few, advancing and retreating, are perhaps a first sketch of the meeting and colloquy between the four kings of the dead and the king of the four seasonal Ember Days. The detail of decapitated shades has a certain relevance in that the soldiers risen from battle who made up the furious horde often appeared as death had overtaken them: "One carried his viscera before him, another bore his head in his hand," Geiler von Kaisersberg wrote only a few years earlier.[42]

The third report describes pigs running onto the field, just as the vision of the phantom combatants in the *Littera de le maravigliose battaglie* ends with "an innumerable quantity of pigs who grunted and rose up into the air, running wildly here and there." In the folk tradition of the furious horde, souls could take the form of animals or be accompanied by animals—horses and dogs above all, but also pigs, particularly in some cantons in Switzerland.[43] A large number of animals appear in the account of the fourth eyewitness as well. He reports that he saw first "several thousand black and white sheep walking on the snow"; next, "a great many red and white oxen"; then, "just as many friars [dressed in] black and white"; finally, as if he had been subjected to pressure from the collective imagination of the crowd around him (he was "led to look where there were many other people as well"), he "thought he saw an infinite number of armed men on foot and on horseback, and many with readied lances, all of them helmeted and all moving and running over those fields with a multitude of hay carts." In a notable qualitative jump that tells us much about the process involved in the creation of visions, this eyewitness reaches the more complex level of elaboration of the first account given in the letter.

The last two reports, relegated to a postscript, are almost completely negative. One "homo da bene" (the term indicates that he was a trustworthy witness, though it is not clear whether it is a judgment of his integrity or his social status) looks for a long time without seeing anything before he finally believes he can distinguish two decapitated shades that advance

[42] Geiler von Kaisersberg, *Zur Geschichte des Volks-Aberglaubens*, p. 22.

[43] See Hans Plischke, *Die Sage vom wilden Heere im deutschen Volke* (Eilenburg: C. W. Offenhauer, 1914), pp. 30–31.

over the snow and then disappear. Some in the crowd gather enough courage to approach the church. They see nothing unusual, but others watching them (from a safe distance) see them surrounded by shades. In conclusion, the writer of the letter adds that "some . . . took such a fright that they became sick, and . . . still others died of it."

Obviously the visions, as reported in this singular text, were extraordinarily fluid, flexible, and susceptible to being adapted to a specific model. This process of adjustment must have been enormously swift, as we can see from the dates of the various reports, which overlap to such an extent that it is nearly impossible to establish a clear, logical, and chronological order among them. Antonio Verdello's letter bears the date of 4 January; Bartolomeo da Villachiara's letter is dated 23 December; on 29 December, Marin Sanudo notes the events in his journal in terms that lead us to suppose that he had at hand a source of information that was already fairly well formalized.[44] Finally, there is a letter dated 28 December from one Marin Saracho or Saracco in Bergamo to Antonio Orefici in Vicenza that seems to represent a last phase in the construction of the myth before it reached its definitive form.[45] The letter speaks of the daily apparition of two friars ("appareno ogni zorno due frati sie miglia lontano di Bergamo"), then of two armed men bearing halberds who come out of a wood to climb a hill ("se levava fuora de quel boscheto dui armati con le labarde et vengono in zima de la colina"), who are finally transformed into two crowned kings conferring together until one of them throws his gauntlet into the air, setting off the battle. Thus we have arrived fairly close to our point of departure—to the *Littera de le maravigliose battaglie* and its presentation of the visions as a manifestation of the furious horde.

At this point we need to consider the cultural environment in which this parallel was drawn. Admittedly, the apparitions must have been seen and believed by people of very different social and cultural levels. We should not forget Caroldo's scornful opinion concerning the "simple people" who thought they had seen men in arms in the fumes rising from a mound of fertilizer; nor should we ignore the social distance separating Caroldo, secretary of the Venetian Republic in the service of the French commander in Italy, the "homo da bene" who saw only "due umbre . . . senza capo, forte obscure," and the "simplice persone" who saw infantry, cavalry, and baggage trains. Still, there seems to have been an inverse relationship between the elaborateness and complexity of the visions and the social level of the viewer. The *Littera de le maravigliose battaglie* (hence the interpretation of the apparitions as a manifestation of the furious horde) had an author whose name is given explicitly and to whom it would thus seem that we

[44] Sanuto, *Diarii*, vol. 25, col. 167.

[45] Ibid., cols. 189–90.

should attribute the elaboration of the visions in their definitive form. He was, as we have seen, a historical personage about whom we have precise information: Bartolomeo Martinengo, the son of Count Vettore, the late Giovan Francesco Martinengo.[46] The Martinengo family had split into a number of branches, the one that interests us here being the Villachiara branch, so called from the castle of that name (parts of which are still standing) east of the Oglio River not far from Crema. Bartolomeo was a military man and had participated in the battles of the Holy League, in particular in the autumn of 1514, when he had fought beside Lorenzo Orsini da Cere, the captain of the Venetian infantry, in the zone between Crema, Bergamo, and Brescia. In recognition of his services, the doge of Venice, with all due solemnity, raised Bartolomeo to count of Villachiara on 16 November 1516, and he held command of Cremona for the Venetian Republic. The letter was sent from the castle of Villachiara, where Bartolomeo probably was at the time. It is also probable that the visions that gave rise to the text printed in letter form under his name were related by one of his men, whether Bartolomeo actually wrote the letter or not. In fact, Marin Sanudo informs us in a journal entry for 29 December that "Count Vetor da Martinengo, or rather, the Contin [literally, the little count] his son, sent one of his serving men who, coming too near these phantasms or spirits or whatever they were, was severely beaten by them."[47] Perhaps it was this unknown "fameglio," to whom Bartolomeo himself probably alludes in his letter when he says that "one or two of our own [men] are sick from fear," who, besieged by his terror of the "phantasms," tipped his own personal experience definitively into the realm of myth.

Letters and Pamphlets in Italy and in Europe

The event had vast notoriety, thanks to the publication of the piece whose genesis I have attempted to reconstruct. It gave rise to another text printed in Italy that gives a somewhat different version of the events at Verdello and thrusts them into an eschatological framework ("I sorely suspect that

[46] On the Martinengo family in general, see Paolo Guerrini, *I conti di Martinengo* (Brescia, 1930), a work that contains inaccuracies, however. On Bartolomeo in particular, see pp. 484–89 of Guerrini, and Carlo Pasero, *Francia, Spagna, Impero a Brescia, 1509–1516*, Supplemento ai Commentari dell'Ateneo di Brescia per il 1957 (Brescia, 1958), pp. 339–40 and 356, to which should be added the many pertinent entries in Sanuto, *Diarii*, vols. 19, 20, 21, 23, *ad indicem*. On the castle of Villachiara, for which Bartolomeo ordered frescoes painted by the Campi brothers, see Adriano Peroni, "L'architettura e la scultura nei secoli XV e XVI," in *Storia di Brescia*, 5 vols. (Brescia: Morcelliana, 1963–1964), vol. 2, pp. 717–19.

[47] Sanuto, *Diarii*, vol. 25, col. 167.

in our times we can rightly say *consummatum est*").[48] This publication must have had a much more restricted circulation than the *Littera de le maravigliose battaglie*, which was certainly used as the basis for a French translation (in at least two different editions) and a German translation.[49] The German translation, destined for a market that might grasp the affair, set the visions explicitly within the myth of the furious horde. Along with the name of the sender and the recipient, as in the Italian original, the letter also bore the indication, "von Dieterichs Bern" (in Italian tradition, the name Dietrich von Bern was one name for King Theodoric of Verona, but in Germanic folklore he had become one of the leaders of the phantom army).[50] The translator thus recognized a formulation of that myth in the text, probably seeing the Ostrogothic king in the king of "ferocissimo aspetto e di poca paciencia armato" who sets off the infernal battle by throwing his mail gauntlet into the air.

Thanks especially to the print piece we have examined, the battle of the spirits of Verdello was thus famous far and wide, its renown reaching into France and Germany. This means that it is possible to reconstruct the progress of its notoriety, the channels that news of it followed, and the time this required, which gives us an opportunity to go beyond strictly oral transmission and to trace one example of the itineraries open to cultural images in Europe of the early modern age. The itineraries for information that circulated by epistolary means and those followed by printed publications should be kept distinct, however. Letters moved more rapidly, but over shorter distances. The visions began toward the middle of December; Marin Saracco could write about them from Bergamo to Vicenza on the 28th, and Marin Sanudo noted them in his journal on 29 December. News must have reached Venice several days before, however, if Antonio Verdello had time to gather information and then answer Paolo Morosini's request for particulars on 4 January. Milan also heard of the

[48] *Copia delle stupende et horribile cose che ne boschi di Bergamo sono a questi giorni apparse* (n.p., n.d.).

[49] *La terrible et merveilleuse bataille que a este veue novellement en la duche de Millan VIII jours durant au pres de la cite de Bergamo: translate de italien en françoys* (n.p., n.d. [Paris, 1518]); *La translacion de italien en francoys de la lettre des merveilleuses et horribles batailles nouvellement apparues au pays de Bergame, translate par maistre Michel du Pont, banquier a Troyes. Lan mil cinq cent et dix sept* [Troyes: Nicolas le Rouge]; *Ein wunderbarlich, grausam und erschrockenlich Geschichte von Streyt woelche ist geschehen und neuwlich gesehen worden In dem land Bargamasca* . . . (n.p., n.d.).

[50] Plischke, *Die Sage vom wilden Heere*, p. 39; Renato Serra, "Su la pena de i dissipatori (*Inferno*, C. XII, vv. 109–129)," *Giornale storico della letteratura italiana* 43 (1904): 278–98; p. 294; Claude Luttrell, "Folk Legend as Source for Arthurian Romance: The Wild Hunt," in Kenneth Varty, ed., *An Arthurian Tapestry* (Glasgow: Published on behalf of the British Branch of the International Arthurian Society at the French Dept. of the University of Scotland, 1981), pp. 94, 99.

apparitions fairly soon because Gian Giacomo Caroldo wrote on the subject to his brother on 12 January but was apparently aware of the events several days earlier.

Thus news moved rapidly within a fairly restricted geographical area, for the most part within the confines of the Venetian Republic. Word reached Rome a bit later, probably in the form of a manuscript copy of Bartolomeo da Villachiara's letter and of other letters. On 21 January 1518, in fact, Leo X read "some letters on the apparitions of Bergamo" to the cardinals assembled in consistory.[51] It was also in Rome that the *Littera de le maravigliose battaglie* was most probably printed (by Gabriele da Bologna), since the anonymous French cleric cited earlier states in his journal that "the aforesaid books were printed in Rome and sold publicly . . . to persons of note and in great favor."[52] It was from Rome, then, that the most complete working out of the news of the battles of the dead made its way, in the form best adapted to wide circulation and over a longer distance, arriving in France and Germany, as we have seen, and Valladolid, as we know from a letter of Pietro Martire d'Anghiera dated 23 February. In the meantime, the pamphlet lost no time circulating within the confines of the Pontifical States. In Cesena, as we have seen, the chronicler Giuliano Fantaguzzi noted in his *Caos* that "books printed about the visions and combats of spirits taking place in the Bergamasco" began to circulate in his city by 20 January (a date that indicates, taking the entire chronology into consideration, that the *Littera* came off Gabriele da Bologna's presses around 14 or 15 January).

From Rome news of the spectral battles rapidly rebounded to northern Italy. Bartolomeo da Villachiara's letter—certainly in the Roman edition, the only one to mention him by name—was put into verse by a Po valley tale singer, and his poem was used to pad out a reprinting of the minstrel's *frottola*, *Memoria delli novi segni*, already mentioned several times. The additions—sixteen quatrains of limping verse—were even clumsier than the doggerel into which they were inserted, but they did give a faithful description of "the signs that have appeared / again in Geradada / where every road was full / of armed men." Ghiaradadda (now Gera d'Adda) confirms the reference to the battle at nearby Agnadello, also referred to in the work's title, now modified to read: *Segni e prodigi spaventosi apparsi in Lombardia nel confino de Trevi e Rivolta seccha: quali appareno doi o tre volte al zorno a combattere in ordenanza e con ferissime artelarie viste visibilmente per el magnifico Bartolomeo da Villa Chiara: et molti altri uomini degni di fede.*[53] Trevi and Rivoltasecca (now Treviglio and Rivolta d'Adda) were in fact

[51] Sanuto, *Diarii*, vol. 25, col. 219.

[52] Biblioteca Apostolica Vaticana, MS Barb. Lat. 3552, fol. 32*v*.

[53] (n.p., n.d.).

fairly pertinent topographical references for the battle called "of Agnadello" or "of la Ghiaradadda." There is no longer any mention of Verdello, and the permanent alteration of the circumstances of the place and the time in which the spectral battles took place is a persuasive confirmation of their definitive assimilation into a mythic model.

From Myth to Propaganda

Rome functioned well as a sounding board of international scale for the prodigious—for the apparitions at Verdello as earlier for the monster of Ravenna. The impression is inescapable that the success of these two events in Rome was due to the circumstances that favored their use for propaganda purposes. In the case of the Verdello apparitions, the political context was furnished by the crusade against the Turks. When Leo X read the letters describing the visions at Verdello to the assembled cardinals, he commented that these prodigious apparitions were "signals that the Turk will soon be attacking Christianity . . . thus we need to make proper provisions and not shilly-shally."[54] As is known, the notion of a crusade against the Turks frequently arose in sixteenth-century Italy, often in quite concrete terms, involving the collection of alms and the establishment of diplomatic contacts. This was precisely the situation during the months in question. As early as the beginning of November 1517, Leo X was considering the organization of a league of Christian princes against the Turk, and after a successful Egyptian campaign the previous spring, Selim I was then at the peak of his dangerous power.

Among the many missives offering advice received by the pope was a Latin epistle from a humanist in Imola, Giovanni Antonio Flaminio, which merits a brief word. Flaminio had spent long periods of his life in Serravalle (now Vittorio Veneto), not far from the eastern borders of Italy. He was there in 1499 when the Turks reached the Tagliamento River, which is probably why he approached the problem of Turkish pressure with particularly intense feeling. From 1514 until 1536, the date of his death, he sent letters to every pope who was elected to urge him to declare a crusade. Aside from the letter of 1517 (in prose), he had already sent Leo X an epistle on the same subject in hexameters in 1514.[55] The 1517 letter dif-

[54] Sanuto, *Diarii*, vol. 25, col. 219.

[55] Biographical and bibliographical information on Giovanni Antonio Flaminio can be found in Alessandro Pastore, *Marcantonio Flaminio. Fortune e sfortune di un chierico nell'Italia del Cinquecento* (Milan: Franco Angeli, 1981), pp. 15–17; the epistles to the popes are in Ioannis Antonii Flaminii, *Silvarum libri II. Eiusdem epigrammatum libri III* (Bologna: per Hieronymum de Benedictis, 1515); Flaminii, *Epistolae familiares*, ed. Fr. Dominico Josepho Capponi (Bologna: ex typographia Sancti Thomae Aquinatis, 1744).

fered from its rather repetitive predecessor in that it gave fuller treatment to the "ingentia prodigia, quae futurae calamitates praenunciant . . . et ad consulendum in commune monere, hortari, impellere non cessant."[56] Flaminio urged the pope to use his authority to mitigate the discord among Christians and to unite their forces under the sign of the cross in order to march against their common Ottoman enemy. Leaving aside its rhetorical scheme, Flaminio's letter is truly singular for its sources, a major portion of which, surprisingly enough, turns out to be a somewhat pedestrian translation into Latin of the *Memoria delli novi segni*,[57] quite evidently in the 1511 version that bore this title (as Flaminio's letter precedes the apparitions at Verdello, it thus also precedes the edition with the title *Segni e prodigi spaventosi* quoting Bartolomeo's *Littera*). In short, Giovanni Antonio Flaminio, a humanist and teacher of Latin, used a text from the culture of the city streets to invite the reigning pontiff to declare a crusade. Not only did he borrow its description; he took over its general thrust, which was, precisely, an invitation to Christian princes to unite for the purpose of liberating the Holy Sepulchre, thus diverting from mankind the divine wrath that was revealed by the prodigies it described—a fine example indeed of the complex relations between humanists and the vernacular.

Given the situation that faced the pope, Flaminio's letter found Leo X well disposed to listen to its arguments. On 7 November a commission of cardinals was formed, which prepared a fairly broad-ranging questionnaire to be sent to Christian rulers so as to know their thoughts on the most opportune strategy to follow and on how to organize the crusade and raise the necessary military forces.[58] Early in January 1518 the pope received word from Constantinople, via Ragusa and Ancona, that the Turks were on the move, which set off a new flurry of preparations. In particular, Leo X sent briefs to all the sovereigns of Europe, and it was precisely to discuss the responses he had already received that the cardinals had been called together on 21 January.[59] Thus the apparitions of combating armies could have been considered premonitory, a warning of the imminent and expected struggle between the Cross and the Crescent (according to the interpretive scheme proposed by both Flaminio and the anonymous tale singer who preceded him) and could prove useful in preparing the way for a request for new taxes. The projected expedition against the Turks never

[56] Flaminii, *Epistolae familiares*, p. 59.

[57] Ibid., p. 60 for the passage in Flaminio closely translating quatrains 6–31 of the *Memoria delli novi segni*.

[58] Sanuto, *Diarii*, vol. 25, cols. 76 and 95–106. On preparations for the crusade of 1517–1518, see Charles Göllner, *Turcica*, 3 vols. (Bucharest: Editura Academiei R.P.R., 1961–1978), vol. 3, *Die Türkenfrage in der öffentlichen Meinung Europas im 16. Jahrhundert*, pp. 73–74.

[59] Sanuto, *Diarii*, vol. 25, cols. 204 and 219.

took place, but in the early months of 1518 the pope worked diligently to raise financial aid, sent out a number of briefs, and urged that ceremonies and penitential processions be organized.[60] The pope was not alone in raising money: Franciscan friars moving about the Venetian *terraferma* also collected funds, at times abusively. To increase the appeal of their requests for alms for St. Peter's they included propaganda for the crusade in their sermons, thus incurring protests from the Venetian Council of Ten.[61]

The propagandistic context into which the visions at Verdello were placed, particularly in Rome, was evident from various facts. The pamphlet about the "the visions and combats of spirits" reached Cesena on 20 January, as we have seen, together with another work entitled *Signuri stupende del grando aparato face il Turco per pasare in cristianità*. In all probability, this print piece, whose title already announces the Turks' large-scale mobilization, contained a letter that both Sanudo and Tommasino Lancellotti report.[62] It gave a highly colored description of the terrifying aspect of the fleet of the Great Turk in the Levant: The ships bore banners with a black cross on a red field; the galley of the Great Turk himself was all black—sails, rigging, oars, and all—with only the banners in gold bearing a red cross placed upside down. All the ships were laden with large wood crosses (clearly, for the eventual martyrdom of captured Christians). That the two pamphlets circulated at exactly the same time might simply reflect the widespread presence of these topics in Roman circles, but it may also have been a deliberate move to prepare people's minds for the collection of funds. Even Francesco Guicciardini, who was at the time serving as pontifical governor of Reggio Emilia, received the two news items together and appears to have made a connection between them. On 19 January he wrote to Goro Gheri in Florence:

> The prodigy has disappeared, but it is confirmed from so many places that, as for me, I cannot laugh at it, above all hearing so much about the Turk's

[60] Scipione Vegio, *Historia rerum Insubribus gestarum sub Gallorum dominio* in *Bibliotheca Historica Italica* (Milan: Brigola, 1876–1901), vol. 1, p. 31; *Bando delle processioni per la unione dei principi Christiani contra Turchi* (Rome, 1518); Giovanni Cambi, "Istorie," in Fr. Ildefonso di San Luigi, ed., *Delizie degli eruditi toscani*, 24 vols. (Florence: Gaetano Cambiagi, 1770–1789), vol. 23 (1786), pp. 138–41; Leonello Beliardi, *Cronaca della città di Modena (1512–1518)*, ed. Albano Biondi and Michele Oppi (Modena: Panini, 1981), p. 142.

[61] Sanuto, *Diarii*, vol. 25, cols. 390–91.

[62] Ibid., cols. 335–36; Tommasino Lancellotti, *Cronaca modenese*, ed. Carlo Borghi, 12 vols. (Parma: P. Fiaccadori, 1863), vol. 1, pp. 438–39. Analogous and dramatic news of the Turkish fleet was also contained in a letter dated Milan, 18 February 1518, from one Fra Giovanni Antonio to the minorite Zaccaria da Ravenna in Cremona, which also gives a description of a number of prodigies interpreted as omens of the imminent arrival of the Turk in Italy, for which see Francesco Novati, ed., "La vita e le opere di Domenico Bordigallo," *Archivio Veneto* 19 (1880): 327–56; pp. 334–35.

preparations, and believing that now is like the past [and] that great things have been signified ahead of time by great prodigies.[63]

The connection that Guicciardini establishes between the "apparati del Turco" (mentioned in a letter dated two days earlier) and "the prodigy" of Verdello does not figure in the news that he received from the place where the apparitions were seen, so we can suppose that he linked the two on the basis of what he heard from Rome. As early as 8 January, Guicciardini sent Gheri a copy of a letter on the visions that he had received from near Brescia, in which (thus differing somewhat from all those examined up to this point) there is no suggestion of any relationship between the prodigy and preparations for war against the Turks.[64] We know of this letter thanks to Giovanni Cambi's summary of it in his *Istorie*, where he states explicitly that Guicciardini was the source of his information:

> On a plain, in the daytime, near certain woods and pastures, [people] saw a great King coming to parley from one side, and from the other another King with six and eight lords, and when they had been there awhile they disappeared; and then two great armies came to parley and to do battle together and stayed an hour fighting together. And this thing happened several times, but there were more than three days from one time to the other: on which the common voice [*la brighata*] judged it a combat of great lords. In that [part of] Lombardy there were some curious [people] who wanted to get close to the said armies to see what they were and who, as they drew near, out of fear and terror immediately fell sick and lay at death's door.[65]

This version of the events—which, obviously, was written independently of Bartolomeo da Villachiara's letter—was sent directly from Lombardy and contains no anti-Turkish sentiments. All that "la brighata" drew from the visions is a generic prognostication of a "combattimento di gran signori." We learn somewhat more about the matter through another source that, although late in date, offers a wealth of particulars. Toward the end of the seventeenth century, Father Gregorio di Valcamonica published a work on the history of the Camuni, the prehistoric inhabitants of the valley and their descendants. In it he relates that in 1518 the rectors of Brescia had manned the castle overlooking Breno, contrary to previous custom, because of "fears conceived because of some prodigious signs [that] appeared in those days in the territory of Bergamo, in the general system of which people saw presented the affairs of Italy." Thus concern for the political situation in Italy was mixed, in the minds of the rectors of

[63] Francesco Guicciardini, *Carteggi*, ed. Roberto Palmarocchi, 17 vols. (Bologna: Nicola Zanichelli, 1938–), vol. 2, p. 240.

[64] Ibid., p. 236.

[65] Cambi, "Istorie," p. 131.

Brescia and of the local population, with a holy terror aroused by "prodigious signs." But just what did the population of the area really think about those signs? "Everyone interpreted them in his own way, but the most sensible ones took them as a prediction that King Francis of France and King Charles of Spain, who was later Emperor Charles V, were to tussle between them in Italy for the Duchy of Milan."[66] Father Gregorio was doubtless using hindsight when he stressed this interpretation over others that he may have had available, but it communicates the sense of alarm (whether or not it was shared) that suggested to the rectors of Brescia that it would be prudent to keep the commander of the castle in Breno on duty. It also contributes to an understanding of what a Lombard meant when he stated that "si faceva giuditio di combattimento di gran signori." These "great lords" were the kings of France and Spain, and what was feared was yet another foreign invasion to seize possession of the Duchy of Milan. Another report, of a different origin, offers an interesting comparison. We know of it from a summary given in the *Journal d'un Bourgeois de Paris*:

> In the said year 1517 [1518] in January, in Rome and like parts, both in the air and on the ground in a wood were heard a great number of armed men fighting (they seemed to be around six or eight thousand men); and [people] heard [something] like cannon, bombards, and arms clashing against one another; which battle lasted a good hour at the most, without [their] seeing anything, however. Afterwards, [they] heard a great many pigs, in equal number, fighting, from which the terrified populace judged that those pigs signified the Mahometan infidels.[67]

The version of events that the Parisian burgher had in hand was substantially different from those we have available (the phantasms are only heard fighting, and nothing is seen), and certainly came from Rome (the visions, in fact, are placed "à Rome et par de là"). In all probability, the Bourgeois had seen the French translation of a Roman print piece other than the *Littera de le maravigliose battaglie* (Leo X, after all, had "some letters" on the apparitions in Bergamo read to the assembled cardinals). In this second piece, the pigs of the vision were interpreted as Muslims. We know well, however, that it would be difficult to impute this interpretation to the "populaire espouvanté"—the equivalent of the *brighata* of the letter forwarded by Guicciardini—to judge from the spontaneous reactions of which we have evidence. From the beginning, all the reports speak of the presence of pigs, but as animals without particular significance who, together with oxen and sheep, painted a picture familiar to Bergamo country dwellers in

[66] Padre Gregorio di Valcamonica, *Curiosj trattenimenti continenti raguagli sacri e profani de' Popoli Camuni* (Venice, 1698; reprint ed., Bologna: Forni, 1965), pp. 561–62.

[67] *Journal d'un Bourgeois de Paris sous le règne de François Premier (1515–1536)*, ed. Ludovic Lalanne (Paris: J. Renouard et c., 1854), p. 62.

those days. The oxen and the sheep disappeared in the mythic tradition of the visions because, unlike the pigs, they had no function in the furious horde. In the final stages, the lost Roman pamphlet definitively removed the visions from their peasant roots by placing the pigs in an ecclesiastical tradition that, as early as the twelfth century, saw pigs as an incarnation of sin and vice.[68] This last shift reworked the visions to serve anti-Turkish ends with the aim of encouraging a broader consensus for the projected crusade.

Twenty years later, in 1538, the Venetian printer Giovanni Andrea Valvassori published a pamphlet entitled *Avisi da Constantinopoli di cose stupende et maravigliose*. The work had two parts, the second of which was a wholly fictional account of the victory of the armada under Andrea Doria over the Turks. The first part, which served as a sort of preamble to the second, was little more than a nearly literal repetition of the *Littera de le maravigliose battaglie*, followed by explanations that the astrologers of the Great Turk were supposed to have given of these prodigies. The last of these to speak, the sage Odobassi, admonishes the sultan in these terms:

> The highly honored king who is seen coming to parley on the field will be that Caesar, emperor of the Christians, so much our enemy, who before he enters into combat will come to meet you in mid-course, and he will ask you whether you want to become a Christian, and you will answer him, no. And then, in a meadow, he will turn around to his men, and will throw the gauntlet in the air as a sign that they should enter into battle, with a face so full of fury that it will strike terror in your men, and in an instant you will see so many arquebuses and so much artillery discharged that it will be impossible to resist them, and at the end they will set your men to flight like pigs, without resistance and in greatest disorder.[69]

The king of the four Ember Days had thus become Charles V. The propagandistic purpose and the aim of supporting anti-Turkish and pro-imperial sentiment that are explicit here reflect elements that were simply latent in the pamphlet's predecessors.[70] One detail should be stressed: The *Avisi* specifically mentions the myth of the furious horde, but only to deny it. One of the wise men whom the Great Turk invites to give his interpretation in fact states that "in ancient days some armed combat must have taken

[68] Lecouteux, "Les Cynocéphales," p. 124.

[69] *Avisi da Constantinopoli di cose stupende, et maravigliose novamente apparse in quelle parti . . . Et unaltro aviso dell'armata del Principe Andrea d'Oria* . . . (Venice: Giovanni Andrea Valvassori, n.d. [1538]), fol. 3*v*.

[70] Although Marcel Bataillon appears unaware of the underlying sources of this and other similar texts, he interprets them correctly; see his "Mythe et connaissance de la Turquie en Occident," in Agostino Pertusi, ed., *Venezia e l'Oriente fra tardo Medioevo e Rinascimento* (Florence: Sansoni, 1966), pp. 451–70.

place in that locality, for which reason those generations still appear in that place with their damned spirits."[71] The ranks of the dead are no longer made up of souls undergoing purification (as in the preceding phase of the Christianization of the myth) but of the damned. Their demonization, in parallel to that of witchcraft, was by then fully achieved.

From Folk Culture to Leo X

One of the many interesting aspects of this entire affair seems to me to be that it confirms connections (postulated before) linking mythology and Germanic folklore with aspects of the cultural and religious life of sixteenth-century Italy, particularly among the subalternate classes.[72] As we have seen, the myth of the furious horde (well defined and widely known in the German world, where, among other things, it was connected with the origins of witchcraft) was sufficiently well known on the plains of Lombardy to be called to mind accurately as a way of dealing with prodigious events in a highly confusing early phase. That we are exceptionally fortunate in being able to follow this development from an unstable visionary creation to a later clear formulation as a specific myth is probably due to an unusually precise and rich documentation.

That is not all, however. This affair also provides an excellent example of the communication of cultural information through social levels that were not only different but notably complex culturally.[73] If we look at the chan-

[71] *Avisi da Constantinopoli*, fol. 2*v*.

[72] More than a century ago, Aleksandr Veselovskii, in an introduction to the *Novella della figlia del re di Dacia* (Pisa: Nistri, 1866), p. xlv (now reprinted in Alexandre Veselovskij, François de Sade, and Giovanni Boccaccio, *La fanciulla perseguitata*, ed. D'Arco Silvio Avalle [Milan: Bompiani, 1977], p. 65), launched the hypothesis that a complex of Nordic traditions, among them the myth of the phantom army, had persisted in Italy at least until the fifteenth century in the territories formerly occupied by the Longobards and, in some parts, also by the Goths. This hypothesis seems confirmed beyond doubt by studies such as Carlo Ginzburg, *The Night Battles*, and Maurizio Bertolotti, "Le ossa e la pelle dei buoi. Un mito popolare tra agiografia e stregoneria," *Quaderni storici* 41 (1947): 470–99. It has even been claimed that Nastagio degli Onesti's novella in the style of Boccaccio is symptomatic of the persistence of the myth, at least until the battle of Ravenna (Boccaccio, *Il Decamerone*, vol. 2, p. 83; Serra, "Su la pena de i dissipatori"; Veselovskij, Sade, and Boccaccio, *La fanciulla perseguitata*, pp. 64–67). This hypothesis finds indirect confirmation, moreover, in the suggestion that the Ravennese dialect word *biatricol* (devil) derives from the name Dietrich von Bern, for which see Manlio Cortelazzo, "Concordanze linguistiche fra Venezia e Ravenna," in Dante Bolognesi, ed., *Ravenna in età veneziana* (Ravenna: Longo, 1986), pp. 188–89.

[73] The importance of investigating both the exchanges between different cultural levels and the various functions of the traditions analyzed is well expressed in Jean-Claude Schmitt, "Les traditions folkloriques dans la culture médiévale. Quelques réflexions de mode," *Archives de Sciences sociales des religions* 52, no. 1 (1981): 5–20.

nels of transmission through which word of this affair traveled between 10 to 15 December 1517 (the hypothetical date of the beginning of the visions) and 23 February 1518 (the date of Pietro Martire d'Anghiera's letter from Valladolid), we see that the time limits are singularly narrow—about two months. Still, we find evidence of a goodly number of means used during those two months: private conversation (oral transmission), private correspondence (written), performance by *cantastorie* (oral again), and printed pamphlets (written). Furthermore, accounts now lost and known only through diaries or chronicles (Giovanni Cambi's *Istorie* and the *Journal d'un Bourgeois de Paris*) allow us to deduce the existence of letters that were manuscript before they appeared in print, but in some fashion no longer fit the category of private correspondence because they were detached from both their sender and their addressee to become "copies of letters" and, in that guise, achieved a wide autonomous, manuscript circulation that often ended up in print publication. This is in all probability what happened with the *Littera de le maravigliose battaglie*. At first a private letter (which was already a written version of an oral account by the "fameglio" who was stricken by the phantasms, according to the reconstruction outlined above), it was then a copy of a letter, and finally a print piece used for propagandistic purposes. Then, however, it was taken up again by a tale singer, and thus was returned to oral transmission.

There are other unknowns superimposed on this already complex picture. As our investigation has progressed, we have found three distinct strata or levels—those of the visions, of the myth, and of propaganda. These three levels stand out clearly in the reconstruction I have attempted and, in my opinion, they are confirmed by the minor but telling detail of the different presentation of the pigs. On the level of the visions, the pigs appear as a reality within the vision, yet they are in some fashion concrete and free of symbolism. The pig, as we know, was a highly important domestic animal between the Middle Ages and the early modern age.[74] For a long time, pigs were allowed to forage in the woods (where the pigs of the vision take refuge), but in early sixteenth-century Lombardy they were more probably kept under a roof. One clear allusion to the presence of pigs or other domestic animals in the area is provided by the heaps of manure, the fumes of which Gian Giacomo Caroldo took as an explanation of the origin of the entire affair. On the mythic level, the pig became an integral part of the myth. We can see this from the fact that the oxen and sheep that accompanied the pigs in the visions of the Bergamo country people no longer have a role in the myth. Finally, at the third level, the pigs acquire a

[74] See *Porci e porcari nel Medioevo. Paesaggio, economia, alimentazione*, ed. Marina Baruzzi and Massimo Montanari (Bologna: IBC: Cooperativa Libraria Universitaria Editrice Bologna, 1981), esp. pp. 29–30 and 72 concerning the raising of pigs in the woods and in pig barns.

symbolic and propagandistic value. They are the Muslim infidels, an emblem of vice, inchoate hordes destined to be routed. In short, the image of the pig remains constant in all versions, but the animal's function varies substantially.

We might well ask, finally, how all these variants fit into the different pigeonholes of social hierarchy. Is there any correspondence between a particular means of communication (oral transmission, letter, print, etc.) and a given social category? What seems to emerge is the interclass character of people whose accounts are on the purely visionary level and, in part, on the mythic level (folklore, as we know, is not exclusively rural or tied to a specific social class).[75] Nonetheless, as the preceding pages have shown, the lower classes (the "simplice persone" and the "fameglio") pay greater attention to the visions and display a greater capacity for elaborating them in complex forms. Those who furnish or who accept a propagandistic interpretation of the apparitions seem to form a much more compact group, not in the channels of communication they use but in their social and cultural status. They are "gens notables et de grant favoir"; they are Francesco Guicciardini or Pope Leo X.

Let me go one step further and add one last variant to the picture outlined thus far, a distinction between two vast territorial and political spheres—Italy of the Po valley, on the one hand, and the Pontifical States, on the other (leaving to one side, for the moment, reverberations of the affair outside Italy). The unknowns in the system I have attempted to construct seem to fall into place. Word of the affair first circulated on the plains of the Po valley within a social context of lay people of middle to lower social status who were receptive to folk influences. The affair received a first political interpretation—that had no sequel, however—in Lombardy, pointing to foreign powers struggling on Italian soil for control of the Milanese state. When Roman circles took over the affair it underwent a radical qualitative shift from the lay realm to the ecclesiastical, from the underclasses to the governing classes, from folk culture to "high" culture (when Guicciardini refers to "cose grande" signified "ora come per el passato" by "prodigi grandi," he is alluding, by implication, to classical divination), from the Italian wars to the crusade against the Turks, and from the visionary and mythic level to that of propaganda. The recasting of folkloric materials as they passed through Rome is, of course, not an isolated fact, as we have seen in connection with the monsters of Ravenna and Bologna. In the early years of the sixteenth century the papal court and circles in Rome tied to it did not refuse "popular" culture, but they did remove

[75] Schmitt, "Les traditions folkloriques," p. 7. See also analogous remarks by D. S. Likhachev cited in Aron Ja. Gurevich, *Categories of Medieval Culture*, tr. G. L. Campbell (London and Boston: Routledge and Kegan Paul, 1985), pp. 59–60.

its constituent parts from their original context and use them in a different sense and for a specific purpose. Certainly in this period exchanges between high and low culture seem extraordinarily rich and frequent: the *Memoria delli novi segni*, translated into Latin by a humanist who offered it, without mention of its origin, to the pope, acquired a second life and more ample telling thanks to the insertion in it of a text—the *Littera de le maravigliose battaglie*—that was given notoriety and further circulation by no less a personage than Pope Leo X. Thanks to the pope, a divinatory interpretation of a folk tradition achieved international fame. Twenty years later it led to an identification of the king of the four Ember Days as Charles V and to a prediction of the rout of the Turks based on the disorderly flight of a herd of pigs.

4

THE APOCALYPTICAL PREACHING OF ANDREA BAURA AND ZACCHERIA DA FIVIZZANO

Was Andrea Baura a Lutheran?

ON CHRISTMAS DAY 1520, Maestro Andrea Baura of Ferrara, a hermit of Saint Augustine, preached in Venice from the balcony of Palazzo Loredan, overlooking Campo Santo Stefano. Marin Sanudo, whose ear was, as always, attuned to every religious event that had social implications, recorded his homily in these terms:

> On Campo San Stephano there was a sermon by Master Andrea of Ferrara that drew a large crowd. The square was full, and he was up on the balcony of the Pontremolis' house . . . and he spoke ill of the pope and of the Roman curia. This man follows the doctrine of Fra Martin Luther, [who] in Germany is a most learned man who follows St. Paul and is much opposed to the pope, for which he is excommunicated by the pope.[1]

Baura's sermon must have been truly extraordinary if it held the attention, out of doors and in the middle of winter, of a larger audience than could fit into the nearby church of Santo Stefano, where he had preached before, as we shall see. It is hardly surprising, then, that echoes of his homily, accompanied by the redoubtable name of Martin Luther, from whom he seemed to take his inspiration, soon reached the ears of Leo X (sharply attacked by Maestro Andrea). The pope was swift to react. Looking upon Baura more as a new Luther than as a Lutheran, he summoned the Venetian ambassador, Alvise Gradenigo, to ask him to see to it that a work Baura had written that was still in manuscript not be printed. Pietro Bembo, who was present as pontifical secretary, later suggested to Gradenigo, privately and on his own initiative, that he have Baura imprisoned,[2] and other requests in the same vein reached the Venetian Signoria from the papacy in the next two weeks. An answer arrived from Venice, through an interlocutor, "that Brother Andrea of Ferrara being no longer in Venice, neither his conclusion nor other things against the Holy See have been or

[1] Marino Sanuto, *Diarii*, 58 vols. (Venice: R. Deputazione Veneta di storia patria, 1879–1903), vol. 29, col. 495.

[2] Ibid., col. 552.

will be printed."[3] In reality, Baura had remained "in secret" in the city, and he later went to Ferrara under the protection of Alfonso d'Este,[4] where, toward the end of the year, he dedicated the work to Cardinal Corner. The piece was, somewhat disconcertingly, entitled *Apostolicae potestatis contra Martinum Lutherum defensio*,[5] and thus was a defense of papal power against Luther. Was this a politic change of mind or a cover-up? In either case, the situation seems to have been resolved, and as early as 23 March 1521 a pontifical brief arrived in Venice authorizing Baura to return to preaching.

These events are well known.[6] If I return to them here it is because these events had another meaning than the one usually suggested for them. Baura, as is known, had already preached in Venice in the churches of Santo Stefano and San Marco in April 1517 and January 1519. Sanudo was certainly present when he gave the homily on Easter Day, 12 April 1517, as he reports:

> After dining, I was urged to go to San Marco for the preacher of San Stefano, Master Andrea da Ferrara of the order of the hermits, who has a great following. He preached a poor sermon, in my judgment, who was there to hear it, reproving vices well, but without adducing any doctor, philosopher, or poet.[7]

Two years later Sanudo offers further information on this and other sermons of Baura:

> [17 January 1519] This morning in San Stefano there preached one of the first of his order, named Master Andrea da Ferrara, who preached two years ago about prophecies, etc. And thus he preached today, saying that her enemies have now begun to group together against Italy (that is, the Turks). He will preach Saturday and Sunday and will say great things about what is going to

[3] Ibid., cols. 561, 609–10, 614, 615.

[4] Fedele Lampertico, "Ricordi storici del palazzo Loredan," *Nuovo archivio veneto* 5 (1893): 250–54.

[5] The work was later published in Milan in 1523. See below.

[6] On Baura, see Lampertico, "Ricordi storici," pp. 249–55; Franco Gaeta, "Baura, Andrea," in DBI, vol. 7, pp. 296–97; David Gutiérrez, "I primi agostiniani italiani che scrissero contro Lutero," *Analecta augustiniana* 39 (1976): 19–38; Silvana Seidel Menchi, "Le traduzioni italiane di Lutero nella prima metà del Cinquecento," *Rinascimento* 17 (1977): 33–108; pp. 34–36; Antonio Samaritani, "Contributo documentario per un profilo spirituale-religioso di Lucrezia Borgia nella Ferrara degli anni 1502–1519," *Analecta Tertii Ordinis Regularis Sancti Francisci* 14 (1981): 975–90, later included in Samaritani, "La 'Defensio' di Pietro Scazano in favore di Andrea Baura contro Lorenzo Castrofranco (*a*. 1520). Ai prodromi della polemica antiluterana in Italia," *Analecta augustiniana* 47 (1984): 7–42.

[7] The transcription of this passage is based on the original manuscript of the *Diarii* (Biblioteca Marciana di Venezia, MS it. VII 252 [= 9239], fol. 90*r*) because the printed edition (vol. 24, col. 158) erroneously reads "maestro Andrea da Franza" rather than "maestro Andrea da Ferrara."

happen, then he will leave to go preach elsewhere. . . . [20 January 1519] That master from Ferrara preached in San Stefano. He had a large crowd. He made some prophecies: This year Italy will be badly smitten; two cities will be preserved, one of them Venice, if [people] resolve to do good.[8]

Thus Bauer had preached *di profetie* in both 1517 and 1519, perhaps also in 1520, foretelling in detail God's punishment for men's vices, with the Turks serving as the instrument of divine wrath. There was a possible way out, however: "volendo far bene"—that is, by amending one's ways. It is quite understandable that this type of apocalyptical preaching based on divine inspiration would scornfully reject learned citations and any "alegation di alcun dotor, philosopho né poeta."

Itinerant Hermits from the Fifteenth to the Sixteenth Centuries

Apocalyptical preaching was an extraordinarily widespread homiletic genre in Italy in those years, and, added to other channels for the diffusion of prophecy, it assured a broad hearing for the prophetic message among a great variety of social strata. The Neapolitan chronicler Angelo Tummulilli noted as early as 1450 that "ceperunt undique insurgere predicatores fratres de ordine minorum et predicare populo penitentiam." Such men threatened terrible chastisement, "nisi fuerimus conversi . . . et non cessabant profetare nisi malum et ve."[9] Nearly fifty years later, in 1496, Giuliano Dati admonished Italy in his *Diluvio di Roma* in the following terms:

Tu hai tanti profeti già veduti
e scribi e sapienti predicare
. . .
O quanti n'è venuti anchor da poi
che gli ha possuti tutti quanti udire!
ma tu se' obstinato come suoi
e non ti vuo' per niente pentire.
. . .
E la voce di molti ancor rimbomba
che portano una croce sempre in mano.

(You have already seen so many prophets and scribes and wise men preaching . . . O! how many have come in recent days

[8] Sanuto, *Diarii*, vol. 26, cols. 363, 378, 386.

[9] Angelo de Tummulillis, *Notabilia temporum*, ed. Costantino Corvisieri (Livorno: Tip. F. Vigo, 1890), pp. 57–58.

> whom you have had to hear! But you are as obstinate as ever and will not repent for anything. . . . And the voice still echoes of many who forever carry a cross in their hand.)[10]

Thus Italy in 1496 had seen "tanti profeti."[11] Indeed, contemporary chronicles give frequent testimony to itinerant hermits who went "preaching and wailing," often in an apocalyptical key, through the same town squares in which the *cantambanchi* declaimed their tales of catastrophes and prodigious happenings. In the prophecies in verse, hermits and prophets often appeared as signs and messengers of the divine will. The *Diluvio di Roma* gives an excellent picture of apocalyptical preaching, and of prophetic tension in general, in Italy during those years. Dati says:

> Non ti ricorda Guglielmo barbato
> che predicò per Roma con la croce
> el prim'anno de Sisto, in ogni lato
> predicendo tutto 'l male ad alta voce?
> Fulli tolta la croce e bastonato,
> ma tristo chi fa 'l male e poi li nuoce:
> el beato Gulielmo da Morano
> ogi lo chiama al mondo alchun christiano.
>
> Un altro che un san Paulo pareva
> che in Campo di Fior pur predicava,
> e tanta longa barba al pecto haveva,
> e vestito d'azuro sempre andava,

[10] Giuliano Dati, *Del diluvio di Roma del MCCCCLXXXXV adi iiii di dicembre et daltre cose di gran meraviglia* (n.p., n.d.), fol. a iii*r–v*.

[11] Melchior de Pobladura, "La 'Severa riprensione' di fra Matteo da Bascio (1495?–1552)," *Archivio italiano per la storia della pietà* 3 (1962): 281–302; Cesare Vasoli, "L'attesa della nuova era in ambienti e gruppi fiorentini del Quattrocento," in *L'attesa dell'età nuova nella spiritualità della fine del Medioevo* (Todi: Accademia tudertina, 1962), pp. 370–432; Giampaolo Tognetti, "Sul romito e profeta Brandano da Petroio," *Rivista storica italiana* 72 (1960): 20–44; Marjorie Reeves, *The Influence of Prophecy in the Late Middle Ages: A Study in Joachimism* (Oxford: Clarendon Press, 1969), pp. 367 and 447–48; Antonio Volpato, "La predicazione penitenziale–apocalittica nell'attività di due predicatori del 1473," *Bullettino dell'Istituto storico italiano per il Medioevo* 82 (1970) [1974]: 113–28; Giovanni Miccoli, "La Storia religiosa," *Storia d'Italia*, 6 vols. (Turin: G. Einaudi, 1972–1977), vol. 2, *Dalla caduta dell'Impero romano al secolo XVIII*, pt. 1, pp. 968–75; Adriano Prosperi, "Il monaco Teodoro. Note su un processo fiorentino del 1515," *Critica storica* 11 (1975): 71–101; Prosperi, "Gian Battista da Bascio e la predicazione dei romiti alla metà del '500," *Bollettino della società di studi valdesi* 138 (1975): 69–79; Giampaolo Tognetti, "Profezie, profeti itineranti e cultura orale," *La cultura* 18 (1980): 427–34; and, in particular, Bernardo Nobile, " 'Romiti' e vita religiosa nella cronachistica italiana fra '400 e '500," *Cristianesimo nella storia* 5 (1984): 303–40. I have taken into account, whenever it seemed to me opportune, the observations in the latter two articles concerning my own previous works, and I now want to thank the two authors, in particular Bernardo Nobile, who has kindly allowed me to read his essay in typescript. Given his ample treatment of the subject, I will not go into hermits in depth here.

el mal che t'è seguito ti dicieva
. . .
Vedi quel che ti dice suor Palomba,
e Margerita, virgo da Magliano,
. . .
e quel da Ginazano, e 'l ferrarese,
e quel che t'ha già detto Caterina,
seconda verginella fu sanese,
che chi l'udì paria proprio divina.

(Do you not remember bearded Guglielmo, who preached through Rome with the cross the first year of Sixtus, in every place predicting all evil at the top of his lungs? The cross was taken away from him and he was beaten, but woe befell those who do evil and did him harm: the blessed Gulielmo da Morano many Christians in the world call him today. Another who seemed a St. Paul, who preached in the Campo dei Fiori and had a long beard down to his chest and always went about dressed in blue, told you of the evil you have done. . . . See what sister Palomba tells you, and Margarita, the virgin from Magliano, . . . and the one from Ginazano and the Ferrarese, and what Caterina told you, [the] second virgin from Siena, who to those who heard her seemed truly divine.)[12]

We can recognize Colomba da Rieti,[13] Mariano da Genazzano, and Girolamo Savonarola on this list, and other lesser-known persons to whom Dati gives equal importance, such as Guglielmo da Morano and Antonio da Padova, who preached throughout Italy and even in Sicily in the winter of 1472–1473.[14] A long list of prophets, beginning with the illustrious name of Joachim of Fiore and extending to other, more recent "messengers of the Almighty" (St. Vincent Ferrer, blessed Anselmus, St. Bridget, blessed Tommasuccio da Foligno, Osanna da Mantova), figure in the appropriately titled *Imminente flagello de Italia*, which presumably appeared about 1510.[15] There was also the anonymous *cantastorie* of the *Memoria delli novi segni*, which gives an admirable picture of the hermit:

un antico romitto
cum barba longa e chioma
va gridando per Roma

[12] Dati, *Del diluvio di Roma*, fol. a. iii*v*.

[13] Dati mentions Colomba of Rieti twice, once giving her name as "suor Palomba," and the second time using the term "second Catherine of Siena," by which she was known.

[14] On these, see Volpato, "La predicazione penitenziale-apocalittica," and Nobile, " 'Romiti' e vita religiosa," pp. 317–21.

[15] *Imminente flagello de Italia* (n.p., n.d.), fol. 2*r*.

"pace, pace"
poi quando che li piace
invisibil va via
e multi ch'el sia Elia
credon fermo.

(an old hermit with long beard and hair goes crying "peace, peace" through Rome, then when he pleases, invisible, he goes away, and many firmly believe that he is Elijah.)[16]

The suggestion in these lines that the "antico romitto" is the prophet Elijah is important for its eschatological tone. There was in fact a well-established pseudo-Joachimite tradition (probably spread through preaching) that Elijah would return to the earth, together with Enoch, in the last days. For example, the expression "fin a che Henoch apparerà et Helya" had the sense of "until the end of the world" in a Venetian sonnet published anonymously in 1509, and in the *Libellus* of Telesphorus of Cosenza, published in Venice in 1516 but well known before that date, Elijah and Enoch are given as the "two witnesses" mentioned in the Apocalypse ("And I will give unto my two witnesses, and they shall prophesy a thousand two hundred sixty days, clothed in sackcloth": Apoc. 11:3).[17] Sackcloth (or even wild animal skins—*pelle salvatica*)[18] was a constant in the dress of itinerant prophets. Added to the cross, the long beard, and the bare head, such clothing produced a faithful imitation of the current iconography of St. John the Baptist and the prophet Elijah.[19] Matthew says

[16] *Memoria delli novi segni et spaventevoli prodigii comparsi in piu loci de Italia et in varie parte del mondo lanno mille cinquecento undese* (n.p., n.d.), fol. 1*v*.

[17] The 1509 sonnet appears in *Laus Venetorum* (Venice, 1509), fol. 4*r*. On Telesphorus, see Emil Donckel, "Studien über die Prophezeiungen des Fr. Telesphorus von Cosenza O.F.M., 1365–1386," *Archivum franciscanum historicum* 26 (1933): 29–104, 282–314; Herbert Grundmann, *Studien über Joachim von Floris* (Leipzig and Berlin: B. G. Teubner, 1927), p. 193, which contains a careful analysis of the publication. See also Dennis E. Rhodes, *Gli annali tipografici di Lazzaro de' Soardi* (Florence: L. S. Olschki, 1978), pp. 76–77, 80; Roberto Rusconi, *L'attesa della fine. Crisi della società, profezia ed Apocalisse in Italia al tempo del grande scisma d'Occidente (1378–1417)* (Rome: Istituto storico italiano per il Medio Evo, 1979), pp. 171–84; Bernard McGinn, *Visions of the End: Apocalyptical Traditions in the Middle Ages* (New York: Columbia University Press, 1979), pp. 246–47. The return at the end of time of Enoch and Elijah, united in the one person of "er Nocchilia," was familiar to the Roman populace of Belli's day: See Giuseppe Gioacchino Belli, *I sonetti*, ed. Maria Teresa Lanza, 4 vols. (Milan: Feltrinelli, 1965), vol. 1, p. 300, no. 274, "La fin der monno."

[18] Niccola della Tuccia, *Cronache di Viterbo e di altre città*, ed. Ignazio Ciampi, in *Cronache e statuti della città di Viterbo* (Florence: Tipi di M. Cellini e c., 1872), p. 106; Bernardino Zambotti, *Diario ferrarese dall'anno 1476 sino al 1504*, ed. Giuseppe Pardi, RIS vol. 24, pt. 7, no. 2 (Bologna: Nicola Zanichelli, 1937), pp. 3–359; p. 191.

[19] See, for example, Antonio de Vascho, *Il diario della città di Roma dall'anno 1480 all'anno 1492*, ed. Giuseppe Chiesa, RIS vol. 23, pt. 3 (Città di Castello: S. Lapi, 1910–1911), pp. 449–546; p. 523; *Continuazione della cronaca di Bologna detta Varignana (Cronaca B) dal*

of John (Matt. 11:14) that "he is Elias that is to come," a parallel that was frequently drawn.[20] In short, they (John the Baptist in particular) were the models and the archetypes for hermits, lent the hermits epithets such as *Missus a Deo*, for example, which derives from John 1:6 ("There was a man sent from God, whose name was John"), or provided them with names, as was the case with Giovanni Novello, which was not, as has been thought, that preacher's given name and family name, but more probably an epithet qualifying Giovanni as a second John the Baptist.[21]

Although these prophets resembled one another in their fidelity to this stereotype and in their itinerancy, they differed widely in their levels of culture and their social status. They could be friars, priests, or laymen, illiterates or *docti*, physicians, doctors, or ex-peasants. Nonetheless, very few sources show traces of any great degree of complexity in the prophetic preaching of the hermits.[22] For the most part, city chronicles repeat monotonously that the prophets foretold "widespread death, famine, and war," "many future ills," "famine, war, and food shortages"—in short, that "they all say, 'Repent, for God intends to punish Italy.' "[23]

1471 al 1500 in *Corpus Chronicarum bononiensium*, ed. Albano Sorbelli, RIS vol. 18, pt. 1, no. 26 (vol. 4 of the text) (Bologna: Nicola Zanichelli, 1924), p. 435; Dati, *Del diluvio di Roma*, fol. a. iii*v* ("e la voce di molti anchor rimbomba / che portano una croce sempre in mano"); Zambotti, *Diario ferrarese*, p. 191; Tommasino Lancellotti, *Cronaca modenese*, ed. Carlo Borghi, 12 vols. (Parma: P. Fiaccadori, 1863), vol. 6, p. 150.

[20] Louis Réau, *Iconographie de l'art chrétienne*, 3 vols. (Paris: Presses Universitaires Françaises, 1955–1959), vol. 2, pt. 1, p. 349; Réau, "L'iconographie du prophète Elie," in *Elie le prophète*, 2 vols. (Tournai and Paris: Desclée de Brouwer, 1956), vol. 1, pp. 236–37. On John the Baptist, see also Marilyn Aronberg Lavin, "Giovannino Battista: A Study in Renaissance Religious Symbolism," *Art Bulletin* 37 (1955): 85–113, and "Giovannino Battista: A Supplement," *Art Bulletin* 43 (1961): 319–26. For the parallel between John the Baptist and Elijah, see Antonio Pinelli, "La 'philosophie des images.' Emblemi e imprese fra Manierismo e Barocco," *Ricerche di storia dell'arte* 1–2 (1976): 12–13, 21. On the Renaissance tradition of the prophet Elijah, see Katharine R. Firth, *The Apocalyptic Tradition in Reformation Britain, 1530–1645* (Oxford and New York: Oxford University Press, 1979), pp. 5–6, and, for a later period, Guy Demerson, "Un mythe des libertins spirituels: le prophète Elie," in *Aspects du libertinisme au XVIe siècle* (Paris: J. Vrin, 1974), pp. 105–120. Bibliography for the medieval period is given in Rusconi, *L'attesa della fine*, p. 40, n. 5 bis. I might also note that John and Elijah are placed facing one another on the double door of the cathedral of Ravello sculpted by Barisano di Trani in 1179.

[21] Prosperi, "Gian Battista da Bascio," p. 69, changes the name Giovanni Novello to Giovanni Novelli, thus turning his nickname into a family name. On Giovanni Novello, see Nobile, " 'Romiti' e vita religiosa," pp. 322–27.

[22] One exception to this rule was Guglielmo da Morano, who preached in a number of Italian cities and demonstrated wide knowledge of the Bible (see Niccola della Tuccia, *Cronache di Viterbo*, p. 106); another was the "homo quidam natione incognitus," who, preaching in Rome some twenty years later, "reducebat ad concordiam testamentum vetus usque ad novum," hence followed Joachimite models (Stefano Infessura, *Diario della città di Roma*, ed. Oreste Tommasini [Rome: Forzani e c., 1890], pp. 264–65).

[23] Tommaso di Silvestro, *Diario*, ed. Luigi Fumi, RIS vol. 15, pt. 5, no. 2 (Bologna: Nicola Zanichelli, 1923), p. 50; Zambotti, *Diario Ferrarese*, p. 191; *Diario ferrarese dall'anno 1409*

Naturally, these reports do not necessarily tell us what the actual contents of the sermons were but only what the hearers could grasp and make their own. In this sense, the problem of context is related to how the prophets were received. The chroniclers do not always offer explicit comment on the question, but in general it would seem that the prediction of calamities had a wide audience. The anonymous chronicler who describes the preaching of one hermit in Bologna (perhaps Guglielmo da Morano) during the winter of 1472 states that he "had a great following of women and of men . . . and most of the citizens revered him and he was held to be almost a saint."[24] A hermit who rode about Rome on a steer in 1485 "aroused great admiration," although, the chronicler adds, "the better people (*gli huomini da bene*) esteemed these things, but not with as much enthusiasm as the common people (*il volgo*)."[25] Thus these preachers had greater success among the lower classes in the cities. The chronicler says of Giovanni Novello of Siena, who preached in Ferrara during the winter of 1487–1488, that he "showed himself to be a man of good life and merciful."[26] To end the series, "a mass of persons thronged" to hear the unnamed prophet who preached in Rome in 1491.[27]

A reverent hearing did not prevent isolated episodes of intolerance, but on the whole respectful attitudes must have been the rule. Giuliano Dati says of Guglielmo of Morano that "the cross was taken away from him and he was beaten," but he adds that at the time he was writing—1495–1496—many Christians called him blessed.[28] Guglielmo's twenty-five years of popular veneration entitle us to suppose that he had a large following and that his hearers believed his words. Such men must still have found it easy to gather a crowd in 1516, when the fathers assembled for the Fifth Lateran Council felt it necessary to place strict controls on prophetic preaching, as seen in the histories, both contemporary and later, of Brandano, Bonaventura, and Theodore (not by chance, the latter two came to a poor end). The situation was radically different after 1530, however. The preacher dressed in sackcloth who spoke in Modena in June 1532 "in the square where there is the market, in front of the bishop's palace, and spoke about great things that are to come" aroused the alarmed attention of the

sino al 1502 di autori incerti, ed. Giuseppe Pardi, RIS vol. 24, pt. 7, no. 1 (Bologna: Nicola Zanichelli, 1928–1933), p. 167; Lancellotti, *Cronaca modenese*, vol. 4, pp. 11–12.

[24] *Continuazione della cronaca di Bologna*, p. 435. On the problem of the identity of this personage (which is not relevant here), see Nobile, " 'Romiti' e vita religiosa," pp. 317–19.

[25] De Vascho, *Il diario della città di Roma*, p. 523. On this same personage, see, aside from Nobile, " 'Romiti' e vita religiosa," p. 322, the *Notationes* of the Roman grammarian Paolo Pompilio in Giovanni Mercati, "Paolo Pompilio e la scoperta del cadavere intatto sull'Appia nel 1485," *Opere minori*, 6 vols. (Vatican City: Biblioteca Apostolica Vaticana, 1937–84), vol. 4, p. 276.

[26] Zambotti, *Diario ferrarese*, p. 191.

[27] "Cum accurrisset ibi copia hominum" (Infessura, *Diario*, p. 264.

[28] Dati, *Del diluvio di Roma*, fol. a. iii*v*.

vicar of Bishop Giovanni Morone, who was away at the time, who ordered him to cease preaching. Not only did the preacher prompt ecclesiastical repression; it is even more interesting that he provoked laughter among the citizenry: "Most people mock them because they are not well dressed and are not even literate."[29] What fifty years earlier had elicited admiration and an attentive hearing—the inspired man's lack of worldly culture and clothing that reflected his qualifications as a precursor and a prophet—were now the objects of ridicule and laughter.

This was certainly not an isolated case. The hermit who passed through Modena in May of 1539 (probably Brandano) had no greater success. Lancellotti tells us:

> A poor man dressed in sackcloth, barefoot, his hair full of ashes, with a cross of Christ in [his] hand, went about the main square of Modena today, crying, "Repent, repent, for God is going to punish you," and every man laughed and he went on his way.[30]

In his appearance, this personage respected all the elements of the traditional stereotype. Dressed in sackcloth, bareheaded, barefoot, and carrying a cross in his hand, he urged the populace to repentance, predicting future afflictions exactly as had the prophets of fifty years before. The people had said of the earlier prophets that they were dressed "like an apostle"; now they said that this man was "a poor man." The earlier men aroused admiration; this man prompted hilarity. The equating of a certain way of dressing and a particular physical appearance with the image of the prophet now seems lost. The religious value of the poor man as the image of Christ also seems to have nearly disappeared during these decades. Here the poor man is no longer either Christ or a prophet, but only a deviant, an outsider to both civil and ecclesiastical society. The hypothesis that repression of the poor paralleled that of hermits finds apparent confirmation in the behavior of Agostino Zanetti, vicar to the bishop of Bologna. That same year, 1539, Monsignor Zanetti meted out exactly the same treatment to two beggars, caught pretending to have been slaves of the Turks and to have had their tongues cut off, who "went around the churches begging" and, several months later, to a hermit who was predicting earthquakes, storms, war, and pestilence in the city's main square. With perfect equity, Monsignor Zanetti had them all given a good flogging and sentenced them to a

[29] Lancellotti, *Cronaca modenese*, vol. 4, pp. 11–12.

[30] Ibid., p. 150. On preaching in Modena in those years, see Susanna Peyronel, "I conventi maschili e il problema della predicazione nella Modena di Giovanni Morone," in *Il rinascimento e le corti padane. Società e cultura* (Bari: De Donato, 1977), pp. 239–56 (Peyronel does not mention the passage cited, however).

few days in prison.[31] From the 1530s on, tighter and more careful control was gradually established over poverty, sanctity, and the presumption of divine inspiration.

Apocalyptical Preaching in the Churches: Francesco da Montepulciano and His Companions

For the most part, the itinerant hermits preached not in churches but in the public squares, rubbing elbows with "the charlatans, the quack dentists, the butcher surgeons" and with "crowd pleasers who, with the lyre and lascivious novellas hoodwinked the common people."[32] Hermits were an integral part of that scene, and they shared not only the audience but the repertory of gestures of the other actors on that stage. Eyewitness accounts agree that this was the general rule, the most illustrious isolated exception certainly being the *Missus a Deo*, who normally preached in the principal church of the city he visited, however "without ringing of the bells"—that is, with no official announcement.[33] Still, there is no lack of evidence of apocalyptical sermons given in church by friars and monks and even by official preachers; indeed, the sources are singularly abundant and are often quite specific. Perhaps because such sources are in better condition, mentions are particularly frequent after the turn of the sixteenth century, while evidence of the hermits' activities is largely (though not exclusively) earlier. It may be that the case of Savonarola encouraged the proliferation of preachers, which does not mean, of course, that prophetic preachers should necessarily be considered Savonarolans.

In this fashion, an Observant Franciscan of Corsican origin arrived in Orvieto in June 1496. We are told that he

[31] Jacopo Rainieri, *Diario bolognese*, ed. Olindo Guerrini and Corrado Ricci (Bologna: R. Deputazione di storia patria per le provincie di Romagna, 1888), pp. 42–48.

[32] The two quotations come, first, from a preacher who prophesied the sack of Rome in the Campo dei Fiori and, second, from Matteo da Bascio, for which see Francisco Delicado, *Portrait of Lozana: The Lusty Andalusian Woman*, tr. Bruno M. Damiani (Potomac, Md.: Scripta Humanistica, 1987), p. 63; and Paulo da Foligno, *Origo et progressus ordinis Fratrum Minorum Capucchinorum*, ed. P. Melchior a Pobladura (Rome: Institutum Historicum Ord. P. Min. Cap., 1955), p. 124. The tradition of gesture in preaching went back to Francis of Assisi: See Raoul Manselli, "Il gesto come predicazione per san Francesco d'Assisi," *Collectanea franciscana* 51 (1981): 5–16. "Merciless competition among jesters and Franciscan orators" is well illustrated in Vittorio Dornetti, "Sulla predicazione popolare francescana: la parodia di Zaffarino da Firenze," *Cristianesimo nella storia* 3 (1982): 83–102, citation on p. 102.

[33] Giovan Francesco Negri, *Annali della patria*, BUB, MS 1107, vol. 7, pt. 1, fol. 163*r*. On this figure, see Nobile, " 'Romiti' e vita religiosa," pp. 328–29. In spite of several discrepancies, I believe that this was the same person who had already appeared in Venice in May and June 1516 (Sanuto, *Diarii*, vol. 22, cols. 195–96, 206–7, 292–93).

always predicted woes—that is, widespread death, famine, and war—such that all, or rather few, would escape. He had [his listeners] cry out "Jesus, Jesus" at all his sermons and go in procession around the streets with the cross before them and the little children behind them, all continually crying, "Jesus, Jesus, God help us!"[34]

This was a penitential sermon, then, in which prediction presumably drew upon acknowledgment of real problems: the end of peace in Italy and the explosive rise of epidemic syphilis. The chronicler does not speak in very precise terms, however. We know somewhat more about several instances of prophetic preaching in Venice, thanks in particular to Marin Sanudo, who was unfailingly sensitive to the possible political implications in religious life and to the need to keep them in hand. Thus on 7 April 1501 he notes:

at San Salvador there preached a friar of San Stephano, of Veronese nationality, who said in his sermon on Palm Sunday that until 1505 Italy will be torn to shreds, and that the French will be broken in Tuscany, and that he could not tell about Venice. He spoke of the pope and the kings of Spain. Then it was told to the heads of the [Council of] Ten, who ordered him to preach no more. And this was done at the request of the ambassador of France.[35]

If this Veronese friar came from the monastery of Santo Stefano, he was presumably an Augustinian. This is far from certain, in spite of the ambiguous title of *heremita* given to another preacher who "said he was a hermit" when he preached on 31 March 1507 in the church of the Servi and who threatened his hearers with "many things of a prophetical sort from the pulpit . . . about plagues and war with the Turks, saying he was a prophet."[36] Three years later, during Lent, another Veronese reeled off a long list of short- and long-term predictions involving bloody wars in Tuscany and Lombardy.[37] Still another Veronese preacher, Fra Girolamo da Verona, *heremito* (in this case, as we shall see, an Augustinian hermit), who had preached at an earlier date in the church of San Salvatore and had been silenced because he predicted "that the king of France will break the faith," preached *per profetia* in Santo Stefano on 20 March 1513, Palm Sunday:

He said that in the Old Testament up to Christ there were sixty-four generations, and after Christ, fifty-one generations, and that [the two periods] corresponded . . . and thus in the seventeen years to come there will be very great things in Italy, and in this land there will be an upheaval *in Ecclesia Dei*, etc., concluding "blessed are those who will not be alive," and [saying] that tomor-

[34] Tommaso di Silvestro, *Diario*, p. 50.
[35] Sanuto, *Diarii*, vol. 4, col. 11.
[36] Ibid., vol. 7, col. 40.
[37] Ibid., vol. 10, cols. 48–49.

row and the day after he will preach on this matter, which sermon, in my opinion, should not be given. The church was completely full.[38]

Several aspects of this report are interesting. First, there is the clear political context of at least the first of the Veronese preacher's sermons. At the time, Venice was concluding the alliance with France from which, as we have seen, Pope Leo X was to seek to dissuade it in the months to come. It is also interesting to note Sanudo's disapproval—the same disapproval that we see nearly every time he records prophetic preaching, here apparently directed in equal measure toward the more strictly political aspects of Fra Girolamo's homily and its apocalyptical aspects and the warm reception they received ("era tuta la chiesia piena"). But the most relevant detail is perhaps the computation of the generations of the New and the Old Testament, counted not according to the indications given in the Bible but according to the calculations that Joachim of Fiore proposed in his *Concordie Novi ac Veteris Testamenti* (still unpublished at that date but quite evidently known to the preacher).[39] The seventeen years of schism and suffering predicted by the friar from Verona exactly matched the number of years remaining until the end of the fifty-first generation ($51 \times 30 = 1530$; $1530 - 1513 = 17$), and, by implication, they refer to the eschatological passage in Matt. 24:23: "This generation shall not pass, till all these things be done."

The anti-French tone of Fra Girolamo's homiletics and the evocation of Matthew the Evangelist recall another and much better-known preacher whose voice had already been heard during the same months, Francesco da Montepulciano. His famous sermon of 18 December 1513 was shot through with reminiscences of the eschatological theme in Matthew, and it predicted (among other things) the collapse of French aspirations in Italy.[40] It is clear from contemporary reports that Francesco's sermon was

[38] Ibid., vol. 16, col. 53.

[39] Joachim of Fiore, *Divini vatis Abbatis Joachim liber Concordie Novi ac Veteris Testamenti* (Venice: Simone da Lovere, 1519), fol. 134*r*: "ab Adam usque ad Jacob fuere generationes viginti una, a Jacob vero usque ad Christum generationes quadraginta duarum." The count of generations is less in Matt. 1: 1–16 (thirty-eight from Jacob to Christ) and greater in Luke 3: 23–38 (seventy-seven from Adam to Christ). For the calculation of thirty years for one generation, "recte spatium generationis in Novo Testamento triginta annorum numero terminatur," see *Liber Concordie*, fol. 12*v*.

[40] On Francesco da Montepulciano, see Cesare Vasoli, "Temi mistici e profetici alla fine del Quattrocento," in his *Studi sulla cultura del Rinascimento* (Manduria: Lacaita, 1968), pp. 217–19; Roberto Ridolfi, *Vita di Niccolò Machiavelli*, 7th ed., rev. (Florence: Sansoni, 1978), p. 516, available in English as *The Life of Niccolò Machiavelli*, tr. Cecil Grayson (Chicago: University of Chicago Press, 1963), p. 259, n. 32; Giampaolo Tognetti, "Note sul profetismo nel Rinascimento e la letteratura relativa," *Bullettino dell'Istituto storico italiano per il Medioevo* 82 (1970) [1974]: 129–57, esp. pp. 143–46; Donald Weinstein, *Savonarola and Florence: Prophecy and Patriotism in the Renaissance* (Princeton: Princeton University Press, 1970), pp.

not an isolated incident but the most significant and most talked-about of a composite series of sermons. Not only do we know that several friars followed his example, among them two non-Florentines who "exclaimed much against Rome and against the present government of the city," but that he inspired others, even women and illiterate common people ("monks, tertiary nuns, young girls, peasants"), to do so as well. Machiavelli wrote to Vettori near the beginning of February 1514 that about Florence "there is nothing to say, except prophecies and announcements of misfortune."[41] Even outside Florence the weeks during December 1513 and January 1514 were filled with prophetic tension in part connected, as we have seen, with the shifting policies of the Holy See. Furthermore, Francesco da Montepulciano himself seems to have had a less specifically Florentine and Tuscan background than has been thought. The Perugian chronicler Teseo Alfani commented, as he noted the sermons that Francesco gave in Perugia between 20 April and 3 May 1513, that "seventeen years ago he was in Perugia studying, then in Padua, and recently [spent] many years in the Kingdom [of Naples] in a hermitage."[42] The *Storia fiorentina* of Jacopo Pitti also records that Francesco was not alone, but was

---

348–49. There is another edition of the sermon of 18 December 1513 not mentioned in these works: *Predica di frate Francesco da Montepulciano de' frati minori conventuali di san Francesco. Fatta in Santa Croce di Fiorenza a di XVIII di dicembre 1513. Raccolta dalla viva voce del predicatore per Ser Lorenzo Vivoli notaio fiorentino, mentre che predicava* (Florence: Stampa ducale, 1569).

[41] Piero Parenti, *Storia fiorentina*, ed. Joseph Schnitzer, in Schnitzer, *Quellen und Forschungen zur Geschichte Savonarolas*, 4 vols. (Munich: J. J. Lentner [E. Stahl, jun.], 1902–1910), vol. 4, *Savonarola nach den Aufzeichnungen des Florentiners Piero Parenti* (Leipzig: Dunker and Humblot, 1910), p. 308; Jacopo Pitti, *Dell'Istoria fiorentina*, *Archivio storico italiano* 1 (1842): 1–208; p. 112. Machiavelli's letter of 4 February 1514 can be found in Niccolò Machiavelli, *Lettere*, ed. Franco Gaeta (Milan: Feltrinelli, 1961), p. 323, and in *The Letters of Machiavelli*, tr. and ed. Allan Gilbert (New York: Capricorn Books, 1961), p. 153 (Gilbert translation used here). Another well-known letter of Machiavelli, dated 19 December 1513, gives an ironic report of the sermon of the previous day, which he himself did not hear, however ("The preaching I did not hear, because I am not given to such doings": Gaeta ed., pp. 308–9; Gilbert trans., p. 148). Vettori answers from Rome on 24 December with prudence: "I shall not respond concerning the hermit because, as you say, Florence is founded under a planet [that makes] such men abound, and they are heard willingly there" (Gaeta ed., p. 313).

[42] Teseo Alfani, *Frammenti inediti delle memorie di Perugia di Teseo Alfani dall'anno 1506 al 1527*, in *Cronache della città di Perugia*, ed. Ariodante Fabretti, 4 vols. (Turin: coi tipi privati dell'editore / dell'autore, 1887–1892), vol. 3, p. 50. Alfani also offers the information that Francesco had preached earlier in the territories of Siena and Florence, and that when he left Perugia "he went to Assisi and then on his trip" (pp. 50–51). The friar's widespread fame is confirmed by Leonello Beliardi, who records that an earthquake occurred in Florence in January 1514, adding that "it had been predicted by a preacher of the Conventual Order of St. Francis, together with many other woes that were supposed to occur in Florence. And that friar nearly died in Florence because of his aversion to the Florentines, and he was held to be a saint. Thousands of people followed after him": Leonello Beliardi, *Cronaca della città di Modena (1512–1518)*, ed. Albano Biondi and Michele Oppi (Modena: Panini, 1981), p. 90.

part of a group of twelve friars—an obviously symbolical number—who "went about Italy, each one in the province assigned to him, preaching and pronouncing on things to come."[43] To judge by the dates of Francesco's itinerant preaching, the group must have formed (perhaps in the hermitage in the south to which Alfani refers) as early as the spring of 1513, and we can suppose that Girolamo da Verona was part of the same group. There are others, however, whom we can place in the same circle, at least hypothetically. There was a Florentine hermit named Giovanni Battista who sent a letter in early May 1513 to the Treasurer of the Patrimony of St. Peter in Orvieto in which he made complex meteorological and political prophesies. We also know that on Christmas Day 1513 a Franciscan preached a sermon in Padua containing predictions that the Venetians would find reassuring, and that he was received "as a saintly man who said many truths about these wars." During the same period, another Franciscan in Naples, "who has a great following among the people, but is held as mad by the principal [citizens]," was forecasting that within two years the Turks would be on Italian soil and the Church would be profoundly shaken and in deep turmoil. He was eventually chased out of the city, but his place was taken by a Carmelite who confirmed this catastrophic picture and added his own prediction that on 2 February 1514 an earthquake would raze Naples. The population spent the night in the streets, quaking with terror and marching in procession, while the Carmelite prudently fled to Sicily.[44]

Even in the context of the intensive preaching activity that was taking place, and even though it is impossible to prove the hypothesis that these preachers were among the companions of Francesco da Montepulciano, it is nonetheless singular that so many instances of prophetic preaching should occur within such a limited time period. The series does not end there, however. In January 1515, the hermit and prophet Bernardino da Parenzo arrived in Venice, accompanied by the Augustinian Anselmo Botturnio.[45] During the same period a friar, Elia da Brescia, who "professed

[43] Pitti, *Dell' Istoria Fiorentina*, p. 112.

[44] Tommaso di Silvestro, *Diario*, pp. 482–83; Sanuto, *Diarii*, vol. 17, cols. 417 and 496; *Cronica anonima dall'anno 1495 all'anno 1519* in *Raccolta di varie croniche, diarj, ed altri opuscoli così italiani come latini appartenenti alla storia del regno di Napoli*, ed. Alessio Aurelio Pelliccia, 5 vols. (Naples: B. Perger, 1780–1782), vol. 1, p. 284.

[45] Sanuto, *Diarii*, vol. 19, cols. 348–49, 383. On Bernardino da Parenzo, see Maria Pia Billanovich, "Una miniera di epigrafi e di antichità. Il Chiostro Maggiore di S. Giustina a Padova," *Italia medioevale e umanistica* 12 (1969): 197–293; Maria Pia Billanovich and Giovanna Mizzon, "Capodistria in età romana e il pittore Bernardino Parenzano," *Italia medioevale e umanistica* 14 (1971): 249–89; Billanovich, "Bernardino da Parenzo pittore e Bernardino (Lorenzo) da Parenzo eremita," *Italia medioevale e umanistica* 24 (1981): 383–404. On Anselmo Botturnio, see Adriano Prosperi, "Botturnio, Anselmo," in DBI, vol. 13, pp. 505–

to be a hermit," preached in the church of the Servites. Fra Elia (whose name alone is indicative) wore the gray mantle of a hermit and preached repentance and fasting to placate the divine wrath directed at Venice. Above all, he organized penitential processions for children that closely recalled other processions through the streets of Orvieto twenty years earlier. In them there were

> little girls and little boys dressed in white with a candle in [their] hands, and there came so many of them that they made more than four hundred, [it was] a terrifying thing to see their agitation, and [there were] many women, and others of the people. . . . And thus with the torches leading them and the cross these boys and girls came out of the church, [followed by] the friars and the preacher, and they went in procession to San Marzilian [San Marziale], Santa Fosca, [and] Rio Terao [Rio Terrà], and went to the bridge of the Axeo [Aseo], returning to the church, singing the litanies, which was terrifying to see and a fearful thing.[46]

Sanudo probably found the procession not to his liking because it offered no chance for political control and because it failed to express the cohesiveness of city life, as was usual in Venetian civic ritual. He spoke of the matter to "someone who can take care of it." In reality, Elia da Brescia had already been called before the Council of Ten two days earlier, along with other preachers, "and they were admonished that in their preaching they not speak of things of state, but only about sins."[47] Prophetic preaching could indeed have political implications and arouse concern among those in charge of public institutions. Sanudo's reservations and those of the Council of Ten did not put a stop to apocalyptical preaching, however. In April 1517 and January 1519, Andrea Baura preached, also prompting Sanudo's disapproval, as we have seen.

One last case that should be mentioned here is that of an unnamed friar who preached in the church of the Friars Minor on Easter Day (4 April) 1518. Sanudo calls him an "homo sanza lettere" and reports his sermon with his usual expressions of disapproval ("he said a thousand crazy things today"). The friar's discourse covered the usual topics, picturing vices and describing divine wrath and consequent castigation ("God is angry with us, soon ruin will be seen . . . God has loosed three million devils and then three thousand"). According to him, the sign of the end would be an earthquake, which could be averted only by the prayers of two saintly men and the good works of the Venetian government.[48]

7; Gutiérrez, "I primi agostiniani italiani," pp. 8–19. In general, see Bernard McGinn, "Circoli gioachimiti veneziani (1450–1530)," *Cristianesimo nella storia* 7 (1986): 19–39.

[46] Sanuto, *Diarii*, vol. 19, col. 462. See also vol. 20, col. 20.

[47] Ibid., vol. 19, col. 460.

[48] Ibid., vol. 25, cols. 338–39.

Condemnation by the Fifth Lateran Council

A clearly defined literary genre emerges from this complex picture. It met with increasing success until 1516, particularly among the *popolari*, and although it faded somewhat with the decrees of the Fifth Lateran Council, it did not cease completely. The Council's decisions, as is known, laid down guidelines for the persecution of preachers who,

> perverting the multiple sense of Holy Scripture . . . preach terrors, threats, imminent catastrophes . . . daring to affirm that they speak through the inspiration and impulse of the Holy Ghost . . . so that simple people, who are the most disposed to be tricked, easily turn to many errors.

Moreover, these preachers inveighed against prelates and even the pope himself, thus giving a scandalous example to the lay population; finally, they pinpointed with undue precision the moment of the advent of the Antichrist and the Day of Judgment.[49]

This picture obviously coincides with what has been outlined in the preceding pages. Significantly, it expresses concern over the success that these preachers encountered among the *semplici*, the *volgo*, and the laity in general. Sanudo repeatedly expresses similar preoccupations, but for somewhat different reasons. For him, prophetic preaching had actual or potential political implications that were difficult to control and could be serious enough to interfere with "le cosse di Stado." Such implications were all the more dangerous because preaching could provide them with a sounding board among a large public of low social status. Sanudo also had little sympathy for the limited literary quality of a homiletics that had no connection with "high" culture.

To judge from the evidence, after 1516 the prophetic preachers toned down their references to the Antichrist and the Day of Judgment and eliminated allusions to precise dates, but they continued to predict approaching calamities (the Turks, earthquakes) and to draw connections between these disasters and the sins of humankind. We have already met Anselmo Botturnio as the companion of the hermit and prophet Bernardino da Parenzo. Botturnio was also credited with the first print edition of Joachimite writings in Venice. During the same period (in 1521) he wrote:

> Est autem duplex prophetia: altera de adventu Salvatoris, et de his quae pertinent ad divinum mysterium; altera vero de futuris comminationibus. Secundam concedunt doctores vigere; priorem vero perfectam esse et completam nullus dubitat.

[49] *Conciliorum Oecumenicorum Decreta*, ed. Giuseppe Alberigo et al. (Bologna: Istituto per le scienze religiose, 1973), pp. 635–37.

He adds:

> Non desunt etiam in Italia, qui divino afflati munere haec et maiora dictitent, et quae futura sint etiam in hoc saeculo in genus christianum maxime ab infidelibus, nisi reges et principes benevolentia et charitate uniti cum Pontifice Max. attentent obviare Dei flagello, et bonis moribus.[50]

A salutary repentance could thus remove the Turkish threat, considered to be the imminent fruit, now ripe ("perfectam . . . et completam"), of divine wrath. There was, of course, no lack of people around Botturnio and within his own order who, "divino afflati munere," had prophesied from the pulpit "de futuris comminationibus." Even Egidio da Viterbo had begun the homily before the Fifth Lateran Council that we have already seen by recalling that for the past twenty years—thus approximately from the start of the Italian wars (once again interpreted as a powerful, though not the only, impetus for the spread of prophecy)—he had worked to explain to the faithful the meaning of prophecies that announced great turmoil for the Church and its ultimate reform. Canisius used similar themes in his preaching as well, even after the decrees of December 1516. In Rome in January 1517 and in Zaragoza in July 1518 he was still preaching "about the things of the Turk and about prophecies."[51]

Andrea Baura's Vocation: A Clarification

Among Botturnio's fellow religious who shared his views and made them their own there was also Andrea Baura. As early as 1513 Baura wrote and published (with a dedication to Lucrezia Borgia) an *Exposition ingeniosa et accomodata a nostri tempi* (the accommodation to "our times" is interesting) of Psalms 14, 15, and 17. This short work noted the *malitia* and the *scandali* present in the Church, even in "ecclesiastical prelates and leaders," and quarreled bitterly, in barely veiled prophetic terms, with Julius II, then at the end of his life and who in fact died ten days after the work was published.[52] Baura states, speaking in the voice of the renewed Church that was to come addressing Christ:

> Other times, when I did not love you, I trusted in terrestrial fortresses, in arms, in soldiers, and in strong walls and ramparts, which I thought invincible; but I was deluding myself, because there is no fortress where you are not.

[50] Anselmo Botturnio, *Christiana de indulcentiis assertio* (Venice: Bernardino Vitali, 1521), fol. O 1*v*.

[51] Sanuto, *Diarii*, vol. 23, cols. 486–88; 25, col. 600.

[52] *Exposition ingeniosa et accomodata a nostri tempi del xiiii. xv. et xvii. Psalmo. Facta per il Sacro Theologo Frate Andrea Ferrarese de lordine de S. Augustino* (Ferrara: Giovanni Mazzocchi, 11 February 1513), fols. A. iii*r*, C. ii*v*, E. ii*v*.

The future pope "chosen according to human will and not according to God" would be no better than his predecessor, and would bring down the severest punishment on the Church. God would of course send preachers throughout the world who, "will speak, preaching and pronouncing on future things" and thus on "the ruin that God has prepared for the Church," but none of them would be believed. Finally, however, Baura continues, the Church would be purged in the most terrible afflictions, the Muslims would be defeated under the sign of the cross, and finally "the peoples who never knew God will be converted just by hearing the divine word pronounced" (an evident echo of reports that had filtered through from the works of Columbus and Vespucci on how easy it was to convert the indigenous populations of the New World). As a final tribulation, the Church would undergo the advent of the Antichrist, but through divine mercy it would be liberated from his seductions and would rule over him and his minions.[53]

Thus by early 1513 Baura had already developed what seem to have been the fundamental motifs of his preaching in 1517 and 1519—the corruption of the Church, especially the vices of the prelates, and prophetic announcement of tremendous divine castigations. Later, and in particular in a sermon given in Ferrara on 21 October 1520, he made a number of affirmations that seemed to his hearers to smack of Lutheranism and he was obliged to retract them.[54] It is improbable, however, that he returned to those statements in the sermon given in Venice on Christmas Day 1520 that aroused the angry reactions of Leo X recorded at the beginning of this chapter: Baura's preaching in Ferrara in 1520 was strictly theological, concerning the nonmeritorious nature of good works and the sinfulness of all mankind, even of the saints, and it contained no criticism of or even any reference whatever to the ecclesiastical hierarchy. Thus it is likely that the sermon preached in Campo Santo Stefano on Christmas Day 1520 was more like the ones Baura had preached in 1517 and 1519, and that the connection with Martin Luther's doctrines was made by his hearers on the basis of information received from Ferrara.

These hypotheses seem confirmed by a work that Baura apparently wrote during the winter of 1520–1521 but that includes a dedication to Cardinal Marco Corner dated Ferrara, 8 November 1521, and was published only in 1523, probably in Milan. It was seen through the press by Anselmo Botturnio, who dedicated it to the general of the Augustinian order, Gabriele della Volta, in a letter dated from San Marco in Milan, 10 April 1523.[55] Baura's work was to be a defense of the apostolic power, as

[53] Ibid., fols. D. ii*r–v*; C. ii*v*; E. iiii*r*; G. ii*r–v* and iiii*r*; H. i*r*.

[54] Gutiérrez, "I primi agostiniani italiani," pp. 27–29.

[55] Andrea Baura, *Apostolice potestatis defensio. Reverendi patris fratris Andree Baurie ordinis Eremitarum Sancti Augustini sacre Theologie Doctoris eximii ac verbi divini predicatoris celeber-*

its title, *Apostolice potestatis defensio*, indicates. It concluded with the affirmation that the pope was the head of the Church, not in an absolute sense, because the only true head of the Church was Christ, but in the sense that the pope was the vicar of the head, Christ the Lord. The hypothesis that the work represented some sort of abjuration of positions that Baura had held or that it attempted to cover them up is invalidated by the dedicatory letter to Corner:

> Since the renewal of this world is imminent, O most reverend sir, the Lord has called upon me, an ignorant and inexpert and unknowing sinner, to speak. He sent me to scourge the multitude of their vices, to announce his wrath at the sunset with word of his power, and at dawn of his mercy; he sent me to sustain the weak, to comfort the afflicted, and to guide the minds of the reprobate. The impetus of the Spirit constrained me to this purpose, and yet I resisted. Jesus Christ, whose servant I am, is my witness to how many times I fled his presence; still, my mind, in his light, gave presage of future things. I went where the Lord called me; I wearied myself with crying until my throat was hoarse, until I saw the word of God transformed into a serpent, and good interpreted as evil. According to the imperious force of my calling, I reproached the vices of this world and detested them, and the world said, "Whoever disdains and detests the power of Rome scorns and condemns the authority of the Roman pontiff!" Yet I have always praised [that authority] and I have always upheld it to the best of my ability, since I knew that it derives from Christ—even if I have always put Christ before it.[56]

This passage offers an excellent grasp both of the ideology that underlay Baura's thought and of the general orientation of prophetic preaching in his time. We should note first that from the start Baura places his text against a background of apocalyptical expectation ("instante iam saeculi mutatione") and that it is a tissue of biblical echoes that add further meaning. What Baura does here is to put himself in the place of the psalmist surrounded by his enemies (Ps. 69:4, "laboravi clamans, raucae factae sunt fauces meae"; "I have labored with crying; my jaws are become hoarse") who says, a few lines later, "For the zeal of thy house hath eaten me up: and the reproaches of them that reproached thee are fallen on me." Even more, he identifies with the image of the Old Testament prophets, Jeremiah in particular, who "does not know how to speak" and on whom Yahweh prevails with force, constraining him to cry out ceaselessly against the iniquities of Jerusalem despite his attempts to contain the fire that burns in

---

rimi. In Lutherum (n.p., n.d.). Botturnio's dedication to Gabriele della Volta is on fols. 1*v*–2*r*, unnumbered; Baura's dedication to Cardinal Marco Corner is on fols. 2*v*–3*r*, also unnumbered.

[56] Ibid., fol. 2*v*, unnumbered. It can be found in Latin in Gutiérrez, "I primi agostiniani italiani," pp. 31–32.

his bones (Jer. 1:5–6 and 20:7–9). In this context, the phrase "Reprehendebam ego secundum imperium vocationis meae vitia orbis" (here translated "according to the imperious force of my calling, I reproached the vices of this world") leaves little room for doubt: It was the prophet's vocation that Baura feels has been imposed on him. Whether he wills it or no, his mind, enlightened by the light of Christ, foresees future things; he feels himself propelled by the force of the Spirit to cry out against reprobates. It is understandable, at this point, why this Ferrarese Augustinian might have spoken "ill of the pope and of the Roman court," but this does not mean that he adhered to Luther's positions. His work, then, was intended to clear up a misunderstanding. Because the pope had prohibited the publication of the work, the dedication continues, Baura was dedicating it to Cardinal Corner in the hope that Corner would transmit his sentiments to the pope, along with his desire to be a defender of power and of the Church of Rome forever, but it would also send word that he was an implacable adversary ("usque ad mortem oppugnator pro viribus infestissimus") of abuses among Christians.[57]

This dedicatory letter must not have been sufficiently reassuring, for the *Apostolice potestatis defensio* remained unpublished for yet another year and a half, until it was published in April 1523 through the good graces of an indefatigable protector of prophets, Anselmo Botturnio.

Friar Girolamo Piumazzo of Verona

In the meantime, during approximately the same weeks, a case was unfolding that involved Baura, albeit indirectly. On 26 March 1523 he wrote to his friend Gaspare Sardi that his teacher, Girolamo "the Bearded" of Verona, had been imprisoned in Piacenza on the accusation of having spread the heresy of Luther.[58] Maestro Girolamo was still in jail on 14 September of that year. In fact, Gabriele della Volta gave orders not to release him "so as not to confirm the calumnies relayed to the pope that the Order was hypocritical in suppressing heretics."[59] This was a rumor that certainly had also been spread at the time of the equivocal affair concerning Baura, whose work Della Volta, the general of the order, had only a few months before agreed to allow Botturnio to dedicate to him, thus in some measure becoming its sponsor. But who could this personage have been? Memory first suggests another Augustinian, Girolamo of Verona, who in 1513 had preached *per profetia* in Venice in the wake of the *Concordie Novi ac Veteris*

[57] Baura, *Apostolice potestatis defensio*, fol. 3*r*, unnumbered.

[58] Biblioteca Estense di Modena, cod. it. 833 (= α.G. I.15 [23]).

[59] Hubert Jedin, *Papal Legate at the Council of Trent, Cardinal Seripando*, tr. Frederic C. Eckhoff (St. Louis: B. Herder, 1947), p. 132, note.

Testamenti of Joachim of Fiore. This is an interesting hypothesis for several reasons. For one, if it were verified it would confirm, as was already apparent in the case of Baura, the complex, multifaceted relations between prophetic preaching and Lutheran preaching (or presumed Lutheran preaching). On the one hand, the emergence of new patterns of analysis and judgment, based on widespread knowledge of Luther and his work, might lead the public (or a part of the public) to judge as "Lutheran" preachers who were not and had no intention of being so. (This misunderstanding of course might also arise as an oblique effect of the diffusion of certain aspects of Lutheran propaganda, such as its antiecclesiastical tone.) On the other hand, familiarity with Lutheran themes could truly lead (as seems likely in the case of Girolamo of Verona) from prophecy to heresy, and all the more easily within an order in which the study of the works of Joachim traditionally accompanied that of the theology of St. Augustine and which identified the hermits of St. Augustine as the *eremiti* of the third age announced by the abbot of Fiore.[60]

A letter sent a few years later by Girolamo Aleandro, at that time papal nuncio in Venice, provides information on other aspects of the personality of Fra Girolamo of Verona. Aleandro says:

> One Friar Girolamo, Veronese, also called Piumazzo . . . was once retained [imprisoned] in Piacenza on the orders of the bishop of Fano [Goro Gheri], then governor of that city, and [was] sentenced to perpetual imprisonment as a Lutheran. He was sent to Bologna, where he remained in jail for six or seven years and then, at the bidding of I know not what important person [*prencipale*] he was pardoned, [and] was no sooner out of prison than he went to Verona, and in spite of the prohibition of the bishop he insisted on preaching, whereupon [he], returning to his vomit, was by the diligence of that bishop [and] the arm of the Signoria sent out of that city and diocese. It appears that now he boasts of planning to come to Rome and, through great people, of obtaining restitution of his citizenship and his preaching, which, if it were to happen, would much displease that good prelate.[61]

[60] Marjorie Reeves, "Joachimist Expectations in the Order of Augustinian Hermits," *Recherches de théologie ancienne et médiévale* 25 (1958): 111–41.

[61] Girolamo Aleandro to the apostolic protonotary Ambrogio Recalcati, Venice, 16 June 1535, in *Nunziature di Venezia*, ed. Franco Gaeta, Fonti per la storia d'Italia (Rome: Istituto storico italiano per l'età moderna e contemporanea, 1958–), vol. 1, pp. 316–17. Goro Gheri moved from Piacenza to Bologna as deputy of the papal legate, Innocenzo Cibo, in the autumn of 1524, and remained in that city until his death in 1528 (Maria Ferretti, "Legati, vicelegati e governatori di Bologna nel sec. XVI," tesi di laurea discussa presso l'Università di Bologna a.a. 1967–1968, relatore Paolo Prodi, p. 108). Consequently we can suppose that Piumazzo's transfer to the prison in Bologna occurred when Gheri moved from Piacenza to Bologna. In this case the dates would be, approximately: Lent 1523, arrest and imprisonment in Piacenza; 1524–1531, imprisonment in Bologna; 1532–1533, preaching in Verona and expulsion by Giberti.

Girolamo of Verona had thus been sentenced to life imprisonment. He must have enjoyed good protection, however, if he was subsequently liberated and if he was sentenced to no worse than exile when he relapsed in Verona. The letter (which is dated 16 June 1535) also tells us his last name, Piumazzo (thus *barbato* must have been an epithet), which enables us to identify him better. We know of the Augustinian Girolamo Piumazzo of Verona that he was a celebrated preacher much in demand, in particular thanks to his promotion of various state funds such as the Monti di Pietà and the matrimonial *monti*.[62] He preached in Venice during Lent in 1513, as we have seen; in 1514 he preached in Salerno;[63] in 1516 he was in Palermo, where in fact he incited the population against the city's Jews (preaching in favor of the Monti di Pietà was often violently anti-Semitic).[64] In 1517 he was invited to Ravenna by the Augustinian community there, and he received permission to accept from Egidio da Viterbo.[65]

A remarkable figure emerges from the picture we have gradually pieced together: a famous preacher requested throughout Italy, a man who until the Fifth Lateran Council adhered to the models of apocalyptical prophecy but who also propagandized for the Monti di Pietà, yet who ended up a Lutheran. Girolamo Piumazzo thus offers another example—with its own specific characteristics, and occurring at a precociously early date—to add to those of other famous preachers of the Augustinian order imprisoned for doctrinal reasons and then liberated, either under the guarantee of influential persons or because of their own ability to plead their own defense.[66] As we read in Aleandro, the affair had a sequel, since Piumazzo returned to Verona to preach, "non ostante la prohibitione del vescovo." We know how jealously Gian Matteo Giberti watched over the preaching in his diocese. The affair of Father Ludovico Mantovano, three and a half years after Aleandro's letter, clearly shows the great care the bishop of Ve-

[62] Onofrio Panvinio, *De urbis Veronae viris doctrina et bellica virtute illustribus* (Verona, 1621). The same information (taken from Panvinio's work in manuscript, however) can be found in Giuseppe Panfilo, *Chronica Ordinis Fratrum Eremitarum Sancti Augustini* (Rome: Georgii Ferrarrii, 1581), pp. 112–13, which gives Piumazzo's place and date of death (incorrectly, as we shall see) as Venice in 1534.

[63] As can be deduced from a letter dated 4 May 1514 from Gabriele della Volta to Ambrogio Flandino, named a commissioner of the order, along with Girolamo da Genazzano, "in decernenda controversia quae est inter magistrum Hieronymym Veronensem et conventum salernitanum super eleemosyna praedicationis," for which see Gutiérrez, "I primi agostiniani italiani," p. 39.

[64] Tommaso Fazello, *Le due deche dell'historia di Sicilia* (Venice: Domenico e Gio. Battist. Guerra, 1574), p. 894.

[65] Luigi Torelli, *Secoli agostiniani, overo Historia generale del Sacro Ordine Eremetano del gran dottore . . . S. Aurelio Agostino*, 8 vols. (Bologna: Giacomo Monti, 1659–1686), vol. 8, pp. 25, 191.

[66] *Nunziature di Venezia*, vol. 1, p. 316; Pio Paschini, "Episodi di lotta contro l'eresia nell'Italia del primo Cinquecento," *Euntes docete* 9 (1956): 497–513.

rona took to avoid any shadow of suspicion among his clergy. He preferred to nip any ambiguous affair in the bud, "considering," as he wrote to Contarini on 25 February 1539, "the place in which I live and the account that I have to give of myself both here and elsewhere."[67]

Giberti's anxieties are less interesting for our purposes than the precedents for the Augustinian's preaching and his ties with Baura. If we accept the hypothesis that Girolamo Piumazzo of Verona, Andrea Baura's teacher, was the same person as the Girolamo da Verona who preached in Venice *per profetia* on 20 March 1513 and who perhaps belonged to the group of twelve prophets connected with Francesco da Montepulciano who preached throughout the Italian peninsula during the course of 1513, several aspects of the work of the Ferrarese Augustinian would clearly take on a more specific meaning. The *Exposition ingeniosa* was in fact written and published at the beginning of 1513, and Baura did indeed speak of the imminent tribulations brought on by the Antichrist and warn that many preachers would "speak throughout the world, preaching, and predicting things to come." Was this a reference to Francesco da Montepulciano and his companions, who were at that very moment beginning their prophetic pilgrimage through Italy? Certainly, those final months of the papacy of Julius II and the first year of that of Leo X, a time of overlapping but changing pontifical policies, were also a time of high prophetic tension, still apocalyptic in tone.[68] In those months there were still some who awaited the end of time; when Baura returned to the same topic at the end of 1520—if indeed he did—people found it disconcerting because the situation had changed too much. Too many alarm bells (still uncoordinated at this point) were all set to ring, even at the touch of the wrong hands. Then in 1523, control over extremist preaching tightened further, and Girolamo Piumazzo spent many long years in prison.

Other Augustinian Prophets

The case of Baura, with all its aftereffects, did not close the era of prophetic preaching, however. In Milan, in the monastery of San Marco (where Botturnio was living at the time) there was between 1521 and 1523 a friar, "a man of very high repute, old, and he had a great beard, and he was of the order of St. Augustine, a hermit."[69] According to Giovan Marco Burigozzo, the chronicler to whom we owe this description, this friar was one

[67] Adriano Prosperi, "Un processo per eresia a Verona verso la metà del Cinquecento," *Quaderni storici* 15 (1970): 773–94; quotation on p. 792.

[68] See chap. 2, and Weinstein, *Savonarola and Florence*, pp. 350, 353–55.

[69] *Cronache milanesi scritte da Giovan Pietro Cagnola, Giovanni Andrea Prato e Giovan Marco Burigozzo, Archivio storico italiano* 3 (1842): 1–598; p. 436.

of the moving forces behind the resistance against the French. (There were a good number of anti-French Augustinian hermits during those years.) He preached during Lent in 1521 and again that year during Advent. On Candlemas in 1522 he led a great procession from the Duomo to the church of Sant'Ambrogio in a snowstorm ("it was snowing terribly that Sunday"). There were children dressed in white, singing; the clergy of Milan followed, first the regular and then the secular clergy. More important, all the able-bodied men from every parish in the city walked in the procession, each delegation with its captain, its banner, its corporals, its militia, and its drums, and all ready, according to Burigozzo, "to offer their lives and their possessions for the defense of the homeland and against the French." This same militia provided the city troops that did in fact fight against the French, along with imperial troops, in the victory over the French at the battle of the Bicocca the following April.

In the months that followed, the Augustinian seems to have played an increasingly important role: "In this time of war he comforted the souls of the Milanese against the French . . . and he had a banner made with a cross on it" that was kept in the Duomo "in order to carry it against the French" in an eventual conflict. Above all, Botturnio's fellow brother (and we cannot exclude the possibility that he was Botturnio himself) enlivened his preaching with prophetic inspiration: "he delighted in striving to seem a prophet and in divining things that were to come." He had a large following, particularly, as Burigozzo says with scorn, among "homenazzi, donazole e poltronaglia" (no-account men, idle women, and riffraff). Some in the ecclesiastical hierarchy were less enthusiastic, as can be seen from an episode that took place one Sunday in Advent in 1523. The bearded friar ("questo frate de Santo Marco della barbassa") was preaching in the Duomo and the sermon "was going on and on." The priests who were to officiate lost patience and while he was still preaching they began to chant the Introit at the high altar, thus provoking wrath and insults from "hangers-on and little women." The chronicler comments that "anyone among them who managed to say ought against these revered priests was lucky."[70]

This episode provides more than an evident case of prophetic preaching in support of political propaganda in the bosom of an order that seems to have been extremely open to such tendencies at the time. It also shows active disagreement within the Church in Milan, a disagreement that was not stilled by the preacher's embrace of the city's cause. Thus on one side we have the Augustinian friar's active supporters—"homenazzi, donazole e poltronaglia," the audience of choice of the prophets; on the other, the Ambrosian secular clergy, who took every opportunity to try to silence him. They got what they needed soon after in a letter dated 12 January 1524 from Clement VII, who enjoined the archbishop of Milan to enforce

[70] Ibid., pp. 443–44.

the Lateran decree of 1516 concerning preaching, a decree that gradually acquired a new urgency after 1520 and the first cases of Lutheran propaganda.[71]

An Umbrian Hermit and the Sack of Rome

Antiprophetic repression found it harder to move against the hermits. As we have seen, they continued to circulate for a decade after the decrees of the Fifth Lateran Council, flanked (after 1525) by the Capuchins, with whom they were for a time confused. Lancellotti says repeatedly that Giuseppe Piantanida went about "dressed as a hermit," and Matteo da Bascio followed the hermits' patterns of itinerant preaching for his entire lifetime.[72] The episode concerning Brandano is well known, so let us turn instead to a hermit who preached in Orvieto in March 1528. According to Giovan Maria della Porta, writing to Eleonora Gonzaga on 9 March, the hermit wore "the dress of St. John the Baptist," was twenty-four years of age, and "preaches in the public squares about other major disasters that are to come to Rome and to Italy, which will last for all XXIX [1529], and in XXX [1530] the Church is to be renewed." According to this man, the Turks would defeat the emperor, the pope, and the king of France in a great battle near Viterbo, but would later convert to Christianity.[73] He was perhaps the same person as the hermit who arrived in Camerino in July and "went through the city crying *misericordia* with the little children."[74] It

[71] Federico Chabod, *Lo stato e la vita religiosa a Milano nell'epoca di Carlo V* (Turin: G. Einaudi, 1971), p. 232. Contrary to Chabod's opinion, however, the provision was not directly correlated with the sermons of the prophet friar, as demonstrated by analogous letters sent at precisely the same time to the papal nuncios in Venice and Naples: See Bartolommeo Fontana, *Documenti vaticani contro l'eresia luterana in Italia* (Rome: R. Società di storia patria, 1892), pp. 12–13 and 16–17. See also below, p. 147.

[72] Lancellotti, *Cronaca modenese*, vol. 5, pp. 296–97, and vol. 6, pp. 237–38; Arsenio da Ascoli, *La predicazione dei cappuccini nel Cinquecento in Italia* (Loreto [Ancona]: Libreria S. Francesco d'Assisi, 1956), p. 244; Melchior de Pobladura, "La 'Severa riprensione' di fra Matteo da Bascio"; Costanzo Cargnoni, "Alcuni aspetti del successo della riforma cappuccina nei primi cinquant'anni (1525–1575)," in *Le origini della riforma cappuccina* (Ancona: Curia provinciale Frati Cappuccini, 1979), pp. 227–28 and 232–34.

[73] Archivio di Stato di Firenze, *Urbino*, cl. I, div. G 266, fol. 68*v*. Given the difference in their ages, it does not seem to me acceptable to identify this personage as Brandano, as in Ludwig von Pastor, *Geschichte der päpste seit dem ausgang des mittelalters*, 16 vols. (Freiburg im Breisgau; St Louis: Herder, 1886–1933). This reference can be found in the English version, *The History of the Popes from the Close of the Middle Ages*, 40 vols. (n.p.: Consortium Books, [1977?]), vol. 9, p. 379.

[74] Bernardino Lilio, *Diario* (at the date 10 July 1528), cited in Melchior de Pobladura, *Historia generalis Ordinis Fratrum Minorum Cappuccinorum*, 3 vols. (Rome: Institutum Historicum Ord. Fr. Min. Cap., 1947–1951), vol. 1, p. 53. To tell the truth, Lilio speaks of a "frate scappucino," but given the confusion between hermits and Capuchins, this may not invalidate the identification proposed.

is even more likely that he was the "hermit dressed in sackcloth" from near Perugia who came to Venice on 18 May 1529:

> This morning in several churches and later today when the Council had convened, a hermit dressed in sackcloth, barefoot and with nothing on his head, with a wooden staff with the cross at the top, also in wood, of Perosan [Perugian] nationality, from Torre, twenty miles from Perosa [Perugia], of [ ] years of age, named [ ], newly come to this land, climbed onto the banns stone and exhorted everyone to repentance and to doing good, saying, "the sentence has been passed, God intends to renew the world, Venice, mend your ways! The Turk has embarked, for the ruination of Christians, and will cross the Arete [Adese?]! Repent!" and other such words, and many wondered who he was. This man does not want money, only [food] to live on, he leads a rude life, and he beats his chest with a large marble stone as St. Jerome did. If someone gives him a *bezo* or two he takes it and gives it to the poor.[75]

What is striking about this account, beyond its most visibly spectacular aspects (the large stone with which the hermit beats his chest, in imitation of current iconography of St. Jerome), is its fidelity to a pattern we have seen several times before. Just like the learned Augustinian, Baura, fifteen years earlier, he promised destruction and castigation to Rome and to Italy, the coming of the Turks and their victory over Christian forces, their eventual conversion, and the renewal of the Church. These themes can also be found in prophetic works in vernacular verse such as the *Prophetia de santo Anselmo* or the *Prophetia trovata in Roma intagliata in marmoro*, which had begun to circulate some twenty years earlier.[76] One could certainly cite other texts that follow the same or an analogous pattern. We could also hypothesize direct knowledge of them on the part of the hermit (we know, for example, that Brandano read and used a Venetian vernacular edition of the *Pronosticatio* of Johannes Lichtenberger).[77] Furthermore, 1530 was the date that completed the fifty-first generation after the birth of Christ in the calculations that Girolamo of Verona presented in 1513 to the faithful of Venice, basing his predictions on Joachim of Fiore. The date had for some years circulated in other contexts as the moment at which the Church was to be totally renewed. In the last analysis, though, it seems more fruitful to place the preaching of this itinerant prophet (in Orvieto in particular)

[75] Sanuto, *Diarii*, vol. 50, cols. 341–42, 345.

[76] Also in circulation, but, from what I can gather, only in manuscript, was a *Profizia dell'anno 1180 nell'indizione nona per il Serenissimo e clarissimo Re di Jerusalem pacifico Signor del Regno di Cipri ad Urbano P.*, which was probably the direct source of the *Prophetia trovata in Roma*. The *Profizia* (which can be dated to the second half of the Quattrocento) is available under that title, edited by P. Fanfani, in *Il Borghini* 1 (1863): 755–57. There is a sixteenth-century copy with a few variants, untitled but bearing the notation "Reperta in antiquo codice scripta," inserted among other texts dated 1521–1522 in the MS Class. 287 of the Biblioteca Classense of Ravenna, Poesie italiane e latine, fols. 9*v*–11*r*.

[77] Tognetti, "Profezie," p. 327.

within the tense and confused atmosphere of Italy after the sack of Rome in 1527 and before the Congress of Bologna in 1529–1530. Both the hermit's words and the letter reporting them betray a greater sense of anxiety than preceding and apparently analogous texts do. They echo a sense of urgency for the immediate reform of the Church, which faced present *ruine* while *altre maggiori* lay in wait for it. In short, even if events in this viscous history are now so remote that they seem identical (or nearly so), we cannot lump them together or view them as equally important. Given that the conditions and circumstances of Italian political history were constantly changing in those early decades of the Cinquecento, such events acquire their full meaning only when we observe them as one would look at a transparent overlay placed on an ever-changing ground.

The Breakdown of Prophetic Preaching: The Story of Zaccheria da Fivizzano

As the imperial army made its way through Italy in 1529–1530, the pressure of events prompted a new rash of prophecy (less energetic than before, however) that even infected official preaching. Such was the case of the Spanish Dominican Tommaso Nieto, who preached in 1529 in the Duomo in Milan when Spanish troops and *Landsknechten* were bivouacked in the city ("whose fury anyone was indeed fortunate to rein in," Burigozzo commented, as he outlined a miserable but all too familiar picture of the violence and indignities to which the people were subjected by the Spanish and the *Lanzi*).[78] In April of that year Nieto organized a general procession to ask God to forsake his castigations, and as the months passed and tension mounted in the city, his sermons assumed a prophetic tone, remaining so vague, however ("for he was considered our prophet by the greater part of the people, and thus he prophesied and said, 'Stay, do not fear, it will not be, or it will be' "), that they give the impression—at least in Burigozzo's report of them—of aiming at little more than social control and quieting a nervous public opinion ("giving them to hear comforting rubbish"). Nieto's message was more pointed in a sermon that he gave on 5 September 1529, after an embassy had left Milan to confer with Charles V at Piacenza ("there they were to settle the affairs of Christendom"). Probably on the basis of that rumor, Nieto

> gave a most desperate sermon with great threats, not so much for Milan as for all Christendom; but he said that Milan would have the beginning of the renovation of the Church, and for this reason it must be the first afflicted and the last renewed; and he said much, particularly about the great carnage that will soon come to pass. And he said that it was not he who was speaking, no, but

[78] On Nieto, see *Cronache milanesi*, pp. 485–500.

by the mouth of the Holy Ghost . . . and [that] there was no cause to marvel at what he said, and furthermore, he said to me, "Write, when you are at home." And at the end of his sermon he had [everyone] cry *misericordia* two times.[79]

The interconnections between politics and prophecy are clear in this passage, particularly in the relationship between the emperor's approach as he traveled toward Bologna and the expectation of "la renovazion de la eclesia." In point of fact, as we shall see in a later chapter, the accent in the last burst of prophecy that occurred, precisely, in 1530 gradually shifted from the imminence of God's chastisement to proclamation of a peaceful reform of the Church by means of a long-awaited emperor who would inaugurate a new Golden Age.

The language of prophecy was wearing thin, however. Discouraged by the ecclesiastical hierarchy, less and less engrossing to the people, no longer able (after the accords of 1529–1530) to draw on the disasters that followed on the heels of military engagements or armies passing through, it lost its efficacy and its bite. One relevant example of how prophetic language lost significance is a sermon given by the Dominican Fra Zaccheria da Fivizzano in the church of Santa Reparata in Florence, on Sunday, 10 January, thus during the city's ten-month siege by the papal and imperial troops before it surrendered on 12 August 1530.[80] We know from Benedetto Varchi that it was the preaching of Fra Zaccheria, together with that of Benedetto da Foiano, that kept up the morale of the Florentines during those months by encouraging and praising the republican government of the city, bitterly criticizing Pope Clement VII and the Medici family, and promising certain victory to the besieged city in the name of God. Fra Zaccheria belonged to the monastery of San Marco and, in Varchi's words, he "followed the discipline of Savonarola."[81] Fra Zaccheria had in fact defended his reputation before the Synod of Florence in 1516 against the accusation of heresy, stating, in particular, that the concept of the renovation of the Church as Savonarola made use of it was not in itself heretical.

[79] Ibid., p. 498.

[80] The sermon, edited by Carlo Gargiolli, is published in *Il Propugnatore* 12, no. 1 (1879): 417–33. Gargiolli based his edition on a contemporary pamphlet in his possession, *Predica fatta la domenica fra loctava della Epiphania dal Reverendo P. fra Zacheria da Lunigiana frate di san Marcho in sancta Reparata Racholta da uno amico* (n.p., n.d.), in octavo, 12 fols.

[81] Benedetto Varchi, *Storia fiorentina*, ed. Lelio Arbib, 3 vols. (Florence: Società delle storie del Nardi e del Varchi, 1838–1841), vol. 1, p. 474, and vol. 2, pp. 258, 414. Benedetto da Foiano had preached in a prophetic vein in Venice, in the church of the Incurabili, in the weeks immediately following the sack of Rome: "He preached four hours; gave a prophecy of the Apocalypse which interpreted all this ruin of Rome; he said much ill of the pope, cardinals, etc. and much good of the emperor, and he talked much too much" (Sanuto, *Diarii*, vol. 45, cols. 321–22). Benedetto da Foiano had also preached in Venice during Lent 1526, but on that occasion he had asked only that "four things be taken care of: blasphemy, the Lutherans, having justice, and having pious places" (Sanuto, *Diarii*, vol. 41, col. 113).

Quite to the contrary, insofar as it signified moral renewal its urgency was even clear in the deliberations of the Council in course, "quia Iulius papa II non nisi pro reformatione Ecclesie concilium generale convocavit."[82] It is interesting that Fra Zaccheria thought it necessary to base this concept on a clearly prophetic passage in Joel ("ecclesiam . . . fore renovandam per abundantiam Spiritus sancti, quem Deus effundet super omnem carnem"). Joel 2:28 continues, "Your sons and your daughters shall prophesy: your old men shall dream dreams, and your young men shall see visions," going on to announce the "great and dreadful day of the Lord," probably the tacit basis for Zaccheria's proposed renewal of the Church.

If we examine the text of Fra Zaccheria's 1530 sermon in the vernacular, however, we realize that at that date not even this Savonarolan still accepted the models of prophetic preaching as they have been described above, and that if he speaks of the renewal of the Church, he does so on a very different basis than was the case in 1516. His homily, in fact, follows an outline that merits close analysis. Judicious men of the world and the timorous say that Florence has been sold out, he declares, but in reality

> when God sends a great scourge to a city that is full of sin, and when for all that reason it does not convert or repent, it is a manifest sign that it will go ill and that it has no remedy. As it happens . . . Florence . . . is filled with sins. . . . It has already been struck by God several times with great tribulations; it has had famine and great pestilence; now it has the war that wounds it to the bone, and nonetheless it will not convert. . . . What is there then to say, if not that it will be destroyed and that there is no remedy. There are still certain prophecies that strongly threaten the city and say that it is given over to fire and will be burned.

The *ragioni dei paurosi* are obviously those of the prophetic preachers of twenty years earlier. To oppose them, Fra Zaccheria continues, there are the reasons of the simple, who have faith in God. The simple know that the Lord can permit reason and justice to be oppressed, yes, but not extinguished; they know that there is sin in Florence, but there are also works of charity and mercy. As for the prophecies, "if we have to depend upon them, we have better, differently founded prophecies than those prudent men had, because we have heard them with our own ears and seen a great many of them come true thus far."

The living memory of Savonarola, whom Fra Zaccheria claims to have heard with his own ears, is thus opposed to a model of prophetic preaching that by that time had become rigid, a model that this Dominican rejected as good only for the timid. Even though he refers obsequiously to the

[82] Alceste Giorgetti, "Fra' Luca Bettini e la sua difesa del Savonarola," *Archivio storico italiano* 47, pt. 2 (1919): 164–231; p. 216. See also Weinstein, *Savonarola and Florence*, pp. 359–61.

prophecies of his master, somehow it was the prophecy practiced day by day in his own time that he denies.

> I am not a prophet, nor do I speak to you as a prophet, because I do not want to arrogate to myself what I do not possess; but I speak to you as a preacher according to Holy Scripture, according to the doctrine of the saints, according to the order of divine providence, insofar as we can know it, and according to reason and natural discourse.

It is precisely on the basis of natural reason that Fra Zaccheria moves on to his final and definitive argument:

> When the world is ruined and has grown old in vice, God is accustomed to renew it and take it back. . . . Now, we see the world more corrupt than ever, because the faith of Christ is nearly reduced to one corner of the world. . . . What shall we say, then? We shall say that God will do what he is accustomed to doing, that is, to renew it and yet another time purge it. Why do you think that he has begun to send so many scourges if not to reform and renew his Church? . . . Because it is nearly totally aged and corrupted by sins, he has begun to purge it with the scourge, and he will not rest until he has set it up again according to his way. . . . Thus believe me, God will take away the old rubbish that is in the Church today and will make a totally renewed house and vineyard.[83]

Taken as a whole, these arguments closely resemble those of Gasparo Contarini fifteen years earlier (in 1516, at a singularly early date), who used the image of the wheel of fortune to state (respectfully, to be sure) his disagreement with Savonarola:

> This renovation of the Church I know not by prophecy, but natural and divine reason dictate it to me. The natural because human things do not go according to an infinite straight line, but go according to a circular line; although all do not make a perfect circle and when they have come to a certain term in their augmentation they then move higher. You apply this. Divine reason also tells me that sometimes God must regulate his Church, the which should [be] highly desired by all Christians.[84]

The substance of the discrepancy between the figure of Savonarola as a symbol of prophecy and the demand for a reform of the Church dictated

[83] *Predica fatta la domenica*, pp. 428, 432, 434, 435–36.

[84] Felix Gilbert, "Contarini on Savonarola: An Unknown Document of 1516," *Archiv für Reformationsgeschichte* 59 (1968): 145–75; p. 149. See also Bartolomeo Cerretani, "Storie in dialogo della mutatione di Firenze," in Joseph Schnitzer, *Quellen und Forschungen zur Geschichte Savonarolas*, 3 vols. (Munich: J. J. Lentner [E. Stahl, jun.], 1902–1904), vol. 3, pp. 91–92, referring to the year 1520. On the image of the wheel of fortune, see Giorgio Stabile, "La ruota della fortuna: tempo ciclico e ricorso storico," in *Scienze, credenze occulte, livelli di cultura. Convegno internazionale di studi (Firenze, 26–30 giugno 1980)* (Florence: L. S. Olschki, 1982), pp. 477–503.

by natural and divine reason reemerges in the words of Fra Zaccheria. Moreover, speaking in the very name of Savonarola, Zaccheria rejects and refutes a model of preaching that for at least the two preceding decades had spread among extremely broad and socially differentiated segments of the population first an eschatological expectation of the end and then the expectation of catastrophes—the Turks, wars—that were human but immediate and terrible. From 1530 on, this channel for the diffusion of prophecy among a popular audience ran dry, as did the others. The hermits no longer found a hearing, *cantastorie* and printers turned to other materials, monsters acquired a different significance, and the pulpit no longer served to predict the future but rather to negate the present or to suggest a wide variety of changes in the Church. In this sense, it is singular and significant that it was precisely the preaching of a Savonarolan that gives us the most comprehensive sign of the end of a culture.

Fra Zaccheria was to preach again. We find him as an official reader (*lettore condotto*) of Sacred Scripture, paid by the Signoria of Venice "with a salary of fifty *ducati* a year for expenses and to buy books," first, in August 1532, in the church of the Trinità and, after June 1533, also in San Zanipolo.[85] He occasionally preached in other churches as well. Sanudo did not like his homilies ("he goes on and on . . . he did not give a good sermon . . . he said a lot of nonsense"),[86] and in fact the Dominican was much more appreciated by the *ignoranti* and the *idioti* than by the *dotti*, in particular in his readings of the epistles of St. Paul held in the church of the Trinità (in San Zanipolo he read Ecclesiastes). As the papal nuncio, Girolamo Aleandro, wrote to Iacopo Salviati, papal secretary, on 15 August 1533:

> [Fra Zaccheria] read . . . the epistles of St. Paul with the exposition always in the vernacular, for which he has an audience of many more ignorant and common people than of the learned, a thing that certainly pleased me little, because sacred doctrine is not subject to being put into the hands of common and simple people, particularly when we know that the Lutheran heresy has multiplied and grown in Germany by this way alone.[87]

Aleandro's fears were well founded. On 8 May a carpenter, Mastro Antonio da Rialto, was arrested as a Lutheran, and it came out in the interrogations that he had assiduously attended the readings from St. Paul at the church of the Trinità and, "after the readings . . . started to speak," denying free will, among other things.[88] The personal position of the reader aside, public readings of the Bible could thus in themselves give

[85] Sanuto, *Diarii*, vol. 56, cols. 777, 846–47, and vol. 58, col. 246.

[86] Ibid., vol. 57, col. 376; vol. 58, col. 22.

[87] *Nunziature di Venezia*, vol. 1, p. 104.

[88] Franco Gaeta, "Documenti da codici vaticani per la storia della riforma in Venezia. Appunti e documenti," *Annuario dell'Istituto storico italiano per l'età moderna e contemporanea* 7 (1955): 27. See also the other interrogations on pp. 25–26.

heretical opinions a chance to jell. Rome reacted with alarm, and on 1 October Tommaso Badia, master of the Sacred Palace, transmitted peremptory orders to Aleandro to prohibit this new custom of reading the Bible in the vernacular in public in the churches unless the preachers involved underwent preliminary examination.[89] Fra Zaccheria continued to preach in spite of everything. The last remaining trace of prophecy in his homiletics was a violent antiecclesiastical and antipapal tone. (Like Andrea Baura fifteen years earlier, he "spoke ill of the pope and of the Roman court," however, with a more specific political and anti-Medicean purpose.) Aleandro shrewdly noted that this was precisely why Zaccheria found favor with the Signoria and with the public, who were thus led to listen more trustingly to the refutation of Lutheran opinions that Aleandro encouraged.[90] Thus prophetic preaching could be taken as Lutheran, as in the case of Baura; it could become Lutheran, as with Girolamo Piumazzo; finally, a reformed Savonarolan could be manipulated and transformed into an anti-Lutheran preacher, as happened with Fra Zaccheria, thanks to Aleandro's political skill.

In the end, the last resistance was vanquished, and Fra Zaccheria was induced to throw himself at the feet of Clement VII and beg his pardon. On the return trip, however, he died unexpectedly, some said of poison.[91]

[89] Fontana, *Documenti vaticani*, pp. 73–74.

[90] Girolamo Aleandro to Pietro Carnesecchi, Venice, 13 March 1534, in *Nunziature di Venezia*, vol. 1, pp. 178–79.

[91] Benedetto Varchi asserts that the meeting with the pope occurred in Perugia, but this seems doubtful because Clement died on 26 September 1534 and had already been sick for many months (Varchi, *Storia fiorentina*, vol. 2, p. 498). The rumor of Zaccheria's death by poison is reported in Roberto Ridolfi, *Vita di Girolamo Savonarola*, 2 vols. (Rome: A. Belardetti, 1952), vol. 2, p. 46, which does not indicate the source of the item, however. In the English version, the reference is on p. 301 of *The Life of Girolamo Savonarola*, tr. Cecil Grayson (New York: Knopf, 1959).

5

ANTI-LUTHERAN PROPHECY: LUTHER AS MONSTER AND PSEUDOPROPHET

More on Monsters

THE PROBLEM of the relationship between prophecy and the spread of the Reformation has come up before in these pages. Thus far, the question has been what happened to prophetic preaching each time that it entered into contact with Lutheranism. There is another side to the problem, however. We might ask whether, and how, and in which of its aspects prophecy was used in Italy during these same years as a polemical weapon in the confessional dispute and, eventually, with what aims and with the use of what techniques.

To begin with, let us recall what has already been said on the combined divinatory and politico-religious meaning that was attributed to the monstrous births in Italy during that period. They were *segni*—generic signs of divine wrath and of God's will, thus warnings of a catastrophic future. But they were also indications that a merciful Providence offered to humankind so that if people were sufficiently inspired by piety they could disentangle themselves from events and read the true significance of history. The monsters display probably the clearest form of one of prophecy's most prominent characteristics during these years. As a global culture, prophecy provided the key to a unified interpretation of nature, of the supernatural, and of human history. This is why contemporary chronicles often ended by pointing to the monsters, which they took to be signs equal to the task of expressing their age. We have already seen this in Johannes Multivallis's continuation of the chronicle of Eusebius of Caesarea, which in fact ends with a description of the monster of Ravenna and its significance. It is also true, for example, of the *Chronica* of Joannes Nauclerus, which ends in the final years of the fifteenth century with a reference to the monsters that had captured the attention of the court of Maximilian I, and of Sebastian Brant in particular:

> Creator et stellas et cometas in caelo, et gladios igneos et dracones creat et apparere facit in sublimi; similiter et portenta in terra et in mari, monstra in hominibus etiam nasci, ut infantulos multorum capitum, propter quod et monstra dicuntur, non solum quod propter admirationem novitatis ea ho-

mines sibi monstrant, sed quoniam iram Dei monstrant imminere hominibus: quod Deus, supplex oro, bene vertat. Finis historiae Joannis Nauclerii tubingensis praepositi, quae a condito mundo in annum christianae salutis millesimum et quingentesimum deducta est feliciter.[1]

The most interesting aspect of this text is obviously not its theory of monsters, which is absolutely concordant with the current literature, but that it is presented, on the whole, as a historical and political comment on the present age. Nauclerus was writing at the very beginning of the sixteenth century; later, the gradual distinction between scientific fields that separated natural history from politics or theology contributed to the dismantling of this sort of prophetic analysis of monsters and, more generally, to the end of prophecy as a cohesive culture.

The two creatures born in Ravenna and Bologna had in fact already produced a great variety in the politico-ecclesiastical and prophetic meanings attributed to the monsters. Ten years later, that wealth of meaning persisted in the descriptions of the other monstrous creatures to which we now turn, and meaning acquired even greater complexity from the context of confessional polemics in which teratological interpretation was set. We need to examine how this context influenced prophetic techniques, first concerning the monsters, and in particular the so-called monk-calf, or the monster of Saxony.

The Monster of Saxony: Luther's Interpretation

The monster of Saxony was a deformed fetus found in the uterus of a cow in Waltersdorf near Freiberg in Saxony on 8 December 1522.[2] The monster, whose most salient characteristic was a large fold of flesh on its neck that might recall a monk's cowl, was dried and sent to Duke Frederick of Saxony ("apud quem nunc visitur," a contemporary witness noted).[3] At

[1] *Cronica d. Johannis Nauclerii praepositi tubingensis succinctim compraendentia res memorabiles saeculorum omnium ac gentium, ab initio mundi usque ad annum Christi nati MCCCCC* (Cologne, 1569), pp. 1121–22.

[2] On this question, see Martin Luther, *D. Martin Luthers Werke. Kritische Gesamtausgabe* (hereafter cited as *WKG*), 97 vols. (Weimar: H. Böhlau, 1883–1987), vol. 1 (1900), pt. 11, pp. 357–61; vol. 4 (1933), pt. 3, p. 10; Eugen Holländer, *Wunder, Wundergeburt und Wundergestalt in Einblattdrucken des fünfzehnten bis achtzehnten Jahrhunderts*, 2nd ed. (Stuttgart: F. Enke, 1922), pp. 322–25; Hartmann Grisar and Franz Heege, *Luthers Kampfbilder*, 4 vols. (Freiburg im Breisgau: Herder, 1921–1923), vol. 3, *Bilderkampf in den Schriften von 1523 bis 1545*, pp. 14–23; Robert W. Scribner, *For the Sake of Simple Folk: Popular Propaganda for the German Reformation* (Cambridge and New York: Cambridge University Press, 1981), pp. 127–32.

[3] Johann Georg Schenck, *Monstrorum historia memorabilis* (Frankfurt, 1609), p. 89. Apparently Schenck was citing a broadsheet similar to a colored drawing conserved in the Univer-

nearly the same time, other illustrated reports on the event appeared and had an immediate and wide distribution. As early as 26 December of the same year Johannes Magenbuch sent a print piece of the sort to Wolfgang Richard in Ulm. He comments:

> Monstrum tibi hic mitto, quod exceptum est e vacca, quam quidam volebat mactare Fribergae, quae civitas est ducis Henrici Misniae. Quid significet, difficile dictu est. Convocavit dux omnes monachos, ut dicerent quid prae se ferret hoc portentum; nihil volebant statuere. Tandem princeps ipse subridens conclusit et dixit vaccam esse matrem omnium monachorum.[4]

Beyond the gratuity of Duke Heinrich von Meissen's insulting remark on the parentage of monks, the final words give an accurate idea of how immediately the monster of Saxony was put into a context of religious polemics. Nor was this a one-way operation. On 5 January 1523, Margrave Georg of Brandenburg wrote to Luther from Prague to make his excuses for a regrettable incident. Several days before, he had received word of the monster of Freiberg, which he had passed on to an astronomer in Prague to get his explanation. Without the margrave's knowledge, the astronomer had printed an interpretation in verse that equated the monster with Luther. The work was sequestered and all the copies were burned.[5] Perhaps in reaction to this episode, Luther determined to furnish his own interpretation of the deformed calf. The piece must have been nearly completed on 16 January, when he wrote to Wenzeslaus Link:

> Gratiam et pacem. Unum monstrorum ego interpretor modo. Omissa generali interpretatione monstrorum quae significant certo rerum publicarum mutationem per bella potissimum, quo et mihi non est dubium Germaniae portendi vel summam belli calamitatem vel extremum diem, ego tantum versor in particulari interpretatione quae ad monachos pertinet.[6]

The monk-calf that Luther interpreted in these terms was only one of the many monsters to crop up in Europe at the time ("monstra cottidie crebrescunt," Luther wrote to Georg Spalatin four days earlier).[7] To balance the picture, Melanchthon commented during the same period on the so-called pope-ass, another monstrous creature known widely since its discovery on the banks of the Tiber in 1496. The two texts were published

---

sitätsbibliotek of Würzburg, cited in *WKG*, vol. 4, pt. 3, p. 10. A sheet containing the same text in French must have fallen into the hands of the Bourgeois of Paris, who describes it in the same terms: *Journal d'un Bourgeois de Paris sous le regne de François Premier (1515–1536)*, ed. Ludovic Lalanne (Paris: J. Renouard et c., 1854), p. 95.

[4] *WKG*, vol. 4, pt. 3, p. 17.

[5] Ibid., pp. 8–9.

[6] Ibid., p. 17.

[7] Ibid., p. 15.

together, splendidly illustrated with two engravings by Lucas Cranach, under the title *Deuttung der zwo grewlichen figuren, Bapstesels zu Rom und Munchkalbs zu Freyerberg in Meyssen funden*, a publication that had later printings, both together and apart, not germane to our concerns here.[8] What we should note is Luther's clear perception of the multiple layers of interpretation of monsters in general and of this one in particular (an interpretive variety that in all probability explains the vast and multifaceted success of this and other "monsters"). Luther makes a clear distinction between a global interpretation of the deformed creatures, used prophetically, and an interpretation in a political key and aimed at one specific topic, not intended to exclude or eliminate the more general meaning, but superimposed upon it. The text says of this type of reading:

> Die prophetische Deuttung dises Munchkalbs wil ich dem Geyst lassen, denn ich kein prophet binn. . . . Ein ander gebe die prophetische Deuttung. Ich will meyn Munchkalb meynem stand zu dienst deutten.[9]

Thus Luther intended to dedicate this work to the service of his *Stand* (in the medieval sense of *ordo monachorum*), or, to put it differently, to the service of the doctrinal and popularizing activities that he was pursuing during these very months regarding the uselessness and even the perniciousness of monastic vows. In the same month of January 1523, the *M. Lutheri ad Brismannum epistola de votis monasticis* appeared; a sermon on 25 January insisted at length on the hypocrisy of good works without faith that permeated monks like leprosy; between April and May he wrote and published the *Ursach und Antwort dass Jungfrauen Klöster göttlich verlassen mögen*, in which he justified his encouragement of twelve nuns who fled the convent of Nimpschen on 7 April and took refuge with him.[10] One of them, in fact, Katharina von Bora, was to become his wife.

The *monstra*, as we have seen, had been linked with divination since classical antiquity, and the connection between divination and Reformation and anti-Reformation propaganda was pointed out some time ago. We should note, though, that in the *Deuttung* Luther was not limiting himself to furnishing propaganda in the form of prophecy. Admittedly, he alludes

[8] On the various editions of the *Deuttung*, see *WKG*, vol. 1, pt. 11, pp. 361–68. On Cranach's engravings, see Fritz Saxl, "Illustrated Pamphlets of the Reformation," in his *Lectures*, 2 vols. (London: Warburg Institute, University of London, 1957), pp. 255–66; Werner Timm, "Notizen zur Graphik Lucas Cranachs," in Peter H. Feist et al., eds., *Lucas Cranach: Künstler und Gesellschaft: Referate des Colloquiums mit internationaler Beteiligung zum 500. Geburtstag Lucas Cranachs d. Ä.* (Wittenberg: Staatliche Lutherhalle, 1973), p. 93; Dieter Koepplin, Tilman Falk et al., *Lukas Cranach: Gemälde, Zeichnungnen, Druckgraphik: Austellung im Kunstmuseum Basel, 15. Juni–8 September 1974*), 2 vols. (Basel: Birkhäuser, 1974), vol. 1, p. 370, nn. 246–47.

[9] *WKG*, vol. 1, pt. 11, pp. 380–81.

[10] Ibid., pp. 284–91; 9–11; 394–400.

to the hidden divinatory meaning of the monster, but then, making good use of the same techniques of argumentation that he ascribes to the brand of prophecy practiced by others ("ein andere gebe die prophetische Deuttung"), he returns to the present, analyzing the meaning of the various parts of the calf (his closed eyes, his long tongue, his mangled thighs, and so forth), concluding that "all sistery and monkery is nothing but false and mendacious appearance." Thus the vague prophecy of catastrophe that was implied by the monster ("rerum publicarum mutationem . . . summam belli calamitatem . . . extremum diem") was a threatening confirmation of his interpretation.

The prophetic and the propagandistic approaches to analysis of the monster were not the only ones. When the Dominican theologian Johannes Cochlaeus, writing in April 1523, answered a piece that Luther had written against him (*Adversus armatum virum Cokleum*, composed early in February of the same year),[11] he did so by imitating the spirit of medieval marginalia and feigning an absurd and ridiculous combat between a snail and the Minotaur.[12] Luther had played on the sense of the word *cochlaea* ("snail," which, incidentally, he translates erroneously as *testudo*, "box turtle") to laugh at the *armatum virum Cokleum* and his useless shell of arguments, placing the Dominican among the "istae testudines, limacae, talpae, lacertae, erucae, locustae, bruci, vespae, imo viperae et stelliones, qui . . . pereunt in immundiciis suis sophisticis."[13] Cochlaeus responded in kind, not only identifying Luther with the monster of Saxony but going so far as to draw a parallel between the deformed calf and the Minotaur. This point of departure had a number of consequences for the composition and the structure of Cochlaeus's work (leaving aside for the moment its doctrinal content, which concerned grace through the sacraments and through faith). First, it forced Cochlaeus into a cultural framework of constant reference to classical mythology, so that along with the Minotaur we get Apis, the sacred bull, which had been known for several decades in connection with the *religio aegyptiaca*, thanks in particular to the popularizing activities of Annio of Viterbo (Giovanni Nanni). A second and perhaps more conspicuous result was that the work was in fact a series of elegant and superficial variations on the theme of the struggle between the

[11] Ibid., pp. 295–306.

[12] Johannes Cochlaeus, *Adversus cucullatum Minotaurum Wittenbergensem*, ed. Joseph Schweitzer, Corpus Catholicorum no. 3 (Münster, 1920). Cochlaeus returned to the topic in his *Historia Ioannis Cochlaei de actis et scriptis Martini Lutheri Saxonis* . . . (Cologne: apud Theodorum Baumium, 1568), fol. 99*r*. On Cochlaeus, see Remigius Bäumer, *Johannes Cochlaeus (1479–1552). Leben und Werk im Dienst der katholischen Reform* (Münster: Aschendorf, 1980); Gotthelf Wiedermann, "Cochlaeus as Polemicist," in *Seven-headed Luther. Essays in Commemoration of a Quincentenary, 1483–1983*, ed. Peter Newman Brooks (Oxford: Oxford University Press and New York: Clarendon Press, 1983), pp. 195–205.

[13] *WKG*, vol. 1, pt. 11, p. 305.

minax Minotaurus and the *parva cochlaea*, to the point that its rhetorical structure ended up getting the better of its theological content.

The text begins with a parody of the first lines of the *Aeneid*:

> Monstra bovemque cano, boreae qui primus ab oris
> Theutonicas terras profugus conspurcat. . . .[14]

The rest of the work continues in the same tone. Luther is called "saxonicus vitulus," "semicucullatus bos," "gloriosus Minotaurus," and finally "that great son of the Bohemian Pasiphae." The insult that Heinrich von Meissen had applied to Freiberg monks' parentage was thus turned against Luther and heightened by a mythological context. Rather than turning the image of the monster to prophetic or specifically propagandistic purposes, Cochlaeus consistently uses it for rhetorical and mythological ends. Only toward the end of his tract does he seem to abandon his pose as a humanist and return to a symbolic and religious interpretation of the monster of Saxony, identifying it, surprisingly enough, with Germany: "Deus optimus maximus resarciat has Germaniae scissuras, et conglutinet vulnera hiantia."[15] The *scissurae* in the body of the monk-calf had now become a physical laceration and a sign of the religious schism that divided Germany.

Luther as Monster

The monk-calf had a belated vogue in treatises on teratology of the latter sixteenth century from Paré to Rueff, Aldrovandi, and Fortunio Liceto,[16] but by that time its prophetic and symbolic connotations had been nearly totally lost and it belonged more in the ideal realm of the *Wunderkammern* than in the domain of doctrinal polemics. More interesting to our purposes is the stabilization and persistence of the image of Luther as the monster of Saxony. A year after the publication of the *Adversus cucullatum Minotaurum*, the Polish astrologer Johannes Ploniscus (Jan z Płonsk) blended the "monstrifica ac ridenda figura" of the monster of Saxony with a polemical position on the universal deluge predicted for 1524, accusing Luther, "hic

[14] Cochlaeus, *Adversus cucullatum Minotaurum*, p. 13.

[15] Ibid., p. 57.

[16] Jakob Rueff, *De conceptu et generatione hominis* . . . (Frankfurt am Main: [S. Feyerabendi], 1587, fol. 4*r*; Conrad Lycosthenes (Conrad Wollfhart), *Prodigiorum ac ostentorum chronicon* (Basel, 1557), p. 528; Ambroise Paré, *Des monstres et prodiges*, ed. Jean Céard (Geneva: Droz, 1971), pp. 36, 165 (available in English as *On Monsters and Marvels*, tr. Janis L. Pallister [Chicago: University of Chicago Press, 1982], pp. 46, 156–57); Pierre Boaistuau et al., *Histoires prodigieuses extraictes de plusieurs fameux autheurs, grecs & latins, sacrez & prophanes, divisées en cinq livres* (Antwerp: G. Ianssens, 1594), pp. 709–20; Fortunio Liceto, *De monstrorum caussis, natura, et differentiis libri duo . . . secunda editio correctior* (Padua: Apud Frambottum, 1634; colophon dated 1633), p. 100; Ulisse Aldrovandi, *Monstrorum historia* (Bologna: Marco Antonio Bernia, 1642), p. 371.

vitulus cucullatus et legislator saxonicus," of having spread fearful expectation of the flood in Germany.[17] Even many years later, Cochlaeus's work found an echo in the *Libri mirabilium septem* of Friedrich Nausea and the *Historia gentium septentrionalium* of Olaus Magnus.[18]

This image lost no time in penetrating Italy, even independently of Cochlaeus's work. As early as February 1523 an anonymous chronicler in Cremona wrote:

> There came a letter from Rome [about] how a peasant in Magna [Germany] had killed a cow, and when he had killed it, he left it that way three days, and after three days [when] the cow was opened he found a monster that had the face of a man and a friar's tonsure, but it was ugly to see and had a hood in front and in back like those of the friars, and had the body of a man, hairy arms and legs, and cleft hands and feet like a pig's, and the letter says that it lived three days.[19]

On 26 May Tommasino Lancellotti made an analogous entry in his chronicle:

> There was brought to Modena a picture of a monster born of a cow in Saxony that has a quasi-human head, and it has a tonsure and scapulary of skin like a friar's scapulary, and arms in front and legs and feet like a pig's and the tail of a pig. It is said that it is a friar who is called Martin Utero, who is dead and who several years ago preached heresy in Lamagna [Germany].[20]

These texts testify to the circulation in Italy of print pieces on "a monster born of a cow in Saxony." Internal evidence tells us several things. First, this is the earliest mention of Luther to be gleaned from Italian chronicles, the *Diarii* of Marin Sanudo excepted. Thus Luther was talked about in northern Italy early in 1523, but his name was distorted, he was reported as dead, and he was identified with an abnormal aborted calf. It is clear that we are in the realm of the most obvious anti-Reformation propaganda. We might also wonder what relationship there was between the *depintura* brought to Modena and the "littere da Roma" mentioned by the Cre-

[17] Johannes Ploniscus, *Judicium maius magnarum coniunctionum anno 1524 evenientium ad annos futuros quadraginta duraturum* (Cracow, n.d.), cited in Paola Zambelli, "Fine del mondo o inizio della propaganda? Astrologia, filosofia della storia e propaganda politico-religiosa nel dibattito sulla congiunzione del 1524," in *Scienze, credenze occulte, livelli di cultura. Convegno internazionale di studi (Firenze, 26–30 giugno 1980)* (Florence: L. S. Olschki, 1982), pp. 291–368, esp. pp. 331–34.

[18] Friedrich Nausea, *Libri mirabilium septum* (Cologne: apud P. Quentell, 1532), fols. xxiv *r–v*; Olaus Magnus, *Historia delle genti e della natura delle cose settentrionali d'Olao Magno goto* (Venice: D. Nicolini [for] gli heredi di Lucantonio Giunta, 1565), fol. 169*v*.

[19] *Cronache cremonesi dall'anno MCCCCIX al MDXXV*, ed. Francesco Robolotti, *Bibliotheca Historica Italica*, 4 vols. (Milan: Brigola, 1876–1901), vol. 1, p. 252.

[20] Tommasino Lancellotti, *Cronaca modenese*, ed. Carlo Borghi, 12 vols. (Parma: P. Fiaccadori, 1863), vol. 1, p. 440.

monese chronicler. It is not too improbable that the latter refers not to a private letter but to a print piece, since the term *littera*, as we have seen, was at the time often included in the titles of short works on prodigious events. It allowed the printer or the sponsor of the publication to claim credibility by referring to the direct testimony of the author, real or imaginary, of the supposed letter. That the terms *littera* and *depintura* might refer to the same publication (more likely a broadsheet than a pamphlet) seems possible from a close comparison of the two passages cited. Both, in fact, speak of a monster born of a cow but with an almost human face, who seemed to have a tonsure and a cowl like a friar's and who had feet and hooves like a pig's. Furthermore, the two chroniclers note these details in the same order. If the *littera* was illustrated, it could have been defined as a *depintura*; conversely, the *depintura* in Modena was most probably accompanied by an explicative text, perhaps even extremely short. We shall soon examine a true broadsheet on the same topic with these very characteristics. We might ask, finally (and this is not clear from the passages cited), whether identifying the monster as Luther and reporting him as dead (only in Lancellotti) were details in the text or texts that the two chroniclers had consulted.

One answer, on a hypothetical level, emerges from a comparison of these texts with a letter written by Pietro Martire d'Anghiera—as always, an indefatigable collector of print pieces on prodigies and monstrosities—several months later, on 25 August, from Valladolid. Anghiera states that two different pictures of monsters of "juvencae formam sub humana specie" had reached that city from Germany, and he comments: "Lutheri heretici et commilitorum eius referre specie populi summurmurant."[21] In this case, as perhaps with the Italian publication or publications, the monster was identified as Luther only by implication. The piece was to be understood and to serve as a warning to those who already knew the name of the German monk, but without furnishing inopportune information to anyone not yet aware of the heresy rife in Germany. As for a possible connection between the Italian print pieces and the German pamphlets from which they took their inspiration, it is clear that the Italian pieces were unrelated to either Luther's text or Cochlaeus's, but derived from one of the earlier, more anodyne accounts that had appeared in Germany as early as December 1522. Their early circulation in Italy (from February 1523) confirms this supposition. If we accept the various hypotheses that have been outlined thus far, we can conclude that the two Italian chroniclers were referring to an illustrated print piece of Roman origin (information traveled easily from Germany to Rome). Its text (presumably brief) was written in the form of a letter; it proposed—but only implicitly—that the monster be

[21] Pietro Martire d'Anghiera, *Opus epistolarum Petri Martyris Anglerii* (Amsterdam: typis Elzevirianis, 1670), p. 459.

equated with Luther; its aims were propagandistic and anti-Reformation. Furthermore, it is more than probable that the *depintura* mentioned in the Modenese chronicle also came from Rome: Modena belonged to the Holy See in this period, and for that reason there was a steady and privileged flow of information and propaganda between the two cities.[22]

The Monster of Castelbaldo

The image of Luther as a monster must have had a notable effect on the greater public in Italy, and even some years later interpretation of a monstrous creature still served anti-Lutheran propagandistic aims. Early in 1526 a broadsheet circulated in Venice (or at least in the territories of the Serenissima) that was printed on one side only, bore a small engraving and a short text printed in fine type, and was presented without title, author's name, or mention of the printer and the place of publication (Figure 9).[23] The incipit follows the conventions for this sort of literature:

> The lack of faith that reigns in the world today, my most illustrious lords, [is] the reason why the Eternal Father sends many monsters that are not believed [unless] we see them; and although they proceed from an ill-disposed, badly organized, or imperfect nature, or from superfluous sperm, nevertheless God the master of nature allows to happen what he could obviate for our most enormous sins, so that, as I said in the other exposition on the monster of Germany, seeing that we are of a perfect nature, we have cause to praise our father and Eternal God and fear him, considering that he could have made [others] similar and more monstrous.

The anonymous writer had thus already published an *Expositione del monstro d'Alemagna*, which, if it resembled this text in having an engraving and a brief text, might correspond to the descriptions of the *depintura* and the *littere* that circulated in Modena and Cremona. This is only a hypothesis, however, open to doubt, because the *littere* in Cremona came from Rome. We must admit the circulation of at least two or three print pieces on the topic in central and northern Italy, thus confirming that the image of Luther as a monster penetrated into this region.[24]

[22] See below, pp. 160–61.

[23] This piece was pasted into the original manuscript of Marin Sanudo's *Diarii* (Biblioteca Marciana di Venezia, ms. it. VII 268 [= 9255], fol. 435*r*). The text is reproduced in the printed edition of Marino Sanuto, *Diarii*, 58 vols. (Venice: R. Deputazione Veneta di storia patria, 1879–1903), vol. 40, cols. 652–53. Sanudo had occasion to see this creature while it was still alive (col. 650).

[24] Further confirmation comes from the recent discovery of an analogous sheet inside the manuscript of the *Historiae senenses* of Sigismondo Tizio: See Paola Zambelli, "Da Giulio II a Paolo III. Come l'astrologo provocatore Luca Gaurico divenne vescovo," in Fabio Tronca-

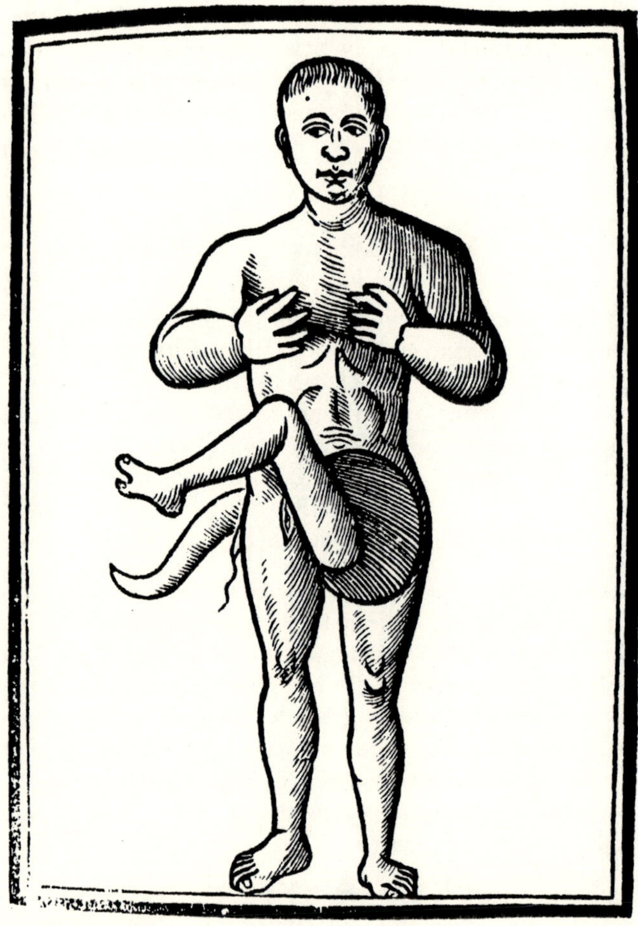

Fig. 9. The Monster of Castelbaldo. Illustration from an Italian broadsheet, Biblioteca Marciana, Venice.

Following the introductory paragraph in the Venetian broadsheet comes word of a creature born

> deformed and monstrous near Castelbaldo at Maxi [Masi, in the province of Padua, between Badia Polesine and Castelbaldo] in M.D.XXV, on the 28th day of December, with three legs, and the third leg between the [other] two, turned upward, and between the right leg and the middle one it had the nature [sexual parts] of a woman and behind it has the male member, and in the body it had [something] like a round ball or a head, and an imperfect arm behind.

---

relli, ed., *La città dei segreti, Magia, astrologia e cultura esoterica a Roma* (*XV–XVIII secolo*), Convegno Roma ermetica (1983: Rome, Italy) (Milan: Franco Angeli, 1985), pp. 311–12.

The anonymous writer then turns to an interpretation of the monster and of the symbolic and divinatory "significance" of every part of his body. The "bala tonda" signifies the vainglory of the world or perhaps the deceiving and hidden "cogitation" of princes; the upturned leg

> signifies a leader or a pseudoprophet who will predict falsely, and since a foot cannot walk turned against nature, so this one will not be able to make his way—that is, will not last long before he is annihilated. The imperfect arm signifies the imperfect works that he will make the holy faith of Jesus Christ display and he will ruin it, and since it is behind, counter to nature, so will he go against the holy faith. And by the woman's nature [we see] that he will promise that lust is no sin. And by the male member, which is turned backward, is meant the very great and putrid sin against nature that reigns in the world today, for which God will promise this false prophet that he will come to scourge Christianity.

Luther is quite obviously the false prophet turned against the body of which he is a member, whose works are imperfect, and who "will promise that lust is no sin." We know, in fact, and these pages offer further confirmation, that one of the most persistent rumors about Luther circulating in Italy was that he favored undue sexual freedom.[25] Thus although the great reformer was not explicitly equated with the monster of Castelbaldo, he was nonetheless tacitly associated with its deformity—a sign of moral deformity—and with lasciviousness, all the more so in that his preaching was taken as a divine punishment for sodomy, "il grandissimo e spuzolente peccato contra natura che ogidì regna al mondo." He is also presented as a false prophet, which makes this text interesting as a point of conjunction between the two different images of Luther as a monster and as a pseudoprophet. In any event, divine wrath would soon take care of him: "non durarà longo tempo che sarà anichilito." The prediction, like the false information of Luther's death given in Lancellotti, functioned as a prophecy, as an omen of things to come, and also as a warning.

An Anti-Lutheran Prophecy

Prophecy could thus be used for propagandistic, anti-Reformation ends when the bodies of deformed creatures were used for baneful predictions of the imminent coming of Luther (or his double) and coupled with pre-

[25] When Gasparo Contarini went to the Diet of Worms in April 1520, he picked up, secondhand, the information that Luther "dicat . . . matrimonium . . . dissolvi posse, fornicationem simplicem peccatum non esse, ac innuit mulierum illam comunitatem de qua Plato in sua Republica": Sanuto, *Diarii*, vol. 30, cols. 211–12. See also, on a totally different level, the *Lamento de Italia contra Martin Lutherano. Opera nuova* (n.p., n.d., but written by a Florentine around 1530), fols. 4*v*–5*r*.

dictions of their ultimate annihilation and death (in some texts, such as the one Lancellotti saw, given as already achieved).[26] It is also interesting to note that, unlike the pieces that circulated at the time of Leo X, which were on a relatively higher cultural scale, the anti-Lutheran broadsides that we have examined or reconstructed were all in the vernacular and seem to have been of the "popular" sort. Thus they were addressed to a broad public who could be thought to be still interested, in the 1520s, in the literary genre of the *monstra* and who had the greatest need (in the eyes of those who put out such texts) to be protected against the lure of Luther's name.

The same propagandistic ends were pursued by means of other materials, again in a prophetic vein and again having a broad circulation. Thus the same popular typology is evident in an octavo-sized text of four leaves, with no indication of place or date of printing but apparently published around 1530, entitled *Vita de santo Angelo carmelitano martyre con la prophetia data a lui per el nostro signor Jesu Christo de tutto quello che e advenuto e advegnira alla christianitade per infedeli et della setta et leze falsa luterina.*[27] The pamphlet's title page bears an engraving taken from the *Pronosticatio* of Johannes Lichtenberger, a text whose extraordinary success in Italy can be traced through the wide distribution of its illustrations in other publications of a "popular" nature. The engraving used here shows Christ as he allots tasks to representatives of the three walks of life—priests, warriors, and peasants. We know, however, that the notion of the tripartite division of society was not common in Italy, where the image in question was interpreted as the Last Judgment, thereby giving it eschatological significance.[28] Thus both the title and the illustration place this short work in a prophetic context. It was, however, only a slightly revamped version of a *Vita sancti Angeli martyris* attributed to Enoch, patriarch of Jerusalem, and later known for the edition of it that Benoît Gonon produced from a fifteenth-century manuscript of the work for the *Vitae Patrum Occidentis* (Lyon, 1625), subsequently reprinted in the *Acta Sanctorum.*[29] The text was clearly biographical and recounted the life of St. Angelus, first on Mount Carmel and then in Rome (where he was supposed to have met St. Francis), his miracles, and his death, which took place in Licata on 5 May 1225 at the hand of one Berengario, a Cathar whom he had reprimanded

[26] The false news of Luther's death was also reported in 1529 in Leonardo and Gregorio Amaseo and Gio. Antonio Azio, *Diarii udinesi, dall'anno 1508 al 1541* (Venice: R. Deputazione di storia patria per le Venezie, 1884), p. 302, and in 1531 in Sanuto, *Diarii*, vol. 50, col. 308 and vol. 55, col. 279. In these cases as well, the news was quite evidently expedient for propagandistic purposes.

[27] See Victor Massena, prince d'Essling, *Etudes sur l'art de la gravure sur bois à Venise: Les livres à figures vénitiens de la fin du XVe siècle et du commencement du XVIe*, 4 vols. (Florence: L. S. Olschki and Paris: H. Leclerc, 1907–1914), vol. 2, pt. 2, p. 646.

[28] See Ottavia Niccoli, *I sacerdoti, i guerrieri, i contadini. Storia di un'immagine della società* (Turin: G. Einaudi, 1979), pp. 58–61.

[29] *Acta sanctorum*, 68 vols. (Paris: V. Palmé, 1863–1919), vol. 15, *Maius*, pp. 15*–47*.

for having an incestuous relationship with his own sister. This last note, which combines the themes of lust and heresy, provides us with a vantage point for understanding the sense of this publication. At the end of the 1520s, when Europe teemed with Reformation propaganda, this text, aimed at a wide audience, promoted the need to oppose, even at risk of one's life, a heresy that was spreading everywhere and was judged to lead to lasciviousness. Another, Latin version of the same *Life* was printed in 1526 under the auspices of Tommaso Bellorosi of Palermo, who added a prophetic note to it, in particular by reading into it a prediction of a Turkish victory in Italy ("de turcali victoria contra Italiam").[30] The *Life* published in the vernacular was addressed to a different public on a lower level (as is clear from the physical characteristics of the work); nonetheless, it too was presented as a prophetic text rooted in the present, especially through the use of one particular passage that deserves closer examination.

Angelus had lived in the Palestinian desert for five years when Christ himself appeared to him and predicted his martyrdom, to be followed by wars with the Turks and subsequent turmoil throughout a good part of Europe (which naturally was the first reason why sixteenth-century printers should have been interested in the *Life* and undoubtedly was what had attracted Bellorosi). At this point in the narrative a passage was inserted, which is given here first in the original Latin (subsequently published by Gonon) and then in the Italian paraphrase in order to show how small changes in the text adapted it to the contemporary scene. The passage runs thus:

Istud erit quando Ecclesia erit saepissime divisa et unusquisque alteri adversabitur, et quando duo vel tres summi Pontifices effici voluerint, et quando Ecclesia erit a multis tyrannis expoliata, et quando Ecclesia plena erit multarum Religionum hypocritarum, populos defraudantium sub colore sanctitatis: qui paucam caritatem erga proximum habebunt, et loco ejus superbiam, avaritiam, invidiam, luxuriam et sodomiam communiter habebunt. Et propter talia peccata permittam Italiam, et quasi omnes Christianos per manus inimicorum meorum castigari.

Et questo sarà come venirà scisma in la chiesa, simonia con altri mali, per li quali serà da diversi tyranni spogliata et malmenata. Et quando si levaranno male gente che sotto specie de sanctitade sedurà el popolo con nove et permixte lege, concorrendogli larga vita et bestial vivere. Onde questi lupi sotto tal manto levaranno ogni bon costume facendo licito lo illicito. Perhò surgerà la ira divina et permetterà che 'l gladi[o] deli inimici de Dio haverà vigore contra il christianesimo, aciò ch'el sequiti vendetta contra li soi inimici per li inimici.[31]

[30] Ibid., p. 13*.

[31] Ibid., p. 34* for the Latin text; *Vita de santo Angelo Carmelitano* (n.p., n.d. [c.1530]), fol. A iii*r*, for the vernacular version.

The reference to "two or three most high pontiffs" allows us, first of all, to date the Latin *Vita* (or at least its later interpolation) with some certainty, as this clearly refers to the years of the Great Schism in the West.[32] The same reference, by then no longer current, is left out of the Italian version, which speaks only of schism and introduces instead the concept of simony, indicated (unlike the Latin text) as the reason why the Church will be "despoiled and mistreated by various tyrants." The elaboration of this idea (the Latin text shows only the participle "expoliata") makes us think that the writer had in mind the sack of Rome. The most skillful and the most important modification, however, comes later, where the phrase "ecclesia plena erit multarum religionum hypocritarum, populos defraudantium sub colore sanctitatis," along with what follows, becomes "bad people will rise up, who under the guise of sanctity will seduce the people with new and mixed laws," and so forth.

In short, a commonplace of the late Middle Ages—deploring the proliferation and decadence of the religious orders—has been transformed into a denunciation of Lutheran preaching. Furthermore, the principal reason for the success of that preaching is seen as being the "broader life and bestial living" that it permitted when "the illicit" was made legitimate. The theme of the sexual license permitted by Reformed doctrine, which we have already encountered and will encounter again, is an extraordinarily tenacious *topos*. To sum up this print piece, however, we find in it signs of the same process that we have witnessed in connection with the verse prophecies published toward the end of the fifteenth century: When a traumatic event—first the arrival of Charles VIII, later the breakup of the unity of the *respublica christiana*—exerted pressure on society, people returned to the old texts, reread them, reworked them in the light of present events, and gave them titles that explained and justified their new currency. This phenomenon had been massive thirty years earlier, however; now it occurred only rarely.

God's Chastisement of Heretics

Another technique of the anti-Lutheran propaganda that also made use of popular print pieces of a prophetic nature was the use of celestial signs to predict horrible calamities as punishment for the rapid spread of heresy. The episode of the universal deluge expected in 1524 (to be discussed in the next chapter) provided an excellent opportunity to identify the feared catastrophic flood with God's castigation for the Lutheran heresy and to

[32] In another, probably earlier *Vita* given in the *Acta sanctorum: Maius*, Christ limits himself to foretelling Angelus's martyrdom when he speaks to him (p. 51*).

use it to try to destroy Lutheranism. It was not unique, however. As late as 1536 a rough and poorly printed octavo-sized leaflet of two leaves appeared, printed in Rome "per Albertin Zanelli" and entitled *El gran prodigio di tre soli apparsi in Franza adi nove de Setembrio a hore tredese. In di de sabbato cosa multo stupenda.* The text is epistolary in form (a technique frequently used for information on prodigious events, as we have seen), but it does not give the name either of the writer of the supposed letter or of its addressee.

The letter speaks of a phenomenon connected with the refraction of light that was often recorded during those years and to which we shall return, parhelia, or "parelia," as the text says: two "accidental suns that surround our natural sun." This phenomenon was, according to the writer, "most cruelly apart from nature," and the three suns were omens of the overturning of states and of bloody battles, earthquakes, pestilence, and famine. What had caused this disturbance? "The Lutheran sect and pagans, who with lasciviousness and their false laws have worked to subject the natural sun—that is, the Christian people, observant of the evangelical law."[33] The author later makes it clear that the natural sun represents the pope and the emperor and that this indivisible dual civil and ecclesiastical power, portrayed as the one true day star, will soon destroy (indeed, "burn up and annihilate") the other duality, the Turks and the Lutherans, "whereupon for one or both will follow the destruction of the leader and his sect . . . [they] and their followers will be punished, burned, and destroyed." Prophecy in the 1520s had stopped at foretelling the end of Luther and his followers by the action of God's wrath and providential catastrophes; now, in 1536, divine chastisement took a more human form, working through the Holy See, seconded by the secular arm, and leading directly to the flaming pyres. It was a significant change of direction in the struggle against heresy. The leaflet concludes with a warning to the "auditori" (can we then presume that the piece was read publicly?) that God would withhold the threatened scourges only if they could join their thoughts and turn their arms against those who sought to destroy the true law of Christ.[34]

One more time, and again in 1536, "lasciviousness" was the way the "Lutheran sect" entrapped the Christian multitudes. As we have seen, this was a truly recurrent theme in anti-Lutheran propaganda in Italy, at least (though not exclusively) in its more rudimentary, less refined forms. Although at first this certainly came of the application of a well-known stereotype connected with heresy, the insistence with which the theme recurs makes one wonder whether in some cases there was not some basis in

[33] *El gran prodigio di tre soli* (Rome: Albertin Zanelli, 1536), fol. 2*r*.

[34] Ibid., fol. 2*v*.

fact—whether, in other words, some defender of the Reformed word, in the fervor of preaching the Christian's newfound liberties, did not choose his examples from the realm of sexual morality as well.

A Case of Reformation Cryptopropaganda

Up to now we have seen that the language of prophecy was used, even after 1530, to combat the "pseudoprophet" of Saxony "who will predict falsities," who "will promise that lust is no sin," who "under the guise of sanctity will seduce the people with new and permissive laws," and with his "lasciviousness and false laws will work to subject . . . the Christian people."

In point of fact, a pseudoprophet had been expected for some time in Italy and in Europe in general, even several decades before Luther began to preach. The great conjunction of Jupiter and Saturn in 1484 (with its various interpretations) and the controversy concerning Antonio Arquato's *De Eversione Europae* are events too well known to merit further discussion here.[35] I might note, however, that when Arquato states (probably still in the Quattrocento), "veniet a septentrione heresiarcha magnus," he was without a doubt basing his prediction on the planetary conjunction, even if he did not say so explicitly. This was also the sense in which contemporary commentators understood him.[36] Andrea Bernardi, the barber chronicler from Forlì, gives living testimony to the circulation of these and other similar prognostications. In the waning days of 1484, Bernardi draws from a prognostication for the year 1485 written by the astrologer Marco Scribanario the disquieting conviction of the imminent rise of "new prophets who will make marvelous demonstrations of faith and of religion," adding that "in many places temples and oratories will be destroyed." Both Scribanario and Andrea Bernardi based their predictions on the conjunction of Jupiter and Saturn in the sign of the Scorpion.[37]

The text that perhaps contributed the most to expectations of a new prophet (still using the great planetary conjunction as a base) was the *Pro-*

[35] In connection with these events, see at least Eugenio Garin, "Il pronostico dell'Arquato sulla distruzione dell'Europa," in his *L'età nuova. Ricerche di storia della cultura dal XII al XVI secolo* (Naples: Morano, 1969), pp. 105–11. Zambelli, "Fine del mondo" reviews the bibliography on the topic (to which I might add Jean Deny, "Les Pseudo-prophéties concernant les Turcs au XVIe siècle," *Revue des études islamiques* 10 [1936]: 201–220, esp. "La Prédiction d'Antonio Torquato," 207–216) and treats the expectation of a pseudoprophet in the context of polemics concerning the flood (pp. 313–23).

[36] See Garin, "Il pronostico dell'Arquato," pp. 110–11.

[37] Andrea Bernardi, *Cronache forlivesi . . . dal 1476 al 1517*, ed. Giuseppe Mazzatinti, 2 vols. (Bologna: R. Deputazione di storia patria, 1895–1897), vol. 1, pt. 1, p. 156.

nosticatio of Johannes Lichtenberger in its fourteen Italian editions.[38] Lichtenberger's work can help us to a correct interpretation of the last text that interests us here, the *Pronosticho de Maestro Alberto Neapolitano sopra lanno 1523 Intitulato al Populo Christiano*, a work of four leaves with no indication of place or date of publication, as was usual for this type of publication. In its general lines the structure of this short work is not very different from that of others of the same sort. There is an astrological and theological introduction, then a few brief predictions relating to the seasons and the harvests, followed by a short note, "De le guerre et de la pace," a more general prediction, and, finally, a page devoted to conjunctions and oppositions of the moon and to the dates of movable feasts during the year.

A closer reading of the text shows, however, that the first part and the long concluding prediction are in reality literal borrowings of two long passages from Lichtenberger's *Pronosticatio*.[39] Worse, they are a plagiarism of a plagiarism in that they use the parts of Lichtenberger's work that he in turn had copied from the *Prognostica ad viginti annos duratura* of the Flemish mathematician (later bishop of Fossombrone) Paul of Middelburg (Paulus Middelburgensis).[40] It goes without saying that in this whirl of references reaching back to ever higher cultural levels, the figure of Maestro Alberto Napoletano dissolves into thin air. As no other notice of such a person can be found, the name obviously was a convenient shield for the unknown compiler of the publication. It would nonetheless be too restrictive to consider this unknown person (whom we shall continue to call Alberto Napoletano, out of convention) merely a plagiarist. The second of

[38] To the thirteen editions cited in Domenico Fava, "La fortuna del pronostico di Giovanni Lichtenberger in Italia nel Quattrocento e nel Cinquecento," *Gutenbergjahrbuch* 5 (1930): 126–48, we should add at least one more, cited in Ugo Baroncelli, "Altri incunabuli bresciani sconosciuti o poco noti," in *Contributi alla storia del libro italiano. Miscellanea in onore di Lamberto Donati* (Florence: L. S. Olschki, 1969), pp. 53–65, esp. 58–60.

[39] The first passage begins with the words "Benedecta sia la maestà del creatore" and ends "et è venuto da lo ascendente insino a duodeci gradi de Scorpione del quale Venere è divisore" (*Pronosticho de Maestro Alberto Neapolitano sopra lanno 1523 Intitulato al Populo Christiano*, fols. A *r*–A ii*r*); the second begins "Bisognera dare nova lege per la humana necessità" and ends "& instituirà epso profeta una nova religione" (ibid., fols. 3*r*–4*r*, unnumbered). The Italian version followed here seems identical (among all the Italian editions of Lichtenberger that I have been able to check) with the *Pronosticatione in vulgare rara et piu non udita* . . . , "Impressa in Venetia nel anno MCCCCCXXV. Adi XIII Septembrio. Cavada da unaltra stampada in Modena per maestro Pietro Francioso nel anno MCCCCLXXXXIj adi XIV de aprile." The passages indicated are on fols. a. iiii*r*–b. i*r*; f. i*r*–f. ii*r*.

[40] Paul of Middelburg's work, in its turn, was a "servile" copy (Warburg's term is "sklavischer Benutzung") of passages from the *De magnis conjunctionibus* of Albumazar (Abū Ma'shar): Aby M. Warburg, *Ausgewälte Schriften und Würdigungen*, ed. Dieter Wuttke (Baden-Baden: Verlag Valentin Koerner, 1980), pp. 234–35; Italian translation of the first edition, *La rinascita del paganesimo antico*, tr. Emma Cantimori Mezzomonti (Florence: La Nuova Italia, 1966), p. 341.

the two passages that he picked up from Lichtenberger (and he from Paulus) predicts the coming of a new prophet from the north, one who would excel in the interpretation of Scripture, belong to a monastic order, found a new religion, and give humanity new laws for its changing needs. It is immediately apparent, then, that this brief work was more than a plagiarism or yet another proof (even another relevant proof) of the success of Lichtenberger's *Pronosticatio* in Italy. Once again, we see an earlier text reinterpreted and reappropriated because there was a profound sentiment that it was again current. It responded to a situation that it had prefigured when it was written, and now, when that situation had taken on concrete form, it cast new light on it to show its hidden potentialities. In short, Alberto Napoletano's text should not be read simply as a cryptorepublication of Lichtenberger. In 1523, it presupposed an awareness (strongly anchored in the compiler's mind) that the prophet had in fact appeared in the person of Luther. It is interesting to note, what is more, that the text is cut so as to reverse the sense of Lichtenberger's prediction. Lichtenberger stated that the prophet who was to come would indeed have an excellent mind and profound knowledge, "but will often speak lies and will have his knowledge cauterized; and will have poison closed up in his tail like a scorpion, where the [planetary] conjunction is made, and will be the cause of the spilling of much blood."[41] He was thus to be a false prophet (and we might well wonder at this point whether the passage was present in the minds of the anonymous anti-Lutheran polemicists discussed above who speak precisely of "a false prophet who will give new and false laws"). The omission of this passage in Alberto Napoletano's text indicates instead a radically different choice—the implicit affirmation that Luther was, to the contrary, a prophet as "true as St. Francis and St. Dominic were" rather than a pseudoprophet like Muhammad.[42] For this reason it seems to me that we can speak of Reform propaganda (hidden, to be sure) in connection with this pamphlet. The point of view and the purpose in repeating some of the most suggestive pages of the *Pronosticatio* are, in the last analysis, not far from Luther's own when he reprinted the same work in 1527 with a preface of his writing in which he recalls that much of what Lichtenberger had stated was erroneous, but that there was still truth in his pages, given that he had written "on the basis of the signs and the warnings of God."[43] When he offered only the pages of the German astrologer that

[41] Lichtenberger, *Pronosticatione in vulgare*, fol. f. ii*v*.

[42] Ibid., fol. f. i*r*; Alberto Napoletano, *Pronosticho*, fol. 3*v*, unnumbered.

[43] Johannes Lichtenberger, *Die weissagunge Johannis Lichtenbergs deudsch, zugericht mit uleys. Sampt einer nutzlichen vorrede und unterricht D. Martini Luthers* (Wittenberg: [Hans Lufft], 1527). Luther's preface is reprinted in Warburg, *La rinascita del paganesimo antico*, pp. 377–82, from which I quote.

appeared to be confirmed by being realized, Alberto Napoletano made a selection that Luther thought unnecessary.

The *Pronosticho de Maestro Alberto Neapolitano* seems to have fulfilled a need for some time, because it was reprinted without changes in 1529, except for retouching the date included in the title and the figures in the lunar calendar on the last page.[44] It is a shame that we cannot know the reactions of the readers of the two pamphlets, although we can reconstruct an echo of them: Fernando Colombo, who had bought the 1523 version of the work, hastened to purchase the 1529 edition (and probably was highly disappointed when he discovered that it was actually identical to the earlier edition). Thus we do not know whether this text aroused suspicion in Church circles. The most probable hypothesis is that this evocation of Luther the prophet—the only text to do so, since the others treated him as a pseudoprophet and a monster—either eluded unfriendly eyes or simply passed unobserved. The name of Luther does not appear in it, it is true, but, as Delio Cantimori wrote about another sixteenth-century episode involving prophecy for propaganda purposes, it is surer and less compromising to let people read between the lines than to say certain things out loud.[45]

[44] *Pronosticho de Maestro Alberto Neapolitano sopra lanno. Mille cinquecento vintinove. Con el Tacuin dela Luna Intitulato al Populo Christiano* (n.p., n.d.).

[45] Delio Cantimori, *Umanesimo e religione nel Rinascimento* (Turin: G. Einaudi, 1975), p. 173.

6

BETWEEN ASTROLOGY AND PROPHECY: THE FLOOD OF 1524

Astrology and Prophecy: The Flood *in piscibus*

AS WE have seen, in the early sixteenth century the divinatory arts, prophecy, and scrutiny of the signs that God had impressed upon nature or transmitted to men through visions seemed to form a complex cultural nucleus somehow perceived as a unit by the *popolari* who participated in that culture. The next problem concerns the relationship between this cultural phenomenon and the astrological science of the time (including areas of possible overlap), which is in turn connected to the broader problem raised some time ago by Eugenio Garin of the diffusion and utilization of astrology outside the confines of the universities and the courts that were its designated seats.[1]

How city dwellers reacted to the flood predicted for February 1524 provides an interesting case in point and throws light on both aspects of the question.[2] The debate was launched by the publication in 1499 of the *Ephemerides* of Johann Stöffler (reprinted in Venice in 1522),[3] which predicted that, due to multiple planetary conjunctions that year in the sign of Pisces, a large number of catastrophes would take place in 1524. As has been observed, the quarrel soon took a nonprofessional turn and involved not only astrologers but also physicians, theologians, and philosophers, all of whom would of course have encountered astrology during the course of their uni-

[1] Eugenio Garin, *Lo zodiaco della vita. La polemica sull'astrologia dal Trecento al Cinquecento* (Rome and Bari: Laterza, 1976), p. 146; available in English as *Astrology in the Renaissance: The Zodiac of Life*, tr. Carolyn Jackson and June Allen, revised by Clare Robertson (London and Boston: Routledge and Kegan Paul, 1983), p. 93.

[2] For the quarrel over the flood, see the ample discussion in Paola Zambelli, "Fine del mondo o inizio della propaganda? Astrologia, filosofia della storia e propaganda politico-religiosa nel dibattito sulla congiunzione del 1524," in *Science, credenze occulte, livelli di cultura. Convegno internazionale di studi (Firenze, 26–30 giugno 1980)* (Florence: L. S. Olschki, 1982), pp. 291–368; Zambelli, "Da Giulio II a Paolo III. Come l'astrologo provocatore Luca Gaurico divenne vescovo," in Fabio Troncarelli, ed., *La città dei segreti. Magia, astrologia e cultura esoterica a Roma (XV–XVIII secolo)*, Convegno Roma ermetica (1983: Rome, Italy) (Milan: Franco Angeli, 1985).

[3] Johann Stöffler, *Almanach nova plurimis annis venturis inservientia* (Venice: Lucantonio Giunta, 1522).

versity studies. What interests us is not so much—or not only—to weigh these people's contributions to the question but rather to measure and characterize, insofar as possible, the involvement in this affair of various social levels and different social circles. This may furnish a first round of data helpful in evaluating the extent to which astrology had penetrated the culture of the urban lower classes, how it was regarded, and, in this specific case, to what extent it was connected with the prophetic tensions that, as we have seen, played such a vital role among these segments of society at the time.

A Case of Collective Panic

Prediction of the flood *in piscibus* had a vast and far-reaching resonance. The sources seem to agree in insisting, albeit in generic terms, on the breadth and universality of the fear it generated. In the Marches the terrifying rumor spread that Mount Conero, which rises by the Adriatic south of Ancona, would be submerged, as would the Guasco hill, the site of the city's cathedral, San Ciriaco.[4] Tommasino Lancellotti wrote that in Modena "everyone is fearful," adding, "there has been great terror in people and perhaps some have died of fear."[5] Marin Sanudo, noting news that he had received from the *terraferma*, states, "The whole land is inclined to devotion for fear of these floods. . . . The entire mainland is in great fear."[6] The astrologer Silvestro Lucarelli reported that in Rome most people, if

[4] See Alessandro Pastore, "Un corrispondente sconosciuto di Pietro Pomponazzi. Il medico Giacomo Tiburzi da Pergola e le sue lettere," *Quaderni per la storia dell'Università di Padova* 17 (1984): 67–88, esp. p. 77, which stresses the widespread expectation of the flood in the region around Ancona. On the same subject, see Carlo Piancastelli, *Pronostici ed almanacchi. Studio di bibliografia romagnola* (Rome: D. Ripamonti, 1913), p. 32. For another example, see *Pronostico di Maestro Constantino de S. Maria in Georgio phisico excellentissimo sopra la significatione de li Eclipsi de la Luna e convento e congregatione de li pianeti nel signo di Pesce*: "Impresso in Ancona: per maestro Bernardino Guiraldo da Vercelli. Anno D.ni MDXXIII a di primo del Mese de Agosto." On this publication and on the efforts of the printer Bernardino Guerralda to publicize the flood, see Filippo M. Giochi and Alessandro Mordenti, *Annali della tipografia in Ancona 1512–1799* (Rome: Edizioni di storia e letteratura, 1980), pp. xxx–xxxvi, 20–22, 30, 32–33.

[5] Tommasino Lancellotti, *Cronica modenese*, Biblioteca Estense di Modena, MS α T1 2, fols. 176*v*–177*v*. In this chapter I have preferred to cite the manuscript version of this work rather than the printed edition cited elsewhere because the latter has a number of elisions and omissions concerning the very events under consideration. For example, Lancellotti's sense of alarm also came from the careful meteorological notes that he kept day by day for the entire month of February, which he subsequently amended in a more optimistic direction. These notations were all omitted from the printed edition.

[6] Marino Sanuto, *Diarii*, 58 vols. (Venice: R. Deputazione veneta di storia patria, 1879–1903), vol. 35, cols. 332 and 341.

not everyone, and people of all social conditions feared the flood: "Plurimos, ne dicam omnes, ac cuiusque conditionis homines, diluvium valde pertimescere."[7]

We shall soon see to what extent we can accept Lucarelli's statement at face value and apply it outside Rome. For now, it is important to note that the channels of communication concerning the expected flood were not the same for all social classes. In descending order of the social and cultural hierarchy, we find Latin treatises, epistolary communications, annual works of prognostication in Latin, brief works and annual prognostications in the vernacular, and, finally, oral transmission. All these means of transmission except the last, which remains hypothetical, can be documented.

We shall return, however, to preaching, an important and ascertainable oral means of communication. Giacomo Tiburzi, a physician in Pergola, in the duchy of Urbino, wrote in November 1523 that in earlier years the flood had been "ab astrologis praenunciato, a circulatoribus in foro decantato, ac a viris religiosis in rostris universo audiente populo divulgato."[8] Astrologers, *cantastorie*, and preachers all contributed to oral communication and to the extremely broad diffusion of diluvial predictions. Tiburzi, on the other hand, stresses the special role of preaching as a "mass medium" ("universo audiente populo"). This special role is confirmed in the journals of Andrea Pietramellara, son of the astrologer Giacomo Pietramellara. According to another source, Giovanni Cambi's *Istorie*, the Conventual Franciscans played a particularly prominent role in preaching about the flood, but "the Observant friars of St. Dominic laughed at the idea."[9] Whether people believed in it or no, the flood had become a commonplace. As early as May 1521, Niccolò Machiavelli included "the flood that is to come . . . and similar stories for tavern benches" in a listing of banal topics of conversation. When Francesco Guicciardini mentions the promised flood in a letter dated 25 January 1524 addressed to Cesare Colombo, his Roman correspondent for matters relating to the governance of Modena, his tone is light and he gives no explanations, taking it for granted that Colombo will understand what he is alluding to: "everything is asleep here; I dearly hope that either the deluge or some explosion in Lombardy will soon wake us up."[10]

[7] Silvestro Lucarelli, *Prognosticon anni MDXXIV quo opiniones pseudoastrologorum diluvium et siccitatem praesentis anni falso praedicentium improbantur* (Rome: [Francesco Minizio Calvo], 1524), fol. A *iv*.

[8] Cited in Pastore, "Un corrispondente sconosciuto," p. 77.

[9] Nerio Malvezzi, "Il diario metereologico di Andrea Pietramellara per l'anno 1524," in *Atti e memorie della R. Deputazione di storia patria per le provincie di Romagna*, ser. 3, no. 2 (1884): p. 445; Giovanni Cambi, *Istorie*, in Fr. Ildefonso di San Luigi, ed., *Delizie degli eruditi toscani*, 24 vols. (Florence: Gaetano Cambiagi, 1770–1789), vol. 23, p. 254.

[10] Niccolò Machiavelli, *Lettere*, ed. Franco Gaeta (Milan: Feltrinelli, 1961), p. 409; avail-

Not only had this particular flood become a commonplace; the very idea of a flood was part of the patrimony of widely held notions and clichés in fifteenth- and sixteenth-century Italy. There was a specific reason for this. *Diluvio*, "deluge," could be, and indeed in this period was, used as a synonym for *alluvione*, "flood,"[11] and, taken in this sense, "deluges" had occurred with unheard-of frequency in recent decades. Toward the end of the fifteenth century the effects of the deforestation practiced in Italy between the Trecento and the Quattrocento began to be felt, and they were disastrous. Data on the Po basin and water courses in Lombardy show that whereas between 1400 and 1450 there had been only two floods and one occasion on which high water broke through the embankments, between 1450 and 1500 there were seven floods and four breakthroughs, and from 1500 to 1550 six floods and three breakthroughs. According to other data, the Modena countryside suffered more than thirty floods, inundations, and washouts between 1493 and 1550.[12] We can find an echo of these disasters in the verse compositions addressed to a general public (and full of prophetic allusions) that were recited by the *cantambanchi* and published in low-cost, broadly distributed fugitive print pieces. Such works brandished the terrifying word in their titles: *Del diluvio di Roma del MCCCCLXXXXV*; *Diluvio successo in Cesena del 1525*; *Diluvio di Roma che fu a dì sette di ottobre lanno del mille cinquecento e trenta.*[13]

This literary genre, mixing poetry, prophecy, and chronicle, undoubtedly had a certain vogue and a sizable circulation, as reflected in Francesco Berni's burlesque imitation of the genre in his *Capitolo del diluvio*, which described the inundations that followed when in 1521 a brook in the Mugello, the Muccione, and the Sieve, a tributary of the Arno, overflowed

---

able in English as *The Letters of Machiavelli*, tr. and ed. Allan Gilbert (New York: Capricorn Books, 1961), p. 201; Francesco Guicciardini, *Carteggi*, ed. Roberto Palmarocchi, 17 vols. (Bologna: Nicola Zanichelli, 1938–), vol. 7, p. 59.

[11] Paul of Middelburg even expressed irritation at the confusion of the two terms: Paulus Middelburgensis, *Prognosticon R.p.d. Pauli de Middelburgo episcopi Forosemproniensis ostendens anno MDXXIV nullum neque universale neque provinciale diluvium futurum* (n.p., n.d. [Venice, 1523]), fol. A. iv*r*.

[12] *Vie d'acqua da Milano al mare. L'avvenire della navigazione interna padana*, catalogue ed. Aldo Giobbio (Ospiate/Bollate: Tip. I.G.A., 1963), p. 66; Gian Luigi Basini, *L'uomo e il pane. Risorse, consumi e carenze alimentari nella popolazione modenese nel Cinque e Seicento* (Milan: A. Giuffrè, 1970), pp. 127–30.

[13] Giuliano Dati, *Del diluvio di Roma del MCCCCLXXXXV adi iiii di dicembre et daltre cose di gran meraviglia* (n.p., n.d.); Cornelio Guasconi, *Diluvio successo in Cesena del 1525 adi 10 de luglio* (Venice: Nicolò di Aristotele detto il Zoppino, 1526); *Diluvio di Roma che fu a dì sette di ottobre lanno del mille cinquecento e trenta* (Venice: "ad instantia de Zoanmaria Lirico Venetiano"). Information on other popular print pieces with verse descriptions of floods can be found in Robert Weiss, "Cesena e il suo diluvio del 1525 in un poemetto poco noto," in *Contributi alla storia del libro italiano. Miscellanea in onore di Lamberto Donati* (Florence: L. S. Olschki, 1969), pp. 359–69.

their banks.[14] Berni used the narrative techniques and the cadences of deluge literature to parody it. Addressing an imaginary audience, he employs buffoonery to evoke the aura of holy terror of inundations that pervaded such compositions. Because floods and inundations—God's castigation par excellence—recalled the Universal Flood of Genesis, they served as warnings and fitted into the complex systems of signs of divine wrath. On occasion they even acquired a prophetic significance. Leandro Alberti, speaking of the Tiber in his *Descrittione di tutta Italia*, calls the river a "true and religious prophet and diviner," and notes that "clearly, never has it been seen to come out of its bed and inundate Rome that it was not followed by some great destruction, war, pestilence, or famine."[15] Thus a flood might be but the first of many tremendous catastrophes sent by God, and this was precisely how the *cantastorie* presented them.

All this helps us to understand what lay behind a fear of floods. I might note that although Stöffler speaks of many calamities, he says not a word about floods. Only gradually did astrological literature begin to predict floods, which were never presented as coming alone, but were given as the first of many disasters. That the planetary conjunction prompting the current danger was to take place in Pisces, the water sign, undoubtedly shaped predictions. Still, we should not forget that floods, whether *diluvio* or *alluvione*, had recently become a more urgent problem and that they had acquired a strong prophetic and divinatory meaning familiar to a vast public. Thus out of the vague congeries of disasters predicted by Stöffler and his imitators the flood came to predominate. We find little echo in the popular consciousness of the forecasts of earthquakes and religious upheavals that took up so much space in the astrologers' predictions.[16]

Awaiting Divine Castigation

In reality, then, the flood of 1524 was viewed less as an exceptional astral catastrophe than as an aggravated version of a situation that was already all

[14] Francesco Berni, *Rime*, ed., Giorgio Barberi Squarotti (Turin: G. Einaudi, 1969), pp. 9–12.

[15] Leandro Alberti, *Descrittione di tutta Italia* (Venice: Domenico de' Farri, 1557), fol. 77*r*. This was a familiar commonplace. Pietro Martire d'Anghiera, writing to Pomponio Leto on 12 May 1499, states that it originated in the tradition of classical antiquity, for which see *Opus epistolarum Petri Martyris Anglerii* (Amsterdam: typis Elzevirianis, 1670), p. 118. Luis Gómez, *De prodigiosis Tyberis inundationibus* (Rome, 1531), reiterates the theme. In a letter sent 22 October 1530 to the marchese Federico II Gonzaga of Mantua, the recent flood in Rome is treated not only as a "judgment of God" but also as "prodigious and indicative of most terrible effects": Sanuto, *Diarii*, vol. 52, cols. 74–76.

[16] See, for example, Lodovico Vitali, *De terremotu* (Bologna: Giovanni Antonio Benedetti, 1508), fol. B ii *v*.

too familiar and that recalled hardships everyone had experienced. Any severe thunderstorm might be a signal and forewarning of its coming. On 17 October 1523, Lunardo Anselmi, consul for the Serenissima in Naples, sent word to the authorities in Venice of disastrous downpours that had inundated Naples four days before, "carrying away along via de san Zenaro [Via San Gennaro] trees [and] houses, with death of males and females, [and] all the mills ruined." Returning to the topic several days later, he drew a connection between the end of the rainfall and some people's opinion that the "prediction of the future deluge known in all the world" had turned out to be false.[17] Consul Anselmi and his circle had thus believed that the deluge *in piscibus* had already begun, and a contingent improvement in meteorological conditions was enough to prompt their disbelief in the astrologers' predictions.

Ways of dealing with the coming flood necessarily included expedients that had already been tried. Giuliano Dati describes in his *Diluvio di Roma* people procuring boats or moving to the upper stories of their houses or to the rooftops. Analogous preparations and systems of defense were put into operation to escape the effects of the sixteen terrible planetary conjunctions. As Eustachio Celebrino, a polygraph and engraver from Udine, stated,

> con victuaglie in cima agli alti monti
> ciascun s'asconde, se rinchiude e serra.
>
> (with victuals on top of the high mountains everyone hides himself, closes himself up, and locks the doors.)[18]

This was not mere poetic exaggeration. Evidence related to the event is so abundant and detailed that it leaves little room for doubt. In Rome and Florence great stores of grain were laid up. Anton Francesco Doni later wrote that in Rome "all fled into the highest rooms of the houses . . . and many left the city, retreating to the mountains." The astrologer Lucarelli, who arrived in Rome from the provincial city of Camerino in December 1523, totally unaware of the excitement, reports that alarm was general, and that in particular many nobles so feared that the Tiber would flood that they used hunting trips as an excuse to take to the hills.[19] Similar behavior was noted in other parts of Italy as well. In Sicily, many people

[17] Sanuto, *Diarii*, vol. 35, col. 171.

[18] Eustachio Celebrino, *La dechiaratione per che non è venuto il diluvio del 1524* (Venice: Francesco Bindoni e Matteo Pasini compagni, n.d. [1524]), fol. D. 2*r*.

[19] Francisco Delicado, *La Lozana andaluza*, ed. L. Orioli (Milan: Adelphi, 1970), p. 222; in English, *Portrait of Lozana: The Lusty Andalusian Woman*, tr. Bruno M. Damiani (Potomac, Md.: Scripta Humanistica, 1987), p. 285; Cambi, *Istorie*, p. 255; [Anton Francesco Doni], *Mondo piccolo dell'Accademia peregrina* (Venice: Francesco Marcolini, 1552), fol. 11*r*; Lucarelli, *Prognosticon*, fol. A i*v*.

fortified the doors of their houses; in Friuli and the Vicenza area, Sanudo reports, people "prepared wooden houses in the mountains with provisions"; elsewhere, houseboats or skiffs were built to ride out the flood.[20]

In short, the rich fled to the country much as they had done in times of pestilence—at least, the social selection involved was much the same. Those who were unable to amass provisions in mountain areas or rent space on upper floors reacted differently. Isidoro Isolani put it quite explicitly: "talia quidem excogitare ad principes spectat, perficere nobilium est. Plebs nempe . . . divinae pietatis opus arbitramur."[21] Thus great collective and civic religious rites were needed, and indeed did take place. There were public recitations of the litany to the Virgin, mass communions, and alms offered "for the community"; in Naples there were spontaneous penitential processions of "many young girls . . . with their hair in disarray and bare feet." More often, such processions were organized by the diocesan authorities, as was the case in France in Besançon or in Italy in Modena and Brescia, where representatives of all segments of associative civic life, "schools and arts [guilds], friars, priests," made their way through the city for three days in a row.[22] Two points need to be stressed. First, these were urban and communitarian patterns of behavior representing a specific contrast to the more private actions of those who moved to higher ground or took to the hills. Second, these collective efforts to ward off the catastrophe were immediately taken over by the ecclesiastical hierarchy, who established rigorous control over them. In theory, religious life should not have been affected by the results of a planetary conjunction that had been predicted on the basis of astrological science. In this case, however, the minute astrology left the inner circle of the specialists, prophecy was superimposed on it. The deluge *in piscibus* appeared to be a catastrophe sent by divine wrath, and as such it was an easy substitute for the Turkish peril in the schemes of the literary genre of prophetic preaching that we have already examined. We have no direct evidence, but it is certainly highly probable that the preachers who gave sermons predicting the flood in Florence, Bo-

[20] Francesco Maurolico, *Sicanarum rerum compendium* (Messina: Petrus Spira, 1562), fol. 200*v*; Sanuto, *Diarii*, vol. 35, col. 341; Agostino Nifo, *De falsa diluvii prognosticatione* (Bologna: Girolamo Benedetti, 1520), fol. a. ii*r*; Isidoro Isolani O.P., *Ex humana divinaque sapientia tractatus de futura nova mundi mutatione* (Bologna: Girolamo Benedetti, 1523), fol. 17*r*.

[21] Isolani, *Ex humana divinaque sapientia tractatus*, fol. 17*r*.

[22] Sanuto, *Diarii*, vol. 35, cols. 163 and 340–41; *Letters and Papers, Foreign and Domestic of the Reign of Henry VIII*, 21 vols. (London: Longman & Co., 1862–1932), vol. 6 (1870), pt. 1, p. 10. Brescia had been braced for the deluge for years: On 20 August 1519 the Brescian notary Girolamo Stella wrote to his brother Antonio that a tornado had devastated the countryside to such an extent that people "thought that all the land would be destroyed and submerged. I think that the deluge that is supposed to come in 1524 is trying to come this year": Sanuto, *Diarii*, vol. 27, col. 591. On Modena, see below.

logna, and the duchy of Urbino followed an outline much like the one in Agostino Nifo's *De falsa diluvii pronosticatione*. Nifo argued that if Noah's flood had been caused by human evil, certainly there should come a flood *now*, when the sins of humankind have never been so great: "futurum diluvium non vi illius contentus tamen, sed vi humani sceleris . . . sit diiudicandum."[23] It was in fact precisely in January 1524, when discussions were at their most heated and fear at its peak, that a series of letters was sent from the Holy See to ecclesiastical authorities in a number of Italian cities to remind them of the decrees concerning preaching established by the Fifth Lateran Council.[24] Why should it have been felt necessary to tighten control over preaching at just this moment? One possible answer is that this was simply a repressive norm from the beginnings of the Reformation, but the timing is so perfect as to suggest that the Church was attempting to control a recrudescence of apocalyptical thought, the prelude to which certainly existed, and probably concrete signs of it as well.

Furthermore, it is significant that in 1523 when Isolani proclaimed an "immutatio futura in omni vivente," basing his argument on the stars, he felt it necessary to confirm this prediction by citing prophecies of the blessed Veronica of Binasco and to conclude that prayer was the only effective way of warding off the flood. In 1524 Paulus Angelus—a well-known star in the prophetic constellation of the sixteenth century—stated his opposition to the "confuse sonans nomen illud praeteritum iam diluvii pro coniunctionibus planetarum" that had been revealed to him personally by means of visions warning that the sword of divine wrath was ready to strike the Christian world.[25]

Thus the idea that divine castigation was imminent in the concrete form of a flood, not because of the planetary conjunction but because of the sins of humankind, was present on different cultural levels. It was a commonplace, but in the specific circumstances it lent itself well to being used as an efficacious instrument of propaganda. During the course of the month of February an epistolary *Avviso* in vernacular, dated from Trent, 6 February, circulated in Italy and was sent through his ambassador to the doge by the marchese of Mantua, Federico II Gonzaga. (Sanudo commented, "non fo creto," "it was not believed.")[26] The letter told of floods and terrible inundations of the Danube and the Rhine that had submerged villages and towns in Germany, "opened and destroyed mountains, and covered many

[23] Nifo, *De falsa diluvii prognosticatione*, fol. a. iiii*r*.

[24] See above, p. 113.

[25] Isolani, *Ex humana divinaque sapientia tractatus*, fols. 15*r–v*; *Epistola Pauli Angeli . . . in Sathan ruinam tyranidis . . . item prefatio eiusdem P.A. . . . cum enucleata veraci apertiorique declaratione perfecta detegendo quid generis diluviorum coniunctio planetarum in anno MDXXIV significare voluerit* (n.p., n.d. [1524]), fols. 3*v*–4*r*.

[26] Sanuto, *Diarii*, vol. 35, col. 450.

villas and castles." The writer then recalled, in a seemingly abrupt shift of topic, that "the Lutheran opinion perseveres and grows" in precisely those regions, and he concludes with a warning that "the lord God will punish this crime with his scourge, *as he has already begun to do*." The thread of his argument is shown by where it leads: The flood, which he posits as already having taken place, thus served as a divine weapon offered to the Catholics for an easy victory over the arrogant Lutherans. The anti-Reformation slant of the sheet is obvious, and it becomes even more so in light of the deliberate falsity of the news given.

The relationship between the flood and the Reformation was not always understood in that key. In Rome, people seemed to allege some sort of connection between Luther and the catastrophe of the flood, seen as God's chastisement of the Church. Iacopo Lopis Stunica (in Spanish, Jaime López de Zúñiga) took the trouble, in an *Epistula . . . super significationibus XVI coniunctionum in signo piscium* addressed to Paul of Middelburg and dated from Rome, 8 January 1524, to counter the hypothesis that Luther was the prophet created by the sixteen great conjunctions, which he attributes to Giannotti. According to Lopis Stunica, this figure was a pseudoprophet who came from the south, not from the north as did the Saxon monk. He seems so intent on denying this hypothesis that we sense an interest in avoiding the image of Luther as a prophet that we have traced earlier. The following day, 9 January, Marino da Pozzo, secretary to Cardinal Francesco Pisani, wrote from Rome to Francesco Spinelli concerning the excitement in the city over Luther. After noting that "it is said that the pope will make him a cardinal so as to silence him," Da Pozzo gives a glimpse of his own opinions: "and I believe that this will be the deluge of the Church, but God will not want to see such destruction of the Church."[27]

"This" refers to Luther, not to the high waters expected in February. Here the deluge is not only divine castigation for the sins of humankind but also the destruction and submersion of the Church, its definitive ruin without hope of correction or ultimate salvation. Isidoro Isolani, reiterating the saving virtues of prayer to combat the flood, added, in like fashion,

[27] [Jaime López de Zúñiga], *Epistola Stunicae ad R.P. Episcopum Forosempronien. super significationibus XVI coniunctionum in signo piscium que future sunt mense Februario huius anni MDXXIIII* (n.p., n.d. [Rome: Marcello Silber, 1524]). See Alberto Tinto, *Gli annali tipografici di Eucario e Marcello Silber (1501–1527)* (Florence: L. S. Olschki, 1968), p. 186; Sanuto, *Diarii*, vol. 35, col. 334. The elector of Saxony was also aware of the rumor that Luther had been offered a cardinalcy: Hartmann Grisar, *Martin Luthers Leben und sein Werk* (Freiburg im Breisgau: B. Herder, 1926), available in English as *Martin Luther, His Life and Work*, adapted from the 2nd German edition by Frank J. Eble, ed. Arthur Preuss (Westminster, Md.: Newman Press, 1950), p. 141. It was reported a few decades later by Cosme de Aldana, *Discorso contro il volgo in cui con buone ragioni si reprovano molte sue false opinioni* (Florence: G. Marescotti, 1578), p. 193.

that only prayer was capable of saving the seat of Peter "ab incursibus tot adversantium, et magis forte internis quam externis."[28] Fear of the Lutherans, of the fragmentation of Christianity, and of the dismantling of ecclesiastical institutions was thus intimately connected with fear of the flood, through which it took on more concrete form. Albrecht Dürer's famous dream can perhaps be interpreted in a similar manner: Several years later (30 May 1525), he dreamed of the universal deluge fifteen days after the defeat of the peasants in the battle of Frankenhausen and four days after the decapitation of Thomas Münzer, and he illustrated his nightmare in a watercolor now in Vienna.[29] The deluge could be elevated to a symbol and provide a focus for the genuine anxiety prompted by the weakening of social structures and of religious unity in Europe at the beginning of the modern era; it could also be proposed as an awe-inspiring phantasm that obligatorily called forth a penitential *animus* and behavior (this is the sense in which processions and other collective rites should be understood) and made it necessary to tighten the reins on traditional orthodox religion.

The Deluge and Church Reform: Jean Albertin

A spiritual and prophetic reading of the deluge as the submersion of the Church can also be found in the work of a singular and isolated figure, Jean Albertin or Albertini, a priest from the Valais. We know little about him except that he was still living in 1542 and served as the administrator of the hospital in Sion.[30] Of his several remaining writings, one is of particular interest for our purposes, the *De mirabili temporis mutatione ac terrene potestatis a loco in locum translatione*, published by the Geneva printer Wygand Köln in 1524. In this brief work, Jean Albertin, who proclaims himself a prophet and doctor of theology, predicts the renewal of the universal Church and the imminent end of time. The Church, Albertin says, was once a precious edifice of sapphires and gems, but with the passage of time useless stones had been added to it. "In presenti mutatione, que est ecclesie reformatio." Those useless stones will be torn down, he continues, and, thanks to the abuses of the Roman curia, the power of Peter will be taken away from Rome and be transferred to the Church of Sion.[31] We might well wonder how Albertin could possibly have reached such a singular con-

[28] Isolani, *Ex humana divinaque sapientia tractatus*, fol. 17*r*.

[29] See A. Rosenthal, "Dürer's Dream of 1525," *Burlington Magazine* 69 (1936): 82–85.

[30] Henri Naef, *Les Origines de la Réforme à Genève: La cité des évêques, l'humanisme, les signes précurseurs* (Geneva: E. Droz, 1936), p. 427. On Albertin in general, see pp. 427–35. To my knowledge, publications in Geneva relating to the flood have not yet been studied.

[31] Johannes Albertinus, *De mirabili temporis mutatione ac terrene potestatis a loco in locum translatione* (Geneva: Wygand Köln, 1524), fols a. iv*r* and a. ii*r*–*v*.

clusion, and it is tempting to conjecture that he had somehow come to know (in whole or in part) the "book" that had appeared eight years earlier in Rome in which a monk named Bonaventura proclaimed the decadence of the Roman See and predicted "se . . . translaturum imperium ecclesiae ad ecclesiam in Syon"—that is, Zion, or Jerusalem.[32] If so, Albertin would have to have interpreted this passage in a highly personal, idiosyncratic manner, which was not impossible in the early decades of the sixteenth century.

In any event, Albertin declares in *De mirabili temporis mutatione* that even the stars show that great turmoil is nigh. The age of Noah has returned, he says, and a deluge (more spiritual than meteorological, however) is approaching: "omnium viciorum suprema inundatio, exorta ex partibus inferioribus" was about to submerge even the highest places (that is, the ecclesiastical hierarchy). As in the age of Noah when only those closed within the ark were saved, so now only those who take refuge in the spiritual ark of the "renewed Holy Mother Church" will be saved. Two signs were given to confirm this transformation of the Church, both taken from 4 Esdras (an apocryphal text that would, incidentally, repay study of its prophetic function at the beginning of the early modern period). The first passage, it seems to me, gives truly singular evidence of the profound impression that the invention of print made on contemporaries, to the point that, like the discovery of America, it acquired eschatological significance. Citing Esdras, Albertin writes that before the end "libri aperientur ante faciem firmamenti, et omnes videbunt simul. Libri per magna parte fuerunt aperti per artem impressoriam: per quam infiniti libri qui fuerent absconditi venerunt ad lucem." The second sign proclaimed in Esdras was that women would be delivered prematurely and the aborted fetus would live. Indeed, Albertin says, this is precisely what has begun to happen in the church of the Virgin "in villa Blise" (Blitzingen), where stillborn infants resuscitate—a detail that tells us that the church in Blitzingen was one of the hundreds of *sanctuaires à répit* that held out hope for the salvation of unbaptized dead infants by arranging for their momentary resurrection. Finally, Jean Albertin concludes, universal peace must be established and a general council must be convoked "propter ecclesiastici status reformationem."[33]

Even in the somewhat confused pages of Albertin's treatise, then, the image of the expected flood played a central role and was inextricably min-

[32] *Exemplum literarum Domini Stephani Rosin Caesareae Majestatis apud S. Sedem sollicitatoris ad Reverendum Principem D. Carolum Gurcensem* in Constantin Höfler, "Analecten zur Geschichte Deutschlands und Italiens," *Abhandlungen der Historischen Klasse der königlich Bayerischen Akademie der Wissenschaften* 4, no. 3 (1846): 56. On Bonaventura, see Giampaolo Tognetti, "Bonaventura," DBI, vol. 11, pp. 611–12.

[33] Albertinus, *De mirabili temporis mutatione*, fols. a. iv*r*; b. ii*v*; b. iii*r*; c. ii*r*.

gled with the notion of the renewal of the Church. Ecclesiastical society was to be profoundly transformed by the flood and would turn to new prophets and heed the prodigies that were omens revealing divine will. What makes the views of this Valais priest important is that they confirm the complexity of the meanings—the religious meanings, in particular—that contemporaries attributed to the diluvial catastrophe. The text is also interesting because it allows us to see that expectation of the deluge was widespread in the Valais and in Geneva. Indeed, in the *Annales de la cité de Genève* attributed to Jean Savion (but probably the work of his brother Jacques) we read that "in that year [1524] a certain fantasy-prone astrologer predicted in public by means of print that in that year a deluge would come like the one of Noah's time, which astonished many people, but events showed the contrary."[34] It is of course difficult, not to say impossible, to establish the identity of the "fantastique astrologue" to whom Savion refers. We might note, however, that in 1526 Wygand Köln, Jean Albertin's publisher, published comic prognostications under the title *Merveilles advenir en cestuy an vingt et sis*, a work structured as a response to predictions of the flood in Geneva. The text of this pamphlet refers to 1524 and not 1526, as is clear from the rhymes, which were distorted in order to update the original text:

Je fais sçavoir que an moys de mars
de cest an courant vingt et sit [quatre]
plouviont nobles, douples ducas,
ecus royaulx, quatre à quatre.

(I tell you that in the month of March of this current year twenty-six [four] noble [coins], double ducats [and] royal *écus* will rain down hand over fist.)

The anonymous author turns prediction of the deluge upside down by listing Lenten foods:

Puis tomberont aulx et oignons,
pleura vinaygre, huille de noix,
molles, aigrefins, estourions,
ambles, anguilles, lavares.

(Then there will fall garlics and onions, it will rain vinegar, walnut oil, mussels, haddock, sturgeon, perch, eels, whitefish.)

In the final hundred lines the poet assails the astrologers as mad perverters of the true faith ("those who fear floods [are] all insane and apostate").

[34] *Annales de la cité de Genève attribuées à Iean Savyon*, ed. Edouard Fick (Geneva, 1858), p. 113.

Who could have believed, he continues, "that magicians, mathematicians and necromancers could have such a wide hearing among us?" All they do is to spread "errors, lies, [and] heretical maxims" against the true faith. The author concludes with the fear that the erroneous calculations of those who had predicted "that we must die by a vast inundation of water" would in the end change the very motion of the great machine of the heavens:

> S'ilz continuent, vous verréz que les cieulx,
> la grant machine et tout le firmament,
> sera rieglé par l'erreur vicieulx
> de quoy ilz usent, d'ung veult ambicieulx,
> et changera l'antique mouvemant.

> (If they continue, you will see that the heavens, the great machine and the entire firmament will be regulated by the depraved error that they pursue with ambitious desire, and will alter the ancient motion.)[35]

We will find voices in Italy not too unlike this anonymous Genevan's, authors whose verse combined an impatient and burlesque parody of astrologers and their calculations with a more serious opposition between the true faith and the claims to decipher the heavens by means of a false and deceiving science.

Carnival Rites in Venice and Rome

The fear that gripped people in 1524 touched a good part of Italy and of Europe, extending from Brescia to Vicenza, Friuli, Trent, Mantua, Rome, Naples, Modena, and Ancona and including vast areas of France, Germany, Spain, and the duchy of Savoy.[36]

In Venice, however, Tommasino Lancellotti reported that "people are talking against the flood."[37] As we have seen, the dramatic announcement that the deluge had already taken place in Germany "was not believed" by the members of the Great Council, and it was only as a joke that Ruzante asked one of his ladyloves to prepare him a garret room in no less a struc-

[35] *Merveilles advenir en cestuy an vingt et sis. Prognostication satirique pour l'année 1526* ([Geneva: Wygand Köln] Geneva, 1893), pp. 27, 33–36.

[36] As discussed above. See also Pierre Bayle, s.v. "Stöffler," in his *Dictionnaire historique et critique*, 4th ed. rev., 4 vols. (Amsterdam: P. Brunel, 1730), vol. 4, pp. 285–87. For Spain, see Juan de Cazalla, bishop of Vera, "Escriptora contra los astrologos judiciarios," in Melquiades Andrés, "Un tratado teologico de Juan de Cazalla contra la astrologia judiciaria (1523)," *Burgense* 16 (1975): 583. Cazalla's brief tract is clearly based on the *Tractato contra li astrologi* of Girolamo Savonarola, though he does not mention the work (see below, n. 64).

[37] Lancellotti, *Cronica*, vol. 1, fol. 176*r*.

ture than the bell tower of St. Mark's.[38] That this was a broad joke (based, however, on farcical exaggeration of an accepted reality) is confirmed by the fact that on the very day of 4 February—the day on which the planetary conjunction was to have reached its most threatening point—Ruzante joined the buffoon Zuan Polo and other friends from the Compagnia degli Ortolani in a masquerade. The revelers were all

> dressed in costumes of crimson velvet with large sleeves of shimmering multicolored silk and with satin and velvet hats on their heads [and] face masks with noses. And each of them had two servants before him, each one with a torch in his hand, dressed as a peasant. One of them had a golden costume and they had great skill: first [came the] buffoons Zuan Polo and others, along with Ruzante of Padua, others dressed as peasants who jumped about and danced very well, and six disguised as young peasants who sang *villote*, and they all had various rustic things in their hands such as hoes, shovels, stakes, spades, rakes, etc., as well as trumpets, pipes, flutes, and deafening horns. And they went around the square of San Marco, then in the evening with their torches lit they went about the [city], and at one o'clock in the evening [7 P.M.] they came to the Palace of the Doge, in the courtyard, to show off their skill.[39]

The fact of the matter was that 4 February was not only "el dì del gran deslubio," as the *Alfabeto dei villani* called it, confusing it with the Day of Judgment,[40] but also *la zobia giota*—Fat Thursday—hence Carnival season. Carnival, which was just as much a collective rite as the religious processions that took place in Brescia, Modena, and Besançon, furnished the second great antidote to fear of the flood. The object of people's terror was transformed into an object of laughter; its real meaning was turned upside down by obscene double meanings; the stars and the planetary conjunctions were brought down to the level of bodily and genital functions. When Carnival, following its normal function, turned the deluge *in piscibus* into a *diluvio d'unto e grasso*, laughter gave it the power to conjure away the looming peril. This was precisely what happened during the first week of February 1524. The flood was chosen as the theme for Carnival floats and masquerades. In Rome, for example, there was a float "that was Noah's ark, on which there was a musical group that sang to signify that the flood had passed, and they loosed birds from the ark, a very lovely idea invented

38 "Lettera qual scrive Ruzante a una so morosa," in *Le lettere di messer Andrea Calmo riprodotte sulle stampe migliori*, ed. Vittorio Rossi (Turin: E. Loescher, 1888), p. cxx and n. pp. cxix–cxxi.

39 Sanuto, *Diarii*, vol. 35, col. 393.

40 Emilio Lovarini, *Studi sul Ruzzante e la letteratura pavana*, ed. Gianfranco Folena (Padua: Antenore, 1965), p. 429.

for Cardinal Cesarino."[41] On another float, the creation of Archbishop Marco Corner, "which was a boat being prepared to flee the deluge, and inside there was a very good musical group with lutes and viols," singers performed a song composed by Agostino Bevazzano that was a tissue of allusions and double meanings, respecting the prescribed patterns of the literary genre of Carnival songs. The singers sang of their flight from the deluge and invited the ladies to join them:

> Belle donne, vi exortamo
> a congiongervi con noi
> perché quel che non possiamo
> soli far, farem con voi;
> non perdete il tempo poi,
> ché il diluvio è per venire.
> Noi portiam certi instrumenti
> da allegrarvi il cor nel petto:
> che li usiate siam contenti
> per magior vostro diletto.
>
> (Lovely women, we exhort you to join with us, because what we cannot do alone, we will do with you; waste no time, for the flood is about to come. We bear certain implements to cheer your hearts in your breasts: we will be happy if you use them for your greater delight.)[42]

Obscene double meanings were expected of Carnival language not only at the popular level but also at the level of the archbishop's *invenzioni*. In Florence, parading hermits invited Florentine women to take to the hills with them

> imperò che ogni astrolago e indovino
> v'han tutti sbigottiti
> (secondo che da molti inteso abbiano)
> che un tempo orrendo e strano
> minaccia a ogni terra
> peste, diluvio e guerra,
> fulgur, tempeste, tremuoti, rovine,
> come se già del monde fussi fine.
> E voglion soprattutto che le stelle
> influssin con tant'acque

[41] Sanuto, *Diarii*, vol. 35, col. 422.

[42] Ibid., col. 423. On Agostino Bevazzano or Beazano, secretary to Cardinal Marco Corner and, later, to Pietro Bembo, see Francesco Tateo, "Beaziano (Beazzano, Bevazzano), Agostino," in DBI, vol. 7, pp. 390–93, and the notes in Baldassare Castiglione, *Il Cortegiano del conte Baldesar Castiglione*, ed. Vittorio Cian (Florence: G. C. Sansoni, 1929), p. 249.

che 'l mondo tutto quanto si ricuopra.
Per questo, donne grazïose e belle,
se mai servir vi piacque
alcuna cosa che vi sia di sopra,
. . .
venitene con noi
sopra la cima de nostri alti sassi.

(because all the astrologers and diviners have bewildered you, according to what many have understood, [by saying] that horrible and strange weather threatens all lands [with] plague, flood, and war, lightning, storms, earthquakes, [and] destruction, as if it were already the end of the world, and they all insist that the stars will overflow with so much water that the whole world will be covered. Thus, graceful and beautiful women, if ever you were pleased to make use of something on top of you . . . come away with us to the top of our high rocks.)[43]

This verse is Machiavelli's, though it is certainly not among his best. Delio Cantimori refers to it, but he fails to grasp fully the specific nature of the song as Carnival poetry or to emphasize its direct connection with the expected flood.[44] This "Canto de' romiti" does indeed contain an echo of the quarrel with prophets and hermits that Machiavelli pursued elsewhere with a good deal more acerbity, but it should also be noted that "hermits" were one of the most frequent Carnival disguises in Florence.[45]

As we have seen, cardinals and famous (and less famous) men of letters suggested themes for such Carnival parades and composed verse for them. We should also remember that verse had a secondary role in this sort of festivity, in the main being used to back up the music, lights, "machines" (floats and special effects mechanisms), and costumes. Nonetheless, Carnival provided an effective means of communication at a moment when people of many social levels rubbed elbows. This was true in general, and it was true in this specific instance. In Rome, where the festivities described took place, fear of the flood gripped people of every social condition, at least according to the astrologer Lucarelli, even if he speaks most about the

[43] Niccolò Machiavelli, *Opere*, ed. Ezio Raimondi (Milan: Mursia, 1976), pp. 958–59.

[44] Delio Cantimori, "Niccolò Machiavelli: il politico e lo storico," *Storia della letteratura italiana*, ed. Emilio Cecchi and Natalino Sapegno, 9 vols. (Milan: Garzanti, 1965–), vol. 4, *Il Cinquecento*, pp. 7–53, esp. p. 32; Cantimori, *Umanesimo e religione nel Rinascimento* (Turin: G. Einaudi, 1975), p. 251.

[45] See Charles Southward Singleton, *Nuovi canti carnascialeschi del rinascimento con un'appendice; Tavola generale dei canti carnascialeschi editi e inediti* (Modena: Società tipografica modenese, 1940).

terror of the nobility. The message may have passed down from high places, but the medium chosen involved lower social strata as well. Elsewhere, as we shall see, this movement was inverted, which means that the message was not the same.

If Rome and Florence chose the deluge as a theme for their Carnival celebrations without rejecting or denying the flood itself, in fact accepting it as logical (in Rome at least; Machiavelli is another affair), in other cities Carnival served as a satirical antidote to panic. This was true of an extraordinary celebration organized on Carnival Sunday by the Venetian "nation" in Constantinople. The Venetian colony passed the night watching "very lascivious" dances by Turkish and Epirote women and nibbling on "cakes and sweetmeats and elaborate dishes," and when their revels had gone "from songs to dances, from one treat to another, the sun rose [showing] its rays before they left the theater." This description comes from a letter from the vice-bailiff of Venice in that city, Carlo Zen, to Giacomo Corner. His description ends with a warning:

> You can pass the word to those most consummate philosophers and astrologers that these provisions were taken against their predictions of the deluge. . . . From here I do not know what may have happened among you; for the love we bear you, we are in the greatest fear that you have not been able to make like provisions.[46]

Thus Carnival and celebration functioned as antidotes to, and as *provisioni* against, astrology, the deluge, and fear. If among the Roman nobility and the cardinals the flood was the object of fear and was evoked in basically respectful terms, even in a Carnival mood, these Venetian merchants viewed both the flood and astrological science with antagonism and treated them with sarcasm. It is difficult to evaluate accurately whether this attitude was owing to their civic allegiance or to their social group—that is, whether it came from their being Venetians or merchants (remembering that where the flood is concerned, Venice was something of an island of indifference and incredulity unique in Italy). All categories of Venetian society seem to have shared this attitude, from the doge, who reacted with disbelief to the false news of the flood in Germany transmitted from Mantua by Federico II Gonzaga, down to the young nobles of the Company of the Ortolani, who, on the day that the flood was supposed to strike, paraded about Piazza San Marco by torchlight, led by the great Ruzante and dressed as peasants, singing and dancing. All Venice, down to the merchants in far-off Constantinople, rejected both astrology and fear. This attitude might well be compared to another, better-known reaction of the political establishment in Venice, when it long held out against panic dur-

[46] Sanuto, *Diarii*, vol. 36, col. 121.

ing periods of epidemic plague and widely shared fear of plague spreaders. We might well wonder whether this reaction to the promised flood was not also a deliberate political choice on the part of the Venetian Republic.

This question is not easy to answer. It is true that response to the flood was strikingly concordant in Venice, whether it came from high culture or street culture. In these same days of Carnival a *cantastorie*, perhaps from the Po valley, who called himself Master Pegasus Neptune was declaiming one of his compositions in a Venetian square (presumably Piazza San Marco) in which the coming flood and the astrologers who had predicted it were subjected to sarcasm a good deal more pointed and language a lot stronger than had been used in Rome or Florence. After the usual invocation to the "Lord whom all the stars obey," the tale singer promised his "benigni auditori" that he would give the lie to the "castronazi" and "frappadori" (gutless, deceiving) astrologers

> che volendo nel ciel troppo mirare
> caschan in gran precepitio d'errori
>
> . . .
>
> un gran diluvio dicono sti tali
> nel anno vintiquattro è per venire,
> e verranno per l'aque tanti mali
> che l'human sesso si haverà a stremire.
>
> (who, looking up at the sky too much fall over a great precipice of errors. . . . They say [that] a great deluge is to come in the year twenty-four and so many evils will come by the waters that humankind will be exhausted.)[47]

Every day during the month of February Pegaso Neptunio discredited such predictions by spouting mocking prophecies about the next Carnival season, the struggle between Carnival and Lent, and the death of Carnival, thus reducing the deluge *in piscibus* to a flood of food and wine. Carnival, as we know from Piero Camporesi's studies, was, by antonomasia, *il diluviante*,[48] an ambiguous epithet that finds its most telling expression and an excellent definition in this fine example of the Carnival genre. Pegaso Neptunio states:

[47] *Pronostico: over diluvio consolatorio composto per lo eximio Dottore Maestro Pegaso Neptunio: el qual dechiara de giorno in giorno quel che sarà nel mese de febraro: Cosa belissima & molto da ridere* (n.p., n.d. [Venice? 1524]), fol. 2*r*. We can suppose that Pegaso Neptunio worked the crowd in Piazza San Marco on the basis of what we know about the habits of charlatans and *cantambanchi*: See Peter Burke, *Popular Culture in Early Modern Europe* (New York: New York University Press, 1978), p. 98.

[48] Piero Camporesi, *La maschera di Bertoldo. G. C. Croce e la letterature carnevalesca* (Turin: G. Einaudi, 1976), p. 144.

Serà un diluvio tra i pollami ancora
nel'acqua cotta dentro i calderoni
. . .
e serà gran diluvio ogni matino
de vin grecho, dalmaticho e latino
. . .
seran venti terribili et horrendi
che se traranno a guisa de bombarde
mandando d'ostro fetori stupendi.

(There will be a deluge of poultry still in the soup cauldrons . . . and there will be a great flood every morning of Greek, Dalmatian, and Latin wine . . . There will be terrible and horrendous winds shot off like bombards sending off stupendous stenches.)

In this transposition into a Carnival key, astral conjunctions become "conjunctions of cheese and lasagna" or, with obvious sexual connotations, "conjunctions of Venus and Mars," and the sign of Pisces is a warning of the monotony of the Lenten diet. The deluge is reduced to the level of bodily and genital functions; it is turned upside down; it is swallowed—hence defeated—by Carnival, personified as "Pazifacio compagnone francho." However, even that merry prankster and boon companion was destined to be defeated and killed by Lent in the person of the onion, the Lenten foodstuff par excellence:

Una regina verrà con gran gente
con la coa verde et con lo capo biancho,
e moverà gran guerra immantinente
a Pazifacio compagnone francho:
per le cevolle et schalogne mordente
el povero signor venirà a mancho.

(A queen will come with many followers, with a green tail and a white head, and she will make sudden war on Merry Prankster, boon companion: by means of stinging onions and shallots will the poor lord come to his end.)

The exceptional event of the flood had no place in a cycle of years in which the seasons decline only to rise again unchanged. The poem concludes by prophesying a series of obvious events, a familiar procedure in comic prognostication:

li gatti et cani inimici serano
meglio de ravi taglieran le spade
campagne et monti al scoperto sarano
et l'hostarie saran ben visitade.

> (cats and dogs will be enemies; swords will cut better than radishes; fields and mountains will be out in the open; and the taverns will be well frequented.)

The world, that is, will remain as it always has been, immutably cyclical. Thus there is no reason to upset oneself with foolish fears; it is better to turn to the ongoing Carnival and "triumph" by giving oneself over to the pleasures of the table, of sex, and of laughter:

> Voi compagnoni contenti restate
> d'altra pioza n'habbiate paura;
> et in questi pochi giorni triomphate,
> ché ve concede la madre natura.
> Questi astrologi matti bertezate
> ché in dir cotal pazie pongon sua cura,
> et se questo ch'io dico voi farette
> in cielo e in terra contenti sarette.

> (You, good companions, stay happy and have no fear of more rain; and in these few days you will triumph, since Mother Nature concedes them to you. Mock those mad astrologers who take such trouble to say such insane things, and if you do what I tell you, you will be content in heaven and on earth.)[49]

The Carnival of Modena versus the Flood, Astrology, and Power

Obviously, a composition like Pegaso Neptunio's poem could have been designed not only to invite listeners to join in the laughter of Carnival but also to calm a public opinion that was subject to panic. Not that a hypothesis of the sort can be proved in connection with this particular text. It is certain, however, that this was a problem that transcended the individual case of Venice, and that revelation of danger needed to be disciplined and fear kept under control. This was why the Bolognese astrologer Giacomo Pietramellara published (just a month apart, 12 November and 10 December 1523) both a short work in Latin promising terrible calamities, *Enunctiationes generales de concursu omnium errantium syderum in signo Piscium*, and a much more reassuring prognostication in the vernacular.[50] In this

[49] *Pronostico: over diluvio consolatorio*, respectively, fols. 2*v*, 3*r*, 3*v*, 3*r*, 4*r*.

[50] Giacomo Pietramellara, *Enunctiationes generales de concursu omnium errantium syderum in signo Piscium futuro mense februario 1524* (Bologna: "per dominum Magistrum Iacobum Petramellarium," 1523). Following the *Enunctiationes*, the colophon for which is dated 12 November (fol. a. iv *r*), there is a *Iacobi Petramellari pronosticon in futuris rerum eventibus anni*

manner, the learned could be advised of the danger, while the vast and heterogeneous public that bought the vernacular yearly prognostications was spared useless terror and fed only crumbs of a truth (or what was believed to be a truth) that was apportioned unevenly according to social level. In other words, fear itself was to be feared and constituted a problem for public order. To speak in still more general terms, the real problem was one of political management. When astrological debate descended to the city streets it became a complex system of opposing and contradictory forces involving fear, ritual, and mockery. These forces had to be channeled. They also lent themselves to being exploited in various ways on the political plane.

This was what happened in Modena, where all the various strands involved in the predicted flood of 1524 were woven into a complex and ongoing whole. The opposing camps of deluge and Carnival became polarized, producing a particularly emblematic expression of political tension in that city. But let us proceed in orderly fashion, following the story as Tommasino Lancellotti relates it. Fear reached Modena "by letters from Rome" on 21 December 1523:

> And on the said day by letters written from Rome we heard how they are afraid of the deluge that it is said there is to be in February of 1524, and that in this hour many persons have set up stocks of provisions up in the hills to flee the deluge.[51]

The papal court in Rome, especially during the Medici papacy, was certainly one of the principal centers of astrological culture in Italy, and this may perhaps be enough to explain why fear of the flood should have arrived in Modena from Rome. There is something else, though. Relations between Modena and Rome were particularly close at the time. After Julius II occupied the city in 1510, it was ceded to Emperor Maximilian, only to be sold back to the Church, which meant that Modena had been in the

---

1524 dated 10 December. The same text appeared in Italian under the same date and printed separately with the title *Pronostico de Maestro Iacomo Petramellara sopra lanno 1524 delle cose in esso accaderanno* (Bologna: "per dominum Magistrum Iacobum Petramellarium," 1523). In the interest of clarity, I must add that the words attributed to me and given between quotation marks in Paola Zambelli, "Fine del mondo," p. 334—"The deluge and astrology are identified . . . with the interests of the dominant classes and a double literature came to be created, alarmist for the learned, reassuring for those who did not know Latin"—are not taken from any published work of mine but from a typescript distributed in preparation for discussion among the participants in the conference "Scienze, credenze occulte, livelli di cultura" held in Florence 26–30 June 1980. I agree with Paola Zambelli that such an "interesting thesis" would "require qualification," which was precisely what I did both in my paper presented at those meetings and in the discussions connected with them.

[51] Lancellotti, *Cronica modenese*, vol 2, in Biblioteca Estense di Modena, MS α T1 3, fol. 85*r*.

papal dominions since 1514 and was to remain under the popes until 1527.[52] Thus channels of communication between the two cities remained open, and it was by that route rather than through the Veneto, Bologna, or Lombardy that word of the expected flood reached Modena. Alarm spread rapidly, and on 31 January, the feast day of St. Geminiano, patron saint of the city, "a great throng came to the pardon of the said saint . . . and many persons confessed and were given absolution, in order to be well with God for anything that might happen." Thus far, the reaction was spontaneous, but on the following day, 1 February, the episcopal authorities took over the organization of religious practices aimed at preventing the flood. Gian Domenico Sigibaldi, vicar to Bishop Ercole Rangoni, spoke out in alarm:

> He exhorted everyone to fast on this first day, which is Monday, [and on] Wednesday and Friday; and Wednesday three processions will take place to pray to God and his Mother and St. Geminiano to defend this city of Modena from the prodigies of the astrologers, who have prognosticated that in February 1524 there is to be the deluge because of the conjunction of the planets in the place they were found at the time of the Flood, when Noah made the ark by God's commandment.[53]

It is not difficult to identify the work to which Sigibaldi refers: *De la vera pronosticatione del diluvio del Mille et cinquecento e vintiquatro. Composta per lo excellentissimo Philosopho Tomaso da Ravenna.*[54] Even in its title, this text was intended as an attack on Agostino Nifo's *De falsa diluvii pronosticatione*, and one of its arguments in favor of the reality of the flood was based on the hypothesis that the planets would be aligned in the sign of Pisces in 1524 exactly as they had been in Noah's time in the sign of Aquarius. The author of this tract was the same Tommaso Giannotti whom we have already met addressing laudatory enigmas to Leo X in a caption for a broadsheet on the monster of Bologna. In 1524 Giannotti was the personal astrologer of Count Guido Rangoni "Il Piccolo," commander of the papal military forces in Modena and a man so passionately interested in astrology that on several occasions Giannotti cites his opinions and suggestions.[55]

[52] Tommaso Sandonnini, *Modena sotto il governo dei papi* (Modena: t. Sociale, 1879).

[53] Lancellotti, *Cronica*, vol. 2, fol. 88*r*; vol. 1, fol. 176*r*.

[54] *De la vera pronosticatione del diluvio del Mille et cinquecento e vintiquatro. Composta per lo excellentissimo Philosopho Tomaso da Ravenna* (n.p., n.d. [Venice? 1522? certainly before the eclipse of the moon on 13 March 1523]). The allusion to Noah's Flood is on fols. 4*r–v*.

[55] On Giannotti, see Carlo Malagola, "Tomaso Filologo da Ravenna, professore nello studio padovano e mecenate," *Nuovo archivio veneto*, n.s. 2 (1901): 249–53; pp. 252–53; Piancastelli, *Pronostici ed almanacchi*, pp. 26–30, 32–34; Andrea Corsini, *Medici ciarlatani e ciarlatani medici* (Bologna: N. Zanichelli, 1922), pp. 76–77; Max Sander, *Le livre à figures italien depuis 1467 jusqu'à 1530. Essai de sa bibliographie et de son histoire*, 6 vols. (New York: G. E. Stechert, 1941; Milan: Heopli, [1942]), vol. 2, pp. 547–48. On Rangoni, see Luigi Rangoni

Giannotti's work thus represents one more link between the deluge and fear of the deluge, on the one hand, and papal power, on the other. Conversely, the bishop's vicar, Sigibaldi, entrusted defense of the city to a series of collective celebrations addressed to God, the Virgin, and St. Geminiano. The role of the city's patron saint, which has no parallel in antidiluvial rites in other cities, is easily explained when we realize that the saint's cult had recently been reinforced by a miracle that took place in 1511 when the French were besieging the city, and that Geminiano had in some manner become emblematic of the city's autonomy.[56]

Using the saint to oppose the astrological predictions might thus imply another source of tension between the city's freedoms and the central power. The following day, 2 February, opposition took an explosive turn when exorcising the flood took the form of Carnival rites and became explicit satire of procedures to enforce papal domination of the city. In the evening after vespers, the municipal trumpeters sounded a call, as if to announce a papal brief, and the people gathered in the main square.

> And when they had sounded, ser Zan Martino di Vechi opened the brief, which went thus: "On the part of the magnificent podestà of Modena. Banish misser Deluge from [this] land and place under pain of rebellion; and all the astrologers who will astrologize the flood in the future are not to be given credence; and may no one print or put forth anything whatsoever concerning the deluge, under pain of rebellion; and banish misser Thomaxo, astrologer of the lord Count Guido Rangon, for having fled to the mountains for fear of the flood," plus certain other things said to mock the said podestà who plays the astrologer, who bears the name misser Paulo di Brunori da Corezo, and also the astrologer of Count Guido.[57]

The joke was aimed, through Giannotti, at Count Rangoni, commander of the papal troops who, I might add, had also fled from Modena when danger seemed imminent. The other person mentioned was Paolo Brunori of Correggio, podestà of Modena from January 1522 to February 1525 and also a man fond of astrology. According to the city statutes, the General Council had the power to elect the podestà, but in reality this post was often filled by the central power, as was the case during the years 1514 to 1527.[58] The tension that this situation produced was so intense that when

---

Machiavelli, *Piccolo sunto storico della famiglia Rangoni di Modena* (Rome: Befani, 1908), pp. 30–42.

[56] Susanna Peyronel Rambaldi, *Speranze e crisi nel Cinquecento modenese. Tensioni religiose e vita cittadina ai tempi di Giovanni Morone* (Milan: Franco Angeli, 1979), pp. 34–36.

[57] Lancellotti, *Cronica*, vol. 1, fols. 176*v* and 177*r*.

[58] On Paolo Brunori, see Emilio Paolo Vicini, *I podestà di Modena. Serie cronologica 1336–1796* (Modena: Società tipografica modenese–Antica tipografia Soliani, 1918), pp. 189–90; on election procedures for the post of podestà, see Vicini, *I podestà di Modena, 1156–1796, Parte Ia (1156–1336)* (Rome: Giornale araldico-storico-genealogico, 1913), p. 14.

Brunori's immediate predecessor, Guerrino Garisendi, was made podestà, as Lancellotti tells us, "despite the Magnificent Community and the citizens," he was killed (in January 1522), and although his assassins were known, they were not brought to justice.[59] Brunori's successor, Angelo Tagliaferri of Parma, also died in office of a violent death (perhaps masked as an accident) on 5 June 1526.[60] All these events make it clear why astrology was linked with power in the eyes of the citizens of Modena, why it was epitomized in the unwelcome figure of Brunori, and why past events gave a further political tint to the Carnival derision aimed at astrologers. On the same day, 2 February,

> certain writings have been attached to the columns against the deluge making fun of the astrologers, saying that they have put a shrimp up in the heavens, a bow, a set of scales, a goat, and other signs; and who knows if they have not put up an owl and a hoot owl, crazy as they are, and other such things in vituperation of astrologers.[61]

The "scrite" to which Lancellotti rather vaguely alludes can be identified as three *sonetti caudati* also mentioned in a chronicle in Cremona.[62] The connection is clear from a passage in the first of these satirical extended sonnets. Paraphrasing Stöffler, it begins "O erigite caput, viri christiani" and continues:

> Ponete in ciel dui gambari, un montone,
> un becco, un'urna, un arco, una saetta,
> una bilancia, un luccio, uno scorpione;
>
> perché non li agiongiete una civetta
> e un barbagiani, pazzi da bastone,
> anzi da ceppi, da catena et cetta?
>
> (Put in the heavens two shrimp, a ram, a billy goat, an urn, a bow, an arrow, scales, a pike, a scorpion; why not add to them an owl and a hoot owl, mad enough to be beaten with a stick, or, better, to be put in logs or in chains, etc.?)

We do not know whether the three sonnets, which must have circulated fairly widely, were written in Modena, Cremona, or elsewhere. In any event, the cultural coordinates of these texts that show through the Carnival mask, particularly in the third sonnet and to some extent in the second, are more interesting to our purposes. The first sonnet expresses the au-

[59] Lancellotti, *Cronica*, vol. 1, fol. 137*v*.

[60] Vicini, *I podestà di Modena. Serie cronologica 1336–1796*, pp. 190–91.

[61] Lancellotti, *Cronica*, vol. 1, fol. 177*r*.

[62] Francesco Novati, "Il diluvio universale profetizzato per il 1524," *Archivio storico lombardo* 29, no. 2 (1902): 191–94.

thor's indignation at the "thieving" astrologers who have dethroned Christ from the heavens and substituted figures from classical antiquity for his "high and divine kingdom" by reading the imaginary figures of the zodiac into the stars. The second sonnet presents the planets as the source of life and as a symbol of cosmic harmony, whereas astrologers, "intent . . . on avarice, on gold," stress their supposed malignant influences. "You are astrologers, not prophets," the poet comments sarcastically, inverting the usual order of terms.

The third sonnet (which begins: "Cazzo! questo è il diluvio universale") is couched in strictly Carnival terms, transforming the astrologer's instruments into pots and pans and other kitchen equipment:

> Questi vostri astrolabi son patelle,
> le sfere balle da far magatelle,
> il quadrante è una pentola, un bochale;
> le tavole son mense apparecchiate
> ove voi vi calcati i buon bocconi.
>
> . . .
>
> Cuius, cuia, coioni,
> havete del profeta e del divino
> quando havete bevuto ben del vino.
> Ite col Tacuino
> nelle cocine, nelle stuffe, in chiasso,
> ove è sempre il diluvio d'unto e grasso.
>
> (These astrolabes of yours are frying pans, your spheres are juggling balls, the quadrant is a pot, a jar; your tables are [dining] tables set, where you put good things to eat. [*Nonsense conjugation*], you are part prophet and part diviner when you have drunk well of wine. Go with your Almanac into the kitchens, to the stoves in the back alley, where there is always a flood of grease and fat.)

The first thing to note is that although the author is obviously an educated man, he knows the forms of Carnival literature and uses them to perfection, which shows how difficult it is to evaluate accurately the social circle in which texts of this sort arose and just how ambiguous the term "popular" can be.[63] In any event, along with Carnival elements and blended with them, we see elements of a very different type that seem to have come from a specific source, the *Tractato contra li astrologi* of Girolamo Savonarola.[64] As is known, in this brief work Savonarola took argu-

[63] For analogous observations, see Burke, *Popular Culture in Early Modern Europe*, pp. 23–25.

[64] Girolamo Savonarola, *Tractato contra li astrologi* (Florence: Bartolomeo de' Libri, 1497),

ments that Giovanni Pico had already used, summarized them, organizing them differently and shifting their meaning, and mixed them with others to adapt them to the specific public of his followers, both among the lower classes and the governing class in Florence, with the aim of urging them to "castigate and punish" astrologers, as he says on the last page of his book. The work contains a good many themes that we have now encountered in the three sonnets. It criticizes the astrologers' greed, it contrasts astrology and prophecy, it affirms Christ's unique sovereignty over the heavens, and, in particular, it satirizes the zodiac, which men have created but which they have ended up by believing to be real. Savonarola declares that "such figures are fictitious" and that

> there is no man who, in such a multitude of stars, coupling them in various manners, cannot imagine whatever figures he wants. . . . Just as men have imagined animal figures, they could have imagined houses, or castles, or trees, or other similar things . . . but to believe that God and nature have drawn in the sky lions, dragons, dogs, scorpions, vases, archers, and monsters is a ridiculous thing.[65]

The verses I have cited as having been paraphrased by Lancellotti seem in turn to derive directly from these lines. Furthermore, it is interesting to note that in order to attack the idea of the deluge, in Modena and Spain alike, people turned to Savonarola when they sought a figure emblematic of the struggle between prophecy and astrology. But let us return to Lancellotti's account of the doings in Modena, which culminated on Fat Thursday, 4 February:

> Two men, masked, were amusing themselves dressed as philosophers. As misser Francesco Guizardino and misser Paulo di Brunori, podestà of Modena, passed along the Canalchiare [Corso Canal Chiaro] in Modena, taking a stroll, they encountered the said two philosophers. One had a sextant, a pencil, and an [armillary] sphere, and went about astrologizing; and in that instant the other astrologer lifted up his robe and showed him his rear, and his companion astrologized his rear with the sextant, and he accomplished this task with such grace that the lord governor and all the others took great pleasure in it, except for misser podestà, because the joke was made on purpose to mock the astrologers and the said podestà, whom they had astrologized on the rear end; and the lord governor took great pleasure in this, but misser Paulo no. You who read [this], do not marvel at what I write because I tell you a timely truth.[66]

Once more, denial of the flood and of astrology was mixed with mockery of the representatives of papal power. This was Lancellotti's reason for sug-

---

now in Savonarola, *Scritti filosofici*, ed. Giancarlo Garfagnini and Eugenio Garin (Rome: A. Belardetti, 1982), pp. 273–370.

[65] Ibid., pp. 370 and 339–40.

[66] Lancellotti, *Cronica*, vol. 1, fols. 177*r* and *v*.

gesting that the reader not be surprised at the vulgarity of his anecdote because it came "a bono proposito." It was not solely out of fondness for a coarse gag that the chronicler lingered over his description of two masked revelers representing the celestial sphere with the aid of a rotundity of a very different sort; it was also because Lancellotti understood and wanted to have his readers understand that a more general symbol was concealed behind that first, crude one—the refusal of the citizens of Modena to tolerate Rome's dual abuse of its power when it deprived the city of its political autonomy and imposed an ideology, astrology, that was both unwelcome and a source of fear.

Prophecy versus Astrology

This raucous scene provides an emblematic ending to our tale, as only a few final considerations remain. At the beginning of this chapter, two problems were posed: What was the relationship between prophecy and astrology, and how broadly distributed and how strong was belief in astrological science outside learned circles, in particular among the urban lower classes. On the first point, we can say that the affair of the deluge expected in 1524 is a good example of how prophetic culture could absorb, envelop, and to some extent annul astrological culture. There is no doubt that announcement of the deluge resounded far and wide, building on a tragically frequent series of inundations in recent years and on a specific tradition placing floods in a prophetic context. Above all, preaching gave prediction of the flood a vast audience (Giacomo Tiburzi deplored the "universo audiente populo") and placed it within an apocalyptical homiletic tradition that had long enjoyed broad popularity and had only recently been reined in by the ecclesiastical authorities (but not snuffed out, if in precisely those years the Church felt the need to remind local ecclesiastics of the decrees for its repression.) The flood was thus accepted and believed in more as a castigation from God for the corruption of the Church or, in another view, for the Lutheran rebellion, than as the effect of an inauspicious planetary conjunction (which in fact swept away the very foundations of astrological science). In confirmation of this hypothesis I might observe that when Carnival ritual merriment reigned and ecclesiastical and penitential rites lost their intensity and their effectiveness, manifestations of disbelief and derision not only became more frequent than displays of fear but overwhelmed and ultimately destroyed them. Two cities fail to fit this pattern: Rome, where panic seems to have been widespread, and Venice, where announcements of the flood, although widely known, were by no means accepted. Modena, finally, which fully conforms to the pattern indicated, indirectly confirms the strong connections that people perceived to exist between astrology and political power, in particular Roman political power. When astrology was mocked, power too was denied.

In short, at least as far as the specific instance examined here is concerned, we seem to be able to say that urban populations were fully aware of astrology, but that they gave it little credit. Popular divination used other means. The failure of the predictions of the flood and their comic inversion in a Carnival key thus had an enormous negative effect on the figure of the astrologer, but not on the image of the preacher, even though preachers had shared fully in that failure. In the end, the figure of the astrologer emerged much diminished by the way popular culture had received the supposed deluge. In the culture of the mass of urban folk, the astrological arts were reduced to the level of a juggler's bag of tricks, and astrological science is denied, derided, and seems ineffectual. As Celebrino said, "vedo dispersa gir l'astrologia."[67]

[67] Celebrino, *La dechiaratione per che non è venuto il diluvio*, fol. D. 2*r*.

7

AWAITING A NEW OCTAVIAN

A Case of Possession and of Propaganda

IN ROME in April 1519 a woman possessed by spirits ("she speaks Latin, predicts things to come, reveals people's secret sins") was taken to the basilica of St. Peter "to the column where they say Christ was bound" and subjected to procedures designed to liberate her.[1] The basilica did indeed boast a "column that casts out spirits," as one pilgrim from Brescia wrote when he was in Rome for the Jubilee of 1475 and had visited it among the other *mirabilia Urbis*.[2] The exorcist began by asking the spirit oppressing the woman to tell his name; it answered that it was not a demon—as it surely would have been some decades later—but a certain messer Agamennone Marescotti, formerly a Roman senator in the pay of the Venetians. He then offered a number of predictions, these among them, according to Marcantonio Michiel, writing to Nicolò Tiepolo:

> The Turk will come this year to Rome, and as victor will fodder his horse on top of the altar of Peter, and [the horse] not eating it, by miracle he will become a Christian. He also says that the king of France will be elected emperor, specifying the electors who will give him their votes and for what reason they will do so.[3]

Ostensibly, these two predictions were unconnected. In reality, the woman possessed by spirits juxtaposed a pro-French political viewpoint of the current struggle over the choice of a successor for Emperor Maximilian I with a specific reminiscence taken from a prophecy in verse that we have already encountered, the title of which, *La vera prophetia . . . la quale declara la venuta de uno imperatore*, clarifies the connection with the imminent

[1] Marino Sanuto, *Diarii*, 58 vols. (Venice: R. Deputazione Veneta di storia patria, 1879–1903), vol. 27, col. 224.

[2] "Cronaca di Corradino Palazzo," in *Le cronache bresciane inedite dei secoli XV–XIX*, ed. Paolo Guerrini, 5 vols. (Brescia: Editrice Brixia Sacra, 1922–1932), vol. 1, p. 220. This column was reputed to have come from the temple of Solomon, and Christ was supposed to have stood beside it. It is also mentioned by Bernardo Portinari in the dedication to Leo X of his *Disputationes II de daemonibus*, the manuscript of which is conserved in the Biblioteca Medicea Laurenziana di Firenze, Pluteo 84, 22. See also Lynn Thorndike, *A History of Magic and Experimental Science*, 8 vols. (New York: Columbia University Press, 1923–1958), vol. 5, p. 85.

[3] Sanuto, *Diarii*, vol. 27, col. 224.

election. The miraculous conversion reported above figures in that prophecy in these terms:

> Poi vigniranno i Turchi
> dentro a la cità de Roma;
> li romani serano spurchi
> per l'alpestra e grave soma.
> La scrittura così noma
> che 'l Turcho farà manzare
> el cavalo sopra l'altare
> quale è del primo pastore.
>
> La gloriosa nostra Donna
> un miracolo mostrarà,
> quel caval in hora bona
> presto si inzenochiarà.
> Quando el Turcho vederà
> tal miracolo per Dio mandato
> presto sarà baptezato
> e pentuto del so errore.
>
> (Then the Turks will come into the city of Rome; the Romans will be bled dry by the rude and heavy burden. The writing thus says that the Turk will have his horse eat on top of the altar that is the first shepherd's. Our glorious Lady will show a miracle: the horse, now meek, will immediately kneel. When the Turk sees this miracle sent by God he will immediately be baptized and will repent of his error.)[4]

This must have been a well-known prophecy. A number of years later, in 1530, Marcantonio Magno, who translated Juan de Valdés's *Alphabeto Cristiano* into Italian, expressed fear that the Turk would come "all the way to Rome . . . so that we shall see him, in our days, fulfill the prophecy told so many times before, that he will have his horse feed on the altar of St. Peter's."[5] The poem contained another important element, however. Its refrain promised, "There will come an emperor who will put all the world in peace," which means that the possessed woman identified the promised peace-making emperor with Francis I, thus connecting the prophecy to a specific political content. This is not explicit in Michiel's letter, as he is

[4] *La vera prophetia prophetizata dal glorioso Santo Anselmo la quale declara la venuta de uno imperatore: el qual mettera pace tra li christiani et conquistara infideli trovata in Roma* (Collicuti: Francesco da Udine), fols. 2*r*–*v*. On the various editions of this prophecy, see chap. 1, nn. 10 and 46.

[5] Sanuto, *Diarii*, vol. 53, col. 425.

more interested in other, more comic aspects of the episode, but it seems obvious, considering that although Leo X's policies were usually ambiguous, he favored the Most Christian king of France over the Most Catholic Spanish. Many aspects of this episode arouse our curiosity to know more. Not only does it confirm the broad propagandistic use made of cases of possession, which have already been studied;[6] it also shows the broad distribution of prophecies in verse. We cannot help wondering whether the possessed woman had gotten her hands on the printed text or whether she had simply heard it declaimed or mentioned. Finally, we see here yet another example of prophecy concerning the emperor, a topic that is certainly well known. It is a singular example, however. Not only was it manifested orally but by a woman in a state of psychological turmoil who quite unconsciously organized into one statement both the rumors that were circulating concerning the elections in course and her reminiscences of a widely distributed text accessible even to the lower levels of the Roman population.

The Emperor of Peace in Popular Print

A good deal of study has been devoted to the vast place that medieval and Renaissance prophecy, from Dante on, reserved for a holy imperial figure who would bring peace and on whose saintliness a beneficent renewal of the papacy in the person of an angelic pope would depend.[7] What is not yet fully understood is the circulation of these themes among the "lower" levels of society, nor in what form and by what paths they were connected with the changing scene in Italian and European history, to which they adapted by shifting the emphasis of their varied parts.

Both in their physical existence and in their utilization, "popular" print pieces on prophecy doubtlessly represent one of the chief signs of and principal media for the "lower" circulation of imperial themes. Indeed, such themes were among the topics most frequent in popular print literature; compared with the medieval tradition of Church reform under an "angelic pope," they represented a current of extraordinary sticking power. It is probable that the crisis in imperial power, by then irreversible, encouraged

[6] See Daniel Pickering Walker, *Unclean Spirits: Possession and Exorcism in France and England in the late Sixteenth and early Seventeenth Centuries* (Philadelphia: University of Pennsylvania Press, 1981). For northern Italy, see Ottavio Franceschini, "L'esorcista," in *Medicina, erbe e magia* (Bologna: Federazione delle Casse di Risparmio e delle Banche del Monte dell'Emilia Romagna, 1981), pp. 99–115.

[7] As an absolute minimum, see Friedrich von Bezold, "Zur deutschen Kaiserage," *Vortrag von Sitzungberichte der Philolosophisch-Philologischen und historischen Klasse der königlich Bayerischen Akademie der Wissenschaften* (1884): 560–606; Marjorie Reeves, *The Influence of Prophecy in the Late Middle Ages: A Study in Joachimism* (Oxford: Clarendon Press, 1969), pp. 347–74.

such publications by contributing to expectations of peace and prosperity projected onto the figure of a *deus ex machina* that was in reality nonexistent but was predicted for a near but indeterminate future. Thus we read, in a random sampling of prophetic print pieces, that an "emperor . . . of the lineage of David will lead all the people back to justice . . . returning the clergy to the way of the apostles."[8] Similarly, we read that

> Farassi un sancto e digno imperatore
> che 'l mondo tenerà sotto a sua alla
> con bona divotione e bono amore.
> *Rex regum* serà lui che già non falla,
> di casa David, dil mondo signore,
> pien di possanza il suo vigor non calla;
> adunarà la christianità tutta
> contro l'infidel, con magna condutta.

> (A saintly and worthy emperor will be made who will hold the world under his wing with good devotion and good love. *Rex regum* will he be who will not fail; of the house of David, lord of the world, full of power, his strength will not decline; he will gather together all Christianity against the infidel with mighty deeds.)[9]

These are fairly generic indications, which do not lend themselves particularly well to association with specific persons or political situations. The same was true of the *Vera prophetia . . . de uno imperatore*, the first edition of which is undated but has been placed at around 1510. Certainly anyone who listened to these lines being declaimed to the sound of a viol in the public square or who acquired for a half *quattrino* the two- or four-page printed version asked nothing better than to find in them the reassuring effigy of a real person, but in order for the connection to be made, some concrete historical connection had to be provided. Thus when in 1512 Emperor Maximilian, who was admittedly gifted with inventiveness but had little charisma, joined the Holy League against the French, the prophetic books opened their pages to him.

> Non convien più dubitare
> nel venir de Maximiano
> che in Italia a mano a mano
> sue bandiere vol spiegare.
> Non convien più dubitare.
> Gli è adempiuto quel ch'àn ditto

[8] *Pronostico overo profecia delanno MCCCCCXCV fina alanno MCCCCCXXXII* (Stampata in Bologna del MCCCCCVII. Die XXIIII Decembris), fol. 3*r*.

[9] *Imminente flagello de Italia* (n.p., n.d.), fol. 6*r*.

le Sybille tutte quante,
quel che Brigida ha poi scritto
gli è finito ad questo instante,
et però gli è quivi astante
per la Italia trapassare.
Non convien più dubitare.

(There is no longer cause to doubt of the coming of Maximilian, who in Italy, bit by bit, intends to unfurl his banners. There is no longer cause to doubt. With him, what all the Sibyls said has been fulfilled; what Bridget later wrote has just ended in this instant, and yet he is here present in order to pass through Italy. There is no longer cause to doubt.)[10]

The Milanese chronicler Ambrogio da Paullo also recorded the prognostication that Maximilian would "make all the world obedient and reform the Church and make [a] new order."[11] These were expectations that went far beyond the person in question. Their deeper roots—the call for reform of the Church and for a new order in Christianity—emerge from even the most generic passages quoted above, but they sprang into operation attached to a real person whenever concrete historical events allowed.

Charles V, the Second Charlemagne

As we have seen, the new imperial election of 1519 was seen as the moment that would finally produce the emperor hailed in the prophecies. Steady pressure from the Turks in the Mediterranean basin probably contributed to this sentiment. Nearly three years had passed since Selim I had invaded Egypt, feeding the worst fears for the fate of Europe, Italy in particular. Conversely, it was part of Charles's electoral propaganda that he "promised to go against infidels,"[12] which was also one of the principal characteristics of the emperor promised in the prophecies. This explains why the prophecy of the second Charlemagne was modified to apply to Charles V immediately after his election. This prophecy, formerly applied to Charles VIII of France, predicted a sovereign, victor over both Europe and Asia, who would end his life on the hill of Calvary, at last liberated from the infidel. Along with the earlier publications of a text beginning

[10] *Questa sie la venuta del Imperatore* (n.p., n.d.), fol. 1*r*. In a similar vein, see also *Questa sie la tregua fata con limperatore e san Marco e con tutti gli altri principi christiani novamente confirmata* (n.p., n.d. [1512]).

[11] *Cronaca milanese dall'anno 1476 al 1515 di Maestro Ambrogio da Paullo*, ed. Antonio Ceruti, *Miscellanea di storia italiana* 13 (1871): 91–353; p. 282.

[12] Sanuto, *Diarii*, vol. 27, col. 446.

"Charolo fiol de Charoli," an edition of the same prophecy now circulated, undated but presumably printed in 1519, entitled *Prophetia Caroli Imperatoris*, the first phrase of which was altered to read "Carolus Philippi filius" (Charles V was the son of Philip the Handsome). The text was in Latin, as if to show that the piece was addressed to the learned, but it also contained three prophecies in the vernacular, which would have guaranteed it a fairly large circulation.[13]

In the years that followed, the prophecy of the second Charlemagne, adapted in this fashion, circulated above all in manuscript, reemerging at crucial moments in Charles's imperial career. In this fashion, one member of the d'Arco family transcribed the prophecy at the time of the battle of Pavia, adding a commentary of his own on that memorable event, which seemed to him to fulfill certain aspects of the prophecy (he connected the many nations that were defeated by Charles at Pavia with the phrase in the prophecy, "educet bella subjugans anglos, gallos, hispanos et longobardos").[14] Later, in January 1527, Tommasino Lancellotti transcribed the same text into his chronicle, stating that he had received it four years earlier but had lost it, finding it again at that time "by God's will" (since the prophecy, according to Lancellotti, was fulfilled precisely in those days).[15] However, during those same months of the battle of Pavia, presumably toward the end of 1524, another publication connected Charles with the great medieval prophetic tradition. This work was a broadsheet from Piedmont entitled *Hystorie nove: dove se contiene la venuta de lo imperatore per incoronarsi: et de le grande cose che hano ad essere*, the text of which reads:

Fugeti et non aspetando el gran furore
ché vene un novo Xerze et novo Marte;
questo he dil vero Cesar sucessore

che vinse il mondo con la sacra mano
facendosi sol primo imperatore;
questo he quel divo e sacro Carlo Mano

[13] *Prophetia Caroli Imperatoris con altre Prophetie di diversi santi huomini* (n.p., n.d.). The hypothesis that this edition of the prophecy was printed in 1519 is based on the text that follows the *Prophetia Caroli Imperatoris*, here given the title *Prophetia stampata nel mille quatrocento nonantaotto: che tratta de la cose passate et che debbeno venire*, the first two lines of which read: "El se movera un gato / anni sete diece e quatro." If we add up the date given in the title with the years indicated in the first lines, we get 1498 + 7 + 10 + 4 = 1519, the presumed year of publication. The compiler undoubtedly had this calculation in mind and would have changed his numbers if he had realized that the date for the fulfillment of the prophecy had passed.

[14] Antonio Medin, "La battaglia di Pavia. Profeti e poeti italiani," *Archivio storico lombardo* 52 (1925): 252–90; p. 254.

[15] Tommasino Lancellotti, *Cronaca modenese*, ed. Carlo Borghi, 12 vols. (Parma: P. Fiaccadori, 1863), vol. 2, p. 170.

qual Brigida predisse in le sue carte
che extinguerebe il furore galicano.
Merlin comprese anchor con la sua arte

che l'ucel di Iove volarebe a tondo,
regnabit ubique, et disse: "in ogni parte
tutte le profetie d'alto e da fondo

volto he rivolto, finalmento trovo
che ha essere sol costui signor dil mondo."
. . .

Per questo tornaran l'aride piante
et reverdire, dicho per ogni deserto
naseran fiori più che mai galante.

Il ciel per soa clementia ne l'hano offerto,
sol per cavarne da le man de Faraone:
ut implent scripture ab experto.

Surget rex magnus a septentrione
qui destruet potentiam omnem Galorum,
nec redibunt in Italia regione

per infinita secula seculorum.
Amen.

(Flee without awaiting the great furor because a new Xerxes and a new Mars is coming; this one is truly the successor of Caesar who won the world with sacred hand, making himself the only first emperor; this one is that divine and holy Charles the Great of whom Bridget predicted in her papers that he would extinguish the Gallican fury. Merlin still understood by his art that Jove's bird would fly back, "he will reign everywhere," and he said, "everywhere, all prophecies high and low has he turned inside out, finally I find that he alone is to be the lord of the world." . . . For this one the dry plants will revive and turn green again, I say, in every desert flowers will be born more beautiful than ever. The heavens have offered him to us out of their clemency, simply to remove him from the hands of the Pharaoh: "So that Scripture may be fulfilled in experience." A great king will rise in the north who will destroy the power of all Frenchmen, and they will never return to Italian lands for all eternity, Amen.)[16]

[16] *Hystorie nove: dove se contiene la venuta de lo imperatore per incoronarsi: et de le grande cose che hano ad essere* (n.p., n.d. [Turin: 1524?]), fols. 1*r–v*.

Thus Bridget and Merlin had already predicted the victory of the imperial forces over the French and the imminent descent of Charles into the Italian peninsula. This tissue of prophecies gradually defined Charles by placing his persona in the sacred and providential context discussed by Frances A. Yates.[17] Elements of the current political scene (the Turkish question, the Lutheran problem) came to be combined with others that belonged to the prophetic realm (the image of the emperor who would come to bring peace to all Christendom when the Church had been reformed and the Holy Sepulchre liberated) and with the portrait of the universal sovereign that Charles was gradually coming to resemble for objective cultural and dynastic reasons. The result of all these combinations was an extraordinarily sturdy image, well adapted to the demands of imperial propaganda, that could be circulated and received with great ease by means of pamphlets and broadsheets, which in turn contributed much to keeping alive hope and expectation.

Prophecies of the Sack of Rome

When on 27 January 1527 Tommasino Lancellotti once again got his hands on a copy of the prophecy of the second Charlemagne, which he had seen four years earlier under the title of *Pronostico dela Maestà delo Imperatore Carolo* and subsequently lost, he thought that this had happened "by God's will"—that is, that God himself had presented him with the best key for understanding and interpreting the present and foreseeing the future.

It was generally true in 1517 and the years immediately following that known prophecies were read again and meditated anew. When Rome was sacked, it was as if a veil had been rent and prophecies that had been obscure had found definitive clarification in events. This sort of attitude is evident in one passage of the *Dialogo di Lattantio et di uno Archidiacono* in which Alfonso de Valdés speaks of the many prophecies that had circulated in Rome during the years preceding the sack:

> LATTANTIO: Oh! Lord help me! I remember that when I was in Rome many prophecies were found there that spoke of this persecution of the clergy that was to come in the time of this emperor.
>
> THE ARCHDEACON: That is the truth. A thousand times have we read them there for our comfort and amusement.[18]

[17] Frances A. Yates, *Astraea: The Imperial Theme in the Sixteenth Century* (London and Boston: Routledge & Kegan Paul, 1975), pp. 20–28. See also Reeves, *The Influence of Prophecy*, pp. 359–74, and (concerning Antonio Arquato in particular) Delio Cantimori, *Umanesimo e religione nel Rinascimento* (Turin: G. Einaudi, 1975), pp. 164–74, 182–92.

[18] Alfonso de Valdés, *Due dialoghi. Traduzione italiana del sec. XVI*, ed. Giuseppe de Gennaro (Naples: Istituto universitario orientale, 1968), p. 396.

Tommasino Lancellotti reread the *Profezia di santa Brigida* in much the same spirit and he reports that it "tells of the widespread death in Rome just as they now say it happened." In fact, Lancellotti was still reflecting on the question several months after the sack of Rome (which seemed to him a well-deserved punishment of Rome, the pope, and the Church), observing that "all these things were predicted many years ago by the preachers and no one believed them."[19] With hindsight and in light of the sack of Rome, the typical themes of apocalyptical preaching—denunciation of the failings of the ecclesiastical hierarchy, warning of divine wrath, prediction of terrible punishment—seemed to have been proved valid.[20]

Prophecies were not only reread but reprinted. Around 1530 or slightly earlier a very short work of four leaves was published without indication of place or date. The title page reads: *Profetie cavate duno opuscolo stampato gia trentanni passati il quale si chiama pronosticatione vera et piu non udita: et io ho tratto fora quelle cose le qual par che ocorra al presente acio che ognun senza comprar el libro possi saciar lapetito suo circha aquesta materia. Laus Deo*. Thus the work was a reprinting (or a partial reprinting) of Lichtenberger's *Pronosticatio*, which it cited only by its title, however, without mention of the author's name. Better, it was an anthology of extracts chosen according to both economic and historical criteria.[21] Thus this brief work offered, at the lowest possible cost, the predictions from the *Pronosticatio* "that seem necessary in the present"—that is, that seemed to have just come true. The statement that thirty years had passed since the publication of the original together with the type of selections made bring the publication without question to the time of the sack of Rome. It reads:

> Here St. Bridget in the book of her Revelations says, "the Church of God will be placed under the great eagle. . . . The eagle will leave the rock of la Magna [Germany] accompanied by many griffins who, coming swiftly into the orchard, will chase away the shepherd of the fifth terrestrial zone into the seventh. . . . O holy mother Church, weep. . . . Thus the root of sin will arise again out of the scorpionists, worse than Antiochus, who overturned the vases of the Temple; worse than Joab, most full of deceit; worse than Ahab who made gardens of sweet-smelling herbs of the vineyard of the Lord Sabaoth; even worse than Appollonius who despoiled the temple of the Lord. . . . He

[19] Lancellotti, *Cronaca modenese*, vol. 2, p. 271.

[20] I do not intend to go into prophecy of the sack of Rome here. See P. Picca, "Il sacco di Roma del 1527. Profezie, previsioni, prodigi," *Nuova Antologia* 345 (1929): 120–25 and, of course, André Chastel, *The Sack of Rome, 1527*, tr. Beth Archer (Princeton: Princeton University Press, 1983), pp. 78–90.

[21] Following the order of the *Profetie cavate duno opuscolo*, these extracts were taken from Lichtenberger, *Pronosticatione*, pt. 1, chap. 3; pt. 2, chaps. 4, 9, 35, 36; and pt. 2, chap. 14, respectively.

> will not be ashamed to smash the holy places, nor will he be ashamed to commit sacrilege . . . thus as the root of sin, you will be punished by God.

The anonymous compiler thus performed the editorial tasks of rereading, selecting, collating, and rethinking prophecies that were already known, just as others were doing on that tragic occasion. Other predictions followed, not concerning the sack. Unlike the earlier ones, they no longer respected the internal order of Lichtenberger's book, thus seeming to shift their main focus to the spread of the Reformation:

> Until such time as the Church is renewed, God will permit a great schism to arise in the Church. . . . Three names of blasphemers preaching heresy will incite the people against the clergy. . . . Take care, you religious from Trier, and you, philosophers from Cologne, that the rapacious wolves do not enter your sheepcote: . . . for in your time will unheard-of woes arise in your churches (which God forbid). Finis.[22]

Even in Lichtenberger's *Pronosticatio*, then, one could find references to the sins of the Church and its punishment, to the religious schism in Germany, and to the "great eagle"—the emperor—whose winged vortex would bring chastisement and renewal to the ecclesiastical hierarchy. If we compare this reading of Lichtenberger to Alberto Napolitano's, we see that by their very nature prophecies had an ambiguous and contradictory life of their own. They could acquire specific meaning (which might change from age to age) only in contact with both the selective eye of a reader and the historical event that somehow guided that eye to locating a continuous and meaningful line in what to an indifferent bystander would seem a vast confusion of vague and superimposed signs. Nor is that all; such a selection could be made directly by the reader, but it could also be the work of others aware of the need for short, easy-to-read, low-cost texts aimed at a mass public. Compilers distilled only a few elements out of the original prophecy—different ones every time—and offered readers passages from Lichtenberger that seemed to speak of Luther as a new prophet or of the sack of Rome and the ambiguous (because both sacrilegious and regenerative) role of the emperor. Naturally, this facilitated all sorts of propagandistic operations.

Leonello Beliardi and His Collection of Predictions

This use of predictions clearly shows how prophecy could construct a charismatic halo around real persons. As we have seen, the medieval image of the emperor of peace that reemerged in support of Maximilian contributed

[22] Ibid., fols A. i*v*, A. ii*r*, A. ii*v*, A. iii*r*–*v*, A. iv*r*.

to the creation of broad-scale expectations concerning the imperial election of 1519 that reached so far down in society that they could even appear in the incoherent statements of a possessed woman. Furthermore, the political status and personal positions of Charles himself (not to mention the ideology fashioned for him by his counselors) created an appealing correspondence between that image and the person of the young emperor. Finally, the sack of Rome led people of a variety of cultural and social levels (Alfonso de Valdés and Tommasino Lancellotti, but also the anonymous purchasers of the *Profetie cavate duno opuscolo*) to reread and rethink prophecies, both the written ones and those transmitted orally by preachers, that spoke of punishments inflicted on the Church for its failings by an emperor sent by God. It seemed strikingly evident that this emperor was Charles.

This mental process is well illustrated by a group of six prophecies appended to the *Cronaca della città di Modena* of Leonello Beliardi, a man of law of that city.[23] The events that Beliardi chronicled occurred from 1512 to 1518, but this corpus of prophetic texts gives the impression that it could have been compiled separately, after the text of the chronicle had been written, hence that it parallels the manuscript collections of prophecies that have already been discussed. The text of the chronicle has not come down to us in an autograph version but through a transcription (apparently a fairly accurate one) that Tiraboschi made in 1785 from the original, then in the hands of Ireneo Affò,[24] and it is plausible to suppose that the texts collected at the end of the chronicle were written in a separate notebook. In fact the first of them, the verse prophecy *Più volte nella mente so' exforzato*, lacks its beginning, indicating that the first page of the notebook of prophecies may have been lost.[25]

These texts are quite varied. They include *Più volte nella mente so' exforzato* without a first page; a *Pronosticon Diaboli D.ni Caroli Suxenae, 1441*; the prophecy, mentioned several times earlier, *Gallorum levitas*, here under the title *Carmina Romae inventa in marmore sculpta apud sanctum Pancratium*; a *Pronosticum* dated "Ex Urbe X Iulij 1511" and attributed to one Panfilo Morano or Moreni, a prophecy known as early as the late thirteenth century; the *Bononia Studium perdet*; and, finally, a *Scriptura quaedam tabula aenea sculpta, quae fuit inventa in partibus Angliae in vetustissimo quodam sepulcro, anno 1456*. Some of these texts are long, some short; their age varies; some of their authors are known, others unknown; they are in

[23] Leonello Beliardi, *Cronaca della città di Modena (1512–1518)*, ed. Albano Biondi and Michele Oppi (Modena: Parini, 1981), pp. 144–55. See also the "Nota al testo" of Albano Biondi, pp. 166–68.

[24] Ibid., pp. 159–60.

[25] On this prophecy, see Roberto Rusconi, *L'attesa della fine. Crisi della società, profezia ed Apocalisse in Italia al tempo del grande scisma d'Occidente (1378–1417)* (Rome: Istituto storico italiano per il Medio Evo, 1979), pp. 156–58.

verse and in prose, in Latin and in the vernacular. Rather than investigating the origin of these texts, it is probably more worthwhile to speculate on the overall interpretation that Leonello Beliardi might have given them and on the meaning they may have had for him as a set of texts.

The poet Girolamo Casio de' Medici sheds light on the question. Immediately after the sack of Rome he composed a "Canzon ove si narra la Strage e il Sacco di Roma diritiva al Catholico re di Spagna & de Romani Carlo Quinto eletto imperatore."[26] Like Lattantio and the Archdeacon in Alfonso de Valdés's dialogue and like Tommasino Lancellotti and so many others of their age, Casio went back to ancient prophecies and attempted to read into them the meaning dictated by current events. One of the prophecies that Casio summarized in verse was the *Scriptura quaedam tabula aenea sculpta*, which proclaimed:

> in varie profetie
> trovassi, e legge iscritto
> e sculto in una tavola di rame
> . . .
> nel Mille e Quatrocento Cinquantasei
> in Anglia trovata
> fu in uno avel.
>
> (in various prophecies there is found and there reads, inscribed and sculpted on a brass tablet. . . . in 1456 it was found in a tomb in England.)

For Casio this prophecy represented both an explanation of the horrors of the sack of Rome and a program for the emperor: "Victory over Rome accomplished, to the Holy Land is he called." Indeed, the sack, which Casio interprets as a purification for the "nefarious sins" of Christians, should be followed by a crusade with Charles V as its predestined hero. Once Charles VIII of France had seemed to embody the prophecy:

> volò la fama, e il disse esser quel Carlo.
> Ma tu quel sei, di cui scrivendo parlo.
>
> (the rumor flew and the saying that it was that Charles. But you are the one, [you] of whom I speak as I write.)

This provides a key for reading at least one of the texts collected by Beliardi. In reality, however, even in their variety, these texts show a singular consonance of themes, which can be reduced, in substance, to impatience

[26] Girolamo Casio de' Medici, *Vita et morte di Giesu Christo* (n.p., n.d. [1527/1528]), fols. +1*r*–+4*v*.

before the arrogance of the clergy ("vana gloria cleri")[27] and, above all, the expectation of the "great eagle,"[28] mentioned in several texts, who "superbos corriget, domabit et affliget,"[29] will bring the Turks to heel, and will vanquish the French[30]—in short, to expectation of the emperor "promised in the law and prophesied":

> poi che saranno distrutti li tiranni
> et li preti cattiati con lor danni
> verrà quellui ch'enfra Lamandi
> serà alevato.
>
> . . .
>
> Custui serà singnore de tuto el mondo
>
> . . .
>
> Costui farà pace in ogni lato.
>
> (after the tyrants are destroyed and the priests chased away with their evil deeds, there will come one who will be raised in Germany. . . . He will be lord of the entire world. . . . He will make peace everywhere.)[31]

He was also to assure the regeneration of the Roman church:

> li santi preti de novello stato
> predecarano
>
> . . .
>
> or te ralegra populo romano.
>
> (the holy priests of the new state will preach. . . . Now will you be happy, people of Rome.)[32]

In Italy, and above all in Rome, there would be "tot clades, tot subversiones, tot suspensiones, decapitationes, depopulationes, depredationes, rapinas, ruinas et incendia . . . usque ad annum 1529." Then, however, there would come a "monarcha nomine Carolus Imperator toto orbi, cujus imperio etiam Christi hostes parebunt et prostrati succumbent."[33]

It seems difficult to deny the sense that underlies these juxtaposed texts,

[27] *Carmina Romae inventa in marmore sculpta apud sanctum Pancratium*, in Beliardi, *Cronaca della città di Modena*, p. 150.

[28] *Pronosticon Diaboli D.ni Caroli Suxenae, 1441*, in ibid., p. 149; *Carmina Romae inventa*, in ibid, p. 150; *Pronosticum*, in ibid., p. 153.

[29] *Pronosticon Diaboli*, in ibid., p. 149.

[30] *Più volte nella mente so' exforzato*, in ibid., p. 147; *Pronosticon Diaboli*, in ibid., p. 150; *Carmina Romae inventa*, in ibid., p. 150.

[31] *Più volte nella mente so' exforzato*, in ibid., pp. 146–47.

[32] Ibid., p. 147.

[33] *Scriptura quaedam tabula aenea sculpta, quae fuit inventa in partibus Angliae in vetustissimo quodam sepulcro, anno 1456*, in ibid., pp. 154–55.

which immediately evoke a precise political and cultural climate in which confounding the evil prelates and heralding the advent of a universal emperor seemed one and the same thing. In that Beliardi died on 24 February 1528,[34] it hardly seems risky to suppose that these prophecies were collected and transcribed during the months immediately following the sack of Rome, when "a monarch of the name of Charles" seemed an instrument for the purification of the Church and even in Modena people were returning to the old prophecies that predicted, in Lancellotti's words, "la mortalità di Roma."

Prognostications and Prophecies for the Congress of Bologna

In this fashion, an atmosphere of prophetic expectation gradually developed to welcome Charles when he finally arrived at the Congress of Bologna in 1529. A generous harvest of print pieces appealing to a broad audience expressed Italy's hope that the emperor and the peace he would make with the pope would bring relief from the wars that had tormented the land until then. One *Historia nova quale trata de la venuta del lo Imperatore* began with these words:

> Italia dati piacere,
> da ti leva ogni gravezza
> convertir sa in alegrezza
> il pasato dispiacere.
> . . .
> Italia dati piacere.
> Bona pace he ordinata
> tanto in mare quanto in terra.
>
> (Italy, take pleasure, chase away all care, may you convert past displeasure into joy. . . . Italy, take pleasure. Good peace is commanded both on the seas and on land.)[35]

Other compositions placed the same ideas in a more strictly prophetic framework:

> Questo è il sacro Imperatore,
> questo è quel profetizato,
> questo è quel vero signore
> che ci harà pacificato.

[34] Lancellotti, *Cronaca modenese*, vol. 2, p. 341.

[35] *Historia nova quale trata de la venuta del lo Imperatore a laude de Italia de Genova et del nobille Andrea Doria* (n.p., n.d. [Savona, J. Berruerio, 1530?]), fols. 1*r–v*.

Or sia donque laudato
questa sua bona arivata.

(This is the holy Emperor, this is the one prophesied, this is that true lord who will bring us peace. Thus may his fortunate arrival be praised.)

Italy herself spoke these words, personified in a pamphlet of four unnumbered leaves and entitled *Alegreza de Italia per la venuta del Sacro Imperatore*.[36] Thus Charles V was the emperor of peace, "quel profetizato." The same idea appears in another anonymous composition of the same year (1530), entitled *Il gran susidio el qual domanda tutta Italia al Imperatore*:

Cercato ò santa Scriptura quasi tuta,
di molte profetie son adimpito,
del suo bell'arbor tolt'ò ciò che fruta:
io trovo esser tu quello sì gradito
che tanti fati farà sua conduta,
che l'alle extenderai in ogni sito,
e sbigottir farai el turco tale
tra lor seguendo d'infiniti male.

(I have searched nearly all of holy Scripture, I am filled with many prophecies, from its fine tree I have taken what was productive: I find that you are the one so welcome that many acts will smooth his way, who will extend your wings in every place and so confound the Turk, infinite afflictions following among them.)[37]

It is understandable, then, that there was no dearth of astrologers and prophets of all sorts in Bologna, all of whom took care to accommodate events and predictions in the form most appropriate to the interests of one party or another. A Latin prophecy that had been known for at least twenty years by its first line, "Veniet de occidente rex magnus et ferus," was particularly popular. It predicted that after a period of suffering and destruction, the sovereign to which its title referred would be crowned in Bologna, followed by a period of joy and universal abundance. Moreover, the prophecy was adjusted to the advantage of the municipality in the sense that in the version distributed on 14 February the phrase "et postea erit civitas imperialis," absent in the original, was added to the phrase "et Bononiae

[36] *Alegreza de Italia per la venuta del Sacro Imperatore con la exortatione. Soneto per Pietro Venetiano* (n.p., n.d. [Venice, 1530?]).

[37] *Il gran susidio el qual domanda tutta Italia al Imperatore cognoscendo che quello è inspirato da Dio e venuto in Italia per liberarla* (n.p., n.d.).

coronabitur."[38] In that way, the city hoped to get something in return for the expense and trouble of welcoming the pontifical and imperial parties and their troops.

The emperor himself was the principal topic of the prophecies, however. Girolamo Balbi published a work entitled *De futuris Caroli Augusti successibus vaticinium* in honor of Charles's arrival in Bologna in November 1529.[39] The work was a pure and simple panegyric in Latin hexameters forecasting the return of the eagles of victory to the Campidoglio and the recuperation of the sacred sites in the Holy Land thanks to Charles. It is nevertheless significant that Balbi's ultra-Ciceronian praises should have been expressed in the form of a prophecy. Astrological prognostication was another sort of prophecy that lent itself well to the praise of political power during these same years. The astrologer had to take into account his debts toward the ruler when he made up his annual *iuditium*, and that gratitude was often part of the logic of simple dependence and patronage is common knowledge and has been clearly demonstrated for astrologers in Ferrara.[40] Furthermore, when the astrologer failed to respect such courtesies he had to suffer the consequences. This is what happened to Luca Gaurico when he predicted "una gran iattura" (a hex cast) on Giovanni Bentivoglio. Gaurico was subjected to torture (he was stretched on the ropes), then turned over to the inquisitor "as an invoker of demons and heretic," and his writings and prognostications were burned in the city square.[41] Another astrologer, Alfonso Pisano, was imprisoned by Pope Clement VII when he predicted the pope's death in 1533. He was kept in jail on bread and water for six months and then exiled.[42]

Relations between the astrologer and the ruler were further complicated when the astrologer took not only his prince's requirements into account as he compiled his predictions but also the needs of the general reading public. He then had to combine praise with propaganda and exhortation,

[38] Matteo Dandolo to Lorenzo Priuli, 25 February 1530, in Sanuto, *Diarii*, vol. 52, col. 638. The text of the prophecy, transcribed during March 1510, is also given in its entirety in Tommaso di Silvestro, *Diario*, ed. Luigi Fumi, in RIS 15, pt. 5 (Bologna: Nicola Zanichelli, 1923), vol. 2, p. 425.

[39] Girolamo Balbi, *De futuris Caroli Augusti successibus vaticinium* (Bologna: Giovan Battista Faelli, November 1529). Balbi published another work as well: *Ad Carolum V imperatorem De coronatione* (Bologna: Giovan Battista Faelli, 1530). On this work and on the symbolism of the coronation in general, see Tiziana Bernardi, "Analisi di una cerimonia pubblica. L'incoronazione di Carlo V a Bologna," *Quaderni storici* 61 (1986): 171–99.

[40] By Cesare Vasoli, *La cultura delle corti* (Bologna: Cappelli, 1980), pp. 129–58.

[41] Cherubino Ghirardacci, *Della historia di Bologna, parte terza*, ed. Albano Sorbelli, RIS 33, pt. 1 (Città di Castello: S. Lapi, 1912–1932), p. 342; Giuliano Fantaguzzi, *Caos. Cronache cesenati del sec. XV*, ed. Dino Bazzocchi (Cesena: Tip. Arturo Bettini, 1915), p. 231.

[42] The episode is narrated in the *Pronostico de lanno del 1538 per lo excellente maistro Alphonso Pisano: in laude del sumo Pontifice papa Paulo terzo vicario de Christo et de tutta la Christianitate* (n.p., n.d. [1538]), fol. 1*v*.

which was precisely what happened during the Congress of Bologna. Luca Gaurico was among the astrologers present,[43] but he does not seem to have written prognostications, nor did he take an active part in setting the date for the coronation (which, as is known, was chosen by Charles himself because it was both his birthday and the anniversary of the battle of Pavia). Still, we can in some fashion hear the voice of the man who was considered the prince of astrologers of his time through the person and pen of one Gasparo Crivelli from Milan, Gaurico's self-proclaimed disciple (to the point that Crivelli joined Gaurico's name to his own twice on the title page of the vernacular prognostications that he compiled and had printed in Bologna on 10 November 1529).[44] The prognostication (during the course of which Guarico's works are cited repeatedly) alternates between predictions of peace and prosperity for Italy, for the pope, and particularly for the emperor, and other more negative predictions concerning Süleyman and the city of Florence. The sultan was to be struck by the plague and every sort of disaster, to the point of losing his state "for the conjunctions of all the planets in Pisces that took place in 1524" (which means that when the sixteen terrible conjunctions had failed to bring on a flood, they were recycled to augur harm to the Turks). As for the Florentines, they were to have a change of government and to suffer "all sorts of misfortunes and so many shipwrecks that they will not know what to do." The predictions aimed at Francis I of France and for the Venetians were more ambiguous. Both were promised, though in equivocal terms, an encounter with the pope and with the emperor, "and thus they will treat of difficult things."[45]

As is evident, these predictions were suffused with propaganda and with adulatory intent, in particular where Charles V was concerned. The imperial fortunes were associated with the fortunes of all those (and only those) who accepted alliance with the emperor and fell in with his aims; when all was said and done, Charles was the sole fixed point of reference in peace or for a just war and the center of a cosmos that was harmonious and content because it revolved around him. Crivelli also repeatedly exhorts the emperor to lead a crusade "against the enemies of and rebels to the Christian name," an expression that apparently covered both the Turks and the Lutherans. In another passage, one might argue, exhortation is concealed as

[43] Sanuto, *Diarii*, vol. 52, col. 503.

[44] *Pronostico De lo Anno M.D.XXX. de Gasparo Crivello Milanese Discipulo di M. Luca gaurico*, "Datum Bononiae die decimo novembris 1529." The title page bears an architectonic framework with cupids, candelabras, and griffins enclosing the title. At the bottom, an oval shield bears the words "Lucae Gaurici Neapoli." My observation is based on the copy conserved in the library of the Archiginnasio di Bologna.

[45] Ibid., fols. 3*r* and 4*r*.

prediction: Crivelli interprets two eclipses to mean "that before the end of four years the Church will be very well reformed."[46]

In predictions of this sort, reform of the Church, the crusade, and punishment of heretics and rebels were lumped together and founded on the idea of empire. They also contributed to that idea, enriching it and giving it added complexity. The vehicle of the annual prognostication in the vernacular guaranteed this ideology a broad distribution and lent it conviction. The prophetic possibilities inherent in the figure of Charles V could easily be made explicit, particularly since his coming to an agreement with the pope seemed likely to generate a solution to the problems that tormented Italy and Christendom.

Three Suns for a New Octavian

The religious and prophetic reading of the encounter between the pope and the emperor in Bologna is demonstrated by another episode as well. On 22 April 1531, Tommasino Lancellotti described in his chronicle a prodigious phenomenon that had appeared in the sky:

> And all the persons who were in the piazza of Modena said that there were three suns; every person marveled much at such a signal in the sky in this age, saying that in the time of Emperor Octavian three suns had appeared, [and] at that time universal peace was made for the entire world. God grant that this be so in the present, because for forty-nine years now there has been no peace in Italy, and never in the days of men who are living in the world has there been greater dearth than there is at present.[47]

The phenomenon of refraction alluded to here, known as parhelion (here triple parhelia), was commonly taken as "a fearful sign," and between 1485 and 1514 we find it noted in contemporary chronicles at least four times, always accompanied by expressions of terror. In 1536 it was called "most cruelly out of nature" in the *Gran prodigio di tre soli apparsi in Franza.*[48] Only in 1531 were the three suns considered an omen of "universal peace for all men" as "in the time of the Emperor Octavian." Tommasino Lancellotti was referring here to what a widespread medieval tra-

[46] Ibid., fols. 2*r* and *v*.

[47] Lancellotti, *Cronaca modenese*, vol. 3, pp. 238–39.

[48] Leone Cobelli, *Cronache forlivesi*, ed. Giosuè Carducci and Enrico Frati (Bologna: Regia tipografia, 1874), pp. 284–85; Andrea Bernardi, *Cronache forlivesi . . . dal 1476 al 1517*, ed. Giuseppe Mazzatinti, 2 vols. (Bologna: R. Deputazione di storia patria, 1895–1897), vol. 1, p. 159; Tommaso di Silvestro, *Diario*, p. 11, Stefano Infessura, *Diario della città di Roma di Stefano Infessura scriba-senato*, ed. Oreste Tommasini (Rome: Forzani, 1890), p. 280. The phrase "un segno spaventoso" comes from Tommaso di Silvestro in the passage cited.

dition, publicized through preaching, considered to be one of the prophetic signs of the coming of Christ.[49] Vincent de Beauvais described it in the thirteenth century in these terms:

> The day after [the death of Caesar] there appeared three suns in the East, which gradually united again into one sun, foretelling that the triumvirate of Lucius Antonius, Mark Antony, and Augustus would be transformed into a monarchy; and above all that the knowledge of a God one and three was then imminent in all the world.[50]

The three suns that appeared after the death of Caesar were thus considered both an imperial sign and a religious sign, the interpretation of which went back to the providential reading of the empire of Augustus given in the Middle Ages as a necessary background of peace for the birth of Christ. That the parhelia could be interpreted as an "imperial" sign explains why they were considered an omen of peace by those who gathered in the main square of Modena. The passage of the new Caesar Augustus and his coronation in Bologna, which had taken place only a few months earlier, seemed to have launched a new Golden Age. That made it necessary to read positively a sign that in all other instances was considered inauspicious.

This interpretation can only be hypothetical, but it is clarified and confirmed by a passage on the three suns that had appeared the year before written by Friedrich Nausea, bishop of Vienna, in his *Libri mirabilium septem* in 1532. Among the many prodigies that had occurred in 1531, Nausea writes, paraphrasing Vincent de Beauvais without mentioning him, the parhelia, or three suns, were of particular interest, because they recalled the suns that appeared after the death of Caesar and that foretold both the advent of a universal monarchy after the triumvirate and the cult of a three-in-one God. Nausea continues:

> And may the heavens grant that in the present circumstances as well the three suns signify that the same cult will become established, even among the Turks, under the most invincible and most Christian princes, Charles V, emperor and Ferdinando, most glorious king of the Romans, God be their highest guide!

Nausea had a few doubts about this. He remembered that in other circumstances the three suns were an inauspicious prodigy. Thus he states

[49] Carlo Delcorno, *Giordano da Pisa e l'antica predicazione volgare* (Florence: L. S. Olschki, 1975), pp. 264–66, demonstrates that the prodigy of the three suns was part of the repertory of *exempla* of late medieval preaching. See also Bernardino da Siena, *Le prediche volgari*, ed. Ciro Cannarozzi, 7 vols. (Pistoia: Alberto Pacinotti, 1934–), vol. 2, p. 278.

[50] Vincentius Bellovacensis, *Bibliotheca Mundi. Tomus qui Speculum Historiale inscribitur* (Douai, 1644), bk. 6, chap. 41, p. 187: "Die sequenti apparuerunt tres soles in oriente, qui paulatim in unum corpus solis redacti sunt, significantes quod dominium Lucii Antonii et Marci Antonii et Augusti in Monarchiam rediret. Vel potius quod notitia trini Dei et unius toti orbi futura imminebat."

(and we thank him for it) that in furnishing these suggestions, he is by no means basing his thought on the canonical laws of augury and astrology ("haud quaquam sim sequuturus leges nec Prophetarum, nec Astronomorum, nec Astrologorum, nec Augurum, nec Auspicum") but only on the traditions handed down by his elders, founded on the oral transmission of certain rules:

> Rather will I follow the criteria of those old men with white hair who, basing themselves on long experience and attentive comparison and reciprocal confrontation of many events past and present, predict future [events] with great certainty and finesse, and evaluate in substantially accurate manner what the greater part of the celestial and terrestrial signs signify and foretell.[51]

Thus we see a hint of the "popular divination" that we have already seen and that was the common fodder of the city dwellers who gathered in the squares to compare the *mirabilia* that appeared in the heavens, or that they were shown for a few pennies at the fairs and the taverns, with the marvels pictured on the broadsheets or described by the *cantastorie*. The very term, "popular divination"—*genus divinationum . . . populare vel plebeium*—was used in this same sense by Kaspar Peucer, Melanchthon's son-in-law. According to Peucer, this was divination that did not look deeply into the cause of events or into the profound relationship between omens and the events they signified, but rather recalled and compared past omens and events, arriving at the establishment of divinatory rules that give foreknowledge of the future "satis foeliciter."[52]

Although Nausea was a bishop and a humanist, then, he was aware of and could manipulate criteria of "common" and "popular" divination. He soon abandoned this terrain, however, to return to the atmosphere of a different and higher culture, citing an epigram of the Neapolitan poet Girolamo Borgia on the three suns. Among the works of Borgia, who lived from 1475 to about 1550, there were an unpublished *Historia de bellis italicis*, a poem with a divinatory background entitled *Incendium ad Avernum Lacum nocte intempesta exortum*, and a number of verse compositions in praise of Charles V.[53] In his epigram on the three suns, Borgia outdid himself, however. After evoking the prodigy of Augustus's days, as tradition dictated, he continues:

[51] Friedrich Nausea, *Libri mirabilium septem* (Cologne: apud P. Quentell, 1532), fols. 33*v* and 30*r*: "Atque utinam ii nostra quoque tempestate tres soles subsinnent eundem vel apud Turcas cultum, sub invictissimis et christianissimis principibus Carolo Imp. V et Ferdinando Rhomanorum [*sic*] rege gloriosissimo, duce Deo rediturum!"; "Sim sequuturus . . . dumtaxat normas canorum senum, qui longo usu et diligenti rerum praeteritarum et praesentium comparatione mutuaque collatione freti nonnunquam certius exquisitiusque presagiunt et signa plerumque caeli et terrae quid haec ipsa nobis velint et portendant non impie diiudicant."

[52] Kaspar Peucer, *Commentarius de praecipuis divinationum generibus* (Wittenberg: Johannes Crato, 1553), fols. 40*r* and *v*.

[53] See Gianni Ballistreri, "Borgia (Borgio), Girolamo," DBI, vol. 12, pp. 721–24.

Pandite, mortales, oculos in caligine mersos
numen et in terris cernite esse novum.

Charles V was thus not only the new Augustus but also a new divinity, and his holy and imperial vocation, his *numen*, was proclaimed to the ends of the earth:

Caesar numen habet radios a margine mundi
victores mittens; omnia iura domat.

Charles V's device, with two columns and the motto *Plus oultre*, expressed a notion similar to the one implied in these hexameters. Furthermore, the discovery and Christianization of new worlds had very clearly defined prophetic implications.[54] It is certain, however, that one of the missions Providence had set the Sun God was to extend his rays to the confines of the world and bring back within the *res publica christiana* the savages of the new Indies, whom Borgia defines as "genus ille ferum." No one could withstand him, because it was God's will that he come, god himself:

Hic est ille deus demissus Numine terris;
longo expectatus tempore Caesar adest,
omnes qui terras teneat ditione sub una,
qui domitet Turcas ac genus ille ferum.
Caesaris imperio populi parete volentes,
caesaris imperium credite iussa Dei.[55]

Thus an exceptional harvest of prophecies common to men of learning and to popular literature (with evident reciprocal influences) accompanied the start of a new Golden Age. The medieval image of the emperor of peace had dissolved into that of the new Caesar Augustus, a transformation, incidentally, that was due not only to reasons of general historical evolution or the mere triumph of classical tradition over the medieval tradition but also to the need to express, albeit in encomiastic form, an urgent and real need for peace and political and economic stability, clearly identifiable through the realization of a concrete model "of Octavian, emperor."[56]

[54] See Adriano Prosperi, "America e Apocalisse. Note sulla 'conquista spirituale' del Nuovo Mondo," *Critica storica* 13 (1976): 1–61 and the bibliography contained in that article; Yates, *Astraea*, p. 31.

[55] Nausea, *Libri mirabilium septem*, fol. 34*r*.

[56] One excellent indication of this attitude is the title of a brief work of four leaves, *Il priegho d'Italia detto su'l Pater Nostro fatto al sommo iddio nel quale il priegha voglia liberarla dalle longhe guerre, miserie et affanni, de i quali per longho tempo e stata afflitta et gli piaccia renderli quella libertà che gia hebbe prima et darli pace universale come hebbe al tempo d'Augusto con altri capitoli. Cosa molto degna et bella di nuovo stampata* (n.p., n.d.).

EPILOGUE

1530: The End of Popular Prophecy: The End of Liberty in Italy

STRANGE TO SAY, after the Congress of Bologna the various forms of prophecy that until then had been so lively among the Italian urban populations died out almost simultaneously. The three years between 1527 and 1530 seem to signal the apex of street-corner prophecy and were soon followed by its collapse. This is particularly true of the forms of prophecy best adapted to oral transmission, which were less standardized and could seek a broader range of means of communication. Prophetic print pieces suddenly disappeared from the market; prophetic preaching from the pulpit had already virtually died out (we have seen the singular case of Zaccheria da Fivizzano); hermits continued to circulate, but with every-increasing difficulty, censured from on high and derided on all sides. It is also interesting to note that the decline of popular prophecy had no parallel in other parts of Europe; indeed, in France and England prophecy began to be established only after 1530 and lasted to the mid-seventeenth century.[1]

The "monsters," for their part, had a curious destiny. In Germany the Reformation saw to it that they continued to fulfill their ominous mission,[2] but in Italy they were gradually transformed into curiosities in museums

[1] See, in particular, Katharine R. Firth, *The Apocalyptic Tradition in Reformation Britain, 1530–1645* (Oxford and New York: Oxford University Press, 1979), pp. 10–13; and Elisabeth Labrousse, *L'Entrée de Saturne au lion. L'éclipse de soleil du 12 août 1654* (The Hague: M. Nijhoff, 1974). See also Anne Jacobson Schutte, " 'Such Monstrous Briths': A Neglected Aspect of the Antinomian Controversy," *Renaissance Quarterly* 38 (1985): 85–106.

[2] That Melanchthon in particular retained an interest in monsters is well known and especially applicable here. See Stefano Caroti, "Comete, portenti, causalità naturale e escatologia in Filippo Melantone," in *Scienze, credenze occulte, livelli di cultura. Convegno internazionale di studi (Firenze, 26–30 giugno 1980)* (Florence: L. S. Olschki, 1982), pp. 293–426. Another interesting case is the collection of *terata* that the Zurich canon Johann Jakob Wick inserted in his journals, at Bullinger's suggestion, precisely in order to reach a better understanding of the "catastrophic times" in which he lived. (The diaries, written between 1560 and 1588, are now conserved in the Zentralbibliothek of Zurich.) See Matthias Senn, *Johann Jakob Wick (1522–1588) und seine Sammlung von Nachrichten zur Zeitgeschichte* (Zurich: Leeman, 1974) and, for the print pieces on monsters under consideration here, Brigitte Schwarz, "Johann Jacob Wick e la sua raccolta di fogli volanti a soggetto mostruoso," tesi di laurea discussa presso l'Università di Bologna, a.a. 1985/86, relatrice Ottavia Niccoli. In general, see Robin Bruce Barnes, *Prophecy and Gnosis: Apocalypticism in the Wake of the Lutheran Reformation* (Stanford, Calif.: Stanford University Press, 1988).

or anatomical exhibits. When in 1550 in Modena a domestic cat gave birth to a deformed kitten, no one thought to draw prognostications from the event. However, one Geminiano de' Rossi, who found the dead kitten, had it embalmed and kept it as "a monstrous thing."[3] The exhibition of deformed creatures was of course no novelty, but here it seems to fit better in a *Wunderkammer* (admittedly of minimal size) than at a village fair. In any event, the divinatory function that abnormalities had once had no longer existed. That is not all. We have seen that between the fifteenth and the sixteenth centuries monsters in some fashion represented the finger of God pointed at the sins of humankind, but predominantly at their political sins and, to some extent, their social sins. They highlighted such matters as the corruption of the ecclesiastical hierarchy, the decline in civic virtue and religion in urban life, or cowardly vacillation before the Turkish menace. Somewhere between 1525 and 1550 an important transformation took place in this area, and around 1550 monsters once again became a sign of sin, but of a private sin—indeed the most private of all sins, because they were held to be clamorous proof of the parents' transgression of sexual taboos, in particular the mother's, whose fault was consenting to sexual relations during menstruation.[4] This was a highly significant shift in the ongoing process of the narrowing of sexual ethics during the latter half of the sixteenth century and an intensification of the negative conception of women and their bodies as a direct source of corruption. Thus monsters were still some sort of sign, but no longer were they to be deciphered by the criteria dictated by orally transmitted lore (as the *divinatio popularis* was transmitted by the elders of the community). They were a manifest result of improper conjugal behavior, visible to all eyes, and needed no help from divinatory science to be understood. Eventually physicians were called upon to decide whether the cause of a "monstrous" conception was this or another. The accent, however, had shifted from a relationship of sign and signified to one of cause and effect.

From Expectation of a New Age to the Age of Repression

Thus far I have sought to interpret a cultural phenomenon as a unified entity and global culture that aimed at encompassing nature, history, and the supernatural in a single act of comprehension. One might well wonder whether the nearly instantaneous end of a cultural phenomenon of this

[3] Tommasino Lancellotti, *Cronaca modenese,* ed. Carlo Borghi, 12 vols. (Parma: P. Fiaccadori, 1863), vol. 9, p. 210.

[4] See Ottavia Niccoli, " 'Menstruum quasi monstruum' parti mostruosi e tabù mestruale nel '500," *Quaderni storici* 44 (1980): 402–28.

importance was connected with a process of exhaustion within that culture, or whether it resulted predominantly from outside repression.

In all probability, the two hypotheses should be combined. I have sought to analyze, particularly in the first and last chapters of this book, the immediate and conscious relationships that operated within the minds of those who transmitted the cultural values of prophecy and linked it to the calamities of the Italian wars. The relationship was complex, but it was stated so explicitly and with so much insistence that it is impossible to doubt its existence. Andrea Bernardi, to pick one example, stated that there had been many forewarnings of the arrival of the French, chief among them "the many prophecies of many saints" that had circulated throughout Italy. He also comments:

> That does not mean that the said prophecies showed no celestial influence: but everyone everywhere among the peoples of Italy prognosticated and wanted to speak of [their] coming for the bad government and great rapine of our said Italian lords, for truly there was nothing left of us but bones, because they had taken the blood and the flesh.[5]

Urban prophecy was thus born of dissatisfaction with the present situation, and it encouraged an openness toward political novelties. These novelties in turn generated prophecies, in an apparently continual exchange of cause and effect. As Matarazzo wrote, "in those times there were found and newly published prophecies without end . . . because in those times Italy began to do new things everywhere."[6] As we have just seen, in one sense the tremendous increase in prophecy in 1529–1530 was a mirror image of the preceding fifty years. Where in the decades before the catastrophe, all prophecy focused on expectation of reform and renewal, afterward it expressed the triumphal fulfillment of those expectations. Prophecy was a language of medieval origin, even though it attempted to emphasize its total embodiment in one real political situation after another, and it is quite comprehensible that by 1530 it should have become somewhat threadbare. Even without considering the wearing out of a tradition, prophecy so to speak signed its own death warrant in 1530, for when all prophecies are fulfilled, prophecy itself has no further reason for being. For that reason widespread acceptance of the notion that Charles V's descent into Italy, his pact with the pope, and his coronation truly signaled fulfillment of the predictions of the advent of a sovereign of peace and the beginning of an era of renewal for both Christendom and the empire could not help but result in a lessening of prophetic tension. There is something

[5] Andrea Bernardi, *Cronache forlivesi . . . dal 1476 al 1517,* ed. Giuseppe Mazzatinti, 2 vols. (Bologna: R. Deputazione di storia patria, 1895–1897), vol. 1, pt. 2, p. 72.

[6] Francesco Matarazzo (detto Maturanzio), *Cronaca della città di Perugia dal 1492 al 1503,* ed. Ariodante Fabretti, *Archivio storico italiano* 16, pt. 2 (1851), p. 16.

else, however. These events seemed to signal the end of a catastrophic period of wars and disasters. To recall the words of Tommasino Lancellotti that have already been cited:

> In the time of Emperor Octavian . . . universal peace was made for the entire world. God grant that this be so in the present, because for forty-nine years now there has been no peace in Italy, and never in the days of men . . . has there been greater universal dearth.

These words go far to explain the sudden decline of public prophecy after 1530. Although armed combat did not cease entirely,[7] there was greater political and military stability in the Italian peninsula and the situation as a whole seemed radically changed. The phase of the "liberty of Italy" had ended, but continual harassment by the horrors of war slackened for people all over Italy. This was why prophecy had run its course. Conversely, the relation between war and prophecy seems confirmed by the fact that in other parts of Europe, where wars of religion still gripped the population, apocalyptical tensions continued to be strong until the end of the Thirty Years War, only to die out with the end of that conflict and the rise of a new balance of power in Europe.[8]

The coronation in Bologna also opened a new period in ecclesiastical life in Italy (and not only in Italy, to tell the truth). The urban prophecy examined here was doubtless an aspect of the strong expectations of a new age that permeated society from the latter half of the fifteenth century.[9] As we have seen, the relationship between novelty and prophecy is clear in both Bernardi and Matarazzo. After 1530 it is clear that pressures for renewal and reform (particularly reform of the Church) tended to peter out, giving way to a period in which the ecclesiastical hierarchy closed ranks and reorganized to combat the spread of heresy. All direct forms of relationship with the supernatural were judged to be dangerous and came under increasingly stringent control. A number of phenomena that had been characteristic of religious life in the fifty years between 1480 and 1530 thus either ground to a halt or were suffocated. We know, for example, that one specific model of female saintliness centering on charisma, with strong prophetic tendencies and demonstrably capable of attracting groups of followers, died out or was repressed precisely around the same time. Supernatural visions, which previously had been accepted as a singular but not anoma-

[7] See Bernardo Nobile, " 'Romiti' e vita religiosa nella cronachistica italiana fra '400 e '500," *Cristianesimo nella storia* 5 (1984): 303-40; p. 337.

[8] See above, note 1, and Josef V. Polisensky, *The Thirty Years War,* tr. Robert Evans (Berkeley: University of California Press, 1971), p. 76.

[9] See, in particular, the studies published in *L'attesa dell'età nuova nella spiritualità della fine del medioevo. Convegno del 16–19 ottobre 1960)* (Todi: Accademia tudertina, 1962); and Eugenio Garin, *"L'età nuova. Ricerche di storia della cultura del XII al XVI secolo* (Naples: Morano, 1969).

lous part of the life of piety and had been repeatedly documented, re-elaborated, and retold, met with constantly increasing mistrust and reprobation.[10]

The forms of prophecy that have been examined in these pages also came under increasingly rigid control, but something else happened as well. We have seen that on various occasions (with the "monsters" of Ravenna and Bologna and the apparitions at Verdello and in the letter of Giovanni Antonio Flaminio to Leo X) ecclesiastical "high" culture manipulated, re-elaborated, and turned to its own purposes elements that more properly belonged to the prophecy of "low" culture. Paradoxically, the classical and Ciceronian culture that flourished at the papal court and in the circles around it during the years of Leo X's papacy and the early years of Clement VII favored this habit. Interest in the world of classical antiquity brought with it a renewed fascination with the *monstra, prodigia,* and *portenta,* a fascination that popular divination, for its part, pursued indefatigably. During the decade between 1520 and 1530 these intense interchanges between high and low culture declined steadily, and after 1530 the elites rejected any sort of involvement with the world of folklore. Models of saintliness, visionary experience, and pious practices that had roots in folk traditions were defined as superstitious; divination in all its aspects, *divinatio popularis* in particular, was rejected more and more decisively. Such attitudes add up to what we would have to call the Counter-Reformation, a conventional but efficacious term.

Divination, An Iniquitous and Female Art

In 1578 a work was published in Florence entitled *Discorso contro il volgo in cui con buone ragioni si reprovano molte sue false opinioni.* It was the work of Cosme de Aldana, a Spaniard. Among other topics that he treated, Aldana reproved a number of popular beliefs (and in some cases, people's failure to believe), for example, that the common people derided astrologers and refused to believe in them, maintaining their own divinatory beliefs

> in which because a dog barks in a certain way . . . you say, if anyone is sick in the neighborhood, he will die. . . . You do not leave anything on earth to which you do not give some significance.[11]

[10] Ottavia Niccoli, "Visioni e racconti di visioni nell'Italia del primo Cinquecento," *Società e storia* 28 (1985): 253–79; Adriano Prosperi, "Dalle 'divine madri' ai 'padri spirituali,' " in *Women and Men in Spiritual Culture: XIV–XVIII Centuries,* ed. Elisja Schulte van Kessel (The Hague; Netherlands Govt. Pub. Office, 1986), pp. 71–90; Gabriella Zarri, "Le sante vive. Per una tipologia della santità femminile nel primo Cinquecento," *Annali dell'Istituto italo-germanico in Trento* 6 (1980): 371–445.

[11] Cosme de Aldana, *Discorso contro il volgo in cui con buone ragioni si reprovano molte sue false opinioni* (Florence: G. Marescotti, 1578), pp. 264-65. On astrology, see pp. 250–63.

The contrast between the learned science of astrology and popular divination was clearly defined, as is evident today and as contemporaries were well aware. It is interesting that Aldana went on to liken this contrast to the one between learned and popular medicine (as he says, between *medici* and *ciarlatani*), in which the physicians were scorned by the common people, who heeded only the charlatans.[12] Still, Aldana's total contempt for the low science of divination is singular; Leo X or Guicciardini, not to mention an artisan, a merchant, or a notary, would never have expressed such a thought fifty or sixty years earlier.

So *divinatio popularis* was rejected. It survived somewhat longer among the common people, however, in particular, as Aldana says, among "certain ignorant and silly old enchantresses and charm purveyors," women who went about "throwing flour on a polished table on St. John's Eve to forecast the husband their daughter would have." The same women, he continues, attempt to heal the sick "with their [spells], part conjuration, part old wives' sayings [*parole da veglia*] or comic expressions, [and] with certain measurements of the palm to be made (they say) with the heart hand."[13] Aldana's criticism reflects an ancient polemic against healers—*vetulae*—that began with Thomas Aquinas.[14] Nonetheless, these words show early traces of a more specific phenomenon that was to take shape during the second half of the sixteenth century and run its course by the end of the century. A work published in Venice in 1599, written by Giuseppe Passi and entitled *I donneschi diffetti* shows that we have returned to the climate of revived misogyny discussed earlier. Some passages of this work merit closer examination, however. Passi deplores the wicked arts—*"arti scellerate"*—proper to women that consist in "wanting to know things that are to come." It was not the learned science of astrology that he had in mind; for that he refers his readers to the *Disputationes contra astrologiam* of Giovanni Pico. He was alluding instead to the "thousand superstitions" of women, such as their custom of observing birds and heeding their cries,

> their casting spells with odd and even numbers, with letters, [and] with figures attributed to the celestial signs . . . like [their] casting straws of uneven length, considering the designs that show in molten lead, drawing points on a tablet or a stone with one's face turned to the moon, selecting beans [blindfolded], and similar folderol and vanities put to use by women. . . . Now it is clear, *madonne,* and there is no "maybe" about whether these spells that you use superstitiously are legitimate, for if you chance to lose as much as a penny,

[12] Ibid., p. 231.

[13] Ibid., pp. 266 and 232.

[14] See Jole Agrimi and Chiara Crisciani, "Medici e 'vetulae' dal Duecento al Quattrocento: problemi di una ricerca," in *Cultura popolare e cultura dotta nel Seicento: Atti del convegno di studi Genova, 23–25 novembre 1982* (Milan: Franco Angeli, 1983), pp. 144–59.

immediately like a dog after a hare you run for the shears and the sieve to see if so-and-so stole it from you . . . with a thousand silly and vain words, thinking that the sieve will move when you pronounce your superstitious words.[15]

By reading between the lines of Passi's reproaches to women we can grasp a number of magic practices, which are corroborated in Inquisitorial trials of the sixteenth and seventeenth centuries. We also see traces of the *libri delle sorti* that were immensely popular during the sixteenth century.[16] Divination in these spell books was increasingly colored by a desire to entertain—though Passi seems not to have been amused. Finally, it is interesting to find the divinatory technique of the movement of a sieve suspended from the point of a pair of shears mentioned here. The procedure was already known to Pomponazzi, Tommaso Campanella had tried it personally, and it was known in England as well.[17]

Passi presents an interesting and varied array of divinatory practices and techniques, but it should be noted that he attributes them solely and in all circumstances to women, in opposition to astrology, which—by implication, to be sure—seems reserved to men. Pomponazzi, by contrast, speaks of the shears and the sieve as a technique practiced by charlatans and tale singers, thus as a predominantly male technique. From a sort of divination exclusive to the subalternate classes—to the *volgo,* to use Aldana's term—we have shifted over to a divination specific to another subalternate world, the world of women. With these women's procedures we have reached the last residue, the last shreds, of the prophetic culture that I have sought to reconstruct in these pages. They are scattered, however, and stripped of any coherence. Tied to purely private concerns, they are powerless to read the supernatural world, the world of nature, or human society (thus politics and history) in any sort of unified manner.

Indeed, the channels of diffusion for prophetic culture had been blocked once and for all. The element that perhaps had given them their greatest breadth—the swift and diversified circulation of cultural entities through a variety of social levels and circles—had stopped quite a while earlier. In all

15 Guiseppe Passi, *I donneschi diffetti* (Venice: Iacobo Antonio Somascho, 1599), pp. 141–45. Scipione Mercurio, who wrote approximately at the same time, considered "this art . . . more exercised by women than by men": Scipione Mercurio, *De gli errori popolari d'Italia libri sette* (Padua: Matteo Cadorino, 1658), p. 311.

16 See Ottavia Niccoli, "Gioco, divinazione, livelli di cultura. Il Triompho di Fortuna di Sigismondo Fanti," *Rivista storica italiana* 96 (1984): 591–99 and the bibliography contained therein.

17 Pietro Pomponazzi, *De naturlium effectuum admirandorum causis, Et de incantationibus liber* (Basel: ex officina Henricpetrina, [1567]), p. 55; Tommaso Campanella, *Del senso delle cose e della magia,* ed. Antonio Bruers (Bari: G. Laterza & figli, 1925), p. 300. For England, see Keith Thomas, *Religion and the Decline of Magic* (New York: Scribner, 1971), pp. 213–14.

probability, prophecy did not totally die out, however. Further study could certainly discover remaining traces even in the late sixteenth century, for example, in the sect of "Benedetto corazzaro" (Benedetto the armorer) in Venice, or among the followers of Giorgio Siculo, or again among the nuns of the convent of San Lorenzo in Bologna.[18] But the political and public use of the prophetic and visionary experience—in short, its civic dimension—had certainly ended. What once took place in the city squares now retired behind closed doors in houses, in the confessional, and in the cloister, isolated and relegated to an exclusively private domain. Expectation of the new age had meant religious, political, and cultural palingenesis, but now there were no more new ages to forecast and await. The time for prophecy had ended; the time for utopias had not yet begun.

[18] Carlo Ginzburg, "Due note sul profetismo cinquecentesco," *Rivista storica italiana* 78 (1966): 184–227; Prosperi, "Dalle 'divine madri.' "

Index

Printed in the United States
21668LVS00001B/215

9 780691 008356

Samples of Student Writing

Exploring Literature

Exploring Literature

Writing and Thinking About Fiction, Poetry, Drama, and the Essay

Frank Madden
SUNY Westchester Community College

New York San Francisco Boston
London Toronto Sydney Tokyo Singapore Madrid
Mexico City Munich Paris Cape Town Hong Kong Montreal

Editor-in-Chief: Joseph Terry
Acquisitions Editor: Erika Berg
Development Editor: Katharine Glynn
Marketing Manager: Melanie Goulet
Supplements Editor: Donna Campion
Media Supplements Editor: Nancy Garcia
Production Manager: Donna DeBenedictis
Project Coordination, Text Design, Art, and Electronic Page Makeup: Elm Street Publishing Services, Inc.
Cover Designer/Manager: John Callahan
Cover Illustration: "Flying People Holding Up Book" by Janet Atkinson, courtesy of The Stock Illustration Source, Inc.
Photo Researcher: Joanne Polster / Photosearch, Inc.
Senior Manufacturing Buyer: Dennis J. Para
Printer and Binder: Quebecor World–Taunton
Cover Printer: Phoenix Color Corp.

For permission to use copyrighted material, grateful acknowledgment is made to the copyright holders on pp. 1500–1508, which are hereby made part of this copyright page.

Library of Congress Cataloging-in-Publication Data

Madden, Frank.
Exploring literature / Frank Madden.
p. cm.
Includes index.
ISBN 0-321-01183-X (alk. paper)
1. Reader-response criticism. 2. Books and reading. 3. Literature—History and criticism—Theory, etc. I. Title.

PN98.R38 M27 2001
808—dc21 00-061366

Please visit our website at http://www.ablongman.com/madden

ISBN 0-321-01183-X

1 2 3 4 5 6 7 8 9 10—RNT—03 02 01 00

For Sharon, Michelle, and Suzanne

❧

BRIEF CONTENTS

DETAILED CONTENTS

CHAPTER 5
Research and Documentation: Writing with Secondary Sources 201

PART III *A Thematic Anthology* 233

FAMILY AND FRIENDS 234

FICTION

POETRY

DRAMA

ESSAYS

Case Studies in Composition

HERITAGE AND IDENTITY 811

FICTION

POETRY

FICTION

POETRY

DRAMA

ESSAYS

Case Studies in Composition

ALTERNATE CONTENTS BY GENRE

FICTION

POETRY

DRAMA

ESSAYS

PAINTING

a rich context for research. A student writer describes his identification with the pull of family in James Joyce's *Eveline* and investigates conditions in Ireland that prompted the vast migration of the Irish. A narrative of the student's process precedes the essay. Finally, the section on Faith and Doubt contains a case study, **"Thinking About Interpretation, Poetry, and Painting"** that includes nine famous paintings and poems written about them. All case studies include a student essay illustrative of the approach.

The Literary Selections

The literature in this book, a broad selection of both classic and contemporary pieces, has been chosen for its quality, diversity, and appeal to students. Of special note are 13 plays, including the classics, *Oedipus Rex, Antigonê, Othello, Hamlet, A Doll's House, The Glass Menagerie, A Raisin in the Sun,* and contemporary plays like August Wilson's *Joe Turner's Come and Gone,* David Mamet's *Oleanna,* and Wendy Wasserstein's *The Man in a Case.*

Writing About Literature

Throughout this text—from journals to formal critical and research essays—students use writing to learn about literature. The use of writing as an important instructional tool in literature classes is well documented. Students who examine their own practices in reading and writing become more self-aware, more independent, and stronger readers and writers.

Samples of Student Writing There are 18 student essays and many other samples of students' writing throughout the chapters and case studies.

Questions and Prompts

Questions and prompts throughout this book tap students' responses without implying right or wrong answers. They help students flesh out, clarify, and support their responses and encourage them to ask their own questions—questions that open up, not shut down, additional possibilities. These prompts respect the reader's role and encourage divergent responses, but emphasize that the value of an assertion lies not in itself but in the nature of its supporting evidence.

Critical Thinking

Whether they are reviewing their own judgments or citing evidence to support a critical essay, students are encouraged to think critically about their responses throughout this book. Of special note is Chapter 4, "Argumentation: Interpreting and Evaluating," which focuses directly on the process of critical thinking and argumentation. Explanations, examples, and exercises guide students through the process of inductive reasoning and substantiation, interpretation and evaluation, and planning and supporting an argument. Issues of purpose, audience, and evidence are central to this discussion. The final section of this chapter exemplifies the process of critical thinking and argumentation by following a student's progress from initial journal entry to a final draft of a critical essay.

Voice

The narrative voice of *Exploring Literature* is informal and conversational. This book is intended to be read by students—to be accessible, friendly, and informative.

ORGANIZATION: USING THIS TEXT

Exploring Literature can be used in many different ways. Its explanations, prompts, and literature are resources to be chosen by instructors and students as needed, in or out of sequence, with maximum flexibility. Although the reading and writing activities in this book are organized in a sequence of increasing complexity, the recursive nature of both writing and responding to literature is emphasized throughout. The construction of a coherent interpretation is a continuous process of responses that frequently change with rereading and reflection.

For instructors who want to emphasize a reader-response approach, have students write journals, reading logs, or response essays about literature. **Part I, "Making Connections,"** provides a rich source of material. These chapters are more than an exploration of literature. They are an exploration of the students who read and write about the literature in these chapters. Students are encouraged to think about the ways that their backgrounds and personalities, their understanding of others, their knowledge of texts and contexts—their "meaning making" processes—influence their responses to literature. Questions that accompany the literature help students clarify their responses and develop them into text-supportable hypotheses and essays. **Chapter 1, "Participation: Personal Response and Critical Thinking,"** helps students develop connections to literature through their backgrounds and experiences. **Chapter 2, "Communication: Writing About Literature,"** introduces students to aspects of literary craft through discussions of voice, description, and comparison—fostering the sensitivity to language necessary for a complete experience with literature. The chapter concludes with a discussion of the writing process, samples of drafts, and a final response essay.

Instructors who favor a more text-based approach may choose to skip Part I and move directly to **Part II, "Analysis, Argumentation, and Research." Chapter 3, "Exploration and Analysis: Genre and the Elements of Literature,"** emphasizes the importance of close reading and analysis. General introductions to fiction, poetry, drama, and the essay are followed by a comprehensive explanation of the elements that make each a distinct form. Carefully chosen literary selections illustrate and support these explanations. The drama section includes background information on Greek, Shakespearean, and Modern Drama, as well as tips on reading the language of Shakespeare. Wherever possible, explanations of the elements are illustrated with reference to students' experiences and are accompanied by specific examples from literature in the text.

Chapter 4, "Argumentation: Interpreting and Evaluating," guides students through the process of critical thinking, reading, writing, and research. Students are reminded of the ways in which they use critical thinking in their lives and how similar methods of analysis and support can be used to interpret and evaluate literature. Inductive thinking, substantiation, interpretation, and evaluation are discussed. The use of argumentation to develop critical essays is presented and supported by student entries, giving students insights into how to develop their own ideas. Based on the elements discussed in Chapter 3, students are provided with questions, prompts, and checklists to help them develop standards. A comprehensive discussion of argumentation helps students see the difference between response and critical essays and suggests specific questions to ask when constructing an effective argument. The chapter concludes with an examination of a student's process and product from journal entry to final draft of a critical essay.

Chapter 5, "Research and Documentation: Writing with Secondary Sources," completes Part II with a discussion of writing using secondary sources. Explanations and exercises help students integrate secondary sources into their writing. This chapter explores popular areas of research to help students choose a research paper topic and gives information about searching for sources in the library and on the Internet, as well as helps students to learn to take notes, document sources, and use MLA format. It concludes with a sample student research essay.

Part III, "A Thematic Anthology," organizes the four genres of literature under five compelling themes: Family and Friends, Women and Men, Heritage and Identity, Culture and Class, and Faith and Doubt. Each category includes the location of a comprehensive introduction to each of the genres. As mentioned earlier, the literature in this book has been chosen for its quality, diversity, and appeal to students. These stories, poems, plays, and essays represent a broad selection of both classic and contemporary literature. For those who prefer a genre approach, an alternative table of contents organizes the literature under the categories of fiction, poetry, drama, and essays. This table of contents follows the Detailed Contents.

Each theme opens with a photograph and a series of short provocative quotations, a "Dialogue Across History," that provide a historical context for the literature that follows. An introductory statement about the theme and a brief statement about the literature included under that theme follow. In each section, one work of literature is highlighted and followed by two student papers written from different perspectives about the selected work. These essays illustrate a diversity of opinion, exemplify ways in which the literature might be "read," and demonstrate how students' experiences, behaviors, values, and opinions are tools for deepening their understanding and appreciation of literature. "Case Studies in Composition" follow the literature in each section. These case studies are a resource for interpretation and biography; interpretation in cultural and historical context; interpretation and performance; interpretation, culture, and research; and interpretation, poetry, and painting.

The **Appendix, "Critical Approaches to Literature,"** is a succinct discussion of major critical theories. The **Glossary** provides a useful reference tool as it outlines literary terms for students.

Supplements

Instructor's Manual An Instructor's Manual with detailed comments and suggestions for teaching each selection is available in print and online. This important resource also contains references to critical articles and books that we have found most useful. ISBN 0-321-02740-X

***Exploring Literature* Website** The *Exploring Literature* website can be found at http://www.ablongman.com/madden. This site includes in-depth information about featured authors, activities for writing about literature, as well as helpful links to literature and research sites.

Audio- and Videotapes For qualified adoptors, an impressive selection of videotapes and Longman audiotapes is available to enrich students' experience of literature.

Penguin Program In cooperation with Penguin Putnam Inc., one of Longman's sibling companies, we are proud to offer a variety of Penguin paperbacks at a significant discount when packaged with any Longman title. Excellent additions to any literature course, Penguin titles give students the opportunity to explore contemporary and classic fiction and drama. Available titles include works by authors as diverse as Julia Alvarez, Mary Shelley, Shakespeare, and Toni Morrison.

Daedalus Online Daedalus Online is an Internet-based collaborative writing environment for students. The program offers prewriting strategies and prompts, computer-mediated conferencing, peer collaboration and review, and comprehensive writing support. For educators, Daedalus Online offers a comprehensive suite of online course management tools. For information, visit http://daedalus.pearsoned.com, or contact your Longman sales representative.

English Pages (http://www.ablongman.com/englishpages) This website provides professors and students with continuously updated resources for reading, writing, and research practice in four areas: composition, literature, technical writing, and basic skills. Features include simulated searches, where students simulate the process of finding and evaluating information on the World Wide Web; first-person essays that show students how everyday men and women have applied what they have learned in composition to a wide variety of writing issues and research topics.

The Longman Guide to Columbia Online Style This 32-page booklet includes an overview of Columbia Online Style (COS), guidelines for finding and evaluating electronic sources and examples for citing electronic sources. COS is a documentation style developed specifically for citing electronic sources. *The Longman Guide to Columbia Online Style* is free when packaged with any Longman text.

***Researching Online,* Fourth Edition** Students will find this companion indispensable to their navigation of the Internet. It includes detailed information on Internet resources such as e-mail, listservs, and Usenet newsgroups; advanced techniques for using search engines; tips on how to assess the validity of electronic sources; and a section on HTML that shows students how to create and post their own Web pages.

Analyzing Literature This brief supplement provides critical reading strategies, writing advice, and sample student papers to help students interpret and discuss literary works in a variety of genres. Suggestions for collaborative activities and online research on literary topics are also featured, as well as numerous exercises and writing assignments.

The Essential Research Guide A handy two-page laminated card, *The Essential Research Guide*, features a table with guidelines for evaluating different kinds of print and online sources, a chart of editing and proofreading symbols, and a list of cross-curricular website resources.

ACKNOWLEDGMENTS

I am indebted to many people over the years who have had a direct and indirect influence on my teaching philosophy—and on the writing of this book. Most notable among these teacher-scholars is Louise Rosenblatt, my teacher at NYU nearly thirty years ago. In addition, John Clifford, Alan Purves, Peter Elbow, Wayne Booth, Robert Scholes, Ann Berthoff, Toby Fulwiler, Robert Berlin, Carl Schmidt, Cindy Onore, John Mayher, Dawn Rodrigues, Judith Stanford, Kathi Blake Yancey, and others have influenced and inspired my work. I am grateful to my generous colleagues at WCC: Bill Costanzo, who read the manuscript in its many stages with great care; Alan Devenish and Liz Gaffney, who contributed their own work; Joanne Falinski, Nick Schevera, Richard Courage, Mira Sakrajda, and others who tried out the materials, contributed ideas, and/or submitted student samples. I am grateful to my students who have taught me so much about teaching and this book, especially those students who contributed their work to this volume: Dierdre Curran, Christine Leibowitz, Suzanne McCloskey, Susan MacNaughten, Michelle McAuliffe, Julie Fitzmaurice, Sara Roell, Marie Tymon, Barbara Pfister, Trisa Hayes, Alejandro Ramos, Debora Van Coughnett, Charles Chiang, William Winters, Jennifer Stelz, Kevin Chamberlain, Janice Bevilacqua, Jacquelyn Webster, and others. I am indebted to President Joseph Hankin for fostering an atmosphere at WCC that made this work possible. And I am especially grateful to my brother John, who early in my life gave me a reason to care about literature, and to my wife, Sharon, who continues to be my most discerning reader and loving supporter.

For their thoughtful and insightful comments to many drafts of manuscript, I am very grateful to the following reviewers: Dr. Roger Arpin, Southeast Missouri State University; Mary Baron, University of North Florida; Jennifer Beech, University of Southern Mississippi; Greg Bernard, Illinois Valley Community College; Paul Bodmer, Bismarck State College; Carol Ann Britt, San Antonio College; James L. Brown, Kansas City Kansas Community College; Lennard Davies, Binghamton University; Ruth Elowtiz, Chabot College; Norma Cruz Gonzalez, San Antonio College; Lila M. Harper, Central Washington University; Cindy Hicks, Chabot College; Melynda Huskey, University of Idaho; Stephen P. M. Howard, Essex Community College; Alex Jakurowski, Orange County Community College; Timothy J. Jones, Oklahoma City Community College; Shawn Liang, Mohawk Valley Community College; Margaret Lindgren, University of Cincinnati; Cecilia Machski, LaGuardia Community College, City University of New York; Zack Miller, Brookhaven College; Dorothy Minor, Tulsa Community College; Nancy Moore, Edmonds Community College; Michael Morris, East Field College; Marsha Nourse, Dean College; Mark Punches, Oklahoma City Community College; Mark Reynolds, Jefferson Davis Community College; Denise Rodgers, University of Louisiana at Lafayette; Dawn Rodriques, University of Texas at Brownsville; Donald Rude, Texas Tech University; Alan Shaw, Monroe Community College; Chenliang Seng, Northern Kentucky University; Edward Smith, University of Central Florida; Dr. John Snyder, College of Staten Island, City University of New York; Margaret Snyder, Bergen Community College; Jacquelynn Sorenson, University of Nebraska at Lincoln; Dorothy Stephens, University of Arkansas; Phillip Sterling, Ferris State University; A. Janice Sumner, Hillsborough Community College; Nancy Taylor, California State at Northridge; Howard Tinberg, Bristol Community College; Carolyn Wall, Spokane Community College; Linda Wells, Boston University, College of General Studies; Evelyn Wilson, Tarrant County Junior College; John Venne, Ball State University; and Paula Dede Yow, Kennesaw State University.

At Longman, I am especially grateful to Katharine Glynn, whose intelligence, insight, experience, judgment, and comfort have meant so much to me throughout this long process. I am indebted to Lisa Moore whose vision and support made this book possible and to Tisha Rossi whose belief in its worth never wavered. I also wish to thank Melanie Goulet for getting the word out about this book so effectively, and Donna DeBenedictis, Ingrid Mount, and Caroline Gloodt for their dedication, fine work, and patience while turning a manuscript into a book.

Frank Madden
SUNY Westchester Community College

• ABOUT THE AUTHOR •

FRANK MADDEN

Frank Madden has a Ph.D. from New York University and is Professor and Chair of the English Department at SUNY Westchester Community College. He has taught in graduate programs at CCNY, Iona College, and the New School for Social Research, and in 1998 was Chair of the NCTE College Section Institute on the Teaching of Literature. He is a recipient of the SUNY Chancellor's Award for Excellence in Teaching, the Foundation for Westchester Community College Faculty Award for Excellence in Scholarship, and the Phi Delta Kappan Educator of the Year Award from Iona College. He was Chair of the College Section of the NCTE from 1995–1998 and has served on the Executive Committees of the NCTE, the MLA-ADE, the SUNY Council on Writing, and as Chair of the MLA ad hoc Committee on Teaching. He was recently elected Associate Chair and will become Chair of TYCA in 2001. His articles and chapters about the teaching of literature have appeared in a variety of books and journals, including *College English, College Literature, English Journal, Computers and Composition, Computers and the Humanities,* and the *ADE Bulletin.*

Exploring Literature

PART I

Making Connections

CHAPTER 1

Participation

Personal Response and Critical Thinking

We begin our exploration of literature with you, the reader. Your engagement creates the literary experience. By itself, the literature in this book, as brilliantly crafted or as famous or critically acclaimed as it may be, is just words on a page. It is your reading of these words through the lenses of your own experiences and beliefs that brings them to life and gives them meaning, a meaning ultimately as unique as you are.

Literature reveals a possible world to us. Our engagement and involvement are the keys to enter this world and to imagine its possibilities. Our backgrounds and personalities, our understanding of others, our prior experience with literature, our knowledge of the world—our sources for making meaning—are important factors in this process. And unlike our busy lives, which sometimes race forward with little time for reflection, literature awaits our examination. We can participate in it as we experience it, and analyze it as we step back and observe it.

The Personal Dimension of Reading Literature

Most literature does not intend to convey a moral or lesson. At its best, it reveals as life reveals. But like life, our *reading* of literature evokes our emotion and judgment. Narrators and literary characters express their beliefs in what they say or do, and as we read, we respond to their words and actions through our own beliefs—comparing their choices with our own, and approving or disapproving as they meet or fail to meet our expectations. While most good literature does not teach or preach, it does explore and reveal what it means to be human and provides us with a substantial opportunity for learning and self-understanding.

Later on in this chapter, and throughout the book, you are asked to think about your responses and to consider how your own experiences and beliefs influence them. Acknowledging, reviewing, and thinking critically about the judgments you make as you read may provide you with valuable insights into literature and yourself.

Personal Response and Critical Thinking

Thinking critically about literature is an outgrowth of our personal responses. It is natural for us to want to comprehend what moves us or has meaning to us. As children, we may have tried to make sense of what we read by making connections with other things we had read or experienced. We might have remembered reading something similar in another story or believed that a particular author would keep us in suspense. We knew which books we liked, and even if we didn't analyze our reading systematically, we may have wondered what made those stories appealing to us.

When we think critically about literature we build on our personal responses—recording them, reviewing them, discussing them, and supporting them. Being engaged is a crucial initial component of a complete literary experience. But once we experience this engagement and believe that literature has something to offer us, it follows that we want to know more about it, to see how it triggers our responses and judgments, to understand the skill with which it was created, and to articulate what it means to us.

Critical thinking does not mean searching for one right answer. There may be as many answers as there are readers. *Your* best answers are those that analyze and articulate your responses in the light of supporting evidence. This is critical thinking, a process that can make your opinions about literature well-informed ones.

Writing to Learn

Writing is an excellent way to learn about literature. Whether you are jotting down notes, writing in a journal, or constructing a formal essay, you're learning. You're learning when you struggle to choose the right words to describe your impressions, and when you revise those words because they are not quite what you mean. And you are learning when you "get it just right" and see your words match what you want to say. In short, writing your responses down helps you learn and articulate what you think and feel more clearly.

Keeping a Journal or Reading Log

One of the best tools for exploring and thinking about your experiences in writing is a journal or reading log, and you may find it helpful to keep one in which to record your responses to the literature in this book. Journals and reading logs can help you view and review your ideas. Writing and reading your words on paper may help you articulate, clarify, and expand your ideas. Use your journal to identify and express your reactions, what moves or bothers you, or what seems intriguing or confusing. Write in your most natural voice and don't worry about sounding wise. Take chances and try out ideas. Unless you decide to share them, you are the only one who will see these entries.

If you use your journal to keep a record of your responses, you can look back for connections later on. These responses, along with subsequent reading and the comments of classmates, can help you develop ideas as you write the essays required by your instructor. If you are conscientious about keeping your journal, your entries will evolve naturally into a statement of the meaning you've constructed from the work. In the long run, the most important ingredient in your essays will not be the position you take, but the support you derive from the literature and your experience with it. Recording these observations in your journal now may provide you with some of this support later.

What you write in your journal or log is your choice. It should be as unique as your experience with the literature itself. You may or may not like what you read. You may find it engaging or filled with meaning. You may find it confusing or boring. Whatever your response, you'll benefit most from keeping a journal or log if your entries honestly reflect your experience.

A variation of the journal is a **literature response sheet**. Like the journal, each response sheet accounts for your first impressions during and after your reading. Your instructor may collect them and use them to initiate class discussion.

There is no one correct way of keeping a journal or log. The student samples that follow are all different, but each is a start and might be built upon to develop a more formal essay. ("Araby" appears on p. 544 and "There's a Certain Slant of Light" on p. 1381.) Even if you are not familiar with these pieces, these samples reflect the kinds of issues that might be addressed in response to any work of literature.

From confusion:

I found the story of "Araby" to be a little confusing. I couldn't really fathom what the actual point of the story was. There is a boy whose name is not mentioned, and he apparently has some sort of infatuation with a nun. He spies on her, peering through a tiny crack in his shades. He ends up talking to her and telling her that if he goes to Araby, the bazaar, he will buy her a present because she cannot go.

I realize this is a very well written and powerful piece of writing not written in modern (today's) terms. The last line of the story intrigued me. "Gazing up into the darkness I saw myself as a creature driven and derided by vanity; and my eyes burned with anguish and anger."

I guess he said this because he did not buy her anything at Araby. I don't exactly know why. Maybe because he got there too late or maybe in the back of his mind he expected her to be there.

To an appreciation of the author's artistry:

The beginning of "Araby" was written with a lot of descriptive words. As soon as I began to read sentence by sentence, the words formed pictures in my mind. I got the feeling of a painting being painted stroke by stroke. The description of the street being blind and quiet except when the school set the boys free gave me a feeling of quiet and then sudden noise, as the boys came rushing through the streets. Describing the air as cold, the space of the sky ever-changing violet allowed me to feel the cold and see the colors.

From identification:

The first time I read the lines "There's a certain slant of light, / Winter Afternoons-- / That oppresses, like the Heft / of Cathedral Tunes--" I had an immediate picture of grayish-white skies and cold, bare ground. It was almost frightening. The first stanza expresses a feeling I've had for a lifetime of hideous, anxiety-filled, depressing Sunday winter afternoons. From childhood, with homework unfinished and school rearing its terrifying Monday-morning head, through adulthood and its end-of-the-weekend, back to work dread, I've experienced that "Seal Despair--."

To complete frustration:

I've read this poem over and over, repeatedly, non-stop, until I finally collapsed from total exhaustion. This must be the most confusing poem I've had the misfortune of stumbling upon.

WHAT DOES IT MEAN!? What light? The winter afternoon light? As heavy as cathedral tunes? Find a scar from what? Internal difference? Meanings? Aggggh!

Help. Could the author be talking about the sun? All I have are questions when it comes to this poem. I do like the choice of words, though. They sounded grand, royal, imperial, and made me feel like there was something to grab from them. I am disappointed in myself, and the people around me, who also couldn't make sense of it.

Double-Entry Journals and Logs

Because you may be asked to read and write comments about your journal or log entries from time to time, an especially effective format is the double-entry journal. By writing on only the front side of each page (or on the right half of each page), you will leave the back of the previous page (or the left half of each page) free for subsequent commentary (new ideas, revisions, summation, etc.) while rereading and reflecting. Leaving this space, you may go back later, read through your comments, circle and make notes about entries you've made, or add additional comments based on subsequent readings or class discussion.

I liked this story. I could tell by the way the author wrote that this was long ago in the early 1900s. It sounded like my grandfather's young life, but it's still timeless. I could relate what Joyce was saying to nowadays. I myself have felt that way. All your words and feelings are jumbled around one person. A crush. It's very stressful and exhilarating at the same time. I do have one question, though. Was the object of Joyce's desire and affection a nun? I thought maybe she was because she was always "clad in brown" and she couldn't go to Araby because her convent was having a meeting. I didn't feel that aspect was presented too clearly. Maybe I'm misreading. Overall, I enjoyed this story very much.

She's not a nun. I found out in class that parochial schools were sometimes called convent schools back then. You didn't have to be a nun to go there. That part of the story makes much more sense to me now.

It's very light compared to Antigone. After that story, everything seems a little happier. I'm pretty sure the girl was a nun, but it's never clearly stated.

The Social Nature of Learning: Collaboration

Writing ideas down is one effective way to learn, but so much of what we learn is also learned through conversation. Sharing our responses with others, and listening to their feedback and ideas, helps us build and clarify our own ideas.

By articulating what you think you know and what you need to know through conversation, you may develop a clearer understanding of the literature. Throughout this text you'll be encouraged to share and exchange your ideas and collaborate with your classmates in pairs and small groups.

Personal, Not Private

Many of the questions that follow in this chapter prompt you to write about personal issues. These questions are not an attempt to invade your privacy or encourage you to write about aspects of your life or experience that may embarrass you or make you feel uncomfortable. What is personal or private is very different for each of us. You may choose to write some responses for your eyes only, some to share or some not at all. That choice is always yours.

Ourselves as Readers

Our early experiences with books may have a significant influence on how we feel about reading. For many of us who enjoy reading, this joy was discovered outside the classroom. We felt free to experience the books we read without fear of having our responses judged as right or wrong. For many who do not like to read, however, reading was often a painful chore, usually an assignment for the classroom with all the accompanying pressures of being evaluated. How often we read now and whether we see ourselves as good readers may have much to do with these earlier experiences.

You might find it worthwhile to write about some of these reading experiences in your journal or share them with others. It may be illuminating to see how much you have in common as a reader with other members of the class.

Different Kinds of Reading

Unfortunately, for many of us, the different types of reading we were given in school were often treated the same way. Reading assignments that primarily dealt with content or factual information were often not distinguished from imaginative literature. We know, however, that different types of reading material require very different kinds of involvement. Reading a science text, for example, requires that we focus on acquiring information for future use, whereas a poem, play, or work of fiction, while requiring our understanding of the facts, seeks to involve us personally in the moment—to have us share an experience, to evoke our feelings.

Read the following paragraph.

> CAUTION—NOT FOR PERSONAL USE—If splashed on skin or in eyes, rinse immediately. If accidentally taken internally give large amounts of milk or water. Call a physician. Point mouth of container away from you when removing cap. AVOID TRANSFER TO FOOD OR BEVERAGE CONTAINERS—KEEP CONTAINER UPRIGHT IN A COOL PLACE TIGHTLY CAPPED.

➤ *GETTING STARTED—YOUR FIRST RESPONSE*

1. What is your response to the paragraph on page 7?
2. Of what use is the information in this statement?

Read the following poem.

PETER MEINKE (b.1932)

ADVICE TO MY SON [1981]

— for Tim

The trick is, to live your days
as if each one may be your last
(for they go fast, and young men lose their lives
in strange and unimaginable ways)
but at the same time, plan long range
(for they go slow: if you survive
the shattered windshield and the bursting shell
you will arrive
at our approximation here below
of heaven or hell).

To be specific, between the peony and the rose
plant squash and spinach, turnips and tomatoes;
beauty is nectar
and nectar, in a desert, saves—
but the stomach craves stronger sustenance
than the honied vine.
Therefore, marry a pretty girl
after seeing her mother;
speak truth to one man,
work with another;
and always serve bread with your wine.

But, son,
always serve wine.

➤ *GETTING STARTED—YOUR FIRST RESPONSE*

1. What is your reaction to this poem?
2. What advice do you think is being given?
3. Do you agree or disagree with this advice?
4. Of what use is the information in this poem?

➤ *QUESTIONS FOR READING AND WRITING*

Compare your response to the warning label paragraph with your response to the poem, "Advice to My Son."

1. Both the poem and the warning label give advice. In what way was your reading experience with each different?
2. Did the physical appearance of each influence *how* you read it? If the warning label were written in verse form would you have read it with different expectations?
3. To what extent can you connect the advice given in the poem to your own background or experience? To what extent can you connect the advice given in the warning label?
4. Did you learn anything from the poem? From the warning label? If so, did the *nature* of what you learned differ in each case? Explain.

The process of reading often raises more questions than it answers. After reading, some of the most important questions to address are the ones you have raised yourself. So before you answer the questions that follow each selection in this chapter, you may want to write down your first impressions and any questions that came to mind during and after your reading.

Making Connections

Among the many factors that influence our response to literature is identification with characters, circumstances, and issues. Our personalities, backgrounds, and experiences can have a strong impact on these connections.

We may identify with characters because we see aspects of our own personalities in them or admire aspects of their personalities and wish we had them ourselves. We might respond negatively to characters because aspects of their personalities are different than ours or similar to ones we don't like in ourselves. We may agree or disagree with what the characters say or do, or ask ourselves if we would have behaved the same way.

Conversely, by showing us a view of life that is different from our own, literature might influence our beliefs and behavior. We may learn from literature as we learn from life itself.

Images of Ourselves

How we view ourselves in relation to the world around us is very complex. We probably have an image of who we are that we carry within ourselves most of the time, but we are likely to project a different personality according to the situations (home, work, school, etc.) in which we find ourselves. Depending on our relationships with them, the people we know are also likely to describe us very differently. Our families, friends, casual acquaintances, employers, and teachers may experience who we are in very different ways.

➤ *MAKING CONNECTIONS—"Not Waving but Drowning"*

Many of us have had the experience of being told by people that once they got to know us they discovered we differed greatly from their earlier impression of us. Can you recall an experience like that in your own life? If so, try to remember how it made you feel to hear that.

STEVIE SMITH (1902–1971)

NOT WAVING BUT DROWNING [1957]

Nobody heard him, the dead man,
But still he lay moaning:
I was much further out than you thought
And not waving but drowning.

Poor chap, he always loved larking
And now he's dead
It must have been too cold for him his heart gave way,
They said.

Oh, no no no, it was too cold always
(Still the dead one lay moaning)
I was much too far out all my life
And not waving but drowning.

➤ *QUESTIONS FOR READING AND WRITING*

1. What do you think is happening in the poem? Who is drowning?
2. There is more than one speaker in this poem. Who are these speakers?
3. To what extent is your response to this poem affected by your own experience?

Culture, Experience, and Values

Who we are and how we respond to literature is also influenced by many other factors. Family, religion, race, gender, friends, other influential people in our lives, and our experiences shape our views in significant ways.

We may come from a family that is strongly connected to its ethnic roots, religious or not religious at all, closely knit or disconnected, warm and welcoming, suffocating, or cold and impersonal. Or we may not have a family at all. Our friends, too, may affect who we are, what we believe, and how we act.

We may be strongly influenced by our race, ethnic background, or gender. If we have never experienced or witnessed discrimination, we might not be able to understand its significance. If we have witnessed prejudice or had it directed against us, we know how devastating it can be. Our gender may affect the expectations others have for us, the encouragement we receive for education and career goals, marriage and family, even our involvement in sports. And it certainly influences our view of the opposite sex.

If we are deeply religious, it might be at the heart of everything we value. If we are not, our religious backgrounds may still exert a strong influence on our lives. What we do for a living, how old we are, our sexual orientation, our disabilities, or other factors may also affect how we see the world—and the literature we read.

➤ *MAKING CONNECTIONS—"Incident"*

If you have ever been called a derogatory name because of your race, ethnic background, gender, or other factor, you know how disturbing that experience can be. If you have ever been in this position or witnessed it happening to someone else, try to recall your reaction. If you've never been in this position, try to imagine how it might make someone feel.

COUNTEE CULLEN (1903–1946)

INCIDENT [1925]

Once riding in old Baltimore,
  Heart-filled, head-filled with glee,
I saw a Baltimorean
  Keep looking straight at me.

Now I was eight and very small,
  And he was no whit bigger,
And so I smiled, but he poked out
  His tongue, and called me, "Nigger."

I saw the whole of Baltimore
  From May until December:
Of all the things that happened there
  That's all that I remember.

➤ *QUESTIONS FOR READING AND WRITING*

1. Can you describe an event in your life that made such a lasting impression on you?
2. If you have experienced or observed an event like the one described in "Incident," how does this influence your response? If you have not experienced or observed an event like this, how does this affect your response to the poem?
3. If the speaker were describing a racist incident he experienced as an adult, how do you think the poem would be different? Why does the speaker say, "That's all that I remember"?
4. In what way does the title of the poem fit the poem's content?
5. How does the rhyme scheme of the poem affect your response to the poem's content?

➤ *MAKING CONNECTIONS—"Those Winter Sundays"*

Most of us can probably identify a person who was "always there" for us and who seemed to do the things that really mattered without being asked and who may often have been taken for granted.

Before you read the following poem, try to recall someone like that in your own life.

ROBERT HAYDEN (1913–1980)

THOSE WINTER SUNDAYS [1962]

Sundays too my father got up early
and put his clothes on in the blueblack cold,
then with cracked hands that ached
from labor in the weekday weather made
banked fires blaze. No one ever thanked him.

I'd wake and hear the cold splintering, breaking.
When the rooms were warm, he'd call,
and slowly I would rise and dress,
fearing the chronic angers of that house,

Speaking indifferently to him,
who had driven out the cold
and polished my good shoes as well.
What did I know, what did I know
of love's austere and lonely offices?

➤ *QUESTIONS FOR READING AND WRITING*

1. Describe the situation in the poem. Who is the speaker?
2. How does the speaker feel? Have you ever had similar feelings?
3. If you could identify a person who was "always there" for you, how does this remembrance influence your understanding of the poem?
4. What does the speaker mean by "love's austere and lonely offices"?
5. What other words, phrases, or parts of the poem had an impact on you? How so?

➤ *MAKING CONNECTIONS—"Barbie Doll"*

In a world that bombards us with images from television, films, and magazines, many of us feel great pressure to look or behave in particular ways. Sometimes this pressure may even make us value our own individual strengths less favorably than what is simply more popular. See if you can recall a time when you felt pressured this way and how you reacted to that pressure.

MARGE PIERCY (b. 1936)

BARBIE DOLL [1969]

This girlchild was born as usual
and presented dolls that did pee-pee
and miniature GE stoves and irons
and wee lipsticks the color of cherry candy.
Then in the magic of puberty, a classmate said:
You have a great big nose and fat legs.

She was healthy, tested intelligent,
possessed strong arms and back,
abundant sexual drive and manual dexterity.
She went to and fro apologizing.
Everyone saw a fat nose on thick legs.

She was advised to play coy,
exhorted to come on hearty,
exercise, diet, smile and wheedle.
Her good nature wore out
Like a fan belt.
So she cut off her nose and her legs
and offered them up.
In the casket displayed on satin she lay
with the undertaker's cosmetics painted on,
a turned-up putty nose,
dressed in a pink and white nightie.
Doesn't she look pretty? everyone said.

Consummation at last.
To every woman a happy ending.

➤ *QUESTIONS FOR READING AND WRITING*

1. To what extent is your response influenced by your own experience? Could you identify with the feelings of the "girlchild" in this poem?
2. The media bombards all of us with images that pressure us to act or look in a certain way. How does your experience with advertisements, television, movies, magazines, or newspapers influence your response to the poem?
3. Do you think a female reader is likely to respond differently to this poem than a male reader? Explain.
4. Do you think the "girlchild" is literally dead at the end of the poem? Explain.

5. What do you think "Consummation at last. / To every woman a happy ending." means?
6. What other words, phrases, or parts of the poem affected you? How so?
7. Compare this poem with "Advice to My Son" (p. 8). If Meinke's poem were called "Advice to My Daughter," do you think the advice would be the same?

The Whole and Its Parts

You've probably come across the statement "The whole is equal to the sum of its parts." Seems to make sense, doesn't it? Well, in some areas of study it does, but it cannot account for our response to literature. In literature and other artistic expressions, there is a whole that is greater than the sum of its parts, a whole that blossoms as the parts come together in our imaginations.

We don't like our favorite music because we identify the parts and add them up to a whole experience; we like it because we experience the sound of the instruments, the rhythms, the voices, the lyrics, all together and all at once. For all of us that means more than the sum of the notes or words we hear, and to each of us that means something different.

Like music, literature cannot be reduced to its parts to account for its meaning. But like music there are parts, and as we become more experienced listeners or readers we want to know how those parts work together. Later on in this book, we will try to comprehend the craft with which the parts are assembled. However, not until we believe the experience of literature has something to offer us will we care about the skill with which it was created, so for now, let's continue to explore how and what it means to us.

Participating, Not Solving

It's essential that we are *active* participants when we read or listen to imaginative literature. But if we look for the parts of a poem before we have experienced the whole, we may shut down the emotions we need to experience it—and miss the *life* of the poem. Placing ourselves *emotionally* inside the poem, rather than examining it *rationally* from the outside, enables us to feel and sense the words and images and lets these impressions wash over us. Poetry sometimes involves an imagining that is like our dreams and reveals things to us that are not always understood in rational ways.

However, like much of the "academic" reading we do, reading poetry occurs most often in school. And school, with its right and wrong answers, has a way of making us tense and rigid (and very rational). If you had heard (studied) some of your favorite songs and music for the first time in school, you might never have loosened up enough to like them at all. Poems are not math problems—they don't have one "correct" answer. They might not even "add up." The right answer is the one that makes the most sense to you, a "sense" supported by your own imagination and the text of the poem itself. Being confused and making mistakes along the way is part of the process of finding your own right answer.

Being in the Moment

We can't get at the heart of our experience with literature by summarizing it. We might account for all that matters on the "Caution" label on the bleach bottle (p. 7) by saying, "This is a very caustic liquid and you could hurt yourself by coming in contact with it." But we couldn't get at the essence of the poem "Incident" by saying, "A kid went to Baltimore, someone called him a name, and he's never forgotten it." We read the warning label for the information we take away with us; the label seeks to inform us. Literature seeks to involve us.

A newspaper article, for example, might relate the "who, what, when, where, and why" of an event, but literature must do much more than that. It may even move us to question events in our own lives and influence us as we make our own decisions. The following newspaper account appeared in The *New York Times* the day after the racially motivated bombing of a church in Birmingham, Alabama, in 1963.

BIRMINGHAM BOMB KILLS 4 NEGRO GIRLS IN CHURCH; RIOTS FLARE; 2 BOYS SLAIN

GUARD SUMMONED

Wallace Acts on City Plea
for Help as 20 Are Injured

By CLAUDE SITTON
Special to *The New York Times*
BIRMINGHAM, Ala., Sept. 15—[1963]

A bomb severely damaged a Negro church today during Sunday school services, killing four Negro girls and setting off racial rioting and other rioting in which two Negro boys were shot to death.

Fourteen Negroes were injured in the explosion. One Negro and five whites were hurt in the disorders that followed.

Some 500 National Guardsman in battle dress stood by at armories here tonight on orders of Gov. George C. Wallace. And 300 state troopers joined the Birmingham police, Jefferson County sheriff's deputies and other law-enforcement units in efforts to restore peace.

Governor Wallace sent the guardsmen and the troopers in response to requests from local authorities.

Sporadic gunfire sounded in Negro neighborhoods tonight, and small bands of residents roamed the streets. Aside from the patrols that cruised the city armed with riot guns, carbines and shotguns, few whites were seen.

Fire Bomb Hurled

At one point, three fires burned

(*continued*)

simultaneously in Negro sections, one at a broom and mop factory, one at a roofing company and a third in another building. An incendiary bomb was tossed into a supermarket, but the flames were extinguished swiftly. Fire marshals investigated blazes at two vacant houses to see if arson was involved.

The explosion at the 16th Street Baptist Church this morning brought hundreds of angry Negroes pouring into the streets. Some attacked the police with stones. The police dispersed them by firing shotguns over their heads. Johnny Robinson, a 16 year old Negro was shot in the back by a policeman with a shotgun this afternoon. Officers said the victim was among a group that hurled stones at white youths driving through the area in cars flying Confederate battle flags.

When the police arrived, the youths fled, and one policeman said he had fired low but that some of the shot had struck the Robinson youth in the back.

Virgil Wade, a 13-year old Negro, was shot and killed just outside Birmingham while riding a bicycle. The Jefferson County sheriff's office said "there apparently was no reason at all" for the killing, but indicated that it was related to the general racial disorders.

Wallace Offers Reward

Governor Wallace, at the request of city officials, offered a $5,000 reward for the arrest and conviction of the bombers.

None of the 50 bombings of Negro property here since World War II have been solved.

The four girls killed in the blast had just heard Mrs. Ellis C. Demand, their teacher, complete the Sunday School lesson for the day. The subject was "The Love That Forgives."

The blast occurred at about 10:25 A.M. (12:25 P.M. New York time).

Church members said they found the girls huddled together beneath a pile of masonry debris.

Parents of 3 Are Teachers

Both parents of each of the victims teach in the city's schools. The dead were identified by University Hospital officials as:

Cynthia Wesley, 14, the only child of Claude A. Wesley, principal of the Lewis Elementary School, and Mrs. Wesley, a teacher there.

Denise McNair, 11, also an only child, whose parents are teachers.

Carol Robertson, 14, whose parents are teachers and whose grandmother, Mrs. Sallie Anderson, is one of the Negro members of a biracial committee established by Mayor Boutwell to deal with racial problems.

Adie Mae Collins, 14, about whom no information was immediately available.

The blast blew gaping holes through walls in the church basement. Floors of offices in the rear of the sanctuary appeared near collapse. Stairways were blocked by splintered window frames, glass, and timbers.

Chief Police Inspector W. J. Haley said the impact of the blast indicated that at least 15 sticks of dynamite might have caused it. He said the police had talked to two witnesses who reported having seen a car drive by the church, slow down and then speed away before the blast.

➤ *GETTING STARTED—YOUR FIRST RESPONSE*

1. What is your response to this newspaper article?
2. Of what use is the information in the article?

3. To what extent does this information imply what is "between the lines"?

Read the following poem about the same event.

DUDLEY RANDALL (b. 1914)

BALLAD OF BIRMINGHAM [1964]

"Mother dear, may I go downtown
Instead of out to play,
And march the streets of Birmingham
In a Freedom March today?"

"No, baby, no, you may not go,
For the dogs are fierce and wild,
And clubs and hoses, guns and jails
Aren't good for a little child."

"But, mother, I won't be alone
Other children will go with me,
And march the streets of Birmingham
To make our country free."

"No, baby, no, you may not go,
For I fear those guns will fire.
But you may go to church instead
And sing in the children's choir.

She has combed and brushed her night-dark hair,
And bathed rose petal sweet,
And drawn white gloves on her small brown hands,
And white shoes on her feet.

The mother smiled to know her child
Was in that sacred place,
But that smile was the last smile
To come upon her face.

For when she heard the explosion,
Her eyes grew wet and wild.
She raced through the streets of Birmingham
Calling for her child.

She clawed through bits of glass and brick,
Then lifted out a shoe.
"O, here's the shoe my baby wore,
But, baby, where are you?"

➤ GETTING STARTED—YOUR FIRST RESPONSE

1. What is your response to this poem?
2. Of what use is the information in the poem?
3. If you were the mother in this poem, how would you have responded to the daughter's request?

➤ QUESTIONS FOR READING AND WRITING

1. Both the newspaper article and the poem recount the bombing. What makes the poem different than the newspaper account?
2. What did you learn from the newspaper account? What did you learn from the poem? How was the *nature* of what you learned different?
3. To what extent is your response to "Ballad of Birmingham" influenced by your own experience?
4. How does the rhyme scheme affect your response to the poem's content? The second and fourth lines of each stanza rhyme. How does this rhyme scheme and the rhythm of the poem affect you? How might it change your response if the first and third lines rhymed instead—or as well?

Imagining Is Believing

When we read, the strength of our emotional involvement is based on our ability to experience scenes as if we were there. If we "surrender" ourselves, we not only imagine the details provided, we create ones that are not. We may occasionally say, or hear people say "I liked the book better than the movie" or "I can't believe so and so was cast in that role." We probably mean, "I liked the movie of the book in my mind better than the movie on the screen" or "That actor is nothing like the character I created in my mind." Unless we complete the picture in our minds by filling in the details, we won't have a satisfying experience with literature.

Where do we get these details? Some of what we imagine is shared and comes from our cultural backgrounds. And some of what we imagine is personal and familiar and is fueled by our own experiences—the people, places, or events in our own lives. For example, it doesn't have to be summer for us to imagine the sun and heat on the beach—or winter for us to imagine snow. Through our "sense" memories, we can "recall" now what we felt and saw then. What we see in our "mind's eye" may also derive from music, television, film and other forms of media, and other things we have read.

➤ QUESTIONS FOR READING AND WRITING

1. How did you picture the house in Robert Hayden's poem "Those Winter Sundays"? What did the mother and the little girl look like in "Ballad of Birmingham"? Think about the pictures in your mind from other poems or stories you have read.
2. Where do your pictures come from?

3. How much of what you picture in each of these scenes come from detail that the author provided and how much completely from your imagination?

➤ *RESPONSE REVIEW*

If you've been keeping a journal or writing down other initial reactions, take a look back at your entries up to this point. Identify the factors that seem most important in your responses. Add any insights that may have occurred since writing or reading these entries.

CHAPTER 2

Communication

Writing About Literature

The goal in this chapter is to develop your initial responses into an essay about literature. We begin by emphasizing the response essay, but the habits of thinking and writing stressed in this chapter apply equally well to the critical essay explored in later chapters. Finding our writing voices; developing a clear thesis statement; showing what we mean through detail, illustration, and comparison; and citing evidence from the text are also core principles for writing a critical essay. Our emphasis on analysis, argumentation, and research in Chapters 3, 4, and 5 will complement and build on our discussion in this chapter.

THE RESPONSE ESSAY

In many ways, writing a response essay is like the journal writing described earlier. You can write in a conversational tone and explore personal connections and associations. You don't have to prove anything, but you do want to say something important enough to share with others.

Why would we want to share our experiences with literature? Perhaps the most compelling reason is the same one we have for communicating any other important event. Why do we discuss our experiences of movies, games, concerts, exhibits, or parties? Why do we chat about dates, meaningful events in our lives, or interesting people we have met?

Although some people need to impress others with their knowledge, accomplishments, or "important" acquaintances, many of us share because we have a need to "review" or "reexperience" with others, to have them say "I see what you mean" or "I understand why you were affected that way." We don't want advice; we want caring listeners. This kind of sharing has a give-and-take to it. We give a rendering of our experience, and we receive other people's understanding, affirmation, and appreciation—their participation. It's not "scoring points" or *proving* we are right; it's an experience in itself.

The purpose of a response essay is to invite readers into our experience with literature—not to win an argument. If the voice in our writing, the reader's sense of who we are, is that of a "sharer," not a prosecuting attorney, the essay will feel like a welcome invitation, not a summons. Readers are better able to see when we *show,* not *show off.* The strength of their involvement is based on how much they care about what we share. Our voice in presenting that experience strongly influences their level of interest. For readers who accept our invitation, "I see what you mean" takes on a literal dimension. The clarity and thoughtfulness with which we write will determine how glad they are that they came.

Voice and Writing

Finding Our Voices Few would question the importance of voice in the realm of speaking and listening. Accurately or not, we often make judgments about people's personalities by the sounds of their voices. It would not be unusual to hear someone say, "She sounds like someone I can trust" or "He sounds like a phony." On the other hand, when we speak to a friend, we know that our own voices will usually sound (and feel) more comfortable and confident than when we inquire about a job, ask someone for a date, or speak to a large audience. The sound of our voices and the style with which we speak are bound to be influenced by our level of comfort, to whom we are speaking, and what we want from the communication. It is not surprising, then, that we give so much attention to how we sound and the words we use when we are concerned about making an impression.

For example, leaving a message for incoming calls on a phone answering machine seems like a very simple procedure. But if you have ever recorded or witnessed someone recording a message of this kind, you know that it usually takes more than one try to "get it right." Getting it right, of course, has a lot to do with our situations and who we think will be calling. The kind of message we might leave to amuse our friends is likely to be very different than the one we would want a prospective employer to hear as we await the results of a job interview.

Voice in Writing We know that the tone of voice we use when speaking is likely to make an impression—that *how* we say the words out loud can convey as much meaning as the words themselves. But speech and writing are different. We can think about and revise most writing, but speech is usually spontaneous, and we don't revise what we say in normal conversation. Spontaneous speech contains lots of stops and false starts and sound fillers that would look silly in writing. Unless we say something especially memorable or inflammatory, we're confident these words won't be heard (or read) over and over again. So, what does voice have to do with writing?

Virtually all of us learned to speak before we learned to read. Throughout our lives, we've been conditioned to hear the words we read. As children, many of us said the words out loud as we read to ourselves. Even if we don't move our lips or say the words out loud now, it's difficult to read them without triggering the nerves that activate speech and help us to "sub-vocalize" and hear the words voiced in our minds.

So, too, readers of our writing want to hear our voices—to get a sense of who we are. As writers we are conscious of this. For example, when writing a letter or an e-mail message our voices may change according to whom we send it, what we want, and how we want to be perceived. In a personal letter to an old friend we are probably free "to be ourselves." Our friends know us, and usually we're not anxious about the impression we will make. We are confident they will recognize our voices in the words. However, when writing a letter "To the Editor," flirting with a new romantic interest, or applying for a job, our voices are likely to be quite different. We may want to convey a sense of responsibility, wisdom, wit, or whatever else we can demonstrate to make a positive impression.

What we write about may also have a strong influence on how we are heard. As you might imagine, we write with more feeling and a clearer, stronger voice about issues that move us. Here too, we write with more confidence when we are sure of our audience. Those entries that are private (and for our eyes only) are likely to be different than those we know will be read by others. Those entries written for our friends or agreeable classmates will probably be different than those written for an unknown audience.

Voice and Response to Literature

Showing and Telling Most of us are best convinced when we see for ourselves. It would certainly seem risky to buy a car "sight unseen." We would probably insist on seeing it, trying it out, getting the "feel" of it before we decided to buy. When we talk with friends about a concert, game, or party, we probably wouldn't settle for "It was great." Again, we would like to get the "feel" of it, to hear the details, to imagine ourselves there, to share the experience.

As readers, we have a similar need. We are not likely to settle for being told an issue is compelling or trivial; an event exciting, suspenseful, or sad; a character fascinating, dull, or manipulative. We want to be moved by the issue, to be present at the event, to know the character for ourselves. Writers' voices are believable when we experience characters and events with them—when the conclusions ("exciting," " sad," "dull") are ours—when we are shown, not simply told.

The entries that follow were written in response to Countee Cullen's "Incident" (p. 11). It's a short poem, so if you haven't read it you might want to do that now and write your own response before you read the entries below.

Nick's Response:

I know how the young boy felt. I was made to feel inferior in the school I attended as a child because I was Italian and poor. He could no longer see the beautiful things in Baltimore. He was hurt so deeply by being called "nigger." I'm sure this affected the rest of his life. His ego had to be smashed now that the other boy made him conscious of prejudice. He must have been very angry and would always remember this incident. It must have caused him to see the color of one's skin as being a bad thing and therefore he felt as though he was bad. I could relate to the hurt that he felt. It makes you feel very inferior and blocks your vision from other things in life because you feel as though you must hide somewhere.

Ellen's Response:

I've witnessed this kind of prejudice. When I was a freshman in high school, there was one black student in my homeroom class. His name was Jon. Our school was about 99.9 percent white. Every morning was hell for Jon. The "in-crowd" football-playing heroes would always harass him. Not just the ones who belonged in my homeroom, even seniors would make the trip to our classroom to call Jon names like "licorice," and "boy," and all the other juicy racial slurs. Jon never seemed to be affected by this ignorance, but he was probably dying inside. He would just turn away.

One morning, one of the football heroes got very personal with his attack toward Jon. Jon turned and leered at him. The white football hero yelled at him, "Boy! Did I say you could look at me?" Then he got up and punched Jon. Jon fought back. (The teacher never saw any of the harassment, I don't know why.) Jon and Mr. Football Hero went to the principal's office. Jon got suspended. Mr. Football Hero didn't get in trouble; he went to lunch.

Doris's Response:

My own experience of being a woman had influence over my response. I once asked a contractor to do some renovations on my home. I was asked to make an appointment to discuss the work and was told to make it "only when your husband is home so we can talk to him."

I felt sadness for the child who was so hurt by the word "nigger." To be so cruel to lash out at another person in a sensitive area. Words can cut like a knife. We are all born equal and do not ask for our sex, race, color, or ethnic backgrounds. We are just born into them. Each of us needs to be sensitive to each other.

Trudy's Response:

I was called a name when I was young at school and didn't know anyone and never spoke to anybody. So a group of girls decided to call me a "Jamaican body scratcher." I knew how he felt and what he was experiencing at the time. At the time he was small and traveling to Baltimore for the first time. He was looking out the window, seeing all kinds of sights, but it so happened that he tried to be friendly and was called a "nigger."

No matter what color or what race you are, you cut a white man, he bleeds red blood. You cut a black man, he bleeds red blood. So I think it's about time racism should stop.

➤ *QUESTIONS FOR READING AND WRITING*

1. How were the responses of Nick, Ellen, Doris, and Trudy influenced by their experiences?
2. Consider your response to the poem. How does it compare to theirs? Does reading their responses affect your own response to the poem? If so, how?
3. To what extent have they "shown" what they've told?
4. Which entries seem most effective to you? What factors seem to make them effective?
5. Read your own response to the poem. How does the voice in your response compare with those you've just read?
6. How would you describe the voice in Countee Cullen's poem "Incident"? What factors make it effective?
7. In what way is "showing" a factor in both the poem and the responses to it? What scenes, details, words, or phrases had the biggest impact on you?

Before you answer the questions after the following selections, you may want to write down your first impressions and any questions that come to mind during and after your reading.

➤ *MAKING CONNECTIONS—"Eleven"*

From our perspectives as adults, many of the problems of childhood may seem relatively unimportant. However, what may seem unimportant to us now may have affected us very differently when we were growing up.

Can you remember what it was like to be an eleven-year-old? See if you can recall an event that you found especially humiliating or embarrassing at that age. Try to remember what you were feeling and what you found especially difficult about the experience.

SANDRA CISNEROS (b. 1954)

ELEVEN [1983]

What they don't understand about birthdays and what they never tell you is that when you're eleven, you're also ten, and nine, and eight, and seven, and six, and five, and four, and three, and two, and one. And when you wake up on your eleventh birthday you expect to feel eleven, but you don't. You open your eyes and everything's just like yesterday, only it's today. And you don't feel eleven at all. You feel like you're still ten. And you are—underneath the year that makes you eleven.

Like some days you might say something stupid, and that's the part of you that's still ten. Or maybe some days you might need to sit on your mama's lap because you're scared, and that's the part of you that's five. And maybe one day when you're all grown up maybe you will need to cry like if you're three, and that's okay. That's what I tell Mama when she's sad and needs to cry. Maybe she's feeling three.

Because the way you grow old is kind of like an onion or like the rings inside a tree trunk or like my little wooden dolls that fit one inside the other, each year inside the next one. That's how being eleven years old is.

You don't feel eleven. Not right away. It takes a few days, weeks even, sometimes even months before you say Eleven when they ask you. And you don't feel smart eleven, not until you're almost twelve. That's the way it is.

5 Only today I wish I didn't have only eleven years rattling inside me like pennies in a tin Band-Aid box. Today I wish I was one hundred and two instead of eleven because if I was one hundred and two I'd have known what to say when Mrs. Price put the red sweater on my desk I would've known how to tell her it wasn't mine instead of just sitting there with that look on my face and nothing coming out of my mouth.

"Whose is this?" Mrs. Price says, and she holds the red sweater up in the air for all the class to see. "Whose? It's been sitting in the coatroom for a month."

"Not mine," says everybody. "Not me."

"It has to belong to somebody," Mrs. Price keeps saying, but nobody can remember. It's an ugly sweater with red plastic buttons and a collar and sleeves all stretched out like you could use them for a jump rope. It's maybe a thousand years old and even if it belonged to me I wouldn't say so.

Maybe because I'm skinny, maybe because she doesn't like me, that stupid Sylvia Saldivar says, "I think it belongs to Rachel." An ugly sweater like that, all raggedy and old, but Mrs. Price believes her; Mrs. Price takes the sweater and puts it right on my desk, but when I open my mouth nothing comes out.

10 "That's not, I don't, you're not . . . Not mine," I finally say in a little voice that was maybe me when I was four.

"Of course it's yours," Mrs. Price says. "I remember you wearing it once." Because she's older and the teacher, she's right and I'm not.

Not mine, not mine, not mine, but Mrs. Price is already turning to page thirty-two and math problem number four. I don't know why but all of a sudden

I'm feeling sick inside, like the part of me that's three wants to come out of my eyes, only I squeeze them shut tight and bite down on my teeth real hard and try to remember today I am eleven, eleven.

Mama is making a cake for me for tonight, and when Papa comes home everybody will sing Happy birthday, happy birthday to you.

But when the sick feeling goes away and I open my eyes, the red sweater's still sitting there like a big red mountain. I move the red sweater to the corner of my desk with my ruler. I move my pencil and books and eraser as far from it as possible. I even move my chair a little to the right. Not mine, not mine, not mine.

15 In my head I'm thinking how long till lunchtime, how long till I can take the red sweater and throw it over the schoolyard fence, or leave it hanging on a parking meter, or bunch it up into a little ball and toss it in the alley. Except when math period ends Mrs. Price says loud and in front of everybody, "Now, Rachel, that's enough," because she sees I've shoved the red sweater to the tippy-tip corner of my desk and it's hanging all over the edge like a waterfall, but I don't care.

"Rachel," Mrs. Price says. She says it like she's getting mad. "You put that sweater on right now and no more nonsense."

"But it's not—"

"Now!" Mrs. Price says.

This is when I wish I wasn't eleven, because all the years inside of me—ten, nine, eight, seven, six, five, four, three, two, and one—are pushing at the back of my eyes when I put one arm through one sleeve of the sweater that smells like cottage cheese, and then the other arm through the other and stand there with my arms apart like if the sweater hurts me and it does, all itchy and full of germs that aren't even mine.

20 That's when everything I've been holding in since this morning, since when Mrs. Price put the sweater on my desk, finally lets go, and all of a sudden I'm crying in front of everybody. I wish I was invisible but I'm not. I'm eleven and it's my birthday today and I'm crying like I'm three in front of everybody. I put my head down on the desk and bury my face in my stupid clown-sweater arms. My face all hot and spit coming out of my mouth because I can't stop the little animal noises from coming out of me, until there aren't any more tears left in my eyes, and it's just my body shaking like when you have the hiccups, and my whole head hurts like when you drink milk too fast.

But the worst part is right before the bell rings for lunch. That stupid Phyllis Lopez, who is even dumber than Sylvia Saldivar, says she remembers the red sweater is hers! I take it off right away and give it to her, only Mrs. Price pretends like everything's okay.

Today I'm eleven. There's a cake Mama's making for tonight, and when Papa comes home from work we'll eat it. There'll be candles and presents and everybody will sing Happy birthday, happy birthday to you, Rachel, only it's too late.

I'm eleven today. I'm eleven, ten, nine, eight, seven, six, five, four, three, two, and one, but I wish I was one hundred and two. I wish I was anything but eleven, because I want today to be far away already, far away like a runaway balloon, like a tiny *o* in the sky, so tiny-tiny you have to close your eyes to see it.

➤ *QUESTIONS FOR READING AND WRITING*

1. If you could recall a childhood event that you found humiliating or embarrassing, how did that memory influence your response to this story?
2. How does the voice of the narrator affect your response?
3. What does the speaker mean when she says, "the way you grow old is kind of like an onion or like the rings inside a tree trunk or like my little wooden dolls that fit one inside the other"?
4. What other passages in the story had an impact on you? How so?
5. If you find the voice of the story convincing, what features of the writing seem to make it effective? To what extent does the story "show" what is told?

➤ *MAKING CONNECTIONS—"Mothers"*

We would all probably like some things in our lives to be different. Before you read the essay that follows, see if you can think of something in your life that you wish was different. If that "something" were different, how might it change your life? Would everything be better? Might anything be worse?

ANNA QUINDLEN (b. 1953)

MOTHERS [1988]

The two women are sitting at a corner table in the restaurant, their shopping bags wedged between their chairs and the wall: Lord & Taylor, Bloomingdale's, something from Ann Taylor for the younger one. She is wearing a bright silk shirt, some good gold jewelry; her hair is on the long side, her makeup faint. The older woman is wearing a suit, a string of pearls, a diamond solitaire, and a narrow band. They lean across the table. I imagine the conversation: Will the new blazer go with the old skirt? Is the dress really right for an afternoon wedding? How is Daddy? How is his ulcer? Won't he slow down just a little bit?

It seems that I see mothers and daughters everywhere, gliding through what I think of as the adult rituals of parent and child. My mother died when I was nineteen. For a long time, it was all you needed to know about me, a kind of vestpocket description of my emotional complexion: "Meet you in the lobby in ten minutes—I have long-brown hair, am on the short side, have on a red coat, and my mother died when I was nineteen."

That's not true anymore. When I see a mother and a daughter having lunch in a restaurant, shopping at Saks, talking together on the crosstown bus, I no longer want to murder them. I just stare a little more than is polite, hoping that I can combine my observations with a half-remembered conversation, some anecdotes, a few old dresses, a photograph or two, and re-create, like an archaeologist of the soul, a relationship that will never exist. Of course, the question is whether it would have ever existed at all. One day at lunch I told two of my closest friends that what I minded most about not having a mother was the absence of that grown-up woman-to-woman relationship that was impossible as a child or adolescent, and that my friends were having with their mothers now. They both looked at me as though my teeth had turned purple. I didn't need to ask why; I've heard so many times about the futility of such relationships, about women with business suits and briefcases reduced to whining children by their mothers' offhand comment about a man, or a dress, or a homemade dinner.

I accept the fact that mothers and daughters probably always see each other across a chasm of rivalries. But I forget all those things when one of my friends is down with the flu and her mother arrives with an overnight bag to manage her household and feed her soup.

5 So now, at the center of my heart there is a fantasy, and a mystery. The fantasy is small, and silly: a shopping trip, perhaps a pair of shoes, a walk, a talk, lunch in a good restaurant, which my mother assumes is the kind of place I eat at all the time. I pick up the check. We take a cab to the train. She reminds me of somebody's birthday. I invite her and my father to dinner. The mystery is whether the fantasy has within it a nugget of fact. Would I really have wanted her to take care of the wedding arrangements, or come and stay for a week after the children were born? Would we have talked on the telephone about this and that? Would she have saved my clippings in a scrapbook? Or would she have meddled in my affairs, volunteering opinions I didn't want to hear about things that were none of her business, criticizing my clothes and my children? Worse still, would we have been strangers with nothing to say to each other? Is all the good I remember about us simply wishful thinking? Is all the bad self-protection? Perhaps it is at best difficult, at worst impossible for children and parents to be adults together. But I would love to be able to know that.

Sometimes I feel like one of those people searching, searching for the mother who gave them up for adoption. I have some small questions for her and I want the answers: How did she get her children to sleep through the night? What was her first labor like? Was there olive oil in her tomato sauce? Was she happy? If she had it to do over again, would she? When we pulled her wedding dress out of the box the other day to see if my sister might wear it, we were shocked to find how tiny it was. "My God," I said, "did you starve yourself to get into this thing?" But there was no one there. And if she had been there, perhaps I would not have asked in the first place. I suspect that we would have been friends, but I don't really know. I was simply a little too young at nineteen to understand the woman inside the mother.

I occasionally pass by one of those restaurant tables and I hear the bickering about nothing: You did so, I did not, don't tell me what you did or didn't do, oh, leave me alone. And I think that my fantasies are better than any reality could be. Then again, maybe not.

➤ *QUESTIONS FOR READING AND WRITING*

1. To what extent is your response to this essay influenced by your own experience?
2. How does the voice of the narrator affect your response? In what way does she "show" what she tells?

3. What does the speaker mean when she says, "My mother died when I was nineteen. For a long time, it was all you needed to know about me"?
4. What other passages in the essay had an impact on you?
5. If you find the voice of the story convincing, what features of the writing seem to make it effective?

➤ *MAKING CONNECTIONS—"Salvation"*

The desire for approval can be a very strong incentive when making important decisions. Making a decision that meets with the disapproval of our parents or others we respect can be difficult and emotionally painful—even if we believe that we've made the right choice. We may even have strong ethical reasons for taking a position, yet feel reluctant to disappoint those with whom we have emotional ties.

Try to recall an event in your life when the pressure of approval was a major factor in an important decision. Try to remember what you were feeling at the time.

LANGSTON HUGHES (1902–1967)

SALVATION [1940]

I was saved from sin when I was going on thirteen. But not really saved. It happened like this. There was a big revival at my Auntie Reed's church. Every night for weeks there had been much preaching, singing, praying, and shouting, and some very hardened sinners had been brought to Christ, and the membership of the church had grown by leaps and bounds. Then just before the revival ended, they held a special meeting for children, "to bring the young lambs to the fold." My aunt spoke of it for days ahead. That night I was escorted to the front row and placed on the mourners' bench with all the other young sinners, who had not yet been brought to Jesus.

My aunt told me that when you were saved you saw a light, and something happened to you inside! And Jesus came into your life! And God was with you from then on! She said you could see and hear and feel Jesus in your soul. I believed her. I had heard a great many old people say the same thing and it seemed to me they ought to know. So I sat there calmly in the hot, crowded church, waiting for Jesus to come to me.

The preacher preached a wonderful rhythmical sermon, all moans and shouts and lonely cries and dire pictures of hell, and then he sang a song about the ninety and nine safe in the fold, but one little lamb was left out in the cold. Then he said: "Won't you come? Won't you come to Jesus? Young lambs, won't you come?" And he held out his arms to all us young sinners there on the mourners' bench. And the little girls cried. And some of them jumped up and went to Jesus right away. But most of us just sat there.

A great many old people came and knelt around us and prayed, old women with jet-black faces and braided hair, old men with work-gnarled hands. And the church sang a song about the lower lights are burning, some poor sinners to be saved. And the whole building rocked with prayer and song.

5 Still I kept waiting to *see* Jesus.

Finally all the young people had gone to the altar and were saved, but one boy and me. He was a rounder's son named Westley. Westley and I were surrounded by sisters and deacons praying. It was very hot in the church, and getting late now. Finally Westley said to me in a whisper: "God damn! I'm tired o' sitting here. Let's get up and be saved." So he got up and was saved.

Then I was left all alone on the mourners' bench. My aunt came and knelt at my knees and cried while prayers and song swirled all around me in the little church. The whole congregation prayed for me alone, in a mighty wail of moans and voices. And I kept waiting serenely for Jesus, waiting, waiting—but he didn't come. I wanted to see him, but nothing happened to me. Nothing! I wanted something to happen to me, but nothing happened.

I heard the songs and the minister saying: "Why don't you come? My dear child, why don't you come to Jesus? Jesus is waiting for you. He wants you. Why don't you come? Sister Reed, what is this child's name?"

"Langston," my aunt sobbed.

10 "Langston, why don't you come? Why don't you come and be saved? Oh, Lamb of God! Why don't you come?"

Now it was really getting late. I began to be ashamed of myself, holding everything up so long. I began to wonder what God thought about Westley, who certainly hadn't seen Jesus either, but who was now sitting proudly on the platform, swinging his knickerbockered legs and grinning down at me, surrounded by deacons and old women on their knees praying. God had not struck Westley dead for taking his name in vain or for lying in the temple. So I decided that maybe to save further trouble, I'd better lie, too, and say, that Jesus had come, and get up and be saved.

So I got up.

Suddenly the whole room broke into a sea of shouting, as they saw me rise. Waves of rejoicing swept the place. Women leaped in the air. My aunt threw her arms around me. The minister took me by the hand and led me to the platform.

When things quieted down, in a hushed silence, punctuated by a few ecstatic "Amens," all the new young lambs were blessed in the name of God. Then joyous singing filled the room.

15 That night, for the last time in my life but one—for I was a big boy twelve years old—I cried. I cried, in bed alone, and couldn't stop. I buried my head under the quilts, but my aunt heard me. She woke up and told my uncle I was crying because the Holy Ghost had come into my life, and because I had seen Jesus. But I was really crying because I couldn't bear to tell her that I had lied, that I had deceived everybody in the church, that I hadn't seen Jesus and that now I didn't believe there was a Jesus any more, since he didn't come to help me.

➤ *QUESTIONS FOR READING AND WRITING*

1. If you could recall an event in your life when the pressure of approval was a major factor in an important decision, how did that memory affect your response to this story?

2. Do you think young Langston made the right decision? Why?
3. How are you affected by the description of the pressure on young Langston as the only unsaved "lamb"?
4. To what extent has Hughes "shown," not just told about, the pressure? What details has he chosen to convey the extent of that pressure?
5. What other passages in this essay affect you the most? What details help to make them effective?

WRITING TO DESCRIBE

An effective description is much more than a summary. A summary has no voice. An engaging description has our voice, impressions, and feelings, as well as relevant details. When someone asks us to describe a person we know very well (a friend, lover, spouse, parent) or a place with which we are very familiar (our home, bedroom, car, or a favorite hangout), we're not likely to respond with factual information alone. A summary of facts (dimensions, features, or colors) will not adequately convey what we feel is most important. Those details support our impression but do not replace it. Important details, however, do help the reader picture what we are describing and clarify *why* we feel the way we do.

Choosing Details

Which details we choose when describing and supporting our responses can make a big difference. Writing "Tanya makes me feel very comfortable" by itself will not be as clear as combining it with examples or details of what she does that shows it is true: "She's very soft spoken, smiles a lot, and is a good listener." We would not include every detail ("She's wants to graduate next year") unless it's relevant ("So she knows the kind of pressure I'm feeling"). Including details not important to our impression will not support, and may even dilute, the impact of ones that are.

Choosing Details from Literature

So, too, the details we choose to clarify and support our responses to literature have an important impact on readers. To describe the young girl's pain in "Eleven" without reference to the red sweater omits a crucial detail and contributing factor to her humiliation. When describing "Mothers," leaving out the imagined conversations between the speaker and her dead mother ignores an important component of her sense of loss and wishful thinking. Those details, those parts, capture the whole of the work in miniature.

➤ *QUESTIONS FOR READING AND WRITING*

1. How do you respond when someone asks you to describe a work of literature that you've read? To what extent does a summary convey what you've

experienced—what you feel is most important? To what extent does it seem inadequate? The following exercise may provide some insight:

a. Choose a favorite work of literature (either from these first two chapters or from past reading).
b. Summarize it.
c. Write down your strongest impressions of that work. Write down the details—from your experience and the literature—that support or clarify those impressions.
d. What is the difference between the summary and your impressions?
e. Which parts of the summary support your impression? Which do not?

Writing to Compare

How many times are we asked to describe something, and our first reaction is "Well, it's like . . ." or "It reminds me of . . . ." In fact it seems hard to describe anything without resorting to comparison somewhere along the way. When we think about our friends, we may compare and contrast them consciously and unconsciously with each other. When we take part in important events, we may compare them to similar events in our past: "This reminds me of the wedding I went to last year" or "My brother's graduation was done very differently."

Comparing and contrasting are also natural ways to describe our responses to literature. We might compare ourselves or others with literary characters, or our own experiences with those in a work of literature. We may compare the choices made by various characters with the choices we would make. We might even be reminded of previous reading experiences and compare the work—or elements of the work—we are reading with one we've read before. We might even compare a work of literature with a work from another form of art, like painting. A good example of both process and product is the student sample of Barbara Pfister (see p. 1481) who compares van Gogh's *Starry Night* with Anne Sexton's poem about the painting.

Comparing and Contrasting Using a Venn Diagram

One effective technique for generating and organizing ideas when writing to compare is a Venn diagram (Figure 2.1). This technique works equally well when comparing personal experience with the work (Figure 2.2) or comparing works or characters with one another (Figure 2.3).

1. Draw two interconnecting circles. Identify each circle.
2. In the common, interconnecting area write down what the subjects have in common.
3. In the separate sections, write down what is different.

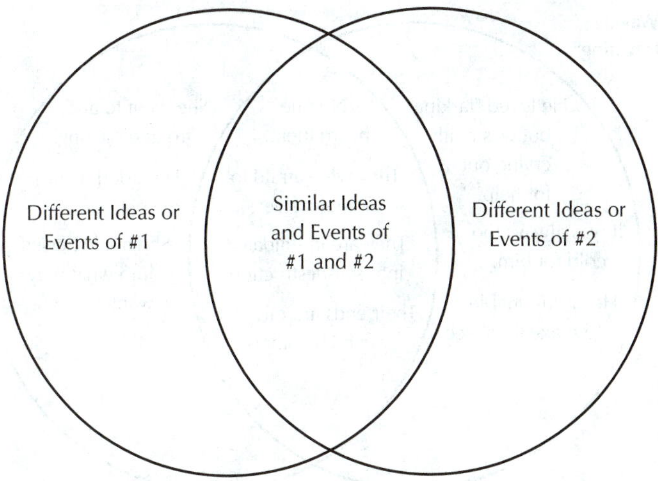

FIGURE 2.1

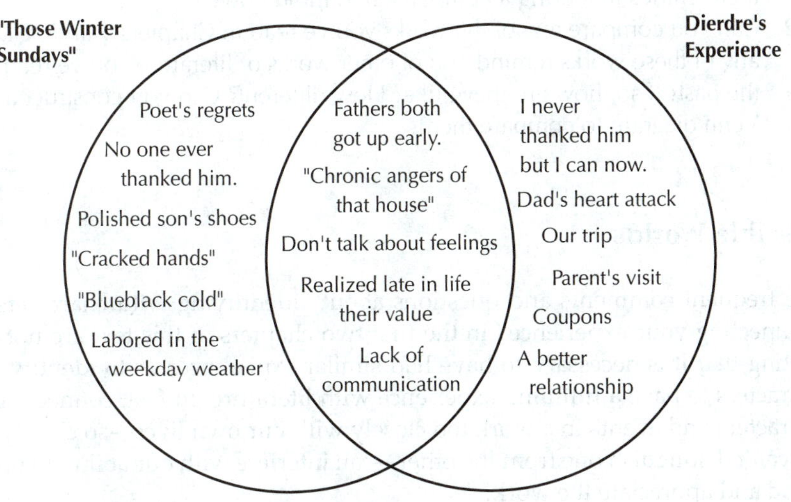

FIGURE 2.2 *Comparing Experience with Literature*

FIGURE 2.3 *Comparing Two Works of Literature*

➤ *QUESTIONS FOR READING AND WRITING*

1. If you are jotting down responses to your reading, take a look back through your entries. How many times did a work remind you of someone or something in your own life? If none did at the time you wrote your response, are there entries that bring a comparison to mind now?
2. Can you compare any of the works you've read in Chapters 1 and 2? Do any of these works remind you of other works of literature you've read in the past? If so, how are they alike? How different? Can you construct a Venn diagram to compare them?

Possible Worlds

The frequent comments and questions about "identifying with characters" or "connecting your experience" in the first two chapters of this text are not suggesting that it is necessary to have had similar experiences or to identify with characters to have a fulfilling experience with literature. In fact, connecting the characters and events in a work too closely with our own lives—so closely that we can't distinguish one from the other—can interfere with our ability to understand and appreciate the work.

When taking us where we have never been, literature has the power to increase the breadth and depth of our vision—to help us learn and grow in the way that all new experiences can. It is not necessary for us to have been embarrassed in school as an eleven-year-old, to have lost our mothers, or to have feigned being "saved" at a church service to be moved by "Eleven, "Mothers," or "Salvation."

The journal responses of Christine Leibowitz below to "Salvation" and "Mothers" illustrate this point. Here is Christine's response to Langston Hughes's "Salvation":

> The essay "Salvation" is wonderful! I remember being saved in ninth grade. There was this boy who went to my church and I thought that he parted the seas, so to speak. One day he invited me to go to Sunday Youth Group with him. I figured that if Shawn went then it couldn't be that bad. And, well, as my parents said, "He was such a nice boy!" So I went.
>
> This essay reminded me of that period of my life. It was funny, as was my own mission. When Langston was kneeling at the altar and everyone was waiting for him to be saved, I thought about how we used to close our eyes in church and the pastor would ask us to raise our hands if we sought salvation and were ready to give our lives to Christ. (Should I raise my hand and get it over with?) It was always a dilemma.
>
> I think Jesus forgave Langston. In fact, I believe that his true salvation was achieved when he lay in bed that night crying for not being honest. He was probably the only lamb of lambs that was truly saved on that blessed day.

Obviously, Christine's ability to identify with young Langston brought this scene vividly to life for her and intensified her reading experience, but this does not mean that she wouldn't have appreciated the essay otherwise.

Here is Christine's response to Anna Quindlen's "Mothers":

> I cannot identify with the speaker of this essay because my mother is alive and well. We share all of the things that the speaker fantasizes about. We laugh together, shop together, share stories and ideas, and give each other advice and criticism (good or bad). I have a wonderful and warm relationship with my mother. She is the first person I call when something good happens in my life and when I need a shoulder to cry on.
>
> The speaker of the essay lost her mother at age nineteen. She dreams about sharing things with her mother that I would normally take for granted. She must feel an incredible void in her life. My mother is an extension of myself. She is so much a part of me that if she were not here, I honestly believe that I would be a different person. She speaks of meeting someone in the lobby and describes herself as "on the short side, have on a red coat, and

my mother died when I was nineteen." That is how I think I would describe myself if I had outlived my mother. It is as if she is somehow not a complete person. She calls it "a vest pocket description of her emotional complexion." And for a while "all any one needed to know about [her]."

How would I go through the rest of my life without my mother? I shudder to think of the possibility. It is as frightening as thinking I, myself, may not wake up tomorrow. I feel compassion for this woman. I want to tell her how sorry I am and then I want to call my mom to make sure she is OK.

The speaker tries to rationalize that "mothers and daughters always see each other across a chasm of rivalries," but I think that she may be trying to compensate for her loss. I am enriched and blessed by my relationship with my mother and what happens in our lives, the love that we share transcends all.

I am so thankful to be able to read this essay knowing that my mother is just a phone call away and waiting to share with me a little bit of everything or a whole bunch of nothing.

In this response, unlike her response to "Salvation," Christine cannot identify with the plight of the speaker in "Mothers" because her own mother is still alive. However, rather than interfering with her response, her different circumstances make Quindlen's essay rich in meaning for her. The essay has taken her to a possible world. Ultimately, it is our intelligence and sensitivity to the human condition, not simply a shared experience, that helps us imagine the possibilities and become engaged with the work.

Response to Literature: Describing and Comparing

You are likely to write with more feeling and a clearer, stronger voice about issues that move you, so your strongest response or impression may provide the best topic to write about, but selecting relevant details to support that response is equally important. You are not only describing how you felt, but what prompted you to feel this way.

Staying Anchored in a Work of Literature

Remember, this is an essay in response to literature. When sharing personal responses, it can be very easy to see the work simply as a prompt to tell our own stories. Seeing and sharing the parallels between our own experiences and those in a work may strengthen our voices and clarify our responses, but the work on the page must remain prominent in the presentation. To write an effective response essay, it is essential to stay "anchored" in the work and balance references to personal experience with references to the literature itself.

➤ *QUESTIONS FOR READING AND WRITING*

In this exercise, you may find it illuminating to share your work with a partner or a small group.

1. Take a look back through your responses and select some of your strongest reactions or impressions.
2. If you wrote down details to support your response, do those details adequately convey it? Do those details include specific references to the text?
3. Are there places where you might have clarified your response through a comparison (with other characters, people you know, other students' responses)?
4. If you did not write down supporting details or if you did not cite the text for support, go back to the work of literature and see if you can.

The entries that follow were written in response to Robert Hayden's "Those Winter Sundays" on page 12. Read (or reread) the poem and write your response before you read the following entries.

LeaAnne's Response:

"Those Winter Sundays" brought to mind my brother Joey. Growing up in a severely dysfunctional home, he always seemed to be the one to have my best interests at heart. He did things for me, and with me without ever being asked, even when he had so many problems of his own to contend with. The poem touched upon the fact that the writer never got around to thanking his father for all he had done, and I was able to relate to that emotion because at the time the age difference between my brother and I made me too young to be able to acknowledge all his efforts and thank him for them. Of course, as an adult I've tried to thank him on many occasions, but the right words never seem to emerge.

Michael's Response:

When I read the poem "Those Winter Sundays" I could not help but think of the relationship I have with my own father. Like the father in the poem, my dad also has "cracked hands that ached from the labor in the weekday." The difference is that my father has a bad back. He injured his back twice in workplace accidents. His second accident forced him to retire.

His job now is taking care of the family. His new role includes driving my younger brother and sister to school, and he also does numerous things around the house. He does all these tasks without complaining about his back.

He does so many things for me during the day. When I have class at night, he makes sure that dinner is ready early so I can eat and also make it to school on time. You want to know something? Just like the writer, I have never thanked him once for all the things he has done for me.

Vincent's Response:

Feelings of loneliness and imagery give you a sense of unsaid things, trying to say what the author realizes now and didn't then. I identify with the author very much. It shows a different form of love, that of "austere office" that goes unrecognized and unappreciated. I love the open expression in the imagery--a sense of feeling the scenario from your own experience.

Ken's Response:

This poem made me think of my father. Even though I don't mean to, I never thank my dad. I appreciate him, but I don't really show that. Reading the poem, I could feel the cold floor turn warm as the author's father put the fire on. Then I could feel the icy cold return in the author's words. This poem was personal.

Dierdre's Response:

I love this poem because I am totally able to relate. It brought so many things back to me about my relationship with my father--some painful, some happy. I grew up in a similar situation, and although there was no love verbally communicated by my gruff father, he always did little things, like getting up early to turn up the heat, digging my car out of the snow and warming it up while I dressed. The day we read this poem in class I got home to find an envelope from my still gruff, uncommunicative father (age has softened him a little). There was no card or letter, just a bunch of coupons, mostly for stuff for my cat, which is his way of sending love. Coupons. It was very nice, and I zipped off a letter of appreciation. I'm glad I still have the opportunity.

➤ *QUESTIONS FOR READING AND WRITING*

1. How were the responses of LeaAnne, Michael, Vincent, Ken, and Dierdre influenced by their backgrounds and experiences?
2. Which entries seem to convey the strongest impressions? How so?
3. Which responses seem more anchored in the literature and which seem to digress more to the reader's own experience?

4. Imagine the entry you like best as the opening of a response essay. Make some suggestions for how it might be supported from the text of "Those Winter Sundays."
5. Consider your own response to the poem and to the questions on page 12. How do your responses compare to theirs? How does reading these journal entries affect your own response to the poem?
6. Take a close look at your own response. What details, quotes, and examples have you used to support your response? To what extent have you anchored your response in the work itself?

✔CHECKLIST • *Developing A Response Essay*

- ❑ Write down your impressions.
- ❑ Write down whatever questions come to mind during and after your reading.
- ❑ What confuses you? What do you want to know more about? How can you find out?
- ❑ Do any of the characters remind you of yourself or people you know? Do any of the events remind you of ones in your own life?
- ❑ Do these associations with the story help or interfere with your response? If so, how?
- ❑ What do you find most interesting or compelling about the work? Why? How can you "show" what made this issue so compelling for you? What details or passages in the work illustrate support for your response?

FROM FIRST RESPONSE TO FINAL DRAFT

In the section that follows, we look at Dierdre Curran's response to Robert Hayden's "Those Winter Sundays" on the previous page and follow its progress through to the final draft of her essay. Though her goal is to write a response essay, the strategies she illustrates work equally well when planning and generating ideas for a critical essay.

The purpose of the strategies that follow is not to move you step by step through a rigid sequence. Whether you are composing a response or a critical essay, writing is a continuous process of moving forward and returning and moving forward again. The best way to organize an essay may occur to you early or late in the process. You may get some of your best new ideas just when you thought you were almost finished. Try to let your ideas flow freely throughout the process. Don't close out ideas by imposing a structure that will keep you from expressing what you would really like to say.

Reading literature encourages a variety of responses—and perhaps more questions than answers. Generate and explore as many of your questions and ideas as possible before you decide on one direction. Free your ideas and follow them where they go. You may be surprised by what you find on your journey.

Using First Responses

If you've been keeping a journal or writing other initial responses to your reading, chances are you have already generated some good ideas for writing an essay. After you read your entries and add any comments based on rereading and class discussion, go back and underline or circle what you believe are your strongest impressions.

Let's look at Dierdre's journal response as an example:

> I love this poem because I am totally able to relate. <u>It brought so many things back to me about my relationship with my father--some painful, some happy</u>. I grew up in a similar situation, and although there was no love verbally communicated by my gruff father, he always did little things, like getting up early to turn up the heat, digging my car out of the snow and warming it up while I dressed. The day we read this poem in class I got home to find an envelope from my still gruff, uncommunicative father (age has softened him a little). There was no card or letter, just a bunch of coupons, mostly for stuff for my cat, which is his way of sending love. Coupons. It was very nice, and I zipped off a letter of appreciation. I'm glad I still have the opportunity.

Making Choices When making a choice or choices about which idea(s) to pursue, you may want to answer two essential questions:

1. Do you care enough about this idea to pursue it further?
   You will write with your strongest voice about issues that have the most meaning to you and about which you believe you want to say something that is important for both you and your readers.
2. Is it "do-able"?
   Can you write an essay about this? No matter how compelling your idea is, you won't be able to write an essay about it unless you have enough to say, or you can support it from both your experience and the work (of literature). Remember, if the point you are trying to make is obvious, abstract, or very general, it may be impossible to develop it into an appealing essay in a reasonable amount of time.

Extending Ideas

Dierdre chose the second sentence (underlined) from the entry above as the core of her response. It's obvious that she cares about this idea very much. And she feels confident that there are many lines in the poem that she can use to support the comparison between her relationship and that in the poem. But a look at her journal entry tells us that she has not identified many of them yet. But her essay seems very "do-able," and her journal entry has given her a start.

Dierdre has already followed her core idea with some specific support from her own experience, but she has not provided much specific support from the text of the poem itself. So if she wants to generate more ideas or extend or expand her support, there are a few other techniques she might use.

Directed Freewriting If you don't have a journal entry or other initial response, or you want to generate more ideas, directed freewriting can be a useful technique. The best time to do this exercise is immediately after you finish reading, while your thoughts and impressions are still fresh. The intention of this exercise is to release what you know without blocking it with pauses for reflection, punctuation, or editing.

1. Write down the name of the topic, phrase, or sentence you want to focus on.
2. Write down (nonstop) everything that comes into your mind for five or ten minutes. If punctuation or capitalization gets in the way, don't even use it.
3. Read what you have written and choose (circle or underline) your strongest responses.

Here is Dierdre Curran's directed freewriting response to Robert Hayden's "Those Winter Sunday's" in response to the sentence from her journal entry: It brought so many things back to me about my relationship with my father--some painful, some happy.

My father does not express his love for us by telling us. He does things instead. Growing up was really hard I wanted him to tell me he loved me. It has taken me years to believe that he really does even though he never says it. Did the poet ever get to tell his own father about these things. I'll bet not. He sounds as if he regrets not understanding that his father was really expressing love in the things he did. I really like Robert Hayden's descriptions of how the house felt. My house felt the same way. Why did he have to be so cold? Could he help it? Did he really love my older brothers more than me? Was I a disappointment to him? But not everything was as bleak as it seems now. There were good times but it just feels not. My father is old now and had a heart attack and only now are we beginning to say what I wish we had said before. I feel much better about now. We seem to have found a way to express our love now. I love him so much. I only hope I will have the chance to express that now before he's gone.

Dierdre's freewriting adds more detail to her earlier statement, and she was able to generate some very compelling ideas about her relationship with her father and her connections to the poem itself. By asking questions about and listing details of the selected statements, she may uncover even more specific material.

Asking Questions Having already narrowed her choice to a particular idea, she might ask as many questions (and subquestions) as she can about some aspect of that idea. Of course, it's useful to ask only questions that will provide new information (and cannot be answered yes or no).

1. Choose an important word, phrase, or sentence from your journal entry and write down as many related questions as you can.
2. Choose and answer the questions that will add to or clarify your support.

My father does not express his love for us by telling us.

How often do we talk?

What do we talk about?

How does he express his love?

Why doesn't he express his love in words?

Where is the similarity in the poem?

I'm glad I still have the opportunity to express appreciation.

Did the speaker in the poem ever get to tell his father what he felt?

Why does it feel like he never did?

How do I/will I express my appreciation?

I really like Robert Hayden's description of the house.

What language does he use?

Why is it effective?

Following up with detailed answers to these questions is likely to provide additional specific support for the original core idea.

Listing

1. Choose key words or sentences from your response (the name of a character, an event, an element of literature, etc.).
2. List as many related details under each as you can. By choosing some key phrases that apply to her identification with the speaker in the poem, Dierdre is able to uncover other specific details.

My father does things for me instead.

He got up early and turned up the heat.

Dug my car out of the snow and warmed it up.

Sent me envelopes with coupons.

Took my sister and me on a trip to Maryland.

On Sundays he always made sure we had the comics and jelly doughnuts.

He comforted me when my dog died.

He sometimes laughed and joked around with me and my sister.

He recently sent me the first letter I have ever received from him.

I really like Robert Hayden's description of the house in the poem.

I could feel the pain of the "blueblack cold."

I could feel and hear the cold "splintering, breaking."

Remembering getting dressed quickly in the cold.

Imagining the rooms getting warm.

The house was like their relationship.

Semantic Mapping, or Clustering

For some of us, it is easier to follow directions by looking at a map than following directions in a printed sequence. Sometimes we need to see the whole picture. When writing in response to literature, too, sometimes we can understand, see relationships, and generate and extend ideas better spatially than linearly. A technique called **semantic mapping** or **clustering** makes it possible to see ideas and relationships this way (Figure 2.4). This is how it works:

1. Write down a question or statement in the center of a blank page in your journal or on another piece of paper. Put a circle around it.
2. Draw lines out from the circle and write a statement or idea related to that central idea.
3. Continue to draw lines out from the central circle and the subcircles. Those from the central circle are subsets of ideas; each circle further along each line is a level of greater specificity.

One of the intriguing things about mapping is that once you get going, it's hard to stop. Seeing a picture of the ideas seems to make the relationships among them clearer.

Finding Connections With any of these strategies, an additional step that might be productive, and which emerges naturally from the mapping exercise, is finding and describing the relationships between and among the ideas (the circles) generated on different lines. When you finish your map, you might draw lines across circles and write statements identifying and examining the relationships. Such statements might go a long way toward answering the central question or identifying a unifying theme for the story. For example, writing a statement about the connection among the circles from Dierdre's map might provide some additional insights (Figure 2.5).

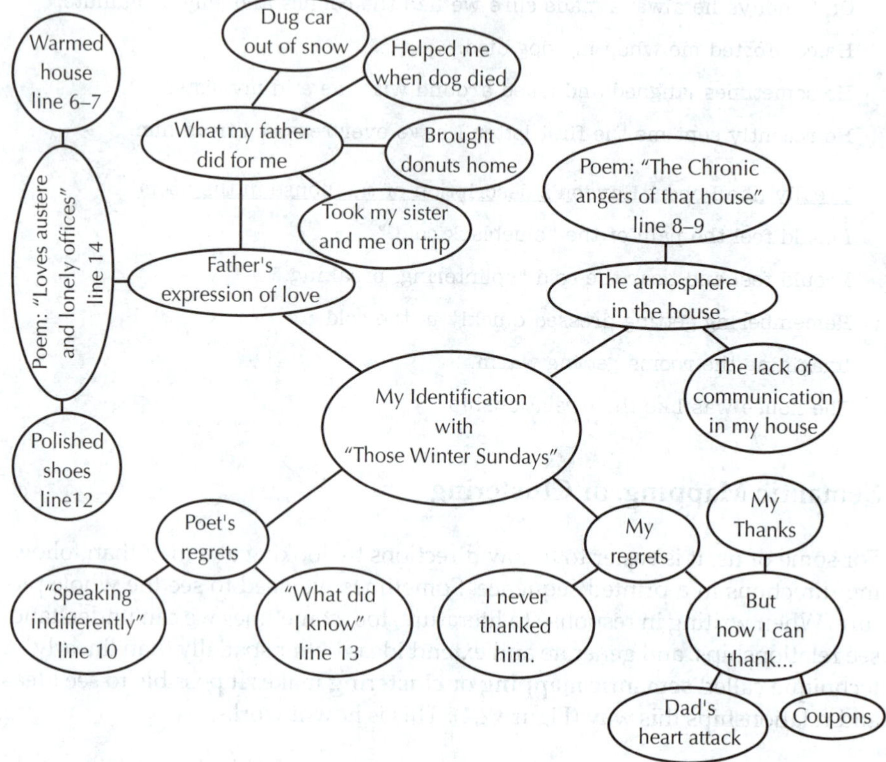

FIGURE 2.4 *Dierdre's Semantic Map*

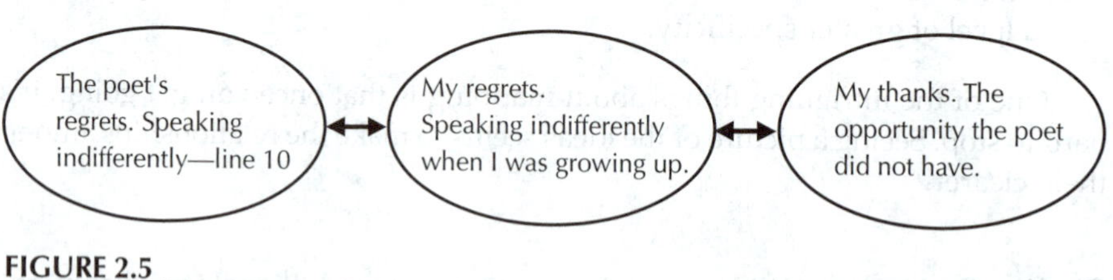

FIGURE 2.5

Mix and Match

The strategies above are not an end in themselves, but simply the means to generate and extend ideas, ask questions, and make choices. They should be used in whatever way they work for you. There is no one "right" way to ask questions or list ideas. If a particular method is working, keep using it. If it is not, try something else. For example, you may find that only the first few circles in a mapping exercise are useful. In order to generate details quickly, you may prefer to list them instead of putting circles around them. So you might want to start with a map, get a few ideas, and then make a list to get at the details. Along with keeping a journal, you may want to freewrite as well. Different ways, combinations, and paces of writing may bring different ideas. What matters in this "prewriting" stage is that you feel free to explore in your most productive way.

Collaboration

Sharing Responses If you are keeping a journal or jotting down responses to your reading, you may find it useful to exchange your writing with a classmate. In addition to sharing responses to the work of literature, you might comment on each other's entries. The biggest advantage to sharing this way is that it gives you an audience and immediate feedback.

Combining Questions After generating your own questions about a particular piece of literature, it might be worthwhile to share these questions in pairs or with a small group. Pool everyone's questions, discuss their strengths and weaknesses, and narrow the list down to the strongest ones.

Connecting Cluster Circles You might work collaboratively on a semantic map, or cluster sheet. In response to a question, topic, or character, each individual in a small group might take responsibility for a line of circles extending from the middle. Then your group might draw lines connecting one line of circles to another line of circles. By discussing these connections, new ideas, directions, and possibilities will emerge.

The Response Essay: Composing a Draft

Once you have settled on your topic and gathered supporting ideas and details, you can begin to write a draft of your essay. Even at this stage you may want to avoid forcing your writing into an inflexible outline. There may be possibilities you haven't thought of, so avoid putting walls around your work just yet.

As in earlier stages of the process, what works best for each of us may be different. Some students may work best by writing this first draft as quickly as possible without stopping and then going back to review and revise when finished. Many students (and probably most experienced writers) find that writing more reflectively at this stage works best for them. And if you have already narrowed your focus to a particular idea and generated lots of details to support it, you may want to proceed with more reflection and review what you have written while you write. You may want to read it out loud to hear how the wording sounds and if the ideas are complete and clear. Evaluating your writing may give you valuable insight into where you need to go.

Once you have narrowed your focus to a particular idea and generated lots of details in support of the idea, you are ready to create a thesis statement. Your thesis statement should incorporate all the evidence that you have, but also be specific enough for you to support. Your thesis statement should also reveal what you intend to show in your essay.

Dierdre's Draft

Earlier in this section, we saw Dierdre Curran's journal entry, freewriting, listing, asking questions, and her semantic map in response to Robert Hayden's "Those Winter Sundays." Let's follow up by looking at a draft of her response essay.

Twice on Sunday

The relationship between parent and child is often a significant one in literature. In his poem "Those Winter Sundays," Robert Hayden illustrates the starkness of one such relationship. The author of this poem is left, as an adult, feeling guilt and regret over never being able to communicate understanding and appreciation of the father's limited demonstrative abilities. I found myself being able to fully relate to the emotions of this poem, as I have a strong personal connection with the situation that is detailed.

The author tells of "fearing the chronic angers of that house." The house I grew up in always seemed filled with anger to me, too. The only communication that ever went on between my parents, myself, and all of my brothers and sisters involved displays of anger; we never had conversations, we had arguments and disagreements. No one in my family ever apologized to one another, or told another that they loved them, or expressed sympathy or support when something was wrong. It was a home filled with much bitterness and stress, presumably brought on by constant financial troubles. There was nothing to ever balance it out, no tangible expressions of love from my parents . . . or so I thought until I got a little older and came to understand more.

The author tells of how the father got up early "in the blueblack cold," and then with "cracked hands that ached" from labor in the weekday weather made banked fires blaze. "No one ever thanked him." My Dad has always been a painfully early riser; he would get up hours before the rest of us had to. In the wintertime, he always made sure that he was up and had turned on the heat so that when the rest of us awoke it was to a warm house. In the winters of my late teens, when I needed his car to get to work, he would always go outside to start it and warm it up. Often he dug it out of a night's snowfall for me, too. I was still reeling from the trauma of my teenage years, so, seething with bitterness, I actually resented him doing me a favor. I never once thanked him for it--I was annoyed by it! My obnoxious, sullen, and ungrateful attitude led me to believe that he was only doing something he was expected to do. My behavior is well described when the author tells how he "spoke indifferently to him, who had driven out the cold."

The poem's author realizes, later in life, that although his father never outwardly expressed his love in so many words, it was expressed through a variety of gestures. Something as simple as shining his son's shoes can be interpreted as an open display of affection. When I think back on my childhood, I realize that although he is a very gruff and restrained man, my father also showed his love in the only ways he knew how. When we were kids, my father spent a lot more time with my brother, throwing the baseball and playing basketball, going to ball games. I think that once we got past a certain age (toddler), he didn't really know what to do with my sister and myself, because we were girls. When I was about six, I remember getting together with my older sister, Lucy, and informing our mother that we resented the fact that Dad always "did stuff with Tighe," but not with us. As a result, we got the treat of spending a weekend with him alone on a road trip (a business trip for him) down to Maryland. He never said, "I love you as much as your brother," or hugged us or kissed us, but he made the effort to spend time with us, and we all enjoyed it (well, I <u>think</u> he did, he seemed to). Upon seeing so many horses on the roadside, I was insistent that I get up close to one. So, intent on getting me to my horses, my Dad came up with a solution . . . he took us to the racetrack!

In retrospect, I realize that my Dad has done many things over the years to convey his affection. When we were very little, I shared a room with my sister Lucy. Sometimes at night if he was in a good mood, right before we went to bed, my Dad would pretend that he was Frankenstein. He would close his eyes and stretch out his arms in front of him, walking like a fictional monster. He would chase us to our beds, approaching slowly, while we shrieked in terrified laughter, running from him. When he finally caught us, we got tickled to the point of hysteria, and then it was time for bed. I also recall how on Sundays (yes, there is a Sunday connection with the poem also), he would go out early to buy the newspapers. On top of making sure that we had the Sunday comics, he always came back with jelly donuts from the bakery, too.

The worst day of my life was when I had to put my fifteen-year-old diabetic dog, Freebie, to sleep. The guilt has never left me. No one in my family would go with me to the vet. When my best friend, John, came to the house that morning to drive me and the dog, my mother wouldn't even come downstairs, but at least my father said goodbye to her. He was the only one that was as upset as I was, and I was crushed, only he never showed it. The day I brought her ashes back to throw around the yard, he found me in the house crying hysterically; I was totally heartbroken. When I first came back from the vet on that awful day (when I held her in my arms and watched the life sink from her beautiful brown eyes, then blued by cataracts), no one hugged me, no one said, "I'm sorry." The day I brought Freebie back home for the last time and fell apart in the backyard, my father's only way of acknowledging my grief was to come outside and yell at me. He just stood there and kept yelling, and I just sat there and kept crying. Finally he got quiet and told me that he missed the dog as much as me, and hadn't gone with me because he didn't have the guts to do what I had done. Then he helped me up and walked me up the driveway, hugging me for the very first time in memory.

My parents came out for a visit last summer. They moved to Indiana, and I had not seen them in almost a year. In the parking lot where I met up with them, I gave my father a big hug and told him that I had really missed him. He, of course, did not hug me back, and (surprised by my open display of affection) could only manage the reply, "Yeah, twice on Sunday!" I understood that this was his best effort, and I still laugh about it because it was so typical.

A few weeks later, my oldest sister called to tell me that my father had suffered a heart attack out in Indiana. I was basically floored, and promptly drank a bottle and a half of Merlot. While I was sucking that down, I was crying hysterically. Two very long days later, I was on a plane to see him, even though he tried to tell me it was not necessary because he was doing so well. I had to see for myself. The plane trip was hellacious. It took twelve hours to get there, and the delays were torture. I finally told the airline people that I didn't care about the inclement weather, or the size of the plane.

I didn't care if it was a bicycle with wings, they had to fly me to South Bend. I made it to the hospital ten minutes before visiting hours ended on my birthday. As I rushed down the hall frantically toward his room, I heard him call out my name in excited surprise and saw him slowly hurrying toward me, pale, be-tubed and in his hospital gown. I could not believe how happy he was to see me; it made the whole trip worth it. He repeatedly held my hand and offered me his cheek for a kiss, every couple of minutes. When he asked me "what in the hell" I was doing out there, my reply was that I had the day off anyway and decided to come see him for my birthday. He had a good laugh at that one. He was a much less gruff man than the last time I had seen him.

Never in my life has my father verbally expressed his love. In younger years I was blind to the fact that he just doesn't know how, but that he shows it in other ways. That used to make me so mad and frustrated. But he has mellowed with the coming of grandchildren and his own older age, and I have opened my eyes and learned to appreciate the gestures and to interpret their meaning. In "Those Winter Sundays," the author tells of the guilt of his own ignorance of "love's austere and lonely offices." While I can't imagine the day either one of us is ever able to actually say "I love you" to the other one, I am secure in the knowledge that it is mutually understood. I had always planned on naming a child after him, but when my brother named his first son John, I had to settle for naming my cat "Dad." While "Dad the Human" is publicly insulted by the feline's moniker, I suspect inside he is touched.

We still don't talk about personal feelings, although now that his health has dealt him a major wake-up call I see that changing a little. This past month has marked the first letter he ever wrote to me--three pages about the weather, constantly interjected with <u>SO THERE!</u> in large, capital underlined letters. I also received my very first birthday card, which not only did he sign himself, he signed it with "Love." Of course, it doesn't say "Love, Dad," it says "Love, J.C."--his initials. I laughed when I read it, and I was thrilled that he has been able to make so much progress.

The author of this poem conveys some universal feelings of guilty realization that I think all children reach as they become adults. I am just thankful that I have been given the time and opportunity in life to establish a bond with my father that I am not sure any of his other children have the privilege of sharing. I love him very much, and I have a relationship with him that may seem comparatively odd to other people, but that I treasure. Luckily I also have the sense of humor that is necessary to appreciate it.

Revision

Rethinking, "re-visioning," and rewriting are just as important for a response essay about literature as they are for any other kind of writing. Having discovered what you want to say, you can now focus on how well you have said it. How well is your draft organized? Does it have unnecessary or redundant information? Are there gaps that need to be filled in? Are there enough details? Is there enough support from the work of literature? Have you expressed yourself as clearly as possible?

Organization and Unity

One of the most effective ways of checking the organization of a draft is by doing an **after-draft outline**. Go back to each paragraph and find the controlling idea. List the main ideas they represent, one after the other. This should give you an outline of your draft.

Let's look at an outline of Dierdre's draft:

1. Introduction and Thesis Statement
   The relationship in the poem reminds me of my own.
2. The house I grew up in always seemed filled with anger too.

3, 4. Both my father and his father expressed their love in the same way.

5. My father has done things to express his love.
6. The worst day of my life is also my fondest memory of my father.
7. My parents visited last year.
8. Two weeks ago, my father had a heart attack.
9. I didn't understand when I was younger—now I know.
10. We still don't talk about personal feelings, but our relationship is better.
11. Conclusion (I'm glad I've had the chance the poet missed).

When Dierdre looked at her list, she was concerned that she might have too many paragraphs. For the most part, the organization of her essay followed the pattern of the poem itself. She compared her relationship with her father to that of the poet's with his father. She took lines from the poem and then commented on how each matched her experience. This pattern made sense to her, but it appeared that several of these paragraphs were too long and unwieldy.

Showing Support

The support Dierdre used in this essay came from two sources: the poem and her personal experience. She supported her references to the text by quoting the poem. She supported references to her experience by giving examples. She believed she had enough support in both cases and that her examples firmly established the connection.

Clarity

Dierdre realized that she would have to tighten up her language by deleting unnecessary words, expressions, and sentences. After cutting and combining, she could decide if some of the paragraphs should be combined as well. She also realized that her choice of words did not always express what she meant. In paragraphs 4 and 5 in particular, she decided that cutting, combining, and reordering some of the examples would strengthen the pace and organization of the essay.

Her most difficult decision was what to cut. She wanted her essay to be clearly expressed and tightly organized, but she didn't want to sacrifice the concrete details and scenes that gave it a strong voice.

Voice

She believed that one of the strengths of this piece was its voice, a voice which "showed" through quotes and examples. Her biggest task was to maintain a strong voice throughout the essay while tightening up her prose overall.

✔CHECKLIST • *Revision*

Organization and Unity

- ❑ Do all the paragraphs relate to the central thesis?
- ❑ Is the organization of those paragraphs within the essay clear?
- ❑ Do each of the sentences within the paragraphs relate to the central idea of the paragraph?

Support

- ❑ Are there enough details to support or clarify your assertions? Have you "shown" what you've told?
- ❑ Are there enough quotes from the work of literature to support your assertions?
- ❑ Are the paragraphs fully developed?
- ❑ Is the essay fully developed? Have you accounted for all aspects of your thesis statement?

Clarity

- ❑ Is the central thesis of the essay clearly stated?
- ❑ Does the title of your essay account for your thesis?
- ❑ Is the language clear?

(*continued*)

- ❑ Are there redundancies, digressions, or meaningless phrases that could be cut?
- ❑ Is the essay written in the format required by your instructor? Have you documented your references to the text and included a list of works cited?

Voice

- ❑ Does it sound like you? When you read it out loud, can you hear your voice and emotion?

Editing or proofreading is a crucial final step in the process of producing an essay. In addition to making any changes that did not occur to you earlier and fine tuning your writing, it's essential to check your essays for correct grammar, spelling, punctuation, and typos.

✔CHECKLIST • *Editing and Proofreading*

- ❑ Are all of your sentences complete sentences?
- ❑ Are all of your sentences punctuated appropriately?
- ❑ Are the words spelled correctly? Have you checked for easily confused words (then/than, your/you're, its/it's, etc.)?
- ❑ Are you sure of the meaning of all the words you've used?
- ❑ Are the titles of works underlined or in quotations as appropriate?
- ❑ Is the title and heading on the first page in the correct format?
- ❑ Have you followed your essay with works cited?
- ❑ Are there particular errors you have a tendency to make? Have you looked for those in this essay?

Remember, computer spell checkers do not make choices about word usage. Confused words (than/then, there/their/they're, etc.) will not be flagged by a spell checker. You will have to use your own eyes and judgment to correct those errors.

Dierdre's Revised Essay

After rewriting her introduction to make it clearer, Dierdre cut many words and phrases, combined many sentences, and shifted some of her examples. After reading this clearer, shorter version, she decided to stay with the same number of paragraphs. She could have combined several of them but decided not to. The resulting paragraphs would have been too long and much more difficult for the reader to absorb.

Dierdre Curran

Dr. Madden

English 102

Fall 200X

Twice on Sunday

In his poem, "Those Winter Sundays," Robert Hayden illustrates the starkness of his relationship with his father. As a child, he was never able to understand or appreciate what his father did for him. As an adult, he feels guilt and regret because it is too late to communicate his appreciation. I have experienced a similar relationship, and I can relate strongly to the emotions expressed in this poem.

The poet tells of "fearing the chronic angers of that house" (9). The house I grew up in always seemed filled with anger to me, too. We never had conversations; we had arguments and disagreements. We never apologized to one another, said "I love you," or expressed sympathy or support when something was wrong. Our home was filled with bitterness and stress. There was nothing to ever balance it out, no tangible expressions of love from my parents . . . or so I thought until I got a little older and came to understand more.

He says his father " . . . got up early / and put his clothes on in the blueblack cold / then with cracked hands that ached / from labor in the week-day weather made / banked fires blaze. No one ever thanked him" (1–5). In the wintertime, my dad was always up before the rest of us and had turned on the heat so that we awoke to a warm house. When I was older and needed his car to get to work, he would always go outside to start and warm it up. Often he dug it out of a night's snowfall. Reeling from the trauma of my teenage years and seething with bitterness, I actually resented his doing me a favor. I never once thanked him for it. I was annoyed and believed that he was only doing something he was expected to do. My behavior is well described when Hayden tells how he spoke "indifferently to him / who had driven out the cold" (10–11).

Later in life, the poet realizes that while his father never expressed his love in words, he expressed it through a variety of gestures, like shining his son's shoes. When I recall my childhood, I realize that my father also showed his love in the only ways he knew how. When we were very little, I shared a room with my sister Lucy. Sometimes at night if he was in a good mood, right before we went to bed, my Dad would pretend that he was Frankenstein. He would close his eyes and stretch out his arms in front of him, walking like the fictional monster, approaching slowly, while we shrieked in terrified laughter, running from him. When he finally caught us, we got tickled to the point of hysteria. On Sundays, he would go out early to buy the newspapers and make sure that we had the comics and jelly donuts, too.

Once, my older sister and I complained that my father spent much more time with my brother than he did with us, so he took us with him on a business trip to Maryland. He never said, "I love you as much as your brother," or hugged us or kissed us, but he made the effort to spend time with us, and we all enjoyed it (well, I think he did; he seemed to). Seeing many horses on the roadside, I was insistent that I get up close to one. So, intent on getting me to my horses, my dad came up with a solution . . . he took us to the racetrack!

The worst day of my life is also my fondest memory of my father. It was the day I had to put my fifteen-year-old, diabetic dog Freebie to sleep. The guilt has never left me. No one in my family would go with me to the vet. At least my father said goodbye to her. He was the only one who was as upset as I was, and I was crushed. He never showed it. When I brought her ashes back to throw around the yard, he found me in the house crying hysterically. I was totally heartbroken. No one hugged me, no one said, "I'm sorry." My father's only way of acknowledging my grief was to come outside and yell at me. He just stood there and kept yelling, and I just sat there and kept crying. Finally, he got quiet and told me that he missed the dog as much as I did, and hadn't gone with me because he didn't have the guts to do what I had done. Then he helped me up and walked me up the driveway, hugging me for the first time I can remember.

After I graduated from high school, my parents moved to Indiana. Last summer they came back for a visit. We had not seen each other in almost a year. In the parking lot where I met them, I gave my father a big hug and told him that I really missed him. He, of course, did not hug me back, and (surprised by my open display of affection) could only manage the reply, "Yeah, twice on Sunday!" I understood that this was his best effort, and I still laugh about it because it was so typical.

A few weeks ago, my oldest sister called to tell me that my father had suffered a heart attack. I was floored. I drank a bottle of wine and cried hysterically. Two very long days later, I was on a plane to see him. The plane trip was horrible. It took twelve hours to get there, and the delays were torture. I didn't care about the inclement weather or the size of the plane. I didn't care about anything but getting to South Bend as soon as I could. I made it to the hospital on my birthday, ten minutes before visiting hours ended. As I rushed down the hall looking frantically for his room, I heard him call out my name in excited surprise and saw him slowly hurrying toward me, pale, be-tubed and in his hospital gown. I could not believe how happy he was to see me. It made the whole trip worth it. He repeatedly held my hand and offered me his cheek for a kiss every couple of minutes. When he asked me "what in the hell" I was doing out there, I replied that I had the day off anyway, and decided to come see him for my birthday. He had a good laugh at that one. He seemed much less gruff than the last time I had seen him.

Never in my life has my father verbally expressed his love. In younger years I was blind to the fact that he just didn't know how, but that he showed it in other ways. That used to make me so mad and frustrated. But he has mellowed with the coming of age and grandchildren, and I have opened my eyes and learned to appreciate his gestures, and to interpret their meaning. In "Those Winter Sundays, " the poet tells of the guilt of his own ignorance "of love's austere and lonely offices" (14). While I can't imagine the day when we will ever be able to actually say "I love you" to each other, I am secure in the knowledge that it is mutually understood.

We still don't talk about personal feelings, but now that his health has dealt him a major wake-up call, I see that changing a little. This past month has marked the first letter he ever wrote to me--three pages about the weather, constantly interjected with SO THERE! in large, capital underlined letters. I also received my very first birthday card. Not only did he sign it himself, but he signed it with love. Of course, it doesn't say "Love, Dad," it says "Love, J.C."--his initials. I laughed when I read it, and I was thrilled that he has been able to make so much progress.

In "Those Winter Sundays," Robert Hayden conveys feelings of guilt that I think most children experience as they become adults. I am just thankful that I have been given the time and the opportunity in life to establish a bond with my father. I love him very much, and I have a relationship with him that may seem comparatively odd to other people, but it's one that I treasure. Luckily, I also have the sense of humor that is necessary to appreciate it.

Work Cited

Hayden, Robert. "Those Winter Sundays." Exploring Literature. Ed. Frank Madden. New York: Longman, 2001, 12.

PART II

Analysis, Argumentation, and Research

CHAPTER 3

Exploration and Analysis

Genre and the Elements of Literature

To analyze anything is to look closely at how it works—to examine its parts. Our intention in this chapter, however, is not to reduce literature to parts. Our goal is to provide you with tools to articulate and develop your responses into effective critical essays. We know that the parts of a literary work alone cannot account for its meaning, a meaning that fully blossoms only as the parts work together. But reading the work carefully and analyzing its parts can tell you a great deal about it—and how it triggered your response. Analysis is an important step in interpreting or evaluating literature, and it is through this process that you may gather the support to make your opinion an informed one.

YOUR FIRST RESPONSE

When you read a work of literature for the first time, relax and give yourself enough time to experience it. Don't try too hard to figure it out. Get impressions. Notice words and phrases. Read them out loud. Listen to the rhythms. Follow the personal associations that come up. Let yourself feel the emotions connected to them. Don't be discouraged if you have difficulty understanding every word or line your first time through. Have a dictionary handy and look up unfamiliar words. Let your unanswered questions stick with you. Write them down if you think you won't remember them later.

Immediately after your first reading, jot down your impressions and the questions that came to mind during your reading. Capture your response while it's fresh. If you wait until later, you may forget. In fact, you may come away from your reading with more questions than answers. So a second or third reading with these questions in mind may clarify much that was confusing the first time through. If you were reminded of people or events in your life, try to think about the difference that those associations made in your response. Did they help? Did they interfere? Does the text of the work support your response?

Before you analyze the work, try to grab hold of what you found most provocative about it. You will write with a stronger voice and more conviction when you write about what interests you most.

✔CHECKLIST • *Your First Response*

- ❑ Write down your first impressions.
- ❑ Write down the questions that come to mind during and after your reading.
- ❑ What confuses you? What do you want to know more about? How can you find out?
- ❑ What words or phrases affect you most?
- ❑ Do any of the characters remind you of yourself or people you know?
- ❑ Do any of the events remind you of ones in your own life?
- ❑ Do these associations help or interfere with your response? If so, how?
- ❑ What do you find most interesting or compelling about the work?

Close Reading

Analysis requires close reading. In a way the term *close reading* means the opposite of what it sounds like. When we read closely, we don't get closer to the literature and our experience with it; rather, we step back. We move from being inside the work to looking at it from the outside, from participating to observing. This process requires a careful reading and a conscious examination of the elements of the work and how they contribute to its overall meaning.

A close reading is not a first reading, it is a rereading. When you return to read the work of literature or your notes again after discussion in class, you are doing a close reading. You have already stepped back from your own views to hear the responses of others. You are reading your notes and the literature informed by what you have learned from those discussions.

Annotating the Text

One effective way to do a close reading of fiction, poetry, drama, or essays is to mark up the text by underlining, circling, highlighting, or making notes in the margins. You may even find it useful to do these annotations in more than one stage. In the first stage you might want to concentrate on your understanding of the text by summarizing, noting words or passages you don't understand, and asking questions—exploring the text. Later on, as you narrow your focus, you may want to identify elements of the text, patterns, evidence, or quotations to support your thesis—analyzing the text. If you don't want to mark up the pages of your book, make a copy of the work and do your annotations on this copy. Or write your annotations on Post-it notes and attach them in the margins of the work.

First Annotation: Exploration

PERCY BYSSHE SHELLEY (1792–1822)

OZYMANDIAS

[1818]

I met a traveler from an antique land
Who said: "Two vast and trunkless legs of stone
Stand in the desert . . . Near them on the sand,
Half-sunk, a shattered visage lies, whose frown
And wrinkled lip, and sneer of cold command,
Tell that its sculptor well those passions read
Which yet survive, stamped on these lifeless things,
The hand that mocked them, and the heart that fed:
And on the pedestal these words appear:
'My name is Ozymandias, king of kings:
Look on my works, ye Mighty, and despair!'
Nothing beside remains. Round the decay
Of that colossal wreck, boundless and bare
The lone and level sands stretch far away"

What does he mean "trunkless legs"?
Look up visage.
"Cold command"–a ruler?
A sculptor–a statue?
Hand-mocked, heart-fed? How does "hand" differ from "heart"?
Summary–He met someone from a far away country who saw an ancient large, broken statue with an arrogant statement on it.

This first annotation is an exploration of your first reading. You may clarify what you understand and ask questions about what you don't understand, or indicate what you need to know more about. You might make guesses, note impressions, summarize, and, in general, give yourself something to think about when you begin a second reading.

Second Annotation: Analysis

PERCY BYSSHE SHELLEY (1792–1822)

How does this compare with other Shelley poems I've read?
What was going on in England at this time? Who was the king?

OZYMANDIAS

[1818]

I met a traveler from an antique land
Who said: "Two vast and trunkless legs of stone
Stand in the desert . . . Near them on the sand,
Half-sunk, a shattered visage lies, whose frown
And wrinkled lip, and sneer of cold command,
Tell that its sculptor well those passions read
Which yet survive, stamped on these lifeless things,
The hand that mocked them, and the heart that fed:
And on the pedestal these words appear:
'My name is Ozymandias, king of kings:
Look on my works, ye Mighty, and despair!'
Nothing beside remains. Round the decay
Of that colossal wreck, boundless and bare
The lone and level sands stretch far away"

Why "antique" and not just "old" or "ancient"?
The rhyme scheme: abab–"stone" and "frown"?
Not just grand but arrogant as well.
"Read" and "fed" rhyme but not "command" and "things."
The hand of the sculptor / the heart of the king?
A powerful image–decayed and worn-out grandeur and arrogance in a desert.
Rhymes: despair/bare–decay/away
What a powerful ironic contrast!

The second annotation is a closer reading and more analytical. Here you might look for some of the elements of literature we discuss in this chapter, try to find patterns, seek evidence to support your early conclusions, or even place the work within a larger historical, social, or biographical context.

Literature in Its Many Contexts

Our focus on textual analysis in this chapter—on genres and their elements—is not an attempt to limit the scope of your writing to types of literature or parts of the work alone. Those parts and those works exist in a larger world—a context framed by personal, cultural, historical, biographical, and other influences. Seeing beyond the work to the contexts that influenced its writing—and your reading—may enliven and enrich your experience of the work and help you produce a more interesting essay.

Your Critical Approach

What you value most about literature, your critical stance, can be an important factor in determining what you analyze and write about when interpreting and evaluating literature. Critical approaches are broadly classified as reader based (emphasizing the reader's response and the text), text based (emphasizing the text), context based (emphasizing the background of the work), and author based (emphasizing connections to the author's life or intentions). Whatever approach you take may determine the strategy and terms you use in your writing. For a more comprehensive explanation of these approaches see the Appendix (p. 1487). Keep in mind that critical approaches may easily overlap, and critics often combine them in their analyses. The difference between one critical stance and another may be more a matter of emphasis than kind, and drawing upon several approaches can yield a rich interpretation.

Interpretive Communities

Stanley Fish, a professor and literary critic, has suggested that groups of readers who value the same approach to analyzing literature belong to "an interpretive community." Although our interpretations are influenced by whatever collaborative group or class we are in at present, we also carry and apply our own individual values and those of the many other communities (family, friends, religion) to which we belong. In this respect, we are members of many interpretive communities, and we are continually refiguring and revising our interpretations and evaluations in the light of our personal beliefs and group discussions. You may find it worthwhile and productive to keep track of this complex mix of personal response and group discussion as you write about the literature you read and discuss.

Reading and Analyzing Fiction

Telling stories and listening to stories seems to be a natural part of our lives. When we meet with friends to hear about an experience, "just the facts" won't do. We want to hear the stories that give meaning to those facts. Why do we read and listen to stories? What kind of experience do we expect to have when we sit down to read a short story or "curl up with a good book"? Many of us might say that we want to "escape" from the stress of everyday life. But in this highly complex world there are many other ways to escape. What is it about the experience of reading a good story that makes it unique and draws us to it?

Beyond an escape, reading a story brings us to a place in our imaginations where we can live through the experience of others. Prompted by the author's words, we imagine the scenes, characters, and conflicts. We take the chances, feel the emotions, and share the insights—but without suffering the risks or consequences that living through them ourselves might bring.

Stories and storytelling have been an important part of every culture since people first roamed the earth. Before there was written language to record them, people shared stories orally and passed them down to their descendants. Even today, these stories convey the "truths" of many cultures and religions and give meaning to the lives of millions of people.

Fiction and Truth

In many ways, the designation "fiction" is misleading. Most fiction tells a story that is "made up"—or at least the specific details of the story probably did not occur in exactly the way described, in this place, at this time, to characters with these names. The most important quality of good fiction, though, is the truth or truths it tells—about being human and struggling to make sense of a complex world. The truth of fiction transcends fact. In it we see a model of our own struggle, a model not limited by the daily news of specific time and place and fact.

Narration

The narrator is the storyteller, the intermediary who shapes and flavors the story for us. Try to distinguish between the author of the story and the narrator, or speaker. The narrator has been created by the author with a particular effect in mind. As you can imagine, *who* tells the story and *how* it is told can make a big difference. The same story told from a different point of view or with a different voice affects everything we experience as we read.

Point of View

Think about the last time you watched a concert or sports event on television. Can you recall how many different camera shots you were shown? When the camera gave you a distant shot, you could see a large part of the arena and most of the performers. You could see what no one performer could see. But you could not experience what it was like to be in the middle of the action. Only a close-up camera shot could help you feel the physical energy, the emotion, and give you the perspective of an individual performer. But, of course, by isolating your view to one performer, you lost the larger view of the entire event. Directors, camera operators, and announcers make choices about which perspectives work best at given times. From any of these distances and angles the event we witness is the same, but the point of view we have makes our experience of it quite different.

In similar fashion, our reading of fiction is strongly influenced by the narrator's point of view. Authors, like directors or camera operators, make choices about which point of view will convey the story most effectively. In Sandra Cisneros's short story "Eleven," for example, we experience the humiliation of the young girl from her perspective—so "close up" that we share what she thinks and feels. The author might have chosen to describe the event through a narrator who was looking on or from the viewpoint of the teacher or another student in her class. But because we see the event through the girl's eyes, we experience her pain as if it is happening to us. From any of these perspectives the event remains the same, but in each case our experience of it is quite different.

Point of view is the perspective from which the narrator tells the story. Generally, the pronoun that dominates the narration signals which point of view is represented. The terms most commonly used to identify point of view are first person, third person, omniscient, objective, and shifting.

First person uses the pronoun *I* and usually places the narrator in the story. We see through the view of that character (as an announcer and camera might isolate what we see to the view of one performer). The narrator sees through that character's eyes (as a camera sees through a performer's eyes). We see what he or she sees. As readers, we will only know what this one person experiences. The brief selections below from two short stories, "A&P" and "The Yellow Wallpaper," are examples of first-person point of view.

From "A&P," by John Updike (See the complete story on p. 296.)

In walks these three girls in nothing but bathing suits. I'm in the third checkout slot, with my back to the door, so I don't see them until they're over by the bread. The one that caught my eye first was the one in the plaid green two-piece. She was a chunky kid with a good tan and a sweet broad soft-looking can with those two crescents of white just under it, where the sun never seems to hit, at the top of the backs of her legs. I stood there with my hand on a box of Hi Ho crackers trying to remember if I rang it up or not. I ring it up again and the customer starts giving me hell. She's one of these cash register watchers, a witch about fifty with rouge on her cheekbones and no eyebrows, and I know it made her day to trip me up. She'd been watching cash registers for fifty years and probably never seen a mistake before.

From "The Yellow Wallpaper," by Charlotte Perkins Gilman (See the complete story on p. 532.)

It is very seldom that mere ordinary people like John and myself secure ancestral halls for the summer.

A colonial mansion, a hereditary estate, I would say a haunted house and reach the height of romantic felicity—but that would be asking too much of fate!

Still I will proudly declare that there is something queer about it.

Else, why should it be let so cheaply? And why have stood so long untenanted?

John laughs at me, of course, but one expects that.

John is practical in the extreme. He has no patience with faith, an intense horror of superstition, and he scoffs openly at any talk of things not to be felt and seen and put down in figures.

John is a physician, and perhaps—(I would not say it to a living soul, of course, but this is dead paper and a great relief to my mind)—*perhaps* that is one reason I do not get well faster.

You see, he does not believe I am sick! And what can one do?

Third person uses the pronouns *he* or *she,* but still usually limits us to one character's view. The narrator does not see through the character's eyes but focuses on the character and what he or she sees and thinks. Specifically, this is called **limited third-person point of view**. The perspective below in Liliana Heker's "Stolen Party" is limited third person. The narrator describes the action and the characters from the distance of a third person, but limits us to the thoughts of one character, Rosaura.

From "The Stolen Party," by Liliana Heker (See the complete story on p. 1128.)

Apart from the girl with the bow, all the others were delightful. The one she liked best was Luciana, with her golden birthday crown; and then the boys. Rosaura won the sack race, and nobody managed to catch her when they played tag. When they split into two teams to play charades, all the boys wanted her for their side. Rosaura felt she had never been so happy in her life.

But the best was still to come. The best came after Luciana blew out the candles. First the cake. Senora Ines had asked her to help pass the cake around, and Rosaura had enjoyed the task immensely, because everyone called out to her shouting, "Me, me!" Rosaura remembered a story in which there was a queen who had the power of life and death over her subjects. She had always loved that, having the power of life and death. To Luciana and the boys she gave the largest pieces, and to the girl with the bow she gave a slice so thin one could see through it.

Omniscient point of view also uses the pronouns *he, she,* and *they,* but the narrator is "all knowing" and able to move in and out of the minds of all the characters, choosing what and when to share. The selection from "The Open

Boat" below is written in an omniscient point of view. Only an omniscient narrator could know that "None of them knew the color of the sky."

From "The Open Boat," by Stephen Crane (See the complete story on p. 1302.)

None of them knew the color of the sky. Their eyes glanced level and were fastened upon the waves that swept toward them. These waves were of the hue of slate, save for the tops, which were of foaming white, and all of the men knew the colors of the sea. The horizon narrowed and widened, and dipped and rose, and at all times its edge was jagged with waves that seemed to thrust up in points like rocks.

Objective point of view minimizes the intervention of the narrator. The setting and the action are described, and we "listen in" on the dialogue, but the narrator does not interpret for us. We must do that ourselves. The selection that follows from "Hills Like White Elephants" is written in objective point of view. The narrator describes the setting, the characters, and the action from a distance while we seem to overhear their conversation from a neighboring table.

From "Hills like White Elephants," by Ernest Hemingway (See the complete story on p. 528.)

The hills across the valley of the Ebro were long and white. On this side there was no shade and no trees and the station was between two lines of rails in the sun. Close against the side of the station there was the warm shadow of the building and a curtain, made of strings of bamboo beads, hung across the open door into the bar, to keep out flies. The American and the girl with him sat at a table in the shade, outside the building. It was very hot and the express from Barcelona would come in forty minutes. It stopped at this junction for two minutes and went on to Madrid.

"What should we drink?" the girl asked. She had taken off her hat and put it on the table.

"It's pretty hot," the man said.

"Let's drink beer."

"Dos cervesas," the man said into the curtain.

"Big ones?" a woman asked from the doorway.

"Yes. Two big ones."

Shifting point of view gives us more than one point of view. It may shift from omniscient to first- or third-person point of view (like an overhead camera view of an arena that shifts focus to one performer). Or it may shift from first or third person to omniscient (like a camera that focuses on one performer, then opens up to show all of the action).

Voice

Voice refers to the narrator's persona, the personality that seems to come alive in the words. It is quite possible to have the same point of view but very different voices. The preceding selections from "A&P" and "The Yellow Wallpaper" both have a first-person point of view, but the voice (and personality) of Sammy in "A&P" is very different from that of the narrator in "The Yellow Wallpaper."

Reliability

Just as we make judgments about the credibility of characters, we should consider the stability and the motives of the narrator—especially if the narrator is a character in the story. If there are discrepancies between what you are being told and your own judgment of the same events or characters in the story, this may be an indication of the narrator's unreliability. For example, our response to a story like "The Yellow Wallpaper" is very dependent on our judgment of the narrator's stability.

✔CHECKLIST • *Narration*

- ❑ Who is the narrator?
- ❑ What is the point of view?
- ❑ How would you describe the narrator's voice?
- ❑ What is the narrator's relationship to the story? Is the narrator reliable? Does the narrator have any questionable motives? Is the narrator confused or emotionally unstable?
- ❑ Does the narration (point of view and voice) effectively convey the story's meaning?

SETTING

In our own lives, the places and company we seek have much to do with how we want to feel. When we want to relax, we go somewhere informal and familiar. When hungry but with little time to eat, we may go to a bare and efficient place where they serve fast food. On a dinner date, however, we are more likely to seek a restaurant with a sophisticated, romantic atmosphere.

If you were asked to describe the setting you are in right now, what factors would go into your description? Would you include more than its physical features? Setting is more than just physical surroundings. It includes the atmosphere, and atmosphere changes regularly. The weather, lighting, and time of day or night may change it. The people present may change it. Who are they? What is our relationship to them? Are we or they happy or sad? Can you "cut the tension with a knife"? Permanent factors, like physical qualities, are a "shell" for this atmosphere, but those factors that vary (people, time, weather, task) strongly influence a setting too.

In literature, setting is the location *and* the atmosphere of the story. It has a direct and indirect impact on character and conflict; it supports and emphasizes the story's meaning. Its most important function is to make us feel present in the world that the characters inhabit. The more we can visualize, the more we participate, the more satisfying the experience.

Location

Location tells us where and when the story is taking place. John Updike's "A&P" (p. 296), set in the 1960s in suburban Massachusetts, has a very different feel to it than James Joyce's "Araby" (p. 544), set in Dublin in the 1890s, or John Steinbeck's "The Chrysanthemums" (p. 1365), set in rural California in the 1930s. Both the *where* and the *when* will strongly influence the values and behavior of the characters and color the rest of the story.

Atmosphere

The **atmosphere** in a story arises from the mix of location and variable circumstances, such as the personalities present, the conflict, time of day, season, and even the weather. An effectively rendered atmosphere helps us see and experience concrete details of the setting as if we were present. It supports and complements the conflict and characters and helps to convey the story's meaning.

✔CHECKLIST • *Setting*

- ❑ What physical location is this? What does it look like?
- ❑ When does the story take place? What difference does it make to the story?
- ❑ What details help us visualize the setting?
- ❑ Can you describe the atmosphere? How is the lighting? What are the dominant colors? How are the people behaving? How are they dressed? What is the weather like? What is the mood like?

CONFLICT AND PLOT

We spend a good portion of every day resolving conflicts. Most of them are so small we don't even think of them as conflicts. We solve them easily without much effort or anxiety. We get up in the morning when we don't feel like it. We wait patiently for the traffic light to change before we go forward. The solutions and consequences are clear. If we stay in bed, we'll lose pay or be overcut in class. If we go through the red light, we might kill someone. There is not much internal strife here. And these dilemmas are not likely to make compelling stories.

As the conflicts become more complex, however, our anxiety increases and the choices seem more difficult: "What classes will I take next semester?" "How will I get to school tomorrow?" "Should I ask that person for a date?" Increase the complexity to another level and we get: "Should I stay in school next semester?" "Will I have to buy a car?" "Should I get married?" As the stakes are raised, our internal conflict increases. As you might imagine, the internal nature of conflict also has a lot to do with the personalities of the people involved. For people who are sensitive and shy, asking for a date may be a major conflict. The possibility of being rejected may cause great anxiety. For someone very depressed, even getting out of bed may seem like a major accomplishment.

In literature, **conflict** is the struggle of opposing external or internal forces. Conflict is at the heart of every story. In fact, without it we don't have a story—at least not one most of us would want to hear or read. The impediments and complications of conflict keep us reading. The more important, challenging, believable, and coherent the conflict is the more we are engaged by the story and want to follow it to its conclusion.

Internal and External Conflict

External conflict may be physical (characters against nature) or social (characters against each other or against society). Internal conflict is a struggle of opposing forces within a character. The best stories contain elements of both types of conflict, but the emphasis is usually on internal conflict.

Conflict and Characterization

Internal conflict has much to do with the makeup of the characters in the story. Consider the personality of each character. What provokes an internal conflict in one person may go unnoticed by another. A character who is insecure and self-conscious is likely to react very differently to some situations than a character who is confident and self-absorbed.

PLOT

When we share our own stories we structure them not only to convey the facts but also to have maximum impact. We might withhold information until later for the effect it will have on our listeners. We don't jump to answer the plea: So what happened!? We might say, "Hold on, I'm getting there, but you have to hear this part first to get a good sense of what happened later." We are naturally sensitive to the way that the arrangement of the details adds suspense or helps the listener "to be there" and feel the experience.

Plot is the structure of the story. It is the pattern of twists and turns the story takes. Most plots spring from conflict. To have a discernible plot, we must have impediments and complications for the work to take the twists and turns necessary to keep us reading.

One traditional arrangement of plot in a short story follows a pattern of exposition, rising action, crisis (sometimes called climax,) falling action, and resolution (sometimes called denouement or untying).

CRISIS/CLIMAX
(The moment of truth, the turning point of the conflict.)

RISING ACTION
(The conflict builds, and our emotional involvement intensifies.)

FALLING ACTION
(The crisis is over, the conflict fades, the intensity subsides.)

EXPOSITION
(We learn about the circumstances, characters, and the conflict.)

RESOLUTION
(Things are wrapped up and we are returned to normalcy.)

The diagram of this structure is a bit misleading. Even stories that contain these elements in their plots are generally not balanced so evenly. The crisis, for example, rarely falls right in the middle of the story. The bulk of most stories is spent building (exposition and rising action) to the crisis. Once the crisis is reached, the story usually winds down (falling action and resolution) quickly.

Many television shows and crime stories are classic examples of this formula. In the early days of TV, Earle Stanley Gardner's *Perry Mason* mysteries were turned into a television series. As seen in the following excerpt, each episode fit this pattern especially well—so well it was easy to work in commercial breaks between stages of the plot as if they were part of the show.

> *Exposition:* A desperate client appears at the office of famous defense attorney Perry Mason, reveals that a hideous crime has been committed (usually murder), indicates that he or she is a suspect, and proclaims innocence. Perry confers with his secretary and confidant Della Street and calls in private detective Paul Burke. In the course of these deliberations, we (the viewers or readers) find out about the circumstances, characters, and conflict of the story. (*Commercial break*)
>
> *Rising Action:* The client is arrested and charged with the hideous crime. The conflict builds as a motive is established and overwhelming circumstantial evidence mounts. Meanwhile, Paul desperately seeks information and other suspects and the setting shifts to the courtroom. The conflict intensifies: the suspense increases. (*Commercial break*)
>
> *The Crisis or Climax:* In the courtroom, the district attorney continues to build an iron-clad case against the defendant. Occasionally private eye Paul enters the courtroom and passes notes to Perry. Perry occasionally sends Della on an errand. The crucial moment occurs when Perry calls the real killer (or an accomplice) to the stand and he or she breaks down under his scrutiny and the weight of the newly discovered evidence (gathered by the relentless Paul) and confesses to the crime. (*Commercial break*)

The Falling Action: The murderer reveals motive and method. (*Commercial break*)

The Resolution: Perry reveals how the good guys found out the truth and shares a joke with Della, Paul, and the grateful, relieved former defendant. Justice is done, and all return to normalcy. (*End of show*)

Consider some of your favorite television shows. Do they have predictable plot structures? Can you describe them? How well do they work?

A major impediment to finding a traditional plot structure is that it doesn't fit some of the best fiction. In many works of fiction, the crisis or climax occurs at the end of the story. Things are not wrapped up for us. There is no intention to provide us with a resolution. Life doesn't come in episodes that resolve conflict so neatly. Stories that intend to capture life as it is don't "wrap up" so neatly either. Joyce's "Araby," Steinbeck's "The Chrysanthemums" (p. 1365), Updike's "A&P" (p. 296), Bobbie Ann Mason's "Shiloh" (p. 549), and many other stories don't fit this pattern. Most of these stories reach their crisis or climax and end when the protagonist or central character sees beyond a comforting illusion and confronts painful reality. After this climax there is no resolution—nor would we want one.

✔ CHECKLIST • *Conflict and Plot*

- ❑ What is the primary external conflict in the story?
- ❑ What is the primary internal conflict?
- ❑ Are there other conflicts? If so, what are they?
- ❑ How would you support your identification of conflict by what is in the text?
- ❑ To what extent do the traits of the characters lead to conflict?
- ❑ Can you identify the plot?
- ❑ Does it conform to the traditional structure? If so, how so? If not, what is the structure?

CHARACTER

Do you remember the first day of class? Surrounded by unfamiliar faces, you may have wondered, Who are these people? Even the instructor may have been unfamiliar to you. By the end of that class, though, you probably formed many impressions. You had some sense of what your classmates were like, perhaps even which ones you might like to know better. Some of those impressions may have come from *what* your classmates said about themselves and *how* they said it. But it's unlikely, even if they described themselves, that they told you what to think or feel about them. That was your decision. You probably decided what to think of them on the basis of their appearances, what they did, what they said, how they said it, and what others said about them. You wouldn't have settled for being told what to think; you wanted to see for yourself.

At its best, **characterization**, the development of characters in a story, gives us the same opportunity. The author brings characters to life and lets us "get to know them" as we know people in our own lives. While the narrator may tell us some things directly about the characters, we find out much of what we know indirectly through action and dialogue. We are not told what to think or feel about them. We observe the characters thinking, speaking, and doing. We hear what others say about them. They seem believable and motivated. And like our responses to people in our own lives, our reactions and judgments are based on our own observations.

The main character in a story is called the **protagonist**. When we find a character or characters who seem to be a major force in opposition to the protagonist, that character or characters is called the **antagonist** or **antagonists**. For example, the protagonist in Sandra Cisneros's short story "Eleven" is the young girl who narrates the story. The antagonist is Mrs. Price, who humiliates her in front of her classmates. In Ralph Ellison's "Battle Royal" (p. 830) the protagonist is the young man who narrates the story. The antagonists are "the town's leading white citizens," who degrade him at their brutally racist ceremony.

When characters lack the development that seems to bring them to life, lack the complexity that lets us know them as we know people in our own lives, and seem to represent "types" more than real personalities they are called **flat** or **stock characters**. When they seem fully developed, with all the complexities of real people, they are described as **round characters**.

✔CHECKLIST • *Character*

- ❑ What is your impression of the characters?
- ❑ What do the characters do that makes you feel this way? What do they say that makes you feel this way? What is said about them by other characters that makes you feel this way?
- ❑ Are the characters motivated and consistent? Are they believable?
- ❑ Are there flat or stock characters in the story?
- ❑ Can you identify the protagonist? One or more antagonists?
- ❑ Can you support your responses from the text of the story?

LANGUAGE AND STYLE

It's not possible to separate language and style from other elements. Language is the vehicle that carries them to you. The formal or informal style of the language is an integral part of narration. The evocative nature of the language used to describe setting has so much to do with our visualization and response to it. The style of the language used by the characters tells us a great deal about who they are. And the symbolic nature of the language may complement and support the story's theme or meaning.

Diction

The type of language they use, their **diction**, tells us a lot about narrators and characters and establishes their voices. Their use of formal vocabulary tells us one thing, their use of informal or nonstandard words or phrases conveys something very different. The frequency of images and figurative language may also have an effect on our reading and response to a story.

Symbol

A **symbol** is something that represents more than itself. Just about anything in a story might be symbolic. In fiction, symbols are most likely to be objects, names, or places, but they might be actions, sounds, or colors as well.

✔ **CHECKLIST** • ***Language and Style***

- ❑ Is the language formal or informal?
- ❑ What does the nature of the language tell you about the narrator or characters?
- ❑ Are there many instances of figurative language (imagery, simile, metaphor)? (See pages 86–93 in this chapter.)
- ❑ Is there a dominant symbol? Are there any symbols? If so, how do they connect to or support the story?

THEME

Theme is the central idea expressed by the story. It is a generalization, an insight about life derived from the work as a whole. Identifying and articulating this meaning is not easy. Although our experience of the theme may be holistic or impressionistic, the analysis and support required for its articulation demand a close look at the parts—the language, events, characters, and outcome of the story.

Theme or Moral?

When writing about literature, a temptation is to reduce what it means to a moral or lesson. Good literature reveals a complex world. Statements like

"Honesty is the best policy" may seem to reverberate with truth until we examine them closely. Is honesty always the best policy? Is it always the most ethical policy? Is it "moral" to tell people things that will hurt them? Didactic stories intend to deliver a moral. A moral preaches; it teaches a lesson or a code of conduct. A theme reveals; it gives us insight into human nature.

Consider the difference between revealing and preaching. If we read a story in which John loves Mary and Mary falls in love with Bill, we might state the simplified theme of the story as: People don't necessarily fall in love with those who are in love with them. To identify this theme, we examine the particulars of the story, come to a conclusion about them, and then expand this conclusion into a generalization about life itself.

A moral, however, is a simple lesson or rule of conduct. If we tried to find a moral in the previous John-Mary-Bill example, we might write, "Fall in love only with people who love you." But we know from our experience of the world that such a statement is much too simple to account for the complex nature of this situation. It would also seem silly to reduce John Steinbeck's story "The Chrysanthemums" to the moral "Don't trust strangers." It's clear that Eliza's unfulfilled desire for appreciation and love reveals a much more complex situation than such a moral could solve. Similarly, the frustration and humiliation of the protagonists in "Eleven" and "Battle Royal," or the intense emotional and ethical dilemma of the couple in "Hills Like White Elephants," cannot be reduced to clear lessons or morals. They reveal, as life reveals, complexity intact. In most modern literature, theme is not usually expressed as a moral, and it will probably take more than a few words to state the theme of a complex work.

✔CHECKLIST • *Theme*

- ❑ What are the major details (characters, conflicts, outcome) of the story?
- ❑ What conclusion about the story did you draw from these details?
- ❑ What generalization about life does this conclusion lead to?
- ❑ What does the story mean? What is the theme of the story?
- ❑ Is the story didactic? Does it preach or give a lesson?

✔SUMMARY CHECKLIST • *Analyzing Fiction*

Narration

- ❑ Who is the narrator?
- ❑ What is the point of view?
- ❑ How would you describe the narrator's voice?
- ❑ What is the narrator's relationship to the story? Is the narrator reliable?

(*continued*)

- ❑ Does the narrator have any questionable motives? Is the narrator confused or emotionally unstable?
- ❑ Does the narration (point of view and voice) effectively convey the story's meaning?

Setting

- ❑ What physical location is this? What does it look like?
- ❑ When does the story take place? What difference does it make to the story?
- ❑ What details help us visualize the setting?
- ❑ Can you describe the atmosphere?
- ❑ How is the lighting? What are the dominant colors?
- ❑ How are the people behaving? How are they dressed?
- ❑ What is the weather like? What is the mood like?

Conflict and Plot

- ❑ What is the primary external conflict in the story?
- ❑ What is the primary internal conflict?
- ❑ Are there other conflicts? If so, what are they?
- ❑ How would you support your identification of conflict by what is in the text?
- ❑ To what extent do the traits of the characters lead to conflict?
- ❑ Can you identify the plot?
- ❑ Does it conform to the traditional structure? If so, how so? If not, what is the structure?

Character

- ❑ What is your impression of the characters?
- ❑ What do the characters do that makes you feel this way?
- ❑ What do they say that makes you feel this way?
- ❑ What is said about them by other characters that makes you feel this way?
- ❑ Are the characters motivated and consistent? Are they believable?
- ❑ Are there flat or stock characters in the story?
- ❑ Can you identify the protagonist? One or more antagonists?
- ❑ Can you support your responses from the text of the story?

Language and Style

- ❑ Is the language formal or informal?
- ❑ What does the nature of the language tell you about the narrator or characters?

(*continued*)

- ❑ Are there many instances of figurative language (imagery, simile, metaphor)?
- ❑ Is there a dominant symbol? Are there any symbols?

Theme

- ❑ What are the major details (characters, conflicts, outcome) of the story?
- ❑ What conclusion about the story did you draw from these details?
- ❑ What generalization about life does this conclusion lead to?
- ❑ Is the story didactic? Does it preach or give a lesson?
- ❑ What is the central idea or theme of the story?

GETTING IDEAS FOR WRITING ABOUT FICTION

Following "One Friday Morning," many of the questions from the summary checklist above are applied to the story, and we consider some of the ways the elements on this list might be used to prompt ideas for a critical essay.

LANGSTON HUGHES (1902–1967)

ONE FRIDAY MORNING [1939]

The thrilling news did not come directly to Nancy Lee, but it came in little indirections that finally added themselves up to one tremendous fact: she had won the prize! But being a calm and quiet young lady, she did not say anything, although the whole high school buzzed with rumors, guesses, reportedly authentic announcements on the part of students who had no right to be making announcements at all—since no student really knew yet who had won this year's art scholarship.

But Nancy Lee's drawing was so good, her lines so sure, her colors so bright and harmonious, that certainly no other student in the senior art class at George Washington High was thought to have very much of a chance. Yet you never could tell. Last year nobody had expected Joe Williams to win the Artist Club scholarship with that funny modernistic water color he had done of the high-level bridge. In fact, it was hard to make out there was a bridge until you had looked at the picture a long time. Still, Joe Williams got the prize, was feted by the community's leading painters, club women, and society folks at a big banquet at the Park-Rose Hotel, and was now an award student at the Art School—the city's only art school.

Nancy Lee Johnson was a colored girl, a few years out of the South. But seldom did her high-school classmates think of her as colored. She was smart, pretty, and brown, and fitted in well with the life of the school. She stood high in scholarship, played a swell game of basketball, had taken part in the senior musical in a soft, velvety voice, and had never seemed to intrude or stand out, except in pleasant ways, so it was seldom even mentioned—her color.

Nancy Lee sometimes forgot she was colored herself. She liked her classmates and her school. Particularly she liked her art teacher, Miss Dietrich, the tall red-haired woman who taught her law and order in doing things; and the beauty of working step by step until a job is done; a picture finished; a design created; or a block print carved out of nothing but an idea and a smooth square of linoleum, inked, proofs made, and finally put down on paper-clean, sharp, beautiful, individual, unlike any other in the world, thus making the paper have a meaning nobody else could give it except Nancy Lee. That was the wonderful thing about true creation. You made something nobody else on earth could make but you.

5 Miss Dietrich was the kind of teacher who brought out the best in her students—but their own best, not anybody else's copied best. For anybody else's best, great though it might be, even Michelangelo's, wasn't enough to please Miss Dietrich, dealing with the creative impulses of young men and women living in an American city in the Middle West, and being American.

Nancy Lee was proud of being American, a Negro American with blood out of Africa a long time ago, too many generations back to count. But her parents had taught her the beauties of Africa, its strength, its songs, its mighty rivers, its early smelting of iron, its building of the pyramids, and its ancient and important civilizations. And Miss Dietrich had discovered for her the sharp and humorous lines of African sculpture, Benin, Congo, Makonde. Nancy Lee's father was a mail carrier, her mother a social worker in a city settlement house. Both parents had been to Negro colleges in the South. And her mother had gotten a further degree in social work from a Northern university. Her parents were, like most Americans, simple, ordinary people who had worked hard and steadily for their education. Now they were trying to make it easier for Nancy Lee to achieve learning than it had been for them. They would be very happy when they heard of the award to their daughter—yet Nancy did not tell them. To surprise them would be better. Besides, there had been a promise.

Casually, one day, Miss Dietrich asked Nancy Lee what color frame she thought would be best on her picture. That had been the first inkling.

"Blue," Nancy Lee said. Although the picture had been entered in the Artist Club contest a month ago, Nancy Lee did not hesitate in her choice of a color for the possible frame, since she could still see her picture clearly in her mind's eye for that picture waiting for the blue frame had come out of her soul, her own life, and had bloomed into miraculous being with Miss Dietrich's help. It was, she knew, the best water color she had painted in her four years as a high-school art student, and she was glad she had made something Miss Dietrich liked well enough to permit her to enter in the contest before she graduated.

It was not a modernistic picture in the sense that you had to look at it a long time to understand what it meant. It was just a simple scene in the city park on a spring day, with the trees still leaflessly lacy against the sky, the new grass fresh and green, a flag on a tall pole in the center, children playing, and an old Negro woman sitting on a bench with her head turned. A lot for one picture, to be sure, but it was not there in heavy and final detail like a calendar. Its charm was that everything was light and airy, happy like spring, with a lot of blue sky, paper-white clouds, and air showing through. You could tell that the old Negro woman was looking at the flag, and that the flag was proud in the spring breeze, and that the breeze helped to make the children's dresses billow as they played.

10 Miss Dietrich had taught Nancy Lee how to paint spring, people, and a breeze on what was only a plain white piece of paper from the supply closet. But Miss Dietrich had not said make it like any other spring-people-breeze ever seen before. She let it remain Nancy Lee's own. That is how the old Negro woman happened to be there looking at the flag—for in her mind the flag, the spring, and the woman formed a kind of triangle holding a dream Nancy Lee wanted to express. White stars on a blue field, spring, children, ever-growing life, and an old woman. Would the judges at the Artist Club like it?

One wet, rainy April afternoon Miss O'Shay, the girls' vice-principal, sent for Nancy Lee to stop by her office as school closed. Pupils without umbrellas or raincoats were clustered in doorways, hoping to make it home between showers. Outside the skies were gray. Nancy Lee's thoughts were suddenly gray, too.

She did not think she had done anything wrong, yet that tight little knot came in her throat just the same as she approached Miss O'Shay's door. Perhaps she had banged her locker too often and too hard. Perhaps the note in French she had written to Sallie halfway across the study hall just for fun had never gotten to Sallie but into Miss O'Shay's hands instead. Or maybe she was failing in some subject and wouldn't be allowed to graduate. Chemistry! A pang went through the pit of her stomach. She knocked on Miss O'Shay's door. That familiarly solid and competent voice said, "Come in."

Miss O'Shay had a way of making you feel welcome, even if you came to be expelled.

"Sit down, Nancy Lee Johnson," said Miss O'Shay. "I have something to tell you." Nancy Lee sat down. "But I must ask you to promise not to tell anyone yet."

15 "I won't, Miss O'Shay," Nancy Lee said, wondering what on earth the principal had to say to her.

"You are about to graduate," Miss O'Shay said. "And we shall miss you. You have been an excellent student, Nancy, and you will not be without honors on the senior list, as I am sure you know."

At that point there was a light knock on the door. Miss O'Shay called out, "Come in," and Miss Dietrich entered. "May I be a part of this, too?" she asked, tall and smiling.

"Of course," Miss O'Shay said. "I was just telling Nancy Lee what we thought of her. But I hadn't gotten around to giving her the news. Perhaps, Miss Dietrich, you'd like to tell her yourself"

Miss Dietrich was always direct. "Nancy Lee," she said, "your picture has won the Artist Club scholarship."

20 The slender brown girl's eyes widened, her heart thumped, then her throat tightened again. She tried to smile, but instead tears came to her eyes.

"Dear Nancy Lee," Miss O'Shay said, "we are so happy for you." The elderly white woman took her hand and shook it warmly while Miss Dietrich beamed with pride.

Nancy Lee must have danced all the way home. She never remembered quite how she got there through the rain. She hoped she had been dignified. But certainly she hadn't stopped to tell anybody her secret on the way. Raindrops, smiles, and tears mingled on her brown cheeks. She hoped her mother hadn't yet gotten home and that the house was empty. She wanted to have time to calm down and look natural before she had to see anyone. She didn't want to be bursting with excitement—having a secret to contain.

Miss O'Shay's calling her to the office had been in the nature of a preparation and a warning. The kind, elderly vice-principal said she did not believe in catching young ladies unawares, even with honors, so she wished her to know about the coming award. In making acceptance speeches she wanted her to be calm, prepared, not nervous, overcome, and frightened. So Nancy Lee was asked to think what she would say when the scholarship was conferred upon her a few days hence, both at the Friday morning high-school assembly hour, when the announcement would be made, and at the evening banquet of the Artist Club. Nancy Lee promised the vice-principal to think calmly about what she would say.

Miss Dietrich had then asked for some facts about her parents, her background, and her life, since such material would probably be desired for the papers. Nancy Lee had told her how, six years before, they had come up from the Deep South, her father having been successful in achieving a transfer from the one post office to another, a thing he had long sought in order to give Nancy Lee a chance to go to school in the North. Now they lived in a modest Negro neighborhood, went to see the best plays when they came to town, and had been saving to send Nancy Lee to art school, in case she were permitted to enter. But the scholarship would help a great deal, for they were not rich people.

"Now Mother can have a new coat next winter," Nancy Lee thought, "because my tuition will all be covered for the first year. And once in art school, there are other scholarships I can win."

Dreams began to dance through her head, plans and ambitions, beauties she would create for herself, her parents, and the Negro people—for Nancy Lee possessed a deep and reverent race pride. She could see the old woman in her picture (really her grandmother in the South) lifting her head to the bright stars on the flag in the distance. A Negro in America! Often hurt, discriminated against, sometimes lynched—but always there were the stars on the blue body of the flag. Was there any other flag in the world that had so many stars? Nancy Lee thought deeply, but she could remember none in all the encyclopedias or geographies she had ever looked into.

"Hitch your wagon to a star," Nancy Lee thought, dancing home in the rain. "Who were our flag-makers?"

Friday morning came, the morning when the world would know—her high-school world, the newspaper world, her mother and dad. Dad could not be there at the assembly to hear the announcement, nor see her prize picture displayed on the stage, nor to listen to Nancy Lee's little speech of acceptance, but Mother would be able to come, although Mother was much puzzled as to why Nancy Lee was so insistent she be at school on that particular Friday morning.

When something is happening, something new and fine, something that will change your very life, it is hard to go to sleep at night for thinking about it, and hard to keep your heart from pounding, or a strange little knot of joy from gathering in your throat. Nancy Lee had taken her bath, brushed her hair until it glowed, and had gone to bed thinking about the next day, the big day, when before three thousand students, she would be the one student honored, her painting the one painting to be acclaimed as the best of the year from all the art classes of the city. Her short speech of gratitude was ready. She went over it in her mind, not word for word (because she didn't want it to sound as if she had learned it by heart), but she let the thoughts flow simply and sincerely through her consciousness many times.

30 When the president of the Artist Club presented her with the medal and scroll of the scholarship award, she would say:

"Judges and members of the Artist Club, I want to thank you for this award that means so much to me personally and through me to my people, the colored people of this city, who, sometimes, are discouraged and bewildered, thinking that color and poverty are against them. I accept this award with gratitude and pride, not for myself alone, but for my race that believes in American opportunity and American fairness—and the bright stars in our flag. I thank Miss Dietrich and the teachers who made it possible for me to have the knowledge and training that lie behind this honor you have conferred upon my painting. When I came here from the South a few years ago, I was not sure how you would receive me. You received me well. You have given me a chance and helped me along the road I wanted to follow. I suppose the judges know that every week here at assembly the students of this school pledge allegiance to the flag. I shall try to be worthy of that pledge, and of the help and friendship and understanding of my fellow citizens of whatever race or creed, and of our American dream of 'Liberty and justice for all!'"

That would be her response before the students in the morning. How proud and happy the Negro pupils would be, perhaps almost as proud as they were of the one colored star on the football team. Her mother would probably cry with happiness. Thus Nancy Lee went to sleep dreaming of a wonderful tomorrow.

The bright sunlight of an April morning woke her. There was breakfast with her parents—their half-amused and puzzled faces across the table, wondering what could be this secret that made her eyes so bright. The swift walk to school; the clock in the tower almost nine; hundreds of pupils streaming into the long, rambling old building that was the city's largest high school; the sudden quiet of the homeroom after the bell rang; then the teacher opening her record book to call the roll. But just before she began, she looked across the room until her eyes located Nancy Lee.

"Nancy," she said, "Miss O'Shay would like to see you in her office, please."

35 Nancy Lee rose and went out while the names were being called and the word *present* added its period to each name. Perhaps, Nancy Lee thought, the reporters from the papers had already come. Maybe they wanted to take her picture before assembly, which wasn't until ten o'clock. (Last year they had had the photograph of the winner of the award in the morning papers as soon as the announcement had been made.)

Nancy Lee knocked at Miss O'Shay's door.

"Come in."

The vice-principal stood at her desk. There was no one else in the room. It was very quiet.

"Sit down, Nancy Lee," she said. Miss O'Shay did not smile. There was a long pause. The seconds went by slowly. "I do not know how to tell you what I have to say," the elderly woman began, her eyes on the papers on her desk. "I am indignant and ashamed for myself and for this city." Then she lifted her eyes and looked at Nancy Lee in the near blue dress, sitting there before her. "You are not to receive the scholarship this morning."

Outside in the hall the electric bells announcing the first period rang, loud and interminably long. Miss O'Shay remained silent. To the brown girl here in the chair, the room grew suddenly smaller, smaller, smaller, and there was no air. She could not speak.

Miss O'Shay said, "When the committee learned that you were colored, they changed their plans."

Still Nancy Lee said nothing, for there was no air to give breath to her lungs.

"Here is the letter from the committee, Nancy Lee." Miss O'Shay picked it up and read the final paragraph to her.

" 'It seems to us wiser to arbitrarily rotate the award among the various high schools of the city from now on. And especially in this case since the student chosen happens to be colored, a circumstance which unfortunately, had we known, might have prevented this embarrassment. But there have never been any Negro students in the local art school, and the presence of one there might create difficulties for all concerned. We have high regard for the quality of Nancy Lee Johnson's talent, but we do not feel it would be fair to honor it with the Artist Club award.' " Miss O'Shay paused. She put the letter down.

"Nancy Lee, I am very sorry to have to give you this message."

"But my speech," Nancy Lee said, "was about. . . ." The words stuck in her throat. ". . . about America. . . ."

Miss O'Shay had risen; she turned her back and stood looking out the window at the spring tulips in the school yard.

"I thought, since the award would be made at assembly right after our oath of allegiance," the words rumbled almost hysterically from Nancy Lee's throat now, "I would put part of the flag salute in my speech. You know, Miss O'Shay, that part about 'liberty and justice for all.'"

"I know," said Miss O'Shay, slowly facing the room again. "But America is only what we who believe in it make it. I am Irish. You may not know, Nancy Lee, but years ago we were called the dirty Irish, and mobs rioted against us in the big cities, and we were invited to go back where we came from. But we didn't go. And we didn't give up, because we believed in the American dream, and in our power to make that dream come true. Difficulties, yes. Mountains to climb, yes. Discouragements to face, yes. Democracy to make, yes. That is it, Nancy Lee! We still have in this world of ours democracy to *make*. You and I, Nancy Lee. But the premise and the base are here, the lines of the Declaration of Independence and the words of Lincoln are here, and the stars in our flag. Those who deny you this scholarship do not know the meaning of those stars, but it's up to us to make them know. As a teacher in the public schools of this city, I myself will go before the school board and ask them to remove from our system the offer of any prizes or awards denied to any student because of race or color."

Suddenly Miss O'Shay stopped speaking. Her clear, clear blue eyes looked into those of the girl before her. The woman's eyes were full of strength and courage. "Lift up your head, Nancy Lee, and smile at me."

Miss O'Shay stood against the open window with the green lawn and the tulips beyond, the sunlight tangled in her gray hair, her voice an electric flow of strength to the hurt spirit of Nancy Lee. The Abolitionists who believed in freedom when there was slavery must have been like that. The first white teachers who went into the Deep South to teach the freed slaves must have been like that. All those who stand against ignorance, narrowness, hate, and mud on stars must be like that.

Nancy Lee lifted her head and smiled. The bell for assembly rang. She went through the long hall filled with students, toward the auditorium.

"There will be other awards," Nancy Lee thought. "There are schools in other cities. This won't keep me down. But when I'm a woman, I'll fight to see that these things don't happen to other girls as this has happened to me. And men and women like Miss O'Shay will help me."

She took her seat among the seniors. The doors of the auditorium closed. As the principal came onto the platform, the students rose and turned their eyes to the flag on the stage.

One hand went to the heart, the other outstretched toward the flag. Three thousand voices spoke. Among them was the voice of a dark girl whose cheeks were suddenly wet with tears, "... one nation indivisible, with liberty and justice for all."

"That is the land we must make," she thought.

GENERATING IDEAS FOR WRITING

One of the best ways to get ideas for an essay is to ask and answer your own most compelling questions. Write down whatever questions come to mind during and after your reading. See if your answers to these questions provide topics for writing. Or choose a compelling idea from a journal entry, draw a Venn diagram to compare elements, characters, or stories (pp. 33–34), use directed freewriting (p. 41), ask questions (p. 42), list, or draw a cluster, or semantic map (pp. 43–44), to loosen up ideas.

Listed below is a much more structured approach based on the elements of fiction discussed earlier in this section. Applying these questions to "One Friday Morning" may demonstrate how the elements might be applied to any work of short fiction.

Getting Started—Your First Response

1. What questions came to mind as you read "One Friday Morning"?

2. To what extent can you connect "One Friday Morning" to your own background or experience?
3. What do you find most compelling or provocative about the story?

Narration

1. Unlike the first-person narrative of Sandra Cisneros's "Eleven" in Chapter 2, this story is told from the third-person point of view. How does this narrative perspective affect your experience of the story?
2. What is the tone of the narration? What is the attitude of the narrator toward Nancy Lee? To what extent is the narrator reliable?
3. If the story were told in the first person by Nancy Lee herself, how would it change the way you experience it? Would you know any more than you do now? If so, what?
4. If the story were told by Miss O'Shay or Miss Dietrich, how would it change the way you experience the story?

Setting

1. Describe the setting of "One Friday Morning." In what location does the story take place? When does it occur?
2. What effect does the setting have on your response to the story?
3. "Outside the skies were gray" is a description of the weather in one scene. In what way does the weather agree with or contrast the action in the story?
4. What other details in Langston Hughes's writing were most effective in conveying the setting? Quote them from the text.
5. This story was originally published in 1939. If the story were written and published recently, would you have responded differently? Explain.

Conflict and Plot

1. What events in "One Friday Morning" lead to the conflict?
2. How would you describe the conflict? Which elements of the conflict are external? Which ones are internal?
3. To what extent does the conflict derive from Nancy Lee, Miss Dietrich, Miss O'Shay, and their beliefs?
4. What is the climax of this story? What is the resolution? To what extent are you satisfied with the resolution?

Character

1. Describe Nancy Lee. How does what she says and does show you who she is? Do you learn about her directly or indirectly? Explain.
2. How would you describe Miss Dietrich? Miss O'Shay? What do they do or say that supports your description? Are they round or flat characters? Why?

3. What quotes from the text support your description of Nancy Lee? Of Miss Deitrich? Of Miss O'Shay?
4. To what extent do Nancy Lee, Miss Deitrich, or Miss O'Shay change or develop in the story?
5. If Nancy Lee is the protagonist, who is the antagonist?

Language and Style

1. Is the language of "One Friday Morning" formal or informal?
2. What does the nature of the language Nancy Lee uses tell you about her? The language of Miss Dietrich? Of Miss O'Shay? Cite examples.
3. How does the language of the narration affect you? For example, the sentence "Raindrops, smiles, and tears mingled on her brown cheeks" paints an especially touching picture. What other images appeal to you and why?
4. Do you see any symbols in "One Friday Morning"? If so, explain.

Theme

1. What conclusion do you draw from "One Friday Morning"?
2. What details and events lead to this conclusion?
3. What is the point of the story? What is the theme?

Topics for Writing

The following list is not exhaustive, but simply illustrative of the kinds of questions that might emerge from more specific analytical questions (and combinations of questions) like those above. Your responses to these questions might provide worthwhile topics for writing.

1. What is the effect of third-person narration on the characterization of Nancy Lee?
2. What would this story be like if told by Nancy Lee?
3. In what way is the school setting a factor in the outcome of "One Friday Morning"?
4. In what way is the larger setting of the Midwest a factor in the outcome?
5. To what extent are Miss Deitrich and Miss O'Shay helpful mentors for Nancy Lee?
6. To what extent are Miss Deitrich and Miss O'Shay cooperating with a racist system?
7. How does Langston Hughes's "One Friday Morning" compare with his poem "A Dream Deferred" (p. 88)? How does it compare to other works of Langston Hughes?
8. What were race relations like in this country in 1939? How does "One Friday Morning" fit within the time period and culture in which it was written? To what extent would the resolution of this story be acceptable today?

Reading and Analyzing Poetry

The subject of poetry is human experience. We are not likely to say of any event, "You can't write a poem about that." Birth, death, youth, old age, love, jealousy, ambition, loyalty, laughter, triumph, defeat—if we can experience it, we can write poetry about it. The more an experience moves us, the more important it seems to record the emotion, sensation, or memory with a poem. Reading poetry is a personal as well as a social experience. It is personal in the way it offers us a reflection of our own interior lives, our thoughts and emotions expressed in the words of others; and it is social in the way it offers us a glimpse of other people's interior lives, the shared expression of their hearts and minds.

Poems are not written to fill textbooks or create academic exercises. They are written to communicate with us. If we reduce our reading to analysis alone, we may "figure out" the poem's structure, its rhyme scheme and rhythm, or how it might be classified, but we may miss the experience of the poem itself. That experience relies on our ability to imagine—the ability to take the "sleeping" poem from the print on the page and "wake it up" through our imagination, senses, and emotions. This is not the kind of reading we might be used to doing in an academic environment, where we often read for information alone. And it may not be the style of reading we are used to in our everyday lives—in a world that bombards us with the exaggerated language of advertising, TV commercials, and talk shows, or reduces everything to sound bites. Given the lack of meaning in so much of that language, we may speed through it or ignore it altogether. We are not used to paying attention to language with our senses and emotions, to forming images; they are so often formed for us.

Poetry invites your engagement and comprehension. To be engaged by a poem, you need the time to read slowly and participate fully with your mind and senses. Once engaged, you have reason to analyze the poem's language, its structure, its rhymes or rhythms—to comprehend *how* it has prompted your response. Reading a poem this way involves your mind, senses, and emotions—and it has the power to change you the way that all meaningful experiences can.

Language and Style

Denotation and Connotation

Faced with an unfamiliar word—dictionary in hand—you might look up its definition and be reasonably satisfied with what you find. But if you are already familiar with that word, a dictionary definition is not likely to account for everything the word means to you. While you might not disagree with the dictionary definition, or **denotation**, of the word, you probably won't be entirely satisfied with it, either. Your own definitions, or **connotations**, for familiar words are flavored with personal associations. Dictionary definitions alone cannot account for this complex response to language.

The compressed nature of language and meaning in poetry makes word choice crucial. Poets are very conscious of the effect that connotations, or suggested meanings, have on readers. Synonyms for the word *thin*, for example, include *slim, slender, lean, skinny*, and *trim*—words that mean almost the same thing. But each of these words has a different connotation and slightly different meaning for each of us—and a different effect on us when we read it. Being conscious of word choices and patterns of language may tell us a great deal about what makes a poem effective and how it triggers our responses.

Voice

Be sure to differentiate between the poet and the speaker in a poem. In some poems the poet and the speaker are virtually the same, and we can assume the thoughts of the speaker are those of the poet as well. In Robert Hayden's poem "Those Winter Sundays" (p. 12), the speaker's remembrance seems to be that of the poet himself. On the other hand, the speaker (the "voice") in a poem may use vocabulary and express attitudes that are not characteristic of the poet. The speaker in Robert Browning's "Porphyria's Lover" (p. 566), a demented, homicidal lover, is clearly not the poet himself. Being able to identify the speaker, the speaker's attitude toward the poem's content, and the speaker's intended audience helps us read the poem more effectively.

Tone

The key to **tone** is voice. When we see or hear a poet speaking, the words, intonations, physical gestures, and facial expressions tell us the attitude of the speaker toward the subject. When we "hear" voice in our reading, we can also sense the intonations. Cues in a printed poem are not always obvious, however, and to sense the tone we must often rely on the pattern and types of words the poet chooses. Sometimes the contradictory nature of the language can give us a strong sense of that tone.

STEPHEN CRANE (1871–1900)

WAR IS KIND [1899]

Do not weep, maiden, for war is kind.
Because your lover threw wild hands toward the sky
And the affrighted steed ran on alone,
Do not weep.
War is kind.

Hoarse, booming drums of the regiment,
Little souls who thirst for fight,
These men were born to drill and die.
The unexplained glory flies above them,
Great is the battle god, great, and his kingdom
A field where a thousand corpses lie.

Do not weep, babe, for war is kind.
Because your father tumbled in the yellow trenches,
Raged at his breast, gulped and died,
Do not weep.
War is kind.

Swift blazing flag of the regiment,
Eagle with crest of red and gold,
These men were born to drill and die.
Point for them the virtue of slaughter,
Make plain for them the excellence of killing
And a field where a thousand corpses lie.

Mother whose heart hung humble as a button
On the bright splendid shroud of your son,
Do not weep.
War is kind.

➤ *QUESTIONS FOR READING AND WRITING*

1. How did your feelings about war influence your response?
2. What do you think about the choice of words Crane uses to describe war?
3. With many poems, being sensitive to the voice of the speaker is crucial to our response. The tone expressed by that voice may change the meaning. How are you affected by the tone in this poem?
4. What indications of tone are there in the text of the poem? Is there a contradiction between the title "War Is Kind" and the details that Crane uses to support it?
5. How does the poet's tone affect the meaning of "War Is Kind"?

Imagery

An **image** is a mental picture prompted by words. Images result from concrete language that appeals to our senses. "Nice image," we've heard people say about particularly striking words or phrases. But images do not exist in words on a page. They exist in our minds. The words on the page may prompt the images in our minds, but it is our own senses and memories that evoke the pictures. Experiments have shown that we use the same parts of our brains when we see or hear the word for an object as we do when encountering the object itself. It is our sense memories that bring a poet's words to life to form an image. We can see (hear, taste, touch, or smell) them in our mind's eye (ear, tongue, hand, or nose).

HELEN CHASSIN (b. 1938)

THE WORD PLUM [1986]

The word *plum* is delicious

pout and push, luxury of
self-love, and savoring murmur

full in the mouth and falling
like fruit

taut skin
pierced, bitten, provoked into
juice, and tart flesh
question
and reply, lip and tongue
of pleasure.

ROBERT BROWNING (1812–1889)

MEETING AT NIGHT [1845]

The gray sea and the long black land:
And the yellow half-moon large and low;
And the startled little waves that leap
In fiery ringlets from their sleep,
As I gain the cove with pushing prow,
And quench its speed in the slushy sand.

Then a mile of warm sea-scented beach;
Three fields to cross till a farm appears;
A tap at the pane, the quick sharp scratch
And blue spurt of a lighted match,
And a voice less loud, through its joys and fears,
Than the two hearts beating each to each!

➤ *QUESTIONS FOR READING AND WRITING*

1. Not all poetry intends to make a serious statement. Some poems simply intend to engage us in an aesthetic or sensory experience. Does "The Word *Plum*" have a different effect on you than "Meeting at Night" or "War Is Kind"? Explain.
2. To what extent can you connect "The Word *Plum*" and "Meeting at Night" to your own experience? How does that connection affect your response to the imagery?

3. In "The Word *Plum*," the senses of taste and touch are primarily the senses we rely on to experience the images in the poem. How many senses do you use to experience the images in "Meeting at Night"?
4. How do these images add to the overall effect of the poems for you?

Figurative Language: Everyday Poetry

There is nothing unusual about figurative language. In fact, we would have a hard time communicating with each other without it. Comparison is at the core of "figures of speech," or figurative language. We use what is already familiar to describe something new, or we describe something familiar in a new way. Used in tandem with concrete language, similes and metaphors can lead to very striking images.

A **simile** is an announced comparison. We announce or introduce this comparison by using the words *like* or *as*. For example, "He's as quiet as a church mouse." or "She swims like a fish." Those things compared usually have only one characteristic in common. Some of the most evocative descriptions in literature are similes. James Joyce's description of a young boy's infatuation, "But my body was like a harp and her words and gestures were like fingers running upon the wires" (see "Araby," page 544) and Marge Piercy's words, "Her good nature wore out like a fan belt" (see "Barbie Doll," page 13) are vivid examples of how simile can evoke lasting images in our minds.

LANGSTON HUGHES (1902–1967)

A DREAM DEFERRED [1951]

What happens to a dream deferred?

Does it dry up
like a raisin in the sun?
Or fester like a sore—
And then run?
Does it stink like rotten meat?
Or crust and sugar over—
like a syrupy sweet?
Maybe it just sags
like a heavy load.

Or does it explode?

N. SCOTT MOMADAY (b. 1934)

SIMILE

[1974]

What did we say to each other
that now we are as the deer
who walk in single file
with heads high
with ears forward
with eyes watchful
with hooves always placed on firm ground
in whose limbs there is latent flight

➤ *QUESTIONS FOR READING AND WRITING*

1. Each of these poems relies on comparison to make its point. To what extent do these comparisons bring personal experiences to mind?
2. There are five announced comparisons (similes) and one implied comparison (metaphor) in "A Dream Deferred." What are they? What images do they prompt in you? What senses do you use to experience them?
3. As its title suggests, there is one announced comparison in "Simile." What is it? What image does it prompt in you?
4. To what extent are you affected differently by the many brief similes of "A Dream Deferred" in comparison to the one extended simile in "Simile"?
5. What is the point of each poem? In each case, how do the similes present it effectively?
6. To what extent is "A Dream Deferred" similar to Hughes's short story "One Friday Morning" (p. 75)?

A **metaphor** is a more direct and more complete comparison than a simile. A metaphor does not announce itself; it states that something *is* something else (My love is a red rose) or implies it (My love has red petals and sharp thorns.). Our everyday language is filled with metaphors. We call attractive-looking people hunks and foxes. Businesses use implied metaphors to name their products. We buy an antiperspirant named Arrid, soap named Irish Spring, computers named Powerbooks, and cars named Jaguars. Sometimes, however, people get carried away and mix metaphors, with curious results. A baseball manager once remarked about a suspended player, that "The ball was in his court now [tennis], so he better not step out of bounds [basketball], or he'd be down for the count [boxing]."

CARL SANDBURG (1878–1967)

FOG [1916]

The fog comes
on little cat feet.
It sits looking
over harbor and city
on silent haunches
and then moves on.

H. D. (HILDA DOOLITTLE) (1886–1961)

OREAD° [1924]

Whirl up, sea—
whirl your pointed pines,
splash your great pines
on our rocks,
hurl your green over us,
cover us with your pools of fir.

oread mountain nymph

Personification is a frequently used form of metaphor. To personify is to give human characteristics or qualities to something not human. Consider how often you personify objects in your everyday use of language.

JAMES STEPHENS (1882–1950)

THE WIND [1915]

The wind stood up and gave a shout.
He whistled on his fingers and

Kicked the withered leaves about
And thumped the branches with his hand

And said he'd kill and kill and kill,
And so he will and so he will.

➤ *QUESTIONS FOR READING AND WRITING*

1. To what extent is your response to "Fog," "Oread," or "The Wind" influenced by your own experience? Support your explanation with reference to the poems.

2. What are the metaphors in each poem?
3. What images do they prompt in you?
4. What senses do you use to experience them?
5. How do these images add to the overall effect of the poems?

Symbol

A **symbol** is something that represents more than itself. Every word we speak is a symbol. Government flags, religious objects, and logos on college sweatshirts are all symbols. We have personal symbols (meaningful objects, special songs), public symbols (flags), and conventional symbols (a road as the journey of life, seasons to represent the stages of our lives). Symbols are subject to personal interpretation. A nation's flag may symbolize truth and justice to one person, but deceit and oppression to another.

ROBERT FROST (1874–1963)

THE ROAD NOT TAKEN [1915]

Two roads diverged in a yellow wood
And sorry I could not travel both
And be one traveler, long I stood
And looked down one as far as I could
To where it bent in the undergrowth;

Then took the other, as just as fair,
Because it was grassy and wanted wear:
Though as for that the passing there
Had worn them really about the same.

And both that morning equally lay
In leaves no step had trodden black.
Oh, I kept the first for another day!
Yet knowing how way leads on to way,
I doubted if I should ever come back.

I shall be telling this with a sigh
somewhere ages and ages hence:
Two roads diverged in a wood, and I—
I took the one less traveled by,
And that has made all the difference.

TESS GALLAGHER (b. 1943)

THE HUG [1987]

A woman is reading a poem on the street
and another woman stops to listen. We stop too,
with our arms around each other. The poem
is being read and listened to out here
in the open. Behind us
no one is entering or leaving the houses.

Suddenly a hug comes over me and I'm
giving it to you, like a variable star shooting light
off to make itself comfortable, then
subsiding. I finish but keep on holding
you. A man walks up to us and we know he hasn't
come out of nowhere, but if he could, he
would have. He looks homeless because of how
he needs. "Can I have one of those?" he asks you,
and I feel you nod. I'm surprised,
surprised you don't tell him how
it is—that I'm yours, only
yours, etc., exclusive as a nose to
its face. Love—that's what we're talking about, love
that nabs you with "for me
only" and holds on.

So I walk over to him and put my
arms around him and try to
hug him like I mean it. He's got an overcoat on
so thick I can't feel
him past it. I'm starting the hug
and thinking, "How big a hug is this supposed to be?
How long should I hold this hug?" Already
we could be eternal, his arms falling over my
shoulders, my hands not
meeting behind his back, he is so big!

I put my head into his chest and snuggle
in. I lean into him. I lean my blood and my wishes
into him. He stands for it. This is his
and he's starting to give it back so well I know he's
getting it. This hug. So truly, so tenderly
we stop having arms and I don't know if
my lover has walked away or what, or
if the woman is still reading the poem, or the houses—
what about them?—the houses.

Clearly, a little permission is a dangerous thing.
But when you hug someone you want it
to be a masterpiece of connection, the way the button
on his coat will leave the imprint of
a planet in my cheek
when I walk away, when I try to find some place
to go back to.

➤ *QUESTIONS FOR READING AND WRITING*

1. To what extent is your response to "The Road Not Taken" or "The Hug" influenced by your own experience?
2. If the road in "The Road Not Taken" is a symbol for the journey of life, what is the symbol in "The Hug" and what does it represent?
3. What images do these poems prompt in you?
4. What senses do you use to experience these images?
5. How does the symbolism add to the overall effect of the poem for you?

✔ CHECKLIST • *Language and Style*

- ❑ How does the poet's choice of words affect your response?
- ❑ How are you affected by the speaker's voice?
- ❑ What images do you experience?
- ❑ Are there similes or metaphors?
- ❑ Is there symbolism?
- ❑ How do word choice, voice, imagery, figurative language, and/or symbolism affect your response?
- ❑ How can you support your responses from the text?

Sound and Structure

Long before we had the ability to speak, we enjoyed making and listening to sounds. As newcomers to the world, we were probably soothed or frightened by the sound of the adult voices around us. The sounds we made helped us develop our vocal chords, but there was much more to it than that. We listened to the sounds we made and adjusted them until we got them just right. We made the leap from gurgles and hisses to new sounds with real syllables like ba-ba, ma-ma, da-da.

The amazing thing is that all of this happened before we could speak and understand words or sentences from the adult language that surrounded us. Those sounds were a universal language we shared with children all over the world. And those sounds, like music, seemed to have an appeal in and of themselves—

an appeal we haven't forgotten. Sometimes we listen to songs and sing along or sing the songs to ourselves—even when we don't know all the words. And sometimes we like the sounds of the words and the rhymes and rhythms of poems just as much as their meanings.

Finding the Beat: Limericks

A light, usually humorous, form of poetry that is helpful for getting the feel of rhyme and rhythm is the **limerick**. Limericks are very common and almost always anonymous (usually for good reason), and we're just as likely to see them scrawled on a wall as on paper.

The limerick packs laughs anatomical
Into space that is quite economical.
    But the good ones I've seen
    So seldom are clean,
And the clean ones so seldom are comical.

Read it out loud several times. Listen to the rhythm. Look at the rhyme pattern or scheme. Which lines rhyme? What is the rhythm like? Can you describe the pattern of a limerick? If you need to, read it out loud again.

Here's another one:

There was a young maid who said, "Why (*a*)
Can't I look in my ear with my eye? (*a*)
    If I put my mind to it, (*b*)
    I'm sure I can do it. (*b*)
You never can tell till you try." (*a*)

Can you figure out the pattern?

Limericks have five lines. The first, second, and fifth lines rhyme (*aaa,* above) and so do the third and fourth (*bb,* above). The first, third, and fifth have the same verbal rhythm (**meter**) and length, and so do the second and fourth.

Sometimes we don't notice what we have until it's gone:

A decrepit old gas man named Peter,
While hunting around for the meter,
    Touched a leak with his light.
    He arose out of sight,
And, as anyone can see by reading this, he also destroyed the meter.

What "destroyed" the meter? Can you fix it by rewriting the fifth line yourself?

Rhyme, Alliteration, Assonance

As kids in school, we may have used rhymes to memorize the number of days in each month or the names of the states or presidents. The most obvious rhymes come at ends of lines when final vowel and consonant sounds in a word at the end of one line match vowel and consonant sounds at the end of another (l*and* and s*and*, th*ings* and k*ings*, b*are* and desp*air*).

Less obvious are repeated initial consonant sounds ("*d*o or *d*ie," "*s*ink or *s*wim," *s*uffering *s*uccotash"), which is called **alliteration**.

Less obvious still are **assonance**, or repeated vowel sounds (t*i*me l*i*ne, fr*ee* and *ea*sy) and **consonance**, or repeated consonant sounds (shor*t* and smar*t*, s*tr*u*ts* and f*r*e*ts*).

When we listen to music, we are moved along (in spirit and time) and can anticipate structure by patterns and combinations of repeated tones. If we listen sensitively to rhyme and rhythm in poetry, we are likely to have a similar experience.

Look at the following quatrains (units of four lines) from two different William Blake poems. This quatrain has an *ab, ab* rhyme scheme:

From "London"

In every cry of every Man, (*a*)
In every Infant's cry of fear, (*b*)
In every voice, in every ban, (*a*)
The mind-forg'd manacles I hear. (*b*)

This quatrain has an *aa, bb* rhyme scheme:

From "The Tyger"

In what distant deeps or skies (*a*)
Burnt the fire of thine eyes? (*a*)
On what wings dare he aspire? (*b*)
What the hand dare seize the fire? (*b*)

Recite each quatrain out loud several times. How does the ordering of rhyme affect your pace? How does it affect the content of the lines and the units of thought you remember?

Examine other poems in this section. For example, Robert Browning's "Meeting at Night" and Robert Frost's "The Road Not Taken" have very different rhyme schemes. Read them out loud and see how the rhyme scheme affects how you hear and organize the content of the poems.

Meter

Some rhythm in poetry is described by the word *meter*. **Meter** refers to the pattern of stressed (/) and unstressed (˘) syllables in a line. The group of syllables making up one metrical unit is called a **foot**. The metrical feet most commonly used are **iambic** (unstressed, stressed), **trochaic** (stressed, unstressed), **anapestic** (two unstressed, one stressed), and **dactylic** (one stressed, two unstressed).

The number of feet in each line is described as **monometer** (one foot), **dimeter** (two feet), **trimeter** (three feet), **tetrameter** (four feet), **pentameter** (five feet), **hexameter** (six feet), **heptameter** (seven feet), and **octometer** (eight feet).

The most common form of meter in poetry written in English is **iambic** (unstressed, stressed) **pentameter** (five feet).

The pair of lines from two sonnets written over three hundred years apart are examples of iambic pentameter: (five feet of iambic per line):

Dĕsír\ĭng thís\ măn's árt \ănd thát\ măn's scópe
Wĭth whát\ Ĭ móst\ ĕnjóy\ cŏntént\ĕd léast,
—William Shakespeare (1609)

Nŏr yét\ ă flóat\ĭng spár\ tŏ mén\ thăt sínk
Ănd ríse\ ănd sínk\ ănd ríse\ ănd sínk\ ăgáin;
—Edna St. Vincent Millay (1931)

Formal Verse: The Sonnet

One of the most popular and enduring formal verse structures is the sonnet. Sonnets are fourteen lines long and are usually written in iambic pentameter. Rhyme schemes will vary according to type. The oldest form of the sonnet is the Italian, or Petrarchan, sonnet (named for its greatest practitioner, Petrarch). Its rhyme scheme is usually an octave (eight lines) and a sestet (six lines). The octave usually follows a pattern of *abbaabba*. The concluding sestet may be *cdecde* or *cdcdcd* or *cdedce*.

In English, the most popular form is the English, or Shakespearean, sonnet (named for its greatest practitioner, Shakespeare, who wrote 154 of them), so we use it here to illustrate formal verse. The Shakespearean sonnet is a fourteen-line poem of three quatrains (four-line units) and a final couplet (a two-line unit) in the rhyme scheme *abab cdcd efef gg*. It is a structure that presents the content of the poem in predictable ways. The first two quatrains often present a problem. The third quatrain is often pivotal and begins a reversal. The final couplet most often suggests a solution.

William Shakespeare (1564–1616)

Sonnet No. 29 [1609]

When, in disgrace with Fortune and men's eyes, (*a*)
I all alone beweep my outcast state, (*b*)
And trouble deaf heaven with my bootless° cries, (*a*)
And look upon myself, and curse my fate, (*b*)
Wishing me like to one more rich in hope, (*c*)
Featured like him, like him with friends possessed, (*d*)
Desiring this man's art and that man's scope, (*c*)
With what I most enjoy contented least: (*d*)
Yet in these thoughts myself almost despising, (*e*)
Haply I think on thee—and then my state, (*f*)
Like to the lark at break of day arising (*e*)
From sullen earth, sings hymns at heaven's gate; (*f*)
For thy sweet love remembered such wealth brings (*g*)
That then I scorn to change my state with kings. (*g*)

[3]**bootless** useless

Edna St. Vincent Millay (1892–1950)

Love Is Not All [1931]

Love is not all; it is not meat nor drink (*a*)
Nor slumber nor a roof against the rain; (*b*)
Nor yet a floating spar to men that sink (*a*)
And rise and sink and rise and sink again; (*b*)
Love cannot fill the thickened lung with breath, (*c*)
Nor clean the blood, nor set the fractured bone; (*d*)
Yet many a man is making friends with death (*c*)
Even as I speak, for lack of love alone. (*d*)
It well may be that in a difficult hour, (*e*)
Pinned down by pain and moaning for release (*f*)
Or nagged by want past resolution's power, (*e*)
I might be driven to sell your love for peace, (*f*)
Or trade the memory of this night for food. (*g*)
It well may be. I do not think I would. (*g*)

➤ QUESTIONS FOR READING AND WRITING

1. Describe the emotions of the speakers in these poems.
2. Do their circumstances bring to mind any of your own experiences? Would you describe love in these terms? How does that affect your response?
3. In what way does the sonnet structure of each affect your response?
4. Can you find a pattern in the structure of each that is connected to the content?

Blank Verse

Another popular form is **blank verse**. Blank verse is unrhymed but follows a regular verse form, usually iambic pentameter. Some of the greatest epic poems and plays (including Milton's *Paradise Lost* and Shakespeare's plays) have been written in blank verse, and it is still a very popular form today.

Here are the first eleven lines from Robert Frost's "Mending Wall." The entire poem is forty-five lines long (see p. 314).

Something there is that doesn't love a wall
That sends the frozen ground swell under it
And spills the upper boulders in the sun,
And makes gaps even two can pass abreast.
The work of hunters is another thing:
I have come after them and made repair
Where they have left not one stone on a stone,
But they would have the rabbit out of hiding,
To please the yelping dogs. The gaps I mean,
No one has seen them made or heard them made,
But at spring mending-time we find them there.

While it does not rhyme, the iambic pentameter still moves us from line to line in a regular predictable rhythm and influences our "hearing" of the poem. Read it out loud several times and see if you can hear and feel the regular beat.

Iambic pentameter is the dominant pattern in blank verse, but every word and every line may not conform to this pattern. For example, "Something," the first word of Frost's poem above, with its emphasis on the first syllable, is trochaic (stressed–unstressed), not iambic (unstressed–stressed). So, too, while the dominant pattern of Shakespeare's sonnets and plays is blank verse, not every foot is iambic, nor every line pentameter. You will find a number of exceptions to this pattern in the sonnets and both *Othello* (p. 588) and *Hamlet* (p. 973) in this text.

Free Verse

As its title implies, this is verse that is not constrained by an imposed form. **Free verse** does not have a rhyme scheme or regular rhythm. It is not formless, however, but relies on its own words and content to determine its best form. The poem which follows was written by Walt Whitman, a celebrated pioneer of free-verse writing.

WALT WHITMAN (1819–1892)

WHEN I HEARD THE LEARN'D ASTRONOMER [1865]

When I heard the learn'd astronomer,
When the proofs, the figures, were ranged in columns before me,
When I was shown the charts and diagrams, to add, divide, and measure them,
When I sitting heard the astronomer where he lectured with applause in the lecture-room,
How soon unaccountable I became tired and sick,
Till rising and gliding out I wander'd off by myself,
In the mystical moist night-air, and from time to time,
Look'd up in perfect silence at the stars.

➤ *QUESTIONS FOR READING AND WRITING*

1. Have you ever been in a situation where the explanation of the experience paled in comparison to the experience itself? Explain.
2. What does the speaker mean when he says, "How soon unaccountable I became tired and sick"?
3. How does the free verse affect your response to the poem?

✔CHECKLIST • *Sound and Structure*

- ❑ Is there a rhyme scheme in the poem? If so, what is its pattern? How does the rhyme scheme add to the overall effect of the poem?
- ❑ Are there other sound devices (alliteration, assonance, consonance)? If so, how do they affect your response?
- ❑ Is there a regular pattern to the verse? If so, what is it? How does it add to the effect of the poem?
- ❑ If there is no regular pattern, how does the unique form of the poem match the content? How did it affect your response?

Interpretation: What Does the Poem Mean?

Theme is the meaning we construct from the poem. It is an insight about life that we derive from the poem as a whole. Identifying and articulating this meaning is not an easy task. While our experience of the poem may be holistic or impressionistic, the analysis and support required for its articulation demand a close look at the parts—the language, events, and outcome of the poem.

Explication

An explication involves a line-by-line analysis of a text. Since works of fiction or drama are usually long, an explication would take quite a bit of time and space and would probably be better left to a lengthy term paper. Most poems, however, are relatively brief and by their nature "packed with meaning." So they present a good opportunity for a very close reading and examination—an opportunity to look closely at sounds, words, images, lines, and how they all work together to deliver the poem's meaning. An explication is not just a summary or translation of the poet's language into your own; it is a detailed interpretation of *how* and *what* you believe the poem means.

Like other forms of literature, poems are not problems to be solved. They don't have one correct answer or interpretation. Remember, what makes an interpretation convincing or defensible is your ability to support it.

Theme or Moral

As with fiction, be wary of reducing what the poem means to a moral or lesson. Good literature reveals a complex world. A moral preaches; it teaches us a lesson or a code of conduct. A theme reveals; it gives us insight into human nature.

✔ CHECKLIST • *Interpretation and Theme*

- ❑ What are the major details (the sounds, words, rhymes, rhythms, etc.) of the poem? What conclusion can you draw from these details?
- ❑ What generalization about life does the conclusion lead to?
- ❑ What does the poem mean? What is the theme of the poem?
- ❑ Is the poem didactic? Does it preach or give a lesson?

Types of Poetry

For the sake of clarification and simplification, poetry may be classified into two types: lyric and narrative. As with other forms of literature, classifications of this kind are not exclusive. There is overlap between the designations lyric and narrative. Poems in each of these categories may have elements characteristic of the other. And both lyric and narrative poetry have dramatic qualities.

Lyric Poetry

Lyric poetry is the most popular form of poetry written today. Lyric poems are characterized by the expression of the speaker's innermost feelings, thoughts, and imagination. The word *lyric* is taken from a stringed musical instrument called the lyre, which was used in classical and medieval times to accompany a singer. In addition to the very subjective stance of the speaker, lyric poems are melodic—a melody not derived from a lyre but from words and their arrangement. It's not mere coincidence that the words that accompany the melody in a song are called lyrics. Most of the poetry in this text can be classified as lyric poetry, but a specific example of this type is Edna St. Vincent Millay's "Love Is Not All" (p. 97).

One kind of lyric poetry that deserves special mention is the **dramatic monologue**. In a dramatic monologue, the poet, like an actor in a play, assumes a different persona and speaks to us through the voice and personality of another person. Robert Browning's "Porphyria's Lover" (p. 566) is an example of a dramatic monologue.

Narrative Poetry

A narrative poem tells a story. The poet takes on a role similar to that of a narrator in a work of fiction. The oldest stories were recorded in poetry and recited by "bards" who used the rhythms of the verse to help them memorize their lines. One difference between the narratives of short stories and those of narrative poems is length. With the exception of epic poems—book-length, narrative poems with lots of room for development of conflict and character—the length of most narrative poems limits the development of conflict and character. The brevity of the poems allows little space for exposition, and the poem usually moves quickly to the "chase," or crisis, beginning virtually in the middle of the story (or *in medias res*). Dudley Randall's "Ballad of Birmingham" (p. 17) and Seamus Heaney's "Mid-Term Break" (p. 320) are examples of narrative poems.

✔CHECKLIST • *Types of Poetry*

- ❏ Is the poem an expression of the poet's thoughts and feelings, or is it telling a story?
- ❏ Is it a narrative or lyric poem, or a dramatic monologue?

✔SUMMARY CHECKLIST • *Analyzing Poetry*

Language and Style

- ❑ How are you affected by the speaker's voice?
- ❑ What images do you experience?
- ❑ Are there similes or metaphors?
- ❑ Is there symbolism?
- ❑ How do voice, imagery, figurative language, and/or symbolism affect your response?
- ❑ How can you support your responses from the text?

Sound and Structure

- ❑ Is there a rhyme scheme in the poem? If so, what is its pattern?
- ❑ How does the rhyme scheme add to the overall effect of the poem?
- ❑ Are there other sound devices (alliteration, assonance, consonance)?
- ❑ If so, how do they affect your response?
- ❑ Is there a regular pattern to the verse? If so, describe it.
- ❑ How does it add to the effect of the poem?
- ❑ If there is no regular pattern, how does the unique form of the poem match the content? How did it affect your response?

Interpretation and Theme

- ❑ What are the major details (images, symbols, rhymes, rhythms, etc.) of the poem?
- ❑ What conclusion can you draw from these details?
- ❑ What generalization about life does the conclusion lead to?
- ❑ What does the poem mean? What is its theme?
- ❑ Is the poem didactic? (Does it preach or give a lesson?)

Types of Poetry

- ❑ Is the poem an expression of the poet's thoughts and feelings, or is it telling a story? Is it a narrative or lyric poem?

GETTING IDEAS FOR WRITING ABOUT POETRY

Following "Pigeon Woman," many of the questions from the summary checklist above are applied to the poem, and we consider some of the ways the elements discussed in this section might be used to prompt ideas for an essay.

MAY SWENSON (1919–1989)

PIGEON WOMAN [1958]

Slate, or dirty-marbled-colored,
or rusty-iron-colored, the pigeons
on the flagstones in front of the
Public Library make a sharp lake

into which the pigeon woman wades
at exactly 1:30. She wears a
plastic pink raincoat with a round
collar (looking like a little

girl, so gay) and flat gym shoes,
her hair square-cut, orange.
Wide-apart feet carefully enter
the spinning, crooning waves

(as if she'd just learned how
to walk, each step conscious,
an accomplishment); blue knots in the
calves of her bare legs (uglied marble),

age in angled cords of jaw
and neck, her pimento-colored hair,
hanging in thin tassels, is gray
around a balding crown.

The day-old bread drops down
from her veined hand dipping out
of a paper sack. Choppy, shadowy ripples,
the pigeons strike around her legs.

Sack empty, she squats and seems to rinse
her hands in them—the rainy greens and
oily purples of their necks. Almost
they let her wet thirsty fingertips—

but drain away in an untouchable tide.
A make-believe trade
she has come to, in her lostness
of illness or age—to treat the motley

city pigeons at 1:30 every day, in all
weathers. It is for them she colors her own
feathers. Ruddy-footed
on the lime stained paving,

purling to meet her when she comes,
they are a lake of love. Retreating
from her hands as soon as empty
they are the flints of love.

GENERATING IDEAS FOR WRITING

One of the best ways to get ideas for an essay is to ask and answer your own most compelling questions. Write down whatever questions come to mind during and after your reading. See if the answers to these questions provide topics for writing. Or choose a compelling idea from a journal entry, draw a Venn diagram to compare elements or other works (pp. 33–34), use directed freewriting (p. 41), ask questions (p. 42), list, or draw a cluster, or semantic map (pp. 43–44), to loosen up ideas.

Listed below is a more structured approach based on the elements of poetry discussed earlier in this section. Applying these questions to "Pigeon Woman" may demonstrate how the elements might be applied to any poem.

Getting Started—Your First Response

1. What questions came to mind as you read "Pigeon Woman"?
2. What words or expressions are not clear to you?
3. To what extent can you connect "Pigeon Woman" to your own background or experience?
4. What do you find most compelling or provocative about the poem?

Language and Style

1. Who is the speaker in "Pigeon Woman"? What kind of voice does (s)he have? What is the speaker's tone? What is the speaker's attitude toward the woman being described?
2. One image in the poem describes the pigeons as making "a sharp lake into which the pigeon woman wades." Where else in the poem is that image supported?
3. What other images in the poem have an effect on you? To what senses do the images appeal?
4. What similes or metaphors do you find in the poem? How do they contribute to the imagery?
5. How does the figurative language in "Pigeon Woman" help to convey its meaning?
6. Is there symbolism in the poem? Explain.

Sound and Structure

1. This poem does not have an obvious rhyme scheme. How does that affect your response?

2. What instances of alliteration or assonance can you identify?
3. To what extent does "Pigeon Woman" have a rhythm or a regular pattern to the verse? How does that influence your reading?
4. How does the form of "Pigeon Woman" match its content? To what extent does it help to convey its meaning?

Interpretation and Theme

1. What does the last line, "they are the flints of love," mean?
2. What are the major details of the poem?
3. What conclusion can you draw from the details? What is the poem about?
4. To what extent does this conclusion lead to a generalization about life?
5. What is the theme of "Pigeon Woman"?

Types of Poetry

1. Is "Pigeon Woman" expressing the poet's innermost thoughts and feelings, or is it telling a story? Is it a narrative or lyric poem? Explain.

Topics for Writing

The following list is not exhaustive, but simply illustrative of the kinds of questions that might emerge from the more specific analytical questions (and combinations of questions) like those above. Your responses to these questions might provide worthwhile topics for writing.

1. To what extent is "Pigeon Woman" a love story?
2. Some poems paint pictures; some make statements. In what way does this poem do both?
3. How do the structure, images, and sounds of the poem convey the meaning of "Pigeon Woman"?
4. To what extent is this poem a comment about human relationships?
5. It is not unusual to see lonely, old people looking for companionship. In what way does "Pigeon Woman" enable us to "be there" and experience what that means?
6. Many people rely on the company of "nature's creatures" for companionship. To what extent is this a poem about this kind of mutual dependency?
7. How necessary was it to understand the social circumstances of the woman to make sense of the poem?
8. Can you compare this poem or the woman in it to another work or character in that work? Explain.

9. This poem was written in 1958. Does it still make sense today? How so?
10. Are you familiar with other poems of May Swenson? If so, how does this poem compare with them?

READING AND ANALYZING DRAMA

Since earliest times, people have had the need to act out and witness stories. Telling them and hearing them was important too, but witnessing the drama of the story as it happened was a different kind of experience. Ancient hunters wore masks of the animals they hunted because they believed that by mimicking their behavior they would come to know, understand, and honor them—and, of course, hunt them more effectively. From the time of the ancient Greeks to the present, however, we have shared a somewhat more idealistic goal. We've believed that by acting out and witnessing the struggle of other human beings, we are enlightened about the nature of our own lives.

To look at the history of drama, to see its development, is to learn a great deal about who people were and what they valued at different times in history. Whatever technological, social, or political developments have changed us over the last several thousand years, it is clear that there are important ties at the core of human experience that still bind us with our ancient ancestors.

Although we have seen dramatists' definitions of a hero or protagonist change over the years, from Aristotle's "characters of a higher type" to Arthur Miller's "common man [and woman]," the focus of drama remains the struggle of characters to face life with a sense of purpose and dignity. From the Greeks to the present, characters struggle with the gods, themselves, each other, and society. They rise to heroic heights or fall from them. Of noble birth, they may fail to be humble, and fall. Of humble birth, they may struggle to be noble, and triumph.

As we witness drama at its best from any period, we see ourselves and recollect the struggle of our own lives. And most of all, we are reminded of the human drama outside the theater, where joy and suffering, courage and cowardice, have been acted out for no audience in particular for thousands of years.

Reading a Play

Drama is meant to be seen and heard, so attending a good performance of a play is almost always preferable to reading it. In addition to what you see and hear onstage, the sense of community you share with the audience can be an integral part of your experience. If you are reading a play, though, there are a few strategies that may enhance your experience.

To read a play effectively , try to create the stage in your mind. Imagine you are sitting in a theater watching a performance. If there are stage directions, read them carefully. Try to imagine the set, props, and action, and hear the voices. Be conscious of what the characters say and how their words can help you picture the scene. If you are not sure who a character is, you may need to go back from time to time to read the list of characters or reread the dialogue.

Point of View

A play does not usually have a narrator to interpret the action for us. Most often we see the play through our own eyes. We observe the actions of the characters, hear what they say and what is said about them, and make our own judgments.

In Greek drama, however, it is the function of the chorus and *Choragos* (the leader of the chorus) to address the audience from time to time to remind us about the cultural and historical context of the play and the significance of the action and dialogue. In Shakespearean drama, the characters themselves will sometimes speak directly to us in asides or soliloquies. In the plays *Hamlet* and *Othello,* for example, the characters Hamlet and Iago share their thoughts directly with us at important times throughout the play. And occasionally in a modern play a character acts as narrator and comments on the action at timely intervals. Such is the role that Tom plays in Tennessee Williams's *The Glass Menagerie.* But generally, whether attending a performance or reading a play, we are on our own.

✔CHECKLIST • *Point of View*

- ❑ Does the play have a narrator? If so, who is it?
- ❑ What effect does this narration have on your response?

Set and Setting

In drama, the immediate setting is the set itself. When attending a play, it's often the first part of the drama we experience. It draws us into another world. We know it's not real, but we are prepared to forget that once the action starts. As we look at the set and wonder what the action will be like, we are already beginning to experience the play.

In the history of theater, sets and settings have varied widely. Greek and Shakespearean plays were originally performed on a bare set, and the setting was sometimes described by the characters themselves or by a narrator, but always imagined by the audience. Over the years, both Greek and Shakespearean drama have often been performed with elaborate sets (particularly in videos and films). In most modern plays, the nature of the setting is spelled out in detail in the script. For example, the printed texts in this volume of the Greek plays *Antigonê* (p. 123) and *Oedipus Rex* (p. 903), and the Shakespearean plays *Othello* (p. 588) and *Hamlet* (p. 973) contain little indication of the nature of the setting beyond a broad reference to location. On the other hand, the texts of modern plays like *A Doll's House* (p. 725), *The Glass Menagerie* (p. 335), and *A Raisin in the Sun* (p. 402) contain very specific details about the nature of the set and setting.

As in fiction, setting is more than the place and time period of the play. It has a direct and indirect impact on character and conflict. It supports and emphasizes the play's meaning. And its most important function is to make us feel present in the world that the characters inhabit.

Location tells us where and when the story is taking place. Both the *where* and the *when* will strongly influence the values and behavior of the characters and color the rest of the play. **Atmosphere** is the mix of location and more changeable circumstances, such as conflict, the characters present, the time of day, the season, and the weather. Its overall effect supports and complements conflict and character and helps to convey the play's meaning.

✔CHECKLIST • *Set and Setting*

- ❑ When is the play set? What role does the setting have? What physical location is this? The country? The city? What does the set look like? What props are present? Can you describe the atmosphere?
- ❑ What time of day is this? What is the lighting? What are the dominant colors? What is the weather? Who is present? How are they dressed?
- ❑ Does the setting support and emphasize the story's meaning?

Conflict and Plot

Conflict is at the heart of every play. The impediments and complications the characters must overcome keep us watching or reading. The more important, challenging, believable, and coherent a conflict is the more we are engaged by the action and dialogue, and the greater our desire to follow it to its conclusion.

Internal and External Conflict

External conflict may be physical (characters against nature) or social (characters against each other or against society). **Internal conflict** is a struggle of opposing forces within a character. The best drama contains elements of both types of conflict, but the emphasis is usually on the internal elements.

Conflict and Characterization

As in fiction, who the characters are, how they feel about themselves, and how they behave are at the core of both external and internal conflict.

Plot

Plot is the structure of the play. It is the pattern of twists and turns that the play takes. Most plots spring from conflict. To have a discernible plot, we must have impediments, complications, and opposition.

The traditional arrangement of plot in drama is virtually the same as it is in fiction. It follows a pattern of exposition, rising action, crisis (sometimes called climax), falling action, and resolution (sometimes called denouement or untying).

The fundamental difference between plot in fiction and drama is how we experience the plot. Without the benefit of a narrator we are limited to action and dialogue, so the plot must develop entirely through what we see and hear onstage.

Exposition: We learn what we need to know about the circumstances, characters, and the potential conflict through dialogue and action.

Rising Action: An event occurs that builds the conflict, and our emotional involvement intensifies.

Crisis, or Climax: The main character is in the moment of truth. The turning point of the conflict (sometimes called a reversal) begins.

Falling Action: The conflict is beyond the crisis, the intensity subsides, and the outcome seems inevitable.

Resolution: The details are wrapped up and we are returned to normalcy.

Applying this pattern to drama can be problematic. Modern playwrights in particular do not limit their work to conform to a pattern that wraps the conflict up so neatly. The structure of many modern plays emerges naturally from the content of the play and bears little resemblance to this classical pattern.

The Poetics

The Poetics of Aristotle is the earliest surviving work of literary criticism in the Western world. Written from 335 to 322 B.C., more than one hundred years after the works of Aeschylus, Sophocles, and Euripides were first produced, it was modeled on plays that Aristotle liked best. It is our earliest written set of standards for dramatic art, and it continues to be influential today. The plays of Sophocles were particularly favored by Aristotle, so both of Sophocles' plays in this text are good models of these standards.

Tragedy

The Poetics emphasizes the nature of the **tragic hero** and the importance of plot in tragedy. Aristotle defines his tragic hero as a character of noble stature who is admired by society but flawed. The flaw (often excessive pride, or hubris) leads directly to a reversal of good fortune (catastrophe). But the punishment usually exceeds the crime, and the character deserves our pity. The tragic fall is not a complete loss, as the character gains in wisdom and self-knowledge. Finally, there is a recognition of the causes and consequences of this reversal, and a resolution returns things to normal. The audience, enlightened by the play, experiences **catharsis** (emotional purging or cleansing).

Comedy

Aristotle does not have as much to say about comedy, which he considers a lower form of drama. He suggests that "characters of a higher type" are fit subjects for tragedy, but "persons inferior" are appropriate for comedy. The traditional plot of comedy is the reverse of tragedy. The protagonist, usually an ordinary person, faces a dilemma. The plot of the play is an extrication from this dilemma and an improvement of circumstances. The reversal of fortune, therefore, is from bad to good; the falling action becomes a rising action with a happy ending.

Although these classifications of tragedy and comedy have been in place since the age of Greek drama, most plays since that time have not strictly conformed to these requirements. Modern plays in particular often contain elements of both tragedy and comedy, a classification called tragicomedy, which is discussed later in the chapter.

✔CHECKLIST • *Conflict and Plot*

- ❑ What is the primary external conflict in the play?
- ❑ What is the primary internal conflict?
- ❑ Are there other conflicts? If so, what are they?
- ❑ How would you support your identification of conflict from the text?
- ❑ In what way do the personality traits of the characters lead to this conflict?
- ❑ Can you identify the plot?
- ❑ Does it conform to the traditional structure? If so, how so? If not, what is the structure?
- ❑ Is it a tragedy or comedy?
- ❑ Does it conform to a traditional plot structure?

CHARACTER

As in fiction, characterization in drama is the development of characters in a story. But unlike fiction, where some characterization is done through description, characterization in most drama is limited to action and dialogue. We find out about the characters indirectly. We are not told what to think or feel about them. We observe them speaking and doing. We hear what other characters have to say about them. If they are well developed, they seem believable and motivated. Like our response to people in our lives, our response to them and our judgments about them is based on our own observations.

The same terms in both drama and fiction are used to describe characters. The main character in a drama is called the *protagonist.* A character who seems to be a major force in opposition to the protagonist is called an *antagonist.* When characters are not fully developed but seem to represent "types" more than real personalities, we call them *flat,* or *stock, characters.* When they seem fully developed with the complexities of real people, they are described as *round characters.*

✔CHECKLIST • *Characterization*

- ❑ How do you feel about the characters ?
- ❑ What did the characters do to make you feel this way?
- ❑ What did the characters say to make you feel this way?
- ❑ What was said about the characters to make you feel this way?
- ❑ Are the characters motivated and consistent? Are they believable?
- ❑ Are there flat or stock characters in the play?
- ❑ Who is the protagonist? An antagonist?
- ❑ Can you support your responses to the characters from the text of the play?

Language and Style

Language is the vehicle that carries the characters to you. The style of language used by the characters tells us a lot about them. And the symbolic nature of the language may complement and support the story's theme or meaning.

Greek and Shakespearean plays are written in verse. This very formal style has a very different effect on the audience than the informal vernacular used in modern drama.

Diction

An important element in establishing characters is the kind of language they use to express themselves. This is especially important in drama, because what we know is usually limited to dialogue and action. Characters are often defined as much by *how* they say something as *what* they say. Diction is particularly important in the naturalistic speech of modern drama, where it tells us a great deal about class and cultural distinctions.

Symbol

A **symbol** is something that represents more than itself. In drama, the set, costumes, and props are often used symbolically. The set (the furniture, the size of the room, the light, and color, etc.) often reflects the content of the play itself. The props (the objects onstage and those used by the characters) often reflect the conflict, characters, and theme of the play. The costumes tell us a great deal about the characters themselves.

✔CHECKLIST • *Language and Style*

- ❑ Is the language used in the play formal or informal?
- ❑ What does the nature of their language tell you about the characters?
- ❑ Are there any symbols? Is the set symbolic? Are the props or the costumes symbolic? If so, how do they connect to or support the story?

THEME

As in fiction and poetry, **theme** is the central idea expressed by the play. It is a generalization, an insight about life, that we derive from the play as a whole. Identifying and articulating this meaning is not an easy task. While our experience of the theme may be holistic or impressionistic, the analysis and support required for its articulation demands a close look at the parts—the language, events, characters, and outcome of the play.

Like fiction and poetry, plays do not have one correct answer or interpretation. What makes an interpretation convincing or defensible is your ability to support it. Your belief about what the play means may change as you move back and forth through the stages of your reading or viewing experience. The first time you experience a play, you may feel one way, but writing down your reflections, rereading the play, and discussing it with others may lead to a different, better-informed understanding and interpretation.

Theme or Moral

A temptation when writing about literature is to reduce what it means to a moral or lesson. Good literature reveals a complex world. A moral preaches; it teaches us a lesson or a code of conduct. A theme reveals; it gives us an insight into human nature.

One of the functions of classical drama is to illuminate the audience spiritually, so it's almost certain that we will be left with a clear message by the end of a play. In this respect, Greek plays tend to be **didactic**, or lesson-giving, in a way that most drama since the time of Shakespeare does not.

✔CHECKLIST • *Theme*

- ❑ What are the major details (characters, conflicts, outcome) of the play?
- ❑ What conclusion about the play did you draw from these details?
- ❑ What generalization about life does this conclusion lead to?
- ❑ What is the central idea or theme of the play?
- ❑ Is the play didactic? Does the theme preach or give a lesson?

PERIODS OF DRAMA: A BRIEF BACKGROUND

Greek Drama

Ancient Greece was a remarkable place. It was a democratic society flourishing in the midst of totalitarian regimes and foreign wars. It was also a place where achievements in art, literature, and philosophy were so great that they are still revered as models today, thousands of years after their creation.

Greek drama emerged from religious rituals of the time, but Greek religion bore little resemblance to the dominant religions of the modern Western world. Modern Western religions acknowledge a single, just, and benevolent God, whereas Greek religion was polytheistic and recognized many gods—deities who were just as likely to be arbitrary and nasty as to be just and benevolent. For the ancient Greeks, this world was a microcosm, or smaller version, of the divine world. And since the deities themselves were capable of both good and evil, the existence of evil in the world did not contradict these beliefs.

The Greeks believed that they had little control of their fate but had much control of and responsibility for how they faced up to it. This view, which espoused dignity and humility in the face of adversity, is at the core of most Greek drama. The Greeks saw life as a series of struggles to be faced with courage and humility.

During the fifth century B.C., dramatic or religious festivals were held each spring to celebrate Dionysus, the god of wine and fertility. These festivals are thought to be the origin of Greek tragedy. Playwrights from all over Greece competed for prizes awarded by wealthy citizens, with each competing playwright presenting a trilogy of tragic plays. Though we know the names of more than 150 of these ancient writers, we have only a small sample of their work. Of the almost three hundred plays from the three most prominent playwrights of this period, Euripides, Aeschylus, and Sophocles, only thirty-two remain. Given the quality of these plays, it is sad to imagine the treasures that have been lost.

Staging and Acting The word *theater* is taken from the Greek *theatron* or "seeing-place," a term used to describe the huge open-air amphitheater that seated the audience during performances. Despite their huge dimensions, these theaters had excellent acoustics that were aided by the small megaphones in the actors' masks and a style of acting more in keeping with religious ritual than real life. The number of actors with individual roles onstage at once was limited to two or three. The set was bare and the actors were stationary. All the roles were played by males who wore ornate costumes and large masks to reflect the mood of the play and represent types as much as individuals. Though the dialogue itself and the choral odes contained references to and descriptions of violent actions, no violence was actually shown.

The Chorus The chorus entered during the **parodos** (the choral ode) and remained onstage throughout the play. The role of the chorus came directly from drama as religious ritual, and dates to a time when there were no individual actors. What the chorus said about the action reflected the traditional values of an Athenian audience. When a passage of dialogue was finished, the characters left the stage and the chorus came forward to comment on it. They chanted their lines together and moved as a unit in one direction, then the other. The chorus explained the action, built anticipation for the upcoming scene, and reminded the audience about the significance of the action or dialogue and the cultural or historical context of the play.

The **choragos** was the leader of the chorus. He acted and spoke as the group's representative, and he was free to speak with both the chorus and the other characters onstage.

Audience Participation An ancient Greek audience would have already known the myths that inspired the plays. They would have been more curious, then, about the play's dramatization (the acting out of the dramatic moments) than the story line. Suspense was based on the tension of the crises, not on the outcome of the plot. According to Aristotle, the tragic nature of a play should not leave its audience depressed or disheartened. Instead, the audience should be enlightened and inspired by what they had witnessed.

The Language of the Script Because the text is a translation into modern English, you should not have too much trouble reading it. The verse form was a convention of the time and a requirement. It is not written as people of this time would have spoken to one another. The diction is formal and represents the exalted speech of nobility.

SHAKESPEAREAN DRAMA

As we enter the twenty first century, it is difficult to see the world in the light (or darkness) of Elizabethan England. Central to the world view of this period was the idea of a vertical hierarchy (God superior to the king, the king superior to nobles, the nobles superior to peasants, etc.). People's places in this hierarchy directly affected their quality of life and the kind of rights they had. The king or queen ruled by "divine right," not as elected leaders, "through the consent of the governed." Although we regularly make claims for equal opportunity as guaranteed by law today, the idea of peasants in the sixteenth century claiming equal rights with people above their rank would have seemed outrageous. People were not free to worship as they chose. They were not even free to dress as they chose. Though the "sumptuary laws" were not always enforced, they prohibited peasants from dressing in other than coarse fabrics and dull colors, with fine fabrics and bright colors reserved for the nobility. What we call science was nonexistent; very little was known about the cause or spread of disease, and very little could be done for those who became ill. For much of the population, the fastest means of transportation was on foot, and life was difficult and short.

And yet, life had never been better. England was emerging as a world power. Trade had opened up with the Continent, providing an exchange of goods, culture, language, and literature never seen before. The printing press was mass producing pamphlets and books, and literacy among the general public was improving dramatically.

It is into this atmosphere that Shakespeare was born in 1564, the year the great Renaissance artist Michelangelo died. It is fitting that Shakespeare was born at the end of the Renaissance. The Renaissance was a "rebirth"—a revival of a golden age—a triumph of classical creation. Shakespeare's art is distinguished by a looking forward. Like the explorers of his time, his is a genius of discovery. He explores what is most essential to individual human experience. Rather than types, he discovers highly individualized characters who struggle with each other and themselves, not with fate, the gods, or heredity. But most of all, he discovers language to express these characters, and their struggles in verse unparalleled for the quality of its poetry and insight.

Staging and Acting

Before the late sixteenth century, acting companies traveled from town to town and rented space in yards of local inns. Plays were produced on a platform at one end of the yard and the audience gathered around the platform. Wealthier members of the audience viewed the action from the balconies of the surrounding rooms of the inn. The major advantages of this arrangement were its informal, festive atmosphere, the attendance of all classes, and the intimate actor-audience relationship that it encouraged. The close proximity of actor and audience allowed for direct eye contact, an ideal situation for the many soliloquies and asides that playwrights of this period included in their plays.

The Globe Theatre, where most of Shakespeare's plays were performed, was built in 1599 and reflected the kind of space that actors were used to—a space that maintained the intimate atmosphere of the innyards. The Globe was typical of theaters of its kind: a tight, enclosed structure with galleries around the periphery, a projecting platform (about as deep as it was wide) with two upstage entrances and at least one balcony. The stage itself was almost bare, with only a few simple props or a table, chair, or throne when appropriate. It was a very versatile acting area; there were two exit and entrance doors in the rear of the platform, a curtained alcove between them, a second-story balcony above the stage, a third-story balcony for musicians, a ceiling or heavens extending over the platform supported by two pillars on the stage, and a trap door in the stage platform from which ghosts or devils might emerge.

Although the costumes were elaborate, they reflected current fashion and were not designed to convey the actual clothing of the different countries or times in history depicted in the plays. As in ancient Greece, all parts were played by males. Violence was depicted onstage and quite realistically. Public executions and an abundance of brutal entertainment gave Elizabethans particular expectations. Actors did their best to meet them.

Audience Participation

Audience members who paid the highest admission prices sat in the three stories of covered galleries that enclosed the theater. Here they were protected from the often inclement English weather. Those who paid the least stood in the open area below and around the stage and were called groundlings, a term meant to disparage their social standing as much as to describe their location in the theater.

Throughout his plays, Shakespeare created opportunities for characters to speak directly with the audience. Delivered by a character alone onstage, these **soliloquies** are a "thinking out loud;" "true to the speaker, they range from philosophical to diabolical in nature." And they are often the highlights of Shakespeare's plays. Sometimes characters address the audience while not alone onstage. These brief comments, usually in the midst of ongoing dialogue, are called **asides**. The close proximity of actor and audience in an Elizabethan theater made both types of "confidences" particularly effective.

Tips on Reading the Language of Shakespeare

Most of the verse in Shakespeare's plays is written in unrhymed iambic pentameter or blank verse (see p. 98 for a detailed description). This pattern of rhythm (alternating unstressed and stressed syllables) is the natural way English is spoken. The predictability of the pattern made it easier for actors of this period to memorize their lines.

Shakespeare wrote in modern English, but it was a relatively early form of modern English. Some of the words he used have disappeared from the language, some have different meanings now than they did then, and some sentences have a syntax, or word order, we no longer recognize.

Look at the following passage from *Othello* (Act III, scene 4).

OTH: That's a fault.
That handkerchief
Did an Egyptian to my mother give;
She was a charmer, and could almost read
The thoughts of people: she told her, while she kept it,
'Twould make her amiable and subdue my father
Entirely to her love, but if she lost it
Or made a gift of it, my father's eye
Should hold her loathed and his spirits should hunt
After new fancies: she, dying, gave it me;
And bid me, when my fate would have me wive,
To give it her.

Although the plays are written in blank verse, don't let the capital letters at the beginning of each line affect your reading. Don't stop at the end of each verse line unless it has punctuation. Use the punctuation to create pauses or stops as you would with language in prose. Let's look at one of the sentences above in prose form, with the capitals removed:

> "She told her, while she kept it, it would make her amiable and subdue my father entirely to her love, but if she lost it or made a gift of it, my father's eye should hold her loathed and his spirits should hunt after new fancies"

Even in prose, this is a long sentence and requires patience and concentration to understand. But by reading it as prose, you can focus on the punctuation. Some of the phrases might still seem a bit elusive, but read it a few times and see if it is easier to understand.

Reading Out Loud

Good actors help the audience understand the language by the tone and pacing of their voices. But when you are reading from the text of the play, you won't have the benefit of hearing an actor's voice. Reading the lines aloud may help. When you read silently, you subvocalize and hear the words in your brain. But the sound and sense of these words will be clearer if you say and hear the word combinations out loud.

Read the verse passage from *Othello* above aloud and see what you learn about its meaning (and your understanding) in the process.

Word Order

Getting used to the language of Shakespeare means adjusting our expectations for word order in a sentence. In today's English, we generally express ourselves in a subject-verb-object pattern. For example: "A girl hit that ball to her brother." But earlier forms of English sometimes used a word order with the verb at the end. In this earlier form our sentence would read: "That ball did a girl to her brother hit." Takes a little longer to figure out, doesn't it? We need to read the whole sentence to get to the verb. And it is only after we get to the verb that we understand what is being said.

If you look at the first sentence of the quote from *Othello* (above), "That handkerchief Did an Egyptian to my mother give," you'll see the same pattern. If those words were written in the subject-verb-object pattern we are used to, they would read: "An Egyptian gave that handkerchief to my mother." Made sense much faster, didn't it? You've seen this older verb pattern before in language carried down through the ages for meaningful rituals, like the marriage ceremony (e.g., "With this ring I thee wed" and "Til death do us part").

Most often, the key to reading unusual word order is patience. The meaning may not be clear until you reach the last word of the sentence—and even then you may have to pause to unravel it.

Words, Words, Words

While many other modern languages still have them, English dropped the second person "familiar" pronoun form some time ago, and uses the "you" form exclusively. When Shakespeare wrote his plays, however, *thou, thee, thy,* and *thine* were the second-person singular "familiar" versions of *you, your,* and *yours.* In general, they indicated a caring relationship with the person addressed—a lover, family member, servant. Dropped as well are verb endings like *st* which agreed with these familiar pronouns (thou dost, thou shalt, thou goest). Other third-person verb endings like *th* ("It *hath* made me ill"; "It *doth* give me heartburn") have simply become obsolete.

It is not unusual to see letters replaced with apostrophes occasionally. ("Whether *'tis* nobler"; "*'twould* make her amiable", "*o'erstep* not the modesty of nature"). By leaving a letter out, Shakespeare often managed to eliminate a beat and keep the blank verse intact. In these cases, the context of the statement will usually tell you that *'tis* means "it is," *'twould* means "it would," and *o'erstep* means "overstep."

In other cases, entire words seem to be left out ("Let's [?] to bed knight"; "My father had a daughter [?] loved a man"). Again in these cases the context of the sentence should tell you that *go* and *who* are the words assumed to be understood.

Shakespeare was a master of making up words too (*assassinate, dislocate, obscene, reliance, submerged,* and hundreds of others we still use), and changing words from one part of speech to another, for example, in the above quote from *Othello,* the use of *wive* instead of *marry:* "And bid me, when my fate would have me wive, To give it her." So don't be surprised when you come across a verb that you're used to as a noun. The meaning is likely to be what you think it is.

You may notice that when a king speaks, he often uses the pronouns *our, us,* and *we* to refer to himself. In the first line of his opening speech in Act

I, scene 2 of Hamlet, Claudius refers to himself this way: "Though yet of Hamlet *our* dear brother's death / The memory be green." This use of the "royal plural," or "imperial we," was common among royalty, who saw themselves as personifying the kingdom and everyone in it.

Finally, it is very helpful to read the notes that accompany the text. You'll need help with words no longer in use and words that had a different meaning than they do now. It will take a little longer to read the text, but remember that patience is a key to having a successful experience with Shakespeare's work.

Modern Drama

Modern drama, like so much else "modern," was born in the nineteenth century. Its emergence was a natural outgrowth and reflection of the profound social, political, and technological changes taking place around it. Like so many other modern movements, it arose as a reaction— to the content, staging, and acting of the neoclassical drama and romantic melodrama so popular in the era that preceded it. As this reaction ran its course, virtually every aspect of theater changed.

The preceding seventeenth and eighteenth centuries were dominated early by neoclassicism (or new classicism), which was notable for its rigid adherence to the forms of classical drama. While there were a number of highly successful comedies, the power and passion of ancient tragedy was missing in an age that seemed to prefer form over substance. Later in this period, melodramas with elaborate but oversimplified plots, flat characters, excessive sentiment, and happy endings were most popular. The physical layout of the theater changed during this period, too: theaters moved indoors. The stage was recessed behind and framed by a **proscenium arch** at the end of a long room or hall. The audience was seated directly in front of the stage and in the surrounding galleries. This layout is the one we still see today in most school auditoriums and many theaters. Settings for each play were painted on canvas backdrops behind the acting area. A scene could be changed simply by changing the backdrop. Both the audience and the actors behaved with great flamboyance. The audience came to the theater as much to be seen as to see the action onstage. Consequently, both audience and actors spent much money on elaborate costumes. And as the size of theaters increased, so did the volume of the actors' voices and the exaggeration of their gestures.

A transformation to what we recognize as modern drama came slowly, and it took much of the nineteenth century to make real progress. But that change and that movement toward **realism** in both content and technique would affect every aspect of drama. Writers depicted the reality of struggling, ordinary people. Set designers produced authentic settings onstage. Actors spoke and behaved like real people.

But even as realism was becoming established, it was generating reactions to its own form and objective view of reality. In the twentieth century, **symbolism** would seek its truth in symbols, myths, and dreams; **expressionism** in the subjectivity of perception; and **surrealism** in the irrationality of the unconscious mind.

Modern drama is a synthesis of many forms and philosophies. More than a single approach, it is characterized by variety and diversity—diversity of content, perspective, and staging. The traditional categories of tragedy and comedy are inadequate to classify most modern drama. Tragic, comic, and absurd views of life often mix together in the same script, side by side, back to back. This diverse combination of views and styles is described as **tragicomedy**.

Staging and Acting

In general, theaters built today have better acoustical, visual, and spatial arrangements than ever before. Interiors with rising tiers of seats give audiences clear sight lines and encourage a more naturalistic style of acting. In many ways the era of modern drama began with the development of the **box set**—a set composed of **flats**, or connected walls enclosing three sides of the stage, with an invisible "fourth wall" open to the audience. Through this invisible fourth wall the audience sees the action and eavesdrops on the conversations of characters, who occupy a room with authentic furniture, rugs, hanging fixtures, and other realistic props.

Today, there are many types of stages. Several variations of the proscenium stage with enclosed box set have evolved. And since the 1940s, thrust stages, a throwback to the Elizabethan platform that extends into the audience, and the arena stage, or theater in the round, a circular acting area surrounded by the audience, have been designed to bring audiences closer to the actors.

Artificial light and sound create realistic stage settings. Lighting can project times, places, and moods, and can even divide the stage into different acting areas. Computerized light boards control hundreds of lights and lighting combinations. Electronic amplification and portable microphones make it easier for actors to speak in their natural voices. Authentic costumes complement the set, support historical authenticity, and enrich characterization.

As the twentieth century approached and the demands for realism increased, the training of actors changed too. The work of Constantin Stanislavski epitomized this movement. Stanislavski's *method* required that actors express the interior lives of the characters they played—to live the role by finding the character's emotions and motivation in themselves. More than a century after he developed his method, it is still the most popular approach used by actors to prepare their roles.

Audience Participation

While realistic staging and lighting highlight a real setting peopled by real characters, they put the audience literally in the dark. Though the box set encourages actors to move more deeply into "character," its fourth wall maintains a distance from the audience. The actors move on a lighted stage very visible to the audience, but the audience often sits in the dark invisible to the actors.

The Language and Style of the Script

Characters in modern drama almost always speak in colloquial language, not verse. What they say sounds like everyday speech. Following the lead of fiction writers in the late nineteenth century, dramatists began to write dialogue in the regional speech of the characters. Having "an ear" for dialogue, for realistic speech and how it sounds, is a crucial skill for any dramatist today.

Stage directions in the text of modern plays are more detailed than ever before. Descriptions of the set, props, movements of the actors, and the lighting are often specified in the script and integrated with action and characterization.

✔SUMMARY CHECKLIST • *Analyzing Drama*

Point of View

- ❑ Does the play have a narrator? If so, who is it?
- ❑ What effect does this narration have on your response?

Set and Setting

- ❑ When is the play set? What role does the setting have? What physical location is this? The country? The city? What does the set look like? What props are present?
- ❑ Can you describe the atmosphere?
- ❑ What time of day is this? What is the lighting? What are the dominant colors?
- ❑ What is the weather?
- ❑ Who is present? How are they dressed?
- ❑ Does the setting support and emphasize the story's meaning?

Conflict and Plot

- ❑ What is the primary external conflict in the play?
- ❑ What is the primary internal conflict?
- ❑ Are there other conflicts? If so, what are they?
- ❑ How would you support your identification of conflict from the text?

(*continued*)

- ❑ In what way do the personality traits of the characters lead to this conflict?
- ❑ Can you identify the plot?
- ❑ Does it conform to the traditional structure? If so, how? If not, what is the structure?
- ❑ Is it a tragedy or a comedy?
- ❑ Does it conform to a traditional plot structure?

Characterization

- ❑ How do you feel about the characters? What do the characters do to make you feel this way? What do the characters say to make you feel this way? What is said about the characters to make you feel this way?
- ❑ Are the characters motivated and consistent? Are they believable? Are there flat, or stock, characters in the play?
- ❑ Who is the protagonist? The antagonist(s)?
- ❑ Can you support your responses to the characters from the text of the play?

Language and Style

- ❑ Is the language used in the play formal or informal?
- ❑ What does the nature of their language use tell you about the characters?
- ❑ Are there any symbols? Is the set symbolic? Are the props or the costumes symbolic? If so, how do they connect to or support the story?

Theme

- ❑ What are the major details (characters, conflicts, outcome) of the play?
- ❑ What conclusion about the play did you draw from these details?
- ❑ What generalization about life does this conclusion lead to?
- ❑ What does the play mean? What is its theme?
- ❑ Is the play didactic? Does the theme preach, or give a lesson?

Getting Ideas for Writing About Drama

Following *Antigonê,* many of the questions from the summary checklist above are applied to the play, and we consider some of the ways the elements discussed in this section might be used to prompt ideas for an essay.

SOPHOCLES (496?–406 B.C.)

ANTIGONÊ [CA. 441 B.C.]

AN ENGLISH VERSION BY DUDLEY FITTS AND ROBERT FITZGERALD

CHARACTERS

ANTIGONÊ
ISMENÊ
EURYDICÊ
CREON
HAIMON
TEIRESIAS
A SENTRY
A MESSENGER
CHORUS

SCENE: *Before the palace of* CREON, *King of Thebes. A central double door, and two lateral doors. A platform extends the length of the facade, and from this platform three steps lead down into the orchestra, or chorus-ground.*
TIME: *Dawn of the day after the repulse of the Argive army from the assault on Thebes.*

PROLOGUE

ANTIGONÊ *and* ISMENÊ *enter from the central door of the palace.*

ANTIGONÊ: Ismenê, dear sister,
You would think that we had already suffered enough
For the curse on Oedipus:°
I cannot imagine any grief
That you and I have not gone through. And now—
Have they told you of the new decree of our King Creon?
ISMENÊ: I have heard nothing: I know
That two sisters lost two brothers, a double death
In a single hour; and I know that the Argive army
Fled in the night; but beyond this, nothing.
ANTIGONÊ: I thought so. And that is why I wanted you
To come out here with me. There is something we must do.
ISMENÊ: Why do you speak so strangely?

3 Oedipus the father of Antigonê, Ismenê and their brothers Polyneicês and Eteoclês, and former king of Thebes. Oedipus unknowingly killed his father, Laios, and married his mother, Iocastê. When he discovered the truth, he blinded himself and left Thebes. After Oedipus abdicated the throne, the two brothers ruled. But they quarreled. Polyneices was defeated but returned to attack Thebes. Both brothers were killed in battle. Creon, who became king, ordered that Polyneicês remain unburied.

ANTIGONÊ: Listen, Ismenê:
Creon buried our brother Eteoclês
With military honors, gave him a soldier's funeral,
And it was right that he should; but Polyneicês,
Who fought as bravely and died as miserably,—
They say that Creon has sworn
No one shall bury him, no one mourn for him,
But his body must lie in the fields, a sweet treasure
For carrion birds to find as they search for food.
That is what they say, and our good Creon is coming here
To announce it publicly; and the penalty—
Stoning to death in the public square!
There it is,
And now you can prove what you are:
A true sister, or a traitor to your family.
ISMENÊ: Antigonê, you are mad! What could I possibly do?
ANTIGONÊ: You must decide whether you will help me or not.
ISMENÊ: I do not understand you. Help you in what?
ANTIGONÊ: Ismenê, I am going to bury him. Will you come?
ISMENÊ: Bury him! You have just said the new law forbids it.
ANTIGONÊ: He is my brother. And he is your brother, too.
ISMENÊ: But think of the danger! Think what Creon will do!
ANTIGONÊ: Creon is not strong enough to stand in my way.
ISMENÊ: Ah sister!
Oedipus died, everyone hating him
For what his own search brought to light, his eyes
Ripped out by his own hand; and Iocastê died,
His mother and wife at once: she twisted the cords
That strangled her life; and our two brothers died,
Each killed by the other's sword. And we are left:
But oh, Antigonê,
Think how much more terrible than these
Our own death would be if we should go against Creon
And do what he has forbidden! We are only women,
We cannot fight with men, Antigonê!
The law is strong, we must give in to the law
In this thing, and in worse. I beg the Dead
To forgive me, but I am helpless: I must yield
To those in authority. And I think it is dangerous business
To be always meddling.
ANTIGONÊ: If that is what you think,
I should not want you, even if you asked to come.
You have made your choice, you can be what you want to be.
But I will bury him; and if I must die,

I say that this crime is holy: I shall lie down
With him in death, and I shall be as dear
To him as he to me.
It is the dead,
Not the living, who make the longest demands:
We die for ever . . .
You may do as you like,
Since apparently the laws of the gods mean nothing to you.

ISMENÊ: They mean a great deal to me; but I have no strength
To break laws that were made for the public good.

ANTIGONÊ: That must be your excuse, I suppose. But as for me,
I will bury the brother I love.

ISMENÊ: Antigonê,
I am so afraid for you!

ANTIGONÊ: You need not be:
You have yourself to consider, after all.

ISMENÊ: But no one must hear of this, you must tell no one!
I will keep it a secret, I promise!

ANTIGONÊ: O tell it! Tell everyone!
Think how they'll hate you when it all comes out
If they learn that you knew about it all the time!

ISMENÊ: So fiery! You should be cold with fear.

ANTIGONÊ: Perhaps. But I am doing only what I must.

ISMENÊ: But you can do it? I say that you cannot.

ANTIGONÊ: Very well: when my strength gives out,
I shall do no more.

ISMENÊ: Impossible things should not be tried at all.

ANTIGONÊ: Go away, Ismenê:
I shall be hating you soon, and the dead will too,
For your words are hateful. Leave me my foolish plan:
I am not afraid of the danger; if it means death,
It will not be the worst of deaths—death without honor.

ISMENÊ: Go then, if you feel that you must.
You are unwise,
But a loyal friend indeed to those who love you.

Exit into the palace. ANTIGONÊ *goes off, left. Enter the Chorus.*

PARODOS°

Strophe 1°

CHORUS: Now the long blade of the sun, lying
Level east to west, touches with glory

Parodos The entrance song of the chorus **Strophe** sung as the chorus moves from stage right to stage left

Thebes of the Seven Gates. Open, unlidded
Eye of golden day! O marching light
Across the eddy and rush of Dircê's stream°
Striking the white shields of the enemy
Thrown headlong backward from the blaze of morning!
CHORAGOS:° Polyneicês their commander
Roused them with windy phrases,
He the wild eagle screaming
Insults above our land,
His wings their shields of snow,
His crest their marshalled helms.

Antistrophe 1°

CHORUS: Against our seven gates in a yawning ring
The famished spears came onward in the night;
But before his jaws were sated with our blood,
Or pinefire took the garland of our towers,
He was thrown back; and as he turned, great Thebes—
No tender victim for his noisy power—
Rose like a dragon behind him, shouting war.
CHORAGOS: For God hates utterly
The bray of bragging tongues;
And when he beheld their smiling,
Their swagger of golden helms,
The frown of his thunder blasted
Their first man from our walls.

Strophe 2

CHORUS: We heard his shout of triumph high in the air
Turn to a scream; far out in a flaming arc
He fell with his windy torch, and the earth struck him.
And others storming in fury no less than his
Found shock of death in the dusty joy of battle.
CHORAGOS: Seven captains at seven gates
Yielded their clanging arms to the god
That bends the battle-line and breaks it.
These two only, brothers in blood,
Face to face in matchless rage,
Mirroring each the other's death,
Clashed in long combat.

5 Dircê's stream a river near Thebes **8 Choragos** the leader of the chorus **Antistrophe** sung as the chorus moves from stage left to stage right

Antistrophe 2

CHORUS: But now in the beautiful morning of victory
Let Thebes of the many chariots sing for joy!
With hearts for dancing we'll take leave of war:
Our temples shall be sweet with hymns of praise,
And the long night shall echo with our chorus.

SCENE I

CHORAGOS: But now at last our new King is coming:
Creon of Thebes, Menoikeus' son.
In this auspicious dawn of his reign
What are the new complexities
That shifting Fate has woven for him?
What is his counsel? Why has he summoned
The old men to hear him?

Enter CREON *from the palace, center. He addresses the Chorus from the top step.*

CREON: Gentlemen: I have the honor to inform you that our Ship of State, which recent storms have threatened to destroy, has come safely to harbor at last, guided by the merciful wisdom of Heaven. I have summoned you here this morning because I know that I can depend upon you: your devotion to King Laïos was absolute; you never hesitated in your duty to our late ruler Oedipus; and when Oedipus died, your loyalty was transferred to his children. Unfortunately, as you know, his two sons, the princes Eteoclês and Polyneicês, have killed each other in battle; and I, as the next in blood, have succeeded to the full power of the throne.

I am aware, of course, that no Ruler can expect complete loyalty from his subjects until he has been tested in office. Nevertheless, I say to you at the very outset that I have nothing but contempt for the kind of Governor who is afraid, for whatever reason, to follow the course that he knows is best for the State; and as for the man who sets private friendship above the public welfare,—I have no use for him, either. I call God to witness that if I saw my country headed for ruin, I should not be afraid to speak out plainly; and I need hardly remind you that I would never have any dealings with an enemy of the people. No one values friendship more highly than I; but we must remember that friends made at the risk of wrecking our Ship are not real friends at all.

These are my principles, at any rate, and that is why I have made the following decision concerning the sons of Oedipus: Eteoclês, who died as a man should die, fighting for his country, is to be buried with full military honors, with all the ceremony that is usual when the greatest heroes die; but his brother Polyneicês, who broke his exile to come back with fire and sword against his native city and the shrines of his fathers' gods, whose one idea was to spill the blood of his blood and sell his own people into slavery—Polyneicês, I say, is to have no burial: no man is to touch him or say the least prayer for him; he shall lie on the plain, unburied; and the birds and the scavenging dogs can do with him whatever they like.

This is my command, and you can see the wisdom behind it. As long as I am King, no traitor is going to be honored with the loyal man. But whoever shows by word and deed that he is on the side of the State,—he shall have my respect while he is living, and my reverence when he is dead.

CHORAGOS: If that is your will, Creon son of Menoikeus,
You have the right to enforce it: we are yours.
CREON: That is my will. Take care that you do your part.
CHORAGOS: We are old men: let the younger ones carry it out.
CREON: I do not mean that: the sentries have been appointed.
CHORAGOS: Then what is it that you would have us do?
CREON: You will give no support to whoever breaks this law.
CHORAGOS: Only a crazy man is in love with death!
CREON: And death it is, yet money talks, and the wisest
Have sometimes been known to count a few coins too many.

Enter SENTRY *from left.*

SENTRY: I'll not say that I'm out of breath from running, King, because every time I stopped to think about what I have to tell you, I felt like going back. And all the time a voice kept saying, "You fool, don't you know you're walking straight into trouble?"; and then another voice: "Yes, but if you let somebody else get the news to Creon first, it will be even worse than that for you!" But good sense won out, at least I hope it was good sense, and here I am with a story that makes no sense at all; but I'll tell it anyhow, because, as they say, what's going to happen's going to happen and—

CREON: Come to the point. What have you to say?
SENTRY: I did not do it. I did not see who did it. You must not punish me for what someone else has done.
CREON: A comprehensive defense! More effective, perhaps,
If I knew its purpose. Come: what is it?
SENTRY: A dreadful thing . . . I don't know how to put it—
CREON: Out with it!
SENTRY: Well, then;
The dead man—
Polyneicês—

Pause. The SENTRY *is overcome, fumbles for words.* CREON *waits impassively.*

out there—
someone,—
New dust on the slimy flesh!

Pause. No sign from CREON.

Someone has given it burial that way, and
Gone . . .

Long pause. CREON *finally speaks with deadly control.*

CREON: And the man who dared do this?
SENTRY: I swear I
Do not know! You must believe me!
Listen:
The ground was dry, not a sign of digging, no,
Not a wheeltrack in the dust, no trace of anyone.
It was when they relieved us this morning: and one of them,
The corporal, pointed to it.
There it was,
The strangest—
Look:
The body, just mounded over with light dust: you see?
Not buried really, but as if they'd covered it
Just enough for the ghost's peace. And no sign
Of dogs or any wild animal that had been there.
And then what a scene there was! Every man of us
Accusing the other: we all proved the other man did it,
We all had proof that we could not have done it.
We were ready to take hot iron in our hands,
Walk through fire, swear by all the gods,
It was not I!
I do not know who it was, but it was not I!

CREON'S *rage has been mounting steadily, but the* SENTRY *is too intent upon his story to notice it.*

And then, when this came to nothing, someone said
A thing that silenced us and made us stare
Down at the ground: you had to be told the news,
And one of us had to do it! We threw the dice,
And the bad luck fell to me. So here I am,
No happier to be here than you are to have me:
Nobody likes the man who brings bad news.
CHORAGOS: I have been wondering, King: can it be that the gods have done this?
CREON [*furiously*]: Stop!
Must you doddering wrecks
Go out of your heads entirely? "The gods"!
Intolerable!
The gods favor this corpse? Why? How had he served them?
Tried to loot their temples, burn their images,

Yes, and the whole State, and its laws with it!
Is it your senile opinion that the gods love to honor bad men?
A pious thought!—
No, from the very beginning
There have been those who have whispered together,
Stiff-necked anarchists, putting their heads together,
Scheming against me in alleys. These are the men,
And they have bribed my own guard to do this thing.
[*Sententiously.*] Money!
There's nothing in the world so demoralizing as money.
Down go your cities,
Homes gone, men gone, honest hearts corrupted,
Crookedness of all kinds, and all for money!

To SENTRY.

But you—!
I swear by God and by the throne of God,
The man who has done this thing shall pay for it!
Find that man, bring him here to me, or your death
Will be the least of your problems: I'll string you up
Alive, and there will be certain ways to make you
Discover your employer before you die;
And the process may teach you a lesson you seem to have missed:
The dearest profit is sometimes all too dear:
That depends on the source. Do you understand me?
A fortune won is often misfortune.

SENTRY: King, may I speak?
CREON: Your very voice distresses me.
SENTRY: Are you sure that it is my voice, and not your conscience?
CREON: By God, he wants to analyze me now!
SENTRY: It is not what I say, but what has been done, that hurts you.
CREON: You talk too much.
SENTRY: Maybe; but I've done nothing.
CREON: Sold your soul for some silver: that's all you've done.
SENTRY: How dreadful it is when the right judge judges wrong!
CREON: Your figures of speech
May entertain you now; but unless you bring me the man,
You will get little profit from them in the end.

Exit CREON *into the palace.*

SENTRY: "Bring me the man"—!
I'd like nothing better than bringing him the man!
But bring him or not, you have seen the last of me here.
At any rate, I am safe!

Exit SENTRY.

ODE I

Strophe 1

CHORUS: Numberless are the world's wonders, but none
More wonderful than man; the stormgray sea
Yields to his prows, the huge crests bear him high;
Earth, holy and inexhaustible, is graven
With shining furrows where his plows have gone
Year after year, the timeless labor of stallions.

Antistrophe 1

The lightboned birds and beasts that cling to cover,
The lithe fish lighting their reaches of dim water,
All are taken, tamed in the net of his mind;
The lion on the hill, the wild horse windy-maned,
Resign to him; and his blunt yoke has broken
The sultry shoulders of the mountain bull.

Strophe 2

Words also, and thought as rapid as air,
He fashions to his good use; statecraft is his,
And his the skill that deflects the arrows of snow,
The spears of winter rain: from every wind
He has made himself secure—from all but one:
In the late wind of death he cannot stand.

Antistrophe 2

O clear intelligence, force beyond all measure!
O fate of man, working both good and evil!
When the laws are kept, how proudly his city stands!
When the laws are broken, what of his city then?
Never may the anárchic man find rest at my hearth,
Never be it said that my thoughts are his thoughts.

SCENE II

Reenter SENTRY *leading* ANTIGONÊ.

CHORAGOS: What does this mean? Surely this captive woman
Is the Princess, Antigonê. Why should she be taken?
SENTRY: Here is the one who did it! We caught her
In the very act of burying him—Where is Creon?
CHORAGOS: Just coming from the house.

Enter CREON, *center.*

CREON: What has happened?
Why have you come back so soon?
SENTRY [*expansively*]: O King,
A man should never be too sure of anything:
I would have sworn
That you'd not see me here again: your anger
Frightened me so, and the things you threatened me with;
But how could I tell then
That I'd be able to solve the case so soon?
No dice-throwing this time: I was only too glad to come!
Here is this woman. She is the guilty one:
We found her trying to bury him.
Take her, then; question her; judge her as you will.
I am through with the whole thing now, and glad of it.
CREON: But this is Antigonê! Why have you brought her here?
SENTRY: She was burying him, I tell you!
CREON: [*severely*] Is this the truth?
SENTRY: I saw her with my own eyes. Can I say more?
CREON: The details: come, tell me quickly!
SENTRY: It was like this:
After those terrible threats of yours, King,
We went back and brushed the dust away from the body.
The flesh was soft by now, and stinking,
So we sat on a hill to windward and kept guard.
No napping this time! We kept each other awake.
But nothing happened until the white round sun
Whirled in the center of the round sky over us:
Then, suddenly,
A storm of dust roared up from the earth, and the sky
Went out, the plain vanished with all its trees
In the stinging dark. We closed our eyes and endured it.
The whirlwind lasted a long time, but it passed;
And then we looked, and there was Antigonê!
I have seen
A mother bird come back to a stripped nest, heard
Her crying bitterly a broken note or two
For the young ones stolen. Just so, when this girl
Found the bare corpse, and all her love's work wasted,
She wept, and cried on heaven to damn the hands
That had done this thing.
And then she brought more dust
And sprinkled wine three times for her brother's ghost.
We ran and took her at once. She was not afraid,

Not even when we charged her with what she had done.
She denied nothing.
And this was a comfort to me,
And some uneasiness: for it is a good thing
To escape from death, but it is no great pleasure
To bring death to a friend.
Yet I always say
There is nothing so comfortable as your own safe skin!

CREON [*slowly, dangerously*]: And you, Antigonê,
You with your head hanging,—do you confess this thing?

ANTIGONÊ: I do. I deny nothing.

CREON [*to* SENTRY]: You may go.

Exit SENTRY.

[*to* ANTIGONÊ] Tell me, tell me briefly:
Had you heard my proclamation touching this matter?

ANTIGONÊ: It was public. Could I help hearing it?

CREON: And yet you dared defy the law.

ANTIGONÊ: I dared.
It was not God's proclamation. That final Justice
That rules the world below makes no such laws.

Your edict, King, was strong,
But all your strength is weakness itself against
The immortal unrecorded laws of God.
They are not merely now: they were, and shall be,
Operative for ever, beyond man utterly.

I knew I must die, even without your decree:
I am only mortal. And if I must die
Now, before it is my time to die,
Surely this is no hardship: can anyone
Living, as I live, with evil all about me,
Think Death less than a friend? This death of mine
Is of no importance; but if I had left my brother
Lying in death unburied, I should have suffered.
Now I do not.
You smile at me. Ah Creon,
Think me a fool, if you like; but it may well be
That a fool convicts me of folly.

CHORAGOS: Like father, like daughter: both headstrong, deaf to reason!
She has never learned to yield.

CREON: She has much to learn.
The inflexible heart breaks first, the toughest iron

Cracks first, and the wildest horses bend their necks
At the pull of the smallest curb.
Pride? In a slave?
This girl is guilty of a double insolence,
Breaking the given laws and boasting of it.
Who is the man here,
She or I, if this crime goes unpunished?
Sister's child, or more than sister's child,
Or closer yet in blood—she and her sister
Win bitter death for this!

[*to* SERVANTS]

Go, some of you,
Arrest Ismenê. I accuse her equally.
Bring her: you will find her sniffling in the house there.

Her mind's a traitor: crimes kept in the dark
Cry for light, and the guardian brain shudders;
But how much worse than this
Is brazen boasting of barefaced anarchy!
ANTIGONÊ: Creon, what more do you want than my death?
CREON: Nothing.
That gives me everything.
ANTIGONÊ: Then I beg you: kill me.
This talking is a great weariness: your words
Are distasteful to me, and I am sure that mine
Seem so to you. And yet they should not seem so:
I should have praise and honor for what I have done.
All these men here would praise me
Were their lips not frozen shut with fear of you.
[*Bitterly.*] Ah the good fortune of kings,
Licensed to say and do whatever they please!
CREON: You are alone here in that opinion.
ANTIGONÊ: No, they are with me. But they keep their tongues in leash.
CREON: Maybe. But you are guilty, and they are not.
ANTIGONÊ: There is no guilt in reverence for the dead.
CREON: But Eteoclês—was he not your brother too?
ANTIGONÊ: My brother too.
CREON: And you insult his memory?
ANTIGONÊ [*softly*]: The dead man would not say that I insult it.
CREON: He would: for you honor a traitor as much as him.
ANTIGONÊ: His own brother, traitor or not, and equal in blood.
CREON: He made war on his country. Eteoclês defended it.
ANTIGONÊ: Nevertheless, there are honors due all the dead.

CREON: But not the same for the wicked as for the just.
ANTIGONÊ: Ah Creon, Creon,
Which of us can say what the gods hold wicked?
CREON: An enemy is an enemy, even dead.
ANTIGONÊ: It is my nature to join in love, not hate.
CREON [*finally losing patience*]: Go join them, then; if you must have your love,
Find it in hell!
CHORAGOS: But see, Ismenê comes:

Enter ISMENÊ, *guarded.*

Those tears are sisterly, the cloud
That shadows her eyes rains down gentle sorrow.
CREON: You too, Ismenê,
Snake in my ordered house, sucking my blood
Stealthily—and all the time I never knew
That these two sisters were aiming at my throne!
Ismenê,
Do you confess your share in this crime, or deny it?
Answer me.
ISMENÊ: Yes, if she will let me say so. I am guilty.
ANTIGONÊ [*coldly*]: No, Ismenê. You have no right to say so.
You would not help me, and I will not have you help me.
ISMENÊ: But now I know what you meant; and I am here
To join you, to take my share of punishment.
ANTIGONÊ: The dead man and the gods who rule the dead
Know whose act this was. Words are not friends.
ISMENÊ: Do you refuse me, Antigonê? I want to die with you:
I too have a duty that I must discharge to the dead.
ANTIGONÊ: You shall not lessen my death by sharing it.
ISMENÊ: What do I care for life when you are dead?
ANTIGONÊ: Ask Creon. You're always hanging on his opinions.
ISMENÊ: You are laughing at me. Why, Antigonê?
ANTIGONÊ: It's a joyless laughter, Ismenê.
ISMENÊ: But can I do nothing?
ANTIGONÊ: Yes. Save yourself. I shall not envy you.
There are those who will praise you; I shall have honor, too.
ISMENÊ: But we are equally guilty!
ANTIGONÊ: No more, Ismenê.
You are alive, but I belong to Death.
CREON [*to the Chorus*]: Gentlemen, I beg you to observe these girls:
One has just now lost her mind; the other,
It seems, has never had a mind at all.
ISMENÊ: Grief teaches the steadiest minds to waver, King.

CREON: Yours certainly did, when you assumed guilt with the guilty!
ISMENÊ: But how could I go on living without her?
CREON: You are.
She is already dead.
ISMENÊ: But your own son's bride!
CREON: There are places enough for him to push his plow.
I want no wicked women for my sons!
ISMENÊ: O dearest Haimon, how your father wrongs you!
CREON: I've had enough of your childish talk of marriage!
CHORAGOS: Do you really intend to steal this girl from your son?
CREON: No; Death will do that for me.
CHORAGOS: Then she must die?
CREON [*ironically*]: You dazzle me.
—But enough of this talk!
[*to* GUARDS] You, there, take them away and guard them well:
For they are but women, and even brave men run
When they see Death coming.

Exeunt ISMENÊ, ANTIGONÊ, *and* GUARDS.

ODE II

Strophe 1

CHORUS: Fortunate is the man who has never tasted God's vengeance!
Where once the anger of heaven has struck, that house is shaken
For ever: damnation rises behind each child
Like a wave cresting out of the black northeast,
When the long darkness under sea roars up
And bursts drumming death upon the windwhipped sand.

Antistrophe 1

I have seen this gathering sorrow from time long past
Loom upon Oedipus' children: generation from generation
Takes the compulsive rage of the enemy god.
So lately this last flower of Oedipus' line
Drank the sunlight! but now a passionate word
And a handful of dust have closed up all its beauty.

Strophe 2

What mortal arrogance
Transcends the wrath of Zeus?
Sleep cannot lull him nor the effortless long months
Of the timeless gods: but he is young for ever,
And his house is the shining day of high Olympos.

All that is and shall be,
And all the past, is his.
No pride on earth is free of the curse of heaven.

Antistrophe 2

The straying dreams of men
May bring them ghosts of joy:
But as they drowse, the waking embers burn them;
Or they walk with fixed eyes, as blind men walk.
But the ancient wisdom speaks for our own time:
Fate works most for woe
With Folly's fairest show.
Man's little pleasure is the spring of sorrow.

SCENE III

CHORAGOS: But here is Haimon, King, the last of all your sons.
Is it grief for Antigonê that brings him here,
And bitterness at being robbed of his bride?

Enter HAIMON.

CREON: We shall soon see, and no need of diviners.
—Son,
You have heard my final judgment on that girl:
Have you come here hating me, or have you come
With deference and with love, whatever I do?
HAIMON: I am your son, father. You are my guide.
You make things clear for me, and I obey you.
No marriage means more to me than your continuing wisdom.
CREON: Good. That is the way to behave: subordinate
Everything else, my son, to your father's will.
This is what a man prays for, that he may get
Sons attentive and dutiful in his house,
Each one hating his father's enemies,
Honoring his father's friends. But if his sons
Fail him, if they turn out unprofitably,
What has he fathered but trouble for himself
And amusement for the malicious?
So you are right
Not to lose your head over this woman.
Your pleasure with her would soon grow cold, Haimon,
And then you'd have a hellcat in bed and elsewhere.
Let her find her husband in Hell!
Of all the people in this city, only she

Has had contempt for my law and broken it.

Do you want me to show myself weak before the people?
Or to break my sworn word? No, and I will not.
The woman dies.
I suppose she'll plead "family ties." Well, let her.
If I permit my own family to rebel,
How shall I earn the world's obedience?
Show me the man who keeps his house in hand,
He's fit for public authority.
I'll have no dealings
With law-breakers, critics of the government:
Whoever is chosen to govern should be obeyed—
Must be obeyed, in all things, great and small,
Just and unjust! O Haimon,
The man who knows how to obey, and that man only,
Knows how to give commands when the time comes.
You can depend on him, no matter how fast
The spears come: he's a good soldier, he'll stick it out.

Anarchy, anarchy! Show me a greater evil!
This is why cities tumble and the great houses rain down,
This is what scatters armies!
No, no: good lives are made so by discipline.
We keep the laws then, and the lawmakers,
And no woman shall seduce us. If we must lose,
Let's lose to a man, at least! Is a woman stronger than we?

CHORAGOS: Unless time has rusted my wits,
What you say, King, is said with point and dignity.

HAIMON [*boyishly earnest*]: Father:
Reason is God's crowning gift to man, and you are right
To warn me against losing mine. I cannot say—
I hope that I shall never want to say!—that you
Have reasoned badly. Yet there are other men
Who can reason, too; and their opinions might be helpful.
You are not in a position to know everything
That people say or do, or what they feel:
Your temper terrifies them—everyone
Will tell you only what you like to hear.
But I, at any rate, can listen; and I have heard them
Muttering and whispering in the dark about this girl.
They say no woman has ever, so unreasonably,
Died so shameful a death for a generous act:

"She covered her brother's body. Is this indecent?
She kept him from dogs and vultures. Is this a crime?
Death?—She should have all the honor that we can give her!"

This is the way they talk out there in the city.

You must believe me:
Nothing is closer to me than your happiness.
What could be closer? Must not any son
Value his father's fortune as his father does his?
I beg you, do not be unchangeable:
Do not believe that you alone can be right.
The man who thinks that,
The man who maintains that only he has the power
To reason correctly, the gift to speak, the soul—
A man like that, when you know him, turns out empty.

It is not reason never to yield to reason!

In flood time you can see how some trees bend,
And because they bend, even their twigs are safe,
While stubborn trees are torn up, roots and all.
And the same thing happens in sailing:
Make your sheet fast, never slacken,—and over you go,
Head over heels and under: and there's your voyage.
Forget you are angry! Let yourself be moved!
I know I am young; but please let me say this:
The ideal condition
Would be, I admit, that men should be right by instinct;
But since we are all too likely to go astray,
The reasonable thing is to learn from those who can teach.

CHORAGOS: You will do well to listen to him, King,
If what he says is sensible. And you, Haimon,
Must listen to your father.—Both speak well.

CREON: You consider it right for a man of my years and experience
To go to school to a boy?

HAIMON: It is not right,
If I am wrong. But if I am young, and right,
What does my age matter?

CREON: You think it right to stand up for an anarchist?

HAIMON: Not at all. I pay no respect to criminals.

CREON: Then she is not a criminal?

HAIMON: The City would deny it, to a man.

CREON: And the City proposes to teach me how to rule?
HAIMON: Ah. Who is it that's talking like a boy now?
CREON: My voice is the one voice giving orders in this City!
HAIMON: It is no City if it takes orders from one voice.
CREON: The State is the King!
HAIMON: Yes, if the State is a desert.

Pause.

CREON: This boy, it seems, has sold out to a woman.
HAIMON: If you are a woman: my concern is only for you.
CREON: So? Your "concern"! In a public brawl with your father!
HAIMON: How about you, in a public brawl with justice?
CREON: With justice, when all that I do is within my rights?
HAIMON: You have no right to trample on God's right.
CREON [*completely out of control*]: Fool, adolescent fool! Taken in by a woman!
HAIMON: You'll never see me taken in by anything vile.
CREON: Every word you say is for her!
HAIMON [*quietly, darkly*]: And for you.
And for me. And for the gods under the earth.
CREON: You'll never marry her while she lives.
HAIMON: Then she must die.—But her death will cause another.
CREON: Another?
Have you lost your senses? Is this an open threat?
HAIMON: There is no threat in speaking to emptiness.
CREON: I swear you'll regret this superior tone of yours!
You are the empty one!
HAIMON: If you were not my father,
I'd say you were perverse.
CREON: You girlstruck fool, don't play at words with me!
HAIMON: I am sorry. You prefer silence.
CREON: Now, by God—!
I swear, by all the gods in heaven above us,
You'll watch it, I swear you shall!

[*To the* SERVANTS.]

Bring her out!
Bring the woman out! Let her die before his eyes!
Here, this instant, with her bridegroom beside her!
HAIMON: Not here, no; she will not die here, King.
And you will never see my face again.
Go on raving as long as you've a friend to endure you.

Exit HAIMON.

CHORAGOS: Gone, gone.
Creon, a young man in a rage is dangerous!

CREON: Let him do, or dream to do, more than a man can.
He shall not save these girls from death.
CHORAGOS: These girls?
You have sentenced them both?
CREON: No, you are right.
I will not kill the one whose hands are clean.
CHORAGOS: But Antigonê?
CREON [*somberly*]: I will carry her far away
Out there in the wilderness, and lock her
Living in a vault of stone. She shall have food,
As the custom is, to absolve the State of her death.
And there let her pray to the gods of hell:
They are her only gods:
Perhaps they will show her an escape from death,
Or she may learn,
though late,
That piety shown the dead is pity in vain.
Exit CREON.

ODE III

Strophe

CHORUS: Love, unconquerable
Waster of rich men, keeper
Of warm lights and all-night vigil
In the soft face of a girl:
Sea-wanderer, forest-visitor!
Even the pure Immortals cannot escape you,
And mortal man, in his one day's dusk,
Trembles before your glory.

Antistrophe

Surely you swerve upon ruin
The just man's consenting heart,
As here you have made bright anger
Strike between father and son—
And none has conquered but Love!
A girl's glance working the will of heaven:
Pleasure to her alone who mocks us,
Merciless Aphroditê.°

16 Aphroditê the goddess of love

SCENE IV

CHORAGOS [*as* ANTIGONÊ *enters guarded*]: But I can no longer stand in awe of this,
Nor, seeing what I see, keep back my tears.
Here is Antigonê, passing to that chamber
Where all find sleep at last.

Strophe 1

ANTIGONÊ: Look upon me, friends, and pity me
Turning back at the night's edge to say
Good-by to the sun that shines for me no longer;
Now sleepy Death
Summons me down to Acheron,° that cold shore:
There is no bridesong there, nor any music.
CHORUS: Yet not unpraised, not without a kind of honor,
You walk at last into the underworld;
Untouched by sickness, broken by no sword.
What woman has ever found your way to death?

Antistrophe 1

ANTIGONÊ: How often I have heard the story of Niobê,
Tantalos's wretched daughter, how the stone
Clung fast about her, ivy-close: and they say
The rain falls endlessly
And sifting soft snow; her tears are never done.
I feel the loneliness of her death in mine.
CHORUS: But she was born of heaven, and you
Are woman, woman-born. If her death is yours,
A mortal woman's, is this not for you
Glory in our world and in the world beyond?

Strophe 2

ANTIGONÊ: You laugh at me. Ah, friends, friends,
Can you not wait until I am dead? O Thebes,
O men many-charioted, in love with Fortune,
Dear springs of Dircê, sacred Theban grove,
Be witnesses for me, denied all pity,
Unjustly judged! and think a word of love
For her whose path turns
Under dark earth, where there are no more tears.

9 Acheron a river of the underworld where death reigns

CHORUS: You have passed beyond human daring and come at last
Into a place of stone where Justice sits.
I cannot tell
What shape of your father's guilt appears in this.

Antistrophe 2

ANTIGONÊ: You have touched it at last: that bridal bed
Unspeakable, horror of son and mother mingling:
Their crime, infection of all our family!
O Oedipus, father and brother!
Your marriage strikes from the grave to murder mine.
I have been a stranger here in my own land:
All my life
The blasphemy of my birth has followed me.
CHORUS: Reverence is a virtue, but strength
Lives in established law: that must prevail.
You have made your choice,
Your death is the doing of your conscious hand.

Epode

ANTIGONÊ: Then let me go, since all your words are bitter,
And the very light of the sun is cold to me.
Lead me to my vigil, where I must have
Neither love nor lamentation; no song, but silence.

CREON *interrupts impatiently.*

CREON: If dirges and planned lamentations could put off death,
Men would be singing for ever.

[*to the* SERVANTS]

Take her, go!
You know your orders: take her to the vault
And leave her alone there. And if she lives or dies,
That's her affair, not ours: our hands are clean.
ANTIGONÊ: O tomb, vaulted bride bed in eternal rock,
Soon I shall be with my own again
Where Persephonê° welcomes the thin ghosts underground:
And I shall see my father again, and you, mother,
And dearest Polyneicês—
dearest indeed
To me, since it was my hand

60 Persephonê the queen of the underworld

That washed him clean and poured the ritual wine:
And my reward is death before my time!

And yet, as men's hearts know, I have done no wrong,
I have not sinned before God. Or if I have,
I shall know the truth in death. But if the guilt
Lies upon Creon who judged me, then, I pray,
May his punishment equal my own.

CHORAGOS: O passionate heart,
Unyielding, tormented still by the same winds!
CREON: Her guards shall have good cause to regret their delaying.
ANTIGONÊ: Ah! That voice is like the voice of death!
CREON: I can give you no reason to think you are mistaken.
ANTIGONÊ: Thebes, and you my fathers' gods,
And rulers of Thebes, you see me now, the last
Unhappy daughter of a line of kings,
Your kings, led away to death. You will remember
What things I suffer, and at what men's hands,
Because I would not transgress the laws of heaven.
[*To the* GUARDS, *simply.*] Come: let us wait no longer.

Exit ANTIGONÊ, *left, guarded.*

ODE IV

Strophe 1

CHORUS: All Danaê's beauty was locked away
In a brazen cell where the sunlight could not come:
A small room still as any grave, enclosed her.
Yet she was a princess too,
And Zeus in a rain of gold poured love upon her.
O child, child,
No power in wealth or war
Or tough sea-blackened ships
Can prevail against untiring Destiny!

Antistrophe 1

And Dryas' son° also, that furious king,
Bore the god's prisoning anger for his pride:
Sealed up by Dionysos in deaf stone,
His madness died among echoes.
So at the last he learned what dreadful power

10 Dryas' son Lycurgus, king of Thrace

His tongue had mocked:
For he had profaned the revels,
And fired the wrath of the nine
Implacable Sisters° that love the sound of the flute.

Strophe 2

And old men tell a half-remembered tale
Of horror where a dark ledge splits the sea
And a double surf beats on the gray shores:
How a king's new woman,° sick
With hatred for the queen he had imprisoned,
Ripped out his two sons' eyes with her bloody hands
While grinning Arês° watched the shuttle plunge
Four times: four blind wounds crying for revenge,

Antistrophe 2

Crying, tears and blood mingled.—Piteously born,
Those sons whose mother was of heavenly birth!
Her father was the god of the North Wind
And she was cradled by gales,
She raced with young colts on the glittering hills
And walked untrammeled in the open light:
But in her marriage deathless Fate found means
To build a tomb like yours for all her joy.

SCENE V

Enter blind TEIRESIAS, *led by a boy. The opening speeches of* TEIRESIAS *should be in singsong contrast to the realistic lines of* CREON.

TEIRESIAS: This is the way the blind man comes, Princes, Princes,
Lockstep, two heads lit by the eyes of one.
CREON: What new thing have you to tell us, old Teiresias?
TEIRESIAS: I have much to tell you: listen to the prophet, Creon.
CREON: I am not aware that I have ever failed to listen.
TEIRESIAS: Then you have done wisely, King, and ruled well.
CREON: I admit my debt to you. But what have you to say?
TEIRESIAS: This, Creon: you stand once more on the edge of fate.
CREON: What do you mean? Your words are a kind of dread.
TEIRESIAS: Listen Creon:

18 Implacable Sisters the Muses of poetry and music, arts and sciences **22 King's new woman** Eidothea, second wife of King Phineas, blinded her stepsons after the king had imprisoned their mother in a cave **25 Arês** the god of war who loves bloodshed

I was sitting in my chair of augury, at the place
Where the birds gather about me. They were all a-chatter,
As is their habit, when suddenly I heard
A strange note in their jangling, a scream, a
Whirring fury; I knew that they were fighting,
Tearing each other, dying
In a whirlwind of wings clashing. And I was afraid.
I began the rites of burnt-offering at the altar,
But Hephaistos° failed me: instead of bright flame,
There was only the sputtering slime of the fat thigh-flesh
Melting: the entrails dissolved in gray smoke,
The bare bone burst from the welter. And no blaze!

This was a sign from heaven. My boy described it,
Seeing for me as I see for others.

I tell you, Creon, you yourself have brought
This new calamity upon us. Our hearths and altars
Are stained with the corruption of dogs and carrion birds
That glut themselves on the corpse of Oedipus' son.
The gods are deaf when we pray to them, their fire
Recoils from our offering, their birds of omen
Have no cry of comfort, for they are gorged
With the thick blood of the dead.
O my son,
These are no trifles! Think: all men make mistakes,
But a good man yields when he knows his course is wrong,
And repairs the evil. The only crime is pride.

Give in to the dead man, then: do not fight with a corpse—
What glory is it to kill a man who is dead?
Think, I beg you:
It is for your own good that I speak as I do.
You should be able to yield for your own good.
CREON: It seems that prophets have made me their especial province.
All my life long
I have been a kind of butt for the dull arrows
Of doddering fortune-tellers!
No, Teiresias:
If your birds—if the great eagles of God himself

19 Hephaistos the god of fire

Should carry him stinking bit by bit to heaven,
I would not yield. I am not afraid of pollution:
No man can defile the gods.
Do what you will,
Go into business, make money, speculate
In India gold or that synthetic gold from Sardis,
Get rich otherwise than by my consent to bury him.
Teiresias, it is a sorry thing when a wise man
Sells his wisdom, lets out his words for hire!
TEIRESIAS: Ah Creon! Is there no man left in the world—
CREON: To do what?—Come, let's have the aphorism!
TEIRESIAS: No man who knows that wisdom outweighs any wealth?
CREON: As surely as bribes are baser than any baseness.
TEIRESIAS: You are sick, Creon! You are deathly sick!
CREON: As you say: it is not my place to challenge a prophet.
TEIRESIAS: Yet you have said my prophecy is for sale.
CREON: The generation of prophets has always loved gold.
TEIRESIAS: The generation of kings has always loved brass.
CREON: You forget yourself! You are speaking to your King.
TEIRESIAS: I know it. You are a king because of me.
CREON: You have a certain skill; but you have sold out.
TEIRESIAS: King, you will drive me to words that—
CREON: Say them, say them!
Only remember: I will not pay you for them.
TEIRESIAS: No, you will find them too costly.
CREON: No doubt. Speak:
Whatever you say, you will not change my will.
TEIRESIAS: Then take this, and take it to heart!
The time is not far off when you shall pay back
Corpse for corpse, flesh of your own flesh.
You have thrust the child of this world into living night,
You have kept from the gods below the child that is theirs:
The one in a grave before her death, the other,
Dead, denied the grave. This is your crime:
And the Furies and the dark gods of Hell
Are swift with terrible punishment for you.

Do you want to buy me now, Creon?
Not many days,
And your house will be full of men and women weeping,
And curses will be hurled at you from far
Cities grieving for sons unburied, left to rot

Before the walls of Thebes.

These are my arrows, Creon: they are all for you.

[*To boy.*] But come, child: lead me home.
Let him waste his fine anger upon younger men.
Maybe he will learn at last
To control a wiser tongue in a better head.

Exit TEIRESIAS.

CHORAGOS: The old man has gone, King, but his words
Remain to plague us. I am old, too,
But I cannot remember that he was ever false.
CREON: That is true. . . . It troubles me.
Oh it is hard to give in! but it is worse
To risk everything for stubborn pride.
CHORAGOS: Creon: take my advice.
CREON: What shall I do?
CHORAGOS: Go quickly: free Antigonê from her vault
And build a tomb for the body of Polyneicês.
CREON: You would have me do this!
CHORAGOS: Creon, yes!
And it must be done at once: God moves
Swiftly to cancel the folly of stubborn men.
CREON: It is hard to deny the heart! But I
Will do it: I will not fight with destiny.
CHORAGOS: You must go yourself, you cannot leave it to others.
CREON: I will go.
—Bring axes, servants:
Come with me to the tomb. I buried her, I
Will set her free.
Oh quickly!
My mind misgives—
The laws of the gods are mighty, and a man must serve them
To the last day of his life!

Exit CREON.

PAEAN°

Strophe 1

CHORAGOS: God of many names

Paean a triumphant song

CHORUS: O Iacchos°
son
of Kadmeian Sémelê°
O born of the Thunder!
Guardian of the West
Regent
of Eleusis' plain
O Prince of maenad Thebes
and the Dragon Field by rippling Ismenos.°

Antistrophe 1

CHORAGOS: God of many names
CHORUS: the flame of torches
flares on our hills
the nymphs of Iacchos
dance at the spring of Castalia.°
from the vine-close mountain
come ah come in ivy:
Evohé evohé! sings through the streets of Thebes

Strophe 2

CHORAGOS: God of many names
CHORUS: Iacchos of Thebes
heavenly Child
of Sémelê bride of the Thunderer!
The shadow of plague is upon us:
come
with clement feet
oh come from Parnasos
down the long slopes
across the lamenting water

Antistrophe 2

CHORAGOS: Iô Fire! Chorister of the throbbing stars!
O purest among the voices of the night!
Thou son of God, blaze for us!
CHORUS: Come with choric rapture of circling Maenads°
Who cry *Iô Iacche!*

1 Iacchos also called Bacchos or Dionysos, god of wine and revelry **2 Sémelê** mother of Iacchos, consort of Zeus **5 Ismenos** a river near Thebes where, legend has it, the ancestors of Thebes sprang from a dragon's teeth **7 Castalia** a spring on Mount Parnassus **18 Maenad** female worshipper, attendant of Iacchos

God of many names!

EXODOS

Enter MESSENGER *from left.*

MESSENGER: Men of the line of Kadmos,° you who live
Near Amphion's citadel,°
I cannot say
Of any condition of human life "This is fixed,
This is clearly good, or bad." Fate raises up,
And Fate casts down the happy and unhappy alike:
No man can foretell his Fate.
Take the case of Creon:
Creon was happy once, as I count happiness:
Victorious in battle, sole governor of the land,
Fortunate father of children nobly born.
And now it has all gone from him! Who can say
That a man is still alive when his life's joy fails?
He is a walking dead man. Grant him rich,
Let him live like a king in his great house:
If his pleasure is gone, I would not give
So much as the shadow of smoke for all he owns.
CHORAGOS: Your words hint at sorrow: what is your news for us?
MESSENGER: They are dead. The living are guilty of their death.
CHORAGOS: Who is guilty? Who is dead? Speak!
MESSENGER: Haimon.
Haimon is dead; and the hand that killed him
Is his own hand.
CHORAGOS: His father's? or his own?
MESSENGER: His own, driven mad by the murder his father had done.
CHORAGOS: Teiresias, Teiresias, how clearly you saw it all!
MESSENGER: This is my news: you must draw what conclusions you can from it.
CHORAGOS: But look: Eurydicê, our Queen:
Has she overheard us?

Enter EURYDICÊ *from the palace, center.*

EURYDICÊ: I have heard something, friends:
As I was unlocking the gate of Pallas'° shrine,
For I needed her help today, I heard a voice
Telling of some new sorrow. And I fainted

1 Kadmos sowed the dragon's teeth and founded Thebes **2 Amphion's citadel** Amphion's lyre playing was so beautiful that he charmed stones to form a wall around Thebes **27 Pallas** Athena, the goddess of wisdom

There at the temple with all my maidens about me.
But speak again: whatever it is, I can bear it:
Grief and I are no strangers.

MESSENGER: Dearest Lady.
I will tell you plainly all that I have seen.
I shall not try to comfort you: what is the use,
Since comfort could lie only in what is not true?
The truth is always best.
I went with Creon
To the outer plain where Polyneicês was lying,
No friend to pity him, his body shredded by dogs.
We made our prayers in that place to Hecatê°
And Pluto,° that they would be merciful. And we bathed
The corpse with holy water, and we brought
Fresh-broken branches to burn what was left of it,
And upon the urn we heaped up a towering barrow
Of the earth of his own land.
When we were done, we ran
To the vault where Antigonê lay on her couch of stone.
One of the servants had gone ahead,
And while he was yet far off he heard a voice
Grieving within the chamber, and he came back
And told Creon. And as the King went closer,
The air was full of wailing, the words lost,
And he begged us to make all haste. "Am I a prophet?"
He said, weeping, "And must I walk this road,
The saddest of all that I have gone before?
My son's voice calls me on. Oh quickly, quickly!
Look through the crevice there, and tell me
If it is Haimon, or some deception of the gods!"

We obeyed; and in the cavern's farthest corner
We saw her lying:
She had made a noose of her fine linen veil
And hanged herself. Haimon lay beside her,
His arms about her waist, lamenting her,
His love lost under ground, crying out
That his father had stolen her away from him.

When Creon saw him the tears rushed to his eyes

39 Hecatê the goddess of witchcraft **40 Pluto** king of the underworld

And he called to him: "What have you done, child? Speak to me.
What are you thinking that makes your eyes so strange?
O my son, my son, I come to you on my knees!"
But Haimon spat in his face. He said not a word,
Staring—
And suddenly drew his sword
And lunged. Creon shrank back, the blade missed; and the boy,
Desperate against himself, drove it half its length
Into his own side, and fell. And as he died
He gathered Antigonê close in his arms again,
Choking, his blood bright red on her white cheek.
And now he lies dead with the dead, and she is his
At last, his bride in the houses of the dead.

Exit EURYDICÊ *into the palace.*

CHORAGOS: She has left us without a word. What can this mean?
MESSENGER: It troubles me, too; yet she knows what is best,
Her grief is too great for public lamentation,
And doubtless she has gone to her chamber to weep
For her dead son, leading her maidens in his dirge.

Pause.

CHORAGOS: It may be so: but I fear this deep silence.
MESSENGER: I will see what she is doing. I will go in.

Exit MESSENGER *into the palace.*

Enter CREON *with attendants, bearing* HAIMON'S *body.*

CHORAGOS: But here is the king himself: oh look at him,
Bearing his own damnation in his arms.
CREON: Nothing you say can touch me any more.
My own blind heart has brought me
From darkness to final darkness. Here you see
The father murdering, the murdered son—
And all my civic wisdom!

Haimon my son, so young, so young to die,
I was the fool, not you; and you died for me.
CHORAGOS: That is the truth; but you were late in learning it.
CREON: This truth is hard to bear. Surely a god
Has crushed me beneath the hugest weight of heaven,
And driven me headlong a barbaric way
To trample out the thing I held most dear.

The pains that men will take to come to pain!

Enter MESSENGER *from the palace.*

MESSENGER: The burden you carry in your hands is heavy,
But it is not all: you will find more in your house.
CREON: What burden worse than this shall I find there?
MESSENGER: The Queen is dead.
CREON: O port of death, deaf world,
Is there no pity for me? And you, Angel of evil,
I was dead, and your words are death again.
Is it true, boy? Can it be true?
Is my wife dead? Has death bred death?
MESSENGER: You can see for yourself.

The doors are opened and the body of EURYDICÊ *is disclosed within.*

CREON: Oh pity!
All true, all true, and more than I can bear!
O my wife, my son!
MESSENGER: She stood before the altar, and her heart
Welcomed the knife her own hand guided,
And a great cry burst from her lips for Megareus° dead,
And for Haimon dead, her sons; and her last breath
Was a curse for their father, the murderer of her sons.
And she fell, and the dark flowed in through her closing eyes.
CREON: O God, I am sick with fear.
Are there no swords here? Has no one a blow for me?
MESSENGER: Her curse is upon you for the deaths of both.
CREON: It is right that it should be. I alone am guilty.
I know it, and I say it. Lead me in,
Quickly, friends.
I have neither life nor substance. Lead me in.
CHORAGOS: You are right, if there can be right in so much wrong.
The briefest way is best in a world of sorrow.
CREON: Let it come,
Let death come quickly, and be kind to me.
I would not ever see the sun again.
CHORAGOS: All that will come when it will; but we, meanwhile,
Have much to do. Leave the future to itself.
CREON: All my heart was in that prayer!
CHORAGOS: Then do not pray any more: the sky is deaf.
CREON: Lead me away. I have been rash and foolish.
I have killed my son and my wife.

114 Megareus the other son of Eurydice and Creon who had sacrificed himself to Ares to save Thebes from the seven who attacked it

I look for comfort; my comfort lies here dead.
Whatever my hands have touched has come to nothing.
Fate has brought all my pride to a thought of dust.

As CREON *is being led into the house, the* CHORAGOS *advances and speaks directly to the audience.*

CHORAGOS: There is no happiness where there is no wisdom;
No wisdom but in submission to the gods.
Big words are always punished,
And proud men in old age learn to be wise.

GENERATING IDEAS FOR WRITING

One of the best ways to get ideas for an essay is to ask and answer your own most compelling questions. Write down whatever questions come to mind during and after your reading. See if the answers to these questions provide topics for writing. Or choose a compelling idea from a journal entry, draw a Venn diagram to compare elements or other works (pp. 33–34), use directed freewriting (p. 41), ask questions (p. 42), list, or draw a cluster, or semantic map (pp. 43–44) to loosen up ideas.

Listed below is a more structured approach based on the elements of drama discussed earlier in this section. Applying these questions to *Antigonê* may demonstrate how the elements might be applied to any work of drama.

Getting Started—Your First Response

1. To what extent is your response to *Antigonê* influenced by your own experience?
2. If you were placed in their positions, would you behave the same way as Antigonê? Creon? Haimon? Ismenê? Explain.
3. Do you think loyalty to your family, religion, or country is more important? Explain.

Language and Style

1. How does the formal language and verse form of the play affect you?
2. What does Creon's use of language tell you about him?
3. Is there symbolism in this play? Explain.

Narration

1. How are you affected by the comments of Choragos and the chorus?
2. How does the nature of what they say differ from what the individual characters say?
3. How does the role of Choragos differ from that of the other characters?

Setting

1. When and where is *Antigonê* set?
2. What is the atmosphere in this play?
3. How does the setting influence the conflict between Antigonê and Creon?
4. To what extent does the setting support and emphasize the play's meaning?
5. There are very few stage directions in *Antigonê.* To what extent did that affect your reading of the play?

Conflict and Plot

1. What is the main conflict in the play? Is it external or internal? Explain.
2. How many other conflicts are there?
3. In what way are they related to the main conflict?
4. To what extent does the plot follow a traditional structure?

Character

1. How does what Antigonê, Ismenê, Creon, and Haimon say tell you about them?
2. How does what they do tell you about them?
3. What is the function of Tieresias in this play?
4. To what extent is conflict in *Antigonê* connected to characterization?
5. Who is the protagonist and who is the antagonist in this play?

Theme

1. What is the theme of *Antigonê?*
2. How do setting, conflict, and character contribute to this theme?
3. To what extent does the play preach as well as reveal?

TOPICS FOR WRITING

The following list is not exhaustive, but simply illustrative of the kinds of questions that might emerge from the more specific analytical questions (and combinations of questions) like those above. Your responses might provide worthwhile topics for writing.

1. Compare the characterizations of Antigonê and Creon. To what extent are they alike or different?
2. To what extent was it possible for Antigonê to achieve the burial of her brother through different means?

3. Is Creon powerless to respond differently to her behavior? Explain.
4. What is the role of Ismenê? To what extent can you justify her behavior?
5. What is the impact of power on the characters in *Antigonê?*
6. What is the impact of pride on the characters in this play?
7. How important is it that a woman broke the law? What does the play tell us about the place of women in that society?
8. What is the connection between the choral odes and the play's meaning?
9. To what extent is *Antigonê* typical of the work of Sophocles? How does this play compare with *Oedipus Rex?*
10. How does it compare to the work of other Greek dramatists of this period?
11. How well does *Antigonê* fulfill Aristotle's requirements for tragedy?
12. In what way is this play a reflection of the cultural beliefs of ancient Greece?
13. In what way does the conflict in *Antigonê* transcend that period and speak to us now?

Reading and Analyzing Essays

Of all forms of literature, you are probably most familiar with the essay. You have read them in newspapers and magazines most of your life. And you have had lots of practice writing them. If reading and writing essays has been a good experience, you already know why they are important. They let us express who we are and what we think—our personal stories, impressions, feelings, ideas, and opinions. They let us know who other people are and what they think. They spring from a basic human need to communicate.

In late-sixteenth-century France, Michel de Montaigne, the first modern essay writer, introduced his book, *Essais,* by writing, "I am myself the subject of my book." Whatever form the essay has taken since then, Montaigne's statement is still at the heart of effective essay writing. Both of the earliest popular essay writers, Montaigne and his English counterpart Francis Bacon were personal and informal. They wrote about whatever intrigued them, usually in a light, speculative way. They didn't write about the strange or unusual; they wrote about everyday topics—conversation, education, friendship, gardening. But they wrote about these topics in such an entertaining and insightful way that their voices, as if in conversation with us, come back to life when we read them three hundred years later. Since that time some of our most prominent writers have expanded the scope of the essay to moral, social, and political criticism, and its tone from bawdy humor and biting satire to great solemnity.

Most of our favorite essay writers today write in newspapers and magazines. We may call them columnists, op-ed writers, or sports writers, but they are in fact essay writers. They don't tell us the news; they tell us what they think of the news. They are emotional, outspoken, and opinionated in predictable ways—and very much the inheritors of Montaigne's "I." They have strong "voices," and we have gotten to know them. Whether we agree or disagree with them, we usually look forward to reading what they have to say.

When you're reading an essay for the first time, imagine you're in a conversation, that the writer is talking to you. Relax and listen. And talk back from time to time by writing down your responses.

TYPES OF ESSAYS

There is no easy or entirely accurate way to classify essays. Instead of giving a clear picture of how each category is different, the discussion of types below blurs distinctions. After all, narrative and expository essays may be argumentative: exposition and argumentation may use narrative to make or to prove their points. Basically, the intention of all essays is to be persuasive, to have readers respond by thinking, "I see what you mean" or "Yes, you're right."

It may be helpful to think of the designations narrative, expository, and argumentative as degrees of emphasis rather than discrete or exclusive types.

Narrative

Narrative essays tell a story. Most essays of this type spring from an event or experience in the writer's life. Beyond sharing an aspect of the writer's life, however, their intention is to make a point, present an idea, or make an argument. They not only recount what's happened, they emphasize the importance of the occurrence. This narration is often "seasoned" with personal comment, reflection, and opinion.

Voice is crucial to this kind of essay. All of the personal narratives in this text rely heavily on the narrator as a participant who feels frustration, pain, or joy; who experiences insight and earns the right to tell the story.

Among the narrative essays in this text are "Salvation" (p. 29), "No Name Woman," (p. 390), and "Graduation in Stamps" (p. 947).

Expository

Expository essays share, explain, suggest, or explore information, emotion, and ideas. You might ask, "What else is there?" This is the broadest category. Many of these essays may seem to be narrative or argumentative; they may use stories as examples or may imply an argument or position. The key to exposition is the emphasis on showing and sharing insight—not primarily on telling a story or making an argument.

A few examples of exposition in this text are "Mothers" (p. 27), Bettleheim's "Cinderella" (p. 706), and "Why I Write" (p. 955).

Argumentative

The intention of a formal argumentative essay is to prove a point by supporting it with evidence. Note that proving and persuading are not the same thing. Proving may persuade or convince us if we are open-minded and have not formed a contrary opinion. If we feel differently about an issue, the amount of logical evidence might not matter. People are often persuaded by advertisements that offer little or no evidence but appeal almost exclusively to their emotions or sense of style.

The most effective argumentative essays do not rely on evidence alone to convince us. While facts and statistics may lie at the foundation of a strong persuasive argument, examples and personal anecdotes often do the real convincing. We think with our heads, but we pay attention with our hearts. When we look at some of the essays in this book that make convincing arguments, we see that they appeal to both head and heart.

A few wide-ranging examples of argumentative essays in this text are "I Want a Wife" (p. 711), "A Modest Proposal" (p. 1266), and "I Have a Dream" (p. 960).

✔CHECKLIST • *Types of Essays*

- ❑ Would you classify the essay as narrative, expository, argumentative? Explain. Is the classification clear? If not, why?

Language, Style, and Structure

Formal or Informal

Formal essays are usually about a serious topic; they have a fairly tight, clear structure and strategy. Their narrative perspective emphasizes objectivity, and the writer's voice is often impersonal and detached. This type of essay is more likely to gather its support from facts, data, or statistics, and to use formal language, not everyday words or phrases.

Though many formal essays have a complex structure, the classic structure of a formal essay has an introduction that involves the reader and states the thesis; a middle that gives details and examples; and a conclusion that restates support for the thesis and (if successful) leaves the reader enlightened and convinced.

Informal essays deal with both lighthearted and serious topics. They generally rely on detail, emotion, narrative, and personal examples for support. The choice of words and sentence structure is more likely to be conversational and informal, with everyday phrases, dialogue, narration, imagery, and figurative language. The overall structure of an informal essay is likely to emerge from the subject matter rather than adhere to a predetermined structure.

Voice

Voice refers to the individual personality that comes alive in the words. It is the key to **tone**, and tone is not always easy to pick up. When we see or hear a person speaking words, their intonations, physical gestures, and facial expressions tell us the attitude of the speaker toward the subject. When we hear "voice" in our reading too, we can also sense the intonations. Cues in a printed text are not always obvious, however, and we must often rely on the pattern and types of words the writer chooses to sense the tone.

Word Choice and Style

Choice of language is an important element in creating voice in an essay. Figurative language brings the writing to life. Concrete details and evocative images pull us into the text. Formal vocabulary evokes a different response from us than informal or nonstandard words. So, too, the frequency of images and figurative language has an effect on our reading and response. Using what you already know about language in fiction, poetry, and drama tells you much about imagery, figurative language, syntax, rhythm, and sound in essays as well.

✔CHECKLIST • *Language, Style, and Structure*

- ❑ In general, is the essay formal or informal? How so?
- ❑ How would you describe the writer's voice?
- ❑ What is the author's relationship to the essay? Do you find the author believable? Why? Was the voice of the author effective in conveying the essay's meaning? Why?
- ❑ Is the language formal or informal?
- ❑ What does the nature of the language tell you about the essay?
- ❑ Are there many instances of imagery and figurative language (simile, metaphor)? If so, how do they connect to or support the essay?

THEME OR THESIS: WHAT'S THE POINT?

The theme, or thesis, of an essay is the insight the writer shares; or the point the writer wants to teach, prove, or convince us of. Because they often have a tight structure and direct writing style, it may be easier to identify and to articulate the theme in a formal essay than in a narrative or informal one.

Inform, Preach, or Reveal

Many formal, expository essays intend to inform or teach us. Likewise, it's the intention of many formal, argumentative essays to teach a lesson or convince us of a particular moral view. Essays of this type are often written in response to a perceived political or social problem. In this respect they have a moral, or message.

At the beginning of the essay, formal-essay writers often announce what they intend to prove or to explain and then remind us again at the end. The predictability of the structure itself is designed to make it clear. Like other forms of literature, however, most good narrative and informal essays share or reveal something insightful about human nature. Our experience of the theme, however, may be holistic or impressionistic—and a bit more elusive.

Regardless of the type of essay, what makes your interpretation convincing or defensible is your ability to support it. Your belief about what the essay means may change as you move back and forth through the stages of your reading experience. The first time you read an essay, you may feel one way. Writing down your reflections, rereading the essay, and discussing it with others may lead to a different, better-informed understanding and interpretation.

✔CHECKLIST • *Theme or Thesis*

❑ What is the intention of the essay? Is it trying to inform us of something? To prove or convince us of something? To share an insight?

❑ What is its theme or thesis?

✔SUMMARY CHECKLIST • *Analyzing Essays*

Types of Essays

❑ Would you classify the essay as narrative, expository, or argumentative? Explain. Is the classification clear? If not, why?

Language, Style, and Structure

❑ In general, is the essay formal or informal? How so?

❑ How would you describe the writer's voice?

❑ What is the author's relationship to the essay? Do you find the author believable? Why?

❑ Was the voice of the author effective in conveying the essay's meaning? Why?

❑ Is the language formal or informal?

❑ What does the nature of the language tell you about the essay?

(*continued*)

- ❑ Are there many instances of imagery and figurative language (simile, metaphor)? If so, how do they connect to or support the essay?

Theme or Thesis

- ❑ What is the intention of the essay? Is it trying to inform us of something? To prove or convince us of something? To share an insight?
- ❑ What is its theme or thesis?

GETTING IDEAS FOR WRITING

Following "Mother Tongue," many of the questions from the summary checklist above are applied to the essay, and we consider some of the ways the elements discussed in this section might be used to prompt ideas for a critical essay.

AMY TAN (b. 1952)

MOTHER TONGUE [1990]

I am not a scholar of English or literature. I cannot give you much more than personal opinions on the English language and its variations in this country or others. I am a writer. And by that definition, I am someone who has always loved language. I am fascinated by language in daily life. I spend a great deal of my time thinking about the power of language—the way it can evoke an emotion, a visual image, a complex idea, or a simple truth. Language is the tool of my trade. And I use them all—all the Englishes I grew up with.

Recently, I was made keenly aware of the different Englishes I do use. I was giving a talk to a large group of people, the same talk I had already given to half a dozen other groups. The nature of the talk was about my writing, my life, and my book, *The Joy Luck Club*. The talk was going along well enough, until I remembered one major difference that made the whole talk sound wrong. My mother was in the room. And it was perhaps the first time she had heard me give a lengthy speech, using the kind of English I have never used with her. I was saying things like, "The intersection of memory upon imagination" and "There is an aspect of my fiction that relates to thus-and-thus"—a speech filled with carefully wrought grammatical phrases, burdened, it suddenly seemed to me, with nominalized forms, past perfect tenses, conditional phrases, all the forms of standard English that I had learned in school and through books, the forms of English I did not use at home with my mother.

Just last week, I was walking down the street with my mother, and I again found myself conscious of the English I was using, the English I do use with her. We were talking about the price of new and used furniture and I heard myself saying this: "Not waste money that way." My husband was with us as well, and he didn't notice any switch in my English. And then I realized why. It's because over the twenty years we've been together I've often used that same kind of English with him, and sometimes he even uses it with me. It has become our language of intimacy, a different sort of English that relates to family talk, the language I grew up with.

So you'll have some idea of what this family talk I heard sounds like, I'll quote what my mother said during a recent conversation which I videotaped and then transcribed. During this conversation, my mother was talking about a political gangster in Shanghai who had the same last name as her family's, Du, and how the gangster in his early years wanted to be adopted by her family, which was rich by comparison. Later, the gangster became more powerful, far richer than my mother's family, and one day showed up at my mother's wedding to pay his respects. Here's what she said in part:

> Du-Yusong having business like fruit stand. Like off the street kind. He is Du like Du Zong-but not Tsung-ming Island people. The local people call putong, the river east side, he belong to that side local people. That man want to ask Du Zong father take him in like become own family. Du Zong father wasn't look down on him, but didn't take seriously, until that man big like become a mafia. Now important person, very hard to inviting him. Chinese way, came only to show respect, don't stay for dinner. Respect for making big celebration, he shows up. Mean gives lots of respect. Chinese custom. Chinese social life that way. If too important won't have to stay too long. He come to my wedding. I didn't see, I heard it. I gone to boy's side, they have YMCA dinner. Chinese age I was nineteen.

You should know that my mother's expressive command of English belies' how much she actually understands. She reads the *Forbes* report, listens to *Wall Street Week,* converses daily with her stockbroker, reads all of Shirley MacLaine's books with ease—all kinds of things I can't begin to understand. Yet some of my friends tell me they understand 50 percent of what my mother says. Some say they understand 80 to 90 percent. Some say they understand none of it, as if she were speaking pure Chinese. But to me, my mother's English is perfectly clear, perfectly natural. It's my mother tongue. Her language, as I hear it, is vivid, direct, full of observation and imagery. That was the language that helped shape the way I saw things, expressed things, made sense of the world.

Lately, I've been giving more thought to the kind of English my mother speaks. Like others, I have described it to people as "broken" or "fractured" English. But I wince when I say that. It has always bothered me that I can think of no way to describe it other than "broken," as if it were damaged and needed to be fixed, as if it lacked a certain wholeness and soundness. I've heard other terms used, "limited English," for example. But they seem just as bad, as if everything is limited, including people's perceptions of the limited English speaker.

I know this for a fact, because when I was growing up, my mother's "limited" English limited my perception of her. I was ashamed of her English. I believed that her English reflected the quality of what she had to say. That is, because she expressed them imperfectly her thoughts were imperfect. And I had plenty of empirical evidence to support me: the fact that people in department stores, at banks, and at restaurants did not take her seriously, did not give her good service, pretended not to understand her, or even acted as if they did not hear her.

My mother had long realized the limitations of her English as well. When I was fifteen, she used to have me call people on the phone to pretend I was she. In this guise, I was forced to ask for information or even to complain and yell at people who had been rude to her. One time it was a call to her stockbroker in New York. She had cashed out her small portfolio and it just so happened we were going to go to New York the next week, our very first trip outside California. I had to get on the phone and say in an adolescent voice that was not very convincing, "This is Mrs. Tan."

And my mother was standing in the back whispering loudly, "Why he don't send me check, already two weeks late. So mad he lie to me, losing me money."

And then I said in perfect English, "Yes, I'm getting rather concerned. You had agreed to send the check two weeks ago, but it hasn't arrived.'

Then she began to talk more loudly. "What he want, I come to New York tell him front of his boss, you cheating me?" And I was trying to calm her down, make her be quiet, while telling the stockbroker, "I can't tolerate any more excuses. If I don't receive the check immediately, I am going to have to speak to your manager when I'm in New York next week." And sure enough, the following week there we were in front of this astonished stockbroker, and I was sitting there red-faced and quiet, and my mother, the real Mrs. Tan, was shouting at his boss in her impeccable broken English.

We used a similar routine just five days ago, for a situation that was far less humorous. My mother had gone to the hospital for an appointment, to find out about a benign brain tumor a CAT scan had revealed a month ago. She said she had spoken very good English, her best English, no mistakes, Still, she said, the hospital did not apologize when they said they had lost the CAT scan and she had come for nothing. She said they did not seem to have any sympathy when she told them she was anxious to know the exact diagnosis, since her husband and son had both died of brain tumors. She said they would not give her any more information until the next time and she would have to make another appointment for that. So she said she would not leave until the doctor called her daughter. She wouldn't budge. And when the doctor finally called her daughter, me, who spoke in perfect English—lo and behold—we had assurances the CAT scan would be found, promises that a conference call on Monday would be held, and apologies for any suffering my mother had gone through for a most regrettable mistake.

I think my mother's English almost had an effect on limiting my possibilities in life as well. Sociologists and linguists probably will tell you that a person developing language skills are more influenced by peers. But I do think that the language spoken in the family, especially in immigrant families which are more insular, plays a large role in shaping the language of the child. And I believe that it affected my results on achievement tests, IQ tests, and the SAT. While my English skills were never judged as poor, compared to math, English could not be considered my strong suit. In grade school I did moderately well, getting perhaps B's, sometimes B-pluses, in English and scoring perhaps in the sixtieth or seventieth percentile on achievement tests. But those scores were not good enough to override the opinion that my true abilities lay in math and science, because in those areas I achieved As and scored in the ninetieth percentile or higher.

This was understandable. Math is precise; there is only one correct answer. Whereas, for me at least, the answers on English tests were always a judgment call, a matter of opinion and personal experience. Those tests were constructed around items like fill-in-the-blank sentence completion, such as, "Even though Tom was—, Mary thought he was—" And the correct answer always seemed to be the most bland combinations of thoughts, for example, "Even though Tom was shy, Mary thought he was charming," with the grammatical structure "even though" limiting the correct answer to some sort of semantic opposites, so you wouldn't get answers like, "Even though Tom was foolish, Mary thought he was ridiculous." Well, according to my mother, there were very few limitations as to what Tom could have been and what Mary might have thought of him. So I never did well on tests like that.

The same was true with word analogies, pairs of words in which you were supposed to find some sort of logical, semantic relationship—for example, "*Sunset* is to *nightfall* as—is to—." And here you would be presented with a list of four possible pairs, one of which showed the same kind of relationship: *red* is to *stoplight, bus* is to *arrival, chills* is to *fever, yawn* is to *boring.* Well, I could never think that way. I knew what the tests were asking, but I could not block out of my mind the images already created by the first pair, *sunset* is to nightfall"—and I would see a burst of colors against a darkening sky, the moon rising, the lowering of a curtain of stars. And all the other pairs of words—red, bus, stoplight, boring—just threw up a mass of confusing images, making it impossible for me to sort out something as logical as saying: "A sunset precedes nightfall" is the same as "a chill precedes a fever." The only way I would have gotten that answer right would have been to imagine an associative situation, for example, my being disobedient and staying out past sunset, catching a chill at night, which turns into feverish pneumonia as punishment, which indeed did happen to me.

I have been thinking about all this lately, about my mother's English, about achievement tests. Because lately I've been asked, as a writer, why there are not more Asian Americans represented in American literature. Why are there few Asian Americans enrolled in creative writing programs? Why do so many Chinese students go into engineering? Well, these are broad sociological questions I can't begin to answer. But I have noticed in surveys—in fact, just last week—that Asian students, as a whole, always do significantly better on math achievement tests than in English. And this makes me think that there are other Asian-American students whose English spoken in the home might also be described as "broken" or "limited." And perhaps they also have teachers who are steering them away from writing and into math and science, which is what happened to me.

Fortunately, I happen to be rebellious in nature and enjoy the challenge of disproving assumptions made about me. I became an English major my first year in college, after being enrolled as pre-med. I started writing nonfiction as a freelancer the week after I was told by my former boss that writing was my worst skill and I should hone my talents toward account management.

But it wasn't until 1985 that I finally began to write fiction. And at first I wrote using what I thought to be wittily crafted sentences, sentences that would finally prove I had mastery over the English language. Here's an example from the first draft of a story that later made its way into *The Joy Luck Club,* but without this line: "That was my mental quandary in its nascent state." A terrible line, which I can barely pronounce.

Fortunately, for reasons I won't get into today, I later decided I should envision a reader for the stories I would write. And the reader I decided upon was my mother, because these were stories about mothers. So with this reader in mind—and in fact she did read my early drafts—I began to write stories using all the Englishes I grew up with: the English I spoke to my mother, which for lack of a better term might be described as "simple"; the English she used with me, which for lack of a better term might be described as "broken"; my translation of her Chinese, which could certainly be described as "watered down"; and what I imagined to be her translation of her Chinese if she could speak in perfect English, her internal language, and for that I sought to preserve the essence, but neither an English nor a Chinese structure. I wanted to capture what language ability tests can never reveal: her intent, her passion, her imagery, the rhythms of her speech and the nature of her thoughts.

Apart from what any critic had to say about my writing, I knew I had succeeded where it counted when my mother finished reading my book and gave me her verdict: "So easy to read."

GENERATING IDEAS FOR WRITING

One of the best ways to get ideas for an essay is to ask and answer your own most compelling questions. Write down whatever questions come to mind during and after your reading. See if the answers to these questions provide topics for writing. Or choose a compelling idea from a journal entry, draw a Venn diagram to compare elements or other works (pp. 33–34), use directed freewriting (p. 41), ask questions (p. 42), list, or draw a cluster, or semantic map (pp. 43–44) to loosen up ideas.

Listed below is a more structured approach based on the elements of drama discussed earlier in this section. Applying these questions to "Mother Tongue" may demonstrate how the elements might be applied to any essay.

First Response

1. To what extent is your response to "Mother Tongue" influenced by your own background or experience?

Type of Essay

1. How does the voice of the writer influence your response?
2. Amy Tan opens her essay by writing "I am not a scholar of English or literature." How does that influence your response to her?
3. Would you classify this as a narrative, expository, or argumentative essay? Why? To what extent is the classification clear?

Language, Style, and Structure

1. In general, is "Mother Tongue" formal or informal? How so?
2. Is Amy Tan's use of language formal or informal?
3. Are there many instances of imagery and figurative language (simile, metaphor)? If so, how do they connect to or support the essay?
4. How would you describe Amy Tan's voice? Do you find her believable? Why?
5. Was she effective in conveying the essay's meaning? How so?

Theme or Thesis

1. Do you gain any insights about yourself or your writing from this essay? If so, explain?
2. What is the intention of the essay? Is it trying to inform us of something? To prove or convince us of something? To share an insight?
3. What do you think the author is trying to say? What is the essay's theme or thesis?

Topics for Writing

The following list is not exhaustive, but simply illustrative of the kinds of questions that might emerge from the more specific analytical questions (and combinations of questions) like those above. Your responses to these questions might provide worthwhile topics for writing.

1. How does the way people use language influence other people's opinion of them?
2. Amy Tan writes, "the language spoken in the family, especially in immigrant families which are more insular, plays a large role in shaping the language of the child." Do you think this is true? Explain.
3. In what way is it possible for someone to be articulate and not have a formal command of the language?
4. To what extent is there an advantage to using "different Englishes" for different occasions?
5. Do you think many people have a "mother tongue"? Do you? Explain.
6. Do you think everyone should learn to use standard English correctly? Why?

CHAPTER 4

Argumentation
Interpreting and Evaluating

The goal in this chapter is to develop your writing and analysis into a critical essay. Writing a critical essay is a natural extension of your earlier work. At their best, your essays should continue to express, in your strongest voice, what you believe is important. There is no need for you to become completely formal or use complicated terminology. But writing a critical essay does require reading and rereading a text carefully, gathering textual evidence, building observations into an interpretation or evaluation, and articulating a sound argument. Convincing others requires clear thinking and writing. We may write with a stronger voice when we feel passionate about an issue, but it is our ability to explain *why* with evidence, not just our passion, that gives clarity and credibility to our arguments.

The Critical Essay

The difference between a response essay and a critical essay is more a matter of emphasis than kind. A response essay describes our experience with literature—how we are personally affected by the work. The primary intention of a response essay is to share our personal experience, not to argue for a position.

A critical essay, while motivated by our experience with literature, shifts the emphasis toward the work itself and builds an argument for what the work or some aspect of it means (an interpretation), or its worth (an evaluation), or both. In addition to analyzing or explicating the text of a work, or making comparisons, a critical essay may address the beliefs or actions of the narrator or characters, or view a work or its elements within a variety of historical, cultural, biographical, or other contexts (see the Appendix for an explanation of these approaches).

Writing a critical essay is a natural extension of your earlier work building details into a conclusion. Beyond this work, however, you must be prepared to offer arguments in support of your views and state them clearly and persuasively. Reading the two journal entries that follow may give you an insight into the difference between a personal and a critical response.

Debra's Response to *Antigonê:*

While reading Antigone I was thinking I had never read anything written like this. It was awkward to stumble on certain words, not sure if I could pronounce them right or understand their meaning.

I thought the story on the whole was beautiful but sad. The love that Antigone had for her brother was touching. She was a strong person who stood up for what she believed in.

The ending was very sad because she died needlessly. The fact that she took her own life was no great surprise. Knowing that she was left for dead, she did what she thought best. I thought it sad that Creon lost his son and wife, but I also think he brought it on himself.

Suzanne's Response to *Antigonê:*

I really liked this play. I thought it was very well written and a lot easier to understand than I expected. The central focus throughout the play seems to be public policy vs. individual conscience. I found it very interesting that even though Antigone was written so long ago it dealt with civil disobedience, which remains a major social issue to this day. I liked the way Antigone stood up for what she felt was right instead of letting Creon force her to live with something she felt was morally wrong. Creon's sexist attitude became his downfall. At first I thought Haimon would side with his father, so I was pretty surprised when they found him dead in Antigone's cave. Everyone tried to reason with Creon, and he had plenty of chances to change his mind, so I thought he got what he deserved. It seemed a little unnecessary for everyone to have to die in order to prove this point, but I guess that's how tragedies go.

Debra writes about how the play affected her—what emotions she felt about characters and scenes, and even what difficulties she had with the text of the play. Her intention seems to be to share her personal experience of the play, not to argue an interpretation or evaluation.

Suzanne also comments about how the play affected her, but she has taken her comments a step further. When she writes, "The central focus throughout the play seems to be public policy vs. individual conscience," she is stating what she believes the play is about—the subject of the play. By going one step further and stating what she believes the play is saying about this subject, she may have a strong proposition, or thesis statement, for a critical essay.

When she writes, "I thought it was very well written," she is making an evaluative statement about the quality of writing in the play. Again, if she defines what she means by well written, and indicates how *Antigonê* fulfills that description, she may have a good proposition, or thesis statement, for a critical essay.

In each case, her support for these propositions (not the propositions themselves) is the crucial factor in building either of these statements into a clear thesis statement and effective critical essay. In both cases, she would have to build an argument by gathering support from the text. To support her interpretation of what *Antigonê* is saying about "public policy vs. individual conscience," she would have to define what she meant by these terms, cite evidence, and identify connecting patterns of this theme in the text of the play. To support her evaluation that "it was very well written," she would have to define her standards for well written and show—with reference to the text—how the play matched them.

Choosing a Topic: Process and Product

Beginning on page 168 of this chapter, we look at Suzanne McCloskey's process in writing a critical essay, from her first response (on page 168) through her first draft to her final essay. The explanations below refer to many other student samples you might consult for additional clarification.

Writing to Analyze or Explicate

To analyze a work of literature is to look closely at how it works—to examine its parts or elements (language, form, conflict, plot, characterization, theme) as they contribute to the work's meaning.

The final draft of Suzanne McCloskey's sample essay at the end of this chapter (p. 197) argues for what she believes is the theme of *Antigonê:* "The arrogance of political power cannot defeat moral justice, for conscience and the will of the gods will always triumph." In her essay about *Othello* on page 696, Ann Linde analyzes the characterizations of Iago, Othello, Desdemona, and Cassio, and argues that their "not being what they seem" leads to the tragedy that envelopes them all.

An **explication** is a detailed analysis, a line-by-line interpretation of *how* and *what* a short work (or brief section of a larger work) means. Because they are longer pieces, works of fiction, drama, and essays usually don't lend themselves to such close reading. Most poems, however, are relatively brief, and by their nature packed with meaning. Poetry presents a good opportunity for a very close reading and an examination of sounds, words, images, lines, and how they all work together to deliver the work's meaning. An explication is not just a summary or translation of the author's language into your own; it is a detailed explanation of *how* the work conveys meaning.

On page 1097, Charles Chiang explicates the text of the "To be or not to be" soliloquy from Shakespeare's *Hamlet* by closely examining each line of the speech and building it into an interpretation of Hamlet's character and Shakespeare's intended effect on the audience.

Writing to Compare

In what way are characters or other aspects of this work comparable to each other? To what extent is the work or some aspect of it comparable to other works or aspects of them? The objective of a comparison is not just to list similarities and differences but to reveal something important about whatever is being compared. Which details you choose as the basis of this comparison can make a difference. To give yourself a clear direction, and an overview of what you have, it may be helpful to make separate lists of similarities and differences before you start to write. Ask yourself what's worth comparing and what's not—and how this comparison might yield an effective essay. One useful method of lining up similarities and differences is the Venn diagram, described in Chapter 2 on pages 33–34.

In her sample essay (p. 1165), Jennifer Stelz compares the "young adult" narration perspective of Langston Hughes's "Theme for English B" with the "adult looking back" perspective of Countee Cullen's "Incident." She concludes that while both poems are about racism, the narrative perspective of each creates a very different impression on the reader. Susan MacNaughten (p. 226) compares two characters from different works, Nora from *A Doll's House* and Antigonê from Sophocles' play, and argues that each in her own way demonstrates the attribute of personal responsibility. And on page 1481, Barbara Pfister compares two different types of art—a Van Gogh painting, *Starry Night*, and an Anne Sexton poem written in response to it.

Writing About the Beliefs or Actions of the Narrator or Characters

As we've discussed, narrators and literary characters often express their beliefs in what they say or do. It's natural for us to judge their words and actions through our own beliefs, compare their choices with our own, and approve or disapprove as they meet or fail to meet our expectations. This is the kind of topic that lends itself well to a response essay—an essay that describes our experience of the work and the emotions we felt—the outrage, frustration, pleasure, or pride we experienced in response to the beliefs expressed. But writing about the beliefs or actions of the narrator or characters can also be a good topic for a critical essay.

Remember, a critical essay shifts the emphasis toward the work and builds an argument for what the work or some aspect of it means (an interpretation) or its worth (an evaluation), or both. To write a critical essay about the beliefs or actions of the narrator or characters, you must clearly identify those beliefs or actions and cite evidence that exemplifies them. Based on your own clearly stated criteria, you might interpret what they mean or build an argument for or against them.

The student essays of Michelle McAuliffe (p. 301) and Julie Fitzmaurice (p. 303) about John Updike's "A&P" illustrate this type of response. Both students comment on the protagonist's decision to quit his job, but they disagree about the wisdom of his decision. Michelle criticizes his decision and believes that he will regret it because of the consequences it will have for him and his family. Julie, however, sees his action as an inspiring statement that he will refuse to sell out and live his life like the store manager in the story. In her essay on "Everyday Use" (page 880), Debora Van Coughnett also writes about beliefs when she criticizes the superficiality of one character's claim to her heritage when compared to the "real" respect it is given as lived every day by her mother and sister.

Writing About Literature in Context

To write about literature in context is to consider the work within a framework of cultural, historical, biographical, or other influences. For a more comprehensive explanation of these approaches (including historical, gender, political-economic, psychoanalytic, archetypal, and biographical criticism), see the Appendix: Critical Approaches to Literature, on page 1487.

In her sample essay on page 694, Marie Tymon writes about the attitudes of the male characters toward women in *Othello* and sees them as typical of a time in history and a culture that encouraged the physical and emotional abuse of women. Trisa Hayes critiques Ibsen's *A Doll's House* and Kate Chopin's "The Story of an Hour" within the historical and social framework of the nineteenth century. And Kevin Chamberlain's essay about James Joyce's "Eveline" on page 1279 examines the cultural imperatives of late-nineteenth-century Ireland as they seem to determine the fate of the story's protagonist.

✔ CHECKLIST • *Choosing a Topic for a Critical Essay*

- ❏ What work or aspect of a work interests you?
- ❏ Is there a work or elements of a work (language, form, conflict, plot, characterization, theme) that you would like to analyze or explicate?
- ❏ Would it be illuminating to compare this work or some aspect of it to another work or works?
- ❏ Are there beliefs or actions of the narrator or characters that you want to interpret or evaluate?
- ❏ Do you want to interpret or evaluate the work or aspects of it within a larger historical, cultural, biographical, or other context?

Critical Thinking: Induction and Substantiation

Have you ever watched a toddler discover the world? The child crawls through the grass, stops to examine it blade by blade, picks it up, feels it, shakes it, tastes it. The child explores the surroundings and tests them piece by piece, and after several tries, probably comes to a conclusion: Grass is good for crawling but not so great for eating. When someone offers you a type of food you've never eaten before, how do you respond? How do you discover if you like it or not? Well, you probably ask for a taste. If you like the taste, you might ask for more. If you don't like the taste, you may or may not try more. This kind of examining, testing, making tentative observations, retesting, and concluding is a fairly common process in our lives. It is called **inductive reasoning**.

When you think or write inductively, you move from specific observations to conclusions. If you try a new food and like it, the next time it's offered you can respond with more certainty. You've tested it and can come to a tentative conclusion. Each subsequent tasting gives you more information and solidifies your conclusion: I like sushi; it tastes good.

Once you arrive at your conclusion, you are ready to make a generalization: Sushi tastes good. The process of supporting this generalization is called **substantiation**. When we substantiate, we support our conclusion with specific observations. This brings the process full circle. We discover how much we like sushi through specific tastings; we explain why sushi is good with support from those tastings: This sushi sits lightly on my tongue; it's soft and moist with a full seafood flavor and pleasant smell. We arrive at our conclusion inductively; we support, defend, and explain it through substantiation.

Developing Standards

As we examine our reasons for liking something, we also identify and develop standards. We know how good this food can be; we now have certain expectations. (Standards for sushi: 1. Soft. 2. Moist. 3. Full seafood flavor. 4. Pleasant smell.) When something meets our expectations, we can identify why. When it doesn't, we can say where and perhaps why it falls short.

Thinking Critically About Literature

In many ways, thinking and writing about literature follows a similar induction and substantiation pattern as that described above. As we initially read, respond, discuss, and write about our experience with literature, we build on our specific observations of the text and arrive at our conclusions inductively. With those conclusions in hand, we substantiate them with reference to our specific observations of the text. Writing an effective, convincing essay requires that we have enough evidence to support our conclusions and that we have clearly explained the connection between the two. Finding the evidence and making the connections requires a close rereading of the text.

Facts and Opinions

All of us have probably been criticized at some time for not being objective or allowing our personal feelings to influence our judgment. It's not possible, of course, to be entirely objective—to separate the facts from who we are and how we see them. Most of our feelings and prejudgments come from our personalities, backgrounds, and experiences, and they form values we have developed unconsciously over time. In the course of our daily lives, we're not usually required to justify our feelings or our opinions. But writing an effective critical essay requires a rationale for our judgments—reasons derived not only from our feelings and values but from ingredients in the work of literature that prompt those judgments. Although there is no guarantee that everyone will agree with our conclusions, we can make sure that our evidence is recognized and respected as valid.

➤ *GETTING STARTED—YOUR FIRST RESPONSE*

1. Read one of your responses to a work of literature.
2. Which parts are fact, which opinion? How can you tell the difference?
3. To what extent can you support your opinions with facts?
4. To what extent can you explain how the facts support your opinions?

➤ *SUPPORTING CONNECTIONS—"EX-BASKETBALL PLAYER"*

Remember, "telling" your views alone will not convince readers. Telling what the literature means or declaring its effectiveness is not convincing unless you support those views by *showing* what led to your conclusion. Identifying details, giving examples, making comparisons, and quoting from the text of the work are means to this end.

JOHN UPDIKE (b. 1932)

EX-BASKETBALL PLAYER [1958]

Pearl Avenue runs past the high-school lot,
Bends with the trolley tracks, and stops, cut off
Before it has a chance to go two blocks,
At Colonel McComsky Plaza. Berth's Garage
Is on the corner facing west, and there,
Most days, you'll find Flick Webb, who helps Berth out.

Flick stands tall among the idiot pumps—
Five on a side, the old bubble-head style,
Their rubber elbows hanging loose and low.
One's nostrils are two S's, and his eyes
An E and O.° And one is squat, without
A head at all—more of a football type.

Once Flick played for the high-school team, the Wizards.
He was good: in fact, the best. In '46
He bucketed three hundred ninety points,
A county record still. The ball loved Flick.
I saw him rack up thirty-eight or forty
In one home game. His hands were like wild birds.

[11]**ESSO** brand of gasoline (now called Exxon)

He never learned a trade, he just sells gas,
Checks oil, and changes flats. Once in a while,
As a gag, he dribbles an inner tube,
But most of us remember anyway.
His hands are fine and nervous on the lug wrench.
It makes no difference to the lug wrench, though.

Off work, he hangs around Mae's luncheonette.
Grease-gray and kind of coiled, he plays pinball,
Smokes those thin cigars, nurses lemon phosphates.
Flick seldom says a word to Mae, just nods
Beyond her face toward bright applauding tiers
Of Necco Wafers, Nibs, and Juju Beads.

➤ *QUESTIONS FOR READING AND WRITING*

Induction

1. Go back and read "Ex-Basketball Player" again.
2. As you read, write down as many details about Flick Webb as you can.
3. Review what you wrote down as you finished the poem, any questions you jotted down, and your list of details.
4. What conclusion does this information lead you to draw about Flick Webb?

Substantiation

1. Write down your conclusion.
2. Support your conclusion through reference to your details.
3. Are all of these details facts? Would everyone agree that they are facts?
4. Explain how these details support your conclusion.
5. Reread what you've written and answer the following questions:
   a. Do you have enough details to support your conclusion?
   b. Do *all* the details about Flick Webb in the poem support your conclusion?
   c. If not, how can you account for these details?
   d. When you consider *all* the details—all the evidence—does your conclusion still hold up? If not, revise your conclusion to match the evidence.

Conclusion

1. Sometimes what seems self-evident to us is not so evident to our readers. Write a statement that explains *how* the details in the poem support your conclusion about Flick Webb.

INTERPRETATION: WHAT DOES IT MEAN?

The idea of coming up with an interpretation may seem a bit overwhelming, but in our everyday lives we hear and respond to this request regularly. "What do you make of that?" "What was that all about?" and "What's your read on that?"

are among the many ways we might be asked for an interpretation. At the core of all these questions is a basic request for an explanation of "meaning." When we construct and articulate that meaning we are giving our interpretation.

What goes into our explanation of meaning, of course, has a lot to do with who we are. Our interpretations are influenced by many personal factors, but what makes an interpretation convincing or credible is our ability to explain *why*—a why not based on unsupported personal opinion but on support with evidence.

An interpretation of literature may involve almost any aspect of work, from the meaning of a single word, image, character, or place to a statement of its overall meaning. It may even involve more than one work, so don't feel that you must limit yourself to choosing from the possibilities discussed here.

A Defensible Interpretation, Not *the* Right Answer

Works of literature are not problems to be solved. They don't have one correct answer or interpretation. Remember, what makes an interpretation convincing or defensible is the quality of its support. Your belief about what a story means may change as you move back and forth through the stages of your reading experience. The first time you read a work you may feel one way, but writing down your reflections, rereading the text, and discussing it with others may lead to a different, better-informed understanding and interpretation.

Developing an Interpretation

As you consider the statements and questions that follow, think about the works you've read and how the language, point of view, setting, conflict, or characterization in those pieces influenced your response. Our brief discussion of these elements below is a carry-over from a more comprehensive explanation of these terms in Chapter 3. *If you have unanswered questions about these elements, you may find it helpful to refer to that discussion beginning on page 62.*

Language and Form

The diction of the narrator or characters, concrete images, similes, metaphors, and symbols may all contribute in crucial ways to the meaning of literature.

Think about the impact of the powerful, concrete imagery in Robert Hayden's "Those Winter Sundays" (p. 12) or Marge Piercy's "Barbie Doll" (p. 13). Consider Sammy's slang and concrete descriptions in John Updike's "A&P" (p. 296) and the effect they have on your reading. Try to imagine less powerful images, vague descriptions, unnatural diction, and how your response to these works might differ.

The sounds and structures of rhyme, rhythm, and verse may also play a vital role in conveying a work's meaning. Consider the rhymes, rhythms and verse form in Countee Cullen's "Incident" (p. 11) or Dudley Randall's "Ballad of

Birmingham" (p. 17)—and in other pieces you've read—and how they influence your response.

Narration: Point of View and Voice

Point of view, the perspective from which the narrator speaks to us, can strongly influence our interpretation. This narrative "lens" controls what we see and know about the setting, the characters, or the conflict in a work. The narrator's *voice* gives us a personality behind the words.

Consider Mama's up-close first person narration and its influence on your interpretation of Alice Walker's "Everyday Use" (p. 871). How is your response to Ernest Hemingway's "Hills like White Elephants" (p. 528) affected by its distanced third person objective narration? How would a first person point of view from either the man or the woman's perspective change Hemingway's story? Can you imagine "Everyday Use" narrated from the distance of third person objective, or from Dee's perspective, and how it might be different?

Recall other works you've read and how point of view or voice influence your response to the setting, conflict, characters, or the story's meaning. Imagine how a shift in narration might change your interpretation.

Setting

Setting is the environment in which the work takes place. It includes location, time, atmosphere, and mood and has a direct and indirect impact on character and conflict. It supports and emphasizes the story's meaning.

Consider the dreary, dark atmosphere in James Joyce's "Araby," and how it contrasts with the warmth of the boy's feelings for Mangan's sister. Picture the overpowering ocean waves and high cold stars in the black sky of Stephen Crane's "The Open Boat" and their effect on the characters and your reading.

Think about the settings of other works you've read and their impact on conflict, characters, or theme. Try to imagine those stories in a different setting and the difference that would make to the conflicts, the characters, and your response.

Conflict and Plot

Conflict is the struggle of opposing external or internal forces. External conflict may be physical or social. Internal conflict is a struggle of opposing forces within a character. Most good literature contains both types of conflict, but places greater emphasis on the internal component.

Think about the extraordinary external and internal conflicts in the brutal, racist humiliation experienced by the young man in Ralph Ellison's "Battle Royal" (p. 830). Or consider the ordinary but painful internal conflict that results from the young girl's humiliation in Sandra Cisneros' "Eleven" (p. 25). The first person point of view has a major impact on our understanding of the characters and conflicts in these stories. While the narrator/protagonists in both pieces are young, they are pre-teen and late-teen and articulate their sense of conflict in very different terms. An oppressive setting in each story increases the pressure and makes them (and us) feel their conflicts more intensely.

Recall other works you've read and look at the ways that conflict is developed or intensified through point of view, voice, setting, or characterization. If any of these elements were changed, imagine how the conflict and your response to it might be affected.

Plot is the structure of the story. Think about the plots of stories you've read. How does the structure of each work convey the setting, the conflict, the characters, and ultimately the story's meaning?

Characterization

Characterization is the creation and development of characters in a work. Well-developed characters come to life. In our own lives, we react to people on the basis of how they look and what they say and do. In most good literature, we're able to observe characters thinking, speaking, and doing—and judge who they are for ourselves.

Consider how much you learn about the characters Antigonê and Ismenê solely from their conversation in the Prologue of Sophocles' *Antigonê* (p. 123). Think about the description, actions, and reactions of Eliza as her character gradually emerges in John Steinbeck's "The Chrysanthemums" (p. 1365). The narration, conversations, settings, and conflicts all provide an opportunity for us to witness these characters thinking, saying, and doing.

Recall other characters in works you've read. How did you get to know them? How did the narrator's point of view, the character's diction, the setting, or their conflicts influence your understanding of who they are?

The Whole: Theme

Theme is the central idea expressed by a work. Identifying and articulating this idea is not always an easy task. It's true that the whole work's theme or meaning is greater than the sum of its parts, but the support required for your justification of it still calls for an analysis of the work's elements—the language, narration, setting, conflicts, characters, and outcome—and their relationship to the whole.

What conclusion about the work can you draw from its elements? Try to expand your conclusion about the work into a generalization or idea that addresses the human condition. What is the work saying about being human? What is its theme?

Beliefs or Actions Expressed by the Narrator or Characters

It is natural for us to respond to the beliefs and actions of characters through the lenses of our own values, so it's not surprising that, as a subset of characterization, this is one of the more popular topics for interpretation. What's your interpretation of the beliefs or actions (or potential actions) expressed by the man or the woman in Ernest Hemingway's "Hills like White Elephants" (p. 528)? What is your understanding of the beliefs expressed by the narrator/protagonist in Langston Hughes" "Salvation"?

Think about the beliefs or actions of other characters in your reading. What are they? How do you feel about them? How are these beliefs exemplified by what the narrator or characters say or do? How would you interpret them?

For a more comprehensive explanation of this option with references to student samples in this text, see page 170 earlier in this chapter.

The Work in Context

To interpret a work in its context successfully, you must be able to identify the contextual framework that surrounds it and articulate the influence that context has on the work or an element of the work. If you're not very knowledgeable about this background, it may be necessary to do additional reading and research before you begin to write your essay.

What are the cultural imperatives that influence the girl in Marge Piercy's "Barbie Doll," or the historical, cultural, and biographical influences on Lorraine Hansberry's *A Raisin in the Sun?*

Think of other works you've read, and the historical, cultural, biographical, or other contextual factors that influenced them. How do these factors affect or enrich your reading and interpretation of those works?

For a more comprehensive explanation of this option with references to student samples in this text, see page 171 earlier in this chapter or the Appendix "Critical Approaches to Literature" on page 1487.

✔ CHECKLIST • *Developing an Interpretation*

Language and Form

- ❑ In what ways are diction, imagery, figurative language, or symbolism important to the work and your understanding of it?
- ❑ What role do rhyme, rhythm, or verse form play in the work?

Narration: Point of View and Voice

- ❑ In what ways do point of view and voice affect what you know about the setting, conflict, or characters?
- ❑ How does the narration influence your understanding of the work's meaning?
- ❑ How would you interpret the impact of narration on the work?

Setting

- ❑ In what ways does the work's setting affect conflict and characterization?
- ❑ How would you interpret the influence of setting on the work's meaning?

Conflict and Plot

- ❑ In what ways is conflict related to setting and characterization?

(*continued*)

- ❑ How does the plot structure convey the conflict and the story's meaning?
- ❑ How would you interpret the conflict or the importance of plot in the work?

Characterization

- ❑ How is characterization related to point of view, setting, and conflict?
- ❑ How do the characters affect your understanding of the work's meaning?
- ❑ How would you interpret the characters in the work?

Theme

- ❑ Describe the elements (language, narration, setting, conflict/plot, characters) of the work ?
- ❑ What conclusion can you draw from these elements?
- ❑ What comment about the human condition—what generalization about life—does this conclusion lead to?
- ❑ What is the central idea expressed by the work? What do you think the work means?

Interpreting the Beliefs or Actions of the Narrator or Characters

- ❑ What beliefs are expressed by the narrator or characters in the work and how does what they say or do exemplify these beliefs or actions?
- ❑ How would you interpret the effect of these beliefs on the work?

Interpreting a Work in Context

- ❑ How is the work influenced by historical, cultural, biographical, or other contextual factors?
- ❑ How would you interpret the work in the light of these contextual factors?

Interpretation or Evaluation?

Like many other classifications in literature, *interpretation* and *evaluation* are not separate and distinct. In our reading, both often occur at the same time. When we write about our reading, however, we can make choices about which to emphasize. Do we want to interpret what the work or an aspect of it means or its worth? While each is a different emphasis, it may be difficult to separate them, and many critical essays are a combination of both.

Evaluation: How Well Does It Work?

Throughout this book you have been encouraged to identify and write about what you value. Those values or standards directly influence your response to literature. Writing an effective evaluative essay requires that you make these standards explicit and account for the ways in which they have led to your evaluation of a work. You become a credible critic by evaluating in the light of these clearly defined standards.

Developing Standards

Each of us has clearly defined standards about some things and not about others. Every day we are bombarded with advertisements that make great claims without support. They assume our lack of standards. They tell us with glitz rather than showing us with facts. Do we always buy products because we know a lot about them? Do we buy cars, stereos, or computers because we know they are quality products or because we like the ads and the attractive people in them? What are our standards for judging?

You've been evaluating literature since you first started reading. You like it or don't like it, believe it's good or bad. How specific you are about "why" may depend on your experience as a reader. Those of us who read often have probably given some thought to why we like to read some things more than others. Experienced readers are likely to respond to "why" by pointing to particular qualities that are present or absent. Those of us who don't read very much might simply say, "I couldn't get into it" or "It was boring" and leave it at that. Our standards, the principles by which we evaluate literature, tend to be developed through experience and over time.

➤ *QUESTIONS FOR THINKING AND WRITING*

Write down your responses to the following questions. You may even find it interesting to share them with other members of the class in pairs or small groups.

1. Choose a topic you know a lot about (music, dance, sports, cars, computers, etc.). How did you learn about it? By yourself? Did someone show you or teach you? Why do you think you know a lot about it?
2. What are your standards or criteria for evaluating the topic you chose in question 1? See if you can make a list and explain the importance of each standard.
3. Think back to a large purchase you made recently (clothes, computer, stereo, etc.). What were your standards or criteria for evaluation? Make a list and explain the importance of each of these standards.
4. Do you feel as if you know a lot about literature? How would you feel if someone asked you to evaluate a poem, story, play, or essay? Explain.
5. What are your standards for evaluating literature? See if you can make a list of standards and explain the importance of each one. If you can't, what difficulties did you encounter?

Developing Standards for Evaluating Literature

Our task in this chapter is not only to help you develop new standards but to identify and build on those you already have. You've been developing and applying standards for evaluating literature throughout your life. They're as familiar to you as your everyday experiences, so familiar you don't usually stop to analyze or spell them out.

We live in the world that literature reveals. We make judgments about the nature of that world—people's biases, our surroundings, difficult circumstances, and the authenticity of people we meet. In this way we have already experienced and developed standards about point of view, setting, conflict, and character. What may not be so familiar, however, is a systematic way of applying these standards to literature.

Your Own Standards: Expectations and Intentions

When we choose entertainment, we usually know what to expect. When we see a fantasy movie like *Alien* or *Star Wars,* we have very different expectations than when we see a realistic film. Listening to a rock song brings different expectations than listening to an opera. We have different expectations for a Stephen King thriller than for a story like James Joyce's "Araby."

The standards we have for evaluating literature are directly affected by our expectations. Is the primary purpose of this literature to thrill or entertain? To make a social comment? To reveal something essential about the human condition? All of these? Some of these? It would be unfair to apply the same standards to a mystery thriller that we would to "Araby." On the other hand, applying our "thrill and entertain" standards to a story that intends to give insight into the human condition seems equally unfair.

Standards for Evaluating Literature

Of course, we may not always be aware of the type and intentions of the literature we read until after we begin reading. Many of the pieces in this book may put you in that position. Almost all of these pieces, however, have been chosen because they seek to reveal something important about the human experience. The expectations and standards discussed below are measured against this intention.

The standards for language, point of view, setting, conflict, character, and theme discussed here are derived from our description of these elements in earlier chapters. The questions and brief explanations that follow are a guide to the kinds of qualities we might look for when evaluating these elements.

Language and Form When language is used effectively it prompts our imaginations and provides us with clear images, rhythm, and insight. Form complements content and effectively conveys meaning to us.

Point of View When point of view is used effectively, we see the characters, setting, and events from a perspective that helps us experience the overall meaning of a work.

Setting An effective setting will help us see and experience the concrete details of a work's environment. We "sense" the sights, sounds, and emotions of the atmosphere as if we were really there. The writer of an effective setting does not settle for vague descriptions. An effective setting complements and clarifies conflict, character, and theme. It seems a natural vehicle to convey the story's meaning.

Conflict and Plot Unless we feel its reality, we are not drawn into the conflict. For this to happen, we must be able to imagine ourselves or others faced with this situation. In many cases, it is our ability to identify with the *internal nature* (the anxiety, frustration, and disappointment) of the conflict, which gives us a feel for it. We may never have faced this kind of external dilemma, but other experiences we have had may give us an idea of what the dilemma feels like inside.

We won't care about the conflict if it's not important to the characters and to us. As we know from our own lives, a conflict doesn't need to be a life-and-death struggle to have an impact on us. We might want to ask ourselves, "If I were in this circumstance, would this be an important conflict for me?" Well-developed conflict and plot, like a game between two evenly matched teams or players, keeps us involved until the outcome is decided.

Characterization Effective characters seem lifelike. Like real people, they are not simple, but have depth and complexity. They are believable. When characters are developed most effectively, we don't have to be told who they are. We "see" and experience them through their words, actions, and what others have to say about them.

As in life, well-developed characters have reasons, or motivations, for behaving as they do. They will act in a relatively consistent pattern. They won't behave one way on one occasion and differently on another without adequate motivation.

Theme An effective theme gives us an insight into human nature. When literature preaches or teaches a lesson, it doesn't usually account for the complexities of the real world. An effective theme transcends the time and place of its setting. It has universal qualities that make it applicable to human nature in any time or place.

Beliefs or Actions of the Narrator or Characters Before you evaluate the beliefs or actions of the narrator or characters, be clear about what they are and be clear about your own standards for judging them. Only when you have clarified both will you be able to evaluate the beliefs in the work measured against your own criteria, take a position, and build an argument for or against those beliefs.

The Work in Context Before you can evaluate the influence of historical, cultural, biographical, or other contextual factors on the work, you must have knowledge of these areas. If you don't have knowledge of these contexts, you must do research and additional reading to give yourself standards and criteria with which to evaluate.

✔ CHECKLIST • *Developing an Evaluation*

Language and Form

- ❑ How well does the language prompt your imagination and engage your emotions?
- ❑ How effective are the language and form in conveying the work's meaning?

Narration

- ❑ How effective is the narrative perspective, or point of view, in helping you understand the work's meaning?

Setting

- ❑ How effective is the setting in presenting the concrete details and enabling you to feel like you're present?
- ❑ How well does the setting complement conflict and character and support and emphasize the work's meaning?

Conflict and Plot

- ❑ How believable is the internal and external conflict?
- ❑ How important is the conflict?
- ❑ How challenging is the struggle?
- ❑ How unified is the conflict? How well do the minor conflicts complement each other and support the major conflicts?
- ❑ How well does the plot's structure convey the conflict and the story's meaning?

Characterization

- ❑ How believable are the characters? How complex?
- ❑ How effectively are the characters developed? Are you shown, not told, who they are? How so?
- ❑ How motivated and consistent are the characters? Does their behavior make sense?

Theme

- ❑ Does the theme *reveal* or *preach?* Is it an insight about life or a lesson?
- ❑ How universal is the theme? Is it limited by time, place, and circumstances?

Beliefs and Actions of the Narrator or Characters

- ❑ What are the beliefs and actions of the narrator or characters in the work?
- ❑ What are your standards for evaluating these beliefs or actions?
- ❑ Why do you agree or disagree with these beliefs or actions?

(*continued*)

The Work in Context

- ❑ How much do you know about the contextual background of the work? What do you need to know? How will you find out more?
- ❑ What are your standards for evaluating this context?
- ❑ How well does the work fulfill these standards?

Argumentation: Writing a Critical Essay

There are many different ways to plan and structure a critical essay. The suggestions that follow represent one approach. The purpose of this discussion is not to move you step by step through a rigid sequence. Constructing an argument is a continuous process of moving forward and returning and moving forward again. The strongest thesis, the most convincing evidence, the most effective structure may occur to you early or late. Let your ideas flow freely throughout the process. Some of your best ideas may come to you when you think you're almost finished.

The Shape of an Argument

The subject

The proposition about the subject (the thesis)

The evidence that supports the proposition about the subject

The explanation that connects the evidence to the proposition about the subject

Planning Your Argument

Determine the Argument's Feasibility Can you write a critical essay about this? No matter how compelling your proposition, you cannot write an essay about it unless you have enough to say and can find enough evidence to support your argument. If the point you want to make is obvious, abstract, or very general, it may be impossible to come up with a solid argument and develop it into a convincing essay in a reasonable amount of time.

Consider Your Own Motivation How much do you care about the subject? Will it sustain your enthusiasm long enough for you to complete the essay? Can you identify strongly with the situation in the work? Do you approve or disapprove of a character's action? Do you believe the work has helped you to understand yourself or inspired you to act in a particular way? Have you learned something about your own life through your experience of the work? Finally, do you feel strongly about your ability to convince an audience of your argument?

You will work with more enthusiasm and write with a stronger voice when you care about the subject.

Clarify Your Proposition: Write a Thesis Statement Do you have a clear understanding of the proposition you are trying to prove? If you don't, you won't be able to express it in a form your readers will understand. Try to put your proposition into the form of a complete sentence that connects it to the subject. This thesis statement will sit at the core of your argument. Everything in your argument must relate back to and support this thesis statement. If you've put it in a form that you and your readers clearly understand, you will know if the evidence you've gathered adequately supports it.

If your thesis is an interpretation, define what you mean by the terms of the proposition or thesis. In her journal entry at the beginning of this chapter, Suzanne has identified the subject of *Antigonê* as "public policy vs. individual conscience." Her proposition about this subject, her thesis statement (what she believes the play is saying about public policy and individual conscience), will not be clear unless she spells out what she means by those terms. What "public policy" and "individual conscience" mean to her may be different than what they mean to other readers.

If your thesis is an evaluation, define your standards. If (like Suzanne) you believe *Antigonê* is well written, what are your standards for a well-written play? If you believe the characters are well developed, what are your standards for effective characterization?

Be careful to distinguish between the *subject* of your essay and your *proposition* about the subject—your thesis statement. Suzanne's subject is "public policy vs. individual conscience." What she believes the play, *Antigonê,* is saying about this subject—her thesis statement—(as reflected in the final draft of her essay) is "The arrogance of political power cannot defeat moral justice, for conscience and the will of the gods will always triumph."

As you consider the evidence you have and gather new evidence, you may discover that your thesis statement must be adjusted to accommodate this new information. Be flexible. Match the statement to the evidence, and the evidence to the statement. Until you submit your final draft, it's never too late to make adjustments to strengthen your thesis.

Know Your Readers What can you assume about your readers? If you're writing this essay to be read by those in your class, you may already have some idea what your classmates and instructor think about your opinion. If so, does your thesis statement agree with the majority of responses you've heard? If not, it's important to "speak to" these contrary views when you present your own view.

No matter how convincing your evidence may be, if you don't address their contrary position, your readers will always wonder "Yes, but what about . . . ." This doesn't mean you must change their minds, but it does mean that you must account for all the evidence, especially the evidence that may seem (to some) to go against your thesis statement. If you cannot account for it, it may be time to reexamine your original proposition.

Remember, many interpretations of a work may be acceptable. The strength of your thesis is in its support, not the thesis itself. So don't offend your readers by being inflexible and suggesting that anyone holding a different view is ignorant. Feeling strongly about what you want to prove gives you a stronger voice, but insulting or overpowering your readers is not likely to be persuasive.

Supporting Your Argument

Arrange Your Support Effectively Substantiation and induction (see "Critical Thinking," pp. 171–173) are the two most common approaches to argumentation. In each case, the order in which the proposition, or thesis statement, and the supporting evidence are presented is different.

You substantiate your argument when you place the thesis statement or proposition at the beginning of the essay and lay out evidence in the rest of the essay to support it. You begin with a generalization and support it with specific examples as evidence. You immediately make it clear to your readers what you intend to prove. Your thesis remains in their minds as they encounter each piece of subsequent evidence. In fact, if what you propose at the outset is interesting enough, your thesis statement may act as a "hook" for your readers and pull them into the essay.

Substantiation
(a = b + b + b + b + b + b)
(Your thesis equals the sum of the evidence.)

This approach may not work well if you are trying to convince skeptical readers, that is, readers who have already made up their minds and hold a contrary view. Encountering a proposition they disagree with at the beginning may interfere with their response through the rest of the essay. Once they know what you want to prove, they may not give you an open-minded reading. They may be predisposed to disagree with you no matter how compelling your evidence.

Inductive argumentation moves from specific examples to a generalization or conclusion. It mimics the process you probably went through when you came up with your proposition to begin with. As the specifics of the work built up in your mind, they moved you toward a conclusion and a proposition. A more effective strategy to convince a skeptical reader may be to withhold your proposition until the end. By first providing support, before readers know what your position is, they may withhold judgment and be more likely to accept your thesis when it comes as the natural conclusion of strong evidence.

Induction
(b + b + b + b + b + b = a)
(The sum of the evidence equals your thesis.)

And, of course, there are variations of these strategies. For example, if you're stating your thesis up front, you may want to provide background information to "educate" the reader before you present your thesis, and then follow with supporting evidence. If you are using an inductive approach, you may want to build your support to a natural conclusion, and then discuss why this conclusion makes sense. In any case, you should consider your audience and your intentions before you decide which strategy will work best.

Support Your Thesis with Facts from the Text Earlier, we discussed the difference between facts and opinions (pp. 172–173). Facts are verifiable. You can cite them in the text. They should be the core of the evidence that supports your argument.

For example, it is a fact that in John Updike's poem "Ex-Basketball Player," Flick Webb was a high school basketball star. You can verify this fact by citing the text of the poem:

> Once Flick played for the high-school team, the Wizards.
> He was good: in fact, the best. In '46
> He bucketed three hundred ninety points,
> A county record still. The ball loved Flick.

And you can verify the fact of his current employment by citing the text:

> He never learned a trade, he just sells gas,
> Checks oil, and changes flats.

But if (based on these few facts) you say that Flick is an "unhappy loser," you are expressing an opinion, not a fact. You may hold this opinion for any number of personal reasons, prompted by a few facts in the poem. But if you want to build an argument to support this opinion, you will need to connect most or all the facts in the poem in a convincing way, and logically demonstrate how they lead to this conclusion. A good critical essay requires reasons for your judgments, factual support derived not only from your feelings and values but from ingredients in the text that logically combine to prompt them. There is no guarantee, of course, that everyone will agree with your conclusions, but you should make sure that your evidence is recognized and respected as valid.

Account for All the Evidence A strong thesis is constructed from all the evidence, not just the parts that agree with your conclusion. A discerning reader sees contrary evidence whether you point it out or not. For example, it is a fact that the speaker in Robert Frost's "The Road Not Taken" (p. 91) has taken the road less traveled, as suggested in the first two lines of this stanza:

> Then took the other, as just as fair,
> Because it was grassy and wanted wear:
> Though as for that the passing there
> Had worn them really about the same.

To suggest that one road was very different from the other, though, is to ignore the last two lines.

It is a fact that he says his choice will make a difference in his life:

I shall be telling this with a sigh
Somewhere ages and ages hence:
Two roads diverged in a wood, and I—
I took the one less traveled by,
And that has made all the difference.

But suggesting that the speaker knows that this choice was the best one and has made him happiest is to ignore other lines in this last stanza that seem to indicate uncertainty. Do we know that "all the difference" means a positive difference? How would you support that from the text?

So too, in Alice Walker's "Everyday Use" (p. 871), if you ignore the fact that the story is told by Dee's mother, you fail to account for the subjectivity of her descriptions. By addressing her subjectivity, however, and demonstrating that she is a reliable narrator by matching her descriptions to Dee's actions in the story, you may establish credibility for her narration and what she tells you.

None of this is to say that the personal meaning you derive from the work is not the most important meaning for you—a meaning that is often based on many factors beyond the text. But for the purposes of a critical essay, you must rely heavily on the text and its factual support to make a convincing case for your reader.

Explain the Connections Sometimes what seems self-evident to us is not so evident to our readers.

In addition to highlighting the facts to support your argument, explain the connections. Explicitly show your readers *how* the chosen evidence supports your conclusion. For example, if your proposition is that "Ismenê is not as courageous as Antigonê," and your evidence is that Ismenê says," . . . . I have no strength / To break the laws that were made for the public good," it is still necessary to explain the connection between the evidence (what Ismenê has said) and the proposition (that Ismenê is not as courageous as Antigonê).

Consider the explanation: "While Antigonê is willing to accept the consequences of her action and suffer death if necessary, Ismenê indicates that she is afraid of Creon's directive and will not join her sister in the burial." This explanation shows the connection between the proposition and the quoted evidence and makes your logic clear to the reader.

Opening, Closing, and Revising Your Argument

Write Your Introduction After You Know Your Argument It may seem strange to wait until you're almost finished with the first draft of an essay before writing its introduction. However, introducing an essay is a bit like introducing a person. In both cases, you can make a more effective introduction when you know who or what you are introducing. This does not mean you have to mention everything you know. It means that you know your subject well enough to say the essential things.

Make your introduction interesting. You want the reader to continue reading beyond the first paragraph. Remember what seemed so interesting to you about the work, and try to pass that interest on to the reader. Make sure that what you say flows smoothly and maintains the same voice used in the rest of the essay. If you're developing your argument through substantiation, this is the place to state your thesis as clearly as possible.

Close Your Argument Reasonably Although there is no need to summarize your essay in the conclusion, it may be helpful to remind the reader of the logic of your argument and explain the basic connections between your support and your thesis. Avoid being too ambitious. Only make claims or take credit for connections you've actually established.

If you've developed your argument inductively, this is the place where you want to state your thesis. Remember not to overstate your case. If you've proved your point, the evidence will carry it.

Revise with a Fresh View If you really want to "re-vision" your essay, to see it again from a fresh perspective, it's best to let some time pass. Try to place yourself in the position of the reader who is reading your essay for the first time.

As with any other essay, it can be very useful to do an after-draft outline. Go back and identify the point of each paragraph. List those points. This should give you a pretty good overview of your essay. How well is your draft organized? Does the sequence make sense? Are there gaps that need to be filled? Is there enough support?

Within the body of the essay have you explained the connections between your support and your thesis? Have you expressed those connections as clearly as possible? Have you maintained a consistent voice throughout the essay?

Check Against Your Intentions and Organization

- State your thesis clearly. Support and clarify your thesis with enough details and examples from the work of literature. *Show* what you have stated.
- Give the essay a title based on your thesis. If you're having trouble thinking of a title, it may be an indication that the thesis itself is not clear.
- Make sure that your essay is fully developed. Account for all aspects of your thesis statement. All your paragraphs must relate to that central thesis, and the organization of those paragraphs within the essay should be clear.
- Each paragraph should be fully developed too; each of the sentences within your paragraphs should relate to the central idea of that paragraph.
- All your statements should add something to the essay. Are there redundancies, digressions, or meaningless phrases that could be cut?

Proofread Carefully

- Proofreading is a crucial final step in the process of producing an essay. In addition to making any changes that did not occur to you earlier and fine tuning your writing, check your essay for correct grammar, spelling, punctuation, and typos.

- Make sure all your sentences are complete and punctuated appropriately.
- Check to see that all of your words are spelled correctly. Check for easily confused words (then/than, your/you're, its/it's, etc.), which computerized spell checkers do not pick up.
- Check on the meaning of any words you are not sure of. Make sure the titles of works are underlined or in quotations, as appropriate.
- If there are types of errors you personally have a tendency to make, look carefully for them.
- Finally, make sure you've followed the *MLA Handbook for Writers of Research Papers* or another documentation format recommended by your instructor. Have you cited and documented your sources correctly? Do you have a "Work(s) Cited" section at the end of your essay?

✔ CHECKLIST • *Writing a Critical Essay*

Planning Your Argument

Determine Its Feasibility

❑ Can you write a critical essay about this?

❑ Do you have enough to say, and can you find enough evidence to support your case?

Consider Your Motivation

❑ Will this topic sustain your interest long enough for you to do a good job?

Clarify Your Thesis

❑ Do you have a clear understanding of the thesis you want to argue? Can you articulate it in a thesis statement?

Know Your Readers

❑ What assumptions can you make about your readers? Are they likely to agree or disagree with your thesis?

Supporting Your Argument

Arrange Your Support Effectively

❑ Is the support for your thesis arranged in the most effective way?

❑ Is it more effective to develop your argument by stating your thesis first and then supporting it with evidence, or by allowing the evidence to build into your thesis?

Support Your Thesis with Facts from the Text

❑ Is your support based on facts or opinions?

❑ Have you supported your opinions with facts and quotes from the text?

Account for All the Evidence

❑ Have you accounted for *all* the evidence in the text?

(*continued*)

- ❑ Have you accounted for evidence that may not support your thesis?

Explain the Connections

- ❑ Have you explained *how* the evidence you've chosen supports your thesis?

Opening, Closing, and Revising

Write or Rewrite Your Introduction After Your First Draft

- ❑ Is your introduction clear, informative, and interesting?
- ❑ If appropriate, does it map out the journey for the reader?

Close Your Argument Reasonably

- ❑ Have you explained the connections between the thesis and your support?
- ❑ Have you claimed anything for which you haven't delivered evidence?

Revise with a Fresh View

- ❑ Have you reread and reviewed your essay?
- ❑ How well is your draft organized? Does the sequence make sense?
- ❑ Are there gaps that need to be filled? Is there enough support?
- ❑ Have you explained the connections between your support and your thesis?
- ❑ Have you expressed those connections as clearly as possible?
- ❑ Have you maintained a consistent "voice" throughout the essay?

Review Your Intentions and Organization

- ❑ Is the central thesis of the essay clearly stated? Does the title account for your thesis?
- ❑ Is the essay fully developed? Have you accounted for all aspects of your thesis statement?
- ❑ Are there enough details to support or clarify your thesis? Have you *shown* what you've told?
- ❑ Are there enough quotes from the work to support your thesis?
- ❑ Do all the paragraphs relate to your thesis? Is the essay fully developed?
- ❑ Is the organization of the paragraphs within the essay clear?
- ❑ Are the paragraphs fully developed?
- ❑ Do each of the sentences within the paragraphs relate to the paragraph's central ideas?
- ❑ Is the language clear?
- ❑ Are there redundancies, digressions, or meaningless phrases that could be cut?

(*continued*)

Proofread Carefully

- ❑ Are all your sentences complete sentences?
- ❑ Are all your sentences punctuated appropriately?
- ❑ Have you checked for easily confused words (then/than, your/you're, its/it's, etc)?
- ❑ Are you sure of the meaning of all the words you've used?
- ❑ Are the titles of works underlined or in quotations, as appropriate?
- ❑ Are there particular errors that you have a tendency to make? Have you looked for those in this essay?
- ❑ Is the essay written in the format required by your instructor? Have you documented your references to the text and included a list of works cited?

From First Response to Critical Essay

The same processes that are so useful in generating ideas for a response essay are just as valuable for giving you ideas and narrowing your topic for a critical essay. Reading literature encourages a variety of responses—and perhaps raises more questions than answers. It is a good idea to generate and explore as many of your questions and ideas as possible before you decide on a topic. Below is a quick review of strategies to get started. For a detailed explanation of these techniques, with examples, see Chapter 2, pages 39–45.

- *Using directed freewriting* can generate ideas. The best time to do this exercise is immediately after you finish reading, while your thoughts and impressions are still fresh. The intention of this exercise is to release what you know without blocking it with pauses for reflection, punctuation, or editing.
- *Asking questions about a general topic* is likely to provide you with new information. Responding with detailed answers to these questions may provide you with ideas for a narrowed thesis and specific support for that thesis.
- By *choosing a few key words or phrases* that apply to your topic and then *listing* as many related details under each as you can, you should be able to generate many concrete details and much specific support for your ideas.
- *Clustering your ideas* or drawing a semantic map may help you discover and understand relationships, and generate and extend ideas better by seeing them spatially rather than linearly.

The Development of a Critical Essay

Earlier in this chapter, we looked at Suzanne's journal entry in response to Sophocles' *Antigonê* (p. 123). Let's follow up as she develops this journal entry into a critical essay.

Planning an Argument

Suzanne's Proposition Suzanne's proposition in her first draft was that the focus of *Antigonê* is public policy versus individual conscience. In addition, she wanted to address Creon's sexism as a feature of that policy.

Feasibility During her own reading and in class discussion, she saw much support for this thesis. Several statements in the play immediately came to mind that would support this idea, and she felt confident that this evidence would provide her with a strong argument.

Motivation Suzanne had strong motivation to write about this issue. She liked the play and felt strongly about its issues, especially individual conscience and women's equality.

Clarity of the Thesis Statement Her thesis statement, "The theme of *Antigonê* is public policy versus individual conscience." seems clear. But, as we will see when she revises, this statement identifies the subject of the play, not what the play is saying about this subject.

Audience Based on general class discussion and the response of her small group, she was confident about her position. Occasionally, someone would sympathize with Creon's position, but in general her classmates were supportive of her views.

Supporting the Argument

Arranging Support In class discussion, Suzanne had already received a generally sympathetic response. She was not trying to convince a hostile audience, so she believed that it would be most effective to state her position at the beginning and substantiate that position with support from the text.

Her plan was to introduce her thesis as clearly as possible, state and connect her beliefs about Creon and Antigonê with support from the play, and conclude by reaffirming her belief and how the text supported it.

Deriving Factual Support from the Text She derived her support from two basic sources: first, her description and interpretation of the actions of Creon and Antigonê; second, what Creon, Antigonê, and Haimon said that confirmed her judgments and her thesis statement.

Accounting for All the Evidence In addition to the evidence that favored her views, she considered views that were more sympathetic to Creon's position. The most common argument sympathetic to Creon was that Antigonê put him in an impossible position through her aggressive stance, that had she approached him in a more reasonable way he might have listened. She intended to use Haimon's experience with Creon to counter this argument.

Explaining the Connections Suzanne knew that she would have to explain the connections between her support (the quotes from the text and the actions of the characters) and her proposition, which was that Creon and Antigonê were representative of "public policy" and "individual conscience," respectively.

Suzanne's Draft

Based on her journal entry and notes, Suzanne wrote the following draft:

Might Against Right

Antigone is a tragic story that deals with the struggles between public policy and individual conscience, and on a lesser level, a woman's conflict with a man. Sophocles broaches the issues of might against right and civil disobedience in this shockingly tragic play.

In this play, Creon stands for public policy and Antigone symbolizes the individual conscience. The major conflict lies between these two headstrong figures. Creon has just been made king of Thebes because his nephews have killed each other in battle. Creon decreed that Eteocles, who died defending Thebes in battle, should be buried with full military honors. Polyneices was to be left to rot in the fields because Creon believed him to be a traitor who didn't deserve to be honored. Creon's law was clear: whoever disobeyed him and buried Polyneices was sentenced to be stoned to death in the public square. Creon is more concerned with forcing everyone to obey his decree than whether or not he has done the right thing. He seems to be an extremely headstrong and stubborn man who has a very hard time admitting that he's wrong. It is these very qualities that cause the chain reaction that dictates the downfall of Creon and all whom he loves.

Antigone is the sister of Eteocles and Polyneices, and she decides that she cannot abide by Creon's law. Polyneices was her brother just as much as Eteocles was, and to leave him to rot in the fields was wrong according to her conscience and God's law. She felt that Creon had no right to try to overstep God's boundaries; kings shouldn't presume to dictate who is privileged enough for a burial. Burial is supposed to be a universal right given to all of mankind. When Creon is informed that it is Antigone who has defied his law, he explodes. Not only has Antigone blatantly disregarded his wishes, she is both smug and righteous about the whole situation: "It was not God's proclamation. That final justice that rules the world below makes no such laws."

This shows the strength of Antigone's convictions. She knows that she will die for what she has done, but she stands firmly behind her decision and just wants it to be over with.

Creon is doubly enraged; Antigone has deliberately defied him and she is a woman. Women are supposed to be timid, weak, and docile creatures who need to be guided by men and their laws. Creon might have considered revoking his decree if it had been anyone else, but a woman has defied him and he can't let a mere woman get the better of him. This has now become, to a smaller degree, a battle of the sexes: "This girl is guilty of a double insolence, breaking the given laws and boasting of it. Who is the man here, she or I, if this crime goes unpunished?" This quote illustrates the lengths to which Creon would go to triumph over Antigone. Antigone defied a man's law and now a man is going to teach her a lesson. Creon's sense was being affected by his discriminatory and condescending attitude toward women. His irrationality is further proven when his son, Haimon, tries to reason with him. Haimon points out the validity of Antigone's actions and the fear that prevents any of the other citizens to voice their support of her: "I have heard them, muttering and whispering in the dark about this girl. They say no woman has ever, so unreasonably, died so shameful a death for a generous act: She covered her brother's body. Is this indecent? She kept him from dogs and vultures. Is this a crime? Death--she should have all the honor that we can give her."

The citizens of Thebes are starting to discreetly voice their disapproval of Creon's condemnation of Antigone's act of mercy. Creon interprets Haimon's speech as a sign that Haimon has chosen Antigone over him and forces Haimon to denounce his own father. This further alienates Creon from his subjects, and the play's atmosphere begins to change. Creon is not in complete control anymore. A woman has managed to disrupt his reign and turn his most precious all, his son, against him. Creon is going to force Antigone to regret her actions against him by sentencing her to a slow, painful death in a sealed cave with no food or water. A quick death would be too easy. Creon wants her to suffer. From this point on, the atmosphere of the play continues to spiral into a whirlwind of chaos and tragedy.

Teiresias, the old prophet who's never wrong, comes to warn Creon that the wrath of the gods will be upon him if he doesn't right his wrongs: "The time is not far off when you shall pay back corpse for corpse, flesh of your own flesh." But by then it's too late. By the time he sees the error of his ways, Creon's course of destruction is already set and the damage has already been done.

Creon's foolish superiority complex led to the downfall of everyone he cared about and his credibility as a king. He let his attitude toward women and his thirst for absolute power cloud his judgment and drove his family into the arms of death and tragedy. Antigone's fight against the unjust decree of the king could be characterized as the beginnings of civil disobedience. She is driven by her firm belief in God's laws and her own views on right and wrong. Antigone believed that a law is not right just because it's a law and that God's law outweighs public policy every time.

Opening, Closing, and Revising

Introduction While her introductory paragraph was adequate to keep her focused throughout the draft, it would have to be revised to integrate Creon's sexism. In addition, she has not defined what she means by "public policy" and "individual conscience." This would be an appropriate place to define her terms.

Finally, she realizes that her "public policy versus individual conscience" statement is only identifying the subject of the play, not *what the play is saying* about that subject. She must come up with a thesis statement that more clearly represents the theme of the play.

Closing Her closing could be more inclusive of her whole argument. Her statement about the "beginnings of civil disobedience" is a nice touch and will leave readers with a sense of its relevance to today.

Revising When Suzanne examined the structure of her draft by creating an after-draft outline from her paragraphs, it took the following form:

Paragraph #1—Introduction (a brief statement of the thesis and comment about Creon's sexism). A statement about the subject (public policy vs. individual conscience) but not what the play was saying about that subject (a thesis statement).
Paragraph #2—Creon's stance as public policy and summary of the major conflict
Paragraph #3—Antigonê's position
Paragraph #4—Creon's sexism
Paragraph #5—Haimon's reasonable approach, Creon's response, and Teiresias's prophecy
Paragraph #6—Conclusion (a brief statement summarizing the conflict, Antigonê's motivation, and its significance then and now)

For the most part, her draft contained the information and support she needed, but the thesis statement could be clearer, some of the paragraphs more tightly structured, and the essay's organization more coherent. By combining her first two paragraphs into a more substantial introduction concluding in a thesis statement, and combining and reorganizing subsequent paragraphs, she came up with the following revised outline:

Paragraph #1—Introduction (explains the basic conflict, defines the terms, and states the thesis)
Paragraph #2—Fleshes out the conflict
Paragraph #3—Antigonê's position
Paragraph #4—Creon's response and its motivation (to include sexism)
Paragraph #5—Haimon's reasoned approach
Paragraph #6—Creon's response
Paragraph #7—The warning and prophecy of Teiresias
Paragraph #8—Conclusion (a more inclusive summary and reminder of the play's thesis)

Checking Against Intentions Her intentions were to explain and support her now clearer thesis that the play's theme is "The arrogance of political power cannot defeat moral justice, for conscience and the will of the gods will always triumph," and that part of Creon's motivation for condemning Antigonê was sexist. She believed that this reorganization and integration would accomplish her goal.

Proofreading In addition to correcting a few minor problems, she would have to cite the line sources of her textual support, format it correctly, and add a "work cited" section at the end of her essay.

Suzanne's Revised Essay

Suzanne McCloskey

Dr. Madden

English 102

November 3, 200X

Might Against Right

Sophocles' tragic play, Antigone, is a powerful example of the struggle between public policy and individual conscience. Throughout history, rulers have imposed and enforced laws for what they claim is the best interest of the public. At times, courageous individuals have refused to obey these laws, despite the consequences, because these policies interfered with their own consciences. Creon stands for public policy in this play, and Antigone represents individual conscience, loyalty to the gods, and civil disobedience.

Sophocles' message is clear: the arrogance of political power cannot defeat moral justice, for conscience and the will of the gods will always triumph.

The major conflict in this play is between Creon and Antigone. Creon has just been made king of Thebes because his nephews have killed each other in battle. He decrees that Eteocles, who died defending Thebes, will be buried with full military honors. The body of Polyneices, however, will be left to rot in the fields. Creon believed that Polyneices was a traitor who didn't deserve to be honored. His law was clear: whoever disobeyed him and buried Polyneices was to be stoned to death in the public square. Creon, however, seems more concerned with forcing everyone to obey his decree than whether or not he has done the right thing. He is an extremely headstrong and stubborn man who has a very hard time admitting that he is wrong. It is these personal weaknesses that begin the chain reaction that destroys Creon and those he loves.

Antigone is the sister of Eteocles and Polyneices, and she decides that she cannot abide by Creon's law. Polyneices was her brother, just as much as Eteocles was. According to her conscience and the laws of the gods, leaving his body to rot in the fields was wrong. She felt that Creon had no right to overstep the boundaries of what the gods decreed. Kings shouldn't presume to dictate who is privileged enough for a burial. Burial is supposed to be a universal right given to all of mankind. When Creon is informed that it is Antigone who has defied his law, he explodes in anger. Not only has Antigone blatantly disregarded his wishes, she is smug and righteous about it. She says, "It was not God's proclamation. That final justice / That rules the world below makes no such laws" (II, 58–59). Her statement shows the strength of her convictions. She knows that she will die for what she has done, but she stands firmly behind her decision.

Creon is doubly enraged; Antigone has deliberately defied him, and she is a woman. In Creon's view, women are supposed to be timid, weak, and docile creatures who need to be guided by men and their laws. He can't let a mere woman get the better of him. He says, "This girl is guilty of a double insolence, / Breaking the given laws and boasting of it. / Who is the man here, she or I, if this crime goes unpunished?" (II, 80–83). Creon's statement illustrates the lengths to which he will go to triumph over Antigone. Antigone defied a man's law, and now a man is going to teach her a lesson. His judgment is clearly affected by his discriminatory and condescending attitude toward women.

Creon's blind stubbornness is demonstrated further when his son, Haimon, tries to reason with him. Haimon points out the validity of Antigone's actions and the fear that prevents any of the other citizens from voicing their support of her:

HAIMON. I have heard them,
Muttering and whispering in the dark about this girl.
They say no woman has ever, so unreasonably,
Died so shameful a death for a generous act:
She covered her brother's body. Is this indecent?
She kept him from dogs and vultures. Is this a crime?
Death--She should have all the honor that we can give her! (III, 61–67)

The citizens of Thebes are discreetly voicing their disapproval of Creon's condemnation of Antigone's act of mercy. Creon interprets Haimon's speech as a sign that Haimon has chosen Antigone over him and forces his own son to denounce him. This further alienates Creon from his subjects, and the play's atmosphere begins to change. Creon is not in complete control anymore. A woman has managed to disrupt his reign and even turn his son against him. He tries to make Antigone regret her actions by sentencing her to a slow, painful death in a sealed cave with no food or water. A quick death would be too easy. Creon wants her to suffer.

From this point on, the atmosphere of the play continues to spiral into a whirlwind of chaos and tragedy. Teiresias, the old prophet who is never wrong, comes to warn Creon that the wrath of the gods will be upon him if he doesn't right his wrongs: "The time is not far off when you shall pay back / Corpse for corpse, flesh of your own flesh." (V, 71–72) But by then it's too late. By the time Creon sees the error of his ways, his course of destruction is already set and the damage has already been done.

Creon's "public policy" destroys his credibility as a king and everyone he cares about. He lets his thirst for absolute power and his condescending attitude toward women cloud his judgment and drives his family into the arms of death and tragedy. Antigone's fight against the unjust decree of the king is an act of civil disobedience. She is driven by her firm belief in her religion and her own views on right and wrong. Antigone believes that a law is not right just because it is a law. Individual conscience and the laws of the gods must always outweigh public policy.

Work Cited

Sophocles. Antigone. Trans. Dudley Fitts and Robert Fitzgerald. Exploring Literature. Ed. Frank Madden. New York: Longman, 2001. 123–154.

CHAPTER 5

Research and Documentation

Writing with Secondary Sources

When you hear the word *research,* you may groan and think of card catalogs, piles of impenetrable books, and late nights at the library. But research is probably a commonplace event in your life. When you call a friend to seek advice about hooking up your stereo you are doing research. When you look up the spelling or meaning of a word in the dictionary, you are doing research. When you ask the opinion of a classmate about a poem, you are doing research. So despite the ominous connotations the word might have for you in an academic setting, it's an activity you already know a lot about.

For the most part, writing a research essay about literature is not a new activity for you either. You are doing research whenever you go to the text of the work itself, the **primary source**, to support your opinions and interpretations. But in this chapter, the range of your research is extended to include **secondary sources**—sources beyond the text of the work and your classroom—sources that may help to clarify, enrich, or add clout to your interpretation. By going to secondary sources, you can also expand the scope of your writing. You might, for example, consult articles or books that were written about the work or its author. You might consult sources that were written about the cultural or historical period in which the work was written. Or you might explore any number of other possibilities. The choices are only limited by your time and imagination.

Creating, Expanding, and Joining Interpretive Communities

Previously, we discussed how your classmates and collaborative groups become "interpretive communities," groups of readers who help to shape your views about how and what literature means. Your initial responses to literature are based on many factors. And through the social and intellectual exchanges of your small and large groups, you confirm, supplement, or change these responses. Of course, the people and what they value about literature are different in each of those groups. In this respect, you already belong to many different interpretive communities. By using secondary sources, however, you join new communities and share the views of many other readers and writers across hundreds of years and around the world.

It Is Your Interpretation

Regardless of how much research you do, this essay should be *your* interpretation in *your* own voice. Remember, what makes an interpretation convincing or defensible is your ability to support it. What the work means to you may change as you move back and forth through the stages of your reading experience. Doing research continues this process and adds to your support. In the same way that writing down your reflections, rereading the text, and discussing it with others informs your response, seeking information and ideas from secondary sources may lead you to a different, better-informed understanding and interpretation. Integrating these sources into your own writing style, however, is not always easy and may take some practice.

➤ *QUESTIONS FOR READING AND WRITING*

1. Look back through your writing and pick out a work of literature that you discussed in class.
2. Try to remember what others in your class said about it.
   a. Did any of their comments help you to see the work in a different way?
   b. Did you disagree with any of their comments?
3. Write a response that includes their comments and your reactions to them.
4. Read your response.
   a. Does it accurately reflect your experience of the group's discussion?
   b. Were you able to integrate others' comments comfortably into your own writing?
   c. If not, what problems did you encounter?

Integrating Sources into Your Writing

When you listen to the views of others in your class, you can still claim your final interpretation as your own. You might refer to someone else's view to support your opinion—or comment on others' views as a point of disagreement. But your interpretation and the support behind it are still your own. Ultimately, this is your essay, not simply the views of other students and the instructor strung together. An essay that uses secondary sources for support should be no different. But it's not always easy to integrate secondary sources into our writing without being too artificial or making the essay look like a list of other people's statements pasted together.

➤ QUESTIONS FOR READING AND WRITING

1. Write a review of a movie you have seen recently.
2. Find a review of that movie in a newspaper or magazine.
3. Does the critic agree with you? Does he or she bring up points that you did not consider in your review? If so, did any of these points make you reconsider your own view?
4. Rewrite your review, but this time make reference to your secondary source, the other critic's review.
5. Read your second review. Were you able to integrate the critic's review smoothly into your own writing? If not, what problems did you encounter?

THE "I-SEARCH" OPTION

One way of guaranteeing your personal involvement in the gathering and writing process is the "I-Search" essay, recommended by Ken Macrorie. The "I-Search" begins with your own natural curiosity about something. In this case, it might be some aspect or element of a piece of literature (a character, the author, the setting). Once you've identified this "something," seek out information and answers by interviewing other students and faculty members. Go to books and articles only after you've talked with people. The "I-Search" essay becomes an account of your search—complete with your thoughts and feelings.

When you write, you'll be writing about your quest, your exploration—sharing the story of both what you found and how you found it. It's a great way to involve yourself personally in the process, maintain your natural writing voice, and make your essay more interesting to write and read.

GROUP RESEARCH PROJECTS

Collaborating with classmates on a research project can also be a great learning experience. For example, several students may decide that they have a common interest in a particular author and form a research group. Each student might focus on a different aspect of the author's life or writing. But in the process, all of the students can share information, point out leads, and combine resources. At the culmination of the project, the group might present its findings and discuss its work with the class as a whole.

GETTING STARTED

Use Journal Entries, Notes, and Consult Your Classmates

If you are choosing your own topic, you might begin by asking yourself the same questions you would about any other kind of essay. If you are keeping a journal or other notes, you've probably already jotted down some potential topics for your research. Look back at your entries. Make sure you feel confident about the details and your understanding of the work. What did you find most interesting about the work? What would you like to know more about?

Remember, you are seeking information from other sources. You are not limited to what you already know. So be flexible. You don't have to decide on your final topic right away. Share your early ideas with other students and your friends. They may give you ideas you haven't considered. In the process of putting your ideas into words and getting feedback, try out and develop the language and strategies you will use later in the essay itself.

Some Popular Areas of Literary Research

A Particular Work, Features of a Work, or Different Critical Views of a Work A research essay on a single work is similar to the critical essays you have been writing, but by going to secondary sources you can tap the views of critics who may give you insights you haven't considered. For example, Sophocles' *Antigonê* contains several complex external and internal conflicts; the attitudes and behavior of Desdemona and Emilia in Shakespeare's *Othello* raise compelling questions about the role of women; the strong narrator in Alice Walker's "Everyday Use" might provide an interesting study of the effect of point of view.

A Particular Author or the Relationship Between the Author's Life and Work Is there something about the work that makes you curious about the person who wrote it? Or about the connection of that person's life to the work? For example, Robert Hayden's "Those Winter Sundays" (p. 12), James Joyce's "Araby" (p. 544), and Liliana Heker's "The Stolen Party" (p. 1128), are very personal pieces about growing up. When you read them you may wonder how closely they are tied to the authors' own experiences. It might be interesting to explore the author's life in search of these connections.

The Social, Historical, or Cultural Background of a Work When was the work written? Under what circumstances was it written? What impact did this background have on the work and its reception by the public? For example, when you read or see Ibsen's *A Doll House,* it may make you curious about the marriage customs that existed when the play was written. You may wonder how audiences of 1879 responded to the play. Shakespeare's *Othello* may arouse your interest in race relations in Elizabethan England (where the play was written) or in Venice (where the play was set).

Political, Philosophical, and Artistic Influences on the Author's Work What political, philosophical, and artistic sources influenced the work or its author? In what way was the author influenced? How did the work of this author influence other authors? For example, how did the philosophical or political atmosphere of the time influence W. H. Auden's "The Unknown Citizen"? How did Sophocles' plays influence Aristotle's writing of *The Poetics?*

A Theme or Characters Compared Across Two or More Works Is there a common theme that is shared by two or more works? Are there characters in different works who share similar traits? How do they compare? How are they alike? How are they different? How do secondary sources describe this theme or these characters? For example, the sample research essay at the end of this chapter (p. 226) considers the theme of responsibility as it affects two characters in different works of literature: Antigonê in Sophocles' play *Antigonê* and Nora in Ibsen's *A Doll's House*. The writer of the essay calls upon secondary sources to support both her description of the characters and her definition of the theme.

➤ *QUESTIONS FOR READING AND WRITING*

Identify some works of literature that appeal to you.

1. What do you find most interesting about them?
2. What would you like to learn more about?
3. What kind of research would help you do that?

YOUR SEARCH

People

Sometimes the best sources to start with are people. If you are struggling to find a topic, share your struggle with your friends, classmates, and teachers. If you have chosen a topic, try it out. Explain why you think it's interesting. See what they think. They may be able to give you ideas you hadn't considered, and spot problems. Use them for support, and cite them in your essay.

The Library

Again, your best initial source here may be people themselves, the librarians. Librarians are specially educated to know about the library's resources. They not only want to help you find what you need for this project, they want to help you learn how to use the library for future projects. Go to the library's information desk. Most libraries have one just inside the front door. Ask if there is a library map or information guide. Learn the location of the reference desk. The reference librarian can help you find the resources you need and show you how to use them.

The On-Line Public Access Catalog

Once you have some idea about what you're looking for, go to the library's on-line or card catalog. Most academic libraries list their books in a computerized on-line public access catalog (OPAC). Here you can look for information under the author's name, the title of the book, the subject of the book, or key words in its title. OPACs provide a quick and efficient guide to books about authors and their work. Most library systems are computerized and share resources with other libraries, so you not only have access to the listings in your library, but others as well. Through on-line services you may have access to the collections of many large public and university research libraries. If you find a source you want in another library, you may be able to use the interlibrary loan service to retrieve it.

Reference Works

A particularly valuable source in your search for literary criticism is the *MLA International Bibliography.* It lists scholarly books and articles published each year, and it's organized by period and author. Reference works like *The Oxford Companion to English Literature, The Oxford Companion to American Literature,* or *The Reader's Encyclopedia* can also be good places to start. The *New York Times* index may be very useful for book and play reviews. Even the *Reader's Guide to Periodical Literature* may contain some useful reviews located in popular magazines like the *Atlantic Monthly, Time, Newsweek,* and the *New Yorker.*

Some Other Encyclopedias and Indexes Useful for Literary Research

Biographical Dictionary of Irish Writers
Black Writers
Cassell's Encyclopedia of World Literature
Columbia Dictionary of Modern European Literature
Contemporary Authors
Contemporary Dramatists
Contemporary Novelists
Contemporary Poets
Dictionary of British Folk-Tales in the English Language
Dictionary of Celtic Myth and Legend
Dictionary of Celtic Mythology
Dictionary of Concepts in Literary Criticism and Theory
Dictionary of Literary Biography
Dictionary of Mythology, Folklore, and Symbols
Dictionary of Native American Mythology
Encyclopedia of Contemporary Literary Theory
Encyclopedia of Continental Women Writers
Encyclopedia of Literature and Criticism
Encyclopedia of World Literature in the Twentieth Century
Encyclopedia of World Theater
Funk and Wagnall's Standard Dictionary of Folklore, Mythology and Legend
Handbook to Literature
Larousse Encyclopedia of Mythology
Larousse World Mythology
Literary History of England
Literary History of the United States
Masterplots

McGraw-Hill Encyclopedia of World Drama
Mythology of All Races
Oxford Companion to American Literature
Oxford Companion to American Theatre
Oxford Companion to Canadian Literature
Oxford Companion to Children's Literature
Oxford Companion to Classical Literature
Oxford Companion to the Theatre
Oxford Guide to British Women Writers
New Princeton Encyclopedia of Poetry and Poetics
New York Times Theater Reviews, 1920–1970
The Reader's Encyclopedia
Reader's Encyclopedia of World Drama
Theater Dictionary
Twentieth-Century Authors

Some Bibliographies, Indexes, and Abstracts Useful for Literary Research

Abstracts of English Studies
American Literature Abstracts
Annual Bibliography of English Language and Literature
Centennial Index
Contemporary Literary Criticism
Cumulated Dramatic Index 1909–1949
Language and Literature
MLA International Bibliography
New Cambridge Bibliography of English Literature
Play Index
Short Story Index
Year's Work in English Studies

The Internet and the World Wide Web

The Internet is a huge system of regional computer networks. It is often called the information superhighway because it functions like a high-speed highway that carries its users to many smaller roads (or computer networks) leading from it. It enables you to tap into vast amounts of knowledge stored in the world's great universities and libraries. It can give you access to books, journals, reference works, databases, and enlightening conversation.

Connecting to the Internet Most colleges and universities have their own Internet connections and provide accounts to students. So check with your school's computer center. Find out if you can use this connection from your home computer or if you can only make the connection from your campus computer center.

For convenience, you may prefer to subscribe to a commercial on-line service, such as America Online, Prodigy, or CompuServe. You will have to pay a monthly charge, but the ease of use and the additional services provided may make it a good investment.

The World Wide Web Most indexes and sources of information about books and periodicals are organized in alphabetical or chronological order. In such a system it is easy to find sources about individual topics, but identifying and exploring relationships between and among these items or topics can be very difficult and time-consuming. The World Wide Web is a hypertext system that moves you from one source to the other. It finds the connections you request between pieces of information and helps to generate new ones. It allows the same set of information to be presented in many different ways. By typing in key words or phrases you request the combinations, and the Web does the legwork. Instead of choosing an item on a menu, you use your mouse to click on a highlighted term or topic on a Web "page."

Most Internet systems provide access to Web browsers, like Netscape Navigator or Microsoft Explorer. By using these programs you can leave "bookmarks," or "favorite places," and move directly to a site without going through many screens to get there. Web browsers also make it easy for you to save or print the information you have uncovered.

Directories and Search Engines Some sites such as Google, Yahoo, Alta Vista, Excite, HotBot, Infoseek, or Lycos act as directories, or search engines. These programs create indexes of key words in the documents they find. They usually provide a long, horizontal box in which you type words that describe your subject. It helps to be as specific as possible. Type in as many key words as you can to narrow your field; otherwise your search will come up with many more sources than you will have time to examine.

Web Addresses A Web site address is called a Uniform Resource Locator, or URL. These addresses can be very long and complicated. But once you store the address in your Web browser, you will probably not have to type it in again.

Web addresses begin with the letters "http," usually followed by "://www" (http://www). When you type this code at the beginning of an address, the computer knows you are searching for a Web site.

The middle of the address is an abbreviation for the specific site. For example, "nyu" is New York University (http://www.nyu); the abbreviation "msu" represents Michigan State University (http://www.msu).

The end of the address indicates the type of organization. The code for a college or university is usually "edu" (http://www.nyu.edu). The addresses of nonprofit organizations end with "org"; commercial organizations with "com"; and government agencies with "gov."

Libraries on the Internet You can find most college and university libraries on the Internet and tap into their on-line public access catalogs (OPAC). If you find the sources you are looking for, you can request them through interlibrary loan. Many libraries also have their own Web pages that will show you how to access their reference works or useful databases through your computer.

Discussion Groups and Newsgroups Two resources for direct, on-line communication with other people who have similar interests are discussion groups and newsgroups. You can join a discussion, or chat, group by subscribing to a mailing list and receiving messages via e-mail.

Newsgroups are like bulletin boards—everyone in the group reads the same messages. They provide information similar to discussion groups but don't send individual messages. Users can post and read messages without subscribing to a list. Newsgroups are joined through a newsreader or a World Wide Web browser.

Evaluating Internet Sources

Prior to publication, books and articles in scholarly journals are usually reviewed and carefully edited by those with expertise in the field. So, too, editors at reputable newspapers and magazines usually ask writers to verify the accuracy of their sources before they will publish their work. But anyone can put information on the Internet.

Always check the source of any information you take from the Internet. This information is not always screened for accuracy. Look for biographical or other data that might tell you something about the author or the author's academic or scholarly affiliation. If the author provides additional links or other sources, check them out to verify the accuracy of the information. Look for publication or revision dates. As with any source, make sure the assertions made are supported with evidence and that you give credit to the author, and correctly cite the information when you quote or paraphrase from a Web site.

Remember, you are ultimately responsible for the accuracy of your support information, not an unknown and potentially unreliable source on the Internet.

✔CHECKLIST • *Evaluating Internet Sources*

- ❑ Make sure that the author of the document or the person or group responsible for the Web site is identified. Is this person or group a credible source? How so?
- ❑ Check to see that the work's sources are indicated. Is there a list of works cited? Does the list seem sufficient?
- ❑ Are there "links" to other sources indicated? Do they seem reliable?
- ❑ Check the dates of the sources. Are they current? Is there a different date for an earlier print source? Have the sources been revised?

Taking Notes

Whether you use slips of paper, note cards, or a computer, you should be able to rearrange your information according to your needs. Cards are easier to move around and rearrange, so most researchers find it convenient to use "3 × 5" or "4 × 6" file or note cards to record documentation information and notes, usually with a separate source on each card. But you may prefer to use sheets of paper or to take notes on the photocopied articles themselves.

Be selective when you go through your sources. Keep the focus of your essay in mind as you take notes. Some material is irrelevant and should be ignored. Those sources that are particularly valuable may provide you with several note cards worth of information and point you to additional sources as well. As you read, be sure to jot down your own ideas as they occur to you. If you wait until later, you may forget them.

Don't forget to copy all the information you will need for documentation later, including page numbers. In fact, whether you are using note cards or a computer, it is a good idea to record the bibliographic information of the books and articles in the form you will be using on the works cited page of your essay. If you are using cards, you can simply rearrange them in alphabetical order so that you will have the appropriate format ready when listing your works cited.

Paraphrasing and Summarizing

Most of your notes should paraphrase (record the material in your own words) or summarize (condense the material to its main points) rather than quote directly (record the author's exact words). In addition to helping you comprehend what you are reading, putting the material into your own words (in your own writing style and in your own voice) will clarify your ideas and help you build the language you will need later when you write your essay.

Quoting

Remember, this is *your* essay. It is *your* argument or point you want to express. It is not other people's points pasted together. Bring in secondary sources only when you need them. Use direct quotes only when the language in your source makes an impact that your own wording would not. Be sure to surround any quotes you use with sufficient support. Give them an adequate introduction, and explain how they work as evidence. Work quotes smoothly into your writing style. Combine what you paraphrase and summarize with brief quotations.

One effective way of working quotations into your writing is by using an **ellipsis**. An ellipsis is three periods with a space before each and a space after the last (. . .). Simply placing quotation marks around a word or a brief phrase usually makes it clear you left out the rest of the sentence. But when you are quoting most (but not all) of a sentence, or you are leaving out unnecessary parts of a long sentence, an ellipsis signals to the reader that the quoted material has been taken out of the context of a sentence. Use three periods with a space before each for an ellipsis *within* a sentence. When an ellipsis comes at the end of a sentence, use four periods—three for the ellipsis and one more to end the sentence. When a parenthetical reference ends the sentence, use three periods followed by the parenthetical reference and a final period.

For example, if you wanted to describe some of the physical characteristics of Maggie in Alice Walker's "Everyday Use," wanted to indicate a larger context, but did not want to quote an entire sentence, you might choose to write: In contrast to her attractive and confident sister Dee, Maggie is described as " . . . homely and ashamed of the burn scars down her arms and legs . . . " (p. 871).

Review

When your note-taking seems complete, look again at your tentative thesis and organization. Have you balanced your essay with adequate secondary support for each section? Do you need more information? If so, you will need to go back and do research in the particular areas that need strengthening.

➤ *QUESTIONS*

1. How familiar are you with the resources you'll need to write your essay? What would you like to know more about? How will you find out?
2. What note-taking method have you used in the past? Has this worked well for you? How do you plan to record your notes for this essay?

Documentation—Some Basics

What Must Be Documented

1. Information that is not common knowledge—knowledge that you or most others would not have without reference to this or a similar source.
2. Information or ideas from another source (text or interview) that you have paraphrased (rephrased in your own words) or summarized (reduced to its essential points).
3. Direct quotations from another source (text or interview).

Where and How

1. In the text of the essay itself, you must indicate the author and page number(s) of borrowed information or quotations.
2. On a separate page at the end of the essay, you must include an alphabetized list of all the sources you have used in the text.

Avoid Plagiarism

Plagiarism is taking someone else's ideas or words and passing them off as your own. The most basic rule of all documentation is that direct quotations and summarized or paraphrased information or ideas from another source must be appropriately credited. To use other people's words and ideas and not give them credit is a serious academic offense.

A Directory of MLA Formatting and Documentation

The Physical Layout of the Research Essay

Citing Sources in the Text of the Essay

Documenting the Works Cited

Books

Periodicals

Electronic Sources

The Physical Layout of the Research Essay

Individual course requirements may vary from this MLA format, so check with your instructor before writing your essay.

Type of Paper Your research essay should be typed on 8 1/2″ x 11″ unlined paper.

Margins Top and bottom margins should be one inch from the edge of the paper.
Left and right margins should be one inch from the edge of the paper.

Spacing The text of your research essay should be double-spaced.
Quotations should be double-spaced.
Your works cited page should be double-spaced.

Page Numbers Number all pages in the upper-right-hand corner about 1/2 inch from the top edge of the paper. If possible, type your name before the page number.

Heading and Title Your research essay does not require a separate title page. At the top and left margin of your first page, print the following:

Your Name
Your Instructor's Name
The Title and Number of the Course
The Date

Center the Title

(Do not underline, place in quotations or capitalize all the letters in your title. Double space between the title and the first line of your writing.)

The Text

of Your

Essay

Works Cited Page The works cited page is a separate page at the end of the essay.

1. Works are listed in alphabetical order.
2. Each listing is double-spaced, and there is double-spacing between listings.
3. The first line of each listing begins at the left margin. All other lines are indented.
4. Only works cited in the text are included.

Documentation—MLA Style

Because it is the most popular form for those who do literary research, the style we use here for documentation is taken from the *MLA Handbook for Writers of Research Papers*.

Citing Sources in the Text of the Essay

The source from which you have taken the information is cited directly in the essay through parenthetic reference in the following ways:

1. Ideas or information rephrased in your own words.

   The author's last name and the page number in parentheses: (Brown 253)

   Example: The conditions in those schools were reported as terrible (Brown 253).

2. Ideas or information put into your own words but with the author's name mentioned in the text.

   Page number in parentheses: (253)

   Example: Brown reported that the conditions in the schools he visited were terrible (253).

3. Direct quotation—prose

   Direct prose quotations of *four lines or less* are put in quotation marks and integrated into the text of your writing.

   Example: "I could not believe the appalling conditions I saw" (Brown 253).

   or

   Brown said, "I could not believe the appalling conditions I saw" (253).

4. Direct prose quotations of *five or more lines* are double-spaced and separated from the text of your writing by starting the quote on a new line and indenting the left margin an inch.

   Example: It was very clear that Dr. Grantly was taking much longer to die than anyone expected:

   > A month since the physicians had named four weeks as the outside period during which breath could be supported within the body of the dying man. At the end of the month the physicians wondered, and named another fortnight. The old man lived on wine alone, but at the end of the fortnight he still lived; and the tidings of the ministry became more frequent. (Trollope 3)

5. Direct quotation—poetry

   Direct quotations of *three lines or fewer* may be put in quotation marks and integrated into the text of your writing. Use a slash (/) with a space on each side to separate the lines of verse.

   Example: I sense deep regret in Robert Hayden's last lines: "What did I know, what did I know / of love's austere and lonely offices?" (13–14).

6. Direct quotations of *more than three lines* should be double-spaced and begin on a new line. Indent all quoted lines one inch from the left margin and use no quotation marks.

   Example: I was deeply affected by the scene described in William Stafford's poem:

   > The car aimed ahead its lowered parking lights;
   > under the hood purred the steady engine.
   > I stood in the glare of the warm exhaust turning red;
   > around our group I could hear the wilderness listen. (13–16)

7. Direct quotation—drama

   Quoted dialogue between two or more characters should be separated from the text. Begin each quote with the character's name indented one inch from the left margin, written in all capital letters, and followed by a period. All additional lines below that first line should be indented three additional spaces. Line-numbered verse plays are cited in parentheses by act, scene, and line numbers; prose plays by page numbers.

Example: In Sophocles' play, Ismene's attempt to talk Antigone out of her defiance is futile:

> ISMENE. But no one must hear of this, you must tell no one! I will keep it
> a secret, I promise!
> ANTIGONE. Oh, tell it! Tell everyone!
> Think how they'll hate you when it all comes out
> If they learn that you knew about it all the time!
> ISMENE. So fiery! You should be cold with fear.
> ANTIGONE. Perhaps. But I am doing what I must. (Pro. 68–75)

Works Cited Documentation

The descriptions and examples below account for many of the sources you are likely to use, but this is not an exhaustive list. If the source you are using is not accounted for, the best source of additional information is Joseph Gibaldi's *MLA Handbook for Writers of Research Papers,* fifth edition, published by the Modern Language Association of America, 1998.

Books

1. A Book By One Author

   Author's Name (reversed). Title of Book (underlined). City of Publication: Publishing Company, Year of Publication.

   Examples:

   Ellmann, Richard. James Joyce. New York: Oxford University Press, 1959.

   Sledge, Linda Ching. A Map of Paradise. New York: Bantam Books, 1997.

2. A Book by Two or Three Authors

   Author's Name (reversed) and Second Author's Name. Title of Book (underlined). City of Publication: Publishing Company, Year of Publication.

   Examples:

   Desmond, Adrian, and James Moore. Darwin. New York: Warner, 1991.

   Gilbert, Sandra, and Susan Gubar. The Madwoman in the Attic: The Woman Writer and the Nineteenth Century Literary Imagination. New Haven: Yale University Press, 1979.

3. A Work in an Anthology

Author's Name (reversed). "Name of the Work" (in quotation marks). Title of the Anthology (underlined). City of Publication: Publishing Company, Year of Publication, Page Range.

Examples:

Chopin, Kate. "The Story of an Hour." Literature for Composition. 4th ed. Ed. Sylvan Barnet, Morton Berman, William Burto, and Marcia Stubbs. New York: HarperCollins, 1996. 14–16.

Valdez, Luis. "Los Vendidos." Exploring Literature. Ed. Frank Madden. New York: Longman, 2001. 1244–1252.

4. A Work in a Collection by the Same Author

Author's Name (reversed). "Title of the Work "(in quotation marks). Title of the Collection (underlined). City of Publication: Publishing Company, Year of Publication. Page Range.

Examples:

Cheever, John. "The Enormous Radio." The Stories of John Cheever. New York: Knopf, 1978. 33–41.

Sontag, Susan, "The Aesthetics of Silence." Styles of Radical Will. New York: Farrar, 1969. 3–34.

5. An Introduction, Foreword, or Afterword

Author's Name. Introduction. Title of Book (underlined). By (author of book's name). City of Publication: Publishing Company, Year of Publication, Page Range.

Examples:

Costanzo, William V. Introduction. Reading the Movies. By William Costanzo. Urbana, IL: NCTE, 1992.

Orne, Martin T. Foreword. Anne Sexton. By Dianne Wood Middlebrook. Boston: Houghton Mifflin, 1991. xii–xxiii.

6. A Reference Book (Encyclopedia, Dictionary, etc.)

Title of Entry (if a person, reverse the name). Title of Reference Book (underlined). Number and/or Year of Edition.

Examples:

"Symbol." The New Encyclopedia Britannica: Micropaedia. 1974 ed.

Sheridan, Richard Brinsley. The Oxford Companion to English Literature. 5th ed. 1985.

7. An Author with Two or More Works

Author's Name (reversed, in first entry of author only). Rest of Publication Information.

In subsequent listings, type three hyphens, followed by a period and the title.

Example:

Costanzo, William V. The Electronic Text. Englewood Cliffs, N.J.: Educational Technology Pub., 1989.

---. Reading the Movies. Urbana, Ill.: NCTE, 1992.

8. A Translated Book

Author's Name (reversed). Title of Book (underlined). Translator. City of Publication: Publishing Company, Year of Publication.

Example:

Homer. The Odyssey. Trans. Robert Fagles. New York: Penguin, 1996.

Periodicals

9. An Article in a Magazine

Author's Name (reversed). "Title of Article" (in quotation marks). Title of Magazine (underlined) Date of Publication (date, month, year): Page Range. If monthly or bimonthly, list month(s) as date. If no author's name appears, begin with the title of the article (but not "a" or "the").

Examples:

Korda, Michael. "The Third Man." New Yorker 25 Mar. 1996: 44–51.

Updike, John. "The Literary Life." Civilization Dec. 1996: 56–73.

10. An Article in a Scholarly Journal

Author's Name (reversed). "Title of Article" (in quotation marks). Title of Journal (underlined) and Volume Number (year of publication, in parentheses): Page Range.

Examples:

Kamps, Ivo. "Possible Pasts: Historiography and Legitimation in Henry VIII." College English 58 (1996): 192–215.

Wilkinson, James. "A Choice of Fictions: Historians, Memory, and Evidence." PMLA 111 (1996): 80–92.

11. An Article in a Newspaper

Author's Name (reversed). "Title of Article" (in quotation marks). Title of Newspaper (underlined) and Date. Edition: Section Letter and Beginning Page Number.

Examples:

Grimes, William. "A Woman of Words That Win Pulitzers." New York Times 4 June 1996: C1.

Wu, Jim. "Authors Praise New Forms." New York Times 8 March 1987, Sec. 2:1.

12. A Review

Reviewer's Name (reversed). "Title of Review" (in quotation marks). Rev. of Title of Work Reviewed, by Author of Work Reviewed. Publication (underlined) Publication Date: Inclusive Page Numbers.

Examples:

Fraser, Kennedy. "Piper Pipe That Song Again." Rev. of Blake, by Peter Ackroyd. New Yorker 27 May 1996: 127–31.

Vendler, Helen. Rev. of Essays on Style, ed. Roger Fowler. Essays in Criticism 16 (1966): 457–63.

Electronic Sources

Electronic sources include databases on CD-ROM, diskette, and magnetic tape, and online sources from the Internet.

13. A Periodical CD-ROM Database

Author's Name (reversed). "Title" (in quotation marks). Name of Source (electronic journal, conference, database, etc., underlined). Number of Volume or Issue. Year or Date of Publication. Publication Medium (CD-ROM, diskette, tape). Vendor. Date of Electronic Publication.

Example:

Barron, James. "After 17 Years, Cicada Emerges for Ritual of Sex and Death." New York Times Ondisc. CD-ROM. UMI-Proquest. 4 June 1996.

14. A Nonperiodical CD-ROM Publication

Author's Name (reversed). Title (underlined). Medium of Publication. City of Publication. Publisher. Date of Publication.

Example:

Shakespeare, William. All's Well That Ends Well. William Shakespeare: The Complete Works on CD-ROM. CD-ROM. Abingdon, Eng.: Andromeda Interactive, 1994.

15. On-line Sources from the Internet

(If print source) Author's Name (reversed). Title (in quotations or underlined as appropriate). Print Source Information (same as print citation). Title of Project, Database, Etc. (underlined). Volume, Issue, or Identifying Number (if available). Date of Electronic Publication. Page, Paragraph, or Section Numbers. Institution or Organization Sponsoring of the Site. Date of Access. Electronic Address (within angle brackets).

Example (on-line print source):

Twain, Mark. The Adventures of Tom Sawyer. Internet Wiretap Online Library. Carnegie-Mellon University. 22 Feb. 1999. <http:www.cs.cs.cmu.edu/Web/people/rgs/sawyr-table.html>.

Example (on-line Web site):

Voice of the Shuttle English Literature. University of California, Santa Barbara. Rev. 1999. 22 Feb. 1999. <http://www.humanitas.ucsb.edu/shuttle/english.html>.

Other Sources

16. A Personal Interview

Person's Name (reversed). Type of Interview (telephone, mail, on-line, personal, etc.). Date.

Examples:

Courage, Richard. E-mail to the author. 10 March 1997. Martin, James. Telephone interview. 3 June 1996.

17. A Lecture

Speaker's Name (reversed). "Title of the Lecture" (in quotation marks). Nature of the Meeting. Location. Date.

Examples:

Haynes, Terry. "The Problematic Essay: Right and Responsibility." Conference on College Composition and Communication. Hyatt Regency, Milwaukee. 28 Mar. 1996.

Worley, Demetrice A. "Telling Tales in School: An African American Woman's Voice in Composition." MLA Convention. Sheraton Washington, Washington, D.C. 28 Dec. 1996.

18. A TV or Radio Program

"Title of Episode or Segment" (in quotation marks). Title of Program (underlined). Name of the Network. Call Letters of the Local Station. Date of Broadcast.

Examples:

"The Irish Question." The Story of English. PBS. WNET, New York. 6 Apr. 1985.

Brideshead Revisited, Episode 4. With Anthony Andrews and Jeremy Irons. PBS. WETA, Washington, D.C. 24 July 1984.

19. A Sound Recording

Name of Person (composer, conductor, performers—whoever should be emphasized). Title of the Recording (underlined). Manufacturer, Year of Issue. Medium (CD, LP, audiocassette, audiotape).

Examples:

Mozart, Wolfgang Amadeus. Symphony no. 40 in G minor. Vienna Philharmonic. Cond. Leonard Bernstein. Deutsche Grammophon, 1984. Audiocassette.

Rea, Stephen. James Joyce's Ulysses. BBC Audio, 1993. Audiocassette.

20. A Film or Video Recording

Title of Film or Video (underlined). Director. Distributor, Year.

Examples:

Agamemnon. By Aeschylus. Dir. Peter Hall. The National Theatre of Great Britain, 1983.

Rozencrantz and Guildenstern Are Dead. Dir. Tom Stoppard. Perf. Gary Oldman, Tim Roth, and Richard Dreyfuss. Cinecom Entertainment, 1990.

Sample Works Cited

Works Cited

Agamemnon. By Aeschylus. dir. Peter Hall. The National Theatre of Great Britain, 1983.

Barron, James. "After 17 Years, Cicada Emerges for Ritual of Sex and Death." New York Times Ondisc. CD-ROM. UMI-Proquest. 4 June 1996.

Cheever, John. "The Enormous Radio." The Stories of John Cheever. New York: Knopf, 1978. 33–41.

Costanzo, William V. The Electronic Text. Englewood Cliffs N.J.: Educational Technology Pub., 1989.

---. Reading the Movies. Urbana, Ill.: NCTE, 1992.

Desmond, Adrian and James Moore. Darwin. New York: Warner, 1991.

Ellmann, Richard. James Joyce. New York: Oxford University Press, 1959.

Fraser, Kennedy. "Piper Pipe That Song Again." Rev. of Blake, by Peter Ackroyd. New Yorker. 27 May 1996: 127–131.

Grimes, William. "A Woman of Words That Win Pulitzers." New York Times 4 June 1996: C1.

Haynes, Terry. "The Problematic Essay: Right and Responsibility." Conference on College Composition and Communication. Hyatt Regency, Milwaukee. 28 Mar. 1996.

Homer. The Odyssey. Trans. Robert Fagles. New York: Penguin, 1996.

"The Irish Question." The Story of English. PBS. WNET, New York. 6 Apr. 1985.

Kamps, Ivo. "Possible Pasts: Historiography and Legitimation in Henry VIII." College English 58 (1996): 192–215.

Korda, Michael. "The Third Man." New Yorker. 25 Mar. 1996: 44–51.

Martin, James. Phone interview, 3 June 1996.

Rea, Stephen. James Joyce's Ulysses. BBC Audio, 1993. Audiocassette.

Sheridan, Richard Brinsley. The Oxford Companion to English Literature. 5th ed., 1985.

Sledge, Linda Ching. A Map of Paradise. New York: Bantam: Books, 1997.

Twain, Mark. The Adventures of Tom Sawyer. Internet Wiretap Online Library. Carnegie-Mellon University. 22 Feb. 1999. <http:www.cs.cs.cmu.edu/Web/people/rgs/sawyr-table.html>.

Valdez, Luis. "Los Vendidos." Exploring Literature. Ed. Frank Madden. New York: Longman, 2001. 1244–1252.

Voice of the Shuttle English Literature. University of California, Santa Barbara. Rev. 1999. 22 Feb. 1999. <http://www.humanitas.ucsb.edu/shuttle/english.html>.

From First Response to Research Essay

The same processes that are so useful in generating ideas for personal or critical essays may be just as valuable for giving you ideas and narrowing your topic for a research essay. Reading literature encourages a variety of responses and perhaps raises more questions than it answers. It is a good idea to generate and explore as many of your questions and ideas as possible before you decide on one direction. Here is a quick review of strategies to get started. For a detailed explanation of these techniques, with examples, see Chapter 2, pages 39–45.

- Employing directed freewriting can be a useful technique for loosening up ideas. The best time to do this exercise is immediately after you finish reading, while your thoughts and impressions are still fresh. The intention of directed freewriting is to release what you know without blocking it with pauses for reflection, punctuation, or editing.
- Asking questions about a general topic is likely to provide you with new information. Responding with detailed answers to these questions may provide you with ideas for a narrowed thesis and specific support for that thesis.
- Choosing a few key words or phrases that apply to your topic and then listing as many related details under each as you can should help you generate many concrete details and much specific support for your ideas.
- Clustering your ideas or drawing a semantic map may help you understand, see relationships, and generate and extend ideas better spatially rather than linearly.

✔ CHECKLIST • *Writing a Research Essay*

Planning Your Essay

Consider Your Motivation

- ❑ Will this topic sustain your interest long enough for you to do a good job?

Determine Its Feasibility

- ❑ Can you write a research essay about this subject?
- ❑ Do you have enough to say and can you find enough evidence to support your case?

Secondary Sources

- ❑ Can you find appropriate secondary sources? Where will you get them? Are you sure of their reliability?
- ❑ Have you given yourself enough time to do the research and to organize your information?

Taking Notes

- ❑ Do you have an effective system to organize your notes? What is it?
- ❑ Have you copied down all the information you will need to document your sources?

(*continued*)

❑ Have you decided which sources to summarize, paraphrase, and quote?

Clarify Your Thesis

❑ Do you have a clear understanding of the thesis you want to argue?

❑ Can you articulate it in a thesis statement?

Know Your Readers

❑ What assumptions can you make about your readers?

❑ Are they likely to agree or disagree with your thesis?

Supporting Your Argument

Arrange Your Support Effectively

❑ Is the support for your thesis arranged in the most effective way?

❑ Is it more effective to develop your argument by stating your thesis first and then supporting it with evidence or by allowing the evidence to build into your thesis?

Integrating Secondary Sources

❑ What is the most effective way to integrate your secondary sources? What should be paraphrased? What should be quoted? Why?

❑ How can you effectively and smoothly integrate your secondary sources into your own writing style?

Support Your Thesis with Facts from the Text and Secondary Sources

❑ Is your support based on facts or opinions?

❑ Have you supported your opinions with facts and quotes from the text?

❑ Do your secondary sources support your view? How?

Account for All the Evidence

❑ Have you accounted for all the evidence in the text?

❑ Have you accounted for evidence that may not support your thesis?

❑ Have you accounted for secondary source material that may not support your thesis?

Explain the Connections

❑ Have you explained *how* the evidence you have chosen supports your thesis?

❑ Are the connections between your secondary sources and your thesis clear?

Opening, Closing, and Revising

Write or Rewrite Your Introduction After Your First Draft

❑ Is your introduction clear, informative, and interesting?

❑ If appropriate, does it map out the journey for the reader?

Close Your Argument Reasonably

❑ Have you explained the connections between the thesis and your primary and secondary source support?

(*continued*)

- ❑ Have you only claimed what you have really delivered?

Revise with a Fresh View

- ❑ Have you reread and reviewed your essay?
- ❑ How well is your draft organized? Does the sequence make sense?
- ❑ Are there gaps that need to be filled? Is there enough support?
- ❑ Have you explained the connections between your support and your thesis?
- ❑ Have you expressed those connections as clearly as possible?
- ❑ Have you maintained a consistent "voice" throughout the essay?

Review Your Intentions and Organization

- ❑ Is the central thesis of the essay clearly stated?
- ❑ Does the title of your essay account for your thesis?
- ❑ Is the essay fully developed? Have you accounted for all aspects of your thesis statement?
- ❑ Do all the paragraphs relate to your thesis? Is the essay fully developed?
- ❑ Is the organization of those paragraphs within the essay clear?
- ❑ Are the paragraphs fully developed?
- ❑ Do each of the sentences within the paragraphs relate to the central idea of the paragraph?
- ❑ Are there enough details to support or clarify your proposition? Have you "shown" what you've "told"?
- ❑ Are there enough quotes from both primary and secondary sources to support your thesis?
- ❑ Are there redundancies, digressions, or meaningless phrases that could be cut?

Proofread Carefully

- ❑ Are all of your sentences complete sentences?
- ❑ Are all of your sentences punctuated appropriately?
- ❑ Are all the words spelled correctly?
- ❑ Have you checked for easily confused words (then/than, your/you're, its/it's, etc.)?
- ❑ Are you sure of the meaning of all the words you've used?
- ❑ Are the titles of works underlined or in quotations as appropriate?
- ❑ Are there particular errors you have a tendency to make?
- ❑ Have you looked for those in this essay?
- ❑ Is the essay written in the format required by your instructor? Have you documented your references to the text and included a list of works cited?

A Sample Research Essay

Susan MacNaughten

Dr. Sakrajda

English 102

April 12, 200X

Antigone, Nora, and Responsibility:

What Did They Do and What Can We Learn from Them?

Nora in Henrik Ibsen's A Doll's House and Antigone in Sophocles' Antigone confront their dilemmas in very different ways and under very different circumstances, but they both take responsibility for their actions and themselves. This theme of personal responsibility, which dominates both plays, is still very relevant for us today.

Sophocles' Antigone opens with Antigone telling her sister, Ismene, of the death of their two brothers, Eteocles and Polyneices, who killed each other during the attack on Thebes. The new ruler, Creon, has given Eteocles a burial with full military honors, as it was he who had defended their cherished city. Polyneices, who had been expelled by his brother, sought revenge by forming an army to attack Thebes. Creon, who has proclaimed Polyneices a traitor, has issued an edict that his body is to be left unburied in the fields, exposed to the elements and the animals. Antigone, feeling cursed by her family's history, believes it is her hereditary responsibility to bury Polyneices. Their conflict arises over this issue. Antigone is split between human law and divine law. She is compelled by the law of personal responsibility, so it is not a question of choosing to follow the law of the king or the unwritten laws of the gods. She has no choice. If she obeys Creon's edict, she will be unable to bear the guilt. After quarreling and parting with Ismene, Antigone carries out her plan on her own, ultimately leading to her death.

Responsibility is very important to Antigone. She wants others to be responsible as well. This is evidenced in the beginning of the play, as Antigone unsuccessfully tries to convince her fear-ridden sister, Ismene, to join her in her plan: "Now you can prove what you are: / A true sister, or a traitor to your family" (Pro. 27–28). But Ismene does not believe in exceeding a woman's position in society. She feels women cannot fight with men, that the very thought is mad. But Antigone perseveres:

> . . . I will bury him; and if I must die,
> I say that this crime is holy: I shall lie down
> With him in death, and I shall be as dear
> To him as he to me. (Pro. 55–58)

But Ismene is afraid of Creon. And while she may agree with Antigone, she believes that in this instance the laws of man outweigh the laws of the gods. Antigone, frustrated with her sister's excuses, tells her, "Go away, Ismene: / I shall be hating you soon, and the dead will too, / For your words are hateful . . . " (Pro. 77–79). This statement shows that Antigone has no tolerance for those who do not wish to accept responsibility. However, Antigone is smart enough to know that she can only be responsible for herself and not others. And so she carries out her plan to bury her brother alone.

Later, in her confrontation with Creon, Antigone remains strong and as sure of her decision as ever:

> . . . This death of mine
> Is of no importance; but if I had left my brother
> Lying in death unburied, I should have suffered.
> Now I do not. (II, 69–72)

This statement exemplifies Antigone's sense of responsibility. It shows that Antigone could not have lived with herself had she not followed her conscience by burying her brother. She had to act responsibly in order to maintain her own sense of self.

In Henrik Ibsen's A Doll's House, we are presented with the marriage of Torvald and Nora Helmer. Torvald is a businessman who expects his wife to take care of the children, but at the same time treats her like a child, making references to her as his "little squirrel" or "little singing bird." Nora is a lighthearted, even childish young woman who likes to spend money and prance around. Her speech and behavior are quite immature.

Many years before, Nora forged her father's name to a promissory note because she needed money to save her husband's life. Eventually, she is blackmailed with this and lives in fear of the day that Torvald will learn the truth. She fantasizes that Torvald will accept her guilt as his own. But when Torvald turns on her, Nora experiences an epiphany. She realizes that she has never had thoughts and ideas of her own; she has only been what Torvald wanted her to be. And so she awakens to her sense of personal responsibility; she leaves Torvald and the children in order to discover who she really is.

Initially Nora appears to be little more than a child in a woman's body. She exhibits little sense of responsibility, yet she speaks of her own responsibility:

> . . . Whenever Torvald gave me money for new clothes and such-like, I never spent more than half. And always I bought the simplest and cheapest things. It's a blessing most things look well on me, so Torvald never noticed anything. But sometimes I did feel it was a bit hard, Kristine, because it is nice to be well dressed, isn't it? (736)

Here we see Nora's egocentric side. Still, we know that Nora went to great lengths to save her husband's life. She managed to acquire a large sum of money (albeit illicitly) and take care of her family. She also felt compelled not to tell her sick father or husband how she acquired this money. Nora knew this was not wise, but she felt that she had to do it. She acted responsibly because she did not have a choice.

Nonetheless, Nora appears to be quite happy, living from moment to moment, until her first confrontation with Krogstad, the blackmailer. Nora confesses that it was she who forged her father's name on the note. This is perhaps the first sign of Nora becoming more responsible. But then, instead of becoming fully responsible and admitting her guilt to her husband, she engages herself in little games and fantasies in the hopes that Krogstad will leave her and her family alone. Her sense of responsibility is short-lived.

Later, after Torvald has read Krogstad's letter, Nora is forced to admit her guilt to her husband. Yet this is not done out of a sense of responsibility to herself. It is not until the end of the play, when Torvald is relieved to have received the forged note, that Nora finally acknowledges her ignorance. But even then, she does not want to be accountable for the person she has become:

> . . . At home, Daddy used to tell me what he thought, then I thought the same. And if I thought differently, I kept quiet about it, because he wouldn't have liked it. He used to call me his baby doll, and he played with me as I used to play with my dolls. Then I came to live in your house--. . . You arranged everything to your tastes, and I

> acquired the same tastes. Or pretended to-- . . . You and daddy did me a great wrong. It's your fault I've never made anything of my life. (780)

This is a very important moment. Nora is still in denial as far as personal accountability is concerned, but at the same time is acknowledging her ignorance. This is the beginning of personal responsibility to herself. She continues to go on with her proclamation, explaining to Torvald that she must leave if she is to educate and discover herself. She believes that she has duties to herself as a human being. Again she speaks of her responsibility, which in turn is making Nora responsible to herself as a human being:

> Listen, Torvald, from what I've heard, when a wife leaves her husband's house as I am doing now, he is absolved by law of all responsibility for her. I can at any rate, free you from all responsibility. You must not feel in any way bound, any more than I shall. There must be freedom on both sides. (784)

And so she frees Torvald of any responsibility, which in turn makes Nora responsible for herself.

Antigone and Nora are very different characters. Antigone has an innate sense of personal responsibility. For Nora, it has to be learned. But where do the similarities lie between Antigone and Nora? Both of them have broken a law for which they have to face the consequences. Eva Le Gallienne, commenting on the character of Nora, writes:

> To Nora it was right and natural to commit forgery to save her husband's life. Any other behavior would have been unthinkable. She would have done anything to save or shield anyone she loved. (Introduction, xiv)

Similarly, in his essay on <u>Antigone</u>, Cedric H. Whitman states:

> Antigone, with her precise and unshakable perception of divine law, is the embodiment of the heroic individual in a world whose institutions cannot change but have usurped a right to existence apart from the justifiable interest of the citizens. (82–83)

Both Antigone and Nora are faced with the dilemma of following their consciences or following public law. They both maintain that their actions are above the law. Nora believes that she will be exonerated of any wrongdoing when people discover the reason for her crime. But Antigone's and Nora's feelings mean nothing in the eyes of the law. Nora is lucky enough to escape the legal consequences--Antigone is not.

Antigone and Nora both have to make difficult decisions. Antigone chooses death, and Nora chooses life on her own without her husband and children. And so, while Antigone and Nora may have come to realize their sense of personal responsibility in different ways, they clearly both share the characteristics of responsibility, as well as bravery.

Paul Tillich has written: "The law of love is the ultimate law because it is the negation of law . . ." (152). His statement applies equally to Antigone and Nora, as they both acted out of love when they violated the law. But what do they offer us today? First, we must give ourselves a working definition of responsibility to oneself. I will use Adrienne Rich's definition of responsibility to oneself in her essay "Claiming an Education":

> Responsibility to yourself means refusing to let others do your thinking, talking, and naming for you; it means learning to respect and use your own brains and instincts; hence grappling with hard work. . . . Responsibility to yourself means that you don't fall for shallow and easy solutions . . . It means that you refuse to sell your talents and aspirations short, simply to avoid conflict and confrontation. (168)

This definition is relevant to the character of Nora. Her inability to let Torvald continue to think and talk for her led to conflict with her sense of self and a confrontation with her husband. This resulted in her using her own brains and instincts, and she became emancipated. While Nora's decision may have been impulsive, since she left her children as well as her husband, many women have followed in her footsteps, as evidenced by the number of successful single women and single mothers in society today.

Antigone refused to sacrifice what she believed in simply for the sake of avoiding confrontation. But her situation was more complicated, the risk factor much higher. What can we learn from her today? If we believe in following our consciences and ignoring the law, we face the consequences of our actions. Conversely, if we maintain that laws and rules are established for the good of society and cannot ever be violated, we run the risk of personal conflict. For example, there are some crimes that take place in our society that many people feel are justifiable. Consider the mother who has depleted all sources of income and prostitutes herself in order to obtain money for her sick child's medical needs, or the husband who assists his terminally ill wife in committing suicide. Should these people go to jail? Where and how do we draw the line between public law and moral law? Joseph Fletcher comments on this issue:

> Legalism always bears down hard on the need for order, putting its premium on obedience to law, even statutory law. It would, if it could immobilize Martin Luther King and the sit-in demonstrators or civil rights protestors, whereas situation ethics gives high-order value to freedom, and to that responsibility for free decision which is the obverse side of the coin of freedom. (138)

There are no easy solutions to these issues, just as there were no easy solutions for Antigone and Nora. Right or wrong, they force us to think about personal accountability and the choices we make for ourselves in today's society.

Works Cited

Fletcher, Joseph. Situation Ethics: The New Morality. Philadelphia: Westminster Press, 1966.

Ibsen, Henrik. A Doll's House. Trans. James Walter McFarlane. Exploring Literature, Ed. Frank Madden. New York: Longman, 2001, 725–786.

Le Gallienne, Eva. Introduction. Henrik Ibsen. Eight Plays. New York: McGraw, 1982. vii–xxxiii.

Rich, Adrienne. "Claiming an Education." Casts of Thought: Writing In and Against Tradition. Eds. George Otte and Linda Palumbo. New York: Macmillan, 1990. 165–170.

Sophocles. Antigone. Trans. Dudley Fitts and Robert Fitzgerald. Exploring Literature. Ed. Frank Madden. New York: Longman, 2001, 123–154.

Tillich, Paul. Systematic Theology. Vol. I. Chicago: University of Chicago Press, 1967.

Whitman, Cedric H. Sophocles: A Study of Heroic Humanism, 3rd ed. Cambridge: Harvard University Press, 1971.

PART III

A Thematic Anthology

Family & Friends

Family & Friends

A Dialogue Across History

Friends have all things in common.
—Plato, *Dialogues,* 428–348 B.C.

He who has a thousand friends has not a / Friend to spare. / And he who has one enemy will meet him / Everywhere.
—Ali ibn-Abi-Talib, c. 602–661

In the misfortune of our best friends we often find something that is not displeasing.
—La Rochefouchaud, *Maxims,* 1665

It is impossible to please all the world and one's father.
—Jean de la Fontaine, 1668

I lay it down as fact that if all men knew what others say of them, there would not be four friends in the world.
—Blaise Pascal, *Pensees,* 1670

Fate chooses our relatives, we choose our friends.
—Jacques Delille, *Malheur et Pitie,* 1803

The only way to have a friend is to be one.
—Ralph Waldo Emerson, *Friendship,* 1841

A friend is a person with whom I may be sincere. Before him, I may think aloud.
—Ralph Waldo Emerson, *Friendship,* 1841

Give a little love to a child, and you get a great deal back.
—John Ruskin, *The Crown of Wild Olive,* 1866

Happy families are all alike; every unhappy family is unhappy in its own way.
—Leo Tostoi, *Anna Karenina,* 1877

So long as we serve; so long as we are loved by others, I would almost say that we are indispensable; and no man is useless while he has a friend.

—Robert Louis Stevenson, *Across the Plains,* 1892

The little world of childhood with its familiar surroundings is a model of the greater world. The more intensely the family has stamped its character upon the child, the more it will tend to feel and see its earlier miniature world again in the bigger world of adult life.

—Carl Jung, *The Theory of Psychoanalysis,* 1913

Home is the place where, when you have to / go there, / They have to take you in.

—Robert Frost, *The Death of the Hired Man,* 1914

Before the Flowers of Friendship Faded Friendship Faded.

—Gertrude Stein, *book title,* 1930

Each friend represents a world in us, a world possibly not born until they arrive, and it is only by this meeting that a new world is born.

—Anaïs Nin, 1937

The more people have studied different methods of bringing up children the more they have come to the conclusion that what good mothers and fathers instinctively feel like doing for their babies is the best after all.

—Benjamin Spock, *The Common Sense Book of Baby and Child Care,* 1946

If we were to see the family as a wealthy source of traditions, stories, characters and values, we might not feel so alone and abandoned to a life that has to be manufactured every day.

—Thomas Moore, *Soul Mates,* 1994

Every parent knows that raising children requires bicycle pumps, Beanie babies, notebook paper, prayers, skill, and plain dumb luck. But what many of us don't ever come to grips with is this: we must take responsibility for the world our children inhabit. We make the world for them. We give it to them. And if we fail them, they will break our hearts ten different ways.

—Amy Dickinson, *Time,* 1999

Family and Friends: Exploring Your Own Experiences and Beliefs

A look at depictions of family life over the last fifty years shows us how much the public image of family has changed. It is a long journey from the stable, wise, supportive families of television shows like *Ozzie and Harriet* or *Father Knows Best* of the 1950s to the chaotic, bumbling families depicted in shows like *The Simpsons* or *Married with Children* of the 1990s. We live in an age that bombards us with traditional "family values" while urging our recovery from "dysfunctional family" experiences. Our families may be large and extend to distant relations or be as small as a single parent and child. Until we have the opportunity to form our own families, we don't have much choice about family membership. "Home," as Robert Frost writes, may be ". . . the place that when you have to / go there,/ They have to take you in." And this same sense of responsibility may also compel us to love our brothers or sisters even when we don't like them very much.

For many of us, friends are a chosen family. We rely on friends to provide the kind of stability, wisdom, and support that make us think of them as "family" in the most favorable sense of the word. We confide in our friends or ask for their help when we're in trouble, and we selflessly rush to help and comfort them when they are most in need.

Our families and friends can have a powerful effect on our lives. They influence and shape our values, our behavior, our aspirations. We may be happy in their company and so attached to them that we have difficulty pulling away. We may be unhappy and disconnected from them and yearn for the warmth we believe we're missing. As we experience the issues of family and friends that we encounter in literature, we will naturally compare them to similar circumstances in our own lives.

Reading and Writing About Family and Friends

At least one aspect of the many stories, poems, plays, and essays in this section is about the impact that family and/or friends have on characters: the heartbreaking father-son conflict over tradition and values in Chinua Achebe's short story, "Marriage Is a Private Affair"; a young man's experience of the death of a sibling in Seamus Heaney's poem "Midterm Break"; the vulnerability of a young woman and her protective family in Tennessee William's play *The Glass Menagerie;* and the abuse and suicide of an aunt in Maxine Hong Kingston's haunting essay, "No Name Woman." The brief quotes that open this section also give you some idea of the number of compelling emotions that are connected to family and friends. Issues of parent-child tension, mutual support, loneliness, loyalty, comfort, personal growth, and parental responsibility head a long list of concerns. Any of these or other related issues might provide a fine topic for an essay.

◆ FICTION ◆

CHINUA ACHEBE (b. 1930)

The son of a mission schoolteacher, Chinua Achebe was born and raised in eastern Nigeria, a British colony that later became the Republic of Nigeria after gaining independence in 1963. Educated both in Africa and England, he first burst into prominence with his 1958 novel Things Fall Apart, *a moving portrayal of the conflicts between traditional tribal customs and European culture in colonial Africa. He has since become one of the most influential African voices of his generation. Much of his later work, including the novels* Man of the People *(1964) and* Anthills of the Savannah *(1988), explores the corruption and conflicts of contemporary Nigeria. He currently resides both in Nigeria and the United States, holding teaching positions at Stanford University, the University of Massachusetts at Amherst, and Bard College.*

MARRIAGE IS A PRIVATE AFFAIR [1972]

Have you written to your dad yet?" asked Nene one afternoon as she sat with Nnaemeka in her room at 16 Kasanga Street, Lagos.

"No. I've been thinking about it. I think it's better to tell him when I get home on leave!"

"But why? Your leave is such a long way off yet—six whole weeks. He should be let into our happiness now."

Nnaemeka was silent for a while, and then began very slowly as if he groped for his words: "I wish I were sure it would be happiness to him."

5 "Of course it must," replied Nene, a little surprised. "Why shouldn't it?"

"You have lived in Lagos all your life, and you know very little about people in remote parts of the country."

"That's what you always say. But I don't believe anybody will be so unlike other people that they will be unhappy when their sons are engaged to marry."

"Yes. They are most unhappy if the engagement is not arranged by them. In our case it's worse—you are not even an Ibo."

This was said so seriously and so bluntly that Nene could not find speech immediately. In the cosmopolitan atmosphere of the city it had always seemed to her something of a joke that a person's tribe could determine whom he married.

10 At last she said, "You don't really mean that he will object to your marrying me simply on that account? I had always thought you Ibos were kindly disposed to other people."

"So we are. But when it comes to marriage, well, its not quite so simple. And this," he added, "is not peculiar to the Ibos. If your father were alive and lived in the heart of lbibio-land he would be exactly like my father."

"I don't know. But anyway, as your father is so fond of you, I'm sure he will forgive you soon enough. Come on then, be a good boy and send him a nice lovely letter. . ."

"It would not be wise to break the news to him by writing. A letter will bring it upon him with a shock. I'm quite sure about that."

"All right, honey, suit yourself. You know your father."

As Nnaemeka walked home that evening he turned over in his mind the different ways of overcoming his father's opposition, especially now that he had gone and found a girl for him. He had thought of showing his letter to Nene but decided on second thought not to, at least for the moment. He read it again when he got home and couldn't help smiling to himself. He remembered Ugoye quite well, an Amazon of a girl who used to beat up all the boys, himself included, on the way to the stream, a complete dunce at school.

> I have found a girl who will suit you admirably—Ugoye Nweke, the eldest daughter of our neighbor, Jacob Nweke. She has a proper Christian upbringing. When she stopped schooling some years ago her father (a man of sound judgment) sent her to live in the house of a pastor where she has received all the training a wife could need. Her Sunday School teacher has told me that she reads her Bible very fluently. I hope we shall begin negotiations when you come home in December.

On the second evening of his return from Lagos Nnaemeka sat with his father under a cassia tree. This was the old man's retreat where he went to read his Bible when the parching December sun had set and a fresh, reviving wind blew on the leaves.

"Father," began Nnaemeka suddenly, "I have come to ask forgiveness."

"Forgiveness? For what, my son?" he asked in amazement.

"It's about this marriage question!"

"Which marriage question."

"I can't—we must—I mean it is impossible for me to marry Nweke's daughter."

"Impossible? Why?" asked his father.

"I don't love her."

"Nobody said you did. Why should you?" he asked.

"Marriage today is different. . ."

"Look here, my son," interrupted his father, "nothing is different. What one looks for in a wife are a good character and a Christian background."

Nnaemeka saw there was no hope along the present line of argument.

"Moreover," he said, "I am engaged to marry another girl who has all of Ugoye's good qualities, and who. . ."

His father did not believe his ears. "What did you say?" he asked slowly and disconcertingly.

"She is a good Christian," his son went on, "and a teacher in a girls' school in Lagos."

"Teacher, did you say? If you consider that a qualification for a good wife I should like to point out to you, Emeka, that no Christian woman should teach. St. Paul in his letter to the Corinthians says that women should keep silence." He rose slowly from his seat and paced forwards and backwards. This was his pet subject, and he condemned vehemently those church leaders who encouraged women to teach in their schools. After he had spent his emotion on a long homily, he at last came back to his son's engagement, in a seemingly milder tone.

"Whose daughter is she, anyway?"

"She is Nene Atang."

"What!" All the mildness was gone again. "Did you say Neneatang? What does that mean?"

"Nene Atang from Calabar. She is the only girl I can marry." This was a very rash reply and Nnaemeka expected the storm to burst. But it did not. His father merely walked away into his room. This was most unexpected and perplexed Nnaemeka. His father's silence was infinitely more menacing than a flood of threatening speech. That night the old man did not eat.

When he sent for Nnaemeka a day later he applied all possible ways of dissuasion. But the young man's heart was hardened, and his father eventually gave him up as lost.

"I owe it to you, my son, as a duty to show you what is right and what is wrong. Whoever put this idea into your head might as well have cut your throat. It is Satan's work." He waved his son away.

"You will change your mind, Father, when you know Nene."

"I shall never see her" was the reply. From that night the father scarcely spoke to his son. He did not, however, cease hoping that he would realize how serious was the danger he was heading for. Day and night he put him in his prayers.

Nnaemeka, for his own part, was very deeply affected by his father's grief. But he kept hoping that it would pass away. If it had occurred to him that never in the history of his people had a man married a woman who spoke a different tongue, he might have been less optimistic. "It has never been heard," was the verdict of an old man speaking a few weeks later. In that short sentence he spoke for all of his people. This man had come with others to commiserate with Okeke when news went round about his son's behavior. By that time the son had gone back to Lagos.

"It has never been heard," said the old man again with a sad shake of his head.

"What did Our Lord say?" asked another gentleman. "Sons shall rise against their Fathers; it is there in the Holy Book."

"It is the beginning of the end," said another.

The discussion thus tending to become theological, Madubogwu, a highly practical man, brought it down once more to the ordinary level.

"Have you thought of consulting a native doctor about your son?" he asked Nnaemeka's father.

"He isn't sick," was the reply.

"What is he then? The boy's mind is diseased and only a good herbalist can bring him back to his right senses. The medicine he requires is *Amalile,* the same that women apply with success to recapture their husbands' straying affection."

"Madubogwu is right," said another gentleman. "This thing calls for medicine."

"I shall not call in a native doctor." Nnaemeka's father was known to be obstinately ahead of his more superstitious neighbors in these matters. "I will not be another Mrs. Ochuba. If my son wants to kill himself let him do it with his own hands. It is not for me to help him."

"But it was her fault," said Madubogwu. "She ought to have gone to an honest herbalist. She was a clever woman, nevertheless."

"She was a wicked murderess," said Jonathan who rarely argued with his neighbors because, he often said, they were incapable of reasoning. "The medicine was prepared for her husband, it was his name they called in its preparation and I am sure it would have been perfectly beneficial to him. It was wicked to put it into the herbalist's food, and say you were only trying it out."

Six months later, Nnaemeka was showing his young wife a short letter from his father:

> It amazes me that you could be so unfeeling as to send me your wedding picture. I would have sent it back. But on further thought I decided just to cut off your wife and sent it back to you because I have nothing to do with her. How I wish that I had nothing to do with you either.

When Nene read through this letter and looked at the mutilated picture her eyes filled with tears, and she began to sob.

"Don't cry, my darling," said her husband. "He is essentially good natured and will one day look more kindly on our marriage." But years passed and that one day did not come.

For eight years, Okeke would have nothing to do with his son, Nnaemeka. Only three times (when Nnaemeka asked to come home and spend his leave) did he write to him.

"I can't have you in my house," he replied on one occasion. "It can be of no interest to me where or how you spend your leave—or your life, for that matter."

The prejudice against Nnaemeka's marriage was not confined to his little village. In Lagos, especially among his people who worked there, it showed itself in a different way. Their women, when they met at their village meeting were not hostile to Nene. Rather, they paid her such excessive deference as to make her feel she was not one of them. But as time went on, Nene gradually broke through some of this prejudice and even began to make friends among them. Slowly and grudgingly they began to admit that she kept her home much better than most of them.

The story eventually got to the little village in the heart of the Ibo country that Nnaemeka and his young wife were a most happy couple. But his father was one of the few people who knew nothing about this. He always displayed so much temper whenever his son's name was mentioned that everyone avoided it in his presence. By a tremendous effort of will he had succeeded in pushing his son to the back of his mind. The strain had nearly killed him but he had persevered, and won.

Then one day he received a letter from Nene, and in spite of himself he began to glance through it perfunctorily until all of a sudden the expression on his face changed and he began to read more carefully.

> . . . Our two sons, from the day they learnt that they have a grandfather, have insisted on being taken to him. I find it impossible to tell them that you will not see them. I implore you to allow Nnaemeka to bring them home for a short time during his leave next month. I shall remain here in Lagos . . .

The old man at once felt the resolution he had built up over so many years falling in. He was telling himself that he must not give in. He tried to steel his heart against all emotional appeals. It was a reenactment of that other struggle. He leaned against a window and looked out. The sky was overcast with heavy black clouds and a high wind began to blow filling the air with dust and dry leaves. It was one of those rare occasions when even Nature takes a hand in a human fight. Very soon it began to rain, the first rain in the year. It came down in large sharp drops and was accompanied by the lightning and thunder which mark a change of season. Okeke was trying hard not to think of his two grandsons. But he knew he was now fighting a losing battle. He tried to hum a favorite hymn but the pattering of large rain drops on the roof broke up the tune. His mind immediately returned to the children. How could he shut his door against them? By a curious mental process he imagined them standing, sad and forsaken, under the harsh angry weather—shut out from his house.

That night he hardly slept, from remorse—and a vague fear that he might die without making it up to them.

➤ *QUESTIONS FOR READING AND WRITING*

1. At the start of the story Nnaemeka has a letter from his father that he doesn't share with Nene. Why does he conceal its contents? Is he justified in not sharing such information with his fiancée?
2. Nnaemeka's father objects to his marriage to Nene because she is not an Ibo. Are there any groups whose members it would be difficult for you to marry?
3. What do you think of the way that Okeke treats his son and daughter-in-law? Is it ever appropriate to disown a child? How does your culture affect how you answer that question?
4. Throughout the story, Nnaemeka seems optimistic that his father will come to accept his marriage. Do Okeke's reactions to Nene's letter at the end of the story validate his son's optimism? Why?
5. What do you think the rain near the end of the story symbolizes?
6. It is commonly assumed that marriages are based upon love, but even in our society people marry for reasons other than love. Is marriage for a motive other than love justifiable? Might it even be preferable? Explain.

JAMES BALDWIN (1924–1987)

James Baldwin grew up in poverty in Harlem with his mother, eight half-brothers and -sisters, and a stepfather whom he hated. He became a preacher at the age of fourteen, but after graduating from high school he left the ministry disillusioned. Turning to writing, he struggled for over ten years to complete his first novel, the autobiographical Go Tell It on the Mountain *(1953), a publication which instantly made Baldwin one of the most important American writers of his time. In his subsequent work, which included numerous novels, plays, and essays, Baldwin continually explored issues of racial and sexual identity, and the problems of the civil rights movement, often writing of his own experiences of his family and Harlem. Unhappy with racial conditions in the United States, Baldwin spent most of his adult life in Paris, returning to the United States only occasionally.*

SONNY'S BLUES [1957]

I read about it in the paper, in the subway, on my way to work. I read it, and I couldn't believe it, and I read it again. Then perhaps I just stared at it, at the newsprint spelling out his name, spelling out the story. I stared at it in the swinging lights of the subway car, and in the faces and bodies of the people, and in my own face, trapped in the darkness which roared outside.

It was not to be believed and I kept telling myself that, as I walked from the subway station to the high school. And at the same time I couldn't doubt it. I was scared, scared for Sonny. He became real to me again. A great block of ice got settled in my belly and kept melting there slowly all day long, while I taught my classes algebra. It was a special kind of ice. It kept melting, sending trickles of ice water all up and down my veins, but it never got less. Sometimes it hardened and seemed to expand until I felt my guts were going to come spilling out or that I was going to choke or scream. This would always be at a moment when I was remembering some specific thing Sonny had once said or done.

When he was about as old as the boys in my classes his face had been bright and open, there was a lot of copper in it; and he'd had wonderfully direct brown eyes, and great gentleness and privacy. I wondered what he looked like now. He had been picked up, the evening before, in a raid on an apartment downtown, for peddling and using heroin.

I couldn't believe it: but what I mean by that is that I couldn't find any room for it anywhere inside me. I had kept it outside me for a long time. I hadn't wanted to know. I had had suspicions, but I didn't name them, I kept putting them away. I told myself that Sonny was wild, but he wasn't crazy. And he'd always been a good boy, he hadn't ever turned hard or evil or disrespectful, the way kids can, so quick, so quick, especially in Harlem. I didn't want to believe that I'd ever see my brother going down, coming to nothing, all that light in his face gone out, in the condition I'd already seen so many others. Yet it had happened and here I was, talking about algebra to a lot of boys who might, every one of them for all I knew, be popping off needles every time they went to the head. Maybe it did more for them than algebra could.

5 I was sure that the first time Sonny had ever had horse, he couldn't have been much older than these boys were now. These boys, now, were living as we'd been living then, they were growing up with a rush and their heads bumped abruptly against the low ceiling of their actual possibilities. They were filled with rage. All they really knew were two darknesses, the darkness of their lives, which was now closing in on them, and the darkness of the movies, which had blinded them to that other darkness, and in which they now, vindictively, dreamed, at once more together than they were at any other time, and more alone.

When the last bell rang, the last class ended, I let out my breath. It seemed I'd been holding it for all that time. My clothes were wet—I may have looked as though I'd been sitting in a steam bath, all dressed up, all afternoon. I sat alone in the classroom a long time. I listened to the boys outside, downstairs, shouting and cursing and laughing. Their laughter struck me for perhaps the first time. It was not the joyous laughter which—God knows why—one associates with children. It was mocking and insular, its intent was to denigrate. It was disenchanted, and in this, also, lay the authority of their curses. Perhaps I was listening to them because I was thinking about my brother and in them I heard my brother. And myself.

One boy was whistling a tune, at once very complicated and very simple, it seemed to be pouring out of him as though he were a bird, and it sounded very cool and moving through all that harsh, bright air, only just holding its own through all those other sounds.

I stood up and walked over to the window and looked down into the courtyard. It was the beginning of the spring and the sap was rising in the boys. A teacher passed through them every now and again, quickly, as though he or she couldn't wait to get out of that courtyard, to get those boys out of their sight and off their minds. I started collecting my stuff. I thought I'd better get home and talk to Isabel.

The courtyard was almost deserted by the time I got downstairs. I saw this boy standing in the shadow of a doorway, looking just like Sonny. I almost called his name. Then I saw that it wasn't Sonny, but somebody we used to know, a boy from around our block. He'd been Sonny's friend. He'd never been mine, having been too young for me, and, anyway, I'd never liked him. And now, even though he was a grown-up man, he still hung around that block, still spent hours on the street corners, was always high and raggy. I used to run into him from time to time and he'd often work around to asking me for a quarter or fifty cents. He always had some real good excuse, too, and I always gave it to him, I don't know why.

10 But now, abruptly, I hated him. I couldn't stand the way he looked at me, partly like a dog, partly like a cunning child. I wanted to ask him what the hell he was doing in the school courtyard.

He sort of shuffled over to me, and he said, "I see you got the papers. So you already know about it."

"You mean about Sonny? Yes, I already know about it. How come they didn't get you?"

He grinned. It made him repulsive and it also brought to mind what he'd looked like as a kid. "I wasn't there. I stay away from them people."

"Good for you." I offered him a cigarette and I watched him through the smoke. "You come all the way down here just to tell me about Sonny?"

15 "That's right." He was sort of shaking his head and his eyes looked strange, as though they were about to cross. The bright sun deadened his damp dark brown skin and it made his eyes look yellow and showed up the dirt in his kinked hair. He smelled funky. I moved a little away from him and I said, "Well, thanks. But I already know about it and I got to get home."

"I'll walk you a little ways," he said. We started walking. There were a couple of kids still loitering in the courtyard and one of them said goodnight to me and looked strangely at the boy beside me.

"What're you going to do?" he asked me. "I mean, about Sonny?"

"Look. I haven't seen Sonny for over a year, I'm not sure I'm going to do anything. Anyway, what the hell *can* I do?"

"That's right," he said quickly, "ain't nothing you can do. Can't much help old Sonny no more, I guess."

20 It was what I was thinking and so it seemed to me he had no right to say it.

"I'm surprised at Sonny, though," he went on—he had a funny way of talking, he looked straight ahead as though he were talking to himself—"I thought Sonny was a smart boy, I thought he was too smart to get hung."

"I guess he thought so too," I said sharply, "and that's how he got hung. And how about you? You're pretty goddamn smart, I bet."

Then he looked directly at me, just for a minute. "I ain't smart," he said. "If I was smart, I'd have reached for a pistol a long time ago."

"Look. Don't tell *me* your sad story, if it was up to me, I'd give you one." Then I felt guilty—guilty, probably, for never having supposed that the poor bastard *had* a story of his own, much less a sad one, and I asked, quickly, "What's going to happen to him now?"

25 He didn't answer this. He was off by himself some place. "Funny thing," he said, and from his tone we might have been discussing the quickest way to get to Brooklyn, "when I saw the papers this morning, the first thing I asked myself was if I had anything to do with it. I felt sort of responsible."

I began to listen more carefully. The subway station was on the corner, just before us, and I stopped. He stopped, too. We were in front of a bar and he ducked slightly, peering in, but whoever he was looking for didn't seem to be there. The juke box was blasting away with something black and bouncy and I half watched the barmaid as she danced her way from the juke box to her place behind the bar. And I watched her face as she laughingly responded to something someone said to her, still keeping time to the music. When she smiled one saw the little girl, one sensed the doomed, still-struggling woman beneath the battered face of the semiwhore.

"I never *give* Sonny nothing," the boy said finally, "but a long time ago I come to school high and Sonny asked me how it felt." He paused, I couldn't bear to watch him, I watched the barmaid, and I listened to the music which seemed to be causing the pavement to shake. "I told him it felt great." The music stopped, the barmaid paused and watched the juke box until the music began again. "It did."

All this was carrying me some place I didn't want to go. I certainly didn't want to know how it felt. It filled everything, the people, the houses, the music, the dark, quicksilver barmaid, with menace; and this menace was their reality.

"What's going to happen to him now?" I asked again.

"They'll send him away some place and they'll try to cure him." He shook his head. "Maybe he'll even think he's kicked the habit. Then they'll let him loose"—he gestured, throwing his cigarette into the gutter. "That's all."

"What do you mean, that's *all?*"

But I knew what he meant.

"I *mean,* that's *all.*" He turned his head and looked at me, pulling down the corners of his mouth. "Don't you know what I mean?" he asked, softly.

"How the hell *would* I know what you mean?" I almost whispered it, I don't know why.

"That's right," he said to the air, "how would *he* know what I mean?" He turned toward me again, patient and calm, and yet I somehow felt him shaking, shaking as though he were going to fall apart. I felt that ice in my guts again, the dread I'd felt all afternoon; and again I watched the barmaid, moving about the bar, washing glasses, and singing. "Listen. They'll let him out and then it'll just start all over again. That's what I mean."

"You mean—they'll let him out. And then he'll just start working his way back in again. You mean he'll never kick the habit. Is that what you mean?"

"That's right," he said, cheerfully. "*You* see what I mean."

"Tell me," I said at last, "why does he want to die? He must want to die, he's killing himself, why does he want to die?"

He looked at me in surprise. He licked his lips. "He don't want to die. He wants to live. Don't nobody want to die, ever."

Then I wanted to ask him—too many things. He could not have answered, or if he had, I could not have borne the answers. I started walking. "Well, I guess it's none of my business."

"It's going to be rough on old Sonny," he said. We reached the subway station. "This is your station?" he asked. I nodded. I took one step down. "Damn!" he said, suddenly. I looked up at him. He grinned again. "Damn it if I didn't leave all my money home. You ain't got a dollar on you, have you? Just for a couple of days, is all."

All at once something inside gave and threatened to come pouring out of me. I didn't hate him any more. I felt that in another moment I'd start crying like a child.

"Sure," I said. "Don't sweat." I looked in my wallet and didn't have a dollar, I only had a five. "Here," I said. "That hold you?"

He didn't look at it—he didn't want to look at it. A terrible closed look came over his face, as though he were keeping the number on the bill a secret from him and me. "Thanks," he said, and now he was dying to see me go. "Don't worry about Sonny. Maybe I'll write him or something."

"Sure," I said. "You do that. So long."

"Be seeing you," he said. I went on down the steps.

And I didn't write Sonny or send him anything for a long time. When I finally did, it was just after my little girl died, he wrote me back a letter which made me feel like a bastard.

Here's what he said:

> Dear brother,
>
> 50 You don't know how much I needed to hear from you. I wanted to write you many a time but I dug how much I must have hurt you and so I didn't write. But now I feel like a man who's been trying to climb up out of some deep, real deep and funky hole and just saw the sun up there, outside. I got to get outside.
>
> I can't tell you much about how I got here. I mean I don't know how to tell you. I guess I was afraid of something or I was trying to escape from something and you know I have never been very strong in the head (smile). I'm glad Mama and Daddy are dead and can't see what's happened to their son and I swear if I'd known what I was doing I would never have hurt you so, you and a lot of other fine people who were nice to me and who believed in me.
>
> I don't want you to think it had anything to do with me being a musician. It's more than that. Or maybe less than that. I can't get anything straight in my head down here and I try not to think about what's going to happen to me when I get outside again. Sometime I think I'm going to flip and *never* get outside and sometime I think I'll come straight back. I tell you one thing, though, I'd rather blow my brains out than go through this again. But that's what they all say, so they tell me. If I tell you when I'm coming to New York and if you could meet me, I sure would appreciate it. Give my love to Isabel and the kids and I was sure sorry to hear about little Gracie. I wish I could be like Mama and say the Lord's will be done, but I don't know it seems to me that trouble is the one thing that never does get stopped and I don't know what good it does to blame it on the Lord. But maybe it does some good if you believe it.
>
> Your brother,
> Sonny

55 Then I kept in constant touch with him and I sent him whatever I could and I went to meet him when he came back to New York. When I saw him many things I thought I had forgotten came flooding back to me. This was because I had begun, finally, to wonder about Sonny, about the life that Sonny lived inside. This life, whatever it was, had made him older and thinner and it had deepened the distant stillness in which he had always moved. He looked very unlike my baby brother. Yet, when he smiled, when we shook hands, the baby brother I'd never known looked out from the depths of his private life, like an animal waiting to be coaxed into the light.

"How you been keeping?" he asked me.

"All right. And you?"

"Just fine." He was smiling all over his face. "It's good to see you again."

"It's good to see you."

The seven years' difference in our ages lay between us like a chasm: I wondered if these years would ever operate between us as a bridge. I was remembering, and it made it hard to catch my breath, that I had been there when he was born; and I had heard the first words he had ever spoken. When he started to walk, he walked from our mother straight to me. I caught him just before he fell when he took the first steps he ever took in this world.

"How's Isabel?"

"Just fine. She's dying to see you."

"And the boys?"

"They're fine, too. They're anxious to see their uncle."

"Oh, come on. You know they don't remember me."

"Are you kidding? Of course they remember you."

He grinned again. We got into a taxi. We had a lot to say to each other, far too much to know how to begin.

As the taxi began to move, I asked, "You still want to go to India?"

He laughed. "You still remember that. Hell, no. This place is Indian enough for me."

"It used to belong to them," I said.

And he laughed again. "They damn sure knew what they were doing when they got rid of it."

Years ago, when he was around fourteen, he'd been all hipped on the idea of going to India. He read books about people sitting on rocks, naked, in all kinds of weather, but mostly bad, naturally, and walking barefoot through hot coals and arriving at wisdom. I used to say that it sounded to me as though they were getting away from wisdom as fast as they could. I think he sort of looked down on me for that.

"Do you mind," he asked, "if we have the driver drive alongside the park? On the west side—I haven't seen the city in so long."

"Of course not," I said. I was afraid that I might sound as though I were humoring him, but I hoped he wouldn't take it that way.

So we drove along, between the green of the park and the stony, lifeless elegance of hotels and apartment buildings, toward the vivid, killing streets of our childhood. These streets hadn't changed, though housing projects jutted up out of them now like rocks in the middle of a boiling sea. Most of the houses in which we had grown up had vanished, as had the stores from which we had stolen, the basements in which we had first tried sex, the rooftops from which we had hurled tin cans and bricks. But houses exactly like the houses of our past yet dominated the landscape, boys exactly like the boys we once had been found themselves smothering in these houses, came down into the streets for light and air and found themselves encircled by disaster. Some escaped the trap, most didn't. Those who got out always left something of themselves behind, as some animals amputate a leg and leave it in the trap. It might be said, perhaps, that I had escaped, after all, I was a school teacher; or that Sonny had, he hadn't lived in Harlem for years. Yet, as the cab moved uptown through streets which seemed, with a rush, to darken with dark people, and as I covertly studied Sonny's face, it came to me that what we both were seeking through our separate cab windows was that part of ourselves which had been left behind. It's always at the hour of trouble and confrontation that the missing member aches.

We hit 110th Street and started rolling up Lenox Avenue. And I'd known this avenue all my life, but it seemed to me again, as it had seemed on the day I'd first heard about Sonny's trouble, filled with a hidden menace which was its very breath of life.

"We almost there," said Sonny.

"Almost." We were both too nervous to say anything more.

We live in a housing project. It hasn't been up long. A few days after it was up it seemed uninhabitably new, now, of course, it's already rundown. It looks like a parody of the good, clean, faceless life—God knows the people who live in it do their best to make it a parody. The beat-looking grass lying around isn't enough to make their lives green, the hedges will never hold out the streets, and they know it. The big windows fool no one, they aren't big enough to make space out of no space. They don't bother with the windows, they watch the TV screen instead. The playground is most popular with the children who don't play at jacks, or skip rope, or roller skate, or swing, and they can be found in it after dark. We moved in partly because it's not too far from where I teach, and partly for the kids; but it's really just like the houses in which Sonny and I grew up. The same things happen, they'll have the same things to remember. The moment Sonny and I started into the house I had the feeling that I was simply bringing him back into the danger he had almost died trying to escape.

Sonny has never been talkative. So I don't know why I was sure he'd be dying to talk to me when supper was over the first night. Everything went fine, the oldest boy remembered him, and the youngest boy liked him, and Sonny had remembered to bring something for each of them; and Isabel, who is really much nicer than I am, more open and giving, had gone to a lot of trouble about dinner and was genuinely glad to see him. And she's always been able to tease Sonny in a way that I haven't. It was nice to see her face so vivid again and to hear her laugh and watch her make Sonny laugh. She wasn't, or, anyway, she didn't seem to be, at all uneasy or embarrassed. She chatted as though there were no subject which had to be avoided and she got Sonny past his first, faint stiffness. And thank God she was there, for I was filled with that icy dread again. Everything I did seemed awkward to me, and everything I said sounded freighted with hidden meaning. I was trying to remember everything I'd heard about dope addiction and I couldn't help watching Sonny for signs. I wasn't doing it out of malice. I was trying to find out something about my brother. I was dying to hear him tell me he was safe.

"Safe!" my father grunted, whenever Mama suggested trying to move to a neighborhood which might be safer for children. "Safe, hell! Ain't no place safe for kids, nor nobody."

He always went on like this, but he wasn't, ever, really as bad as he sounded, not even on weekends, when he got drunk. As a matter of fact, he was always on the lookout for "something a little better," but he died before he found it. He died suddenly, during a drunken weekend in the middle of the war, when Sonny was fifteen.

He and Sonny hadn't ever got on too well. And this was partly because Sonny was the apple of his father's eye. It was because he loved Sonny so much and was frightened for him, that he was always fighting with him. It doesn't do any good to fight with Sonny. Sonny just moves back, inside himself, where he can't be reached. But the principal reason that they never hit it off is that they were so much alike. Daddy was big and rough and loud-talking, just the opposite of Sonny, but they both had—that same privacy.

Mama tried to tell me something about this, just after Daddy died. I was home on leave from the army.

This was the last time I ever saw my mother alive. Just the same, this picture gets all mixed up in my mind with pictures I had of her when she was younger. The way I always see her is the way she used to be on a Sunday afternoon, say, when the old folks were talking after the big Sunday dinner. I always see her wearing pale blue. She'd be sitting on the sofa. And my father would be sitting in the easy chair, not far from her. And the living room would be full of church folks and relatives. There they sit, in chairs all around the living room, and the night is creeping up outside, but nobody knows it yet. You can see the darkness growing against the windowpanes and you hear the street noises every now and again, or maybe the jangling beat of a tambourine from one of the churches close by, but it's real quiet in the room. For a moment nobody's talking, but every face looks darkening, like the sky outside. And my mother rocks a little from the waist, and my father's eyes are closed. Everyone is looking at something a child can't see. For a minute they've forgotten the children. Maybe a kid is lying on the rug, half asleep. Maybe somebody's got a kid in his lap and is absent-mindedly stroking the kid's head. Maybe there's a kid, quiet and big-eyed, curled up in a big chair in the corner. The silence, the darkness coming, and the darkness in the faces frightens the child obscurely. He hopes that the hand which strokes his forehead will never stop—will never die. He hopes that there will never come a time when the old folks won't be sitting around the living room, talking about where they've come from, and what they've seen, and what's happened to them and their kinfolk.

85 But something deep and watchful in the child knows that this is bound to end, is already ending. In a moment someone will get up and turn on the light. Then the old folks will remember the children and they won't talk any more that day. And when light fills the room, the child is filled with darkness. He knows that every time this happens he's moved just a little closer to that darkness outside. The darkness outside is what the old folks have been talking about. It's what they've come from. It's what they endure. The child knows that they won't talk any more because if he knows too much about what's happened to *them,* he'll know too much too soon, about what's going to happen to *him.*

The last time I talked to my mother, I remember I was restless. I wanted to get out and see Isabel. We weren't married then and we had a lot to straighten out between us.

There Mama sat, in black, by the window. She was humming an old church song, *Lord, you brought me from a long ways off.* Sonny was out somewhere. Mama kept watching the streets.

"I don't know," she said, "if I'll ever see you again, after you go off from here. But I hope you'll remember the things I tried to teach you."

"Don't talk like that," I said, and smiled. "You'll be here a long time yet."

She smiled, too, but she said nothing. She was quiet for a long time. And I said, "Mama, don't you worry about nothing. I'll be writing all the time, and you be getting the checks. . . ."

"I want to talk to you about your brother," she said, suddenly. "If anything happens to me he ain't going to have nobody to look out for him."

"Mama," I said, "ain't nothing going to happen to you *or* Sonny. Sonny's all right. He's a good boy and he's got good sense."

"It ain't a question of his being a good boy," Mama said, "nor of his having good sense. It ain't only the bad ones, nor yet the dumb ones that gets sucked under." She stopped, looking at me. "Your Daddy once had a brother," she said, and she smiled in a way that made me feel she was in pain. "You didn't never know that, did you?"

"No," I said, "I never knew that," and I watched her face.

"Oh, yes," she said, "your Daddy had a brother." She looked out of the window again. "I know you never saw your Daddy cry. But I did—many a time, through all these years."

I asked her, "What happened to his brother? How come nobody's ever talked about him?"

This was the first time I ever saw my mother look old.

"His brother got killed," she said, "when he was just a little younger than you are now. I knew him. He was a fine boy. He was maybe a little full of the devil, but he didn't mean nobody no harm."

Then she stopped and the room was silent, exactly as it had sometimes been on those Sunday afternoons. Mama kept looking out into the streets.

"He used to have a job in the mill," she said, "and, like all young folks, he just liked to perform on Saturday nights. Saturday nights, him and your father would drift around to different places, go to dances and things like that, or just sit around with people they knew, and your father's brother would sing, he had a fine voice, and play along with himself on his guitar. Well, this particular Saturday night, him and your father was coming home from some place, and they were both a little drunk and there was a moon that night, it was bright like day. Your father's brother was feeling kind of good, and he was whistling to himself, and he had his guitar slung over his shoulder. They was coming down a hill and beneath them was a road that turned off from the highway. Well, your father's brother, being always kind of frisky, decided to run down this hill, and he did, with that guitar banging and clanging behind him, and he ran across the road, and he was making water behind a tree. And your father was sort of amused at him and he was still coming down the hill, kind of slow. Then he heard a car motor and that same minute his brother stepped from behind the tree, into the road, in the moonlight. And he started to cross the road. And your father started to run down the hill, he says he don't know why. This car was full of white men. They was all drunk, and when they seen your father's brother they let out a great whoop and holler and they aimed the car straight at him. They was having fun, they just wanted to scare him, the way they do sometimes, you know. But they was drunk. And I guess the boy, being drunk, too, and scared, kind of lost his head. By the time he jumped it was too late. Your father says he heard his brother scream when the car rolled over him, and he heard the wood of that guitar when it give, and he heard them strings go flying, and he heard them white men shouting, and the car kept on a-going and it ain't stopped till this day. And, time your father got down the hill, his brother weren't nothing but blood and pulp."

Tears were gleaming on my mother's face. There wasn't anything I could say.

"He never mentioned it," she said, "because I never let him mention it before you children. Your Daddy was like a crazy man that night and for many a night thereafter. He says he never in his life seen anything as dark as that road after the lights of that car had gone away. Weren't nothing, weren't nobody on that road, just your Daddy and his brother and that busted guitar. Oh, yes. Your Daddy never did really get right again. Till the day he died he weren't sure but that every white man he saw was the man that killed his brother."

She stopped and took out her handkerchief and dried her eyes and looked at me.

"I ain't telling you all this," she said, "to make you scared or bitter or to make you hate nobody. I'm telling you this because you got a brother. And the world ain't changed."

105 I guess I didn't want to believe this. I guess she saw this in my face. She turned away from me, toward the window again, searching those streets.

"But I praise my Redeemer," she said at last, "that He called your Daddy home before me. I ain't saying it to throw no flowers at myself, but, I declare, it keeps me from feeling too cast down to know I helped your father get safely through this world. Your father always acted like he was the roughest, strongest man on earth. And everybody took him to be like that. But if he hadn't had *me* there—to see his tears!"

She was crying again. Still, I couldn't move. I said, "Lord, Lord, Mama, I didn't know it was like that."

"Oh, honey," she said, "there's a lot that you don't know. But you are going to find it out." She stood up from the window and came over to me. "You got to hold on to your brother," she said, "and don't let him fall, no matter what it looks like is happening to him and no matter how evil you gets with him. You going to be evil with him many a time. But don't you forget what I told you, you hear?"

"I won't forget," I said. "Don't you worry, I won't forget. I won't let nothing happen to Sonny."

110 My mother smiled as though she were amused at something she saw in my face. Then, "You may not be able to stop nothing from happening. But you got to let him know you's *there.*"

Two days later I was married, and then I was gone. And I had a lot of things on my mind and I pretty well forgot my promise to Mama until I got shipped home on a special furlough for her funeral.

And, after the funeral, with just Sonny and me alone in the empty kitchen, I tried to find out something about him.

"What do you want to do?" I asked him.

"I'm going to be a musician," he said.

115 For he had graduated, in the time I had been away, from dancing to the juke box to finding out who was playing what, and what they were doing with it, and he had bought himself a set of drums.

"You mean, you want to be a drummer?" I somehow had the feeling that being a drummer might be all right for other people but not for my brother Sonny.

"I don't think," he said, looking at me very gravely, "that I'll ever be a good drummer. But I think I can play a piano."

I frowned. I'd never played the role of the older brother quite so seriously before, had scarcely ever, in fact, *asked* Sonny a damn thing. I sensed myself in the presence of something I didn't really know how to handle, didn't understand. So I made my frown a little deeper as I asked: "What kind of musician do you want to be?"

He grinned. "How many kinds do you think there are?"

120 "Be *serious,*" I said.

He laughed, throwing his head back, and then looked at me. "I *am* serious."

"Well, then, for Christ's sake, stop kidding around and answer a serious question. I mean, do you want to be a concert pianist, you want to play classical music and all that, or—or what?" Long before I finished he was laughing again. "For Christ's *sake,* Sonny!"

He sobered, but with difficulty. "I'm sorry. But you sound so—*scared!*" and he was off again.

"Well, you may think it's funny now, baby, but it's not going to be so funny when you have to make your living at it, let me tell you *that.*" I was furious because I knew he was laughing at me and I didn't know why.

125 "No," he said, very sober now, and afraid, perhaps, that he'd hurt me, "I don't want to be a classical pianist. That isn't what interests me. I mean—" he paused, looking hard at me, as though his eyes would help me to understand, and then gestured helplessly, as though perhaps his hand would help—"I mean, I'll have a lot of studying to do, and I'll have to study *everything,* but, I mean, I want to play *with*—jazz musicians." He stopped. "I want to play jazz," he said.

Well, the word had never before sounded as heavy, as real, as it sounded that afternoon in Sonny's mouth. I just looked at him and I was probably frowning a real frown by this time. I simply couldn't see why on earth he'd want to spend his time hanging around nightclubs, clowning around on bandstands, while people pushed each other around a dance floor. It seemed—beneath him, somehow. I had never thought about it before, had never been forced to, but I suppose I had always put jazz musicians in a class with what Daddy called "good-time people."

"Are you *serious?*"

"Hell, *yes,* I'm serious."

He looked more helpless than ever, and annoyed, and deeply hurt.

130 I suggested, helpfully: "You mean—like Louis Armstrong?"

His face closed as though I'd struck him. "No. I'm not talking about none of that old-time, down home crap."

"Well, look, Sonny, I'm sorry, don't get mad. I just don't altogether get it, that's all. Name somebody—you know, a jazz musician you admire."

"Bird."

"Who?"

135 "Bird! Charlie Parker! Don't they teach you nothing in the goddamn army?"

I lit a cigarette. I was surprised and then a little amused to discover that I was trembling. "I've been out of touch," I said. "You'll have to be patient with me. Now. Who's this Parker character?"

"He's just one of the greatest jazz musicians alive," said Sonny, sullenly, his hands in his pockets, his back to me. "Maybe *the* greatest," he added, bitterly, "that's probably why you never heard of him."

"All right," I said, "I'm ignorant. I'm sorry. I'll go out and buy all the cat's records right away, all right?"

"It don't," said Sonny, with dignity, "make any difference to me. I don't care what you listen to. Don't do me no favors."

140 I was beginning to realize that I'd never seen him so upset before. With another part of my mind I was thinking that this would probably turn out to be one of those things kids go through and that I shouldn't make it seem important by pushing it too hard. Still, I didn't think it would do any harm to ask: "Doesn't all this take a lot of time? Can you make a living at it?"

He turned back to me and half leaned, half sat, on the kitchen table. "Everything takes time," he said, "and—well, yes, sure, I can make a living at it. But what I don't seem to be able to make you understand is that it's the only thing I want to do."

"Well, Sonny," I said, gently, "you know people can't always do exactly what they *want* to do—"

"*No*, I don't know that," said Sonny, surprising me. "I think people *ought* to do what they want to do, what else are they alive for?"

"You getting to be a big boy," I said desperately, "it's time you started thinking about your future."

145 "I'm thinking about my future," said Sonny, grimly. "I think about it all the time."

I gave up. I decided, if he didn't change his mind, that we could always talk about it later. "In the meantime," I said, "you got to finish school." We had already decided that he'd have to move in with Isabel and her folks. I knew this wasn't the ideal arrangement because Isabel's folks are inclined to be dicty and they hadn't especially wanted Isabel to marry me. But I didn't know what else to do. "And we have to get you fixed up at Isabel's."

There was a long silence. He moved from the kitchen table to the window. "That's a terrible idea. You know it yourself."

"Do you have a *better* idea?"

He just walked up and down the kitchen for a minute. He was as tall as I was. He had started to shave. I suddenly had the feeling that I didn't know him at all.

150 He stopped at the kitchen table and picked up my cigarettes. Looking at me with a kind of mocking, amused defiance, he put one between his lips. "You mind?"

"You smoking already?"

He lit the cigarette and nodded, watching me through the smoke. "I just wanted to see if I'd have the courage to smoke in front of you." He grinned and blew a great cloud of smoke to the ceiling. "It was easy." He looked at my face. "Come on, now. I bet you was smoking at my age, tell the truth."

I didn't say anything but the truth was on my face, and he laughed. But now there was something very strained in his laugh. "Sure. And I bet that ain't all you was doing."

He was frightening me a little. "Cut the crap," I said. "We already decided that you was going to go and live at Isabel's. Now what's got into you all of a sudden?"

"*You* decided it," he pointed out. "*I* didn't decide nothing." He stopped in front of me, leaning against the stove, arms loosely folded. "Look, brother. I don't want to stay in Harlem no more, I really don't." He was very earnest. He looked at me, then over toward the kitchen window. There was something in his eyes I'd never seen before, some thoughtfulness, some worry all his own. He rubbed the muscle of one arm. "It's time I was getting out of here."

"Where do you want to go, Sonny?"

"I want to join the army. Or the navy, I don't care. If I say I'm old enough, they'll believe me."

Then I got mad. It was because I was so scared. "You must be crazy. You goddamn fool, what the hell do you want to go and join the *army* for?"

"I just told you. To get out of Harlem."

"Sonny, you haven't even finished *school.* And if you really want to be a musician, how do you expect to study if you're in the *army?*"

He looked at me, trapped, and in anguish. "There's ways. I might be able to work out some kind of deal. Anyway, I'll have the G.I. Bill when I come out."

"*If* you come out." We stared at each other. "Sonny, please. Be reasonable. I know the setup is far from perfect. But we got to do the best we can."

"I ain't learning nothing in school," he said. "Even when I go." He turned away from me and opened the window and threw his cigarette out into the narrow alley. I watched his back. "At least, I ain't learning nothing you'd want me to learn." He slammed the window so hard I thought the glass would fly out, and turned back to me. "And I'm sick of the stink of these garbage cans!"

"Sonny," I said, "I know how you feel. But if you don't finish school now, you're going to be sorry later that you didn't." I grabbed him by the shoulders. "And you only got another year. It ain't so bad. And I'll come back and I swear I'll help you do *whatever* you want to do. Just try to put up with it till I come back. Will you please do that? For me?"

He didn't answer and he wouldn't look at me.

"Sonny. You hear me?"

He pulled away. "I hear you. But you never hear anything I say."

I didn't know what to say to that. He looked out of the window and then back at me. "OK," he said, and sighed. "I'll try."

Then I said, trying to cheer him up a little, "They got a piano at Isabel's. You can practice on it."

170 And as a matter of fact, it did cheer him up for a minute. "That's right," he said to himself. "I forgot that." His face relaxed a little. But the worry, the thoughtfulness, played on it still, the way shadows play on a face which is staring into the fire.

But I thought I'd never hear the end of that piano. At first, Isabel would write me, saying how nice it was that Sonny was so serious about his music and how, as soon as he came in from school, or wherever he had been when he was supposed to be at school, he went straight to that piano and stayed there until suppertime. And, after supper, he went back to that piano and stayed there until everybody went to bed. He was at the piano all day Saturday and all day Sunday. Then he bought a record player and started playing records. He'd play one record over and over again, all day long sometimes, and he'd improvise along with it on the piano. Or he'd play one section of the record, one chord, one change, one progression, then he'd do it on the piano. Then back to the record. Then back to the piano.

Well, I really don't know how they stood it. Isabel finally confessed that it wasn't like living with a person at all, it was like living with sound. And the sound didn't make any sense to her, didn't make any sense to any of them—naturally. They began, in a way, to be afflicted by this presence that was living in their home. It was as though Sonny were some sort of god, or monster. He moved in an atmosphere which wasn't like theirs at all. They fed him and he ate, he washed himself, he walked in and out of their door; he certainly wasn't nasty or unpleasant or rude, Sonny isn't any of those things; but it was as though he were all wrapped up in some cloud, some fire, some vision all his own; and there wasn't any way to reach him.

At the same time, he wasn't really a man yet, he was still a child, and they had to watch out for him in all kinds of ways. They certainly couldn't throw him out. Neither did they dare to make a great scene about that piano because even they dimly sensed, as I sensed, from so many thousands of miles away, that Sonny was at that piano playing for his life.

But he hadn't been going to school. One day a letter came from the school board and Isabel's mother got it—there had, apparently, been other letters but Sonny had torn them up. This day, when Sonny came in, Isabel's mother showed him the letter and asked where he'd been spending his time. And she finally got it out of him that he'd been down in Greenwich Village, with musicians and other characters, in a white girl's apartment. And this scared her and she started to scream at him and what came up, once she began—though she denies it to this day—was what sacrifices they were making to give Sonny a decent home and how little he appreciated it.

175 Sonny didn't play the piano that day. By evening, Isabel's mother had calmed down but then there was the old man to deal with, and Isabel herself. Isabel says she did her best to be calm but she broke down and started crying. She says she just watched Sonny's face. She could tell, by watching him, what was happening with him. And what was happening was that they penetrated his cloud, they had reached him. Even if their fingers had been a thousand times more gentle than human fingers ever are, he could hardly help feeling that they had stripped him naked and were spitting on that nakedness. For he also had to see that his presence, that music, which was life or death to him, had been torture for them and that they had endured it, not at all for his sake, but only for mine. And Sonny couldn't take that.

He can take it a little better today than he could then but he's still not very good at it and, frankly, I don't know anybody who is.

The silence of the next few days must have been louder than the sound of all the music ever played since time began. One morning, before she went to work, Isabel was in his room for something and she suddenly realized that all of his records were gone. And she knew for certain that he was gone. And he was. He went as far as the navy would carry him. He finally sent me a postcard from some place in Greece and that was the first I knew that Sonny was still alive. I didn't see him any more until we were both back in New York and the war had long been over.

He was a man by then, of course, but I wasn't willing to see it. He came by the house from time to time, but we fought almost every time we met. I didn't like the way he carried himself, loose and dreamlike all the time, and I didn't like his friends, and his music seemed to be merely an excuse for the life he led. It sounded just that weird and disordered.

Then we had a fight, a pretty awful fight, and I didn't see him for months. By and by I looked him up, where he was living, in a furnished room in the Village, and I tried to make it up. But there were lots of people in the room and Sonny just lay on his bed, and he wouldn't come downstairs with me, and he treated these other people as though they were his family and I weren't. So I got mad and then he got mad, and then I told him that he might just as well be dead as live the way he was living. Then he stood up and he told me not to worry about him any more in life, that he *was* dead as far as I was concerned. Then he pushed me to the door and the other people looked on as though nothing were happening, and he slammed the door behind me. I stood in the hallway, staring at the door. I heard somebody laugh in the room and then the tears came to my eyes. I started down the steps, whistling to keep from crying, I kept whistling to myself, *You going to need me, baby, one of these cold, rainy days.*

I read about Sonny's trouble in the spring. Little Grace died in the fall. She was a beautiful little girl. But she only lived a little over two years. She died of polio and she suffered. She had a slight fever for a couple of days, but it didn't seem like anything and we just kept her in bed. And we would certainly have called the doctor, but the fever dropped, she seemed to be all right. So we thought it had just been a cold. Then, one day, she was up, playing, Isabel was in the kitchen fixing lunch for the two boys when they'd come in from school, and she heard Grace fall down in the living room. When you have a lot of children you don't always start running when one of them falls, unless they start screaming or something. And, this time, Grace was quiet. Yet, Isabel says that when she heard that *thump* and then that silence, something happened in her to make her afraid. And she ran to the living room and there was little Grace on the floor, all twisted up, and the reason she hadn't screamed was that she couldn't get her breath. And when she did scream, it was the worst sound, Isabel says, that she'd ever heard in all her life, and she still hears it sometimes in her dreams. Isabel will sometimes wake me up with a low, moaning, strangled sound and I have to be quick to awaken her and hold her to me and where Isabel is weeping against me seems a mortal wound.

I think I may have written Sonny the very day that little Grace was buried. I was sitting in the living room in the dark, by myself, and I suddenly thought of Sonny. My trouble made his real.

One Saturday afternoon, when Sonny had been living with us, or, anyway, been in our house, for nearly two weeks, I found myself wandering aimlessly about the living room, drinking from a can of beer, and trying to work up the courage to search Sonny's room. He was out, he was usually out whenever I was home, and Isabel had taken the children to see their grandparents. Suddenly I was standing still in front of the living room window, watching Seventh Avenue. The idea of searching Sonny's room made me still. I scarcely dared to admit to myself what I'd be searching for. I didn't know what I'd do if I found it. Or if I didn't.

On the sidewalk across from me, near the entrance to a barbecue joint, some people were holding an old-fashioned revival meeting. The barbecue cook, wearing a dirty white apron, his conked hair reddish and metallic in the pale sun, and a cigarette between his lips, stood in the doorway, watching them. Kids and older people paused in their errands and stood there, along with some older men and a couple of very tough-looking women who watched everything that happened on the avenue, as though they owned it, or were maybe owned by it. Well, they were watching this, too. The revival was being carried on by three sisters in black, and a brother. All they had were their voices and their Bibles and a tambourine. The brother was testifying and while he testified two of the sisters stood together, seeming to say, amen, and the third sister walked around with the tambourine outstretched and a couple of people dropped coins into it. Then the brother's testimony ended and the sister who had been taking up the collection dumped the coins into her palm and transferred them to the pocket of her long black robe. Then she raised both hands, striking the tambourine against the air, and then against one hand, and she started to sing. And the two other sisters and the brother joined in.

It was strange, suddenly, to watch, though I had been seeing these street meetings all my life. So, of course, had everybody else down there. Yet, they paused and watched and listened and I stood still at the window. "*Tis the old ship of Zion,*" they sang, and the sister with the tambourine kept a steady, jangling beat, "*it has rescued many a thousand!*" Not a soul under the sound of their voices was hearing this song for the first time, not one of them had been rescued. Nor had they seen much in the way of rescue work being done around them. Neither did they especially believe in the holiness of the three sisters and the brother, they knew too much about them, knew where they lived, and how. The woman with the tambourine, whose voice dominated the air, whose face was bright with joy, was divided by very little from the woman who stood watching her, a cigarette between her heavy, chapped lips, her hair a cuckoo's nest, her face scarred and swollen from many beatings, and her black eyes glittering like coal. Perhaps they both knew this, which was why, when, as rarely, they addressed each other, they addressed each other as Sister. As the singing filled the air the watching, listening faces underwent a change, the eyes focusing on something within; the music seemed to soothe a poison out of them; and time seemed, nearly, to fall away from the sullen, belligerent, battered faces, as though they were fleeing back to their first condition, while dreaming of their last. The barbecue cook half shook his head and smiled, and dropped his cigarette and disappeared into his joint. A man fumbled in his pockets for change and stood holding it in his hand impatiently, as though he had just remembered a pressing appointment further up the avenue. He looked furious. Then I saw Sonny, standing on the edge of the crowd. He was carrying a wide, flat notebook with a green cover, and it made him look, from where I was standing, almost like a schoolboy. The coppery sun brought out the copper in his skin, he was very faintly smiling, standing very still. Then the singing stopped, the tambourine turned into a collection plate again. The furious man dropped in his coins and vanished, so did a couple of the women, and Sonny dropped some change in the plate, looking directly at the woman with a little smile. He started across the avenue, toward the house. He has a slow, loping walk, something like the way Harlem hipsters walk, only he's imposed on this his own half-beat. I had never really noticed it before.

I stayed at the window, both relieved and apprehensive. As Sonny disappeared from my sight, they began singing again. And they were still singing when his key turned in the lock.

"Hey," he said.

"Hey, yourself. You want some beer?"

"No. Well, maybe." But he came up to the window and stood beside me, looking out. "What a warm voice," he said.

They were singing *If I could only hear my mother pray again!*

"Yes," I said, "and she can sure beat that tambourine."

"But what a terrible song," he said, and laughed. He dropped his notebook on the sofa and disappeared into the kitchen. "Where's Isabel and the kids?"

"I think they went to see their grandparents. You hungry?"

"No." He came back into the living room with his can of beer. "You want to come some place with me tonight?"

I sensed, I don't know how, that I couldn't possibly say no. "Sure. Where?"

He sat down on the sofa and picked up his notebook and started leafing through it. "I'm going to sit in with some fellows in a joint in the Village."

"You mean, you're going to play, tonight?"

"That's right." He took a swallow of his beer and moved back to the window. He gave me a sidelong look. "If you can stand it."

"I'll try," I said.

He smiled to himself and we both watched as the meeting across the way broke up. The three sisters and the brother, heads bowed, were singing *God be with you till we meet again.* The faces around them were very quiet. Then the song ended. The small crowd dispersed. We watched the three women and the lone man walk slowly up the avenue.

"When she was singing before," said Sonny, abruptly, "her voice reminded me for a minute of what heroin feels like sometimes—when it's in your veins. It makes you feel sort of warm and cool at the same time. And distant. And—and sure." He sipped his beer, very deliberately not looking at me. I watched his face. "It makes you feel—in control. Sometimes you've got to have that feeling."

"Do you?" I sat down slowly in the easy chair.

"Sometimes." He went to the sofa and picked up his notebook again. "Some people do."

"In order," I asked, "to play?" And my voice was very ugly, full of contempt and anger.

"Well"—he looked at me with great, troubled eyes, as though, in fact, he hoped his eyes would tell me things he could never otherwise say—"they *think* so. And *if* they think so—!"

"And what do *you* think?" I asked.

205 He sat on the sofa and put his can of beer on the floor. "I don't know," he said, and I couldn't be sure if he were answering my question or pursuing his thoughts. His face didn't tell me. "It's not so much to *play.* It's to *stand* it, to be able to make it at all. On any level." He frowned and smiled: "In order to keep from shaking to pieces."

"But these friends of yours," I said, "they seem to shake themselves to pieces pretty goddamn fast."

"Maybe." He played with the notebook. And something told me that I should curb my tongue, that Sonny was doing his best to talk, that I should listen. "But of course you only know the ones that've gone to pieces. Some don't—or at least they haven't *yet* and that's just about all *any* of us can say." He paused. "And then there are some who just live, really, in hell, and they know it and they see what's happening and they go right on. I don't know." He sighed, dropped the notebook, folded his arms. "Some guys, you can tell from the way they play, they on something *all* the time. And you can see that, well, it makes something real for them. But of course," he picked up his beer from the floor and sipped it and put the can down again, "they *want* to, too, you've got to see that. Even some of them that say they don't—*some,* not all."

"And what about you?" I asked—I couldn't help it. "What about you? Do *you* want to?"

He stood up and walked to the window and remained silent for a long time. Then he sighed. "Me," he said. Then: "While I was downstairs before, on my way here, listening to that woman sing, it struck me all of a sudden how much suffering she must have had to go through—to sing like that. It's *repulsive* to think you have to suffer that much."

210 I said: "But there's no way not to suffer—is there, Sonny?"

"I believe not," he said and smiled, "but that's never stopped anyone from trying." He looked at me. "Has it?" I realized, with this mocking look, that there stood between us, forever, beyond the power of time or forgiveness, the fact that I had held silence—so long!—when he had needed human speech to help him. He turned back to the window. "No, there's no way not to suffer. But you try all kinds of ways to keep from drowning in it, to keep on top of it, and to make it seem—well, like *you.* Like you did something, all right, and now you're suffering for it. You know?" I said nothing. "Well you know," he said, impatiently, "Why *do* people suffer? Maybe it's better to do something to give it a reason, *any* reason."

"But we just agreed," I said "that there's no way not to suffer. Isn't it better, then, just to—take it?"

"But nobody just takes it," Sonny cried, "that's what I'm telling you! *Everybody* tries not to. You're just hung up on the *way* some people try—it's not *your* way!"

The hair on my face began to itch, my face felt wet. "That's not true," I said, "that's not true. I don't give a damn what other people do, I don't even care how they suffer. I just care how *you* suffer." And he looked at me. "Please believe me," I said, "I don't want to see you—die—trying not to suffer."

"I won't," he said, flatly, "die trying not to suffer. At least, not any faster than anybody else."

"But there's no need," I said, trying to laugh, "is there? in killing yourself."

I wanted to say more, but I couldn't. I wanted to talk about will power and how life could be—well, beautiful. I wanted to say that it was all within; but was it? or, rather, wasn't that exactly the trouble? And I wanted to promise that I would never fail him again. But it would all have sounded—empty words and lies.

So I made the promise to myself and prayed that I would keep it.

"It's terrible sometimes, inside," he said, "that's what's the trouble. You walk these streets, black and funky and cold, and there's not really a living ass to talk to, and there's nothing shaking, and there's no way of getting it out—that storm inside. You can't talk it and you can't make love with it, and when you finally try to get with it and play it, you realize *nobody's* listening. So *you've* got to listen. You got to find a way to listen."

And then he walked away from the window and sat on the sofa again, as though all the wind had suddenly been knocked out of him. "Sometimes you'll do *anything* to play, even cut your mother's throat." He laughed and looked at me. "Or your brother's." Then he sobered. "Or your own." Then: "Don't worry. I'm all right now and I think I'll *be* all right. But I can't forget-where I've been. I don't mean just the physical place I've been, I mean where I've *been*. And *what* I've been."

"What have you been, Sonny?" I asked.

He smiled—but sat sideways on the sofa, his elbow resting on the back, his fingers playing with his mouth and chin, not looking at me. "I've been something I didn't recognize, didn't know I could be. Didn't know anybody could be." He stopped, looking inward, looking helplessly young, looking old. "I'm not talking about it now because I feel *guilty* or anything like that—maybe it would be better if I did, I don't know. Anyway, I can't really talk about it. Not to you, not to anybody," and now he turned and faced me. "Sometimes, you know, and it was actually when I was most *out* of the world, I felt that I was in it, that I was *with* it, really, and I could play or I didn't really have to *play*, it just came out of me, it was there. And I don't know how I played, thinking about it now, but I know I did awful things, those times, sometimes, to people. Or it wasn't that I *did* anything to them—it was that they weren't real." He picked up the beer can; it was empty; he rolled it between his palms: "And other times—well, I needed a fix, I needed to find a place to lean, I needed to clear a space to *listen*—and I couldn't find it, and I—went crazy, I did terrible things to *me*, I was terrible *for* me." He began pressing the beer can between his hands, I watched the metal begin to give. It glittered, as he played with it, like a knife, and I was afraid he would cut himself, but I said nothing. "Oh well. I can never tell you. I was all by myself at the bottom of something, stinking and sweating and crying and shaking, and I smelled it, you know? *my* stink, and I thought I'd die if I couldn't get away from it and yet, all the same, I knew that everything I was doing was just locking me in with it. And I didn't know," he paused, still flattening the beer can, "I didn't know, I still *don't* know, something kept telling me that maybe it was good to smell your own stink, but I didn't think that *that* was what I'd been trying to do—and—who can stand it?" and he abruptly dropped the ruined beer can, looking at me with a small, still smile, and then rose, walking to the window as though it were the lodestone rock. I watched his face, he watched the avenue. "I couldn't tell you when Mama died—but the reason I wanted to leave Harlem so bad was to get away from drugs. And then, when I ran away, that's what I was running from—really. When I came back, nothing had changed, I hadn't changed, I was just—older." And he stopped, drumming with his fingers on the windowpane. The sun had vanished, soon darkness would fall. I watched his face. "It can come again," he said, almost as though speaking to himself. Then he turned to me. "It can come again," he repeated. "I just want you to know that."

"All right," I said, at last. "So it can come again. All right."

He smiled, but the smile was sorrowful. "I had to try to tell you," he said.

"Yes," I said. "I understand that."

"You're my brother," he said, looking straight at me, and not smiling at all.

"Yes," I repeated, "yes. I understand that."

He turned back to the window, looking out. "All that hatred down there," he said, "all that hatred and misery and love. It's a wonder it doesn't blow the avenue apart."

We went to the only nightclub on a short, dark street, downtown. We squeezed through the narrow, chattering, jam-packed bar to the entrance of the big room, where the bandstand was. And we stood there for a moment, for the lights were very dim in this room and we couldn't see. Then, "Hello, boy," said a voice and an enormous black man, much older than Sonny or myself, erupted out of all that atmospheric lighting and put an arm around Sonny's shoulder. "I been sitting right here," he said, "waiting for you."

He had a big voice, too, and heads in the darkness turned toward us.

Sonny grinned and pulled a little away, and said, "Creole, this is my brother. I told you about him."

Creole shook my hand. "I'm glad to meet you, son," he said, and it was clear that he was glad to meet me *there*, for Sonny's sake. And he smiled, "You got a real musician in *your* family," and he took his arm from Sonny's shoulder and slapped him, lightly, affectionately, with the back of his hand.

"Well. Now I've heard it all," said a voice behind us. This was another musician, and a friend of Sonny's, a coal-black, cheerful-looking man, built close to the ground. He immediately began confiding to me, at the top of his lungs, the most terrible things about Sonny, his teeth gleaming like a lighthouse and his laugh coming up out of him like the beginning of an earthquake. And it turned out that everyone at the bar knew Sonny, or almost everyone; some were musicians, working there, or nearby, or not working, some were simply hangers-on, and some were there to hear Sonny play. I was introduced to all of them and they were all very polite to me. Yet, it was clear that, for them, I was only Sonny's brother. Here, I was in Sonny's world. Or, rather: his kingdom. Here, it was not even a question that his veins bore royal blood.

They were going to play soon and Creole installed me, by myself, at a table in a dark corner. Then I watched them, Creole, and the little black man, and Sonny, and the others, while they horsed around, standing just below the bandstand. The light from the bandstand spilled just a little short of them and, watching them laughing and gesturing and moving about, I had the feeling that they, nevertheless, were being most careful not to step into that circle of light too suddenly: that if they moved into the light too suddenly, without thinking, they would perish in flame. Then, while I watched, one of them, the small, black man, moved into the light and crossed the bandstand and started fooling around with his drums. Then—being funny and being, also, extremely ceremonious—Creole took Sonny by the arm and led him to the piano. A woman's voice called Sonny's name and a few hands started clapping. And Sonny, also being funny and being ceremonious, and so touched, I think, that he could have cried, but neither hiding it nor showing it, riding it like a man, grinned, and put both hands to his heart and bowed from the waist.

Creole then went to the bass fiddle and a lean, very bright-skinned brown man jumped up on the bandstand and picked up his horn. So there they were, and the atmosphere on the bandstand and in the room began to change and tighten. Someone stepped up to the microphone and announced them. Then there were all kinds of murmurs. Some people at the bar shushed others. The waitress ran around, frantically getting in the last orders, guys and chicks got closer to each other, and the lights on the bandstand, on the quartet, turned to a kind of indigo. Then they all looked different there. Creole looked about him for the last time, as though he were making certain that all his chickens were in the coop, and then he—jumped and struck the fiddle. And there they were.

All I know about music is that not many people ever really hear it. And even then, on the rare occasions when something opens within, and the music enters, what we mainly hear, or hear corroborated, are personal, private, vanishing evocations. But the man who creates the music is hearing something else, is dealing with the roar rising from the void and imposing order on it as it hits the air. What is evoked in him, then, is of another order, more terrible because it has no words, and triumphant, too, for that same reason. And his triumph, when he triumphs, is ours. I just watched Sonny's face. His face was troubled, he was working hard, but he wasn't with it. And I had the feeling that, in a way, everyone on the bandstand was waiting for him, both waiting for him and pushing him along. But as I began to watch Creole, I realized that it was Creole who held them all back. He had them on a short rein. Up there, keeping the beat with his whole body, wailing on the fiddle, with his eyes half closed, he was listening to everything, but he was listening to Sonny. He was having a dialogue with Sonny. He wanted Sonny to leave the shoreline and strike out for the deep water. He was Sonny's witness that deep water and drowning were not the same thing—he had been there, and he knew. And he wanted Sonny to know. He was waiting for Sonny to do the things on the keys which would let Creole know that Sonny was in the water.

And, while Creole listened, Sonny moved, deep within, exactly like someone in torment. I had never before thought of how awful the relationship must be between the musician and his instrument. He has to fill it, this instrument, with the breath of life, his own. He has to make it do what he wants it to do. And a piano is just a piano. It's made out of so much wood and wires and little hammers and big ones, and ivory. While there's only so much you can do with it, the only way to find this out is to try; to try and make it do everything.

And Sonny hadn't been near a piano for over a year. And he wasn't on much better terms with his life, not the life that stretched before him now. He and the piano stammered, started one way, got scared, stopped; started another way, panicked, marked time, started again; then seemed to have found a direction, panicked again, got stuck. And the face I saw on Sonny I'd never seen before. Everything had been burned out of it, and, at the same time, things usually hidden were being burned in, by the fire and fury of the battle which was occurring in him up there.

Yet, watching Creole's face as they neared the end of the first set, I had the feeling that something had happened, something I hadn't heard. Then they finished, there was scattered applause, and then, without an instant's warning, Creole started into something else, it was almost sardonic, it was *Am I Blue.* And, as though he commanded, Sonny began to play. Something began to happen. And Creole let out the reins. The dry, low, black man said something awful on the drums, Creole answered, and the drums talked back. Then the horn insisted, sweet and high, slightly detached perhaps, and Creole listened, commenting now and then, dry, and driving, beautiful and calm and old. Then they all came together again, and Sonny was part of the family again. I could tell this from his face. He seemed to have found, right there beneath his fingers, a damn brand-new piano. It seemed that he couldn't get over it. Then, for awhile, just being happy with Sonny, they seemed to be agreeing with him that brand-new pianos certainly were a gas.

240 Then Creole stepped forward to remind them that what they were playing was the blues. He hit something in all of them, he hit something in me, myself, and the music tightened and deepened, apprehension began to beat the air. Creole began to tell us what the blues were all about. They were not about anything very new. He and his boys up there were keeping it new, at the risk of ruin, destruction, madness, and death, in order to find new ways to make us listen. For, while the tale of how we suffer, and how we are delighted, and how we may triumph is never new, it always must be heard. There isn't any other tale to tell, it's the only light we've got in all this darkness.

And this tale, according to that face, that body, those strong hands on those strings, has another aspect in every country, and a new depth in every generation. Listen, Creole seemed to be saying, listen. Now these are Sonny's blues. He made the little black man on the drums know it, and the bright, brown man on the horn. Creole wasn't trying any longer to get Sonny in the water. He was wishing him Godspeed. Then he stepped back, very slowly, filling the air with the immense suggestion that Sonny speak for himself.

Then they all gathered around Sonny and Sonny played. Every now and again one of them seemed to say, amen. Sonny's fingers filled the air with life, his life. But that life contained so many others. And Sonny went all the way back, he really began with the spare, flat statement of the opening phrase of the song. Then he began to make it his. It was very beautiful because it wasn't hurried and it was no longer a lament. I seemed to hear with what burning he had made it his, with what burning we had yet to make it ours, how we could cease lamenting. Freedom lurked around us and I understood, at last, that he could help us to be free if we would listen, that he would never be free until we did. Yet, there was no battle in his face now. I heard what he had gone through, and would continue to go through until he came to rest in earth. He had made it his: that long line, of which we knew only Mama and Daddy. And he was giving it back, as everything must be given back, so that, passing through death, it can live forever. I saw my mother's face again, and felt, for the first time, how the stones of the road she had walked on must have bruised her feet. I saw the moonlit road where my father's brother died. And it brought something else back to me, and carried me past it. I saw my little girl again and felt Isabel's tears again, and I felt my own tears begin to rise. And I was yet aware that this was only a moment, that the world waited outside, as hungry as a tiger, and that trouble stretched above us, longer than the sky.

Then it was over. Creole and Sonny let out their breath, both soaking wet, and grinning. There was a lot of applause and some of it was real. In the dark, the girl came by and I asked her to take drinks to the bandstand. There was a long pause, while they talked up there in the indigo light and after awhile I saw the girl put a Scotch and milk on top of the piano for Sonny. He didn't seem to notice it, but just before they started playing again, he sipped from it and looked toward me, and nodded. Then he put it back on top of the piano. For me, then, as they began to play again, it glowed and shook above my brother's head like the very cup of trembling.

➤ *QUESTIONS FOR READING AND WRITING*

1. Who is the narrator? What kind of relationship does he have with Sonny?
2. How does the tale of the narrator's father and his father's brother shed light on this story?
3. How would you interpret the statement: "All they knew were two darknesses, the darkness of their lives, which was now closing in on them, and the darkness of the movies, which had blinded them to that other darkness?"
4. Why do you think the narrator writes to Sonny after his daughter, Gracie, dies? What does he mean, "My trouble made his real"?
5. Describe the relationship between Sonny and his music? Why does it mean so much to him?
6. The relationship between Sonny and his brother changes. What helps the narrator to understand Sonny better?
7. In what way do you think "Sonny's Blues" is an appropriate title for this story?

LOUISE ERDRICH (b. 1954)

The daughter of a Chippewa Indian mother and a German-American father, Louise Erdrich was raised in Wahpeton, North Dakota, near the Turtle Mountain Reservation. Her parents both worked in the Bureau of Indian Affairs boarding school. From an early age, she was encouraged to write stories (she says: "My father used to give me a nickel for every story I wrote"). She graduated from Dartmouth College in 1976 and earned an M.A. from Johns Hopkins University in 1979. Her works include Love Medicine *(1984, and an expanded edition, 1993),* The Beet Queen *(1986),* Tracks *(1988),* The Crown of Columbus *(1991), which she coauthored with her late husband, Michael Dorris, and* The Bingo Palace *(1995). Her most recent novel* The Antelope Wife *was published in 1998.*

THE RED CONVERTIBLE [1984]

Lyman Lamartine

I was the first one to drive a convertible on my reservation. And of course it was red, a red Olds. I owned that car along with my brother Henry Junior. We owned it together until his boots filled with water on a windy night and he bought out my share. Now Henry owns the whole car, and his youngest brother Lyman (that's myself), Lyman walks everywhere he goes.

How did I earn enough money to buy my share in the first place? My own talent was I could always make money. I had a touch for it, unusual in a Chippewa. From the first I was different that way, and everyone recognized it. I was the only kid they let in the American Legion Hall to shine shoes, for example, and one Christmas I sold spiritual bouquets for the mission door to door. The nuns let me keep a percentage. Once I started, it seemed the more money I made the easier the money came. Everyone encouraged it. When I was fifteen I got a job washing dishes at the Joliet Café, and that was where my first big break happened.

It wasn't long before I was promoted to busing tables, and then the order-order cook quit and I was hired to take her place. No sooner than you know it I was managing the Joliet. The rest is history. I went on managing. I soon became part owner, and of course there was no stopping me then. It wasn't long before the whole thing was mine.

After I'd owned the Joliet for one year, it blew over in the worst tornado ever seen around here. The whole operation was smashed to bits. A total loss. The fryalator was up in a tree, the grill torn in half like it was paper. I was only sixteen. I had it all in my mother's name, and I lost it quick, but before I lost it I had every one of my relatives, and their relatives, to dinner, and I also bought that red Olds I mentioned, along with Henry.

The first time we saw it! I'll tell you when we first saw it. We had gotten a ride up to Winnipeg, and both of us had money. Don't ask me why, because we never mentioned a car or anything, we just had all our money. Mine was cash, a big bankroll from the Joliet's insurance. Henry had two checks—a week's extra pay for being laid off, and his regular check from the Jewel Bearing Plant.

We were walking down Portage anyway, seeing the sights, when we saw it. There it was, parked, large as life. Really as *if* it was alive. I thought of the word *repose,* because the car wasn't simply stopped, parked, or whatever. That car reposed, calm and gleaming, a FOR SALE sign in its left front window. Then, before we had thought it over at all, the car belonged to us and our pockets were empty. We had just enough money for gas back home.

We went places in that car, me and Henry. We took off driving all one whole summer. We started off toward the Little Knife River and Mandaree in Fort Berthold and then we found ourselves down in Wakpala somehow, and then suddenly we were over in Montana on the Rocky Boy, and yet the summer was not even half over. Some people hang on to details when they travel, but we didn't let them bother us and just lived our everyday lives here to there.

I do remember this one place with willows. I remember I laid under those trees and it was comfortable. So comfortable. The branches bent down all around me like a tent or a stable. And quiet, it was quiet, even though there was a powwow close enough so I could see it going on. The air was not too still, not too windy either. When the dust rises up and hangs in the air around the dancers like that, I feel good. Henry was asleep with his arms thrown wide. Later on, he woke up and we started driving again. We were somewhere in Montana, or maybe on the Blood Reserve—it could have been anywhere. Anyway it was where we met the girl.

All her hair was in buns around her ears, that's the first thing I noticed about her. She was posed alongside the road with her arm out, so we stopped. That girl was short, so short her lumber shirt looked comical on her, like a nightgown. She had jeans on and fancy moccasins and she carried a little suitcase.

"Hop on in," says Henry. So she climbs in between us.

"We'll take you home," I says. "Where do you live?"

"Chicken," she says.

"Where the hell's that?" I ask her.

"Alaska."

"Okay," says Henry, and we drive.

We got up there and never wanted to leave. The sun doesn't truly set there in summer, and the night is more of soft dusk. You might doze off, sometimes, but before you know it you're up again, like an animal in nature. You never feel like you have to sleep hard or put away the world. And things would grow up there. One day just dirt or moss, the next day flowers and long grass. The girl's name was Susy. Her family really took to us. They fed us and put us up. We had our own tent to live in by their house, and the kids would be in and out of there all day and night. They couldn't get over me and Henry being brothers, we looked so different. We told them we know we had the same mother, anyway.

One night Susy came in to visit us. We sat around in the tent talking of this and that. The season was changing. It was getting darker by that time, and the cold was even getting just a little mean. I told her it was time for us to go. She stood up on a chair.

"You never seen my hair," Susy said.

That was true. She was standing on a chair, but still, when she unclipped her buns the hair reached all the way to the ground. Our eyes opened. You couldn't tell how much hair she had when it was rolled up so neatly. Then my brother Henry did something funny. He went up to the chair and said, "Jump on my shoulders." So she did that, and her hair reached down past his waist, and he started twirling, this way and that, so her hair was flung out from side to side.

"I always wondered what it was like to have long pretty hair," Henry says. Well we laughed. It was a funny sight, the way he did it. The next morning we got up and took leave of those people.

On to greener pastures, as they say. It was down through Spokane and across Idaho then Montana and very soon we were racing the weather right along under the Canadian border through Columbus, Des Lacs, and then we were in Bottineau County and soon home. We'd made most of the trip, that summer, without putting up the car hood at all. We got home just in time, it turned out, for the army to remember Henry had signed up to join it.

I don't wonder that the army was so glad to get my brother that they turned him into a Marine. He was built like a brick outhouse anyway. We liked to tease him that they really wanted him for his Indian nose. He had a nose big and sharp as a hatchet, like the nose on Red Tomahawk, the Indian who killed Sitting Bull, whose profile is on signs all along the North Dakota highways. Henry went off to training camp, came home once during Christmas, then the next thing you know we got an overseas letter from him. It was 1970, and he said he was stationed up in the northern hill country. Whereabouts I did not know. He wasn't such a hot letter writer, and only got off two before the enemy caught him. I could never keep it straight, which direction those good Vietnam soldiers were from.

I wrote him back several times, even though I didn't know if those letters would get through. I kept him informed all about the car. Most of the time I had it up on blocks in the yard or half taken apart, because that long trip did a hard job on it under the hood.

I always had good luck with numbers, and never worried about the draft myself. I never even had to think about what my number was. But Henry was never lucky in the same way as me. It was at least three years before Henry came home. By then I guess the whole war was solved in the government's mind, but for him it would keep on going. In those years I'd put his car into almost perfect shape. I always thought of it as his car while he was gone, even though when he left he said, "Now it's yours," and threw me his key.

25 "Thanks for the extra key," I'd said. "I'll put it up in your drawer just in case I need it." He laughed.

When he came home, though, Henry was very different, and I'll say this: the change was no good. You could hardly expect him to change for the better, I know. But he was quiet, so quiet, and never comfortable sitting still anywhere but always up and moving around. I thought back to times we'd sat still for whole afternoons, never moving a muscle, just shifting our weight along the ground, talking to whoever sat with us, watching things. He'd always had a joke, then, too, and now you couldn't get him to laugh, or when he did it was more the sound of a man choking, a sound that stopped up the throats of other people around him. They got to leaving him alone most of the time, and I didn't blame them. It was a fact: Henry was jumpy and mean.

I'd bought a color TV set for my mom and the rest of us while Henry was away. Money still came very easy. I was sorry I'd ever bought it though, because of Henry. I was also sorry I'd bought color, because with black-and-white pictures seem older and farther away. But what are you going to do? He sat in front of it, watching it, and that was the only time he was completely still. But it was the kind of stillness that you see in a rabbit when it freezes and before it will bolt. He was not easy. He sat in his chair gripping the armrests with all his might, as if the chair itself was moving at a high speed and if he let go at all he would rocket forward and maybe crash right through the set.

Once I was in the room watching TV with Henry and I heard his teeth click at something. I looked over, and he'd bitten through his lip. Blood was going down his chin. I tell you right then I wanted to smash that tube to pieces. I went over to it but Henry must have known what I was up to. He rushed from his chair and shoved me out of the way, against the wall. I told myself he didn't know what he was doing.

My mom came in, turned the set off real quiet, and told us she had made something for supper. So we went and sat down. There was still blood going down Henry's chin, but he didn't notice it and no one said anything, even though every time he took a bite of his bread his blood fell onto it until he was eating his own blood mixed in with the food.

30 While Henry was not around we talked about what was going to happen to him. There were no Indian doctors on the reservation, and my mom couldn't come around to trusting the old man, Moses Pillager, because he courted her long ago and was jealous of her husbands. He might take revenge through her son. We were afraid that if we brought Henry to a regular hospital they would keep him.

"They don't fix them in those places," Mom said; "they just give them drugs."

"We wouldn't get him there in the first place," I agree, "so let's just forget about it."

Then I thought about the car.

Henry had not even looked at the car since he'd gotten home, though like I said, it was in tip-top condition and ready to drive. I thought the car might bring the old Henry back somehow. So I bided my time and waited for my chance to interest him in the vehicle.

35 One night Henry was off somewhere. I took myself a hammer. I went out to that car and I did a number on its underside. Whacked it up. Bent the tail pipe double. Ripped the muffler loose. By the time I was done with the car it looked worse than any typical Indian car that has been driven all its life on reservation roads, which they always say are like government promises—full of holes. It just about hurt me, I'll tell you that! I threw dirt in the carburetor and I ripped all the electric tape off the seats. I made it look just as beat up as I could. Then I sat back and waited for Henry to find it.

Still, it took him over a month. That was all right, because it was just getting warm enough, not melting, but warm enough to work outside.

"Lyman," he says, walking in one day, "that red car looks like shit."

"Well it's old," I says. "You got to expect that."

"No way!" says Henry. "That car's a classic! But you went and ran the piss right out of it, Lyman, and you know it don't deserve that. I kept that car in A-one shape. You don't remember. You're too young. But when I left, that car was running like a watch. Now I don't even know if I can get it to start again, let alone get it anywhere near its old condition."

40 "Well you try," I said, like I was getting mad, "but I say it's a piece of junk."

Then I walked out before he could realize I knew he'd strung together more than six words at once.

After that I thought he'd freeze himself to death working on that car. He was out there all day, and at night he rigged up a little lamp, ran a cord out the window, and had himself some light to see by while he worked. He was better than he had been before, but that's still not saying much. It was easier for him to do the things the rest of us did. He ate more slowly and didn't jump up and down during the meal to get this or that or look out the window. I put my hand in the back of the TV set, I admit, and fiddled around with it good, so that it was almost impossible now to get a clear picture. He didn't look at it very often anyway. He was always out with that car or going off to get parts for it. By the time it was really melting outside, he had it fixed.

I had been feeling down in the dumps about Henry around this time. We had always been together before. Henry and Lyman. But he was such a loner now that I didn't know how to take it. So I jumped at the chance one day when Henry seemed friendly. It's not that he smiled or anything. He just said, "Let's take that old shitbox for a spin." Just the way he said it made me think he could be coming around.

We went out to the car. It was spring. The sun was shining very bright. My only sister, Bonita, who was just eleven years old, came out and made us stand together for a picture. Henry leaned his elbow on the red car's windshield, and he took his other arm and put it over my shoulder, very carefully, as though it was heavy for him to lift and he didn't want to bring the weight down all at once.

45 "Smile," Bonita said, and he did.

That picture. I never look at it anymore. A few months ago, I don't know why, I got his picture out and tacked it on the wall. I felt good about Henry at the time, close to him. I felt good having his picture on the wall, until one night when I was looking at television. I was a little drunk and stoned. I looked up at the wall and Henry was staring at me. I don't know what it was, but his smile had changed, or maybe it was gone. All I know is I couldn't stay in the same room with that picture. I was shaking. I got up, closed the door, and went into the kitchen. A little later my friend Ray came over and we both went back into that room. We put the picture in a brown bag, folded the bag over and over tightly, then put it way back in a closet.

I still see that picture now, as if it tugs at me, whenever I pass that closet door. The picture is very clear in my mind. It was so sunny that day Henry had to squint against the glare. Or maybe the camera Bonita held flashed like a mirror, blinding him, before she snapped the picture. My face is right out in the sun, big and round. But he might have drawn back, because the shadows on his face are deep as holes. There are two shadows curved like little hooks around the ends of his smile, as if to frame it and try to keep it there—that one, first smile that looked like it might have hurt his face. He has his field jacket on and the worn-in clothes he'd come back in and kept wearing ever since. After Bonita took the picture, she went into the house and we got into the car. There was a full cooler in the trunk. We started off, east, toward Pembina and the Red River because Henry said he wanted to see the high water.

The trip over there was beautiful. When everything starts changing, drying up, clearing off, you feel like your whole life is starting. Henry felt it, too. The top was down and the car hummed like a top. He'd really put it back in shape, even the tape on the seats was very carefully put down and glued back in layers. It's not that he smiled again or even joked, but his face looked to me as if it was clear, more peaceful. It looked as though he wasn't thinking of anything in particular except the bare fields and windbreaks and houses we were passing.

The river was high and full of winter trash when we got there. The sun was still out, but it was colder by the river. There were still little clumps of dirty snow here and there on the banks. The water hadn't gone over the banks yet, but it would, you could tell. It was just at its limit, hard swollen, glossy like an old gray scar. We made ourselves a fire, and we sat down and watched the current go. As I watched it I felt something squeezing inside me and tightening and trying to let go all at the same time. I knew I was not just feeling it myself; I knew I was feeling what Henry was going through at that moment. Except that I couldn't stand it, the closing and opening. I jumped to my feet. I took Henry by the shoulders and I started shaking him. "Wake up," I says, "wake up, wake up, wake up!" I didn't know what had come over me. I sat down beside him again.

His face was totally white and hard. Then it broke, like stones break all of a sudden when water boils up inside them.

"I know it," he says. "I know it. I can't help it. It's no use."

We start talking. He said he knew what I'd done with the car. It was obvious it had been whacked out of shape and not just neglected. He said he wanted to give the car to me for good now, it was no use. He said he'd fixed it just to give it back and I should take it.

"No way," I says. "I don't want it."

"That's okay," he says, "you take it."

55 "I don't want it, though," I says back to him, and then to emphasize, just to emphasize, you understand, I touch his shoulder. He slaps my hand off.

"Take that car," he says.

"No," I say. "Make me," I say, and then he grabs my jacket and rips the arm loose. That jacket is a class act, suede with tags and zippers. I push Henry backwards, off the log. He jumps up and bowls me over. We go down in a clinch and come up swinging hard, for all we're worth, with our fists. He socks my jaw so hard I feel like it swings loose. Then I'm at his rib cage and land a good one under his chin so his head snaps back. He's dazzled. He looks at me and I look at him and then his eyes are full of tears and blood and at first I think he's crying. But no, he's laughing. "Ha! Ha!" he says. "Ha! Ha! Take good care of it."

"Okay," I says. "Okay, no problem. Ha! Ha!"

I can't help it, and I start laughing, too. My face feels fat and strange, and after a while I get a beer from the cooler in the trunk, and when I hand it to Henry he takes his shirt and wipes my germs off. "Hoof and mouth disease," he says. For some reason this cracks me up, and so we're really laughing for a while, and then we drink all the rest of the beers one by one and throw them in the river and see how far, how fast, the current takes them before they fill up and sink.

60 "You want to go on back?" I ask after a while. "Maybe we could snag a couple nice Kashpaw girls."

He says nothing. But I can tell his mood is turning again.

"They're all crazy, the girls up here, every damn one of them."

"You're crazy too," I say, to jolly him up. "Crazy Lamartine boys!"

He looks as though he will take this wrong at first. His face twists, then clears. And he jumps up on his feet. "That's right!" he says. "Crazier 'n hell. Crazy Indians!"

65 I think it's the old Henry again. He throws off his jacket and starts springing his legs up from the knees like a fancy dancer. He's doing something between a grass dance and a bunny hop, no kind of dance I ever saw before, but neither has anyone else on all this green growing earth. He's wild. He wants to pitch whoopee! He's up and at me and all over. All this time I'm laughing so hard, so hard my belly is getting tied up in a knot.

"Got to cool me off!" he shouts all of a sudden. Then he runs over to the river and jumps in.

There's boards and other things in the current. It's so high. No sound comes from the river after the splash he makes, so I run right over. I look around. It's getting dark. I see he's halfway across the water already, and I know he didn't swim there but the current took him. It's far. I hear his voice, though, very clearly across it.

"My boots are filling," he says.

He says this in a normal voice, like he just noticed and he doesn't know what to think of it. Then he's gone. A branch comes by. Another branch. And I go in.

70 By the time I get out of the river, off the snag I pulled myself onto, the sun is down. I walk back to the car, turn on the high beams, and drive it up the bank. I put

it in first gear and then I take my foot off the clutch. I get out, close the door, and watch it plow softly into the water. The headlights reach in as they go down, searching, still lighted even after the water swirls over the back end. I wait. The wires short out. It is all finally dark. And then there is only the water, the sound of it going and running and going and running and running.

➤ QUESTIONS FOR READING AND WRITING

1. In the first paragraph the narrator, Lyman, says of the red convertible: "We owned it together until his boots filled up with water." Were you puzzled by this comment? In what way does it make sense at the end of the story?
2. Why do you suppose Lyman refers to himself in the third person at the end of the first paragraph?
3. What do you think happened to Henry in Vietnam that changed him?
4. Why is the red convertible so important to Lyman? To Henry? To their relationship?
5. Why does Lyman push the car into the water after Henry?

D. H. LAWRENCE (1885–1930)

D[avid] H[erbert] Lawrence was born in Nottinghamshire, England. In the largely autobiographical novel Sons and Lovers *(1913), Lawrence wrote about his difficult childhood as the son of a coarse (and often drunken) coal miner and an overprotective and demanding mother. After earning a teaching degree while on a scholarship at Nottingham University College in 1908, Lawrence taught school while he worked on his first novel,* The White Peacock *(1910) and published his first poems and short stories in the* English Review. *In 1912, he quit teaching after meeting and falling in love with Frieda von Richthofen, the sister of the German flying ace, the Red Baron. They were married in 1914, following her divorce. In 1915, Lawrence published his novel,* The Rainbow, *the story of three generations of a family in Nottinghamshire. Like much of his following work, the novel was extremely controversial for its frank depiction of sexual relationships and was banned by the English courts. Lawrence spent the rest of his life in self-imposed exile with his wife, traveling around the world. Though he wrote numerous novels, poems, and essays, many critics consider Lawrence's best work to be his short stories.*

The Horse Dealer's Daughter [1922]

"Well, Mabel, and what are you going to do with yourself?" asked Joe, with foolish flippancy. He felt quite safe himself. Without listening for an answer, he turned aside, worked a grain of tobacco to the tip of his tongue and spat it out. He did not care about anything, since he felt safe himself.

The three brothers and the sister sat round the desolate breakfast table, attempting some sort of desultory consultation. The morning's post had given the final tap to the family fortune, and all was over. The dreary dining room itself, with its heavy mahogany furniture, looked as if it were waiting to be done away with.

But the consultation amounted to nothing. There was a strange air of ineffectuality about the three men, as they sprawled at table, smoking and reflecting vaguely on their own condition. The girl was alone, a rather short, sullen-looking young woman of twenty-seven. She did not share the same life as her brothers. She would have been good-looking, save for the impassive fixity of her face, "bull-dog," as her brothers called it.

There was a confused tramping of horses' feet outside. The three men all sprawled round in their chairs to watch. Beyond the dark hollybushes that separated the strip of lawn from the highroad, they could see a cavalcade of shire horses swinging out of their own yard, being taken for exercise. This was the last time. These were the last horses that would go through their hands. The young men watched with critical, callous looks. They were all frightened at the collapse of their lives, and the sense of disaster in which they were involved left them no inner freedom.

5 Yet they were three fine, well-set fellows enough. Joe, the eldest, was a man of thirty-three, broad and handsome in a hot, flushed way. His face was red, he twisted his black moustache over a thick finger, his eyes were shallow and restless. He had a sensual way of uncovering his teeth when he laughed, and his bearing was stupid. Now he watched the horses with a glazed look of helplessness in his eyes, a certain stupor of downfall.

The great draught-horses swung past. They were tied head to tail, four of them, and they heaved along to where a lane branched off from the highroad, planting their great hoofs floutingly in the fine black mud, swinging their great rounded haunches sumptuously, and trotting a few sudden steps as they were led into the lane, round the corner. Every movement showed a massive, slumbrous strength, and a stupidity which held them in subjection. The groom at the head looked back, jerking the leading rope. And the cavalcade moved out of sight up the lane, the tail of the last horse, bobbed up tight and stiff, held out taut from the swinging great haunches as they rocked behind the hedges in a motion like sleep.

Joe watched with glazed hopeless eyes. The horses were almost like his own body to him. He felt he was done for now. Luckily he was engaged to a woman as old as himself, and therefore her father, who was steward of a neighboring estate, would provide him with a job. He would marry and go into harness. His life was over, he would be a subject animal now.

He turned uneasily aside, the retreating steps of the horses echoing in his ears. Then, with foolish restlessness, he reached for the scraps of bacon-rind from the plates, and making a faint whistling sound, flung them to the terrier that lay against the fender. He watched the dog swallow them, and waited till the creature looked into his eyes. Then a faint grin came on his face, and in a high, foolish voice he said:

"You won't get much more bacon, shall you, you little bitch?"

The dog faintly and dismally wagged its tail, then lowered its haunches, circled round, and lay down again.

There was another helpless silence at the table. Joe sprawled uneasily in his seat, not willing to go till the family conclave was dissolved. Fred Henry, the second brother, was erect, clean-limbed, alert. He had watched the passing of the horses with more sangfroid. If he was an animal, like Joe, he was an animal which controls, not one which is controlled. He was master of any horse, and he carried himself with a well-tempered air of mastery. But he was not master of the situations of life. He pushed his coarse brown moustache upwards, off his lip, and glanced irritably at his sister, who sat impassive and inscrutable.

"You'll go and stop with Lucy for a bit, shan't you?" he asked. The girl did not answer.

"I don't see what else you can do," persisted Fred Henry.

"Go as a skivvy," Joe interpolated laconically.

The girl did not move a muscle.

"If I was her, I should go in for training for a nurse," said Malcolm, the youngest of them all. He was the baby of the family, a young man of twenty-two, with a fresh, jaunty *museau.*[1]

But Mabel did not take any notice of him. They had talked at her and round her for so many years, that she hardly heard them at all.

The marble clock on the mantelpiece softly chimed the half-hour, the dog rose uneasily from the hearthrug and looked at the party at the breakfast table. But still they sat on in ineffectual conclave.

"Oh, all right," said Joe suddenly, apropos of nothing. "I'll get a move on."

He pushed back his chair, straddled his knees with a downward jerk, to get them free, in horsey fashion, and went to the fire. Still he did not go out of the room; he was curious to know what the others would do or say. He began to charge his pipe, looking down at the dog and saying, in a high, affected voice:

"Going wi' me? Going wi' me are ter? Tha'rt goin' further than tha counts on just now, dost hear?"

The dog faintly wagged its tail, the man stuck out his jaw and covered his pipe with his hands, and puffed intently, losing himself in the tobacco, looking down all the while at the dog with an absent brown eye. The dog looked at him in mournful distrust. Joe stood with his knees stuck out, in real horsey fashion.

"Have you had a letter from Lucy?" Fred Henry asked of his sister.

"Last week," came the neutral reply.

"And what does she say?"

There was no answer.

"Does she *ask* you to go and stop there?" persisted Fred Henry.

"She says I can if I like."

[1] **museau** muzzle or snout; slang for "face"

"Well, then, you'd better. Tell her you'll come on Monday."

This was received in silence.

"That's what you'll do then, is it?" said Fred Henry, in some exasperation.

But she made no answer. There was a silence of futility and irritation in the room. Malcolm grinned fatuously.

"You'll have to make up your mind between now and next Wednesday," said Joe loudly, "or else find yourself lodgings on the kurbstone."

The face of the young woman darkened, but she sat on immutable.

"Here's Jack Fergusson!" exclaimed Malcolm, who was looking aimlessly out of the window.

"Where?" exclaimed Joe, loudly.

"Just gone past."

"Coming in?"

Malcolm craned his neck to see the gate.

"Yes," he said.

There was a silence. Mabel sat on like one condemned, at the head of the table. Then a whistle was heard from the kitchen. The dog got up and barked sharply. Joe opened the door and shouted:

"Come on."

After a moment a young man entered. He was muffled up in overcoat and a purple woolen scarf, and his tweed cap, which he did not remove, was pulled down on his head. He was of medium height, his face was rather long and pale, his eyes looked tired.

"Hello, Jack! Well, Jack!" exclaimed Malcolm and Joe. Fred Henry merely said, "Jack."

"What's doing?" asked the newcomer, evidently addressing Fred Henry.

"Same. We've got to be out by Wednesday. Got a cold?"

"I have—got it bad, too."

"Why don't you stop in?"

"*Me* stop in? When I can't stand on my legs, perhaps I shall have a chance." The young man spoke huskily. He had a slight Scotch accent.

"It's a knock-out, isn't it," said Joe, boisterously, "if a doctor goes round croaking with a cold. Looks bad for the patients, doesn't it?"

The young doctor looked at him slowly.

"Anything the matter with *you,* then?" he asked sarcastically.

"Not as I know of. Damn your eyes. I hope not. Why?"

"I thought you were very concerned about the patients, wondered if you might be one yourself."

"Damn it, no, I've never been patient to no flaming doctor, and hope I never shall be," returned Joe.

At this point Mabel rose from the table, and they all seemed to become aware of her existence. She began putting the dishes together. The young doctor looked at her, but did not address her. He had not greeted her. She went out of the room with the tray, her face impassive and unchanged.

"When are you off then, all of you?" asked the doctor.

"I'm catching the eleven-forty," replied Malcolm. "Are you goin down wi' th' trap, Joe?"

"Yes, I've told you I am going down wi' th' trap, haven't I?"

"We'd better be getting her in then. So long, Jack, if I don't see you before I go," said Malcolm, shaking hands.

He went out, followed by Joe, who seemed to have his tail between his legs.

"Well, this is the devil's own," exclaimed the doctor, when he was left alone with Fred Henry. "Going before Wednesday, are you?"

"That's the orders," replied the other.

"Where, to Northampton?"

"That's it."

"The devil!" exclaimed Fergusson, with quiet chagrin.

And there was silence between the two.

"All settled up, are you?" asked Fergusson.

"About."

There was another pause.

"Well, I shall miss yer, Freddy, boy," said the young doctor.

"And I shall miss thee, Jack," returned the other.

"Miss you like hell," mused the doctor.

Fred Henry turned aside. There was nothing to say. Mabel came in again, to finish clearing the table.

"What are *you* going to do, then, Miss Pervin?" asked Fergusson. "Going to your sister's, are you?"

Mabel looked at him with her steady, dangerous eyes, that always made him uncomfortable, unsettling his superficial ease.

"No," she said.

"Well, what in the name of fortune are *you* going to do? Say what you mean to do," cried Fred Henry, with futile intensity.

But she only averted her head, and continued her work. She folded the white table-cloth, and put on the chenile cloth.

"The sulkiest bitch that ever trod!" muttered her brother.

But she finished her task with perfectly impassive face, the young doctor watching her interestedly all the while. Then she went out.

Fred Henry stared after her, clenching his lips, his blue eyes fixing in sharp antagonism, as he made a grimace of sour exasperation.

"You could bray her into bits, and that's all you'd get out of her," he said in a small, narrowed tone.

The doctor smiled faintly.

"What's she *going* to do, then?" he asked.

"Strike me if I know!" returned the other.

There was a pause. Then the doctor stirred.

"I'll be seeing you to-night, shall I?" he said to his friend.

"Ay—where's it to be? Are we going over to Jessdale?"

"I don't know. I've got such a cold on me. I'll come round to the Moon and Stars, anyway."

"Let Lizzie and May miss their night for once, eh?"

"That's it—if I feel as I do now."

"All's one—"

The two young men went through the passage and down to the back door together. The house was large, but it was servantless now, and desolate. At the back was a small bricked house-yard, and beyond that a big square, graveled fine and red, and having stables on two sides. Sloping, dank, winter-dark fields stretched away on the open sides.

But the stables were empty. Joseph Pervin, the father of the family, had been a man of no education, who had become a fairly large horse dealer. The stables had been full of horses, there was a great turmoil and come-and-go of horses and of dealers and grooms. Then the kitchen was full of servants. But of late things had declined. The old man had married a second time, to retrieve his fortunes. Now he was dead and everything was gone to the dogs, there was nothing but debt and threatening.

For months, Mabel had been servantless in the big house, keeping the home together in penury for her ineffectual brothers. She had kept house for ten years. But previously it was with unstinted means. Then, however brutal and coarse everything was, the sense of money had kept her proud, confident. The men might be foul-mouthed, the women in the kitchen might have bad reputations, her brothers might have illegitimate children. But so long as there was money, the girl felt herself established, and brutally proud, reserved.

No company came to the house, save dealers and coarse men. Mabel had no associates of her own sex, after her sister went away. But she did not mind. She went regularly to church, she attended to her father. And she lived in the memory of her mother, who had died when she was fourteen, and whom she had loved. She had loved her father, too, in a different way, depending upon him, and feeling secure in him, until at the age of fifty-four he married again. And then she had set hard against him. Now he had died and left them all hopelessly in debt.

She had suffered badly during the period of poverty. Nothing, however, could shake the curious sullen, animal pride that dominated each member of the family. Now, for Mabel, the end had come. Still she would not cast about her. She would follow her own way just the same. She would always hold the keys of her own situation. Mindless and persistent, she endured from day to day. Why should she think? Why should she answer anybody? It was enough that this was the end, and there was no way out. She need not pass any more darkly along the main street of the small town, avoiding every eye. She need not demean herself any more, going into the shops and buying the cheapest food. This was at an end. She thought of nobody, not even of herself. Mindless and persistent, she seemed in a sort of ecstasy to be coming nearer to her fulfillment, her own glorification, approaching her dead mother, who was glorified.

In the afternoon she took a little bag, with shears and sponge and a small scrubbing brush, and went out. It was a gray, wintry day, with saddened, dark green fields and an atmosphere blackened by the smoke of foundries not far off. She went quickly, darkly along the causeway, heeding nobody, through the town to the churchyard.

100 There she always felt secure, as if no one could see her, although as a matter of fact she was exposed to the stare of every one who passed along under the churchyard wall. Nevertheless, once under the shadow of the great looming church, among the graves, she felt immune from the world, reserved within the thick churchyard wall as in another country.

Carefully she clipped the grass from the grave, and arranged the pinky white, small chrysanthemums in the tin cross. When this was done, she took an empty jar from a neighboring grave, brought water, and carefully, most scrupulously sponged the marble head-stone and the coping-stone.

It gave her sincere satisfaction to do this. She felt in immediate contact with the world of her mother. She took minute pains, went through the park in a state bordering on pure happiness, as if in performing this task she came into a subtle, intimate connection with her mother. For the life she followed here in the world was far less real than the world of death she inherited from her mother.

The doctor's house was just by the church. Fergusson, being a mere hired assistant, was slave to the country-side. As he hurried now to attend to the out-patients in the surgery, glancing across the graveyard with his quick eyes, he saw the girl at her task at the grave. She seemed so intent and remote, it was like looking into another world. Some mystical element was touched in him. He slowed down as he walked, watching her as if spellbound.

She lifted her eyes, feeling him looking. Their eyes met. And each looked away again at once, each feeling, in some way, found out by the other. He lifted his cap and passed on down the road. There remained distinct in his consciousness, like a vision, the memory of her face, lifted from the tombstone in the churchyard, and looking at him with slow, large, portentous eyes. It *was* portentous, her face. It seemed to mesmerize him. There was a heavy power in her eyes which laid hold of his whole being, as if he had drunk some powerful drug. He had been feeling weak and done before. Now the life came back into him, he felt delivered from his own fretted, daily self.

105 He finished his duties at the surgery as quickly as might be, hastily filling up the bottles of the waiting people with cheap drugs. Then, in perpetual haste, he set off again to visit several cases in another part of his round, before tea-time. At all times he preferred to walk if he could, but particularly when he was not well. He fancied the motion restored him.

The afternoon was falling. It was gray, deadened, and wintry, with a slow, moist, heavy coldness sinking in and deadening all the faculties. But why should he think or notice? He hastily climbed the hill and turned across the dark green fields, following the black cindertrack. In the distance, across a shallow dip in the country, the small town was clustered like smouldering ash, a tower, a spire, a heap of low, raw, extinct houses. And on the nearest fringe of the town, sloping into the dip, was Oldmeadow, the Pervins's house. He could see the stables and the outbuildings distinctly, as they lay towards him on the slope. Well, he would not go there many more times! Another resource would be lost to him, another place gone: the only company he cared for in the alien, ugly little town he was losing. Nothing but work, drudgery, constant hastening from dwelling to dwelling among the colliers and the ironworkers. It wore him out, but at the same time he had a craving for it. It was a stimulant to him to be in the homes of the working people, moving as it were through the innermost body of their life. His nerves were excited and gratified. He could come so near, into the very lives of the rough, inarticulate, powerfully emotional men and women. He grumbled, he said he hated the hellish hole. But as a matter of fact it excited him, the contact with the rough, strongly-feeling people was a stimulant applied direct to his nerves.

Below Oldmeadow, in the green, shallow, soddened hollow of fields, lay a square, deep pond. Roving across the landscape, the doctor's quick eye detected a figure in black passing through the gate of the field, down towards the pond. He looked again. It would be Mabel Pervin. His mind suddenly became alive and attentive.

Why was she going down there? He pulled up on the path on the slope above, and stood staring. He could just make sure of the small black figure moving in the hollow of the failing day. He seemed to see her in the midst of such obscurity, that he was like a clairvoyant, seeing rather with the mind's eye than with ordinary sight. Yet he could see her positively enough, while he kept his eye attentive. He felt, if he looked away from her, in the thick, ugly falling dusk, he would lose her altogether.

He followed her minutely as she moved, direct and intent, like something transmitted rather than stirring in voluntary activity, straight down the field towards the pond. There she stood on the bank for a moment. She never raised her head. Then she waded slowly into the water.

110 He stood motionless as the small black figure walked slowly and deliberately towards the center of the pond, very slowly, gradually moving deeper into the motionless water, and still moving forward as the water got up to her breast. Then he could see her no more in the dusk of the dead afternoon.

"There!" he exclaimed. "Would you believe it?"

And he hastened straight down, running over the wet soddened fields, pushing through the hedges, down into the depression of callous wintry obscurity. It took him several minutes to come to the pond. He stood on the bank, breathing heavily. He could see nothing. His eyes seemed to penetrate the dead water. Yes, perhaps that was the dark shadow of her black clothing beneath the surface of the water.

He slowly ventured into the pond. The bottom was deep, soft clay, he sank in, and the water clasped dead cold round his legs. As he stirred he could smell the cold, rotten clay that fouled up into the water. It was objectionable in his lungs. Still, repelled and yet not heeding, he moved deeper into the pond. The cold water rose over his thighs, over his loins, upon his abdomen. The lower part of his body was all sunk in the hideous cold element. And the bottom was so deeply soft and uncertain he was afraid of pitching with his mouth underneath. He could not swim, and was afraid.

He crouched a little, spreading his hands under the water and moving them round, trying to feel for her. The dead cold pond swayed upon his chest. He moved again, a little deeper, and again, with his hands underneath, he felt all around under the water. And he touched her clothing. But it evaded his fingers. He made a desperate effort to grasp it.

115 And so doing he lost his balance and went under, horribly, suffocating in the foul earthy water, struggling madly for a few moments. At last, after what seemed an

eternity, he got his footing, rose again into the air and looked around. He gasped, and knew he was in the world. Then he looked at the water. She had risen near him. He grasped her clothing, and drawing her nearer, turned to take his way to land again.

He went very slowly, carefully, absorbed in the slow progress. He rose higher, climbing out of the pond. The water was now only about his legs: he was thankful, full of relief to be out of the clutches of the pond. He lifted her and staggered on to the bank, out of the horror of wet, gray clay.

He laid her down on the bank. She was quite unconscious and running with water. He made the water come from her mouth, he worked to restore her. He did not have to work very long before he could feel the breathing begin again in her: she was breathing naturally. He worked a little longer. He could feel her live beneath his hands: she was coming back. He wiped her face, wrapped her in his overcoat, looked round into the dim, dark gray world, then lifted her and staggered down the bank and across the fields.

It seemed an unthinkably long way, and his burden so heavy he felt he would never get to the house. But at last he was in the stable-yard, and then in the house-yard. He opened the door and went into the house. In the kitchen he laid her down on the hearthrug, and called. The house was empty. But the fire was burning in the grate.

Then again he kneeled to attend to her. She was breathing regularly, her eyes were wide open and as if conscious, but there seemed something missing in her look. She was conscious in herself, but unconscious of her surroundings.

120 He ran upstairs, took blankets from a bed, and put them before the fire to warm. Then he removed her saturated, earthy-smelling clothing, rubbed her dry with a towel, and wrapped her naked in the blankets. Then he went into the dining-room, to look for spirits. There was a little whisky. He drank a gulp himself, and put some into her mouth.

The effect was instantaneous. She looked full into his face, as if she had been seeing him for some time, and yet had only just become conscious of him.

"Dr. Fergusson?" she said.

"What?" he answered.

He was divesting himself of his coat, intending to find some dry clothing upstairs. He could not bear the smell of the dead, clayey water, and he was mortally afraid of his own health.

125 "What did I do?" she asked.

"Walked into the pond," he replied. He had begun to shudder like one sick, and could hardly attend to her. Her eyes remained full on him, he seemed to be going dark in his mind, looking back at her helplessly. The shuddering became quieter in him, his life came back in him, dark and unknowing, but strong again.

"Was I out of my mind?" she asked, while her eyes were fixed on him all the time.

"Maybe, for the moment," he replied. He felt quiet, because his strength came back. The strange fretful strain had left him.

"Am I out of my mind now?" she asked.

130 "Are you?" he reflected a moment. "No." he answered truthfully. "I don't see that you are." He turned his face aside. He was afraid now, because he felt dazed, and felt

dimly that her power was stronger than his, in this issue. And she continued to look at him fixedly all the time. "Can you tell me where I shall find some dry things to put on?" he asked.

"Did you dive into the pond for me?" she asked.

"No," he answered. "I walked in. But I went in overhead as well."

There was silence for a moment. He hesitated. He very much wanted to go upstairs to get into dry clothing. But there was another desire in him. And she seemed to hold him. His will seemed to have gone to sleep, and left him, standing there slack before her. But he felt warm inside himself. He did not shudder at all, though his clothes were sodden on him.

"Why did you?" she asked.

"Because I didn't want you to do such a foolish thing," he said.

"It wasn't foolish," she said, still gazing at him as she lay on the floor, with a sofa cushion under her head. "It was the right thing to do. *I* knew best, then."

"I'll go and shift these wet things," he said. But still he had not the power to move out of her presence, until she sent him. It was as if she had the life of his body in her hands, and he could not extricate himself. Or perhaps he did not want to.

Suddenly she sat up. Then she became aware of her own immediate condition. She felt the blankets about her, she knew her own limbs.

For a moment it seemed as if her reason were going. She looked round, with wild eye, as if seeking something. He stood still with fear. She saw her clothing lying scattered.

"Who undressed me?" she asked, her eyes resting full and inevitable on his face.

"I did," he replied, "to bring you round."

For some moments she sat and gazed at him awfully, her lips parted.

"Do you love me, then?" she asked.

He only stood and stared at her, fascinated. His soul seemed to melt.

She shuffled forward on her knees, and put her arms round him, round his legs, as he stood there, pressing her breasts against his knees and thighs, clutching him with strange, convulsive certainty, pressing his thighs against her, drawing him to her face, her throat, as she looked up at him with flaring, humble eyes of transfiguration, triumphant in first possession.

"You love me," she murmured, in strange transport, yearning and triumphant and confident. "You love me. I know you love me, I know."

And she was passionately kissing his knees, through the wet clothing, passionately and indiscriminately kissing his knees, his legs, as if unaware of everything.

He looked down at the tangled wet hair, the wild, bare, animal shoulders. He was amazed, bewildered, and afraid. He had never thought of loving her. He had never wanted to love her. When he rescued her and restored her, he was a doctor, and she was a patient. He had had no single personal thought of her. Nay, this introduction of the personal element was very distasteful to him, a violation of his professional honor. It was horrible to have her there embracing his knees. It was horrible. He revolted from it, violently. And yet—and yet—he had not the power to break away.

She looked at him again, with the same supplication of powerful love, and that same transcendent, frightening light of triumph. In view of the delicate flame which seemed to come from her face like a light, he was powerless. And yet he had never intended to love her. He had never intended. And something stubborn in him could not give way.

"You love me," she repeated, in a murmur of deep, rhapsodic assurance. "You love me."

Her hands were drawing him, drawing him down to her. He was afraid, even a little horrified. For he had, really, no intention of loving her. Yet her hands were drawing him towards her. He put out his hand quickly to steady himself, and grasped her bare shoulder. A flame seemed to burn the hand that grasped her soft shoulder. He had no intention of loving her: his whole will was against his yielding. It was horrible. And yet wonderful was the touch of her shoulders, beautiful the shining of her face. Was she perhaps mad? He had a horror of yielding to her. Yet something in him ached also.

He had been staring away at the door, away from her. But his hand remained on her shoulder. She had gone suddenly very still. He looked down at her. Her eyes were now wide with fear, with doubt, the light was dying from her face, a shadow of terrible grayness was returning. He could not bear the touch of her eyes' question upon him, and the look of death behind the question.

With an inward groan he gave way, and let his heart yield towards her. A sudden gentle smile came on his face. And her eyes, which never left his face, slowly, slowly filled with tears. He watched the strange water rise in her eyes, like some slow fountain coming up. And his heart seemed to burn and melt away in his breast.

He could not bear to look at her any more. He dropped on his knees and caught her head with his arms and pressed her face against his throat. She was very still. His heart, which seemed to have broken, was burning with a kind of agony in his breast. And he felt her slow, hot tears wetting his throat. But he could not move.

He felt the hot tears wet his neck and the hollows of his neck, and he remained motionless, suspended through one of man's eternities. Only now it had become indispensable to him to have her face pressed close to him; he could never let her go again. He could never let her head go away from the close clutch of his arm. He wanted to remain like that for ever, with his heart hurting him in a pain that was also life to him. Without knowing, he was looking down on her damp, soft brown hair.

Then, as it were suddenly, he smelt the horrid stagnant smell of that water. And at the same moment she drew away from him and looked at him. Her eyes were wistful and unfathomable. He was afraid of them, and he fell to kissing her, not knowing what he was doing. He wanted her eyes not to have that terrible, wistful, unfathomable look.

When she turned her face to him again, a faint delicate flush was glowing, and there was again dawning that terrible shining of joy in her eyes, which really terrified him, and yet which he now wanted to see, because he feared the look of doubt still more.

"You love me?" she said, rather faltering.

"Yes." The word cost him a painful effort. Not because it wasn't true. But because it was too newly true, the *saying* seemed to tear open again his newly torn heart. And he hardly wanted it to be true, even now.

160 She lifted her face to him, and he bent forward and kissed her on the mouth, gently, with the one kiss that is an eternal pledge. And as he kissed her his heart strained again in his breast. He never intended to love her. But now it was over. He had crossed over the gulf to her, and all that he had left behind had shriveled and become void.

After the kiss, her eyes again slowly filled with tears. She sat still, away from him, with her face drooped aside, and her hands folded in her lap. The tears fell very slowly. There was complete silence. He too sat there motionless and silent on the hearthrug. The strange pain of his heart that was broken seemed to consume him. That he should love her? That this was love! That he should be ripped open in this way! Him, a doctor! How they would all jeer if they knew! It was agony to him to think they might know.

In the curious naked pain of the thought he looked again to her. She was sitting there drooped into a muse. He saw a tear fall, and his heart flared hot. He saw for the first time that one of her shoulders was quite uncovered, one arm bare, he could see one of her small breasts; dimly, because it had become almost dark in the room.

"Why are you crying?" he asked, in an altered voice.

She looked up at him, and behind her tears the consciousness of her situation for the first time brought a dark look of shame to her eyes.

165 "I'm not crying, really," she said, watching him half frightened.

He reached his hand, and softly closed it on her bare arm.

"I love you! I love you!" he said in a soft, low vibrating voice, unlike himself.

She shrank, and dropped her head. The soft, penetrating grip of his hand on her arm distressed her. She looked up at him.

"I want to go," she said. "I want to go and get you some dry things."

170 "Why?" he said. "I'm all right."

"But I want to go," she said. "And I want you to change your things."

He released her arm, and she wrapped herself in the blanket, looking at him rather frightened. And still she did not rise.

"Kiss me," she said wistfully.

He kissed her, but briefly, half in anger.

175 Then, after a second, she rose nervously, all mixed up in the blanket. He watched her in her confusion, as she tried to extricate herself and wrap herself up so that she could walk. He watched her relentlessly, as she knew. And as she went, the blanket trailing, and as he saw a glimpse of her feet and her white leg, he tried to remember her as she was when he had wrapped her in the blanket. But then he didn't want to remember, because she had been nothing to him then, and his nature revolted from remembering her as she was when she was nothing to him.

A tumbling, muffled noise from within the dark house startled him. Then he heard her voice:—"There are clothes." He rose and went to the foot of the stairs, and gathered up the garments she had thrown down. Then he came back to the fire, to rub himself down and dress. He grinned at his own appearance when he had finished.

The fire was sinking, so he put on coal. The house was now quite dark, save for the light of a street-lamp that shone in faintly from beyond the holly trees. He lit the gas with matches he found on the mantelpiece. Then he emptied the pockets of his own clothes, and threw all his wet things in a heap into the scullery. After which he gathered up her sodden clothes, gently, and put them in a separate heap on the copper-top in the scullery.

It was six o'clock on the clock. His own watch had stopped. He ought to go back to the surgery. He waited, and still she did not come down. So he went to the foot of the stairs and called:

"I shall have to go."

Almost immediately he heard her coming down. She had on her best dress of black voile, and her hair was tidy, but still damp. She looked at him—and in spite of herself, smiled.

"I don't like you in those clothes," she said.

"Do I look a sight?" he answered.

They were shy of one another.

"I'll make you some tea," she said.

"No, I must go."

"Must you?" And she looked at him again with the wide, strained, doubtful eyes. And again, from the pain of his breast, he knew how he loved her. He went and bent to kiss her, gently, passionately, with his heart's painful kiss.

"And my hair smells so horrible," she murmured in distraction. "And I'm so awful, I'm so awful! Oh, no, I'm too awful." And she broke into bitter, heart-broken sobbing. "You can't want to love me, I'm horrible."

"Don't be silly, don't be silly," he said, trying to comfort her, kissing her, holding her in his arms. "I want you, I want to marry you, we're going to be married, quickly, quickly—tomorrow if I can."

But she only sobbed terribly, and cried:

"I feel awful. I feel awful. I feel I'm horrible to you."

"No, I want you, I want you," was all he answered, blindly, with that terrible intonation which frightened her almost more than her horror lest he should *not* want her.

➤ *QUESTIONS FOR READING AND WRITING*

1. In what way is the setting of the story a factor? How would you describe the surroundings and their effect on Mabel and Fergusson?
2. Describe Mabel. What is her everyday existence like? How is she treated by her father and brothers? In what ways does she differ from them?
3. Describe Fergusson. What is his everyday existence like?
4. What is the conflict in this story? To what extent is it related to setting and characterization?
5. At the end of the story Fergusson cries out, "I want you, I want you." Why does he seem to want Mabel so much? Do you think they are really in love? Explain.

TILLIE OLSEN (b. 1913)

Tillie Olsen was born in Omaha, Nebraska. Her parents had immigrated from Russia, fleeing czarist persecution for their socialist views. Forced to quit school after the eleventh grade, she went to work to help support her family. Olsen married in 1936, and she spent the following twenty years raising her four children and working full-time in a series of secretarial jobs. She wrote at odd moments at work, or late at night after her children had gone to bed. Except for a few poems and a short story published before her marriage, Olsen published nothing until "I Stand here Ironing" appeared in 1954. Though her stories have appeared in numerous publications, her only volume of short stories to date, Tell Me a Riddle, *was published in 1961. In 1974, she completed a novel,* Yonnonido, *which she started when she was nineteen and had put aside for over thirty years. Olsen has held teaching positions at many institutions, including UCLA, Stanford, the Massachusetts Institute of Technology, and Kenyon College.*

I STAND HERE IRONING [1961]

I stand here ironing, and what you asked me moves tormented back and forth with the iron.

"I wish you would manage the time to come in and talk with me about your daughter. I'm sure you can help me understand her. She's a youngster who needs help and whom I'm deeply interested in helping."

"Who needs help." . . . Even if I came, what good would it do? You think because I am her mother I have a key, or that in some way you could use me as a key? She has lived for nineteen years. There is all that life that has happened outside of me, beyond me.

And when is there time to remember, to sift, to weigh, to estimate, to total? I will start and there will be an interruption and I will have to gather it all together again. Or I will become engulfed with all I did or did not do, with what should have been and what cannot be helped.

5 She was a beautiful baby. The first and only one of our five that was beautiful at birth. You do not guess how new and uneasy her tenancy in her now-loveliness. You did not know her all those years she was thought homely, or see her poring over her baby pictures, making me tell her over and over how beautiful she had been—and would be, I would tell her—and was now, to the seeing eye. But the seeing eyes were few or nonexistent. Including mine.

I nursed her. They feel that's important nowadays. I nursed all the children, but with her, with all the fierce rigidity of first motherhood, I did like the books then said. Though her cries battered me to trembling and my breasts ached with swollenness, I waited till the clock decreed.

Why do I put that first? I do not even know if it matters, or if it explains anything.

She was a beautiful baby. She blew shining bubbles of sound. She loved motion, loved light, loved color and music and textures. She would lie on the floor in her blue overalls patting the surface so hard in ecstasy her hands and feet would blur. She was a miracle to me, but when she was eight months old I had to leave her daytimes with the woman downstairs to whom she was no miracle at all, for I worked or looked for work and for Emily's father, who "could no longer endure" (he wrote in his good-bye note) "sharing want with us."

I was nineteen. It was the pre-relief, pre-WPA world of the depression. I would start running as soon as I got off the streetcar, running up the stairs, the place smelling sour, and awake or asleep to startle awake, when she saw me she would break into a clogged weeping that could not be comforted, a weeping I can hear yet.

10 After a while I found a job hashing at night so I could be with her days, and it was better. But it came to where I had to bring her to his family and leave her.

It took a long time to raise the money for her fare back. Then she got chicken pox and I had to wait longer. When she finally came, I hardly knew her, walking quick and nervous like her father, looking like her father, thin, and dressed in a shoddy red that yellowed her skin and glared at the pockmarks. All the baby loveliness gone.

She was two. Old enough for nursery school they said, and I did not know then what I know now—the fatigue of the long day, and the lacerations of group life in the kinds of nurseries that are only parking places for children.

Except that it would have made no difference if I had known. It was the only place there was. It was the only way we could be together, the only way I could hold a job.

And even without knowing, I knew. I knew the teacher that was evil because all these years it has curdled into my memory, the little boy hunched in the corner, her rasp, "why aren't you outside, because Alvin hits you? that's no reason, go out, scaredy." I knew Emily hated it even if she did not clutch and implore "don't go Mommy" like the other children, mornings.

15 She always had a reason why we should stay home. Momma, you look sick. Momma, I feel sick. Momma, the teachers aren't there today, they're sick. Momma, we can't go, there was a fire there last night. Momma, it's a holiday today, no school, they told me.

But never a direct protest, never rebellion. I think of our others in their three-, four-year-oldness—the explosions, the tempers, the denunciations, the demands—and I feel suddenly ill. I put the iron down. What in me demanded that goodness in her? And what was the cost, the cost to her of such goodness?

The old man living in the back once said in his gentle way: "You should smile at Emily more when you look at her." What *was* in my face when I looked at her? I loved her. There were all the acts of love.

It was only with the others I remembered what he said, and it was the face of joy, and not of care or tightness or worry I turned to them—too late for Emily. She does not smile easily, let alone almost always as her brothers and sisters do. Her face is closed and somber, but when she wants, how fluid. You must have seen it in her pantomimes, you spoke of her rare gift for comedy on the stage that rouses laughter out of the audience so dear they applaud and applaud and do not want to let her go.

Where does it come from, that comedy? There was none of it in her when she came back to me that second time, after I had had to send her away again. She had a new daddy now to learn to love, and I think perhaps it was a better time.

20 Except when we left her alone nights, telling ourselves she was old enough.

"Can't you go some other time, Mommy, like tomorrow?" she would ask. "Will it be just a little while you'll be gone? Do you promise?"

The time we came back, the front door open, the clock on the floor in the hall. She rigid awake. "It wasn't just a little while. I didn't cry. Three times I called you, just three times, and then I ran downstairs to open the door so you could come faster. The clock talked loud. I threw it away, it scared me what it talked."

She said the clock talked loud again that night I went to the hospital to have Susan. She was delirious with the fever that comes from red measles, but she was fully conscious all the week I was gone and the week after we were home when she could not come near the new baby or me.

She did not get well. She stayed skeleton thin, not wanting to eat, and night after night she had nightmares. She would call for me, and I would rouse from exhaustion to sleepily call back: "You're all right, darling, go to sleep, it's just a dream," and if she still called, in a sterner voice, "now go to sleep, Emily, there's nothing to hurt you." Twice, only twice, when I had to get up for Susan anyhow, I went in to sit with her.

25 Now when it is too late (as if she would let me hold and comfort her like I do the others) I get up and go to her at once at her moan or restless stirring. "Are you awake, Emily? Can I get you something?" And the answer is always the same: "No, I'm all right, go back to sleep, Mother."

They persuaded me at the clinic to send her away to a convalescent home in the country where "she can have the kind of food and care you can't manage for her, and you'll be free to concentrate on the new baby." They still send children to that place. I see pictures on the society page of sleek young women planning affairs to raise money for it, or dancing at the affairs, or decorating Easter eggs or filling Christmas stockings for the children.

They never have a picture of the children so I do not know if the girls still wear those gigantic red bows and the ravaged looks on the every other Sunday when parents can come to visit "unless otherwise notified"—as we were notified the first six weeks.

Oh it is a handsome place, green lawns and tall trees and fluted flower beds. High up on the balconies of each cottage the children stand, the girls in their red bows and white dresses, the boys in white suits and giant red ties. The parents stand below shrieking up to be heard and the children shriek down to be heard, and between them the invisible wall: "Not to Be Contaminated by Parental Germs or Physical Affection."

There was a tiny girl who always stood hand in hand with Emily. Her parents never came. One visit she was gone. "They moved her to Rose Cottage," Emily shouted in explanation. "They don't like you to love anybody here."

30 She wrote once a week, the labored writing of a seven-year-old. "I am fine. How is the baby. If I write my letter nicely I will have a star. Love." There never was a star. We wrote every other day, letters she could never hold or keep but only hear read—

once. “We simply do not have room for children to keep any personal possessions,” they patiently explained when we pieced one Sunday’s shrieking together to plead how much it would mean to Emily, who loved so to keep things, to be allowed to keep her letters and cards.

Each visit she looked frailer. “She isn’t eating,” they told us.

(They had runny eggs for breakfast or mush with lumps, Emily said later, I’d hold it in my mouth and not swallow. Nothing ever tasted good, just when they had chicken.)

It took us eight months to get her released home, and only the fact that she gained back so little of her seven lost pounds convinced the social worker.

I used to try to hold and love her after she came back, but her body would stay stiff, and after a while she’d push away. She ate little. Food sickened her, and I think much of life too. Oh she had physical lightness and brightness, twinkling by on skates, bouncing like a ball up and down up and down over the jump rope, skimming over the hill: but these were momentary.

She fretted about her appearance, thin and dark and foreign-looking at a time when every little girl was supposed to look or thought she should look a chubby blonde replica of Shirley Temple. The doorbell sometimes rang for her, but no one seemed to come and play in the house or be a best friend. Maybe because we moved so much.

There was a boy she loved painfully through two school semesters. Months later she told me how she had taken pennies from my purse to buy him candy. “Licorice was his favorite and I brought him some every day, but he still liked Jennifer better’n me. Why, Mommy?” The kind of question for which there is no answer.

School was a worry to her. She was not glib or quick in a world where glibness and quickness were easily confused with ability to learn. To her overworked and exasperated teachers she was an over conscientious “slow learner” who kept trying to catch up and was absent entirely too often.

I let her be absent, though sometimes the illness was imaginary. How different from my now-strictness about attendance with the others. I wasn’t working. We had a new baby, I was home anyhow. Sometimes, after Susan grew old enough, I would keep her home from school, too, to have them all together.

Mostly Emily had asthma, and her breathing, harsh and labored, would fill the house with a curiously tranquil sound. I would bring the two old dresser mirrors and her boxes of collections to her bed. She would select beads and single earrings, bottle tops and shells, dried flowers and pebbles, old postcards and scraps, all sorts of oddments; then she and Susan would play Kingdom, setting up landscapes and furniture, peopling them with action.

Those were the only times of peaceful companionship between her and Susan. I have edged away from it, that poisonous feeling between them, that terrible balancing of hurts and needs I had to do between the two, and did so badly, those earlier years.

Oh there are conflicts between the others too, each one human, needing, demanding, hurting, taking—but only between Emily and Susan, no, Emily toward Susan that corroding resentment. It seems so obvious on the surface, yet it is not obvious. Susan, the second child, Susan, golden- and curly-haired and chubby, quick and articulate and assured, everything in appearance and manner Emily was not; Susan, not able to resist Emily's precious things, losing or sometimes clumsily breaking them; Susan telling jokes and riddles to company for applause while Emily sat silent (to say to me later: that was *my* riddle, Mother, I told it to Susan); Susan, who for all the five years' difference in age was just a year behind Emily in developing physically.

I am glad for that slow physical development that widened the difference between her and her contemporaries, though she suffered over it. She was too vulnerable for that terrible world of youthful competition, of preening and parading, of constant measuring of yourself against every other, of envy, "If I had the copper hair," "If I had that skin . . . ." She tormented herself enough about not looking like the others, there was enough of the unsureness, the having to be conscious of words before you speak, the constant caring—what are they thinking of me? without having it all magnified by the merciless physical drives.

Ronnie is calling. He is wet and I change him. It is rare there is such a cry now. That time of motherhood is almost behind me when the ear is not one's own but must always be racked and listening for the child cry, the child call. We sit for a while and I hold him, looking out over the city spread in charcoal with its soft aisles of light. "*Shoogily,*" he breathes and curls closer. I carry him back to bed, asleep. *Shoogily.* A funny word, a family word, inherited from Emily, invented by her to say: *comfort.*

In this and other ways she leaves her seal, I say aloud. And startle at my saying it. What do I mean? What did I start to gather together, to try and make coherent? I was at the terrible, growing years. War years. I do not remember them well. I was working, there were four smaller ones now, there was not time for her. She had to help be a mother, and housekeeper, and shopper. She had to set her seal. Mornings of crisis and near hysteria trying to get lunches packed, hair combed, coats and shoes found, everyone to school or Child Care on time, the baby ready for transportation. And always the paper scribbled on by a smaller one, the book looked at by Susan then mislaid, the homework not done. Running out to that huge school where she was one, she was lost, she was a drop; suffering over the unpreparedness, stammering and unsure in her classes.

There was so little time left at night after the kids were bedded down. She would struggle over books, always eating (it was in those years she developed her enormous appetite that is legendary in our family) and I would be ironing, or preparing food for the next day, or writing V-mail to Bill, or tending the baby. Sometimes, to make me laugh, or out of her despair, she would imitate happenings or types at school.

I think I said once: "Why don't you do something like this in the school amateur show?" One morning she phoned me at work, hardly understandable through the weeping: "Mother, I did it. I won, I won; they gave me first prize; they clapped and clapped and wouldn't let me go."

Now suddenly she was Somebody, and as imprisoned in her difference as she had been in anonymity.

She began to be asked to perform at other high schools, even in colleges, then at city and statewide affairs. The first one we went to, I only recognized her that first moment when thin, shy, she almost drowned herself into the curtains. Then: Was this Emily? The control, the command, the convulsing and deadly clowning, the spell, then the roaring, stamping audience, unwilling to let this rare and precious laughter out of their lives.

Afterwards: You ought to do something about her with a gift like that—but without money or knowing how, what does one do? We have left it all to her, and the gift has as often eddied inside, clogged and clotted, as been used and growing.

50 She is coming. She runs up the stairs two at a time with her light graceful step, and I know she is happy tonight. Whatever it was that occasioned your call did not happen today.

"Aren't you ever going to finish the ironing, Mother? Whistler painted his mother in a rocker. I'd have to paint mine standing over an ironing board." This is one of her communicative nights and she tells me everything and nothing as she fixes herself a plate of food out of the icebox.

She is so lovely. Why did you want me to come in at all? Why were you concerned? She will find her way.

She starts up the stairs to bed. "Don't get me up with the rest in the morning." "But I thought you were having midterms." "Oh, those," she comes back in, kisses me, and says quite lightly, "in a couple of years when we'll all be atom-dead they won't matter a bit."

She has said it before. She *believes* it. But because I have been dredging the past, and all that compounds a human being is so heavy and meaningful in me, I cannot endure it tonight.

55 I will never total it all. I will never come in to say: She was a child seldom smiled at. Her father left me before she was a year old. I had to work her first six years when there was work, or I sent her home and to his relatives. There were years she had care she hated. She was dark and thin and foreign-looking in a world where the prestige went to blondeness and curly hair and dimples, she was slow where glibness was prized. She was a child of anxious, not proud, love. We were poor and could not afford for her the soil of easy growth. I was a young mother, I was a distracted mother. There were other children pushing up, demanding. Her younger sister seemed all that she was not. There were years she did not want me to touch her. She kept too much in herself, her life was such she had to keep too much in herself. My wisdom came too late. She has much to her and probably little will come of it. She is a child of her age, of depression, of war, of fear.

Let her be. So all that is in her will not bloom—but in how many does it? There is still enough left to live by. Only help her to know—help make it so there is cause for her to know—that she is more than this dress on the ironing board, helpless before the iron.

➤ *QUESTIONS FOR READING AND WRITING*

1. The story opens with a reference to "you." Who is this "you" supposed to be?
2. The protagonist is the narrator of the story. How do you feel about her? How do you think her daughter Emily would tell this story?

3. What kind of relationship does the narrator have with her daughter? In what ways has the narrator shown her love for Emily?
4. To what extent do you think the economic circumstances, the physical conditions of her life, influence the narrator's attitude?

LUIGI PIRANDELLO (1867–1936)

Luigi Pirandello was born in Sicily to well-to-do parents. He attended the University of Rome and the University of Bonn, where he first began writing poetry and fiction. In 1896, he married the daughter of his father's business partner. The marriage was a happy one, and Pirandello pursued a career as a writer until the collapse of the family business in 1904 left him impoverished. The stress of these events drove his wife insane, and for the next fifteen years Pirandello took care of her, until finally committing her to an institution in 1919. Though he accepted a position as a teacher at a girl's school in order to support his family, Pirandello continued to write and publish novels, stories, and plays. In 1924, he became the director of his own company, the Art Theatre of Rome, which eventually toured throughout the world, influencing a generation of directors, playwrights, and actors. In 1934, he was awarded the Nobel Prize for literature. Questions about the perception of reality, truth, and the self are at the center of much of his work. Nowhere are his concerns more clearly presented than in his most famous work, the play Six Characters in Search of an Author, *which created a sensation when it appeared in 1922.*

WAR [1939]

The passengers who had left Rome by the night express had had to stop until dawn at the small station of Fabriano in order to continue their journey by the small old-fashioned local joining the main line with Sulmona.

At dawn, in a stuffy and smoky second-class carriage in which five people had already spent the night, a bulky woman in deep mourning was hoisted in—almost like a shapeless bundle. Behind her, puffing and moaning, followed her husband—a tiny man, thin and weakly, his face death-white, his eyes small and bright and looking shy and uneasy.

Having at last taken a seat he politely thanked the passengers who had helped his wife and who had made room for her; then he turned round to the woman trying to pull down the collar of her coat, and politely inquired:

"Are you all right, dear?"

5 The wife, instead of answering, pulled up her collar again to her eyes, so as to hide her face.

"Nasty world," muttered the husband with a sad smile.

And he felt it his duty to explain to his traveling companions that the poor woman was to be pitied, for the war was taking away from her her only son, a boy of twenty to whom both had devoted their entire life, even breaking up their home at Sulmona to follow him to Rome, where he had to go as a student, then allowing him to volunteer for war with an assurance, however, that at least for six months he would not be sent to the front and now, all of a sudden, receiving a wire saying that he was due to leave in three days' time and asking them to go and see him off.

The woman under the big coat was twisting and wriggling, at times growling like a wild animal, feeling certain that all those explanations would not have aroused even a shadow of sympathy from those people who—most likely—were in the same plight as herself. One of them, who had been listening with particular attention, said:

"You should thank God that your son is only leaving now for the front. Mine has been sent there the first day of the war. He has already come back twice wounded and been sent back again to the front."

10 "What about me? I have two sons and three nephews at the front," said another passenger.

"Maybe, but in our case it is our *only* son," ventured the husband.

"What difference can it make? You may spoil your only son with excessive attentions, but you cannot love him more than you would all your other children if you had any. Paternal love is not like bread that can be broken into pieces and split amongst the children in equal shares. A father gives *all* his love to each one of his children without discrimination, whether it be one or ten, and if I am suffering now for my two sons, I am not suffering half for each of them but double . . ."

"True . . . true . . ." sighed the embarrassed husband, "but suppose (of course we all hope it will never be your case) a father has two sons at the front and he loses one of them, there is still one left to console him . . . while . . . "

"Yes," answered the other, getting cross, "a son left to console him but also a son left for whom he must survive, while in the case of the father of an only son if the son dies the father can die too and put an end to his distress. Which of the two positions is the worse? Don't you see how my case would be worse than yours?"

15 "Nonsense," interrupted another traveler, a fat, red-faced man with bloodshot eyes of the palest gray.

He was panting. From his bulging eyes seemed to spurt inner violence of an uncontrolled vitality which his weakened body could hardly contain.

"Nonsense," he repeated, trying to cover his mouth with his hand so as to hide the two missing front teeth. "Nonsense. Do we give life to our children for our own benefit?"

The other travelers stared at him in distress. The one who had had his son at the front since the first day of the war sighed: "You are right. Our children do not belong to us. They belong to the Country . . . "

"Bosh," retorted the fat traveler. "Do we think of the Country when we give life to our children? Our sons are born because . . . well, because they must be born and when they come to life they take our own life with them. This is the truth. We belong to them but they never belong to us. And when they reach twenty they are exactly what we were at their age. We too had a father and mother, but there were so many other things as well . . . girls, cigarettes, illusions, new ties . . . and the Country, of course, whose call we would have answered—when we were twenty—even if father and mother had said no. Now at our age, the love of our Country is still great, of course, but stronger than it is the love for our children. Is there any one of us here who wouldn't gladly take his son's place at the front if the could?"

There was a silence all round, everybody nodding as to approve.

"Why then," continued the fat man, "shouldn't we consider the feelings of our children when they are twenty? Isn't it natural that at their age they should consider the love for their Country (I am speaking of decent boys, of course) even greater than the love for us? Isn't it natural that it should be so, as after all they must look upon us as upon old boys who cannot move any more and must stay at home? If Country exists, if Country is a natural necessity, like bread, of which each of us must eat in order not to die of hunger, somebody must go to defend it. And our sons go, when they are twenty, and they don't want tears, because if they die, they die inflamed and happy (I am speaking, of course, of decent boys). Now, if one dies young and happy, without having the ugly sides of life, the boredom of it, the pettiness, the bitterness of disillusion . . . what more can we ask for him? Everyone should stop crying; everyone should laugh, as I do . . . or at least thank God—as I do—because my son, before dying, sent me a message saying that he was dying satisfied at having ended his life in the best way he could have wished. That is why, as you see, I do not even wear mourning . . ."

He shook his light fawn coat as to show it; his livid lip over his missing teeth was trembling, his eyes were watery and motionless, and soon after he ended with a shrill laugh which might well have been a sob.

"Quite so . . . quite so . . ." agreed the others.

The woman who, bundled in a corner under her coat, had been sitting and listening had—for the last three months—tried to find in the words of her husband and her friends something to console her in her deep sorrow, something that might show her how a mother should resign herself to send her son not even to death but to a probably dangerous life. Yet not a word had she found amongst the many which had been said . . . and her grief had been greater in seeing that nobody—as the thought—could share her feelings.

But now the words of the traveler amazed and almost stunned her. She suddenly realized that it wasn't the others who were wrong and could not understand her but herself who could not rise up to the same height of those fathers and mothers willing to resign themselves, without crying, not only to the departure of their sons but even to their death.

She lifted her head, she bent over from her corner trying to listen with great attention to the details which the fat man was giving to his companions about the way his son had fallen as a hero, for his King and his Country, happy and without regrets. It seemed to her that she had stumbled into a world she had never dreamt of, a world so far unknown to her and she was so pleased to hear everyone joining in congratulating that brave father who could so stoically speak of his child's death.

Then suddenly, just as if she had heard nothing of what had been said and almost as if waking up from a dream, she turned to the old man, asking him:

"Then . . . is your son really dead?"

Everybody stared at her. The old man, too, turned to look at her, fixing his great, bulging, horribly watery light gray eyes, deep in her face. For some little time he tried to answer, but words failed him. He looked and looked at her, almost as if only then—at that silly, incongruous question—he had suddenly realized at last that his son was really dead—gone for ever—for ever. His face contracted, became horribly distorted, then he snatched in haste a handkerchief from his pocket and, to the amazement of everyone, broke into harrowing, heart-rending, uncontrollable sobs.

➤ *QUESTIONS FOR READING AND WRITING*

1. How do you feel about sacrificing a family member or loved one to war?
2. At one point the red-faced man says, "I do not even wear mourning." How does the narrator's description of him bear this out?
3. What is your reaction to the ending of the story? Why do you think the red-faced man begins to sob when the woman asks him, "Then . . . is your son really dead?"
4. Do you think this is a story about war or about parents' love for their children, or something else? Explain.

TWO READERS ~ TWO CHOICES

■ *EXPLORING "A&P"*

Making Connections There is nothing extraordinary about the setting, the characters, or the conflict of John Updike's short story "A&P." The setting, an A&P supermarket in suburban Massachusetts in the 1960s, is as commonplace as it gets. And we experience this setting and the story's conflict through the eyes and mind of the protagonist, Sammy, an ordinary young man enduring the monotony of working a checkout slot. But Sammy checks out more than groceries. Through his narration we view the customers and employees of the supermarket, and witness his conflict, an ordinary conflict, but one that leaves him feeling "how hard the world was going to be to me hereafter."

What is extraordinary about this story is the quality of John Updike's description and his characterization of Sammy and his dilemma. Sammy, the supermarket, the customers, his boss, and his parents come to life for us. Whether we agree or disagree with Sammy's decision, we are reminded of our own choices and their consequences. In the tradition of some of the best fiction, Updike finds the "extraordinary in the ordinary" and reveals a great deal about the hard choices of growing up.

Your Experiences and Beliefs Before you read "A&P," it may be helpful to think about your own experiences and beliefs in relation to issues that emerge from this story: pleasing or disappointing parents, teachers, employers, or other people you respect; or staying in a job, in school, or in a relationship to avoid disappointing others; or taking responsibility for your actions. If you have ever worked in a supermarket, department store, fast-food restaurant, or similar business, try to remember what that experience was like for you. If you have ever been in charge of other employees, try to recall how that responsibility made you feel.

John Updike (b. 1932)

John Updike was born in Shillington, Pennsylvania. His father was a teacher, and his mother a writer. After graduating from Harvard University in 1954, Updike spent two years in England, where he studied at the Ruskin School of Drawing and Fine Art. After returning to the United States in 1955, he worked as a reporter for the New Yorker, *leaving the magazine two years later to become a full-time writer. Though he is an accomplished critic, essayist, and poet, Updike is best known for his novels, which include* The Centaur *(1963),* Couples *(1968),* S. *(1988), and* Rabbit is Rich, *which was awarded the Pulitzer Prize in 1982. His novel* The Witches of Eastwick *(1984) was turned into a film starring Susan Sarandon and Jack Nicholson in 1987. His latest novel,* Gertrude and Cladius, *was published in 2000. Michiko Kakutani, a long-time critic for the* New York Times, *has said of Updike's fiction: "His heroes over the years, have all suffered from 'the tension and guilt of being human.' Torn between vestigial spiritual yearnings and the new imperatives of self-fulfillment, they hunger for salvation even as they submit to importunate demands of the flesh."*

A&P

[1962]

In walks these three girls in nothing but bathing suits. I'm in the third check-out slot, with my back to the door, so I don't see them until they're over by the bread. The one that caught my eye first was the one in the plaid green two-piece. She was a chunky kid, with a good tan and a sweet broad soft-looking can with those two crescents of white just under it, where the sun never seems to hit, at the top of the backs of her legs. I stood there with my hand on a box of HiHo crackers trying to remember if I rang it up or not. I ring it up again and the customer starts giving me hell. She's one of these cash-register-watchers, a witch about fifty with rouge on her cheekbones and no eyebrows, and I know it made her day to trip me up. She'd been watching cash registers for fifty years and probably never seen a mistake before.

By the time I got her feathers smoothed and her goodies into a bag—she gives me a little snort in passing, if she'd been born at the right time they would have burned her over in Salem—by the time I get her on her way the girls had circled around the bread and were coming back, without a pushcart, back my way along the counters, in the aisle between the check-outs and the Special bins. They didn't even have shoes on. There was this chunky one, with the two-piece—it was bright green and the seams on the bra were still sharp and her belly was still pretty pale so I guessed she just got it (the suit)—there was this one, with one of those chubby berry-faces, the lips all bunched together under her nose, this one, and a tall one, with black hair that hadn't quite frizzed right, and one of these sunburns right across under the eyes, and a chin that was too long—you know, the kind of girl other girls think is very "striking" and "attractive" but never quite makes it, as they very well know, which is why they like her so much—and then the third one, that wasn't quite so tall. She was the queen. She kind of led them, the other two peeking around and making their shoulders round. She didn't look around, not this queen, she just walked straight on slowly, on these long white prima donna legs. She came down a little hard on her heels, as if she didn't walk in her bare feet that much, putting down her heels and then letting the weight move along to her toes as if she was testing the floor with every step, putting a little deliberate, extra action into it. You never know for sure how girls' minds work (do you really think it's a mind in there or just a little buzz like a bee in a glass jar?), but you got the idea she had talked the other two into coming in here with her, and now she was showing them how to do it, walk slow and hold yourself straight.

She had on a kind of dirty-pink—beige maybe, I don't know—bathing suit with a little nubble all over it and, what got me, the straps were down. They were off her shoulders looped loose around the cool tops of her arms, and I guess as a result the suit had slipped a little on her, so all around the top of the cloth there was this shining rim. If it hadn't been there you wouldn't have known there could have been anything whiter than those shoulders. With the straps pushed off, there was nothing between the top of the suit and the top of her head except just *her,* this clean bare plane of the top of her chest down from the shoulder bones like a dented sheet of metal tilted in the light. I mean, it was more than pretty.

She had sort of oaky hair that the sun and salt had bleached, done up in a bun that was unraveling, and a kind of prim face. Walking into the A&P with your straps down, I suppose it's the only kind of face you *can* have. She held her head so high her neck, coming up out of those white shoulders, looked kind of stretched, but I didn't mind. The longer her neck was, the more of her there was.

5 She must have felt in the corner of her eye me and over my shoulder Stokesie in the second slot watching, but she didn't tip. Not this queen. She kept her eyes moving across the racks, and stopped, and turned so slow it made my stomach rub the inside of my apron, and buzzed to the other two, who kind of huddled against her for relief, and they all three of them went up the cat-and-dog-food-breakfast-cereal-macaroni-rice-raisins-seasonings-spreads-spaghetti-soft-drinks-crackers-and-cookies aisle. From the third slot I look straight up this aisle to the meat counter, and I watched them all the way. The fat one with the tan sort of fumbled with the cookies, but on second thought she put the packages back. The sheep pushing their carts down the aisle—the girls were walking against the usual traffic (not that we have one-way signs or anything)—were pretty hilarious. You could see them, when Queenie's white shoulders dawned on them, kind of jerk, or hop, or

hiccup, but their eyes snapped back to their own baskets and on they pushed. I bet you could set off dynamite in an A&P and the people would by and large keep reaching and checking oatmeal off their lists and muttering "Let me see, there was a third thing, began with A, asparagus, no, ah yes, applesauce!" or whatever it is they do mutter. But there was no doubt, this jiggled them. A few houseslaves in pin curlers even looked around after pushing their carts past to make sure what they had seen was correct.

You know, it's one thing to have a girl in a bathing suit down on the beach, where what with the glare nobody can look at each other much anyway, and another thing in the cool of the A&P, under the fluorescent lights, against all those stacked packages, with her feet paddling along naked over our checkerboard green-and-cream rubber-tile floor.

"Oh Daddy," Stokesie said beside me. "I feel so faint."

"Darling," I said. "Hold me tight." Stokesie's married, with two babies chalked up on his fuselage already, but as far as I can tell that's the only difference. He's twenty-two, and I was nineteen this April.

"Is it done?" he asks, the responsible married man finding his voice. I forgot to say he thinks he's going to be manager some sunny day, maybe in 1990 when it's called the Great Alexandrov and Petrooshki Tea Company or something.

10 What he meant was, our town is five miles from a beach, with a big summer colony out on the Point, but we're right in the middle of town, and the women generally put on a shirt or shorts or something before they get out of the car into the street. And anyway these are usually women with six children and varicose veins mapping their legs and nobody, including them, could care less. As I say, we're right in the middle of town, and if you stand at our front doors you can see two banks and the Congregational church and the newspaper store and three real-estate offices and about twenty-seven old freeloaders tearing up Central Street because the sewer broke again. It's not as if we're on the Cape; we're north of Boston and there's people in this town haven't seen the ocean for twenty years.

The girls had reached the meat counter and were asking McMahon something. He pointed, they pointed, and they shuffled out of sight behind a pyramid of Diet Delight peaches. All that was left for us to see was old McMahon patting his mouth and looking after them sizing up their joints. Poor kids, I began to feel sorry for them, they couldn't help it.

Now here comes the sad part of the story, at least my family says it's sad but I don't think it's sad myself. The store's pretty empty, it being Thursday afternoon, so there was nothing much to do except lean on the register and wait for the girls to show up again. The whole store was like a pinball machine and I didn't know which tunnel they'd come out of. After a while they come around out of the far aisle, around the light bulbs, records at discount of the Caribbean Six or Tony Martin Sings or some such gunk you wonder they waste the wax on, sixpacks of candy bars, and plastic toys done up in cellophane that fall apart when a kid looks at them anyway. Around they come, Queenie still leading the way, and holding a little gray jar in her hand. Slots Three through Seven are unmanned, and I could see her wondering between Stokes and me, but Stokesie with his usual luck, draws an old party in baggy gray pants who stumbles up with four giant cans of pineapple juice (what do these bums *do* with all that pineapple juice? I've often asked myself) so the girls come to me. Queenie puts down the jar and I take it into my fingers icy cold. Kingfish Fancy Herring Snacks in Pure Sour Cream: 49¢. Now her hands are empty, not a ring or a bracelet, bare as God made them, and I wonder where the money's coming from. Still with that prim look she lifts a folded dollar bill out of the hollow at the center of her nubbled pink top. The jar went heavy in my hand. Really, I thought that was so cute.

Then everybody's luck begins to run out. Lengel comes in from haggling with a truck full of cabbages on the lot and is about to scuttle into that door marked MANAGER behind which he hides all day when the girls touch his eye. Lengel's pretty dreary, teaches Sunday school and the rest, but he doesn't miss that much. He comes over and says, "Girls, this isn't the beach."

Queenie blushes, though maybe it's just a brush of sunburn I was noticing for the first time, now that she was so close. "My mother asked me to pick up a jar of herring snacks." Her voice kind of startled me, the way voices do when you see the people first, coming out so flat and dumb yet kind of tony, too, the way it ticked over "pick up" and "snacks." All of a sudden I slid right down her voice into her living room. Her father and the other men were standing around in ice-cream coats and bow ties and the women were in sandals picking up herring snacks on toothpicks off a big plate and they were all holding drinks the color of water with olives and sprigs of mint in them. When my parents have somebody over they get lemonade and if it's a real racy affair Schlitz in tall glasses with "They'll Do It Every Time" cartoons stenciled on.

15 "That's all right," Lengel said. "But this isn't the beach." His repeating this struck me as funny, as if it had just occurred to him, and he had been thinking all these years the A&P was a great big dune and he was the head lifeguard. He didn't like my smiling—as I say he doesn't miss much—but he concentrates on giving the girls that sad Sunday-school-superintendent stare.

Queenie's blush is no sunburn now, and the plump one in plaid, that I liked better from the back—a really sweet can—pipes up, "We weren't doing any shopping. We just came in for the one thing."

"That makes no difference," Lengel tells her, and I could see from the way his eyes went that he hadn't noticed she was wearing a two-piece before. "We want you decently dressed when you come in here."

"We *are* decent," Queenie says suddenly, her lower lip pushing, getting sore now that she remembers her place, a place from which the crowd that runs the A&P must look pretty crummy. Fancy Herring Snacks flashed in her very blue eyes.

"Girls, I don't want to argue with you. After this come in here with your shoulders covered. It's our policy." He turns his back. That's policy for you. Policy is what the kingpins want. What the others want is juvenile delinquency.

20 All this while, the customers had been showing up with their carts but, you know, sheep, seeing a scene, they had all bunched up on Stokesie, who shook open a paper bag as gently as peeling a peach, not wanting to miss a word. I could feel in the silence everybody getting nervous, most of all Lengel, who asks me, "Sammy, have you rung up this purchase?"

I thought and said, "No" but it wasn't about that I was thinking. I go through the punches, 4, 9, GROC, TOT—it's more complicated than you think, and after you do it often enough, it begins to make a little song, that you hear words to, in my case "Hello (*bing*) there, you (*gung*) hap-py pee-pul (splat)!"—the splat being the drawer flying out. I uncrease the bill, tenderly as you may imagine, it just having come from between the two smoothest scoops of vanilla I had ever known were there, and pass a half and a penny into her narrow pink palm, and nestle the herrings in a bag and twist its neck and hand it over, all the time thinking.

The girls, and who'd blame them, are in a hurry to get out, so I say "I quit" to Lengel quick enough for them to hear, hoping they'll stop and watch me, their unsuspected hero. They keep right on going, into the electric eye; the door flies open and they flicker across the lot to their car, Queenie and Plaid and Big Tall Goony-Goony (not that as raw material she was so bad), leaving me with Lengel and a kink in his eyebrow.

"Did you say something, Sammy?"

"I said I quit."

"I thought you did."

"You didn't have to embarrass them."

"It was they who were embarrassing us."

I started to say something that came out "Fiddle-de-doo." It's a saying of my grandmother's, and I know she would have been pleased.

"I don't think you know what you're saying," Lengel said.

"I know you don't," I said. "But I do." I pull the bow at the back of my apron and start shrugging it off my shoulders. A couple customers that had been heading for my slot begin to knock against each other, like scared pigs in a chute.

Lengel sighs and begins to look very patient and old and gray. He's been a friend of my parents for years. "Sammy, you don't want to do this to your Mom and Dad," he tells me. It's true, I don't. But it seems to me that once you begin a gesture it's fatal not to go through with it. I fold the apron, "Sammy" stitched in red on the pocket, and put it on the counter, and drop the bow tie on top of it. The bow tie is theirs, if you've ever wondered. "You'll feel this for the rest of your life," Lengel says, and I know that's true, too, but remembering how he made that pretty girl blush makes me so scrunchy inside I punch the No Sale tab and the machine whirs "pee-pul" and the drawer splats out. One advantage to this scene taking place in summer, I can follow this up with a clean exit, there's no fumbling around getting your coat and galoshes, I just saunter into the electric eye in my white shirt that my mother ironed the night before, and the door heaves itself open, and outside the sunshine is skating around on the asphalt.

I look around for my girls, but they're gone, of course. There wasn't anybody but some young married screaming with her children about some candy they didn't get by the door of a powder-blue Falcon station wagon. Looking back in the big windows, over the bags of peat moss and aluminum lawn furniture stacked on the pavement, I could see Lengel in my place in the slot, checking the sheep through. His face was dark gray and his back stiff, as if he'd just had an injection of iron, and my stomach kind of fell as I felt how hard the world was going to be to me hereafter.

➤ *QUESTIONS FOR READING AND WRITING*

1. To what extent can you connect "A&P" with your own background and experience? How did this influence your response?
2. How would you describe the narrator, Sammy? What is your reaction to his description of the girls and what he says about the customers?
3. How are you affected by the concrete description of the setting?
4. What do you think Sammy means when he says, "Now here comes the sad part of the story, at least my family says it's sad but I don't think it's sad myself"?
5. If you were in his position, would you have made the same decision?
6. What does Sammy mean at the end of the story when he says, ". . . my stomach kind of fell as I felt how hard the world was going to be to me hereafter"?

~ TWO STUDENT PAPERS

Depending on your experience of it, "A&P" is a story about many different things. You may experience it as a story about family pressure, rebellion, loss of innocence, immaturity, or any number of other issues.

In the student essays that follow, Michelle and Julie both emphasize the importance of Sammy's decision to quit, but come to different conclusions about what it means. Michelle sees it as a loss of innocence—a realization by Sammy that his actions will have negative consequences for him and his family. Julie also sees Sammy's action as significant, but as a defining moment for the rest of his life, a clear statement that Sammy will refuse to live his life like Lengel.

Michelle McAuliffe

Dr. Madden

English 102

April 10, 200X

Ironed Shirts and Bathing Suits

We all have moments in our lives when we find ourselves alone and forced to see the world and ourselves in a new and painful light. In the short story "A&P," John Updike illustrates how a seemingly unimportant experience becomes this kind of moment in the life of his main character, Sammy.

Sammy is a lively, cynical, young guy who seems more than familiar with the grocery sciences, anatomy of the store, and psychology of the customer mind: "The girls had circled around the bread and were coming back, without a pushcart, back my way along the counters, in the aisle between the checkouts and the Special bins" (296–297). Sammy spends a lot of time analyzing the store and the people in it: "I bet you could set off dynamite in an A&P and the people would by and large keep reaching and checking oatmeal off their lists and muttering, 'Let me see, there was a third thing, began with an A, asparagus, no ah yes, applesauce!' or whatever it is they do mutter." (298). He doesn't hesitate to pass judgment on them either: "What do these bums do with all that pineapple juice" (299). This seems to be the primary mental activity of his day.

On this particular day, Sammy's focus is on three young girls who enter the store wearing bathing suits. Besides ogling their every move, he gets a kick out of how they are dressed and people's reactions to it: "You could see them, when Queenie's white shoulders dawned on them, kind of jerk, or hop, or hiccup, but their eyes snapped back to their own baskets and on they pushed" (297–298). But Lengel, the store manager, is not so amused. He exclaims, "Girls, this isn't the beach" (299). And the fun begins.

When the confrontation with the girls and the manager occurs, Sammy sees it as time to act instead of watching passively. We can't really say what motivates his action. It may be something noble, or simply an excuse to be rid of a stifling job. Even Sammy might not be able to tell us. He has the initial urge to quit in the presence of the girls, but when they're gone, he still feels strongly about something. Once he says he quits, it's too late to turn back. Even though Lengel, the store manager, is giving him the chance to stay, "You don't want to do this to your Mom and Dad" (300), his decision is final. Sammy admits to us that he doesn't want to do this to his parents, but adds, "It seems to me that once you begin a gesture it's fatal not to go through with it" (300). He has his personal dignity to consider. Lengel speaks prophetically when he says, "You'll feel this for the rest of your life" (300). Sammy knows this too, but feels his decision is one of liberation. He even likes the idea of this taking place in the summertime, so he can make a quick exit.

Sammy, however, is also aware of Lengel's reaction. He notices that "Lengel sighs and begins to look very patient and gray" (300). His need for a quick exit is a result of feeling some shame and guilt in the face of a family friend and an understanding man. When Sammy gets outside, the desolation of the parking lot takes away the glory of his act in the war between youth and responsibility. His righteous decision is not so simple anymore. Without something to rebel against he feels alone. Sammy may be expressing his sympathy for Lengel when he says, "I could see Lengel in my place in the slot, checking the sheep through. His face was dark gray and his back stiff, as if he'd just had an injection of iron, and my stomach kind of fell as I felt how hard the world was going to be to me hereafter" (300). He feels that Lengel and his parents, and perhaps the entire adult world, must be disappointed in him. He has let them down.

Although we can't say what immediate consequence Sammy will face, we know that he recognizes the effects of his action beyond himself. This realization of how we affect others through our actions is not a lesson to be learned in books; we must experience it. We are often surprised when we see how what we do, say, or think affects others. At moments like this we know we have learned something valuable. Although we don't always understand it, we know that it's something that will influence our outlook on life. At the end of this story, Sammy is all alone to contemplate a decision and thoughts that only a half hour before were very far from his mind. Such is the introduction of insight and wisdom into our lives--when we least expect it, and in the most unlikely situations.

Work Cited

Updike, John. "A&P." Exploring Literature. Ed. Frank Madden. New York: Longman, 2001. 296–300.

Julie Fitzmaurice

Dr. Madden

English 102

April 6, 200X

What Makes Sammy Quit?

In John Updike's short story "A&P," we see the world through the eyes of a nineteen-year-old. Sammy, the main character, is also the narrator, and his narration creates the tone and atmosphere of the story. When Sammy quits his job for no obvious reason we are left with a question: Why? Was it his impatience with older people, rebellion against authority, or just boredom? It was not one of these alone that made him quit, but the synergy of them all which, once in motion, could not be stopped.

First, let us consider Sammy and what we learn about his character in the story. Updike doesn't actually give us many details about him. From the text we learn that Sammy is nineteen years old and lives in a small town north of Boston, five miles from the beach. The most important key to Sammy's character, however, is how he sees everyone else.

Virtually everything we learn in this story, we learn through Sammy's thoughts. Sammy comes from a working-class background: "When my parents have somebody over they get lemonade and if it's a real racy affair Schlitz in tall glasses with 'They'll Do It Every Time' cartoons stenciled on" (299). Another indication of a working-class background is in his comment, "Now here comes the sad part of the story, at least my family says it's sad, but I don't think it's sad myself" (298). This statement tells us that Sammy's parents placed importance on his job at the A&P.

His comments about Lengel tell us more about Sammy than they do about his boss at the A&P. Lengel is older and the manager of the A&P. He teaches Sunday school and has been a friend of Sammy's parents for years. Sammy thinks Lengel is "pretty dreary," and "doesn't miss that much" (299), and describes him as giving the girls that "sad Sunday-school-superintendent stare" (299). His descriptions of the customers also tell us a lot about him: "one of these cash-register-watchers, a witch about fifty" (296), "The sheep pushing their carts down the aisle" (297), and "A few houseslaves in pin curlers" (298). These comments reveal Sammy's impatience with adults and his rebellious streak.

Sammy's description of the A&P itself turns the store into a quasi character. The A&P has its own pulse and comes alive for us. He tells us what the store looks and sounds like. The cash register even sings a song as Sammy tediously pushes its keys: "Hello (bing) there, you (gung) hap-py pee-pul (splat)!" (300). Almost everyone has experienced the setting of a food store. There is a certain universality about them. But Sammy's description of the "cat-and-dog-food-breakfast-cereal-macaroni-rice-raisins-seasonings-spreads-spaghetti-soft-drinks-crackers-and-cookies aisle" (297) brings this familiar place to dull but fresh life.

Sammy goes into great detail about the girls, too. Had he been busy he would not have noticed so much about them. The store was slow, and Sammy leans on the register looking at the girls. He is so bored that he sees the store as a pinball machine. The girls are the balls, and the aisles are the chutes that the balls travel through.

His detailed description has a strong impact on our reading of the story. It makes it easy for us to imagine being nineteen and working in a store on a hot summer day. Sammy describes what the atmosphere is like: "The store's pretty empty, it being Thursday afternoon, so there was nothing much to do except lean on the register and wait for the girls to show up again" (298).

At the climax of the story, when Lengel confronts the girls about their bathing suits, Sammy is already bored and frustrated to exhaustion. He thinks that Lengel is a pompous bag of wind, so he says, "I quit" (300). He says this to Lengel to save himself, not the girls. The girls are simply the final impetus for Sammy's quitting, he needs them as his excuse. He would like to have the girls think that he is quitting his job in indignation over the way Lengel treated them.

At this moment, Lengel is everything that Sammy detests. He represents all the things that Sammy wants to rebel against: age, authority, his working-class background, Sunday school teachers, and the voice of righteousness. He realizes that if he stays at the A&P he will become a Lengel. In one brief moment all his emotions synergize. The two words "I quit" leave his lips, and Sammy changes the course of his life forever.

Work Cited

Updike, John. "A&P." Exploring Literature. Ed. Frank Madden. New York: Longman, 2001, 296–300.

EUDORA WELTY (b. 1909)

The daughter of an insurance salesman, Eudora Welty graduated from the University of Wisconsin in 1929 and studied advertising at the Columbia University Graduate School of Business. She lives today in Jackson, Mississippi, the town where she was born and where she has spent most of her life. Welty has written many novels, including The Optimist's Daughter, *which won the Pulitzer Prize in 1972, and numerous essays, but she is best known for her short stories. Though the stories are almost invariably set in a specific geographic locale—the small towns of the Mississippi delta—Welty's best stories uncover aspects of the human experience that are universal.*

A WORN PATH

[1941]

It was December—a bright frozen day in the early morning. Far out in the country there was an old Negro woman with her head tied in a red rag, coming along a path through the pinewoods. Her name was Phoenix Jackson. She was very old and small and she walked slowly in the dark pine shadows, moving a little from side to side in her steps, with the balanced heaviness and lightness of a pendulum in a grandfather clock. She carried a thin, small cane made from an umbrella, and with this she kept tapping the frozen earth in front of her. This made a grave and persistent noise in the still air, that seemed meditative like the chirping of a solitary little bird.

She wore a dark striped dress reaching down to her shoe tops, and an equally long apron of bleached sugar sacks, with a full pocket: all neat and tidy, but every time she took a step she might have fallen over her shoelaces, which dragged from her unlaced shoes. She looked straight ahead. Her eyes were blue with age. Her skin had a pattern all its own of numberless branching wrinkles and as though a whole little tree stood in the middle of her forehead, but a golden color ran underneath, and the two knobs of her cheeks were illuminated by a yellow burning under the dark. Under the red rag her hair came down on her neck in the frailest of ringlets, still black, and with an odor like copper.

Now and then there was a quivering in the thicket. Old Phoenix said, "Out of my way, all you foxes, owls, beetles, jack rabbits, coons, and wild animals! . . . Keep out from under these feet, little bob-whites. . . . Keep the big wild hogs out of my path. Don't let none of those come running my direction. I got a long way." Under her small black-freckled hand her cane, limber as a buggy whip, would switch at the brush as if to rouse up any hiding things.

On she went. The woods were deep and still. The sun made the pine needles almost too bright to look at, up where the wind rocked. The cones dropped as light as feathers. Down in the hollow was the mourning dove—it was not too late for him.

5 The path ran up a hill. "Seem like there is chains about my feet, time I get this far," she said, in the voice of argument old people keep to use with themselves. "Something always take a hold of me on this hill—pleads I should stay."

After she got to the top she turned and gave a full, severe look behind her where she had come. "Up through pines," she said at length. "Now down through oaks."

Her eyes opened their widest, and she started down gently. But before she got to the bottom of the hill a bush caught her dress.

Her fingers were busy and intent, but her skirts were full and long, so that before she could pull them free in one place they were caught in another. It was not possible to allow the dress to tear. "I in the thorny bush," she said. "Thorns, you doing your appointed work. Never want to let folks pass, no sir. Old eyes thought you was a pretty little *green* bush."

Finally, trembling all over, she stood free, and after a moment dared to stoop for her cane.

10 "Sun so high!" she cried, leaning back and looking, while the thick tears went over her eyes. "The time getting all gone here."

At the foot of this hill was a place where a log was laid across the creek.

"Now comes the trial," said Phoenix.

Putting her right foot out, she mounted the log and shut her eyes. Lifting her skirt, leveling her cane fiercely before her, like a festival figure in some parade, she began to march across. Then she opened her eyes and she was safe on the other side.

"I wasn't as old as I thought," she said.

15 But she sat down to rest. She spread her skirts on the bank around her and folded her hands over her knees. Up above her was a tree in a pearly cloud of mistletoe. She did not dare to close her eyes, and when a little boy brought her a little plate with a slice of marble-cake on it she spoke to him. "That would be acceptable," she said. But when she went to take it there was just her own hand in the air.

So she left that tree, and had to go through a barbed-wire fence. There she had to creep and crawl, spreading her knees and stretching her fingers like a baby trying to climb the steps. But she talked loudly to herself: she could not let her dress be torn now, so late in the day, and she could not pay for having her arm or leg sawed off if she got caught fast where she was.

At last she was safe through the fence and risen up out in the clearing. Big dead trees, like black men with one arm, were standing in the purple stalks of the withered cotton field. There sat a buzzard.

"Who you watching?"

In the furrow she made her way along.

20 "Glad this not the season for bulls," she said, looking sideways, "and the good Lord made his snakes to curl up and sleep in the winter. A pleasure I don't see no

two-headed snake coming around that tree, where it come once. It took a while to get by him, back in the summer."

She passed through the old cotton and went into a field of dead corn. It whispered and shook and was taller than her head. "Through the maze now," she said, for there was no path.

Then there was something tall, black, and skinny there, moving before her.

At first she took it for a man. It could have been a man dancing in the field. But she stood still and listened, and it did not make a sound. It was as silent as a ghost.

"Ghost," she said sharply, "who be you the ghost of? For I have heard of nary death close by."

25 But there was no answer—only the ragged dancing in the wind.

She shut her eyes, reached out her hand, and touched a sleeve. She found a coat and inside that an emptiness, cold as ice.

"You scarecrow," she said. Her face lighted. "I ought to be shut up for good," she said with laughter. "My senses is gone. I too old. I the oldest people I ever know. Dance, old scarecrow," she said, "while I dancing with you."

She kicked her foot over the furrow, and with mouth drawn down, shook her head once or twice in a little strutting way. Some husks blew down and whirled in streamers about her skirts.

Then she went on, parting her way from side to side with the cane, through the whispering field. At last she came to the end, to a wagon track where the silver grass blew between the red ruts. The quail were walking around like pullets, seeming all dainty and unseen.

30 "Walk pretty," she said. "This the easy place. This the easy going."

She followed the track, swaying through the quiet bare fields, through the little strings of trees silver in their dead leaves, past cabins silver from weather, with the doors and windows boarded shut, all like old women under a spell sitting there. "I walking in their sleep," she said, nodding her head vigorously.

In a ravine she went where a spring was silently flowing through a hollow log. Old Phoenix bent and drank. "Sweet-gum makes the water sweet," she said, and drank more. "Nobody know who made this well, for it was here when I was born."

The track crossed a swampy part where the moss hung as white as lace from every limb. "Sleep on, alligators, and blow your bubbles." Then the track went into the road.

Deep, deep the road went down between the high green-colored banks. Overhead the live-oaks met, and it was as dark as a cave.

35 A black dog with a lolling tongue came up out of the weeds by the ditch. She was meditating, and not ready, and when he came at her she only hit him a little with her cane. Over she went in the ditch, like a little puff of milk-weed.

Down there, her senses drifted away. A dream visited her, and she reached her hand up, but nothing reached down and gave her a pull. So she lay there and presently went to talking. "Old woman," she said to herself, "that black dog come up out of the weeds to stall you off, and now there he sitting on his fine tail, smiling at you."

A white man finally came along and found her—a hunter, a young man, with his dog on a chain.

"Well, Granny!" he laughed. "what are you doing there?"

"Lying on my back like a June-bug waiting to be turned over, mister," she said, reaching up her hand.

He lifted her up, gave her a swing in the air, and set her down. "Anything broken, Granny?"

"No sir, them old dead weeds is springy enough," said Phoenix, when she had got her breath. "I thank you for your trouble."

"Where do you live, Granny?" he asked, while the two dogs were growling at each other.

"Away back yonder, sir, behind the ridge. You can't even see it from here."

"On your way home?"

"No, sir, I going to town."

"Why, that's too far! That's as far as I walk when I come out myself, and I get something for my trouble." He patted the stuffed bag he carried, and there hung down a little closed claw. It was one of the bob-whites, with its beak hooked bitterly to show it was dead. "Now you go on home, Granny!"

"I bound to go to town, mister," said Phoenix. "The time come around."

He gave another laugh, filling the whole landscape. "I know you old colored people! Wouldn't miss going to town to see Santa Claus!"

But something held old Phoenix very still. The deep lines in her face went into a fierce and different radiation. Without warning, she had seen with her own eyes a flashing nickel fall out of the man's pocket onto the ground.

"How old are you, Granny?" he was saying.

"There is no telling, mister," she said, "no telling."

Then she gave a little cry and clapped her hands and said, "Git on away from here, dog! Look! Look at that dog!" She laughed as if in admiration. "He ain't scared of nobody. He a big black dog." She whispered, "Sic him!"

"Watch me get rid of that cur," said the man. "Sic him, Pete! Sic him!"

Phoenix heard the dogs fighting, and heard the man running and throwing sticks. She even heard a gunshot. But she was slowly bending forward by that time, further and further forward, the lids stretched down over her eyes, as if she were doing this in her sleep. Her chin was lowered almost to her knees. The yellow palm of her hand came out from the fold of her apron. Her fingers slid down and along the ground under the piece of money with the grace and care they would have in lifting an egg from under a sitting hen. Then she slowly straightened up, she stood erect, and the nickel was in her apron pocket. A bird flew by. Her lips moved. "God watching me the whole time. I come to stealing."

The man came back, and his own dog panted about them. "Well, I scared him off that time," he said, and then he laughed and lifted his gun and pointed it at Phoenix.

She stood straight and faced him.

"Doesn't the gun scare you?" he said, still pointing it.

"No, sir, I seen plenty go off closer by, in my day, and for less than what I done," she said, holding utterly still.

He smiled, and shouldered the gun. "Well, Granny," he said, "you must be a hundred years old, and scared of nothing. I'd give you a dime if I had any money with me. But you take my advice and stay home, and nothing will happen to you."

60 "I bound to go on my way, mister," said Phoenix. She inclined her head in the red rag. Then they went in different directions, but she could hear the gun shooting again and again over the hill.

She walked on. The shadows hung from the oak trees to the road like curtains. Then she smelled wood-smoke, and smelled the river, and she saw a steeple and the cabins on their steep steps. Dozens of little black children whirled around her. There ahead was Natchez shining. Bells were ringing. She walked on.

In the paved city it was Christmas time. There were red and green electric lights strung and crisscrossed everywhere, and all turned on in the daytime. Old Phoenix would have been lost if she had not distrusted her eyesight and depended on her feet to know where to take her.

She paused quietly on the sidewalk where people were passing by. A lady came along in the crowd, carrying an armful of red-, green-, and silver-wrapped presents; she gave off perfume like the red roses in hot summer, and Phoenix stopped her.

"Please, missy, will you lace up my shoe?" She held up her foot.

65 "What do you want, Grandma?"

"See my shoe," said Phoenix. "Do all right for out in the country, but wouldn't look right to go in a big building."

"Stand still then, Grandma," said the lady. She put her packages down on the sidewalk beside her and laced and tied both shoes tightly.

"Can't lace 'em with a cane," said Phoenix. "Thank you, missy, I doesn't mind asking a nice lady to tie up my shoe, when I gets out on the street."

Moving slowly and from side to side, she went into the big building and into a tower of steps, where she walked up and around and around until her feet knew to stop.

70 She entered a door, and there she saw nailed up on the wall the document that had been stamped with the gold seal and framed in the gold frame, which matched the dream that was hung up in her head.

"Here I be," she said. There was a fixed and ceremonial stiffness over her body.

"A charity case, I suppose," said an attendant who sat at the desk before her.

But Phoenix only looked above her head. There was sweat on her face, the wrinkles in her skin shone like a bright net.

"Speak up, Grandma," the woman said. "What's your name? We must have your history, you know. Have you been here before? What seems to be the trouble with you?"

75 Old Phoenix only gave a twitch to her face as if a fly were bothering her.

"Are you deaf?" cried the attendant.

But then the nurse came in.

"Oh, that's just old Aunt Phoenix," she said. "She doesn't come for herself—she has a little grandson. She makes these trips just as regular as clockwork. She lives away back off the old Natchez Trace." She bent down. "Well, Aunt Phoenix, why don't you just take a seat? We won't keep you standing after your long trip." She pointed.

The old woman sat down, bolt upright in the chair.

80 "Now, how is the boy?" asked the nurse.

Old Phoenix did not speak.

"I said, how is the boy?"

But Phoenix only waited and stared straight ahead, her face very solemn and withdrawn into rigidity.

"Is his throat any better?" asked the nurse. "Aunt Phoenix, don't you hear me? Is your grandson's throat any better since the last time you came for the medicine?"

With her hands on her knees, the old woman waited, silent, erect and motionless, just as if she were in armor.

"You mustn't take up our time this way, Aunt Phoenix," the nurse said. "Tell us quickly about your grandson, and get it over. He isn't dead, is he?"

At last there came a flicker and then a flame of comprehension across her face, and she spoke.

"My grandson. It was my memory had left me. There I sat and forgot why I made my long trip."

"Forgot?" The nurse frowned. "After you came so far?"

Then Phoenix was like an old woman begging a dignified forgiveness for waking up frightened in the night. "I never did go to school, I was too old at the Surrender," she said in a soft voice. "I'm an old woman without an education. It was my memory fail me. My little grandson, he is just the same, and I forgot it in the coming."

"Throat never heals, does it?" said the nurse, speaking in a loud, sure voice to Old Phoenix. By now she had a card with something written on it, a little list. "Yes. Swallowed lye. When was it—January—two—three years ago—"

Phoenix spoke unasked now. "No, missy, he not dead, he just the same. Every little while his throat begin to close up again, and he not able to swallow. He not get his breath. He not able to help himself. So the time come around, and I go on another trip for the soothing medicine."

"All right. The doctor said as long as you came to get it, you could have it," said the nurse. "But it's an obstinate case."

"My little grandson, he sit up there in the house all wrapped up, waiting by himself," Phoenix went on. "We is the only two left in the world. He suffer and it don't seem to put him back at all. He got a sweet look. He going to last. He wear a little patch quilt and peep out holding his mouth open like a little bird. I remembers so plain now. I not going to forget him again, no, the whole enduring time. I could tell him from all the others in creation."

"All right." The nurse was trying to hush her now. She brought her a bottle of medicine. "Charity," she said, making a check mark in a book.

Old Phoenix held the bottle close to her eyes and then carefully put it into her pocket.

"I thank you," she said.

"It's Christmas time, Grandma," said the attendant. "Could I give you a few pennies out of my purse?"

"Five pennies is a nickel," said Phoenix stiffly.

"Here's a nickel," said the attendant.

Phoenix rose carefully and held out her hand. She received the nickel and then fished the other nickel out of her pocket and laid it beside the new one. She stared at her palm closely, with her head on one side.

Then she gave a tap with her cane on the floor.

"This is what come to me to do," she said. "I going to the store and buy my child a little windmill they sells, made out of paper. He going to find it hard to believe there such a thing in the world. I'll march myself back where he waiting, holding it straight up in this hand."

She lifted her free hand, gave a little nod, turned round, and walked out of the doctor's office. Then her slow step began on the stairs, going down.

➤ *QUESTIONS FOR READING AND WRITING*

1. The Phoenix is a bird that, according to legend, lived for hundreds of years, burned itself to ashes on a funeral pyre, and then rose from the ashes to live again. Why do you think the protagonist of "A Worn Path" is named Phoenix?
2. Based on what you learn about Phoenix in the story, what is her background?
3. What is your response to the hunter she meets on the path? What is his role in the story?
4. What is the central conflict or struggle in this story? What are the obstacles against Phoenix? How does she overcome them?
5. In what way is "A Worn Path" an appropriate title for this story?

◆ POETRY ◆

JULIA ALVAREZ (b. 1950)

Though Julia Alvarez was born in New York City, she spent her childhood in the Dominican Republic. When she was ten, she returned with her parents to New York City, where she attended public schools. Confused and lonely (she spoke only Spanish), she struggled until high school, where she encountered an English teacher who encouraged her to write of her experiences as a stranger to the United States and its language. This experience was transforming, and she discovered her love of writing. She went on to study at Middlebury College, where she currently teaches, and later earned an M.F.A. from Syracuse University. She has published two books of poetry, Homecoming *(1984) and* The Other Side/El Otro Lado *(1995), and four novels,* How the Garcia Girls Lost Their Accents *(1991),* In the Time of the Butterflies *(1994),* !Yo! *(1996), and* In the Name of Salome *(2000).*

DUSTING [1984]

Each morning I wrote my name
On the dusty cabinet, then crossed
The dining table in script, scrawled
In capitals on the backs of chairs,
Practicing signatures like scales
While mother followed, squirting
Linseed from a burping can
Into a crumpled-up flannel.

She erased my fingerprints
From the bookshelf and rocker,
Polished mirrors on the desk
Scribbled with my alphabets.
My name was swallowed in the towel
With which she jewelled the table tops.
The grain surfaced in the oak
And the pine grew luminous.
But I refused with every mark
To be like her, anonymous.

➤ *QUESTIONS FOR READING AND WRITING*

1. The speaker's attitude toward her mother seems to be revealed in the poem's final word. What effect did the speaker's final comment have on you? Were you expecting the poem to end this way?
2. In what sense is the mother "anonymous"? Why do you think the speaker refuses to be like her?
3. How else might this poem have ended? Generate a list of words that could have been chosen to describe the mother, and consider how each would change the overall effect of the poem.

JUDITH ORTIZ COFER (b. 1952)

The daughter of a Puerto Rican mother and a United States mainland father, Judith Ortiz Cofer was born in Puerto Rico but immigrated to the mainland in 1956. Educated at the Augusta College and Florida Atlantic University, Cofer did further graduate work at Oxford University in 1977 and then worked as an English teacher and bilingual instructor in Florida. Due to her bilingual upbringing, much of Cofer's work is concerned with the power of language and its uses. She has published several volumes of poetry, and a novel, The Line of the Sun *(1989).*

My Father in the Navy: A Childhood Memory [1987]

Stiff and immaculate
in the white cloth of his uniform
and a round cap on his head like a halo,
he was an apparition on leave from a shadow-world
and only flesh and blood when he rose from below
the waterline where he kept watch over the engines
and dials making sure the ship parted the waters
on a straight course.
Mother, brother, and I kept vigil
on the nights and dawns of his arrivals,
watching the corner beyond the neon sign of a quasar
for the flash of white our father like an angel
heralding a new day.
His homecomings were the verses
we composed over the years making up
the siren's song that kept him coming back
from the bellies of iron whales
and into our nights
like the evening prayer.

➤ *QUESTIONS FOR READING AND WRITING*

1. To what extent is your response to this poem affected by your own experience?
2. What does the speaker in the poem look forward to about her father? What lines in the poem indicate that?
3. What does the speaker mean by "he was an apparition on leave from a shadow-world"?

Robert Frost (1874–1963)

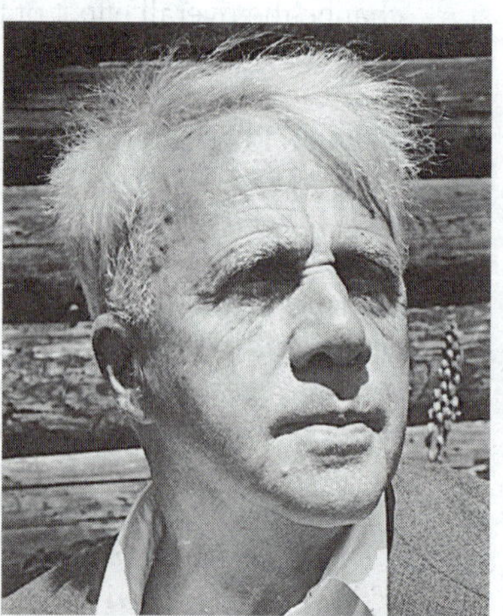

Robert Frost was born in San Francisco, California, to a headmaster and schoolteacher who met at a tiny private school in Pennsylvania. When his father died of tuberculosis in 1885, his mother returned the family to New England. Frost attended a local high school where, together with the woman he would eventually marry, Elinor White, he served as class valedictorian. It was in high school, where he was known as the class poet, that Frost seriously began writing poetry. In the many years that followed, Frost continued to write while he attended college (short stints

at Dartmouth and Harvard) and held a series of odd jobs, including work as a cobbler, journalist, teacher, and at a cotton mill. From 1900 to 1905, he lived on a farm in Derry, New Hampshire, purchased for him by his grandfather, but financial hardships—he and Elinor had five children by this point—forced him to return to teaching. In 1912, frustrated by his inability to publish in the United States, Frost moved his family to England, where he published his first two books of poetry A Boy's Will *(1913) and* North of Boston *(1914). By the time he returned to the United States in 1915, he was well on his way to becoming the most famous American poet of the century. In 1961, an infirm Frost read his poem "The Gift Outright" at the inauguration of President John F. Kennedy. His poetry, which takes much of its inspiration from the countryside of New England, is often deceptively simple, as it artfully and effortlessly weaves together traditional metrical forms with colloquial American speech.*

Mending Wall [1914]

Something there is that doesn't love a wall,
That sends the frozen-ground-swell under it,
And spills the upper boulders in the sun;
And makes gaps even two can pass abreast.
The work of hunters is another thing:
I have come after them and made repair
Where they have left not one stone on a stone,
But they would have the rabbit out of hiding,
To please the yelping dogs. The gaps I mean,
No one has seen them made or heard them made,
But at spring mending-time we find them there.
I let my neighbor know beyond the hill;
And on a day we meet to walk the line
And set the wall between us once again.
We keep the wall between us as we go.
To each the boulders that have fallen to each.
And some are loaves and some so nearly balls
We have to use a spell to make them balance:
"Stay where you are until our backs are turned!"
We wear our fingers rough with handling them.
Oh, just another kind of outdoor game,
One on a side. It comes to little more:
There where it is we do not need the wall:
He is all pine and I am apple orchard.
My apple trees will never get across
And eat the cones under his pines, I tell him.
He only says, "Good fences make good neighbors."
Spring is the mischief in me, and I wonder
If I could put a notion in his head:
"*Why* do they make good neighbors? Isn't it

Where there are cows? But here there are no cows.
Before I built a wall I'd ask to know
What I was walling in or walling out,
And to whom I was like to give offense.
Something there is that doesn't love a wall,
That wants it down." I could say "Elves" to him,
But it's not elves exactly, and I'd rather
He said it for himself. I see him there
Bringing a stone grasped firmly by the top
In each hand, like an old-stone savage armed.
He moves in darkness as it seems to me,
Not of woods only and the shade of trees.
He will not go behind his father's saying,
And he likes having thought of it so well
He says again, "Good fences make good neighbors."

➤ *QUESTIONS FOR READING AND WRITING*

1. Have you ever felt walled in or out? Explain.
2. What is the "Something" in "Something there is that doesn't love a wall"?
3. What does the line "He moves in darkness as it seems to me" mean to you?
4. Does the speaker in the poem agree that "Good fences make good neighbors"? Do you?

ELIZABETH GAFFNEY (b. 1953)

Elizabeth Gaffney's poems have appeared in Wordsmith, Southern Poetry Review, College English, Descant, Wind *and other publications. A graduate of Fordham University, she has a Ph.D. from the State University of New York at Stony Brook and teaches at SUNY Westchester Community College. She lives in Pelham, New York with her husband and three children.*

LOSSES THAT TURN UP IN DREAMS [1992]

The notebook I left on a windowsill
in Keating Hall two years ago
floats back to me full of poems.
The silver pin shaped like a bird's wings,

my mother's gold chain
stolen with the burnished purse I loved,
its leather worn to smoothness
from years of use—in dreams
appear again my homing pigeons.

Their familiar feel reassures me
that nothing's ever gone for good;
the sunglasses, pens, umbrellas,
the scarf of red and blue challis,
the lost socks, the trivial objects
I weep for are losses so palpable,

all equal in the land of dreams,
where the baby I lost one October night
comes home to nest, poor ghost,
and my mother, grandmother, uncles
crowd small rooms, and I am one
with the tree that bloomed on my birthday,
a daughter, filling up with milk and love.

➤ *QUESTIONS FOR READING AND WRITING*

1. What losses is the speaker talking about?
2. In what way are the objects that she mentions "homing pigeons"? Can you think of objects in your own life that are "homing pigeons"?
3. What does she mean "I am one / with the tree that bloomed on my birthday"?

NIKKI GIOVANNI (b. 1943)

One of the most prominent poets to emerge from the black literary movement of the 1960s, Nikki Giovanni was born in Knoxville, Tennessee. Her father was a probation officer, and her mother a social worker. Growing up, she was particularly close to her maternal grandmother and spent summers with her in Knoxville even after her family moved to Cincinnati, Ohio. It was while she was at Fisk University in Nashville that she grew politically aware, serving in Fisk's chapter of the SNCC (Student Non-Violent Coordinating Committee), which promoted the concept of "black power" in confronting the social and economic problems of the time. Her first

books of poetry, Black Feeling and Black Talk *(1968),* Black Judgment *(1968), and* Re: Creation *(1970) were enormously successful and brought her much acclaim. A vibrant personality, she has toured the United States giving lectures and reading her poetry, and has recorded numerous albums of her poetry, including* Truth Is on Its Way, *which was the best-selling spoken-word album of 1971. Though her more recent work is more introspective and less political, she remains deeply committed to the transforming power of poetry. She has said: "If everybody became a poet, the world would be so much better." Her latest book of poetry,* Love Poems, *was published in 1997.*

Nikki-Rosa [1968]

childhood remembrances are always a drag
if you're Black
you already remember things like living in Woodlawn
with no inside toilet
and if you become famous for or something
they never talk about how happy you were to have your mother
all to yourself and
how good the water felt when you got your batch from one of those
big tubs that folk in chicago barbecue in
and somehow when you talk about home
it never gets across how much you
understood their feelings
as the whole family attended meetings about Hollydale
and even though you remember
your biographers never understood
your father's pain as he sells his stock
and another dream goes
and though you're poor it isn't poverty that
concern you
and though they fought a lot
it isn't your father's drinking that makes any difference
but only that everybody is together and you
and your sister have happy birthdays and very good christmasses
and I really hope no white person ever has cause to write about me
because they never understood Black love is Black wealth and they'll
probably talk about my hard childhood and never understand that
all the while I was quite happy

➤ *QUESTIONS FOR READING AND WRITING*

1. The poem opens with "childhood remembrances are always a drag." Are childhood remembrances a drag for you? Explain.
2. Do you think there is a difference between "childhood remembrances" and childhood itself? Explain.
3. Why does the speaker say, "I really hope no white person ever has cause to write about me"?

SEAMUS HEANEY (b. 1969)

Sometimes referred to as Ireland's greatest poet since Yeats, Seamus Heaney was born on a farm in County Derry in Northern Ireland. He graduated from Queen's University in Belfast in 1961. He published his first book of poetry, Eleven Poems, *in 1965.* The Midnight Verdict *(1993) is his most recent. He was awarded the Nobel Prize in 1995. Currently he divides his time between Dublin and the United States, where he holds a teaching position at Harvard University. The rich, and often violent, history of Ireland and its people is the concern of much of his poetry. His latest book, a critically acclaimed verse translation of* Beowulf, *was published in 2000.*

DIGGING [1965]

Between my finger and my thumb
The squat pen rests; snug as a gun.

Under my window, a clean rasping sound
When the spade sinks into gravelly ground:
My father, digging. I look down

Till his straining rump among the flowerbeds
Bends low, comes up twenty years away
Stooping in rhythm through potato drills
Where he was digging.

The coarse boot nestled on the lug, the shaft
Against the inside knee was levered firmly.
He rooted out tall tops, buried the bright edge deep
To scatter new potatoes that we picked
Loving their cool hardness in our hands.

By God, the old man could handle a spade.
Just like his old man.

My grandfather cut more turf in a day
Than any other man on Toner's bog.
Once I carried him milk in a bottle
Corked sloppily with paper. He straightened up
To drink it, then fell to right away

Nicking and slicing neatly, heaving sods
Over his shoulder, going down and down
For the good turf. Digging.

The cold smell of potato mould, the squelch and slap
Of soggy peat, the curt cuts of an edge
Through living roots awaken in my head.
But I've no spade to follow men like them.

Between my finger and my thumb
The squat pen rests.
I'll dig with it.

➤ *QUESTIONS FOR READING AND WRITING*

1. What kind of work did the speaker's father and grandfather do? To what extent is your response to this poem influenced by your own background?
2. The speaker begins the poem by saying, "The squat pen rests; snug as a gun." But in the last stanza he says of the squat pen, "I'll dig with it." What kind of work does he do and what does he mean?

Mid-Term Break [1965]

I sat all morning in the college sick bay
Counting bells knelling classes to a close.
At two o'clock our neighbors drove me home.

In the porch I met my father crying—
He had always taken funerals in his stride—
And Big Jim Evans saying it was a hard blow.

The baby cooed and laughed and rocked the pram
When I came in, and I was embarrassed
By old men standing up to shake my hand

And tell me they were "sorry for my trouble."
Whispers informed strangers I was the eldest,
Away at school, as my mother held my hand

In hers and coughed out angry tearless sighs.
At ten o'clock the ambulance arrived
With the corpse, stanched and bandaged by the nurses.

Next morning I went up into the room. Snowdrops
And candles soothed the bedside; I saw him
For the first time in six weeks. Paler now,

Wearing a poppy bruise on his left temple.
He lay in the four foot box as in his cot.
No gaudy scars, the bumper knocked him clear.

A four foot box, a foot for every year.

➤ QUESTIONS FOR READING AND WRITING

1. The boy is told by the old men that they are "sorry for my trouble." What trouble is that? What's happened here?
2. To what extent is your response to this poem affected by your own experience?
3. The last line of the poem, "A four foot box, a foot for every year," stands by itself. What is your reaction to it. In what ways is it appropriate to wrap up the poem?

PHILIP LARKIN (1922–1985)

Philip Larkin was born to a working-class family in Coventry, an industrial city in northern England. He attended Oxford University on a scholarship, and afterward served for many years as the librarian at the University of Hull. Though he wrote novels and was an astute critic of both music—jazz, in particular—and literature, Larkin is remembered today as one of England's most influential postwar poets. In his poems, which are often called anti-Romantic, Larkin takes a witty, sophisticated, and tough-minded approach to traditional poetic subjects.

THIS BE THE VERSE [1971]

They fuck you up, your mum and dad.
  They may not mean to, but they do.
They fill you with the faults they had
  And add some extra, just for you.

But they were fucked up in their turn
  By fools in old-style hats and coats,
Who half the time were soppy-stern
  And half at one another's throats.

Man hands on misery to man.
  It deepens like a coastal shelf.
Get out as early as you can.
  And don't have any kids yourself.

➤ QUESTIONS FOR READING AND WRITING

1. What is the tone of this poem? Were you surprised by it, and the message? Why?
2. Is the advice at the end realistic? Do you agree with it? Explain.

MICHAEL LASSELL (b. 1947)

Michael Lassell is the author of six books of poetry, fiction, and nonfiction, including A Flame for the Touch That Matters *(1998) and* Decade Dance *(1990), which won a Lambda Literary Award. He is also the editor of five books, including (with Elena Georgiou)* The World in U.S.: Lesbian and Gay Poetry of the Next Wave *(St. Martin's Press, 2000) and* Elton John and Tim Rice's Adia: The Making of a Broadway Show *(Disney Editions, 2000). He holds degrees from Colgate University, California Institute of the Arts, and Yale, and lives in New York City, where he is the features editor of* Metropolitan Home *magazine.*

HOW TO WATCH YOUR BROTHER DIE [1990]

for Carl Morse

When the call comes, be calm.
Say to your wife, "My brother is dying. I have to fly
to California."
Try not to be shocked that he already looks like
a cadaver.
Say to the young man sitting by your brother's side,
"I'm his brother."
Try not to be shocked when the young man says,
"I'm his lover. Thanks for coming."

Listen to the doctor with a steel face on.
Sign the necessary forms.
Tell the doctor you will take care of everything.
Wonder why doctors are so remote.

Watch the lover's eyes as they stare into
your brother's eyes as they stare into
space.
Wonder what they see there.
Remember the time he was jealous and
opened your eyebrow with a sharp stick.
Forgive him out loud
even if he can't
understand you.
Realize the scar will be
all that's left of him.

Over coffee in the hospital cafeteria
say to the lover, "You're an extremely good-looking
young man."
Hear him say,
"I never thought I was good enough looking to
deserve your brother."

Watch the tears well up in his eyes. Say,
"I'm sorry, I don't know what it means to be
the lover of another man."
Hear him say,
"It's just like a wife, only the commitment is
deeper because the odds against you are so much
greater."
Say nothing, but
take his hand like a brother's.

Drive to Mexico for unproved drugs that might
help him live longer.
Explain what they are to the border guard.
Fill with rage when he informs you,
"You can't bring those across."

Begin to grow loud.
Feel the lover's hand on your arm
restraining you. See in the guard's eye
how much a man can hate another man.
Say to the lover, "How can you stand it?"
Hear him say, "You get used to it."
Think of one of your children getting used to
another man's hatred.

Call your wife on the telephone. Tell her,
"He hasn't much time.
I'll be home soon." Before you hang up, say,
"How could anyone's commitment be deeper than
a husband and wife?" Hear her say,
"Please. I don't want to know all the details."

When he slips into an irrevocable coma,
hold his lover in your arms while he sobs,
no longer strong. Wonder how much longer
you will be able to be strong.
Feel how it feels to hold a man in your arms
whose arms are used to holding men.
Offer God anything to bring your brother back.
Know you have nothing God could possibly want.
Curse God, but do not
abandon Him.

Stare at the face of the funeral director
when he tells you he will not
embalm the body for fear of
contamination. Let him see in your eyes
how much a man can hate another man.

Stand beside a casket covered in flowers,
white flowers. Say,
"Thank you for coming," to each of several
hundred men
who file past in tears, some of them
holding hands. Know that your brother's life
was not what you imagined. Overhear two
mourners say, "I wonder who'll be next?" and
"I don't care anymore,
as long as it isn't you."

Arrange to take an early flight home,
his lover will drive you to the airport.
When your flight is announced say,
awkwardly, "If I can do anything, please
let me know." Do not flinch when he says,
"Forgive yourself for not wanting to know him
after he told you. He did."
Stop and let it soak in. Say,
"He forgave me, or he knew himself?"
"Both," the lover will say, not knowing what else
to do. Hold him like a brother while he
kisses you on the cheek. Think that
you haven't been kissed by a man since
your father died. Think,
"This is no moment not to be strong."

Fly first class and drink Scotch. Stroke
your split eyebrow with a finger and
think of your brother alive. Smile
at the memory and think
how your children will feel in your arms,
warm and friendly and without challenge.

➤ *QUESTIONS FOR READING AND WRITING*

1. What do you think of the title of the poem? Is this how to watch your brother die? Explain.
2. Who is the "you" to whom the speaker addresses himself?
3. What does the speaker mean by "See in the guard's eye how much a man can hate another man." What other images of love or hate can you find in the poem?

4. The poem concludes with "think how your children will feel in your arms, / warm and friendly and without challenge." Is this a fitting conclusion? Explain.

LI-YOUNG LEE (b. 1957)

Li-Young Lee was born in Jakarta, Indonesia. He came to the United States in 1964 at the age of seven, when his father, a physician and minister, was forced to flee Indonesia due to political persecution. He attended the University of Pittsburgh, the University of Arizona, and the State University of New York at Brockport. His volumes of poetry include Rose *(1986) and* The City in Which I Love You *(1990). In 1994, he published a book of his memoirs,* The Winged Seed. *He currently lives in Chicago.*

THE GIFT [1986]

To pull the metal splinter from my palm
my father recited a story in a low voice.
I watched his lovely face and not the blade.
Before the story ended he removed
the iron sliver I thought I'd die from.

I can't remember the tale
but hear his voice still, a well
of dark water, a prayer.
And I recall his hands,
two measures of tenderness
he laid against my face,
the flames of discipline
he raised above my head.

Had you entered that afternoon
you would have thought you saw a man
planting something in a boy's palm,
a silver tear, a tiny flame.
Had you followed that boy
you would have arrived here,
where I bend over my wife's right hand.

Look how I shave her thumbnail down
so carefully she feels no pain.

Watch as I lift the splinter out.
I was seven when my father
took my hand like this,
and I did not hold that shard
between my fingers and think,
Metal that will bury me,
christen it Little Assassin,
Ore Going Deep for My Heart,
And I did not lift up my wound and cry,

Death visited here!
I did what a child does
when he's given something to keep,
I kissed my father.

➤ QUESTIONS FOR READING AND WRITING

1. What is "the" gift?
2. How do you think the italicized phrases "*Metal that will bury me*" and "*Death visited here!*" fit in this poem? Are there any other phrases that stand out for you?
3. Can you remember a time when someone gave you a "gift" like this? Explain.

EDNA ST. VINCENT MILLAY

(1892–1950)

Edna St. Vincent Millay was born in Rockland, Maine, and began writing poetry as a child. After graduating from Vassar College in 1917, she moved to New York City, where she quickly became a noted figure in the bustling arts scene of Greenwich Village. She published her first book of poetry, the acclaimed Renascence and Other Poems, *that same year. In 1923, she won the Pulitzer Prize for* The Harp Weaver and Other Poems. *Her later poetry, which became increasingly political, never received the same acclaim as her early work, and, after 1940, when she suffered a nervous breakdown, she wrote very little. She died of a heart attack in 1950, feeling that she had been largely forgotten. After her death, the publication of her collected poems in 1956 restored her position as one of the most accomplished poets of the century.*

LAMENT [1921]

Listen, children:
Your father is dead.

From his old coats
I'll make you little jackets;
I'll make you little trousers
From his old pants.
There'll be in his pockets
Things he used to put there,
Keys and pennies
Covered with tobacco;
Dan shall have the pennies
To save in his bank;
Anne shall have the keys
To make a pretty noise with.
Life must go on,
And the dead be forgotten;
Life must go on,
Though good men die;
Anne, eat your breakfast;
Dan, take your medicine;
Life must go on;
I forget just why.

➤ *QUESTIONS FOR READING AND WRITING*

1. What is your reaction to the first two lines? To what extent does your own experience affect your response to this poem?
2. What is the tone of the poem? What does the last line "I forget just why" tell you about the speaker's real feelings?
3. Compare this poem to "Mid-Term Break" on page 320.

JANICE MIRIKITANI (b. 1938)

Like many Japanese-Americans of her generation, Janice Mirikitani was incarcerated with her family in an internment camp during World War II. She was educated at UCLA and the University of California of Berkeley, where she first developed her interests in the arts, both from a creative and administrative perspective. During her career, she has managed numerous social and arts programs, public and private, including San Francisco's famous Glide Foundation. She has published three collections of poetry: Awake in the River *(1978),* Shedding Silence *(1987), and* We, the Dangerous *(1994).*

For My Father

[1987]

He came over the ocean
carrying Mt. Fuji on
his back/Tule Lake on his chest
hacked through the brush
of deserts
and made them grow
strawberries

we stole berries
from the stem
we could not afford them
for breakfast

his eyes held
nothing
as he whipped us
for stealing.

the desert had dried
his soul.

wordless
he sold
the rich,
full berries
to hakujin°
whose children
pointed at our eyes

they ate fresh
strawberries
on corn flakes.

Father,
i wanted to scream
at your silence.
Your strength
was a stranger
i could never touch.

iron
in your eyes
to shield
the pain
to shield desert-like wind

22 **hakujin** white people

from patches
of strawberries
grown
from
tears.

➤ *QUESTIONS FOR READING AND WRITING*

1. The speaker says that her father "came over the ocean / carrying Mt. Fuji on his back." What do you think she means?
2. Later in the poem, she addresses her father directly and says, "Your strength / was a stranger / I could never touch." What do you think she is saying about their relationship? What has she been missing?
3. Have you ever had this kind of response to a parent or authority figure in your life? Explain.

SHARON OLDS (b. 1942)

Born in San Francisco, California, Sharon Olds graduated from Stanford University in 1964 and earned a Ph.D. from Columbia University in 1972. She published her first book of poetry, Satan Says, *in 1980, but it was not until her second,* The Dead and the Living, *which won the National Book Critics Circle Award in 1985, that her reputation as an important voice was firmly established. Her poetry, which is often intensely personal, is noted for its candor and power. Her latest book of poems,* Blood, Tin, and Straw *was published in 1999. She teaches creative writing at New York University.*

35/10

[1984]

Brushing out my daughter's dark
silken hair before the mirror
I see the grey gleaming on my head,
the silver-haired servant behind her. Why is it
just as we begin to go
they begin to arrive, the fold in my neck
clarifying as the fine bones of her
hips sharpen? As my skin shows
its dry pitting, she opens like a small
pale flower on the tip of a cactus;
as my last chances to bear a child
are falling through my body, the duds among them,

her purse of eggs, round and
firm as hard-boiled yolks, is about
to snap its clasp. I brush her tangled
fragrant hair at bedtime. It's an old
story—the oldest we have on our planet—
the story of replacement.

➤ *QUESTIONS FOR READING AND WRITING*

1. What does the title of the poem refer to? How do the numbers "35/10" match the specific comparisons of the poem?
2. In what way is it "an old / story—the oldest we have on our planet"? How does it play itself out in your own life?
3. Compare this poem to "Dusting" on page 313.

LINDA PASTAN (b.1932)

Linda Pastan was born in New York City and has degrees from Radcliffe College and Brandeis University. Her books of poetry include A Perfect Circle of Sun *(1971),* Five Stages of Grief *(1978),* PM/AM *(1982), which was nominated for the American Book Award,* Imperfect Paradise *(1988), and* Heroes in Disguise *(1991). She has been honored with grants from the National Endowment for the Arts and by being named poet laureate of the state of Maryland.*

MARKS [1978]

My husband gives me an A
for last night's supper,
an incomplete for my ironing,
a B plus in bed.
My son says I am average,
an average mother, but if
I put my mind to it
I could improve.
My daughter believes
In Pass / Fail and tells me
I pass. Wait 'til they learn
I'm dropping out.

➤ *QUESTIONS FOR READING AND WRITING*

1. What kind relationship does the speaker have with her family?

2. What does she mean by "Wait 'til they learn / I'm dropping out"?
3. How does the speaker compare with the mothers in "Dusting" (p. 313) or "35/10" (p. 329)?

THEODORE ROETHKE (1908–1963)

Theodore Roethke was a native of Saginaw, Michigan where his father owned a greenhouse. The poem "My Papa's Waltz" is taken from his second volume of poems, The Lost Son *(1948). During the course of a long career, he won two National Book Awards, and in 1954 received the Pulitzer Prize for his book of poems* The Waking: Poems 1933–1953.

MY PAPA'S WALTZ [1942]

The whiskey on your breath
Could make a small boy dizzy;
But I hung on like death
Such waltzing was not easy.

We romped until the pans
Slid from the kitchen shelf;
My mother's countenance
Could not unfrown itself.

The hand that held my wrist
Was battered on one knuckle;
At every step you missed
My right ear scraped a buckle.

You beat time on my head
With a palm caked hard by dirt,
Then waltzed me off to bed
Still clinging to your shirt.

➤ *QUESTIONS FOR READING AND WRITING*

1. To what extent is your response to this poem affected by your own experience?
2. What is the mother's response to the dancing? Why?
3. How does this father compare with the fathers in "Those Winter Sundays," on page 12? or "For My Father" on page 328?

Cathy Song (b. 1955)

Cathy Song was born in Honolulu, Hawaii, to a Korean father and a Chinese mother. She graduated from Wellesley College in 1975, and received an M.A. from Boston College in 1981. She currently lives in Hawaii, when she is not teaching creative writing on the mainland. Her first book, The Picture Bride, *from which "The Youngest Daughter" is taken, was published in 1983.* Frameless Windows, Squares of Light, *her second, was published in 1991. Her latest book of poems* School Figures *appeared in 1994.*

The Youngest Daughter [1983]

The sky has been dark
for many years.
My skin has become as damp
and pale as rice paper
and feels the way
mother's used to before the drying sun
parched it out there in the fields.

Lately, when I touch my eyelids,
my hands react as if
I had just touched something
hot enough to burn.
My skin, aspirin colored,
tingles with migraine. Mother
has been massaging the left side of my face
especially in the evenings
when the pain flares up.

This morning
her breathing was graveled,
her voice gruff with affection
when I wheeled her into the bath.
She was in a good humor,
making jokes about her great breasts,
floating in the milky water
like two walruses,
flaccid and whiskered around the nipples.
I scrubbed them with a sour taste
in my mouth, thinking:
six children and an old man
have sucked from these brown nipples.

I was almost tender
when I came to the blue bruises
that freckle her body,
places where she has been injecting insulin
for thirty years. I soaped her slowly,
she sighed deeply, her eyes closed.
It seems it has always
been like this: the two of us
in this sunless room,
the splashing of the bathwater.

In the afternoons
when she has rested,
she prepares our ritual of tea and rice,
garnished with a shred of gingered fish,
a slice of pickled turnip,
a token for my white body.
We eat in the familiar silence.
She knows I am not to be trusted,
even now planning my escape.
As I toast to her health
with the tea she has poured,
a thousand cranes curtain the window,
fly up in a sudden breeze.

➤ *QUESTIONS FOR READING AND WRITING*

1. How would you describe the relationship between the speaker and her mother? What lines in the poem support your view?
2. What does she mean by "She knows I am not to be trusted, / even now planning my escape"?
3. Compare this poem to "Dusting" on page 313 and "35/10" on page 329.

PAUL ZIMMER (b. 1934)

Paul Zimmer was born in Canton, Ohio, and attended Kent State University. He has spent most of his career in publishing, beginning as a manager of the book department at Macy's department store in San Francisco. He worked for many years as the director of the University of Iowa Press until his retirement in 1998. His books of poetry include The Great Bird of Love *(1989), and* Crossing to Sunlight *(1996). "Zimmer in Grade School" is part of a series of poems in which a semiautobiographical figure, Zimmer, is the primary persona.*

Zimmer in Grade School [1983]

In grade school I wondered
Why I had been born
To wrestle in the ashy puddles,
With my square nose
Streaming mucus and blood.
My knuckles puffed from combat
And the old nun's ruler,
I feared everything: God,
Learning and my schoolmates.
I could not count, spell or read.
My report card proclaimed
These scarlet failures.
My parents wrang their loving hands.
My guardian angel wept constantly.

But I could never hide anything.
If I peed my pants in class
The puddle was always quickly evident.
My worst mistakes were at
The blackboard for Jesus and all
The saints to see.
Even now
When I hide behind elaborate mask
It is always known that I am Zimmer,
The one who does the messy papers
And fractures all his crayons,
Who spits upon the radiators
And sits all day in shame
Outside the office of the principal.

➤ *QUESTIONS FOR READING AND WRITING*

1. What did you wonder about yourself in grade school? To what extent do you still wonder the same things?
2. What does the speaker mean by "When I hide behind elaborate mask / It is always known that I am Zimmer"? Who is Zimmer?

• DRAMA •

TENNESSEE WILLIAMS (1911–1983)

Tennessee Williams was born in Columbus, Mississippi, and moved with his family to St. Louis, Missouri, when he was twelve. The troubled family of The Glass Menagerie *resembles William's own—his mother was a faded southern beauty, his sister suffered from intense shyness, and Williams himself, a frustrated writer, worked at a series of low-paying, unsatisfying jobs. After years of struggling,* The Glass Menagerie *opened on Broadway to tremendous acclaim in 1945, and Williams was instantly established as an important new voice in the theater. Lonely women inhabiting a world of dreams, much like Amanda in* The Glass Menagerie, *are central figures in many of his greatest plays, including* A Streetcar Named Desire, *which won the Pulitzer Prize in 1947, and* Summer and Smoke *(1948). His other major works include the Pulitzer Prize-winning* Cat on a Hot Tin Roof *(1955),* The Rose Tattoo *(1951),* Orpheus Descending *(1957),* Sweet Bird of Youth *(1959), and* The Night of the Iguana *(1961). Though he continued to write until his death, his later plays were less successful. Nevertheless, Williams remains one of the giants of twentieth-century drama.*

THE GLASS MENAGERIE [1945]

CHARACTERS

AMANDA WINGFIELD, *the mother. A little woman of great but confused vitality clinging frantically to another time and place. Her characterization must be carefully created, not copied from type. She is not paranoiac, but her life is paranoia. There is much to admire in* AMANDA, *and as much to love and pity as there is to laugh at. Certainly she has endurance and a kind of heroism, and though her foolishness makes her unwittingly cruel at times, there is tenderness in her slight person.*

LAURA WINGFIELD, *her daughter.* AMANDA, *having failed to establish contact with reality, continues to live vitally in her illusions, but* LAURA'S *situation is even graver. A childhood illness has left her crippled, one leg slightly shorter than the other, and held in a brace. This defect need not be more than suggested on the stage. Stemming from this,* LAURA'S *separation increases till she is like a piece of her own glass collection, too exquisitely fragile to move from the shelf.*

TOM WINGFIELD, *her son. And the narrator of the play. A poet with a job in a warehouse. His nature is not remorseless, but to escape from a trap he has to act without pity.*

JIM O'CONNOR, *the gentleman caller. A nice, ordinary, young man.*

SCENE: *An alley in St. Louis.*
PART I: *Preparation for a Gentleman Caller.*
PART II: *The Gentleman Calls.*
TIME: *Now and the Past.*

SCENE I

The Wingfield apartment is in the rear of the building, one of those vast hive-like conglomerations of cellular living-units that flower as warty growths in over-crowded urban centers of lower middle-class population and are symptomatic of the impulse of this largest and fundamentally enslaved section of American society to avoid fluidity and differentiation and to exist and function as one interfused mass of automatism.

The apartment faces an alley and is entered by a fire escape, a structure whose name is a touch of accidental poetic truth, for all of these huge buildings are always burning with the slow and implacable fires of human desperation. The fire escape is included in the set—that is, the landing of it and steps descending from it.

The scene is memory and is therefore nonrealistic. Memory takes a lot of poetic license. It omits some details; others are exaggerated, according to the emotional value of the articles it touches, for memory is seated predominantly in the heart. The interior is therefore rather dim and poetic.

At the rise of the curtain, the audience is faced with the dark, grim rear wall of the Wingfield tenement. This building, which runs parallel to the footlights, is flanked on both sides by dark, narrow alleys which run into murky canyons of tangled clotheslines, garbage cans and the sinister latticework of neighboring fire escapes. It is up and down these side alleys that exterior entrances and exits are made, during the play. At the end of TOM'S *opening commentary, the dark tenement wall slowly reveals (by means of a transparency) the interior of the ground floor Wingfield apartment.*

Downstage is the living room, which also serves as a sleeping room for LAURA, *the sofa unfolding to make her bed. Upstage, center, and divided by a wide arch or second proscenium with transparent faded portieres (or second curtain), is the dining room. In an old-fashioned what-not in the living room are seen scores of transparent glass animals. A blown-up photograph of the father hangs on the wall of the living room, facing the audience, to the left of the archway. It is the face of a very handsome young man in a doughboy's First World War cap. He is gallantly smiling, ineluctably smiling, as if to say, "I will be smiling forever."*

The audience hears and sees the opening scene in the dining room through both the transparent fourth wall of the building and the transparent gauze portieres of the dining room arch. It is during this revealing scene that the fourth wall slowly ascends, out of sight. This transparent exterior wall is not brought down again until the very end of the play, during TOM'S *final speech.*

The narrator is an undisguised convention of the play. He takes whatever license with dramatic convention as is convenient to his purposes.

TOM *enters dressed as a merchant sailor from alley, stage left, and strolls across the front of the stage to the fire escape. There he stops and lights a cigarette. He addresses the audience.*

TOM: Yes, I have tricks in my pocket, I have things up my sleeve. But I am the opposite of a stage magician. He gives you illusion that has the appearance of truth. I give you truth in the pleasant disguise of illusion. To begin with, I turn back time. I reverse it to that quaint period, the thirties, when the huge middle class of America was matriculating in a school for the blind. Their eyes had failed them, or they had failed their eyes, and so they were having their fingers pressed forcibly down on the fiery Braille alphabet of a dissolving economy. In Spain there was revolution. Here there was only shouting and confusion. In Spain there was Guernica. Here there were disturbances of labor, sometimes pretty violent, in otherwise peaceful cities such as Chicago, Cleveland, Saint Louis. . . . This is the social background of the play.

[*Music.*]

The play is memory.

Being a memory play, it is dimly lighted, it is sentimental, it is not realistic. In memory everything seems to happen to music. That explains the fiddle in the wings. I am the narrator of the play, and also a character in it. The other characters are my mother, Amanda, my sister, Laura, and a gentleman caller who appears in the final scenes. He is the most realistic character in the play, being an emissary from a world of reality that we were somehow set apart from. But since I have a poet's weakness for symbols, I am using this character also as a symbol; he is the long delayed but always expected something that we live for. There is a fifth character in the play who doesn't appear except in this larger-than-life photograph over the mantel. This is our father who left us a long time ago. He was a telephone man who fell in love with long distances; he gave up his job with the telephone company and skipped the light fantastic out of town. . . . The last we heard of him was a picture postcard from Mazatlan, on the Pacific coast of Mexico, containing a message of two words—"Hello—Goodbye!" and no address. I think the rest of the play will explain itself. . . .

AMANDA'S *voice becomes audible through the portieres.*

[Legend on screen: "Où Sont les Neiges."[1]]

He divides the portieres and enters the upstage area.

[1] **Où Sont les Neiges [d'antan]** "Where are the snows of yesteryear? A quotation from the French poet Francois Villon to be projected on a screen at the back of the stage.

AMANDA *and* LAURA *are seated at a drop-leaf table. Eating is indicated by gestures without food or utensils.* AMANDA *faces the audience.* TOM *and* LAURA *are seated in profile.*

The interior has lit up softly and through the scrim we see AMANDA *and* LAURA *seated at the table in the upstage area.*

AMANDA [*calling*]: Tom?

TOM: Yes, Mother.

AMANDA: We can't say grace until you come to the table!

TOM: Coming, Mother. [*He bows slightly and withdraws, reappearing a few moments later in his place at the table.*]

AMANDA [*to her son*]: Honey, don't *push* with your *fingers.* If you have to push with something, the thing to push with is a crust of bread. And chew—chew! Animals have sections in their stomachs which enable them to digest food without mastication, but human beings are supposed to chew their food before they swallow it down. Eat food leisurely, son, and really enjoy it. A well-cooked meal has lots of delicate flavors that have to be held in the mouth for appreciation. So chew your food and give your salivary glands a chance to function!

TOM *deliberately lays his imaginary fork down and pushes his chair back from the table.*

TOM: I haven't enjoyed one bite of this dinner because of your constant directions on how to eat it. It's you that makes me rush through meals with your hawklike attention to every bite I take. Sickening—spoils my appetite—all this discussion of animals' secretion—salivary glands—mastication!

AMANDA [*lightly*]: Temperament like a Metropolitan star! [*He rises and crosses downstage.*] You're not excused from the table.

TOM: I am getting a cigarette.

AMANDA: You smoke too much.

LAURA *rises.*

LAURA: I'll bring in the blanc mange.

He remains standing with his cigarette by the portieres during the following.

AMANDA [*rising*]: No, sister, no, sister—you be the lady this time and I'll be the darky.

LAURA: I'm already up.

AMANDA: Resume your seat, little sister—I want you to stay fresh and pretty—for gentlemen callers!

LAURA: I'm not expecting any gentlemen callers.

AMANDA [*crossing out to kitchenette. Airily*]: Sometimes they come when they are least expected! Why, I remember one Sunday afternoon in Blue Mountain—[*enters kitchenette.*]

TOM: I know what's coming!

LAURA: Yes. But let her tell it.
TOM: Again?
LAURA: She loves to tell it.

AMANDA *returns with bowl of dessert.*

AMANDA: One Sunday afternoon in Blue Mountain—your mother received—*seventeen*—gentlemen callers! Why, sometimes there weren't chairs enough to accommodate them all. We had to send the nigger over to bring in folding chairs from the parish house.
TOM [*remaining at portieres*]: How did you entertain those gentlemen callers?
AMANDA: I understood the art of conversation!
TOM: I bet you could talk.
AMANDA: Girls in those days *knew* how to talk, I can tell you.
TOM: Yes?

[Image: AMANDA *as a girl on a porch greeting callers.]*

AMANDA: They knew how to entertain their gentlemen callers. It wasn't enough for a girl to be possessed of a pretty face and a graceful figure—although I wasn't slighted in either respect. She also needed to have a nimble wit and a tongue to meet all occasions.
TOM: What did you talk about?
AMANDA: Things of importance going on in the world! Never anything coarse or common or vulgar. [*She addresses* TOM *as though he were seated in the vacant chair at the table though be remains by portieres. He plays this scene as though he held the book.*] My callers were gentlemen—all! Among my callers were some of the most prominent young planters of the Mississippi Delta—planters and sons of planters!

TOM *motions for music and a spot of light on* AMANDA: *Her eyes lift, her face glows, her voice becomes rich and elegiac.*

[Screen legend: "Où Sont les Neiges."]

There was young Champ Laughlin who later became vice president of the Delta Planters Bank. Hadley Stevenson who was drowned in Moon Lake and left his widow one hundred and fifty thousand in Government bonds. There were the Cutrere brothers, Wesley and Bates. Bates was one of my bright particular beaux! He got in a quarrel with that wild Wainright boy. They shot it out on the floor of Moon Lake Casino. Bates was shot through the stomach. Died in the ambulance on his way to Memphis. His widow was also well-provided for, came into eight or ten thousand acres, that's all. She married him on the rebound—never loved her—carried my picture on him the night he died! And there was that boy that every girl in Delta had set her cap for! That beautiful, brilliant young Fitzhugh boy from Green County!
TOM: What did he leave his widow?

AMANDA: He never married! Gracious, you talk as though all of my old admirers had turned up their toes to the daisies!

TOM: Isn't this the first you mentioned that still survives?

AMANDA: That Fitzhugh boy went North and made a fortune—came to be known as the Wolf of Wall Street! He had the Midas touch, whatever he touched turned to gold! And I could have been Mrs. Duncan J. Fitzhugh, mind you! But—I picked your *father!*

LAURA [*rising*]: Mother, let me clear the table.

AMANDA: No dear, you go in front and study your typewriter chart. Or practice your shorthand a little. Stay fresh and pretty—It's almost time for our gentlemen callers to start arriving. [*She flounces girlishly toward the kitchenette.*] How many do you suppose we're going to entertain this afternoon?

TOM *throws down the paper and jumps up with a groan.*

LAURA [*alone in the dining room*]: I don't believe we're going to receive any, Mother.

AMANDA [*reappearing, airily*]: What? No one—not one? You must be joking! [LAURA *nervously echoes her laugh. She slips in a fugitive manner through the half-open portieres and draws them gently behind her. A shaft of very clear light is thrown on her face against the faded tapestry of the curtains.*] [*Music: "The Glass Menagerie" under faintly.*] [*lightly.*] Not one gentleman caller? It can't be true! There must be a flood, there must have been a tornado!

LAURA: It isn't a flood, it's not a tornado, Mother. I'm just not popular like you were in Blue Mountain. . . . [TOM *utters another groan.* LAURA *glances at him with a faint, apologetic smile. Her voice catching a little.*] Mother's afraid I'm going to be an old maid.

[The scene dims out with "The Glass Menagerie" music.]

SCENE 2

"Laura, Haven't You Ever Liked Some Boy?"

On the dark stage the screen is lighted with the image of blue roses. Gradually LAURA'S *figure becomes apparent and the screen goes out. The music subsides.*

LAURA *is seated in the delicate ivory chair at the small clawfoot table.*

She wears a dress of soft violet material for a kimono—her hair tied back from her forehead with a ribbon.

She is washing and polishing her collection of glass.

AMANDA *appears on the fire-escape steps. At the sound of her ascent,* LAURA *catches her breath, thrusts the bowl of ornaments away and seats herself stiffly before the diagram of the typewriter keyboard as though it held her spellbound. Something has happened to* AMANDA. *It is written in her face as she climbs to the landing: a look that is grim and hopeless and a little absurd.*

She has on one of those cheap or imitation velvety-looking cloth coats with imitation fur collar. Her hat is five or six years old, one of those dreadful cloche hats that were worn in the late twenties, and she is clasping an enormous black patent-leather pocketbook with nickel clasp and initials. This is her full-dress outfit, the one she usually wears to the D.A.R.

Before entering she looks through the door.

She purses her lips, opens her eyes wide, rolls them upward and shakes her head.

Then she slowly lets herself in the door. Seeing her mother's expression LAURA *touches her lips with a nervous gesture.*

LAURA: Hello, Mother, I was—[*She makes a nervous gesture toward the chart on the wall.* AMANDA *leans against the shut door and stares at* LAURA *with a martyred look.*]

AMANDA: Deception? Deception? [*She slowly removes her hat and gloves, continuing the swift suffering stare. She lets the bat and gloves fall on the floor—a bit of acting.*]

LAURA [*shakily*]: How was the D.A.R. meeting? [AMANDA *slowly opens her purse and removes a dainty white handkerchief which she shakes out delicately and delicately touches to her lips and nostrils.*] Didn't you go to the D.A.R. meeting, Mother?

AMANDA [*faintly, almost inaudibly*]: —No.—No. [*then more forcibly.*] I did not have the strength—to go to the D.A.R. In fact, I did not have the courage! I wanted to find a hole in the ground and hide myself in it forever! [*She crosses slowly to the wall and removes the diagram of the typewriter keyboard. She holds it in front of her for a second, staring at it sweetly and sorrowfully—then bites her lips and tears it in two pieces.*]

LAURA [*faintly*]: Why did you do that, Mother? [AMANDA *repeats the same procedure with the chart of the Gregg alphabet.*] Why are you—

AMANDA: Why? Why? How old are you, Laura?

LAURA: Mother, you know my age.

AMANDA: I thought that you were an adult; it seems that I was mistaken. [*She crosses slowly to the sofa and sinks down and stares at* LAURA.]

LAURA: Please don't stare at me, Mother.

AMANDA *closes her eyes and lowers her head. Count ten.*

AMANDA: What are we going to do, what is going to become of us, what is the future?

Count ten.

LAURA: Has something happened, Mother? [*AMANDA draws a long breath and takes out the handkerchief again. Dabbing process.*] Mother, has—something happened?

AMANDA: I'll be all right in a minute. I'm just bewildered—[*count five*]—by life. . . .

LAURA: Mother, I wish that you would tell me what's happened.

AMANDA: As you know, I was supposed to be inducted into my office at the D.A.R. this afternoon. [*Image: A swarm of typewriters.*] But I stopped off at Rubicam's Business College to speak to your teachers about your having a cold and ask them what progress they thought you were making down there.

LAURA: Oh. . . .

AMANDA: I went to the typing instructor and introduced myself as your mother. She didn't know who you were. Wingfield, she said. We don't have any such student enrolled at the school! I assured her she did, that you had been going to classes since early in January. "I wonder," she said, "if you could be talking about that terribly shy little girl who dropped out of school after only a few days' attendance?" "No," I said, "Laura, my daughter, has been going to school every day for the past six weeks!" "Excuse me," she said. She took the attendance book out and there was your name, unmistakably printed, and all the dates you were absent until they decided that you had dropped out of school. I still said, "No, there must have been some mistake! There must have been some mix-up in the records!" And she said, "No—I remember her perfectly now. Her hand shook so that she couldn't hit the right keys! The first time we gave a speed-test, she broke down completely—was sick at the stomach and almost had to be carried into the wash-room! After that morning she never showed up any more. We phoned the house but never got any answer"—while I was working at Famous and Barr, I suppose, demonstrating those—Oh! I felt so weak I could barely keep on my feet. I had to sit down while they got me a glass of water! Fifty dollars tuition, all of our plans—my hopes and ambitions for you—just gone up the spout, just gone up the spout like that. [LAURA *draws a long breath and gets awkwardly to her feet. She crosses to the victrola and winds it up.*] What are you doing?

LAURA: Oh! [*She releases the handle and returns to her seat.*]

AMANDA: Laura, where have you been going when you've gone out pretending that you were going to business college?

LAURA: I've just been going out walking.

AMANDA: That's not true.

LAURA: It is. I just went walking.

AMANDA: Walking? Walking? In winter? Deliberately courting pneumonia in that light coat? Where did you walk to, Laura?

LAURA: It was the lesser of two evils, Mother. [*Image: Winter scene in park.*] I couldn't go back up. I—threw up—on the floor!

AMANDA: From half past seven till after five every day you mean to tell me you walked around in the park, because you wanted to make me think that you were still going to Rubicam's Business College?

LAURA: It wasn't as bad as it sounds. I went inside places to get warmed up.

AMANDA: Inside where?

LAURA: I went in the art museum and the bird-houses at the zoo. I visited the penguins every day! Sometimes I did without lunch and went to the movies. Lately I've been spending most of my afternoons in the Jewel box, that big glass house where they raise the tropical flowers.

AMANDA: You did all this to deceive me, just for the deception? [LAURA *looks down.*] Why?

LAURA: Mother, when you're disappointed, you get that awful suffering look on your face, like the picture of Jesus' mother in the museum!

AMANDA: Hush!

LAURA: I couldn't face it.

Pause. A whisper of strings.

[Legend: "The Crust of Humility."]

AMANDA [*hopelessly fingering the huge pocketbook*]: So what are we going to do the rest of our lives? Stay home and watch the parades go by? Amuse ourselves with the glass menagerie, darling? Eternally play those worn-out phonograph records your father left as a painful reminder of him? We won't have a business career—we've given that up because it gave us nervous indigestion! [*laughs wearily.*] What is there left but dependency all our lives? I know so well what becomes of unmarried women who aren't prepared to occupy a position. I've seen such pitiful cases in the South—barely tolerated spinsters living upon the grudging patronage of sister's husband or brother's wife!—stuck away in some little mousetrap of a room—encouraged by one in-law to visit another—little birdlike women without any nest—eating the crust of humility all their life! Is that the future that we've mapped out for ourselves? I swear it's the only alternative I can think of! It isn't a very pleasant alternative, is it? Of course—some girls *do marry.* [LAURA *twists her hands nervously.*] Haven't you ever liked some boy?

LAURA: Yes. I liked one once. [*rises.*] I came across his picture a while ago.

AMANDA [*with some interest*]: He gave you his picture?

LAURA: No, it's in the year-book.

AMANDA [*disappointed*]: Oh—a high-school boy.

[Screen Image: JIM *as a high-school hero bearing a silver cup.]*

LAURA: Yes. His name was Jim. [LAURA *lifts the heavy annual from the clawfoot table.*] Here he is in *The Pirates of Penzance.*

AMANDA [*absently*]: The what?

LAURA: The operetta the senior class put on. He had a wonderful voice and we sat across the aisle from each other Mondays, Wednesdays and Fridays in the Aud. Here he is with the silver cup for debating! See his grin?

AMANDA [*absently*]: He must have had a jolly disposition.

LAURA: He used to call me—Blue Roses.

[Image: Blue roses.]

AMANDA: Why did he call you such a name as that?

LAURA: When I had that attack of pleurosis—he asked me what was the matter when I came back. I said pleurosis—he thought that I said Blue Roses! So that's what he always called me after that. Whenever he saw me, he'd holler, "Hello, Blue Roses!" I didn't care for the girl that he went out with. Emily Meisenbach. Emily was the best-dressed girl at Soldan. She never struck me, though, as being sincere. . . . It says in the Personal Section—they're engaged. That's—six years ago! They must be married by now.

AMANDA: Girls that aren't cut out for business careers usually wind up married to some nice man. [*gets up with a spark of revival.*] Sister, that's what you'll do!

LAURA *utters a startled, doubtful laugh. She reaches quickly for a piece of glass.*

LAURA: But, Mother—

AMANDA: Yes? [*crossing to photograph.*]

LAURA [*in a tone of frightened apology*]: I'm—crippled!

[Image: Screen.]

AMANDA: Nonsense! Laura, I've told you never, never to use that word. Why, you're not crippled, you just have a little defect—hardly noticeable, even! When people have some slight disadvantage like that, they cultivate other things to make up for it—develop charm—and vivacity—and—*charm!* That's all you have to do! [*She turns again to the photograph.*] One thing your father had *plenty of—was charm!*

TOM *motions to the fiddle in the wings.*

[The scene fades out with music.]

SCENE 3

[Legend on screen: "After the Fiasco—"]

TOM *speaks from the fire escape landing.*

TOM: After the fiasco at Rubicam's Business College, the idea of getting a gentleman caller for Laura began to play a more important part in Mother's calculations. It became an obsession. Like some archetype of the universal unconscious, the image of the gentleman caller haunted our small apartment. . . . [*Image: Young man at door with flowers.*] An evening at home rarely passed without some allusion to this image, this specter, this hope. . . . Even when he wasn't mentioned, his presence hung in Mother's preoccupied look and in my sister's frightened, apologetic manner—hung like a sentence passed upon the Wingfields! Mother was a woman of action as well as words. She began to take logical steps in the planned direction. Late that winter and in the early spring—realizing that extra money would be needed to properly feather the nest and plume the bird—she conducted a vigorous campaign on the telephone, roping in subscribers to one of those magazines for matrons called *The Homemaker's Companion,* the type of journal that features the serialized sublimations of ladies of letters who think in terms of delicate cuplike breasts, slim, tapering waists, rich, creamy thighs, eyes like wood smoke in autumn, fingers that soothe and caress like strains of music, bodies as powerful as Etruscan sculpture.

[Screen image: Glamor *magazine cover.]*

AMANDA *enters with phone on long extension cord. She is spotted in the dim stage.*

AMANDA: Ida Scott? This is Amanda Wingfield! We *missed* you at the D.A.R. last Monday! I said to myself: She's probably suffering with that sinus condition! How is that sinus condition? Horrors! Heaven have mercy!—You're a Christian martyr, yes, that's what you are, a Christian martyr! Well, I just now happened to notice that your subscription to the *Companion's* about to expire! Yes, it expires with the next issue, honey!—just when that wonderful new serial by Bessie Mae Hopper is getting off to such an exciting start. Oh, honey, it's something that you can't miss! You remember how *Gone with the Wind* took everybody by storm? You simply couldn't go out if you hadn't read it. All everybody *talked* was Scarlett O'Hara. Well, this is a book that critics already compare to *Gone with the Wind.* It's the *Gone with the Wind* of the post–World War generation!—What?—Burning?—Oh, honey, don't let them burn, go take a look in the oven and I'll hold the wire! Heavens—I think she's hung up!

[Dim out.]

[Legend on screen: "You Think I'm in Love with Continental Shoemakers?"]

Before the stage is lighted, the violent voices of TOM *and* AMANDA *are heard. They are quarreling behind the portieres. In front of them stands* LAURA *with clenched hands and panicky expression.*

A clear pool of light on her figure throughout this scene.

TOM: What in Christ's name am I—

AMANDA [*shrilly*]: Don't you use that—

TOM: Supposed to do!

AMANDA: Expression! Not in my—

TOM: Ohhh!

AMANDA: Presence! Have you gone out of your senses?

TOM: I have, that's true, *driven* out!

AMANDA: What is the matter with you, you—big—big—IDIOT!

TOM: Look—I've got *no thing,* no single thing—

AMANDA: Lower your voice!

TOM: In my life here that I can call my OWN! Everything is—

AMANDA: Stop that shouting!

TOM: Yesterday you confiscated my books! You had the nerve to—

AMANDA: I took that horrible novel back to the library—yes! That hideous book by that insane Mr. Lawrence. [TOM *laughs wildly.*] I cannot control the output of diseased minds or people who cater to them—[TOM *laughs still more wildly.*] BUT I WON'T ALLOW SUCH FILTH BROUGHT INTO MY HOUSE! No, no, no, no, no!

TOM: House, house! Who pays rent on it, who makes a slave of himself to—

AMANDA [*fairly screeching*]: Don't you DARE to—

TOM: No, no, *I* mustn't say things! *I've* got to just—

AMANDA: Let me tell you—

TOM: I don't want to hear any more! [*He tears the portieres open. The upstage area is lit with a turgid smoky red glow.*]

AMANDA'S *hair is in metal curlers and she wears a very old bathrobe, much too large for her slight figure, a relic of the faithless Mr. Wingfield.*

An upright typewriter and a wild disarray of manuscripts are on the dropleaf table. The quarrel was probably precipitated by AMANDA'S *interruption of his creative labor. A chair lying overthrown on the floor.*

Their gesticulating shadows are cast on the ceiling by the fiery glow.

AMANDA: You *will* hear more, you—

TOM: No, I won't hear more, I'm going out!

AMANDA: You come right back in—

TOM: Out, out, out! Because I'm—

AMANDA: Come back here, Tom Wingfield! I'm not through talking to you!

TOM: Oh, go—

LAURA [*desperately*]: Tom!

AMANDA: You're going to listen, and no more insolence from you! I'm at the end of my patience! [*He comes back toward her.*]

TOM: What do you think I'm at? Aren't I supposed to have any patience to reach the end of, Mother? I know, I know. It seems unimportant to you, what I'm *doing*—what I *want* to do—having a little *difference* between them! You don't think that—

AMANDA: I think you've been doing things that you're ashamed of. That's why you act like this. I don't believe that you go every night to the movies. Nobody goes to the movies night after night. Nobody in their right minds goes to the movies as often as you pretend to. People don't go to the movies at nearly midnight, and movies don't let out at two A.M. Come in stumbling. Muttering to yourself like a maniac! You get three hours' sleep and then go to work. Oh, I can picture the way you're doing down there. Moping, doping, because you're in no condition.

TOM [*wildly*]: No, I'm in no condition!

AMANDA: What right have you got to jeopardize your job? Jeopardize the security of us all? How do you think we'd manage if you were—

TOM: Listen! You think I'm crazy *about* the *warehouse?* [*He bends fiercely toward her slight figure.*] You think I'm in love with the Continental Shoemakers? You think I want to spend fifty-five *years* down there in that—*celotex interior!* with—*fluorescent—tubes!* Look! I'd rather somebody picked up a crowbar and battered out my brains—than go back mornings! I *go!* Every time you come in yelling that God damn "*Rise and Shine!*" "*Rise and Shine!*" I say to myself "How *lucky dead* people are!" But I get up. I *go!* For sixty-five dollars a month I give up all that I dream of doing and being *ever!* And you say self—*self's* all I ever think of. Why, listen, if self is what I thought of, Mother, I'd be where he is—GONE! [*pointing to father's picture.*] As far as the system of transportation reaches! [*He starts past her. She grabs his arm.*] Don't grab at me, Mother!

AMANDA: Where are you going?

TOM: I'm going to the *movies!*

AMANDA: I don't believe that lie!

TOM [*Crouching toward her, overtowering her tiny figure. She backs away, gasping*]: I'm going to opium dens! Yes, opium dens, dens of vice and criminals' hangouts, Mother. I've joined the Hogan gang, I'm a hired assassin, I carry a tommy-gun in a violin case! I run a string of cathouses in the valley! They call me Killer, Killer Wingfield, I'm leading a doublelife, a simple, honest warehouse worker by day, by night a dynamic *czar* of the *underworld, Mother.* I go to gambling casinos, I spin away fortunes on the roulette table! I wear a patch over one eye and a false mustache, sometimes I put on green whiskers. On those occasions they call me—*El Diablo!* Oh, I could tell you things to make you sleepless! My enemies plan to dynamite this place. They're going to blow us all sky high some night! I'll be glad, very happy, and so will you! You'll go up, up on a broomstick, over Blue Mountain with seventeen gentlemen callers! You ugly—babbling old—*witch*. . . .

[He goes through a series of violent, clumsy movements, seizing his overcoat, lunging to the door, pulling it fiercely open. The women watch him, aghast. His arm catches in the sleeve of the coat as he struggles to pull it on. For a moment he is pinioned by the bulky garment. With an outraged groan he tears the coat off again, splitting the shoulders of it and hurls it across the room. It strikes against the shelf of LAURA*'s glass collection, there is a tinkle of shattering glass.* LAURA *cries out as if wounded.]*

[Music legend: "The Glass Menagerie."]

LAURA [*shrilly*]: *My glass!*—menagerie. . . . [*She covers her face and turns away.*] *But* AMANDA *is still stunned and stupefied by the "ugly witch" so that she barely notices this occurrence. Now she recovers her speech.*

AMANDA [*in an awful voice*]: I won't speak to you—until you apologize!

[She crosses through portieres and draws them together behind her. TOM *is left with* LAURA. LAURA *clings weakly to the mantel with her face averted.* TOM *stares at her stupidly for a moment. Then he crosses to shelf. Drops, awkwardly to his knees to collect the fallen glass, glancing at* LAURA *as if he would speak but couldn't.]*

"The Glass Menagerie" steals in as

[The scene dims out.]

SCENE 4

The interior is dark. Faint light in the alley.

A deep-voiced bell in a church is tolling the hour of five as the scene commences.

TOM *appears at the top of the alley. After each solemn boom of the bell in the tower, he shakes a little noise-maker or rattle as if to express the tiny spasm of man in contrast to the sustained power and dignity of the Almighty. This and the unsteadiness of his advance make it evident that he has been drinking.*

As he climbs the few steps to the fire-escape landing light steals up inside. LAURA *appears in nightdress, observing* TOM'S *empty bed in the front room.*

TOM *fishes in his pockets for the door key, removing a motley assortment of articles in the search, including a perfect shower of movie ticket stubs and an empty bottle. At last he finds the key, but just as he is about to insert it, it slips from his fingers. He strikes a match and crouches below the door.*

TOM [*bitterly*]: One crack—and it falls through!

LAURA *opens the door.*

LAURA: Tom! Tom, what are you doing?

TOM: Looking for a door key.

LAURA: Where have you been all this time?

TOM: I have been to the movies.

LAURA: All this time at the movies?

TOM: There was a very long program. There was a Garbo picture and a Mickey Mouse and a travelogue and a newsreel and a preview of coming attractions. And there was an organ solo and a collection for the milk fund—simultaneously—which ended up in a terrible fight between a fat lady and an usher!

LAURA [*innocently*]: Did you have to stay through everything?

TOM: Of course! And, oh, I forgot! There was a big stage show! The headliner on this stage show was Malvolio the Magician. He performed wonderful tricks, many of them, such as pouring water back and forth between pitchers. First it turned to wine and then it turned to beer and then it turned to whiskey. I know it was whiskey it finally turned into because he needed somebody to come up out of the audience to help him, and I came up—both shows! It was Kentucky Straight Bourbon. A very generous fellow, he gave souvenirs. [*He pulls from his back pocket a shimmering rainbow-colored scarf.*] He gave me this. This is his magic scarf. You can have it, Laura. You wave it over a canary cage and you get a bowl of goldfish. You wave it over the goldfish bowl and they fly away canaries. . . . But the wonderfullest trick of all was the coffin trick. We nailed him into a coffin and he got out of the coffin without removing one nail. [*He has come inside.*] There is a trick that would come in handy for me—get me out of this two-by-four situation! [*flops onto bed and starts removing shoes.*]

LAURA: Tom—Shhh!

TOM: What you shushing me for?

LAURA: You'll wake up Mother.

TOM: Goody, goody! Pay 'er back for all those "Rise an' shines." [*lies down, groaning.*] You know it don't take much intelligence to get yourself into a nailed-up coffin, Laura. But who in hell ever got himself out of one without removing one nail?

As if in answer, the father's grinning photograph lights up.

[Scene dims out.]

Immediately following: The church bell is heard striking six. At the sixth stroke the alarm clock goes off in AMANDA'S *room, and after a few moments we hear her calling: "Rise and shine! Rise and shine! Laura, go tell your brother to rise and shine!"*

TOM: [*sitting up slowly*]: I'll rise—but I won't shine.

The light increases.

AMANDA: Laura, tell your brother his coffee is ready.

LAURA *slips into front room.*

LAURA: Tom! it's nearly seven. Don't make Mother nervous. [*He stares at her stupidly. Beseechingly.*] Tom, speak to Mother this morning. Make up with her, apologize, speak to her!

TOM: She won't to me. It's her that started not speaking.

LAURA: If you just say you're sorry she'll start speaking.

TOM: Her not speaking—is that such a tragedy?

LAURA: Please—please!

AMANDA [*calling from kitchenette*]: Laura, are you going to do what I asked you to do, or do I have to get dressed and go out myself?

LAURA: Going, going—soon as I get on my coat! [*She pulls on a shapeless felt hat with nervous, jerky movement, pleadingly glancing at* TOM. *Rushes awkwardly for coat. The coat is one of* AMANDA'S, *inaccurately made-over, the sleeves too short for* LAURA.] Butter and what else?

AMANDA [*entering upstage*]: Just butter. Tell them to charge it.

LAURA: Mother, they make such faces when I do that.

AMANDA: Sticks and stones may break my bones, but the expression on Mr. Garfinkel's face won't harm us! Tell your brother his coffee is getting cold.

LAURA [*at door*]: Do what I asked you, will you, will you, Tom?

He looks sullenly away.

AMANDA: Laura, go now or just don't go at all!

LAURA [*rushing out*]: Going—going! [*A second later she cries out.* TOM *springs up and crosses to the door.* AMANDA *rushes anxiously in.* TOM *opens the door.*]

TOM: Laura?

LAURA: I'm all right. I slipped, but I'm all right.

AMANDA [*peering anxiously after her*]: If anyone breaks a leg on those fire escape steps, the landlord ought to be sued for every cent he possesses!

[She shuts door. Remembers she isn't speaking and returns to other room.]

As TOM *enters listlessly for his coffee, she turns her back to him and stands rigidly facing the window on the gloomy gray vault of the areaway. Its light on her face with its aged but childish features is cruelly sharp, satirical as a Daumier*[2] *print.*

[Music Under: "Ave Maria."]

TOM *glances sheepishly but sullenly at her averted figure and slumps at the table. The coffee is scalding hot; he sips it and gasps and spits it back in the cup. At his gasp,* AMANDA *catches her breath and half turns. Then catches herself and turns back to window.*

TOM *blows on his coffee, glancing sidewise at his mother. She clears her throat.* TOM *clears his. He starts to rise. Sinks back down again, scratches his head, clears his throat again.* AMANDA *coughs.* TOM *raises his cup in both hands to blow on it, his eyes staring over the rim of it at his mother for several moments. Then he slowly sets the cup down and awkwardly and hesitantly rises from the chair.*

TOM [*hoarsely*]: Mother. I—I apologize. Mother. [AMANDA *draws a quick, shuddering breath. Her face works grotesquely. She breaks into childlike tears.*] I'm sorry for what I said, for everything that I said, I didn't mean it.

AMANDA [*sobbingly*]: My devotion has made me a witch and so I make myself hateful to my children!

TOM: No you *don't.*

AMANDA: I worry so much, don't sleep, it makes me nervous!

TOM [*gently*]: I understand that.

AMANDA: I've had to put up a solitary battle all these years. But you're my right-hand bower! Don't fall down, don't fail!

TOM [*gently*]: I try, Mother.

[2]**Honoré Daumier** (1808–1879) French caricaturist, painter, and sculptor who was known for the lithographs he created to mock middle class society.

AMANDA [*with great enthusiasm*]: Try and you will SUCCEED! [*The notion makes her breathless.*] Why, you—you're just *full* of natural endowments! Both of my children—they're *unusual* children! Don't you think I know it? I'm so—*proud!* Happy and—feel I've—so much to be thankful for but—promise me one thing, son!

TOM: What, Mother?

AMANDA: Promise, son, you'll—never be a drunkard!

TOM [*turns to her grinning*]: I will never be a drunkard, Mother.

AMANDA: That's what frightened me so, that you'd be drinking! Eat a bowl of Purina!

TOM: Just coffee, Mother.

AMANDA: Shredded wheat biscuit?

TOM: No. No, Mother, just coffee.

AMANDA: You can't put in a day's work on an empty stomach. You've got ten minutes—don't gulp! Drinking too-hot liquids makes cancer of the stomach.... Put cream in.

TOM: No, thank you.

AMANDA: To cool it.

TOM: No! No, thank you, I want it black.

AMANDA: I know, but it's not good for you. We have to do all that we can to build ourselves up. In these trying times we live in, all that we have to cling to is—each other.... That's why it's so important to—Tom, I—I sent out your sister so I could discuss something with you. If you hadn't spoken I would have spoken to you. [*sits down.*]

TOM [*gently*]: What is it, Mother, that you want to discuss?

AMANDA: Laura!

TOM *puts his cup down slowly.*

[Legend on screen: "Laura."]

[Music: "The Glass Menagerie."]

TOM: —Oh.—Laura...

AMANDA [*touching his sleeve*]: You know how Laura is. So quiet but—still water runs deep! She notices things and I think she—broods about them. [TOM *looks up.*] A few days ago I came in and she was crying.

TOM: What about?

AMANDA: You.

TOM: Me?

AMANDA: She has an idea that you're not happy here.

TOM: What gave her that idea?

AMANDA: What gives her any idea? However, you do act strangely. I—I'm not criticizing, understand *that!* I know your ambitions do not lie in the warehouse, that like everybody in the whole wide world—you've had to—make sacrifices, but—Tom—Tom—life's not easy, it calls for—Spartan endurance! There's so many things in my heart that I cannot describe to you! I've never told you but I—*loved* your father. . . .

TOM [*gently*]: I know that, Mother.

AMANDA: And you—when I see you taking after his ways! Staying out late—and—well, you *had* been drinking the night you were in that—terrifying condition! Laura says that you hate the apartment and that you go out nights to get away from it! Is that true, Tom?

TOM: No. You say there's so much in your heart that you can't describe to me. That's true of me, too. There's so much in my heart that I can't describe to *you!* So let's respect each other's—

AMANDA: But, why—*why,* Tom—are you always so *restless?* Where do you go to, nights?

TOM: I—go to the movies.

AMANDA: Why do you go to the movies so much, Tom?

TOM: I go to the movies because—I like adventure. Adventure is something I don't have much of at work, so I go to the movies.

AMANDA: But, Tom, you go to the movies *entirely* too *much!*

TOM: I like a lot of adventure.

AMANDA *looks baffled, then hurt. As the familiar inquisition resumes he becomes hard and impatient again.* AMANDA *slips back into her querulous attitude toward him.*

[Image on screen: Sailing vessel with Jolly Roger.]

AMANDA: Most young men find adventure in their careers.

TOM: Then most young men are not employed in a warehouse.

AMANDA: The world is full of young men employed in warehouses and offices and factories.

TOM: Do all of them find adventure in their careers?

AMANDA: They do or they do without it! Not everybody has a craze for adventure.

TOM: Man is by instinct a lover, a hunter, a fighter, and none of those instincts are given much play at the warehouse!

AMANDA: Man is by instinct! Don't quote instinct to me! Instinct is something that people have got away from! It belongs to animals! Christian adults don't want it!

TOM: What do Christian adults want, then, Mother?

AMANDA: Superior things! Things of the mind and the spirit! Only animals have to satisfy instincts! Surely your aims are somewhat higher than theirs! Than monkeys—pigs—

TOM: I reckon they're not.

AMANDA: You're joking. However, that isn't what I wanted to discuss.

TOM [*rising*]: I haven't much time.

AMANDA [*pushing his shoulders*]: Sit down.

TOM: You want me to punch in red at the warehouse, Mother?

AMANDA: You have five minutes. I want to talk about Laura.

[Legend: "Plans and Provisions."]

TOM: All right! What about Laura?

AMANDA: We have to be making plans and provisions for her. She's older than you, two years, and nothing has happened. She just drifts along doing nothing. It frightens me terribly how she just drifts along.

TOM: I guess she's the type that people call home girls.

AMANDA: There's no such type, and if there is, it's a pity! That is unless the home is hers, with a husband!

TOM: What?

AMANDA: Oh, I can see the handwriting on the wall as plain as I see the nose in the front of my face! It's terrifying! More and more you remind me of your father! He was out all hours without explanation—Then *left! Goodbye!* And me with the bag to hold. I saw that letter you got from the merchant marine. I know what you're dreaming of. I'm not standing here blindfolded. Very well, then. Then *do* it! But not till there's somebody to take your place.

TOM: What do you mean?

AMANDA: I mean that as soon as Laura has got somebody to take care of her, married, a home of her own, independent—why, then you'll be free to go wherever you please, on land, on sea, whichever way the wind blows! But until that time you've got to look out for your sister. I don't say me because I'm old and don't matter! I say for your sister because she's young and dependent. I put her in business college—a dismal failure! Frightened her so it made her sick to her stomach. I took her over to the Young People's League at the church. Another fiasco. She spoke to nobody, nobody spoke to her. Now all she does is fool with those pieces of glass and play those worn-out records. What kind of a life is that for a girl to lead!

TOM: What can I do about it?

AMANDA: Overcome selfishness! Self, self, self is all that you ever think of! [TOM *springs up and crosses to get his coat. It is ugly and bulky. He pulls on a cap with earmuffs.*] Where is your muffler? Put your wool muffler on! [*He snatches it angrily from the closet and tosses it around his neck and pulls both ends tight.*] Tom! I haven't said what I had in mind to ask you.

TOM: I'm too late to—

AMANDA [*catching his arms—very importunately. Then shyly*]: Down at the warehouse, aren't there some—nice young men?

TOM: No!

AMANDA: There must be—*some.*

TOM: Mother—

Gesture.

AMANDA: Find out one that's clean-living—doesn't drink and—ask him out for sister!

TOM: What?

AMANDA: For *sister!* To *meet!* Get *acquainted!*

TOM [*stamping to door*]: Oh, my *go-osh!*

AMANDA: Will you? [*He opens door. Imploringly.*] Will you? [*He starts down*] Will you? Will you, dear?

TOM [*calling back*]: YES!

AMANDA *closes the door hesitantly and with a troubled but faintly hopeful expression.*

[*Screen image:* Glamor *magazine cover.*]

Spot AMANDA *at phone.*

AMANDA: Ella Cartwright? This is Amanda Wingfield! How are you, honey? How is that kidney condition? [*count five.*] *Horrors!* [*count five.*] You're a Christian martyr, yes, honey, that's what you are, a Christian martyr! Well, I just happened to notice in my little red book that your subscription to the *Companion* has just run out! I knew that you wouldn't want to miss out on the wonderful serial starting in this new issue. It's by Bessie Mae Hopper, the first thing she's written since *Honeymoon for Three.* Wasn't that a strange and interesting story? Well, this one is even lovelier, I believe. It has a sophisticated society background. It's all about the horsey set on Long Island!

[*Fade out.*]

SCENE 5

[*Legend on screen: "Annunciation."*] *Fade with music.*

It is early dusk of a spring evening. Supper has just been finished at the Wingfield apartment. AMANDA *and* LAURA *in light colored dresses are removing dishes from the table, in the upstage area, which is shadowy, their movements formalized almost as a dance or ritual, their moving forms as pale and silent as moths.*

TOM, *in white shirt and trousers, rises from the table and crosses toward the fire escape.*

AMANDA [*as he passes her*]: Son, will you do me a favor?

TOM: What?

AMANDA: Comb your hair! You look so pretty when your hair is combed! [TOM *slouches on sofa with evening paper. Enormous caption: "Franco Triumphs."*] There is only one respect in which I would like you to emulate your father.

TOM: What respect is that?

AMANDA: The care he always took of his appearance. He never allowed himself to look untidy. [*He throws down the paper and crosses to fire escape.*] Where are you going?

TOM: I'm going out to smoke.

AMANDA: You smoke too much. A pack a day at fifteen cents a pack. How much would that amount to in a month? Thirty times fifteen is how much, Tom? Figure it out and you will be astounded at what you could save. Enough to give you a night-school course in accounting at Washington U! Just think what a wonderful thing that would be for you, son!

TOM *is unmoved by the thought.*

TOM: I'd rather smoke. [*He steps out on landing, letting the screen door slam.*]

AMANDA [*sharply*]: I know! That's the tragedy of it. . . . [*Alone, she turns to look at her husband's picture.*]

[*Dance music: "All the World Is Waiting for the Sunrise!"*]

TOM [*to the audience*]: Across the alley from us was the Paradise Dance Hall. On evenings in spring the windows and doors were open and the music came outdoors. Sometimes the lights were turned out except for a large glass sphere that hung from the ceiling. It would turn slowly about and filter the dusk with delicate rainbow colors. Then the orchestra played a waltz or a tango, something that had a slow and sensuous rhythm. Couples would come outside, to the relative privacy of the alley. You could see them kissing behind ash pits and telephone poles. This was the compensation for lives that passed like mine, without any change or adventure. Adventure and change were imminent in this year. They were waiting around the corner for all these kids. Suspended in the mist over Berchtesgaden[3], caught in the folds of Chamberlain's[4] umbrella—In Spain there was Guernica! But here there was only hot swing music and liquor, dance halls, bars, and movies, and sex that hung in the gloom like a chandelier and flooded the world with brief, deceptive rainbows. . . . All the world was waiting for bombardments!

AMANDA *turns from the picture and comes outside.*

AMANDA [*sighing*]: A fire escape landing's a poor excuse for a porch. [*She spreads a newspaper on a step and sits down, gracefully and demurely as if she were settling into a swing on a Mississippi veranda.*] What are you looking at?

TOM: The moon.

AMANDA: Is there a moon this evening?

[3] **Berchtesgaden** A resort town in Bavaria, Germany, where Hitler met with the leaders of the Third Reich to plan strategy. [4] **Neville Chamberlain** (1969–1940) British prime minister who believed that Hitler could be appeased, a policy that many thought led to World War II.

TOM: It's rising over Garfinkel's Delicatessen.

AMANDA: So it is! A little silver slipper of a moon. Have you made a wish on it yet?

TOM: Um-hum.

AMANDA: What did you wish for?

TOM: That's a secret.

AMANDA: A secret, huh? Well, I won't tell mine either. I will be just as mysterious as you.

TOM: I bet I can guess what yours is.

AMANDA: Is my head so transparent?

TOM: You're not a sphinx.

AMANDA: No, I don't have secrets. I'll tell you what I wished for on the moon. Success and happiness for my precious children! I wish for that whenever there's a moon, and when there isn't a moon, I wish for it, too.

TOM: I thought perhaps you wished for a gentleman caller.

AMANDA: Why do you say that?

TOM: Don't you remember asking me to fetch one?

AMANDA: I remember suggesting that it would be nice for your sister if you brought some nice young man from the warehouse. I think I've made that suggestion more than once.

TOM: Yes, you have made it repeatedly.

AMANDA: Well?

TOM: We are going to have one.

AMANDA: What?

TOM: A gentleman caller!

[The Annunciation Is Celebrated with Music.]

AMANDA *rises.*

[Image on screen: Caller with bouquet.]

AMANDA: You mean you have asked some nice young man to come over?

TOM: Yep. I've asked him to dinner.

AMANDA: You really did?

TOM: I did!

AMANDA: You did, and did he—*accept?*

TOM: He did!

AMANDA: Well, well—well, well! That's—lovely!

TOM: I thought that you would be pleased.

AMANDA: It's definite, then?

TOM: Very definite.

AMANDA: Soon?

TOM: Very soon.

AMANDA: For heaven's sake, stop putting on and tell me some things, will you?

TOM: What things do you want me to tell you?

AMANDA: Naturally I would like to know when he's *coming!*

TOM: He's coming tomorrow.

AMANDA: *Tomorrow?*

TOM: Yep. Tomorrow.

AMANDA: But, Tom!

TOM: Yes, Mother?

AMANDA: Tomorrow gives me no time!

TOM: Time for what?

AMANDA: Preparations! Why didn't you phone me at once, as soon as you asked him, the minute that he accepted? Then, don't you see, I could have been getting ready!

TOM: You don't have to make any fuss.

AMANDA: Oh, Tom, Tom, Tom, of course I have to make a fuss! I want things nice, not sloppy! Not thrown together. I'll certainly have to do some fast thinking, won't I?

TOM: I don't see why you have to think at all.

AMANDA: You just don't know. We can't have a gentleman caller in a pigsty! All my wedding silver has to be polished, the monogrammed table linen ought to be laundered! The windows have to be washed and fresh curtains put up. And how about clothes? We have to *wear* something, don't we?

TOM: Mother, this boy is no one to make a fuss over!

AMANDA: Do you realize he's the first young man we've introduced to your sister? It's terrible, dreadful, disgraceful that poor little sister has never received a single gentleman caller! Tom, come inside! [*She opens the screen door.*]

TOM: What for?

AMANDA: I want to ask you some things.

TOM: If you're going to make such a fuss, I'll call it off, I'll tell him not to come.

AMANDA: You certainly won't do anything of the kind. Nothing offends people worse than broken engagements. It simply means I'll have to work like a Turk! We won't be brilliant, but we'll pass inspection. Come on inside. [TOM *follows, groaning.*] Sit down.

TOM: Any particular place you would like me to sit?

AMANDA: Thank heavens I've got that new sofa! I'm also making payments on a floor lamp I'll have sent out! And put the chintz covers on, they'll brighten things up! Of course I'd hoped to have these walls repapered . . . . What is the young man's name?

TOM: His name is O'Connor.

AMANDA: That, of course, means fish—tomorrow is Friday! I'll have that salmon loaf—with Durkee's dressing! What does he do? He works at the warehouse?

TOM: Of course! How else would I—

AMANDA: Tom, he—doesn't drink?

TOM: Why do you ask me that?

AMANDA: Your father *did!*

TOM: Don't get started on that!

AMANDA: He *does* drink, then?

TOM: Not that I know of!

AMANDA: Make sure, be certain! The last thing I want for my daughter's a boy who drinks!

TOM: Aren't you being a little premature? Mr. O'Connor has not yet appeared on the scene!

AMANDA: But will tomorrow. To meet your sister, and what do I know about his character? Nothing! Old maids are better off than wives of drunkards!

TOM: Oh, my God!

AMANDA: Be still!

TOM [*leaning forward to whisper*]: Lots of fellows meet girls whom they don't marry!

AMANDA: Oh, talk sensibly, Tom—and don't be sarcastic! [*She has gotten a hair-brush.*]

TOM: What are you doing?

AMANDA: I'm brushing that cowlick down! What is this young man's position at the warehouse?

TOM [*submitting grimly to the brush and the interrogation*]: This young man's position is that of a shipping clerk, Mother.

AMANDA: Sounds to me like a fairly responsible job, the sort of a job *you* would be in if you just had more *get-up.* What is his salary? Have you got any idea?

TOM: I would judge it to be approximately eighty-five dollars a month.

AMANDA: Well—not princely, but—

TOM: Twenty more than I make.

AMANDA: Yes, how well I know! But for a family man, eighty-five dollars a month is not much more than you can just get by on. . . .

TOM: Yes, but Mr. O'Connor is not a family man.

AMANDA: He might be, mightn't he? Some time in the future?

TOM: I see. Plans and provisions.

AMANDA: You are the only young man that I know of who ignores the fact that the future becomes the present, the present the past, and the past turns into everlasting regret if you don't plan for it!

TOM: I will think that over and see what I can make of it.

AMANDA: Don't be supercilious with your mother! Tell me some more about this—what do you call him?

TOM: James D. O'Connor. The D. is for Delaney.

AMANDA: Irish on *both* sides! *Gracious!* And doesn't drink?

TOM: Shall I call him up and ask him right this minute?

AMANDA: The only way to find out about those things is to make discreet inquiries at the proper moment. When I was a girl in Blue Mountain and it was suspected that a young man drank, the girl whose attentions he had been receiving, if any girl *was,* would sometimes speak to the minister of his church, or rather her father would if her father was living, and sort of feel him out on the young man's character. That is the way such things are discreetly handled to keep a young woman from making a tragic mistake!

TOM: Then how did you happen to make a tragic mistake?

AMANDA: That innocent look of your father's had everyone fooled! He *smiled*—the world was *enchanted!* No girl can do worse than put herself at the mercy of a handsome appearance! I hope that Mr. O'Connor is not too good-looking.

TOM: No, he's not too good-looking. He's covered with freckles and hasn't too much of a nose.

AMANDA: He's not right-down homely, though?

TOM: Not right-down homely. Just medium homely, I'd say.

AMANDA: Character's what to look for in a man.

TOM: That's what I've always said, Mother.

AMANDA: You've never said anything of the kind and I suspect you would never give it a thought.

TOM: Don't be suspicious of me.

AMANDA: At least I hope he's the type that's up and coming.

TOM: I think he really goes in for self-improvement.

AMANDA: What reason have you to think so?

TOM: He goes to night school.

AMANDA [*beaming*]: Splendid! What does he do, I mean study?

TOM: Radio engineering and public speaking!

AMANDA: Then he has visions of being advanced in the world! Any young man who studies public speaking is aiming to have an executive job some day! And radio engineering? A thing for the future! Both of these facts are very illuminating. Those are the sort of things that a mother should know concerning any young man who comes to call on her daughter. Seriously or—not.

TOM: One little warning. He doesn't know about Laura. I didn't let on that we had dark ulterior motives. I just said, why don't you come have dinner with us? He said okay and that was the whole conversation.

AMANDA: I bet it was! You're eloquent as an oyster. However, he'll know about Laura when he gets here. When he sees how lovely and sweet and pretty she is, he'll thank his lucky stars he was asked to dinner.

TOM: Mother, you mustn't expect too much of Laura.

AMANDA: What do you mean?

TOM: Laura seems all those things to you and me because she's ours and we love her. We don't even notice she's crippled any more.

AMANDA: Don't say crippled! You know that I never allow that word to be used!

TOM: But face facts, Mother. She is and—that's not all—

AMANDA: What do you mean "not all"?

TOM: Laura is very different from other girls.

AMANDA: I think the difference is all to her advantage.

TOM: Not quite all—in the eyes of others—strangers—she's terribly shy and lives in a world of her own and those things make her seem a little peculiar to people outside the house.

AMANDA: Don't say peculiar.

TOM: Face the facts. She is.

[The dance-Hall music changes to a tango that has a minor and somewhat ominous tone.]

AMANDA: In what way is she peculiar—may I ask?

TOM [*gently*]: She lives in a world of her own—a world of—little glass ornaments, Mother. . . . [*Gets up.* AMANDA *remains holding brush, looking at him, troubled.*] She plays old phonograph records and—that's about all—[*He glances at himself in the mirror and crosses to door.*]

AMANDA [*sharply*]: Where are you going?

TOM: I'm going to the movies. [*out screen door.*]

AMANDA: Not to the movies, every night to the movies! [*follows quickly to screen door.*] I don't believe you always go to the movies! [*He is gone.* AMANDA *looks worriedly after him for a moment. Then vitality and optimism return and she turns from the door. Crossing to portieres.*] Laura! Laura! [LAURA *answers from kitchenette.*]

LAURA: Yes, Mother.

AMANDA: Let those dishes go and come in front! [LAURA *appears with dish towel. Gaily.*] Laura, come here and make a wish on the moon!

LAURA [*entering*]: Moon—moon?

AMANDA: A little silver slipper of a moon. Look over your left shoulder, Laura, and make a wish! [LAURA *looks faintly puzzled as if called out of sleep.* AMANDA *seizes her shoulders and turns her at angle by the door.*] Now! Now, darling, *wish!*

LAURA: What shall I wish for, Mother?

AMANDA: [*her voice trembling and her eyes suddenly filling with tears*]: Happiness! Good fortune!

The violin rises and the stage dims out.

SCENE 6

[Image: High school hero.]

TOM: And so the following evening I brought Jim home to dinner. I had known Jim slightly in high school. In high school Jim was a hero. He had tremendous Irish good nature and vitality with the scrubbed and polished look of white chinaware. He seemed to move in a continual spotlight. He was a star in basketball, captain of the debating club, president of the senior class and the glee club and he sang the male lead in the annual light operas. He was always running or bounding, never just walking. He seemed always at the point of defeating the law of gravity. He was shooting with such velocity through his adolescence that you would logically expect him to arrive at nothing short of the White House by the time he was thirty. But Jim apparently ran into more interference after his graduation from Soldan. His speed had definitely slowed. Six years after he left high school he was holding a job that wasn't much better than mine.

[Image: Clerk.]

He was the only one at the warehouse with whom I was on friendly terms. I was valuable to him as someone who could remember his former glory, who had seen him win basketball games and the silver cup in debating. He knew of my secret practice of retiring to a cabinet of the washroom to work on poems when business was slack in the warehouse. He called me Shakespeare. And while the other boys in the warehouse regarded me with suspicious hostility, Jim took a humorous attitude toward me. Gradually his attitude affected the others, their hostility wore off and they also began to smile at me as people smile at an oddly fashioned dog who trots across their path at some distance.

I knew that Jim and Laura had known each other at Soldan, and I had heard Laura speak admiringly of his voice. I didn't know if Jim remembered her or not. In high school Laura had been as unobtrusive as Jim had been astonishing. If he did remember Laura, it was not as my sister, for when I asked him to dinner, he grinned and said, "You know, Shakespeare, I never thought of you as having folks!"

He was about to discover that I did. . . .

[Light upstage]

[Legend on screen: "The Accent of a Coming Foot."]

Friday evening. It is about five o'clock of a late spring evening which comes "scattering poems in the sky."

A delicate lemony light is in the Wingfield apartment.

AMANDA *has worked like a Turk in preparation for the gentleman caller. The results are astonishing. The new floor lamp with its rose-silk shade is in place, a colored paper lantern conceals the broken light fixture in the ceiling, new billowing white curtains are at the windows, chintz covers are on chairs and sofa, a pair of new sofa pillows make their initial appearance.*

Open boxes and tissue paper are scattered on the floor.

LAURA *stands in the middle with lifted arms while* AMANDA *crouches before her, adjusting the hem of the new dress, devout and ritualistic. The dress is colored and designed by memory. The arrangement of* LAURA'S *hair is changed; it is softer and more becoming. A fragile, unearthly prettiness has come out in* LAURA: *she is like a piece of translucent glass touched by light, given a momentary radiance, not actual, not lasting.*

AMANDA [*impatiently*]: Why are you trembling?

LAURA: Mother, you've made me so nervous!

AMANDA: How have I made you nervous?

LAURA: By all this fuss! You make it seem so important!

AMANDA: I don't understand you, Laura. You couldn't be satisfied with just sitting home, and yet whenever I try to arrange something for you, you seem to resist it. [*She gets up.*] Now take a look at yourself. No, wait! Wait just a moment—I have an idea!

LAURA: What is it now?

AMANDA *produces two powder puffs which she wraps in handkerchiefs and stuffs in* LAURA'S *bosom.*

LAURA: Mother, what are you doing?

AMANDA: They call them "Gay Deceivers!"

LAURA: I won't wear them!

AMANDA: You will!

LAURA: Why should I?

AMANDA: Because, to be painfully honest, your chest is flat.

LAURA: You make it seem like we were setting a trap.

AMANDA: All pretty girls are a trap, a pretty trap, and men expect them to be. [*Legend: "A Pretty Trap."*] Now look at yourself, young lady. This is the prettiest you will ever be! I've got to fix myself now! You're going to be surprised by your mother's appearance! [*She crosses through portieres, humming gaily.*]

LAURA *moves slowly to the long mirror and stares solemnly at herself.*

A wind blows the white curtains inward in a slow, graceful motion and with a faint sorrowful sighing.

AMANDA [*off stage*]: It isn't dark enough yet. [*She turns slowly before the mirror with a troubled look.*]

[Legend on screen: "This Is My Sister: Celebrate Her with Strings!" Music.]

AMANDA [*laughing, off*]: I'm going to show you something. I'm going to make a spectacular appearance!

LAURA: What is it, Mother?

AMANDA: Possess your soul in patience—you will see! Something I've resurrected from that old trunk! Styles haven't changed so terribly much after all.... [*She parts the portieres.*] Now just look at your mother! [*She wears a girlish frock of yellowed voile with a blue silk sash. She carries a bunch of jonquils—the legend of her youth is nearly revived. Feverishly.*] This is the dress in which I led the cotillion. Won the cakewalk twice at Sunset Hill, wore one spring to the governor's ball in Jackson! See how I sashayed around the ballroom, Laura? [*She raises her skirt and does a mincing step around the room.*] I wore it on Sundays for my gentlemen callers! I had it on the day I met your father—I had malaria fever all that spring. The change of climate from East Tennessee to the Delta—weakened resistance—I had a little temperature all the time—not enough to be serious—just enough to make me restless and giddy! Invitations poured in—parties all over the Delta!—"Stay in bed," said Mother, "you have fever!"—but I just wouldn't.—I took quinine but kept on going, going!—Evenings, dances!—Afternoons, long, long rides! Picnics—lovely!—So lovely, that country in May.—All lacy with dogwood, literally flooded with jonquils!—That was the spring I had the craze for jonquils. Jonquils became an absolute obsession. Mother said, "Honey, there's no more room for jonquils." And still I kept bringing in more jonquils. Whenever, wherever I saw them, I'd say, "Stop! Stop! I see jonquils!" I made the young men help me gather the jonquils! It was a joke, Amanda and her jonquils! Finally there were no more vases to hold them, every available space was filled with jonquils. No vases to hold them? All right, I'll hold them myself! And then I—[*She stops in front of the picture. Music.*] met your father! Malaria fever and jonquils and then—this—boy. . . . [*She switches on the rose-colored lamp.*] I hope they get here before it starts to rain. [*She crosses upstage and places the jonquils in bowl on table.*] I gave your brother a little extra change so he and Mr. O'Connor could take the service car home.

LAURA [*with altered look*]: What did you say his name was?

AMANDA: O'Connor.

LAURA: What is his first name?

AMANDA: I don't remember. Oh, yes, I do. It was—Jim!

LAURA *sways slightly and catches hold of a chair.*

[Legend on screen: "Not Jim!"]

LAURA [*faintly*]: Not—Jim!

AMANDA: Yes, that was it, it was Jim! I've never known a Jim that wasn't nice!

[Music: Ominous.]

LAURA: Are you sure his name is Jim O'Connor?

AMANDA: Yes. Why?

LAURA: Is he the one that Tom used to know in high school?

AMANDA: He didn't say so. I think he just got to know him at the warehouse.

LAURA: There was a Jim O'Connor we both knew in high school—[*Then, with effort.*] If that is the one that Tom is bringing to dinner—you'll have to excuse me, I won't come to the table.

AMANDA: What sort of nonsense is this?

LAURA: You asked me once if I'd ever liked a boy. Don't you remember I showed you this boy's picture?

AMANDA: You mean the boy you showed me in the year book?

LAURA: Yes, that boy.

AMANDA: Laura, Laura, were you in love with that boy?

LAURA: I don't know, Mother. All I know is I couldn't sit at the table if it was him!

AMANDA: It won't be him! It isn't the least bit likely. But whether it is or not, you will come to the table. You will not be excused.

LAURA: I'll have to be, Mother.

AMANDA: I don't intend to humor your silliness, Laura. I've had too much from you and your brother, both! So just sit down and compose yourself till they come. Tom has forgotten his key so you'll have to let them in, when they arrive.

LAURA [*panicky*]: Oh, Mother—*you* answer the door!

AMANDA [*lightly*]: I'll be in the kitchen—busy!

LAURA: Oh, Mother, please answer the door, don't make me do it!

AMANDA [*crossing into kitchenette*]: I've got to fix the dressing for the salmon. Fuss, fuss—silliness!—over a gentleman caller!

Door swings shut. LAURA *is left alone.*

[Legend: "Terror!"]

She utters a low moan and turns off the lamp—sits stiffly on the edge of the sofa, knotting her fingers together.

[Legend on screen: "The Opening of a Door!"]

TOM *and* JIM *appear on the fire escape steps and climb to landing. Hearing their approach,* LAURA *rises with a panicky gesture. She retreats to the portieres.*

The doorbell. LAURA *catches her breath and touches her throat. Low drums.*

AMANDA [*calling*]: Laura, sweetheart! The door!

LAURA *stares at it without moving.*

JIM: I think we just beat the rain.

TOM: Uh-huh. [*He rings again, nervously.* JIM *whistles and fishes for a cigarette.*]

AMANDA [*very, very gaily*]: Laura, that is your brother and Mr. O'Connor! Will you let them in, darling?

LAURA *crosses toward kitchenette door.*

LAURA [*breathlessly*]: Mother—you go to the door!

AMANDA *steps out of kitchenette and stares furiously at* LAURA: *She points imperiously at the door.*

LAURA: Please, please!

AMANDA [*in a fierce whisper*]: What is the matter with you, you silly thing?

LAURA [*desperately*]: Please, you answer it, *please!*

AMANDA: I told you I wasn't going to humor you, Laura. Why have you chosen this moment to lose your mind?

LAURA: Please, please, please, you go!

AMANDA: You'll have to go to the door because I can't!

LAURA [*despairingly*]: I can't either!

AMANDA: Why?

LAURA: I'm *sick!*

AMANDA: I'm sick, too—of your nonsense! Why can't you and your brother be normal people? Fantastic whims and behavior! [TOM *gives a long ring.*] Preposterous goings on! Can you give me one reason—[*calls out lyrically.*] COMING! JUST ONE SECOND!—why should you be afraid to open a door? Now you answer it, Laura!

LAURA: Oh, oh, oh . . . [*She returns through the portieres. Darts to the victrola and winds it frantically and turns it on.*]

AMANDA: Laura Wingfield, you march right to that door!

LAURA: Yes—yes, Mother!

A faraway, scratchy rendition of "Dardanella" softens the air and gives her strength to move through it. She slips to the door and draws it cautiously open. TOM *enters with caller,* JIM O'CONNOR.

TOM: Laura, this is Jim. Jim, this is my sister, Laura.

JIM [*stepping inside*]: I didn't know that Shakespeare had a sister!

LAURA [*retreating stiff and trembling from the door*]: How—how do you do?

JIM [*heartily extending his hand*]: Okay!

LAURA *touches it hesitantly with hers.*

JIM: Your hand's *cold,* Laura!

LAURA: Yes, well—I've been playing the victrola. . . .

JIM: Must have been playing classical music on it! You ought to play a little hot swing music to warm you up!

LAURA: Excuse me—I haven't finished playing the victrola. . . .

She turns awkwardly and hurries into the front room. She pauses a second by the victrola. Then catches her breath and darts through the portieres like a frightened deer.

JIM [*grinning*]: What was the matter?

TOM: Oh—with Laura? Laura is—terribly shy.

JIM: Shy, huh? It's unusual to meet a shy girl nowadays. I don't believe you ever mentioned you had a sister.

TOM: Well, now you know. I have one. Here is the *Post Dispatch.* You want a piece of it?

JIM: Uh-huh.

TOM: What piece? The comics?

JIM: Sports! [*glances at it*] Ole Dizzy Dean is on his bad behavior.

TOM [*disinterest*] Yeah? [*lights cigarette and crosses back to fire escape door.*]

JIM: Where are *you* going?

TOM: I'm going out on the terrace.

JIM [*goes after him*]: You know, Shakespeare—I'm going to sell you a bill of goods!

TOM: What goods?

JIM: A course I'm taking.

TOM: Huh?

JIM: In public speaking! You and me, we're not the warehouse type.

TOM: Thanks—that's good news. But what has public speaking got to do with it?

JIM: It fits you for—executive positions!

TOM: Awww.

JIM: I tell you it's done a helluva lot for me.

[Image: Executive at desk.]

TOM: In what respect?

JIM: In every! Ask yourself what is the difference between you an' me and men in the office down front? Brains?—No!—Ability?—No! Then what? Just one little thing—

TOM: What is that one little thing?

JIM: Primarily it amounts to—social poise! Being able to square up to people and hold your own on any social level!

AMANDA [*off stage*]: Tom?

TOM: Yes, Mother?

AMANDA: Is that you and Mr. O'Connor?

TOM: Yes, Mother.

AMANDA: Well, you just make yourselves comfortable in there.

TOM: Yes, Mother.

AMANDA: Ask Mr. O'Connor if he would like to wash his hands.

JIM: Aw—no—no—thank you—I took care of that at the warehouse. Tom—

TOM: Yes?

JIM: Mr. Mendoza was speaking to me about you.

TOM: Favorably?

JIM: What do you think?

TOM: Well—

JIM: You're going to be out of a job if you don't wake up.

TOM: I am waking up—

JIM: You show no signs.

TOM: The signs are interior.

[Image on screen: The sailing vessel with Jolly Roger again.]

TOM: I'm planning to change. [*He leans over the rail speaking with quiet exhilaration. The incandescent marquees and signs of the first-run movie houses light his face from across the alley. He looks like a voyager.*] I'm right at the point of committing myself to a future that doesn't include the warehouse and Mr. Mendoza or even a night-school course in public speaking.

JIM: What are you gassing about?

TOM: I'm tired of the movies.

JIM: Movies!

TOM: Yes, movies! Look at them—[*a wave toward the marvels of Grand Avenue.*] All of those glamorous people—having adventures—hogging it all, gobbling the whole thing up! You know what happens? People go to the *movies* instead of *moving!* Hollywood characters are supposed to have all the adventures for everybody in America, while everybody in America sits in a dark room and watches them have them! Yes, until there's a war. That's when adventure becomes available to the masses! *Everyone's* dish, not only Gable's! Then the people in the dark room come out of the dark room to have some adventures themselves—Goody, goody—It's our turn now, to go to the South Sea Island—to make a safari—to be exotic, far off—But I'm not patient. I don't want to wait till then. I'm tired of the movies and I am *about to move!*

JIM [*incredulously*]: Move?

TOM: Yes.

JIM: When?

TOM: Soon!

JIM: Where? Where?

Theme three music Seems to Answer the Question, while TOM *thinks it over. He Searches among his pockets.*

TOM: I'm starting to boil inside. I know I seem dreamy, but inside—well, I'm boiling! Whenever I pick up a shoe, I shudder a little thinking how short life is and what I am doing!—Whatever that means. I know it doesn't mean shoes—except as something to wear on a traveler's feet [*finds paper.*] Look—

JIM: What?

TOM: I'm a member.

JIM [*reading*]: The Union of Merchant Seamen.

TOM: I paid my dues this month, instead of the light bill.

JIM: You will regret it when they turn the lights off.

TOM: I won't be here.

JIM: How about your mother?

TOM: I'm like my father. The bastard son of a bastard! See how he grins? And he's been absent going on sixteen years!

JIM: You're just talking, you drip. How does your mother feel about it?

TOM: Shhh—Here comes Mother! Mother is not acquainted with my plans!

AMANDA [*enters portieres*]: Where are you all?

TOM: On the terrace, Mother.

They start inside. She advances to them. TOM *is distinctly shocked at her appearance. Even* JIM *blinks a little. He is making his first contact with girlish Southern vivacity and in spite of the night-school course in public speaking is somewhat thrown off the beam by the unexpected outlay of social charm.*

Certain responses are attempted by JIM *but are swept aside by* AMANDA'*s gay laughter and chatter.* TOM *is embarrassed but after the first shock* JIM *reacts very warmly. Grins and chuckles, is altogether won over.*

[Image: AMANDA *as a girl.]*

AMANDA [*coyly smiling, shaking her girlish ringlets*]: Well, well, well, so this is Mr. O'Connor. Introductions entirely unnecessary. I've heard so much about you from my boy. I finally said to him, Tom—good gracious!—why don't you bring this paragon to supper? I'd like to meet this nice young man at the warehouse!—Instead of just hearing him sing your praises so much! I don't know why my son is so standoffish—that's not Southern behavior! Let's sit down and—I think we could stand a little more air in here! Tom, leave the door open. I felt a nice fresh breeze a moment ago. Where has it gone? Mmm, so warm already! And not quite summer, even. We're going to burn up when summer really gets started. However, we're having—we're having a very light supper. I think light things are better fo' this time of year. The same as light clothes are. Light clothes an' light food are what warm weather calls fo'. You know our blood gets so thick during th' winter—it takes a while fo' us to *adjust* ou'selves—when the season changes. . . . It's come so quick this year, I wasn't prepared. All of a sudden—heavens! Already summer!—I ran to the trunk an' pulled out this light dress—Terribly old! Historical almost! But feels so good—so good an' co-ol, y'know. . . .

TOM: Mother—

AMANDA: Yes, honey?

TOM: How about—supper?

AMANDA: Honey, you go ask Sister if supper is ready! You know that Sister is in full charge of supper! Tell her you hungry boys are waiting for it. [*to* JIM] Have you met Laura?

JIM: She—

AMANDA: Let you in? Oh, good, you've met already! It's rare for a girl as sweet an' pretty as Laura to be domestic! But Laura is, thank heavens, not only pretty but also very domestic. I'm not at all. I never was a bit. I never could make a thing but angel-food cake. Well, in the South we had so many servants. Gone, gone, gone. All vestiges of gracious living! Gone completely! I wasn't prepared for what the future brought me. All of my gentlemen callers were sons of planters and so of course I assumed that I would be married to one and raise my family on a large piece of land with plenty of servants. But man proposes—and woman accepts the proposal!—To vary that old, old saying a little bit—I married no planter! I married a man who worked for the telephone company!—that gallantly smiling gentleman over there! [*points to the picture.*] A telephone man who—fell in love with long distance!—Now he travels and I don't even know where!—But what am I going on for about my—tribulations! Tell me yours—I hope you don't have any! Tom?

TOM [*returning*]: Yes, Mother?

AMANDA: Is supper nearly ready?

TOM: It looks to me like supper is on the table.

AMANDA: Let me look—[*She rises prettily and looks through portieres.*] Oh, lovely—But where is Sister?

TOM: Laura is not feeling well and she says that she thinks she'd better not come to the table.

AMANDA: What?—Nonsense!—Laura? Oh, Laura!

LAURA [*off stage, faintly*]: Yes, Mother.

AMANDA: You really must come to the table. We won't be seated until you come to the table! Come in, Mr. O'Connor. You sit over there and I'll—Laura? Laura Wingfield! You're keeping us waiting, honey! We can't say grace until you come to the table!

The back door is pushed weakly open and LAURA *comes in. She is obviously quite faint, her lips trembling, her eyes wide and staring. She moves unsteadily toward the table.*

[Legend: "Terror!"]

Outside a summer storm is coming abruptly. The white curtains billow inward at the windows and there is a sorrowful murmur and deep blue dusk.

LAURA *suddenly stumbles—She catches a chair with a faint moan.*

TOM: Laura!

AMANDA: Laura! [*There is a clap of thunder.*] [*Legend: "Ah!"*] [*despairingly.*] Why, Laura, you are sick, darling! Tom, help you sister into the living room, dear! Sit in the living room, Laura—rest on the sofa. Well! [*to the gentleman caller.*] Standing over the hot stove made her ill!—I told her that it was just too warm this evening, but—[TOM *comes back in.* LAURA *is on the sofa.*] Is Laura all right now?

TOM: Yes.

AMANDA: What *is* that? Rain? A nice cool rain has come up! [*She gives the gentleman caller a frightened look.*] I think we may—have grace—now . . . [TOM *looks at her stupidly.*] Tom, honey—you say grace!

TOM: Oh . . . "For these and all thy mercies—" [*They bow their heads.* AMANDA *stealing a nervous glance at* JIM. *IN THE LIVING ROOM* LAURA, *stretched on the sofa, clenches her hand to her lips, to hold back a shuddering sob.*] God's Holy Name be praised—

[The scene dims out.]

SCENE 7

A Souvenir

Half an hour later. Dinner is just being finished in the upstage area which is concealed by the drawn portieres.

As the curtain rises LAURA *is still huddled upon the sofa, her feet drawn under her, her head resting on a pale blue pillow, her eyes wide and mysteriously watchful. The new floor lamp with its shade of rose-colored silk gives a soft, becoming light to her face, bringing out the fragile, unearthly prettiness which usually escapes attention. There is a steady murmur of rain, but it is slackening and stops soon after the scene begins; the air outside becomes pale and luminous as the moon breaks out.*

A moment after the curtain rises, the lights in both rooms flicker and go out.

JIM: Hey, there, Mr. Light Bulb!

AMANDA *laughs nervously.*

[Legend: "Suspension of a Public Service."]

AMANDA: Where was Moses when the lights went out? Ha-ha. Do you know the answer to that one, Mr. O'Connor?

JIM: No, ma'am, what's the answer?

AMANDA: In the dark! [JIM *laughs appreciatively.*] Everybody sit still. I'll light the candles. Isn't it lucky we have them on the table? Where's a match? Which of you gentlemen can provide a match?

JIM: Here.

AMANDA: Thank you, sir.

JIM: Not at all, Ma'am!

AMANDA: I guess the fuse has burnt out. Mr. O'Connor, can you tell a burnt-out fuse? I know I can't and Tom is a total loss when it comes to mechanics. [*Sound: Getting up: Voices recede a little to kitchenette.*] Oh, be careful you don't bump into something. We don't want our gentleman caller to break his neck. Now wouldn't that be a fine howdy-do?

JIM: Ha-ha! Where is the fuse box?

AMANDA: Right here next to the stove. Can you see anything?

JIM: Just a minute.

AMANDA: Isn't electricity a mysterious thing? Wasn't it Benjamin Franklin who tied a key to a kite? We live in such a mysterious universe, don't we? Some people say that science clears up all the mysteries for us. In my opinion it only creates more! Have you found it yet?

JIM: No, Ma'am. All these fuses look okay to me.

AMANDA: Tom!

TOM: Yes, Mother?

AMANDA: That light bill I gave you several days ago. The one I told you we got the notices about?

TOM: Oh.—Yeah.

[Legend: "Ha!"]

AMANDA: You didn't neglect to pay it by any chance?

TOM: Why, I—

AMANDA: Didn't! I might have known it!

JIM: Shakespeare probably wrote a poem on that light bill, Mrs. Wingfield.

AMANDA: I might have known better than to trust him with it! There's such a high price for negligence in this world!

JIM: Maybe the poem will win a ten-dollar prize.

AMANDA: We'll just have to spend the remainder of the evening in the nineteenth century, before Mr. Edison made the Mazda[6] lamp!

JIM: Candlelight is my favorite kind of light.

AMANDA: That shows you're romantic! But that's no excuse for Tom. Well, we got through dinner. Very considerate of them to let us get through dinner before they plunged us into everlasting darkness, wasn't it, Mr. O'Connor?

JIM: Ha-ha!

AMANDA: Tom, as a penalty for your carelessness you can help me with the dishes.

JIM: Let me give you a hand.

AMANDA: Indeed you will not!

JIM: I ought to be good for something.

AMANDA: Good for something? [*Her tone is rhapsodic.*] *You?* Why, Mr. O'Connor, nobody, *nobody's* given me this much entertainment in years—as you have!

[6] **Mazda lamp** electric lamp

JIM: Aw, now, Mrs. Wingfield!

AMANDA: I'm not exaggerating, not one bit! But Sister is all by her lonesome. You go keep her company in the parlor! I'll give you this lovely old candelabrum that used to be on the altar at the church of the Heavenly Rest. It was melted a little out of shape when the church burnt down. Lightning struck it one spring. Gypsy Jones was holding a revival at the time and he intimated that the church was destroyed because the Episcopalians gave card parties.

JIM: Ha-ha.

AMANDA: And how about coaxing Sister to drink a little wine? I think it would be good for her! Can you carry both at once?

JIM: Sure. I'm Superman!

AMANDA: Now, Thomas, get into this apron!

The door of kitchenette swings closed on AMANDA'S *gay laughter; the flickering light approaches the portieres.*

LAURA *sits up nervously as he enters. Her speech at first is low and breathless from the almost intolerable strain of being alone with a stranger.*

[Legend: "I Don't Suppose You Remember Me at All!"]

In her first speeches in this scene, before JIM'S *warmth overcomes her paralyzing shyness,* LAURA'S *voice is thin and breathless as though she has run up a steep flight of stairs.*

JIM'S *attitude is gently humorous. In playing this scene it should be stressed that while the incident is apparently unimportant, it is to* LAURA *the climax of her secret life.*

JIM: Hello, there, Laura.

LAURA [*faintly*]: Hello. [*She clears her throat.*]

JIM: How are you feeling now? Better?

LAURA: Yes. Yes, thank you.

JIM: This is for you. A little dandelion wine. [*He extends it toward her with extravagant gallantry.*]

LAURA: Thank you.

JIM: Drink it—but don't get drunk! [*He laughs heartily.* LAURA *takes the glass uncertainly; laughs shyly.*] Where shall I set the candles?

LAURA: Oh—oh, anywhere . . .

JIM: How about here on the floor? Any objections?

LAURA: No.

JIM: I'll spread a newspaper under to catch the drippings. I like to sit on the floor. Mind if I do?

LAURA: Oh, no.

JIM: Give me a pillow?

LAURA: What?

JIM: A pillow!

LAURA: Oh . . . [*hands him one quickly.*]

JIM: How about you? Don't you like to sit on the floor?

LAURA: Oh—yes.

JIM: Why don't you, then?

LAURA: I—will.

JIM: Take a pillow! [LAURA *does. Sits on the other side of the candelabrum.* JIM *crosses his legs and smiles engagingly at her.*] I can't hardly see you sitting way over there.

LAURA: I can—see you.

JIM: I know, but that's not fair, I'm in the limelight. [LAURA *moves her pillow closer.*] Good! Now I can see you! Comfortable?

LAURA: Yes.

JIM: So am I. Comfortable as a cow. Will you have some gum?

LAURA: No, thank you.

JIM: I think that I will indulge, with your permission [*musingly unwraps it and holds it up.*] Think of the fortune made by the guy that invented the first piece of chewing gum. Amazing, huh? The Wrigley Building is one of the sights of Chicago.—I saw it summer before last when I went up to the Century of Progress. Did you take in the Century of Progress?

LAURA: No, I didn't.

JIM: Well, it was quite a wonderful exposition. What impressed me most was the Hall of Science. Gives you an idea of what the future will be in America, even more wonderful than the present time is! [*Pause, Smiling at her.*] Your brother tells me you're shy. Is that right, Laura?

LAURA: I—don't know.

JIM: I judge you to be an old-fashioned type of girl. Well, I think that's a pretty good type to be. Hope you don't think I'm being too personal—do you?

LAURA [*hastily, out of embarrassment*]: I believe I *will* take a piece of gum, if you—don't mind. [*clearing her throat.*] Mr. O'Connor, have you—kept up with your singing?

JIM: Singing? Me?

LAURA: Yes. I remember what a beautiful voice you had.

JIM: When did you hear me sing?

[Voice offstage in the pause]

VOICE [*offstage*].

O blow, ye winds, heigh-ho.
A-roving I will go!
I'm off to my love
With a boxing glove—
Ten thousand miles away!

JIM: You say you've heard me sing?

LAURA: Oh, yes! Yes, very often . . . I—don't suppose you remember me—at all?

JIM [*smiling doubtfully*]: You know I have an idea I've seen you before. I had that idea soon as you opened the door. It seemed almost like I was about to remember your name. But the name that I started to call you—wasn't a name! And so I stopped myself before I said it.

LAURA: Wasn't it—Blue Roses?

JIM [*springs up, grinning*]: Blue Roses! My gosh, yes—Blue Roses! That's what I had on my tongue when you opened the door! Isn't it funny what tricks your memory plays? I didn't connect you with the high school somehow or other. But that's where it was; it was high school. I didn't even know you were Shakespeare's sister! Gosh, I'm sorry.

LAURA: I didn't expect you to. You—barely knew me!

JIM: But we did have a speaking acquaintance, huh?

LAURA: Yes, we—spoke to each other.

JIM: When did you recognize me?

LAURA: Oh, right away!

JIM: Soon as I came in the door?

LAURA: When I heard your name I thought it was probably you. I knew that Tom used to know you a little in high school. So when you came in the door—Well, then I was—sure.

JIM: Why didn't you *say* something, then?

LAURA [*breathlessly*]: I didn't know what to say, I was—too surprised!

JIM: For goodness' sakes! You know, this sure is funny!

LAURA: Yes! Yes, isn't it, though. . . .

JIM: Didn't we have a class in something together?

LAURA: Yes, we did.

JIM: What class was that?

LAURA: It was—singing—Chorus!

JIM: Aw!

LAURA: I sat across the aisle from you in the Aud.

JIM: Aw.

LAURA: Mondays, Wednesdays, and Fridays.

JIM: Now I remember—you always came in late.

LAURA: Yes, it was so hard for me, getting upstairs. I had a brace on my leg—it clumped so loud!

JIM: I never heard any clumping.

LAURA [*wincing at the recollection*]: To me it sounded like—thunder!

JIM: Well, well, well. I never even noticed.

LAURA: And everybody was seated before I came in. I had to walk in front of all those people. My seat was in the back row. I had to go clumping all the way up the aisle with everyone watching!

JIM: You shouldn't have been self-conscious.

LAURA: I know, but I was. It was always such a relief when the singing started.

JIM: Aw, yes, I've placed you now! I used to call you Blue Roses. How was it that I got started calling you that?

LAURA: I was out of school a little while with pleurosis. When I came back you asked me what was the matter. I said I had pleurosis—you thought I said Blue Roses. That's what you always called me after that!

JIM: I hope you didn't mind.

LAURA: Oh, no—I liked it. You see, I wasn't acquainted with many—people. . . .

JIM: As I remember you sort of stuck by yourself.

LAURA: I—I—never had much luck at—making friends.

JIM: I don't see why you wouldn't.

LAURA: Well, I—started out badly.

JIM: You mean being—

LAURA: Yes, it sort of—stood between me—

JIM: You shouldn't have let it!

LAURA: I know, but it did, and—

JIM: You were shy with people!

LAURA: I tried not to be but never could—

JIM: Overcome it?

LAURA: No, I—I never could!

JIM: I guess being shy is something you have to work out of kind of gradually.

LAURA [*sorrowfully*]: Yes—I guess it—

JIM: Takes time!

LAURA: Yes—

JIM: People are not so dreadful when you know them. That's what you have to remember! And everybody has problems, not just you, but practically everybody has got some problems. You think of yourself as having the only problems, as being the only one who is disappointed. But just look around you and you will see lots of people as disappointed as you are. For instance, I hoped when I was going to high school that I would be further along at this time, six years later, than I am now—You remember that wonderful write-up I had in *The Torch?*

LAURA: Yes! [*She rises and crosses to table.*]

JIM: It said I was bound to succeed in anything I went into! [LAURA *returns with the annual.*] Holy Jeez! The Torch! [*He accepts it reverently. They smile across it with mutual wonder.* LAURA *crouches beside him and they begin to turn through it.* LAURA'*s shyness is dissolving in his warmth.*]

LAURA: Here you are in Pirates of Penzance!

JIM [*wistfully*]: I sang the baritone lead in that operetta.

LAURA [*rapidly*]: So—*beautifully!*

JIM [*protesting*]: Aw—

LAURA: Yes, yes—beautifully—beautifully!

JIM: You heard me?

LAURA: All three times!

JIM: No!

LAURA: Yes!

JIM: All three performances?

LAURA [*looking down*]: Yes.

JIM: Why?

LAURA: I—wanted to ask you to—autograph my program.

JIM: Why didn't you ask me to?

LAURA: You were always surrounded by your own friends so much that I never had a chance to.

JIM: You should have just—

LAURA: Well, I—thought you might think I was—

JIM: Thought I might think you was—what?

LAURA: Oh—

JIM [*with reflective relish*]: I was beleaguered by females in those days.

LAURA: You were terribly popular!

JIM: Yeah—

LAURA: You had such a—friendly way—

JIM: I was spoiled in high school.

LAURA: Everybody—liked you!

JIM: Including you?

LAURA: I—yes, I—I did, too—[*She gently closes the book in her lap.*]

JIM: Well, well, well!—Give me that program, Laura. [*She hands it to him. He signs it with a flourish.*] There you are—better late than never!

LAURA: Oh, I—what a—surprise!

JIM: My signature isn't worth very much right now. But some day—maybe—it will increase in value! Being disappointed is one thing and being discouraged is something else. I am disappointed but I'm not discouraged. I'm twenty-three years old. How old are you?

LAURA: I'll be twenty-four in June.

JIM: That's not old age!

LAURA: No, but—

JIM: You finished high school?

LAURA [*with difficulty*]: I didn't go back.

JIM: You mean you dropped out?

LAURA: I made bad grades in my final examinations. [*She rises and replaces the book and the program. Her voice strained.*] How is—Emily Meisenbach getting along?

JIM: Oh, that kraut-head!

LAURA: Why do you call her that?

JIM: That's what she was.

LAURA: You're not still—going with her?

JIM: I never see her.

LAURA: It said in the Personal Section that you were—engaged!

JIM: I know, but I wasn't impressed by that—propaganda!

LAURA: It wasn't—the truth?

JIM: Only in Emily's optimistic opinion!

LAURA: Oh—

[Legend: "What Have You Done Since High School?"]

JIM *lights a cigarette and leans indolently back on his elbows smiling at* LAURA *with a warmth and charm which light her inwardly with altar candles. She remains by the table and turns in her hands a piece of glass to cover her tumult.*

JIM [*after several reflective puffs on a cigarette*]: What have you done since high school? [*She seems not to hear him.*] Huh? [LAURA *looks up.*] I said what have you done since high school, Laura?

LAURA: Nothing much.

JIM: You must have been doing something these six long years.

LAURA: Yes.

JIM: Well, then, such as what?

LAURA: I took a business course at business college—

JIM: How did that work out?

LAURA: Well, not very—well—I had to drop out, it gave me—indigestion—

JIM laughs gently.

JIM: What are you doing now?

LAURA: I don't do anything—much. Oh, please don't think I sit around doing nothing! My glass collection takes up a good deal of my time. Glass is something you have to take good care of.

JIM: What did you say—about glass?

LAURA: Collection I said—I have one—[*She clears her throat and turns away again, acutely shy.*]

JIM [*abruptly*]: You know what I judge to be the trouble with you? Inferiority complex! Know what that is? That's what they call it when someone low rates himself! I understand it because I had it, too. Although my case was not so aggravated as yours seems to be. I had it until I took up public speaking, developed my voice, and learned that I had an aptitude for science. Before that time I never thought of myself as being outstanding in any way whatsoever! Now I've never made a regular study of it, but I have a friend who says I can analyze people better than doctors that make a profession of it. I don't claim that to be necessarily true, but I can sure guess a person's psychology, Laura! [*takes out his gum.*] Excuse me, Laura. I always take it out when the flavor is gone. I'll use this scrap of paper to wrap it in. I know how it is to get it stuck on a shoe. Yep—that's what I judge to be your principal trouble. A lack of confidence in yourself as a person. You don't have the proper amount of faith in yourself. I'm basing that fact on a number of your remarks and also on certain observations

I've made. For instance that clumping you thought was so awful in high school. You say that you even dreaded to walk into class. You see what you did? You dropped out of school, you gave up an education because of a clump, which as far as I know was practically nonexistent! A little physical defect is what you have. Hardly noticeable even! Magnified thousands of times by imagination! You know what my strong advice to you is? Think of yourself as *superior* in some way!

LAURA: In what way would I think?

JIM: Why, man alive, Laura! Just look about you a little. What do you see? A world full of common people! All of 'em born and all of 'em going to die! Which of them has one-tenth of your good points! Or mine! Or anyone else's, as far as that goes—Gosh! Everybody excels in some one thing. Some in many! [*unconsciously glances at himself in the mirror.*] All you've got to do is discover in *what!* Take me, for instance. [*He adjusts his tie at the mirror.*] My interest happens to lie in electro-dynamics. I'm taking a course in radio engineering at night school, Laura, on top of a fairly responsible job at the warehouse. I'm taking that course and studying public speaking.

LAURA: Ohhhh.

JIM: Because I believe in the future of television! [*turning back to her.*] I wish to be ready to go up right along with it. Therefore I'm planning to get in on the ground floor. In fact, I've already made the right connections and all that remains is for the industry itself to get under way! Full steam—[*His eyes are starry.*] *Knowledge*—Zzzzzp! *Money*—Zzzzzzp!—*Power!* That's the cycle democracy is built on! [*His attitude is convincingly dynamic. LAURA stares at him, even her shyness eclipsed in her absolute wonder. He suddenly grins.*] I guess you think I think a lot of myself!

LAURA: No-o-o-o, I—

JIM: Now how about you? Isn't there something you take more interest in than anything else?

LAURA: Well, I do—as I said—have my—glass collection—

A peal of girlish laughter from the kitchen.

JIM: I'm not right sure I know what you're talking about. What kind of glass is it?

LAURA: Little articles of it, they're ornaments mostly! Most of them are little animals made out of glass, the tiniest little animals in the world. Mother calls them a glass menagerie! Here's an example of one, if you'd like to see it! This one is one of the oldest. It's nearly thirteen. [*He stretches out his hand.*] [*Music: "The Glass Menagerie."*] Oh, be careful—if you breathe, it breaks!

JIM: I'd better not take it. I'm pretty clumsy with things.

LAURA: Go on, I trust you with him! [*places it in his palm.*] There now—you're holding him gently! Hold him over the light, he loves the light! You see how the light shines through him?

JIM: It sure does shine!

LAURA: I shouldn't be partial, but he is my favorite one.

JIM: What kind of a thing is this one supposed to be?

LAURA: Haven't you noticed the single horn on his forehead?

JIM: A unicorn, huh?

LAURA: Mmm-hmmm!

JIM: Unicorns, aren't they extinct in the modern world?

LAURA: I know!

JIM: Poor little fellow, he must feel sort of lonesome.

LAURA [*smiling*]: Well, if he does he doesn't complain about it. He stays on a shelf with some horses that don't have horns and all of them seem to get along nicely together.

JIM: How do you know?

LAURA [*lightly*]: I haven't heard any arguments among them!

JIM [*grinning*]: No arguments, huh? Well, that's a pretty good sign! Where shall I set him?

LAURA: Put him on the table. They all like a change of scenery once in a while!

JIM [*stretching*]: Well, well, well, well—Look how big my shadow is when I stretch!

LAURA: Oh, oh, yes—it stretches across the ceiling!

JIM [*crossing to door*]: I think it's stopped raining. [*opens fire escape door.*] Where does the music come from?

LAURA: From the Paradise Dance Hall across the alley.

JIM: How about cutting the rug a little, Miss Wingfield?

LAURA: Oh, I—

JIM: Or is your program filled up? Let me have a look at it. [*grasps imaginary card.*] Why, every dance is taken! I'll just have to scratch some out.

[Waltz music: "La Golondrina."] Ahhh, a waltz! [He executes some sweeping turns by himself then holds his arms toward LAURA.*]*

LAURA [*breathlessly*]: I—can't dance!

JIM: There you go, that inferiority stuff!

LAURA: I've never danced in my life!

JIM: Come on, try!

LAURA: Oh, but I'd step on you!

JIM: I'm not made out of glass.

LAURA: How—how—how do we start?

JIM: Just leave it to me. You hold your arms out a little.

LAURA: Like this?

JIM: A little bit higher. Right. Now don't tighten up, that's the main thing about it—relax.

LAURA [*laughing breathlessly*]: It's hard not to.

JIM: Okay.

LAURA: I'm afraid you can't budge me.

JIM: What do you bet I can't? [*He swings her into motion.*]

LAURA: Goodness, yes, you can!

JIM: Let yourself go, now, Laura, just let yourself go.

LAURA: I'm—

JIM: Come on!

LAURA: Trying?

JIM: Not so stiff—Easy does it!

LAURA: I know but I'm—

JIM: Loosen th' backbone! There now, that's a lot better.

LAURA: Am I?

JIM: Lots, lots better! [*He moves her about the room in a clumsy waltz.*]

LAURA: Oh, my!

JIM: Ha-ha!

LAURA: Goodness, yes you can!

JIM: Ha-ha-ha! [*They suddenly bump into the table.* JIM *stops.*] What did we hit on?

LAURA: Table.

JIM: Did something fall off it? I think—

LAURA: Yes.

JIM: I hope that it wasn't the little glass horse with the horn!

LAURA: Yes.

JIM: Aw, aw, aw. Is it broken?

LAURA: Now it is just like all the other horses.

JIM: It's lost its—

LAURA: Horn! It doesn't matter. Maybe it's a blessing in disguise.

JIM: You'll never forgive me. I bet that that was your favorite piece of glass.

LAURA: I don't have favorites much. It's no tragedy, Freckles. Glass breaks so easily. No matter how careful you are. The traffic jars the shelves and things fall off them.

JIM: Still I'm awfully sorry that I was the cause.

LAURA [*smiling*]: I'll just imagine he had an operation. The horn was removed to make him feel less—freakish! [*They both laugh.*] Now he will feel more at home with the other horses, the ones that don't have horns . . .

JIM: Ha-ha, that's very funny! [*suddenly serious.*] I'm glad to see that you have a sense of humor. You know—you're—well—very different! Surprisingly different from anyone else I know! [*His voice becomes soft and hesitant with a genuine feeling.*] Do you mind me telling you that? [LAURA *is abashed beyond speech.*] You make me feel sort of—I don't know how to put it! I'm usually pretty good at expressing things, but—This is something that I don't know how to say! LAURA *touches her throat and clears it—turns the broken unicorn in her hands.*] [*even softer*] Has anyone ever told you that you were pretty? [*Pause: Music.*] [LAURA *looks up slowly, with wonder, and shakes her head.*] Well, you are! In a very different way from anyone else. And all the nicer because of the difference, too. [*His voice becomes low and husky.* LAURA *turns away, nearly faint with the novelty of her emotions.*] I wish that you were my sister. I'd teach you to have some confidence in yourself. The different people are not like other people, but being different is nothing to be ashamed of. Because other people are not such wonderful people. They're one hundred times one thousand. You're one times one! They walk all over the earth. You just stay here. They're common as—weeds, but—you—well, you're—*Blue Roses!*

[Image on screen: Blue Roses.]

[Music changes.]

LAURA: But blue is wrong for—roses . . .

JIM: It's right for you—You're—pretty!

LAURA: In what respect am I pretty?

JIM: In all respects—believe me! Your eyes—your hair—are pretty! Your hands are pretty! [*He catches hold of her hand.*] You think I'm making this up because I'm invited to dinner and have to be nice. Oh, I could do that! I could put on an act for you, Laura, and say lots of things without being very sincere. But this time I am. I'm talking to you sincerely. I happened to notice you had this inferiority complex that keeps you from feeling comfortable with people. Somebody needs to build your confidence up and make you proud instead of shy and turning away and—blushing—Somebody ought to—ought to—kiss you. Laura! [*His hand slips slowly up her arm to her shoulder.*] [*Music Swells Tumultuously.*] [*He suddenly turns her about and kisses her on the lips. When he releases her* LAURA *sinks on the sofa with a bright, dazed look.* JIM *backs away and fishes in his pocket for a cigarette.*] [*Legend on screen: "Souvenir."*] Stumble-john! [*He lights the cigarette, avoiding her look. There is a peal of girlish laughter from* AMANDA *in the kitchen.* LAURA *slowly raises and opens her hand. It still contains the little broken glass animal. She looks at it with a tender, bewildered expression.*] Stumble-john! I shouldn't have done that—That was way off the beam. You don't smoke, do you? [*She looks up, smiling, not hearing the question. He sits beside her a little gingerly. She looks at him speechlessly—waiting. He coughs decorously and moves a little farther aside as he considers the situation and senses her feelings, dimly, with perturbation. Gently.*] Would you—care for a—mint? [*She doesn't seem to hear him but her look grows brighter even.*] Peppermint—Life Saver? My pocket's a regular drug store—wherever I go . . . [*He pops a mint in his mouth. Then gulps and decides to make a clean breast of it. He speaks slowly and gingerly.*] Laura, you know, if I had a sister like you, I'd do the same thing as Tom. I'd bring out fellows—introduce her to them. The right type of boys of a type to—appreciate her. Only—well—he made a mistake about me. Maybe I've got no call to be saying this. That may not have been the idea in having me over. But what if it was? There's nothing wrong about that. The only trouble is that in my case—I'm not in a situation to—do the right thing. I can't take down your number and say I'll phone. I can't call up next week and—ask for a date. I thought I had better explain the situation in case you misunderstood it and—hurt your feelings. . . . [*Pause. Slowly, very slowly,* LAURA'*s look changes, her eyes returning slowly from his to the ornament in her palm.*]

AMANDA *utters another gay laugh in the kitchen.*

LAURA [*faintly*]: You—won't—call again?

JIM: No, Laura, I can't [*He rises from the sofa.*] As I was just explaining, I've—got strings on me, Laura, I've—been going steady! I go out all the time with a girl named Betty. She's a home-girl like you, and Catholic, and Irish, and in a great many ways we—get along fine. I met her last summer on a moonlight boat trip up the river to Alton, on the Majestic. Well—right away from the start it was—love! [*Legend: Love!*] [LAURA *sways slightly forward and grips the arm of the sofa. He fails to notice, now enrapt in his own comfortable being.*] Being in love has made a new man of me! [*Leaning stiffly forward, clutching the arm of the sofa,* LAURA *struggles visibly with her storm. But* JIM *is oblivious, she is a long way off.*] The power of love is really pretty tremendous! Love is something that—changes the whole world, Laura! [*The storm abates a little and* LAURA *leans back. He notices her again.*] It happened that Betty's aunt took sick, she got a wire and had to go to Centralia. So Tom—when he asked me to dinner—I naturally just accepted the invitation, not knowing that you—that he—that I—[*He stops awkwardly.*] Huh—I'm a stumble-john! [*He flops back on the sofa. The holy candles in the altar of* LAURA'*s face have been snuffed out! There is a look of almost infinite desolation.* JIM *glances at her uneasily.*] I wish that you would—say something. [*She bites her lip which was trembling and then bravely smiles. She opens her hand again on the broken glass ornament. Then she gently takes his hand and raises it level with her own. She carefully places the unicorn in the palm of his hand, then pushes his fingers closed upon it.*] What are you—doing that for? You want me to have him?—Laura? [*She nods.*] What for?

LAURA: A—souvenir . . .

She rises unsteadily and crouches beside the victrola to wind it up.

[Legend on screen: "Things Have a Way of Turning Out So Badly."]

[Or image: "Gentleman Caller Waving Goodbye!—Gaily."]

At this moment AMANDA *rushes brightly back in the front room. She bears a pitcher of fruit punch in an old-fashioned cut-glass pitcher and a plate of macaroons. The plate has a gold border and poppies painted on it.*

AMANDA: Well, well, well! Isn't the air delightful after the shower? I've made you children a little liquid refreshment. [*turns gaily to the gentleman caller.*] Jim, do you know that song about lemonade?
"Lemonade, lemonade
Made in the shade and stirred with a spade—
Good enough for any old maid!"

JIM [*uneasily*]: Ha-ha! No—I never heard it.

AMANDA: Why, Laura! You look so serious!

JIM: We were having a serious conversation.

AMANDA: Good! Now you're better acquainted!

JIM [*uncertainly*]: Ha-ha! Yes.

AMANDA: You modern young people are much more serious-minded than my generation. I was so gay as a girl!

JIM: You haven't changed, Mrs. Wingfield.

AMANDA: Tonight I'm rejuvenated! The gaiety of the occasion, Mr. O'Connor! [*She tosses her head with a peal of laughter. Spills lemonade.*] Oooo! I'm baptizing myself!

JIM: Here—let me—

AMANDA [*setting the pitcher down*]: There now. I discovered we had some maraschino cherries. I dumped them in, juice and all!

JIM: You shouldn't have gone to that trouble, Mrs. Wingfield.

AMANDA: Trouble, trouble? Why it was loads of fun! Didn't you hear me cutting up in the kitchen? I bet your ears were burning! I told Tom how outdone with him I was for keeping you to himself so long a time! He should have brought you over much, much sooner! Well, now that you've found your way, I want you to be a very frequent caller! Not just occasional but all the time. Oh, we're going to have a lot of gay times together! I see them coming! Mmm, just breathe that air! So fresh, and the moon's so pretty! I'll skip back out—I know where my place is when young folks are having a—serious conversation!

JIM: Oh, don't go out, Mrs. Wingfield. The fact of the matter is I've got to be going.

AMANDA: Going, now? You're joking! Why, it's only the shank of the evening, Mr. O'Connor!

JIM: Well, you know how it is.

AMANDA: You mean you're a young workingman and have to keep workingmen's hours. We'll let you off early tonight. But only on the condition that next time you stay later. What's the best night for you? Isn't Saturday night the best night for you workingmen?

JIM: I have a couple of time clocks to punch, Mrs. Wingfield. One at morning, another one at night!

AMANDA: My, but you *are* ambitious! You work at night, too?

JIM: No, Ma'am, not work but—Betty! [*He crosses deliberately to pick up his hat. The band at the Paradise Dance Hall goes into a tender waltz.*]

AMANDA: Betty? Betty? Who's—Betty! [*There is an ominous cracking sound in the sky.*]

JIM: Oh, just a girl. The girl I go steady with! [*He smiles charmingly. The sky falls.*]

[Legend: "The Sky Falls."]

AMANDA [*a long-drawn exhalation*]: Ohhh . . . Is it a serious romance, Mr. O'Connor?

JIM: We're going to be married the second Sunday in June.

AMANDA: Ohhhh—how nice! Tom didn't mention that you were engaged to be married.

JIM: The cat's not out of the bag at the warehouse yet. You know how they are. They call you Romeo and stuff like that. [*He stops at the oval mirror to put on his hat. He carefully shapes the brim and the crown to give a discreetly dashing effect.*] It's been a wonderful evening, Mrs. Wingfield. I guess this is what they mean by Southern hospitality.

AMANDA: It really wasn't anything at all.

JIM: I hope it don't seem like I'm rushing off. But I promised Betty I'd pick her up at the Wabash depot, an' by the time I get my jalopy down there her train'll be in. Some women are pretty upset if you keep 'em waiting.

AMANDA: Yes, I know—The tyranny of women! [*extends her hand.*] Goodbye, Mr. O'Connor. I wish you luck—and happiness—and success! All three of them, and so does Laura!—Don't you, Laura?

LAURA: Yes!

JIM [*taking her hand*]: Goodbye, Laura. I'm certainly going to treasure that souvenir. And don't you forget the good advice I gave you. [*raises his voice to a cheery shout.*] So long, Shakespeare! Thanks again, ladies—good night!

He grins and ducks jauntily out.

Still bravely grimacing, AMANDA *closes the door on the gentleman caller. Then she turns back to the room with a puzzled expression. She and* LAURA *don't dare to face each other.* LAURA *crouches beside the victrola to wind it.*

AMANDA [*faintly*]: Things have a way of turning out so badly. I don't believe that I would play the victrola. Well, well—well—Our gentleman caller was engaged to be married! Tom!

TOM [*from back*]: Yes, Mother?

AMANDA: Come in here a minute. I want to tell you something awfully funny.

TOM [*enters with macaroon and a glass of lemonade*]: Has the gentleman caller gotten away already?

AMANDA: The gentleman caller has made an early departure. What a wonderful joke you played on us!

TOM: How do you mean?

AMANDA: You didn't mention that he was engaged to be married.

TOM: Jim? Engaged?

AMANDA: That's what he just informed us.

TOM: I'll be jiggered! I didn't know about that.

AMANDA: That seems very peculiar.

TOM: What's peculiar about it?

AMANDA: Didn't you call him your best friend down at the warehouse?

TOM: He is, but how did I know?

AMANDA: It seems extremely peculiar that you wouldn't know your best friend was going to be married!

TOM: The warehouse is where I work, not where I know things about people!

AMANDA: You don't know things anywhere! You live in a dream; you manufacture illusions! [*He crosses to door.*] Where are you going?

TOM: I'm going to the movies.

AMANDA: That's right, now that you've had us make such fools of ourselves. The effort, the preparations, all the expense! The new floor lamp, the rug, the clothes for Laura! All for what? To entertain some other girl's fiancé! Go to the movies, go! Don't think about us, a mother deserted, an unmarried sister who's crippled and has no job! Don't let anything interfere with your selfish pleasure! Just go, go, go—to the movies!

TOM: All right, I will! The more you shout about my selfishness to me the quicker I'll go, and I won't go to the movies!

AMANDA: Go, then! Then go to the moon—you selfish dreamer!

TOM *smashes his glass on the floor. He plunges out on the fire escape, slamming the door.* LAURA *screams—cut by door.*

Dance-hall music up. TOM *goes to the rail and grips it desperately, lifting his face in the chill white moonlight penetrating the narrow abyss of the alley.*

[Legend on screen: "And So Good-bye . . ."]

TOM'S *closing speech is timed with the interior pantomime. The interior scene is played as though viewed through sound-proof glass.* AMANDA *appears to be making a comforting speech to* LAURA *who is huddled upon the sofa. Now that we cannot hear the mother's speech, her silliness is gone and she has dignity and tragic beauty.* LAURA'S *dark hair hides her face until at the end of the speech she lifts it to smile at her mother.* AMANDA'S *gestures are slow and graceful, almost dance-like, as she comforts the daughter. At the end of her speech she glances a moment at the father's picture—then withdraws through the portieres. At close of* TOM'S *speech,* LAURA *blows out the candles, ending the play.*

TOM: I didn't go to the moon, I went much further—for time is the longest distance between two places—Not long after that I was fired for writing a poem on the lid of a shoe box. I left Saint Louis. I descended the steps of this fire-escape for a last time and followed, from then on, in my father's footsteps, attempting to find in motion what was lost in space—I traveled around a great deal. The cities swept about me like dead leaves, leaves that were brightly colored but torn away from the branches. I would have stopped, but I was pursued by something. It always came upon me unawares, taking me altogether by surprise. Perhaps it was a familiar bit of music. Perhaps it was only a piece of transparent glass. Perhaps I am walking along a street at night, in some strange city, before I have found companions. I pass the lighted window of a shop where perfume is sold. The window is filled with pieces of colored glass, tiny transparent bottles in delicate colors, like bits of a shattered rainbow. Then all at once my sister touches my shoulder. I turn around and look into her eyes . . . Oh, Laura, Laura, I tried to leave you behind me, but I am more faithful than I intended to be! I reach for a cigarette, I cross the street, I run into the movies or a bar, I buy a drink, I speak to the nearest stranger—anything that can blow your candles out! [LAURA *bends over the candles.*]—for nowadays the world is lit by lightning! Blow out your candles, Laura—and so goodbye . . .

She blows the candles out.

[The scene dissolves.]

➤ *QUESTIONS FOR READING AND WRITING*

1. Who is the central character in this play? What criteria do you use to make your determination?
2. Plays are meant to be seen more than read. Nevertheless, Williams provides detailed and vivid descriptions of the setting, characters, and stage action. Carefully reread his descriptions of the three Wingfields at the start of the play. Could you learn this much about each character solely by reading the scenes that follow? Does the play deliver the characters that Williams promises?
3. A central issue in the play is whether Tom will obey his mother's wishes and stay in St. Louis with her and his sister. Yet, when Tom addresses us at the start of the play, he wears a merchant marine uniform, signaling that he will not choose to remain at home. Does this visual clue influence your understanding of Tom as the play develops? Instead of suspense as to whether Tom will obey his mother's wishes, what effect does this create?
4. It is presented as a fact that Laura is the recluse of the family. Yet, does it seem to you that either Amanda or Tom have many friends and acquaintances? How has Laura garnered this reputation? Is it fair or unfair?

5. Which Wingfield changes the most over the course of the play? Which one changes the least?
6. Over and over, Jim tells Laura what he would do if she were his sister. Is this an indictment of Tom as a brother? Do you think Tom does his duty by his family?
7. As Laura reveals herself to Jim, does he react in the way you expect him too? Do his reactions to Laura change what you think of Amanda and Tom?
8. In what ways is Jim different from the Wingfields? Why is Laura able to give Jim the broken horse? Do you see this as an unselfish act or as an exchange for something she has received from him?
9. Why does Tom leave home? Is either Amanda or Laura responsible? Could they have done anything to make him stay?
10. Do you think *The Glass Menagerie* is an appropriate title for this play? Explain.

◆ ESSAYS ◆

DORIS KEARNS GOODWIN (b. 1943)

Doris Kearns Goodwin is best known as a scholar and the author of several outstanding biographies. She wrote Lyndon Johnson and the American Dream *(1976),* The Fitzgeralds and the Kennedys, An American Saga *(1987), and won a Pulitzer Prize for* No Ordinary Time: Franklin and Eleanor Roosevelt *(1994). She addressed the topic she explores here, her love of baseball and her relationship with her father in* Wait Till Next Year *(1997). She teaches at Harvard University.*

FROM FATHER, WITH LOVE [1986]

The game of baseball has always been linked in my mind with the mystic texture of childhood, with the sounds and smells of summer nights and with the memories of my father.

My love for baseball was born on the first day my father took me to Ebbets Field in Brooklyn. Riding in the trolley car, he seemed as excited as I was, and he never stopped talking; now describing for me the street in Brooklyn where he had grown up, now recalling the first game he had been taken to by his own father, now recapturing for me his favorite memories from the Dodgers of his youth—the Dodgers of Casey Stengel, Zach Wheat, and Jimmy Johnston.

In the evenings, when my dad came home from work, we would sit together on our porch and relive the events of that afternoon's game which I had so carefully preserved in the large, red scorebook I'd been given for my seventh birthday. I can still remember how proud I was to have mastered all those strange and wonderful symbols that permitted me to recapture, in miniature form, the every movement of Jackie Robinson and Pee Wee Reese, Duke Snider and Gil Hodges. But the real power of that scorebook lay in the responsibility it entailed. For all through my childhood, my father kept from me the knowledge that the daily papers printed daily box scores, allowing me to believe that without my personal renderings of all those games he missed while he was at work, he would be unable to follow our team in the only proper way a team should be followed, day by day, inning by inning. In other words, without me, his love for baseball would be forever incomplete.

To be sure, there were risks involved in making a commitment as boundless as mine. For me, as for all too many Brooklyn fans, the presiding memory of "the boys of summer" was the memory of the final playoff game in 1951 against the Giants. Going into the ninth, the Dodgers held a 4–1 lead. Then came two singles and a double, placing the winning run at the plate with Bobby Thomson at bat. As Dressen replaced Erskine with Branca, my older sister, with maddening foresight, predicted the forever famous Thomson homer—a prediction that left me so angry with her, imagining that with her words she had somehow brought it about, that I would not speak to her for days.

5 So the seasons of my childhood passed until that miserable summer when the Dodgers were taken away to Los Angeles by the unforgivable O'Malley, leaving all our rash hopes and dreams of glory behind. And then came a summer of still deeper sadness when my father died. Suddenly my feelings for baseball seemed an aspect of my departing youth, along with my childhood freckles and my favorite childhood haunts, to be left behind when I went away to college and never came back.

Then one September day, having settled into teaching at Harvard, I agreed, half reluctantly, to go to Fenway Park. There it was again: the cozy ballfield scaled to human dimensions so that every word of encouragement and every scornful yell could be heard on the field; the fervent crowd that could, with equal passion, curse a player for today's failures after cheering his heroics the day before; the team that always seemed to break your heart in the last week of the season. It took only a matter of minutes before I found myself directing all my old intensities toward my new team—the Boston Red Sox.

I am often teased by my women friends about my obsession, but just as often, in the most unexpected places—in academic conferences, in literary discussions, at the most elegant dinner parties—I find other women just as crazily committed to baseball as I am, and the discovery creates an instant bond between us. All at once, we are deep in conversation, mingling together the past and the present, as if the history of the Red Sox had been our history too.

There we stand, one moment recollecting the unparalleled performance of Yaz[1] in '67, the next sharing ideas on how the present lineup should be changed; one

[1] **Yaz** Red Sox star Carl Yastremski

moment recapturing the splendid career of "the Splendid Splinter,"[2] the next complaining about the manager's decision to pull the pitcher the night before. And then, invariably, comes the most vivid memory of all, the frozen image of Carlton Fisk as he rounded first in the sixth game of the '75 World Series, an image as intense in its evocation of triumph as the image of Ralph Branca weeping in the dugout is in its portrayal of heartache.

There is another, more personal memory associated with Carlton Fisk, for he was, after all the years I had followed baseball, the first player I actually met in person. Apparently, he had read the biography I had written on Lyndon Johnson and wanted to meet me. Yet when the meeting took place, I found myself reduced to the shyness of childhood. There I was, a professor at Harvard, accustomed to speaking with presidents of the United States, and yet, standing beside this young man in a baseball uniform, I was speechless.

10 Finally, Fisk said that it must have been an awesome experience to work with a man of such immense power as President Johnson—and with that, I was at last able to stammer out, with a laugh, "Not as awesome as the thought that I am really standing here talking with you."

Perhaps I have circled back to my childhood, but if this is so, I am certain that my journey through time is connected in some fundamental way to the fact that I am now a parent myself, anxious to share with my three sons the same ritual I once shared with my father.

For in this linkage between the generations rests the magic of baseball, a game that has defied the ravages of modern life, a game that is still played today by the same basic rules and at the same pace as it was played one hundred years ago. There is something deeply satisfying in the knowledge of this continuity.

And there is something else as well which I have experienced sitting in Fenway Park with my small boys on a warm summer's day. If I close my eyes against the sun, all at once I am back at Ebbets Field, a young girl once more in the presence of my father, watching the players of my youth on the grassy field below. There is magic in this moment, for when I open my eyes and see my sons in the place where my father once sat, I feel an invisible bond between our three generations, an anchor of loyalty linking my sons to the grandfather whose face they never saw but whose person they have already come to know through this most timeless of all sports, the game of baseball.

➤ *QUESTIONS FOR READING AND WRITING*

1. Can you think of activities that you have shared with those close to you—as an opportunity to communicate with them?
2. In what way is the author's love for baseball connected to her father?
3. As a person who has worked with important people, including a president of the United States, why is she so overwhelmed when she meets Carlton Fisk?
4. What is her father's legacy to her? To what extent do you think she has passed this legacy on to her own children?

[2] **"the Splendid Splinter"** Ted Williams another famous Red Sox player

MAXINE HONG KINGSTON (b. 1940)

Maxine Hong Kingston was born in Stockton, California, to Chinese immigrant parents. Her parents held many jobs. Her father was a scholar, a manager of a gambling house, and a laundry worker. Her mother worked as a midwife, a practitioner of Chinese medicine, a field hand, and a laundry worker. Kingston attended the University of California at Berkeley, where she is currently a member of the faculty. Equally at home in Chinese, American, and Chinese-American culture, she draws on all three in her writing, which is often autobiographical. Her works include China Men *(1980),* Hawaii One Summer *(1987), and* Through the Black Curtain *(1988). "No Name Woman" is taken from her book* The Woman Warrior: Memoirs of a Girlhood Among Ghosts, *which won a National Book Critics Circle Award for general nonfiction in 1976.*

NO NAME WOMAN [1976]

"You must not tell anyone," my mother said, "what I am about to tell you. In China your father had a sister who killed herself. She jumped into the family well. We say that your father has all brothers because it is as if she had never been born.

"In 1924 just a few days after our village celebrated seventeen hurry-up weddings—to make sure that every young man who went 'out on the road' would responsibly come home—your father and his brothers and your grandfather and his brothers and your aunt's new husband sailed for America, the Gold Mountain. It was your grandfather's last trip. Those lucky enough to get contracts waved goodbye from the decks. They fed and guarded the stowaways and helped them off in Cuba, New York, Bali, Hawaii. 'We'll meet in California next year,' they said. All of them sent money home.

"I remember looking at your aunt one day when she and I were dressing; I had not noticed before that she had such a protruding melon of a stomach. But I did not think, 'She's pregnant,' until she began to look like other pregnant women, her shirt pulling and the white tops of her black pants showing. She could not have been pregnant, you see, because her husband had been gone for years. No one said anything. We did not discuss it. In early summer she was ready to have the child, long after the time when it could have been possible.

"The village had also been counting. On the night the baby was to be born the villagers raided our house. Some were crying. Like a great saw, teeth strung with lights, files of people walked zigzag across our land, tearing the rice. Their lanterns doubled in the disturbed black water, which drained away through the broken bunds. As the villagers closed in, we could see that some of them, probably men and women we knew well, wore white masks. The people with long hair hung it over their faces. Women with short hair made it stand up on end. Some had tied white bands around their foreheads, arms, and legs.

5 "At first they threw mud and rocks at the house. Then they threw eggs and began slaughtering our stock. We could hear the animals scream their deaths—the roosters, the pigs, a last great roar from the ox. Familiar wild heads flared in our night windows; the villagers encircled us. Some of the faces stopped to peer at us, their eyes rushing like searchlights. The hands flattened against the panes, framed heads, and left red prints.

"The villagers broke in the front and the back doors at the same time, even though we had not locked the doors against them. Their knives dripped with the blood of our animals. They smeared blood on the doors and walls. One woman swung a chicken, whose throat she had slit, splattering blood in red arcs about her. We stood together in the middle of our house, in the family hall with the pictures and tables of the ancestors around us, and looked straight ahead.

"At that time the house had only two wings. When the men came back, we would build two more to enclose our courtyard and a third one to begin a second courtyard. The villagers pushed through both wings, even your grandparents' rooms, to find your aunt's, which was also mine until the men returned. From this room a new wing for one of the younger families would grow. They ripped up her clothes and shoes and broke her combs, grinding them underfoot. They tore her work from the loom. They scattered the cooking fire and rolled the new weaving in it. We could hear them in the kitchen breaking our bowls and banging the pots. They overturned the great waist-high earthenware jugs; duck eggs, pickled fruits, vegetables burst out and mixed in acrid torrents. The old woman from the next field swept a broom through the air and loosed the spirits-of-the-broom over our heads. 'Pig.' 'Ghost.' 'Pig,' they sobbed and scolded while they ruined our house.

"When they left, they took sugar and oranges to bless themselves. They cut pieces from the dead animals. Some of them took bowls that were not broken and clothes that were not torn. Afterward we swept up the rice and sewed it back up into sacks. But the smells from the spilled preserves lasted. Your aunt gave birth in the pigsty that night. The next morning when I went for the water, I found her and the baby plugging up the family well.

"Don't let your father know what I told you. He denies her. Now that you have started to menstruate, what happened to her could happen to you. Don't humiliate us. You wouldn't like to be forgotten as if you had never been born. The villagers are watchful."

10 Whenever she had to warn us about life, my mother told stories that ran like this one, a story to grow up on. She tested our strength to establish realities. Those in the emigrant generations who could not reassert brute survival died young and far from home. Those of us in the first American generations have had to figure out how the invisible world the emigrants built around our childhoods fit in solid America.

The emigrants confused the gods by diverting their curses, misleading them with crooked streets and false names. They must try to confuse their offspring as well, who, I suppose, threaten them in similar ways—always trying to get things straight, always trying to name the unspeakable. The Chinese I know hide their names; sojourners take new names when their lives change and guard their real names with silence.

Chinese-Americans, when you try to understand what things in you are Chinese, how do you separate what is peculiar to childhood, to poverty, insanities, one family, your mother who marked your growing with stories, from what is Chinese? What is Chinese tradition and what is the movies?

If I want to learn what clothes my aunt wore, whether flashy or ordinary, I would have to begin, "Remember Father's drowned-in-the-well sister?" I cannot ask that. My mother has told me once and for all the useful parts. She will add nothing unless powered by Necessity, a riverbank that guides her life. She plants vegetable gardens rather than lawns; she carries the odd-shaped tomatoes home from the fields and eats food left for the gods.

Whenever we did frivolous things, we used up energy; we flew high kites. We children came up off the ground over the melting cones our parents brought home from work and the American movie on New Year's Day—*Oh, You Beautiful Doll* with Betty Grable one year, and *She Wore a Yellow Ribbon* with John Wayne another year. After the one carnival ride each, we paid in guilt; our tired father counted his change on the dark walk home.

15 Adultery is extravagance. Could people who hatch their own chicks and eat the embryos and the heads for delicacies and boil the feet in vinegar for party food, leaving only the gravel, eating even the gizzard lining—could such people engender a prodigal aunt? To be a woman, to have a daughter in starvation time was a waste enough. My aunt could not have been the lone romantic who gave up everything for sex. Women in the old China did not choose. Some man had commanded her to lie with him and be his secret evil. I wonder whether he masked himself when he joined the raid on her family.

Perhaps she encountered him in the fields or on the mountain where the daughters-in-law collected fuel. Or perhaps he first noticed her in the marketplace. He was not a stranger because the village housed no strangers. She had to have dealings with him other than sex. Perhaps he worked an adjoining field, or he sold her the cloth for the dress she sewed and wore. His demand must have surprised, then terrified her. She obeyed him; she always did as she was told.

When the family found a young man in the next village to be her husband, she stood tractably beside the best rooster, his proxy, and promised before they met that she would be his forever. She was lucky that he was her age and she would be the first wife, an advantage secure now. The night she first saw him, he had sex with her. Then he left for America. She had almost forgotten what he looked like. When she tried to envision him, she only saw the black and white face in the group photograph the men had had taken before leaving.

The other man was not, after all, much different from her husband. They both gave orders: she followed. "If you tell your family, I'll beat you. I'll kill you. Be here again next week." No one talked sex, ever. And she might have separated the rapes from the rest of living if only she did not have to buy her oil from him or gather wood in the same forest. I want her fear to have lasted just as long as rape lasted so that the fear could have been contained. No drawn-out fear. But women at sex hazarded birth and hence lifetimes. The fear did not stop but permeated everywhere. She told the man, "I think I'm pregnant." He organized the raid against her.

On nights when my mother and father talked about their life back home, sometimes they mentioned an "outcast table" whose business they still seemed to be settling, their voices tight. In a commensal tradition, where food is precious, the powerful older people made wrongdoers eat alone. Instead of letting them start separate new lives like the Japanese, who could become samurais and geishas, the Chinese family, faces averted but eyes glowering sideways, hung on to the offenders and fed them leftovers. My aunt must have lived in the same house as my parents and eaten at an outcast table. My mother spoke about the raid as if she had seen it, when she and my aunt, a daughter-in-law to a different household, should not have been living together at all. Daughters-in-law lived with their husbands' parents, not their own; a synonym for marriage in Chinese is "taking a daughter-in-law." Her husband's parents could have sold her, mortgaged her, stoned her. But they had sent her back to her own mother and father, a mysterious act hinting at disgraces not told me. Perhaps they had thrown her out to deflect the avengers.

She was the only daughter; her four brothers went with her father, husband, and uncles "out on the road" and for some years became western men. When the goods were divided among the family, three of the brothers took land, and the youngest, my father, chose an education. After my grandparents gave their daughter away to her husband's family, they had dispensed all the adventure and all the property. They expected her alone to keep the traditional ways, which her brothers, now among the barbarians, could fumble without detection. The heavy, deep-rooted women were to maintain the past against the flood, safe for returning. But the rare urge west had fixed upon our family, and so my aunt crossed boundaries not delineated in space.

The work of preservation demands that the feelings playing about in one's guts not be turned into action. Just watch their passing like cherry blossoms. But perhaps my aunt, my forerunner, caught in a slow life, let dreams grow and fade and after some months or years went toward what persisted. Fear at the enormities of the forbidden kept her desires delicate, wire and bone. She looked at a man because she liked the way the hair was tucked behind his ears, or she liked the question-mark line of a long torso curving at the shoulder and straight at the hip. For warm eyes or a soft voice or a slow walk—that's all—a few hairs, a line, a brightness, a sound, a pace, she gave up family. She offered us up for a charm that vanished with tiredness, a pigtail that didn't toss when the wind died. Why, the wrong lighting could erase the dearest thing about him.

It could very well have been, however, that my aunt did not take subtle enjoyment of her friend, but, a wild woman, kept rollicking company. Imagining her free with sex doesn't fit, though. I don't know any women like that, or men either. Unless I see her life branching into mine, she gives me no ancestral help.

To sustain her being in love, she often worked at herself in the mirror, guessing at the colors and shapes that would interest him, changing them frequently in order to hit on the right combination. She wanted him to look back.

On a farm near the sea, a woman who tended her appearance reaped a reputation for eccentricity. All the married women blunt-cut their hair in flaps about their ears or pulled it back in tight buns. No nonsense. Neither style blew easily into heart-catching tangles. And at their weddings they displayed themselves in their long hair for the last time. "It brushed the backs of my knees," my mother tells me. "It was braided, and even so, it brushed the backs of my knees."

25 At the mirror my aunt combed individuality into her bob. A bun could have been contrived to escape into black streamers blowing in the wind or in quiet wisps about her face, but only the older women in our picture album wear buns. She brushed her hair back from her forehead, tucking the flaps behind her ears. She looped a piece of thread, knotted into a circle between her index fingers and thumbs, and ran the double strand across her forehead. When she closed her fingers as if she were making a pair of shadow geese bite, the string twisted together catching the little hairs. Then she pulled the thread away from her skin, ripping the hairs out neatly, her eyes watering from the needles of pain. Opening her fingers, she cleaned the thread, then rolled it along her hairline and the tops of her eyebrows. My mother did the same to me and my sisters and herself. I used to believe that the expression "caught by the short hairs" meant a captive held with a depilatory string. It especially hurt at the temples, but my mother said we were lucky we didn't have to have our feet bound when we were seven. Sisters used to sit on their beds and cry together, she said, as their mothers or their slaves removed the bandages for a few minutes each night and let the blood gush back into their veins. I hope that the man my aunt loved appreciated a smooth brow, that he wasn't just a tits-and-ass man.

Once my aunt found a freckle on her chin, at a spot that the almanac said predestined her for unhappiness. She dug it out with a hot needle and washed the wound with peroxide.

More attention to her looks than these pullings of hairs and pickings at spots would have caused gossip among the villagers. They owned work clothes and good clothes, and they wore good clothes for feasting the new seasons. But since a woman combing her hair hexes beginnings, my aunt rarely found an occasion to look her best. Women looked like great sea snails—the corded wood, babies, and laundry they carried were the whorls on their backs. The Chinese did not admire a bent back; goddesses and warriors stood straight. Still there must have been a marvelous freeing of beauty when a worker laid down her burden and stretched and arched.

Such commonplace loveliness, however, was not enough for my aunt. She dreamed of a lover for the fifteen days of New Year's, the time for families to exchange visits, money, and food. She plied her secret comb. And sure enough she cursed the year, the family, the village, and herself.

Even as her hair lured her imminent lover, many other men looked at her. Uncles, cousins, nephews, brothers would have looked, too, had they been home between journeys. Perhaps they had already been restraining their curiosity, and they left, fearful that their glances, like a field of nesting birds, might be startled and caught. Poverty hurt, and that was their first reason for leaving. But another, final reason for leaving the crowded house was the never-said.

30 She may have been unusually beloved, the precious only daughter, spoiled and mirror gazing because of the affection the family lavished on her. When her husband left, they welcomed the chance to take her back from the in-laws; she could live like the little daughter for just a while longer. There are stories that my grandfather was different from other people, "crazy ever since the little Jap bayoneted him in the head." He used to put his naked penis on the dinner table, laughing. And one day he brought home a baby girl, wrapped up inside his brown western-style greatcoat. He had traded one of his sons, probably my father, the youngest, for her. My

grandmother made him trade back. When he finally got a daughter of his own, he doted on her. They must have all loved her, except perhaps my father, the only brother who never went back to China, having once been traded for a girl.

Brothers and sisters, newly men and women, had to efface their sexual color and present plain miens. Disturbing hair and eyes, a smile like no other threatened the ideal of five generations living under one roof. To focus blurs, people shouted face to face and yelled from room to room. The immigrants I know have loud voices, unmodulated to American tones even after years away from the village where they called their friendships out across the fields. I have not been able to stop my mother's screams in public libraries or over telephones. Walking erect (knees straight, toes pointed forward, not pigeon-toed, which is Chinese-feminine) and speaking in an inaudible voice, I have tried to turn myself American-feminine. Chinese communication was loud, public. Only sick people had to whisper. But at the dinner table, where the family members came nearest one another, no one could talk, not the outcasts nor any eaters. Every word that falls from the mouth is a coin lost. Silently they gave and accepted food with both hands. A preoccupied child who took his bowl with one hand got a sideways glare. A complete moment of total attention is due everyone alike. Children and lovers have no singularity here, but my aunt used a secret voice, a separate attentiveness.

She kept the man's name to herself throughout her labor and dying; she did not accuse him that he be punished with her. To save her inseminator's name she gave silent birth.

He may have been somebody in her own household, but intercourse with a man outside the family would have been no less abhorrent. All the village were kinsmen, and the titles shouted in loud country voices never let kinship be forgotten. Any man within visiting distance would have been neutralized as a lover—"brother," "younger brother," "older brother"—one hundred and fifteen relationship titles. Parents researched birth charts probably not so much to assure good fortune as to circumvent incest in a population that has but one hundred surnames. Everybody has eight million relatives. How useless then sexual mannerisms, how dangerous.

As if it came from an atavism deeper than fear, I used to add "brother" silently to boys' names. It hexed the boys, who would or would not ask me to dance, and made them less scary and as familiar and deserving of benevolence as girls.

But, of course, I hexed myself also—no dates. I should have stood up, both arms waving, and shouted out across libraries, "Hey, you! Love me back." I had no idea, though, how to make attraction selective, how to control its direction and magnitude. If I made myself American-pretty so that the five or six Chinese boys in the class fell in love with me, everyone else—the Caucasian, Negro, and Japanese boys—would too. Sisterliness, dignified and honorable, made much more sense.

Attraction eludes control so stubbornly that whole societies designed to organize relationships among people cannot keep order, not even when they bind people to one another from childhood and raise them together. Among the very poor and the wealthy, brothers married their adopted sisters, like doves. Our family allowed some romance, paying adult brides' prices and providing dowries so that their sons and daughters could marry strangers. Marriage promises to turn strangers into friendly relatives—a nation of siblings.

In the village structure, spirits shimmered among the live creatures, balanced and held in equilibrium by time and land. But one human being flaring up into violence could open up a black hole, a maelstrom that pulled in the sky. The frightened villagers, who depended on one another to maintain the real, went to my aunt to show her a personal, physical representation of the break she had made in the "roundness." Misallying couples snapped off the future, which was to be embodied in true offspring. The villagers punished her for acting as if she could have a private life, secret and apart from them.

If my aunt had betrayed the family at a time of large grain yields and peace, when many boys were born, and wings were being built on many houses, perhaps she might have escaped such severe punishment. But the men—hungry, greedy, tired of planting in dry soil, cuckolded—had had to leave the village in order to send food-money home. There were ghost plagues, bandit plagues, wars with the Japanese, floods. My Chinese brother and sister had died of an unknown sickness. Adultery, perhaps only a mistake during good times, became a crime when the village needed food.

The round moon cakes and round doorways, the round tables of graduated size that fit one roundness inside another, round windows and rice bowls—these talismen had lost their power to warn this family of the law: a family must be whole, faithfully keeping the descent line by having sons to feed the old and the dead, who in turn look after the family. The villagers came to show my aunt and her lover-in-hiding a broken house. The villagers were speeding up the circling of events because she was too shortsighted to see that her infidelity had already harmed the village, that waves of consequences would return unpredictably, sometimes in disguise, as now, to hurt her. This roundness had to be made coin-sized so that she would see its circumference: punish her at the birth of her baby. Awaken her to the inexorable. People who refused fatalism because they could invent small resources insisted on culpability. Deny accidents and wrest fault from the stars.

After the villagers left, their lanterns now scattering in various directions toward home, the family broke their silence and cursed her. "Aiaa, we're going to die. Death is coming. Death is coming. Look what you've done. You've killed us. Ghost! Dead ghost! Ghost! You've never been born." She ran out into the fields, far enough from the house so that she could no longer hear their voices, and pressed herself against the earth, her own land no more. When she felt the birth coming, she thought that she had been hurt. Her body seized together. "They've hurt me too much," she thought. "This is gall, and it will kill me." Her forehead and knees against the earth, her body convulsed and then released her onto her back. The black well of sky and stars went out and out and out forever; her body and her complexity seemed to disappear. She was one of the stars, a bright dot in blackness, without home, without a companion, in eternal cold and silence. An agoraphobia rose in her, speeding higher and higher, bigger and bigger; she would not be able to contain it; there would be no end to fear.

Flayed, unprotected against space, she felt pain return, focusing her body. This pain chilled her—a cold, steady kind of surface pain. Inside, spasmodically, the other pain, the pain of the child, heated her. For hours she lay on the ground, alternately body and space. Sometimes a vision of normal comfort obliterated reality:

she saw the family in the evening gambling at the dinner table, the young people massaging their elders' backs. She saw them congratulating one another, high joy on the mornings the rice shoots came up. When these pictures burst, the stars drew yet further apart. Black space opened.

She got to her feet to fight better and remembered that old-fashioned women gave birth in their pigsties to fool the jealous, pain-dealing gods, who do not snatch piglets. Before the next spasms could stop her, she ran to the pigsty, each step a rushing out into emptiness. She climbed over the fence and knelt in the dirt. It was good to have a fence enclosing her, a tribal person alone.

Laboring, this woman who had carried her child as a foreign growth that sickened her every day, expelled it at last. She reached down to touch the hot, wet, moving mass, surely smaller than anything human, and could feel that it was human after all—fingers, toes, nails, nose. She pulled it up on to her belly, and it lay curled there, butt in the air, feet precisely tucked one under the other. She opened her loose shirt and buttoned the child inside. After resting, it squirmed and thrashed and she pushed it up to her breast. It turned its head this way and that until it found her nipple. There, it made little snuffling noises. She clenched her teeth at its preciousness, lovely as a young calf, a piglet, a little dog.

She may have gone to the pigsty as a last act of responsibility: she would protect this child as she had protected its father. It would look after her soul, leaving supplies on her grave. But how would this tiny child without family find her grave when there would be no marker for her anywhere, neither in the earth nor the family hall? No one would give her a family hall name. She had taken the child with her into the wastes. At its birth the two of them had felt the same raw pain of separation, a wound that only the family pressing tight could close. A child with no descent line would not soften her life but only trail after her, ghostlike, begging her to give it purpose. At dawn the villagers on their way to the fields would stand around the fence and look.

45 Full of milk, the little ghost slept. When it awoke, she hardened her breasts against the milk that crying loosens. Toward morning she picked up the baby and walked to the well.

Carrying the baby to the well shows loving. Otherwise abandon it. Turn its face into the mud. Mothers who love their children take them along. It was probably a girl; there is some hope of forgiveness for boys.

"Don't tell anyone you had an aunt. Your father does not want to hear her name. She has never been born." I have believed that sex was unspeakable and words so strong and fathers so frail that "aunt" would do my father mysterious harm. I have thought that my family, having settled among immigrants who had also been their neighbors in the ancestral land, needed to clean their name, and a wrong word would incite the kinspeople even here. But there is more to this silence: they want me to participate in her punishment. And I have.

In the twenty years since I heard this story I have not asked for details nor said my aunt's name; I do not know it. People who can comfort the dead can also chase after them to hurt them further—a reverse ancestor worship. The real punishment was not the raid swiftly inflicted by the villagers, but the family's deliberately forgetting her. Her betrayal so maddened them, they saw to it that she would suffer forever, even after death. Always hungry, always needing, she would have to beg food from other ghosts, snatch and steal it from those whose living descendants give them gifts. She would have to fight the ghosts massed at crossroads for the buns a few thoughtful citizens leave to decoy her away from village and home so that the ancestral spirits could feast unharassed. At peace, they could act like gods, not ghosts, their descent lines providing them with paper suits and dresses, spirit money, paper houses, paper automobiles, chicken, meat, and rice into eternity—essences delivered up in smoke and flames, steam and incense rising from each rice bowl. In an attempt to make the Chinese care for people outside the family, Chairman Mao encourages us now to give our paper replicas to the spirits of outstanding soldiers and workers, no matter whose ancestors they may be. My aunt remains forever hungry. Goods are not distributed evenly among the dead.

My aunt haunts me—her ghost drawn to me because now, after fifty years of neglect, I alone devote pages of paper to her, though not origamied into houses and clothes. I do not think she always means me well. I am telling on her, and she was a spite suicide, drowning herself in the drinking water. The Chinese are always very frightened of the drowned one, whose weeping ghost, wet hair hanging and skin bloated, waits silently by the water to pull down a substitute.

➤ *QUESTIONS FOR READING AND WRITING*

1. Are there things most families want to keep quiet? To what extent does your own background or experience affect your response to "No Name Woman?"
2. What does the author mean by "Adultery, perhaps only a mistake during good times, became a crime when the village needed food"?
3. Why is the author "haunted" by her aunt? Would you be? Explain.

MARK TWAIN (1835–1910)

Born Samuel Longhorne Clemens in Florida, Missouri, Mark Twain was raised along the Mississippi River, in the town of Hannibal. He left school at the age of twelve, worked first in the printing trade, where he wrote occasional news stories and sketches, and then, in 1859, fulfilled his childhood dream of becoming a riverboat pilot. The Civil War put an end to commercial traffic on the river, and after a short and uncomfortable time in the Confederate army, Twain headed West to Colorado, Nevada, and finally California to seek his fortune. It was there, while working as a reporter, that he decided on his vocation as a writer and began publishing a series of popular humorous writings, including "The Celebrated Jumping Frog of Calaveras County" (1865). The publication of The Innocents Abroad *in 1869, a humorous*

account of his travels in Europe, established his reputation as an important literary figure, and he spent the rest of his life as one of America's most recognizable personalities. His novels include The Adventures of Tom Sawyer *(1876).* The Prince and the Pauper *(1882),* A Connecticut Yankee in King Arthur's Court *(1889), and his masterpiece* The Adventures of Huckleberry Finn *(1884), which Ernest Hemingway called "the best book we've had."*

Advice to Youth [1882]

Being told I would be expected to talk here, I inquired what sort of a talk I ought to make. They said it should be something suitable to youth—something didactic, instructive, or something in the nature of good advice. Very well. I have a few things in my mind which I have often longed to say for the instruction of the young; for it is in one's tender early years that such things will best take root and be most enduring and most valuable. First, then, I will say to you, my young friends—and I say it beseechingly, urgingly—

Always obey your parents, when they are present. This is the best policy in the long run, because if you don't they will make you. Most parents think they know better than you do, and you can generally make more by humoring that superstition than you can by acting on your own better judgment.

Be respectful to your superiors, if you have any, also to strangers, and sometimes to others. If a person offend you, and you are in doubt as to whether it was intentional or not, do not resort to extreme measures; simply watch your chance and hit him with a brick. That will be sufficient. If you shall find that he had not intended any offense, come out frankly and confess yourself in the wrong when you struck him; acknowledge it like a man and say you didn't mean to. Yes, always avoid violence; in this age of charity and kindliness, the time has gone by for such things. Leave dynamite to the low and unrefined.

Go to bed early, get up early—this is wise. Some authorities say get up with the sun; some others say get up with one thing, some with another. But a lark is really the best thing to get up with. It gives you a splendid reputation with everybody to know that you get up with the lark; and if you get the right kind of a lark, and work at him right, you can easily train him to get up at half past nine, every time—it is no trick at all.

5 Now as to the matter of lying. You want to be very careful about lying; otherwise you are nearly sure to get caught. Once caught, you can never again be, in the eyes of the good and the pure, what you were before. Many a young person has injured himself permanently through a single clumsy and illfinished lie, the result of carelessness born of incomplete training. Some authorities hold that the young ought not to lie at all. That, of course, is putting it rather stronger than necessary; still, while I cannot go quite so far as that, I do maintain, and I believe I am right, that the young ought to be temperate in the use of this great art until practice and experience shall give them that confidence, elegance, and precision which alone can make the accomplishment graceful and profitable. Patience, diligence, painstaking attention to detail—these are the requirements; these, in time, will make the student perfect; upon these, and upon these only, may he rely as the sure foundation for

future eminence. Think what tedious years of study, thought, practice, experience, went to the equipment of that peerless old master who was able to impose upon the whole world the lofty and sounding maxim that "truth is mighty and will prevail"—the most majestic compound fracture of fact which any of woman born has yet achieved. For the history of our race, and each individual's experience, are sown thick with evidence that a truth is not hard to kill and that a lie told well is immortal. There is in Boston a monument of the man who discovered anaesthesia; many people are aware, in these latter days, that that man didn't discover it at all, but stole the discovery from another man. Is this truth mighty, and will it prevail? Ah no, my hearers, the monument is made of hardy material, but the lie it tells will outlast it a million years. An awkward, feeble, leaky lie is a thing which you ought to make it your unceasing study to avoid; such a lie as that has no more real permanence than an average truth. Why, you might as well tell the truth at once and be done with it. A feeble, stupid, preposterous lie will not live two years—except it be a slander upon somebody. It is indestructible, then, of course, but that is no merit of yours. A final word: begin your practice of this gracious and beautiful art early—begin now. If I had begun earlier, I could have learned how.

Never handle firearms carelessly. The sorrow and suffering that have been caused through the innocent out heedless handling of firearms by the young! Only four days ago, right in the next farmhouse to the one where I am spending the summer, a grandmother, old and gray and sweet, one of the loveliest spirits in the land, was sitting at her work, when her young grandson crept in and got down an old, battered, rusty gun which had not been touched for many years and was supposed not to be loaded, and pointed it at her, laughing and threatening to shoot. In her fright she ran screaming and pleading toward the door on the other side of the room; but as she passed him he placed the gun almost against her very breast and pulled the trigger! He had supposed it was not loaded. And he was right—it wasn't. So there wasn't any harm done. It is the only case of that kind I ever heard of. Therefore, just the same, don't you meddle with old unloaded firearms; they are the most deadly and unerring things that have ever been created by man. You don't have to take any pains at all with them; you don't have to have a rest, you don't have to have any sights on the gun, you don't have to take aim, even. No, you just pick out a relative and bang away, and you are sure to get him. A youth who can't hit a cathedral at thirty yards with a Gatling gun in three-quarters of an hour, can take up an old empty musket and bag his grandmother every time, at a hundred. Think what Waterloo would have been if one of the armies had been boys armed with old muskets supposed not to be loaded, and the other army had been composed of their female relations. The very thought of it makes one shudder.

There are many sorts of books; but good ones are the sort for the young to read. Remember that. They are a great, an inestimable, an unspeakable means of improvement. Therefore be careful in your selection, my young friends; be very careful; confine yourselves exclusively to Robertson's Sermons, Baxter's *Saint's Rest, The Innocents Abroad,* and works of that kind.

But I have said enough. I hope you will treasure up the instructions which I have given you, and make them a guide to your feet and a light to your understanding. Build your character thoughtfully and painstakingly upon these precepts, and by and by, when you have got it built, you will be surprised and gratified to see how nicely and sharply it resembles everybody else's.

➤ *QUESTIONS FOR READING AND WRITING*

1. What is the tone of this essay? To what extent does Twain mean what he says?
2. Have you ever received advice like this? If so, did you always take it seriously? Explain.
3. Do you think there is wisdom in this essay? Explain.

Case Studies in Composition

Thinking About Interpretation and Biography

Lorraine Hansberry and *A Raisin in the Sun*

Lorraine Hansberry (1930–1965)

Lorraine Hansberry was born in Chicago, Illinois, to middle-class black parents who lived on the city's South Side. When she was still a child, her father was barred from purchasing a house in a white neighborhood. He sued and pursued the case all the way to the Supreme Court, which ruled in his favor. Hansberry attended the University of Wisconsin as an undergraduate. Following college, she pursued a career as a painter studying at the Art Institute of Chicago and in Mexico before she decided to move to New York to pursue her interest in writing. There she wrote for Freedom, *a magazine founded by the great singer-actor turned political activist, Paul Robeson. When her first play,* A Raisin in the Sun, *premiered at the Ethel Barrymore Theater in 1959, it was the first play written by an African-American woman to be performed on Broadway. She wrote only one other play,* The Sign in Sidney Brustien's Window *(1965), before she died of cancer at the age of thirty-four. The title of* A Raisin in the Sun *is taken from the poem "A Dream Deferred," by Langston Hughes (p. 88).*

A Raisin in the Sun [1958]

CHARACTERS IN ORDER OF APPEARANCE
RUTH YOUNGER *Walter's wife, about thirty*
TRAVIS YOUNGER *her son and Walter's*
WALTER LEE YOUNGER (brother) *RUTH's husband, mid-thirties*
BENEATHA YOUNGER *Walter's sister, about twenty*
LENA YOUNGER (Mama) *mother of Walter and Beneatha*
JOSEPH ASAGAI *Nigerian, Beneatha's suitor*
GEORGE MURCHISON *Beneatha's date, wealthy*
KARL LINDNER *white, chairman of the Clybourne Park New Neighbors Orientation* Committee

BOBO *one of Walter's business partners*
MOVING MEN

The action of the play is set in Chicago's South Side, sometime between World War II and the present.

ACT I
Scene 1. Friday morning
Scene 2. The following morning

ACT II
Scene 1. Later, the same day
Scene 2. Friday night, a few weeks later
Scene 3. Moving day, one week later

ACT III
An hour later

ACT I
SCENE 1

The Younger living room would be a comfortable and well-ordered room if it were not for a number of indestructible contradictions to this state of being. Its furnishings are typical and undistinguished and their primary feature now is that they have clearly had to accommodate the living of too many people for too many years—and they are tired. Still, we can see that at some time, a time probably no longer remembered by the family (except perhaps for MAMA*) the furnishings of this room were actually selected with care and love and even hope—and brought to this apartment and arranged with taste and pride.*

That was a long time ago. Now the once loved pattern of the couch upholstery has to fight to show itself from under acres of crocheted doilies and couch covers which have themselves finally come to be more important than the upholstery. And here a table or a chair has been moved to disguise the worn places in the carpet; but the carpet has fought back by showing its weariness, with depressing uniformity, elsewhere on its surface.

Weariness has, in fact, won in this room. Everything has been polished, washed, sat on, used, scrubbed too often. All pretenses but living itself have long since vanished from the very atmosphere of this room.

Moreover, a section of this room, for it is not really a room unto itself, though the landlord's lease would make it seem so, slopes backward to provide a small kitchen area, where the family prepares the meals that are eaten in the living room proper, which must also serve as dining room. The single window that has been provided for these "two" rooms is located in this kitchen area. The sole natural light the family may enjoy in the course of a day is only that which fights its way through this little window.

At left, a door leads to a bedroom which is shared by MAMA *and her daughter,* BENEATHA. *At right, opposite, is a second room (which in the beginning of the life of this apartment was probably a breakfast room) which serves as a bedroom for Walter and his wife,* RUTH.

Time: Sometime between World War II and the present.

Place: Chicago's South Side.

At rise: It is morning dark in the living room. TRAVIS *is asleep on the make-down bed at center. An alarm clock sounds from within the bedroom at right, and presently* RUTH *enters from that room and closes the door behind her. She crosses sleepily toward the window. As she passes her sleeping son she reaches down and shakes him a little. At the window she raises the shade and a dusky South Side morning light comes in feebly. She fills a pot with water and puts it on to boil. She calls to the boy, between yawns, in a slightly muffled voice.*

RUTH *is about thirty. We can see that she was a pretty girl, even exceptionally so, but now it is apparent that life has been little that she expected, and disappointment has already begun to hang in her face. In a few years, before thirty-five even, she will be known among her people as a "settled woman."*

She crosses to her son and gives him a good, final, rousing shake.

RUTH: Come on now, boy, it's seven thirty! [*Her son sits up at last, in a stupor of sleepiness.*] I say hurry up, Travis! You ain't the only person in the world got to use a bathroom! [*The child, a sturdy, handsome little boy of ten or eleven, drags himself out of the bed and almost blindly takes his towels and "today's clothes" from drawers and a closet and goes out to the bathroom, which is in an outside hall and which is shared by another family or families on the same floor.* RUTH *crosses to the bedroom door at right and opens it and calls in to her husband.*] Walter Lee! . . . It's after seven thirty! Lemme see you do some waking up in there now! [*She waits.*] You better get up from there, man! It's after seven thirty I tell you. [*She waits again.*] All right, you just go ahead and lay there and next thing you know Travis be finished and Mr. Johnson'll be in there and you'll be fussing and cussing round here like a mad man! And be late too! [*She waits, at the end of patience.*] Walter Lee—it's time for you to get up! [*She waits another second and then starts to go into the bedroom, but is apparently satisfied that her husband has begun to get up. She stops, pulls the door to, and returns to the kitchen area. She wipes her face with a moist cloth and runs her fingers through her sleep-disheveled hair in a vain effort and ties an apron around her housecoat. The bedroom door at right opens and her husband stands in the doorway in his pajamas, which are rumpled and mismated. He is a lean, intense young man in his middle thirties, inclined to quick nervous movements and erratic speech habits—and always in his voice there is a quality of indictment.*]

WALTER: Is he out yet?

RUTH: What you mean *out*? He ain't hardly got in there good yet.

WALTER [*wandering in, still more oriented to sleep than to a new day*]: Well, what was you doing all that yelling for if I can't even get in there yet? [*stopping and thinking*] Check coming today?

RUTH: They *said* Saturday and this is just Friday and I hopes to God you ain't going to get up here first thing this morning and start talking to me 'bout no money—'cause I 'bout don't want to hear it.

WALTER: Something the matter with you this morning?

RUTH: No—I'm just sleepy as the devil. What kind of eggs you want?

WALTER: Not scrambled. [*RUTH starts to scramble eggs.*] Paper come? [*RUTH points impatiently to the rolled up* Tribune *on the table, and he gets it and spreads it out and vaguely reads the front page.*] Set off another bomb yesterday.

RUTH [*maximum indifference*]: Did they?

WALTER [*looking up*]: What's the matter with you?

RUTH: Ain't nothing the matter with me. And don't keep asking me that this morning.

WALTER: Ain't nobody bothering you. [*reading the news of the day absently again*] Say Colonel McCormick is sick.

RUTH [*affecting tea-party interest*]: Is he now? Poor thing.

WALTER [*Sighing and looking at his watch*]: Oh, me. [*He waits.*] Now what is that boy doing in that bathroom all this time? He just going to have to start getting up earlier. I can't be being late to work on account of him fooling around in there.

RUTH [*turning on him*]: Oh, no he ain't going to be getting up earlier no such thing! It ain't his fault that he can't get to bed no earlier nights 'cause he got a bunch of crazy good-for-nothing clowns sitting up running their mouths in what is supposed to be his bedroom after ten o'clock at night . . .

WALTER: That's what you mad about, ain't it? The things I want to talk about with my friends just couldn't be important in your mind, could they? [*He rises and finds a cigarette in her handbag on the table and crosses to the little window and looks out, smoking and deeply enjoying this first one.*]

RUTH [*almost matter of factly, a complaint too automatic to deserve emphasis*]: Why you always got to smoke before you eat in the morning?

WALTER [*at the window*]: Just look at 'em down there. . . . Running and racing to work . . . [*He turns and faces his wife and watches her a moment at the stove, and then, suddenly.*] You look young this morning, baby.

RUTH [*indifferently*]: Yeah?

WALTER: Just for a second—stirring them eggs. It's gone now—just for a second it was—you looked real young again. [*then, drily*] It's gone now—you look like yourself again.

RUTH: Man, if you don't shut up and leave me alone.

WALTER [*looking out to the street again*]: First thing a man ought to learn in life is not to make love to no colored woman first thing in the morning. You all some evil people at eight o'clock in the morning. [*TRAVIS appears in the hall doorway, almost fully dressed and quite wide awake now, his towels and pajamas across his shoulders. He opens the door and signals for his father to make the bathroom in a hurry.*]

TRAVIS [*watching the bathroom*]: Daddy, come on! [*WALTER gets his bathroom utensils and flies out to the bathroom.*]

RUTH: Sit down and have your breakfast, Travis.

TRAVIS: Mama, this is Friday. [*gleefully*] Check coming tomorrow, huh?

RUTH: You get your mind off money and eat your breakfast.

TRAVIS [*eating*]: This is the morning we supposed to bring the fifty cents to school.

RUTH: Well, I ain't got no fifty cents this morning.

TRAVIS: Teacher say we have to.

RUTH: I don't care what teacher say. I ain't got it. Eat your breakfast, Travis.

TRAVIS: I *am* eating.

RUTH: Hush up now and just eat! [*The boy gives her an exasperated look for her lack of understanding, and eats grudgingly.*]

TRAVIS: You think Grandmama would have it?

RUTH: No! And I want you to stop asking your grandmother for money, you hear me?

TRAVIS [*outraged*]: Gaaaleee! I don't ask her, she just gimme it sometimes!

RUTH: Travis Willard Younger—I got too much on me this morning to be—

TRAVIS: Maybe Daddy—

RUTH: *Travis!* [*The boy hushes abruptly. They are both quiet and tense for several seconds.*]

TRAVIS [*presently*]: Could I maybe go carry some groceries in front of the supermarket for a little while after school then?

RUTH: Just hush, I said. [*TRAVIS jabs his spoon into his cereal bowl viciously, and rests his head in anger upon his fists.*] If you through eating, you can get over there and make up your bed. [*The boy obeys stiffly and crosses the room, almost mechanically, to the bed and more or less carefully folds the covering. He carries the bedding into his mother's room and returns with his books and cap.*]

TRAVIS [*sulking and standing apart from her unnaturally*]: I'm gone.

RUTH [*looking up from the stove to inspect him automatically*]: Come here. [*He crosses to her and she studies his head.*] If you don't take this comb and fix this here head, you better! [*TRAVIS puts down his books with a great sigh of oppression, and crosses to the mirror. His mother mutters under her breath about his "stubbornness."*] 'Bout to march out of here with that head looking just like chickens slept in it! I just don't know where you get your stubborn ways . . . And get your jacket, too. Looks chilly out this morning.

TRAVIS [*with conspicuously brushed hair and jacket*]: I'm gone.

RUTH: Get carfare and milk money—[*waving one finger*]—and not a single penny for no caps, you hear me?

TRAVIS [*with sullen politeness*]: Yes'm. [*He turns in outrage to leave. His mother watches after him as in his frustration he approaches the door almost comically. When she speaks to him, her voice has become a very gentle tease.*]

RUTH [*mocking, as she thinks he would say it*]: Oh, Mama makes me so mad sometimes, I don't know what to do! [*She waits and continues to his back as he stands stock-still in front of the door.*] I wouldn't kiss that woman good-bye for nothing in this world this morning! [*The boy finally turns around and rolls his eyes at her, knowing the mood has changed and he is vindicated; he does not, however, move toward her yet.*] Not for nothing in this world! [*She finally laughs aloud at him and holds out her arms to him and we see that it is a way between them, very old and practiced. He crosses to her and allows her to embrace him warmly but keeps his face fixed with masculine rigidity. She holds him back from her presently and looks at him and runs her fingers over the features of his face. With utter gentleness—*] Now—whose little old angry man are you?

TRAVIS [*The masculinity and gruffness start to fade at last.*]: Aw gaalee—Mama . . .

RUTH [*mimicking*]: Aw—gaaaaalleeeee, Mama! [*She pushes him, with rough playfulness and finality, toward the door.*] Get on out of here or you going to be late.

TRAVIS [*in the face of love, new aggressiveness*]: Mama, could I *please* go carry groceries?

RUTH: Honey, it's starting to get so cold evenings.

WALTER [*coming in from the bedroom and drawing a make-believe gun from a make-believe holster and shooting at his son*]: What is it he wants to do?

RUTH: Go carry groceries after school at the supermarket.

WALTER: Well, let him go . . .

TRAVIS [*quickly, to the ally*]: I *have* to—she won't gimme the fifty cents . . .

WALTER [*to his wife only*]: Why not?

RUTH [*simply, and with flavor*]: 'Cause we don't have it.

WALTER [*to* RUTH *only*]: What you tell the boy things like that for? [*reaching down into his pants with a rather important gesture*] Here, son—[*He hands the boy the coin, but his eyes are directed to his wife's.* TRAVIS *takes the money happily.*]

TRAVIS: Thanks, Daddy. [*He starts out.* RUTH *watches both of them with murder in her eyes.* WALTER *stands and stares back at her with defiance, and suddenly reaches into his pocket again on an afterthought.*]

WALTER [*without even looking at his son, still staring hard at his wife*]: In fact, here's another fifty cents . . . Buy yourself some fruit today—or take a taxicab to school or something!

TRAVIS: Whoopee—[*He leaps up and clasps his father around the middle with his legs, and they face each other in mutual appreciation; slowly* WALTER LEE *peeks around the boy to catch the violent rays from his wife's eyes and draws his head back as if shot.*]

WALTER: You better get down now—and get to school, man.

TRAVIS [*at the door*]: O.K. Good-bye. [*He exits.*]

WALTER [*after him, pointing with pride*]: That's *my* boy. [*She looks at him in disgust and turns back to her work.*] You know what I was thinking 'bout in the bathroom this morning?

RUTH: No.

WALTER: How come you always try to be so pleasant!

RUTH: What is there to be pleasant 'bout!

WALTER: You want to know what I was thinking 'bout in the bathroom or not!

RUTH: I know what you thinking 'bout.

WALTER [*ignoring her*]: 'Bout what me and Willy Harris was talking about last night.

RUTH [*immediately—a refrain*]: Willy Harris is a good-for-nothing loudmouth.

WALTER: Anybody who talks to me has got to be a good-for-nothing loudmouth, ain't he? And what you know about who is just a good-for-nothing loudmouth? Charlie Atkins was just a "good-for-nothing loudmouth" too, wasn't he! When he wanted me to go in the dry-cleaning business with him. And now—he's grossing a hundred thousand a year. A hundred thousand dollars a year! You still call *him* a loudmouth!

RUTH [*bitterly*]: Oh, Walter Lee . . . [*She folds her head on her arms over the table.*]

WALTER [*rising and coming to her and standing over her*]: You tired, ain't you? Tired of everything. Me, the boy, the way we live—this beat-up hole—everything. Ain't you? [*She doesn't look up, doesn't answer.*] So tired—moaning and groaning all the time, but you wouldn't do nothing to help, would you? You couldn't be on my side that long for nothing, could you?

RUTH: Walter, please leave me alone.

WALTER: A man needs for a woman to back him up . . .

RUTH: Walter—

WALTER: Mama would listen to you. You know she listen to you more than she do me and Bennie. She think more of you. All you have to do is just sit down with her when you drinking your coffee one morning and talking 'bout things like you do and—[*He sits down beside her and demonstrates graphically what he thinks her methods and tone should be.*]—you just sip your coffee, see, and say easy like that you been thinking 'bout that deal Walter Lee is so interested in, 'bout the store and all, and sip some more coffee, like what you saying ain't really that important to you—And the next thing you know, she be listening good and asking you questions and when I come home—I can tell her the details. This ain't no fly-by-night proposition, baby. I mean we figured it out, me and Willy and Bobo.

RUTH [*with a frown*]: Bobo?

WALTER: Yeah. You see, this little liquor store we got in mind cost seventy-five thousand and we figured the initial investment on the place be 'bout thirty thousand, see. That be ten thousand each. Course, there's a couple of hundred you got to pay so's you don't spend your life just waiting for them clowns to let your license get approved—

RUTH: You mean graft?

WALTER [*frowning impatiently*]: Don't call it that. See there, that just goes to show you what women understand about the world. Baby, don't *nothing* happen for you in this world 'less you pay *somebody* off!

RUTH: Walter, leave me alone! [*She raises her head and stares at him vigorously—then says, more quietly.*] Eat your eggs, they gonna be cold.

WALTER [*straightening up from her and looking off*]: That's it. There you are. Man say to his woman: I got me a dream. His woman say: Eat your eggs. [*sadly, but gaining in power*] Man say: I got to take hold of this here world, baby! And a woman will say: Eat your eggs and go to work. [*passionately now*] Man say: I got to change my life, I'm choking to death, baby! And his woman say—[*in utter anguish as he brings his fists down on his thighs*]—Your eggs is getting cold!

RUTH [*softly*]: Walter, that ain't none of our money.

WALTER [*not listening at all or even looking at her*]: This morning, I was lookin' in the mirror and thinking about it . . . I'm thirty-five years old; I been married eleven years and I got a boy who sleeps in the living room—[*very, very quietly*]—and all I got to give him is stories about how rich white people live . . .

RUTH: Eat your eggs, Walter.

WALTER: *Damn my eggs . . . damn all the eggs that ever was!*

RUTH: Then go to work.

WALTER [*looking up at her*]: See—I'm trying to talk to you 'bout myself—[*shaking his head with the repetition*]—and all you can say is eat them eggs and go to work.

RUTH [*wearily*]: Honey, you never say nothing new. I listen to you every day, every night and every morning, and you never say nothing new. [*shrugging*] So you would rather *be* Mr. Arnold than be his chauffeur. So—I would *rather* be living in Buckingham Palace.

WALTER: That is just what is wrong with the colored woman in this world . . . Don't understand about building their men up and making 'em feel like they somebody. Like they can do something.

RUTH [*drily, but to hurt*]: There *are* colored men who do things.

WALTER: No thanks to the colored woman.

RUTH: Well, being a colored woman, I guess I can't help myself none. [*She rises and gets the ironing board and sets it up and attacks a huge pile of rough-dried clothes, sprinkling them in preparation for the ironing and then rolling them into tight fat balls.*]

WALTER [*mumbling*]: We one group of men tied to a race of women with small minds. [*his sister* BENEATHA *enters. She is about twenty, as slim and intense as her brother. She is not as pretty as her sister-in-law, but her lean, almost intellectual face has a handsomeness of its own. She wears a bright-red flannel nightie, and her thick hair stands wildly about her head. Her speech is a mixture of many things; it is different from the rest of the family's insofar as education has permeated her sense of English—and perhaps the Midwest rather than the South has finally—at last—won out in her inflection; but not altogether, because over all of it is a soft slurring and transformed use of vowels which is the decided influence of the South Side. She passes through the room without looking at either* RUTH *or* WALTER *and goes to the outside door and looks, a little blindly, out to the bathroom. She sees that it has been lost to the Johnsons. She closes the door with a sleepy vengeance and crosses to the table and sits down a little defeated.*]

BENEATHA: I am going to start timing those people.

WALTER: You should get up earlier.

BENEATHA [*Her face in her hands. She is still fighting the urge to go back to bed*]: Really—would you suggest dawn? Where's the paper?

WALTER [*pushing the paper across the table to her as he studies her almost clinically, as though he has never seen her before*]: You a horrible-looking chick at this hour.

BENEATHA [*drily*]: Good morning, everybody.

WALTER [*senselessly*]: How is school coming?

BENEATHA [*in the same spirit*]: Lovely, Lovely. And you know, biology is the greatest. [*looking up at him*] I dissected something that looked just like you yesterday.

WALTER: I just wondered if you've made up your mind and everything.

BENEATHA [*gaining in sharpness and impatience*]: And what did I answer yesterday morning—and the day before that?

RUTH [*from the ironing board, like someone disinterested and old*]: Don't be so nasty, Bennie.

BENEATHA [*still to her brother*]: And the day before that and the day before that!

WALTER [*defensively*]: I'm interested in you. Something wrong with that? Ain't many girls who decide—

WALTER and BENEATHA [*in unison*]: —"to be a doctor." [*silence*]

WALTER: Have we figured out yet just exactly how much medical school is going to cost?

RUTH: Walter Lee, why don't you leave that girl alone and get out of here to work?

BENEATHA [*exits to the bathroom and bangs on the door*]: Come on out of there, please! [*She comes back into the room.*]

WALTER [*looking at his sister intently*]: You know the check is coming tomorrow.

BENEATHA [*turning on him with a sharpness all her own*]: That money belongs to Mama, Walter, and it's for her to decide how she wants to use it. I don't care if she wants to buy a house or a rocket ship or just nail it up somewhere and look at it. It's hers. Not ours—hers.

WALTER [*bitterly*]: Now ain't that fine! You just got your mother's interest at heart, ain't you, girl? You such a nice girl—but if Mama got that money she can always take a few thousand and help you through school too—can't she?

BENEATHA: I have never asked anyone around here to do anything for me!

WALTER: No! And the line between asking and just accepting when the time comes is big and wide—ain't it!

BENEATHA [*with fury*]: What do you want from me, Brother—that I quit school or just drop dead, which!

WALTER: I don't want nothing but for you to stop acting holy 'round here. Me and Ruth done made some sacrifices for you—why can't you do something for the family?

RUTH: Walter, don't be dragging me in it.

WALTER: You are in it—Don't you get up and go work in somebody's kitchen for the last three years to help put clothes on her back?

RUTH: Oh, Walter—that's not fair . . .

WALTER: It ain't that nobody expects you to get on your knees and say thank you, Brother; thank you, Ruth; thank you, Mama—and thank you, Travis, for wearing the same pair of shoes for two semesters—

BENEATHA [*dropping to her knees*]: Well—I do—all right?—thank everybody . . . and forgive me for ever wanting to be anything at all . . . forgive me, forgive me!

RUTH: Please stop it! Your mama'll hear you.

WALTER: Who the hell told you you had to be a doctor? If you so crazy 'bout messing 'round with sick people—then go be a nurse like other women—or just get married and be quiet . . .

BENEATHA: Well—you finally got it said . . . It took you three years but you finally got it said. Walter, give up; leave me alone—it's Mama's money.

WALTER: *He was my father, too!*

BENEATHA: So what? He was mine, too—and Travis' grandfather—but the insurance money belongs to Mama. Picking on me is not going to make her give it to you to invest in any liquor stores—[*under breath, dropping into a chair*]—and I for one say, God bless Mama for that!

WALTER [*To RUTH*]: See—did you hear? Did you hear!

RUTH: Honey, please go to work.

WALTER: Nobody in this house is ever going to understand me.

BENEATHA: Because you're a nut.

WALTER: Who's a nut?

BENEATHA: You—you are a nut. Thee is mad, boy.

WALTER [*looking at his wife and his sister from the door, very sadly*]: The world's most backward race of people, and that's a fact.

BENEATHA [*turning slowly in her chair*]: And then there are all those prophets who would lead us out of the wilderness—[*WALTER slams out of the house.*]—into the swamps!

RUTH: Bennie, why you always gotta be pickin' on your brother? Can't you be a little sweeter sometimes? [*Door opens. WALTER walks in.*]

WALTER [*to RUTH*]: I need some money for carfare.

RUTH [*looks at him, then warms; teasing, but tenderly*]: Fifty cents? [*She goes to her bag and gets money.*] Here, take a taxi. [*WALTER exits. MAMA enters. She is a woman in her early sixties, full-bodied and strong. She is one of those women of a certain grace and beauty who wear it so unobtrusively that it takes a while to notice. Her dark-brown face is surrounded by the total whiteness of her hair, and, being a woman who has adjusted to many things in life and overcome many more, her face is full of strength. She has, we can see, wit and faith of a kind that keep her eyes lit and full of interest and expectancy. She is, in a word, a beautiful woman. Her bearing is perhaps most like the noble bearing of the women of the Hereros of Southwest Africa—rather as if she imagines that as she walks she still bears a basket or a vessel upon her head. Her speech, on the other hand, is as careless as her carriage is precise—she is inclined to slur everything—but her voice is perhaps not so much quiet as simply soft.*]

MAMA: Who that 'round here slamming doors at this hour? [*She crosses through the room, goes to the window, opens it, and brings in a feeble little plant growing doggedly in a small pot on the window sill. She feels the dirt and puts in back out.*]

RUTH: That was Walter Lee. He and Bennie was at it again.

MAMA: My children and they tempers. Lord, if this little old plant don't get more sun that it's been getting it ain't never going to see spring again. [*She turns from the window.*] What's the matter with you this morning, Ruth? You looks right peaked. You aiming to iron all them things? Leave some for me. I'll get to 'em this afternoon. Bennie honey, it's too drafty for you to be sitting 'round half dressed. Where's your robe?

BENEATHA: In the cleaners.

MAMA: Well, go get mine and put it on.

BENEATHA: I'm not cold, Mama, honest.

MAMA: I know—but you so thin . . .

BENEATHA [*irritably*]: Mama, I'm not cold.

MAMA [*seeing the make-down bed as TRAVIS has left it*]: Lord have mercy, look at that poor bed. Bless his heart—he tries, don't he? [*She moves to the bed TRAVIS has sloppily made up.*]

RUTH: No—he don't half try at all 'cause he knows you going to come along behind him and fix everything. That's just how come he don't know how to do nothing right now—you done spoiled that boy so.

MAMA: Well—he's a little boy. Ain't supposed to know 'bout housekeeping. My baby, that's what he is. What you fix for his breakfast this morning?

RUTH [*angrily*]: I feed my son, Lena!

MAMA: I ain't meddling—[*under breath, busy-bodyish*]: I just noticed all last week he had cold cereal, and when it starts getting this chilly in the fall a child ought to have some hot grits or something when he goes out in the cold—

RUTH [*furious*]: I gave him hot oats—is that all right!

MAMA: I ain't meddling. [*pause*] Put a lot of nice butter on it? [*RUTH shoots her an angry look and does not reply.*] He likes lots of butter.

RUTH [*exasperated*]: Lena—

MAMA [*To BENEATHA: MAMA is inclined to wander conversationally sometimes*]: What was you and your brother fussing 'bout this morning?

BENEATHA: It's not important, Mama. [*She gets up and goes to look out at the bathroom, which is apparently free, and she picks up her towels and rushes out.*]

MAMA: What was they fighting about?

RUTH: Now you know as well as I do.

MAMA [*shaking her head*]: Brother still worrying hisself sick about that money?

RUTH: You know he is.

MAMA: You had breakfast?

RUTH: Some coffee.

MAMA: Girl, you better start eating and looking after yourself better. You almost thin as Travis.

RUTH: Lena—

MAMA: Uh-hunh?

RUTH: What are you going to do with it?

MAMA: Now don't you start, child. It's too early in the morning to be talking about money. It ain't Christian.

RUTH: It's just that he got his heart set on that store—

MAMA: You mean that liquor store that Willy Harris want him to invest in?

RUTH: Yes—

MAMA: We ain't no business people, Ruth. We just plain working folks.

RUTH: Ain't nobody business people till they go into business. Walter Lee say colored people ain't never going to start getting ahead till they start gambling on some different kinds of things in the world—investments and things.

MAMA: What done got into you, girl? Walter Lee done finally sold you on investing.

RUTH: No. Mama, something is happening between Walter and me. I don't know what it is—but he needs something—something I can't give him any more. He needs this chance, Lena.

MAMA [*frowning deeply*]: But liquor, honey—

RUTH: Well—like Walter say—I spec people going to always be drinking themselves some liquor.

MAMA: Well—whether they drinks it or not ain't none of my business. But whether I go into business selling it to 'em is, and I don't want that on my ledger this late in life. [*stopping suddenly and studying her daughter-in-law*] Ruth Younger, what's the matter with you today? You look like you could fall over right there.

RUTH: I'm tired.

MAMA: Then you better stay home from work today.

RUTH: I can't stay home. She'd be calling up the agency and screaming at them, "My girl didn't come in today—send me somebody! My girl didn't come in!" Oh, she just have a fit . . .

MAMA: Well, let her have it. I'll just call her up and say you got the flu—

RUTH [*laughing*]: Why the flu?

MAMA: 'Cause it sounds respectable to 'em. Something white people get, too. They know 'bout the flu. Otherwise they think you been cut up or something when you tell 'em you sick.

RUTH: I got to go in. We need the money.

MAMA: Somebody would of thought my children done all but starved to death the way they talk about money here late. Child, we got a great big old check coming tomorrow.

RUTH [*sincerely, but also self-righteously*]: Now that's your money. It ain't got nothing to do with me. We all feel like that—Walter and Bennie and me—even Travis.

MAMA [*thoughtfully, and suddenly very far away*]: Ten thousand dollars—

RUTH: Sure is wonderful.

MAMA: Ten thousand dollars.

RUTH: You know what you should do, Miss Lena? You should take yourself a trip somewhere. To Europe or South America or someplace—

MAMA [*throwing up her hands at the thought*]: Oh, child!

RUTH: I'm serious. Just pack up and leave! Go on away and enjoy yourself some. Forget about the family and have yourself a ball for once in your life—

MAMA [*drily*]: You sound like I'm just about ready to die. Who'd go with me? What I look like wandering 'round Europe by myself?

RUTH: Shoot—these here rich white women do it all the time. They don't think nothing of packing up they suitcases and piling on one of them big steamships and—swoosh!—they gone, child.

MAMA: Something always told me I wasn't no rich white woman.

RUTH: Well—what are you going to do with it then?

MAMA: I ain't rightly decided. [*Thinking. She speaks now with emphasis.*] Some of it got to be put away for BENEATHA and her schoolin'—and ain't nothing going to touch that part of it. Nothing. [*She waits several seconds, trying to make up her mind about something, and looks at* RUTH *little tentatively before going on.*] Been thinking that we maybe could meet the notes on a little old two-story somewhere, with a yard where Travis could play in the summertime, if we use part of the insurance for a down payment and everybody kind of pitch in. I could maybe take on a little day work again, few days a week—

RUTH [*studying her mother-in-law furtively and concentrating on her ironing, anxious to encourage without seeming to*]: Well, Lord knows, we've put enough rent into this here rat trap to pay for four houses by now . . .

MAMA [*looking up at the words "rat trap" and then looking around and leaning back and sighing—in a suddenly reflective mood—*]: "Rat trap"—yes, that's all it is. [*smiling*] I remember just as well the day me and Big Walter moved in here. Hadn't been married but two weeks and wasn't planning on living here no more than a year. [*She shakes her head at the dissolved dream.*] We was going to set away, little by little, don't you know, and buy a little place out in Morgan Park. We had even picked out the house. [*chuckling a little*] Looks right dumpy today. But Lord, child, you should know all the dreams I had 'bout buying that house and fixing it up and making me a little garden in the back—[*She waits and stops smiling.*] And didn't none of it happen. [*dropping her hands in a futile gesture*]

RUTH [*keeps her head down, ironing*]: Yes, life can be a barrel of disappointments, sometimes.

MAMA: Honey, Big Walter would come in here some nights back then and slump down on that couch there and just look at the rug, and look at me and look at the rug and then back at me—and I'd know he was down then . . . really down. [*After a second very long and thoughtful pause; she is seeing back to times that only she can see.*] And then, Lord, when I lost that baby—little Claude—I almost thought I was going to lose Big Walter too. Oh, that man grieved hisself! He was one man to love his children.

RUTH: Ain't nothin' can tear at you like losin' your baby.

MAMA: I guess that's how come that man finally worked hisself to death like he done. Likely he was fighting his own war with this here world that took his baby from him.

RUTH: He sure was a fine man, all right. I always liked Mr. Younger.

MAMA: Crazy 'bout his children! God knows there was plenty wrong with Walter Younger—hard-headed, mean, kind of wild with women—plenty wrong with him. But he sure loved his children. Always wanted them to have something—be something. That's where Brother gets all these notions, I reckon. Big Walter used to say, he'd get right wet in the eyes sometimes, lean his head back with the water standing in his eyes and say, "Seem like God didn't see fit to give the black man nothing but dreams—

but He did give us children to make them dreams seem worth while." [*She smiles.*] He could talk like that, don't you know.

RUTH: Yes, he sure could. He was a good man, Mr. Younger.

MAMA: Yes, a fine man—just couldn't never catch up with his dreams, that's all. [*BENEATHA comes in, brushing her hair and looking up to the ceiling, where the sound of a vacuum cleaner has started up.*]

BENEATHA: What could be so dirty on that woman's rugs that she has to vacuum them every single day?

RUTH: I wish certain young women 'round here who I could name would take inspiration about certain rugs in a certain apartment I could also mention.

BENEATHA [*shrugging*]: How much cleaning can a house need, for Christ's sakes?

MAMA [*not liking the Lord's name used thus*]: Bennie!

RUTH: Just listen to her—just listen!

BENEATHA: Oh, God!

MAMA: If you use the Lord's name just one more time—

BENEATHA [*a bit of a whine*]: Oh, Mama—

RUTH: Fresh—just fresh as salt, this girl!

BENEATHA [*drily*]: Well—if the salt loses its savor—

MAMA: Now that will do. I just ain't going to have you 'round here reciting the scriptures in vain—you hear me?

BENEATHA: How did I manage to get on everybody's wrong side by just walking into a room?

RUTH: If you weren't so fresh—

BENEATHA: Ruth, I'm twenty years old.

MAMA: What time you be home from school today?

BENEATHA: Kind of late. [*with enthusiasm*] Madeline is going to start my guitar lessons today. [*MAMA and RUTH look up with the same expression.*]

MAMA: Your *what* kind of lessons?

BENEATHA: Guitar.

RUTH: Oh, Father!

MAMA: How come you done taken it in your mind to learn to play the guitar?

BENEATHA: I just want to, that's all.

MAMA [*smiling*]: Lord, child, don't you know what to do with yourself? How long it going to be before you get tired of this now—like you got tired of that little play-acting group you joined last year? [*looking at RUTH*] And what was it the year before that?

RUTH: The horseback-riding club for which she bought that fifty-five-dollar riding habit that's been hanging in the closet ever since!

MAMA [*to BENEATHA*]: Why you got to flit so from one thing to another, baby?

BENEATHA [*sharply*]: I just want to learn to play the guitar. Is there anything wrong with that?

MAMA: Ain't nobody trying to stop you. I just wonders sometimes why you has to flit so from one thing to another all the time. You ain't never done nothing with all that camera equipment you brought home—

BENEATHA: I don't flit! I—I experiment with different forms of expression—
RUTH: Like riding a horse?
BENEATHA: —People have to express themselves one way or another.
MAMA: What is it you want to express?
BENEATHA [*angrily*]: Me! [*MAMA and RUTH look at each other and burst into raucous laughter*] Don't worry—I don't expect you to understand.
MAMA [*to change the subject*]: Who you going out with tomorrow night?
BENEATHA [*with displeasure*]: George Murchison again.
MAMA [*pleased*]: Oh—you getting a little sweet on him?
RUTH: You ask me, this child ain't sweet on nobody but herself—[*under breath*] Express herself! [*They laugh.*]
BENEATHA: Oh—I like George all right, Mama. I mean I like him enough to go out with him and stuff, but—
RUTH [*for devilment*]: What does and stuff mean?
BENEATHA: Mind your own business.
MAMA: Stop picking at her now, Ruth. [*s thoughtful pause, and then a suspicious sudden look at her daughter as she turns in her chair for emphasis*] What does it mean?
BENEATHA [*wearily*]: Oh, I just mean I couldn't ever really be serious about George. He's—he's so shallow.
RUTH: Shallow—what do you mean he's shallow? He's *Rich!*
MAMA: Hush, Ruth.
BENEATHA: I know he's rich. He knows he's rich, too.
RUTH: Well—what other qualities a man got to have to satisfy you, little girl?
BENEATHA: You wouldn't even begin to understand. Anybody who married WALTER could not possibly understand.
MAMA [*outraged*]: What kind of way is that to talk about your brother?
BENEATHA: Brother is a flip—let's face it.
MAMA [*to RUTH, helplessly*]: What's a flip?
RUTH [*glad to add kindling*]: She's saying he's crazy.
BENEATHA: Not crazy. Brother isn't really crazy yet—he—he's an elaborate neurotic.
MAMA: Hush your mouth!
BENEATHA: As for George. Well. George looks good—he's got a beautiful car and he takes me to nice places and, as my sister-in-law says, he is probably the richest boy I will ever get to know and I even like him sometimes—but if the Youngers are sitting around waiting to see if their little Bennie is going to tie up the family with the Murchisons, they are wasting their time.
RUTH: You mean you wouldn't marry George Murchison if he asked you someday? That pretty, rich thing? Honey, I knew you was odd—
BENEATHA: No I would not marry him if all I felt for him was what I feel now. Besides, George's family wouldn't really like it.
MAMA: Why not?

BENEATHA: Oh, Mama—The Murchisons are honest-to-God-real-*live*-rich colored people, and the only people in the world who are more snobbish than rich white people are rich colored people. I thought everybody knew that. I've met Mrs. Murchison. She's a scene!

MAMA: You must not dislike people 'cause they well off, honey.

BENEATHA: Why not? It makes just as much sense as disliking people 'cause they are poor, and lots of people do that.

RUTH [*a wisdom-of-the-ages manner. To Mama*]: Well, she'll get over some of this—

BENEATHA: Get over it? What are you talking about, Ruth? Listen, I'm going to be a doctor. I'm not worried about who I'm going to marry yet—if I ever get married.

MAMA and RUTH: *If!*

MAMA: Now, Bennie—

BENEATHA: Oh, I probably will . . . but first I'm going to be a doctor, and George, for one, still thinks that's pretty funny. I couldn't be bothered with that. I am going to be a doctor and everybody around here better understand that!

MAMA [*kindly*]: 'Course you going to be a doctor, honey, God willing.

BENEATHA [*drily*]: God hasn't got a thing to do with it.

MAMA: Beneatha—that just wasn't necessary.

BENEATHA: Well—neither is God. I get sick of hearing about God.

MAMA: Beneatha!

BENEATHA: I mean it! I'm just tired of hearing about God all the time. What has He got to do with anything? Does he pay tuition?

MAMA: You 'bout to get your fresh little jaw slapped!

RUTH: That's just what she needs, all right!

BENEATHA: Why? Why can't I say what I want to around here, like everybody else?

MAMA: It don't sound nice for a young girl to say things like that—you wasn't brought up that way. Me and your father went to trouble to get you and Brother to church every Sunday.

BENEATHA: Mama, you don't understand. It's all a matter of ideas, and God is just one idea I don't accept. It's not important. I am not going out and be immoral or commit crimes because I don't believe in God. I don't even think about it. It's just that I get tired of Him getting credit for all the things the human race achieves through its own stubborn effort. There simply is no blasted God—there is only man and it is he who makes miracles! [*MAMA absorbs this speech, studies her daughter and rises slowly and crosses to BENEATHA and slaps her powerfully across the face. After, there is only silence and the daughter drops her eyes from her mother's face, and MAMA is very tall before her.*]

MAMA: Now—you say after me, in my mother's house there is still God. [*There is a long pause and* BENEATHA *stares at the floor wordlessly.* MAMA *repeats the phrase with precision and cool emotion.*] In my mother's house there is still God.

BENEATHA: In my mother's house there is still God. [*a long pause*]

MAMA [*Walking away from* BENEATHA, *too disturbed for triumphant posture. Stopping and turning back to her daughter.*]: There are some ideas we ain't going to have in this house. Not long as I am at the head of this family.

BENEATHA: Yes, ma'am. [MAMA *walks out of the room.*]

RUTH [*almost gently, with profound understanding*]: You think you a woman, Bennie—but you still a little girl. What you did was childish—so you got treated like a child.

BENEATHA: I see. [*quietly*] I also see that everybody thinks it's all right for MAMA to be a tyrant. But all the tyranny in the world will never put a God in the heavens! [*She picks up her books and goes out.*]

RUTH [*goes to Mama's door*]: She said she was sorry.

MAMA [*coming out, going to her plant*]: They frightens me, Ruth. My children.

RUTH: You got good children, Lena. They just a little off sometimes—but they're good.

MAMA: No—There's something come down between me and them that don't let us understand each other and I don't know what it is. One done almost lost his mind thinking 'bout money all the time and the other done commence to talk about things I can't seem to understand in no form or fashion. What is it that's changing, Ruth?

RUTH [*soothingly, older than her years*]: Now . . . you taking it all too seriously. You just got strong-willed children and it takes a strong woman like you to keep 'em in hand.

MAMA [*looking at her plant and sprinkling a little water on it*]: They spirited all right, my children. Got to admit they got spirit—Bennie and Walter. Like this little old plant that ain't never had enough sunshine or nothing—and look at it . . . [*She has her back to* RUTH, *who has had to stop ironing and lean against something and put the back of her hand to her forehead.*]

RUTH [*trying to keep* MAMA *from noticing*]: You . . . sure . . . loves that little old thing, don't you? . . .

MAMA: Well, I always wanted me a garden like I used to see sometimes at the back of the houses down home. This plant is close as I ever got to having one. [*She looks out of the window as she replaces the plant.*] Lord, ain't nothing as dreary as the view from this window on a dreary day, is there? Why ain't you singing this morning, Ruth? Sing that "No Ways Tired." That song always lifts me up so—[*She turns at last to see that* RUTH *has slipped quietly into a chair, in a state of semiconsciousness.*] Ruth! Ruth honey—what's the matter with you . . . Ruth!

CURTAIN

SCENE 2

It is the following morning; a Saturday morning, and house cleaning is in progress at the Youngers. Furniture has been shoved hither and yon and MAMA *is giving the kitchen-area walls a washing down.* BENEATHA, *in dungarees, with a handkerchief tied around her face, is spraying insecticide into the cracks in the walls. As they work, the radio is on and a South Side disk jockey program is inappropriately filling the house with a rather exotic saxophone blues.* TRAVIS, *the sole idle one, is leaning on his arms, looking out of the window.*

TRAVIS: Grandmama, that stuff Bennie is using smells awful. Can I go downstairs, please?

MAMA: Did you get all them chores done already? I ain't seen you doing much.

TRAVIS: Yes'm—finished early. Where did MAMA go this morning?

MAMA [*looking at* BENEATHA]: She had to go on a little errand.

TRAVIS: Where?

MAMA: To tend to her business.

TRAVIS: Can I go outside then?

MAMA: Oh, I guess so. You better stay right in front of the house, though . . . and keep a good lookout for the postman.

TRAVIS: Yes'm. [*He starts out and decides to give his* AUNT BENEATHA *a good swat on the legs as he passes her.*] Leave them poor little old cockroaches alone, they ain't bothering you none. [*He runs as she swings the spray gun at him both viciously and playfully.* WALTER *enters from the bedroom and goes to the phone.*]

MAMA: Look out there, girl, before you be spilling some of that stuff on that child!

TRAVIS [*teasing*]: That's right—look out now! [*He exits.*]

BENEATHA [*drily*]: I can't imagine that it would hurt him—it has never hurt the roaches.

MAMA: Well, little boys' hides ain't as tough as South Side roaches.

WALTER [*into phone*]: Hello—Let me talk to Willy Harris.

MAMA: You better get over there behind the bureau. I seen one marching out of there like Napoleon yesterday.

WALTER: Hello, Willy? It ain't come yet. It'll be here in a few minutes. Did the lawyer give you the papers?

BENEATHA: There's really only one way to get rid of them, Mama—

MAMA: How?

BENEATHA: Set fire to this building.

WALTER: Good. Good. I'll be right over.

BENEATHA: Where did Ruth go, WALTER?

WALTER: I don't know. [*He exits abruptly.*]

BENEATHA: Mama, where did Ruth go?

MAMA [*looking at her with meaning*]: To the doctor, I think.

BENEATHA: The doctor? What's the matter? [*They exchange glances.*] You don't think—

MAMA [*with her sense of drama*]: Now I ain't saying what I think. But I ain't never been wrong 'bout a woman neither. [*The phone rings.*]

BENEATHA [*at the phone*]: Hay-lo . . . [*pause, and a moment of recognition*] Well—when did you get back! . . . And how was it? . . . Of course I've missed you—in my way . . . This morning? No . . . house cleaning and all that and Mama hates it if I let people come over when the house is like this . . . You *have?* Well, that's different . . . What is it—Oh, what the hell, come on over . . . Right, see you then.

[*She hangs up.*]

MAMA [*who has listened vigorously, as is her habit*]: Who is that you inviting over here with this house looking like this? You ain't got the pride you was born with!

BENEATHA: Asagai doesn't care how houses look, Mama—he's an intellectual.

MAMA: *Who?*

BENEATHA: Asagai—Joseph Asagai. He's an African boy I met on campus. He's been studying in Canada all summer.

MAMA: What's his name?

BENEATHA: Asagai, Joseph. Ah-sah-guy . . . He's from Nigeria.

MAMA: Oh, that's the little country that was founded by slaves way back . . .

BENEATHA: No, Mama—that's Liberia.

MAMA: I don't think I never met no African before.

BENEATHA: Well, do me a favor and don't ask him a whole lot of ignorant questions about Africans. I mean, do they wear clothes and all that—

MAMA: Well, now, I guess if you think we so ignorant 'round here maybe you shouldn't bring your friends here—

BENEATHA: It's just that people ask such crazy things. All anyone seems to know about when it comes to Africa is Tarzan—

MAMA [*indignantly*]: Why should I know anything about Africa?

BENEATHA: Why do you give money at church for the missionary work?

MAMA: Well, that's to help save people.

BENEATHA: You mean save them from *heathenism*—

MAMA [*innocently*]: Yes.

BENEATHA: I'm afraid they need more salvation from the British and the French. [*RUTH comes in forlornly and pulls off her coat with dejection. They both turn to look at her.*]

RUTH [*Dispiritedly*]: Well, I guess from all the happy faces—everybody knows.

BENEATHA: You pregnant?

MAMA: Lord have mercy, I sure hope it's a little old girl. Travis ought to have a sister. [*BENEATHA and RUTH give her a hopeless look for this grandmotherly enthusiasm*]

BENEATHA: How far along are you?

RUTH: Two months.

BENEATHA: Did you mean to? I mean did you plan it or was it an accident?

MAMA: What do you know about planning or not planning?

BENEATHA: Oh, Mama.

RUTH [*wearily*]: She's twenty years old, Lena.

BENEATHA: Did you plan it, Ruth?

RUTH: Mind your own business.

BENEATHA: It is my business—where is he going to live, on the roof? [*There is silence following the remark as the three women react to the sense of it.*] Gee—I didn't mean that, Ruth, honest. Gee, I don't feel like that at all. I—I think it is wonderful.

RUTH [*dully*]: Wonderful.

BENEATHA: Yes—really.

MAMA [*looking at* RUTH, *worried*]: Doctor say everything going to be all right?

RUTH [*far away*]: Yes—she says everything is going to be fine . . .

MAMA [*Immediately suspicious*]: "She"—What doctor you went to? [RUTH *folds over, near hysteria*]

MAMA [*worriedly hovering over* RUTH]: Ruth, honey—what's the matter with you—you sick? [RUTH *has her fists clenched on her thighs and is fighting hard to suppress a scream that seems to be rising in her.*]

BENEATHA: What's the matter with her, Mama?

MAMA [*working her fingers in* RUTH*'s shoulder to relax her*]: She be all right. Women gets right depressed sometimes when they get her way. [*speaking softly, expertly, rapidly*] Now you just relax. That's right . . . just lean back, don't think 'bout nothing at all . . . nothing at all—

RUTH: I'm all right . . . [*The glassy-eyed look melts and then she collapses into a fit of heavy sobbing. The bell rings.*]

BENEATHA: Oh, my God—that must be Asagai.

MAMA [*to* RUTH]: Come on now, honey. You need to lie down and rest awhile . . . then have some nice hot food. [*They exit,* RUTH*'s weight on her mother-in-law.* BENEATHA, *herself profoundly disturbed, opens the door to admit a rather dramatic-looking young man with a large package.*]

ASAGAI: Hello, Alaiyo—

BENEATHA [*holding the door open and regarding him with pleasure*]: Hello . . . [*long pause*] Well—come in. And please excuse everything. My mother was very upset about my letting anyone come here with the place like this.

ASAGAI [*coming into the room*]: You look disturbed too . . . Is something wrong?

BENEATHA [*still at the door, absently*]: Yes . . . we've all got acute ghetto-itus. [*She smiles and comes toward him, finding a cigarette and sitting.*] So—sit down! How was Canada?

ASAGAI [*a sophisticate*]: Canadian.

BENEATHA [*looking at him*]: I'm very glad you are back.

ASAGAI [*looking back at her in turn*]: Are you really?

BENEATHA: Yes—very.

ASAGAI: Why—you were quite glad when I went away. What happened?

BENEATHA: You went away.

ASAGAI: Ahhhhhhhh.

BENEATHA: Before—you wanted to be so serious before there was time.

ASAGAI: How much time must there be before one knows what one feels?

BENEATHA [*Stalling this particular conversation. Her hands pressed together, in a deliberately childish gesture*]: What did you bring me?

ASAGAI [*handing her the package*]: Open it and see.

BENEATHA [*eagerly opening the package and drawing out some records and the colorful robes of a Nigerian woman*]: Oh, Asagai! . . . You got them for me! . . . How beautiful . . . and the records too! [*She lifts out the robes and runs to the mirror with them and holds the drapery up in front of herself.*]

ASAGAI [*coming to her at the mirror*]: I shall have to teach you how to drape it properly. [*He flings the material about her for the moment and stands back to look at her.*] Ah—*Oh-pay-gay-day, oh-gbah-mu-shay.* [*a Yoruba exclamation for admiration*] You wear it well . . . very well . . . mutilated hair and all.

BENEATHA [*turning suddenly*]: My hair—what's wrong with my hair?

ASAGAI [*shrugging*]: Were you born with it like that?

BENEATHA [*reaching up to touch it*]: No . . . of course not. [*She looks back to the mirror, disturbed.*]

ASAGAI [*smiling*]: How then?

BENEATHA: You know perfectly well how . . . as crinkly as yours . . . that's how.

ASAGAI: And it is ugly to you that way?

BENEATHA [*quickly*]: Oh, no—not ugly . . . [*more slowly, apologetically*] But it's so hard to manage when it's, well—raw.

ASAGAI: And so to accommodate that—you mutilate it every week?

BENEATHA: It's not mutilation!

ASAGAI [*laughing aloud at her seriousness*]: Oh . . . please! I am only teasing you because you are so very serious about these things. [*He stands back from her and folds his arms across his chest as he watches her pulling at her hair and frowning in the mirror.*] Do you remember the first time you met me at school? . . . [*He laughs.*] You came up to me and said—and I thought you were the most serious little thing I had ever seen—you said: [*He imitates her.*] "Mr. Asagai—I want very much to talk with you. About Africa. You see, Mr. Asagai, I am looking for my *identity!*" [*He laughs.*]

BENEATHA [*turning to him, not laughing*]: Yes—[*Her face is quizzical, profoundly disturbed.*]

ASAGAI [*still teasing and reaching out and taking her face in his hands and turning her profile to him*]: Well . . . it is true that this is not so much a profile of a Hollywood queen as perhaps a queen of the Nile—[*a mock dismissal of the importance of the question*] But what does it matter? Assimilationism is so popular in your country.

BENEATHA [*wheeling, passionately, sharply*]: I am not an assimilationist!

ASAGAI [*The protest hangs in the room for a moment and* ASAGAI *studies her, his laughter fading.*]: Such a serious one. [*There is a pause.*] So—you like the robes? You must take excellent care of them—they are from my sister's personal wardrobe.

BENEATHA [*with incredulity*]: You—you sent all the way home—for me?

ASAGAI [*with charm*]: For you—I would do much more . . . Well, that is what I came for. I must go.

BENEATHA: Will you call me Monday?

ASAGAI: Yes . . . We have a great deal to talk about. I mean about identity and time and all that.

BENEATHA: Time?

ASAGAI: Yes. About how much time one needs to know what one feels.

BENEATHA: You never understood that there is more than one kind of feeling which can exist between a man and a woman—or, at least, there should be.

ASAGAI [*shaking his head negatively but gently*]: No. Between a man and a woman there need be only one kind of feeling. I have that for you . . . Now even . . . right this moment . . .

BENEATHA: I know—and by itself—it won't do. I can find that anywhere.

ASAGAI: For a woman it should be enough.

BENEATHA: I know—because that's what it says in all the novels that men write. But it isn't. Go ahead and laugh—but I'm not interested in being someone's little episode in America or—[*with feminine vengeance*]—one of them! [ASAGAI *has burst into laughter again.*] That's funny as hell, huh!

ASAGAI: It's just that every American girl I have known has said that to me. White—black—in this you are all the same. And the same speech, too!

BENEATHA [*angrily*]: Yuk, yuk, yuk!

ASAGAI: It's how you can be sure that the world's most liberated women are not liberated at all. You all talk about it too much! [MAMA *enters and is immediately all social charm because of the presence of a guest.*]

BENEATHA: Oh—Mama—this is Mr. Asagai.

MAMA: How do you do?

ASAGAI [*total politeness to an elder*]: How do you do, Mrs. Younger. Please forgive me for coming at such an outrageous hour on a Saturday.

MAMA: Well, you are quite welcome. I just hope you understand that our house don't always look like this. [*chatterish*] You must come again. I would love to hear all about—[*not sure of the name*]—your country. I think it's so sad the way our American Negroes don't know nothing about Africa 'cept Tarzan and all that. And all that money they pour into these churches when they ought to be helping you people over there drive out them French and Englishmen done taken away your land. [*The mother flashes a slightly superior look at her daughter upon completion of the recitation.*]

ASAGAI [*taken aback by this sudden and acutely unrelated expression of sympathy*]: Yes . . . yes . . .

MAMA [*smiling at him suddenly and relaxing and looking him over*]: How many miles is it from here to where you come from?

ASAGAI: Many thousands.

MAMA [*looking at him as she would WALTER*]: I bet you don't half look after yourself, being away from your mama either. I spec you better come 'round here from time to time and get yourself some decent home-cooked meals . . .

ASAGAI [*moved*]: Thank you. Thank you very much. [*They are all quiet, then—*] Well . . . I must go. I will call you Monday, Alaiyo.

MAMA: What's that he call you?

ASAGAI: Oh—"Alaiyo." I hope you don't mind. It is what you would call a nickname, I think. It is a Yoruba word. I am a Yoruba.

MAMA [*looking at BENEATHA*]: I—I thought he was from—

ASAGAI [*understanding*]: Nigeria is my country. Yoruba is my tribal origin—

BENEATHA: You didn't tell us what Alaiyo means . . . for all I know, you might be calling me Little Idiot or something . . .

ASAGAI: Well . . . let me see . . . I do not know how just to explain it . . . The sense of a thing can be so different when it changes languages.

BENEATHA: You're evading.

ASAGAI: No—really it is difficult . . . [*thinking*] It means . . . it means One for Whom Bread—Food—Is Not Enough. [*He looks at her.*] Is that all right?

BENEATHA [*understanding, softly*]: Thank you.

MAMA [*looking from one to the other and not understanding any of it*]: Well . . . that's nice . . . You must come see us again—Mr.—

ASAGAI: Ah-sah-guy . . .

MAMA: Yes . . . Do come again.

ASAGAI: Good-bye. [*He exits.*]

MAMA [*after him*]: Lord, that's a pretty thing just went out here! [*insinuatingly, to her daughter*] Yes, I guess I see why we done commence to get so interested in Africa 'round here. Missionaries my aunt Jenny! [*She exits.*]

BENEATHA: Oh, Mama! . . . [*She picks up the Nigerian dress and holds it up to her in front of the mirror again. She sets the headdress on haphazardly and then notices her hair again and clutches at it and then replaces the headdress and frowns at herself. Then she starts to wriggle in front of the mirror as she thinks a Nigerian woman might. TRAVIS enters and regards her.*]

TRAVIS: You cracking up?

BENEATHA: Shut up. [*She pulls the headdress off and looks at herself in the mirror and clutches at her hair again and squinches her eyes as if trying to imagine something. Then, suddenly, she gets her raincoat and kerchief and hurriedly prepares for going out.*]

MAMA [*coming back into the room*]: She's resting now. Travis, baby, run next door and ask Miss Johnson to please let me have a little kitchen cleanser. This here can is empty as Jacob's kettle.

TRAVIS: I just came in.

MAMA: Do as you told. [*He exits and she looks at her daughter.*] Where you going?

BENEATHA [*halting at the door*]: To become a queen of the Nile! [*She exits in a breathless blaze of glory. RUTH appears in the bedroom doorway.*]

MAMA: Who told you to get up?

RUTH: Ain't nothing wrong with me to be lying in no bed for. Where did Bennie go?

MAMA [*drumming her fingers*]: Far as I could make out—to Egypt. [*RUTH just looks at her.*] What time is it getting to?

RUTH: Ten twenty. And the mailman going to ring that bell this morning just like he done every morning for the last umpteen years. [*TRAVIS comes in with the cleanser can.*]

TRAVIS: She say to tell you that she don't have much.

MAMA [*angrily*]: Lord, some people I could name sure is tight-fisted! [*directing her grandson*] Mark two cans of cleanser down on the list there. If she that hard up for kitchen cleanser, I sure don't want to forget to get her none!

RUTH: Lena—maybe the woman is just short on cleanser—

MAMA [*not listening*]:—Much baking powder as she done borrowed from me all these years, she could of done gone into the baking business! [*The bell sounds suddenly and sharply and all three are stunned—serious and silent—mid-speech. In spite of all the other conversation and distractions of the morning, this is what they have been waiting for, even TRAVIS, who looks helplessly from his mother to his grandmother. RUTH is the first to come to life again.*]

RUTH [*to TRAVIS*]: Get down them steps, boy! [*TRAVIS snaps to life and flies out to get the mail.*]

MAMA [*her eyes wide, her hand to her breast*]: You mean it done really come?

RUTH [*excited*]: Oh, Miss Lena!

MAMA [*collecting herself*]: Well . . . I don't know what we all so excited about 'round here for. We known it was coming for months.

RUTH: That's a whole lot different from having it come and being able to hold it in your hands . . . a piece of paper worth ten thousand dollars . . . [*TRAVIS bursts back into the room. He holds the envelope high above his head, like a little dancer, his face is radiant and he is breathless. He moves to his grandmother with sudden slow ceremony and puts the envelope into her hands. She accepts it, and then merely holds it and looks at it.*] Come on! Open it . . . Lord have mercy, I wish Walter Lee was here!

TRAVIS: Open it, Grandmama!

MAMA [*staring at it*]: Now you all be quiet. It's just a check.

RUTH: Open it . . .

MAMA [*still staring at it*]: Now don't act silly . . . We ain't never been no people to act silly 'bout no money—

RUTH [*swiftly*]: We ain't never had none before—*open it!* [*MAMA finally makes a good strong tear and pulls out the thin blue slice of paper and inspects it closely. The boy and his mother study it raptly over MAMA's shoulders.*]

MAMA: Travis! [*She is counting off with doubt.*] Is that the right number of zeros?

TRAVIS: Yes'm . . . ten thousand dollars. Gaalee, Grandmama, you rich.

MAMA [*She holds the check away from her, still looking at it. Slowly her face sobers into a mask of unhappiness.*]: Ten thousand dollars. [*She hands it to Ruth.*] Put it away somewhere, Ruth. [*She does not look at RUTH; her eyes seem to be seeing something somewhere very far off.*] Ten thousand dollars they give you. Ten thousand dollars.

TRAVIS [*to his mother, sincerely*]: What's the matter with Grandmama—don't she want to be rich?

RUTH [*distractedly*]: You go on out and play now, baby. [*TRAVIS exits. MAMA starts wiping dishes absently, humming intently to herself. RUTH turns to her, with kind exasperation.*] You've gone and got yourself upset.

MAMA [*not looking at her*]: I spec if it wasn't for you all . . . I would just put that money away or give it to the church or something.

RUTH: Now what kind of talk is that. Mr. Younger would just be plain mad if he could hear you talking foolish like that.

MAMA [*stopping and staring off*]: Yes . . . he sure would. [*sighing*] We got enough to do with that money, all right. [*She halts then, and turns and looks at her daughter-in-law hard; RUTH avoids her eyes and MAMA wipes her hands with finality and starts to speak firmly to RUTH.*] Where did you go today, girl?

RUTH: To the doctor.

MAMA [*impatiently*]: Now, Ruth . . . you know better than that. Old Doctor Jones is strange enough in his way but there ain't nothing 'bout him make somebody slip and call him "she"—like you done this morning.

RUTH: Well, that's what happened—my tongue slipped.

MAMA: You went to see that woman, didn't you?

RUTH [*defensively, giving herself away*]: What woman you talking about?

MAMA [*angrily*]: That woman who—[*WALTER enters in great excitement.*]

WALTER: Did it come?

MAMA [*quietly*]: Can't you give people a Christian greeting before you start asking about money?

WALTER [*to RUTH*]: Did it come? [*RUTH unfolds the check and lays it quietly before him, watching him intently with thoughts of her own. WALTER sits down and grasps it close and counts off the zeros.*] Ten thousand dollars—[*He turns suddenly, frantically to his mother and draws some papers out of his breast pocket.*] Mama—look. Old Willy Harris put everything on paper—

MAMA: Son—I think you ought to talk to your wife . . . I'll go on out and leave you alone if you want—

WALTER: I can talk to her later—Mama, look—

MAMA: Son—

WALTER: WILL SOMEBODY PLEASE LISTEN TO ME TODAY!

MAMA [*quietly*]: I don't 'low no yellin' in this house, Walter Lee, and you know it—[*WALTER stares at them in frustration and starts to speak several times.*] And there ain't going to be no investing in no liquor stores. I don't aim to have to speak on that again. [*a long pause*]

WALTER: Oh—so you don't aim to have to speak on that again? So you have decided . . . [*crumpling his papers*] Well, *you* tell that to my boy tonight when you put him to sleep on the living-room couch . . . [*turning to MAMA and speaking directly to her*]: Yeah—and tell it to my wife, Mama, tomorrow when she has to go out of here to look after somebody else's kids. And tell it to *me*, Mama, every time we need a new pair of curtains and I have to watch *you* go out and work in somebody's kitchen. Yeah, you tell me then! [*WALTER starts out*]

RUTH: Where you going?

WALTER: I'm going out!

RUTH: Where?

WALTER: Just out of this house somewhere—

RUTH [*getting her coat*]: I'll come too.

WALTER: I don't want you to come!

RUTH: I got something to talk to you about, Walter.

WALTER: That's too bad.

MAMA [*still quietly*]: Walter Lee—[*She waits and he finally turns and looks at her.*] Sit down.

WALTER: I'm a grown man, Mama.

MAMA: Ain't nobody said you wasn't grown. But you still in my house and my presence. And as long as you are—you'll talk to your wife civil. Now sit down.

RUTH [*suddenly*]: Oh, let him go on out and drink himself to death! He makes me sick to my stomach! [*She flings her coat against him.*]

WALTER [*violently*]: And you turn mine, too, baby! [*RUTH goes into their bedroom and slams the door behind her.*] That was my greatest mistake—

MAMA [*still quietly*]: Walter, what is the matter with you?

WALTER: Matter with me? Ain't nothing the matter with *me!*

MAMA: Yes there is. Something eating you up like a crazy man. Something more than me not giving you this money. The past few years I been watching it happen to you. You get all nervous acting and kind of wild in the eyes—[*WALTER jumps up impatiently at her words.*] I said sit there now, I'm talking to you!

WALTER: Mama—I don't need no nagging at me today.

MAMA: Seem like you getting to a place where you always tied up in some kind of knot about something. But if anybody ask you 'bout it you just yell at 'em and bust out the house and go out and drink somewheres. Walter Lee, people can't live with that. Ruth's a good, patient girl in her way—but you getting to be too much. Boy, don't make the mistake of driving that girl away from you.

WALTER: Why—what she do for me?

MAMA: She loves you.

WALTER: Mama—I'm going out. I want to go off somewhere and be by myself for a while.

MAMA: I'm sorry 'bout your liquor store, son. It just wasn't the thing for us to do. That's what I want to tell you about—

WALTER: I got to go out, Mama—[*He rises.*]

MAMA: It's dangerous, son.

WALTER: What's dangerous?

MAMA: When a man goes outside his home to look for peace.

WALTER [*beseechingly*]: Then why can't there never be no peace in this house then?

MAMA: You done found it in some other house?

WALTER: No—there ain't no woman! Why do women always think there's a woman somewhere when a man gets restless. [*coming to her*] Mama—Mama—I want so many things . . .

MAMA: Yes, son—

WALTER: I want so many things that they are driving me kind of crazy . . . Mama—look at me.

MAMA: I'm looking at you. You a good-looking boy. You got a job, a nice wife, a fine boy and—

WALTER: A job. [*looks at her*] Mama, a job? I open and close car doors all day long. I drive a man around in his limousine and I say, "Yes, sir; no, sir; very good, sir; shall I take the Drive, sir?" Mama, that ain't no kind of job . . . that ain't nothing at all. [*very quietly*] Mama, I don't know if I can make you understand.

MAMA: Understand what, baby?

WALTER [*quietly*]: Sometimes it's like I can see the future stretched out in front of me—just plain as day. The future, Mama. Hanging over there at the edge of my days. Just waiting for me—a big, looming blank space—full of *nothing*. Just waiting for *me*. [*pause*] Mama—sometimes when I'm downtown and I pass them cool, quiet-looking restaurants where them white boys are sitting back and talking 'bout things . . . sitting there turning deals worth millions of dollars . . . sometimes I see guys don't look much older than me—

MAMA: Son—how come you talk so much 'bout money?

WALTER [*with immense passion*]: Because it is life, Mama!

MAMA [*quietly*]: Oh—[*very quietly*] So now it's life. Money is life. Once upon a time freedom used to be life—now it's money. I guess the world really do change . . .

WALTER: No—it was always money, Mama. We just didn't know about it.

MAMA: No . . . something has changed. [*She looks at him.*] You something new, boy. In my time we was worried about not being lynched and getting to the North if we could and how to stay alive and still have a pinch of dignity too . . . Now here come you and Beneatha—talking 'bout things we ain't never even thought about hardly, me and your daddy. You ain't satisfied or proud of nothing we done. I mean that you had a home; that we kept you out of trouble till you was grown; that you don't have to ride to work on the back of nobody's streetcar—You my children—but how different we done become.

WALTER: You just don't understand, Mama, you just don't understand.

MAMA: Son—do you know your wife is expecting another baby? [*WALTER stands, stunned, and absorbs what his mother has said.*] That's what she wanted to talk to you about. [*WALTER sinks down into a chair.*] This ain't for me to be telling—but you ought to know. [*She waits*] I think Ruth is thinking 'bout getting rid of that child.

WALTER [*slowly understanding*]: No—no—Ruth wouldn't do that.

MAMA: When the world gets ugly enough—a woman will do anything for her family. *The part that's already living.*

WALTER: You don't know Ruth, Mama, if you think she would do that. [*RUTH opens the bedroom door and stands there a little limp.*]

RUTH [*beaten*]: Yes I would too, Walter, [*pause*] I gave her a five-dollar down payment. [*There is total silence as the man stares at his wife and the mother stares at her son.*]

MAMA [*presently*]: Well—[*tightly*] Well—son, I'm waiting to hear you say something . . . I'm waiting to hear how you be your father's son. Be the man he was . . . [*pause*] Your wife say she going to destroy your child. And I'm waiting to hear you talk like him and say we a people who give children life, not who destroys them—[*She rises.*] I'm waiting to see you stand up and look like your daddy and say we done give up one baby to poverty and that we ain't going to give up nary another one . . . I'm waiting.

WALTER: Ruth—

MAMA: If you a son of mine, tell her! [*WALTER turns, looks at her and can say nothing. She continues, bitterly.*] You . . . you are a disgrace to your father's memory. Somebody get me my hat.

CURTAIN

ACT II

SCENE 1

Time: Later the same day.

At rise: RUTH is ironing again. She has the radio going. Presently BENEATHA's bedroom door opens and RUTH's mouth falls and she puts down the iron in fascination.

RUTH: What have we got on tonight!

BENEATHA [*emerging grandly from the doorway so that we can see her thoroughly robed in the costume ASAGAI brought.*]: You are looking at what a well-dressed Nigerian woman wears—[*She parades for RUTH, her hair completely hidden by the headdress; she is coquettishly fanning herself with an ornate oriental fan, mistakenly more like Butterfly than any Nigerian that ever was.*] Isn't it beautiful? [*She promenades to the radio and, with an arrogant flourish, turns off the good loud blues that is playing.*] Enough of this assimilationist junk! [*RUTH follows her with her eyes as she goes to the phonograph and puts on a record and turns and waits ceremoniously for the music to come up. Then with a shout—*] OCOMOGOSIAY! [*RUTH jumps. The music comes up, a lovely Nigerian melody. BENEATHA listens, enraptured, her eyes far away—"back to the past." She begins to dance. RUTH is dumbfounded.*]

RUTH: What kind of dance is that?

BENEATHA: A folk dance.

RUTH [*Pearl Bailey*]: What kind of folks do that, honey?

BENEATHA: It's from Nigeria. It's a dance of welcome.

RUTH: Who you welcoming?

BENEATHA: The men back to the village.

RUTH: Where they been?

BENEATHA: How should I know—out hunting or something. Anyway, they are coming back now . . .

RUTH: Well, that's good.

BENEATHA [*with the record*]: *Alundi, alundi*
Alundi alunya
Jop pu a jeepua
Ang gu soooooooooo
Ai yai yae . . .

Ayehaye—alundi . . . [*WALTER comes in during this performance; he has obviously been drinking. He leans against the door heavily and watches his sister, at first with distaste. Then his eyes look off—"back to the past"—as he lifts both his fists to the roof, screaming.*]

WALTER: YEAH . . . AND ETHIOPIA STRETCH FORTH HER HANDS AGAIN! . . .

RUTH [*drily, looking at him*]: Yes—and Africa sure is claiming her own tonight. [*She gives them both up and starts ironing again.*]

WALTER [*all in a drunken, dramatic shout*]: Shut up! . . . I'm digging them drums . . . them drums move me! . . . [*He makes his weaving way to his wife's face and leans in close to her.*] In my heart of hearts—[*He thumps his chest.*]—I am much warrior!

RUTH [*without even looking up*]: In your heart of hearts you are much drunkard.

WALTER [*coming away from her and starting to wander around the room, shouting*]: Me and Jomo . . . [*Intently, in his sister's face. She has stopped dancing to watch him in this unknown mood.*] That's my man, Kenyatta. [*Shouting and thumping his chest.*] FLAMING SPEAR! HOT DAMN! [*He is suddenly in possession of an imaginary spear and actively spearing enemies all over the room.*] OCOMOGOSIAY . . . THE LION IS WAKING . . . OWIMOWEH! [*He pulls his shirt open and leaps up on a table and gestures with his spear. The bell rings.* RUTH *goes to answer.*]

BENEATHA [*to encourage Walter, thoroughly caught up with this side of him*]: OCOMOGOSIAY, FLAMING SPEAR!

WALTER [*On the table, very far gone, his eyes pure glass sheets. He sees what we cannot, that he is a leader of his people, a great chief, a descendant of Chaka, and that the hour to march has come.*]: Listen, my black brothers—

BENEATHA: OCOMOGOSIAY!

WALTER: —Do you hear the waters rushing against the shores of the coastlands—

BENEATHA: OCOMOGOSIAY!

WALTER: —Do you hear the screeching of the cocks in yonder hills beyond where the chiefs meet in council for the coming of the mighty war—

BENEATHA: OCOMOGOSIAY!

WALTER: —Do you hear the beating of the wings of the birds flying low over the mountains and the low places of our land—[RUTH *opens the door,* GEORGE *Murchison enters.*]

BENEATHA: OCOMOGOSIAY!

WALTER: —Do you hear the singing of the women, singing the war songs of our fathers to the babies in the great houses . . . singing the sweet war songs? OH, DO YOU HEAR, MY BLACK BROTHERS?

BENEATHA [*completely gone*]: We hear you, Flaming Spear—

WALTER: Telling us to prepare for the greatness of the time— [*to* GEORGE] Black Brother! [*He extends his hand for the fraternal clasp.*]

GEORGE: Black Brother, hell!

RUTH [*having had enough, and embarrassed for the family*]: Beneatha, you got company—what's the matter with you? Walter Lee Younger, get down off that table and stop acting like a fool . . . [WALTER *comes down off the table suddenly and makes a quick exit to the bathroom.*]

RUTH: He's had a little to drink . . . I don't know what her excuse is.

GEORGE [*to* BENEATHA]: Look honey, we're going *to* the theatre—we're not going to be *in* it . . . so go change, huh?

RUTH: You expect this boy to go out with you looking like that?

BENEATHA [*looking at* GEORGE]: That's up to George. If he's ashamed of his heritage—

GEORGE: Oh, don't be so proud of yourself, Bennie—just because you look eccentric.

BENEATHA: How can something that's natural be eccentric?

GEORGE: That's what being eccentric means—being natural. Get dressed.

BENEATHA: I don't like that, George.

RUTH: Why must you and your brother make an argument out of everything people say?

BENEATHA: Because I hate assimilationist Negroes!

RUTH: Will somebody please tell me what assimila-who-ever means!

GEORGE: Oh, it's just a college girl's way of calling people Uncle Toms—but that isn't what it means at all.

RUTH: Well, what does it mean?

BENEATHA [*cutting* GEORGE *off and staring at him as she replies to* RUTH]: It means someone who is willing to give up his own culture and submerge himself completely in the dominant, and in this case, *oppressive* culture!

GEORGE: Oh, dear, dear, dear! Here we go! A lecture on the African past! On our Great West African Heritage! In one second we will hear all about the great Ashanti empires; the great Songhay civilizations; and the great sculpture of Benin—and then some poetry in the Bantu—and the whole monologue will end with the word *heritage!* [*nastily*] Let's face it, baby, your heritage is nothing but a bunch of raggedy-assed spirituals and some grass huts!

BENEATHA: *Grass huts!* [*RUTH crosses to her and forcibly pushes her toward the bedroom.*] See there . . . you are standing there in your splendid ignorance talking about people who were the first to smelt iron on the face of the earth! [*RUTH is pushing her through the door.*] The Ashanti were performing surgical operations when the English—[*RUTH pulls the door to, with BENEATHA on the other side, and smiles graciously at GEORGE. BENEATHA opens the door and shouts the end of the sentence defiantly at GEORGE.*]—were still tattooing themselves with blue dragons . . . [*She goes back inside.*]

RUTH: Have a seat, George. [*They both sit. RUTH folds her hands rather primly on her lap, determined to demonstrate the civilization of the family.*] Warm, ain't it? I mean for September. [*pause*] Just like they always say about Chicago weather: If it's too hot or cold for you, just wait a minute and it'll change. [*She smiles happily at this cliché, of clichés.*] Everybody say it's got to do with them bombs and things they keep setting off. [*pause*] Would you like a nice cold beer?

GEORGE: No, thank you. I don't care for beer. [*He looks at his watch.*] I hope she hurries up.

RUTH: What time is the show?

GEORGE: It's an eight-thirty curtain. That's just Chicago, though. In New York standard curtain time is eight forty. [*He is rather proud of this knowledge.*]

RUTH [*properly appreciating it*]: You get to New York a lot?

GEORGE [*offhand*]: Few times a year.

RUTH: Oh—that's nice. I've never been to New York. [*WALTER enters. We feel he has relieved himself, but the edge of unreality is still with him.*]

WALTER: New York ain't got nothing Chicago ain't. Just a bunch of hustling people all squeezed up together—being "Eastern." [*He turns his face into a screw of displeasure.*]

GEORGE: Oh—you've been?

WALTER: Plenty of times.

RUTH [*shocked at the lie*]: Walter Lee Younger!

WALTER [*staring her down*]: Plenty! [*pause*] What we got to drink in this house? Why don't you offer this man some refreshment. [*to GEORGE*] They don't know how to entertain people in this house, man.

GEORGE: Thank you—I don't really care for anything.

WALTER [*feeling his head; sobriety coming*]: Where's Mama?

RUTH: She ain't come back yet.

WALTER [*looking Murchison over from head to toe, scrutinizing his carefully casual tweed sports jacket over cashmere V-neck sweater over soft eyelet shirt and tie, and soft slacks, finished off with white buckskin shoes*]: Why all you college boys wear them fairyish-looking white shoes?

RUTH: Walter Lee! [*GEORGE MURCHISON ignores the remark.*]

WALTER [*to RUTH*]: Well, they look crazy as hell—white shoes, cold as it is.

RUTH [*crushed*]: You have to excuse him—

WALTER: No he don't! Excuse me for what? What you always excusing me for! I'll excuse myself when I needs to be excused! [*a pause*] They look as funny as them black knee socks Beneatha wears out of here all the time.

RUTH: It's the college *style*, Walter.

WALTER: Style, hell. She looks like she got burnt legs or something!

RUTH: Oh, Walter—

WALTER [*an irritable mimic*]: Oh, Walter! Oh, Walter! [*to MURCHISON*] How's your old man making out? I understand you all going to buy that big hotel on the Drive?[1] [*He finds a beer in the refrigerator, wanders over to MURCHISON, sipping and wiping his lips with the back of his hand, and straddling a chair backwards to talk to the other man.*] Shrewd move. Your

[1] **Drive** Chicago's Outer Drive running along Lake Michigan

old man is all right, man. [*tapping his head and half winking for emphasis*] I mean he knows how to operate. I mean he thinks big, you know what I mean, I mean for a home,[2] you know? But I think he's kind of running out of ideas now. I'd like to talk to him. Listen, man, I got some plans that could turn this city upside down. I mean I think like he does. *Big.* Invest big, gamble big, hell, lose *big* if you have to, you know what I mean. It's hard to find a man on this whole Southside who understands my kind of thinking—you dig? [*He scrutinizes* MURCHISON *again, drinks his beer, squints his eyes and leans in close, confidential, man to man.*] Me and you ought to sit down and talk sometimes, man. Man, I got me some ideas . . .

MURCHISON [*with boredom*]: Yeah—sometimes we'll have to do that, Walter.

WALTER [*understanding the indifference, and offended*]: Yeah—well, when you get the time, man. I know you a busy little boy.

RUTH: Walter, please—

WALTER [*bitterly, hurt*]: I know ain't nothing in this world as busy as you colored college boys with your fraternity pins and white shoes . . .

RUTH [*covering her face with humiliation*]: Oh, Walter Lee—

WALTER: I see you all all the time—with the books tucked under your arms—going to your [*British* A—*a mimic*] "clahsses." And for what! What the hell you learning over there? Filling up your heads—[*counting off on his fingers*]—with the sociology and the psychology—but they teaching you how to be a man? How to take over and run the world? They teaching you how to run a rubber plantation or a steel mill? Naw—just to talk proper and read books and wear white shoes . . .

GEORGE [*looking at him with distaste, a little above it all*]: You're all wacked up with bitterness, man.

WALTER [*intently, almost quietly, between the teeth, glaring at the boy*]: And you—ain't you bitter, man? Ain't you just about had it yet? Don't you see no stars gleaming that you can't reach out and grab? You happy?—You contented son-of-a-bitch—you happy? You got it made? Bitter? Man, I'm a volcano. Bitter? Here I am a giant—surrounded by ants! Ants who can't even understand what it is the giant is talking about.

RUTH [*passionately and suddenly*]: Oh, Walter—ain't you with nobody!

WALTER [*violently*]: No! 'Cause ain't nobody with me! Not even my own mother!

RUTH: Walter, that's a terrible thing to say! [BENEATHA *enters, dressed for the evening in a cocktail dress and earrings.*]

GEORGE: Well—hey, you look great.

BENEATHA: Let's go, George. See you all later.

[2] **home** home-boy; one of us

RUTH: Have a nice time.

GEORGE: Thanks. Good night. [*to* WALTER, *sarcastically*] Good night, *Prometheus.* [*BENEATHA and GEORGE exit.*]

WALTER [*to RUTH*]: Who is Prometheus?

RUTH: I don't know. Don't worry about it.

WALTER [*in fury, pointing after GEORGE*]: See there—they get to a point where they can't insult you man to man—they got to go talk about something ain't nobody never heard of!

RUTH: How do you know it was an insult? [*to humor him*] Maybe Prometheus is a nice fellow.

WALTER: Prometheus! I bet there ain't even no such thing! I bet that simple-minded clown—

RUTH: Walter—[*She stops what she is doing and looks at him.*]

WALTER [*yelling*]: Don't start!

RUTH: Start what?

WALTER: Your nagging! Where was I? Who was I with? How much money did I spend?

RUTH [*plaintively*]: Walter Lee—why don't we just try to talk about it . . .

WALTER [*not listening*]: I been out talking with people who understand me. People who care about the things I got on my mind.

RUTH [*wearily*]: I guess that means people like Willy Harris.

WALTER: Yes, people like Willy Harris.

RUTH [*with a sudden flash of impatience*]: Why don't you all just hurry up and go into the banking business and stop talking about it!

WALTER: Why? You want to know why? 'Cause we all tied up in a race of people that don't know how to do nothing but moan, pray and have babies! [*The line is too bitter even for him and he looks at her and sits down.*]

RUTH: Oh, Walter . . . [*softy*] Honey, why can't you stop fighting me?

WALTER [*without thinking*]: Who's fighting you? Who even cares about you? [*This line begins the retardation of his mood.*]

RUTH: Well—[*She waits a long time, and then with resignation starts to put away her things.*] I guess I might as well go on to bed . . . [*more or less to herself*] I don't know where we lost it . . . but we have . . . [*Then, to him.*] I—I'm sorry about this new baby, Walter. I guess maybe I better go on and do what I started . . . I guess I just didn't realize how bad things was with us . . . I guess I just didn't really realize—[*She starts out to the bedroom and stops.*] You want some hot milk?

WALTER: Hot milk?

RUTH: Yes—hot milk.

WALTER: Why hot milk?

RUTH: 'Cause after all that liquor you come home with you ought to have something hot in your stomach.

WALTER: I don't want no milk.

RUTH: You want some coffee then?

WALTER: No, I don't want no coffee. I don't want nothing hot to drink. [*almost plaintively*] Why you always trying to give me something to eat?

RUTH [*standing and looking at him helplessly*]: What else can I give you, Walter Lee Younger? [*She stands and looks at him and presently turns to go out again. He lifts his head and watches her going away from him in a new mood which began to emerge when he asked her, "Who cares about you?"*]

WALTER: It's been rough, ain't it, baby? [*She hears and stops but does not turn around and he continues to her back.*] I guess between two people there ain't never as much understood as folks generally thinks there is. I mean like between me and you—[*She turns to face him.*] How we gets to the place where we scared to talk softness to each other. [*He waits, thinking hard himself.*] Why you think it got to be like that? [*He is thoughtful, almost as a child would be.*] Ruth, what is it gets into people ought to be close?

RUTH: I don't know, honey. I think about it a lot.

WALTER: On account of you and me, you mean? The way things are with us. The way something done come down between us.

RUTH: There ain't so much between us, Walter . . . Not when you come to me and try to talk to me. Try to be with me . . . a little even.

WALTER [*total honesty*]: Sometimes . . . sometimes . . . I don't even know how to try.

RUTH: Walter—

WALTER: Yes?

RUTH [*coming to him, gently and with misgiving, but coming to him*]: Honey . . . life don't have to be like this. I mean sometimes people can do things so that things are better . . . You remember how we used to talk when Travis was born . . . about the way we were going to live . . . the kind of house . . . [*She is stroking his head.*] Well, it's all starting to slip away from us . . . [*MAMA enters, and WALTER jumps up and shouts at her.*]

WALTER: Mama, where have you been?

MAMA: My—them steps is longer than they used to be. Whew! [*She sits down and ignores him.*] How you feeling this evening, Ruth! [*RUTH shrugs, disturbed some at having been prematurely interrupted and watching her husband knowingly.*]

WALTER: Mama, where have you been all day?

MAMA [*still ignoring him and leaning on the table and changing to more comfortable shoes*]: Where's Travis?

RUTH: I let him go out earlier and he ain't come back yet. Boy, is he going to get it!

WALTER: Mama!

MAMA [*as if she has heard him for the first time*]: Yes, son?

WALTER: Where did you go this afternoon?

MAMA: I went downtown to tend to some business that I had to tend to.

WALTER: What kind of business?

MAMA: You know better than to question me like a child, Brother.

WALTER [*rising and bending over the table*]: Where were you, Mama? [*bringing his fists down and shouting*] Mama, you didn't go do something with that insurance money, something crazy? [*The front door opens slowly, interrupting him, and* TRAVIS *peeks his head in, less than hopefully.*]

TRAVIS [*to his mother*]: Mama, I—

RUTH: "Mama I" nothing! You're going to get it, boy! Get on in that bedroom and get yourself ready!

TRAVIS: But I—

MAMA: Why don't you all never let the child explain hisself.

RUTH: Keep out of it now, Lena. [MAMA *clamps her lips together, and* RUTH *advances toward her son menacingly.*]

RUTH: A thousand times I have told you not to go off like that—

MAMA [*holding out her arms to her grandson*]: Well—at least let me tell him something. I want him to be the first one to hear . . . Come here, Travis. [*the boy obeys, gladly*] Travis—[*She takes him by the shoulder and looks into his face.*]—you know that money we got in the mail this morning?

TRAVIS: Yes'm—

MAMA: Well—what you think your grandmama gone and done with that money?

TRAVIS: I don't know, Grandmama.

MAMA [*putting her finger on his nose for emphasis*]: She went out and she bought you a house! [*The explosion comes from* WALTER *at the end of the revelation and he jumps up and turns away from all of them in a fury.* MAMA *continues, to* TRAVIS.] You glad about the house? It's going to be yours when you get to be a man.

TRAVIS: Yeah—I always wanted to live in a house.

MAMA: All right, gimme some sugar then—[TRAVIS *puts his arms around her neck as she watches her son over the boy's shoulder. Then, to* TRAVIS, *after the embrace.*] Now when you say your prayers tonight, you thank God and your grandfather—'cause it was him who give you the house—in his way.

RUTH [*taking the boy from* MAMA *and pushing him toward the bedroom*]: Now you get out of here and get ready for your beating.

TRAVIS: Aw, Mama—

RUTH: Get on in there—[*closing the door behind him and turning radiantly to her mother-in-law*] So you went and did it!

MAMA [*quietly, looking at her son with pain*]: Yes, I did.

RUTH [*raising both arms classically*]: *Praise God!* [*Looks at* WALTER *a moment, who says nothing. She crosses rapidly to her husband.*] Please, honey—let me be glad . . . you be glad too. [*She has laid her hands on his shoulders, but he shakes himself free of her roughly, without turning to face her.*] Oh, Walter . . . a home . . . *a home.* [*She comes back to* MAMA.] Well—where is it? How big is it? How much it going to cost?

MAMA: Well—

RUTH: When we moving?

MAMA [*smiling at her*]: First of the month.

RUTH [*throwing back her head with jubilance*]: *Praise God!*

MAMA [*tentatively, still looking at her son's back turned against her and* RUTH]: It's—it's a nice house too . . . [*She cannot help speaking directly to him. An imploring quality in her voice, her manner, makes her almost like a girl now.*] Three bedrooms—nice big one for you and Ruth . . . Me and Beneatha still have to share our room, but Travis have one of his own—and [*with difficulty*] I figure if the—new baby—is a boy, we could get one of them double-decker outfits . . . And there's a yard with a little patch of dirt where I could maybe get to grow me a few flowers . . . And a nice big basement . . .

RUTH: Walter honey, be glad—

MAMA [*still to his back, fingering things on the table*]: 'Course I don't want to make it sound fancier than it is . . . It's just a plain little old house—but it's made good and solid—and it will be *ours.* Walter Lee—it makes a difference in a man when he can walk on floors that belong to *him* . . .

RUTH: Where is it?

MAMA [*frightened at this telling*]: Well—well—it's out there in Clybourne Park—[*RUTH's radiance fades abruptly, and WALTER finally turns slowly to face his mother with incredulity and hostility.*]

RUTH: Where?

MAMA [*matter-of-factly*]: Four o six Clybourne Street, Clybourne Park.

RUTH: Clybourne Park? Mama, there ain't no colored people living in Clybourne Park.

MAMA [*almost idiotically*]: Well, I guess there's going to be some now.

WALTER [*bitterly*]: So that's the peace and comfort you went out and bought for us today!

MAMA [*raising her eyes to meet his finally*]: Son—I just tried to find the nicest place for the least amount of money for my family.

RUTH [*trying to recover from the shock*]: Well—well—'course I ain't one never been 'fraid of no crackers, mind you—but—well, wasn't there no other houses nowhere?

MAMA: Them houses they put up for colored in them areas way out all seem to cost twice as much as other houses. I did the best I could.

RUTH [*Struck senseless with the news, in its various degrees of goodness and trouble, she sits a moment, her fists propping her chin in thought, and then she starts to rise, bringing her fists down with vigor, the radiance spreading from cheek to cheek again.*]: Well—well!—All I can say is—if this is my time in life—my time—to say good-bye—[*And she builds with momentum as she starts to circle the room with an exuberant, almost tearfully happy release.*]—to these Goddamned cracking walls!—[*She pounds the walls*]—and these marching roaches!—[*She wipes at an imaginary army of marching roaches.*]—and this cramped little closet which ain't now or never was no kitchen! . . . then I say it loud and good, *Hallelujah! and good-bye misery . . . I don't never want to see your ugly face again!* [*She laughs joyously, having practically destroyed the apartment, and flings her arms up and lets them come down happily, slowly, reflectively, over her abdomen, aware for the first time perhaps that the life therein pulses with happiness and not despair.*] Lena?

MAMA [*moved, watching her happiness*]: Yes, honey?

RUTH [*looking off*]: Is there—is there a whole lot of sunlight?

MAMA [*understanding*]: Yes, child, there's a whole lot of sunlight. [*long pause*]

RUTH [*collecting herself and going to the door of the room* TRAVIS *is in*]: Well—I guess I better see 'bout Travis. [*to* MAMA] Lord, I sure don't feel like whipping nobody today! [*she exits*]

MAMA [*The mother and son are left alone now and the mother waits a long time, considering deeply, before she speaks.*]: Son—you—you understand what I done, don't you? [WALTER *is silent and sullen.*] I—I just seen my family falling apart today . . . just falling to pieces in front of my eyes . . . We couldn't of gone on like we was today. We was going backwards 'stead of forwards—talking 'bout killing babies and wishing each other was dead . . . When it gets like that in life—you just got to do something different, push on out and do something bigger . . . [*She waits.*] I wish you say something, son . . . I wish you'd say how deep inside you you think I done the right thing—

WALTER [*crossing slowly to his bedroom door and finally turning there and speaking measuredly*]: What you need me to say you done right for? You the head of this family. You run our lives like you want to. It was your money and you did what you wanted with it. So what you need for me to say it was all right for? [*bitterly, to hurt her as deeply as he knows is possible*] So you butchered up a dream of mine—you—who always talking 'bout your children's dreams . . .

MAMA: Walter Lee—[*He just closes the door behind him.* MAMA *sits alone, thinking heavily.*]

CURTAIN

SCENE 2

TIME: *Friday night. A few weeks later.*

At rise: Packing crates mark the intention of the family to move. BENEATHA *and* GEORGE *come in, presumably from an evening out again.*

GEORGE: O.K.... O.K., whatever you say ... [*They both sit on the couch. He tries to kiss her. She moves away.*] Look, we've had a nice evening; let's not spoil it, huh? ... [*He again turns her head and tries to nuzzle in and she turns away from him, not with distaste but with momentary lack of interest; in a mood to pursue what they were talking about.*]

BENEATHA: I'm trying to talk to you.

GEORGE: We always talk.

BENEATHA: Yes—and I love to talk.

GEORGE [*exasperated; rising*]: I know it and I don't mind it sometimes... I want you to cut it out, see—The moody stuff, I mean. I don't like it. You're a nice-looking girl... all over. That's all you need, honey, forget the atmosphere. Guys aren't going to go for the atmosphere—they're going to go for what they see. Be glad for that. Drop the Garbo routine. It doesn't go with you. As for myself, I want a nice—[*groping*]—simple [*thoughtfully*]—sophisticated girl... not a poet—O.K.? [*She rebuffs him again and he starts to leave.*]

BENEATHA: Why are you angry?

GEORGE: Because this is stupid! I don't go out with you to discuss the nature of "quiet desperation" or to hear all about your thoughts—because the world will go on thinking what it thinks regardless—

BENEATHA: Then why read books? Why go to school?

GEORGE [*with artificial patience, counting on his fingers*]: It's simple. You read books—to learn facts—to get grades—to pass the course—to get a degree. That's all—it has nothing to do with thoughts. [*a long pause*]

BENEATHA: I see. [*a longer pause as she looks at him*] Good night, George. [*GEORGE looks at her a little oddly, and starts to exit. He meets MAMA coming in.*]

GEORGE: Oh—hello, Mrs. Younger.

MAMA: Hello, George, how you feeling?

GEORGE: Fine—fine, how are you?

MAMA: Oh, a little tired. You know them steps can get you after a day's work. You all have a nice time tonight?

GEORGE: Yes—a fine time. Well, good night.

MAMA: Good night. [*He exits. MAMA closes the door behind her.*] Hello, honey. What you sitting like that for?

BENEATHA: I'm just sitting.

MAMA: Didn't you have a nice time?

BENEATHA: No.

MAMA: No? What's the matter?

BENEATHA: Mama, George is a fool—honest. [*She rises.*]

MAMA [*Hustling around unloading the packages she has entered with. She stops.*]: Is he, baby?

BENEATHA: Yes. [*BENEATHA makes up TRAVIS' bed as she talks.*]

MAMA: You sure?

BENEATHA: Yes.

MAMA: Well—I guess you better not waste your time with no fools. [*BENEATHA looks up at her mother, watching her put groceries in the refrigerator. Finally she gathers up her things and starts into the bedroom. At the door she stops and looks back at her mother.*]

BENEATHA: Mama—

MAMA: Yes, baby—

BENEATHA: Thank you.

MAMA: For what?

BENEATHA: For understanding me this time. [*She exits quickly and the mother stands, smiling a little, looking at the place where BENEATHA had stood. RUTH enters.*]

RUTH: Now don't you fool with any of this stuff, Lena—

MAMA: Oh, I just thought I'd sort a few things out. [*The phone rings. RUTH answers.*]

RUTH [*at the phone*]: Hello—Just a minute. [*goes to door*] Walter, it's Mrs. Arnold. [*Waits. Goes back to the phone. Tense.*] Hello. Yes, this is his wife speaking . . . He's lying down now. Yes . . . well, he'll be in tomorrow. He's been very sick. Yes—I know we should have called, but we were so sure he'd be able to come in today. Yes—yes, I'm very sorry. Yes . . . Thank you very much. [*She hangs up. WALTER is standing in the doorway of the bedroom behind her.*] That was Mrs. Arnold.

WALTER [*indifferently*]: Was it?

RUTH: She said if you don't come in tomorrow that they are getting a new man . . .

WALTER: Ain't that sad—ain't that crying sad.

RUTH: She said Mr. Arnold has had to take a cab for three days . . . Walter, you ain't been to work for three days! [*This is a revelation to her.*] Where you been, Walter Lee Younger? [*WALTER looks at her and starts to laugh.*] You're going to lose your job.

WALTER: That's right . . .

RUTH: Oh, Walter, and with your mother working like a dog every day—

WALTER: That's sad too—Everything is sad.

MAMA: What you been doing for these three days, son?

WALTER: Mama—you don't know all the things a man what got leisure can find to do in this city . . . What's this—Friday night? Well—Wednesday I borrowed Willy Harris' car and I went for a drive . . . just me and myself and I drove and drove . . . Way out . . . way past South Chicago, and I parked the car and I sat and looked at the steel mills all day long. I just sat in the car and looked at them big black chimneys for hours. Then I drove back and I went to the Green Hat. [*pause*] And Thursday—Thursday I borrowed the car again and I got in it and I pointed it the other way and I drove the other way—for hours—way, way up to Wisconsin, and I looked at the farms. I just drove and looked at the farms. Then I drove back and I went to the Green Hat. [*pause*] And today—today I didn't get the car. Today I just walked. All over the Southside. And I looked at the Negroes and they looked at me and finally I just sat down on the curb at Thirty-ninth and South Parkway and I just sat there and watched the Negroes go by. And then I went to the Green Hat. You all sad? You all depressed? And you know where I am going right now—[*RUTH goes out quietly.*].

MAMA: Oh, Big Walter, is this the harvest of our days?

WALTER: You know what I like about the Green Hat? [*He turns the radio on and a steamy, deep blues pours into the room.*] I like this little cat they got there who blows a sax . . . He blows. He talks to me. He ain't but 'bout five feet tall and he's got a conked head and his eyes is always closed and he's all music—

MAMA [*rising and getting some papers out of her handbag*]: Walter—

WALTER: And there's this other guy who plays the piano . . . and they got a sound. I mean they can work on some music . . . They got the best little combo in the world in the Green Hat . . . You can just sit there and drink and listen to them three men play and you realize that don't nothing matter worth a damn, but just being there—

MAMA: I've helped do it to you, haven't I, son? Walter, I been wrong.

WALTER: Naw—you ain't never been wrong about nothing, Mama.

MAMA: Listen to me, now. I say I been wrong, son. That I been doing to you what the rest of the world been doing to you. [*She stops and he looks up slowly at her and she meets his eyes pleadingly.*] Walter—what you ain't understood is that I ain't got nothing, don't own nothing, ain't never really wanted nothing that wasn't for you. There ain't nothing as precious to me . . . There ain't nothing worth holding on to, money, dreams, nothing else—if it means—if it means it's going to destroy my boy. [*She puts her papers in front of him and he watches her without speaking or moving.*] I paid the man thirty-five hundred dollars down on the house. That leaves sixty-five hundred dollars. Monday morning I want you to take this money and take three thousand dollars and put it in a savings account for Beneatha's medical schooling. The rest you put in a checking account—with your name on it. And from now on any penny that come out of it or that go in it is for you to look after. For you to decide. [*She drops her hands a little helplessly.*] It ain't much, but it's all I got in the world and I'm putting it in your hands. I'm telling you to be the head of this family from now on like you supposed to be.

WALTER [*stares at the money*]: You trust me like that, Mama?

MAMA: I ain't never stop trusting you. Like I ain't never stop loving you. [*She goes out, and WALTER sits looking at the money on the table as the music *continues in its idiom, pulsing in the room. Finally, in a decisive gesture, he gets up, and, in mingled joy and desperation, picks up the money. At the same moment,* TRAVIS *enters for bed.*]

TRAVIS: What's the matter, Daddy? You drunk?

WALTER [*sweetly, more sweetly than we have ever known him*]: No, Daddy ain't drunk. Daddy ain't going to never be drunk again. . . .

TRAVIS: Well, good night, Daddy. [*The father has come from behind the couch and leans over, embracing his son.*]

WALTER: Son, I feel like talking to you tonight.

TRAVIS: About what?

WALTER: Oh, about a lot of things. About you and what kind of man you going to be when you grow up. . . . Son—son, what do you want to be when you grow up?

TRAVIS: A bus driver.

WALTER [*laughing a little*]: A what? Man, that ain't nothing to want to be!

TRAVIS: Why not?

WALTER: 'Cause, man—it ain't big enough—you know what I mean.

TRAVIS: I don't know then. I can't make up my mind. Sometimes Mama asks me that too. And sometimes when I tell her I just want to be like you—she says she don't want me to be like that and sometimes she says she does . . .

WALTER [*gathering him up in his arms*]: You know what, Travis? In seven years you going to be seventeen years old. And things is going to be very different with us in seven years, Travis. . . . One day when you are seventeen I'll come home—home from my office downtown somewhere—

TRAVIS: You don't work in no office, Daddy.

WALTER: No—but after tonight. After what your daddy gonna do tonight, there's going to be offices—a whole lot of offices. . . .

TRAVIS: What you gonna do tonight, Daddy?

WALTER: You wouldn't understand yet, son, but your daddy's gonna make a transaction . . . a business transaction that's going to change our lives . . . That's how come one day when you 'bout seventeen years old I'll come home and I'll be pretty tired, you know what I mean, after a day of conferences and secretaries getting things wrong the way they do . . . 'cause an executive's life is hell, man—[*The more he talks the farther away he gets.*] And I'll pull the car up on the driveway . . . just a plain black Chrysler, I think, with white walls—no—black tires. More elegant. Rich people don't have to be flashy . . . though I'll have to get something a little sportier for Ruth—maybe a Cadillac convertible to do her shopping in. . . . And I'll come up the steps to the house and the gardener will be clipping away at the hedges and he'll say, "Good evening, Mr. Younger." And I'll say, "Hello, Jefferson, how are you this evening?" And I'll go inside and Ruth will come downstairs and meet me at the door and we'll kiss each other and she'll take my arm and we'll go up to your room to see you sitting on the floor with the catalogues of all the great schools in America around you. . . . All the great schools in the world! And—and I'll say, all right son—it's your seventeenth birthday, what is it you've decided? . . . Just tell me where you want to go to school and you'll *go*. Just tell me, what it is you want to be—and you'll be it. . . . Whatever you want to be—Yessir! [*He holds his arms open for* TRAVIS.] You just name it, son . . . [TRAVIS *leaps into them*] and I hand you the world! [WALTER'S *voice has risen in pitch and hysterical promise and on the last line he lifts* TRAVIS *high.*]

BLACKOUT

SCENE 3

TIME: *Saturday, moving day, one week later.*

Before the curtain rises, RUTH'S *voice, a strident, dramatic church alto, cuts through the silence.*

It is, in the darkness, a triumphant surge, a penetrating statement of expectation: "Oh, Lord, I don't feel no ways tired! Children, oh, glory hallelujah!"

As the curtain rises we see that RUTH *is alone in the living room, finishing up the family's packing. It is moving day. She is nailing crates and tying cartons.* BENEATHA *enters, carrying a guitar case, and watches her exuberant sister-in-law.*

RUTH: Hey!

BENEATHA [*putting away the case*]: Hi.

RUTH [*pointing at a package*]: Honey—look in that package there and see what I found on sale this morning at the South Center. [RUTH *gets up and moves to the package and draws out some curtains.*] Lookahere—hand-turned hems!

BENEATHA: How do you know the window size out there?

RUTH [*who hadn't thought of that*]: Oh—Well, they bound to fit something in the whole house. Anyhow, they was too good a bargain to pass up. [RUTH *slaps her head, suddenly remembering something.*] Oh, Bennie—I meant to put a special note on that carton over there. That's your mama's good china and she wants 'em to be very careful with it.

BENEATHA: I'll do it. [BENEATHA *finds a piece of paper and starts to draw large letters on it.*]

RUTH: You know what I'm going to do soon as I get in that new house?

BENEATHA: What?

RUTH: Honey—I'm going to run me a tub of water up to here . . . [*with her fingers practically up to her nostrils*] And I'm going to get in it—and I am going to sit . . . and sit . . . and sit in that hot water and the first person who knocks to tell *me* to hurry up and come out—

BENEATHA: Gets shot at sunrise.

RUTH [*laughing happily*]: You said it, sister! [*noticing how large BENEATHA is absent-mindedly making the note*] Honey, they ain't going to read that from no airplane.

BENEATHA [*laughing herself*]: I guess I always think things have more emphasis if they are big, somehow.

RUTH [*looking up at her and smiling*]: You and your brother seem to have that as a philosophy of life. Lord, that man—done changed so 'round here. You know—you know what we did last night? Me and Walter Lee?

BENEATHA: What?

RUTH [*smiling to herself*]: We went to the movies. [*looking at BENEATHA to see if she understands*] We went to the movies. You know the last time me and Walter went to the movies together?

BENEATHA: No.

RUTH: Me neither. That's how long it been. [*smiling again*] But we went last night. The picture wasn't much good, but that didn't seem to matter. We went—and we held hands.

BENEATHA: Oh, Lord!

RUTH: We held hands—and you know what?

BENEATHA: What?

RUTH: When we come out of the show it was late and dark and all the stores and things was closed up . . . and it was kind of chilly and there wasn't many people on the streets . . . and we was still holding hands, me and Walter.

BENEATHA: You're killing me. [*WALTER enters with a large package. His happiness is deep in him; he cannot keep still with his new-found exuberance. He is singing and wiggling and snapping his fingers. He puts his package in a corner and puts a phonograph record, which he has brought in with him, on the record player. As the music comes up he dances over to RUTH and tries to get her to dance with him. She gives in at last to his raunchiness and in a fit of giggling allows herself to be drawn into his mood and together they deliberately burlesque an old social dance of their youth.*]

BENEATHA [*Regarding them a long time as they dance, then drawing in her breath for a deeply exaggerated comment which she does not particularly mean.*]: Talk about—olddddddddddd—fashionedddddd—Negroes!

WALTER [*stopping momentarily*]: What kind of Negroes? [*He says this in fun. He is not angry with her today, nor with anyone. He starts to dance with his wife again.*]

BENEATHA: Old-fashioned.

WALTER [*as he dances with RUTH*]: You know, when these *New Negroes* have their convention—[*pointing at his sister*]—that is going to be the chairman of the Committee on Unending Agitation. [*He goes on dancing, then stops.*] Race, race, race! . . . Girl, I do believe you are the first person in the history of the entire human race to successfully brainwash yourself.

[BENEATHA *breaks up and he goes on dancing. He stops again, enjoying his tease.*] Damn, even the N double A C P takes a holiday sometimes! [BENEATHA *and* RUTH *laugh. He dances with* RUTH *some more and starts to laugh and stops and pantomimes someone over an operating table.*] I can just see that chick someday looking down at some poor cat on an operating table before she starts to slice him, saying . . . [*pulling his sleeves back maliciously*] "By the way, what are your views on civil rights down there? . . ." [*He laughs at her again and starts to dance happily. The bell sounds.*]

BENEATHA: Sticks and stones may break my bones but . . . words will never hurt me! [BENEATHA *goes to the door and opens it as* WALTER *and* RUTH *go on with the clowning.* BENEATHA *is somewhat surprised to see a quiet-looking middle-aged white man in a business suit holding his hat and a briefcase in his hand and consulting a small piece of paper.*]

MAN: Uh—how do you do, miss. I am looking for a Mrs.—[*He looks at the slip of paper.*] Mrs. Lena Younger?

BENEATHA [*smoothing her hair with slight embarrassment*]: Oh—yes, that's my mother. Excuse me. [*She closes the door and turns to quiet the other two.*] Ruth! Brother! Somebody's here. [*Then she opens the door. The man casts a curious quick glance at all of them.*] Uh—come in please.

MAN [*coming in*]: Thank you.

BENEATHA: My mother isn't here just now. Is it business?

MAN: Yes . . . well, of a sort.

WALTER [*freely, the Man of the House*]: Have a seat. I'm Mrs. Younger's son. I look after most of her business matters. [RUTH *and* BENEATHA *exchange amused glances.*]

MAN [*regarding* WALTER, *and sitting*]: Well—My name is Karl Lindner . . .

WALTER [*stretching out his hand*]: Walter Younger. This is my wife—[RUTH *nods politely.*]—and my sister.

LINDNER: How do you do.

WALTER [*amiably, as he sits himself easily on a chair, leaning with interest forward on his knees and looking expectantly into the newcomer's face*]: What can we do for you, Mr. Lindner!

Lindner [*some minor shuffling of the hat and briefcase on his knees*]: Well—I am a representative of the Clybourne Park Improvement Association—

WALTER [*pointing*]: Why don't you sit your things on the floor?

LINDNER: Oh—yes. Thank you. [*He slides the briefcase and hat under the chair.*] And as I was saying—I am from the Clybourne Park Improvement Association and we have had it brought to our attention at the last meeting that you people—or at least your mother—has bought a piece of residential property at—[*He digs for the slip of paper again.*]—four o six at Clybourne Street . . .

WALTER: That's right. Care for something to drink? Ruth, get Mr. Lindner a beer.

LINDNER [*upset for some reason*]: Oh—no, really, I mean thank you very much, but no thank you.

RUTH [*innocently*]: Some coffee?

LINDNER: Thank you, nothing at all. [*BENEATHA is watching the man carefully.*]

LINDNER: Well, I don't know how much you folks know about our organization. [*He is a gentle man; thoughtful and somewhat labored in his manner.*] It is one of these community organizations set up to look after—oh, you know, things like block upkeep and special projects and we also have what we call our New Neighbors Orientation Committee . . .

BENEATHA [*drily*]: Yes—and what do they do?

LINDNER [*turning a little to her and then returning the main force to WALTER*]: Well—it's what you might call a sort of welcoming committee, I guess. I mean they, we, I'm the chairman of the committee—go around and see the new people who move into the neighborhood and sort of give them the lowdown on the way we do things out in Clybourne Park.

BENEATHA [*with appreciation of the two meanings, which escape RUTH and WALTER*]: Uh-huh.

LINDNER: And we also have the category of what the association calls—[*He looks elsewhere.*]—uh—special community problems . . .

BENEATHA: Yes—and what are some of those?

WALTER: Girl, let the man talk.

LINDNER [*with understated relief*]: Thank you. I would sort of like to explain this thing in my own way. I mean I want to explain to you in a certain way.

WALTER: Go ahead.

LINDNER: Yes. Well. I'm going to try to get right to the point. I'm sure we'll all appreciate that in the long run.

BENEATHA: Yes.

WALTER: Be still now!

LINDNER: Well—

RUTH [*still innocently*]: Would you like another chair—you don't look comfortable.

LINDNER [*more frustrated than annoyed*]: No, thank you very much. Please. Well—to get right to the point I—[*a great breath, and he is off at last*] I am sure you people must be aware of some of the incidents which have happened in various parts of the city when colored people have moved into certain areas—[*BENEATHA exhales heavily and starts tossing a piece of fruit up and down in the air.*] Well—because we have what I think is going to be a unique type of organization in American community life—not only do we deplore that kind of thing—but we are trying to do something about it. [*BENEATHA stops tossing and turns with a new and quizzical interest to the man.*] We feel—[*gaining confidence in his mission because of the interest in the faces of the people he is talking to*]—we feel that most of the trouble in this world, when you come right down to it—[*He hits his knee for emphasis.*]—most of the trouble exists because people just don't sit down and talk to each other.

RUTH [*nodding as she might in church, pleased with the remark*]: You can say that again, mister.

LINDNER [*more encouraged by such affirmation*]: That we don't try hard enough in this world to understand the other fellow's problem. The other guy's point of view.

RUTH: Now that's right. [*BENEATHA and WALTER merely watch and listen with genuine interest.*]

LINDNER: Yes—that's the way we feel out in Clybourne Park. And that's why I was elected to come here this afternoon and talk to you people. Friendly like, you know, the way people should talk to each other and see if we couldn't find some way to work this thing out. As I say, the whole business is a matter of caring about the other fellow. Anybody can see that you are a nice family of folks, hard working and honest I'm sure. [*BENEATHA frowns slightly, quizzically, her head tilted regarding him.*] Today everybody knows what it means to be on the outside of *something*. And of course, there is always somebody who is out to take the advantage of people who don't always understand.

WALTER: What do you mean?

LINDNER: Well—you see our community is made of people who've worked hard as the dickens for years to build up that little community. They're not rich and fancy people; just hardworking, honest people who don't really have much but those little homes and a dream of the kind of community they want to raise their children in. Now, I don't say we are perfect and there is a lot wrong in some of the things they want. But you've got to admit that a man, right or wrong, has the right to want to have the neighborhood he lives in a certain kind of way. And at the moment the overwhelming majority of our people out there feel that people get along better, take more of a common interest in the life of the community, when they share a common background. I want you to believe me when I tell you that race prejudice simply doesn't enter into it. It is a matter of the people of Clybourne Park believing, rightly or wrongly, as I say, that for the happiness of all concerned that our Negro families are happier when they live in their *own* communities.

BENEATHA [*with a grand and bitter gesture*]: This, friends, is the Welcoming Committee!

WALTER [*dumbfounded, looking at LINDNER*]: Is this what you came marching all the way over here to tell us?

LINDNER: Well, now we've been having a fine conversation. I hope you'll hear me all the way through.

WALTER [*tightly*]: Go ahead, man.

LINDNER: You see—in the face of all things I have said, we are prepared to make your family a very generous offer . . .

BENEATHA: Thirty pieces and not a coin less!

WALTER: Yeah?

LINDNER [*putting on his glasses and drawing a form out of the briefcase*]: Our association is prepared, through the collective effort of our people, to buy the house from you at a financial gain to your family.

RUTH: Lord have mercy, ain't this the living gall!

WALTER: All right, you through?

LINDNER: Well, I want to give you the exact terms of the financial arrangement—

WALTER: We don't want to hear no exact terms of no arrangements. I want to know if you got any more to tell us 'bout getting together?

LINDNER [*taking off his glasses*]: Well—I don't suppose that you feel . . .

WALTER: Never mind how I feel—you got any more to say 'bout how people ought to sit down and talk to each other? . . . Get out of my house, man. [*He turns his back and walks to the door.*]

LINDNER [*looking around at the hostile faces and reaching and assembling his hat and briefcase*]: Well—I don't understand why you people are reacting this way. What do you think you are going to gain by moving into a neighborhood where you just aren't wanted and where some elements—well—people can get awful worked up when they feel that their whole way of life and everything they've ever worked for is threatened.

WALTER: Get out.

LINDNER [*at the door, holding a small card*]: Well—I'm sorry it went like this.

WALTER: Get out.

LINDNER [*almost sadly regarding WALTER*]: You just can't force people to change their hearts, son. [*He turns and put his card on a table and exits. WALTER pushes the door to with stinging hatred, and stands looking at it. RUTH just sits and BENEATHA just stands. They say nothing. MAMA and TRAVIS enter.*]

MAMA: Well—this all the packing got done since I left out of here this morning. I testify before God that my children got all the energy of the dead. What time the moving men due?

BENEATHA: Four o'clock. You had a caller, Mama. [*She is smiling, teasingly.*]

MAMA: Sure enough—who?

BENEATHA [*her arms folded saucily*]: The Welcoming Committee. [*WALTER and RUTH giggle.*]

MAMA [*innocently*]: Who?

BENEATHA: The Welcoming Committee. They said they're sure going to be glad to see you when you get there.

WALTER [*devilishly*]: Yeah, they said they can't hardly wait to see your face. [*laughter*]

MAMA [*sensing their facetiousness*]: What's the matter with you all?

WALTER: Ain't nothing the matter with us. We just telling you 'bout the gentleman who came to see you this afternoon. From the Clybourne Park Improvement Association.

MAMA: What he want?

RUTH [*in the same mood as BENEATHA and WALTER*]: To welcome you, honey.

WALTER: He said they can't hardly wait. He said the one thing they don't have, that they just dying to have out there is a fine family of colored people! [*to RUTH and BENEATHA*] Ain't that right!

RUTH and BENEATHA [*mockingly*]: Yeah! He left his card in case—[*They indicate the card, and MAMA picks it up and throws it on the floor—understanding and looking off as she draws her chair up to the table on which she has put her plant and some sticks and some cord.*]

MAMA: Father, give us strength. [*knowingly—and without fun*] Did he threaten us?

BENEATHA: Oh—Mama—they don't do it like that any more. He talked Brotherhood. He said everybody ought to learn how to sit down and hate each other with good Christian fellowship. [*She and WALTER shake hands to ridicule the remark.*]

MAMA [*sadly*]: Lord, protect us . . .

RUTH: You should hear the money those folks raised to buy the house from us. All we paid and then some.

BENEATHA: What they think we going to do—eat 'em?

RUTH: No, honey, marry 'em.

MAMA [*shaking her head*]: Lord, Lord, Lord . . .

RUTH: Well—that's the way the crackers crumble. Joke.

BENEATHA [*laughingly noticing what her mother is doing*]: Mama, what are you doing?

MAMA: Fixing my plant so it won't get hurt none on the way . . .

BENEATHA: Mama, you going to take that to the new house?

MAMA: Un-huh—

BENEATHA: That raggedy-looking old thing?

MAMA [*stopping and looking at her*]: It expresses *me*.

RUTH [*with delight, to BENEATHA*]: So there, Miss Thing! [*WALTER comes to MAMA suddenly and bends down behind her and squeezes her in his arms with all his strength. She is overwhelmed by the suddenness of it and, though delighted, her manner is like that of RUTH with TRAVIS.*]

MAMA: Look out now, boy! You make me mess up my thing here!

WALTER [*His face lit, he slips down on his knees beside her, his arms still about her.*]: Mama . . . you know what it means to climb up in the chariot?

MAMA [*gruffly, very happy*]: Get on away from me now . . .

RUTH [*near the gift-wrapped package, trying to catch WALTER's eye*]: Psst—

WALTER: What the old song say, Mama . . .

RUTH: Walter—Now? [*She is pointing at the package.*]

WALTER [*speaking the lines, sweetly, playfully, in his mother's face*]:
I got wings . . . you got wings . . .
All God's children got wings . . .

MAMA: Boy—get out of my face and do some work . . .

WALTER: *When I get to heaven gonna put on my wings,*
Gonna fly all over God's heaven . . .

BENEATHA [*teasingly, from across the room*]: Everybody talking 'bout heaven ain't going there!

WALTER [*to RUTH, who is carrying the box across to them*]: I don't know, you think we ought to give her that . . . Seems to me she ain't been very appreciative around here.

MAMA [*eying the box, which is obviously a gift*]: What is that?

WALTER [*taking it from RUTH and putting it on the table in front of MAMA*]: Well—what you all think? Should we give it to her?

RUTH: Oh—she was pretty good today.

MAMA: I'll good you—[*She turns her eyes to the box again.*]

BENEATHA: Open it, Mama. [*She stands up, looks at it, turns and looks at all of them, and then presses her hands together and does not open the package.*]

WALTER [*sweetly*]: Open it, Mama. It's for you. [*MAMA looks in his eyes. It is the first present in her life without its being Christmas. Slowly she opens her package and lifts out, one by one, a brand-new sparkling set of gardening tools. WALTER continues, prodding.*] Ruth made up the note—read it . . .

MAMA [*picking up the card and adjusting her glasses*]: "To our own Mrs. Miniver—Love from Brother, Ruth and Beneatha." Ain't that lovely . . .

TRAVIS [*tugging at his father's sleeve*]: Daddy, can I give her mine now?

WALTER: All right, son. [*TRAVIS flies to get his gift.*] Travis didn't want to go in with the rest of us, Mama. He got his own. [*somewhat amused*] We don't know what it is . . .

TRAVIS [*racing back in the room with a large hatbox and putting it in front of his grandmother*]: Here!

MAMA: Lord have mercy, baby. You done gone and bought your grandmother a hat?

TRAVIS [*very proud*]: Open it! [*She does and lifts out an elaborate, but very elaborate, wide gardening hat, and all the adults break up at the sight of it.*]

RUTH: Travis, honey, what is that?

TRAVIS [*who thinks it is beautiful and appropriate*]: It's a gardening hat! Like the ladies always have on in the magazines when they work in their gardens.

BENEATHA [*giggling fiercely*]: Travis—we were trying to make Mama Mrs. Miniver—not Scarlett O'Hara!

MAMA [*indignantly*]: What's the matter with you all! This here is a beautiful hat! [*absurdly*] I always wanted me one just like it! [*She pops it on her head to prove it to her grandson, and the hat is ludicrous and considerably oversized.*]

RUTH: Hot dog! Go, Mama!

WALTER [*doubled over with laughter*]: I'm sorry, Mama—but you look like you ready to go out and chop you some cotton sure enough! [*They all laugh except MAMA, out of deference to TRAVIS's feelings.*]

MAMA [*gathering the boy up to her*]: Bless your heart—this is the prettiest hat I ever owned—[*WALTER, RUTH and BENEATHA chime in—noisily, festively and insincerely congratulating TRAVIS on his gift.*] What are we all standing around here for? We ain't finished packin' yet. Bennie, you ain't packed one book. [*The bell rings.*]

BENEATHA: That couldn't be the movers . . . it's not hardly two o'clock yet—[*BENEATHA goes into her room. MAMA starts for door.*]

WALTER [*turning, stiffening*]: Wait—wait—I'll get it. [*He stands and looks at the door.*]

MAMA: You expecting company, son?

WALTER [*just looking at the door*]: Yeah—yeah . . . [*MAMA looks at RUTH, and they exchange innocent and unfrightened glances.*]

MAMA [*not understanding*]: Well, let them in, son.

BENEATHA [*from her room*]: We need some more string.

MAMA: Travis—you run to the hardware and get me some string cord. [*MAMA goes out and WALTER turns and looks at RUTH. TRAVIS goes to a dish for money.*]

RUTH: Why don't you answer the door, man?

WALTER [*suddenly bounding across the floor to her*]: 'Cause sometimes it hard to let the future begin! [*stooping down in her face*]

I got wings! You got wings!
All God's children got wings!

[He crosses to the door and throws it open. Standing there is a very slight little man in a not too prosperous business suit and with haunted frightened eyes and a bat pulled down tightly, brim up, around his forehead. TRAVIS passes between the men and exits. WALTER leans deep in the man's face, still in his jubilance.]

When I get to heaven gonna put on my wings,
Gonna fly all over God's heaven . . .

[The little man just stares at him]

Heaven—
[*Suddenly he stops and looks past the little man into the empty hallway.*]
Where's Willy, man?

BOBO: He ain't with me.

WALTER [*not disturbed*]: Oh—come on in. You know my wife.

BOBO [*dumbly, taking off his hat*]: Yes—h'you, Miss Ruth.

RUTH [*quietly, a mood apart from her husband already, seeing BOBO*]: Hello, Bobo.

WALTER: You right on time today . . . Right on time. That's the way! [*He slaps* BOBO *on his back.*] Sit down . . . lemme hear. [RUTH *stands stiffly and quietly in back of them, as though somehow she senses death, her eyes fixed on her husband.*]

BOBO [*his frightened eyes on the floor, his hat in his hands*]: Could I please get a drink of water, before I tell you about it, Walter Lee? [WALTER *does not take his eyes off the man.* RUTH *goes blindly to the tap and gets a glass of water and brings it to* BOBO.]

WALTER: There ain't nothing wrong, is there?

BOBO: Lemme tell you—

WALTER: Man—didn't nothing go wrong?

BOBO: Lemme tell you—Walter Lee. [*Looking at* RUTH *and talking to her more than to* WALTER.] You know how it was. I got to tell you how it was. I mean first I got to tell you how it was all the way . . . I mean about the money I put in, Walter Lee . . .

WALTER [*with taut agitation now*]: What about the money you put in?

BOBO: Well—it wasn't much as we told you—me and Willy—[*He stops.*] I'm sorry, Walter. I got a bad feeling about it. I got a real bad feeling about it . . .

WALTER: Man, what you telling me about all this for? . . . Tell me what happened in Springfield . . .

BOBO: Springfield.

RUTH [*like a dead woman*]: What was supposed to happen in Springfield?

BOBO [*to her*]: This deal that me and Walter went into with Willy—Me and Willy was going to go down to Springfield and spread some money 'round so's we wouldn't have to wait so long for the liquor license . . . That's what we were going to do. Everybody said that was the way you had to do, you understand, Miss Ruth?

WALTER: Man—what happened down there?

BOBO [*a pitiful man, near tears*]: I'm trying to tell you, Walter.

WALTER [*screaming at him suddenly*]: THEN TELL ME, GODDAMMIT . . . WHAT'S THE MATTER WITH YOU?

BOBO: Man . . . I didn't go to no Springfield, yesterday.

WALTER [*halted, life hanging in the moment*]: Why not?

BOBO [*the long way, the hard way to tell*]: 'Cause I didn't have no reasons to . . .

WALTER: Man, what are you talking about!

BOBO: I'm talking about the fact that when I got to the train station yesterday morning—eight o'clock like we planned . . . Man—*Willy didn't never show up.*

WALTER: Why . . . where was he . . . where is he?

BOBO: That's what I'm trying to tell you . . . I don't know . . . I waited six hours . . . I called his house . . . and I waited . . . six hours . . . I waited in that train station six hours . . . [*breaking into tears*] That was all the extra money I had in the world . . . [*looking up at* WALTER *with the tears running down his face*] Man, *Willy is gone.*

WALTER: Gone, what you mean Willy is gone? Gone where? You mean he went by himself. You mean he went off to Springfield by himself—to take care of getting the license—[*turns and looks anxiously at* RUTH] You mean maybe he didn't want too many people in on the business down there? [*looks to* RUTH *again, as before*] You know Willy got his own ways. [*looks back to* BOBO] Maybe you was late yesterday and he just went on down there without you. Maybe—maybe—he's been callin' you at home tryin' to tell you what happened or something. Maybe—maybe—he just got sick. He's somewhere—he's got to be somewhere. We just got to find him—me and you got to find him. [*grabs* BOBO *senselessly by the collar and starts to shake him*] We got to!

BOBO [*in sudden angry, frightened agony*]: What's the matter with you, Walter! *When a cat take off with your money he don't leave you no maps!*

WALTER [*turning madly, as though he is looking for Willy in the very room*]: Willy! . . . Willy . . . don't do it . . . Please don't do it . . . Man, not with that money . . . Man, please, not with that money . . . Oh, God . . . Don't let it be true . . . [*He is wandering around, crying out for Willy and looking for him or perhaps for help from God.*] Man . . . I trusted you . . . Man, I put my life in your hands . . . [*He starts to crumple down on the floor as* RUTH *just covers her face in horror,* MAMA *opens the door and comes into the room, with* BENEATHA *behind her.*] Man . . . [*He starts to pound the floor with his fists, sobbing wildly.*] *That money is made out of my father's flesh . . .*

BOBO [*standing over him helplessly*]: I'm sorry, Walter . . . [*Only* WALTER*'s sobs reply.* BOBO *puts on his hat.*] I had my life staked on this deal, too . . . [*He exits.*]

MAMA [*to* WALTER]: Son—[*She goes to him, bends down to him, talks to his bent head.*] Son . . . Is it gone? Son, I gave, you sixty-five hundred dollars. Is it gone? All of it? Beneatha's money too?

WALTER [*lifting his head slowly*]: Mama . . . I never . . . went to the bank at all

MAMA [*not wanting to believe him*]: You mean . . . your sister's school money . . . you used that too . . . Walter? . . .

WALTER: Yessss! . . . All of it . . . It's all gone . . .

[*There is total silence.* RUTH *stands with her face covered with her hands;* BENEATHA *leans forlornly against a wall, fingering a piece of red ribbon from the mother's gift.* MAMA *stops and looks at her son without recognition and then, quite without thinking about it, starts to beat him senselessly in the face.* BENEATHA *goes to them and stops it.*]

BENEATHA: Mama! [MAMA *stops and looks at both of her children and rises slowly and wanders vaguely, aimlessly away from them.*]

MAMA: I seen . . . him . . . night after night . . . come in . . . and look at that rug . . . and then look at me . . . the red showing in his eyes . . . the veins moving in his head . . . I seen him grow thin and old before he was forty . . . working and working and working like somebody's old horse . . . killing himself . . . and you—you give it all away in a day . . .

BENEATHA: Mama—

MAMA: Oh, God . . . [*She looks up to Him.*] Look down here—and show me the strength.

BENEATHA: Mama—

MAMA [*folding over*]: Strength . . .

BENEATHA [*plaintively*]: MAMA . . .

MAMA: Strength!

CURTAIN

ACT III

An hour later.

At curtain, there is a sullen light of gloom in the living room, gray light not unlike that which began the first scene of Act I. At left we can see WALTER *within his room, alone with himself. He is stretched out on the bed, his shirt out and open, his arms under his head. He does not smoke, he does not cry out, he merely lies there, looking up at the ceiling, much as if he were alone in the world.*

In the living room BENEATHA *sits at the table, still surrounded by the now almost ominous packing crates. She sits looking off. We feel that this is a mood struck perhaps an hour before, and it lingers now, full of the empty sound of profound disappointment. We see on a line from her brother's bedroom the sameness of their attitudes. Presently the bell rings and* BENEATHA *rises without ambition or interest in answering. It is* ASAGAI, *smiling broadly, striding into the room with energy and happy expectation and conversation.*

ASAGAI: I came over . . . I had some free time. I thought I might help with the packing. Ah, I like the look of packing crates! A household in preparation for a journey! It depresses some people . . . but for me . . . it is another feeling. Something full of the flow of life, do you understand? Movement, progress . . . It makes me think of Africa.

BENEATHA: Africa!

ASAGAI: What kind of a mood is this? Have I told you how deeply you move me?

BENEATHA: He gave away the money, Asagai . . .

ASAGAI: Who gave away what money?

BENEATHA: The insurance money. My brother gave it away.

ASAGAI: Gave it away?

BENEATHA: He made an investment! With a man even Travis wouldn't have trusted.

ASAGAI: And it's gone?

BENEATHA: Gone!

ASAGAI: I'm very sorry . . . And you, now?

BENEATHA: Me? . . . Me? . . . Me, I'm nothing . . . Me. When I was very small . . . we used to take our sleds out in the wintertime and the only hills we had were the ice-covered stone steps of some houses down the street. And we used to fill them in with snow and make them smooth and slide down them all day . . . and it was very dangerous you know . . . far too steep . . . and sure enough one day a kid named Rufus came down too fast and hit the sidewalk . . . and we saw his face just split open right there in front of us . . . And I remember standing there looking at his bloody open face thinking that was the end of Rufus. But the ambulance came and they took him to the hospital and they fixed the broken bones and they sewed it all up . . . and the next time I saw Rufus he just had a little line down the middle of his face . . . I never got over that . . . [*WALTER sits up, listening on the bed. Throughout this scene it is important that we feel his reaction at all times, that he visibly respond to the words of his sister and ASAGAI.*]

ASAGAI: What?

BENEATHA: That that was what one person could do for another, fix him up—sew up the problem, make him all right again. That was the most marvelous thing in the world . . . I wanted to do that. I always thought it was the one concrete thing in the world that a human being could do. Fix up the sick, you know—and make them whole again. This was truly being God . . .

ASAGAI: You wanted to be God?

BENEATHA: No—I wanted to cure. It used to be so important to me. I wanted to cure. It used to matter. I used to care. I mean about people and how their bodies hurt . . .

ASAGAI: And you've stopped caring?

BENEATHA: Yes—I think so.

ASAGAI: Why? [*WALTER rises, goes to the door of his room and is about to open it, then stops and stands listening, leaning on the door jamb.*]

BENEATHA: Because it doesn't seem deep enough, close enough to what ails mankind—I mean this thing of sewing up bodies or administering drugs. Don't you understand? It was a child's reaction to the world. I thought that doctors had the secret to all the hurts . . . That's the way a child sees things—or an idealist.

ASAGAI: Children see things very well sometimes—and idealists even better.

BENEATHA: I know that's what you think. Because you are still where I left off—you still care. This is what you see for the world, for Africa. You with the dreams of the future will patch up all Africa—you are going to cure the Great Sore of colonialism with Independence—

ASAGAI: Yes!

BENEATHA: Yes—and you think that one word is the penicillin of the human spirit: "Independence!" But then what?

ASAGAI: That will be the problem for another time. First we must get there.

BENEATHA: And where does it end?

ASAGAI: End? Who even spoke of an end? To life? To living?

BENEATHA: An end to misery!

ASAGAI [*smiling*]: You sound like a French intellectual.

BENEATHA: No! I sound like a human being who just had her future taken right out of her hands! While I was sleeping in my bed in there, things were happening in this world that directly concerned me—and nobody asked me, consulted me—they just went out and did things—and changed my life. Don't you see there isn't any real progress, Asagai, there is only one large circle that we march in, around and around, each of us with our own little picture—in front of us—our own little mirage that we think is the future.

ASAGAI: That is the mistake.

BENEATHA: What?

ASAGAI: What you just said—about the circle. It isn't a circle—it is simply a long line—as in geometry, you know, one that reaches into infinity. And because we cannot see the end—we also cannot see how it changes. And it is very odd but those who see the changes are called "idealists"—and those who cannot, or refuse to think, they are the "realists." It is very strange, and amusing too, I think.

BENEATHA: You—you are almost religious.

ASAGAI: Yes . . . I think I have the religion of doing what is necessary in the world—and of worshipping man—because he is so marvelous, you see.

BENEATHA: Man is foul! And the human race deserves its misery!

ASAGAI: You see: *you* have become the religious one in the old sense. Already, and after such a small defeat, you are worshipping despair.

BENEATHA: From now on, I worship the truth—and the truth is that people are puny, small and selfish . . .

ASAGAI: Truth? Why is it that you despairing ones always think that only you have the truth? I never thought to see *you* like that. You! Your brother made a stupid, childish mistake—and you are grateful to him. So that now you can give up the ailing human race on account of it. You talk about what good is struggle; what good is anything? Where are we all going? And why are we bothering?

BENEATHA: *And you cannot answer it!* All your talk and dreams about Africa and Independence. Independence and then what? What about all the crooks and petty thieves and just plain idiots who will come into power to steal and plunder the same as before—only now they will be black and do it in the name of the new Independence—You cannot answer that.

ASAGAI [*shouting over her*]: *I live the answer!* [*pause*] In my village at home it is the exceptional man who can even read a newspaper . . . or who ever *sees* a book at all. I will go home and much of what I will have to say will seem strange to the people of my village. . . . But I will teach and work and things will happen, slowly and swiftly. At times it will seem that nothing changes at all . . . and then again . . . the sudden dramatic events which make history leap into the future. And then quiet again. Retrogression even. Guns, murder, revolution. And I even will have moments when I wonder if the quiet was not better than all that death and hatred. But I will look about my village at the illiteracy and disease and ignorance and I will not wonder long. And perhaps . . . perhaps I will be a great man . . . I mean perhaps I will hold on to the substance of truth and find my way always with the right course . . . and perhaps for it I will be butchered in my bed some night by the servants of empire . . .

BENEATHA: *The martyr!*

ASAGAI: . . . or perhaps I shall live to be a very old man, respected and esteemed in my new nation . . . And perhaps I shall hold office and this is what I'm trying to tell you, Alaiyo; perhaps the things I believe now for my country will be wrong and outmoded, and I will not understand and do terrible things to have things my way or merely to keep my power. Don't you see that there will be young men and women, not British soldiers then, but my own black countrymen . . . to step out of the shadows some evening and slit my then useless throat? Don't you see they have always been there . . . that they always will be. And that such a thing as my own death will be an advance? They who might kill me even . . . actually replenish me!

BENEATHA: Oh, Asagai, I know all that.

ASAGAI: Good! Then stop moaning and groaning and tell me what you plan to do.

BENEATHA: Do?

ASAGAI: I have a bit of a suggestion.

BENEATHA: What?

ASAGAI [*rather quietly for him*]: That when it is all over—that you come home with me—

BENEATHA [*slapping herself on the forehead with exasperation born of misunderstanding*]: Oh—Asagai—at this moment you decide to be romantic!

ASAGAI [*quickly understanding the misunderstanding*]: My dear, young creature of the New World—I do not mean across the city—I mean across the ocean; home—to Africa.

BENEATHA [*slowly understanding and turning to him with murmured amazement*]: To—to Nigeria?

ASAGAI: Yes! . . . [*smiling and lifting his arms playfully*]. Three hundred years later the African Prince rose up out of the seas and swept the maiden back across the middle passage over which her ancestors had come—

BENEATHA [*unable to play*]: Nigeria?

ASAGAI: Nigeria. Home. [*coming to her with genuine romantic flippancy*] I will show you our mountains and our stars; and give you cool drinks from gourds and teach you the old songs and the ways of our people—and, in time, we will pretend that—[*very softly*]—you have only been away for a day—[*She turns her back to him, thinking. He swings her around and takes her full in his arms in a long embrace which proceeds to passion*]

BENEATHA [*pulling away*]: You're getting me all mixed up—

ASAGAI: Why?

BENEATHA: Too many things—too many things have happened today. I must sit down and think. I don't know what I feel about anything right this minute. [*She promptly sits down and props her chin on her fist.*]

ASAGAI [*charmed*]: All right, I shall leave you. No—don't get up. [*touching her, gently, sweetly*] Just sit awhile and think . . . Never be afraid to sit awhile and think. [*He goes to door and looks at her.*] How often I have looked at you and said, "Ah—so this is what the New World hath finally wrought . . ." [*He exits. BENEATHA sits on alone. Presently WALTER enters from his room and starts to rummage through things, feverishly looking for something. She looks up and turns in her seat.*]

BENEATHA [*hissingly*]: Yes—just look at what the New World hath wrought! . . . Just look! [*She gestures with bitter disgust.*] There he is! *Monsieur le petit bougeois noir*—himself! There he is—Symbol of a Rising Class! Entrepreneur! Titan of the system! [*WALTER ignores her completely and continues frantically and destructively looking for something and hurling things to the floor and tearing things out of their place in his search. BENEATHA ignores the eccentricity of his actions and goes on with the monologue of insult.*] Did you dream of yachts on Lake Michigan, Brother? Did you see yourself on that Great Day sitting down at the Conference Table, surrounded by all the mighty bald-headed men in America? All halted, waiting, breathless, waiting for your pronouncements on industry? Waiting for you—Chairman of the Board? [*WALTER finds what he is looking for—a small piece of white paper—and pushes it in his pocket and puts on his coat and rushes out without ever having looked at her. She shouts after him.*] I look at you and I see the final triumph of stupidity in the world! [*The door slams and she returns to just sitting again. RUTH comes quickly out of MAMA's room.*]

RUTH: Who was that?

BENEATHA: Your husband.

RUTH: Where did he go?

BENEATHA: Who knows—maybe he has an appointment at U.S. Steel.

RUTH [*anxiously, with frightened eyes*]: You didn't say nothing bad to him, did you?

BENEATHA: Bad? Say anything bad to him? No—I told him he was a sweet boy and full of dreams and everything is strictly peachy keen, as the ofay[3] kids say!

[MAMA enters from her bedroom. She is lost, vague, trying to catch hold, to make some sense of her former command of the world, but it still eludes her. A sense of waste overwhelms her gait; a measure of apology rides on her shoulders. She goes to her plant, which has remained on the table, looks at it, picks it up and takes it to the window sill and sets it outside, and she stands and looks at it a long moment. Then she closes the window, straightens her body with effort and turns around to her children.]

MAMA: Well—ain't it a mess in here, though? [*a false cheerfulness, a beginning of something*] I guess we all better stop moping around and get some work done. All this unpacking and everything we got to do. [*RUTH raises her head slowly in response to the sense of the line; and BENEATHA in similar manner turns very slowly to look at her mother.*] One of you all better call the moving people and tell 'em not to come.

RUTH: Tell 'em not to come?

MAMA: Of course, baby. Ain't no need in 'em coming all the way here and having to go back. They charges for that too. [*She sits down, fingers to her brow, thinking.*] Lord, ever since I was a little girl, I always remembers people saying, "Lena—Lena Eggleston, you aims too high all the time. You needs to slow down and see life a little more like it is. Just slow down some." That's what they always used to say down home—"Lord, that Lena Eggleston is a high-minded thing. She'll get her due one day!"

RUTH: No, Lena . . .

MAMA: Me and Big Walter just didn't never learn right.

RUTH: Lena, no! We gotta go. Bennie—tell her . . . [*She rises and crosses to BENEATHA with her arms outstretched. BENEATHA doesn't respond.*] Tell her we can still move . . . the notes ain't but a hundred and twenty-five a month. We got four grown people in this house—we can work . . .

MAMA [*to herself*]: Just aimed too high all the time—

RUTH [*turning and going to MAMA fast—the words pouring out with urgency and desperation*]: Lena—I'll work . . . I'll work twenty hours a day in all the kitchens in Chicago . . . I'll strap my baby on my back if I have to and scrub all the floors in America and wash all the sheets in America if I have to—but we got to move . . . We got to get out of here . . . [*MAMA reaches out absently and pats RUTH's hand.*]

MAMA: No—I sees things differently now. Been thinking 'bout some of the things we could do to fix this place up some. I seen a second-hand bureau over on Maxwell Street just the other day that could fit right there. [*She*

[3] **ofay** white (pig Latin meaning "foe")

points to where the new furniture might go. RUTH *wanders away from her.*] Would need some new handles on it and then a little varnish and then it look like something brand-new. And—we can put up them new curtains in the kitchen . . . Why this place be looking fine. Cheer us all up so that we forget trouble ever came . . . [*to* RUTH] And you could get some nice screens to put up in your room round the baby's bassinet . . . [*She looks at both of them, pleadingly.*] Sometimes you just got to know when to give up some things . . . and hold on to what you got. [WALTER *enters from the outside, looking spent and leaning against the door, his coat hanging from him.*]

MAMA: Where you been, son?

WALTER [*breathing hard*]: Made a call.

MAMA: To who, son?

WALTER: To the Man.

MAMA: What man, baby?

WALTER: The Man, Mama. Don't you know who The Man is?

RUTH: Walter Lee?

WALTER: *The Man.* Like the guys in the street say—*the Man.* Captain Boss—Mistuh Charley . . . Old Captain Please Mr. Bossman . . .

BENEATHA [*suddenly*]: Lindner!

WALTER: That's right! That's good. I told him to come right over.

BENEATHA [*fiercely, understanding*]: For what? What do you want to see him for?

WALTER [*looking at his sister*]: We are going to do business with him.

MAMA: What you talking 'bout, son?

WALTER: Talking 'bout life, Mama. You all always telling me to see life like it is. Well—I laid in there on my back today . . . and I figured it out. Life just like it is. Who gets and who don't get. [*He sits down with his coat on and laughs.*] Mama, you know it's all divided up. Life is. Sure enough. Between the takers and the "tooken." [*He laughs.*] I've figured it out finally. [*He looks around at them.*] Yeah. Some of us always getting "tooken." [*He laughs.*] People like Willy Harris, they don't never get "tooken." And you know why the rest of us do? 'Cause we all mixed up. Mixed up bad. We get to looking 'round for the right and the wrong; and we worry about it and cry about it and stay up nights trying to figure out 'bout the wrong and the right of things all the time . . . And all the time, man, them takers is out there operating, just taking and taking. Willy Harris? Shoot—Willy Harris don't even count. He don't even count in the big scheme of things. But I'll say one thing for old Willy Harris . . . he's taught me something. He's taught me to keep my eye on what counts in this world. Yeah—[*shouting out a little*] Thanks, Willy!

RUTH: What did you call that man for, Walter Lee!

WALTER: Called him to tell him to come on over to the show. Gonna put on a show for the man. Just what he wants to see. You see, Mama, the man came here today and he told us that them people out there where you want us to move—well they so upset they willing to pay us not to move out there. [*He laughs again.*] And—and oh, Mama—you would of been proud of the way me and Ruth and Bennie acted. We told him to get out . . . Lord have mercy! We told the man to get out. Oh, we was some proud folks this afternoon, yeah. [*He lights a cigarette.*] We were still full of that old-time stuff . . .

RUTH [*coming toward him slowly*]: You talking 'bout taking them people's money to keep us from moving in that house?

WALTER: I ain't just talking 'bout it, baby—I'm telling you that's what's going to happen.

BENEATHA: Oh, God! Where is the bottom! Where is the real honest-to-God bottom so he can't go any farther!

WALTER: See—that's the old stuff. You and that boy that was here today. You all want everybody to carry a flag and a spear and sing some marching songs, huh? You wanna spend your life looking into things and trying to find the right and the wrong part, huh? Yeah. You know what's going to happen to that boy someday—he'll find himself sitting in a dungeon, locked in forever—and the takers will have the key! Forget it, baby! There ain't no causes—there ain't nothing but taking in this world, and he who takes most is smartest—and it don't make a damn bit of difference *how*.

MAMA: You making something inside me cry, son. Some awful pain inside me.

WALTER: Don't cry, Mama. Understand. That white man is going to walk in that door able to write checks for more money than we ever had. It's important to him and I'm going to help him . . . I'm going to put on the show, Mama.

MAMA: Son—I come from five generations of people who was slaves and sharecroppers—but ain't nobody in my family never let nobody pay 'em no money that was a way of telling us we wasn't fit to walk the earth. We ain't never been that poor. [*raising her eyes and looking at him*] We ain't never been that dead inside.

BENEATHA: Well—we are dead now. All the talk about dreams and sunlight that goes on in this house. All dead.

WALTER: What's the matter with you all! I didn't make this world! It was give to me this way! Hell, yes, I want me some yachts someday! Yes, I want to hang some real pearls 'round my wife's neck. Ain't she supposed to wear no pearls? Somebody tell me—tell me, who decides which women is suppose to wear pearls in this world. I tell you I am a *man*—and I think my wife should wear some pearls in this world! [*This last line hangs a good while and* WALTER *begins to move about the room. The word "Man" has penetrated his consciousness; he mumbles it to himself repeatedly between strange agitated pauses as he moves about.*]

MAMA: Baby, how you going to feel on the inside?

WALTER: Fine! . . . Going to feel fine . . . a man . . .

MAMA: You won't have nothing left then, Walter Lee.

WALTER [*coming to her*]: I'm going to feel fine, Mama. I'm going to look that son-of-a-bitch in the eyes and say—[*He falters.*]—and say, "All right, Mr. Lindner—[*He falters even more.*]—that's your neighborhood out there. You got the right to keep it like you want. You got the right to have it like you want. Just write the check and—the house is yours." And, and I am going to say—[*His voice almost breaks.*] And you—you people just put the money in my hand and you won't have to live next to this bunch of stinking niggers! . . . [*He straightens up and moves away from his mother, walking around the room.*] Maybe—maybe I'll just get down on my black knees . . . [*He does so; RUTH and BENNIE and MAMA watch him in frozen horror.*] Captain, Mistuh, Bossman. [*He starts crying.*] A-hee-hee-hee! [*wringing his hands in profoundly anguished imitation*] Yasssssuh! Great White Father, just gi' ussen de money, fo' God's sake, and we's ain't gwine come out deh and dirty up yo' white folks neighborhood . . . [*He breaks down completely, then gets up and goes into the bedroom.*]

BENEATHA: That is not a man. That is nothing but a toothless rat.

MAMA: Yes—death done come in this here house. [*She is nodding, slowly, reflectively.*] Done come walking in my house. On the lips of my children. You what supposed to be my beginning again. You—what supposed to be my harvest. [*to BENEATHA*] You—you mourning your brother?

BENEATHA: He's no brother of mine.

MAMA: What you say?

BENEATHA: I said that that individual in that room is no brother of mine.

MAMA: That's what I thought you said. You feeling like you better than he is today? [*BENEATHA does not answer.*] Yes? What you tell him a minute ago? That he wasn't a man? Yes? You give him up for me? You done wrote his epitaph too—like the rest of the world? Well, who give you the privilege?

BENEATHA: Be on my side for once! You saw what he just did, Mama! You saw him—down on his knees. Wasn't it you who taught me—to despise any man who would do that? Do what he's going to do.

MAMA: Yes—I taught you that. Me and your daddy. But I thought I taught you something else too . . . I thought I taught you to love him.

BENEATHA: Love him? There is nothing left to love.

MAMA: There is always something left to love. And if you ain't learned that, you ain't learned nothing. [*looking at her*] Have you cried for that boy today? I don't mean for yourself and for the family 'cause we lost the money. I mean for him; what he been through and what it done to him. Child, when do you think is the time to love somebody the most; when they done good and made things easy for everybody? Well then, you ain't through learning—because that ain't the time at all. It's when he's at his lowest and can't believe in hisself 'cause the world done whipped him so.

When you starts measuring somebody, measure him right, child, measure him right. Make sure you done taken into account what hills and valleys he come through before he got to wherever he is. [*TRAVIS bursts into the room at the end of the speech, leaving the door open.*]

TRAVIS: Grandmama—the moving men are downstairs! The truck just pulled up.

MAMA [*turning and looking at him*]: Are they, baby? They downstairs? [*She sighs and sits. LINDNER appears in the doorway. He peers in and knocks lightly, to gain attention, and comes in. All turn to look at him.*]

LINDNER [*hat and briefcase in hand*]: Uh—hello . . . [*RUTH crosses mechanically to the bedroom door and opens it and lets it swing open freely and slowly as the lights come up on WALTER within, still in his coat, sitting at the far corner of the room. He looks up and out through the room to LINDNER.*]

RUTH: He's here. [*A long minute passes and WALTER slowly gets up.*]

LINDNER [*coming to the table with efficiency, putting his briefcase on the table and starting to unfold papers and unscrew fountain pens*]: Well, I certainly was glad to hear from you people. [*WALTER has begun the trek out of the room, slowly and awkwardly, rather like a small boy, passing the back of his sleeve across his mouth from time to time.*] Life can really be so much simpler than people let it be most of the time. Well—with whom do I negotiate? You, Mrs. Younger, or your son here? [*MAMA sits with her hands folded on her lap and her eyes closed as WALTER advances. TRAVIS goes close to LINDNER and looks at the papers curiously.*] Just some official papers, sonny.

RUTH: Travis, you go downstairs.

MAMA [*opening her eyes and looking into WALTER's*]: No. Travis, you stay right here. And you make him understand what you doing. Walter Lee. You teach him good. Like Willy Harris taught you. You show where our five generations done come to. Go ahead, son—

WALTER [*Looks down into his boy's eyes. TRAVIS grins at him merrily and WALTER draws him beside him with his arm lightly around his shoulders.*]: Well, Mr. Lindner. [*BENEATHA turns away.*] We called you—[*There is a profound, simple groping quality in his speech.*]—because, well, me and my family [*He looks around and shifts from one foot to the other.*] Well—we are very plain people . . .

LINDNER: Yes—

WALTER: I mean—I have worked as a chauffeur most of my life—and my wife here, she does domestic work in people's kitchens. So does my mother. I mean—we are plain people . . .

LINDNER: Yes, Mr. Younger—

WALTER [*really like a small boy, looking down at his shoes and then up at the man*]: And—uh—well, my father, well, he was a laborer most of his life.

LINDNER [*absolutely confused*]: Uh, yes—

WALTER [*looking down at his toes once again*]: My father almost beat a man to death once because this man called him a bad name or something, you know what I mean?

LINDNER: No, I'm afraid I don't.

WALTER [*finally straightening up*]: Well, what I mean is that we come from people who had a lot of pride. I mean—we are very proud people. And that's my sister over there and she's going to be a doctor—and we are very proud—

LINDNER: Well—I am sure that is very nice, but—

WALTER [*Starting to cry and facing the man eye to eye*]: What I am telling you is that we called you over here to tell you that we are very proud and that this is—this is my son, who makes the sixth generation of our family in this country, and that we have all thought about your offer and we have decided to move into our house because my father—my father—he earned it. [*MAMA has her eyes closed and is rocking back and forth as though she were in church, with her head nodding the amen yes.*] We don't want to make no trouble for nobody or fight no causes—but we will try to be good neighbors. That's all we got to say. [*He looks the man absolutely in the eyes.*] We don't want your money. [*He turns and walks away from the man.*]

LINDNER [*looking around at all of them*]: I take it then that you have decided to occupy.

BENEATHA: That's what the man said.

LINDNER [*to MAMA in her reverie*]: Then I would like to appeal to you, Mrs. Younger. You are older and wiser and understand things better I am sure . . .

MAMA [*rising*]: I am afraid you don't understand. My son said we was going to move and there ain't nothing left for me to say. [*Shaking her head with double meaning.*] You know how these young folks is nowadays, mister. Can't do a thing with 'em. Good-bye.

LINDNER [*folding up his materials*]: Well—if you are that final about it . . . There is nothing left for me to say. [*He finishes. He is almost ignored by the family, who are concentrating on WALTER LEE. At the door LINDNER halts and looks around.*] I sure hope you people know what you're doing. [*He shakes his head and exits.*]

RUTH [*looking around and coming to life*]: Well, for God's sake—if the moving men are here—LET'S GET THE HELL OUT OF HERE!

MAMA [*into action*]: Ain't it the truth! Look at all this here mess. Ruth, put Travis' good jacket on him . . . Walter Lee, fix your tie and tuck your shirt in, you look just like somebody's hoodlum. Lord have mercy, where is my plant? [*She flies to get it amid the general bustling of the family, who are deliberately trying to ignore the nobility of the past moment.*] You all start on down . . . Travis child, don't go empty-handed . . . Ruth, where did I put that box with my skillets in it? I want to be in charge of it myself . . . I'm going to make us the biggest dinner we ever ate tonight . . . Beneatha, what's the matter with them stockings? Pull them things up, girl . . . [*The family starts to file out as two moving men appear and begin to carry out the heavier pieces of furniture, bumping into the family as they move about.*]

BENEATHA: Mama, Asagai—asked me to marry him today and go to Africa—

MAMA [*in the middle of her getting-ready activity*]: He did? You ain't old enough to marry nobody—[*Seeing the moving men lifting one of her chairs precariously.*] Darling, that ain't no bale of cotton, please handle it so we can sit in it again. I had that chair twenty-five years . . . [*The movers sigh with exasperation and go on with their work.*]

BENEATHA [*girlishly and unreasonably trying to pursue the conversation*]: To go to Africa, Mama—be a doctor in Africa . . .

MAMA [*distracted*]: Yes, baby—

WALTER: Africa! What he want to go to Africa for?

BENEATHA: To practice there . . . .

WALTER: Girl, if you don't get all them silly ideas out your head! You better marry yourself a man with some loot . . .

BENEATHA [*angrily, precisely as in the first scene of the play*]: What have you go to do with who I marry!

WALTER: Plenty. Now I think George Murchison—[*He and BENEATHA go out yelling at each other vigorously; BENEATHA is heard saying that she would not marry GEORGE MURCHISON if he were Adam and she were Eve, etc. The anger is loud and real till their voices diminish. RUTH stands at the door and turns to MAMA and smiles knowingly.*]

MAMA [*fixing her hat at last*]: Yeah—they something all right, my children . . .

RUTH: Yeah—they're something. Let's go, Lena.

MAMA [*stalling, starting to look around at the house*]: Yes—I'm coming. Ruth—

RUTH: Yes?

MAMA [*quietly, woman to woman*]: He finally come into his manhood today, didn't he? Kind of like a rainbow after the rain . . .

RUTH [*biting her lip lest her own pride explode in front of MAMA*]: Yes, Lena. [*WALTER's voice calls for them raucously.*]

MAMA [*waving RUTH out vaguely*]: All right, honey—go on down. I be down directly. [*RUTH hesitates, then exits. MAMA stands, at last alone in the living room, her plant on the table before her as the lights start to come down. She looks around at all the walls and ceilings and suddenly, despite herself, while the children call below, a great heaving thing rises in her and she puts her fist to her mouth, takes a final desperate look, pulls her coat about her, pats her hat and goes out. The lights dim down. The door opens and she comes back in, grabs her plant, and goes out for the last time.*]

CURTAIN

➤ QUESTIONS FOR READING AND WRITING

1. The title of the play is taken from a line in Langston Hughes's poem "A Dream Deferred" (page 88). Do you think *A Raisin in the Sun* is an appropriate title? Explain.
2. How are sunlight and Mama's plant used as symbols in this play? How do these objects also serve to set the mood?
3. The main characters all have different plans for the insurance money. What do you think of the process the Younger's follow in making the decision? Do you think the decision might have been made differently?
4. Does the Younger family share a common heritage with Asagai? Explain your answer with examples from the play.
5. What purpose do the scenes between George and Beneatha serve? Compare their different ideas about education, race, heritage, and the future.
6. Do you think it is necessary for Mama to entrust Walter with all the money? Why doesn't she split the money, giving Beneatha her share?
7. Do you agree with Walter's decision at the end of the play? What does he gain? What would be gained or lost by selling to Lindner? What kind of life do you expect the Youngers to find in Clybourne Park?
8. Ruth is very eager for the family to move into a house. Have you ever lived somewhere that you didn't consider a home? How does that affect a person—or a family—psychologically?
9. To what extent are the family's problems a question of bad luck, bad timing, or forces beyond their control? Provide examples.

LORRAINE HANSBERRY

Knowing about the author's life or intentions is not a prerequisite for understanding and appreciating a work of literature. Good literature stands on its own and appeals to us through its own merit. Of greatest importance, for our purposes, is your reading and interpretation of these texts. But discovering and exploring connections between an author's background and the literature may enrich and expand your response.

Our focus in this casebook is on playwright Lorraine Hansberry. Her story is both inspiring and tragically sad. By the time she was twenty-nine years old *A Raisin in the Sun* was an award-winning play on Broadway, and this brilliant young playwright seemed to have a remarkable future in front of her. Before she was thirty-five years old, however, she was dead from cancer.

The passages that follow contain the comments of both Lorraine Hansberry and others about her life and work. Many of her own comments, taken largely from interviews and public presentations, were organized and reprinted by her husband in a production and publication called *To Be Young, Gifted, and Black* (*YGB*). The rest of her comments are taken from speeches and television interviews with Mike Wallace and Studs Terkel shortly after the Broadway debut of *A Raisin in the Sun.* The commentary of others includes a biographical tribute by friend and fellow writer James Baldwin, and critical and biographical commentary about the play by Julius Lester, Anne Cheney, Steven R. Carter, and Margaret B. Wilkerson. The casebook concludes with a 1999 article by Michael Anderson that celebrates the fortieth anniversary of the play's opening.

How has Lorraine Hansberry's background, her artistic philosophy, and the influence of other writers affected her writing of *A Raisin in the Sun?* Does the play seem to fulfill her own artistic requirements? Do the characters have within them the "elements of profundity, of profound anguish"? Does the play seem to "tell the truth about people"? How do her own comments about herself compare with what others say? Is there anything in her background, for example, that may account for what Steven R. Carter in his comments calls her "artistic misstep"?

In Her Own Words

On Growing Up "I was born May 19, 1930, the last of four children. Of love and my parents there is little to be written: their relationship to their children was utilitarian. We were fed and housed and dressed and outfitted with more cash than our associates and that was all. We were also vaguely taught certain vague absolutes: that we were better than no one but infinitely superior to everyone; that we were products of the proudest and most mistreated of the races of man; that there was nothing enormously difficult about life; that one succeeded as a matter of course."

"Life was not a struggle—it was something that one *did*. One won an argument because, if facts gave out, one invented them—with color! The only sinful people in the world were dull people. And above all, there were two things which were never to be betrayed: the family and the race. But of love, there was nothing ever said." (*YGB*, p. 17–18)

"Seven years separated the nearest of my brothers and sisters and myself; I wear, I am sure, the earmarks of that familial station to this day. Little has been written or thought to my knowledge about children who occupy that place: the last born separated by an uncommon length of time from the next youngest. I suspect we are probably a race apart." (*YGB*, p. 18)

"I was given, during my grade school years, one-half the amount of education prescribed by the Board of Education of my city. This was so because the children of the Chicago ghetto were jammed into a segregated school system. I am a product of that system and one result is that—to this day—I cannot count properly. I do not add, subtract, or multiply with ease. Our teachers, devoted and indifferent alike, had to sacrifice something to make the system work at all—and in my case it was arithmetic that got put aside most often. Thus, the mind which was able to grasp university-level reading materials in the sixth and seventh grades had not been sufficiently exposed to elementary arithmetic to make even simple change in a grocery store."

"This is what is meant when we speak of the scars, the marks that the ghettoized child carries through life. To be imprisoned in the ghetto is to be forgotten—or deliberately cheated of one's birthright—at best." (*YGB*, p. 36)

"But we are all shaped, are we not, by that particular rim of the soup bowl where we swim, and I have remained throughout the balance of my life a creature formed in a community atmosphere where I was known as a "rich" girl."

"In any case, my mother sent me to kindergarten in white fur in the middle of the depression; the kids beat me up; and I think it was from that moment I became—a rebel . . ." (*YGB*, p. 36)

"Above all, there had been an aspect of the society of the kids from the ghetto which demanded utmost respect: they fought. The girls as well as the boys. THEY FOUGHT. If you were not right with them, or sometimes even if you were, there they were of an afternoon after school, standing waiting for you in the sunshine; a little gang of them in their gym shoes, milling close together, blocking off the sidewalk, daring you to break for it and try to run to the other side of the street where, if luck prevailed, one might gain the protection of some chance passing adult. That, ultimately, was the worst thing of all to do because they always got you after that. *Always.* It was better to continue on right in their midst, feigning the courage or at least nonchalance." (*YGB*, p. 38)

"[My father] was the sort of a man who put a great deal of his money, a great deal of his extraordinary talents, and a great deal of passion into everything that we say is the American way of going after gold. He moved his family into a restricted area where no Negroes were supposed to live and proceeded to fight the case in the courts, all the way to the Supreme Court of the United States. This cost a great deal of money and involved the assistance of the NAACP attorneys and so on. It is the way of struggling that everyone says is the proper way. And it individually resulted in a decision against restrictive covenance, which is a famous case known as Hansberry vs. Lee." (From a speech at Town Hall, New York City, 1964)

On Her Motivation To Become a Playwright "My high school yearbook bears the dedication: "Englewood High trains for citizenship in a world of many different peoples. Who could better appreciate this wonderful country than our forefathers who traveled hundreds of miles from every known nation, seeking a land of freedom from discrimination of race, color, or creed." And in illustration, there is this:

> *The Great Branches of Man at Englewood High:* in front, Mangolia Ali of East Indian Mohammedan descent; second couple, Nancy Diagre and Harold Bradley, Negroid; middle couple, Rosalind Sherr and William Krugman, Jewish religion, not a racial stock; next, Eleanor Trester and Theodore Flood, Caucasoid; extreme right, Lois Lee and Barbara Nomura, Mongoloid; rear, left, Mr. Thompson, principal.

I was reminded of Englewood by a questionnaire which came from *Show* magazine the other day . . .

THE SHAKESPEAREAN EXPERIENCE
SHOW POLL #5, February 1964

Some Questions Answered by: Robert Bolt, Jean Cocteau, T. S. Eliot, Tyrone Guthrie, Lorraine Hansberry, Joan Littlewood, Harold Pinter, Alain Robbe-Grillet, Igor Stravinsky, Harry S. Truman

QUESTION: *What was your first contact with Shakespeare?*

High school English literature classwork. We had to read and memorize speeches from *Macbeth* and *Julius Caesar* all under the auspices of a strange and bewigged teacher who we, after this induction, naturally and cruelly christened "Pale Hecate"—God rest her gentle, enraptured and igniting soul!

Pale Hecate enters, ruler in hand, and takes her place in the classroom. She surveys the class. They come to attention as her eye falls on each in turn.

PALE HECATE: Y'do not read, nor speak, nor write the English language! I suspect that y'do not even *think* in it! God only knows in what language y'do think, or if you think at all. 'Tis true that the *English* have done little enough with the tongue, but being the English I expect it was the best they could do. [*They giggle.*] In any case, I'll have it learned properly beMiss—as for you, indeed, surely you will recognize the third letter of the alphabet when y'have seen it?

STUDENT: C.

PALE HECATE: Aye, a C it 'tis! You're a bright and clever one now after all, aren't y'lass? [*The class snickers.*] And now, my brilliance, would you also be informing us as to what a grade signifies when it is thus put upon the page?

STUDENT: Average.

PALE HECATE: "Average." Yes, yes—and what else in your case, my iridescence? Well the, I'll be tellin' you in fine order. It stands for "cheat," my luminous one! [*The class sobers.*] For them that will do *half* when *all* is called for; for them that will slip and slide through life at the edge of their minds, never once pushing into the interior to see what wonders are hiding there—content to drift along on whatever gets them by, *cheating* themselves, *cheating* the world, *cheating* Nature! That is what the C means, my dear child—[*She smiles.*]—my pet [*they giggle; in rapid order she raps each on the head with her ruler.*]—my laziest *Queen of the Ethiopes!*

She exits or dims out.

QUESTION: *Which is your favorite Shakespeare play and why?*

"Favorite? It is like choosing the "superiority" of autumn days; mingling titles permits a reply: *Othello* and *Hamlet.* Why? There is a sweetness in the former that lingers long after the tragedy is done. A kind of possibility that we suspect in man wherein even its flaw is a tribute. The latter because there remains a depth in the prince that, as we all know, constantly reengages as we mature. And it does seem that the wit remains the brightest and most instructive in all dramatic literature."

QUESTION: *What is the most important result of your familiarity with Shakespeare? What has he given you?*

"Comfort and agitation so bound together that they are inseparable. Man, as set down in the plays, is large. Enormous. Capable of anything at all. And yet fragile, too, this view of the human spirit; one feels it ought be respected and protected and loved rather fiercely.

Rollicking times, Shakespeare has given me. I love to laugh and his humor is that of everyday; of every man's foible at no man's expense. Language. At thirteen a difficult and alien tedium, those Elizabethan cadences; but soon a balm, a thrilling source of contact with life." (*YGB*, pp. 43–44)

(At seventeen years old, sitting in on a rehearsal of Sean O'Casey's *Juno and the Paycock*)"I remember rather clearly that my coming had been an accident. Also that I sat in the orchestra close to the stage: the orchestra of the great modern building which is the main theater plant of the University of Wisconsin. The woman's voice, the howl, the shriek of misery fitted to a wail of poetry that consumed all my senses and all my awareness of human pain, endurance and the futility of it— "Now Mrs. Madigan reappeared with her compassionate shawl and the wail rose and hummed through the tenement, through Dublin, through Ireland itself and then mingled with seas and became something born of the Irish wail that was all of us. I remember sitting there stunned with a melody that I thought might have been sung in a different meter. The play was *Juno,* the writer Sean O'Casey—but the melody was one that I had known for a very long while."

"I was seventeen and I did not think then of *writing* the melody as *I* knew it—in a different key; but I believe it entered my consciousness and stayed there . . ." (*YGB*, p. 65)

"I love Sean O'Casey. This, to me, is the playwright of the twentieth century accepting and using the most obvious instruments of Shakespeare, which is the human personality in its totality. O'Casey never fools you about the Irish, you see . . . the Irish drunkard, the Irish braggart, the Irish liar . . . and the genuine heroism which must naturally emerge when you tell the truth about people. This, to me, is the height of artistic perception and is the most rewarding kind of thing that can happen in drama, because when you believe people so completely—because *everybody* has their drunkards and their braggarts and their cowards, you know—then you also believe them in their moments of heroic assertion; you don't doubt them." (*YGB*, p. 69)

"I happen to believe that the most ordinary human being . . . has within him elements of profundity, of profound anguish. You don't have to go to the kings and queens of the earth—I think the Greeks and the Elizabethans did this because it was a logical concept—but every human being is in enormous conflict about something, even if it's how to get to work in the morning and all that . . ." (Studs Terkel interview, 1959)

"I'm particularly attracted to a medium where not only do you get to do what we do in life every day—you know, talk to people—but to be very selective about the nature of the conversation. It's an opportunity to treat character in the most absolute relief, one against the other, so that everything, sympathy and conflict, is played so sharply, you know—even a little more than a novel. And I suppose it's my own private sense of drama that makes *that* appeal to me." (Studs Terkel interview, 1959)

"There's no contradiction between protest art and good art. That's an artificial argument. You either write a good play or bad play. It doesn't have too much to do with what it is about. People say that this or that minority group is so preoccupied with their problem that it diminishes their art. I've always been very pleased, and my husband also, to note that for the last two hundred years the only writers in the English language we've had to boast about are the Irish writers—who reflect an oppressed culture." (Mike Wallace interview, 1959)

***On* A Raisin in the Sun** "Months before I had turned the last page out of the typewriter and pressed all the sheets neatly together in a pile, and gone and stretched out face down on the living room floor. I had finished a play; a play I had no reason to think or not think would ever be done; a play that I was sure no one would quite understand . . ."

"I cannot any longer remember if I liked it or not. I have said to some that it was not my 'kind' of play; and yet it moved me to read it sometimes—and once I wept at a performance."

"I have been tongue-tied and glib and fatuous trying to answer questions which must always seem strange to a writer: 'Why did you write it?' and 'How did it come to be?'"

"The truly relevant and revealing answers are always too diffuse, too vague in time and place and specific meaning to quite try and share with people. I know—but how can I tell it." (*YGB*, p. 104)

Hotel Taft
New Haven, Conn.
January 19, 1959

Dear Mother:

Well—here we are. I am sitting alone in a nice hotel room in New Haven, Conn. Downstairs, next door in the Shubert Theatre, technicians are putting the finishing touches on a living room that is supposed to be a Chicago living room. Wednesday the curtain goes up at 8 P.M. The next day the New Haven papers will say what they think of our efforts. A great deal of money has been spent and a lot of people have done some hard, hard work, and it may be the beginning of many different careers.

The actors are very good and the director is a very talented man—so if it is a poor show I won't be able to blame a soul but your youngest daughter.

Mama, it is a play that tells the truth about people, Negroes and life and I think it will help a lot of people to understand how we are just as complicated as they are—and just as mixed up—but above all, that we have among our miserable and downtrodden ranks—people who are the very essence of human dignity. That is what, after all the laughter and tears, the play is supposed to say. I hope it will make you very proud. See you soon. Love to all. (*YGB*, p. 91)

> QUESTION:*Is there a character in the play who represents Lorraine Hansberry?*

"The college student—Beneatha. I had a great deal of fun with this character. First of all I knew if the play ever got to Broadway, she would be the kind of character that people had never seen before—a Negro girl with actual pretensions of any sort—it's just unknown to theater and I also had a great deal of fun making fun of her a little bit because it's a pleasure to sit back eight years later and see yourself as you think you were. What she reflects symbolically is a very legitimate and active sentiment among American Negro intellectuals and among much larger sections of Negro life, that repudiates much of what has come to us through cultural experience and historical experience that we think is not necessarily as valid as we have been told that it is. And since the 1930s there has been quite a movement that feels that what we want now is a recognition of the beauty of things African and the beauty of things black, and this girl represents part of this development—as I do, I think." (Mike Wallace interview, 1959)

On Walter Lee's comment: "We're all tied up in a race of people who don't know how to do nothing but moan, pray and have babies."

"He's an individual. He's one character in a play—representative of a good many people. This is inner group bitterness. When one can't speak against anyone else, one indicts one's own. It's very common. People have done this always. And he means this to hurt. It's a line that's directed toward his wife in the play. It's a way of turning the attack within for his own personal reasons. I think if you had a conversation with Walter Lee Younger, he'd have other things to tell you. But in that moment, he is trying to hurt her." (Mike Wallace interview, 1959)

On what people of any race can learn from this play:

"I have a suspicion of the universal humanity of all people. I think it is possible to reach it. And I think in the moment when they are sitting in the theater and they murmur in favor of the family and they applaud a particular action, I believe that almost every human being there genuinely wishes it to happen. To what extent that any member of the audience comes out of the theater at any time and retains the emotion of a moment within the theater I certainly couldn't begin to guess. In a much larger way, it may have affirmative effects." (Mike Wallace interview, 1959)

On the affirmative ending of the play:

"For me this is one of the most affirmative periods in history. I'm very pleased that those peoples in the world that I feel closest to, the colonial peoples, the African peoples, the Asian peoples, are in an insurgent mood. They are in the process of transforming the world, and I think for the better. I can't quite understand pessimism at this moment. Unless, of course, one is wedded to things that are dying out like colonialism, like racism. Walter Lee Younger and his family are necessarily tied to this international movement, whether they have consciousness of it or not, they belong to an affirmative movement in history. Anything that he does that is the least positive has implications that embrace all of us. I feel that his moving into the new house, his decision, is in a way a reply to those who say all guilt is equal, all questions lack clarity that it's hard to know what you should fight for or against, that there are things to do—that the new house has many shapes, and we must make some decisions in this country as this man does." (Mike Wallace interview, 1959)

On Mama:

"This is a very strong woman. This is a woman who keeps her authority in any way that she has to, emotionally, physically, however. I think she's a great woman. But she can be wrong—terribly wrong." (Mike Wallace interview, 1959)

On what Joseph Asagai represents in this play:

"He represents two things: he represents, first of all, the true intellectual. This is a young man who is so absolutely confident in his understanding and his perception about the world that he has no need of any of the façade of pseudo intellectuality—for any of the pretenses and the nonsense. He can already kid about all the features of intense nationalism because he's been there and he understands beyond that point. He's already concerned about the human race on a new level. He's a true, genuine intellectual. So that he doesn't have time or interest except for amusement in useless passion, in useless promenading of ideas. That's partially what he represents. The other thing that he represents is much more overt. I was aware that on a Broadway stage they have never seen an African who didn't have his shoes hanging around his neck and a bone through his nose or his ears or something. And I thought that even just theatrically speaking this would most certainly be refreshing, and what this fellow represents in the play is the emergence of an articulate and deeply conscious colonial intelligentsia in the world." (Studs Terkel interview, 1959)

In Others' Words

James Baldwin

Sweet Lorraine [1969]

That's the way I always felt about her, and so I won't apologize for calling her that now. *She* understood it: in that far too brief a time when we walked and talked and laughed and drank together, sometimes in the streets and bars and restaurants of the Village, sometimes at her house, sometimes at my house, sometimes gracelessly fleeing the houses of others; and sometimes seeming, for anyone who didn't know us, to be having a knockdown, drag-out battle. We spent a lot of time arguing about history and tremendously related subjects in her Bleecker Street and, later Waverly Place flat. And often, just when I was certain that she was about to throw me out, as being altogether too rowdy a type, she would stand up, her hands on her hips (for these down-home sessions she always wore slacks) and pick up my empty glass as though she intended to throw it at me. Then she would walk into the kitchen, saying, with a haughty toss of her head, "Really, Jimmy. You ain't *right*, child!" With which stern put down, she would hand me another drink and launch into a brilliant analysis of just why I wasn't "right." I would often stagger down her stairs as the sun came up, usually in the middle of a paragraph and always in the middle of a laugh. That marvelous laugh. That marvelous face. I loved her, she was my sister and my comrade. Her going did not so much make me lonely as make me realize how lonely we were. We had that respect for each other which perhaps is only felt by people on the same side of the barricades, listening to the accumulating thunder of the hooves of horses and the threads of tanks.

The first time I ever saw Lorraine was at the Actors' Studio, in the winter of '57–58. She was there as an observer of the Workshop Production of *Giovanni's Room.*[1] She was way up in the bleachers, taking on some of the biggest names in the American theater because she had liked the play and they, in the main, hadn't. I was enormously grateful to her, she seemed to speak for me; and afterwards she talked to me with a gentleness and generosity never to be forgotten. A small, shy, determined

[1] **Giovanni's Room** a novel by James Baldwin published in 1956

person, with that strength dictated by absolutely impersonal ambition: she was not trying to "make it"—she was trying to keep the faith.

We really met, however, in Philadelphia, in 1959, when *A Raisin in the Sun* was at the beginning of its amazing career. Much has been written about this play; I personally feel that it will demand a far less guilty and constricted people than the present-day Americans to be able to assess it at all; as an historical achievement, anyway, no one can gainsay its importance. What is relevant here is that I had never in my life seen so many black people in the theater. And the reason was that never before, in the entire history of the American theater, had so much of the truth of black people's lives been seen on the stage. Black people ignored the theater because the theater had always ignored them.

But, in *Raisin,* black people recognized that house and all the people in it—the mother, the son, the daughter, and the daughter-in-law, and supplied the play with an interpretative element which could not be present in the minds of white people: a kind of claustrophobic terror, created not only by their knowledge of the house but by their knowledge of the streets. And when the curtain came down, Lorraine and I found ourselves in the backstage alley, where she was immediately mobbed. I produced a pen and Lorraine handed me her handbag and began signing autographs. "It only happens once," she said. I stood there and watched. I watched the people, who loved Lorraine for what she had brought to them; and watched Lorraine, who loved the people for what they brought to *her.* It was not, for her, a matter of being admired. She was being corroborated and confirmed. She was wise enough and honest enough to recognize that black American artists are a very special case. One is not merely an artist and one is not judged merely as an artist: the black people crowding around Lorraine, whether or not they considered her an artist, assuredly considered her a witness. This country's concept of art and artists has the effect, scarcely worth mentioning by now, of isolating the artist from the people. One can see the effect of this in the irrelevance of so much of the work produced by celebrated white artists; but the effect of this isolation on a black artist is absolutely fatal. He *is,* already, as a black American citizen, isolated from most of his white countrymen. At the crucial hour, he can hardly look to his artistic peers for help, for they do not know enough about him to be able to correct him. To continue to grow, to remain in touch with himself, he needs the support of that community from which, however, all of the pressures of American life incessantly conspire to remove him. And when he is effectively removed, he falls silent—and the people have lost another hope.

5 Much of the strain under which Lorraine worked was produced by her knowledge of this reality, and her determined refusal to be destroyed by it. She was a very young woman, with an overpowering vision, and fame had come to her early—she must certainly have wished, often enough, that fame had seen fit to drag its feet a little. For fame and recognition are not synonymous, especially not here, and her fame was to cause her to be criticized very harshly, very loudly, and very often by both black and white people who were unable to believe, apparently, that a really serious intention could be contained in so glamorous a frame. She took it all with a kind of astringent good humor, refusing, for example, even to consider defending herself when she was being accused of being a "slum-lord" because of her family's real-estate holdings in Chicago. I called her during that

time, and all she said—with a wry laugh—was, "My God, Jimmy, do you realize you're only the second person who's called me today? And you know how my phone kept ringing *before!*" She was not surprised. She was devoted to the human race, but she was not romantic about it.

JULIUS LESTER

THE HEROIC DIMENSION IN A RAISIN IN THE SUN [1972]

A Raisin in the Sun is no intellectual abstraction about upward mobility and conspicuous consumption. It goes right to the core of practically every black family in the ghettos of Chicago, New York, Los Angeles, and elsewhere. Whether they have a picture of Jesus, Martin Luther King, or Malcolm X on the lead-painted walls of their rat-infested tenement, all of them want to get the hell out of there as quickly as they can. Maybe black militants don't know it, or don't want to admit it, but Malcolm X made a down payment on a house in a suburban community a few weeks before he was murdered. And one surely can't accuse Malcolm of bourgeois aspirations. He merely wanted what every black wants—a home of his own adequate to his needs, at a minimum, and the fulfillment of his desires, at the most. . . . *A Raisin in the Sun* is most definitely about "human dignity" because Lorraine Hansberry is concerned with the attitude we must have toward material things if we are to be their master and not their slave. Is that attitude to be Mama's? Or is it to be Walter's? And, for blacks, locked out from these things for so long, the question is a crucial one. As blacks acquire more and more of America's material offerings, are they, too, going to be transformed by their acquisitions into mindless consumers like the majority of whites? Or are they going to continue to walk in the path of righteousness like their forebears? Lorraine Hansberry summarized it well when, in a letter, she wrote of the play:

> . . . we cannot . . . very well succumb to monetary values and know the survival of certain interior aspects of man which . . . must remain if we are to loom larger than other creatures on this planet. . . . Our people fight daily and magnificently for a more comfortable material base for their lives; they desperately need and hourly sacrifice for clean homes, decent food, personal and group dignity and the abolition of terroristic violence as their children's heritage. So, in that sense, I am certainly a materialist in the first order.
>
> However, the distortion of this aspiration surrounds us in the form of an almost maniacal lusting for "acquisitions." It seems to have absorbed the national mentality and Negroes, to be sure, have certainly been affected by it. The young man in the play, Walter Lee, is meant to symbolize their number. Consequently, in the beginning, he dreams not so much of being comfortable and imparting the most meaningful gifts to his son (education in depth, humanist values, a worship of dignity) but merely of being what it seems to him the "success" portion of humankind is—"rich." Toward

> this end he is willing to make an old trade; urgently willing. On the fact that some aspect of his society has brought him to this point, the core of the drama hangs.

Walter blames himself, his wife, and his mother for what he sees as his personal failure. And only at the end of the play does it become possible for him to realize that there is a puppeteer manipulating him, a puppeteer who brought him dangerously close to destroying his family and himself.

5 The climax of the play comes after Walter's deal to get a liquor license falls through. Mama Younger has made a $3,500 down payment on a house and gives the remaining money to Walter to do with as he wishes after he deposits $2,500 in a savings account for Beneatha's education. Walter, however, takes the entire $6,500 and gives it to one of his two future "partners." One of the "partners" absconds with the money. A Mr. Lindner, a white man from the neighborhood into which they are to move, comes and offers to buy the house from them for more than they would eventually pay. The whites in the neighborhood do not want a black family moving in. Previously, Walter had scornfully turned the man down. However, when he learns that his money has been stolen, he calls Mr. Lindner on the phone and tells him that they will sell the house. Mr. Lindner comes over and Walter finds that he is unable to go through with it. There is something in him—a little bit of self-respect is still left; he tells Mr. Lindner that they are going to move in. And with Walter making his first step toward being a man, a *black* man, the play ends.

Few see the heroism in Walter's simple act of assertion. Indeed, how many who have seen the play or the movie have not thought that Walter was a fool for *not* accepting the money? How one views Walter's act is a direct reflection of how much one accepts the American dream. And there is the significance of the fact that the play ends with the Youngers moving into a "white" neighborhood. To see this as a confirmation of the American dream is to accept the myth that blacks have wanted nothing more than to be integrated with whites. In actuality, the fact that the neighborhood is white is the least important thing about it. It merely happened to be the neighborhood in which Mama Younger could find a nice house she could afford. And it is this simple, practical element which has always been mistaken by whites as a desire on the part of blacks to be "integrated." But why, the question could be raised, would the Youngers persist in moving into a neighborhood where they are not wanted, where they may be subjected to harassment or even physical violence? They persist, as all blacks persist, not because it is any great honor to live among whites, but because one cannot consider himself a human being as long as he acquiesces to restrictions placed upon him by others, particularly if those restrictions are based solely on race or religion. If Walter had accepted the money, he would have been saying, in graphic language, You are right, we are niggers and don't have the right to live where we can afford to. But, with that earthy eloquence of a black still close to his roots, Walter says, "We have decided to move into our house because my father—my father—he earned it." And, in that realization, Walter learns also that it was not a black woman who castrated him. It was America and his own acceptance of America's values. No woman can make him a man. He has to do it himself.

He is a hero, a twentieth-century hero. We still long, of course, for the heroes who seemed to ride history as if it were a bronco and they were champion rodeo riders. But those heroes—if they were ever real—come from a time when life, perhaps, was somewhat less complex. But the problems that face man in the latter twentieth century are large, larger than any one of us, and the sword of a knight in armor is laughable to the dragons roaming our countryside. Our heroes are more difficult to recognize only because they appear so small beside the overwhelming enemies they must slay. But because they appear small does not mean that they are, and it does not make their acts less heroic. Walter Lee Younger has his contemporary historic counterpart in the person of a mall, quiet black woman named Roas Parks who refused to get out of a seat on a bus in Montgomery, Alabama. It would have been so easy for her to have relinquished her seat to a white person that day—as it would have been easy for Walter to have taken the money. But something in her, as in him, said No. And in that quiet dissent, both of them said Yes to human dignity. They said No to those who would define them and thereby deny their existence, and by saying No, they began to define themselves. There have been many Rosa Parks, but few of them have mysteriously set in motion a whole movement for social change. Walter Lee Younger is one of those whose act probably set nothing in motion. And that only increases its heroic dimension. In an article in *The Village Voice,* which compared Walter to Willy Loman, Lorraine Hansberry described the hero she saw in Walter Younger.

> For if there are no waving flags and marching songs at the barricades as Walter marches out with his little battalion, it is not because the battle lacks nobility. On the contrary, he has picked up in his way, still imperfect and wobbly in his small view of human destiny, what I believe Arthur Miller once called "the golden thread of history." He becomes, in spite of those who are too intrigued with despair and hatred of man to see it, King Oedipus refusing to tear out his eyes, but attacking the Oracle instead. He is that last Jewish patriot manning his rifle in the burning ghetto at Warsaw; he is that young girl who swam into sharks to save a friend a few weeks ago; he is Anne Frank, still believing in people; he is the nine small heroes of Little Rock; he is Michelangelo creating David, and Beethoven bursting forth with the Ninth Symphony. He is all those things because he has finally reached out in his tiny moment and caught that sweet essence which is human dignity, and it shines like the old star-touched dream that is in his eyes.

ANNE CHENEY

THE AFRICAN HERITAGE IN A RAISIN IN THE SUN [1984]

A moving testament to the strength and endurance of the human spirit, *A Raisin in the Sun* is a quiet celebration of the black family, the importance of African roots, the equality of women, the vulnerability of marriage, the true value of money, the survival of the individual, and the nature of man's dreams. A well-made play, *Raisin* at first seems a plea for racial tolerance or a fable of man's overcoming an insensitive society, but the simple eloquence of the characters elevates the play into a universal representation of all people's hopes, fears, and dreams.

On January 19, 1959, a timid Lorraine Hansberry wrote her mother about *Raisin:* "Mama, it is a play that tells the truth about people, Negroes and life and I think it will help a lot of people to understand how we are just as complicated as they are . . . people who are the very essence of human dignity. . . . I hope it will make you very proud." Indeed, *A Raisin in the Sun* made not only Nannie Perry Hansberry proud but also artists—both black and white. *Raisin* was the first play by a black writer ever to win the prestigious New York Drama Critics' Circle Award. The play would become "an American classic, published and produced in some thirty languages abroad and in thousands of productions across the country. . . . James Baldwin [said]: "Never before in the entire history of the American theatre had so much of the truth of Black people's lives been seen on the stage." Despite the earlier contributions of Langston Hughes, David Littlejohn wrote, "It would not be unfair in dating the emergence of a serious and mature Negro theatre in America from 1959, the date of Lorraine Hansberry's *A Raisin in the Sun. . . .*"

Today some black critics feel that *A Raisin in the Sun* is a play whose time has passed—a simplistic, halting treatment of race relations. Some are confused by Hansberry's professed nationalism, when she seems to favor integration. Harold Cruse even calls *Raisin* a "cleverly written piece of glorified soap opera." Hansberry used the traditional form of the well-made play in *Raisin,* especially observing the unities of action, place, and time. The action of the play is carefully delineated: act 1 serves as the beginning, act 2 as the middle, and act 3 as the tightly knit end. Furthermore, all action is carefully and causally related. Hansberry strictly abides by the unity of place: all action transpires in one room of the Youngers' South Side Chicago apartment. Stretching the unity of time from one day to one month (not unusual for a modern dramatist), Hansberry still maintains unity of impression with the central emotional concerns of the Younger family: Walter's search for a dream, Lena's faith in God and the family, Beneatha's hope for a new world.

Hansberry needed this rather traditional form to control the innovative ideas and themes of *Raisin.* Far from being a stereotyped or romanticized treatment of black life, the play embodies ideas that have been uncommon on the Broadway stage in any period. Resurrecting the ideas of the Harlem renaissance and anticipating the new thinking of the 1960s, Hansberry examines the importance of African roots, traditional versus innovative women, the nature of marriage, the real meaning of money, the search for human dignity. Most significantly, she addresses the sensitive question of to what extent people, in liberating themselves from the burdens of discrimination, should aspire to a white middle-class way of life.

5 During her *Freedom* years, Lorraine Hansberry continued to study African history with encouragement from Paul Robeson, W.E.B. Du Bois, and Louis Burnham. "She had spent hours of her younger years poring over maps of the African continent. . . . She was at one, texture, blood . . . with the sound of a mighty

Congo drum." She imaginatively knew the lions, drumbeats, quiet sandy nights, respected the antiquity of Ethiopia founded in 1000 B.C. Stirred by Kenya and Ghana wresting control from Europe and England, Hansberry inevitably incorporated her knowledge of Africa in her first play. More than earlier playwrights, Hansberry made Africa a serious, yet natural, issue on Broadway.

In *Raisin* even George Murchison, Beneatha's beau, has an awareness of his African past. In the fever of Walter Lee's and Beneatha's mock African dance in act 2, George remarks sarcastically: "In one second we will hear all about the great Ashanti empires; the great Songhay civilizations; and the great sculpture of Benin—and then some poetry in the Bantu." George had probably learned in a college atmosphere that the Songhai empire was a powerful western African kingdom, which garnered wealth from its export of ivory and gold between 850 and 1500 A.D. (Mali and Ghana—not to be confused with the modern state of Ghana—were equally old and powerful empires.) Along the coast of Nigeria, Benin was another expansive empire, noted for its bronze and gold art objects, that came to power around 1500. Coming to power about 1700, Ashanti was still another western kingdom famous for its heroic warriors.

In the stage direction, Hansberry writes that Lena has "the noble bearing of the women of the Hereros of Southwest Africa," who were essentially a pastoral people. Thus Hansberry identifies Lena as an "earth mother," one who nurtures both her family and her plant as well as she can. But Lena reveals her total ignorance of African history by a parroting of Beneatha's earlier remarks in her politely naïve, unwittingly humorous speech to Joseph Asagai, the young Nigerian visitor: "I think it's so sad the way our American Negroes don't know nothing about Africa 'cept Tarzan and all that. And all that money they pour into these churches when they ought to be helping you people over there drive out them French and Englishmen done taken away your Land."

Most of the African material in *A Raisin in the Sun,* however, surfaces in conversations between Beneatha and Joseph Asagai. Touched by Beneatha's beauty and idealism, Asagai lovingly nicknames her Alaiyo—a Yoruban word for "One for Whom Bread—Food—Is Not Enough." In act 3, after Walter Lee has been duped out of his $6,500, Asagai visits an embittered, distraught Beneatha. Speaking of his beloved Nigeria, Asagai reveals his basic philosophy of life, of Africa: "A household in preparation of a journey . . . it is another feeling. Something full of the flow of life. . . . Movement, progress. . . . It makes me think of Africa." Perhaps he sees in Beneatha a microcosmic America—one struggling to overthrow the limitations imposed on her by an alien culture.

Asagai's village in Nigeria is one where most people cannot read, where many have not even seen a book. In the village, there are mountains and stars, cool drinks from gourds at the well, old songs, people who move slowly, anciently. But Nigeria also has guns, murder, revolution, illiteracy, disease, ignorance. Asagai understands the inevitability of change and progress in Africa; he imagines for a moment the consequences should he betray the movement. "Don't you see that . . . young men and women . . . my own black countrymen . . . [may] . . . step out of the shadows some evening and slit my then useless throat?" Rebuking Beneatha for becoming discouraged over one small frustration (Walter's losing the money), Asagai views his possible death as an advance toward freedom for himself and his people. "They who might kill me even . . . actually replenish me." Asagai's beliefs certainly contribute to Beneatha's transition from brittle idealist to a more tolerant human being.

In an interview with Studs Terkel (Chicago, May 2, 1959), Lorraine Hansberry referred to Joseph Asagai as her "favorite character" in *Raisin.* He represents the "true intellectual" with no pretense, no illusions. A revolutionary and nationalist, he realizes that initially black African leaders may be as corrupt as their white predecessors (Idi Amin of Uganda bore out this theory in the 1970s). Nevertheless, he shares Hansberry's conviction that "before you can start talking about what's wrong with independence, get it." More the idealist than the practical, effective leader—compared to Kenyatta and Nkrumah—Asagai is willing to die at the hands of his countrymen for the general good and freedom. (Harold Issacs suggests that his name derives from the Zulu word *asegai,* "sawed-off spear.") On a more obvious level, Asagai certainly refutes the stage stereotype of the African with "a bone through his nose, or his ears."

In *A Raisin in the Sun,* then, Africa becomes a symbol of a proud heritage and a troublesome but hopeful future. To Hansberry's great credit, Africa is a natural, at times humorous, element in the Younger family—as Walter Lee shouts "HOT DAMN! FLAMING SPEAR," as Beneatha dresses in Nigerian robes, as Mama speaks of Tarzan, churches, and Englishmen.

STEVEN R. CARTER

HANSBERRY'S ARTISTIC MISSTEP [1994]

Unfortunately, Hansberry's vigorous, sharp, and usually intriguing characterization of Beneatha is slightly marred by her one serious artistic misstep in *A Raisin in the Sun.* This occurs when Beneatha tells Lena and Ruth about the guitar lessons she has just started and they remind her about "the horseback-riding club for which she bought that fifty-five dollar riding habit that's been hanging in the closet ever since!" On the whole, this scene portrays Beneatha's striving for self-expression with warm humor and a touch of self-mockery that almost always pleases the audiences. The problem is that only a short time earlier Walter had angrily demanded that Beneatha show more gratitude for the financial sacrifices he and Ruth have made for her, and Ruth had denied her son the fifty cents he requested for school. It is inconceivable that a woman who could refuse such a small sum to a dearly beloved son would so casually accept the squandering of a much larger contribution to a mere sister-in-law, and even if, by some miracle, she were able to accept it out of an all-embracing feminist sisterhood (which doesn't fit Ruth's overall character), she could not do so with such ease. Worse still, lightly tossing away all this money in the face of the family's dire need makes Beneatha seem monstrously selfish rather than mildly selfish as Hansberry had intended. Granted, Hansberry's main concern in the scene was the general relationship between the two older women and Beneatha, particularly their fond amusement at the younger woman's forms of self-expression, which are so different from anything they have ever done, and their vicarious delight at her ability to break free from restrictions, including that of having to weigh the cost of everything. However, on this rare occasion, by concentrating exclusively on the moment and neglecting to see its relation to previous parts of the play, Hansberry, to a small but disconcerting extent, damages the whole.

Margaret B. Wilkerson

Hansberry's Awareness of Culture and Gender [1994]

As a black writer, Hansberry was caught in a paradox of expectations. She was expected to write about that which she "knew best," the black experience, and yet that expression was doomed to be called parochial and narrow. Hansberry, however, challenged these facile categories and forced a redefinition of the term "universality," one which would include the dissonant voice of an oppressed American minority. As a young college student, she had wandered into a rehearsal of Sean O'Casey's *Juno and the Paycock.* Hearing in the wails and moans of the Irish characters a universal cry of human misery, she determined to capture that sound in the idiom of her own people—so that it could be heard by all. "One of the most sound ideas in dramatic writing," she would later conclude, "is that in order to create the universal, you must pay very great attention to the specific. Universality, I think, emerges from truthful identity of what is. . . . In other words, I think people, to the extent we accept them and believe them as who they're supposed to be, to that extent they can become everybody." Such a choice by a black writer posed an unusual challenge to the literary establishment and a divided society ill-prepared to comprehend its meaning.

"All art is ultimately social: that which agitates and that which prepares the mind for slumber," Hansberry argued, attacking another basic tenet held by traditional critics. One of the most fundamental illusions of her time and culture, she believed, is the idea that art is not and should not make a social statement. The belief in "l'art pour l'art" permeates literary and theatrical criticism, denying the integral relationship between society and art. "The writer is deceived who thinks he has some other choice. The question is not whether one will make a social statement in one's work—but only *what* the statement will say, for if it says anything at all, it will be social."

It would have been impossible for a person of her background and sensitivity to divorce herself from the momentous social and political events of the 1950s and 1960s. This period witnessed the beginning of a Cold War between the U.S. and Soviet superpowers, a rising demand by blacks for civil rights at home, and a growing intransigence by colonized peoples throughout the world. Isolation is the enemy of black writers, Hansberry believed; they are obligated to participate in the intellectual and social affairs of humankind everywhere.

This abhorrence for narrowness and parochialism led her to examine the hidden alliance between racism and sexism long before it was popular to do so, and to shape a vision cognizant of the many dimensions of colonialism and oppression. Anticipating the women's movement of the 1970s, Hansberry was already aware of the peculiar oppression under which women lived and the particular devastation visited upon women of color.

With the statement "I was born black and a female," Hansberry immediately established the basis for a tension that informed her world view. Her consciousness, of both ethnicity and gender from the very beginning, brought awareness of two key forces of conflict and oppression in the contemporary world. Because she embraced these dual truths despite their implicit competition for her attention (a competition exacerbated by external pressures), her vision was expansive enough to contain and even synthesize what to others would be contradictions. Thus, she was amused in 1955 at progressive friends who protested whenever she posed "so much as an itsy-bitsy analogy between the situation, say, of the Negro people in the U.S.—and women." She was astonished to be accused by a woman of being bitter and of thinking that men are beasts simply because she expressed the view that women are oppressed. "Must I hate 'men' any more than I hate 'white people'—because some of them are savage and others commit savage acts," she asked herself. "Of course not!" she answered vehemently.

This recognition of the tension implicit in her blackness and femaleness was the starting point for her philosophical journey from the South Side of Chicago to the world community. The following quote charts the journey and the expansion of Hansberry's consciousness, which is unconstrained by culture and gender, but which at the same time refuses to diminish the importance of either.

> I was born on the South Side of Chicago. I was born black and a female. I was born in a depression after one world war, and came into my adolescence during another. While I was still in my teens the first atom bombs were dropped on human beings at Nagasaki and Hiroshima. And by the time I was twenty-three years old, my government and that of the Soviet Union had entered actively into the worst conflict of nerves in human history—the Cold War.
>
> I have lost friends and relatives through cancer, lynching, and war. I have been personally the victim of physical attack which was the offspring of racial and political hysteria. I have worked with the handicapped and seen the ravages of congenital diseases that we have not yet conquered, because we spend our time and ingenuity in far less purposeful wars; I have known persons afflicted with drug addiction and alcoholism and mental illness. I see daily on the streets of New York, street gangs and prostitutes and beggars. I have, like all of you, on a thousand occasions seen indescribable displays of man's very real inhumanity to man, and I have come to maturity, as we all must, knowing that greed and malice and indifference to human misery and bigotry and corruption, brutality, and perhaps above all else, ignorance—the prime ancient and persistent enemy of man—abound in this world.
>
> I say all of this to say that one cannot live with sighted eyes and feeling heart and not know and react to the miseries which afflict this world.

Her "sighted eyes and feeling heart" were what enabled her to hear the wail of her own people in O'Casey's *Juno and the Paycock,* a play steeped in Irish history and tradition. And those eloquent moans sent her forth to capture that collective cry in a black idiom.

Hansberry's cognizance of being black and female formed the basis for her comprehensive world view. Just as she could accept fully the implications and responsibility of both blackness and femaleness, so was she also aware of the many other competing and equally legitimate causes which grow out of humankind's misery. The one issue that deeply concerned her but that she did not address publicly was homosexuality. The repressive atmosphere of the 1950s, coupled with the homophobia of the general society, including politically left organizations, caused her to suppress her writings that explored issues of sexuality and gender relations. Nevertheless, she pushed and teased boundaries by probing the nature of the individual within the specifics of culture, ethnicity, and gender. In the midst of her expansiveness, she refused to diminish the pain, suffering, or truths of any one group in order to benefit another, a factor which made her plays particularly rich and her characters thoroughly complex. Hence, she could write authentically about a black family in *A Raisin in the Sun* and yet produce, in the same instance, a play which appealed to both blacks and whites, bridging for a moment the historical and cultural gaps between them.

Her universalism, which redefines that much abused term, grew out of a deep, complex encounter with the specific terms of human experience as it occurs for blacks, women, whites, and many other groups of people. Her universalism was not facile, nor did it gloss over the things that divide people. She engaged those issues, worked through them to find whatever may be, *a priori,* the human commonality that lies beneath. It was as if she believed that one can understand and embrace the human family (with all its familial warfare) only to the extent that one can engage the truths (however partisan they may seem) of a social, cultural individual. "We must turn our eyes outward," she wrote, "but to do so we must also turn them inward toward our people and their complex and still transitory culture." When she turned inward, she saw not only color but gender as well—a prism of humanity.

MICHAEL ANDERSON

A RAISIN IN THE SUN: *A LANDMARK LESSON IN BEING BLACK* [1999]

They had never seen anything like it. The theater critics, hurrying down the aisles under the pressure of deadline, paused at the rear of the Ethel Barrymore Theater. The date was March 11, 1959. For a few moments they stopped considering the words with which they would salute this poetically named play, *A Raisin in the Sun.* Instead, they watched the first-night audience deliver its own verdict: on its feet and willing to applaud, it seemed, for eternity.

The cast took its curtain calls—Sidney Poitier, Claudia McNeil, Ruby Dee, Diana Sands, Lonne Elder 3d, Lou Gossett Jr., Ivan Dixon, Glynn Turman, John

Fiedler, Ed Hall, Douglas Turner—as the applause engulfed the theater. The stage manager opened and closed the curtain. The director, Lloyd Richards, joined his players, but the ovations swelled ever louder and more insistent: "Author! Author! Author!"

Finally, Mr. Poitier descended to a fourth-row aisle seat, where the twenty-eight-year-old playwright sat, thrilled rigid at the reception of her first produced play. On the arm of her leading man, Lorraine Hansberry took the stage.

"It was as if the audience that night uniquely understood that they had not just seen a play but had attended a historical event," the play's coproducer, Philip Rose, said recently, reminiscing about the opening on the eve of its fortieth anniversary this Thursday.

5 In that remarkable theatrical season of 1958–59, Broadway had seen Paul Newman and Geraldine Page open (the previous night) in Tennessee Williams's *Sweet Bird of Youth,* directed by Elia Kazan; Helen Hayes and Kim Stanley in *A Touch of the Poet* by Eugene O'Neill, directed by Harold Clurman, and Christopher Plummer and Raymond Massey in Archibald MacLeish's *J.B.,* also directed by Mr. Kazan.

But until that evening, Broadway had never seen a play written by a black woman, nor a play with a black director, nor a commercially produced drama about black life, rather than musicals or comedy. The Broadway premiere of *A Raisin in the Sun* was as much a milestone in the nation's social history as it was in American theater. "Never before," commented James Baldwin, "had so much of the truth of black people's lives been seen onstage."

Hansberry's story—about the black Younger family's decision to risk moving from their "rat-trap" on the South Side of Chicago to a three-bedroom house in an all-white neighborhood—interwove prescient observations about identity, feminism, and personal ethics. Unlike the wooden "problem plays" about blacks that preceded it, *A Raisin in the Sun* seemed steeped in human drama. The cruelties of racism—"What happens to a dream deferred/ Does it dry up/ Like a raisin in the sun?" in the words of the Langston Hughes poem that gave the play its title—are illuminated through the dynamics of conflict and love between mother and son, husband and wife, brother and sister.

Kenneth Tynan remarked in his review of *A Raisin in the Sun* in *The New Yorker* that "a play is not an entity in itself, it is a part of history." In that sense, the presence of the play on Broadway appeared to be a triumph of determined idealism for those involved. The 1960s would see productions of *The Blacks,* the drama by Jean Genet about racism, as well as works by the black playwrights LeRoi Jones (later Amiri Baraka) and Ed Bullins. Lonne Elder 3rd would go on to write the acclaimed 1969 play *Ceremonies in Dark Old Men.*

But in the 1950s, before the acclaim that greeted *A Raisin in the Sun,* "Broadway was not ready for a play about a black family," Mr. Richards, the director, said.

10 What Broadway knew about black people, Hansberry once told a reporter, involved "cardboard characters, cute dialect bits, or hip-swinging musicals from exotic scores." (And few enough of those: in the seventy-seven productions of the

1958–59 season, Actors Equity reported that the number of Broadway parts for black actors totaled twenty-four.)

The inspiration for *A Raisin in the Sun*, its author said, came after she had seen a play in 1956 that left her "disgusted with a whole body of material about Negroes." That night, she told her husband, Robert Nemiroff, "I'm going to write a social drama about Negroes that will be good art." But since devoting herself full-time to playwriting in 1955, she had accomplished little—drafts of three plays had gone nowhere beyond sympathetic readings by her husband and friends.

She expected much the same in the late summer of 1957, when she and Nemiroff invited company for a dinner of spaghetti and banana cream pie to their fourth-floor walk-up on Bleecker Street in Greenwich Village.

Then Nemiroff began to read from the work that had possessed his wife for nearly a year. This time it was different. "The feeling was one of excitement," Mr. Rose said, during an interview in his office on the Upper West Side of Manhattan. After an animated discussion that went on into the night, Mr. Rose called Hansberry early the next morning. "I told her," he said, " 'this play has to get done, and it has to get done on Broadway.' "

Mr. Rose would end up as a producer of nearly two dozen plays, including *Purlie Victorious* (1961), *The Owl and the Pussycat* (1964), and the musical *Shenandoah* (1975). But at the time, he was thirty-six years old and in the music business, producing and publishing. He said he had assumed that there would be difficulties in getting a work by a first-time playwright on the boards, but not that raising the money would take nearly fifteen agonizing months.

15 Networking among his friends brought a response "somewhere between admiration and pity," he said, along with donations of $50 toward what they regarded as a lost cause. Established theatrical backers were equally skeptical. "Much as some expressed admiration," Nemiroff wrote in his introduction to the Modern Library edition of *A Raisin in the Sun,* the play "was turned down by virtually every established name in the business."

The conventional wisdom was that "nobody was going to pay those prices to see "a bunch of Negroes emoting," Hansberry later said in a letter included in *To Be Young, Gifted and Black,* a collection of her writings. (Nemiroff assembled the book after Hansberry's death from cancer at thirty-four in 1965, during the run of her second Broadway play, *The Sign in Sidney Brustein's Window;* Nemiroff died in 1991.)

"Very often, the professionals were respectful, even admiring that I would think of trying to get the play on," said Mr. Rose, who is writing a book about the production. "However, they could not see where it would make any money."

He did have one ace: his friend Sidney Poitier. Already a movie star, the actor had agreed to join the cast after being "overwhelmed by the power of the material," as he wrote in his own memoir, *This Life.* "Without Sidney Poitier," Mr. Rose said, "the play would never have seen the light of day."

Mr. Poitier was also responsible for the director. "I had a pact with Sidney Poitier," Mr. Richards said in an interview at his home on the Upper West Side. It dated to their time as students of the director and drama teacher Paul Mann. "One day, after class, Sidney said, 'If I ever do anything on Broadway, I want you to direct it.' "

20 In December 1957, Mr. Poitier introduced Mr. Richards, already known as an actor, teacher, and director, to Mr. Rose and Hansberry. They clicked.

"There was no question that I wanted to do the play," Mr. Richards said, remembering that when he and his wife first read it, "We laughed and cried; it was a wonderful evening reading." Still, it was the work of a neophyte, and he and Hansberry struggled until opening night to develop her script. Although not autobiographical, the story originated from an incident in Hansberry's childhood.

Her parents, politically and socially prominent in Chicago's black upper-middle class, agreed in 1938 to take the lead in the fight against housing segregation by buying a home in an all-white neighborhood near the University of Chicago. Hansberry would always remember being an eight-year-old who was "spat at, cursed and pummeled in the daily trek to and from school." She also remembered the nights her mother patrolled their house with a loaded pistol against the "literally howling mobs" that surrounded their home and once threw bricks through their windows.

But the real story of the play, Mr. Rose said, was not the family's move to the unreceptive white neighborhood but Walter Lee Younger, the character portrayed by Mr. Poitier, "and his development, his being able to accept certain responsibilities." With this as the goal, playwright and director began their work.

Meanwhile, the tasks of production went on, including casting.

25 "*Raisin* was a big breakthrough," said Ruby Dee. "The mainstream was not welcoming for African-American actors." She signed on even though she would not have the ingenue role of Walter Lee's sister that she desired; Diana Sands got the part, while Claudia McNeil portrayed his mother. Instead, Ms. Dee would play his wife, Ruth. "Another one of those put-upon wives. And they always seemed to be named Ruth!" But, she added: "I dusted off my disappointment. This was very important. It was going to be a Broadway show."

It would be, that is, if the money could be raised. Throughout 1958, Mr. Rose sought big-money angels. "The smart money on Broadway was not involved and would not be involved," Mr. Richards said. The $75,000 budget (equivalent to more than $420,000 today) would eventually come from a group of 147 investors—"more than any play on Broadway had had up to that time," Mr. Richards said. Mr. Poitier's wife, Juanita, invested $4,000 and "about two or three people, including Harry Belafonte, put in $2,000 each," Mr. Rose said. But the most significant investor was the playwright William Gibson, whose *Two for the Seesaw* had opened a successful run with Anne Bancroft and Henry Fonda in January 1958.

"I sent him the play," Mr. Rose recalled. "He called me and said: 'This play must get on Broadway.' " With that endorsement (and Mr. Gibson's own stake of $750), his tax consultant, David J. Cogan, a previous Broadway investor who initially had rejected *A Raisin in the Sun*, signed on as coproducer, and the financing was complete. Rehearsals began on December 27, 1958.

There was only one problem: no theater on Broadway would agree to rent to *A Raisin in the Sun*. The same arguments were repeated: a white audience would not pay to see a nonmusical about blacks. The possibility of black theatergoers was dismissed out of hand. And if they did come, would white patrons stay away—perhaps even boycott other shows? In 1958, the Supreme Court's landmark school desegregation decision was four years old; not until February 1960 would the student sit-ins put the racial equality movement permanently before the nation's conscience. Even in the relatively urbane climate of the Village, an interracial couple like Hansberry and Nemiroff could expect stares and denial of service in some restaurants.

Mr. Rose said he was advised to terminate the production until he could obtain a theater. Instead, he took a gamble: he booked the traditional tryout theaters in New Haven and Philadelphia. "And I prayed a lot," he said. "But I knew if we didn't do it, nothing was going to get done. The hope was that we had something so spectacular, Broadway couldn't ignore us." His daring paid off. The rave reviews for the four-night engagement in New Haven were matched during the two-week run in Philadelphia.

30 *A Raisin in the Sun* ended up playing for nineteen months at the Ethel Barrymore on Broadway. Hansberry won the New York Drama Critics Circle Award for best play, and most of the original cast starred in the 1961 film version, directed by Daniel Petrie. The 1973 musical *Raisin* was adapted from the play and produced by Nemiroff. The play has been translated into thirty languages.

In retrospect, Mr. Rose can joke that during the prolonged incubation of *A Raisin in the Sun* he was discouraged "only about half the time." But his explanation for his stubborn determination is simple: "I believed in it. I loved the play."

A Student Essay

Sara Roell

Dr. Madden

English 102

December 12, 200X

Lorraine Hansberry and the Realism of <u>A Raisin in the Sun</u>

The issue of racism and the emergence of civil rights among black men and women is evident in Lorraine Hansberry's <u>A Raisin in the Sun</u>. The play, written in 1959, is an interesting and at times wrenching depiction of a black family's struggle to achieve the American dream and escape the constraints of poverty. When the play first opened, in the early years of the civil rights movement, there was a great deal of controversy surrounding it because it was written realistically. Situations such as a black family moving into an all-white neighborhood were not common before this time period; they were just beginning to emerge. But disagreement exists about the motivation and the goals Lorraine Hansberry had in mind when she wrote the play. Hansberry has been praised by many critics, but also widely criticized.

Harold Cruse questions Hansberry's intentions for writing the play. "She intended to write a Negro play because she could not make her stage debut with anything else" (270). During that time the theater was primarily white, forcing authors to direct their writing to reflect white ideas or beliefs. He calls Hansberry evasive about her intentions and thinks she visualizes the Negro world through a "quasi-white orientation." Essentially, Cruse believes that the author is not a force for the black community, but rather supports the drive for racial integration in which the Negro working class must give up its ethnicity. Racism is portrayed in this play, but whether or not it is displayed realistically is also questioned.

The fact that Hansberry grew up as a middle-class African American rather than a "Harlem Negro" (Cruse 270), led many people to criticize her writing as unrealistic not only with reference to racism, but to the experiences of the working-class black American as well.

Walter is a middle-aged, black man who works as a chauffeur and becomes obsessed with his dreams of a business venture to give him financial independence. Living in overcrowded conditions and unable to provide adequately for his family, he feels that as an independent business owner he will attain economic gains as well as heightened value as a human being. "It can be asked, if A Raisin in the Sun is oriented to reality, why does Walter willingly give up those things, i.e., independence and economic success" (Adams 109). Adams believes that this is not a black play, that the conditions of the Younger family are universal and represent many ethnic groups.

The reality of the play, however, was never a question for me. Hansberry depicted the Youngers very realistically. In the late 1950s, it would have been very unusual for a black male to escape the poverty of an urban ghetto and its resulting oppression. Uneducated and with few available resources, Walter's dream is understandable, and although it turns out to be an unwise venture, it is just this obsession that helps him to escape his oppression even before it is realized. In fact, Walter is so taken with his idealized self that he is unable to alter his plan even when faced with his mother's moral reservations. I am struck with the importance that the family's newfound money represented for them and what this must have meant to a black male trapped by racism in south Chicago. While Walter seems superficial on one level, it is understandable how this windfall could contribute to his dreams of providing for himself and his family. An example of this is his statement that he wants to provide pearls for his wife, Ruth, as other men do for their wives: ". . . Who decides which women is supposed to wear pearls in this world. I tell you I am a man. . ." (Hansberry 463).

Racism in this play is overtly expressed through the white character, Lindner, who represents the white majority of the time and in all likelihood a white minority even now. A less obvious representation of the impact of racism is portrayed in the internal, racial conflicts of the black characters themselves, especially Walter Lee Younger and his untrustworthy friend Willy.

Walter's growth is evident as his focus changes from materialism to his conviction that his family should move into an all-white neighborhood where blacks aren't wanted. At this juncture, Walter realizes that what really gives his life worth is standing up for the principle that should be basic to all people, that every individual has a basic right to choose where and how they live. Walter's decision to go forward with the move to the all-white neighborhood represents a victory for himself as a person and a black male.

Walter finally tells Lindner that his family will move despite protests and monetary incentives. "Few see the heroism in Walter's simple act of assertion in rejecting the white neighborhood association's offer to buy them out" (Lester 479). Lindner is representative of the white majority of this time period. However, in his initial meeting with the Younger family his discomfort is evident when he realizes that the family members are open and likable. An example of this is when Ruth says, "Would you like another chair--you don't took comfortable" (Hansberry 448). Lindner was stumbling on his words and could not get directly to the point. It is interesting that Hansberry portrayed this character as polite and unthreatening, although his message was racially motivated. Given the climate of the times and the subsequent racial strife that occurred in the United States during the 1960s, creating a character in this way took what could have been an even more politically charged issue and softened it so that a white majority could be more reflective about their own prejudices.

Although we never see or meet him, we know that Willy has a background similar to Walter's. He is a black man living in a racially oppressed ghetto. Despite the fact that he has a similar background and has the same wants and needs as his friends, he steals the money. Racism and poverty provoke thinking like this by clouding a person's vision and making him feel entitled to have something he has never had an opportunity to acquire. Willy has no illusions about getting rich through Walter's liquor store. "You know Willy got his own ways" (Hansberry 454). He is street smart and is not bound by traditional moral codes or religious ideals that probably never worked in the past for him anyway. He has never worked in a neighborhood where if you need something, for the most part, you either do without it or get it any way you can.

These three characters, Walter Younger, Lindner, and Willy, are all dealing with racial issues that impact on them both globally and individually. In some ways Willy and Lindner are more similar to each other than to Walter. They have learned to negotiate the racism in their environments differently, but both with narrow focus. Walter Younger, while initially focused on escaping his situation and the effect that racism had on it, ultimately rose to hurdle his internal conflicts and stand up for beliefs that he felt gave him his individual worth.

"A Raisin in the Sun is most definitely about human dignity," writes Julius Lester. "Lorraine Hansberry is concerned with the attitude we must have toward material things if we are to be their master and not their slave" (478). The play was introduced into a society just beginning to become aware of many flaws, and people were forced to change their actions and feelings about the controversial issues of that time period. The debatable issues surrounding this play are not important when considering the issues within the play. They are universal.

The struggle of Walter Lee and his family can be understood by everyone. The public reaction to the play when it was first produced is evidence of the ignorance that people had toward its issues. The embarrassing issue of racism was something America didn't want to face, but civil rights leaders, dramatists like Hansberry, or the people themselves who were suffering from it forced us to see what we didn't want to or know how to deal with. Anne Cheney suggests how Americans should view A Raisin in the Sun: "Raisin at first seems a plea for racial tolerance or a fable of man's overcoming an insensitive society, but the simple eloquence of the characters elevates the play into a universal representation of all people's hopes, fears, and dreams" (481).

Works Cited

Adams, George R. "Black Literature: Black Militant Drama," American Imago. New York: Association for Applied Psychoanalysis, Inc., 1971. Vol. 28, No. 2.107–28.

Cheney, Anne. "The African Heritage in A Raisin in the Sun." Exploring Literature. Ed. Frank Madden. New York: Longman, 2001. 480–483.

Cruse, Harold. Lorraine Hansberry, The Crisis of the Negro Intellectual. New York: William Morrow & Company, Inc., 1967. 267–84.

Hansberry, Lorraine. A Raisin in the Sun. Exploring Literature. Ed. Frank Madden. New York: Longman, 2001. 402–468.

Lester, Julius. "The Heroic Dimension in A Raisin in the Sun." Exploring Literature. Ed. Frank Madden. New York: Longman, 2001. 478–480.

Exploring the Literature of Family and Friends: Options for Writing and Research

Some Options for Writing About Family and Friends

1. Consider the ways in which your family or friends have affected your life. Do any of the stories, poems, plays, or essays in this section remind you of your relationships with family or friends?

    Choose one or more of these works and write a response essay that compares your experience or circumstances with those in the literature.
2. Our families and friends can influence and shape our values, our behavior, our aspirations. These values can also strongly influence our response to literature. We may agree or disagree with what an author says or what characters say or do. So, too, literature may influence us and the formation of our values about family and friends.

    Choose one or more works in this section and write an essay about the ways in which this literature either provoked your moral judgment or enabled you to learn something that influenced your values.
3. In his *Theory of Psychoanalysis,* Carl Jung, a pioneer and influential theorist in the field of psychology, wrote: "The little world of childhood with its familiar surroundings is a model of the greater world. The more intensely the family has stamped its character upon the child, the more it will tend to feel and see its earlier miniature world again in the bigger world of adult life."

Consider this quote and write an essay about the way in which one or more works in this section exemplify the way that early family experiences influence how we see and experience the world.

4. Over two thousand years ago, Plato wrote in *Dialogues:* "Friends have all things in common." What do you think he meant?

   Are any of the selections in this section good examples of this adage about friendship?

   Write about this quote as it applies to one or more works in this section.

5. Choose a quote (or quotes) in the introduction to this section, "Family and Friends" (pp. 235–236) and pair it (or them) with one of the longer pieces in this section that either supports it or argues against it. For example, Benjamin Spock's statement about the instincts of parents to do what is best for their children might be paired with Tennessee Williams's *The Glass Menagerie,* which might be seen as an argument against it. If we chose Jean de la Fontaine's comment about the impossibility of pleasing all the world and one's father, we might choose Janice Mirikitani's poem "For My Father" to qualify and to support la Fontaine's statement.

   Write an essay that compares or contrasts a quote (or quotes) from the introduction with a story, poem, play, or essay that supports or argues against it.

A Research Option

Janice Mirikitani's poem "For My Father," Tennessee Williams's play *The Glass Menagerie* and Doris Kearns Goodwin's *From Father with Love* all have something important to say about family and friends. However, each of these works springs from a very different historical, social, or political context.

Expanding our exploration of literature to include the context in which these works were produced can be an enriching and enlightening experience. Choose one or more of these or other works in this section and write a research essay that includes secondary source material about the historical, social, or political background that influenced the creation of this literature.

Collaboration: Writing and Revising with Your Peers

In addition to applying your own values and standards to writing about the literature in this section, you may find it beneficial to share and discuss your work with classmates. Getting feedback from others can help you generate and clarify your ideas and revise and edit your writing more effectively.

Choose a work, a topic, or one of the options for writing about family and friends above, and work with a partner or in a small group. Exchange journal entries or response sheets, generate questions together, do a group semantic map (see pp. 40–45), or simply share and respond to each other's ideas.

After you have written a rough draft of your essay, share it with a partner or your group. Respondents should function primarily as sensitive readers and give honest, constructive responses. They should try to be aware of each writer's purpose, discuss concerns particular to each writer, and comment on the effectiveness of the essay's organization, support, clarity, and voice (for a checklist for revision, see pp. 51–52).

In the final stage of your writing, editing and proofreading might be done in a similar fashion. A partner or group of readers might help you check for correct grammar, spelling, punctuation, and typos (a checklist for editing is on p. 52).

A Writing/Research Portfolio Option

A portfolio is a collection of your work, related materials, and commentary about your work collected over time. Gathering materials in a portfolio will provide you with resources for research and development. You can use your portfolio to collect your writing about the literature in this section, find a topic to write about, revise or add to your work, or keep multiple drafts and monitor the changes you make as you revise. Among the resources you might include:

- Your responses to the quotes and prompts about family and friends at the beginning of this section, the questions you had right after you finished reading each piece of literature, or your journal entries.
- What your classmates, instructor, or published critics had to say about the literature and how their comments may have influenced your interpretation.
- Information you've gathered from the library and the Internet about the historical, social, and political context of the work or its author.

Women & Men

WOMEN & MEN

A DIALOGUE ACROSS HISTORY

The gate of the subtle and profound female / Is the root of Heaven and Earth. / It is continuous, and seems to be always existing. / Use it and you will never wear out.

—Lao-tzu, *Tao te Ching,* c. 550 B.C.

A woman is always a fickle, unstable thing.

—Vergil, Eclogues, 37 B.C.

The education of women should always be relative to that of men. To please, to be useful to us, to make us love and esteem them, to educate us when young, to take care of us when grown up; to advise, to console us, to render our lives easy and agreeable. These are the duties of women at all times, and what they should be taught in their infancy.

—Jean Jacques Rousseau, *Emile,* 1762

It would be an endless task to trace the variety of meannesses, cares, and sorrows into which women are plunged by the prevailing opinion that they were created rather to feel than reason, and that all power they obtain must be obtained by their charms and weakness.

—Mary Wollstonecraft, *A Vindication of the Rights of Women,* 1792

We hold these truths to be self-evident, that all men and women *are created equal.*

—Elizabeth Cady Stanton, *Declaration of Sentiments,* 1848

With women the heart argues, not the mind.

—Matthew Arnold, *Merope,* 1858

The great question . . . which I have not been able to answer, despite my thirty years of research into the feminine soul, is 'What does a woman want?'

—Sigmund Freud, 1930

The usual masculine disillusionment is discovering that a woman has a brain.

—Margaret Mitchell, *Gone with the Wind,* 1936

We know of no culture that has said articulately, that there is no difference between men and women except in the way they contribute to the creation of the next generation.

—Margaret Mead, *Male and Female,* 1948

This has always been a man's world, and none of the reasons hitherto brought forward in explanation of this fact has seemed adequate.

—Simone de Beauvoir, *The Second Sex,* 1949

A girl should not expect special privileges because of her sex, but neither should she 'adjust' to prejudice and discrimination. She must learn to compete . . . not as a woman, but as a human being.

—Betty Friedan, *The Feminine Mystique,* 1963

If women had wives to keep house for them, to stay home with vomiting children, to get the car fixed, fight with the painters, run to the supermarket, reconcile the bank statements, listen to everyone's problems, cater the dinner parties, and nourish the spirit each night, just imagine the possibilities for expansion—the number of books that would be written, companies started, professorships filled, political offices that would be held, by women.

—Gail Sheehy, *Passages,* 1976

Depriving millions of gay American adults the marriages of their choice, and the rights that flow from marriage, denies equal protection of the law. They, their families and friends, together with fair-minded people everywhere, should demand an end to this monstrous injustice.

—Thomas Stoddard, *Gay Marriages: Make Them Legal,* 1988

We have defective mythologies that ignore masculine depth of feeling, assign men a place in the sky instead of earth, teach obedience to the wrong powers, and entangle men and women in systems of industrial domination.

—Robert Bly, *Iron John,* 1990

We all want , above all, to be heard—but not merely to be heard. We want to be understood—heard for what we think we are saying, for what we know we meant. With increased understanding of the ways women and men use language should come a decrease in the frequency of the complaint, You just don't understand.

—Deborah Tannen, *You Just Don't Understand,* 1990

Women and Men: Exploring Your Experiences and Beliefs

"Can't live with them, can't live without them." We've heard this statement directed at both men and women. What is more compelling, more passionate, or more divisive than a debate about women and men? It's a debate that has been going on since humans have existed. Beyond our reproductive functions, are there significant differences between men and women? Are we intellectually and emotionally different? Should there be a different role for each gender?

Throughout most of history, women have been treated as inferior to men. It is only within the past two-hundred years or so that women have had a voice loud enough to be acknowledged. While Elizabeth Cady Stanton's statement of 150 years ago, "We hold these truths to be self-evident, that all *men and women* are created equal," may seem "self-evident" to us today, it has been less than one-hundred years since women have even had the right to vote in this country. Although it is still not clear that women have been given equal opportunity in all areas, it is obvious how far women have come. Many men, however, now find themselves confused, frustrated, and even "bashed" by the emergence of women and the blurring of gender roles. If women's roles have been redefined, what about the roles of men?

Your gender has a lot to do with many aspects of your life. It may influence your aspirations or the expectations others have for you, the encouragement you receive for education and career goals, marriage and family, even your involvement in sports. It probably influences the formation of your values. And it certainly influences your view of the opposite sex. As a preparation for reading the literature in this section, you may find it helpful to think about your own values and beliefs about gender.

Reading and Writing About Women and Men

At least one aspect of the many stories, poems, plays, and essays that follow is about the ways that gender determines how men and women define themselves and each other—and the impact that has on their relationships: a young boy's overwhelming crush on his friend's older sister in James Joyce's short story "Araby," a demented lover in Robert Browning's poem "Porphyria's Lover," a woman's discovery that her marriage has kept her a child in Henrik Ibsen's drama "A Doll's House," and a tribute to the mothers and grandmothers who kept the creative spark alive despite the enduring horror and hardship of slavery and bigotry in Alice Walker's essay "In Search of Our Mother's Gardens." The brief quotes that open this section also give you some idea of the number of compelling ethical, political, and social arguments connected to gender. Equal rights and opportunity, intellectual equality, stereotyping, bigotry, arrogance, and styles of communication head a long list of concerns. Any of these or other related issues would provide a fine topic for an essay.

◆ FICTION ◆

ANTON CHEKHOV (1860–1904)

Considered the father of the modern short story and the modern play, Anton Pavlovich Chekhov was born in the town of Taganrog, near the Black Sea, in Russia. His grandfather was a serf who bought his family's freedom. Chekhov attended the University of Moscow on a scholarship, eventually earning a degree in medicine. In an effort to support himself and his impoverished family during this period, Chekhov began writing short pieces, first sketches and jokes, and later short stories for newspapers and journals. By 1886, Chekhov had gained enough recognition to make writing his chief interest and occupation. His long association with the famed Moscow Arts Theater began with its acclaimed production of The Seagull *in 1898 (which had a disastrous premiere two years earlier in St. Petersburg), and continued with productions of his greatest plays,* The Three Sisters, Uncle Vanya, *and* The Cherry Orchard. *In his later years, which were plagued by ill-health, Chekhov married Olga Knipper, a star of the theater company. He died in 1904 of tuberculosis. His short stories, which he continued to write even after he became a successful playwright, are characterized not only by their economical prose style, but by a love of humanity that is often set against a pervading mood of sadness.*

THE LADY WITH THE PET DOG [1899]

Translated by Avrahm Yarmolinsky

I

A new person, it was said, had appeared on the esplanade: a lady with a pet dog. Dmitry Dmitrich Gurov, who had spent a fortnight at Yalta and had got used to the place, had also begun to take an interest in new arrivals. As he sat in Vernet's confectionery shop, he saw, walking on the esplanade, a fair-haired young woman of medium height, wearing a beret; a white Pomeranian was trotting behind her.

And afterwards he met her in the public garden and in the square several times a day. She walked alone, always wearing the same beret and always with the white dog; no one knew who she was and everyone called her simply "the lady with the pet dog."

"If she is here alone without husband or friends," Gurov reflected, "it wouldn't be a bad thing to make her acquaintance."

He was under forty, but he already had a daughter twelve years old, and two sons at school. They had found a wife for him when he was very young, a student in his second year, and by now she seemed half as old again as he. She was a tall, erect woman with dark eyebrows, stately and dignified and, as she said of herself, intellectual. She read a great deal, used simplified spelling in her letters, called her husband, not Dmitry, but Dimitry, while he privately considered her of limited intelligence, narrow-minded, dowdy, was afraid of her, and did not like to be at home. He had begun being unfaithful to her long ago—had been unfaithful to her often and, probably for that reason, almost always spoke ill of women, and when they were talked of in his presence used to call them "the inferior race."

It seemed to him that he had been sufficiently tutored by bitter experience to call them what he pleased, and yet he could not have lived without "the inferior race" for two days together. In the company of men he was bored and ill at ease, he was chilly and uncommunicative with them; but when he was among women he felt free, and knew what to speak to them about and how to comport himself; and even to be silent with them was no strain on him. In his appearance, in his character, in his whole make-up there was something attractive and elusive that disposed women in his favor and allured them. He knew that, and some force seemed to draw him to them, too.

Oft-repeated and really bitter experience had taught him long ago that with decent people—particularly Moscow people—who are irresolute and slow to move, every affair which at first seems a light and charming adventure inevitably grows into a whole problem of extreme complexity, and in the end a painful situation is created. But at every new meeting with an interesting woman this lesson of experience seemed to slip from his memory, and he was eager for life, and everything seemed so simple and diverting.

One evening while he was dining in the public garden the lady in the beret walked up without haste to take the next table. Her expression, her gait, her dress, and the way she did her hair told him that she belonged to the upper class, that she was married, that she was in Yalta for the first time and alone, and that she was bored there. The stories told of the immorality in Yalta are to a great extent untrue; he despised them, and knew that such stories were made up for the most part by persons who would have been glad to sin themselves if they had had the chance; but when the lady sat down at the next table three paces from him, he recalled these stories of easy conquests, of trips to the mountains, and the tempting thought of a swift, fleeting liaison, a romance with an unknown woman of whose very name he was ignorant suddenly took hold of him.

He beckoned invitingly to the Pomeranian, and when the dog approached him, shook his finger at it. The Pomeranian growled; Gurov threatened it again.

The lady glanced at him and at once dropped her eyes.

"He doesn't bite," she said and blushed.

"May I give him a bone?" he asked; and when she nodded he inquired affably, "Have you been in Yalta long?"

"About five days."

"And I am dragging out the second week here."

There was a short silence.

"Time passes quickly, and yet it is so dull here!" she said, not looking at him.

"It's only the fashion to say it's dull here. A provincial will live in Belyov or Zhizdra and not be bored, but when he comes here it's 'Oh, the dullness! Oh, the dust!' One would think he came from Granada."

She laughed. Then both continued eating in silence, like strangers, but after dinner they walked together and there sprang up between them the light banter of people who are free and contented, to whom it does not matter where they go or what they talk about. They walked and talked of the strange light on the sea: the water was a soft, warm, lilac color, and there was a golden band of moonlight upon it. They talked of how sultry it was after a hot day. Gurov told her that he was a native of Moscow, that he had studied languages and literature at the university, but had a post in a bank; that at one time he had trained to become an opera singer but had given it up, that he owned two houses in Moscow. And he learned from her that she had grown up in Petersburg, but had lived in S______ since her marriage two years previously, that she was going to stay in Yalta for about another month, and that her husband, who needed a rest, too, might perhaps come to fetch her. She was not certain whether her husband was a member of a Government Board or served on a Zemstvo Council, and this amused her. And Gurov learned that her name was Anna Sergeyevna.

Afterwards in his room at the hotel he thought about her—and was certain that he would meet her the next day. It was bound to happen. Getting into bed he recalled that she had been a schoolgirl only recently, doing lessons like his own daughter; he thought how much timidity and angularity there was still in her laugh and her manner of talking with a stranger. It must have been the first time in her life that she was alone in a setting in which she was followed, looked at, and spoken to for one secret purpose alone, which she could hardly fail to guess. He thought of her slim, delicate throat, her lovely gray eyes.

"There's something pathetic about her, though," he thought, and dropped off.

II

A week had passed since they had struck up an acquaintance. It was a holiday. It was close indoors, while in the street the wind whirled the dust about and blew people's hats off. One was thirsty all day, and Gurov often went into the restaurant and offered Anna Sergeyevna a soft drink or ice cream. One did not know what to do with oneself.

In the evening when the wind had abated they went out on the pier to watch the steamer come in. There were a great many people walking about the dock; they had come to welcome someone and they were carrying bunches of flowers. And two peculiarities of a festive Yalta crowd stood out: the elderly ladies were dressed like young ones and there were many generals.

Owing to the choppy sea, the steamer arrived late, after sunset, and it was a long time tacking about before it put in at the pier. Anna Sergeyevna peered at the steamer and the passengers through her lorgnette as though looking for acquaintances, and whenever she turned to Gurov her eyes were shining. She talked a great deal and asked questions jerkily, forgetting the next moment what she had asked; then she lost her lorgnette in the crush.

The festive crowd began to disperse; it was now too dark to see people's faces; there was no wind any more, but Gurov and Anna Sergeyevna still stood as though waiting to see someone else come off the steamer. Anna Sergeyevna was silent now, and sniffed her flowers without looking at Gurov.

"The weather has improved this evening," he said. "Where shall we go now? Shall we drive somewhere?"

25 She did not reply.

Then he looked at her intently, and suddenly embraced her and kissed her on the lips, and the moist fragrance of her flowers enveloped him; and at once he looked round him anxiously, wondering if anyone had seen them.

"Let us go to your place," he said softly. And they walked off together rapidly.

The air in her room was close and there was the smell of the perfume she had bought at the Japanese shop. Looking at her, Gurov thought: "What encounters life offers!" From the past he preserved the memory of carefree, good-natured women whom love made gay and who were grateful to him for the happiness he gave them, however brief it might be; and of women like his wife who loved without sincerity, with too many words, affectedly, hysterically, with an expression that it was not love or passion that engaged them but something more significant; and of two or three others, very beautiful, frigid women, across whose faces would suddenly flit a rapacious expression—an obstinate desire to take from life more than it could give, and these were women no longer young, capricious, unreflecting, domineering, unintelligent, and when Gurov grew cold to them their beauty aroused his hatred, and the lace on their lingerie seemed to him to resemble scales.

But here there was the timidity, the angularity of inexperienced youth, a feeling of awkwardness; and there was a sense of embarrassment, as though someone had suddenly knocked at the door. Anna Sergeyevna, "the lady with the pet dog," treated what had happened in a peculiar way, very seriously, as though it were her fall—so it seemed, and this was odd and inappropriate. Her features drooped and faded, and her long hair hung down sadly on either side of her face; she grew pensive and her dejected pose was that of a Magdalene in a picture by an old master.

30 "It's not right," she said. "You don't respect me now, you first of all."

There was a watermelon on the table. Gurov cut himself a slice and began eating it without haste. They were silent for at least half an hour.

There was something touching about Anna Sergeyevna; she had the purity of a well-bred, naive woman who has seen little of life. The single candle burning on the table barely illuminated her face, yet it was clear that she was unhappy.

"Why should I stop respecting you, darling?" asked Gurov. "You don't know what you're saying."

"God forgive me," she said, and her eyes filled with tears. "It's terrible."

35 "It's as though you were trying to exonerate yourself."

"How can I exonerate myself? No. I am a bad, low woman; I despise myself and I have no thought of exonerating myself. It's not my husband but myself I have deceived. And not only just now; I have been deceiving myself for a long time. My husband may be a good, honest man, but he is a flunkey! I don't know what he does, what his work is, but I know he is a flunkey! I was twenty when I married him. I was tormented by curiosity; I wanted something better. 'There must be a different sort of life,' I said to myself. I wanted to live! To live, to live! Curiosity kept eating at me—you don't understand, but I swear to God I could no longer control myself; something was going on in me; I could not be held back. I told my husband I was ill, and came here. And here I have been walking about as though in a daze, as though I were mad; and now I have become a vulgar, vile woman whom anyone may despise."

Gurov was already bored with her; he was irritated by her naive tone, by her repentance, so unexpected and so out of place, but for the tears in her eyes he might have thought she was joking or play-acting.

"I don't understand, my dear," he said softly. "What do you want?"

She hid her face on his breast and pressed close to him.

"Believe me, believe me, I beg you," she said, "I love honesty and purity, and sin is loathsome to me; I don't know what I'm doing. Simple people say, 'The Evil One has led me astray.' And I may say of myself now that the Evil One has led me astray."

"Quiet, quiet," he murmured.

He looked into her fixed, frightened eyes, kissed her, spoke to her softly and affectionately, and by degrees she calmed down, and her gaiety returned; both began laughing.

Afterwards when they went out there was not a soul on the esplanade. The town with its cypresses looked quite dead, but the sea was still sounding as it broke upon the beach; a single launch was rocking on the waves and on it a lantern was blinking sleepily.

They found a cab and drove to Oreanda.

"I found out your surname in the hall just now; it was written on the board—von Dideritz," said Gurov. "Is your husband German?"

"No; I believe his grandfather was German, but he is Greek Orthodox himself."

At Oreanda they sat on a bench not far from the church, looked down at the sea, and were silent. Yalta was barely visible through the morning mist; white clouds rested motionlessly on the mountaintops. The leaves did not stir on the trees, cicadas twanged, and the monotonous muffled sound of the sea that rose from below spoke of the peace, the eternal sleep awaiting us. So it rumbled below when there was no Yalta, no Oreanda here; so it rumbles now, and it will rumble as indifferently and as hollowly when we are no more. And in this constancy, in this complete indifference to the life and death of each of us, there lies, perhaps, a pledge of our eternal salvation, of the unceasing advance of life upon earth, of unceasing movement towards perfection. Sitting beside a young woman who in the dawn seemed so lovely, Gurov, soothed and spellbound by these magical surroundings—the sea, the mountains, the clouds, the wide sky—thought how everything is really beautiful in this world when one reflects: everything except what we think or do ourselves when we forget the higher aims of life and our own human dignity.

A man strolled up to them—probably a guard—looked at them and walked away. And this detail, too, seemed so mysterious and beautiful. They saw a steamer arrive from Feodosia, its lights extinguished in the glow of dawn.

"There is dew on the grass," said Anna Sergeyevna, after a silence.

"Yes, it's time to go home."

They returned to the city.

Then they met every day at twelve o'clock on the esplanade, lunched and dined together, took walks, admired the sea. She complained that she slept badly, that she had palpitations, asked the same questions, troubled now by jealousy and now by the fear that he did not respect her sufficiently. And often in the square or the public garden, when there was no one near them, he suddenly drew her to him and kissed her passionately. Complete idleness, these kisses in broad daylight exchanged furtively in dread of someone's seeing them, the heat, the smell of the sea, and the continual flitting before his eyes of idle, well-dressed, well-fed people, worked a complete change in him; he kept telling Anna Sergeyevna how beautiful she was, how seductive, was urgently passionate; he would not move a step away from her, while she was often pensive and continually pressed him to confess that he did not respect her, did not love her in the least, and saw in her nothing but a common woman. Almost every evening rather late they drove somewhere out of town, to Oreanda or to the waterfall; and the excursion was always a success, the scenery invariably impressed them as beautiful and magnificent.

They were expecting her husband, but a letter came from him saying that he had eye-trouble, and begging his wife to return home as soon as possible. Anna Sergeyevna made haste to go.

"It's a good thing I am leaving," she said to Gurov. "It's the hand of Fate!"

55 She took a carriage to the railway station, and he went with her. They were driving the whole day. When she had taken her place in the express, and when the second bell had rung, she said, "Let me look at you once more—let me look at you again. Like this."

She was not crying but was so sad that she seemed ill and her face was quivering.

"I shall be thinking of you—remembering you," she said. "God bless you; be happy. Don't remember evil against me. We are parting forever—it has to be, for we ought never to have met. Well, God bless you."

The train moved off rapidly, its lights soon vanished, and a minute later there was no sound of it, as though everything had conspired to end as quickly as possible that sweet trance, that madness. Left alone on the platform, and gazing into the dark distance, Gurov listened to the twang of the grasshoppers and the hum of the telegraph wires, feeling as though he had just waked up. And he reflected, musing, that there had now been another episode or adventure in his life, and it, too, was at an end, and nothing was left of it but a memory. He was moved, sad, and slightly remorseful: this young woman whom he would never meet again had not been happy with him; he had been warm and affectionate with her, but yet in his manner, his tone, and his caresses there had been a shade of light irony, the slightly coarse arrogance of a happy male who was, besides, almost twice her age. She had constantly called him kind, exceptional, high-minded; obviously he had seemed to her different from what he really was, so he had involuntarily deceived her.

Here at the station there was already a scent of autumn in the air; it was a chilly evening.

60 "It is time for me to go north, too," thought Gurov as he left the platform. "High time!"

III

At home in Moscow the winter routine was already established; the stoves were heated, and in the morning it was still dark when the children were having breakfast and getting ready for school, and the nurse would light the lamp for a short time. There were frosts already. When the first snow falls, on the first day the sleighs are out, it is pleasant to see the white earth, the white roofs; one draws easy, delicious breaths, and the season brings back the days of one's youth. The old limes and birches, white with hoar-frost, have a good-natured look; they are closer to one's heart than cypresses and palms, and near them one no longer wants to think of mountains and the sea.

Gurov, a native of Moscow, arrived there on a fine frosty day, and when he put on his fur coat and warm gloves and took a walk along Petrovka, and when on Saturday night he heard the bells ringing, his recent trip and the places he had visited lost all charm for him. Little by little he became immersed in Moscow life, greedily read three newspapers a day, and declared that he did not read the Moscow papers on principle. He already felt a longing for restaurants, clubs, formal dinners, anniversary celebrations, and it flattered him to entertain distinguished lawyers and actors, and to play cards with a professor at the physicians' club. He could eat a whole portion of meat stewed with pickled cabbage and served in a pan, Moscow style.

A month or so would pass and the image of Anna Sergeyevna, it seemed to him, would become misty in his memory, and only from time to time he would dream of her with her touching smile as he dreamed of others. But more than a month went by, winter came into its own, and everything was still clear in his memory as though he had parted from Anna Sergeyevna only yesterday. And his memories glowed more and more vividly. When in the evening stillness the voices of his children preparing their lessons reached his study, or when he listened to a song or to an organ playing in a restaurant, or when the storm howled in the chimney, suddenly everything would rise up in his memory; what had happened on the pier and the early morning with the mist on the mountains, and the steamer coming from Feodosia, and the kisses. He would pace about his room a long time, remembering and smiling; then his memories passed into reveries, and in his imagination the past would mingle with what was to come. He did not dream of Anna Sergeyevna, but she followed him about everywhere and watched him. When he shut his eyes he saw her before him as though she were there in the flesh, and she seemed to him lovelier, younger, tenderer than she had been, and he imagined himself a finer man than he had been in Yalta. Of evenings she peered out at him from the bookcase, from the fireplace, from the corner—he heard her breathing, the caressing rustle of her clothes. In the street he followed the women with his eyes, looking for someone who resembled her.

Already he was tormented by a strong desire to share his memories with someone. But in his home it was impossible to talk of his love, and he had no one to talk to outside; certainly he could not confide in his tenants or in anyone at the bank. And what was there to talk about? He hadn't loved her then, had he? Had there been anything beautiful, poetical, edifying, or simply interesting in his relations with Anna Sergeyevna? And he was forced to talk vaguely of love, of women, and no one guessed what he meant; only his wife would twitch her black eyebrows and say, "The part of a philanderer does not suit you at all, Dimitry."

One evening, coming out of the physicians' club with an official with whom he had been playing cards, he could not resist saying:

"If you only knew what a fascinating woman I became acquainted with at Yalta!"

The official got into his sledge and was driving away, but turned suddenly and shouted:

"Dmitry Dmitrich!"

"What is it?"

"You were right this evening: the sturgeon was a bit high."

These words, so commonplace, for some reason moved Gurov to indignation, and struck him as degrading and unclean. What savage manners, what mugs! What stupid nights, what dull, humdrum days! Frenzied gambling, gluttony, drunkenness, continual talk always about the same thing! Futile pursuits and conversations always about the same topics take up the better part of one's time, the better part of one's strength, and in the end there is left a life clipped and wingless, an absurd mess, and there is no escaping or getting away from it—just as though one were in a madhouse or a prison.

Gurov, boiling with indignation, did not sleep all night. And he had a headache all the next day. And the following nights too he slept badly; he sat up in bed, thinking, or paced up and down his room. He was fed up with his children, fed up with the bank; he had no desire to go anywhere or to talk of anything.

In December during the holidays he prepared to take a trip and told his wife he was going to Petersburg to do what he could for a young friend—and he set off for S______. What for? He did not know, himself. He wanted to see Anna Sergeyevna and talk with her, to arrange a rendezvous if possible.

He arrived at S______ in the morning, and at the hotel took the best room, in which the floor was covered with gray army cloth, and on the table there was an inkstand, gray with dust and topped by a figure on horseback, its hat in its raised hand and its head broken off. The porter gave him the necessary information: von Dideritz lived in a house of his own on Staro-Goncharnaya Street, not far from the hotel: he was rich and lived well and kept his own horses; everyone in the town knew him. The porter pronounced the name: "Dridiritz."

Without haste Gurov made his way to Staro-Goncharnaya Street and found the house. Directly opposite the house stretched a long gray fence studded with nails.

"A fence like that would make one run away," thought Gurov, looking now at the fence, now at the windows of the house.

He reflected: this was a holiday, and the husband was apt to be at home. And in any case, it would be tactless to go into the house and disturb her. If he were to send her a note, it might fall into her husband's hands, and that might spoil everything. The best thing was to rely on chance. And he kept walking up and down the street and along the fence, waiting for the chance. He saw a beggar go in at the gate and heard the dogs attack him; then an hour later he heard a piano, and the sound came to him faintly and indistinctly. Probably it was Anna Sergeyevna playing. The front door opened suddenly, and an old woman came out, followed by the familiar white Pomeranian. Gurov was on the point of calling to the dog, but his heart began beating violently, and in his excitement he could not remember the Pomeranian's name.

He kept walking up and down, and hated the gray fence more and more, and by now he thought irritably that Anna Sergeyevna had forgotten him, and was perhaps already diverting herself with another man, and that that was very natural in a young woman who from morning till night had to look at that damn fence. He went back to his hotel room and sat on the couch for a long while, not knowing what to do, then he had dinner and a long nap.

"How stupid and annoying all this is!" he thought when he woke and looked at the dark windows: it was already evening. "Here I've had a good sleep for some reason. What am I going to do at night?"

He sat on the bed, which was covered with a cheap gray blanket of the kind seen in hospitals, and he twitted himself in his vexation:

"So there's your lady with the pet dog. There's your adventure. A nice place to cool your heels in."

That morning at the station a playbill in large letters had caught his eye. *The Geisha* was to be given for the first time. He thought of this and drove to the theater.

"It's quite possible that she goes to first nights," he thought.

The theater was full. As in all provincial theaters, there was a haze above the chandelier, the gallery was noisy and restless; in the front row, before the beginning of the performance the local dandies were standing with their hands clasped behind their backs; in the Governor's box the Governor's daughter, wearing a boa, occupied the front seat, while the Governor himself hid modestly behind the portiere and only his hands were visible; the curtain swayed; the orchestra was a long time tuning up. While the audience was coming in and taking their seats, Gurov scanned the faces eagerly.

Anna Sergeyevna, too, came in. She sat down in the third row, and when Gurov looked at her his heart contracted, and he understood clearly that in the whole world there was no human being so near, so precious, and so important to him; she, this little, undistinguished woman, lost in a provincial crowd, with a vulgar lorgnette in her hand, filled his whole life now, was his sorrow and his joy, the only happiness that he now desired for himself, and to the sounds of the bad orchestra, of the miserable local violins, he thought how lovely she was. He thought and dreamed.

A young man with small side-whiskers, very tall and stooped, came in with Anna Sergeyevna and sat down beside her; he nodded his head at every step and seemed to be bowing continually. Probably this was the husband whom at Yalta, in an access of bitter feeling, she had called a flunkey. And there really was in his lanky figure, his side-whiskers, his small bald patch, something of a flunkey's retiring manner; his smile was mawkish, and in his buttonhole there was an academic badge like a waiter's number.

During the first intermission the husband went out to have a smoke; she remained in her seat. Gurov, who was also sitting in the orchestra, went up to her and said in a shaky voice, with a forced smile:

"Good evening!"

She glanced at him and turned pale, then looked at him again in horror, unable to believe her eyes, and gripped the fan and the lorgnette tightly together in her hands, evidently trying to keep herself from fainting. Both were silent. She was sitting, he was standing, frightened by her distress and not daring to take a seat beside her. The violins and the flute that were being tuned up sang out. He suddenly felt frightened: it seemed as if all the people in the boxes were looking at them. She got up and went hurriedly to the exit; he followed her, and both of them walked blindly along the corridors and up and down stairs, and figures in the uniforms prescribed for magistrates, teachers, and officials of the Department of Crown Lands, all wearing badges, flitted before their eyes, as did also ladies, and fur coats on hangers; they were conscious of drafts and the smell of stale tobacco. And Gurov, whose heart was beating violently, thought:

90 "Oh, Lord! Why are these people here and this orchestra!"

And at that instant he suddenly recalled how when he had seen Anna Sergeyevna off at the station he had said to himself that all was over between them and that they would never meet again. But how distant the end still was!

On the narrow, gloomy staircase over which it said "To the Amphitheatre," she stopped.

"How you frightened me!" she said, breathing hard, still pale and stunned. "Oh, how you frightened me! I am barely alive. Why did you come? Why?"

"But do understand, Anna, do understand—" he said hurriedly, under his breath. "I implore you, do understand—"

95 She looked at him with fear, with entreaty, with love; she looked at him intently, to keep his features more distinctly in her memory.

"I suffer so," she went on, not listening to him. "All this time I have been thinking of nothing but you; I live only by the thought of you. And I wanted to forget, to forget; but why, oh, why have you come?"

On the landing above them two high school boys were looking down and smoking, but it was all the same to Gurov; he drew Anna Sergeyevna to him and began kissing her face and hands.

"What are you doing, what are you doing!" she was saying in horror, pushing him away. "We have lost our senses. Go away today; go away at once—I conjure you by all that is sacred, I implore you—People are coming this way!"

Someone was walking up the stairs.

100 "You must leave," Anna Sergeyevna went on in a whisper. "Do you hear, Dmitry Dmitrich? I will come and see you in Moscow. I have never been happy; I am unhappy now, and I never, never shall be happy, never! So don't make me suffer still more! I swear I'll come to Moscow. But now let us part. My dear, good, precious one, let us part!"

She pressed his hand and walked rapidly downstairs, turning to look round at him, and from her eyes he could see that she really was unhappy. Gurov stood for a while, listening, then when all grew quiet, he found his coat and left the theater.

IV

And Anna Sergeyevna began coming to see him in Moscow. Once every two or three months she left S______ telling her husband that she was going to consult a doctor about a woman's ailment from which she was suffering—and her husband did and did not believe her. When she arrived in Moscow she would stop at the Slavyansky Bazar Hotel, and at once send a man in a red cap to Gurov. Gurov came to see her, and no one in Moscow knew of it.

Once he was going to see her in this way on a winter morning (the messenger had come the evening before and not found him in). With him walked his daughter, whom he wanted to take to school; it was on the way. Snow was coming down in big wet flakes.

"It's three degrees above zero,[1] and yet it's snowing," Gurov was saying to his daughter. "But this temperature prevails only on the surface of the earth; in the upper layers of the atmosphere there is quite a different temperature."

"And why doesn't it thunder in winter, papa?"

He explained that, too. He talked, thinking all the while that he was on his way to a rendezvous, and no living soul knew of it, and probably no one would ever know. He had two lives, an open one, seen and known by all who needed to know it, full of conventional truth and conventional falsehood, exactly like the lives of his friends and acquaintances; and another life that went on in secret. And through some strange, perhaps accidental, combination of circumstances, everything that was of interest and importance to him, everything that was essential to him, everything about which he felt sincerely and did not deceive himself, everything that constituted the core of his life, was going on concealed from others; while all that was false, the shell in which he hid to cover the truth—his work at the bank, for instance, his discussions at the club, his references to the "inferior race," his appearances at anniversary celebrations with his wife—all that went on in the open. Judging others by himself, he did not believe what he saw, and always fancied that every man led his real, most interesting life under cover of secrecy as under cover of night. The personal life of every individual is based on secrecy, and perhaps it is partly for that reason that civilized man is so nervously anxious that personal privacy should be respected.

Having taken his daughter to school, Gurov went on to the Slavyansky Bazar Hotel. He took off his fur coat in the lobby, went upstairs, and knocked gently at the door. Anna Sergeyevna, wearing his favorite gray dress, exhausted by the journey and by waiting, had been expecting him since the previous evening. She was pale, and looked at him without a smile, and had hardly entered when she flung herself on his breast. That kiss was a long, lingering one, as though they had not seen one another for two years.

[1]**three degrees above zero** about 37 degrees Fahrenheit

"Well, darling, how are you getting on there?" he asked. "What news?"

"Wait; I'll tell you in a moment—I can't speak."

110 She could not speak; she was crying. She turned away from him, and pressed her handkerchief to her eyes.

"Let her have her cry; meanwhile I'll sit down," he thought, and he seated himself in an armchair.

Then he rang and ordered tea, and while he was having his tea she remained standing at the window with her back to him. She was crying out of sheer agitation, in the sorrowful consciousness that their life was so sad; that they could only see each other in secret and had to hide from people like thieves! Was it not a broken life?

"Come, stop now, dear!" he said.

It was plain to him that this love of theirs would not be over soon, that the end of it was not in sight. Anna Sergeyevna was growing more and more attached to him. She adored him, and it was unthinkable to tell her that their love was bound to come to an end some day; besides, she would not have believed it!

115 He went up to her and took her by the shoulders, to fondle her and say something diverting, and at that moment he caught sight of himself in the mirror.

His hair was already beginning to turn gray. And it seemed odd to him that he had grown so much older in the last few years, and lost his looks. The shoulders on which his hands rested were warm and heaving. He felt compassion for this life, still so warm and lovely, but probably already about to begin to fade and wither like his own. Why did she love him so much? He always seemed to women different from what he was, and they loved in him not himself, but the man whom their imagination created and whom they had been eagerly seeking all their lives; and afterwards, when they saw their mistake, they loved him nevertheless. And not one of them had been happy with him. In the past he had met women, come together with them, parted from them, but he had never once loved; it was anything you please, but not love. And only now when his head was gray he had fallen in love, really, truly—for the first time in his life.

Anna Sergeyevna and he loved each other as people do who are very close and intimate, like man and wife, like tender friends; it seemed to them that Fate itself had meant them for one another, and they could not understand why he had a wife and she a husband; and it was as though they were a pair of migratory birds, male and female, caught and forced to live in different cages. They forgave each other what they were ashamed of in their past, they forgave everything in the present, and felt that this love of theirs had altered them both.

Formerly in moments of sadness he had soothed himself with whatever logical arguments came into his head, but now he no longer cared for logic; he felt profound compassion, he wanted to be sincere and tender.

"Give it up now, my darling," he said. "You've had your cry; that's enough. Let us have a talk now, we'll think up something."

120 Then they spent a long time taking counsel together, they talked of how to avoid the necessity for secrecy, for deception, for living in different cities, and not seeing one another for long stretches of time. How could they free themselves from these intolerable fetters?

"How? How?" he asked, clutching his head. "How?"

And it seemed as though in a little while the solution would be found, and then a new and glorious life would begin; and it was clear to both of them that the end was still far off, and that what was to be most complicated and difficult for them was only just beginning.

➤ *QUESTIONS FOR READING AND WRITING*

1. Why do you think that most of the action takes place away from Moscow?
2. What attracts Gurov to Anna Sergeyevna in the first place? During their time in Yalta, she is concerned with whether or not he respects her. Does he?
3. There are no scenes between Gurov and his wife. Why? Would it change how you feel about Gurov and Anna Sergeyevna if you knew more about his wife?
4. Is there a sense in which the central characters behave nobly? Do you think that infidelity is ever justified? Is love for a mistress the same as love for a wife?
5. What does the last paragraph mean? What has happened to make the time ahead "to be most complicated and difficult"? Explain.

KATE CHOPIN (1851–1906)

Kate Chopin was born in St. Louis, Missouri. Her father, an Irish immigrant, became a successful businessman. Her mother was a prominent member of the French-Creole community and traveled in exclusive social circles. Chopin attended Catholic school and, before her marriage at nineteen to Creole cotton broker Oscar Chopin, was much admired for her beauty and wit. The couple settled first in New Orleans and, following the collapse of Oscar's business, moved to his family's plantations in Natchitoches Parish. Following his unexpected death in 1883, at a doctor's suggestion, Chopin began writing. Her stories, which are set among the Creole people of the Louisiana bayou, were collected and published in two anthologies, Bayou Folk *(1894) and* A Night in Arcadie *(1899). Her greatest work, the novel* The Awakening *(1899), which tells the story of an extramarital affair, was denounced as obscene and was largely ignored until it was reevaluated by critics, beginning in the 1930s, who praised it for its emotional honesty and beautiful prose.*

The Story of an Hour [1891]

Knowing that Mrs. Mallard was afflicted with a heart trouble, great care was taken to break to her as gently as possible the news of her husband's death.

It was her sister Josephine who told her, in broken sentences, veiled hints that revealed in half concealing. Her husband's friend Richards was there, too, near her. It was he who had been in the newspaper office when intelligence of the railroad disaster was received, with Brently Mallard's name leading the list of "killed." He had only taken the time to assure himself of its truth by a second telegram, and had hastened to forestall any less careful, less tender friend in bearing the sad message.

She did not hear the story as many women have heard the same, with a paralyzed inability to accept its significance. She wept at once, with sudden, wild abandonment, in her sister's arms. When the storm of grief had spent itself she went away to her room alone. She would have no one follow her.

There stood, facing the open window, a comfortable, roomy armchair. Into this she sank, pressed down by a physical exhaustion that haunted her body and seemed to reach into her soul.

5 She could see in the open square before her house the tops of trees that were all aquiver with the new spring life. The delicious breath of rain was in the air. In the street below a peddler was crying his wares. The notes of a distant song which some one was singing reached her faintly, and countless sparrows were twittering in the eaves.

There were patches of blue sky showing here and there through the clouds that had met and piled above the other in the west facing her window.

She sat with her head thrown back upon the cushion of the chair quite motionless, except when a sob came up into her throat and shook her, as a child who has cried itself to sleep continues to sob in its dreams.

She was young, with a fair, calm face, whose lines bespoke repression and even a certain strength. But now there was a dull stare in her eyes, whose gaze was fixed away off yonder on one of those patches of blue sky. It was not a glance of reflection, but rather indicated a suspension of intelligent thought.

There was something coming to her and she was waiting for it, fearfully. What was it? She did not know; it was too subtle and elusive to name. But she felt it, creeping out of the sky, reaching toward her through the sounds, the scents, the color that filled the air.

10 Now her bosom rose and fell tumultuously. She was beginning to recognize this thing that was approaching to possess her, and she was striving to beat it back with her will—as powerless as her two white slender hands would have been.

When she abandoned herself a little whispered word escaped her slightly parted lips. She said it over and over under her breath: "Free, free, free!" The vacant stare and the look of terror that had followed it went from her eyes. They stayed keen and bright. Her pulses beat fast, and the coursing blood warmed and relaxed every inch of her body.

She did not stop to ask if it were not a monstrous joy that held her. A clear and exalted perception enabled her to dismiss the suggestion as trivial.

She knew that she would weep again when she saw the kind, tender hands folded in death; the face that had never looked save with love upon her, fixed and gray and dead. But she saw beyond that bitter moment a long procession of years to come that would belong to her absolutely. And she opened and spread her arms out to them in welcome.

There would be no one to live for her during those coming years; she would live for herself. There would be no powerful will bending her in that blind persistence with which men and women believe they have a right to impose a private will upon a fellow creature. A kind intention or a cruel intention made the act seem no less a crime as she looked upon it in that brief moment of illumination.

15 And yet she had loved him—sometimes. Often she had not. What did it matter! What could love, the unsolved mystery, count for in face of this possession of self-assertion which she suddenly recognized as the strongest impulse of her being.

"Free! Body and soul free!" she kept whispering.

Josephine was kneeling before the closed door with her lips to the keyhole, imploring for admission. "Louise, open the door! I beg; open the door—you will make yourself ill. What are you doing, Louise? For heaven's sake open the door."

"Go away. I am not making myself ill." No; she was drinking in a very elixir of life through that open window.

Her fancy was running riot along those days ahead of her. Spring days, and summer days, and all sorts of days that would be her own. She breathed a quick prayer that life might be long. It was only yesterday she had thought with a shudder that life might be long.

20 She arose at length and opened the door to her sister's importunities. There was a feverish triumph in her eyes, and she carried herself unwittingly like a goddess of Victory. She clasped her sister's waist, and together they descended the stairs. Richards stood waiting for them at the bottom.

Some one was opening the front door with a latchkey. It was Brently Mallard who entered, a little travel-stained, composedly carrying his grip-sack and umbrella. He had been far from the scene of accident, and did not even know there had been one. He stood amazed at Josephine's piercing cry; at Richards' quick motion to screen him from the view of his wife.

But Richards was too late.

When the doctors came they said she had died of heart disease—of joy that kills.

➤ *QUESTIONS FOR READING AND WRITING*

1. Of what significance is the first sentence of this story?
2. How did you feel about Louise's first response to her husband's death? What is she struggling with? What is her conflict?
3. What do you know about her husband?
4. The doctors said Louise died of "joy that kills." Do you agree? Explain.
5. This story was published in 1891. Does that matter? Could the same story be written about a wife today? Explain.

WILLIAM FAULKNER (1897–1962)

William Faulkner was born into a genteel Southern family and was raised in Oxford, Mississippi, where he attended the University of Mississippi. Following World War I, during which he served in the Canadian air force, he settled in Oxford, Mississippi, and worked for a time in the post office until he was forced to resign—he was lax in his duties and often became absorbed in writing or reading. By 1930 he had published a book of verse and a number of novels, including two of his greatest, The Sound and The Fury *(1929) and* As I Lay Dying *(1930), but he did not reach a wide readership until the publication of the novel* Sanctuary, *in 1931. Fifteen of his novels, as well as many of his short stories, are set in fictional Yoknapatawpha County, Mississippi, and concern themselves with the interconnected fortunes of a group of families of different social classes from the Civil War to modern times. Other major works include:* Light in August *(1931),* Absalom! Absalom! *(1939),* The Hamlet *(1940), and* Collected Stories *(1950). Faulkner was awarded the Nobel Prize in 1950. When asked about his inspiration for "A Rose for Emily," which originally appeared in* These Thirteen *(1931), a collection of short stories, Faulkner said: "That came from a picture of the strand of hair on the pillow. It was a ghost story. Simply a picture of a strand of hair on the pillow in the abandoned house."*

A ROSE FOR EMILY [1931]

I

When Miss Emily Grierson died, our whole town went to her funeral: the men through a sort of respectful affection for a fallen monument, the women mostly out of curiosity to see the inside of her house, which no one save an old manservant—a combined gardener and cook—had seen in at least ten years.

It was a big, squarish frame house that had once been white, decorated with cupolas and spires and scrolled balconies in the heavily lightsome style of the seventies, set on what had once been our most select street. But garages and cotton gins had encroached and obliterated even the august names of that neighborhood; only Miss Emily's house was left, lifting its stubborn and coquettish decay above the cotton wagons and the gasoline pumps—an eyesore among eyesores. And now Miss Emily had gone to join the representatives of those august names where they lay in the cedar-bemused cemetery among the ranked and anonymous graves of Union and Confederate soldiers who fell at the battle of Jefferson.

Alive, Miss Emily had been a tradition, a duty, and a care; a sort of hereditary obligation upon the town, dating from that day in 1894 when Colonel Sartoris, the mayor—he who fathered the edict that no Negro woman should appear on the streets without an apron—remitted her taxes, the dispensation dating from the death of her father on into perpetuity. Not that Miss Emily would have accepted charity. Colonel Sartoris invented an involved tale to the effect that Miss Emily's father had loaned money to the town, which the town, as a matter of business, preferred this way of repaying. Only a man of Colonel Sartoris' generation and thought could have invented it, and only a woman could have believed it.

When the next generation, with its more modern ideas, became mayors and aldermen, this arrangement created some little dissatisfaction. On the first of the year they mailed her a tax notice. February came, and there was no reply. They wrote her a formal letter, asking her to call at the sheriff's office at her convenience. A week later the mayor wrote her himself, offering to call or to send his car for her, and received in reply a note on paper of an archaic shape, in a thin, flowing calligraphy in faded ink, to the effect that she no longer went out at all. The tax notice was also enclosed, without comment.

5 They called a special meeting of the Board of Aldermen. A deputation waited upon her, knocked at the door through which no visitor had passed since she ceased giving china-painting lessons eight or ten years earlier. They were admitted by the old Negro into a dim hall from which a staircase mounted into still more shadow. It smelled of dust and disuse—a close, dank smell. The Negro led them into the parlor. It was furnished in heavy, leather-covered furniture. When the Negro opened the blinds of one window, they could see that the leather was cracked; and when they sat down, a faint dust rose sluggishly about their thighs, spinning with slow motes in the single sunray. On a tarnished gilt easel before the fireplace stood a crayon portrait of Miss Emily's father.

They rose when she entered—a small, fat woman in black, with a thin gold chain descending to her waist and vanishing into her belt, leaning on an ebony cane with a tarnished gold head. Her skeleton was small and spare; perhaps that was why what would have been merely plumpness in another was obesity in her. She looked bloated, like a body long submerged in motionless water, and of that pallid hue. Her eyes, lost in the fatty ridges of her face, looked like two small pieces of coal pressed into a lump of dough as they moved from one face to another while the visitors stated their errand.

She did not ask them to sit. She just stood in the door and listened quietly until the spokesman came to a stumbling halt. Then they could hear the invisible watch ticking at the end of the gold chain.

Her voice was dry and cold. "I have no taxes in Jefferson. Colonel Sartoris explained it to me. Perhaps one of you can gain access to the city records and satisfy yourselves."

"But we have. We are the city authorities, Miss Emily. Didn't you get a notice from the sheriff, signed by him?"

10 "I received a paper, yes," Miss Emily said. "Perhaps he considers himself the sheriff . . . . I have no taxes in Jefferson."

"But there is nothing on the books to show that, you see. We must go by the—"

"See Colonel Sartoris. I have no taxes in Jefferson."

"But, Miss Emily—"

"See Colonel Sartoris." (Colonel Sartoris had been dead almost ten years.) "I have no taxes in Jefferson. Tobe!" The Negro appeared. "Show these gentlemen out."

II

15 So she vanquished them, horse and foot, just as she had vanquished their fathers thirty years before about the smell. That was two years after her father's death and a short time after her sweetheart—the one we believed would marry her—had deserted her. After her father's death she went out very little; after her sweetheart went away, people hardly saw her at all. A few of the ladies had the temerity to call, but were not received, and the only sign of life about the place was the Negro man—a young man then—going in and out with a market basket.

"Just as if a man—any man—could keep a kitchen properly," the ladies said; so they were not surprised when the smell developed. It was another link between the gross, teeming world and the high and mighty Griersons.

A neighbor, a woman, complained to the mayor, Judge Stevens, eighty years old.

"But what will you have me do about it, madam?" he said.

"Why, send her word to stop it," the woman said. "Isn't there a law?"

20 "I'm sure that won't be necessary," Judge Stevens said. "It's probably just a snake or a rat that nigger of hers killed in the yard. I'll speak to him about it."

The next day he received two more complaints, one from a man who came in diffident deprecation. "We really must do something about it, Judge, I'd be the last one in the world to bother Miss Emily, but we've got to do something." That night the Board of Aldermen met—three gray-beards and one younger man, a member of the rising generation.

"It's simple enough," he said. "Send her word to have her place cleaned up. Given her a certain time to do it in, and if she don't . . . "

"Dammit, sir," Judge Stevens said, "will you accuse a lady to her face of smelling bad?"

So the next night, after midnight, four men crossed Miss Emily's lawn and slunk about the house like burglars, sniffing along the base of the brickwork and at the cellar openings while one of them performed a regular sowing motion with his hand out of a sack slung from his shoulder. They broke open the cellar door and sprinkled lime there, and in all the outbuildings. As they recrossed the lawn, a window that had been dark was lighted and Miss Emily sat in it, the light behind her, and her upright torso motionless as that of an idol. They crept quietly across the lawn and into the shadow of the locusts that lined the street. After a week or two the smell went away.

25 That was when people had begun to feel really sorry for her. People in our town remembering how old lady Wyatt, her great-aunt, had gone completely crazy at last, believed that the Griersons held themselves a little too high for what they really were. None of the young men were quite good enough for Miss Emily and such. We had long thought of them as a tableau; Miss Emily a slender figure in white in the background, her father a spraddled silhouette in the foreground, his back to her and clutching a horsewhip, the two of them framed by the backflung front door. So when she got to be thirty and was still single, we were not pleased exactly, but vin-

dicated; even with insanity in the family she wouldn't have turned down all of her chances if they had really materialized.

When her father died, it got about that the house was all that was left to her; and in a way, people were glad. At last they could pity Miss Emily. Being left alone, and a pauper, she had become humanized. Now she too would know the old thrill and the old despair of a penny more or less.

The day after his death all the ladies prepared to call at the house and offer condolence and aid, as is our custom. Miss Emily met them at the door, dressed as usual and with no trace of grief on her face. She told them that her father was not dead. She did that for three days, with the ministers calling on her, and the doctors, trying to persuade her to let them dispose of the body. Just as they were about to resort to law and force, she broke down, and they buried her father quickly.

We did not say she was crazy then. We believed she had to do that. We remembered all the young men her father had driven away, and we knew that with nothing left, she would have to cling to that which had robbed her, as people will.

III

She was sick for a long time. When we saw her again, her hair was cut short, making her look like a girl, with a vague resemblance to those angels in colored church windows—sort of tragic and serene.

30 The town had just let the contracts for paving the sidewalks, and in the summer after her father's death they began to work. The construction company came with niggers and mules and machinery, and a foreman named Homer Barron, a Yankee—a big, dark, ready man, with a big voice and eyes lighter than his face. The little boys would follow in groups to hear him cuss the niggers, and the niggers singing in time to the rise and fall of picks. Pretty soon he knew everybody in town. Whenever you heard a lot of laughing anywhere about the square, Homer Barron would be in the center of the group. Presently we began to see him and Miss Emily on Sunday afternoons driving in the yellow-wheeled buggy and the matched team of bays from the livery stable.

At first we were glad that Miss Emily would have an interest, because the ladies all said, "Of course a Grierson would not think seriously of a Northerner, a day laborer." But there were still others, older people, who said that even grief could not cause a real lady to forget *noblesse oblige*—without calling it *noblesse oblige.* They just said, "Poor Emily. Her kinsfolk should come to her." She had some kin in Alabama; but years ago her father had fallen out with them over the estate of old lady Wyatt, the crazy woman, and there was no communication between the two families. They had not even been represented at the funeral.

And as soon as the old people said, "Poor Emily," the whispering began. "Do you suppose it's really so?" they said to one another. "Of course it is. What else could . . . ." This behind their hands; rustling of craned silk and satin behind jalousies closed upon the sun of Sunday afternoon as the thin, swift clop-clop-clop of the matched team passed: "Poor Emily."

She carried her head high enough—even when we believed that she was fallen. It was as if she demanded more than ever the recognition of her dignity as the last

Grierson; as if it had wanted that touch of earthiness to reaffirm her imperviousness. Like when she bought the rat poison, the arsenic. That was over a year after they had begun to say "Poor Emily," and while the two female cousins were visiting her.

"I want some poison," she said to the druggist. She was over thirty then, still a slight woman, though thinner than usual, with cold, haughty black eyes in a face the flesh of which was strained across the temples and about the eyesockets as you imagine a lighthouse-keeper's face ought to look. "I want some poison," she said.

35 "Yes, Miss Emily. What kind? For rats and such? I'd recom—"

"I want the best you have. I don't care what kind."

The druggist named several. "They'll kill anything up to an elephant. But what you want is—"

"Arsenic." Miss Emily said. "Is that a good one?"

"Is . . . arsenic? Yes ma'am. But what you want—"

40 "I want arsenic."

The druggist looked down at her. She looked back at him, erect, her face like a strained flag. "Why, of course," the druggist said. "If that's what you want. But the law requires you to tell what you are going to use it for."

Miss Emily just stared at him, her head tilted back in order to look him eye for eye, until he looked away and went and got the arsenic and wrapped it up. The Negro delivery boy brought her the package; the druggist didn't come back. When she opened the package at home there was written on the box, under the skull and bones: "For rats."

IV

So the next day we all said. "She will kill herself"; and we said it would be the best thing. When she had first begun to be seen with Homer Barron, we had said, "She will marry him." Then we said, "She will persuade him yet," because Homer himself had remarked—he liked men, and it was known that he drank with the younger men in the Elks' Club—that he was not a marrying man. Later we said, "Poor Emily," behind the jalousies as they passed on Sunday afternoon in the glittering buggy, Miss Emily with her head high and Homer Barron with his hat cocked and a cigar in his teeth, reins and whip in a yellow glove.

Then some of the ladies began to say that it was a disgrace to the town and a bad example to the young people. The men did not want to interfere, but at last the ladies forced the Baptist minister—Miss Emily's people were Episcopal—to call upon her. He would never divulge what happened during that interview, but he refused to go back again. The next Sunday they again drove about the streets, and the following day the minister's wife wrote to Miss Emily's relations in Alabama.

45 So she had blood-kin under her roof again and we sat back to watch developments. At first nothing happened. Then we were sure that they were to be married. We learned that Miss Emily had been to the jeweler's and ordered a man's toilet set in silver, with the letters H.B. on each piece. Two days later we learned that she had bought a complete outfit of men's clothing, including a nightshirt, and we said, "They are married." We were really glad. We were glad because the two female cousins were even more Grierson than Miss Emily had ever been.

So we were surprised when Homer Barron—the streets had been finished some time since—was gone. We were a little disappointed that there was not a public blowing-off, but we believed that he had gone on to prepare for Miss Emily's coming, or to give her a chance to get rid of the cousins. (By that time it was a cabal, and we were all Miss Emily's allies to help circumvent the cousins.) Sure enough, after another week they departed. And, as we had expected all along, within three days Homer Barron was back in town. A neighbor saw the Negro man admit him at the kitchen door at dusk one evening.

And that was the last we saw of Homer Barron. And of Miss Emily for some time. The Negro man went in and out with the market basket, but the front door remained closed. Now and then we would see her at a window for a moment, as the men did that night when they sprinkled the lime, but for almost six months she did not appear on the streets. Then we knew that this was to be expected too; as if that quality of her father which had thwarted her woman's life so many times had been too virulent and too furious to die.

When we next saw Miss Emily, she had grown fat and her hair was turning gray. During the next few years it grew grayer and grayer until it attained an even pepper-and-salt iron-gray, when it ceased turning. Up to the day of her death at seventy-four it was still that vigorous iron-gray, like the hair of an active man.

From that time on her front door remained closed, save for a period of six or seven years, when she was about forty, during which she gave lessons in china-painting. She fitted up a studio in one of the downstairs rooms, where the daughters and granddaughters of Colonel Sartoris' contemporaries were sent to her with the same regularity and in the same spirit that they were sent on Sundays with a twenty-five cent piece for the collection plate. Meanwhile her taxes had been remitted.

Then the newer generation became the backbone and the spirit of the town, and the painting pupils grew up and fell away and did not send their children to her with boxes of color and tedious brushes and pictures cut from the ladies' magazines. The front door closed upon the last one and remained closed for good. When the town got free postal delivery, Miss Emily alone refused to let them fasten the metal numbers above her door and attach a mailbox to it. She would not listen to them.

Daily, monthly, yearly we watched the Negro grow grayer and more stooped, going in and out with the market basket. Each December we sent her a tax notice, which would be returned by the post office a week later, unclaimed. Now and then we could see her in one of the downstairs windows—she had evidently shut up the top floor of the house—like the carven torso of an idol in a niche, looking or not looking at us, we could never tell which. Thus she passed from generation to generation—dear, inescapable, impervious, tranquil, and perverse.

And so she died. Fell ill in the house filled with dust and shadows, with only a doddering Negro man to wait on her. We did not even know she was sick; we had long since given up trying to get any information from the Negro. He talked to no one, probably not even to her, for his voice had grown harsh and rusty, as if from disuse.

She died in one of the downstairs rooms, in a heavy walnut bed with a curtain, her gray head propped on a pillow yellow and moldy with age and lack of sunlight.

V

The Negro met the first of the ladies at the front door and let them in, with their hushed, sibilant voices and their quick, curious glances, and then he disappeared. He walked right through the house and out the back and was not seen again.

55 The two female cousins came at once. They held the funeral on the second day, with the town coming to look at Miss Emily beneath a mass of bought flowers, with the crayon face of her father musing profoundly above the bier and the ladies sibilant and macabre; and the very old men—some in their brushed Confederate uniforms—on the porch and the lawn, talking of Miss Emily as if she had been a contemporary of theirs, believing that they had danced with her and courted her perhaps, confusing time with its mathematical progression, as the old do, to whom all the past is not a diminishing road, but, instead, a huge meadow which no winter ever quite touches, divided from them now by the narrow bottleneck of the most recent decade of years.

Already we knew that there was one room in that region above stairs which no one had seen in forty years, and which would have to be forced. They waited until Miss Emily was decently in the ground before they opened it.

The violence of breaking down the door seemed to fill this room with pervading dust. A thin, acrid pall as of the tomb seemed to lie everywhere upon this room decked and furnished as for a bridal: upon the valance curtains of faded rose color, upon the rose-shaded lights, upon the dressing table, upon the delicate array of crystal and the man's toilet things backed with tarnished silver, silver so tarnished that the monogram was obscured. Among them lay a collar and tie, as if they had just been removed, which, lifted, left upon the surface a pale crescent in the dust. Upon a chair hung the suit, carefully folded; beneath it the two mute shoes and the discarded socks.

The man himself lay in the bed.

For a long while we just stood there, looking down at the profound and fleshless grin. The body had apparently once lain in the attitude of an embrace, but now the long sleep that outlasts love, that conquers even the grimace of love, had cuckolded him. What was left of him, rotted beneath what was left of the nightshirt, had become inextricable from the bed in which he lay; and upon him and upon the pillow beside him lay that even coating of the patient and biding dust.

60 Then we noticed that in the second pillow was the indentation of a head. One of us lifted something from it, and leaning forward, that faint and invisible dust dry and acrid in the nostrils, we saw a long strand of iron-gray hair.

➤ *QUESTIONS FOR READING AND WRITING*

1. Who is the narrator? How does the narrator's point of view influence what you know in the story? What difference does it make that the story is told in flashbacks instead of from beginning to end? What is the narrator's attitude toward Emily?
2. How do you feel about Emily Grierson? What is her conflict?
3. Who is Homer Barron? How does his characterization differ from Emily's?

4. At the end of the story, what is the significance of the iron-gray strand of hair on the second pillow? Are there indications earlier in the story that foreshadow this outcome?
5. Why is Emily such a formidable force in the town? Why does she seem to get away with so much?
6. In what way is the setting (the house, the town, Mississippi) of this story important? What is the relationship between the setting and the characters?
7. To what extent is this a story about change—or the inability to change?

JACOB LUDWIG CARL GRIMM
(1785–1863)

AND WILHELM CARL GRIMM
(1786–1859)

The Brothers Grimm are best known today for their collection of children's tales known popularly as Grimm's fairy tales, though during their lifetime they were both renowned as scholars of the German language. They derived most of the fairy tales in their volume, not from written sources, but by interviewing German peasants.

CINDERELLA [1812]

Translated by Margaret Hunt and James Stern

The wife of a rich man fell sick, and as she felt that her end was drawing near, she called her only daughter to her bedside and said: "Dear child, be good and pious, and then the good God will always protect you, and I will look down on you from heaven and be near you." Thereupon she closed her eyes and departed. Every day the maiden went out to her mother's grave and wept, and she remained pious and good. When winter came the snow spread a white sheet over the grave, and by the time the spring sun had drawn it off again, the man had taken another wife.

The woman had brought with her into the house two daughters, who were beautiful and fair of face, but vile and black of heart. Now began a bad time for the poor step-child. "Is the stupid goose to sit in the parlor with us?" they said. "He who wants to eat bread must earn it; out with the kitchen-wench." They took her pretty clothes away from her, put an old grey bedgown on her, and gave her wooden shoes. "Just look at the proud princess, how decked out she is!" they cried, and laughed, and led her into the kitchen. There she had to do hard work from morning till night, get up before daybreak, carry water, light fires, cook and wash. Besides this, the sisters did her every imaginable injury—they mocked her and emptied her peas and lentils into the ashes, so that she was forced to sit and pick them out again. In the evening when she had worked till she was weary she had no bed to go to, but had to sleep by the hearth in the cinders. And as on that account she always looked dusty and dirty, they called her Cinderella.

It happened that the father was once going to the fair, and he asked his two step-daughters what he should bring back for them. "Beautiful dresses," said one, "pearls and jewels," said the second. "And you, Cinderella," said he, "what will you have?" "Father, break off for me the first branch which knocks against your hat on your way home." So he bought beautiful dresses, pearls and jewels for his two step-daughters, and on his way home, as he was riding through a green thicket, a hazel twig brushed against him and knocked off his hat. Then he broke off the branch and took it with him. When he reached home he gave his step-daughters the things which they had wished for, and to Cinderella he gave the branch from the hazel bush. Cinderella thanked him, went to her mother's grave and planted the branch on it, and wept so much that the tears fell down on it and watered it. And it grew and became a handsome tree. Thrice a day Cinderella went and sat beneath it, and wept and prayed, and a little white bird always came on the tree, and if Cinderella expressed a wish, the bird threw down to her what she had wished for.

It happened, however, that the King gave orders for a festival which was to last three days, and to which all the beautiful young girls in the county were invited, in order that his son might choose himself a bride. When the two step-sisters heard that they too were to appear among the number, they were delighted, called Cinderella and said: "Comb our hair for us, brush our shoes and fasten our buckles, for we are going to the wedding at the King's palace." Cinderella obeyed, but wept, because she too would have liked to go with them to the dance, and begged her step-mother to allow her to do so. "You go, Cinderella!" said she; "covered in dust and dirt as you are, and would go to the festival? You have no clothes and shoes, and yet would dance!" As, however, Cinderella went on asking, the step-mother said at last: "I have emptied a dish of lentils into the ashes for you, if you have picked them out again in two hours, you shall go with us." The maiden went through the backdoor into the garden, and called: "You tame pigeons, you turtle-doves, and all you birds beneath the sky, come and help me to pick

The good into the pot,
The bad into the crop."

5 Then two white pigeons came in by the kitchen-window, and afterwards the turtle-doves, and at last all the birds beneath the sky, came whirring and crowding in, and alighted amongst the ashes. And the pigeons nodded with their heads and began pick, pick, pick, pick, and the rest began also pick, pick, pick, pick, and gathered all the good grains into the dish. Hardly had one hour passed before they had finished, and all flew out again. Then the girl took the dish to her step-mother, and was glad, and believed that now she would be allowed to go with them to the festival. But the stepmother said: "No, Cinderella, you have no clothes and you cannot dance; you would only be laughed at." And as Cinderella wept at this, the step-mother said: "If you can pick two dishes of lentils out of the ashes for me in one

hour, you shall go with us." And she thought to herself: "That she most certainly cannot do again." When the step-mother had emptied the two dishes of lentils amongst the ashes, the maiden went through the back-door into the garden and cried: "You tame pigeons, you turtle-doves, and all you birds beneath the sky, come and help me to pick

The good into the pot,
The bad into the crop."

Then two white pigeons came in by the kitchen-window, and afterwards the turtle-doves, and at length all the birds beneath the sky, came whirring and crowding in, and alighted amongst the ashes. And the doves nodded with their heads and began pick, pick, pick, pick, and the others began also pick, pick, pick, pick, and gathered all the good seeds into the dishes, and before half an hour was over they had already finished, and all flew out again. Then the maiden carried the dishes to the step-mother and was delighted, and believed that she might now go with them to the festival. But the step-mother said: "All this will not help; you cannot go with us, for you have no clothes and can not dance; we should be ashamed of you!" On this she turned her back on Cinderella, and hurried away with her two proud daughters.

As no one was now at home, Cinderella went to her mother's grave beneath the hazel tree, and cried:

"Shiver and quiver, little tree,
Silver and gold throw down over me."

Then the bird threw a gold and silver dress down to her, and slippers embroidered with silk and silver. She put on the dress with all speed, and went to the festival. Her step-sisters and the step-mother however did not know her, and thought she must be a foreign princess, for she looked so beautiful in the golden dress. They never once thought of Cinderella, and believed that she was sitting at home in the dirt, picking lentils out of the ashes. The prince approached her, took her by the hand and danced with her. He would dance with no other maiden, and never let loose of her hand, and if any one else came to invite her, he said: "This is my partner."

She danced till it was evening, and then she wanted to go home. But the King's son said: "I will go with you and bear you company," for he wished to see to whom the beautiful maiden belonged. She escaped from him, however, and sprang into the pigeon-house. The King's son waited until her father came, and then he told him that the unknown maiden had leapt into the pigeon-house. The old man thought: "Can it be Cinderella?" and they had to bring him an axe and a pickaxe that he might hew the pigeon-house to pieces, but no one was inside it. And when they got home Cinderella lay in her dirty clothes among the ashes, and a dim little oil-lamp was burning on the mantle-piece, for Cinderella had jumped quickly down from the back of the pigeon-house and had run to the little hazel-tree, and there she had taken off her beautiful clothes and laid them on the grave, and the bird had taken them away again, and then she had seated herself in the kitchen amongst the ashes in her grey gown.

10 Next day when the festival began afresh, and her parents and the stepsisters had gone once more, Cinderella went to the hazel-tree and said:

> "Shiver and quiver, little tree,
> Silver and gold throw down over me."

Then the bird threw down a much more beautiful dress than on the preceding day. And when Cinderella appeared at the festival in this dress, every one was astonished at her beauty. The King's son had waited until she came, and instantly took her by the hand and danced with no one but her. When others came and invited her he said: "This is my partner." When evening came she wished to leave, and the King's son followed her and wanted to see into which house she went. But she sprang away from him, and into the garden behind the house. Therein stood a beautiful tall tree on which hung the most magnificent pears. She clambered so nimbly between the branches like a squirrel that the King's son did not know where she was gone. He waited until her father came, and said to him: "The unknown maiden has escaped from me, and I believe she has climbed up the pear-tree." The father thought: "Can it be Cinderella?" and had an axe brought and cut the tree down, but no one was on it. And when they got into the kitchen, Cinderella lay there among the ashes, as usual, for she had jumped down on the other side of the tree, had taken the beautiful dress to the bird on the little hazel-tree, and put on her grey gown.

On the third day, when the parents and sisters had gone away, Cinderella went once more to her mother's grave and said to the little tree:

> "Shiver and quiver, little tree,
> Silver and gold throw down over me."

And now the bird threw down to her a dress which was more splendid and magnificent than any she had yet had, and the slippers were golden. And when she went to the festival in the dress, no one knew how to speak for astonishment. The King's son danced with her only, and if any one invited her to dance, he said: "This is my partner."

When evening came, Cinderella wished to leave, and the King's son was anxious to go with her, but she escaped from him so quickly that he could not follow her. The King's son, however, had employed a ruse, and had caused the whole staircase to be smeared with pitch, and there, when she ran down, had the maiden's left slipper remained stuck. The King's son picked it up, and it was small and dainty, and all golden. Next morning, he went with it to the father, and said to him: "No one shall be my wife but she whose foot this golden slipper fits." Then were the two sisters glad, for they had pretty feet. The eldest went with the shoe into her room and wanted to try it on, and her mother stood by. But she could not get her big toe into it, and the shoe was too small for her. Then her mother gave her a knife and said: "Cut the toe off; when you are Queen you will no more need to go on foot." The maiden cut the toe off, forced the foot into the shoe, swallowed the pain, and went out to the King's son. Then he took her on his horse as his bride and rode away with her. They were obliged, however, to pass the grave, and there, on the hazel-tree, the two little pigeons sat on it and cried:

"Turn and peep, turn and peep,
There's blood within the shoe,
The shoe it is too small for her,
The true bride waits for you."

Then he looked at her foot and saw how the blood was trickling from it. He turned his horse round and took the false bride home again, and said she was not the true one, and that the other sister was to put the shoe on. Then this one went into her chamber and got her toes safely into the shoe, but her heel was too large. So her mother gave her a knife and said: "Cut a bit off your heel; when you are Queen you will have no more need to go on foot." The maiden cut a bit off her heel, forced her foot into the shoe, swallowed the pain, and went out to the King's son. He took her on his horse as his bride, and rode away with her, but when they passed by the hazel-tree, the two little pigeons sat on it and cried:

"Turn and peep, turn and peep,
There's blood within the shoe,
The shoe it is too small for her,
The true bride waits for you."

He looked down at her foot and saw how the blood was running out of her shoe, and how it had stained her white stocking quite red. Then he turned his horse and took the false bride home again. "This also is not the right one," said he, "have you no other daughter?" "No," said the man, "there is still a little stunted kitchen-wench which my late wife left behind her, but she cannot possibly be the bride." The King's son said he was to send her up to him; but the mother answered: "Oh no, she is much too dirty, she cannot show herself!" But he absolutely insisted on it, and Cinderella had to be called. She first washed her hands and face clean, and then went and bowed down before the King's son, who gave her the golden shoe. Then she seated herself on a stool, drew her foot out of the heavy wooden shoe, and put it into the slipper, which fitted like a glove. And when she rose up and the King's son looked at her face he recognized the beautiful maiden who had danced with him and cried: "That is the true bride!" The step-mother and the two sisters were horrified and became pale with rage; he, however, took Cinderella on his horse and rode away with her. As they passed by the hazel tree, the two white doves cried:

"Turn and peep, turn and peep,
No blood is in the shoe,
The shoe is not too small for her,
The true bride rides with you,"

and when they had cried that, the two came flying down and placed themselves on Cinderella's shoulders, one on the right, the other on the left, and remained sitting there.

15 When the wedding with the King's son was to be celebrated, the two false sisters came and wanted to get into favor with Cinderella and share her good fortune. When the betrothed couple went to church, the elder was at the right side and the younger at the left, and the pigeons pecked out one eye from each of them. Afterwards as they came back, the elder was at the left, and the younger at

the right, and then the pigeons pecked out the other eye from each. And thus, for their wickedness and falsehood, they were punished with blindness all their days.

➤ *QUESTIONS FOR READING AND WRITING*

1. Did you find anything different about this version of Cinderella than the one you are used to reading or viewing?
2. How are you affected by the harsh punishment that Cinderella's stepsisters receive? Do you think they deserve it?
3. Do these gruesome details change the impact of the story? Why do you think they have been removed from the modern version of this fairy tale?

ERNEST HEMINGWAY (1899–1961)

Ernest Hemingway was born in Oak Park, Illinois, and began his writing career as a newspaper reporter. He was an active participant in World War I, the Spanish Civil War, and World War II, and often used his personal experiences as the source of his work. His direct, spare writing style was a major influence on many writers in the twentieth century. His writing includes A Farewell to Arms *(1929),* For Whom the Bell Tolls *(1940), and* The Old Man and the Sea *(1954). He received the Nobel Prize for literature in 1954.*

HILLS LIKE WHITE ELEPHANTS [1927]

The hills across the valley of the Ebro were long and white. On this side there was no shade and no trees and the station was between two lines of rails in the sun. Close against the side of the station there was the warm shadow of the building and a curtain, made of strings of bamboo beads, hung across the open door into the bar, to keep out flies. The American and the girl with him sat at a table in the shade, outside the building. It was very hot and the express from Barcelona would come in forty minutes. It stopped at this junction for two minutes and went on to Madrid.

"What should we drink?" the girl asked. She had taken off her hat and put it on the table.

"It's pretty hot," the man said.

"Let's drink beer."

5 "Dos cervezas," the man said into the curtain.

"Big ones?" a woman asked from the doorway.

"Yes. Two big ones."

The woman brought two glasses of beer and two felt pads. She put the felt pads and the beer glasses on the table and looked at the man and the girl. The girl was looking off at the line of hills. They were white in the sun and the country was brown and dry.

"They look like white elephants," she said.

"I've never seen one," the man drank his beer.

"No, you wouldn't have."

"I might have," the man said. "Just because you say I wouldn't have doesn't prove anything."

The girl looked at the bead curtain. "They've painted something on it," she said. "What does it say?"

"Anis del Toro. It's a drink."

"Could we try it?"

The man called "Listen" through the curtain. The woman came out from the bar.

"Four reales."

"We want two Anis del Toro."

"With water?"

"Do you want it with water?"

"I don't know," the girl said. "Is it good with water?"

"It's all right."

"You want them with water?" asked the woman.

"Yes, with water."

"It tastes like licorice," the girl said and put the glass down.

"That's the way with everything."

"Yes," said the girl. "Everything tastes of licorice. Especially all the things you've waited so long for, like absinthe."

"Oh, cut it out."

"You started it," the girl said. "I was being amused. I was having a fine time."

"Well, let's try and have a fine time."

"All right. I was trying. I said the mountains looked like white elephants. Wasn't that bright?"

"That was bright."

"I wanted to try this new drink. That's all we do, isn't it—look at things and try new drinks?"

"I guess so."

The girl looked across at the hills.

"They're lovely hills," she said. "They don't really look like white elephants. I just meant the coloring of their skin through the trees."

"Should we have another drink?"

"All right."

The warm wind blew the bead curtain against the table.

"The beer's nice and cool," the man said.

"It's lovely," the girl said.

"It's really an awfully simple operation, Jig," the man said. "It's not really an operation at all."

The girl looked at the ground the table legs rested on.

"I know you wouldn't mind it, Jig. It's really not anything. It's just to let the air in."

The girl did not say anything.

"I'll go with you and I'll stay with you all the time. They just let the air in and then it's all perfectly natural."

"Then what will we do afterward?"

"We'll be fine afterward. Just like we were before."

"What makes you think so?"

"That's the only thing that bothers us. It's the only thing that's made us unhappy."

The girl looked at the bead curtain, put her hand out and took hold of two of the strings of beads.

"And you think then we'll be all right and be happy."

"I know we will. You don't have to be afraid. I've known lots of people that have done it."

"So have I," said the girl. "And afterward they were all so happy."

"Well," the man said, "if you don't want to you don't have to. I wouldn't have you do it if you didn't want to. But I know it's perfectly simple."

"And you really want to?"

"I think it's the best thing to do. But I don't want you to do it if you don't really want to."

"And if I do it you'll be happy and things will be like they were and you'll love me?"

"I love you now. You know I love you."

"I know. But if I do it, then it will be nice again if I say things are like white elephants, and you'll like it?"

"I'll love it. I love it now but I just can't think about it. You know how I get when I worry."

"If I do it you won't ever worry?"

"I won't worry about that because it's perfectly simple."

"Then I'll do it. Because I don't care about me."

"What do you mean?"

"I don't care about me."

"Well, I care about you."

"Oh, yes. But I don't care about me. And I'll do it and then everything will be fine."

"I don't want you to do it if you feel that way."

The girl stood up and walked to the end of the station. Across, on the other side, were fields of grain and trees along the banks of the Ebro. Far away, beyond the river, were mountains. The shadow of a cloud moved across the field of grain and she saw the river through the trees.

"And we could have all this," she said. "And we could have everything and every day we make it more impossible."

"What did you say?"

"I said we could have everything."

"We can have everything."

"No, we can't."

"We can have the whole world."

"No, we can't."

"We can go everywhere."

"No, we can't. It isn't ours any more."

"It's ours."

"No, it isn't. And once they take it away, you never get it back."

"But they haven't taken it away."

"We'll wait and see."

"Come on back in the shade," he said. "You mustn't feel that way."

"I don't feel any way," the girl said. "I just know things."

"I don't want you to do anything that you don't want to do—"

"Nor that isn't good for me," she said. "I know. Could we have another beer?"

"All right. But you've got to realize—"

"I realize," the girl said. "Can't we maybe stop talking?"

They sat down at the table and the girl looked across at the hills on the dry side of the valley and the man looked at her and at the table.

"You've got to realize," he said, "that I don't want you to do it if you don't want to. I'm perfectly willing to go through with it if it means anything to you."

"Doesn't it mean anything to you? We could get along."

"Of course it does. But I don't want anybody but you. I don't want any one else. And I know it's perfectly simple."

"Yes, you know it's perfectly simple."

"It's all right for you to say that, but I do know it."

"Would you do something for me now?"

"I'd do anything for you."

"Would you please please please please please please please stop talking?"

He did not say anything but looked at the bags against the wall of the station. There were labels on them from all the hotels where they had spent nights.

"But I don't want you to," he said, "I don't care anything about it."

"I'll scream," the girl said.

The woman came out through the curtains with two glasses of beer and put them down on the damp felt pads. "The train comes in five minutes," she said.

"What did she say?" asked the girl.

"That the train is coming in five minutes."

The girl smiled brightly at the woman, to thank her.

"I'd better take the bags over to the other side of the station," the man said. She smiled at him.

"All right. Then come back and we'll finish the beer."

He picked up the two heavy bags and carried them around the station to the other tracks. He looked up the tracks but could not see the train. Coming back, he walked through the barroom, where people waiting for the train were drinking. He drank an Anis at the bar and looked at the people. They were all waiting reasonably for the train. He went out through the bead curtain. She was sitting at the table and smiled at him.

"Do you feel better?" he asked.

"I feel fine," she said. "There's nothing wrong with me. I feel fine."

➤ *QUESTIONS FOR READING AND WRITING*

1. What are the man and woman discussing? Do you have strong feelings about this topic? If so, how does that influence your response? If you were placed in this situation, what would you say or do?
2. From what point of view is the story told? How does that affect your response?
3. What is the conflict in the story? Is it external, internal, both?
4. Some researchers have suggested that men and women talk to each other with different intentions. Do you see any indication of this in the story? How are you affected by the language of the conversation?
5. What does their conversation tell you about these characters and their relationship? Do you think this relationship has a positive future? Why?

Charlotte Perkins Gilman

(1860–1935)

Charlotte Perkins Gilman was born in Hartford, Connecticut. Because her father, the writer Frederick Beecher Perkins, abandoned the family when she was only an infant, she was often left in the company of relatives, who included Harriet Beecher Stowe, the author of Uncle Tom's Cabin, *and the feminist activists Isabella Beecher Hooker and Catherine Beecher. These women instilled in Gilman the ideas of equality and independence, which formed the basis for the political activism that made her famous later in life. Though she wrote numerous works about the conditions of women, her reputation as a writer of literature rests almost solely on her short story "The Yellow Wallpaper," which adds a feminist twist to the psychological horror story pioneered by Edgar Allen Poe. The story, written in 1899, was based on her own experiences. During her unhappy first marriage, Gilman suffered a severe depression following the birth of her daughter. A noted doctor of the time prescribed a regimen of bed rest and minimal intellectual stimulation. Her condition only worsened. Eventually she rebelled, and taking responsibility for her own cure, separated from her husband and moved to California. In 1900, she married again, this time happily to her cousin George Houghton Gilman. She remained active politically until she took her own life in 1935, after fighting a losing battle with breast cancer.*

The Yellow Wallpaper [1899]

It is very seldom that mere ordinary people like John and myself secure ancestral halls for the summer.

A colonial mansion, a hereditary estate, I would say a haunted house and reach the height of romantic felicity—but that would be asking too much of fate!

Still I will proudly declare that there is something queer about it.

Else, why should it be let so cheaply? And why have stood so long untenanted?

5 John laughs at me, of course, but one expects that.

John is practical in the extreme. He has no patience with faith, an intense horror of superstition, and he scoffs openly at any talk of things not to be felt and seen and put down in figures.

John is a physician, and *perhaps*—(I would not say it to a living soul, of course, but this is dead paper and a great relief to my mind)—*perhaps* that is one reason I do not get well faster.

You see, he does not believe I am sick! And what can one do?

If a physician of high standing, and one's own husband, assures friends and relatives that there is really nothing the matter with one but temporary nervous depression—a slight hysterical tendency—what is one to do?

10 My brother is also a physician, and also of high standing, and he says the same thing.

So I take phosphates or phosphites—whichever it is—and tonics, and air and exercise, and journeys, and am absolutely forbidden to "work" until I am well again.

Personally, I disagree with their ideas.

Personally, I believe that congenial work, with excitement and change, would do me good.

But what is one to do?

15 I did write for a while in spite of them: but it *does* exhaust me a good deal—having to be so sly about it, or else meet with heavy opposition.

I sometimes fancy that in my condition, if I had less opposition and more society and stimulus—but John says the very worst thing I can do is to think about my condition, and I confess it always makes me feel bad.

So I will let it alone and talk about the house.

The most beautiful place! It is quite alone, standing well back from the road, quite three miles from the village. It makes me think of English places that you read about, for there are hedges and walls and gates that lock, and lots of separate little houses for the gardeners and people.

There is a *delicious* garden! I never saw such a garden—large and shady, full of box-bordered paths, and lined with long grape-covered arbors with seats under them.

20 There were greenhouses, but they are all broken now.

There was some legal trouble, I believe, something about the heirs and coheirs; anyhow, the place has been empty for years.

That spoils my ghostliness, I am afraid, but I don't care—there is something strange about the house—I can feel it.

I even said so to John one moonlight evening, but he said what I felt was a draught, and shut the window.

I get unreasonably angry with John sometimes. I'm sure I never used to be so sensitive. I think it is due to this nervous condition.

But John says if I feel so I shall neglect proper self-control; so I take pains to control myself—before him, at least, and that makes me very tired.

I don't like our room a bit. I wanted one downstairs that opened onto the piazza and had roses all over the window, and such pretty old-fashioned chintz hangings! But John would not hear of it.

He said there was only one window and not room for two beds, and no near room for him if he took another.

He is very careful and loving, and hardly lets me stir without special direction.

I have a schedule prescription for each hour in the day; he takes all care from me, and so I feel basely ungrateful not to value it more.

He said he came here solely on my account, that I was to have perfect rest and all the air I could get. "Your exercise depends on your strength, my dear," said he, "and your food somewhat on your appetite; but air you can absorb all the time." So we took the nursery at the top of the house.

It is a big, airy room, the whole floor nearly, with windows that look all ways, and air and sunshine galore. It was nursery first, and then playroom and gymnasium, I should judge, for the windows are barred for little children, and there are rings and things in the walls.

The paint and paper look as if a boys' school had used it. It is stripped off—the paper—in great patches all around the head of my bed, about as far as I can reach, and in a great place on the other side of the room low down. I never saw a worse paper in my life. One of those sprawling, flamboyant patterns committing every artistic sin.

It is dull enough to confuse the eye in following, pronounced enough to constantly irritate and provoke study, and when you follow the lame uncertain curves for a little distance they suddenly commit suicide—plunge off at outrageous angles, destroy themselves in unheard-of contradictions.

The color is repellent, almost revolting: a smouldering unclean yellow, strangely faded by the slow-turning sunlight. It is a dull yet lurid orange in some places, a sickly sulphur tint in others.

No wonder the children hated it! I should hate it myself if I had to live in this room long.

There comes John, and I must put this away—he hates to have me write a word.

We have been here two weeks, and I haven't felt like writing before, since that first day.

I am sitting by the window now, up in this atrocious nursery, and there is nothing to hinder my writing as much as I please, save lack of strength.

John is away all day, and even some nights when his cases are serious.

I am glad my case is not serious!

But these nervous troubles are dreadfully depressing.

John does not know how much I really suffer. He knows there is no reason to suffer, and that satisfies him.

Of course it is only nervousness. It does weigh on me so not to do my duty in any way!

I meant to be such a help to John, such a real rest and comfort, and here I am a comparative burden already!

Nobody would believe what an effort it is to do what little I am able—to dress and entertain, and order things.

It is fortunate Mary is so good with the baby. Such a dear baby!

And yet I *cannot* be with him, it makes me so nervous.

I suppose John never was nervous in his life. He laughs at me so about this wallpaper!

At first he meant to repaper the room, but afterward he said that I was letting it get the better of me, and that nothing was worse for a nervous patient than to give way to such fancies.

He said that after the wallpaper was changed it would be the heavy bedstead, and then the barred windows, and then that gate at the head of the stairs, and so on.

"You know the place is doing you good," he said, "and really, dear, I don't care to renovate the house just for a three months' rental."

"Then do let us go downstairs," I said, "there are such pretty rooms there."

Then he took me in his arms and called me a blessed little goose, and said he would go down to the cellar, if I wished, and have it whitewashed into the bargain.

But he is right enough about the beds and windows and things.

It is as airy and comfortable a room as anyone need wish, and, of course, I would not be so silly as to make him uncomfortable just for a whim.

I'm really getting quite fond of the big room, all but that horrid paper.

Out of one window I can see the garden—those mysterious deep-shaded arbors, the riotous old-fashioned flowers, and bushes and gnarly trees.

Out of another I get a lovely view of the bay and a little private wharf belonging to the estate. There is a beautiful shaded lane that runs down there from the house. I always fancy I see people walking in these numerous paths and arbors, but John has cautioned me not to give way to fancy in the least. He says that with my imaginative power and habit of story-making, a nervous weakness like mine is sure to lead to all manner of excited fancies, and that I ought to use my will and good sense to check the tendency. So I try.

I think sometimes that if I were only well enough to write a little it would relieve the press of ideas and rest me.

But I find I get pretty tired when I try.

It is so discouraging not to have any advice and companionship about my work. When I get really well, John says we will ask Cousin Henry and Julia down for a long visit; but he says he would as soon put fireworks in my pillow-case as to let me have those stimulating people about now.

I wish I could get well faster.

But I must not think about that. This paper looks to me as if it *knew* what a vicious influence it had!

There is a recurrent spot where the pattern lolls like a broken neck and two bulbous eyes stare at you upside down.

65 I get positively angry with the impertinence of it and the everlastingness. Up and down and sideways they crawl, and those absurd, unblinking eyes are everywhere. There is one place where two breadths didn't match, and the eyes go all up and down the line, one a little higher than the other.

I never saw so much expression in an inanimate thing before, and we all know how much expression they have! I used to lie awake as a child and get more entertainment and terror out of blank walls and plain furniture than most children could find in a toystore.

I remember what a kindly wink the knobs of our big, old bureau used to have, and there was one chair that always seemed like a strong friend.

I used to feel that if any of the other things looked too fierce I could always hop into that chair and be safe.

The furniture in this room is no worse than inharmonious, however, for we had to bring it all from downstairs. I suppose when this was used as a playroom they had to take the nursery things out, and no wonder! I never saw such ravages as the children have made here.

70 The wallpaper, as I said before, is torn off in spots, and it sticketh closer than a brother—they must have had perseverance as well as hatred.

Then the floor is scratched and gouged and splintered, the plaster itself is dug out here and there, and this great heavy bed which is all we found in the room, looks as if it had been through the wars.

But I don't mind it a bit—only the paper.

There comes John's sister. Such a dear girl as she is, and so careful of me! I must not let her find me writing.

She is a perfect and enthusiastic housekeeper, and hopes for no better profession. I verily believe she thinks it is the writing which made me sick!

75 But I can write when she is out, and see her a long way off from these windows.

There is one that commands the road, a lovely shaded winding road, and one that just looks off over the country. A lovely country, too, full of great elms and velvet meadows.

This wallpaper has a kind of sub-pattern in a different shade, a particularly irritating one, for you can only see it in certain lights, and not clearly then.

But in the places where it isn't faded and where the sun is just so—I can see a strange, provoking, formless sort of figure that seems to skulk about behind that silly and conspicuous front design.

There's sister on the stairs!

80 Well, the Fourth of July is over! The people are all gone and I am tired out. John thought it might do me good to see a little company, so we just had Mother and Nellie and the children down for a week.

Of course I didn't do a thing. Jennie sees to everything now.

But it tired me all the same.

John says if I don't pick up faster he shall send me to Weir Mitchell[1] in the fall.

But I don't want to go there at all. I had a friend who was in his hands once, and she says he is just like John and my brother, only more so!

85 Besides, it is such an undertaking to go so far.

[1]**Weir Mitchell** a physician known for his "rest cure" for psychoneuroses

I don't feel as if it was worth while to turn my hand over for anything, and I'm getting dreadfully fretful and querulous.

I cry at nothing, and cry most of the time.

Of course I don't when John is here, or anybody else, but when I am alone.

And I am alone a good deal just now. John is kept in town very often by serious cases, and Jennie is good and lets me alone when I want her to.

So I walk a little in the garden or down that lovely lane, sit on the porch under the roses, and lie down up here a good deal.

I'm getting really fond of the room in spite of the wallpaper. Perhaps *because* of the wallpaper.

It dwells in my mind so!

I lie here on this great immovable bed—it is nailed down. I believe—and follow that pattern about by the hour. It is as good as gymnastics, I assure you. I start, we'll say, at the bottom, down in the corner over there where it has not been touched, and I determine for the thousandth time that I *will* follow that pointless pattern to some sort of a conclusion.

I know a little of the principle of design, and I know this thing was not arranged on any laws of radiation, or alternation, or repetition, or symmetry, or anything else that I ever heard of.

It is repeated, of course, by the breadths, but not otherwise.

Looked at in one way each breadth stands alone; the bloated curves and flourishes—a kind of "debased Romanesque" with delirium tremens go waddling up and down in isolated columns of fatuity.

But, on the other hand, they connect diagonally, and the sprawling outlines run off in great slanting waves of optic horror, like a lot of wallowing sea-weeds in full chase.

The whole thing goes horizontally, too, at least it seems so, and I exhaust myself in trying to distinguish the order of its going in that direction.

They have used a horizontal breadth for a frieze, and that adds wonderfully to the confusion.

There is one end of the room where it is almost intact, and there, when the crosslights fade and the low sun shines directly upon it, I can almost fancy radiation after all—the interminable grotesque seems to form around a common center and rush off in headlong plunges of equal distraction.

It makes me tired to follow it. I will take a nap, I guess.

I don't know why I should write this.

I don't want to.

I don't feel able.

And I know John would think it absurd. But I *must* say what I feel and think in some way—it is such a relief.

But the effort is getting to be greater than the relief!

Half the time now I am awfully lazy, and lie down ever so much. John says I mustn't lose my strength, and has me take cod liver oil and lots of tonics and things, to say nothing of ale and wine and rare meat.

Dear John! He loves me very dearly, and hates to have me sick. I tried to have a real earnest reasonable talk with him the other day, and tell him how I wish he would let me go and make a visit to Cousin Henry and Julia.

But he said I wasn't able to go, nor able to stand it after I got there: and I did not make out a very good case for myself, for I was crying before I had finished.

110 It is getting to be a great effort for me to think straight. Just this nervous weakness, I suppose.

And dear John gathered me up in his arms, and just carried me upstairs and laid me on the bed, and sat by me and read to me till it tired my head.

He said I was his darling and his comfort and all he had, and that I must take care of myself for his sake, and keep well.

He says no one but myself can help me out of it, that I must use my will and self-control and not let any silly fancies run away with me.

There's one comfort—the baby is well and happy, and does not have to occupy this nursery with the horrid wallpaper.

115 If we had not used it, that blessed child would have! What a fortunate escape! Why, I wouldn't have a child of mine, an impressionable little thing, live in such a room for worlds.

I never thought of it before, but it is lucky that John kept me here after all. I can stand it so much easier than a baby, you see.

Of course I never mention it to them any more—I am too wise—but I keep watch for it all the same.

There are things in that paper that nobody knows but me, or ever will.

Behind that outside pattern the dim shapes get clearer every day.

120 It is always the same shape, only very numerous.

And it is like a woman stooping down and creeping about behind that pattern. I don't like it a bit. I wonder—I begin to think—I wish John would take me away from here!

It is so hard to talk with John about my case, because he is so wise, and because he loves me so.

But I tried last night.

It was moonlight. The moon shines in all around just as the sun does.

125 I hate to see it sometimes, it creeps so slowly, and always comes in by one window or another.

John was asleep and I hated to waken him, so I kept still and watched the moonlight on that undulating wallpaper till I felt creepy.

The faint figure behind seemed to shake the pattern, just as if she wanted to get out.

I got up softly and went to feel and see if the paper *did* move, and when I came back John was awake.

"What is it, little girl?" he said. "Don't go walking about like that—you'll get cold."

130 I thought it was a good time to talk, so I told him that I really was not gaining here, and that I wished he would take me away.

"Why darling!" said he, "our lease will be up in three weeks, and I can't see how to leave before."

"The repairs are not done at home, and I cannot possibly leave town just now. Of course if you were in any danger, I could and would, but you really are better, dear, whether you can see it or not. I am a doctor, dear, and I know. You are gaining flesh and color, your appetite is better, I feel really much easier about you."

"I don't weigh a bit more," said I, "nor as much; and my appetite may be better in the evening when you are here but it is worse in the morning when you are away!"

"Bless her little heart!" said he with a big hug, "She shall be as sick as she pleases! But now let's improve the shining hours by going to sleep, and talk about it in the morning!"

135 "And you won't go away?" I asked gloomily.

"Why, how can I, dear? It is only three weeks more and then we will take a nice little trip of a few days while Jennie is getting the house ready. Really, dear, you are better!"

"Better in body perhaps—" I began, and stopped short, for he sat up straight and looked at me with such a stern, reproachful look that I could not say another word.

"My darling," said he, "I beg of you, for my sake and for our child's sake, as well as for your own, that you will never for one instant let that idea enter your mind! There is nothing so dangerous, so fascinating, to a temperament like yours. It is a false and foolish fancy. Can you not trust me as a physician when I tell you so?"

So of course I said no more on that score, and we went to sleep before long. He thought I was asleep first, but I wasn't and lay there for hours trying to decide whether that front pattern and the back pattern really did move together or separately.

140 On a pattern like this, by daylight, there is a lack of sequence, a defiance of law, that is a constant irritant to a normal mind.

The color is hideous enough, and unreliable enough, and infuriating enough, but the pattern is torturing.

You think you have mastered it, but just as you get well under way in following, it turns a back-somersault and there you are. It slaps you in the face, knocks you down, and tramples upon you. It is like a bad dream.

The outside pattern is a florid arabesque, reminding one of a fungus. If you can imagine a toadstool in joints, an interminable string of toadstools, budding and sprouting in endless convolutions—why, that is something like it.

That is, sometimes!

145 There is one marked peculiarity about this paper, a thing nobody seems to notice but myself, and that is that it changes as the light changes.

When the sun shoots in through the east window—I always watch for that first long, straight ray—it changes so quickly that I never can quite believe it.

That is why I watch it always.

By moonlight—the moon shines in all night when there is a moon—I wouldn't know it was the same paper.

At night in any kind of light, in twilight, candlelight, lamplight, and worst of all by moonlight, it becomes bars! The outside pattern, I mean, and the woman behind it is as plain as can be.

150 I didn't realize for a long time what the thing was that showed behind, that dim sub-pattern, but now I am quite sure it is a woman.

By daylight she is subdued, quiet. I fancy it is the pattern that keeps her so still. It is so puzzling. It keeps me quiet by the hour.

I lie down ever so much now. John says it is good for me, and to sleep all I can.

Indeed he started the habit by making me lie down for an hour after each meal.

It is a very bad habit, I am convinced, for you see, I don't sleep.

155 And that cultivates deceit, for I don't tell them I'm awake—oh, no!

The fact is I am getting a little afraid of John.

He seems very queer sometimes, and even Jennie has an inexplicable look.

It strikes me occasionally, just as a scientific hypothesis, that perhaps it is the paper!

I have watched John when he did not know I was looking, and come into the room suddenly on the most innocent excuses, and I've caught him several times *looking at the paper!* And Jennie too. I caught Jennie with her hand on it once.

160 She didn't know I was in the room, and when I asked her in a quiet, a very quiet voice, with the most restrained manner possible, what she was doing with the paper, she turned around as if she had been caught stealing, and looked quite angry—asked me why I should frighten her so!

Then she said that the paper stained everything it touched, that she had found yellow smooches on all my clothes and John's, and she wished we would be more careful!

Did not that sound innocent? But I know she was studying that pattern, and I am determined that nobody shall find it out but myself!

Life is very much more exciting now than it used to be. You see I have something more to expect, to look forward to, to watch. I really do eat better, and am more quiet than I was.

John is so pleased to see me improve! He laughed a little the other day, and said I seemed to be flourishing in spite of my wallpaper.

165 I turned it off with a laugh. I had no intention of telling him it was *because* of the wallpaper—he would make fun of me. He might even want to take me away.

I don't want to leave now until I have found it out. There is a week more, and I think that will be enough.

I'm feeling so much better!

I don't sleep much at night, for it is so interesting to watch developments, but I sleep a good deal during the daytime.

In the daytime it is tiresome and perplexing.

170 There are always new shoots on the fungus, and new shades of yellow all over it. I cannot keep count of them, though I have tried conscientiously.

It is the strangest yellow, that wallpaper! It makes me think of all the yellow things I ever saw—not beautiful ones like buttercups, but old foul, bad yellow things.

But there is something else about that paper—the smell! I noticed it the moment we came into the room, but with so much air and sun it was not bad. Now we have had a week of fog and rain, and whether the windows are open or not, the smell is here.

It creeps all over the house.

I find it hovering in the dining-room, skulking in the parlor, hiding in the hall, lying in wait for me on the stairs.

175 It gets into my hair.

Even when I go to ride, if I turn my head suddenly and surprise it—there is that smell!

Such a peculiar odor, too! I have spent hours in trying to analyze it, to find what it smelled like.

It is not bad—at first—and very gentle, but quite the subtlest, most enduring odor I ever met.

In this damp weather it is awful, I wake up in the night and find it hanging over me.

180 It used to disturb me at first. I thought seriously of burning the house—to reach the smell.

But now I am used to it. The only thing I can think of that it is like is the *color* of the paper! A yellow smell.

There is a very funny mark on this wall, low down, near the mopboard. A streak that runs round the room. It goes behind every piece of furniture, except the bed, a long, straight, even *smooch,* as if it had been rubbed over and over.

I wonder how it was done and who did it, and what they did it for. Round and round and round—round and round and round—it makes me dizzy!

I really have discovered something at last.

185 Through watching so much at night, when it changes so, I have finally found out.

The front pattern *does* move—and no wonder! The woman behind shakes it!

Sometimes I think there are a great many women behind, and sometimes only one, and she crawls around fast, and her crawling shakes it all over.

Then in the very bright spots she keeps still, and in the very shady spots she just takes hold of the bars and shakes them hard.

And she is all the time trying to climb through. But nobody could climb through that pattern—it strangles so: I think that is why it has so many heads.

190 They get through, and then the pattern strangles them off and turns them upside down, and makes their eyes white!

If those heads were covered or taken off it would not be half so bad.

I think that woman gets out in the daytime!

And I'll tell you why—privately—I've seen her!

I can see her out of every one of my windows!

195 It is the same woman, I know, for she is always creeping, and most women do not creep by daylight.

I see her in that long shaded lane, creeping up and down. I see her in those dark grape arbors, creeping all around the garden.

I see her on that long road under the trees, creeping along, and when a carriage comes she hides under the blackberry vines.

I don't blame her a bit. It must be very humiliating to be caught creeping by daylight!

I always lock the door when I creep by daylight. I can't do it at night, for I know John would suspect something at once.

200 And John is so queer now, that I don't want to irritate him. I wish he would take another room! Besides, I don't want anybody to get that woman out at night but myself.

I often wonder if I could see her out of all the windows at once.

But, turn as fast as I can, I can only see out of one at one time.

And though I always see her, she *may* be able to creep faster than I can turn! I have watched her sometimes away off in the open country, creeping as fast as a cloud shadow in a wind.

If only that top pattern could be gotten off from the under one! I mean to try it, little by little.

205 I have found out another funny thing, but I shan't tell it this time! It does not do to trust people too much.

There are only two more days to get this paper off, and I believe John is beginning to notice. I don't like the look in his eyes.

And I heard him ask Jennie a lot of professional questions about me. She had a very good report to give.

She said I slept a good deal in the daytime.

John knows I don't sleep very well at night, for all I'm so quiet!

210 He asked me all sorts of questions, too, and pretended to be very loving and kind.

As if I couldn't see through him!

Still, I don't wonder he acts so, sleeping under this paper for three months.

It only interests me, but I feel sure John and Jennie are affected by it.

Hurrah! This is the last day, but it is enough. John is to stay in town over night, and won't be out until this evening.

215 Jennie wanted to sleep with me—the sly thing; but I told her I should undoubtedly rest better for a night all alone.

That was clever, for really I wasn't alone a bit! As soon as it was moonlight and that poor thing began to crawl and shake the pattern, I got up and ran to help her.

I pulled and she shook. I shook and she pulled, and before morning we had peeled off yards of that paper.

A strip about as high as my head and half around the room.

And then when the sun came and that awful pattern began to laugh at me, I declared I would finish it today!

220 We go away tomorrow, and they are moving all my furniture down again to leave things as they were before.

Jennie looked at the wall in amazement, but I told her merrily that I did it out of pure spite at the vicious thing.

She laughed and said she wouldn't mind doing it herself, but I must not get tired.

How she betrayed herself that time!

But I am here, and no person touches this paper but Me—not *alive!*

225 She tried to get me out of the room—it was too patent! But I said it was so quiet and empty and clean now that I believed I would lie down again and sleep all I could, and not to wake me even for dinner—I would call when I woke.

So now she is gone, and the servants are gone, and the things are gone, and there is nothing left but that great bedstead nailed down, with the canvas mattress we found on it.

We shall sleep downstairs tonight, and take the boat home tomorrow.

I quite enjoy the room, now it is bare again.

How those children did tear about here!

This bedstead is fairly gnawed!

But I must get to work.

I have locked the door and thrown the key down into the front path.

I don't want to go out, and I don't want to have anybody come in, till John comes.

I want to astonish him.

I've got a rope up here that even Jennie did not find. If that woman does get out, and tries to get away, I can tie her!

But I forgot I could not reach far without anything to stand on!

This bed will *not* move!

I tried to lift and push it until I was lame, and then I got so angry I bit off a little piece at one corner—but it hurt my teeth.

Then I peeled off all the paper I could reach standing on the floor. It sticks horribly and the pattern just enjoys it! All those strangled heads and bulbous eyes and waddling fungus growths just shriek with derision!

I am getting angry enough to do something desperate. To jump out of the window would be admirable exercise, but the bars are too strong even to try.

Besides I wouldn't do it. Of course not. I know well enough that a step like that is improper and might be misconstrued.

I don't like to *look* out of the windows even—there are so many of those creeping women, and they creep so fast.

I wonder if they all come out of that wallpaper as I did?

But I am securely fastened now by my well-hidden rope—you don't get *me* out in the road there!

I suppose I shall have to get back behind the pattern when it comes night, and that is hard!

It is so pleasant to be out in this great room and creep around as I please!

I don't want to go outside. I won't, even if Jennie asks me to.

For outside you have to creep on the ground, and everything is green instead of yellow.

But here I can creep smoothly on the floor, and my shoulder just fits in that long smooch around the wall, so I cannot lose my way.

Why, there's John at the door!

It is no use, young man, you can't open it!

How he does call and pound!

Now he's crying to Jennie for an axe.

It would be a shame to break down that beautiful door!

"John, dear!" said I in the gentlest voice, "The key is down by the front steps, under a plantain leaf!"

That silenced him for a few moments.

Then he said, very quietly indeed, "Open the door, my darling!"

"I can't," said I. "The key is down by the front door under a plantain leaf!" And then I said it again, several times, very gently and slowly, and said it so often that he had to go and see, and he got it of course, and came in. He stopped short by the door.

"What is the matter?" he cried. "For God's sake, what are you doing!"

260 I kept on creeping just the same, but I looked at him over my shoulder.

"I've got out at last," said I, "in spite of you and Jane. And I've pulled off most of the paper, so you can't put me back!"

Now why should that man have fainted? But he did, and right across my path by the wall, so that I had to creep over him every time!

➤ *QUESTIONS FOR READING AND WRITING*

1. The narrator is the main character in the story. To what extent does this influence what you are told in this story? Can you describe the narrator? Do you think she is reliable? Explain
2. Describe her relationship with her husband, John. What is he like? How does he treat her?
3. What kind of illness does the narrator say she has? What does her physician-husband prescribe as a cure? Do you think it's an appropriate cure? Why or why not?
4. In what way is the yellow wallpaper symbolic in this story? To what extent does the narrator's description of it change as the story progresses? Do you see any other symbols in the story?
5. To what extent does the narrator change as the story progresses? What are the indications of that in the story?
6. Near the end of the story, the narrator says, "I've got out at last." Has she? Explain.

JAMES JOYCE (1882–1941)

James Joyce was one of ten children born into a middle-class family of declining fortunes in a suburb of Dublin, Ireland. In spite of an unhappy childhood dominated by a drunken father, Joyce managed to receive a thorough classical education, first in Jesuit schools and then at University College, Dublin. Though he spent most of his adult life living outside of Ireland, Dublin is the backdrop for nearly all of his work. His three innovative novels, Portrait of the Artist as a Young Man *(1916),* Ulysses *(1922), and* Finnegans Wake *(1939), established him as one of the greatest writers of modern times. "Araby" is taken from his collection of short stories,* Dubliners, *which appeared in 1914 after an eight-year battle with publishers who feared it would offend important residents of the city.*

Araby [1914]

North Richmond Street, being blind, was a quiet street except at the hour when the Christian Brothers' School set the boys free. An uninhabited house of two stories stood at the blind end, detached from its neighbors in a square ground. The other houses of the street, conscious of decent lives within them, gazed at one another with brown imperturbable faces.

The former tenant of our house, a priest, had died in the back drawing-room. Air, musty from having been long enclosed, hung in all the rooms, and the waste room behind the kitchen was littered with old useless papers. Among these I found a few paper-covered books, the pages of which were curled and damp: *The Abbot*[1], by Walter Scott, *The Devout Communicant*[2] and *The Memoirs of Vidocq*[3]. I liked the last best because its leaves were yellow. The wild garden behind the house contained a central apple-tree and a few straggling bushes under one of which I found the late tenant's rusty bicycle-pump. He had been a very charitable priest; in his will he had left all his money to institutions and the furniture of his house to his sister.

When the short days of winter came dusk fell before we had well eaten our dinners. When we met in the street the houses had grown sombre. The space of sky above us was the colour of ever-changing violet and towards it the lamps of the street lifted their feeble lanterns. The cold air stung us and we played till our bodies glowed. Our shouts echoed in the silent street. The career of our play brought us through the dark muddy lanes behind the houses where we ran the gauntlet of the rough tribes from the cottages, to the back doors of the dark dripping gardens where odours arose from the ashpits, to the dark odorous stables where a coachman smoothed and combed the horse or shook music from the buckled harness. When we returned to the street light from the kitchen windows had filled the areas. If my uncle was seen turning the corner we hid in the shadow until we had seen him safely housed. Or if Mangan's sister came out on the doorstep to call her brother in to his tea we watched her from our shadow peer up and down the street. We waited to see whether she would remain or go in and, if she remained, we left our shadow and walked up to Mangan's steps resignedly. She was waiting for us, her figure defined by the light from the half-opened door. Her brother always teased her before he obeyed and I stood by the railings looking at her. Her dress swung as she moved her body and the soft rope of her hair tossed from side to side.

Every morning I lay on the floor in the front parlour watching her door. The blind was pulled down to within an inch of the sash so that I could not be seen. When she came out on the doorstep my heart leaped. I ran to the hall, seized my books and followed her. I kept her brown figure always in my eye and, when we came near the point at which our ways diverged, I quickened my pace and passed her. This happened morning after morning. I had never spoken to her, except for a few casual words, and yet her name was like a summons to all my foolish blood.

5 Her image accompanied me even in places the most hostile to romance. On Saturday evenings when my aunt went marketing I had to go to carry some of the parcels. We walked through the flaring streets, jostled by drunken men and bar-

[1]**The Abbot** an early nineteenth century romantic novel [2]**The Devout Communicant** a religious text [3]**The Memoirs of Vidocq** the memoirs of a French secret service agent

gaining women, amid the curses of labourers, the shrill litanies of shop-boys who stood on guard by the barrels of pigs' cheeks, the nasal chanting of street-singers, who sang a *come-all-you* about O'Donovan Rossa, or a ballad about the troubles in our native land. These noises converged in a single sensation of life for me: I imagined that I bore my chalice safely through a throng of foes. Her name sprang to my lips at moments in strange prayers and praises which I myself did not understand. My eyes were often full of tears (I could not tell why) and at times a flood from my heart seemed to pour itself out into my bosom. I thought little of the future. I did not know whether I would ever speak to her or not or, if I spoke to her, how I could tell her of my confused adoration. But my body was like a harp and her words and gestures were like fingers running upon the wires.

One evening I went into the back drawing-room in which the priest had died. It was a dark rainy evening and there was no sound in the house. Through one of the broken panes I heard the rain impinge upon the earth, the fine incessant needles of water playing in the sodden beds. Some distant lamp or lighted window gleamed below me. I was thankful that I could see so little. All my senses seemed to desire to veil themselves and, feeling that I was about to slip from them, I pressed the palms of my hands together until they trembled, murmuring: "*O love! O love!*" many times.

At last she spoke to me. When she addressed the first words to me I was so confused that I did not know what to answer. She asked me was I going to Araby. I forget whether I answered yes or no. It would be a splendid bazaar, she said; she would love to go.

"And why can't you? I asked.

While she spoke she turned a silver bracelet round and round her wrist. She could not go, she said, because there would be a retreat that week in her convent.[4] Her brother and two other boys were fighting for their caps and I was alone at the railings. She held one of the spikes, bowing her head towards me. The light from the lamp opposite our door caught the white curve of her neck, lit up her hair that rested there and, falling, lit up the hand upon the railing. It fell over one side of her dress and caught the white border of a petticoat, just visible as she stood at ease.

"It's well for you," she said.

"If I go," I said, "I will bring you something."

What innumerable follies laid waste my waking and sleeping thoughts after that evening! I wished to annihilate the tedious intervening days. I chafed against the work of school. At night in my bedroom and by day in the classroom her image came between me and the page I strove to read. The syllables of the word *Araby* were called to me through the silence in which my soul luxuriated and cast an Eastern enchantment over me. I asked for leave to go to the bazaar on Saturday night. My aunt was surprised and hoped it was not some Freemason affair. I answered few questions in class. I watched my master's face pass from amiability to sternness; he hoped I was not beginning to idle. I could not call my wandering thoughts together. I had hardly any patience with the serious work of life which,

[4]**convent** in this case a parochial school for girls

now that it stood between me and my desire, seemed to me child's play, ugly monotonous child's play.

On Saturday morning I reminded my uncle that I wished to go to the bazaar in the evening. He was fussing at the hall-stand, looking for the hat-brush, and answered me curtly:

"Yes, boy, I know."

15 As he was in the hall I could not go into the front parlour and lie at the window. I left the house in bad humour and walked slowly towards the school. The air was pitilessly raw and already my heart misgave me.

When I came home to dinner my uncle had not yet been home. Still it was early. I sat staring at the clock for some time and, when its ticking began to irritate me, I left the room. I mounted the staircase and gained the upper part of the house. The high cold empty gloomy rooms liberated me and I went from room to room singing. From the front window I saw my companions playing below in the street. Their cries reached me weakened and indistinct and, leaning my forehead against the cool glass, I looked over at the dark house where she lived. I may have stood there for an hour, seeing nothing but the brown-clad figure cast by my imagination, touched discreetly by the lamplight at the curved neck, at the hand upon the railings and at the border below the dress.

When I came downstairs again I found Mrs. Mercer sitting at the fire. She was an old garrulous woman, a pawnbroker's widow, who collected used stamps for some pious purpose. I had to endure the gossip of the tea-table. The meal was prolonged beyond an hour and still my uncle did not come. Mrs Mercer stood up to go: she was sorry she couldn't wait any longer, but it was after eight o'clock and she did not like to be out late, as the night air was bad for her. When she had gone I began to walk up and down the room, clenching my fists. My aunt said:

"I'm afraid you may put off your bazaar for this night of Our Lord."

At nine o'clock I heard my uncle's latchkey in the halldoor. I heard him talking to himself and heard the hallstand rocking when it had received the weight of his overcoat. I could interpret these signs. When he was midway through his dinner I asked him to give me the money to go to the bazaar. He had forgotten.

20 "The people are in bed and after their first sleep now," he said.

I did not smile. My aunt said to him energetically:

"Can't you give him the money and let him go? You've kept him late enough as it is."

My uncle said he was very sorry he had forgotten. He said he believed in the old saying: "All work and no play makes Jack a dull boy." He asked me where I was going and, when I had told him a second time he asked me did I know *The Arab's Farewell to His Steed.* When I left the kitchen he was about to recite the opening lines of the piece to my aunt.

I held a florin tightly in my hand as I strode down Buckingham Street towards the station. The sight of the streets thronged with buyers and glaring with gas recalled to me the purpose of my journey. I took my seat in a third-class carriage of a deserted train. After an intolerable delay the train moved out of the station slowly. It crept onward among ruinous houses and over the twinkling river. At Westland Row Station a crowd of people pressed to the carriage doors; but the porters moved them back, saying that it was a special train for the bazaar. I remained alone in the bare carriage. In a few minutes the train drew up beside an improvised wooden platform. I passed out on to the road and saw by the lighted dial of a clock that it was ten minutes to ten. In front of me was a large building which displayed the magical name.

I could not find any sixpenny entrance and, fearing that the bazaar would be closed, I passed in quickly through a turnstile, handing a shilling to a weary-looking man. I found myself in a big hall girdled at half its height by a gallery. Nearly all the stalls were closed and the greater part of the hall was in darkness. I recognized a silence like that which pervades a church after a service. I walked into the center of the bazaar timidly. A few people were gathered about the stalls which were still open. Before a curtain, over which the words *Café Chantant* were written in coloured lamps, two men were counting money on a salver. I listened to the fall of the coins.

Remembering with difficulty why I had come I went over to one of the stalls and examined porcelain vases and flowered tea-sets. At the door of the stall a young lady was talking and laughing with two young gentlemen. I remarked their English accents and listened vaguely to their conversation.

"O, I never said such a thing!"

"O, but you did!"

"O, but I didn't!"

"Didn't she say that?"

"Yes. I heard her."

"O, there's a . . . fib!"

Observing me the young lady came over and asked me did I wish to buy anything. The tone of her voice was not encouraging; she seemed to have spoken to me out of a sense of duty. I looked humbly at the great jars that stood like eastern guards at either side of the dark entrance to the stall and murmured:

"No, thank you."

The young lady changed the position of one of the vases and went back to the two young men. They began to talk of the same subject. Once or twice the young lady glanced at me over her shoulder.

I lingered before her stall, though I knew my stay was useless, to make my interest in her wares seem the more real. Then I turned away slowly and walked down the middle of the bazaar. I allowed the two pennies to fall against the sixpence in my pocket. I heard a voice call from one end of the gallery that the light was out. The upper part of the hall was now completely dark.

Gazing up into the darkness I saw myself as a creature driven and derided by vanity; and my eyes burned with anguish and anger.

➤ *QUESTIONS FOR READING AND WRITING*

1. To what extent does your own experience influence your response to this story?
2. Describe the setting of the story. How are you affected by the personification in the first paragraph? Is North Richmond street "blind" only because

it's a dead-end street? Do you think the setting is an appropriate background for the boy's feelings? Explain.

3. Who is the narrator? How old is he at the time of the story? Is the story told in the "voice" of a child or an adult? What difference does that make in the telling and in your response?
4. What aspects of the boy's reactions illustrate his feelings for Mangan's sister? Do you think the boy's crush is believable? Do people behave like this when they are "smitten"? Explain.
5. To what extent is the Araby bazaar symbolic of the boy's crush on Mangan's sister?
6. At the end of the story, why do you think the boy sees himself "as a creature driven and derided by vanity"?

BOBBIE ANN MASON (b. 1940)

Bobbie Ann Mason grew up in rural Kentucky on a dairy farm. An excellent student, Mason was encouraged in her studies by her parents, who never finished high school. She attended college at the University of Kentucky, where she majored in journalism and later earned an M.A. from the State University of Kentucky, where she majored in journalism, an M.A. from the State University of New York at Binghamton, and a Ph.D. from the University of Connecticut. Her first collection of short stories, Shiloh and Other Stories *(1982), was enormously well received, winning the Ernest Hemingway Foundation Award in 1982 for the year's most distinguished work of fiction. Her 1985 novel,* In Country, *was made into a film. Her most recent novel,* Clear Springs, *appeared in 2000. Mason has described her work, which is usually set in the South and filled with popular culture references, as "southern Gothic going to the supermarket."*

SHILOH [1982]

Leroy Moffitt's wife, Norma Jean, is working on her pectorals. She lifts three-pound dumbbells to warm up, then progresses to a twenty-pound barbell. Standing with her legs apart, she reminds Leroy of Wonder Woman.

"I'd give anything if I could just get these muscles to where they're real hard," says Norma Jean. "Feel this arm. It's not as hard as the other one."

"That's 'cause you're right-handed," says Leroy, dodging as she swings the barbell in an arc.

"Do you think so?"

5 "Sure."

Leroy is a truckdriver. He injured his leg in a highway accident four months ago, and his physical therapy, which involves weights and a pulley, prompted Norma Jean to try building herself up. Now she is attending a body-building class. Leroy has been collecting temporary disability since his tractor-trailer jackknifed in Missouri, badly twisting his left leg in its socket. He has a steel pin in his hip. He will probably not be able to drive his rig again. It sits in the backyard, like a gigantic bird that has flown home to roost. Leroy has been home in Kentucky for three months, and his leg is almost healed, but the accident frightened him and he does not want to drive any more long hauls. He is not sure what to do next. In the meantime, he makes things from craft kits. He started by building a miniature log cabin from notched Popsicle sticks. He varnished it and placed it on the TV set, where it remains. It reminds him of a rustic Nativity scene. Then he tried string art (sailing ships on black velvet), a macramé owl kit, a snap-together B-17 Flying Fortress, and a lamp made out of a model truck, with a light fixture screwed in the top of the cab. At first the kits were diversions, something to kill time, but now he is thinking about building a full-scale log house from a kit. It would be considerably cheaper than building a regular house, and besides, Leroy has grown to appreciate how things are put together. He has begun to realize that in all the years he was on the road he never took time to examine anything. He was always flying past scenery.

"They won't let you build a log cabin in any of the new subdivisions," Norma Jean tells him.

"They will if I tell them it's for you," he says, teasing her. Ever since they were married, he has promised Norma Jean he would build her a new home one day. They have always rented, and the house they live in is small and nondescript. It does not even feel like a home, Leroy realizes now.

Norma Jean works at the Rexall drugstore, and she has acquired an amazing amount of information about cosmetics. When she explains to Leroy the three stages of complexion care, involving creams, toners, and moisturizers, he thinks happily of other petroleum products—axle grease, diesel fuel. This is a connection between him and Norma Jean. Since he has been home, he has felt unusually tender about his wife and guilty over his long absences. But he can't tell what she feels about him. Norma Jean has never complained about his traveling; she has never made hurt remarks, like calling his truck a "widow-maker." He is reasonably certain she has been faithful to him, but he wishes she would celebrate his permanent homecoming more happily. Norma Jean is often startled to find Leroy at home, and he thinks she seems a little disappointed about it. Perhaps he reminds her too much of the early days of their marriage, before he went on the road. They had a child who died as an infant, years ago. They never speak about their memories of Randy, which have almost faded, but now that Leroy is home all the time, they sometimes feel awkward around each other, and Leroy wonders if one of them should mention the child. He has the feeling that they are waking up out of a dream together—that they must create a new marriage, start afresh. They are lucky they are still married. Leroy has read that for most people losing a child destroys the marriage—or else he heard this on *Donahue.* He can't always remember where he learns things anymore.

10 At Christmas, Leroy bought an electric organ for Norma Jean. She used to play the piano when she was in high school. “It don’t leave you,” she told him once. “It’s like riding a bicycle.”

The new instrument had so many keys and buttons that she was bewildered by it at first. She touched the keys tentatively, pushed some buttons, then pecked out “Chopsticks.” It came out in an amplified fox-trot rhythm, with marimba sounds.

“It’s an orchestra!” she cried.

The organ had a pecan-look finish and eighteen preset chords, with optional flute, violin, trumpet, clarinet, and banjo accompaniments. Norma Jean mastered the organ almost immediately. At first she played Christmas songs. Then she bought *The Sixties Songbook* and learned every tune in it, adding variations to each with the rows of brightly colored buttons.

“I didn’t like these old songs back then,” she said. “But I have this crazy feeling I missed something.”

15 “You didn’t miss a thing,” said Leroy.

Leroy likes to lie on the couch and smoke a joint and listen to Norma Jean play “Can’t Take My Eyes Off You” and “I’ll Be Back.” He is back again. After fifteen years on the road, he is finally settling down with the woman he loves. She is still pretty. Her skin is flawless. Her frosted curls resemble pencil trimmings.

Now that Leroy has come home to stay, he notices how much the town has changed. Subdivisions are spreading across western Kentucky like an oil slick. The sign at the edge of town says “Pop: 11,500”—only seven hundred more than it said twenty years before. Leroy can’t figure out who is living in all the new houses. The farmers who used to gather around the courthouse square on Saturday afternoons to play checkers and spit tobacco juice have gone. It has been years since Leroy has thought about the farmers, and they have disappeared without his noticing.

Leroy meets a kid named Stevie Hamilton in the parking lot at the new shopping center. While they pretend to be strangers meeting over a stalled car, Stevie tosses an ounce of marijuana under the front seat of Leroy’s car. Stevie is wearing orange jogging shoes and a T-shirt that says CHATTAHOOCHEE SUPER-RAT. His father is a prominent doctor who lives in one of the expensive subdivisions in a new white-columned brick house that looks like a funeral parlor. In the phone book under his name there is a separate number, with the listing “Teenagers.”

“Where do you get this stuff?” asks Leroy. “From your pappy?”

20 “That’s for me to know and you to find out,” Stevie says. He is slit-eyed and skinny.

“What else you got?”

“What you interested in?”

“Nothing special. Just wondered.”

Leroy used to take speed on the road. Now he has to go slowly. He needs to be mellow. He leans back against the car and says. “I’m aiming to build me a log house, soon as I get time. My wife, though, I don’t think she likes the idea.”

25 “Well, let me know when you want me again,” Stevie says. He has a cigarette in his cupped palm, as though sheltering it from the wind. He takes a long drag, then stomps it on the asphalt and slouches away.

Stevie's father was two years ahead of Leroy in high school. Leroy is thirty-four. He married Norma Jean when they were both eighteen, and their child Randy was born a few months later, but he died at the age of four months and three days. He would be about Stevie's age now. Norma Jean and Leroy were at the drive-in, watching a double feature (*Dr. Strangelove* and *Lover Come Back*), and the baby was sleeping in the back seat. When the first movie ended, the baby was dead. It was the sudden infant death syndrome. Leroy remembers handing Randy to a nurse at the emergency room, as though he were offering her a large doll as a present. A dead baby feels like a sack of flour. "It just happens sometimes," said the doctor, in what Leroy always recalls as a nonchalant tone. Leroy can hardly remember the child anymore, but he still sees vividly a scene from *Dr. Strangelove* in which the President of the United States was talking in a folksy voice on the hot line to the Soviet premier about the bomber accidentally headed toward Russia. He was in the War Room, and the world map was lit up. Leroy remembers Norma Jean standing catatonically beside him in the hospital and himself thinking: Who is this strange girl? He had forgotten who she was. Now scientists are saying that crib death is caused by a virus. Nobody knows anything, Leroy thinks. The answers are always changing.

When Leroy gets home from the shopping center. Norma Jean's mother, Mabel Beasley, is there. Until this year. Leroy has not realized how much time she spends with Norma Jean. When she visits, she inspects the closets and then the plants, informing Norma Jean when a plant is droopy or yellow. Mabel calls the plants "flowers," although there are never any blooms. She also notices if Norma Jean's laundry is piling up. Mabel is a short, overweight woman whose tight, brown-dyed curls look more like a wig than the actual wig she sometimes wears. Today she has brought Norma Jean an off-white dust ruffle she made for the bed; Mabel works in a custom-upholstery shop.

"This is the tenth one I made this year," Mabel says. "I got started and couldn't stop."

"It's real pretty," says Norma Jean.

30 "Now we can hide things under the bed," says Leroy, who gets along with his mother-in-law primarily by joking with her. Mabel has never really forgiven him for disgracing her by getting Norma Jean pregnant. When the baby died, she said that fate was mocking her.

"What's that thing?" Mabel says to Leroy in a loud voice, pointing to a tangle of yarn on a piece of canvas.

Leroy holds it up for Mabel to see. "It's my needlepoint," he explains. "This is a *Star Trek* pillow cover."

"That's what a woman would do," says Mabel. "Great day in the morning!"

"All the big football players on TV do it," he says.

35 "Why, Leroy, you're always trying to fool me. I don't believe you for one minute. You don't know what to do with yourself—that's the whole trouble. Sewing!"

"I'm aiming to build us a log house," says Leroy. "Soon as my plans come."

"Like *heck* you are," says Norma Jean. She takes Leroy's needlepoint and shoves it into a drawer. "You have to find a job first. Nobody can afford to build now anyway."

Mabel straightens her girdle and says. "I still think before you get tied down y'all ought to take a little run to Shiloh."

"One of these days, Mama," Norma Jean says impatiently.

Mabel is talking about Shiloh, Tennessee. For the past few years, she has been urging Leroy and Norma Jean to visit the Civil War battleground there. Mabel went there on her honeymoon—the only real trip she ever took. Her husband died of a perforated ulcer when Norma Jean was ten, but Mabel, who was accepted into the United Daughters of the Confederacy in 1975, is still preoccupied with going back to Shiloh.

"I've been to kingdom come and back in that truck out yonder," Leroy says to Mabel, "but we never yet set foot in that battleground. Ain't that something? How did I miss it?"

"It's not even that far," Mabel says.

After Mabel leaves, Norma Jean reads to Leroy from a list she has made. "Things you could do," she announces. "You could get a job as a guard at Union Carbide, where they'd let you set on a stool. You could get on at the lumberyard. You could do a little carpenter work, if you want to build so bad. You could—"

"I can't do something where I'd have to stand up all day."

"You ought to try standing up all day behind a cosmetics counter. It's amazing that I have strong feet, coming from two parents that never had strong feet at all." At the moment Norma Jean is holding on to the kitchen counter, raising her knees one at a time as she talks. She is wearing two-pound ankle weights.

"Don't worry," says Leroy. "I'll do something."

"You could truck calves to slaughter for somebody. You wouldn't have to drive any big old truck for that."

"I'm going to build you this house," says Leroy. "I want to make you a real home."

"I don't want to live in any log cabin."

"It's not a cabin. It's a house."

"I don't care. It looks like a cabin."

"You and me together could lift those logs. It's just like lifting weights."

Norma Jean doesn't answer. Under her breath, she is counting. Now she is marching through the kitchen. She is doing goose steps.

Before his accident, when Leroy came home he used to stay in the house with Norma Jean, watching TV in bed and playing cards. She would cook fried chicken, picnic ham, chocolate pie—all his favorites. Now he is home alone much of the time. In the mornings, Norma Jean disappears, leaving a cooling place in the bed. She eats a cereal called Body Buddies, and she leaves the bowl on the table, with the soggy tan balls floating in a milk puddle. He sees things about Norma Jean that he never realized before. When she chops onions, she stares off into a corner, as if she can't bear to look. She puts on her house slippers almost precisely at nine o'clock every evening and nudges her jogging shoes under the couch. She saves bread heels for the birds. Leroy watches the birds at the feeder. He notices the peculiar way goldfinches fly past the window. They close their wings, then fall, then spread their wings to catch and lift themselves. He wonders if they close their eyes when they fall. Norma Jean closes her eyes when they are in bed. She wants the lights turned out. Even then, he is sure she closes her eyes.

55 He goes for long drives around town. He tends to drive a car rather carelessly. Power steering and an automatic shift make a car feel so small and inconsequential that his body is hardly involved in the driving process. His injured leg stretches out comfortably. Once or twice he has almost hit something, but even the prospect of an accident seems minor in a car. He cruises the new subdivisions, feeling like a criminal rehearsing for a robbery. Norma Jean is probably right about a log house being inappropriate here in the new subdivision. All the houses look grand and complicated. They depress him.

One day when Leroy comes home from a drive he finds Norma Jean in tears. She is in the kitchen making a potato and mushroom-soup casserole, with grated cheese topping. She is crying because her mother caught her smoking.

"I didn't hear her coming. I was standing here puffing away pretty as you please," Norma Jean says, wiping her eyes.

"I knew it would happen sooner or later," says Leroy, putting his arm around her.

"She don't know the meaning of the word 'knock,'" says Norma Jean. "It's a wonder she hadn't caught me years ago."

60 "Think of it this way," Leroy says. "What if she caught me with a joint?"

"You better not let her!" Norma Jean shrieks. "I'm warning you, Leroy Moffitt!"

"I'm just kidding. Here, play me a tune. That'll help you relax."

Norma Jean puts the casserole in the oven and sets the timer. Then she plays a ragtime tune, with horns and banjo, as Leroy lights up a joint and lies on the couch, laughing to himself about Mabel's catching him at it. He thinks of Stevie Hamilton—a doctor's son pushing grass. Everything is funny. The whole town seems crazy and small. He is reminded of Virgil Mathis, a boastful policeman Leroy used to shoot pool with. Virgil recently led a drug bust in a back room at a bowling alley, where he seized ten thousand dollars' worth of marijuana. The newspaper had a picture of him holding up the bags of grass and grinning widely. Right now, Leroy can imagine Virgil breaking down the door and arresting him with a lungful of smoke. Virgil would probably have been alerted to the scene because of all the racket Norma Jean is making. Now she sounds like a hard-rock band. Norma Jean is terrific. When she switches to a Latin-rhythm version of "Sunshine Superman," Leroy hums along. Norma Jean's foot goes up and down, up and down.

"Well, what do you think?" Leroy says, when Norma Jean pauses to search through her music.

65 "What do I think about what?"

His mind has gone blank. Then he says. "I'll sell my rig and build us a house." That wasn't what he wanted to say. He wanted to know what she thought—what she *really* thought—about them.

"Don't start in on that again," says Norma Jean. She begins playing "Who'll Be the Next in Line?"

Leroy used to tell hitchhikers his whole life story—about his travels, his hometown, the baby. He would end with a question: "Well, what do you think?" It was just a rhetorical question. In time, he had the feeling that he'd been telling the same story over and over to the same hitchhikers. He quit talking to hitchhikers when he realized how his voice sounded—whining and self-pitying, like some teenage-tragedy song. Now Leroy has the sudden impulse to tell Norma Jean about himself, as if he had just met her. They have known each other so long they have forgotten a lot about each other. They could become reacquainted. But when the oven timer goes off and she runs to the kitchen, he forgets why he wants to do this.

The next day, Mabel drops by. It is Saturday and Norma Jean is cleaning. Leroy is studying the plans of his log house, which have finally come in the mail. He has them spread out on the table—big sheets of stiff blue paper, with diagrams and numbers printed in white. While Norma Jean runs the vacuum, Mabel drinks coffee. She sets her coffee cup on a blueprint.

70 "I'm just waiting for time to pass," she says to Leroy, drumming her fingers on the table.

As soon as Norma Jean switches off the vacuum, Mabel says in a loud voice. "Did you hear about the datsun dog that killed the baby?"

Norma Jean says, "The word is 'dachshund.'"

"They put the dog on trial. It chewed the baby's legs off. The mother was in the next room all the time." She raises her voice. "They thought it was neglect."

Norma Jean is holding her ears. Leroy manages to open the refrigerator and get some Diet Pepsi to offer Mabel. Mabel still has some coffee and she waves away the Pepsi.

75 "Datsuns are like that," Mabel says. "They're jealous dogs. They'll tear a place to pieces if you don't keep an eye on them."

"You better watch out what you're saying, Mabel," says Leroy.

"Well, facts is facts."

Leroy looks out the window at his rig. It is like a huge piece of furniture gathering dust in the backyard. Pretty soon it will be an antique. He hears the vacuum cleaner. Norma Jean seems to be cleaning the living room rug again.

Later, she says to Leroy. "She just said that about the baby because she caught me smoking. She's trying to pay me back."

80 "What are you talking about?" Leroy says, nervously shuffling blueprints.

"You know good and well," Norma Jean says. She is sitting in a kitchen chair with her feet up and her arms wrapped around her knees. She looks small and helpless. She says. "The very idea, her bringing up a subject like that! Saying it was neglect."

"She didn't mean that," Leroy says.

"She might not have *thought* she meant it. She always says things like that. You don't know how she goes on."

"But she didn't really mean it. She was just talking."

85 Leroy opens a king-sized bottle of beer and pours it into two glasses, dividing it carefully. He hands a glass to Norma Jean and she takes it from him mechanically. For a long time, they sit by the kitchen window watching the birds at the feeder.

Something is happening. Norma Jean is going to night school. She has graduated from her six-week body-building course and now she is taking an adult-education course in composition at Paducah Community College. She spends her evenings outlining paragraphs.

"First, you have a topic sentence," she explains to Leroy. "Then you divide it up. Your secondary topic has to be connected to your primary topic."

To Leroy, this sounds intimidating. "I never was any good in English," he says.

"It makes a lot of sense."

90 "What are you doing this for, anyhow?"

She shrugs. "It's something to do." She stands up and lifts her dumbbells a few times.

"Driving a rig, nobody cared about my English."

"I'm not criticizing your English."

Norma Jean used to say, "If I lose ten minutes' sleep, I just drag all day." Now she stays up late, writing compositions. She got a B on her first paper—a how-to theme on soup-based casseroles. Recently Norma Jean has been cooking unusual foods—tacos, lasagna, Bombay chicken. She doesn't play the organ anymore, though her second paper was called "Why Music Is Important to Me." She sits at the kitchen table, concentrating on her outlines, while Leroy plays with his log house plans, practicing with a set of Lincoln Logs. The thought of getting a truckload of notched, numbered logs scares him, and he wants to be prepared. As he and Norma Jean work together at the kitchen table, Leroy has the hopeful thought that they are sharing something, but he knows he is a fool to think this. Norma Jean is miles away. He knows he is going to lose her. Like Mabel, he is just waiting for time to pass.

95 One day, Mabel is there before Norma Jean gets home from work, and Leroy finds himself confiding in her. Mabel, he realizes, must know Norma Jean better than he does.

"I don't know what's got into that girl," Mabel says. "She used to go to bed with the chickens. Now you say she's up all hours. Plus her a-smoking. I like to died."

"I want to make her this beautiful home," Leroy says, indicating the Lincoln Logs. "I don't think she even wants it. Maybe she was happier with me gone."

"She don't know what to make of you, coming home like this."

"Is that it?"

100 Mabel takes the roof off his Lincoln Log cabin. "You couldn't get *me* in a log cabin," she says. "I was raised in one. It's no picnic, let me tell you."

"They're different now," says Leroy.

"I tell you what," Mabel says, smiling oddly at Leroy.

"What?"

"Take her on down to Shiloh. Y'all need to get out together, stir a little. Her brain's all balled up over them books."

105 Leroy can see traces of Norma Jean's features in her mother's face. Mabel's worn face has the texture of crinkled cotton, but suddenly she looks pretty. It occurs

to Leroy that Mabel has been hinting all along that she wants them to take her with them to Shiloh.

"Let's all go to Shiloh," he says. "You and me and her. Come Sunday."

Mabel throws up her hand in protest. "Oh, no, not me. Young folks want to be by theirselves."

When Norma Jean comes in with groceries, Leroy says excitedly. "Your mama here's been dying to go to Shiloh for thirty-five years. It's about time we went, don't you think?"

"I'm not going to butt in on anybody's second honeymoon," Mabel says.

"Who's going on a honeymoon, for Christ's sake?" Norma Jean says loudly.

"I never raised no daughter of mine to talk that-a-way," Mabel says.

"You ain't seen nothing yet," says Norma Jean. She starts putting away boxes and cans, slamming cabinet doors.

"There's a log cabin at Shiloh," Mabel says. "It was there during the battle. There's bullet holes in it."

"When are you going to *shut up* about Shiloh, Mama?" asks Norma Jean.

"I always thought Shiloh was the prettiest place, so full of history," Mabel goes on. "I just hoped y'all could see it once before I die, so you could tell me about it." Later, she whispers to Leroy. "You do what I said. A little change is what she needs."

"Your name means 'the king,'" Norma Jean says to Leroy that evening. He is trying to get her to go to Shiloh, and she is reading a book about another century.

"Well, I reckon I ought to be right proud."

"I guess so."

"Am I still king around here?"

Norma Jean flexes her biceps and feels them for hardness. "I'm not fooling around with anybody, if that's what you mean," she says.

"Would you tell me if you were?"

"I don't know."

"What does your name mean?"

"It was Marilyn Monroe's real name."

"No kidding!"

"Norma comes from the Normans. They were invaders," she says. She closes her book and looks hard at Leroy. "I'll go to Shiloh with you if you'll stop staring at me."

On Sunday, Norma Jean packs a picnic and they go to Shiloh. To Leroy's relief Mabel says she does not want to come with them. Norma Jean drives, and Leroy, sitting beside her, feels like some boring hitchhiker she has picked up. He tries some conversation, but she answers him in monosyllables. At Shiloh, she drives aimlessly through the park, past bluffs and trails and steep ravines. Shiloh is an immense place, and Leroy cannot see it as a battleground. It is not what he expected. He thought it would look like a golf course. Monuments are everywhere, showing through the thick clusters of trees. Norma Jean passes the log cabin Mabel mentioned. It is surrounded by tourists looking for bullet holes.

"That's not the kind of log house I've got in mind," says Leroy apologetically.

"I know *that*."

130 "This is a pretty place. Your mama was right."

"It's O.K.," says Norma Jean. "Well, we've seen it. I hope she's satisfied."

They burst out laughing together.

At the park museum, a movie on Shiloh is shown every half hour, but they decide that they don't want to see it. They buy a souvenir Confederate flag for Mabel, and then they find a picnic spot near the cemetery. Norma Jean has brought a picnic cooler, with pimento sandwiches, soft drinks, and Yodels. Leroy eats a sandwich and then smokes a joint, hiding it behind the picnic cooler. Norma Jean has quit smoking altogether. She is picking cake crumbs from the cellophane wrapper, like a fussy bird.

Leroy says, "So the boys in gray ended up in Corinth. The Union soldiers zapped 'em finally. April 7, 1862."

135 They both know that he doesn't know any history. He is just talking about some of the historical plaques they have read. He feels awkward, like a boy on a date with an older girl. They are still just making conversation.

"Corinth is where Mama eloped to," says Norma Jean.

They sit in silence and stare at the cemetery for the Union dead and, beyond, at a tall cluster of trees. Campers are parked nearby, bumper to bumper, and small children in bright clothing are cavorting and squealing. Norma Jean wads up the cake wrapper and squeezes it tightly in her hand. Without looking at Leroy, she says, "I want to leave you."

Leroy takes a bottle of Coke out of the cooler and flips off the cap. He holds the bottle poised near his mouth but cannot remember to take a drink. Finally he says. "No, you don't."

"Yes, I do."

140 "I won't let you."

"You can't stop me."

"Don't do me that way."

Leroy knows Norma Jean will have her own way. "Didn't I promise to be home from now on?" he says.

"In some ways, a woman prefers a man who wanders," says Norma Jean. "That sounds crazy, I know."

145 "You're not crazy."

Leroy remembers to drink from his Coke. Then he says, "Yes, you *are* crazy. You and me could start all over again. Right back at the beginning.

"We *have* started all over again," says Norma Jean. "And this is how it turned out."

"What did I do wrong?"

"Nothing."

150 "Is this one of those women's lib things?" Leroy asks.

"Don't be funny."

The cemetery, a green slope dotted with white markers, looks like a subdivision site. Leroy is trying to comprehend that his marriage is breaking up, but for some reason he is wondering about white slabs in a graveyard.

"Everything was fine till Mama caught me smoking," says Norma Jean, standing up. "That set something off."

"What are you talking about?"

155 "She won't leave me alone—*you* won't leave me alone." Norma Jean seems to be crying, but she is looking away from him. "I feel eighteen again. I can't face that all over again." She starts walking away. "No, it *wasn't* fine. I don't know what I'm saying. Forget it."

Leroy takes a lungful of smoke and closes his eyes as Norma Jean's words sink in. He tries to focus on the fact that thirty-five hundred soldiers died on the grounds around him. He can only think of that war as a board game with plastic soldiers. Leroy almost smiles, as he compares the Confederates' daring attack on the Union camps and Virgil Mathis's raid on the bowling alley. General Grant, drunk and furious, shoved the Southerners back to Corinth, where Mabel and Jet Beasley were married years later, when Mabel was still thin and good-looking. The next day, Mabel and Jet visited the battleground, and then Norma Jean was born, and then she married Leroy and they had a baby, which they lost, and now Leroy and Norma Jean are here at the same battleground. Leroy knows he is leaving out a lot. He is leaving out the insides of history. History was always just names and dates to him. It occurs to him that building a house of logs is similarly empty—too simple. And the real inner workings of a marriage, like most of history, have escaped him. Now he sees that building a log house is the dumbest idea he could have had. It was clumsy of him to think Norma Jean would want a log house. It was a crazy idea. He'll have to think of something else, quickly. He will wad the blueprints into tight balls and fling them into the lake. Then he'll get moving again. He opens his eyes. Norma Jean has moved away and is walking through the cemetery, following a serpentine brick path.

Leroy gets up to follow his wife, but his good leg is asleep and his bad leg still hurts him. Norma Jean is far away, walking rapidly toward the bluff by the river, and he tries to hobble toward her. Some children run past him, screaming noisily. Norma Jean has reached the bluff, and she is looking out over the Tennessee River. Now she turns toward Leroy and waves her arms. Is she beckoning to him? She seems to be doing an exercise for her chest muscles. The sky is unusually pale—the color of the dust ruffle Mabel made for their bed.

➤ *QUESTIONS FOR READING AND WRITING*

1. To what extent does your own background or experience influence your response to this story? Have you ever had the experience of "growing away" from someone? Explain.
2. The two main characters, Leroy and Norma Jean, seem to change as the story progresses. What do you think is happening to each of them? To their relationship?
3. Norma Jean and Leroy don't seem to have much to say to each other. Why? Are there times when you expect them to say more? What do you think remains unsaid?
4. Shiloh was the site of a major Civil War battle won by Union forces. Do you think this is an appropriate setting for this story? Explain.
5. What do you think is the theme of this story? To what extent does the title of the story account for that theme?

Rosario Morales

With her daughter Aurora Levins Morales, Rosario Morales coauthored Getting Home Alive, *a collection of poetry and prose published in 1986 and described by one critic as the most important book to come out of the Puerto Rican diaspora in a generation. "The Day It Happened" was published in* Callaloo.

The Day It Happened

[1992]

The day it happened I was washing my hair. I had long hair then that went halfway down my back and I washed it once a week and rinsed it with lemon juice "to bring out the blond highlights" Mami said. Then I'd set it into pincurls that took an age to do because there was so much to wind around and around my finger. But if Mami was in a good mood, and she looked like she might be that day, she curled the back for me. I usually did all this on Saturday so I would look great for church on Sunday, and for a date Saturday night if I ever had one. ¡ojala!

Naturally the moment when it all began I was rinsing the big soapy mess. Nosy Maria was leaning out the window drying her dark red fingernails in the breeze when Josie stepped out of our apartment house doorway with a suitcase in her hand. Maria sucked in her breath so hard the sound brought my mother who took one look, crossed herself, or so Maria says, and started praying. Someone needed to pray for Josie. It was five o'clock and Ramón was due home any minute.

I wouldn't have known anything about any of this if Olga next door hadn't rung our doorbell and banged on the door just when Mami was too deep in prayer to hear and Maria was leaning out over the sill with her eyes bugging out. I cursed, very quietly of course, because if Mami or Papi heard me curse I'd get a slap across my face. I wrapped my sopping head in a towel and opened the door to Olga's "Oh my goodness, oh my dear. Oh honey, did you see? Look out the window this minute. I wouldn't have believed it if I hadn't seen it with my own two eyes. That poor little kid. I hate to think . . ." and on and on as we crossed the apartment to look out on the street.

Little Mikey from across the way was telling the rest of the kids how he'd found a taxi for Josie the minute he'd hit Southern Boulevard and how he'd hailed it and how the driver had let him ride back to Brook Street in the front seat—even though all of them had seen him arrive and step out with his back stiff with pride. Meantime Josie was back down in the street with Doña Toña from across the hall and Betty Murphy upstairs right behind her, all of them loaded down with two lamps, a typewriter and a big box of books. Doña Toña was muttering something we couldn't hear up here on the second story but it was probably either the prayer I was hearing on my right or the " . . . hurry oh hurry oh God he'll be here any minute are you mad girl, are you mad" that came at me from the left.

It was hard not to be scared as well as glad that Josie was packing up and leaving Ramón. They'd been married only six months but already they were in a pattern, like the Garcias down the block who did everything the same way on the same day, all year. Ramón worked late till seven every week day and five on Saturday. When he arrived he expected a good dinner to be on the table at the right temperature exactly five minutes after he walked in the door. He yelled if she didn't get it right and sometimes even if she did.

Saturday evening they went out to a party or the bar down the avenue, both of them dressed up and Ramón looking proud and cheerful for a change. Josie always looked great. She's so cute. Small and plump with long lashes on her dark eyes and, get this, naturally curly hair. She smiled a lot when she was happy but she hadn't been happy much lately and not at all since she got pregnant. I wasn't supposed to know this. God, I was almost thirteen! But Maria, who was fourteen and a half and thought she was twenty, listened in on conversations in the living room by opening the door a sliver and she told me all about it.

Saturday nights there was sure to be a fight. Either it was that Josie was "no fun, a man can't be a man with such a wet rag around." Or it was that Josie was "a tramp. Why else was that guy staring at you, eating you up with his eyes?" The first time it happened, soon after they moved in, it woke me up from a deep sleep and I was so scared I crept into Maria's bed. I'd never heard such yelling in my life. When my parents fight it's during the day and in angry whispers. It sounds like a snake convention in my parents' bedroom. That's bad enough. Maria and I get real nervous and nothing's right until they make up and talk in normal voices again. But Ramón could be heard right through the floor at two in the morning. And then he took to throwing things and then he started hitting her. The first time that happened Josie didn't go to morning mass at St. Francis and Mami went down to her apartment to see if she was sick or something. Josie came to the door with a big bruise on her face. After that Mami went to fetch her every Sunday and stayed with her if she was too ashamed to go to church.

After she found out she was pregnant Josie had talked it over with Doña Toña and Doña Toña had talked it over with Mami and by and by we all knew she was scared he would hurt the little baby growing inside of her and worried about the child growing up with Ramón for a father. He expected too much of everyone and little kids hurt so when a parent thinks whatever they do is all wrong. Ha! Tell that to Mami and Papi, will you.

I don't think there was anyone in the neighborhood on Ramón's side not even Joe who liked to bully his wife and daughters but didn't realize he did or Tito who talked all the time about "wearing the pants in this family." Ramón was too much, even for them. Josie was so clearly a fine person, a quiet homebody, a sweetypie. Ramón was out of his mind, that's what most of us thought. I mean you had to be to be so regularly mean to a person who adored you. And she did, at least at first. You could see it in the way she looked at him, boasted about his strength, his good job, his brains. The way she excused his temper. "He can't help himself. He doesn't mean it."

10 And now she was packed up and sitting in the taxi. Waiting for him to come home, I guess. That was too much for Mami and she scooted out the door with Olga, Maria, Papi, no less, and me right behind her with that soaked blue towel wrapped sloppily around my head. "Ai Mamita! Jesus, Maria y José. Jesus Maria y José," came faintly up the stairs in the front of the hurrying line. I knew Mami and I knew she meant to stand in front of Josie to protect her from that bully and, sure as shooting, Papi was going to protect Mami who was going so fast in her house slippers she almost fell down except that Olga gripped her hard and kept her upright.

When we streamed out the door into the small crowd that had gathered by now it was to see Ramón coming down the street with a sour look on his face. He looked up once or twice but mostly just stared at his feet as he strode up the block. He swept past us and almost into the house the way he did when he came home weary from the shipyard and the long ride home. He would have missed seeing Josie for sure, as I was praying he would, except that she called to him.

"Ramón," she said in her soft voice, stepping out of the taxi. "Ramón." He looked up and around then, took in the crowd, the taxi with a tall lamp lying on the back seat and Josie in her good suit. He stood looking at all this and especially at Josie for a long time. When he spoke it was only to Josie, as if we weren't there at all. He had to clear his throat to say "Josie?"

I was totally surprised and confused. He sounded so small, you know. So uncertain. It was Josie looked tall now and hard. If I hadn't known what I knew I would've said Josie was the bully in the family. She looked him straight in the eye and said stiffly, as if they were lines someone had given her to memorize, "I warned you. I said I would leave if you ever hit me again. I am not safe with you. Our child is not safe with you. I'm going now. I left arroz con pollo on the stove and the electric bill on the table." He didn't answer so she turned to hug Doña Toña and Mami before sitting herself back down. It was then that Ramón acted. Before I could blink he'd hurled himself at her, thrown himself on his knees and gripped her around her stockinged legs. "No! No te vayas. Tu no comprendes. Eres muy joven para comprender. Tu no puedes dejarme asi. Estamos casados para la vida. Te amo para siempre, para siempre. Josita, mi amor, no te vayas. Si te vas me mato. Te lo juro. No te puedes ir. No te puedes ir . . . " and on and on in a hoarse voice while Josie stood there frozen, fear on her face. There was no sound but Maria whispering occasional translations into Olga's impatient ear "Don't go." "You're too young to understand." "We're married for life." "I'll love you always." "I'll kill myself, I swear it."

It went on forever, Josie standing there, Ramón kneeling, all of us listening, tears running down my face, Josie's face, Mami's face. It was Olga who ended it, who walked up to Ramón, knelt down beside him, put an arm around him, and started talking, telling him Josie was a mother now and had to think about what was best for her baby, that it was his baby too, that he had to let her go now so she could bear a baby healthy in body and soul, that she knew he loved Josie, that his love would let him do what was best for them all. He was crying now, arguing with her while he slowly let go while he said he never could let her go that she was his whole life, that he would die without her, while Josie kissed Toña quickly on the cheek and climbed in next to the taxi driver who sat there looking the way I probably looked, dazed, like he'd stumbled into a movie screen and couldn't get out. She had to tell him to drive off.

➤ *QUESTIONS FOR READING AND WRITING*

1. Who is the narrator? How does her point of view influence your response to the story?
2. Describe Ramón. Why is Josie leaving him? Why is Josie upset that she is pregnant?
3. Why does Ramón sound so small when he realizes Josie is leaving? Do you believe what he says in response? Explain.
4. Do you think Josie will eventually take Ramón back? Do you think she should? Why or why not?

◆ POETRY ◆

MAYA ANGELOU (b. 1928)

Maya Angelou was born (Marguerite Johnson) in St. Louis, Missouri, and lived with her grandmother in Stamps, Arkansas. She studied music, dance, and drama, and also became a writer. She became very involved in the black civil rights movement, and from 1963 to 1966 she lived in Ghana. Angelou is known for her many volumes of autobiographical novels, the first of which is I Know Why the Caged Bird Sings *(1969). Her six works of poetry are* Just Give Me a Cool Drink of Water for I Die *(1971),* Oh Pray My Wings Are Gonna Fit Me Well *(1975),* And Still I Rise *(1978),* Shaker, Why Don't You Sing? *(1983),* Now Sheba Sings the Song *(1987), and* I Shall Not Be Moved *(1990). She read her poem "On the Pulse of Morning" at the inauguration ceremony for President Bill Clinton in 1993. In the same year, a collection of Angelou's essays,* Wouldn't Take Nothing for My Journey, *was published. She teaches at Wake Forest University.*

Phenomenal Woman [1978]

Pretty women wonder where my secret lies.
I'm not cute or built to suit a fashion model's size
But when I start to tell them,
They think I'm telling lies.
I say,
It's in the reach of my arms,
The span of my hips,
The stride of my step,
The curl of my lips.
I'm a woman
Phenomenally.
Phenomenal woman,
That's me.

I walk into a room
Just as cool as you please,
And to a man,
The fellows stand or
Fall down on their knees.
Then they swarm around me,
A hive of honey bees.
I say,
It's the fire in my eyes,
And the flash of my teeth,
The swing in my waist,
And the joy in my feet.
I'm a woman
Phenomenally.
Phenomenal woman,
That's me.

Men themselves have wondered
What they see in me.
They try so much
But they can't touch
My inner mystery.
When I try to show them
They say they still can't see.
I say,
It's in the arch of my back,
The sun of my smile,
The ride of my breasts,
The grace of my style.
I'm a woman
Phenomenally.

Phenomenal woman,
That's me.

Now you understand
Just why my head's not bowed.
I don't shout or jump about
Or have to talk real loud.
When you see me passing
It ought to make you proud.
I say,
It's in the click of my heels,
The bend of my hair,
The palm of my hand,
The need for my care.
'Cause I'm a woman
Phenomenally.
Phenomenal woman,
That's me.

➤ *QUESTIONS FOR READING AND WRITING*

1. What is so "phenomenal" about the speaker? What lines in the poem indicate that?
2. Compare this poem with Marge Piercy's "Barbie Doll" on page 13. Do you think the "girlchild" might have become a phenomenal woman? Explain.

MARGARET ATWOOD (b. 1939)

Margaret Atwood was born in Ottawa, Canada, and took extensive trips during her childhood through the wilds of Canada with her father, an entomologist. In 1962, the same year she graduated from the University of Toronto, she published her first book of poetry, Double Persephone. *She has since published numerous works of fiction, poetry, and criticism, including the novels* Surfacing *(1972),* Cat's Eye *(1988), and the futuristic* The Handmaid's Tale *(1985), which was made into a film. Her most recent novel is* Alias Grace *(1996). A fierce proponent of Canadian literature as well as an ardent feminist, Atwood has been instrumental in forging a Canadian cultural identity separate from that of England and the United States. She told an interviewer in* Ms. *magazine, "I began as a profoundly apolitical writer, but then I began to do what all novelists and some poets do: I began to describe the world around me."*

You Fit into Me [1971]

you fit into me
like a hook into an eye

a fish hook
an open eye

➤ *QUESTIONS FOR READING AND WRITING*

1. The first stanza introduces the second. The second is an abrupt shift. How do they differ?
2. How would you describe this relationship? Have you ever had one like it?

Robert Browning (1812–1889)

The son of a banker, Robert Browning was born in a suburb of London, and first learned the joy of reading in his father's vast library. He published his first collection of poems, Pauline, *in 1833, and over the next thirty years followed it with numerous other volumes, which, though they contained some of his greatest works, were financially unsuccessful. In 1846, in one of the most famous matches in literary history, he married the celebrated poet Elizabeth Barrett, who wrote the sonnet that begins "How do I love thee? Let me count the ways" to him. Because of her ill health and to escape her overbearing father, the couple moved to Italy. After her death in 1861, he returned to England and wrote* The Ring and the Book *(1868–1869), a long narrative poem about a famous seventeenth-century murder case. The poem was Brownings' first major success and brought him the wide recognition and respect that had thus far eluded him. Many of his best regarded poems, including* Porphyria's Lover, *take the form of dramatic monologues, in which the poet creates a character who reveals himself or herself while delivering an extended speech, often to a silent listener.*

Porphyria's Lover [1834]

The rain set early in tonight,
    The sullen wind was soon awake,
It tore the elm-tops down for spite,
    And did its worst to vex the lake:
I listened with heart fit to break.

When glided in Porphyria; straight
She shut the cold out and the storm,
And kneeled and made the cheerless grate
Blaze up, and all the cottage warm;
Which done, she rose, and from her form
Withdrew the dripping cloak and shawl,
And laid her soiled gloves by, untied
Her hat and let the damp hair fall,
And, last, she sat down by my side
And called me. When no voice replied,
She put my arm about her waist,
And made her smooth white shoulder bare,
And all her yellow hair displaced,
And, stooping, made my cheek lie there,
And spread, o'er all, her yellow hair,
Murmuring how she loved me-she
Too weak, for all her heart's endeavor,
To set its struggling passion free
From pride, and vainer ties dissever,
And give herself to me forever.
But passion sometimes would prevail,
Nor could tonight's gay feast restrain
A sudden thought of one so pale
For love of her, and all in vain:
So, she was come through wind and rain.
Be sure I looked up at her eyes
Happy and proud; at last I knew
Porphyria worshiped me: surprise
Made my heart swell, and still it grew
While I debated what to do.
That moment she was mine, mine, fair,
Perfectly pure and good: I found
A thing to do, and all her hair
In one long yellow string I wound
Three times her little throat around,
And strangled her. No pain felt she;
I am quite sure she felt no pain.
As a shut bud that holds a bee,
I warily opened her lids: again
Laughed the blue eyes without a stain.
And I untightened next the tress
About her neck; her cheek once more
Blushed bright beneath my burning kiss:
I propped her head up as before,
Only, this time my shoulder bore

Her head, which droops upon it still:
  The smiling rosy little head,
So glad it has its utmost will,
  That all it scorned at once is fled,
And I, its love, am gained instead!
  Porphyria's love: she guessed not how
Her darling one wish would be heard.
  And thus we sit together now,
And all night long we have not stirred,
  And yet God has not said a word!

QUESTIONS FOR READING AND WRITING

1. What details set the mood early in the poem?
2. Paraphrase the speaker's argument. According to him, why is it appropriate to strangle Porphyria?
3. Interpret the last line of the poem. Is the speaker showing consciousness of guilt?
4. Compare this poem to William Faulkner's "A Rose for Emily." How are Miss Emily and the speaker of this poem similar and different?

JOHN DONNE (1572–1631)

John Donne was born into a Roman Catholic family and attended Oxford and Cambridge. As a young man, in response to the rabid anti-Catholic sentiments of Elizabethan England, he abandoned his faith and determined to make his way in the court of Queen Elizabeth I using his charm, learning, and poetic abilities. In 1601, he destroyed his chances for serious advancement after secretly marrying Ann More, the niece of Sir Thomas Egerton, his employer. Donne then struggled to make ends meet, publishing treatises and poetry only occasionally. In 1615, after years of resistance, he converted to Anglicanism and became a priest. Donne became renowned for his preaching, and was soon considered one of the greatest preachers of the age. In 1621, he was appointed Dean of St. Paul's Cathedral, a post he held until his death. His poetry, most of which was published posthumously, is usually divided into two periods: his love poetry is said to date from the beginning of his career, while his religious poems are said to date from his later years. The greatest of the so-called metaphysical school of poets, Donne's poetry is

remarkable for its elaborate conceits (extended metaphors), unconventional imagery, and highly compressed meanings.

THE FLEA [1633]

Mark but this flea, and mark in this
How little that which thou deny'st me is;
It sucked me first, and now sucks thee,
And in this flea our two bloods mingled be;
Thou know'st that this cannot be said
A sin, nor shame, nor loss of maidenhead;
Yet this enjoys before it woo,
And pampered swells with one blood made of two,
And this, alas, is more than we would do.

Oh stay, three lives in one flea spare,
Where we almost, yea, more than married are.
This flea is you and I, and this
Our marriage bed and marriage temple is;
Though parents grudge, and you, we are met
And cloistered in these living walls of jet.
Though use make you apt to kill me,
Let not to that, self-murder added be,
And sacrilege, three sins in killing three.

Cruel and sudden, hast thou since
Purpled thy nail in blood of innocence?
Wherein could this flea guilty be,
Except in that drop which it sucked from thee?
Yet thou triumph'st and say'st that thou
Find'st not thyself, nor me the weaker now.
'Tis true. Then learn how false fears be:
Just so much honor, when thou yield'st to me,
Will waste, as this flea's death took life from thee.

➤ *QUESTIONS FOR READING AND WRITING*

1. What does the speaker in the poem want? Are you convinced he should get it?
2. Why does he believe that the flea unites him with his love? What does he mean by "Let not to that, self-murder added be, / And sacrilege, three sins in killing three"?
3. Each stanza begins with three rhyming pairs of lines or couplets and ends with three rhyming lines. How is your reading affected by this? Do you think this form conveys the meaning of the poem effectively?

JUDY GRAHN (b. 1940)

Judy Grahn was born in Chicago, Illinois. Her father worked as a cook, and her mother was a photographer's assistant. In her twenties, she worked in a series of odd jobs, including short-order cook, artist's model, and nurses aid before starting the Women's Press Collective with artist Wendy Cadden in Oakland, California, in 1969. In the 1980s, although she was already a well-established poet, she returned to school at San Francisco State University and earned a B.A. degree. She currently teaches in the New College of California in San Francisco, where she helped create the Gay and Lesbian Studies department. Her publications include: The Work of a Common Woman: The Collected Poetry of Judy Grahn, 1964–1977 *(1978),* The Queen of Wands *(1982), and a collection of nonfiction,* Blood and Bread and Roses *(1986).*

ELLA, IN A SQUARE APRON, ALONG HIGHWAY 80 [1971]

She's a copperheaded waitress,
tired and sharp-worded, she hides
her bad brown tooth behind a wicked
smile, and flicks her ass
out of habit, to fend off the pass
that passes for affection.
She keeps her mind the way men
keep a knife—keen to strip the game
down to her size. She has a thin spine,
swallows her eggs cold, and tells lies.
She slaps a wet rag at the truck drivers
if they should complain. She understands
the necessity for pain, turns away
the smaller tips, out of pride, and
keeps a flask under the counter. Once,
she shot a lover who misused her child.
Before she got out of jail, the courts had pounced
and given the child away. Like some isolated lake,
her flat blue eyes take care of their own stark
bottoms. Her hands are nervous, curled, ready
to scrape.
The common woman is as common
as a rattlesnake.

➤ QUESTIONS FOR READING AND WRITING

1. Who is Ella? What words or phrases in the poem help you to see her?
2. What does the speaker mean by "The common woman is as common / as a rattlesnake"?

A. E. HOUSMAN (1859–1936)

An important scholar of Latin as well as a celebrated poet, A[lfred] E[dward] Housman was born in the village of Fockbury in Worcestershire, England. A brilliant student at Oxford University, Housman inexplicably failed his final exams. Determined to redeem himself after his poor showing, he wrote scholarly articles while working at night as a civil servant in the patent office. His brilliant scholarship eventually won him positions at the University of London and Cambridge University. During his life he published only two slim volumes of poetry, A Shropshire Lad *(1898) and* Last Poems *(1922). His poems are tinged with melancholy, often dealing with themes of lost love and youth. His* Complete Poems, *which includes verses that were published posthumously, was published in 1956.*

WHEN I WAS ONE-AND-TWENTY [1898]

When I was one-and-twenty
  I heard a wise man say,
'Give crowns and pounds and guineas
  But not your heart away;
Give pearls away and rubies
  But keep your fancy free.'
But I was one-and-twenty,
  No use to talk to me.

When I was one-and-twenty
  I heard him say again,
'The heart out of the bosom
  Was never given in vain;
'Tis paid with sighs a plenty
  And sold for endless rue.'
And I am two-and-twenty,
  And oh, 'tis true, 'tis true.

➤ QUESTIONS FOR READING AND WRITING

1. What do you think of the wise man's advice in the first stanza?
2. Would you have taken his advice? Explain.
3. What's happened to the speaker? Does he regret his decision? Would you?

MAXINE KUMIN (b. 1925)

Maxine Kumin was born in Philadelphia, Pennsylvania, and currently lives on a farm in New Hampshire. She attended Radcliffe College, earning a B.A. degree in 1946 and an M.A. in 1948. Though Kumin was always interested in writing poetry, she did not begin to write seriously until, frustrated in her role as a suburban housewife, she began taking workshops at the Boston Center for Adult Education. At one of these workshops she met Anne Sexton, then also a housewife, and the two women became close friends. Over the following years, the women, who collaborated on three children's books, were important influences on each other, often providing suggestions, critiques, and support. Kumin's poetry, less confessional and more optimistic than Sexton's, often finds its subject matter in the details of everyday life in rural New England. Her works include four novels, numerous works for children, two collections of short stories, two collections of critical essays, and numerous volumes of poetry, including Up Country: Poems of New England, *which was awarded the Pulitzer Prize in 1973. Her most recent work,* Connecting the Dots: Poems, *appeared in 1996.*

AFTER LOVE [1972]

Afterwards, the compromise.
Bodies resume their boundaries.

These legs, for instance, mine.
Your arms take you back in.

Spoons of our fingers, lips
admit their ownership.

The bedding yawns, a door
blows aimlessly ajar

and overhead, a plane
singsongs coming down.

Nothing is changed, except
there was a moment when

the wolf, the mongering wolf
who stands outside the self

lay lightly down, and slept.

➤ QUESTIONS FOR READING AND WRITING

1. What does the speaker mean by "Afterwards, the compromise"?
2. Who is "the mongering wolf / who stands outside the self"?

Christopher Marlowe

(1564–1593)

Christopher Marlowe was a contemporary of Shakespeare and one of the most successful playwrights and poets of the Elizabethan era, but his career was cut short when he was murdered in a tavern brawl. His major plays include Tamburlaine the Great *(1587),* Dr. Faustus *(1588), and* Edward II *(1592). Walter Raleigh's response to "A Passionate Shepherd to His Love" appears on page 578.*

The Passionate Shepherd to His Love

Come live with me and be my love
And we will all the pleasures prove
That valleys, groves, hills, and fields
Woods, or steepy mountain yields.

And we will sit upon the rocks,
Seeing the shepherds feed their flocks,
By shallow rivers to whose falls
Melodious birds sing madrigals.

And I will make thee beds of roses
And a thousand fragrant posies,
A cap of flowers, and a kirtle°
Embroidered with leaves of myrtle;

A gown made of the finest wool
Which from our pretty lambs we pull;
Fair lined slippers for the cold,
With buckles of the purest gold;

[11]**kirtle** a long gown

A belt of straw and ivy buds,
With coral clasps and amber studs:
And if these pleasures may thee move
Come live with me and be my love.

The shepherds' swains° shall dance and sing
For thy delight each May morning:
If these delights thy mind may move
Then live with me and be my love.

[21]**swains** boy servants

➤ *QUESTIONS FOR READING AND WRITING*

1. What does the shepherd want? What does he offer?
2. Do you think he is being realistic? Explain.
3. Compare this poem with "The Nymph's Reply to the Shepherd" on page 578.

ANDREW MARVELL (1621–1678)

Andrew Marvell was born in the town of Hull and attended Cambridge University, graduating in 1638. During the English civil war, he held posts as a tutor in the family of an important general on the Parliamentary side, and as a secretary to the poet Milton. During the war, in 1659, Marvell was elected to Parliament and served, even after the Restoration, as a well-regarded member until his death. Marvell, who was known only for the few satires he published during his lifetime, was recognized as an important lyric poet only after his death, when his Miscellaneous Poems *were published in 1681. "To His Coy Mistress" is widely considered one of the greatest English love poems.*

TO HIS COY MISTRESS [1641]

Had we but world enough, and time,
This coyness, lady, were no crime.
We would sit down, and think which way
To walk, and pass our long love's day.
Thou by the Indian Ganges' side
Shoudst rubies find: I by the tide
Of Humber° would complain. I would
Love you ten years before the flood,

[7]**Humber** the river that runs through Marvell's native town, Hull

And you should, if you please, refuse
Till the conversion of the Jews°.
My vegetable love° should grow
Vaster than empires and more slow;
An hundred years should go to praise
Thine eyes, and on thy forehead gaze;
Two hundred to adore each breast,
But thirty thousand to the rest;
An age at least to every part,
And the last age should show your heart.
For, lady, you deserve this state,
Nor would I love at lower rate.
    But at my back I always hear
Time's winged chariot hurrying near;
And yonder all before us lie
Deserts of vast eternity.
Thy beauty shall no more be found;
Nor, in thy marble vault, shall sound
My echoing song, then worms shall try
That long-preserved virginity,
And your quaint honor turn to dust,
And into ashes all my lust:
The grave's a fine and private place,
But none, I think, do there embrace.
    Now therefore, while the youthful hue
Sits on thy skin like morning dew
And while thy willing soul transpires°
At every pore with instant fires,
Now let us sport us while we may,
And now, like amorous birds of prey,
Rather at once our time devour
Than languish in his slow-chapped° power.
Let us roll all our strength and all
Our sweetness up into one ball,
And tear our pleasures with rough strife
Thorough the iron gates of life:
Thus, though we cannot make our sun
Stand still, yet we will make him run.

➤ *QUESTIONS FOR READING AND WRITING*

1. What does the speaker in the poem want? Why does he think he should have it?

10 **the conversion of the Jews** supposedly to occur at the end of time   11 **vegetable love** growing slowly
35 **transpires** breathes   40 **slow-chapped** devouring slowly

2. The poem is divided into three parts. Discuss the speaker's logic as he moves through each of these parts.
3. What images does the speaker use to dramatize his points?
4. Do you find his argument sincere or convincing? Explain.
5. Do you find any of the language exaggerated? Explain.
6. How do you think Ella in "Ella, in a square apron, along Highway 80" (see page 570) would respond to this argument?

SHARON OLDS (b. 1942)

(See biography on page 329.)

SEX WITHOUT LOVE [1984]

How do they do it, the ones who make love
without love? Beautiful as dancers,
gliding over each other like ice-skaters
over the ice, fingers hooked
inside each other's bodies, faces
red as steak, wine, wet as the
children at birth whose mothers are going to
give them away. How do they come to the
come to the come to the God come to the
still waters, and not love
the one who came there with them, light
rising slowly as steam off their joined
skin? These are the true religious,
the purists, the pros, the ones who will not
accept a false Messiah, love the
priest instead of the God. They do not
mistake the lover for their own pleasure,
they are like great runners, they know they are alone
with the road surface, the cold, the wind,
the fit of their shoes, their over-all cardio-
vascular health—just factors; like the partner
in the bed, and not the truth, which is the
single body alone in the universe
against its own best time.

➤ *QUESTIONS FOR READING AND WRITING*

1. What is the tone of this poem?
2. In what way do the lovers "glide over each other like ice-skaters / over the ice"?
3. What is the purpose of the stammered "come to the" in lines 8 and 9?

SYLVIA PLATH (1932–1963)

Encouraged by her mother, Sylvia Plath began writing poetry as a precocious child in Boston, publishing her first poem in the Boston Traveller *when she was only eight years old. That same year her father died, an event that haunted her for the rest of her life. Like the protagonist in her autobiographical novel* The Bell Jar *(1963), she was a star student at Smith College, became a guest editor of a fashion magazine, and moved for a short time to New York City. When she returned home, she suffered the first of her serious mental breakdowns and attempted suicide. She was institutionalized for over a year and received electric shock treatments. When she returned to Smith she again excelled, winning a Fulbright scholarship to England after her final year. While studying at Cambridge she met and fell in love with the English poet Ted Hughes. Married in 1956, the couple eventually settled in the English countryside and produced two children. The marriage was a difficult one, and the couple separated in 1962. Once again Plath entered a severe depression, committing suicide in 1963. Her greatest work dates to the tortured final years of her life, when she was able to channel her energies into highly personal, ironic, and often terrifying poems. Her* Collected Poems, *edited by Ted Hughes, appeared in 1981 and was awarded the Pulitzer Prize.*

MIRROR [1963]

I am silver and exact. I have no preconceptions.
Whatever I see I swallow immediately
Just as it is, unmisted by love or dislike.
I am not cruel, only truthful—
The eye of a little god, four-cornered.
Most of the time I meditate on the opposite wall.
It is pink, with speckles. I have looked at it so long
I think it is a part of my heart. But it flickers.
Faces and darkness separate us over and over.

Now I am a lake. A woman bends over me.
Searching my reaches for what she really is.
Then she turns to those liars, the candles or the moon.
I see her back, and reflect it faithfully.
She rewards me with tears and an agitation of hands.
I am important to her. She comes and goes.
Each morning it is her face that replaces the darkness.
In me she has drowned a young girl, and in me an old woman
Rises toward her day after day, like a terrible fish.

➤ *QUESTIONS FOR READING AND WRITING*

1. Who is the speaker in this poem?
2. To what extent is the mirror honest? In what way are "the candles or the moon" liars?
3. Who and what is being mirrored? In what way does it "rise to the surface like a terrible fish"?

WALTER RALEIGH (1552–1618)

Walter Raleigh is best known as an adventurer, explorer, and adviser to Queen Elizabeth I. He organized expeditions to North America, founded a settlement in Virginia, and introduced tobacco to Europe. Involved in political intrigue for much of his career, he was imprisoned for thirteen years in the Tower of London and was eventually executed by James I. "The Nymph's Reply to the Shepherd" was written in response to Christopher Marlowe's "The Passionate Shepherd to His Love," on page 573.

THE NYMPH'S REPLY TO THE SHEPHERD [1600]

If all the world were young,
And truth in every shepherd's tongue,
These pretty pleasures might me move
To live with thee and be thy love.

Time drives the flocks from field to fold
When rivers rage and rocks grow cold,
And Philomel° becometh dumb;
The rest complains of cares to come.

The flowers do fade, and wanton fields
To wayward winter reckoning yields;
A honey tongue, a heart of gall,
Is fancy's spring, but sorrow's fall.

Thy gowns, thy shoes, thy bed of roses,
Thy cap, thy kirtle°, and thy posies
Soon break, soon winter, soon forgotten-
In folly ripe, in season rotten.

7 **Philomel** nightingale bird 14 **kirtle** a long gown

Thy belt of straw and ivy buds,
Thy coral clasps and amber studs,
All these in me no means can move
To come to thee and be thy love.

But could youth last and love still breed,
Had joys no date nor age no need,
Then these delights my mind might move
To come with thee and be thy love.

➤ *QUESTIONS FOR READING AND WRITING*

1. Do you agree with this reply to "The Passionate Shepherd to His Love" (p. 573)? Explain.
2. Why doesn't the speaker give the shepherd what he wants? How does her vision of reality differ from his? What reality does she recognize that he does not?
3. How would you imagine this speaker might respond to the argument in "To His Coy Mistress" (p. 574).

ADRIENNE RICH (b. 1929)

Adrienne Rich was born into a well-to-do family in Baltimore, Maryland. Her father was a doctor, and her mother, prior to her marriage, had been a musician. While attending Radcliffe College, Rich was selected by W. H. Auden for the prestigious Yale Younger Poets series, publishing her first volume of poetry A Change of World *(1951). In 1953 she married an accountant and soon had three sons. In her enormously influential book* Of Woman Born *(1976), she wrote of her experiences of motherhood and her eventual rejection of the traditional role that society thrust upon her. Her poetry, as well as her prose, has always been overtly political, reflecting first her participation in the antiwar protests of the 1960s and 1970s, and later as a leading voice in the feminist movement. Her works include:* Leaflets: Poems 1965–1968 *(1969),* The Will to Change: Poems, 1968–1970 *(1971),* Blood, Bread and Poetry: Selected Prose 1979–1986 *(1986), and* What Is Found There: Notebooks on Poetry and Politics *(1995). "Rape" is taken from* Diving into the Wreck: Poems, 1971–1972 *(1973), which was awarded the National Book Award. Rich declined the honor as an individual, but accepted it on behalf of women everywhere whose voices had been silenced.*

RAPE [1973]

There is a cop who is both prowler and father:
he comes from your block, grew up with your brothers,

had certain ideals.

You hardly know him in his boots and silver badge,
on horseback, one hand touching his gun.

You hardly know him but you have to get to know him:
he has access to machinery that could kill you.
He and his stallion clop like warlords among the trash,
his ideals stand in the air, a frozen cloud
from between his unsmiling lips.

And so, when the time comes, you have to turn to him,
the maniac's sperm still greasing your thighs,
your mind whirling like crazy. You have to confess
to him, you are guilty of the crime
of having been forced.

And you see his blue eyes, the blue eyes of all the family
whom you used to know, grow narrow and glisten,
his hand types out the details
and he wants them all
but the hysteria in your voice pleases him best.

You hardly know him but now he thinks he knows you:
he has taken down your worst moment
on a machine and filed it in a file.
He knows, or thinks he knows, how much you imagined;
he knows, or thinks he knows, what you secretly wanted.

He has access to machinery that could get you put away;
and if, in the sickening light of the precinct,
and if, in the sickening light of the precinct,
your details sound like a portrait of your confessor,
will you swallow, will you deny them, will you lie your way home?

ALBERTO RIOS (b. 1952)

Alberto Rios is a native of Nogales, Arizona, and is the product of Mexican-American and British parents. His books of poetry include Whispering to Fool the Wind *(1981), for which he won the Walt Whitman Award,* The Live Orchard Woman *(1990), and* Pig Cookies and Other Stories *(1995). He teaches at Arizona State University.*

The Purpose of Altar Boys [1982]

Tonio told me at catechism
the big part of the eye
admits good, and the little
black part is for seeing
evil—his mother told him
who was a widow and so
an authority on such things.
That's why at night
the black part gets bigger.
That's why kids can't go out
at night, and at night
girls take off their clothes
and walk around their
bedrooms or jump on their
beds or wear only sandals
and stand in their windows.
I was the altar boy
who knew about these things,
whose mission on some Sundays
was to remind people of
the night before as they
knelt for Holy Communion.
To keep Christ from falling
I held the metal plate
under chins,
while on the thick
red carpet of the altar
I dragged my feet
and waited for the precise
moment: plate to chin
I delivered without expression
the Holy Electric Shock,
the kind that produces
a really large swallowing
and makes people think.
I thought of it as justice.
But on other Sundays the fire
in my eyes was different,
my mission somehow changed.
I would hold the metal plate
a little too hard
against those certain same
nervous chins, and I
I would look
with authority down
the tops of white dresses.

➤ QUESTIONS FOR READING AND WRITING

1. Who is the speaker? What is the tone of the poem?
2. What does he mean in lines 19 to 21, that his "mission on some Sundays / was to remind people of / the night before"?
3. He says that on other Sundays his mission changed? How so?

ANNE SEXTON (1928–1974)

Born and raised in New England, Anne Sexton attended Garland Junior College and was married at the age of twenty. She suffered the first of many mental breakdowns following the birth of her first child in 1954. After a breakdown following the birth of her second child, she began writing poetry at the suggestion of a therapist. To Bedlam and Part Way Back, *her first book of poems, was published in 1960. Her 1967 volume,* Live or Die, *was awarded the Pulitzer Prize. Though she became extraordinarily successful, Sexton continually struggled with depression. Following her divorce, she committed suicide in 1974. Like her contemporary Sylvia Plath, Sexton's powerful and often startling work has been characterized as confessional poetry, in which deeply personal topics once considered taboo in modern poetry—mental illness, religious guilt, therapy—are openly discussed.*

CINDERELLA [1970]

You always read about it:
the plumber with twelve children
who wins the Irish Sweepstakes.
From toilets to riches.
That story.

Or the nursemaid,
some luscious sweet from Denmark
who captures the oldest son's heart.
From diapers to Dior.
That story.

Or a milkman who serves the wealthy,
eggs, cream, butter, yogurt, milk,
the white truck like an ambulance
who goes into real estate
and makes a pile.

From homogenized to martinis at lunch.

Or the charwoman
who is on the bus when it cracks up
and collects enough from the insurance.
From mops to Bonwit Teller.
That story.

Once
the wife of a rich man was on her deathbed
and she said to her daughter Cinderella:
Be devout. Be good. Then I will smile
down from heaven in the seam of a cloud.
The man took another wife who had
two daughters, pretty enough
but with hearts like blackjacks.
Cinderella was their maid.
She slept on the sooty hearth each night
and walked around looking like Al Jolson.
Her father brought presents home from town,
jewels and gowns for the other women
but the twig of a tree for Cinderella.
She planted that twig on her mother's grave
and it grew to a tree where a white dove sat.
Whenever she wished for anything the dove
would drop it like an egg upon the ground.
The bird is important, my dears, so heed him.

Next came the ball, as you all know.
It was a marriage market.
The prince was looking for a wife.
All but Cinderella were preparing
and gussying up for the big event.
Cinderella begged to go too.
Her stepmother threw a dish of lentils
into the cinders and said: Pick them
up in an hour and you shall go.
The white dove brought all his friends;
all the warm wings of the fatherland came,
and picked up the lentils in a jiffy.
No, Cinderella, said the stepmother,
you have no clothes and cannot dance.
That's the way with stepmothers.

Cinderella went to the tree at the grave
and cried forth like a gospel singer:
Mama! Mama! My turtledove,
send me to the prince's ball!

The bird dropped down a golden dress
and delicate little gold slippers.
Rather a large package for a simple bird.
So she went. Which is no surprise.
Her stepmother and sisters didn't
recognize her without her cinder face
and the prince took her hand on the spot
and danced with no other the whole day.

As nightfall came she thought she'd better
get home. The prince walked her home
and she disappeared into the pigeon house
and although the prince took an axe and broke
it open she was gone. Back to her cinders.
These events repeated themselves for three days.
However on the third day the prince
covered the palace steps with cobbler's wax
and Cinderella's gold shoe stuck upon it.
Now he would find whom the shoe fit
and find his strange dancing girl for keeps.
He went to their house and the two sisters
were delighted because they had lovely feet.
The eldest went into a room to try the slipper on
but her big toe got in the way so she simply
sliced it off and put on the slipper;
The prince rode away with her until the white dove
told him to look at the blood pouring forth.
That is the way with amputations.
They don't just heal up like a wish.
The other sister cut off her heel
but the blood told as blood will.
The prince was getting tired.

He began to feel like a shoe salesman.
But he gave it one last try.
This time Cinderella fit into the shoe
like a love letter into its envelope.
At the wedding ceremony
he two sisters came to curry favor
and the white dove pecked their eyes out.
Two hollow spots were left
like soup spoons.

Cinderella and the prince
lived, they say, happily ever after,
like two dolls in a museum case

never bothered by diapers or dust,
never arguing over the timing of an egg,
never telling the same story twice,
never getting a middle-aged spread,
their darling smiles pasted on for eternity
Regular Bobbsey Twins.
That story.

➤ *QUESTIONS FOR READING AND WRITING*

1. Compare this version of Cinderella with the Grimm Brothers version on page 523.
2. Who is the speaker in this version? How does the speaker's "voice" differ from that of the narrator in the Grimm version? What words of phrases exemplify that difference? How are you affected by the repetition of the phrase, "That story"?
3. The last stanza is a variation on the usual ending of a fairy tale. What is its tone? To what extent does it emphasize the tone of the entire poem?

WILLIAM SHAKESPEARE (1564–1616)

Though William Shakespeare is the most famous writer ever to have written in English, details of his life are surprisingly sketchy. It is known that he was born in the town of Stratford-on-Avon, where he probably attended the local grammar school, and that he married Anne Hathaway in 1582. By 1592, he was an actor and playwright in London, associated with the Lord Chamberlain's Men, the most successful acting troupe of the time. In 1593 and 1594, he published two long mythological poems, Venus and Adonis *and* The Rape of Lucrece. *His astonishing sequence of sonnets, some of the most beautiful poetry ever created, were published in 1609, though they were probably written from 1592–1594, when the theaters were shut because of the plague. By 1597, he was able to buy a large house in Stratford and apparently retired there in 1610. His works for the theater, which were not published until after his death, number thirteen comedies (including* A Midsummer's Night Dream, Twelfth Night, *and* The Merchant of Venice*), ten tragedies (including* Romeo and Juliet, Macbeth, Julius Caesar, Othello, *and* Hamlet*), ten history plays, and four romances (including* The Tempest*). Ben Jonson, a playwright who was Shakespeare's contemporary and rival, wrote of him: "He was not of an age, but for all time!"*

Shall I Compare Thee to a Summer's Day? (Sonnet No. 18) [1609]

Shall I compare thee to a summer's day?
Thou art more lovely and more temperate:
Rough winds do shake the darling buds of May,
And summer's lease hath all too short a date;
Sometime too hot the eye of heaven shines,
And often is his gold complexion dimm'd;
And every fair from fair sometime declines,
By chance or nature's changing course untrimm'd;
But thy eternal summer shall not fade
Nor lose possession of that fair thou ow'st;
Nor shall Death brag thou wand'rest in his shade,
When in eternal lines to time thou grow'st;
So long as men can breathe or eyes can see,
So long lives this, and this gives life to thee.

➤ *QUESTIONS FOR READING AND WRITING*

1. Do you think he should compare his beloved to a summer's day? Why or why not?
2. Compare this sonnet to "My Mistress' Eyes are Nothing Like the Sun" below.
3. In many of Shakespeare's sonnets, a dilemma is presented in the first eight lines—a turning point and solution in the next six. To what extent is that the case here?

My Mistress' Eyes are Nothing Like the Sun (Sonnet No. 130) [1609]

My mistress' eyes are nothing like the sun;
Coral is far more red than her lips' red;
If snow be white, why then her breasts are dun;
If hairs be wires, black wires grow on her head.
I have seen roses damasked,° red and white,
But no such roses see I in her cheeks;
And in some perfumes is there more delight
Than in the breath that from my mistress reeks.
I love to hear her speak, yet well I know
That music hath a far more pleasing sound;
I grant I never saw a goddess go°;
My mistress, when she walks, treads on the ground.
And yet, by heaven, I think my love as rare
As any she belied with false compare.

[5]**damasked** of mingled red and white [11]**go** walk

➤ *QUESTIONS FOR READING AND WRITING*

1. According to the speaker, his mistress's eyes, lips, breasts, hair, cheeks, breath, voice, and walk don't stand up to nature very well. Do you think he is insulting her? Explain.
2. In what way do the last two lines reverse the first ten?
3. To what extent is this poem about the use of language?

WHEN MY LOVE SWEARS THAT SHE IS MADE OF TRUTH (SONNET NO. 138)

[1609]

When my love swears that she is made of truth,
I do believe her, though I know she lies,
That she might think me some untutor'd youth,
Unlearned in the world's false subtleties.
Thus vainly thinking that she thinks me young,
Although she knows my days are past the best,
Simply I credit her false-speaking tongue:
On both sides thus is simple truth suppress'd.
But wherefore says she not she is unjust?
And wherefore say not I that I am old?
O, love's best habit is in seeming trust,
And age in love loves not to have years told:
  Therefore I lie with her, and she with me,
  And in our faults by lies we flatter'd be.

➤ *QUESTIONS FOR READING AND WRITING*

1. If the speaker knows his love "lies," why do you think he believes her?
2. Do you agree that "love's best habit is in seeming trust"? Why or why not?
3. Compare this sonnet with the previous two sonnets.

◆ DRAMA ◆

TWO READERS ~ TWO CHOICES

■ *EXPLORING "OTHELLO"*

Making Connections *Othello* is one of Shakespeare's most powerful plays. It grabs us and repels us at the same time. We may find ourselves repulsed by

Iago's calculated evil yet fascinated by his charming, brilliant manipulation. We may admire the nobility of Othello but find ourselves disgusted by his jealousy and lack of faith in Desdemona. We may be drawn to the generosity and unconditional love of Desdemona, yet feel disappointed and frustrated by her persistent, unquestioning deference to Othello. With its larger than life characters, intrigue, treachery, and improbable plot, it may seem like a modern soap opera; but its relentless pursuit of the destructive nature of jealousy, its rich characterization, and the beauty and insight of its poetry reveal much more about the human condition than any "soap" can.

Like most drama, *Othello* was written to be performed. The best way to understand and appreciate it is to experience a production of it. The verse, however, is so rich with poetic language that it may be difficult to fully grasp during a performance. It may also be difficult to understand archaic words and sort out the word order without explanatory notes and the text in front of you. The ideal combination then, is to see a performance of *Othello* and to read the text of the play.

Your Experiences and Beliefs Before you read or view *Othello,* you may want to consider your own beliefs and experiences as they apply to some of the issues that emerge from this play: loyalty in relationships, jealousy, revenge, interracial marriage, romantic relationships between older men and younger women, the role of men and women in a marriage. If you had to choose, would you trust a good friend of many years or someone with whom you were having a romantic relationship? Do you think that trusting people is naive or foolish? Do you think that some people are naturally evil? Do you think good people are capable of evil acts?

WILLIAM SHAKESPEARE (1564–1616)

(See biography on page 585.)

OTHELLO, THE MOOR OF VENICE [1604]

CHARACTERS

OTHELLO, the Moor
BRABANTIO, [a SENATOR,] father to DESDEMONA
CASSIO, an honorable lieutenant [to Othello]
IAGO, [Othello's ancient,] a villain
RODERIGO, a gulled gentleman
DUKE of VENICE
SENATORS [of Venice]
MONTANO, governor of Cyprus
GENTLEMEN of Cyprus
LODOVICO and GRATIANO, [kinsmen to Brabantio,] two noble Venetians

SAILORS
CLOWN
DESDEMONA, [daughter to Brabantio and] wife to Othello
EMILIA, wife to IAGO
BIANCA, a courtesan [and mistress to Cassio]
A MESSENGER
A HERALD
A MUSICIAN
SERVANTS, ATTENDANTS, OFFICERS, SENATORS, MUSICIANS, GENTLEMEN

SCENE: *Venice; a seaport in Cyprus*

ACT I

SCENE I [Venice. A Street.]

[Enter RODERIGO and IAGO.]

RODERIGO: Tush, never tell me!° I take it much unkindly
That thou, IAGO, who hast had my purse
As if the strings were thine, shouldst know of this.°
IAGO: 'Sblood,° but you'll not hear me.
If ever I did dream of such a matter,
Abhor me.
RODERIGO: Thou toldst me thou didst hold him in thy hate.
IAGO: Despise me
If I do not. Three great ones of the city,
In personal suit to make me his lieutenant,
Off-capped to him;° and by the faith of man,
I know my price, I am worth no worse a place.
But he, as loving his own pride and purposes,
Evades them with a bombast circumstance°
Horribly stuffed with epithets of war,°
And, in conclusion,
Nonsuits° my mediators. For, "Certes,"° says he,
"I have already chose my officer."
And what was he?
Forsooth, a great arithmetician,°
One Michael Cassio, a Florentine,

1 **never tell me** an expression of incredulity, like "tell me another one" 3 **this** i.e., Desdemona's elopement 4 **'Sblood** by His (Christ's) blood 11 **him** i.e., Othello 14 **bombast circumstance** wordy evasion (bombast is cotton padding) 15 **epithets of war** military expressions 17 **Nonsuits** rejects the petition of **Certes** certainly 20 **arithmetician** i.e., a man whose military knowledge is merely theoretical, based on books of tactics

A fellow almost damned in a fair wife,°
That never set a squadron in the field
Nor the division of a battle° knows
More than a spinster°—unless the bookish theoric,°
Wherein the togaed° consuls° can propose°
As masterly as he. Mere prattle without practice
Is all his soldiership. But he, sir, had th' election;
And I, of whom his° eyes had seen the proof
At Rhodes, at Cyprus, and on other grounds
Christened° and heathen, must be beleed and calmed°
By debitor and creditor.° This countercaster,°
He, in good time,° must his lieutenant be,
And I—God bless the mark!°—his Moorship's ancient.°

RODERIGO: By heaven, I rather would have been his hangman.°

IAGO: Why, there's no remedy. 'Tis the curse of service;
Preferment° goes by letter and affection,°
And not by old gradation,° where each second
Stood heir to th' first. Now, sir, be judge yourself
Whether I in any just term° am affined°
To love the Moor.

RODERIGO: I would not follow him then.

IAGO: O sir, content you.°
I follow him to serve my turn upon him.
We cannot all be masters, nor all masters
Cannot be truly° followed. You shall mark
Many a duteous and knee-crooking knave
That, doting on his own obsequious bondage,
Wears out his time, much like his master's ass,
For naught but provender, and when he's old, cashiered.°
Whip me° such honest knaves. Others there are
Who, trimmed in forms and visages of duty,°

22 **A . . . wife** Cassio does not seem to be married, but his counterpart in Shakespeare's source does have a woman in his house. See also Act IV, Scene i, line 127. 24 **division of a battle** disposition of a military unit 25 **a spinster** i.e., a housewife, one whose regular occupation is spinning **theoric** theory 26 **togaed** wearing the toga **consuls** counselors, Senators **propose** discuss 29 **his** i.e., Othello's 31 **Christened** Christian **beleed and calmed** left to leeward without wind, becalmed. (a sailing metaphor) 32 **debitor and creditor** a name for a system of bookkeeping, here used as a contemptuous nickname for Cassio **countercaster** i.e., bookkeeper, one who tallies with **counters,** or "metal disks" (said contemptuously) 33 **in good time** opportunely, i.e., forsooth 34 **God bless the mark** perhaps originally a formula to ward off evil; here an expression of impatience **ancient** standard-bearer, ensign 35 **his hangman** the executioner of him 37 **Preferment** promotion **letter and affection** personal influence and favoritism 38 **old gradation** step-by-step seniority, the traditional way 40 **term** respect **affined** bound 43 **content you** don't you worry about that 46 **truly** faithfully 50 **cashiered** dismissed from service 51 **Whip me** whip, as far as I'm concerned 52 **trimmed . . . duty** dressed up in the mere form and show of dutifulness

Keep yet their hearts attending on themselves,
And, throwing but shows of service on their lords,
Do well thrive by them, and when they have lined their coats,°
Do themselves homage.° These fellows have some soul,
And such a one do I profess myself. For, sir,
It is as sure as you are Roderigo,
Were I the Moor I would not be Iago.°
In following him, I follow but myself—
Heaven is my judge, not I for love and duty,
But seeming so for my peculiar° end.
For when my outward action doth demonstrate
The native° act and figure° of my heart
In compliment extern,° 'tis not long after
But I will wear my heart upon my sleeve
For daws° to peck at. I am not what I am.°

RODERIGO: What a full° fortune does the thick-lips° owe°
If he can carry 't thus!°

IAGO: Call up her father.
Rouse him, make after him, poison his delight,
Proclaim him in the streets; incense her kinsmen,
And, though he in a fertile climate dwell,
Plague him with flies.° Though that his joy be joy,°
Yet throw such changes of vexation° on 't
As it may° lose some color.°

RODERIGO: Here is her father's house. I'll call aloud.

IAGO: Do, with like timorous° accent and dire yell
As when, by night and negligence,° the fire
Is spied in populous cities.

RODERIGO: What ho, Brabantio! Signor Brabantio, ho!

IAGO: Awake! What ho, Brabantio! Thieves, thieves, thieves!
Look to your house, your daughter, and your bags!
Thieves, thieves!

55 **lined their coats** i.e., stuffed their purses 56 **Do themselves homage** i.e., attend to self-interest solely 59 **Were . . . Iago** i.e., if I were able to assume command, I certainly would not choose to remain a subordinate, or, I would keep a suspicious eye on a flattering subordinate 62 **peculiar** particular, personal 64 **native** innate **figure** shape, intent 65 **compliment extern** outward show. Conforming in this case to the inner workings and intention of the heart 67 **daws** small crowlike birds, proverbially stupid and avaricious **I am not what I am** i.e., I am not one who wears his heart on his sleeve 68 **full** swelling **thick-lips** Elizabethans often applied the term "Moor" to Negroes **owe** own 69 **carry 't thus** carry this off 72–73 **though . . . flies** though he seems prosperous and happy now, vex him with misery 73 **Though . . . be joy** although he seems fortunate and happy (repeats the idea of line 72) 74 **changes of vexation** vexing changes 75 **As it may** that may cause it to **some color** some of its fresh gloss 77 **timorous** frightening 78 **and negligence** i.e., by negligence

[BRABANTIO [enters] above [at a window].°]

BRABANTIO: What is the reason of this terrible summons?
What is the matter° there?
RODERIGO: Signor, is all your family within?
IAGO: Are your doors locked?
BRABANTIO: Why, wherefore ask you this?
IAGO: Zounds,° sir, you're robbed. For shame, put on your gown!
Your heart is burst; you have lost half your soul.
Even now, now, very now, an old black ram
Is tupping° your white ewe. Arise, arise!
Awake the snorting° citizens with the bell,
Or else the devil° will make a grandsire of you.
Arise, I say!
BRABANTIO: What, have you lost your wits?
RODERIGO: Most reverend signor, do you know my voice?
BRABANTIO: Not I. What are you?
RODERIGO: My name is Roderigo.
BRABANTIO: The worser welcome.
I have charged thee not to haunt about my doors.
In honest plainness thou hast heard me say
My daughter is not for thee; and now, in madness,
Being full of supper and distempering° drafts,
Upon malicious bravery° dost thou come
To start° my quiet.
RODERIGO: Sir, sir, sir—
BRABANTIO: But thou must needs be sure
My spirits and my place° have in° their power
To make this bitter to thee.
RODERIGO: Patience, good sir.
BRABANTIO: What tell'st thou me of robbing? This is Venice;
My house is not a grange.°
RODERIGO: Most grave Brabantio,
In simple° and pure soul I come to you.
IAGO: Zounds, sir, you are one of those that will not serve God if the devil bid you. Because we come to do you service and you think we are ruffians,

83 s.d. **at a window** this stage direction, from the Quarto, probably calls for an appearance on the gallery above and rearstage 85 **the matter** your business 88 **Zounds** by His (Christ's) wounds 91 **tupping** covering, copulating with (said of sheep) 92 **snorting** snoring 93 **the devil** the devil was conventionally pictured as black 102 **distempering** intoxicating 103 **Upon malicious bravery** with hostile intent to defy me 104 **start** startle, disrupt 106 **My spirits and my place** my temperament and my authority of office **have in** have it in 109 **grange** isolated country house 110 **simple** sincere

you'll have your daughter covered with a Barbary° horse; you'll have your nephews° neigh to you; you'll have coursers° for cousins° and jennets° for germans.°

BRABANTIO: What profane wretch art thou?

IAGO: I am one, sir, that comes to tell you your daughter and the Moor are now making the beast with two backs.

BRABANTIO: Thou art a villain.

IAGO: You are—a senator.°

BRABANTIO: This thou shalt answer.° I know thee, Roderigo.

RODERIGO: Sir, I will answer anything. But I beseech you,
If't be your pleasure and most wise° consent—
As partly I find it is—that your fair daughter,
At this odd-even° and dull watch o' the night,
Transported with° no worse nor better guard
But with a knave° of common hire, a gondolier,
To the gross clasps of a lascivious Moor—
If this be known to you and your allowance°
We then have done you bold and saucy° wrongs.
But if you know not this, my manners tell me
We have your wrong rebuke. Do not believe
That, from° the sense of all civility,°
I thus would play and trifle with your reverence.°
Your daughter, if you have not given her leave,
I say again, hath made a gross revolt,
Tying her duty, beauty, wit,° and fortunes
In an extravagant° and wheeling° stranger°
Of here and everywhere. Straight° satisfy yourself.
If she be in her chamber or your house,
Let loose on me the justice of the state
For thus deluding you.

BRABANTIO: Strike on the tinder,° ho!
Give me a taper! Call up all my people!
This accident° is not unlike my dream.
Belief of it oppresses me already.
Light, I say, light!

113 **Barbary** from northern Africa (and hence associated with Othello) 114 **nephews** i.e., grandsons **coursers** powerful horses **cousins** kinsmen **jennets** small Spanish horses 115 **germans** near relatives 119 a **senator** said with mock politeness, as though the word itself were an insult 120 **answer** be held accountable for 122 **wise** well-informed 124 **odd-even** between one day and the next, i.e., about midnight 125 **with** by 126 **But with a knave** than by a low fellow, a servant 128 **allowance** permission 129 **saucy** insolent 132 **from** contrary to **civility** good manners, decency 133 **your reverence** the respect due to you 136 **wit** intelligence 137 **extravagant** expatriate, wandering far from home **wheeling** roving about, vagabond **stranger** foreigner 138 **Straight** straightway 142 **tinder** charred linen ignited by a spark from flint and steel, used to light torches or **tapers** (lines 143, 168) 144 **accident** occurrence, event

[Exit [above].]

IAGO: Farewell, for I must leave you.
It seems not meet° nor wholesome to my place°
To be producted° —as, if I stay, I shall—
Against the Moor. For I do know the state,
However this may gall° him with some check,°
Cannot with safety cast° him, for he's embarked°
With such loud reason° to the Cyprus wars,
Which even now stands in act,° that, for their souls,°
Another of his fathom° they have none
To lead their business; in which regard,°
Though I do hate him as I do hell pains,
Yet for necessity of present life°
I must show out a flag and sign of love,
Which is indeed but sign. That you shall surely find him,
Lead to the Sagittary° the raisèd search,°
And there will I be with him. So farewell.

[Exit.]

[Enter [below] BRABANTIO [in his nightgown°] with servants and torches.]

BRABANTIO: It is too true an evil. Gone she is;
And what's to come of my despisèd time°
Is naught but bitterness. Now, Roderigo,
Where didst thou see her?—O unhappy girl!—
With the Moor, sayst thou?—Who would be a father!—
How didst thou know 'twas she?—O, she deceives me
Past thought!—What said she to you?—Get more tapers.
Raise all my kindred.—Are they married, think you?
RODERIGO: Truly, I think they are.
BRABANTIO: O heaven! How got she out? O treason of the blood!
Fathers, from hence trust not your daughters' minds
By what you see them act. Is there not charms°
By which the property° of youth and maidhood
May be abused?° Have you not read, Roderigo,
Of some such thing?

147 **meet** fitting **place** position (as ensign) 148 **producted** produced (as a witness) 150 **gall** rub; oppress **check** rebuke 151 **cast** dismiss **embarked** engaged 152 **loud reason** unanimous shout of confirmation (in the Senate) 153 **stands in act** are going on **for their souls** to save themselves 154 **fathom** i.e., ability, depth of experience 155 **in which regard** out of regard for which 157 **life** livelihood 160 **Sagittary** an inn or house where Othello and Desdemona are staying, named for its sign of Sagittarius, or Centaur **raisèd search** search party roused out of sleep 161 s.d. **nightgown** dressing gown (this costuming is specified in the Quarto text) 163 **time** i.e., remainder of life 173 **charms** spells 174 **property** special quality, nature 175 **abused** deceived

RODERIGO: Yes, sir, I have indeed.
BRABANTIO: Call up my brother.—O, would you had had her!—
Some one way, some another.—Do you know
Where we may apprehend her and the Moor?
RODERIGO: I think I can discover° him, if you please
To get good guard and go along with me.
BRABANTIO: Pray you, lead on. At every house I'll call;
I may command° at most.—Get weapons, ho!
And raise some special officers of night.—
On, good Roderigo. I will deserve° your pains.

[Exeunt.]

SCENE II [Venice. Another Street, Before Othello's Lodgings.]

[Enter OTHELLO, IAGO, attendants with torches.]

IAGO: Though in the trade of war I have slain men,
Yet do I hold it very stuff° o' the conscience
To do no contrived° murder. I lack iniquity
Sometimes to do me service. Nine or ten times
I had thought t' have yerked° him° here under the ribs.
OTHELLO: 'Tis better as it is.
IAGO: Nay, but he prated,
And spoke such scurvy and provoking terms
Against your honor
That, with the little godliness I have,
I did full hard forbear him.° But, I pray you, sir,
Are you fast married? Be assured of this,
That the magnifico° is much beloved,
And hath in his effect° a voice potential°
As double as the Duke's. He will divorce you,
Or put upon you what restraint or grievance
The law, with all his might to enforce it on,
Will give him cable.°
OTHELLO: Let him do his spite.
My services which I have done the seigniory°
Shall out-tongue his complaints. 'Tis yet to know°—
Which, when I know that boasting is an honor,
I shall promulgate—I fetch my life and being

180 **discover** reveal, uncover 183 **command** demand assistance 185 **deserve** show gratitude for
2 **very stuff** essence, basic material (continuing the metaphor of **trade** from line 1) 3 **contrived** premeditated 5 **yerked** stabbed **him** i.e., Roderigo 10 **I . . . him** I restrained myself with great difficulty from assaulting him 12 **magnifico** Venetian grandee, i.e., Brabantio 13 **in his effect** at his command **potential** powerful 17 **cable** i.e., scope 18 **seigniory** Venetian government
19 **yet to know** not yet widely known

From men of royal siege,° and my demerits°
May speak unbonneted° to as proud a fortune
As this that I have reached. For know, Iago,
But that I love the gentle Desdemona,
I would not my unhousèd° free condition
Put into circumscription and confine°
For the sea's worth.° But look, what lights come yond?

[Enter CASSIO *[and certain officers°] with torches.]*

IAGO: Those are the raisèd father and his friends.
You were best go in.
OTHELLO: Not I. I must be found.
My parts, my title, and my perfect soul°
Shall manifest me rightly. Is it they?
IAGO: By Janus,° I think no.
OTHELLO: The servants of the Duke? And my lieutenant?
The goodness of the night upon you, friends!
What is the news?
CASSIO: The Duke does greet you, General,
And he requires your haste-post-haste appearance
Even on the instant.
OTHELLO: What is the matter,° think you?
CASSIO: Something from Cyprus, as I may divine.°
It is a business of some heat.° The galleys
Have sent a dozen sequent° Messengers
This very night at one another's heels,
And many of the consuls,° raised and met,
Are at the Duke's already. You have been hotly called for;
When, being not at your lodging to be found,
The Senate hath sent about° three several° quests
To search you out.
OTHELLO: 'Tis well I am found by you.
I will but spend a word here in the house
And go with you.

[Exit.]

22 **siege** i.e., rank (literally, a seat used by a person of distinction) **demerits** deserts 23 **unbonneted** without removing the hat, i.e., on equal terms (or "with hat off," "in all due modesty") 26 **unhousèd** unconfined, undomesticated 27 **circumscription and confine** restriction and confinement 28 **the sea's worth** all the riches at the bottom of the sea s.d. **officers** the Quarto text calls for "Cassio with lights, officers with torches" 31 **My . . . soul** my natural gifts, my position or reputation, and my unflawed conscience 33 **Janus** Roman two-faced god of beginnings 38 **matter** business 39 **divine** guess 40 **heat** urgency 41 **sequent** successive 43 **consuls** senators 46 **about** all over the city **several** separate

CASSIO: Ancient, what makes° he here?
IAGO: Faith, he tonight hath boarded° a land carrack.°
If it prove lawful prize,° he's made forever.
CASSIO: I do not understand.
IAGO: He's married.
CASSIO: To who?

[Enter OTHELLO.]

IAGO: Marry,° to—Come, Captain, will you go?
OTHELLO: Have with you.°
CASSIO: Here comes another troop to seek for you.

[Enter BRABANTIO, RODERIGO, with officers and torches.°]

IAGO: It is Brabantio. General, be advised.°
He comes to bad intent.
OTHELLO: Holla! Stand there!
RODERIGO: Signor, it is the Moor.
BRABANTIO: Down with him, thief!

[They draw on both sides.]

IAGO: You, Roderigo! Come, sir, I am for you.
OTHELLO: Keep up° your bright swords, for the dew will rust them.
Good signor, you shall more command with years
Than with your weapons.
BRABANTIO: O thou foul thief, where hast thou stowed my daughter?
Damned as thou art, thou hast enchanted her!
For I'll refer me° to all things of sense,°
If she in chains of magic were not bound
Whether a maid so tender, fair, and happy,
So opposite to marriage that she shunned
The wealthy curlèd darlings of our nation,
Would ever have, t' incur a general mock,
Run from her guardage° to the sooty bosom
Of such a thing as thou—to fear, not to delight.
Judge me the world if 'tis not gross in sense°
That thou hast practiced on her with foul charms,
Abused her delicate youth with drugs or minerals°

49 **makes** does 50 **boarded** gone aboard and seized as an act of piracy (with sexual suggestion) **carrack** large merchant ship 51 **prize** booty 53 **Marry** an oath, originally "by the Virgin Mary"; here used with wordplay on **married** 54 **Have with you** i.e., let's go 55 s.d. **officers and torches** the Quarto text calls for "others with lights and weapons" 56 **be advised** be on your guard 60 **Keep up** keep in the sheath 65 **refer me** submit my case **things of sense** commonsense understandings, or, creatures possessing common sense 71 **her guardage** my guardianship of her 73 **gross in sense** obvious 75 **minerals** i.e., poisons

That weakens motion.° I'll have't disputed on;°
'Tis probable and palpable to thinking.
I therefore apprehend and do attach° thee
For an abuser of the world, a practicer
Of arts inhibited° and out of warrant.°
Lay hold upon him! If he do resist,
Subdue him at his peril.

OTHELLO: Hold your hands,
Both you of my inclining° and the rest.
Were it my cue to fight, I should have known it
Without a prompter.—Whither will you that I go
To answer this your charge?

BRABANTIO: To prison, till fit time
Of law and course of direct session°
Call thee to answer.

OTHELLO: What if I do obey?
How may the Duke be therewith satisfied,
Whose Messengers are here about my side
Upon some present business of the state
To bring me to him?

OFFICER: 'Tis true, most worthy signor.
The Duke's in council, and your noble self,
I am sure, is sent for.

BRABANTIO: How? The Duke in council?
In this time of the night? Bring him away.°
Mine's not an idle° cause. The Duke himself,
Or any of my brothers of the state,
Cannot but feel this wrong as 'twere their own;
For if such actions may have passage free,°
Bondslaves and pagans shall our statesmen be.

[Exeunt.]

SCENE III [Venice. A Council Chamber.]

[Enter DUKE [and] SENATORS [and sit at a table, with lights], and OFFICERS.° The DUKE and SENATORS are reading dispatches.]

DUKE: There is no composition° in these news
That gives them credit.

76 **weakens motion** impair the vital faculties **disputed** on argued in court by professional counsel, debated by experts 78 **attach** arrest 80 **arts inhibited** prohibited arts, black magic **out of warrant** illegal 83 **inclining** following, party 88 **course of direct session** regular or specially convened legal proceedings 96 **away** right along 97 **idle** trifling 100 **have passage free** are allowed to go unchecked s.d. **Enter... officers** the Quarto text calls for the Duke and Senators to "sit at a table with lights and attendants" 1 **composition** consistency

FIRST SENATOR: Indeed, they are disproportioned.°
My letters say a hundred and seven galleys.
DUKE: And mine, a hundred forty.
SECOND SENATOR: And mine, two hundred.
But though they jump° not on a just° account—
As in these cases, where the aim° reports
'Tis oft with difference—yet do they all confirm
A Turkish fleet, and bearing up to Cyprus.
DUKE: Nay, it is possible enough to judgment.
I do not so secure me in the error
But the main article I do approve°
In fearful sense.
SAILOR (within): What ho, what ho, what ho!

[Enter SAILOR.]

OFFICER: A Messenger from the galleys.
DUKE: Now, what's the business?
SAILOR: The Turkish preparation° makes for Rhodes.
So was I bid report here to the state
By Signor Angelo.
DUKE: How say you by° this change?
FIRST SENATOR: This cannot be
By no assay° of reason. 'Tis a pageant°
To keep us in false gaze.° When we consider
Th' importancy of Cyprus to the Turk,
And let ourselves again but understand
That, as it more concerns the Turk than Rhodes,
So may he with more facile question bear it,°
For that° it stands not in such warlike brace,°
But altogether lacks th' abilities°
That Rhodes is dressed in°—if we make thought of this,
We must not think the Turk is so unskillful°
To leave that latest° which concerns him first,
Neglecting an attempt of ease and gain
To wake° and wage° a danger profitless.
DUKE: Nay, in all confidence, he's not for Rhodes.
OFFICER: Here is more news.

3 **disproportioned** inconsistent 6 **jump** agree **just** exact 7 **the aim** conjecture 11–12 **I do not . . . approve** I do not take such (false) comfort in the discrepancies that I fail to perceive the main point, i.e., that the Turkish fleet is threatening 16 **preparation** fleet prepared for battle 19 **by** about 20 **assay** test **pageant** mere show 21 **in false gaze** looking the wrong way 25 **So may . . . it** so also he (the Turk) can more easily capture it (Cyprus) 26 **For that** since **brace** state of defense 27 **abilities** means of self-defense 28 **dressed in** equipped with 29 **unskillful** deficient in judgment 30 **latest** last 32 **wake** stir up **wage** risk

[Enter a MESSENGER.]

MESSENGER: The Ottomites, reverend and gracious,
Steering with due course toward the isle of Rhodes,
Have there injointed them° with an after° fleet.
FIRST SENATOR: Ay, so I thought. How many, as you guess?
MESSENGER: Of thirty sail; and now they do restem
Their backward course,° bearing with frank appearance°
Their purposes toward Cyprus. Signor Montano,
Your trusty and most valiant servitor,°
With his free duty° recommends° you thus,
And prays you to believe him.
DUKE: 'Tis certain then for Cyprus.
Marcus Luccicos, is not he in town?
FIRST SENATOR: He's now in Florence.
DUKE: Write from us to him, post-post-haste. Dispatch.
FIRST SENATOR: Here comes Brabantio and the valiant Moor.

[Enter BRABANTIO, OTHELLO, CASSIO, IAGO, RODERIGO, and OFFICERS.]

DUKE: Valiant Othello, we must straight° employ you
Against the general enemy° Ottoman.
[*To BRABANTIO.*] I did not see you; welcome, gentle° signor.
We lacked your counsel and your help tonight.
BRABANTIO: So did I yours. Good Your Grace, pardon me;
Neither my place° nor aught I heard of business
Hath raised me from my bed, nor doth the general care
Take hold on me, for my particular° grief
Is of so floodgate° and o'erbearing nature
That it engluts° and swallows other sorrows
And it is still itself.°
DUKE: Why, what's the matter?
BRABANTIO: My daughter! O, my daughter!
DUKE and SENATORS: Dead?
BRABANTIO: Ay, to me.
She is abused,° stol'n from me, and corrupted
By spells and medicines bought of mountebanks;
For nature so preposterously to err,

37 **injointed them** joined themselves **after** second, following 39–40 **restem . . . course** retrace their original course 40 **frank appearance** undisguised intent 42 **servitor** officer under your command 43 **free duty** freely given and loyal service **recommends** commends himself and reports to 50 **straight** straightway 51 **general enemy** universal enemy to all Christendom 52 **gentle** noble 55 **place** official position 57 **particular** personal 58 **floodgate** i.e., overwhelming (as when floodgates are opened) 59 **engluts** engulfs 60 **is still itself** remains undiminished 62 **abused** deceived

Being not deficient,° blind, or lame of sense,°
Sans° witchcraft could not.

DUKE: Whoe'er he be that in this foul proceeding
Hath thus beguiled your daughter of herself,
And you of her, the bloody book of law
You shall yourself read in the bitter letter
After your own sense°—yea, though our proper° son
Stood in your action.°

BRABANTIO: Humbly I thank Your Grace.
Here is the man, this Moor, whom now it seems
Your special mandate for the state affairs
Hath hither brought.

ALL: We are very sorry for 't.

DUKE [*to OTHELLO*]: What, in your own part, can you say to this?

BRABANTIO: Nothing, but this is so.

OTHELLO: Most potent, grave, and reverend signors,
My very noble and approved° good masters:
That I have ta'en away this old man's daughter,
It is most true; true, I have married her.
The very head and front° of my offending
Hath this extent, no more. Rude° am I in my speech,
And little blessed with the soft phrase of peace;
For since these arms of mine had seven years' pith,°
Till now some nine moons wasted,° they have used
Their dearest° action in the tented field;
And little of this great world can I speak
More than pertains to feats of broils and battle,
And therefore little shall I grace my cause
In speaking for myself. Yet, by your gracious patience,
I will a round° unvarnished tale deliver
Of my whole course of love—what drugs, what charms,
What conjuration, and what mighty magic,
For such proceeding I am charged withal,°
I won his daughter.

BRABANTIO: A maiden never bold;
Of spirit so still and quiet that her motion

65 **deficient** defective **lame of sense** deficient in sensory perception 66 **Sans** without 71 **After . . . sense** according to your own interpretation **our proper** my own 72 **Stood . . . action** were under your accusation 79 **approved** proved, esteemed 82 **head and front** height and breadth, entire extent 83 **Rude** unpolished 85 **since . . . pith** i.e., since I was seven **pith** strength, vigor 86 **Till . . . wasted** until some nine months ago (since when Othello has evidently not been on active duty, but in Venice) 87 **dearest** most valuable 92 **round** plain 95 **withal** with

Blushed at herself;° and she, in spite of nature,
Of years,° of country, credit,° everything,
To fall in love with what she feared to look on!
It is a judgment maimed and most imperfect
That will confess° perfection so could err
Against all rules of nature, and must be driven
To find out practices° of cunning hell
Why this should be. I therefore vouch° again
That with some mixtures powerful o'er the blood,°
Or with some dram conjured to this effect,°
He wrought upon her.

DUKE: To vouch this is no proof,
Without more wider° and more overt test°
Than these thin habits° and poor likelihoods°
Of modern seeming° do prefer° against him.

FIRST SENATOR: But Othello, speak.
Did you by indirect and forcèd courses°
Subdue and poison this young maid's affections?
Or came it by request and such fair question°
As soul to soul affordeth?

OTHELLO: I do beseech you,
Send for the lady to the Sagittary
And let her speak of me before her father.
If you do find me foul in her report,
The trust, the office I do hold of you
Not only take away, but let your sentence
Even fall upon my life.

DUKE: Fetch Desdemona hither.

OTHELLO: Ancient, conduct them. You best know the place.

[Exeunt IAGO and attendants.]

And, till she come, as truly as to heaven
I do confess the vices of my blood,°
So justly° to your grave ears I'll present
How I did thrive in this fair lady's love,
And she in mine.

97–98 **her . . . herself** i.e., she blushed easily at herself (**motion** can suggest the impulse of the soul or of the emotions, or physical movement) 99 **years** i.e., difference in age **credit** virtuous reputation 102 **confess** concede (that) 104 **practices** plots 105 **vouch** assert 106 **blood** passions 107 **dram . . . effect** dose made by magical spells to have this effect 109 **more wider** fuller **test** testimony 110 **habits** garments, i.e., appearances **poor likelihoods** weak inferences 111 **modern seeming** commonplace assumption **prefer** bring forth 113 **forcèd courses** means used against her will 115 **question** conversation 125 **blood** passions, human nature 126 **justly** truthfully, accurately

DUKE: Say it, Othello.
OTHELLO: Her father loved me, oft invited me,
Still° questioned me the story of my life
From year to year—the battles, sieges, fortunes
That I have passed.
I ran it through, even from my boyish days
To th' very moment that he bade me tell it,
Wherein I spoke of most disastrous chances,
Of moving accidents° by flood and field,
Of hairbreadth scapes i' th' imminent deadly breach,°
Of being taken by the insolent foe
And sold to slavery, of my redemption thence,
And portance° in my travels' history,
Wherein of antres° vast and deserts idle,°
Rough quarries,° rocks, and hills whose heads touch heaven,
It was my hint° to speak—such was my process—
And of the Cannibals that each other eat,
The Anthropophagi,° and men whose heads
Do grow beneath their shoulders. These things to hear
Would Desdemona seriously incline;
But still the house affairs would draw her thence,
Which ever as she could with haste dispatch
She'd come again, and with a greedy ear
Devour up my discourse. Which I, observing,
Took once a pliant° hour, and found good means
To draw from her a prayer of earnest heart
That I would all my pilgrimage dilate,°
Whereof by parcels° she had something heard,
But not intentively.° I did consent,
And often did beguile her of her tears,
When I did speak of some distressful stroke
That my youth suffered. My story being done,
She gave me for my pains a world of sighs.
She swore, in faith, 'twas strange, 'twas passing° strange,
'Twas pitiful, 'twas wondrous pitiful.
She wished she had not heard it, yet she wished
That heaven had made her° such a man. She thanked me,

131 **Still** continually 137 **moving accidents** stirring happenings 138 **imminent . . . breach** death-threatening gaps made in a fortification 141 **portance** conduct 142 **antres** caverns **idle** barren, desolate 143 **Rough quarries** rugged rock formations 144 **hint** occasion, opportunity 146 **Anthropophagi** man-eaters (A term from Pliny's *Natural History.*) 153 **pliant** well-suiting 155 **dilate** relate in detail 156 **by parcels** piecemeal 157 **intentively** with full attention, continuously 162 **passing** exceedingly 165 **made her** created her to be

And bade me, if I had a friend that loved her,
I should but teach him how to tell my story,
And that would woo her. Upon this hint° I spake.
She loved me for the dangers I had passed,
And I loved her that she did pity them.
This only is the witchcraft I have used.
Here comes the lady. Let her witness it.

[Enter DESDEMONA, IAGO, *[and] attendants.]*

DUKE: I think this tale would win my daughter too.
Good Brabantio,
Take up this mangled matter at the best.°
Men do their broken weapons rather use
Than their bare hands.

BRABANTIO: I pray you, hear her speak.
If she confess that she was half the wooer,
Destruction on my head if my bad blame
Light on the man!—Come hither, gentle mistress.
Do you perceive in all this noble company
Where most you owe obedience?

DESDEMONA: My noble Father,
I do perceive here a divided duty.
To you I am bound for life and education;°
My life and education both do learn° me
How to respect you. You are the lord of duty;°
I am hitherto your daughter. But here's my husband,
And so much duty as my mother showed
To you, preferring you before her father,
So much I challenge° that I may profess
Due to the Moor my lord.

BRABANTIO: God be with you! I have done.
Please it Your Grace, on to the state affairs.
I had rather to adopt a child than get° it.
Come hither, Moor. *[He joins the hands of* OTHELLO *and* DESDEMONA.*]*
I here do give thee that with all my heart°
Which, but thou hast already, with all my heart°
I would keep from thee.—For your sake,° jewel,

168 **hint** opportunity (Othello does not mean that she was dropping hints.) 175 **Take . . . best** make the best of a bad bargain 184 **education** upbringing 185 **learn** teach 186 **of duty** to whom duty is due 190 **challenge** claim 194 **get** beget 196 **with all my heart** wherein my whole affection has been engaged 197 **with all my heart** willingly, gladly 198 **For your sake** on your account

I am glad at soul I have no other child,
For thy escape° would teach me tyranny,
To hang clogs° on them.—I have done, my lord.

DUKE: Let me speak like yourself,° and lay a sentence°
Which, as a grece° or step, may help these lovers
Into your favor.
When remedies° are past, the griefs are ended
By seeing the worst, which late on hopes depended.°
To mourn a mischief° that is past and gone
Is the next° way to draw new mischief on.
What° cannot be preserved when fortune takes,
Patience her injury a mockery makes.°
The robbed that smiles steals something from the thief;
He robs himself that spends a bootless grief.°

BRABANTIO: So let the Turk of Cyprus us beguile,
We lose it not, so long as we can smile.
He bears the sentence well that nothing bears
But the free comfort which from thence he hears,
But he bears both the sentence and the sorrow
That, to pay grief, must of poor patience borrow.°
These sentences, to sugar or to gall,
Being strong on both sides, are equivocal.°
But words are words. I never yet did hear
That the bruised heart was piercèd through the ear.°
I humbly beseech you, proceed to th' affairs of state.

DUKE: The Turk with a most mighty preparation makes for Cyprus. Othello, the fortitude° of the place is best known to you; and though we have there a substitute° of most allowed° sufficiency, yet opinion,° a sovereign mistress of effects, throws a more safer voice on you.° You must therefore be

200 **escape** elopement 201 **clogs** literally, blocks of wood fastened to the legs of criminals or convicts to inhibit escape 202 **like yourself** i.e., as you would, in your proper temper **lay a sentence** apply a maxim 203 **grece** step 205 **remedies** hopes of remedy 206 **which . . . depended** which griefs were sustained until recently by hopeful anticipation 207 **mischief** misfortune, injury 208 **next** nearest 209 **What** whatever 210 **Patience . . . makes** patience laughs at the injury inflicted by fortune (and thus eases the pain) 212 **spends a bootless grief** indulges in unavailing grief 215–218 **He bears . . . borrow** a person well bears out your maxim who can enjoy its platitudinous comfort, free of all genuine sorrow, but anyone whose grief bankrupts his poor patience is left with your saying and his sorrow, too (**bears the sentence** also plays on the meaning, "receives judicial sentence") 219–220 **These . . . equivocal** these fine maxims are equivocal, either sweet or bitter in their application 222 **piercèd . . . ear** i.e., surgically lanced and cured by mere words of advice 225 **fortitude** strength 226 **substitute** deputy **allowed** acknowledged 226–227 **opinion . . . on you** general opinion, an important determiner of affairs, chooses you as the best man

content to slubber° the gloss of your new fortunes with this more stubborn° and boisterous expedition

OTHELLO: The tyrant custom, most grave senators,
Hath made the flinty and steel couch of war
My thrice-driven° bed of down. I do agnize°
A natural and prompt alacrity
I find in hardness,° and do undertake
These present wars against the Ottomites.
Most humbly therefore bending to your state,°
I crave fit disposition for my wife,
Due reference of place and exhibition,°
With such accommodation° and besort°
As levels° with her breeding.°

DUKE: Why, at her father's.

BRABANTIO: I will not have it so.

OTHELLO: Nor I.

DESDEMONA: Nor I. I would not there reside,
To put my father in impatient thoughts
By being in his eye. Most gracious Duke,
To my unfolding° lend your prosperous ° ear,
And let me find a charter° in your voice,
T' assist my simpleness.

DUKE: What would you, Desdemona?

DESDEMONA: That I did love the Moor to live with him,
My downright violence and storm of fortunes°
May trumpet to the world. My heart's subdued
Even to the very quality of my lord.°
I saw Othello's visage in his mind,
And to his honors and his valiant parts°
Did I my soul and fortunes consecrate.
So that, dear lords, if I be left behind
A moth° of peace, and he go to the war,
The rites° for why I love him are bereft me,
And I a heavy interim shall support

228 **slubber** soil, sully 229 **stubborn** harsh, rough 232 **thrice-driven** thrice sifted, winnowed **agnize** know in myself, acknowledge 234 **hardness** hardship 235 **bending . . . state** bowing or kneeling to your authority 237 **reference . . . exhibition** provision of appropriate place to live and allowance of money 239 **accommodation** suitable provision. besort attendance 240 **levels** equals, suits **breeding** social position, upbringing 245 **unfolding** explanation, proposal **prosperous** propitious 246 **charter** privilege, authorization 250 **My . . . fortunes** my plain and total breach of social custom, taking my future by storm and disrupting my whole life 251–252 **My heart's . . . lord** my heart is brought wholly into accord with Othello's virtues; I love him for his virtues 254 **parts** qualities 257 **moth** i.e., one who consumes merely 258 **rites** rites of love (with a suggestion, too, of "rights," sharing)

By his dear° absence. Let me go with him.
OTHELLO: Let her have your voice.°
Vouch with me, heaven, I therefor beg it not
To please the palate of my appetite,
Nor to comply with heat°—the young affects°
In me defunct—and proper° satisfaction,
But to be free° and bounteous to her mind.
And heaven defend° your good souls that you think°
I will your serious and great business scant
When she is with me. No, when light-winged toys
Of feathered Cupid seel° with wanton dullness
My speculative and officed instruments,°
That° my disports° corrupt and taint° my business,
Let huswives make a skillet of my helm,
And all indign° and base adversities
Make head° against my estimation!°
DUKE: Be it as you shall privately determine,
Either for her stay or going. Th' affair cries haste,
And speed must answer it.
A SENATOR: You must away tonight.
DESDEMONA: Tonight, my lord?
DUKE: This night.
OTHELLO: With all my heart.
DUKE: At nine i' the morning here we'll meet again.
Othello, leave some Officer behind,
And he shall our commission bring to you,
With such things else of quality and respect°
As doth import° you.
OTHELLO: So please Your Grace, my ancient;
A man he is of honesty and trust.
To his conveyance I assign my wife,
With what else needful Your Good Grace shall think
To be sent after me.
DUKE: Let it be so.
Good night to everyone. [*To BRABANTIO.*] And, noble signor,

260 **dear** (1) heartfelt (2) costly 261 **voice** consent 264 **heat** sexual passion **young affects** passions of youth, desires 265 **proper** personal 266 **free** generous 267 **defend** forbid **think** should think 270 **seel** i.e., make blind (as in falconry, by sewing up the eyes of the hawk during training) 271 **speculative . . . instruments** eyes and other faculties used in the performance of duty 272 **That** so that **disports** sexual pastimes **taint** impair 274 **indign** unworthy, shameful 275 **Make head** raise an army **estimation** reputation 283 **of quality and respect** of importance and relevance 284 **import** concern

If virtue no delighted° beauty lack,
Your son-in-law is far more fair than black.

FIRST SENATOR: Adieu, brave Moor. Use Desdemona well.

BRABANTIO: Look to her, Moor, if thou hast eyes to see.
She has deceived her father, and may thee.

[Exeunt (DUKE, BRABANTIO, CASSIO, SENATORS, and OFFICERS).]

OTHELLO: My life upon her faith! Honest Iago,
My Desdemona must I leave to thee.
I prithee, let thy wife attend on her,
And bring them after in the best advantage.°
Come, Desdemona. I have but an hour
Of love, of worldly matters and direction,°
To spend with thee. We must obey the time.°

[Exit (with DESDEMONA).]

RODERIGO: Iago—

IAGO: What sayst thou, noble heart?

RODERIGO: What will I do, think'st thou?

IAGO: Why, go to bed and sleep.

RODERIGO: I will incontinently° drown myself.

IAGO: If thou dost, I shall never love thee after. Why, thou silly gentleman?

RODERIGO: It is silliness to live when to live is torment; and then have we a prescription° to die when death is our physician.

IAGO: O villainous!° I have looked upon the world for four times seven years, and, since I could distinguish betwixt a benefit and an injury, I never found man that knew how to love himself. Ere I would say I would drown myself for the love of a guinea hen,° I would change my humanity with a baboon.

RODERIGO: What should I do? I confess it is my shame to be so fond,° but it is not in my virtue° to amend it.

IAGO: Virtue? A fig!° 'Tis in ourselves that we are thus or thus. Our bodies are our gardens, to the which our wills are gardeners; so that if we will plant nettles or sow lettuce, set hyssop° and weed up thyme, supply it with one gender° of herbs or distract it with° many, either to have it sterile with idleness° or manured with industry—why, the power and corrigible authority° of this lies in our wills. If the beam° of our lives had not one

290 **delighted** capable of delighting 298 **in . . . advantage** at the most favorable opportunity 300 **direction** instructions 301 **the time** the urgency of the present crisis 306 **incontinently** immediately, without self-restraint **prescription** (1) right based on long-established custom (2) doctor's prescription 310 **villainous** i.e., what perfect nonsense 312 **guinea hen** a slang term for a prostitute 315 **fond** infatuated 316 **virtue** strength, nature 317 **fig** to give a fig is to thrust the thumb between the first and second fingers in a vulgar and insulting gesture 319 **hyssop** an herb of the mint family 320 **gender** kind **distract it with** divide it among 321 **idleness** want of cultivation 321–322 **corrigible authority** power to correct 322 **beam** balance

scale of reason to poise[o] another of sensuality, the blood[o] and baseness of our natures would conduct us to most preposterous conclusions. But we have reason to cool our raging motions,[o] our carnal stings, our unbitted[o] lusts, whereof I take this that you call love to be a sect or scion.[o]

RODERIGO: It cannot be.

IAGO: It is merely a lust of the blood and a permission of the will. Come, be a man. Drown thyself? Drown cats and blind puppies. I have professed me thy friend, and I confess me knit to thy deserving with cables of perdurable[o] toughness. I could never better stead[o] thee than now. Put money in thy purse. Follow thou the wars; defeat thy favor[o] with an usurped[o] beard. I say, put money in thy purse. It cannot be long that Desdemona should continue her love to the Moor—put money in thy purse—nor he his to her. It was a violent commencement in her, and thou shalt see an answerable sequestration[o] —put but money in thy purse. These Moors are changeable in their wills[o] —fill thy purse with money. The food that to him now is as luscious as locusts[o] shall be to him shortly as bitter as coloquintida.[o] She must change for youth; when she is sated with his body, she will find the error of her choice. She must have change, she must. Therefore put money in thy purse. If thou wilt needs damn thyself, do it a more delicate way than drowning. Make[o] all the money thou canst. If sanctimony[o] and a frail vow betwixt an erring[o] barbarian and a supersubtle Venetian be not too hard for my wits and all the tribe of hell, thou shalt enjoy her. Therefore make money. A pox of drowning thyself! It is clean out of the way.[o] Seek thou rather to be hanged in compassing[o] thy joy than to be drowned and go without her.

RODERIGO: Wilt thou be fast[o] to my hopes if I depend on the issue?[o]

IAGO: Thou art sure of me. Go, make money. I have told thee often, and I retell thee again and again, I hate the Moor. My cause is hearted;[o] thine hath no less reason. Let us be conjunctive[o] in our revenge against him. If thou canst cuckold him, thou dost thyself a pleasure, me a sport. There are many events in the womb of time which will be delivered. Traverse,[o] go, provide thy money. We will have more of this tomorrow. Adieu.

323 **poise** counterbalance **blood** natural passions 325 **motions** appetites **unbitted** unbridled, uncontrolled 326 **sect or scion** cutting or offshoot 330–331 **perdurable** very durable 331 **stead** assist 332 **defeat thy favor** disguise your face **usurped** the suggestion is that Roderigo is not man enough to have a beard of his own 335–336 **an answerable sequestration** a corresponding separation or estrangement 337 **wills** carnal appetites 338 **locusts** fruit of the carob tree (see Matthew 3:4), or perhaps honeysuckle 339 **coloquintida** colocynth or bitter apple, a purgative 342 **Make** raise, collect 343 **sanctimony** sacred ceremony **erring** wandering, vagabond, unsteady 346 **clean . . . way** entirely unsuitable as a course of action **compassing** encompassing, embracing 348 **fast** true **issue** (successful) outcome 350 **hearted** fixed in the heart, heartfelt 351 **conjunctive** united 353 **Traverse** a military marching term

RODERIGO: Where shall we meet i' the morning?
IAGO: At my lodging.
RODERIGO: I'll be with thee betimes.°

[He starts to leave.]

IAGO: Go to, farewell.—Do you hear, Roderigo?
RODERIGO: What say you?
IAGO: No more of drowning, do you hear?
RODERIGO: I am changed.
IAGO: Go to, farewell. Put money enough in your purse.
RODERIGO: I'll sell all my land.

[Exit.]

IAGO: Thus do I ever make my fool my purse;
For I mine own gained knowledge should profane
If I would time expend with such a snipe°
But for my sport and profit. I hate the Moor;
And it is thought abroad° that twixt my sheets
He's done my office.° I know not if 't be true;
But I, for mere suspicion in that kind,
Will do as if for surety.° He holds me well;°
The better shall my purpose work on him.
Cassio's a proper° man. Let me see now:
To get his place and to plume up° my will
In double knavery—How, how?—Let's see:
After some time, to abuse° Othello's ear
That he° is too familiar with his wife.
He hath a person and a smooth dispose°
To be suspected, framed to make women false.
The Moor is of a free° and open° nature,
That thinks men honest that but seem to be so,
And will as tenderly° be led by the nose
As asses are.
I have 't. It is engendered. Hell and night
Must bring this monstrous birth to the world's light.

[Exit.]

357 **betimes** early **snipe** woodcock, i.e., fool 368 **it is thought abroad** it is rumored 369 **my office** i.e., my sexual function as husband 371 **do . . . surety** act as if on certain knowledge. **holds me well** regards me favorably 373 **proper** handsome 374 **plume up** put a feather in the cap of, i.e., glorify, gratify 376 **abuse** deceive 377 **he** i.e., Cassio 378 **dispose** disposition 380 **free** frank, generous. **open** unsuspicious 382 **tenderly** readily

ACT II

SCENE I [A Seaport in Cyprus. An Open Place Near the Quay.]

[Enter MONTANO and two GENTLEMEN.]

MONTANO: What from the cape can you discern at sea?
FIRST GENTLEMAN: Nothing at all. It is a high-wrought flood.°
I cannot, twixt the heaven and the main,°
Descry a sail.
MONTANO: Methinks the wind hath spoke aloud at land;
A fuller blast ne'er shook our battlements.
If it hath ruffianed° so upon the sea,
What ribs of oak, when mountains° melt on them,
Can hold the mortise?° What shall we hear of this?
SECOND GENTLEMAN: A segregation° of the Turkish fleet.
For do but stand upon the foaming shore,
The chidden° billow seems to pelt the clouds;
The wind-shaked surge, with high and monstrous mane,°
Seems to cast water on the burning Bear°
And quench the guards of th' ever-fixèd pole.
I never did like molestation° view
On the enchafèd° flood.
MONTANO: If that° the Turkish fleet
Be not ensheltered and embayed,° they are drowned;
It is impossible to bear it out.°

[Enter a (Third) GENTLEMAN.]

THIRD GENTLEMAN: News, lads! Our wars are done.
The desperate tempest hath so banged the Turks
That their designment° halts.° A noble ship of Venice
Hath seen a grievous wreck° and sufferance°
On most part of their fleet.
MONTANO: How? Is this true?
THIRD GENTLEMAN: The ship is here put in,
A Veronesa;° Michael Cassio,

2 **high-wrought flood** very agitated sea 3 **main** ocean (also at line 41) 7 **ruffianed** raged 8 **mountains** i.e., of water 9 **hold the mortise** hold their joints together (A **mortise** is the socket hollowed out in fitting timbers.) 10 **segregation** dispersal 12 **chidden** i.e., rebuked, repelled (by the shore), and thus shot into the air 13 **monstrous mane** the surf is like the mane of a wild beast 14 **the burning Bear** i.e., the constellation Ursa Minor or the Little Bear, which includes the polestar (and hence regarded as the **guards of th' ever-fixèd pole** in the next line; sometimes the term **guards** is applied to the two "pointers" of the Big Bear or Dipper, which may be intended here.) 16 **like molestation** comparable disturbance 17 **enchafèd** angry 18 **If that** if 19 **embayed** sheltered by a bay 20 **bear it out** survive, weather the storm 23 **designment** design, enterprise **halts** is lame 24 **wreck** shipwreck **sufferance** damage, disaster 28 **Veronesa** i.e., fitted out in Verona for Venetian service, or possibly Verennessa (the Folio spelling), i.e., **verrinessa,** a cutter (from **verrinare,** "to cut through")

Lieutenant to the warlike Moor Othello,
Is come on shore; the Moor himself at sea,
And is in full commission here for Cyprus.

MONTANO: I am glad on 't. 'Tis a worthy governor.

THIRD GENTLEMAN: But this same Cassio, though he speak of comfort
Touching the Turkish loss, yet he looks sadly°
And prays the Moor be safe, for they were parted
With foul and violent tempest.

MONTANO: Pray heaven he be,
For I have served him, and the man commands
Like a full° soldier. Let's to the seaside, ho!
As well to see the vessel that's come in
As to throw out our eyes for brave Othello,
Even till we make the main and th' aerial blue°
An indistinct regard.°

THIRD GENTLEMAN: Come, let's do so,
For every minute is expectancy°
Of more arrivance.°

[Enter CASSIO.]

CASSIO: Thanks, you the valiant of this warlike isle,
That so approve° the Moor! O, let the heavens
Give him defense against the elements,
For I have lost him on a dangerous sea.

MONTANO: Is he well shipped?

CASSIO: His bark is stoutly timbered, and his pilot
Of very expert and approved allowance;°
Therefore my hopes, not surfeited to death,°
Stand in bold cure.°

[*A cry*] within: "A sail, a sail, a sail!"

CASSIO: What noise?

A GENTLEMAN: The town is empty. On the brow o' the sea°
Stand ranks of people, and they cry "A sail!"

CASSIO: My hopes do shape him for° the governor.

[A shot within.]

SECOND GENTLEMAN: They do discharge their shot of courtesy;°
Our friends at least.

34 **sadly** gravely 38 **full** perfect 41 **the main . . . blue** the sea and the sky 42 **An indistinct regard** indistinguishable in our view 43 **is expectancy** gives expectation 44 **arrivance** arrival 46 **approve** admire, honor 51 **approved allowance** tested reputation 52 **surfeited to death** i.e., overextended, worn thin through repeated application or delayed fulfillment 53 **in bold cure** in strong hopes of fulfillment 55 **brow o' the sea** cliff-edge 57 **My . . . for** I hope it is 58 **discharge . . . courtesy** fire a salute in token of respect and courtesy

CASSIO: I pray you, sir, go forth,
And give us truth who 'tis that is arrived.
SECOND GENTLEMAN: I shall.

[Exit.]

MONTANO: But, good Lieutenant, is your general wived?
CASSIO: Most fortunately. He hath achieved a maid
That paragons° description and wild fame,°
One that excels the quirks° of blazoning° pens,
And in th' essential vesture of creation
Does tire the enginer.°

[Enter (Second) GENTLEMAN.°]

How now? Who has put in?°
SECOND GENTLEMAN: 'Tis one Iago, ancient to the General.
CASSIO: He's had most favorable and happy speed.
Tempests themselves, high seas, and howling winds,
The guttered° rocks and congregated sands—
Traitors ensteeped° to clog the guiltless keel—
As° having sense of beauty, do omit°
Their mortal° natures, letting go safely by
The divine Desdemona.
MONTANO: What is she?
CASSIO: She that I spake of, our great captain's captain,
Left in the conduct of the bold Iago,
Whose footing° here anticipates our thoughts
A sennight's° speed. Great Jove, Othello guard,
And swell his sail with thine own powerful breath,
That he may bless this bay with his tall° ship,
Make love's quick pants in Desdemona's arms,
Give renewed fire to our extincted spirits,
And bring all Cyprus comfort!

[Enter DESDEMONA, IAGO, RODERIGO, and EMILIA.]

O, behold,
The riches of the ship is come on shore!
You men of Cyprus, let her have your knees.

[The gentlemen make curtsy to DESDEMONA.]

64 **paragons** surpasses **wild fame** extravagant report 65 **quirks** witty conceits **blazoning** setting forth as though in heraldic language 66–67 **in . . . enginer** in her real, God-given, beauty, (she) defeats any attempt to praise her **enginer** engineer, i.e., poet, one who devises s.d. **Second Gentleman** (So identified in the Quarto text here and in lines 58, 61, 68, and 97; the Folio calls him a gentleman.) 67 **put in** i.e., to harbor 71 **guttered** jagged, trenched 72 **ensteeped** lying under water 73 **As** as if **omit** forbear to exercise 74 **mortal** deadly 78 **footing** landing 79 **sennight's** week's 81 **tall** splendid, gallant

Hail to thee, lady! And the grace of heaven
Before, behind thee, and on every hand
Enwheel thee round!
DESDEMONA: I thank you, valiant Cassio.
What tidings can you tell me of my lord?
CASSIO: He is not yet arrived, nor know I aught
But that he's well and will be shortly here.
DESDEMONA: O, but I fear—How lost you company?
CASSIO: The great contention of the sea and skies
Parted our fellowship.
(*Within*) "A sail, a sail!"
[A shot.]
But hark. A sail!
SECOND GENTLEMAN: They give their greeting to the citadel.
This likewise is a friend.
CASSIO: See for the news.
[Exit SECOND GENTLEMAN.]
Good Ancient, you are welcome. [*Kissing EMILIA.*] Welcome, mistress.
Let it not gall your patience, good Iago,
That I extend° my manners; 'tis my breeding°
That gives me this bold show of courtesy.
IAGO: Sir, would she give you so much of her lips
As of her tongue she oft bestows on me,
You would have enough.
DESDEMONA: Alas, she has no speech!°
IAGO: In faith, too much.
I find it still,° when I have list° to sleep.
Marry, before your ladyship, I grant,
She puts her tongue a little in her heart
And chides with thinking.°
EMILIA: You have little cause to say so.
IAGO: Come on, come on. You are pictures out of doors,°
Bells° in your parlors, wildcats in your kitchens,°
Saints° in your injuries, devils being offended,
Players° in your huswifery,° and huswives° in your beds.
DESDEMONA: O, fie upon thee, slanderer!

101 **extend** give scope to **breeding** training in the niceties of etiquette 106 **she has no speech** i.e., she's not a chatterbox, as you allege 108 **still** always **list** desire 111 **with thinking** i.e., in her thoughts only 112 **pictures out of doors** i.e., silent and well-behaved in public 113 **Bells** i.e., jangling, noisy, and brazen **in your kitchens** i.e., in domestic affairs (Ladies would not do the cooking.) 114 **Saints** martyrs 115 **Players** idlers, triflers, or deceivers **huswifery** housekeeping **huswives** hussies (i.e., women are "busy" in bed, or unduly thrifty in dispensing sexual favors)

IAGO: Nay, it is true, or else I am a Turk.°
You rise to play, and go to bed to work.
EMILIA: You shall not write my praise.
IAGO: No, let me not.
DESDEMONA: What wouldst write of me, if thou shouldst praise me?
IAGO: O gentle lady, do not put me to 't,
For I am nothing if not critical.°
DESDEMONA: Come on, essay.°—There's one gone to the harbor?
IAGO: Ay, madam.
DESDEMONA: I am not merry, but I do beguile
The thing I am° by seeming otherwise.
Come, how wouldst thou praise me?
IAGO: I am about it, but indeed my invention
Comes from my pate as birdlime° does from frieze°—
It plucks out brains and all. But my Muse labors,°
And thus she is delivered:
If she be fair and wise, fairness and wit,
The one's for use, the other useth it.°
DESDEMONA: Well praised! How if she be black° and witty?
IAGO: If she be black, and thereto have a wit,
She'll find a white° that shall her blackness fit.°
DESDEMONA: Worse and worse.
EMILIA: How if fair and foolish?
IAGO: She never yet was foolish that was fair,
For even her folly° helped her to an heir.°
DESDEMONA: These are old fond° paradoxes to make fools laugh i' th' alehouse. What miserable praise hast thou for her that's foul and foolish?
IAGO: There's none so foul° and foolish thereunto,°
But does foul° pranks which fair and wise ones do.
DESDEMONA: O heavy ignorance! Thou praisest the worst best. But what praise couldst thou bestow on a deserving woman indeed, one that, in the authority of her merit, did justly put on the vouch° of very malice itself?

117 **a Turk** an infidel, not to be believed 122 **critical** censorious 123 **essay** try 126 **The thing I am** i.e., my anxious self 129 **birdlime** sticky substance used to catch small birds **frieze** coarse woolen cloth 130 **labors** (1) exerts herself (2) prepares to deliver a child (with a following pun on **delivered** in line 131) 133 **The one's . . . it** i.e., her cleverness will make use of her beauty 134 **black** dark-complexioned, brunette 136 **a white** a fair person (with word-play on "wight," a person) **fit** (with sexual suggestion of mating) 139 **folly** (with added meaning of "lechery, wantonness") **to an heir** i.e., to bear a child 140 **fond** foolish 142 **foul** ugly **thereunto** in addition 143 **foul** sluttish 146 **put . . . vouch** compel the approval

IAGO: She that was ever fair, and never proud,
Had tongue at will, and yet was never loud,
Never lacked gold and yet went never gay,°
Fled from her wish, and yet said, "Now I may,"°
She that being angered, her revenge being nigh,
Bade her wrong stay° and her displeasure fly,
She that in wisdom never was so frail
To change the cod's head for the salmon's tail,°
She that could think and ne'er disclose her mind,
See suitors following and not look behind,
She was a wight, if ever such wight were—

DESDEMONA: To do what?

IAGO: To suckle fools° and chronicle small beer.°

DESDEMONA: O most lame and impotent conclusion! Do not learn of him, Emilia, though he be thy husband. How say you, Cassio? Is he not a most profane° and liberal° counselor?

CASSIO: He speaks home,° madam. You may relish° him more in° the soldier than in the scholar.

[CASSIO and DESDEMONA stand together, conversing intimately.]

IAGO [*aside*]: He takes her by the palm. Ay, well said,° whisper. With as little a web as this will I ensnare as great a fly as Cassio. Ay, smile upon her, do; I will gyve° thee in thine own courtship.° You say true;° 'tis so, indeed. If such tricks as these strip you out of your lieutenantry, it had been better you had not kissed your three fingers so oft, which now again you are most apt to play the sir° in. Very good; well kissed! An excellent courtesy! 'Tis so, indeed. Yet again your fingers to your lips? Would they were clyster pipes° for your sake! [*Trumpet within.*] The Moor! I know his trumpet.

CASSIO: 'Tis truly so.

DESDEMONA: Let's meet him and receive him.

CASSIO: Lo, where he comes!

[Enter OTHELLO and attendants.]

OTHELLO: O my fair warrior!

149 **gay** extravagantly clothed 150 **Fled . . . may** avoided temptation where the choice was hers 152 **Bade . . . stay** i.e., resolved to put up with her injury patiently 154 **To . . . tail** i.e., to exchange a lackluster husband for a sexy lover (**Cod's head** is slang for "penis," and **tail,** for "pudendum.") 159 **suckle fools** breastfeed babies **chronicle small beer** i.e., keep petty household accounts, keep track of trivial matters 162 **profane** irreverent, ribald **liberal** licentious, free-spoken 163 **home** right to the target (A term from fencing.) **relish** appreciate **in** in the character of 165 **well said** well done 167 **gyve** fetter, shackle **courtship** courtesy, show of courtly manners **You say true** i.e., that's right, go ahead 170 **the sir** i.e., the fine gentleman 172 **clyster pipes** tubes used for enemas and douches

DESDEMONA: My dear Othello!
OTHELLO: It gives me wonder great as my content
To see you here before me. O my soul's joy,
If after every tempest come such calms,
May the winds blow till they have wakened death,
And let the laboring bark climb hills of seas
Olympus-high, and duck again as low
As hell's from heaven! If it were now to die,
'Twere now to be most happy, for I fear
My soul hath her content so absolute
That not another comfort like to this
Succeeds in unknown fate.[o]
DESDEMONA: The heavens forbid
But that our loves and comforts should increase
Even as our days do grow!
OTHELLO: Amen to that, sweet powers!
I cannot speak enough of this content.
It stops me here; it is too much of joy.
And this, and this, the greatest discords be

[They kiss.[o]]

That e'er our hearts shall make!
IAGO [*aside*]: O, you are well tuned now!
But I'll set down[o] the pegs that make this music,
As honest as I am.[o]
OTHELLO: Come, let us to the castle.
News, friends! Our wars are done, the Turks are drowned.
How does my old acquaintance of this isle?—
Honey, you shall be well desired[o] in Cyprus;
I have found great love amongst them. O my sweet,
I prattle out of fashion,[o] and I dote
In mine own comforts.—I prithee, good Iago,
Go to the bay and disembark my coffers.[o]
Bring thou the master[o] to the citadel;
He is a good one, and his worthiness
Does challenge[o] much respect.—Come, Desdemona.—
Once more, well met at Cyprus!

188 **Succeeds . . . fate** i.e., can follow in the unknown future 194 s.d. **They kiss** (The direction is from the Quarto.) 197 **set down** loosen (and hence untune the instrument) 198 **As . . . I am** for all my supposed honesty 202 **desired** welcomed 204 **out of fashion** irrelevantly, incoherently 206 **coffers** chests, baggage 207 **master** ship's captain 209 **challenge** lay claim to, deserve

[Exeunt Othello and Desdemona (and all but Iago and Roderigo).]

Iago [*to an attendant*]: Do thou meet me presently at the harbor. [*To Roderigo.*] Come hither. If thou be'st valiant—as, they say, base men° being in love have then a nobility in their natures more than is native to them—list° me. The Lieutenant tonight watches on the court of guard.° First, I must tell thee this: Desdemona is directly in love with him.

Roderigo: With him? Why, 'tis not possible.

Iago: Lay thy finger thus,° and let thy soul be instructed. Mark me with what violence she first loved the Moor, but° for bragging and telling her fantastical lies. To love him still for prating? Let not thy discreet heart think it. Her eye must be fed; and what delight shall she have to look on the devil? When the blood is made dull with the act of sport,° there should be, again to inflame it and to give satiety a fresh appetite, loveliness in favor,° sympathy° in years, manners, and beauties—all which the Moor is defective in. Now, for want of these required conveniences,° her delicate tenderness will find itself abused,° begin to heave the gorge,° disrelish and abhor the Moor. Very nature° will instruct her in it and compel her to some second choice. Now, sir, this granted—as it is a most pregnant° and unforced position—who stands so eminent in the degree of° this fortune as Cassio does? A knave very voluble,° no further conscionable° than in putting on the mere form of civil and humane° seeming for the better compassing of his salt° and most hidden loose affection.° Why, none, why, none. A slipper° and subtle knave, a finder out of occasions, that has an eye can stamp° and counterfeit advantages,° though true advantage never present itself; a devilish knave. Besides, the knave is handsome, young, and hath all those requisites in him that folly° and green° minds look after. A pestilent complete knave, and the woman hath found him° already.

Roderigo: I cannot believe that in her. She's full of most blessed condition.°

Iago: Blessed fig's end!° The wine she drinks is made of grapes. If she had been blessed, she would never have loved the Moor. Blessed pudding!° Didst thou not see her paddle with the palm of his hand? Didst not mark that?

212 **base men** even lowly born men 214 **list** listen to **court of guard** guardhouse (Cassio is in charge of the watch.) 217 **thus** i.e., on your lips 218 **but** only 221 **the act of sport** sex 222 **favor** appearance 222–223 **sympathy** correspondence, similarity 224 **required conveniences** things conducive to sexual compatibility 225 **abused** cheated, revolted **heave the gorge** experience nausea 226 **Very nature** her very instincts 227 **pregnant** evident, cogent 228 **in . . . of** as next in line for 229 **voluble** facile, glib **conscionable** conscientious, conscience-bound 230 **humane** polite, courteous 231 **salt** licentious **affection** passion 231–232 **slipper** slippery 232 **an eye can stamp** an eye that can coin, create 233 **advantages** favorable opportunities 235 **folly** wantonness **green** immature 236 **found him** sized him up, perceived his intent 237 **condition** disposition 238 **fig's end** (See Act I, Scene iii, line 317 for the vulgar gesture of the fig.) 239 **pudding** sausage

RODERIGO: Yes, that I did; but that was but courtesy.

IAGO: Lechery, by this hand. An index° and obscure° prologue to the history of lust and foul thoughts. They met so near with their lips that their breaths embraced together. Villainous thoughts, Roderigo! When these mutualities° so marshal the way, hard at hand° comes the master and main exercise, th' incorporate° conclusion. Pish! But, sir, be you ruled by me. I have brought you from Venice. Watch you° tonight; for the command, I'll lay 't upon you.° Cassio knows you not. I'll not be far from you. Do you find some occasion to anger Cassio, either by speaking too loud, or tainting° his discipline, or from what other course you please, which the time shall more favorably minister.°

RODERIGO: Well.

IAGO: Sir, he's rash and very sudden in choler,° and haply° may strike at you. Provoke him that he may, for even out of that will I cause these of Cyprus to mutiny,° whose qualification° shall come into no true taste° again but by the displanting of Cassio. So shall you have a shorter journey to your desires by the means I shall then have to prefer° them, and the impediment most profitably removed, without the which there were no expectation of our prosperity.

RODERIGO: I will do this, if you can bring it to any opportunity.

IAGO: I warrant° thee. Meet me by and by° at the citadel. I must fetch his necessaries ashore. Farewell.

RODERIGO: Adieu.

[Exit.]

IAGO: That Cassio loves her, I do well believe 't;
That she loves him, 'tis apt° and of great credit.°
The Moor, howbeit that I endure him not,
Is of a constant, loving, noble nature,
And I dare think he'll prove to Desdemona
A most dear husband. Now, I do love her too,
Not out of absolute lust—though peradventure
I stand accountant° for as great a sin—
But partly led to diet° my revenge
For that I do suspect the lusty Moor

243 **index** table of contents **obscure** i.e., the **lust and foul thoughts** in line 244 are secret, hidden from view 245–246 **mutualities** exchanges, intimacies **hard at hand** closely following 247 **incorporate** carnal 248 **Watch you** stand watch 248–249 **for the command . . . you** I'll arrange for you to be appointed, given orders 250–251 **tainting** disparaging 252 **minister** provide 254 **choler** wrath **haply** perhaps 256 **mutiny** riot **qualification** appeasement **true taste** i.e., acceptable state 258 **prefer** advance 262 **warrant** assure **by and by** immediately 266 **apt** probable **credit** credibility 272 **accountant** accountable 273 **diet** feed

Hath leaped into my seat, the thought whereof
Doth, like a poisonous mineral, gnaw my innards;
And nothing can or shall content my soul
Till I am evened with him, wife for wife,
Or failing so, yet that I put the Moor
At least into a jealousy so strong
That judgment cannot cure. Which thing to do,
If this poor trash of Venice, whom I trace°
For° his quick hunting, stand the putting on,°
I'll have our Michael Cassio on the hip,°
Abuse° him to the Moor in the rank garb—°
For I fear Cassio with my nightcap° too—
Make the Moor thank me, love me, and reward me
For making him egregiously an ass
And practicing upon° his peace and quiet
Even to madness. 'Tis here, but yet confused.
Knavery's plain face is never seen till used.

[Exit.]

SCENE II [Cyprus. A Street.]

[Enter OTHELLO'S HERALD *with a proclamation.]*

HERALD: It is Othello's pleasure, our noble and valiant general, that, upon certain tidings now arrived, importing the mere° perdition° of the Turkish fleet, every man put himself into triumph:° some to dance, some to make bonfires, each man to what sport and revels his addiction° leads him. For, besides these beneficial news, it is the celebration of his nuptial. So much was his pleasure should be proclaimed. All offices° are open, and there is full liberty of feasting from this present hour of five till the bell have told eleven. Heaven bless the isle of Cyprus and our noble general Othello!

[Exit.]

SCENE III [Cyprus. The Citadel.]

[Enter OTHELLO, DESDEMONA, CASSIO, *and attendants.]*

OTHELLO: Good Michael, look you to the guard tonight.
Let's teach ourselves that honorable stop°

282 **trace** i.e., train, or follow, or perhaps trash, a hunting term, meaning to put weights on a hunting dog in order to slow him down 283 **For** to make more eager **stand . . . on** respond properly when I incite him to quarrel 284 **on the hip** at my mercy, where I can throw him (A wrestling term.) 285 **Abuse** slander **rank garb** coarse manner, gross fashion 286 **with my nightcap** i.e., as a rival in my bed, as one who gives me cuckold's horns 289 **practicing upon** plotting against 2 **mere perdition** complete destruction 3 **triumph** public celebration 4 **addiction** inclination 6 **offices** rooms where food and drink are kept 2 **stop** restraint

Not to outsport° discretion.

CASSIO: Iago hath direction what to do,
But notwithstanding, with my personal eye
Will I look to 't.

OTHELLO: Iago is most honest.
Michael, good night. Tomorrow with your earliest°
Let me have speech with you. [*To* DESDEMONA.]
Come, my dear love,
The purchase made, the fruits are to ensue;
That profit's yet to come 'tween me and you.°—
Good night.

*[Exit (*OTHELLO*, with* DESDEMONA *and attendants).]*

[Enter IAGO.*]*

CASSIO: Welcome, Iago. We must to the watch.

IAGO: Not this hour,° Lieutenant; 'tis not yet ten o' the clock. Our general cast° us thus early for the love of his Desdemona; who° let us not therefore blame. He hath not yet made wanton the night with her, and she is sport for Jove.

CASSIO: She's a most exquisite lady.

IAGO: And, I'll warrant her, full of game.

CASSIO: Indeed, she's a most fresh and delicate creature.

IAGO: What an eye she has! Methinks it sounds a parley° to provocation.

CASSIO: An inviting eye, and yet methinks right modest.

IAGO: And when she speaks, is it not an alarum° to love?

CASSIO: She is indeed perfection.

IAGO: Well, happiness to their sheets! Come, Lieutenant, I have a stoup° of wine, and here without° are a brace° of Cyprus gallants that would fain have a measure° to the health of black Othello.

CASSIO: Not tonight, good Iago. I have very poor and unhappy brains for drinking. I could well wish courtesy would invent some other custom of entertainment.

IAGO: O, they are our friends. But one cup! I'll drink for you.°

CASSIO: I have drunk but one cup tonight, and that was craftily qualified° too, and behold what innovation° it makes here.° I am unfortunate in the infirmity and dare not task my weakness with any more.

3 **outsport** celebrate beyond the bounds of 7 **with your earliest** at your earliest convenience 9–10 **The purchase . . . you** i.e., though married, we haven't yet consummated our love 13 **Not this hour** not for an hour yet **cast** dismissed 14 **who** i.e., Othello 20 **sounds a parley** calls for a conference, issues an invitation 22 **alarum** signal calling men to arms (continuing the military metaphor of **parley,** line 20) 24 **stoup** measure of liquor, two quarts 25 **without** outside **brace** pair 25–26 **fain have a measure** gladly drink a toast 30 **for you** in your place (Iago will do the steady drinking to keep the gallants company while Cassio has only one cup.) 31 **qualified** diluted 32 **innovation** disturbance, insurrection **here** i.e., in my head

IAGO: What, man? 'Tis a night of revels. The gallants desire it.
CASSIO: Where are they?
IAGO: Here at the door. I pray you, call them in.
CASSIO: I'll do 't, but it dislikes me.°

[Exit.]

IAGO: If I can fasten but one cup upon him,
With that which he hath drunk tonight already,
He'll be as full of quarrel and offense°
As my young mistress' dog. Now, my sick fool Roderigo,
Whom love hath turned almost the wrong side out,
To Desdemona hath tonight caroused°
Potations pottle-deep;° and he's to watch.°
Three lads of Cyprus—noble swelling° spirits,
That hold their honors in a wary distance,°
The very elements° of this warlike isle—
Have I tonight flustered with flowing cups,
And they watch° too. Now, 'mongst this flock of drunkards
Am I to put our Cassio in some action
That may offend the isle.—But here they come.

[Enter CASSIO, MONTANO, and gentlemen; (servants following with wine).]

If consequence do but approve my dream,°
My boat sails freely both with wind and stream.°

CASSIO: 'Fore God, they have given me a rouse° already.
MONTANO: Good faith, a little one; not past a pint, as I am a soldier.
IAGO: Some wine, ho! [*He sings.*]

"And let me the cannikin° clink, clink,
And let me the cannikin clink.
A soldier's a man,
O, man's life's but a span° ;
Why, then, let a soldier drink."

Some wine, boys!

CASSIO: 'Fore God, an excellent song.
IAGO: I learned it in England, where indeed they are most potent in potting.° Your Dane, your German, and your swag-bellied Hollander—drink, ho!—are nothing to your English.

37 **it dislikes me** i.e., I'm reluctant 40 **offense** readiness to take offense 43 **caroused** drunk off 44 **pottle-deep** to the bottom of the tankard **watch** stand watch 45 **swelling** proud 46 **hold . . . distance** i.e., are extremely sensitive of their honor 47 **very elements** typical sort 49 **watch** are members of the guard 52 **If . . . dream** if subsequent events will only substantiate my scheme 53 **stream** current 54 **rouse** full draft of liquor 57 **cannikin** small drinking vessel 60 **span** brief span of time (Compare Psalm 39:6 as rendered in the 1928 Book of Common Prayer: "Thou hast made my days as it were a span long.") 64 **potting** drinking

CASSIO: Is your Englishman so exquisite in his drinking?

IAGO: Why, he drinks you,° with facility, your Dane° dead drunk; he sweats not° to overthrow your Almain;° he gives your Hollander a vomit ere the next pottle can be filled.

CASSIO: To the health of our general!

MONTANO: I am for it, Lieutenant, and I'll do you justice.°

IAGO: O sweet England! [*He sings.*]

"King Stephen was and-a worthy peer,
His breeches cost him but a crown;
He held them sixpence all too dear,
With that he called the tailor lown.°

He was a wight of high renown,
And thou art but of low degree.
'Tis pride° that pulls the country down;
Then take thy auld° cloak about thee."

Some wine, ho!

CASSIO: 'Fore God, this is a more exquisite song than the other.

IAGO: Will you hear 't again?

CASSIO: No, for I hold him to be unworthy of his place that does those things. Well, God's above all; and there be souls must be saved, and there be souls must not be saved.

IAGO: It's true, good Lieutenant.

CASSIO: For mine own part—no offense to the General, nor any man of quality° —I hope to be saved.

IAGO: And so do I too, Lieutenant.

CASSIO: Ay, but, by your leave, not before me; the lieutenant is to be saved before the ancient. Let's have no more of this; let's to our affairs —God forgive us our sins!—Gentlemen, let's look to our business. Do not think, gentlemen, I am drunk. This is my ancient; this is my right hand, and this is my left. I am not drunk now. I can stand well enough, and speak well enough.

GENTLEMEN: Excellent well.

CASSIO: Why, very well then; you must not think then that I am drunk.

[Exit.]

MONTANO: To th' platform, masters. Come, let's set the watch.°

[Exeunt Gentlemen.]

IAGO: You see this fellow that is gone before.

68 **drinks you** drinks **your Dane** your typical Dane **sweats not** i.e., need not exert himself 69 **Almain** German 72 **I'll . . . justice** i.e., I'll drink as much as you 77 **lown** lout, rascal 80 **pride** i.e., extravagance in dress 81 **auld** old 89–90 **quality** rank 100 **set the watch** mount the guard

He's a soldier fit to stand by Caesar
And give direction; and do but see his vice.
'Tis to his virtue a just equinox,°
The one as long as th' other. 'Tis pity of him.
I fear the trust Othello puts him in,
On some odd time of his infirmity,
Will shake this island.

MONTANO: But is he often thus?

IAGO: 'Tis evermore the prologue to his sleep.
He'll watch the horologe a double set,°
If drink rock not his cradle.

MONTANO: It were well
The General were put in mind of it.
Perhaps he sees it not, or his good nature
Prizes the virtue that appears in Cassio
And looks not on his evils. Is not this true?

[Enter RODERIGO.]

IAGO [*aside to him*]: How now, Roderigo?
I pray you, after the Lieutenant; go.

[Exit RODERIGO.]

MONTANO: And 'tis great pity that the noble Moor
Should hazard such a place as his own second
With° one of an engraffed° infirmity.
It were an honest action to say so
To the Moor.

IAGO: Not I, for this fair island.
I do love Cassio well and would do much
To cure him of this evil.

[Cry within: "Help! Help!"]

But, hark! What noise?

[Enter CASSIO, pursuing° RODERIGO.]

CASSIO: Zounds, you rogue! You rascal!

MONTANO: What's the matter, Lieutenant?

CASSIO: A knave teach me my duty? I'll beat the knave into a twiggen° bottle.

104 **just equinox** exact counterpart (**equinox** is an equal length of days and nights) 110 **watch... set** stay awake twice around the clock or **horologe** 119–120 **hazard... With** risk giving such an important position as his second in command to 120 **engraffed** engrafted, inveterate 124 s.d. **pursuing** (The Quarto text reads, "driving in.") 127 **twiggen** wicker-covered (Cassio vows to assail Roderigo until his skin resembles wickerwork or until he has driven Roderigo through the holes in a wickerwork.)

RODERIGO: Beat me?
CASSIO: Dost thou prate, rogue?
[He strikes RODERIGO.]
MONTANO: Nay, good Lieutenant. [*Restraining him.*] I pray you, sir, hold your hand.
CASSIO: Let me go, sir, or I'll knock you o'er the mazard.°
MONTANO: Come, come, you're drunk.
CASSIO: Drunk?
[They fight.]
IAGO [*aside to RODERIGO*]: Away, I say. Go out and cry a mutiny.°
[Exit RODERIGO.]
Nay, good Lieutenant—God's will, gentlemen—
Help, ho!—Lieutenant—sir—Montano—sir—
Help, masters!° —Here's a goodly watch indeed!
[A bell rings.]°
Who's that which rings the bell?—Diablo,° ho!
The town will rise.° God's will, Lieutenant, hold!
You'll be ashamed forever.
[Enter Othello and attendants (with weapons).]
OTHELLO: What is the matter here?
MONTANO: Zounds, I bleed still.
I am hurt to th' death. He dies! [*He thrusts at CASSIO.*]
OTHELLO: Hold, for your lives!
IAGO: Hold, ho! Lieutenant—sir—Montano—gentlemen—
Have you forgot all sense of place and duty?
Hold! The General speaks to you. Hold, for shame!
OTHELLO: Why, how now, ho! From whence ariseth this?
Are we turned Turks, and to ourselves do that
Which heaven hath forbid the Ottomites?°
For Christian shame, put by this barbarous brawl!
He that stirs next to carve for° his own rage
Holds his soul light;° he dies upon his motion.°
Silence that dreadful bell. It frights the isle
From her propriety.° What is the matter, masters?

132 **mazard** i.e., head (Literally, a drinking vessel.) 135 **mutiny** riot 138 **masters** sirs s.d. **A bell rings** (This direction is from the Quarto, as are **Exit Roderigo** at line 135, They fight at line 139, and **with weapons** at line 141.) 139 **Diablo** the devil 140 **rise** grow riotous 148–149 **to ourselves . . . Ottomites** inflict on ourselves the harm that heaven has prevented the Turks from doing (by destroying their fleet) 151 **carve for** i.e., indulge, satisfy with his sword 152 **Holds . . . light** i.e., places little value on his life **upon his motion** if he moves 154 **propriety** proper state or condition

Honest Iago, that looks dead with grieving,
Speak. Who began this? On thy love, I charge thee.
IAGO: I do not know. Friends all but now, even now,
In quarter° and in terms° like bride and groom
Devesting them° for bed; and then, but now—
As if some planet had unwitted men—
Swords out, and tilting one at others' breasts
In opposition bloody. I cannot speak°
Any beginning to this peevish odds;°
And would in action glorious I had lost
Those legs that brought me to a part of it!
OTHELLO: How comes it, Michael, you are thus forgot?°
CASSIO: I pray you, pardon me. I cannot speak.
OTHELLO: Worthy Montano, you were wont be° civil;
The gravity and stillness° of your youth
The world hath noted, and your name is great
In mouths of wisest censure.° What's the matter
That you unlace° your reputation thus
And spend your rich opinion° for the name
Of a night-brawler? Give me answer to it.
MONTANO: Worthy Othello, I am hurt to danger.
Your officer, Iago, can inform you—
While I spare speech, which something° now offends° me—
Of all that I do know; nor know I aught
By me that's said or done amiss this night,
Unless self-charity be sometimes a vice,
And to defend ourselves it be a sin
When violence assails us.
OTHELLO: Now, by heaven,
My blood° begins my safer guides° to rule,
And passion, having my best judgment collied,°
Essays° to lead the way. Zounds, if I stir,
Or do but lift this arm, the best of you
Shall sink in my rebuke. Give me to know
How this foul rout° began, who set it on;
And he that is approved in° this offense,

158 **In quarter** in friendly conduct, within bounds **in terms** on good terms 159 **Devesting them** undressing themselves 162 **speak** explain 163 **peevish odds** childish quarrel 166 **are thus forgot** have forgotten yourself thus 168 **wont be** accustomed to be 167 **stillness** sobriety 171 **censure** judgment 172 **unlace** undo, lay open (as one might loose the strings of a purse containing reputation) 173 **opinion** reputation 177 **something** somewhat **offends** pains 183 **blood** passion (of anger) **guides** i.e., reason 184 **collied** darkened 185 **Essays** undertakes 188 **rout** riot 189 **approved in** found guilty of

Though he had twinned with me, both at a birth,
Shall lose me. What? In a town of[o] war
Yet wild, the people's hearts brim full of fear,
To manage[o] private and domestic quarrel?
In night, and on the court and guard of safety?[o]
'Tis monstrous. Iago, who began 't?

MONTANO [*to IAGO*]: If partially affined,[o] or leagued in office,[o]
Thou dost deliver more or less than truth,
Thou art no soldier.

IAGO: Touch me not so near.
I had rather have this tongue cut from my mouth
Than it should do offense to Michael Cassio;
Yet, I persuade myself, to speak the truth
Shall nothing wrong him. Thus it is, General.
Montano and myself being in speech,
There comes a fellow crying out for help,
And Cassio following him with determined sword
To execute[o] upon him. Sir, this gentleman

[indicating MONTANO]

Steps in to Cassio and entreats his pause.[o]
Myself the crying fellow did pursue,
Lest by his clamor—as it so fell out—
The town might fall in fright. He, swift of foot,
Outran my purpose, and I returned, the rather[o]
For that I heard the clink and fall of swords
And Cassio high in oath, which till tonight
I ne'er might say before. When I came back—
For this was brief—I found them close together
At blow and thrust, even as again they were
When you yourself did part them.
More of this matter cannot I report.
But men are men; the best sometimes forget.[o]
Though Cassio did some little wrong to him,
As men in rage strike those that wish them best,[o]
Yet surely Cassio, I believe, received

191 **town of** town garrisoned for 193 **manage** undertake 194 **on . . . safety** at the main guardhouse or headquarters and on watch 196 **partially affined** made partial by some personal relationship **leagued in office** in league as fellow officers 206 **execute** give effect to (his anger) 207 **his pause** him to stop 211 **rather** sooner 219 **forget** forget themselves 221 **those . . . best** i.e., even those who are well disposed

From him that fled some strange indignity,
Which patience could not pass.°

OTHELLO: I know, Iago,
Thy honesty and love doth mince this matter,
Making it light to Cassio. Cassio, I love thee,
But nevermore be Officer of mine.

[Enter DESDEMONA, *attended.]*

Look if my gentle love be not raised up.
I'll make thee an example.

DESDEMONA: What is the matter, dear?

OTHELLO: All's well now, sweeting;
Come away to bed. [*To* MONTANO.] Sir, for your hurts,
Myself will be your surgeon.° —Lead him off.

*[*MONTANO *is led off.]*

Iago, look with care about the town
And silence those whom this vile brawl distracted.
Come, Desdemona. 'Tis the soldiers' life
To have their balmy slumbers waked with strife.

[Exit (with all but IAGO *and* CASSIO*).]*

IAGO: What, are you hurt, Lieutenant?

CASSIO: Ay, past all surgery.

IAGO: Marry, God forbid!

CASSIO: Reputation, reputation, reputation! O, I have lost my reputation! I have lost the immortal part of myself, and what remains is bestial. My reputation, Iago, my reputation!

IAGO: As I am an honest man, I thought you had received some bodily wound; there is more sense in that than in reputation. Reputation is an idle and most false imposition,° oft got without merit and lost without deserving. You have lost no reputation at all, unless you repute yourself such a loser. What, man, there are more ways to recover° the General again. You are but now cast in his mood° -a punishment more in policy° than in malice, even so as one would beat his offenseless dog to affright an imperious lion.° Sue° to him again and he's yours.

224 **pass** pass over, overlook 232 **be your surgeon** i.e., make sure you receive medical attention 245 **false imposition** thing artificially imposed and of no real value 247 **recover** regain favor with 248 **cast in his mood** dismissed in a moment of anger **in policy** done for expediency's sake and as a public gesture 249–250 **would . . . lion** i.e., would make an example of a minor offender in order to deter more important and dangerous offenders 250 **Sue** petition

Cassio: I will rather sue to be despised than to deceive so good a commander with so slight,° so drunken, and so indiscreet an Officer. Drunk? And speak parrot?° And squabble? Swagger? Swear? And discourse fustian with one's own shadow? O thou invisible spirit of wine, if thou hast no name to be known by, let us call thee devil!

Iago: What was he that you followed with your sword? What had he done to you?

Cassio: I know not.

Iago: Is 't possible?

Cassio: I remember a mass of things, but nothing distinctly; a quarrel, but nothing wherefore.° O God, that men should put an enemy in their mouths to steal away their brains! That we should, with joy, pleasance, revel, and applause° transform ourselves into beasts!

Iago: Why, but you are now well enough. How came you thus recovered?

Cassio: It hath pleased the devil drunkenness to give place to the devil wrath. One unperfectness shows me another, to make me frankly despise myself.

Iago: Come, you are too severe a moraler.° As the time, the place, and the condition of this country stands, I could heartily wish this had not befallen; but since it is as it is, mend it for your own good.

Cassio: I will ask him for my place again; he shall tell me I am a drunkard. Had I as many mouths as Hydra,° such an answer would stop them all. To be now a sensible man, by and by a fool, and presently a beast! O, strange! Every inordinate cup is unblessed, and the ingredient is a devil.

Iago: Come, come, good wine is a good familiar creature, if it be well used. Exclaim no more against it. And, good Lieutenant, I think you think I love you.

Cassio: I have well approved° it, sir. I drunk!

Iago: You or any man living may be drunk at a time,° man. I'll tell you what you shall do. Our general's wife is now the general—I may say so in this respect, for that° he hath devoted and given up himself to the contemplation, mark, and denotement° of her parts° and graces. Confess yourself freely to her; importune her help to put you in your place again. She is of so free,° so kind, so apt, so blessed a disposition, she holds it a vice in her goodness not to do more than she is requested. This broken joint between you and her husband entreat her to splinter;° and, my fortunes against any lay° worth naming, this crack of your love shall grow stronger than it was before.

252 **slight** worthless 253 **speak parrot** talk nonsense, rant 261 **wherefore** why 263 **applause** desire for applause 267 **moraler** moralizer 271 **Hydra** the Lernaean Hydra, a monster with many heads and the ability to grow two heads when one was cut off, slain by Hercules as the second of his twelve labors 277 **approved** proved 278 **at a time** at one time or another 279–280 **in . . . that** in view of this fact, that 281 **mark, and denotement** both words mean "observation" **parts** qualities 283 **free** generous 285 **splinter** bind with splints **lay** stake, wager

CASSIO: You advise me well.

IAGO: I protest,° in the sincerity of love and honest kindness.

CASSIO: I think it freely;° and betimes in the morning I will beseech the virtuous Desdemona to undertake for me. I am desperate of my fortunes if they check° me here.

IAGO: You are in the right. Good night, Lieutenant. I must to the watch.

CASSIO: Good night, honest Iago.

[Exit CASSIO.]

IAGO: And what's he then that says I play the villain,
When this advice is free° I give, and honest,
Probal° to thinking, and indeed the course
To win the Moor again? For 'tis most easy
Th' inclining° Desdemona to subdue°
In any honest suit; she's framed as fruitful°
As the free elements.° And then for her
To win the Moor—were 't to renounce his baptism,
All seals and symbols of redeemèd sin—
His soul is so enfettered to her love
That she may make, unmake, do what she list,
Even as her appetite° shall play the god
With his weak function.° How am I then a villain,
To counsel Cassio to this parallel° course
Directly to his good? Divinity of hell!°
When devils will the blackest sins put on,°
They do suggest° at first with heavenly shows,
As I do now. For whiles this honest fool
Plies Desdemona to repair his fortune,
And she for him pleads strongly to the Moor,
I'll pour this pestilence into his ear,
That she repeals him° for her body's lust;
And by how much she strives to do him good,
She shall undo her credit with the Moor.
So will I turn her virtue into pitch,°
And out of her own goodness make the net

289 **protest** insist, declare 290 **freely** unreservedly 292 **check** repulse 296 **free** (1) free from guile (2) freely given 297 **Probal** probable, reasonable 299 **inclining** favorably disposed **subdue** persuade 300 **framed as fruitful** created as generous 301 **free elements** i.e., earth, air, fire, and water, unrestrained and spontaneous 306 **her appetite** her desire, or, perhaps, his desire for her 307 **function** exercise of faculties (weakened by his fondness for her) 308 **parallel** corresponding to these facts and to his best interests 309 **Divinity of hell** inverted theology of hell (which seduces the soul to its damnation) 310 **put on** further, instigate 311 **suggest** tempt 316 **repeals him** attempts to get him restored 319 **pitch** i.e., (1) foul blackness (2) a snaring substance

That shall enmesh them all.

[Enter RODERIGO.*]*

How now, Roderigo?

RODERIGO: I do follow here in the chase, not like a hound that hunts, but one that fills up the cry.° My money is almost spent; I have been tonight exceedingly well cudgeled; and I think the issue will be I shall have so much° experience for my pains, and so, with no money at all and a little more wit, return again to Venice.

IAGO: How poor are they that have not patience!
What wound did ever heal but by degrees?
Thou know'st we work by wit, and not by witchcraft,
And wit depends on dilatory time.
Does 't not go well? Cassio hath beaten thee,
And thou, by that small hurt, hast cashiered° Cassio.
Though other things grow fair against the sun,
Yet fruits that blossom first will first be ripe.°
Content thyself awhile. By the Mass, 'tis morning!
Pleasure and action make the hours seem short.
Retire thee; go where thou art billeted.
Away, I say! Thou shalt know more hereafter.
Nay, get thee gone.

[Exit RODERIGO.*]*

Two things are to be done.
My wife must move° for Cassio to her mistress;
I'll set her on;
Myself the while to draw the Moor apart
And bring him jump° when he may Cassio find
Soliciting his wife. Ay, that's the way.
Dull not device° by coldness° and delay.

[Exit.]

ACT III

SCENE I [Before the Chamber of OTHELLO and DESDEMONA.]

[Enter CASSIO *(and)* MUSICIANS.*]*

CASSIO: Masters, play here—I will content your pains°—
Something that's brief, and bid "Good morrow, General."

323 **fills up the cry** merely takes part as one of the pack 324–325 **so much** just so much and no more 332 **cashiered** dismissed from service 333–334 **Though . . . ripe** i.e., plans that are well prepared and set expeditiously in motion will soonest ripen into success 340 **move** plead 343 **jump** precisely 345 **device** plot **coldness** lack of zeal 1 **content your pains** reward your efforts

[They play.]

[Enter CLOWN.]

CLOWN: Why, masters, have your instruments been in Naples, that they speak i' the nose° thus?

A MUSICIAN: How, sir, how?

CLOWN: Are these, I pray you, wind instruments?

A MUSICIAN: Ay, marry, are they, sir.

CLOWN: O, thereby hangs a tail.

A MUSICIAN: Whereby hangs a tale, sir?

CLOWN: Marry, sir, by many a wind instrument° that I know. But, masters, here's money for you. [*He gives money.*] And the General so likes your music that he desires you, for love's sake,° to make no more noise with it.

A MUSICIAN: Well, sir, we will not.

CLOWN: If you have any music that may not° be heard, to 't again; but, as they say, to hear music the General does not greatly care.

A MUSICIAN: We have none such, sir.

CLOWN: Then put up your pipes in your bag, for I'll away.° Go, vanish into air, away!

[Exeunt MUSICIANS.]

CASSIO: Dost thou hear, mine honest friend?

CLOWN: No, I hear not your honest friend; I hear you.

CASSIO: Prithee, keep up° thy quillets.° There's a poor piece of gold for thee. [*He gives money.*] If the gentle-woman that attends the General's wife be stirring, tell her there's one Cassio entreats her a little favor of speech.° Wilt thou do this?

CLOWN: She is stirring, sir. If she will stir° hither, I shall seem° to notify unto her.

CASSIO: Do, good my friend.

[Exit CLOWN.]

[Enter IAGO.]

In happy time,° Iago.

3–4 **speak i' the nose** (1) sound nasal (2) sound like one whose nose has been attacked by syphilis (Naples was popularly supposed to have a high incidence of venereal disease.) 10 **wind instrument** (With a joke on flatulence. The **tail,** line 8, that hangs nearby the **wind instrument** suggests the penis.) 12 **for love's sake** (1) out of friendship and affection (2) for the sake of lovemaking in Othello's marriage 14 **may not** cannot 17 **I'll away** (Possibly a misprint, or a snatch of song?) 21 **keep up** do not bring out, do not use **quillets** quibbles, puns 23 **a little . . . speech** the favor of a brief talk 25 **stir** bestir herself (with a play on stirring, "rousing herself from rest") **seem** deem it good, think fit 27 **In happy time** i.e., well met

IAGO: You have not been abed, then?
CASSIO: Why, no. The day had broke
Before we parted. I have made bold, Iago,
To send in to your wife. My suit to her
Is that she will to virtuous Desdemona
Procure me some access.
IAGO: I'll send her to you presently;
And I'll devise a means to draw the Moor
Out of the way, that your converse and business
May be more free.
CASSIO: I humbly thank you for 't.

[Exit IAGO.]

I never knew
A Florentine° more kind and honest.

[Enter EMILIA.]

EMILIA: Good morrow, good Lieutenant. I am sorry
For your displeasure;° but all will sure be well.
The General and his wife are talking of it,
And she speaks for you stoutly.° The Moor replies
That he you hurt is of great fame° in Cyprus
And great affinity,° and that in wholesome wisdom
He might not but refuse you; but he protests° he loves you
And needs no other suitor but his likings
To take the safest occasion by the front°
To bring you in again.
CASSIO: Yet I beseech you,
If you think fit, or that it may be done,
Give me advantage of some brief discourse
With Desdemon alone.
EMILIA: Pray you, come in.
I will bestow you where you shall have time
To speak your bosom° freely.
CASSIO: I am much bound to you.

[Exeunt.]

39 **Florentine** i.e., even a fellow Florentine (Iago is a Venetian; Cassio is a Florentine.) 41 **displeasure** fall from favor 43 **stoutly** spiritedly 44 **fame** reputation, importance 45 **affinity** kindred, family connection 46 **protests** insists 48 **occasion . . . front** opportunity by the forelock 54 **bosom** inmost thoughts

SCENE II [The Citadel.]

[Enter OTHELLO, IAGO, *and* GENTLEMEN.*]*

OTHELLO [*giving letters*]: These letters give, Iago, to the pilot,
And by him do my duties° to the Senate.
That done, I will be walking on the works;°
Repair° there to me.
IAGO: Well, my good lord, I'll do 't.
OTHELLO: This fortification, gentlemen, shall we see 't?
GENTLEMEN: We'll wait upon° your lordship.

[Exeunt.]

SCENE III [The Garden of the Citadel.]

[Enter DESDEMONA, CASSIO, *and* EMILIA.*]*

DESDEMONA: Be thou assured, good Cassio, I will do
All my abilities in thy behalf.
EMILIA: Good madam, do. I warrant it grieves my husband
As if the cause were his.
DESDEMONA: O, that's an honest fellow. Do not doubt, Cassio,
But I will have my lord and you again
As friendly as you were.
CASSIO: Bounteous madam,
Whatever shall become of Michael Cassio,
He's never anything but your true servant.
DESDEMONA: I know 't. I thank you. You do love my lord;
You have known him long, and be you well assured
He shall in strangeness° stand no farther off
Than in a politic° distance.
CASSIO: Ay, but, lady,
That policy may either last so long,
Or feed upon such nice and waterish diet,°
Or breed itself so out of circumstance,°
That, I being absent and my place supplied,°
My general will forget my love and service.
DESDEMONA: Do not doubt° that. Before Emilia here
I give thee warrant° of thy place. Assure thee,

2 **do my duties** convey my respects 3 **works** breastworks, fortifications 4 **Repair** return, come 6 **wait upon** attend 12 **strangeness** aloofness 13 **politic** required by wise policy 15 **Or . . . diet** or sustain itself at length upon such trivial and meager technicalities 16 **breed . . . circumstance** continually renew itself so out of chance events, or yield so few chances for my being pardoned 17 **supplied** filled by another person 19 **doubt** fear 20 **warrant** guarantee

If I do vow a friendship I'll perform it
To the last article. My lord shall never rest.
I'll watch him tame° and talk him out of patience;°
His bed shall seem a school, his board° a shrift;°
I'll intermingle everything he does
With Cassio's suit. Therefore be merry, Cassio,
For thy solicitor° shall rather die
Than give thy cause away.°

[Enter OTHELLO *and* IAGO *(at a distance).]*

EMILIA: Madam, here comes my lord.
CASSIO: Madam, I'll take my leave.
DESDEMONA: Why, stay, and hear me speak.
CASSIO: Madam, not now. I am very ill at ease,
Unfit for mine own purposes.
DESDEMONA: Well, do your discretion.°

[Exit CASSIO.*]*

IAGO: Ha? I like not that.
OTHELLO: What dost thou say?
IAGO: Nothing, my lord; or if—I know not what.
OTHELLO: Was not that Cassio parted from my wife?
IAGO: Cassio, my lord? No, sure, I cannot think it,
That he would steal away so guiltylike,
Seeing you coming.
OTHELLO: I do believe 'twas he.
DESDEMONA: How now, my lord?
I have been talking with a suitor here,
A man that languishes in your displeasure.
OTHELLO: Who is 't you mean?
DESDEMONA: Why, your lieutenant, Cassio. Good my lord,
If I have any grace or power to move you,
His present reconciliation take;°
For if he be not one that truly loves you,
That errs in ignorance and not in cunning,°
I have no judgment in an honest face.
I prithee, call him back.
OTHELLO: Went he hence now?
DESDEMONA: Yes, faith, so humbled

23 **watch him tame** tame him by keeping him from sleeping (A term from falconry.) **out of patience** past his endurance 24 **board** dining table **shrift** confessional 27 **solicitor** advocate 28 **away** up 34 **do your discretion** act according to your own discretion 49 **His . . . take** let him be reconciled to you right away 51 **in cunning** wittingly

That he hath left part of his grief with me
To suffer with him. Good love, call him back.
OTHELLO: Not now, sweet Desdemon. Some other time.
DESDEMONA: But shall 't be shortly?
OTHELLO: The sooner, sweet, for you.
DESDEMONA: Shall 't be tonight at supper?
OTHELLO: No, not tonight.
DESDEMONA: Tomorrow dinner,° then?
OTHELLO: I shall not dine at home.
I meet the captains at the citadel.
DESDEMONA: Why, then, tomorrow night, or Tuesday morn,
On Tuesday noon, or night, on Wednesday morn.
I prithee, name the time, but let it not
Exceed three days. In faith, he's penitent;
And yet his trespass, in our common reason°—
Save that, they say, the wars must make example
Out of her best°— is not almost° a fault
T' incur a private check.° When shall he come?
Tell me, Othello. I wonder in my soul
What you would ask me that I should deny,
Or stand so mammering on.° What? Michael Cassio,
That came a-wooing with you, and so many a time,
When I have spoke of you dispraisingly,
Hath ta'en your part—to have so much to do
To bring him in!° By 'r Lady, I could do much—
OTHELLO: Prithee, no more. Let him come when he will;
I will deny thee nothing.
DESDEMONA: Why, this is not a boon.
'Tis as I should entreat you wear your gloves,
Or feed on nourishing dishes, or keep you warm,
Or sue to you to do a peculiar° profit
To your own person. Nay, when I have a suit
Wherein I mean to touch° your love indeed,
It shall be full of poise° and difficult weight,
And fearful to be granted.
OTHELLO: I will deny thee nothing.

63 **dinner** (The noontime meal.) 70 **common reason** everyday judgments 71–72 **Save . . . best** were it not that, as the saying goes, military discipline requires making an example of the very best men (Her refers to **wars** as a singular concept.) 72 **not almost** scarcely 73 **private check** even a private reprimand 76 **mammering on** wavering about 80 **bring him in** restore him to favor 86 **peculiar** particular, personal 88 **touch** test 89 **poise** weight, heaviness; or equipoise, delicate balance involving hard choice

Whereon,° I do beseech thee, grant me this,
To leave me but a little to myself.
DESDEMONA: Shall I deny you? No. Farewell, my lord.
OTHELLO: Farewell, my Desdemona. I'll come to thee straight.°
DESDEMONA: Emilia, come.—Be as your fancies° teach you;
Whate'er you be, I am obedient.

[Exit (with EMILIA).]

OTHELLO: Excellent wretch! ° Perdition catch my soul
But I do love thee! And when I love thee not,
Chaos is come again.°
IAGO: My noble lord—
OTHELLO: What dost thou say, Iago?
IAGO: Did Michael Cassio, when you wooed my lady,
Know of your love?
OTHELLO: He did, from first to last. Why dost thou ask?
IAGO: But for a satisfaction of my thought;
No further harm.
OTHELLO: Why of thy thought, Iago?
IAGO: I did not think he had been acquainted with her.
OTHELLO: O, yes, and went between us very oft.
IAGO: Indeed?
OTHELLO: Indeed? Ay, indeed. Discern'st thou aught in that?
Is he not honest?
IAGO: Honest, my lord?
OTHELLO: Honest. Ay, honest.
IAGO: My lord, for aught I know.
OTHELLO: What dost thou think?
IAGO: Think, my lord?
OTHELLO: "Think, my lord?" By heaven, thou echo'st me,
As if there were some monster in thy thought
Too hideous to be shown. Thou dost mean something.
I heard thee say even now, thou lik'st not that,
When Cassio left my wife. What didst not like?
And when I told thee he was of my counsel°
In my whole course of wooing, thou criedst "Indeed?"
And didst contract and purse° thy brow together
As if thou then hadst shut up in thy brain
Some horrible conceit.° If thou dost love me,

92 **Whereon** in return for which 95 **straight** straightway 96 **fancies** inclinations 98 **wretch** (A term of affectionate endearment.) 99–100 **And . . . again** i.e., my love for you will last forever, until the end of time when chaos will return (But with an unconscious, ironic suggestion that, if anything should induce Othello to cease loving Desdemona, the result would be chaos.) 123 **of my counsel** in my confidence 125 **purse** knit 127 **conceit** fancy

Show me thy thought.
IAGO: My lord, you know I love you.
OTHELLO: I think thou dost;
And, for° I know thou'rt full of love and honesty,
And weigh'st thy words before thou giv'st them breath,
Therefore these stops° of thine fright me the more;
For such things in a false disloyal knave
Are tricks of custom,° but in a man that's just
They're close dilations,° working from the heart
That passion cannot rule.°
IAGO: For° Michael Cassio,
I dare be sworn I think that he is honest.
OTHELLO: I think so too.
IAGO: Men should be what they seem;
Or those that be not, would they might seem none!°
OTHELLO: Certain, men should be what they seem.
IAGO: Why, then, I think Cassio's an honest man.
OTHELLO: Nay, yet there's more in this.
I prithee, speak to me as to thy thinkings,
As thou dost ruminate, and give thy worst of thoughts
The worst of words.
IAGO: Good my lord, pardon me.
Though I am bound to every act of duty,
I am not bound to that° all slaves are free to.
Utter my thoughts? Why, say they are vile and false,
As where's the palace whereinto foul things
Sometimes intrude not? Who has that breast so pure
But some uncleanly apprehensions
Keep leets and law days,° and in sessions sit
With° meditations lawful?°
OTHELLO: Thou dost conspire against thy friend,° Iago,
If thou but think'st him wronged and mak'st his ear
A stranger to thy thoughts.
IAGO: I do beseech you,
Though I perchance am vicious° in my guess—

131 **for** because 133 **stops** pauses 135 **of custom** customary 136 **close dilations** secret or involuntary expressions or delays 137 **That passion cannot rule** i.e., that are too passionately strong to be restrained (referring to the workings), or, that cannot rule its own passions (referring to the heart) **For** as for 140 **none** i.e., not to be men, or not seem to be honest 148 **that** that which **free to** free with respect to 153 **Keep leets and law days** i.e., hold court, set up their authority in one's heart (**Leets** are a kind of manor court; **law days** are the days courts sit in session, or those sessions.) 154 **With** along with **lawful** innocent 155 **thy friend** i.e., Othello 159 **vicious** wrong

As I confess it is my nature's plague
To spy into abuses, and oft my jealousy°
Shapes faults that are not—that your wisdom then,°
From one° that so imperfectly conceits,°
Would take no notice, nor build yourself a trouble
Out of his scattering° and unsure observance.
It were not for your quiet nor your good,
Nor for my manhood, honesty, and wisdom,
To let you know my thoughts.

OTHELLO: What dost thou mean?

IAGO: Good name in man and woman, dear my lord,
Is the immediate° jewel of their souls.
Who steals my purse steals trash; 'tis something, nothing;
'Twas mine, 'tis his, and has been slave to thousands;
But he that filches from me my good name
Robs me of that which not enriches him
And makes me poor indeed.

OTHELLO: By heaven, I'll know thy thoughts.

IAGO: You cannot, if° my heart were in your hand,
Nor shall not, whilst 'tis in my custody.

OTHELLO: Ha?

IAGO: O, beware, my lord, of jealousy.
It is the green-eyed monster which doth mock
The meat it feeds on.° That cuckold lives in bliss
Who, certain of his fate, loves not his wronger;°
But O, what damnèd minutes tells° he o'er
Who dotes, yet doubts, suspects, yet fondly loves!

OTHELLO: O misery!

IAGO: Poor and content is rich, and rich enough,°
But riches fineless° is as poor as winter
To him that ever fears he shall be poor.
Good God, the souls of all my tribe defend
From jealousy!

OTHELLO: Why, why is this?
Think'st thou I'd make a life of jealousy,
To follow still the changes of the moon

161 **jealousy** suspicious nature 162 **then** on that account 163 **one** i.e., myself, Iago **conceits** judges, conjectures 165 **scattering** random 170 **immediate** essential, most precious 177 **if** even if 180–181 **doth mock . . . on** mocks and torments the heart of its victim, the man who suffers jealousy 182 **his wronger** i.e., his faithless wife (The unsuspecting cuckold is spared the misery of loving his wife only to discover she is cheating on him.) 183 **tells** counts 186 **Poor . . . enough** to be content with what little one has is the greatest wealth of all (proverbial) 187 **fineless** boundless

With fresh suspicions?° No! To be once in doubt
Is once° to be resolved.° Exchange me for a goat
When I shall turn the business of my soul
To such exsufflicate and blown° surmises
Matching thy inference.° 'Tis not to make me jealous
To say my wife is fair, feeds well, loves company,
Is free of speech, sings, plays, and dances well;
Where virtue is, these are more virtuous.
Nor from mine own weak merits will I draw
The smallest fear or doubt of her revolt,°
For she had eyes, and chose me. No, Iago,
I'll see before I doubt; when I doubt, prove;
And on the proof, there is no more but this—
Away at once with love or jealousy.

IAGO: I am glad of this, for now I shall have reason
To show the love and duty that I bear you
With franker spirit. Therefore, as I am bound,
Receive it from me. I speak not yet of proof.
Look to your wife; observe her well with Cassio.
Wear your eyes thus, not° jealous nor secure.°
I would not have your free and noble nature,
Out of self-bounty,° be abused.° Look to 't.
I know our country disposition well;
In Venice they do let God see the pranks
They dare not show their husbands; their best conscience
Is not to leave 't undone, but keep 't unknown.

OTHELLO: Dost thou say so?

IAGO: She did deceive her father, marrying you;
And when she seemed to shake and fear your looks,
She loved them most.

OTHELLO: And so she did.

IAGO: Why, go to,° then!
She that, so young, could give out such a seeming,°
To seel° her father's eyes up close as oak,°
He thought 'twas witchcraft! But I am much to blame.
I humbly do beseech you of your pardon

193–194 **To follow . . . suspicions** to be constantly imagining new causes for suspicion, changing incessantly like the moon 195 **once** once and for all **resolved** free of doubt, having settled the matter 197 **exsufflicate and blown** inflated and blown up, rumored about, or, spat out and fly-blown, hence, loathsome, disgusting 198 **inference** description or allegation 203 **doubt . . . revolt** fear of her unfaithfulness 213 **not** neither **secure** free from uncertainty 215 **self-bounty** inherent or natural goodness and generosity **abused** deceived 222 **go to** an expression of impatience 224 **seeming** false appearance 225 **seel** blind (A term from falconry.) **oak** a close-grained wood

For too much loving you.
OTHELLO: I am bound° to thee forever.
IAGO: I see this hath a little dashed your spirits.
OTHELLO: Not a jot, not a jot.
IAGO: I' faith, I fear it has.
I hope you will consider what is spoke
Comes from my love. But I do see you're moved.
I am to pray you not to strain my speech
To grosser issues° nor to larger reach°
Than to suspicion.
OTHELLO: I will not.
IAGO: Should you do so, my lord,
My speech should fall into such vile success°
Which my thoughts aimed not. Cassio's my worthy friend.
My lord, I see you're moved.
OTHELLO: No, not much moved.
I do not think but Desdemona's honest.°
IAGO: Long live she so! And long live you to think so!
OTHELLO: And yet, how nature erring from itself—
IAGO: Ay, there's the point! As—to be bold with you—
Not to affect° many proposèd matches
Of her own clime, complexion, and degree,°
Whereto we see in all things nature tends—
Foh! One may smell in such a will° most rank,
Foul disproportion,° thoughts unnatural.
But pardon me. I do not in position°
Distinctly speak of her, though I may fear
Her will, recoiling° to her better° judgment,
May fall to match you with her country forms°
And happily° repent.
OTHELLO: Farewell, farewell!
If more thou dost perceive, let me know more.
Set on thy wife to observe. Leave me, Iago.
IAGO [*going*]: My lord, I take my leave.
OTHELLO: Why did I marry? This honest creature doubtless

229 **bound** indebted (but perhaps with ironic sense of "tied") 235 **issues** significances **reach** meaning, scope 239 **success** effect, result 242 **honest** chaste 246 **affect** prefer, desire 247 **clime . . . degree** country, color, and social position 249 **will** sensuality, appetite 250 **disproportion** abnormality 251 **position** argument, proposition 253 **recoiling** reverting **better** i.e., more natural and reconsidered 254 **fall . . . forms** undertake to compare you with Venetian norms of handsomeness 255 **happily repent** haply repent her marriage

Sees and knows more, much more, than he unfolds.
IAGO [*returning*]: My Lord, I would I might entreat your honor
To scan° this thing no farther. Leave it to time.
Although 'tis fit that Cassio have his place—
For, sure, he fills it up with great ability—
Yet, if you please to hold him off awhile,
You shall by that perceive him and his means.°
Note if your lady strain his entertainment°
With any strong or vehement importunity;
Much will be seen in that. In the meantime,
Let me be thought too busy° in my fears—
As worthy cause I have to fear I am—
And hold her free,° I do beseech your honor.
OTHELLO: Fear not my government.°
IAGO: I once more take my leave.
[Exit.]
OTHELLO: This fellow's of exceeding honesty,
And knows all qualities,° with a learnèd spirit,
Of human dealings. If I do prove her haggard,°
Though that her jesses° were my dear heartstrings,
I'd whistle her off and let her down the wind°
To prey at fortune.° Haply, for° I am black
And have not those soft parts of conversation°
That chamberers° have, or for I am declined
Into the vale of years—yet that's not much—
She's gone. I am abused,° and my relief
Must be to loathe her. O curse of marriage,
That we can call these delicate creatures ours
And not their appetites! I had rather be a toad
And live upon the vapor of a dungeon
Than keep a corner in the thing I love
For others' uses. Yet, 'tis the plague of great ones;
Prerogatived° are they less than the base.°

262 **scan** scrutinize 266 **his means** the method he uses (to regain his post) 267 **strain his entertainment** urge his reinstatement 270 **busy** interfering 272 **hold her free** regard her as innocent 273 **government** self-control, conduct 276 **qualities** natures, types 277 **haggard** wild (like a wild female hawk) 278 **jesses** straps fastened around the legs of a trained hawk 279 **I'd . . . wind** i.e., I'd let her go forever (To release a hawk downwind was to invite it not to return.) 280 **prey at fortune** fend for herself in the wild **Haply, for** perhaps because 281 **soft . . . conversation** pleasing graces of social behavior 282 **chamberers** gallants 284 **abused** deceived 291 **Prerogatived** privileged (to have honest wives) **the base** ordinary citizens (Socially prominent men are especially prone to the unavoidable destiny of being cuckolded and to the public shame that goes with it.)

'Tis destiny unshunnable, like death.
Even then this forkèd[o] plague is fated to us
When we do quicken.[o] Look where she comes.

[Enter DESDEMONA and EMILIA.]

If she be false, O, then heaven mocks itself!
I'll not believe 't.

DESDEMONA: How now, my dear Othello?
Your dinner, and the generous[o] islanders
By you invited, do attend[o] your presence.

OTHELLO: I am to blame.

DESDEMONA: Why do you speak so faintly?
Are you not well?

OTHELLO: I have a pain upon my forehead here.

DESDEMONA: Faith, that's with watching.[o] 'Twill away again.

[She offers her handkerchief.]

Let me but bind it hard, within this hour
It will be well.

OTHELLO: Your napkin[o] is too little.
Let it alone.[o] Come, I'll go in with you.

[He puts the handkerchief from him, and it drops.]

DESDEMONA: I am very sorry that you are not well.

[Exit (with OTHELLO).]

EMILIA [*picking up the handkerchief*]: I am glad I have found this napkin.
This was her first remembrance from the Moor.
My wayward[o] husband hath a hundred times
Wooed me to steal it, but she so loves the token—
For he conjured her she should ever keep it—
That she reserves it evermore about her
To kiss and talk to. I'll have the work ta'en out,[o]
And give 't Iago. What he will do with it
Heaven knows, not I;
I nothing but to please his fantasy,[o]

[Enter IAGO.]

293 **forkèd** an allusion to the horns of the cuckold 294 **quicken** receive life (Quicken may also mean to swarm with maggots as the body festers, as in Act IV, Scene ii, line 69, in which case line 293 suggests that **even then,** in death, we are cuckolded by **forkèd** worms.) 297 **generous** noble 298 **attend** await 302 **watching** too little sleep 304 **napkin** handkerchief 305 **Let it alone** i.e., never mind 309 **wayward** capricious 313 **work ta'en out** design of the embroidery copied 316 **fantasy** whim

IAGO: How now? What do you here alone?
EMILIA: Do not you chide. I have a thing for you.
IAGO: You have a thing for me? It is a common thing°—
EMILIA: Ha?
IAGO: To have a foolish wife.
EMILIA: O, is that all? What will you give me now
 For that same handkerchief?
IAGO: What handkerchief?
EMILIA: What handkerchief?
 Why, that the Moor first gave to Desdemona;
 That which so often you did bid me steal.
IAGO: Hast stolen it from her?
EMILIA: No, faith. She let it drop by negligence,
 And to th' advantage° I, being here, took 't up.
 Look, here 'tis.
IAGO: A good wench! Give it me.
EMILIA: What will you do with 't, that you have been so earnest
 To have me filch it?
IAGO [*snatching it*]: Why, what is that to you?
EMILIA: If it be not for some purpose of import,
 Give 't me again. Poor lady, she'll run mad
 When she shall lack° it.
IAGO: Be not acknown on 't.°
 I have use for it. Go, leave me.
[Exit EMILIA.*]*
 I will in Cassio's lodging lose° this napkin
 And let him find it. Trifles light as air
 Are to the jealous confirmations strong
 As proofs of Holy Writ. This may do something.
 The Moor already changes with my poison.
 Dangerous conceits° are in their natures poisons,
 Which at the first are scarce found to distaste,°
 But with a little act° upon the blood
 Burn like the mines of sulfur.
[Enter OTHELLO.*]*
 I did say so.

319 **common thing** with bawdy suggestion; **common** suggests coarseness and availability to all comers, and **thing** is a slang term for the pudendum 330 **to th' advantage** taking the opportunity 336 **lack** miss **Be . . . on't** do not confess knowledge of it 338 **lose** (The Folio spelling, **loose,** is a normal spelling for "lose," but it may also contain the idea of "let go," "release.") 343 **conceits** fancies, ideas 344 **distaste** be distasteful 345 **act** action, working

Look where he comes! Not poppy nor mandragora°
Nor all the drowsy syrups of the world
Shall ever medicine thee to that sweet sleep
Which thou owedst° yesterday.

OTHELLO: Ha, ha, false to me?

IAGO: Why, how now, General? No more of that.

OTHELLO: Avaunt! Begone! Thou hast set me on the rack.
I swear 'tis better to be much abused
Than but to know 't a little.

IAGO: How now, my lord?

OTHELLO: What sense had I of her stolen hours of lust?
I saw 't not, thought it not, it harmed not me.
I slept the next night well, fed well, was free° and merry;
I found not Cassio's kisses on her lips.
He that is robbed, not wanting° what is stolen,
Let him not know 't and he's not robbed at all.

IAGO: I am sorry to hear this.

OTHELLO: I had been happy if the general camp,
Pioners° and all, had tasted her sweet body,
So° I had nothing known. O, now, forever
Farewell the tranquil mind! Farewell content!
Farewell the plumèd troops and the big° wars
That makes ambition virtue! O, farewell!
Farewell the neighing steed and the shrill trump,
The spirit-stirring drum, th' ear-piercing fife,
The royal banner, and all quality,°
Pride,° pomp, and circumstance° of glorious war!
And O, you mortal engines,° whose rude throats
Th' immortal Jove's dread clamors° counterfeit,
Farewell! Othello's occupation's gone.

IAGO: Is 't possible, my lord?

OTHELLO: Villain, be sure thou prove my love a whore!
Be sure of it. Give me the ocular proof,
Or, by the worth of mine eternal soul,
Thou hadst been better have been born a dog
Than answer my waked wrath!

347 **mandragora** an opiate made of the mandrake root 350 **thou owedst** you did own 357 **free** carefree 359 **wanting** missing 363 **Pioners** diggers of mines, the lowest grade of soldiers 364 **So** provided 366 **big** stately 370 **quality** character, essential nature 371 **Pride** rich display **circumstance** pageantry 372 **mortal engines** i.e., cannon (**Mortal** means "deadly.") 373 **Jove's dread clamors** i.e., thunder

IAGO: Is 't come to this?
OTHELLO: Make me to see 't, or at the least so prove it
That the probation° bear no hinge nor loop
To hang a doubt on, or woe upon thy life!
IAGO: My noble lord—
OTHELLO: If thou dost slander her and torture me,
Never pray more; abandon all remorse;°
On horror's head horrors accumulate;°
Do deeds to make heaven weep, all earth amazed;°
For nothing canst thou to damnation add
Greater than that.
IAGO: O grace! O heaven forgive me!
Are you a man? Have you a soul or sense?
God b' wi' you; take mine office. O wretched fool,°
That lov'st to make thine honesty a vice!°
O monstrous world! Take note, take note, O world,
To be direct and honest is not safe.
I thank you for this profit,° and from hence°
I'll love no friend, sith° love breeds such offense.°
OTHELLO: Nay, stay. Thou shouldst be° honest.
IAGO: I should be wise, for honesty's a fool
And loses that° it works for.
OTHELLO: By the world,
I think my wife be honest and think she is not;
I think that thou art just and think thou art not.
I'll have some proof. My name, that was as fresh
As Dian's° visage, is now begrimed and black
As mine own face. If there be cords, or knives,
Poison, or fire, or suffocating streams,
I'll not endure it. Would I were satisfied!
IAGO: I see, sir, you are eaten up with passion.
I do repent me that I put it to you.
You would be satisfied?
OTHELLO: Would? Nay, and I will.
IAGO: And may; but how? How satisfied, my lord?

382 **probation** proof 386 **remorse** pity, penitent hope for salvation 387 **horrors accumulate** add still more horrors 388 **amazed** confounded with horror 393 **O wretched fool** Iago addresses himself as a fool for having carried honesty too far 394 **vice** failing, something overdone 397 **profit** profitable instruction **hence** henceforth 398 **sith** since **offense** i.e., harm to the one who offers help and friendship 399 **Thou shouldst be** it appears that you are (But Iago replies in the sense of "ought to be.") 401 **that** what 405 **Dian** Diana, goddess of the moon and of chastity

Would you, the supervisor,[o] grossly gape on?
Behold her topped?
OTHELLO: Death and damnation! O!
IAGO: It were a tedious difficulty, I think,
To bring them to that prospect. Damn them then,[o]
If ever mortal eyes do see them bolster[o]
More[o] than their own.[o] What then? How then?
What shall I say? Where's satisfaction?
It is impossible you should see this,
Were they as prime[o] as goats, as hot as monkeys,
As salt[o] as wolves in pride,[o] and fools as gross
As ignorance made drunk. But yet I say,
If imputation and strong circumstances[o]
Which lead directly to the door of truth
Will give you satisfaction, you might have 't.
OTHELLO: Give me a living reason she's disloyal.
IAGO: I do not like the office.
But sith[o] I am entered in this cause so far,
Pricked[o] to 't by foolish honesty and love,
I will go on. I lay with Cassio lately,
And being troubled with a raging tooth
I could not sleep. There are a kind of men
So loose of soul that in their sleeps will mutter
Their affairs. One of this kind is Cassio.
In sleep I heard him say, "Sweet Desdemona,
Let us be wary, let us hide our loves!"
And then, sir, would he grip and wring my hand,
Cry "O sweet creature!", then kiss me hard,
As if he plucked up kisses by the roots
That grew upon my lips; then laid his leg
Over my thigh, and sighed, and kissed, and then
Cried, "Cursèd fate that gave thee to the Moor!"
OTHELLO: O monstrous! Monstrous!
IAGO: Nay, this was but his dream.
OTHELLO: But this denoted a foregone conclusion.[o]
'Tis a shrewd doubt,[o] though it be but a dream.
IAGO: And this may help to thicken other proofs
That do demonstrate thinly.

413 **supervisor** onlooker 416 **Damn them then** i.e., they would have to be really incorrigible 417 **bolster** go to bed together, share a bolster 418 **More** other **own** own eyes 421 **prime** lustful 422 **salt** wanton, sensual **pride** heat 424 **imputation . . . circumstances** strong circumstantial evidence 429 **sith** since 430 **Pricked** spurred 445 **foregone conclusion** concluded experience or action 446 **shrewd doubt** suspicious circumstance

OTHELLO: I'll tear her all to pieces.
IAGO: Nay, but be wise. Yet we see nothing done;
She may be honest yet. Tell me but this:
Have you not sometimes seen a handkerchief
Spotted with strawberries° in your wife's hand?
OTHELLO: I gave her such a one. 'Twas my first gift.
IAGO: I know not that; but such a handkerchief—
I am sure it was your wife's—did I today
See Cassio wipe his beard with.
OTHELLO: If it be that—
IAGO: If it be that, or any that was hers,
It speaks against her with the other proofs.
OTHELLO: O, that the slave° had forty thousand lives!
One is too poor, too weak for my revenge.
Now do I see 'tis true. Look here, Iago,
All my fond° love thus do I blow to heaven.
'Tis gone.
Arise, black vengeance, from the hollow hell!
Yield up, O love, thy crown and hearted° throne
To tyrannous hate! Swell, bosom, with thy freight,°
For 'tis of aspics'° tongues!
IAGO: Yet be content.°
OTHELLO: O, blood, blood, blood!
IAGO: Patience, I say. Your mind perhaps may change.
OTHELLO: Never, Iago. Like to the Pontic Sea,°
Whose icy current and compulsive course
Ne'er feels retiring ebb, but keeps due on
To the Propontic° and the Hellespont,°
Even so my bloody thoughts with violent pace
Shall ne'er look back, ne'er ebb to humble love,
l that a capable° and wide revenge
Swallow them up. Now, by yond marble° heaven,
[*Kneeling*] In the due reverence of a sacred vow
I here engage my words.
IAGO: Do not rise yet.
[*He kneels.*]° Witness, you ever-burning lights above,

452 **Spotted with strawberries** embroidered with a strawberry pattern 459 **the slave** i.e., Cassio 462 **fond** foolish (but also suggesting "affectionate") 465 **hearted** fixed in the heart 466 **freight** burden 467 **aspics'** venomous serpents' 468 **content** calm 471 **Pontic Sea** Black Sea 474 **Propontic** Sea of Marmara, between the Black Sea and the Aegean **Hellespont** Dardanelles, straits where the Sea of Marmara joins with the Aegean 477 **capable** ample, comprehensive 478 **marble** i.e., gleaming like marble and unrelenting 481 s.d. **He kneels** (In the Quarto text, Iago kneels here after Othello has knelt at line 479.)

You elements that clip° us round about,
Witness that here Iago doth give up
The execution° of his wit,° hands, heart,
To wronged Othello's service. Let him command,
And to obey shall be in me remorse,°
What bloody business ever.°

[They rise.]

OTHELLO: I greet thy love,
Not with vain thanks, but with acceptance bounteous,
And will upon the instant put thee to 't.°
Within these three days let me hear thee say
That Cassio's not alive.

IAGO: My friend is dead;
'Tis done at your request. But let her live.

OTHELLO: Damn her, lewd minx!° O, damn her, damn her!
Come, go with me apart. I will withdraw
To furnish me with some swift means of death
For the fair devil. Now art thou my lieutenant.

IAGO: I am your own forever.

[Exeunt]

SCENE IV [Before the Citadel.]

[Enter DESDEMONA, EMILIA, and CLOWN.]

DESDEMONA: Do you know, sirrah,° where Lieutenant Cassio lies?°

CLOWN: I dare not say he lies anywhere.

DESDEMONA: Why, man?

CLOWN: He's a soldier, and for me to say a soldier lies, 'tis stabbing.

DESDEMONA: Go to. Where lodges he?

CLOWN: To tell you where he lodges is to tell you where I lie.

DESDEMONA: Can anything be made of this?

CLOWN: I know not where he lodges, and for me to devise a lodging and say he lies here, or he lies there, were to lie in mine own throat.°

DESDEMONA: Can you inquire him out, and be edified by report?

CLOWN: I will catechize the world for him; that is, make questions, and by them answer.

DESDEMONA: Seek him, bid him come hither. Tell him I have moved° my lord on his behalf and hope all will be well.

482 **clip** encompass 484 **execution** exercise, action **wit** mind 486 **remorse** pity (for Othello's wrongs) 487 **ever** soever 489 **to 't** to the proof 493 **minx** wanton 1 **sirrah** form of address to an inferior **lies** lodges (but the CLOWN makes the obvious pun) 9 **lie . . . throat** (1) lie egregiously and deliberately (2) use the windpipe to speak a lie 13 **moved** petitioned

CLOWN: To do this is within the compass of man's wit, and therefore I will attempt the doing it.

[Exit CLOWN.*]*

DESDEMONA: Where should I lose that handkerchief, Emilia?
EMILIA: I know not, madam.
DESDEMONA: Believe me, I had rather have lost my purse
Full of crusadoes;° and but my noble Moor
Is true of mind and made of no such baseness
As jealous creatures are, it were enough
To put him to ill thinking.
EMILIA: Is he not jealous?
DESDEMONA: Who, he? I think the sun where he was born
Drew all such humors° from him.
EMILIA: Look where he comes.

[Enter OTHELLO.*]*

DESDEMONA: I will not leave him now till Cassio
Be called to him.—How is 't with you, my lord?
OTHELLO: Well, my good lady. [*Aside.*] O, hardness to dissemble!—
How do you, Desdemona?
DESDEMONA: Well, my good lord.
OTHELLO: Give me your hand. [*She gives her hand.*] This hand is moist, my lady.
DESDEMONA: It yet hath felt no age nor known no sorrow.
OTHELLO: This argues° fruitfulness° and liberal° heart.
Hot, hot, and moist. This hand of yours requires
A sequester° from liberty, fasting and prayer,
Much castigation,° exercise devout;°
For here's a young and sweating devil here
That commonly rebels. 'Tis a good hand,
A frank° one.
DESDEMONA: You may indeed say so,
For 'twas that hand that gave away my heart.
OTHELLO: A liberal hand. The hearts of old gave hands,°
But our new Heraldry is hands, not hearts.°
DESDEMONA: I cannot speak of this. Come now, your promise.

20 **crusadoes** Portuguese gold coins 24 **humors** refers to the four bodily fluids thought to determine temperament 33 **argues** gives evidence of **fruitfulness** generosity, amorousness, and fecundity **liberal** generous and sexually free 35 **sequester** separation, sequestration 36 **castigation** corrective discipline **exercise devout** i.e., prayer, religious meditation, etc. 39 **frank** generous, open (with sexual suggestion) 41 **The hearts . . . hands** i.e., in former times, people would give their hearts when they gave their hands to something 42 **But . . . hearts** i.e., in our decadent times, the joining of hands is no longer a badge to signify the giving of hearts

OTHELLO: What promise, chuck?°
DESDEMONA: I have sent to bid Cassio come speak with you.
OTHELLO: I have a salt and sorry rheum° offends me;
  Lend me thy handkerchief.
DESDEMONA: Here, my lord.

[She offers a handkerchief.]

OTHELLO: That which I gave you.
DESDEMONA: I have it not about me.
OTHELLO: Not?
DESDEMONA: No, faith, my lord.
OTHELLO: That's a fault. That handkerchief
  Did an Egyptian to my mother give.
  She was a charmer,° and could almost read
  The thoughts of people. She told her, while she kept it
  'Twould make her amiable° and subdue my father
  Entirely to her love, but if she lost it
  Or made a gift of it, my father's eye
  Should hold her loathèd and his spirits should hunt
  After new fancies.° She, dying, gave it me,
  And bid me, when my fate would have me wived,
  To give it her.° I did so; and take heed on 't;
  Make it a darling like your precious eye.
  To lose 't or give 't away were such perdition°
  As nothing else could match.
DESDEMONA: Is 't possible?
OTHELLO: 'Tis true. There's magic in the web° of it.
  A sibyl, that had numbered in the world
  The sun to course two hundred compasses,°
  In her prophetic fury° sewed the work;°
  The worms were hallowed that did breed the silk,
  And it was dyed in mummy° which the skillful
  Conserved of° maidens' hearts.
DESDEMONA: I' faith! Is 't true?
OTHELLO: Most veritable. Therefore look to 't well.

44 **chuck** a term of endearment 46 **salt . . . rheum** distressful head cold or watering of the eyes 54 **charmer** sorceress 56 **amiable** desirable 60 **fancies** loves 62 **her** i.e., to my wife 64 **perdition** loss 66 **web** fabric, weaving 68 **compasses** annual circlings (The **sibyl,** or prophetess, was two hundred years old.) 69 **prophetic fury** frenzy of prophetic inspiration **work** embroidered pattern 71 **mummy** medicinal or magical preparation drained from mummified bodies 72 **Conserved of** prepared or preserved out of

DESDEMONA: Then would to God that I had never seen 't!
OTHELLO: Ha? Wherefore?
DESDEMONA: Why do you speak so startingly and rash?°
OTHELLO: Is 't lost? Is 't gone? Speak, is 't out o' the way?°
DESDEMONA: Heaven bless us!
OTHELLO: Say you?
DESDEMONA: It is not lost; but what an if° it were?
OTHELLO: How?
DESDEMONA: I say it is not lost.
OTHELLO: Fetch 't, let me see 't.
DESDEMONA: Why, so I can, sir, but I will not now.
This is a trick to put me from my suit.
Pray you, let Cassio be received again.
OTHELLO: Fetch me the handkerchief! My mind misgives.
DESDEMONA: Come, come,
You'll never meet a more sufficient° man.
OTHELLO: The handkerchief!
DESDEMONA: I pray, talk° me of Cassio.
OTHELLO: The handkerchief!
DESDEMONA: A man that all his time°
Hath founded his good fortunes on your love,
Shared dangers with you—
OTHELLO: The handkerchief!
DESDEMONA: I' faith, you are to blame.
OTHELLO: Zounds!
[Exit OTHELLO.]
EMILIA: Is not this man jealous?
DESDEMONA: I ne'er saw this before.
Sure, there's some wonder in this handkerchief.
I am most unhappy in the loss of it.
EMILIA: 'Tis not a year or two shows us a man.°
They are all but stomachs, and we all but° food;
They eat us hungerly,° and when they are full
They belch us.
[Enter IAGO and CASSIO.]
Look you, Cassio and my husband.
IAGO [*to CASSIO*]: There is no other way; 'tis she must do 't.

76 **startingly and rash** disjointedly and impetuously, excitedly 77 **out o' the way** lost, misplaced 80 **an if** if 88 **sufficient** able, complete 89 **talk** talk to 90 **all his time** throughout his career 100 **'Tis . . . man** i.e., you can't really know a man even in a year or two of experience, or, real men come along seldom 101 **but** nothing but 102 **hungerly** hungrily

And, lo, the happiness!° Go and importune her.
DESDEMONA: How now, good Cassio? What's the news with you?
CASSIO: Madam, my former suit. I do beseech you
That by your virtuous° means I may again
Exist and be a member of his love
Whom I, with all the office° of my heart,
Entirely honor. I would not be delayed.
If my offense be of such mortal° kind
That nor my service past, nor° present sorrows,
Nor purposed merit in futurity
Can ransom me into his love again,
But to know so must be my benefit;°
So shall I clothe me in a forced content,
And shut myself up in° some other course,
To fortune's alms.°
DESDEMONA: Alas, thrice-gentle Cassio,
My advocation° is not now in tune.
My lord is not my lord; nor should I know him,
Were he in favor° as in humor° altered.
So help me every spirit sanctified
As I have spoken for you all my best
And stood within the blank° of his displeasure
For my free speech! You must awhile be patient.
What I can do I will, and more I will
Than for myself I dare. Let that suffice you.
IAGO: Is my lord angry?
EMILIA: He went hence but now,
And certainly in strange unquietness.
IAGO: Can he be angry? I have seen the cannon
When it hath blown his ranks into the air,
And like the devil from his very arm
Puffed his own brother—and is he angry?
Something of moment° then. I will go meet him.
There's matter in 't indeed, if he be angry.
DESDEMONA: I prithee, do so.

105 **the happiness** in happy time, fortunately met 108 **virtuous** efficacious 110 **office** loyal service 112 **mortal** fatal 113 **nor . . . nor** neither . . . nor 116 **But . . . benefit** merely to know that my case is hopeless will have to content me (and will be better than uncertainty) 118 **shut . . . in** confine myself to 119 **To fortune's alms** throwing myself on the mercy of fortune 120 **advocation** advocacy 122 **favor** appearance **humor** mood 125 **within the blank** within point-blank range (The **blank** is the center of the target.) 135 **of moment** of immediate importance, momentous

[Exit Iago.]

Something, sure, of state,°
Either from Venice, or some unhatched practice°
Made demonstrable here in Cyprus to him,
Hath puddled° his clear spirit; and in such cases
Men's natures wrangle with inferior things,
Though great ones are their object. 'Tis even so;
For let our finger ache, and it indues°
Our other, healthful members even to a sense
Of pain. Nay, we must think men are not gods,
Nor of them look for such observancy°
As fits the bridal.° Beshrew me° much, Emilia,
I was, unhandsome° warrior as I am,
Arraigning his unkindness with° my soul;
But now I find I had suborned the witness,°
And he's indicted falsely.

Emilia: Pray heaven it be
State matters, as you think, and no conception
Nor no jealous toy° concerning you.

Desdemona: Alas the day! I never gave him cause.

Emilia: But jealous souls will not be answered so;
They are not ever jealous for the cause,
But jealous for° they're jealous. It is a monster
Begot upon itself,° born on itself.

Desdemona: Heaven keep that monster from Othello's mind!

Emilia: Lady, amen.

Desdemona: I will go seek him. Cassio, walk hereabout.
If I do find him fit, I'll move your suit
And seek to effect it to my uttermost.

Cassio: I humbly thank your ladyship.

[Exit (Desdemona with Emilia).]

[Enter Bianca.]

Bianca: Save° you, friend Cassio!

Cassio: What make° you from home?
How is 't with you, my most fair Bianca?

137 **of state** concerning state affairs 138 **unhatched practice** as yet unexecuted or undiscovered plot 140 **puddled** muddied 143 **indues** brings to the same condition 146 **observancy** attentiveness 147 **bridal** wedding (when a bridegroom is newly attentive to his bride) **Beshrew me** a mild oath 148 **unhandsome** insufficient, unskillful 149 **with** before the bar of 150 **suborned the witness** induced the witness to give false testimony 153 **toy** fancy 157 **for** because 158 **Begot upon itself** generated solely from itself 164 **Save** God save 165 **make** do

I' faith, sweet love, I was coming to your house.
BIANCA: And I was going to your lodging, Cassio.
What, keep a week away? Seven days and nights?
Eightscore-eight° hours? And lovers' absent hours
More tedious than the dial° eightscore times?
O weary reckoning!
CASSIO: Pardon me, Bianca.
I have this while with leaden thoughts been pressed;
But I shall, in a more continuate° time,
Strike off this score° of absence. Sweet Bianca,
[giving her DESDEMONA's handkerchief]
Take me this work out.°
BIANCA: O Cassio, whence came this?
This is some token from a newer friend.°
To the felt absence now I feel a cause.
Is 't come to this? Well, well.
CASSIO: Go to, woman!
Throw your vile guesses in the devil's teeth,
From whence you have them. You are jealous now
That this is from some mistress, some remembrance.
No, by my faith, Bianca.
BIANCA: Why, whose is it?
CASSIO: I know not, neither. I found it in my chamber.
I like the work well. Ere it be demanded°—
As like° enough it will—I would have it copied.
Take it and do 't, and leave me for this time.
BIANCA: Leave you? Wherefore?
CASSIO: I do attend here on the General,
And think it no addition,° nor my wish,
To have him see me womaned.
BIANCA: Why, I pray you?
CASSIO: Not that I love you not.
BIANCA: But that you do not love me.
I pray you, bring° me on the way a little,
And say if I shall see you soon at night.
CASSIO: 'Tis but a little way that I can bring you,
For I attend here; but I'll see you soon.

170 **Eightscore-eight** one hundred sixty-eight, the number of hours in a week 171 **the dial** a complete revolution of the clock 174 **continuate** uninterrupted 175 **Strike . . . score** settle this account 176 **Take . . . out** copy this embroidery for me 177 **friend** mistress 185 **demanded** inquired for 186 **like** likely 190 **addition** i.e., addition to my reputation 195 **bring** accompany

BIANCA: 'Tis very good. I must be circumstanced.°

[Exeunt omnes.]

ACT IV

SCENE I [Before the Citadel.]

[Enter OTHELLO and IAGO.]

IAGO: Will you think so?
OTHELLO: Think so, Iago?
IAGO: What,
To kiss in private?
OTHELLO: An unauthorized kiss!
IAGO: Or to be naked with her friend in bed
An hour or more, not meaning any harm?
OTHELLO: Naked in bed, Iago, and not mean harm?
It is hypocrisy against the devil.
They that mean virtuously and yet do so,
The devil their virtue tempts, and they tempt heaven.
IAGO: If they do nothing, 'tis a venial° slip.
But if I give my wife a handkerchief—
OTHELLO: What then?
IAGO: Why then, 'tis hers, my lord, and being hers,
She may, I think, bestow 't on any man.
OTHELLO: She is protectress of her honor too.
May she give that?
IAGO: Her honor is an essence that's not seen;
They have it° very oft that have it not.
But, for the handkerchief—
OTHELLO: By heaven, I would most gladly have forgot it.
Thou saidst—O, it comes o'er my memory
As doth the raven o'er the infectious house,°
Boding to all—he had my handkerchief.
IAGO: Ay, what of that?
OTHELLO: That's not so good now.
IAGO: What
If I had said I had seen him do you wrong?
Or heard him say—as knaves be such abroad,°

199 **be circumstanced** be governed by circumstance, yield to your conditions 9 **venial** pardonable 17 **They have it** i.e., they enjoy a reputation for it 21 **raven . . . house** allusion to the belief that the raven hovered over a house of sickness or infection, such as one visited by the plague 25 **abroad** around about

Who having, by their own importunate suit,
Or voluntary dotage° of some mistress,
Convincèd or supplied° them, cannot choose
But they must blab—

OTHELLO: Hath he said anything?

IAGO: He hath, my lord; but, be you well assured,
No more than he'll unswear.

OTHELLO: What hath he said?

IAGO: Faith, that he did-I know not what he did.

OTHELLO: What? What?

IAGO: Lie—

OTHELLO: With her?

IAGO: With her, on her; what you will.

OTHELLO: Lie with her? Lie on her? We say "lie on her" when they belie° her. Lie with her? Zounds, that's fulsome.°—Handkerchief—confessions—handkerchief!—To confess and be hanged for his labor—first to be hanged and then to confess.° I tremble at it. Nature would not invest herself in such shadowing passion without some instruction.° It is not words° that shakes me thus. Pish! Noses, ears, and lips.—Is 't possible?—Confess-handkerchief!—O devil!

[Falls in a trance.]

IAGO: Work on,
My medicine, work! Thus credulous fools are caught,
And many worthy and chaste dames even thus,
All guiltless, meet reproach.—What, ho! My lord!
My lord, I say! Othello!

[Enter CASSIO.]

How now, Cassio?

CASSIO: What's the matter?

IAGO: My lord is fall'n into an epilepsy.
This is his second fit. He had one yesterday.

CASSIO: Rub him about the temples.

IAGO: No, forbear.
The lethargy° must have his° quiet course.

27 **voluntary dotage** willing infatuation 28 **Convincèd or supplied** seduced or sexually gratified 36 **belie** slander 37 **fulsome** foul 38–39 **first . . . to confess** Othello reverses the proverbial **confess** and be **hanged;** Cassio is to be given no time to confess before he dies 39–40 **Nature . . . instruction** i.e., without some foundation in fact, nature would not have dressed herself in such an overwhelming passion that comes over me now and fills my mind with images, or in such a lifelike fantasy as Cassio had in his dream of lying with Desdemona 40 **words** mere words 52 **lethargy** coma **his** its

If not, he foams at mouth, and by and by
Breaks out to savage madness. Look, he stirs.
Do you withdraw yourself a little while.
He will recover straight. When he is gone,
I would on great occasion° speak with you.

[Exit CASSIO.]

How is it, General? Have you not hurt your head?

OTHELLO: Dost thou mock me?°

IAGO: I mock you not, by heaven.
Would you would bear your fortune like a man!

OTHELLO: A hornèd man's a monster and a beast.

IAGO: There's many a beast then in a populous city,
And many a civil° monster.

OTHELLO: Did he confess it?

IAGO: Good sir, be a man.
Think every bearded fellow that's but yoked°
May draw with you.° There's millions now alive
That nightly lie in those unproper° beds
Which they dare swear peculiar.° Your case is better.°
O, 'tis the spite of hell, the fiend's arch-mock,
To lip° a wanton in a secure° couch
And to suppose her chaste! No, let me know,
And knowing what I am,° I know what she shall be.°

OTHELLO: O, thou art wise. 'Tis certain.

IAGO: Stand you awhile apart;
Confine yourself but in a patient list.°
Whilst you were here o'erwhelmèd with your grief—
A passion most unsuiting such a man—
Cassio came hither. I shifted him away,°
And laid good 'scuse upon your ecstasy,°
Bade him anon return and here speak with me,
The which he promised. Do but encave° yourself
And mark the fleers,° the gibes, and notable° scorns
That dwell in every region of his face;

57 **on great occasion** on a matter of great importance 59 **mock me** Othello takes Iago's question about hurting his head to be a mocking reference to the cuckold's horns 63 **civil** i.e., dwelling in a city 66 **yoked** (1) married (2) put into the yoke of infamy and cuckoldry 67 **draw with you** pull as you do, like oxen who are yoked, i.e., share your fate as cuckold 68 **unproper** not exclusively their own 69 **peculiar** private, their own **better** i.e., because you know the truth 71 **lip** kiss **secure** free from suspicion 73 **what I am** i.e., a cuckold **she shall be** will happen to her 76 **in . . . list** within the bounds of patience 79 **shifted him away** used a dodge to get rid of him 80 **ecstasy** trance 82 **encave** conceal 83 **fleers** sneers **notable** obvious

For I will make him tell the tale anew,
Where, how, how oft, how long ago, and when
He hath and is again to cope° your wife.
I say, but mark his gesture. Marry, patience!
Or I shall say you're all-in-all in spleen,°
And nothing of a man.

OTHELLO: Dost thou hear, Iago?
I will be found most cunning in my patience;
But—dost thou hear?—most bloody.

IAGO: That's not amiss;
But yet keep time° in all. Will you withdraw?

[OTHELLO stands apart.]

Now will I question Cassio of Bianca,
A huswife° that by selling her desires
Buys herself bread and clothes. It is a creature
That dotes on Cassio—as 'tis the strumpet's plague
To beguile many and be beguiled by one.
He, when he hears of her, cannot restrain°
From the excess of laughter. Here he comes.

[Enter CASSIO.]

As he shall smile, Othello shall go mad;
And his unbookish° jealousy must conster°
Poor Cassio's smiles, gestures, and light behaviors
Quite in the wrong.—How do you now, Lieutenant?

CASSIO: The worser that you give me the addition°
Whose want° even kills me.

IAGO: Ply Desdemona well and you are sure on 't.
[*Speaking lower.*] Now, if this suit lay in Bianca's power,
How quickly should you speed!

CASSIO [*laughing*]: Alas, poor caitiff!°

OTHELLO [*aside*]: Look how he laughs already!

IAGO: I never knew a woman love man so.

CASSIO: Alas, poor rogue! I think, i' faith, she loves me.

OTHELLO: Now he denies it faintly, and laughs it out.

IAGO: Do you hear, Cassio?

OTHELLO: Now he importunes him
To tell it o'er. Go to!° Well said,° well said.

IAGO: She gives it out that you shall marry her.

87 **cope** encounter with, have sex with 89 **all-in-all in spleen** utterly governed by passionate impulses 93 **keep time** keep yourself steady (as in music) 95 **huswife** hussy 99 **restrain** refrain 102 **unbookish** uninstructed **conster** construe 105 **addition** title 106 **Whose want** the lack of which 110 **caitiff** wretch 116 **Go to** an expression of remonstrance **Well said** well done

Do you intend it?

CASSIO: Ha, ha, ha!

OTHELLO: Do you triumph, Roman?° Do you triumph?

CASSIO: I marry her? What? A customer?° Prithee, bear some charity to my wit;° do not think it so unwholesome. Ha, ha, ha!

OTHELLO: So, so, so, so! They laugh that win.°

IAGO: Faith, the cry° goes that you shall marry her.

CASSIO: Prithee, say true.

IAGO: I am a very villain else.°

OTHELLO: Have you scored me?° Well.

CASSIO: This is the monkey's own giving out. She is persuaded I will marry her out of her own love and flattery,° not out of my promise.

OTHELLO: Iago beckons me.° Now he begins the story.

CASSIO: She was here even now; she haunts me in every place. I was the other day talking on the seabank° with certain Venetians, and thither comes the bauble,° and, by this hand,° she falls me thus about my neck—

[He embraces IAGO.]

OTHELLO: Crying, "O dear Cassio!" as it were; his gesture imports it.

CASSIO: So hangs and lolls and weep upon me, so shakes and pulls me. Ha, ha, ha!

OTHELLO: Now he tells how she plucked him to my chamber. O, I see that nose of yours, but not that dog I shall throw it to.°

CASSIO: Well, I must leave her company.

IAGO: Before me,° look where she comes.

[Enter BIANCA (with OTHELLO's handkerchief).]

CASSIO: 'Tis such another fitchew!° Marry, a perfumed one.—What do you mean by this haunting of me?

BIANCA: Let the devil and his dam° haunt you! What did you mean by that same handkerchief you gave me even now? I was a fine fool to take it. I must take out the work? A likely piece of work,° that you should find it in your chamber and know not who left it there! This is some minx's token, and I must take out the work? There; give it your hobbyhorse.° [*She gives him the handkerchief.*] Wheresoever you had it, I'll take out no work on 't.

120 **Roman** the Romans were noted for their **triumphs** or triumphal processions 121 **customer** i.e., prostitute **bear . . . wit** be more charitable to my judgment 123 **They . . . win** i.e., they that laugh last laugh best 124 **cry** rumor 126 **I . . . else** call me a complete rogue if I'm not telling the truth 127 **scored me** scored off me, beaten me, made up my reckoning, branded me 129 **flattery** self-flattery, self-deception 130 **beckons** signals 132 **seabank** seashore 133 **bauble** plaything **by this hand** I make my vow 138 **not . . . to** Othello imagines himself cutting off Cassio's nose and throwing it to a dog 140 **Before me** i.e., on my soul 141 **'Tis . . . fitchew** what a polecat she is! Just like all the others (Polecats were often compared with prostitutes because of their rank smell and presumed lechery.) 143 **dam** mother 145 **A likely . . . work** a fine story 147 **hobbyhorse** harlot

CASSIO: How now, my sweet Bianca? How now? How now?

OTHELLO: By heaven, that should be° my handkerchief!

BIANCA: If you'll come to supper tonight, you may; if you will not, come when you are next prepared for.°

[Exit.]

IAGO: After her, after her.

CASSIO: Faith, I must. She'll rail in the streets else.

IAGO: Will you sup there?

CASSIO: Faith, I intend so.

IAGO: Well, I may chance to see you, for I would very fain speak with you.

CASSIO: Prithee, come. Will you?

IAGO: Go to.° Say no more.

[Exit CASSIO.]

OTHELLO [*advancing*]: How shall I murder him, Iago?

IAGO: Did you perceive how he laughed at his vice?

OTHELLO: O, Iago!

IAGO: And did you see the handkerchief?

OTHELLO: Was that mine?

IAGO: Yours, by this hand. And to see how he prizes the foolish woman your wife! She gave it him, and he hath given it his whore.

OTHELLO: I would have him nine years a-killing. A fine woman! A fair woman! A sweet woman!

IAGO: Nay, you must forget that.

OTHELLO: Ay, let her rot and perish, and be damned tonight, for she shall not live. No, my heart is turned to stone; I strike it, and it hurts my hand. O, the world hath not a sweeter creature! She might lie by an emperor's side and command him tasks.

IAGO: Nay, that's not your way.°

OTHELLO: Hang her! I do but say what she is. So delicate with her needle! An admirable musician! O, she will sing the savageness out of a bear. Of so high and plenteous wit and invention!°

IAGO: She's the worse for all this.

OTHELLO: O, a thousand, a thousand times! And then, of so gentle a condition!°

IAGO: Ay, too gentle.°

OTHELLO: Nay, that's certain. But yet the pity of it, Iago! O, Iago, the pity of it, Iago!

150 **should be** must be 152 **when . . . for** when I'm ready for you (i.e., never) 159 **Go to** an expression of remonstrance 174 **your way** i.e., the way you should think of her 177 **invention** imagination 179–180 **gentle a condition** wellborn and well-bred 181 **gentle** generous, yielding (to other men)

IAGO: If you are so fond° over her iniquity, give her patent° to offend, for if it touch not you it comes near nobody.

OTHELLO: I will chop her into messes.° Cuckold me?

IAGO: O, 'tis foul in her.

OTHELLO: With mine officer?

IAGO: That's fouler.

OTHELLO: Get me some poison, Iago, this night. I'll not expostulate with her, lest her body and beauty unprovide° my mind again. This night, Iago.

IAGO: Do it not with poison. Strangle her in her bed, even the bed she hath contaminated.

OTHELLO: Good, good! The justice of it pleases. Very good.

IAGO: And for Cassio, let me be his undertaker.° You shall hear more by midnight.

OTHELLO: Excellent good. [*A trumpet within.*] What trumpet is that same?

IAGO: I warrant, something from Venice.

[Enter LODOVICO, DESDEMONA, *and attendants.]*

'Tis Lodovico. This comes from the Duke.
See, your wife's with him.

LODOVICO: God save you, worthy General!

OTHELLO: With all my heart,° sir.

LODOVICO [*giving him a letter*]: The Duke and the senators of Venice greet you.

OTHELLO: I kiss the instrument of their pleasures.

[He opens the letter, and reads.]

DESDEMONA: And what's the news, good cousin Lodovico?

IAGO: I am very glad to see you, signor.
Welcome to Cyprus.

LODOVICO: I thank you. How does Lieutenant Cassio?

IAGO: Lives, sir.

DESDEMONA: Cousin, there's fall'n between him and my lord
An unkind° breach; but you shall make all well.

OTHELLO: Are you sure of that?

DESDEMONA: My lord?

OTHELLO [*reads*]: "This fail you not to do, as you will—"

LODOVICO: He did not call; he's busy in the paper.
Is there division twixt my lord and Cassio?

DESDEMONA: A most unhappy one. I would do much
T' atone°, for the love I bear to Cassio.

184 **fond** foolish **patent** license 186 **messes** portions of meat, i.e., bits 191 **unprovide** weaken, render unfit 195 **be his undertaker** undertake to dispatch him 202 **With all my heart** i.e., I thank you most heartily 212 **unkind** unnatural, contrary to their natures; hurtful 219 **atone** reconcile

OTHELLO: Fire and brimstone!
DESDEMONA: My lord?
OTHELLO: Are you wise?
DESDEMONA: What, is he angry?
LODOVICO: Maybe the letter moved him;
For, as I think, they do command him home,
Deputing Cassio in his government.°
DESDEMONA: By my troth, I am glad on 't.°
OTHELLO: Indeed?
DESDEMONA: My lord?
OTHELLO: I am glad to see you mad.°
DESDEMONA: Why, sweet Othello—
OTHELLO [*striking her*]: Devil!
DESDEMONA: I have not deserved this.
LODOVICO: My lord, this would not be believed in Venice,
Though I should swear I saw 't. 'Tis very much.°
Make her amends; she weeps.
OTHELLO: O devil, devil!
If that the earth could teem° with woman's tears,
Each drop she falls would prove a crocodile.°
Out of my sight!
DESDEMONA: I will not stay to offend you. [*Going.*]
LODOVICO: Truly, an obedient lady.
I do beseech your lordship, call her back.
OTHELLO: Mistress!
DESDEMONA [*returning*]: My lord?
OTHELLO: What would you with her, sir?°
LODOVICO: Who, I, my lord?
OTHELLO: Ay, you did wish that I would make her turn.
Sir, she can turn, and turn, and yet go on
And turn again; and she can weep, sir, weep;
And she's obedient,° as you say, obedient,
Very obedient.—Proceed you in your tears.—
Concerning this, sir—O well-painted passion!°—
I am commanded home.—Get you away;
I'll send for you anon.—Sir, I obey the mandate

225 **government** office 226 **on 't** of it 229 **I am . . . mad** i.e., I am glad to see that you are insane enough to rejoice in Cassio's promotion (Othello bitterly plays on Desdemona's **I am glad.**) 233 **very much** too much, outrageous 236 **teem** breed, be impregnated 237 **falls . . . crocodile** crocodiles were supposed to weep hypocritical tears for their victims 243 **What . . . sir** Othello implies that Desdemona is pliant and will do a **turn**, lines 245–247, for any man 248 **obedient** with much the same sexual connotation as **turn** in lines 245–247 250 **passion** i.e., grief

And will return to Venice.—Hence, avaunt!

[Exit DESDEMONA.]

Cassio shall have my place. And, sir, tonight
I do entreat that we may sup together.
You are welcome, sir, to Cyprus.—Goats and monkeys!°

[Exit.]

LODOVICO: Is this the noble Moor whom our full Senate
Call all in all sufficient? Is this the nature
Whom passion could not shake? Whose solid virtue
The shot of accident nor dart of chance
Could neither graze nor pierce?

IAGO: He is much changed.

LODOVICO: Are his wits safe? Is he not light of brain?

IAGO: He's that he is. I may not breathe my censure
What he might be. If what he might he is not,
I would to heaven he were!°

LODOVICO: What, strike his wife?

IAGO: Faith, that was not so well; yet would I knew
That stroke would prove the worst!

LODOVICO: Is it his use?°
Or did the letters work upon his blood°
And new-create his fault?

IAGO: Alas, alas!
It is not honesty in me to speak
What I have seen and known. You shall observe him,
And his own courses will denote° him so
That I may save my speech. Do but go after,
And mark how he continues.

LODOVICO: I am sorry that I am deceived in him.

[Exeunt.]

SCENE II [The Citadel.]

[Enter OTHELLO and EMILIA.]

OTHELLO: You have seen nothing then?

EMILIA: Nor ever heard, nor ever did suspect.

OTHELLO: Yes, you have seen Cassio and she together.

EMILIA: But then I saw no harm, and then I heard

256 **Goats and monkeys** (See Act III, Scene iii, line 421.) 263–265 **I may . . . were** i.e., I dare not venture an opinion as to whether he's of unsound mind, as you suggest, but, if he isn't, then it might be better to wish he were in fact insane, since only that could excuse his wild behavior 267 **use** custom 268 **blood** passions 272 **courses will denote** actions will reveal

Each syllable that breath made up between them.
OTHELLO: What, did they never whisper?
EMILIA: Never, my lord.
OTHELLO: Nor send you out o' the way?
EMILIA: Never.
OTHELLO: To fetch her fan, her gloves, her mask, nor nothing?
EMILIA: Never, my lord.
OTHELLO: That's strange.
EMILIA: I durst, my lord, to wager she is honest,
Lay down my soul at stake.° If you think other,
Remove your thought; it doth abuse your bosom.°
If any wretch have put this in your head,
Let heaven requite it with the serpent's curse!°
For if she be not honest, chaste, and true,
There's no man happy; the purest of their wives
Is foul as slander.
OTHELLO: Bid her come hither. Go.
[Exit EMILIA.]
She says enough; yet she's a simple bawd
That cannot say as much.° This° is a subtle whore,
A closet lock and key° of villainous secrets.
And yet she'll kneel and pray; I have seen her do 't.
[Enter DESDEMONA and EMILIA.]
DESDEMONA: My lord, what is your will?
OTHELLO: Pray you, chuck, come hither.
DESDEMONA: What is your pleasure?
OTHELLO: Let me see your eyes.
Look in my face.
DESDEMONA: What horrible fancy's this?
OTHELLO [*to EMILIA*]: Some of your function,° mistress.
Leave procreants° alone and shut the door;
Cough or cry "hem" if anybody come.
Your mystery, your mystery!° Nay, dispatch.
[Exit EMILIA.]

14 **at stake** as the wager 15 **abuse your bosom** deceive you 17 **the serpent's curse** the curse pronounced by God on the serpent for deceiving Eve, just as some man has done to Othello and Desdemona (See Genesis 3:14.) 21–22 **she's . . . much** i.e., any procuress or go-between who couldn't make up as plausible a story as Emilia's would have to be pretty stupid 22 **This** i.e., Desdemona 23 **closet lock and key** i.e., concealer 29 **Some . . . function** i.e., practice your chosen profession, that of bawd (by guarding the door) 30 **procreants** mating couples 32 **mystery** trade, occupation

DESDEMONA [*kneeling*]: Upon my knees, what doth your speech import?
I understand a fury in your words,
But not the words.
OTHELLO: Why, what art thou?
DESDEMONA: Your wife, my lord, your true
And loyal wife.
OTHELLO: Come, swear it, damn thyself,
Lest, being like one of heaven,° the devils themselves
Should fear to seize thee. Therefore be double damned:
Swear thou art honest.
DESDEMONA: Heaven doth truly know it.
OTHELLO: Heaven truly knows that thou art false as hell.
DESDEMONA: To whom, my lord? With whom? How am I false?
OTHELLO [*weeping*]: Ah, Desdemon! Away, away, away!
DESDEMONA: Alas the heavy day! Why do you weep?
Am I the motive° of these tears, my lord?
If haply you my father do suspect
An instrument of this your calling back,
Lay not your blame on me. If you have lost him,
I have lost him too.
OTHELLO: Had it pleased heaven
To try me with affliction, had they° rained
All kinds of sores and shames on my bare head,
Steeped me in poverty to the very lips,
Given to captivity me and my utmost hopes,
I should have found in some place of my soul
A drop of patience. But, alas, to make me
A fixèd figure for the time of scorn°
To point his° slow and moving finger° at!
Yet could I bear that too, well, very well.
But there where I have garnered° up my heart,
Where either I must live or bear no life,
The fountain° from the which my current runs
Or else dries up—to be discarded thence!
Or keep it as a cistern° for foul toads
To knot° and gender° in! Turn thy complexion there,°

38 **being . . . heaven** looking like an angel 45 **motive** cause 50 **they** i.e., heavenly powers 56 **time of scorn** i.e., scornful world 57 **his** its **slow and moving finger** i.e., hour hand of the clock, moving so slowly it seems hardly to move at all (Othello envisages himself as being eternally pointed at by the scornful world as the numbers on a clock are pointed at by the hour hand.) 59 **garnered** stored 61 **fountain** spring 63 **cistern** cesspool 64 **knot** couple **gender** engender **Turn . . . there** change your color, grow pale, at such a sight

Patience, thou young and rose-lipped cherubin—
Ay, there look grim as hell!°
DESDEMONA: I hope my noble lord esteems me honest.°
OTHELLO: O, ay, as summer flies are in the shambles,°
That quicken° even with blowing.° O thou weed,
Who art so lovely fair and smell'st so sweet
That the sense aches at thee, would thou hadst ne'er been born!
DESDEMONA: Alas, what ignorant° sin have I committed?
OTHELLO: Was this fair paper, this most goodly book,
Made to write "whore" upon? What committed?
Committed? O thou public commoner!°
I should make very forges of my cheeks,
That would to cinders burn up modesty,
Did I but speak thy deeds. What committed?
Heaven stops the nose at it and the moon winks;°
The bawdy° wind, that kisses all it meets,
Is hushed within the hollow mine° of earth
And will not hear 't. What committed?
Impudent strumpet!
DESDEMONA: By heaven, you do me wrong.
OTHELLO: Are not you a strumpet?
DESDEMONA: No, as I am a Christian.
If to preserve this vessel° for my lord
From any other foul unlawful touch
Be not to be a strumpet, I am none.
OTHELLO: What, not a whore?
DESDEMONA: No, as I shall be saved.
OTHELLO: Is 't possible?
DESDEMONA: O, heaven forgive us!
OTHELLO: I cry you mercy,° then.
I took you for that cunning whore of Venice
That married with Othello. [*Calling out.*] You, mistress,
That have the office opposite to Saint Peter
And keep the gate of hell!

65–66 **Patience . . . hell** even Patience, that rose-lipped cherub, will look grim and pale at this spectacle 67 **honest** chaste 68 **shambles** slaughterhouse 69 **quicken** come to life **with blowing** i.e., with the puffing up of something rotten in which maggots are breeding 72 **ignorant sin** sin in ignorance 75 **commoner** prostitute 79 **winks** closes her eyes (The moon symbolizes chastity.) 80 **bawdy** kissing one and all 81 **mine** cave (where the winds were thought to dwell) 86 **vessel** body 92 **cry you mercy** beg your pardon

[Enter EMILIA.*]*

You, you, ay, you!
We have done our course.° There's money for your pains. *[He gives money.]*
I pray you, turn the key and keep our counsel.

[Exit.]

EMILIA: Alas, what does this gentleman conceive?°
How do you, madam? How do you, my good lady?
DESDEMONA: Faith, half asleep.°
EMILIA: Good madam, what's the matter with my lord?
DESDEMONA: With who?
EMILIA: Why, with my lord, madam.
DESDEMONA: Who is thy lord?
EMILIA: He that is yours, sweet lady.
DESDEMONA: I have none. Do not talk to me, Emilia.
I cannot weep, nor answers have I none
But what should go by water.° Prithee, tonight
Lay on my bed my wedding sheets, remember;
And call thy husband hither.
EMILIA: Here's a change indeed!

[Exit.]

DESDEMONA: 'Tis meet I should be used so, very meet.°
How have I been behaved, that he might stick°
The small'st opinion° on my least misuse?°

[Enter IAGO *and* EMILIA.*]*

IAGO: What is your pleasure, madam? How is 't with you?
DESDEMONA: I cannot tell. Those that do teach young babes
Do it with gentle means and easy tasks.
He might have chid me so, for, in good faith,
I am a child to chiding.
IAGO: What is the matter, lady?
EMILIA: Alas, Iago, my lord hath so bewhored her,
Thrown such despite and heavy terms upon her,
That true hearts cannot bear it.
DESDEMONA: Am I that name, Iago?
IAGO: What name, fair lady?

97 **course** business (with an indecent suggestion of "trick," turn at sex) 99 **conceive** suppose, think 101 **half asleep** i.e., dazed 108 **go by water** be expressed by tears 112 **meet** fitting 113 **stick** attach 114 **opinion** censure **least misuse** slightest misconduct

Desdemona: Such as she said my lord did say I was.
Emilia: He called her whore. A beggar in his drink
Could not have laid such terms upon his callet.°
Iago: Why did he so?
Desdemona [*weeping*]: I do not know. I am sure I am none such.
Iago: Do not weep, do not weep. Alas the day!
Emilia: Hath she forsook so many noble matches,
Her father and her country and her friends,
To be called whore? Would it not make one weep?
Desdemona: It is my wretched fortune.
Iago: Beshrew° him for 't!
How comes this trick° upon him?
Desdemona: Nay, heaven doth know.
Emilia: I will be hanged if some eternal° villain,
Some busy and insinuating° rogue,
Some cogging,° cozening° slave, to get some office,
Have not devised this slander. I will be hanged else.
Iago: Fie, there is no such man. It is impossible.
Desdemona: If any such there be, heaven pardon him!
Emilia: A halter° pardon him! And hell gnaw his bones!
Why should he call her whore? Who keeps her company?
What place? What time? What form?° What likelihood?
The Moor's abused by some most villainous knave,
Some base notorious knave, some scurvy fellow.
O heaven, that° such companions° thou'dst unfold,°
And put in every honest hand a whip
To lash the rascals naked through the world
Even from the east to th' west!
Iago: Speak within door.°
Emilia: O, fie upon them! Some such squire° he was
That turned your wit the seamy side without°
And made you to suspect me with the Moor.
Iago: You are a fool. Go to.°
Desdemona: Alas, Iago,
What shall I do to win my lord again?
Good friend, go to him; for, by this light of heaven,

128 **callet** whore 135 **Beshrew** curse 136 **trick** strange behavior, delusion 137 **eternal** inveterate 138 **insinuating** ingratiating, fawning, wheedling 139 **cogging** cheating **cozening** defrauding 143 **halter** hangman's noose 145 **form** appearance, circumstance 148 **that** would that **companions** fellows **unfold** expose 151 **within door** i.e., not so loud 152 **squire** fellow 153 **seamy side without** wrong side out 155 **Go to** i.e., that's enough

I know not how I lost him. Here I kneel. [*She kneels.*]
If e'er my will did trespass 'gainst his love,
Either in discourse° of thought or actual deed,
Or that° mine eyes, mine ears, or any sense
Delighted them° in any other form;
Or that I do not yet,° and ever did,
And ever will—though he do shake me off
To beggarly divorcement—love him dearly,
Comfort forswear° me! Unkindness may do much,
And his unkindness may defeat° my life,
But never taint my love. I cannot say "whore."
It does abhor° me now I speak the word;
To do the act that might the addition° earn
Not the world's mass of vanity° could make me.

[She rises.]

IAGO: I pray you, be content. 'Tis but his humor.°
The business of the state does him offense,
And he does chide with you.

DESDEMONA: If 'twere no other—

IAGO: It is but so, I warrant.

[Trumpets within.]

Hark, how these instruments summon you to supper!
The Messengers of Venice stays the meat.°
Go in, and weep not. All things shall be well.

[Exeunt DESDEMONA and EMILIA.]

[Enter RODERIGO.]

How now, Roderigo?

RODERIGO: I do not find that thou deal'st justly with me.

IAGO: What in the contrary?

RODERIGO: Every day thou daff'st me° with some device,° Iago, and rather, as it seems to me now, keep'st from me all conveniency° than suppliest me with the least advantage° of hope. I will indeed no longer endure it, nor am I yet persuaded to put up° in peace what already I have foolishly suffered.

160 **discourse of thought** process of thinking 161 **that** if (Also in line 163.) 162 **Delighted them** took delight 163 **yet** still 166 **Comfort forswear** may heavenly comfort forsake 167 **defeat** destroy 169 **abhor** (1) fill me with abhorrence (2) make me whorelike 170 **addition** title 171 **vanity** showy splendor 172 **humor** mood 178 **stays the meat** are waiting to dine 183 **thou daff'st me** you put me off **device** excuse, trick 184 **conveniency** advantage, opportunity 185 **advantage** increase 186 **put up** submit to, tolerate

Iago: Will you hear me, Roderigo?

Roderigo: Faith, I have heard too much, for your words and performances are no kin together.

Iago: You charge me most unjustly.

Roderigo: With naught but truth. I have wasted myself out of my means. The jewels you have had from me to deliver° Desdemona would half have corrupted a votarist.° You have told me she hath received them and returned me expectations and comforts of sudden respect° and acquaintance, but I find none.

Iago: Well, go to, very well.

Roderigo: "Very well"! "Go to"! I cannot go to,° man, nor 'tis not very well. By this hand, I think it is scurvy, and begin to find myself fopped° in it.

Iago: Very well.

Roderigo: I tell you 'tis not very well.° I will make myself known to Desdemona. If she will return me my jewels, I will give over my suit and repent my unlawful solicitation; if not, assure yourself I will seek satisfaction° of you.

Iago: You have said now?°

Roderigo: Ay, and said nothing but what I protest intendment° of doing.

Iago: Why, now I see there's mettle in thee, and even from this instant do build on thee a better opinion than ever before. Give me thy hand, Roderigo. Thou hast taken against me a most just exception; but yet I protest I have dealt most directly in thy affair.

Roderigo: It hath not appeared.

Iago: I grant indeed it hath not appeared, and your suspicion is not without wit and judgment. But, Roderigo, if thou hast that in thee indeed which I have greater reason to believe now than ever—I mean purpose, courage, and valor—this night show it. If thou the next night following enjoy not Desdemona, take me from this world with treachery and devise engines° for my life.

Roderigo: Well, what is it? Is it within reason and compass?

Iago: Sir, there is especial commission come from Venice to depute Cassio in Othello's place.

Roderigo: Is that true? Why, then Othello and Desdemona return again to Venice.

193 **deliver** deliver to 194 **votarist** nun 195 **sudden respect** immediate consideration 198 **I cannot go to** (Roderigo changes Iago's **go to**, an expression urging patience, to **I cannot go to**, "I have no opportunity for success in wooing.") 199 **fopped** fooled, duped 201 **not very well** (Roderigo changes Iago's **very well**, "all right, then," to **not very well**, "not at all good.") 203–204 **satisfaction** repayment (The term normally means settling of accounts in a duel.) 205 **You . . . now** have you finished? 206 **intendment** intention 216 **engines for** plots against

IAGO: O, no; he goes into Mauritania and takes away with him the fair Desdemona, unless his abode be lingered here by some accident; wherein none can be so determinate° as the removing of Cassio.

RODERIGO: How do you mean, removing of him?

IAGO: Why, by making him uncapable of Othello's place—knocking out his brains.

RODERIGO: And that you would have me to do?

IAGO: Ay, if you dare do yourself a profit and a right. He sups tonight with a harlotry,° and thither will I go to him. He knows not yet of his honorable fortune. If you will watch his going thence, which I will fashion to fall out° between twelve and one, you may take him at your pleasure. I will be near to second your attempt, and he shall fall between us. Come, stand not amazed at it, but go along with me. I will show you such a necessity in his death that you shall think yourself bound to put it on him. It is now high° suppertime, and the night grows to waste.° About it.

RODERIGO: I will hear further reason for this.

IAGO: And you shall be satisfied.

[Exeunt.]

SCENE III [The Citadel.]

[Enter OTHELLO, LODOVICO, DESDEMONA, EMILIA, and attendants.]

LODOVICO: I do beseech you, sir, trouble yourself no further.

OTHELLO: O, pardon me; 'twill do me good to walk.

LODOVICO: Madam, good night. I humbly thank your ladyship.

DESDEMONA: Your honor is most welcome.

OTHELLO: Will you walk, sir?
O, Desdemona!

DESDEMONA: My lord?

OTHELLO: Get you to bed on th' instant.
I will be returned forthwith. Dismiss your attendant there. Look 't be done.

DESDEMONA: I will, my lord.

[Exit (OTHELLO, with LODOVICO and attendants).]

EMILIA: How goes it now? He looks gentler than he did.

DESDEMONA: He says he will return incontinent,°
And hath commanded me to go to bed,
And bid me to dismiss you.

EMILIA: Dismiss me?

225 **determinate** conclusive 230–231 **harlotry** slut 232–233 **fall out** occur 237 **high** fully **grows to waste** wastes away 12 **incontinent** immediately

DESDEMONA: It was his bidding. Therefore, good Emilia,
Give me my nightly wearing, and adieu.
We must not now displease him.
EMILIA: I would you had never seen him!
DESDEMONA: So would not I. My love doth so approve him
That even his stubbornness,° his checks,° his frowns—
Prithee, unpin me—have grace and favor in them.

[EMILIA prepares DESDEMONA for bed.]

EMILIA: I have laid those sheets you bade me on the bed.
DESDEMONA: All's one.° Good faith, how foolish are our minds!
If I do die before thee, prithee shroud me
In one of these same sheets.
EMILIA: Come, come, you talk.°
DESDEMONA: My mother had a maid called Barbary.
She was in love, and he she loved proved mad°
And did forsake her. She had a song of "Willow."
An old thing 'twas, but it expressed her fortune,
And she died singing it. That song tonight
Will not go from my mind; I have much to do
But to go hang° my head all at one side
And sing it like poor Barbary. Prithee, dispatch.
EMILIA: Shall I go fetch your nightgown?°
DESDEMONA: No, unpin me here.
This Lodovico is a proper° man.
EMILIA: A very handsome man.
DESDEMONA: He speaks well.
EMILIA: I know a lady in Venice would have walked barefoot to Palestine for a touch of his nether lip.
DESDEMONA [*singing*]:
"The poor soul sat sighing by a sycamore tree,
Sing all a green willow;°
Her hand on her bosom, her head on her knee,
Sing willow, willow, willow.
The fresh streams ran by her and murmured her moans;
Sing willow, willow, willow;
Her salt tears fell from her, and softened the stones—"
Lay by these.
[*Singing.*] "Sing willow, willow, willow—"

21 **stubbornness** roughness **checks** rebukes 24 **All's one** all right; it doesn't really matter 26 **talk** i.e., prattle 28 **mad** wild, i.e., faithless 32–33 **I . . . hang** I can scarcely keep myself from hanging 35 **nightgown** dressing gown 37 **proper** handsome 43 **willow** a conventional emblem of disappointed love

Prithee, hie thee.° He'll come anon.°
[*Singing.*] "Sing all a green willow must be my garland.
Let nobody blame him; his scorn I approve—"
Nay, that's not next.—Hark! Who is 't that knocks?

EMILIA: It's the wind.

DESDEMONA [*singing*]:
"I called my love false love; but what said he then?
Sing willow, willow, willow;
If I court more women, you'll couch with more men."
So, get thee gone. Good night. Mine eyes do itch;
Doth that bode weeping?

EMILIA: 'Tis neither here nor there.

DESDEMONA: I have heard it said so. O, these men, these men!
Dost thou in conscience think—tell me, Emilia—
That there be women do abuse° their husbands
In such gross kind?

EMILIA: There be some such, no question.

DESDEMONA: Wouldst thou do such a deed for all the world?

EMILIA: Why, would not you?

DESDEMONA: No, by this heavenly light!

EMILIA: Nor I neither by this heavenly light;
I might do 't as well i' the dark.

DESDEMONA: Wouldst thou do such a deed for all the world?

EMILIA: The world's a huge thing. It is a great price
For a small vice.

DESDEMONA: Good troth, I think thou wouldst not.

EMILIA: By my troth, I think I should, and undo 't when I had done. Marry, I would not do such a thing for a joint ring,° nor for measures of lawn,° nor for gowns, petticoats, nor caps, nor any petty exhibition.° But for all the whole world! Uds° pity, who would not make her husband a cuckold to make him a monarch? I should venture purgatory for 't.

DESDEMONA: Beshrew me if I would do such a wrong
For the whole world.

EMILIA: Why, the wrong is but a wrong i' the world, and having the world for your labor, 'tis a wrong in your own world, and you might quickly make it right.

DESDEMONA: I do not think there is any such woman.

EMILIA: Yes, a dozen, and as many
To th' vantage° as would store° the world they played° for.

51 **hie thee** hurry **anon** right away 63 **abuse** deceive 74 **joint ring** a ring made in separate halves **lawn** fine linen 75 **exhibition** gift 76 **Uds** God's 85 **To th' vantage** in addition, to boot **store** populate **played** (1) gambled (2) sported sexually

But I do think it is their husbands' faults
If wives do fall. Say that they slack their duties°
And pour our treasures into foreign laps,°
Or else break out in peevish jealousies,
Throwing restraint upon us? Or say they strike us,°
Or scant our former having in despite?°
Why, we have galls,° and though we have some grace,
Yet have we some revenge. Let husbands know
Their wives have sense° like them. They see, and smell,
And have their palates both for sweet and sour,
As husbands have. What is it that they do
When they change us for others? Is it sport?°
I think it is. And doth affection° breed it?
I think it doth. Is 't frailty that thus errs?
It is so, too. And have not we affections,
Desires for sport, and frailty, as men have?
Then let them use us well; else let them know,
The ills we do, their ills instruct us so.

DESDEMONA: Good night, good night. God me such uses° send
Not to pick bad from bad, but by bad mend!°

[Exeunt.]

ACT V

SCENE I [A Street in Cyprus.]

[Enter IAGO and RODERIGO.]

IAGO: Here stand behind this bulk.° Straight will he come.
Wear thy good rapier bare,° and put it home.
Quick, quick! Fear nothing. I'll be at thy elbow.
It makes us or it mars us. Think on that,
And fix most firm thy resolution.

RODERIGO: Be near at hand. I may miscarry in 't.

IAGO: Here, at thy hand. Be bold, and take thy stand.

87 **duties** marital duties 88 **pour . . . laps** i.e., are unfaithful, give what is rightfully ours (semen) to other women 90 **Throwing . . . us** i.e., jealously restricting our freedom to see other men 91 **scant . . . despite** reduce our allowance to spite us 92 **have galls** i.e., are capable of resenting injury and insult 94 **sense** physical sense 97 **sport** sexual pastime 98 **affection** passion 104 **uses** habit, practice 105 **Not . . . mend** i.e., not to learn bad conduct from others' badness (as Emilia has suggested women learn from men), but to mend my ways by perceiving what badness is, making spiritual benefit out of evil and adversity 1 **bulk** framework projecting from the front of a shop 2 **bare** unsheathed

[IAGO stands aside. RODERIGO conceals himself.]

RODERIGO: I have no great devotion to the deed;
And yet he hath given me satisfying reasons.
'Tis but a man gone. Forth, my sword! He dies.

[He draws.]

IAGO: I have rubbed this young quat° almost to the sense,°
And he grows angry. Now, whether he kill Cassio
Or Cassio him, or each do kill the other,
Every way makes my gain. Live Roderigo,°
He calls me to a restitution large
Of gold and jewels that I bobbed° from him
As gifts to Desdemona.
It must not be. If Cassio do remain,
He hath a daily beauty in his life
That makes me ugly; and besides, the Moor
May unfold° me to him; there stand I in much peril.
No, he must die. Be 't so. I hear him coming.

[Enter CASSIO.]

RODERIGO [*coming forth*]: I know his gait, 'tis he.—Villain, thou diest!

[He attacks CASSIO.]

CASSIO: That thrust had been mine enemy indeed,
But that my coat° is better than thou know'st.
I will make proof° of thine.

[He draws, and wounds RODERIGO.]

RODERIGO: O, I am slain!

[He falls.]

[IAGO, from behind, wounds CASSIO in the leg, and exits.]

CASSIO: I am maimed forever. Help, ho! Murder! Murder!

[Enter OTHELLO.]

OTHELLO: The voice of Cassio! Iago keeps his word.
RODERIGO: O, villain that I am!
OTHELLO: It is even so.
CASSIO: O, help, ho! Light! A surgeon!
OTHELLO: 'Tis he. O brave Iago, honest and just,
That hast such noble sense of thy friend's wrong!
Thou teachest me. Minion,° your dear lies dead,

11 **quat** pimple, pustule **to the sense** to the quick 14 **Live Roderigo** if Roderigo lives 16 **bobbed** swindled 21 **unfold** expose 25 **coat** possibly a garment of mail under the outer clothing, or simply a tougher coat than Roderigo expected 26 **proof** a test 34 **Minion** hussy (i.e., Desdemona)

And your unblest fate hies.° Strumpet, I come.
Forth of° my heart those charms, thine eyes, are blotted;
Thy bed, lust-stained, shall with lust's blood be spotted.

[Exit OTHELLO.*]*

[Enter LODOVICO *and* GRATIANO.*]*

CASSIO: What ho! No watch? No passage?° Murder! Murder!
GRATIANO: 'Tis some mischance. The voice is very direful.
CASSIO: O, help!
LODOVICO: Hark!
RODERIGO: O wretched villain!
LODOVICO: Two or three groan. 'Tis heavy° night;
These may be counterfeits. Let's think 't unsafe
To come in to° the cry without more help.

[They remain near the entrance.]

RODERIGO: Nobody come? Then shall I bleed to death.

[Enter IAGO *(in his shirtsleeves, with a light).]*

LODOVICO: Hark!
GRATIANO: Here's one comes in his shirt, with light and weapons.
IAGO: Who's there? Whose noise is this that cries on° murder?
LODOVICO: We do not know.
IAGO: Did not you hear a cry?
CASSIO: Here, here! For heaven's sake, help me!
IAGO: What's the matter?

[He moves toward CASSIO.*]*

GRATIANO [*to* LODOVICO]: This is Othello's ancient, as I take it.
LODOVICO [*to* GRATIANO]: The same indeed, a very valiant fellow.
IAGO [*to* CASSIO]: What° are you here that cry so grievously?
CASSIO: Iago? O, I am spoiled,° undone by villains!
Give me some help.
IAGO: O me, Lieutenant! What villains have done this?
CASSIO: I think that one of them is hereabout,
And cannot make° away.
IAGO: O treacherous villains!

[To LODOVICO *and* GRATIANO.*]*

What are you there? Come in, and give some help.

[They advance.]

35 **hies** hastens on 36 **Forth of** from out 38 **passage** people passing by 43 **heavy** thick, dark 45 **come in to** approach 49 **cries on** cries out 54 **What** who (also at lines 60 and 66) 55 **spoiled** ruined, done for 59 **make** get

RODERIGO: O, help me there!

CASSIO: That's one of them.

IAGO: O murderous slave! O villain!

[He stabs RODERIGO.]

RODERIGO: O damned Iago! O inhuman dog!

IAGO: Kill men i' the dark?—Where be these bloody thieves?—
How silent is this town!—Ho! Murder, murder!—
[To LODOVICO and GRATIANO.] What may you be? Are you of good or evil?

LODOVICO: As you shall prove us, praise° us.

IAGO: Signor Lodovico?

LODOVICO: He, sir.

IAGO: I cry you mercy.° Here's Cassio hurt by villains.

GRATIANO: Cassio?

IAGO: How is 't, brother?

CASSIO: My leg is cut in two.

IAGO: Marry, heaven forbid!
Light, gentlemen! I'll bind it with my shirt.

[He hands them the light, and tends to CASSIO's wound.]

[Enter BIANCA.]

BIANCA: What is the matter, ho? Who is 't that cried?

IAGO: Who is 't that cried?

BIANCA: O my dear Cassio!
My sweet Cassio! O Cassio, Cassio, Cassio!

IAGO: O notable strumpet! Cassio, may you suspect
Who they should be that have thus mangled you?

CASSIO: No.

GRATIANO: I am sorry to find you thus. I have been to seek you.

IAGO: Lend me a garter. [*He applies a tourniquet.*] So.—O, for a chair,°
To bear him easily hence!

BIANCA: Alas, he faints! O Cassio, Cassio, Cassio!

IAGO: Gentlemen all, I do suspect this trash
To be a party in this injury.—
Patience awhile, good Cassio.—Come, come;
Lend me a light. [*He shines the light on RODERIGO.*]
Know we this face or no?
Alas, my friend and my dear countryman

68 **praise** appraise 71 **I cry you mercy** I beg your pardon 84 **chair** litter

Roderigo! No.—Yes, sure.—O heaven! Roderigo!
GRATIANO: What, of Venice?
IAGO: Even he, sir. Did you know him?
GRATIANO: Know him? Ay.
IAGO: Signor Gratiano? I cry your gentle° pardon.
These bloody accidents° must excuse my manners
That so neglected you.
GRATIANO: I am glad to see you.
IAGO: How do you, Cassio? O, a chair, a chair!
GRATIANO: Roderigo!
IAGO: He, he, 'tis he. [*A litter is brought in.*] O, that's well said;° the chair.
Some good man bear him carefully from hence;
I'll fetch the General's surgeon. [*To* BIANCA.] For you, mistress,
Save you your labor.°—He that lies slain here, Cassio,
Was my dear friend. What malice° was between you?
CASSIO: None in the world, nor do I know the man.
IAGO [*to* BIANCA]: What, look you pale?—O, bear him out o' th' air.°
[*CASSIO and RODERIGO are borne off.*]
Stay you,° good gentlemen.—Look you pale, mistress?—
Do you perceive the gastness° of her eye?—
Nay, if you stare,° we shall hear more anon.—
Behold her well; I pray you, look upon her.
Do you see, gentlemen? Nay, guiltiness
Will speak, though tongues were out of use.
[*Enter EMILIA.*]
EMILIA: 'Las, what's the matter? What's the matter, husband?
IAGO: Cassio hath here been set on in the dark
By Roderigo and fellows that are scaped.
He's almost slain, and Roderigo dead.
EMILIA: Alas, good gentleman! Alas, good Cassio!
IAGO: This is the fruits of whoring. Prithee, Emilia,
Go know° of Cassio where he supped tonight.
[*To* BIANCA.] What, do you shake at that?
BIANCA: He supped at my house, but I therefore shake not.
IAGO: O, did he so? I charge you go with me.
EMILIA: O, fie upon thee, strumpet!

97 **gentle** noble 98 **accidents** sudden events 102 **well said** well done 105 **Save . . . labor** i.e., never you mind tending Cassio 106 **malice** enmity 108 **bear . . . air** fresh air was thought to be dangerous for a wound 109 **Stay you** Lodovico and Gratiano are evidently about to leave 110 **gastness** terror 111 **stare** Iago pretends to interpret Bianca's wild looks as an involuntary confession of guilt 121 **know** learn

BIANCA: I am no strumpet, but of life as honest°
As you that thus abuse me.
EMILIA: As I? Faugh! Fie upon thee!
IAGO: Kind gentlemen, let's go see poor Cassio dressed.°—
Come, mistress, you must tell's another tale.
Emilia, run you to the citadel
And tell my lord and lady what hath happed.—
Will you go on afore? [*Aside.*] This is the night
That either makes me or fordoes° me quite.

[Exeunt.]

SCENE II [A Bedchamber in the Citadel.]

[Enter OTHELLO (with a light), and DESDEMONA in her bed.]°

OTHELLO: It is the cause,° it is the cause, my soul.
Let me not name it to you, you chaste stars!
It is the cause. Yet I'll not shed her blood,
Nor scar that whiter skin of hers than snow,
And smooth as monumental° alabaster.
Yet she must die, else she'll betray more men.
Put out the light, and then put out the light.°
If I quench thee, thou flaming minister,°
I can again thy former light restore,
Should I repent me;° but once put out thy light,
Thou cunning'st pattern° of excelling nature,
I know not where is that Promethean heat°
That can thy light relume.° When I have plucked thy rose,
I cannot give it vital growth again;
It needs must wither. I'll smell thee on the tree.

[He kisses her.]

O balmy breath, that dost almost persuade
Justice to break her sword! One more, one more.
Be thus when thou art dead, and I will kill thee,
And love thee after. One more, and that's the last.

[He kisses her.]

126 **honest** chaste 129 **Cassio dressed** Cassio's wounds dressed 134 **fordoes** undoes, ruins s.d. **in her bed** (Either the curtains are drawn back to reveal the bed in a recessed area backstage, or the bed is "thrust out" onstage as the scene begins.) 1 **cause** i.e., cause of justice, the offense itself, which Othello must correct as an agent of justice 5 **monumental** i.e., used in making tombs and funeral monuments 7 **the light . . . light** the torch or lamp . . . Desdemona's life 8 **flaming minister** torch or lamp that serves me 10 **repent me** change my mind 11 **Thou . . . pattern** you skillfully wrought perfect example 12 **Promethean heat** divine fire (Alluding to the theft of fire from heaven by Prometheus.) 13 **relume** rekindle

So sweet was ne'er so fatal. I must weep,
But they are cruel° tears. This sorrow's heavenly;
It strikes where it doth love.° She wakes.
DESDEMONA: Who's there? Othello?
OTHELLO: Ay, Desdemona.
DESDEMONA: Will you come to bed, my lord?
OTHELLO: Have you prayed tonight, Desdemon?
DESDEMONA: Ay, my lord.
OTHELLO: If you bethink yourself of any crime°
Unreconciled as yet to heaven and grace,
Solicit° for it straight.°
DESDEMONA: Alack, my lord, what may you mean by that?
OTHELLO: Well, do it, and be brief. I will walk by.
I would not kill thy unpreparèd spirit.
No, heaven forfend!° I would not kill thy soul.
DESDEMONA: Talk you of killing?
OTHELLO: Ay, I do.
DESDEMONA: Then heaven
Have mercy on me!
OTHELLO: Amen, with all my heart!
DESDEMONA: If you say so, I hope you will not kill me.
OTHELLO: Humh!
DESDEMONA: And yet I fear you; for you're fatal then
When your eyes roll so. Why I should fear I know not,
Since guiltiness I know not; but yet I feel I fear.
OTHELLO: Think on thy sins.
DESDEMONA: They are loves I bear to you.°
OTHELLO: Ay, and for that thou diest.
DESDEMONA: That death's unnatural that kills for loving.
Alas, why gnaw you so your nether lip?
Some bloody passion shakes your very frame.
These are portents; but yet I hope, I hope,
They do not point on° me.
OTHELLO: Peace, and be still!
DESDEMONA: I will so. What's the matter?
OTHELLO: That handkerchief which I so loved and gave thee
Thou gav'st to Cassio.

21 **cruel** unrelenting 22 **It . . . love** compare Hebrews 12:6: "For whom the Lord loveth he chasteneth" 28 **crime** sin 30 **Solicit** petition, pray **straight** immediately 34 **forfend** forbid
42 **They are . . . you** i.e., if I sinned, it was in loving you more than my father or more than God
48 **point on** point at, predict what is to happen to

DESDEMONA: No, by my life and soul!
Send for the man and ask him.
OTHELLO: Sweet soul, take heed, take heed of perjury.
Thou art on thy deathbed.
DESDEMONA: Ay, but not yet to die.
OTHELLO: Yes, presently.°
Therefore confess thee freely of thy sin;
For to deny each article with oath
Cannot remove nor choke the strong conception°
That I do groan withal.° Thou art to die.
DESDEMONA: Then Lord have mercy on me!
OTHELLO: I say, amen.
DESDEMONA: And have you mercy too! I never did
Offend° you in my life; never loved Cassio
But with such general warranty° of heaven
As I might love. I never gave him token.
OTHELLO: By heaven, I saw my handkerchief in 's hand.
O perjured woman! Thou dost stone° my heart,
And makes me call what I intend to do
A murder, which I thought a sacrifice.
I saw the handkerchief.
DESDEMONA: He found it, then.
I never gave it him. Send for him hither;
Let him confess a truth.
OTHELLO: He hath confessed.
DESDEMONA: What, my lord?
OTHELLO: That he hath used thee.
DESDEMONA: How? Unlawfully?
OTHELLO: Ay.
DESDEMONA: He will not say so.
OTHELLO: No, his mouth is stopped;
Honest Iago hath ta'en order° for 't.
DESDEMONA: O, my fear interprets. What, is he dead?
OTHELLO: Had all his hairs been lives, my great revenge
Had stomach for them all.
DESDEMONA: Alas, he is betrayed and I undone!
[She weeps.]
OTHELLO: Out, strumpet! Weep'st thou for him to my face?

56 **presently** immediately 59 **conception** (1) belief in your guilt (2) plan in my mind 60 **groan withal** (1) groan at in sorrow (2) as in giving birth 63 **Offend** wrong 64 **warranty** sanction 67 **stone** turn to stone, harden 76 **ta'en order** taken measures

DESDEMONA: O, banish me, my lord, but kill me not!
OTHELLO: Down, strumpet!
DESDEMONA: Kill me tomorrow; let me live tonight!
OTHELLO: Nay, if you strive—
DESDEMONA: But half an hour!
OTHELLO: Being done,° there is no pause.
DESDEMONA: But while I say one prayer!
OTHELLO: It is too late.

[Smothers her.]

EMILIA *[at the door]*: My lord, my lord! What, ho! My lord, my lord!
OTHELLO: What noise is this? Not dead? Not yet quite dead?
I that am cruel am yet merciful;
I would not have thee linger in thy pain.

[He dispatches her.]

So, so.
EMILIA *[within]*: What, ho! My lord, my lord!
OTHELLO: Who's there?
EMILIA *[within]*: O, good my lord, I would speak a word with you!
OTHELLO: Yes, 'tis Emilia.—By and by.—She's dead.
'Tis like° she comes to speak of Cassio's death.—
The noise was here.° Ha! No more moving?
Still as the grave. Shall she come in? Were 't good?—
I think she stirs again. No. What's best to do?
If she come in, she'll sure speak to my wife.
My wife! My wife! What wife? I have no wife.
O, insupportable! O heavy hour!
Methinks it should be now a huge eclipse
Of sun and moon, and that th' affrighted globe
Should yawn° at alteration.°
EMILIA *[within]*: I do beseech you
That I may speak with you, O, good my lord!
OTHELLO: I had forgot thee. O, come in, Emilia.—
Soft,° by and by. Let me the curtains draw.—

[He closes the bed-curtains and opens the door.]

Where art thou?

87 **Being done** i.e., since justice has begun its relentless course 95 **like** likely that 96 **here** the Folio's **high** is possible, suggesting that the commotion of the attack on Cassio was loud 104 **yawn** gape in amazement, i.e., move in an earthquake (According to Pliny, earthquakes often happen during eclipses.) **at alteration** at these cataclysmic events in nature, well suited to express the horror of Desdemona's death 107 **Soft** wait a minute

[Enter EMILIA.]

What's the matter with thee now?
EMILIA: O, my good lord, yonder's foul murders done!
OTHELLO: What, now?
EMILIA: But now, my lord.
OTHELLO: It is the very error° of the moon;
She comes more nearer earth than she was wont,
And makes men mad.
EMILIA: Cassio, my lord, hath killed a young Venetian
Called Roderigo.
OTHELLO: Roderigo killed?
And Cassio killed?
EMILIA: No, Cassio is not killed.
OTHELLO: Not Cassio killed? Then murder's out of tune,
And sweet revenge grows harsh.
DESDEMONA: O, falsely, falsely murdered!
EMILIA: O Lord, what cry is that?
OTHELLO: That? What?
EMILIA: Out° and alas, that was my lady's voice.

[She opens the bed-curtains.]

Help, help, ho, help! O lady, speak again!
Sweet Desdemona! O sweet mistress, speak!
DESDEMONA: A guiltless death I die.
EMILIA: O, who hath done this deed?
DESDEMONA: Nobody; I myself. Farewell.
Commend me to my kind lord. O, farewell!

[She dies.]

OTHELLO: Why, how should she be murdered?
EMILIA: Alas, who knows?
OTHELLO: You heard her say herself it was not I.
EMILIA: She said so. I must needs report the truth.
OTHELLO: She's like a liar gone to burning hell!
'Twas I that killed her.
EMILIA: O, the more angel she,
And you the blacker devil!
OTHELLO: She turned to folly,° and she was a whore.
EMILIA: Thou dost belie° her, and thou art a devil.

112 **error** aberration, irregularity 123 **Out** a cry of dismay, intensifying **alas** 136 **folly** i.e., wantonness, fleshly sin 137 **belie** slander

OTHELLO: She was false as water.
EMILIA: Thou art rash as fire to say
That she was false. O, she was heavenly true!
OTHELLO: Cassio did top her. Ask thy husband else.°
O, I were damned beneath all depth in hell
But that I did proceed upon just grounds
To this extremity. Thy husband knew it all.
EMILIA: My husband?
OTHELLO: Thy husband.
EMILIA: That she was false to wedlock?
OTHELLO: Ay, with Cassio. Nay, had she been true,
If heaven would make me such another world
Of one entire and perfect chrysolite,°
I'd not have sold her for it.
EMILIA: My husband?
OTHELLO: Ay, 'twas he that told me on her first.
An honest man he is, and hates the slime
That sticks on filthy deeds.
EMILIA: My husband?
OTHELLO: What needs this iterance,° woman? I say thy husband.
EMILIA: O mistress, villainy hath made mocks with° love!
My husband say she was false?
OTHELLO: He, woman;
I say thy husband. Dost understand the word?
My friend, thy husband, honest, honest Iago.
EMILIA: If he say so, may his pernicious soul
Rot half a grain a day! He lies to th' heart.
She was too fond of her most filthy bargain.
OTHELLO: Ha?

[He draws.]

EMILIA: Do thy worst!
This deed of thine is no more worthy heaven
Than thou wast worthy her.
OTHELLO: Peace, you were best.°
EMILIA: Thou hast not half that power to do me harm
As I have to be hurt.° O gull!° O dolt!
As ignorant as dirt! Thou hast done a deed—
I care not for thy sword; I'll make thee known,

141 **else** i.e., if you don't believe me 150 **chrysolite** precious topaz 157 **iterance** iteration, repetition 158 **made mocks with** derided, made sport of 168 **you were best** it would be best for you 170 **to be hurt** i.e., to endure hurt **gull** dupe

Though I lost twenty lives.—Help! Help, ho, help!
The Moor hath killed my mistress! Murder, murder!

[Enter MONTANO, GRATIANO, *and* IAGO.*]*

MONTANO: What is the matter? How now, General?
EMILIA: O, are you come, Iago? You have done well,
That men must lay their murders on your neck.
GRATIANO: What is the matter?
EMILIA [*to* IAGO]: Disprove this villain, if thou be'st a man.
He says thou toldst him that his wife was false.
I know thou didst not; thou'rt not such a villain.
Speak, for my heart is full.
IAGO: I told him what I thought, and told no more
Than what he found himself was apt° and true.
EMILIA: But did you ever tell him she was false?
IAGO: I did.
EMILIA: You told a lie, an odious, damnèd lie!
Upon my soul, a lie, a wicked lie.
She false with Cassio? Did you say with Cassio?
IAGO: With Cassio, mistress. Go to, charm° your tongue.
EMILIA: I will not charm my tongue; I am bound to speak.
My mistress here lies murdered in her bed—
ALL: O heavens forfend!
EMILIA: And your reports have set the murder on.
OTHELLO: Nay, stare not, masters. It is true indeed.
GRATIANO: 'Tis a strange truth.
MONTANO: O monstrous act!
EMILIA: Villainy, villainy, villainy!
I think upon 't—I think I smell 't! O villainy!
I thought so then° —I'll kill myself for grief—
O villainy, villainy!
IAGO: What, are you mad? I charge you, get you home.
EMILIA: Good gentlemen, let me have leave to speak.
'Tis proper I obey him, but not now.
Perchance, Iago, I will ne'er go home.
OTHELLO: O! O! O!

*[*OTHELLO *falls on the bed.°]*

EMILIA: Nay, lay thee down and roar,
For thou hast killed the sweetest innocent

184 **apt** plausible 190 **charm** keep silent (as though by a magic spell) 199 **then** (Perhaps at Act III, Scene iii, lines 331–332 and Act IV, Scene ii, lines 137–154.) 204 s.d. **Othello . . . bed** (This direction is from the Quarto, as also **He kisses her** at line 19 and **She dies** at line 129.)

That e'er did lift up eye.°
OTHELLO [*rising*]: O, she was foul!
I scarce did know you, uncle. There lies your niece,
Whose breath indeed these hands have newly stopped.
I know this act shows° horrible and grim.
GRATIANO: Poor Desdemon! I am glad thy father's dead.
Thy match was mortal to him, and pure grief
Shore his old thread° in twain. Did he live now,
This sight would make him do a desperate turn,°
Yea, curse his better angel from his side,
And fall to reprobance.°
OTHELLO: 'Tis pitiful. But yet Iago knows
That she with Cassio hath the act of shame
A thousand times committed. Cassio confessed it;
And she did gratify° his amorous works
With that recognizance° and pledge of love
Which I first gave her. I saw it in his hand;
It was a handkerchief, an antique token
My father gave my mother.
EMILIA: O God! O heavenly God!
IAGO: Zounds, hold your peace.
EMILIA: 'Twill out, 'twill out! I peace?
No, I will speak as liberal as the north.°
Let heaven and men and devils, let them all,
All, all, cry shame against me, yet I'll speak.
IAGO: Be wise, and get you home.
EMILIA: I will not.
[IAGO threatens EMILIA.]
GRATIANO: Fie
Your sword upon a woman?
EMILIA: O thou dull Moor! That handkerchief thou speak'st of
I found by fortune and did give my husband;
For often, with a solemn earnestness,
More than indeed belonged° to such a trifle,
He begged of me to steal 't.
IAGO: Villainous whore!

207 **lift up eye** i.e., lift her eyes to heaven 210 **shows** looks 213 **Shore . . . thread** sheared the thread of his old age (as Atropos, one of the three Fates, was thought to do) 214 **turn** deed 216 **reprobance** damnation, i.e., suicide 220 **gratify** reward 221 **recognizance** token 228 **liberal as the north** freely as the north wind (blows) 235 **belonged** was appropriate

EMILIA: She give it Cassio? No, alas! I found it,
And I did give't my husband.
IAGO: Filth, thou liest!
EMILIA: By heaven, I do not, I do not, gentlemen.
O murderous coxcomb!° What should such a fool
Do with so good a wife?
OTHELLO: Are there no stones° in heaven
But what serves for the thunder?—Precious° villain!

[He runs at IAGO; MONTANO disarms OTHELLO. IAGO, from behind, stabs EMILIA.°]

GRATIANO: The woman falls! Sure he hath killed his wife.
EMILIA: Ay, ay. O, lay me by my mistress' side.

[Exit IAGO.]

GRATIANO: He's gone, but his wife's killed.
MONTANO: 'Tis a notorious villain. Take you this weapon,
Which I have here recovered from the Moor.
Come, guard the door without. Let him not pass,
But kill him rather. I'll after that same villain,
For 'tis a damnèd slave.

[Exit (with all but OTHELLO and EMILIA, who has been laid by DESDEMONA's side).]

OTHELLO: I am not valiant neither,
But every puny whipster° gets my sword.
But why should honor° outlive honesty?°
Let it go all.
EMILIA: What did thy song bode, lady?
Hark, canst thou hear me? I will play the swan,
And die in music. [*She sings.*] "Willow, willow, willow."
Moor, she was chaste. She loved thee, cruel Moor.
So come my soul to bliss as I speak true.
So speaking as I think, alas, I die.

[She dies.]

OTHELLO: I have another weapon in this chamber;
It was a sword of Spain, the ice-brook's temper°—
O, here it is. [*He finds a sword.*] Uncle, I must come forth.

240 **coxcomb** fool (Addressed to Othello.) 242 **stones** bolts, such as those used for thunderbolts 243 **Precious** i.e., arrant, utter. s.d. **He . . . Emilia** (The Quarto text reads, "The Moor runs at Iago. Iago kills his wife." The Quarto also specifies the exit of Iago at line 245 and the death of Emilia at line 260.) 253 **whipster** contemptible fellow (one who is always ready to whip out his sword) 254 **honor** i.e., the bravery for which one enjoys a soldier's reputation **honesty** true integrity 262 **the ice-brook's temper** tempered in ice-cold water

GRATIANO [*within*]: If thou attempt it, it will cost thee dear.
Thou hast no weapon, and perforce must suffer.
OTHELLO: Look in upon me then and speak with me,
Or, naked° as I am, I will assault thee.

[Enter GRATIANO.]

GRATIANO: What is the matter?
OTHELLO: Behold, I have a weapon;
A better never did itself sustain
Upon a soldier's thigh. I have seen the day
That, with this little arm and this good sword,
I have made my way through more impediments
Than twenty times your stop.° But O, vain boast!
Who can control his fate? 'Tis not so now.
Be not afraid, though you do see me weaponed;
Here is my journey's end, here is my butt°
And very seamark° of my utmost sail.

[GRATIANO steps back.]

Do you go back dismayed? 'Tis a lost° fear;
Man but a rush° against Othello's breast
And he retires. Where should Othello go?

[He turns to DESDEMONA.]

Now, how dost thou look now? O ill-starred wench!
Pale as thy smock! When we shall meet at compt,°
This look of thine will hurl my soul from heaven,
And fiends will snatch at it. Cold, cold, my girl?
Even like thy chastity. O cursèd, cursèd slave!°
Whip me, ye devils,
From the possession of this heavenly sight!
Blow me about in winds! Roast me in sulfur!
Wash me in steep-down gulfs of liquid fire!
O Desdemon! Dead, Desdemon! Dead! O! O!

[Enter LODOVICO, CASSIO (carried in a litter°), MONTANO, and IAGO (prisoner), with OFFICERS.]

LODOVICO: Where is this rash and most unfortunate man?
OTHELLO: That's he that was Othello. Here I am.
LODOVICO: Where is that viper? Bring the villain forth.

267 **naked** unarmed 273 **stop** power (to stop) 276 **butt** goal, limit (An archery term.) 277 **seamark** beacon (marking his destination or limit) 278 **lost** wasted, unneeded 279 **Man . . . rush** wield no more than a reed 382 **compt** account, judgment day 285 **slave** i.e., Othello himself 290 s.d. **in a litter** (The Quarto specifies that Cassio is "in a chair.")

[IAGO is led forward.]

OTHELLO: I look down towards his feet;° but that's a fable.
If that thou be'st a devil, I cannot kill thee.

[He wounds IAGO.]

LODOVICO: Wrench his sword from him.

[OTHELLO is disarmed.]

IAGO: I bleed, sir, but not killed.

OTHELLO: I am not sorry neither. I'd have thee live,
For in my sense° 'tis happiness to die.

LODOVICO: O thou Othello, that was once so good,
Fall'n in the practice° of a cursèd slave,°
What shall be said to thee?

OTHELLO: Why, anything.
An honorable murderer, if you will,
For naught I did in hate, but all in honor.

LODOVICO: This wretch hath part confessed his villainy.
Did you and he consent° in Cassio's death?

OTHELLO: Ay.

CASSIO: Dear General, I never gave you cause.

OTHELLO: I do believe it, and I ask your pardon.
Will you, I pray, demand that demi-devil
Why he hath thus ensnared my soul and body?

IAGO: Demand me nothing. What you know, you know.
From this time forth I never will speak word.

LODOVICO: What, not to pray?

GRATIANO: Torments° will ope your lips.

OTHELLO: Well, thou dost best.

LODOVICO: Sir, you shall understand what hath befall'n,
Which, as I think, you know not. Here is a letter
Found in the pocket of the slain Roderigo;
And here another. [*He produces letters.*] The one of them imports
The death of Cassio, to be undertook
By Roderigo.

OTHELLO: O villain!

CASSIO: Most heathenish and most gross!°

LODOVICO [*showing another paper*]: Now here's another discontented° paper

294 **towards his feet** i.e., to see if they are cloven, as the devil's are fabled to be 298 **in my sense** to one who feels as I do 300 **in the practice** through the plotting, into the snare **slave** villain 305 **consent** agree 314 **Torments** torture 322 **gross** monstrous

Found in his pocket too. And this, it seems,
Roderigo meant t' have sent this damnèd villain;
But that belike° Iago in the interim
Came in and satisfied him.°

OTHELLO: O thou pernicious caitiff!—
How came you, Cassio, by that handkerchief
That was my wife's?

CASSIO: I found it in my chamber;
And he himself confessed but even now
That there he dropped it for a special purpose
Which wrought to his desire.°

OTHELLO: O fool, fool, fool!

CASSIO: There is besides in Roderigo's letter
How he upbraids Iago, that he made him
Brave° me upon the watch, whereon it came°
That I was cast;° and even but now he spake,
After long seeming dead, Iago hurt him,
Iago set him on.

LODOVICO [*to OTHELLO*]: You must forsake this room and go with us.
Your power and your command is taken off,°
And Cassio rules in Cyprus. For this slave,
If there be any cunning cruelty
That can torment him much and hold him long,°
It shall be his. You shall close prisoner rest°
Till that the nature of your fault be known
To the Venetian state.—Come, bring away.

OTHELLO: Soft you;° a word or two before you go.
I have done the state some service, and they know 't.
No more of that. I pray you, in your letters,
When you shall these unlucky° deeds relate,
Speak of me as I am; nothing extenuate,
Nor set down aught in malice. Then must you speak
Of one that loved not wisely but too well;
Of one not easily jealous but, being wrought,°
Perplexed° in the extreme; of one whose hand,

326 **belike** most likely 327 **Came . . . him** interposed and gave him satisfactory explanation 333 **wrought . . . desire** worked out as he wished, fitted in with his plan 336 **Brave** defy **whereon it came** whereof it came about 337 **cast** dismissed 341 **taken off** taken away 344 **hold him long** keep him alive a long time (during his torture) 345 **rest** remain 348 **Soft you** one moment 351 **unlucky** unfortunate 355 **wrought** worked upon, worked into a frenzy 356 **Perplexed** distraught

Like the base Indian,° threw a pearl away
Richer than all his tribe; of one whose subdued° eyes,
Albeit unusèd to the melting mood,
Drops tears as fast as the Arabian trees
Their medicinable gum.° Set you down this;
And say besides that in Aleppo once,
Where a malignant and a turbaned Turk
Beat a Venetian and traduced the state,
I took by th' throat the circumcisèd dog
And smote him, thus.

[He stabs himself.°]

LODOVICO: O bloody period!°
GRATIANO: All that is spoke is marred.
OTHELLO: I kissed thee ere I killed thee. No way but this,
Killing myself, to die upon a kiss.

[He kisses DESDEMONA and dies.]

CASSIO: This did I fear, but thought he had no weapon;
For he was great of heart.
LODOVICO [*to IAGO*]: O Spartan dog,°
More fell° than anguish, hunger, or the sea!
Look on the tragic loading of this bed.
This is thy work. The object poisons sight;
Let it be hid.° Gratiano, keep° the house,

[The bed curtains are drawn]

And seize upon° the fortunes of the Moor,
For they succeed on° you. [*To CASSIO.*] To you, Lord Governor,
Remains the censure° of this hellish villain,
The time, the place, the torture. O, enforce it!
Myself will straight aboard, and to the state
This heavy act with heavy heart relate.

[Exeunt.]

357 **Indian** (This reading from the Quarto pictures an ignorant savage who cannot recognize the value of a precious jewel. The Folio reading, **Iudean** or **Judean,** i.e., infidel or disbeliever, may refer to Herod, who slew Miriamne in a fit of jealousy, or to Judas Iscariot, the betrayer of Christ.) 358 **subdued** i.e., overcome by grief 361 **gum** i.e., myrrh 366 s.d. **He stabs himself** (This direction is in the Quarto text.) 367 **period** termination, conclusion 373 **Spartan dog** (Spartan dogs were noted for their savagery and silence.) 374 **fell** cruel 376 **Let it be hid** i.e., draw the bed curtains. (No stage direction specifies that the dead are to be carried offstage at the end of the play.) **keep** remain in 377 **seize upon** take legal possession of 378 **succeed on** pass as though by inheritance to 379 **censure** sentencing

QUESTIONS FOR READING AND WRITING

1. To what extent do your own beliefs or experiences influence your response to this play?
2. How is it possible for so noble a character as Othello to become so jealous and so gullible? Why doesn't he approach Desdemona about his suspicions earlier?
3. Why do you think that Othello trusts Iago rather than Desdemona? Does it seem reasonable that he succumbs to Iago's treachery?
4. What motivates Iago? Why isn't he satisfied when he gets the lieutenancy?
5. What do you think of Desdemona's response to Othello's abusive behavior? Should she have responded differently? If so, how?
6. How would you describe the roles of men and women in this play?
7. Shakespeare is known for his development of minor characters. How important a role does Brabantio, Roderigo, Cassio, or Emilia play in this tragedy? Could different behavior on the part of any one of these change the outcome of the play?
8. Do you agree that Othello has "loved not wisely but too well."? Are there other reasons for this tragedy? Explain.
9. Choose a scene from the play and discuss why this scene is important in the light of the whole play.
10. Like all of Shakespeare's plays, most of this play is dramatic poetry. Choose examples of poetic language from *Othello* that are especially effective in evoking emotion, developing character, or advancing the conflict or plot. Discuss what makes this language work so well.

TWO STUDENT PAPERS

Depending on your experience of it, *Othello* may be a play about many different things. You may experience it as a play about jealousy, loyalty, trust, friendship, love, treachery, racism, wife abuse, or any number of other issues.

In her contextual critical essay, Marie Tymon writes about the play from the perspective of cultural or feminist criticism. She shares what she feels can be learned from the play by addressing the issue of physical and psychological abuse of women—how the arrogant and demeaning attitudes expressed toward women in *Othello* were typical of the seventeenth century and still represent a primary cause of spouse abuse. Ann Linde's critical essay analyzes the characterizations of Iago, Othello, Desdemona, Cassio, and Emilia, and concludes that none of these characters "are what they seem"—and that these misleading appearances lead to the play's tragic outcome.

Marie Tymon

Dr. Madden

English 102

December 10, 200X

The Truth About Us

Culture and tradition play an important role in our lives. Many cultures have an unwritten code that husbands can command and abuse their wives. Personal fear is only one of many factors that makes women tolerate this abuse. Cultural acceptance is also a major contributing factor. The question arises why the women in this play, Desdemona, Emilia, and Bianca, tolerate the abuse and violence inflicted upon them by their men. A critical conflict in Othello turns on this question. Are today's women any different? Is the best about us the truth about us? Or is the worst about us the truth about us?

The women in Othello have an emotional commitment that the men seem incapable of reciprocating. Their attitudes and feelings toward the men in their lives, however, sharpen the focus on the male treatment of women. Desdemona's absolute devotion to Othello emphasizes his cruel treatment of her; Emilia's absolute devotion to Iago likewise underscores his hatred of her and all women. Othello, Iago, and Cassio are men who hunger for power. Male competition shows itself in a series of sexual offenses and revenges that makes each of the men either "cuckold," "cuckoldee," or both. They appear to be in sexual competition with each other. Desdemona is linked in some real or imaginary way to almost every man in the play--Brabantio, Othello, Roderigo, Cassio, and even Iago.

There is a tendency to both idealize and devalue women and to be obsessed with female chastity and male honor. Iago knows what will upset Brabantio most when he tells him his "daughter and the Moor are now making the beast with two backs / . . . an old black ram is tupping your white ewe" (1.118–19). Women exist not to love but to satisfy men's appetites. Both publicly and privately women are exploited and abused in this play. In Act I, Brabantio is publicly humiliated by his daughter. First he lies about her attraction to the Moor and calls her a "whore."

At the time this play was written, patriarchal marriages granted the father control of the daughter's sexuality until she was married. Then her sexuality became the possession and responsibility of her husband. A man's honor was called into question if it was known that he could not control the sexuality of a daughter or wife. Sexual references of this kind are seen throughout the play. Iago says he "hate[s] the Moor; / And it is thought abroad that 'twixt my sheets / Has done my office" (1.3.367–369). Iago plays along with the rumor that Othello has slept with Emilia. Men in Othello are concerned with honor in a way that women are not. A double standard dictates that men sew "wild oats" while women may not. Obviously, the women they marry must be different in kind than those with whom they sew their oats.

This male brand of sexuality is accompanied by violence and abuse. We see Emilia presenting the handkerchief to Iago "to please his fantasy" (3.3.316). Iago shows his appreciation by calling her "a common thing" (3.3.320). Bianca is likewise abused by Cassio, who calls her "another fitchew," (4.1.140) or wanton woman. At the beginning of the play, Othello is absolutely enraptured by his love for Desdemona. This is in strong contrast to his outbursts later when he calls her "A public commoner," (4.1.75) a whore, and "as false as water" (5.2.138). He follows this with public, physical violence and eventually murder. The obedience of Emilia and Bianca mirrors Desdemona's compliant devotion to Othello.

In today's world, too, women stay in abusive relationships. The question is why. There are many families in which male power and abuse, and female helplessness, abound. Leaving an abusive marriage is an enormous psychological and practical undertaking. A woman tends to question herself, not the man, when a relationship turns ugly. I have worked in an assault treatment unit. Many of the victims ask if they are codependent--as if this was about women who love too much, or about love at all instead of power and control.

Further trapping a battered woman is her emotional dependency on her husband. Like Emilia and Desdemona, a battered wife identifies with her violent husband because she feels responsible for choosing this person as a lifetime partner. Often these women become so isolated that their only reality is what their abuser is telling them rather than what might be the truth.

In Shakespeare's day, patriarchal marriages prevailed because there was no escape from violent relationships. Women had to accept them because the culture would not protect them. It is only in the last twenty years that feminists have made progress in the courts, legislatures, and health care institutions to change our attitudes about male violence toward women. But we are still a long way from seeing the "truth about us." Many men still follow in the footsteps of Iago and Othello as they mock the women they claim to love. The media has a history of glamorizing male violence and distorting its social and emotional realities. We have yet to see images of male violence in mass media that accurately target these sources and hold its perpetrators accountable. There is much to be learned about this in the tragedy of Othello. Those of us who respect the rights of all human beings must not look away. Society cannot continue to tolerate violence against women.

Work Cited

Shakespeare, William. Othello. Exploring Literature. Ed. Frank Madden. New York: Longman, 2001, 588–692.

Ann Linde

Dr. Madden

English 102

April 12, 200X

Appearances May Be Deceiving

Throughout Othello, it becomes very apparent that things and characters are not what they appear to be. The characters are perceived in different ways by the audience and by each other, and this affects their interaction during the play. Deception is a major theme throughout the play and is seen in many forms and through many of the characters.

The first character that displays this conflict is Iago. He appears to Roderigo, as well as Othello later in the play, to be honest and acting in friendship. Iago is in truth a villainous and greedy character bent on revenge and shows loyalty and true friendship to no one. In Act I he even says this outright to Roderigo. Iago shows his true form when he says, "Were I the Moor I would not be Iago. / In following him, I follow but myself" (1.1.59–60). Iago even goes so far as to actually say to Roderigo "I am not what I am" (1.1.67), yet the unfailingly gullible Roderigo still follows him and places his trust in Iago.

As Iago and Roderigo go to Brabantio's house, Iago appears to be trying to help Brabantio save his daughter as he says, "Zounds, sir, you're robbed"

(1.1.88) and "Your heart is burst; you have lost half your soul" (1.1.89). Meanwhile, his true motive is to cause trouble for Othello by revealing the elopement and rousing her father's anger. As Brabantio searches for Othello, Iago appears to be a supportive and protective friend. Ironically, Iago is hinting at his own deception as he swears, "By Janus" that it is not Brabantio who has found them, but Cassio instead. Janus is a Roman god with two faces, and Iago shows that he also has two faces, first causing the conflict, then appearing to be supportive and helpful to Othello.

In Act 3, Iago tells Othello, "Men should be what they seem; / Or those that be not, would they might seem none!" (3.3.139–140). Iago is not at all what he seems, and is, in fact, the exact opposite of what he seems to be. Appearing reluctant to display Desdemona's infidelity, Iago says, "I should be wise, for honesty's a fool / And loses that it works for" (3.3.400–401). Honesty is not included in his agenda as he continues with his deception.

Othello is also a character who may not be what he appears to be. After his entrance in the play, the duke greets him as "Valiant Othello." He appears to be a brave warrior, self-controlled and confident. Othello remains calm when confronted by Brabantio even as swords are drawn, and he appeals to Brabantio's sense of reason. Even as Brabantio demands his arrest for using witchcraft or charms to steal his daughter, Othello remains apparently unshakable.

Othello displays his love and trust in his new bride, Desdomona, after they are reunited at the beginning of Act 2, saying, "If it were now to die,/'Twere now to be most happy," (2.1.184–185). In these lines, he comments that he would battle any storm to be with her. Unfortunately, it will soon become evident that this great warrior will lose the battle with the storm of jealousy. As we move into Act 3, Iago begins to plant doubt in his mind. Othello shows that his trust in Iago is growing and his faith in his wife is diminishing when he says, "By the world, / I think my wife be honest and think she is not;" (3.3.401–402). In this change, I see the man who initially appeared to be calm and in control now being controlled himself by jealousy. I also find it ironic that the mighty Othello is being duped and deceived in much the same way that the obviously gullible and naïve Roderigo is.

As the roots of jealousy take hold in Othello's mind, he becomes increasingly out of control and violent. He declares that he wants Cassio executed, and says of Desdemona, "I will withdraw / To furnish me with some swift means of death / For the fair devil" (3.3.494–496). At this point in the play, Othello's character is the direct opposite of how he appeared in Act I.

The storm of his rage reaches its full fury when he kills Desdemona. After he realizes that it was Iago who deceived him and not his loving wife, he again appears to be noble and in control. Even though he is preparing to kill himself, he explains himself to Lodovico and the others. In his attempt to explain his actions, he says, "Speak of me as I am; nothing extenuate, / Nor set down aught in malice. Then must you speak / Of one that loved not wisely but too well" (5.2.352–354), to relate to them that he was consumed by jealousy. In his suicide, I feel that he is taking responsibility for his actions. He is also once again showing the depth of his love for Desdemona, because dying is the only way he can be with her once more.

Desdemona's appearance in the play is also deceiving. Her father portrays her as deceptive and false when he says, "Look to her, Moor, if thou hast eyes to see. / She has deceived her father, and may thee." (1.3.293–294). By disobeying her father, Desdemona appears able to betray the person she is supposed to love and obey. The phrase "look to her" suggests that she needs to be watched. As Iago plots and schemes, Desdemona is believed to be guilty of infidelity when in fact she remained completely faithful to Othello. The portrayal of her as unfaithful will prove to be incorrect by the end of the play. Ironically, her love for her husband and her attempts to soothe him are what provide Iago with the ammunition to make her appear unfaithful, the handkerchief.

Another character that is not what she seems to be is Emilia. She appears to be completely subservient to and controlled by her husband, Iago. This is evident in their exchange during Act 2, when he says that her only use is "To suckle fools and chronicle small beer" (2.1.159). After Emilia finds the handkerchief that Desdemona has dropped, Iago once again demonstrates his domination over his wife. Although Emilia knows that Desdemona will "run mad / When she shall lack it" (3.3.335–336), she doesn't tell anyone he took the handkerchief. The image of Emilia being a dominated and subservient woman is shattered at the end of the play. When Emilia finds that her mistress has been killed by Othello and later that her husband is responsible, she confronts both men. Although she loves and wants to obey her husband, she still takes a stand for what is right.

Throughout the play, Cassio is perceived by the audience to be a generally goodhearted, fairly upbeat individual, with a good sense of honor and duty. He shows true admiration and respect for Desdemona when he says, "The riches of the ship is come on shore!" (2.1.85) to announce her arrival. His devotion and loyalty to Othello are easily seen when he shows his concern for Othello's safety, saying, "Great Jove, Othello guard, / And swell his sail with thine own powerful breath" (2.1.79–80).

His appearance to other characters is a different story. To Othello, he initially appears to be trustworthy. Iago changed the way Cassio was seen in Othello's eyes. Iago set the scene so convincingly that Cassio was wrongly accused and punished for fighting with Roderigo. After Iago plants the seeds of doubt about Desdemona in Othello's mind, Cassio appears to Othello to be the worst kind of traitor, one who would steal his new bride. During the controversy that ensues, Cassio's appearance to his girlfriend Bianca also changes. At the instant he gave her the handkerchief, he appeared to be unfaithful to her. In her eyes, the only way he could have gotten it was from another woman.

The handkerchief is also an object that appears to have different meanings for different people. For Othello, the handkerchief is a symbol of fidelity and love. He explains this when he says it belonged to his mother and "while she kept it, / 'Twould make her amiable and subdue my father / Entirely to her love," (3.4.55–57). In Desdemona's eyes, the handkerchief is cherished because it was a gift from Othello. Before he explains its origins, she seems to know nothing of its history or proposed powers. After the handkerchief is out of Desdemona's hands, its meaning changes for everyone involved. To Iago, the handkerchief symbolizes the culmination of his evil plans. Without it, he has no concrete evidence for Othello to see. Desdemona, seeing how it enraged her husband and hearing of its magical powers, begins to fear the handkerchief and says, "Then would to God that I had never seen 't!" (3.4.74). To Bianca, it means that her lover, Cassio, was in love with someone else, because he is so taken by the embroidery that she assumes it had to belong to a new love. The greatest change in the perception of the handkerchief occurs with Othello. Initially a symbol of love and passion, after it is lost it becomes a sign of her infidelity.

The handkerchief is symbolic of the volatile relationships between the characters in the play. In reality it is just a common object, a piece of cloth, but its appearance and meaning change depending on who is holding it. This is the same way the characters are perceived in different ways at different times. As we find out at the end of the play, appearances and deception lead to jealousy and rage. This goes to show that appearances can be deceiving, and deadly too.

Work Cited

Shakespeare, William. Othello. Exploring Literature. Ed. Frank Madden. New York: Longman, 2001. 588–692.

WENDY WASSERSTEIN (b. 1950)

Wendy Wasserstein is a native of Brooklyn, New York. In 1989, her play The Heidi Chronicles *won both a Tony Award for Best Play and a Pulitzer Prize for drama. Another play,* The Sisters Rosenweig *(1993), won an Outer Circle Critics Award and a Tony nomination.* The Man in a Case *is based on a short story by one of her favorite writers, Anton Chekhov. Wasserstein writes frequently for public television and film and lives in New York City.*

THE MAN IN A CASE [1986]

CHARACTERS
BYELINKOV
VARINKA

SCENE: *A small garden in the village of Mironitski, 1898*

[BYELINKOV is pacing. Enter VARINKA out of breath.]

BYELINKOV: You are ten minutes late.

VARINKA: The most amazing thing happened on my way over here. You know the woman who runs the grocery store down the road. She wears a black wig during the week, and a blond wig on Saturday nights. And she has the daughter who married an engineer in Moscow who is doing very well thank you and is living, God bless them, in a three-room apartment. But he really is the most boring man in the world. All he talks about is his future and his station in life. Well, she heard we were to be married and she gave me this basket of apricots to give to you.

BYELINKOV: That is a most amazing thing!

VARINKA: She said to me, "Varinka, you are marrying the most honorable man in the entire village. In this village he is the only man fit to speak with my son-in-law."

BYELINKOV: I don't care for apricots. They give me hives.

VARINKA: I can return them. I'm sure if I told her they give you hives she would give me a basket of raisins or a cake.

BYELINKOV: I don't know this woman or her pompous son-in-law. Why would she give me her cakes?

VARINKA: She adores you!

BYELINKOV: She is emotionally loose.

VARINKA: She adores you by reputation. Everyone adores you by reputation. I tell everyone I am to marry Byelinkov, the finest teacher in the country.

BYELINKOV: You tell them this?

VARINKA: If they don't tell me first.

BYELINKOV: Pride can be an imperfect value.

VARINKA: It isn't pride. It is the truth. You are a great man!

BYELINKOV: I am the master of Greek and Latin at a local school at the end of the village of Mironitski.

[VARINKA kisses him.]

VARINKA: And I am to be the master of Greek and Latin's wife!

BYELINKOV: Being married requires a great deal of responsibility. I hope I am able to provide you with all that a married man must properly provide a wife.

VARINKA: We will be very happy.

BYELINKOV: Happiness is for children. We are entering into a social contract, an amicable agreement to provide us with a secure and satisfying future.

VARINKA: You are so sweet! You are the sweetest man in the world!

BYELINKOV: I'm a man set in his ways who saw a chance to provide himself with a small challenge.

VARINKA: Look at you! Look at you! Your sweet round spectacles, your dear collar always starched, always raised, your perfectly pressed pants always creasing at right angles perpendicular to the floor, and my most favorite part, the sweet little galoshes, rain or shine, just in case. My Byelinkov, never taken by surprise. Except by me.

BYELINKOV: You speak about me as if I were your pet.

VARINKA: You are my pet! My little school mouse.

BYELINKOV: A mouse?

VARINKA: My sweetest dancing bear with galoshes, my little stale babka.

BYELINKOV: A stale babka?

VARINKA: I am not Pushkin.[1]

BYELINKOV [*laughs*]: That depends what you think of Pushkin.

VARINKA: You're smiling. I knew I could make you smile today.

BYELINKOV: I am a responsible man. Every day I have for breakfast black bread, fruit, hot tea, and every day I smile three times. I am halfway into my translation of the *Aeneid*[2] from classical Greek hexameter[3] into Russian alexandrines.[4] In twenty years I have never been late to school. I am a responsible man, but no dancing bear.

VARINKA: Dance with me.

BYELINKOV: Now? It is nearly four weeks before the wedding!

VARINKA: It's a beautiful afternoon. We are in your garden. The roses are in full bloom.

BYELINKOV: The roses have beetles.

VARINKA: Dance with me!

BYELINKOV: You are a demanding woman.

VARINKA: You chose me. And right. And left. And turn. And right. And left.

BYELINKOV: And turn. Give me your hand. You dance like a school mouse. It's a beautiful afternoon! We are in my garden. The roses are in full bloom! And turn. And turn. [*twirls* VARINKA *around*]

*[*BYELINKOV *stops dancing.]*

BYELINKOV: To place a lilac in your hair. Every year on this day I will place a lilac in your hair.

VARINKA: Will you remember?

BYELINKOV: I will write it down. [*takes a notebook from his pocket*] Dear Byelinkov, don't forget the day a young lady, your bride, entered your garden, your peace, and danced on the roses. On that day every year you are to place a lilac in her hair.

VARINKA: I love you.

BYELINKOV: It is convenient we met.

VARINKA: I love you.

BYELINKOV: You are a girl.

VARINKA: I am thirty.

BYELINKOV: But you think like a girl. That is an attractive attribute.

VARINKA: Do you love me?

BYELINKOV: We've never spoken about housekeeping.

VARINKA: I am an excellent housekeeper. I kept house for my family on the farm in Gadyatchsky. I can make a beetroot soup with tomatoes and aubergines which is so nice. Awfully, awfully nice.

BYELINKOV: You are fond of expletives.

VARINKA: My beet soup, sir, is excellent!

[1] **Alexander Pushkin** a famous Russian poet and dramatist (1799–1837) [2] **Aeneid** epic poem written by Vergil (70–19 B.C.) [3] **hexameter** a line of verse having six metric units [4] **alexandrine** a line of verse having six metric units

BYELINKOV: Please don't be cross. I too am an excellent housekeeper. I have a place for everything in the house. A shelf for each pot, a cubby for every spoon, a folder for favorite recipes. I have cooked for myself for twenty years. Though my beet soup is not outstanding, it is sufficient.

VARINKA: I'm sure it's very good.

BYELINKOV: No. It is awfully, awfully not. What I am outstanding in, however, what gives me greatest pleasure, is preserving those things which are left over. I wrap each tomato slice I haven't used in a wet cloth and place it in the coolest corner of the house. I have had my shoes for seven years because I wrap them in the galoshes you are so fond of and every night before I go to sleep I wrap my bed in quilts and curtains so I never catch a draft.

VARINKA: You sleep with curtains on your bed?

BYELINKOV: I like to keep warm.

VARINKA: I will make you a new quilt.

BYELINKOV: No. No new quilt. That would be hazardous.

VARINKA: It is hazardous to sleep under curtains.

BYELINKOV: Varinka, I don't like change very much. If one works out the arithmetic, the final fraction of improvement is at best less than an eighth of value over the total damage caused by disruption. I never thought of marrying till I saw your eyes dancing among the familiar faces at the headmaster's tea. I assumed I would grow old preserved like those which are left over, wrapped suitably in my case of curtains and quilts.

VARINKA: Byelinkov, I want us to have dinners with friends and summer country visits. I want people to say, "Have you spent time with Varinka and Byelinkov? He is so happy now that they are married. She is just what he needed."

BYELINKOV: You have already brought me some happiness. But I never was a sad man. Don't ever think I thought I was a sad man.

VARINKA: My sweetest darling, you can be whatever you want! If you are sad, they'll say she talks all the time, and he is soft-spoken and kind.

BYELINKOV: And if I am difficult?

VARINKA: Oh, they'll say he is difficult because he is highly intelligent. All great men are difficult. Look at Lermontov, Tchaikovsky, Peter the Great.

BYELINKOV: Ivan the Terrible.

VARINKA: Yes, him too.

BYELINKOV: Why are you marrying me? I am none of these things.

VARINKA: To me you are.

BYELINKOV: You have imagined this. You have constructed an elaborate romance for yourself. Perhaps you are the great one. You are the one with the great imagination.

VARINKA: Byelinkov, I am a pretty girl of thirty. You're right, I am not a woman. I have not made myself into a woman because I do not deserve that honor. Until I came to this town to visit my brother I lived on my family's farm. As the years passed I became younger and younger in fear that I would never marry. And it wasn't that I wasn't pretty enough or sweet enough, it was just that no man ever looked at me and saw a wife. I was not the woman who would be there when he came home. Until I met you I thought I would lie all my life and say I never married because I never met a man I loved. I will love you, Byelinkov. And I will help you to love me. We deserve the life everyone else has. We deserve not to be different.

BYELINKOV: Yes. We are the same as everyone else.

VARINKA: Tell me you love me.

BYELINKOV: I love you.

VARINKA [*takes his hands*]: We will be very happy. I am very strong. [*pauses*] It is time for tea.

BYELINKOV: It is too early for tea. Tea is at half past the hour.

VARINKA: Do you have heavy cream? It will be awfully nice with apricots.

BYELINKOV: Heavy cream is too rich for teatime.

VARINKA: But today is special. Today you placed a lilac in my hair. Write in your note pad. Every year we will celebrate with apricots and heavy cream. I will go to my brother's house and get some.

BYELINKOV: But your brother's house is a mile from here.

VARINKA: Today it is much shorter. Today my brother gave me his bicycle to ride. I will be back very soon.

BYELINKOV: You rode to my house by bicycle! Did anyone see you?

VARINKA: Of course. I had such fun. I told you I saw the grocery store lady with the son-in-law who is doing very well thank you in Moscow, and the headmaster's wife.

BYELINKOV: You say the headmaster's wife!

VARINKA: She smile at me.

BYELINKOV: Did she laugh or smile?

VARINKA: She laughed a little. She said, "My dear, you are very progressive to ride a bicycle." She said, "You and your fiancé Byelinkov must ride together sometime. I wonder if he'll take off his galoshes when he rides a bicycle."

BYELINKOV: She said that?

VARINKA: She adores you. We had a good giggle.

BYELINKOV: A woman can be arrested for riding a bicycle. That is not progressive, it is a premeditated revolutionary act. Your brother must be awfully, awfully careful on behalf of your behavior. He has been careless—oh so careless—in giving you the bicycle.

BYELINKOV: Dearest Byelinkov, you are wrapping yourself under curtains and quilts! I made friends on the bicycle.

BYELINKOV: You saw more than the headmaster's wife and the idiot grocery woman.

VARINKA: She is not an idiot.

BYELINKOV: She is a potato-vending, sausage-armed fool!

VARINKA: Shhh! My school mouse. Shhh!

BYELINKOV: What other friends did you make on this bicycle.

VARINKA: I saw students from my brother's classes. They waved and shouted, "Anthropos in love! Anthropos in love!!"

BYELINKOV: Where is that bicycle?

VARINKA: I left it outside the gate. What are you doing?

BYELINKOV [*muttering as he exits*]: Anthropos in love, anthropos in love.

VARINKA: They were cheering me on. Careful, you'll trample the roses.

BYELINKOV [*returning with the bicycle*]: Anthopos is the Greek singular for man. Anthropos in love translates as the Greek and Latin master in love. Of course they cheered you. Their instructor, who teaches them the discipline and contained beauty of the classics, is in love with a sprite on a bicycle. It is a good giggle, isn't it? A very good giggle! I am returning this bicycle to your brother.

VARINKA: But it is teatime.

BYELINKOV: Today we will not have tea.

VARINKA: But you will have to walk back a mile.

BYELINKOV: I have my galoshes on. [*gets on the bicycle*] Varinka, we deserve not to be different. [*Begins to pedal. The bicycle doesn't move.*]

VARINKA: Put the kickstand up.

BYELINKOV: I beg your pardon.

VARINKA [*giggling*]: Byelinkov, to make the bicycle move, you must put the kickstand up.

*[*BYELINKOV *puts it up and awkwardly falls off the bicycle as it moves.]*

[*laughing*] Ha ha ha. My little school mouse. You look so funny! You are the sweetest dearest man in the world. Ha ha ha!

[pause]

BYELINKOV: Please help me up. I'm afraid my galosh is caught.

VARINKA [*trying not to laugh*]: Your galosh is caught! [*explodes in laughter again*] Oh, you are so funny! I do love you so. [*helps* BYELINKOV *up*] You were right, my pet, as always. We don't need heavy cream for tea. The fraction of improvement isn't worth the damage caused by the disruption.

BYELINKOV: Varinka, it is still too early for tea. I must complete two stanzas of my translation before late afternoon. That is my regular schedule.

VARINKA: Then I will watch while you work.

BYELINKOV: No. You had a good giggle. That is enough.

VARINKA: Then while you work I will work too. I will make lists of guests for our wedding.

BYELINKOV: I can concentrate only when I am alone in my house. Please take your bicycle home to your brother.

VARINKA: But I don't want to leave you. You look so sad.

BYELINKOV: I never was a sad man. Don't ever think I was a sad man.

VARINKA: Byelinkov, it's a beautiful day, we are in your garden. The roses are in bloom.

BYELINKOV: Allow me to help you on to your bicycle. [*takes* VARINKA*'s hand as she gets on the bike*]

VARINKA: You are such a gentleman. We will be very happy.

BYELINKOV: You are very strong. Good day, Varinka.

*[*VARINKA *pedals off.* BYELINKOV, *alone in the garden, takes out his pad and rips up the note about the lilac, strews it over the garden, then carefully picks up each piece of paper and places them all in a small envelope as lights fade to black.]*

➤ *QUESTIONS FOR READING AND WRITING*

1. It doesn't take long in this comedy to identify the basic personality traits of Byelinkov and Varinka. To what extent does their relationship remind you of people you know?
2. In what way is Byelinkov's response to Varinka's riding the bicycle typical of all his responses?
3. How does the time (1898) and place (Russia) of the setting influence your response? Do you think it makes the play more humorous? Why or why not?
4. Which of these characters do you prefer? Why?
5. Is this a good match? Can you predict what this relationship will be like in five years? Do you think it will last that long? Explain.

◆ ESSAYS ◆

BRUNO BETTLEHEIM (1903–1996)

Austrian-born psychologist, educator, and author Bruno Bettleheim came to the United States in 1939, after surviving a series of German concentration camps. He wrote about his experience in the widely read and enormously influential Individual and Mass Behavior in Extreme Situations *(1943). Once in America, Bettleheim established himself as an expert on the psychology of children, publishing works such as* Love is Not Enough *(1950),* The Children of the Dream *(1969),* A Home for the Heart *(1974), and* Surviving and Other Essays *(1979). Cinderella is taken from* The Uses of Enchantment *(1976), in which Bettleheim discusses the psychosocial importance of fairy tales.*

CINDERELLA

[1976]

By all accounts, "Cinderella" is the best-known fairy tale, and probably also the best-liked. It is quite an old story; when first written down in China during the ninth century A.D., it already had a history. The unrivaled tiny foot size as a mark of extraordinary virtue, distinction, and beauty, and the slipper made of precious material are facets which point to an Eastern, if not necessarily Chinese, origin. The modern hearer does not connect sexual attractiveness and beauty in general with extreme smallness of the foot, as the ancient Chinese did, in accordance with their practice of binding women's feet.

"Cinderella," as we know it, is experienced as a story about the agonies and hopes which form the essential content of sibling rivalry; and about the degraded heroine winning out over her siblings who abused her. Long before Perrault gave "Cinderella" the form in which it is now widely known, "having to live among the ashes" was a symbol of being debased in comparison to one's siblings, irrespective of sex. In Germany, for example, there were stories in which such an ash-boy later becomes king, which parallels Cinderella's fate. "Aschenputtel" is the title of the Brothers Grimm's version of the tale. The term originally designated a lowly, dirty kitchenmaid who must tend to the fireplace ashes.

There are many examples in the German language of how being forced to dwell among the ashes was a symbol not just of degradation, but also of sibling rivalry, and of the sibling who finally surpasses the brother or brothers who have debased him. Martin Luther[1] in his *Table Talks* speaks about Cain as the God-forsaken evildoer who is powerful, while pious Abel is forced to be his ash-brother (*Aschebrüdel*), a mere nothing, subject to Cain; in one of Luther's sermons he says that Esau was forced into the role of Jacob's ash-brother. Cain and Abel, Jacob and Esau are Biblical examples of one brother being suppressed or destroyed by the other.

The fairy tale replaces sibling relations with relations between step-siblings—perhaps a device to explain and make acceptable an animosity which one wishes would not exist among true siblings. Although sibling rivalry is universal and "natural" in the sense that it is the negative consequence of being a sibling, this same relation also generates equally as much positive feeling between siblings, highlighted in fairy tales such as "Brother and Sister."

5 No other fairy tale renders so well as the "Cinderella" stories the inner experiences of the young child in the throes of sibling rivalry, when he feels hopelessly outclassed by his brothers and sisters. Cinderella is pushed down and degraded by her stepsisters; her interests are sacrificed to theirs by her (step)mother; she is expected to do the dirtiest work and although she performs it well, she receives no credit for it; only more is demanded of her. This is how the child feels when devastated by the miseries of sibling rivalry. Exaggerated though Cinderella's tribulations and degradations may seem to the adult, the child carried away by sibling rivalry feels, "That's me; that's how they mistreat me, or would want to; that's how little they think of me." And there are moments—often long time periods—when for inner reasons a child feels this way even when his position among his siblings may seem to give him no cause for it.

When a story corresponds to how the child feels deep down—as no realistic narrative is likely to do—it attains an emotional quality of "truth" for the child. The events of "Cinderella" offer him vivid images that give body to his overwhelming

[1]**Martin Luther** (1483–1546) German leader of the Protestant Reformation and Lutheranism

but nevertheless often vague and nondescript emotions; so these episodes seem more convincing to him than his life experiences.

The term "sibling rivalry" refers to a most complex constellation of feelings and their causes. With extremely rare exceptions, the emotions aroused in the person subject to sibling rivalry are far out of proportion to what his real situation with his sisters and brothers would justify, seen objectively. While all children at times suffer greatly from sibling rivalry, parents seldom sacrifice one of the children to the others, nor do they condone the other children's persecuting one of them. Difficult as objective judgments are for the young child—nearly impossible when his emotions are aroused—even he in his more rational moments "knows" that he is not treated as badly as Cinderella. But the child often feels mistreated, despite all his "knowledge" to the contrary. That is why he believes in the inherent truth of "Cinderella," and then he also comes to believe in her eventual deliverance and victory. From her triumph he gains the exaggerated hopes for his future which he needs to counteract the extreme misery he experiences when ravaged by sibling rivalry.

Despite the name "sibling rivalry," this miserable passion has only incidentally to do with a child's actual brothers and sisters. The real source of it is the child's feelings about his parents. When a child's older brother or sister is more competent than he, this arouses only temporary feelings of jealousy. Another child being given special attention becomes an insult only if the child fears that, in contrast, he is thought little of by his parents, or feels rejected by them. It is because of such an anxiety that one or all of a child's sisters or brothers may become a thorn in his flesh. Fearing that in comparison to them he cannot win his parents' love and esteem is what inflames sibling rivalry. This is indicated in stories by the fact that it matters little whether the siblings actually possess greater competence. The Biblical story of Joseph tells that it is jealousy of parental affection lavished on him which accounts for the destructive behavior of his brothers. Unlike Cinderella's, Joseph's parent does not participate in degrading him, and, on the contrary, prefers him to his other children. But Joseph, like Cinderella, is turned into a slave, and, like her, he miraculously escapes and ends by surpassing his siblings.

Telling a child who is devastated by sibling rivalry that he will grow up to do as well as his brothers and sisters offers little relief from his present feelings of dejection. Much as he would like to trust our assurances, most of the time he cannot. A child can see things only with subjective eyes, and comparing himself on this basis to his siblings, he has no confidence that he, on his own, will someday be able to fare as well as they. If he could believe more in himself, he would not feel destroyed by his siblings no matter what they might do to him, since then he could trust that time would bring about a desired reversal of fortune. But since the child cannot, on his own, look forward with confidence to some future day when things will turn out all right for him, he can gain relief only through fantasies of glory—a domination over his siblings—which he hopes will become reality through some fortunate event.

10 Whatever our position within the family, at certain times in our lives we are beset by sibling rivalry in some form or other. Even an only child feels that other children have some great advantages over him, and this makes him intensely jealous. Further, he may suffer from the anxious thought that if he did have a sibling, his parents would prefer this other child to him. "Cinderella" is a fairy tale which makes nearly as strong an appeal to boys as to girls, since children of both sexes

suffer equally from sibling rivalry, and have the same desire to be rescued from their lowly position and surpass those who seem superior to them.

On the surface, "Cinderella" is as deceptively simple as the story of Little Red Riding Hood, with which it shares greatest popularity. "Cinderella" tells about the agonies of sibling rivalry, of wishes coming true, of the humble being elevated, of true merit being recognized even when hidden under rags, of virtue rewarded and evil punished—a straightforward story. But under this overt content is concealed a welter of complex and largely unconscious material, which details of the story allude to just enough to set our unconscious associations going. This makes a contrast between surface simplicity and underlying complexity which arouses deep interest in the story and explains its appeal to the millions over centuries. To begin gaining an understanding of these hidden meanings, we have to penetrate behind the obvious sources of sibling rivalry discussed so far.

As mentioned before, if the child could only believe that it is the infirmities of his age which account for his lowly position, he would not have to suffer so wretchedly from sibling rivalry, because he could trust the future to right matters. When he thinks that his degradation is deserved, he feels his plight is utterly hopeless. Djuna Barnes's perceptive statement about fairy tales—that the child knows something about them which he cannot tell (such as that he likes the idea of Little Red Riding Hood and the wolf being in bed together)—could be extended by dividing fairy tales into two groups: one group where the child responds only unconsciously to the inherent truth of the story and thus cannot tell about it; and another large number of tales where the child preconsciously or even consciously knows what the "truth" of the story consists of and thus could tell about it, but does not want to let on that he knows. Some aspects of "Cinderella" fall into the latter category. Many children believe that Cinderella probably deserves her fate at the beginning of the story, as they feel they would, too; but they don't want anyone to know it. Despite this, she is worthy at the end to be exalted, as the child hopes he will be too, irrespective of his earlier shortcomings.

Every child believes at some period of his life—and this is not only at rare moments—that because of his secret wishes, if not also his clandestine actions, he deserves to be degraded, banned from the presence of others, relegated to a netherworld of smut. He fears this may be so, irrespective of how fortunate his situation may be in reality. He hates and fears those others—such as his siblings—whom he believes to be entirely free of similar evilness, and he fears that they or his parents will discover what he is really like, and then demean him as Cinderella was by her family. Because he wants others—most of all, his parents—to believe in his innocence, he is delighted that "everybody" believes in Cinderella's. This is one of the great attractions of this fairy tale. Since people give credence to Cinderella's goodness, they will also believe in his, so the child hopes. And "Cinderella" nourishes this hope, which is one reason it is such a delightful story.

Another aspect which holds large appeal for the child is the vileness of the stepmother and stepsisters. Whatever the shortcomings of a child may be in his own eyes, these pale into insignificance when compared to the stepsisters' and stepmother's falsehood and nastiness. Further, what these stepsisters do to Cinderella justifies whatever nasty thoughts one may have about one's siblings: they are so vile that anything one may wish would happen to them is more than justified.

Compared to their behavior, Cinderella is indeed innocent. So the child, on hearing her story, feels he need not feel guilty about his angry thoughts.

15 On a very different level—and reality considerations coexist easily with fantastic exaggerations in the child's mind—as badly as one's parents or siblings seem to treat one, and much as one thinks one suffers because of it, all this is nothing compared to Cinderella's fate. Her story reminds the child at the same time how lucky he is, and how much worse things could be. (Any anxiety about the latter possibility is relieved, as always in fairy tales, by the happy ending.)

The behavior of a five-and-a-half-year-old girl, as reported by her father, may illustrate how easily a child may feel that she is a "Cinderella." This little girl had a younger sister of whom she was very jealous. The girl was very fond of "Cinderella," since the story offered her material with which to act out her feelings, and because without the story's imagery she would have been hard pressed to comprehend and express them. This little girl had used to dress very neatly and liked pretty clothes, but she became unkempt and dirty. One day when she was asked to fetch some salt, she said as she was doing so, "Why do you treat me like Cinderella?"

Almost speechless, her mother asked her, "Why do you think I treat you like Cinderella?"

"Because you make me do all the hardest work in the house!" was the little girl's answer. Having thus drawn her parents into her fantasies, she acted them out more openly, pretending to sweep up all the dirt, etc. She went even further, playing that she prepared her little sister for the ball. But she went the "Cinderella" story one better, based on her unconscious understanding of the contradictory emotions fused into the "Cinderella" role, because at another moment she told her mother and sister, "You shouldn't be jealous of me just because I am the most beautiful in the family."

This shows that behind the surface humility of Cinderella lies the conviction of her superiority to mother and sisters, as if she would think: "You can make me do all the dirty work, and I pretend that I am dirty, but within me I know that you treat me this way because you are jealous of me because I am so much better than you." This conviction is supported by the story's ending, which assures every "Cinderella" that eventually she will be discovered by her prince.

20 Why does the child believe deep within himself that Cinderella deserves her dejected state? This question takes us back to the child's state of mind at the end of the oedipal period. Before he is caught in oedipal entanglements, the child is convinced that he is lovable, and loved, if all is well within his family relationships. Psychoanalysis describes this stage of complete satisfaction with oneself as "primary narcissism." During this period the child feels certain that he is the center of the universe, so there is no reason to be jealous of anybody.

The oedipal disappointments which come at the end of this developmental stage cast deep shadows of doubt on the child's sense of his worthiness. He feels that if he were really as deserving of love as he had thought, then his parents would never be critical of him or disappoint him. The only explanation for parental criticism the child can think of is that there must be some serious flaw in him which accounts for what he experiences as rejection. If his desires remain unsatisfied and his parents disappoint him, there must be something wrong with him or his desires, or both. He cannot yet accept that reasons other than those residing within him could have an impact on his fate. In his oedipal jealousy, wanting to get rid of the parent of the same sex had seemed the most natural thing in the world, but now the child realizes that he cannot have his own way, and that maybe this is so because the desire was wrong. He is no longer so sure that he is preferred to his siblings, and he begins to suspect that this may be due to the fact that *they* are free of any bad thoughts or wrongdoing such as his.

All this happens as the child is gradually subjected to ever more critical attitudes as he is being socialized. He is asked to behave in ways which run counter to his natural desires, and he resents this. Still he must obey, which makes him very angry. This anger is directed against those who make demands, most likely his parents; and this is another reason to wish to get rid of them, and still another reason to feel guilty about such wishes. This is why the child also feels that he deserves to be chastised for his feelings, a punishment he believes he can escape only if nobody learns what he is thinking when he is angry. The feeling of being unworthy to be loved by his parents at a time when his desire for their love is very strong leads to the fear of rejection, even when in reality there is none. This rejection fear compounds the anxiety that others are preferred and also maybe preferable—the root of sibling rivalry.

➤ *QUESTIONS FOR READING AND WRITING*

1. Do you agree with Bettleheim that *Cinderella* is a tale "about the agonies and hopes which form the essential content of sibling rivalry"? Why or why not? What else might Cinderella be about?
2. Bettleheim argues that children without siblings—as well as older siblings—respond to the Cinderella story in the same way that younger siblings do. Explain his argument. Do you find it convincing? Or do you think that if *Cinderella* is about sibling rivalry, then younger siblings, older siblings, and "only" children would respond to the story in different ways?
3. Do you think that boys respond to Cinderella's plight in the same way that girls do? Why or why not?
4. Read Ann Sexton's poem "Cinderella," which appears earlier in this section (p. 582). Do you think Bettleheim's interpretation of the Cinderella tale pertains to this poem as well? Why or why not? Does Sexton seem to think that the tale is about sibling rivalry?

JUDY BRADY (b. 1937)

Judy Brady was born in San Francisco, California, and attended the University of Iowa, where she earned a B.F.A. in painting. Brady, now divorced, has worked as an author, editor and secretary. "I Want a Wife," one of the best-known popular essays among feminist writings, first appeared in the 1972 spring issue of Ms. *magazine. In 1991, she edited an anthology of women writers entitled* 1 in 3: Women with Cancer Confront an Epidemic.

I Want a Wife [1971]

I belong to that classification of people known as wives. I am A Wife. And, not altogether incidentally, I am a mother.

Not too long ago a male friend of mine appeared on the scene fresh from a recent divorce. He had one child, who is, of course, with his ex-wife. He is looking for another wife. As I thought about him while I was ironing one evening, it suddenly occurred to me that I, too, would like to have a wife. Why do I want a wife?

I would like to go back to school so that I can become economically independent, support myself, and, if need be, support those dependent upon me. I want a wife who will work and send me to school. And while I am going to school I want a wife to take care of my children. I want a wife to keep track of the children's doctor and dentist appointments. And to keep track of mine, too. I want a wife to make sure my children eat properly and are kept clean. I want a wife who will wash the children's clothes and keep them mended. I want a wife who is a good nurturant attendant to my children, who arranges for their schooling, makes sure that they have an adequate social life with their peers, takes them to the park, the zoo, etc. I want a wife who takes care of the children when they are sick, a wife who arranges to be around when the children need special care, because, of course, I cannot miss classes at school. My wife must arrange to lose time at work and not lose the job. It may mean a small cut in my wife's income from time to time, but I guess I can tolerate that. Needless to say, my wife will arrange and pay for the care of the children while my wife is working.

I want a wife who will take care of my physical needs. I want a wife who will keep my house clean. A wife who will pick up after my children, a wife who will pick up after me. I want a wife who will keep my clothes clean, ironed, mended, replaced when need be, and who will see to it that my personal things are kept in their proper place so that I can find what I need the minute I need it. I want a wife who cooks the meals, a wife who is a *good* cook. I want a wife who will plan the menus, do the necessary grocery shopping, prepare the meals, serve them pleasantly, and then do the cleaning up while I do my studying. I want a wife who will care for me when I am sick and sympathize with my pain and loss of time from school. I want a wife to go along when our family takes a vacation so that someone can continue to care for me and my children when I need a rest and change of scene.

5 I want a wife who will not bother me with rambling complaints about a wife's duties. But I want a wife who will listen to me when I feel the need to explain a rather difficult point I have come across in my course of studies. And I want a wife who will type my papers for me when I have written them.

I want a wife who will take care of the details of my social fife. When my wife and I are invited out by my friends, I want a wife who will take care of the babysitting arrangements. When I meet people at school that I like and want to entertain, I want a wife who will have the house clean, will prepare a special meal, serve it to me and my friends, and not interrupt when I talk about things that interest me and my friends. I want a wife who will have arranged that the children are fed and ready for bed before my guests arrive so that the children do not bother us. I want a wife who takes care of the needs of my guests so that they feel comfortable, who makes sure that they have an ashtray, that they are passed the hors d'oeuvres, that they are offered a second helping of the food, that their wine glasses are replenished when necessary, that their coffee is served to them as they like it. And I want a wife who knows that sometimes I need a night out by myself.

I want a wife who is sensitive to my sexual needs, a wife who makes love passionately and eagerly when I feel like it, a wife who makes sure that I am satisfied. And, of course, I want a wife who will not demand sexual attention when I am not in the mood for it. I want a wife who assumes the complete responsibility for birth control, because I do not want more children. I want a wife who will remain sexually faithful to me so that I do not have to clutter up my intellectual life with jealousies. And I want a wife who understands that my sexual needs may entail more than strict adherence to monogamy. I must, after all, be able to relate to people as fully as possible.

If by chance, I find another person more suitable as a wife than the wife I already have, I want the liberty to replace my present wife with another one. Naturally, I will expect a fresh, new life: my wife will take the children and be solely responsible for them so that I am left free.

When I am through with school and have a job, I want my wife to quit worrying and remain at home so that my wife can more fully and completely take care of a wife's duties.

My god, who *wouldn't* want a wife?

QUESTIONS FOR READING AND WRITING

1. To what extent do your own beliefs or experiences influence your response to this essay?
2. How is *wife* defined in the essay? What constitutes a wife? Does the word have a legal or spiritual meaning in this essay?
3. At the end of the essay the author asks, "Who *wouldn't* want a wife?" Think about the flip side of that question. Who would want to be a wife? Is the role appealing at all? To the essayist? To you?
4. From this essay, is there any reason to want a husband? Why or why not? By implication, do husbands have any redeeming qualities?
5. How do you think Nora in Ibsen's *A Doll's House* (p. 725) would respond to this essay? Does she want a wife? Are her complaints the same as the ones voiced by Judy Brady?

SEI SHŌNAGAN (c. 966–c. 1017)

Sei Shōnagan was a lady-in-waiting at the court of the Japanese empress during the end of the tenth century. Renowned for her beauty and wit, she left the court following the death of the empress and married a provincial governor. Following his death, she became a Buddist nun. "A Lover's Departure" is taken from The Pillow Book, *her famous "notebook," filled with over three-hundred entries made up of anecdotes, poems, and reflections of life in the royal court.*

A Lover's Departure [c. 990]

A lover who is leaving at dawn announces that he has to find his fan and his paper. "I know I put them somewhere last night," he says. Since it is pitch dark, he gropes about the room, bumping into the furniture and muttering, "Strange! Where on earth can they be?" Finally he discovers the objects. He thrusts the paper into the breast of his robe with a great rustling sound; then he snaps open his fan and busily fans away with it. Only now is he ready to take his leave. What charmless behavior! "Hateful" is an understatement.

Equally disagreeable is the man who, when leaving in the middle of the night, takes care to fasten the cord of his headdress. This is quite unnecessary; he could perfectly well put it gently on his head without tying the cord. And why must he spend time adjusting his cloak or hunting costume? Does he really think someone may see him at this time of night and criticize him for not being impeccably dressed?

A good lover will behave as elegantly at dawn as at any other time. He drags himself out of bed with a look of dismay on his face. The lady urges him on: "Come, my friend, it's getting light. You don't want anyone to find you here." He gives a deep sigh, as if to say that the night has not been nearly long enough and that it is agony to leave. Once up, he does not instantly pull on his trousers. Instead he comes close to the lady and whispers whatever was left unsaid during the night. Even when he is dressed, he still lingers, vaguely pretending to be fastening his sash.

Presently he raises the lattice, and the two lovers stand together by the side door while he tells her how he dreads the coming day, which will keep them apart; then he slips away. The lady watches him go, and this moment of parting will remain among her most charming memories.

5 Indeed, one's attachment to a man depends largely on the elegance of his leave-taking. When he jumps out of bed, scurries about the room, tightly fastens his trouser-sash, rolls up the sleeves of his Court cloak, overrobe, or hunting costume, stuffs his belongings into the breast of his robe and then briskly secures the outer sash—one really begins to hate him.

➤ *QUESTIONS FOR READING AND WRITING*

1. This piece is more than a thousand years old. Does it seem old and out of date to you? Explain.
2. What do you think of the statement "one's attachment to a man depends largely on the elegance of his leave-taking"?

ALICE WALKER (b. 1944)

Alice Walker was one of eight children born in rural Georgia to sharecropper parents and was particularly close to her mother. Walker first attended Spelman College, and then transferred to Sarah Lawrence, where she earned a B.A. degree in 1965. In 1967, she married a white civil rights lawyer (they have since divorced), and the couple settled in Jackson, Mississippi, where they were the first legally married interracial couple

in the city. The following year, while she was teaching at Jackson State University, she published the first of her seven volumes of concise and unsentimental verse, Once. *Though she first attracted national attention with her edition of* I Love Myself When I Am Laughing *(1979), an anthology of essays about Zora Neale Hurston, it was her novel,* The Color Purple, *the story of a black woman's struggle in the early twentieth century, that made her the literary equivalent of a superstar. Her other novels include* The Temple of My Familiar *(1989) and* Possessing the Secret of Joy *(1992). Her most recent novel is* By the Light of My Father's Smile *(1999). Walker currently resides in southern California. "In Search of Our Mothers' Gardens," taken from a 1983 book of essays of the same name, describes the effect that her mother and other female relatives had on her development as a woman and an artist.*

In Search of Our Mothers' Gardens [1983]

I described her own nature and temperament. Told how they needed a larger life for their expression. . . . I pointed out that in lieu of proper channels, her emotions had overflowed into paths that dissipated them. I talked, beautifully I thought, about an art that would be born, an art that would open the way for women the likes of her. I asked her to hope, and build up an inner life against the coming of that day. . . . I sang, with a strange quiver in my voice, a promise song.

—"Avey," Jean Toomer, Cane

The poet speaking to a prostitute who falls asleep while he's talking

When the poet Jean Toomer walked through the South in the early twenties, he discovered a curious thing: black women whose spirituality was so intense, so deep, so *unconscious,* that they were themselves unaware of the richness they held. They stumbled blindly through their lives; creatures so abused and mutilated in body, so dimmed and confused by pain, that they considered themselves unworthy even of hope. In the selfless abstractions their bodies became to the men who used them, they became more than "sexual objects," more even than mere women: they became "Saints." Instead of being perceived as whole persons, their bodies became shrines: what was thought to be their minds became temples suitable for worship. These crazy Saints stared out at the world, wildly, like lunatics—or quietly, like suicides; and the "God" that was in their gaze was as mute as a great stone.

Who were these Saints? These crazy, loony, pitiful women?

Some of them, without a doubt, were our mothers and grandmothers.

In the still heat of the post-Reconstruction South, this is how they seemed to Jean Toomer: exquisite butterflies trapped in an evil honey, toiling away their lives in an era, a century, that did not acknowledge them, except as "the *mule* of the world." They dreamed dreams that no one knew—not even themselves, in any coherent fashion—and saw visions no one could understand. They wandered or sat about the countryside crooning lullabies to ghosts, and drawing the mother of Christ in charcoal on courthouse walls.

5 They forced their minds to desert their bodies and their striving spirits sought to rise, like frail whirlwinds from the hard red clay. And when those frail whirlwinds fell, in scattered particles, upon the ground, no one mourned. Instead, men lit candles to celebrate the emptiness that remained, as people do who enter a beautiful but vacant space to resurrect a God.

Our mothers and grandmothers, some of them: moving to music not yet written. And they waited.

They waited for a day when the unknown thing that was in them would be made known; but guessed, somehow in their darkness, that on the day of their revelation they would be long dead. Therefore to Toomer they walked, and even ran, in slow motion. For they were going nowhere immediate, and the future was not yet within their grasp. And men took our mothers and grandmothers, "but got no pleasure from it." So complex was their passion and their calm.

To Toomer, they lay vacant and fallow as autumn fields, with harvest time never in sight: and he saw them enter loveless marriages, without joy; and become prostitutes, without resistance; and become mothers of children, without fulfillment.

For these grandmothers and mothers of ours were not Saints, but Artists; driven to a numb and bleeding madness by the springs of creativity in them for which there was no release. They were Creators, who lived lives of spiritual waste, because they were so rich in spirituality—which is the basis of Art—that the strain of enduring their unused and unwanted talent drove them insane. Throwing away this spirituality was their pathetic attempt to lighten the soul to a weight their work-worn, sexually abused bodies could bear.

10 What did it mean for a black woman to be an artist in our grandmothers' time? In our great-grandmothers' day? It is a question with an answer cruel enough to stop the blood.

Did you have a genius of a great-great-grandmother who died under some ignorant and depraved white overseer's lash? Or was she required to bake biscuits for a lazy backwater tramp, when she cried out in her soul to paint watercolors of sunsets, or the rain falling on the green and peaceful pasturelands? Or was her body broken and forced to bear children (who were more often than not sold away from her)—eight, ten, fifteen, twenty children—when her one joy was the thought of modeling heroic figures of rebellion, in stone or clay?

How was the creativity of the black woman kept alive, year after year and century after century, when for most of the years black people have been in America, it was a punishable crime for a black person to read or write? And the freedom to paint, to sculpt, to expand the mind with action did not exist. Consider, if you can bear to imagine it, what might have been the result if singing, too, had been forbidden by law. Listen to the voices of Bessie Smith, Billie Holiday, Nina Simone, Roberta Flack, and Aretha Franklin, among others, and imagine those voices muzzled for life. Then you may begin to comprehend the lives of our "crazy," "Sainted" mothers and grandmothers. The agony of the lives of women who might have been Poets, Novelists, Essayists, and Short-Story Writers (over a period of centuries) who died with their great gifts stifled within them.

And, if this were the end of the story, we would have cause to cry out in my paraphrase of Okot p'Bitek's great poem:

O, my clanswomen
Let us all cry together!
Come,
Let us mourn the death of our mother,
The death of a Queen
The ash that was produced
By a great fire!
O, this homestead is utterly dead
Close the gates
With *lacari* thorns,
For our mother
The creator of the Stool is lost!
And all the young women
Have perished in the wilderness!

But this is not the end of the story, for all the young women—our mothers and grandmothers, *ourselves*—have not perished in the wilderness. And if we ask ourselves why, and search for and find the answer, we will know beyond all efforts to erase it from our minds, just exactly who, and of what, we black American women are.

15 One example, perhaps the most pathetic, most misunderstood one, can provide a backdrop for our mothers' work: Phillis Wheatley, a slave in the 1700s.

Virginia Woolf, in her book *A Room of One's Own,* wrote that in order for a woman to write fiction she must have two things, certainly: a room of her own (with key and lock) and enough money to support herself.

What then are we to make of Phillis Wheatley, a slave, who owned not even herself? This sickly, frail black girl who required a servant of her own at times—her health was so precarious—and who, had she been white, would have been easily considered the intellectual superior of all the women and most of the men in the society of her day.

Virginia Woolf wrote further, speaking of course not of our Phillis, that "any woman born with a great gift in the sixteenth century" [insert "eighteenth century," insert "black woman," insert "born or made a slave"] would certainly have gone crazed, shot herself, or ended her days in some lonely cottage outside the village, half witch, half wizard [insert "Saint,"], feared and mocked at. For it needs little skill and psychology to be sure that a highly gifted girl who had tried to use her gift for poetry would have been so thwarted and hindered by contrary instincts [add "chains, guns, the lash, the ownership of one's body by someone else, submission to an alien religion"], that she must have lost her health and sanity to a certainty."

The key words, as they relate to Phillis, are "contrary instincts." For when we read the poetry of Phillis Wheatley—as when we read the novels of Nella Larsen or the oddly false-sounding autobiography of that freest of all black women writers, Zora Hurston—evidence of "contrary instincts" is everywhere. Her loyalties were completely divided, as was, without question, her mind.

20 But how could this be otherwise? Captured at seven, a slave of wealthy, doting whites who instilled in her the "savagery" of the Africa they "rescued" her from . . . one wonders if she was even able to remember her homeland as she had known it, or as it really was.

Yet, because she did try to use her gift for poetry in a world that made her a slave, she was "so thwarted and hindered by . . . contrary instincts, that she . . . lost her health. . . ." In the last years of her brief life, burdened not only with the need to express her gift but also with a penniless, friendless "freedom" and several small children for whom she was forced to do strenuous work to feed, she lost her health, certainly. Suffering from malnutrition and neglect and who knows what mental agonies, Phillis Wheatley died.

So torn by "contrary instincts" was black, kidnapped, enslaved Phillis that her description of "the Goddess"—as she poetically called the Liberty she did not have—is ironically, cruelly humorous. And, in fact, has held Phillis up to ridicule for more than a century. It is usually read prior to hanging Phillis's memory as that of a fool. She wrote:

> The Goddess comes, she moves divinely fair,
> Olive and laurel binds her *golden* hair.
> Wherever shines this native of the skies,
> Unnumber'd charms and recent graces rise. [My italics]

It is obvious that Phillis, the slave, combed the "Goddess's" hair every morning; prior, perhaps, to bringing in the milk, or fixing her mistress's lunch. She took her imagery from the one thing she saw elevated above all others.

With the benefit of hindsight we ask, "How could she?"

25 But at last, Phillis, we understand. No more snickering when your stiff, struggling, ambivalent lines are forced on us. We know now that you were not an idiot or a traitor; only a sickly little black girl, snatched from your home and country and made a slave; a woman who still struggled to sing the song that was your gift, although in a land of barbarians who praised you for your bewildered tongue. It is not so much what you sang, as that you kept alive, in so many of our ancestors, *the notion of song.*

Black women are called, in the folklore that so aptly identifies one's status in society, "the *mule* of the world," because we have been handed the burdens that everyone else—*everyone* else—refused to carry. We have also been called "Matriarchs," "Superwomen," and "Mean and Evil Bitches." Not to mention "Castraters" and "Sapphire's Mama." When we have pleaded for understanding, our character has been distorted; when we have asked for simple caring, we have been handed empty inspirational appellations, then stuck in the farthest corner. When we have asked for love, we have been given children. In short, even our plainer gifts, our labors of fidelity and love, have been knocked down our throats. To be an artist and a black woman, even today, lowers our status in many respects, rather than raises it: and yet, artists we will be.

Therefore we must fearlessly pull out of ourselves and look at and identify with our lives the living creativity *some* of our great-grandmothers were not allowed to know. I stress *some* of them because it is well known that the majority of our great-grandmothers knew, even without "knowing" it, the reality of their spirituality, even if they didn't recognize it beyond what happened in the singing at church—and they never had any intention of giving it up.

How they did it—those millions of black women who were not Phillis Wheatley, or Lucy Terry or Frances Harper or Zora Hurston or Nella Larsen or Bessie Smith; or Elizabeth Catlett, or Katherine Dunham, either—brings me to the title of this essay, "In Search of Our Mothers' Gardens," which is a personal account that is yet shared, in its theme and its meaning, by all of us. I found, while thinking about the far-reaching world of the creative black woman, that often the truest answer to a question that really matters can be found very close.

In the late 1920s my mother ran away from home to marry my father. Marriage, if not running away, was expected of seventeen-year-old girls. By the time she was twenty, she had two children and was pregnant with a third. Five children later, I was born. And this is how I came to know my mother: she seemed a large, soft, loving-eyed woman who was rarely impatient in our home. Her quick, violent temper was on view only a few times a year, when she battled with the white landlord who had the misfortune to suggest to her that her children did not need to go to school.

30 She made all the clothes we wore, even my brothers' overalls. She made all the towels and sheets we used. She spent the summers canning vegetables and fruits. She spent the winter evenings making quilts enough to cover all our beds.

During the "working" day, she labored beside—not behind—my father in the fields. Her day began before sunup, and did not end until late at night. There was never a moment for her to sit down, undisturbed, to unravel her own private thoughts; never a time free from interruption—by work or the noisy inquiries of her many children. And yet, it is to my mother—and all our mothers who were not famous—that I went in search of the secret of what has fed that muzzled and often mutilated, but vibrant, creative spirit that the black woman has inherited, and that pops out in wild and unlikely places to this day.

But when, you will ask, did my overworked mother have time to know or care about feeding the creative spirit?

The answer is so simple that many of us have spent years discovering it. We have constantly looked high, when we should have looked high—and low.

For example: in the Smithsonian Institution in Washington, D.C., there hangs a quilt unlike any other in the world. In fanciful, inspired, and yet simple and identifiable figures, it portrays the story of the Crucifixion. It is considered rare, beyond price. Though it follows no known pattern of quilt-making, and though it is made of bits and pieces of worthless rags, it is obviously the work of a person of powerful imagination and deep spiritual feeling. Below this quilt I saw a note that says it was made by "an anonymous Black woman in Alabama, a hundred years ago."

35 If we could locate this "anonymous" black woman from Alabama, she would turn out to be one of our grandmothers—an artist who left her mark in the only materials she could afford, and in the only medium her position in society allowed her to use.

As Virginia Woolf wrote further, in *A Room of One's Own:*

> Yet genius of a sort must have existed among women as it must have existed among the working class. [Change this to "slaves" and "the wives and daughters of sharecroppers."] Now and again an Emily Brontë or a Robert Burns [change this to "a Zora Hurston or a Richard Wright"] blazes out and proves its presence. But certainly it never got itself on to paper. When, however, one reads of a witch being ducked, of a woman possessed by devils [or "Sainthood"], of a wise woman selling herbs [our root workers], or even a very remarkable man who had a mother, then I think we are on the track of a lost novelist, a suppressed poet, of some mute and inglorious Jane Austen. . . . Indeed, I would venture to guess that Anon, who wrote so may poems without signing them, was often a woman. . . .

And so our mothers and grandmothers have, more often than not anonymously, handed on the creative spark, the seed of the flower they themselves never hoped to see; or like a sealed letter they could not plainly read.

And so it is, certainly, with my own mother. Unlike "Ma" Rainey's songs, which retained their creator's name even while blasting forth from Bessie Smith's mouth, no song or poem will bear my mother's name. Yet so many of the stories that I write, that we all write, are my mother's stories. Only recently did I fully realize this: that through years of listening to my mother's stories of her life, I have absorbed not only the stories themselves, but something of the manner in which she spoke, something of the urgency that involves the knowledge that her stories—like her life—must be recorded. It is probably for this reason that so much of what I have written is about characters whose counterparts in real life are so much older than I am.

But the telling of these stories, which came from my mother's lips as naturally as breathing, was not the only way my mother showed herself as an artist. For stories, too, were subject to being distracted, to dying without conclusion. Dinners must be started, and cotton must be gathered before the big rains. The artist that was and is my mother showed itself to me only after many years. This is what I finally noticed:

40 Like Mem, a character in *The Third Life of Grange Copeland,* my mother adorned with flowers whatever shabby house we were forced to live in. And not just your typical straggly country stand of zinnias, either. She planted ambitious gardens—and still does—with over fifty different varieties of plants that bloom profusely from early March until late November. Before she left home for the fields, she watered her flowers, chopped up the grass, and laid out new beds. When she returned from the fields she might divide clumps of bulbs, dig a cold pit, uproot and replant roses, or prune branches from her taller bushes or trees—until night came and it was too dark to see.

Whatever she planted grew as if by magic, and her fame as a grower of flowers spread over three counties. Because of her creativity with her flowers, even my memories of poverty are seen through a screen of blooms—sunflowers, petunias, roses, dahlias, forsythia, spirea, delphiniums, verbena . . . and on and on.

And I remember people coming to my mother's yard to be given cuttings from her flowers; I hear again the praise showered on her because whatever rocky soil she landed on, she turned into a garden. A garden so brilliant with colors, so original in its design, so magnificent with life and creativity, that to this day people drive by our house in Georgia—perfect strangers and imperfect strangers—and ask to stand or walk among my mother's art.

I notice that it is only when my mother is working in her flowers that she is radiant, almost to the point of being invisible—except as Creator: hand and eye. She is involved in work her soul must have. Ordering the universe in the image of her personal conception of Beauty.

Her face, as she prepares the Art that is her gift, is a legacy of respect she leaves to me, for all that illuminates and cherishes life. She has handed down respect for the possibilities—and the will to grasp them.

For her, so hindered and intruded upon in so many ways, being an artist has still been a daily part of her life. This ability to hold on, even in very simple ways, is work black women have done for a very long time.

This poem is not enough, but it is something, for the woman who literally covered the holes in our walls with sunflowers:

They were women then
My mama's generation
Husky of voice—Stout of
Step
With fists as well as
Hands
How they battered down
Doors
And ironed
Starched white
Shirts
How they led
Armies
Headragged Generals
Across mined
Fields
Booby-trapped
Kitchens
To discover books
Desks
A place for us
How they knew what we
Must know
Without knowing a page
Of it
Themselves.

Guided by my heritage of a love of beauty and a respect for stength—in search of my mother's garden, I found my own.

And perhaps in Africa over two hundred years ago, there was just such a mother; perhaps she painted vivid and daring decorations in oranges and yellows and greens on the walls of her hut; perhaps she sang—in a voice like Roberta Flack's—*sweetly* over the compounds of her village; perhaps she wove the most stunning mats or told the most ingenious stories of all the village storytellers. Perhaps she was herself a poet—though only her daughter's name is signed to the poems that we know.

Perhaps Phillis Wheatley's mother was also an artist.

Perhaps in more than Phillis Wheatley's biological life is her mother's signature made clear.

➤ *QUESTIONS FOR READING AND WRITING*

1. What kinds of suffering were black women in the South subjected to? To what extent did this force them to turn to different means of artistic expression?
2. Walker describes these women as "exquisite butterflies trapped in evil honey." How does that metaphor capture their plight?
3. In her description of the "fortune that so aptly identifies one's status in society," Walter says that black women have been called everything from "superwomen" to "mean and evil bitches." How can you account for this?
4. Where has Walker discovered her mother's artistry?
5. Compare this essay to Alice Walker's short story "Everyday Use," on page 870, or Virginia Woolf's "If Shakespeare Had a Sister," on page 723.

VIRGINIA WOOLF (1882–1941)

Virginia Woolf was born in London, England. Her father, Leslie Stephen, was a prominent scholar, and through him Woolf was introduced to many of the leading lights of the Victorian age. Unlike her brothers who were sent to college, she was educated at home in her father's massive library. After his death, she and her sister, Vanessa Bell, moved to London, where they became the center of the so-called "Bloomsbury Group," informal gatherings of the era's most important intellectuals, including E. M. Forster and John Maynard Keynes. Throughout her life, Woolf was acutely aware of what she felt was the inferior status accorded her as a woman, and this theme runs throughout much of her work. A pioneer in the technique of "stream of consciousness," she is best known for her experimental novels, including Mrs. Dalloway *(1925),* To The Lighthouse *(1927),* Orlando *(1928), and* The Waves *(1931). After suffering a series of nervous breakdowns during which she feared she was going insane, Woolf committed suicide in 1941. "If Shakespeare Had a Sister" is taken from her 1929 classic feminist work,* A Room of One's Own.

If Shakespeare Had a Sister [1929]

It would have been impossible, completely and entirely, for any woman to have written the plays of Shakespeare in the age of Shakespeare. Let me imagine, since facts are so hard to come by, what would have happened had Shakespeare had a wonderfully gifted sister, called Judith, let us say. Shakespeare himself went, very probably—his mother was an heiress—to the grammar school, where he may have learnt Latin—Ovid, Virgil and Horace—and the elements of grammar and logic. He was, it is well known, a wild boy who poached rabbits, perhaps shot a deer, and had, rather sooner than he should have done, to marry a woman in the neighborhood, who bore him a child rather quicker than was right. That escapade sent him to seek his fortune in London. He had, it seemed, a taste for the theatre; he began by holding horses at the stage door. Very soon he got work in the theatre, became a successful actor, and lived at the hub of the universe, meeting everybody, knowing everybody, practicing his art on the boards, exercising his wits in the streets, and even getting access to the palace of the queen. Meanwhile his extraordinarily gifted sister, let us suppose, remained at home. She was as adventurous, as imaginative, as agog to see the world as he was. But she was not sent to school. She had no chance of learning grammar and logic, let alone of reading Horace and Virgil. She picked up a book now and then, one of her brother's perhaps, and read a few pages. But then her parents came in and told her to mend the stockings or mind the stew and not moon about with books and papers. They would have spoken sharply but kindly, for they were substantial people who knew the conditions of life for a woman and loved their daughter—indeed, more likely than not she was the apple of her father's eye. Perhaps she scribbled some pages up in an apple loft on the sly, but was careful to hide them or set fire to them. Soon, however, before she was out of her teens, she was to be betrothed to the son of a neighboring woolstapler. She cried out that marriage was hateful to her, and for that she was severely beaten by her father. Then he ceased to scold her. He begged her instead not to hurt him, not to shame him in this matter of her marriage. He would give her a chain of beads or a fine petticoat, he said; and there were tears in his eyes. How could she disobey him? How could she break his heart? The force of her own gift alone drove her to it. She made up a small parcel of her belongings, let herself down by a rope one summer's night and took the road to London. She was not seventeen. The birds that sang in the hedge were not more musical than she was. She had the quickest fancy, a gift like her brother's, for the tune of words. Like him, she had a taste for the theatre. She stood at the stage door; she wanted to act, she said. Men laughed in her face. The manager—a fat, loose-lipped man—guffawed. He bellowed something about poodles dancing and women acting—no woman, he said, could possibly be an actress. He hinted—you can imagine what. She could get no training in her craft. Could she even seek her dinner in a tavern or roam the streets at midnight? Yet her genius was for fiction and lusted to feed abundantly upon the lives of men and women and the study of their ways. At last—for she was very young, oddly like Shakespeare the poet in her face, with the same grey eyes and rounded brows—at last Nick Greene the actor-manager took pity on her; she found herself with child by that gentleman and so—who shall measure the heat and violence of the poet's heart when caught and tangled in a woman's body?—killed herself one winter's night and lies buried at some cross-roads where the omnibuses now stop outside the Elephant and Castle.

That, more or less, is how the story would run, I think, if a woman in Shakespeare's day had had Shakespeare's genius. But for my part, I agree with the deceased bishop, if such he was—it is unthinkable that any woman in Shakespeare's day should have had Shakespeare's genius. For genius like Shakespeare's is not born among labouring, uneducated, servile people. It was not born in England among the Saxons and the Britons. It is not born today among the working classes. How, then, could it have been born among women whose work began, according to Professor Trevelyan, almost before they were out of the nursery, who were forced to it by their parents and held to it by all the power of law and custom? Yet genius of a sort must have existed among women as it must have existed among the working classes. Now and again an Emily Brontë or a Robert Burns blazes out and proves its presence. But certainly it never got itself on to paper. When, however, one reads of a witch being ducked, of a woman possessed by devils, of a wise woman selling herbs, or even of a very remarkable man who had a mother, then I think we are on the track of a lost novelist, a suppressed poet, of some mute and inglorious Jane Austen, some Emily Brontë who dashed her brains out on the moor or mopped and mowed about the highways crazed with the torture that her gift had put her to. Indeed, I would venture to guess that Anon, who wrote so many poems without signing them, was often a woman.

➤ *QUESTIONS FOR READING AND WRITING*

1. Why does Woolf create a sister for Shakespeare? What basic point is she trying to make?
2. In what ways does she indicate that Judith would have been deprived of the opportunities that William had?
3. If Shakespeare were alive today and had a sister, do you think her opportunities would be different? If so, how?

CASE STUDIES IN COMPOSITION

Thinking About Interpretation in Cultural and Historical Contexts

Henrik Ibsen and *A Doll's House*

Henrik Ibsen was born in the seaport town of Skien, Norway. When he was still a child, his father, once a prosperous businessman, lost his fortune and the family was reduced to poverty. As a teenager, Ibsen was apprenticed to a pharmacist and briefly studied medicine, but soon found himself employed as a stage manager in a small regional theater. He turned to writing historical plays, and enjoyed some success. Moving to the capital city of Christiania (now Oslo), Ibsen managed the Norwegian Theater. When the theater failed in 1864, due in part to lack of government support, a disillusioned Ibsen left Norway and spent over twenty years living in continental Europe. His greatest plays, including A Doll's House, Ghosts, An Enemy of the People, The Wild Duck, *and* Hedda Gabler, *date to this period. These highly realistic plays revolutionized modern drama by wedding characters of psychological depth to thoughtful plots concerning the age's most pressing social problems. His later plays,* John Gabriel Borkman *(1896), and* When We Dead Awaken *(1899), which he wrote after his triumphant return to Norway in 1891, were heavily symbolic and poetic. Ibsen suffered a stroke in 1900, which left him unable to write.*

A DOLL'S HOUSE [1879]

TRANSLATED BY JAMES MCFARLANE

CHARACTERS

TORVALD HELMER, a lawyer
NORA, his wife

DR. RANK
MRS. KRISTINE LINDE
NILS KROGSTAD
ANNE MARIE, the nursemaid
HELENE, the maid
THE HELMERS' THREE CHILDREN
THE HELMERS' THREE CHILDREN
A PORTER

The action takes place in the Helmers' flat.

ACT I

A pleasant room, tastefully but not expensively furnished. On the back wall, one door on the right leads to the entrance hall, a second door on the left leads to Helmer's study. Between these two doors, a piano. In the middle of the left wall, a door; and downstage from it, a window. Near the window a round table with armchairs and a small sofa. In the right wall, upstage, a door; and on the same wall downstage, a porcelain stove with a couple of armchairs and a rocking chair. Between the stove and the door a small table. Etchings on the walls. A whatnot with china and other small objects d'art; a small bookcase with books in handsome bindings. Carpet on the floor; a fire burns in the stove. A winter's day.

The front doorbell rings in the hall; a moment later, there is the sound of the front door being opened. Nora comes into the room, happily humming to herself. She is dressed in her outdoor things, and is carrying lots of parcels which she then puts down on the table, right. She leaves the door into the hall standing open; a Porter can be seen outside holding a Christmas tree and a basket; he hands them to the Maid who has opened the door for them.

NORA: Hide the Christmas tree away carefully, Helene. The children mustn't see it till this evening when it's decorated. [*To the Porter, taking out her purse.*] How much?

PORTER: Fifty öre.

NORA: There's a crown. Keep the change.

[The Porter thanks her and goes. Nora shuts the door. She continues to laugh quietly and happily to herself as she takes off her things. She takes a bag of macaroons out of her pocket and eats one or two; then she walks stealthily across and listens at her husband's door.]

NORA: Yes, he's in.

[She begins humming again as she walks over to the table, right.]

HELMER [*in his study*]: Is that my little skylark chirruping out there?

NORA [*busy opening some of the parcels*]: Yes, it is.

HELMER: Is that my little squirrel frisking about?

NORA: Yes!

HELMER: When did my little squirrel get home?

NORA: Just this minute. [*She stuffs the bag of macaroons in her pocket and wipes her mouth.*] Come on out, Torvald, and see what I've bought.

HELMER: I don't want to be disturbed! [*A moment later, he opens the door and looks out, his pen in his hand.*] "Bought," did you say? All that? Has my little spendthrift been out squandering money again?

NORA: But, Torvald, surely this year we can spread ourselves just a little. This is the first Christmas we haven't had to go carefully.

HELMER: Ah, but that doesn't mean we can afford to be extravagant, you know.

NORA: Oh yes, Torvald, surely we can afford to be just a little bit extravagant now, can't we? Just a teeny-weeny bit. You are getting quite a good salary now, and you are going to earn lots and lots of money.

HELMER: Yes, after the New Year. But it's going to be three whole months before the first pay cheque comes in.

NORA: Pooh! We can always borrow in the meantime.

HELMER: Nora! [*Crosses to her and takes her playfully by the ear.*] Here we go again, you and your frivolous ideas! Suppose I went and borrowed a thousand crowns today, and you went and spent it all over Christmas, then on New Year's Eve a slate fell and hit me on the head and there I was. . . .

NORA [*putting her hand over his mouth*]: Sh! Don't say such horrid things.

HELMER: Yes, but supposing something like that did happen . . . what then?

NORA: If anything as awful as that did happen, I wouldn't care if I owed anybody anything or not.

HELMER: Yes, but what about the people I'd borrowed from?

NORA: Them? Who cares about them! They are only strangers!

HELMER: Nora, Nora! Just like a woman! Seriously though, Nora, you know what I think about these things. No debts! Never borrow! There's always something inhibited, something unpleasant, about a home built on credit and borrowed money. We two have managed to stick it out so far, and that's the way we'll go on for the little time that remains.

NORA [*walks over to the stove*]: Very well, just as you say, Torvald.

HELMER [*following her*]: There, there! My little singing bird mustn't go drooping her wings, eh? Has it got the sulks, that little squirrel of mine? [*Takes out his wallet.*] Nora, what do you think I've got here?

NORA [*quickly turning round*]: Money!

HELMER: There! [*He hands her some notes*]. Good heavens, I know only too well how Christmas runs away with the housekeeping.

NORA [*counts*]: Ten, twenty, thirty, forty. Oh, thank you, thank you, Torvald! This will see me quite a long way.

HELMER: Yes, it'll have to.

NORA: Yes, yes, I'll see that it does. But come over here, I want to show you all the things I've bought. And so cheap! Look, some new clothes for Ivar . . . and a little sword. There's a horse and a trumpet for Bob. And a doll and a doll's cot for Emmy. They are not very grand but she'll have them all broken before long anyway. And I've got some dress material and some handkerchiefs for the maids. Though, really, dear old Anne Marie should have had something better.

HELMER: And what's in this parcel here?

NORA [*shrieking*]: No, Torvald! You mustn't see that till tonight!

HELMER: All right. But tell me now, what did my little spendthrift fancy for herself?

NORA: For me? Puh, I don't really want anything.

HELMER: Of course you do. Anything reasonable that you think you might like, just tell me.

NORA: Well, I don't really know. As a matter of fact, though, Torvald . . .

HELMER: Well?

NORA [*toying with his coat buttons, and without looking at him*]: If you did want to give me something, you could . . . you could always . . .

HELMER: Well, well, out with it!

NORA [*quickly*]: You could always give me money, Torvald. Only what you think you could spare. And then I could buy myself something with it later on.

HELMER: But Nora. . . .

NORA: Oh, please, Torvald dear! Please! I beg you. Then I'd wrap the money up in some pretty gilt paper and hang it on the Christmas tree. Wouldn't that be fun?

HELMER: What do we call my pretty little pet when it runs away with all the money?

NORA: I know, I know, we call it a spendthrift. But please let's do what I said, Torvald. Then I'll have a bit of time to think about what I need most. Isn't that awfully sensible, now, eh?

HELMER [*smiling*]: Yes, it is indeed—that is, if only you really could hold on to the money I gave you, and really did buy something for yourself with it. But it just gets mixed up with the housekeeping and frittered away on all sorts of useless things, and then I have to dig into my pocket all over again.

NORA: Oh but, Torvald. . . .

HELMER: You can't deny it, Nora dear. [*Puts his arm round her waist.*] My pretty little pet is very sweet, but it runs away with an awful lot of money. It's incredible how expensive it is for a man to keep such a pet.

NORA: For shame! How can you say such a thing? As a matter of fact I save everything I can.

HELMER [*laughs*]: Yes, you are right there. Everything you *can.* But you simply can't.

NORA [*hums and smiles quietly and happily*]: Ah, if you only knew how many expenses the likes of us skylarks and squirrels have, Torvald!

HELMER: What a funny little one you are! Just like your father. Always on the lookout for money, wherever you can lay your hands on it; but as soon as you've got it, it just seems to slip through your fingers. You never seem to know what you've done with it. Well, one must accept you as you are. It's in the blood. Oh yes, it is, Nora. That sort of thing is hereditary.

NORA: Oh, I only wish I'd inherited a few more of Daddy's qualities.

HELMER: And I wouldn't want my pretty little songbird to be the least bit different from what she is now. But come to think of it, you look rather . . . rather . . . how shall I put it? . . . rather guilty today. . . .

NORA: Do I?

HELMER: Yes, you do indeed. Look me straight in the eye.

NORA [*looks at him*]: Well?

HELMER [*wagging his finger at her*]: My little sweet-tooth surely didn't forget herself in town today?

NORA: No, whatever makes you think that?

HELMER: She didn't just pop into the confectioner's for a moment?

NORA: No, I assure you, Torvald . . . !

HELMER: Didn't try sampling the preserves?

NORA: No, really I didn't.

HELMER: Didn't go nibbling a macaroon or two?

NORA: No, Torvald, honestly, you must believe me . . . !

HELMER: All right then! It's really just my little joke. . . .

NORA [*crosses to the table*]: I would never dream of doing anything you didn't want me to.

HELMER: Of course not, I know that. And then you've given me your word. . . . [*Crosses to her.*] Well then, Nora dearest, you shall keep your little Christmas secrets. They'll all come out tonight, I dare say, when we light the tree.

NORA: Did you remember to invite Dr. Rank?

HELMER: No. But there's really no need. Of course he'll come and have dinner with us. Anyway, I can ask him when he looks in this morning. I've ordered some good wine. Nora, you can't imagine how I am looking forward to this evening.

NORA: So am I. And won't the children enjoy it, Torvald!

HELMER: Oh, what a glorious feeling it is, knowing you've got a nice, safe job, and a good fat income. Don't you agree? Isn't it wonderful, just thinking about it?

NORA: Oh, it's marvelous!

HELMER: Do you remember last Christmas? Three whole weeks beforehand you shut yourself up every evening till after midnight making flowers for the Christmas tree and all the other splendid things you wanted to surprise us with. Ugh, I never felt so bored in all my life.

NORA: I wasn't the least bit bored.

HELMER [*smiling*]: But it turned out a bit of an anticlimax, Nora.

NORA: Oh, you are not going to tease me about that again! How was I to know the cat would get in and pull everything to bits?

HELMER: No, of course you weren't. Poor little Nora! All you wanted was for us to have a nice time—and it's the thought behind it that counts, after all. All the same, it's a good thing we've seen the back of those lean times.

NORA: Yes, really it's marvelous.

HELMER: Now there's no need for me to sit here all on my own, bored to tears. And you don't have to strain your dear little eyes, and work those dainty little fingers to the bone. . . .

NORA [*clapping her hands*]: No, Torvald, I don't, do I? Not any more. Oh, how marvelous it is to hear that! [*Takes his arm.*] Now I want to tell you how I've been thinking we might arrange things, Torvald. As soon as Christmas is over. . . . [*The door-bell rings in the hall.*] Oh, there's the bell. [*Tidies one or two things in the room.*] It's probably a visitor. What a nuisance!

HELMER: Remember I'm not at home to callers.

MAID [*in the doorway*]: There's a lady to see you, ma'am.

NORA: Show her in, please.

MAID [*to Helmer*]: And the doctor's just arrived, too, sir.

HELMER: Did he go straight into my room?

MAID: Yes, he did, sir.

[Helmer goes into his study. The Maid shows in Mrs. Linde, who is in traveling clothes, and closes the door after her.]

MRS. LINDE [*subdued and rather hesitantly*]: How do you do, Nora?

NORA [*uncertainly*]: How do you do?

MRS. LINDE: I'm afraid you don't recognize me.

NORA: No, I don't think I . . . And yet I seem to. . . . [*Bursts out suddenly.*] Why! Kristine! Is it really you?

MRS. LINDE: Yes, it's me.

NORA: Kristine! Fancy not recognizing you again! But how was I to, when . . . [*Gently.*] How you've changed, Kristine!

MRS. LINDE: I dare say I have. In nine . . . ten years . . . .

NORA: Is it so long since we last saw each other? Yes, it must be. Oh, believe me these last eight years have been such a happy time. And now you've come up to town, too? All that long journey in wintertime. That took courage.

MRS. LINDE: I just arrived this morning on the steamer.

NORA: To enjoy yourself over Christmas, of course. How lovely! Oh, we'll have such fun, you'll see. Do take off your things. You are not cold, are you? [*Helps her.*] There now! Now let's sit down here in comfort beside the stove. No, here, you take the armchair, I'll sit here on the rocking chair. [*Takes her hands.*] Ah, now you look a bit more like your old self again. It was just that when I first saw you. . . . But you are a little paler, Kristine . . . and perhaps even a bit thinner!

MRS. LINDE: And much, much older, Nora.

NORA: Yes, perhaps a little older . . . very, very little, not really very much. [*Stops suddenly and looks serious.*] Oh, what a thoughtless creature I am, sitting here chattering on like this! Dear, sweet Kristine, can you forgive me?

MRS. LINDE: What do you mean, Nora?

NORA [*gently*]: Poor Kristine, of course you're a widow now.

MRS. LINDE: Yes, my husband died three years ago.

NORA: Oh, I remember now. I read about it in the papers. Oh, Kristine, believe me I often thought at the time of writing to you. But I kept putting it off, something always seemed to crop up.

MRS. LINDE: My dear Nora, I understand so well.

NORA: No, it wasn't very nice of me, Kristine. Oh, you poor thing, what you must have gone through. And didn't he leave you anything?

MRS. LINDE: No.

NORA: And no children?

MRS. LINDE: No.

NORA: Absolutely nothing?

MRS. LINDE: Nothing at all . . . not even a broken heart to grieve over.

NORA [*looks at her incredulously*]: But, Kristine, is that possible?

MRS. LINDE [*smiles sadly and strokes Nora's hair*]: Oh, it sometimes happens, Nora.

NORA: So utterly alone. How terribly sad that must be for you. I have three lovely children. You can't see them for the moment, because they're out with their nanny. But now you must tell me all about yourself. . . .

MRS. LINDE: No, no, I want to hear about you.

NORA: No, you start. I won't be selfish today. I must think only about your affairs today. But there's just one thing I really must tell you. Have you heard about the great stroke of luck we've had in the last few days?

MRS. LINDE: No. What is it?

NORA: What do you think? My husband has just been made Bank Manager!

MRS. LINDE: Your husband? How splendid!

NORA: Isn't it tremendous! It's not a very steady way of making a living, you know, being a lawyer, especially if he refuses to take on anything that's the least bit shady—which of course is what Torvald does, and I think he's quite right. You can imagine how pleased we are! He starts at the Bank straight after New Year, and he's getting a big salary and lots of commission. From now on we'll be able to live quite differently . . . we'll do just what we want. Oh, Kristine, I'm so happy and relieved. I must say it's lovely to have plenty of money and not have to worry. Isn't it?

MRS. LINDE: Yes. It must be nice to have enough, at any rate.

NORA: No, not just enough, but pots and pots of money.

MRS. LINDE [*smiles*]: Nora, Nora, haven't you learned any sense yet? At school you used to be an awful spendthrift.

NORA: Yes, Torvald still says I am. [*Wags her finger.*] But little Nora isn't as stupid as everybody thinks. Oh, we haven't really been in a position where I could afford to spend a lot of money. We've both had to work.

MRS. LINDE: You too?

NORA: Yes, odd jobs—sewing, crochetwork, embroidery and things like that. [*Casually.*] And one or two other things, besides. I suppose you know that Torvald left the Ministry when we got married. There weren't any prospects of promotion in his department, and of course he needed to earn more money than he had before. But the first year he wore himself out completely. He had to take on all kinds of extra jobs, you know, and he found himself working all hours of the day and night. But he couldn't go on like that; and he became seriously ill. The doctors said it was essential for him to go South.

MRS. LINDE: Yes, I believe you spent a whole year in Italy, didn't you?

NORA: That's right. It wasn't easy to get away, I can tell you. It was just after I'd had Ivar. But of course we had to go. Oh, it was an absolutely marvelous trip. And it saved Torvald's life. But it cost an awful lot of money, Kristine.

MRS. LINDE: That I can well imagine.

NORA: Twelve hundred dollars. Four thousand eight hundred crowns. That's a lot of money, Kristine.

MRS. LINDE: Yes, but in such circumstances, one is very lucky if one has it.

NORA: Well, we got it from Daddy, you see.

MRS. LINDE: Ah, that was it. It was just about then your father died, I believe, wasn't it?

NORA: Yes, Kristine, just about then. And do you know, I couldn't even go and look after him. Here was I expecting Ivar any day. And I also had poor Torvald, gravely ill, on my hands. Dear, kind Daddy! I never saw him again, Kristine. Oh, that's the saddest thing that has happened to me in all my married life.

MRS. LINDE: I know you were very fond of him. But after that you left for Italy?

NORA: Yes, we had the money then, and the doctors said it was urgent. We left a month later.

MRS. LINDE: And your husband came back completely cured?

NORA: Fit as a fiddle!

MRS. LINDE: But . . . what about the doctor?

NORA: How do you mean?

MRS. LINDE: I thought the maid said something about the gentleman who came at the same time as me being a doctor.

NORA: Yes, that was Dr. Rank. But this isn't a professional visit. He's our best friend and he always looks in at least once a day. No, Torvald has never had a day's illness since. And the children are fit and healthy, and so am I. [*Jumps up and claps her hands.*] Oh God, oh God, isn't it marvelous to be alive, and to be happy, Kristine! . . . Oh, but I ought to be ashamed of myself . . . Here I go on talking about nothing but myself. [*She sits on a low stool near Mrs. Linde and lays her arms on her lap.*] Oh, please, you mustn't be angry with me! Tell me, is it really true that you didn't love your husband? What made you marry him, then?

MRS. LINDE: My mother was still alive; she was bedridden and helpless. And then I had my two young brothers to look after as well. I didn't think I would be justified in refusing him.

NORA: No, I dare say you are right. I suppose he was fairly wealthy then?

MRS. LINDE: He was quite well off, I believe. But the business was shaky. When he died, it went all to pieces, and there just wasn't anything left.

NORA: What then?

MRS. LINDE: Well, I had to fend for myself, opening a little shop, running a little school, anything I could turn my hand to. These last three years have been one long relentless drudge. But now it's finished, Nora. My poor dear mother doesn't need me any more, she's passed away. Nor the boys either; they're at work now, they can look after themselves.

NORA: What a relief you must find it. . . .

MRS. LINDE: No, Nora! Just unutterably empty. Nobody to live for any more. [*Stands up restless.*] That's why I couldn't stand it any longer being cut off up there. Surely it must be a bit easier here to find something to occupy your mind. If only I could manage to find a steady job of some kind, in an office perhaps. . . .

NORA: But, Kristine, that's terribly exhausting; and you look so worn out even before you start. The best thing for you would be a little holiday at some quiet little resort.

MRS. LINDE [*crosses to the window*]: I haven't any father I can fall back on for the money, Nora.

NORA [*rises*]: Oh, please, you mustn't be angry with me!

MRS. LINDE [*goes to her*]: My dear Nora, you mustn't be angry with me either. That's the worst thing about people in my position, they become so bitter. One has nobody to work for, yet one has to be on the look-out all the time. Life has to go on, and one starts thinking only of oneself. Believe it or not, when you told me the good news about your step up, I was pleased not so much for your sake as for mine.

NORA: How do you mean? Ah, I see. You think Torvald might be able to do something for you.

MRS. LINDE: Yes, that's exactly what I thought.

NORA: And so he shall, Kristine. Just leave things to me. I'll bring it up so cleverly . . . I'll think up something to put him in a good mood. Oh, I do so much want to help you.

MRS. LINDE: It is awfully kind of you, Nora, offering to do all this for me, particularly in your case, where you haven't known much trouble or hardship in your own life.

NORA: When I . . . ? I haven't known much . . . ?

MRS. LINDE [*smiling*]: Well, good heavens, a little bit of sewing to do and a few things like that. What a child you are, Nora!

NORA [*tosses her head and walks across the room*]: I wouldn't be too sure of that, if I were you.

MRS. LINDE: Oh?

NORA: You're just like the rest of them. You all think I'm useless when it comes to anything really serious. . . .

MRS. LINDE: Come, come. . . .

NORA: You think I've never had anything much to contend with in this hard world.

MRS. LINDE: Nora dear, you've only just been telling me all the things you've had to put up with.

NORA: Pooh! They were just trivialities! [*Softly.*] I haven't told you about the really big thing.

MRS. LINDE: What big thing? What do you mean?

NORA: I know you rather tend to look down on me, Kristine. But you shouldn't, you know. You are proud of having worked so hard and so long for your mother.

MRS. LINDE: I'm sure I don't look down on anybody. But it's true what you say: I am both proud and happy when I think of how I was able to make Mother's life a little easier towards the end.

NORA: And you are proud when you think of what you have done for your brothers, too.

MRS. LINDE: I think I have every right to be.

NORA: I think so too. But now I'm going to tell you something, Kristine. I too have something to be proud and happy about.

MRS. LINDE: I don't doubt that. But what is it you mean?

NORA: Not so loud. Imagine if Torvald were to hear! He must never on any account . . . nobody must know about it, Kristine, nobody but you.

MRS. LINDE: But what is it?

NORA: Come over here. [*She pulls her down on the sofa beside her.*] Yes, Kristine, I too have something to be proud and happy about. I was the one who saved Torvald's life.

MRS. LINDE: Saved . . . ? How . . . ?

NORA: I told you about our trip to Italy. Torvald would never have recovered but for that. . . .

MRS. LINDE: Well? Your father gave you what money was necessary. . . .

NORA [*smiles*]: That's what Torvald thinks, and everybody else. But . . .

MRS. LINDE: But . . . ?

NORA: Daddy never gave us a penny. I was the one who raised the money.

MRS. LINDE: You? All that money?

NORA: Twelve hundred dollars. Four thousand eight hundred crowns. What do you say to that!

MRS. LINDE: But, Nora, how was it possible? Had you won a sweepstake or something?

NORA [*contemptuously*]: A sweepstake? Pooh! There would have been nothing to it then.

MRS. LINDE: Where did you get it from, then?

NORA [*hums and smiles secretively*]: H'm, tra-la-la!

MRS. LINDE: Because what you couldn't do was borrow it.

NORA: Oh? Why not?

MRS. LINDE: Well, a wife can't borrow without her husband's consent.

NORA [*tossing her head*]: Ah, but when it happens to be a wife with a bit of a sense for business . . . a wife who knows her way about things, then. . . .

MRS. LINDE: But, Nora, I just don't understand. . . .

NORA: You don't have to. I haven't said I did borrow the money. I might have got it some other way. [*Throws herself back on the sofa.*] I might even have got it from some admirer. Anyone as reasonably attractive as I am. . . .

MRS. LINDE: Don't be so silly!

NORA: Now you must be dying of curiosity, Kristine.

MRS. LINDE: Listen to me now, Nora dear—you haven't done anything rash, have you?

NORA [*sitting up again*]: Is it rash to save your husband's life?

MRS. LINDE: I think it was rash to do anything without telling him. . . .

NORA: But the whole point was that he mustn't know anything. Good heavens, can't you see! He wasn't even supposed to know how desperately ill he was. It was me the doctors came and told his life was in danger, that the only way to save him was to go South for a while. Do you think I didn't try talking him into it first? I began dropping hints about how nice it would be if I could be taken on a little trip abroad, like other young wives. I wept, I pleaded. I told him he ought to show some consideration for my condition, and let me have a bit of my own way. And then I suggested he might take out a loan. But at that he nearly lost his temper, Kristine. He said I was being frivolous, that it was his duty as a husband not to give in to all these whims and fancies of mine—as I do believe he called them. All right, I thought, somehow you've got to be saved. And it was then I found a way . . . .

MRS. LINDE: Did your husband never find out from your father that the money hadn't come from him?

NORA: No, never. It was just about the time Daddy died. I'd intended letting him into the secret and asking him not to give me away. But when he was so ill . . . I'm sorry to say it never became necessary.

MRS. LINDE: And you never confided in your husband?

NORA: Good heavens, how could you ever imagine such a thing! When he's so strict about such matters! Besides, Torvald is a man with a good deal of pride—it would be terribly embarrassing and humiliating for him if he thought he owed anything to me. It would spoil everything between us; this happy home of ours would never be the same again.

MRS. LINDE: Are you never going to tell him?

NORA [*reflectively, half smiling*]: Oh yes, some day perhaps . . . in many years time, when I'm no longer as pretty as I am now. You mustn't laugh! What I mean of course is when Torvald isn't quite so much in love with me as he is now, when he's lost interest in watching me dance, or get dressed up, or recite. Then it might be a good thing to have something in reserve . . . .[*Breaks off.*] What nonsense! That day will never come. Well, what have you got to say to my big secret, Kristine? Still think I'm not much good for anything? One thing, though, it's meant a lot of worry for me, I can tell you. It hasn't always been easy to meet my obligations when the time came. You know in business there is something called quarterly interest, and other things called instalments, and these are always terribly difficult things to cope with. So what I've had to do is save a little here and there, you see, wherever I could. I couldn't really save anything out of the housekeeping, because Torvald has to live in decent style. I couldn't let the children go about badly dressed either—I felt any money I got for them had to go on them alone. Such sweet little things!

MRS. LINDE: Poor Nora! So it had to come out of your own allowance?

NORA: Of course. After all, I was the one it concerned most. Whenever Torvald gave me money for new clothes and such-like, I never spent more than half. And always I bought the simplest and cheapest things. It's a blessing most things look well on me, so Torvald never noticed anything. But sometimes I did feel it was a bit hard, Kristine, because it is nice to be well dressed, isn't it?

MRS. LINDE: Yes, I suppose it is.

NORA: I have had some other sources of income, of course. Last winter I was lucky enough to get quite a bit of copying to do. So I shut myself up every night and sat and wrote through to the small hours of the morning. Oh, sometimes I was so tired, so tired. But it was tremendous fun all the same, sitting there working and earning money like that. It was almost like being a man.

MRS. LINDE: And how much have you been able to pay off like this?

NORA: Well, I can't tell exactly. It's not easy to know where you are with transactions of this kind, you understand. All I know is I've paid off just as much as I could scrape together. Many's the time I was at my wit's end. [*Smiles.*] Then I used to sit here and pretend that some rich old gentleman had fallen in love with me. . . .

MRS. LINDE: What! What gentleman?

NORA: Oh, rubbish! . . . and that now he had died, and when they opened his will, there in big letters were the words: "My entire fortune is to be paid over, immediately and in cash, to charming Mrs. Nora Helmer."

MRS. LINDE: But my dear Nora—who is this man?

NORA: Good heavens, don't you understand? There never was any old gentleman; it was just something I used to sit here pretending, time and time again, when I didn't know where to turn next for money. But it doesn't make very much difference; as far as I'm concerned, the old boy can do what he likes, I'm tired of him; I can't be bothered any more with him or his will. Because now all my worries are over. [*Jumping up.*] Oh God, what a glorious thought, Kristine! No more worries! Just think of being without a care in the world . . . being able to romp with the children, and making the house nice and attractive, and having things just as Torvald likes to have them! And then spring will soon be here, and blue skies. And maybe we can go away somewhere. I might even see something of the sea again. Oh, yes! When you're happy, life is a wonderful thing!

[The doorbell is heard in the hall.]

MRS. LINDE [*gets up*]: There's the bell. Perhaps I'd better go.

NORA: No, do stay, please. I don't suppose it's for me; it's probably somebody for Torvald . . .

MAID [*in the doorway*]: Excuse me, ma'am, but there's a gentleman here wants to see Mr. Helmer, and I didn't quite know . . . because the doctor is in there. . . .

NORA: Who is the gentleman?

KROGSTAD [*in the doorway*]: It's me, Mrs. Helmer.

[Mrs. Linde starts, then turns away to the window.]

NORA [*tense, takes a step towards him and speaks in a low voice*]: You? What is it? What do you want to talk to my husband about?

KROGSTAD: Bank matters . . . in a manner of speaking. I work at the bank, and I hear your husband is to be the new manager. . . .

NORA: So it's . . .

KROGSTAD: Just routine business matters, Mrs. Helmer. Absolutely nothing else.

NORA: Well then, please go into his study.

[She nods impassively and shuts the hall door behind him; then she walks across and sees to the stove.]

MRS. LINDE: Nora . . . who was that man?

NORA: His name is Krogstad.

MRS. LINDE: So it really was him.

NORA: Do you know the man?

MRS. LINDE: I used to know him . . . a good many years ago. He was a solicitor's clerk in our district for a while.

NORA: Yes, so he was.

MRS. LINDE: How he's changed!

NORA: His marriage wasn't a very happy one, I believe.

MRS. LINDE: He's a widower now, isn't he?

NORA: With a lot of children. There, it'll burn better now.

[She closes the stove door and moves the rocking chair a little to one side.]

MRS. LINDE: He does a certain amount of business on the side, they say?

NORA: Oh? Yes, it's always possible. I just don't know. . . . But let's not think about business . . . it's all so dull.

[Dr. Rank comes in from Helmer's study.]

DR. RANK [*still in the doorway*]: No, no, Torvald, I won't intrude. I'll just look in on your wife for a moment. [*Shuts the door and notices Mrs. Linde.*] Oh, I beg your pardon. I'm afraid I'm intruding here as well.

NORA: No, not at all! [*Introduces them.*] Dr. Rank . . . Mrs. Linde.

RANK: Ah! A name I've often heard mentioned in this house. I believe I came past you on the stairs as I came in.

MRS. LINDE: I have to take things slowly going upstairs. I find it rather a trial.

RANK: Ah, some little disability somewhere, eh?

MRS. LINDE: Just a bit run down, I think, actually.

RANK: Is that all? Then I suppose you've come to town for a good rest—doing the rounds of the parties?

MRS. LINDE: I have come to look for work.

RANK: Is that supposed to be some kind of sovereign remedy for being run down?

MRS. LINDE: One must live, Doctor.

RANK: Yes, it's generally thought to be necessary.

NORA: Come, come, Dr. Rank. You are quite as keen to live as anybody.

RANK: Quite keen, yes. Miserable as I am, I'm quite ready to let things drag on as long as possible. All my patients are the same. Even those with a moral affliction are no different. As a matter of fact, there's a bad case of that kind in talking with Helmer at this very moment . . .

MRS. LINDE [*softly*]: Ah!

NORA: Whom do you mean?

RANK: A person called Krogstad—nobody you would know. He's rotten to the core. But even he began talking about having to *live*, as though it were something terribly important.

NORA: Oh? And what did he want to talk to Torvald about?

RANK: I honestly don't know. All I heard was something about the Bank.

NORA: I didn't know that Krog . . . that this Mr. Krogstad had anything to do with the Bank.

RANK: Oh yes, he's got some kind of job down there. [*To Mrs. Linde.*] I wonder if you've got people in your part of the country too who go rushing round sniffing out cases of moral corruption, and then installing the individuals concerned in nice, well-paid jobs where they can keep them under observation. Sound, decent people have to be content to stay out in the cold.

MRS. LINDE: Yet surely it's the sick who most need to be brought in.

RANK [*shrugs his shoulders*]: Well, there we have it. It's that attitude that's turning society into a clinic.

[Nora, lost in her own thoughts, breaks into smothered laughter and claps her hands.]

RANK: Why are you laughing at that? Do you know in fact what society is?

NORA: What do I care about your silly old society? I was laughing about something quite different . . . something frightfully funny. Tell me, Dr. Rank, are all the people who work at the Bank dependent on Torvald now?

RANK: Is that what you find so frightfully funny?

NORA [*smiles and hums*]: Never you mind! Never you mind! [*Walks about the room.*] Yes, it really is terribly amusing to think that we . . . that Torvald now has power over so many people. [*She takes the bag out of her pocket.*] Dr. Rank, what about a little macaroon?

RANK: Look at this, eh? Macaroons. I thought they were forbidden here.

NORA: Yes, but these are some Kristine gave me.

MRS. LINDE: What? I . . . ?

NORA: Now, now, you needn't be alarmed. You weren't to know that Torvald had forbidden them. He's worried in case they ruin my teeth, you know. Still . . . what's it matter once in a while! Don't you think so, Dr. Rank? Here! [*She pops a macaroon into his mouth.*] And you too, Kristine. And I shall have one as well; just a little one . . . or two at the most. [*She walks about the room again.*] Really I am so happy. There's just one little thing I'd love to do now.

RANK: What's that?

NORA: Something I'd love to say in front of Torvald.

RANK: Then why can't you?

NORA: No, I daren't. It's not very nice.

MRS. LINDE: Not very nice?

RANK: Well, in that case it might not be wise. But to us, I don't see why. . . . What is this you would love to say in front of Helmer?

NORA: I would simply love to say: "Damn."

RANK: Are you mad!

MRS. LINDE: Good gracious, Nora . . . !

RANK: Say it! Here he is!

NORA [*hiding the bag of macaroons*]: Sh! Sh!

[Helmer comes out of his room, his overcoat over his arm and his hat in his hand.]

NORA [*going over to him*]: Well, Torvald dear, did you get rid of him?

HELMER: Yes, he's just gone.

NORA: Let me introduce you. This is Kristine, who has just arrived in town. . . .

HELMER: Kristine . . . ? You must forgive me, but I don't think I know . . .

NORA: Mrs. Linde, Torvald dear. Kristine Linde.

HELMER: Ah, indeed. A school friend of my wife's, presumably.

MRS. LINDE: Yes, we were girls together.

NORA: Fancy, Torvald, she's come all this long way just to have a word with you.

HELMER: How is that?

MRS. LINDE: Well, it wasn't really . . .

NORA: The thing is, Kristine is terribly clever at office work, and she's frightfully keen on finding a job with some efficient man, so that she can learn even more. . . .

HELMER: Very sensible, Mrs. Linde.

NORA: And then when she heard you'd been made Bank Manager—there was a bit in the paper about it—she set off at once. Torvald please! You *will* try and do something for Kristine, won't you? For my sake?

HELMER: Well, that's not altogether impossible. You are a widow, I presume?

MRS. LINDE: Yes.

HELMER: And you've had some experience in business?

MRS. LINDE: A fair amount.

HELMER: Well, it's quite probable I can find you a job, I think. . . .

NORA [*clapping her hands*]: There, you see!

HELMER: You have come at a fortunate moment, Mrs. Linde . . .

MRS. LINDE: Oh, how can I ever thank you . . . ?

HELMER: Not a bit. [*He puts on his overcoat.*] But for the present I must ask you to excuse me. . . .

RANK: Wait. I'm coming with you.

[He fetches his fur coat from the hall and warms it at the stove.]

NORA: Don't be long, Torvald dear.

HELMER: Not more than an hour, that's all.

NORA: Are you leaving too, Kristine?

MRS. LINDE [*putting on her things*]: Yes, I must go and see if I can't find myself a room.

HELMER: Perhaps we can all walk down the road together.

NORA [*helping her*]: What a nuisance we are so limited for space here. I'm afraid it just isn't possible. . . .

MRS. LINDE: Oh, you mustn't dream of it! Goodbye, Nora dear, and thanks for everything.

NORA: Goodbye for the present. But . . . you'll be coming back this evening, of course. And you too, Dr. Rank? What's that? If you are up to it? Of course you'll be up to it. Just wrap yourself up well.

[They go out, talking, into the hall; children's voices can be heard on the stairs.]

NORA: Here they are! Here they are! [*She runs to the front door and opens it. Anne Marie, the nursemaid, enters with the children.*] Come in! Come in! [*She bends down and kisses them.*] Ah! my sweet little darlings. . . . You see them, Kristine? Aren't they lovely!

RANK: Don't stand here chattering in this draught!

HELMER: Come along, Mrs. Linde. The place now becomes unbearable for anybody except mothers.

[Dr. Rank, Helmer and Mrs. Linde go down the stairs: the Nursemaid comes into the room with the children, then Nora, shutting the door behind her.]

NORA: How fresh and bright you look! My, what red cheeks you've got! Like apples and roses. [*During the following, the children keep chattering away to her.*] Have you had a nice time? That's splendid. And you gave Emmy and Bob a ride on your sledge? Did you now! Both together! Fancy that! There's a clever boy, Ivar. Oh, let me take her a little while, Anne Marie. There's my sweet little babydoll! [*She takes the youngest of the children from the nursemaid and dances with her.*] All right, Mummy will dance with Bobby too. What? You've been throwing snowballs? Oh, I wish I'd been there. No, don't bother, Anne Marie, I'll help them off with their things. No, please, let me—I like doing it. You go on in, you look frozen. You'll find some hot coffee on the stove. [*The nursemaid goes into the room, left. Nora takes off the children's coats and hats and throws them down anywhere, while the children all talk at once.*] Really! A great big dog came running after you? But he didn't bite. No, the doggies wouldn't bite my pretty little dollies. You mustn't touch the parcels, Ivar! What are they? Wouldn't you like to know! No, no, that's nasty. Now? Shall we play something? What shall we play? Hide and seek? Yes, let's play hide and seek. Bob can hide first. Me first? All right, let me hide first.

[She and the children play, laughing and shrieking, in this room and in the adjacent room on the right. Finally Nora hides under the table; the children come rushing in to look for her but cannot find her; they hear her stifled laughter, rush to the table, lift up the tablecloth and find her. Tremendous shouts of delight. She creeps out and pretends to frighten them. More shouts. Meanwhile there has been a knock at the front door, which nobody has heard. The door half opens, and Krogstad can be seen. He waits a little; the game continues.]

KROGSTAD: I beg your pardon, Mrs. Helmer. . . .

NORA [*turns with a stifled cry and half jumps up*]: Ah! What do you want?

KROGSTAD: Excuse me. The front door was standing open. Somebody must have forgotten to shut it. . . .

NORA [*standing up*]: My husband isn't at home, Mr. Krogstad.

KROGSTAD: I know.

NORA: Well . . . what are you doing here?

KROGSTAD: I want a word with you.

NORA: With . . . ? [*Quietly, to the children.*] Go to Anne Marie. What? No, the strange man won't do anything to Mummy. When he's gone we'll have another game. [*She leads the children into the room, left, and shuts the door after them; tense and uneasy.*] You want to speak to me?

KROGSTAD: Yes, I do.

NORA: Today? But it isn't the first of the month yet. . . .

KROGSTAD: No, it's Christmas Eve. It depends entirely on you what sort of Christmas you have.

NORA: What do you want? Today I can't possibly . . .

KROGSTAD: Let's not talk about that for the moment. It's something else. You've got a moment to spare?

NORA: Yes, I suppose so, though . . .

KROGSTAD: Good. I was sitting in Olsen's café, and I saw your husband go down the road . . .

NORA: Did you?

KROGSTAD: . . . with a lady.

NORA: Well?

KROGSTAD: May I be so bold as to ask whether that lady was a Mrs. Linde?

NORA: Yes.

KROGSTAD: Just arrived in town?

NORA: Yes, today.

KROGSTAD: And she's a good friend of yours?

NORA: Yes, she is. But I can't see . . .

KROGSTAD: I also knew her once.

NORA: I know.

KROGSTAD: Oh? So you know all about it. I thought as much. Well, I want to ask you straight: is Mrs. Linde getting a job in the Bank?

NORA: How dare you cross-examine me like this, Mr. Krogstad? You, one of my husband's subordinates? But since you've asked me, I'll tell you. Yes, Mrs. Linde has got a job. And I'm the one who got it for her, Mr. Krogstad. Now you know.

KROGSTAD: So my guess was right.

NORA [*walking up and down*]: Oh, I think I can say that some of us have a little influence now and again. Just because one happens to be a woman, that doesn't mean. . . . People in subordinate positions, ought to take care they don't offend anybody . . . who . . . him . . .

KROGSTAD: . . . has influence?

NORA: Exactly.

KROGSTAD [*changing his tone*]: Mrs. Helmer, will you have the goodness to use your influence on my behalf?

NORA: What? What do you mean?

KROGSTAD: Will you be so good as to see that I keep my modest little job at the Bank?

NORA: What do you mean? Who wants to take it away from you?

KROGSTAD: Oh, you needn't try and pretend to me you don't know. I can quite see that this friend of yours isn't particularly anxious to bump up against me. And I can also see now whom I can thank for being given the sack.

NORA: But I assure you. . . .

KROGSTAD: All right, all right. But to come to the point: there's still time. And I advise you to use your influence to stop it.

NORA: But, Mr. Krogstad, I *have* no influence.

KROGSTAD: Haven't you? I thought just now you said yourself...

NORA: I didn't mean it that way, of course. Me? What makes you think I've got any influence of that kind over my husband?

KROGSTAD: I know your husband from our student days. I don't suppose he is any more steadfast than other married men.

NORA: You speak disrespectfully of my husband like that and I'll show you the door.

KROGSTAD: So the lady's got courage.

NORA: I'm not frightened of you any more. After New Year's I'll soon be finished with the whole business.

KROGSTAD [*controlling himself*]: Listen to me, Mrs. Helmer. If necessary I shall fight for my little job in the Bank as if I were fighting for my life.

NORA: So it seems.

KROGSTAD: It's not just for the money, that's the last thing I care about. There's something else . . . well, I might as well out with it. You see it's like this. You know as well as anybody that some years ago I got myself mixed up in a bit of trouble.

NORA: I believe I've heard something of the sort.

KROGSTAD: It never got as far as the courts; but immediately it was as if all paths were barred to me. So I started going in for the sort of business you know about. I had to do something, and I think I can say I haven't been one of the worst. But now I have to get out of it. My sons are growing up; for their sake I must try and win back what respectability I can. That job in the Bank was like the first step on the ladder for me. And now your husband wants to kick me off the ladder again, back into the mud.

NORA: But in God's name, Mr. Krogstad, it's quite beyond my power to help you.

KROGSTAD: That's because you haven't the will to help me. But I have ways of making you.

NORA: You wouldn't go and tell my husband I owe you money?

KROGSTAD: Suppose I did tell him?

NORA: It would be a rotten shame. [*Half choking with tears.*] That secret is all my pride and joy—why should he have to hear about it in this nasty, horrid way . . . hear about it from *you*. You would make things horribly unpleasant for me. . . .

KROGSTAD: Merely unpleasant?

NORA [*vehemently*]: Go on, do it then! It'll be all the worse for you. Because then my husband will see for himself what a bad man you are, and then you certainly won't be able to keep your job.

KROGSTAD: I asked whether it was only a bit of domestic unpleasantness you were afraid of?

NORA: If my husband gets to know about it, he'll pay off what's owing at once. And then we'd have nothing more to do with you.

KROGSTAD [*taking a pace towards her*]: Listen, Mrs. Helmer, either you haven't a very good memory, or else you don't understand much about business. I'd better make the position a little bit clearer for you.

NORA: How do you mean?

KROGSTAD: When your husband was ill, you came to me for the loan of twelve hundred dollars.

NORA: I didn't know of anybody else.

KROGSTAD: I promised to find you the money. . . .

NORA: And you did find it.

KROGSTAD: I promised to find you the money on certain conditions. At the time you were so concerned about your husband's illness, and so anxious to get the money for going away with, that I don't think you paid very much attention to all the incidentals. So there is perhaps some point in reminding you of them. Well, I promised to find you the money against an IOU which I drew up for you.

NORA: Yes, and which I signed.

KROGSTAD: Very good. But below that I added a few lines, by which your father was to stand security. This your father was to sign.

NORA: Was to . . . ? He did sign it.

KROGSTAD: I had left the date blank. The idea was that your father was to add the date himself when he signed it. Remember?

NORA: Yes, I think. . . .

KROGSTAD: I then gave you the IOU to post to your father. Wasn't that so?

NORA: Yes.

KROGSTAD: Which of course you did at once. Because only about five or six days later you brought it back to me with your father's signature. I then paid out the money.

NORA: Well? Haven't I paid the installments regularly?

KROGSTAD: Yes, fairly. But . . . coming back to what we were talking about . . . that was a pretty bad period you were going through then, Mrs. Helmer.

NORA: Yes, it was.

KROGSTAD: Your father was seriously ill, I believe.

NORA: He was very near the end.

KROGSTAD: And died shortly afterwards?

NORA: Yes.

KROGSTAD: Tell me, Mrs. Helmer, do you happen to remember which day your father died? The exact date, I mean.

NORA: Daddy died on 29 September.

KROGSTAD: Quite correct. I made some inquiries. Which brings up a rather curious point [*takes out a paper*] which I simply cannot explain.

NORA: Curious . . . ? I don't know . . .

KROGSTAD: The curious thing is, Mrs. Helmer, that your father signed this document three days after his death.

NORA: What? I don't understand. . . .

KROGSTAD: Your father died on 29 September. But look here. Your father has dated his signature 2 October. Isn't that rather curious, Mrs. Helmer? [*Nora remains silent.*] It's also remarkable that the words '2 October' and the year are not in your father's handwriting, but in a handwriting I rather think I recognize. Well, perhaps that could be explained. Your father might have forgotten to date his signature, and then somebody else might have made a guess at the date later, before the fact of your father's death was known. There is nothing wrong in that. What really matters is the signature. And *that* is of course genuine, Mrs. Helmer? It really was your father who wrote his name here?

NORA [*after a moment's silence, throws her head back and looks at him defiantly*]: No, it wasn't. It was me who signed father's name.

KROGSTAD: Listen to me. I suppose you realize that that is a very dangerous confession?

NORA: Why? You'll soon have all your money back.

KROGSTAD: Let me ask you a question: why didn't you send that document to your father?

NORA: It was impossible. Daddy was ill. If I'd asked him for his signature, I'd have to tell him what the money was for. Don't you see, when he was as ill as that I couldn't go and tell him that my husband's life was in danger. It was simply impossible.

KROGSTAD: It would have been better for you if you had abandoned the whole trip.

NORA: No, that was impossible. This was the thing that was to save my husband's life. I couldn't give it up.

KROGSTAD: But did it never strike you that this was fraudulent . . . ?

NORA: That wouldn't have meant anything to me. Why should I worry about you? I couldn't stand you, not when you insisted on going through with all those cold-blooded formalities, knowing all the time what a critical state my husband was in.

KROGSTAD: Mrs. Helmer, it's quite clear you still haven't the faintest idea what it is you've committed. But let me tell you, my own offence was no more and no worse than that, and it ruined my entire reputation.

NORA: You? Are you trying to tell me that you once risked everything to save your wife's life?

KROGSTAD: The law takes no account of motives.

NORA: Then they must be very bad laws.

KROGSTAD: Bad or not, if I produce this document in court, you'll be condemned according to them.

NORA: I don't believe it. Isn't a daughter entitled to try and save her father from worry and anxiety on his deathbed? Isn't a wife entitled to save her husband's life? I might not know very much about the law, but I feel sure of one thing: it must say somewhere that things like this are allowed. You mean to say you don't know that—you, when it's your job? You must be a rotten lawyer, Mr. Krogstad.

KROGSTAD: That may be. But when it comes to business transactions—like the sort between us two-perhaps you'll admit I know something about them? Good. Now you must please yourself. But I tell you this: if I'm pitched out a second time, you are going to keep me company.

[He bows and goes out through the hall.]

NORA [*stands thoughtfully for a moment, then tosses her head*]: Rubbish! He's just trying to scare me. I'm not such a fool as all that. [*Begins gathering up the children's clothes; after a moment she stops.*] Yet . . . ? No, it's impossible! I did it for love, didn't I?

THE CHILDREN [*in the doorway, left*]: Mummy, the gentleman's just gone out of the gate.

NORA: Yes, I know. But you mustn't say anything to anybody about that gentleman. You hear? Not even to Daddy!

THE CHILDREN: All right, Mummy. Are you going to play again?

NORA: No, not just now.

THE CHILDREN: But Mummy, you promised!

NORA: Yes, but I can't just now. Off you go now, I have a lot to do. Off you go, my darlings. [*She herds them carefully into the other room and shuts the door behind them. She sits down on the sofa, picks up her embroidery and works a few stitches, but soon stops.*] No! [*She flings her work down, stands up, goes to the hall door and calls out.*] Helene! Fetch the tree in for me, please. [*She walks across to the table, left, and opens the drawer; again pauses.*] No, really, it's quite impossible!

MAID [*with the Christmas tree*]: Where shall I put it, ma'am?

NORA: On the floor there, in the middle.

MAID: Anything else you want me to bring?

NORA: No, thank you. I've got what I want.

[The maid has put the tree down and goes out.]

NORA [*busy decorating the tree*]: Candles here . . . and flowers here—Revolting man! It's all nonsense! There's nothing to worry about. We'll have a lovely Christmas tree. And I'll do anything you want me to, Torvald; I'll sing for you, dance for you. . . .

[Helmer, with a bundle of documents under his arm, comes in by the hall door.]

NORA: Ah, back again already?
HELMER: Yes. Anybody been?
NORA: Here? No.
HELMER: That's funny. I just saw Krogstad leave the house.
NORA: Oh? O yes, that's right. Krogstad was here a minute.
HELMER: Nora, I can tell by your face he's been asking you to put a good word in for him.
NORA: Yes.
HELMER: And you were to pretend it was your own idea? You were to keep quiet about his having been here. He asked you to do that as well, didn't he?
NORA: Yes, Torvald. But . . .
HELMER: Nora, Nora, what possessed you to do a thing like that? Talking to a person like him, making him promises? And then on top of everything, to tell me a lie!
NORA: A lie . . . ?
HELMER: Didn't you say that nobody had been here? [*Wagging his finger at her.*] Never again must my little song-bird do a thing like that! Little song-birds must keep their pretty little beaks out of mischief; no chirruping out of tune! [*Puts his arm round her waist.*] Isn't that the way we want things to be? Yes, of course it is. [*Lets her go.*] So let's say no more about it. [*Sits down by the stove.*] Ah, nice and cozy here!

[He glances through his papers.]

NORA [*busy with the Christmas tree, after a short pause*]: Torvald!
HELMER: Yes.
NORA: I'm so looking forward to the fancy dress ball at the Stenborgs on Boxing Day.
HELMER: And I'm terribly curious to see what sort of surprise you've got for me.
NORA: Oh, it's too silly.
HELMER: Oh?
NORA: I just can't think of anything suitable. Everything seems so absurd, so pointless.
HELMER: Has my little Nora come to that conclusion?
NORA [*behind his chair, her arms on the chair-back*]: Are you very busy, Torvald?
HELMER: Oh. . . .
NORA: What are all those papers?
HELMER: Bank matters.
NORA: Already?
HELMER: I have persuaded the retiring manager to give me authority to make any changes in organization or personnel I think necessary. I have to

work on it over the Christmas week. I want everything straight by the New Year.

NORA: So that was why that poor Krogstad. . . .

HELMER: Hm!

NORA [*still leaning against the back of the chair, running her fingers through his hair*]: If you hadn't been so busy, Torvald, I'd have asked you to do me an awfully big favor.

HELMER: Let me hear it. What's it to be?

NORA: Nobody's got such good taste as you. And the thing is I do so want to look my best at the fancy dress ball. Torvald, couldn't you give me some advice and tell me what you think I ought to go as, and how I should arrange my costume?

HELMER: Aha! So my impulsive little woman is asking for somebody to come to her rescue, eh?

NORA: Please, Torvald, I never get anywhere without your help.

HELMER: Very well, I'll think about it. We'll find something.

NORA: That's sweet of you. [*She goes across to the tree again; pause.*] How pretty these red flowers look.—Tell me, was it really something terribly wrong this man Krogstad did?

HELMER: Forgery. Have you any idea what that means?

NORA: Perhaps circumstances left him no choice?

HELMER: Maybe. Or perhaps, like so many others, he just didn't think. I am not so heartless that I would necessarily want to condemn a man for a single mistake like that.

NORA: Oh no, Torvald, of course not!

HELMER: Many a man might be able to redeem himself, if he honestly confessed his guilt and took his punishment.

NORA: Punishment?

HELMER: But that wasn't the way Krogstad chose. He dodged what was due to him by a cunning trick. And that's what has been the cause of his corruption.

NORA: Do you think it would . . . ?

HELMER: Just think how a man with a thing like that on his conscience will always be having to lie and cheat and dissemble; he can never drop the mask, not even with his own wife and children. And the children—that's the most terrible part of it, Nora.

NORA: Why?

HELMER: A fog of lies like that in a household, and it spreads disease and infection to every part of it. Every breath the children take in that kind of house is reeking with evil germs.

NORA [*closer behind him*]: Are you sure of that?

HELMER: My dear Nora, as a lawyer I know what I'm talking about. Practically all juvenile delinquents come from homes where the mother is dishonest.

NORA: Why mothers particularly?

HELMER: It's generally traceable to the mothers, but of course fathers can have the same influence. Every lawyer knows that only too well. And yet there's Krogstad been poisoning his own children for years with lies and deceit. That's the reason I call him morally depraved. [*Holds out his hands to her.*] That's why my sweet little Nora must promise me not to try putting in any more good words for him. Shake hands on it. Well? What's this? Give me your hand. There now! That's settled. I assure you I would have found it impossible to work with him. I quite literally feel physically sick in the presence of such people.

NORA [*draws her hand away and walks over to the other side of the Christmas tree*]: How hot it is in here! And I still have such a lot to do.

HELMER [*stands up and collects his papers together*]: Yes, I'd better think of getting some of this read before dinner. I must also think about your costume. And I might even be able to lay my hands on something to wrap in gold paper and hang on the Christmas tree. [*He lays his hand on her head.*] My precious little singing bird.

[*He goes into his study and shuts the door behind him.*]

NORA [*quietly, after a pause*]: Nonsense! It can't be. It's impossible. It *must* be impossible.

MAID [*in the doorway, left*]: The children keep asking so nicely if they can come in and see Mummy.

NORA: No, no, don't let them in! You stay with them, Anne Marie.

MAID: Very well, ma'am.

[*She shuts the door.*]

NORA [*pale with terror*]: Corrupt my children . . . ! Poison my home? [*Short pause; she throws back her head.*] It's not true! It could never, never be true!

ACT II

The same room. In the corner beside the piano stands the Christmas tree, stripped, bedraggled and with its candles burnt out. Nora's outdoor things lie on the sofa. Nora, alone there, walks about restlessly; at last she stops by the sofa and picks up her coat.

NORA [*putting her coat down again*]: Somebody's coming! [*Crosses to the door, listens.*] No, it's nobody. Nobody will come today, of course, Christmas Day—nor tomorrow, either. But perhaps. . . .[*She opens the door and looks out.*] No, nothing in the letter box; quite empty. [*Comes forward.*] Oh, nonsense! He didn't mean it seriously. Things like that can't happen. It's impossible. Why, I have three small children.

[*The nursemaid comes from the room, left, carrying a big cardboard box.*]

NURSE MAID: I finally found it, the box with the fancy dress costumes.

NORA: Thank you. Put it on the table, please.

NURSE MAID [*does this*]: But I'm afraid they are in an awful mess.

NORA: Oh, if only I could rip them up into a thousand pieces!

NURSE MAID: Good heavens, they can be mended all right, with a bit of patience.

NORA: Yes, I'll go over and get Mrs. Linde to help me.

NURSE MAID: Out again? In this terrible weather? You'll catch your death of cold, Ma'am.

NORA: Oh, worse things might happen.—How are the children?

NURSE MAID: Playing with their Christmas presents, poor little things, but . . .

NORA: Do they keep asking for me?

NURSE MAID: They are so used to being with their Mummy.

NORA: Yes, Anne Marie, from now on I can't be with them as often as I was before.

NURSE MAID: Ah well, children get used to anything in time.

NORA: Do you think so? Do you think they would forget their Mummy if she went away for good?

NURSE MAID: Good gracious—for good?

NORA: Tell me, Anne Marie—I've often wondered—how on earth could you bear to hand your child over to strangers?

NURSE MAID: Well, there was nothing else for it when I had to come and nurse my little Nora.

NORA: Yes but . . . how could you *bring* yourself to do it?

NURSE MAID: When I had the chance of such a good place? When a poor girl's been in trouble she must make the best of things. Because *he* didn't help, the rotter.

NORA: But your daughter will have forgotten you.

NURSE MAID: Oh no, she hasn't. She wrote to me when she got confirmed, and again when she got married.

NORA [*putting her arms round her neck*]: Dear old Anne Marie, you were a good mother to me when I was little.

NURSE MAID: My poor little Nora never had any other mother but me.

NORA: And if my little ones only had you, I know you would. . . .Oh, what am I talking about! [*She opens the box.*] Go in to them. I must . . . Tomorrow I'll let you see how pretty I am going to look.

NURSE MAID: Ah, there'll be nobody at the ball as pretty as my Nora.

[She goes into the room, left.]

NORA [*begins unpacking the box, but soon throws it down*]: Oh, if only I dare go out. If only I could be sure nobody would come. And that nothing would happen in the meantime here at home. Rubbish—nobody's going to come. I mustn't think about it. Brush this muff. Pretty gloves, pretty gloves! I'll put it right out of my mind. One, two, three, four, five, six. . . . [*Screams.*] Ah, they are coming. . . .[*She starts towards the door, but stops irresolute. Mrs. Linde comes from the hall, where she has taken off her things.*] Oh, it's you, Kristine. There's nobody else out there, is there? I'm so glad you've come.

MRS. LINDE: I heard you'd been over looking for me.

NORA: Yes, I was just passing. There's something you must help me with. Come and sit beside me on the sofa here. You see, the Stenborgs are having a fancy dress party upstairs tomorrow evening, and now Torvald wants me to go as a Neapolitan fisher lass and dance the tarantella. I learned it in Capri, you know.

MRS. LINDE: Well, well! So you are going to do a party piece?

NORA: Torvald says I should. Look, here's the costume, Torvald had it made for me down there. But it's got all torn and I simply don't know. . . .

MRS. LINDE: We'll soon have that put right. It's only the trimming come away here and there. Got a needle and thread? Ah, here's what we are after.

NORA: It's awfully kind of you.

MRS. LINDE: So you are going to be all dressed up tomorrow, Nora? Tell you what—I'll pop over for a minute to see you in all your finery. But I'm quite forgetting to thank you for the pleasant time we had last night.

NORA [*gets up and walks across the room*]: Somehow I didn't think yesterday was as nice as things generally are.—You should have come to town a little earlier, Kristine.—Yes, Torvald certainly knows how to make things pleasant about the place.

MRS. LINDE: You too, I should say. You are not your father's daughter for nothing. But tell me, is Dr. Rank always as depressed as he was last night?

NORA: No, last night it was rather obvious. He's got something seriously wrong with him, you know. Tuberculosis of the spine, poor fellow. His father was a horrible man, who used to have mistresses and things like that. That's why the son was always ailing, right from being a child.

MRS. LINDE [*lowering her sewing*]: But my dear Nora, how do you come to know about things like that?

NORA [*walking about the room*]: Huh! When you've got three children, you get these visits from . . . women who have had a certain amount of medical training. And you hear all sorts of things from them.

MRS. LINDE [*begins sewing again; short silence*]: Does Dr. Rank call in every day?

NORA: Every single day. He was Torvald's best friend as a boy, and he's a good friend of mine, too. Dr. Rank is almost like one of the family.

MRS. LINDE: But tell me—is he really genuine? What I mean is: doesn't he sometimes rather turn on the charm?

NORA: No, on the contrary. What makes you think that?

MRS. LINDE: When you introduced me yesterday, he claimed he'd often heard my name in this house. But afterwards I noticed your husband hadn't the faintest idea who I was. Then how is it that Dr. Rank should. . . .

NORA: Oh yes, it was quite right what he said, Kristine. You see Torvald is so terribly in love with me that he says he wants me all to himself. When we were first married, it even used to make him sort of jealous if I only as much as mentioned any of my old friends from back home. So of course I stopped doing it. But I often talk to Dr. Rank about such things. He likes hearing about them.

MRS. LINDE: Listen, Nora! In lots of ways you are still a child. Now, I'm a good deal older than you, and a bit more experienced. I'll tell you something: I think you ought to give up all this business with Dr. Rank.

NORA: Give up what business?

MRS. LINDE: The whole thing, I should say. Weren't you saying yesterday something about a rich admirer who was to provide you with money. . . .

NORA: One who's never existed, I regret to say. But what of it?

MRS. LINDE: Has Dr. Rank money?

NORA: Yes, he has.

MRS. LINDE: And no dependents?

NORA: No, nobody. But . . . ?

MRS. LINDE: And he comes to the house every day?

NORA: Yes, I told you.

MRS. LINDE: But how can a man of his position want to pester you like this?

NORA: I simply don't understand.

MRS. LINDE: Don't pretend, Nora. Do you think I don't see now who you borrowed the twelve hundred from?

NORA: Are you out of your mind? Do you really think that? A friend of ours who comes here every day? The whole situation would have been absolutely intolerable.

MRS. LINDE: It *really* isn't him?

NORA: No, I give you my word. It would never have occurred to me for one moment. . . . Anyway, he didn't have the money to lend then. He didn't inherit it till later.

MRS. LINDE: Just as well for you, I'd say, my dear Nora.

NORA: No, it would never have occurred to me to ask Dr. Rank. . . . All the same I'm pretty certain if I were to ask him . . .

MRS. LINDE: But of course you won't.

NORA: No, of course not. I can't ever imagine it being necessary. But I'm quite certain if ever I were to mention it to Dr. Rank. . . .

MRS. LINDE: Behind your husband's back?

NORA: I have to get myself out of that other business. That's also behind his back. I must get myself out of that.

MRS. LINDE: Yes, that's what I said yesterday. But . . .

NORA [*walking up and down*]: A man's better at coping with these things than a woman. . . .

MRS. LINDE: Your own husband, yes.

NORA: Nonsense! [*Stops.*] When you've paid everything you owe, you do get your IOU back again, don't you?

MRS. LINDE: Of course.

NORA: And you can tear it up into a thousand pieces and burn it—the nasty, filthy thing!

MRS. LINDE [*looking fixedly at her, puts down her sewing and slowly rises*]: Nora, you are hiding something from me.

NORA: Is it so obvious?

MRS. LINDE: Something has happened to you since yesterday morning. Nora, what is it?

NORA [*going towards her*]: Kristine! [*Listens.*] Hush! There's Torvald back. Look, you go and sit in there beside the children for the time being. Torvald can't stand the sight of mending lying about. Get Anne Marie to help you.

MRS. LINDE [*gathering a lot of the things together*]: All right, but I'm not leaving until we have thrashed this thing out.

[She goes into the room, left; at the same time Helmer comes in from the hall.]

NORA [*goes to meet him*]: I've been longing for you to be back, Torvald, dear.

HELMER: Was that the dressmaker . . . ?

NORA: No, it was Kristine; she's helping me with my costume. I think it's going to look very nice . . .

HELMER: Wasn't that a good idea of mine, now?

NORA: Wonderful! But wasn't it also nice of me to let you have your way?

HELMER [*taking her under the chin*]: Nice of you—because you let your husband have his way? All right, you little rogue, I know you didn't mean it that way. But I don't want to disturb you. You'll be wanting to try the costume on, I suppose.

NORA: And I dare say you've got work to do?

HELMER: Yes. [*Shows her a bundle of papers.*] Look at this. I've been down at the Bank. . . .

[He turns to go into his study.]

NORA: Torvald!

HELMER [*stopping*]: Yes.

NORA: If a little squirrel were to ask ever so nicely . . . ?

HELMER: Well?

NORA: Would you do something for it?

HELMER: Naturally I would first have to know what it is.

NORA: Please, if only you would let it have its way, and do what it wants, it'd scamper about and do all sorts of marvelous tricks.

HELMER: What is it?

NORA: And the pretty little skylark would sing all day long. . . .

HELMER: Huh! It does that anyway.

NORA: I'd pretend I was an elfin child and dance a moonlight dance for you, Torvald.

HELMER: Nora—I hope it's not that business you started on this morning?

NORA [*coming closer*]: Yes, it is, Torvald. I implore you!

HELMER: You have the nerve to bring that up again?

NORA: Yes, yes, you *must* listen to me. You must let Krogstad keep his job at the Bank.

HELMER: My dear Nora, I'm giving his job to Mrs. Linde.

NORA: Yes, it's awfully sweet of you. But couldn't you get rid of somebody else in the office instead of Krogstad?

HELMER: This really is the most incredible obstinacy! Just because you go and make some thoughtless promise to put in a good word for him, you expect me . . .

NORA: It's not that, Torvald. It's for your own sake. That man writes in all the nastiest papers, you told me that yourself. He can do you no end of harm. He terrifies me to death. . . .

HELMER: Aha, now I see. It's your memories of what happened before that are frightening you.

NORA: What do you mean?

HELMER: It's your father you are thinking of.

NORA: Yes . . . yes, that's right. You remember all the nasty insinuations those wicked people put in the papers about Daddy? I honestly think they would have had him dismissed if the Ministry hadn't sent you down to investigate, and you hadn't been so kind and helpful.

HELMER: My dear little Nora, there is a considerable difference between your father and me. Your father's professional conduct was not entirely above suspicion. Mine is. And I hope it's going to stay that way as long as I hold this position.

NORA: But nobody knows what some of these evil people are capable of. Things could be so nice and pleasant for us here, in the peace and quiet of our home—you and me and the children, Torvald! That's why I implore you. . . .

HELMER: The more you plead for him, the more impossible you make it for me to keep him on. It's already known down at the Bank that I am going to give Krogstad his notice. If it ever got around that the new manager had been talked over by his wife. . . .

NORA: What of it?

HELMER: Oh, nothing! As long as the little woman gets her own stubborn way . . . ! Do you want me to make myself a laughing stock in the office? . . . Give people the idea that I am susceptible to any kind of outside pressure? You can imagine how soon I'd feel the consequences of that! Anyway, there's one other consideration that makes it impossible to have Krogstad in the Bank as long as I am manager.

NORA: What's that?

HELMER: At a pinch I might have overlooked his past lapses. . . .

NORA: Of course you could, Torvald!

HELMER: And I'm told he's not bad at his job, either. But we knew each other rather well when we were younger. It was one of those rather rash friendships that prove embarrassing in later life. There's no reason why you shouldn't know we were once on terms of some familiarity. And he, in his tactless way, makes no attempt to hide the fact, particularly when other people are present. On the contrary, he thinks he has every right to treat me as an equal, with his "Torvald this" and "Torvald that" every time he opens his mouth. I find it extremely irritating, I can tell you. He would make my position at the Bank absolutely intolerable.

NORA: Torvald, surely you aren't serious?

HELMER: Oh? Why not?

NORA: Well, it's all so petty.

HELMER: What's that you say? Petty? Do you think I'm petty?

NORA: No, not at all, Torvald dear! And that's why . . .

HELMER: Doesn't make any difference! . . . You call my motives petty; so I must be petty too. Petty! Indeed! Well, we'll put a stop to that, once and for all. [*He opens the hall door and calls.*] Helene!

NORA: What are you going to do?

HELMER [*searching among his papers*]: Settle things. [*The maid comes in.*] See this letter? I want you to take it down at once. Get hold of a messenger and get him to deliver it. Quickly. The address is on the outside. There's the money.

MAID: Very good, sir.

[She goes with the letter.]

HELMER [*putting his papers together*]: There now, my stubborn little miss.

NORA [*breathless*]: Torvald . . . what was that letter?

HELMER: Krogstad's notice.

NORA: Get it back, Torvald! There's still time! Oh, Torvald, get it back! Please for my sake, for your sake, for the sake of the children! Listen, Torvald, please! You don't realize what it can do to us.

HELMER: Too late.

NORA: Yes, too late.

HELMER: My dear Nora, I forgive you this anxiety of yours, although it is actually a bit of an insult. Oh, but it is, I tell you! It's hardly flattering to suppose that anything this miserable pen-pusher wrote could frighten *me!*

But I forgive you all the same, because it is rather a sweet way of showing how much you love me. [*He takes her in his arms.*] This is how things must be, my own darling Nora. When it comes to the point, I've enough strength and enough courage, believe me, for whatever happens. You'll find I'm man enough to take everything on myself.

NORA [*terrified*]: What do you mean?

HELMER: Everything, I said. . . .

NORA [*in command of herself*]: That is something you shall never, never do.

HELMER: All right, then we'll share it, Nora—as man and wife. That's what we'll do. [*Caressing her.*] Does that make you happy now? There, there, don't look at me with those eyes, like a little frightened dove. The whole thing is sheer imagination.—Why don't you run through the tarantella and try out the tambourine? I'll go into my study and shut both the doors, then I won't hear anything. You can make all the noise you want. [*Turns in the doorway.*] And when Rank comes, tell him where he can find me.

[He nods to her, goes with his papers into his room, and shuts the door behind him.]

NORA [*wild-eyed with terror, stands as though transfixed*]: He's quite capable of doing it! He would do it! No matter what, he'd do it.—No, never in this world! Anything but that! Help? Some way out . . . ? [*The doorbell rings in the hall.*] Dr. Rank . . . ! Anything but that, anything! [*She brushes her hands over her face, pulls herself together and opens the door into the hall. Dr. Rank is standing outside hanging up his fur coat. During what follows it begins to grow dark.*] Hello, Dr. Rank. I recognized your ring. Do you mind not going in to Torvald just yet, I think he's busy.

RANK: And you?

[Dr. Rank comes into the room and she closes the door behind him.]

NORA: Oh, you know very well I've always got time for you.

RANK: Thank you. A privilege I shall take advantage of as long as I am able.

NORA: What do you mean-as long as you are able?

RANK: Does that frighten you?

NORA: Well, it's just that it sounds so strange. Is anything likely to happen?

RANK: Only what I have long expected. But I didn't think it would come quite so soon.

NORA [*catching at his arm*]: What have you found out? Dr. Rank, you must tell me!

RANK: I'm slowly sinking. There's nothing to be done about it.

NORA [*with a sigh of relief*]: Oh, it's *you* you're . . . ?

RANK: Who else? No point in deceiving oneself. I am the most wretched of all my patients, Mrs. Helmer. These last few days I've made a careful analysis of my internal economy. Bankrupt! Within a month I shall probably be lying rotting up there in the churchyard.

NORA: Come now, what a ghastly thing to say!

RANK: The whole damned thing is ghastly. But the worst thing is all the ghastliness that has to be gone through first. I only have one more test to make; and when that's done I'll know pretty well when the final disintegration will start. There's something I want to ask you. Helmer is a sensitive soul; he loathes anything that's ugly. I don't want him visiting me. . . .

NORA: But Dr. Rank. . . .

RANK: On no account must he. I won't have it. I'll lock the door on him.—As soon as I'm absolutely certain of the worst, I'll send you my visiting card with a black cross on it. You'll know then the final horrible disintegration has begun.

NORA: Really, you are being quite absurd today. And here was I hoping you would be in a thoroughly good mood.

RANK: With death staring me in the face? Why should I suffer for another man's sins? What justice is there in that? Somewhere, somehow, every single family must be suffering some such cruel retribution. . . .

NORA [*stopping up her ears*]: Rubbish! Do cheer up!

RANK: Yes, really the whole thing's nothing but a huge joke. My poor innocent spine must do penance for my father's gay subaltern life.

NORA [*by the table, left*]: Wasn't he rather partial to asparagus and *pàté de foie gras?*

RANK: Yes, he was. And truffles.

NORA: Truffles, yes. And oysters, too, I believe?

RANK: Yes, oysters, oysters, of course.

NORA: And all the port and champagne that goes with them. It does seem a pity all these delicious things should attack the spine.

RANK: Especially when they attack a poor spine that never had any fun out of them.

NORA: Yes, that is an awful pity.

RANK [*looks at her sharply*]: Hm. . . .

NORA [*after a pause*]: Why did you smile?

RANK: No, it was you who laughed.

NORA: No, it was you who smiled, Dr. Rank!

RANK [*getting up*]: You are a bigger rascal than I thought you were.

NORA: I feel full of mischief today.

RANK: So it seems.

NORA [*putting her hands on his shoulders*]: Dear, dear Dr. Rank, you mustn't go and die on Torvald and me.

RANK: You wouldn't miss me for long. When you are gone, you are soon forgotten.

NORA [*looking at him anxiously*]: Do you think so?

RANK: People make new contacts, then . . .

NORA: Who make new contacts?

RANK: Both you and Helmer will, when I'm gone. You yourself are already well on the way, it seems to me. What was this Mrs. Linde doing here last night?

NORA: Surely you aren't jealous of poor Kristine?

RANK: Yes, I am. She'll be my successor in this house. When I'm done for, I can see this woman. . . .

NORA: Hush! Don't talk so loud, she's in there.

RANK: Today as well? There you are, you see!

NORA: Just to do some sewing on my dress. Good Lord, how absurd you are! [*She sits down on the sofa.*] Now Dr. Rank, cheer up. You'll see tomorrow how nicely I can dance. And you can pretend I'm doing it just for you—and for Torvald as well, of course. [*She takes various things out of the box.*] Come here, Dr. Rank. I want to show you something.

RANK [*sits*]: What is it?

NORA: Look!

RANK: Silk stockings.

NORA: Flesh-coloured! Aren't they lovely! Of course, it's dark here now, but tomorrow . . . . No, no, no, you can only look at the feet. Oh well, you might as well see a bit higher up, too.

RANK: Hm. . . .

NORA: Why are you looking so critical? Don't you think they'll fit?

RANK: I couldn't possibly offer any informed opinion about that.

NORA [*looks at him for a moment*]: Shame on you. [*Hits him lightly across the ear with the stockings.*] Take that! [*Folds them up again.*]

RANK: And what other delights am I to be allowed to see?

NORA: Not another thing. You are too naughty. [*She hums a little and searches among her things.*]

RANK [*after a short pause*]: Sitting here so intimately like this with you, I can't imagine . . . I simply cannot conceive what would have become of me if I had never come to this house.

NORA [*smiles*]: Yes, I rather think you do enjoy coming here.

RANK [*in a low voice, looking fixedly ahead*]: And the thought of having to leave it all . . .

NORA: Nonsense. You aren't leaving.

RANK [*in the same tone*]: . . . without being able to leave behind even the slightest token of gratitude, hardly a fleeting regret even . . . nothing but an empty place to be filled by the first person that comes along.

NORA: Supposing I were to ask you to . . . ? No . . .

RANK: What?

NORA: . . . to show me the extent of your friendship . . .

RANK: Yes?

NORA: I mean . . . to do me a tremendous favor. . . .

RANK: Would you really, for once, give me that pleasure?

NORA: You have no idea what it is.

RANK: All right, tell me.

NORA: No, really I can't, Dr. Rank. It's altogether too much to ask . . . because I need your advice and help as well. . . .

RANK: The more the better. I cannot imagine what you have in mind. But tell me anyway. You do trust me, don't you?

NORA: Yes, I trust you more than anybody I know. You are my best and my most faithful friend. I know that. So I will tell you. Well then, Dr. Rank, there is something you must help me to prevent. You know how deeply, how passionately Torvald is in love with me. He would never hesitate for a moment to sacrifice his life for my sake.

RANK [*bending towards her*]: Nora . . . do you think he's the only one who . . . ?

NORA [*stiffening slightly*]: Who . . . ?

RANK: Who wouldn't gladly give his life for your sake.

NORA [*sadly*]: Oh!

RANK: I swore to myself you would know before I went. I'll never have a better opportunity. Well, Nora! Now you know. And now you know too that you can confide in me as in nobody else.

NORA [*rises and speaks evenly and calmly*]: Let me past.

RANK [*makes way for her, but remains seated*]: Nora. . . .

NORA [*in the hall doorway*]: Helene, bring the lamp in, please. [*Walks over to the stove.*] Oh, my dear Dr. Rank, that really was rather horrid of you.

RANK [*getting up*]: That I have loved you every bit as much as anybody? Is *that* horrid?

NORA: No, but that you had to go and tell me. When it was all so unnecessary. . . .

RANK: What do you mean? Did you know . . . ?

[The maid comes in with the lamp, puts it on the table, and goes out again.]

RANK: Nora . . . Mrs. Helmer . . . I'm asking you if you knew?

NORA: How can I tell whether I did or didn't. I simply can't tell you. . . . Oh, how could you be so clumsy, Dr. Rank! When everything was so nice.

RANK: Anyway, you know now that I'm at your service, body and soul. So you can speak out.

NORA [*looking at him*]: After this?

RANK: I beg you to tell me what it is.

NORA: I can tell you nothing now.

RANK: You must. You can't torment me like this. Give me a chance—I'll do anything that's humanly possible.

NORA: You can do nothing for me now. Actually, I don't really need any help. It's all just my imagination, really it is. Of course! [*She sits down in the rock-*

ing chair, looks at him and smiles.] I must say, you are a nice one, Dr. Rank! Don't you feel ashamed of yourself, now the lamp's been brought in?

RANK: No, not exactly. But perhaps I ought to go—for good?

NORA: No, you mustn't do that. You must keep coming just as you've always done. You know very well Torvald would miss you terribly.

RANK: And *you?*

NORA: I always think it's tremendous fun having you.

RANK: That's exactly what gave me wrong ideas. I just can't puzzle you out. I often used to feel you'd just as soon be with me as with Helmer.

NORA: Well, you see, there are those people you love and those people you'd almost rather *be* with.

RANK: Yes, there's something in that.

NORA: When I was a girl at home, I loved Daddy best, of course. But I also thought it great fun if I could slip into the maids' room. For one thing they never preached at me. And they always talked about such exciting things.

RANK: Aha! So it's their role I've taken over!

NORA [*jumps up and crosses to him*]: Oh, my dear, kind Dr. Rank, I didn't mean that at all. But you can see how it's a bit with Torvald as it was with Daddy. . . .

[The maid comes in from the hall.]

MAID: Please, ma'am . . . !

[She whispers and hands her a card.]

NORA [*glances at the card*]: Ah!

[She puts it in her pocket.]

RANK: Anything wrong?

NORA: No, no, not at all. It's just . . . it's my new costume. . . .

RANK: How is that? There's your costume in there.

NORA: That one, yes. But this is another one. I've ordered it. Torvald mustn't hear about it. . . .

RANK: Ah, so that's the big secret, is it!

NORA: Yes, that's right. Just go in and see him, will you? He's in the study. Keep him occupied for the time being. . . .

RANK: Don't worry. He shan't escape me.

[He goes into Helmer's study.]

NORA [*to the maid*]: Is he waiting in the kitchen?

MAID: Yes, he came up the back stairs. . . .

NORA: But didn't you tell him somebody was here?

MAID: Yes, but it was no good.

NORA: Won't he go?

MAID: No, he won't till he's seen you.

NORA: Let him in, then. But quietly. Helene, you mustn't tell anybody about this. It's a surprise for my husband.

MAID: I understand, ma'am. . . .

[She goes out.]

NORA: Here it comes! What I've been dreading! No, no, it can't happen, it *can't* happen.

[She walks over and bolts Helmer's door. The maid opens the hall door for Krogstad and shuts it again behind him. He is wearing a fur coat, overshoes, and a fur cap.]

NORA [*goes towards him*]: Keep your voice down, my husband is at home.

KROGSTAD: What if he is?

NORA: What do you want with me?

KROGSTAD: To find out something.

NORA: Hurry, then. What is it?

KROGSTAD: You know I've been given notice.

NORA: I couldn't prevent it, Mr. Krogstad, I did my utmost for you, but it was no use.

KROGSTAD: Has your husband so little affection for you? He knows what I can do to you, yet he dares. . . .

NORA: You don't imagine he knows about it!

KROGSTAD: No, I didn't imagine he did. It didn't seem a bit like my good friend Torvald Helmer to show that much courage. . . .

NORA: Mr. Krogstad, I must ask you to show some respect for my husband.

KROGSTAD: Oh, sure! All due respect! But since you are so anxious to keep this business quiet, Mrs. Helmer, I take it you now have a rather clearer idea of just what it is you've done, than you had yesterday.

NORA: Clearer than *you* could ever have given me.

KROGSTAD: Yes, being as I am such a rotten lawyer. . . .

NORA: What do *you* want with me?

KROGSTAD: I just wanted to see how things stood, Mrs. Helmer. I've been thinking about you all day. Even a mere money-lender, a hack journalist, a—well, even somebody like me has a bit of what you might call feeling.

NORA: Show it then. Think of my little children.

KROGSTAD: Did you or your husband think of mine? But what does it matter now? There was just one thing I wanted to say: you needn't take this business too seriously. I shan't start any proceedings, for the present.

NORA: Ah, I knew you wouldn't.

KROGSTAD: The whole thing can be arranged quite amicably. Nobody need know. Just the three of us.

NORA: My husband must never know.

KROGSTAD: How can you prevent it? Can you pay off the balance?

NORA: No, not immediately.

KROGSTAD: Perhaps you've some way of getting hold of the money in the next few days.

NORA: None I want to make use of.

KROGSTAD: Well, it wouldn't have been very much help to you if you had. Even if you stood there with the cash in your hand and to spare, you still wouldn't get your IOU back from me now.

NORA: What are you going to do with it?

KROGSTAD: Just keep it—have it in my possession. Nobody who isn't implicated need know about it. So if you are thinking of trying any desperate remedies . . .

NORA: Which I am. . . .

KROGSTAD: . . . if you happen to be thinking of running away . . .

NORA: Which I am!

KROGSTAD: . . . or anything worse . . .

NORA: How did you know?

KROGSTAD: . . . forget it!

NORA: How did you know I was thinking of *that?*

KROGSTAD: Most of us think of *that,* to begin with. I did, too; but I didn't have the courage. . . .

NORA [*tonelessly*]: I haven't either.

KROGSTAD [*relieved*]: So you haven't the courage either, eh?

NORA: No, I haven't! I haven't!

KROGSTAD: It would also be very stupid. There'd only be the first domestic storm to get over. . . . I've got a letter to your husband in my pocket here. . . .

NORA: And it's all in there?

KROGSTAD: In as tactful a way as possible.

NORA [*quickly*]: He must never read that letter. Tear it up. I'll find the money somehow.

KROGSTAD: Excuse me, Mrs. Helmer, but I've just told you. . . .

NORA: I'm not talking about the money I owe you. I want to know how much you are demanding from my husband, and I'll get the money.

KROGSTAD: I want no money from your husband.

NORA: What do you want?

KROGSTAD: I'll tell you. I want to get on my feet again, Mrs. Helmer; I want to get to the top. And your husband is going to help me. For the last eighteen months I've gone straight; all that time it's been hard going; I was content to work my way up, step by step. Now I'm being kicked out, and I won't stand for being taken back again as an act of charity. I'm going to get to the top, I tell you. I'm going back into that Bank—with a better job. Your husband is going to create a new vacancy, just for me. . . .

NORA: He'll never do that!

KROGSTAD: He will do it. I know him. He'll do it without so much as a whimper.

And once I'm in there with him, you'll see what's what. In less than a year I'll be his right-hand man. It'll be Nils Krogstad, not Torvald Helmer, who'll be running that Bank.

NORA: You'll never live to see that day!

KROGSTAD: You mean you . . . ?

NORA: Now I have the courage.

KROGSTAD: You can't frighten me! A precious pampered little thing like you. . . .

NORA: I'll show you! I'll show you!

KROGSTAD: Under the ice, maybe? Down in the cold, black water? Then being washed up in the spring, bloated, hairless, unrecognizable. . . .

NORA: You can't frighten me.

KROGSTAD: You can't frighten me, either. People don't do that sort of thing, Mrs. Helmer. There wouldn't be any point to it, anyway, I'd still have him right in my pocket.

NORA: Afterwards? When I'm no longer . . .

KROGSTAD: Aren't you forgetting that your reputation would then be entirely in my hands? [*Nora stands looking at him, speechless.*] Well, I've warned you. Don't do anything silly. When Helmer gets my letter, I expect to hear from him. And don't forget: it's him who is forcing me off the straight and narrow again, your own husband! That's something I'll never forgive him for. Goodbye, Mrs. Helmer.

[He goes out through the hall. NORA crosses to the door, opens it slightly, and listens.]

NORA: He's going. He hasn't left the letter. No, no, that would be impossible! [*Opens the door further and further.*] What's he doing? He's stopped outside. He's not going down the stairs. Has he changed his mind? Is he . . . ? [*A letter falls into the letter box. Then Krogstad's footsteps are heard receding as he walks downstairs. Nora gives a stifled cry, runs across the room to the sofa table; pause.*] In the letter box! [*She creeps stealthily across to the hall door.*] There it is! Torvald, Torvald! It's hopeless now!

MRS. LINDE: [*comes into the room, left, carrying the costume*]: There, I think that's everything. Shall we try it on?

NORA [*in a low, hoarse voice*]: Kristine, come here.

MRS. LINDE [*throws the dress down on the sofa*]: What's wrong with you? You look upset.

NORA: Come here. Do you see that letter? There, look! Through the glass in the letter box.

MRS. LINDE: Yes, yes, I can see it.

NORA: It's a letter from Krogstad.

MRS. LINDE: Nora! It was Krogstad who lent you the money!

NORA: Yes. And now Torvald will get to know everything.

MRS. LINDE: Believe me, Nora, it's best for you both.

NORA: But there's more to it than that. I forged a signature. . . .

MRS. LINDE: Heavens above!

NORA: Listen, I want to tell you something, Kristine, so you can be my witness.

MRS. LINDE: What do you mean, "witness"? What do you want me to . . . ?

NORA: If I should go mad . . . which might easily happen . . .

MRS. LINDE: Nora!

NORA: Or if anything happened to me . . . which meant I couldn't be here. . . .

MRS. LINDE: Nora, Nora! Are you out of your mind?

NORA: And if somebody else wanted to take it all upon himself, the whole blame, you understand. . . .

MRS. LINDE: Yes, yes. But what makes you think . . . ?

NORA: Then you must testify that it isn't true, Kristine. I'm not out of my mind; I'm quite sane now. And I tell you this: nobody else knew anything, I alone was responsible for the whole thing. Remember that!

MRS. LINDE: I will. But I don't understand a word of it.

NORA: Why should you? You see something miraculous is going to happen.

MRS. LINDE: Something miraculous?

NORA: Yes, a miracle. But something so terrible as well, Kristine—oh, it must never happen, not for anything.

MRS. LINDE: I'm going straight over to talk to Krogstad.

NORA: Don't go. He'll only do you harm.

MRS. LINDE: There was a time when he would have done anything for me.

NORA: Him!

MRS. LINDE: Where does he live?

NORA: How do I know . . . ? Wait a minute. [She feels in her pocket.] Here's his card. But the letter, the letter . . . !

HELMER [*from his study, knocking on the door*]: Nora!

NORA [*cries out in terror*]: What's that? What do you want?

HELMER: Don't be frightened. We're not coming in. You've locked the door. Are you trying on?

NORA: Yes, yes, I'm trying on. It looks so nice on me, Torvald.

MRS. LINDE [*who has read the card*]: He lives just round the corner.

NORA: It's no use. It's hopeless. The letter is there in the box.

MRS. LINDE: Your husband keeps the key?

NORA: Always.

MRS. LINDE: Krogstad must ask for his letter back unread, he must find some sort of excuse. . . .

NORA: But this is just the time that Torvald generally . . .

MRS. LINDE: Put him off! Go in and keep him busy. I'll be back as soon as I can.

[She goes out hastily by the hall door. Nora walks over to Helmer's door, opens it and peeps in.]

NORA: Torvald!

HELMER [*in the study*]: Well, can a man get into his own living room again now? Come along, Rank, now we'll see . . . [*In the doorway.*] But what's this?

NORA: What, Torvald dear?

HELMER: Rank led me to expect some kind of marvelous transformation.

RANK [*in the doorway*]: That's what I thought too, but I must have been mistaken.

NORA: I'm not showing myself off to anybody before tomorrow.

HELMER: Nora dear, you look tired. You haven't been practising too hard?

NORA: No, I haven't practiced at all yet.

HELMER: You'll have to, though.

NORA: Yes, I certainly must, Torvald. But I just can't get anywhere without your help: I've completely forgotten it.

HELMER: We'll soon polish it up.

NORA: Yes, do help me, Torvald. Promise? I'm so nervous. All those people. . . . You must devote yourself exclusively to me this evening. Pens away! Forget all about the office! Promise me, Torvald dear!

HELMER: I promise. This evening I am wholly and entirely at your service . . . helpless little thing that you are. Oh, but while I remember, I'll just look first . . .

[He goes towards the hall door.]

NORA: What do you want out there?

HELMER: Just want to see if there are any letters.

NORA: No, don't, Torvald!

HELMER: Why not?

NORA: Torvald, *please!* There aren't any.

HELMER: Just let me see.

[He starts to go. Nora, at the piano, plays the opening bars of the tarantella.]

HELMER [*at the door, stops*]: Aha!

NORA: I shan't be able to dance tomorrow if I don't rehearse it with you.

HELMER [*walks to her*]: Are you really so nervous, Nora dear?

NORA: Terribly nervous. Let me run through it now. There's still time before supper. Come and sit here and play for me, Torvald dear. Tell me what to do, keep me right—as you always do.

HELMER: Certainly, with pleasure, if that's what you want.

[He sits at the piano. Nora snatches the tambourine out of the box, and also a long gaily coloured shawl which she drapes round herself, then with a bound she leaps forward.]

NORA [*shouts*]: Now play for me! Now I'll dance!

[Helmer plays and Nora dances; Dr. Rank stands at the piano behind Helmer and looks on.]

HELMER [*playing*]: Not so fast! Not so fast!

NORA: I can't help it.

HELMER: Not so wild, Nora!

NORA: This is how it has to be.

HELMER [*stops*]: No, no, that won't do at all.

NORA [*laughs and swings the tambourine*]: Didn't I tell you?

RANK: Let me play for her.

HELMER [*gets up*]: Yes, do. Then I'll be better able to tell her what to do.

[Rank sits down at the piano and plays. Nora dances more and more wildly. Helmer stands by the stove giving her repeated directions as she dances; she does not seem to hear them. Her hair comes undone and falls about her shoulders; she pays no attention and goes on dancing. Mrs. Linde enters.]

MRS. LINDE [*standing as though spellbound in the doorway*]: Ah . . . !

NORA [*dancing*]: See what fun we are having, Kristine.

HELMER: But my dear darling Nora, you are dancing as though your life depended on it.

NORA: It does.

HELMER: Stop, Rank! This is sheer madness. Stop, I say.

[Rank stops playing and Nora comes to a sudden halt.]

HELMER [*crosses to her*]: I would never have believed it. You have forgotten everything I ever taught you.

NORA [*throwing away the tambourine*]: There you are, you see.

HELMER: Well, some more instruction is certainly needed there.

NORA: Yes, you see how necessary it is. You must go on coaching me right up to the last minute. Promise me, Torvald?

HELMER: You can rely on me.

NORA: You mustn't think about anything else but me until after tomorrow. . . mustn't open any letters . . . mustn't touch the letter box.

HELMER: Ah, you are still frightened of what that man might . . .

NORA: Yes, yes, I am.

HELMER: I can see from your face there's already a letter there from him.

NORA: I don't know. I think so. But you mustn't read anything like that now. We don't want anything horrid coming between us until all this is over.

RANK [*softly to Helmer*]: I shouldn't cross her.

HELMER [*puts his arm round her*]: The child must have her way. But tomorrow night, when your dance is done. . . .

NORA: Then you are free.

MAID [*in the doorway, right*]: Dinner is served, madam.

NORA: We'll have champagne, Helene.

MAID: Very good, madam.

[She goes.]

HELMER: Aha! It's to be quite a banquet, eh?

NORA: With champagne flowing until dawn. [*Shouts.*] And some macaroons, Helene . . . lots of them, for once in a while.

HELMER [*seizing her hands*]: Now, now, not so wild and excitable! Let me see you being my own little singing bird again.

NORA: Oh yes, I will. And if you'll just go in . . . you, too, Dr. Rank. Kristine, you must help me to do my hair.

RANK [*softly, as they leave*]: There isn't anything . . . anything as it were, impending, is there?

HELMER: No, not at all, my dear fellow. It's nothing but these childish fears I was telling you about.

[They go out to the right.]

NORA: Well?

MRS. LINDE: He's left town.

NORA: I saw it in your face.

MRS. LINDE: He's coming back tomorrow evening. I left a note for him.

NORA: You shouldn't have done that. You must let things take their course. Because really it's a case for rejoicing, waiting like this for the miracle.

MRS. LINDE: What is it you are waiting for?

NORA: Oh, you wouldn't understand. Go and join the other two. I'll be there in a minute.

[Mrs. Linde goes into the dining-room. Nora stands for a moment as though to collect herself, then looks at her watch.]

NORA: Five. Seven hours to midnight. Then twenty-four hours till the next midnight. Then the tarantella will be over. Twenty-four and seven? Thirty-one hours to live.

HELMER [*in the doorway, right*]: What's happened to our little sky-lark?

NORA [*running towards him with open arms*]: Here she is!

ACT III

The same room. The round table has been moved to the center of the room, and the chairs placed round it. A lamp is burning on the table. The door to the hall stands open. Dance music can be heard coming from the floor above. Mrs. Linde is sitting by the table, idly turning over the pages of a book; she tries to read, but does not seem able to concentrate. Once or twice she listens, tensely, for a sound at the front door.

MRS. LINDE [*looking at her watch*]: Still not here. There isn't much time left. I only hope he hasn't . . . [*She listens again.*] Ah, there he is. [*She goes out into the hall, and cautiously opens the front door. Soft footsteps can be heard on the stairs. She whispers.*] Come in. There's nobody here.

KROGSTAD [*in the doorway*]: I found a note from you at home. What does it all mean?

MRS. LINDE: I *had* to talk to you.

KROGSTAD: Oh? And did it have to be here, in this house?

MRS. LINDE: It wasn't possible over at my place, it hasn't a separate entrance. Come in. We are quite alone. The maid's asleep and the Helmers are at a party upstairs.

KROGSTAD [*comes into the room*]: Well, well! So the Helmers are out dancing tonight! Really?

MRS. LINDE: Yes, why not?

KROGSTAD: Why not indeed!

MRS. LINDE: Well then, Nils. Let's talk.

KROGSTAD: Have we two anything more to talk about?

MRS. LINDE: We have a great deal to talk about.

KROGSTAD: I shouldn't have thought so.

MRS. LINDE: That's because you never really understood me.

KROGSTAD: What else was there to understand, apart from the old, old story? A heartless woman throws a man over the moment something more profitable offers itself.

MRS. LINDE: Do you really think I'm so heartless? Do you think I found it easy to break it off.

KROGSTAD: Didn't you?

MRS. LINDE: You didn't really believe that?

KROGSTAD: If that wasn't the case, why did you write to me as you did?

MRS. LINDE: There was nothing else I could do. If I had to make the break, I felt in duty bound to destroy any feeling that you had for me.

KROGSTAD [*clenching his hands*]: So that's how it was. And all that . . . was for money!

MRS. LINDE: You mustn't forget I had a helpless mother and two young brothers. We couldn't wait for you, Nils. At that time you hadn't much immediate prospect of anything.

KROGSTAD: That may be. But you had no right to throw me over for somebody else.

MRS. LINDE: Well, I don't know. Many's the time I've asked myself whether I was justified.

KROGSTAD [*more quietly*]: When I lost you, it was just as if the ground had slipped away from under my feet. Look at me now: a broken man clinging to the wreck of his life.

MRS. LINDE: Help might be near.

KROGSTAD: It was near. Then you came along and got in the way.

MRS. LINDE: Quite without knowing, Nils. I only heard today it's you I'm supposed to be replacing at the Bank.

KROGSTAD: If you say so, I believe you. But now you do know, aren't you going to withdraw?

MRS. LINDE: No, that wouldn't benefit you in the slightest.

KROGSTAD: Benefit, benefit . . . ! I would do it just the same.

MRS. LINDE: I have learned to go carefully. Life and hard, bitter necessity have taught me that.

KROGSTAD: And life has taught me not to believe in pretty speeches.

MRS. LINDE: Then life has taught you a very sensible thing. But deeds are something you surely must believe in?

KROGSTAD: How do you mean?

MRS. LINDE: You said you were like a broken man clinging to the wreck of his life.

KROGSTAD: And I said it with good reason.

MRS. LINDE: And I am like a broken woman clinging to the wreck of her life. Nobody to care about, and nobody to care for.

KROGSTAD: It was your own choice.

MRS. LINDE: At the time there was no other choice.

KROGSTAD: Well, what of it?

MRS. LINDE: Nils, what about us two castaways joining forces.

KROGSTAD: What's that you say?

MRS. LINDE: Two of us on one wreck surely stand a better chance than each on his own.

KROGSTAD: Kristine!

MRS. LINDE: Why do you suppose I came to town?

KROGSTAD: You mean, you thought of me?

MRS. LINDE: Without work I couldn't live. All my life I have worked, for as long as I can remember; that has always been my one great joy. But now I'm completely alone in the world, and feeling horribly empty and forlorn. There's no pleasure in working only for yourself. Nils, give me somebody and something to work for.

KROGSTAD: I don't believe all this. It's only a woman's hysteria, wanting to be all magnanimous and self-sacrificing.

MRS. LINDE: Have you ever known me hysterical before?

KROGSTAD: Would you really do this? Tell me—do you know all about my past?

MRS. LINDE: Yes.

KROGSTAD: And you know what people think about me?

MRS. LINDE: Just now you hinted you thought you might have been a different person with me.

KROGSTAD: I'm convinced I would.

MRS. LINDE: Couldn't it still happen?

KROGSTAD: Kristine! You know what you are saying, don't you? Yes, you do. I can see you do. Have you really the courage . . . ?

MRS. LINDE: I need someone to mother, and your children need a mother. We two need each other. Nils, I have faith in what, deep down, you are. With you I can face anything.

KROGSTAD [*seizing her hands*]: Thank you, thank you, Kristine. And I'll soon have everybody looking up to me, or I'll know the reason why. Ah, but I was forgetting. . . .

MRS. LINDE: Hush! The tarantella! You must go!

KROGSTAD: Why? What is it?

MRS. LINDE: You hear that dance upstairs? When it's finished they'll be coming.

KROGSTAD: Yes, I'll go. It's too late to do anything. Of course, you know nothing about what steps I've taken against the Helmers.

MRS. LINDE: Yes, Nils, I do know.

KROGSTAD: Yet you still want to go on. . . .

MRS. LINDE: I know how far a man like you can be driven by despair.

KROGSTAD: Oh, if only I could undo what I've done!

MRS. LINDE: You still can. Your letter is still there in the box.

KROGSTAD: Are you sure?

MRS. LINDE: Quite sure. But . . .

KROGSTAD [*regards her searchingly*]: Is that how things are? You want to save your friend at any price? Tell me straight. Is that it?

MRS. LINDE: When you've sold yourself *once* for other people's sake, you don't do it again.

KROGSTAD: I shall demand my letter back.

MRS. LINDE: No, no.

KROGSTAD: Of course I will, I'll wait here till Helmer comes. I'll tell him he has to give me my letter back . . . that it's only about my notice . . . that he mustn't read it. . . .

MRS. LINDE: No, Nils, don't ask for it back.

KROGSTAD: But wasn't that the very reason you got me here?

MRS. LINDE: Yes, that was my first terrified reaction. But that was yesterday, and it's quite incredible the things I've witnessed in this house in the last twenty-four hours. Helmer must know everything. This unhappy secret must come out. Those two must have the whole thing out between them. All this secrecy and deception, it just can't go on.

KROGSTAD: Well, if you want to risk it . . . .But one thing I can do, and I'll do it at once. . . .

MRS. LINDE [*listening*]: Hurry! Go, go! The dance has stopped. We aren't safe a moment longer.

KROGSTAD: I'll wait for you downstairs.

MRS. LINDE: Yes, do. You must see me home.

KROGSTAD: I've never been so incredibly happy before.

[He goes out by the front door. The door out into the hall remains standing open.]

MRS. LINDE [*tidies the room a little and gets her hat and coat ready*]: How things change! How things change! Somebody to work for . . . to live for. A home to bring happiness into. Just let me get down to it. . . .I wish they'd come. . . .[*Listens.*] Ah, there they are. . . .Get my things.

[She takes her coat and hat. The voices of Helmer and Nora are heard outside. A key is turned and Helmer pushes Nora almost forcibly into the hall. She is dressed in the Italian costume, with a big black shawl over it. He is in evening dress, and over it a black cloak, open.]

NORA [*still in the doorway, reluctantly*]: No, no, not in here! I want to go back up again. I don't want to leave so early.

HELMER: But my dearest Nora . . .

NORA: Oh, please, Torvald, I beg you. . . . *Please,* just for another hour.

HELMER: Not another minute, Nora my sweet. You remember what we agreed. There now, come along in. You'll catch cold standing there.

[He leads her, in spite of her resistance, gently but firmly into the room.]

MRS. LINDE: Good evening.

NORA: Kristine!

HELMER: Why, Mrs. Linde. You here so late?

MRS. LINDE: Yes. You must forgive me but I did so want to see Nora all dressed up.

NORA: Have you been sitting here waiting for me?

MRS. LINDE: Yes, I'm afraid I wasn't in time to catch you before you went upstairs. And I felt I couldn't leave again without seeing you.

HELMER [*removing Nora's shawl*]: Well take a good look at her. I think I can say she's worth looking at. Isn't she lovely, Mrs. Linde?

MRS. LINDE: Yes, I must say. . . .

HELMER: Isn't she quite extraordinarily lovely? That's what everybody at the party thought, too. But she's dreadfully stubborn . . . the sweet little thing! And what shall we do about that? Would you believe it, I nearly had to use force to get her away.

NORA: Oh Torvald, you'll be sorry you didn't let me stay, even for half an hour.

HELMER: You hear that, Mrs. Linde? She dances her tarantella, there's wild applause—which was well deserved, although the performance was perhaps rather realistic . . . I mean, rather more so than was strictly necessary from the artistic point of view. But anyway! The main thing is she was a success, a tremendous success. Was I supposed to let her stay after that? Spoil the effect? No thank you! I took my lovely little Capri girl—my capricious little Capri girl, I might say—by the arm, whisked her once round the room, a curtsey all round, and then—as they say in novels—the beautiful vision vanished. An exit should always be effective, Mrs. Linde. But I just can't get Nora to see that. Phew! It's warm in here. [*He throws his cloak over a chair and opens the door to his study.*] What? It's dark. Oh yes, of course. Excuse me. . . .

[He goes in and lights a few candles.]

NORA [*quickly, in a breathless whisper*]: Well?

MRS. LINDE [*softly*]: I've spoken to him.

NORA: And . . . ?

MRS. LINDE: Nora . . . you must tell your husband everything.

NORA [*tonelessly*]: I knew it.

MRS. LINDE: You've got nothing to fear from Krogstad. But you must speak.

NORA: I won't.

MRS. LINDE: Then the letter will.

NORA: Thank you, Kristine. Now I know what's to be done. Hush . . . !

HELMER [*comes in again*]: Well, Mrs. Linde, have you finished admiring her?

MRS. LINDE: Yes. And now I must say good night.

HELMER: Oh, already? Is this yours, this knitting?

MRS. LINDE [*takes it*]: Yes, thank you. I nearly forgot it.

HELMER: So you knit, eh?

MRS. LINDE: Yes.

HELMER: You should embroider instead, you know.

MRS. LINDE: Oh? Why?

HELMER: So much prettier. Watch! You hold the embroidery like this in the left hand, and then you take the needle in the right hand, like this, and you describe a long, graceful curve. Isn't that right?

MRS. LINDE: Yes, I suppose so. . . .

HELMER: Whereas knitting on the other hand just can't help being ugly. Look! Arms pressed into the sides, the knitting needles going up and down—there's something Chinese about it. . . . Ah, that was marvelous champagne they served tonight.

MRS. LINDE: Well, good night, Nora! And stop being so stubborn.

HELMER: Well said, Mrs. Linde!

MRS. LINDE: Good night, Mr. Helmer.

HELMER [*accompanying her to the door*]: Good night, good night! You'll get home all right, I hope? I'd be only too pleased to. . . . But you haven't far to walk. Good night, good night! [*She goes; he shuts the door behind her and comes in again.*] There we are, got rid of her at last. She's a frightful bore, that woman.

NORA: Aren't you very tired, Torvald?

HELMER: Not in the least.

NORA: Not sleepy?

HELMER: Not at all. On the contrary, I feel extremely lively. What about you? Yes, you look quite tired and sleepy.

NORA: Yes, I'm very tired. I just want to fall straight off to sleep.

HELMER: There you are, you see! Wasn't I right in thinking we shouldn't stay any longer.

NORA: Oh, everything you do is right.

HELMER [*kissing her forehead*]: There's my little sky-lark talking common sense. Did you notice how gay Rank was this evening?

NORA: Oh, was he? I didn't get a chance to talk to him.

HELMER: I hardly did either. But it's a long time since I saw him in such a good mood. [*Looks at Nora for a moment or two, then comes nearer her.*] Ah, it's wonderful to be back in our own home again, and quite alone with you. How irresistibly lovely you are, Nora!

NORA: Don't look at me like that, Torvald!

HELMER: Can't I look at my most treasured possession? At all this loveliness that's mine and mine alone, completely and utterly mine.

NORA [*walks round to the other side of the table*]: You mustn't talk to me like that tonight.

HELMER [*following her*]: You still have the tarantella in your blood, I see. And that makes you even more desirable. Listen! The guests are beginning to leave now. [*Softly.*] Nora . . . soon the whole house will be silent.

NORA: I should hope so.

HELMER: Of course you do, don't you, Nora my darling? You know, whenever I'm out at a party with you . . . do you know why I never talk to you very much, why I always stand away from you and only steal a quick glance at you now and then . . . do you know why I do that? It's because I'm pretending we are secretly in love, secretly engaged and nobody suspects there is anything between us.

NORA: Yes, yes. I know your thoughts are always with me, of course.

HELMER: And when it's time to go, and I lay your shawl round those shapely, young shoulders, round the exquisite curve of your neck . . . I pretend that you are my young bride, that we are just leaving our wedding, that I am taking you to our new home for the first time . . . to be alone with you for the first time . . . quite alone with your young and trembling loveliness! All evening I've been longing for you, and nothing else. And as I watched you darting and swaying in the tarantella, my blood was on fire . . . I couldn't bear it any longer . . . and that's why I brought you down here with me so early . . . .

NORA: Go away, Torvald! Please leave me alone. I won't have it.

HELMER: What's this? It's just your little game isn't it, my little Nora. Won't! Won't! Am I not your husband . . . ?

[There is a knock on the front door.]

NORA [*startled*]: Listen . . . !

HELMER [*going towards the hall*]: Who's there?

RANK [*outside*]: It's me. Can I come in for a minute?

HELMER [*in a low voice, annoyed*]: Oh, what does he want now? [*Aloud*] Wait a moment. [*He walks across and opens the door.*] How nice of you to look in on your way out.

RANK: I fancied I heard your voice and I thought I would just look in. [*He takes a quick glance round.*] Ah yes, this dear, familiar old place! How cozy and comfortable you've got things here, you two.

HELMER: You seemed to be having a pretty good time upstairs yourself.

RANK: Capital! Why shouldn't I? Why not make the most of things in this world? At least as much as one can, and for as long as one can. The wine was excellent. . . .

HELMER: Especially the champagne.

RANK: You noticed that too, did you? It's incredible the amount I was able to put away.

NORA: Torvald also drank a lot of champagne this evening.

RANK: Oh?

NORA: Yes, and that always makes him quite merry.

RANK: Well, why shouldn't a man allow himself a jolly evening after a day well spent?

HELMER: Well spent? I'm afraid I can't exactly claim that.

RANK [*clapping him on the shoulder*]: But I can, you see!

NORA: Dr. Rank, am I right in thinking you carried out a certain laboratory test today?

RANK: Exactly.

HELMER: Look at our little Nora talking about laboratory tests!

NORA: And may I congratulate you on the result?

RANK: You may indeed.

NORA: So it was good?

RANK: The best possible, for both doctor and patient—certainty!

NORA [*quickly and searchingly*]: Certainty?

RANK: Absolute certainty. So why shouldn't I allow myself a jolly evening after that?

NORA: Quite right, Dr. Rank.

HELMER: I quite agree. As long as you don't suffer for it in the morning.

RANK: Well, you never get anything for nothing in this life.

NORA: Dr. Rank . . . you are very fond of masquerades, aren't you?

RANK: Yes, when there are plenty of amusing disguises. . . .

NORA: Tell me, what shall we two go as next time?

HELMER: There's frivolity for you . . . thinking about the next time already!

RANK: We two? I'll tell you. You must go as Lady Luck . . . .

HELMER: Yes, but how do you find a costume to suggest *that?*

RANK: Your wife could simply go in her everyday clothes. . . .

HELMER: That was nicely said. But don't you know what you would be?

RANK: Yes, my dear friend, I know exactly what I shall be.

HELMER: Well?

RANK: At the next masquerade, I shall be invisible.

HELMER: That's a funny idea!

RANK: There's a big black cloak . . . haven't you heard of the cloak of invisibility? That comes right down over you, and then nobody can see you.

HELMER [*suppressing a smile*]: Of course, that's right.

RANK: But I'm clean forgetting what I came for. Helmer, give me a cigar, one of the dark Havanas.

HELMER: With the greatest of pleasure.

[He offers his case.]

RANK [*takes one and cuts the end off*]: Thanks.

NORA [*strikes a match*]: Let me give you a light.

RANK: Thank you. [*She holds out the match and he lights his cigar.*] And now, goodbye!

HELMER: Goodbye, goodbye, my dear fellow!

NORA: Sleep well, Dr. Rank.

RANK: Thank you for that wish.

NORA: Wish me the same.

RANK: You? All right, if you want me to. . . . Sleep well. And thanks for the light.

[He nods to them both, and goes.]

HELMER [*subdued*]: He's had a lot to drink.

NORA [*absently*]: Very likely.

[Helmer takes a bunch of keys out of his pocket and goes out into the hall.]

NORA: Torvald . . . what do you want there?

HELMER: I must empty the letter box, it's quite full. There'll be no room for the papers in the morning. . . .

NORA: Are you going to work tonight?

HELMER: You know very well I'm not. Hello, what's this? Somebody's been at the lock.

NORA: At the lock?

HELMER: Yes, I'm sure of it. Why should that be? I'd hardly have thought the maids . . . ? Here's a broken hairpin. Nora, it's one of yours. . . .

NORA [*quickly*]: It must have been the children . . . .

HELMER: Then you'd better tell them not to. Ah . . . there . . . I've managed to get it open. [*He takes the things out and shouts into the kitchen.*] Helene! . . . Helene, put the light out in the hall. [*He comes into the room again with the letters in his hand and shuts the hall door.*] Look how it all mounts up. [*Runs through them.*] What's this?

NORA: The letter! Oh no, Torvald, no!

HELMER: Two visiting cards . . . from Dr. Rank.

NORA: From Dr. Rank?

HELMER [*looking at them*]: Dr. Rank, Medical Practitioner. They were on top. He must have put them in as he left.

NORA: Is there anything on them?

HELMER: There's a black cross above his name. Look. What an uncanny idea. It's just as if he were announcing his own death.

NORA: He is.

HELMER: What? What do you know about it? Has he said anything to you?

NORA: Yes. He said when these cards came, he would have taken his last leave of us. He was going to shut himself up and die.

HELMER: Poor fellow! Of course I knew we couldn't keep him with us very long. But so soon. . . . And hiding himself away like a wounded animal.

NORA: When it has to happen, it's best that it should happen without words. Don't you think so, Torvald?

HELMER [*walking up and down*]: He had grown so close to us. I don't think I can imagine him gone. His suffering and his loneliness seemed almost to provide a background of dark cloud to the sunshine of our lives. Well, perhaps it's all for the best. For him at any rate. [*Pauses.*] And maybe for us as well, Nora. Now there's just the two of us. [*Puts his arms round her.*] Oh, my darling wife, I can't hold you close enough. You know, Nora . . . many's the time I wish you were threatened by some terrible danger so I could risk everything, body and soul, for your sake.

NORA [*tears herself free and says firmly and decisively*]: Now you must read your letters, Torvald.

HELMER: No, no, not tonight. I want to be with you, my darling wife.

NORA: Knowing all the time your friend is dying . . . ?

HELMER: You are right. It's been a shock to both of us. This ugly thing has come between us . . . thoughts of death and decay. We must try to free ourselves from it. Until then . . . we shall go our separate ways.

NORA [*her arms round his neck*]: Torvald . . . good night! Good night!

HELMER [*kisses her forehead*]: Goodnight, my little singing bird. Sleep well, Nora, I'll just read through my letters.

[He takes the letters into his room and shuts the door behind him.]

NORA [*gropes around her, wild-eyed, seizes Helmer's cloak, wraps it round herself, and whispers quickly, hoarsely, spasmodically*]: Never see him again. Never, never, never. [*Throws her shawl over her head.*] And never see the children again either. Never, never. Oh, that black icy water. Oh, that bottomless . . . ! If only it were all over! He's got it now. Now he's reading it. Oh no, no! Not yet! Torvald, goodbye . . . and my children. . . .

[She rushes out in the direction of the hall; at the same moment Helmer flings open his door and stands there with an open letter in his hand.]

HELMER: Nora!

NORA [*shrieks*]: Ah!

HELMER: What is this? Do you know what is in this letter?

NORA: Yes, I know. Let me go! Let me out!

HELMER [*holds her back*]: Where are you going?

NORA [*trying to tear herself free*]: You mustn't try to save me, Torvald!

HELMER [*reels back*]: True! Is it true what he writes? How dreadful! No, no, it can't possibly be true.

NORA: It *is* true. I loved you more than anything else in the world.

HELMER: Don't come to me with a lot of paltry excuses!

NORA [*taking a step towards him*]: Torvald . . . !

HELMER: Miserable woman . . . what is this you have done?

NORA: Let me go. I won't have you taking the blame for me. You mustn't take it on yourself.

HELMER: Stop play-acting! [*Locks the front door.*] You are staying here to give an account of yourself. Do you understand what you have done? Answer me! Do you understand?

NORA [*looking fixedly at him, her face hardening*]: Yes, now I'm really beginning to understand.

HELMER [*walking up and down*]: Oh, what a terrible awakening this is. All these eight years . . . this woman who was my pride and joy . . . a hypocrite, a liar, worse than that, a criminal! Oh, how utterly squalid it all is! Ugh! Ugh! [*Nora remains silent and looks fixedly at him.*] I should have realized something like this would happen. I should have seen it coming. All your father's irresponsible ways. . . . Quiet! All your father's irresponsible ways are coming out in you. No religion, no morals, no sense of duty. . . . Oh, this is my punishment for turning a blind eye to him. It was for your sake I did it, and this is what I get for it.

NORA: Yes, this.

HELMER: Now you have ruined my entire happiness, jeopardized my whole future. It's terrible to think of. Here I am, at the mercy of a thoroughly unscrupulous person; he can do whatever he likes with me, demand anything he wants, order me about just as he chooses . . . and I daren't even whimper. I'm done for, a miserable failure, and it's all the fault of a feather-brained woman!

NORA: When I've left this world behind, you will be free.

HELMER: Oh, stop pretending! Your father was just the same, always ready with fine phrases. What good would it do me if you left this world behind, as you put it? Not the slightest bit of good. He can still let it all come out, if he likes; and if he does, people might even suspect me of being an accomplice in these criminal acts of yours. They might even think I was the one behind it all, that it was I who pushed you into it! And it's you I have to thank for this . . . and when I've taken such good care of you, all our married life. Now do you understand what you have done to me?

NORA [*coldly and calmly*]: Yes.

HELMER: I just can't understand it, it's so incredible. But we must see about putting things right. Take that shawl off. Take it off, I tell you! I must see if I can't find some way or other of appeasing him. The thing must be hushed up at all costs. And as far as you and I are concerned, things must appear to go on exactly as before. But only in the eyes of the world, of course. In other words you'll go on living here; that's understood. But you will not be allowed to bring up the children, I can't trust you with them. . . . Oh, that I should have to say this to the woman I loved so dearly, the woman I still. . . . Well, that must be all over and done with. From now on, there can be no question of happiness. All we can do is save the bits and pieces from the wreck, preserve appearances. . . . [*The front door-bell rings. Helmer gives a start.*] What's that? So late? How terrible, supposing. . . . If he should . . . ? Hide, Nora! Say you are not well.

[Nora stands motionless. Helmer walks across and opens the door into the hall.]

MAID [*half dressed, in the hall*]: It's a note for Mrs. Helmer.

HELMER: Give it to me. [*He snatches the note and shuts the door.*] Yes, it's from him. You can't have it. I want to read it myself.

NORA: You read it then.

HELMER [*by the lamp*]: I hardly dare. Perhaps this is the end, for both of us. Well, I must know. [*He opens the note hurriedly, reads a few lines, looks at another enclosed sheet, and gives a cry of joy.*] Nora! [*Nora looks at him inquiringly.*] Nora! I must read it again. Yes, yes, it's true! I am saved! Nora, I am saved!

NORA: And me?

HELMER: You too, of course, we are both saved, you as well as me. Look, he's sent your IOU back. He sends his regrets and apologies for what he has done. . . .His luck has changed. . . . Oh, what does it matter what he says. We are saved, Nora! Nobody can do anything to you now. Oh, Nora, Nora . . . but let's get rid of this disgusting thing first. Let me see. . . . [*He glances at the IOU.*] No, I don't want to see it. I don't want it to be anything but a dream. [*He tears up the IOU and both letters, throws all the pieces into the stove and watches them burn.*] Well, that's the end of that. He said in his note you'd known since Christmas Eve. . . . You must have had three terrible days of it, Nora.

NORA: These three days haven't been easy.

HELMER: The agonies you must have gone through! When the only way out seemed to be. . . . No, let's forget the whole ghastly thing. We can rejoice and say: It's all over! It's all over! Listen to me, Nora! You don't seem to understand: it's all over! Why this grim look on your face? Oh, poor little Nora, of course I understand. You can't bring yourself to believe I've forgiven you. But I have, Nora, I swear it. I forgive you everything. I know you did what you did because you loved me.

NORA: That's true.

HELMER: You loved me as a wife should love her husband. It was simply that you didn't have the experience to judge what was the best way of going about things. But do you think I love you any the less for that; just because you don't know how to act on your own responsibility? No, no, you just lean on me, I shall give you all the advice and guidance you need. I wouldn't be a proper man if I didn't find a woman doubly attractive for being so obviously helpless. You mustn't dwell on the harsh things I said in that first moment of horror, when I thought everything was going to come crashing down about my ears. I have forgiven you, Nora, I swear it! I have forgiven you!

NORA: Thank you for your forgiveness.

[She goes out through the door, right.]

HELMER: No, don't go! [He looks through the doorway.] What are you doing in the spare room?

NORA: Taking off this fancy dress.

HELMER [*standing at the open door*]: Yes, do. You try and get some rest, and set your mind at peace again, my frightened little songbird. Have a good long sleep; you know you are safe and sound under my wing. [*Walks up and down near the door.*] What a nice, cozy little home we have here, Nora! Here you can find refuge. Here I shall hold you like a hunted dove I have rescued unscathed from the cruel talons of the hawk, and calm your poor beating heart. And that will come, gradually, Nora, believe me. Tomorrow you'll see everything quite differently. Soon everything will be just as it was before. You won't need me to keep on telling you I've forgiven you; you'll feel convinced of it in your own heart. You don't really imagine me ever thinking of turning you out, or even of reproaching you? Oh, a real man isn't made that way, you know, Nora. For a man, there's something indescribably moving and very satisfying in knowing that he has forgiven his wife—forgiven her, completely and genuinely, from the depths of his heart. It's as though it made her his property in a double sense: he has, as it were, given her a new life, and she becomes in a way both his wife and at the same time his child. That is how you will seem to me after today, helpless, perplexed little thing that you are. Don't you worry your pretty little head about anything, Nora. Just you be frank with me, and I'll take all the decisions for you. . . . What's this? Not in bed? You've changed your things?

NORA [*in her everyday dress*]: Yes, Torvald, I've changed.

HELMER: What for? It's late.

NORA: I shan't sleep tonight.

HELMER: But my dear Nora. . . .

NORA [*looks at her watch*]: It's not so terribly late. Sit down, Torvald. We two have a lot to talk about.

[She sits down at one side of the table.]

HELMER: Nora, what is all this? Why so grim?

NORA: Sit down. It'll take some time. I have a lot to say to you.

HELMER [*sits down at the table opposite her*]: You frighten me, Nora. I don't understand you.

NORA: Exactly. You don't understand me. And I have never understood you, either—until tonight. No, don't interrupt. I just want you to listen to what I have to say. We are going to have things out, Torvald.

HELMER: What do you mean?

NORA: Isn't there anything that strikes you about the way we two are sitting here?

HELMER: What's that?

NORA: We have now been married eight years. Hasn't it struck you this is the first time you and I, man and wife, have had a serious talk together?

HELMER: Depends what you mean by "serious."

NORA: Eight whole years—no, more, ever since we first knew each other—and never have we exchanged one serious word about serious things.

HELMER: What did you want me to do? Get you involved in worries that you couldn't possibly help me to bear?

NORA: I'm not talking about worries. I say we've never once sat down together and seriously tried to get to the bottom of anything.

HELMER: But, my dear Nora, would that have been a thing for you?

NORA: That's just it. You have never understood me . . . I've been greatly wronged, Torvald. First by my father, and then by you.

HELMER: What! Us two! The two people who loved you more than anybody?

NORA [*shakes her head*]: You two never loved me. You only thought how nice it was to be in love with me.

HELMER: But, Nora, what's this you are saying?

NORA: It's right, you know, Torvald. At home, Daddy used to tell me what he thought, then I thought the same. And if I thought differently, I kept quiet about it, because he wouldn't have liked it. He used to call me his baby doll, and he played with me as I used to play with my dolls. Then I came to live in your house. . . .

HELMER: What way is that to talk about our marriage?

NORA [*imperturbably*]: What I mean is: I passed out of Daddy's hands into yours. You arranged everything to your tastes, and I acquired the same tastes. Or I pretended to . . . I don't really know . . . I think it was a bit of both, sometimes one thing and sometimes the other. When I look back, it seems to me I have been living here like a beggar, from hand to mouth. I lived by doing tricks for you, Torvald. But that's the way you wanted it. You and Daddy did me a great wrong. It's your fault that I've never made anything of my life.

HELMER: Nora, how unreasonable . . . how ungrateful you are! Haven't you been happy here?

NORA: No, never. I thought I was, but I wasn't really.

HELMER: Not . . . not happy!

NORA: No, just gay. And you've always been so kind to me. But our house has never been anything but a playroom. I have been your doll wife, just as at home I was Daddy's doll child. And the children in turn have been my dolls. I thought it was fun when you came and played with me, just as they thought it was fun when I went and played with them. That's been our marriage, Torvald.

HELMER: There is some truth in what you say, exaggerated and hysterical though it is. But from now on it will be different. Playtime is over; now comes the time for lessons.

NORA: Whose lessons? Mine or the children's?

HELMER: Both yours and the children's, my dear Nora.

NORA: Ah, Torvald, you are not the man to teach me to be a good wife for you.

HELMER: How can you say that?

NORA: And what sort of qualifications have I to teach the children?

HELMER: Nora!

NORA: Didn't you say yourself, a minute or two ago, that you couldn't trust me with that job.

HELMER: In the heat of the moment! You shouldn't pay any attention to that.

NORA: On the contrary, you were quite right. I'm not up to it. There's another problem needs solving first. I must take steps to educate myself. You are not the man to help me there. That's something I must do on my own. That's why I'm leaving you.

HELMER [*jumps up*]: What did you say?

NORA: If I'm ever to reach any understanding of myself and the things around me, I must learn to stand alone. That's why I can't stay here with you any longer.

HELMER: Nora! Nora!

NORA: I'm leaving here at once. I dare say Kristine will put me up for tonight. . . .

HELMER: You are out of your mind! I won't let you! I forbid you!

NORA: It's no use forbidding me anything now. I'm taking with me my own personal belongings. I don't want anything of yours, either now or later.

HELMER: This is madness!

NORA: Tomorrow I'm going home—to what used to be my home, I mean. It will be easier for me to find something to do there.

HELMER: Oh, you blind, inexperienced . . .

NORA: I must set about *getting* experience, Torvald.

HELMER: And leave your home, your husband and your children? Don't you care what people will say?

NORA: That's no concern of mine. All I know is that this is necessary for me.

HELMER: This is outrageous! You are betraying your most sacred duty.

NORA: And what do you consider to be my most sacred duty?

HELMER: Does it take me to tell you that? Isn't it your duty to your husband and your children?

NORA: I have another duty equally sacred.

HELMER: You have not. What duty might *that* be?

NORA: My duty to myself.

HELMER: First and foremost, you are a wife and mother.

NORA: That I don't believe any more. I believe that first and foremost I am an individual, just as much as you are—or at least I'm going to try to be. I know most people agree with you, Torvald, and that's also what it says in books. But I'm not content any more with what most people say, or with what it says in books. I have to think things out for myself, and get things clear.

HELMER: Surely you are clear about your position in your own home? Haven't you an infallible guide in questions like these? Haven't you your religion?

NORA: Oh, Torvald, I don't really know what religion is.

HELMER: What do you say!

NORA: All I know is what Pastor Hansen said when I was confirmed. He said religion was this, that and the other. When I'm away from all this and on my own, I'll go into that, too. I want to find out whether what Pastor Hansen told me was right—or at least whether it's right for *me.*

HELMER: This is incredible talk from a young woman! But if religion cannot keep you on the right path, let me at least stir your conscience. I suppose you do have some moral sense? Or tell me—perhaps you don't?

NORA: Well, Torvald, that's not easy to say. I simply don't know. I'm really very confused about such things. All I know is my ideas about such things are very different from yours. I've also learnt that the law is different from what I thought; but I simply can't get it into my head that that particular law is right. Apparently a woman has no right to spare her old father on his deathbed, or to save her husband's life, even. I just don't believe it.

HELMER: You are talking like a child. You understand nothing about the society you live in.

NORA: No, I don't. But I shall go into that too. I must try to discover who is right, society or me.

HELMER: You are ill, Nora. You are delirious. I'm half inclined to think you are out of your mind.

NORA: Never have I felt so calm and collected as I do tonight.

HELMER: Calm and collected enough to leave your husband and children?

NORA: Yes.

HELMER: Then only one explanation is possible.

NORA: And that is?

HELMER: You don't love me any more.

NORA: Exactly.

HELMER: Nora! Can you say that!

NORA: I'm desperately sorry, Torvald. Because you have always been so kind to me. But I can't help it. I don't love you any more.

HELMER [*struggling to keep his composure*]: Is that also a "calm and collected" decision you've made?

NORA: Yes, absolutely calm and collected. That's why I don't want to stay here.

HELMER: And can you also account for how I forfeited your love?

NORA: Yes, very easily. It was tonight, when the miracle didn't happen. It was then I realized you weren't the man I thought you were.

HELMER: Explain yourself more clearly. I don't understand.

NORA: For eight years I have been patiently waiting. Because, heavens, I knew miracles didn't happen every day. Then this devastating business started, and I became absolutely convinced the miracle *would* happen. All the time Krogstad's letter lay there, it never so much as crossed my mind that you would ever submit to that man's conditions. I was absolutely convinced you would say to him: Tell the whole wide world if you like. And when that was done . . .

HELMER: Yes, then what? After I had exposed my own wife to dishonor and shame . . . !

NORA: When that was done, I was absolutely convinced you would come forward and take everything on yourself, and say: I am the guilty one.

HELMER: Nora!

NORA: You mean I'd never let you make such a sacrifice for my sake? Of course not. But what would my story have counted for against yours?—That was the miracle I went in hope and dread of. It was to prevent it that I was ready to end my life.

HELMER: I would gladly toil day and night for you, Nora, enduring all manner of sorrow and distress. But nobody sacrifices his *honor* for the one he loves.

NORA: Hundreds and thousands of women have.

HELMER: Oh, you think and talk like a stupid child.

NORA: All right. But you neither think nor talk like the man I would want to share my life with. When you had got over your fright—and you weren't concerned about me but only about what might happen to you—and when all danger was past, you acted as though nothing had happened. I was your little skylark again, your little doll, exactly as before; except you would have to protect it twice as carefully as before, now that it had shown itself to be so weak and fragile. [*Rises.*] Torvald, that was the moment I realized that for eight years I'd been living with a stranger, and had borne him three children. . . . Oh, I can't bear to think about it! I could tear myself to shreds.

HELMER [*sadly*]: I see. I see. There is a tremendous gulf dividing us. But, Nora, is there no way we might bridge it?

NORA: As I am now, I am no wife for you.

HELMER: I still have it in me to change.

NORA: Perhaps . . . if you have your doll taken away.

HELMER: And be separated from you! No, no, Nora, the very thought of it is inconceivable.

NORA [*goes into the room, right*]: All the more reason why it must be done.

[She comes back with her outdoor things and a small traveling bag, which she puts on the chair beside the table.]

HELMER: Nora, Nora, not now! Wait till the morning.

NORA [*putting on her coat*]: I can't spend the night in a strange man's room.

HELMER: Couldn't we go on living here like brother and sister . . . ?

NORA [*tying on her hat*]: You know very well that wouldn't last. [*She draws the shawl round her.*] Goodbye, Torvald. I don't want to see the children. I know they are in better hands than mine. As I am now, I can never be anything to them.

HELMER: But some day, Nora, some day . . . ?

NORA: How should I know? I've no idea what I might turn out to be.

HELMER: But you are my wife, whatever you are.

NORA: Listen, Torvald, from what I've heard, when a wife leaves her husband's house as I am doing now, he is absolved by law of all responsibility for her. I can at any rate free you from all responsibility. You must not feel in any way bound, any more than I shall. There must be full freedom on both sides. Look, here's your ring back. Give me mine.

HELMER: That too?

NORA: That too.

HELMER: There it is.

NORA: Well, that's the end of that. I'll put the keys down here. The maids know where everything is in the house—better than I do, in fact. Kristine will come in the morning after I've left to pack up the few things I brought with me from home. I want them sent on.

HELMER: The end! Nora, will you never think of me?

NORA: I dare say I'll often think about you and the children and this house.

HELMER: May I write to you, Nora?

NORA: No, never. I won't let you.

HELMER: But surely I can send you . . .

NORA: Nothing, nothing.

HELMER: Can't I help you if ever you need it?

NORA: I said no. I don't accept things from strangers.

HELMER: Nora, can I never be anything more to you than a stranger?

NORA [*takes her bag*]: Ah, Torvald, only by a miracle of miracles . . .

HELMER: Name it, this miracle of miracles!

NORA: Both you and I would have to change to the point where. . . . Oh, Torvald, I don't believe in miracles any more.

HELMER: But I *will* believe. Name it! Change to the point where . . . ?

NORA: Where we could make a real marriage of our lives together. Goodbye!

[She goes out through the hall door.]

HELMER [*sinks down on a chair near the door, and covers his face with his hands*]: Nora! Nora! [*He rises and looks round.*] Empty! She's gone! [*With sudden hope.*] The miracle of miracles . . . ?

[The heavy sound of a door being slammed is heard from below.]

➤ *QUESTIONS FOR READING AND WRITING*

1. To what extent was your response to this play influenced by your own background or experience?
2. What kind of relationship do the Helmers' have? In what way do their conversations early in the play tell us almost everything there is to know about their relationship?
3. To what extent is Nora a victim of society? Of Torvald? Of herself?
4. Who is Mrs. Linde and how does she differ from Nora?
5. What is your response to Krogstad? To what extent is he a victim of society?
6. What kind of relationship do Krogstad and Mrs. Linde have? Compare it to the Helmers' relationship.
7. What is the role of Dr. Rank in the play? To what extent does he know her better than Torvald? Why is Nora so upset when he confesses his love for her?
8. How do you feel about Nora leaving Torvald and their children at the end of the play? Do you think she has a choice? Consider Ibsen's changed ending on page 791. Which ending do you prefer?
9. What is the theme of the play? What objects or actions in the play seem symbolic of the play's theme?
10. Is the play still relevant? Are there relationships like this today? Explain.
11. What conventions of society are being criticized in the play? Consider Ibsen's statements on pages 791–792. What is your response to his views in light of your response to the play?

Women in Cultural and Historical Context

The best literature has a universal, timeless quality. It speaks to us across time and culture and appeals to our humanity. But being aware of the historical and cultural context from which literature springs can enrich our understanding of it and lead to greater insight.

A number of the stories and plays in this section depict the lives of women in the late nineteenth and early twentieth centuries. Their actions and reactions are strongly motivated by the cultural imperatives of their time. Though we still struggle with issues of social justice at the turn of the twenty-first century, it is impossible for us to fully appreciate the impact of these imperatives on people who lived in these times. But a look at some sample letters, notes, newspaper columns, and excerpts from speeches and essays—the historical and cultural artifacts—may give us a better feel for the assumptions about women that dominated that era.

With the exception of our final essay, "The Rest of the Story," published by Natalie Zemon Davis and Jill Ker Conway in 1999, all of the selections that follow are more than a century old. The letters of John and Abigail Adams are more than two hundred years old, and seem to draw the battle lines for the prolonged struggle for women's rights that followed. On the eve of one rebellion, Abigail Adams forecasts another if the men creating the new "code of laws" are not "more generous and favorable" to women than their ancestors have been. In its own way, each of the other selections acts for or against that rebellion. A German husband's letter to his uncooperative wife illustrates the righteousness and arrogance of the male role in marriage. Having severed one bond of slavery herself, Sojourner Truth encourages and inspires women to overcome another in her speech to a women's rights meeting in Ohio.

Adding to their earlier pieces in this section, Henrik Ibsen and Charlotte Perkins Gilman show us their views of women's rights from another angle. Ibsen's "notes" for the play *A Doll's House*, a changed ending he wrote reluctantly for a German production of the play, and his speech to the Norwegian League for Women's Rights inject some interesting complications into our understanding of his intentions. Charlotte Perkins Gilman (Stetson), writing in a very different voice than the speaker in her short story "The Yellow Wallpaper," makes her case for women's rights in an excerpt from her scholarly essay "Women and Economics."

Elizabeth Cady Stanton writes about the compelling need for women to be given their "birthright of self-sovereignty." And in the latest of the nineteenth century pieces, two journalists, Wibur Fisk Tillet and Dorothy Dix, assess the progress made by women in the nineteenth century. Tillet believes much progress has been made—as long as women don't develop masculine qualities and wander outside the home. Dix, a pioneer advice-to-women columnist for a New Orleans newspaper *The Daily Picayune,* is a bit more feisty and realistic with her assessment.

At the end of the nineteenth century, 134 years after Abigail Adams's letter, it's clear that her prophesied rebellion was still going strong. It's sobering to realize, however, that twenty more years would pass before women even had the right to vote.

You can inform your response to the pieces that follow by considering essays that appeared earlier in this section: the twentieth-century pieces, Virginia Woolf's "If Shakespeare Had a Sister," Alice Walker's "In Search of Our Mother's Garden," and Judy Brady's "I Want a Wife." Each of these essays complement and, in the last two cases, bring up to date similar concerns expressed so long ago.

THE ADAMS LETTERS [1776]

From Abigail to John
Braintree
March 31, 1776

——I long to hear that you have declared an independancy (sic)—and by the way in the new Code of Laws which I suppose it will be necessary for you to make I desire you would Remember the Ladies and be more generous and favorable to them than your ancestors. Do not put such unlimited powers into the hands of the Husbands. Remember all Men would be tyrants if they could. If perticular (sic) care and attention is not paid to the Laidies (sic) we are determined to foment a Rebellion, and will not hold ourselves bound by any Laws in which we have no voice, or Representation.

That your Sex are Naturally Tyrannical is a Truth so thoroughly established as to admit of no dispute, but such of you as wish to be happy willingly give up the harsh title of Master for the more tender and endearing one of Friend. Why then, not put it out of power of the vicious and the Lawless to use us with cruelty and indignity with impunity. Men of Sense in all Ages abhor those customs which treat us only as the vassals of your Sex. Regard us then as Beings placed by providence under your protection and in imitation of the Supreem (sic) Being make use of that power only for our happiness.

From John to Abigail
April 14, 1776

As to your extraordinary Code of Laws, I cannot but laugh. We have been told that our Struggle has loosened the bands of Government everywhere. The Children and Apprentices were disobedient—that schools and Colledges (sic) were grown turbulent—that Indians slighted their Guardians and Negroes grew insolent to their Masters. But your Letter was the first Intimation that another Tribe more numerous and powerfull (sic) than all the rest were grown discontented.—This is rather too coarse a Compliment but you are so saucy, I won't blot it out.

Depend upon it, We know better than to repeal our Masculine systems. Altho (sic) they are in full Force, you know they are little more than Theory. We dare not exert our Power in its full Latitude. We are obliged to go fair, and softly, and in Practice you know We are the subjects. We have only the Name of Masters, and rather than give this, which would compleatly (sic) subject us to the Despotism of the Peticoat, I hope General Washington, and all our Brave Heroes would fight.

A Husband's Letter to His Wife [1844]

June 23, 1844

Dear Wife,

You have sinned greatly—and maybe I too; but this much is certain: Adam sinned after Eve had already sinned. So it is with us; you, alone, carry the guilt of all the misfortune which, however, I helped to enlarge later by my behavior. Listen now, since I still believe certain things to be necessary in order that we may have a peaceful life. If we want not only to be content for a day but forever, you will have to follow my wishes. So examine yourself and determine if you are strong enough to conquer your false ambitions and your stubbornness to submit to all the conditions, the fulfillment of which I cannot ignore. Every sensible person will tell you that all I ask of you is what is easily understood. If you insist on remaining stubborn, then do not return to my house, for you will never be happy with me; your husband, children, and the entire city threaten indifference or even contempt.

But if you decide to act *sensibly and correctly, that is justly and kindly,* then be certain that many in the world will envy you.

I am including here the paper which I read to you in front of the rabbi; ask anyone in your residence if the wishes expressed by me are not quite reasonable, and are of a kind to which every wife can agree for the welfare of domestic happiness. In any case, act in a way you think best.

When you decide to return, write to tell me on which day and hour you depart from Berlin and give me your itinerary whether by way of Kuestrin and Pinne or by way of Wollstein. I will then meet you at Wollstein or Pinne. I expect you will bring Solomon with you.

Don't travel unprepared. If you need money, ask your father.

May God enlighten your heart and mind.

I remain your so far unhappy, [Marcus]

Greetings to my parents, brothers, and sisters; also your brother. Show them what you wish, this letter, the enclosure, whatever you want. The children are fortunately healthy,

If you want to return with joy and peace, write me by return mail. In that case, I would rather send you a carriage. Maybe Madam Fraenkel will come along. . . .

(*Enclosure*)

My wife promises—for which every wife is obligated to her husband—to follow my wishes in everything and to strictly obey my orders. It is already self-evident that our marital relations have often been disturbed by the fact that my wife does not follow my wishes but believes herself to be entitled to act on her own, even if this is totally against my orders. In order not to have to remind my wife every second what my wishes are regarding homemaking and public conduct—wishes which I have often expressed—I want to make here a few rules which shall serve as a code of conduct. A home is best run if the work for each hour is planned ahead of time, if possible.

Servants get up no later than 5:00 A.M. in summer and 6:00 A.M. in winter, the children an hour later. The cook prepares breakfast. The nursemaid puts out clothes for every child, prepares water and sponge, cleans the combs, etc. The cook should stay in the kitchen unless there is time to clean the rooms. At least once a week the rooms should be cleaned whenever possible, but not all on the same day.

Every Wednesday, the people in the house should do a laundry. Every last Wednesday in the month, there shall be a large laundry with an outside washer-woman. At least every Monday, the seamstress shall come into the house to fix what is necessary.

Every Thursday or Friday, bread is baked for the week; I think it is best to buy grain and have it ground, but to knead it at home.

Every Friday special bread (Barches) should be bought for the evening meal.

The kitchen list will be prepared and discussed every Thursday evening, jointly, by me and my wife; but my wish is to be decisive.

After this, provisions are to be bought every Friday at the market. For this purpose, my wife, herself, will go to the market on Fridays, accompanied by a servant; she can substitute a special woman who does errands (*Faktorfrau*) if she wishes, but not a servant.

All expenditures have to be written down daily and punctually.

The children receive a bath every Thursday evening. The children's clothes must be kept in a specially appointed chest, with a separate compartment for each child with the child's name upon it. The boys' suits and girls' dresses are to be kept separately. To keep used laundry, there must be a hamper easily accessible. Equally important is the food storage box in which provisions are kept in order, locked and safe from vermin.

The kitchen should be kept in order. Once a week all woodwork and copper must be scoured. The lights and lamps have to be cleaned daily. Toward servants, one has to be strict and just. Therefore, one should not call them names which aren't suitable for a decent wife. One should give them enough nourishing food. Disobedience and obstinacy are to be referred to me.

My wife will never make visits in my absence. However, she should visit the synagogue every Saturday—at least once a month; also she should go for a walk with the children at least once a week.

SOJOURNER TRUTH

AIN'T I A WOMAN [1851]

This impromptu speech given by Sojourner Truth, a freed slave, was recorded with her own commentary by Frances Gage at a woman's rights convention in Ohio.

"WALL, CHILERN, WHAR DAR IS SO MUCH racket dar must be somethin' out o' kilter. I tink dat 'twixt de niggers of de Souf and de womin at de Norf, all talkin' 'bout rights, de white men will be in a fix pretty soon. But what's all dis here talkin' 'bout?

"Dat man ober dar say dat womin needs to be helped into carriages, and lifted ober ditches, and to hab de best place everywhar. Nobody eber helps me into carriages, or ober mud puddles, or gibs me any best place!" And raising herself to her full height, and her voice to a pitch like rolling thunder, she asked, 'And an't I a woman? Look at me! Look at my arm! (and she bared her right arm to the shoulder, showing her tremendous muscular power). I have ploughed, and planted, and gathered into barns, and no man could head me! And an't I a woman? I could work as much and eat as much as a man—when I could get it—and bear de lash as well! And an't I a woman? I have borne thirteen chilern, and seen 'em mos' all sold off to slavery, and when I cried out with my mother's grief, none but Jesus heard me! And an't I a woman?

"Den dey talks 'bout dis ting in de head; what dis dey call it?" ("Intellect," whispered someone near.) "Dat's it, honey. What's dat got to do wid womin's rights or nigger's rights? If my cup won't hold but a pint, and yourn holds a quart, wouldn't ye be mean not to let me have my little half-measure full?" And she pointed her significant finger, and sent a keen glance at the minister who had made the argument. The cheering was long and loud.

"Den dat little man in black dar, he say women can't have as much rights as men, 'cause Christ wan't a woman! Whar did your Christ come from?" Rolling thunder couldn't have stilled that crowd, as did those deep, wonderful tones, as she stood there with outstretched arms and eyes of fire. Raising her voice still louder, she repeated, "Whar did your Christ come from? From God and a, woman! Man had nothin' to do wid Him." Oh, what a rebuke that was to that little man.

Turning again to another objector, she took up the defense of Mother Eve. I cannot follow her through it all. It was pointed, and witty, and solemn; eliciting at almost every sentence deafening applause; and she ended by asserting: "If de fust woman God ever made was strong enough to turn de world upside down all alone, dese women togedder (and she glanced her eye over the platform) ought to be able to turn it back, and get it right side up again! And now dey is asking to do it, de men better let 'em." Long-continued cheering greeted this. "'Bleeged to ye for hearin' on me, and now ole Sojourner han't got nothin' more to say."

Amid roars of applause, she returned to her corner, leaving more than one of us with streaming eyes, and hearts beating with gratitude. She had taken us up in her strong arms and carried us safely over the slough of difficulty turning the whole tide in our favor. I have never in my life seen anything like the magical influence that subdued the mobbish spirit of the day, and turned the sneers and jeers of an excited crowd into notes of respect and admiration. Hundreds rushed up to shake hands with her, and congratulate the glorious old mother, and bid her God-speed on her mission of "testifyin' agin concerning the wickedness of this 'ere people."

HENRIK IBSEN

NOTES FOR THE MODERN TRAGEDY [1878]

There are two kinds of spiritual law, two kinds of conscience, one in man and another, altogether different, in woman. They do not understand each other; but in practical life the woman is judged by man's law, as though she were not a woman but a man.

The wife in the play ends by having no idea of what is right or wrong; natural feeling on the one hand and belief in authority on the other have altogether bewildered her.

A woman cannot be herself in the society of the present day, which is an exclusively masculine society, with laws framed by men and with a judicial system that judges feminine conduct from a masculine point of view.

She has committed forgery, and she is proud of it; for she did it out of love for her husband, to save his life. But this husband with his commonplace principles of honor is on the side of the law and looks at the question from the masculine point of view.

Spiritual conflicts. Oppressed and bewildered by the belief in authority, she loses faith in her moral right and ability to bring up her children. Bitterness. A mother in modern society, like certain insects who go away and die when she has done her duty in the propagation of the race. Love of life, of home, of husband and children and family. Now and then a womanly shaking off of her thoughts. Sudden return of anxiety and terror. She must bear it all alone. The catastrophe approaches, inexorably, inevitably. Despair, conflict, and destruction.

THE CHANGED ENDING OF A DOLL'S HOUSE *FOR A GERMAN PRODUCTION* [1880]

NORA: . . . . Where we could make a real marriage out of our lives together. Goodbye. [*Begins to go.*]

HELMER: Go then! [*Seizes her arm.*] But first you shall see your children for the last time!

NORA: Let me go! I will not see them! I cannot!

HELMER [*draws her over to the door, left*]: You shall see them. [*Opens the door and says softly.*] Look, there they are asleep, peaceful and carefree. Tomorrow, when they wake up and call for their mother, they will be—motherless.

NORA: [*trembling*] Motherless . . . !

HELMER: As you once were.

NORA: Motherless! [*Struggles with herself, lets her traveling bag fall, and says.*] Oh, this is a sin against myself, but I cannot leave them. [*Half sinks down by the door.*]

HELMER [*joyfully, but softly*]: Nora!

[*The Curtain Falls.*]

Speech at the Banquet of the Norwegian League for Women's Rights

[1898]

Christiania, May 26, 1898

I am not a member of the Women's Rights League. Whatever I have written has been without any conscious thought of making propaganda. I have been more the poet and less the social philosopher than people generally seem inclined to believe. I thank you for the toast, but must disclaim the honor of having consciously worked for the women's rights movement. I am not even quite clear as to just what this women's rights movement really is. To me it has seemed a problem of mankind in general. And if you read my books carefully you will understand this. True enough, it is desirable to solve the woman problem, along with all the others; but that has not been the whole purpose. My task has been the *description of humanity.* To be sure, whenever such a description is felt to be reasonably true, the reader will read his own feelings and sentiments into the work of the poet. These are then attributed to the poet; but incorrectly so. Every reader remolds the work beautifully and neatly, each according to his own personality. Not only those who write but also those who read are poets. They are collaborators. They are often more poetical than the poet himself.

Elizabeth Cady Stanton

Excerpt from "The Solitude of Self"

[1892]

The strongest reason for giving woman all the opportunities for higher education, for the full development of her faculties, her forces of mind and body; for giving her the most enlarged freedom of thought and action; a complete emancipation from all forms of bondage, of custom, dependence, superstition; from all the crippling influences of fear—is the solitude and personal responsibility of her own individual life. The strongest reason why we ask for woman a voice in the government under which she lives; in the religion she is asked to believe; equality in social life, where she is the chief factor; a place in the trades and professions, where she may earn her bread, is because of her birthright to self-sovereignty; because, as an individual, she must rely on herself. No matter how much women prefer to lean, to be protected and supported, nor how much men desire to have them do so, they must make the voyage of life alone, and for safety in an emergency, they must know something of the laws of navigation. To guide our own craft, we must be captain, pilot, engineer; with chart and compass to stand at the wheel; to watch the winds and waves, and know when to take in the sail, and to read the signs in the firmament over all. It matters not whether the solitary voyager is man or woman; nature, having endowed them equally, leaves them to their own skill and judgment in the hour of danger, and, if not equal to the occasion, alike they perish.

To appreciate the importance of fitting every human soul for independent action, think for a moment of the immeasurable solitude of self. We come into the world alone, unlike all who have gone before us, we leave it alone, under circumstances peculiar to ourselves. No mortal ever has been, no mortal ever will be like the soul just launched on the sea of life. There can never again be just such a combination of prenatal influences; never again just such environments as make up the infancy, youth and manhood of this one. Nature never repeats herself, and the possibilities of one human soul will never be found in another. No one has ever found two blades of ribbon grass alike, and no one will ever find two human beings alike. Seeing, then, that what must be the infinite diversity in human character, we can in a measure appreciate the loss to a nation when any class of the people is uneducated and unrepresented in the government.

WILBUR FISK TILLETT

EXCERPT FROM "SOUTHERN WOMANHOOD" [1891]

The growing respectability of self-support in woman is everywhere recognized as one of the healthiest signs of the times. The number of vocations open to women is constantly on the increase. Some modes of self-support are, and always will be, socially more respectable than others. In the report for 1888 of the Commissioner of Labor concerning the number and condition of working-women in the large cities is the following concerning Charleston, South Carolina:

> In no other Southern city has the exclusion of women from business been so rigid and the tradition that respectability is forfeited by manual labor so influential and powerful. Proud and well-born women have practised great self-denial at ill-paid conventional pursuits in preference to independence in untrodden paths. The embargo against self-support, however, has to some extent been lifted, and were there a larger number of remunerative occupations open to women, the rush to avail of them would show how ineffectual the old traditions have become.

A similar report of 1890 would show rapid changes and advances in public sentiment concerning the respectability of self-support in women, and would reveal that the "embargo" had, in most parts of the South at least, been entirely removed.

If we look at the South as a whole, and not at individual portions of it, it is unquestionably true that the great changes which the past thirty years have witnessed have wrought most favorably upon the intellectual life of Southern womanhood. The conditions under which Southern women now live are far more favorable for developing literary women than those existing in the days of slavery. In 1869 a volume was published by Mr. James Wood Davidson entitled "The Living Writers of the South," in which 241 writers are noticed, of which number 75 are women and 166 are men. Of the 241 named, 40 had written only for newspapers and magazines, while 201 had published one or more volumes, aggregating 739 in all. Although this book was published only four years after the close of the war, it was even then true that from two thirds to three fourths of the volumes mentioned in it as having been published by women—not to speak of the others—had been written and published after the opening of the war. They had been called forth by the war and the trying experiences following it. Whether the changed conditions under which we live have anything to do with it, it is nevertheless certainly true that there have been more literary women developed in the South in the thirty years since the war than in all our previous history.

It is Victor Hugo who has called this "the century of woman." It is certainly an age that has witnessed great changes in the life, education, and labor of women everywhere; and these changes have all been in the direction of enlarging the sphere of woman's activities, increasing her liberties, and opening up possibilities to her life hitherto restricted to man. It is a movement limited to no land and to no race. So far as this movement may have any tendency to take woman out of her true place in the home, to give her man's work to do and to develop masculine qualities in her, it finds no sympathy in the South. The Southern woman loves the retirement of home, and shrinks from everything that would tend to bring her into the public gaze.

Dorothy Dix

"The American Wife" [1898]

It always seems to the American woman that the wives of other countries, who are held up for her admiration and imitation, have rather the easiest time of it. It would be comparatively simple to make yourself a decorative object to adorn a man's house, if that were all that was expected of you. It would be simple enough to accomplish marvels of cooking and housekeeping if that were the chief end of life. It is when one attempts to combine the useful and the ornamental—to be a Dresden statuette in the parlor and a reliable range in the kitchen—that the situation becomes trying, and calls for genuine ability. Yet this is what we expect of the average American wife, merely as a matter of course. She must be a paragon of domesticity, an ornament in society, a wonder in finance and a light in the literary circle to which she belongs.

In our curious social system, many things are left to her that the men attend to in other countries. For one thing, her husband expects her to assume all authority and management of the home and family. He doesn't want to be bothered about it. When he makes the money he feels he has done his whole duty, and he leaves the rest to her. When he comes home, tired out, after a day's work, he wants to rest, to read his paper, to think out some scheme in which he is interested. If his wife has any idea of leaning on his superior judgment and asking his advice about domestic problems she is very soon undeceived. "Great Scotts, Mary," is the impatient reply, "can't you manage your own affairs? I haven't got time to see about it. Settle it yourself."

It is the same way about the children. The American father is generally a devoted parent, but he wants his wife to do the managing and disciplining. In the brief hours he is at home, the little ones are his playthings, and he spoils them, and indulges them with a happy sense that he has no responsibility about it and that their mother will have to do the subsequent disciplining. She is responsible for their mental and physical well-being. She decides on the schools, and what they shall study, what colleges they shall attend, and all the rest of it. The average American John has a well-founded belief that his Mary is the smartest woman in the world, and knows what she is about, and so, at last, when she announces that the children need to go to Europe to study this or that, he consents through mere force of habit. He is so much in the way of letting her decide things it doesn't occur to him he could raise a dissenting voice.

To her, too, he leaves the matter of society. She dominates it, and runs it, and an American married man's social position depends entirely on his wife. If she is ambitious he climbs meekly up the social ladder in her wake; if she is not ambitious, they sit comfortably and contentedly down on the lower rungs, and stay there. He feels that he would be a bungler in the game of society, and he simply backs her hand for all it is worth. He pays for the house in the fashionable neighborhood of her choice, and for her entertainments, but he leaves all the rest to "mother and the girls." They must attend to the intricate social machinery, that he admits is a necessity, and is perfectly willing to support with anything but his own presence.

"*Women and Suicide*" [1899]

The claim recently put boldly forth by a distinguished lawyer that a person has a right to die, when by means of disease or misfortune life becomes a burden, has provoked renewed discussion of the suicide question, and it is interesting, in this connection, to note that by far the larger number of suicides are among men. Women seldom take their own lives, and so we have the curious and contradictory spectacle of the sex that is universally accounted the braver and stronger, flinging themselves out of the world to avoid its troubles, while the weaklings patiently bear theirs on to the bitter end.

Nothing is more common than for the man who has speculated with other people's money and lost, and so brought ruin and disgrace on his family, to commit suicide. In fact, after reading of the trusted cashier going wrong, in one column, we almost expect to read in the next that he shot himself. No thought apparently comes to him of having any duty to stay and help lift the misery he brought on innocent people. In times of great financial stress, when a rich man has everything swept away, he, too, often solves the question of the future for himself by suicide, leaving his wife and little children to face a situation for which they are wholly unprepared. You never hear of a woman committing suicide and leaving her little children to the cruel mercies of the world, because she has lost her property. Instead, she feels more than ever that they need her care, and her help, and that she would be incapable of the unmentionable baseness of deserting them in such a crisis.

Yet if suicide is ever justifiable, it is for woman far more than men. She is always handicapped in the race of life. Sometimes with bodily infirmities, sometimes with mental idiosyncrasies, always by lack of training and business experience. Hard as poverty is for a man, it is harder still for a woman. Desperate as the struggle for existence is for him, it is still more desperate for her, limited by narrower opportunities, and rewarded with lesser pay. Terrible as are the tortures suffered by many a poor wretch, they are no worse than the life-long martyrdom that many a woman endures with never a thought of doing anything but bearing them with Christian fortitude and resignation until God's own hand sets her free.

There are many reasons why this state of affairs should exist. Woman's whole life is one long lesson in patience and submission. She must always give in. Men feel that they are born to command, to force circumstances to their will, and when circumstances can no longer be forced or bent, and they must yield to untoward fate, too many yield to the desire to avoid the misery they see before them by sneaking out of life. It is always a coward's deed. The babe salutes life with a wail, and the dying man takes leave of it with a groan. Between there is no time that has not its own troubles, and cares, and sorrows, and it is our part to bear them with courage, and it should be part of our pride in our sex that so many women sustain this brave attitude towards life under circumstances that might well tempt them to play the coward's part.

Charlotte Perkins Stetson (Gilman)

Excerpt from "Women and Economics" [1899]

Worse than the check set upon the physical activities of women has been the restriction of their power to think and judge for themselves. The extended use of the human will and its decisions is conditioned upon free, voluntary action. In her rudimentary position, woman was denied the physical freedom which underlies all knowledge, she was denied the mental freedom which is the path to further wisdom, she was denied the moral freedom of being mistress of her own action and of learning by the merciful law of consequences what was right and what was wrong; and she has remained, perforce, undeveloped in the larger judgment of ethics.

Her moral sense is large enough, morbidly large, because in this tutelage she is always being praised or blamed for her conduct. She lives in a forcing-bed of sensitiveness to moral distinctions, but the broad judgment that alone can guide and govern this sensitiveness she has not. Her contribution to moral progress has added to the anguish of the world the fierce sense of sin and shame, the desperate desire to do right, the fear of wrong; without giving it the essential help of a practical wisdom and a regulated will. Inheriting with each generation the accumulating forces of our social nature, set back in each generation by the conditions of the primitive human female, women have become vividly self-conscious centres of moral impulse, but poor guides as to the conduct which alone can make that impulse useful and build the habit of morality into the constitution of the race.

Recognizing her intense feeling on moral lines, and seeing in her the rigidly preserved virtues of faith, submission, and self-sacrifice,—qualities which in the Dark Ages were held to be the first of virtues,—we have agreed of late years to call woman the moral superior of man. But the ceaseless growth of human life, social life, has developed in him new virtues, later, higher, more needful; and the moral nature of woman, as maintained in this rudimentary stage by her economic dependence, is a continual check to the progress of the human soul. The main feature of her life—the restriction of her range of duty to the love and service of her own immediate family—acts upon us continually as a retarding influence, hindering the expansion of the spirit of social love and service on which our very lives depend. It keeps the moral standard of the patriarchal era still before us, and blinds our eyes to the full duty of man.

An intense self-consciousness, born of the ceaseless contact of close personal relation; an inordinate self-interest, bred by the constant personal attention and service of this relation; a feverish, torturing, moral sensitiveness, without the width and clarity of vision of a full-grown moral sense; a thwarted will, used to meek surrender, cunning evasion, or futile rebellion; a childish, wavering, short-range judgment, handicapped by emotion; a measureless devotion to one's own sex relatives, and a maternal passion swollen with the full strength of the great social heart, but denied social expression,—such psychic qualities as these, born in us all, are the inevitable result of the sexuo-economic relation.

It is not alone upon woman, and, through her, upon the race, that the ill-effects may be observed. Man, as master, has suffered from his position also. The lust for power and conquest, natural to the male of any species, has been fostered in him to an enormous degree by this cheap and easy lordship. His dominance is not that of one chosen as best fitted to rule or of one ruling by successful competition with "foemen worthy of his steel"; but it is a sovereignty based on the accident of sex, and holding over such helpless and inferior dependants as could not question or oppose. The easy superiority that needs no striving to maintain it; the temptation to cruelty always begotten by irresponsible power; the pride and self-will which surely accompany it,—these qualities have been bred into the souls of men by their side of the relation. When man's place was maintained by brute force, it made him more brutal: when his place was maintained by purchase, by the power of economic necessity, then he grew into the merciless use of such power as distinguishes him to-day.

Yet here, as in the other evil results of the sexuo-economic relation, we can see the accompanying good that made the condition necessary in its time; and we can follow the beautiful results of our present changes with comforting assurance. A healthy, normal moral sense will be ours, freed from its exaggerations and contradictions; and, with that clear perception, we shall no longer conceive of the ethical process as something outside of and against nature, but as the most natural thing in the world.

Where now we strive and agonize after impossible virtues, we shall then grow naturally and easily into those very qualities; and we shall not even think of them as especially commendable. Where our progress hitherto has been warped and hindered by the retarding influence of surviving rudimentary forces, it will flow on smoothly and rapidly when both men and women stand equal in economic relation. When the mother of the race is free, we shall have a better world, by the easy right of birth and by the calm, slow, friendly forces of social evolution.

Natalie Zemon Davis and Jill Ker Conway

The Rest of the Story [1999]

For all their drama and insight, traditional histories of the last thousand years fall short. Written mostly by men, they introduced women into the standard parade of wars, revolutions, monarchs and parliaments only at moments like their ascension to inherited thrones or religious authority. In the nineteenth century, most male historians compounded the problem by making women's history sound as though women had only then begun making headway.

Women's history has more to it than that. Women have always questioned their subordination and often found ways around it. Further, some institutions important in the lives of women that seem timeless, like monogamous marriage, are in fact rooted in the last thousand years; some ostensibly modern movements reach far back in time. Indeed, many turning points on the thousand-year time line of women's history are little known or little understood. The following brief account of that history describes the rest of the story.

Who Says Men Are Closer to God?

Are women and men more alike than they are different? And where they are different, are women inferior or superior? Such questions have been debated since biblical times, and especially in the years after 1000. Some medieval theologians—male, that is—taught that woman was not created in God's image. But that could not be true, abbesses and nuns objected, for they had felt Christ's "imprint of resemblance" on them. Hildegard of Bingen, a nun in the Rhineland in the twelfth century, insisted that women's "weakness" did not refer to spiritual capacities. A woman could mortify the flesh and draw close to God as well as any man.

Such women accepted the general view that the universe was organized into realms of higher and lower: angels over humans, humans over animals, nobles over commoners, soul over body. But when it came to men over women, women balked. Christine de Pizan, poet and moralist at the French court, said in her "Book of the City of Ladies" of 1405 that God had created men and women with equal potential. If men had stronger bodies, women had freer and sharper minds, if they were just educated. Against the old medical idea that women had a hungry womb—that is, a sexual appetite less controllable than men's—Christine countered that women were by nature virtuous and modest.

The hottest debates about male-female relations in medieval Europe turned on celibacy. In the tenth and eleventh centuries, many priests were married, and their wives had access to the sacred. In a turning point in women's history, the eleventh-century reforms of Pope Gregory VII did away with clerical marriage in the Roman Church. These reforms inaugurated ten centuries in which sexually active males—and all women—were forbidden to perform important liturgical functions. A spiritual demotion it may have been, but it also confirmed an ideal of the celibate life, leaving nuns like Hildegard of Bingen scope for high ascetic devotions.

One Man, One Wife

The church put all its force behind insisting on monogamous, permanent marriage. An important step was declaring the full doctrine of marriage as a religious sacrament in 1215. Getting the doctrine accepted by lay people was another matter. Among the landed classes, men lived with concubines instead of, or along with, wives and cast their women aside at will. Only when the great families decided that the church's rule would help keep feudal property together did they go along.

Then in the sixteenth century, the Protestant Reformation did away with marriage as a religious sacrament and allowed for divorce. Yet it legitimated marriage all the more by allowing clergymen to wed and doing away with celibate nunneries and monasteries. In Europe, prostitution was made illegal in both Catholic and Protestant cities. It was still practiced, of course, as was concubinage, especially between European settlers in America and their female slaves. But monogamous marriage remained the triumphant cultural ideal.

According to religious teaching and secular law, the wife was "subject" to her husband, and her property was under his control. He was to rule her justly and not be cruel. Moderate beating was permissible, though some Protestant pastors preached against using it at all, and Ashkenazic rabbis disagreed about whether it was grounds for divorce. Divorce was not an easy out: a single woman with children could scarcely survive. Marriage was a frame that most women accepted, hoping for affectionate unions. What we today would call lesbian couples lived as married partners in the seventeenth and eighteenth centuries, one cross-dressing as a man. Protofeminists chronicled abuses in marriage, but did not reject the notion of "subjection" outright until the eighteenth century. A seventeenth-century male feminist said that wives should defer to their husbands not because the men were truly superior, but to keep the peace.

Nine Babies, Three Adults

More worrisome to women than subjection was procreation. For most of the millennium, the pattern was many births, many deaths. Given the poor food and poor health, it was not always easy to get and stay pregnant. Many infants, even among the wealthy, died at birth. In seventeenth-century France, a long-lived peasant mother might bring nine children to term; half might survive till age five, and she could rejoice if two or three reached adulthood. Under these circumstances, the local midwife was consulted much more often for medicines to conceive than for those to abort. Only in the late seventeenth century, when a better food supply in Western Europe allowed more children to survive, did couples start to limit the number of their children.

The model of man over woman had some effect in every sphere, forcing women to find means to cope or resist. Female wage earners were paid less than men; the women improvised new ways to stitch, smuggle, peddle or beg. Male surgeons began to deliver babies in the wealthy families in the seventeenth century; midwives defended their female turf in the village, claiming their dexterous hands would do better than the surgeon's forceps.

Does "Man" Include Woman?

Since the days of Hildegard of Bingen, women had tried for a larger role in religion. The witchcraft prosecutions that swept Europe and then New England in the fifteenth through seventeenth centuries threatened that initiative: among the many thousands executed, women outnumbered men everywhere, at least four to one. To rulers and churchmen seeking control, the sorceress with her pact with the devil was the symbol of secret revolt. Out of jealousy, infertile village women even accused other women. Meanwhile, during the Counter Reformation, energetic women founded teaching orders that brought instruction to many girls other than nuns; contemplative orders were reformed by leaders like Teresa of Avila. Her autobiography, a profound account of a woman's interior and mystical life, was read as eagerly as Augustine's "Confessions."

Jewish women followed their own leader in the women's gallery of the synagogue; one Yiddish prayer visualized women studying Torah in Paradise. Protestant women expanded their Bible reading, but it was especially radical sects like the Quakers who challenged the limits on women. Margaret Fell wrote her 1666 tract, "Women's Speaking Justified," against Paul's admonition that women should keep silent in church. Women "led by the Spirit of God" could preach "Christ in the Male and Female is one."

For centuries, women had been queens, some of whom, like Elizabeth I of England, sustained authority by combining "masculine" and "feminine" styles of rulership. But no woman served in the law courts or chancelleries of late medieval and early modern monarchies. If a woman wanted to fight in the royal army, she had to do so disguised as a man. Joan of Arc, openly leading soldiers into battle to save France, was an exception in her day—and she ended up burned at the stake.

Most political action of women was taken informally through conversations and coquetry at court and as sponsors of the salons that arose in many cities in the seventeenth century. More open influence came about through increased literacy and printing. By the eighteenth century, women of diverse views were contributing to the abundant pamphlet literature on public affairs. The English historian Catharine Sawbridge Macaulay published tracts defending authors' copyright, frequently elected parliaments and the rights of the American colonies. As for the illiterate women of the lower classes in England, France and the Netherlands, their only lever of protest was joining in street riots.

All these forms of political action came together in the French Revolution, and some new ones were added as women made public political speeches and joined the army openly. The new philosophy of rational natural rights placed all men on an equal footing in regard to citizenship and the law. But did "men" include women? The French playwright Olympe de Gouges insisted that it did in her "Declaration of the Rights of Woman," in 1791, as did Mary Wollstonecraft the following year in "A Vindication of the Rights of Woman." Others did not want women to have so much of a share in political life. Men of the revolution said that women should stay home and rear their sons to be good citizens. Even evangelical women encouraged their sisters to seek reform through religion and leave matters of state to men. It would be the new American republic where the issues of women's status would play out most vigorously over the next century.

"The Slavery of Marriage"

When enlightenment ideas came to America, the debate about women's rights found a new context, since the most powerful form of social hierarchy there was not gender but race. And the American Constitution, by dispensing with hereditary rank and monarchical institutions, immediately granted women a new role: teaching republican values to young Americans. The new republic opened many avenues to women: social, economic, political, educational and religious. Evangelical Christianity made the home, not the church, the site of religious instruction.

As women increasingly assumed this responsibility, they also began teaching outside the home and stressed the need for women's schools. In the first half of the nineteenth century, Emma Willard's Troy Female Seminary and Catharine Beecher's Hartford Female Seminary became thriving institutions, followed by Mary Lyon's Mount Holyoke Female Seminary. By midcentury, it was clear that tax revenues should be spent to educate girls as well as boys, at least in New York and New England. By the 1870s, many public universities admitted women, and elite women's colleges like Smith and Wellesley were established. In 1894, feminist donors to Johns Hopkins Medical School used their gifts to compel the admission of women.

Still, far into the first half of the twentieth century, many professional schools continued to bar women, and when they were admitted, discrimination drove them to lower-status professional fields. Female doctors were steered toward public health, lawyers to social work, language scholars to library cataloguing, scientists to high-school teaching.

Within the white middle-class family, education and religious responsibility for children improved women's status through the nineteenth century. By the 1830s, magazines analyzing life from a woman's point of view began to flourish in North America. In Europe, female writers of philosophical insight, from George Eliot to Virginia Woolf in the early twentieth century and on up to Simone de Beauvoir, steadily clarified women's issues. But mostly, wives were still considered their husbands' subordinates.

American feminists wishing to convey their critique of marriage often did so through the lens of slavery, the most volatile public issue of the mid- and late nineteenth century. "The investigation of the rights of the slave has led me to a better understanding of my own," wrote Angelina Grimk, a Southern abolitionist. "I have found the Anti-Slavery cause to be the high school of morals in our land. Now if rights are founded in the nature of our moral being, then the mere circumstance of sex does not give to man higher rights and responsibilities than to woman."

Though they didn't participate in elections, American women believed that they had access to the political system through the right to petition Congress. But as the conflict over abolition escalated, it became clear that women's petitions were not being heard. The right to vote was moved to the top of the list. Female reformers like Elizabeth Cady Stanton and Anna Howard Shaw combined spellbinding oratory with noisy street politics. Stanton was well known, for instance, for her lecture The Slavery of Marriage. The argument for suffrage then became more expedient: white women's votes would balance those of newly enfranchised black males and immigrants. The majority that ratified the nineteenth Amendment in 1920 was built on these racist grounds.

New Experts in Mothering: Men

Meanwhile, biological science was replacing theology as the language for discussing the differences between women and men. The popularity of Darwinian thought and the discovery of the endocrine system anchored the discussion firmly in science. Nor were such discussions purely theoretical, for by the 1920s women and men began to inhabit the same workplace. Even so, the young women taking clerical jobs in corporate offices were considered little threat, for it was thought that their hormones would drive them to maternity and service rather than wealth and power.

The new economic forces at work in America radically altered the role of women as workers, mothers and wives. Industrialization had created jobs for women in factories and textile mills in the mid-1800s. At the same time, the fruits of industrialization—mass-produced clothing and foods—gave middle-class mothers a new role: manager of household consumption. But many female responsibilities were subject to male guidance at the turn of the century. In the new field of child studies, male experts like G. Stanley Hall even tried to make mothering a science.

Isolation made mothers willing recipients of such expertise. The middle class had begun its flight from the city in the mid-nineteenth century, and by its close servants were being replaced by new labor-saving household equipment. So suburban women were alone with their children. Whereas in the eighteenth century the family was a partnership for spouses and children, the twentieth-century family became based on intimacy. Greater life expectancy meant that marriages lasted longer, well past a woman's childbearing years. As infant mortality declined, the family became more child-centered, and private insurance and pensions, as well as governmental assistance, made older parents less dependent on working children.

The emotional tone of marriages also changed with the rise of the corporation and the profession. Increasingly, the vocations of middle-class men excluded their families. This prompted a movement for more accessible divorce, along with longer marriages, increased mobility and the growing ideal of emotional and sexual fulfillment between spouses.

Not-So-Equal Rights

Sigmund Freud and other pioneers of psychology profoundly affected the status of women by arguing that an acceptance of gender difference was a prerequisite for mental health. From the 1920s through the 1970s, women with political, scientific or intellectual interests were stigmatized as neurotic, while men involved in the more feminine realms like the arts were considered less than fully male. The family dynamic laid out by Freud, based on latent erotic attachments, encouraged sons to overcome their mother complexes by becoming strong and independent. Daughters, meanwhile, were encouraged to replace their love for their fathers by finding a male romantic partner rather than by developing an independent self. In time, however, feminist interpretations of difference developed. In the 1970s, Nancy Chodorow reworked Freud's Oedipal system to point out that the strongest erotic gratification a female infant receives comes from a same-sex relationship with her mother, raising questions about the inevitability of female dependence on males.

In the political sphere, meanwhile, female voting didn't change party power structures, and women began developing parallel institutions like the National Woman's Party, in 1916. Its 1923 drive for an equal rights amendment failed, just as its successor failed in the 1970s, partly because Americans, including women, remained resistant to the idea of a woman as President. Once again, feminists created parallel structures to support female candidates, like Emily's List (Early Money Is Like Yeast). Where once the rare women elected to public office were typically the widows of male officeholders, the election of women became unremarkable, though even now they comprise only a fraction of Congress and high state officials.

In the 1960s, feminists began to focus on changing the composition of high-status professions. Once access to graduate education was won, feminist scholars pushed to change patterns of research and teaching so that women were no longer regarded as a failed model of the male norm, but as a norm themselves. In so doing, they helped ignite the culture wars of the 1980s and 90s. And by the end of the 90s, women constituted 60 percent of college graduates. Even so, on leaving school they still face the continuing reality of the glass ceiling.

Inflation, rising economic expectations and women's quest for professional equality after World War II produced the reinvention of the nanny—a movement promptly challenged by the argument that only birth mothers could care effectively for their children. A successful dual-track life as mother and professional, therefore, required heroic energy or a flouting of this conventional wisdom. Two careers within one family often meant a commuter marriage, which may have seemed new but which echoed the old aristocratic pattern: spouses parted by attendance at court and by journeys to distant estates or remote colonies. But now there is a big difference: a woman's property and income do not necessarily belong to her husband.

While feminist interpretations of gender difference gained favor in the 1970s, and while lesbian feminists argued in the 1980s for difference with a difference, claiming the superiority of same-sex relationships, a strong backlash arose in conservative quarters. This was marked not only by a denigration of feminism but also by an elevation of macho versions of male power and fresh assertions of difference. Such arguments were once again located in theology by Christian, Jewish and Islamic fundamentalists. Meanwhile, new debates about gender difference emerged in brain research. While female and male synapses might fire the same way, doubters insisted that there must surely be a difference in the circuitry. Questions about differences in wiring are a new form of debate that goes back to the medieval question about whether women have souls.

The New Terrain

So what has happened to women over the past thousand years? Western women and their children have made astonishing gains in health and life expectancy, though most of their non-Western sisters have not yet shared those benefits. The scope of women's work has expanded vastly, much of it paying well enough so that women with children can survive. Women in the West have secured access to education beyond the wildest dreams of their medieval counterparts. Women's athletic prowess has captured public imagination, and a female general is no longer a novelty.

But what of the mixed outcomes? Feminist spirituality today provides a powerful leaven within some Christian, Jewish and Islamic communities, but others still forbid female participation, and the loss of the institutional structure once provided by female religious orders has shrunk the territory controlled by women. The reduced number of women's colleges has had a similar effect. Women's reproductive lives, though, are now managed by technologies subject to male control. The ability to detect the sex of a fetus can result in higher abortion rates for female infants, whereas in medieval society the girl babies at least had a chance to be born. Sexual freedoms have enlarged the sphere of pleasure, but with them have come unresolved problems about sexual behavior.

What will be the new terrain for addressing the issues of likeness and difference? What new strategies will women develop to dismantle exclusively male hierarchies? The cognitive sciences will most likely inherit the role of theology in arguing about differences between male and female. Still, the global rise of religious fundamentalism will counter women's efforts to secure equal footing. And among women worldwide there will remain stark differences about how to achieve a better life.

But argument—and laughter—about the relationship between women and men will never end. Our physical bodies are cultural texts that are constantly revised, and no single formulation of the relationship between the sexes can last.

A Student Essay

Trisa Hayes

Dr. Madden

English 102

December 20, 200X

The Age of Living Dolls: A Doll's House, "The Story of an Hour"

and the Rights of Married Women in the Nineteenth Century

When I was a little girl, I desperately wanted a doll house. After my persistent begging, whining, and promise making, my parents finally gave in and bought me one. I spent hours playing with my doll, the new house, and all its tiny furniture. I loved it simply because I had sole control over all aspects of my doll's life: when she would eat, where she would shop, what she would wear, what time she would go to bed. These were things my parents had control over in my life.

Playing with my doll was fun until the newness wore off; after that I only played with her when I was bored. The rest of the time she just sat in her house, lifeless and waiting patiently for the next string of activities I would plan for her.

Over the years my parents and others encouraged me to make my own decisions no matter how big they were, and having the freedom to do so is something I'll never take for granted again. After reading Henrik Ibsen's A Doll's House and Kate Chopin's "The Story of an Hour," I saw what life could be like through the eyes of women who are treated like dolls. These stories are an illustration of women's roles and the dilemmas they faced in society during the nineteenth century.

The protagonist in A Doll's House is Nora, a simple housewife who is treated like a five-year-old by her husband Torvald. It appears at first that the only thing Nora is capable of is mirroring what her husband wishes to see in her. Because he expects her to be like a pet, she flutters and twitters about the room like a helpless bird, or takes on the characteristics of a small woodland creature that relies entirely on a much larger beast for its safety. As I continued to read about her incomprehensible submissiveness, I found myself getting angrier and angrier. First she hides her macaroons because Torvald doesn't want her to have sweets. Then there's my favorite example; Nora tells Torvald, "Oh, everything you do is right" (772). Her spineless actions are infuriating.

Torvald's overwhelming male chauvinistic attitude only intensified my frustrations. When Nora approaches him on Krogstad's behalf, Torvald insists he will have to replace him and gives this revealing excuse: "If it ever got around that the new bank manager had been talked over by his wife . . ." (754). And when Nora tells him he is always right, he responds, "There's my little skylark talking common sense" (773).

But this is 1879, and Nora and Torvald are only filling the female/male roles that are socially acceptable at that time. It is a man's world, with only male views and male rules. What gives men the right to tell women how to behave? Nothing. They are just the physically stronger of the two sexes. As Charlotte Perkin's Stetson says in "Women and Economics," published in 1899, a man's role in relation to women is "a sovereignty based on the accident of sex." But Nora is growing tired of being treated like mindless property and snaps to Mrs. Linde, "You're just like the rest of them. You all think I'm useless when it comes to anything really serious" (734).

When Torvald opens Krogstad's letter, she is so terrified of him, she wants to escape from the house before he has a chance to confront her. He grabs her arm and declares with great despair and rage, "I'm done for, a miserable failure, and it's all the fault of a featherbrained woman" (3.395–396). This is hardly a way for him to show his gratitude to the woman who saved his life. As soon as Torvald receives the next letter and returned IOU from Krogstad, he cries "I am saved" (3.427) and digs himself into a deeper hole in Nora's eyes when he adds, "There is something indescribably moving and very satisfying in knowing that he has forgiven his wife. . . . It's as though it made her his property in a double sense: he has, as it were, given her new life, and she becomes in a way both his wife and at the same time his child" (779). Torvald's response has provided Nora with a revelation about Torvald and about herself. She begins to discover how very little she knows about herself and the world around her. She isn't even aware of her own interests because she has always been so eager to please her husband.

His unsavory responses present her with a new dilemma. Should she abandon her family and comfortable home for a sense of self-worth? Or should she stay and sacrifice any future prospects of happiness? I can't imagine being forced to believe that it's a woman's duty to maintain a man's happiness even if it costs her her own. Furthermore, Nora had to consider how others would treat her if she left, for back then women absolutely, positively did not go against the grain of society's expectations unless they were fully prepared to endure vicious slurs and be shunned by respected members of the community, lifelong friends, and in some instances even their own families.

Then, with a mature demeanor, Nora sits down with her husband to have a serious discussion for the first time. The tide of power shifts as she reveals her observations of their life together. She explains to him how both he and her father have treated her like a doll, and that now she is certain of what she needs to do. She announces to Torvald that she is leaving him. He is dumbfounded but attempts to reason with her by reminding him of her "sacred duty" to him and their children, but she unleashes her pent up feelings on him: "I'm not content anymore with what most people say, or what it says in books. I have to think things out for myself, and get things clear" (782). "I must try to discover who is right, society or me" (782). And she leaves to try to discover the choices and opportunities for those who are not confined to a child's boundaries.

Kate Chopin, who was born in 1851 and died in 1904, probably witnessed such struggles firsthand. The sign of her times were expressed through her writing, specifically through "The Story of an Hour." It's evident that throughout history many women have walked in Nora's shoes, thus the fight for the right to vote. But most women of her time didn't dare acknowledge the slightest dissatisfaction with their roles as wives and mothers, much less have the courage to leave. "The Story of an Hour" is the story of such a woman.

Her story is about a woman who has just found out that her husband has died in a railroad disaster. At first she is in shock, void of all emotion. And then without warning she begins to cry hysterically. After her sister Josephine succeeds in calming her somewhat, she retreats to the solitude of her room to collect her thoughts. Then, after a sincere struggle to maintain the specific emotions that society expects her to have over the loss of her husband, she finally succumbs to her true feelings by uttering softly to herself, "Free, free, free!" (514).

Her sister, out of concern, begs her to open the door. She "breathed a quick prayer that life might be long. It was only yesterday she had thought with a shudder that life might be long" (515). Then, almost in a tranquil state, she rises to let Josephine in and agrees to accompany her downstairs. But as they descend the front door unlocks and in walks her husband, completely unscathed and very much alive. She instantly dies of a heart attack at the sight of her husband. The doctors said she died from a "joy that kills," but nothing could be further from the truth. She and Nora, though worlds apart in some ways, share a common bond. They both have a burning desire to be free, to break the mold of their doll-like lives.

It's frightening to read about all the stifling rules and regulations women had to follow back then. Just thinking about it makes me claustrophobic. The sad part is that there are still an astounding number of women in our country who are forced to obey each and every command given to them by their husbands, no matter how humiliating or dehumanizing. The ability to think as an individual is gradually stripped and they become more and more lifeless, mindless dolls every day.

I am deeply grateful to the women who believed that they deserved more in life than that. Because of these two stories, I have a new respect and understanding of the women that lived in the nineteenth century, a time I think of as "the age of the living dolls." For without these pioneering women who struggled through and endured many hardships to obtain basic human rights, life for women now would only be something to be endured and not enjoyed.

Works Cited

Chopin, Kate. "The Story of an Hour." Exploring Literature. Ed. Frank Madden. New York: Longman, 2001. 513–516.

Ibsen, Henrik. "A Doll's House." Exploring Literature. Ed. Frank Madden. New York: Longman, 2001. 725–786.

Stetson (Gilman), Charlotte Perkins. Excerpt from "Women and Economics." Exploring Literature. Ed. Frank Madden. New York: Longman, 2001. 796.

Exploring the Literature of Women and Men: Options for Writing and Research

Some Options for Writing About Women and Men

1. Consider the ways your gender or the gender of those you know has affected your life. Do any of the stories, poems, plays, or essays in this section remind you of your own experiences or the circumstances of your life? Choose one or more of these works and write a response essay that compares your experience or circumstances with those in the literature.
2. Our own values about gender can affect how we see the world and strongly influence our response to literature. We may agree or disagree with what an author says or what characters say or do. So too, literature may influence us and the formation of our values about gender. Write an essay about the ways in which one or more works in this section either provoked a moral judgment on your part or helped you learn something.
3. Over two hundred years ago, Mary Wollstonecraft in *A Vindication of the Rights of Women* wrote: "It would be an endless task to trace the variety of meannesses, cares, and sorrows into which women are plunged by the prevailing opinion that they were created rather to feel than reason, and that all power they obtain must be obtained by their charms and weakness."

Consider this quote, and write an essay about how this kind of stereotyping has influenced the way women are treated or behave in one or more works in this section.

4. In a best selling book, *Iron John,* Robert Bly wrote: We have defective mythologies that ignore masculine depth of feeling, assign men a place in the sky instead of earth, teach obedience to the wrong powers, and entangle men and women in systems of industrial domination." Write about this quote as it applies to the roles of men in one or more works in this section.

5. Choose a quote (or quotes) in the introduction to this section, "Women and Men" (p. 498) and pair it (or them) with one of the longer pieces in this section that either supports it or argues against it. For example, Rousseau's quote about the education (training) of women might be paired with Judy Brady's essay "I Want a Wife," which argues against it. On the other hand, if we chose Gail Sheehy's quote about the plight of the modern married woman, we might choose the Brady essay to exemplify and support the point Sheehy is making.

   Write an essay which compares or contrasts a quote (or quotes) from the introduction with a story, poem, play, or essay that supports or argues against it.

A Research Option

Anton Chekhov's "The Lady with the Pet Dog," Andrew Marvell's poem "To His Coy Mistress," Henrik Ibsen's play *A Doll's House,* and Judy Brady's essay "I Want a Wife" all have something important to say about relationships between men and women. Each of these works, however, springs from a very different historical, social, or political context. Expanding our exploration of literature to include the context in which these works were produced can be an enriching and enlightening experience.

Choose one or more of these or other works in this section and write a research essay that includes secondary source material about the historical, social, or political background of the literature.

Collaboration: Writing and Revising with Your Peers

In addition to applying your own values and standards to writing about the literature in this section, you may find it beneficial to share and discuss your work with classmates. Getting feedback from others can help you generate and clarify your ideas and revise and edit your writing more effectively.

Choose a work, topic, or one of the options for writing about women and men above, and work with a partner or in a small group. Exchange journal entries or response sheets, generate questions together, do a group semantic map (see pp. 40–45), or simply share and respond to each other's ideas.

After you have written a rough draft of your essay, share it with a partner or your group. Respondents should function primarily as sensitive readers and give honest, constructive responses. They should try to be aware of each writer's purpose, discuss concerns particular to each writer, and comment on the effectiveness of the essay's organization, support, clarity, and voice (for a comprehensive checklist for revision, see p. 51).

In the final stage of your writing, editing and proofreading might be done in a similar fashion. A partner or a group of readers might help you check for correct grammar, spelling, punctuation, and typos (a comprehensive checklist for editing is on p. 52).

A Writing/Research Portfolio Option

A portfolio is a collection of your work, related materials, and commentary about your work collected over time. Gathering materials in a portfolio will provide you with resources for research and development. You can use your portfolio to collect your writing about the literature in this section, to find a topic to write about, to revise or add to your work, or to keep multiple drafts and monitor the changes you make as you revise. Among the resources you might include:

- Your responses to the quotes and prompts about women and men at the beginning of this section, the questions you had right after you finished reading each work of literature, and your journal entries.
- What your classmates, instructor, or published critics had to say about the literature and how their comments may have influenced your interpretation.
- Information you've gathered from the library and the Internet about the historical, social, and political context of the work or its author.

Heritage & Identity

HERITAGE & IDENTITY

A DIALOGUE ACROSS HISTORY

Better one's own duty, [though] imperfect, / Than another's duty well performed.

—from the *Bhagavad Gita,* c. 250 B.C.–250 A.D.

I must study politics and war that my sons may have liberty to study mathematics and philosophy. My sons ought to study mathematics and philosophy, geography, natural history, naval architecture, navigation, commerce, and agriculture, in order to give their children a right to study painting, poetry, music, architecture, statuary, tapestry, and porcelain.

—John Adams, letter to Abigail, 1780

People will not look forward to posterity who never look backward to their ancestors.

—Edmund Burke, *Reflections on the Revolution in France,* 1790

These lands are ours. No one has a right to remove us because we were the first owners. The Great Spirit above us has appointed this place for us, on which to light our fires, and here we will remain. As to boundaries, the Great Spirit knows no boundaries, nor will his red children acknowledge any.

—Chief Tecumseh, 1810

Our country is the world—our countrymen are all mankind.

—William Lloyd Garrison, *The Liberator,* 1831

Instead of boiling up individuals into the species, I would draw a chalk line round every individuality, and preach to it to keep within that, and preserve and cultivate its identity.

—Jane Welsh Carlyle, letter, 1845

If a man does not keep pace with his companions, perhaps it is because he hears a different drummer. Let him step to the music which he hears, however measured or far away.

—Henry David Thoreau, *Walden,* 1854

I'm Nobody! Who are you? / Are you—Nobody—too?

—Emily Dickinson, c. 1861

When I found that I had crossed that line [during her first escape from slavery], I looked at my hands to see if I was the same person. There was such a glory over everything.

—Harriet Tubman, her biography, 1868

It is worthwhile for anyone to have behind him a few generations of honest, hard-working ancestry.

—John P. Marquand, *The Late George Apley*, 1937

Men can starve from a lack of self-realization as much as . . . from a lack of bread.

—Richard Wright, *Native Son*, 1940

It is thus with most of us; we are what other people say we are. We know ourselves chiefly by hearsay.

—Eric Hoffer, *The Passionate State of Mind*, 1954

We become what we are only by the radical and profound rejection of what others have said about us.

—Jean Paul Sartre, preface to Frantz Fanon's *Wretched of the Earth*, 1961

I have a dream that one day on the red hills of Georgia the sons of former slaves and the sons of former slaveowners will be able to sit down together at the table of brotherhood.

—Martin Luther King Jr., speech, 1963

How many roads must a man walk down / Before you call him a man?

—Bob Dylan, "Blowin' in the Wind," 1962

If you write about the things and the people you know best, you discover your roots. Even if they are new roots, fresh roots . . . they are better than . . . no roots.

—Isaac Bashevis Singer, interview, 1978

Our genetic heritage endows each of us with a series of emotional setpoints that determines our temperament. But the brain circuitry involved is extraordinarily malleable. . . . This means that childhood and adolescence are critical windows of opportunity for setting down the essential emotional habits that will govern our lives.

—Daniel Goleman, *Emotional Intelligence*, 1995

Heritage and Identity: Exploring Your Experiences and Beliefs

Who we are and how we got to be this way seems to be of interest to all of us. Are we who we are because of our roots, the nature and nurture of our ancestors? Or are we who we are because of conscious choices we make as individuals? Are we responsible only to ourselves for our actions, or do we have a special responsibility to our posterity?

The elusive answers to these questions are at the heart of our search for identity. Whether we seek our personal identity by marching to the beat of Thoreau's "different drummer," celebrate our common humanity at Martin Luther King's "table of brotherhood," or recognize in ourselves the features, traits, or gestures that we inherit from our ancestors, we spend much of our lives finding our place in the world and our sense of who we are.

How we respond to literature, too, is often influenced by our sense of heritage and personal identity—how we see ourselves, our backgrounds, and our circumstances reflected in what we read. Though we probably have an image of ourselves that we carry within us most of the time, we are likely to project a different personality according to the situations in which we find ourselves. So, too, our sense of heritage may affect our personal identity. If our friends and family members find their ethnic background or heritage to be a central issue in their daily lives, then we probably feel the same way. As a preparation for reading the literature in this section, you may find it helpful to think about your own values and beliefs about heritage and identity.

Reading and Writing About Heritage and Identity

At least one aspect of the many stories, poems, plays, and essays in this section is about the impact that heritage or identity have on the characters: a high school boy's depression and desperate escape to another life in Willa Cather's short story "Paul's Case"; W.H. Auden's satirical tribute to an identityless hero in his poem "The Unknown Citizen"; and Neil Miller's exploration of the lives of residents in a rural gay community in his essay "In Search of Gay America." The brief quotes that open this section also give you some idea of the number of compelling ethical, political, and social arguments that are connected to heritage and identity. Ancestry and posterity, social pressure and individual conscience, community and anonymity, and responsibility and self-realization head a long list of concerns. Any of these or other related issues would provide a fine topic for an essay.

• FICTION •

JULIA ALVAREZ (b. 1954)

(See biography on page 312.)

SNOW

[1991]

Our first year in New York we rented a small apartment with a Catholic school nearby, taught by the Sisters of Charity, hefty women in long black gowns and bonnets that made them look peculiar, like dolls in mourning. I liked them a lot, especially my grandmotherly fourth grade teacher, Sister Zoe. I had a lovely name, she said, and she had me teach the whole class how to pronounce it. *Yo-lan-da.* As the only immigrant in my class, I was put in a special seat in the first row by the window, apart from the other children so that Sister Zoe could tutor me without disturbing them. Slowly, she enunciated the new words I was to repeat: *laundromat, cornflakes, subway, snow.*

Soon I picked up enough English to understand holocaust was in the air. Sister Zoe explained to a wide-eyed classroom what was happening in Cuba. Russian missiles were being assembled, trained supposedly on New York City. President Kennedy, looking worried too, was on the television at home, explaining we might have to go to war against the Communists. At school, we had air-raid drills: an ominous bell would go off and we'd file into the hall, fall to the floor, cover our heads with our coats, and imagine our hair falling out, the bones in our arms going soft. At home, Mami and my sisters and I said a rosary for world peace. I heard new vocabulary: *nuclear bomb, radioactive fallout, bomb shelter.* Sister Zoe explained how it would happen. She drew a picture of a mushroom on the blackboard and dotted a flurry of chalkmarks for the dusty fallout that would kill us all.

The months grew cold, November, December. It was dark when I got up in the morning, frosty when I followed my breath to school. One morning as I sat at my desk daydreaming out the window, I saw dots in the air like the ones Sister Zoe had drawn—random at first, then lots and lots. I shrieked, "Bomb! Bomb!" Sister Zoe jerked around, her full black skirt ballooning as she hurried to my side. A few girls began to cry.

But then Sister Zoe's shocked look faded. "Why, Yolanda dear, that's snow!" She laughed. "Snow."

5 "Snow," I repeated. I looked out the window warily. All my life I had heard about the white crystals that fell out of American skies in the winter. From my desk I watched the fine powder dust the sidewalk and parked cars below. Each flake was different, Sister Zoe said, like a person, irreplaceable and beautiful.

➤ *QUESTIONS FOR READING AND WRITING*

1. Why is the snowfall such a shocking experience for the narrator?
2. At the end of this brief story, Sister Zoe tries to calm Yolanda by describing the "fallout" that frightened her. Do you think her explanation of snow is effective? Why?

WILLA CATHER (1873–1947)

Willa Cather was born in the Shenandoah Valley of Virginia, but moved with her family to Red Cloud, Nebraska, a young community made up primarily of European immigrants, when she was nine years old. She attended the University of Nebraska, and after graduation in 1895 moved back East, first to Pittsburgh and then to New York City, where she worked as a reporter, high school teacher, and editor, writing and publishing occasional poems and short stories. In 1912, following the publication of her first novel, Alexander's Bridge, *Cather left her job as managing editor of* McClure's *magazine, deciding to devote herself exclusively to writing fiction. Much of her greatest work, including the novels* O Pioneers! *(1913),* The Song of the Lark *(1915), and* My Antonia *(1918), is set in the rural frontier of her childhood. "Paul's Case," which explores the artistic temperament and power of the human imagination in an inhospitable world, is taken from* The Troll Garden *(1905), Cather's first collection of short stories.*

PAUL'S CASE

[1905]

A Study in Temperament

It was Paul's afternoon to appear before the faculty of the Pittsburgh High School to account for his various misdemeanors. He had been suspended a week ago, and his father had called at the Principal's office and confessed his perplexity about his son. Paul entered the faculty room suave and smiling. His clothes were a trifle outgrown and the tan velvet on the collar of his open overcoat was frayed and worn; but for all that there was something of the dandy about him, and he wore an opal pin in his neatly knotted black four-in-hand, and a red carnation in his buttonhole. This latter adornment the faculty somehow felt was not properly significant of the contrite spirit befitting a boy under the ban of suspension.

Paul was tall for his age and very thin, with high, cramped shoulders and a narrow chest. His eyes were remarkable for a certain hysterical brilliancy, and he continually used them in a conscious, theatrical sort of way, peculiarly offensive in a boy. The pupils were abnormally large, as though he were addicted to belladonna, but there was a glassy glitter about them which that drug does not produce.

When questioned by the Principal as to why he was there, Paul stated, politely enough, that he wanted to come back to school. This was a lie, but Paul was quite accustomed to lying; found it, indeed, indispensable for overcoming friction. His teachers were asked to state their respective charges against him, which they did with such a rancor and aggrievedness as evinced that this was not a usual case. Disorder and impertinence were among the offenses named, yet each of his instructors felt that it was scarcely possible to put into words the real cause of the trouble, which lay in a sort of hysterically defiant manner of the boy's; in the contempt which they all knew he felt for them, and which he seemingly made not the least effort to conceal. Once, when he had been making a synopsis of a paragraph at the blackboard, his English teacher had stepped to his side and attempted to guide his hand. Paul had started back with a shudder and thrust his hands violently behind him. The astonished woman could scarcely have been more hurt and embarrassed had he struck at her. The insult was so involuntary and definitely personal as to be unforgettable. In one way and another, he had made all his teachers, men and women alike, conscious of the same feeling of physical aversion. In one class he habitually sat with his hand shading his eyes; in another he always looked out of the window during the recitation; in another he made a running commentary on the lecture, with humorous intention.

His teachers felt this afternoon that his whole attitude was symbolized by his shrug and his flippantly red carnation flower, and they fell upon him without mercy, his English teacher leading the pack. He stood through it smiling, his pale lips parted over his white teeth. (His lips were continually twitching, and he had a habit of raising his eyebrows that was contemptuous and irritating to the last degree.) Older boys than Paul had broken down and shed tears under that ordeal, but his set smile did not once desert him, and his only sign of discomfort was the nervous trembling of the fingers that toyed with the buttons of his overcoat, and an occasional jerking of the other hand which held his hat. Paul was always smiling, always glancing about him, seeming to feel that people might be watching him and trying to detect something. This conscious expression, since it was as far as possible from boyish mirthfulness, was usually attributed to insolence or "smartness."

5 As the inquisition proceeded, one of his instructors repeated an impertinent remark of the boy's, and the Principal asked him whether he thought that a courteous speech to make to a woman. Paul shrugged his shoulders slightly and his eyebrows twitched.

"I don't know," he replied. "I didn't mean to be polite or impolite, either. I guess it's a sort of way I have of saying things regardless."

The Principal asked him whether he didn't think that a way it would be well to get rid of. Paul grinned and said he guessed so. When he was told that he could go, he bowed gracefully and went out. His bow was but a repetition of the scandalous red carnation.

His teachers were in despair, and his drawing master voiced the feeling of them all when he declared there was something about the boy which none of them understood. He added: "I don't really believe that smile of his comes altogether from insolence; there's something sort of haunted about it. The boy is not strong, for one thing. There is something wrong about the fellow."

The drawing master had come to realize that, in looking at Paul, one saw only his white teeth and the forced animation of his eyes. One warm afternoon the boy had gone to sleep at his drawing board, and his master had noted with amazement what a white, blue-veined face it was; drawn and wrinkled like an old man's about the eyes, the lips twitching even in his sleep.

10 His teachers left the building dissatisfied and unhappy; humiliated to have felt so vindictive toward a mere boy, to have uttered this feeling in cutting terms, and to have set each other on, as it were, in the gruesome game of intemperate reproach. Some of them remembered having seen a miserable street cat set at bay by a ring of tormentors.

As for Paul, he ran down the hill whistling the Soldiers' Chorus from *Faust*,[1] looking wildly behind him now and then to see whether some of his teachers were not there to witness his light-heartedness. As it was now late in the afternoon and Paul was on duty that evening as usher at Carnegie Hall[2], he decided that he would not go home to supper.

When he reached the concert hall the doors were not yet open and, as it was chilly outside, he decided to go up into the picture gallery—always deserted at this hour—where there were some of Raffaëlli's[3] gay studies of Paris streets and an airy blue Venetian scene or two that always exhilarated him. He was delighted to find no one in the gallery but the old guard, who sat in one corner, a newspaper on his knee, a black patch over one eye and the other closed. Paul possessed himself of the place and walked confidently up and down, whistling under his breath. After a while he sat down before a blue Rico[4] and lost himself. When he bethought him to look at his watch, it was after seven o'clock, and he rose with a start and ran downstairs, making a face at Augustus, Caesar[5], peering out from the cast-room, and an evil gesture at the Venus of Milo as he passed her on the stairway.

When Paul reached the ushers' dressing-room half-a-dozen boys were there already, and he began excitedly to tumble into his uniform. It was one of the few that at all approached fitting, and Paul thought it very becoming—though he knew that the tight, straight coat accentuated his narrow chest, about which he was exceedingly sensitive. He was always excited while he dressed, twanging all over to the tuning of the strings and the preliminary flourishes of the horns in the music-room; but tonight he seemed quite beside himself, and he teased and plagued the boys until, telling him that he was crazy, they put him down on the floor and sat on him.

Somewhat calmed by his suppression, Paul dashed out to the front of the house to seat the early comers. He was a model usher. Gracious and smiling he ran up and down the aisles. Nothing was too much trouble for him; he carried messages and brought programs as though it were his greatest pleasure in life, and all the people in his section thought him a charming boy, feeling that he remembered and admired them. As the house filled, he grew more and more vivacious and animated, and the color came to his cheeks and lips. It was very much as though this were a great reception and Paul were the host. Just as the musicians came out to take their places, his English teacher arrived with checks for the seats which a prominent manufacturer had taken for the season. She betrayed some embarrassment when she handed Paul the tickets, and a *hauteur* which subsequently made her feel very foolish. Paul was startled for a moment, and had the feeling of wanting to put her out; what business had she here among all these fine people and gay colors? He looked her over and decided that she was not appropriately dressed and must be a fool to sit downstairs in such togs. The tickets had probably been sent her out of kindness, he reflected as he put down a seat for her, and she had about as much right to sit there as he had.

15 When the symphony began Paul sank into one of the rear seats with a long sigh of relief, and lost himself as he had done before the Rico. It was not that sym-

[1] **Faust** a popular opera [2] **Carnegie Hall** in Pittsburgh, not New York [3] **Raffaëlli** an impressionist painter, sculptor, and engraver [4] **Rico** a Spanish landscape painter [5] **Caesar . . . Milo** copies of the famous statues of Augustus and the Venus de Milo

phonies, as such, meant anything in particular to Paul, but the first sigh of the instruments seemed to free some hilarious spirit within him; something that struggled there like the Genius in the bottle found by the Arab fisherman[6]. He felt a sudden zest of life; the lights danced before his eyes and the concert hall blazed into unimaginable splendor. When the soprano soloist came on, Paul forgot even the nastiness of his teacher's being there, and gave himself up to the peculiar intoxication such personages always had for him. The soloist chanced to be a German woman, by no means in her first youth, and the mother of many children; but she wore an elaborate gown and a tiara, and she had that indefinable air of achievement, that world-shine upon her, which always blinded Paul to any possible defects.

After a concert was over, Paul was always irritable and wretched until he got to sleep—and tonight he was even more than usually restless. He had the feeling of not being able to let down, of its being impossible to give up this delicious excitement which was the only thing that could be called living at all. During the last number he withdrew and, after hastily changing his clothes in the dressing-room, slipped out to the side door where the singer's carriage stood. Here he began pacing rapidly up and down the walk, waiting to see her come out.

Over yonder the Schenley, in its vacant stretch, loomed big and square through the fine rain, the windows of its twelve stories glowing like those of a lighted cardboard house under a Christmas tree. All the actors and singers of any importance stayed there when they were in the city, and a number of the big manufacturers of the place lived there in the winter. Paul had often hung about the hotel, watching the people go in and out, longing to enter and leave schoolmasters and dull care behind him forever.

At last the singer came out, accompanied by the conductor, who helped her into her carriage and closed the door with a cordial *auf Wiedersehen*[7]—which set Paul to wondering whether she were not an old sweetheart of his. Paul followed the carriage over to the hotel, walking so rapidly as not to be far from the entrance when the singer alighted and disappeared behind the swinging glass doors which were opened by a Negro in a tall hat and a long coat. In the moment that the door was ajar, it seemed to Paul that he, too, entered. He seemed to feel himself go after her up the steps, into the warm, lighted building, into an exotic, a tropical world of shiny, glistening surfaces and basking ease. He reflected upon the mysterious dishes that were brought into the dining-room, the green bottles in buckets of ice, as he had seen them in the supper party pictures of the Sunday supplement. A quick gust of wind brought the rain down with sudden vehemence, and Paul was startled to find that he was still outside in the slush of the gravel driveway; that his boots were letting in the water and his scanty overcoat was clinging wet about him; that the lights in front of the concert hall were out, and that the rain was driving in sheets between him and the orange glow of the windows above him. There it was, what he wanted—tangibly before him, like the fairy world of a Christmas pantomime; as the rain beat in his face, Paul wondered whether he were destined always to shiver in the black night outside, looking up at it.

He turned and walked reluctantly toward the car[8] tracks. The end had to come sometime; his father in his night-clothes at the top of the stairs, explanations that

[6] **Arab fisherman** reference to a tale from *The Arabian Nights* [7] **auf Wiedersehen** German for "goodbye" [8] **car** streetcar

did not explain, hastily improvised fictions that were forever tripping him up, his upstairs room and its horrible yellow wallpaper, the creaking bureau with the greasy plush collar-box, and over his painted wooden bed the pictures of George Washington and John Calvin[9], and the framed motto, "Feed my Lambs,"[10] which had been worked in red worsted by his mother, whom Paul could not remember.

Half an hour later, Paul alighted from the Negley Avenue car and went slowly down one of the side streets off the main thoroughfare. It was a highly respectable street, where all the houses were exactly alike, and where businessmen of moderate means begot and reared large families of children, all of whom went to Sabbath-school and learned the shorter catechism, and were interested in arithmetic; all of whom were as exactly alike as their homes, and of a piece with the monotony in which they lived. Paul never went up Cordelia Street without a shudder of loathing. His home was next to the house of the Cumberland[11] minister. He approached it tonight with the nerveless sense of defeat, the hopeless feeling of sinking back forever into ugliness and commonness that he had always had when he came home. The moment he turned into Cordelia Street he felt the waters close above his head. After each of these orgies of living, he experienced all the physical depression which follows a debauch; the loathing of respectable beds, of common food, of a house permeated by kitchen odors; a shuddering repulsion for the flavorless, colorless mass of everyday existence; a morbid desire for cool things and soft lights and fresh flowers.

The nearer he approached the house, the more absolutely unequal Paul felt to the sight of it all; his ugly sleeping chamber; the cold bathroom with the grimy zinc tub, the cracked mirror, the dripping spigots; his father, at the top of the stairs, his hairy legs sticking out from his nightshirt, his feet thrust into carpet slippers. He was so much later than usual that there would certainly be inquiries and reproaches. Paul stopped short before the door. He felt that he could not be accosted by his father tonight; that he could not toss again on that miserable bed. He would not go in. He would tell his father that he had no car fare, and it was raining so hard he had gone home with one of the boys and stayed all night.

Meanwhile, he was wet and cold. He went around to the back of the house and tried one of the basement windows, found it open, raised it cautiously, and scrambled down the cellar wall to the floor. There he stood, holding his breath, terrified by the noise he had made; but the floor above him was silent, and there was no creak on the stairs. He found a soap-box, and carried it over to the soft ring of light that streamed from the furnace door, and sat down. He was horribly afraid of rats, so he did not try to sleep, but sat looking distrustfully at the dark, still terrified lest he might have awakened his father. In such reactions, after one of the experiences which made days and nights out of the dreary blanks of the calendar, when his senses were deadened, Paul's head was always singularly clear. Suppose his father had heard him getting in at the window and had come down and shot him for a burglar? Then, again, suppose his father had come down, pistol in hand, and he had cried out in time to save himself, and his father had been horrified to think how nearly he had killed him? Then, again, suppose a day should come when his father

[9] **John Calvin** an early leader of the Protestant Reformation [10] **"Feed my Lambs"** from John 21:15–17
[11] **Cumberland** an Evangelical branch of the Presbyterian church

would remember that night, and wish there had been no warning cry to stay his hand? With this last supposition Paul entertained himself until daybreak.

The following Sunday was fine; the sodden November chill was broken by the last flash of autumnal summer. In the morning Paul had to go to church and Sabbath-school, as always. On seasonable Sunday afternoons the burghers of Cordelia Street usually sat out on their front "stoops," and talked to their neighbors on the next stoop, or called to those across the street in neighborly fashion. The men sat placidly on gay cushions placed upon the steps that led down to the sidewalk, while the women, in their Sunday "waists,"[12] sat in rockers on the cramped porches, pretending to be greatly at their ease. The children played in the streets; there were so many of them that the place resembled the recreation grounds of a kindergarten. The men on the steps—all in their shirt sleeves, their vests unbuttoned—sat with their legs well apart, their stomachs comfortably protruding, and talked of the prices of things, or told anecdotes of the sagacity of their various chiefs and overlords. They occasionally looked over the multitude of squabbling children, listened affectionately to their high-pitched, nasal voices, smiling to see their own proclivities reproduced in their offspring, and interspersed their legends of the iron kings with remarks about their sons' progress at school, their grades in arithmetic, and the amounts they had saved in their toy banks. On this last Sunday of November, Paul sat all the afternoon on the lowest step of his "stoop," staring into the street, while his sisters, in their rockers, were talking to the minister's daughters next door about how many shirtwaists they had made in the last week, and how many waffles someone had eaten at the last church supper. When the weather was warm, and his father was in a particularly jovial frame of mind, the girls made lemonade, which was always brought out in a red-glass pitcher, ornamented with forget-me-nots in blue enamel. This the girls thought very fine, and the neighbors always joked about the suspicious color of the pitcher.

Today Paul's father sat on the top step, talking to a young man who shifted a restless baby from knee to knee. He happened to be the young man who was daily held up to Paul as a model, and after whom it was his father's dearest hope that he would pattern. This young man was of a ruddy complexion, with a compressed, red mouth, and faded, nearsighted eyes, over which he wore thick spectacles, with gold bows that curved about his ears. He was clerk to one of the magnates of a great steel corporation, and was looked upon in Cordelia Street as a young man with a future. There was a story that, come five years ago—he was now barely twenty-six—he had been a trifle 'dissipated,' but in order to curb his appetites and save the loss of time and strength that a sowing of wild oats might have entailed, he had taken his chief's advice, oft reiterated to his employees, and at twenty-one had married the first woman whom he could persuade to share his fortunes. She happened to be an angular school mistress, much older than he, who also wore thick glasses, and who had now borne him four children, all nearsighted, like herself.

The young man was relating how his chief, now cruising in the Mediterranean, kept in touch with all the details of the business, arranging his office hours on his yacht just as though he were at home, and "knocking off work enough to keep two stenographers busy." His father told, in turn, the plan his corporation was consid-

[12] **waists** laced, close-fitting vests or jackets

ering, of putting in an electric railway plant at Cairo. Paul snapped his teeth; he had an awful apprehension that they might spoil it all before he got there. Yet he rather liked to hear these legends of the iron kings, that were told and retold on Sundays and holidays; these stories of palaces in Venice, yachts on the Mediterranean, and high play at Monte Carlo appealed to his fancy, and he was interested in the triumphs of these cash boys[13] who had become famous, though he had no mind for the cash-boy stage.

After supper was over, and he had helped to dry the dishes, Paul nervously asked his father whether he could go to George's to get some help in his geometry, and still more nervously asked for car fare. This latter request he had to repeat, as his father, on principle, did not like to hear requests for money, whether much or little. He asked Paul whether he could not go to some boy who lived nearer, and told him that he ought not to leave his school work until Sunday; but he gave him the dime. He was not a poor man, but he had a worthy ambition to come up in the world. His only reason for allowing Paul to usher was that he thought a boy ought to be earning a little.

Paul bounded upstairs, scrubbed the greasy odor of the dishwater from his hands with the ill-smelling soap he hated, and then shook over his fingers a few drops of violet water from the bottle he kept hidden in his drawer. He left the house with his geometry conspicuously under his arm, and the moment he got out of Cordelia Street and boarded a downtown car, he shook off the lethargy of two deadening days, and began to live again.

The leading juvenile of the permanent stock company which played at one of the downtown theatres was an acquaintance of Paul's, and the boy had been invited to drop in at the Sunday night rehearsals whenever he could. For more than a year Paul had spent every available moment loitering about Charley Edwards's dressing-room. He had won a place among Edward's following not only because the young actor, who could not afford to employ a dresser, often found him useful, but because he recognized in Paul something akin to what churchmen term "vocation."

It was at the theatre and at Carnegie Hall that Paul really lived; the rest was but a sleep and a forgetting. This was Paul's fairy tale, and it had for him all the allurement of a secret love. The moment he inhaled the gassy, painty, dusty odor behind the scenes, he breathed like a prisoner set free, and felt within him the possibility of doing or saying splendid, brilliant things. The moment the cracked orchestra beat out the overture from *Martha*[14], or jerked at the serenade from *Rigoletto*[15], all stupid and ugly things slid from him, and his senses were deliciously, yet delicately fired.

Perhaps it was because, in Paul's world, the natural nearly always wore the guise of ugliness, that a certain element of artificiality seemed to him necessary in beauty. Perhaps it was because his experience of life elsewhere was so full of Sabbath-school picnics, petty economies, wholesome advice as to how to succeed in life, and the unescapable odors of cooking, that he found this existence so alluring, these smartly-clad men and women so attractive, that he was so moved by these starry apple orchards that bloomed perennially under the limelight.

[13] **cash boys** *The Cash Boy*, a "rags to riches" novel by Horatio Alger [14] ***Martha*** opera by Friedrick von Flotow and the source of "The Last Rose of Summer" [15] ***Rigoletto*** a well-known opera by Giuseppe Verdi

It would be difficult to put it strongly enough how convincingly the stage entrance of that theatre was for Paul the actual portal of Romance. Certainly none of the company ever suspected it, least of all Charley Edwards. It was very like the old stories that used to float about London of fabulously rich Jews, who had subterranean halls, with palms, and fountains, and soft lamps and richly apparelled women who never saw the disenchanting light of London day. So, in the midst of that smoke-palled city, enamored of figures and grimy toil, Paul had his secret temple, his wishing carpet, his bit of blue-and-white Mediterranean shore bathed in perpetual sunshine.

Several of Paul's teachers had a theory that his imagination had been perverted by garish fiction, but the truth was, he scarcely ever read at all. The books at home were not such as would either tempt or corrupt a youthful mind, and as for reading the novels that some of his friends urged upon him—well, he got what he wanted much more quickly from music; any sort of music, from an orchestra to a barrel organ. He needed only the spark, the indescribable thrill that made his imagination master of his senses, and he could make plots and pictures enough of his own. It was equally true that he was not stage-struck—not, at any rate, in the usual acceptation of that expression. He had no desire to become an actor, any more than he had to become a musician. He felt no necessity to do any of these things; what he wanted was to see, to be in the atmosphere, float on the wave of it, to be carried out, blue league after blue league, away from everything.

After a night behind the scenes, Paul found the school-room more than ever repulsive; the bare floors and naked walls; the prosy men who never wore frock coats, or violets in their buttonholes; the women with their dull gowns, shrill voices, and pitiful seriousness about prepositions that govern the dative. He could not bear to have the other pupils think, for a moment, that he took these people seriously; he must convey to them that he considered it all trivial, and was there only by way of a joke, anyway. He had autographed pictures of all the members of the stock company which he showed his classmates, telling them the most incredible stories of his familiarity with these people, of his acquaintance with the soloists who came to Carnegie Hall, his suppers with them and the flowers he sent them. When these stories lost their effect, and his audience grew listless, he would bid all the boys good-bye, announcing that he was going to travel for a while; going to Naples, to California, to Egypt. Then, next Monday, he would slip back, conscious and nervously smiling; his sister was ill, and he should have to defer his voyage until spring.

Matters went steadily worse with Paul at school. In the itch to let his instructors know how heartily he despised them and how thoroughly he was appreciated elsewhere, he mentioned once or twice that he had no time to fool with theorems; adding—with a twitch of the eyebrows and a touch of that nervous bravado which so perplexed them—that he was helping the people down at the stock company; they were old friends of his.

The upshot of the matter was, that the Principal went to Paul's father, and Paul was taken out of school and put to work. The manager at Carnegie Hall was told to get another usher in his stead; the door-keeper at the theatre was warned not to admit him to the house; and Charley Edwards remorsefully promised the boy's father not to see him again.

The members of the stock company were vastly amused when some of Paul's stories reached them—especially the women. They were hard-working women, most of them supporting indigent husbands or brothers, and they laughed rather bitterly at having stirred the boy to such fervid and florid inventions. They agreed with the faculty and with his father, that Paul's was a bad case.

The east-bound train was ploughing through a January snowstorm; the dull dawn was beginning to show gray when the engine whistled a mile out of Newark[16]. Paul started up from the seat where he had lain curled in uneasy slumber, rubbed the breath-misted window glass with his hand, and peered out. The snow was whirling in curling eddies above the white bottom lands, and the drifts lay already deep in the fields and along the fences, while here and there the long dead grass and dried weed stalks protruded black above it. Lights shone from the scattered houses, and a gang of laborers who stood beside the track waved their lanterns.

Paul had slept very little, and he felt grimy and uncomfortable. He had made the all-night journey in a day coach because he was afraid if he took a Pullman he might be seen by some Pittsburgh business man who had noticed him in Denny & Carson's office. When the whistle woke him, he clutched quickly at his breast pocket, glancing about him with an uncertain smile. But the little, clay-bespattered Italians were still sleeping, the slatternly women across the aisle were in open-mouthed oblivion, and even the crumby, crying babies were for the nonce stilled. Paul settled back to struggle with his impatience as best as he could.

When he arrived at the Jersey City station, he hurried through his breakfast, manifestly ill at ease and keeping a sharp eye about him. After he reached the Twenty-third Street station[17], he consulted a cabman, and had himself driven to a men's furnishing establishment that was just opening for the day. He spent upward of two hours there, buying with endless reconsidering and great care. His new street suit he put on in the fitting-room; the frock coat and dress clothes he had bundled into the cab with his shirts. Then he drove to a hatter's and a shoe house. His next errand was at Tiffany's, where he selected his silver-mounted brushes[18] and a scarf-pin. He would not wait to have his silver marked, he said. Lastly, he stopped at a trunk shop on Broadway, and had his purchases packed into various traveling bags.

It was a little after one-o'clock when he drove up to the Waldorf, and after settling with the cabman, went into the office. He registered from Washington; said his mother and father had been abroad, and that he had come down to await the arrival of their steamer. He told his story plausibly and had no trouble, since he volunteered to pay for them in advance, in engaging his rooms; a sleeping-room, sitting room and bath.

Not once, but a hundred times Paul had planned this entry into New York. He had gone over every detail of it with Charley Edwards, and in his scrap book at home there were pages of description about New York hotels, cut from the Sunday papers.

When he was shown to his sitting-room on the eighth floor, he saw at a glance that everything was as it should be; there was but one detail in his mental picture that the place did not realize, so he rang for the bell boy and sent him down for flowers. He moved about nervously until the boy returned, putting away his new

[16] **Newark** New Jersey city about twenty miles from New York [17] **Twenty-third Street station** Paul's destination in Manhattan [18] **brushes** hairbrushes

linen and fingering it delightedly as he did so. When the flowers came, he put them hastily into water, and then tumbled into a hot bath. Presently he came out of his white bathroom, resplendent in his new silk underwear, and playing with the tassels of his red robe. The snow was whirling so fiercely outside his windows that he could scarcely see across the street; but within the air was deliciously soft and fragrant. He put the violets and jonquils on the tabouret beside the couch, and threw himself down, with a long sigh, covering himself with a Roman blanket. He was thoroughly tired; he had been in such haste, he had stood up to such a strain, covered so much ground in the last twenty-four hours, that he wanted to think how it had all come about. Lulled by the sound of the wind, the warm air, and the cool fragrance of the flowers, he sank into deep, drowsy retrospection.

It had been wonderfully simple; when they had shut him out of the theatre and concert hall, when they had taken away his bone, the whole thing was virtually determined. The rest was a mere matter of opportunity. The only thing that at all surprised him was his own courage—for he realized well enough that he had always been tormented by fear, a sort of apprehensive dread that, of late years, as the meshes of the lies he had told closed about him, had been pulling the muscles of his body tighter and tighter. Until now, he could not remember the time when he had not been dreading something. Even when he was a little boy, it was always there—behind him, or before, or on either side. There had always been the shadowed corner, the dark place into which he dared not look, but from which something seemed always to be watching him—and Paul had done things that were not pretty to watch, he knew.

But now he had a curious sense of relief, as though he had at last thrown down the gauntlet to the thing in the corner.

Yet it was but a day since he had been sulking in the traces; but yesterday afternoon that he had been sent to the bank with Denny & Carson's deposit, as usual—but this time he was instructed to leave the book to be balanced. There was above two thousand dollars in checks, and nearly a thousand in the bank notes which he had taken from the book and quietly transferred to his pocket. At the bank he had made out a new deposit slip. His nerves had been steady enough to permit of his returning to the office, where he had finished his work and asked for a full day's holiday tomorrow, Saturday, giving a perfectly reasonable pretext. The bank book, he knew, would not be returned before Monday or Tuesday, and his father would be out of town for the next week. From the time he slipped the bank notes into his pocket until he boarded the night train for New York, he had not known a moment's hesitation.

How astonishingly easy it had all been; here he was, the thing done; and this time there would be no awakening, no figure at the top of the stairs. He watched the snow flakes whirling by his window until he fell asleep.

When he awoke, it was four o'clock in the afternoon. He bounded up with a start; half of one of his precious days gone already! He spent nearly an hour in dressing, watching every stage of his toilet carefully in the mirror. Everything was quite perfect; he was exactly the kind of boy he had always wanted to be.

When he went downstairs, Paul took a carriage and drove up Fifth Avenue toward the Park.[19] The snow had somewhat abated; carriages and tradesmen's

[19] **the Park** Central Park

wagons were hurrying soundlessly to and fro in the winter twilight; boys in woolen mufflers were shoveling off the doorsteps; the avenue stages[20] made fine spots of color against the white street. Here and there on the corners whole flower gardens blooming behind windows, against which the snow flakes stuck and melted; violets, roses, carnations, lilies of the valley—somewhat vastly more lovely and alluring that they blossomed thus unnaturally in the snow. The Park itself was a wonderful stage winter-piece.

When he returned, the pause of the twilight had ceased, and the tune of the streets had changed. The snow was falling faster, lights streamed from the hotels that reared their dozen stories fearlessly up into the storm, defying the raging Atlantic winds. A long, black stream of carriages poured down the avenue, intersected here and there by other streams, tending horizontally. There were a score of cabs about the entrance of his hotel, and his driver had to wait. Boys in livery were running in and out of the awning stretched across the sidewalk, up and down the red velvet carpet laid from the door to the street. Above, about, within it all was the rumble and roar, the hurry and toss of thousands of human beings as hot for pleasure as himself, and on every side of him towered the glaring affirmation of the omnipotence of wealth.

The boy set his teeth and drew his shoulders together in a spasm of realization; the plot of all dramas, the text of all romances, the nerve-stuff of all sensations was whirling about him like the snow flakes. He burnt like a faggot in a tempest.

When Paul went down to dinner, the music of the orchestra floated up the elevator shaft to greet him. As he stepped into the thronged corridor, he sank back into one of the chairs against the wall to get his breath. The lights, the chatter, the perfumes, the bewildering medley of color—he had, for a moment, the feeling of not being able to stand it. But only for a moment; these were his own people, he told himself. He went slowly about the corridors, through the writing-rooms, smoking-rooms, reception-rooms, as though he were exploring the chambers of an enchanted palace, built and peopled for him alone.

When he reached the dining room he sat down at a table near a window. The flowers, the white linen, the many-colored wine glasses, the gay toilettes of the women, the low popping of corks, the undulating repetitions of the *Blue Danube*[21] from the orchestra, all flooded Paul's dream with bewildering radiance. When the roseate tinge of his champagne was added—that cold, precious, bubbling stuff that creamed and foamed in his glass—Paul wondered that there were honest men in the world at all. This was what all the world was fighting for, he reflected; this was what all the struggle was about. He doubted the reality of his past. Had he ever known a place called Cordelia Street, a place where fagged-looking business men got on the early car. Mere rivets in a machine they seemed to Paul—sickening men, with combings of children's hair always hanging to their coats, and the smell of cooking in their clothes. Cordelia Street—Ah! that belonged to another time and country! Had he not always been thus, had he not sat here night after night, from as far back as he could remember, looking pensively over just such shimmering tex-

[20] **avenue stages** shop display windows [21] ***Blue Danube*** "The Blue Danube" is the best-known waltz of composer Johann Strauss

tures, and slowly twirling the stem of a glass like this one between his thumb and middle finger? He rather thought he had.

He was not in the least abashed or lonely. He had no especial desire to meet or to know any of these people; all he demanded was the right to look on and conjecture, to watch the pageant. The mere stage properties were all he contended for. Nor was he lonely later in the evening, in his loge at the Opera. He was entirely rid of his nervous misgivings, of his forced aggressiveness, of the imperative desire to show himself different from his surroundings. He felt now that his surroundings explained him. Nobody questioned the purple;[22] he had only to wear it passively. He had only to glance down at his attire to reassure himself that here it would be impossible for anyone to humiliate him.

He found it hard to leave his beautiful sitting room to go to bed that night, and sat long watching the raging storm from his turret window. When he went to sleep, it was with the lights turned on in his bedroom; partly because of his old timidity, and partly so that, if he should wake in the night, there would be no wretched moment of doubt, no horrible suspicion of yellow wallpaper, or of Washington and Calvin above his bed.

55 On Sunday morning the city was practically snow-bound. Paul breakfasted late, and in the afternoon he fell in with a wild San Francisco boy, a freshman at Yale, who said he had run down for a "little flyer" over Sunday. The young man offered to show Paul the night side of the town, and the two boys went off together after dinner, not returning to the hotel until seven o'clock the next morning. They had started out in the confiding warmth of a champagne friendship, but their parting in the elevator was singularly cool. The freshman pulled himself together to make his train, and Paul went to bed. He awoke at two o'clock in the afternoon, very thirsty and dizzy, and rang for ice-water, coffee, and the Pittsburgh papers.

On the part of the hotel management, Paul excited no suspicion. There was this to be said for him, that he wore his spoils with dignity and in no way made himself conspicuous. His chief greediness lay in his ears and eyes, and his excesses were not offensive ones. His dearest pleasures were the gray winter twilights in his sitting room; his quiet enjoyment of his flowers, his clothes, his wide divan, his cigarette, and his sense of power. He could not remember a time when he had felt so at peace with himself. The mere release from the necessity of petty lying, lying every day and every day, restored his self-respect. He had never lied for pleasure, even at school; but to make himself noticed and admired, to assert his difference from other Cordelia Street boys; and he felt a good deal more manly, more honest, even, now that he had no need for boastful pretensions, now that he could, as his actor friends used to say, "dress the part." It was characteristic that remorse did not occur to him. His golden days went by without a shadow, and he made each as perfect as he could.

On the eighth day after his arrival in New York, he found the whole affair exploited in the Pittsburgh papers, exploited with a wealth of detail which indicated that local news of a sensational nature was at a low ebb. The firm of Denny & Carson announced that the boy's father had refunded the full amount of the theft,

[22] **purple** a color fit for royalty

and that they had no intention of prosecuting. The Cumberland minister had been interviewed, and expressed his hope of yet reclaiming the motherless lad, and his Sabbath-school teacher declared that she would spare no effort to that end. The rumor had reached Pittsburgh that the boy had been seen in a New York hotel, and his father had gone East to find him and bring him home.

Paul had just come in to dress for dinner; he sank into a chair, weak in the knees, and clasped his head in his hands. It was to be worse than jail, even; the tepid waters of Cordelia Street were to close over him finally and forever. The gray monotony stretched before him in hopeless, unrelieved years; Sabbath-school, Young People's Meeting, the yellow-papered room, the damp dish-towels; it all rushed back upon him with a sickening vividness. He had the old feeling that the orchestra had suddenly stopped, the sinking sensation that the play was over. The sweat broke out on his face, and he sprang to his feet, looked about him with his white, conscious smile, and winked at himself in the mirror. With something of the old childish belief in miracles with which he had so often gone to class, all his lessons unlearned, Paul dressed and dashed whistling down the corridor to the elevator.

He had no sooner entered the dining room and caught the measure of the music, than his remembrance was lightened by his old elastic power of claiming the moment, mounting with it, and finding it all sufficient. The glare and glitter about him, the mere scenic accessories had again, and for the last time, their old potency. He would show himself that he was game, he would finish the thing splendidly. He doubted, more than ever, the existence of Cordelia Street, and for the first time he drank his wine recklessly. Was he not, after all, one of those fortunate beings? He drummed a nervous accompaniment to the music and looked about him, telling himself over and over that it had paid.

He reflected drowsily, to the swell of the violin and the chill sweetness of his wine, that he might have done it more wisely. He might have caught an outbound steamer and been well out of their clutches before now. But the other side of the world had seemed too far away and too uncertain then; he could not have waited for it; his need had been too sharp. If he had to choose over again, he would do the same thing tomorrow. He looked affectionately about the dining room, now gilded with a soft mist. Ah, it has paid indeed!

Paul was awakened next morning by a painful throbbing in his head and feet. He had thrown himself across the bed without undressing, and had slept with his shoes on. His limbs and hands were lead heavy, and his tongue and throat were parched. There came upon him one of those fateful attacks of clear-headedness that never occurred except when he was physically exhausted and his nerves hung loose. He lay still and closed his eyes and let the tide of things wash over him.

His father was in New York: "stopping at some joint or other," he told himself. The memory of successive summers on the front stoop fell upon him like a weight of black water. He had not a hundred dollars left, and he knew now, more than ever, that money was everything, the wall that stood between all he loathed and all he wanted. The thing was winding itself up; he had thought of that on his first glorious day in New York, and had even provided a way to snap the threat. It lay on his dressing-table now; he had got it out last night when he came blindly up from dinner—but the shiny metal hurt his eyes, and he disliked the look of it, anyway.

He rose and moved about with a painful effort, succumbing now and again to attacks of nausea. It was the old depression exaggerated; all the world had become Cordelia Street. Yet somehow he was not afraid of anything, was absolutely calm; perhaps because he had looked into the dark corner at last and knew. It was bad enough, what he saw there, but somehow not so bad as his long fear of it had been. He saw everything clearly now. He had a feeling that he had made the best of it, that he had lived the sort of life he was meant to live, and for half an hour he sat staring at the revolver. But he told himself that was not the way, so he went downstairs and took a cab to the ferry.

When Paul arrived at Newark, he got off the train and took another cab, directing the driver to follow the Pennsylvania tracks out of the town. The snow lay heavy on the roadways and had drifted deep in the open fields. Only here and there the dead grass or dried weed stalks projected, singularly black, above it. Once well into the country, Paul dismissed the carriage and walked, floundering along the tracks, his mind a medley of irrelevant things. He seemed to hold in his brain an actual picture of everything he had seen that morning. He remembered every feature of both his drivers, of the toothless old woman from whom he had bought the red flowers in his coat, the agent from whom he had got his ticket, and all of his fellow-passengers on the ferry. His mind, unable to cope with vital matters near at hand, worked feverishly and deftly at sorting and grouping these images. They made for him a part of the ugliness of the world, of the ache in his head, and the bitter burning on his tongue. He stooped and put a handful of snow into his mouth as he walked, but that, too, seemed hot. When he reached a little hillside, where the tracks ran through a cut some twenty feet below him, he stopped and sat down.

The carnations in his coat were drooping with the cold, he noticed; all their red glory over. It occurred to him that all the flowers he had seen in the show windows that first night must have gone the same way, long before this. It was only one splendid breath they had, in spite of their brave mockery at the winter outside the glass. It was a losing game in the end, it seemed, this revolt against the homilies by which the world is run. Paul took one of the blossoms carefully from his coat and scooped a little hole in the snow, where he covered it up. Then he dozed a while, from his weak condition, seemingly insensible to the cold.

The sound of an approaching train woke him, and he started to his feet, remembering only his resolution, and afraid lest he should be too late. He stood watching the approaching locomotive, his teeth chattering, his lips drawn away from them in a frightened smile; once or twice he glanced nervously sidewise, as though he were being watched. When the right moment came, he jumped. As he fell, the folly of his haste occurred to him with merciless clearness, the vastness of what he had left undone. There flashed through his brain, clearer than ever before, the blue of Adriatic water, the yellow of Algerian sands.

He felt something strike his chest—his body was being thrown swiftly through the air, on and on, immeasurably far and fast, while his limbs gently relaxed. Then, because the picture-making mechanism was crushed, the disturbing visions flashed into black, and Paul dropped back into the immense design of things.

➤ *QUESTIONS FOR READING AND WRITING*

1. Early in the story the teachers gather to reprimand Paul. What are their motives? Although they don't have the effect on Paul that they intend, they still feel strange about what they have done. Why?
2. What do the theater and concert hall offer Paul that school and home don't? How does Paul's enthusiasm for these arts differ from the enthusiasm of typical supporters?
3. Is Paul antisocial, or is there a sense in which he needs other people? What sort of relationships does he form? Cite evidence from the story.
4. Many people think they know what is in Paul's best interest—including Paul. Who really knows what's best? Should Paul be trusted to pursue his interests, or are his father and teachers right to seek ways to make him conform?
5. Is Paul's an avoidable tragedy? Who is to blame for Paul's fate? Are there some people who just can't be helped?
6. If you were a character in this story or if Paul were a real person in your life, you'd probably respond much less sympathetically to the act of his stealing money from his father's firm. What is different for you as a reader of this story? How does fiction allow you to see events from a different point of view? As you read the story, where do your sympathies lie?
7. Near the end of the story, Paul has a number of options open to him. For one, he could turn himself in; he could also resolve to identify and pursue a career that would allow him to lead the life he desires. What prevents him from exploring these options? What do you think he realized in his last moment?

RALPH ELLISON (1914–1994)

Ralph Ellison was born in Oklahoma. "Battle Royal" is an excerpt from his novel Invisible Man, *which won the National Book Award in 1953 and was widely praised for its depiction of the plight of African-Americans. In addition to his fiction writing, Ellison frequently wrote essays and gave interviews about race relations, and was Albert Schweitzer Professor of the Humanities at New York University. The* Collected Essays of Ralph Ellison *was published in 1995, and an unfinished novel,* Juneteenth *(completed by John Callahan) was published in 1999.*

Battle Royal [1953]

It goes a long way back, some twenty years. All my life I had been looking for something, and everywhere I turned someone tried to tell me what it was. I accepted their answers too, though they were often in contradiction and even self-contradictory. I was naïve. I was looking for myself and asking everyone except myself questions which I, and only I, could answer. It took me a long time and much painful boomeranging of my expectations to achieve a realization everyone else appears to have been born with: That I am nobody but myself. But first I had to discover that I am an invisible man!

And yet I am no freak of nature, nor of history. I was in the cards, other things having been equal (or unequal) eighty-five years ago. I am not ashamed of my grandparents for having been slaves. I am only ashamed of myself for having at one time been ashamed. About eighty-five years ago they were told that they were free, united with others of our country in everything pertaining to the common good, and, in everything social, separate like the fingers of the hand. And they believed it. They exulted in it. They stayed in their place, worked hard, and brought up my father to do the same. But my grandfather is the one. He was an odd old guy, my grandfather, and I am told I take after him. It was he who caused the trouble. On his deathbed he called my father to him and said, "Son, after I'm gone I want you to keep up the good fight. I never told you, but our life is a war and I have been a traitor all my born days, a spy in the enemy's country ever since I give up my gun back in the Reconstruction. Live with your head in the lion's mouth. I want you to overcome 'em with yeses, undermine 'em with grins, agree 'em to death and destruction, let 'em swoller you till they vomit or bust wide open." They thought the old man had gone out of his mind. He had been the meekest of men. The younger children were rushed from the room, the shades drawn and the flame of the lamp turned so low that it sputtered on the wick like the old man's breathing. "Learn it to the younguns," he whispered fiercely; then he died.

But my folks were more alarmed over his last words than over his dying. It was as though he had not died at all, his words caused so much anxiety. I was warned emphatically to forget what he had said and, indeed, this is the first time it has been mentioned outside the family circle. It had a tremendous effect upon me, however. I could never be sure of what he meant. Grandfather had been a quiet old man who never made any trouble, yet on his deathbed he had called himself a traitor and a spy, and he had spoken of his meekness as a dangerous activity. It became a constant puzzle which lay unanswered in the back of my mind. And whenever things went well for me I remembered my grandfather and felt guilty and uncomfortable. It was as though I was carrying out his advice in spite of myself. And to make it worse, everyone loved me for it. I was praised by the most lily-white men of the town. I was considered an example of desirable conduct—just as my grandfather had been. And what puzzled me was that the old man had defined it as *treachery.* When I was praised for my conduct I felt a guilt that in some way I was doing something that was really against the wishes of the white folks, that if they had understood they would have desired me to act just the opposite, that I should have been sulky and mean, and that that really would have been what they wanted, even though they were fooled and thought they wanted me to act as I did. It made me afraid that some day they would look upon me as a traitor and I would be lost. Still I was more afraid to act any other way because they didn't like that at all. The old man's words were like a curse. On my graduation day I delivered an oration in which I showed that humility was the secret, indeed, the very essence of progress. (Not that I believed this—how could I, remembering my grandfather?—I only believed that it worked.) It was a great success. Everyone praised me and I was invited to give the speech at a gathering of the town's leading white citizens. It was a triumph for our whole community.

It was in the main ballroom of the leading hotel. When I got there I discovered that it was on the occasion of a smoker, and I was told that since I was to be there anyway I might as well take part in the battle royal to be fought by some of my schoolmates as part of the entertainment. The battle royal came first.

5 All of the town's big shots were there in their tuxedoes, wolfing down the buffet foods, drinking beer and whiskey and smoking black cigars. It was a large room with a high ceiling. Chairs were arranged in neat rows around three sides of a portable boxing ring. The fourth side was clear, revealing a gleaming space of polished floor. I had some misgivings over the battle royal, by the way. Not from a distaste for fighting, but because I didn't care too much for the other fellows who were to take part. They were tough guys who seemed to have no grandfather's curse worrying their minds. No one could mistake their toughness. And besides, I suspected that fighting a battle royal might detract from the dignity of my speech. In those pre-invisible days I visualized myself as a potential Booker T. Washington. But the other fellows didn't care too much for me either, and there were nine of them. I felt superior to them in my way, and I didn't like the manner in which we were all crowded together into the servants' elevator. Nor did they like my being there. In fact, as the warmly lighted floors flashed past the elevator we had words over the fact that I, by taking part in the fight, had knocked one of their friends out of a night's work.

We were led out of the elevator through a rococo hall into an anteroom and told to get into our fighting togs. Each of us was issued a pair of boxing gloves and ushered out into the big mirrored hall, which we entered looking cautiously about us and whispering, lest we might accidentally be heard above the noise of the room. It was foggy with cigar smoke. And already the whiskey was taking effect. I was shocked to see some of the most important men of the town quite tipsy. They were all there—bankers, lawyers, judges, doctors, fire chiefs, teachers, merchants. Even one of the more fashionable pastors. Something we could not see was going on up front. A clarinet was vibrating sensuously and the men were standing up and moving eagerly forward. We were a small tight group, clustered together, our bare upper bodies touching and shining with anticipatory sweat; while up front the big shots were becoming increasingly excited over something we still could not see. Suddenly I heard the school superintendent, who had told me to come, yell. "Bring up the shines, gentlemen! Bring up the little shines!"

We were rushed up to the front of the ballroom, where it smelled even more strongly of tobacco and whiskey. Then we were pushed into place. I almost wet my pants. A sea of faces, some hostile, some amused, ringed around us, and in the center, facing us, stood a magnificent blonde—stark naked. There was dead silence. I felt a blast of cold air chill me. I tried to back away, but they were behind me and around me. Some of the boys stood with lowered heads, trembling. I felt a wave of irrational guilt and fear. My teeth chattered, my skin turned to goose flesh, my knees knocked. Yet I was strongly attracted and looked in spite of myself. Had the price of looking been blindness, I would have looked. The hair was yellow like that of a circus kewpie doll, the face heavily powdered and rouged, as though to form an abstract mask, the eyes hollow and smeared a cool blue, the color of a baboon's butt. I felt a desire to spit upon her as my eyes brushed slowly over her body. Her breasts were firm and round as the domes of East Indian temples, and I stood so close as to see the fine skin texture and beads of pearly perspiration glistening like dew around the pink and erected buds of her nipples. I wanted at one and the same time to run from the room, to sink through the floor, or go to her and cover her from my eyes and the eyes of the others with my body; to feel the soft thighs, to caress her and destroy her, to love her and murder her, to hide from her, and yet to stroke where below the small American flag tattooed upon her belly her thighs formed a capital V. I had a notion that of all in the room she saw only me with her impersonal eyes.

And then she began to dance, a slow sensuous movement; the smoke of a hundred cigars clinging to her like the thinnest of veils. She seemed like a fair bird-girl girdled in veils calling to me from the angry surface of some gray and threatening sea. I was transported. Then I became aware of the clarinet playing and the big shots yelling at us. Some threatened us if we looked and others if we did not. On my right I saw one boy faint. And now a man grabbed a silver pitcher from a table and stepped close as he dashed ice water upon him and stood him up and forced two of us to support him as his head hung and moans issued from his thick bluish lips. Another boy began to plead to go home. He was the largest of the group, wearing dark red fighting trunks much too small to conceal the erection which projected from him as though in answer to the insinuating low-registered moans of the clarinet. He tried to hide himself with his boxing gloves.

And all the while the blonde continued dancing, smiling faintly at the big shots who watched her with fascination, and faintly smiling at our fear. I noticed a certain merchant who followed her hungrily, his lips loose and drooling. He was a large man who wore diamond studs in a shirtfront which swelled with the ample paunch underneath, and each time the blonde swayed her undulating hips he ran his hand through the thin hair of his bald head and, with his arms upheld, his posture clumsy like that of an intoxicated panda, wound his belly in a slow and obscene grind. This creature was completely hypnotized. The music had quickened. As the dancer flung herself about with a detached expression on her face, the men began reaching out to touch her. I could see their beefy fingers sink into her soft flesh. Some of the others tried to stop them and she began to move around the floor in graceful circles, as they gave chase, slipping and sliding over the polished floor. It was mad. Chairs went crashing, drinks were spilt, as they ran laughing and howling after her. They caught her just as she reached a door, raised her from the floor, and tossed her as college boys are tossed at a hazing, and above her red, fixed-smiling lips I saw the terror and disgust in her eyes, almost like my own terror and that which I saw in some of the other boys. As I watched, they tossed her twice and her soft breasts seemed to flatten against the air and her legs flung wildly as she spun. Some of the more sober ones helped her to escape. And I started off the floor, heading for the anteroom with the rest of the boys.

10 Some were still crying and in hysteria. But as we tried to leave we were stopped and ordered to get into the ring. There was nothing to do but what we were told. All ten of us climbed under the ropes and allowed ourselves to be blindfolded with broad bands of white cloth. One of the men seemed to feel a bit sympathetic and tried to cheer us up as we stood with our backs against the ropes. Some of us tried to grin. "See that boy over there?" one of the men said. "I want you to run across at the bell and give it to him right in the belly. If you don't get him, I'm going to get you. I don't like his looks." Each of us was told the same. The blindfolds were put on. Yet even then I had been going over my speech. In my mind each word was as bright as flame. I felt the cloth pressed into place, and frowned so that it would be loosened when I relaxed.

But now I felt a sudden fit of blind terror. I was unused to darkness. It was as though I had suddenly found myself in a dark room filled with poisonous cottonmouths. I could hear the bleary voices yelling insistently for the battle royal to begin.

"Get going in there!"

"Let me at that big nigger!"

I strained to pick up the school superintendent's voice, as though to squeeze some security out of that slightly more familiar sound.

15 "Let me at those black sonsabitches!" someone yelled.

"No, Jackson, no!" another voice yelled. "Here, somebody, help me hold Jack."

"I want to get at that ginger-colored nigger. Tear him limb from limb," the first voice yelled.

I stood against the ropes trembling. For in those days I was what they called ginger-colored, and he sounded as though he might crunch me between his teeth like a crisp ginger cookie.

Quite a struggle was going on. Chairs were being kicked about and I could hear voices grunting as with a terrific effort. I wanted to see, to see more desperately than ever before. But the blindfold was as tight as a thick skin-puckering scab and when I raised my gloved hands to push the layers of white aside a voice yelled, "Oh, no you don't, black bastard! Leave that alone!"

20 "Ring the bell before Jackson kills him a coon!" someone boomed in the sudden silence. And I heard the bell clang and the sound of the feet scuffling forward.

A glove smacked against my head. I pivoted, striking out stiffly as someone went past, and felt the jar ripple along the length of my arm to my shoulder. Then it seemed as though all nine of the boys had turned upon me at once. Blows pounded me from all sides while I struck out as best I could. So many blows landed upon me that I wondered if I were not the only blindfolded fighter in the ring, or if the man called Jackson hadn't succeeded in getting me after all.

Blindfolded, I could no longer control my motions. I had no dignity. I stumbled about like a baby or a drunken man. The smoke had become thicker and with each new blow it seemed to sear and further restrict my lungs. My saliva became like hot bitter glue. A glove connected with my head, filling my mouth with warm blood. It was everywhere. I could not tell if the moisture I felt upon my body was sweat or blood. A blow landed hard against the nape of my neck. I felt myself going over, my head hitting the floor. Streaks of blue light filled the black world behind the blindfold. I lay prone, pretending that I was knocked out, but felt myself seized by hands and yanked to my feet. "Get going, black boy! Mix it up!" My arms were like lead, my head smarting from blows. I managed to feel my way to the ropes and held on, trying to catch my breath. A glove landed in my midsection and I went over again, feeling as though the smoke had become a knife jabbed into my guts. Pushed this way and that by the legs milling around me, I finally pulled erect and discovered that I could see the black, sweat-washed forms weaving in the smoky-blue atmosphere like drunken dancers weaving to the rapid drum-like thuds of blows.

Everyone fought hysterically. It was complete anarchy. Everybody fought everybody else. No group fought together for long. Two, three, four, fought one, then turned to fight each other, were themselves attacked. Blows landed below the belt and in the kidney, with the gloves open as well as closed, and with my eye partly opened now there was not so much terror. I moved carefully, avoiding blows, although not too many to attract attention, fighting from group to group. The boys groped about like blind, cautious crabs crouching to protect their mid-sections, their heads pulled in short against their shoulders, their arms stretched nervously before them, with their fists testing the smoke-filled air like the knobbed feelers of hypersensitive snails. In one corner I glimpsed a boy violently punching the air and heard him scream in pain as he smashed his hand against a ring post. For a second I saw him bent over holding his hand, then going down as a blow caught his unprotected head. I played one group against the other, slipping and throwing a punch then stepping out of range while pushing the others into the melee to take the blows blindly aimed at me. The smoke was agonizing and there were no rounds, no bells at three minute intervals to relieve our exhaustion. The room spun round me, a swirl of lights, smoke, sweating bodies surrounded by tense white faces. I bled from both nose and mouth, the blood spattering upon my chest.

The men kept yelling, "Slug him, black boy! Knock his guts out!"

25 "Uppercut him! Kill him! Kill that big boy!"

Taking a fake fall, I saw a boy going down heavily beside me as though we were felled by a single blow, saw a sneaker-clad foot shoot into his groin as the two who had knocked him down stumbled upon him. I rolled out of range, feeling a twinge of nausea.

The harder we fought the more threatening the men became. And yet, I had begun to worry about my speech again. How would it go? Would they recognize my ability? What would they give me?

I was fighting automatically and suddenly I noticed that one after another of the boys was leaving the ring. I was surprised, filled with panic, as though I had been left alone with an unknown danger. Then I understood. The boys had arranged it among themselves. It was the custom for the two men left in the ring to slug it out for the winner's prize. I discovered this too late. When the bell sounded two men in tuxedoes leaped into the ring and removed the blindfold. I found myself facing Tatlock, the biggest of the gang. I felt sick at my stomach. Hardly had the bell stopped ringing in my ears than it clanged again and I saw him moving swiftly toward me. Thinking of nothing else to do I hit him smash on the nose. He kept coming, bringing the rank sharp violence of stale sweat. His face was a black bank of a face, only his eyes alive—with hate of me and aglow with a feverish terror from what had happened to us all. I became anxious. I wanted to deliver my speech and he came at me as though he meant to beat it out of me. I smashed him again and again, taking his blows as they came. Then on a sudden impulse I struck him lightly as we clinched, I whispered, "Fake like I knocked you out, you can have the prize."

"I'll break your behind," he whispered hoarsely.

"For *them?*"

"For *me,* sonofabitch!"

They were yelling for us to break it up and Tatlock spun me half around with a blow, and as a joggled camera sweeps in a reeling scene, I saw the howling red faces crouching tense beneath the cloud of blue-gray smoke. For a moment the world wavered, unraveled, flowed, then my head cleared and Tatlock bounced before me. That fluttering shadow before my eyes was his jabbing left hand. Then falling forward, my head against his damp shoulder, I whispered,

"I'll make it five dollars more."

"Go to hell!"

But his muscles relaxed a trifle beneath my pressure and I breathed, "Seven!"

"Give it to your ma," he said, ripping me beneath the heart.

And while I still held him I butted him and moved away. I felt myself bombarded with punches. I fought back with hopeless desperation. I wanted to deliver my speech more than anything else in the world, because I felt that only these men could judge truly my ability, and now this stupid clown was ruining my chances. I began fighting carefully now, moving in to punch him and out again with my greater speed. A lucky blow to his chin and I had him going too—until I heard a loud voice yell, "I got my money on the big boy."

Hearing this, I almost dropped my guard. I was confused: Should I try to win against the voice out there? Would not this go against my speech, and was not this a moment for humility, for nonresistance? A blow to my head as I danced about sent my right eye popping like a jack-in-the-box and settled my dilemma. The room went red as I fell. It was a dream fall, my body languid and fastidious as to where to land, until the floor became impatient and smashed up to meet me. A moment later I came to. An hypnotic voice said FIVE emphatically. And I lay there, hazily watching a dark red spot of my own blood shaping itself into a butterfly, glistening and soaking into the soiled gray world of the canvas.

When the voice drawled TEN I was lifted up and dragged to a chair. I sat dazed. My eye pained and swelled with each throb of my pounding heart and I wondered if now I would be allowed to speak. I was wringing wet, my mouth still bleeding. We were grouped along the wall now. The other boys ignored me as they congratulated Tatlock and speculated as to how much they would be paid. One boy whimpered over his smashed hand. Looking up front, I saw attendants in white jackets rolling the portable ring away and placing a small square rug in the vacant space surrounded by chairs. Perhaps, I thought, I will stand on the rug to deliver my speech.

Then the M.C. called to us, "Come on up here boys and get your money." We ran forward to where the men laughed and talked in their chairs, waiting. Everyone seemed friendly now.

"There it is on the rug," the man said. I saw the rug covered with coins of all dimensions and a few crumpled bills. But what excited me, scattered here and there, were the gold pieces.

"Boys, it's all yours," the man said. "You get all you grab."

"That's right, Sambo," a blond man said, winking at me confidentially.

I trembled with excitement, forgetting my pain. I would get the gold and the bills, I thought. I would use both hands. I would throw my body against the boys nearest me to block them from the gold.

"Get down around the rug now," the man commanded, "and don't anyone touch it until I give the signal."

"This ought to be good," I heard.

As told, we got around the square rug on our knees. Slowly the man raised his freckled hand as we followed it upward with our eyes.

I heard, "These niggers look like they're about to pray!"

Then, "Ready," the man said. "Go!"

I lunged for a yellow coin lying on the blue design of the carpet, touching it and sending a surprised shriek to join those rising around me. I tried frantically to remove my hand but could not let go. A hot, violent force tore through my body, shaking me like a wet rat. The rug was electrified. The hair bristled up on my head as I shook myself free. My muscles jumped, my nerves jangled, writhed. But I saw that this was not stopping the other boys. Laughing in fear and embarrassment, some were holding back and scooping up the coins knocked off by the painful contortions of the others. The men roared above us as we struggled.

"Pick it up, goddamnit, pick it up!" someone called like a bass-voiced parrot. "Go on, get it!"

I crawled rapidly around the floor, picking up the coins, trying to avoid the coppers and to get greenbacks and the gold. Ignoring the shock by laughing, as I brushed the coins off quickly, I discovered that I could contain the electricity—a contradiction, but it works. Then the men began to push us onto the rug. Laughing embarrassedly, we struggled out of their hands and kept after the coins. We were all wet and slippery and hard to hold. Suddenly I saw a boy lifted into the air, glistening with sweat like a circus seal, and dropped, his wet back landing flush upon the charged rug, heard him yell and saw him literally dance upon his back, his elbows beating a frenzied tattoo upon the floor, his muscles twitching like the flesh of a horse stung by many flies. When he finally rolled off, his face was gray and no one stopped him when he ran from the floor amid booming laughter.

"Get the money," the M.C. called. "That's good hard American cash!"

And we snatched and grabbed, snatched and grabbed. I was careful not to come too close to the rug now, and when I felt the hot whiskey breath descend upon me like a cloud of foul air I reached out and grabbed the leg of a chair. It was occupied and I held on desperately.

55 "Leggo, nigger! Leggo!"

The huge face wavered down to mine as he tried to push me free. But my body was slippery and he was too drunk. It was Mr. Colcord, who owned a chain of movie houses and "entertainment palaces." Each time he grabbed me I slipped out of his hands. It became a real struggle. I feared the rug more than I did the drunk, so I held on, surprising myself for a moment by trying to topple *him* upon the rug. It was such an enormous idea that I found myself actually carrying it out. I tried not to be obvious, yet when I grabbed his leg, trying to tumble him out of the chair, he raised up roaring with laughter, and, looking at me with soberness dead in the eye, kicked me viciously in the chest. The chair leg flew out of my hand. I felt myself going and rolled. It was as though I had rolled through a bed of hot coals. It seemed a whole century would pass before I would roll free, a century in which I was seared through the deepest levels of my body to the fearful breath within me and the breath seared and heated to the point of explosion. It'll all be over in a flash, I thought as I rolled clear. It'll all be over in a flash.

But not yet, the men on the other side were waiting, red faces swollen as though from apoplexy as they bent forward in their chairs. Seeing their fingers coming toward me I rolled away as a fumbled football rolls off the receiver's fingertips, back into the coals. That time I luckily sent the rug sliding out of place and heard the coins ringing against the floor and the boys scuffling to pick them up and the M.C. calling, "All right, boys, that's all. Go get dressed and get your money."

I was limp as a dish rag. My back felt as though it had been beaten with wires.

When we had dressed the M.C. came in and gave us each five dollars, except Tatlock, who got ten for being the last in the ring. Then he told us to leave. I was not to get a chance to deliver my speech, I thought. I was going out into the dim alley in despair when I was stopped and told to go back. I returned to the ballroom, where the men were pushing back their chairs and gathering in groups to talk.

60 The M.C. knocked on a table for quiet. "Gentlemen," he said, "we almost forgot an important part of the program. A most serious part, gentlemen. This boy was brought here to deliver a speech which he made at his graduation yesterday. . . ."

"Bravo!"

"I'm told that he is the smartest boy we've got out there in Greenwood. I'm told that he knows more big words than a pocket-sized dictionary."

Much applause and laughter.

"So now, gentlemen, I want you to give him your attention."

65 There was still laughter as I faced them, my mouth dry, my eye throbbing. I began slowly, but evidently my throat was tense, because they began shouting, "Louder! Louder!"

"We of the younger generation extol the wisdom of that great leader and educator," I shouted. "who first spoke these flaming words of wisdom: 'A ship lost at sea for many days suddenly sighted a friendly vessel. From the mast of the unfortunate vessel was seen a signal: "Water, water; we die of thirst!" The answer from the friendly vessel came back: "Cast down your bucket where you are." The captain of the distressed vessel, at last heeding the injunction, cast down his bucket, and it came up full of fresh sparkling water from the mouth of the Amazon River.' And like him I say, and in his words. 'To those of my race who depend upon bettering their condition in a foreign land, or who underestimate the importance of cultivating friendly relations with the Southern white man, who is his next-door neighbor, I would say: "Cast down your bucket where you are"—cast it down in making friends in every manly way of the people of all races by whom we are surrounded. . . .'"

I spoke automatically and with such fervor that I did not realize that the men were still talking and laughing until my dry mouth, filling up with blood from the cut, almost strangled me. I coughed, wanting to stop and go to one of the tall brass, sand-filled spittoons to relieve myself, but a few of the men, especially the superintendent, were listening and I was afraid. So I gulped it down, blood, saliva and all, and continued. (What powers of endurance I had during those days! What enthusiasm! What a belief in the rightness of things!) I spoke even louder in spite of the pain. But still they talked and still they laughed, as though deaf with cotton in dirty ears. So I spoke with greater emotional emphasis. I closed my ears and swallowed blood until I was nauseated. The speech seemed a hundred times as long as before, but I could not leave out a single word. All had to be said, each memorized nuance considered, rendered. Nor was that all. Whenever I uttered a word of three or more syllables a group of voices would yell for me to repeat it. I used the phrase "social responsibility" and they yelled:

"What's the word you say, boy?"

"Social responsibility," I said.

"What?"

"Social . . . "

"Louder."

" . . . responsibility."

"More!"

"Respon—"

"Repeat!"

"—sibility."

The room filled with the uproar of laughter until, no doubt, distracted by having to gulp down my blood, I made a mistake and yelled a phrase I had often seen denounced in newspaper editorials, heard debated in private.

"Social . . . "

"What?" they yelled.

" . . . equality—"

The laughter hung smokelike in the sudden stillness. I opened my eyes, puzzled. Sounds of displeasure filled the room. The M.C. rushed forward. They shouted hostile phrases at me. But I did not understand.

A small dry mustached man in the front row blared out, "Say that slowly, son!"

"What sir?"

"What you just said!"

"Social responsibility, sir." I said.

"You weren't being smart, were you, boy?" he said, not unkindly.

"No, sir!"

"You sure that about 'equality' was a mistake?"

"Oh, yes, sir," I said. "I was swallowing blood."

"Well, you had better speak more slowly so we can understand. We mean to do right by you, but you've got to know your place at all times. All right, now, go on with your speech."

I was afraid. I wanted to leave but I wanted also to speak and I was afraid they'd snatch me down.

"Thank you, sir," I said, beginning where I had left off, and having them ignore me as before.

Yet when I finished there was a thunderous applause. I was surprised to see the superintendent come forth with a package wrapped in white tissue paper, and gesturing for quiet, address the men.

95 "Gentlemen, you see that I did not overpraise this boy. He makes a good speech and some day he'll lead his people in the proper paths. And I don't have to tell you that that is important in these days and times. This is a good, smart boy, and so to encourage him in the right direction, in the name of the Board of Education I wish to present him a prize in the form of this . . ."

He paused, removing the tissue paper and revealing a gleaming calfskin brief case.

" . . . in the form of this first-class article from Shad Whitmore's shop."

"Boy," he said, addressing me, "take this prize and keep it well. Consider it a badge of office. Prize it. Keep developing as you are and some day it will be filled with important papers that will help shape the destiny of your people."

I was so moved that I could hardly express my thanks. A rope of bloody saliva forming a shape like an undiscovered continent drooled upon the leather and I wiped it quickly away. I felt an importance that I had never dreamed.

100 "Open it and see what's inside," I was told.

My fingers a-tremble, I complied, smelling the fresh leather and finding an official-looking document inside. It was a scholarship to the state college for Negroes. My eyes filled with tears and I ran awkwardly off the floor.

I was overjoyed; I did not even mind when I discovered that the gold pieces I had scrambled for were brass pocket tokens advertising a certain make of automobile.

When I reached home everyone was excited. Next day the neighbors came to congratulate me. I even felt safe from grandfather, whose deathbed curse usually spoiled my triumphs. I stood beneath his photograph with my brief case in hand and smiled triumphantly into his stolid black peasant's face. It was a face that fascinated me. The eyes seemed to follow everywhere I went.

That night I dreamed I was at a circus with him and that he refused to laugh at the clowns no matter what they did. Then later he told me to open my brief case and read what was inside and I did, finding an official envelope stamped with the state seal; and inside the envelope I found another and another, endlessly, and I thought I would fall of weariness: "Them's years," he said, "Now open that one." And I did and in it I found an engraved document containing a short message in letters of gold. "Read it," my grandfather said. "Out loud."

105 "To Whom It May Concern," I intoned. "Keep This Nigger-Boy Running."

I awoke with the old man's laughter ringing in my ears.

(It was a dream I was to remember and dream again for many years after. But at the time I had no insight into its meaning. First I had to attend college.)

➤ *QUESTIONS FOR READING AND WRITING*

1. Have you ever found yourself in a humiliating circumstance and were afraid to protest? If so, how did that experience affect your response to this story?
2. The narrator is the protagonist. In what way does this point of view influence how you experience the story?
3. If you were placed in the same situation as the narrator, would you have acted the same way? Explain.
4. Describe the setting of the story. What aspects of the description were most effective in conveying the atmosphere?
5. Why does the audience react so strongly to the narrator's use of the terms "social responsibility" and "social equality"?
6. What is the primary conflict in the story? Is it external, internal, both? Explain.
7. What is the theme of "Battle Royal"?

JAMAICA KINCAID (b. 1949)

Jamaica Kincaid, whose given name was Elaine Potter Richardson, was born in St. John's Antigua, an island in the West Indies. She left the rural island when she was seventeen and came to New York City to work as an au pair. She studied photography at the New School in New York and attended Franconia College in New Hampshire. Much of her work is drawn for her own experiences, both as a child in Antigua and as an immigrant in the United States. Her works include a collection of short stories, At the Bottom of the River *(1983), two novels,* Annie John *(1985) and* Lucy *(1990), and a book of essays,* A Small Place *(1988). Her most recent work,* Autobiography of My Mother, *appeared in 1995. She currently divides her time between New York City, where she has worked for many years as a staff writer for the* New Yorker, *and Bennington College in Vermont, where she is a lecturer.*

GIRL [1978]

Wash the white clothes on Monday and put them on the stone heap; wash the color clothes on Tuesday and put them on the clothes-line to dry; don't walk barehead in the hot sun; cook pumpkin fritters in very hot sweet oil; soak your little clothes right after you take them off; when buying cotton to make yourself a nice blouse, be sure that it doesn't have gum on it, because that way it won't hold up well after a wash; soak salt fish overnight before you cook it; is it true that you sing benna in Sunday school? always eat your food in such a way that it won't turn someone else's stomach; on Sundays try to walk like a lady and not like the slut you are so bent on becoming; don't sing benna in Sunday school; you mustn't speak to wharf-rat boys, not even to give directions; don't eat fruits on the street—flies will follow you; *but I don't sing benna on Sundays at all and never in Sunday school;* this is how to sew on a button; this is how to make a buttonhole for the button you have just sewed on; this is how to hem a dress when you see the hem coming down and so to prevent yourself from looking like the slut I know you are so bent on becoming; this is how you iron your father's khaki shirt so that it doesn't have a crease; this is how you iron your fathers' khaki pants so that they don't have a crease; this is how you grow okra—far from the house, because okra tree harbors red ants; when you are growing dasheen, make sure it gets plenty of water or else it makes your throat itch when you are eating it; this is how you sweep a corner; this is how you sweep a whole house; this is how you sweep a yard; this is how you smile to someone you don't like too much; this is how you smile at someone you don't like at all; this is how you smile to someone you like completely; this is how you set a table for tea; this is how you set a table for dinner; this is how you set a table for dinner with an important guest; this is how you set a table for lunch; this is how you set a table for breakfast; this is how to behave in the presence of men who don't know you very well, and this way they won't recognize immediately the slut I have warned you against becoming; be sure to wash every day, even if it is with your own spit; don't squat down to play marbles—you are not a boy, you know; don't pick people's flowers—you might catch something; don't throw stones at blackbirds, because it might not be a blackbird at all; this is how to make a bread pudding; this is how to make doukona; this is how to make pepper pot; this is how to make a good medicine for a cold; this is how to make a good medicine to throw away a child before it even becomes a child; this is how to catch a fish; this is how to throw back a fish you don't like, and that way something bad won't fall on you; this is how to bully a man; this is how a man bullies you; this is how to love a man, and if this doesn't work there are other ways, and if they don't work don't feel too bad about giving up; this is how to spit up in the air if you feel like it, and this is how to move quick so that it doesn't fall on you; this is how to make ends meet; always squeeze bread to make sure it's fresh; *but what if the baker won't let me feel the bread?* you mean to say that after all you are really going to be the kind of woman who the baker won't let near the bread?

➤ *QUESTIONS FOR READING AND WRITING*

1. Describe the point of view and voice in this story. Who is the narrator? What effect does the nonstop advice—in a nonstop paragraph—have on you?
2. Who is making the italicized comments. What difference do they make to you?
3. How would you describe this relationship?

ALICE MUNRO (b. 1931)

*One of the most important voices in modern Canadian literature, Alice Munro was born on a farm in Wingham, Ontario, and attended the University of Western Ontario, earning her B.A. degree in 1952. She has so far written only short stories, publishing ten critically acclaimed collections—*The Love of a Good Woman *(1998) is her latest—often set in the small towns of southwestern Ontario or among people reared in those towns who have been transplanted elsewhere. She said in a* New York Times *interview: "I never intended to be a short story writer. I started writing them because I didn't have time to write anything else—I had three children. And then I got used to writing stories, so I saw my material that way, and I don't think I'll ever write a novel."*

BOYS AND GIRLS [1968]

My father was a fox farmer. That is, he raised silver foxes, in pens; and in the fall and early winter, when their fur was prime, he killed them and skinned them and sold their pelts to the Hudson's Bay Company or the Montreal Fur Traders. These companies supplied us with heroic calendars to hang, one on each side of the kitchen door. Against a background of cold blue sky and black pine forests and treacherous northern rivers, plumed adventurers planted the flags of England or of France; magnificent savages bent their backs to the portage.

For several weeks before Christmas, my father worked after supper in the cellar of our house. The cellar was whitewashed, and lit by a hundred-watt bulb over the worktable. My brother Laird and I sat on the top step and watched. My father removed the pelt inside-out from the body of the fox, which looked surprisingly small, mean and rat-like, deprived of its arrogant weight of fur. The naked, slippery bodies were collected in a sack and buried at the dump. One time the hired man, Henry Bailey, had taken a swipe at me with this sack, saying, "Christmas present!" My mother thought that was not funny. In fact she disliked the whole pelting operation—that was what the killing, skinning, and preparation of the furs was called—and wished it did not have to take place in the house. There was the smell. After the pelt had been stretched inside-out on a long board my father scraped away delicately, removing the little clotted webs of blood vessels, the bubbles of fat; the smell of blood and animal fat, with the strong primitive odor of the fox itself, penetrated all parts of the house. I found it reassuringly seasonal, like the smell of oranges and pine needles.

Henry Bailey suffered from bronchial troubles. He would cough and cough until his narrow face turned scarlet, and his light blue, derisive eyes filled up with tears; then he took the lid off the stove, and, standing well back, shot out a great clot of phlegm—hsss—straight into the heart of the flames. We admired him for this performance and for his ability to make his stomach growl at will, and for his laughter, which was full of high whistlings and gurglings and involved the whole faulty machinery of his chest. It was sometimes hard to tell what he was laughing at, and always possible that it might be us.

After we had been sent to bed we could still smell fox and still hear Henry's laugh, but these things, reminders of the warm, safe, brightly lit downstairs world, seemed lost and diminished, floating on the stale cold air upstairs. We were afraid at night in the winter. We were not afraid of *outside* though this was the time of year when snowdrifts curled around our house like sleeping whales and the wind harassed us all night, coming up from the buried fields, the frozen swamp, with its old bugbear chorus of threats and misery. We were afraid of *inside,* the room where we slept. At this time the upstairs of our house was not finished. A brick chimney went up one wall. In the middle of the floor was a square hole, with a wooden railing around it; that was where the stairs came up. On the other side of the stairwell were the things that nobody had any use for any more—a soldiery roll of linoleum, standing on end, a wicker baby carriage, a fern basket, china jugs and basins with cracks in them, a picture of the Battle of Balaclava, very sad to look at. I had told Laird, as soon as he was old enough to understand such things, that bats and skeletons lived over there; whenever a man escaped from the county jail, twenty miles away, I imagined that he had somehow let himself in the window and was hiding behind the linoleum. But we had rules to keep us safe. When the light was on, we were safe as long as we did not step off the square of worn carpet which defined our bedroom-space; when the light was off no place was safe but the beds themselves. I had to turn out the light kneeling on the end of my bed, and stretching as far as I could to reach the cord.

5 In the dark we lay on our beds, our narrow life rafts, and fixed our eyes on the faint light coming up the stairwell, and sang songs. Laird sang "Jingle Bells," which he would sing any time, whether it was Christmas or not, and I sang "Danny Boy." I loved the sound of my own voice, frail and supplicating, rising in the dark. We could make out the tall frosted shapes of the windows now, gloomy and white. When I came to the part, *When I am dead, as dead I well may be*—a fit of shivering caused not by the cold sheets but by pleasurable emotion almost silenced me. *You'll kneel and say, an Ave there above me*—What was an Ave? Every day I forgot to find out.

Laird went straight from singing to sleep. I could hear his long, satisfied, bubbly breaths. Now for the time that remained to me, the most perfectly private and perhaps the best time of the whole day, I arranged myself tightly under the covers and went on with one of the stories I was telling myself from night to night. These stories were about myself, when I had grown a little older; they took place in a world that was recognizably mine, yet one that presented opportunities for courage, boldness and self-sacrifice, as mine never did. I rescued people from a bombed building (it discouraged me that the real war had gone on so far away from Jubilee). I shot two rabid wolves who were menacing the schoolyard (the teachers cowered terrified at my back). I rode a fine horse spiritedly down the main street of Jubilee, acknowledging the townspeople's gratitude for some yet-to-be-worked-out piece of heroism (nobody ever rode a horse there, except King Billy in the Orangemen's Day parade). There was always riding and shooting in these stories, though I had only been on a horse twice—bareback because we did not own a saddle—and the second time I had slid right around and dropped under the horse's feet; it had stepped placidly over me. I really was learning to shoot, but I could not hit anything yet, not even tin cans on fence posts.

Alive, the foxes inhabited a world my father made for them. It was surrounded by a high guard fence, like a medieval town, with a gate that was padlocked at night. Along the streets of this town were ranged large, sturdy pens. Each of them had a real door that a man could go through, a wooden ramp along the wire, for the foxes to run up and down on, and a kennel—something like a clothes chest with airholes—where they slept and stayed in winter and had their young. There were feeding and watering dishes attached to the wire in such a way that they could be emptied and cleaned from the outside. The dishes were made of old tin cans, and the ramps and kennels of odds and ends of old lumber. Everything was tidy and ingenious; my father was tirelessly inventive and his favorite book in the world was Robinson Crusoe. He had fitted a tin drum on a wheelbarrow, for bringing water to the pens. This was my job in summer, when the foxes had to have water twice a day. Between nine and ten o'clock in the morning, and again after supper, I filled the drum at the pump and trundled it down through the barnyard to the pens, where I parked it, and filled my watering can and went along the streets. Laird came too, with his little cream and green gardening can, filled too full and knocking against his legs and slopping water on his canvas shoes. I had the real watering can, my father's, though I could only carry it three-quarters full.

The foxes all had names, which were printed on a tin plate and hung beside their doors. They were not named when they were born, but when they survived the first year's pelting and were added to the breeding stock. Those my father had named were called names like Prince, Bob, Wally and Betty. Those I had named were called Star or Turk, or Maureen or Diana. Laird named one Maud after a hired girl we had when he was little, one Harold after a boy at school, and one Mexico, he did not say why.

Naming them did not make pets out of them, or anything like it. Nobody but my father ever went into the pens, and he had twice had blood-poisoning from bites. When I was bringing them their water they prowled up and down on the paths they had made inside their pens, barking seldom—they saved that for nighttime, when they might get up a chorus of community frenzy—but always watching me, their eyes burning, clear gold, in their pointed, malevolent faces. They were beautiful for their delicate legs and heavy, aristocratic tails and the bright fur sprinkled on dark down their backs—which gave them their name—but especially for their faces, drawn exquisitely sharp in pure hostility, and their golden eyes.

10 Besides carrying water I helped my father when he cut the long grass, and the lamb's quarter and flowering money-musk, that grew between the pens. He cut with

the scythe and I raked into piles. Then he took a pitchfork and threw fresh-cut grass all over the top of the pens to keep the foxes cooler and shade their coats, which were browned by too much sun. My father did not talk to me unless it was about the job we were doing. In this he was quite different from my mother, who, if she was feeling cheerful, would tell me all sorts of things—the name of a dog she had had when she was a little girl, the names of boys she had gone out with later on when she was grown up, and what certain dresses of hers had looked like—she could not imagine now what had become of them. Whatever thoughts and stories my father had were private, and I was shy of him and would never ask him questions. Nevertheless I worked willingly under his eyes, and with a feeling of pride. One time a feed salesman came down into the pens to talk to him and my father said, "Like to have you meet my new hired man." I turned away and raked furiously, red in the face with pleasure.

"Could of fooled me," said the salesman. "I thought it was only a girl."

After the grass was cut, it seemed suddenly much later in the year. I walked on stubble in the earlier evening, aware of the reddening skies, the entering silences, of fall. When I wheeled the tank out of the gate and put the padlock on, it was almost dark. One night at this time I saw my mother and father standing on the little rise of ground we called the gangway, in front of the barn. My father had just come from the meathouse; he had his stiff bloody apron on, and a pail of cut-up meat in his hand.

It was an odd thing to see my mother down at the barn. She did not often come out of the house unless it was to do something—hang out the wash or dig potatoes in the garden. She looked out of place, with her bare lumpy legs, not touched by the sun, her apron still on and damp across the stomach from the supper dishes. Her hair was tied up in a kerchief, wisps of it falling out. She would tie her hair up like this in the morning, saying she did not have time to do it properly, and it would stay tied up all day. It was true, too; she really did not have time. These days our back porch was piled with baskets of peaches and grapes and pears, bought in town, and onions and tomatoes and cucumbers grown at home, all waiting to be made into jelly and jam and preserves, pickles and chili sauce. In the kitchen there was a fire in the stove all day, jars clinked in boiling water, sometimes a cheesecloth bag was strung on a pole between two chairs straining blue-black grape pulp for jelly. I was given jobs to do and I would sit at the table peeling peaches that had been soaked in the hot water, or cutting up onions, my eyes smarting and streaming. As soon as I was done I ran out of the house, trying to get out of earshot before my mother thought of what she wanted me to do next. I hated the hot dark kitchen in summer, the green blinds and the flypapers, the same old oilcloth table and wavy mirror and bumpy linoleum. My mother was too tired and preoccupied to talk to me, she had no heart to tell about the Normal School Graduation Dance; sweat trickled over her face and she was always counting under her breath, pointing at jars, dumping cups of sugar. It seemed to me that work in the house was endless, dreary and peculiarly depressing; work done out of doors, and in my father's service, was ritualistically important.

I wheeled the tank up to the barn, where it was kept, and I heard my mother saying, "Wait till Laird gets a little bigger, then you'll have a real help."

15 What my father said I did not hear. I was pleased by the way he stood listening, politely as he would to a salesman or a stranger, but with an air of wanting to get on with his real work. I felt my mother had no business down here and I wanted him to feel the same way. What did she mean about Laird? He was no help to anybody. Where was he now? Swinging himself sick on the swing, going around in circles, or trying to catch caterpillars. He never once stayed with me till I was finished.

"And then I can use her more in the house," I heard my mother say. She had a dead-quiet, regretful way of talking about me that always made me uneasy. "I just get my back turned and she runs off. It's not like I had a girl in the family at all."

I went and sat on a feed bag in the corner of the barn, not wanting to appear when this conversation was going on. My mother, I felt, was not to be trusted. She was kinder than my father and more easily fooled, but you could not depend on her, and the real reasons for the things she said and did were not to be known. She loved me, and she sat up late at night making a dress of the difficult style I wanted, for me to wear when school started, but she was also my enemy. She was always plotting. She was plotting now to get me to stay in the house more, although she knew I hated it (*because* she knew I hated it) and keep me from working for my father. It seemed to me she would do this simply out of perversity, and to try her power. It did not occur to me that she could be lonely, or jealous. No grown-up could be; they were too fortunate. I sat and kicked my heels monotonously against a feed bag, raising dust, and did not come out till she was gone.

At any rate, I did not expect my father to pay any attention to what she said. Who could imagine Laird doing my work—Laird remembering the padlock and cleaning out the watering dishes with a leaf on the end of a stick, or even wheeling the tank without it tumbling over? It showed how little my mother knew about the way things really were.

I have forgotten to say what the foxes were fed. My father's bloody apron reminded me. They were fed horsemeat. At this time most farmers still kept horses, and when a horse got too old to work, or broke a leg or got down and would not get up, as they sometimes did, the owner would call my father, and he and Henry went out to the farm in the truck. Usually they shot and butchered the horse there, paying the farmer from five to twelve dollars. If they had already too much meat on hand, they would bring the horse back alive, and keep it for a few days or weeks in our stable, until the meat was needed. After the war the farmers were buying tractors and gradually getting rid of horses altogether, so it sometimes happened that we got a good healthy horse, that there was just no use for any more. If this happened in the winter we might keep the horse in our stable till spring, for we had plenty of hay and if there was a lot of snow—and the plow did not always get our road cleared—it was convenient to be able to go to town with a horse and cutter.

20 The winter I was eleven years old we had two horses in the stable. We did not know what names they had had before, so we called them Mack and Flora. Mack was an old black workhorse, sooty and indifferent. Flora was a sorrel mare, a driver. We took them both out in the cutter. Mack was slow and easy to handle. Flora was given to fits of violent alarm, veering at cars and even at other horses, but we loved her speed and high-stepping, her general air of gallantry and abandon. On

Saturdays we went down to the stable and as soon as we opened the door on its cosy, animal-smelling darkness Flora threw up her head, rolled her eyes, whinnied despairingly and pulled herself through a crisis of nerves on the spot. It was not safe to go into her stall; she would kick.

This winter also I began to hear a great deal more on the theme my mother had sounded when she had been talking in front of the barn. I no longer felt safe. It seemed that in the minds of the people around me there was a steady undercurrent of thought, not to be deflected, on this one subject. The word girl had formerly seemed to me innocent and unburdened, like the word *child;* now it appeared that it was no such thing. A girl was not, as I had supposed, simply what I was; it was what I had to become. It was a definition, always touched with emphasis, with reproach and disappointment. Also it was a joke on me. Once Laird and I were fighting, and for the first time ever I had to use all my strength against him; even so, he caught and pinned my arm for a moment, really hurting me. Henry saw this, and laughed, saying, "Oh, that there Laird's gonna show you, one of these days!" Laird was getting a lot bigger. But I was getting bigger too.

My grandmother came to stay with us for a few weeks and I heard other things. "Girls don't slam doors like that." "Girls keep their knees together when they sit down." And worse still, when I asked some questions, "That's none of girls' business." I continued to slam the doors and sit as awkwardly as possible, thinking by such measures I kept myself free.

When spring came, the horses were let out in the barnyard. Mack stood against the barn wall trying to scratch his neck and haunches, but Flora trotted up and down and reared at the fences, clattering her hooves against the rails. Snow drifts dwindled quickly, revealing the hard gray and brown earth, the familiar rise and fall of the ground, plain and bare after the fantastic landscape of winter. There was a great feeling of opening-out, of release. We just wore rubbers now, over our shoes; our feet felt ridiculously light. One Saturday we went to the stable and found all the doors open, letting in the unaccustomed sunlight and fresh air. Henry was there, just idling around looking at his collection of calendars which were tacked up behind the stalls in a part of the stable my mother had probably never seen.

"Come to say goodbye to your old friend Mack?" Henry said. "Here, you give him a taste of oats." He poured some oats in Laird's cupped hands and Laird went to feed Mack. Mack's teeth were in bad shape. He ate very slowly, patiently shifting the oats around in his mouth, trying to find a stump of a molar to grind it on. "Poor old Mac," said Henry mournfully. "When a horse's teeth's gone, he's gone. That's about the way."

"Are you going to shoot him today?" I said. Mack and Flora had been in the stable so long I had almost forgotten they were going to be shot.

Henry didn't answer me. Instead he started to sing in a high, trembly, mocking-sorrowful voice. *Oh, there's no more work, for poor Uncle Ned, he's gone where the good darkies go.* Mack's thick, blackish tongue worked diligently at Laird's hand. I went out before the song was ended and sat down on the gangway.

I had never seen them shoot a horse, but I knew where it was done. Last summer Laird and I had come upon a horse's entrails before they were buried. We had thought it was a big black snake, coiled up in the sun. That was around in the field that ran up beside the barn. I thought that if we went inside the barn, and found a wide crack or a knothole to look through, we would be able to see them do it. It was not something I wanted to see; just the same, if a thing really happened, it was better to see, and know.

My father came down from the house, carrying the gun.

"What are you doing here?" he said.

"Nothing."

"Go on up and play around the house."

He sent Laird out of the stable. I said to Laird. "Do you want to see them shoot Mack?" and without waiting for an answer led him around to the front door of the barn, opened it carefully, and went in. "Be quiet or they'll hear us," I said. We could hear Henry and my father talking in the stable; then the heavy, shuffling steps of Mack being backed out of his stall.

In the loft it was cold and dark. Thin crisscrossed beams of sunlight fell through the cracks. The hay was low. It was a rolling country, hills and hollows, slipping under our feet. About four feet up was a beam going around the walls. We piled hay up in one corner and I boosted Laird up and hoisted myself. The beam was not very wide; we crept along it with our hands flat on the barn walls. There were plenty of knotholes, and I found one that gave me the view I wanted—a corner of the barnyard, the gate, part of the field. Laird did not have a knothole and began to complain.

I showed him a widened crack between two boards. "Be quiet and wait. If they hear you you'll get us in trouble."

My father came in sight carrying the gun. Henry was leading Mack by the halter. He dropped it and took out his cigarette papers and tobacco; he rolled cigarettes for my father and himself. While this was going on Mack nosed around in the old, dead grass along the fence. Then my father opened the gate and they took Mack through. Henry led Mack away from the path to a patch of ground and they talked together, not loud enough for us to hear. Mack again began searching for a mouthful of fresh grass, which was not to be found. My father walked away in a straight line, and stopped short at a distance which seemed to suit him. Henry was walking away from Mack too, but sideways, still negligently holding on to the halter. My father raised the gun and Mack looked up as if he had noticed something and my father shot him.

Mack did not collapse at once but swayed, lurched sideways and fell, first on his side; then he rolled over on his back and, amazingly, kicked his legs for a few seconds in the air. At this Henry laughed, as if Mack had done a trick for him. Laird, who had drawn a long, groaning breath of surprise when the shot was fired, said out loud, "He's not dead." And it seemed to me it might be true. But his legs stopped, he rolled on his side again, his muscles quivered and sank. The two men walked over and looked at him in a businesslike way; they bent down and examined his forehead where the bullet had gone in, and now I saw his blood on the brown grass.

"Now they just skin him and cut him up," I said. "Let's go." My legs were a little shaky and I jumped gratefully down into the hay. "Now you've seen how they shoot a horse," I said in a congratulatory way, as if I had seen it many times before. "Let's see if any barn cat's had kittens in the hay." Laird jumped. He seemed young and obedient again. Suddenly I remembered how, when he was little, I had brought him into the barn and told him to climb the ladder to the top beam. That was in the spring, too, when the hay was low. I had done it out of a need for excitement, a desire for something to happen so that I could tell about it. He was wearing a little bulky brown and white checked coat, made down from one of mine. He went all the way up just as I told him, and sat down on the top beam with the hay far below him on one side, and the barn floor and some old machinery on the other. Then I ran screaming to my father. "Laird's up on the top beam!" My father came, my mother came, my father went up the ladder talking very quietly and brought Laird down under his arm, at which my mother leaned against the ladder and began to cry. They said to me, "Why weren't you watching him?" but nobody ever knew the truth. Laird did not know enough to tell. But whenever I saw the brown and white checked coat hanging in the closet, or at the bottom of the rag bag, which was where it ended up, I felt a weight in my stomach, the sadness of unexorcised guilt.

I looked at Laird, who did not even remember this, and I did not like the look on this thin, winter-pale face. His expression was not frightened or upset, but remote, concentrating. "Listen," I said, in an unusually bright and friendly voice, "you aren't going to tell, are you?"

"No," he said absently.

"Promise."

"Promise," he said. I grabbed the hand behind his back to make sure he was not crossing his fingers. Even so, he might have a nightmare; it might come out that way. I decided I had better work hard to get all thoughts of what he had seen out of his mind—which, it seemed to me, could not hold very many things at a time. I got some money I had saved and that afternoon we went into Jubilee and saw a show, with Judy Canova, at which we both laughed a great deal. After that I thought it would be all right.

Two weeks later I knew they were going to shoot Flora. I knew from the night before, when I heard my mother ask if the hay was holding out all right, and my father said, "Well, after tomorrow there'll just be the cow, and we should be able to put her out to grass in another week." So I knew it was Flora's turn in the morning.

This time I didn't think of watching it. That was something to see just one time. I had not thought about it very often since, but sometimes when I was busy, working at school, or standing in front of the mirror combing my hair and wondering if I would be pretty when I grew up, the whole scene would flash into my mind: I would see the easy, practiced way my father raised the gun, and hear Henry laughing when Mack kicked his legs in the air. I did not have any great feeling of horror and opposition, such as a city child might have had; I was too used to seeing the death of animals as a necessity by which we lived. Yet I felt a little ashamed, and there was a new wariness, a sense of holding-off, in my attitude to my father and his work.

It was a fine day, and we were going around the yard picking up tree branches that had been torn off in winter storms. This was something we had been told to do, and also we wanted to use them to make a teepee. We heard Flora whinny, and then my father's voice and Henry's shouting, and we ran down to the barnyard to see what was going on.

45 The stable door was open. Henry had just brought Flora out, and she had broken away from him. She was running free in the barnyard, from one end to the other. We climbed up on the fence. It was exciting to see her running, whinnying, going up on her hind legs, prancing and threatening like a horse in a Western movie, an unbroken ranch horse, though she was just an old driver, an old sorrel mare. My father and Henry ran after her and tried to grab the dangling halter. They tried to work her into a corner, and they had almost succeeded when she made a run between them, wild-eyed, and disappeared around the corner of the barn. We heard the rails clatter down as she got over the fence, and Henry yelled. "She's into the field now!"

That meant she was in the long L-shaped field that ran up by the house. If she got around the center, heading towards the lane, the gate was open; the truck had been driven into the field this morning. My father shouted to me, because I was on the other side of the fence, nearest the lane. "Go shut the gate!"

I could run very fast. I ran across the garden, past the tree where our swing was hung, and jumped across a ditch into the lane. There was the open gate. She had not got out, I could not see her up the road; she must have run to the other end of the field. The gate was heavy, I lifted it out of the gravel and carried it across the roadway. I had it halfway across when she came in sight, galloping straight toward me. There was just time to get the chain on. Laird came scrambling through the ditch to help me.

Instead of shutting the gate, I opened it as wide as I could. I did not make any decision to do this, it was just what I did. Flora never slowed down; she galloped straight past me, and Laird jumped up and down, yelling "Shut it, shut it!" even after it was too late. My father and Henry appeared in the field a moment too late to see what I had done. They only saw Flora heading for the township road. They would think I had not got there in time.

They did not waste any time asking about it. They went back to the barn and got the gun and the knives they used, and put these in the truck; then they turned the truck around and came bouncing up the field toward us. Laird called to them, "Let me go too, let me go too!" and Henry stopped the truck and they took him in. I shut the gate after they were all gone.

50 I supposed Laird would tell. I wondered what would happen to me. I had never disobeyed my father before, and I could not understand why I had done it. Flora would not really get away. They would catch up with her in the truck. Or if they did not catch her this morning somebody would see her and telephone us this afternoon or tomorrow. There was no wild country here for her to run to, only farms. What was more, my father had paid for her, we needed the meat to feed the foxes, we needed the foxes to make our living. All I had done was make more work for my father who worked hard enough already. And when my father found out about it he was not going to trust me any more; he would know that I was not entirely on his side. I was on Flora's side, and that made me no use to anybody, not even to her. Just the same, I did not regret it; when she came running at me and I held the gate open, that was the only thing I could do.

I went back to the house, and my mother said. "What's all the commotion?" I told her that Flora had kicked down the fence and got away. "Your poor father," she said, "now he'll have to go chasing over the countryside. Well, there isn't any use planning dinner before one." She put up the ironing board. I wanted to tell her, but thought better of it and went upstairs and sat on my bed.

Lately I had been trying to make my part of the room fancy, spreading the bed with old lace curtains, and fixing myself a dressing table with some leftovers of cretonne for a skirt. I planned to put up some kind of barricade between my bed and Laird's, to keep my section separate from his. In the sunlight, the lace curtains were just dusty rags. We did not sing at night any more. One night when I was singing Laird said, "You sound silly," and I went right on but the next night I did not start. There was not so much need to anyway, we were no longer afraid. We knew it was just old furniture over there, old jumble and confusion. We did not keep to the rules. I still stayed awake after Laird was asleep and told myself stories, but even in these stories something different was happening, mysterious alterations took place. A story might start off in the old way, with a spectacular danger, a fire or wild animals, and for a while I might rescue people; then things would change around, and instead, somebody would be rescuing me. It might be a boy from our class at school, or even Mr. Campbell, our teacher, who tickled girls under the arms. And at this point the story concerned itself at great length with what I looked like—how long my hair was, and what kind of dress I had on; by the time I had these details worked out the real excitement of the story was lost.

It was later than one o'clock when the truck came back. The tarpaulin was over the back, which meant there was meat in it. My mother had to heat dinner up all over again. Henry and my father had changed from their bloody overalls into ordinary working overalls in the barn, and they washed their arms and necks and faces at the sink, and splashed water on their hair and combed it. Laird lifted his arm to show off a streak of blood. "We shot old Flora," he said, "and cut her up in fifty pieces."

"Well I don't want to hear about it," my mother said. "And don't come to my table like that."

My father made him go and wash the blood off.

We sat down and my father said grace and Henry pasted his chewing-gum on the end of his fork, the way he always did; when he took it off he would have us admire the pattern. We began to pass the bowls of steaming, overcooked vegetables. Laird looked across the table at me and said proudly, distinctly. "Anyway it was her fault Flora got away."

"What?" my father said.

"She could of shut the gate and she didn't. She just open' it up and Flora run out."

"Is that right?" my father said.

Everybody at the table was looking at me. I nodded, swallowing food with great difficulty. To my shame, tears flooded my eyes.

My father made a curt sound of disgust. "What did you do that for?"

I did not answer. I put down my fork and waited to be sent from the table, still not looking up.

But this did not happen. For some time nobody said anything, then Laird said matter-of-factly, "She's crying."

"Never mind," my father said. He spoke with resignation, even good humor, the words which absolved and dismissed me for good. "She's only a girl," he said. I didn't protest that, even in my heart. Maybe it was true.

➤ *QUESTIONS FOR READING AND WRITING*

1. To what extent does your own experience influence your response to this story?
2. What is the narrator's conflict? Is it external? Internal? Both?
3. What is the importance of the setting in this story? To what extent does it form the characters? In what ways might they be different if they were living in the city or the suburbs?
4. At the end of the story, the narrator's father excuses her action by saying, "She's only a girl." What does he mean? How do you suppose he would define "a boy"? What does his definition of his daughter say about him?
5. The narrator reacts to her father's statement by saying, "Maybe it was true." What do you think she means? Is she agreeing with what he means? Explain.

FRANK O'CONNOR (1903–1966)

Frank O'Connor was the adopted pen name of Michael Donovan, who was born in Cork, Ireland. When he was only in the fourth grade, his impoverished parents were forced to take him out of school so he could go to work. Nevertheless, while toiling at numerous odd jobs, he developed a lifelong love of reading and writing. During the "troubles" of 1918–1921, which led to an independent Ireland, O'Connor was a soldier of the Irish Republican Army. He later wrote about his experiences in his 1931 collection of short stories, Guest of the Nation. *Following the war, O'Connor worked first as a librarian, and later as a director of the famous Abbey Theatre in Dublin. He then moved to the United States, where he held teaching positions at Harvard University and Northwestern University, and achieved some celebrity appearing on Sunday morning television telling stories. His work—which includes stories, novels, plays, poetry and criticism—is noted for its humor, poetic sensibility, and superb craftsmanship.*

MY OEDIPUS COMPLEX [1950]

Father was in the army all through the war—the first war, I mean—so, up to the age of five, I never saw much of him, and what I saw did not worry me. Sometimes I woke and there was a big figure in khaki peering down at me in the candlelight. Sometimes in the early morning I heard the slamming of the front door and the clatter of nailed boots down the cobbles of the lane. These were Father's entrances and exits. Like Santa Claus he came and went mysteriously.

In fact, I rather liked his visits, though it was an uncomfortable squeeze between Mother and him when I got into the big bed in the early morning. He smoked, which gave him a pleasant musty smell, and shaved, an operation of astounding interest. Each time he left a trail of souvenirs—model tanks and Gurkha knives with handles made of bullet cases, and German helmets and cap badges and buttonsticks, and all sorts of military equipment—carefully stowed away in a long box on top of the wardrobe, in case they ever came in handy. There was a bit of the magpie about Father; he expected everything to come in handy. When his back was turned, Mother let me get a chair and rummage through his treasures. She didn't seem to think so highly of them as he did.

The war was the most peaceful period of my life. The window of my attic faced southeast. My mother had curtained it, but that had small effect. I always woke with the first light and, with all the responsibilities of the previous day melted, feeling myself rather like the sun, ready to illumine and rejoice. Life never seemed so simple and clear and full of possibilities as then. I put my feet out from under the clothes—I called them Mrs. Left and Mrs. Right—and invented dramatic situations for them in which they discussed the problems of the day. At least Mrs. Right did; she was very demonstrative, but I hadn't the same control of Mrs. Left, so she mostly contented herself with nodding agreement.

They discussed what Mother and I should do during the day, what Santa Claus should give a fellow for Christmas, and what steps should be taken to brighten the home. There was that little matter of the baby, for instance. Mother and I could never agree about that. Ours was the only house in the terrace without a new baby, and Mother said we couldn't afford one till Father came back from the war because they cost seventeen and six. That showed how simple she was. The Geneys up the road had a baby, and everyone knew they couldn't afford seventeen and six. It was probably a cheap baby, and Mother wanted something really good, but I felt she was too exclusive. The Geneys' baby would have done us fine.

5 Having settled my plans for the day, I got up, put a chair under the attic window, and lifted the frame high enough to stick out my head. The window overlooked the front gardens of the terrace behind ours, and beyond these it looked over a deep valley to the tall, red-brick houses terraced up the opposite hillside, which were all still in shadow, while those at our side of the valley were all lit up, though with long strange shadows that made them seem unfamiliar; rigid and painted.

After that I went into Mother's room and climbed into the big bed. She woke and I began to tell her of my schemes. By this time, though I never seem to have noticed it, I was petrified in my nightshirt, and I thawed as I talked until, the last frost melted, I fell asleep beside her and woke again only when I heard her below in the kitchen, making the breakfast.

After breakfast we went into town; heard Mass at St. Augustine's and said a prayer for Father, and did the shopping. If the afternoon was fine we either went for a walk in the country or a visit to Mother's great friend in the convent, Mother St. Dominic. Mother had them all praying for Father, and every night, going to bed, I asked God to send him back safe from the war to us. Little, indeed, did I know what I was praying for!

One morning, I got into the big bed, and there, sure enough, was Father in his usual Santa Claus manner, but later, instead of uniform, he put on his best blue suit, and Mother was as pleased as anything. I saw nothing to be pleased about, because, out of uniform, Father was altogether less interesting, but she only beamed, and explained that our prayers had been answered, and off we went to Mass to thank God for having brought Father safely home.

The irony of it! That very day when he came in to dinner he took off his boots and put on his slippers, donned the dirty old cap he wore about the house to save him from colds, crossed his legs, and began to talk gravely to Mother, who looked anxious. Naturally, I disliked her looking anxious, because it destroyed her good looks, so I interrupted him.

10 "Just a moment, Larry!" she said gently.

This was only what she said when we had boring visitors, so I attached no importance to it and went on talking.

"Do be quiet, Larry!" she said impatiently. "Don't you hear me talking to Daddy?"

This was the first time I had heard those ominous words, "talking to Daddy," and I couldn't help feeling that if this was how God answered prayers, he couldn't listen to them very attentively.

"Why are you talking to Daddy?" I asked with as great a show of indifference as I could muster.

15 "Because Daddy and I have business to discuss. Now, don't interrupt again!"

In the afternoon, at Mother's request, Father took me for a walk. This time we went into town instead of out the country, and I thought at first, in my usual optimistic way, that it might be an improvement. It was nothing of the sort. Father and I had quite different notions of a walk in town. He had no proper interest in trams, ships, and horses, and the only thing that seemed to divert him was talking to fellows as old as himself. When I wanted to stop he simply went on, dragging me behind him by the hand; when he wanted to stop I had no alternative but to do the same. I noticed that it seemed to be a sign that he wanted to stop for a long time whenever he leaned against a wall. The second time I saw him do it I got wild. He seemed to be settling himself forever. I pulled him by the coat and trousers, but, unlike Mother who, if you were too persistent, got into a wax and said: "Larry, if you don't behave yourself, I'll give you a good slap," Father had an extraordinary capacity for amiable inattention. I sized him up and wondered would I cry, but he seemed to be too remote to be annoyed even by that. Really, it was like going for a walk with a mountain! He either ignored the wrenching and pummelling entirely, or else glanced down with a grin of amusement from his peak. I had never met anyone so absorbed in himself as he seemed.

At teatime, "talking to Daddy" began again, complicated this time by the fact that he had an evening paper, and every few minutes he put it down and told Mother something new out of it. I felt this was foul play. Man for man, I was prepared to compete with him anytime for Mother's attention, but when he had it all made up for him by other people it left me no chance. Several times I tried to change the subject without success.

"You must be quiet while Daddy is reading, Larry," Mother said impatiently.

It was clear that she either genuinely liked talking to Father better than talking to me, or else that he had some terrible hold on her which made her afraid to admit the truth.

"Mummy," I said that night when she was tucking me up, "do you think if I prayed hard God would send Daddy back to the war?"

She seemed to think about that for a moment.

"No, dear," she said with a smile. "I don't think he would."

"Why wouldn't he, Mummy?"

"Because there isn't a war any longer, dear."

"But, Mummy, couldn't God make another war, if He liked?"

"He wouldn't like to, dear. It's not God who makes wars, but bad people."

"Oh!" I said.

I was disappointed about that. I began to think that God wasn't quite what he was cracked up to be.

Next morning I woke at my usual hour, feeling like a bottle of champagne. I put out my feet and invented a long conversation in which Mrs. Right talked of the trouble she had with her own father till she put him in the Home. I didn't quite know what the Home was but it sounded the right place for Father. Then I got my chair and stuck my head out of the attic window. Dawn was just breaking, with a guilty air that made me feel I had caught it in the act. My head bursting with stories and schemes, I stumbled in next door, and in the half-darkness scrambled into the big bed. There was no room at Mother's side so I had to get between her and Father. For the time being I had forgotten about him, and for several minutes I sat bolt upright, racking my brains to know what I could do with him. He was taking up more than his fair share of the bed, and I couldn't get comfortable, so I gave him several kicks that made him grunt and stretch. He made room all right, though. Mother waked and felt for me. I settled back comfortably in the warmth of the bed with my thumb in my mouth.

"Mummy!" I hummed, loudly and contentedly. "Sssh! dear," she whispered. "Don't wake Daddy!"

This was a new development, which threatened to be even more serious than "talking to Daddy." Life without my early-morning conferences was unthinkable.

"Why?" I asked severely.

"Because poor Daddy is tired."

This seemed to me a quite inadequate reason, and I was sickened by the sentimentality of her "poor Daddy." I never liked that sort of gush; it always struck me as insincere.

"Oh!" I said lightly. Then in my most winning tone: "Do you know where I want to go with you today, Mummy?"

"No, dear," she sighed.

"I want to go down the Glen and fish for thornybacks with my new net, and then I want to go out to the Fox and Hounds, and—"

"Don't-wake-daddy!" she hissed angrily, clapping her hand across my mouth.

But it was too late. He was awake, or nearly so. He grunted and reached for the matches. Then he stared incredulously at his watch.

"Like a cup of tea, dear?" asked Mother in a meek, hushed voice I had never heard her use before. It sounded almost as though she were afraid.

"Tea?" he exclaimed indignantly. "Do you know what the time is?"

"And after that I want to go up the Rathcooney Road," I said loudly, afraid I'd forget something in all those interruptions.

"Go to sleep at once, Larry!" she said sharply.

I began to snivel. I couldn't concentrate, the way that pair went on, and smothering my early-morning schemes was like burying a family from the cradle.

Father said nothing, but lit his pipe and sucked it, looking out into the shadows without minding Mother or me. I knew he was mad. Every time I made a remark Mother hushed me irritably. I was mortified. I felt it wasn't fair; there was even something sinister in it. Every time I had pointed out to her the waste of making two beds when we could both sleep in one, she had told me it was healthier like that, and now here was this man, this stranger, sleeping with her without the least regard for her health!

He got up early and made tea, but though he brought Mother a cup he brought none for me.

"Mummy," I shouted, "I want a cup of tea, too."

"Yes, dear," she said patiently. "You can drink from Mummy's saucer."

That settled it. Either Father or I would have to leave the house. I didn't want to drink from Mother's saucer; I wanted to be treated as an equal in my own home, so, just to spite her, I drank it all and left none for her. She took that quietly, too.

But that night when she was putting me to bed she said gently:

"Larry, I want you to promise me something."

"What is it?" I asked.

"Not to come in and disturb poor Daddy in the morning. Promise?"

"Poor Daddy" again! I was becoming suspicious of everything involving that quite impossible man.

"Why?" I asked.

"Because poor Daddy is worried and tired and he doesn't sleep well."

"Why doesn't he, Mummy?"

"Well, you know, don't you, that while he was at the war Mummy got the pennies from the Post Office?"

"From Miss MacCarthy?"

"That's right. But now, you see, Miss MacCarthy hasn't any more pennies, so Daddy must go out and find us some. You know what would happen if he couldn't?"

"No," I said, "tell us."

"Well, I think we might have to go out and beg for them like the poor old woman on Fridays. We wouldn't like that, would we?"

"No," I agreed. "We wouldn't."

"So you'll promise not to come in and wake him?"

"Promise."

Mind you, I meant that. I knew pennies were a serious matter, and I was all against having to go out and beg like the old woman on Fridays. Mother laid out all my toys in a complete ring around the bed so that, whatever way I got out, I was bound to fall over one of them.

When I woke I remembered my promise all right. I got up and sat on the floor and played—for hours, it seemed to me. Then I got my chair and looked out the attic window for more hours. I wished it was time for Father to wake; I wished someone would make me a cup of tea. I didn't feel in the least like the sun; instead, I was bored and so very, very cold! I simply longed for the warmth and depth of the big featherbed.

At last I could stand it no longer. I went into the next room. As there was still no room at Mother's side I climbed over her and she woke with a start.

"Larry," she whispered, gripping my arm very tightly, "what did you promise?"

"But I did Mummy," I wailed, caught in the very act. "I was quiet for ever so long."

"Oh, dear, and you're perished!" she said sadly, feeling me all over. "Now, if I let you stay will you promise not to talk?"

"But I want to talk, Mummy," I wailed.

"That has nothing to do with it," she said with a firmness that was new to me. "Daddy wants to sleep. Now, do you understand that?"

I understood it only too well. I wanted to talk, he wanted to sleep—whose house was it, anyway?

"Mummy," I said with equal firmness, "I think it would be healthier for Daddy to sleep in his own bed."

That seemed to stagger her, because she said nothing for a while.

"Now, once for all," she went on, "you're to be perfectly quiet or go back to your own bed. Which is it to be?"

The injustice of it got me down. I had convicted her out of her own mouth of inconsistency and unreasonableness, and she hadn't even attempted to reply. Full of spite, I gave Father a kick, which she didn't notice but which made him grunt and open his eyes in alarm.

"What time is it?" he asked in a panic-stricken voice, not looking at Mother but at the door, as if he saw someone there.

"It's early yet," she replied soothingly. "It's only the child. Go to sleep again.... Now, Larry," she added, getting out of bed, "you've wakened Daddy and you must go back."

This time, for all her quiet air, I knew she meant it, and knew that my principal rights and privileges were as good as lost unless I asserted them at once. As she lifted me, I gave a screech, enough to wake the dead, not to mind Father. He groaned.

"That damn child! Doesn't he ever sleep?"

"It's only a habit, dear," she said quietly, though I could see she was vexed.

"Well, it's time he got out of it," shouted Father, beginning to heave in the bed. He suddenly gathered all the bedclothes about him, turned to the wall, and then looked back over his shoulder with nothing showing only two small, spiteful, dark eyes. The man looked very wicked.

85 To open the bedroom door, Mother had to let me down, and I broke free and dashed for the farthest corner, screeching. Father sat bolt upright in bed.

"Shut up, you little puppy!" he said in a choking voice.

I was so astonished that I stopped screeching. Never, never had anyone spoken to me in that tone before. I looked at him incredulously and saw his face convulsed with rage. It was only then that I fully realized how God had codded me, listening to my prayers for the safe return of this monster.

"Shut up, you!" I bawled, beside myself.

"What's that you said?" shouted Father, making a wild leap out of the bed.

90 "Mick, Mick!" cried Mother. "Don't you see the child isn't used to you?"

"I see he's better fed than taught," snarled Father, waving his arms wildly. "He wants his bottom smacked."

All his previous shouting was as nothing to these obscene words referring to my person. They really made my blood boil.

"Smack your own!" I screamed hysterically. "Smack your own! Shut up! Shut up!"

At this he lost his patience and let fly at me. He did it with the lack of conviction you'd expect of a man under Mother's horrified eyes, and it ended up as a mere tap, but the sheer indignity of being struck at all by a stranger, a total stranger who had cajoled his way back from the war into our big bed as a result of my innocent intercession, made me completely dotty. I shrieked and shrieked, and danced in my bare feet, and Father, looking awkward and hairy in nothing but a short gray army shirt, glared down at me like a mountain out for murder. I think it must have been then that I realized he was jealous too. And there stood Mother in her nightdress, looking as if her heart was broken between us. I hoped she felt as she looked. It seemed to me that she deserved it all.

95 From that morning out my life was a hell. Father and I were enemies, open and avowed. We conducted a series of skirmishes against one another, he trying to steal my time with Mother and I his. When she was sitting on my bed, telling me a story, he took to looking for some pair of old boots which he alleged he had left behind him at the beginning of the war. While he talked to Mother I played loudly with my toys to show my total lack of concern. He created a terrible scene one evening when he came in from work and found me at his box, playing with his regimental badges, Gurkha knives and buttonsticks. Mother got up and took the box from me.

"You mustn't play with Daddy's toys unless he lets you, Larry," she said severely. "Daddy doesn't play with yours."

For some reason Father looked at her as if she had struck him and then turned away with a scowl.

"Those are not toys," he growled, taking down the box again to see had I lifted anything. "Some of those curios are very rare and valuable."

But as time went on I saw more and more how he managed to alienate Mother and me. What made it worse was that I couldn't grasp his method or see what attraction he had for Mother. In every possible way he was less winning than I. He had a common accent and made noises at his tea. I thought for a while that it might be the newspapers she was interested in, so I made up bits of news on my own to read to her. Then I thought it might be the smoking, which I personally thought attractive, and took his pipes and went round the house dribbling into them till he caught me. I even made noises at my tea, but Mother only told me I was disgusting. It all seemed to hinge round that unhealthy habit of sleeping together, so I made a point of dropping into their bedroom and nosing round, talking to myself, so that they wouldn't know I was watching them, but they were never up to anything that I could see. In the end it beat me. It seemed to depend on being grown-up and giving people rings, and I realized I'd have to wait.

100 But at the same time I wanted him to see that I was only waiting, not giving up the fight. One evening when he was being particularly obnoxious, chattering away well above my head, I let him have it.

"Mummy," I said, "do you know what I'm going to do when I grow up?"

"No, dear," she replied. "What?"

"I'm going to marry you," I said quietly.

Father gave a great guffaw out of him, but he didn't take me in. I knew it must only be pretense. And Mother, in spite of everything, was pleased. I felt she was probably relieved to know that one day Father's hold on her would be broken.

105 "Won't that be nice?" she said with a smile.

"It'll be very nice," I said confidently. "Because we're going to have lots and lots of babies."

"That's right, dear," she said placidly. "I think we'll have one soon, and then you'll have plenty of company."

I was no end pleased about that because it showed that in spite of the way she gave in to Father she still considered my wishes. Besides, it would put the Geneys in their place.

It didn't turn out like that, though. To begin with, she was very preoccupied—I supposed about where she would get the seventeen and six—and though Father took to staying out late in the evenings it did me no particular good. She stopped taking me for walks, became as touchy as blazes, and smacked me for nothing at all. Sometimes I wished I'd never mentioned the confounded baby—I seemed to have a genius for bringing calamity on myself.

110 And calamity it was! Sonny arrived in the most appalling hullabaloo—even that much he couldn't do without a fuss—and from the first moment I disliked him. He was a difficult child—so far as I was concerned he was always difficult—and demanded far too much attention. Mother was simply silly about him, and couldn't see when he was only showing off. As company he was worse than useless. He slept all day, and I had to go round the house on tiptoe to avoid waking him. It wasn't any longer a question of not waking Father. The slogan now was "Don't-wake-Sonny!" I couldn't understand why the child wouldn't sleep at the proper time, so whenever Mother's back was turned I woke him. Sometimes to keep him awake I pinched him as well. Mother caught me at it one day and gave me a most unmerciful flaking.

One evening, when Father was coming in from work, I was playing trains in the front garden. I let on not to notice him; instead, I pretended to be talking to myself, and said in a loud voice: "If another bloody baby comes into this house, I'm going out."

Father stopped dead and looked at me over his shoulder.

"What's that you said?" he asked sternly.

"I was only talking to myself," I replied, trying to conceal my panic. "It's private."

115 He turned and went in without a word. Mind you, I intended it as a solemn warning, but its effect was quite different. Father started being quite nice to me. I could understand that, of course. Mother was quite sickening about Sonny. Even at mealtimes she'd get up and gawk at him in the cradle with an idiotic smile, and tell Father to do the same. He was always polite about it, but he looked so puzzled you could see he didn't know what she was talking about. He complained of the way Sonny cried at night, but she only got cross and said that Sonny never cried except when there was something up with him—which was a flaming lie, because Sonny never had anything up with him, and only cried for attention. It was really painful to see how simple-minded she was. Father wasn't attractive, but he had a fine intelligence. He saw through Sonny, and now he knew that I saw through him as well.

One night I woke with a start. There was someone beside me in the bed. For one wild moment I felt sure it must be Mother, having come to her senses and left Father for good, but then I heard Sonny in convulsions in the next room, and Mother saying: "There! There! There!" and I knew it wasn't she. It was Father. He was lying beside me, wide awake, breathing hard and apparently as mad as hell.

After awhile it came to me what he was mad about. It was his turn now. After turning me out of the big bed, he had been turned out himself. Mother had no consideration now for anyone but that poisonous pup, Sonny. I couldn't help feeling sorry for Father. I had been through it all myself, and even at that age I was magnanimous. I began to stroke him down and say: "There! There!" He wasn't exactly responsive.

"Aren't you asleep either?" he snarled.

"Ah, come on and put your arm around us, can't you?" I said, and he did, in a sort of way. Gingerly, I suppose, is how you'd describe it. He was very bony but better than nothing.

120 At Christmas he went out of his way to buy me a really nice model railway.

➤ *QUESTIONS FOR READING AND WRITING*

1. What is an Oedipus complex? Do you think "My Oedipus Complex" is an appropriate title for this story? Explain.
2. Who is the narrator in this story? How does the narrator's point of view establish the tone? What makes the story humorous?
3. How does the relationship between the narrator and his father change as the story develops?
4. In what way is the ending, like much of the story, ironic?

Amy Tan (b. 1952)

Amy Tan was born in Oakland, California, several years after her mother and father immigrated from China. Upon the deaths of her brother and father in 1967 and 1968, the family began a haphazard journey through Europe, before settling in Switzerland. For the next seven years, Tan attended five schools before graduating with honors from San Jose State University, where she later earned an M.A. in Linguistics. In 1989, The Joy Luck Club *(from which "Two Kinds" is taken) was published and, through word-of-mouth endorsements by independent booksellers, became a surprise bestseller. Though Tan wrote the book as a collection of linked short stories, reviewers enthusiastically and erroneously referred to the book as an intricately woven "novel." It was nominated for the National Book Award and the National Book Critics Award and was adapted into a film for Hollywood Pictures in 1994 with Tan as a co-screenwriter. Tan's second novel,* The Kitchen God's Wife *was published in 1991, followed by* The Hundred Secret Senses *in 1995. Her short stories and essays have appeared in* The Atlantic, Harper's, The New Yorker, *and other publications. Her essay, "Mother Tongue" (p. 161) was chosen for best American Essays 1991. She was the guest editor for the* 1999 Best American Short Stories.

Two Kinds [1989]

My mother believed you could be anything you wanted to be in America. You could open a restaurant. You could work for the government and get good retirement. You could buy a house with almost no money down. You could become rich. You could become instantly famous.

"Of course you can be prodigy, too," my mother told me when I was nine. "You can be best anything. What does Auntie Lindo know? Her daughter, she is only best tricky."

America was where all my mother's hopes lay. She had come here in 1949 after losing everything in China: her mother and father, her family home, her first husband, and two daughters, twin baby girls. But she never looked back with regret. There were so many ways for things to get better.

We didn't immediately pick the right kind of prodigy. At first my mother thought I could be a Chinese Shirley Temple. We'd watch Shirley's old movies on TV as though they were training films. My mother would poke my arm and say, "*Ni kan.*" —You watch. And I would see Shirley tapping her feet, or singing a sailor song, or pursing her lips into a very round O while saying "Oh, my goodness."

5 "*Ni kan,*" said my mother as Shirley's eyes flooded with tears. "You already know how. Don't need talent for crying!"

Soon after my mother got this idea about Shirley Temple, she took me to a beauty training school in the Mission district and put me in the hands of a student who could barely hold the scissors without shaking. Instead of getting big fat curls, I emerged with an uneven mass of crinkly black fuzz. My mother dragged me off to the bathroom and tried to wet down my hair.

"You look like Negro Chinese," she lamented, as if I had done this on purpose.

The instructor of the beauty training school had to lop off these soggy clumps to make my hair even again. "Peter Pan is very popular these days," the instructor assured my mother. I now had hair the length of a boy's, with straight-across bangs that hung at a slant two inches above my eyebrows. I liked the haircut and it made me actually look forward to my future fame.

In fact, in the beginning, I was just as excited as my mother, maybe even more so. I pictured this prodigy part of me as many different images, trying each one on for size. I was a dainty ballerina girl standing by the curtains, waiting to hear the music that would send me floating on my tiptoes. I was like the Christ child lifted out of the straw manger, crying with holy indignity. I was Cinderella stepping from her pumpkin carriage with sparkly cartoon music filling the air.

10 In all of my imaginings, I was filled with a sense that I would soon become *perfect.* My mother and father would adore me. I would be beyond reproach. I would never feel the need to sulk for anything.

But sometimes the prodigy in me became impatient. "If you don't hurry up and get me out of here, I'm disappearing for good," it warned. "And then you'll always be nothing."

Every night after dinner, my mother and I would sit at the Formica kitchen table. She would present new tests, taking her examples from stories of amazing children she had read in *Ripley's Believe It or Not,* or *Good Housekeeping, Reader's Digest,* and a dozen other magazines she kept in a pile in our bathroom. My mother got these magazines from people whose houses she cleaned. And since she cleaned many houses each week, we had a great assortment. She would look through them all, searching for stories about remarkable children.

The first night she brought out a story about a three-year-old boy who knew the capitals of all the states and even most of the European countries. A teacher was quoted as saying the little boy could also pronounce the names of the foreign cities correctly.

"What's the capital of Finland?" my mother asked me, looking at the magazine story.

15 All I knew was the capital of California, because Sacramento was the name of the street we lived on in Chinatown. "Nairobi!" I guessed, saying the most foreign word I could think of. She checked to see if that was possibly one way to pronounce "Helsinki" before showing me the answer.

The tests got harder—multiplying numbers in my head, finding the queen of hearts in a deck of cards, trying to stand on my head without using my hands, predicting the daily temperatures in Los Angeles, New York, and London.

One night I had to look at a page from the Bible for three minutes and then report everything I could remember. "Now Jehoshaphat had riches and honor in abundance and . . . that's all I remember, Ma," I said.

And after seeing my mother's disappointed face once again, something inside of me began to die. I hated the tests, the raised hopes and failed expectations. Before going to bed that night, I looked in the mirror above the bathroom sink and when I saw only my face staring back—and that it would always be this ordinary face—I began to cry. Such a sad, ugly girl! I made high-pitched noises like a crazed animal, trying to scratch out the face in the mirror.

And then I saw what seemed to be the prodigy side of me—because I had never seen that face before. I looked at my reflection, blinking so I could see more clearly. The girl staring back at me was angry, powerful. This girl and I were the same. I had new thoughts, willful thoughts, or rather thoughts filled with lots of won'ts. I won't let her change me, I promised myself. I won't be what I'm not.

20 So now on nights when my mother presented her tests, I performed listlessly, my head propped on one arm. I pretended to be bored. And I was. I got so bored I started counting the bellows of the foghorns out on the bay while my mother drilled me in other areas. The sound was comforting and reminded me of the cow jumping over the moon. And the next day, I played a game with myself, seeing if my mother would give up on me before eight bellows. After a while I usually counted only one, maybe two bellows at most. At last she was beginning to give up hope.

Two or three months had gone by without any mention of my being a prodigy again. And then one day my mother was watching *The Ed Sullivan Show* on TV. The TV was old and the sound kept shorting out. Every time my mother got halfway up from the sofa to adjust the set, the sound would go back on and Ed would be talking. As soon as she sat down, Ed would go silent again. She got up, the TV broke into loud piano music. She sat down. Silence. Up and down, back and forth, quiet and loud. It was like a stiff embraceless dance between her and the TV set. Finally she stood by the set with her hand on the sound dial.

She seemed entranced by the music, a little frenzied piano piece with this mesmerizing quality, sort of quick passages and then teasing lilting ones before it returned to the quick playful parts.

"*Ni kan*," my mother said, calling me over with hurried hand gestures, "Look here."

I could see why my mother was fascinated by the music. It was being pounded out by a little Chinese girl, about nine years old, with a Peter Pan haircut. The girl had the sauciness of a Shirley Temple. She was proudly modest like a proper Chinese child. And she also did this fancy sweep of a curtsy, so that the fluffy skirt of her white dress cascaded slowly to the floor like the petals of a large carnation.

25 In spite of these warning signs, I wasn't worried. Our family had no piano and we couldn't afford to buy one, let alone reams of sheet music and piano lessons. So I could be generous in my comments when my mother bad-mouthed the little girl on TV.

"Play note right, but doesn't sound good! No singing sound," my mother complained.

"What are you picking on her for?" I said carelessly. "She's pretty good. Maybe she's not the best, but she's trying hard." I knew almost immediately I would be sorry I said that.

"Just like you," she said. "Not the best. Because you not trying." She gave a little huff as she let go of the sound dial and sat down on the sofa.

The little Chinese girl sat down also to play an encore of "Anitra's Dance," by Grieg. I remember the song, because later on I had to learn how to play it.

Three days after watching *The Ed Sullivan Show,* my mother told me what my schedule would be for piano lessons and piano practice. She had talked to Mr. Chong, who lived on the first floor of our apartment building. Mr. Chong was a retired piano teacher and my mother had traded housecleaning services for weekly lessons and a piano for me to practice on every day, two hours a day, from four until six.

When my mother told me this, I felt as though I had been sent to hell. I whined and then kicked my foot a little when I couldn't stand it anymore.

"Why don't you like me the way I am? I'm *not* a genius! I can't play the piano. And even if I could, I wouldn't go on TV if you paid me a million dollars!" I cried.

My mother slapped me. "Who ask you be genius?" she shouted. "Only ask you be your best. For you sake. You think I want you be genius? Hnnh! What for! Who ask you!"

"So ungrateful," I heard her mutter in Chinese. "If she had as much talent as she has temper, she would be famous now."

Mr. Chong, whom I secretly nicknamed Old Chong, was very strange, always tapping his fingers to the silent music of an invisible orchestra. He looked ancient in my eyes. He had lost most of the hair on top of his head and he wore thick glasses and had eyes that always looked tired and sleepy. But he must have been younger than I thought, since he lived with his mother and was not yet married.

I met Old Lady Chong once and that was enough. She had this peculiar smell like a baby that had done something in its pants. And her fingers felt like a dead person's, like an old peach I once found in the back of the refrigerator; the skin just slid off the meat when I picked it up.

I soon found out why Old Chong had retired from teaching piano. He was deaf. "Like Beethoven!" he shouted to me. "We're both listening only in our head!" And he would start to conduct his frantic silent sonatas.

Our lessons went like this. He would open the book and point to different things, explaining their purpose: "Key! Treble! Bass! No sharps or flats! So this is C major! Listen now and play after me!"

And then he would play the C scale a few times, a simple chord, and then, as if inspired by an old, unreachable itch, he gradually added more notes and running trills and a pounding bass until the music was really something quite grand.

I would play after him, the simple scale, the simple chord, and then I just played some nonsense that sounded like a cat running up and down on top of garbage cans. Old Chong smiled and applauded and then said, "Very good! But now you must learn to keep time!"

So that's how I discovered that Old Chong's eyes were too slow to keep up with the wrong notes I was playing. He went through the motions in half-time. To help me keep rhythm, he stood behind me, pushing down on my right shoulder for every beat. He balanced pennies on top of my wrists so I would keep them still as I slowly played scales and arpeggios. He had me curve my hand around an apple and keep that shape when playing chords. He marched stiffly to show me how to make each finger dance up and down, staccato like an obedient little soldier.

He taught me all these things, and that was how I also learned I could be lazy and get away with mistakes, lots of mistakes. If I hit the wrong notes because I hadn't practiced enough, I never corrected myself. I just kept playing in rhythm. And Old Chong kept conducting his own private reverie.

So maybe I never really gave myself a fair chance. I did pick up the basics pretty quickly, and I might have become a good pianist at that young age. But I was so determined not to try, not to be anybody different that I learned to play only the most ear-splitting preludes, the most discordant hymns.

Over the next year I practiced like this, dutifully in my own way. And then one day I heard my mother and her friend Lindo Jong both talking in a loud bragging tone of voice so others could hear. It was after church, and I was leaning against the brick wall wearing a dress with stiff white petticoats. Auntie Lindo's daughter, Waverly, who was about my age, was standing farther down the wall about five feet away. We had grown up together and shared all the closeness of two sisters squabbling over crayons and dolls. In other words, for the most part, we hated each other. I thought she was snotty. Waverly Jong had gained a certain amount of fame as "Chinatown's Littlest Chinese Chess Champion."

"She bring home too many trophy," lamented Auntie Lindo that Sunday. "All day she play chess. All day I have no time do nothing but dust off her winnings." She threw a scolding look at Waverly, who pretended not to see her.

"You lucky you don't have this problem," said Auntie Lindo with a sigh to my mother.

And my mother squared her shoulders and bragged: "Our problem worser than yours. If we ask Jing-mei wash dish, she hear nothing but music. It's like you can't stop this natural talent."

And right then, I was determined to put a stop to her foolish pride.

A few weeks later, Old Chong and my mother conspired to have me play in a talent show which would be held in the church hall. By then, my parents had saved up enough to buy me a secondhand piano, a black Wurlitzer spinet with a scarred bench. It was the showpiece of our living room.

For the talent show, I was to play a piece called "Pleading Child" from Schumann's *Scenes from Childhood.* It was a simple, moody piece that sounded more difficult than it was. I was supposed to memorize the whole thing, playing the repeat parts twice to make the piece sound longer. But I dawdled over it, playing a few bars and then cheating, looking up to see what notes followed. I never really listened to what I was playing. I daydreamed about being somewhere else, about being someone else.

The part I liked to practice best was the fancy curtsy: right foot out, touch the rose on the carpet with a pointed foot, sweep to the side, left leg bends, look up and smile.

My parents invited all the couples from the Joy Luck Club to witness my debut. Auntie Lindo and Uncle Tin were there. Waverly and her two older brothers had also come. The first two rows were filled with children both younger and older than I was. The littlest ones got to go first. They recited simple nursery rhymes, squawked out tunes on miniature violins, twirled Hula Hoops, pranced in pink ballet tutus, and when they bowed or curtsied, the audience would sigh in unison, "Awww," and then clap enthusiastically.

When my turn came, I was very confident. I remember my childish excitement. It was as if I knew, without a doubt, that the prodigy side of me really did exist. I had no fear whatsoever, no nervousness. I remember thinking to myself, This is it! This is it! I looked out over the audience, at my mother's blank face, my father's yawn, Auntie Lindo's stiff-lipped smile, Waverly's sulky expression. I had on a white dress layered with sheets of lace, and a pink bow in my Peter Pan haircut. As I sat down I envisioned people jumping to their feet and Ed Sullivan rushing up to introduce me to everyone on TV.

And I started to play. It was so beautiful. I was so caught up in how lovely I looked that at first I didn't worry how I would sound. So it was a surprise to me when I hit the first wrong note and I realized something didn't sound quite right. And then I hit another and another followed that. A chill started at the top of my head and began to trickle down. Yet I couldn't stop playing, as though my hands were bewitched. I kept thinking my fingers would adjust themselves back, like a train switching to the right track. I played this strange jumble through two repeats, the sour notes staying with me all the way to the end.

When I stood up, I discovered my legs were shaking. Maybe I had just been nervous and the audience, like Old Chong, had seen me go through the right motions and had not heard anything wrong at all. I swept my right foot out, went down on my knee, looked up and smiled. The room was quiet, except for Old Chong, who was beaming and shouting, "Bravo! Bravo! Well done!" But then I saw my mother's face, her stricken face. The audience clapped weakly, and as I walked back to my chair, with my whole face quivering as I tried not to cry, I heard a little boy whisper loudly to his mother, "That was awful," and the mother whispered back, "Well, she certainly tried."

And now I realized how many people were in the audience, the whole world it seemed. I was aware of eyes burning into my back. I felt the shame of my mother and father as they sat stiffly throughout the rest of the show.

We could have escaped during intermission. Pride and some strange sense of honor must have anchored my parents to their chairs. And so we watched it all: the eighteen-year-old boy with a fake moustache who did a magic show and juggled flaming hoops while riding a unicycle. The breasted girl with white makeup who sang from *Madame Butterfly* and got honorable mention. And the eleven-year-old boy who won first prize playing a tricky violin song that sounded like a busy bee.

After the show, the Hsus, the Jongs, and the St. Clairs from the Joy Luck Club, came up to my mother and father.

"Lots of talented kids," Auntie Lindo said vaguely, smiling broadly.

"That was somethin' else," said my father, and I wondered if he was referring to me in a humorous way, or whether he even remembered what I had done.

Waverly looked at me and shrugged her shoulders. "You aren't a genius like me," she said matter-of-factly. And if I hadn't felt so bad, I would have pulled her braids and punched her stomach.

But my mother's expression was what devastated me: a quiet, blank look that said she had lost everything. I felt the same way, and it seemed as if everybody were now coming up, like gawkers at the scene of an accident, to see what parts were actually missing. When we got on the bus to go home, my father was humming the busy-bee tune and my mother was silent. I kept thinking she wanted to wait until we got home before shouting at me. But when my father unlocked the door to our apartment, my mother walked in and then went to the back, into the bedroom. No accusations. No blame. And in a way, I felt disappointed. I had been waiting for her to start shouting, so I could shout back and cry and blame her for all my misery.

I assumed my talent-show fiasco meant I never had to play the piano again. But two days later, after school, my mother came out of the kitchen and saw me watching TV.

"Four clock," she reminded me as if it were any other day. I was stunned, as though she were asking me to go through the talent-show torture again. I wedged myself more tightly in front of the TV.

"Turn off TV," she called from the kitchen five minutes later.

I didn't budge. And then I decided. I didn't have to do what my mother said anymore. I wasn't her slave. This wasn't China. I had listened to her before and look what happened. She was the stupid one.

She came out from the kitchen and stood in the arched entryway of the living room. "Four clock," she said once again, louder.

"I'm not going to play anymore," I said nonchalantly. "Why should I? I'm not a genius."

She walked over and stood in front of the TV. I saw her chest was heaving up and down in an angry way.

"No!" I said, and I now felt stronger, as if my true self had finally emerged. So this was what had been inside me all along.

"No! I won't!" I screamed.

She yanked me by the arm, pulled me off the floor, snapped off the TV. She was frighteningly strong, half pulling, half carrying me toward the piano as I kicked the throw rugs under my feet. She lifted me up and onto the hard bench. I was sobbing by now, looking at her bitterly. Her chest was heaving even more and her mouth was open, smiling crazily as if she were pleased I was crying.

"You want me to be someone that I'm not!" I sobbed. "I'll never be the kind of daughter you want me to be!"

"Only two kinds of daughters," she shouted in Chinese. "Those who are obedient and those who follow their own mind! Only one kind of daughter can live in this house. Obedient daughter!"

"Then I wish I wasn't your daughter. I wish you weren't my mother," I shouted. As I said these things I got scared. It felt like worms and toads and slimy things crawling out of my chest, but it also felt good, as if this awful side of me had surfaced, at last.

"Too late change this," said my mother shrilly.

And I could sense her anger rising to its breaking point. I wanted to see it spill over. And that's when I remembered the babies she had lost in China, the ones we never talked about. "Then I wish I'd never been born!" I shouted. "I wish I were dead! Like them."

It was as if I had said the magic words. Alakazam!—and her face went blank, her mouth closed, her arms went slack, and she backed out of the room, stunned, as if she were blowing away like a small brown leaf, thin, brittle, lifeless.

It was not the only disappointment my mother felt in me. In the years that followed, I failed her so many times, each time asserting my own will, my right to fall short of expectations. I didn't get straight As. I didn't become class president. I didn't get into Stanford. I dropped out of college.

For unlike my mother, I did not believe I could be anything I wanted to be. I could only be me.

And for all those years, we never talked about the disaster at the recital or my terrible accusations afterward at the piano bench. All of that remained unchecked, like a betrayal that was now unspeakable. So I never found a way to ask her why she had hoped for something so large that failure was inevitable.

And even worse, I never asked her what frightened me the most: Why had she given up hope?

For after our struggle at the piano, she never mentioned my playing again. The lessons stopped. The lid to the piano was closed, shutting out the dust, my misery, and her dreams.

So she surprised me. A few years ago, she offered to give me the piano, for my thirtieth birthday. I had not played in all those years. I saw the offer as a sign of forgiveness, a tremendous burden removed.

"Are you sure?" I asked shyly. "I mean, won't you and Dad miss it?"

"No, this your piano," she said firmly. "Always your piano. You only one can play."

"Well, I probably can't play anymore," I said. "It's been years."

"You pick up fast," said my mother, as if she knew this was certain. "You have natural talent. You could been genius if you want to."

"No I couldn't."

"You just not trying," said my mother. And she was neither angry nor sad. She said it as if to announce a fact that could never be disproved. "Take it," she said.

But I didn't at first. It was enough that she had offered it to me. And after that, every time I saw it in my parents' living room, standing in front of the bay windows, it made me feel proud, as if it were a shiny trophy I had won back.

Last week I sent a tuner over to my parents' apartment and had the piano reconditioned, for purely sentimental reasons. My mother had died a few months before and I had been getting things in order for my father, a little bit at a time. I put the jewelry in special silk pouches. The sweaters she had knitted in yellow, pink, bright orange—all the colors I hated—I put those in moth-proof boxes. I found some old Chinese silk dresses, the kind with little slits up the sides. I rubbed the old silk against my skin, then wrapped them in tissue and decided to take them home with me.

After I had the piano tuned, I opened the lid and touched the keys. It sounded even richer than I remembered. Really, it was a very good piano. Inside the bench were the same exercise notes with handwritten scales, the same secondhand music books with their covers held together with yellow tape.

I opened up the Schumann book to the dark little piece I had played at the recital. It was on the left-hand side of the page, "Pleading Child." It looked more difficult than I remembered. I played a few bars, surprised at how easily the notes came back to me.

95 And for the first time, or so it seemed, I noticed the piece on the right-hand side. It was called "Perfectly Contented." I tried to play this one as well. It had a lighter melody but the same flowing rhythm and turned out to be quite easy. "Pleading Child" was shorter but slower; "Perfectly Contented" was longer, but faster. And after I played them both a few times, I realized they were two halves of the same song.

➤ *QUESTIONS FOR READING AND WRITING*

1. The narrator, Jing-Mei, is the protagonist in this story. How does her point of view affect how and what we are told?
2. Describe Jing-Mei. What is the primary conflict she struggles with? Is it external? Internal? Both? Explain. Why is she so resistant to her mother's wishes?
3. To what extent does your background or experience affect your response to the story?
4. Describe her mother. How would she characterize Jing-Mei? What does she want for her daughter? How does her own background influence that?
5. When Jing-Mei shouts at her mother that she wishes she was not her daughter, she recalls, "As I said [this] I got scared. It felt like worms and toads and slimy things crawling out of my chest, but it also felt good, as if this awful side of me had surfaced, at last." What do you think she means?
6. After her mother dies, Jing-Mei is reunited with her piano. What does she realize about herself, her mother, and their relationship?

TWO READERS ~ TWO CHOICES

■ *EXPLORING "Everyday Use"*

Making Connections One of the more compelling aspects of Alice Walker's short story "Everyday Use" is its reminder that heritage is much more than a coat of arms or a display of historical artifacts. The legacy most of us inherit from our ancestors has been shaped not by glorious and noteworthy achievement but by quiet courage and everyday struggle.

The story reminds us, too, that in the shift from one generation to the next there is often a clash of values and a breaking away. Mama, the story's narrator, has learned and taught her lessons in the school of practical experience, a school where dirt floors and tin roofs dictate the values of physical strength, simple dignity, and humility. For one daughter, Maggie, this environment and its old-time values are a comforting refuge. But for her other daughter, Dee, these conditions are something to escape from, a reference point for how far she has come as she makes her way up through a world of formal education and the values of modern living .

Your Experiences and Beliefs Before you read "Everyday Use", you may want to consider your own experiences and beliefs as they apply to some of the issues that emerge from this story. How do you feel about your own heritage? Is it a major factor in your identity? Have you ever felt embarrassed by your family? Would you be satisfied to live the life your parents or other close family members have lived? If you have brothers or sisters, do you think of yourself as more or less ambitious than they are? What do you consider to be the measure of success? Do you think there is more to be learned through formal education or practical experience? Do you feel in control of forging your own identity?

ALICE WALKER (b. 1944)

(See biography on page 714.)

EVERYDAY USE [1973]

For Your Grandmama

I will wait for her in the yard that Maggie and I made so clean and wavy yesterday afternoon. A yard like this is more comfortable than most people know. It is not just a yard. It is like an extended living room. When the hard clay is swept clean as a floor and the fine sand around the edges lined with tiny, irregular grooves anyone can come and sit and look up into the elm tree and wait for the breezes that never come inside the house.

Maggie will be nervous until: after her sister goes: she will stand hopelessly in corners homely and ashamed of the burn scars down her arms and legs, eyeing her sister with a mixture of envy and awe. She thinks her sister has held life always in the palm of one hand, that "no" is a word the world never learned to say to her.

You've no doubt seen those TV shows where the child who has "made it" is confronted, as a surprise, by her own mother and father, tottering in weakly from backstage. (A pleasant surprise, of course: What would they do if parent and child came on the show only to curse out and insult each other?) On TV mother and child embrace and smile into each other's faces. Sometimes the mother and father weep, the child wraps them in her arms and leans across the table to tell how she would not have made it without their help. I have seen these programs.

Sometimes I dream a dream in which Dee and I are suddenly brought together on a TV program of this sort. Out of a dark and soft-seated limousine I am ushered into a bright room filled with many people. There I meet a smiling, gray, sporty man like Johnny Carson who shakes my hand and tells me what a fine girl I have. Then we are on the stage and Dee is embracing me with tears in her eyes. She pins on my dress a large orchid, even though she has told me once that she thinks orchids are tacky flowers.

5 In real life I am a large, big-boned woman with rough, man-working hands. In the winter I wear flannel nightgowns to bed and overalls during the day. I can kill and clean a hog as mercilessly as a man. My fat keeps me hot in zero weather. I can work outside all day, breaking ice to get water for washing; I can eat pork liver cooked over the open fire minutes after it comes steaming from the hog. One winter I knocked a bull calf straight in the brain between the eyes with a sledge hammer and had the meat hung up to chill before nightfall. But of course all this does not show on television. I am the way my daughter would want me to be: a hundred pounds lighter, my skin like an uncooked barley pancake. My hair glistens in the hot bright lights. Johnny Carson has much to do to keep up with my quick and witty tongue.

But that is a mistake. I know even before I wake up. Who ever knew a Johnson with a quick tongue? Who can even imagine me looking a strange white man in the eye? It seems to me I have talked to them always with one foot raised in flight, with my head turned in whichever way is farthest from them. Dee, though. She would always look anyone in the eye. Hesitation was no part of her nature.

"How do I look, Mama?" Maggie says, showing just enough of her thin body enveloped in pink skirt and red blouse for me to know she's there, almost hidden by the door.

"Come out into the yard," I say.

Have you ever seen a lame animal, perhaps a dog run over by some careless person rich enough to own a car, sidle up to someone who is ignorant enough to be kind to him? That is the way my Maggie walks. She has been like this, chin on chest, eyes on ground, feet in shuffle, ever since the fire that burned the other house to the ground.

10 Dee is lighter than Maggie, with nicer hair and a fuller figure. She's a woman now, though sometimes I forget. How long ago was it that the other house burned? Ten, twelve years? Sometimes I can still hear the flames and feel Maggie's arms sticking to me, her hair smoking and her dress falling off her in little black papery flakes. Her eyes seemed stretched open, blazed open by the flames reflected in them. And Dee. I see her standing off under the sweet gum tree she used to dig gum out of, a look of concentration on her face as she watched the last dingy gray board of the house fall in toward the red-hot brick chimney. Why don't you do a dance around the ashes? I'd wanted to ask her. She had hated the house that much.

I used to think she hated Maggie, too. But that was before we raised the money, the church and me, to send her to Augusta to school. She used to read to us without pity; forcing words, lies, other folks' habits, whole lives upon us two, sitting trapped and ignorant underneath her voice. She washed us in a river of make-believe, burned us with a lot of knowledge we didn't necessarily need to know. Pressed us to her with the serious way she read, to shove us away at just the moment, like dimwits, we seemed about to understand.

Dee wanted nice things. A yellow organdy dress to wear to her graduation from high school; black pumps to match a green suit she'd made from an old suit somebody gave me. She was determined to stare down any disaster in her efforts. Her eyelids would not flicker for minutes at a time. Often I fought off the temptation to shake her. At sixteen she had a style of her own: and knew what style was.

I never had an education myself. After second grade the school was closed down. Don't ask me why: in 1927 colored asked fewer questions than they do now. Sometimes Maggie reads to me. She stumbles along good-naturedly but can't see well. She knows she is not bright. Like good looks and money, quickness passed her by. She will marry John Thomas (who has mossy teeth in an earnest face) and then I'll be free to sit here and I guess just sing church songs to myself. Although I never was a good singer. Never could carry a tune. I was always better at a man's job. I used to love to milk till I was hooked in the side in '49. Cows are soothing and slow and don't bother you, unless you try to milk them the wrong way.

I have deliberately turned my back on the house. It is three rooms, just like the one that burned, except the roof is tin; they don't make shingle roofs any more. There are no real windows, just some holes cut in the sides, like the portholes in a ship, but not round and not square, with rawhide holding the shutters up on the outside. This house is in a pasture, too, like the other one. No doubt when Dee sees it she will want to tear it down. She wrote me once that no matter where we "choose" to live, she will manage to come see us. But she will never bring her friends. Maggie and I thought about this and Maggie asked me, "Mama, when did Dee ever *have* any friends?"

15 She had a few. Furtive boys in pink shirts hanging about on washday after school. Nervous girls who never laughed. Impressed with her they worshiped the well-turned phrase, the cute shape, the scalding humor that erupted like bubbles in lye. She read to them.

When she was courting Jimmy T she didn't have much time to pay to us, but turned all her faultfinding power on him. *He flew* to marry a cheap gal from a family of ignorant flashy people. She hardly had time to recompose herself.

When she comes I will meet—but there they are!

Maggie attempts to make a dash for the house, in her shuffling way, but I stay her with my hand. "Come back here," I say. And she stops and tries to dig a well in the sand with her toe.

It is hard to see them clearly through the strong sun. But even the first glimpse of leg out of the car tells me it is Dee. Her feet were always neat-looking, as if God himself had shaped them with a certain style. From the other side of the car comes a short, stocky man. Hair is all over his head a foot long and hanging from his chin like a kinky mule tail. I hear Maggie suck in her breath. "Uhnnnh," is what it sounds like. Like when you see the wriggling end of a snake just in front of your foot on the road. "Uhnnnh."

20 Dee next. A dress down to the ground, in this hot weather. A dress so loud it hurts my eyes. There are yellows and oranges enough to throw back the light of the sun. *I* feel my whole face warming from the heat waves it throws out. Earrings

gold, too, and hanging down to her shoulders. Bracelets dangling and making noises when she moves her arm up to shake the folds of the dress out of her armpits. The dress is loose and flows, and as she walks closer, I like it. I hear Maggie go "Uhnnnh" again. It is her sister's hair. It stands straight up like the wool on a sheep. It is black as night and around the edges are two long pigtails that rope about like small lizards disappearing behind her ears.

"Wa-su-zo-Tean-o!" she says, coming on in that gliding way the dress makes her move. The short stocky fellow with the hair to his navel is all grinning and he follows up with "Asalamalakim, my mother and sister!" He moves to hug Maggie but she falls back, right up against the back of my chair. I feel her trembling there and when I look up I see the perspiration falling off her chin.

"Don't get up," says Dee. Since I am stout it takes something of a push. You can see me trying to move a second or two before I make it. She turns, showing white heels through her sandals, and goes back to the car. Out she peeks next with a Polaroid. She stoops down quickly and lines up picture after picture of me sitting there in front of the house with Maggie cowering behind me. She never takes a shot without making sure the house is included. When a cow comes nibbling around the edge of the yard she snaps it and me and Maggie *and* the house. Then she puts the Polaroid in the back seat of the car, and comes up and kisses me on the forehead.

Meanwhile Asalamalakim is going through the motions with Maggie's hand. Maggie's hand is as limp as a fish, and probably as cold, despite the sweat, and she keeps trying to pull it back. It looks like Asalamalakim wants to shake hands but wants to do it fancy. Or maybe he don't know how people shake hands. Anyhow, he soon gives up on Maggie.

"Well," I say. "Dee."

"No, Mama," she says. "Not Dee, Wangero Leewanika Kemanjo!"

"What happened to 'Dee'?" I wanted to know.

"She's dead," Wangero said. "I couldn't bear it any longer being named after the people who oppress me."

"You know as well as me you was named after your aunt Dicie," I said. Dicie is my sister. She named Dee. We called her "Big Dee" after Dee was born.

"But who was *she* named after?" asked Wangero.

"I guess after Grandma Dee," I said.

"And who was she named after?" asked Wangero.

"Her mother," I said, and saw Wangero was getting tired. "That's about as far back as I can trace it," I said. Though, in fact, I probably could have carried it back beyond the Civil War through the branches.

"Well," said Asalamalakim, "there you are."

"Uhnnnh," I heard Maggie say.

"There I was not," I said, "before 'Dicie' cropped up in our family, so why should I try to trace it that far back?"

He just stood there grinning, looking down on me like somebody inspecting Model A car. Every once in a while he and Wangero sent eye signals over my head.

"How do you pronounce this name?" I asked.

"You don't have to call me by it if you don't want to," said Wangero.

Why shouldn't 1?" I asked. "If that's what you want us to call you, we'll call you."

40 "I know it might sound awkward at first," said Wangero.

"I'll get used to it," I said. "Ream it out again."

Well, soon we got the name out of the way. Asalamalakim had a name twice as long and three times as hard. After I tripped over it two or three times he told me to just call him Hakim-a-barber. I wanted to ask him was he a barber, but I didn't really think he was, so I didn't ask.

"You must belong to those beef-cattle peoples down the road," I said. They said "Asalamalakim" when they met you, too, but they didn't shake hands. Always too busy: feeding the cattle, fixing the fences, putting up saltlick shelters, throwing down hay. When the white folks poisoned some of the herd the men stayed up all night with rifles in their hands. I walked a mile and a half just to see the sight.

Hakim-a-barber said, "I accept some of their doctrines, but farming and raising cattle is not my style." (They didn't tell me, and I didn't ask, whether Wangero [Dee] had really gone and married him.)

45 We sat down to eat and right away he said he didn't eat collards and pork was unclean. Wangero, though, went on through the chitlins and corn bread, the greens and everything else. She talked a blue streak over the sweet potatoes. Everything delighted her. Even the fact that we still used the benches her daddy made for the table when we couldn't afford to buy chairs.

"Oh, Mama!" she cried. Then turned to Hakim-a-barber. "I never knew how lovely these benches are. You can feel the rump prints," she said, running her hands underneath her and along the bench.

Then she gave a sigh and her hand closed over Grandma Dee's butter dish. "That's it!" she said. "I knew there was something I wanted to ask you if I could have." She jumped up from the table and went over in the corner where the chum stood, the milk in it clabber by now. She looked at the churn and looked at it.

"This churn top is what I need," she said. "Didn't Uncle Buddy whittle it out of a tree you all used to have?"

"Yes," I said.

50 "Uh huh," she said happily. "And I want the dasher, too."

"Uncle Buddy whittle that, too?" asked the barber.

Dee (Wangero) looked up at me.

"Aunt Dee's first husband whittled the dash," said Maggie so low you almost couldn't hear her. "His name was Henry, but they called him Stash."

"Maggie's brain is like an elephant's," Wangero said, laughing. "I can use the chum top as a centerpiece for the alcove table," she said, sliding a plate over the chum, "and I'll think of something artistic to do with the dasher."

55 When she finished wrapping the dasher the handle stuck out. I took it for a moment in my hands. You didn't even have to look close to see where hands pushing the dasher up and down to make butter had left a kind of sink in the wood. In fact, there were a lot of small sinks; you could see where thumbs and fingers had sunk into the wood. It was beautiful light yellow wood, from a tree that grew in the yard where Big Dee and Stash had lived.

After dinner Dee (Wangero) went to the trunk at the foot of my bed and started rifling through it. Maggie hung back in the kitchen over the dishpan. Out came Wangero with two quilts. They had been pieced by Grandma Dee and then

Big Dee and me had hung them on the quilt frames on the front porch and quilted them. One was in the Lone Star pattern. The other was Walk Around the Mountain. In both of them were scraps of dresses Grandma Dee had worn fifty and more years ago. Bits and pieces of Grandpa Jarrell's Paisley shirts. And one teeny faded blue piece, about the size of a penny matchbox, that was from Great Grandpa Ezra's uniform that he wore in the Civil War.

"Mama," Wangero said sweet as a bird. "Can I have these old quilts?"

I heard something fall in the kitchen, and a minute later the kitchen door slammed.

"Why don't you take one or two of the others?" I asked. "These old things was just done by me and Big Dee from some tops your grandma pieced before she died."

60 "That'll make them last better," I said.

"That's not the point," said Wangero. "These are all pieces of dresses Grandma used to wear. She did all this stitching by hand. Imagine!" She held the quilts securely in her arms, stroking them.

"Some of the pieces, like those lavender ones, come from old clothes her mother handed down to her," I said, moving up to touch the quilts. Dee (Wangero) moved back just enough so that I couldn't reach the quilts. They already belonged to her.

"Imagine!" she breathed again, clutching them closely to her bosom.

"The truth is," I said, "I promised to give them quilts to Maggie, for when she marries John Thomas."

65 She gasped like a bee had stung her.

"Maggie can't appreciate these quilts!" she said. "She'd probably be backward enough to put them to everyday use."

"I reckon she would," I said. "God knows I been saving 'em for long enough with nobody using 'em. I hope she will!" I didn't want to bring up how I had offered Dee (Wangero) a quilt when she went away to college. Then she had told me they were old-fashioned, out of style.

"But they're *priceless!*" she was saying now, furiously; for she has a temper. "Maggie would put them on the bed and in five years they'd be in rags. Less than that!"

"She can always make some more," I said. "Maggie knows how to quilt."

70 Dee (Wangero) looked at me with hatred. "You just will not understand. The point is these quilts, *these* quilts!"

"Well," I said, stumped. "What would you do with them?"

"Hang them," she said. As if that was the only thing you could do with quilts.

Maggie by now was standing in the door. I could almost hear the sound her feet made as they scraped over each other.

"She can have them, Mama," she said, like somebody used to never winning anything, or having anything reserved for her. "I can 'member Grandma Dee without the quilts."

75 I looked at her hard. She had filled her bottom lip with checkerbeny snuff and it gave her face a kind of dopey, hangdog look. It was Grandma Dee and Big Dee who taught her how to quilt herself. She stood there with her scarred hands hidden

in the folds of her skirt. She looked at her sister with something like fear but she wasn't mad at her. This was Maggie's portion. This was the way she knew God to work.

When I looked at her like that something hit me in the top of my head and ran down to the soles of my feet. just like when I'm in church and the spirit of God touches me and I get happy and shout. I did something I never had done before: hugged Maggie to me, then dragged her on into the room, snatched the quilts out of Miss Wangero's hands and dumped them into Maggie's lap. Maggie just sat there on my bed with her mouth open.

"Take one or two of the others," I said to Dee.

But she turned without a word and went out to Hakim-a-barber.

"You just don't understand," she said, as Maggie and I came out to the car.

80 "What don't I understand?" I wanted to know.

"Your heritage," she said. And then she turned to Maggie, kissed her, and said, "You ought to try to make something of yourself, too, Maggie. It's really a new day for us. But from the way you and Mama still live you'd never know it."

She put on some sunglasses that hid everything above the tip of her nose and her chin.

Maggie smiled; maybe at the sunglasses. But a real smile, not scared. After we watched the car dust settle I asked Maggie to bring me a dip of snuff. And then the two of us sat there just enjoying, until it was time to go in the house and go to bed.

➤ *QUESTIONS FOR READING AND WRITING*

1. To what extent does your own background or experience influence your response to "Everyday Use"?
2. This story is told from Mama's point of view. In what way does that affect how and what you are told? If the story were told from Dee's point of view, how would it differ? Cite some examples from the text.
3. The setting of "Everyday Use" seems to mean something different to each of the characters. What does it mean to Mama? To Dee? To Maggie?
4. If you were in Dee's situation, would you have acted differently? Would you see the quilt as a valuable artifact or something to be used every day? Explain.
5. Is the title of the story appropriate? How so? How would you define *everyday use?*

~ TWO STUDENT PAPERS

Depending on your experience of it, "Everyday Use" is a story about many different things. You may experience it as a story about heritage and identity, tradition versus change, lack of communication between generations, ingratitude, formal education versus experience, or any number of other issues.

In his response essay, Alejandro Ramos identifies with Dee's search to find her heritage and compares it to his own struggle to find his ethnic identity in his Hispanic and African-American roots. In her critical essay, Debora VanCoughnett, disagrees with the beliefs expressed by Dee, and argues that Dee has learned much less about her heritage through her formal education than Mama and Maggie know and understand through their experience. She criticizes the superficiality of Dee's claim to her heritage when compared with the "real" respect it is given as lived every day by her mother and sister.

Alejandro Ramos Jr.

Dr. Madden

English 102

October 15, 200X

The Conflict of Change

History has shown us that as time wears on traditions give way to change. Along with change, conflicts have always emerged between two great forces: the forces of the old and tradition and the forces of the new and change. This conflict is often seen between parents and their children. An excellent example of this conflict of old and new between parent and child is seen in Alice Walker's story "Everyday Use." At the core of this conflict is a search for heritage and identity.

Mama and Maggie represent the old way of living. They live off the land, do things for themselves, and accept life the way it has always been. However, Mama's other daughter Dee (Wangero Leewanika Kemanjo) represents a new way of living and thinking. She is educated and believes in fighting for her rights. She has gone through an identity crisis and says she has found herself. When she is asked by her mother what happened to "Dee," the name she was given at birth (and a name that had been in her family since before the Civil War) she says, "She's dead. I couldn't bear it any longer, being named after the people who oppress me" (874). She not only changed her name, but she changed her hairstyle and way of dressing. She has new ideas, too, and a different attitude toward the world. Mama says, "Who can even imagine me looking a strange white man in the eye? It seems to me I have talked to them always with one foot raised in flight, with my head turned in whichever way is farthest from them. Dee, though. She would always look anyone in the eye. Hesitation was no part of her nature" (872).

Dee is not willing to accept things as they have been, especially the old relationship between whites and blacks.

Unlike Dee, Mama and Maggie are not educated. Mama says, "I never had an education myself. After second grade the school was closed down. Don't ask me why: in 1927 colored asked fewer questions than they do now. Sometimes Maggie reads to me. She stumbles along good-naturedly but can't see well. She knows she is not bright" (873). But Dee is bright and educated and won't settle for the life that Mama and Maggie have accepted.

This story reminds me of my own identity crisis. Like Dee's mother, my father believed that life is a certain way and one just accepted it. He was easygoing and believed in working hard and making sure that everything was in order. He was amused by my "identity crisis" and wondered what the fuss was all about.

To me, however, my ethnic identity was very important. My crisis, whether I was African-American or Spanish, came about primarily because of my friends. My Spanish friends said that I was African-American, and my African-American friends claimed that I was Spanish. Since each group defined me as being from the other, I felt very isolated and alone. I didn't feel like I really belonged to either group. Unlike Dee, I didn't resolve my conflict by changing my name, hairstyle, or style of dress. I finally accepted the fact that I was both Spanish and African-American and learned to enjoy being bicultural.

I am sure that Dee's identification problem was not brought about entirely by herself, either. She was influenced by people, like Hakim-a-barber, who were her friends. She was also influenced by her education. Mama identifies the source of her conflict with Dee best when she says that Dee " . . . used to read to us without pity; forcing words, lies, other folks' habits, whole lives upon us two, sitting trapped and ignorant underneath her voice. She washed us in a river of make believe, burned us with a lot of knowledge we didn't necessarily need to know" (872). To Mama, this book knowledge is "lies" and "knowledge we didn't . . . need to know." To Dee this knowledge is the source of her heritage and very important to her.

Mama and Maggie don't have sophisticated, knowledgeable friends or a formal education. Their identity is connected to everyday living and the way things have always been—even if some of these things are not as they should be. They represent the forces of the old and tradition. Dee's identity and her sense of heritage come from books and an appreciation of her African culture, not as she has lived them, but as she has read about them. She represents the forces of the new and change. As is usually the case in conflicts between the forces of old and new, both sides would benefit a great deal by listening to and learning from each other.

Work Cited

Walker, Alice. "Everyday Use." Exploring Literature. Ed. Frank Madden. New York: Longman, 2001, 871-877.

Debora VanCoughnett

Dr. Madden

English 102

October 16, 200X

Using Heritage Every Day

In the short story "Everyday Use," by Alice Walker, Dee accuses her mother of not understanding her heritage, yet Dee herself denies her own true roots. Not only does she change her name, trying to become someone she isn't, but she criticizes her mother and sister for living the way they do. Maggie and her mother, however, are the only ones in this family who can truly grasp their heritage.

When Dee comes back home after being educated and modernized, she tells her mother that the old "Dee" is dead and that her new name is "Wangero Leewanika Kemanjo." She says "I couldn't bear it any longer being named after the people who oppress me" (874). Despite her educated comment, Dee didn't even know the origin of her own name. Her mother tells her she was named for her aunt and generations of ancestors going back before the Civil War, not a white slaveholder. The name Dee has chosen may be connected to her African ancestry, but it is not connected to her personal heritage. It is she who doesn't understand her heritage, not her mother.

As Mama describes her, Dee seems only concerned with appearances: "At sixteen she had a style of her own: and knew what style was" (873). She is much more physically attractive than Maggie who moves like a " . . . lame animal, perhaps a dog run over by some careless person . . . . [she] walks . . . chin on chest, eyes on the ground, feet in shuffle" (872). This is obviously not a style Dee would find acceptable. Mama's style and appearance are no doubt an embarrassment to her as well. Mama describes herself as " . . . a large big boned woman with rough, man-working hands. In the winter I wear flannel nightgowns to bed and overalls during the day. I can kill and clean a hog as mercilessly as a man. My fat keeps me hot in zero weather" (872). It's no wonder that Dee wrote to her once that " . . . no matter where we 'choose' to live, she will manage to come see us. But she will never bring her friends" (873). It's obvious that she is ashamed of Mama and Maggie and doesn't want anyone else to know about them except under her terms.

Dee concerns herself too much with appearances. She dresses so others have to take notice. She wears a " . . . dress so loud it hurt [Mama's] eyes" (873). She takes Polaroids of her family, making sure that the house or even a cow was in each shot. She is not taking these pictures because she is proud of where she is from; she only wants to show off—to let her friends know how pitiful her family home is and far she has come to get where she is.

When Dee asks her mother for the quilts, she comments that Maggie would " . . . probably be backward enough to put them to everyday use" (876). She also wants the churn and the dasher that her mother still uses on a daily basis, but Dee wants to use them " . . . as a centerpiece for the alcove table" (875). That was not what Uncle Biddy whittled them for, or why Grandma stitched the quilts. They are meant for everyday use, not merely for display. It is Dee's total misconception of the real meaning behind the quilts that points to her ignorance, not her family's. In this respect, Mama and Maggie are the educated ones. Her grandmother made them to be used, not to be hung on the wall and admired.

It is very ironic for Dee (Wangero) to have the audacity to tell her mother that she (Mama) does not understand her heritage. It is true that her mother and Maggie do not have a formal education and are not attractive nor stylish, but they experience their heritage every day. No matter what Dee has learned from books and schooling, or how stylish she is with her African name or dress, it was she, not her family, who didn't have a clue to what her heritage was really like.

Work Cited

Walker, Alice. "Everyday Use." Exploring Literature. Ed. Frank Madden. New York: Longman, 2001, 871-877.

◆ **POETRY** ◆

SHERMAN ALEXIE (b. 1966)

Sherman Alexie achieved a goal by having ten books of poetry and fiction published before he turned thirty. In 2000, he's added another two.

His very first book, The Business of Fancydancing *(Hanging Loose Press, 1992) was chosen as a New York Times Notable Book of the Year and reviewer James R. Kincaid wrote: "Mr. Alexie's is one of the major lyric voices of our time." Alexie's latest poetry collection is* One Stick Song *(Hanging Loose) and his latest fiction collection is* The Toughest Indian in the World *(Atlantic Monthly Press). A film,* Smoke Signals, *for which he wrote a script adapted from one of the short stories in his book* The Lone Ranger and Tonto Fistfight in Heaven, *has won rave reviews and large audiences. He is presently involved with new film projects and a new novel. He has also written criticism and articles.*

Alexie's poems and stories have appeared very widely, and he has read from his work in virtually every state as well as in several European countries. Among many awards, he has won a Lila Wallace-Reader's Digest Writer's Award, an American Book Award, and a Creative Writing Fellowship from the National Endowment for the Arts.

An enrolled Spokane/Coeur d'Alene Indian, Alexie was born on the Spokane reservation in Wellpinit, Washington, in 1966. He is very active in the American Indian community and frequently gives workshops. He now lives in Seattle with his wife and infant son.

ON THE AMTRAK FROM BOSTON TO NEW YORK CITY [1993]

The white woman across the aisle from me says, "Look,
look at all the history, that house
on the hill there is over two hundred years old,"
as she points out the window past me

into what she has been taught. I have learned
little more about American history during my few days
back East than what I expected and far less
of what we should all know of the tribal stories

whose architecture is 15,000 years older
than the corners of the house that sits
museumed on the hill. "Walden Pond,"°
the woman on the train asks, "Did you see Walden Pond?"

and I don't have a cruel enough heart to break
her own by telling her there are five Walden Ponds
on my little reservation out West
and at least a hundred more surrounding Spokane,

the city I pretend to call my home. "Listen,
"I could have told her. "I don't give a shit
about Walden. I know the Indians were living stories
around that pond before Walden's grandparents were born.

and before his grandparents' grandparents were born
I'm tired of hearing about Don-fucking-Henley° saving it too,
because that's redundant. If Don Henley's brothers and sisters
and mothers and fathers hadn't come here in the first place

then nothing would need to be saved."
But I didn't say a word to the woman about Walden
Pond because she smiled so much and seemed delighted
that I thought to bring her an orange juice

back from the food car. I respect elders
of every color. All I really did was eat
my tasteless sandwich, drink my Diet Pepsi
and nod my head whenever the woman pointed out

another little piece of her country's history
while I, as all Indians have done
since this war began, made plans
for what I would do and say the next time

somebody from the enemy thought I was one of their own.

[11]**Walden Pond** the place where Henry David Thoreau (1817–1862) lived and about which he wrote his most famous book, *Walden* (1854) [22]**Don Henley** a rock singer who helped protect Walden from commercial development

➤ *QUESTIONS FOR READING AND WRITING*

1. What is the significance of the title? Do you think the Amtrak between Boston and New York is an appropriate setting? Why or why not?
2. In what way is the speaker's Native-American heritage a factor in this poem? Why does he refer to the white woman as "the enemy"?

Gloria Anzaldúa (b. 1942)

Gloria Anzaldúa was born in southern Texas of Mexican, Native-American, and Anglo ancestry. Her mixed background has served as the major influence on her writing. She has taught at the University of Texas at Austin, San Francisco State University, the University of California at Santa Cruz, and Vermont College. "To Live in the Borderlands Means You" is taken from her critically acclaimed book Borderlands / LaFrontera: The New Mestiza.

To Live in the Borderlands Means You [1987]

[To live in the Borderlands means you]
are neither *hispana india negra española*
ni gabacha,° *eres mestiza, mulata,* half-breed
caught in the crossfire between camps
while carrying all five races on your back
not knowing which side to turn to, run from;

To live in the Borderlands means knowing
  that the *india* in you,
  betrayed for 500 years,
  is no longer speaking to you,
  that *mexicanas* call you *rajetas,*°
  that denying the Anglo inside you
  is as bad as having denied
  the Indian or Black;

Cuando vives en la frontera
  people walk through you, the wind steals your voice,
  you're a *burra, buey,* scapegoat,
  forerunner of a new race,
  half and half—both woman and man, neither—
  a new gender;

To live in the Borderlands means to
  put *chile* in the borscht,
  eat whole wheat *tortillas,*
  speak Tex-Mex with a Brooklyn accent;
  be stopped by *la migra* at the border checkpoints;

3 **gabacha** a white woman   11 **rajetas** "split"

Living in the Borderlands means you fight hard to
resist the gold elixir beckoning from the bottle,
the pull of the gun barrel,
the rope crushing the hollow of your throat;

In the Borderlands
you are the battleground
where enemies are kin to each other;
you are at home, a stranger,
the border disputes have been settled
the volley of shots have shattered the truce
you are wounded, lost in action
dead, fighting back;

To live in the Borderlands means
the mill with the razor white teeth wants to shred off
your olive-red skin, crush out the kernel, your heart
pound you pinch you roll you out
smelling like white bread but dead;

To survive the Borderlands
you must live *sin fronteras*
be a crossroads.

QUESTIONS FOR READING AND WRITING

1. What are the "Borderlands"? Is this solely a geographical location? To what extent do you, your family, or friends live in the Borderlands?
2. In the last stanza, what does the speaker mean by "to survive the Borderlands / you must . . . / be a crossroads"?

MARGARET ATWOOD (b. 1939)

(See biography on page 565.)

THIS IS A PHOTOGRAPH OF ME [1966]

It was taken some time ago.
At first it seems to be
a smeared
print: blurred lines and grey flecks
blended with the paper;

then, as you scan
it, you see in the left-hand corner
a thing that is like a branch: part of a tree
(balsam or spruce) emerging
and, to the right, halfway up
what ought to be a gentle
slope, a small frame house.

In the background there is a lake,
and beyond that, some low hills.
(The photograph was taken
the day after I drowned.

I am in the lake, in the center
of the picture, just under the surface.

it is difficult to say where
precisely, or to say
how large or small I am:
the effect of water
on light is a distortion

but if you look long enough,
eventually
you will be able to see me.)

➤ *QUESTIONS FOR READING AND WRITING*

1. The title also serves as the first line of the poem. What is the effect of this device? If there were no title, what would be lost?
2. What is the mood of this poem? What is the speaker's attitude to the photograph? Why do you think that she wants you to look at it? Why do you think the picture is so hard to see clearly?
3. What do you think the speaker means she says she is " . . . just under the surface. / it is difficult to say where"?

W. H. AUDEN (1907–1973)

W[ystan] H[ugh] Auden was born in York, England, and educated at Oxford University. Like many intellectuals of his generation, his left-wing politics led him to serve on the loyalist side of the Spanish Civil War, but Auden quickly became disillusioned after witnessing the destruction and looting of Roman Catholic churches and returned to England. He immigrated to America in 1939, becoming a citizen in 1946. In 1947, he coined the term "the Age of Anxiety" in a long poem of the same name, which has since served as a shorthand term for the intellectual mood of the mid-twentieth century. His early work is characterized by his sharp wit and facility with elaborate verse forms. His later work, influenced by his reawakening interest in Christianity, became increasingly religious in tone.

The Unknown Citizen [1940]

To
SOCIAL SECURITY ACCOUNT NUMBER 067-01-9818
THIS MARBLE MONUMENT IS ERECTED BY THE STATE

He was found by the Bureau of Statistics to be
One against whom there was no official complaint,
And all the reports on his conduct agree
That, in the modern sense of an old-fashioned word, he was a saint,
For in everything he did he served the Greater Community.
Except for the war, till the day he retired
He worked in one factory and never got fired,
But satisfied his employers, Fudge Motors, Inc.,
Yet was neither a scab nor odd in his views,
For his Union reports that he paid his dues
(Our report on his Union says it was sound),
And our Social Psychology workers found
He was popular with his mates and liked a drink.
The Press are convinced that he bought a paper every day,
And that his reactions to advertisements were normal in every way.
Policies taken out in his name prove that he was fully insured,
And a certificate shows that he was once in hospital but left it cured.
Both *Producer's Research* and *High Grade Living* declare
He was fully sensible to the advantages of the Installment Plan,
And had everything necessary to the Modern Man—
A victrola, a radio, a car, and a frigidaire.
Our investigators into Public Opinion are content
That he held the proper opinions for the time of year;
When there was peace, he was for peace; when there was war, he went.
He was married and added five children to the population,
Which, our eugenist says, was the right number for a parent of his generation,
And our teachers report that he never interfered with their education.
Was he free? Was he happy? The question is absurd;
Had anything been wrong, we should certainly have heard.

➤ *QUESTIONS FOR READING AND WRITING*

1. What is the tone of this poem? What lines in the poem indicate this?
2. This poem was written in 1940, so a few of the unknown citizen's possessions are not state-of-the-art. Can you update them to present-day equivalents?
3. Based on what is said about him, who is "the Unknown Citizen"? Was he "free"? Was he "happy"? Is the question absurd?

GWENDOLYN BROOKS (b. 1917)

Born in Topeka, Kansas, Gwendolyn Brooks was raised on the South Side of Chicago. She graduated from Wilson Junior College in 1936, and married in 1939. Though Brooks began writing poetry as a child she did not find her vocation until she entered a poetry workshop at a local community arts center in the early 1940s. Influenced by Langston Hughes and other poets of the Harlem Renaissance, Brooks attempted to wed the familiar idiom and rhythms of the colloquial speech of Chicago's South Side to the traditional poetic forms she encountered in the workshop. Her first collection of poetry, A Street in Bronzeville, *appeared in 1945. In 1949, with the publication of* Annie Allen, *she became the first African-American woman awarded the Pulitzer Prize. After attending a conference of African-American writers at Fisk University in 1967, Brooks became convinced that "black poets should write as blacks, about blacks, and address themselves to blacks." As a result, she became a devoted teacher of writing, particularly in the African-American community, and abandoned her New York publisher in favor of small African-American presses. In addition to numerous volumes of poetry, she has published children's books. a novel,* Maud Martha *(1953), and an autobiography* Report from Part I *(1972). Brooks, who has received over fifty honorary degrees, still resides on Chicago's South Side.*

WE REAL COOL

[1960]

The Pool Players.
Seven at the Golden Shovel.

We real cool. We
Left school. We

Lurk late. We
Strike straight. We

Sing sin. We
Thin gin. We

Jazz June. We
Die soon.

➤ *QUESTIONS FOR READING AND WRITING*

1. Who is the speaker in this poem?
2. What is the relationship between rhyme and rhythm and meaning in this poem?
3. Were you surprised by the last line? Explain.

E.E. CUMMINGS (1894–1962)

E[dwin] E[stlin] Cummings was born in Cambridge, Massachusetts. He began writing poetry as a child, and claimed that he wrote at least one poem a day between the ages of eight and twenty-two. He attended Harvard University, earning a B.A. degree in 1915 and an M.A. in 1916. During World War I, he served as an ambulance driver and was confined for a time in a French internment camp for what proved to be a mistaken suspicion of treason. In 1922, he wrote of these experiences in his novel The Enormous Room, *which proved to be a great critical success. In the 1920s, he published the collections of poetry—including* & *(1925),* XLI Poems *(1925), and* is 5 *(1926)—that would establish him as America's foremost avant-garde poet. His* Complete Poems: 1910 to 1962 *was published in 1980. Though his poems employ slang, dialect, and all kinds of typographical games, they are often much more accessible than they immediately appear.*

anyone lived in a pretty how town [1940]

anyone lived in a pretty how town
(with up so floating many bells down)
spring summer autumn winter
he sang his didn't he danced his did.

Women and men (both little and small)
cared for anyone not at all
they sowed their isn't they reaped their same
sun moon stars rain

children guessed (but only a few
and down they forgot as up they grew
autumn winter spring summer)
that noone loved him more by more

when by now and tree by leaf
she laughed his joy she cried his grief,
bird by snow and stir by still
anyone's any was all to her

someones married their everyones
laughed their cryings and did their dance
(sleep wake hope and then) they
said their nevers they slept their dream

stars rain sun moon
(and only the snow can begin to explain
how children are apt to forget to remember
with up so floating many bells down)

one day anyone died i guess
(and noone stooped to kiss his face)
busy folk buried them side by side
little by little and was by was

all by all and deep by deep
and more by more they dream their sleep
noone and anyone earth by april
wish by spirit and if by yes.

Women and men (both dong and ding)
summer autumn winter spring
reaped their sowing and went their came
sun moon stars rain

➤ *QUESTIONS FOR READING AND WRITING*

1. How was your reading affected by the unusual style of the writing? Pick out some lines and describe what you think they mean.
2. Who is "anyone"?
3. What do you think the poem means?

Paul Laurence Dunbar

(1872–1906)

Paul Laurence Dunbar was born and raised in Dayton, Ohio. Both of his parents had been slaves. Dunbar excelled in high school, where he was the only African-American in his class, and served both as the class president and class poet. While in high school, he worked as an editor at the Dayton Tattler, *a short-lived newspaper for blacks. His widowed mother's financial situation ruled out college, and, unable to find a position as a writer because of his race, he found work at a number of jobs (including one as an elevator operator), which allowed him the leisure to continue writing and publishing poems. By 1892 he had earned enough recognition that he could pursue a literary career. He wrote prolifically but was plagued by ill health. In 1906, at the age of thirty-three, he died of tuberculosis. Though he is best know for his poems, which were the first to incorporate African-American speech, Dunbar published numerous novels, short stories, and essays.*

We Wear the Mask [1895]

We wear the mask that grins and lies,
It hides our cheeks and shades our eyes—
This debt we pay to human guile;
With torn and bleeding hearts we smile,
And mouth with myriad subtleties.

Why should the world be over-wise,
In counting all our tears and sighs?
Nay, let them only see us, while
    We wear the mask.

We smile, but, O great Christ, our cries
To thee from tortured souls arise.
We sing, but oh the clay is vile

Beneath our feet, and long the mile;
But let the world dream otherwise,
    We wear the mask!

➤ *QUESTIONS FOR READING AND WRITING*

1. Who is the "we" the speaker refers to?
2. What does the "mask" look like? What are the different forms it takes?
3. To what extent does the year in which the poem was published amplify its content?

T. S. Eliot (1888–1965)

Born to a wealthy family in St. Louis, Missouri, T[homas] S[tearns] Eliot attended Harvard University, where he studied literature as an undergraduate, and, as a graduate student, Sanskrit and philosophy. After further studies at the Sorbonne and Oxford University, he settled in England in 1915, taking a job first at an insurance company and later in publishing, becoming a British citizen in 1926. Eliot, with his first volume of poetry, Prufrock and Other Observations *(1917), and the 1922 publication of "The Waste Land," transformed the landscape of modern poetry, shattering literary conventions in order to give voice to what he felt was the spiritual emptiness of the modern world. An influential critic, he also wrote verse plays, including* Murder in the Cathedral *(1935) and* The Cocktail Party *(1949). He was awarded the Nobel Prize in 1948. Recent biographies of Eliot have not always treated him kindly, and there is*

much scholarly debate on the extent and importance of his anti-Semitism. Nevertheless, Eliot remains perhaps the most influential poet of the twentieth century.

THE LOVE SONG OF J. ALFRED PRUFROCK [1917]

S'io credessi che mia risposta fosse
A persona che mai tornasse al mondo,
Questa fiamma staria senza più scosse.
Ma per ciò che giammai di questo fondo
Non tornò vivo alcun, s'i'odo il vero,
Senza tema d'infamia ti rispondo.°

Let us go then, you and I,
When the evening is spread out against the sky
Like a patient etherised upon a table;
Let us go, through certain half-deserted streets,
The muttering retreats
Of restless nights in one-night cheap hotels
And sawdust restaurants with oyster-shells:
Streets that follow like a tedious argument
Of insidious intent
To lead you to an overwhelming question . . .
Oh, do not ask, "What is it?"
Let us go and make our visit.

In the room the women come and go
Talking of Michelangelo.°

The yellow fog that rubs its back upon the window-panes,
The yellow smoke that rubs its muzzle on the window-panes,
Licked its tongue into the corners of the evening,
Lingered upon the pools that stand in drains,
Let fall upon its back the soot that falls from chimneys,
Slipped by the terrace, made a sudden leap,
And seeing that it was a soft October night,
Curled once about the house, and fell asleep.

And indeed there will be time
For the yellow smoke that slides along the street
Rubbing its back upon the window-panes;
There will be time, there will be time
To prepare a face to meet the faces that you meet;
There will be time to murder and create,

[6]The statement introducing the confession of the poet Guido da Montefeltro in Dante's *Inferno* (1321). canto xxcii, 61–66. "If I thought I was speaking to someone who would go back to the world, this flame would shake no more. But since nobody has ever gone back alive from this place, if what I hear is true. I answer you without fear of infamy." [20]**Michelangelo** (1474–1564) the most famous artist of the Italian Renaissance

And time for all the works and days° of hands
That lift and drop a question on your plate;
Time for you and time for me,
And time yet for a hundred indecisions,
And for a hundred visions and revisions,
Before the taking of a toast and tea.

In the room the women come and go
Talking of Michelangelo.

And indeed there will be time
To wonder, "Do I dare?" and, "Do I dare?"
Time to turn back and descend the stair,
With a bald spot in the middle of my hair—
[They will say: "How his hair is growing thin!"]
My morning coat, my collar mounting firmly to the chin,
My necktie rich and modest, but asserted by a simple pin—
[They will say: "But how his arms and legs are thin!"]
Do I dare
Disturb the universe?
In a minute there is time
For decisions and revisions which a minute will reverse.

For I have known them all already, known them all—
Have known the evenings, mornings, afternoons,
I have measured out my life with coffee spoons;
I know the voices dying with a dying fall
Beneath the music from a farther room.
  So how should I presume?

And I have known the eyes already, known them all—
The eyes that fix you in a formulated phrase,
And when I am formulated, sprawling on a pin,
When I am pinned and wriggling on the wall,
Then how should I begin
To spit out all the butt-ends of my days and ways?
  And how should I presume?

And I have known the arms already, known them all—
Arms that are braceleted and white and bare
[But in the lamplight, downed with light brown hair!°]
Is it perfume from a dress
That makes me so digress?

[35]**works and days** possibly an allusion to *Works and Days,* a poem giving practical advice on farming by the Greek poet Hestod (8th Century B.C.) [70]see Shakespeare's *Twelfth Night* (1623), Act I Scene I 1–4

Arms that lie along a table, or wrap about a shawl.
    And should I then presume?
    And how should I begin?

. . . . .

Shall I say, I have gone at dusk through narrow streets
And watched the smoke that rises from the pipes
Of lonely men in shirt-sleeves, leaning out of windows? . . .

I should have been a pair of ragged claws
Scuttling across the floors of silent seas.

. . . . .

And the afternoon, the evening, sleeps so peacefully!
Smoothed by long fingers,
Asleep . . . tired . . . or it malingers,
Stretched on the floor, here beside you and me.
Should I, after tea and cakes and ices,
Have the strength to force the moment to its crisis?
But though I have wept and fasted, wept and prayed,
Though I have seen my head [grown slightly bald] brought in upon a platter°,
I am no prophet—and here's no great matter;
I have seen the moment of my greatness flicker,
And I have seen the eternal Footman hold my coat, and snicker,
And in short, I was afraid.

And would it have been worth it, after all,
After the cups, the marmalade, the tea,
Among the porcelain, among some talk of you and me,
Would it have been worth while,
To have bitten off the matter with a smile,
To have squeezed the universe into a ball°
To roll it toward some overwhelming question,
To say: "I am Lazarus°, come from the dead.
Come back to tell you all, I shall tell you all"—
If one, settling a pillow by her head,
    Should say: "That is not what I meant at all.
    That is not it, at all."

And would it have been worth it, after all,
Would it have been worth while,
After the sunsets and the dooryards and the sprinkled streets,
After the novels, after the teacups, after the skirts that trail along the floor—
And this, and so much more?—

[88] An allusion to John the Baptist, the New Testament prophet, whose head was presented to Queen Herodias on a charger Matthew 14:3–11. [98]see Andrew Marvell's "To His Coy Mistress" (1681), lines 41–42, p. 574. [100]**Lazarus** the man raised by Jesus from the dead. John 11:1–44.

It is impossible to say just what I mean!
But as if a magic lantern threw the nerves in patterns on a screen:
Would it have been worth while
If one, settling a pillow or throwing off a shawl,
And turning toward the window, should say:
"That is not it at all,
That is not what I meant, at all."

. . . . .

No! I am not Prince Hamlet, nor was meant to be;
Am an attendant lord, one that will do
To swell a progress, start a scene or two,
Advise the prince; no doubt, an easy tool,
Deferential, glad to be of use,
Politic, cautious, and meticulous;
Full of high sentence, but a bit obtuse;
At times, indeed, almost ridiculous—
Almost, at times, the Fool.

I grow old . . . I grow old . . .
I shall wear the bottoms of my trousers rolled.

Shall I part my hair behind? Do I dare to eat a peach?
I shall wear white flannel trousers, and walk upon the beach.
I have heard the mermaids singing, each to each.

I do not think that they will sing to me.

I have seen them riding seaward on the waves
Combing the white hair of the waves blown back
When the wind blows the water white and black.

We have lingered in the chambers of the sea
By sea-girls wreathed with seaweed red and brown
Till human voices wake us, and we drown.

➤ *QUESTIONS FOR READING AND WRITING*

1. What is the tone of the poem? How does the language in the poem convey that tone? Is this a love song, as the title indicates?
2. Who is J. Alfred Prufrock? What is his world like? He says, "I have measured out my life with coffee spoons." What do you think he means? Find other images in the poem that convey his self-image.
3. What does he mean when he says, "Do I dare / Disturb the universe?" What is he afraid of?
4. Do you ever feel like you have "To prepare a face to meet the faces that you meet."? If so, to what extent does that help you understand J. Alfred Prufrock—and this poem?

MARTIN ESPADA (b. 1957)

Martin Espada was born in Brooklyn, New York, of Puerto Rican ancestry. In 1991, he received the Peterson poetry Prize for Rebellion in the Circle of a Lover's Hands. *In addition to writing poetry, he works as a lawyer and often defends the civil rights of immigrants. He lives in Boston.*

LATIN NIGHT AT THE PAWN SHOP

Chelsea, Massachusetts
Christmas, 1987

[1987]

The apparition of a salsa band
gleaming in the Liberty Loan
pawnshop window:

Golden trumpet.
silver trombone,
congas, maracas, tambourine,
all with price tags dangling
like the city morgue ticket
on a dead man's toe.

➤ QUESTIONS FOR READING AND WRITING

1. In what way does Christmas provide an important context for this poem?
2. How do the images in the pawn shop window reflect people's lives—and deaths?

LANGSTON HUGHES (1902–1967)

One of the most important figures of the Harlem Renaissance,—a movement of African-American artists, writers, poets, and musicians in the 1920s and 1930s centered in the Harlem neighborhood of New York City—Langston Hughes was born in Joplin, Missouri, and graduated from Lincoln University in Pennsylvania. As a young man, he traveled the world as a merchant seaman, visiting Africa and living for a time in Paris and Rome. A poet, writer of fiction, playwright, lyricist,

editor, critic, and essayist, Hughes published two volumes of autobiography, The Big Sea *(1940) and* I Wonder as I Wander *(1956). Hughes's work, which is filled with the sounds and music of the African-American experience, has influenced generations of American writers.*

I, Too [1925]

I, too, sing America.

I am the darker brother.
They send me to eat in the kitchen
When company comes,
But I laugh,
And eat well,
And grow strong.

Tomorrow,
I'll sit at the table
When company comes.
Nobody'll dare
Say to me,
"Eat in the kitchen,"
Then.

Besides,
They'll see how beautiful I am
And be ashamed—

I, too, am America.

➤ *QUESTIONS FOR READING AND WRITING*

1. Who is the speaker in this poem? What does he mean by "I, Too"? Who else is he referring to?
2. Compare this poem to Dunbar's "We Wear the Mask" on page 890 or other Hughes's works in this book: "Theme for English B" on page 1164, "A Dream Deferred" on page 88, or "One Friday Morning" on page 75.
3. What other works have you read that speak to the same issue?

CLAUDE MCKAY (1889–1948)

Claude McKay was born to peasant farmers in Sunny Ville, Jamaica. Encouraged by his older brother, who was a schoolteacher, he turned to writing poetry when he was just a boy. He won an award for his first volume of poetry, Songs of Jamaica, *published in London in 1912. The award money allowed McKay to travel to the United States, where he studied for a time at the Tuskegee Institute and at Kansas State University before settling in New York City. Energized by the racism he encountered, McKay continued to write poetry, much of it political, as he became active in a number of social causes. In the 1920s, together with writers such as Langston Hughes and Zora Neale Hurston, McKay became one of the leading features of the movement known as the Harlem Renaissance.* Home to Harlem, *his 1928 novel about a black soldier's return home following World War I, was a tremendous commercial success. His other works include two novels,* Banjo: A Story Without a Plot *(1929) and* Banana Bottom *(1933), and an autobiography,* A Long Way from Home *(1937).*

America

[1921]

Although she feeds me bread of bitterness,
And sinks into my throat her tiger's tooth,
Stealing my breath of life, I will confess
I love this cultured hell that tests my youth!
Her vigor flows like tides into my blood,
Giving me strength erect against her hate.
Her bigness sweeps my being like a flood.
Yet as a rebel fronts a king in state,
I stand within her walls with not a shred
Of terror, malice, not a word of jeer.
Darkly I gaze into the days ahead,
And see her might and granite wonders there,
Beneath the touch of Time's unerring hand,
Like priceless treasures sinking in the sand.

➤ *QUESTIONS FOR READING AND WRITING*

1. Despite the abuse he experiences, the speaker says, "I love this cultured hell." Why?
2. What does he mean when he says that he sees [America] "like priceless treasures sinking in the sand"?

Pat Mora (b. 1942)

Pat Mora was born in El Paso, Texas. Her father was an ophthalmologist and her mother, a homemaker. Mora earned her B.A. degree from Texas Western College in

1963, and an M.A. in 1967 from the University of Texas at El Paso. She taught for many years at both the high school and university level, but now devotes herself completely to her poetry. Chants, *her first volume of verse, was published in 1984, and she has since published three additional collections:* Borders *(1986),* Communion *(1991), and* Holy Water *(1995). "For a variety of complex reasons," she told* Contemporary Authors, *"anthologized American literature does not reflect the ethnic diversity of the United States. I write, in part, because Hispanic perspectives need to be part of our literary heritage; I want to be part of that validation process. I also write because I am fascinated by the pleasure and power of words."*

IMMIGRANTS [1986]

wrap their babies in the American flag,
feed them mashed hot dogs and apple pie,
name them Bill and Daisy,
buy them blonde dolls that blink blue
eyes or a football and tiny cleats
before the baby can even walk,
speak to them in thick English,
        hallo, babee, hallo,
whisper in Spanish or Polish
when the babies sleep, whisper
in a dark parent bed, that dark
parent fear, "Will they like
our boy, our girl, our fine american
boy, our fine american girl?"

➤ *QUESTIONS FOR READING AND WRITING*

1. To whom is the speaker saying, "wrap their babies in the American flag"?
2. What does she mean by "that dark parent fear"?
3. Compare this poem to the short story "Two Kinds," on page 862.

WILLIAM WORDSWORTH (1770–1850)

William Wordsworth was born in Cockermouth on the northern tip of England's Lake District and spent much of his childhood exploring the natural sights of this region, which later served as the setting for many of his greatest poems. In 1791, after attending

Cambridge University he traveled to France, where he became a supporter of the French Revolution and met and fell in love with a French woman, Annette Vallon, with whom he had a daughter. Due to the political situation, Wordsworth was forced to flee France and the couple never married. Together with his sister Dorothy, an accomplished writer herself and his later editor, Wordsworth settled first in a rent-free cottage in Dorsetshire, and then moved to Somersetshire to be near his friend, the poet Samuel Taylor Coleridge. In 1798, the two men collaborated to produce Lyrical Ballads *(which Wordsworth revised in 1800), a collection of poetry credited with bringing the Romantic movement to England. The enormously influential volume was a commercial success, and Wordsworth and his sister were able to live comfortably for the rest of their lives. In 1843, he was appointed poet laureate. Today, Wordsworth is best remembered for his deeply-felt depiction of the English countryside and of the customs and common speech of its people.*

Composed upon Westminster Bridge, September 3, 1802 [1807]

Earth has not anything to show more fair:
Dull would he be of soul who could pass by
A sight so touching in its majesty;
This City now doth, like a garment, wear
The beauty of the morning; silent, bare,
Ships, towers, domes, theaters, and temples lie
Open unto the fields, and to the sky;
All bright and glittering in the smokeless air.
Never did sun more beautifully steep
In his first splendor, valley, rock, or hill;
Ne'er saw I, never felt, a calm so deep!
The river glideth at his own sweet will:
Dear God! the very houses seem asleep;
And all that mighty heart is lying still!

➤ *QUESTIONS FOR READING AND WRITING*

1. Much of Wordsworth's verse depicts the countryside, but this is a city scene in early morning. To what extent is the beauty depicted here just as majestic as—but different than—nature?
2. Have you ever been so "taken" by a "human-made" sight? Explain.
3. Compare this poem to William Blake's "London" on page 1155.

MITSUYE YAMADA (b. 1923)

Mitsuye Yamada was born to Japanese parents (already official U.S. residents) who were visiting Fukuoka, Japan. She spent most of her childhood in Seattle, where her father was an interpreter and her mother a seamstress. During World War II, she and her family were interned at the Minidoka Relocation Center in Idaho. She attended New York University and the University of Chicago, and currently teaches in the Department of English at Cypress College in California. She has written: "Poetry to me means making connections . . . I can express in poetry what is happening to me better than any other genre, because what is happening now is invariably closely linked with what has happened in the past. Poetry then is a continuous process of making connections as I live my life. It holds my life together."

THE QUESTION OF LOYALTY [1976]

I met the deadline
for alien registration
once before
was numbered fingerprinted
and ordered not to travel
without permit.

But alien still they said I must
forswear allegiance to the emperor,
for me that was easy
I didn't even know him
but my mother who did cried out
    If I sign this
    What will I be?
    I am doubly loyal
    to my American children
    also to my own people.
    How can double mean nothing?
    I wish no one to lose this war
    Everyone does.

    I was poor
    at math.
    I signed
    my only ticket out.

➤ *QUESTIONS FOR READING AND WRITING*

1. Why is the speaker being asked to "forswear allegiance to the emperor"?
2. What does she mean by "I was poor at math"? Was she? Explain.

WILLIAM BUTLER YEATS (1865–1939)

Considered one of the greatest poets of the twentieth century, William Butler Yeats was born in Dublin, Ireland. Following in the footsteps of his father, a well-known painter, Yeats studied art for a time in Dublin and London, but gradually turned his focus to writing. While still a young man, perhaps influenced by what would turn out to be his almost lifelong affair with the actress and fervent nationalist Maud Gonne, Yeats became politically active in the movement for an independent Ireland. In 1899, he was an instrumental figure in the formation of the Irish National Theatre (now the Abbey Theatre), writing a number of verse plays for the theater and encouraging other important playwrights, including John Synge, to do likewise. Discouraged by the Irish reaction to the theater and his works in particular, Yeats lived in London for a time, but positive political events and his marriage to Georgie Hyde Lees, a spiritual medium, led to his return. He served as a senator in the newly established Irish Free State from 1922 to 1928. In 1923, he became the first Irishman awarded the Nobel Prize. Though he wrote poetry filled with the sights, sounds, and folklore of his native land throughout his life, much of his greatest work dates to his final years, when he combined his Irish perspective with a deeply-felt spiritual sense and symbolic system. "The Lake Isle of Innisfree" was written in 1893 and, like much of Yeats's early poetry, is deeply Romantic in its outlook.

THE LAKE ISLE OF INNISFREE [1893]

I will arise and go now, and go to Innisfree,
And a small cabin build there, of clay and wattles° made:
Nine bean-rows will I have there, a hive for the honey-bee,
And live alone in the bee-loud glade.

And I shall have some peace there, for peace comes dropping slow,
Dropping from the veils of the morning to where the cricket sings;
There midnight's all a glimmer, and noon a purple glow,
And evening full of the linnet's wings.

I will arise and go now, for always night and day
I hear lake water lapping with low sounds by the shore;
While I stand on the roadway, or on the pavements gray,
I hear it in the deep heart's core.

[2]**wattles** twigs woven together

➤ *QUESTIONS FOR READING AND WRITING*

1. Yeats was a student living in the city of London when he wrote this poem. To what extent do you think that might have influenced the intensity of the speaker's images? Explain.
2. What does he mean by "I hear it in the deep heart's core"? Do you ever hear things in "the deep heart's core"? Explain.
3. In what way does the alternating rhyme scheme of the lines in each stanza affect your response to the content?

◆ DRAMA ◆

SOPHOCLES (c. 496–406 B.C.)

*Considered during his lifetime one of the three great Athenian tragic playwrights (the other two being Aeschylus and Euripides), Sophocles is believed to have written over one hundred and twenty plays, though only seven of his tragedies have survived to modern times (*Ajax, Antigonê, Oedipus the King, Electra, Philoctetes, The Trachinian Women, *and* Oedipus at Colonus*). A popular figure throughout his long life, he served in a series of public offices, including those of general and priest, during a century that witnessed Athens' rise to power and its subsequent decline.* Oedipus Rex *(sometimes called* Oedipus Tyrannus *or* Oedipus the King*), Sophocles' retelling of the legend of Oedipus, was probably written in 429 B.C. The play has been held in high esteem since ancient times, when Aristotle cited the play as the perfect example of tragedy in his famous treatise on poetry, the* Poetics.

OEDIPUS REX [C. 429 B.C.]

AN ENGLISH VERSION BY DUDLEY FITTS AND ROBERT FITZGERALD

CHARACTERS

OEDIPUS
A PRIEST
CREON
TEIRESIAS
IOCASTÊ
MESSENGER
SHEPHERD OF LAÏOS
SECOND MESSENGER
CHORUS OF THEBAN ELDERS

SCENE: *Before the palace of* OEDIPUS, *king of Thebes. A central door and two lateral doors open onto a platform which runs the length of the facade. On the platform, right and left, are altars; and three steps lead down into the "orchestra," or chorus ground. At the beginning of the action these steps are crowded by* SUPPLIANTS *who have brought branches and chaplets of olive leaves and who lie in various attitudes of despair.* OEDIPUS *enters.*

PROLOGUE

OEDIPUS: My children, generations of the living
In the line of Kadmos,° nursed at his ancient hearth;
Why have you strewn yourselves before these altars
In supplication, with your boughs and garlands?
The breath of incense rises from the city
With a sound of prayer and lamentation.
Children,
I would not have you speak through messengers,
And therefore I have come myself to hear you—
I, Oedipus who bear the famous name.
[*To a* PRIEST.] You, there, since you are eldest in the company,
Speak for them all, tell me what preys upon you,
Whether you come in dread, or crave some blessing:
Tell me, and never doubt that I will help you
In every way I can; I should be heartless
Were I not moved to find you suppliant here.
PRIEST: Great Oedipus, O powerful King of Thebes!
You see how all the ages of our people
Cling to your altar steps: here are boys
Who can barely stand alone, and here are priests
By weight of age, as I am a priest of God,
And young men chosen from those yet unmarried;
As for the others, all that multitude,
They wait with olive chaplets in the squares,
At the two shrines of Pallas,° and where Apollo°
Speaks in the glowing embers.
Your own eyes
Must tell you: Thebes is in her extremity
And cannot lift her head from the surge of death.
A rust consumes the buds and fruits of the earth;
The herds are sick; children die unborn,
And labor is vain. The god of plague and pyre
Raids like detestable lightning through the city,

2 Kadmos according to legend, the founder of Thebes. **24 Pallas** Athena, Zeus's daughter and the goddess of wisdom **Apollo** Zeus' son and the god of poetry and prophecy

And all the house of Kadmos is laid waste,
All emptied, and all darkened: Death alone
Battens upon the misery of Thebes.
You are not one of the immortal gods, we know;
Yet we have come to you to make our prayer
As to the man of all men best in adversity
And wisest in the ways of God. You saved us
From the Sphinx,° that flinty singer, and the tribute
We paid to her so long; yet you were never
Better informed than we, nor could we teach you:
It was some god breathed in you to set us free.

Therefore, O mighty King, we turn to you:
Find us our safety, find us a remedy,
Whether by counsel of the gods or the men.
A king of wisdom tested in the past
Can act in a time of troubles, and act well.
Noblest of men, restore
Life to your city! Think how all men call you
Liberator for your triumph long ago;
Ah, when your years of kingship are remembered,
Let them not say *We rose, but later fell—*
Keep the State from going down in the storm!
Once, years ago, with happy augury,
You brought us fortune; be the same again!
No man questions your power to rule the land:
But rule over men, not over a dead city!
Ships are only hulls, citadels are nothing,
When no life moves in the empty passageways.

OEDIPUS: Poor children! You may be sure I know
All that you longed for in your coming here.
I know that you are deathly sick; and yet,
Sick as you are, not one is as sick as I.
Each of you suffers in himself alone
His anguish, not another's; but my spirit
Groans for the city, for myself, for you.

I was not sleeping, you are not waking me.
No, I have been in tears for a long while
And in my restless thought walked many ways.
In all my search, I found one helpful course,

39 The Sphinx a monster with a lion's body, bird's wings, and woman's face

And that I have taken: I have sent Creon,
Son of Menoikeus, brother of the Queen,
To Delphi, Apollo's place of revelation,
To learn there, if he can,
What act or pledge of mine may save the city.
I have counted the days, and now, this very day,
I am troubled, for he has overstayed his time.
What is he doing? He has been gone too long.
Yet whenever he comes back, I should do ill
To scant whatever hint the god may give.

PRIEST: It is a timely promise. At this instant
They tell me Creon is here.

OEDIPUS: O Lord Apollo!
May his news be fair as his face is radiant!

PRIEST: It could not be otherwise: he is crowned with bay,
The chaplet is thick with berries.

OEDIPUS: We shall soon know;
He is near enough to hear us now.

[*Enter* CREON.]

O Prince:
Brother: son of Menoikeus:
What answer do you bring us from the god?

CREON: It is favorable. I can tell you, great afflictions
Will turn out well, if they are taken well.

OEDIPUS: What was the oracle? These vague words
Leave me still hanging between hope and fear.

CREON: Is it your pleasure to hear me with all these
Gathered around us? I am prepared to speak,
But should we not go in?

OEDIPUS: Let them all hear it.
It is for them I suffer, more than myself.

CREON: Then I will tell you what I heard at Delphi.

In plain words
The god commands us to expel from the land of Thebes
An old defilement that it seems we shelter.
It is a deathly thing, beyond expiation.
We must not let it feed upon us longer.

OEDIPUS: What defilement? How shall we rid ourselves of it?

CREON: By exile or death, blood for blood. It was
Murder that brought the plague-wind on the city.

OEDIPUS: Murder of whom? Surely the god has named him?

CREON: My lord: long ago Laïos was our king,
  Before you came to govern us.
OEDIPUS: I know;
  I learned of him from others; I never saw him.
CREON: He was murdered; and Apollo commands us now
  To take revenge upon whoever killed him.
OEDIPUS: Upon whom? Where are they? Where shall we find a clue
  To solve that crime, after so many years?
CREON: Here in this land, he said.
  If we make enquiry,
  We may touch things that otherwise escape us.
OEDIPUS: Tell me: Was Laïos murdered in his house,
  Or in the fields, or in some foreign country?
CREON: He said he planned to make a pilgrimage.
  He did not come home again.
OEDIPUS: And was there no one,
  No witness, no companion, to tell what happened?
CREON: They were all killed but one, and he got away
  So frightened that he could remember one thing only.
OEDIPUS: What was that one thing? One may be the key
  To everything, if we resolve to use it.
CREON: He said that a band of highwaymen attacked them.
  Outnumbered them, and overwhelmed the King.
OEDIPUS: Strange, that a highwayman should be so daring—
  Unless some faction here bribed him to do it.
CREON: We thought of that. But after Laïos' death
  New troubles arose and we had no avenger.
OEDIPUS: What troubles could prevent your hunting down the killers?
CREON: The riddling Sphinx's song
  Made us deaf to all mysteries but her own.
OEDIPUS: Then once more I must bring what is dark to light.
  It is most fitting that Apollo shows,
  As you do, this compunction for the dead.
  You shall see how I stand by you, as I should,
  To avenge the city and the city's god,
  And not as though it were for some distant friend,
  But for my own sake, to be rid of evil.
  Whoever killed King Laïos might—who knows?—
  Decide at any moment to kill me as well.
  By avenging the murdered king I protect myself.
  Come, then, my children: leave the altar steps,
  Lift up your olive boughs!
  One of you go

And summon the people of Kadmos to gather here.
I will do all that I can; you may tell them that.

[Exit a PAGE.*]*

So, with the help of God,
We shall be saved—or else indeed we are lost.

PRIEST: Let us rise, children. It was for this we came,
And now the King has promised it himself.
Phoibos° has sent us an oracle; may he descend
Himself to save us and drive out the plague.

[Exeunt OEDIPUS *and* CREON *into the palace by the central door. The* PRIEST *and the* SUPPLIANTS *disperse right and left. After a short pause the Chorus enters the orchestra.]*

PÁRODOS°

Strophe° 1

CHORUS: What is God singing in his profound
Delphi of gold and shadow?
What oracle for Thebes, the sunwhipped city?
Fear unjoints me, the roots of my heart tremble.
Now I remember, O Healer, your power, and wonder;
Will you send doom like a sudden cloud, or weave it
Like nightfall of the past?
Speak, speak to us, issue of holy sound:
Dearest to our expectancy: be tender!

Antistrophe° 1

Let me pray to Athenê, the immortal daughter of Zeus,
And to Artemis her sister
Who keeps her famous throne in the market ring,
And to Apollo, bowman at the far butts of heaven—

O gods, descend! Like three streams leap against
The fires of our grief, the fires of darkness;
Be swift to bring us rest!

As in the old time from the brilliant house
Of air you stepped to save us, come again!

152 Phoibos Phoebus Apollo **s.d. Párodos** the entrance song of the chorus **s.d. Strophe** sung as the chorus moves from stage left to stage right **s.d. Antistrophe** sung as the chorus moves from stage left to stage right

Strophe 2

Now our afflictions have no end,
Now all our stricken host lies down
And no man fights off death with his mind;

The noble plowland bears no grain,
And groaning mothers cannot bear—

See, how our lives like birds take wing,
Like sparks that fly when a fire soars,
To the shore of the god of evening.

Antistrophe 2

The plague burns on, it is pitiless
Though pallid children laden with death
Lie unwept in the stony ways,
And old gray women by every path
Flock to the strand about the altars

There to strike their breasts and cry
Worship of Phoibos in wailing prayers:
Be kind, God's golden child!

Strophe 3

There are no swords in this attack by fire,
No shields, but we are ringed with cries.
Send the besieger plunging from our homes
Into the vast sea-room of the Atlantic
Or into the waves that foam eastward of Thrace—
For the day ravages what the night spares—

Destroy our enemy, lord of the thunder!
Let him be riven by lightning from heaven!

Antistrophe 3

Phoibos Apollo, stretch the sun's bowstring,
That golden cord, until it sing for us,
Flashing arrows in heaven!
Artemis,° Huntress,

45 Artemis the goddess of the hunt

Race with flaring lights upon our mountains!
O scarlet god, O golden-banded brow,
O Theban Bacchos° in a storm of Maenads,°

[Enter OEDIPUS, *center.]*

Whirl upon Death, that all the Undying hate!
Come with blinding cressets, come in joy!

SCENE I

OEDIPUS: Is this your prayer? It may be answered. Come,
Listen to me, act as the crisis demands,
And you shall have relief from all these evils.

Until now I was a stranger to this tale,
As I had been a stranger to the crime.
Could I track down the murderer without a clue?
But now, friends,
As one who became a citizen after the murder,
I make this proclamation to all Thebans:
If any man knows by whose hand Laïos, son of Labdakos,
Met his death, I direct that man to tell me everything,
No matter what he fears for having so long withheld it.
Let it stand as promised that no further trouble
Will come to him, but he may leave the land in safety.

Moreover: If anyone knows the murderer to be foreign,
Let him not keep silent: he shall have his reward from me.
However, if he does conceal it, if any man
Fearing for his friend or for himself disobeys this edict,
Hear what I propose to do:
I solemnly forbid the people of this country,
Where power and throne are mine, ever to receive that man
Or speak to him, no matter who he is, or let him
Join in sacrifice, lustration, or in prayer.
I decree that he be driven from every house,

Being, as he is, corruption itself to us: the Delphic
Voice of Zeus has pronounced this revelation.
Thus I associate myself with the oracle
And take the side of the murdered king.

As for the criminal, I pray to God—

48 Bacchos . . . Maenads the god of wine and revelry with his female attendants

Whether it be a lurking thief, or one of a number—
I pray that that man's life be consumed in evil and
wretchedness.
And as for me, this curse applies no less
If it should turn out that the culprit is my guest here,
Sharing my hearth.
You have heard the penalty.
I lay it on you now to attend to this
For my sake, for Apollo's, for the sick
Sterile city that heaven has abandoned.
Suppose the oracle had given you no command:
Should this defilement go uncleansed for ever?
You should have found the murderer: your king,
A noble king, had been destroyed!
Now I,
Having the power that he held before me,
Having his bed, begetting children there
Upon his wife, as he would have, had he lived—
Their son would have been my children's brother,
If Laïos had had luck in fatherhood!
(But surely ill luck rushed upon his reign)—
I say I take the son's part, just as though
I were his son, to press the fight for him
And see it won! I'll find the hand that brought
Death to Labdakos' and Polydoros' child,
Heir of Kadmos' and Agenor's line.
And as for those who fail me,
May the gods deny them the fruit of the earth,
Fruit of the womb, and may they rot utterly!
Let them be wretched as we are wretched, and worse!
For you, for loyal Thebans, and for all
Who find my actions right, I pray the favor
Of justice, and of all the immortal gods.

CHORAGOS: Since I am under oath, my lord, I swear
I did not do the murder, I cannot name
The murderer. Might not the oracle
That has ordained the search tell where to find him?

OEDIPUS: An honest question. But no man in the world
Can make the gods do more than the gods will.

CHORAGOS: There is one last expedient—

OEDIPUS: Tell me what it is.
Though it seem slight, you must not hold it back.

CHORAGOS: A lord clairvoyant to the lord Apollo,
As we all know, is the skilled Teiresias.

One might learn much about this from him, Oedipus.
OEDIPUS: I am not wasting time:
Creon spoke of this, and I have sent for him—
Twice, in fact; it is strange that he is not here.
CHORAGOS: The other matter—that old report—seems useless.
OEDIPUS: Tell me. I am interested in all reports.
CHORAGOS: The King was said to have been killed by highwaymen.
OEDIPUS: I know. But we have no witnesses to that.
CHORAGOS: If the killer can feel a particle of dread,
Your curse will bring him out of hiding!
OEDIPUS: No.
The man who dared that act will fear no curse

[Enter the blind seer TEIRESIAS *led by a* PAGE.*]*

CHORAGOS: But there is one man who may detect the criminal.
This is Teiresias, this is the holy prophet
In whom, alone of all men, truth was born.
OEDIPUS: Teiresias: seer: student of mysteries,
Of all that's taught and all that no man tells,
Secrets of Heaven and secrets of the earth:
Blind though you are, you know the city lies
Sick with plague; and from this plague, my lord,
We find that you alone can guard or save us.

Possibly you did not hear the messengers?
Apollo, when we sent to him,
Sent us back word that this great pestilence
Would lift, but only if we established clearly
The identity of those who murdered Laïos.
They must be killed or exiled.
Can you use
Bird flight or any art of divination
To purify yourself, and Thebes, and me
From this contagion? We are in your hands.
There is no fairer duty
Than that of helping others in distress.
TEIRESIAS: How dreadful knowledge of the truth can be
When there's no help in truth! I knew this well,
But did not act on it: else I should not have come.
OEDIPUS: What is troubling you? Why are your eyes so cold?
TEIRESIAS: Let me go home. Bear your own fate, and I'll
Bear mine. It is better so: trust what I say.

OEDIPUS: What you say is ungracious and unhelpful
To your native country. Do not refuse to speak.
TEIRESIAS: When it comes to speech, your own is neither temperate
Nor opportune. I wish to be more prudent.
OEDIPUS: In God's name, we all beg you—
TEIRESIAS: You are all ignorant.
No; I will never tell you what I know.
Now it is my misery; then, it would be yours.
OEDIPUS: What! You do know something, and will not tell us?
You would betray us all and wreck the State?
TEIRESIAS: I do not intend to torture myself, or you.
Why persist in asking? You will not persuade me.
OEDIPUS: What a wicked man you are! You'd try a stone's
Patience! Out with it! Have you no feeling at all?
TEIRESIAS: You call me unfeeling. If you could only see
The nature of your feelings . . .
OEDIPUS: Why,
Who would not feel as I do? Who could endure
Your arrogance toward the city?
TEIRESIAS: What does it matter!
Whether I speak or not, it is bound to come.
OEDIPUS: Then, if "it" is bound to come, you are bound
to tell me.
TEIRESIAS: No, I will not go on. Rage as you please.
OEDIPUS: Rage? Why not!
And I'll tell you what I think:
You planned it, you had it done, you all but
Killed him with your own hands: if you had eyes,
I'd say the crime was yours, and yours alone.
TEIRESIAS: So? I charge you, then,
Abide by the proclamation you have made.
From this day forth
Never speak again to these men or to me;
You yourself are the pollution of this country.
OEDIPUS: You dare say that! Can you possibly think you have
Some way of going free, after such insolence?
TEIRESIAS: I have gone free. It is the truth sustains me.
OEDIPUS: Who taught you shamelessness? It was not your craft.
TEIRESIAS: You did. You made me speak. I did not want to.
OEDIPUS: Speak what? Let me hear it again more clearly.
TEIRESIAS: Was it not clear before? Are you tempting me?
OEDIPUS: I did not understand it. Say it again.
TEIRESIAS: I say that you are the murderer whom you seek.

OEDIPUS: Now twice you have spat out infamy. You'll
pay for it!
TEIRESIAS: Would you care for more? Do you wish to be really angry?
OEDIPUS: Say what you will. Whatever you say is worthless.
TEIRESIAS: I say you live in hideous shame with those
Most dear to you. You cannot see the evil.
OEDIPUS: It seems you can go on mouthing like this for ever.
TEIRESIAS: I can, if there is power in truth.
OEDIPUS: There is:
But not for you, not for you,
You sightless, witless, senseless, mad old man!
TEIRESIAS: You are the madman. There is no one here
Who will not curse you soon, as you curse me.
OEDIPUS: You child of endless night! You cannot hurt me
Or any other man who sees the sun.
TEIRESIAS: True: it is not from me your fate will come.
That lies within Apollo's competence,
As it is his concern.
OEDIPUS: Tell me:
Are you speaking for Creon, or for yourself?
TEIRESIAS: Creon is no threat. You weave your own doom.
OEDIPUS: Wealth, power, craft of statesmanship!
Kingly position, everywhere admired!
What savage envy is stored up against these,
If Creon, whom I trusted, Creon my friend,
For this great office which the city once
Put in my hands unsought—if for this power
Creon desires in secret to destroy me!

He has brought this decrepit fortune-teller, this
Collector of dirty pennies, this prophet fraud—
Why, he is no more clairvoyant than I am!
Tell us:
Has your mystic mummery ever approached the truth?
When that hellcat the Sphinx was performing here,
What help were you to these people?
Her magic was not for the first man who came along:
It demanded a real exorcist. Your birds—
What good were they? or the gods, for the matter of that?
But I came by,
Oedipus, the simple man, who knows nothing—
I thought it out for myself, no birds helped me!
And this is the man you think you can destroy,

That you may be close to Creon when he's king!
Well, you and your friend Creon, it seems to me,
Will suffer most. If you were not an old man,
You would have paid already for your plot.
CHORAGOS: We cannot see that his words or yours
Have spoken except in anger, Oedipus,
And of anger we have no need. How can God's will
Be accomplished best? That is what most concerns us.
TEIRESIAS: You are a king. But where argument's concerned
I am your man, as much a king as you.
I am not your servant, but Apollo's.
I have no need of Creon to speak for me.

Listen to me. You mock my blindness, do you?
But I say that you, with both your eyes, are blind:
You cannot see the wretchedness of your life,
Not in whose house you live, no, nor with whom.
Who are your father and mother? Can you tell me?
You do not even know the blind wrongs
That you have done them, on earth and in the world below.
But the double lash of your parents' curse will whip you
Out of this land some day, with only night
Upon your precious eyes.
Your cries then—where will they not be heard?
What fastness of Kithairon will not echo them?
And that bridal-descant of yours—you'll know it then,
The song they sang when you came here to Thebes
And found your misguided berthing.
All this, and more, that you cannot guess at now,
Will bring you to yourself among your children.
Be angry, then. Curse Creon. Curse my words.
I tell you, no man that walks upon the earth
Shall be rooted out more horribly than you.
OEDIPUS: Am I to bear this from him?—Damnation
Take you! Out of this place! Out of my sight!
TEIRESIAS: I would not have come at all if you had not asked me.
OEDIPUS: Could I have told that you'd talk nonsense, that
You'd come here to make a fool of yourself, and of me?
TEIRESIAS: A fool? Your parents thought me sane enough.
OEDIPUS: My parents again!—Wait: who were my parents?
TEIRESIAS: This day will give you a father, and break your heart.
OEDIPUS: Your infantile riddles! Your damned abracadabra!
TEIRESIAS: You were a great man once at solving riddles.

OEDIPUS: Mock me with that if you like; you will find it true.
TEIRESIAS: It was true enough. It brought about your ruin.
OEDIPUS: But if it saved this town?
TEIRESIAS [*to the PAGE*]. Boy, give me your hand.
OEDIPUS: Yes, boy; lead him away.
—While you are here
We can do nothing. Go; leave us in peace.
TEIRESIAS: I will go when I have said what I have to say.
How can you hurt me? And I tell you again:
The man you have been looking for all this time,
The damned man, the murderer of Laïos,
That man is in Thebes. To your mind he is foreignborn,
But it will soon be shown that he is a Theban,
A revelation that will fail to please.
A blind man,
Who has his eyes now; a penniless man, who is rich now;
And he will go tapping the strange earth with his staff;
To the children with whom he lives now he will be
Brother and father—the very same; to her
Who bore him, son and husband—the very same
Who came to his father's bed, wet with his father's blood.

Enough. Go think that over.
If later you find error in what I have said,
You may say that I have no skill in prophecy.

[Exit TEIRESIAS, led by his PAGE; OEDIPUS goes into the palace.]

ODE 1°

Strophe 1

CHORUS: The Delphic stone of prophecies
Remembers ancient regicide
And a still bloody hand.
That killer's hour of flight has come.
He must be stronger than riderless
Coursers of untiring wind,
For the son of Zeus° armed with his father's thunder
Leaps in lightning after him;
And the Furies° follow him, the sad Furies.

Antistrophe 1

Holy Parnossos' peak of snow

s.d. Ode a poetic song **7 son of Zeus** Apollo **9 the Furies** women spirits who punished those guilty of evil

Flashes and blinds that secret man,
That all shall hunt him down:
Though he may roam the forest shade
Like a bull gone wild from pasture
To rage through glooms of stone.
Doom comes down on him; flight will not avail him;
For the world's heart calls him desolate,
And the immortal Furies follow, for ever follow.

Strophe 2

But now a wilder thing is heard
From the old man skilled at hearing Fate in the wingbeat of a bird.
Bewildered as a blown bird, my soul hovers and cannot find
Foothold in this debate, or any reason or rest of mind.
But no man ever brought—none can bring
Proof of strife between Thebes' royal house,
Labdakos' line° and the son of Polybos;°
And never until now has any man brought word
Of Laïos' dark death staining Oedipus the King.

Antistrophe 2

Divine Zeus and Apollo hold
Perfect intelligence alone of all tales ever told;
And well though this diviner works, he works in his own night;
No man can judge that rough unknown or trust in second sight,
For wisdom changes hands among the wise.
Shall I believe my great lord criminal
At a raging word that a blind old man let fall?
I saw him, when the carrion woman faced him of old,
Prove his heroic mind! These evil words are lies.

SCENE 2

CREON: Men of Thebes:
I am told that heavy accusations

Have been brought against me by King Oedipus.
I am not the kind of man to bear this tamely.

If in these present difficulties
He holds me accountable for any harm to him
Through anything I have said or done—why, then,

26 Labdakos' line descendants of Labdakos **Polybos** king of Corinth, foster father of Oedipus

I do not value life in this dishonor.
It is not as though this rumor touched upon
Some private indiscretion. The matter is grave.
The fact is that I am being called disloyal
To the State, to my fellow citizens, to my friends.

CHORAGOS: He may have spoken in anger, not from his mind.

CREON: But did you hear him say I was the one
Who seduced the old prophet into lying?

CHORAGOS: The thing was said; I do not know how seriously.

CREON: But you were watching him! Were his eyes steady?
Did he look like a man in his right mind?

CHORAGOS: I do not know.
I cannot judge the behavior of great men.
But here is the King himself.

[Enter OEDIPUS.]

OEDIPUS: So you dared come back.
Why? How brazen of you to come to my house,
You murderer!
Do you think I do not know
That you plotted to kill me, plotted to steal my throne?
Tell me, in God's name: am I coward, a fool,
That you should dream you could accomplish this?
A fool who could not see your slippery game?
A coward, not to fight back when I saw it?
You are the fool, Creon, are you not? hoping
Without support or friends to get a throne?
Thrones may be won or bought: you could do neither.

CREON: Now listen to me. You have talked; let me talk; too.
You cannot judge unless you know the facts.

OEDIPUS: You speak well: there is one fact; but I find it hard
To learn from the deadliest enemy I have.

CREON: That above all I must dispute with you.

OEDIPUS: That above all I will not hear you deny.

CREON: If you think there is anything good in being stubborn
Against all reason, then I say you are wrong.

OEDIPUS: If you think a man can sin against his own kind
And not be punished for it, I say you are mad.

CREON: I agree. But tell me: what have I done to you?

OEDIPUS: You advised me to send for that wizard, did you not?

CREON: I did. I should do it again.

OEDIPUS: Very well. Now tell me:
How long has it been since Laïos—

CREON: What of Laïos?

OEDIPUS: Since he vanished in that onset by the road?
CREON: It was long ago, a long time.
OEDIPUS: And this prophet,
Was he practicing here then?
CREON: He was; and with honor, as now.
OEDIPUS: Did he speak of me at that time?
CREON: He never did;
At least, not when I was present.
OEDIPUS: But . . . the enquiry?
I suppose you held one?
CREON: We did, but we learned nothing.
OEDIPUS: Why did the prophet not speak against me then?
CREON: I do not know; and I am the kind of man
Who holds his tongue when he has no facts to go on.
OEDIPUS: There's one fact that you know, and you could tell it.
CREON: What fact is that? If I know it, you shall have it.
OEDIPUS: If he were not involved with you, he could not say
That it was I who murdered Laïos.
CREON: If he says that, you are the one that knows it!—
But now it is my turn to question you.
OEDIPUS: Put your questions. I am no murderer.
CREON: First, then: You married my sister?
OEDIPUS: I married your sister.
CREON: And you rule the kingdom equally with her?
OEDIPUS: Everything that she wants she has from me.
CREON: And I am the third, equal to both of you?
OEDIPUS: That is why I call you a bad friend.
CREON: No. Reason it out, as I have done.
Think of this first. Would any sane man prefer
Power, with all a king's anxieties,
To that same power and the grace of sleep?
Certainly not I.
I have never longed for the king's power—only his rights.
Would any wise man differ from me in this?
As matters stand, I have my way in everything
With your consent, and no responsibilities.
If I were king, I should be a slave to policy.
How could I desire a scepter more
Than what is now mine—untroubled influence?
No, I have not gone mad; I need no honors,
Except those with the perquisites I have now.
I am welcome everywhere; every man salutes me,
And those who want your favor seek my ear,

Since I know how to manage what they ask.
Should I exchange this ease for that anxiety?
Besides, no sober mind is treasonable.
I hate anarchy
And never would deal with any man who likes it.

Test what I have said. Go to the priestess
At Delphi, ask if I quoted her correctly.
And as for this other thing: if I am found
Guilty of treason with Teiresias,
Then sentence me to death! You have my word
It is a sentence I should cast my vote for—
But not without evidence!
                    You do wrong
When you take good men for bad, bad men for good.
A true friend thrown aside—why, life itself
Is not more precious!
                    In time you will know this well:
For time, and time alone, will show the just man,
Though scoundrels are discovered in a day.

CHORAGOS: This is well said, and a prudent man would ponder it.
Judgments too quickly formed are dangerous.

OEDIPUS: But is he not quick in his duplicity?
And shall I not be quick to parry him?
Would you have me stand still, hold my peace, and let
This man win everything, through my inaction?

CREON: And you want—what is it, then? To banish me?

OEDIPUS: No, not exile. It is your death I want,
So that all the world may see what treason means.

CREON: You will persist, then? You will not believe me?

OEDIPUS: How can I believe you?

CREON: Then you are a fool.

OEDIPUS: To save myself?

CREON: In justice, think of me.

OEDIPUS: You are evil incarnate.

CREON: But suppose that you are wrong?

OEDIPUS: Still I must rule.

CREON: But not if you rule badly.

OEDIPUS: O city, city!

CREON: It is my city, too!

CHORAGOS: Now, my lords, be still. I see the Queen,
Iocastê, coming from her palace chambers;
And it is time she came, for the sake of you both.

This dreadful quarrel can be resolved through her.

[Enter IOCASTÊ.]

IOCASTÊ: Poor foolish men, what wicked din is this?
With Thebes sick to death, is it not shameful
That you should rake some private quarrel up?

[To OEDIPUS.]

Come into the house.
—And you, Creon, go now:
Let us have no more of this tumult over nothing.

CREON: Nothing? No, sister: what your husband plans for me
Is one of two great evils: exile or death.

OEDIPUS: He is right.
Why, woman, I have caught him squarely
Plotting against my life.

CREON: No! Let me die
Accurst if ever I have wished you harm!

IOCASTÊ: Ah, believe it, Oedipus!
In the name of the gods, respect this oath of his
For my sake, for the sake of these people here!

Strophe 1

CHORAGOS: Open your mind to her, my lord. Be ruled by her, I beg you!

OEDIPUS: What would you have me do?

CHORAGOS: Respect Creon's word. He has never spoken like a fool,
And now he has sworn an oath.

OEDIPUS: You know what you ask?

CHORAGOS: I do.

OEDIPUS: Speak on, then.

CHORAGOS: A friend so sworn should not be baited so,
In blind malice, and without final proof.

OEDIPUS: You are aware, I hope, that what you say
Means death for me, or exile at the least.

Strophe 2

CHORAGOS: No, I swear by Helios, first in Heaven!
May I die friendless and accurst,
The worst of deaths, if ever I meant that!
It is the withering fields
That hurt my sick heart:
Must we bear all these ills,
And now your bad blood as well?

OEDIPUS: Then let him go. And let me die, if I must,
Or be driven by him in shame from the land of Thebes.
It is your unhappiness, and not his talk,
That touches me.
As for him—
Wherever he is, I will hate him as long as I live.
CREON: Ugly in yielding, as you were ugly in rage!
Natures like yours chiefly torment themselves.
OEDIPUS: Can you not go? Can you not leave me?
CREON: I can.
You do not know me; but the city knows me,
And in its eyes I am just, if not in yours.
[Exit CREON.]

Antistrophe 1

CHORAGOS: Lady Iocastê, did you not ask the King
to go to his chambers?
IOCASTÊ: First tell me what has happened.
CHORAGOS: There was suspicion without evidence; yet it rankled
As even false charges will.
IOCASTÊ: On both sides?
CHORAGOS: On both.
IOCASTÊ: But what was said?
CHORAGOS: Oh let it rest, let it be done with!
Have we not suffered enough?
OEDIPUS: You see to what your decency has brought you:
You have made difficulties where my heart saw none.

Antistrophe 2

CHORAGOS: Oedipus, it is not once only I have told you—
You must know I should count myself unwise
To the point of madness, should I now forsake you—
You, under whose hand,
In the storm of another time,
Our dear land sailed out free,
But now stand fast at the helm!
IOCASTÊ: In God's name, Oedipus, inform your wife as well:
Why are you so set in this hard anger?
OEDIPUS: I will tell you, for none of these men deserves
My confidence as you do. It is Creon's work,
His treachery, his plotting against me.
IOCASTÊ: Go on, if you can make this clear to me.

OEDIPUS: He charges me with the murder of Laïos.
IOCASTÊ: Has he some knowledge? Or does he speak from hearsay?
OEDIPUS: He would not commit himself to such a charge,
But he has brought in that damnable soothsayer
To tell his story.
IOCASTÊ: Set your mind at rest.
If it is a question of soothsayers, I tell you
That you will find no man whose craft gives knowledge
Of the unknowable.
Here is my proof:

An oracle was reported to Laïos once
(I will not say from Phoibos himself, but from
His appointed ministers, at any rate)
That his doom would be death at the hands of his own son—
His son, born of his flesh and of mine!
Now, you remember the story: Laïos was killed
By marauding strangers where three highways meet;
But his child had not been three days in this world
Before the King had pierced the baby's ankles
And left him to die on a lonely mountainside.

Thus, Apollo never caused that child
To kill his father, and it was not Laïos' fate
To die at the hands of his son, as he had feared.
This is what prophets and prophecies are worth!
Have no dread of them.
It is God himself
Who can show us what he wills, in his own way.
OEDIPUS: How strange a shadowy memory crossed my mind,
Just now while you were speaking; it chilled my heart.
IOCASTÊ: What do you mean? What memory do you speak of?
OEDIPUS: If I understand you, Laïos was killed
At a place where three roads meet.
IOCASTÊ: So it was said;
We have no later story.
OEDIPUS: Where did it happen?
IOCASTÊ: Phokis, it is called: at a place where the Theban Way
Divides into the roads towards Delphi and Daulia.
OEDIPUS: When?
IOCASTÊ: We had the news not long before you came
And proved the right to your succession here.
OEDIPUS: Ah, what net has God been weaving for me?

IOCASTÊ: Oedipus! Why does this trouble you?
OEDIPUS: Do not ask me yet.
First, tell me how Laïos looked, and tell me
How old he was.
IOCASTÊ: He was tall, his hair just touched
With white; his form was not unlike your own.
OEDIPUS: I think that I myself may be accurst
By my own ignorant edict.
IOCASTÊ: You speak strangely.
It makes me tremble to look at you, my King.
OEDIPUS: I am not sure that the blind man cannot see.
But I should know better if you were to tell me—
IOCASTÊ: Anything—though I dread to hear you ask it.
OEDIPUS: Was the King lightly escorted, or did he ride
With a large company, as a ruler should?
IOCASTÊ: There were five men with him in all: one was a herald;
And a single chariot, which he was driving.
OEDIPUS: Alas, that makes it plain enough!
But who—
Who told you how it happened?
IOCASTÊ: A household servant,
The only one to escape.
OEDIPUS: And is he still
A servant of ours?
IOCASTÊ: No; for when he came back at last
And found you enthroned in the place of the dead king,
He came to me, touched my hand with his, and begged
That I would send him away to the frontier district
Where only the shepherds go—
As far away from the city as I could send him.
I granted his prayer; for although the man was a slave,
He had earned more than this favor at my hands.
OEDIPUS: Can he be called back quickly?
IOCASTÊ: Easily.
But why?
OEDIPUS: I have taken too much upon myself
Without enquiry; therefore I wish to consult him.
IOCASTÊ: Then he shall come.
But am I not one also
To whom you might confide these fears of yours!
OEDIPUS: That is your right; it will not be denied you,
Now least of all; for I have reached a pitch
Of wild foreboding. Is there anyone

To whom I should sooner speak?
Polybos of Corinth is my father.
My mother is a Dorian: Meropê.
I grew up chief among the men of Corinth
Until a strange thing happened—
Not worth my passion, it may be, but strange.

At a feast, a drunken man maundering in his cups
Cries out that I am not my father's son!

I contained myself that night, though I felt anger
And a sinking heart. The next day I visited
My father and mother, and questioned them. They stormed,
Calling it all the slanderous rant of a fool;
And this relieved me. Yet the suspicion
Remained always aching in my mind;
I knew there was talk; I could not rest;
And finally, saying nothing to my parents,
I went to the shrine at Delphi.
The god dismissed my question without reply;
He spoke of other things.
Some were clear,
Full of wretchedness, dreadful, unbearable:
As, that I should lie with my own mother, breed
Children from whom all men would turn their eyes;
And that I should be my father's murderer.

I heard all this, and fled. And from that day
Corinth to me was only in the stars
Descending in that quarter of the sky,
As I wandered farther and farther on my way
To a land where I should never see the evil
Sung by the oracle. And I came to this country
Where, so you say, King Laïos was killed.
I will tell you all that happened there, my lady.

There were three highways
Coming together at a place I passed;
And there a herald came towards me, and a chariot
Drawn by horses, with a man such as you describe
Seated in it. The groom leading the horses
Forced me off the road at his lord's command;
But as this charioteer lurched over towards me

I struck him in my rage. The old man saw me
And brought his double goad down upon my head
As I came abreast.
He was paid back, and more!
Swinging my club in this right hand I knocked him
Out of his car, and he rolled on the ground.
I killed him.

I killed them all.
Now if that stranger and Laïos were—kin,
Where is a man more miserable than I?
More hated by the gods? Citizen and alien alike
Must never shelter me or speak to me—
I must be shunned by all.
And I myself
Pronounced this malediction upon myself!

Think of it: I have touched you with these hands,
These hands that killed your husband. What defilement!

Am I all evil, then? It must be so,
Since I must flee from Thebes, yet never again
See my own countrymen, my own country,
For fear of joining my mother in marriage
And killing Polybos, my father.
Ah,
If I was created so, born to this fate,
Who could deny the savagery of God?
O holy majesty of heavenly powers!
May I never see that day! Never!
Rather let me vanish from the race of men
Than know the abomination destined me!

CHORAGOS: We too, my lord, have felt dismay at this.
But there is hope: you have yet to hear the shepherd.

OEDIPUS: Indeed, I fear no other hope is left me.

IOCASTÊ: What do you hope from him when he comes?

OEDIPUS: This much:
If his account of the murder tallies with yours,
Then I am cleared.

IOCASTÊ: What was it that I said
Of such importance?

OEDIPUS: Why, "marauders," you said,
Killed the King, according to this man's story.

If he maintains that still, if there were several,
Clearly the guilt is not mine: I was alone.
But if he says one man, singlehanded, did it,
Then the evidence all points to me.

IOCASTÊ: You may be sure that he said there were several;
And can he call back that story now? He cannot.
The whole city heard it as plainly as I.
But suppose he alters some detail of it:
He cannot ever show that Laïos' death
Fulfilled the oracle: for Apollo said
My child was doomed to kill him; and my child—
Poor baby!—it was my child that died first.

No. From now on, where oracles are concerned,
I would not waste a second thought on any.

OEDIPUS: You may be right.
But come: let someone go
For the shepherd at once. This matter must be settled.

IOCASTÊ: I will send for him.
I would not wish to cross you in anything,
And surely not in this.—Let us go in.

[Exeunt into the palace.]

ODE II

Strophe 1

CHORUS: Let me be reverent in the ways of right,
Lowly the paths I journey on;
Let all my words and actions keep
The laws of the pure universe
From highest Heaven handed down.
For Heaven is their bright nurse,
Those generations of the realms of light;
Ah, never of mortal kind were they begot,
Nor are they slaves of memory, lost in sleep:
Their Father is greater than Time, and ages not.

Antistrophe 1

The tyrant is a child of Pride
Who drinks from his great sickening cup
Recklessness and vanity,
Until from his high crest headlong

He plummets to the dust of hope.
That strong man is not strong.
But let no fair ambition be denied;
May God protect the wrestler for the State
In government, in comely policy,
Who will fear God, and on His ordinance wait.

Strophe 2

Haughtiness and the high hand of disdain
Tempt and outrage God's holy law;
And any mortal who dares hold
No immortal Power in awe
Will be caught up in a net of pain:
The price for which his levity is sold.
Let each man take due earnings, then,
And keep his hands from holy things,
And from blasphemy stand apart—
Else the crackling blast of heaven
Blows on his head, and on his desperate heart;
Though fools will honor impious men,
In their cities no tragic poet sings.

Antistrophe 2

Shall we lose faith in Delphi's obscurities,
We who have heard the world's core
Discredited, and the sacred wood
Of Zeus at Elis praised no more?
The deeds and the strange prophecies
Must make a pattern yet to be understood.
Zeus, if indeed you are lord of all,
Throned in light over night and day,
Mirror this in your endless mind:
Our masters call the oracle
Words on the wind, and the Delphic vision blind!
Their hearts no longer know Apollo,
And reverence for the gods has died away.

SCENE 3

[Enter IOCASTÊ.*]*

IOCASTÊ: Princes of Thebes, it has occurred to me
To visit the altars of the gods, bearing
These branches as a suppliant, and this incense.

Our King is not himself: his noble soul
Is overwrought with fantasies of dread,
Else he would consider
The new prophecies in the light of the old.
He will listen to any voice that speaks disaster,
And my advice goes for nothing.

[She approaches the altar, right.]

To you, then, Apollo,
Lycean lord, since you are nearest, I turn in prayer.
Receive these offerings, and grant us deliverance
From defilement. Our hearts are heavy with fear
When we see our leader distracted, as helpless sailors
Are terrified by the confusion of their helmsman.

[Enter MESSENGER.]

MESSENGER: Friends, no doubt you can direct me:
Where shall I find the house of Oedipus,
Or, better still, where is the King himself?
CHORAGOS: It is this very place, stranger; he is inside.
This is his wife and mother of his children.
MESSENGER: I wish her happiness in a happy house,
Blest in all the fulfillment of her marriage.
IOCASTÊ: I wish as much for you: your courtesy
Deserves a like good fortune. But now, tell me:
Why have you come? What have you to say to us?
MESSENGER: Good news, my lady, for your house and your husband.
IOCASTÊ What news? Who sent you here?
MESSENGER: I am from Corinth.
The news I bring ought to mean joy for you,
Though it may be you will find some grief in it.
IOCASTÊ: What is it? How can it touch us in both ways?
MESSENGER: The people of Corinth, they say,
Intend to call Oedipus to be their king.
IOCASTÊ: But old Polybos—is he not reigning still?
MESSENGER: No. Death holds him in his sepulchre.
IOCASTÊ: What are you saying? Polybos is dead?
MESSENGER: If I am not telling the truth, may I die myself.
IOCASTÊ: [*to a MAIDSERVANT*] Go in, go quickly; tell this to your master.
O riddlers of God's will, where are you now!
This was the man whom Oedipus, long ago,
Feared so, fled so, in dread of destroying him—
But it was another fate by which he died.

[Enter OEDIPUS, center.]

OEDIPUS: Dearest Iocastê, why have you sent for me?
IOCASTÊ: Listen to what this man says, and then tell me
 What has become of the solemn prophecies.
OEDIPUS: Who is this man? What is his news for me?
IOCASTÊ: He has come from Corinth to announce your father's death!
OEDIPUS: Is it true, stranger? Tell me in your own words.
MESSENGER: I cannot say it more clearly: the king is dead.
OEDIPUS: Was it by treason? Or by an attack of illness?
MESSENGER: A little thing brings old men to their rest.
OEDIPUS: It was sickness, then?
MESSENGER: Yes, and his many years.
OEDIPUS: Ah!
 Why should a man respect the Pythian hearth,° or
 Give heed to the birds that jangle above his head?
 They prophesied that I should kill Polybos,
 Kill my own father; but he is dead and buried,
 And I am here—I never touched him, never,
 Unless he died in grief for my departure,
 And thus, in a sense, through me. No Polybos
 Has packed the oracles off with him underground.
 They are empty words.
IOCASTÊ: Had I not told you so?
OEDIPUS: You had; it was my faint heart that betrayed me.
IOCASTÊ: From now on never think of those things again.
OEDIPUS: And yet—must I not fear my mother's bed?
IOCASTÊ: Why should anyone in this world be afraid,
 Since Fate rules us and nothing can be foreseen?
 A man should live only for the present day.
 Have no more fear of sleeping with your mother.
 How many men, in dreams, have lain with their mothers!
 No reasonable man is troubled by such things.
OEDIPUS: That is true; only—
 If only my mother were not still alive!
 But she is alive. I cannot help my dread.
IOCASTÊ: Yet this news of your father's death is wonderful.
OEDIPUS: Wonderful. But I fear the living woman.
MESSENGER: Tell me, who is this woman that you fear?
OEDIPUS: It is Meropê, man; the wife of King Polybos.
MESSENGER: Meropê? Why should you be afraid of her?
OEDIPUS: An oracle of the gods, a dreadful saying.

52 Pythian hearth an alternate name for Delphi. It came from Python, the dragon that guarded Delphi until Apollo killed it and established his oracle there.

MESSENGER: Can you tell me about it or are you sworn to silence?
OEDIPUS: I can tell you, and I will.
Apollo said through his prophet that I was the man
Who should marry his own mother, shed his father's blood
With his own hands. And so, for all these years
I have kept clear of Corinth, and no harm has come—
Though it would have been sweet to see my parents again.
MESSENGER: And is this the fear that drove you out of Corinth?
OEDIPUS: Would you have me kill my father?
MESSENGER: As for that
You must be reassured by the news I gave you.
OEDIPUS: If you could reassure me, I would reward you.
MESSENGER: I had that in mind, I will confess: I thought
I could count on you when you returned to Corinth.
OEDIPUS: No: I will never go near my parents again.
MESSENGER: Ah, son, you still do not know what you are doing—
OEDIPUS: What do you mean? In the name of God tell me!
MESSENGER: —If these are your reasons for not going home.
OEDIPUS: I tell you, I fear the oracle may come true.
MESSENGER: And guilt may come upon you through your parents?
OEDIPUS: That is the dread that is always in my heart.
MESSENGER: Can you not see that all your fears are groundless?
OEDIPUS: How can you say that? They are my parents, surely?
MESSENGER: Polybos was not your father.
OEDIPUS: Not my father?
MESSENGER: No more your father than the man speaking to you.
OEDIPUS: But you are nothing to me!
MESSENGER: Neither was he.
OEDIPUS: Then why did he call me son?
MESSENGER: I will tell you:
Long ago he had you from my hands, as a gift.
OEDIPUS: Then how could he love me so, if I was not his?
MESSENGER: He had no children, and his heart turned to you.
OEDIPUS: What of you? Did you buy me? Did you find me by chance?
MESSENGER: I came upon you in the crooked pass of Kithairon.
OEDIPUS: And what were you doing there?
MESSENGER: Tending my flocks.
OEDIPUS: A wandering shepherd?
MESSENGER: But your savior, son, that day.
OEDIPUS: From what did you save me?
MESSENGER: Your ankles should tell you that.
OEDIPUS: Ah, stranger, why do you speak of that childhood pain?
MESSENGER: I cut the bonds that tied your ankles together.

OEDIPUS: I have had the mark as long as I can remember.
MESSENGER: That was why you were given the name you bear.°
OEDIPUS: God! Was it my father or my mother who did it?
  Tell me!
MESSENGER: I do not know. The man who gave you to me
  Can tell you better than I.
OEDIPUS: It was not you that found me, but another?
MESSENGER: It was another shepherd gave you to me.
OEDIPUS: Who was he? Can you tell me who he was?
MESSENGER: I think he was said to be one of Laïos' people.
OEDIPUS: You mean the Laïos's who was king here years ago?
MESSENGER: Yes; King Laïos; and the man was one of his herdsmen.
OEDIPUS: Is he still alive? Can I see him?
MESSENGER: These men here
  Know best about such things.
OEDIPUS: Does anyone here
  Know this shepherd that he is talking about?
  Have you seen him in the fields, or in the town?
  If you have, tell me. It is time things were made plain.
CHORAGOS: I think the man he means is that same shepherd
  You have already asked to see. Iocastê perhaps
  Could tell you something.
OEDIPUS: Do you know anything
  About him, Lady? Is he the man we have summoned?
  Is that the man this shepherd means?
IOCASTÊ: Why think of him?
  Forget this herdsman. Forget it all.
  This talk is a waste of time.
OEDIPUS: How can you say that,
  When the clues to my true birth are in my hands?
IOCASTÊ: For God's love, let us have no more questioning!
  Is your life nothing to you?
  My own is pain enough for me to bear.
OEDIPUS: You need not worry. Suppose my mother a slave,
  And born of slaves: no baseness can touch you.
IOCASTÊ: Listen to me, I beg you: do not do this thing!
OEDIPUS: I will not listen; the truth must be made known.
IOCASTÊ: Everything that I say is for your own good!
OEDIPUS: My own good

116 name you bear the name "Oedipus" means "swollen-foot"

Snaps my patience, then: I want none of it.
IOCASTÊ: You are fatally wrong! May you never learn who you are!
OEDIPUS: Go, one of you, and bring the shepherd here.
Let us leave this woman to brag of her royal name.
IOCASTÊ: Ah, miserable!
That is the only word I have for you now.
That is the only word I can ever have.

[Exit into the palace.]

CHORAGOS: Why has she left us, Oedipus? Why has she gone
In such a passion of sorrow? I fear this silence:
Something dreadful may come of it.
OEDIPUS: Let it come!
However base my birth, I must know about it.
The Queen, like a woman, is perhaps ashamed
To think of my low origin. But I
Am a child of luck; I cannot be dishonored.
Luck is my mother; the passing months, my brothers,
Have seen me rich and poor.
If this is so,
How could I wish that I were someone else?
How could I not be glad to know my birth?

ODE III

Strophe

CHORUS: If ever the coming time were known
To my heart's pondering,
Kithairon, now by Heaven I see the torches
At the festival of the next full moon,
And see the dance, and hear the choir sing
A grace to your gentle shade:
Mountain where Oedipus was found,
O mountain guard of a noble race!
May the god who heals us lend his aid,
And let that glory come to pass
For our king's cradling-ground.

Antistrophe

Of the nymphs that flower beyond the years.
Who bore you, royal child,
To Pan of the hills or the timberline Apollo,

Cold in delight where the upland clears,
Or Hermês for whom Kyllenê's heights° are piled?
Or flushed as evening cloud,
Great Dionysos,° roamer of mountains,
He—was it he who found you there,
And caught you up in his own proud
Arms from the sweet god-ravisher
Who laughed by the Muses'° fountains?

SCENE 4

OEDIPUS: Sirs: though I do not know the man,
I think I see him coming, this shepherd we want:
He is old, like our friend here, and the men
Bringing him seem to be servants of my house.
But you can tell, if you have ever seen him

[Enter SHEPHERD escorted by servants.]

CHORAGOS: I know him, he was Laïos' man. You can trust him.
OEDIPUS: Tell me first, you from Corinth: is this the shepherd
We were discussing?
MESSENGER: This is the very man.
OEDIPUS: [*to SHEPHERD*] Come here. No, look at me. You must answer
Everything I ask.—You belonged to Laïos?
SHEPHERD: Yes: born his slave, brought up in his house.
OEDIPUS: Tell me: what kind of work did you do for him?
SHEPHERD: I was a shepherd of his, most of my life.
OEDIPUS: Where mainly did you go for pasturage?
SHEPHERD: Sometimes Kithairon, sometimes the hills nearby.
OEDIPUS: Do you remember ever seeing this man out there?
SHEPHERD: What would he be doing there? This man?
OEDIPUS: This man standing here. Have you ever seen him before?
SHEPHERD: No. At least, not to my recollection.
MESSENGER: And that is not strange, my lord. But I'll refresh
His memory: he must remember when we two
Spent three whole seasons together, March to September,
On Kithairon or thereabouts. He had two flocks;
I had one. Each autumn I'd drive mine home
And he would go back with his to Laïos' sheepfold.—
Is this not true, just as I have described it?
SHEPHERD: True, yes; but it was all so long ago.
MESSENGER: Well, then: do you remember, back in those days

16 Kyllenê's heights a holy mountain, the birthplace of Hermes **18 Dionysos** god of wine and revelry also called Bacchos **22 The Muses** sisters who inspire poetry and music, arts and sciences

That you gave me a baby boy to bring up as my own?
SHEPHERD: What if I did? What are you trying to say?
MESSENGER: King Oedipus was once that little child.
SHEPHERD: Damn you, hold your tongue!
OEDIPUS: No more of that!
It is your tongue needs watching, not this man's.
SHEPHERD: My King, my Master, what is it I have done wrong?
OEDIPUS: You have not answered his question about the boy,
SHEPHERD: He does not know . . . He is only making trouble . . .
OEDIPUS: Come, speak plainly, or it will go hard with you.
SHEPHERD: In God's name, do not torture an old man!
OEDIPUS: Come here, one of you; bind his arms behind him.
SHEPHERD: Unhappy king! What more do you wish to learn?
OEDIPUS: Did you give this man the child he speaks of?
SHEPHERD: I did.
And I would to God I had died that very day.
OEDIPUS: You will die now unless you speak the truth.
SHEPHERD: Yet if I speak the truth, I am worse than dead.
OEDIPUS: Very well; since you insist upon delaying—
SHEPHERD: No! I have told you already that I gave him the boy.
OEDIPUS: Where did you get him? From your house?
From somewhere else?
SHEPHERD: Not from mine, no. A man gave him to me.
OEDIPUS: Is that man here? Do you know whose slave he was?
SHEPHERD: For God's love, my King, do not ask me any more!
OEDIPUS: You are a dead man if I have to ask you again.
SHEPHERD: Then . . . Then the child was from the palace of Laïos.
OEDIPUS: A slave child? or a child of his own line?
SHEPHERD: Ah, I am on the brink of dreadful speech!
OEDIPUS: And I of dreadful hearing. Yet I must hear.
SHEPHERD: If you must be told, then . . .
They said it was Laïos' child,
But it is your wife who can tell you about that.
OEDIPUS: My wife!—Did she give it to you?
SHEPHERD: My lord, she did.
OEDIPUS: Do you know why?
SHEPHERD: I was told to get rid of it.
OEDIPUS: An unspeakable mother!
SHEPHERD: There had been prophecies . . .
OEDIPUS: Tell me.
SHEPHERD: It was said that the boy would kill his own father.
OEDIPUS: Then why did you give him over to this old man?
SHEPHERD: I pitied the baby, my King,
And I thought that this man would take him far away

To his own country.
He saved him—but for what a fate!
For if you are what this man says you are,
No man living is more wretched than Oedipus.
OEDIPUS: Ah God!
It was true!
All the prophecies!
—Now,
O light, may I look on you for the last time!
I, Oedipus,
Oedipus, damned in his birth, in his marriage damned,
Damned in the blood he shed with his own hand!
[He rushes into the palace.]

ODE IV

Strophe 1

CHORUS: Alas for the seed of men.
What measure shall I give these generations
That breathe on the void and are void
And exist and do not exist?

Who bears more weight of joy
Than mass of sunlight shifting in images,
Or who shall make his thought stay on
That down time drifts away?

Your splendor is all fallen.

O naked brow of wrath and tears,
O change of Oedipus!
I who saw your days call no man blest—
Your great days like ghosts gone.

Antistrophe 1

That mind was a strong bow.
Deep, how deep you drew it then, hard archer,
At a dim fearful range,
And brought dear glory down!

You overcame the stranger—
The virgin with her hooking lion claws—
And though death sang, stood like a tower

To make pale Thebes take heart.

Fortress against our sorrow!

Divine king, giver of laws,
Majestic Oedipus!
No prince in Thebes had ever such renown,
No prince won such grace of power.

Strophe 2

And now of all men ever known
Most pitiful is this man's story:
His fortunes are most changed, his state
Fallen to a low slave's
Ground under bitter fate.

O Oedipus, most royal one!
The great door that expelled you to the light
Gave it night—ah, gave night to your glory:
As to the father, to the fathering son.

All understood too late.

How could that queen whom Laïos won,
The garden that he harrowed at his height,
Be silent when that act was done?

Antistrophe 2

But all eyes fail before time's eye.
All actions come to justice there.
Though never willed, though far down the deep past,
Your bed, your dread sirings,
Are brought to book at last.
Child by Laïos doomed to die,
Then doomed to lose that fortunate little death,
Would God you never took breath in this air
That with my wailing lips I take to cry:

For I weep the world's outcast.

I was blind, and now I can tell why:
Asleep, for you had given ease of breath

To Thebes, while the false years went by.

EXODOS

[Enter, from the palace, the SECOND MESSENGER.*]*

SECOND MESSENGER: Elders of Thebes, most honored in this land,
What horrors are yours to see and hear, what weight
Of sorrow to be endured, if, true to your birth,
You venerate the line of Labdakos!
I think neither Istros nor Phasis, those great rivers,
Could purify this place of the corruption
It shelters now, or soon must bring to light—
Evil not done unconsciously, but willed.

The greatest griefs are those we cause ourselves.
CHORAGOS: Surely, friend, we have grief enough already;
What new sorrow do you mean?
SECOND MESSENGER: The Queen is dead.
CHORAGOS: Iocastê? Dead? But at whose hand?
SECOND MESSENGER: Her own.
The full horror of what happened you cannot know,
For you did not see it; but I, who did, will tell you
As clearly as I can how she met her death.

When she had left us,
In passionate silence, passing through the court,
She ran to her apartment in the house,
Her hair clutched by the fingers of both hands.
She closed the doors behind her; then, by that bed
Where long ago the fatal son was conceived—
That son who should bring about his father's death—
We heard her call upon Laïos, dead so many years,
And heard her wail for the double fruit of her marriage,
A husband by her husband, children by her child.

Exactly how she died I do not know:
For Oedipus burst in moaning and would not let us
Keep vigil to the end: it was by him
As he stormed about the room that our eyes were caught.
From one to another of us he went, begging a sword,
Cursing the wife who was not his wife, the mother
Whose womb had carried his own children and himself.
I do not know: it was none of us aided him,
But surely one of the gods was in control!

For with a dreadful cry
He hurled his weight, as though wrenched out of himself,
At the twin doors: the bolts gave, and he rushed in.
And there we saw her hanging, her body swaying
From the cruel cord she had noosed about her neck.
A great sob broke from him heartbreaking to hear,
As he loosed the rope and lowered her to the ground.

I would blot out from my mind what happened next!
For the King ripped from her gown the golden brooches
That were her ornament, and raised them, and plunged them down
Straight into his own eyeballs, crying, "No more,
No more shall you look on the misery about me,
The horrors of my own doing! Too long you have known
The faces of those whom I should never have seen,
Too long been blind to those for whom I was searching!
From this hour, go in darkness!" And as he spoke,
He struck at his eyes—not once, but many times;
And the blood spattered his beard,
Bursting from his ruined sockets like red hail.

So from the unhappiness of two this evil has sprung,
A curse on the man and woman alike. The old
Happiness of the house of Labdakos
Was happiness enough: where is it today?
It is all wailing and ruin, disgrace, death—all
The misery of mankind that has a name—
And it is wholly and for ever theirs.

CHORAGOS: Is he in agony still? Is there no rest for him?

SECOND MESSENGER: He is calling for someone to lead him to the gates
So that all the children of Kadmos may look upon
His father's murderer, his mother's—no,
I cannot say it!
And then he will leave Thebes,
Self-exiled, in order that the curse
Which he himself pronounced may depart from the house.
He is weak, and there is none to lead him,
So terrible is his suffering.
But you will see:
Look, the doors are opening; in a moment
You will see a thing that would crush a heart of stone.

[The central door is opened; OEDIPUS, blinded, is led in.]

CHORAGOS: Dreadful indeed for men to see.

Never have my own eyes
Looked on a sight so full of fear.

Oedipus!
What madness came upon you, what daemon
Leaped on your life with heavier
Punishment than a mortal man can bear?
No: I cannot even
Look at you, poor ruined one.
And I would speak, question, ponder,
If I were able. No.
You make me shudder.

OEDIPUS: God. God.
Is there a sorrow greater?
Where shall I find harbor in this world?
My voice is hurled far on a dark wind.
What has God done to me?

CHORAGOS: Too terrible to think of, or to see.

Strophe 1

OEDIPUS: O cloud of night,
Never to be turned away: night coming on,
I cannot tell how: night like a shroud!
My fair winds brought me here.
Oh God. Again
The pain of the spikes where I had sight,
The flooding pain
Of memory, never to be gouged out.

CHORAGOS: This is not strange.
You suffer it all twice over, remorse in pain,
Pain in remorse.

Antistrophe 1

OEDIPUS: Ah dear friend
Are you faithful even yet, you alone?
Are you still standing near me, will you stay here,
Patient, to care for the blind?
The blind man!
Yet even blind I know who it is attends me,
By the voice's tone—
Though my new darkness hide the comforter.

CHORAGOS: Oh fearful act!
What god was it drove you to rake black
Night across your eyes?

Strophe 2

OEDIPUS: Apollo. Apollo. Dear
Children, the god was Apollo.
He brought my sick, sick fate upon me.
But the blinding hand was my own!
How could I bear to see
When all my sight was horror everywhere?
CHORAGOS: Everywhere; that is true.
OEDIPUS: And now what is left?
Images? Love? A greeting even,
Sweet to the senses? Is there anything?
Ah, no, friends: lead me away
Lead me away from Thebes.
Lead the great wreck
And hell of Oedipus, whom the gods hate.
CHORAGOS: Your fate is clear, you are not blind to that.
Would God you had never found it out!

Antistrophe 2

OEDIPUS: Death take the man who unbound
My feet on that hillside
And delivered me from death to life! What life?
If only I had died,
This weight of monstrous doom
Could not have dragged me and my darlings down.
CHORAGOS: I would have wished the same.
OEDIPUS: Oh never to have come here
With my father's blood upon me! Never
To have been the man they call his mother's husband!
Oh accurst! O child of evil,
To have entered that wretched bed—
the selfsame one!
More primal than sin itself, this fell to me.
CHORAGOS: I do not know how I can answer you.
You were better dead than alive and blind.
OEDIPUS: Do not counsel me any more. This punishment
That I have laid upon myself is just.

If I had eyes,
I do not know how I could bear the sight
Of my father, when I came to the house of Death,
Or my mother: for I have sinned against them both
So vilely that I could not make my peace
By strangling my own life.
Or do you think my children,
Born as they were born, would be sweet to my eyes?
Ah never, never! Nor this town with its high walls,
Nor the holy images of the gods.
For I,
Thrice miserable—Oedipus, noblest of all the line
Of Kadmos, have condemned myself to enjoy
These things no more, by my own malediction
Expelling that man whom the gods declared
To be a defilement in the house of Laïos.
After exposing the rankness of my own guilt,
How could I look men frankly in the eyes?
No, I swear it,
If I could have stifled my hearing at its source,
I would have done it and made all this body
A tight cell of misery, blank to light and sound:
So I should have been safe in a dark agony
Beyond all recollection.
Ah Kithairon!
Why did you shelter me? When I was cast upon you,
Why did I not die? Then I should never
Have shown the world my execrable birth.

Ah Polybos! Corinth, city that I believed
The ancient seat of my ancestors: how fair
I seemed, your child! And all the while this evil
Was cancerous within me!
For I am sick
In my daily life, sick in my origin.

O three roads, dark ravine, woodland and way
Where three roads met you, drinking my father's blood,
My own blood, spilled by my own hand: can you remember
The unspeakable things I did there, and the things
I went on from there to do?

O marriage, marriage!
The act that engendered me, and again the act
Performed by the son in the same bed—
Ah, the net
Of incest, mingling fathers, brothers, sons,
With brides, wives, mothers: the last evil
That can be known by men: no tongue can say
How evil!
No. For the love of God, conceal me
Somewhere far from Thebes; or kill me; or hurl me
Into the sea, away from men's eyes for ever.
Come, lead me. You need not fear to touch me.
Of all men, I alone can bear this guilt.

[Enter Creon.]

Choragos: We are not the ones to decide; but Creon here
May fitly judge of what you ask. He only
Is left to protect the city in your place.
Oedipus: Alas, how can I speak to him? What right have I
To beg his courtesy whom I have deeply wronged?
Creon: I have not come to mock you, Oedipus,
Or to reproach you, either.

[To Attendants.]

—You, standing there:
If you have lost all respect for man's dignity,
At least respect the flame of Lord Helios:
Do not allow this pollution to show itself
Openly here, an affront to the earth
And Heaven's rain and the light of day. No, take him
Into the house as quickly as you can.
For it is proper
That only the close kindred see his grief.
Oedipus: I pray you in God's name, since your courtesy
Ignores my dark expectation, visiting
With mercy this man of all men most execrable:
Give me what I ask—for your good, not for mine.
Creon: And what is it that you would have me do?
Oedipus: Drive me out of this country as quickly as may be
To a place where no human voice can ever greet me.
Creon: I should have done that before now—only,
God's will had not been wholly revealed to me.

OEDIPUS: But his command is plain: the parricide
Must be destroyed. I am that evil man.
CREON: That is the sense of it, yes; but as things are,
We had best discover clearly what is to be done.
OEDIPUS: You would learn more about a man like me?
CREON: You are ready now to listen to the god.
OEDIPUS: I will listen. But it is to you
That I must turn for help. I beg you, hear me.

The woman in there—
Give her whatever funeral you think proper:
She is your sister.
—But let me go, Creon!
Let me purge my father's Thebes of the pollution
Of my living here, and go out to the wild hills,
To Kithairon, that has won such fame with me,
The tomb my mother and father appointed for me,
And let me die there, as they willed I should.
And yet I know
Death will not ever come to me through sickness
Or in any natural way: I have been preserved
For some unthinkable fate. But let that be.
As for my sons, you need not care for them.
They are men, they will find some way to live.
But my poor daughters, who have shared my table,
Who never before have been parted from their father—
Take care of them, Creon; do this for me.
And will you let me touch them with my hands
A last time, and let us weep together?
Be kind, my lord,
Great prince, be kind!
Could I but touch them,
They would be mine again, as when I had my eyes.

[Enter ANTIGONÊ and ISMENE, attended.]

Ah, God!
Is it my dearest children I hear weeping?
Has Creon pitied me and sent my daughters?
CREON: Yes, Oedipus: I knew that they were dear to you
In the old days, and know you must love them still.
OEDIPUS: May God bless you for this—and be a friendlier
Guardian to you than he has been to me!

Children, where are you?
Come quickly to my hands: they are your brother's—
Hands that have brought your father's once clear eyes
To this way of seeing—
Ah dearest ones,
I had neither sight nor knowledge then, your father
By the woman who was the source of his life!
And I weep for you—having no strength to see you—,
I weep for you when I think of the bitterness
That men will visit upon you all your lives.
What homes, what festivals can you attend
Without being forced to depart again in tears?
And when you come to marriageable age,
Where is the man, my daughters, who would dare
Risk the bane that lies on all my children?
Is there any evil wanting? Your father killed
His father; sowed the womb of her who bore him;
Engendered you at the fount of his own existence!
That is what they will say of you.
Then, whom
Can you ever marry? There are no bridegrooms for you,
And your lives must wither away in sterile dreaming.
O Creon, son of Menoikeus!
You are the only father my daughters have,
Since we, their parents, are both of us gone for ever.
They are your own blood: you will not let them
Fall into beggary and loneliness;
You will keep them from the miseries that are mine!
Take pity on them; see, they are only children,
Friendless except for you. Promise me this,
Great Prince, and give me your hand in token of it.

[CREON clasps his right hand.]

Children:
I could say much, if you could understand me,
But as it is, I have only this prayer for you:
Live where you can, be as happy as you can—
Happier, please God, than God has made your father!

CREON: Enough. You have wept enough. Now go within.
OEDIPUS: I must; but it is hard.
CREON: Time eases all things.
OEDIPUS: But you must promise—

CREON: Say what you desire.
OEDIPUS: Send me from Thebes!
CREON: God grant that I may!
OEDIPUS: But since God hates me . . .
CREON: No, he will grant your wish.
OEDIPUS: You promise?
CREON: I cannot speak beyond my knowledge.
OEDIPUS: Then lead me in.
CREON: Come now, and leave your children.
OEDIPUS: No! Do not take them from me!
CREON: Think no longer
That you are in command here, but rather think
How, when you were, you served your own destruction.

[Exeunt into the house all but the CHORUS; the CHORAGOS chants directly to the audience.]

CHORAGOS: Men of Thebes: look upon Oedipus.
This is the king who solved the famous riddle
And towered up, most powerful of men.
No mortal eyes but looked on him with envy,
Yet in the end ruin swept over him.
Let every man in mankind's frailty
Consider his last day; and let none
Presume on his good fortune until he find
Life, at his death, a memory without pain.

➤ QUESTIONS FOR READING AND WRITING

1. Do you believe Oedipus is to blame for what happens to him? Is his fate inescapable? Explain.
2. What is the primary conflict of the play?
3. Oedipus opens the play by initiating a search for whoever has defiled the honor of Thebes. How does his search change as detail after detail comes to light? How does the attitude of the chorus change? Why do you think Iocastê becomes less aggressive about pursuing the truth?
4. Why is Oedipus so nasty to Creon and Teiresias?
5. How is Oedipus behaving at the end of the play? To what extent does he maintain his nobility despite the horror of his earlier predicament?
6. What do the choragus and the chorus bring to the play? Do the choral odes add anything? If so, what?
7. While violence, like Iocastê's suicide and Oedipus's blinding, is reported by messengers, ancient Greek playwrights did not believe it was appropriate to show violence onstage. Do you think this is a good idea? What difference does it make in this play?

◆ ESSAYS ◆

MAYA ANGELOU

(See biography on page 563.)

GRADUATION IN STAMPS [1969]

The children in Stamps trembled visibly with anticipation. Some adults were excited too, but to be certain the whole young population had come down with graduation epidemic. Large classes were graduating from both the grammar school and the high school. Even those who were years removed from their own day of glorious release were anxious to help with preparations as a kind of dry run. The junior students who were moving into the vacating classes' chairs were tradition-bound to show their talents for leadership and management. They strutted through the school and around the campus exerting pressure on the lower grades. Their authority was so new that occasionally if they pressed a little too hard it had to be overlooked. After all, next term was coming, and it never hurt a sixth grader to have a play sister in the eighth grade, or a tenth-year student to be able to call a twelfth grader Bubba. So all was endured in a spirit of shared understanding. But the graduating classes themselves were the nobility. Like travelers with exotic destinations on their minds, the graduates were remarkably forgetful. They came to school without their books, or tablets or even pencils. Volunteers fell over themselves to secure replacements for the missing equipment. When accepted, the willing workers might or might not be thanked, and it was of no importance to the pregraduation rites. Even teachers were respectful of the now quiet and aging seniors, and tended to speak to them, if not as equals, as beings only slightly lower than themselves. After tests were returned and grades given, the student body, which acted like an extended family, knew who did well, who excelled, and what piteous ones had failed.

Unlike the white high school, Lafayette County Training School distinguished itself by having neither lawn, nor hedges, nor tennis court, nor climbing ivy. Its two buildings (main classrooms, the grade school and home economics) were set on a dirt hill with no fence to limit either its boundaries or those of bordering farms. There was a large expanse to the left of the school which was used alternately as a baseball diamond or a basketball court. Rusty hoops on the swaying poles represented the permanent recreational equipment, although bats and balls could be borrowed from the PE teacher if the borrower was qualified and if the diamond wasn't occupied.

Over this rocky area relieved by a few shady tall persimmon trees the graduating class walked. The girls often held hands and no longer bothered to speak to the lower students. There was a sadness about them, as if this old world was not their home and they were bound for higher ground. The boys, on the other hand, had become more friendly, more outgoing. A decided change from the closed attitude they projected while studying for finals. Now they seemed not ready to give up the old school, the familiar paths and classrooms. Only a small percentage would be continuing on to college—one of the South's A&M (agricultural and mechanical) schools, which trained Negro youths to be carpenters, farmers, handymen, masons, maids, cooks and baby nurses. Their future rode heavily on their shoulders, and blinded them to the collective joy that had pervaded the lives of the boys and girls in the grammar school graduating class.

Parents who could afford it had ordered new shoes and ready-made clothes for themselves from Sears and Roebuck or Montgomery Ward. They also engaged the best seamstresses to make the floating graduating dresses and to cut down second-hand pants which would be pressed to a military slickness for the important event.

5 Oh, it was important, all right. Whitefolks would attend the ceremony, and two or three would speak of God and home, and the Southern way of life, and Mrs. Parsons, the principal's wife, would play the graduation march while the lower-grade graduates paraded down the aisles and took their seats below the platform. The high school seniors would wait in empty classrooms to make their dramatic entrance.

In the store I was the person of the moment. The birthday girl. The center. Bailey had graduated the year before, although to do so he had had to forfeit all pleasures to make up for his time lost in Baton Rouge.

My class was wearing butter-yellow piqué dresses, and Momma launched out on mine. She smocked the yoke into tiny crisscrossing puckers, then shirred the rest of the bodice. Her dark fingers ducked in and out of the lemony cloth as she embroidered raised daisies around the hem. Before she considered herself finished she had added a crocheted cuff on the puff sleeves, and a pointy crocheted collar.

I was going to be lovely. A walking model of all the various styles of fine hand sewing and it didn't worry me that I was only twelve years old and merely graduating from the eighth grade. Besides, many teachers in Arkansas Negro schools had only that diploma and were licensed to impart wisdom.

The days had become longer and more noticeable. The faded beige of former times had been replaced with strong and sure colors. I began to see my classmates' clothes, their skin tones, and the dust that waved off pussy willows. Clouds that lazed across the sky were objects of great concern to me. Their shiftier shapes might have held a message that in my new happiness and with a little bit of time I'd soon decipher. During that period I looked at the arch of heaven so religiously my neck kept a steady ache. I had taken to smiling more often, and my jaws hurt from the unaccustomed activity. Between the two physical sore spots, I suppose I could have been uncomfortable, but that was not the case. As a member of the winning team (the graduating class of 1940) I had outdistanced unpleasant sensations by miles. I was headed for the freedom of open fields.

10 Youth and social approval allied themselves with me and we trammeled memories of slights and insults. The wind of our swift passage remodeled my features. Lost tears were pounded to mud and then to dust. Years of withdrawal were brushed aside and left behind, as hanging ropes of parasitic moss.

My work alone had awarded me a top place and I was going to be one of the first called in the graduating ceremonies. On the classroom blackboard, as well as on the bulletin board in the auditorium, there were blue stars and white stars and red stars. No absences, no tardinesses, and my academic work was among the best of the year. I could say the preamble to the Constitution even faster than Bailey. We timed ourselves often: "WethepeopleoftheUnitedStatesinordertoformamoreperfectunion . . ." I had memorized the Presidents of the United States from Washington to Roosevelt in chronological as well as alphabetical order.

My hair pleased me too. Gradually the black mass had lengthened and thickened, so that it kept at last to its braided pattern, and I didn't have to yank my scalp off when I tried to comb it.

Louise and I had rehearsed the exercises until we tired out ourselves. Henry Reed was class valedictorian. He was a small, very black boy with hooded eyes, a long, broad nose and an oddly shaped head. I had admired him for years because each term he and I vied for the best grades in our class. Most often he bested me, but instead of being disappointed I was pleased that we shared top places between us. Like many Southern Black children, he lived with his grandmother, who was as strict as Momma and as kind as she knew how to be. He was courteous, respectful and soft-spoken to elders, but on the playground he chose to play the roughest games. I admired him. Anyone, I reckoned, sufficiently afraid or sufficiently dull could be polite. But to be able to operate at a top level with both adults and children was admirable.

His valedictory speech was entitled "To Be or Not To Be." The rigid tenth-grade teacher had helped him to write it. He'd been working on the dramatic stresses for months.

15 The weeks until graduation were filled with heady activities. A group of small children were to be presented in a play about buttercups and daisies and bunny rabbits. They could be heard throughout the building practicing their hops and their little songs that sounded like silver bells. The older girls (non-graduates, of course) were assigned the task of making refreshments for the night's festivities. A tangy scent of ginger, cinnamon, nutmeg and chocolate wafted around the home economics building as the budding cooks made samples for themselves and their teachers.

In every corner of the workshop, axes and saws split fresh timber as the woodshop boys made sets and stage scenery. Only the graduates were left out of the general bustle. We were free to sit in the library at the back of the building or look in quite detachedly, naturally, on the measures being taken for our event.

Even the minister preached on graduation the Sunday before. His subject was, "Let your light so shine that men will see your good works and praise your Father, Who is in Heaven." Although the sermon was purported to be addressed to us, he used the occasion to speak to backsliders, gamblers, and general ne'er-do-wells. But since he had called our names at the beginning of the service we were mollified.

Among Negroes the tradition was to give presents to children going only from one grade to another. How much more important this was when the person was graduating at the top of the class. Uncle Willie and Momma had sent away for a Mickey Mouse watch like Bailey's. Louise gave me four embroidered handkerchiefs. (I gave her three crocheted doilies.) Mrs. Sneed, the minister's wife, made me an underskirt to wear for graduation, and nearly every customer gave me a nickel or maybe even a dime with the instruction "Keep on moving to high ground," or some such encouragement.

Amazingly the great day finally dawned and I was out of bed before I knew it. I threw open the back door to see it more clearly, but Momma said, "Sister, come away from that door and put your robe on."

20 I hoped the memory of that morning would never leave me. Sunlight was itself still young, and the day had none of the insistence maturity would bring it in a few hours. In my robe and barefoot in the backyard, under cover of going to see about my new beans, I gave myself up to the gentle warmth and thanked God that no matter what evil I had done in my life He had allowed me to live to see this day. Somewhere in my fatalism I had expected to die, accidentally, and never have the chance to walk up the stairs in the auditorium and gracefully receive my hard-earned diploma. Out *of* God's merciful bosom I had won reprieve.

Bailey came out in his robe and gave me a box wrapped in Christmas paper. He said he had saved his money for months to pay for it. It felt like a box of chocolates, but I knew Bailey wouldn't save money to buy candy when we had all we could want under our noses.

He was as proud of the gift as I. It was a soft-leather-bound copy of a collection of poems by Edgar Allan Poe, or, as Bailey and I called him, "Eap." I turned to "Annabel Lee" and we walked up and down the garden rows, the cool dirt between our toes, reciting the beautifully sad lines.

Momma made a Sunday breakfast although it was only Friday. After we finished the blessing, I opened my eyes to find the watch on my plate. It was a dream of a day. Everything went smoothly and to my credit, I didn't have to be reminded or scolded for anything. Near even'ng I was too jittery to attend to chores, so Bailey volunteered to do all before his bath.

Days before, we had made a sign for the Store and as we turned out the lights Momma hung the cardboard over the doorknob. It read clearly: CLOSED. GRADUATION.

25 My dress fitted perfectly and everyone said that I looked like a sunbeam in it. On the hill, going toward the school, Bailey walked behind with Uncle Willie, who muttered, "Go on, Ju." He wanted him to walk ahead with us because it embarrassed him to have to walk so slowly. Bailey said he'd let the ladies walk together, and the men would bring up the rear. We all laughed, nicely.

Little children dashed by out of the dark like fireflies. Their crepe-paper dresses and butterfly wings were not made for running and we heard more than one rip, dryly, and the regretful "uh uh" that followed.

The school blazed without gaiety. The windows seemed cold and unfriendly from the lower hill. A sense of ill-fated timing crept over me, and if Momma hadn't reached for my hand I would have drifted back to Bailey and Uncle Willie, and possibly beyond. She made a few slow jokes about my feet getting cold, and tugged me along to the now-strange building.

Around the front steps, assurance came back. There were my fellow "greats," the graduating class. Hair brushed back, legs oiled, new dresses and pressed pleats, fresh pocket handkerchiefs and little handbags, all homesewn. Oh, we were up to snuff, all right. I joined my comrades and didn't even see my family go in to find seats in the crowded auditorium.

The school band struck up a march and all classes filed in as had been rehearsed. We stood in front of our seats, as assigned, and on a signal from the choir director, we sat. No sooner had this been accomplished than the band started to play the national anthem. We rose again and sang the song, after which we recited the pledge of allegiance. We remained standing for a brief minute before the choir director and the principal signaled to us, rather desperately I thought, to take our seats. The command was so unusual that our carefully rehearsed and smooth-running machine was thrown off. For a full minute we fumbled for our chairs and bumped into each other awkwardly. Habits change or solidify under pressure, so in our state of nervous tension we had been ready to follow our usual assembly pattern: the American National Anthem, then the pledge of allegiance, then the song every Black person I knew called the Negro National Anthem. All done in the same key, with the same passion and most often standing on the same foot.

30 Finding my seat at last, I was overcome with a presentiment of worse things to come. Something unrehearsed, unplanned, was going to happen, and we were going to be made to look bad. I distinctly remember being explicit in the choice of pronoun. It was "we," the graduating class, the unit, that concerned me then.

The principal welcomed "parents and friends" and asked the Baptist minister to lead us in prayer. His invocation was brief and punchy, and for a second I thought we were getting back on the high road to right action. When the principal came back to the dais, however, his voice had changed. Sounds always affected me profoundly and the principal's voice was one of my favorites. During assembly it melted and lowed weakly into the audience. It had not been in my plan to listen to him, but my curiosity was piqued and I straightened up to give him my attention.

He was talking about Booker T. Washington, our "late great leader," who said we can be as close as the fingers on the hand, etc. . . . Then he said a few vague things about friendship and the friendship of kindly people to those less fortunate than themselves. With that his voice nearly faded, thin, away. Like a river diminishing to a stream and then to a trickle. But he cleared his throat and said, "Our speaker tonight, who is also our friend, came from Texarkana to deliver the commencement address, but due to the irregularity of the train schedule, he's going to, as they say, 'speak and run.'" He said that we understood and wanted the man to know that we were most grateful for the time he was able to give us and then something about how we were willing always to adjust to another's program, and without more ado—"I give you Mr. Edward Donleavy."

Not one but two white men came through the door offstage. The shorter one walked to the speaker's platform, and the tall one moved over to the center seat and sat down. But that was our principal's seat, and already occupied. The dislodged gentleman bounced around for a long breath or two before the Baptist minister gave him his chair, then with more dignity than the situation deserved, the minister walked off the stage.

Donleavy looked at the audience once (on reflection, I'm sure that he wanted only to reassure himself that we were really there), adjusted his glasses and began to read from a sheaf of papers.

35 He was glad "to be here and to see the work going on just as it was in the other schools."

At the first "Amen" from the audience I willed the offender to immediate death by choking on the word. But "Amen's" and "Yes, sir's" began to fall around the room like rain through a ragged umbrella.

He told us of the wonderful changes we children in Stamps had in store. The Central School (naturally, the white school was Central) had already been granted improvements that would be in use in the fall. A well-known artist was coming from Little Rock to teach art to them. They were going to have the newest microscopes and chemistry equipment for their laboratory. Mr. Donleavy didn't leave us long in the dark over who made these improvements available to Central High. Nor were we to be ignored in the general betterment scheme he had in mind.

He said that he had pointed out to people at a very high level that one of the first-line football tacklers at Arkansas Agricultural and Mechanical College had graduated from good old Lafayette County Training School. Here fewer Amen's were heard. Those few that did break through lay dully in the air with the heaviness of habit.

He went on to praise us. He went on to say how he had bragged that "one of the best basketball players at Fisk sank his first ball right here at Lafayette County Training School."

40 The white kids were going to have a chance to become Galileos and Madame Curies and Edisons and Gauguins, and our boys (the girls weren't even in on it) would try to be Jesse Owenses and Joe Louises.

Owens and the Brown Bomber were great heroes in our world, but what school official in the white-goddom of Little Rock had the right to decide that those two men must be our only heroes? Who decided that for Henry Reed to become a scientist he had to work like George Washington Carver, as a bootblack, to buy a lousy microscope? Bailey was obviously always going to be too small to be an athlete, so which concrete angel glued to what country seat had decided that if my brother wanted to become a lawyer he had to first pay penance for his skin by picking cotton and hoeing corn and studying correspondence books at night for twenty years?

The man's dead words fell like bricks around the auditorium and too many settled in my belly. Constrained by hard-learned manners I couldn't look behind me, but to my left and right the proud graduating class of 1940 had dropped their heads. Every girl in my row had found something new to do with her handkerchief. Some folded the tiny squares into love knots, some into triangles, but most were wadding them, then pressing them flat on their yellow laps.

On the dais, the ancient tragedy was being replayed. Professor Parsons sat, a sculptor's reject, rigid. His large, heavy body seemed devoid of will or willingness, and his eyes said he was no longer with us. The other teachers examined the flag (which was draped stage right) or their notes, or the windows which opened on our now-famous playing diamond.

Graduation, the hush-hush magic time of frills and gifts and congratulations and diplomas, was finished for me before my name was called. The accomplishment was nothing. The meticulous maps, drawn in three colors of ink, learning and spelling decasyllabic words, memorizing the whole of *The Rape of Lucrece*—it was nothing. Donleavy had exposed us.

45 We were maids and farmers, handymen and washerwomen, and anything higher that we aspired to was farcical and presumptuous.

Then I wished that Gabriel Prosser and Nat Turner had killed all whitefolks in their beds and that Abraham Lincoln had been assassinated before the signing of the Emancipation Proclamation, and that Harriet Tubman had been killed by that blow on her head and Christopher Columbus had drowned in the *Santa Maria.*

It was awful to be Negro and have no control over my life. It was brutal to be young and already trained to sit quietly and listen to charges brought against my color and no chance of defense. We should all be dead. I thought I should like to see us all dead, one on top of the other. A pyramid of flesh with the whitefolks on the bottom, as the broad base, then the Indians with their silly tomahawks and teepees and wigwams and treaties, the Negroes with their mops and recipes and cotton sacks and spirituals sticking out of their mouths. The Dutch children should all stumble in their wooden shoes and break their necks. The French should choke to death on the Louisiana Purchase (1803) while silkworms ate all the Chinese with their stupid pigtails. As a species, we were an abomination. All of us.

Donleavy was running for election, and assured our parents that if he won we could count on having the only colored paved playing field in that part of Arkansas. Also—he never looked up to acknowledge the grunts of acceptance—also, we were bound to get some new equipment for the home economics building and the workshop.

He finished, and since there was no need to give any more than the most perfunctory thank-you's, he nodded to the men on the stage, and the tall white man who was never introduced joined him at the door. They left with the attitude that now they were off to something really important. (The graduation ceremonies at Lafayette County Training School had been a mere preliminary.)

50 The ugliness they left was palpable. An uninvited guest who wouldn't leave. The choir was summoned and sang a modern arrangement of "Onward, Christian Soldiers," with new words pertaining to graduates seeking their place in the world. But it didn't work. Elouise, the daughter of the Baptist minister, recited "Invictus," and I could have cried at the impertinence of "I am the master of my fate, I am the captain of my soul."

My name had lost its ring of familiarity and I had to be nudged to go and receive my diploma. All my preparations had fled. I neither marched up to the stage like a conquering Amazon, nor did I look in the audience for Bailey's nod of approval. Marguerite Johnson, I heard the name again, my honors were read, there were noises in the audience of appreciation, and I took my place on the stage as rehearsed.

I thought about colors I hated: ecru, puce, lavender, beige and black.

There was shuffling and rustling around me, then Henry Reed was giving his valedictory address, "To Be or Not to Be." Hadn't he heard the whitefolks? We couldn't be, so the question was a waste of time. Henry's voice came out clear and strong. I feared to look at him. Hadn't he got the message? There was no "nobler in the mind" for Negroes because the world didn't think we had minds, and they let us know it. "Outrageous fortune"? Now, that was a joke. When the ceremony was over I had to tell Henry Reed some things. That is, if I still cared. Not "rub," Henry, "erase." "Ah, there's the erase." Us.

Henry had been a good student in elocution. His voice rose on tides of promise and fell on waves of warnings. The English teacher had helped him to create a sermon winging through Hamlet's soliloquy. To be a man, a doer, a builder, a leader, or to be a tool, an unfunny joke, a crusher of funky toadstools. I marveled that Henry could go through with the speech as if we had a choice.

55 I had been listening and silently rebutting each sentence with my eyes closed; then there was a hush, which in an audience warns that something unplanned is happening. I looked up and saw Henry Reed, the conservative, the proper, the 'A' student, turn his back to the audience and turn to us (the proud graduating class of 1940) and sing, nearly speaking,

> Lift ev'ry voice and sing
> Till earth and heaven ring
> Ring with the harmonies of Liberty . . .

It was the poem written by James Weldon Johnson. It was the music composed by J. Rosamond Johnson. It was the Negro National Anthem. Out of habit we were singing it.

Our mothers and fathers stood in the dark hall and joined the hymn of encouragement. A kindergarten teacher led the small children onto the stage and the buttercups and daisies and bunny rabbits marked time and tried to follow:

> Stony the road we trod
> Bitter the chastening rod
> Felt in the days when hope, unborn, had died.
> Yet with a steady beat
> Have not our weary feet
> Come to the place for which our fathers sighed?

Every child I knew had learned that song with his ABC's and along with "Jesus Loves Me This I Know." But I personally had never heard it before. Never heard the words, despite the thousands of times I had sung them. Never thought they had anything to do with me.

On the other hand, the words of Patrick Henry had made such an impression on me that I had been able to stretch myself tall and trembling and say, "I know not what course others may take, but as for me, give me liberty or give me death." And now I heard, really for the first time:

> We have come over a way that with tears has been watered,
> We have come, treading our path through the blood of the slaughtered.

While echoes of the song shivered in the air, Henry Reed bowed his head, said "Thank you," and returned to his place in the line. The tears that slipped down many faces were not wiped away in shame.

60 We were on top again. As always, again. We survived. The depths had been icy and dark, but now a bright sun spoke to our souls. I was no longer simply a member

of the proud graduating class of 1940; I was a proud member of the wonderful, beautiful Negro race.

➤ *QUESTIONS FOR READING AND WRITING*

1. To what extent was your response to "Graduation in Stamps" influenced by your own experience? Have you ever felt belittled by someone who thought he or she was giving you advice? Explain.
2. Why does Marguerite Johnson feel disappointed and belittled by the words of Mr. Donleavy?
3. In what way is Henry Reed's "To Be or Not to Be" speech both ironic and timely—as it follows the words of Donleavy?
4. How does the series of events at the end of the essay restore Marguerite to being "a proud member of the wonderful beautiful Negro race?"

JOAN DIDION (b. 1934)

Joan Didion was born in Sacramento, California, and attended the University of California at Berkeley, graduating in 1956. She began her writing career as a promotional copywriter at Vogue magazine, eventually becoming an associate feature editor. Following the publication of her first novel, Run River, *in 1963, she moved to California and earned her living as a freelance reporter. In 1968, she collected her work in* Slouching towards Bethlehem, *which, with its unsentimental tone and precise prose, became a commercial and critical success. She has since written numerous essays, novels—*The Last Thing He Wanted *(1996) is her latest—and screenplays. When asked about her relatively low output as a writer, Didion responded that she constantly revises and hones her writing: "I'm not much interested in spontaneity, what concerns me is total control."*

WHY I WRITE [1976]

Of course I stole the title for this talk, from George Orwell.[1] One reason I stole it was that I like the sound of the words: Why I Write. There you have three short unambiguous words that share a sound, and the sound they share is this:

I
I
I

[1]**George Orwell** a prominent British writer

In many ways writing is the act of saying *I*, of imposing oneself upon other people, of saying *listen to me, see it my way, change your mind.* It's an aggressive, even a hostile act. You can disguise its aggressiveness all you want with veils of subordinate clauses and qualifiers and tentative subjunctives, with ellipses and evasions—with the whole manner of intimating rather than claiming, of alluding rather than stating—but there's no getting around the fact that setting words on paper is the tactic of a secret bully, an invasion, an imposition of the writer's sensibility on the reader's most private space.

I stole the title not only because the words sounded right but because they seemed to sum up, in a no-nonsense way, all I have to tell you. Like many writers I have only this one "subject," this one "area": the act of writing. I can bring you no reports from any other front. I may have other interests: I am "interested," for example, in marine biology, but I don't flatter myself that you would come out to hear me talk about it. I am not a scholar. I am not in the least an intellectual, which is not to say that when I hear the word "intellectual" I reach for my gun, but only to say that I do not think in abstracts. During the years when I was an undergraduate at Berkeley I tried, with a kind of hopeless late-adolescent energy, to buy some temporary visa into the world of ideas, to forge for myself a mind that could deal with the abstract.

In short I tried to think. I failed. My attention veered inexorably back to the specific, to the tangible, to what was generally considered, by everyone I knew then and for that matter have known since, the peripheral. I would try to contemplate the Hegelian dialectic[2] and would find myself concentrating instead on a flowering pear tree outside my window and the particular way the petals fell on my floor. I would try to read linguistic theory and would find myself wondering instead if the lights were on in the bevatron up the hill. When I say that I was wondering if the lights were on in the bevatron you might immediately suspect, if you deal in ideas at all, that I was registering the bevatron as a political symbol, thinking in shorthand about the military-industrial complex and its role in the university community, but you would be wrong. I was only wondering if the lights were on in the bevatron, and how they looked. A physical fact.

5 I had trouble graduating from Berkeley, not because of this inability to deal with ideas—I was majoring in English, and I could locate the house-and-garden imagery in *The Portrait of a Lady*[3] as well as the next person, "imagery" being by definition the kind of specific that got my attention—but simply because I had neglected to take a course in Milton[4]. For reasons which now sound baroque I needed a degree by the end of that summer, and the English department finally agreed, if I would come down from Sacramento every Friday and talk about the cosmology of *Paradise Lost,* to certify me proficient in Milton. I did this. Some Fridays I took the Greyhound bus, other Fridays I caught the Southern Pacific's City of San Francisco on the last leg of its transcontinental trip. I can no longer tell you whether Milton put the sun or the earth at the center of his universe in

[2]**Hegelian dialectic** trying to find the truth by synthesizing an idea with its opposite [3]**The Portrait of a Lady** a late nineteenth century novel by Henry James [4]**Milton** a seventeenth-century English poet

Paradise Lost, the central question of at least one century and a topic about which I wrote 10,000 words that summer, but I can still recall the exact rancidity of the butter in the City of San Francisco's dining car, and the way the tinted windows on the Greyhound bus cast the oil refineries around Carquinez Straits into a grayed and obscurely sinister light. In short my attention was always on the periphery, on what I would see and taste and touch, on the butter, and the Greyhound bus. During those years I was traveling on what I knew to be a very shaky passport, forged papers: I knew that I was no legitimate resident in any world of ideas. I knew I couldn't think. All I knew then was what I couldn't do. All I knew then was what I wasn't, and it took me some years to discover what I was.

Which was a writer.

By which I mean not a "good" writer or a "bad" writer but simply a writer, a person whose most absorbed and passionate hours are spent arranging words on pieces of paper. Had my credentials been in order I would never have become a writer. Had I been blessed with even limited access to my own mind there would have been no reason to write. I write entirely to find out what I'm thinking, what I'm looking at, what I see and what it means. What I want and what I fear. Why did the oil refineries around Carquinez Straits seem sinister to me in the summer of 1956? Why have the night lights in the bevatron burned in my mind for twenty years? *What is going on in these pictures in my mind?*

When I talk about pictures in my mind I am talking, quite specifically, about images that shimmer around the edges. There used to be an illustration in every elementary psychology book showing a cat drawn by a patient in varying stages of schizophrenia. This cat had a shimmer around it. You could see the molecular structure breaking down at the very edges of the cat: the cat became the background and the background the cat, everything interacting, exchanging ions. People on hallucinogens describe the same perception of objects. I'm not a schizophrenic, nor do I take hallucinogens, but certain images do shimmer for me. Look hard enough, and you can't miss the shimmer. It's there. You can't think too much about these pictures that shimmer. You just lie low and let them develop. You stay quiet. You don't talk to many people and you keep your nervous system from shorting out and you try to locate the cat in the shimmer, the grammar in the picture.

Just as I meant "shimmer" literally I mean "grammar" literally. Grammar is a piano I play by ear, since I seem to have been out of school the year the rules were mentioned. All I know about grammar is its infinite power. To shift the structure of a sentence alters the meaning of that sentence, as definitely and inflexibly as the position of a camera alters the meaning of the object photographed. Many people know about camera angles now, but not so many know about sentences. The arrangement of the words matters, and the arrangement you want can be found in the picture in your mind. The picture dictates the arrangement. The picture dictates whether this will be a sentence with or without clauses, a sentence that ends hard or a dying-fall sentence, long or short, active or passive. The picture tells you how to arrange the words and the arrangement of the words tells you, or tells me, what's going on in the picture. *Nota bene:*[5]

10 It tells you.

You don't tell it.

Let me show you what I mean by pictures in the mind. I began *Play It as It Lays* just as I have begun each of my novels, with no notion of "character" or "plot" or even "incident." I had only two pictures in my mind, more about which later, and a technical intention, which was to write a novel so elliptical and fast that it would be over before you noticed it, a novel so fast that it would scarcely exist on the page at all. About the pictures: the first was of white space. Empty space. This was clearly the picture that dictated the narrative intention of the book—a book in which anything that happened would happen off the page, a "white" book to which the reader would have to bring his or her own bad dreams—and yet this picture told me no "story," suggested no situation. The second picture did. This second picture was of something actually witnessed. A young woman with long hair and a short white halter dress walks through the casino at the Riviera in Las Vegas at one in the morning. She crosses the casino alone and picks up a house telephone. I watch her because I have heard her paged, and recognize her name: she is a minor actress I see around Los Angeles from time to time, in places like Jax and once in a gynecologist's office in the Beverly Hills Clinic, but have never met. I know nothing about her. Who is paging her? Why is she here to be paged? How exactly did she come to this? It was precisely this moment in Las Vegas that made *Play It as It Lays* begin to tell itself to me, but the moment appears in the novel only obliquely, in a chapter which begins:

"Maria made a list of things she would never do. She would never: walk through the Sands or Caesar's alone after midnight. She would never: ball at a party, do S-M unless she wanted to, borrow furs from Abe Lipsey, deal. She would never: carry a Yorkshire in Beverly Hills."

That is the beginning of the chapter and that is also the end of the chapter, which may suggest what I meant by "white space."

15 I recall having a number of pictures in my mind when I began the novel I just finished, *A Book of Common Prayer*. As a matter of fact one of these pictures was of that bevatron I mentioned, although I would be hard put to tell you a story in which nuclear energy figured. Another was a newspaper photograph of a hijacked 707 burning on the desert in the Middle East. Another was the night view from a room in which I once spent a week with paratyphoid, a hotel room on the Colombian coast. My husband and I seemed to be on the Colombian coast representing the United States of America at a film festival (I recall invoking the name "Jack Valenti"[6] a lot, as if its reiteration could make me well), and it was a bad place to have fever, not only because my indisposition offended our hosts but because every night in this hotel the generator failed. The lights went out. The elevator stopped. My husband would go to the event of the evening and

[5]**Nota bene** Latin for "note well" [6]**Jack Valenti** President of the Motion Picture Association of America

make excuses for me and I would stay alone in this hotel room, in the dark. I remember standing at the window trying to call Bogotá (the telephone seemed to work on the same principle as the generator) and watching the night wind come up and wondering what I was doing eleven degrees off the equator with a fever of 103. The view from that window definitely figures in *A Book of Common Prayer,* as does the burning 707, and yet none of these pictures told me the story I needed.

The picture that did, the picture that shimmered and made these other images coalesce, was the Panama airport at 6 A.M. I was in this airport only once, on a plane to Bogotá that stopped for an hour to refuel, but the way it looked that morning remained superimposed on everything I saw until the day I finished *A Book of Common Prayer.* I lived in that airport for several years. I can still feel the hot air when I step off the plane, can see the heat already rising off the tarmac at 6 A.M. I can feel my skirt damp and wrinkled on my legs. I can feel the asphalt stick to my sandals. I remember the big tail of a Pan American plane floating motionless down at the end of the tarmac. I remember the sound of a slot machine in the waiting room. I could tell you that I remember a particular woman in the airport, an American woman, a *norteamericana,* a thin *norteamericana* about 40 who wore a big square emerald in lieu of a wedding ring, but there was no such woman there.

I put this woman in the airport later. I made this woman up, just as I later made up a country to put the airport in, and a family to run the country. This woman in the airport is neither catching a plane nor meeting one. She is ordering tea in the airport coffee shop. In fact she is not simply "ordering" tea but insisting that the water be boiled, in front of her, for twenty minutes. Why is this woman in this airport? Why is she going nowhere, where has she been? Where did she get that big emerald? What derangement, or disassociation, makes her believe that her will to see the water boiled can possibly prevail?

"She had been going to one airport or another for four months, one could see it, looking at the visas on her passport. All those airports where Charlotte Douglas's passport had been stamped would have looked alike. Sometimes the sign on the tower would say "Bienvenidos" and sometimes the sign on the tower would say "Bienvenue," some places were wet and hot and others dry and hot, but at each of these airports the pastel concrete walls would rust and stain and the swamp off the runway would be littered with the fuselages of cannibalized Fairchild F-227's and the water would need boiling.

"I knew why Charlotte went to the airport even if Victor did not."

20 "I knew about airports."

These lines appear about halfway through *A Book of Common Prayer,* but I wrote them during the second week I worked on the book, long before I had any idea where Charlotte Douglas had been or why she went to airports. Until I wrote these lines I had no character called "Victor" in mind: the necessity for mentioning a name, and the name "Victor," occurred to me as I wrote the sentence. *I knew why Charlotte went to the airport* sounded incomplete. *I knew why Charlotte went to the airport even if Victor did not* carried a little more narrative drive. Most important of all, until I wrote these lines I did not know who "I" was, who was telling the story. I had intended until that moment that the "I" be no more than the voice of the author, a nineteenth-century omniscient narrator. But there it was:

"I knew why Charlotte went to the airport even if Victor did not."

"I knew about airports."

This "I" was the voice of no author in my house. This "I" was someone who not only knew why Charlotte went to the airport but also knew someone called "Victor." Who was Victor? Who was this narrator? Why was this narrator telling me this story? Let me tell you one thing about why writers write: had I known the answer to any of these questions I would never have needed to write a novel.

➤ *QUESTIONS FOR READING AND WRITING*

1. In your own words, answer the central question of this essay: Why does Joan Didion write?
2. Do any of the revelations made in this essay surprise you? What, for example, do you think of Didion's saying she writes, in part, because she is not an abstract thinker?
3. Do you agree that writing is in itself necessarily a selfish act? Why or why not?
4. Are there any ideas contained in this essay that you might put to use in your own writing? Which ones? How?

Martin Luther King, Jr.

(1929–1968)

Martin Luther King Jr. was born in Atlanta, Georgia. His father was a minister, and his mother, a teacher. He received a B.A. degree from Morehouse College in 1951, a Ph.D. from Boston University in 1955, and a D.D. from the Chicago Theological Seminary in 1957. King embraced the teachings of Indian leader Mahatma Gandhi, who preached nonviolence as a route to social reform. In 1955 and 1956, applying Gandhi's teaching, King became a national celebrity after organizing a successful boycott of Montgomery, Alabama's, segregated bus system. In the following years, King moved to the forefront of the movement to dismantle all forms of desegregation in the United States, organizing the march on Washington in 1963 and challenging the voting laws in Selma, Alabama, in 1965. In 1964, he became the youngest man ever to win the Nobel Peace Prize. During his lifetime his publications included Stride Toward Freedom: The Montgomery Story *(1958),* Why We Can't Wait *(1964), and his famous open-letter in which he defended his nonviolent philosophy,* Letter from Birmingham City Jail *(1963), written while he*

was imprisoned for organizing protests. King was assassinated on April 4, 1968. "I Have a Dream" was delivered on August 28, 1963, to an audience of over 250,000 who had gathered at the Lincoln Memorial as part of the march on Washington.

I Have a Dream [1963]

Five score years ago, a great American, in whose symbolic shadow we stand, signed the Emancipation Proclamation. This momentous decree came as a great beacon light of hope to millions of Negro slaves who had been seared in the flames of withering injustice. It came as a joyous daybreak to end the long night of captivity.

But one hundred years later, we must face the tragic fact that the Negro is still not free. One hundred years later, the life of the Negro is still sadly crippled by the manacles of segregation and the chains of discrimination. One hundred years later, the Negro lives on a lonely island of poverty in the midst of a vast ocean of material prosperity. One hundred years later, the Negro is still languishing in the corners of American society and finds himself an exile in his own land. So we have come here today to dramatize an appalling condition.

In a sense we have come to our nation's Capitol to cash a check. When the architects of our republic wrote the magnificent words of the Constitution and the Declaration of Independence, they were signing a promissory note to which every American was to fall heir. This note was a promise that all men would be guaranteed the unalienable rights of life, liberty, and the pursuit of happiness.

It is obvious today that America has defaulted on this promissory note insofar as her citizens of color are concerned. Instead of honoring this sacred obligation, America has given the Negro people a bad check; a check which has come back marked "insufficient funds." But we refuse to believe that the bank of justice is bankrupt. We refuse to believe that there are insufficient funds in the great vaults of opportunity of this nation. So we have come to cash this check—a check that will give us upon demand the riches of freedom and the security of justice. We have also come to this hallowed spot to remind America of the fierce urgency of *now.* This is no time to engage in the luxury of cooling off or to take the tranquilizing drug of gradualism. *Now* is the time to make real the promises of Democracy. *Now* is the time to rise from the dark and desolate valley of segregation to the sunlit path of racial justice. *Now* is the time to open the doors of opportunity to all of God's children. *Now* is the time to lift our nation from the quicksands of racial injustice to the solid rock of brotherhood.

5 It would be fatal for the nation to overlook the urgency of the moment and to underestimate the determination of the Negro. This sweltering summer of the Negro's legitimate discontent will not pass until there is an invigorating autumn of freedom and equality. 1963 is not an end, but a beginning. Those who hope that the Negro needed to blow off steam and will now be content will have a rude awakening if the nation returns to business as usual. There will be neither rest nor tranquility in America until the Negro is granted his citizenship rights. The whirlwinds of revolt will continue to shake the foundations of our nation until the bright day of justice emerges.

But there is something I must say to my people who stand on the warm threshold which leads into the palace of justice. In the process of gaining our rightful place we must not be guilty of wrongful deeds. Let us not seek to satisfy our thirst for freedom by drinking from the cup of bitterness and hatred. We must forever conduct our struggle on the high plane of dignity and discipline. We must not allow our creative protest to degenerate into physical violence. Again and again we must rise to the majestic heights of meeting physical force with soul force. The marvelous new militancy which has engulfed the Negro community must not lead us to a distrust of all white people, for many of our white brothers, as evidenced by their presence here today, have come to realize that their destiny is tied up with our destiny and their freedom is inextricably bound to our freedom. We cannot walk alone.

And as we walk, we must make the pledge that we shall march ahead. We cannot turn back. There are those who are asking the devotees of civil rights, "When will you be satisfied?" We can never be satisfied as long as the Negro is the victim of the unspeakable horrors of police brutality. We can never be satisfied as long as our bodies, heavy with the fatigue of travel, cannot gain lodging in the motels of the highways and the hotels of the cities. We cannot be satisfied as long as the Negro's basic mobility is from a smaller ghetto to a larger one. We can never be satisfied as long as a Negro in Mississippi cannot vote and a Negro in New York believes he has nothing for which to vote. No, no, we are not satisfied, and we will not be satisfied until justice rolls down like waters and righteousness like a mighty stream.

I am not unmindful that some of you have come here out of great trials and tribulations. Some of you have come fresh from narrow jail cells. Some of you have come from areas where your quest for freedom left you battered by the storms of persecution and staggered by the winds of policy brutality. You have been the veterans of creative suffering. Continue to work with the faith that unearned suffering is redemptive.

Go back to Mississippi, go back to Alabama, go back to South Carolina, go back to Georgia, go back to Louisiana, go back to the slums and ghettoes of our northern cities, knowing that somehow this situation can and will be changed. Let us not wallow in the valley of despair.

10 I say to you today, my friends, that in spite of the difficulties and frustrations of the moment I still have a dream. It is a dream deeply rooted in the American dream.

I have a dream that one day this nation will rise up and live out the true meaning of its creed: "We hold these truths to be self-evident; that all men are created equal."

I have a dream that one day on the red hills of Georgia the sons of former slaves and the sons of former slaveowners will be able to sit down together at the table of brotherhood.

I have a dream that the state of Mississippi, a desert state sweltering with the heat of injustice and oppression, will be transformed into an oasis of freedom and justice.

I have a dream that my four little children will one day live in a nation where they will not be judged by the color of their skin but by the content of their character.

15 I have a dream today.

I have a dream that the state of Alabama, whose governor's lips are presently dripping with the words of interposition and nullification, will be transformed into a situation where little black boys and black girls will be able to join hands with little white boys and white girls and walk together as sisters and brothers.

I have a dream today.

I have a dream that one day every valley shall be exalted, every hill and mountain shall be made low, the rough places will be made plain, and the crooked places will be made straight, and the glory of the Lord shall be revealed, and all flesh shall see it together.

This is our hope. This is the faith with which I return to the South. With this faith we will be able to hew out of the mountain of despair a stone of hope. With this faith we will be able to transform the jangling discords of our nation into a beautiful symphony of brotherhood. With this faith we will be able to work together, to pray together, to struggle together, to go to jail together, to stand up for freedom together, knowing that we will be free one day.

This will be the day when all of God's children will be able to sing with new meaning.

My country, tis of thee
Sweet land of liberty,
    Of thee I sing:
Land where my fathers died,
Land of the pilgrims' pride,
From every mountainside
    Let freedom ring.

And if America is to be a great nation this must become true. So let freedom ring from the prodigious hilltops of New Hampshire. Let freedom ring from the mighty mountains of New York. Let freedom ring from the heightening Alleghenies of Pennsylvania!

Let freedom ring from the snowcapped Rockies of Colorado!

Let freedom ring from the curvaceous peaks of California!

But not only that; let freedom ring from Stone Mountain of Georgia!

Let freedom ring from Lookout Mountain of Tennessee!

Let freedom ring from every hill and molehill of Mississippi. From every mountainside, let freedom ring.

When we let freedom ring, when we let it ring from every village and every hamlet, from every state and every city, we will be able to speed up that day when all of God's children, black men and white men, Jews and Gentiles, Protestants and Catholics, will be able to join hands and sing in the words of the old Negro spiritual, "Free at last! Free at last! Thank God almighty, we are free at last!"

➤ *QUESTIONS FOR READING AND WRITING*

1. What is the dream of Martin Luther King?
2. He says his dream is derived from the "American Dream." What is the American Dream?

3. What does he mean by "this will be the day when all God's children will be able to sing with new meaning 'My country 'tis of the, / Sweet land of liberty',"?
4. What is the tone of this essay? Who is the intended audience? What is its objective?
5. To what extent are the style, structure, and use of figurative language inspirational?

NEIL MILLER

Neil Miller is author of Gay and Lesbian Life from Buenos Aires to Bangkok *and* In Search of Gay America *(1989). He has traveled through small towns, rural areas, mid-sized cities, suburbs, and large urban centers in search of what it means and is like to be gay in America and overseas. His writing is dedicated to exploring the enormous changes that are taking place in the lives of lesbians and gay men.*

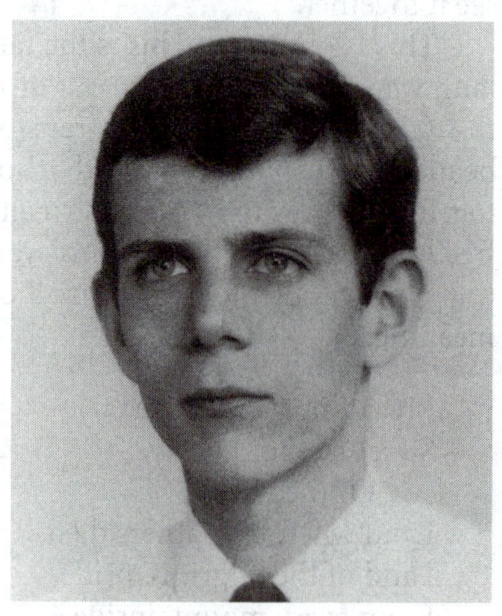

IN SEARCH OF GAY AMERICA: OGILVIE, MINNESOTA (POPULATION 374)

[1989]

I missed the Minnesota State Fair by three weeks. As an easterner living in a large urban area, I am not particularly conscious of state fairs. And I never assumed that the beef and poultry barn or the cattle barn of a state fair would be a particularly good place to observe gay and lesbian life.

I was wrong. At the Minnesota State Fair, held at the end of August at the St. Paul fairgrounds, a brown and white fifteen hundred pound bull belonging to Al Philipi and John Ritter was named the 1987 state champion. Al and John are two gay dairy farmers who live sixty-five miles north of the Twin Cities. At the awards ceremony, they received a wooden plaque in the shape of the state of Minnesota with the state seal embossed in gold. Tears were streaming down Al's face, John told me.

In the Twin Cities of Minneapolis and St. Paul, you can't help but be aware of the state's agricultural roots. The farm is always just a generation away, despite the air of urban sophistication, the experimental theatre and the recording studios and the take-out Szechuan restaurants, the punk rockers and the long-haired graduate students pedalling their ten-speeds down Hennepin Avenue as if it were Harvard Square. The connection to the land is as true for gay people as anyone else. Karen Clark, the openly lesbian state representative from an inner-city district of

Minneapolis, told me with pride that she had grown up on a farm in southwestern Minnesota; she advertised her rural background in her campaign literature. On the office wall of Allan Spear, the gay state senator and chairman of the Minnesota Senate Judiciary Committee, were large framed photographs of Floyd Olson and Elmer Benson, the two agrarian reforming governors of the thirties elected on the ticket of the Farmer Labor party. So when the managing editor of *Equal Time,* the gay newspaper in Minneapolis, suggested I interview one of their editors who lived on a farm and whose lover was a full-time dairy farmer, I was eager to do so. Orwell[1] had written that the coal miner was second in importance to the man who plowed the soil. I had found the first after such travail; two genuine dairy farmers were as close as I expected to get to the second.

When I arrived at Al and John's farm, late on a Saturday afternoon, autumn was beginning to wane, though it was only September. The leaves had turned to dull yellows and oranges, the cornfields along the side of the road were a russet brown, the days were crisp and clear, and the nights felt colder. Al and John were in high spirits. They had just returned from an overnight trip to the Guernsey Breeders Association cattle sale in Hutchinson, Minnesota, a few hours' drive away. Their friend Paul Leach, a gay dairy farmer who lived an hour to the north, had come by to do the milking and keep an eye on things. Al and John had bought three new cows in Hutchinson, and their prize-winning bull had been displayed on the cover of the auction catalog. John told me later that Al hadn't slept for the entire week before the auction.

5 Al didn't tend to sleep much anyway. He had put his cows on an unusual schedule, milking and feeding five times in each two-day period, at nine and a half hour intervals, with the schedule changing every other day. The cycle began with a milking at midnight; other milkings followed at nine thirty the next morning and seven in the evening. The next day he milked at four thirty in the morning, at two in the afternoon, and once again at midnight. (Most farmers had a saner schedule, milking regularly at five in the morning and five in the evening.) Al started on this routine to increase cash flow. "Your operation can either get larger and generate more product," he said, "or you can generate more product per unit." Buying more cows was just too expensive, with prices ranging from $750 to $1,600 a head, so Al opted for getting more milk out of the cows he had. The arrangement seemed to work, with production up eighteen percent since they had started on the new schedule. One result was that Al and John had a coffee pot going twenty-four hours a day, and Al took frequent catnaps.

I had never been on a dairy farm before and didn't realize how demanding the work could be. John and Al had fifty cows, twenty of which were milking. Almost all their livestock was brown and white Guernseys, and the two farmers were extremely partial to the breed. Guernsey cattle, they told me, tended to produce higher solids in their milk, which was good for making cheese. Their farm produced six hundred pounds of milk each day, which John and Al sold to a dairy cooperative that resold it to small cheese plants in Wisconsin. Each milking and feeding lasted about two and a half hours.

[1]**Orwell** George Orwell (1903–1950) prominent British writer

The evening I arrived, I fell asleep before the midnight milking (or "melking," as John and Al pronounce it) but was at the barn promptly at nine thirty the following morning. There, in a sweatshirt, jeans, and high galoshes, John was lugging a forty-five pound steel milking unit from cow to cow and transferring the milk to a big steel vat at the entrance to the barn; then he washed and cleaned the cows' teats, swept the stalls, and shoveled manure. Paul, the visiting farmer, was in charge of the feeding. Al was shoring up a broken stall and giving the cows a dessert of beet pulp.

Like a proud father, Al introduced me to every cow by name, personality, and production value. First came Lilly, lone Brown Swiss among Guernseys, a cow Al described as "heavy, aggressive, good producing. She will finish with 21,000 to 22,000 pounds of milk this year." Then, Honors: "a people cow." Isabel: "on her first lactation." Teardrop: "Our gay friends love her. She has incredibly beautiful eyes." And so on, through fifty cows, eight crested Polish chickens (whose coloration made them look as if they were wearing hats), sixteen lambs (Al hoped to increase that number to one or two hundred soon; both the wool and lamb market had been up recently), two lavender angora rabbits (whose fur could be spun into yarn), and three horses. Never far away was Nellie, a diminutive white poodle who made a rather humorous farm dog.

Al compared looking after his cows to bringing up fifty children. "They are very dependent on humans and very individual," he said. "With them, there are tremendous difficulties and tremendous disappointments. They can have structural problems, heart attacks. You play doctor and nurse to them. They can lay down and die one day for no apparent reason. In this business, the profit margins are slim, the tension and stress can be awful." The rewards made it all worthwhile, nonetheless: "the renewing experience" of calving, the "tremendous joy" of working with animals.

10 Al was an unusual combination of urban camp sensibility and country style and values. He wore two earrings in his left ear and a bangle on his wrist; his shirt was open almost to his navel. He gave his cows names like "You Tell 'Em Dorothy" and "Fashion Design" and called one sheep "Dottie of Fergus Falls" (after an ice-cream commercial). He divided the cows that weren't milking into three categories: "debs, minnies, and nymphettes." Inside the farmhouse, gay paperback gothics and mysteries filled the shelves. Three movie-theatre seats provided living room furniture, someone's idea of trendy but not particularly comfortable "gay" decor. On the dining room wall was a photograph of someone standing in the barn dressed in black stockings, lace panties, and black jacket, with a cow looking on incredulously in the background. On closer inspection, the person in the photograph turned out to bear a striking resemblance to Al. Also on that wall was the wooden plaque Al and John's bull won at the State Fair. "1987 Minnesota State Fair Grand Champion," it read.

Al, at thirty-seven, was the dreamer, the impractical one, living out his passion—his love of animals. John, at thirty-two, complemented him—he was solid and forthright, bringing sense, balance, and some hard-headed financial realism to the operation and to their life together. When Al described the cows as "a commodity," John assured me, "He doesn't really mean that. He picked up that phrase from me." Unlike Al, John had a life beyond the farm. He commuted five days a week to the Twin Cities, where he worked as a reporter-editor for *The Farmer,* a monthly magazine that covers midwestern agriculture. He also worked part-time as regional news editor for *Equal Time,* the gay and lesbian paper. While Al called dairy farming "my career," John considered himself a journalist first and a farmer second.

Weekdays, John left for work at seven in the morning, often not returning until as late as eleven in the evening, especially if he was doing a story for *Equal Time.* Sometimes he could be gone for days at a stretch covering South Dakota, his beat. John's absences left the management of the farm almost completely in Al's hands. Al became the one to negotiate with the banks and the dairy cooperative and the salesmen who came to the farm to sell feed and semen, to talk to the veterinarian and the county agent. He spent his days like most other dairy farmers in the Midwest: milking and feeding cows, cleaning barns, hauling manure, mowing lawns, confronting crises, and grabbing a few hours of sleep when he could.

Al and John had been dairy farmers for four years and lovers for eight and a half. They leased a five-acre farm near the town of Ogilvie, where the exurbia of Minneapolis gives way to the bait shops and mobile homes of Kanabec County. One demographer recently anointed the county the next area for growth in Minnesota, but there were few signs of development yet, at least in the area where Al and John lived. Ogilvie, the nearest town and where the two did their shopping, looks as if it is out of a painting by Edward Hopper. The country is flat and cheerless, crossed by Highway 65, the route that hunters and fishermen from the Twin Cities take to their cabins on the lakes farther north. The farms are poor and relatively small; the visitor misses the intimacy of the rolling country of Iowa to the south or the dramatic expanses of the wheat belt of the Dakotas to the west.

There was nothing particularly bucolic about John and Al's Blue Spur Farm. They didn't grow their own feed or even have a vegetable garden. The farmhouse, located virtually on the highway, was plain and slightly rundown. Just behind the house, the cattle barn, with its characteristic grey-shingled silo, was badly in need of paint. Connected to it was a tin-roofed, functional structure for the dry cows and baby heifers and a shed for the lambs. A few acres of pasture behind the barn completed the picture.

15 I went off with John and Paul, the visiting farmer, in John's pickup to have dinner at the Sportsman's Cafe, the nearest watering hole, about ten minutes down the road at Mora. Sportsman's was a joint with a large counter in the middle and booths along the side wall. It was open twenty-four hours a day to serve fishermen and hunters and state troopers, and John knew all the waitresses, women in their forties and fifties who have spent their lives standing on their feet. "Where's your friend?" one of them asked John as soon as we walked in. "I haven't seen either one of you in weeks."

At Sportsman's, we ate homemade oyster stew and pecan pie, and John drank several cups of coffee to keep awake for the late-night milking. John told me that he and Al had both grown up on dairy farms—Al in northern Minnesota, sixty miles from the Canadian border, where his father raised Guernseys; John to the west of the Twin Cities, where his family still raised Holsteins. John had always intended to get away from farming; the work was too hard. He met Al at the wedding of a mutual friend in Grand Forks, North Dakota. At the time, John was living in the

Twin Cities and working on a newspaper; Al was farming with his father. Soon after, Al moved down to St. Paul to live with John, working in retail clothing stores.

But the attractions of urban life dwindled, and the focus of their lives began to shift back towards the farm. John moved into ag-journalism, writing for *The Farmer,* partly because he was frustrated by the long hours of news writing but also because of Al's continuing interest in the subject. More and more, they began to fantasize about returning to a rural setting, if not to farming itself. Their friends refused to take them seriously, dismissing the idea as "cute" or "a nice little dream." Al and John bought some horses and moved just outside St. Paul. A few cows wouldn't be too much trouble, they decided, and then they moved out even farther. John was somewhat reluctant; he is the cautious one, after all, and also the one who really wanted to get away from farming. But Al pressed, and John gave in.

John stressed that in returning to the farm, he and Al had made a conscious effort to do things differently from most gay farmers in the past. Traditionally, he said, in order to stay in agriculture, gay farmers either married someone of the opposite sex or completely sacrificed any possibility of a relationship. Whatever their strategy for survival, they remained in the closet. Although John and Al weren't going to advertise their homosexuality, they were determined not to hide it either, letting people draw their own conclusions instead. "I have run into people in town who thought we were brothers, even though our names are different," said John. "They are more comfortable thinking that way." Some people were suspicious, he admitted, and others knew they were gay and didn't approve, sometimes telling them so directly. But he thought that to half of them, the possibility of his and Al's homosexuality "doesn't occur at all."

Al agreed. "Most farmers are more interested in how the livestock in our farming operation performs," he told me later. When a story about them as gay farmers (including photos) appeared on the front page of the daily newspaper in nearby St. Cloud, there was no visible reaction from their neighbors.

20 Their friend Paul had had a more traditionally closeted experience, however. He was a sweet and unassuming man in his late twenties, with curly brown hair and a neatly clipped beard. Four and a half years ago, while living in the Twin Cities, he became the lover of an older man. The two bought a farm together in a predominantly Finnish area about two and a half hours north of Minneapolis. The older man had died of lung cancer a few months before; Paul still spoke of his lover in the present tense. Paul stayed on at the farm with only three small calves, rebuilding a barn and hoping to establish a viable livestock business. Paul said the main issue for the neighbors had not been the couple's homosexuality but the fact that he and his lover were German Catholics, not Finnish Protestants. "First they thought my lover was my father until they realized we didn't have the same last name," he said. "Then they thought I was just his hired man." Now, his neighbors were beginning to wonder. "They are thinking, 'This is weird. The hired man is still living there,'" Paul observed. Just a week before, in the small town nearby, he had heard someone mutter "There goes a queer," as he was leaving a store. "I presume they were talking about me," he said. "I guess I'm 'out' now."

For their part, Al and John had not been particularly active in the organization of local Guernsey farmers, but this was changing. The award their bull received at the state fair and the fact they were advertising their livestock in the Guernsey breeders' magazine had given them increased visibility among local farmers. Now, "people notice us," said John. "The ad gave people an opportunity to say something to us." In fact, the following week Al and John were holding a potluck picnic at their farm for the Northeast District Guernsey Breeders Association. They expected about twenty dairy farmers to attend.

There had been one disturbing episode, however. Al had been coaching the 4-H county dairy cattle judging team, composed of kids aged fourteen to sixteen. One parent complained to the county agent who supervises the 4-H that Al was gay. The agent apparently failed to back Al up, and Al resigned as coach. He hoped to be invited back the following year, noting that the kids involved in the organization had been supportive. But John, always the more realistic one, was doubtful this would happen.

In the process of living in the country, they had increasingly discovered other farmers like themselves—a gay male couple nearby who raised sheep, a lesbian couple who had dairy goats, and two other men with a hog farm. Three years ago, Al and John took out a classified advertisement in *Equal Time,* announcing they would be at the state fair and inviting other gay people to stop by the cattle barn and say hello. They were startled by the constant stream of visitors. This summer, *Equal Time* published John's "Gay Guide to the State Fair" as its cover article. One result was that Paul came by the cattle barn, introduced himself to them, and all three became fast friends.

The fact that John and Al were open about their sexuality put them in a pivotal spot in helping to develop a close-knit rural gay community in Minnesota. (John and Al, it should be noted, were not the first gay farmers in the state to come out publicly. Dick Hanson, farmer, farm activist, and member of the Democratic National Committee, was openly gay and quite well-known. Hanson died of AIDS in late July 1987.) "Unless you are willing to be 'out,' it is hard to connect with people," John observed. "A lot of these gay farmers thought they were the only ones doing this." Now Al and John's social circle was shifting. Although they remained close with many of their urban gay friends, especially those who were interested in what they were doing, only a special occasion could persuade them to trek into the Twin Cities.

25 To me, one of the most interesting aspects of John and Al's return to the farm was that it had brought about a reconciliation with their parents. Several years ago, when John first told his parents he was gay, they were traumatized, he said. But out of seven sons of a farm family, John was the only one currently involved in agriculture. For his father, who was still operating the family farm, the return of his gay son to the land was "the least expected thing," said John. His father had been supportive of their operation and both father and son tried to help each other whenever possible, trading advice and material assistance. As John noted, they were both in the same business and faced the "same questions and troubles."

None of Al's two brothers and two sisters were farming either, and his parents had retired. But family ties to the land remained strong. One sister, who lived in Denver, was "absolutely thrilled," he said, when their bull won the state fair championship. Although she lived in a city, she was eager for her children to have some connection with the family's rural roots. "And it just so happens that in our family Uncle Al and Uncle John are the only ones who are farming," her brother pointed out.

The ability of both sets of parents to identify with Al and John's occupation appeared to provide a counterweight to their difficulties in accepting their sons' homosexuality. If they had lived in the Twin Cities and worked at jobs their parents couldn't identify with, the gay issue might loom larger between the generations, Al and John thought. John noted that from the time he went to college until he began farming, he had had little in common with his family. That certainly wasn't true these days. "As far as sexuality goes, they accept it but they are not supportive," he said. "But they are supportive of the rest of my life."

Al and John maintained that living on the farm had strengthened their own relationship as well, and noted that they had been together the longest in their circle of gay couples. John believed that doing what they wanted to do with their lives—in Al's case, farming, in John's, a combination of farming and journalism—gave their relationship a strength it might not have had if they had sacrificed their aspirations and opted for a more conventional urban gay life. The fact they were business partners as well as lovers provided another tie; it would take months to dissolve their financial bonds. "This is not just a personal relationship, but an economic one, too," Al said.

Although they had left the big city behind, they were reluctant to cut their links to the larger gay world. They had been exploring the notion of combining farming with managing a gay-oriented bed and breakfast. (By the end of my travels, I was convinced that running a B and B is the dream of half the gay men in the United States.) The farm they currently leased wouldn't be appropriate, so they were looking at property slightly closer to the Twin Cities. "It is a dream," John admitted. He also conceded that combining milking cows and raising sheep with changing sheets and cooking breakfast for guests might turn out to be more than they could handle. Nonetheless, they were just not the kind of farmers who want to be "isolated and secluded," as John put it. The presence of a large and active gay community in the Twin Cities offered them a connection and a potential for involvement that other gay farmers who lived farther away didn't have.

Few urban gays were following in Al and John's footsteps. The dismal state of the farm economy argued against any major migration back to the farm; large numbers of farmers, both gay and straight, were packing up and leaving the land, as it was. And many gay men and lesbians who grew up on farms and in rural areas didn't necessarily recall their formative years with fondness. "You grow up on the farm and as you realize your sexuality, you feel you just don't fit," Al told me. "You don't fit in at Sunday church dinners or the PTA or picnics. You become frustrated and you search for others like yourself, and they are not real visible in a rural area. So you tend to leave."

But the pull of one's roots is a powerful thing. "As you mature," Al added, "you tend to go back."

➤ *QUESTIONS FOR READING AND WRITING*

1. Why do you think the writer was surprised to find "gay and lesbian life" in Ogilvie, Minnesota? Were you? Explain.
2. What do you think has been the key to Al and John's acceptance in the farm community?
3. The author indicates that few urban gays are following the path of Al and John. Why?
4. This article was published in 1989. Do you think gays are more accepted as fixtures in suburban and rural life today? Explain.

MAY SARTON (1912–1995)

May Sarton was born in Belgium and raised in Cambridge, Massachusetts. Her father was the prominent historian of science, George Sarton. After attending schools locally and in Belgium, she settled in New York City and was a member of Eva Le Gallienne's Civic Repertory Theatre from 1929 to 1934, before founding and directing her own experimental company, the Associated Actors Theatre, from 1934 to 1937. She gradually turned her interests to creative writing, publishing her first book of poetry, Encounter, *in 1937, following it with numerous other volumes of poetry, novels, and autobiography. She is particularly well-known for her journals that depict her often solitary life in rural New Hampshire. She continued to keep journals into her old age, publishing them periodically—*At Seventy: A Journal *(1984),* After the Stroke: A Journal *(1988), and* At Eighty-Two: A Journal *(1996). Her final collection of poetry,* Coming into Eighty, *was published in 1994.*

THE REWARDS OF LIVING A SOLITARY LIFE [1974]

The other day an acquaintance of mine, a gregarious and charming man, told me he had found himself unexpectedly alone in New York for an hour or two between appointments. He went to the Whitney and spent the "empty" time looking at things in solitary bliss. For him it proved to be a shock nearly as great as falling in love to discover that he could enjoy himself so much alone.

What had he been afraid of, I asked myself? That, suddenly alone, he would discover that he bored himself, or that there was, quite simply, no self there to meet? But having taken the plunge, he is now on the brink of adventure; he is about to be launched into his own inner space, space as immense, unexplored, and sometimes frightening as outer space to the astronaut. His every perception will come to him with a new freshness and, for a time, seem startlingly original. For anyone who can see things for himself with a naked eye becomes, for a moment or two, something of a genius. With another human being present vision becomes double vision, inevitably. We are busy wondering, what does my companion see or think of this, and what do I think of it? The original impact gets lost, or diffused.

"Music I heard with you was more than music." Exactly. And therefore music *itself* can only be heard alone. Solitude is the salt of personhood. It brings out the authentic flavor of every experience.

"Alone one is never lonely: the spirit adventures, walking/In a quiet garden, in a cool house, abiding single there."

5 Loneliness is most acutely felt with other people, for with others, even with a lover sometimes, we suffer from our differences of taste, temperament, mood. Human intercourse often demands that we soften the edge of perception, or withdraw at the very instant of personal truth for fear of hurting, or of being inappropriately present, which is to say naked, in a social situation. Alone we can afford to be wholly whatever we are, and to feel whatever we feel absolutely. That is a great luxury!

For me the most interesting thing about a solitary life, and mine has been that for the last twenty years, is that it becomes increasingly rewarding. When I can wake up and watch the sun rise over the ocean, as I do most days, and know that I have an entire day ahead, uninterrupted, in which to write a few pages, take a walk with my dog, lie down in the afternoon for a long think (why does one think better in a horizontal position?), read and listen to music, I am flooded with happiness.

I am lonely only when I am overtired, when I have worked too long without a break, when for the time being I feel empty and need filling up. And I am lonely sometimes when I come back home after a lecture trip, when I have seen a lot of people and talked a lot, and am full to the brim with experience that needs to be sorted out.

Then for a little while the house feels huge and empty, and I wonder where my self is hiding. It has to be recaptured slowly by watering the plants, perhaps, and looking again at each one as though it were a person, by feeding the two cats, by cooking a meal.

It takes a while, as I watch the surf blowing up in fountains at the end of the field, but the moment comes when the world falls away, and the self emerges again from the deep unconscious, bringing back all I have recently experienced to be explored and slowly understood, when I can converse again with my hidden powers, and so grow, and so be renewed, till death do us part.

➤ *QUESTIONS FOR READING AND WRITING*

1. What are the rewards of living a solitary life?
2. What is the difference between "solitude" and "loneliness"?
3. What evidence does the author give to support her view? How does the strategy and structure of the essay amplify that support?

CASE STUDIES IN COMPOSITION

Thinking About Interpretation and Performance

William Shakespeare and *Hamlet*

WILLIAM SHAKESPEARE (1564–1616)

HAMLET, PRINCE OF DENMARK

DRAMATIS PERSONAE
GHOST of Hamlet, the former King of Denmark
CLAUDIUS, King of Denmark, the former King's brother
GERTRUDE, Queen of Denmark, widow of the former King and now wife of Claudius
HAMLET, Prince of Denmark, son of the late King and of Gertrude
POLONIUS, *councillor to the King*
LAERTES, *his son*
OPHELIA, *his daughter*
REYNALDO, *his servant*
HORATIO, *Hamlet's friend and fellow student*

VOLTIMAND,
CORNELIUS,
ROSENCRANTZ,
GUILDENSTERN,
OSRIC,
A GENTLEMAN,
A LORD,
} *members of the Danish court*

BERNARDO,
FRANCISCO,
MARCELLUS,
} *officers and soldiers on watch*

FORTINBRAS, *Prince of Norway*
CAPTAIN *in his army*
Three or Four PLAYERS, *taking the roles of* PROLOGUE, PLAYER KING, PLAYER QUEEN, and LUCIANUS

Two MESSENGERS
FIRST SAILOR
Two CLOWNS, *a gravedigger and his companion*
PRIEST
FIRST AMBASSADOR *from England*
Lords, Soldiers, Attendants, Guards, other Players, Followers of Laertes, other Sailors, another Ambassador or Ambassadors from England

SCENE: *Denmark*

[1.1 *Enter* BERNARDO *and* FRANCISCO, *two sentinels (meeting)*].°

BERNARDO: Who's there?
FRANCISCO: Nay, answer me.° Stand and unfold yourself.°
BERNARDO: Long live the King!
FRANCISCO: Bernardo?
BERNARDO: He.
FRANCISCO: You come most carefully upon your hour.
BERNARDO: 'Tis now struck twelve. Get thee to bed, Francisco.
FRANCISCO: For this relief much thanks. 'Tis bitter cold,
And I am sick at heart.
BERNARDO: Have you had quiet guard?
FRANCISCO: Not a mouse stirring.
BERNARDO: Well, good night.
If you do meet Horatio and Marcellus,
The rivals° of my watch, bid them make haste.

[Enter HORATIO *and* MARCELLUS.*]*

FRANCISCO: I think I hear them.—Stand, ho! Who is there?
HORATIO: Friends to this ground.°
MARCELLUS: And liegemen to the Dane.°
FRANCISCO: Give° you good night.
MARCELLUS: O, farewell, honest soldier. Who hath relieved you?
FRANCISCO: Bernardo hath my place. Give you good night.

[Exit FRANCISCO.*]*

MARCELLUS: Holla! Bernardo!
BERNARDO: Say, what, is Horatio there?
HORATIO: A piece of him.
BERNARDO: Welcome, Horatio. Welcome, good Marcellus.
HORATIO: What, has this thing appeared again tonight?

1.1 s.d. **Location: Elsinore castle. A guard platform.** 2 **me** (Francisco emphasizes that he is the sentry currently on watch.) **unfold yourself** reveal your identity 14 **rivals** partners 16 **ground** country, land 17 **liegemen to the Dane** men sworn to serve the Danish king 18 **Give** i.e., may God give

BERNARDO: I have seen nothing.
MARCELLUS: Horatio says 'tis but our fantasy,°
And will not let belief take hold of him
Touching this dreaded sight twice seen of us.
Therefore I have entreated him along°
With us to watch° the minutes of this night,
That if again this apparition come
He may approve° our eyes and speak to it.
HORATIO: Tush, tush, 'twill not appear.
BERNARDO: Sit down awhile,
And let us once again assail your ears,
That are so fortified against our story,
What° we have two nights seen.
HORATIO: Well, sit we down,
And let us hear Bernardo speak of this.
BERNARDO: Last night of all,°
When yond same star that's westward from the pole°
Had made his° course t' illume° that part of heaven
Where now it burns, Marcellus and myself,
The bell then beating one—

[Enter GHOST.]

MARCELLUS: Peace, break thee off! Look where it comes again!
BERNARDO: In the same figure like the King that's dead.
MARCELLUS: Thou art a scholar.° Speak to it, Horatio.
BERNARDO: Looks 'a° not like the King? Mark it, Horatio.
HORATIO: Most like. It harrows me with fear and wonder.
BERNARDO: It would be spoke to.°
MARCELLUS: Speak to it, Horatio.
HORATIO: What art thou that usurp'st° this time of night,
Together with that fair and warlike form
In which the majesty of buried Denmark°
Did sometime° march? By heaven, I charge thee, speak!
MARCELLUS: It is offended.
BERNARDO: See, it stalks away.
HORATIO: Stay! Speak, speak! I charge thee, speak!

[Exit GHOST.]

27 **fantasy** imagination 30 **along** to come along 31 **watch** keep watch during 33 **approve** corroborate 37 **What** with what 39 **Last . . . all** i.e., this *very* last night (Emphatic.) 40 **pole** polestar, north star 41 **his** its **illume** illuminate 46 **scholar** one learned enough to know how to question a ghost properly 47 **'a** he 49 **It . . . to** (It was commonly believed that a ghost could not speak until spoken to.) 50 **usurp'st** wrongfully takes over 52 **buried Denmark** the buried King of Denmark 53 **sometime** formerly

MARCELLUS: 'Tis gone and will not answer.
BERNARDO: How now, Horatio? You tremble and look pale.
Is not this something more than fantasy?
What think you on 't?°
HORATIO: Before my God, I might not this believe
Without the sensible° and true avouch°
Of mine own eyes.
MARCELLUS: Is it not like the King?
HORATIO: As thou art to thyself.
Such was the very armor he had on
When he the ambitious Norway° combated.
So frowned he once when, in an angry parle,°
He smote the sledded° Polacks° on the ice.
'Tis strange.
MARCELLUS: Thus twice before, and jump° at this dead hour,
With martial stalk° hath he gone by our watch.
HORATIO: In what particular thought to work° I know not,
But in the gross and scope° of mine opinion
This bodes some strange eruption to our state.
MARCELLUS: Good now,° sit down, and tell me, he that knows,
Why this same strict and most observant watch
So nightly toils° the subject° of the land,
And why such daily cast° of brazen cannon
And foreign mart° for implements of war,
Why such impress° of shipwrights, whose sore task
Does not divide the Sunday from the week.
What might be toward,° that this sweaty haste
Doth make the night joint-laborer with the day?
Who is 't that can inform me?
HORATIO: That can I;
At least, the whisper goes so. Our last king,
Whose image even but now appeared to us,
Was, as you know, by Fortinbras of Norway,
Thereto pricked on° by a most emulate° pride,°
Dared to the combat; in which our valiant Hamlet—
For so this side of our known world° esteemed him—

59 **on't** of it 61 **sensible** confirmed by the senses **avouch** warrant, evidence 65 **Norway** King of Norway 66 **parle** parley 67 **sledded** traveling on sleds **Polacks** Poles 69 **jump** exactly 70 **stalk** stride 71 **to work** i.e., to collect my thoughts and try to understand this 72 **gross and scope** general drift 74 **Good now** (An expression denoting entreaty or expostulation.) 76 **toils** causes to toil **subject** subjects 77 **cast** casting 78 **mart** buying and selling 79 **impress** impressment, conscription 81 **toward** in preparation 87 **pricked on** incited **emulate** emulous, ambitious **Thereto . . . pride** (Refers to old Fortinbras, not the Danish King.) 89 **this . . . world** i.e., all Europe, the Western world

Did slay this Fortinbras; who by a sealed° compact
Well ratified by law and heraldry
Did forfeit, with his life, all those his lands
Which he stood seized° of, to the conqueror;
Against the° which a moiety competent°
Was gagèd° by our king, which had returned°
To the inheritance° of Fortinbras
Had he been vanquisher, as, by the same cov'nant°
And carriage of the article designed,°
His fell to Hamlet. Now, sir, young Fortinbras,
Of unimprovèd mettle° hot and full,
Hath in the skirts° of Norway here and there
Sharked up° a list° of lawless resolutes°
For food and diet° to some enterprise
That hath a stomach° in 't, which is no other—
As it doth well appear unto our state—
But to recover of us, by strong hand
And terms compulsatory, those foresaid lands
So by his father lost. And this, I take it,
Is the main motive of our preparations,
The source of this our watch, and the chief head°
Of this posthaste and rummage° in the land.

BERNARDO: I think it be no other but e'en so.
Well may it sort° that this portentous figure
Comes armèd through our watch so like the King
That was and is the question° of these wars.

HORATIO: A mote° it is to trouble the mind's eye.
In the most high and palmy° state of Rome,
A little ere the mightiest Julius fell,
The graves stood tenantless, and the sheeted° dead
Did squeak and gibber in the Roman streets;
As° stars with trains° of fire and dews of blood,
Disasters° in the sun; and the moist star°

90 **sealed** certified, confirmed 93 **seized** possessed 94 **Against the** in return for **moiety** competent corresponding portion 95 **gagèd** engaged, pledged **had returned** would have passed 96 **inheritance** possession 97 **cov'nant** i.e., the *sealed compact* of line 90 98 **carriage . . . designed** carrying out of the article or clause drawn up to cover the point 100 **unimprovèd mettle** untried, undisciplined spirits 101 **skirts** outlying regions, outskirts 102 **Sharked up** gathered up, as a shark takes fish **list** i.e., troop **resolutes** desperadoes 103 **For food and diet** i.e., they are to serve as *food,* or "means," *to some enterprise;* also they serve in return for the rations they get 104 **stomach** (1) a spirit of daring (2) an appetite that is fed by the *lawless resolutes* 110 **head** source 111 **rummage** bustle, commotion 113 **sort** suit 115 **question** focus of contention 116 **mote** speck of dust 117 **palmy** flourishing 119 **sheeted** shrouded 121 **As** (This abrupt transition suggests that matter is possibly omitted between lines 120 and 121.) **trains** trails 122 **Disasters** unfavorable signs or aspects **moist star** i.e., moon, governing tides

Upon whose influence Neptune's° empire stands°
Was sick almost to doomsday° with eclipse.
And even the like precurse° of feared events,
As harbingers° preceding still° the fates
And prologue to the omen° coming on,
Have heaven and earth together demonstrated
Unto our climatures° and countrymen.

[Enter GHOST.*]*

But soft,° behold! Lo, where it comes again!
I'll cross° it, though it blast° me. [*It spreads his° arms.*]
Stay, *illusion!*
If thou hast any sound or use of voice,
Speak to me!
If there be any good thing to be done
That may to thee do ease and grace to me,
Speak to me!
If thou art privy to° thy country's fate,
Which, happily,° foreknowing may avoid,
O, speak!
Or if thou hast uphoarded in thy life
Extorted treasure in the womb of earth,
For which, they say, you spirits oft walk in death,
Speak of it! [*The cock crows.*] Stay and speak!—Stop it, Marcellus.

MARCELLUS: Shall I strike at it with my partisan?°

HORATIO: Do, if it will not stand. [*They strike at it.*]

BERNARDO: 'Tis here!

HORATIO: 'Tis here!

[Exit GHOST.*]*

MARCELLUS: 'Tis gone.
We do it wrong, being so majestical,
To offer it the show of violence,
For it is as the air invulnerable,
And our vain blows malicious mockery.

BERNARDO: It was about to speak when the cock crew.

HORATIO: And then it started like a guilty thing
Upon a fearful summons. I have heard
The cock, that is the trumpet° to the morn,

123 **Neptune** god of the sea **stands** depends 124 **sick . . . doomsday** (See Matthew 24:29 and Revelation 6:12.) 125 **precurse** heralding, foreshadowing 126 **harbingers** forerunners **still** continually 127 **omen** calamitous event 129 **climatures** regions 130 **soft** i.e., enough, break off 131 **cross** stand in its path, confront **blast** wither, strike with a curse s.d. **his** its 137 **privy to** in on the secret of 138 **happily** haply, perchance 144 **partisan** long-handled spear 156 **trumpet** trumpeter

Doth with his lofty and shrill-sounding throat
Awake the god of day, and at his warning,
Whether in sea or fire, in earth or air,
Th' extravagant and erring° spirit hies°
To his confine; and of the truth herein
This present object made probation.°

MARCELLUS: It faded on the crowing of the cock.
Some say that ever 'gainst° that season comes
Wherein our Savior's birth is celebrated,
This bird of dawning singeth all night long,
And then, they say, no spirit dare stir abroad;
The nights are wholesome, then no planets strike,°
No fairy takes,° nor witch hath power to charm,
So hallowed and so gracious° is that time.

HORATIO: So have I heared and do in part believe it.
But, look, the morn in russet mantle clad
Walks o'er the dew of yon high eastward hill.
Break we our watch up, and by my advice
Let us impart what we have seen tonight
Unto young Hamlet; for upon my life,
This spirit, dumb to us, will speak to him.
Do you consent we shall acquaint him with it,
As needful in our loves, fitting our duty?

MARCELLUS: Let's do 't, I pray, and I this morning know
Where we shall find him most conveniently.

[Exeunt.]

[1.2 Flourish. Enter CLAUDIUS, *King of Denmark,* GERTRUDE *the Queen, (the) Council, as°* POLONIUS *and his son* LAERTES, HAMLET, *cum aliis° (including* VOLTIMAND *and* CORNELIUS*).]°*

KING: Though yet of Hamlet our° dear brother's death
The memory be green, and that it us befitted
To bear our hearts in grief and our whole kingdom
To be contracted in one brow of woe,
Yet so far hath discretion fought with nature
That we with wisest sorrow think on him
Together with remembrance of ourselves.
Therefore our sometime° sister, now our queen,
Th' imperial jointress° to this warlike state,

160 **extravagant and erring** wandering beyond bounds (The words have similar meaning.) **hies** hastens 162 **probation** proof 164 **'gainst** just before 168 **strike** destroy by evil influence 169 **takes** bewitches 170 **gracious** full of grace 1.2 s.d. **Location: The castle. as** i.e., such as, including **cum aliis** with others 1 **our** my (The royal "we"; also in the following lines.) 8 **sometime** former 9 **jointress** woman possessing property with her husband

Have we, as 'twere with a defeated joy—
With an auspicious and a dropping eye,°
With mirth in funeral and with dirge in marriage,
In equal scale weighing delight and dole°—
Taken to wife: Nor have we herein barred
Your better wisdoms, which have freely gone
With this affair along. For all, our thanks.
Now follows that you know° young Fortinbras,
Holding a weak supposal° of our worth,
Or thinking by our late dear brother's death
Our state to be disjoint and out of frame,
Co-leaguèd with° this dream of his advantage,°
He hath not failed to pester us with message
Importing° the surrender of those lands
Lost by his father, with all bonds° of law,
To our most valiant brother. So much for him.
Now for ourself and for this time of meeting.
Thus much the business is: we have here writ
To Norway, uncle of young Fortinbras—
Who, impotent° and bed-rid, scarcely hears
Of this his nephew's purpose—to suppress
His° further gait° herein, in that the levies,
The lists, and full proportions are all made
Out of his subject;° and we here dispatch
You, good Cornelius, and you, Voltimand,
For bearers of this greeting to old Norway,
Giving to you no further personal power
To business with the King more than the scope
Of these dilated° articles allow. [*He gives a paper.*]
Farewell, and let your haste commend your duty.°

CORNELIUS, VOLTIMAND: In that, and all things, will we show our duty.

KING: We doubt it nothing.° Heartily farewell.

[Exeunt VOLTIMAND *and* CORNELIUS.*]*

And now, Laertes, what's the news with you?
You told us of some suit; what is 't, Laertes?

11 **With . . . eye** with one eye smiling and the other weeping 13 **dole** grief 17 **that you know** what you know already, that; or, that you be informed as follows 18 **weak supposal** low estimate 21 **Co-leaguèd with** joined to, allied with **dream . . . advantage** illusory hope of having the advantage (His only ally is this hope.) 23 **Importing** pertaining to 24 **bonds** contracts 29 **impotent** helpless 31 **His** i.e., Fortinbras' **gait** proceeding 31–33 **in that . . . subject** since the levying of troops and supplies is drawn entirely from the King of Norway's own subjects 38 **dilated** set out at length 39 **let . . . duty** let your swift obeying of orders, rather than mere words, express your dutifulness 41 **nothing** not at all

You cannot speak of reason to the Dane°
And lose your voice.° What wouldst thou beg, Laertes,
That shall not be my offer, not thy asking?
The head is not more native° to the heart,
The hand more instrumental° to the mouth,
Than is the throne of Denmark to thy father.
What wouldst thou have, Laertes?
LAERTES: My dread lord,
Your leave and favor° to return to France,
From whence though willingly I came to Denmark
To show my duty in your coronation,
Yet now I must confess, that duty done,
My thoughts and wishes bend again toward France
And bow them to your gracious leave and pardon.°
KING: Have you your father's leave? What says Polonius?
POLONIUS: H'ath,° my lord, wrung from me my slow leave
By laborsome petition, and at last
Upon his will I sealed° my hard° consent.
I do beseech you, give him leave to go.
KING: Take thy fair hour,° Laertes. Time be thine,
And thy best graces spend it at thy will!°
But now, my cousin° Hamlet, and my son—
HAMLET: A little more than kin, and less than kind.°
KING: How is it that the clouds still hang on you?
HAMLET: Not so, my lord. I am too much in the sun.°
QUEEN: Good Hamlet, cast thy nighted color° off,
And let thine eye look like a friend on Denmark.°
Do not forever with thy vailèd lids°
Seek for thy noble father in the dust.
Thou know'st 'tis common,° all that lives must die,

44 **the Dane** the Danish king 45 **lose your voice** waste your speech 47 **native** closely connected, related 48 **instrumental** serviceable 51 **leave and favor** kind permission 56 **bow . . . pardon** entreatingly make a deep bow, asking your permission to depart 58 **H'ath** he has 60 **sealed** (as if sealing a legal document) **hard** reluctant 62 **Take thy fair hour** enjoy your time of youth 63 **And . . . will** and may your finest qualities guide the way you choose to spend your time 64 **cousin** any kin not of the immediate family 65 **A little . . . kind** i.e., closer than an ordinary nephew (since I am stepson), and yet more separated in natural feeling (with pun on *kind* meaning "affectionate" and "natural," "lawful." This line is often read as an aside, but it need not be. The King chooses perhaps not to respond to Hamlet's cryptic and bitter remark.) 67 **the sun** i.e., the sunshine of the King's royal favor (with pun on *son*) 68 **nighted color** (1) mourning garments of black (2) dark melancholy 69 **Denmark** the King of Denmark 70 **vailèd lids** lowered eyes 72 **common** of universal occurrence (But Hamlet plays on the sense of "vulgar" in line 74.)

Passing through nature to eternity.
HAMLET: Ay, madam, it is common.
QUEEN: If it be,
Why seems it so particular° with thee?
HAMLET: Seems, madam? Nay, it is. I know not "seems."
'Tis not alone my inky cloak, good Mother,
Nor customary° suits of solemn black,
Nor windy suspiration° of forced breath,
No, nor the fruitful° river in the eye,
Nor the dejected havior° of the visage,
Together with all forms, moods,° shapes of grief,
That can denote me truly. These indeed seem,
For they are actions that a man might play.
But I have that within which passes show;
These but the trappings and the suits of woe.
KING: 'Tis sweet and commendable in your nature, Hamlet,
To give these mourning duties to your father.
But you must know your father lost a father,
That father lost, lost his, and the survivor bound
In filial obligation for some term
To do obsequious° sorrow. But to persever°
In obstinate condolement° is a course
Of impious stubbornness. 'Tis unmanly grief.
It shows a will most incorrect to heaven,
A heart unfortified,° a mind impatient,
An understanding simple° and unschooled.
For what we know must be and is as common
As any the most vulgar thing to sense,°
Why should we in our peevish opposition
Take it to heart? Fie, 'tis a fault to heaven,
A fault against the dead, a fault to nature,
To reason most absurd, whose common theme
Is death of fathers, and who still° hath cried,
From the first corpse° till he that died today,
"This must be so." We pray you, throw to earth
This unprevailing° woe and think of us

75 **particular** personal 78 **customary** (1) socially conventional (2) habitual with me 79 **suspiration** sighing 80 **fruitful** abundant 81 **havior** expression 82 **moods** outward expression of feeling 92 **obsequious** suited to obsequies or funerals **persever** persevere 93 **condolement** sorrowing 96 **unfortified** i.e., against adversity 97 **simple** ignorant 99 **As . . . sense** as the most ordinary experience 104 **still** always 105 **the first corpse** (Abel's) 107 **unprevailing** unavailing, useless

As of a father; for let the world take note,
You are the most immediate° to our throne,
And with no less nobility of love
Than that which dearest father bears his son
Do I impart toward° you. For° your intent
In going back to school° in Wittenberg,°
It is most retrograde° to our desire,
And we beseech you bend you° to remain
Here in the cheer and comfort of our eye,
Our chiefest courtier, cousin, and our son.
QUEEN: Let not thy mother lose her prayers, Hamlet.
I pray thee, stay with us, go not to Wittenberg.
HAMLET: I shall in all my best° obey you, madam.
KING: Why, 'tis a loving and a fair reply.
Be as ourself in Denmark. Madam, come.
This gentle and unforced accord of Hamlet
Sits smiling to° my heart, in grace° whereof
No jocund° health that Denmark drinks today
But the great cannon to the clouds shall tell,
And the King's rouse° the heaven shall bruit again,°
Respeaking earthly thunder.° Come away.

[Flourish. Exeunt all but HAMLET.]

HAMLET: O, that this too too sullied° flesh would melt,
Thaw, and resolve itself into a dew!
Or that the Everlasting had not fixed
His canon° 'gainst self-slaughter! O God, God,
How weary, stale, flat, and unprofitable
Seem to me all the uses° of this world!
Fie on 't, ah fie! 'Tis an unweeded garden
That grows to seed. Things rank and gross in nature
Possess it merely.° That it should come to this!
But two months dead—nay, not so much, not two.
So excellent a king, that was to° this
Hyperion° to a satyr,° so loving to my mother
That he might not beteem° the winds of heaven

109 **most immediate** next in succession 112 **impart toward** i.e., bestow my affection on **For** as for 113 **to school** i.e., to your studies **Wittenberg** famous German university founded in 1502 114 **retrograde** contrary 115 **bend you** incline yourself 120 **in all my best** to the best of my ability 124 **to** i.e., at **grace** thanksgiving 125 **jocund** merry 127 **rouse** drinking of a draft of liquor **bruit again** loudly echo 128 **thunder** i.e., of trumpet and kettledrum, sounded when the King drinks; see 1.4.8-12 129 **sullied** defiled (The early quartos read *sallied;* the Folio, *solid.*) 132 **canon** law 134 **all the uses** the whole routine 137 **merely** completely 139 **to** in comparison to 140 **Hyperion** Titan sun-god, father of Helios **satyr** a lecherous creature of classical mythology, half-human but with a goat's legs, tail, ears, and horns 141 **beteem** allow

Visit her face too roughly. Heaven and earth,
Must I remember? Why, she would hang on him
As if increase of appetite had grown
By what it fed on, and yet within a month—
Let me not think on 't; frailty, thy name is woman!—
A little month, or ere° those shoes were old
With which she followed my poor father's body,
Like Niobe;° all tears, why she, even she—
O God, a beast, that wants discourse of reason,°
Would have mourned longer—married with my uncle,
My father's brother, but no more like my father
Than I to Hercules. Within a month,
Ere yet the salt of most unrighteous tears
Had left the flushing in her gallèd° eyes,
She married. O, most wicked speed, to post°
With such dexterity to incestuous° sheets!
It is not, nor it cannot come to good.
But break, my heart, for I must hold my tongue.

[Enter HORATIO, MARCELLUS and BERNARDO.]

HORATIO: Hail to your lordship!
HAMLET: I am glad to see you well.
Horatio!—or I do forget myself.
HORATIO: The same, my lord, and your poor servant ever.
HAMLET: Sir, my good friend; I'll change that name° with you.
And what make you from° Wittenberg, Horatio?
Marcellus.
MARCELLUS: My good lord.
HAMLET: I am very glad to see you. [*To BERNARDO.*] Good even, sir.—
But what in faith make you from Wittenberg?
HORATIO: A truant disposition, good my lord.
HAMLET: I would not hear your enemy say so,
Nor shall you do my ear that violence
To make it truster of your own report
Against yourself. I know you are no truant.
But what is your affair in Elsinore?
We'll teach you to drink deep ere you depart.

147 **or ere** even before 149 **Niobe** Tantalus' daughter, Queen of Thebes, who boasted that she had more sons and daughters than Leto; for this, Apollo and Artemis, children of Leto, slew her fourteen children. She was turned by Zeus into a stone that continually dropped tears. 150 **wants . . . reason** lacks the faculty of reason 155 **gallèd** irritated, inflamed 156 **post** hasten 157 **incestuous** (In Shakespeare's day, the marriage of a man like Claudius to his deceased brother's wife was considered incestuous.) 163 **change that name** i.e., give and receive reciprocally the name of "friend" (rather than talk of "servant") 164 **make you from** are you doing away from

Horatio: My lord, I came to see your father's funeral.
Hamlet: I prithee, do not mock me, fellow student;
I think it was to see my mother's wedding.
Horatio: Indeed, my lord, it followed hard° upon.
Hamlet: Thrift, thrift, Horatio! The funeral baked meats°
Did coldly° furnish forth the marriage tables.
Would I had met my dearest° foe in heaven
Or ever° I had seen that day, Horatio!
My father!—Methinks I see my father.
Horatio: Where, my lord?
Hamlet: In my mind's eye, Horatio.
Horatio: I saw him once. 'A° was a goodly king.
Hamlet: 'A was a man. Take him for all in all,
I shall not look upon his like again.
Horatio: My lord, I think I saw him yesternight.
Hamlet: Saw? Who?
Horatio: My lord, the King your father.
Hamlet: The King my father?
Horatio: Season your admiration° for a while
With an attent° ear till I may deliver,
Upon the witness of these gentlemen,
This marvel to you.
Hamlet: For God's love, let me hear!
Horatio: Two nights together had these gentlemen,
Marcellus and Bernardo, on their watch,
In the dead waste° and middle of the night,
Been thus encountered. A figure like your father,
Armèd at point° exactly, cap-á-pie,°
Appears before them, and with solemn march
Goes slow and stately by them. Thrice he walked
By their oppressed and fear-surprisèd eyes
Within his truncheon's° length, whilst they, distilled°
Almost to jelly with the act° of fear,
Stand dumb and speak not to him. This to me
In dreadful° secrecy impart they did,
And I with them the third night kept the watch,
Where, as they had delivered, both in time,
Form of the thing, each word made true and good,

179 **hard** close 180 **baked meats** meat pies 181 **coldly** i.e., as cold leftovers 182 **dearest** closest (and therefore deadliest) 183 **Or ever** before 186 **'A** he 193 **Season your admiration** restrain your astonishment 194 **attent** attentive 199 **dead waste** desolate stillness 201 **at point** correctly in every detail **cap-á-pie** from head to foot 205 **truncheon** officer's staff **distilled** dissolved 206 **act** action, operation 208 **dreadful** full of dread

The apparition comes. I knew your father;
These hands are not more like.

HAMLET: But where was this?

MARCELLUS: My lord, upon the platform where we watch.

HAMLET: Did you not speak to it?

HORATIO: My lord, I did,
But answer made it none. Yet once methought
It lifted up its head and did address
Itself to motion, like as it would speak;°
But even then° the morning cock crew loud,
And at the sound it shrunk in haste away
And vanished from our sight.

HAMLET: 'Tis very strange.

HORATIO: As I do live, my honored lord, 'tis true,
And we did think it writ down in our duty
To let you know of it.

HAMLET: Indeed, indeed, sirs. But this troubles me.
Hold you the watch tonight?

ALL: We do, my lord.

HAMLET: Armed, say you?

ALL: Armed, my lord.

HAMLET: From top to toe?

ALL: My lord, from head to foot.

HAMLET: Then saw you not his face?

HORATIO: O, yes, my lord, he wore his beaver° up.

HAMLET: What° looked he, frowningly?

HORATIO: A countenance more in sorrow than in anger.

HAMLET: Pale or red?

HORATIO: Nay, very pale.

HAMLET: And fixed his eyes upon you?

HORATIO: Most constantly.

HAMLET: I would I had been there.

HORATIO: It would have much amazed you.

HAMLET: Very like, very like. Stayed it long?

HORATIO: While one with moderate haste might tell° a hundred.

MARCELLUS, BERNARDO: Longer, longer.

HORATIO: Not when I saw 't.

HAMLET: His beard was grizzled°—no?

HORATIO: It was, as I have seen it in his life,

217–218 **did . . . speak** began to move as though it were about to speak 219 **even then** at that very instant 232 **beaver** visor on the helmet 233 **What** how 242 **tell** count 245 **grizzled** gray

A sable silvered.°
HAMLET: I will watch tonight.
Perchance 'twill walk again.
HORATIO: I warrant° it will.
HAMLET: If it assume my noble father's person,
I'll speak to it though hell itself should gape
And bid me hold my peace. I pray you all,
If you have hitherto concealed this sight,
Let it be tenable° in your silence still,
And whatsoever else shall hap tonight,
Give it an understanding but no tongue.
I will requite your loves. So, fare you well.
Upon the platform twixt eleven and twelve
I'll visit you.
ALL: Our duty to your honor.
HAMLET: Your loves, as mine to you. Farewell.

[Exeunt (all but HAMLET).]

My father's spirit in arms! All is not well.
I doubt° some foul play. Would the night were come!
Till then sit still, my soul. Foul deeds will rise,
Though all the earth o'erwhelm them, to men's eyes.

[Exit.]

[1.3 Enter LAERTES and OPHELIA, his sister.]°

LAERTES: My necessaries are embarked. Farewell.
And, sister, as the winds give benefit
And convoy is assistant,° do not sleep
But let me hear from you.
OPHELIA: Do you doubt that?
LAERTES: For Hamlet, and the trifling of his favor,
Hold it a fashion and a toy in blood,°
A violet in the youth of primy° nature,
Forward,° not permanent, sweet, not lasting,
The perfume and suppliance° of a minute—
No more.
OPHELIA: No more but so?
LAERTES: Think it no more.
For nature crescent° does not grow alone

247 **sable silvered** black mixed with white 248 **warrant** assure you 253 **tenable** held 261 **doubt** suspect 1.3 s.d. **Location: Polonius' chambers** 3 **convoy is assistant** means of conveyance are available 6 **toy in blood** passing amorous fancy 7 **primy** in its prime, springtime 8 **Forward** precocious 9 **suppliance** supply, filler 11 **crescent** growing, waxing

In thews° and bulk, but as this temple° waxes
The inward service of the mind and soul
Grows wide withal.° Perhaps he loves you now,
And now no soil° nor cautel° doth besmirch
The virtue of his will,° but you must fear,
His greatness weighed,° his will is not his own.
For he himself is subject to his birth.
He may not, as unvalued persons do,
Carve° for himself, for on his choice depends
The safety and health of this whole state,
And therefore must his choice be circumscribed
Unto the voice and yielding° of that body
Whereof he is the head. Then if he says he loves you,
It fits your wisdom so far to believe it
As he in his particular act and place°
May give his saying deed, which is no further
Than the main voice° of Denmark goes withal.°
Then weigh what loss your honor may sustain
If with too credent° ear you list° his songs,
Or lose your heart, or your chaste treasure open
To his unmastered importunity.
Fear it, Ophelia, fear it, my dear sister,
And keep you in the rear of your affection,°
Out of the shot and danger of desire.
The chariest° maid is prodigal enough
If she unmask° her beauty to the moon.°
Virtue itself scapes not calumnious strokes.
The canker galls° the infants of the spring
Too oft before their buttons° be disclosed,°
And in the morn and liquid dew° of youth
Contagious blastments° are most imminent.
Be wary then; best safety lies in fear.
Youth to itself rebels,° though none else near.

OPHELIA: I shall the effect of this good lesson keep

12 **thews** bodily strength **temple** i.e., body 14 **Grows wide withal** grows along with it 15 **soil** blemish **cautel** deceit 16 **will** desire 17 **His greatness weighed** if you take into account his high position 20 **Carve** i.e., choose 23 **voice and yielding** assent, approval 26 **in . . . place** in his particular restricted circumstances 28 **main voice** general assent **withal** along with 30 **credent** credulous **list** listen to 34 **keep . . . affection** don't advance as far as your affection might lead you (A military metaphor.) 36 **chariest** most scrupulously modest 37 **If she unmask** if she does no more than show her beauty **moon** (Symbol of chastity.) 39 **canker galls** canker-worm destroys 40 **buttons** buds **disclosed** opened 41 **liquid dew** i.e., time when dew is fresh and bright 42 **blastments** blights 44 **Youth . . . rebels** youth is inherently rebellious

As watchman to my heart. But, good my brother,
Do not, as some ungracious° pastors do,
Show me the steep and thorny way to heaven,
Whiles like a puffed° and reckless libertine
Himself the primrose path of dalliance treads,
And recks° not his own rede.°

[Enter Polonius.*]*

Laertes: O, fear me not.°
I stay too long. But here my father comes.
A double° blessing is a double grace;
Occasion smiles upon a second leave.°

Polonius: Yet here, Laertes? Aboard, aboard, for shame!
The wind sits in the shoulder of your sail,
And you are stayed for. There—my blessing with thee!
And these few precepts in thy memory
Look° thou character.° Give thy thoughts no tongue,
Nor any unproportioned° thought his° act.
Be thou familiar,° but by no means vulgar.°
Those friends thou hast, and their adoption tried,°
Grapple them unto thy soul with hoops of steel,
But do not dull thy palm° with entertainment
Of each new-hatched, unfledged courage.° Beware
Of entrance to a quarrel, but being in,
Bear 't that° th' opposèd may beware of thee.
Give every man thy ear, but few thy voice;
Take each man's censure,° but reserve thy judgment.
Costly thy habit° as thy purse can buy,
But not expressed in fancy;° rich, not gaudy,
For the apparel oft proclaims the man,
And they in France of the best rank and station
Are of a most select and generous chief in that.°
Neither a borrower nor a lender be,

47 **ungracious** ungodly 49 **puffed** bloated, or swollen with pride 51 **recks** heeds **rede** counsel **fear me not** don't worry on my account 53 **double** (Laertes has already bid his father good-bye.) 54 **Occasion . . . leave** happy is the circumstance that provides a second leave-taking (The goddess Occasion, or Opportunity, smiles.) 59 **Look** be sure that **character** inscribe 60 **unproportioned** badly calculated, intemperate **his** its 61 **familiar** sociable **vulgar** common 62 **and their adoption tried** and also their suitability for adoption as friends having been tested 64 **dull thy palm** i.e., shake hands so often as to make the gesture meaningless 65 **courage** young man of spirit 67 **Bear 't that** manage it so that 69 **censure** opinion, judgment 70 **habit** clothing 71 **fancy** excessive ornament, decadent fashion 74 **Are . . . that** are of a most refined and well-bred preeminence in choosing what to wear

For loan oft loses both itself and friend,
And borrowing dulleth edge of husbandry.°
This above all: to thine own self be true,
And it must follow, as the night the day,
Thou canst not then be false to any man.
Farewell. My blessing season° this in thee!
LAERTES: Most humbly do I take my leave, my lord.
POLONIUS: The time invests° you. Go, your servants tend.°
LAERTES: Farewell, Ophelia, and remember well
What I have said to you.
OPHELIA: 'Tis in my memory locked,
And you yourself shall keep the key of it.
LAERTES: Farewell.
[Exit LAERTES.]
POLONIUS: What is 't, Ophelia, he hath said to you?
OPHELIA: So please you, something touching the Lord Hamlet.
POLONIUS: Marry,° well bethought.
'Tis told me he hath very oft of late
Given private time to you, and you yourself
Have of your audience been most free and bounteous.
If it be so—as so 'tis put on° me,
And that in way of caution—I must tell you
You do not understand yourself so clearly
As it behooves° my daughter and your honor.
What is between you? Give me up the truth.
OPHELIA: He hath, my lord, of late made many tenders°
Of his affection to me.
POLONIUS: Affection? Pooh! You speak like a green girl,
Unsifted° in such perilous circumstance.
Do you believe his tenders, as you call them?
OPHELIA: I do not know, my lord, what I should think.
POLONIUS: Marry, I will teach you. Think yourself a baby
That you have ta'en these tenders for true pay
Which are not sterling.° Tender° yourself more dearly,
Or—not to crack the wind° of the poor phrase,
Running it thus—you'll tender me a fool.°

77 **husbandry** thrift 81 **season** mature 83 **invests** besieges, presses upon **tend** attend, wait 91 **Marry** i.e., by the Virgin Mary (A mild oath.) 95 **put on** impressed on, told to 98 **behooves** befits 100 **tenders** offers 103 **Unsifted** i.e., untried 108 **sterling** legal currency **Tender** hold, look after, offer 109 **crack the wind** i.e., run it until it is broken-winded 110 **tender me a fool** (1) show yourself to me as a fool (2) show me up as a fool (3) present me with a grandchild (*Fool* was a term of endearment for a child.)

OPHELIA: My lord, he hath importuned me with love
In honorable fashion.
POLONIUS: Ay, fashion° you may call it. Go to,° go to.
OPHELIA: And hath given countenance° to his speech, my lord,
With almost all the holy vows of heaven.
POLONIUS: Ay, springes° to catch woodcocks.° I do know,
When the blood burns, how prodigal° the soul
Lends the tongue vows. These blazes, daughter,
Giving more light than heat, extinct in both
Even in their promise as it° is a-making,
You must not take for fire. From this time
Be something° scanter of your maiden presence.
Set your entreatments° at a higher rate
Than a command to parle.° For Lord Hamlet,
Believe so much in him° that he is young,
And with a larger tether may he walk
Than may be given you. In few,° Ophelia,
Do not believe his vows, for they are brokers,°
Not of that dye° which their investments° show,
But mere implorators° of unholy suits,
Breathing° like sanctified and pious bawds,
The better to beguile. This is for all:°
I would not, in plain terms, from this time forth
Have you so slander° any moment° leisure
As to give words or talk with the Lord Hamlet.
Look to 't, I charge you. Come your ways.°
OPHELIA: I shall obey, my lord.

[Exeunt.]

[1.4 Enter HAMLET, HORATIO, and MARCELLUS.]°
HAMLET: The air bites shrewdly,° it is very cold.
HORATIO: It is a nipping and an eager° air.
HAMLET: What hour now?
HORATIO: I think it lacks of° twelve.
MARCELLUS: No, it is struck.

113 **fashion** mere form, pretense **Go to** (An expression of impatience.) 114 **countenance** credit, confirmation 116 **springes** snares **woodcocks** birds easily caught; here used to connote gullibility 117 **prodigal** prodigally 120 **it** i.e., the promise 122 **something** somewhat 123 **entreatments** negotiations for surrender (A military term.) 124 **parle** discuss terms with the enemy (Polonius urges his daughter, in the metaphor of military language, not to meet with Hamlet and consider giving in to him merely because he requests an interview.) 125 **so . . . him** this much concerning him 127 **In few** briefly 128 **brokers** go-betweens, procurers 129 **dye** color or sort **investments** clothes (The vows are not what they seem.) 130 **mere implorators** out and out solicitors 131 **Breathing** speaking 132 **for all** once for all, in sum 134 **slander** abuse, misuse **moment** moment's 136 **Come your ways** come along 1.4 s.d. **Location: The guard platform** 1 **shrewdly** keenly, sharply 2 **eager** biting 3 **lacks of** is just short of

HORATIO: Indeed? I heard it not.
It then draws near the season°
Wherein the spirit held his wont° to walk.
[A flourish of trumpets, and two pieces° go off (within).]
What does this mean, my lord?
HAMLET: The King doth wake° tonight and takes his rouse,°
Keeps wassail,° and the swaggering upspring° reels,°
And as he drains his drafts of Rhenish° down,
The kettledrum and trumpet thus bray out
The triumph of his pledge.°
HORATIO: It is a custom?
HAMLET: Ay, marry, is't,
But to my mind, though I am native here
And to the manner° born, it is a custom
More honored in the breach than the observance.°
This heavy-headed revel east and west°
Makes us traduced and taxed of° other nations.
They clepe° us drunkards, and with swinish phrase°
Soil our addition;° and indeed it takes
From our achievements, though performed at height,°
The pith and marrow of our attribute.°
So, oft it chances in particular men,
That for° some vicious mole of nature° in them,
As in their birth—wherein they are not guilty,
Since nature cannot choose his° origin—
By their o'ergrowth of some complexion,°
Oft breaking down the pales° and forts of reason,
Or by some habit that too much o'erleavens°
The form of plausive° manners, that these men,
Carrying, I say, the stamp of one defect,
Being nature's livery° or fortune's star,°
His virtues else,° be they as pure as grace,

5 **season** time 6 **held his wont** was accustomed s.d. **pieces** i.e., of ordnance, cannon 8 **wake** stay awake and hold revel **takes his rouse** carouses 9 **wassail** carousal **upspring** wild German dance **reels** dances 10 **Rhenish** Rhine wine 12 **The triumph . . . pledge** i.e., his feat in draining the wine in a single draft 15 **manner** custom (of drinking) 16 **More . . . observance** better neglected than followed 17 **east and west** i.e., everywhere 18 **taxed of** censured by 19 **clepe** call **with swinish phrase** i.e., by calling us swine 20 **addition** reputation 21 **at height** outstandingly 22 **The pith . . . attribute** the essence of the reputation that others attribute to us 24 **for** on account of **mole of nature** natural blemish in one's constitution 26 **his** its 27 **their o'ergrowth . . . complexion** the excessive growth in individuals of some natural trait 28 **pales** palings, fences (as of a fortification) 29 **o'erleavens** induces a change throughout (as yeast works in dough) 30 **plausive** pleasing 32 **nature's livery** sign of one's servitude to nature **fortune's star** the destiny that chance brings 33 **His virtues else** i.e., the other qualities of *these men* (line 30)

As infinite as man may undergo,°
Shall in the general censure° take corruption
From that particular fault. The dram of evil
Doth all the noble substance often dout
To his own scandal.°

[Enter GHOST.*]*

HORATIO: Look, my lord, it comes!
HAMLET: Angels and ministers° of grace defend us!
Be thou° a spirit of health° or goblin damned,
Bring° with thee airs from heaven or blasts from hell,
Be thy intents° wicked or charitable,
Thou com'st in such a questionable° shape
That I will speak to thee. I'll call thee Hamlet,
King, father, royal Dane. O, answer me!
Let me not burst in ignorance, but tell
Why thy canonized° bones, hearsèd° in death,
Have burst their cerements;° why the sepulcher
Wherein we saw thee quietly inurned°
Hath oped his ponderous and marble jaws
To cast thee up again. What may this mean,
That thou, dead corpse, again in complete steel,°
Revisits thus the glimpses of the moon,°
Making night hideous, and we fools of nature°
So horridly to shake our disposition°
With thoughts beyond the reaches of our souls?
Say, why is this? Wherefore? What should we do?

[The GHOST *beckons* HAMLET.*]*

HORATIO: It beckons you to go away with it,
As if it some impartment° did desire
To you alone.
MARCELLUS: Look with what courteous action
It wafts you to a more removèd ground.
But do not go with it.

34 **may undergo** can sustain 35 **general censure** general opinion that people have of him 36–38 **The dram . . . scandal** i.e., the small drop of evil blots out or works against the noble substance of the whole and brings it into disrepute. To *dout* is to blot out. (A famous crux.) 39 **ministers of grace** messengers of God 40 **Be thou** whether you are **spirit of health** good angel 41 **Bring** whether you bring 42 **Be thy intents** whether your intentions are 43 **questionable** inviting question 47 **canonized** buried according to the canons of the church **hearsèd** coffined 48 **cerements** grave clothes 49 **inurned** entombed 52 **complete steel** full armor 53 **glimpses of the moon** pale and uncertain moonlight 54 **fools of nature** mere men, limited to natural knowledge and subject to nature 55 **So . . . disposition** to distress our mental composure so violently 59 **impartment** communication

HORATIO: No, by no means.
HAMLET: It will not speak. Then I will follow it.
HORATIO: Do not, my lord!
HAMLET: Why, what should be the fear?
I do not set my life at a pin's fee,°
And for my soul, what can it do to that,
Being a thing immortal as itself?
It waves me forth again. I'll follow it.
HORATIO: What if it tempt you toward the flood,° my lord,
Or to the dreadful summit of the cliff
That beetles o'er° his° base into the sea,
And there assume some other horrible form
Which might deprive your sovereignty of reason°
And draw you into madness? Think of it.
The very place puts toys of desperation,°
Without more motive, into every brain
That looks so many fathoms to the sea
And hears it roar beneath.
HAMLET: It wafts me still.—Go on, I'll follow thee.
MARCELLUS: You shall not go, my lord. [*They try to stop him.*]
HAMLET: Hold off your hands!
HORATIO: Be ruled. You shall not go.
HAMLET: My fate cries out,°
And makes each petty° artery° in this body
As hardy as the Nemean lion's° nerve.°
Still am I called. Unhand me, gentlemen.
By heaven, I'll make a ghost of him that lets° me!
I say, away!—Go on, I'll follow thee.
[*Exeunt GHOST and HAMLET.*]
HORATIO: He waxes desperate with imagination.
MARCELLUS: Let's follow. 'Tis not fit thus to obey him.
HORATIO: Have after.° To what issue° will this come?
MARCELLUS: Something is rotten in the state of Denmark.
HORATIO: Heaven will direct it.°
MARCELLUS: Nay, let's follow him.

65 **fee** value 69 **flood** sea 71 **beetles o'er** overhangs threateningly (like bushy eyebrows) **his** its 73 **deprive . . . reason** take away the rule of reason over your mind 75 **toys of desperation** fancies of desperate acts, i.e., suicide 81 **My fate cries out** my destiny summons me 82 **petty** weak **artery** (through which the vital spirits were thought to have been conveyed) 83 **Nemean lion** one of the monsters slain by Hercules in his twelve labors **nerve** sinew 85 **lets** hinders 89 **Have after** let's go after him **issue** outcome 91 **it** i.e., the outcome

[Exeunt.]

[1.5 Enter GHOST *and* HAMLET.*]*°

HAMLET: Whither wilt thou lead me? Speak. I'll go no further.
GHOST: Mark me.
HAMLET: I will.
GHOST: My hour is almost come,
When I to sulfurous and tormenting flames
Must render up myself.
HAMLET: Alas, poor ghost!
GHOST: Pity me not, but lend thy serious hearing
To what I shall unfold.
HAMLET: Speak. I am bound° to hear.
GHOST: So art thou to revenge, when thou shalt hear.
HAMLET: What?
GHOST: I am thy father's spirit,
Doomed for a certain term to walk the night,
And for the day confined to fast° in fires,
Till the foul crimes° done in my days of nature°
Are burnt and purged away. But that° I am forbid
To tell the secrets of my prison house,
I could a tale unfold whose lightest word
Would harrow up° thy soul, freeze thy young blood,
Make thy two eyes like stars start from their spheres,°
Thy knotted and combinèd locks° to part,
And each particular hair to stand on end
Like quills upon the fretful porcupine.
But this eternal blazon° must not be
To ears of flesh and blood. List, list, O, list!
If thou didst ever thy dear father love—
HAMLET: O God!
GHOST: Revenge his foul and most unnatural murder.
HAMLET: Murder?
GHOST: Murder most foul, as in the best° it is,
But this most foul, strange, and unnatural.
HAMLET: Haste me to know't, that I, with wings as swift

1.5 s.d. **Location: The battlements of the castle** 7 **bound** (1) ready (2) obligated by duty and fate (The Ghost, in line 8, answers in the second sense.) 12 **fast** do penance by fasting 13 **crimes** sins **of nature** as a mortal 14 **But that** were it not that 17 **harrow up** lacerate, tea 18 **spheres** i.e., eye-sockets, here compared to the orbits or transparent revolving spheres in which, according to Ptolemaic astronomy, the heavenly bodies were fixed 19 **knotted . . . locks** hair neatly arranged and confined 22 **eternal blazon** revelation of the secrets of eternity 28 **in the best** even at best

As meditation or the thoughts of love,
May sweep to my revenge.
GHOST: I find thee apt;
And duller shouldst thou be° than the fat° weed
That roots itself in ease on Lethe° wharf,
Wouldst thou not stir in this. Now, Hamlet, hear.
'Tis given out that, sleeping in my orchard,°
A serpent stung me. So the whole ear of Denmark
Is by a forgèd process° of my death
Rankly abused.° But know, thou noble youth,
The serpent that did sting thy father's life
Now wears his crown.
HAMLET: O, my prophetic soul! My uncle!
GHOST: Ay, that incestuous, that adulterate° beast,
With witchcraft of his wit, with traitorous gifts°—
O wicked wit and gifts, that have the power
So to seduce!—won to his shameful lust
The will of my most seeming-virtuous queen.
O Hamlet, what a falling off was there!
From me, whose love was of that dignity
That it went hand in hand even with the vow°
I made to her in marriage, and to decline
Upon a wretch whose natural gifts were poor
To° those of mine!
But virtue, as it° never will be moved,
Though lewdness court it in a shape of heaven,°
So lust, though to a radiant angel linked,
Will sate itself in a celestial bed°
And prey on garbage.
But soft, methinks I scent the morning air.
Brief let me be. Sleeping within my orchard,
My custom always of the afternoon,
Upon my secure° hour thy uncle stole,
With juice of cursèd hebona° in a vial,
And in the porches of my ears° did pour

33 **shouldst thou be** you would have to be **fat** torpid, lethargic 34 **Lethe** the river of forgetfulness in Hades 36 **orchard** garden 38 **forgèd process** falsified account 39 **abused** deceived 43 **adulterate** adulterous 44 **gifts** (1) talents (2) presents 50 **even with the vow** with the very vow 53 **To** compared to 54 **virtue, as it** as virtue 55 **shape of heaven** heavenly form 57 **sate . . . bed** cease to find sexual pleasure in a virtuously lawful marriage 62 **secure** confident, unsuspicious 63 **hebona** a poison (The word seems to be a form of *ebony,* though it is thought perhaps to be related to *benbane,* a poison, or to *ebenus,* "yew.") 64 **porches of my ears** ears as a porch or entrance of the body

The leprous distillment,° whose effect
Holds such an enmity with blood of man
That swift as quicksilver it courses through
The natural gates and alleys of the body,
And with a sudden vigor it doth posset°
And curd, like eager° droppings into milk,
The thin and wholesome blood. So did it mine,
And a most instant tetter° barked° about,
Most lazar-like,° with vile and loathsome crust,
All my smooth body.
Thus was I, sleeping, by a brother's hand
Of life, of crown, of queen at once dispatched,°
Cut off even in the blossoms of my sin,
Unhouseled,° disappointed,° unaneled,°
No reckoning° made, but sent to my account
With all my imperfections on my head.
O, horrible! O, horrible, most horrible!
If thou hast nature° in thee, bear it not.
Let not the royal bed of Denmark be
A couch for luxury° and damnèd incest.
But, howsoever thou pursues this act,
Taint not thy mind nor let thy soul contrive
Against thy mother aught. Leave her to heaven
And to those thorns that in her bosom lodge,
To prick and sting her. Fare thee well at once.
The glowworm shows the matin° to be near,
And 'gins to pale his° uneffectual fire.
Adieu, adieu, adieu! Remember me.

[Exit.]

HAMLET: O all you host of heaven! O earth! What else?
And shall I couple° hell? O, fie! Hold,° hold, my heart,
And you, my sinews, grow not instant° old,
But bear me stiffly up. Remember thee?
Ay, thou poor ghost, whiles memory holds a seat
In this distracted globe.° Remember thee?

65 **leprous distillment** distillation causing leprosylike disfigurement 69 **posset** coagulate, curdle 70 **eager** sour, acid 72 **tetter** eruption of scabs **barked** recovered with a rough covering, like bark on a tree 73 **lazar-like** leperlike 76 **dispatched** suddenly deprived 78 **Uphouseled** without having received the Sacrament **disappointment** unready (spiritually) for the last journey **unaneled** without having received extreme unction 79 **reckoning** settling of accounts 82 **nature** i.e., the promptings of a son 84 **luxury** lechery 90 **matin** morning 91 **his** its 94 **couple** add **Hold** hold together 95 **instant** instantly 98 **globe** (1) head (2) world

Yea, from the table[o] of my memory
I'll wipe away all trivial fond[o] records,
All saws[o] of books, all forms,[o] all pressures[o] past
That youth and observation copied there,
And thy commandment all alone shall live
Within the book and volume of my brain,
Unmixed with baser matter. Yes, by heaven!
O most pernicious woman!
O villain, villain, smiling, damnèd villain!
My tables[o]—meet it is[o] I set it down
That one may smile, and smile, and be a villain.
At least I am sure it may be so in Denmark.

[Writing.]

So uncle, there you are.[o] Now to my word:
It is "Adieu, adieu! Remember me."
I have sworn't.

[Enter HORATIO *and* MARCELLUS.*]*

HORATIO: My lord, my lord!
MARCELLUS: Lord Hamlet!
HORATIO: Heavens secure him![o]
HAMLET: So be it.
MARCELLUS: Hilo, ho, ho, my lord!
HAMLET: Hilo, ho, ho, boy! Come, bird, come.[o]
MARCELLUS: How is 't, my noble lord?
HORATIO: What news, my lord?
HAMLET: O, wonderful!
HORATIO: Good my lord, tell it.
HAMLET: No, you will reveal it.
HORATIO: Not I, my lord, by heaven.
MARCELLUS: Nor I, my lord.
HAMLET: How say you, then, would heart of man once[o] think it?
But you'll be secret?
HORATIO, MARCELLUS: Ay, by heaven, my lord.
HAMLET: There's never a villain dwelling in all Denmark
But he's an arrant[o] knave.
HORATIO: There needs no ghost, my lord, come from the grave

99 **table** tablet, slate 100 **fond** foolish 101 **saws** wise sayings **forms** shapes or images copied onto the slate; general ideas **pressures** impressions stamped 108 **tables** writing tablets **meet it is** it is fitting 111 **there you are** i.e., there, I've written that down against you 116 **secure him** keep him safe 119 **Hilo . . . come** (A falconer's call to a hawk in air. Hamlet mocks the hallooing as though it were a part of hawking.) 127 **once** ever 130 **arrant** thoroughgoing

To tell us this.
HAMLET: Why, right, you are in the right.
And so, without more circumstance° at all,
I hold it fit that we shake hands and part,
You as your business and desire shall point you—
For every man hath business and desire,
Such as it is—and for my own poor part,
Look you, I'll go pray,
HORATIO: These are but wild and whirling words, my lord.
HAMLET: I am sorry they offend you, heartily;
Yes, faith, heartily.
HORATIO: There's no offense, my lord.
HAMLET: Yes, but Saint Patrick,° but there is, Horatio,
And much offense° too. Touching this vision here,
It is an honest ghost,° that let me tell you.
For your desire to know what is between us,
O'ermaster 't as you may. And now, good friends,
As you are friends, scholars, and soldiers,
Give me one poor request.
HORATIO: What is 't, my lord? We will.
HAMLET: Never make known what you have seen tonight.
HORATIO, MARCELLUS: My lord, we will not.
HAMLET: Nay, but swear 't.
HORATIO: In faith, my lord, not I.°
MARCELLUS: Nor I, my lord, in faith.
HAMLET: Upon my sword.° [*He holds out his sword.*]
MARCELLUS: We have sworn, my lord, already.°
HAMLET: Indeed, upon my sword, indeed.
GHOST: [*cries under the stage*] Swear.
HAMLET: Ha, ha, boy, sayst thou so? Art thou there, truepenny?°
Come on, you hear this fellow in the cellarage.
Consent to swear.
HORATIO: Propose the oath, my lord.
HAMLET: Never to speak of this that you have seen,
Swear by my sword.
GHOST: [*beneath*] Swear. [*They swear.°*]

133 **circumstance** ceremony, elaboration 142 **Saint Patrick** The keeper of Purgatory and patron saint of all blunders and confusion.) 143 **offense** (Hamlet deliberately changes Horatio's "no offense taken" to "an offense against all decency.") 144 **an honest ghost** i.e., a real ghost and not an evil spirit 153 **In faith . . . I** i.e., I swear not to tell what I have seen (Horatio is not refusing to swear.) 155 **sword** i.e., the hilt in the form of a cross 156 **We . . . already** i.e., we swore in *faith* 159 **truepenny** honest old fellow 164 **s.d. They swear** (Seemingly they swear here, and at lines 170 and 190, as they lay their hands on Hamlet's sword. Triple oaths would have particular force; these three oaths deal with what they have seen, what they have heard, and what they promise about Hamlet's *antic disposition.*

HAMLET: *Hic et ubique?*° Then we'll shift our ground.
[He moves to another spot.]
Come hither, gentlemen,
And lay your hands again upon my sword.
Swear by my sword
Never to speak of this that you have heard.
GHOST: [*beneath*] Swear by his sword. [*They swear.*]
HAMLET: Well said, old mole. Canst work i' th' earth so fast?
A worthy pioneer!°—Once more removed, good friends.
[He moves again.]
HORATIO: O day and night, but this is wondrous strange!
HAMLET: And therefore as a stranger° give it welcome.
There are more things in heaven and earth, Horatio,
Than are dreamt of in your philosophy.°
But come;
Here, as before, never, so help you mercy,°
How strange or odd soe'er I bear myself—
As I perchance hereafter shall think meet
To put an antic° disposition on—
That you, at such times seeing me, never shall,
With arms encumbered° thus, or this headshake,
Or by pronouncing of some doubtful phrase
As "Well, we know," or "We could, an if° we would,"
Or "If we list° to speak," or "There be, an if they might,"
Or such ambiguous giving out,° to note°
That you know aught° of me—this do swear,
So grace and mercy at your most need help you.
GHOST: [*beneath*] Swear. [*They swear.*]
HAMLET: Rest, rest, perturbèd spirit! So, gentlemen,
With all my love I do commend me to you;°
And what so poor a man as Hamlet is
May do t' express his love and friending° to you,
God willing, shall not lack.° Let us go in together,
And still° your fingers on your lips, I pray.
The time° is out of joint. O cursèd spite°

165 ***Hic et ubique*** here and everywhere (Latin.) 172 **pioneer** foot soldier assigned to dig tunnels and excavations 174 **as a stranger** i.e., needing your hospitality 176 **your philosophy** this subject called "natural philosophy" or "science" that people talk about 178 **so help you mercy** as you hope for God's mercy when you are judged 181 **antic** fantastic 183 **encumbered** folded 185 **an if** if 186 **list** wished **There . . . might** i.e., there are people here (we, in fact) who could tell news if we were at liberty to do so 187 **giving out** intimation **note** draw attention to the fact 188 **aught** i.e., something secret 192 **do . . . you** entrust myself to you 194 **friending** friendliness 195 **lack** be lacking 196 **still** always 197 **The time** the state of affairs **spite** i.e., the spite of Fortune

That ever I was born to set it right!
[They wait for him to leave first.]
Nay, come, let's go together.°
[Exeunt.]

[2.1 *Enter old* POLONIUS *with his man* (REYNALDO).]°

POLONIUS: Give him this money and these notes, Reynaldo.
[He gives money and papers.]
REYNALDO: I will, my lord.
POLONIUS: You shall do marvelous° wisely, good Reynaldo,
Before you visit him, to make inquire°
Of his behavior.
REYNALDO: My lord, I did intend it.
POLONIUS: Marry, well said, very well said. Look you, sir,
Inquire me first what Danskers° are in Paris,
And how, and who, what means,° and where they keep,°
What company, at what expense; and finding
By this encompassment° and drift° of question
That they do know my son, come you more nearer
Than your particular demands will touch it.°
Take you,° as 'twere, some distant knowledge of him,
As thus, "I know his father and his friends,
And in part him." Do you mark this, Reynaldo?
REYNALDO: Ay, very well, my lord.
POLONIUS: "And in part him, but," you may say, "not well.
But if 't be he I mean, he's very wild,
Addicted so and so," and there put on° him
What forgeries° you please—marry, none so rank°
As may dishonor him, take heed of that,
But, sir, such wanton,° wild, and usual slips
As are companions noted and most known
To youth and liberty.
REYNALDO: As gaming, my lord.
POLONIUS: Ay, or drinking, fencing, swearing,
Quarreling, drabbing°—you may go so far.
REYNALDO: My lord, that would dishonor him.

199 **let's go together** (Probably they wait for him to leave first, but he refuses this ceremoniousness.) 2.1 s.d. **Location: Polonius' chambers** 3 **marvelous** marvelously 4 **inquire** inquiry 7 **Danskers** Danes 8 **what means** what wealth (they have) **keep** dwell 10 **encompassment** roundabout talking **drift** gradual approach or course 11–12 **come . . . it** you will find out more this way than by asking pointed questions (*particular demands*) 13 **Take you** assume, pretend 19 **put on** impute to 20 **forgeries** invented tales **rank** gross 22 **wanton** sportive, unrestrained 27 **drabbing** whoring

POLONIUS: Faith, no, as you may season° it in the charge.
You must not put another scandal on him
That he is open to incontinency;°
That's not my meaning. But breathe his faults so quaintly°
That they may seem the taints of liberty,°
The flash and outbreak of a fiery mind,
A savageness in unreclaimèd blood,
Of general assault.°
REYNALDO: But, my good lord—
POLONIUS: Wherefore should you do this?
REYNALDO: Ay, my lord, I would know that.
POLONIUS: Marry, sir, here's my drift,
And I believe it is a fetch of warrant.°
You laying these slight sullies on my son,
As 'twere a thing a little soiled wi' the working,°
Mark you,
Your party in converse,° him you would sound,°
Having ever° seen in the prenominate crimes°
The youth you breathe° of guilty, be assured
He closes with you in this consequence:°
"Good sir," or so, or "friend," or "gentleman,"
According to the phrase or the addition°
Of man and country.
REYNALDO: Very good, my lord.
POLONIUS: And then, sir, does 'a this—'a does—what was I about to say? By the Mass, I was about to say something. Where did I leave?
REYNALDO: At "closes in the consequence."
POLONIUS: At "closes in the consequence," ay, marry.
He closes thus: "I know the gentleman,
I saw him yesterday," or "th' other day,"
Or then, or then, with such or such, "and as you say,
There was 'a gaming," "there o'ertook in 's rouse,"°
"There falling out° at tennis," or perchance
"I saw him enter such a house of sale,"

29 **season** temper, soften 31 **incontinency** habitual sexual excess 32 **quaintly** artfully, subtly 33 **taints of liberty** faults resulting from free living 35–36 **A savageness . . . assault** a wildness in untamed youth that assails all indiscriminately 41 **fetch of warrant** legitimate trick 43 **soiled wi' the working** soiled by handling while it is being made, i.e., by involvement in the ways of the world 45 **converse** conversation **sound** i.e., sound out 46 **Having ever** if he has ever **prenominate crimes** before-mentioned offenses 47 **breathe** speak 48 **closes . . . consequence** takes you into his confidence in some fashion, as follows 50 **addition** title 60 **o'er-took in 's rouse** overcome by drink 61 **falling out** quarreling

Videlicet° a brothel, or so forth. See you now,
Your bait of falsehood takes this carp° of truth;
And thus do we of wisdom and of reach,°
With windlasses° and with assays of bias,°
By indirections find directions° out.
So by my former lecture and advice
Shall you my son. You have° me, have you not?

REYNALDO: My lord, I have.

POLONIUS: God b'wi'° ye; fare ye well.

REYNALDO: Good my lord.

POLONIUS: Observe his inclination in yourself.°

REYNALDO: I shall, my lord.

POLONIUS: And let him ply his music.

REYNALDO: Well, my lord.

POLONIUS: Farewell.

[Exit REYNALDO.]

[Enter OPHELIA.]

How now, Ophelia, what's the matter?

OPHELIA: O my lord, my lord, I have been so affrighted!

POLONIUS: With what, i' the name of God?

OPHELIA: My lord, as I was sewing in my closet,°
Lord Hamlet, with his doublet° all unbraced,°
No hat upon his head, his stockings fouled,
Ungartered, and down-gyvèd° to his ankle,
Pale as his shirt, his knees knocking each other,
And with a look so piteous in purport°
As if he had been loosèd out of hell
To speak of horrors—he comes before me.

POLONIUS: Mad for thy love?

OPHELIA: My lord, I do not know,
But truly I do fear it.

POLONIUS: What said he?

OPHELIA: He took me by the wrist and held me hard.
Then goes he to the length of all his arm,
And, with his other hand thus o'er his brow
He falls to such perusal of my face
As° 'a would draw it. Long stayed he so.

63 **Videlicet** namely 64 **carp** a fish 65 **reach** capacity, ability 66 **windlasses** i.e., circuitous paths. (Literally, circuits made to head off the game in hunting.) **assays of bias** attempts through indirection (like the curving path of the bowling ball, which is biased or weighted to one side) 67 **directions** i.e., the way things really are 69 **have** understand 70 **b' wi'** be with 72 **in yourself** in your own person (as well as by asking questions) 79 **closet** private chamber 80 **doublet** close-fitting jacket **unbraced** unfastened 82 **down-gyvèd** fallen to the ankles (like gyves or fetters) 84 **in purport** in what it expressed 93 **As** as if (also in line 97)

At last, a little shaking of mine arm
And thrice his head thus waving up and down,
He raised a sigh so piteous and profound
As it did seem to shatter all his bulk°
And end his being. That done, he lets me go,
And with his head over his shoulder turned
He seemed to find his way without his eyes,
For out o' doors he went without their helps,
And to the last bended their light on me.

POLONIUS: Come, go with me. I will go seek the King.
This is the very ecstasy° of love,
Whose violent property° fordoes° itself
And leads the will to desperate undertakings
As oft as any passion under heaven
That does afflict our natures. I am sorry.
What, have you given him any hard words of late?

OPHELIA: No, my good lord, but as you did command
I did repel his letters and denied
His access to me.

POLONIUS: That hath made him mad.
I am sorry that with better heed and judgment
I had not quoted° him. I feared he did but trifle
And meant to wrack° thee. But beshrew my jealousy!°
By heaven, it is as proper to our age°
To cast beyond° ourselves in our opinions
As it is common for the younger sort
To lack discretion. Come, go we to the King.
This must be known,° which, being kept close,° might move
More grief to hide than hate to utter love.°
Come.

[Exeunt.]

[2.2 Flourish. Enter KING *and* QUEEN, ROSENCRANTZ, *and* GUILDENSTERN *(with others).]°*

KING: Welcome, dear Rosencrantz and Guildenstern.
Moreover that° we much did long to see you,
The need we have to use you did provoke

97 **bulk** body 104 **ecstasy** madness 105 **property** nature **fordoes** destroys 114 **quoted** observed 115 **wrack** ruin, seduce **beshrew my jealousy** a plague upon my suspicious nature 116 **proper . . . age** characteristic of us (old) men 117 **cast beyond** overshoot, miscalculate (A metaphor from hunting.) 120 **known** made known (to the King) **close** secret 120–121 **might . . . love** i.e., might cause more grief (because of what Hamlet might do) by hiding the knowledge of Hamlet's strange behavior to Ophelia than unpleasantness by telling it 2.2 s.d. **Location: The castle** 2 **Moreover that** besides the fact that

Our hasty sending. Something have you heard
Of Hamlet's transformation—so call it,
Sith nor° th' exterior nor the inward man
Resembles that° it was. What it should be,
More than his father's death, that thus hath put him
So much from th' understanding of himself,
I cannot dream of. I entreat you both
That, being of so young days° brought up with him,
And sith so neighbored to° his youth and havior,°
That you vouchsafe your rest° here in our court
Some little time, so by your companies
To draw him on to pleasures, and to gather
So much as from occasion° you may glean,
Whether aught to us unknown afflicts him thus
That, opened,° lies within our remedy.

QUEEN: Good gentlemen, he hath much talked of you,
And sure I am two men there is not living
To whom he more adheres. If it will please you
To show us so much gentry° and good will
As to expend your time with us awhile
For the supply and profit of our hope,°
Your visitation shall receive such thanks
As fits a king's remembrance.°

ROSENCRANTZ: Both Your Majesties
Might, by the sovereign power you have of° us,
Put your dread° pleasures more into command
Than to entreaty.

GUILDENSTERN: But we both obey,
And here give up ourselves in the full bent°
To lay our service freely at your feet,
To be commanded.

KING: Thanks, Rosencrantz and gentle Guildenstern.

QUEEN: Thanks, Guildenstern and gentle Rosencrantz.
And I beseech you instantly to visit
My too much changèd son. Go, some of you,
And bring these gentlemen where Hamlet is.

6 **Sith nor** since neither 7 **that** what 11 **of . . . days** from such early youth 12 **And sith so neighbored to** and since you are (or, and since that time you are) intimately acquainted with **havior** demeanor 13 **vouchsafe your rest** please to stay 16 **occasion** opportunity 18 **opened** being revealed 22 **gentry** courtesy 24 **supply . . . hope** aid and furtherance of what we hope for 26 **As fits . . . remembrance** as would be a fitting gift of a king who rewards true service 27 **of** over 28 **dread** inspiring awe 30 **in . . . bent** to the utmost degree of our capacity (An archery metaphor.)

GUILDENSTERN: Heavens make our presence and our practices°
Pleasant and helpful to him!
QUEEN: Ay, amen!

[Exeunt ROSENCRANTZ and GUILDENSTERN (with some attendants).]

[Enter POLONIUS.]

POLONIUS: Th' ambassadors from Norway, my good lord,
Are joyfully returned.
KING: Thou still° hast been the father of good news.
POLONIUS: Have I, my lord? I assure my good liege
I hold° my duty, as° I hold my soul,
Both to my God and to my gracious king;
And I do think, or else this brain of mine
Hunts not the trail of policy° so sure
As it hath used to do, that I have found
The very cause of Hamlet's lunacy.
KING: O, speak of that! That do I long to hear.
POLONIUS: Give first admittance to th' ambassadors.
My news shall be the fruit° to that great feast.
KING: Thyself do grace° to them and bring them in.

[Exit POLONIUS.]

He tells me, my dear Gertrude, he hath found
The head and source of all your son's distemper.
QUEEN: I doubt° it is no other but the main,°
His father's death and our o'erhasty marriage.

[Enter Ambassadors VOLTIMAND and CORNELIUS, with POLONIUS.]

KING: Well, we shall sift him.°—Welcome, my good friends!
Say, Voltimand, what from our brother° Norway?
VOLTIMAND: Most fair return of greetings and desires.°
Upon our first,° he sent out to suppress
His nephew's levies, which to him appeared
To be a preparation 'gainst the Polack,
But, better looked into, he truly found
It was against Your Highness. Whereat grieved
That so his sickness, age, and impotence°
Was falsely borne in hand,° sends out arrests°

38 **practices** doings 42 **still** always 44 **hold** maintain **as** firmly as 47 **policy** sagacity 52 **fruit** dessert 53 **grace** honor (punning on *grace* said before a *feast,* line 52) 56 **doubt** fear, suspect **main** chief point, principal concern 58 **sift him** question Polonius closely 59 **brother** fellow king 60 **desires** good wishes 61 **Upon our first** at our first words on the business 66 **impotence** helplessness 67 **borne in hand** deluded, taken advantage of **arrests** orders to desist

On Fortinbras, which he, in brief, obeys,
Receives rebuke from Norway, and in fine°
Makes vow before his uncle never more
To give th' assay° of arms against Your Majesty.
Whereon old Norway, overcome with joy,
Gives him three thousand crowns in annual fee
And his commission to employ those soldiers,
So levied as before, against the Polack,
With an entreaty, herein further shown, *[giving a paper]*
That it might please you to give quiet pass
Through your dominions for this enterprise
On such regards of safety and allowance°
As therein are set down.

KING: It likes° us well,
And at our more considered° time we'll read,
Answer, and think upon this business.
Meantime we thank you for your well-took labor.
Go to your rest; at night we'll feast together.
Most welcome home!

[Exeunt Ambassadors.]

POLONIUS: This business is well ended.
My liege, and madam, to expostulate°
What majesty should be, what duty is,
Why day is day, night night, and time is time,
Were nothing but to waste night, day, and time.
Therefore, since brevity is the soul of wit,°
And tediousness the limbs and outward flourishes,
I will be brief. Your noble son is mad.
Mad call I it, for, to define true madness.
What is't but to be nothing else but mad?
But let that go.

QUEEN: More matter, with less art.

POLONIUS: Madam. I swear I use no art at all.
That he's mad, 'tis true; 'tis true 'tis pity.
And pity 'tis 'tis true—a foolish figure,°
But farewell it, for I will use no art.
Mad let us grant him, then, and now remains
That we find out the cause of this effect,
Or rather say, the cause of this defect,

69 **in fine** in conclusion 71 **give th' assay** make trial of strength, challenge 78 **On . . . allowance** i.e., with such considerations for the safety of Denmark and permission for Fortinbras 80 **likes** pleases 81 **considered** suitable for deliberation 86 **expostulate** expound, inquire into 90 **wit** sense or judgment 98 **figure** figure of speech

For this effect defective comes by cause.°
Thus it remains, and the remainder thus.
Perpend.°
I have a daughter—have while she is mine—
Who, in her duty and obedience, mark,
Hath given me this. Now gather and surmise.°
[*He reads the letter.*] "To the celestial and my soul's idol, the most beautified Ophelia"—
That's an ill phrase, a vile phrase; "beautified" is a vile phrase. But you shall hear. Thus: [*He reads.*]
"In her excellent white bosom,° these,° etc."

QUEEN: Came this from Hamlet to her?

POLONIUS: Good madam, stay° awhile, I will be faithful.° [*He reads.*]

"Doubt thou the stars are fire,
    Doubt that the sun doth move,
Doubt° truth to be a liar,
    But never doubt I love.

O dear Ophelia, I am ill at these numbers.° I have not art to reckon° my groans. But that I love thee best, O most best, believe it. Adieu.
Thine evermore, most dear lady, whilst this machine° is to him,
Hamlet."

This in obedience hath my daughter shown me,
And, more above,° hath his solicitings,
As they fell out° by° time, by means, and place,
All given to mine ear.°

KING: But how hath she
Received his love?

POLONIUS: What do you think of me?

KING: As of a man faithful and honorable.

POLONIUS: I would fain° prove so. But what might you think,
When I had seen this hot love on the wing—
As I perceived it, I must tell you that,
Before my daughter told me—what might you,
Or my dear Majesty your queen here, think,

103 **For . . . cause** i.e., for this defective behavior, tis madness, has a cause 105 **Perpend** consider 108 **gather and surmise** draw your own conclusions 113 **In . . . bosom** (The letter is poetically addressed to her heart.) **these** i.e., the letter 115 **stay** wait **faithful** i.e., in reading the letter accurately 118 **Doubt** suspect 120 **ill . . . numbers** unskilled at writing verses 121 **reckon** (1) count (2) number metrically, scan 123 **machine** i.e., body 126 **more above** moreover 127 **fell out** occurred **by** according to 128 **given . . . ear** i.e., told me about 131 **fain** gladly

If I had played the desk or table book,°
Or given my heart a winking,° mute and dumb,
Or looked upon this love with idle sight?°
What might you think? No, I went round° to work,
And my young mistress thus I did bespeak:°
"Lord Hamlet is a prince out of thy star;°
This must not be." And then I prescripts° gave her,
That she should lock herself from his resort,°
Admit no messengers, receive no tokens.
Which done, she took the fruits of my advice;
And he, repellèd—a short tale to make—
Fell into a sadness, then into a fast,
Thence to a watch,° thence into a weakness,
Thence to a lightness,° and by this declension°
Into the madness wherein now he raves,
And all we° mourn for.

KING: [*to the* QUEEN.] Do you think 'tis this?

QUEEN: It may be, very like.

POLONIUS: Hath there been such a time—I would fain know that—
That I have positively said "'Tis so,"
When it proved otherwise?

KING: Not that I know.

POLONIUS: Take this from this,° if this be otherwise.
If circumstances lead me, I will find
Where truth is hid, though it were hid indeed
Within the center.°

KING: How may we try° it further?

POLONIUS: You know sometimes he walks four hours together
Here in the lobby.

QUEEN: So he does indeed.

POLONIUS: At such a time I'll loose° my daughter to him.
Be you and I behind an arras° then.
Mark the encounter. If he love her not
And be not from his reason fall'n thereon,°
Let me be no assistant for a state,

136 **played . . . table book** i.e., remained shut up, concealing the information 137 **given . . . winking** closed the eyes of my heart to this 138 **with idle sight** complacently or incomprehendingly 139 **round** roundly, plainly 140 **bespeak** address 141 **out of thy star** above your sphere, position 142 **prescripts** orders 143 **his resort** his visits 148 **watch** state of sleeplessness 149 **lightness** lightheadedness **declension** decline, deterioration (with a pun on the grammatical sense) 151 **all we** all of us, or, into everything that we 156 **Take this from this** (The actor probably gestures, indicating that he means his head from his shoulders, or his staff of office or chain from his hands or neck, or something similar.) 159 **center** middle point of the earth (which is also the center of the Ptolemaic universe) **try** test, judge 162 **loose** (as one might release an animal that is being mated) 163 **arras** handing, tapestry 165 **thereon** on that account

But keep a farm and carters.°

KING: We will try it.

[Enter HAMLET (reading on a book).]

QUEEN: But look where sadly° the poor wretch comes reading.

POLONIUS: Away, I do beseech you both, away.
I'll board° him presently.° O, give me leave.°

[Exeunt KING and QUEEN (with attendants).]

How does my good Lord Hamlet?

HAMLET: Well, God-a-mercy.°

POLONIUS: Do you know me, my lord?

HAMLET: Excellent well. You are a fishmonger.°

POLONIUS: Not I, my lord.

HAMLET: Then I would you were so honest a man.

POLONIUS: Honest, my lord?

HAMLET: Ay, sir. To be honest, as this world goes, is to be one man picked out of ten thousand.

POLONIUS: That's very true, my lord.

HAMLET: For if the sun breed maggots in a dead dog, being a good kissing carrion°—Have you a daughter?

POLONIUS: I have, my lord.

HAMLET: Let her not walk i' the sun.° Conception° is a blessing, but as your daughter may conceive, friend, look to 't.

POLONIUS: [*aside*] How say you by that? Still harping on my daughter. Yet he knew me not at first; 'a° said I was a fishmonger. 'A is far gone. And truly in my youth I suffered much extremity for love, very near this. I'll speak to him again.—What do you read, my lord?

HAMLET: Words, words, words.

POLONIUS: What is the matter,° my lord?

HAMLET: Between who?

POLONIUS: I mean, the matter that you read, my lord.

HAMLET: Slanders, sir; for the satirical rogue says here that old men have gray beards, that their faces are wrinkled, their eyes purging° thick amber° and plum-tree gum, and that they have a plentiful lack of wit,° together with most weak hams. All which, sir, though I most powerfully and potently

167 **carters** wagon drivers 168 **sadly** seriously 170 **board** accost **presently** at once **give me leave** i.e., excuse me, leave me alone (Said to those he hurries offstage, including the King and Queen.) 172 **God-a-mercy** God have mercy, i.e., thank you 174 **fishmonger** fish merchant 181–182 **a good kissing carrion** i.e., a good piece of flesh for kissing, or for the sun to kiss 184 **i' the sun** in public (with additional implication of the sunshine of princely favors) **Conception** (1) understanding (2) pregnancy 187 **'a** he 191 **matter** substance (But Hamlet plays on the sense of "basis for a dispute.") 195 **purging** discharging **amber** i.e., resin, like the resinous **plum-tree gum** 197 **wit** understanding

believe, yet I hold it not honesty° to have it thus set down, for yourself, sir, shall grow old° as I am, if like a crab you could go backward.

POLONIUS: [*aside*] Though this be madness, yet there is method in 't.—Will you walk out of the air,° my lord?

HAMLET: Into my grave.

POLONIUS: Indeed, that's out of the air. [*Aside.*] How pregnant° sometimes his replies are! A happiness° that often madness hits on, which reason and sanity could not so prosperously° be delivered of. I will leave him and suddenly° contrive the means of meeting between him and my daughter.—My honorable lord, I will most humbly take my leave of you.

HAMLET: You cannot, sir, take from me anything that I will more willingly part withal°—except my life, except my life, except my life.

[Enter GUILDENSTERN and ROSENCRANTZ.]

POLONIUS: Fare you well, my lord.

HAMLET: These tedious old fools!°

POLONIUS: You go to seek the Lord Hamlet. There he is.

ROSENCRANTZ: [*to POLONIUS*] God save you, sir!

[Exit POLONIUS.]

GUILDENSTERN: My honored lord!

ROSENCRANTZ: My most dear lord!

HAMLET: My excellent good friends! How dost thou, Guildenstern? Ah, Rosencrantz! Good lads, how do you both?

ROSENCRANTZ: As the indifferent° children of the earth.

GUILDENSTERN: Happy in that we are not overhappy.
On Fortune's cap we are not the very button.

HAMLET: Nor the soles of her shoe?

ROSENCRANTZ: Neither, my lord.

HAMLET: Then you live about her waist, or in the middle of her favors?°

GUILDENSTERN: Faith, her privates we.°

HAMLET: In the secret parts of Fortune? O, most true, she is a strumpet.° What news?

ROSENCRANTZ: None, my lord, but the world's grown honest.

HAMLET: Then is doomsday near. But your news is not true. Let me question more in particular. What have you, my good friends, deserved at the hands of Fortune that she sends you to prison hither?

198 **honesty** decency, decorum 199 **old** as old 201 **out of the air** (The open air was considered dangerous for sick people.) 203 **pregnant** quick-witted, full of meaning 204 **happiness** felicity of expression 205 **prosperously** successfully 206 **suddenly** immediately 209 **withal** with 211 **old fools** i.e., old men like Polonius 218 **indifferent** ordinary, at neither extreme of fortune or misfortune 223 **favors** i.e., sexual favors 224 **her privates we** i.e., (1) we are sexually intimate with Fortune, the fickle goddess who bestows her favors indiscriminately (2) we are her private citizens 225 **strumpet** prostitute (A common epithet for indiscriminate Fortune; see line 439.)

GUILDENSTERN: Prison, my lord?

HAMLET: Denmark's a prison.

ROSENCRANTZ: Then is the world one.

HAMLET: A goodly one, in which there are many confines,° wards,° and dungeons, Denmark being one o' the worst.

ROSENCRANTZ: We think not so, my lord.

HAMLET: Why then 'tis none to you, for there is nothing either good or bad but thinking makes it so. To me it is a prison.

ROSENCRANTZ: Why then, your ambition makes it one. 'Tis too narrow for your mind.

HAMLET: O God, I could be bounded in a nutshell and count myself a king of infinite space, were it not that I have bad dreams.

GUILDENSTERN: Which dreams indeed are ambition, for the very substance of the ambitious° is merely the shadow of a dream.

HAMLET: A dream itself is but a shadow.

ROSENCRANTZ: Truly, and I hold ambition of so airy and light a quality that it is but a shadow's shadow.

HAMLET: Then are our beggars bodies,° and our monarchs and outstretched° heroes the beggars' shadows. Shall we to the court? For, by my fay,° I cannot reason.

ROSENCRANTZ, GUILDENSTERN: We'll wait upon° you.

HAMLET: No such matter. I will not sort° you with the rest of my servants, for, to speak to you like an honest man, I am most dreadfully attended.° But, in the beaten way° of friendship, what make° you at Elsinore?

ROSENCRANTZ: To visit you, my lord, no other occasion.

HAMLET: Beggar that I am, I'am even poor in thanks; but I thank you, and sure, dear friends, my thanks are too dear a halfpenny.° Were you not sent for? Is it your own inclining? Is it a free° visitation? Come, come, deal justly with me. Come, come. Nay, speak.

GUILDENSTERN: What should we say; my lord?

HAMLET: Anything but to the purpose.° You were sent for, and there is a kind of confession in your looks which your modesties° have not craft enough to color.° I know the good King and Queen have sent for you.

234 **confines** places of confinement **wards** cells 243–244 **the very . . . ambitious** that seemingly very substantial thing that the ambitious pursue 248 **bodies** i.e., solid substances rather than shadows (since beggars are not ambitious) **outstretched** (1) far-reaching in their ambition (2) elongated as shadows 249 **fay** faith 251 **wait upon** accompany, attend (But Hamlet uses the phrase in the sense of providing menial service.) 252 **sort** class, categorize 253 **dreadfully attended** waited upon in slovenly fashion 254 **beaten way** familiar path, tried-and-true course **make** do 257 **too dear a halfpenny** (1) too expensive at even a halfpenny, i.e., of little worth (2) too expensive *by* a halfpenny in return for worthless kindness 258 **free** voluntary 261 **Anything but to the purpose** anything except a straightforward answer (Said ironically.) 262 **modesties** sense of shame 263 **color** disguise

ROSENCRANTZ: To what end, my lord?

HAMLET: That you must teach me. But let me conjure° you, by the rights of our fellowship, by the consonancy of our youth,° by the obligation of our ever-preserved love, and by what more dear a better° proposer could charge° you withal, be even° and direct with me whether you were sent for or no.

ROSENCRANTZ: [*aside to GUILDENSTERN*] What say you?

HAMLET [*aside*]: Nay, then, I have an eye of° you.—If you love me, hold not off.°

GUILDENSTERN: My lord, we were sent for.

HAMLET: I will tell you why; so shall my anticipation prevent your discovery,° and your secrecy to the King and Queen molt no feather,° I have of late—but wherefore I know not—lost all my mirth, forgone all custom of exercises; and indeed it goes so heavily with my disposition that this goodly frame, the earth, seems to me a sterile promontory; this most excellent canopy, the air, look you, this brave° o'erhanging firmament, this majestical roof fretted° with golden fire, why, it appeareth nothing to me but a foul and pestilent congregation° of vapors. What a piece of work° is a man! How noble in reason, how infinite in faculties, in form and moving how express° and admirable, in action how like an angel, in apprehension° how like a god! The beauty of the world, the paragon of animals! And yet, to me, what is this quintessence° of dust? Man delights not me—no, nor woman neither, though by your smiling you seem to say so.

ROSENCRANTZ: My lord, there was no such stuff in my thoughts.

HAMLET: Why did you laugh, then, when I said man delights not me?

ROSENCRANTZ: To think, my lord, if you delight not in man, what Lenten entertainment° the players shall receive from you. We coted° them on the way, and hither are they coming to offer you service.

HAMLET: He that plays the king shall be welcome; His Majesty shall have tribute° of° me. The adventurous knight shall use his foil and target,° the lover shall not sigh gratis,° the humorous man° shall end his part in

265 **conjure** adjure, entreat 266 **the consonancy of our youth** our closeness in our younger days 267 **better** more skillful 268 **charge** urge **even** straight, honest 271 **of** on **hold not off** don't hold back 273 **so . . . discovery** in that way my saying it first will spare you from revealing the truth 274 **molt no feather** i.e., not diminish in the least 278 **brave** splendid **fretted** adorned (with fretwork, as in a vaulted ceiling) 280 **congregation** mass **piece of work** masterpiece 282 **express** well-framed, exact, expressive 282–283 **apprehension** power of comprehending 284 **quintessence** the fifth essence of ancient philosophy, beyond earth, water, air, and fire, supposed to be the substance of the heavenly bodies and to be latent in all things 288–289 **Lenten entertainment** meager reception (appropriate to Lent) 289 **coted** over-took and passed by 291–292 **tribute** (1) applause (2) homage paid in money 292 **of** from **foil and target** sword and shield 293 **gratis** for nothing **humorous man** eccentric character, dominated by one trait or "humor"

peace,° the clown shall make those laugh whose lungs are tickle o' the sear,° and the lady shall say her mind freely, or the blank verse shall halt° for 't. What players are they?

ROSENCRANTZ: Even those you were wont to take such delight in, the tragedians° of the city.

HAMLET: How chances it they travel? Their residence,° both in reputation and profit, was better both ways.

ROSENCRANTZ: I think their inhibition° comes by the means of the late° innovation.°

HAMLET: Do they hold the same estimation they did when I was in the city? Are they so followed?

ROSENCRANTZ: No, indeed are they not.

HAMLET: How comes it? Do they grow rusty?

ROSENCRANTZ: Nay, their endeavor keeps° in the wonted° pace. But there is, sir, an aerie° of children, little eyases,° that cry out on the top of question° and are most tyrannically° clapped for 't. These are now the fashion, and so berattle° the common stages°—so they call them—that many wearing rapiers° are afraid of goose quills° and dare scarce come thither.

HAMLET: What, are they children? Who maintains 'em? How are they escoted?° Will they pursue the quality° no longer than they can sing?° Will they not say afterwards, if they should grow themselves to common° players-as it is most like,° if their means are no better°—their writers do them wrong to make them exclaim against their own succession?°

ROSENCRANTZ: Faith, there has been much to-do° on both sides, and the nation holds it no sin to tar° them to controversy. There was for a while no money bid for argument unless the poet and the player went to cuffs in the question.°

HAMLET: Is 't possible?

293–294 **in peace** i.e., with full license 294–295 **tickle o' the sear** easy on the trigger, ready to laugh easily (A sear is part of a gunlock.) 295 **halt** limp 297 **tragedians** actors 299 **residence** remaining in their usual place, i.e., in the city 301 **inhibition** formal prohibition (from acting plays in the city) **late** recent 301–302 **innovation** i.e., the new fashion in satirical plays performed by boy actors in the "private" theaters; or possibly a political uprising; or the strict limitations set on the theaters in London in 1600 307 **keeps** continues **wonted** usual 308 **aerie** nest **eyases** young hawks **cry . . . question** speak shrilly, dominating the controversy (in decrying the public theaters) 309 **tyrannically** outrageously 310 **berattle** berate, clamor against **common stages** public theaters 310–311 **many wearing rapiers** i.e., many men of fashion, afraid to patronize the common players for fear of being satirized by the poets writing for the boy actors **goose quills** i.e., pens of satirists 312 **escoted** maintained 313 **quality** (acting) profession **no longer . . . sing** i.e., only until their voices change 314 **common** regular, adult 315 **like** likely **if . . . better** if they find no better way to support themselves 316 **succession** i.e., future careers 317 **to-do** ado 318 **tar** set on (as dogs) 318–320 **There . . . question** i.e., for a while, no money was offered by the acting companies to playwrights for the plot to a play unless the satirical poets who wrote for the boys and the adult actors came to blows in the play itself

GUILDENSTERN: O, there has been much throwing about of brains.

HAMLET: Do the boys carry it away?°

ROSENCRANTZ: Ay, that they do, my lord—Hercules and his load° too.°

HAMLET: It is not very strange; for my uncle is King of Denmark, and those that would make mouths° at him while my father lived give twenty, forty, fifty, a hundred ducats° apiece for his picture in little.° 'Sblood,° there is something in this more than natural, if philosophy° could find it out.

[A flourish (of trumpets within).]

GUILDENSTERN: There are the players.

HAMLET: Gentlemen, you are welcome to Elsinore. Your hands, come then. Th' appurtenance° of welcome is fashion and ceremony. Let me comply° with you in this garb,° lest my extent° to the players, which, I tell you, must show fairly outwards,° should more appear like entertainment° than yours. You are welcome. But my uncle-father and aunt-mother are deceived.

GUILDENSTERN: In what, my dear lord?

HAMLET: I am but mad north-north-west.° When the wind is southerly I know a hawk from a handsaw.°

[Enter POLONIUS.]

POLONIUS: Well be with you, gentlemen!

HAMLET: Hark you, Guildenstern, and you too; at each ear a hearer. That great baby you see there is not yet out of his swaddling clouts.°

ROSENCRANTZ: Haply° he is the second time come to them, for they say an old man is twice a child.

HAMLET: I will prophesy he comes to tell me of the players. Mark it.—You say right, sir, o' Monday morning, 'twas then indeed.

POLONIUS: My lord, I have news to tell you.

HAMLET: My lord, I have news to tell you. When Roscius° was an actor in Rome—

POLONIUS: The actors are come hither, my lord.

HAMLET: Buzz,° buzz!

323 **carry it away** i.e., win the day 324 **Hercules . . . load** (Thought to be an allusion to the sign of the Globe Theatre, which was Hercules bearing the world on his shoulders.) 312–324 **How . . . load too** (The passage, omitted from the early quartos, alludes to the so-called War of the Theaters, 1599–1602, the rivalry between the children's companies and the adult actors.) 326 **mouths** faces 327 **ducats** gold coins **in little** in miniature **'Sblood** by God's (Christ's) blood 328 **philosophy** i.e., scientific inquiry 331 **appurtenance** proper accompaniment **comply** observe the formalities of courtesy 332 **garb** i.e., manner **my extent** that which I extend, i.e., my polite behavior 333 **show fairly outwards** show every evidence of cordiality **entertainment** a (warm) reception 337 **north-north-west** just off true north, only partly 338 **hawk, handsaw** i.e., two very different things, though also perhaps meaning a mattock (or *hack*) and a carpenter's cutting tool, respectively; also birds, with a play on *hernshaw,* or heron 341 **swaddling clouts** cloths in which to wrap a newborn baby 342 **Haply** perhaps 347 **Roscius** a famous Roman actor who died in 62 B.C. 350 **Buzz** (An interjection used to denote stale news.)

POLONIUS: Upon my honor—
HAMLET: Then came each actor on his ass.
POLONIUS: The best actors in the world, either for tragedy, comedy, history, pastoral, pastoral-comical, historical-pastoral, tragical-historical, tragical-comical-historical-pastoral, scene individable,° or poem unlimited.° Seneca° cannot be too heavy, nor Plautus° too light. For the law of writ and the liberty,° these° are the only men.
HAMLET: O Jephthah, judge of Israel,° what a treasure hadst thou!
POLONIUS: What a treasure had he, my lord?
HAMLET: Why,
"One fair daughter, and no more,
The which he lovèd passing° well."
POLONIUS: [*aside*] Still on my daughter.
HAMLET: Am I not i' the right, old Jephthah?
POLONIUS: If you call me Jephthah, my lord, I have a daughter that I love passing well.
HAMLET: Nay, that follows not.
POLONIUS: What follows then, my lord?
HAMLET: Why,
"As by lot,° God wot,"°
and then, you know,
"It came to pass, as most like° it was"—
the first row° of the pious chanson° will show you more, for look where my abridgement° comes.

[Enter the PLAYERS.*]*

You are welcome, masters; welcome, all. I am glad to see thee well. Welcome, good friends. O, old friend! Why, thy face is valanced° since I saw thee last. Com'st thou to beard° me in Denmark? What, my young lady° and mistress! By 'r Lady,° your ladyship is nearer to heaven than when I saw you last, by the altitude of a chopine.° Pray God your voice, like a piece of uncurrent° gold, be not cracked within the ring.° Masters,

355 **scene individable** a play observing the unity of place; or perhaps one that is unclassifiable, or performed without intermission **poem unlimited** a play disregarding the unities of time and place; one that is all-inclusive **Seneca** writer of Latin tragedies **Plautus** writer of Latin comedy 356–357 **law . . . liberty** dramatic composition both according to the rules and disregarding the rules **these** i.e., the actors 358 **Jephthah . . . Israel** (Jephthah had to sacrifice his daughter; see Judges 11. Hamlet goes on to quote from a ballad on the theme.) 362 **passing** surpassingly 370 **lot** chance **wot** knows 372 **like** likely, probable 373 **row** stanza **chanson** ballad, song 374 **my abridgment** something that cuts short my conversation; also, a diversion 376 **valanced** fringed (with a beard) 377 **beard** confront, challenge (with obvious pun) 377–378 **young lady** i.e., boy playing women's parts **By 'r Lady** by Our Lady 379 **chopine** thick-soled shoe of Italian fashion 380 **uncurrent** not passable as lawful coinage **cracked . . . ring** i.e., changed from adolescent to male voice, no longer suitable for women's roles (Coins featured rings enclosing the sovereign's head; if the coin was cracked within this ring, it was unfit for currency.)

you are all welcome. We'll e'en to 't° like French falconers, fly at anything we see. We'll have a speech straight.° Come, give us a taste of your quality.° Come, a passionate speech.

First Player: What speech, my good lord?

Hamlet: I heard thee speak me a speech once, but it was never acted, or if it was, not above once, for the play, I remember, pleased not the million; 'twas caviar to the general.° But it was—as I received it, and others, whose judgments in such matters cried in the top of° mine—an excellent play, well digested° in the scenes, set down with as much modesty° as cunning.° I remember one said there were no sallets° in the lines to make the matter savory, nor no matter in the phrase that might indict° the author of affectation, but called it an honest method, as wholesome as sweet, and by very much more handsome° than fine.° One speech in 't I chiefly loved: 'twas Aeneas' tale to Dido, and thereabout of it especially when he speaks of Priam's slaughter.° If it live in your memory, begin at this line: let me see, let me see—

"The rugged Pyrrhus,° like th' Hyrcanian° beast"—

'Tis not so. It begins with Pyrrhus:

"The rugged° Pyrrhus, he whose sable° arms,
Black as his purpose, did the night resemble
When he lay couchèd° in the ominous horse,°
Hath now this dread and black complexion smeared
With heraldry more dismal.° Head to foot
Now is he total gules,° horridly tricked°
With blood of fathers, mothers, daughters, sons,
Baked and impasted° with the parching streets,°
That lend a tyrannous° and a damnèd light
To their lord's° murder. Roasted in wrath and fire,

381 **e'en to 't** go at it 382 **straight** at once 382–383 **quality** professional skill 387 **caviar to the general** caviar to the multitude, i.e., a choice dish too elegant for coarse tastes 388 **cried in the top of** i.e., spoke with greater authority than 389 **digested** arranged, ordered **modesty** moderation, restraint 389–390 **cunning** skill 390 **sallets** i.e., something savory, spicy improprieties 391 **indict** convict 393 **handsome** well-proportioned **fine** elaborately ornamented, showy 395 **Priam's slaughter** the slaying of the ruler of Troy, when the Greeks finally took the city 397 **Pyrrhus** a Greek hero in the Trojan War, also known as Neoptolemus, son of Achilles—another avenging son **Hyrcanian beast** i.e., tiger (On the death of Priam, see Virgil, *Aeneid,* 2.506 ff.; compare the whole speech with Marlowe's *Dido Queen of Carthage,* 2.1.214. ff. On the *Hyrcanian* tiger, see *Aeneid,* 4.366-367. Hyrcania is on the Caspian Sea.) 399 **rugged** shaggy, savage **sable** black (for reasons of camouflage during the episode of the Trojan horse) 401 **couchèd** concealed **ominous horse** fateful Trojan horse, by which the Greeks gained access to Troy 403 **dismal** ill-omened 404 **total gules** entirely red (A heraldic term.) **tricked** spotted and smeared (Heraldic.) 406 **impasted** crusted, like a thick paste **with . . . streets** by the parching heat of the streets (because of the fires everywhere) 407 **tyrannous** cruel 408 **their lord's** i.e., Priam's

And thus o'ersizèd° with coagulate gore,
With eyes like carbuncles,° the hellish Pyrrhus
Old grandsire Priam seeks."
So proceed you.

POLONIUS: 'Fore God, my lord, well spoken, with good accent and good discretion.

FIRST PLAYER: "Anon he finds him
Striking too short at Greeks. His antique° sword,
Rebellious to his arm, lies where it falls,
Repugnant° to command. Unequal matched,
Pyrrhus at Priam drives, in rage strikes wide,
But with the whiff and wind of his fell° sword
Th' unnervèd° father falls. Then senseless Ilium,°
Seeming to feel this blow, with flaming top
Stoops to his° base, and with a hideous crash
Takes prisoner Pyrrhus' ear. For, lo! His sword,
Which was declining° on the milky° head
Of reverend Priam, seemed i' th' air to stick.
So as a painted° tyrant Pyrrhus stood,
And, like a neutral to his will and matter,°
Did nothing.
But as we often see against° some storm
A silence in the heavens, the rack° stand still,
The bold winds speechless, and the orb° below
As hush as death, anon the dreadful thunder
Doth rend the region,° so, after Pyrrhus' pause,
A rousèd vengeance sets him new a-work
And never did the Cyclops'° hammers fall
On Mars's armor forged for proof eterne°
With less remorse° than Pyrrhus' bleeding sword
Now falls on Priam.
Out, out, thou strumpet Fortune! All you gods
In general synod° take away her power!
Break all the spokes and fellies° from her wheel,

409 **o'ersizèd** covered as with size or glue 410 **carbuncles** large fiery-red precious stones thought to emit their own light 415 **antique** ancient, long-used 417 **Repugnant** disobedient, resistant 419 **fell** cruel 420 **unnervèd** strengthless **senseless Ilium** inanimate citadel of Troy 422 **his** its 424 **declining** descending **milky** white-haired 426 **painted** i.e., painted in a picture **like . . . matter** i.e., as though suspended between his intention and its fulfillment 429 **against** just before 430 **rack** mass of clouds 431 **orb** globe, earth 433 **region** sky 435 **Cyclops** giant armor makers in the smithy of Vulcan 436 **proof eterne** eternal resistance to assault 437 **remorse** pity 440 **synod** assembly 441 **fellies** pieces of wood forming the rim of a wheel

And bowl the round nave° down the hill of heaven°
As low as to the fiends!"

POLONIUS: This is too long.

HAMLET: It shall to the barber's with your beard.—Prithee, say on. He's for a jig° or a tale of bawdry, or he sleeps. Say on; come to Hecuba.°

FIRST PLAYER: "But who, ah woe! had° seen the mobléd° queen"—

HAMLET: "The mobléd queen?"

POLONIUS: That's good. "Mobléd queen" is good.

FIRST PLAYER: "Run barefoot up and down, threat'ning the flames°
With bisson rheum,° a clout° upon that head
Where late° the diadem stood, and, for a robe,
About her lank and all o'erteemèd° loins
A blanket, in the alarm of fear caught up—
Who this had seen, with tongue in venom steeped,
'Gainst Fortune's state° would treason have pronounced.°
But if the gods themselves did see her then
When she saw Pyrrhus make malicious sport
In mincing with his sword her husband's limbs,
The instant burst of clamor that she made,
Unless things mortal move them not at all,
Would have made milch° the burning eyes of heaven,°
And passion° in the gods."

POLONIUS: Look whe'er° he has not turned his color and has tears in 's eyes. Prithee, no more.

HAMLET: 'Tis well; I'll have thee speak out the rest of this soon.—Good my lord, will you see the players well bestowed?° Do you hear, let them be well used, for they are the abstract° and brief chronicles of the time. After your death you were better have a bad epitaph than their ill report while you live.

POLONIUS: My lord, I will use them according to their desert.

HAMLET: God's bodikin,° man, much better. Use every man after his desert, and who shall scape whipping? Use them after° your own honor and dignity. The less they deserve, the more merit is in your bounty. Take them in.

442 **nave** hub **hill of heaven** Mount Olympus 446 **jig** comic song and dance often given at the end of a play 447 **Hecuba** wife of Priam 448 **who . . . had** anyone who had (also in line 456) **mobléd** muffled 451 **threat'ning the flames** i.e., weeping hard enough to dampen the flames 452 **bisson rheum** blinding tears **clout** cloth 453 **late** lately 454 **all o'erteemèd** utterly worn out with bearing children 457 **state** rule, managing **pronounced** proclaimed 463 **milch** milky, moist with tears **burning eyes of heaven** i.e., heavenly bodies 464 **passion** overpowering emotion 465 **whe'er** whether 468 **bestowed** lodged 469 **abstract** summary account 473 **God's bodikin** by God's (Christ's) little body, *bodykin* (Not to be confused with *bodkin*, "dagger.") 474 **after** according to

POLONIUS: Come, sirs.

[Exit.]

HAMLET: Follow him, friends. We'll hear a play tomorrow. [*As they start to leave,* HAMLET *detains the* FIRST PLAYER.] Dost thou hear me, old friend? Can you play *The Murder of Gonzago*?

FIRST PLAYER: Ay, my lord.

HAMLET: We'll ha 't° tomorrow night. You could, for a need, study° a speech of some dozen or sixteen lines which I would set down and insert in 't, could you not?

FIRST PLAYER: Ay, my lord.

HAMLET: Very well. Follow that lord, and look you mock him not. [*Exeunt* PLAYERS.] My good friends, I'll leave you till night. You are welcome to Elsinore.

ROSENCRANTZ: Good my lord!

*[Exeunt (*ROSENCRANTZ *and* GUILDENSTERN*).]*

HAMLET: Ay, so, goodbye to you.—Now I am alone.
O, what a rogue and peasant slave am I!
Is it not monstrous that this player here,
But° in a fiction, in a dream of passion,
Could force his soul so to his own conceit°
That from her working° all his visage wanned,°
Tears in his eyes, distraction in his aspect,°
A broken voice, and his whole function suiting
With forms to his conceit?° And all for nothing!
For Hecuba!
What's Hecuba to him, or he to Hecuba,
That he should weep for her? What would he do
Had he the motive and the cue for passion
That I have? He would drown the stage with tears
And cleave the general ear° with horrid° speech,
Make mad the guilty and appall° the free,°
Confound the ignorant,° and amaze° indeed
The very faculties of eyes and ears. Yet I,
A dull and muddy-mettled° rascal, peak°

481 **ha 't** have it **study** memorize 492 **But** merely 493 **force . . . conceit** bring his innermost being so entirely into accord with his conception (of the role) 494 **from her working** as a result of, or in response to, his soul's activity **wanned** grew pale 495 **aspect** look, glance 496–497 **his whole . . . conceit** all his bodily powers responding with actions to suit his thought 503 **the general ear** everyone's ear **horrid** horrible 504 **appall** (literally, make pale.) **free** innocent 505 **Confound the ignorant** i.e., dumbfound those who know nothing of the crime that has been committed **amaze** stun 507 **muddy-mettled** dull-spirited **peak** mope, pine

Like John-a-dreams,° unpregnant of° my cause,
And can say nothing—no, not for a king
Upon whose property° and most dear life
A damned defeat° was made. Am I a coward?
Who calls me villain? Breaks my pate° across?
Plucks off my beard and blows it in my face?
Tweaks me by the nose? Gives me the lie i' the throat°
As deep as to the lungs? Who does me this?
Ha, 'swounds,° I should take it; for it cannot be
But I am pigeon-livered° and lack gall
To make oppression bitter,° or ere this
I should ha' fatted all the region kites°
With this slave's offal.° Bloody, bawdy villain!
Remorseless,° treacherous, lecherous, kindless° villain!
O, vengeance!
Why, what an ass am I! This is most brave,°
That I, the son of a dear father murdered,
Prompted to my revenge by heaven and hell,
Must like a whore unpack my heart with words
And fall a-cursing, like a very drab,°
A scullion!° Fie upon 't, foh! About,° my brains!
Hum, I have heard
That guilty creatures sitting at a play
Have by the very cunning° of the scene°
Been struck so to the soul that presently°
They have proclaimed their malefactions;
For murder, though it have no tongue, will speak
With most miraculous organ. I'll have these players
Play something like the murder of my father
Before mine uncle. I'll observe his looks;
I'll tent° him to the quick.° If 'a do blench,°
I know my course. The spirit that I have seen
May be the devil, and the devil hath power
T' assume a pleasing shape; yea, and perhaps,
Out of my weakness and my melancholy,

508 **John-a-dreams** a sleepy, dreaming idler **unpregnant of** not quickened by 510 **property** i.e., the crown; also character, quality 511 **damned defeat** damnable act of destruction 512 **pate** head 514 **Gives . . . throat** calls me an out-and-out liar 516 **'swounds** by his (Christ's) wounds 517 **pigeon-livered** (The pigeon or dove was popularly supposed to be mild because it secreted no gall.) 518 **bitter** i.e., bitter to me 519 **region kites** kites (birds of prey) of the air 520 **offal** entrails 521 **Remorseless** pitiless **kindless** unnatural 523 **brave** fine, admirable (Said ironically.) 527 **drab** whore 528 **scullion** menial kitchen servant (apt to be foul-mouthed) **About** about it, to work 531**cunning** art, skill **scene** dramatic presentation 532 **presently** at once 538 **tent** probe **the quick** the tender part of a wound, the core **blench** quail, flinch

As he is very potent with such spirits,°
Abuses° me to damn me. I'll have grounds
More relative° than this. The play's the thing
Wherein I'll catch the conscience of the King.

[Exit.]

[3.1 Enter KING, QUEEN, POLONIUS, OPHELIA, ROSENCRANTZ, GUILDERNSTERN, *lords.]*°

KING: And can you by no drift of conference°
Get from him why he puts on this confusion,
Grating so harshly all his days of quiet
With turbulent and dangerous lunacy?

ROSENCRANTZ: He does confess he feels himself distracted,
But from what cause 'a will by no means speak.

GUILDENSTERN: Nor do we find him forward° to be sounded,°
But with a crafty madness keeps aloof
When we would bring him on to some confession
Of his true state.

QUEEN: Did he receive you well?

ROSENCRANTZ: Most like a gentleman.

GUILDENSTERN: But with much forcing of his disposition.°

ROSENCRANTZ: Niggard° of question,° but of our demands
Most free in his reply.

QUEEN: Did you assay° him
To any pastime?

ROSENCRANTZ: Madam, it so fell out that certain players
We o'erraught° on the way. Of these we told him,
And there did seem in him a kind of joy
To hear of it. They are here about the court,
And, as I think, they have already order
This night to play before him.

POLONIUS: 'Tis most true,
And he beseeched me to entreat Your Majesties
To hear and see the matter.

KING: With all my heart, and it doth much content me
To hear him so inclined.
Good gentlemen, give him a further edge°
And drive his purpose into these delights.

ROSENCRANTZ: We shall, my lord.

[Exeunt ROSENCRANTZ *and* GUILDENSTERN.*]*

542 **spirits** humors (of melancholy) 543 **Abuses** deludes 545 **relative** cogent, pertinent 3.1 s.d. **Location: The castle** 1 **drift of conference** directing of conversation 7 **forward** willing **sounded** questioned 12 **disposition** inclination 13 **Niggard** stingy **question** conversation 14 **assay** try to win 17 **o'erraught** overtook 26 **edge** incitement

KING: Sweet Gertrude, leave us too,
For we have closely° sent for Hamlet hither,
That he, as 'twere by accident, may here
Affront° Ophelia.
Her father and myself, lawful espials,°
Will so bestow ourselves that seeing, unseen,
We may of their encounter frankly judge,
And gather by him, as he is behaved,
If't be th' affliction of his love or no
That thus he suffers for.

QUEEN: I shall obey you.
And for your part, Ophelia, I do wish
That your good beauties be the happy cause
Of Hamlet's wildness. So shall I hope your virtues
Will bring him to his wonted° way again,
To both your honors.

OPHELIA: Madam, I wish it may.

[Exit QUEEN.]

POLONIUS: Ophelia, walk you here.—Gracious,° so please you,
We will bestow° ourselves. [*To OPHELIA.*] Read on this book,
[*giving her a book*]
That show of such an exercise° may color°
Your loneliness.° We are oft to blame in this—
'Tis too much proved°—that with devotion's visage
And pious action we do sugar o'er
The devil himself.

KING [aside]: O 'tis too true!
How smart a lash that speech doth give my conscience!
The harlot's cheek, beautied with plastering art,
Is not more ugly to° the thing° that helps it
Than is my deed to my most painted word.
O heavy burden!

POLONIUS: I hear him coming. Let's withdraw, my lord.

[The KING and POLONIUS withdraw.°]

[Enter HAMLET. (OPHELIA pretends to read a book.)]

HAMLET: To be, or not to be, that is the question:
Whether 'tis nobler in the mind to suffer

29 **closely** privately 31 **Affront** confront, meet 32 **espials** spies 41 **wonted** accustomed 43 **Gracious** Your Grace (i.e., the King) 44 **bestow** conceal 45 **exercise** religious exercise (The book she reads is one of devotion.) **color** give a plausible appearance to 46 **loneliness** being alone 47 **too much proved** too often shown to be true, too often practiced 53 **to** compared to **the thing** i.e., the cosmetic 56 **s.d. withdraw** (The King and Polonius may retire behind an arras. The stage directions specify that they "enter" again near the end of the scene.)

The slings° and arrows of outrageous fortune,
Or to take arms against a sea of troubles
And by opposing end them. To die, to sleep—
No more—and by a sleep to say we end
The heartache and the thousand natural shocks
That flesh is heir to. 'Tis a consummation
Devoutly to be wished. To die, to sleep;
To sleep, perchance to dream. Ay, there's the rub,°
For in that sleep of death what dreams may come,
When we have shuffled° off this mortal coil,°
Must give us pause. There's the respect°
That makes calamity of so long life.°
For who would bear the whips and scorns of time,
Th' oppressor's wrong, the proud man's contumely,°
The pangs of disprized° love, the law's delay,
The insolence of office,° and the spurns°
That patient merit of th' unworthy takes,°
When he himself might his quietus° make
With a bare bodkin?° Who would fardels° bear,
To grunt and sweat under a weary life,
But that the dread of something after death,
The undiscovered country from whose bourn°
No traveler returns, puzzles the will,
And makes us rather bear those ills we have
Than fly to others that we know not of?
Thus conscience does make cowards of us all;
And thus the native hue° of resolution
Is sicklied o'er with the pale cast° of thought,
And enterprises of great pitch° and moment°
With this regard° their currents° turn awry
And lose the name of action.—Soft you° now,
The fair Ophelia. Nymph, in thy orisons°
Be all my sins remembered.

59 **slings** missiles 66 **rub** (Literally, an obstacle in the game of bowls.) 68 **shuffled** sloughed, cast **coil** turmoil 69 **respect** consideration 70 **of . . . life** so long-lived, something we willingly endure for so long (also suggesting that long life is itself a calamity) 72 **contumely** insolent abuse 73 **disprized** unvalued 74 **office** officialdom **spurns** insults 75 **of . . . takes** receives from unworthy persons 76 **quietus** acquittance; here, death 77 **a bare bodkin** a mere dagger, unsheathed **fardels** burdens 80 **bourn** frontier, boundary 85 **native hue** natural color, complexion 86 **cast** tinge, shade of color 87 **pitch** height (as of a falcon's flight) **moment** importance 88 **regard** respect, consideration **currents** courses 89 **Soft you** i.e., wait a minute, gently 90 **orisons** prayers

OPHELIA: Good my lord,
How does your honor for this many a day?
HAMLET: I humbly thank you; well, well, well.
OPHELIA: My lord, I have remembrances of yours,
That I have longèd long to redeliver.
I pray you, now receive them. [*She offers tokens.*]
HAMLET: No, not I, I never gave you aught.
OPHELIA: My honored lord, you know right well you did,
And with them words of so sweet breath composed
As made the things more rich. Their perfume lost,
Take these again, for to the noble mind
Rich gifts wax poor when givers prove unkind.
There, my lord. [*She gives tokens.*]
HAMLET: Ha, ha! Are you honest?°
OPHELIA: My lord?
HAMLET: Are you fair?°
OPHELIA: What means your lordship?
HAMLET: That if you be honest and fair, your honesty° should admit no discourse° to your beauty.
OPHELIA: Could beauty, my lord, have better commerce° than with honesty?
HAMLET: Ay, truly, for the power of beauty will sooner transform honesty from what it is to a bawd than the force of honesty can translate beauty into his° likeness. This was sometime° a paradox,° but now the time° gives it proof. I did love you once.
OPHELIA: Indeed, my lord, you made me believe so.
HAMLET: You should not have believed me, for virtue cannot so inoculate° our old stock but we shall relish of it.° I loved you not.
OPHELIA: I was the more deceived.
HAMLET: Get thee to a nunnery.° Why wouldst thou be a breeder of sinners? I am myself indifferent honest,° but yet I could accuse me of such things that it were better my mother had not borne me: I am very proud, revengeful, ambitious, with more offenses at my beck° than I have thoughts to put them in, imagination to give them shape, or time to act them in. What should such fellows as I do crawling between earth and heaven? We are arrant knaves all; believe none of us. Go thy ways to a nunnery. Where's your father?

104 **honest** (1) truthful (2) chaste 106 **fair** (1) beautiful (2) just, honorable 108 **your honesty** your chastity 109 **discourse** to familiar dealings with 110 **commerce** dealings, intercourse 113 **his** its **sometime** formerly **a paradox** a view opposite to commonly held opinion **the time** the present age 116 **inoculate** graft, be engrafted to 117 **but . . . it** that we do not still have about us a taste of the old stock. i.e., retain our sinfulness 119 **nunnery** convent (with possibly an awareness that the word was also used derisively to denote a brothel) 120 **indifferent honest** reasonably virtuous 122 **beck** command

OPHELIA: At home, my lord.

HAMLET: Let the doors be shut upon him, that he may play the fool nowhere but in's own house. Farewell.

OPHELIA: O, help him, you sweet heavens!

HAMLET: If thou dost marry, I'll give thee this plague for thy dowry: be thou as chaste as ice, as pure as snow, thou shalt not escape calumny. Get thee to a nunnery, farewell. Or, if thou wilt needs marry, marry a fool, for wise men know well enough what monsters° you° make of them. To a nunnery, go, and quickly too. Farewell.

OPHELIA: Heavenly powers, restore him!

HAMLET: I have heard of your paintings too, well enough. God hath given you one face, and you make yourselves another. You jig,° you amble,° and you lisp, you nickname God's creatures,° and make your wantonness your ignorance.° Go to, I'll no more on 't;° it hath made me mad. I say we will have no more marriage. Those that are married already—all but one—shall live. The rest shall keep as they are. To a nunnery, go.

[Exit.]

OPHELIA: O, what a noble mind is here o'erthrown!
The courtier's, soldier's, scholar's, eye, tongue, sword,
Th' expectancy° and rose° of the fair state,
The glass of fashion and the mold of form,°
Th' observed of all observers,° quite, quite down!
And I, of ladies most deject and wretched,
That sucked the honey of his music° vows,
Now see that noble and most sovereign reason
Like sweet bells jangled out of tune and harsh,
That unmatched form and feature of blown° youth
Blasted° with ecstasy.° O, woe is me,
T' have seen what I have seen, see what I see!

[Enter KING and POLONIUS.]

KING: Love? His affections° do not that way tend;
Nor what he spake, though it lacked form a little,
Was not like madness. There's something in his soul
O'er which his melancholy sits on brood,°

134 **monsters** (An illusion to the horns of a cuckold.) **you** i.e., you women 138 **jig** dance **amble** move coyly 139 **you nickname . . . creatures** i.e., you give trendy names to things in place of their God-given names 139–140 **make . . . ignorance** i.e., excuse your affectation on the grounds of pretended ignorance **on 't** of it 145 **expectancy** hope **rose** ornament 146 **The glass . . . form** the mirror of true fashioning and the pattern of courtly behavior 147 **Th' observed . . . observers** i.e., the center of attention and honor in the court 149 **music** musical, sweetly uttered 152 **blown** blooming 153 **Blasted** withered **ecstasy** madness 155 **affections** emotions, feelings 158 **sits on brood** sits like a bird on a nest, about to *hatch* mischief (line 159)

And I do doubt° the hatch and the disclose°
Will be some danger; which for to prevent,
I have in quick determination
Thus set it down:° he shall with speed to England
For the demand of° our neglected tribute.
Haply the seas and countries different
With variable objects° shall expel
This something-settled matter in his heart,°
Whereon his brains still° beating puts him thus
From fashion of himself.° What think you on 't

POLONIUS: It shall do well. But yet do I believe
The origin and commencement of his grief
Sprung from neglected love.—How now, Ophelia?
You need not tell us what Lord Hamlet said;
We heard it all.—My lord, do as you please,
But, if you hold it fit, after the play
Let his queen-mother° all alone entreat him
To show his grief. Let her be round° with him;
And I'll be placed, so please you, in the ear
Of all their conference. If she find him not,°
To England send him, or confine him where
Your wisdom best shall think.

KING: It shall be so.
Madness in great ones must not unwatched go.

[Exeunt.]

[3.2 Enter HAMLET and three of the PLAYERS.]°

HAMLET: Speak the speech, I pray you, as I pronounced it to you, trippingly on the tongue. But if you mouth it, as many of our players° do, I had as lief° the town crier spoke my lines. Nor do not saw the air too much with your hand, thus, but use all gently; for in the very torrent, tempest, and, as I may say, whirlwind of your passion, you must acquire and beget a temperance that may give it smoothness. O, it offends me to the soul to hear a robustious° periwig-pated° fellow tear a passion to tatters, to very rags, to split the ears of the groundlings,° who for the most part are capable of° nothing but inexplicable dumb shows° and noise. I would have such a

159 **doubt** fear **disclose** disclosure, hatching 162 **set it down** resolved 163 **For . . . of** to demand 165 **variable objects** various sights and surroundings to divert him 166 **This something . . . heart** the strange matter settled in his heart 167 **still** continually 168 **From . . . himself** out of his natural manner 175 **queen-mother** queen and mother 176 **round** blunt 178 **find him not** fails to discover what is troubling him 3.2 s.d. **Location: The castle** 2 **our players** players nowadays **I had as lief** I would just as soon 7 **robustious** violent, boisterous **periwig-pated** wearing a wig 8 **groundlings** spectators who paid least and stood in the yard of the theater **capable of** able to understand 9 **dumb shows** mimed performances, often used before Shakespeare's time to precede a play or each act

fellow whipped for o'erdoing Termagant.° It out-Herods Herod.° Pray you, avoid it.

FIRST PLAYER: I warrant your honor.

HAMLET: Be not too tame neither, but let your own discretion be your tutor. Suit the action to the word, the word to the action, with this special observance, that you o'erstep not the modesty° of nature. For anything so o'erdone is from° the purpose of playing, whose end, both at the first and now, was and is to hold as 't were the mirror up to nature, to show virtue her feature, scorn° her own image, and the very age and body of the time° his° form and pressure.° Now this overdone or come tardy off,° though it makes the unskillful° laugh, cannot but make the judicious grieve, the censure of the which one° must in your allowance° o'erweigh a whole theater of others. O, there be players that I have seen play, and heard others praise, and that highly, not to speak it profanely,° that, neither having th' accent of Christians° nor the gait of Christian, pagan, nor man,° have so strutted and bellowed that I have thought some of nature's journeymen° had made men and not made them well, they imitated humanity so abominably.°

FIRST PLAYER: I hope we have reformed that indifferently° with us, sir.

HAMLET: O, reform it altogether. And let those that play your clowns speak no more than is set down for them; for there be of them° that will themselves laugh, to set on some quantity of barren° spectators to laugh too, though in the meantime some necessary question of the play be then to be considered. That's villainous, and shows a most pitiful ambition in the fool that uses it. Go make you ready.

[Exeunt PLAYERS.]

[Enter POLONIUS, GUILDENSTERN and ROSENCRANTZ.]

How now, my lord, will the King hear this piece of work?

POLONIUS: And the Queen too, and that presently.°

HAMLET: Bid the players make haste.

[Exit POLONIUS.]

10 **Termagant** a supposed deity of the Mohammedans, not found in any English medieval play but elsewhere portrayed as violent and blustering **Herod** Herod of Jewry (A character in *The Slaughter of the Innocents* and other cycle plays. The part was played with great noise and fury.) 15 **modesty** restraint, moderation 16 **from** contrary to 18 **scorn** i.e., something foolish and deserving of scorn 18–19 **the very . . . time** i.e., the present state of affairs 19 **his** its **pressure** stamp, impressed character **come tardy off** inadequately done 20 **the unskillful** those lacking in judgment 21 **the censure . . . one** the judgment of even one of whom **your allowance** your scale of values 23 **not . . . profanely** (Hamlet anticipates his idea in lines 25–27 that some men were not made by God at all.) 24 **Christians** i.e., ordinary decent folk 25 **nor man** i.e., nor any human being at all 26 **journeymen** laborers who are not yet masters in their trade 27 **abominably** (Shakespeare's usual spelling, *abhominably*, suggests a literal though etymologically incorrect meaning, "removed from human nature.") 28 **indifferently** tolerably 30 **of them** some among them 31 **barren** i.e., of wit 36 **presently** at once

Will you two help to hasten them?
ROSENCRANTZ: Ay, my lord.
[Exeunt they two.]
HAMLET: What ho, Horatio!
[Enter HORATIO.]
HORATIO: Here, sweet lord, at your service.
HAMLET: Horatio, thou art e'en as just a man
As e'er my conversation coped withal.°
HORATIO: O, my dear lord—
HAMLET: Nay, do not think I flatter,
For what advancement may I hope from thee
That no revenue hast but thy good spirits
To feed and clothe thee? Why should the poor be flattered?
No, let the candied° tongue lick absurd pomp,
And crook the pregnant° hinges of the knee
Where thrift° may follow fawning. Dost thou hear?
Since my dear soul was mistress of her choice
And could of men distinguish her election,°
Sh' hath sealed thee° for herself, for thou hast been
As one, in suffering all, that suffers nothing,
A man that Fortune's buffets and rewards
Hast ta'en with equal thanks; and blest are those
Whose blood° and judgment are so well commeddled°
That they are not a pipe for Fortune's finger
To sound what stop° she please. Give me that man
That is not passion's slave, and I will wear him
In my heart's core, ay, in my heart of heart,
As I do thee.—Something too much of this.—
There is a play tonight before the King.
One scene of it comes near the circumstance
Which I have told thee of my father's death.
I prithee, when thou seest that act afoot,
Even with the very comment of thy soul°
Observe my uncle. If his occulted° guilt
Do not itself unkennel° in one speech,
It is a damnèd° ghost that we have seen,

42 **my . . . withal** my dealings encountered 47 **candied** sugared, flattering 48 **pregnant** compliant 49 **thrift** profit 51 **could . . . election** could make distinguishing choices among persons 52 **sealed thee** (Literally, as one would seal a legal document to mark possession.) 56 **blood** passion **commeddled** commingled 58 **stop** hole in a wind instrument for controlling the sound 66 **very . . . soul** your most penetrating observation and consideration 67 **occulted** hidden 68 **unkennel** (As one would say of a fox driven from its lair.) 69 **damnèd** in league with Satan

And my imaginations are as foul
As Vulcan's stithy.° Give him heedful note,
For I mine eyes will rivet to his face,
And after we will both our judgments join
In censure of his seeming.°

HORATIO: Well, my lord.
If 'a steal aught° the whilst this play is playing
And scape detecting, I will pay the theft.

[(Flourish.) Enter trumpets and kettledrums, KING, QUEEN, POLONIUS, OPHELIA, *(*ROSENCRANTZ, GUILDENSTERN, *and other lords, with guards carrying torches).]*

HAMLET: They are coming to the play. I must be idle.°
Get you a place. [*The* KING, QUEEN, *and courtiers sit.*]

KING: How fares our cousin° Hamlet?

HAMLET: Excellent, i' faith, of the chameleon's dish:° I eat the air, promise-crammed. You cannot feed capons° so.

KING: I have nothing with° this answer, Hamlet. These words are not mine.°

HAMLET: No, nor mine now.° [*To* POLONIUS.] My lord, you played once i' th' university, you say?

POLONIUS: That did I, my lord, and was accounted a good actor.

HAMLET: What did you enact?

POLONIUS: I did enact Julius Caesar. I was killed i' the Capitol; Brutus killed me.

HAMLET: It was a brute° part° of him to kill so capital a calf° there.—Be the players ready?

ROSENCRANTZ: Ay, my lord. They stay upon° your patience.

QUEEN: Come hither, my dear Hamlet, sit by me.

HAMLET: No, good Mother, here's metal° more attractive.

POLONIUS: [*to the* KING] O, ho, do you mark that?

HAMLET: Lady, shall I lie in your lap?

[Lying down at OPHELIA*'s feet.]*

OPHELIA: No, my lord.

HAMLET: I mean, my head upon your lap?

OPHELIA: Ay, my lord.

71 **stithy** smithy, place of stiths (anvils) 74 **censure of his seeming** judgment of his appearance or behavior 75 **If 'a steal aught** if he gets away with anything 77 **idle** (1) unoccupied (2) mad 79 **cousin** i.e., close relative 80 **chameleon's dish** (Chameleons were supposed to feed on air. Hamlet deliberately misinterprets the King's *fares* as "feeds." By his phrase *eat the air* he also plays on the idea of feeding himself with the promise of succession, of being the *heir.*) 81 **capons** roosters castrated and *crammed* with feed to make them succulent 82 **have . . . with** make nothing of, or gain nothing from **are not mine** do not respond to what I asked 83 **nor mine now** (Once spoken, words are proverbially no longer the speaker's own—and hence should be uttered warily.) 88 **brute** (The Latin meaning of *brutus,* "stupid," was often used punningly with the name Brutus.) **part** (1) deed (2) role **calf** fool 90 **stay upon** await 92 **metal** substance that is *attractive,* i.e., magnetic, but with suggestion also of *mettle,* "disposition"

HAMLET: Do you think I meant country matters?°

OPHELIA: I think nothing, my lord.

HAMLET: That's a fair thought to lie between maids' legs.

OPHELIA: What is, my lord?

HAMLET: Nothing.°

OPHELIA: You are merry, my lord.

HAMLET: Who, I?

OPHELIA: Ay, my lord.

HAMLET: O God, your only jig maker.° What should a man do but be merry? For look you how cheerfully my mother looks, and my father died within 's° two hours.

OPHELIA: Nay, 'tis twice two months, my lord.

HAMLET: So long? Nay then, let the devil wear black, for I'll have a suit of sables.° O heavens! Die two months ago, and not forgotten yet? Then there's hope a great man's memory may outlive his life half a year. But, by 'r Lady, 'a must build churches, then, or else shall 'a suffer not thinking on,° with the hobbyhorse, whose epitaph is "For O, for O, the hobbyhorse is forgot."°

[The trumpets sound. Dumb show follows.]

[Enter a King and a Queen [very lovingly]; the Queen embracing him, and he her. (She kneels, and makes show of protestation unto him.) He takes her up, and declines his head upon her neck. He lies him down upon a bank of flowers. She, seeing him asleep, leaves him. Anon comes in another man, takes off his crown, kisses it, pours poison in the sleeper's ears, and leaves him. The Queen returns, finds the King dead, makes passionate action. The Poisoner with some three or four come in again, seem to condole with her. The dead body is carried away. The Poisoner woos the Queen with gifts; she seems harsh awhile, but in the end accepts love.]

[Exeunt PLAYERS.]

OPHELIA: What means this, my lord?

HAMLET: Marry, this' miching mallico;° it means mischief.

OPHELIA: Belike° this show imports the argument° of the play.

98 **country matters** sexual intercourse (making a bawdy pun on the first syllable of *country*) 102 **Nothing** the figure zero or naught, suggesting the female sexual anatomy. (*Thing* not infrequently has a bawdy connotation of male or female anatomy, and the reference here could be male.) 106 **only jig maker** very best composer of jigs, i.e., pointless merriment (Hamlet replies sardonically to Ophelia's observation that he is merry by saying, "If you're looking for someone who is really merry, you've come to the right person.") 107 **within 's** within this (i.e., these) 109-110 **suit of sables** garments trimmed with the fur of the sable and hence suited for a wealthy person, not a mourner (but with a pun on *sable*, "black," ironically suggesting mourning once again) 112–113 **suffer . . . on** undergo oblivion 113–114 **For . . . forgot** (verse of a song occurring also in *Love's Labor's Lost*, 3.1.27–28. The hobbyhorse was a character made up to resemble a horse and rider, appearing in the morris dance and such May-game sports. This song laments the disappearance of such customs under pressure from the Puritans.) 116 **this' miching mallico** this is sneaking mischief 117 **Belike** probably **argument** plot

[Enter Prologue.*]*

Hamlet: We shall know by this fellow. The players cannot keep counsel;° they'll tell all.

Ophelia: Will 'a tell us what this show meant?

Hamlet: Ay, or any show that you will show him. Be not you° ashamed to show, he'll not shame to tell you what it means.

Ophelia: You are naught,° you are naught. I'll mark the play.

Prologue: For us, and for our tragedy,
Here stooping° to your clemency,
We beg your hearing patiently.

[Exit.]

Hamlet: Is this a prologue, or the posy of a ring?°

Ophelia: 'Tis brief, my lord.

Hamlet: As woman's love.

[Enter (two Players *as) King and Queen.]*

Player King: Full thirty times hath Phoebus' cart° gone round
Neptune's salt wash° and Tellus'° orbèd ground,
And thirty dozen moons with borrowed° sheen
About the world have times twelve thirties been,
Since love our hearts and Hymen° did our hands
Unite commutual° in most sacred bands.°

Player Queen: So many journeys may the sun and moon
Make us again count o'er ere love be done!
But, woe is me, you are so sick of late,
So far from cheer and from your former state,
That I distrust° you. Yet, though I distrust,°
Discomfort° you, my lord, it nothing° must.
For women's fear and love hold quantity;°
In neither aught, or in extremity.°
Now, what my love is, proof° hath made you know,
And as my love is sized,° my fear is so.
Where love is great, the littlest doubts are fear;
Where little fears grow great, great love grows there.

Player King: Faith, I must leave thee, love, and shortly too;

118 **counsel** secret 121 **Be not you** provided you are not 123 **naught** indecent (Ophelia is reacting to Hamlet's pointed remarks about not being ashamed to show all.) 125 **stooping** bowing 127 **posy . . . ring** brief motto in verse inscribed in a ring 130 **Phoebus' cart** the sun-god's chariot, making its yearly cycle 131 **salt wash** the sea **Tellus** goddess of the earth, of the *orbèd ground* 132 **borrowed** i.e., reflected 134 **Hymen** god of matrimony 135 **commutual** mutually **bands** bonds 140 **distrust** am anxious about 141 **Discomfort** distress **nothing** not at all 142 **hold quantity** keep proportion with one another 143 **In . . . extremity** i.e., women fear and love either too little or too much, but the two, fear and love, are equal in either case 144 **proof** experience 145 **sized** in size

My operant powers° their functions leave to do.°
And thou shalt live in this fair world behind,°
Honored, beloved; and haply one as kind
For husband shalt thou—

PLAYER QUEEN: O, confound the rest!
Such love must needs be treason in my breast.
In second husband let me be accurst!
None° wed the second but who° killed the first.

HAMLET: Wormwood,° wormwood.

PLAYER QUEEN: The instances° that second marriage move°
Are base respects of thrift,° but none of love.
A second time I kill my husband dead
When second husband kisses me in bed.

PLAYER KING: I do believe you think what now you speak,
But what we do determine oft we break.
Purpose is but the slave to memory,°
Of violent birth, but poor validity,°
Which° now, like fruit unripe, sticks on the tree,
But fall unshaken when they mellow be.
Most necessary 'tis that we forget
To pay ourselves what to ourselves is debt.°
What to ourselves in passion we propose,
The passion ending, doth the purpose lose.
The violence of either grief or joy
Their own enactures° with themselves destroy.
Where joy most revels, grief doth most lament;
Grief joys, joy grieves, on slender accident.°
This world is not for aye,° nor 'tis not strange
That even our loves should with our fortunes change;
For 'tis a question left us yet to prove,
Whether love lead fortune, or else fortune love.
The great man down,° you mark his favorite flies;
The poor advanced makes friends of enemies.°
And hitherto° doth love on fortune tend;°

149 **operant powers** vital functions **leave to do** cease to perform 150 **behind** after I have gone 155 **None** i.e., let no woman **but who** except the one who 156 **Wormwood** i.e., how bitter. (Literally, a bitter-tasting plant.) 157 **instances** motives **move** motivate 158 **base . . . thrift** ignoble considerations of material prosperity 163 **Purpose . . . memory** our good intentions are subject to forgetfulness 164 **validity** strength, durability 165 **Which** i.e., purpose 167–168 **Most . . . debt** it's inevitable that in time we forget the obligations we have imposed on ourselves 172 **enactures** fulfillments 173–174 **Where . . . accident** the capacity for extreme joy and grief go together, and often one extreme is instantly changed into its opposite on the slightest provocation 175 **aye** ever 179 **down** fallen in fortune 180 **The poor . . . enemies** when one of humble station is promoted, you see his enemies suddenly becoming his friends 181 **hitherto** up to this point in the argument, or, to this extent **tend** attend

For who not needs° shall never lack a friend,
And who in want° a hollow friend doth try°
Directly seasons him° his enemy.
But, orderly to end where I begun,
Our wills and fates do so contrary run°
That our devices still° are overthrown;
Our thoughts are ours, their ends° none of our own.
So think thou wilt no second husband wed,
But die thy thoughts when thy first lord is dead.

PLAYER QUEEN: Nor° earth to me give food, nor heaven light,
Sport and repose lock from me day and night,°
To desperation turn my trust and hope,
An anchor's cheer° in prison be my scope!°
Each opposite that blanks° the face of joy
Meet what I would have well and it destroy!°
Both here and hence° pursue me lasting strife
If, once a widow, ever I be wife!

HAMLET: If she should break it now!

PLAYER KING: 'Tis deeply sworn. Sweet, leave me here awhile;
My spirits° grow dull, and fain I would beguile
The tedious day with sleep.

PLAYER QUEEN: Sleep rock thy brain,
And never come mischance between us twain!

[(He sleeps.) Exit (PLAYER QUEEN).]

HAMLET: Madam, how like you this play?

QUEEN: The lady doth protest too much,° methinks.

HAMLET: O, but she'll keep her word.

KING: Have you heard the argument?° Is there no offense in 't?

HAMLET: No, no, they do but jest,° poison in jest. No offense° i' the world.

KING: What do you call the play?

HAMLET: *The Mousetrap.* Marry, how? Tropically.° This play is the image of a murder done in Vienna. Gonzago is the Duke's° name, his wife, Baptista.

182 **who not needs** he who is not in need (of wealth) 183 **who in want** he who, being in need **try** test (his generosity) 184 **seasons him** ripens him into 186 **Our . . . run** what we want and what we get go so contrarily 187 **devices still** intentions continually 188 **ends** results 191 **Nor** let neither 192 **Sport . . . night** may day deny me its pastimes and night its repose 194 **anchor's cheer** anchorite's or hermit's fare **my scope** the extent of my happiness 195 **blanks** causes to blanch or grow pale 195–196 **Each . . . destroy** may every adverse thing that causes the face of joy to turn pale meet and destroy everything that I desire to see prosper 197 **hence** in the life hereafter 201 **spirits** vital spirits 205 **doth . . . much** makes too many promises and protestations 207 **argument** plot 208 **jest** make believe 207–208 **offense . . . offense** cause for objection . . . actual injury, crime 210 **Tropically** figuratively (The First Quarto reading, *trapically,* suggests a pun on *trap* in *Mousetrap.*) 211 **Duke's** i.e., King's (A slip that may be due to Shakespeare's possible source, the alleged murder of the Duke of Urbino by Luigi Gonzaga in 1538.)

You shall see anon. 'Tis a knavish piece of work, but what of that? Your Majesty, and we that have free° souls, it touches us not. Let the galled jade° wince, our withers° are unwrung.°

[Enter LUCIANUS.*]*

This is one Lucianus, nephew to the King.

OPHELIA: You are as good as a chorus,° my lord.

HAMLET: I could interpret° between you and your love, if I could see the puppets dallying.°

OPHELIA: You are keen,° my lord, you are keen.

HAMLET: It would cost you a groaning to take off mine edge.

OPHELIA: Still better, and worse.°

HAMLET: So° you mis-take° your husbands. Begin, murder; leave thy damnable faces and begin. Come, the croaking raven doth bellow for revenge.

LUCIANUS: Thoughts black, hands apt, drugs fit, and time agreeing,
Confederate season,° else° no creature seeing,°
Thou mixture rank, of midnight weeds collected,
With Hecate's ban° thrice blasted, thrice infected,
Thy natural magic and dire property°
On wholesome life usurp immediately.

[He pours the poison into the sleeper's ear.]

HAMLET: 'A poisons him i' the garden for his estate.° His° name's Gonzago. The story is extant, and written in very choice Italian. You shall see anon how the murderer gets the love of Gonzago's wife.

*[*CLAUDIUS *rises.]*

OPHELIA: The King rises.

HAMLET: What, frighted with false fire?°

QUEEN: How fares my lord?

POLONIUS: Give o'er the play.

KING: Give me some light. Away!

POLONIUS: Lights, lights, lights!

[Exeunt all but HAMLET *and* HORATIO.*]*

213 **free** guiltless 213–214 **galled jade** horse whose hide is rubbed by saddle or harness 214 **withers** the part between the horse's shoulder blades **unwrung** not rubbed sore 216 **chorus** (In many Elizabethan plays, the forthcoming action was explained by an actor known as the "chorus"; at a puppet show, the actor who spoke the dialogue was known as an "interpreter," as indicated by the lines following.) 217 **interpret** (1) ventriloquize the dialogue, as in puppet show (2) act as pander 217–218 **puppets dallying** (With suggestion of sexual play, continued in *keen,* "sexually aroused," *groaning,* "moaning in pregnancy," and *edge,* "sexual desire" or "impetuosity.") 219 **keen** sharp, bitter 221 **Still . . . worse** more keen, always *bettering* what other people say with witty wordplay, but at the same time more offensive 222 **So** even thus (in marriage) **mis-take** take falseheartedly and cheat on (The marriage vows say "for better, for worse.") 225 **Confederate season** the time and occasion conspiring (to assist the murderer) **else** otherwise **seeing** seeing me 227 **Hecate's ban** the curse of Hecate, the goddess of witchcraft 228 **dire property** baleful quality 230 **estate** i.e., the kingship **His** i.e., the King's 234 **false fire** the blank discharge of a gun loaded with powder but no shot

HAMLET: "Why,° let the strucken deer go weep,
The hart ungallèd° play.
For some must watch,° while some must sleep;
Thus runs the world away."°
Would not this,° sir, and a forest of feathers°—if the rest of my fortunes turn Turk with° me—with two Provincial roses° on my razed° shoes, get me a fellowship in a cry° of players?°

HORATIO: Half a share.

HAMLET: A whole one, I.
"For thou dost know, O Damon° dear,
This realm dismantled° was
Of Jove himself, and now reigns here
A very, very—pajock."°

HORATIO: You might have rhymed.

HAMLET: O good Horatio, I'll take the ghost's word for a thousand pound. Didst perceive?

HORATIO: Very well, my lord.

HAMLET: Upon the talk of the poisoning?

HORATIO: I did very well note him.

[Enter ROSENCRANTZ and GUILDENSTERN.]

HAMLET: Aha! Come, some music! Come, the recorders.°
"For if the King like not the comedy,
Why then, belike, he likes it not, perdy."°
Come, some music.

GUILDENSTERN: Good my lord, vouchsafe me a word with you.

HAMLET: Sir, a whole history.

GUILDENSTERN: The King, sir—

HAMLET: Ay, sir, what of him?

GUILDENSTERN: Is in his retirement° marvelous distempered.°

HAMLET: With drink, sir?

239–242 **Why . . . away** (Probably from an old ballad, with allusion to the popular belief that a wounded deer retires to weep and die; compare with *As You Like It*, 2.1.33-66.) 240 **ungallèd** unafflicted 241 **watch** remain awake 242 **Thus . . . away** thus the world goes 243 **this** i.e., the play **feathers** (Allusion to the plumes that Elizabethan actors were fond of wearing.) 244 **turn Turk with** turn renegade against, go back on **Provincial roses** rosettes of ribbon, named for roses grown in a part of France **razed** with ornamental slashing **cry** pack (of hounds) **fellowship . . . players** partnership in a theatrical company 248 **Damon** the friend of Pythias, as Horatio is friend of Hamlet; or, a traditional pastoral name 249 **dismantled** stripped, divested 249–251 **This realm . . . pajock** i.e., Jove, representing divine authority and justice, has abandoned this realm to its own devices, leaving in his stead only a peacock or vain pretender to virtue (though the rhyme-word expected in place of *pajock* or "peacock" suggests that the realm is now ruled over by an "ass") 258 **recorders** wind instruments of the flute kind 260 **perdy** (A corruption of the French *par dieu*, "by God") 266 **retirement** withdrawal to his chambers **distempered** out of humor (But Hamlet deliberately plays on the wider application to any illness of mind or body, as in line 296, especially to drunkenness.)

GUILDENSTERN: No, my lord, with choler.[o]

HAMLET: Your wisdom should show itself more richer to signify this to the doctor, for for me to put him to his purgation[o] would perhaps plunge him into more choler.

GUILDENSTERN: Good my lord, put your discourse into some frame[o] and start[o] not so wildly from my affair.

HAMLET: I am tame, sir. Pronounce.

GUILDENSTERN: The Queen, your mother, in most great affliction of spirit, hath sent me to you.

HAMLET: You are welcome.

GUILDENSTERN: Nay, good my lord, this courtesy is not of the right breed.[o] If it shall please you to make me a wholesome answer, I will do your mother's commandment; if not, your pardon[o] and my return shall be the end of my business.

HAMLET: Sir, I cannot.

ROSENCRANTZ: What, my lord?

HAMLET: Make you a wholesome answer; my wit's diseased. But, sir, such answer as I can make, you shall command, or rather, as you say, my mother. Therefore no more, but to the matter. My mother, you say—

ROSENCRANTZ: Then thus she says: your behavior hath struck her into amazement and admiration.[o]

HAMLET: O wonderful son, that can so stonish a mother! But is there no sequel at the heels of this mother's admiration? Impart.

ROSENCRANTZ: She desires to speak with you in her closet[o] ere you go to bed.

HAMLET: We shall obey, were she ten times our mother. Have you any further trade with us?

ROSENCRANTZ: My lord, you once did love me.

HAMLET: And do still, by these pickers and stealers.[o]

ROSENCRANTZ: Good my lord, what is your cause of distemper? You do surely bar the door upon your own liberty[o] if you deny[o] your griefs to your friend.

HAMLET: Sir, I lack advancement.

ROSENCRANTZ: How can that be, when you have the voice of the King himself for your succession in Denmark?

HAMLET: Ay, sir, but "While the grass grows"[o]—the proverb is something[o] musty.

268 **choler** anger (But Hamlet takes the word in its more basic humoral sense of "bilious disorder.") 270 **purgation** (Hamlet hints at something going beyond medical treatment to bloodletting and the extraction of confession.) 272 **frame** order **start** shy or jump away (like a horse; the opposite of *tame* in line 274) 278 **breed** (1) kind (2) breeding, manners 280 **pardon** permission to depart 288 **admiration** bewilderment 291 **closet** private chamber 295 **pickers and stealers** i.e., hands (So called from the catechism, "to keep my hands from picking and stealing.") 297 **liberty** i.e., being freed from *distemper,* line 296; but perhaps with a veiled threat as well **deny** refuse to share 302 **While . . . grows** (The rest of the proverb is "the silly horse starves"; Hamlet may not live long enough to succeed to the kingdom.) **something** somewhat

[Enter the PLAYERS° *with recorders.]*

O, the recorders. Let me see one. [*He takes a recorder.*] To withdraw° with you: why do you go about to recover the wind° of me, as if you would drive me into a toil?°

GUILDENSTERN: O, my lord, if my duty be too bold, my love is too unmannerly.°

HAMLET: I do not well understand that.° Will you play upon this pipe?

GUILDENSTERN: My lord, I cannot.

HAMLET: I pray you.

GUILDENSTERN: Believe me, I cannot.

HAMLET: I do beseech you.

GUILDENSTERN: I know no touch of it, my lord.

HAMLET: It is as easy as lying. Govern these ventages° with your fingers and thumb, give it breath with your mouth, and it will discourse most eloquent music. Look you, these are the stops.

GUILDENSTERN: But these cannot I command to any utterance of harmony. I have not the skill.

HAMLET: Why, look you now, how unworthy a thing you make of me! You would play upon me, you would seem to know my stops, you would pluck out the heart of my mystery, you would sound° me from my lowest note to the top of my compass,° and there is much music, excellent voice, in this little organ,° yet cannot you make it speak. 'Sblood, do you think I am easier to be played on than a pipe? Call me what instrument you will, though you can fret° me, you cannot play upon me.

[Enter POLONIUS.*]*

God bless you, sir!

POLONIUS: My lord, the Queen would speak with you, and presently.°

HAMLET: Do you see yonder cloud that's almost in shape of a camel?

POLONIUS: By the Mass and 'tis, like a camel indeed.

HAMLET: Methinks it is like a weasel.

POLONIUS: It is backed like a weasel.

HAMLET: Or like a whale.

POLONIUS: Very like a whale.

HAMLET: Then I will come to my mother by and by.° [*Aside.*] They fool me° to the top of my bent.°—I will come by and by.

303 s.d. **Players** actors 305 **withdraw** speak privately **recover the wind** get to the windward side (thus driving the game into the *toil,* or "net") 306 **toil** snare 307–308 **If . . .unmannerly** if I am using an unmannerly boldness, it is my love that occasion it 309 **I . . . that** i.e., I don't understand how genuine love can be unmannerly 315 **ventages** finger-holes or *stops* (line 317) of the recorder 322 **sound** (1) fathom (2) produce sound in 323 **compass** range (of voice) 324 **organ** musical instrument 326 **fret** irritate (with a quibble on *fret,* meaning the piece of wood, gut, or metal that regulates the fingering on an instrument) 328 **presently** at once 335 **by and by** quite soon **fool me** trifle with me, humor my fooling 336 **top of my bent** limit of my ability or endurance (Literally, the extent to which a bow may be bent.)

POLONIUS: I will say so.
[Exit.]
HAMLET: "By and by" is easily said. Leave me, friends.
[Exeunt all but HAMLET.]
'Tis now the very witching time° of night,
When churchyards yawn and hell itself breathes out
Contagion to this world. Now could I drink hot blood
And do such bitter business as the day
Would quake to look on. Soft, now to my mother.
O heart, lose not thy nature!° Let not ever
The soul of Nero° enter this firm bosom.
Let me be cruel, not unnatural;
I will speak daggers to her, but use none.
My tongue and soul in this be hypocrites:
How in my words soever° she be shent,°
To give them seals° never my soul consent!
[Exit.]
[3.3 Enter KING, ROSENCRANTZ, and GUILDENSTERN.]°
KING: I like him° not, nor stands it safe with us
To let his madness range. Therefore prepare you.
I your commission will forthwith dispatch,°
And he to England shall along with you.
The terms of our estate° may not endure
Hazard so near 's as doth hourly grow
Out of his brows.°
GUILDENSTERN: We will ourselves provide.
Most holy and religious fear° it is
To keep those many many bodies safe
That live and feed upon Your Majesty.
ROSENCRANTZ: The single and peculiar° life is bound
With all the strength and armor of the mind
To keep itself from noyance,° but much more
That spirit upon whose weal depends and rests
The lives of many. The cess° of majesty
Dies not alone, but like a gulf° doth draw

339 **witching time** time when spells are cast and evil is abroad 344 **nature** natural feeling 345 **Nero** murderer of his mother, Agrippina 349 **How . . . soever** however much by my words **shent** rebuked 350 **give them seals** i.e., confirm them with deeds 3.3 s.d. **Location: The castle** 1 **him** i.e., his behavior 3 **dispatch** prepare, cause to be drawn up 5 **terms of our estate** circumstances of my royal position 7 **Out of his brows** i.e., from his brain, in the form of plots and threats 8 **religious fear** sacred concern 11 **single and peculiar** individual and private 13 **noyance** harm 15 **cess** decease, cessation 16 **gulf** whirlpool

What's near it with it; or it is a massy° wheel
Fixed on the summit of the highest mount,
To whose huge spokes ten thousand lesser things
Are mortised° and adjoined, which, when it falls,°
Each small annexment, petty consequence,°
Attends° the boisterous ruin. Never alone
Did the King sigh, but with a general groan.

KING: Arm° you, I pray you, to this speedy voyage,
For we will fetters put about this fear,
Which now goes too free-footed.

ROSENCRANTZ: We will haste us.

[Exeunt gentlemen (ROSENCRANTZ and GUILDENSTERN).]

[Enter POLONIUS.]

POLONIUS: My lord, he's going to his mother's closet.
Behind the arras° I'll convey myself
To hear the process.° I'll warrant she'll tax him home,°
And, as you said—and wisely was it said—
'Tis meet° that some more audience than a mother,
Since nature makes them partial, should o'erhear
The speech, of vantage.° Fare you well, my liege.
I'll call upon you ere you go to bed
And tell you what I know.

KING: Thanks, dear my lord.

[Exit (POLONIUS).]

O, my offense is rank! It smells to heaven.
It hath the primal eldest curse° upon't,
A brother's murder. Pray can I not,
Though inclination be as sharp as will;°
My stronger guilt defeats my strong intent,
And like a man to double business bound°
I stand in pause where I shall first begin,
And both neglect. What if this cursèd hand
Were thicker than itself with brother's blood,
Is there not rain enough in the sweet heavens

17 **massy** massive 20 **mortised** fastened (as with a fitted joint) **when it falls** i.e., when it descends, like the wheel of Fortune, bringing a king down with it 21 **Each . . . consequence** i.e., every hanger-on and unimportant person or thing connected with the King 22 **Attends** participates in 24 **Arm** prepare 28 **arras** screen of tapestry placed around the walls of household apartments (On the Elizabethan stage, the arras was presumably over a door or discovery space in the tiring-house facade.) 29 **process** proceedings **tax him home** reprove him severely 31 **meet** fitting 33 **of vantage** from an advantageous place, or, in addition 37 **the primal eldest curse** the curse of Cain, the first murderer; he killed his brother Abel 39 **Though . . . will** though my desire is as strong as my determination 41 **bound** (1) destined (2) obliged (The King wants to repent and still enjoy what he has gained.)

To wash it white as snow? Whereto serves mercy
But to confront the visage of offense?[o]
And what's in prayer but this twofold force,
To be forestallèd[o] ere we come to fall,
Or pardoned being down? Then I'll look up.
My fault is past. But O, what form of prayer
Can serve my turn? "Forgive me my foul murder"?
That cannot be, since I am still possessed
Of those effects for which I did the murder:
My crown, mine own ambition, and my Queen.
May one be pardoned and retain th' offense?[o]
In the corrupted currents[o] of this world
Offense's gilded hand[o] may shove by[o] justice,
And oft 'tis seen the wicked prize[o] itself
Buys out the law. But 'tis not so above.
There[o] is no shuffling,[o] there the action lies[o]
In his[o] true nature, and we ourselves compelled,
Even to the teeth and forehead[o] of our faults,
To give in[o] evidence. What then? What rests?[o]
Try what repentance can. What can it not?
Yet what can it, when one cannot repent?
O wretched state, O bosom black as death,
O limèd[o] soul that, struggling to be free,
Art more engaged![o] Help, angels! Make assay.[o]
Bow, stubborn knees, and heart with strings of steel,
Be soft as sinews of the newborn babe!
All may be well.

[He kneels.]

[Enter HAMLET.*]*

HAMLET: Now might I do it pat,[o] now 'a is a-praying;
And now I'll do 't. [*He draws his sword.*] And so 'a goes to heaven,
And so am I revenged. That would be scanned:[o]
A villain kills my father, and for that,
I, his sole son, do this same villain send
To heaven.
Why, this is hire and salary, not revenge.

46–47 **Whereto . . . offense** what function does mercy serve other than to meet sin face to face? 49 **forestallèd** prevented (from sinning) 56 **th' offense** the thing for which one offended 57 **currents** courses 58 **gilded hand** hand offering gold as a bribe **shove by** thrust aside 59 **wicked prize** prize won by wickedness 61 **There** i.e., in heaven **shuffling** escape by trickery **the action lies** the accusation is made manifest (A legal metaphor.) 62 **his** its 63 **to the teeth and forehead** face to face, concealing nothing 64 **give in** provide **rests** remains 68 **limèd** caught as with birdlime, a sticky substance used to ensnare birds 69 **engaged** entangled **assay** trial (Said to himself.) 73 **pat** opportunely 75 **would be scanned** needs to be looked into, or, would be interpreted as follows

'A took my father grossly, full of bread,°
With all his crimes broad blown,° as flush° as May;
And how his audit° stands who knows save° heaven?
But in our circumstance and course of thought°
'Tis heavy with him. And am I then revenged,
To take him in the purging of his soul,
When he is fit and seasoned° for his passage?
No!
Up, sword, and know thou a more horrid hent.°

[He puts up his sword.]

When he is drunk asleep, or in his rage,°
Or in th' incestuous pleasure of his bed,
At game,° a-swearing, or about some act
That has no relish° of salvation in 't—
Then trip him, that his heels may kick at heaven,
And that his soul may be as damned and black
As hell, whereto it goes. My mother stays.°
This physic° but prolongs thy sickly days.

[Exit.]

KING: My words fly up, my thoughts remain below.
Words without thoughts never to heaven go.

[Exit.]

[3.4 Enter (QUEEN) GERTRUDE and POLONIUS.]°

POLONIUS: 'A will come straight. Look you lay home° to him.
Tell him his pranks have been too broad° to bear with,
And that Your Grace hath screened and stood between
Much heat° and him. I'll shroud° me even here.
Pray you, be round° with him.

HAMLET: [*within*] Mother, Mother, Mother!

QUEEN: I'll warrant you, fear me not.
Withdraw, I hear him coming.

[POLONIUS hides behind the arras.]

[Enter HAMLET.]

80 **grossly, full of bread** i.e., enjoying his worldly pleasures rather than fasting (See Ezekiel 16:49.) 81 **crimes broad blown** sins in full bloom **flush** vigorous 82 **audit** account **save** except for 83 **in . . . thought** as we see it from our mortal perspective 86 **seasoned** matured, readied 88 **know . . . hent** await to be grasped by me on a more horrid occasion **hent** act of seizing 89 **drunk . . . rage** dead drunk, or in a fit of sexual passion 91 **game** gambling 92 **relish** trace, savor 95 **stays** awaits (me) 96 **physic** purging (by prayer), or, Hamlet's postponement of the killing 3.4 s.d. **Location: The Queen's private chamber** 1 **lay home** thrust to the heart, reprove him soundly 2 **broad** unrestrained 4 **Much heat** i.e., the King's anger **shroud** conceal (with ironic fitness to Polonius' imminent death. The word is only in the First Quarto: the Second Quarto and the Folio read "silence.") 5 **round** blunt

HAMLET: Now, Mother, what's the matter?
QUEEN: Hamlet, thou hast thy father° much offended.
HAMLET: Mother, you have my father much offended.
QUEEN: Come, come, you answer with an idle° tongue.
HAMLET: Go, go, you question with a wicked tongue.
QUEEN: Why, how now, Hamlet?
HAMLET: What's the matter now?
QUEEN: Have you forgot me?°
HAMLET: No, by the rood,° not so:
You are the Queen your husband's brother's wife,
And—would it were not so!—you are my mother.
QUEEN: Nay, then, I'll set those to you that can speak.°
HAMLET: Come, come, and sit you down; you shall not budge.
You go not till I set you up a glass
Where you may see the inmost part of you.
QUEEN: What wilt thou do? Thou wilt not murder me?
Help, ho!
POLONIUS: [*behind the arras*] What ho! Help!
HAMLET: [*drawing*] How now? A rat? Dead for a ducat,° dead!
[*He thrusts his rapier through the arras.*]

POLONIUS: [*behind the arras*] O, I am slain! [*He falls and dies.*]
QUEEN: O me, what hast thou done?
HAMLET: Nay, I know not. Is it the King?
QUEEN: O, what a rash and bloody deed is this!
HAMLET: A bloody deed—almost as bad, good Mother,
As kill a King, and marry with his brother.
QUEEN: As kill a King!
HAMLET: Ay, lady, it was my word.
[*He parts the arras and discovers* POLONIUS.]

Thou wretched, rash, intruding fool, farewell!
I took thee for thy better. Take thy fortune.
Thou find'st to be too busy° is some danger.—
Leave wringing of your hands. Peace, sit you down,
And let me wring your heart, for so I shall,
If it be made of penetrable stuff,
If damnèd custom° have not brazed° it so
That it be proof° and bulwark against sense.°

10 **thy father** i.e., your stepfather, Claudius 12 **idle** foolish 14 **forgot me** i.e., forgotten that I am your mother 15 **rood** cross of Christ 18 **speak** i.e., to someone so rude 25 **Dead for a ducat** i.e., I bet a ducat he's dead; or, a ducat is his life's fee 34 **busy** nosey 38 **damnèd custom** habitual wickedness **brazed** brazened, hardened 39 **proof** armor **sense** feeling

QUEEN: What have I done, that thou dar'st wag thy tongue
In noise so rude against me?
HAMLET: Such an act
That blurs the grace and blush of modesty,
Calls virtue hypocrite, takes off the rose
From the fair forehead of an innocent love
And sets a blister° there, makes marriage vows
As false as dicers' oaths. O, such a deed
As from the body of contraction° plucks
The very soul, and sweet religion makes°
A rhapsody° of words. Heaven's face does glow
O'er this solidity and compound mass
With tristful visage, as against the doom,
Is thought-sick at the act.°
QUEEN: Ay me, what act,
That roars so loud and thunders in the index?°
HAMLET: [*showing her two likenesses*] Look here upon this picture, and on this,
The counterfeit presentment° of two brothers.
See what a grace was seated on this brow:
Hyperion's° curls, the front° of Jove himself,
An eye like Mars° to threaten and command,
A station° like the herald Mercury°
New-lighted° on a heaven-kissing hill—
A combination and a form indeed
Where every god did seem to set his seal°
To give the world assurance of a man.
This was your husband. Look you now what follows:
Here is your husband, like a mildewed ear,°
Blasting° his wholesome brother. Have you eyes?
Could you on this fair mountain leave° to feed
And batten° on this moor?° Ha, have you eyes?
You cannot call it love, for at your age
The heyday° in the blood° is tame, it's humble,
And waits upon the judgment, and what judgment
Would step from this to this? Sense,° sure, you have,

45 **sets a blister** i.e., brands as a harlot 47 **contraction** the marriage contract 48 **sweet religion makes** i.e., makes marriage vows 49 **rhapsody** senseless string 49–52 **Heaven's . . . act** heaven's face blushes at this solid world compounded of the various elements, with sorrowful face as though the day of doom were near, and is sick with horror at the deed (i.e., Gertrude's marriage) 53 **index** table of contents, prelude or preface 55 **counterfeit presentment** portrayed representation 57 **Hyperion's** the sungod's **front** brow 58 **Mars** god of war 59 **station** manner of standing **Mercury** winged messenger of the gods 60 **New-lighted** newly alighted 62 **set his seal** i.e., affix his approval 65 **ear** i.e., of grain 66 **Blasting** blighting 67 **leave** cease 68 **batten** gorge **moor** barren or marshy ground (suggesting also "dark-skinned") 70 **heyday** state of excitement **blood** passion 72 **Sense** perception through the five senses (the functions of the middle or sensible soul)

Else could you not have motion, but sure that sense
Is apoplexed,° for madness would not err,°
Nor sense to ecstasy was ne'er so thralled,
But° it reserved some quantity of choice
To serve in such a difference.° What devil was 't
That thus hath cozened° you at hoodman-blind?°
Eyes without feeling, feeling without sight,
Ears without hands or eyes, smelling sans° all,
Or but a sickly part of one true sense
Could not so mope.° O shame, where is thy blush?
Rebellious hell,
If thou canst mutine° in a matron's bones,
To flaming youth let virtue be as wax
And melt in her own fire.° Proclaim no shame
When the compulsive ardor gives the charge,
Since frost itself as actively doth burn,
And reason panders will.°

QUEEN: O Hamlet, speak no more!
Thou turn'st mine eyes into my very soul,
And there I see such black and grainèd° spots
As will not leave their tinct.°

HAMLET: Nay, but to live
In the rank sweat of an enseamèd° bed,
Stewed° in corruption, honeying and making love
Over the nasty sty!

QUEEN: O, speak to me no more!
These words like daggers enter in my ears.
No more, sweet Hamlet!

HAMLET: A murderer and a villain,
A slave that is not twentieth part the tithe°
Of your precedent lord,° a vice° of kings,

74 **apoplexed** paralyzed (Hamlet goes on to explain that, without such a paralysis of will, mere madness would not so err, nor would the five senses so enthrall themselves to *ecstasy* or lunacy; even such deranged states of mind would be able to make the obvious choice between Hamlet Senior and Claudius.) **err** so err 76 **But** but that 77 **To . . . difference** to help in making a choice between two such men 78 **cozened** cheated **hoodman-blind** blindman's buff (In this game, says Hamlet, the devil must have pushed Claudius toward Gertrude while she was blindfolded.) 80 **sans** without 82 **mope** be dazed, act aimlessly 84 **mutine** incite mutiny 85–86 **be as wax . . . fire** melt like a candle or stick of sealing wax held over the candle flame 86–89 **Proclaim . . . will** call it no shameful business when the compelling ardor of youth delivers the attack, i.e., commits lechery, since the *frost* of advanced age burns with as active a fire of lust and reason perverts itself by fomenting lust rather than restraining it 92 **grainèd** dyed in grain, indelible 93 **leave their tinct** surrender their color 94 **enseamèd** saturated in the grease and filth of passionate lovemaking 95 **Stewed** soaked, bathed (with a suggestion of "stew," brothel) 100 **tithe** tenth part 101 **precedent lord** former husband **vice** buffoon (A reference to the Vice of the morality plays.)

A cutpurse of the empire and the rule,
That from a shelf the precious diadem stole
And put it in his pocket!
QUEEN: No more!
[Enter GHOST (in his nightgown).]
HAMLET: A king of shreds and patches°—
Save me, and hover o'er me with your wings,
You heavenly guards! What would your gracious figure?
QUEEN: Alas, he's mad!
HAMLET: Do you not come your tardy son to chide,
That, lapsed° in time and passion, lets go by
Th' important° acting of your dread command?
O, say!
GHOST: Do not forget. This visitation
Is but to whet thy almost blunted purpose.
But look, amazement° on thy mother sits.
O, step between her and her fighting soul!
Conceit° in weakest bodies strongest works.
Speak to her, Hamlet.
HAMLET: How is it with you, lady?
QUEEN: Alas, how is 't with you,
That you do bend your eye on vacancy,
And with th' incorporal° air do hold discourse?
Forth at your eyes your spirits wildly peep,
And, as the sleeping soldiers in th' alarm,°
Your bedded° hair, like life in excrements,°
Start up and stand on end. O gentle son,
Upon the heat and flame of thy distemper°
Sprinkle cool patience. Whereon do you look?
HAMLET: On him, on him! Look you how pale he glares!
His form and cause conjoined,° preaching to stones,
Would make them capable.°—Do not look upon me,
Lest with this piteous action you convert
My stern effects.° Then what I have to do

106 **shreds and patches** i.e., motley, the traditional costume of the clown or fool 111 **lapsed** delaying 112 **important** importunate, urgent 116 **amazement** distraction 118 **Conceit** imagination 122 **incorporal** immaterial 124 **as . . . alarm** like soldiers called out of sleep by an alarum 125 **bedded** laid flat **like life in excrements** i.e., as though hair, an outgrowth of the body, had a life of its own (Hair was thought to be lifeless because it lacks sensation, and so its standing on end would be unnatural and ominous.) 127 **distemper** disorder 130 **His . . . conjoined** his appearance joined to his cause for speaking 131 **capable** receptive 132–133 **convert . . . effects** divert me from my stern duty

Will want true color—tears perchance for blood.°
QUEEN: To whom do you speak this?
HAMLET: Do you see nothing there?
QUEEN: Nothing at all, yet all that is I see.
HAMLET: Nor did you nothing hear?
QUEEN: No, nothing but ourselves.
HAMLET: Why, look you there, look how it steals away!
My father, in his habit° as° he lived!
Look where he goes even now out at the portal!

[Exit GHOST.]

QUEEN: This is the very° coinage of your brain.
This bodiless creation ecstasy
Is very cunning in.°
HAMLET: Ecstasy?
My pulse as yours doth temperately keep time,
And makes as healthful music. It is not madness
That I have uttered. Bring me to the test,
And I the matter will reword,° which madness
Would gambol° from. Mother, for love of grace,
Lay not that flattering unction° to your soul
That not your trespass but my madness speaks.
It will but skin° and film the ulcerous place,
Whiles rank corruption, mining° all within,
Infects unseen. Confess yourself to heaven,
Repent what's past, avoid what is to come,
And do not spread the compost° on the weeds
To make them ranker. Forgive me this my virtue;°
For in the fatness° of these pursy° times
Virtue itself of vice must pardon beg,
Yea, curb° and woo for leave° to do him good.
QUEEN: O Hamlet, thou hast cleft my heart in twain.
HAMLET: O, throw away the worser part of it,
And live the purer with the other half.
Good night. But go not to my uncle's bed;
Assume a virtue, if you have it not.
That monster, custom, who all sense doth eat,°

134 **want . . . blood** lack plausibility so that (with a play on the normal sense of *color*) I shall shed colorless tears instead of blood 141 **habit** clothes **as** as when 143 **very** mere 144–145 **This . . . in** madness is skillful in creating this kind of hallucination 150 **reword** repeat word for word 151 **gambol** skip away 152 **unction** ointment 154 **skin** grow a skin for 155 **mining** working under the surface 158 **compost** manure 159 **this my virtue** my virtuous talk in reproving you 160 **fatness** grossness **pursy** flabby, out of shape 162 **curb** bow, bend the knee **leave** permission 168 **who . . . eat** which consumes all proper or natural feeling, all sensibility

Of habits devil,° is angel yet in this,
That to the use of actions fair and good
He likewise gives a frock or livery°
That aptly° is put on. Refrain tonight,
And that shall lend a kind of easiness
To the next abstinence; the next more easy;
For use° almost can change the stamp of nature,°
And either° . . . the devil, or throw him out
With wondrous potency. Once more, good night;
And when you are desirous to be blest,
I'll blessing beg of you.° For this same lord,
[pointing to Polonius.]
I do repent; but heaven hath pleased it so
To punish me with this, and this with me,
That I must be their scourge and minister.°
I will bestow° him, and will answer° well
The death I gave him. So, again, good night.
I must be cruel only to be kind.
This° bad begins, and worse remains behind.°
One word more, good lady.

QUEEN: What shall I do?

HAMLET: Not this by no means that I bid you do:
Let the bloat° King tempt you again to bed,
Pinch wanton° on your cheek, call you his mouse,
And let him, for a pair of reechy° kisses,
Or paddling° in your neck with his damned fingers,
Make you to ravel all this matter out°
That I essentially am not in madness,
But mad in craft.° 'Twere good° you let him know,
For who that's but a Queen, fair, sober, wise,
Would from a paddock,° from a bat, a gib,°
Such dear concernings° hide? Who would do so?

169 **Of habits devil** devil-like in prompting evil habits 171 **livery** an outer appearance, a customary garb (and hence a predisposition easily assumed in time of stress) 172 **aptly** readily 175 **use** habit **the stamp of nature** our inborn traits 176 **And either** (A defective line, usually emended by inserting the word *master* after *either,* following the Fourth Quarto and early editors.) 178–179 **when . . . you** i.e., when you are ready to be penitent and seek God's blessing, I will ask your blessing as a dutiful son should 182 **their scourge and minister** i.e., agent of heavenly retribution (By *scourge,* Hamlet also suggests that he himself will eventually suffer punishment in the process of fulfilling heaven's will.) 183 **bestow** stow, dispose of **answer** account or pay for 186 **This** i.e., the killing of Polonius **behind** to come 189 **bloat** bloated 190 **Pinch wanton** i.e., leave his love pinches on your cheeks, branding you as wanton 191 **reechy** dirty, filthy 192 **paddling** fingering amorously 193 **ravel . . . out** unravel, disclose 195 **in craft** by cunning **good** (Said sarcastically; also the following eight lines.) 197 **paddock** toad **gib** tomcat 198 **dear concernings** important affairs

No, in despite of sense and secrecy,°
Unpeg the basket° on the house's top,
Let the birds fly, and like the famous ape,°
To try conclusions,° in the basket creep
And break your own neck down.°

QUEEN: Be thou assured, if words be made of breath,
And breath of life, I have no life to breathe
What thou hast said to me.

HAMLET: I must to England. You know that?

QUEEN: Alack,
I had forgot. 'Tis so concluded on.

HAMLET: There's letters sealed, and my two schoolfellows,
Whom I will trust as I will adders fanged,
They bear the mandate; they must sweep my way
And marshal me to knavery.° Let it work.°
For 'tis the sport to have the enginer°
Hoist with° his own petard,° and 't shall go hard
But I will° delve one yard below their mines°
And blow them at the moon. O, 'tis most sweet
When in one line° two crafts° directly meet.
This man shall set me packing.°
I'll lug the guts into the neighbor room.
Mother, good night indeed. This counselor
Is now most still, most secret, and most grave,
Who was in life a foolish prating knave.—
Come, sir, to draw toward an end° with you.—
Good night, Mother.

[Exeunt (separately, HAMLET dragging in POLONIUS).]

[4.1 *Enter KING and QUEEN,° with ROSENCRANTZ and GUILDENSTERN.]*°

199 **sense and secrecy** secrecy that common sense requires 200 **Unpeg the basket** open the cage, i.e., let out the secret 201 **famous ape** (In a story now lost.) 202 **try conclusions** test the outcome (in which the ape apparently enters a cage from which birds have been released and then tries to fly out of the cage as they have done, falling to its death) 203 **down** in the fall; utterly 211–212 **sweep . . . knavery** sweep a path before me and conduct me to some *knavery* or treachery prepared for me 212 **work** proceed 213 **enginer** maker of military contrivances 214 **Hoist with** blown up by **petard** an explosive used to blow in a door or make a breach 214–215 **'t shall . . . will** unless luck is against me, I will 215 **mines** tunnels used in warfare to undermine the enemy's emplacements; Hamlet will countermine by going under their mines 217 **in one line** i.e., mines and countermines on a collision course, or the countermines directly below the mines **crafts** acts of guile, plots 218 **set me packing** set me to making schemes, and set me to lugging (him), and, also, send me off in a hurry 223 **draw . . . end** finish up (with a pun on *draw,* "pull") 4.1 s.d **Location: The castle** s.d. **Enter . . . Queen** (Some editors argue that Gertrude never exits in 3.4 and that the scene is continuous here, as suggested in the Folio, but the Second Quarto marks an entrance for her and at line 35 Claudius speaks of Gertrude's *closet* as though it were elsewhere. A short time has elapsed, during which the King has become aware of her highly wrought emotional state.)

KING: There's matter° in these sighs, these profound heaves.°
You must translate; 'tis fit we understand them.
Where is your son?
QUEEN: Bestow this place on us a little while.
[Exeunt ROSENCRANTZ and GUILDENSTERN.]
Ah, mine own lord, what have I seen tonight!
KING: What, Gertrude? How does Hamlet?
QUEEN: Mad as the sea and wind when both contend
Which is the mightier. In his lawless fit,
Behind the arras hearing something stir,
Whips out his rapier, cries, "A rat, a rat!"
And in this brainish apprehension° kills
The unseen good old man.
KING: O heavy° deed!
It had been so with us,° had we been there.
His liberty is full of threats to all—
To you yourself, to us, to everyone.
Alas, how shall this bloody deed be answered?°
It will be laid to us, whose providence°
Should have kept short,° restrained, and out of haunt°
This mad young man. But so much was our love,
We would not understand what was most fit,
But, like the owner of a foul disease,
To keep it from divulging,° let it feed
Even on the pith of life. Where is he gone?
QUEEN: To draw apart the body he hath killed,
O'er whom his very madness, like some ore°
Among a mineral° of metals base,
Shows itself pure: 'a weeps for what is done.
KING: O Gertrude, come away!
The sun no sooner shall the mountains touch
But we will ship him hence, and this vile deed
We must with all our majesty and skill
Both countenance° and excuse.—Ho, Guildenstern!
[Enter ROSENCRANTZ and GUILDENSTERN.]
Friends both, go join you with some further aid.
Hamlet in madness hath Polonius slain,

1 **matter** significance **heaves** heavy sighs 11 **brainish apprehension** headstrong conception 12 **heavy** grievous 13 **us** i.e., me (The royal "we"; also in line 15.) 16 **answered** explained 17 **providence** foresight 18 **short** i.e., on a short tether **out of haunt** secluded 22 **divulging** becoming evident 25 **ore** vein of gold 26 **mineral** mine 32 **countenance** put the best face on

And from his mother's closet hath he dragged him.
Go seek him out, speak fair, and bring the body
Into the chapel. I pray you, haste in this.

[Exeunt ROSENCRANTZ *and* GUILDENSTERN.*]*

Come, Gertrude, we'll call up our wisest friends
And let them know both what we mean to do
And what's untimely done°
Whose whisper o'er the world's diameter,°
As level° as the cannon to his blank,°
Transports his poisoned shot, may miss our name
And hit the woundless° air. O, come away!
My soul is full of discord and dismay.

[Exeunt.]

[4.2 Enter HAMLET.*]*°

HAMLET: Safely stowed.

ROSENCRANTZ, GUILDENSTERN *[within]*: Hamlet! Lord Hamlet!

HAMLET: But soft, what noise? Who calls on Hamlet? O, here they come.

[Enter ROSENCRANTZ *and* GUILDENSTERN.*]*

ROSENCRANTZ: What have you done, my lord, with the dead body?

HAMLET: Compounded it with dust, whereto 'tis kin.

ROSENCRANTZ: Tell us where 'tis, that we may take it thence
And bear it to the chapel.

HAMLET: Do not believe it.

ROSENCRANTZ: Believe what?

HAMLET: That I can keep your counsel and not mine own.° Besides, to be demanded of° a sponge, what replication° should be made by the son of a king?

ROSENCRANTZ: Take you me for a sponge, my lord?

HAMLET: Ay, sir, that soaks up the King's countenance,° his rewards, his authorities.° But such officers do the King best service in the end. He keeps them, like an ape, an apple, in the corner of his jaw, first mouthed to be last swallowed. When he needs what you have gleaned, it is but squeezing you, and, sponge, you shall be dry again.

ROSENCRANTZ: I understand you not, my lord.

HAMLET: I am glad of it. A knavish speech sleeps in° a foolish ear.

40 **And . . . done** (A defective line; conjectures as to the missing words include *So, haply, slander* [Capell and others]; *For, haply, slander* [Theobald and others]; and *So envious slander* [Jenkins].) 41 **diameter** extent from side to side 42 **As level** with as direct aim **his blank** its target at point-blank range 44 **woundless** invulnerable 4.2 s.d. **Location: The castle** 10 **That . . . own** i.e., that I can follow your advice (by telling where the body is) and still keep my own secret 11 **demanded of** questioned by **replication** reply 14 **countenance** favor 15 **authorities** delegated power, influence 20 **sleeps in** has no meaning to

ROSENCRANTZ: My lord, you must tell us where the body is and go with us to the King.

HAMLET: The body is with the King, but the King is not with the body.° The King is a thing—

GUILDENSTERN: A thing, my lord?

HAMLET: Of nothing.° Bring me to him. Hide fox, and all after!°

[Exeunt (running).]

[4.3 Enter KING, and two or three.]°

KING: I have sent to seek him, and to find the body.
How dangerous is it that this man goes loose!
Yet must not we put the strong law on him.
He's loved of° the distracted° multitude,
Who like not in their judgment, but their eyes,°
And where 'tis so, th' offender's scourge° is weighed,°
But never the offense. To bear all smooth and even,°
This sudden sending him away must seem
Deliberate pause.° Diseases desperate grown
By desperate appliance° are relieved,
Or not at all.

[Enter ROSENCRANTZ, GUILDENSTERN, and all the rest.]

How now, what hath befall'n?

ROSENCRANTZ: Where the dead body is bestowed, my lord,
We cannot get from him.

KING: But where is he?

ROSENCRANTZ: Without, my lord; guarded, to know your pleasure.

KING: Bring him before us.

ROSENCRANTZ: Ho! Bring in the lord.

[They enter (with HAMLET).]

KING: Now, Hamlet, where's Polonius?

HAMLET: At supper.

KING: At supper? Where?

23 **The . . . body** (Perhaps alludes to the legal commonplace of "the king's two bodies," which drew a distinction between the sacred office of kingship and the particular mortal who possessed it at any given time. Hence, although Claudius' body is necessarily a part of him, true kingship is not contained in it. Similarly, Claudius will have Polonius' body when it is found, but there is no kingship in this business either.) 26 **Of nothing** (1) of no account (2) lacking the essence of kingship, as in lines 23–24 and note **Hide . . . after** (An old signal cry in the game of hide-and-seek, suggesting that Hamlet now runs away from them.) 4.3 s.d. **Location: The castle** 4 **of** by **distracted** fickle, unstable 5 **Who . . . eyes** who choose not by judgment but by appearance 6 **scourge** punishment (Literally, blow with a whip.) **weighed** sympathetically considered 7 **To . . . even** to manage the business in an unprovocative way 9 **Deliberate pause** carefully considered action 10 **appliance** remedies

HAMLET: Not where he eats, but where 'a is eaten. A certain convocation of politic worms° are e'en° at him. Your worm° is your only emperor for diet.° We fat all creatures else to fat us, and we fat ourselves for maggots. Your fat king and your lean beggar is but variable service°—two dishes, but to one table. That's the end.

KING: Alas, alas!

HAMLET: A man may fish with the worm that hath eat° of a king, and eat of the fish that hath fed of that worm.

KING: What dost thou mean by this?

HAMLET: Nothing but to show you how a king may go a progress° through the guts of a beggar.

KING: Where is Polonius?

HAMLET: In heaven. Send thither to see. If your messenger find him not there, seek him i' th' other place yourself. But if indeed you find him not within this month, you shall nose him as you go up the stairs into the lobby.

KING: [*to some attendants*] Go seek him there.

HAMLET: 'A will stay till you come.

[Exeunt attendants.]

KING: Hamlet, this deed, for thine especial safety—
Which we do tender,° as we dearly° grieve
For that which thou hast done—must send thee hence
With fiery quickness. Therefore prepare thyself.
The bark° is ready, and the wind at help,
Th' associates tend,° and everything is bent°
For England.

HAMLET: For England!

KING: Ay, Hamlet.

HAMLET: Good.

KING: So is it, if thou knew'st our purposes.

HAMLET: I see a cherub° that sees them. But come, for England!
Farewell, dear mother.

KING: Thy loving father, Hamlet.

HAMLET: My mother. Father and mother is man and wife, man and wife is one flesh, and so, my mother. Come, for England!

[Exit.]

21 **politic worms** crafty worms (suited to a master spy like Polonius) **e'en** even now **Your worm** your average worm (Compare *your fat king and your lean beggar* in line 23.) 22 **diet** food, eating (with a punning reference to the Diet of Worms, a famous *convocation* held in 1521) 23 **variable service** different courses of a single meal 26 **eat** eaten (Pronounced et.) 29 **progress** royal journey of state 38 **tender** regard, hold dear **dearly** intensely 41 **bark** sailing vessel 42 **tend** wait **bent** in readiness 48 **cherub** (Cherubim are angels of knowledge. Hamlet hints that both he and heaven are onto Claudius' tricks.)

KING: Follow him at foot;° tempt him with speed aboard.
Delay it not. I'll have him hence tonight.
Away! For everything is sealed and done
That else leans on° th' affair. Pray you, make haste.

[Exeunt all but the KING.]

And, England,° if my love thou hold'st at aught°—
As my great power thereof may give thee sense,°
Since yet thy cicatrice° looks raw and red
After the Danish sword, and thy free awe°
Pays homage to us—thou mayst not coldly set°
Our sovereign process,° which imports at full,°
By letters congruing° to that effect,
The present° death of Hamlet. Do it, England,
For like the hectic° in my blood he rages,
And thou must cure me. Till I know 'tis done,
Howe'er my haps,° my joys were ne'er begun.

[Exit.]

[4.4 Enter FORTINBRAS with his army over the stage.]°

FORTINBRAS: Go, Captain, from me greet the Danish king.
KING: Tell him that by his license° Fortinbras
Craves the conveyance of° a promised march
Over his kingdom. You know the rendezvous.
If that His Majesty would aught with us,
We shall express our duty° in his eye;°
And let him know so.
CAPTAIN: I will do 't, my lord.
FORTINBRAS: Go softly° on.

[Exeunt all but the CAPTAIN.]

[Enter HAMLET, ROSENCRANTZ, (GUILDENSTERN,) etc.]

HAMLET: Good sir, whose powers° are these?
CAPTAIN: They are of Norway, sir.
HAMLET: How purposed, sir, I pray you?
CAPTAIN: Against some part of Poland.

53 **at foot** close behind, at heel 56 **leans on** bears upon, is related to 57 **England** i.e., King of England **at aught** at any value 58 **As . . . sense** for so my great power may give you a just appreciation of the importance of valuing my love 59 **cicatrice** scar 60 **free awe** voluntary show of respect 61 **coldly set** regard with indifference 62 **process** command **imports at full** conveys specific directions for 63 **congruing** agreeing 64 **present** immediate 65 **hectic** persistent fever 67 **haps** fortunes 4.4 s.d. **Location: The coast of Denmark** 2 **license** permission 3 **the conveyance of** escort during 6 **duty** respect **eye** presence 9 **softly** slowly, circumspectly 10 **powers** forces

HAMLET: Who commands them, sir?
CAPTAIN: The nephew to old Norway, Fortinbras.
HAMLET: Goes it against the main° of Poland, sir,
Or for some frontier?
CAPTAIN: Truly to speak, and with no addition,°
We go to gain a little patch of ground
That hath in it no profit but the name.
To pay° five ducats, five, I would not farm it;°
Nor will it yield to Norway or the Pole
A ranker° rate, should it be sold in fee.°
HAMLET: Why, then the Polack never will defend it.
CAPTAIN: Yes, it is already garrisoned.
HAMLET: Two thousand souls and twenty thousand ducats
Will not debate° the question of this straw.°
This is th' impostume° of much wealth and peace,
That inward breaks, and shows no cause without
Why the man dies. I humbly thank you, sir.
CAPTAIN: God b' wi' you, sir.
[Exit.]
ROSENCRANTZ: Will 't please you go, my lord?
HAMLET: I'll be with you straight. Go a little before.
[Exeunt all except HAMLET.]

How all occasions do inform against° me
And spur my dull revenge! What is a man,
If his chief good and market of° his time
Be but to sleep and feed? A beast, no more.
Sure he that made us with such large discourse,°
Looking before and after,° gave us not
That capability and godlike reason
To fust° in us unused. Now, whether it be
Bestial oblivion,° or some craven° scruple
Of thinking too precisely° on th' event°—
A thought which, quartered, hath but one part wisdom
And ever three parts coward—I do not know
Why yet I live to say "This thing's to do,"

16 **main** main part 18 **addition** exaggeration 21 **To pay** i.e., for a yearly rental of **farm it** take a lease of it 23 **ranker** higher **in fee** fee simple, outright 27 **debate . . . straw** settle this trifling matter 28 **impostume** abscess 33 **inform against** denounce, betray; take shape against 35 **market of** profit of, compensation for 37 **discourse** power of reasoning 38 **Looking before and after** able to review past events and anticipate the future 40 **fust** grow moldy 41 **oblivion** forgetfulness **craven** cowardly 42 **precisely** scrupulously **event** outcome

Sith° I have cause, and will, and strength, and means
To do 't. Examples gross° as earth exhort me:
Witness this army of such mass and charge,°
Led by a delicate and tender° prince,
Whose spirit with divine ambition puffed
Makes mouths° at the invisible event,°
Exposing what is mortal and unsure
To all that fortune, death, and danger dare,°
Even for an eggshell. Rightly to be great
Is not to stir without great argument,
But greatly to find quarrel in a straw
When honor's at the stake.° How stand I, then,
That have a father killed, a mother stained,
Excitements of° my reason and my blood,
And let all sleep, while to my shame I see
The imminent death of twenty thousand men
That for a fantasy° and trick° of fame
Go to their graves like beds, fight for a plot°
Whereon the numbers cannot try the cause,°
Which is not tomb enough and continent°
To hide the slain? O, from this time forth
My thoughts be bloody or be nothing worth!

[Exit.]

[4.5 *Enter* HORATIO, (QUEEN) GERTRUDE, *and a* GENTLEMAN.]

QUEEN: I will not speak with her.
GENTLEMAN: She is importunate,
Indeed distract.° Her mood will needs be pitied.
QUEEN: What would she have?
GENTLEMAN: She speaks much of her father, says she hears
There's tricks° i' the world, and hems,° and beats her heart,°
Spurns enviously at straws,° speaks things in doubt°
That carry but half sense. Her speech is nothing,

46 **Sith** since 47 **gross** obvious 48 **charge** expense 49 **delicate and tender** of fine and youthful qualities 51 **Makes mouths** makes scornful faces **invisible event** unforeseeable outcome 53 **dare** could do (to him) 54–57 **Rightly . . . stake** true greatness does not normally consist of rushing into action over some trivial provocation; however, when one's honor is involved, even a trifling insult requires that one respond greatly 57 **at the stake** (A metaphor from gambling or bear-baiting.) 59 **Excitements of** promptings by 62 **fantasy** fanciful caprice, illusion **trick** trifle, deceit 63 **plot** plot of ground 64 **Whereon . . . cause** on which there is insufficient room for the soldiers needed to engage in a military contest 65 **continent** receptacle; container 4.5 s.d. **Location: The castle** 2 **distract** distracted 5 **tricks** deceptions **hems** makes "hmm" sounds **heart** i.e., breast 6 **Spurns . . . straws** kicks spitefully, takes offense at trifles **in doubt** obscurely

Yet the unshapèd use° of it doth move
The hearers to collection;° they yawn° at it,
And botch° the words up fit to their own thoughts,
Which,° as her winks and nods and gestures yield° them,
Indeed would make one think there might be thought,°
Though nothing sure, yet much unhappily.°

HORATIO: 'Twere good she were spoken with, for she may strew
Dangerous conjectures in ill-breeding° minds.

QUEEN: Let her come in. *[Exit GENTLEMAN.]*
[*Aside.*] To my sick soul, as sin's true nature is,
Each toy° seems prologue to some great amiss.°
So full of artless jealousy is guilt,
It spills itself in fearing to be spilt.°

[Enter OPHELIA° (distracted).]

OPHELIA: Where is the beauteous majesty of Denmark?

QUEEN: How now, Ophelia?

OPHELIA [*she sings*]:
"How should I your true love know
From another one?
By his cockle hat° and staff,
And his sandal shoon."°

QUEEN: Alas, sweet lady, what imports this song?

OPHELIA: Say you? Nay, pray you, mark.
"He is dead and gone, lady, [*Song.*]
He is dead and gone;
At his head a grass-green turf,
At his heels a stone."
O, ho!

QUEEN: Nay, but Ophelia—

OPHELIA: Pray you, mark. [*Sings.*]
"White his shroud as the mountain snow"—

[Enter KING.]

QUEEN: Alas, look here, my lord.

8 **unshapèd use** incoherent manner 9 **collection** inference, a guess at some sort of meaning **yawn** gape, wonder; grasp (The Folio reading, *aim*, is possible.) 10 **botch** patch 11 **Which** which words **yield** deliver, represent 12 **thought** intended 13 **unhappily** unpleasantly near the truth, shrewdly 15 **ill-breeding** prone to suspect the worst and to make mischief 18 **toy** trifle **amiss** calamity 19–20 **So . . . split** guilt is so full of suspicion that it unskillfully betrays itself in fearing betrayal 20 **s.d. Enter Ophelia** (In the First Quarto, Ophelia enters, "playing on a lute, and her hair down, singing.") 25 **cockle hat** hat with cockle-shell stuck in it as a sign that the wearer had been a pilgrim to the shrine of Saint James of Compostela in Spain 26 **shoon** shoes

OPHELIA: "Larded° with sweet flowers; [*Song.*]
Which bewept to the ground did not go
With true-love showers."°

KING: How do you, pretty lady?

OPHELIA: Well, God 'ild° you! They say the owl° was a baker's daughter. Lord, we know what we are, but know not what we may be. God be at your table!

KING: Conceit° upon her father.

OPHELIA: Pray let's have no words of this; but when they ask you what it means, say you this:
"Tomorrow is Saint Valentine's day, [*Song.*]
All in the morning betime,°
And I a maid at your window,
To be your Valentine.
Then up he rose, and donned his clothes,
And dupped° the chamber door,
Let in the maid, that out a maid
Never departed more."

KING: Pretty Ophelia—

OPHELIA: Indeed, la, without an oath, I'll make an end on 't: [*Sings.*]
"By Gis° and by Saint Charity,
Alack, and fie for shame!
Young men will do 't, if they come to 't;
By Cock,° they are to blame.
Quoth she, 'Before you tumbled me,
You promised me to wed.'"
He answers:
"'So would I ha' done, by yonder sun,
An° thou hadst not come to my bed.'"

KING: How long hath she been thus?

OPHELIA: I hope all will be well. We must be patient, but I cannot choose but weep to think they would lay him i' the cold ground. My brother shall know of it. And so I thank you for your good counsel. Come, my coach! Good night, ladies, good night, sweet ladies, good night, good night.

[*Exit.*]

KING: [*to* HORATIO] Follow her close. Give her good watch, I pray you.

[*Exit* HORATIO.]

38 **Larded** decorated 40 **showers** i.e., tears 42 **God 'ild** God yield or reward **owl** (Refers to a legend about a baker's daughter who was turned into an owl for being ungenerous when Jesus begged a loaf of bread.) 45 **Conceit** brooding 49 **betime** early 53 **dupped** did up, opened 58 **Gis** Jesus 61 **Cock** (A perversion of "God" in oaths; here also with a quibble on the slang word for penis.) 66 **An** if

O, this is the poison of deep grief; it springs
All from her father's death—and now behold!
O Gertrude, Gertrude,
When sorrows come, they come not single spies,°
But in battalions. First, her father slain;
Next, your son gone, and he most violent author
Of his own just remove;° the people muddied,°
Thick and unwholesome in their thoughts and whispers
For good Polonius' death—and we have done but greenly,°
In hugger-mugger° to inter him; poor Ophelia
Divided from herself and her fair judgment,
Without the which we are pictures or mere beasts;
Last, and as much containing° as all these,
Her brother is in secret come from France,
Feeds on this wonder, keeps himself in clouds,°
And wants° not buzzers° to infect his ear
With pestilent speeches of his father's death,
Wherein necessity,° of matter beggared,°
Will nothing stick our person to arraign
In ear and ear.° O my dear Gertrude, this,
Like to a murdering piece,° in many places
Gives me superfluous death.° *[A noise within.]*

QUEEN: Alack, what noise is this?

KING: Attend!°
Where is my Switzers?° Let them guard the door.

[Enter MESSENGER.]

What is the matter?

MESSENGER: Save yourself, my lord!
The ocean, overpeering of his list,°
Eats not the flats° with more impetuous° haste
Than young Laertes, in a riotous head,°
O'erbears your officers. The rabble call him lord,
And, as° the world were now but to begin,
Antiquity forgot, custom not known,

76 **spies** scouts sent in advance of the main force 79 **remove** removal **muddied** stirred up, confused 81 **greenly** in an inexperienced way, foolishly 82 **hugger-mugger** secret haste 85 **as much containing** as full of serious matter 87 **Feeds . . . clouds** feeds his resentment or shocked grievance, holds himself inscrutable and aloof amid all this rumor 88 **wants** lacks **buzzers** gossipers, informers 90 **necessity** i.e., the need to invent some plausible explanation **of matter beggared** unprovided with facts 91–92 **Will . . . ear** will not hesitate to accuse my (royal) person in everybody's ears 93 **murdering piece** cannon loaded so as to scatter its shot 94 **Gives . . . death** kills me over and over 96 **Attend** i.e., guard me 97 **Switzers** Swiss guards, mercenaries 99 **overpeering of his list** overflowing its shore, boundary 100 **flats** i.e., flatlands near shore **impetuous** violent (perhaps also with the meaning of *impiteous* [*impitious,* Q2], "pitiless.") 101 **head** insurrection 103 **as** as if

The ratifiers and props of every word,°
They cry, "Choose we! Laertes shall be king!"
Caps,° hands, and tongues applaud it to the clouds,
"Laertes shall be king, Laertes king!"
QUEEN: How cheerfully on the false trail they cry!
[A noise within.]
O, this is counter,° you false Danish dogs!
[Enter LAERTES *with others.]*
KING: The doors are broke.
LAERTES: Where is this King?—Sirs, stand you all without.
ALL: No, let's come in.
LAERTES: I pray you, give me leave.
ALL: We will, we will.
LAERTES: I thank you. Keep the door. *[Exeunt followers.]* O thou vile king,
Give me my father!
QUEEN: *[restraining him]* Calmly, good Laertes.
LAERTES: That drop of blood that's calm proclaims me bastard,
Cries cuckold to my father, brands the harlot
Even here, between° the chaste unsmirchèd brow
Of my true mother.
KING: What is the cause, Laertes,
That thy rebellion looks so giantlike?
Let him go, Gertrude. Do not fear our° person.
There's such divinity doth hedge° a king
That treason can but peep to what it would,°
Acts little of his will.° Tell me, Laertes,
Why thou art thus incensed. Let him go, Gertrude.
Speak, man.
LAERTES: Where is my father?
KING: Dead.
QUEEN: But not by him.
KING: Let him demand his fill.
LAERTES: How came he dead? I'll not be juggled with.°
To hell, allegiance! Vows, to the blackest devil!
Conscience and grace, to the profoundest pit!
I dare damnation. To this point I stand,°

105 **The ratifiers . . . word** i.e., *antiquity* (or tradition) and *custom* ought to confirm (*ratify*) and underprop our every word or promise 107 **Caps** (The caps are thrown in the air.) 110 **counter** (A hunting term, meaning to follow the trail in a direction opposite to that which the game has taken.) 121 **between** in the middle of 124 **fear our** fear for my 125 **hedge** protect, as with a surrounding barrier 126 **can . . . would** can only peep furtively, as through a barrier, at what it would intend 127 **Acts . . . will** (but) performs little of what it intends 131 **juggled with** cheated, deceived 134 **To . . . stand** I am resolved in this

That both the worlds I give to negligence,°
Let come what comes, only I'll be revenged
Most throughly° for my father.

KING: Who shall stay you?

LAERTES: My will, not all the world's.°
And for° my means, I'll husband them so well
They shall go far with little.

KING: Good Laertes,
If you desire to know the certainty
Of your dear father, is 't writ in your revenge
That, swoopstake,° you will draw both friend and foe,
Winner and loser?

LAERTES: None but his enemies.

KING: Will you know them, then?

LAERTES: To his good friends thus wide I'll ope my arms,
And like the kind life-rendering pelican°
Repast° them with my blood.

KING: Why, now you speak
Like a good child and a true gentleman.
That I am guiltless of your father's death,
And am most sensibly° in grief for it,
It shall as level° to your judgment 'pear
As day does to your eye. *[A noise within.]*

LAERTES: How now, what noise is that?

[Enter OPHELIA.*]*

KING: Let her come in.

LAERTES: O heat, dry up my brains! Tears seven times salt
Burn out the sense and virtue° of mine eye!
By heaven, thy madness shall be paid with weight°
Till our scale turn the beam.° O rose of May!
Dear maid, kind sister, sweet Ophelia!
O heavens, is 't possible a young maid's wits
Should be as mortal as an old man's life?
Nature is fine in° love, and where 'tis fine
It sends some precious instance° of itself
After the thing it loves.°

135 **both . . . negligence** i.e., both this world and the next are of no consequence to me 137 **throughly** thoroughly 139 **My will . . . world's** I'll stop (*stay*) when my will is accomplished, not for anyone else's 140 **for** as for 144 **swoopstake** i.e., indiscriminately (Literally, taking all stakes on the gambling table at once. *Draw* is also a gambling term, meaning "take from.") 149 **pelican** (Refers to the belief that the female pelican fed its young with its own blood.) 150 **Repast** feed 153 **sensibly** feelingly 154 **level** plain 158 **virtue** faculty, power 159 **paid with weight** repaid, avenged equally or more 160 **beam** crossbar of a balance 164 **fine in** refined by 165 **instance** token 166 **After . . . loves** i.e., into the grave, along with Polonius

OPHELIA: [*Song.*]

"They bore him barefaced on the bier,
Hey non nonny, nonny, hey nonny,
And in his grave rained many a tear—"
Fare you well, my dove!

LAERTES: Hadst thou thy wits and didst persuade° revenge,
It could not move thus.

OPHELIA: You must sing "A-down a-down," and you "call him a-down-a."° O, how the wheel° becomes it! It is the false steward° that stole his master's daughter.

LAERTES: This nothing's more than matter.°

OPHELIA: There's rosemary,° that's for remembrance; pray you, love, remember. And there is pansies;° that's for thoughts.

LAERTES: A document° in madness, thoughts and remembrance fitted.

OPHELIA: There's fennel° for you, and columbines.° There's rue° for you, and here's some for me; we may call it herb of grace o' Sundays. You must wear your rue with a difference.° There's a daisy.°
I would give you some violets,° but they withered all when my father died. They say 'a made a good end—
[*Sings.*] "For bonny sweet Robin is all my joy."

LAERTES: Thought° and affliction, passion,° hell itself,
She turns to favor° and to prettiness.

OPHELIA: [*Song.*]

"And will 'a not come again?
And will 'a not come again?
No, no, he is dead.
Go to thy deathbed,
He never will come again.

"His beard was as white as snow,
All flaxen was his poll.°
He is gone, he is gone,
And we cast away moan.
God ha' mercy on his soul!"

171 **persuade** argue cogently for 173 **You . . . a-down-a** (Ophelia assigns the singing of refrains, like her own "Hey non nonny," to others present.) 174 **wheel** spinning wheel as accompaniment to the song, or refrain **false steward** (The story is unknown.) 176 **This . . . matter** this seeming nonsense is more eloquent than sane utterance 177 **rosemary** (Used as a symbol of remembrance both at weddings and at funerals.) 178 **pansies** (Emblems of love and courtship; perhaps from French *pensées,* "thoughts.") 179 **document** instruction, lesson 180 **fennel** (Emblem of flattery.) **columbines** (Emblems of unchastity or ingratitude.) **rue** (Emblem of repentance—a signification that is evident in its popular name, *herb of grace.*) 182 **with a difference** (A device used in heraldry to distinguish one family from another on the coat of arms, here suggesting that Ophelia and the others have different causes of sorrow and repentance; perhaps with a play on rue in the sense of "ruth," "pity.") **daisy** (Emblem of dissembling, faithlessness.) 183 **violets** (Emblems of faithfulness.) 186 **Thought** melancholy **passion** suffering 187 **favor** grace, beauty 194 **poll** head

And of all Christian souls, I pray God. God b' wi' you.
[Exit, followed by GERTRUDE.*]*

LAERTES: Do you see this, O God?
KING: Laertes, I must commune with your grief,
Or you deny me right. Go but apart,
Make choice of whom° your wisest friends you will,
And they shall hear and judge twixt you and me.
If by direct or by collateral hand°
They find us touched,° we will our kingdom give,
Our crown, our life, and all that we call ours
To you in satisfaction; but if not,
Be you content to lend your patience to us,
And we shall jointly labor with your soul
To give it due content.
LAERTES: Let this be so.
His means of death, his obscure funeral—
No trophy,° sword, nor hatchment° o'er his bones,
No noble rite, nor formal ostentation°—
Cry to be heard, as 'twere from heaven to earth,
That° I must call 't in question.°
KING: So you shall,
And where th' offense is, let the great ax fall.
I pray you, go with me.

[Exeunt.]

[4.6 Enter HORATIO *and others.]*
HORATIO: What are they that would speak with me?
GENTLEMAN: Seafaring men, sir. They say they have letters for you.
HORATIO: Let them come in.
[Exit GENTLEMAN.*]*

I do not know from what part of the world
I should be greeted, if not from Lord Hamlet.

[Enter SAILORS.*]*

FIRST SAILOR: God bless you, sir.
HORATIO: Let him bless thee too.
FIRST SAILOR: 'A shall, sir, an 't° please him. There's a letter for you, sir—it came from th' ambassador° that was bound for England—if your name be Horatio, as I am let to know it is. *[He gives a letter.]*

202 **whom** whichever of 204 **collateral hand** indirect agency 205 **us touched** me implicated 211 **trophy** memorial **hatchment** tablet displaying the armorial bearings of a deceased person 212 **ostentation** ceremony 214 **That** so that **call 't in question** demand an explanation 4.6 s.d. **Location: The castle** 8 **an 't** if it 9 **th' ambassador** (Evidently Hamlet. The sailor is being circumspect.)

HORATIO [*reads*]: "Horatio, when thou shalt have overlooked° this, give these fellows some means° to the King; they have letters for him. Ere we were two days old at sea, a pirate of very warlike appointment° gave us chase. Finding ourselves too slow of sail, we put on a compelled valor, and in the grapple I boarded them. On the instant they got clear of our ship, so I alone became their prisoner. They have dealt with me like thieves of mercy,° but they knew what they did: I am to do a good turn for them. Let the King have the letters I have sent, and repair° thou to me with as much speed as thou wouldest fly death. I have words to speak in thine ear will make thee dumb, yet are they much too light for the bore° of the matter. These good fellows will bring thee where I am. Rosencrantz and Guildenstern hold their course for England. Of them I have much to tell thee. Farewell.

He that thou knowest thine, Hamlet."

Come, I will give you way° for these your letters,
And do 't the speedier that you may direct me
To him from whom you brought them.

[*Exeunt.*]

[4.7 *Enter* KING *and* LAERTES.]

KING: Now must your conscience my acquittance seal,°
And you must put me in your heart for friend,
Sith° you have heard, and with a knowing ear,
That he which hath your noble father slain
Pursued my life.

LAERTES: It well appears. But tell me
Why you proceeded not against these feats°
So crimeful and so capital° in nature,
As by your safety, greatness, wisdom, all things else,
You mainly° were stirred up.

KING: O, for two special reasons,
Which may to you perhaps seem much unsinewed,°
But yet to me they're strong. The Queen his mother
Lives almost by his looks, and for myself—
My virtue or my plague, be it either which—
She is so conjunctive° to my life and soul
That, as the star moves not but in his° sphere,°

11 **overlooked** looked over 12 **means** means of access 13 **appointment** equipage 16–17 **thieves of mercy** merciful thieves 18 **repair** come 20 **bore** caliber, i.e., importance 24 **way** means of access 4.7 s.d. **Location: The castle** 1 **my acquittance seal** confirm or acknowledge my innocence 3 **Sith** since 6 **feats** acts 7 **capital** punishable by death 9 **mainly** greatly 11 **unsinewed** weak 15 **conjunctive** closely united (An astronomical metaphor.) 16 **his** its **sphere** one of the hollow spheres in which, according to Ptolematic astronomy, the planets were supposed to move

I could not but by her. The other motive
Why to a public count° I might not go
Is the great love the general gender° bear him,
Who, dipping all his faults in their affection,
Work° like the spring° that turneth wood to stone,
Convert his gyves° to graces, so that my arrows,
Too slightly timbered° for so loud° a wind,
Would have reverted° to my bow again
But not where I had aimed them.

LAERTES: And so have I a noble father lost,
A sister driven into desperate terms,°
Whose worth, if praises may go back° again,
Stood challenger on mount° of all the age
For her perfections. But my revenge will come.

KING: Break not your sleeps for that. You must not think
That we are made of stuff so flat and dull
That we can let our beard be shook with danger
And think it pastime. You shortly shall hear more.
I loved your father, and we love ourself;
And that, I hope, will teach you to imagine—

[Enter MESSENGER with letters.]

How now? What news?

MESSENGER: Letters, my lord, from Hamlet:
This to Your Majesty, this to the Queen.

[He gives letters.]

KING: From Hamlet? Who brought them?

MESSENGER: Sailors, my lord, they say. I saw them not.
They were given me by Claudio. He received them
Of him that brought them.

KING: Laertes, you shall hear them.—
Leave us.

[Exit MESSENGER.]

[*He reads.*] "High and mighty, you shall know I am set naked° on your kingdom. Tomorrow shall I beg leave to see your kingly eyes, when I shall, first asking your pardon,° thereunto recount the occasion of my sudden and more strange return. Hamlet."

18 **count** account, reckoning, indictment 19 **general gender** common people 21 **Work** operate, act **spring** i.e., a spring with such a concentration of lime that it coats a piece of wood with limestone, in effect gilding and petrifying it 22 **gyves** fetters (which, gilded by the people's praise, would look like badges of honor) 23 **slightly timbered** light **loud** (suggesting public outcry on Hamlet's behalf) 24 **reverted** returned 27 **terms** state, condition 28 **go back** i.e., recall what she was 29 **on mount** set up on high 45 **naked** destitute, unarmed, without following 47 **pardon** permission

What should this mean? Are all the rest come back?
Or is it some abuse,° and no such thing?°

LAERTES: Know you the hand?

KING: 'Tis Hamlet's character.° "Naked!"
And in a postscript here he says "alone."
Can you devise° me?

LAERTES: I am lost in it, my lord. But let him come.
It warms the very sickness in my heart
That I shall live and tell him to his teeth,
"Thus didst thou."°

KING: If it be so, Laertes—
As how should it be so? How otherwise?°—
Will you be ruled by me?

LAERTES: Ay, my lord,
So° you will not o'errule me to a peace.

KING: To thine own peace. If he be now returned,
As checking at° his voyage, and that° he means
No more to undertake it, I will work him
To an exploit, now ripe in my device,°
Under the which he shall not choose but fall;
And for his death no wind of blame shall breathe,
But even his mother shall uncharge the practice°
And call it accident.

LAERTES: My lord, I will be ruled,
The rather if you could devise it so
That I might be the organ.°

KING: It falls right.
You have been talked of since your travel much,
And that in Hamlet's hearing, for a quality
Wherein they say you shine. Your sum of parts°
Did not together pluck such envy from him
As did that one, and that, in my regard,
Of the unworthiest siege.°

LAERTES: What part is that, my lord?

KING: A very ribbon in the cap of youth,
Yet needful too, for youth no less becomes°

50 **abuse** deceit **no such thing** not what it appears 51 **character** handwriting 53 **devise** explain to 57 **Thus didst thou** i.e., here's for what you did to my father 58 **As . . . otherwise** how can this (Hamlet's return) be true? Yet how otherwise than true (since we have the evidence of his letter)? 60 **So** provided that 62 **checking at** i.e., turning aside from (like a falcon leaving the quarry to fly at a chance bird) **that** if 64 **device** devising, invention 67 **uncharge the practice** acquit the stratagem of being a plot 70 **organ** agent, instrument 73 **Your . . . parts** i.e., all your other virtues 76 **unworthiest siege** least important rank 79 **no less becomes** is no less suited by

The light and careless livery that it wears
Than settled age his sables° and his weeds°
Importing health and graveness.° Two months since
Here was a gentleman of Normandy.
I have seen myself, and served against, the French,
And they can well° on horseback, but this gallant
Had witchcraft in 't; he grew unto his seat,
And to such wondrous doing brought his horse
As had he been incorpsed and demi-natured°
With the brave beast. So far he topped° my thought
That I in forgery° of shapes and tricks
Come short of what he did.

LAERTES: A Norman was 't?

KING: A Norman.

LAERTES: Upon my life, Lamord.

KING: The very same.

LAERTES: I know him well. He is the brooch° indeed
And gem of all the nation.

KING: He made confession° of you,
And gave you such a masterly report
For art and exercise in your defense,°
And for your rapier most especial,
That he cried out 'twould be a sight indeed
If one could match you. Th' escrimers° of their nation,
He swore, had neither motion, guard, nor eye
If you opposed them. Sir, this report of his
Did Hamlet so envenom with his envy
That he could nothing do but wish and beg
Your sudden° coming o'er, to play° with you.
Now, out of this—

LAERTES: What out of this, my lord?

KING: Laertes, was your father dear to you?
Or are you like the painting of a sorrow,
A face without a heart?

LAERTES: Why ask you this?

KING: Not that I think you did not love your father,
But that I know love is begun by time,°

81 **his sables** its rich robes furred with sable **weeds** garments 82 **Importing . . . graveness** signifying a concern for health and dignified prosperity; also, giving an impression of comfortable prosperity 85 **can well** are skilled 88 **As . . . demi-natured** as if he had been of one body and nearly of one nature (like the centaur) 89 **topped** surpassed 90 **forgery** imagining 94 **brooch** ornament 96 **confession** testimonial, admission of superiority 98 **For . . . defense** with respect to your skill and practice with your weapon 101 **escrimers** fencers 106 **sudden** immediate **play** fence 112 **begun by time** i.e., created by the right circumstance and hence subject to change

And that I see, in passages of proof,°
Time qualifies° the spark and fire of it.
There lives within the very flame of love
A kind of wick or snuff° that will abate it,
And nothing is at a like goodness still,°
For goodness, growing to a pleurisy,°
Dies in his own too much.° That° we would do,
We should do when we would; for this "would" changes
And hath abatements° and delays as many
As there are tongues, are hands, are accidents,°
And then this "should" is like a spendthrift sigh,°
That hurts by easing.° But, to the quick o' th' ulcer:°
Hamlet comes back. What would you undertake
To show yourself in deed your father's son
More than in words?

LAERTES: To cut his throat i' the church.

KING: No place, indeed, should murder sanctuarize;°
Revenge should have no bounds. But good Laertes,
Will you do this,° keep close within your chamber.
Hamlet returned shall know you are come home.
We'll put on those shall° praise your excellence
And set a double varnish on the fame
The Frenchman gave you, bring you in fine° together,
And wager on your heads. He, being remiss,°
Most generous,° and free from all contriving,
Will not peruse the foils, so that with ease,
Or with a little shuffling, you may choose
A sword unbated,° and in a pass of practice°
Requite him for your father.

LAERTES: I will do 't,
And for that purpose I'll anoint my sword.
I bought an unction° of a mountebank°

113 **passages of proof** actual instances that prove it 114 **qualifies** weakens, moderates 116 **snuff** the charred part of a candlewick 117 **nothing . . . still** nothing remains at a constant level of perfection 118 **pleurisy** excess, plethora (Literally, a chest inflammation.) 119 **in . . . much** of its own excess **That** that which 121 **abatements** diminutions 122 **As . . . accidents** as there are tongues to dissuade, hands to prevent, and chance events to intervene 123 **spendthrift sigh** (An allusion to the belief that sighs draw blood from the heart.) 124 **hurts by easing** i.e., costs the heart blood and wastes precious opportunity even while it affords emotional relief **quick o' th' ulcer i.e.,** heart of the matter 128 **sanctuarize** protect from punishment (Alludes to the right of sanctuary with which certain religious places were invested.) 130 **Will you do this** if you wish to do this 132 **put on those shall** arrange for some to 134 **in fine** finally 135 **remiss** negligently unsuspicious 136 **generous** noble-minded 139 **unbated** not blunted having no button **pass of practice** treacherous thrust 142 **unction** ointment **mountebank** quack doctor

So mortal that, but dip a knife in it,
Where it draws blood no cataplasm° so rare,
Collected from all simples° that have virtue°
Under the moon,° can save the thing from death
That is but scratched withal. I'll touch my point
With this contagion, that if I gall° him slightly,
It may be death.

KING: Let's further think of this,
Weigh what convenience both of time and means
May fit us to our shape.° If this should fail,
And that our drift look through our bad performance,°
'Twere better not assayed. Therefore this project
Should have a back or second, that might hold
If this did blast in proof.° Soft, let me see.
We'll make a solemn wager on your cunnings°—
I ha 't!
When in your motion you are hot and dry—
As° make your bouts more violent to that end—
And that he calls for drink, I'll have prepared him
A chalice for the nonce,° whereon but sipping,
If he by chance escape your venomed stuck,°
Our purpose may hold there. [*A cry within.*] But stay, what noise?

[Enter QUEEN.*]*

QUEEN: One woe doth tread upon another's heel,
So fast they follow. Your sister's drowned, Laertes.

LAERTES: Drowned! O, where?

QUEEN: There is a willow grows askant° the brook,
That shows his hoar leaves° in the glassy stream;
Therewith fantastic garlands did she make
Of crowflowers, nettles, daisies, and long purples,°
That liberal° shepherds give a grosser name,°
But our cold° maids do dead men's fingers call them.
There on the pendent° boughs her crownet° weeds

144 **cataplasm** plaster or poultice 145 **simples** herbs **virtue** potency 146 **Under the moon** i.e., anywhere (with reference perhaps to the belief that herbs gathered at night had a special power) 148 **gall** graze, wound 151 **shape** part we propose to act 152 **drift . . . performance** intention should be made visible by our bungling 155 **blast in proof** burst in the test (like a cannon) 156 **cunnings** respective skills 159 **As** i.e., and you should 161 **nonce** occasion 162 **stuck** thrust (From *stoccado,* a fencing term.) 167 **askant** aslant 168 **hoar leaves** white or gray undersides of the leaves 170 **long purples** early purple orchids 171 **liberal** free-spoken **a grosser name** (The testicle-resembling tubers of the orchid, which also in some cases resemble *dead men's fingers,* have earned various slang names like "dogstones" and "cullions.") 172 **cold** chaste 173 **pendent** over-hanging **crownet** made into a chaplet or coronet

Clamb'ring to hang, an envious sliver° broke,
When down her weedy° trophies and herself
Fell in the weeping brook. Her clothes spread wide,
And mermaidlike awhile they bore her up,
Which time she chanted snatches of old lauds,°
As one incapable of° her own distress,
Or like a creature native and endued°
Unto that element. But long it could not be
Till that her garments, heavy with their drink,
Pulled the poor wretch from her melodious lay
To muddy death.

LAERTES: Alas, then she is drowned?

QUEEN: Drowned, drowned.

LAERTES: Too much of water hast thou, poor Ophelia,
And therefore I forbid my tears. But yet
It is our trick;° nature her custom holds,
Let shame say what it will. [*He weeps.*] When these are gone,
The woman will be out.° Adieu, my lord.
I have a speech of fire that fain would blaze,
But that this folly douts° it. [*Exit.*]

KING: Let's follow, Gertrude.
How much I had to do to calm his rage!
Now fear I this will give it start again;
Therefore let's follow.

[*Exeunt.*]

[5.1 *Enter two* CLOWNS° *(with spades and mattocks).*]°

FIRST CLOWN: Is she to be buried in Christian burial, when she willfully seeks her own salvation?°

SECOND CLOWN: I tell thee she is; therefore make her grave straight.° The crowner° hath sat on her,° and finds it° Christian burial.

FIRST CLOWN: How can that be, unless she drowned herself in her own defense?

SECOND CLOWN: Why, 'tis found so.°

174 **envious sliver** malicious branch 175 **weedy** i.e., of plants 178 **lauds** hymns 179 **incapable of** lacking capacity to apprehend 180 **endued** adapted by nature 188 **It is our trick** i.e., weeping is our natural way (when sad) 189–190 **When . . . out** when my tears are all shed, the woman in me will be expended, satisfied 192 **douts** extinguishes (The Second Quarto reads "drowns.") 5.1 s.d. **Location: A churchyard** s.d. **Clowns** rustics 2 **salvation** (A blunder for "damnation," or perhaps a suggestion that Ophelia was taking her own shortcut to heaven.) 3 **straight** straightway, immediately (But with a pun on *strait,* "narrow.") 4 **crowner** coroner **sat on her** conducted an inquest on her case **finds it** gives his official verdict that her means of death was consistent with 6 **found so** determined so in the coroner's verdict

FIRST CLOWN: It must be *se offendendo*,° it cannot be else. For here lies the point: if I drown myself wittingly, it argues an act, and an act hath three branches—it is to act, to do, and to perform. Argal,° she drowned herself wittingly.

SECOND CLOWN: Nay, but hear you, goodman° delver—

FIRST CLOWN: Give me leave. Here lies the water; good. Here stands the man; good. If the man go to this water and drown himself, it is, will he, nill he,° he goes, mark you that. But if the water come to him and drown him, he drowns not himself. Argal, he that is not guilty of his own death shortens not his own life.

SECOND CLOWN: But is this law?

FIRST CLOWN: Ay, marry, is 't—crowner's quest° law.

SECOND CLOWN: Will you ha' the truth on 't? If this had not been a gentlewoman, she should have been buried out o' Christian burial.

FIRST CLOWN: Why, there thou sayst.° And the more pity that great folk should have countenance° in this world to drown or hang themselves, more than their even—Christian.° Come, my spade. There is no ancient° gentlemen but gardeners, ditchers, and grave makers. They hold up° Adam's profession.

SECOND CLOWN: Was he a gentleman?

FIRST CLOWN: 'A was the first that ever bore arms.°

SECOND CLOWN: Why, he had none.

FIRST CLOWN: What, art a heathen? How dost thou understand the Scripture? The Scripture says Adam digged. Could he dig without arms?° I'll put another question to thee. If thou answerest me not to the purpose, confess thyself°—

SECOND CLOWN: Go to.

FIRST CLOWN: What is he that builds stronger than either the mason, the shipwright, or the carpenter?

SECOND CLOWN: The gallows maker, for that frame° outlives a thousand tenants.

FIRST CLOWN: I like thy wit well, in good faith. The gallows does well.° But how does it well? It does well to those that do ill. Now thou dost ill to say the gallows is built stronger than the church. Argal, the gallows may do well to thee. To 't again, come.

7 ***se offendendo*** (A comic mistake for *se defendendo,* a term used in verdicts of justifiable homicide.) 9 **Argal** (Corruption of ergo, "therefore.") 11 **goodman** (An honorific title often used with the name of a profession or craft.) 13 **will he, nill he** whether he will or no, willy-nilly 18 **quest** inquest 21 **there thou sayst** i.e., that's right 22 **countenance** privilege 23 **even-Christian** fellow Christians **ancient** going back to ancient times 25 **hold up** maintain 27 **bore arms** (To be entitled to bear a coat of arms would make Adam a gentleman, but as one who bore a spade, our common ancestor was an ordinary delver in the earth.) 30 **arms** i.e., the arms of the body 32 **confess thyself** (The saying continues, "and be hanged.") 36 **frame** (1) gallows (2) structure 37 **does well** (1) is an apt answer (2) does a good turn

SECOND CLOWN: "Who builds stronger than a mason, a shipwright, or a carpenter?"

FIRST CLOWN: Ay, tell me that, and unyoke.°

SECOND CLOWN: Marry, now I can tell.

FIRST CLOWN: To 't.

SECOND CLOWN: Mass,° I cannot tell.

[Enter HAMLET and HORATIO (at a distance).]

FIRST CLOWN: Cudgel thy brains no more about it, for your dull ass will not mend his pace with beating; and when you are asked this question next, say "a grave maker." The houses he makes lasts till doomsday. Go get thee in and fetch me a stoup° of liquor.

[Exit SECOND CLOWN. FIRST CLOWN digs.]

[Song.]

"In youth, when I did love, did love,°
Methought it was very sweet,
To contract—O—the time for—a—my behove,°
O, methought there—a—was nothing—a—meet."°

HAMLET: Has this fellow no feeling of his business, 'a° sings in gravemaking?

HORATIO: Custom hath made it in him a property of easiness.°

HAMLET: 'Tis e'en so. The hand of little employment hath the daintier sense.°

FIRST CLOWN: *[Song.]*

"But age with his stealing steps
Hath clawed me in his clutch,
And hath shipped me into the land,°
As if I had never been such."

[He throws up a skull.]

HAMLET: That skull had a tongue in it and could sing once. How the knave jowls° it to the ground, as if 'twere Cain's jawbone, that did the first murder! This might be the pate of a politician,° which this ass now o'erreaches,° one that would circumvent God, might it not?

HORATIO: It might, my lord.

HAMLET: Or of a courtier, which could say, "Good morrow, sweet lord! How dost thou, sweet lord?" This might be my Lord Such-a-one, that praised my Lord Such-a-one's horse when 'a meant to beg it, might it not?

HORATIO: Ay, my lord.

43 **unyoke** i.e., after this great effort, you may unharness the team of your wits 46 **Mass** by the Mass 50 **stoup** two-quart measure 51 **In . . . love** (This and the two following stanzas, with nonsensical variations, are from a poem attributed to Lord Vaux and printed in *Tottel's Miscellany*, 1557. The O and *a* [for "ah"] seemingly are the grunts of the digger.) 53 **To contract . . . behove** i.e., to shorten the time for my own advantage (Perhaps he means to *prolong* it.) 54 **meet** suitable, i.e., more suitable 55 **'a** that he 56 **property of easiness** something he can do easily and indifferently 57 **daintier sense** more delicate sense of feeling 60 **into the land** i.e., toward my grave (But note the lack of rhyme in *steps, land.*) 62 **jowls** dashes (with a pun on *jowl*, "jawbone") 64 **politician** schemer, plotter 64–65 **o'erreaches** circumvents, gets the better of (with a quibble on the literal sense)

HAMLET: Why, e'en so, and now my Lady Worm's, chapless,° and knocked about the mazard° with a sexton's spade. Here's fine revolution,° an° we had the trick to see° 't. Did these bones cost no more the breeding but° to play at loggets° with them? Mine ache to think on 't.

FIRST CLOWN: [Song.]

"A pickax and a spade, a spade,
For and° a shrouding sheet;
O, a pit of clay for to be made
For such a guest is meet."

[He throws up another skull.]

HAMLET: There's another. Why may not that be the skull of a lawyer? Where be his quiddities° now, his quillities,° his cases, his tenures,° and his tricks? Why does he suffer this mad knave now to knock him about the sconce° with a dirty shovel, and will not tell him of his action of battery?° Hum, this fellow might be in 's time a great buyer of land, with his statutes, his recognizances,° his fines, his double° vouchers,° his recoveries.° Is this the fine of his fines and the recovery of his recoveries, to have his fine pate full of fine dirt?° Will his vouchers vouch him no more of his purchases, and double ones too, than the length and breadth of a pair of indentures?° The very conveyances° of his lands will scarcely lie in this box,° and must th' inheritor° himself have no more, ha?

HORATIO: Not a jot more, my lord.

HAMLET: Is not parchment made of sheepskins?

HORATIO: Ay, my lord, and of calves' skins too.

HAMLET: They are sheep and calves which seek out assurance in that.° I will speak to this fellow.—Whose grave's this, sirrah?°

FIRST CLOWN: Mine, sir. [Sings.]

"O, pit of clay for to be made
For such a guest is meet."

71 **chapless** having no lower jaw 72 **mazard** i.e., head (Literally, a drinking vessel.) **revolution** turn of Fortune's wheel, change **an** if 73 **trick to see** knack of seeing **cost . . . but** involve so little expense and care in upbringing that we may 74 **loggets** a game in which pieces of hard wood shaped like Indian clubs or bowling pins are thrown to lie as near as possible to a stake 76 **For and** and moreover 80 **quiddities** subtleties, quibbles (From Latin *quid,* "a thing.") **quillities** verbal niceties, subtle distinctions (Variation of *quiddities.*) **tenures** the holding of a piece of property or office, or the conditions or period of such holding 81 **sconce** head 82 **action of battery** lawsuit about physical assault 84 **double** signed by two signatories **vouchers** guarantees of the legality of a title to real estate 84–85 **statutes, recognizances** legal documents guaranteeing a debt by attaching land and property 85 **fines, recoveries** ways of converting entailed estates into "fee simple" or freehold 85–86 **fine of his fines . . . fine pate . . . fine dirt** end of his legal maneuvers...elegant head . . . minutely sifted dirt 87 **pair of indentures** legal document drawn up in duplicate on a single sheet and then cut apart on a zigzag line so that each pair was uniquely matched (Hamlet may refer to two rows of teeth or dentures.) 88 **conveyances** deeds **box** (1) deed box (2) coffin ("Skull" has been suggested.) 89 **inheritor** possessor, owner 93 **assurance in that** safety in legal parchments 94 **sirrah** (A term of address to inferiors.)

HAMLET: I think it be thine, indeed, for thou liest in 't.

FIRST CLOWN: You lie out on 't, sir, and therefore 'tis not yours. For my part, I do not lie in 't, yet it is mine.

HAMLET: Thou dost lie in 't, to be in 't and say it is thine. 'Tis for the dead, not for the quick;° therefore thou liest.

FIRST CLOWN: 'Tis a quick lie, sir; 'twill away again from me to you.

HAMLET: What man dost thou dig it for?

FIRST CLOWN: For no man, sir.

HAMLET: What woman, then?

FIRST CLOWN: For none, neither.

HAMLET: Who is to be buried in 't?

FIRST CLOWN: One that was a woman, sir, but, rest her soul, she's dead.

HAMLET: How absolute° the knave is! We must speak by the card,° or equivocation° will undo us. By the Lord, Horatio, this three years I have took° note of it: the age is grown so picked° that the toe of the peasant comes so near the heel of the courtier, he galls his kibe.°—How long hast thou been grave maker?

FIRST CLOWN: Of all the days i' the year, I came to 't that day that our last king Hamlet overcame Fortinbras.

HAMLET: How long is that since?

FIRST CLOWN: Cannot you tell that? Every fool can tell that. It was that very day that young Hamlet was born—he that is mad and sent into England.

HAMLET: Ay, marry, why was he sent into England?

FIRST CLOWN: Why, because 'a was mad. 'A shall recover his wits there, or if 'a do not, 'tis no great matter there.

HAMLET: Why?

FIRST CLOWN: 'Twill not be seen in him there. There the men are as mad as he.

HAMLET: How came he mad?

FIRST CLOWN: Very strangely, they say.

HAMLET: How strangely?

FIRST CLOWN: Faith, e'en with losing his wits.

HAMLET: Upon what ground?°

FIRST CLOWN: Why, here in Denmark. I have been sexton here, man and boy, thirty years.

HAMLET: How long will a man lie i' th' earth ere he rot?

101 **quick** living 110 **absolute** strict, precise **by the card** i.e., with precision (Literally, by the mariner's compass-card, on which the points of the compass were marked.) 110–111 **equivocation** ambiguity in the use of terms 111 **took** taken 112 **picked** refined, fastidious 113 **galls his kibe** chafes the courtier's chilblain 129 **ground** cause (But, in the next line, the gravedigger takes the word in the sense of "land," "country.")

First Clown: Faith, if 'a be not rotten before 'a die—as we have many pocky° corpses nowadays, that will scarce hold the laying in°—'a will last you° some eight year or nine year. A tanner will last you nine year.

Hamlet: Why he more than another?

First Clown: Why, sir, his hide is so tanned with his trade that 'a will keep out water a great while, and your water is a sore° decayer of your whoreson° dead body. [*He picks up a skull.*] Here's a skull now hath lien you° i' th' earth three-and-twenty years.

Hamlet: Whose was it?

First Clown: A whoreson mad fellow's it was. Whose do you think it was?

Hamlet: Nay, I know not.

First Clown: A pestilence on him for a mad rogue! 'A poured a flagon of Rhenish° on my head once. This same skull, sir, was, sir, Yorick's skull, the King's jester.

Hamlet: This?

First Clown: E'en that.

Hamlet: Let me see. [*He takes the skull.*] Alas, poor Yorick! I knew him, Horatio, a fellow of infinite jest, of most excellent fancy. He hath bore° me on his back a thousand times, and now how abhorred in my imagination it is! My gorge rises° at it. Here hung those lips that I have kissed I know not how oft. Where be your gibes now? Your gambols, your songs, your flashes of merriment that were wont° to set the table on a roar? Not one now, to mock your own grinning?° Quite chopfallen?° Now get you to my lady's chamber and tell her, let her paint an inch thick, to this favor° she must come. Make her laugh at that. Prithee, Horatio, tell me one thing.

Horatio: What's that, my lord?

Hamlet: Dost thou think Alexander looked o' this fashion i' th' earth?

Horatio: E'en so.

Hamlet: And smelt so? Pah! [*He throws down the skull.*]

Horatio: E'en so, my lord.

Hamlet: To what base uses we may return, Horatio! Why may not imagination trace the noble dust of Alexander till 'a find it stopping a bunghole?°

Horatio: 'Twere to consider too curiously° to consider so.

Hamlet: No, faith, not a jot, but to follow him thither with modesty° enough, and likelihood to lead it. As thus: Alexander died, Alexander was buried, Alexander returneth to dust, the dust is earth, of earth we make loam,°

133 **pocky** rotten, diseased (Literally, with the pox, or syphilis.) 134 **hold the laying in** hold together long enough to be interred **last you** last (*You* is used colloquially here and in the following lines.) 138 **sore** i.e., terrible, great **whoreson** i.e., vile, scurvy 139 **lien you** lain (See the note at line 134.) 145 **Rhenish** Rhine wine 150 **bore** borne 152 **My gorge rises** i.e., I feel nauseated 154 **were wont** used 155 **mock your own grinning** mock at the way your skull seems to be grinning (just as you used to mock at yourself and those who grinned at you) **chopfallen** (1) lacking the lower jaw (2) dejected 156 **favor** aspect, appearance 164 **bunghole** hole for filling or emptying a cask 165 **curiously** minutely 166 **modesty** plausible moderation 168 **loam** mortar consisting chiefly of moistened clay and straw

and why of that loam whereto he was converted might they not stop a beer barrel?
Imperious° Caesar, dead and turned to clay,
Might stop a hole to keep the wind away.
O, that that earth which kept the world in awe
Should patch a wall t' expel the winter's flaw!°

[Enter KING, QUEEN, LAERTES, and the corpse (of OPHELIA, in procession, with PRIEST, lords, etc.).]

But soft,° but soft awhile! Here comes the King,
The Queen, the courtiers. Who is this they follow?
And with such maimèd° rites? This doth betoken
The corpse they follow did with desperate hand
Fordo° its own life. 'Twas of some estate.°
Couch we° awhile and mark.

[He and HORATIO conceal themselves. OPHELIA's body is taken to the grave.]

LAERTES: What ceremony else?
HAMLET: [*to HORATIO*] That is Laertes, a very noble youth. Mark.
LAERTES: What ceremony else?
PRIEST: Her obsequies have been as far enlarged
As we have warranty.° Her death was doubtful,
And but that great command o'ersways the order°
She should in ground unsanctified been lodged°
Till the last trumpet. For° charitable prayers,
Shards,° flints, and pebbles should be thrown on her.
Yet here she is allowed her virgin crants,°
Her maiden strewments,° and the bringing home
Of bell and burial.°
LAERTES: Must there no more be done?
PRIEST: No more be done.
We should profane the service of the dead
To sing a requiem and such rest° to her
As to peace-parted souls.°
LAERTES: Lay her i' th' earth,
And from her fair and unpolluted flesh
May violets° spring! I tell thee, churlish priest,

171 **Imperious** imperial 174 **flaw** gust of wind 175 **soft** i.e., wait, be careful 177 **maimèd** mutilated, incomplete 179 **Fordo** destroy **estate** rank 180 **Couch we** let's hide, lie low 185 **warranty** i.e., ecclesiastical authority 186 **great . . . order** orders from on high overrule the prescribed procedures 187 **She should . . . lodged** she should have been buried in unsanctified ground 188 **For** in place of 189 **Shards** broken bits of pottery 190 **crants** garlands betokening maidenhood 191 **strewments** flowers strewn on a coffin 191–192 **bringing . . . burial** laying the body to rest, to the sound of the bell 195 **such rest** i.e., to pray for such rest 196 **peace-parted souls** those who have died at peace with God 198 **violets** (See 4.5.183 and note)

A ministering angel shall my sister be
When thou liest howling.°
HAMLET: [*to HORATIO*] What, the fair Ophelia!
QUEEN: [*scattering flowers*] Sweets to the sweet! Farewell.
I hoped thou shouldst have been my Hamlet's wife.
I thought thy bride-bed to have decked, sweet maid,
And not t' have strewed thy grave.
LAERTES: O, treble woe
Fall ten times treble on that cursèd head
Whose wicked deed thy most ingenious sense°
Deprived thee of! Hold off the earth awhile,
Till I have caught her once more in mine arms.
[*He leaps into the grave and embraces* OPHELIA.]
Now pile your dust upon the quick and dead,
Till of this flat a mountain you have made
T' o'ertop old Pelion or the skyish head
Of blue Olympus.°
HAMLET: [*coming forward*] What is he whose grief
Bears such an emphasis,° whose phrase of sorrow
Conjures the wandering stars° and makes them stand
Like wonder-wounded° hearers? This is I,
Hamlet the Dane.°
LAERTES: [*grappling with him*°] The devil take thy soul!
HAMLET: Thou pray'st not well.
I prithee, take thy fingers from my throat,
For though I am not splenitive° and rash,
Yet have I in me something dangerous,
Which let thy wisdom fear. Hold off thy hand.
KING: Pluck them asunder.
QUEEN: Hamlet, Hamlet!
ALL: Gentlemen!
HORATIO: Good my lord, be quiet.
[*HAMLET and LAERTES are parted.*]

200 **howling** i.e., in hell 206 **ingenious sense** a mind that is quick, alert, of fine qualities 211–212 **Pelion, Olympus** sacred mountains in the north of Thessaly; see also *Ossa*, below, at line 257 214 **emphasis** i.e., rhetorical and florid emphasis (*Phrase* has a similar rhetorical connotation.) 215 **wandering stars** planets 216 **wonder-wounded** struck with amazement 217 **the Dane** (This title normally signifies the King; see 1.1.17 and note.) s.d. **grappling with him** The testimony of the First Quarto that "*Hamlet leaps in after Laertes*" and the "Elegy on Burbage" ("Oft have I seen him leap into the grave") seem to indicate one way in which this fight was staged; however, the difficulty of fitting two contenders and Ophelia's body into a confined space (probably the trapdoor) suggests to many editors the alternative, that Laertes jumps out of the grave to attack Hamlet.) 221 **splenitive** quick-tempered

HAMLET: Why, I will fight with him upon this theme
Until my eyelids will no longer wag.°
QUEEN: O my son, what theme?
HAMLET: I loved Ophelia. Forty thousand brothers
Could not with all their quantity of love
Make up my sum. What wilt thou do for her?
KING: O, he is mad, Laertes.
QUEEN: For love of God, forbear him.°
HAMLET: 'Swounds,° show me what thou'lt do.
Woo't° weep? Woo't fight? Woo't fast? Woo't tear thyself?
Woo't drink up° eisel?° Eat a crocodile?°
I'll do 't. Dost come here to whine?
To outface me with leaping in her grave?
Be buried quick° with her, and so will I.
And if thou prate of mountains, let them throw
Millions of acres on us, till our ground,
Singeing his pate° against the burning zone,°
Make Ossa° like a wart! Nay, an° thou'lt mouth,°
I'll rant as well as thou.
QUEEN: This is mere° madness,
And thus awhile the fit will work on him;
Anon, as patient as the female dove
When that her golden couplets° are disclosed,°
His silence will sit drooping.
HAMLET: Hear you, sir,
What is the reason that you use me thus?
I loved you ever. But it is no matter.
Let Hercules himself do what he may,
The cat will mew, and dog will have his day.°
[Exit HAMLET.]

KING: I pray thee, good Horatio, wait upon him.
[(Exit) HORATIO.]

229 **wag** move (A fluttering eyelid is a conventional sign that life has not yet gone.) 235 **forbear him** leave him alone 236 **'Swounds** by His (Christ's) wounds 237 **Woo't** wilt thou 238 **drink up** drink deeply **eisel** vinegar **crocodile** (Crocodiles were tough and dangerous, and were supposed to shed hypocritical tears.) 241 **quick** alive 244 **his pate** its head, i.e., top **burning zone** zone in the celestial sphere containing the sun's orbit, between the tropics of Cancer and Capricorn 245 **Ossa** another mountain in Thessaly (In their war against the Olympian gods, the giants attempted to heap Ossa on Pelion to scale Olympus.) **an** if **mouth** i.e., rant 246 **mere** utter 249 **golden couplets** two baby pigeons, covered with yellow down **disclosed** hatched 254 **Let . . . day** i.e., (1) even Hercules couldn't stop Laertes' theatrical rant (2) I, too, will have my turn; i.e., despite any blustering attempts at interference, every person will sooner or later do what he or she must do

[*To* LAERTES.] Strengthen your patience in° our last night's speech;
We'll put the matter to the present push.°—
Good Gertrude, set some watch over your son.—
This grave shall have a living° monument.
An hour of quiet° shortly shall we see;
Till then, in patience our proceeding be.

[Exeunt.]

[5.2 *Enter* HAMLET *and* HORATIO.]

HAMLET: So much for this, sir; now shall you see the other.°
You do remember all the circumstance?
HORATIO: Remember it, my lord!
HAMLET: Sir, in my heart there was a kind of fighting
That would not let me sleep. Methought I lay
Worse than the mutines° in the bilboes.° Rashly,°
And praised be rashness for it—let us know°
Our indiscretion° sometimes serves us well
When our deep plots do pall,° and that should learn° us
There's a divinity that shapes our ends,
Rough-hew° them how we will—
HORATIO: That is most certain.
HAMLET: Up from my cabin,
My sea-gown° scarfed° about me, in the dark
Groped I to find out them,° had my desire,
Fingered° their packet, and in fine° withdrew
To mine own room again, making so bold,
My fears forgetting manners, to unseal
Their grand commission; where I found, Horatio—
Ah, royal knavery!—an exact command,
Larded° with many several° sorts of reasons
Importing° Denmark's health and England's too,
With, ho! such bugs° and goblins in my life,°
That on the supervise,° no leisure bated,°
No, not to stay° the grinding of the ax,
My head should be struck off.

256 **in** i.e., by recalling 257 **present push** immediate test 259 **living** lasting (For Laertes' private understanding, Claudius also hints that Hamlet's death will serve as such a monument.) 260 **hour of quiet** time free of conflict 5.2 s.d. **Location: The castle** 1 **see the other** hear the other news 6 **mutines** mutineers **bilboes** shackles **rashly** on impulse (This adverb goes with lines 12 ff.) 7 **know** acknowledge 8 **indiscretion** lack of foresight and judgment (not an indiscreet act) 9 **pall** fail, falter, go stale **learn** teach 11 **Rough-hew** shape roughly 13 **sea-gown** seaman's coat **scarfed** loosely wrapped 14 **them** i.e., Rosencrantz and Guildenstern 15 **Fingered** pilfered, pinched **in fine** finally, in conclusion 20 **Larded** garnished **several** different 21 **Importing** relating to 22 **bugs** bugbears, hobgoblins **in my life** i.e., to be feared if I were allowed to live 23 **supervise** reading **leisure bated** delay allowed 24 **stay** await

HORATIO: Is't possible?
HAMLET: [*giving a document*]
Here's the commission. Read it at more leisure.
But wilt thou hear now how I did proceed?
HORATIO: I beseech you.
HAMLET: Being thus benetted round with villainies—
Ere I could make a prologue to my brains,
They had begun the play°—I sat me down,
Devised a new commission, wrote it fair.°
I once did hold it, as our statists° do,
A baseness° to write fair, and labored much
How to forget that learning; but, sir, now
It did me yeoman's° service. Wilt thou know
Th' effect° of what I wrote?
HORATIO: Ay, good my lord.
HAMLET: An earnest conjuration° from the King,
As England was his faithful tributary,
As love between them like the palm° might flourish,
As peace should still° her wheaten garland° wear
And stand a comma° 'tween their amities,
And many suchlike "as"es° of great charge,°
That on the view and knowing of these contents,
Without debatement further more or less,
He should those bearers put to sudden death,
Not shriving time° allowed.
HORATIO: How was this sealed?
HAMLET: Why, even in that was heaven ordinant.°
I had my father's signet° in my purse,
Which was the model° of that Danish seal;
Folded the writ° up in the form of th' other,
Subscribed° it, gave 't th' impression,° placed it safely,
The changeling° never known. Now, the next day
Was our sea fight, and what to this was sequent°
Thou knowest already.

30–31 **Ere . . . play** before I could consciously turn my brain to the matter, it had started working on a plan 32 **fair** in a clear hand 33 **statists** statesmen 34 **baseness** i.e., lower-class trait 36 **yeoman's** i.e., substantial, faithful, loyal 37 **effect** purport 38 **conjuration** entreaty 40 **palm** (An image of health; see Psalm 92:12) 41 **still** always **wheaten garland** (Symbolic of fruitful agriculture, of peace and plenty.) 42 **comma** (Indicating continuity, link.) 43 **"as"es** (1) the "whereases" of a formal document (2) asses **charge** (1) import (2) burden (appropriate to asses) 47 **shriving time** time for confession and absolution 48 **ordinant** directing 49 **signet** small seal 50 **model** replica 51 **writ** writing 52 **Subscribed** signed (with forged signature) **impression** i.e., with a wax seal 53 **changeling** i.e., substituted letter (Literally, a fairy child substituted for a human one.) 54 **was sequent** followed

HORATIO: So Guildenstern and Rosencrantz go to 't.
HAMLET: Why, man, they did make love to this employment.
They are not near my conscience. Their defeat°
Does by their own insinuation° grow.
'Tis dangerous when the baser° nature comes
Between the pass° and fell° incensèd points
Of mighty opposites.°
HORATIO: Why, what a king is this!
HAMLET: Does it not, think thee, stand me now upon°—
He that hath killed my king and whored my mother,
Popped in between th' election° and my hopes,
Thrown out his angle° for my proper° life,
And with such cozenage°—is 't not perfect conscience
To quit° him with this arm? And is 't not to be damned
To let this canker° of our nature come
In° further evil?
HORATIO: It must be shortly known to him from England
What is the issue of the business there.
HAMLET: It will be short. The interim is mine,
And a man's life's no more than to say "one."°
But I am very sorry, good Horatio,
That to Laertes I forgot myself,
For by the image of my cause I see
The portraiture of his. I'll court his favors.
But, sure, the bravery° of his grief did put me
Into a tow'ring passion.
HORATIO: Peace, who comes here?

[Enter a Courtier (OSRIC).]

OSRIC: Your lordship is right welcome back to Denmark.
HAMLET: I humbly thank you, sir. [*To HORATIO.*] Dost know this water fly?
HORATIO: No, my good lord.
HAMLET: Thy state is the more gracious, for 'tis a vice to know him. He hath much land, and fertile. Let a beast be lord of beasts, and his crib° shall stand at the King's mess.° 'Tis a chuff,° but, as I say, spacious in the possession of dirt.

58 **defeat** destruction 59 **insinuation** intrusive intervention, sticking their noses in my business 60 **baser** of lower social station 61 **pass** thrust **fell** fierce 62 **opposites** antagonists 63 **stand me now upon** become incumbent on me now 65 **election** (The Danish monarch was "elected" by a small number of high-ranking electors.) 66 **angle** fishhook **proper** very 67 **cozenage** trickery 68 **quit** requite, pay back 69 **canker** ulcer 69–70 **come In** grow into 74 **a man's . . . "one"** one's whole life occupies such a short time, only as long as it takes to count to 1 79 **bravery** bravado 85 **crib** manger 86–87 **Let . . . mess** i.e., if a man, no matter how beastlike, is as rich in livestock and possessions as Osric, he may eat at the King's table 86 **chuff** boor, churl (The Second Quarto spelling, *chough*, is a variant spelling that also suggests the meaning here of "chattering jackdaw.")

Osric: Sweet lord, if your lordship were at leisure, I should impart a thing to you from His Majesty.

Hamlet: I will receive it, sir, with all diligence of spirit.
Put your bonnet° to his° right use; 'tis for the head.

Osric: I thank your lordship, it is very hot.

Hamlet: No, believe me, 'tis very cold. The wind is northerly.

Osric: It is indifferent° cold, my lord, indeed.

Hamlet: But yet methinks it is very sultry and hot for my complexion.°

Osric: Exceedingly, my lord. It is very sultry, as 'twere—I cannot tell how. My lord, His Majesty bade me signify to you that 'a has laid a great wager on your head. Sir, this is the matter—

Hamlet: I beseech you, remember.

[Hamlet moves him to put on his hat.]

Osric: Nay, good my lord; for my ease,° in good faith. Sir, here is newly come to court Laertes—believe me, an absolute° gentleman, full of most excellent differences,° of very soft society° and great showing.° Indeed, to speak feelingly° of him, he is the card° or calendar° of gentry,° for you shall find in him the continent of what part a gentleman would see.°

Hamlet: Sir, his definement° suffers no perdition° in you,° though I know to divide him inventorially° would dozy° th' arithmetic of memory, and yet but yaw° neither° in respect of° his quick sail. But, in the verity of extolment,° I take him to be a soul of great article,° and his infusion° of such dearth and rareness° as, to make true diction° of him, his semblable° is his mirror and who else would trace° him his umbrage,° nothing more.

Osric: Your lordship speaks most infallibly of him.

Hamlet: The concernancy,° sir? Why do we wrap the gentleman in our more rawer breath?°

Osric: Sir?

91 **bonnet** any kind of cap or hat **his** its 94 **indifferent** somewhat 95 **complexion** temperament 100 **for my ease** (A conventional reply declining the invitation to put his hat back on.) 101 **absolute** perfect 102 **differences** special qualities **soft society** agreeable manners **great showing** distinguished appearance 103 **feelingly** with just perception **card** chart, map **calendar** guide **gentry** good breeding 104 **the continent . . . see** one who contains in him all the qualities a gentleman would like to see (A *continent* is that which contains.) 105 **definement** definition (Hamlet proceeds to mock Osric by throwing his lofty diction back at him.) **perdition** loss, diminution **you** your description 106 **divide him inventorially** enumerate his graces **dozy** dizzy 107 **yaw** swing unsteadily off course (Said of a ship.) **neither** for all that **in respect of** in comparison with 107–108 **in . . . extolment** in true praise (of him) 108 **of great article** one with many articles in his inventory **infusion** essence, character infused into him by nature 109 **dearth and rareness** rarity **make true diction** speak truly **semblable** only true likeness 110 **who . . . trace** any other person who would wish to follow **umbrage** shadow 112 **concernancy** import, relevance 113 **rawer breath** unrefined speech that can only come short in praising him

HORATIO: Is 't not possible to understand in another tongue?° You will do 't,° sir, really.

HAMLET: What imports the nomination° of this gentleman?

OSRIC: Of Laertes?

HORATIO: [*to* HAMLET] His purse is empty already; all 's golden words are spent.

HAMLET: Of him, sir.

OSRIC: I know you are not ignorant—

HAMLET: I would you did, sir. Yet in faith if you did, it would not much approve° me. Well, sir?

OSRIC: You are not ignorant of what excellence Laertes is—

HAMLET: I dare not confess that, lest I should compare with him in excellence. But to know a man well were to know himself.°

OSRIC: I mean, sir, for° his weapon; but in the imputation laid on him by them,° in his meed° he's unfellowed.°

HAMLET: What's his weapon?

OSRIC: Rapier and dagger.

HAMLET: That's two of his weapons—but well.°

OSRIC: The King, sir, hath wagered with him six Barbary horses, against the which he° has impawned,° as I take it, six French rapiers and poniards,° with their assigns,° as girdle, hangers,° and so.° Three of the carriages,° in faith, are very dear to fancy,° very responsive° to the hilts, most delicate° carriages, and of very liberal conceit.°

HAMLET: What call you the carriages?

HORATIO: [to HAMLET] I knew you must be edified by the margent° ere you had done.

OSRIC: The carriages, sir, are the hangers.

HAMLET: The phrase would be more germane to the matter if we could carry a cannon by our sides; I would it might be hangers till then. But, on: six Barbary horses against six French swords, their assigns, and three liberal-

115 **to understand . . . tongue** i.e., for you, Osric, to understand when someone else speaks your language. (Horatio twits Osric for not being able to understand the kind of flowery speech he himself uses, when Hamlet speaks in such a vein. Alternatively, all this could be said to Hamlet.) **You will do 't** i.e., you can if you try, or, you may well have to try (to speak plainly) 117 **nomination** naming 123 **approve** commend 125–126 **I dare . . . himself** I dare not boast of knowing Laertes' excellence lest I seem to imply a comparable excellence in myself. Certainly, to know another person well, one must know oneself. 127 **for** i.e., with **imputation . . . them** reputation given him by others 128 **meed** merit **unfellowed** unmatched 131 **but well** but never mind 133 **he** i.e., Laertes **impawned** staked, wagered **poniards** daggers **assigns** appurtenances **hangers** straps on the sword belt (*girdle*), from which the sword hung **and so** and so on 134 **carriages** (An affected way of saying *hangers;* literally, gun carriages.) 135 **dear to fancy** delightful to the fancy **responsive** corresponding closely, matching or well adjusted **delicate** (i.e., in workmanship.) 136 **liberal conceit** elaborate design 138 **margent** margin of a book, place for explanatory notes

conceited carriages; that's the French bet against the Danish. Why is this impawned, as you call it?

Osric: The King, sir, hath laid,° sir, that in a dozen passes° between yourself and him, he shall not exceed you three hits. He hath laid on twelve for nine, and it would come to immediate trial, if your lordship would vouchsafe the answer.°

Hamlet: How if I answer no?

Osric: I mean, my lord, the opposition of your person in trial.

Hamlet: Sir, I will walk here in the hall. If it please His Majesty, it is the breathing time° of day with me. Let° the foils be brought, the gentleman willing, and the King hold his purpose. I will win for him an I can; if not, I will gain nothing but my shame and the odd hits.

Osric: Shall I deliver you° so?

Hamlet: To this effect, sir—after what flourish your nature will.

Osric: I commend° my duty to your lordship.

Hamlet: Yours, yours. [*Exit* Osric.] 'A does well to commend it himself; there are no tongues else for 's turn.°

Horatio: This lapwing° runs away with the shell on his head.

Hamlet: 'A did comply with his dug° before 'a sucked it. Thus has he—and many more of the same breed that I know the drossy° age dotes on—only got the tune° of the time and, out of an habit of encounter,° a kind of yeasty° collection,° which carries them through and through the most fanned and winnowed opinions;° and do° but blow them to their trial, the bubbles are out.°

[Enter a Lord.*]*

146 **laid** wagered **passes** bouts (The odds of the betting are hard to explain. Possibly the King bets that Hamlet will win at least five out of twelve, at which point Laertes raises the odds against himself by betting he will win nine.) 149 **vouchsafe the answer** be so good as to accept the challenge (Hamlet deliberately takes the phrase in its literal sense of replying.) 153 **breathing time** exercise period **Let** i.e., if 156 **deliver you** report what you say 158 **commend** commit to your favor (A conventional salutation, but Hamlet wryly uses a more literal meaning, "recommend," "praise," in line 164.) 160 **for 's turn** for his purposes, i.e., to do it for him 161 **lapwing** (A proverbial type of youthful forwardness. Also, a bird that draws intruders away from its nest and was thought to run about with its head in the shell when newly hatched; a seeming reference to Osric's hat.) 162 **comply . . . dug** observe ceremonious formality toward his nurse's or mother's teat 163 **drossy** laden with scum and impurities, frivolous 164 **tune** temper, mood, manner of speech **an habit of encounter** a demeanor in conversing (with courtiers of his own kind) 165 **yeasty** frothy **collection** i.e., of current phrases 165–166 **carries . . . opinions** sustains them right through the scrutiny of persons whose opinions are select and refined (Literally, like grain separated from its chaff. Osric is both the chaff and the bubbly froth on the surface of the liquor that is soon blown away.) 166 **and do** yet do **blow . . . out** test them by merely blowing on them, and their bubbles burst

LORD: My lord, His Majesty commended him to you by young Osric, who brings back to him that you attend him in the hall. He sends to know if your pleasure hold to play with Laertes, or that° you will take longer time.

HAMLET: I am constant to my purposes; they follow the King's pleasure. If his fitness speaks, mine is ready;° now or whensoever, provided I be so able as now.

LORD: The King and Queen and all are coming down.

HAMLET: In happy time.°

LORD: The Queen desires you to use some gentle entertainment° to Laertes before you fall to play.

HAMLET: She well instructs me. *[Exit LORD.]*

HORATIO: You will lose, my lord.

HAMLET: I do not think so. Since he went into France, I have been in continual practice; I shall win at the odds. But thou wouldst not think how ill all's here about my heart; but it is no matter.

HORATIO: Nay, good my lord—

HAMLET: It is but foolery, but it is such a kind of gaingiving° as would perhaps trouble a woman.

HORATIO: If your mind dislike anything, obey it. I will forestall their repair° hither and say you are not fit.

HAMLET: Not a whit, we defy augury. There is special providence in the fall of a sparrow. If it be now, 'tis not to come; if it be not to come, it will be now; if it be not now, yet it will come. The readiness is all. Since no man of aught he leaves knows, what is 't to leave betimes? Let be.°

[A table prepared. (Enter) trumpets, drums, and officers with cushions; KING, QUEEN, (OSRIC,) and all the state; foils, daggers, (and wine borne in;) and LAERTES.]

KING: Come, Hamlet, come and take this hand from me.
[The KING puts LAERTES' hand into HAMLET's.]

HAMLET: [*to LAERTES*] Give me your pardon, sir. I have done you wrong,
But pardon 't as you are a gentleman.
This presence° knows,
And you must needs have heard, how I am punished°
With a sore distraction. What I have done
That might your nature, honor, and exception°

170 **that** if 172–173 **If . . . ready** if he declares his readiness, my convenience waits on his 176 **In happy time** (A phrase of courtesy indicating that the time is convenient.) 177 **entertainment** greeting 185 **gaingiving** misgiving 187 **repair** coming 191–192 **Since . . . Let be** since no one has knowledge of what he is leaving behind, what does an early death matter after all? Enough; don't struggle against it 196 **presence** royal assembly 197 **punished** afflicted 199 **exception** disapproval

Roughly awake, I here proclaim was madness.
Was 't Hamlet wronged Laertes? Never Hamlet.
If Hamlet from himself be ta'en away,
And when he's not himself does wrong Laertes,
Then Hamlet does it not, Hamlet denies it.
Who does it, then? His madness. If 't be so,
Hamlet is of the faction° that is wronged;
His madness is poor Hamlet's enemy.
Sir, in this audience
Let my disclaiming from a purposed evil
Free me so far in your most generous thoughts
That I have° shot my arrow o'er the house
And hurt my brother.

LAERTES: I am satisfied in nature,°
Whose motive° in this case should stir me most
To my revenge. But in my terms of honor
I stand aloof, and will no reconcilement
Till by some elder masters of known honor
I have a voice° and precedent of peace°
To keep my name ungored.° But till that time
I do receive your offered love like love,
And will not wrong it.

HAMLET: I embrace it freely,
And will this brothers' wager frankly° play.—
Give us the foils. Come on.

LAERTES: Come, one for me.

HAMLET: I'll be your foil,° Laertes. In mine ignorance
Your skill shall, like a star i' the darkest night,
Stick fiery off° indeed.

LAERTES: You mock me, sir.

HAMLET: No, by this hand.

KING: Give them the foils, young Osric. Cousin Hamlet,
You know the wager?

HAMLET: Very well, my lord.
Your Grace has laid the odds o'° the weaker side.

KING: I do not fear it; I have seen you both.
But since he is bettered,° we have therefore odds.

206 **faction** party 211 **That I have** as if I had 212 **in nature** i.e., as to my personal feelings 213 **motive** prompting 217 **voice** authoritative pronouncement **of peace** for reconciliation 218 **name ungored** reputation unwounded 221 **frankly** without ill feeling or the burden of rancor 223 **foil** thin metal background which sets a jewel off (with pun on the blunted rapier for fencing) 225 **Stick fiery off** stand out brilliantly 229 **laid the odds o'** bet on, backed 231 **is bettered** has improved; is the odds-on favorite (Laertes' handicap is the "three hits" specified in line 147.)

LAERTES: This is too heavy. Let me see another.
[He exchanges his foil for another.]
HAMLET: This likes me° well. These foils have all a length?
[They prepare to play.]
OSRIC: Ay, my good lord.
KING: Set me the stoups of wine upon that table.
If Hamlet give the first or second hit,
Or quit in answer of the third exchange,°
Let all the battlements their ordnance fire.
The King shall drink to Hamlet's better breath,°
And in the cup an union° shall he throw
Richer than that which four successive kings
In Denmark's crown have worn. Give me the cups,
And let the kettle° to the trumpet speak,
The trumpet to the cannoneer without,
The cannons to the heavens, the heaven to earth,
"Now the King drinks to Hamlet." Come, begin.
[Trumpets the while.]
And you, the judges, bear a wary eye.
HAMLET: Come on, sir.
LAERTES: Come, my lord. *[They play. HAMLET scores a hit.]*
HAMLET: One.
LAERTES: No.
HAMLET: Judgment.
OSRIC: A hit, a very palpable hit.
[Drum, trumpets, and shot. Flourish. A piece goes off.]
LAERTES: Well, again.
KING: Stay, give me drink. Hamlet, this pearl is thine.
[He drinks, and throws a pearl in HAMLET's cup.]
Here's to thy health. Give him the cup.
HAMLET: I'll play this bout first. Set it by awhile.
Come. [*They play.*] Another hit; what say you?
LAERTES: A touch, a touch, I do confess 't.
KING: Our son shall win.
QUEEN: He's fat° and scant of breath.
Here, Hamlet, take my napkin,° rub thy brows.
The Queen carouses° to thy fortune, Hamlet.

233 **likes me** pleases me 237 **Or . . . exchange** i.e., or requites Laertes in the third bout for having won the first two 239 **better breath** improved vigor 240 **union** pearl (So called, according to Pliny's *Natural History*, 9, because pearls are *unique*, never identical.) 243 **kettle** kettledrum 259 **fat** not physically fit, out of training 260 **napkin** handkerchief 261 **carouses** drinks a toast

HAMLET: Good, madam!
KING: Gertrude, do not drink.
QUEEN: I will, my lord, I pray you pardon me. [*She drinks.*]
KING: [*aside*] It is the poisoned cup. It is too late.
HAMLET: I dare not drink yet, madam; by and by.
QUEEN: Come, let me wipe thy face.
LAERTES: [*to KING*] My lord, I'll hit him now.
KING: I do not think 't.
LAERTES: [*aside*] And yet it is almost against my conscience.
HAMLET: Come, for the third, Laertes. You do but dally.
I pray you, pass° with your best violence;
I am afeard you make a wanton of me.°
LAERTES: Say you so? Come on. [*They play.*]
OSRIC: Nothing neither way.
LAERTES: Have at you now!

[*LAERTES wounds HAMLET; then, in scuffling, they change rapiers,° and HAMLET wounds LAERTES.*]

KING: Part them! They are incensed.
HAMLET: Nay, come, again. [*The QUEEN falls.*]
OSRIC: Look to the Queen there, ho!
HORATIO: They bleed on both sides. How is it, my lord?
OSRIC: How is 't, Laertes?
LAERTES: Why, as a woodcock° to mine own springe,° Osric;
I am justly killed with mine own treachery.
HAMLET: How does the Queen?
KING: She swoons to see them bleed.
QUEEN: No, no, the drink, the drink—O my dear Hamlet—
The drink, the drink! I am poisoned. [*She dies.*]
HAMLET: O villainy! Ho, let the door be locked!
Treachery! Seek it out.

[*LAERTES falls. Exit OSRIC.*]

LAERTES: It is here, Hamlet. Hamlet, thou art slain.
No med'cine in the world can do thee good;
In thee there is not half an hour's life.
The treacherous instrument is in thy hand,
Unbated° and envenomed. The foul practice°
Hath turned itself on me. Lo, here I lie,

271 **pass** thrust 272 **make . . . me** i.e., treat me like a spoiled child, trifle with me 275 s.d. **in scuffling, they change rapiers** (This stage direction occurs in the Folio. According to a widespread stage tradition, Hamlet receives a scratch, realizes that Laertes' sword is unbated, and accordingly forces an exchange.) 279 **woodcock** a bird, a type of stupidity or as a decoy **springe** trap, snare 290 **Unbated** not blunted with a button **practice** plot

Never to rise again. Thy mother's poisoned.
I can no more. The King, the King's to blame.
HAMLET: The point envenomed too? Then, venom, to thy work.

[He stabs the KING.]

ALL: Treason! Treason!
KING: O, yet defend me, friends! I am but hurt.
HAMLET: *[forcing the KING to drink.]*
Here, thou incestuous, murderous, damnèd Dane,
Drink off this potion. Is thy union° here?
Follow my mother. *[The KING dies.]*
LAERTES: He is justly served.
It is a poison tempered° by himself.
Exchange forgiveness with me, noble Hamlet.
Mine and my father's death come not upon thee,
Nor thine on me! *[He dies.]*
HAMLET: Heaven make thee free of it! I follow thee.
I am dead, Horatio. Wretched Queen, adieu!
You that look pale and tremble at this chance,°
That are but mutes° or audience to this act,
Had I but time—as this fell° sergeant,° Death,
Is strict° in his arrest°—O, I could tell you—
But let it be. Horatio, I am dead;
Thou livest. Report me and my cause aright
To the unsatisfied.
HORATIO: Never believe it.
I am more an antique Roman° than a Dane.
Here's yet some liquor left.

[He attempts to drink from the poisoned cup. HAMLET prevents him.]

HAMLET: As thou'rt a man,
Give me the cup! Let go! By heaven, I'll ha 't.
O God, Horatio, what a wounded name,
Things standing thus unknown, shall I leave behind me!
If thou didst ever hold me in thy heart,
Absent thee from felicity awhile,
And in this harsh world draw thy breath in pain
To tell my story. *[A march afar off (and a volley within).]*
What warlike noise is this?

[Enter OSRIC.]

298 **union** pearl (See line 240; with grim puns on the word's other meanings: marriage, shared death.) 300 **tempered** mixed 306 **chance** mischance 307 **mutes** silent observers (Literally, actors with non-speaking parts.) 308 **fell** cruel **sergeant** sheriffs officer 309 **strict** (1) severely just (2) unavoidable **arrest** (1) taking into custody (2) stopping my speech 313 **Roman** (Suicide was an honorable choice for many Romans as an alternative to a dishonorable life.)

OSRIC: Young Fortinbras, with conquest come from Poland,
To th' ambassadors of England gives
This warlike volley.
HAMLET: O, I die, Horatio!
The potent poison quite o'ercrows° my spirit.
I cannot live to hear the news from England,
But I do prophesy th' election lights
On Fortinbras. He has my dying voice.°
So tell him, with th' occurents° more and less
Which have solicited°—the rest is silence. *[He dies.]*
HORATIO: Now cracks a noble heart. Good night, sweet prince,
And flights of angels sing thee to thy rest!
[March within.]
Why does the drum come hither?

[Enter FORTINBRAS, with the (English) Ambassadors (with drum, colors, and attendants).]

FORTINBRAS: Where is this sight?
HORATIO: What is it you would see?
If aught of woe or wonder, cease your search.
FORTINBRAS: This quarry° cries on havoc.° O proud Death,
What feast° is toward° in thine eternal cell,
That thou so many princes at a shot
So bloodily hast struck?
FIRST AMBASSADOR: The sight is dismal,
And our affairs from England come too late.
The ears are senseless that should give us hearing,
To tell him his commandment is fulfilled,
That Rosencrantz and Guildenstern are dead.
Where should we have our thanks?
HORATIO: Not from his° mouth,
Had it th' ability of life to thank you.
He never gave commandment for their death.
But since, so jump° upon this bloody question,°
You from the Polack wars, and you from England,
And here arrived, give order that these bodies
High on a stage° be placèd to the view,

326 **o'ercrows** triumphs over (like the winner in a cockfight) 329 **voice** vote 330 **occurrents** events, incidents 331 **solicited** moved, urged (Hamlet doesn't finish saying what the events have prompted—presumably, his acts of vengeance, or his reporting of those events to Fortinbras.) 337 **quarry** heap of dead **cries on havoc** proclaims a general slaughter 338 **feast** i.e., Death feasting on those who have fallen **toward** in preparation 345 **his** i.e., Claudius' 348 **jump** precisely, immediately **question** dispute, affair 351 **stage** platform

And let me speak to th' yet unknowing world
How these things came about. So shall you hear
Of carnal, bloody, and unnatural acts,
Of accidental judgments,° casual° slaughters,
Of deaths put on° by cunning and forced cause,°
And, in this upshot, purposes mistook
Fall'n on th' inventors' heads. All this can I
Truly deliver.

FORTINBRAS: Let us haste to hear it,
And call the noblest to the audience.
For me, with sorrow I embrace my fortune.
I have some rights of memory° in this kingdom,
Which now to claim my vantage° doth invite me.

HORATIO: Of that I shall have also cause to speak,
And from his mouth whose voice will draw on more.°
But let this same be presently° performed,
Even while men's minds are wild, lest more mischance
On° plots and errors happen.

FORTINBRAS: Let four captains
Bear Hamlet, like a soldier, to the stage,
For he was likely, had he been put on,°
To have proved most royal; and for his passage,°
The soldiers' music and the rite of war
Speak° loudly for him.
Take up the bodies. Such a sight as this
Becomes the field,° but here shows much amiss.
Go bid the soldiers shoot.

[Exeunt (marching, bearing off the dead bodies; a peal of ordnance is shot off).]

➤ QUESTIONS FOR READING AND WRITING

1. What is your reaction to Hamlet at the beginning of the play? Do you think his response to his father's death and mother's marriage is excessive? Explain.
2. If you were in his situation, do you think you would have responded in the same way? Why or why not?

355 **judgments** retributions **casual** occurring by chance 356 **put on** instigated **forced cause** contrivance 362 **of memory** traditional, remembered, unforgotten 363 **vantage** favorable opportunity 365 **voice . . . more** vote will influence still others 366 **presently** immediately 368 **On** on the basis of; on top of 370 **put on** i.e., invested in royal office and so put to the test 371 **passage** i.e., from life to death 373 **Speak** (let them) speak 375 **Becomes the field** suits the field of battle

3. What is your response to Claudius at the beginning of the play? Does he seem to be an effective leader, loving stepfather to Hamlet, loving husband to Gertrude? Explain.
4. What is your response to Hamlet's mother Gertrude? Does she seem to be a loving mother to Hamlet? Do you think she understands why he is so angry? Explain.
5. Describe Polonius, Laertes, and Ophelia. To what extent is this a loving family? A dysfunctional family?
6. Pick out Hamlet's soliloquies throughout the play. Is there a pattern in what Hamlet says about himself and his dilemma?
7. Do you think Hamlet procrastinates too much? Is the play he arranges necessary? Should he have killed Claudius at his first opportunity? Explain.
8. Is Hamlet all good? Do you think that his treatment of Ophelia was fair? Are any of his other actions questionable? Explain.
9. At the beginning of the play we are told, "Something is rotten in the state of Denmark." Is all well at the end of the play? Explain.
10. Choose a scene from the play and discuss why it is important in the light of the whole play.
11. Like *Othello* and Shakespeare's other plays, most of this play is dramatic poetry. Choose examples of poetic language from *Hamlet* that are particularly evocative in prompting strong emotion, developing character, building conflict, or advancing the plot. Discuss why the language is so effective.

Interpretation and Performance

An emphasis throughout this book is that literature prompts multiple interpretations. Nowhere is this more apparent than in great works of drama and the process actors go through as they prepare to "interpret" the characters they play.

As readers of literature, we may interpret characters by asking who they are and what they say and do. We can distance ourselves from the work, examine the facts, judge the characters and their actions, and see them as part of a coherent whole. Actors, too, may begin with an objective analysis of characters they play, but rather than distancing themselves from the action and observing characters from outside, they must move inside the play and the characters and immerse themselves in the action.

For an actor, reading a play requires a much closer look—so close that it means looking from the inside out. Questions about characterization shift from "Who is he or she?" to "Who Am I?" "When is this occurring in my life?" How do I feel about being here?" Answering questions like this requires a great deal of work, but it results in a comprehensive analysis and thorough interpretation of character—an interpretation that links actor and playwright in the creative process.

Multiple Interpretations of *Hamlet*

It is hard to imagine any character in dramatic literature who is discussed, interpreted or performed more often than Hamlet. And yet no two Hamlets are identical. From the time of Shakespeare and the first actor who played the role, Richard Burbage, to the present, we are just as likely to identify the character Hamlet with the actor playing the role as with the playwright. Hamlet's words may belong to Shakespeare, but the interpretation of the character belongs to Laurence Olivier, Derek Jacobi, Mel Gibson, Kenneth Branagh, and many other actors who have played the role. While we are likely to say that we prefer one or some of these interpretations more than others, we are not likely to say that one interpretation is right and the others wrong. In this respect, examining different but supportable interpretations can give us an insight into the many views possible when reading other forms of literature as well.

Desperately Seeking Hamlet: Four Interpretations

Over the past fifty years, some of the best performances of Hamlet have been recorded on film and video. Perhaps the four most popular of these productions are Laurence Olivier's 1948 film, which won the Academy Award for best picture; Derek Jacobi's 1979 Hamlet, produced as part of the monumental BBC Shakespeare series; Mel Gibson's portrayal in a popular 1990 Franco Zeffirelli production; and Kenneth Branagh's 1996 star-studded extravaganza. Their performances—their different, but justifiable interpretations—illustrate the complexities of the character and demonstrate the validity of multiple perspectives.

Let's look briefly at these four versions and examine each actor's interpretation of the famous "To be, or not to be" soliloquy. Because this soliloquy is so familiar to the general public, even to those who have never seen the play, it is a major challenge for an actor. Like the role of Hamlet itself, this soliloquy demands a unique interpretation. Both actors and audience often recognize in its rendering a microcosm of the character himself.

Olivier's Hamlet

The oldest, but not the most traditional, of these versions is Laurence Olivier's 1948 film. Revered by many purists as the definitive version, it is in many ways the least pure. The film opens with a reductive voice-over that claims, "This is the story of a man who could not make up his mind." While it is not unusual for directors to cut lines in this four hour long play, Olivier has, in addition, cut two important characters, Rosencrantz and Guildenstern. The fog shrouded setting and powerful orchestral music seem omnipresent. And instead of preceding Hamlet's encounter with Ophelia with his "To be or not to be" soliloquy, Olivier has switched the order of

Shakespeare's text. In this version, Hamlet's speech follows and seems influenced by their painful meeting.

We move into his soliloquy as we move away from a sobbing disconsolate Ophelia who has thrown herself at the foot of the castle steps where Hamlet has just exited. The camera follows the path of her extended arm up the winding, cold, stone stairs—higher and higher—as the music rises and we are hurled into the swirling dark clouds above the castle, then down to the crashing sea and jagged rocks below. The camera shifts slowly to the back of Hamlet's head and seems to bore deeper and deeper into his skull as we hear powerful string music and see an impression of the pulsing, swirling chaos of the sea embedded on the lobes of his brain. And he has not even begun to speak.

When he does speak, he is accompanied by the sounds of the chaotic sea below and powerful orchestral music in the background. He delivers the first part of the speech looking out over the castle wall to the sea below and seems mesmerized by what he sees and says. He produces a dagger and closes his eyes while we hear the "To die, to sleep . . . " section as a voice-over. He snaps out of his reverie when he cries out, "perchance to dream." The music stops and he delivers the rest of the soliloquy to the crashing of the waves beneath him. While he speaks he peruses the sea and points the dagger at himself. As he concludes the soliloquy, he drops the dagger and it falls ominously to the rocks far below. He rises from his precarious perch on the castle wall, finishes the speech, and walks off into the fog.

Jacobi's Hamlet

The BBC video production of 1979 is a very complete version of the play and follows the original order of Shakespeare's text. For Derek Jacobi this means starting the "To be, or not to be" soliloquy from scratch without the momentum of the previous scene to build on. As he begins his soliloquy, therefore, Hamlet remains unaware of the interloping Polonius and Claudius and the "by chance" encounter with Ophelia they have planned for him.

Jacobi enters a quiet empty room, notices us (the audience), and approaches to speak with us. There is no music in the background—just Jacobi and Shakespeare's words. He looks at us, confides in us. He is earnest and philosophical. He seems to ask questions with his statements, and to seek answers while feeling our concern. His is a youthful sadness and confusion—not a deep obsessive depression like Olivier's. Halfway through the soliloquy, we catch a glimpse of Ophelia approaching in the background. But

Jacobi's eyes remain on us throughout. Like Olivier, he shows us his dagger as he contemplates death but looks, too, at the picture of his dead father.

On "lose the name of action," he returns the dagger to its case and greets the "fair Ophelia"—first with enthusiasm and affection, then with disappointment and suspicion as he notices the book she is reading is upside-down.

Gibson's Hamlet

Like Olivier's *Hamlet,* Franco Zeffirelli's 1989 film of the play with Mel Gibson as Hamlet takes a few liberties with Shakespeare's text. Here too, the Ophelia encounter and the "To be, or not to be" soliloquy are reversed from their original order. Hamlet's painful scene with Ophelia precedes his speech, and his realization that "it hath made me mad," seems to say more about his anger than his sanity.

Mel Gibson takes his soliloquy "on the run"—busying himself with other tasks while he speaks to us—not entirely surprising for an actor who is not used to doing Shakespeare. Perhaps the most difficult task in performing Shakespeare's work is delivering a soliloquy head-on with the audience—with nothing between the actor and the audience but the words. Having Gibson keep physically busy while he relates his thoughts fits the energy of this Hamlet. His is a visceral, physical Hamlet who doesn't sit still for much. As he enters a large family crypt below the castle, his perusal of the tombs seems "to give him pause" even before he speaks. Rather than confiding in us as Jacobi does, he seems to be thinking out loud to himself. While he speaks and moves, he pauses to view and touch the reclining statues on top of the tombs. He leans against them, kneels at them, sits on the floor by them as he ponders the big questions of life or death. He seems energized by his musings and almost bounds up the stairs toward the light as he finishes his soliloquy and leaves the crypt.

Branagh's Hamlet

Kenneth Branagh's 1996 four-hour-long production of *Hamlet* is lavish. The play is set in the nineteenth century at a magnificent palace (actually England's Blenheim Palace). The indoor scenes include a throne room surrounded by mirrored walls, overlooked by a gallery and divided by an elevated walkway. There are two-way mirrors and concealed chambers and corridors. There are movie stars galore. And this production definitively answers the question "Was Ophelia sleeping with Hamlet?" by showing Ophelia sleeping with Hamlet.

Like the production itself, the setting for Branagh's "To be, or not to be" soliloquy is opulent—a glorious mirrored-in throne room. Like Shakespeare's text and the BBC production, and unlike the Olivier and Zeffirelli versions, this scene precedes the Ophelia encounter. Branagh enters the huge, empty room and walks slowly across it, footsteps echoing loudly. He turns, looks directly at a mirror—behind which Claudius and Polonius are hiding to listen in on the subsequent Ophelia encounter. He speaks quickly but clearly, his voice almost a whisper. He moves closer and closer to the mirror as he speaks—thus moving closer and closer to the hiding interlopers, who see him clearly through the two-way mirror. Is he speaking to himself or them? He unsheaths a dagger on "bare bodkin" and points it at his reflection in the mirror and Claudius on the other side of the mirror—now only a hand's length away. Claudius shudders.

As the soliloquy ends, Ophelia crosses the long hall. Hamlet approaches her with affection and a gentle hug and kiss, which gradually turns to anger as she tries to return his gifts and he suspects her duplicity.

From Part to Whole, From Whole to Part

Thinking about and analyzing the interpretations of these actors and directors can tell us much about interpreting literature. Many legitimate interpretations are possible. We would not say that one was correct and the others wrong. We might say that we preferred one to the others—or preferred a different one to any presented here.

But we might also conclude that no one scene could show us all of a character. Olivier's interpretation of this soliloquy seems to show us an obsessed, deeply depressed Hamlet close to suicide. Though we can say that this speech tells us a lot about Hamlet, we cannot say that that is all there is to this Hamlet unless we place the speech in the context of all his other speeches and actions. And so it is with Jacobi's earnest and likable Hamlet, Gibson's energetic and sad Hamlet, or Branagh's quick and angry Hamlet. If we characterize any of these Hamlets solely on his behavior as he delivers this one soliloquy, we may be ignoring evidence in other parts of the play that tells us about aspects of the character not revealed in this scene.

So, too, our interpretation of this soliloquy, like an actor's preparation and interpretation of this speech, should be informed by our whole vision of Hamlet—the whole character as we have seen him throughout the play.

A Student Essay—Explication and Analysis

Charles Chiang

Dr. Madden

English 102

November 16, 200X

Hamlet: Connecting with the Audience

In this play, the emotional impact of Hamlet's death results less from his nobility than from his fragility and humanity. It is the human side of Hamlet that touches us and thereby makes his death seem more tragic. Shakespeare creates empathy between Hamlet and the audience in a number of ways but accomplishes the task best with the "To be or not to be" soliloquy. In this speech, which best demonstrates Hamlet's humanity, Shakespeare connects Hamlet to his audience with thoughts that cross the mind of every person at one time or another.

Even without the obvious closeness between the character of Hamlet and the audience that comes from the very nature of the soliloquy, the "To be or not to be" soliloquy is so ingeniously crafted to appeal to the audience that we ignore the minor discrepancies that might come from careful analysis.

For who would bear the whips and scorns of time,
Th'oppressor's wrong, the proud man's contumely,
The pangs of disprized love, the laws delay,
The insolence of office, and the spurns
That patient merit of the'unworthy takes, (3.1.71-76)

In this passage, Shakespeare (through Hamlet) is able to connect with us by using the tactic of a common denominator. Unreturned love ("disprized love"), injustice ("law's delay"), and bureaucracy ("insolence of office") are all experiences that are familiar even to us today. However, are these really experiences that Hamlet has suffered himself? The answer is no.

Hamlet was the prince of Denmark and lived a life of privilege. His only known romantic interest was Ophelia, who obviously returned his affections. Throughout the play almost every request he makes is granted. People are constantly doting on him and waiting on him hand and foot. While this may seem to be a burden to him, it is one the average person is unfamiliar with and one that would naturally distance Hamlet from us. Yet we ignore this reality because the soliloquy is so superbly written.

Shakespeare first manages to manipulate us with the brilliant introduction of the soliloquy:

> To be, or not to be; that is the question:
> Whether 'tis nobler in the mind to suffer
> The slings and arrows of outrageous fortune,
> Or to take arms against a sea of troubles,
> And by opposing, end them. (3.1.58-62)

When first contemplating the subject, Hamlet weighs what choices are involved in suicide. On one side, there are "the slings and arrows of outrageous fortune," which we probably interpret as the death of Hamlet's father, the subsequent marriage of his uncle and mother, the appearance of the ghost, and the revelation that his uncle killed his father.

This series of events, added to the betrayal of Hamlet's childhood friends Rosencrantz and Guildenstern, would qualify as both "outrageous fortune" and "a sea of troubles" to most people because they are not everyday occurrences to anyone. However, there is no resemblance between these events and the common experiences described in the passage above, yet Shakespeare is somehow able to join these two different sets of experiences together and create a bond between Hamlet and the audience.

Shakespeare does this by using logic and a subtle shift in language in the intervening passage between the two sections:

> To die, to sleep--
> No more--and by a sleep to say we end
> The heartache and the thousand natural shocks
> That flesh is heir to. 'Tis a consummation
> Devoutly to be wished. To die, to sleep;
> To sleep, perchance to dream. Ay, there's the rub,
> For in that sleep of death what dreams may come,
> When we have shuffled off this mortal coil,
> Must give us pause. There's the respect

That makes calamity of so long life (3.1.62-71)

First, Shakespeare has Hamlet take a commonsense and almost childlike approach to suicide by comparing it to sleep, an everyday experience. We buy into this argument because death is like a "no more" sleep, a sleep without any waking. Hamlet continues with his logic by asking: If death is like sleep, are there dreams in death? Moreover, he implies there might be nightmares in death, thereby making suicide not an escape from unpleasant experiences.

However, in this progression of logic, Hamlet takes a more familiar tone with the audience. It is not "I" but "we," and Hamlet is no longer ending "the slings and arrows of outrageous fortune" or "a sea of troubles," but now refers to the end of "the heartache and the thousand natural shocks that flesh is heir to." Thus Shakespeare has shifted our thoughts from Hamlet's situation and mortality to our own.

As if he is still trying to distract us from the true topic, himself, Hamlet continues with the logic and reasoning of suicide:

But that the dread of something after death,
The undiscover'd country from whose bourn
No traveler returns, puzzles the will
And makes us rather bear those ills we have
Than fly to others that we know not of?
Thus conscience does make cowards of us all;
And thus the native hue of resolution
Is sicklied o'er with the pale cast of thought,
And enterprises of great pith and moment
With this regard their currents turn awry
And lose the name of action. (3.1.80-90)

Hamlet, like the audience, is afraid of the great unknown of death and that is why he will not commit suicide. However, Hamlet does suspect what death is like because of his experience with his father's ghost. If Hamlet does kill himself without first avenging his father's death, a terrible fate may await him in the afterlife. Though not addressed in this speech, there is also the Christian taboo against suicide and the punishment of going to hell for committing the sin.

It can be suggested that Hamlet knows that death is a fate worse than living, and that his true dilemma lies with deciding to act or go against his uncle. Instead, Hamlet is trying in a roundabout way to tell us that he is a coward for not acting. Like a real person trying to reveal a personal secret and shame, Hamlet hems and haws around the topic, hints at, and then hopes we can guess what he is really talking about. With either explanation, Hamlet still connects and bonds with us.

What the "To be or not to be" soliloquy accomplishes is to bring Hamlet to the level of the audience by allowing both audience and prince to connect with a common interest--suicide. When subtext and nuances are combined, the audience (and reader) is able to sympathize with the character, thereby making his death seem more tragic.

Hamlet's death, unlike the deaths of most fictional characters, and even some real people, evokes an authentic response from us because of the emotional and personal connection. I think this was best demonstrated in our class, where our initial response to the ending was more numbness than sadness. It was only in hindsight that I realized that this reaction was like the initial reaction to a real death--numbness, disbelief, and denial.

Despite the fact that the play is a tragedy, there is a sense of disbelief and denial when Hamlet dies, and not because he died so senselessly. Shakespeare defies the conventions of the time and his own standards because Hamlet lacked the tragic flaw that doomed other tragic heroes. Hamlet's only flaw was to be human.

So if Hamlet can die just because he is all too human, isn't Shakespeare forcing us to confront our own mortality? In "denying" Hamlet's death, the audience is denying its own mortality as if a real person has died, and that's why Hamlet is such a great and memorable play.

Work Cited

Shakespeare, William. Hamlet. Exploring Literature. Ed. Frank Madden. New York: Longman, 2001, 973-1091.

Exploring the Literature of Heritage and Identity: Options for Writing and Research

Some Options for Writing About Heritage and Identity

1. Consider the ways in which your heritage and identity have influenced your life. Do any of the stories, poems, plays, or essays in this section remind you of your own experiences or the circumstances of your life?

   Choose one or more of these works and write a response essay that compares your experience or circumstances with those the literature.

2. Our backgrounds, personalities, and sense of heritage can affect how we see the world and the formation of our values. These values can strongly influence our response to literature. We may agree or disagree with what an author says or what characters say or do. So, too, this literature may influence us and help to form our values about heritage and identity.

   Write an essay about the ways in which one or more works in this section either provoked a moral judgment on your part or helped you learn something.

3. Over two hundred years ago, in *Reflections on the Revolution in France,* Edmund Burke wrote: "People will not look forward to posterity who never look backward to their ancestors." Do you agree?

   Consider this quote, and write an essay about the impact of heritage or the search for heritage in one or more works in this section.

4. In his influential work *Walden,* Henry David Thoreau wrote: "If a man does not keep pace with his companions, perhaps it is because he hears a different drummer. Let him step to the music which he hears, however measured or far away."

   Write about this quote as it applies to the search for identity experienced in one or more works in this section.

5. Choose a quote (or quotes) in the introduction to this section, "Heritage and Identity" and pair it (or them) with one of the longer pieces in this section that either supports or argues against it. For example, Emily Dickinson's poem "I'm Nobody. Who are you?" might be compared with W. H. Auden's "The Unknown Citizen." Or Sartre's quote about finding ourselves by rejecting "what others have said about us" might be compared with the issues of personal identity in Paul Laurence Dunbar's poem "We Wear the Mask."

A Research Option

Willa Cather's story "Paul's Case," T.S. Eliot's "The Love Song of J. Alfred Prufrock," Sophocles' play *Oedipus Rex,* and Neil Miller's essay "In Search of Gay America" all have something important to say about the search for heritage and identity. Each of these works, however, springs from a very different historical, social, or political context.

Expanding our exploration of literature to include the context in which these works were produced can be an enriching and enlightening experience. Choose one or more of these or other works in this section and write a research essay that includes secondary source material about the historical, social, or political background of the literature.

Collaboration: Writing and Revising with Your Peers

In addition to applying your own values and standards to writing about the literature in this section, you may find it beneficial to share and discuss your work with classmates. Getting feedback from others can help you generate and clarify your ideas and revise and edit your writing more effectively.

Choose a work, a topic, or one of the above options for writing about heritage and identity, and work with a partner or in a small group. Exchange journal entries or response sheets, generate questions together, do a group semantic map (see pp. 40–45), or simply share and respond to each other's ideas.

After you have written a rough draft of your essay, share it with a partner or your group. Respondents should function primarily as sensitive readers and give honest, constructive responses. They should try to be aware of each writer's purpose, discuss concerns particular to each writer, and comment on the effectiveness of the essay's organization, support, clarity, and voice. (For a comprehensive checklist for revision, see pp. 51–52).

In the final stage of your writing, editing and proofreading might be done in a similar fashion. A partner or group readers might help you check for correct grammar, spelling, punctuation, and typos. (A comprehensive checklist for editing is on p. 52).

A Writing/Research Portfolio Option

A portfolio is a collection of your work, related materials, and commentary about your work collected over time. Gathering materials in a portfolio will provide you with resources for research and development. You can use your portfolio to collect your writing about the literature in this section, find a topic to write about, revise or add to your work, or keep multiple drafts and monitor the changes you make as you revise.

Among the resources you might include:

- Your responses to the quotes and prompts about heritage and identity at the beginning of this section, the questions you had right after you finished reading each piece of literature, and your journal entries.
- What your classmates, instructor, or published critics had to say about the literature and how their comments may have influenced your interpretation.
- Information you've gathered from the library and the Internet about the historical, social, and political context of the work or its author.

Culture & Class

Culture & Class

A Dialogue Across History

Man is born a barbarian, and only raises himself above the beast by culture.

—Baltasar Gracian, *The Art of Worldly Wisdom,* 1647

Men are seldom more innocently employed than when they are honestly making money.

—Samuel Johnson, letter, 1770

The great law of culture is: Let each become all that he was created capable of being.

—Thomas Carlyle, *Critical Essays,* 1827

Morality knows nothing of geographical boundaries or distinctions of race.

—Herbert Spencer, *Social Statics,* 1851

It is not the consciousness of men that determines their existence, but on the contrary it is their social existence that determines their consciousness.

—Karl Marx, *Critique of Political Economy,* 1859

That which in England we call the middle class is in America virtually the nation.

—Matthew Arnold, *A Word About America,* 1882

Where justice is denied, where poverty is enforced, where ignorance prevails, and where any one class is made to feel that society is in an organized conspiracy to oppress, rob, and degrade them, neither persons nor property will be safe.

—Frederick Douglas, speech, 1883

While there is a lower class I am in it, while there is a criminal element I am of it; while there is a soul in prison, I am not free.

—Eugene Debs, speech, 1900

Money is the most important thing in the world. It represents health, strength, honor, generosity and beauty as conspicuously as the want of it represents illness, weakness, disgrace, meanness and ugliness.

—George Bernard Shaw, *Major Barbara,* 1907

Knowledge of [another] culture should sharpen our ability to scrutinize more steadily, to appreciate more lovingly, our own.

—Margaret Mead, *Coming of Age in Somoa,* 1928

The engine which drives Enterprise is not Thrift, but Profit.

—John Maynard Keynes, *A Treatise on Money,* 1930

The most powerful obstacle to culture . . . is the tendency to aggression, [which is] an innate, independent, instinctual disposition in man.

—Sigmund Freud, *Civilization and Its Discontents,* 1930

I wouldn't want to belong to any club that would accept me as a member.

—Groucho Marx, c. 1935

From the moment of his birth the customs into which [an individual] is born shape his experience and behavior. By the time he can talk, he is the little creature of his culture.

—Ruth Benedict, *Patterns of Culture,* 1934

If we had been allowed to participate in the vital processes of America's national growth, what would have been the textures of our lives, the pattern of our traditions, the routine of our customs, the state of our arts, the code of our laws, the function of our government! . . . We black folk say that America would have been stronger and greater.

—Richard Wright, *Twelve Million Black Voices,* 1941

[Culture] is a product of man: he projects himself into it, he recognizes himself in it; that critical mirror alone offers him his image.

—John Paul Sartre, *The Words,* 1964

A revolution is not the same as inviting people to dinner, or writing an essay, or painting a picture . . . A revolution is an insurrection, an act of violence by which one class overthrows another.

—Mao Tse-tung, *Selected Works,* 1965

No poor, rural, weak, or black person should ever again have to bear the additional burden of being deprived of the opportunity for an education, a job, or simple justice.

—Jimmy Carter, speech, 1971

. . . every historic effort to forge a democratic project has been undermined by two fundamental realities: poverty *and* paranoia. *The persistence of poverty generates levels of* despair *that deepen social conflict; the escalation of paranoia produces levels of* distrust *that reinforce cultural division.*

—Cornel West, *Race Matters,* 1994

Culture and Class: Exploring Your Experiences and Beliefs

What comes to mind when you hear the words *culture* or *class?* In everyday conversation, these words are often used to evaluate people rather than identify their backgrounds or economic status. So it's common to hear people depicted as "cultured" or having "class" as being praised for their good taste, aesthetic appreciation, behavior, or character. But our use of the terms *culture* and *class* here, as reflected in the quotes above and the literature that follows, is based on a more formal definition. For our purposes, *culture* represents the shared attitudes, the values, or the behavioral patterns of a social or ethnic group while *class* refers to categories of economic, occupational, or social status. Though culture and class are often related to and have an important influence on each other, people who share the same cultural background may belong to different economic or social classes. Conversely, people who belong to the same economic or social class may come from very different cultures.

Whether we like to admit it or not, most of us are influenced by the culture or class to which we belong. Where we grow up, our family's background and economic resources, and the nature of our work influence our view of the world. In turn, these factors are likely to affect our aspirations and the way others treat us.

Do you think of yourself as following the customs of a particular culture? Do you see yourself as belonging to an economic or social class within that culture? How would you define your social class? As a preparation for reading the literature in this section, you may find it helpful to think about these questions and consider your own values and beliefs about culture and class.

Reading and Writing About Culture and Class

At least one aspect of the many stories, poems, plays, and essays in this section is about the impact that culture and class have on the characters: a young girl's disillusionment as she realizes her "place" at a birthday party in Liliana Heker's short story "The Stolen Party," the class struggle of migrant farm workers in Luis Valdez's play *Los Vendidos,* and Frederick Douglas's valiant efforts to educate himself in the hostile atmosphere of slavery in the essay "Learning to Read and Write." The brief quotes that open this section also give you some idea of the number of compelling ethical, political, and social arguments that are connected to culture and class. Civil rights, equal opportunity, stereotyping, bigotry, and oppression head a long list of concerns. Any of these or other related issues would provide a fine topic for an essay.

• FICTION •

Toni Cade Bambara (1939–1995)

Toni Cade Bambara was born in New York City and raised in the impoverished neighborhoods of Harlem and Bedford-Stuyvesant, New York, and Jersey City, New Jersey. Born Toni Cade, she added the name Bambara after discovering it as part of a signature in her great-grandmother's sketchbook. She attended Queen's College, where she majored in theater arts and English, graduating in 1959. Before turning to writing, she worked for the New York Department of Welfare, served as a director of recreation in a psychiatric ward, studied theater at the famous Commedia dell'Arte in Italy, ran a local community center, and earned an M.A. from the City University of New York. She began her writing career editing anthologies of black women writers and African-American stories, but first attracted attention with her collections of short stories Gorilla, My Love *(1972) and* The Sea Birds are Still Alive *(1977). She died of cancer in 1995. Her most recent publication,* Deep Sightings and Rescue Missions: Fiction, Essays, and Conversations *(1996), was published posthumously. In an interview in* Black Women Writers at Work, *she said: "It's a tremendous responsibility—responsibility and honor—to be a writer, an artist, a cultural worker . . . One's got to see what the factory worker sees, what the prisoner sees, what the welfare children see, what the scholar sees, got to see what the ruling-class mythmakers see as well, in order to tell the truth and not get trapped."*

The Lesson [1972]

Back in the days when everyone was old and stupid or young and foolish and me and Sugar were the only ones just right, this lady moved on our block with nappy hair and proper speech and no makeup. And quite naturally we laughed at her, laughed the way we did at the junk man who went about his business like he was some big-time president and his sorryass horse his secretary. And we kinda hated her too, hated the way we did the winos who cluttered up our parks and pissed on our handball walls and stank up our hallways and stairs so you couldn't-halfway play hide-and-seek without a goddamn gas mask. Miss Moore was her name. The only woman on the block with no first name. And she was black as hell, cept for her feet, which were fish-white and spooky. And she was always planning these boring-ass things for us to do, us being my cousin, mostly, who lived on the block cause we all moved North the same time and to the same apartment then spread out gradual to breathe. And our parents would yank our heads into some kinda shape and crisp up our clothes so we'd be presentable for travel with Miss Moore, who always looked like she was going to church, though she never did. Which is just one of the things the grownups talked about when they talked behind her back like a dog. But when she came calling, with some sachet she'd sewed up or some gingerbread she'd made or some book, why then they'd still be too embarrassed to turn her down and we'd get handed over all spruced up. She'd been to college and said it was only right that she should take responsibility for the young ones' education, and she not even related by marriage or blood. So they'd go for it. Specially Aunt Gretchen. She was the main gofer in the family. You got some ole dumb shit foolishness you want somebody to go for, you send for Aunt Gretchen. She been screwed into the go-along for so long, it's a blood-deep natural thing with her. Which is how she got saddled with me and Sugar and junior in the first place while our mothers were in a la-de-da apartment up the block having a good ole time.

So this one day Miss Moore rounds us all up at the mailbox and it's puredee hot and she's knockin herself out about arithmetic. And school suppose to let up in summer I heard, but she don't never let up. And the starch in my pinafore scratching the shit outta me and I'm really hating this nappy-head bitch and her goddamn college degree. I'd much rather go to the pool or to the show where it's cool. So me and Sugar leaning on the mailbox being surly, which is a Miss Moore word. And Flyboy checking out what everybody brought for lunch. And Fat Butt already wasting his peanut butter-and-jelly sandwich like the pig he is. And Junebug punchin on Q.T's arm for potato chips. And Rosie Giraffe shifting from one hip to the other waiting for somebody to step on her foot or ask her if she from Georgia so she can kick ass, preferably Mercedes'. And Miss Moore asking us do we know what money is, like we a bunch of retards. I mean real money, she say, like it's only poker chips or monopoly papers we lay on the grocer. So right away I'm tired of this and say so. And would much rather snatch Sugar and go to the Sunset and terrorize the West Indian kids and take their hair ribbons and their money too. And Miss Moore files that remark away for next week's lesson on brotherhood, I can tell. And finally I say we oughta get to the subway cause it's cooler and besides we might meet some cute boys. Sugar done swiped her mama's lipstick, so we ready.

So we heading down the street and she's boring us silly about what things cost and what our parents make and how much goes for rent and how money ain't divided up right in this country. And then she gets to the part about we all poor and live in the slums, which I don't feature. And I'm ready to speak on that, but she steps out in the street and hails two cabs just like that. Then she hustles half the crew in with her and hands me a five-dollar bill and tells me to calculate 10 percent tip for the driver. And we're off. Me and Sugar and Junebug and Flyboy hangin out the window and hollering to everybody, putting lipstick on each other cause Flyboy a faggot anyway, and making farts with our sweaty armpits. But I'm mostly trying to figure how to spend this money. But they all fascinated with the meter ticking and Junebug starts laying bets as to how much it'll read when Flyboy can't hold his breath no more. Then Sugar lays bets as to how much it'll be when we get there. So I'm stuck. Don't nobody want to go for my plan, which is to jump out at the next light and run off to the first bar-b-que we can find. Then the driver tells us to get the hell out cause we there already. And the meter reads eighty-five cents. And I'm stalling to figure out the tip and Sugar say give him a dime. And I decide he don't need it bad as I do, so later for him. But then he tries to take off with Junebug foot still in the door so we talk about his mama something ferocious. Then we check out that we on Fifth Avenue and everybody dressed up in stockings. One lady in a fur coat, hot as it is. White folks crazy.

"This is the place," Miss Moore say, presenting it to us in the voice she uses at the museum. "Let's look in the windows before we go in."

"Can we steal?" Sugar asks very serious like she's getting the ground rules squared away before she plays. "I beg your pardon," say Miss Moore, and we fall out. So she leads us around the windows of the toy store and me and Sugar screamin, "This is mine, that's mine, I gotta have that, that was made for me, I was born for that," till Big Butt drowns us out.

"Hey, I'm going to buy that there."

"That there? You don't even know what it is, stupid."

"I do so," he say punchin on Rosie Giraffe. "It's a microscope."

"Whatcha gonna do with a microscope, fool?"

"Look at things."

"Like what, Ronald?" ask Miss Moore. And Big Butt ain't got the first notion. So here go Miss Moore gabbing about the thousands of bacteria in a drop of water and the somethin or other in a speck of blood and the million and one living things in the air around us is invisible to the naked eye. And what she say that for? Junebug go to town on that "naked" and we rolling. Then Miss Moore ask what it cost. So we all jam into the window smudgin it up and the price tag say $300. So then she ask how long'd take for Big Butt and Junebug to save up their allowances. "Too long," I say. "Yeh," adds Sugar, "outgrown it by that time." And, Miss Moore say no, you never outgrow learning instruments. "Why, even medical students and interns and," blah, blah, blah. And we ready to choke Big Butt for bringing it up in the first damn place.

"This here costs four hundred eighty dollars," say Rosie Giraffe. So we pile up all over her to see what she pointin out. My eyes tells me it's a chunk of glass cracked with something heavy, and different-color inks dripped into the splits, then the whole thing put into a oven or something. But for $480 it don't make sense.

"That's a paperweight made of semi-precious stones fused together under tremendous pressure," she explains slowly, with her hands doing the mining and all the factory work.

"So what's a paperweight?" asks Rosie Giraffe.

"To weigh paper with, dumbbell," say Flyboy, the wise man from the East.

"Not exactly," say Miss Moore, which is what she say when you warm or way off too. "It's to weigh paper down so it won't scatter and make your desk untidy." So right away me and Sugar curtsy to each other and then to Mercedes who is more the tidy type.

"We don't keep paper on top of the desk in my class," say Junebug, figuring Miss Moore crazy or lyin one.

"At home, then," she say. "Don't you have a calendar and a pencil case and a blotter and a letter-opener on your desk at home where you do your homework?"

And she know damn well what our homes look like cause she nosys around in them every chance she gets.

"I don't even have a desk," say Junebug. "Do we?"

20 "No. And I don't get no homework neither," says Big Butt.

"And I don't even have a home," say Flyboy like he do at school to keep the white folks off his back and sorry for him. Send this poor kid to camp posters, is his specialty.

"I do," says Mercedes. "I have a box of stationery on my desk and a picture of my cat. My godmother bought the stationery and the desk. There's a big rose on each sheet and the envelopes smell like roses."

"Who wants to know about your smelly-ass stationery," say Rosie Giraffe fore I can get my two cents in.

"It's important to have a work area all your own so that . . .

25 "Will you look at this sailboat, please," say Flyboy, cuttin her off and pointin to the thing like it was his.

So once again we tumble all over each other to gaze at this magnificent thing in the toy store which is just big enough to maybe sail two kittens across the pond if you strap them to the posts tight. We all start reciting the price tag like we in assembly. "Hand-crafted sailboat of fiberglass at one thousand one hundred ninety-five dollars."

"Unbelievable," I hear myself say and am really stunned. I read it again for myself just in case the group recitation put me in a trance. Same thing. For some reason this pisses me off. We look at Miss Moore and she lookin at us, waiting for I dunno what.

"Who'd pay all that when you can buy a sailboat set for a quarter at Pop's, a tube of glue for a dime, and a ball of string for eight cents? It must have a motor and a whole lot else besides," I say. "My sailboat cost me about fifty cents."

"But will it take water?" say Mercedes with her smart ass.

30 "Took mine to Alley Pond Park once," say Flyboy. "String broke. Lost it. Pity."

"Sailed mine in Central Park and it keeled over and sank. Had to ask my father for another dollar."

"And you got the strap," laugh Big Butt, "The jerk didn't even have a string on it. My old man wailed on his behind."

Little Q.T. was staring hard at the sailboat and you could see he wanted it bad. But he too little and somebody'd just take it from him. So what the hell. "This boat for kids, Miss Moore?"

"Parents silly to buy something like that just to get all broke up," say Rosie Giraffe.

"That much money it should last forever," I figure.

35 "My father'd buy it for me if I wanted it."

"Your father, my ass," say Rosie Giraffe getting a chance to finally push Mercedes.

"Must be rich people shop here," say Q.T.

"You are a very bright boy," say Flyboy. "What was your first clue?" And he rap him on the head with the back of his knuckles, since Q.T. the only one he could get away with. Though Q.T. liable to come up behind you years later and get his licks in when you half expect it.

"What I want to know is," I says to Miss Moore though I never talk to her, I wouldn't give the bitch that satisfaction, "is how much a real boat costs? I figure a thousand'd get you a yacht any day."

40 "Why don't you check that out," she says, "and report back to the group?" Which really pains my ass. If you gonna mess up a perfectly good swim day least you could do is have some answers. "Let's go in," she say like she got something up her sleeve. Only she don't lead the way. So me and Sugar turn the corner to where the entrance is, but when we get there I kinda hang back. Not that I'm scared, what's there to be afraid of, just a toy store. But I feel funny, shame. But what I got to be shamed about? Got as much right to go in as anybody. But somehow I can't seem to get hold of the door, so I step away for Sugar to lead. But she hangs back too. And I look at her and she looks at me and this is ridiculous. I mean, damn, I have never ever been shy about doing nothing or going nowhere. But then Mercedes steps up and then Rosie Giraffe and Big Butt crowd in behind and shove, and next thing we all stuffed into the doorway with only Mercedes squeezing past us, smoothing out her jumper and walking right down the aisle. Then the rest of us tumble in like a glued-together jigsaw done all wrong. And people lookin at us. And it's like the time me and Sugar crashed into the Catholic church on a dare. But once we got in there and everything so hushed and holy and the candles and the bowin and the handkerchiefs on all the drooping heads, I just couldn't go through with the plan. Which was for me to run up to the altar and do a tap dance while Sugar played the nose flute and messed around in the holy water. And Sugar kept given me the elbow. Then later teased me so bad I tied her up in the shower and turned it on and locked her in. And she'd be there till this day if Aunt Gretchen hadn't finally figured I was lyin about the boarder takin a shower.

Same thing in the store. We all walkin on tiptoe and hardly touchin the games and puzzles and things. And I watched Miss Moore who is steady watchin us like she waitin for a sign. Like Mama Drewery watches the sky and sniffs the air and takes note of just how much slant is in the bird formation. Then me and Sugar bump smack into each other, so busy gazing at the toys, 'specially the sailboat. But we don't laugh and go into our fat-lady bump-stomach routine. We just stare at that price tag. Then Sugar run a finger over the whole boat. And I'm jealous and want to hit her. Maybe not her, but I sure want to punch somebody in the mouth.

"Watcha bring us here for, Miss Moore?"

"You sound angry, Sylvia. Are you mad about something?" Given me one of them grins like she tellin a grown-up joke that never turns out to be funny. And she's lookin very closely at me like maybe she plannin to do my portrait from memory. I'm mad, but I won't give her that satisfaction. So I slouch around the store bein very bored and say, "Let's go."

Me and Sugar at the back of the train watchin the tracks whizzin by large then small then gettin gobbled up in the dark. I'm thinkin about this tricky toy I saw in the store. A clown that somersaults on a bar then does chin-ups just cause you yank lightly at his leg. Cost $35. I could see me askin my mother for a $35 birthday clown. "You wanna who that costs what?" she'd say, cocking her head to the side to get a better view of the hole in my head. Thirty-five dollars could buy new bunk beds for junior and Gretchen's boy. Thirty-five dollars and the whole household could go visit Granddaddy Nelson in the country. Thirty-five dollars would pay for the rent and the piano bill too. Who are these people that spend that much for performing clowns and $1000 for toy sailboats? What kinda work they do and how they live and how come we ain't in on it? Where we are is who we are, Miss Moore always pointin out. But it don't necessarily have to be that way, she always adds then waits for somebody to say that poor people have to wake up and demand their share of the pie and don't none of us know what kind of pie she talking about in the first damn place. But she ain't so smart cause I still got her four dollars from the taxi and she sure ain't gettin it. Messin up my day with this shit. Sugar nudges me in my pocket and winks.

45 Miss Moore lines us up in front of the mailbox where we started from, seem like years ago, and I got a headache for thinkin so hard. And we lean all over each other so we can hold up under the draggy-ass lecture she always finishes us off with at the end before we thank her for borin us to tears. But she just looks at us like she readin tea leaves. Finally she say, "Well, what did you think of F.A.O. Schwartz?"

Rosie Giraffe mumbles, "White folks crazy."

"I'd like to go there again when I get my birthday money," says Mercedes, and we shove her out the pack so she has to lean on the mailbox by herself.

"I'd like a shower. Tiring day," say Flyboy.

Then Sugar surprises me by sayin, "You know, Miss Moore, I don't think all of us here put together eat in a year what that sailboat costs." And Miss Moore lights up like somebody goosed her. "And?" she say, urging Sugar on. Only I'm standin on her foot so she don't continue.

50 "Imagine for a minute what kind of society it is in which some people can spend on a toy what it would cost to feed a family of six or seven. What do you think?"

"I think," say Sugar pushing me off her feet like she never done before, cause I whip her ass in a minute, "that this is not much of a democracy if you ask me. Equal chance to pursue happiness means an equal crack at the dough, don't it?" Miss Moore is beside herself and I am disgusted with Sugar's treachery. So I stand on her foot one more time to see if she'll shove me. She shuts up, and Miss Moore looks at me, sorrowfully I'm thinkin. And somethin weird is goin on, I can feel it in my chest.

"Anybody else learn anything today?" lookin dead at me. I walk away and Sugar has to run to catch up and don't even seem to notice when I shrug her arm off my shoulder.

"Well, we got four dollars anyway," she says.

"Uh hunh."

55 "We could go to Hascombs and get half a chocolate layer and then go to the Sunset and still have plenty money for potato chips and ice cream sodas."

"Uh hunh."

"Race you to Hascombs," she say.

We start down the block and she gets ahead which is O.K. by me cause I'm going to the West End and then over to the Drive to think this day through. She can run if she want to and even run faster. But ain't nobody gonna beat me at nuthin.

➤ QUESTIONS FOR READING AND WRITING

1. Think about the final paragraph of the story. Has the narrator changed? If so, why? What does she tell us about herself and her future?
2. You might say that this story is told from the point of view of a "hostile witness." How did you respond to the speaker? To the events she describes? How would the story change if told from Miss Moore's point of view?
3. Describe the narrator's relationship to Sugar. In what ways is this relationship important to the narrator? How is the relationship developed throughout the story?
4. What is Miss Moore's central message? Why does she bring poor inner-city adolescents to a store where they can't afford anything? Do you think this is an effective lesson?

ROBERT OLEN BUTLER (b. 1945)

Robert Olen Butler was born in Granite City, Illinois. He learned the Vietnamese language and culture when he served in the Vietnam War from 1969 to 1972. He has received grants from the National Endowment for the Arts and a Guggenheim Fellowship. "Snow" is taken from a collection of stories, A Good Scent from a Strange Mountain, *which earned Butler Pulitzer Prize for Fiction in 1993. His most recent collection of stories* Tabloid Dreams *was published in 1996. He lives in Louisiana and teaches at McNeese State University.*

SNOW [1992]

I wonder how long he watched me sleeping. I still wonder that. He sat and he did not wake me to ask about his carry-out order. Did he watch my eyes move as I dreamed? When I finally knew he was there and I turned to look at him, I could not make out his whole face at once. His head was turned a little to the side. His beard was neatly trimmed, but the jaw it covered was long and its curve was like a sampan sail and it held my eyes the way a sail always did when I saw one on the sea. Then I raised my eyes and looked at his nose. I am Vietnamese, you know, and we have a different sense of these proportions. Our noses are small and his was long and it also curved, gently, a reminder of his jaw, which I looked at again. His beard was dark gray, like he'd crawled out of a charcoal kiln. I make these comparisons to things from my country and village, but it is only to clearly say what this face was like. It is not that he reminded me of home. That was the farthest thing from my mind when I first saw Mr. Cohen. And I must have stared at him in those first moments with a strange look because when his face turned full to me and I could finally lift my gaze to his eyes, his eyebrows made a little jump like he was asking me, What is it? What's wrong?

I was at this same table before the big window at the front of the restaurant. The Plantation Hunan does not look like a restaurant, though. No one would give it a name like that unless it really was an old plantation house. It's very large and full of antiques. It's quiet right now. Not even five, and I can hear the big clock—I had never seen one till I came here. No one in Vietnam has a clock as tall as a man. Time isn't as important as that in Vietnam. But the clock here is very tall and they call it Grandfather, which I like, and Grandfather is ticking very slowly right now, and he wants me to fall asleep again. But I won't.

This plantation house must feel like a refugee. It is full of foreign smells, ginger and Chinese pepper and fried shells for wonton, and there's a motel on one side and a gas station on the other, not like the life the house once knew, though there are very large oak trees surrounding it, trees that must have been here when this was still a plantation. The house sits on a busy street and the Chinese family who owns it changed it from Plantation Seafood into a place that could hire a Vietnamese woman like me to be a waitress. They are very kind, this family, though we know we are different from each other. They are Chinese and I am Vietnamese and they are very kind, but we are both here in Louisiana and they go somewhere with the other Chinese in town—there are four restaurants and two laundries and some people, I think, who work as engineers at the oil refinery. They go off to themselves and they don't seem to even notice where they are.

I was sleeping that day he came in here. It was late afternoon of the day before Christmas. Almost Christmas Eve. I am not a Christian. My mother and I are Buddhist. I live with my mother and she is very sad for me because I am thirty-four years old and I am not married. There are other Vietnamese here in Lake Charles, Louisiana, but we are not a community. We are all too sad, perhaps, or too tired. But maybe not. Maybe that's just me saying that. Maybe the others are real Americans already. My mother has two Vietnamese friends, old women like her, and her two friends look at me with the same sadness in their faces because of what they see as my life. They know that once I might have been married, but the fiancé I had in my town in Vietnam went away in the Army and though he is still alive in Vietnam, the last I heard, he is driving a cab in Hô Chí Minh City and he is married to someone else. I never really knew him, and I don't feel any loss. It's just that he's the only boy my mother ever speaks of when she gets frightened for me.

5 I get frightened for me, too, sometimes, but it's not because I have no husband. That Christmas Eve afternoon I woke slowly. The front tables are for cocktails and for waiting for carry-out, so the chairs are large and stuffed so that they are soft. My head was very comfortable against one of the high wings of the chair and I opened my eyes without moving. The rest of me was still sleeping, but my eyes opened and the sky was still blue, though the shreds of cloud were turning pink. It looked like a warm sky. And it was. I felt sweat on my throat and I let my eyes move just a little and the live oak in front of the restaurant was quivering—all its leaves were shaking and you might think that it would look cold doing that, but it was a warm wind, I knew. The air was thick and wet, and cutting through the ginger and pepper smell was the fuzzy smell of mildew.

Perhaps it was from my dream but I remembered my first Christmas Eve in America. I slept and woke just like this, in a Chinese restaurant. I was working there. But it was in a distant place, in St. Louis. And I woke to snow. The first snow I had ever seen. It scared me. Many Vietnamese love to see their first snow, but it frightened me in some very deep way that I could not explain, and even remembering that moment—especially as I woke from sleep at the front of another restaurant—frightened me. So I turned my face sharply from the window in the Plantation Hunan and that's when I saw Mr. Cohen.

I stared at those parts of his face, like I said, and maybe this was a way for me to hide from the snow, maybe the strangeness that he saw in my face had to do with the snow. But when his eyebrows jumped and I did not say anything to explain what was going on inside me, I could see him wondering what to do. I could feel him thinking: Should I ask her what is wrong or should I just ask her for my carry-out? I am not an especially shy person, but I hoped he would choose to ask for the carry-out. I came to myself with a little jolt and I stood up and faced him—he was sitting in one of the stuffed chairs at the next table. "I'm sorry," I said, trying to turn us both from my dreaming. "Do you have an order?"

He hesitated, his eyes holding fast on my face. These were very dark eyes, as dark as the eyes of any Vietnamese, but turned up to me like this, his face seemed so large that I had trouble taking it in. Then he said, "Yes. For Cohen," His voice was deep, like a movie actor who is playing a grandfather, the kind of voice that if he asked what it was that I had been dreaming, I would tell him at once.

But he did not ask anything more. I went off to the kitchen and the order was not ready. I wanted to complain to them. There was no one else in the restaurant, and everyone in the kitchen seemed like they were just hanging around. But I don't make any trouble for anybody. So I just went back out to Mr. Cohen. He rose when he saw me, even though he surely also saw that I had no carry-out with me.

"It's not ready yet," I said. "I'm sorry."

"That's okay," he said, and he smiled at me, his gray beard opening and showing teeth that were very white.

"I wanted to scold them," I said. "You should not have to wait for a long time on Christmas Eve."

"It's okay," he said. "This is not my holiday."

I tilted my head, not understanding. He tilted his own head just like mine, like he wanted to keep looking straight into my eyes. Then he said, "I am Jewish."

I straightened my head again, and I felt a little pleasure at knowing that his straightening his own head was caused by me. I still didn't understand, exactly, and he clearly read that in my face. He said, "A Jew doesn't celebrate Christmas."

"I thought all Americans celebrated Christmas," I said.

"Not all. Not exactly." He did a little shrug with his shoulders, and his eyebrows rose like the shrug, as he tilted his head to the side once more, for just a second. It all seemed to say, What is there to do, it's the way the world is and I know it and it all makes me just a little bit weary. He said, "We all stay home, but we don't all celebrate."

He said no more, but he looked at me and I was surprised to find that I had no words either on my tongue or in my head. It felt a little strange to see this very

American man who was not celebrating the holiday. In Vietnam we never miss a holiday and it did not make a difference if we were Buddhist or Cao Đái or Catholic. I thought of this Mr. Cohen sitting in his room tonight alone while all the other Americans celebrated Christmas Eve. But I had nothing to say and he didn't either and he kept looking at me and I glanced down at my hands twisting at my order book and I didn't even remember taking the book out. So I said, "I'll check on your order again," and I turned and went off to the kitchen and I waited there till the order was done, though I stood over next to the door away from the chatter of the cook and the head waiter and the mother of the owner.

Carrying the white paper bag out to the front, I could not help but look inside to see how much food there was. There was enough for two people. So I did not look into Mr. Cohen's eyes as I gave him the food and rang up the order and took his money. I was counting his change into his palm—his hand, too, was very large—and he said, "You're not Chinese, are you?"

20 I said, "No. I am Vietnamese," but I did not raise my face to him, and he went away.

Two days later, it was even earlier in the day when Mr. Cohen came in. About four-thirty. The Grandfather had just chimed the half hour like a man who is really crazy about one subject and talks of it at any chance he gets. I was sitting in my chair at the front once again and my first thought when I saw Mr. Cohen coming through the door was that he would think I am a lazy girl. I started to jump up, but he saw me and he motioned with his hand for me to stay where I was, a single heavy pat in the air, like he'd just laid this large hand of his on the shoulder of an invisible child before him. He said, "I'm early again."

"I am not a lazy girl," I said.

"I know you're not," he said and he sat down in the chair across from me.

"How do you know I'm not?" This question just jumped out of me. I can be a cheeky girl sometimes. My mother says that this was one reason I am not married, that this is why she always talks about the boy I was once going to marry in Vietnam, because he was a shy boy, a weak boy, who would take whatever his wife said and not complain. I myself think this is why he is driving a taxi in Hô Chí Minh City. But as soon as this cheeky thing came out of my mouth to Mr. Cohen, I found that I was afraid. I did not want Mr. Cohen to hate me.

25 But he was smiling. I could even see his white teeth in this smile. He said, "You're right. I have no proof."

"I am always sitting here when you come in," I said, even as I asked myself, Why are you rubbing on this subject?

I saw still more teeth in his smile, then he said, "And the last time you were even sleeping."

I think at this I must have looked upset, because his smile went away fast. He did not have to help me seem a fool before him. "It's all right," he said. "This is a slow time of day. I have trouble staying awake myself. Even in court."

I looked at him more closely, leaving his face. He seemed very prosperous. He was wearing a suit as gray as his beard and it had thin blue stripes, almost invisible, running through it. "You are a judge?"

"A lawyer," he said.

"You will defend me when the owner fires me for sleeping."

This made Mr. Cohen laugh, but when he stopped, his face was very solemn. He seemed to lean nearer to me, though I was sure he did not move. "You had a bad dream the last time," he said.

How did I know he would finally come to ask about my dream? I had known it from the first time I'd heard his voice. "Yes," I said. "I think I was dreaming about the first Christmas Eve I spent in America. I fell asleep before a window in a restaurant in St. Louis, Missouri. When I woke, there was snow on the ground. It was the first snow I'd ever seen. I went to sleep and there was still only a gray afternoon, a thin little rain, like a mist. I had no idea things could change like that. I woke and everything was covered and I was terrified."

I suddenly sounded to myself like a crazy person. Mr. Cohen would think I was lazy and crazy both. I stopped speaking and I looked out the window. A jogger went by in the street, a man in shorts and a T-shirt, and his body glistened with sweat. I felt beads of sweat on my own forehead like little insects crouching there and I kept my eyes outside, wishing now that Mr. Cohen would go away.

"Why did it terrify you?" he said.

"I don't know," I said, though this wasn't really true. I'd thought about it now and then, and though I'd never spoken them, I could imagine reasons.

Mr. Cohen said, "Snow frightened me, too, when I was a child. I'd seen it all my life, but it still frightened me."

I turned to him and now he was looking out the window.

"Why did it frighten you?" I asked, expecting no answer.

But he turned from the window and looked at me and smiled just a little bit, like he was saying that since he had asked this question of me, I could ask him, too. He answered, "It's rather a long story. Are you sure you want to hear it?"

"Yes," I said. Of course I did.

"It was far away from here," he said. "My first home and my second one. Poland and then England. My father was a professor in Warsaw. It was early in 1939. I was eight years old and my father knew something was going wrong. All the talk about the corridor to the sea was just the beginning. He had ears. He knew. So he sent me and my mother to England. He had good friends there. I left that February and there was snow everywhere and I had my own instincts, even at eight. I cried in the courtyard of our apartment building. I threw myself into the snow there and I would not move. I cried like he was sending us away from him forever. He and my mother said it was only for some months, but I didn't believe it. And I was right. They had to lift me bodily and carry me to the taxi. But the snow was in my clothes and as we pulled away and I scrambled up to look out the back window at my father, the snow was melting against my skin and I began to shake. It was as much from my fear as from the cold. The snow was telling me he would die. And he did. He waved at me in the street and he grew smaller and we turned a corner and that was the last I saw of him."

Maybe it was foolish of me, but I thought not so much of Mr. Cohen losing his father. I had lost a father, too, and I knew that it was something that a child lives through. In Vietnam we believe that our ancestors are always close to us, and I could tell that about Mr. Cohen, that his father was still close to him. But what I thought about was Mr. Cohen going to another place, another country, and living with his mother. I live with my mother, just like that. Even still.

He said, "So the snow was something I was afraid of. Every time it snowed in England I knew that my father was dead. It took a few years for us to learn this from others, but I knew it whenever it snowed."

"You lived with your mother?" I said.

"Yes. In England until after the war and then we came to America. The others from Poland and Hungary and Russia that we traveled with all came in through New York City and stayed there. My mother loved trains and she'd read a book once about New Orleans, and so we stayed on the train and we came to the South. I was glad to be in a place where it almost never snowed."

I was thinking how he was a foreigner, too. Not an American, really. But all the talk about the snow made this little chill behind my thoughts. Maybe I was ready to talk about that. Mr. Cohen had spoken many words to me about his childhood and I didn't want him to think I was a girl who takes things without giving something back. He was looking out the window again, and his lips pinched together so that his mouth disappeared in his beard. He seemed sad to me. So I said, "You know why the snow scared me in St. Louis?"

He turned at once with a little humph sound and a crease on his forehead between his eyes and then a very strong voice saying, "Tell me," and it felt like he was scolding himself inside for not paying attention to me. I am not a vain girl, always thinking that men pay such serious attention to me that they get mad at themselves for ignoring me even for a few moments. This is what it really felt like and it surprised me. If I was a vain girl, it wouldn't have surprised me. He said it again: "Tell me why it scared you."

I said, "I think it's because the snow came so quietly and everything was underneath it, like this white surface was the real earth and everything had died—all the trees and the grass and the streets and the houses—everything had died and was buried. It was all lost. I knew there was snow above me, on the roof, and I was dead, too."

"Your own country was very different," Mr. Cohen said.

It pleased me that he thought just the way I once did. You could tell that he wished there was an easy way to make me feel better, make the dream go away. But I said to him, "This is what I also thought. If I could just go to a warm climate, more like home. So I came down to New Orleans, with my mother, just like you, and then we came over to Lake Charles. And it is something like Vietnam here. The rice fields and the heat and the way the storms come in. But it makes no difference. There's no snow to scare me here, but I still sit alone in this chair in the middle of the afternoon and I sleep and I listen to the Grandfather over there ticking."

I stopped talking and I felt like I was making no sense at all, so I said, "I should check on your order."

Mr. Cohen's hand came out over the table. "May I ask your name?"

"I'm Miss Giàu," I said.

55 "Miss Giàu?" he asked, and when he did that, he made a different word, since Vietnamese words change with the way your voice sings them.

I laughed. "My name is Giàu, with the voice falling. It means 'wealthy' in Vietnamese. When you say the word like a question, you say something very different. You say I am Miss Pout."

Mr. Cohen laughed and there was something in the laugh that made me shiver just a little, like a nice little thing, like maybe stepping into the shower when you are covered with dust and feeling the water expose you. But in the back of my mind was his carry-out and there was a bad little feeling there, something I wasn't thinking about, but it made me go off now with heavy feet to the kitchen. I got the bag and it was feeling different as I carried it back to the front of the restaurant. I went behind the counter and I put it down and I wished I'd done this a few moments before, but even with his eyes on me, I looked into the bag. There was one main dish and one portion of soup.

Then Mr. Cohen said, "Is this a giau I see on your face?" And he pronounced the word exactly right, with the curling tone that made it "pout."

I looked up at him and I wanted to smile at how good he said the word, but even wanting to do that made the pout worse. I said, "I was just thinking that your wife must be sick. She is not eating tonight."

60 He could have laughed at this. But he did not. He laid his hand for a moment on his beard, he smoothed it down. He said, "The second dinner on Christmas Eve was for my son passing through town. My wife died some years ago and I am not remarried."

I am not a hard-hearted girl because I knew that a child gets over the loss of a father and because I also knew that a man gets over the loss of a wife. I am a good girl, but I did not feel sad for Mr. Cohen. I felt very happy. Because he laid his hand on mine and he asked if he could call me. I said yes, and as it turns out, New Year's Eve seems to be a Jewish holiday. Vietnamese New Year comes at a different time, but people in Vietnam know to celebrate whatever holiday comes along. So tonight Mr. Cohen and I will go to some restaurant that is not Chinese, and all I have to do now is sit here and listen very carefully to Grandfather as he talks to me about time.

➤ *QUESTIONS FOR READING AND WRITING*

1. Who is the narrator of this story? Why is her background important?
2. Describe Mr. Cohen.
3. In what way does the setting of this story matter?
4. Why is the narrator's mother frightened for her? Why is she frightened for herself?
5. Why do you think the first snowfall she saw frightened her "in some very deep way"? Why does snow frighten Mr. Cohen?
6. It's clear at the end of the story that a spark has been lit between the narrator and Mr. Cohen. Do you think they make a good couple? Explain.

JOHN CHEEVER (1912–1982)

John Cheever was born in Quincy, Massachusetts, and published his first story, "Expelled" in the New Republic *shortly after he was expelled from prep school at the age of eighteen. Instead of attending college, Cheever moved to New York City and devoted himself to writing. His stories, which often appeared in the* New Yorker, *gradually earned him a reputation as a master short-story writer, and, as they were usually set among upper-middle-class suburbanites, led one critic to dub Cheever the "Chekhov of the Suburbs." Though his reputation rests mainly on his short stories, Cheever published a number of well-received novels, most notably* The Wapshot Scandal *(1965), which won the National Book Award. His best-selling* Stories of John Cheever *was awarded the Pulitzer Prize in 1978.*

THE ENORMOUS RADIO

[1947]

Jim and Irene Westcott were the kind of people who seem to strike that satisfactory average of income, endeavor, and respectability that is reached by the statistical reports in college alumni bulletins. They were the parents of two young children, they had been married nine years, they lived on the twelfth floor of an apartment house near Sutton Place,[1] they went to the theatre on an average of 10.3 times a year, and they hoped someday to live in Westchester.[2] Irene Westcott was a pleasant, rather plain girl with soft brown hair and a wide, fine forehead upon which nothing at all had been written, and in the cold weather she wore a coat of fitch skins died to resemble mink. You could not say that Jim Westcott looked younger than he was, but you could at least say of him that he seemed to feel younger. He wore his graying hair cut very short, he dressed in the kind of clothes his class had worn at Andover,[3] and his manner was earnest, vehement, and intentionally naïve. The Westcotts differed from their friends, their classmates, and their neighbors only in an interest they shared in serious music. They went to a great many concerts—although they seldom mentioned this to anyone—and they spent a good deal of time listening to music on the radio.

Their radio was an old instrument, sensitive, unpredictable, and beyond repair. Neither of them understood the mechanics of radio—or of any of the other appliances that surrounded them—and when the instrument faltered, Jim would strike the side of the cabinet with his hand. This sometimes helped. One Sunday afternoon, in the middle of a Schubert quartet, the music faded away altogether. Jim

[1] **Sutton Place** an upscale location in New York City [2] **Westchester** a wealthy suburb of N.Y.C.
[3] **Andover** a prestigious boarding school

struck the cabinet repeatedly, but there was no response; the Schubert was lost to them forever. He promised to buy Irene a new radio, and on Monday when he came home from work he told her that he had got one. He refused to describe it, and said it would be a surprise for her when it came.

The radio was delivered at the kitchen door the following afternoon, and with the assistance of her maid and the handyman Irene uncrated it and brought it into the living room. She was struck at once with the physical ugliness of the large gumwood cabinet. Irene was proud of her living room, she had chosen its furnishings and colors as carefully as she chose her clothes, and now it seemed to her that the new radio stood among her intimate possessions like an aggressive intruder. She was confounded by the number of dials and switches on the instrument panel, and she studied them thoroughly before she put the plug into a wall socket and turned the radio on. The dials flooded with a malevolent green light, and in the distance she heard the music of a piano quintet. The quintet was in the distance for only an instant; it bore down upon her with a speed greater than light and filled the apartment with the noise of music amplified so mightily that it knocked a china ornament from a table to the floor. She rushed to the instrument and reduced the volume. The violent forces that were snared in the ugly gumwood cabinet made her uneasy. Her children came home from school then, and she took them to the Park. It was not until later in the afternoon that she was able to return to the radio.

The maid had given the children their suppers and was supervising their baths when Irene turned on the radio, reduced the volume, and sat down to listen to a Mozart quintet that she knew and enjoyed. The music came through clearly. The new instrument had a much purer tone, she thought, than the old one. She decided that tone was most important and that she could conceal the cabinet behind a sofa. But as soon as she had made her peace with the radio, the interference began. A crackling sound like the noise of a burning powder fuse began to accompany the singing of the strings. Beyond the music, there was a rustling that reminded Irene unpleasantly of the sea, and as the quintet progressed, these noises were joined by many others. She tried all the dials and switches but nothing dimmed the interference, and she sat down, disappointed and bewildered, and tried to trace the flight of the melody. The elevator shaft in her building ran beside the living-room wall, and it was the noise of the elevator that gave her a clue to the character of the static. The rattling of the elevator cables and the opening and closing of the elevator doors were reproduced in her loudspeaker, and, realizing that the radio was sensitive to electrical currents of all sorts, she began to discern through the Mozart the ringing of telephone bells, the dialing of phones, and the lamentation of a vacuum cleaner. By listening more carefully, she was able to distinguish doorbells, elevator bells, electric razors, and Waring mixers, whose sounds had been picked up from the apartments that surrounded hers and transmitted through her loudspeaker. The powerful and ugly instrument, with its mistaken sensitivity to discord, was more than she could hope to master, so she turned the thing off and went into the nursery to see her children.

5 When Jim Westcott came home that night, he went to the radio confidently and worked the controls. He had the same sort of experience Irene had had. A man was

speaking on the station Jim had chosen, and his voice swung instantly from the distance into a force so powerful that it shook the apartment. Jim turned the volume control and reduced the voice. Then, a minute or two later, the interference began. The ringing of telephones and doorbells set in, joined by the rasp of the elevator doors and the whir of cooking appliances. The character of the noise had changed since Irene had tried the radio earlier; the last of the electric razors was being unplugged, the vacuum cleaners had all been returned to their closets, and the static reflected that change in pace that overtakes the city after the sun goes down. He fiddled with the knobs but couldn't get rid of the noises, so he turned the radio off and told Irene that in the morning he'd call the people who had sold it to him and give them hell.

The following afternoon, when Irene returned to the apartment from a luncheon date, the maid told her that a man had come and fixed the radio. Irene went into the living room before she took off her hat or her furs and tried the instrument. From the loudspeaker came a recording of the "Missouri Waltz." It reminded her of the thin, scratchy music from an old-fashioned phonograph that she sometimes heard across the lake where she spent her summers. She waited until the waltz had finished, expecting an explanation of the recording, but there was none. The music was followed by silence, and then the plaintive and scratchy record was repeated. She turned the dial and got a satisfactory burst of Caucasian music—the thump of bare feet in the dust and the rattle of coin jewelry—but in the background she could hear the ringing of bells and a confusion of voices. Her children came home from school then, and she turned off the radio and went to the nursery.

When Jim came home that night, he was tired, and he took a bath and changed his clothes. Then he joined Irene in the living room. He had just turned on the radio when the maid announced dinner, so he left it on, and he and Irene went to the table.

Jim was too tired to make even pretense of sociability, and there was nothing about the dinner to hold Irene's interest, so her attention wandered from the food to the deposits of silver polish on the candlesticks and from there to the music in the other room. She listened for a few minutes to a Chopin prelude and then was surprised to hear a man's voice break in. "For Christ's sake, Kathy," he said, "do you always have to play the piano when I get home?" The music stopped abruptly. "It's the only chance I have," a woman said. "I'm at the office all day." "So am I," the man said. He added something obscene about an upright piano, and slammed a door. The passionate and melancholy music began again.

"Did you hear that?" Irene asked.

10 "What?" Jim was eating his dessert.

"The radio. A man said something while the music was still going on—something dirty."

"It's probably a play."

"I don't think it *is* a play," Irene said.

They left the table and took their coffee into the living room. Irene asked Jim to try another station. He turned the knob. "Have you seen my garters?" a man asked. "Button me up," a woman said. "Have you seen my garters?" the man said again. "Just button me up and I'll find your garters," the woman said. Jim shifted to another station. "I wish you wouldn't leave apple cores in the ashtrays," a man said. "I hate the smell."

"This is strange," Jim said.

"Isn't it?" Irene said.

Jim turned the knob again. "'On the coast of Coromandel where the early pumpkins blow,'" a woman with a pronounced English accent said, "'in the middle of the woods lived the Yonghy-Bonghy-Bò. Two old chairs, and half a candle, one old jug without a handle. . . .'"

"My God!" Irene cried. "That's the Sweeneys' nurse."

"'These were all his worldly goods,'" the British voice continued.

"Turn that thing off," Irene said. "Maybe they can hear *us*." Jim switched the radio off. "That was Miss Armstrong, the Sweeneys' nurse," Irene said. "She must be reading to the little girl. They live in 17-B. I've talked with Miss Armstrong in the Park. I know her voice very well. We must be getting other people's apartments."

"That's impossible," Jim said.

"Well, that was the Sweeneys' nurse," Irene said hotly. "I know her voice. I know it very well. I'm wondering if they can hear us."

Jim turned the switch. First from a distance and then nearer, nearer, as if borne on the wind, came the pure accents of the Sweeneys' nurse again: "'*Lady Jingly! Lady Jingly!*'" she said, "'*sitting where the pumpkins blow, will you come and be my wife?* said the Yonghy-Bonghy-Bò. . . .'"

Jim went over to the radio and said "Hello" loudly into the speaker.

"'*I am tired of living singly,*'" the nurse went on, "'*on this coast so wild and shingly, I'm a-weary of my life; if you'll come and be my wife, quite serene would be my life. . . .*'"

"I guess she can't hear us," Irene said. "Try something else."

Jim turned to another station, and the living room was filled with the uproar of a cocktail party that had overshot its mark. Someone was playing the piano and singing the "Whiffenpoof Song," and the voices that surrounded the piano were vehement and happy. "Eat some more sandwiches," a woman shrieked. There were screams of laughter and a dish of some sort crashed to the floor.

"Those must be the Fullers, in 11-E," Irene said. "I knew they were giving a party this afternoon. I saw her in the liquor store. Isn't this too divine? Try something else. See if you can get those people in 18-C."

The Westcotts overheard that evening a monologue on salmon fishing in Canada, a bridge game, running comments on home movies of what had apparently been a fortnight at Sea Island, and a bitter family quarrel about an overdraft at the bank. They turned off their radio at midnight and went to bed, weak with laughter. Sometime in the night, their son began to call for a glass of water and Irene got one and took it to his room. It was very early. All the lights in the neighborhood were extinguished, and from the boy's window she could see the empty street. She went into the living room and tried the radio. There was some faint coughing, a moan, and then a man spoke. "Are you all right, darling?" he asked. "Yes," a woman said wearily. "Yes, I'm all right, I guess," and then she added with great feeling, "But, you know, Charlie, I don't feel like myself any more. Sometimes there are about fifteen or twenty minutes in the week when I feel like myself. I don't like to go to another doctor, because the doctor's bills are so awful already, but I just don't feel like myself, Charlie. I just never feel like myself." They were not young, Irene thought. She guessed from the timbre of their voices that they were middle-aged. The restrained melancholy of the dialogue and the draft from the bedroom window made her shiver, and she went back to bed.

The following morning, Irene cooked breakfast for the family—the maid didn't come up from her room in the basement until ten—braided her daughter's hair, and waited at the door until her children and her husband had been carried away in the elevator. Then she went into the living room and tried the radio. "I don't want to go to school," a child screamed. "I hate school. I won't go to school. I hate school." "You will go to school," an enraged woman said. "We paid eight hundred dollars to get you into that school and you'll go if it kills you." The next number on the dial produced the worn record of the "Missouri Waltz." Irene shifted the control and invaded the privacy of several breakfast tables. She overheard demonstrations of indigestion, carnal love, abysmal vanity, faith, and despair. Irene's life was nearly as simple and sheltered as it appeared to be, and the forthright and sometimes brutal language that came from the loudspeaker that morning astonished and troubled her. She continued to listen until her maid came in. Then she turned off the radio quickly, since this insight, she realized, was a furtive one.

Irene had a luncheon date with a friend that day, and she left her apartment at a little after twelve. There were a number of women in the elevator when it stopped at her floor. She stared at their handsome and impassive faces, their furs, and the cloth flowers in their hats. Which one of them had been to Sea Island? she wondered. Which one had overdrawn her bank account? The elevator stopped at the tenth floor and a woman with a pair of Skye terriers joined them. Her hair was rigged high on her head and she wore a mink cape. She was humming the "Missouri Waltz."

30 Irene had two Martinis at lunch, and she looked searchingly at her friend and wondered what her secrets were. They had intended to go shopping after lunch, but Irene excused herself and went home. She told the maid that she was not to be disturbed; then she went into the living room, closed the doors, and switched on the radio. She heard, in the course of the afternoon, the halting conversation of a woman entertaining her aunt, the hysterical conclusion of a luncheon party, and a hostess briefing her maid about some cocktail guests. "Don't give the best Scotch to anyone who hasn't white hair," the hostess said. "See if you can get rid of that liver paste before you pass those hot things, and could you lend me five dollars? I want to tip the elevator man."

As the afternoon waned, the conversations increased in intensity. From where Irene sat, she could see the open sky above the East River. There were hundreds of clouds in the sky, as though the south wind had broken the winter into pieces and were blowing it north, and on her radio she could hear the arrival of cocktail guests and the return of children and businessmen from their schools and offices. "I found a good-sized diamond on the bathroom floor this morning," a woman said. "It must have fallen out of that bracelet Mrs. Dunston was wearing last night." "We'll sell it," a man said. "Take it down to the jeweler on Madison Avenue and sell it. Mrs. Dunston won't know the difference, and we could use a couple of hundred bucks.

. . ." "'Oranges and lemons, say the bells of St. Clement's,'" the Sweeneys' nurse sang. "'Halfpence and farthings, say the bells of St. Martin's. When will you pay me? say the bells at old Bailey. . . .'" "It's not a hat," a woman cried, and at her back roared a cocktail party. "It's not a hat, it's a love affair. That's what Walter Florell said. He said it's not a hat, it's a love affair," and then, in a lower voice, the same woman added, "Talk to somebody, for Christ's sake, honey, talk to somebody. If she catches you standing here not talking to anybody, she'll take us off her invitation list, and I love these parties."

The Westcotts were going out for dinner that night, and when Jim came home, Irene was dressing. She seemed sad and vague, and he brought her a drink. They were dining with friends in the neighborhood, and they walked to where they were going. The sky was broad and filled with light. It was one of those splendid spring evenings that excite memory and desire, and the air that touched their hands and faces felt very soft. A Salvation Army band was on the corner playing "Jesus Is Sweeter." Irene drew on her husband's arm and held him there for a minute, to hear the music. "They're really such nice people, aren't they?" she said. "They have such nice faces. Actually, they're so much nicer than a lot of the people we know." She took a bill from her purse and walked over and dropped it into the tambourine. There was in her face, when she returned to her husband, a look of radiant melancholy that he was not familiar with. And her conduct at the dinner party that night seemed strange to him, too. She interrupted her hostess rudely and stared at the people across the table from her with an intensity for which she would have punished her children.

It was still mild when they walked home from the party, and Irene looked up at the spring stars. "'How far that little candle throws its beams,'" she exclaimed. "'So shines a good deed in a naughty world.'" She waited that night until Jim had fallen asleep, and then went into the living room and turned on the radio.

Jim came home at about six the next night. Emma, the maid, let him in, and he had taken off his hat and was taking off his coat when Irene ran into the hall. Her face was shining with tears and her hair was disordered. "Go up to 16-C, Jim!" she screamed. "Don't take off your coat. Go up to 16-C. Mr. Osborn's beating his wife. They've been quarreling since four o'clock, and now he's hitting her. Go up there and stop him."

From the radio in the living room, Jim heard screams, obscenities, and thuds. "You know you don't have to listen to this sort of thing," he said. He strode into the living room and turned the switch. "It's indecent," he said. "It's like looking in windows. You know you don't have to listen to this sort of thing. You can turn it off."

"Oh, it's so horrible, it's so dreadful," Irene was sobbing. "I've been listening all day, and it's so depressing."

"Well, if it's so depressing, why do you listen to it? I bought this damned radio to give you pleasure," he said. "I paid a great deal of money for it. I thought it might make you happy. I wanted to make you happy."

"Don't, don't don't, don't quarrel with me," she moaned, and laid her head on his shoulder. "All the others have been quarreling all day. Everybody's been quarreling. They're all worried about money. Mrs. Hutchinson's mother is dying of cancer in Florida and they don't have enough money to send her to the Mayo Clinic. At least, Mr. Hutchinson says they don't have enough money. And some woman in this building is having an affair with the handyman—with that hideous handyman. It's too disgusting. And Mrs. Melville has heart trouble and Mr. Hendricks is going to lose his job in April and Mrs. Hendricks is horrid about the whole thing and that girl who plays the 'Missouri Waltz' is a whore, a common whore, and the elevator man has tuberculosis and Mr. Osborn has been beating Mrs. Osborn." She wailed, she trembled with grief and checked the stream of tears down her face with the heel of her palm.

"Well, why do you have to listen?" Jim asked again. "Why do you have to listen to this stuff if it makes you so miserable?"

"Oh, don't, don't, don't," she cried. "Life is too terrible, too sordid and awful. But we've never been like that, have we, darling? Have we? I mean, we've always been good and decent and loving to one another, haven't we? And we have two children, two beautiful children. Our lives aren't sordid, are they, darling? Are they?" She flung her arms around his neck and drew his face down to hers. "We're happy, aren't we, darling? We are happy, aren't we?"

"Of course we're happy," he said tiredly. He began to surrender his resentment. "Of course we're happy. I'll have that damned radio fixed or taken away tomorrow." He stroked her soft hair. "My poor girl," he said.

"You love me, don't you?" she asked. "And we're not hypercritical or worried about money or dishonest, are we?"

"No, darling," he said.

A man came in the morning and fixed the radio. Irene turned it on cautiously and was happy to hear a California-wine commercial and a recording of Beethoven's Ninth Symphony, including Schiller's "Ode to Joy." She kept the radio on all day and nothing untoward come from the speaker.

A Spanish suite was being played when Jim came home. "Is everything all right?" he asked. His face was pale, she thought. They had some cocktails and went in to dinner to the "Anvil Chorus" from *Il Trovatore.* This was followed by Debussy's "La Mer."

"I paid the bill for the radio today," Jim said, "It cost four hundred dollars. I hope you'll get some enjoyment out of it."

"Oh, I'm sure I will," Irene said.

"Four hundred dollars is a good deal more than I can afford," he went on. "I wanted to get something that you'd enjoy. It's the last extravagance we'll be able to indulge in this year. I see that you haven't paid your clothing bills yet. I saw them on your dressing table." He looked directly at her. "Why did you tell me you'd paid them? Why did you lie to me?"

"I just didn't want you to worry, Jim," she said. She drank some water. "I'll be able to pay my bills out of this month's allowance. There were the slipcovers last month, and that party."

"You've got to learn to handle the money I give you a little more intelligently, Irene," he said. "You've got to understand that we won't have as much money this year as we had last. I had a very sobering talk with Mitchell today. No one is buying anything. We're spending all our time promoting new issues, and you know how long that takes. I'm not getting any younger, you know. I'm thirty-seven. My hair will be gray next year. I haven't done as well as I'd hoped to do. And I don't suppose things will get any better."

"Yes, dear," she said.

"We've got to start cutting down," Jim said. "We've got to think of the children. To be perfectly frank with you, I worry about money a great deal. I'm not at all sure of the future. No one is. If anything should happen to me, there's the insurance, but that wouldn't go very far today. I've worked awfully hard to give you and the children an comfortable life," he said bitterly. "I don't like to see all of my energies, all of my youth, wasted in fur coats and radios and slipcovers and—"

"Please, Jim," she said. "Please. They'll hear us."

"*Who'll hear us?* Emma can't hear us."

55 "The radio."

"Oh, I'm sick!" he shouted. "I'm sick to death of your apprehensiveness. The radio can't hear us. Nobody can hear us. And what if they can hear us? Who cares?"

Irene got up from the table and went into the living room. Jim went to the door and shouted at her from there. "Why are you so Christly all of a sudden? What's turned you overnight into a convent girl? You stole your mother's jewelry before they probated her will. You never gave your sister a cent of that money that was intended for her—not even when she needed it. You made Grace Howland's life miserable, and where was all your piety and your virtue when you went to that abortionist? I'll never forget how cool you were. You packed your bag and went off to have that child murdered as if you were going to Nassau. If you'd had any reasons, if you'd had any good reasons—"

Irene stood for a minute before the hideous cabinet, disgraced and sickened, but she held her hand on the switch before she extinguished the music and the voices, hoping that the instrument might speak to her kindly, that she might hear the Sweeneys' nurse. Jim continued to shout at her from the door. The voice on the radio was suave and noncommittal. "An early-morning railroad disaster in Tokyo," the loudspeaker said, "killed twenty-nine people. A fire in a Catholic hospital near Buffalo for the care of blind children was extinguished early this morning by nuns. The temperature is forty-seven. The humidity is eighty-nine."

➤ *QUESTIONS FOR READING AND WRITING*

1. Why is the story titled "The Enormous Radio"? Is the radio enormous? Explain.
2. Who are the Westcotts? What is the narrator's attitude toward them? What language does he use to describe them?
3. If they are disappointed that their radio does not get better reception—and invades the privacy of their neighbors—why do they keep listening?
4. After this experience, do you think the Westcotts will ever be the same? Explain.
5. Update this story to the present and give the Westcott's an "enormous television." Would this change the story? Explain.

LILIANA HEKER (b. 1943)

Liliana Heker is a native of Argentina. "The Stolen Party" was published in Spanish in 1982 and translated into English by Alberto Manguel. It was also published in 1985 in a collection of short stories, Other Fires: Short Fiction by Latin American Women.

THE STOLEN PARTY

[1982]

As soon as she arrived she went straight to the kitchen to see if the monkey was there. It was: what a relief! She wouldn't have liked to admit that her mother had been right. *Monkeys at a birthday?* her mother had sneered. *Get away with you, believing any nonsense you're told!* She was cross, but not because of the monkey, the girl thought; it's just because of the party.

"I don't like you going," she told her. "It's a rich people's party."

"Rich people go to Heaven too," said the girl, who studied religion at school.

"Get away with Heaven," said the mother. "The problem with you, young lady, is that you like to fart higher than your ass."

5 The girl didn't approve of the way her mother spoke. She was barely nine, and one of the best in her class.

"I'm going because I've been invited," she said. "And I've been invited because Luciana is my friend. So there."

"Ah yes, your friend," her mother grumbled. She paused. "Listen, Rosaura," she said at last. "That one's not your friend. You know what you are to them? The maid's daughter, that's what."

Rosaura blinked hard: she wasn't going to cry. Then she yelled: "Shut up! You know nothing about being friends!"

Every afternoon she used to go to Luciana's house and they would both finish their homework while Rosaura's mother did the cleaning. They had their tea in the kitchen and they told each other secrets. Rosaura loved everything in the big house, and she also loved the people who lived there.

10 "I'm going because it will be the most lovely party in the whole world, Luciana told me it would. There will be a magician, and he will bring a monkey and everything."

The mother swung around to take a good look at her child, and pompously put her hands on her hips.

"Monkeys at a birthday?" she said. "Get away with you, believing any nonsense you're told!"

Rosaura was deeply offended. She thought it unfair of her mother to accuse other people of being liars simply because they were rich. Rosaura too wanted to be rich, of course. If one day she managed to live in a beautiful palace, would her mother stop loving her? She felt very sad. She wanted to go to that party more than anything else in the world.

"I'll die if I don't go," she whispered, almost without moving her lips.

And she wasn't sure whether she had been heard, but on the morning of the party she discovered that her mother had starched her Christmas dress. And in the afternoon, after washing her hair, her mother rinsed it in apple vinegar so that it would be all nice and shiny. Before going out, Rosaura admired herself in the mirror, with her white dress and glossy hair, and thought she looked terribly pretty.

Señora Ines also seemed to notice. As soon as she saw her, she said:

"How lovely you look today, Rosaura."

Rosaura gave her starched skirt a slight toss with her hands and walked into the party with a firm step. She said hello to Luciana and asked about the monkey. Luciana put on a secretive look and whispered into Rosaura's ear: "He's in the kitchen. But don't tell anyone, because it's a surprise."

Rosaura wanted to make sure. Carefully she entered the kitchen and there she saw it: deep in thought, inside its cage. It looked so funny that the girl stood there for a while, watching it, and later, every so often, she would slip out of the party unseen and go and admire it. Rosaura was the only one allowed into the kitchen. Señora Ines had said: "You yes, but not the others, they're much too boisterous, they might break something." Rosaura had never broken anything. She even managed the jug of orange juice, carrying it from the kitchen into the dining room. She held it carefully and didn't spill a single drop. And Señora Ines had said: "Are you sure you can manage a jug as big as that?" Of course she could manage. She wasn't a butterfingers, like the others. Like that blonde girl with the bow in her hair. As soon as she saw Rosaura, the girl with the bow had said:

"And you? Who are you?"

"I'm a friend of Luciana," said Rosaura.

"No," said the girl with the bow, "you are not a friend of Luciana because I'm her cousin and I know all her friends. And I don't know you."

"So what," said Rosaura. "I come here every afternoon with my mother and we do our homework together."

"You and your mother do your homework together?" asked the girl, laughing.

"I and Luciana do our homework together," said Rosaura, very seriously.

The girl with the bow shrugged her shoulders.

"That's not being friends," she said. "Do you go to school together?"

"No."

"So where do you know her from?" said the girl, getting impatient.

Rosaura remembered her mother's words perfectly. She took a deep breath.

"I'm the daughter of the employee," she said.

Her mother had said very clearly: "If someone asks, you say you're the daughter of the employee; that's all." She also told her to add: "And proud of it." But Rosaura thought that never in her life would she dare say something of the sort.

"What employee?" said the girl with the bow. "Employee in a shop?"

"No," said Rosaura angrily. "My mother doesn't sell anything in any shop, so there."

"So how come she's an employee?" said the girl with the bow.

Just then Señora Ines arrived saying *shh shh,* and asked Rosaura if she wouldn't mind helping serve out the hotdogs, as she knew the house so much better than the others.

"See?" said Rosaura to the girl with the bow, and when no one was looking she kicked her in the shin.

Apart from the girl with the bow, all the others were delightful. The one she liked best was Luciana, with her golden birthday crown; and then the boys. Rosaura won the sack race, and nobody managed to catch her when they played tag. When they split into two teams to play charades, all the boys wanted her for their side. Rosaura felt she had never been so happy in all her life.

But the best was still to come. The best came after Luciana blew out the candles. First the cake. Señora Ines had asked her to help pass the cake around, and Rosaura had enjoyed the task immensely, because everyone called out to her, shouting "Me, me!" Rosaura remembered a story in which there was a queen who had the power of life or death over her subjects. She had always loved that, having the power of life or death. To Luciana and the boys she gave the largest pieces, and to the girl with the bow she gave a slice so thin one could see through it.

After the cake came the magician, tall and bony, with a fine red cape. A true magician: he could untie handkerchiefs by blowing on them and make a chain with links that had no openings. He could guess what cards were pulled out from a pack, and the monkey was his assistant. He called the monkey "partner." "Let's see here, partner," he would say, "turn over a card." And, "Don't run away, partner: time to work now."

The final trick was wonderful. One of the children had to hold the monkey in his arms and the magician said he would make him disappear.

"What, the boy?" they all shouted.

"No, the monkey!" shouted back the magician.

Rosaura thought that this was truly the most amusing party in the whole world.

The magician asked a small fat boy to come and help, but the small fat boy got frightened almost at once and dropped the monkey on the floor. The magician picked him up carefully, whispered something in his ear, and the monkey nodded almost as if he understood.

"You mustn't be so unmanly, my friend," the magician said to the fat boy.

"What's unmanly?" said the fat boy.

The magician turned around as if to look for spies.

"A sissy," said the magician. "Go sit down."

Then he stared at all the faces, one by one. Rosaura felt her heart tremble.

"You, with the Spanish eyes," said the magician. And everyone saw that he was pointing at her.

She wasn't afraid. Neither holding the monkey, nor when the magician made him vanish; not even when, at the end, the magician flung his red cape over

Rosaura's head and uttered a few magic words . . . and the monkey reappeared, chattering happily, in her arms. The children clapped furiously. And before Rosaura returned to her seat, the magician said:

"Thank you very much, my little countess."

She was so pleased with the compliment that a while later, when her mother came to fetch her, that was the first thing she told her.

"I helped the magician and he said to me, 'Thank you very much, my little countess.'"

It was strange because up to then Rosaura had thought that she was angry with her mother. All along Rosaura had imagined that she would say to her: "See that the monkey wasn't a lie?" But instead she was so thrilled that she told her mother all about the wonderful magician.

Her mother tapped her on the head and said: "So now we're a countess!"

But one could see that she was beaming.

And now they both stood in the entrance, because a moment ago Señora Ines, smiling, had said: "Please wait here a second."

Her mother suddenly seemed worried.

"What is it?" she asked Rosaura.

"What is what?" said Rosaura. "It's nothing; she just wants to get the presents for those who are leaving, see?"

She pointed at the fat boy and at a girl with pigtails who were also waiting there, next to their mothers. And she explained about the presents. She knew, because she had been watching those who left before her. When one of the girls was about to leave, Señora Ines would give her a bracelet. When a boy left, Señora Ines gave him a yo-yo. Rosaura preferred the yo-yo because it sparkled, but she didn't mention that to her mother. Her mother might have said: "So why don't you ask for one, you blockhead?" That's what her mother was like. Rosaura didn't feel like explaining that she'd be horribly ashamed to be the odd one out. Instead she said:

"I was the best-behaved at the party."

And she said no more because Señora Ines came out into the hall with two bags, one pink and one blue.

First she went up to the fat boy, gave him a yo-yo out of the blue bag, and the fat boy left with his mother. Then she went up to the girl and gave her a bracelet out of the pink bag, and the girl with the pigtails left as well.

Finally she came up to Rosaura and her mother. She had a big smile on her face and Rosaura liked that. Señora Ines looked down at her, then looked up at her mother, and then said something that made Rosaura proud:

"What a marvelous daughter you have, Herminia."

For an instant, Rosaura thought that she'd give her two presents: the bracelet and the yo-yo. Señora Ines bent down as if about to look for something. Rosaura also leaned forward, stretching out her arm. But she never completed the movement.

Señora Ines didn't look in the pink bag. Nor did she look in the blue bag. Instead she rummaged in her purse. In her hand appeared two bills.

"You really and truly earned this," she said handing them over. "Thank you for all your help, my pet."

Rosaura felt her arms stiffen, stick close to her body, and then she noticed her mother's hand on her shoulder. Instinctively she pressed herself against her mother's body. That was all. Except her eyes. Rosaura's eyes had a cold, clear look that fixed itself on Señora Ines's face.

Señora Ines, motionless, stood there with her hand outstretched. As if she didn't dare draw it back. As if the slightest change might shatter an infinitely delicate balance.

➤ *QUESTIONS FOR READING AND WRITING*

1. To what extent is your response to this story affected by your experience?
2. Why do you think the story is called "The Stolen Party"? What has been "stolen"? Explain.
3. What is the point of view of this story? What impact does this narrative perspective have on the story? If the story were told by Señora Ines, how would it be different?

FLANNERY O'CONNOR (1925–1964)

Flannery O'Connor was born in Savannah, Georgia, and at the age of twelve, moved with her family to nearby Midgeville. After graduating from the local women's College of Georgia, O'Connor attended the University of Iowa, earning an M.F.A. in 1947. Following graduation, she stayed for a short time at Yaddo, a prestigious writer's colony in Saratoga Springs, New York, and then with friends in New York City and Connecticut. In 1950, after she was diagnosed with Lupus, an incurable degenerative blood disease, she returned to Midgeville, where she spent the rest of her life. O'Connor was a devout Roman Catholic. A profound faith permeates her work which, with its blend of grotesque characterizations and religious faith, is often characterized as Southern gothic. About her stories she wrote: "My subject in fiction is the action of grace in a territory held largely by the devil."

EVERYTHING THAT RISES MUST CONVERGE [1965]

Her doctor had told Julian's mother that she must lose twenty pounds on account of her blood pressure, so on Wednesday nights Julian had to take her downtown on the bus for a reducing class at the Y. The reducing class was designed for working girls over fifty, who weighed from 165 to 200 pounds. His mother was one of the slimmer ones, but she said ladies did not tell their age or weight. She would not ride the buses by herself at night since they had been integrated, and because the reducing class was one of her few pleasures, necessary for her health, and *free,* she said Julian could at least put himself out to take her, considering all she did for him. Julian did not like to consider all she did for him, but every Wednesday night he braced himself and took her.

She was almost ready to go, standing before the hall mirror, putting on her hat, while he, his hands behind him, appeared pinned to the door frame, waiting like Saint Sebastian for the arrows to begin piercing him.[1] The hat was new and had cost her seven dollars and a half. She kept saying, "Maybe I shouldn't have paid that for it. No, I shouldn't have. I'll take it off and return it tomorrow. I shouldn't have bought it."

Julian raised his eyes to heaven. "Yes, you should have bought it," he said. "Put it on and let's go." It was a hideous hat. A purple velvet flap came down on one side of it and stood up on the other; the rest of it was green and looked like a cushion with the stuffing out. He decided it was less comical than jaunty and pathetic. Everything that gave her pleasure was small and depressed him.

She lifted the hat one more time and set it down slowly on top of her head. Two wings of gray hair protruded on either side of her florid face, but her eyes, sky-blue, were as innocent and untouched by experience as they must have been when she was ten. Were it not that she was a widow who had struggled fiercely to feed and clothe and put him through school and who was supporting him still, "until he got on his feet," she might have been a little girl that he had to take to town.

5 "It's all right, it's all right," he said. "Let's go." He opened the door himself and started down the walk to get her going. The sky was a dying violet and the houses stood out darkly against it, bulbous liver-colored monstrosities of a uniform ugliness though no two were alike. Since this had been a fashionable neighborhood forty years ago, his mother persisted in thinking they did well to have an apartment in it. Each house had a narrow collar of dirt around it in which sat, usually, a grubby child. Julian walked with his hands in his pockets, his head down and thrust forward and his eyes glazed with the determination to make himself completely numb during the time he would be sacrificed to her pleasure.

The door closed and he turned to find the dumpy figure, surmounted by the atrocious hat, coming toward him. "Well," she said, "you only live once and paying a little more for it, I at least won't meet myself coming and going."

"Some day I'll start making money," Julian said gloomily—he knew he never would—"and you can have one of those jokes whenever you take the fit." But first they would move. He visualized a place where the nearest neighbors would be three miles away on either side.

"I think you're doing fine," she said, drawing on her gloves. "You've only been out of school a year. Rome wasn't built in a day."

[1]**Sebastian** a Christian martyr, was tied to a tree and shot with arrows

She was one of the few members of the Y reducing class who arrived in hat and gloves and who had a son who had been to college: "It takes time," she said, "and the world is in such a mess. This hat looked better on me than any of the others, though when she brought it out I said, 'Take that thing back. I wouldn't have it on my head,' and she said, 'Now wait till you see it on,' and when she put it on me, I said, 'We-ull,' and she said, 'If you ask me, that hat does something for you and you do something for the hat, and besides,' she said, 'with that hat, you won't meet yourself coming and going.'"

Julian thought he could have stood his lot better if she had been selfish, if she had been an old hag who drank and screamed at him. He walked along, saturated in depression, as if in the midst of his martyrdom he had lost his faith. Catching sight of his long, hopeless, irritated face, she stopped suddenly with a grief-stricken look, and pulled back on his arm. "Wait on me," she said. "I'm going back to the house and take this thing off and tomorrow I'm going to return it. I was out of my head. I can pay the gas bill with that seven-fifty."

He caught her arm in a vicious grip. "You are not going to take it back," he said. "I like it."

"Well," she said, "I don't think I ought . . ."

"Shut up and enjoy it," he muttered, more depressed than ever.

"With the world in the mess it's in," she said, "it's a wonder we can enjoy anything. I tell you, the bottom rail is on the top."

Julian sighed.

"Of course," she said, "if you know who you are, you can go anywhere." She said this every time he took her to the reducing class. "Most of them in it are not our kind of people," she said, "but I can be gracious to anybody. I know who I am."

"They don't give a damn for your graciousness," Julian said savagely. "Knowing who you are is good for one generation only. You haven't the foggiest idea where you stand now or who you are."

She stopped and allowed her eyes to flash at him. "I most certainly do know who I am," she said, "and if you don't know who you are, I'm ashamed of you."

"Oh hell," Julian said.

"Your great-grandfather was a former governor of this state," she said. "Your grandfather was a prosperous landowner. Your grandmother was a Godhigh."

"Will you look around you," he said tensely, "and see where you are now?" and he swept his arm jerkily out to indicate the neighborhood, which the growing darkness at least made less dingy.

"You remain what you are," she said. "Your great-grandfather had a plantation and two hundred slaves."

"There are no more slaves," he said irritably.

"They were better off when they were," she said. He groaned to see that she was off on that topic. She rolled onto it every few days like a train on an open track. He knew every stop, every junction, every swamp along the way, and knew the exact point at which her conclusion would roll majestically into the station: "It's ridiculous. It's simply not realistic. They should rise, yes, but on their own side of the fence."

"Let's skip it," Julian said.

"The ones I feel sorry for," she said, "are the ones that are half white. They're tragic."

"Will you skip it?"

"Suppose we were half white. We would certainly have mixed feelings."

"I have mixed feelings now," he groaned.

30 "Well let's talk about something pleasant," she said. "I remember going to Grandpa's when I was a little girl. Then the house had double stairways that went up to what was really the second floor—all the cooking was done on the first. I used to like to stay down in the kitchen on account of the way the walls smelled. I would sit with my nose pressed against the plaster and take deep breaths. Actually the place belonged to the Godhighs but your grandfather Chestny paid the mortgage and saved it for them. They were in reduced circumstances," she said, "but reduced or not, they never forgot who they were."

"Doubtless that decayed mansion reminded them," Julian muttered. He never spoke of it without contempt or thought of it without longing. He had seen it once when he was a child before it had been sold. The double stairways had rotted and been torn down. Negroes were living in it. But it remained in his mind as his mother had known it. It appeared in his dreams regularly. He would stand on the wide porch, listening to the rustle of oak leaves, then wander through the high-ceilinged hall into the parlor that opened onto it and gaze at the worn rugs and faded draperies. It occurred to him that it was he, not she, who could have appreciated it. He preferred its threadbare elegance to anything he could name and it was because of it that all the neighborhoods they had lived in had been a torment to him—whereas she had hardly known the difference. She called her insensitivity "being adjustable."

"And I remember the old darky who was my nurse, Caroline. There was no better person in the world. I've always had a great respect for my colored friends," she said. "I'd do anything in the world for them and they'd . . ."

"Will you for God's sake get off that subject?" Julian said. When he got on a bus by himself, he made it a point to sit down beside a Negro, in reparation as it were for his mother's sins.

"You're mighty touchy tonight," she said. "Do you feel all right?"

35 "Yes I feel all right," he said. "Now lay off."

She pursed her lips. "Well, you certainly are in a vile humor," she observed. "I just won't speak to you at all."

They had reached the bus stop. There was no bus in sight and Julian, his hands still jammed in his pockets and his head thrust forward, scowled down the empty street. The frustration of having to wait on the bus as well as ride on it began to creep up his neck like a hot hand. The presence of his mother was borne in upon him as she gave a pained sigh. He looked at her bleakly. She was holding herself very erect under the preposterous hat, wearing it like a banner of her imaginary dignity. There was in him an evil urge to break her spirit. He suddenly unloosened his tie and pulled it off and put it in his pocket.

She stiffened. "Why must you look like *that* when you take me to town?" she said. "Why must you deliberately embarrass me?"

"If you'll never learn where you are," he said, "you can at least learn where I am."

"You look like a—thug," she said.

"Then I must be one," he murmured.

"I'll just go home," she said. "I will not bother you. If you can't do a little thing like that for me . . ."

Rolling his eyes upward, he put his tie back on. "Restored to my class," he muttered. He thrust his face toward her and hissed, "True culture is in the mind, the *mind*," he said, and tapped his head, "the mind."

"It's in the heart," she said, "and in how you do things and how you do things is because of who you *are*."

"Nobody in the damn bus cares who you are."

"I care who I am," she said icily.

The lighted bus appeared on top of the next hill and as it approached, they moved out into the street to meet it. He put his hand under her elbow and hoisted her up on the creaking step. She entered with a little smile, as if she were going into a drawing room where everyone had been waiting for her. While he put in the tokens, she sat down on one of the broad front seats for three which faced the aisle. A thin woman with protruding teeth and long yellow hair was sitting on the end of it. His mother moved up beside her and left room for Julian beside herself. He sat down and looked at the floor across the aisle where a pair of thin feet in red and white canvas sandals were planted.

His mother immediately began a general conversation meant to attract anyone who felt like talking. "Can it get any hotter?" she said and removed from her purse a folding fan, black with a Japanese scene on it, which she began to flutter before her.

"I reckon it might could," the woman with the protruding teeth said, "but I know for a fact my apartment couldn't get no hotter."

"It must get the afternoon sun," his mother said. She sat forward and looked up and down the bus. It was half filled. Everybody was white. "I see we have the bus to ourselves," she said. Julian cringed.

"For a change," said the woman across the aisle, the owner of the red and white canvas sandals. "I come on one the other day and they were thick as fleas—up front and all through."

"The world is in a mess everywhere," his mother said. "I don't know how we've let it get in this fix."

"What gets my goat is all those boys from good families stealing automobile tires," the woman with the protruding teeth said. "I told my boy, I said you may not be rich but you been raised right and if I ever catch you in any such mess, they can send you on to the reformatory. Be exactly where you belong."

"Training tells," his mother said. "Is your boy in high school?"

"Ninth grade," the woman said.

"My son just finished college last year. He wants to write but he's selling typewriters until he gets started," his mother said.

The woman leaned forward and peered at Julian. He threw her such a malevolent look that she subsided against the seat. On the floor across the aisle there was an abandoned newspaper. He got up and got it and opened it out in front of him. His mother discreetly continued the conversation in a lower tone but the woman across the aisle said in a loud voice, "Well that's nice. Selling typewriters is close to writing. He can go right from one to the other."

"I tell him," his mother said, "that Rome wasn't built in a day."

Behind the newspaper Julian was withdrawing into the inner compartment of his mind where he spent most of his time. This was a kind of mental bubble in which he established himself when he could not bear to be a part of what was going on around him. From it he could see out and judge but in it he was safe from any kind of penetration from without. It was the only place where he felt free of the general idiocy of his fellows. His mother had never entered it but from it he could see her with absolute clarity.

60 The old lady was clever enough and he thought that if she had started from any of the right premises, more might have been expected of her. She lived according to the laws of her own fantasy world, outside of which he had never seen her set foot. The law of it was to sacrifice herself for him after she had first created the necessity to do so by making a mess of things. If he had permitted her sacrifices, it was only because her lack of foresight had made them necessary. All of her life had been a struggle to act like a Chestny without the Chestny goods, and to give him everything she thought a Chestny ought to have; but since, said she, it was fun to struggle, why complain? And when you had won, as she had won, what fun to look back on the hard times! He could not forgive her that she had enjoyed the struggle and that she thought *she* had won.

What she meant when she said she had won was that she had brought him up successfully and had sent him to college and that he had turned out so well—good looking (her teeth had gone unfilled so that his could be straightened), intelligent (he realized he was too intelligent to be a success), and with a future ahead of him (there was of course no future ahead of him). She excused his gloominess on the grounds that he was still growing up and his radical ideas on his lack of practical experience. She said he didn't yet know a thing about "life," that he hadn't even entered the real world—when already he was as disenchanted with it as a man of fifty.

The further irony of all this was that in spite of her, he had turned out so well. In spite of going to only a third-rate college, he had, on his own initiative, come out with a first-rate education; in spite of growing up dominated by a small mind, he had ended up with a large one; in spite of all her foolish views, he was free of prejudice and unafraid to face facts. Most miraculous of all, instead of being blinded by love for her as she was for him, he had cut himself emotionally free of her and could see her with complete objectivity. He was not dominated by his mother.

The bus stopped with a sudden jerk and shook him from his meditation. A woman from the back lurched forward with little steps and barely escaped falling in his newspaper as she righted herself. She got off and a large Negro got on. Julian kept his paper lowered to watch. It gave him a certain satisfaction to see injustice in daily operation. It confirmed his view that with a few exceptions there was no one worth knowing within a radius of three hundred miles. The Negro was well dressed and carried a briefcase. He looked around and then sat down on the other end of the seat where the woman with the red and white canvas sandals was sitting. He immediately unfolded a newspaper and obscured himself behind it. Julian's mother's elbow at once prodded insistently into his ribs. "Now you see why I won't ride on these buses by myself," she whispered.

The woman with the red and white canvas sandals had risen at the same time the Negro sat down and had gone further back in the bus and taken the seat of the woman who had got off. His mother leaned forward and cast her an approving look.

65 Julian rose, crossed the aisle, and sat down in the place of the woman with the canvas sandals. From this position, he looked serenely across at his mother. Her face had turned an angry red. He stared at her, making his eyes the eyes of a stranger. He felt his tension suddenly lift as if he had openly declared war on her.

He would have liked to get in conversation with the Negro and to talk with him about art or politics or any subject that would be above the comprehension of those around them, but the man remained entrenched behind his paper. He was either ignoring the change of seating or had never noticed it. There was no way for Julian to convey his sympathy.

His mother kept her eyes fixed reproachfully on his face. The woman with the protruding teeth was looking at him avidly as if he were a type of monster new to her.

"Do you have a light?" he asked the Negro.

Without looking away from his paper, the man reached in his pocket and handed him a packet of matches.

70 "Thanks," Julian said. For a moment he held the matches foolishly. A NO SMOKING sign looked down upon him from over the door. This alone would not have deterred him; he had no cigarettes. He had quit smoking some months before because he could not afford it. "Sorry," he muttered and handed back the matches. The Negro lowered the paper and gave him an annoyed look. He took the matches and raised the paper again.

His mother continued to gaze at him but she did not take advantage of his momentary discomfort. Her eyes retained their battered look. Her face seemed to be unnaturally red, as if her blood pressure had risen. Julian allowed no glimmer of sympathy to show on his face. Having got the advantage, he wanted desperately to keep it and carry it through. He would have liked to teach her a lesson that would last her a while, but there seemed no way to continue the point. The Negro refused to come out from behind his paper.

Julian folded his arms and looked stolidly before him, facing her but as if he did not see her, as if he had ceased to recognize her existence. He visualized a scene in which, the bus having reached their stop, he would remain in his seat and when she said, "Aren't you going to get off?" he would look at her as at a stranger who had rashly addressed him. The corner they got off on was usually deserted, but it was well lighted and it would not hurt her to walk by herself the four blocks to the Y. He decided to wait until the time came and then decide whether or not he would let her get off by herself. He would have to be at the Y at ten to bring her back, but he could leave her wondering if he was going to show up. There was no reason for her to think she could always depend on him.

He retired again into the high-ceilinged room sparsely settled with large pieces of antique furniture. His soul expanded momentarily but then he became aware of his mother across from him and the vision shriveled. He studied her coldly. Her feet in little pumps dangled like a child's and did not quite reach the floor. She was training on him an exaggerated look of reproach. He felt completely detached from her. At that moment he could with pleasure have slapped her as he would have slapped a particularly obnoxious child in his charge.

He began to imagine various unlikely ways by which he could teach her a lesson. He might make friends with some distinguished Negro professor or lawyer and bring him home to spend the evening. He would be entirely justified but her blood pressure would rise to 300. He could not push her to the extent of making her have a stroke, and moreover, he had never been successful at making any Negro friends. He had tried to strike up an acquaintance on the bus with some of the better types, with ones that looked like professors or ministers or lawyers. One morning he had sat down next to a distinguished-looking dark brown man who had answered his questions with a sonorous solemnity but who had turned out to be an undertaker. Another day he had sat down beside a cigar-smoking Negro with a diamond ring on his finger, but after a few stilted pleasantries, the Negro had rung the buzzer and risen, slipping two lottery tickets into Julian's hand as he climbed over him to leave.

75 He imagined his mother lying desperately ill and his being able to secure only a Negro doctor for her. He toyed with that idea for a few minutes and then dropped it for a momentary vision of himself participating as a sympathizer in a sit-in demonstration. This was possible but he did not linger with it. Instead, he approached the ultimate horror. He brought home a beautiful suspiciously Negroid woman. Prepare yourself, he said. There is nothing you can do about it. This is the woman I've chosen. She's intelligent, dignified, even good, and she's suffered and she hasn't thought it *fun.* Now persecute us, go ahead and persecute us. Drive her out of here, but remember, you're driving me too. His eyes were narrowed and through the indignation he had generated, he saw his mother across the aisle, purple-faced, shrunken to the dwarf-like proportions of her moral nature, sitting like a mummy beneath the ridiculous banner of her hat.

He was tilted out of his fantasy again as the bus stopped. The door opened with a sucking hiss and out of the dark a large, gaily dressed, sullen-looking colored woman got on with a little boy. The child, who might have been four, had on a short plaid suit and a Tyrolean hat with a blue feather in it. Julian hoped that he would sit down beside him and that the woman would push in beside his mother. He could think of no better arrangement.

As she waited for her tokens, the woman was surveying the seating possibilities —he hoped with the idea of sitting where she was least wanted. There was something familiar-looking about her but Julian could not place what it was. She was a giant of a woman. Her face was set not only to meet opposition but to seek it out. The downward tilt of her large lower lip was like a warning sign: DON'T TAMPER WITH ME. Her bulging figure was encased in a green crepe dress and her feet overflowed in red shoes. She had on a hideous hat. A purple velvet flap came down on one side of it and stood up on the other; the rest of it was green and looked like a cushion with the stuffing out. She carried a mammoth red pocketbook that bulged throughout as if it were stuffed with rocks.

To Julian's disappointment, the little boy climbed up on the empty seat beside his mother. His mother lumped all children, black and white, into the common category, "cute," and she thought little Negroes were on the whole cuter than little white children. She smiled at the little boy as he climbed on the seat.

Meanwhile the woman was bearing down upon the empty seat beside Julian. To his annoyance, she squeezed herself into it. He saw his mother's face change as the woman settled herself next to him and he realized with satisfaction that this was more objectionable to her than it was to him. Her face seemed almost gray and there was a look of dull recognition in her eyes, as if suddenly she had sickened at some awful confrontation. Julian saw that it was because she and the woman had, in a sense, swapped sons. Though his mother would not realize the symbolic significance of this, she would feel it. His amusement showed plainly on his face.

80 The woman next to him muttered something unintelligible to herself. He was conscious of a kind of bristling next to him, a muted growling like that of an angry cat. He could not see anything but the red pocketbook upright on the bulging green thighs. He visualized the woman as she had stood waiting for her tokens—the ponderous figure, rising from the red shoes upward over the solid hips, the mammoth bosom, the haughty face, to the green and purple hat.

His eyes widened.

The vision of the two hats, identical, broke upon him with the radiance of a brilliant sunrise. His face was suddenly lit with joy. He could not believe that Fate had thrust upon his mother such a lesson. He gave a loud chuckle so that she would look at him and see that he saw. She turned her eyes on him slowly. The blue in them seemed to have turned a bruised purple. For a moment he had an uncomfortable sense of her innocence, but it lasted only a second before principle rescued him. Justice entitled him to laugh. His grin hardened until it said to her as plainly as if he were saying aloud: Your punishment exactly fits your pettiness. This should teach you a permanent lesson.

Her eyes shifted to the woman. She seemed unable to bear looking at him and to find the woman preferable. He became conscious again of the bristling presence at his side. The woman was rumbling like a volcano about to become active. His mother's mouth began to twitch slightly at one corner. With a sinking heart, he saw incipient signs of recovery on her face and realized that this was going to strike her suddenly as funny and was going to be no lesson at all. She kept her eyes on the woman and an amused smile came over her face as if the woman were a monkey that had stolen her hat. The little Negro was looking up at her with large fascinated eyes. He had been trying to attract her attention for some time.

"Carver!" the woman said suddenly. "Come heah!"

85 When he saw that the spotlight was on him at last, Carver drew his feet up and turned himself toward Julian's mother and giggled.

"Carver!" the woman. "You heah me? Come heah!"

Carver slid down from the seat but remained squatting with his back against the base of it, his head turned slyly around toward Julian's mother, who was smiling at him. The woman reached a hand across the aisle and snatched him to her. He righted himself and hung backwards on her knees, grinning at Julian's mother. "Isn't he cute?" Julian's mother said to the woman with the protruding teeth.

"I reckon he is," the woman said without conviction.

The Negress yanked him upright but he eased out of her grip and shot across the aisle and scrambled, giggling wildly, onto the seat beside his love.

90 "I think he likes me," Julian's mother said, and smiled at the woman. It was the smile she used when she was being particularly gracious to an inferior. Julian saw everything lost. The lesson had rolled off her like rain on a roof.

The woman stood up and yanked the little boy off the seat as if she were snatching him from contagion. Julian could feel the rage in her at having no weapon like his mother's smile. She gave the child a sharp slap across his leg. He howled once and then thrust his head into her stomach and kicked his feet against her shins. "Behave," she said vehemently.

The bus stopped and the Negro who had been reading the newspaper got off. The woman moved over and set the little boy down with a thump between herself and Julian. She held him firmly by the knee. In a moment he put his hands in front of his face and peeped at Julian's mother through his fingers.

"I see yoooooooo!" she said and put her hand in front of her face and peeped at him.

The woman slapped his hand down. "Quit yo' foolishness," she said, "before I knock the living Jesus out of you!"

95 Julian was thankful that the next stop was theirs. He reached up and pulled the cord. The woman reached up and pulled it at the same time. Oh my God, he thought. He had the terrible intuition that when they got off the bus together, his mother would open her purse and give the little boy a nickel. The gesture would be as natural to her as breathing. The bus stopped and the woman got up and lunged to the front, dragging the child, who wished to stay on, after her. Julian and his mother got up and followed. As they neared the door, Julian tried to relieve her of her pocketbook.

"No," she murmured. "I want to give the little boy a nickel."

"No!" Julian hissed. "No!"

She smiled down at the child and opened her bag. The bus door opened and the woman picked him up by the arm and descended with him, hanging at her hip. Once in the street she set him down and shook him.

Julian's mother had to close her purse while she got down the bus step but as soon as her feet were on the ground, she opened it again and began to rummage inside. "I can't find but a penny," she whispered, "but it looks like a new one."

100 "Don't do it!" Julian said fiercely between his teeth. There was a streetlight on the corner and she hurried to get under it so that she could better see into her pocketbook. The woman was heading off rapidly down the street with the child still hanging backward on her hand.

"Oh little boy!" Julian's mother called and took a few quick steps and caught up with them just beyond the lamppost. "Here's a bright new penny for you," and she held out the coin, which shone bronze in the dim light.

The huge woman turned and for a moment stood, her shoulders lifted and her face frozen with frustrated rage, and stared at Julian's mother. Then all at once she seemed to explode like a piece of machinery that had been given one ounce of pressure too much. Julian saw the black fist swing out with the red pocketbook. He shut his eyes and cringed as he heard the woman shout, "He don't take nobody's pennies!" When he opened his eyes, the woman was disappearing down the street with the little boy staring wide-eyed over her shoulder. Julian's mother was sitting on the sidewalk.

"I told you not to do that," Julian said angrily. "I told you not to do that!"

He stood over her for a minute, gritting his teeth. Her legs were stretched out in front of her and her hat was on her lap. He squatted down and looked her in the face. It was totally expressionless. "You got exactly what you deserved," he said. "Now get up."

105 He picked up her pocketbook and put what had fallen out back in it. He picked the hat up off her lap. The penny caught his eye on the sidewalk and he picked that up and let it drop before her eyes into the purse. Then he stood up and leaned over and held his hands out to pull her up. She remained immobile. He sighed. Rising above them on either side were black apartment buildings, marked with irregular rectangles of light. At the end of the block a man came out of a door and walked off in the opposite direction. "All right," he said, "suppose somebody happens by and wants to know why you're sitting on the sidewalk?"

She took the hand and, breathing hard, pulled heavily up on it and then stood for a moment, swaying slightly as if the spots of light in the darkness were circling around her. Her eyes, shadowed and confused, finally settled on his face. He did not try to conceal his irritation. "I hope this teaches you a lesson," he said. She leaned forward and her eyes raked his face. She seemed trying to determine his identity. Then, as if she found nothing familiar about him, she started off with a headlong movement in the wrong direction.

"Aren't you going on to the Y?" he asked.

"Home," she muttered.

"Well, are we walking?"

110 For answer she kept going. Julian followed along, his hands behind him. He saw no reason to let the lesson she had had go without backing it up with an explanation of its meaning. She might as well be made to understand what had happened to her. "Don't think that was just an uppity Negro woman," he said. "That was the whole colored race which will no longer take your condescending pennies. That was your black double. She can wear the same hat as you, and to be sure," he added gratuitously (because he thought it was funny), "it looked better on her than it did on you. What all this means," he said, "is that the old world is gone. The old manners are obsolete and your graciousness is not worth a damn." He thought bitterly of the house that had been lost for him. "You aren't who you think you are," he said.

She continued to plow ahead, paying no attention to him. Her hair had come undone on one side. She dropped her pocketbook and took no notice. He stooped and picked it up and handed it to her but she did not take it.

"You needn't act as if the world had come to an end," he said, "because it hasn't. From now on you've got to live in a new world and face a few realities for a change. Buck up," he said, "it won't kill you."

She was breathing fast.

"Let's wait on the bus," he said.

"Home," she said thickly.

"I hate to see you behave like this," he said. "Just like a child. I should be able to expect more of you." He decided to stop where he was and make her stop and wait for a bus. "I'm not going any farther," he said, stopping. "We're going on the bus."

She continued to go on as if she had not heard him. He took a few steps and caught her arm and stopped her. He looked into her face and caught his breath. He was looking into a face he had never seen before. "Tell Grandpa to come get me," she said.

He stared, stricken.

"Tell Caroline to come get me," she said.

Stunned, he let her go and she lurched forward again, walking as if one leg were shorter than the other. A tide of darkness seemed to be sweeping her from him. "Mother!" he cried. "Darling, sweetheart, wait!" Crumpling, she fell to the pavement. He dashed forward and fell at her side, crying, "Mamma, Mamma!" He turned her over. Her face was fiercely distorted. One eye, large and staring, moved slightly to the left as if it had become unmoored. The other remained fixed on him, raked his face again, found nothing and closed.

"Wait here, wait here!" he cried and jumped up and began to run for help toward a cluster of lights he saw in the distance ahead of him. "Help, help!" he shouted, but his voice was thin, scarcely a thread of sound. The lights drifted farther away the faster he ran and his feet moved numbly as if they carried him nowhere. The tide of darkness seemed to sweep him back to her, postponing from moment to moment his entry into the world of guilt and sorrow.

➤ *QUESTIONS FOR READING AND WRITING*

1. Who do you find yourself favoring? Julian or Julian's mother? Why? If this were your own mother, how would you deal with her?
2. Describe Julian's mother. What shapes her as a character?
3. Describe Julian. What shapes him as a character? He claims he is "free of prejudice." Do you think he is? Julian describes his mother as living "in her own fantasy world." Do you think he lives in the "real" world? Explain.
4. Julian tells his mother that "true culture is in the mind." She responds, "It's in the heart and in how you do things." What do you think?
5. What was your response when Julian's mother offered Carver a penny? Did you think it was bigotry?
6. What is Julian's reaction when he discovers that his mother and Carver's mother are wearing the same hat? What is your reaction to the final scene, when Julian's mother collapses?
7. What is the theme of this story? Why do you think it's called "Everything That Rises Must Converge"?

Estela Portillo Trambley

(1936–1998)

Estela Portillo Trambley was born in El Paso, Texas, of Mexican-American ancestry. She received an M.A. in English and American literature from the University of Texas at El Paso. "The Pilgrim" is taken from a collection of stories, Rain of Scorpion, *which was first published in 1975, then expanded and revised in 1991. Other works include,* The Day of the Swallows *(1970),* Trini *(1983), and* Sor Juana and Other Plays *(1983).*

The Pilgrim

[1991]

Trini walked with stumbling feet behind La Chaparra. They had followed a network of alleys through El Barrio de la Bola overlooking the western bank of the Río Grande. The adobe choza on top of the sandhill gaped empty, roofless, without windows or door. A gaunt cat sitting on a pile of adobe stared at them with the frugal blank eyes of starvation. It was unusual to see a cat in this barrio. They were usually eaten by the starving people who lived in the makeshift cardboard and tin huts scattered along the hill. La Chaparra, her back against the wall, slid down to the ground, out of breath. The barrio ended on top of a hill that overlooked the smelter across the river on the United States side. Trini, tired, brooding, followed the path that led to the river with her eyes, shading them against the harsh sun. La Chaparra had brought her to the easiest crossing. The boundary between Juárez and Smeltertown in El Paso was no more than a series of charcos extending about fifty feet.

"You sure you want to do it?" La Chaparra's voice was skeptical. She muttered under her breath, "You're crazy, no money, having a baby in a strange land—you're crazy."

Trini turned to reassure the seasoned wetback, though her body was feeling the strain of the climb. "Everything will be fine, now that I know the way, thanks to you." She would wait for the pains of birth, then her pilgrimage would begin to the Virgin across the river. Somewhere in El Paso was a church, el Sagrado Corazón. She would be led. Things had been taken care of haphazardly. Tonio had sent her forty American dollars which she promptly gave to Elia for Linda's keep. This time, Linda, she promised, this time will be the last time I shall leave you behind. I will find land, and there we'll stay. The dream stifled her guilt. For her, destiny was an intuitive pull, a plan with a dream, sometimes without practical considerations. But practical considerations were luxuries in life. She could not afford to think of the dangers ahead, the suffering. She must just go. Pull, pull through a dark hole, Perla had said.

On the way back home, La Chaparra cautioned her of the dangers—watch out for la migra, stay away from the highway. If they catch you, you might have the baby in jail if they don't process you back soon enough. Day crossings were easier through El Barrio de la Bola. La Chaparra wished her well and left her at the entrance to El Arroyo Colorado.

5 The birth pains came before dawn a few days later, a soft, late autumn dawn that wove its mysteries for her between pains. She took a streetcar at six that left her on the edge of El Barrio de la Bola. From there she walked all the way down the sandhill through the arrabales leading to the river. The river was not a threat. Most of the water had been banked upstream into irrigation ditches that followed newfound fields converted into farmland from the desert.

This was the point of safe crossing, safe from deep water, if not completely safe from the border patrols who made their morning rounds on the highway that followed the river. Still, her chances were good. Her pains were coming with regularity, but at distant intervals. From the Juárez side of the river she could see the small, humble homes scattered in the hills of Smeltertown. She rested under a tree on the edge of the river, her pores feeling the chill of the coming winter. She leaned her head against the tree, a lilac tree, of all things, in the middle of nowhere! For an instant, she seemed to feel a force from the earth, from her hold on the tree. She laughed, then pain cut sharply through her body. It sharpened and focused her instinct. Failure was impossible.

She took off her shoes and waded across a shallow area until she came to a place where the water was flowing uniformly downstream. She made her way carefully, looking for sure footing, her toes clutching at cold sand. Brown mimosa seeds floated on the surface of the water. Then, without warning, she felt herself slipping into the river. As she fell, a pain broke crimson, a red pain that mixed and swirled with the mud water that was up to her breasts now. She had lost the shoes she was carrying. Her feet sank into the deep soft sand, and she kicked forward to free herself. The steady flow of water helped pull her toward a dry section of riverbed. She was but a few feet away from the American side. Then, she was across.

Shoeless, drenched through and through, holding a wet rebozo around her, she made her way, breathless and cold, to a dirt road leading to the main highway. She looked both ways for any sign of a patrol car, but saw none. She sighed with relief, searching around for a place to rest. Ahead, she saw an abandoned gas station with a rusty broken-down car by its side. She could hide there until a bus arrived. She sat behind the car with the highway before her; looming across the highway was a mountain carved by the machinery of the smelter, contoured by time, veined with the colors of a past life. Its granite silence gave her comfort. She understood mountains. Like trees and the earth, they bound her, gave her their strength. Pain again. It consumed her as she clutched the edge of a fender, the metal cutting into her palm.

While the pain still wavered, she saw a bus approaching far away along the stretch of highway. She wiped the perspiration from her face with the wet rebozo, her body shivering, her vision hazed as she fixed her eyes on the moving, yellow hope that came toward her. Her blood was singing birth, a fading and then a sharpening of her senses. She felt weak as she raised her heavy, tortured body and made her way to the edge of the highway. She stood, feet firm, arms waving. Oh, Sweet Virgin, make it stop! She waited, eyes closed, until she heard the grinding stop. Thank you, Sweet Mother. She opened her eyes to see the door of the bus swing open. When she got on, she saw the driver's eyes questioning. Words came out of her mouth; the clearness of her voice surprised her. "I have no money, but I must get to a church."

10 For a second, the bus driver stared at the pregnant woman, muddied and unkempt, standing her ground. He simply nodded, and the bus went on its way. She saw that the people on the bus were mostly Mexican like herself. Their eyes were frankly and curiously staring. A woman came up and helped her to a seat. She asked with concern, "Is there anything I can do?"

Trini looked at her with pleading eyes. "Where is the church?" She was breathing hard against the coming of another pain.

"A Catholic church?"

Trini nodded. The pain came in purple streaks. She bent her head, her face perspiring freely.

"It's your time," the woman whispered. "There's a hospital near."

15 "No, no, no, the church." Trini's plea swirled with the pain. She whispered, "The Virgin told me."

"¡Jesucristo!"

It seemed that the bus driver was going faster without making his usual stops. No one protested. The church was the destination now. Trini leaned her head against the window, hardly conscious of buildings interlacing light and sounds. At a distance, a church steeple rose south of the maze of city buildings. Someone said, "Over there, El Sagrado Corazón."

Joy danced on the brink of Trini's pain. El Sagrado Corazón! She had been led. She had been helped. She was certain now that her child was meant to be born in the church. The pain pierced, bounced, and dispersed. Then she breathed freely. The bus had stopped. The driver was pointing out directions. "Just go all the way down the street, then turn left."

The woman helped Trini off the bus as voices called out words of sympathy and good luck. As the bus took off again, Trini's legs gave way. She fell on bended knee on the sidewalk. The pains were almost constant now. She looked up at the woman with pleading eyes as the woman cleansed her brow, encouraging, "Just a little way now, pobrecita."

20 "I have to find the Virgin . . ." The words were dry in her throat.

"The rectory . . ."

"No, the church." Trini shook her head in desperation, breathing hard. "The Virgin."

The woman said no more, bracing herself to hold Trini's weight. Through a wave of nausea, Trini saw the church before her. Ave María, Madre de Dios, bendita seas entre todas las mujeres. The prayer came like a flowing relief. They were climbing the steps slowly. Happy moans broke from Trini's throat as her legs wavered and her body shook in pain. She could feel herself leaning heavily on the woman. The woman opened the door of the church, and they walked into its silence. Before them were the long aisles leading up to the altar, a long, quiet, shadowy path. The woman whispered, "Can you make it?"

Trini looked up and saw what seemed like miles before her, but in front of the altar to the right was the Virgin Mary holding out her arms to her. The same smile on Her face as when she had looked down at Trini in the Juárez church. The pain was now one thin tightrope made of colored ribbons that went round and round, swirls of red and black. Reflections from the stained glass windows pulsed their colors, hues of mystery, creation. Colors wavered and swam before her eyes, the Virgin's heartbeat. Yes, she would make it. She stretched out her hand, feeling for the side of a pew to support herself. There was peace now in spite of the pain. The candles flickered, dancing a happiness before the Virgin. But now her body made its own demand, one drumming blow of pain. She fell back in a faint, and the woman broke her fall to the floor as two priests ran down the aisle to see what the matter was. Yes, the Virgin had been right all along . . .

Trini held the piece of paper in her shaking hand. It was in English so the words meant little to her, but the name Ricardo Esconde written in black ink stood out bold and strong. Her eyes, radiant in her triumph, looked for a second into the unconcerned eyes of the clerk, then flickered away. "Gracias."

Thank you, God—thank you, clerk—it was all over. Her son's birth had been registered. She walked away unsteadily, the weight of the baby in her arms, the paper held tightly in her hand. She made her way to a chair in the corner of the office, a queasiness commanding, stomach churning, the taste of vomit in her mouth. She let herself fall into the chair as she tightened her hold on the baby. Her breath came in spurts. She raised her head, throwing it back, mouth half-open to draw in air, her body withstanding many things—fear, hunger, fatigue. She had run away from the priests. Her mind retraced the time of her escape as her shaking hands carefully folded the birth certificate.

It was now in the pocket of her skirt. She had run away, not because the priests had been unkind. They had helped with the birth on the floor of the church, angry questions lost among sympathetic murmurings. After that, sleep overtook the pain. When she awoke, the priests placed a son in her arms, clean, wrapped in a kitchen towel. She had smiled her gratitude and had gone back to sleep. Later, she eagerly drank the hot soup and ate the bread they offered her, the baby close and warm by her side. But then the priest who spoke Spanish told her that the immigration people had to be notified. It was the law. The woman had told them that she had crossed the river.

When they had left her alone, she had simply taken the baby and walked away, out of a side door into an empty street in the early afternoon. She had walked south. When she could walk no more, she sat on a corner bench to rest. A Mexican woman sat next to her, waiting for a bus. She looked at Trini and the baby with interested eyes but said nothing until Trini asked, "Where do I register my baby as a citizen?"

Instantly, the woman understood. She shook her head as if to push away the futility of things, but answered, "City-county building." The woman was pointing north. "It's closed now."

30 "How far?"

"About twelve, thirteen blocks north, on San Antonio Street." The woman's eyes were troubled. "Just walk up, then turn left, but watch out for la migra. You look like you just came out of the river."

The bus stopped before them, and the woman disappeared behind its doors. Trini looked around and saw warehouses with closed doors, parking lots yawning their emptiness. She had the urge to cry, to give up, but the sun was falling in the west, and the baby in her arms told her differently. She sat numb, without plan, without thought as buses came and went, loading and unloading passengers. She sat on the bench until dark, putting the baby to her breast before she set out again. How insatiable was her drowsy, grey fatigue. She set one foot before the other without direction as gauze clouds were swallowed by the night. The night had swallowed her and the baby too. She made her way to an alley, away from the wind, and there in a corner slept, the baby clasped tightly in her arms.

That had been yesterday. Now it was all over. She had found the building—the baby was registered. A thought came to her like the climbing of a mountain, steep and harsh. What now? What now? She caught the stare of a woman waiting for the clerk. Then Trini noticed the clerk's eyes on the baby. The man was clasping his hands, then unclasping them, then tapping his fingers on the counter as if he were deciding to call the authorities.

Wan and pale, Trini drew the baby closely to her and made her way to the door marked "Vital Statistics." Her hands were trembling out of weakness and fear. The baby began to cry as Trini made her way out of the building, shouldering her way through people, avoiding eyes. She was a curious sight, a muddied, barefoot woman with wild hair and feverish eyes, holding a baby, running for dear life. She ran along the streets that took her away from tall buildings, from uniforms, from American people. She was going south again. Her mouth felt dry and raw, and the towel the baby was wrapped in was soaking wet. Oh, my baby, I have to change you, feed you, her heart cried. But still, she ran until she could run no more, standing against the wall of a building to catch her breath, avoiding the curious stares of people. Before her was a street sign. The words were distended images, visions of hope: "Santa Fe."

35 Holy Faith! The name of the street was Holy Faith! An omen—a guiding force—a new decision. The hope was as feverish as her body. She would follow the street to its very end. She started on her way again, feet heavy, body numb, the baby now crying lustily in her arms. People had been left behind. Only one man passed her, unconcerned. Before her was a railroad yard, across the street a bar, beyond that an old familiar bridge, El Puente Negro! Strange, the circle of her life. The end of Santa Fe had brought her to a dead end. She did not want to cross the bridge. She

did not want to go back. She had to find a place nearby to rest, to look after the baby's needs.

Behind a warehouse was a lumberyard fenced off with sagging, rusty wire. She made her way through one section where the fence had sagged to the ground, her feet stepping over a desiccated piece of lumber, half-buried in dry mud. She sat down against the wall of the building and hushed her baby with soft tones of love. The baby had to be changed. She raised her skirt and jerked at the cotton slip underneath. It did not give. The baby lay on the ground crying harder. She pulled at a shoulder strap, tearing it, repeating the process until both straps gave. She pulled the garment from the knees, stepped out of it, then tore it in pieces to make a diaper. With quick fingers she unpinned the wet towel, flinging it over a pile of lumber. Afterwards she placed the dry pieces of cloth on the ground and lifted the baby onto them. He was whimpering in tired, spasmodic little sobs. Her breasts were hard and sore in their fullness. Now she rested against the building, picking up the baby and turning him tenderly toward her. The nipple touched his lips. He took it eagerly, drops of milk forming on the sides of his little mouth. Then she dozed with the baby at her breast.

After a while she awoke with a start, aware of the greyness of the day. She sat quite still, the baby fast asleep. Her arms felt cramped and stiff, so she laid the child low on her lap and stretched out her legs.

Through half-closed lids she saw El Puente Negro at a great distance, like a blot against the greyness of the day. Her mind was a greyness too, things not yet clear or distinct. Thoughts ran: a world in circles, a black bridge standing, pulling through a dark hole, Santa Fe—faith, faith and the burning of a fire, a plan. Perhaps it was all useless, this trying. She felt as if she were a blot lost in space. All she wanted was a chance, a way to stay in the United States, to find a piece of land, to have the family together.

It had taken Celestina fifteen years to buy a thirsty, ungiving piece of land in Mexico—fifteen years! No, there was a better way in the United States where the poor and hungry did not have to stay poor and hungry. Something had pulled her to this country of miracles. It was all still shapeless, meaningless, beyond her. But things would take shape. She would give them shape. A blot in space was the beginning of many things in all directions. She looked down at the sleeping child, Sabochi's child, a son, Rico.

QUESTIONS FOR READING AND WRITING

1. Trini is an illegal immigrant. Do you think she is wrong to try to stay in the United States? Why?
2. Imagine that you are in her situation. Would you try to stay in this country? Explain.
3. Why does she want to give birth in the United States? What do you think will happen to her and her child?
4. What is the central idea or theme of "The Pilgrim"?

LESLIE MARMON SILKO (b. 1948)

Of mixed Native-American, Mexican, and Caucasian descent, Leslie Marmon Silko was raised on the Laguna Pueblo reservation in New Mexico. After graduating from the University of New Mexico, she studied the law for a short time before deciding to pursue writing as a career. Her first novel, Ceremony *(1977), told the story of a young Native American's return to the reservation following World War II. In addition, she has written collections of poems and short stories, as well as* Yellow Woman *and* A Beauty of the Spirit, *a collection of essays about modern Native-American life. Her latest novel,* Almanac of the Dead, *was published in 1991. In her work, Silko often draws upon the rich storytelling tradition of her Pueblo Indian heritage to explore the conflict between Native-American values and the dominant white culture.*

THE MAN TO SEND RAIN CLOUDS

One

They found him under a big cottonwood tree. His Levi jacket and pants were faded light-blue so that he had been easy to find. The big cottonwood tree stood apart from a small grove of winterbare cottonwoods which grew in the wide, sandy arroyo. He had been dead for a day or more, and the sheep had wandered and scattered up and down the arroyo. Leon and his brother-in-law, Ken, gathered the sheep and left them in the pen at the sheep camp before they returned to the cottonwood tree. Leon waited under the tree while Ken drove the truck through the deep sand to the edge of the arroyo. He squinted up at the sun and unzipped his jacket—it sure was hot for this time of year. But high and northwest the blue mountains were still deep in snow. Ken came sliding down the low, crumbling bank about fifty yards down, and he was bringing the red blanket.

Before they wrapped the old man, Leon took a piece of string out of his pocket and tied a small gray feather in the old man's long white hair. Ken gave him the paint. Across the brown wrinkled forehead he drew a streak of white and along the high cheekbones he drew a strip of blue paint. He paused and watched Ken throw pinches of corn meal and pollen into the wind that fluttered the small gray feather. Then Leon painted with yellow under the old man's broad nose, and finally, when he had painted green across the chin, he smiled.

"Send us rain clouds, Grandfather." They laid the bundle in the back of the pickup and covered it with a heavy tarp before they started back to the pueblo.

They turned off the highway onto the sandy pueblo road. Not long after they passed the store and post office they saw Father Paul's car coming toward them. When he recognized their faces he slowed his car and waved for them to stop. The young priest rolled down the car window.

5 "Did you find old Teofilo?" he asked loudly.

Leon stopped the truck. "Good morning, Father. We were just out to the sheep camp. Everything is O.K. now."

"Thank God for that. Teofilo is a very old man. You really shouldn't allow him to stay at the sheep camp alone."

"No, he won't do that any more now."

"Well, I'm glad you understand. I hope I'll be seeing you at Mass this week—we missed you last Sunday. See if you can get old Teofilo to come with you." The priest smiled and waved at them as they drove away.

Two

10 Louise and Teresa were waiting. The table was set for lunch, and the coffee was boiling on the black iron stove. Leon looked at Louise and then at Teresa.

"We found him under a cottonwood tree in the big arroyo near sheep camp. I guess he sat down to rest in the shade and never got up again." Leon walked toward the old man's bed. The red plaid shawl had been shaken and spread carefully over the bed, and a new brown flannel shirt and pair of stiff new Levis were arranged neatly beside the pillow. Louise held the screen door open while Leon and Ken carried in the red blanket. He looked small and shriveled, and after they dressed him in the new shirt and pants he seemed more shrunken.

It was noontime now because the church bells rang the Angelus. They ate the beans with hot bread, and nobody said anything until after Teresa poured the coffee.

Ken stood up and put on his jacket. "I'll see about the gravediggers. Only the top layer of soil is frozen. I think it can be ready before dark."

Leon nodded his head and finished his coffee. After Ken had been gone for a while, the neighbors and clanspeople came quietly to embrace Teofilo's family and to leave food on the table because the gravediggers would come to eat when they were finished.

Three

15 The sky in the west was full of pale-yellow light. Louise stood outside with her hands in the pockets of Leon's green army jacket that was too big for her. The funeral was over, and the old men had taken their candles and medicine bags and were gone. She waited until the body was laid into the pickup before she said anything to Leon. She touched his arm, and he noticed that her hands were still dusty from the corn meal that she had sprinkled around the old man. When she spoke, Leon could not hear her.

"What did you say? I didn't hear you."

"I said that I had been thinking about something."

"About what?"

"About the priest sprinkling holy water for Grandpa. So he won't be thirsty."

20 Leon stared at the new moccasins that Teofilo had made for the ceremonial dances in the summer. They were nearly hidden by the red blanket. It was getting colder, and the wind pushed gray dust down the narrow pueblo road. The sun was approaching the long mesa where it disappeared during the winter. Louise stood there shivering and watching his face. Then he zipped up his jacket and opened the truck door. "I'll see if he's there."

Four

Ken stopped the pickup at the church, and Leon got out; and then Ken drove down the hill to the graveyard where people were waiting. Leon knocked at the old carved door with its symbols of the Lamb. While he waited he looked up at the twin bells from the king of Spain with the last sunlight pouring around them in their tower.

The priest opened the door and smiled when he saw who it was. "Come in! What brings you here this evening?"

The priest walked toward the kitchen, and Leon stood with his cap in his hand, playing with the earflaps and examining the living room—the brown sofa, the green armchair, and the brass lamp that hung down from the ceiling by links of chain. The priest dragged a chair out of the kitchen and offered it to Leon.

"No thank you, Father. I only came to ask you if you would bring your holy water to the graveyard."

The priest turned away from Leon and looked out the window at the patio full of shadows and the dining-room windows of the nuns' cloister across the patio. The curtains were heavy, and the light from within faintly penetrated; it was impossible to see the nuns inside eating supper. "Why didn't you tell me he was dead? I could have brought the Last Rites anyway."

Leon smiled. "It wasn't necessary, Father."

The priest stared down at his scuffed brown loafers and the worn hem of his cassock. "For a Christian burial it was necessary."

His voice was distant, and Leon thought that his blue eyes looked tired.

"It's O.K., Father, we just want him to have plenty of water."

The priest sank down in the green chair and picked up a glossy missionary magazine. He turned the colored pages full of lepers and pagans without looking at them.

"You know I can't do that, Leon. There should have been the Last Rites and a funeral Mass at the very least."

Leon put on his green cap and pulled the flaps down over his ears. "It's getting late, Father. I've got to go."

When Leon opened the door Father Paul stood up and said, "Wait." He left the room and came back wearing a long brown overcoat. He followed Leon out the door and across the dim churchyard to the adobe steps in front of the church. They both stooped to fit through the low adobe entrance. And when they started down the hill to the graveyard only half of the sun was visible above the mesa.

The priest approached the grave slowly, wondering how they had managed to dig into the frozen ground; and then he remembered that this was New Mexico, and saw the pile of cold loose sand beside the hole. The people stood close to each other with little clouds of steam puffing from their faces. The priest looked at them and saw a pile of jackets, gloves, and scarves in the yellow, dry tumbleweeds that grew in the graveyard. He looked at the red blanket, not sure that Teofilo was so small, wondering if it wasn't some perverse Indian trick—something they did in March to ensure a good harvest—wondering if maybe old Teofilo was actually at sheep camp corraling the sheep for the night. But there he was, facing into a cold dry wind and squinting at the last sunlight, ready to bury a red wool blanket while the faces of the parishioners were in shadow with the last warmth of the sun on their backs.

His fingers were stiff, and it took them a long time to twist the lid off the holy water. Drops of water fell on the red blanket and soaked into dark icy spots. He sprinkled the grave and the water disappeared almost before it touched the dim, cold sand; it reminded him of something—he tried to remember what it was, because he thought if he could remember he might understand this. He sprinkled more water; he shook the container until it was empty, and the water fell through the light from sundown like August rain that fell while the sun was still shining, almost evaporating before it touched the wilted squash flowers.

The wind pulled at the priest's brown Franciscan robe and swirled away the corn meal and pollen that had been sprinkled on the blanket. They lowered the bundle into the ground, and they didn't bother to untie the stiff pieces of new rope that were tied around the ends of the blanket. The sun was gone, and over on the highway the eastbound lane was full of headlights. The priest walked away slowly. Leon watched him climb the hill, and when he had disappeared within the tall, thick walls, Leon turned to look up at the high blue mountains in the deep snow that reflected a faint red light from the west. He felt good because it was finished, and he was happy about the sprinkling of the holy water, now the old man could send them big thunderclouds for sure.

➤ *QUESTIONS FOR READING AND WRITING*

1. What motivates Leon to paint Teofilo's face and put a feather in his hair?
2. Why don't they tell the priest that Teofilo is dead?
3. Why does the narrator mention that the twin church bells are from the king of Spain?
4. Why do you think the priest changes his mind about sprinkling the holy water on Teofilo's body?
5. What does the narrator mean by "now the old man could send them big thunderclouds for sure"?

◆ POETRY ◆

WILLIAM BLAKE (1757–1827)

The son of a London haberdasher, William Blake received very little formal education. When he was ten he entered a drawing school, and later studied for a few months at the Royal Academy of Art. At the age of fourteen he was apprenticed to an engraver, and, after seven years, he was able to earn his living illustrating books. From his early twenties to his sixties, when he chose to devote himself exclusively to pictorial art, Blake produced books of his own poetry, which were painstakingly illustrated and handcolored, often with the help of his wife. His early books of poetry, Songs of

Innocence *(1789) and* Songs of Experience *(1794), from which the following poems are taken, express Blake's rage at the social injustices of England. His later work, the so-called* Prophetic Works, *are much more difficult. In these highly symbolic and often cryptic poems, Blake created his own complicated mythological system based on his deeply held religious and spiritual beliefs. (His wife said of him: "I have very little of Mr. Blake's company; he is always in Paradise.") His now famous verses were not very well-known during his lifetime, and it is only in the past century that he has earned a wider readership.*

THE CHIMNEY SWEEPER [1789]

When my mother died I was very young,
And my father sold me while yet my tongue
Could scarcely cry "'weep! 'weep! 'weep!"
So your chimneys I sweep, and in soot I sleep.

There's little Tom Dacre, who cried when his head,
That curled like a lamb's back, was shaved: so I said
"Hush, Tom! Never mind it, for when your head's bare
You know the soot cannot spoil your white hair."

And so he was quiet, and that very night,
As Tom was a-sleeping, he had such a sight!
That thousands of sweepers, Dick, Joe, Ned, and Jack,
Were all of them locked up in coffins of black.

And by came an Angel who had a bright key,
And he opened the coffins and set them all free;
Then down a green plain leaping, laughing, they run,
And wash in a river, and shine in the sun.

Then naked and white, all their bags left behind
They rise upon clouds and *sport* in the wind;
And the Angel told Tom, if he'd be a good boy,
He'd have God for his father, and never want joy.

And so Tom awoke, and we rose in the dark,
And go with our bags and our brushes to work.
Though the morning was cold, Tom was happy and warm;
So if all do their duty they need not fear harm.

QUESTIONS FOR READING AND WRITING

1. Describe the tone and rhythm of this poem. How does it shape your response to the story of the chimney sweeper?
2. Interpret Tom's dream. Does religion play a useful role in his life? Explain.
3. Reread the last line of the poem. Do you think this is really the message of the poem? Why or why not?
4. Can you imagine a similar poem being written about the poor that exist in the world today? Explain.

LONDON [1794]

I wander through each chartered street,
Near where the chartered Thames does flow,
And mark in every face I meet
Marks of weakness, marks of woe.

In every cry of every man,
In every infant's cry of fear,
In every voice, in every ban,
The mind-forged manacles I hear.

How the chimney-sweeper's cry
Every black'ning church appalls
And the hapless soldier's sigh
Runs in blood down palace walls.

But most through midnight streets I hear
How the youthful harlot's curse
Blasts the new born infant's tear
And blights with plagues the marriage hearse.

➤ *QUESTIONS FOR READING AND WRITING*

1. What are "mind-forged manacles"? Can you think of any "mind-forged manacles" that exist today?
2. What is the "youthful harlot's curse" and what does it have to do with blasting "the new born infant's tear" or plaguing "the marriage hearse"?
3. Compare this vision of the city with that of Wordsworth as expressed in "Composed on Westminster Bridge" (p. 899).

WANDA COLEMAN (b. 1946)

Wanda Coleman has received fellowships from the National Endowment for the Arts and the Guggenheim Foundation and was awarded the 1999 Lenore Marshall Poetry Prize. Her most recent books of poetry included Bathwater Wine *(1998),* Native in a Strange Land *(1996), and* Hand Dance *(1993). When not writing, she hosts an interview program on Pacific Radio. She told* Contemporary Authors: *"Words seem inadequate in expressing the anger and outrage I feel at the persistent racism that permeates every aspect of black American life. Since words are what I am best at, I concern myself with this as an urban actuality as best I can."*

Sweet Mama Wanda Tells Fortunes for a Price

dark stairs
me walking up them
the room
is cold
i am here to fuck
then go back
to the streets

he sighs
touches
likes my lips
my cocoa thighs
we lay down
the bed yields
he comes off calling mama

outside
i count my cash
it's been a good night
the street is cold
i head east

➤ *QUESTIONS FOR READING AND WRITING*

1. Who is the speaker in this poem? What kind of "fortunes" does she tell?
2. What is the tone of the poem? What indicates that?
3. What does the speaker mean by "the street is cold"?

Billy Collins (b. 1941)

Billy Collins is the author of six books of poetry, and his work has appeared in a variety of publications, including Poetry, American Poetry Review, American Scholar, Harper's, Paris Review, *and the* New Yorker. *He has received fellowships from the National Endowment for the Arts and the Guggenheim Foundation, and in 1992 he was chosen to serve as "Literary Lion" by the New York Public Library. He teaches at Lehman College, of the City University of New York, and lives in Somers, New York.*

Victoria's Secret [1998]

The one in the upper left-hand corner
is giving me a look
that says I know you are here
and I have nothing better to do
for the remainder of human time
than return your persistent but engaging stare.
She is wearing a deeply scalloped
flame-stitch halter top
with padded push-up styling
and easy side-zip tap pants.

The one on the facing page, however,
who looks at me over her bare shoulder,
cannot hide the shadow of annoyance in her brow.
You have interrupted me,
she seems to be saying,
with your coughing and your loud music.
Now please leave me alone;
let me finish whatever it was I was doing
in my organza-trimmed
whisperweight camisole with
keyhole closure and a point d'esprit mesh back.

I wet my thumb and flip the page.
Here, the one who happens to be reclining
in a satin and lace merry window
with an inset lace-up front,
decorated underwire cups and bodice
with lace ruffles along the bottom
and hook-and-eye closure in the back,
is wearing a slightly contorted expression,
her head thrust back, mouth partially open,
a confusing mixture of pain and surprise
as if she had stepped on a tack
just as I was breaking down
her bedroom door with my shoulder.

Nor does the one directly beneath her
look particularly happy to see me.
She is arching one eyebrow slightly
as if to say, so what if I am wearing nothing
but this stretch panne velvet bodysuit
with a low sweetheart neckline
featuring molded cups and adjustable straps.
Do you have a problem with that?!

The one on the far right is easier to take,
her eyes half-closed
as if she were listening to a medley
of lullabies playing faintly on a music box.
Soon she will drop off to sleep,
her head nestled in the soft crook of her arm,
and later she will wake up in her
Spandex slip dress with the high side slit,
deep scoop neckline, elastic shirring,
and concealed back zip and vent.

But opposite her,
stretched out catlike on a couch
in the warm glow of a paneled library,
is one who wears a distinctly challenging expression,
her face tipped up, exposing
her long neck, her perfectly flared nostrils.
Go ahead, her expression tells me,
take off my satin charmeuse gown
with a sheer, jacquard bodice
decorated with a touch of shimmering Lurex.
Go ahead, fling it into the fireplace.
What do I care, her eyes say, we're all going to hell anyway.

I have other mail to open,
but I cannot help noticing her neighbor
whose eyes are downcast,
her head ever so demurely bowed to the side
as if she were the model who sat for Coreggio
when he painted "The Madonna of St. Jerome,"
only, it became so ungodly hot in Parma
that afternoon, she had to remove
the traditional blue robe
and pose there in his studio
in a beautifully shaped satin teddy
with an embossed V-front,
princess seaming to mold the bodice,
and puckered knit detail.

And occupying the whole facing page
is one who displays that expression
we have come to associate with photographic beauty.
Yes, she is pouting about something,
all lower lip and cheekbone.
Perhaps her ice cream has tumbled
out of its cone onto the parquet floor.
Perhaps she has been waiting all day
for a new sofa to be delivered,

waiting all day in a stretch lace hipster
with lattice edging, sating frog closures,
velvet scrollwork, cuffed ankles,
flare silhouette, and knotted shoulder straps
available in black, champagne, almond,
cinnabar, plum, bronze, mocha,
peach, ivory, carmel, blush, butter, rose, and periwinkle.
It is, of course, impossible to say,
impossible to know what she is thinking,
why her mouth is the shape of petulance.

But this is already too much.
Who has the time to linger on these delicate
lures, these once unmentionable things?
Life is rushing by like a mad, swollen river.
One minute roses are opening in the garden
and the next, snow is flying past my window.
Plus the phone is ringing.
The dog is whining at the door.
Rain is beating on the roof.
And as always there is a list of things I have to do
before the night descends, black and silky,
and the dark hours begin to hurtle by,
before the little doors of the body swing shut
and I ride to sleep, my closed eyes
still burning from all the glossy lights of day.

➤ *QUESTIONS FOR READING AND WRITING*

1. The title of the poem, "Victoria's Secret," is a reference to a well-known store catalog that features women modeling lingerie. What do you think makes the speaker's commentary so humorous as he peruses the pictures?
2. His descriptions of what the models are wearing are very detailed. Why?
3. To what extent is this poem a commentary on American culture? What is Victoria's secret?
4. In what way does the tone of the last stanza differ from the rest? What point do you think the speaker is trying to make?

LAWRENCE FERLINGHETTI (b. 1919)

Lawrence Ferlinghetti was born in Yonkers, New York. His father died before he was born, and his mother was institutionalized following a severe mental breakdown. Shuttled between relatives, he lived in France and a public orphanage before settling with a rich family in Bronxville, New York, where his aunt was working as a governess. After attending the University of North Carolina, where he majored in journalism, Ferlinghetti enlisted in the navy. During World War II, he served as a commander in

the Normandy invasion, and afterward took advantage of the G.I. Bill, earning an M.A. from Columbia University in 1948 and a Ph.D. from the Sorbonne in Paris in 1951. Returning to the United States, he settled in San Francisco where he cofounded City Lights *magazine, the City Lights Pocket Book Shop, and the City Lights Press. The store—the first in the country to specialize in paperbacks—and the press became the focal point of the Beat Generation—a group of enormously influential American writers and artists that included Allen Ginsberg, Jack Kerouac, and William Burroughs. A prolific poet, playwright, and editor, Ferlinghetti's most famous work continues to be his collection of poems* A Coney Island of the Mind *(1958), which, with its embrace of open-form and colloquial speech, is considered one of the key works of the Beat movement. Today, Ferlinghetti continues to operate the City Lights bookstore when he is not traveling giving poetry readings. "Constantly Risking Absurdity" is taken from* A Coney Island of the Mind.

Constantly Risking Absurdity [1958]

Constantly risking absurdity
and death
whenever he performs
above the heads
of his audience
the poet like an acrobat
climbs on rime
to a high wire of his own making
and balancing on eyebeams
above a sea of faces
paces his way
to the other side of day
performing entrechats
and sleight-of-foot tricks
and other high theatrics
and all without mistaking
any thing
for what it may not be
For he's the super realist
who must perforce perceive
taut truth
before the taking of each stance or step
in his supposed advance

toward that still higher perch
where Beauty stands and waits
with gravity
to start her death-defying leap

And he
a little charleychaplin man
who may or may not catch
her fair eternal form
spreadeagled in the empty air
of existence

➤ *QUESTIONS FOR READING AND WRITING*

1. The speaker compares a poet to an acrobat. In what way is the structure of the poem like acrobatics? Does the comparison work for you?
2. To what extent is the poet a "super realist" who tries to catch "Beauty"?

ROBERT FRANCIS (1901–1987)

Robert Francis was born in Upland, Pennsylvania, and graduated from Harvard University in 1923. A professional writer his entire life, he toured throughout the United States teaching writing workshops and delivering lectures. His collections of poetry include: Stand With Me *(1936),* The Sound I Listened For *(1944), and* Robert Francis: Collected Poems 1936–1976 *(1976). His autobiography* The Trouble with Francis *was published in 1971.*

PITCHER [1960]

His art is eccentricity, his aim
How not to hit the mark he seems to aim at,

His passion how to avoid the obvious,
His technique how to vary the avoidance.

The others throw to be comprehended. He
Throws to be a moment misunderstood.

Yet not too much. Not errant, arrant, wild,
But every seeming aberration willed.

Not to, yet still, still to communicate
Making the batter understand too late.

➤ *QUESTIONS FOR READING AND WRITING*

1. In what way is the pitcher's "aim / How not to hit the mark he seems to aim at"?
2. Why would he want to make "the batter understand too late"?

THOMAS HARDY (1840–1928)

Thomas Hardy was born near Dorchester in southwestern England. Apprenticed to an architect at the age of fifteen, Hardy received very little formal schooling outside of the local schools he attended as a boy, but improved himself by reading in his spare time. Unhappy as an architect, he began writing fiction and poetry and, though his first novel was not a success, the success of his second, Under the Greenwood Tree *(1872), allowed him to devote himself to a literary career. Hardy followed this with a string of eleven remarkable novels set in his native Dorchester (called Wessex in the novels), including* Far from the Madding Crowd *(1874),* The Return of the Native *(1879),* The Mayor of Casterbridge *(1887), and* Tess of the D'Ubervilles *(1891). These often bleak novels share a common theme—that human destiny is controlled not by human will but by forces beyond humankind's control. Disillusioned after the hostile reception to* Jude the Obscure *(1895), considered by many modern critics to be his greatest work, Hardy turned to writing highly original poetry that often explored the same themes as his novels. His* Collected Poems *was published in 1931.*

THE MAN HE KILLED [1902]

Had he and I but met
By some old ancient inn,
We should have sat us down to wet
Right many a nipperkin!

But ranged as infantry,
And staring face to face,
I shot at him as he at me,
And killed him in his place.

I shot him dead because—
Because he was my foe.
Just so: my foe of course he was;
That's clear enough; although

He thought he'd list, perhaps,
Off-hand like—just as I—
Was out of work—had sold his traps—
No other reason why.

Yes; quaint and curious war is!
You shoot a fellow down
You'd treat, if met where any bar is,
Or help to half-a-crown.

➤ *QUESTIONS FOR READING AND WRITING*

1. Who is the speaker in the poem? What does his speech tell you about him?
2. Do you think he is trying to justify his actions? Explain.
3. What do you think he concludes? To what extent do you agree?
4. Compare this poem to "War Is Kind" on page 85.

TWO READERS ~ TWO CHOICES

■ *EXPLORING "THEME FOR ENGLISH B"*

In the student essays that follow, two students compare Langston Hughes's poem with a poem they have read earlier, Countee Cullen's "Incident" (see p. 11). Both student essays address the issue of race in these poems, but what the students write and the way they organize their comparisons are quite different. In the first essay, William Winters writes about one poem and then the other—but compares both poems to his own experience—using that experience with racial prejudice as an entry point and source of identification. Jennifer Stelz, on the other hand, compares and contrasts point by point, finding similarities and differences throughout while explicating the poems' common theme of racism.

Making Connections The title of Hughes's poem probably strikes a familiar chord. After all, what could be more usual in an English class than being asked to write a theme or an essay? But for the speaker in this poem, the only African-American in his class, the assigned topic, to "let that page come out of you," presents a particular dilemma. He says, "I wonder if it's that simple." In response to that question, this poem raises a number of compelling issues about racism, commonality, and difference.

Your Experiences and Beliefs Before you read "Theme for English B" it may be helpful to think about your own beliefs and experiences as they apply to some of the issues that emerge from this poem. If you were asked to write about who you are—your own sense of identity—what would you write? Would your comments include ethnic, cultural, or class differences? When you meet other people for the first time, what do you notice first? What characteristics are most important to you ? Have you ever prejudged or felt prejudged by those around you because of ethnic, cultural, or class differences?

LANGSTON HUGHES (1902–1967)

(See biography on page 896.)

THEME FOR ENGLISH B [1951]

The instructor said,

Go home and write
A page tonight.

And let that page come out of you—
Then, it will be true.

I wonder if it's that simple?

I am twenty-two, colored, born in Winston-Salem.
I went to school there, then Durham, then here
To this college on the hill above Harlem.
I am the only colored student in my class.
The steps from the hill lead down to Harlem,
Through a park, then I cross St. Nicholas,
Eighth Avenue, Seventh, and I come to the Y,
The Harlem Branch Y, where I take the elevator
Up to my room, sit down, and write this page:

It's not easy to know what is true for you or me
At twenty-two, my age. But I guess I'm what
I feel and see and hear. Harlem, I hear you:
Hear you, hear me—we two—you, me talk on this page.
(I hear New York, too.) Me—who?
Well, I like to eat, sleep, drink, and be in love.
I like to work, read, learn, and understand life.
I like a pipe for a Christmas present,
Or records—Bessie, bop, or Bach.

I guess being colored doesn't make me not like
The same things other folks like who are other races.
So will my page be colored that I write?
Being me, it will not be white.
But it will be
A part of you instructor.
You are white—
Yet a part of me, as I am part of you.
That's American.

Sometimes perhaps you don't want to be a part of me.
Nor do I often want to be a part of you.
But we are, that's true!
As I learn from you,
I guess you learn from me—
Although you're older—and white—
And somewhat more free.

This is my page for English B.

➤ QUESTIONS FOR READING AND WRITING

1. To what extent does your background or experience influence your response to "Theme for English B"?
2. If you were asked to write an assignment that "let that page come out of you," what would you write about?
3. Has the speaker in the poem "let that page come out of" him? Explain.
4. This poem was first published in 1951. How would it be different if written today?

~ TWO STUDENT PAPERS

William Winters

Dr. Madden

English 102

November 16, 200X

Black and White

The poems "Incident" and "Theme for English B" provide us with a unique understanding of racism. When someone passes judgment on someone else based on that person's race or ethnicity we call it racism. These two poems by Countee Cullen and Langston Hughes gave me an entirely new perspective on racism. I have been fortunate enough not to be the subject of racist remarks. I never thought about what it would be like to have someone direct racist comments at me--except once, which I will return to later. Even though I feel that we cannot understand how it feels to be a victim of racism unless we experience it in real life, these two poems have given me a small taste of it.

"Incident" is short, simple, and to the point. Here we have an innocent eight-year-old child whose heart and head are "filled with glee" (2) because he is excited about visiting the city of Baltimore. The child sees a man and smiles at him. The man then points to him and calls the child a "nigger."

When the speaker describes this happening, I could feel the child's heart sink. And my heart sank too. The child must have felt he was not wanted in this new place. Countee Cullen does an excellent job of letting the reader see the world through the child's eyes.

I could picture myself in this situation because I have also had the feeling of not being wanted in a new place for racist reasons. My family and I were looking at a college in New Haven last year. I was driving around a street outside the campus when a black man casually approached our car. When I slowed down to chat with him, he made an obscene gesture at us. My heart sank, and I was disturbed that this man did this to us for no reason except that we were white. Then, as we were getting on the highway to leave the city, a car with several young black men in it pulled up beside us. One of them rolled down his window and threw a softball at our car. Fortunately, the ball bounced off one of our windows, but any good thoughts I had about the school I had visited or the city of New Haven were shattered. Whenever I hear the words "New Haven" that's all that I remember. This is similar to the child's memory of Baltimore.

I believe that racism is not something we are born with. Instead, it is something we learn from others. The child in the story did not judge the man by the color of his skin. When the child smiled at him, the color of the man's skin did not even cross his young mind. However, the bigot has now made the child aware that people feel strongly about the color of his skin. That bigot was probably not a racist at one time. He learned to hate by observing the behavior of others. This brief, simple poem is very powerful and says a lot with a few words.

"Theme for English B" also deals with the topic of racism. It gets its message across very well, too, but in a slightly different way. Unlike "Incident," it did not put me in the shoes of the main character. I felt more like I was having a conversation with the speaker in the poem. The message I got from this poem is that people are generally the same, but the color of their skin does separate them.

Evidently the main character is very aware of his ethnicity. He describes himself as "twenty-two, colored, born in Winston-Salem" (7). He also tells us that he is the only "colored" student in his class. This contrasts with the poem "Incident," in which the speaker, who is only eight years old, has not yet learned to see the world in black and white. The speaker says he likes to "eat, sleep, drink, and be in love" (21). He also tells us of other "normal" things that he likes. He does this to show that his interests are the same as white people's. I guess some people might be surprised by this!

He continues, however, by saying, "So my page will be colored that I write / Being me, it will not be white" (27-28). Here I think he is telling us that even though he enjoys many of the same things that white people enjoy, his paper will be different because he is black. For him, this is an excellent segue into another thought: "Sometimes perhaps you do not want to be a part of me. / Nor do I want to be a part of you" (34-35). Here, too, he indicates that though we share the same humanity, there are things that make us different. Our ethnic backgrounds, where we grew up, our families, our individual personalities make us different. But this difference is good. It is not something negative. It is good for all of us to have pride in our backgrounds. It gives us the opportunity to learn something from each other. As the speaker in the poem says, "That's American" (33). It is the abuse of these differences that separates ethnicity from racism.

We are all different. We come from different races, cultures, classes, families. These differences, however, are good. They make us unique and give us something to have pride in. Much too often our ethnicity is looked upon as something negative and this results in racism. Unlike our ethnicity, racism is not something we are born with, but something we learn by observing others and living our lives. Racism is not logical; it is stupid. How can we dislike someone just because of the color of their skin? Yes, there are evil people in all races, yet there are good people too. The poems "Incident" and "Theme for English B" are a very good reflection of my own views on this troubling issue.

Works Cited

Cullen, Countee. "Incident." <u>Exploring Literature</u>. Ed. Frank Madden. New York: Longman, 2001, 11.

Hughes, Langston. "Theme for English B." <u>Exploring Literature</u>. Ed. Frank Madden. New York: Longman, 2001, 1164–1165.

Jennifer Stelz

Dr. Madden

English 102

November 15, 200X

Racism

The theme of both "Theme for English B" by Langston Hughes and "Incident" by Countee Cullen is racism. While the two poems are similar in this way, however, they convey their messages very differently. The speaker in "Theme for English B" comments from the point of view of a young adult, while in "Incident" the narrator's perspective is that of an adult looking back into his childhood. Despite this difference, we can see that both speakers are equally affected by the pain that prejudice inflicts. Though the poems were written twenty six-years apart, the strong message about racism in each continues to have a strong impact.

The most obvious difference in the poems is that their speakers are telling their stories from the perspective of very different ages. In "Theme for English B," the speaker is a twenty-two-year-old student who is attending a predominantly white university. "Incident" is told as a memory of a child's visit to Baltimore. In "Theme for English B," the speaker seems reminded every day of the fact that he is "colored" in a "white" university:

> I am twenty-two, colored, born in Winston-Salem.
> I went to school there, then Durham then here
> To this college on the hill above Harlem.
> I am the only colored student in my class. (7-10)

In "Incident," the young boy has only visited Baltimore for a short time, yet racism is branded into his mind forever. The speaker suggests that he does not experience prejudice every day:

> I saw the whole of Baltimore
>   From May until December;
> Of all the things that happened there
>   That's all that I remember. (9-12)

In "Theme for English B," Langston Hughes gives us an image of this twenty-two-year-old slowly and gradually. He describes his similarities, not his differences with whites:

Well I like to eat, sleep, drink and be in love.
I like to work, read, learn, and understand life.
I like a pipe for a Christmas present,
or records--Bessie, Bop, or Bach.
I guess being colored doesn't make me not like
the same things other folks who are other
races. (21-26)

By listening to this young man we get into his mind; we begin to understand who he is. We think of him as being no different than a brother or a best friend. As this image develops in our mind, it helps us identify with the speaker and makes us sympathetic to him. His goal is to convince us not to judge others by the color of their skin.

In the poem "Incident, "the poet takes a different route entirely to get his message across to the reader. Countee Cullen uses shocking, hurtful words coming from a child's mouth to show how painful racism is:

Now I was eight and very small,
  And he was no whit bigger,
And so I smiled, but he poked out
  His tongue, and called me, "Nigger." (5-8)

That one word "nigger" is enough to grab our attention and get a reaction. Not much building up by the speaker is needed to spark strong feelings. That he was only a small boy in particular was enough to make our hearts race with emotion.

The final difference that I noticed between the two poems was the choice of words the poets use. In "Incident" we can see that the speaker has a positive outlook on being an African-American. Although he used the word "nigger" to make his point clear, he also used the word Baltimorean rather than the word "white." His word choice shows that he knows there is racism in the world but that he is not going to inflict it upon others even though it has been inflicted on him.

In "Theme for English B," the speaker calls himself "colored" and says that his instructor is white. He is acknowledging their differences yet emphasizing that we are all American, which makes us the same:

So will my page be colored that I write?
Being me, it will not be white.

But it will be
a part of you instructor.
You are white--
yet a part of me, as I am a part of you.
That's American. (27-33)

He suggests that we not forget our races but learn to accept and appreciate our differences.

While both poems express a similar theme, they deliver their messages in different ways. Both "Theme for English B" and "Incident" emphasize the importance of respecting people of all races, not just blacks and whites. While the poems are different, they have the same purpose--to stop senseless hate.

Works Cited

Cullen, Countee. "Incident." Exploring Literature. Ed. Frank Madden. New York: Longman, 2001. 11.

Hughes, Langston. "Theme for English B." Exploring Literature. Ed. Frank Madden. New York: Longman, 2001. 1164–1165.

ARCHIBALD MACLEISH (1892–1982)

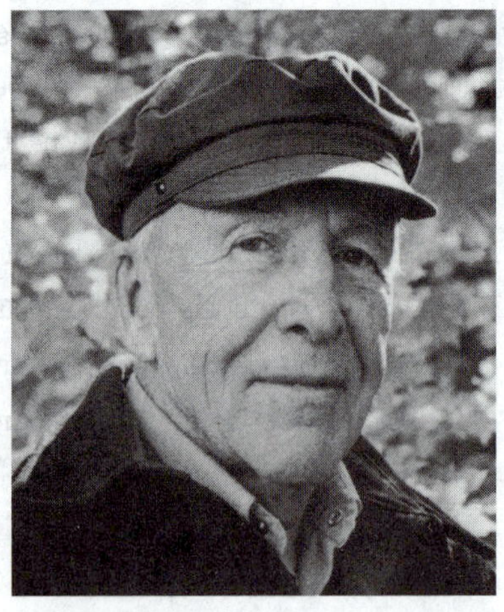

Born in Glencoe, Illinois, Archibald MacLeish attended Yale University as an undergraduate, where he published poems in the Yale Review, *though he later earned a law degree from Harvard University. In 1923, he abandoned his lucrative law career and moved to Paris with his young family to pursue writing. In Paris, he came into contact with many of the greatest poets of the age including Ezra Pound and T. S. Eliot, who greatly influenced his work. In 1932, after returning to the United States, he won the first of his three Pulitzer Prizes for "Conquistador" (1932), an epic poem about Cortez's sixteenth-century expedition to Mexico. In 1939, MacLeish was appointed Librarian of Congress, and during World War II, held a number of important political posts, including assistant secretary of state. In his later years he won two more Pulitzer Prizes, the first for his* New and Collected Poems 1917–1952 *(1952), and the second for his verse drama* J. B. *(1958), a modern retelling of the story of Job. In his later years, MacLeish taught at Harvard before retiring to Amherst, Massachusetts. "Ars Poetica" is Latin for "the art of poetry."*

ARS POETICA [1926]

A poem should be palpable and mute
As a globed fruit,

Dumb
As old medallions to the thumb,

Silent as the sleeve-worn stone
Of casement ledges where the moss has grown—

A poem should be wordless
As the flight of birds.

A poem should be motionless in time
As the moon climbs,

Leaving, as the moon releases
Twig by twig the night-entangled trees,

Leaving, as the moon behind the winter leaves,
Memory by memory the mind—

A poem should be motionless in time
As the moon climbs.

A poem should be equal to:
Not true.

For all the history of grief
An empty doorway and a maple leaf

For love
The leaning grasses and two lights above the sea—

A poem should not mean
But be.

➤ *QUESTIONS FOR READING AND WRITING*

1. Summarize each of the three things that the speaker says "a poem should be."
2. Do you agree with this definition? Explain.
3. Compare MacLeish's definition of poetry with Marianne Moore's on page 1172.

MARIANNE MOORE (1887–1972)

Marianne Moore was born in Kirkwood, Missouri. In 1894, she moved with her mother and brother (she never knew her father) to Pennsylvania, where she later attended Bryn Mawr University. Following graduation in 1910, she taught business courses at the U.S. Indian School in Carlisle, Pennsylvania. The family then moved to Brooklyn, where

Moore lived for the rest of her life, becoming a beloved figure (and devoted Brooklyn Dodger's fan) in her old age. By 1915, she was publishing her first poems, already displaying the wit, verbal skill, and metrical dexterity that later made her famous. Her first volume of poetry, Poems *(1921), was published by her friends (the poet H.D. among them) without her knowledge, and Moore soon found herself with a devoted audience, the poets T. S. Eliot and William Carlos Williams among them. From 1921 to 1925, Moore edited the* Dial, *one of the most important arts journals of the day. Her publications include:* Selected Poems *(1935),* Pangolin, and Other Verse *(1936),* Nevertheless *(1944), and* Collected Poems *(1951), for which she was awarded a Pulitzer Prize. In 1967, she published what is now considered the definitive edition of her poems,* The Complete Poems of Marianne Moore.

POETRY [1921]

I, too, dislike it: there are things that are important beyond
all this fiddle.
Reading it, however, with a perfect contempt for it, one
discovers in
it after all, a place for the genuine.
Hands that can grasp, eyes
that can dilate, hair that can rise
if it must, these things are important not because a

high-sounding interpretation can be put upon them but because they are
useful. When they become so derivative as to become
unintelligible,
the same thing may be said for all of us, that we
do not admire what
we cannot understand: the bat
holding on upside down or in quest of something to

eat, elephants pushing, a wild horse taking a roll, a tireless
wolf under
a tree, the immovable critic twitching his skin like a horse
that feels a flea, the base-
ball fan, the statistician—
nor is it valid
to discriminate against "business documents and

schoolbooks"; all these phenomena are important. One
        must make a distinction
however: when dragged into prominence by half poets,
        the result is not poetry,
nor till the poets among us can be
    "literalists of
    the imagination"—above
        insolence and triviality and can present

for inspection, "imaginary gardens with real toads in them,"
        shall we have
it. In the meantime, if you demand on the one hand,
the raw material of poetry in
    all its rawness and
    that which is on the other hand
            genuine, you are interested in poetry.

➤ *QUESTIONS FOR READING AND WRITING*

1. At the beginning of the poem, the speaker says, "I, too, dislike it." What assumption is she making about her readers? Do you think she is correct in her assumption? Explain.
2. To what extent can poetry be described as "imaginary gardens with real toads in them"?
3. This poem is printed here as it first appeared. In a later 1967 version, it was reduced to its first two sentences. Which version do you prefer? Why?
4. How would you define poetry?

MARGE PIERCY (b. 1936)

Born in Detroit, Michigan, to a working-class family, Marge Piercy attended the University of Michigan (B.A. 1957) and Northwestern University (M.A. 1958). Piercy began writing poems as a result of her involvement in the antiwar movement of the 1960s. In 1969, in reaction to what she considered the misogyny of many activists, she changed her focus to the growing women's movement. She has published many volumes of poetry, beginning with Breaking Camp *in 1968, and many novels. Her most recent* City of Darkness, City of Light: A Novel *appeared in 1996. Much of her work is political, and she has expressed a desire for her writing to be "useful." She has written: "To find ourselves spoken for in art gives dignity to our pain, our anger, our lust, our losses. We can hear what we hope for and what we most fear in the small release of cadenced utterance."*

To Be of Use [1973]

The people I love the best
jump into work head first
without dallying in the shallows
and swim off with sure strokes almost out of sight.
They seem to become natives of that element,
the black sleek heads of seals
bouncing like half-submerged balls.

I love people who harness themselves, an ox to a heavy cart,
who pull like water buffalo, with massive patience,
who strain in the mud and the muck to move things forward,
who do what has to be done, again and again.

I want to be with people who submerge
in the task, who go into the fields to harvest
and work in a row and pass the bags along,
who are not parlor generals and field of deserters
but move in common rhythm
when the food must come in or the fire be put out.

The work of the world is common as mud,
Botched, it smears the hands, crumbles to dust.
But the thing worth doing well done
has a shape that satisfies, clean and evident.
Greek amphoras for wine or oil,
Hopi vases that held corn, are put in museums
but you know they were made to be used.
The pitcher cries for water to carry
and a person for work that is real.

➤ *QUESTIONS FOR READING AND WRITING*

1. Do you think it's important "to be of use"? Why?
2. The speaker says that Greek amphoras and Hopi vases "are put in museums / but you know they were made to be used." What does she mean?
3. Compare this poem to Alice Walker's story "Everyday Use" on page 871.

Edwin Arlington Robinson (1869–1935)

Born into a wealthy New England family, Edwin Arlington Robinson was raised in Gardiner, Maine, a small town that later served as the model for "Tilbury Town," the setting for many of his most famous poems. Encouraged by a neighbor, he developed an interest in poetry and wrote numerous original poems, as well as diligently translating the great Greek and Roman poets. He spent two years at Harvard University, and after failing to get his poems published he decided to print copies of his first collection, The Torrent and The Night Before *(1896), himself. He mailed copies to publishers and received some favorable responses, though some found his subject matter bleak.*

Encouraged, he published The Children of the Night *(1896), which contained many of what were to become his best-known Tilbury poems (including "Richard Cory"). The collection was considered a failure, and Robinson descended into poverty and alcoholism. In 1902, in a stroke of luck, President Roosevelt stumbled onto a copy of* The Children of the Night *and was taken with it, (saying, "I am not sure I understand. . . . but I'm entirely sure that I like it"). Roosevelt found Robinson a post with very few duties in the customs office in New York City, and Robinson was free to devote himself to his poetry. He stepped down from the post following the success of his 1910 collection,* The Town Down the River. *In 1921, Robinson was awarded the first Pulitzer Prize for poetry for his* Collected Poems, *and was awarded two more for* The Man Who Died Twice *(1924) and* Tristam *(1927). After Robinson's death in 1935, Robert Frost, who listed Robinson as one his greatest influences, wrote of him and his often unhappy life: "His theme was unhappiness itself, but his skill was as happy as it was playful. There is that comforting thought for those who suffered to see him suffer."*

RICHARD CORY [1896]

Whenever Richard Cory went downtown,
We people on the pavement looked at him;
He was a gentleman from sole to crown,
Clean favored, and imperially slim,

And he was always quietly arrayed,
And he was always human when he talked;
But still he fluttered pulses when he said,
"Good-morning," and he glittered when he walked.

And he was rich—yes, richer than a king—
And admirably schooled in every grace:
In fine, we thought that he was everything
To make us wish that we were in his place.

So on we worked, and waited for the light,
And went without the meat, and cursed the bread;
And Richard Cory, one calm summer night,
Went home and put a bullet through his head.

➤ *QUESTIONS FOR READING AND WRITING*

1. Who is the speaker in this poem?

2. Who are "we"? Who is Richard Cory to us? What lines in the poem indicate these things?
3. What effect does the last line have on you? Were you surprised? Why?

Mr. Flood's Party [1896]

Old Eben Flood, climbing alone one night
Over the hill between the town below
And the forsaken upland hermitage
That held as much as he should ever know
On earth again of home, paused warily.
The road was his with not a native near;
And Eben, having leisure, said aloud,
For no man else in Tilbury Town to hear:

"Well, Mr. Flood, we have the harvest moon
Again, and we may not have many more;
The bird is on the wing, the poet says,
And you and I have said it here before.
Drink to the bird." He raised up to the light
The jug that he had gone so far to fill,
And answered huskily: "Well, Mr. Flood,
Since you propose it, I believe I will."

Alone, as if enduring to the end
A valiant armor of scarred hopes outworn,
He stood there in the middle of the road
Like Roland's ghost winding a silent horn.
Below him, in the town among the trees,
Where friends of other days had honored him,
A phantom salutation of the dead
Rang thinly till old Eben's eyes were dim.

Then, as a mother lays her sleeping child
Down tenderly, fearing it may awake,
He set the jug down slowly at his feet
With trembling care, knowing that most things break;
And only when assured that on firm earth
It stood, as the uncertain lives of men
Assuredly did not, he paced away,
And with his hand extended paused again:

"Well, Mr. Flood, we have not met like this
In a long time; and many a change has come
To both of us, I fear, since last it was
We had a drop together. Welcome home!"
Convivially returning with himself,
Again he raised the jug up to the light:

And with an acquiescent quaver said:
"Well, Mr. Flood, if you insist, I might.

"Only a very little, Mr. Flood—
For auld lang syne. No more, sir; that will do."
So, for the time, apparently it did,
And Eben evidently thought so too;
For soon amid the silver loneliness
Of night he lifted up his voice and sang,
Secure, with only two moons listening,
Until the whole harmonious landscape rang—

"For auld lang syne." The weary throat gave out,
The last word wavered; and the song being done,
He raised again the jug regretfully
And shook his head, and was again alone.
There was not much that was ahead of him,
And there was nothing in the town below—
Where strangers would have shut the many doors
That many friends had opened long ago.

➤ *QUESTIONS FOR READING AND WRITING*

1. Who is the audience for Mr. Flood's oration?
2. Why do you think "strangers would have shut the doors / That many friends had opened long ago"?
3. Does this poem remind you of anyone you know or of people you've seen or met? Explain.

WOLE SOYINKA (b. 1934)

Wole Soyinka (pronounced "Woh-leh Shaw-yin-ka"), the pen name of Akinwanda Oluwole, was born in Isara, Nigeria. In a memoir, Ake: The Years of Childhood *(1981), Soyinka has written movingly about his early childhood, where he was influenced both by the Christianity of his parents and the traditional tribal culture of his grandfather. While attending the University of Ibadan in Nigeria, he began publishing his first poems in Nigerian literary magazines. He soon transferred to the University of Leeds in England, graduating in 1959. He worked as a script reader for the Royal Court Theater in London, which produced his play* The Swamp Dwellers *in 1955, and returned to Nigeria in 1960 following its independence. While teaching at a*

number of Nigerian universities he continued to write, and during this period produced some of his most important works, including the plays The Lion and the Jewel *(1962),* The Strong Breed *(1963), and* The Dance of the Forests *(1964). In 1965, following the publication of his first novel,* The Interpreters *(1965), he suffered the first of many arrests by the Nigerian police for political reasons. From 1967 to 1969, during the Nigerian-Biafran war, he was held mostly in solitary confinement, and though he was not permitted to read or write, he managed to keep a journal on fragments of packages, toilet paper, and between the lines of books he secretly obtained. Following his release in 1969, he fled Nigeria, returning in 1975 following a change in the political climate. In 1986, he was awarded the Nobel Prize for literature. He fled Nigeria again in 1994 to avoid arrest and was convicted of treason in absentia; a change in the political climate allowed him to return from exile in 1998.*

TELEPHONE CONVERSATION [1960]

The price seemed reasonable, location
Indifferent. The landlady swore she lived
Off premises. Nothing remained
But self-confession. 'Madam,' I warned,
'I hate a wasted journey—I am African.'
Silence. Silenced transmission of
Pressurized good-breeding. Voice, when it came,
Lipstick coated, long gold-rolled
Cigarette-holder pipped. Caught I was, foully.
'HOW DARK?' . . . I had not misheard. . . . 'ARE YOU LIGHT
OR VERY DARK?' Button B. Button A. Stench
Of rancid breath of public hide-and-speak.
Red booth. Red pillar-box. Red double-tiered
Omnibus squelching tar. It *was* real! Shamed
By ill-mannered silence, surrender
Pushed dumbfoundment to beg simplification.
Considerate she was, varying the emphasis—
'ARE YOU DARK? OR VERY LIGHT?' Revelation came.
'You mean—like plain or milk chocolate?'
Her assent was clinical, crushing in its light
Impersonality. Rapidly, wave-length adjusted.
I chose. 'West African sepia'—and as afterthought,
'Down in my passport.' Silence for spectroscopic
Flight of fancy, till truthfulness clanged her accent
Hard on the mouthpiece. 'WHAT'S THAT?' conceding
'DON'T KNOW WHAT THAT IS.' 'Like brunette.'
'THAT'S DARK, ISN'T IT?' 'Not altogether.
Facially, I am brunette, but madam, you should see
The rest of me. Palm of my hand, soles of my feet
Are a peroxide blonde. Friction, caused—
Foolishly madam—by sitting down, has turned
My bottom raven black—One moment madam!'—sensing

Her receiver rearing on the thunderclap
About my ears—'Madam,' I pleaded, 'wouldn't you rather
See for yourself?'

➤ *QUESTIONS FOR READING AND WRITING*

1. Who is the speaker in this poem? What are the circumstances of the call?
2. Who is he speaking to? Describe her. What lines in the poem characterize her?
3. What does the speaker mean at the end of the poem by "wouldn't you rather / See for yourself?"

JEAN TOOMER (1894–1967)

One of the important figures of the Harlem Renaissance, Jean Toomer was born in Washington D.C. Toomer, who was of mixed racial heritage, was raised in the house of his grandfather, who had been governor of Louisiana during Reconstruction. After attending a series of universities without taking a degree, he worked at a series of odd jobs while reading and writing, as he wrote later, "at all possible times." In 1921, Toomer held a position for a few months as principal of a technical institute in Sparta, Georgia, traveling to the Deep South for the first time in his life. The experience inspired him to write his great masterpiece Cane *(1923), an experimental novel made up of the poems, songs, and stories he encountered among the African-Americans of the region. The novel established Toomer's reputation, and throughout the twenties his work appeared in many of the leading African-American and avante-garde journals of the day. In the late 1920s, Toomer became involved with the teachings of a Russian mystic, and eventually stopped writing. He was largely forgotten until the republication of* Cane *in 1969 reawakened interest in his life and works.*

REAPERS [1923]

Black reapers with the sound of steel on stones
Are sharpening scythes. I see them place the hones
In their hip-pockets as a thing that's done,
And start their silent swinging, one by one.

Black horses drive a mower through the weeds,
And there, a field rat, started squealing bleeds,
His belly close to ground. I see the blade,
Blood-stained, continue cutting weeds and shade.

➤ *QUESTIONS FOR READING AND WRITING*

1. How does the poem's rhythm and rhyme scheme affect your response?
2. Describe the images in the poem. How do they emphasize the plight of the reapers?

WILLIAM CARLOS WILLIAMS

(1883–1961)

William Carlos Williams was born in Rutherford, New Jersey. While attending high school in New York City, where he focused most of his energies on math and science, he first discovered his love for writing poetry. He skipped a traditional college education at his parents insistence and went directly to medical school at the University of Pennsylvania. While completing his studies, he came into contact with Ezra Pound, then a graduate student, who would become his lifelong friend and critic, and Hilda Doolitle (the poet H.D.). Pound and H.D. introduced Williams to the imagist movement, which rejected rigid and ordered poetry in favor of simple phrases and an embrace of the ordinary. Over the next forty years, though he practiced medicine full time, Williams wrote volumes of poetry, often finding inspiration in the stories of his patients, jotting poems on prescription pads or between appointments turning to a typewriter he kept in his office. His publications include Collected Poems *(1934),* Later Collected Poems *(1950), a five-volume poem about a nearby city in New Jersey, Paterson (1946–1958), a collection of experimental plays,* Many Loves and Other Plays *(1961), a series of novels, as well as numerous short stories and essays. His final book of poems,* Pictures from Brueghel and Other Poems, *was awarded the Pulitzer Prize in 1963. With his innovative use of free verse, his embrace of American speech, and insistence on the importance of the commonplace, Williams profoundly influenced the course of American poetry.*

AT THE BALL GAME [1923]

The crowd at the ball game
is moved uniformly

by a spirit of uselessness
which delights them—

all the exciting detail
of the chase

and the escape, the error
the flash of genius—

all to no end save beauty
the eternal—

So in detail they, the crowd,
are beautiful

for this
to be warned against

saluted and defied—
It is alive, venomous

it smiles grimly
its words cut—

The flashy female with her
mother, gets it—

The Jew gets it straight—it
is deadly, terrifying—

It is the Inquisition, the
Revolution

It is the beauty itself
that lives

day by day in them
idly—

This is
the power of their faces

It is summer, it is the solstice
the crowd is

cheering, the crowd is laughing
in detail

permanently, seriously
without thought

➤ *QUESTIONS FOR READING AND WRITING*

1. The setting of this poem is a baseball game. Is this a poem about baseball? Explain.
2. What do you think the references to "the flashy female," "the Jew," "the Inquisition," and "the Revolution" mean?
3. What does the speaker mean by "The crowd is laughing / in detail / permanently, seriously / without thought"?

◆ DRAMA ◆

SUSAN GLASPELL (1882–1948)

Susan Keating Glaspell was born in Davenport, Iowa, and attended Drake University. After working for a time as a reporter, she decided to devote herself to writing fiction, publishing two well-regarded novels, the Glory of the Conquered *(1909) and* The Visioning *(1911). In 1913, she married George Cram Cook, a stage director. Together, they moved to Provincetown, Massachusetts, and founded the Provincetown Players, one of the first influential noncommercial theaters in the country. The theater provided an artistic home to many illustrious writers of the time, including Edna St. Vincent Millay and Eugene O'Neill. Glaspell wrote a number of plays for the Players, often with feminist themes. In her later years she wrote, among other works, a biography of her husband,* The Road to the Temple *(1927), and* Alison's House, *which won the Pulitzer Prize in 1930. In the original Provincetown Players production of her best-known play,* Trifles *(1916), Susan Glaspell took the role of Mrs. Hale.*

TRIFLES [1916]

SCENE: *The kitchen in the now abandoned farmhouse of* JOHN WRIGHT, *a gloomy kitchen, and left without having been put in order—unwashed pans under the sink, a loaf of bread outside the breadbox, a dish towel on the table—other signs of incompleted work. At the rear the outer door opens, and the* SHERIFF *comes in, followed by the* COUNTY ATTORNEY *and* HALE: *The* SHERIFF *and* HALE *are men in middle life, the* COUNTY ATTORNEY *is a young man; all are much bundled up and go at once to the stove. They are followed by the two women—the* SHERIFF'S *wife,* MRS. PETERS, *first; she is a slight wiry woman, a thin nervous face.* MRS. HALE *is larger and would ordinarily be called more comfortable looking, but she is disturbed now and looks fearfully about as she enters. The women have come in slowly and stand close together near the door.*

COUNTY ATTORNEY [*at the stove rubbing his hands*]: This feels good. Come up to the fire, ladies.

MRS. PETERS [*after taking a step forward*]: I'm not—cold.

SHERIFF [*unbuttoning his overcoat and stepping away from the stove as if to the beginning of official business*]: Now, Mr. Hale, before we move things about, you explain to Mr. Henderson just what you saw when you came here yesterday morning.

COUNTY ATTORNEY [*crossing down to left of the table*]: By the way, has anything been moved? Are things just as you left them yesterday?

SHERIFF [*looking about*]: It's just the same. When it dropped below zero last night, I thought I'd better send Frank out this morning to make a fire for us—[*sits right of center table*] no use getting pneumonia with a big case on, but I told him not to touch anything except the stove—and you know Frank.

COUNTY ATTORNEY: Somebody should have been left here yesterday.

SHERIFF: Oh—yesterday. When I had to send Frank to Morris Center for that man who went crazy—I want you to know I had my hands full yesterday. I knew you could get back from Omaha by today, and as long as I went over everything here myself—

COUNTY ATTORNEY: Well, Mr. Hale, tell just what happened when you came here yesterday morning.

HALE [*crossing down to above table*]: Harry and I had started to town with a load of potatoes. We came along the road from my place and as I got here, I said, "I'm going to see if I can't get John Wright to go in with me on a party telephone." I spoke to Wright about it once before and he put me off, saying folks talked too much anyway, and all he asked was peace and quiet—I guess you know about how much he talked himself; but I thought maybe if I went to the house and talked about it before his wife, though I said to Harry that I didn't know as what his wife wanted made much difference to John—

COUNTY ATTORNEY: Let's talk about that later, Mr. Hale. I do want to talk about that, but tell now just what happened when you got to the house.

HALE: I didn't hear or see anything; I knocked at the door, and still it was all quiet inside. I knew they must be up, it was past eight o'clock. So I knocked again, and I thought I heard somebody say, "Come in." I wasn't sure, I'm not sure yet, but I opened the door—this door [*indicating the door by which the two women are still standing*] and there in that rocker—[*pointing to it*] sat Mrs. Wright.

[They all look at the rocker.]

COUNTY ATTORNEY: What—was she doing?

HALE: She was rockin' back and forth. She had her apron in her hand and was kind of—pleating it.

COUNTY ATTORNEY: And how did she—look?

HALE: Well, she looked queer.

COUNTY ATTORNEY: How do you mean—queer?

HALE: Well, as if she didn't know what she was going to do next. And kind of done up.

COUNTY ATTORNEY: How did she seem to feel about your coming?

HALE: Why, I don't think she minded—one way or other. She didn't pay much attention. I said, "How do, Mrs. Wright, it's cold, ain't it?" And she said, "Is it?"—and went on kind of pleating at her apron. Well, I was surprised; she didn't ask me to come up to the stove, or to set down, but just sat there, not even looking at me, so I said, "I want to see John." And then she—laughed. I guess you would call it a laugh. I thought of Harry and the team outside, so I said a little sharp: "Can't I see John?" "No," she says, kind o' dull like. "Ain't he home?" says I. "Yes," says she, "he's home." "Then why can't I see him?" I asked her, out of patience. "'Cause he's dead," says she. "*Dead?*" says I. She just nodded her head, not getting a bit excited, but rockin' back and forth. "Why—where is he?" says I, not knowing what to say. She just pointed upstairs—like that [*himself pointing to the room above*]. I got up, with the idea of going up there. I walked from there to here—then I says, "Why, what did he die of?" "He died of a rope around his neck," says she, and just went on pleatin' at her apron. Well, I went out and called Harry. I thought I might—need help. We went upstairs, and there he was lyin'—

COUNTY ATTORNEY: I think I'd rather have you go into that upstairs, where you can point it all out. Just go on now with the rest of the story.

HALE: Well, my first thought was to get that rope off. I looked . . . [*stops, his face twitches.*] . . . but Harry, he went up to him, and he said, "No, he's dead all right, and we'd better not touch anything." So we went back downstairs. She was still sitting that same way. "Has anybody been notified?" I asked. "No," says she, unconcerned. "Who did this, Mrs. Wright?" said Harry. He said it businesslike—and she stopped pleatin' of her apron. "I don't know," she says. "You don't *know?*" says Harry. "No," says she, "Weren't you sleepin' in the bed with him?" says Harry. "Yes," says she, "but I was on the inside." "Somebody slipped a rope round his neck and strangled him, and you didn't wake up?" says Harry. "I didn't wake up," she said after him. We must 'a looked as if we didn't see how that could be, for after a minute she said, "I sleep sound." Harry was going to ask her more questions but I said maybe we ought to let her tell her story first to the coroner, or the sheriff, so Harry went fast as he could to Rivers' place, where there's a telephone.

COUNTY ATTORNEY: And what did Mrs. Wright do when she knew that you had gone for the coroner?

HALE: She moved from that chair to this one over here [*pointing to a small chair in the corner*] and just sat there with her hands held together and looking down. I got a feeling that I ought to make some conversation, so I said I had come in to see if John wanted to put in a telephone, and at that she started to laugh, and then she stopped and looked at me—scared. [*The COUNTY ATTORNEY, who has had his notebook out, makes a note.*] I dunno, maybe it wasn't scared. I wouldn't like to say it was. Soon Harry got back, and then Dr. Lloyd came, and you, Mr. Peters, and so I guess that's all I know that you don't.

COUNTY ATTORNEY [*looking around*]: I guess we'll go upstairs first—and then out to the barn and around there. [*to the SHERIFF*] You're convinced that there was nothing important here—nothing that would point to any motive?

SHERIFF: Nothing here but kitchen things.

[The COUNTY ATTORNEY, *after again looking around the kitchen, opens the door of a cupboard closet. He gets up on a chair and looks on a shelf. Pulls his hand away, sticky.]*

COUNTY ATTORNEY: Here's a nice mess.

[The women draw nearer.]

MRS. PETERS [*to the other woman*]: Oh, her fruit; it did freeze. [*to the* COUNTY ATTORNEY] She worried about that when it turned so cold. She said the fire'd go out and her jars would break.

SHERIFF: Well, can you beat the women! Held for murder and worryin' about her preserves.

COUNTY ATTORNEY: I guess before we're through she may have something more serious than preserves to worry about.

HALE: Well, women are used to worrying over trifles.

[The two women move a little closer together.]

COUNTY ATTORNEY *[with the gallantry of a young politician]:* And yet, for all their worries, what would we do without the ladies? *[The women do not unbend. He goes to the sink, takes a dipperful of water from the pail and pouring it into a basin, washes his hands. Starts to wipe them on the roller towel, turns it for a cleaner place.]* Dirty towels! *[kicks his foot against the pans under the sink.]* Not much of a housekeeper, would you say: ladies?

MRS. HALE *[stiffly]:* There's a great deal of work to be done on a farm.

COUNTY ATTORNEY: To be sure. And yet *[with a little bow to her]* I know there are some Dickson county farmhouses which do not have such roller towels.

[He gives it a pull to expose its full length again.]

MRS. HALE: Those towels get dirty awful quick. Men's hands aren't always as clean as they might be.

COUNTY ATTORNEY: Ah, loyal to your sex, I see. But you and Mrs. Wright were neighbors. I suppose you were friends, too.

MRS. HALE [*shaking her head*]: I've not seen much of her of late years. I've not been in this house—it's more than a year.

COUNTY ATTORNEY: And why was that? You didn't like her?

MRS. HALE: I liked her all well enough. Farmers' wives have their hands full, Mr. Henderson. And then—

COUNTY ATTORNEY: Yes—?

MRS. HALE [*looking about*]: It never seemed a very cheerful place.

COUNTY ATTORNEY: No—it's not cheerful. I shouldn't say she had the homemaking instinct.

MRS. HALE: Well, I don't know as Wright had, either.

COUNTY ATTORNEY: You mean that they didn't get on very well?

MRS. HALE: No, I don't mean anything. But I don't think a place'd be any cheerfuler for John Wright's being in it.

COUNTY ATTORNEY: I'd like to talk more of that a little later. I want to get the lay of things upstairs now.

[He goes to the left, where three steps lead to a stair door.]

SHERIFF: I suppose anything Mrs. Peters does'll be all right. She was to take in some clothes for her, you know, and a few little things. We left in such a hurry yesterday.

COUNTY ATTORNEY: Yes, but I would like to see what you take, Mrs. Peters, and keep an eye out for anything that might be of use to us.

MRS. PETERS: Yes, Mr. Henderson.

[The women listen to the men's steps on the stairs, then look about the kitchen.]

MRS. HALE: I'd hate to have men coming into my kitchen, snooping around and criticizing.

[She arranges the pans under sink which the COUNTY ATTORNEY *had shoved out of place.]*

MRS. PETERS: Of course it's no more than their duty.

MRS. HALE: Duty's all right, but I guess that deputy sheriff that came out to make the fire might have got a little of this on. *[gives the roller towel a pull]* Wish I'd thought of that sooner. Seems mean to talk about her for not having things slicked up when she had to come away in such a hurry.

MRS. PETERS *[who has gone to a small table in the left rear corner of the room, and lifted one end of a towel that covers a pan]:* She had bread set.

[Stands still.]

MRS. HALE [*Eyes fixed on a loaf of bread beside the breadbox, which is on a low shelf at the other side of the room, moves slowly toward it.*]: She was going to put this in there. [*Picks up loaf, then abruptly drops it. In a manner of returning to familiar things.*] It's a shame about her fruit. I wonder if it's all gone. [*gets up on the chair and looks.*] I think there's some here that's all right, Mrs. Peters. Yes—here; [*holding it toward the window*] this is cherries, too. [*looking again*] I declare I believe that's the only one. [*Gets down, bottle in her hand. Goes to the sink and wipes it off on the outside.*] She'll feel awful bad after all her hard work in the hot weather. I remember the afternoon I put up my cherries last summer.

[She puts the bottle on the big kitchen table, center of the room. With a sigh, is about to sit down in the rocking-chair. Before she is seated realizes what chair it is; with a slow look at it, steps back. The chair which she has touched rocks back and forth.]

MRS. PETERS: Well, I must get those things from the front room closet. [*She goes to the door at the right, but after looking into the other room, steps back.*] You coming with me, Mrs. Hale? You could help me carry them.

[They go into the other room; reappear, MRS. PETERS *carrying a dress and skirt,* MRS. HALE *following with a pair of shoes.]*

MRS. PETERS: My, it's cold in there.

[She puts the clothes on the big table, and hurries to the stove.]

MRS. HALE [*examining the skirt*]: Wright was close. I think maybe that's why she kept so much to herself. She didn't even belong to the Ladies Aid. I suppose she felt she couldn't do her part, and then you don't enjoy things when you feel shabby. She used to wear pretty clothes and be lively, when she was Minnie Foster, one of the town girls singing in the choir. But that—oh, that was thirty years ago. This all you was to take in?

MRS. PETERS: She said she wanted an apron. Funny thing to want, for there isn't much to get you dirty in jail, goodness knows. But I suppose just to make her feel more natural. She said they was in the top drawer in this cupboard. Yes, here. And then her little shawl that always hung behind the door. [*opens stair door and looks*] Yes, here it is.

[Quickly shuts door leading upstairs.]

MRS. HALE [*abruptly moving toward her*]: Mrs. Peters?

MRS. PETERS: Yes, Mrs. Hale?

MRS. HALE: Do you think she did it?

MRS. PETERS [*in a frightened voice*]: Oh, I don't know.

MRS. HALE: Well, I don't think she did. Asking for an apron and her little shawl. Worrying about her fruit.

MRS. PETERS [*starts to speak, glances up, where footsteps are heard in the room above. In a low voice*]: Mr. Peters says it looks bad for her. Mr. Henderson is awful sarcastic in speech and he'll make fun of her sayin' she didn't wake up.

MRS. HALE: Well, I guess John Wright didn't wake when they was slipping that rope under his neck.

MRS. PETERS: No, it's strange. It must have been done awful crafty and still. They say it was such a—funny way to kill a man, rigging it all up like that.

MRS. HALE: That's just what Mr. Hale said. There was a gun in the house. He says that's what he can't understand.

MRS. PETERS: Mr. Henderson said coming out that what was needed for the case was a motive; something to show anger, or—sudden feeling.

MRS. HALE [*who is standing by the table*]: Well, I don't see any signs of anger around here. [*She puts her band on the dish towel which lies on the table, stands looking down at the table, one half of which is clean, the other half messy.*] It's wiped to here. [*Makes a move as if to finish work, then turns and looks at loaf of bread outside the breadbox. Drops towel. In that voice of coming back to familiar things.*] Wonder how they are finding things upstairs? I hope she had it a little more red-up up there. You know, it seems kind of *sneaking.* Locking her up in town and then coming out here and trying to get her own house to turn against her!

MRS. PETERS: But, Mrs. Hale, the law is the law.

MRS. HALE: I s'pose 'tis. [*unbuttoning her coat*] Better loosen up your things, Mrs. Peters. You won't feel them when you go out.

[MRS. PETERS takes off her fur tippet, goes to hang it on hook at the back of room, stands looking at the under part of the small corner table.]

MRS. PETERS: She was piecing a quilt.

[She brings the large sewing basket and they look at the bright pieces.]

MRS. HALE: It's log cabin pattern. Pretty, isn't it? I wonder if she was goin' to quilt or just knot it?

[Footsteps have been heard coming down the stairs. The SHERIFF enters, followed by HALE and the COUNTY ATTORNEY.]

SHERIFF: They wonder if she was going to quilt it or just knot it.

[The men laugh; the women look abashed.]

COUNTY ATTORNEY [*rubbing his hands over the stove*]: Frank's fire didn't do much up there, did it? Well, let's go out to the barn and get that cleared up.

[The men go outside.]

MRS. HALE [*resentfully*]: I don't know as there's anything so strange, our takin' up our time with little things while we're waiting for them to get the evidence. [*She sits down at the big table, smoothing out a block with decision.*] I don't see as it's anything to laugh about.

MRS. PETERS [*apologetically*]: Of course they've got awful important things on their minds.

[Pulls up a chair and joins MRS. HALE at the table.]

MRS. HALE [*examining another block*]: Mrs. Peters, look at this one. Here, this is the one she was working on, and look at the sewing! All the rest of it has been so nice and even. And look at this! It's all over the place! Why, it looks as if she didn't know what she was about!

[After she has said this, they look at each other, then started to glance back at the door. After an instant MRS. HALE has pulled at a knot and ripped the sewing.]

MRS. PETERS: Oh, what are you doing, Mrs. Hale?

MRS. HALE [*mildly*]: Just pulling out a stitch or two that's not sewed very good. [*threading a needle*] Bad sewing always made me fidgety.

MRS. PETERS [*nervously*]: I don't think we ought to touch things.

MRS. HALE: I'll just finish up this end. [*suddenly stopping and leaning forward*] Mrs. Peters?

MRS. PETERS: Yes, Mrs. Hale?

MRS. HALE: What do you suppose she was so nervous about?

MRS. PETERS: Oh—I don't know. I don't know as she was nervous. I sometimes sew awful queer when I'm just tired. [*MRS. HALE starts to say something, looks at* MRS. PETERS, *then goes on sewing.*] Well, I must get these things wrapped up. They may be through sooner than we think. [*putting apron and other things together*] I wonder where I can find a piece of paper, and string.

MRS. HALE: In that cupboard, maybe.

MRS. PETERS [*looking in cupboard*]: Why, here's a birdcage. [*holds it up*] Did she have a bird, Mrs. Hale?

MRS. HALE: Why, I don't know whether she did or not—I've not been here for so long. There was a man around last year selling canaries cheap, but I don't know as she took one; maybe she did. She used to sing real pretty herself.

MRS. PETERS [*glancing around*]: Seems funny to think of a bird here. But she must have had one, or why should she have a cage? I wonder what happened to it.

MRS. HALE: I s'pose maybe the cat got it.

MRS. PETERS: No, she didn't have a cat. She's got that feeling some people have about cats—being afraid of them. My cat got in her room, and she was real upset and asked me to take it out.

MRS. HALE: My sister Bessie was like that. Queer, ain't it?

MRS. PETERS [*examining the cage*]: Why, look at this door. It's broke. One hinge is pulled apart.

MRS. HALE [*looking, too*]: Looks as if someone must have been rough with it.

MRS. PETERS: Why, yes.

[She brings the cage forward and puts it on the table.]

MRS. HALE: I wish if they're going to find any evidence they'd be about it. I don't like this place.

MRS. PETERS: But I'm awful glad you came with me, Mrs. Hale. It would be lonesome for me sitting here alone.

MRS. HALE: It would, wouldn't it? [*dropping her sewing*] But I tell you what I do wish, Mrs. Peters. I wish I had come over sometimes when *she* was here. I—[*looking around the room*]—wish I had.

MRS. PETERS: But of course you were awful busy, Mrs. Hale—your house and your children.

MRS. HALE: I could've come. I stayed away because it weren't cheerful—and that's why I ought to have come. I—I've never liked this place. Maybe because it's down in a hollow and you don't see the road. I dunno what it is, but it's a lonesome place and always was. I wish I had come over to see Minnie Foster sometimes. I can see now—

[Shakes her head.]

MRS. PETERS: Well, you mustn't reproach yourself, Mrs. Hale. Somehow we just don't see how it is with other folks until—something comes up.

MRS. HALE: Not having children makes less work—but it makes a quiet house, and Wright out to work all day, and no company when he did come in. Did you know John Wright, Mrs. Peters?

MRS. PETERS: Not to know him; I've seen him in town. They say he was a good man.

MRS. HALE: Yes—good; he didn't drink, and kept his word as well as most, I guess, and paid his debts. But he was a hard man, Mrs. Peters. Just to pass the time of day with him—[*shivers*] Like a raw wind that gets to the bone. [*pauses, her eye falling on the cage*] I should think she would 'a wanted a bird. But what do you suppose went with it?

MRS. PETERS: I don't know, unless it got sick and died.

[She reaches over and swings the broken door, swings it again; both women watch it.]

MRS. HALE: You weren't raised round here, were you? [*MRS. PETERS shakes her head.*] You didn't know—her?

MRS. PETERS: Not till they brought her yesterday.

MRS. HALE: She—come to think of it, she was kind of like a bird herself—real sweet and pretty, but kind of timid and—fluttery. How—she—did—change. [*silence; then as if struck by a happy thought and relieved to get back to everyday things.*] Tell you what, Mrs. Peters; why don't you take the quilt in with you? It might take up her mind.

MRS. PETERS: Why, I think that's a real nice idea, Mrs. Hale. There couldn't possibly be any objection to it, could there? Now, just what would I take? I wonder if her patches are in here—and her things.

[They look in the sewing basket.]

MRS. HALE: Here's some red. I expect this has got sewing things in it [*brings out a fancy box*] What a pretty box. Looks like something somebody would give you. Maybe her scissors are in here. [*Opens box. Suddenly puts her hand to her nose.*] Why—[*MRS. PETERS bends nearer, then turns her face away.*] There's something wrapped up in this piece of silk.

MRS. PETERS: Why, this isn't her scissors.

MRS. HALE [*lifting the silk*]: Oh, Mrs. Peters—it's—

[MRS. PETERS bends closer.]

MRS. PETERS: It's the bird.

MRS. HALE [*jumping up*]: But, Mrs. Peters—look at it. Its neck! Look at its neck! It's all—other side to.

MRS. PETERS: Somebody—wrung—its neck.

[Their eyes meet. A look of growing comprehension, of horror. Steps are heard outside. MRS. HALE slips box under quilt pieces, and sinks into her chair. Enter SHERIFF and COUNTY ATTORNEY. MRS. PETERS rises.]

COUNTY ATTORNEY [*as one turning from serious things to little pleasantries*]: Well, ladies, have you decided whether she was going to quilt it or knot it?

MRS. PETERS: We think she was going to—knot it.

COUNTY ATTORNEY: Well, that's interesting, I'm sure. [*seeing the birdcage*] Has the bird flown?

MRS. HALE [*putting more quilt pieces over the box*]: We think the—cat got it.

COUNTY ATTORNEY [*preoccupied*]: Is there a cat?

[MRS. HALE glances in a quick covert way at MRS. PETERS.]

MRS. PETERS: Well, not *now.* They're superstitious, you know. They leave.

COUNTY ATTORNEY [*to SHERIFF PETERS, continuing an interrupted conversation*]: No sign at all of anyone having come from the outside. Their own rope. Now let's go up again and go over it piece by piece. [*They start upstairs.*] It would have to have been someone who knew just the—

[MRS. PETERS sits down. The two women sit there not looking at one another, but as if peering into something and at the same time holding back. When they talk now it is the manner of feeling their way over strange ground, as if afraid of what they are saying, but as if they cannot help saying it.]

MRS. HALE: She liked the bird. She was going to bury it in that pretty box.

MRS. PETERS [*in a whisper*]: When I was a girl—my kitten—there was a boy took a hatchet, and before my eyes—and before I could get there—[*covers her face an instant*] If they hadn't held me back, I would have—[*catches herself, looks upstairs where steps are heard, falters weakly*]—hurt him.

MRS. HALE [*with a slow look around her*]: I wonder how it would seem never to have had any children around. [*pause*] No, Wright wouldn't like the bird—a thing that sang. She used to sing. He killed that, too.

MRS. PETERS [*moving uneasily*]: We don't know who killed the bird.

MRS. HALE: I knew John Wright.

MRS. PETERS: It was an awful thing was done in this house that night, Mrs. Hale. Killing a man while he slept, slipping a rope around his neck that choked the life out of him.

MRS. HALE: His neck. Choked the life out of him.

[Her hand goes out and rests on the birdcage.]

MRS. PETERS [*with a rising voice*]: We don't know who killed him. We don't know.

MRS. HALE [*her own feeling not interrupted*]: If there'd been years and years of nothing, then a bird to sing to you, it would be awful—still, after the bird was still.

MRS. PETERS [*something within her speaking*]: I know what stillness is. When we homesteaded in Dakota, and my first baby died—after he was two years old, and me with no other then—

MRS. HALE [*moving*]: How soon do you suppose they'll be through, looking for evidence?

MRS. PETERS: I know what stillness is. [*pulling herself back—*] The law has got to punish crime, Mrs. Hale.

MRS. HALE [*not as if answering that*]: I wish you'd seen Minnie Foster when she wore a white dress with blue ribbons and stood up there in the choir and sang. [*a look around the room*] Oh, I *wish* I'd come over here once in a while! That was a crime! That was a crime! Who's going to punish that?

MRS. PETERS [*looking upstairs*]: We mustn't—take on.

MRS. HALE: I might have known she needed help! I know how things can be—for women. I tell you, it's queer, Mrs. Peters. We live close together and we live far apart. We all go through the same things—it's all just a different kind of the same thing. [*brushes her eyes, noticing the bottle of fruit, reaches out for it*] If I was you, I wouldn't tell her her fruit was gone. Tell her it *ain't.* Tell her it's all right. Take this in to prove it to her. She—she may never know whether it was broke or not.

MRS. PETERS [*Takes the bottle, looks about for something to wrap it in; takes petticoat from the clothes brought from the other room, very nervously begins winding this around the bottle. In a false voice.*]: My, it's a good thing the men couldn't hear us. Wouldn't they just laugh! Getting all stirred up over a little thing like a—dead canary. As if that could have anything to do with—with—wouldn't they *laugh!*

[The men are heard coming downstairs.]

MRS. HALE [*under her breath*]: Maybe they would—maybe they wouldn't.

COUNTY ATTORNEY: No, Peters, it's all perfectly clear except a reason for doing it. But you know juries when it comes to women. If there was some definite thing. Something to show—something to make a story about—a thing that would connect up with this strange way of doing it—

[The women's eyes meet for an instant. Enter HALE from outer door.]

HALE: Well, I've got the team around. Pretty cold out there.

COUNTY ATTORNEY: I'm going to stay here awhile by myself. [*to the SHERIFF*] You can send Frank out for me, can't you? I want to go over everything. I'm not satisfied that we can't do better.

SHERIFF: Do you want to see what Mrs. Peters is going to take in? [*The LAWYER goes to the table, picks up the apron, laughs.*]

COUNTY ATTORNEY: Oh, I guess they're not very dangerous things the ladies have picked up. [*Moves a few things about, disturbing the quilt pieces which cover the box. Steps back.*] No, Mrs. Peters doesn't need supervising. For that matter, a sheriff's wife is married to the law. Ever think of it that way, Mrs. Peters?

MRS. PETERS: Not—just that way.

SHERIFF [*chuckling*]: Married to the law. [*moves down right door to the other room*] I just want you to come in here a minute, George. We ought to take a look at these windows.

COUNTY ATTORNEY [*scoffingly*]: Oh windows!

SHERIFF: We'll be right out, Mr. Hale. [*HALE goes outside. The SHERIFF follows the COUNTY ATTORNEY into the other room. Then MRS. HALE rises, hands tight together, looking intensely at MRS. PETERS, whose eyes take a slow turn, finally meeting MRS. HALE's. A moment MRS. HALE holds her, then her own eyes point the way to where the box is concealed. Suddenly MRS. PETERS throws back quilt pieces and tries to put the box in the bag she is carrying. It is too big. She opens box, starts to take the bird out, cannot touch it, goes to pieces, stands there helpless. Sound of a knob turning in the other room.* MRS. HALE *snatches the box and puts it in the pocket of her big coat. Enter* COUNTY ATTORNEY *and* SHERIFF.]

COUNTY ATTORNEY [*crosses to up left door facetiously*]: Well, Henry, at least we found out that she was not going to quilt it. She was going to—what is it you call it, ladies?

MRS. HALE [*standing center below table facing front, her hand against her pocket*]: We call it—knot it, Mr. Henderson.

CURTAIN

➤ QUESTIONS FOR READING AND WRITING

1. Explain the multiple ironies of the play's title. Who is looking for clues? Who finds them?
2. In many ways, the central characters of this play are John Wright and his wife, neither of whom appear onstage. What is the effect of learning about them through other characters? How would this play be different if it included the scenes leading up to the death of John Wright?
3. Why don't Mrs. Peters and Mrs. Hale reveal the evidence they discover? Do they think it would help or hinder Mrs. Wright's case?
4. If all the evidence were to come to light, do you think that it would matter whether or not Mrs. Wright were tried by a jury composed of all women versus a jury composed of all men? Explain.
5. Given the attitudes of the men in this play, how would you describe the values of this culture? What are these women supposed to know? What do they really know?

AUGUST WILSON (b. 1945)

August Wilson was born in Pittsburgh. His early influences were the writers Richard Wright, Langston Hughes, Ralph Ellison, and Amiri Baraka. His play Ma Rainey's Black Bottom, *won the New York Drama Critic's Circle Award as best play in 1985, and in 1987 his play* Fences *won the Pulitzer Prize for drama.* The Piano Lesson *won Wilson a second Pultizer Prize in 1990. His most recent play is* Seven Guitars *(1995). He lives in St. Paul, Minnesota.*

JOE TURNER'S COME AND GONE [1988]

CHARACTERS

SETH HOLLY, *owner of the boardinghouse*

BERTHA HOLLY, his wife
BYNUM WALKER, a rootworker
RUTHERFORD SELIG, a peddler
JEREMY FURLOW, a resident
HERALD LOOMIS, a resident
ZONIA LOOMIS, his daughter
MATTIE CAMPBELL, a resident
REUBEN SCOTT, boy who lives next door
MOLLY CUNNINGHAM, a resident
MARTHA LOOMIS, Herald Loomis's wife

SETTING

August, 1911. A boardinghouse in Pittsburgh. At right is a kitchen. Two doors open off the kitchen. One leads to the outhouse and SETH's workshop. The other to SETH's and BERTHA's bedroom. At left is a parlor. The front door opens into the parlor, which gives access to the stairs leading to the upstairs rooms. There is a small outside playing area.

THE PLAY

It is August in Pittsburgh, 1911. The sun falls out of heaven like a stone. The fires of the steel mill rage with a combined sense of industry and progress. Barges loaded with coal and iron ore trudge up the river to the mill towns that dot the Monongahela and return with fresh, hard, gleaming steel. The city flexes its muscles. Men throw countless bridges across the river, lay roads and carve tunnels through the hills sprouting with houses.

From the deep and the near South the sons and daughters of newly freed African slaves wander into the city. Isolated, cut off from memory, having forgotten the names of the gods and only guessing at their faces, they arrive dazed and stunned, their heart kicking in their chest with a song worth singing. They arrive carrying Bibles and guitars, their pockets lined with dust and fresh hope, marked men and women seeking to scrape from the narrow, crooked cobbles and the fiery blasts of the coke furnace a way of bludgeoning and shaping the malleable parts of themselves into a new identity as free men of definite and sincere worth.

Foreigners in a strange land, they carry as part and parcel of their baggage a long line of separation and dispersement which informs their sensibilities and marks their conduct as they search for ways to reconnect, to reassemble, to give clear and luminous meaning to the song which is both a wail and a whelp of joy.

ACT I

SCENE 1

The lights come up on the kitchen. BERTHA busies herself with breakfast preparations. SETH stands looking out the window at BYNUM in the yard. SETH is in his early fifties. Born of Northern free parents, a skilled craftsman, and owner of the boardinghouse, he has a stability that none of the other characters have. BERTHA is five years his junior. Married for over twenty-five years, she has learned how to negotiate around SETH'S *apparent orneriness.*

SETH [at the window, laughing]: If that ain't the damndest thing I seen. Look here, Bertha.

BERTHA: I done seen Bynum out there with them pigeons before.

SETH: Naw . . . naw . . . look at this. That pigeon flopped out of Bynum's hand and he about to have a fit.

[BERTHA crosses over to the window.]

He down there on his hands and knees behind that bush looking all over for that pigeon and it on the other side of the yard. See it over there?

BERTHA: Come on and get your breakfast and leave that man alone.

SETH: Look at him . . . he still looking. He ain't seen it yet. All that old mumbo jumbo nonsense. I don't know why I put up with it.

BERTHA: You don't say nothing when he bless the house.

SETH: I just go along with that 'cause of you. You around here sprinkling salt all over the place . . . got pennies lined up across the threshold . . . all that heebie-jeebie stuff. I just put up with that 'cause of you. I don't pay that kind of stuff no mind. And you going down there to the church and wanna come home and sprinkle salt all over the place.

BERTHA: It don't hurt none. I can't say if it help . . . but it don't hurt none.

SETH: Look at him. He done found that pigeon and now he's talking to it.

BERTHA: These biscuits be ready in a minute.

SETH: He done drew a big circle with that stick and now he's dancing around. I know he'd better not . . .

[SETH bolts from the window and rushes to the back door.]

Hey, Bynum! Don't be hopping around stepping in my vegetables. Hey, Bynum . . . Watch where you stepping!

BERTHA: SETH, leave that man alone.

SETH [*coming back into the house*]: I don't care how much he be dancing around . . . just don't be stepping in my vegetables. Man got my garden all messed up now . . . planting them weeds out there . . . burying them pigeons and whatnot.

BERTHA: Bynum don't bother nobody. He ain't even thinking about your vegetables.

SETH: I know he ain't! That's why he out there stepping on them.

BERTHA: What Mr. Johnson say down there?

SETH: I told him if I had the tools I could go out here and find me four or five fellows and open up my own shop instead of working for Mr. Olowski. Get me four or five fellows and teach them how to make pots and pans. One man making ten pots is five men making fifty. He told me he'd think about it.

BERTHA: Well, maybe he'll come to see it your way.

SETH: He wanted me to sign over the house to him. You know what I thought of that idea.

BERTHA: He'll come to see you're right.

SETH: I'm going up and talk to Sam Green. There's more than one way to skin a cat. I'm going up and talk to him. See if he got more sense that Mr. Johnson. I can't get nowhere working for Mr. Olowski and selling Selig five or six pots on the side. I'm going up and see Sam Green. See if he loan me the money.

[SETH crosses back to the window.]

Now he got that cup. He done killed that pigeon and now he's putting its blood in that little cup. I believe he drink that blood.

BERTHA: Seth Holly, what is wrong with you this morning? Come on and get your breakfast so you can go to bed. You know Bynum don't be drinking no pigeon blood.

SETH: I don't know what he do.

BERTHA: Well, watch him, then. He's gonna dig a little hole and bury that pigeon. Then he's gonna pray over that blood . . . pour it on top . . . mark out his circle and come on into the house.

SETH: That's what he doing . . . he pouring that blood on top.

BERTHA: When they gonna put you back working daytime? Told me two months ago he was gonna put you back working daytime.

SETH: That's what Mr. Olowski told me. I got to wait till he say when. He tell me what to do. I don't tell him. Drive me crazy to speculate on the man's wishes when he don't know what he want to do himself.

BERTHA: Well, I wish he go ahead and put you back working daytime. This working all hours of the night don't make no sense.

SETH: It don't make no sense for that boy to run out of here and get drunk so they lock him up either.

BERTHA: Who? Who they got locked up for being drunk?

SETH: That boy that's staying upstairs . . . Jeremy. I stopped down there on Logan Street on my way home from work and one of the fellows told me about it. Say he seen it when they arrested him.

BERTHA: I was wondering why I ain't seen him this morning.

SETH: You know I don't put up with that. I told him when he came . . .

[BYNUM enters from the yard carrying some plants. He is a short, round man in his early sixties. A conjure man, or rootworker, he gives the impression of always being in control of everything. Nothing ever bothers him. He seems to be lost in a world of his own making and to swallow any adversity or interference with his grand design.]

What you doing bringing them weeds in my house? Out there stepping on my vegetables and now wanna carry them weeds in my house.

BYNUM: Morning, Seth. Morning, Sister Bertha.

SETH: Messing up my garden growing them things out there. I ought to go out there and pull up all them weeds.

BERTHA: Some gal was by here to see you this morning, Bynum. You was out there in the yard . . . I told her to come back later.

BYNUM [*to SETH*]: You look sick. What's the matter, you ain't eating right?

SETH: What if I was sick? You ain't getting near me with none of that stuff.

[BERTHA sets a plate of biscuits on the table.]

BYNUM: My . . . my . . . Bertha, your biscuits getting fatter and fatter.

[BYNUM takes a biscuit and begins to eat.]

Where Jeremy? I don't see him around this morning. He usually be around riffing and raffing on Saturday morning.

SETH: I know where he at. I know just where he at. They got him down there in the jail. Getting drunk and acting a fool. He down there where he belong with all that foolishness.

BYNUM: Mr. Piney's boys got him, huh? They ain't gonna do nothing but hold on to him for a little while. He's gonna be back here hungrier than a mule directly.

SETH: I don't go for all that carrying on and such. This is a respectable house. I don't have no drunkards or fools around here.

BYNUM: That boy got a lot of country in him. He ain't been up here but two weeks. It's gonna take a while before he can work that country out of him.

SETH: These niggers coming up here with that old backward country style of living. It's hard enough now without all that ignorant kind of acting. Ever since slavery got over with there ain't been nothing but foolish-acting niggers. Word get out they need men to work in the mill and put in these roads . . . and niggers drop everything and head North looking for freedom. They don't know the white fellows looking too. White fellows coming from all over the world. White fellow come over and in six months got more than what I got. But these niggers keep on coming. Walking . . . riding . . . carrying their Bibles. That boy done carried a guitar all the way from North Carolina. What he gonna find out? What he gonna do with that guitar? This the city.

[There is a knock on the door.]

Niggers coming up here from the backwoods . . . coming up here from the country carrying Bibles and guitars looking for freedom. They got a rude awakening.

[SETH goes to answer the door. RUTHERFORD SELIG enters. About SETH's age, he is a thin white man with greasy hair. A peddler, he supplies SETH with the raw materials to make pots and pans which he then peddles door to door in the mill towns along the river. He keeps a list of his customers as they move about and is known in the various communities as the People Finder. He carries squares of sheet metal under his arm.]

Ho! Forgot you was coming today. Come on in.

BYNUM: If it ain't Rutherford Selig . . . the People Finder himself.

SELIG: What say there, Bynum?

BYNUM: I say about my shiny man. You got to tell me something. I done give you my dollar . . . I'm looking to get a report.

SELIG: I got eight here, Seth.

SETH [*taking the sheet metal*]: What is this? What you giving me here? What I'm gonna do with this?

SELIG: I need some dustpans. Everybody asking me about dustpans.

SETH: Gonna cost you fifteen cents apiece. And ten cents to put a handle on them.

SELIG: I'll give you twenty cents apiece with the handles.

SETH: Alright. But I ain't gonna give you but fifteen cents for the sheet metal.

SELIG: It's twenty-five cents apiece for the metal. That's what we agreed on.

SETH: This low-grade sheet metal. They ain't worth but a dime. I'm doing you a favor giving you fifteen cents. You know this metal ain't worth no twenty-five cents. Don't come talking that twenty-five cent stuff to me over no low-grade sheet metal.

SELIG: Alright, fifteen cents apiece. Just make me some dustpans out of them.

[SETH exits with the sheet metal out the back door.]

BERTHA: Sit on down there, Selig. Get you a cup of coffee and a biscuit.

BYNUM: Where you coming from this time?

SELIG: I been upriver. All along the Monongahela. Past Rankin and all up around Little Washington.

BYNUM: Did you find anybody?

SELIG: I found Sadie Jackson up in Braddock. Her mother's staying down there in Scotchbottom say she hadn't heard from her and she didn't know where she was at. I found her up in Braddock on Enoch Street. She bought a frying pan from me.

BYNUM: You around here finding everybody how come you ain't found my shiny man?

SELIG: The only shiny man I saw was the Nigras working on the road gang with the sweat glistening on them.

BYNUM: Naw, you'd be able to tell this fellow. He shine like new money.

SELIG: Well, I done told you I can't find nobody without a name.

BERTHA: Here go one of these hot biscuits, Selig.

BYNUM: This fellow don't have no name. I call him John 'cause it was up around Johnstown where I seen him. I ain't even so sure he's one special fellow. That shine could pass on to anybody. He could be anybody shining.

SELIG: Well, what's he look like beside being shiny? There's lots of shiny Nigras.

BYNUM: He's just a man I seen out on the road. He ain't had no special look. Just a man walking toward me on the road. He come up and asked me which way the road went. I told him everything I knew about the road, where it went and all, and he asked me did I have anything to eat 'cause he was hungry. Say he ain't had nothing to eat in three days. Well, I never be out there on the road without a piece of fried meat. Or an orange or an apple. So I give this fellow an orange. He take and eat that orange and told me to come and go along the road a little ways with him, that he had something he wanted to show me. He had a look about him made me wanna go with him, see what he gonna show me.

We walked on a bit and it's getting kind of far from where I met him when it come up on me all of a sudden, we wasn't going the way he had come from, we was going back my way. Since he said he ain't knew nothing about the road, I asked him about this. He say he had a voice inside him telling him which way to go and if I come and go along with him he was gonna show me the Secret of Life. Quite naturally I followed him. A fellow that's gonna show you the Secret of Life ain't to be taken lightly. We get near this bend in the road . . .

[SETH enters with an assortment of pots.]

SETH: I got six here, Selig.

SELIG: Wait a minute, Seth. Bynum's telling me about the secret of life. Go ahead, Bynum, I wanna hear this.

[SETH sets the pots down and exits out the back.]

BYNUM: We get near this bend in the road and he told me to hold out my hands. Then he rubbed them together with his and I looked down and see they got blood on them. Told me to take and rub it all over me . . . say that was a way of cleaning myself. Then we went around the bend in that road. Got around that bend and it seem like all of a sudden we ain't in the same place. Turn around that bend and everything look like it was twice as big as it was. The trees and everything bigger than life! Sparrows big as eagles! I turned around to look at this fellow and he had this light coming out of him. I had to cover up my eyes to keep from being blinded. He shining like new money with that light. He shined until all the light seemed like it seeped out of him and then he was gone and I was by myself in this strange place where everything was bigger than life.

I wandered around there looking for that road, trying to find my way back from this big place . . . and I looked over and seen my daddy standing there. He was the same size he always was, except for his hands and his mouth. He had a great big old mouth that look like it took up his whole face and his hands were as big as hams. Look like they was too big to carry around. My daddy called me to him. Said he had been thinking about me and it grieved him to see me in the world carrying other people's songs and not having one of my own. Told me he was gonna show me how to find my song. Then he carried me further into this big place until we come to this ocean. Then he showed me something I ain't got words to tell you. But if you stand to witness it, you done seen something there. I stayed in that place awhile and my daddy taught me the meaning of this thing that I had seen and showed me how to find my song. I asked him about the shiny man and he told me he was the One Who Goes Before and Shows the Way. Said there was lots of shiny men and if I ever saw one again before I died then I would know that my song had been accepted and worked its full power in the world and I could lay down and die a happy man. A man who done left his mark on life. On the way people cling to each other out of the truth they find in themselves. Then he showed me how to get back to the road. I came out where everything was its own size and I had my song. I had the Binding Song. I choose that song because that's what I seen most when I was traveling . . . people walking away and leaving one another. So I takes the power of my song and binds them together.

*[*SETH *enters from the yard carrying cabbages and tomatoes.]*

Been binding people ever since. That's why they call me Bynum Just like glue I sticks people together.

SETH: Maybe they ain't supposed to be stuck sometimes. You ever think of that?

BYNUM: Oh, I don't do it lightly. It cost me a piece of myself every time I do. I'm a Binder of What Clings. You got to find out if they cling first. You can't bind what don't cling.

SELIG: Well, how is that the Secret of Life? I thought you said he was gonna show you the secret of life. That's what I'm waiting to find out.

BYNUM: Oh, he showed me alright. But you still got to figure it out. Can't nobody figure it out for you. You got to come to it on your own. That's why I'm looking for the shiny man.

SELIG: Well, I'll keep my eye out for him. What you got there, Seth?

SETH: Here go some cabbage and tomatoes. I got some green beans coming in real nice. I'm gonna take and start me a grapevine out there next year. Butera says he gonna give me a piece of his vine and I'm gonna start that out there.

SELIG: How many of them pots you got?

SETH: I got six. That's six dollars minus eight on top of fifteen for the sheet metal come to a dollar twenty out the six dollars leave me four dollars and eighty cents.

SELIG *[counting out the money]*: There's four dollars . . . and . . . eighty cents.

SETH: How many of them dustpans you want?

SELIG: As many as you can make out them sheets.

SETH: You can use that many? I get to cutting on them sheets figuring how to make them dustpans . . . ain't no telling how many I'm liable to come up with.

SELIG: I can use them and you can make me some more next time.

SETH: Alright, I'm gonna hold you to that, now.

SELIG: Thanks for the biscuit, Bertha.

BERTHA: You know you welcome anytime, Selig.

SETH: Which way you heading?

SELIG: Going down to Wheeling. All through West Virginia there. I'll be back Saturday. They putting in new roads down that way. Makes traveling easier.

SETH: That's what I hear. All up around here too. Got a fellow staying here working on that road by the Brady Street Bridge.

SELIG: Yeah, it's gonna make traveling real nice. Thanks for the cabbage, Seth I'll see you on Saturday.

[SELIG exits.]

SETH [*to BYNUM*]: Why you wanna start all that nonsense talk with that man? All that shiny man nonsense.

BYNUM: You know it ain't no nonsense. Bertha know it ain't no nonsense. I don't know if Selig know or not.

BERTHA: Seth, when you get to making them dustpans make me a coffeepot.

SETH: What's the matter with your coffee? Ain't nothing wrong with your coffee. Don't she make some good coffee, Bynum?

BYNUM: I ain't worried about the coffee. I know she makes some good biscuits.

SETH: I ain't studying no coffeepot, woman. You heard me tell the man I was gonna cut as many dustpans as them sheets will make . . . and all of a sudden you want a coffeepot.

BERTHA: Man, hush up and go on and make me that coffeepot.

[JEREMY enters the front door. About twenty-five, he gives the impression that he has the world in his hand, that he can meet life's challenges head on. He smiles a lot. He is a proficient guitar player, though his spirit has yet to be molded into song.]

BYNUM: I hear Mr. Piney's boys had you.

JEREMY: Fined me two dollars for nothing! Ain't done nothing.

SETH: I told you when you come on here everybody know my house. Know these is respectable quarters. I don't put up with no foolishness. Everybody know Seth Holly keep a good house. Was my daddy's house. This house been a decent house for a long time.

JEREMY: I ain't done nothing, Mr. Seth. I stopped by the Workmen's Club and got me a bottle. Me and Roper Lee from Alabama. Had us a half pint. We was fixing to cut that half in two when they came up on us. Asked us if we was working. We told them we was putting in the road over yonder and that it was our payday. They snatched hold of us to get that two dollars. Me and Roper Lee ain't even had a chance to take a drink when they grabbed us.

SETH: I don't go for all that kind of carrying on.

BERTHA: Leave the boy alone, Seth. You know the police do that. Figure there's too many people out on the street they take some of them off. You know that.

SETH: I ain't gonna have folks talking.

BERTHA: Ain't nobody talking nothing. That's all in your head. You want some grits and biscuits, Jeremy?

JEREMY: Thank you, Miss Bertha. They didn't give us a thing to eat last night. I'll take one of them big bowls if you don't mind.

[There is a knock at the door. SETH goes to answer it. Enter HERALD LOOMIS and his eleven-year-old daughter, ZONIA. HERALD LOOMIS is thirty-two years old. He is at times possessed. A man driven not by the hellhounds that seemingly bay at his heels, but by his search for a world that speaks to something about himself. He is unable to harmonize the forces that swirl around him, and seeks to recreate the world into one that contains his image. He wears a hat and a long wool coat.]

LOOMIS: Me and my daughter looking for a place to stay, mister. You got a sign say you got rooms.

[SETH stares at Loomis, sizing him up.]

Mister, if you ain't got no rooms we can go somewhere else.

SETH: How long you plan on staying?

LOOMIS: Don't know. Two weeks or more maybe.

SETH: It's two dollars a week for the room. We serve meals twice a day. It's two dollars for room and board. Pay up in advance.

[LOOMIS reaches into his pocket.]

It's a dollar extra for the girl.

LOOMIS: The girl sleep in the same room.

SETH: Well, do she eat off the same plate? We serve meals twice a day. That's a dollar extra for food.

LOOMIS: Ain't got no extra dollar. I was planning on asking your missus if she could help out with the cooking and cleaning and whatnot.

SETH: Her helping out don't put no food on the table. I need that dollar to buy some food.

LOOMIS: I'll give you fifty cents extra. She don't eat much.

SETH: Okay . . . but fifty cents don't buy but half a portion.

BERTHA: Seth, she can help me out. Let her help me out. I can use some help.

SETH: Well, that's two dollars for the week. Pay up in advance. Saturday to Saturday. You wanna stay on then it's two more come Saturday.

[LOOMIS pays SETH the money.]

BERTHA: My name's Bertha. This my husband, Seth. You got Bynum and Jeremy over there.

LOOMIS: Ain't nobody else live here?

BERTHA: They the only ones live here now. People come and go. They the only ones here now. You want a cup of coffee and a biscuit?

LOOMIS: We done ate this morning.

BYNUM: Where you coming from, Mister . . . I didn't get your name.

LOOMIS: Name's Herald Loomis. This my daughter, Zonia.

BYNUM: Where you coming from?

LOOMIS: Come from all over. Whicheverway the road take us that's the way we go.

JEREMY: If you looking for a job, I'm working putting in that road down there by the bridge. They can't get enough mens. Always looking to take somebody on.

LOOMIS: I'm looking for a woman named Martha Loomis. That's my wife. Got married legal with the papers and all.

SETH: I don't know nobody named Loomis. I know some Marthas but I don't know no Loomis.

BYNUM: You got to see Rutherford Selig if you wanna find somebody. Selig's the People Finder. Rutherford Selig's a first-class People Finder.

JEREMY: What she look like? Maybe I seen her.

LOOMIS: She a brownskin woman. Got long pretty hair. About five feet from the ground.

JEREMY: I don't know. I might have seen her.

BYNUM: You got to see Rutherford Selig. You give him one dollar to get her name on his list . . . and after she get her name on his list Rutherford Selig will go right on out there and find her. I got him looking for somebody for me.

LOOMIS: You say he find people. How you find him?

BYNUM: You just missed him. He's gone downriver now. You got to wait till Saturday. He's gone downriver with his pots and pans. He come to see Seth on Saturdays. You got to wait till then.

SETH: Come on, I'll show you to your room.

[SETH, LOOMIS, and ZONIA exit up the stairs.]

JEREMY: Miss Bertha, I'll take that biscuit you was gonna give that fellow, if you don't mind. Say, Mr. Bynum, they got somebody like that around here sure enough? Somebody that find people?

BYNUM: Rutherford Selig. He go around selling pots and pans and every house he come to he write down the name and address of whoever lives there. So if you looking for somebody, quite naturally you go and see him . . . 'cause he's the only one who know where everybody live at.

JEREMY: I ought to have him look for this old gal I used to know. It be nice to see her again.

BERTHA [*giving JEREMY a biscuit*]: Jeremy, today's the day for you to pull them sheets off the bed and set them outside your door. I'll set you out some clean ones.

BYNUM: Mr. Piney's boys done ruined your good time last night, Jeremy . . . what you planning for tonight?

JEREMY: They got me scared to go out, Mr. Bynum. They might grab me again.

BYNUM: You ought to take your guitar and go down to Seefus. Seefus got a gambling place down there on Wylie Avenue. You ought to take your guitar and go down there. They got guitar contest down there.

JEREMY: I don't play no contest, Mr. Bynum. Had one of them white fellows cure me of that. I ain't been nowhere near a contest since.

BYNUM: White fellow beat you playing guitar?

JEREMY: Naw, he ain't beat me. I was sitting at home just fixing to sit down and eat when somebody come up to my house and got me. Told me there's a white fellow say he was gonna give a prize to the best guitar player he could find. I take up my guitar and go down there and somebody had gone up and got Bobo Smith and brought him down there. Him and another fellow called Hooter. Old Hooter couldn't play no guitar, he do more hollering than playing, but Bobo could go at it awhile.

This fellow standing there say he the one that was gonna give the prize and me and Bobo started playing for him. Bobo play something and then I'd try to play something better than what he played. Old Hooter, he just holler and bang at the guitar. Man was the worst guitar player I ever seen. So me and Bobo played and after a while I seen where he was getting the attention of this white fellow. He'd play something and while he was playing it he be slapping on the side of the guitar, and that made it sound like he was playing more than he was. So I started doing it too. White fellow ain't knew no difference. He ain't knew as much about guitar playing as Hooter did. After we play awhile, the white fellow called us to him and said he couldn't make up his mind, say all three of us was the best guitar player and we'd have to split the prize between us. Then he give us twenty-five cents. That's eight cents apiece and a penny on the side. That cured me of playing contest to this day.

BYNUM: Seefus ain't like that. Seefus give a whole dollar and a drink of whiskey.

JEREMY: What night they be down there?

BYNUM: Be down there every night. Music don't know no certain night.

BERTHA: You go down to Seefus with them people and you liable to end up in a raid and go to jail sure enough. I don't know why Bynum tell you that.

BYNUM: That's where the music at. That's where the people at. The people down there making music and enjoying themselves. Some things is worth taking the chance going to jail about.

BERTHA: Jeremy ain't got no business going down there.

JEREMY: They got some women down there, Mr. Bynum?

BYNUM: Oh, they got women down there, sure. They got women everywhere. Women be where the men is so they can find each other.

JEREMY: Some of them old gals come out there where we be putting in that road. Hanging around there trying to snatch somebody.

BYNUM: How come some of them ain't snatched hold of you?

JEREMY: I don't want them kind. Them desperate kind. Ain't nothing worse than a desperate woman. Tell them you gonna leave them and they get to crying and carrying on. That just make you want to get away quicker. They get to cutting up your clothes and things trying to keep you staying. Desperate women ain't nothing but trouble for a man.

[SETH enters from the stairs.]

SETH: Something ain't setting right with that fellow.

BERTHA: What's wrong with him? What he say?

SETH: I take him up there and try to talk to him and he ain't for no talking. Say he been traveling . . . coming over from Ohio. Say he a deacon in the church. Say he looking for Martha Pentecost. Talking about that's his wife.

BERTHA: How you know it's the same Martha? Could be talking about anybody. Lots of people named Martha.

SETH: You see that little girl? I didn't hook it up till he said it, but that little girl look just like her. Ask Bynum. [*to* BYNUM] Bynum. Don't that little girl look just like Martha Pentecost?

BERTHA: I still say he could be talking about anybody.

SETH: The way he described her wasn't no doubt who he was talking about. Described her right down to her toes.

BERTHA: What did you tell him?

SETH: I ain't told him nothing. The way that fellow look I wasn't gonna tell him nothing. I don't know what he looking for her for.

BERTHA: What else he have to say?

SETH: I told you he wasn't for no talking. I told him where the outhouse was and to keep that gal off the front porch and out of my garden. He asked if you'd mind setting a hot tub for the gal and that was about the gist of it.

BERTHA: Well, I wouldn't let it worry me if I was you. Come on get your sleep.

BYNUM: He says he looking for Martha and he a deacon in the church.

SETH: That's what he say. Do he look like a deacon to you?

BERTHA: He might be, you don't know. Bynum ain't got no special say on whether he a deacon or not.

SETH: Well, if he the deacon I'd sure like to see the preacher.

BERTHA: Come on get your sleep. Jeremy, don't forget to set them sheets outside the door like I told you.

[BERTHA exits into the bedroom.]

SETH: Something ain't setting right with that fellow, Bynum. He's one of them mean-looking niggers look like he done killed somebody gambling over a quarter.

BYNUM: He ain't no gambler. Gamblers wear nice shoes. This fellow got on clod-hoppers. He been out there walking up and down them roads.

[ZONIA enters from the stairs and looks around.]

BYNUM: You looking for the back door, sugar? There it is. You can go out there and play. It's alright.

SETH [*showing her the door*]: You can go out there and play. Just don't get in my garden. And don't go messing around in my workshed.

[SETH exits into the bedroom. There is a knock on the door.]

JEREMY: Somebody at the door.

*[*JEREMY *goes to answer the door. Enter* MATTIE CAMPBELL. *She is a young woman of twenty-six whose attractiveness is hidden under the weight and concerns of a dissatisfied life. She is a woman in an honest search for love and companionship. She has suffered many defeats in her search, and though not always uncompromising, still believes in the possibility of love.]*

MATTIE: I'm looking for a man named Bynum. Lady told me to come back later.

JEREMY: Sure, he here. Mr. Bynum, somebody here to see you.

BYNUM: Come to see me, huh?

MATTIE: Are you the man they call Bynum? The man folks say can fix things?

BYNUM: Depend on what need fixing. I can't make no promises. But I got a powerful song in some matters.

MATTIE: Can you fix it so my man come back to me?

BYNUM: Come on in . . . have a sit down.

MATTIE: You got to help me. I don't know what else to do.

BYNUM: Depend on how all the circumstances of the thing come together. How all the pieces fit.

MATTIE: I done everything I knowed how to do. You got to make him come back to me.

BYNUM: It ain't nothing to make somebody come back. I can fix it so he can't stand to be away from you. I got my roots and powders, I can fix it so wherever he's at this thing will come up on him and he won't be able to sleep for seeing your face. Won't be able to eat for thinking of you.

MATTIE: That's what I want. Make him come back.

BYNUM: The roots is a powerful thing. I can fix it so one day he'll walk out his front door . . . won't be thinking of nothing. He won't know what it is. All he knows is that a powerful dissatisfaction done set in his bones and can't nothing he do make him feel satisfied. He'll set his foot down on the road and the wind in the trees be talking to him and everywhere he step on the road, that road'll give back your name and something will pull him right up to your doorstep. Now, I can do that. I can take my roots and fix that easy. But maybe he ain't supposed to come back. And if he ain't supposed to come back . . . then he'll be in your bed one morning and it'll come up on him that he's in the wrong place. That he's lost outside of time from his place that he's supposed to be in. Then both of you be lost and trapped outside of life and ain't no way for you to get back into it. 'Cause you lost from yourselves and where the places come together, where you're supposed to be alive, your heart kicking in your chest with a song worth singing.

MATTIE: Make him come back to me. Make his feet say my name on the road. I don't care what happens. Make him come back.

BYNUM: What's your man's name?

MATTIE: He go by Jack Carper. He was born in Alabama then he come to West Texas and find me and we come here. Been here three years before he left.

Say I had a curse prayer on me and he started walking down the road and ain't never come back. Somebody told me, say you can fix things like that.

BYNUM: He just got up one day, set his feet on the road, and walked away?

MATTIE: You got to make him come back, mister.

BYNUM: Did he say goodbye?

MATTIE: Ain't said nothing. Just started walking. I could see where he disappeared. Didn't look back. Just keep walking. Can't you fix it so he come back? I ain't got no curse prayer on me. I know I ain't.

BYNUM: What made him say you had a curse prayer on you?

MATTIE: 'Cause the babies died. Me and Jack had two babies. Two little babies that ain't lived two months before they died. He say it's because somebody cursed me not to have babies.

BYNUM: He ain't bound to you if the babies died. Look like somebody trying to keep you from being bound up and he's gone on back to whoever it is 'cause he's already bound up to her. Ain't nothing to be done. Somebody else done got a powerful hand in it and ain't nothing to be done to break it. You got to let him go find where he's supposed to be in the world.

MATTIE: Jack done gone off and you telling me to forget about him. All my life I been looking for somebody to stop and stay with me. I done already got too many things to forget about. I take Jack Carper's hand and it feel so rough and strong. Seem like he's the strongest man in the world the way he hold me. Like he's bigger than the whole world and can't nothing bad get to me. Even when he act mean sometimes he still make everything seem okay with the world. Like there's part of it that belongs just to you. Now you telling me to forget about him?

BYNUM: Jack Carper gone off to where he belong. There's somebody searching for your doorstep right now. Ain't no need you fretting over Jack Carper. Right now he's a strong thought in your mind. But every time you catch yourself frettin over Jack Carper you push that thought away. You push it out your mind and that thought will get weaker and weaker till you wake up one morning and you won't even be able to call him up on your mind.

[BYNUM gives her a small cloth packet.]

Take this and sleep with it under your pillow and it'll bring good luck to you. Draw it to you like a magnet. It won't be long before you forget all about Jack Carper.

MATTIE: How much . . . do I owe you?

BYNUM: Whatever you got there . . . that'll be alright.

[MATTIE hands BYNUM two quarters. She crosses to the door.]

You sleep with that under your pillow and you'll be alright.

[MATTIE opens the door to exit and JEREMY crosses over to her. BYNUM overhears the first part of their conversation, then exits out the back.]

JEREMY: I overheard what you told Mr. Bynum Had me an old gal did that to me. Woke up one morning and she was gone. Just took off to parts unknown. I woke up that morning and the only thing I could do was look around for my shoes. I woke up and got out of there. Found my shoes and took off. That's the only thing I could think of to do.

MATTIE: She ain't said nothing?

JEREMY: I just looked around for my shoes and got out of there.

MATTIE: Jack ain't said nothing either. He just walked off.

JEREMY: Some mens do that. Womens too. I ain't gone off looking for her. I just let her go. Figure she had a time to come to herself. Wasn't no use of me standing in the way. Where you from?

MATTIE: Texas. I was born in Georgia but I went to Texas with my mama. She dead now. Was picking peaches and fell dead away. I come up here with Jack Carper.

JEREMY: I'm from North Carolina. Down around Raleigh where they got all that tobacco. Been up here about two weeks. I likes it fine except I still got to find me a woman. You got a nice look to you. Look like you have mens standing in your door. Is you got mens standing in your door to get a look at you?

MATTIE: I ain't got nobody since Jack left.

JEREMY: A woman like you need a man. Maybe you let me be your man. I got a nice way with the women. That's what they tell me.

MATTIE: I don't know. Maybe Jack's coming back.

JEREMY: I'll be your man till he come. A woman can't be by her lonesome. Let me be your man till he come.

MATTIE: I just can't go through life piecing myself out to different mens. I need a man who wants to stay with me.

JEREMY: I can't say what's gonna happen. Maybe I'll be the man. I don't know. You wanna go along the road a little ways with me?

MATTIE: I don't know. Seem like life say it's gonna be one thing and end up being another. I'm tired of going from man to man.

JEREMY: Life is like you got to take a chance. Everybody got to take a chance. Can't nobody say what's gonna be. Come on . . . take a chance with me and see what the year bring. Maybe you let me come and see you. Where you staying?

MATTIE: I got me a room up on Bedford. Me and Jack had a room together.

JEREMY: What's the address? I'll come by and get you tonight and we can go down to Seefus. I'm going down there and play my guitar.

MATTIE: You play guitar?

JEREMY: I play guitar like I'm born to it.

MATTIE: I live at 1727 Bedford Avenue. I'm gonna find out if you can play guitar like you say.

JEREMY: I plays it sugar, and that ain't all I do. I got a ten-pound hammer and I knows how to drive it down. Good god . . . you ought to hear my hammer ring!

MATTIE: Go on with that kind of talk, now. If you gonna come by and get me I got to get home and straighten up for you.

JEREMY: I'll be by at eight o'clock. How's eight o'clock? I'm gonna make you forget all about Jack Carper.

MATTIE: Go on, now. I got to get home and fix up for you.

JEREMY: Eight o'clock, sugar.

[The lights go down in the parlor and come up on the yard outside. ZONIA is singing and playing a game.]

ZONIA:

I went downtown
To get my grip
I came back home
Just a pullin' the skiff

I went upstairs
To make my bed
I made a mistake
And I bumped my head
Just a pullin' the skiff

I went downstairs
To milk the cow
I made a mistake
And I milked the sow
Just a pullin' the skiff

Tomorrow, tomorrow
Tomorrow never comes
The marrow the marrow
The marrow in the bone.

[REUBEN enters.]

REUBEN: Hi.

ZONIA: Hi.

REUBEN: What's your name?

ZONIA: Zonia.

REUBEN: What kind of name is that?

ZONIA: It's what my daddy named me.

REUBEN: My name's Reuben. You staying in Mr. Seth's house?

ZONIA: Yeah.

REUBEN: That your daddy I seen you with this morning?

ZONIA: I don't know. Who you see me with?

REUBEN: I saw you with some man had on a great big old coat. And you was walking up to Mr. Seth's house. Had on a hat too.

ZONIA: Yeah, that's my daddy.

REUBEN: You like Mr. Seth?

ZONIA: I ain't see him much.

REUBEN: My grandpap say he a great big old windbag. How come you living in Mr. Seth's house? Don't you have no house?

ZONIA: We going to find my mother.

REUBEN: Where she at?

ZONIA: I don't know. We got to find her. We just go all over.

REUBEN: Why you got to find her? What happened to her?

ZONIA: She ran away.

REUBEN: Why she run away?

ZONIA: I don't know. My daddy say some man named Joe Turner did something bad to him once and that made her run away.

REUBEN: Maybe she coming back and you don't have to go looking for her.

ZONIA: We ain't there no more.

REUBEN: She could have come back when you wasn't there.

ZONIA: My daddy said she ran off and left us so we going looking for her.

REUBEN: What he gonna do when he find her?

ZONIA: He didn't say. He just say he got to find her.

REUBEN: Your daddy say how long you staying in Mr. Seth's house?

ZONIA: He don't say much. But we never stay too long nowhere. He say we got to keep moving till we find her.

REUBEN: Ain't no kids hardly live around here. I had me a friend but he died. He was the best friend I ever had. Me and Eugene used to keep secrets. I still got his pigeons. He told me to let them go when he died. He say, "Reuben, promise me when I die you'll let my pigeons go." But I keep them to remember him by. I ain't never gonna let them go. Even when I get to be grown up. I'm just always gonna have Eugene's pigeons.

[Pause.]

Mr. Bynum a conjure man. My grandpap scared of him. He don't like me to come over here too much. I'm scared of him too. My grandpap told me not to let him get close enough to where he can reach out his hand and touch me.

ZONIA: He don't seem scary to me.

REUBEN: He buys pigeons from me . . . and if you get up early in the morning you can see him out in the yard doing something with them pigeons. My grandpap say he kill them. I sold him one yesterday. I don't know what he do with it. I just hope he don't spook me up.

ZONIA: Why you sell him pigeons if he's gonna spook you up?

REUBEN: I just do like Eugene do. He used to sell Mr. Bynum pigeons. That's how he got to collecting them to sell to Mr. Bynum. Sometime he give me a nickel and sometime he give me a whole dime.

[LOOMIS enters from the house.]

LOOMIS: Zonia!

ZONIA: Sir?

LOOMIS: What you doing?

ZONIA: Nothing.

LOOMIS: You stay around this house, you hear? I don't want you wandering off nowhere.

ZONIA: I ain't wandering off nowhere.

LOOMIS: Miss Bertha set that hot tub and you getting a good scrubbing. Get scrubbed up good. You ain't been scrubbing.

ZONIA: I been scrubbing.

LOOMIS: Look at you. You growing too fast. Your bones getting bigger everyday. I don't want you getting grown on me. Don't you get grown on me too soon. We gonna find your mamma. She around here somewhere. I can smell her. You stay on around this house now. Don't you go nowhere.

ZONIA: Yes, sir.

[LOOMIS exits into the house.]

REUBEN: Wow, your daddy's scary!

ZONIA: He is not! I don't know what you talking about.

REUBEN: He got them mean-looking eyes!

ZONIA: My daddy ain't got no mean-looking eyes!

REUBEN: Aw, girl, I was just messing with you. You wanna go see Eugene's pigeons? Got a great big coop out the back of my house. Come on, I'll show you.

[REUBEN and ZONIA exit as the lights go down.]

SCENE 2

[It is Saturday morning, one week later. The lights come up on the kitchen. BERTHA is at the stove preparing breakfast while SETH sits at the table.]

SETH: Something ain't right about that fellow. I been watching him all week. Something ain't right, I'm telling you.

BERTHA: Seth Holly, why don't you hush up about that man this morning?

SETH: I don't like the way he stare at everybody. Don't look at you natural like. He just be staring at you. Like he trying to figure out something about you. Did you see him when he come back in here?

BERTHA: That man ain't thinking about you.

SETH: He don't work nowhere. Just go out and come back. Go out and come back.

BERTHA: As long as you get your boarding money it ain't your cause about what he do. He don't bother nobody.

SETH: Just go and come back. Going around asking everybody about Martha. Like Henry Allen seen him down at the church last night.

BERTHA: The man's allowed to go to church if he want. He say he a deacon. Ain't nothing wrong about him going to church.

SETH: I ain't talking about him going to church. I'm talking about him hanging around *outside* the church.

BERTHA: Henry Allen say that?

SETH: Say he be standing around outside the church. Like he be watching it.

BERTHA: What on earth he wanna be watching the church for, I wonder?

SETH: That's what I'm trying to figure out. Looks like he fixing to rob it.

BERTHA: Seth, now do he look like the kind that would rob the church?

SETH: I ain't saying that. I ain't saying how he look. It's how he do. Anybody liable to do anything as far as I'm concerned. I ain't never thought about how no church robbers look . . . but now that you mention it, I don't see where they look no different than how he look.

BERTHA: Herald Loomis ain't the kind of man who would rob no church.

SETH: I ain't even so sure that's his name.

BERTHA: Why the man got to lie about his name?

SETH: Anybody can tell anybody anything about what their name is. That's what you call him . . . Herald Loomis. His name is liable to be anything.

BERTHA: Well, until he tell me different that's what I'm gonna call him. You just getting yourself all worked up about the man for nothing.

SETH: Talking about Loomis: Martha's name wasn't no Loomis nothing. Martha's name is Pentecost.

BERTHA: How you so sure that's her right name? Maybe she changed it.

SETH: Martha's a good Christian woman. This fellow here look like he owe the devil a day's work and he's trying to figure out how he gonna pay him. Martha ain't had a speck of distrust about her the whole time she was living here. They moved the church out there to Rankin and I was sorry to see her go.

BERTHA: That's why he be hanging around the church. He looking for her.

SETH: If he looking for her, why don't he go inside and ask? What he doing hanging around outside the church acting sneaky like?

[BYNUM enters from the yard.]

BYNUM: Morning, Seth. Morning, Sister Bertha.

[BYNUM continues through the kitchen and exits up the stairs.]

BERTHA: That's who you should be asking the questions. He been out there in that yard all morning. He was out there before the sun come up. He didn't even come in for breakfast. I don't know what he's doing. He had three of them pigeons line up out there. He dance around till he get tired. He sit down awhile then get up and dance some more. He come through here a little while ago looking like he was mad at the world.

SETH: I don't pay Bynum no mind. He don't spook me up with all that stuff.

BERTHA: That's how Martha come to be living here. She come to see Bynum She come to see him when she first left from down South.

SETH: Martha was living here before Bynum. She ain't come on here when she first left from down there. She come on here after she went back to get her little girl. That's when she come on here.

BERTHA: Well, where was Bynum? He was here when she came.

SETH: Bynum ain't come till after her. That boy Hiram was staying up there in Bynum's room.

BERTHA: Well, how long Bynum been here?

SETH: Bynum ain't been here no longer than three years. That's what I'm trying to tell you. Martha was staying up there and sewing and cleaning for Doc Goldblum when Bynum came. This the longest he ever been in one place.

BERTHA: How you know how long the man been in one place?

SETH: I know Bynum. Bynum ain't no mystery to me. I done seen a hundred niggers like him. He's one of them fellows never could stay in one place. He was wandering all around the country till he got old and settled here. The only thing different about Bynum is he bring all this heebie-jeebie stuff with him.

BERTHA: I still say he was staying here when she came. That's why she came . . . to see him.

SETH: You can say what you want. I know the facts of it. She come on here four years ago all heartbroken 'cause she couldn't find her little girl. And Bynum wasn't nowhere around. She got mixed up in that old heebie-jeebie nonsense with him after he came.

BERTHA: Well, if she came on before Bynum I don't know where she stayed. 'Cause she stayed up there in Hiram's room. Hiram couldn't get along with Bynum and left out of here owing you two dollars. Now, I know you ain't forgot about that!

SETH: Sure did! You know Hiram ain't paid me that two dollars yet. So that's why he be ducking and hiding when he see me down on Logan Street. You right. Martha did come on after Bynum. I forgot that's why Hiram left.

BERTHA: Him and Bynum never could see eye to eye. They always rubbed each other the wrong way. Hiram got to thinking that Bynum was trying to put a fix on him and he moved out. Martha came to see Bynum and ended up taking Hiram's room. Now, I know what I'm talking about. She stayed on here three years till they moved the church.

SETH: She out there in Rankin now. I know where she at. I know where they moved the church to. She right out there in Rankin in that place used to be shoe store. Used to be Wolf's shoe store. They moved to a bigger place and they put that church in there. I know where she at. I know just where she at.

BERTHA: Why don't you tell the man? You see he looking for her.

SETH: I ain't gonna tell that man where that woman is! What I wanna do that for? I don't know nothing about that man. I don't know why he looking for her.

He might wanna do her a harm. I ain't gonna carry that on my hands. He looking for her, he gonna have to find her for himself. I ain't gonna help him. Now, if he had come and presented himself as a gentleman—the way Martha Pentecost's husband would have done—then I would have told him. But I ain't gonna tell this old wild-eyed mean-looking nigger nothing!

BERTHA: Well, why don't you get a ride with Selig and go up there and tell her where he is? See if she wanna see him. If that's her little girl . . . you say Martha was looking for her.

SETH: You know me, Bertha. I don't get mixed up in nobody's business.

[BYNUM enters from the stairs.]

BYNUM: Morning, Seth. Morning, Bertha. Can I still get some breakfast? Mr. Loomis been down here this morning?

SETH: He done gone out and come back. He up there now. Left out of here early this morning wearing that coat. Hot as it is, the man wanna walk around wearing a big old heavy coat. He come back in here paid me for another week, sat down there waiting on Selig. Got tired of waiting and went on back upstairs.

BYNUM: Where's the little girl?

SETH: She out there in the front. Had to chase her and that Reuben off the front porch. She out there somewhere.

BYNUM: Look like if Martha was around here he would have found her by now. My guess is she ain't in the city.

SETH: She ain't! I know where she at. I know just where she at. But I ain't gonna tell him. Not the way he look.

BERTHA: Here go your coffee, Bynum.

BYNUM: He says he gonna get Selig to find her for him.

SETH: Selig can't find her. He talk all that . . . but unless he get lucky and knock on her door he can't find her. That's the only way he find anybody. He got to get lucky. But I know just where she at.

BERTHA: Here go some biscuits, Bynum.

BYNUM: What else you got over there, Sister Bertha? You got some grits and gravy over there? I could go for some of that this morning.

BERTHA [*sets a bowl on the table*]: Seth, come on and help me turn this mattress over. Come on.

SETH: Something ain't right with that fellow, Bynum. I don't like the way he stare at everybody.

BYNUM: Mr. Loomis alright, Seth. He just a man got something on his mind. He just got a straightforward mind, that's all.

SETH: What's that fellow that they had around here? Moses, that's Moses Houser. Man went crazy and jumped off the Brady Street Bridge. I told you when I seen him something wasn't right about him. And I'm telling you about this fellow now.

[There is a knock on the door. SETH goes to answer it. Enter RUTHERFORD SELIG.]

Ho! Come on in, Selig.

BYNUM: If it ain't the People Finder himself.

SELIG: Bynum, before you start . . . I ain't seen no shiny man now.

BYNUM: Who said anything about that? I ain't said nothing about that. I just called you a first-class People Finder.

SELIG: How many dustpans you get out of that sheet metal, Seth?

SETH: You walked by them on your way in. They sitting out there on the porch. Got twenty-eight. Got four out of each sheet and made Bertha a coffeepot out the other one. They a little small but they got nice handles.

SELIG: That was twenty cents apiece, right? That's what we agreed on.

SETH: That's five dollars and sixty cents. Twenty on top of twenty-eight. How many sheets you bring me?

SELIG: I got eight out there. That's a dollar twenty makes me owe you . . .

SETH: Four dollars and forty cents.

SELIG [*paying him*]: Go on and make me some dustpans. I can use all you can make.

[LOOMIS enters from the stairs.]

LOOMIS: I been watching for you. He say you find people.

BYNUM: Mr. Loomis here wants you to find his wife.

LOOMIS: He say you find people. Find her for me.

SELIG: Well, let see here . . . find somebody, is it?

[SELIG rummages through his pockets. He has several notebooks and he is searching for the right one.]

Alright now . . . what's the name?

LOOMIS: Martha Loomis. She my wife. Got married legal with the paper and all.

SELIG [*writing*]: Martha . . . Loomis. How tall is she?

LOOMIS: She five feet from the ground.

SELIG: Five feet . . . tall. Young or old?

LOOMIS: She a young woman. Got long pretty hair.

SELIG: Young . . . long . . . pretty . . . hair. Where did you last see her?

LOOMIS: Tennessee. Nearby Memphis.

SELIG: When was that?

LOOMIS: Nineteen hundred and one.

SELIG: Nineteen . . . hundred and one. I'll tell you, mister . . . you better off without them. Now you take me . . . old Rutherford Selig could tell you a thing or two about these women. I ain't met one yet I could understand. Now, you take Sally out there. That's all a man needs is a good horse. I say giddup and she go. Say whoa and she stop. I feed her some oats and she carry me wherever I want to go. Ain't had a speck of trouble out of her since I had her. Now, I been married. A long time ago down in Kentucky. I got up one morning and I saw this look on my wife's face. Like way down deep inside her she was wishing I was dead. I walked around that morning and every time I looked at her she had that look on her face. It seem like she knew I could see it on her. Every time I looked at her I got smaller and smaller. Well, I wasn't gonna stay around there and just shrink away. I walked out on the porch and closed the door behind me. When I closed the door she locked it. I went out and bought me a horse. And I ain't been without one since! Martha Loomis, huh? Well, now I'll do the best I can do. That's one dollar.

LOOMIS [*holding out dollar suspiciously*]: How you find her?

SELIG: Well now, it ain't no easy job like you think. You can't just go out there and find them like that. There's a lot of little tricks to it. It's not an easy job keeping up with you Nigras the way you move about so. Now you take this woman you looking for . . . this Martha Loomis. She could be anywhere. Time I find her, if you don't keep your eye on her, she'll be gone off someplace else. You'll be thinking she over here and she'll be over there. But like I say there's lot of little tricks to it.

LOOMIS: You say you find her.

SELIG: I can't promise anything but we been finders in my family for a long time. Bringers and finders. My great-granddaddy used to bring Nigras across the ocean on ships. That's wasn't no easy job either. Sometimes the winds would blow so hard you'd think the hand of God was set against the sails. But it set him well in pay and he settled in this new land and found him a wife of good Christian charity with a mind for kids and the like and well . . . here I am, Rutherford Selig. You're in good hands, mister. Me and my daddy have found plenty Nigras. My daddy, rest his soul, used to find runaway slaves for the plantation bosses. He was the best there was at it. Jonas B. Selig. Had him a reputation stretched clean across the country. After Abraham Lincoln give you all Nigras your freedom papers and with you all looking all over for each other . . . we started finding Nigras for Nigras. Of course, it don't pay as much. But the People Finding business ain't so bad.

LOOMIS [*hands him the dollar*]: Find her. Martha Loomis. Find her for me.

SELIG: Like I say, I can't promise you anything. I'm going back upriver, and if she's around in them parts I'll find her for you. But I can't promise you anything.

LOOMIS: When you coming back?

SELIG: I'll be back on Saturday. I come and see Seth to pick up my order on Saturday.

BYNUM: You going upriver, huh? You going up around my way. I used to go all up through there. Blawknox . . . Clairton. Used to go up to Rankin and take that first righthand road. I wore many a pair of shoes out walking around that way. You'd have thought I was a missionary spreading the gospel the way I wandered all around them parts.

SELIG: Okay, Bynum. See you on Saturday.

SETH: Here, let me walk out with you. Help you with them dustpans.

[SETH and SELIG exit out the back. BERTHA enters from the stairs carrying a bundle of sheets.]

BYNUM: Herald Loomis got the People Finder looking for Martha.

BERTHA: You can call him a People Finder if you want to. I know Rutherford Selig carries people away too. He done carried a whole bunch of them away from here. Folks plan on leaving plan by Selig's timing. They wait till he get ready to go, then they hitch a ride on his wagon. Then he charge folks a dollar to tell them where he took them. Now, that's the truth of Rutherford Selig. This old People Finding business is for the birds. He ain't never found nobody he ain't took away. Herald Loomis, you just wasted your dollar.

[BERTHA exits into the bedroom.]

LOOMIS: He say he find her. He say he find her by Saturday. I'm gonna wait till Saturday.

[The lights fade to black.]

SCENE 3

[It is Sunday morning, the next day. The lights come up on the kitchen. SETH sits talking to BYNUM: The breakfast dishes have been cleared away.]

SETH: They can't see that. Neither one of them can see that. Now, how much sense it take to see that? All you got to do is be able to count. One man making ten pots is five men making fifty pots. But they can't see that. Asked where I'm gonna get my five men. Hell, I can teach anybody how to make a pot. I can teach you. I can take you out there and get you started right now. Inside of two weeks you'd know how to make a pot. All you got to do is want to do it. I can get five men. I ain't worried about getting no five men.

BERTHA [*calls from the bedroom*]: Seth. Come on and get ready now. Reverend Gates ain't gonna be holding up his sermon 'cause you sitting out there talking.

SETH: Now, you take the boy, Jeremy. What he gonna do after he put in that road? He can't do nothing but go put in another one somewhere. Now, if he let me show him how to make some pots and pans . . . then he'd have something can't nobody take away from him. After a while he could get his own tools and go off somewhere and make his own pots and pans. Find him somebody to sell them to. Now, Selig can't make no pots and pans. He can sell them but he can't make them. I get me five men with some tools and we'd make him so many pots and pans he'd have to open up a store somewhere. But they can't see that. Neither Mr. Cohen nor Sam Green.

BERTHA [*calls from the bedroom*]: Seth . . . time be wasting. Best be getting on.

SETH: I'm coming, woman! [*to BYNUM*] Want me to sign over the house to borrow five hundred dollars. I ain't that big a fool. That's all I got. Sign it over to them and then I won't have nothing.

[JEREMY enters waving a dollar and carrying his guitar.]

JEREMY: Look here, Mr. Bynum . . . won me another dollar last night down at Seefus! Me and that Mattie Campbell went down there again and I played contest. Ain't no guitar players down there. Wasn't even no contest. Say, Mr. Seth, I asked Mattie Campbell if she wanna come by and have Sunday dinner with us. Get some fried chicken.

SETH: It's gonna cost you twenty-five cents.

JEREMY: That's alright. I got a whole dollar here. Say Mr. Seth . . . me and Mattie Campbell talked it over last night and she gonna move in with me. If that's alright with you.

SETH: Your business is your business . . . but it's gonna cost her a dollar a week for her board. I can't be feeding nobody for free.

JEREMY: Oh, she know that, Mr. Seth. That's what I told her, say she'd have to pay for her meals.

SETH: You say you got a whole dollar there . . . turn loose that twenty-five cents.

JEREMY: Suppose she move in today, then that make seventy-five cents more, so I'll give you the whole dollar for her now till she gets here.

[SETH pockets the money and exits into the bedroom.]

BYNUM: So you and that Mattie Campbell gonna take up together?

JEREMY: I told her she don't need to be by her lonesome, Mr. Bynum. Don't make no sense for both of us to be by our lonesome. So she gonna move in with me.

BYNUM: Sometimes you got to be where you supposed to be. Sometimes you can get all mixed up in life and come to the wrong place.

JEREMY: That's just what I told her, Mr. Bynum. It don't make no sense for her to be all mixed up and lonesome. May as well come here and be with me. She a fine woman too. Got them long legs. Knows how to treat a fellow too. Treat you like you wanna be treated.

BYNUM: You just can't look at it like that. You got to look at the whole thing. Now, you take a fellow go out there, grab hold to a woman and think he got something 'cause she sweet and soft to the touch. Alright. Touching's part of life. It's in the world like everything else. Touching's nice. It feels good. But you can lay your hand upside a horse or a cat, and that feels good too. What's the difference? When you grab hold to a woman, you got something there. You got a whole world there. You got a way of life kicking up under your hand. That woman can take and make you feel like something. I ain't just talking about in the way of jumping off into bed together and rolling around with each other. Anybody can do that. When you grab hold to that woman and look at the whole thing and see what you got . . . why, she can take and make something out of you. Your mother was a woman. That's enough right there to show you what a woman is. Enough to show you what she can do. She made something out of you. Taught you converse, and all about how to take care of yourself, how to see where you at and where you going tomorrow, how to look out to see what's coming in the way of eating, and what to do with yourself when you get lonesome. That's a mighty thing she did. But you just can't look at a woman to jump off into bed with her. That's a foolish thing to ignore a woman like that.

JEREMY: Oh, I ain't ignoring her, Mr. Bynum. It's hard to ignore a woman got legs like she got.

BYNUM: Alright. Let's try it this way. Now, you take a ship. Be out there on the water traveling about. You out there on that ship sailing to and from. And then you see some land. Just like you see a woman walking down the street. You see that land and it don't look like nothing but a line out there on the horizon. That's all it is when you first see it. A line that cross your path out there on the horizon. Now, a smart man know when he see that land, it ain't just a line setting out there. He know that if you get off the water to go take a good look . . . why, there's a whole world right there. A whole world with everything imaginable under the sun. Anything you can think of you can find on that land. Same with a woman. A woman is everything a man need. To a smart man she water and berries. And that's all a man need. That's all he need to live on. You give me some water and berries and if there ain't nothing else I can live a hundred years. See, you just like a man looking at the horizon from a ship. You just seeing a part of it. But it's a blessing when you learn to look at a woman and see in maybe just a few strands of her hair, the way her cheek curves . . . to see in that everything there is out of life to be gotten. It's a blessing to see that. You know you done right and proud by your mother to see that. But you got to learn it. My telling you ain't gonna mean nothing. You got to learn how to come to your own time and place with a woman.

JEREMY: What about your woman, Mr. Bynum? I know you done had some woman.

BYNUM: Oh, I got them in memory time. That lasts longer than any of them ever stayed with me.

JEREMY: I had me an old gal one time . . .

[There is a knock on the door, JEREMY goes to answer it. Enter MOLLY CUNNINGHAM She is about twenty-six, the kind of woman that "could break in on a dollar anywhere she goes." She carries a small cardboard suitcase, and wears a colorful dress of the fashion of the day. JEREMY's heart jumps out of his chest when he sees her.]

MOLLY: You got any rooms here? I'm looking for a room.

JEREMY: Yeah . . . Mr. Seth got rooms. Sure . . . wait till I get Mr. Seth. [*calls*] Mr. Seth! Somebody here to see you! [*to MOLLY*] Yeah, Mr. Seth got some rooms. Got one right next to me. This is a nice place to stay, too. My name's Jeremy. What's yours?

[SETH enters dressed in his Sunday clothes.]

SETH: Ho!

JEREMY: This here woman looking for a place to stay. She say you got any rooms.

MOLLY: Mister, you got any rooms? I seen your sign say you got rooms.

SETH: How long you plan to staying?

MOLLY: I ain't gonna be here long. I ain't looking for no home or nothing. I'd be in Cincinnati if I hadn't missed my train.

SETH: Rooms cost two dollars a week.

MOLLY: Two dollars!

SETH: That includes meals. We serve two meals a day. That's breakfast and dinner.

MOLLY: I hope it ain't on the third floor.

SETH: That's the only one I got. Third floor to the left. That's pay up in advance week to week.

MOLLY [*going into her bosom*]: I'm gonna pay you for one week. My name's Molly. Molly Cunningham.

SETH: I'm Seth Holly. My wife's name is Bertha. She do the cooking and take care of around here. She got sheets on the bed. Towels twenty-five cents a week extra if you ain't got none. You get breakfast and dinner. We got fried chicken on Sundays.

MOLLY: That sounds good. Here's two dollars and twenty-five cents. Look here, Mister . . . ?

SETH: Holly. Seth Holly.

MOLLY: Look here, Mr. Holly. I forgot to tell you. I likes me some company from time to time. I don't like being by myself.

SETH: Your business is your business. I don't meddle in nobody's business. But this is a respectable house. I don't have no riffraff around here. And I don't have no women hauling no men up to their rooms to be making their living. As long as we understand each other then we'll be alright with each other.

MOLLY: Where's the outhouse?

SETH: Straight through the door over yonder.

MOLLY: I get my own key to the front door?

SETH: Everybody get their own key. If you come in late just don't be making no whole lot of noise and carrying on. Don't allow no fussing and fighting around here.

MOLLY: You ain't got to worry about that, mister. Which way you say that outhouse was again?

SETH: Straight through that door over yonder.

[MOLLY exits out the back door. JEREMY crosses to watch her.]

JEREMY: Mr. Bynum, you know what? I think I know what you was talking about now.

[The lights go down on the scene.]

SCENE 4

[The lights come up on the kitchen. It is later the same evening. MATTIE *and all the residents of the house, except* LOOMIS, *sit around the table. They have finished eating and most of the dishes have been cleared.]*

MOLLY: That sure was some good chicken.

JEREMY: That's what I'm talking about. Miss Bertha, you sure can fry some chicken. I thought my mama could fry some chicken. But she can't do half as good as you.

SETH: I know it. That's why I married her. She don't know that, though. She think I married her for something else.

BERTHA: I ain't studying you, Seth. Did you get your things moved in alright, Mattie?

MATTIE: I ain't had that much. Jeremy helped me with what I did have.

BERTHA: You'll get to know your way around here. If you have any questions about anything just ask me. You and Molly both. I get along with everybody. You'll find I ain't no trouble to get along with.

MATTIE: You need some help with the dishes?

BERTHA: I got me a helper. Ain't I, Zonia? Got me a good helper.

ZONIA: Yes, ma'am.

SETH: Look at Bynum sitting over there with his belly all poked out. Ain't saying nothing. Sitting over there half asleep. Ho, Bynum!

BERTHA: If Bynum ain't saying nothing what you wanna start him up for?

SETH: Ho, Bynum!

BYNUM: What you hollering at me for? I ain't doing nothing.

SETH: Come on, we gonna Juba.

BYNUM: You know me, I'm always ready to Juba.

SETH: Well, come on, then.

*[*SETH *pulls out a harmonica and blows a few notes.]*

Come on there, Jeremy. Where's your guitar? Go get your guitar. Bynum says he's ready to Juba.

JEREMY: Don't need no guitar to Juba. Ain't you never Juba without a guitar?

*[*JEREMY *begins to drum on the table.]*

SETH: It ain't that. I ain't never Juba with one! Figured to try it and see how it worked.

BYNUM *[drumming on the table]*: You don't need no guitar. Look at Molly sitting over there. She don't know we Juba on Sunday. We gonna show you something tonight. You and Mattie Campbell both. Ain't that right, Seth?

SETH: You said it! Come on, Bertha, leave them dishes be for a while. We gonna Juba.

BYNUM: Alright. Let's Juba down!

[The Juba is reminiscent of the Ring Shouts of the African slaves. It is a call and response dance. BYNUM sits at the table and drums. He calls the dance as others clap hands, shuffle and stomp around the table. It should be as African as possible, with the performers working themselves up into a near frenzy. The words can be improvised, but should include some mention of the Holy Ghost. In the middle of the dance HERALD LOOMIS enters.]

LOOMIS [*in a rage*]: Stop it! Stop!

[They stop and turn to look at him.]

You all sitting up here singing about the Holy Ghost. What's so holy about the Holy Ghost? You singing and singing. You think the Holy Ghost coming? You singing for the Holy Ghost to come? What he gonna do, huh? He gonna come with tongues of fire to burn up your woolly heads? You gonna tie onto the Holy Ghost and get burned up? What you got then? Why God got to be so big? Why he got to be bigger than me? How much big is there? How much big do you want?

[LOOMIS starts to unzip his pants.]

SETH: Nigger, you crazy!

LOOMIS: How much big you want?

SETH: You done plumb lost your mind!

[LOOMIS begins to speak in tongues and dance around the kitchen. SETH starts after him.]

BERTHA: Leave him alone, Seth. He ain't in his right mind.

LOOMIS [*stops suddenly*]: You all don't know nothing about me. You don't know what I done seen. Herald Loomis done seen some things he ain't got words to tell you.

[LOOMIS starts to walk out the front door and is thrown back and collapses, terror-stricken by his vision. BYNUM crawls to him.]

BYNUM: What you done seen, Herald Loomis?

LOOMIS: I done seen bones rise up out the water. Rise up and walk across the water. Bones walking on top of the water.

BYNUM: Tell me about them bones, Herald Loomis. Tell me what you seen.

LOOMIS: I come to this place . . . to this water that was bigger than the whole world. And I looked out . . . and I seen these bones rise up out the water. Rise up and begin to walk on top of it.

BYNUM: Wasn't nothing but bones and they walking on top of the water.

LOOMIS: Walking without sinking down. Walking on top of the water.

BYNUM: Just marching in a line.

LOOMIS: A whole heap of them. They come up out the water and started marching.

BYNUM: Wasn't nothing but bones and they walking on top of the water.

LOOMIS: One after the other. They just come up out the water and start to walking.

BYNUM: They walking on the water without sinking down. They just walking and walking. And then . . . what happened, Herald Loomis?

LOOMIS: They just walking across the water.

BYNUM: What happened, Herald Loomis? What happened to the bones?

LOOMIS: They just walking across the water . . . and then . . . they sunk down.

BYNUM: The bones sunk into the water. They all sunk down.

LOOMIS: All at one time! They just all fell in the water at one time.

BYNUM: Sunk down like anybody else.

LOOMIS: When they sink down they made a big splash and this here wave come up . . .

BYNUM: A big wave, Herald Loomis. A big wave washed over the land.

LOOMIS: It washed them out of the water and up on the land. Only . . . only . . .

BYNUM: Only they ain't bones no more.

LOOMIS: They got flesh on them! Just like you and me!

BYNUM: Everywhere you look the waves is washing them up on the land right on top of one another.

LOOMIS: They black. Just like you and me. Ain't no difference.

BYNUM: Then what happened, Herald Loomis?

LOOMIS: They ain't moved or nothing. They just laying there.

BYNUM: You just laying there. What you waiting on, Herald Loomis?

LOOMIS: I'm laying there . . . waiting.

BYNUM: What you waiting on, Herald Loomis?

LOOMIS: I'm waiting on the breath to get into my body.

BYNUM: The breath coming into you, Herald Loomis. What you gonna do now?

LOOMIS: The wind's blowing the breath into my body. I can feel it. I'm starting to breathe again.

BYNUM: What you gonna do, Herald Loomis?

LOOMIS: I'm gonna stand up. I got to stand up. I can't lay here no more. All the breath coming into my body and I got to stand up.

BYNUM: Everybody's standing up at the same time.

LOOMIS: The ground's starting to shake. There's a great shaking. The world's busting half in two. The sky's splitting open. I got to stand up.

[LOOMIS attempts to stand up.]

My legs . . . my legs won't stand up!

BYNUM: Everybody's standing and walking toward the road. What you gonna do, Herald Loomis?

LOOMIS: My legs won't stand up.

BYNUM: They shaking hands and saying good-bye to each other and walking every whichaway down the road.

LOOMIS: I got to stand up!

BYNUM: They walking around here now. Mens. Just like you and me. Come right up out the water.

LOOMIS: Got to stand up.

BYNUM: They walking, Herald Loomis. They walking around here now.

LOOMIS: I got to stand up. Get up on the road.

BYNUM: Come on, Herald Loomis.

[LOOMIS tries to stand up.]

LOOMIS: My legs won't stand up! My legs won't stand up!

[LOOMIS collapses on the floor as the lights go down to black.]

ACT II

SCENE 1

[The lights come up on the kitchen. BERTHA busies herself with breakfast preparations. SETH sits at the table.]

SETH: I don't care what his problem is! He's leaving here!

BERTHA: You can't put the man out and he got that little girl. Where they gonna go then?

SETH: I don't care where he go. Let him go back where he was before he come here. I ain't asked him to come here. I knew when I first looked at him something wasn't right with him. Dragging that little girl around with him. Looking like he be sleeping in the woods somewhere. I knew all along he wasn't right.

BERTHA: A fellow get a little drunk he's liable to say or do anything. He ain't done no big harm.

SETH: I just don't have all that carrying on in my house. When he come down here I'm gonna tell him. He got to leave here. My daddy wouldn't stand for it and I ain't gonna stand for it either.

BERTHA: Well, if you put him out you have to put Bynum out too. Bynum right there with him.

SETH: If it wasn't for Bynum ain't no telling what would have happened. Bynum talked to that fellow just as nice and calmed him down. If he wasn't here ain't no telling what would have happened. Bynum ain't done nothing but talk to him and kept him calm. Man acting all crazy with that foolishness. Naw, he's leaving here.

BERTHA: What you gonna tell him? How you gonna tell him to leave?

SETH: I'm gonna tell him straight out. Keep it nice and simple. Mister, you got to leave here!

[MOLLY enters from the stairs.]

MOLLY: Morning.

BERTHA: Did you sleep alright in that bed?

MOLLY: Tired as I was I could have slept anywhere. It's a real nice room, though. This is a nice place.

SETH: I'm sorry you had to put up with all that carrying on last night.

MOLLY: It don't bother me none. I done seen that kind of stuff before.

SETH: You won't have to see it around here no more.

[BYNUM is heard singing offstage.]

I don't put up with all that stuff. When that fellow come down here I'm gonna tell him.

BYNUM [*singing*]:

Soon my work will all be done
Soon my work will all be done
Soon my work will all be done

I'm going to see the king.

BYNUM [*enters*]: Morning, Seth. Morning, Sister Bertha. I see we got Molly Cunningham down here at breakfast.

SETH: Bynum, I wanna thank you for talking to that fellow last night and calming him down. If you hadn't been here ain't no telling what might have happened.

BYNUM: Mr. Loomis alright, Seth. He just got a little excited.

SETH: Well, he can get excited somewhere else 'cause he leaving here.

[MATTIE enters from the stairs.]

BYNUM: Well, there's Mattie Campbell.

MATTIE: Good morning.

BERTHA: Sit on down there, Mattie. I got some biscuits be ready in a minute. The coffee's hot.

MATTIE: Jeremy gone already?

BYNUM: Yeah, he leave out of here early. He got to be there when the sun come up. Most working men got to be there when the sun come up. Everybody but Seth. Seth work at night. Mr. Olowski so busy in his shop he got fellows working at night.

[LOOMIS enters from the stairs.]

SETH: Mr. Loomis, now . . . I don't want no trouble. I keeps me a respectable house here. I don't have no carrying on like what went on last night. This has been a respectable house for a long time. I'm gonna have to ask you to leave.

LOOMIS: You got my two dollars. That two dollars say we stay till Saturday.

[LOOMIS and SETH glare at each other.]

SETH: Alright. Fair enough. You stay till Saturday. But come Saturday you got to leave here.

LOOMIS [*continues to glare at Seth. He goes to the door and calls*]: Zonia. You stay around this house, you hear? Don't you go anywhere.

[LOOMIS exits out the front door.]

SETH: I knew it when I first seen him. I knew something wasn't right with him.

BERTHA: Seth, leave the people alone to eat their breakfast. They don't want to hear that. Go on out there and make some pots and pans. That's the only time you satisfied is when you out there. Go on out there and make some pots and pans and leave them people alone.

SETH: I ain't bothering anybody. I'm just stating the facts. I told you, Bynum.

[BERTHA shoos SETH out the back door and exits into the bedroom.]

MOLLY [*to BYNUM*]: You one of them voo-doo people?

BYNUM: I got a power to bind folks if that what you talking about.

MOLLY: I thought so. The way you talked to that man when he started all that spooky stuff. What you say you had the power to do to people? You ain't the cause of him acting like that, is you?

BYNUM: I binds them together. Sometimes I help them find each other.

MOLLY: How do you do that?

BYNUM: With a song. My daddy taught me how to do it.

MOLLY: That's what they say. Most folks be what they daddy is. I wouldn't want to be like my daddy. Nothing ever set right with him. He tried to make the world over. Carry it around with him everywhere he go. I don't want to be like that. I just take life as it come. I don't be trying to make it over.

[Pause.]

Your daddy used to do that too, huh? Make people stay together?

BYNUM: My daddy used to heal people. He had the Healing Song. I got the Binding Song.

MOLLY: My mama used to believe in all that stuff. If she got sick she would have gone and saw your daddy. As long as he didn't make her drink nothing. She wouldn't drink nothing nobody give her. She was always afraid somebody was gonna poison her. How your daddy heal people?

BYNUM: With a song. He healed people by singing over them. I seen him do it. He sung over this little white girl when she was sick. They made a big to-do about it. They carried the girl's bed out in the yard and had all her kinfolk standing around. The little girl laying up there in the bed. Doctors standing around can't do nothing to help her. And they had my daddy come up and sing his song. It didn't sound no different than any other song. It was just somebody singing. But the song was its own thing and it come out and took upon this little girl with its power and it healed her.

MOLLY: That's sure something else. I don't understand that kind of thing. I guess if the doctor couldn't make me well I'd try it. But otherwise I don't wanna be bothered with that kind of thing. It's too spooky.

BYNUM: Well, let me get on out here and get to work.

[BYNUM gets up and heads out the back door.]

MOLLY: I ain't meant to offend you or nothing. What's your name . . . Bynum? I ain't meant to say nothing to make you feel bad now.

[BYNUM exits out the back door.]

[*to MATTIE*]: I hope he don't feel bad. He's a nice man. I don't wanna hurt nobody's feelings or nothing.

MATTIE: I got to go on up to Doc Goldblum's and finish this ironing.

MOLLY: Now, that's something I don't never wanna do. Iron no clothes. Especially somebody else's. That's what I believe killed my mama. Always ironing and working, doing somebody else's work. Not Molly Cunningham.

MATTIE: It's the only job I got. I got to make it someway to fend for myself.

MOLLY: I thought Jeremy was your man. Ain't he working?

MATTIE: We just be keeping company till maybe Jack come back.

MOLLY: I don't trust none of these men. Jack or nobody else. These men liable to do anything. They wait just until they get one woman tied and locked up with them . . . then they look around to see if they can get another one. Molly don't pay them no mind. One's just as good as the other if you ask me. I ain't never met one that meant nobody no good. You got any babies?

MATTIE: I had two for my man, Jack Carper. But they both died.

MOLLY: That be the best. These men make all these babies, then run off and leave you to take care of them. Talking about they wanna see what's on the other side of the hill. I make sure I don't get no babies. My mama taught me how to do that.

MATTIE: Don't make me no mind. That be nice to be a mother.

MOLLY: Yeah? Well, you go on, then. Molly Cunningham ain't gonna be tied down with no babies. Had me a man one time who I thought had some love in him. Come home one day and he was packing his trunk. Told me the time come when even the best of friends must part. Say he was gonna send me a Special Delivery some old day. I watched him out the window when he carried that trunk out and down to the train station. Said if he was gonna send me a Special Delivery I wasn't gonna be there to get it. I done found out the harder you try to hold onto them, the easier it is for some gal to pull them away. Molly done learned that. That's why I don't trust nobody but the good Lord above, and I don't love nobody but my mama.

MATTIE: I got to get on. Doc Goldblum gonna be waiting.

[MATTIE exits out the front door. SETH enters from his workshop with his apron, gloves, goggles, etc. He carries a bucket and crosses to the sink for water.]

SETH: Everybody gone but you, huh?

MOLLY: That little shack out there by the outhouse . . . that's where you make them pots and pans and stuff?

SETH: Yeah, that's my workshed. I go out there . . . take these hands and make something out of nothing. Take that metal and bend and twist it whatever way I want. My daddy taught me that. He used to make pots and pans. That's how I learned it.

MOLLY: I never knew nobody made no pots and pans. My uncle used to shoe horses.

[JEREMY enters at the front door.]

SETH: I thought you was working? Ain't you working today?

JEREMY: Naw, they fired me. White fellow come by told me to give him fifty cents if I wanted to keep working. Going around to all the colored making them give him fifty cents to keep hold to their jobs. Them other fellows, they was giving it to him. I kept hold to mine and they fired me.

SETH: Boy, what kind of sense that make? What kind of sense it make to get fired from a job where you making eight dollars a week and all it cost you is fifty cents. That's seven dollars and fifty cents profit! This way you ain't got nothing.

JEREMY: It didn't make no sense to me. I don't make but eight dollars. Why I got to give him fifty cents of it? He go around to all the colored and he got ten dollars extra. That's more than I make for a whole week.

SETH: I see you gonna learn the hard way. You just looking at the facts of it. See, right now, without the job, you ain't got nothing. What you gonna do when you can't keep a roof over your head? Right now, come Saturday, unless you come up with another two dollars, you gonna be out there in the streets. Down up under one of them bridges trying to put some food in your belly and wishing you had given that fellow that fifty cents.

JEREMY: Don't make me no difference. There's a big road out there. I can get my guitar and always find me another place to stay. I ain't planning on staying in one place for too long noway.

SETH: We gonna see if you feel like that come Saturday!

[SETH exits out the back. JEREMY sees MOLLY.]

JEREMY: Molly Cunningham. How you doing today, sugar?

MOLLY: You can go on back down there tomorrow and go back to work if you want. They won't even know who you is. Won't even know it's you. I had me a fellow did that one time. They just went ahead and signed him up like they never seen him before.

JEREMY: I'm tired of working anyway. I'm glad they fired me. You sure look pretty today.

MOLLY: Don't come telling me all that pretty stuff. Beauty wanna come in and sit down at your table asking to be fed. I ain't hardly got enough for me.

JEREMY: You know you pretty. Ain't no sense in you saying nothing about that. Why don't you come on and go away with me?

MOLLY: You tied up with that Mattie Campbell. Now you talking about running away with me.

JEREMY: I was just keeping her company 'cause she lonely. You ain't the lonely kind. You the kind that know what she want and how to get it. I need a woman like you to travel around with. Don't you wanna travel around and look at some places with Jeremy? With a woman like you beside him, a man can make it nice in the world.

MOLLY: Molly can make it nice by herself too. Molly don't need nobody leave her cold in hand. The world rough enough as it is.

JEREMY: We can make it better together. I got my guitar and I can play. Won me another dollar last night playing guitar. We can go around and I can play at the dances and we can just enjoy life. You can make it by yourself alright, I agrees with that. A woman like you can make it anywhere she go. But you can make it better if you got a man to protect you.

MOLLY: What places you wanna go around and look at?

JEREMY: All of them! I don't want to miss nothing. I wanna go everywhere and do everything there is to be got out of life. With a woman like you it's like having water and berries. A man got everything he need.

MOLLY: You got to be doing more than playing that guitar. A dollar a day ain't hardly what Molly got in mind.

JEREMY: I gambles real good. I got a hand for it.

MOLLY: Molly don't work. And Molly ain't up for sale.

JEREMY: Sure, baby. You ain't got to work with Jeremy.

MOLLY: There's one more thing.

JEREMY: What's that, sugar?

MOLLY: Molly ain't going South.

[The lights go down on the scene.]

SCENE 2

[The lights come up on the parlor. SETH and BYNUM sit playing a game of dominoes. BYNUM sings to himself.]

BYNUM [*singing*]:

They tell me Joe Turner's come and gone
Ohhh Lordy
They tell me Joe Turner's come and gone
Ohhh Lordy
Got my man and gone

Come with forty links of chain
Ohhh Lordy
Come with forty links of chain
Ohhh Lordy
Got my man and gone

SETH: Come on and play if you gonna play.

BYNUM: I'm gonna play. Soon as I figure out what to do.

SETH: You can't figure out if you wanna play or you wanna sing.

BYNUM: Well sir, I'm gonna do a little bit of both.

[playing]

There. What you gonna do now?

[singing]

They tell me Joe Turner's come and gone
Ohhh Lordy
They tell me Joe Turner's come and gone
Ohhh Lordy

SETH: Why don't you hush up that noise.

BYNUM: That's a song the women sing down around Memphis. The women down there made up that song. I picked it up down there about fifteen years ago.

[LOOMIS enters from the front door.]

BYNUM: Evening, Mr. Loomis.

SETH: Today's Monday, Mr. Loomis. Come Saturday your time is up. We done ate already. My wife roasted up some yams. She got your plate sitting in there on the table. [*to BYNUM*] Whose play is it?

BYNUM: Ain't you keeping up with the game? I thought you was a domino player. I just played so it got to be your turn.

[LOOMIS goes into the kitchen, where a plate of yams is covered and set on the table. He sits down and begins to eat with his hands.]

SETH [*plays*]: Twenty! Give me twenty! You didn't know I had that ace five. You was trying to play around that. You didn't know I had that lying there for you.

BYNUM: You ain't done nothing. I let you have that to get mine.

SETH: Come on and play. You ain't doing nothing but talking. I got a hundred and forty points to your eighty. You ain't doing nothing but talking. Come on and play.

BYNUM [*singing*]:

They tell me Joe Turner's come and gone
Ohhh Lordy
They tell me Joe Turner's come and gone
Ohhh Lordy
Got my man and gone

He come with forty links of chain
Ohhh Lordy

LOOMIS: Why you singing that song? Why you singing about Joe Turner?

BYNUM: I'm just singing to entertain myself.

SETH: You trying to distract me. That's what you trying to do.

BYNUM [*singing*]:

Come with forty links of chain
Ohhh Lordy
Come with forty links of chain

Ohhh Lordy

Loomis: I don't like you singing that song, mister!

Seth: Now, I ain't gonna have no more disturbance around here, Herald Loomis. You start any more disturbance and you leavin' here, Saturday or no Saturday.

Bynum: The man ain't causing no disturbance, Seth. He just say he don't like the song.

Seth: Well, we all friendly folk. All neighborly like. Don't have no squabbling around here. Don't have no disturbance. You gonna have to take that someplace else.

Bynum: He just say he don't like the song. I done sung a whole lot of songs people don't like. I respect everybody. He here in the house too. If he don't like the song, I'll sing something else. I know lots of songs. You got "I Belong to the Band," "Don't You Leave Me Here." You got "Praying on the Old Campground," "Keep Your Lamp Trimmed and Burning" . . . I know lots of songs.

[*sings*]

Boys, I'll be so glad when payday come
Captain, Captain, when payday comes
Gonna catch that Illinois Central
Going to Kankakee

Seth: Why don't you hush up that hollering and come on and play dominoes.

Bynum: You ever been to Johnstown, Herald Loomis? You look like a fellow I seen around there.

Loomis: I don't know no place with that name.

Bynum: That's around where I seen my shiny man. See, you looking for this woman. I'm looking for a shiny man. Seem like everybody looking for something.

Seth: I'm looking for you to come and play these dominoes. That's what I'm looking for.

Bynum: You a farming man, Herald Loomis? You look like you done some farming.

Loomis: Same as everybody. I done farmed some, yeah.

Bynum: I used to work at farming . . . picking cotton. I reckon everybody done picked some cotton.

Seth: I ain't! I ain't never picked no cotton. I was born up here in the North. My daddy was a freedman. I ain't never even seen no cotton!

Bynum: Mr. Loomis done picked some cotton. Ain't you, Herald Loomis? You done picked a bunch of cotton.

Loomis: How you know so much about me? How you know what I done? How much cotton I picked?

Bynum: I can tell from looking at you. My daddy taught me how to do that. Say when you look at a fellow, if you taught yourself to look for it, you can see his song written on him. Tell you what kind of man he is in the world. Now, I can look at you, Mr. Loomis, and see you a man who done forgot his song. Forgot how to sing it. A fellow forget that and he forget who he is. Forget how he's supposed to mark down life. Now, I used to travel all up and down this road and that . . . looking here and there. Searching. Just like you, Mr. Loomis. I didn't know what I was searching for. The only thing I knew was something was keeping me dissatisfied. Something wasn't making my heart smooth and easy. Then one day my daddy gave me a song. That song had a weight to it that was hard to handle. That song was hard to carry. I fought against it. Didn't want to accept that song. I tried to find my daddy to give him back the song. But I found out it wasn't his song. It was my song. It had come from way deep inside me. I looked long back in memory and gathered up pieces and snatches of things to make that song. I was making it up out of myself. And that song helped me on the road. Made it smooth to where my footsteps didn't bite back at me. All the time that song getting bigger and bigger. That song growing with each step of the road. It got so I used all of myself up in the making of that song. Then I was the song in search of itself. That song rattling in my throat and I'm looking for it. See, Mr. Loomis, when a man forgets his song he goes off in search of it . . . till he find out he's got it with him all the time. That's why I can tell you one of Joe Turner's niggers. 'Cause you forgot how to sing your song.

LOOMIS: You lie! How you see that? I got a mark on me? Joe Turner done marked me to where you can see it? You telling me I'm a marked man. What kind of mark you got on you?

[BYNUM begins singing.]

BYNUM:

They tell me Joe Turner's come and gone
Ohhh Lordy
They tell me Joe Turner's come and gone
Ohhh Lordy
Got my man and gone

LOOMIS: Had a whole mess of men he catched. Just go out hunting regular like you go out hunting possum. He catch you and go home to his wife and family. Ain't thought about you going home to yours. Joe Turner catched me when my little girl was just born. Wasn't nothing but a little baby sucking on her mama's titty when he catched me. Joe Turner catched me in nineteen hundred and one. Kept me seven years until nineteen hundred and eight. Kept everybody seven years. He'd go out hunting and bring back forty men at a time. And keep them seven years.

I was walking down this road in this little town outside of Memphis. Come up on these fellows gambling. I was a deacon in the Abundant Life Church. I stopped to preach to these fellows to see if maybe I could turn some of them from their sinning when Joe Turner, brother of the Governor of the great sovereign state of Tennessee, swooped down on us and grabbed everybody there. Kept us all seven years.

My wife Martha gone from me after Joe Turner catched me. Got out from under Joe Turner on his birthday. Me and forty other men put in our seven years and he let us go on his birthday. I made it back to Henry Thompson's place where me and Martha was sharecropping and Martha's gone. She taken my little girl and left her with her mama and took off North. We been looking for her ever since. That's been going on four years now we been looking. That's the only thing I know to do. I just wanna see her face so I can get me a starting place in the world. The world got to start somewhere. That's what I been looking for. I been wandering a long time in somebody else's world. When I find my wife that be the making of my own.

BYNUM: Joe Turner tell why he caught you? You ever asked him that?

LOOMIS: I ain't never seen Joe Turner. Seen him to where I could touch him. I asked one of them fellows one time why he catch niggers. Asked him what I got he want? Why don't he keep on to himself? Why he got to catch me going down the road by my lonesome? He told me I was worthless. Worthless is something you throw away. Something you don't bother with. I ain't seen him throw me away. Wouldn't even let me stay away when I was by my lonesome. I ain't tried to catch him when he going down the road. So I must got something he want. What I got?

SETH: He just want you to do his work for him. That's all.

LOOMIS: I can look at him and see where he big and strong enough to do his own work. So it can't be that. He must want something he ain't got.

BYNUM: That ain't hard to figure out. What he wanted was your song. He wanted to have that song to be his. He thought by catching you he could learn that song. Every nigger he catch he's looking for the one he can learn that song from. Now he's got you bound up to where you can't sing your own song. Couldn't sing it them seven years 'cause you was afraid he would snatch it from under you. But you still got it. You just forgot how to sing it.

LOOMIS [*to BYNUM*]: I know who you are. You one of them bones people.

[The lights go down to black.]

SCENE 3

[The lights come up on the kitchen. It is the following morning. MATTIE and BYNUM sit at the table. BERTHA busies herself at the stove.]

BYNUM: Good luck don't know no special time to come. You sleep with that up under your pillow and good luck can't help but come to you. Sometimes it come and go and you don't even know it's been there.

BERTHA: Bynum, why don't you leave that gal alone? She don't wanna be hearing all that. Why don't you go on and get out the way and leave her alone?

BYNUM [*getting up*]: Alright, alright. But you mark what I'm saying. It'll draw it to you just like a magnet.

[BYNUM exits up the stairs and LOOMIS enters.]

BERTHA: I got some grits here, Mr. Loomis.

[BERTHA sets a bowl on the table.]

If I was you, Mattie, I wouldn't go getting all tied up with Bynum in that stuff. That kind of stuff, even if it do work for a while, it don't last. That just get people more mixed up than they is already. And I wouldn't waste my time fretting over Jeremy either. I seen it coming. I seen it when she first come here. She that kind of woman run off with the first man got a dollar to spend on her. Jeremy just young. He don't know what he getting into. That gal don't mean him no good. She's just using him to keep from being by herself. That's the worst use of a man you can have. You ought to be glad to wash him out of your hair. I done seen all kind of men. I done seen them come and go through here. Jeremy ain't had enough to him for you. You need a man who's got some understanding and who willing to work with that understanding to come to the best he can. You got your time coming. You just tries too hard and can't understand why it don't work for you. Trying to figure it out don't do nothing but give you a troubled mind. Don't no man want a woman with a troubled mind.

You get all that trouble off your mind and just when it look like you ain't never gonna find what you want . . . you look up and it's standing right there. That's how I met my Seth. You gonna look up one day and find everything you want standing right in front of you. Been twenty-seven years now since that happened to me. But life ain't no happy-go-lucky time where everything be just like you want it. You got your time coming. You watch what Bertha's saying.

[SETH enters.]

SETH: Ho!

BERTHA: What you doing come in here so late?

SETH: I was standing down there on Logan Street talking with the fellows. Henry Allen tried to sell me that old piece of horse he got.

[He sees LOOMIS.]

Today's Tuesday, Mr. Loomis.

BERTHA [*pulling him toward the bedroom*]: Come on in here and leave that man alone to eat his breakfast.

SETH: I ain't bothering nobody. I'm just reminding him what day it is.

[SETH and BERTHA exit into the bedroom.]

LOOMIS: That dress got a color to it.

MATTIE: Did you really see them things like you said? Them people come up out the ocean?

LOOMIS: It happened just like that, yeah.

MATTIE: I hope you find your wife. It be good for your little girl for you to find her.

LOOMIS: Got to find her for myself. Find my starting place in the world. Find me a world I can fit in.

MATTIE: I ain't never found no place for me to fit. Seem like all I do is start over. It ain't nothing to find no starting place in the world. You just start from where you find yourself.

LOOMIS: Got to find my wife. That be my starting place.

MATTIE: What if you don't find her? What you gonna do then if you don't find her?

LOOMIS: She out there somewhere. Ain't no such thing as not finding her.

MATTIE: How she got lost from you? Jack just walked away from me.

LOOMIS: Joe Turner split us up. Joe Turner turned the world upside-down. He bound me on to him for seven years.

MATTIE: I hope you find her. It be good for you to find her.

LOOMIS: I been watching you. I been watching you watch me.

MATTIE: I was just trying to figure out if you seen things like you said.

LOOMIS [*getting up*]: Come here and let me touch you. I been watching you. You a full woman. A man needs a full woman. Come on and be with me.

MATTIE: I ain't got enough for you. You'd use me up too fast.

LOOMIS: Herald Loomis got a mind seem like you a part of it since I first seen you. It's been a long time since I seen a full woman. I can smell you from here. I know you got Herald Loomis on your mind, can't keep him apart from it. Come on and be with Herald Loomis.

[LOOMIS has crossed to MATTIE. He touches her awkwardly, gently, tenderly. Inside he howls like a lost wolf pup whose hunger is deep. He goes to touch her but finds he cannot.]

I done forgot how to touch.

[The lights fade to black.]

SCENE 4

[It is early the next morning. The lights come up on ZONIA and REUBEN in the yard.]

REUBEN: Something spooky going on around here. Last night Mr. Bynum was out in the yard singing and talking to the wind . . . and the wind it just be talking back to him. Did you hear it?

ZONIA: I heard it. I was scared to get up and look. I thought it was a storm.

REUBEN: That wasn't no storm. That was Mr. Bynum. First he say something . . . and the wind it say back to him.

ZONIA: I heard it. Was you scared? I was scared.

REUBEN: And then this morning . . . I seen Miss Mabel!

ZONIA: Who Miss Mabel?

REUBEN: Mr. Seth's mother. He got her picture hanging up in the house. She been dead.

ZONIA: How you seen her if she been dead?

REUBEN: Zonia . . . if I tell you something you promise you won't tell anybody?

ZONIA: I promise.

REUBEN: It was early this morning . . . I went out to the coop to feed the pigeons. I was down on the ground like this to open up the door to the coop . . . when all of a sudden I seen some feets in front of me. I looked up . . . and there was Miss Mabel standing there.

ZONIA: Reuben, you better stop telling that! You ain't seen nobody!

REUBEN: Naw, it's the truth. I swear! I seen her just like I see you. Look . . . you can see where she hit me with her cane.

ZONIA: Hit you? What she hit you for?

REUBEN: She says, "Didn't you promise Eugene something?" Then she hit me with her cane. She say, "Let them pigeons go." Then she hit me again. That's what made them marks.

ZONIA: Jeez man . . . get away from me. You done see a haunt!

REUBEN: Shhhh. You promised, Zonia!

ZONIA: You sure it wasn't Miss Bertha come over there and hit you with her hoe?

REUBEN: It wasn't no Miss Bertha. I told you it was Miss Mabel. She was standing right there by the coop. She had this light coming out of her and then she just melted away.

ZONIA: What she had on?

REUBEN: A white dress. Ain't even had no shoes or nothing. Just had on that white dress and them big hands . . . and that cane she hit me with.

ZONIA: How you reckon she knew about the pigeons? You reckon Eugene told her?

REUBEN: I don't know. I sure ain't asked her none. She say Eugene was waiting on them pigeons. Say he couldn't go back home till I let them go. I couldn't get the door to the coop open fast enough.

ZONIA: Maybe she an angel? From the way you say she look with that white dress. Maybe she an angel.

REUBEN: Mean as she was . . . how she gonna be an angel? She used to chase us out her yard and frown up and look evil all the time.

ZONIA: That don't mean she can't be no angel 'cause of how she looked and 'cause she wouldn't let no kids play in her yard. It go by if you got any spots on your heart and if you pray and go to church.

REUBEN: What about she hit me with her cane? An angel wouldn't hit me with her cane.

ZONIA: I don't know. She might. I still say she was an angel.

REUBEN: You reckon Eugene the one who sent old Miss Mabel?

ZONIA: Why he send her? Why he don't come himself?

REUBEN: Figured if he send her maybe that'll make me listen. 'Cause she old.

ZONIA: What you think it feel like?

REUBEN: What?

ZONIA: Being dead.

REUBEN: Like being sleep only you don't know nothing and can't move no more.

ZONIA: If Miss Mabel can come back . . . then maybe Eugene can come back too.

REUBEN: We can go down to the hideout like we used to! He could come back everyday! It be just like he ain't dead.

ZONIA: Maybe that ain't right for him to come back. Feel kinda funny to be playing games with a haunt.

REUBEN: Yeah . . . what if everybody came back? What if Miss Mabel came back just like she ain't dead? Where you and your daddy gonna sleep then?

ZONIA: Maybe they go back at night and don't need no place to sleep.

REUBEN: It still don't seem right. I'm sure gonna miss Eugene. He's the bestest friend anybody ever had.

ZONIA: My daddy say if you miss somebody too much it can kill you. Say he missed me till it liked to killed him.

REUBEN: What if your mama's already dead and all the time you looking for her?

ZONIA: Naw, she ain't dead. My daddy say he can smell her.

REUBEN: You can't smell nobody that ain't here. Maybe he smelling old Miss Bertha. Maybe Miss Bertha your mama?

ZONIA: Naw, she ain't. My mama got long pretty hair and she five feet from the ground!

REUBEN: Your daddy say when you leaving?

[ZONIA doesn't respond.]

Maybe you gonna stay in Mr. Seth's house and don't go looking for your mama no more.

ZONIA: He say we got to leave on Saturday.

REUBEN: Dag! You just only been here for a little while. Don't seem like nothing ever stay the same.

ZONIA: He say he got to find her. Find him a place in the world.

REUBEN: He could find him a place in Mr. Seth's house.

ZONIA: It don't look like we never gonna find her.

REUBEN: Maybe he find her by Saturday then you don't have to go.

ZONIA: I don't know.

REUBEN: You look like a spider!

ZONIA: I ain't no spider!

REUBEN: Got them long skinny arms and legs. You look like one of them Black Widows.

ZONIA: I ain't no Black Window nothing! My name is Zonia!

REUBEN: That's what I'm gonna call you . . . Spider.

ZONIA: You can call me that, but I don't have to answer.

REUBEN: You know what? I think maybe I be your husband when I grow up.

ZONIA: How you know?

REUBEN: I ask my grandpap how you know and he say when the moon falls into a girl's eyes that how you know.

ZONIA: Did it fall into my eyes?

REUBEN: Not that I can tell. Maybe I ain't old enough. Maybe you ain't old enough.

ZONIA: So there! I don't know why you telling me that lie!

REUBEN: That don't mean nothing 'cause I can't see it. I know it's there. Just the way you look at me sometimes look like the moon might have been in your eyes.

ZONIA: That don't mean nothing if you can't see it. You supposed to see it.

REUBEN: Shucks, I see it good enough for me. You ever let anybody kiss you?

ZONIA: Just my daddy. He kiss me on the cheek.

REUBEN: It's better on the lips. Can I kiss you on the lips?

ZONIA: I don't know. You ever kiss anybody before?

REUBEN: I had a cousin let me kiss her on the lips one time. Can I kiss you?

ZONIA: Okay.

[REUBEN kisses her and lays his head against her chest.]

What you doing?

REUBEN: Listening. Your heart singing!

ZONIA: It is not.

REUBEN: Just beating like a drum. Let's kiss again.

[They kiss again.]

Now you mine, Spider. You my girl, okay?

ZONIA: Okay.

REUBEN: When I get grown, I come looking for you.

ZONIA: Okay.

[The lights fade to black.]

SCENE 5

[The lights come up on the kitchen. It is Saturday. BYNUM, LOOMIS, and ZONIA sit at the table. BERTHA prepares breakfast. ZONIA has on a white dress.]

BYNUM: With all this rain we been having he might have ran into some washed-out roads. If that wagon got stuck in the mud he's liable to be still upriver somewhere. If he's upriver then he ain't coming until tomorrow.

LOOMIS: Today's Saturday. He say he be here on Saturday.

BERTHA: Zonia, you gonna eat your breakfast this morning.

ZONIA: Yes, ma'am.

BERTHA: I don't know how you expect to get any bigger if you don't eat. I ain't never seen a child that didn't eat. You about as skinny as a bean pole.

[Pause.]

Mr. Loomis, there's a place down on Wylie. Zeke Mayweather got a house down there. You ought to see if he got any rooms.

*[*LOOMIS *doesn't respond.]*

Well, you're welcome to some breakfast before you move on.

*[*MATTIE *enters from the stairs.]*

MATTIE: Good morning.

BERTHA: Morning, Mattie. Sit on down there and get you some breakfast.

BYNUM: Well, Mattie Campbell, you been sleeping with that up under your pillow like I told you?

BERTHA: Bynum, I done told you to leave that gal alone with all that stuff. You around here meddling in other people's lives. She don't want to hear all that. You ain't doing nothing but confusing her with that stuff.

MATTIE [*to Loomis*]: You all fixing to move on?

LOOMIS: Today's Saturday. I'm paid up till Saturday.

MATTIE: Where you going to?

LOOMIS: Gonna find my wife.

MATTIE: You going off to another city?

LOOMIS: We gonna see where the road take us. Ain't no telling where we wind up.

MATTIE: Eleven years is a long time. Your wife . . . she might have taken up with someone else. People do that when they get lost from each other.

LOOMIS: Zonia. Come on, we gonna find your mama.

*[*LOOMIS *and* ZONIA *cross to the door.]*

MATTIE [*to* ZONIA]: Zonia, Mattie got a ribbon here match your dress. Want Mattie to fix your hair with her ribbon?

*[*ZONIA *nods.* MATTIE *ties the ribbon in her hair.]*

There . . . it got a color just like your dress. [*to* LOOMIS] I hope you find her. I hope you be happy.

LOOMIS: A man looking for a woman be lucky to find you. You a good woman, Mattie. Keep a good heart.

*[*LOOMIS *and* ZONIA *exit.]*

BERTHA: I been watching that man for two weeks . . . and that's the closest I come to seeing him act civilized. I don't know what's between you all, Mattie . . . but the only thing that man needs is somebody to make him laugh. That's all you need in the world is love and laughter. That's all anybody needs. To have love in one hand and laughter in the other.

*[*BERTHA *moves about the kitchen as though blessing it and chasing away the huge sadness that seems to envelop it. It is a dance and demonstration of her own magic, her own remedy that is centuries old and to which she is connected by the muscles of her heart and the blood's memory.]*

You hear me, Mattie? I'm talking about laughing. The kind of laugh that comes from way deep inside. To just stand and laugh and let life flow right through you. Just laugh to let yourself know you're alive.

[She begins to laugh. It is a near-hysterical laughter that is a celebration of life, both its pain and its blessing. MATTIE *and* BYNUM *join in the laughter.* SETH *enters from the front door.]*

SETH: Well, I see you all having fun.

*[*SETH *begins to laugh with them.]*

That LOOMIS fellow standing up there on the corner watching the house. He standing right up there on Manila Street.

BERTHA: Don't you get started on him. The man done left out of here and that's the last I wanna hear of it. You about to drive me crazy with that man.

SETH: I just say he standing up there on the corner. Acting sneaky like he always do. He can stand up there all he want. As long as he don't come back in here.

[There is a knock on the door. SETH *goes to answer it. Enter* MARTHA LOOMIS *(Pentecost). She is a young woman about twenty-eight. She is dressed as befitting a member of an Evangelist church.* RUTHERFORD SELIG *follows.]*

SETH: Look here, Bertha. It's Martha Pentecost. Come on in, Martha. Who that with you? Oh . . . that's Selig. Come on in, Selig.

BERTHA: Come on in, Martha. It's sure good to see you.

BYNUM: Rutherford Selig, you a sure enough first-class People Finder!

SELIG: She was right out there in Rankin. You take that first righthand road . . . right there at that church on Wooster Street. I started to go right-past and something told me to stop at the church and see if they needed any dust-pans.

SETH: Don't she look good, Bertha.

BERTHA: Look all nice and healthy.

MARTHA: Mr. Bynum . . . Selig told me my little girl was here.

SETH: There's some fellow around here say he your husband. Say his name is Loomis. Say you his wife.

MARTHA: Is my little girl with him?

SETH: Yeah, he got a little girl with him. I wasn't gonna tell him where you was. Not the way this fellow look. So he got Selig to find you.

MARTHA: Where they at? They upstairs?

SETH: He was standing right up there on Manila Street. I had to ask him to leave 'cause of how he was carrying on. He come in here one night—

[The door opens and LOOMIS *and* ZONIA *enter.* MARTHA *and* LOOMIS *stare at each other.]*

LOOMIS: Hello, Martha.

MARTHA: Herald . . . Zonia?

LOOMIS: You ain't waited for me, Martha. I got out the place looking to see your face. Seven years I waited to see your face.

MARTHA: Herald, I been looking for you. I wasn't but two months behind you when you went to my mama's and got Zonia. I been looking for you ever since.

LOOMIS: Joe Turner let me loose and I felt all turned around inside. I just wanted to see your face to know that the world was still there. Make sure everything still in its place so I could reconnect myself together. I got there and you was gone, Martha.

MARTHA: Herald . . .

LOOMIS: Left my little girl motherless in the world.

MARTHA: I didn't leave her motherless, Herald. Reverend Tolliver wanted to move the church up North 'cause of all the trouble the colored folks was having down there. Nobody knew what was gonna happen traveling them roads. We didn't even know if we was gonna make it up here or not. I left her with my mama so she be safe. That was better than dragging her out on the road having to duck and hide from people. Wasn't no telling what was gonna happen to us. I didn't leave her motherless in the world. I been looking for you.

LOOMIS: I come up on Henry Thompson's place after seven years of living in hell, and all I'm looking to do is see your face.

MARTHA: Herald, I didn't know if you was ever coming back. They told me Joe Turner had you and my whole world split half in two. My whole life shattered. It was like I had poured it in a cracked jar and it all leaked out the bottom. When it go like that there ain't nothing you can do to put it back together. You talking about Henry Thompson's place like I'm still gonna be working the land by myself. How I'm gonna do that? You wasn't gone but two months and Henry Thompson kicked me off his land and I ain't had no place to go but to my mama's. I stayed and waited there for five years before I woke up one morning and decided that you was dead. Even if you weren't, you was dead to me. I wasn't gonna carry you with me no more. So I killed you in my heart. I buried you. I mourned you. And then I picked up what was left and went on to make life without you. I was a young woman with life at my beckon. I couldn't drag you behind me like a sack of cotton.

LOOMIS: I just been waiting to look on your face to say my goodbye. That goodbye got so big at times, seem like it was gonna swallow me up. Like Jonah in the whale's belly I sat up in that goodbye for three years. That goodbye kept me out on the road searching. Not looking on women in their houses. It kept me bound up to the road. All the time that goodbye swelling up in my chest till I'm about to bust. Now that I see your face I can say my goodbye and make my own world.

[LOOMIS takes ZONIA's hand and presents her to MARTHA.]

Martha . . . here go your daughter. I tried to take care of her. See that she had something to eat. See that she was out of the elements. Whatever I know I tried to teach her. Now she need to learn from her mother whatever you got to teach her. That way she won't be no one-sided person.

[LOOMIS stoops to ZONIA.]

Zonia, you go live with your mama. She a good woman. You go on with her and listen to her good. You my daughter and I love you like a daughter. I hope to see you again in the world somewhere. I'll never forget you.

ZONIA [*throws her arms around LOOMIS in a panic*]: I won't get no bigger! My bones won't get no bigger! They won't! I promise! Take me with you till we keep searching and never finding. I won't get no bigger! I promise!

LOOMIS: Go on and do what I told you now.

MARTHA [*goes to ZONIA and comforts her*]: It's alright, baby. Mama's here. Mama's here. Don't worry. Don't cry.

[MARTHA turns to BYNUM.]

Mr. Bynum, I don't know how to thank you. God bless you.

LOOMIS: It was you! All the time it was you that bind me up! You bound me to the road!

BYNUM: I ain't bind you, Herald Loomis. You can't bind what don't cling.

LOOMIS: Everywhere I go people wanna bind me up. Joe Turner wanna bind me up! Reverend Tolliver wanna bind me up. You wanna bind me up. Everybody wanna bind me up. Well, Joe Turner's come and gone and Herald Loomis ain't for no binding. I ain't gonna let nobody bind me up!

[LOOMIS pulls out a knife.]

BYNUM: It wasn't you, Herald Loomis. I ain't bound you. I bound the little girl to her mother. That's who I bound. You binding yourself. You bound onto your song. All you got to do is stand up and sing it, Herald Loomis. It's right there kicking at your throat. All you got to do is sing it. Then you be free.

MARTHA: Herald . . . look at yourself! Standing there with a knife in your hand. You done gone over to the devil. Come on . . . put down the knife. You got to look to Jesus. Even if you done fell away from the church you can be saved again. The Bible say, "The Lord is my shepherd I shall not want. He maketh me to lie down in green pastures. He leads me beside the still water. He restoreth my soul. He leads me in the path of righteousness for His name's sake. Even though I walk through the shadow of death—"

LOOMIS: That's just where I be walking!

MARTHA: "I shall fear no evil. For Thou art with me. Thy rod and thy staff, they comfort me."

LOOMIS: You can't tell me nothing about no valleys. I done been all across the valleys and the hills and the mountains and the oceans.

MARTHA: "Thou preparest a table for me in the presence of my enemies."

LOOMIS: And all I seen was a bunch of niggers dazed out of their woolly heads. And Mr. Jesus Christ standing there in the middle of them, grinning.

MARTHA: "Thou anointest my head with oil, my cup runneth over."

LOOMIS: He grin that big old grin . . . and niggers wallowing at his feet.

MARTHA: "Surely goodness and mercy shall follow me all the days of my life, and I shall dwell in the house of the Lord forever."

LOOMIS: Great big old white man . . . your Mr. Jesus Christ. Standing there with a whip in one hand and tote board in another, and them niggers swimming in a sea of cotton. And he counting. He tallying up the cotton. "Well, Jeremiah . . . what's the matter, you ain't picked but two hundred pounds of cotton today? Got to put you on half rations." And Jeremiah go back and lay up there on his half rations and talk about what a nice man Mr. Jesus Christ is 'cause he give him salvation after he die. Something wrong here. Something don't fit right!

MARTHA: You got to open up your heart and have faith, Herald. This world is just a trial for the next. Jesus offers you salvation.

LOOMIS: I been wading in the water. I been walking all over the River Jordan. But what it get me, huh? I done been baptized with blood of the lamb and the fire of the Holy Ghost. But what I got, huh? I got salvation? My enemies all around me picking the flesh from my bones. I'm choking on my own blood and all you got to give me is salvation?

MARTHA: You got to be clean, Herald. You got to be washed with the blood of the lamb.

LOOMIS: Blood make you clean? You clean with blood?

MARTHA: Jesus bled for you. He's the Lamb of God who takest away the sins of the world.

LOOMIS: I don't need nobody to bleed for me! I can bleed for myself.

MARTHA: You got to be something, Herald. You just can't be alive. Life don't mean nothing unless it got a meaning.

LOOMIS: What kind of meaning you got? What kind of clean you got, woman? You want blood? Blood make you clean? You clean with blood?

[LOOMIS slashes himself across the chest. He rubs the blood over his face and comes to a realization.]

I'm standing! I'm standing. My legs stood up! I'm standing now!

[Having found his song, the song of self-sufficiency, fully resurrected, cleansed and given breath, free from any encumbrance other than the workings of his own heart and the bonds of the flesh, having accepted the responsibility for his own presence in the world, he is free to soar above the environs that weighed and pushed his spirit into terrifying contractions.]

Goodbye, Martha.

[LOOMIS turns and exits, the knife still in his hands. MATTIE looks about the room and rushes out after him.]

BYNUM: Herald Loomis, you shining! You shining like new money!

[The lights go down to black.]

➤ QUESTIONS FOR READING AND WRITING

1. The play's author, August Wilson, has said, "All over the world, nobody has a God who doesn't resemble them except black Americans." Do you think his comment provides an insight into this play? Do you agree with it?

2. What do you think Martha means when she tells Loomis, "You got to be clean, Herald. You got to be washed with the blood of the lamb"?
3. What does Loomis mean when he replies, "I don't need nobody to bleed for me. I can bleed for myself"?
4. Why do you think Loomis is able to stand at the end of the play when he was unable to earlier? What does Bynum mean when he says to Loomis, "You shining like new money"?
5. Why does Bynum encourage others to find their songs? What is Bynum's song? Bertha's? Seth's? What is yours?
6. How does the speech, or diction, of the characters in this play affect your response? Does it help or hinder? Explain.
7. What is the central idea expressed by this play?

LUIS VALDEZ (b. 1940)

Playwright and film maker Luis Valdez was born in Delano, California, to farm worker parents. In 1964, after graduating from San Jose State University, where he first began writing and directing plays, Valdez joined the United Farm Workers Union, staging improvisations and short scenes meant to educate union members, who were mostly migrant workers, about labor issues. These experiences resulted in his founding of the El Teatro Campesino, a theater company devoted to exploring aspects of the Chicano experience. The company, which over the years has earned an enviable reputation in the theater world, has remained Valdez's artistic home throughout his career. In addition to his work in the theater, Valdez has written and directed a number of films, most notably La Bamba *(1987), the story of the Chicano pop musician, Ritchie Valens.* Los Vendidos, *one of his first efforts at playwriting, was written in 1967. The title can be translated as "The Sellouts."*

LOS VENDIDOS [1967]

CHARACTERS

HONEST SANCHO
SECRETARY
FARM WORKER
JOHNNY
REVOLUCIONARIO
MEXICAN-AMERICAN

SCENE *Honest Sancho's Used Mexican Lot and Mexican Curio Shop. Three models are on display in Honest Sancho's shop: to the right, there is a Revolucionario, complete with sombrero, carrilleras and carabina. At center, on the floor, there is the Farm Worker, under a broad straw sombrero. At stage left is the Pachuco, filero in hand. Honest Sancho is moving among his models, dusting them off and preparing for another day of business.*

SANCHO: *Bueno, bueno, mis monos, vamos a ver a quien vendemos ahora, ¿no?* [*to audience*] *¡Quihubo!* I'm Honest Sancho and this is my shop. *Antes fui contratista pero ahora logré tener mi negocito.* All I need now is a customer. [*A bell rings offstage.*] Ay, a customer!

SECRETARY [*entering*]: Good morning, I'm Miss Jiménez from—

SANCHO: *¡Ah, una chicana!* Welcome, welcome *Señorita* Jiménez.

SECRETARY [*Anglo pronunciation*]: JIM-enez.

SANCHO: *¿Qué?*

SECRETARY: My name is Miss JIM-enez. Don't you speak English? What's wrong with you?

SANCHO: Oh, nothing, Señorita JIM-enez. I'm here to help you.

SECRETARY: That's better. As I was starting to say, I'm a secretary from Governor Reagan's office, and we're looking for a Mexican type for the administration.

SANCHO: Well, you come to the right place, lady. This is Honest Sancho's Used Mexican Lot, and we got all types here. Any particular type you want?

SECRETARY: Yes, we were looking for somebody suave—

SANCHO: Suave.

SECRETARY: Debonair.

SANCHO: *De buen aire.*

SECRETARY: Dark.

SANCHO: *Prieto.*

SECRETARY: But of course not too dark.

SANCHO: *No muy prieto.*

SECRETARY: Perhaps, beige.

SANCHO: Beige, just the tone. *Así como cafecito con leche, ¿no?*

SECRETARY: One more thing. He must be hardworking.

SANCHO: That could only be one model. Step right over here to the center of the shop, lady. [*They cross to the Farm Worker.*] This is our standard farm worker model. As you can see, in the words of our beloved Senator George Murphy, he is "built close to the ground." Also take special notice of his four-ply Goodyear *huaraches,* made from the rain tire. This wide-brimmed sombrero is an extra added feature—keeps off the sun, rain, and dust.

SECRETARY: Yes, it does look durable.

SANCHO: And our farm worker model is friendly. *Muy amable.* Watch. [*snaps his fingers*]

FARM WORKER [*lifts up head*]: *Buenos días, señorita.* [*His head drops.*]

SECRETARY: My, he's friendly.

SANCHO: Didn't I tell you? Loves his *patrones!* But his most attractive feature is that he's hard working. Let me show you. [*Snaps fingers.* FARM WORKER *stands.*]

FARM WORKER: *¡El jale!* [*He begins to work.*]

SANCHO: As you can see, he is cutting grapes.

SECRETARY: Oh, I wouldn't know.

SANCHO: He also picks cotton. [*Snap. FARM WORKER begins to pick cotton.*]

SECRETARY: Versatile isn't he?

SANCHO: He also picks melons. [*Snap. FARM WORKER picks melons.*] That's his slow speed for late in the season. Here's his fast speed. [*Snap. Farm Worker picks faster.*]

SECRETARY: *¡Chihuahua!* . . . I mean, goodness, he sure is a hard worker.

SANCHO [*pulls the FARM WORKER to his feet*]: And that isn't the half of it. Do you see these little holes on his arms that appear to be pores? During those hot sluggish days in the field, when the vines or the branches get so entangled, it's almost impossible to move; these holes emit a certain grease that allow our model to slip and slide right through the crop with no trouble at all.

SECRETARY: Wonderful. But is he economical?

SANCHO: Economical? *Señorita,* you are looking at the Volkswagen of Mexicans. Pennies a day is all it takes. One plate of beans and tortillas will keep him going all day. That, and chile. Plenty of chile. *Chile jalapeños, chile verde, chile colorado.* But, of course, if you do give him chile [*Snap. FARM WORKER turns left face. Snap. FARM WORKER bends over.*] then you have to change his oil filter once a week.

SECRETARY: What about storage?

SANCHO: No problem. You know these new farm labor camps our Honorable Governor Reagan has built out by Parlier or Raisin City? They were designed with our model in mind. Five, six, seven, even ten in one of those shacks will give you no trouble at all. You can also put him in old barns, old cars, river banks. You can even leave him out in the field overnight with no worry!

SECRETARY: Remarkable.

SANCHO: And here's an added feature: Every year at the end of the season, this model goes back to Mexico and doesn't return, automatically, until next spring.

SECRETARY: How about that. But tell me: does he speak English?

SANCHO: Another outstanding feature is that last year this model was programmed to go out on STRIKE! [*Snap.*]

FARM WORKER: *¡HUELGA! ¡HUELGA! Hermanos, sálganse de esos files.* [*Snap. He stops.*]

SECRETARY: No! Oh no, we can't strike in the state capitol.

SANCHO: Well, he also scabs. [*Snap.*]

FARM WORKER: *Me vendo barato, ¿y qué?* [*Snap.*]

SECRETARY: That's much better, but you didn't answer my question. Does he speak English?

SANCHO: *Bueno . . . no, pero* he has other—

SECRETARY: No.

SANCHO: Other features.
SECRETARY: NO! He just won't do!
SANCHO: Okay, okay *pues.* We have other models.
SECRETARY: I hope so. What we need is something a little more sophisticated.
SANCHO: Sophisti—*¿qué?*
SECRETARY: An urban model.
SANCHO: Ah, from the city! Step right back. Over here in this corner of the shop is exactly what you're looking for. Introducing our new 1969 JOHNNY PACHUCO model! This is our fast-back model. Streamlined. Built for speed, low-riding, city life. Take a look at some of these features. Mag shoes, dual exhausts, green chartreuse paint-job, dark-tint windshield, a little poof on top. Let me just turn him on. [*Snap.* JOHNNY *walks to stage center with a* pachuco *bounce.*]
SECRETARY: What was that?
SANCHO: That, *señorita,* was the Chicano shuffle.
SECRETARY: Okay, what does he do?
SANCHO: Anything and everything necessary for city life. For instance, survival: He knife fights. [*Snap.* JOHNNY *pulls out switchblade and swings at* SECRETARY.]

[SECRETARY *screams.*]

SANCHO: He dances. [*Snap.*]
JOHNNY [*singing*]: "Angel Baby, my Angel Baby . . ." [*Snap.*]
SANCHO: And here's a feature no city model can be without. He gets arrested, but not without resisting, of course. [*Snap.*]
JOHNNY: *¡En la madre, la placa!* I didn't do it! I didn't do it! [JOHNNY *turns and stands up against an imaginary wall, legs spread out, arms behind his back.*]
SECRETARY: Oh no, we can't have arrests! We must maintain law and order.
SANCHO: But he's bilingual!
SECRETARY: Bilingual?
SANCHO: *Simón que yes.* He speaks English! Johnny, give us some English. [*Snap.*]
JOHNNY [*comes downstage*]: Fuck you!
SECRETARY [*gasps*]: Oh! I've never been so insulted in my whole life!
SANCHO: Well, he learned it in your school.
SECRETARY: I don't care where he learned it.
SANCHO: But he's economical!
SECRETARY: Economical?
SANCHO: Nickels and dimes. You can keep Johnny running on hamburgers, Taco Bell tacos, Lucky Lager beer, Thunderbird wine, *yesca*—
SECRETARY: *Yesca?*
SANCHO: *Mota.*
SECRETARY: *Mota?*
SANCHO: *Leños . . . Marijuana.* [*Snap;* JOHNNY *inhales on an imaginary joint.*]
SECRETARY: That's against the law!

JOHNNY [*big smile, holding his breath*]: Yeah.

SANCHO: He also sniffs glue. [*Snap. JOHNNY inhales glue, big smile.*]

JOHNNY: That's too much man, *ése.*

SECRETARY: No, Mr. Sancho, I don't think this—

SANCHO: Wait a minute, he has other qualities I know you'll love. For example, an inferiority complex. [*Snap.*]

JOHNNY [*to SANCHO*]: You think you're better than me, huh *ése?* [*swings switchblade.*]

SANCHO: He can also be beaten and he bruises, cut him and he bleeds; kick him and he—[*He beats, bruises and kicks PACHUCO.*] would you like to try it?

SECRETARY: Oh, I couldn't.

SANCHO: Be my guest. He's a great scapegoat.

SECRETARY: No, really.

SANCHO: Please.

SECRETARY: Well, all right. Just once. [*She kicks PACHUCO.*] Oh, he's so soft.

SANCHO: Wasn't that good? Try again.

SECRETARY [*kicks PACHUCO*]: Oh, he's so wonderful! [*She kicks him again.*]

SANCHO: Okay, that's enough, lady. You ruin the merchandise. Yes, our Johnny Pachuco model can give you many hours of pleasure. Why, the L.A.P.D. just bought twenty of these to train their rookie cops on. And talk about maintenance. Señorita, you are looking at an entirely self-supporting machine. You're never going to find our Johnny Pachuco model on the relief rolls. No, sir, this model knows how to liberate.

SECRETARY: Liberate?

SANCHO: He steals. [*Snap. JOHNNY rushes the SECRETARY and steals her purse.*]

JOHNNY: *¡Dame esa bolsa, vieja!* [*He grabs the purse and runs. Snap by SANCHO: He stops.*]

[SECRETARY runs after JOHNNY and grabs purse away from him, kicking him as she goes.]

SECRETARY: No, no, no! We can't have any *more* thieves in the state administration. Put him back.

SANCHO: Okay, we still got other models. Come on, Johnny, we'll sell you to some old lady. [*SANCHO takes JOHNNY back to his place.*]

SECRETARY: Mr. Sancho, I don't think you quite understand what we need. What we need is something that will attract the women voters. Something more traditional, more romantic.

SANCHO: Ah, a lover. [*He smiles meaningfully.*] Step right over here, *señorita.* Introducing our standard Revolucionario and/or Early California Bandit type. As you can see he is well built, sturdy, durable. This is the International Harvester of Mexicans.

SECRETARY: What does he do?

SANCHO: You name it, he does it. He rides horses, stays in the mountains, crosses deserts, plains, rivers, leads revolutions, follows revolutions, kills, can be killed, serves as a martyr, hero, movie star—did I say movie star? Did you ever see *Viva Zapata? Viva Villa? Villa Rides? Pancho Villa Returns? Pancho Villa Goes Back? Pancho Villa Meets Abbott and Costello*—

SECRETARY: I've never seen any of those.

SANCHO: Well, he was in all of them. Listen to this. [*Snap.*]

REVOLUCIONARIO [*scream*]: *¡VIVA VILLAAAAA!*

SECRETARY: That's awfully loud.

SANCHO: He has a volume control. [*He adjusts volume. Snap.*]

REVOLUCIONARIO [*mousey voice*]: *¡Viva Villa!*

SECRETARY: That's better.

SANCHO: And even if you didn't see him in the movies, perhaps you saw him on TV. He makes commercials. [*Snap.*]

REVOLUCIONARIO: Is there a Frito Bandito in your house?

SECRETARY: Oh yes, I've seen that one!

SANCHO: Another feature about this one is that he is economical. He runs on raw horsemeat and tequila!

SECRETARY: Isn't that rather savage?

SANCHO: *Al contrario,* it makes him a lover. [*Snap.*]

REVOLUCIONARIO [*to SECRETARY*]: *¡Ay, mamasota, cochota, ven pa'ca!* [*He grabs SECRETARY and folds her back—Latin-lover style.*]

SANCHO [*Snap. REVOLUCIONARIO goes back upright.*]: Now wasn't that nice?

SECRETARY: Well, it was rather nice.

SANCHO: And finally, there is one outstanding feature about this model I KNOW the ladies are going to love: He's a GENUINE antique! He was made in Mexico in 1910!

SECRETARY: Made in Mexico?

SANCHO: That's right. Once in Tijuana, twice in Guadalajara, three times in Cuernavaca.

SECRETARY: Mr. Sancho, I thought he was an American product.

SANCHO: No, but—

SECRETARY: No, I'm sorry. We can't buy anything but American-made products. He just won't do.

SANCHO: But he's an antique!

SECRETARY: I don't care. You still don't understand what we need. It's true we need Mexican models such as these, but it's more important that he be *American.*

SANCHO: American?

SECRETARY: That's right, and judging from what you've shown me, I don't think you have what we want. Well, my lunch hour's almost over, I better-

SANCHO: Wait a minute! Mexican but American?

SECRETARY: That's correct.

SANCHO: Mexican but . . . [*a sudden flash.*] AMERICAN! Yeah, I think we've got exactly what you want. He just came in today! Give me a minute. [*He exits. Talks from backstage.*] Here he is in the shop. Let me just get some papers off. There. Introducing our new 1970 Mexican-American! Ta-ra-ra-ra-ra-ra-RA-RAAA!

[SANCHO brings out the MEXICAN-AMERICAN model, a clean-shaven middle-class type in a business suit, with glasses.]

SECRETARY *[impressed]:* Where have you been hiding this one?

SANCHO: He just came in this morning. Ain't he a beauty? Feast your eyes on him! Sturdy US STEEL frame, streamlined, modern. As a matter of fact, he is built exactly like our Anglo models except that he comes in a variety of darker shades: naugahyde, leather, or leatherette.

SECRETARY: Naugahyde.

SANCHO: Well, we'll just write that down. Yes, *señorita,* this model represents the apex of American engineering! He is bilingual, college educated, ambitious! Say the word "acculturate" and he accelerates. He is intelligent, well-mannered, clean—did I say clean? *[Snap. MEXICAN-AMERICAN raises his arm.]* Smell.

SECRETARY *[smells]:* Old Sobaco, my favorite.

SANCHO *[Snap. MEXICAN-AMERICAN turns toward SANCHO]:* Eric! *[to SECRETARY]* We call him Eric García. *[to ERIC]* I want you to meet Miss JIM-enez, Eric.

MEXICAN-AMERICAN: Miss JIM-enez, I am delighted to make your acquaintance. *[He kisses her hand.]*

SECRETARY: Oh, my, how charming!

SANCHO: Did you feel the suction? He has seven especially engineered suction cups right behind his lips. He's a charmer all right!

SECRETARY: How about boards? Does he function on boards?

SANCHO: You name them, he is on them. Parole boards, draft boards, school boards, taco quality control boards, surf boards, two-by-fours.

SECRETARY: Does he function in politics?

SANCHO: *Señorita,* you are looking at a political MACHINE. Have you ever heard of the OEO, EOC, COD, WAR ON POVERTY? That's our model! Not only that, he makes political speeches.

SECRETARY: May I hear one?

SANCHO: With pleasure. *[Snap.]* Eric, give us a speech.

MEXICAN-AMERICAN: Mr. Congressman, Mr. Chairman, members of the board, honored guests, ladies and gentlemen. *[SANCHO and SECRETARY applaud.]* Please, please. I come before you as a Mexican-American to tell you about the problems of the Mexican. The problems of the Mexican stem from one thing and one thing alone: He's stupid. He's uneducated. He needs to stay in school. He needs to be ambitious, forward-looking, harder-working. He needs to think American, American, American, AMERICAN, AMERICAN, AMERICAN. GOD BLESS AMERICA! GOD BLESS AMERICA! GOD BLESS AMERICA!! *[He goes out of control.]*

[SANCHO snaps frantically and the MEXICAN-AMERICAN finally slumps forward, bending at the waist.]

SECRETARY: Oh my, he's patriotic too!

SANCHO: *Sí, señorita,* he loves his country. Let me just make a little adjustment here. *[Stands MEXICAN-AMERICAN up.]*

SECRETARY: What about upkeep? Is he economical?

SANCHO: Well, no, I won't lie to you. The Mexican-American costs a little bit more, but you get what you pay for. He's worth every extra cent. You can keep him running on dry Martinis, Langendorf bread.

SECRETARY: Apple pie?

SANCHO: Only Mom's. Of course, he's also programmed to eat Mexican food on ceremonial functions, but I must warn you: an overdose of beans will plug up his exhaust.

SECRETARY: Fine! There's just one more question: HOW MUCH DO YOU WANT FOR HIM?

SANCHO: Well, I tell you what I'm gonna do. Today and today only, because you've been so sweet, I'm gonna let you steal this model from me! I'm gonna let you drive him off the lot for the simple price of—let's see taxes and license included—$15,000.

SECRETARY: Fifteen thousand DOLLARS? For a MEXICAN!

SANCHO: Mexican? What are you talking, lady? This is a Mexican-AMERICAN! We had to melt down two *pachucos,* a farm worker and three *gabachos* to make this model! You want quality, but you gotta pay for it! This is no cheap run-about. He's got class!

SECRETARY: Okay, I'll take him.

SANCHO: You will?

SECRETARY: Here's your money.

SANCHO: You mind if I count it?

SECRETARY: Go right ahead.

SANCHO: Well, you'll get your pink slip in the mail. Oh, do you want me to wrap him up for you? We have a box in the back.

SECRETARY: No, thank you. The governor is having a luncheon this afternoon, and we need a brown face in the crowd. How do I drive him?

SANCHO: Just snap your fingers. He'll do anything you want.

[SECRETARY snaps. MEXICAN-AMERICAN steps forward.]

MEXICAN-AMERICAN: *RAZA QUERIDA, ¡VAMOS LEVANTANDO ARMAS PARA LIBERANOS DE ESTOS DESGRACIADOS GABACHOS QUE NOS EXPLOTAN¡ VAMOS.*

SECRETARY: What did he say?

SANCHO: Something about lifting arms, killing white people, etc.
SECRETARY: But he's not supposed to say that!
SANCHO: Look, lady, don't blame me for bugs from the factory. He's your Mexican-American; you bought him, now drive him off the lot!
SECRETARY: But he's broken!
SANCHO: Try snapping another finger.

[SECRETARY snaps. MEXICAN-AMERICAN comes to life again.]

MEXICAN-AMERICAN: ¡ESTA GRAN HUMANIDAD HA DICHO BASTA! Y SE HA PUESTO EN MARCHA! ¡BASTA! ¡BASTA! ¡VIVA LA RAZA! ¡VIVA LA CAUSA! ¡VIVA LA HUELGA! ¡VIVAN LOS BROWN BERETS! ¡VIVAN LOS ESTUDIANTES! ¡CHICANO POWER!

[The MEXICAN-AMERICAN turns toward the SECRETARY, who gasps and backs up. He keeps turning toward the PACHUCO, FARM WORKER, and REVOLUCIONARIO, snapping his fingers and turning each of them on, one by one.]

PACHUCO [*Snap. To SECRETARY*]: I'm going to get you, baby! *¡Viva La Raza!*
FARM WORKER [*Snap. To SECRETARY*]: *¡Viva la huelga! ¡Viva la Huelga! ¡VIVA LA HUELGA!*
REVOLUCIONARIO [Snap. To SECRETARY]: *¡Viva la revolución! ¡VIVA LA REVOLUCIÓN!*

[The three models join together and advance toward the SECRETARY, who backs up and runs out of the shop screaming. SANCHO is at the other end of the shop holding his money in his hand. All freeze. After a few seconds of silence, the PACHUCO moves and stretches, shaking his arms and loosening up. The FARM WORKER and REVOLUCIONARIO do the same. SANCHO stays where he is, frozen to his spot.]

JOHNNY: Man, that was a long one, *ése.* [*Others agree with him.*]
FARM WORKER: How did we do?
JOHNNY: Perty good, look at all that *lana,* man! [*He goes over to SANCHO and removes the money from his hand. SANCHO stays where he is.*]
REVOLUCIONARIO: *En la madre,* look at all the money.
JOHNNY: We keep this up, we're going to be rich.
FARM WORKER: They think we're machines.
REVOLUCIONARIO: *Burros.*
JOHNNY: Puppets.
MEXICAN-AMERICAN: The only thing I don't like is—how come I always got to play the goddamn Mexican-American?
JOHNNY: That's what you get for finishing high school.
FARM WORKER: How about our wages, *ése?*
JOHNNY: Here it comes right now. Three-thousand dollars for you, three-thousand dollars for you, three-thousand dollars for you, and three-thousand dollars for me. The rest we put back into the business.
MEXICAN-AMERICAN: Too much, man. Heh, where you *vatos* going tonight?
FARM WORKER: I'm going over to Concha's. There's a party.

JOHNNY: Wait a minute, *vatos.* What about our salesman? I think he needs an oil job.

REVOLUCIONARIO: Leave him to me.

[The PACHUCO, FARM WORKER, and MEXICAN-AMERICAN exit, talking loudly about their plans for the night. The REVOLUCIONARIO goes over to SANCHO, removes his derby hat and cigar, lifts him up and throws him over his shoulder. SANCHO hangs loose, lifeless.]

REVOLUCIONARIO *[to audience]:* He's the best model we got! *¡Ajua! [Exit.]*

➤ QUESTIONS FOR READING AND WRITING

1. How would you characterize this play? Is it surrealistic? Political? A parable? Does it have a moral? If so, what is it?
2. What do you think is the significance of the different ways Sancho and the Secretary pronounce "Jimenez"? What do we learn about the Secretary through her pronunciation of her name?
3. How are the Farm Worker, Johnny, and the Revolucionario different? Why does the Secretary reject each?
4. What happens at the end of the play? Why are the four "models" ultimately more real than Sancho?
5. Does our society tend to treat people as merchandise? Are immigrants treated differently than the rest of society? Explain.

◆ ESSAYS ◆

FREDERICK DOUGLASS (1818–1895)

Frederick Douglass was born a slave on a plantation in Maryland. His father was probably a white overseer. After being separated from his mother at the age of eight, Douglass worked first in the household of a wealthy family, and then as a field hand, where he suffered brutal beatings. In 1838, when he was twenty-one, Douglass escaped to the North. Fearful because of his fugitive slave status, Douglass nevertheless attracted public notice after delivering a powerful antislavery speech at an abolitionist convention in Nantucket, and he was subsequently asked to become a full-time speaker on behalf of the Massachusetts Anti-Slavery Society. In 1845, he published his harrowing and inspiring Narrative of the Life of Frederick Douglass, an American Slave, *which he later revised and titled the* Life and Times of Frederick Douglass. *The book made*

him famous, and consequently, more at risk. He moved to England, where he lectured extensively, eventually earning enough money to buy his freedom and return to the United States. A tireless advocate for the rights of African-Americans and women, he spent the rest of life in the public eye, holding a number of governmental and political positions and publishing his own newspaper, The North Star.

Learning to Read and Write [1845]

I lived in Master Hugh's family about seven years. During this time, I succeeded in learning to read and write. In accomplishing this, I was compelled to resort to various stratagems. I had no regular teacher. My mistress, who had kindly commenced to instruct me, had, in compliance with the advice and direction of her husband, not only ceased to instruct, but had set her face against my being instructed by any one else. It is due, however, to my mistress to say of her, that she did not adopt this course of treatment immediately. She at first lacked the depravity indispensable to shutting me up in mental darkness. It was at least necessary for her to have some training in the exercise of irresponsible power, to make her equal to the task of treating me as though I were a brute.

My mistress was, as I have said, a kind and tender-hearted woman; and in the simplicity of her soul she commenced, when I first went to live with her, to treat me as she supposed one human being ought to treat another. In entering upon the duties of a slaveholder, she did not seem to perceive that I sustained to her the relation of a mere chattel, and that for her to treat me as a human being was not only wrong, but dangerously so. Slavery proved as injurious to her as it did to me. When I went there, she was a pious, warm, and tender-hearted woman. There was no sorrow or suffering for which she had not a tear. She had bread for the hungry, clothes for the naked, and comfort for every mourner that came within her reach. Slavery soon proved its ability to divest her of these heavenly qualities. Under its influence, the tender heart became stone, and the lamblike disposition gave way to one of tiger-like fierceness. The first step in her downward course was in her ceasing to instruct me. She now commenced to practice her husband's precepts. She finally became even more violent in her opposition than her husband himself. She was not satisfied with simply doing as well as he had commanded; she seemed anxious to do better. Nothing seemed to make her more angry than to see me with a newspaper. She seemed to think that here lay the danger. I have had her rush at me with a face made all up of fury, and snatch from me a newspaper, in a manner that fully revealed her apprehension. She was an apt woman; and a little experience soon demonstrated, to her satisfaction, that education and slavery were incompatible with each other.

From this time I was most narrowly watched. If I was in a separate room any considerable length of time, I was sure to be suspected of having a book, and was at once called to give an account of myself. All this, however, was too late. The first step had been taken. Mistress, in teaching me the alphabet, had given me the *inch,* and no precaution could prevent me from taking the *ell.*

The plan which I adopted, and the one by which I was most successful, was that of making friends of all the little white boys whom I met in the street. As many of these as I could, I converted into teachers. With their kindly aid, obtained at different times and in different places, I finally succeeded in learning to read. When I was sent on errands, I always took my book with me, and by going one part of my errand quickly, I found time to get a lesson before my return. I used also to carry bread with me, enough of which was always in the house, and to which I was always welcome; for I was much better off in this regard than many of the poor white children in our neighborhood. This bread I used to bestow upon the hungry little urchins, who, in return, would give me that more valuable bread of knowledge. I am strongly tempted to give the names of two or three of those little boys, as a testimonial of the gratitude and affection I bear them; but prudence forbids; not that it would injure me, but it might embarrass them; for it is almost an unpardonable offence to teach slaves to read in this Christian country. It is enough to say of the dear little fellows, that they lived on Philpot Street, very near Durgin and Bailey's ship-yard. I used to talk this matter of slavery over with them. I would sometimes say to them, I wished I could be as free as they would be when they got to be men. "You will be free as soon as you are twenty-one, *but I am a slave for life!* Have not I as good a right to be free as you have?" These words used to trouble them; they would express for me the liveliest sympathy, and console me with the hope that something would occur by which I might be free.

5 I was now about twelve years old, and the thought of being *a slave for life* began to bear heavily upon my heart. Just about this time, I got hold of a book entitled "The Columbian Orator." Every opportunity I got, I used to read this book. Among much of other interesting matter, I found in it a dialogue between a master and his slave. The slave was represented as having run away from his master three times. The dialogue represented the conversation which took place between them, when the slave was retaken the third time. In this dialogue, the whole argument in behalf of slavery was brought forward by the master, all of which was disposed of by the slave. The slave was made to say some very smart as well as impressive things in reply to his master—things which had the desired though unexpected effect; for the conversation resulted in the voluntary emancipation of the slave on the part of the master.

In the same book, I met with one of Sheridan's mighty speeches on and in behalf of Catholic emancipation. These were choice documents to me, I read them over and over again with unabated interest. They gave tongue to interesting thoughts of my own soul, which had frequently flashed through my mind, and died away for want of utterance. The moral which I gained from the dialogue was the power of truth over the conscience of even a slaveholder. What I got from Sheridan was a bold denunciation of slavery, and a powerful vindication of human rights. The reading of these documents enabled me to utter my thoughts, and to meet the arguments brought forward to sustain slavery; but while they relieved me of one difficulty, they brought on another even more painful than the one of which I was relieved. The more I read, the more I was led to abhor and detest my enslavers. I could regard them in no other light than a band of successful robbers, who had left their homes, and gone to Africa, and stolen us from our homes, and in a strange land reduced us to slavery. I loathed them as being the meanest as well as the most wicked of men. As I read and contemplated the subject, behold! that very discontentment which Master Hugh had predicted would follow my learning to read had already come, to torment and sting my soul to unutterable anguish. As I writhed under it, I would at times feel that learning to read had been a curse rather than a blessing. It had given me a view of my wretched condition, without the remedy. It opened my eyes to the horrible pit, but to no ladder upon which to get out. In moments of agony, I envied my fellow-slaves for their stupidity. I have often wished myself a beast. I preferred the condition of the meanest reptile to my own. Any thing, no matter what, to get rid of thinking! It was this everlasting thinking of my condition that tormented me. There was no getting rid of it. It was pressed upon me by every object within sight or hearing, animate or inanimate. The silver trump of freedom had roused my soul to eternal wakefulness. Freedom now appeared, to disappear no more forever. It was heard in every sound, and seen in every thing. It was ever present to torment me with a sense of my wretched condition. I saw nothing without seeing it, I heard nothing without hearing it, and felt nothing without feeling it. It looked from every star, it smiled in every calm, breathed in every wind, and moved in every storm.

I often found myself regretting my own existence, and wishing myself dead; and but for the hope of being free, I have no doubt but that I should have killed myself, or done something for which I should have been killed. While in this state of mind, I was eager to hear any one speak of slavery. I was a ready listener. Every little while, I could hear something about the abolitionists. It was some time before I found what the word meant. It was always used in such connections as to make it an interesting word to me. If a slave ran away and succeeded in getting clear, or if a slave killed his master, set fire to a barn, or did any thing very wrong in the mind of a slaveholder, it was spoken of as the fruit of *abolition.* Hearing the word in this connection very often, I set about learning what it meant. The dictionary afforded me little or no help. I found it was "the act of abolishing"; but then I did not know what was to be abolished. Here I was perplexed. I did not dare to ask any one about its meaning, for I was satisfied that it was something they wanted me to know very little about. After a patient waiting, I got one of our city papers, containing an account of the number of petitions from the north, praying for the abolition of slavery in the District of Columbia, and of the slave trade between the States. From this time I understood the words *abolition* and *abolitionist,* and always drew near when that word was spoken, expecting to hear something of importance to myself and fellow-slaves. The light broke in upon me by degrees. I went one day down on the wharf of Mr. Waters; and seeing two Irishmen unloading a scow of stone, I went, unasked, and helped them. When we had finished, one of them came to me and asked me if I were a slave. I told him I was. He asked, "Are ye a slave for life?" I told him that I was. The good Irishman seemed to be deeply affected by the statement. He said to the other that it was a pity so fine a little fellow as myself should be a slave for life. He said it was a shame to hold me. They both advised me to run away to the north; that I should find friends there, and that I should be free. I pretended not to be interested in what they said, and treated them as if I did not understand them; for I feared they might be treacherous. White men have been known to encourage slaves to escape, and then, to get the reward, catch them and return them to their masters. I was afraid that these seemingly good men might use me so; but I nevertheless remembered their advice, and from that time I resolved to run away. I looked forward to a time at which it would be safe for me to escape. I was too young to think of doing so immediately; besides, I wished to learn how to write, as I might have occasion to write my own pass. I consoled myself with the hope that I should one day find a good chance. Meanwhile, I would learn to write.

The idea as to how I might learn to write was suggested to me by being in Durgin and Bailey's ship-yard, and frequently seeing the ship carpenters, after hewing, and getting a piece of timber ready to use, write on the timber the name of that part of the ship for which it was intended. When a piece of timber was intended for the larboard side, it would be marked thus—"L." When a piece was for the starboard side, it would be marked thus—"S." A piece for the larboard side forward, would be marked thus—"L. F." When a piece was for starboard side forward, it would be marked thus—"S. F" For larboard aft, it would be marked thus—"L. A." For starboard aft, it would be marked thus—"S. A." I soon learned the names of these letters, and for what they were intended when placed upon a piece of timber in the ship-yard. I immediately commenced copying them, and in a short time was able to make the four letters named. After that, when I met with any boy who I knew could write, I would tell him I could write as well as he. The next word would be, "I don't believe you. Let me see you try it." I would then make the letters which I had been so fortunate as to learn, and ask him to beat that. In this way I got a good many lessons in writing, which it is quite possible I should never have gotten in any other way. During this time, my copy-book was the board fence, brick wall, and pavement; my pen and ink was a lump of chalk. With these, I learned mainly how to write. I then commenced and continued copying the Italics in Webster's Spelling Book, until I could make them all without looking on the book. By this time, my little Master Thomas had gone to school, and learned how to write, and had written over a number of copy-books. These had been brought home, and shown to some of our near neighbors, and then laid aside. My mistress used to go to class meeting at the Wilk Street meetinghouse every Monday afternoon, and leave me to take care of the house. When left thus, I used to spend the time in writing in the spaces left in Master Thomas's copy-book, copying what he had written. I continued to do this until I could write a hand very similar to that of Master Thomas. Thus, after a long, tedious effort for years, I finally succeeded in learning how to write.

➤ *QUESTIONS FOR READING AND WRITING*

1. Imagine yourself in Frederick Douglass's position as a slave. Would you run away as he did or would you accept your plight? Explain.
2. Imagine yourself as a person who was in a position to help a runaway slave. How would you respond?
3. Why does Master Hugh's wife change her mind about helping Douglass to read and write?
4. What similarities does Douglass find between his own situation and the struggle for Catholic emancipation in Ireland? What does he learn from *The Columbian Orator?*
5. In what way is Douglass's learning to read and write a powerful statement against the evil of slavery?

GUILLERMO GÓMEZ-PEÑA (b. 1955)

Guillermo Gómez-Peña was born in Mexico City and immigrated to the United States in 1978. Since then he has investigated border culture and transcultural identity. Through journalism, performance, radio, video, poetry, and installations he has explored the relationship between Latinos and the United States. From 1984 to 1990 he founded and participated in the Border Arts Workshop, and contributed to the national radio program Crossroads. *He has received the Prix de la Parole at the International Theatre Festival of the Americas (1989), the Bessie prize in New York (1989) and a MacArthur Fellowship (1991), among other awards. His book* The New World Border *(1997) received the American Book Award.*

DOCUMENTED/UNDOCUMENTED [1988]

I live smack in the fissure between two worlds, in the infected wound: half a block from the end of Western Civilization and four miles from the start of the Mexican-American border, the northernmost point of Latin America. In my fractured reality, but a reality nonetheless, there cohabit two histories, languages, cosmologies, artistic traditions, and political systems which are drastically counterposed. Many "deterritorialized" Latin American artists in Europe and the U.S. have opted for "internationalism" (a cultural identity based upon the "most advanced" of the ideas originating out of New York or Paris). I, on the other hand, opt for "borderness" and assume my role: My generation, the *chilangos* [slang term for a Mexico City native], who came to "el norte" fleeing the imminent ecological and social catastrophe of Mexico City, gradually integrated itself into otherness, in search of that other Mexico grafted onto the entrails of the et cetera . . . became Chicano-ized. We de-Mexicanized ourselves to Mexi-understand ourselves, some without wanting to, others on purpose. And one day, the border became our house, laboratory, and ministry of culture (or counterculture).

Today, eight years after my departure [from Mexico], when they ask me for my nationality or ethnic identity, I can't respond with one word, since my "identity" now possesses multiple repertories: I am Mexican but I am also Chicano and Latin American. At the border they call me *chilango* or *mexiquillo;* in Mexico City it's *pocho* or *norteño;* and in Europe it's *sudaca.* The Anglos call me "Hispanic" or "Latino," and the Germans have, on more than one occasion, confused me with Turks or Italians. I walk amid the rubble of the Tower of Babel of our American post-modernity.

The recapitulation of my personal and collective topography has become my cultural obsession since I arrived in the United States. I look for the traces of my generation, whose distance stretches not only from Mexico City to California, but also from the past to the future, from pre-Columbian America to high technology and from Spanish to English, passing through "Spanglish."

As a result of this process I have become a cultural topographer, border-crosser, and hunter of myths. And it doesn't matter where I find myself, in Califas or Mexico City, in Barcelona or West Berlin; I always have the sensation that I belong to the same species: the migrant tribe of fiery pupils.

5 My work, like that of many border artists, comes from two distinct traditions, and because of this has dual, or on occasion multiple, referential codes. One strain comes from Mexican popular culture, the Latin American literary "boom," and the Mexico City counterculture of the '70s . . . the other comes directly from fluxus (a late '60s international art movement that explored alternative means of production and distribution), concrete poetry, conceptual art, and performance art. These two traditions converge in my border experience and they fuse together.

In my intellectual formation, Carlos Fuentes, Gabriel García Márquez, Oscar Chávez, Felipe Ehrenberg, José, Agustín, and Enrique Cisneros were as important as Burroughs, Foucault, Fassbinder, Lacan, Vito Aconci, and Joseph Beuys.

My "artistic space" is the intersection where the new Mexican urban poetry and the colloquial Anglo poetry meet; the intermediate stage somewhere between Mexican street theater and multimedia performance; the silence that snaps in between the *corrido* and punk; the wall that divides *"neográfica"* (a 1970s Mexico City art movement involved in the production of low-budget book art and graphics) and graffiti; the highway that joins Mexico City and Los Angeles; and the mysterious thread of thought and action that puts pan-Latin Americanism in touch with the Chicano movement, and both of these in touch with other international vanguards.

I am a child of crisis and cultural syncretism, half hippie and half punk. My generation grew up watching movies about *charros* and science fiction, listening to *cumbias* and tunes from the Moody Blues, constructing altars and filming in Super-8, reading the *Corno Emplumado* and *Artforum,* traveling to Tepoztlán and San Francisco, creating and de-creating myths. We went to Cuba in search of political illumination, to Spain to visit the crazy grandmother and to the U.S. in search of the instantaneous musico-sexual Paradise. We found nothing. Our dreams wound up getting caught in the webs of the border.

Our generation belongs to the world's biggest floating population: the weary travelers, the dislocated, those of us who left because we didn't fit anymore, those of us who still haven't arrived because we don't know where to arrive at, or because we can't go back anymore.

10 Our deepest generational emotion is that of loss, which comes from our having left. Our loss is total and occurs at multiple levels: loss of our country (culture and national rituals) and our class (the "illustrious" middle class and upper middle). Progressive loss of language and literary culture in our native tongue (those of us who live in non-Spanish-speaking countries); loss of ideological meta-horizons (the repression against and division of the left) and of metaphysical certainty.

In exchange, what we won was a vision of a more experimental culture, that is to say, a multi-focal and tolerant one. Going beyond nationalisms, we established cultural alliances with other places, and we won a true political conscience (declassicization and consequent politicization) as well as new options in social, sexual, spiritual, and aesthetic behavior.

Our artistic product presents hybrid realities and colliding visions within coalition. We practice the epistemology of multiplicity and a border semiotics. We share certain thematic interests, like the continual clash with cultural otherness, the crisis of identity, or, better said, access to trans- or multiculturalism, and the destruction of borders therefrom; the creation of alternative cartographies, a ferocious critique of the dominant culture of both countries, and, lastly, a proposal for new creative languages.

We witness the borderization of the world, by-product of the "deterritorialization" of vast human sectors. The borders either expand or are shot full of holes. Cultures and languages mutually invade one another. The South rises and melts, while the North descends dangerously with its economic and military pincers. The East moves west and vice-versa. Europe and North America daily receive uncontainable migrations of human beings, a majority of whom are being displaced involuntarily. This phenomenon is the result of multiple factors: regional wars, unemployment, overpopulation, and especially in the enormous disparity in North/South relations.

The demographic facts are staggering: The Middle East and Black Africa are already in Europe, and Latin America's heart now beats in the U.S. New York and Paris increasingly resemble Mexico City and São Paulo. Cities like Tijana and Los ANgeles, once socio-urban abberations are becoming models of a new hybrid culture, full of uncertainty and vitality. And border youth—the fearsome "cholopunks," children of the chasm that is opening between the "first" and the "third" worlds, become the indisputable heirs to a new *mestizaje* (the fusion of the Amerindian and European races).

In this context, concepts like "high culture," "ethnic purity," "cultural identity," "beauty," and "fine arts" are absurdities and anachronisms. Like it or not, we are attending the funeral of modernity and the birth of a new culture.

In 1988, the unigeneric and monocultural vision of the world is insufficient. Syncretism, interdisciplinarianism, and multi-ethnicity are sine qua nons of contemporary art. And the artist or intellectual who doesn't comprehend this will be banished and his or her work will not form part of the great cultural debates of the continent.

Art is conceptual territory where everything is possible, and by the same token there do not exist certainties nor limitations within it. In 1988, all the creative possibilities have been explored, and therefore they are all within our reach.

Thanks to the discoveries and advancements of many artists over the last fifteen years, the concept of *metier* is so wide and the parameters of art so flexible that they include practically every imaginable alternative art as political negotiation (Felipe Ehrenberg—Mexico), as social reform (Joseph Beuys—Germany), as an instrument of multicultural organization (Judy Baca—Los Angeles), or as alternative communication, (*Post Arte* —Mexico, and Kit Galloway & Sherri Rabinowitz—USA). Others conceive art as a strategy of intervention aimed at mass media, or as citizen-diplomacy, social chronicle, a popular semiotics, or personal anthropology.

In 1988, our artistic options in terms of the medium, methodology, system of communication, and channels of distribution for our ideas and images are greater and more diverse than ever. Not understanding and practicing this freedom implies operating outside of history, or, worse yet, blindly accepting the restrictions imposed by cultural bureaucracies.

Our experience as Latino border artists and intellectuals in the U.S. fluctuates between legality and illegality, between partial citizenship and full. For the Anglo community we are simply "an ethnic minority," a subculture, that is to say, some kind of pre-industrial tribe with a good consumerist appente. For the art world, we are practitioners of distant languages that, in the best of cases, are perceived as exotic.

20 In general, we are perceived through the folkloric prisms of Hollywood, fad literature and publicity; or through the ideological filters of mass media. For the average Anglo, we are nothing but "images," "symbols," "metaphors." We lack ontological existence and anthropological concreteness. We are perceived indistinctly as magic creatures with shamanistic powers, happy bohemians with pretechnological sensibilities, or as romantic revolutionaries born in a Cuban poster from the '70s. All this without mentioning the more ordinary myths, which link us with drugs, supersexuality, gratuitous violence, and terrorism, myths that serve to justify racism and disguise the fear of cultural otherness.

These mechanisms of mythification generate semantic interference and obstruct true intercultural dialogue. To make border art implies to reveal and subvert said mechanisms. The term *Hispanic,* coined by techno-marketing experts and by the designers of political campaigns, homogenizes our cultural diversity (Chicanos, Cubans, and Puerto Ricans become indistinguishable), avoids our indigenous cultural heritage and links us directly with Spain. Worse yet, it possesses connotations of upward mobility and political obedience.

The terms *Third World culture, ethnic art,* and *minority art* are openly ethnocentric and necessarily imply an axiological vision of the world at the service of Anglo-European culture. Confronted with them, one can't avoid asking the following questions: Besides possessing more money and arms, is it that the "First World" is qualitatively better in any other way than our "underdeveloped" countries? That the Anglos themselves aren't also an "ethnic group," one of the most violent and antisocial tribes on this planet? That the five hundred million Latin American *mestizos* that inhabit the Americas are a "minority"?

Between Chicanos, Mexicans, and Anglos there is a heritage of relations poisoned by distrust and resentment. For this reason, my cultural work (especially in the camps of performance art and journalism) has concentrated itself upon the destruction of the myths and the stereotypes that each group has invented to rationalize the other two.

With the dismantling of this mythology, I look, if not to create an instantaneous space for intercultural communication, at least to contribute to the creation of the groundwork and theoretical principles for a future dialogue that is capable of transcending the profound historical resentments that exist between the communities on either side of the border.

25 Within the framework of the false amnesty of the Immigration Reform and Control Act and the growing influence of the North American ultra-right, which seeks to close (militarize) the border because of supposed motives of "national security," the collaboration among Chicano, Mexican, and Anglo artists has become indispensable.

Anglo artists can contribute their technical ability, their comprehension of the new mediums of expression and information (video and audio), and their altruist/internationalist tendencies. In turn, Latinos (whether Mexican, Chicano, Caribbean, Central or South American) can contribute the originality of their cultural models, their spiritual strength, and their political understanding of the world.

Together, we can collaborate in surprising cultural projects but without forgetting that *both should retain control of the product,* from the planning stages up through to distribution. If this doesn't occur, then intercultural collaboration isn't authentic. We shouldn't confuse true collaboration with political paternalism, cultural vampirism, voyeurism, economic opportunism, and demogogic multiculturalism.

We should clear up this matter once and for all:

We (Latinos in the United States) don't want to be a mere ingredient of the melting pot. What we want is to participate actively in a humanistic, pluralistic and politicized dialogue, continuous and not sporadic, and that this occur between equals that enjoy the same power of negotiation.

30 For this "intermediate space" to open, first there has to be a pact of mutual cultural understanding and acceptance, and it is precisely in this that the border artist can contribute. In this very delicate historical moment, Mexican artists and intellectuals as well as Chicanos and Anglos should try to "recontextualize" ourselves, that is to say, search for a "common cultural territory," and within it put into practice new models of communication and association.

➤ *QUESTIONS FOR READING AND WRITING*

1. Why does the author refer to where he lives as an "infected wound"?
2. The author refers to himself as a "border artist." What do you think he means? What is a border artist?
3. Compare this essay to Gloria Anzaldúa's "To Live in the Borderlands Means You," on page 884.

RICHARD RODRIGUEZ (b. 1944)

Richard Rodriguez was born in San Francisco, the son of Mexican immigrants. He received a Ph.D. in English Renaissance literature from the University of California at Berkeley. His essays have appeared in a variety of publications, and he has published several books, including Hunger of Memory *(1981),* The Ethics of Change *(1992), and* Days of Obligation *(1993). He is a lecturer, freelance writer, educational consultant, and a frequent contributor to the Lehrer News Hour on public television. He lives in San Francisco.*

WORKERS

[1982]

It was at Stanford, one day near the end of my senior year, that a friend told me about a summer construction job he knew was available. I was quickly alert. Desire uncoiled within me. My friend said that he knew I had been looking for summer employment. He knew I needed some money. Almost apologetically he explained: It was something I probably wouldn't be interested in, but a friend of his, a contractor, needed someone for the summer to do menial jobs. There would be lots of shoveling and raking and sweeping. Nothing too hard. But nothing more interesting either. Still, the pay would be good. Did I want it? Or did I know someone who did?

I did. Yes, I said, surprised to hear myself say it.

In the weeks following, friends cautioned that I had no idea how hard physical labor really is. ("You only *think* you know what it is like to shovel for eight hours straight.") Their objections seemed to me challenges. They resolved the issue. I became happy with my plan. I decided, however, not to tell my parents. I wouldn't tell my mother because I could guess her worried reaction. I would tell my father only after the summer was over, when I could announce that, after all, I did know what "real work" is like.

The day I met the contractor (a Princeton graduate, it turned out), he asked me whether I had done any physical labor before. "In high school, during the summer," I lied. And although he seemed to regard me with skepticism, he decided to give me a try. Several days later, expectant, I arrived at my first construction site. I would take off my shirt to the sun. And at last grasp desired sensation. No longer afraid. At last become like a *bracero.*[1] "We need those tree stumps out of here by tomorrow," the contractor said. I started to work.

5 I labored with excitement that first morning—and all the days after. The work was harder than I could have expected. But it was never as tedious as my friends had warned me it would be. There was too much physical pleasure in the labor. Especially early in the day, I would be most alert to the sensations of movement and straining. Beginning around seven each morning (when the air was still damp but the scent of weeds and dry earth anticipated the heat of the sun), I would feel my body resist the first thrusts of the shovel. My arms, tightened by sleep, would gradually loosen; after only several minutes, sweat would gather in beads on my forehead and then—a short while later—I would feel my chest silky with sweat in the breeze. I would return to my work. A nervous spark of pain would fly up my arm and settle to burn like an ember in the thick of my shoulder. An hour, two passed. Three. My whole body would assume regular movements; my shoveling would be described by identical, even movements. Even later in the day, my enthusiasm for primitive sensation would survive the heat and the dust and the insects pricking my back. I would strain wildly for sensation as the day came to a close. At three-thirty, quitting time, I would stand upright and slowly let my head fall back, luxuriating in the feeling of tightness relieved.

[1] **bracero** laborer

Some of the men working nearby would watch me and laugh. Two or three of the older men took the trouble to teach me the right way to use a pick, the correct way to shovel. "You're doing it wrong, too fucking hard," one man scolded. Then proceeded to show me—what persons who work with their bodies all their lives quickly learn—the most economical way to use one's body in labor.

"Don't make your back do so much work," he instructed. I stood impatiently listening, half listening, vaguely watching, then noticed his work-thickened fingers clutching the shovel. I was annoyed. I wanted to tell him that I enjoyed shoveling the wrong way. And I didn't want to learn the right way. I wasn't afraid of back pain. I liked the way my body felt sore at the end of the day.

I was about to, but, as it turned out, I didn't say a thing. Rather it was at that moment I realized that I was fooling myself if I expected a few weeks of labor to gain me admission to the world of the laborer. I would not learn in three months what my father had meant by "real work." I was not bound to this job; I could imagine its rapid conclusion. For me the sensations of exertion and fatigue could be savored. For my father or uncle, working at comparable jobs when they were my age, such sensations were to be feared. Fatigue took a different toll on their bodies—and minds.

It was, I know, a simple insight. But it was with this realization that I took my first step that summer toward realizing something even more important about the "worker." In the company of carpenters, electricians, plumbers, and painters at lunch, I would often sit quietly, observant. I was not shy in such company. I felt easy, pleased by the knowledge that I was casually accepted, my presence taken for granted by men (exotics) who worked with their hands. Some days the younger men would talk and talk about sex, and they would howl at women who drove by in cars. Other days the talk at lunchtime was subdued; men gathered in separate groups. It depended on who was around. There were rough, good-natured workers. Others were quiet. The more I remember that summer, the more I realize that there was no single *type* of worker. I am embarrassed to say I had not expected such diversity. I certainly had not expected to meet, for example, a plumber who was an abstract painter in his off hours and admired the work of Mark Rothko. Nor did I expect to meet so many workers with college diplomas. (They were the ones who were not surprised that I intended to enter graduate school in the fall.) I suppose what I really want to say here is painfully obvious, but I must say it nevertheless: The men of that summer were middle-class Americans. They certainly didn't constitute an oppressed society. Carefully completing their work sheets; talking about the fortunes of local football teams; planning Las Vegas vacations; comparing the gas mileage of various makes of campers—they were not *los pobres*[2] my mother had spoken about.

10 On two occasions, the contractor hired a group of Mexican aliens. They were employed to cut down some trees and haul off debris. In all, there were six men of varying age. The youngest in his late twenties; the oldest (his father?) perhaps sixty years old. They came and they left in a single old truck. Anonymous men. They were never introduced to the other men at the site. Immediately upon their arrival, they

[2]**los pobres** the poor

would follow the contractor's directions, start working—rarely resting—seemingly driven by a fatalistic sense that work which had to be done was best done as quickly as possible.

I watched them sometimes. Perhaps they watched me. The only time I saw them pay me much notice was one day at lunchtime when I was laughing with the other men. The Mexicans sat apart when they ate, just as they worked by themselves. Quiet. I rarely heard them say much to each other. All I could hear were their voices calling out sharply to one another, giving directions. Otherwise, when they stood briefly resting, they talked among themselves in voices too hard to overhear.

The contractor knew enough Spanish, and the Mexicans—or at least the oldest of them, their spokesman—seemed to know enough English to communicate. But because I was around, the contractor decided one day to make me his translator. (He assumed I could speak Spanish.) I did what I was told. Shyly I went over to tell the Mexicans that the *patrón*[3] wanted them to do something else before they left for the day. As I started to speak, I was afraid with my old fear that I would be unable to pronounce the Spanish words. But it was a simple instruction I had to convey. I could say it in phrases.

The dark sweating faces turned toward me as I spoke. They stopped their work to hear me. Each nodded in response. I stood there. I wanted to say something more. But what could I say in Spanish, even if I could have pronounced the words right? Perhaps I just wanted to engage them in small talk, to be assured of their confidence, our familiarity. I thought for a moment to ask them where in Mexico they were from. Something like that. And maybe I wanted to tell them (a lie, if need be) that my parents were from the same part of Mexico.

I stood there.

15 Their faces watched me. The eyes of the man directly in front of me moved slowly over my shoulder, and I turned to follow his glance toward *el patrón* some distance away. For a moment I felt swept up by that glance into the Mexicans' company. But then I heard one of them returning to work. And then the others went back to work. I left them without saying anything more.

When they had finished, the contractor went over to pay them in cash. (He later told me that he paid them collectively—"for the job," though he wouldn't tell me their wages. He said something quickly about the good rate of exchange "in their own country.") I can still hear the loudly confident voice he used with the Mexicans. It was the sound of the *gringo*[4] I had heard as a very young boy. And I can still hear the quiet, indistinct sounds of the Mexican, the oldest, who replied. At hearing that voice I was sad for the Mexicans. Depressed by their vulnerability. Angry at myself. The adventure of the summer seemed suddenly ludicrous. I would not shorten the distance I felt from *los pobres* with a few weeks of physical labor. I would not become like them. They were different from me. . . .

That summer I worked in the sun may have made me physically indistinguishable from the Mexicans working nearby. (My skin was actually darker because, unlike them, I worked without wearing a shirt. By late August my hands were probably as tough as theirs.) But I was not one of *los pobres.* What made me different from them was an attitude of *mind,* my imagination of myself. . . .

[3]**patrón** boss [4]**gringo** Yankee

In the end, my father was right—though perhaps he did not know how right or why—to say that I would never know what real work is. I will never know what he felt at his last factory job. If tomorrow I worked at some kind of factory, it would go differently for me. My long education would favor me. I could act as a public person—able to defend my interests, to unionize, to petition, to speak up—to challenge and demand. (I will never know what real work is.) I will never know what the Mexicans knew, gathering their shovels and ladders and saws.

Their silence stays with me now. The wages those Mexicans received for their labor were only a measure of their disadvantaged condition. Their silence is more telling. They lack a public identity. They remain profoundly alien. Persons apart. People lacking a union obviously, people without grounds. They depend upon the relative good will or fairness of their employers each day. For such people, lacking a better alternative, it is not such an unreasonable risk.

20 Their silence stays with me. I have taken these many words to describe its impact. Only: the quiet. Something uncanny about it. Its compliance. Vulnerability. Pathos. As I heard their truck rumbling away, I shuddered, my face mirrored with sweat. I had finally come face to face with *los pobres*.

➤ *QUESTIONS FOR READING AND WRITING*

1. What does the writer mean by "Their objections seemed to be challenges"?
2. To what extent have you experienced hard, physical labor? Does your experience of it match the writer's? Could you say, "I liked the way my body felt at the end of the day"? Explain.
3. The writer says, "I would learn in three months what my father had meant by 'real work.' Does he? Explain.
4. With reference to the Mexican workers, the writer says, "What made me different from them was an attitude of mind, my imagination of myself . . . . "What does he mean?

JONATHAN SWIFT (1667–1745)

Jonathan Swift was born to English parents in Ireland and attended Trinity College in Dublin. Forced to flee Ireland during the period of turmoil that followed the abdication of James II, Swift lived ten years in the household of a wealthy relative, where he spent his time reading and where he first discovered his talent as a writer of satire. After many years of indecision, Swift decided on a career in the Church of England, which in turn led to his involvement in politics, where he was an active member of the Tory party. In 1713, he reluctantly returned to Ireland following his appointment as dean of St. Patrick's Cathedral in Dublin, and eventually became a fervent Irish patriot in the struggle for Irish independence. Swift wrote "A Modest

Proposal" (1729), widely considered the greatest satire produced in English, in response to his disgust with the heartless policies of the English government toward the poor in Ireland.

A Modest Proposal

[1729]

For preventing the Children of Poor People in Ireland from Being a Burden to Their Parents or Country, and for Making Them Beneficial to the Public

It is a melancholy object to those who walk through this great town or travel in the country, when they see the streets, the roads and cabindoors crowded with beggars of the female sex, followed by three, four, or six children, all in rags, and importuning every passenger for an alms. These mothers, instead of being able to work for their honest livelihood, are forced to employ all their time in strolling to beg sustenance for their helpless infants: who as they grow up either turn thieves for want of work, or leave their dear native country to fight for the pretender in Spain, or sell themselves to the Barbadoes.

I think it is agreed by all parties that this prodigious number of children in the arms, or on the backs, or at the heels of their mothers, and frequently of their fathers, is in the present deplorable state of the kingdom a very great additional grievance; and, therefore, whoever could find out a fair, cheap, and easy method of making these children sound, and useful members of the commonwealth, would deserve so well of the public as to have his statue set up for a preserver of the nation.

But my intention is very far from being confined to provide only for the children of professed beggars; it is of a much greater extent, and shall take in the whole number of infants at a certain age who are born of parents in effect as little able to support them as those who demand our charity in the streets.

As to my own part, having turned my thoughts for many years upon this important subject, and maturely weighed the several schemes of other projectors,[1] I have always found them grossly mistaken in their computation. It is true a child just dropped from its dam may be supported by her milk for a solar year, with little other nourishment; at most not above the value of 2s,[2] which the mother may certainly get, or the value in scraps, by her lawful occupation of begging; and it is exactly at one year old that I propose to provide for them in such a manner as, instead of being a charge upon their parents or the parish, or wanting food and raiment for the rest of their lives, they shall on the contrary contribute to the feeding, and partly to the clothing of many thousands.

5 There is likewise another great advantage in my scheme, that it will prevent those voluntary abortions, and that horrid practice of women murdering their bastard children, alas! too frequent among us! sacrificing the poor innocent babes I doubt more to avoid the expense than the shame, which would move tears and pity in the most savage and inhuman breast.

The number of souls in this kingdom being usually reckoned one million and a half, of these I calculate there may be about 200,000 couples whose wives are

[1]**projectors** planners [2]**2s** two shillings

breeders; from which number I subtract 30,000 couples who are able to maintain their own children (although I apprehend there cannot be so many, under the present distresses of the kingdom); but this being granted, there will remain 170,000 breeders. I again subtract 50,000 for those women who miscarry, or whose children die by accident or disease within the year. There only remain 120,000 children of poor parents annually born. The question therefore is, how this number shall be reared and provided for, which, as I have already said, under the present situation of affairs, is utterly impossible by all the methods hitherto proposed. For we can neither employ them in handicraft or agriculture; we neither build houses (I mean in the country) nor cultivate land; they can very seldom pick up a livelihood by stealing, until they arrive at six years old, except where they are of towardly parts; although I confess they learn the rudiments much earlier; during which time they can, however, be properly looked upon only as probationers; as I have been informed by a principal gentleman in the County of Cavan, who protested to me that he never knew above one or two instances under the age of six, even in a part of the kingdom so renowned for the quickest proficiency in that art.

I am assured by our merchants, that a boy or a girl before twelve years old is no saleable commodity; and even when they come to this age they will not yield above or 3£[3]or 3£. 2s. 6d.[4] at most on the exchange; which cannot turn to account either to the parents or the kingdom, the charge of nutriment and rags having been at least four times that value.

I shall now therefore humbly propose my own thoughts, which I hope will not be liable to the least objection.

I have been assured by a very knowing American of my acquaintance in London, that a young healthy child well nursed is at a year old a most delicious, nourishing, and wholesome food, whether stewed, roasted, baked, or boiled; and I make no doubt that it will equally serve in a fricassee, or a ragout.

10 I do therefore humbly offer it to public consideration that of the 120,000 children already computed, 20,000 may be reserved for breed, whereof only one-fourth part to be males; which is more than we allow to sheep, black-cattle, or swine; and my reason is, that these children are seldom the fruits of marriage, a circumstance not much regarded by our savages; therefore one male will be sufficient to serve four females. That the remaining 100,000 may, at a year old, be offered in sale to the persons of quality and fortune through the kingdom, always advising the mother to let them suck plentifully in the last month, so as to render them plump and fat for a good table. A child will make two dishes at an entertainment for friends; and when the family dines alone, the fore or hind quarter will make a reasonable dish, and seasoned with a little pepper or salt will be very good boiled on the fourth day, especially in winter.

I have reckoned upon a medium that a child just born will weigh 12 pounds, and in a solar year, if tolerably nursed, increaseth to 28 pounds.

I grant this food will be somewhat dear, and therefore very proper for landlords, who, as they have already devoured most of the parents, seem to have the best title to the children.

[3]**3£** three pounds [4]**6d** six pence

Infant's flesh will be in season throughout the year, but more plentiful in March, and a little before and after: for we are told by a grave author, an eminent French physician, that fish being a prolific diet, there are more children born in Roman Catholic countries about nine months after Lent than at any other season; therefore, reckoning a year after Lent, the markets will be more glutted than usual, because the number of popish infants is at least three to one in this kingdom: and therefore it will have one other collateral advantage, by lessening the number of papists among us.

I have already computed the charge of nursing a beggar's child (in which list I reckon all cottagers, laborers, and four-fifths of the farmers) to be about 2s per annum, rags included; and I believe no gentleman would repine to give 10s for the carcass of a good fat child, which, as I have said, will make four dishes of excellent nutritive meat, when he hath only some particular friend or his own family to dine with him. Thus the squire will learn to be a good landlord, and grow popular among his tenants; the mother will have 8s net profit, and be fit for work until she produces another child.

Those who are more thrifty (as I must confess the times require) may flay the carcass; the skin of which artificially dressed, will make admirable gloves for ladies, and summer boots for fine gentlemen.

As to our city of Dublin, shambles[5] may be appointed for this purpose in the most convenient parts of it, and butchers we may be assured will not be wanting: although I rather recommend buying the children alive, and dressing them hot from the knife as we do roasting pigs.

A very worthy person, a true lover of his country, and whose virtues I highly esteem, was lately pleased in discoursing on this matter to offer a refinement upon my scheme. He said that many gentlemen of this kingdom, having of late destroyed their deer, he conceived that the want of venison might be well supplied by the bodies of young lads and maidens, not exceeding fourteen years of age nor under twelve; so great a number of both sexes in every county being now ready to starve for want of work and service; and these to be disposed of by their parents, if alive, or otherwise by their nearest relations. But with due deference to so excellent a friend and so deserving a patriot, I cannot be altogether in his sentiments; for as to the males, my American acquaintance assured me from frequent experience that their flesh was generally tough and lean, like that of our schoolboys by continual exercise, and their taste disagreeable; and to fatten them would not answer the charge. Then as to the females, it would, I think with humble submission be a loss to the public, because they soon would become breeders themselves: and besides, it is not improbable that some scrupulous people might be apt to censure such a practice (although indeed very unjustly), as a little bordering upon cruelty; which, I confess, hath always been with me the strongest objection against any project, how well soever intended.

But in order to justify my friend, he confessed that this expedient was put into his head by the famous Psalmanazar[6], a native of the island Formosa, who came

[5]**shambles** slaughterhouses [6]**Psalmanazar** George Psalmanazar (c. 1679–1763), wrote *An Historical and Geographical Description of Formosa* (1704). He had never been to Formosa and his book was quickly discovered to be fraudulent.

from thence to London above twenty years ago; and in conversation told my friend that in his country when any young person happened to be put to death, the executioner sold the carcass to persons of quality as a prime dainty; and that in his time the body of a plump girl of fifteen, who was crucified for an attempt to poison the emperor, was sold to his imperial majesty's prime minister of state, and other great mandarins of the court, in joints from the gibbet, at 400 crowns. Neither indeed can I deny, that if the same use were made of several plump young girls in this town, who without one single groat to their fortunes cannot stir abroad without a chair, and appear at the playhouse and assemblies in foreign fineries which they never will pay for, the kingdom would not be the worse.

Some persons of a desponding spirit are in great concern about the vast number of poor people, who are aged, diseased, or maimed, and I have been desired to employ my thoughts what course may be taken to ease the nation of so grievous an encumbrance. But I am not in the least pain upon that matter, because it is very well known that they are every day dying and rotting by cold and famine, and filth and vermin, as fast as can be reasonably expected. And as to the younger laborers, they are now in as hopeful a condition: they cannot get work, and consequently pine away from want of nourishment, to a degree that if at any time they are accidentally hired to common labor, they have not strength to perform it; and thus the country and themselves are delivered from the evils to come.

20 I have too long digressed, and therefore shall return to my subject. I think the advantages by the proposal which I have made are obvious and many, as well as of the highest importance.

For first, as I have already observed, it would greatly lessen the number of papists, with whom we are yearly overrun, being the principal breeders of the nation; as well as our most dangerous enemies; and who stay at home on purpose to deliver the kingdom to the Pretender, hoping to take their advantage by the absence of so many good Protestants, who have chosen rather to leave their country than stay at home and pay tithes against their conscience to an Episcopal curate.

Secondly, The poorer tenants will have something valuable of their own, which by law may be made liable to distress and help to pay their landlord's rent, their corn and cattle being already seized, and money a thing unknown.

Thirdly, Whereas the maintenance of 100,000 children from two years old and upwards, cannot be computed at less than 10s. a-piece per annum, the nation's stock will be thereby increased £50,000 per annum, besides the profit of a new dish introduced to the tables of all gentlemen of fortune in the kingdom who have any refinement in taste. And the money will circulate among ourselves, the goods being entirely of our own growth and manufacture.

Fourthly, The constant breeders beside the gain of 8s sterling per annum by the sale of their children, will be rid of the charge of maintaining them after the first year.

25 Fifthly, This food would likewise bring great custom to taverns, where the vintners will certainly be so prudent as to procure the best receipts for dressing it to perfection, and consequently have their houses frequented by all the fine gentlemen, who justly value themselves upon their knowledge in good eating; and a skilful

cook, who understands how to oblige his guests, will contrive to make it as expensive as they please.

Sixthly, This would be a great inducement to marriage, which all wise nations have either encouraged by rewards or enforced by laws and penalties. It would increase the care and tenderness of mothers towards their children, when they were sure of a settlement for life to the poor babes, provided in some sort by the public, to their annual profit instead of expense. We should soon see an honest emulation among the married women, which of them could bring the fattest child to the market. Men would become as fond of their wives during the time of their pregnancy as they are now of their mares in foal, their cows in calf, or sows when they are ready to farrow; nor offer to beat or kick them (as it is too frequent a practice) for fear of a miscarriage.

Many other advantages might be enumerated. For instance, the addition of some thousand carcasses in our exportation of barreled beef, the propagation of swine's flesh, and improvement in the art of making good bacon, so much wanted among us by the great destruction of pigs, too frequent at our tables, which are no way comparable in taste or magnificence to a well-grown, fat, yearling child, which roasted whole will make a considerable figure at a lord mayor's feast or any other public entertainment. But this and many others I omit, being studios of brevity.

Supposing that 1,000 families in this city would be constant customers for infants' flesh, besides others who might have it at merry-meetings, particularly weddings and christenings, I compute that Dublin would take off annually about 20,000 carcasses; and the rest of the kingdom (where probably they will be sold somewhat cheaper) the remaining 80,000.

I can think of no one objection that will possibly be raised against this proposal, unless it should be urged that the number of people will be thereby much lessened in the kingdom. This I freely own, and it was indeed one principal design in offering it to the world. I desire the reader will observe, that I calculate my remedy for this one individual kingdom of Ireland and for no other that ever was, is, or I think ever can be upon earth. Therefore let no man talk to me of other expedients: of taxing our absentees at 5s. a pound: of using neither clothes, nor household furniture except what is of our own growth and manufacture: of utterly rejecting the materials and instruments that promote foreign luxury: of curing the expensiveness of pride, vanity, idleness, and gaming in our women: of introducing a vein of parsimony, prudence, and temperance: of learning to love our country, in the want of which we differ even from Laplanders and the inhabitants of Topinamboo: of quitting our animosities and factions, nor act any longer like the Jews, who were murdering one another at the very moment their city was taken: of being a little cautious not to sell our country and conscience for nothing: of teaching landlords to have at least one degree of mercy towards their tenants: lastly, of putting a spirit of honesty, industry, and skill into our shopkeepers; who, if a resolution could now be taken to buy only our native goods, would immediately unite to cheat and exact upon us in the price, the measure, and the goodness, nor could ever yet be brought to make one fair proposal of just dealing, though often and earnestly invited to it.

30 Therefore I repeat, let no man talk to me of these and the like expedients, till he hath at least a glimpse of hope that there will ever be some hearty and sincere attempt to put them in practice.

But as to myself, having been wearied out for many years with offering vain, idle, visionary thoughts, and at length utterly despairing of success, I fortunately fell upon this proposal; which, as it is wholly new, so it has something solid and real, of no expense and little trouble, full in our own power, and whereby we can incur no danger in disobliging England. For this kind of commodity will not bear exportation, the flesh being of too tender a consistence to admit a long continuance in salt, although perhaps I could name a country which would be glad to eat up our whole nation without it.

After all, I am not so violently bent upon my own opinion as to reject any offer proposed by wise men, which shall be found equally innocent, cheap, easy, and effectual. But before something of that kind shall be advanced in contradiction to my scheme, and offering a better, I desire the author or authors will be pleased maturely to consider two points. First, as things now stand, how they will be able to find food and raiment for 100,000 useless mouths and backs. And secondly, there being a round million of creatures in human figure throughout this kingdom, whose whole subsistence put into a common stock would leave them in debt 2,000,000£ sterling, adding those who are beggars by profession to the bulk of farmers, cottagers, and laborers with their wives and children who are beggars in effect; I desire those politicians who dislike my overture, and may perhaps be so bold to attempt an answer, that they will first ask the parents of these mortals, whether they would not at this day think it a great happiness to have been sold for food at a year old in the manner I prescribe, and thereby have avoided such a perpetual scene of misfortunes as they have since gone through, by the oppression of landlords, the impossibility of paying rent without money or trade, the want of common sustenance, with neither house nor clothes to cover them from the inclemencies of weather, and the most inevitable prospect of entailing the like or greater miseries upon their breed for ever.

I profess in the sincerity of my heart; that I have not the least personal interest in endeavoring to promote this necessary work, having no other motive than the public good of my country, by advancing our trade, providing for infants, relieving the poor, and giving some pleasure to the rich. I have no children by which I can propose to get a single penny; the youngest being nine years old, and my wife past child-bearing.

➤ *QUESTIONS FOR READING AND WRITING*

1. What is the tone of this essay? How do you know?
2. According to the narrator, what are the advantages of his proposal?
3. If Swift doesn't really mean the exaggerated things he proposes, why do you think he proposes them? What's the point of this essay?

Case Studies in Composition

Thinking About Interpretation, Culture, and Research

James Joyce and *Eveline*

James Joyce (1882–1941)

(See biography on page 544.)

Eveline [1914]

She sat at the window watching the evening invade the avenue. Her head was leaned against the window curtains and in her nostrils was the odour cretonne. She was tired.

Few people passed. The man out of the last house passed on his way home; she heard his footsteps clacking along the concrete pavement and afterwards crunching on the cinder path before the new red houses. One time there used to be a field there in which they used to play every evening with other people's children. Then a man from Belfast bought the field and built houses in it—not like their little brown houses but bright brick houses with shining roofs. The children of the avenue used to play together in that field—the Devines, the Waters, the Dunns, little Keogh the cripple, she and her brothers and sisters. Ernest, however, never played: he was too grown up. Her father used often to hunt them in out of the field with his blackthorn stick; but usually little Keogh used to keep *nix* and call out when he saw her father coming. Still they seemed to have been rather happy then. Her father was not so bad then; and besides, her mother was alive. That was a long time ago; she and her brothers and sisters were all grown up; her mother was dead. Tizzie Dunn was dead, too, and the Waters had gone back to England. Everything changes. Now she was going to go away like the others, to leave her home.

Home! She looked around the room, reviewing all its familiar objects which she had dusted once a week for so many years, wondering where on earth all the dust came from. Perhaps she would never see again those familiar objects from which she had never dreamed of being divided. And yet during all those years she had never found out the name of the priest whose yellowing photograph hung on the wall above the broken harmonium beside the coloured print of the promises made to Blessed Margaret Mary Alacoque. He had been a school friend of her father.

Whenever he showed the photograph to a visitor her father used to pass it with a casual word:

—He is in Melbourne now.

5 She had consented to go away, to leave her home. Was that wise? She tried to weigh each side of the question. In her home anyway she had shelter and food; she had those whom she had known all her life about her. Of course she had to work hard both in the house and at business. What would they say of her in the Stores when they found out that she had run away with a fellow? Say she was a fool, perhaps; and her place would be filled up by advertisement. Miss Gavan would be glad. She had always had an edge on her, especially whenever there were people listening.

—Miss Hill, don't you see these ladies are waiting?

—Look lively, Miss Hill, please.

She would not cry many tears at leaving the Stores.

But in her new home, in a distant unknown country, it would not be like that. Then she would be married—she, Eveline. People would treat her with respect then. She would not be treated as her mother had been. Even now, though she was over nineteen, she sometimes felt herself in danger of her father's violence. She knew it was that that had given her the palpitations. When they were growing up he had never gone for her, like he used to go for Harry and Ernest, because she was a girl; but latterly he had begun to threaten her and say what he would do to her only for her dead mother's sake. And now she had nobody to protect her. Ernest was dead and Harry, who was in the church decorating business, was nearly always down somewhere in the country. Besides, the invariable squabble for money on Saturday nights had begun to weary her unspeakably. She always gave her entire wages—seven shillings—and Harry always sent up what he could but the trouble was to get any money from her father. He said she used to squander the money, that she had no head, that he wasn't going to give her his hard-earned money to throw about the streets, and much more, for he was usually fairly bad of a Saturday night. In the end he would give her the money and ask her had she any intention of buying Sunday's dinner. Then she had to rush out as quickly as she could and do her marketing, holding her black leather purse tightly in her hand as she elbowed her way through the crowds and returning home late under her load of provisions. She had hard work to keep the house together and to see that the two young children who had been left to her charge went to school regularly and got their meals regularly. It was hard work—a hard life—but now that she was about to leave it she did not find it a wholly undesirable life.

10 She was about to explore another life with Frank. Frank was very kind, manly, open-hearted. She was to go away with him by the night-boat to be his wife and to live with him in Buenos Ayres where he had a home waiting for her. How well she remembered the first time she had seen him; he was lodging in a house on the main road where she used to visit. It seemed a few weeks ago. He was standing at the gate, his peaked cap pushed back on his head and his hair tumbled forward over a face of bronze. Then they had come to know each other. He used to meet her outside the Stores every evening and see her home. He took her to see *The Bohemian Girl* and she felt elated as she sat in an unaccustomed part of the theatre with him. He was awfully fond of music and sang a little. People knew that they were courting and,

when he sang about the lass that loves a sailor, she always felt pleasantly confused. He used to call her Poppens out of fun. First of all it had been an excitement for her to have a fellow and then she had begun to like him. He had tales of distant countries. He had started as a deck boy at a pound a month on a ship of the Allan Line going out to Canada. He told her the names of the ships he had been on and the names of the different services. He had sailed through the Straits of Magellan and he told her stories of the terrible Patagonians. He had fallen on his feet in Buenos Ayres, he said, and had come over to the old country just for a holiday. Of course, her father had found out the affair and had forbidden her to have anything to say to him.

—I know these sailor chaps, he said.

One day he had quarreled with Frank and after that she had to meet her lover secretly.

The evening deepened in the avenue. The white of two letters in her lap grew indistinct. One was to Harry; the other was to her father. Ernest had been her favourite but she liked Harry too. Her father was becoming old lately, she noticed; he would miss her. Sometimes he could be very nice. Not long before, when she had been laid up for a day, he had read her out a ghost story and made toast for her at the fire. Another day, when their mother was alive, they had all gone for a picnic to the Hill of Howth. She remembered her father putting on her mother's bonnet to make the children laugh.

Her time was running out but she continued to sit by the window, leaning her head against the window curtain, inhaling the odour of dusty cretonne. Down far in the avenue she could hear a street organ playing. She knew the air. Strange that it should come that very night to remind her of the promise to her mother, her promise to keep the home together as long as she could. She remembered the last night of her mother's illness; she was again in the close dark room at the other side of the hall and outside she heard a melancholy air of Italy. The organ-player had been ordered to go away and given sixpence. She remembered her father strutting back into the sickroom saying.

15 —Damned Italians! Coming over here!

As she mused the pitiful vision of her mother's life laid its spell on the very quick of her being—that life of commonplace sacrifices closing in final craziness. She trembled as she heard again her mother's voice saying constantly with foolish insistence:

—Derevaun Seraun! Derevaun Seraun!

She stood up in a sudden impulse of terror. Escape! She must escape! Frank would save her. He would give her life, perhaps love, too. But she wanted to live. Why should she be unhappy? She had a right to happiness. Frank would take her in his arms, fold her in his arms. He would save her.

She stood among the swaying crowd in the station at the North Wall. He held her hand and she knew that he was speaking to her, saying something about the passage over and over again. The station was full of soldiers with brown baggages. Through the wide doors of the sheds she caught a glimpse of the black mass of the boat, lying in beside the quay wall, with illumined portholes. She answered nothing.

She felt her cheek pale and cold and, out of a maze of distress, she prayed to God to direct her, to show her what was her duty. The boat blew a long mournful whistle into the mist. If she went, to-morrow she would be on the sea with Frank, steaming towards Buenos Ayres. Their passage had been booked. Could she still draw back after all he had done for her? Her distress awoke a nausea in her body and she kept moving her lips in silent fervent prayer.

A bell clanged upon her heart. She felt him seize her hand:

—Come!

All the seas of the world tumbled about her heart. He was drawing her into them: he would drown her. She gripped with both hands at the iron railing.

—Come!

No! No! No! It was impossible. Her hands clutched the iron in frenzy. Amid the seas she sent a cry of anguish!

—Eveline! Evvy!

He rushed beyond the barrier and called to her to follow. He was shouted at to go on but he still called to her. She set her white face to him, passive, like a helpless animal. Her eyes gave him no sign of love or farewell or recognition.

➤ *QUESTIONS FOR READING AND WRITING*

1. To what extent is your response to this story influenced by your own background or experience?
2. Were you hoping that Eveline would leave or stay? Why?
3. Describe Frank. What does he represent to Eveline?
4. To what extent is Eveline a prisoner of her setting? Of her own culture?
5. Do you think Eveline really has a choice at the end of the story? Explain.

Interpretation, Culture, and Research

As we have emphasized throughout this book, writing an effective essay is not always a straightforward process. Many factors may influence the choices we make along the way. This is particularly true when using secondary source research in our writing. One possible topic, and a rich source for research, may be the connection we find between our own backgrounds or culture and that presented in the work. The best research springs from our need to know more—to fill in the gaps in our knowledge. This research is not imposed on our writing but evolves naturally from it.

Below is the commentary of Prof. Alan Devenish, followed by the research essay of his student, Kevin Chamberlain. Dr. Devenish recalls their conferences and the process Kevin experienced while writing his research essay. He explains that Kevin did not set out to do research. While reading James Joyce's short story "Eveline," Kevin found similarities between himself and the protagonist.

He started to write a personal essay, but his interest in her as a character inspired him to want to know more. He sought information about the conditions of her background. This, in turn, led him to do research about the author and to read more of Joyce's work. What began as a personal response developed naturally into an informative and personally meaningful research essay.

All readers may not have such a strong personal identification with the work or, like Kevin, follow up their reading of one work by reading other works by the same author. But the process Kevin followed is a strong model for anyone doing secondary source research. He did not begin by gathering all the information he could and refashioning it into an essay. He began by writing a draft of his own response. In the process, he identified the issues he wanted to explore and generated the questions he needed to answer to make this exploration successful. The objective of his search was not to gather the most information, but to gather answers to his questions. His search was motivated by his "need to know," and it was only through his early writing and reflection that *what* he needed to know became clear to him.

Professor Devenish's Commentary

Before beginning my commentary on his essay "Leaving Home," I met with Kevin Chamberlain to discuss his paper. In preparation for our informal interview I asked him to write a short "process reflection" describing the researching, writing, and revising of his essay. I am tempted to delete this last phrase—"researching, writing, and revising"—because Kevin's actual process did not follow this neat, if unnatural, progression of discrete steps or stages. His process was rich in recursions and excursions, in rethinkings that led to new inquiries, which in turn led to further thinking and writing. The finished essay is not the one Kevin thought he was going to write when he started out.

So, how *did* he start out? Why did he choose to write on James Joyce's "Eveline," a story about a young woman's unsuccessful struggle to leave home, when he had any number of literary works and authors from which to select? "I was drawn to this story because I, too, am attached to my home and family," Kevin writes in his essay, "I have lived in the same house all of my life and I often dread the thought of leaving." In his process reflection Kevin writes similarly: "I was able to empathize with Eveline because I am at a similar point in my life—too long in the nest." Kevin's impetus for this paper was at heart a personal one. He responded emotionally to the title character's fears and desires, to the terrible conflict between home and self. Kevin also notes that he had read other works by Joyce and enjoyed his "writing style." Clearly, however, "Eveline" struck a special chord.

In our conversation, Kevin spoke of his initial impatience with the character Eveline, how he felt "anxious to push this person out of her home—to do what I would do." On further reading and research, however, he tempered this impulse, as he looked more closely at the conditions and culture that gave rise to Eveline's quandary. Reading Joyce's *Portrait of the Artist as a Young Man* and *Dubliners,* along with relevant critical research on the author and Ireland itself, brought Kevin to a more complex and empathetic understanding of the character. No doubt, too, rereading the story reminded Kevin of his own unresolved tensions between loyalties to home and family on one hand, and change and "beginning my own life" on the other.

Along with Kevin's intimate connection with the story's protagonist must be added another: culture. Eveline is not only a person struggling with fierce inner conflicts, she is a person living in a particular place and time, Ireland of the early twentieth century. Again, in his process, Kevin writes of "being part Irish" and how this cultural heritage leads him to share similar values with Eveline in regard to family, religion, and change. At the same time, he realized that he needed to know more of the particular Ireland of Joyce's "Eveline" and how the author "intertwines political, social, religious, and economic themes into his writing . . . That is where the research began."

Cultural relevance, then, became a starting point for inquiry into the important complexities that form the backdrop of Joyce's story. Interestingly, Kevin did not presume that his own Irish heritage gave him a satisfactory understanding of the character or story. Being part Irish did, however, stir his interest in the Ireland that gave rise to Eveline, and indeed to Joyce himself. In our interview, Kevin made the surprising assertion that in Joyce the characters are "the least important things in the story. The characters show one whole side of life, are representative of a whole class of people." What Kevin meant by this, I believe, is that "Eveline," far from being the idiosyncratic story of a particularly troubled young woman, is the story of many an Irish woman of Joyce's day, these Evelines holding fast to the dock railing as their figurative or real ships left for distant ports. In his essay, Kevin makes amply clear the enormous historical, economic, religious, and familial forces that converged into a sort of paralysis in Eveline and so many like her, and how these selfsame forces acted more centrifugally on Joyce and others like him who broke from home, and "the old sow" of Ireland "that eats her farrow," as Kevin quotes Joyce's biting indictment. Most notable in this analysis is that Kevin undertook his research from a need to know more of the very culture whose personal relevance first connected him to the story.

Here I would like to quote Kevin's description of how his initial intent to write an interpretive essay relying solely on his reading of "Eveline" evolved rather organically into a more complex inquiry:

> My first step was to respond to the story, writing an essay that examined the primary source [the story "Eveline"] without any outside influences such as literary criticism. Once the draft was completed I made a list of things in the story that I did not understand but felt were important to understanding the work as a whole . . . By making a list of things I did not understand, I had something to look for in the outside sources. . . . Once I felt I had enough information to revise my first draft, I added in the research to my already existing essay. . . . without letting my research write the paper for me. I simply used the research to support my already existing thesis.

Clearly, Kevin did not start out with either the requirement or the intention of writing a research paper. His method was not to get books out of the library and then figure out a way to incorporate all the research into a readable—or writable—essay. Rather, as his process reflection here and his finished essay demonstrate, he *grew* into the research, beginning with that important personal connection, that moment of recognition between himself and the text. He saw something of himself in Eveline, as he did in the Ireland that lived in her. From this recognition he wrote his first draft, a draft that led him to other questions. These questions, in turn, led him to further reading and writing, thereby strengthening the original connection between himself and the story. He repeated this process through several revisions, each time returning to the library when he felt "there were things that were still not strong enough," until he had satisfied the questions raised by his reading and writing. What started, then, as a response to a short story related to his own life grew to a larger inquiry into cultural contexts, literary criticism, and the author's work. That initial personal response, however, was not simply a starting point for the "real" work of research and writing. From Kevin's process reflections, as from his completed essay, I am convinced that his ongoing—indeed deepened—connection with the character and culture of this story sustained his research, writing, and revision throughout.

By citing Kevin's approach to writing about a literary work I am not claiming that students need to share a cultural identity with an author or text, or find exact parallels with the circumstances of their own lives. What I do believe Kevin's example illustrates is the importance of a personal connection with the work. Clearly, Kevin did not need a male protagonist in a familiar, contemporary setting in order to "relate." He did, however, feel a need to find in the work something that touched him. As it happened, he found this through cultural and psychological perspectives. More important, he then broadened these perspectives, questioning what he read and wrote, adding to it, seeing what was previously unseen. In the process, he learned about women in Joyce's Ireland; he read other works by the author; he saw historical and political patterns in Eveline's painful stasis; he deciphered religious references as significant symbols; he studied the human heart through the particulars of one fictive but very human creation. As important, I think, is that Kevin came to experience this story and his response to it as integral to his own life.

A Student Essay—Research and Culture

Kevin Chamberlain

Dr. Devenish

English 102

March 20, 200X

Leaving Home

James Joyce's short story "Eveline" is the story of a girl who turns down a marriage proposal because of her attachment to her home and family. I was drawn to this story because I, too, am attached to my home and family. I have lived in the same house all of my life, and I often dread the thought of leaving. I live alone with my mother and we depend on each other in many ways. I take care of the house, inside and out, in return for room and board. The problem is that if I were to move out, my mother would not be able to maintain the house. Such a change would alter both our lives in different ways. It would be the beginning of my own life but the end of hers. I know that this must happen sooner or later, but I sometimes feel it is my duty to stay and help out even if it only prolongs the inevitable. Eveline, the main character in Joyce's story, is faced with a similar dilemma. Should she abandon her father and begin her own life? Or should she stay home and take care of her father, but give up her own future in the process?

Eveline's devotion to her father stems from a promise to her deceased mother to keep her home together. Even after the home falls apart, Eveline feels that she must stay. On the surface, it is Eveline's tale of how and why she can not leave. Beneath the surface, the story is a metaphor for womens' conditions in turn-of-the-century Ireland. There are many factors that influence Eveline's decision, but the most compelling are religion, family, and fear of change.

There is not much to the story on the surface. It appears to be nothing more than the story of a girl who makes a bad decision, but Joyce has neatly interwoven a metaphor for what keeps Irish people in an idle state. He is using his story to point out how Irish people, especially women, let themselves be trapped. He does not entirely blame the individual, because conditions gave people a poor foundation to build on. Finally, when there is some certainty, they cling to it and are reluctant to change. This is the plight of Eveline.

In the 1890s, when this story was set, Ireland was still suffering the effects of the potato famine of the 1840s. Around this time, the country had lost millions of its people to starvation and emigration. The people left behind suffered many effects. "For a full century after 1845, poverty was widespread, jobs few and precarious, salaries meager, and opportunities for advancement rare" (Walzl 33). This was especially true for women, who were relegated to more traditional roles.

Lack of financial resources led people to put off marriage. Postponing marriages kept women with their families longer, causing them to become dependent on that lifestyle. As one becomes more devoted to family, the option of marriage becomes less likely. Eveline's chance to marry Frank, her fiancé, is important because it may be her only chance to marry and leave the country. By deciding not to marry Frank, she identifies herself as one woman who will not leave her homeland. In this sense, Eveline is representative of many of her fellow citizens. "Even when emigration had become established as an almost automatic part of rural life, it conflicted sharply with the high value that Irish country people put upon communalism, kinship and a sense of place. To leave here meant a psychic disruption" (Foster 351).

The story opens with Eveline sitting motionless, contemplating leaving the home she has known. After her mother's death, Eveline takes over her duties in the home and tends to her abusive father. "Growing up he had never gone for her, but latterly he had begun to threaten her" (Dubliners 38). Usually, his rage is about money and the idea that she squanders it. The truth is that after working at her job all week, she gives her wages to him, ultimately to support his drinking habits. A family that has a minimal income should treat alcohol as a luxury, yet "he was usually fairly bad of a Saturday night." (38).

This kind of life should create a fear of remaining at home, yet Eveline feels that the unknown is much more frightening. It is clear that her social paralysis is self-inflicted and reinforced by her beliefs. Perhaps it is the thought that her father cannot survive without her that keeps her from leaving. She expends herself and her earnings just to support him. In a way she is acting more like a wife or mother than like a daughter: "She had to work hard both in the house and at business" (37), but her marriage to Frank would change all that. He offers to take her to Buenos Aires, where she could live a comfortable life, but she finally chooses not to go with him because of her attachment to the life she has known. She is paralyzed by her fear of change and her devotion to her family.

During the scene that depicts her mother's final moments, when the promise to keep the home together is made, Eveline muses that her mother's life is a "life of common-place sacrifices closing in final craziness" (40). This describes Eveline's life as well. Her own commonplace sacrifice is staying in her home and tending to her father. To her, it is a necessary sacrifice for her family's sake not to take interest in her own future. Her final craziness happens when she tries to escape. In the final scene at the station, she "clutched the iron [railing] in frenzy" trying to hold on to the life she has known" (41).

Her decision could mark the end of her social existence. She will probably never have this kind of opportunity again. Even if the opportunity again were to arise she would most likely act the same way.

It is obvious that religion plays a role in Eveline's decision as well. In his description of her home, Joyce includes a "colored print of the promises made to Blessed Margaret Mary Alacoque" (37). This is a symbol of devotion to home and family in the Catholic church. The promises that are made by Jesus himself include, "I will establish peace in their homes. / I will comfort them in all their afflictions. / I will be their secure refuge during life, and above all in death" (Gifford 49). Joyce refers to this in his narration because Eveline's promise to her mother parallels these promises. He does this to show how religion only increases the guilt felt by someone who leaves home to make a life for herself. Since Eveline's promise was to keep her family together, it becomes impossible for her to leave. In the final scene, she stands at the station, unable to board the boat: "she prayed to God to direct her, to show her what was her duty" (40). It is clear that she feels it is her duty to stay at home and give up her only chance at starting a life of her own.

There is great emphasis on the promise that Eveline made to her mother, "to keep the home together as long as she could" (40). This might be seen, metaphorically, as the people of Ireland promising to stay together as long as possible because their own country has been taken from them. Weakened by the famine and exploited by the British, the country was in shambles. Although Ireland did not have control of its own government, the people maintained collective unity.

During this time, one of the country's worst periods, people depended on each other to survive. Afterward, the people had trouble getting back on their feet and relied mostly on religion to guide them. Joyce reacted against this. He felt that people should get out of Ireland and writes that "Ireland is the old sow that eats her farrow" (Portrait 220). He makes his feelings very clear in this story by drawing on Eveline's promise to her mother.

Throughout the story, Eveline is tormented by the thought of leaving her home and it ultimately consumes her. Her home life is not at all desirable, yet she stays. It is a condition often depicted by Joyce in his stories: "[Joyce] expresses the fragmentation experienced by individuals unable to rely on old certainties, whether religious, economic, or political" (Werner 27).

It is these certainties that Eveline and many others were unable to part with. Her faith and bond to her family helped instill a fear of change that, for her, is too great to overcome.

I know from my own experience that this is true. One of the main reasons that I still live at home is that I am dependent on the security and simplicity of being where I have always been. By living with what little family I have, I know that I will never go hungry or worry about where I will sleep. I know what is around every corner because I most likely put it there. I am also concerned about what will happen to my home and family when I am gone. There is always the proud fear that people cannot survive without me, and the belittling fear that I can't survive without them. Perhaps it is one or both of these fears that influence Eveline's actions and ultimately control them.

Works Cited

Foster, Roy F. Modern Ireland 1600-1972. London: Penguin, 1988.

Gifford, Don. Joyce Annotated. Calif.: University of California Press, 1982. 48-52.

Joyce, James. Dubliners. Text, Criticism, and Notes. ed. Robert Scholes and A. Walton Litz. New York: Penguin, 1969.

---. Portrait of the Artist as a Young Man. New York: Penguin, 1987.

Walzl, Florence L. "Dubliners: Women in Irish Society." Women in Joyce. Suzette Hanke and Elaine Unkless. Champaign-Urbana, Illinois: University of Illinois Press, 1982. 31-54.

Werner, Craig Hanson. Dubliners. A Student's Companion to the Stories. Robert Lecker. Boston: Twayne Publishers, 1988.

Exploring the Literature of Culture and Class: Options for Writing and Research

Some Options for Writing About Culture and Class

1. Consider the ways in which your culture and class have affected your life. Do any of the stories, poems, plays, or essays in this section remind you of your own experiences or the circumstances in your life?

Choose one or more of these works and write a response essay that compares your experience or circumstances with those in the literature.

2. Where we grew up, the social class and culture we grew up in, and similar factors can influence how we see the world and our response to literature. Based on these values, we may agree or disagree with what an author says or what characters say or do. So too, the ideas expressed about culture and class in literature may influence us and the formation of our values.

   Write an essay about the ways in which one or more works in this section either provoked a moral judgment on your part or helped you learn something.

3. In her book *Patterns of Culture,* anthropologist Ruth Benedict wrote: "From the moment of his birth the customs into which [an individual] is born shape his experience and behavior. By the time he can talk, he is the little creature of his culture."

   Consider this quote, and write an essay about how an author or a character is influenced by his or her culture in one or more works in this section.

4. In his 1859 book *Critique of Political Economy,* political and economic philosopher Karl Marx wrote: "It is not the consciousness of men that determines their existence, but on the contrary it is their social existence that determines their consciousness."

   Write about this quote as it affects the way a character or an author sees the world in one or more works in this section.

5. Choose a quote (or quotes) in the introduction to this section, "Culture and Class" (pp. 1104–1105) and pair it (or them) with one of the longer pieces in this section that either supports it or argues against it. For example, Matthew Arnold's comment about America as one middle class might be paired with Liliana Heker's "The Stolen Party," which might be seen as an argument against it. If we chose Karl Marx's statement about social existence determining consciousness, we might choose Luis Valdez's *Los Vendidos* to support it.

   Write an essay that compares or contrasts a quote (or quotes) from the introduction with a story, poem, play, or essay that supports or argues against it.

A Research Option

William Blake's poem "London," Luis Valdez's play *Los Vendidos,* and Frederick Douglass's essay "Learning to Read and Write" all have something important to say about the impact of culture and class. Each of these works, however, springs from a very different historical, social, or political context.

Expanding our exploration of literature to include the context in which these works were produced can be an enriching and enlightening experience. Choose one or more of these or other works in this section and write a research essay that includes secondary source material about the historical, social, or political background of the literature.

Collaboration: Writing and Revising with Your Peers

In addition to applying your own values and standards to writing about the literature in this section, you may find it beneficial to share and discuss your work with classmates. Getting feedback from others can help you generate and clarify your ideas and revise and edit your writing more effectively.

Choose a work, topic, or one of the options for writing about culture and class above, and work with a partner or in a small group. Exchange journal entries or response sheets, generate questions together, do a group semantic map (see pp. 41–44), or simply share and respond to each other's ideas.

After you have written a rough draft of your essay, share it with a partner or your group. Respondents should function primarily as sensitive readers and give honest, constructive responses. They should try to be aware of each writer's purpose, discuss concerns particular to each writer, and comment on the effectiveness of the essay's organization, support, clarity, and voice. (For a comprehensive checklist for revision, see p. 51).

In the final stage of your writing, editing and proofreading might be done in a similar fashion. A partner or group of readers might help you check for correct grammar, spelling, punctuation, and typos. (A comprehensive checklist for editing is on p. 52).

A Writing/Research Portfolio Option

A portfolio is a collection of your work, related materials, and commentary about your work collected over time. Gathering materials in a portfolio will provide you with resources for research and development. You can use your portfolio to collect your writing about the literature in this section, find a topic to write about, revise or add to your work, or keep multiple drafts and monitor the changes you make as you revise.

Among the resources you might include:

- Your responses to the quotes and prompts about culture and class at the beginning of this section, the questions you had right after you finished reading, each piece of literature, or your journal entries.
- What your classmates, instructor, or published critics had to say about the literature and how their comments may have influenced your interpretation.
- Information you've gathered from the library and the Internet about the historical, social, and political context of the work or its author.

Faith & Doubt

A Dialogue Across History

The life which is unexamined is not worth living.
—Plato, 428–348 B.C., *Symposium*

All men know the utility of useful things; but they do not know the utility of futility.
—Chuang-tzu, 369–286 B.C.

Make money, money by fair means if you can, if not, by any means money.
—Horace (Quintus Horatius Flaccus), The Epistles ca. 10 B.C.

The business of the samurai consists in reflecting on his own station in life, in discharging loyal service to his master if he has one, in deepening his fidelity in associations with friends, and with due consideration of his own position, in devoting himself to duty above all.
—Yamaga Soko, ca. 1650

The mind is always the dupe of the heart.
—Duke Francois de La Rochefoucauld, *Maxims*, 1665

Men never do evil so completely and cheerfully as when they do it from religious conviction.
—Blaise Pascal, *Pensees*, 1670

In the Affairs of this World, Men are saved not by Faith but by the want of it.
—Benjamin Franklin, *Poor Richard's Almanac*, 1757

Morality is not properly the doctrine of how we may make ourselves happy, but how we make ourselves worthy of happiness.
—Immanuel Kant, 1788

The only thing necessary for the triumph of evil is for good men to do nothing.
—Edmund Burke, c. 1800

Life can only be understood backwards; but it must be lived forwards.
—Soren Kierkegard, c. 1850

There lives more faith in honest doubt, / Believe me, than in half the creeds.
—Alfred Lord Tennyson, *In Memoriam,* 1850

The mass of men lead lives of quiet desperation.
—Henry David Thoreau, *Walden,* 1854

So long as man remains free he strives for nothing so incessantly and so painfully as to find someone to worship.
—Fedor Dostoevski, *The Brothers Karamazov,* 1879

Like all weak men he laid an exaggerated stress on not changing one's mind.
—Somerset Maugham, *Of Human Bondage,* 1915

The certainties of one age are the problems of the next.
—R. H. Tawney, *Religion and the Rise of Capitalism,* 1926

Truth has no special time of its own. Its hour is now—always.
—Albert Schweitzer, *Out of My Life and Thought,* 1949

Liberty is the possibility of doubting, the possibility of making a mistake, the possibility of searching and experimenting, the possibility of saying "No" to any authority—literary, artistic, philosophic, religious, social, and even political.
—Ignazio Silone, essay in *The God That Failed,* 1950

I cannot and will not cut my conscience to fit this year's fashions.
—Lillian Hellman, letter, 1952

We are born into a world where alienation awaits us.
—R. D. Laing, *The Politics of Experience,* 1967

We all want to know why. *Man is the asking animal. And while the finding, the belief that we have found the* Answer, *can separate us and make us forget our humanity, it is the seeking that continues to bring us together, that makes and keeps us human.*
—Daniel Boorstin, *The Seekers,* 1998

Faith and Doubt: Exploring Your Experiences and Beliefs

We all want something to believe in—something to give our lives meaning. But we seek and act out our beliefs in many different ways. Many people join communities that share a common religious, ethical, ethnic, or political belief. Others see individual conscience as the most important guide for their beliefs and actions.

The certainty of your beliefs can have an important influence on how you perceive the world. If you are deeply religious, that's probably at the heart of almost everything you value. If you are not religious, the nature of your experiences, the values you grew up with, influential people in your life, what you read, or other factors may strongly influence your perspective. Before you respond to the literature in this section, you may want to think about your own beliefs and/or doubts and how they affect your point of view.

Reading and Writing About Faith and Doubt

At least one aspect of the many stories, poems, plays, and essays in this section is concerned with the conflict of faith and doubt: young soldiers struggling to stay connected with life back home in the midst of the horror and absurdity of war in Tim O'Brien's story "The Things They Carried," the random senselessness of a boy's sudden death in Robert Frost's poem "Out, Out . . . ," and a disturbing look at perspective and truth in David Mamet's *Oleanna.* The brief quotes that open this section also give you some idea of the number of compelling ethical, political, and social arguments that are connected to faith and doubt. Religion, conscience, self-reflection, self-interest, and emotion versus intellect head a long list of concerns. Any of these or other related issues might provide a fine topic for an essay.

◆ FICTION ◆

Thomas Bulfinch (1796–1867)

Thomas Bulfinch was born in Newton, Massachusetts, the son of one of the most prominent architects of the time. During most of his life he worked as a clerk at the Merchant's Bank of Boston, a post that allowed him the leisure to pursue his many other interests, which included writing. His most enduring works are his three collections of myths and fables, The Age of Fables *(1855),* The Age of Chivalry *(1858), and* Legends of Charlemagne *(1863), which are now reprinted under the title*

Bulfinch's Mythology. *Bulfinch's approach to the ancient myths may seem dated by twentieth-century standards, but his learned and vigorous retellings of these tales remain timeless.*

THE MYTH OF DAEDALUS AND ICARUS [1855]

The labyrinth from which Theseus escaped, by means of the clew of Ariadne was built by Daedalus, a most skilful artificer. It was an edifice with numberless winding passages and turnings opening into one another, and seeming to have neither beginning nor end, like the river Maeander, which returns on itself, and flows now onward, now backward, in its course to the sea. Daedalus built the labyrinth for King Minos, but afterwards lost the favor of the king, and was shut up in a tower. He contrived to make his escape from his prison, but could not leave the island by sea, as the king kept strict watch on all the vessels, and permitted none to sail without being carefully searched. "Minos may control the land and sea," said Daedalus, "but not the regions of the air. I will try that way." So he set to work to fabricate wings for himself and his young son Icarus. He wrought feathers together, beginning with the smallest and adding larger, so as to form an increasing surface. The larger ones he secured with thread and the smaller with wax, and gave the whole a gentle curvature like the wings of a bird. Icarus, the boy, stood and looked on, sometimes running to gather up the feathers which the wind had blown away, and then handling the wax and working it over with his fingers, by his play impeding his father in his labors. When at last the work was done, the artist, waving his wings, found himself buoyed upward, and hung suspended, poising himself on the beaten air. He next equipped his son in the same manner, and taught him how to fly, as a bird tempts her young ones from the lofty nest into the air. When all was prepared for flight he said, "Icarus, my son, I charge you to keep at a moderate height, for if you fly too low the damp will clog your wings, and if too high the heat will melt them. Keep near me and you will be safe." While he gave him these instructions and fitted the wings to his shoulders, the face of the father was wet with tears, and his hands trembled. He kissed the boy, not knowing that it was for the last time. Then rising on his wings, he flew off, encouraging him to follow, and looked back from his own flight to see how his son managed his wings. As they flew the ploughman stopped his work to gaze, and the shepherd leaned on his staff and watched them, astonished at the sight, and thinking they were gods who could thus cleave the air.

They passed Samos and Delos on the left and Lebynthos on the right, when the boy, exulting in his career, began to leave the guidance of his companion and soar upward as if to reach heaven. The nearness of the blazing sun softened the wax which held the feathers together, and they came off. He fluttered with his arms, but no feathers remained to hold the air. While his mouth uttered cries to his father it was submerged in the blue waters of the sea, which thenceforth was called by his name. His father cried, "Icarus, Icarus, where are you?" At last he saw the feathers floating on the water, and bitterly lamenting his own arts, he buried the body and called the land Icaria in memory of his child. Daedalus arrived safe in Sicily where he built a Temple to Apollo, and hung up his wings, an offering to the gods.

➤ QUESTIONS FOR READING AND WRITING

1. Is there a lesson in this myth? Explain.
2. Daedalus warned Icarus about flying too high. Why does he bitterly lament his own arts?
3. Compare this myth with Brueghel's painting of it, *Landscape with the Fall of Icarus,* on page 1462. Does the painting capture what you felt after reading "The Myth of Daedalus and Icarus"?

RAYMOND CARVER (1933–1988)

Raymond Carver was born in Clatskanie, Oregon, and raised in Yakima, Washington. After working at a series of low-paying jobs, he entered Humboldt State University in 1963, where he first began to write poetry and short stories, and then went on to earn an M.F.A. from the University of Iowa in 1966. Usually set among working-class people, his stories, like "Cathedral," often hinge on moments of sudden insight. His collections include Put Yourself in My Shoes *(1974),* Will You Please Be Quiet, Please? *(1977),* What We Talk About When We Talk About Love *(1981),* Cathedral *(1984), and* Where I'm Calling from: New and Collected Stories *(1988). His stories inspired* Short Takes, *the critically acclaimed 1993 film directed by Robert Altman. Carver died of lung cancer in 1988. Unlike many writers who came of age in the 1970s, Carver did not see the writing of fiction as a political act: "It just has to be there for the pleasure we take in doing it, and the different kind of pleasure that's taken in reading something that's durable and made to last, as well as beautiful in and of itself. Something that throws off these sparks—a persistent and steady glow, however dim."*

CATHEDRAL

[1981]

This blind man, an old friend of my wife's, he was on his way to spend the night. His wife had died. So he was visiting the dead wife's relatives in Connecticut. He called my wife from his in-laws'. Arrangements were made. He would come by train, a five-hour trip, and my wife would meet him at the station. She hadn't seen him since she worked for him one summer in Seattle ten years ago. But she and the blind man had kept in touch. They made tapes and mailed them back and forth. I wasn't enthusiastic about his visit. He was no one I knew. And his being blind bothered me. My idea of blindness came from the movies. In the movies, the blind moved slowly and never laughed. Sometimes they were led by seeing-eye dogs. A blind man in my house was not something I looked forward to.

That summer in Seattle she had needed a job. She didn't have any money. The man she was going to marry at the end of the summer was in officers' training school. He didn't have any money, either. But she was in love with the guy, and he was in love with her, etc. She'd seen something in the paper: HELP WANTED—*Reading to Blind Man,* and a telephone number. She phoned and went over, was hired on the spot. She'd worked with this blind man all summer. She read stuff to him, case studies, reports, that sort of thing. She helped him organize his little office in the county social-service department. They'd become good friends, my wife and the blind man. How do I know these things? She told me. And she told me something else. On her last day in the office, the blind man asked if he could touch her face. She agreed to this. She told me he touched his fingers to every part of her face, her nose—even her neck! She never forgot it. She even tried to write a poem about it. She was always trying to write a poem. She wrote a poem or two every year, usually after something really important had happened to her.

When we first started going out together, she showed me the poem. In the poem, she recalled his fingers and the way they had moved around over her face. In the poem, she talked about what she had felt at the time, about what went through her mind when the blind man touched her nose and lips. I can remember I didn't think much of the poem. Of course, I didn't tell her that. Maybe I just don't understand poetry. I admit it's not the first thing I reach for when I pick up something to read.

Anyway, this man who'd first enjoyed her favors, the officer-to-be, he'd been her childhood sweetheart. So okay. I'm saying that at the end of the summer she let the blind man run his hands over her face, said goodbye to him, married her childhood etc., who was now a commissioned officer, and she moved away from Seattle. But they'd kept in touch, she and the blind man. She made the first contact after a year or so. She called him up one night from an Air Force base in Alabama. She wanted to talk. They talked. He asked her to send him a tape and tell him about her life. She did this. She sent the tape. On the tape, she told the blind man about her husband and about their life together in the military. She told the blind man she loved her husband but she didn't like it where they lived and she didn't like it that he was part of the military-industrial thing. She told the blind man she'd written a poem and he was in it. She told him that she was writing a poem about what it was like to be an Air Force officer's wife. The poem wasn't finished yet. She was still writing it. The blind man made a tape. He sent her the tape. She made a tape. This went on for years. My wife's officer was posted to one base and then another. She sent tapes from Moody AFB, McGuire, McConnell, and finally Travis, near Sacramento, where one night she got to feeling lonely and cut off from people she kept losing in that moving-around life. She got to feeling she couldn't go it another step. She went in and swallowed all the pills and capsules in the medicine chest and washed them down with a bottle of gin. Then she got into a hot bath and passed out.

5 But instead of dying, she got sick. She threw up. Her officer—why should he have a name? he was the childhood sweetheart, and what more does he want?—came home from somewhere, found her, and called the ambulance. In time, she put it all on a tape and sent the tape to the blind man. Over the years, she put all kinds of stuff on tapes and sent the tapes off lickety-split. Next to writing a poem every

year, I think it was her chief means of recreation. On one tape, she told the blind man she'd decided to live away from her officer for a time. On another tape, she told him about her divorce. She and I began going out, and of course she told her blind man about it. She told him everything, or so it seemed to me. Once she asked me if I'd like to hear the latest tape from the blind man. This was a year ago. I was on the tape, she said. So I said okay, I'd listen to it. I got us drinks and we settled down in the living room. We made ready to listen. First she inserted the tape into the player and adjusted a couple of dials. Then she pushed a lever. The tape squeaked and someone began to talk in this loud voice. She lowered the volume. After a few minutes of harmless chitchat, I heard my own name in the mouth of this stranger, this blind man I didn't even know! And then this: "From all you've said about him, I can only conclude—" But we were interrupted, a knock at the door, something, and we didn't ever get back to the tape. Maybe it was just as well. I'd heard all I wanted to.

Now this same blind man was coming to sleep in my house.

"Maybe I could take him bowling," I said to my wife. She was at the draining board doing scalloped potatoes. She put down the knife she was using and turned around.

"If you love me," she said, "you can do this for me. If you don't love me, okay. But if you had a friend, any friend, and the friend came to visit, I'd make him feel comfortable." She wiped her hands with the dish towel.

"I don't have any blind friends," I said.

10 "You don't have *any* friends," she said. "Period. Besides," she said, "goddamn it, his wife's just died! Don't you understand that? The man's lost his wife!"

I didn't answer. She'd told me a little about the blind man's wife. Her name was Beulah. Beulah! That's a name for a colored woman.

"Was his wife a Negro?" I asked.

"Are you crazy?" my wife said. "Have you just flipped or something?" She picked up a potato. I saw it hit the floor, then roll under the stove. "What's wrong with you?" she said. "Are you drunk?"

"I'm just asking," I said.

15 Right then my wife filled me in with more detail than I cared to know. I made a drink and sat at the kitchen table to listen. Pieces of the story began to fall into place.

Beulah had gone to work for the blind man the summer after my wife had stopped working for him. Pretty soon Beulah and the blind man had themselves a church wedding. It was a little wedding—who'd want to go to such a wedding in the first place?—just the two of them, plus the minister and the minister's wife. But it was a church wedding just the same. It was what Beulah had wanted, he'd said. But even then Beulah must have been carrying the cancer in her glands. After they had been inseparable for eight years—my wife's word, *inseparable* —Beulah's health went into rapid decline. She died in a Seattle hospital room, the blind man sitting beside the bed and holding on to her hand. They'd married, lived and worked together, slept together—had sex, sure—and then the blind man had to bury her. All this without his having ever seen what the goddamned woman looked like. It was beyond my understanding. Hearing this, I felt sorry for the blind man for a little bit. And then I found myself thinking what a pitiful life this woman must have led.

Imagine a woman who could never see herself as she was seen in the eyes of her loved one. A woman who could go on day after day and never receive the smallest compliment from her beloved. A woman whose husband could never read the expression on her face, be it misery or something better. Someone who could wear makeup or not—what difference to him? She could, if she wanted, wear green eyeshadow around one eye, a straight pin in her nostril, yellow slacks and purple shoes, no matter. And then to slip off into death, the blind man's hand on her hand, his blind eyes streaming tears—I'm imagining now—her last thought maybe this: that he never even knew what she looked like, and she on an express to the grave. Robert was left with a small insurance policy and half of a twenty-peso Mexican coin. The other half of the coin went into the box with her. Pathetic.

So when the time rolled around, my wife went to the depot to pick him up. With nothing to do but wait—sure, I blamed him for that—I was having a drink and watching the TV when I heard the car pull into the drive. I got up from the sofa with my drink and went to the window to have a look.

I saw my wife laughing as she parked the car. I saw her get out of the car and shut the door. She was still wearing a smile. Just amazing. She went around to the other side of the car to where the blind man was already starting to get out. This blind man, feature this, he was wearing a full beard! A beard on a blind man! Too much, I say. The blind man reached into the back seat and dragged out a suitcase. My wife took his arm, shut the car door, and, talking all the way, moved him down the drive and then up the steps to the front porch. I turned off the TV. I finished my drink, rinsed the glass, dried my hands. Then I went to the door.

My wife said, "I want you to meet Robert. Robert, this is my husband. I've told you all about him." She was beaming. She had this blind man by his coat sleeve.

20 The blind man let go of his suitcase and up came his hand.

I took it. He squeezed hard, held my hand, and then he let it go.

"I feel like we've already met," he boomed.

"Likewise," I said. I didn't know what else to say. Then I said, "Welcome. I've heard a lot about you." We began to move then, a little group, from the porch into the living room, my wife guiding him by the arm. The blind man was carrying his suitcase in his other hand. My wife said things like, "To your left here, Robert. That's right. Now watch it, there's a chair. That's it. Sit down right here. This is the sofa. We just bought this sofa two weeks ago."

I started to say something about the old sofa. I'd liked that old sofa. But I didn't say anything. Then I wanted to say something else, small-talk, about the scenic ride along the Hudson. How going *to* New York, you should sit on the right-hand side of the train, and coming *from* New York, the left-hand side.

25 "Did you have a good train ride?" I said. "Which side of the train did you sit on, by the way?"

"What a question, which side!" my wife said. "What's it matter which side?" she said.

"I just asked," I said.

"Right side," the blind man said. "I hadn't been on a train in nearly forty years. Not since I was a kid. With my folks. That's been a long time. I'd nearly forgotten the sensation. I have winter in my beard now," he said. "So I've been told, anyway. Do I look distinguished, my dear?" the blind man said to my wife.

"You look distinguished, Robert," she said. "Robert," she said. "Robert, it's just so good to see you."

30 My wife finally took her eyes off the blind man and looked at me. I had the feeling she didn't like what she saw. I shrugged.

I've never met, or personally known, anyone who was blind. This blind man was late forties, a heavy-set, balding man with stooped shoulders, as if he carried a great weight there. He wore brown slacks, brown shoes, a light-brown shirt, a tie, a sports coat. Spiffy. He also had this full beard. But he didn't use a cane and he didn't wear dark glasses. I'd always thought dark glasses were a must for the blind. Fact was, I wished he had a pair. At first glance, his eyes looked like anyone else's eyes. But if you looked close, there was something different about them. Too much white in the iris, for one thing, and the pupils seemed to move around in the sockets without his knowing it or being able to stop it. Creepy. As I stared at his face, I saw the left pupil turn in toward his nose while the other made an effort to keep in one place. But it was only an effort, for that eye was on the roam without his knowing it or wanting it to be.

I said, "Let me get you a drink. What's your pleasure? We have a little of everything. It's one of our pastimes."

"Bub. I'm a Scotch man myself," he said fast enough in this big voice.

"Right," I said. Bub! "Sure you are. I knew it."

35 He let his fingers touch his suitcase, which was sitting alongside the sofa. He was taking his bearings. I didn't blame him for that.

"I'll move that up to your room," my wife said.

"No, that's fine," the blind man said loudly. "It can go up when I go up."

"A little water with the Scotch?" I said.

"Very little," he said.

40 "I knew it." I said.

He said, "Just a tad. The Irish actor, Barry Fitzgerald? I'm like that fellow. When I drink water, Fitzgerald said, I drink water. When I drink whiskey, I drink whiskey." My wife laughed. The blind man brought his hand up under his beard. He lifted his beard slowly and let it drop.

I did the drinks, three big glasses of Scotch with a splash of water in each. Then we made ourselves comfortable and talked about Robert's travels. First the long flight from the West Coast to Connecticut, we covered that. Then from Connecticut up here by train. We had another drink concerning that leg of the trip.

I remembered having read somewhere that the blind didn't smoke because, as speculation had it, they couldn't see the smoke they exhaled. I thought I knew that much and that much only about blind people. But this blind man smoked his cigarette down to the nubbin and then lit another one. This blind man filled his ashtray and my wife emptied it.

When we sat down at the table for dinner, we had another drink. My wife heaped Robert's plate with cube steak, scalloped potatoes, green beans. I buttered him up two slices of bread. I said, "Here's bread and butter for you." I swallowed some of my drink. "Now let us pray," I said, and the blind man lowered his head. My wife looked at me, her mouth agape. "Pray the phone won't ring and the food doesn't get cold," I said.

45 We dug in. We ate everything there was to eat on the table. We ate like there was no tomorrow. We didn't talk. We ate. We scarfed. We grazed that table. We were into serious eating. The blind man had right away located his foods, he knew just where everything was on his plate. I watched with admiration as he used his knife and fork on the meat. He'd cut two pieces of meat, fork the meat into his mouth and then go all out for the scalloped potatoes, the beans next, and then he'd tear off a hunk of buttered bread and eat that. He'd follow this up with a big drink of milk. It didn't seem to bother him to use his fingers once in a while, either.

We finished everything, including half a strawberry pie. For a few moments, we sat as if stunned. Sweat beaded on our faces. Finally, we got up from the table and left the dirty plates. We didn't look back. We took ourselves into the living room and sank into our places again. Robert and my wife sat on the sofa. I took the big chair. We had us two or three more drinks while they talked about the major things that had come to pass for them in the past ten years. For the most part, I just listened. Now and then I joined in. I didn't want him to think I'd left the room, and I didn't want her to think I was feeling left out. They talked of things that had happened to them—to them—these past ten years. I waited in vain to hear my name on my wife's sweet lips: "And then my dear husband came into my life"—something like that. But I heard nothing of the sort. More talk of Robert. Robert had done a little of everything, it seemed, a regular blind jack-of-all-trades. But most recently he and his wife had had an Amway distributorship, from which, I gathered, they'd earned their living, such as it was. The blind man was also a ham radio operator. He talked in his loud voice about conversations he'd had with fellow operators in Guam, in the Philippines, in Alaska, and even in Tahiti. He said he'd have a lot of friends there if he ever wanted to go visit those places. From time to time, he'd turn his blind face toward me, put his hand under his beard, ask me something. How long had I been in my present position? (Three years.) Did I like my work? (I didn't.) Was I going to stay with it? (What were the options?) Finally, when I thought he was beginning to run down, I got up and turned on the TV.

My wife looked at me with irritation. She was heading toward a boil. Then she looked at the blind man and said, "Robert, do you have a TV?"

The blind man said, "My dear, I have two TVs. I have a color set and a black-and-white thing, an old relic. It's funny, but if I turn the TV on, and I'm always turning it on, I turn on the color set. It's funny, don't you think?"

I didn't know what to say to that. I had absolutely nothing to say to that. No opinion. So I watched the news program and tried to listen to what the announcer was saying.

50 "This is a color TV," the blind man said. "Don't ask me how, but I can tell."

"We traded up a while ago," I said.

The blind man had another taste of his drink. He lifted his beard, sniffed it, and let it fall. He leaned forward on the sofa. He positioned his ashtray on the coffee table, then put the lighter to his cigarette. He leaned back on the sofa and crossed his legs at the ankles.

My wife covered her mouth, and then she yawned. She stretched. She said. "I think I'll go upstairs and put on my robe. I think I'll change into something else. Robert, you make yourself comfortable," she said.

"I'm comfortable," the blind man said.

55 "I want you to feel comfortable in this house," she said.

"I am comfortable," the blind man said.

After she'd left the room, he and I listened to the weather report and then to the sports roundup. By that time, she'd been gone so long I didn't know if she was going to come back. I thought she might have gone to bed. I wished she'd come back downstairs. I didn't want to be left alone with a blind man. I asked him if he wanted another drink, and he said sure. Then I asked if he wanted to smoke some dope with me. I said I'd just rolled a number. I hadn't, but I planned to do so in about two shakes. "I'll try some with you," he said.

"Damn right," I said. "That's the stuff."

I got our drinks and sat down on the sofa with him. Then I roll us two fat numbers. I lit one and passed it. I brought it to his fingers. He took it and inhaled.

60 "Hold it as long as you can," I said. I could tell he didn't know the first thing.

My wife came back downstairs wearing her pink robe and her pink slippers.

"What do I smell?" she said.

"We thought we'd have us some cannabis," I said.

My wife gave me a savage look. Then she looked at the blind man and said, "Robert, I didn't know you smoked."

65 He said, "I do now, my dear. There's a first time for everything. But I don't feel anything yet."

"This stuff is pretty mellow," I said. "This stuff is mild. It's dope you can reason with," I said. "It doesn't mess you up."

"Not much it doesn't, bub," he said, and laughed.

My wife sat on the sofa between the blind man and me. I passed her the number. She took it and toked and then passed it back to me. "Which way is this going?" she said. Then she said, "I shouldn't be smoking this. I can hardly keep my eyes open as it is. That dinner did me in. I shouldn't have eaten so much."

"It was the strawberry pie," the blind man said. "That's what did it," he said, and he laughed his big laugh. Then he shook his head.

70 "There's more strawberry pie," I said.

"Do you want some more, Robert?" my wife said.

"Maybe in a little while," he said.

We gave our attention to the TV. My wife yawned again. She said, "Your bed is made up when you feel like going to bed, Robert. I know you must have had a long day. When you're ready to go to bed, say so." She pulled his arm. "Robert?"

He came to and said, "I've had a real nice time. This beats tapes, doesn't it?"

75 I said, "Coming at you," and I put the number between his fingers. He inhaled, held the smoke, and then let it go. It was like he'd been doing it since he was nine years old.

"Thanks, bub," he said. "But I think this is all for me. I think I'm beginning to feel it," he said. He held the burning roach out for my wife.

"Same here," she said. "Ditto. Me, too." She took the roach and passed it to me. "I may just sit here for a while between you two guys with my eyes closed. But don't let me bother you, okay? Either one of you. If it bothers you, say so. Otherwise, I may just sit here with my eyes closed until you're ready to go to bed," she said. "Your bed's made up, Robert, when you're ready. It's right next to our room at the top of the stairs. We'll show you up when you're ready. You wake me up now, you guys, if I fall asleep." She said that and then she closed her eyes and went to sleep.

The news program ended. I got up and changed the channel. I sat back down on the sofa. I wished my wife hadn't pooped out. Her head lay across the back of the sofa, her mouth open. She'd turned so that her robe had slipped away from her legs, exposing a juicy thigh. I reached to draw her robe back over her, and it was then that I glanced at the blind man. What the hell! I flipped the robe open again.

"You say when you want some strawberry pie," I said.

80 "I will," he said.

I said, "Are you tired? Do you want me to take you up to your bed? Are you ready to hit the hay?"

"Not yet," he said. "No, I'll stay up with you bub. If that's all right. I'll stay up until you're ready to turn in. We haven't had a chance to talk. Know what I mean? I feel like me and her monopolized the evening." He lifted his beard and he let it fall. He picked up his cigarettes and his lighter.

"That's all right," I said. Then I said, "I'm glad for the company."

And I guess I was. Every night I smoked dope and stayed up as long as I could before I fell asleep. My wife and I hardly ever went to bed at the same time. When I did go to sleep, I had these dreams. Sometimes I'd wake up from one of them, my heart going crazy.

85 Something about the church and the Middle Ages was on the TV. Not your run-of-the-mill TV fare. I wanted to watch something else. I turned to the other channels. But there was nothing on them, either. So I turned back to the first channel and apologized.

"Bub, it's all right," the blind man said. "It's fine with me. Whatever you want to watch is okay. I'm always learning something. Learning never ends. It won't hurt me to learn something tonight. I got ears," he said.

We didn't say anything for a time. He was leaning forward with his head turned at me, his right ear aimed in the direction of the set. Very disconcerting. Now and then his eyelids drooped and then they snapped open again. Now and then he put his fingers into his beard and tugged, like he was thinking about something he was hearing on the television.

On the screen, a group of men wearing cowls was being set upon and tormented by men dressed in skeleton costumes and men dressed as devils. The men dressed as devils wore devil masks, horns, and long tails. This pageant was part of a procession. The Englishman who was narrating the thing said it took place in Spain once a year. I tried to explain to the blind man what was happening.

"Skeletons," he said. "I know about skeletons," he said, and he nodded.

90 The TV showed this one cathedral. Then there was a long, slow look at another one. Finally, the picture switched to the famous one in Paris, with its flying buttresses

and its spires reaching up to the clouds. The camera pulled away to show the whole of the cathedral rising above the skyline.

There were times when the Englishman who was telling the thing would shut up, would simply let the camera move around over the cathedrals. Or else the camera would tour the countryside, men in fields walking behind oxen. I waited as long as I could. Then I felt I had to say something. I said, "They're showing the outside of this cathedral now, Gargoyles. Little statues carved to look like monsters. Now I guess they're in Italy. Yeah, they're in Italy. There's paintings on the walls of this one church."

"Are those fresco paintings, bub?" he asked, and he sipped from his drink.

I reached for my glass. But it was empty. I tried to remember what I could remember. "You're asking me are those frescoes?" I said. "That's a good question. I don't know."

The camera moved to a cathedral outside Lisbon. The differences in the Portuguese cathedral compared with the French and Italian were not that great. But they were there. Mostly the interior stuff. Then something occurred to me, and I said, "Something has occurred to me. Do you have any idea what a cathedral is? What they look like, that is? Do you follow me? If somebody says cathedral to you, do you have any notion what they're talking about? Do you know the difference between that and a Baptist church, say?"

He let the smoke dribble from his mouth. "I know they took hundreds of workers fifty or a thousand years to build," he said. "I just heard the man say that, of course. I know generations of the same families worked on a cathedral. I heard him say that, too. The men who began their life's work on them, they never lived to see the completion of their work. In that wise, bub, they're no different from the rest of us, right?" He laughed. Then his eyelids drooped again. His head nodded. He seemed to be snoozing. Maybe he was imagining himself in Portugal. The TV was showing another cathedral now. This one was in Germany. The Englishman's voice droned on. "Cathedrals," the blind man said. He sat up and rolled his head back and forth. "If you want the truth, bub, that's about all I know. What I just said. What I heard him say. But maybe you could describe one to me? I wish you'd do it. I'd like that. If you want to know, I really don't have a good idea."

I stared hard at the shot of the cathedral on the TV. How could I even begin to describe it? But say my life depended on it. Say my life was being threatened by an insane guy who said I had to do it or else.

I stared some more at the cathedral before the picture flipped off into the countryside. There was no use. I turned to the blind man and said, "To begin with, they're very tall." I was looking around the room for clues. "They reach way up. Up and up. Toward the sky. They're so big, some of them, they have to have these supports. To help hold them up, so to speak. These supports are called buttresses. They remind me of viaducts, for some reason. But maybe you don't know viaducts, either? Sometimes the cathedrals have devils and such carved into the front. Sometimes lords and ladies. Don't ask me why this is," I said.

He was nodding. The whole upper part of his body seemed to be moving back and forth.

"I'm not doing so good, am I?" I said.

100 He stopped nodding and leaned forward on the edge of the sofa. As he listened to me, he was running his fingers through his beard. I wasn't getting through to him, I could see that. But he waited for me to go on just the same. He nodded, like he was trying to encourage me. I tried to think what else to say. "They're really big," I said. "They're massive. They're built of stone. Marble, too, sometimes. In those olden days, when they built cathedrals, men wanted to be close to God. In those olden days, God was an important part of everyone's life. You could tell this from their cathedral-building. I'm sorry," I said, "but it looks like that's the best I can do for you. I'm just no good at it."

"That's all right, bub," the blind man said. "Hey, listen. I hope you don't mind my asking you. Can I ask you something? Let me ask you a simple question, yes or no. I'm just curious and there's no offense. You're my host. But let me ask if you are in any way religious? You don't mind my asking?"

I shook my head. He couldn't see that, though. A wink is the same as a nod to a blind man. "I guess I don't believe in it. In anything. Sometimes it's hard. You know what I'm saying?"

"Sure, I do," he said.

"Right," I said.

105 The Englishman was still holding forth. My wife sighed in her sleep. She drew a long breath and went on with her sleeping.

"You'll have to forgive me," I said. "But I can't tell you what a cathedral looks like. It just isn't in me to do it. I can't do any more than I've done."

The blind man sat very still, his head down, as he listened to me.

I said, "The truth is, cathedrals don't mean anything special to me. Nothing. Cathedrals. They're something to look at on late-night TV. That's all they are."

It was then that the blind man cleared his throat. He brought something up. He took a handkerchief from his back pocket. Then he said, "I get it, bub. It's okay. It happens. Don't worry about it," he said. "Hey, listen to me. Will you do me a favor? I got an idea. Why don't you find us some heavy paper? And a pen. We'll do something. We'll draw one together. Get us a pen and some heavy paper. Go on, bub, get the stuff," he said.

110 So I went upstairs. My legs felt like they didn't have any strength in them. They felt like they did after I'd done some running. In my wife's room, I looked around. I found some ballpoints in a little basket on her table. And then I tried to think where to look for the kind of paper he was talking about.

Downstairs, in the kitchen, I found a shopping bag with onion skins in the bottom of the bag. I emptied the bag and shook it. I brought it into the living room and sat down with it near his legs. I moved some things, smoothed the wrinkles from the bag, spread it out on the coffee table.

The blind man got down from the sofa and sat next to me on the carpet.

He ran his fingers over the paper. He went up and down the sides of the paper. The edges, even the edges. He fingered the corners.

"All right," he said. "All right, let's do her."

115 He found my hand, the hand with the pen. He closed his hand over my hand. "Go ahead, bub, draw," he said. "Draw. You'll see. I'll follow along with you. It'll be okay. Just begin now like I'm telling you. You'll see. Draw," the blind man said.

So I began. First I drew a box that looked like a house. It could have been the house I lived in. Then I put a roof on it. At either end of the roof, I drew spires. Crazy.

"Swell," he said. "Terrific. You're doing fine," he said. "Never thought anything like this could happen in your lifetime, did you, bub? Well, it's a strange life, we all know that. Go on now. Keep it up."

I put in windows with arches. I drew flying buttresses. I hung great doors. I couldn't stop. The TV station went off the air. I put down the pen and closed and opened my fingers. The blind man felt around over the paper. He moved the tips of his fingers over the paper, all over what I had drawn, and he nodded.

"Doing fine," the blind man said.

I took up the pen again, and he found my hand. I kept at it. I'm no artist. But I kept drawing just the same.

My wife opened up her eyes and gazed at us. She sat up on the sofa, her robe hanging open. She said, "What are you doing? Tell me, I want to know."

I didn't answer her.

The blind man said, "We're drawing a cathedral. Me and him are working on it. Press hard," he said to me. "That's right. That's good," he said. "Sure. You got it, bub, I can tell. You didn't think you could. But you can, can't you? You're cooking with gas now. You know what I'm saying? We're going to really have us something here in a minute. How's the old arm?" he said. "Put some people in there now. What's a cathedral without people?"

My wife said, "What's going on? Robert, what are you doing? What's going on?"

"It's all right," he said to her. "Close your eyes now," the blind man said to me.

I did it. I closed them just like he said.

"Are they closed?" he said. "Don't fudge."

"They're closed," I said.

"Keep them that way," he said. he said, "Don't stop now. Draw."

So we kept on with it. His fingers rode my fingers as my hand went over the paper. It was like nothing else in my life up to now.

Then he said, "I think that's it. I think you got it," he said. "Take a look. What do you think?"

But I had my eyes closed. I thought I'd keep them that way for a little longer. I thought it was something I ought to do.

"Well?" he said. "Are you looking?"

My eyes were still closed. I was in my house. I knew that. But I didn't feel like I was inside anything.

"It's really something," I said.

➤ *QUESTIONS FOR READING AND WRITING*

1. Why does the narrator consistently refer to Robert as "the blind man?" Why doesn't he use his name?
2. The narrator states, "A blind man in my house was not something I looked forward to." What does the narrator have against blind people? Or do you

think he objects to something specific about Robert? If so, what might that be?

3. How does the wife's relationship with her husband differ from her relationship with Robert? It there anything that Robert offers her that her husband doesn't?
4. Are there things you need to see to understand? What do you think contributes more to understanding: seeing or experiencing? Explain.
5. Does Robert learn what a cathedral is in this story? Prior to their drawing together, does the narrator know much more about cathedrals than Robert does? What does the narrator learn to "see?"

STEPHEN CRANE (1871–1900)

Stephen Crane was the youngest of fourteen children born to a Methodist minister in Newark, New Jersey. After briefly attending LaFayette College and Syracuse University, Crane moved to New York City to work as a freelance journalist. He lived a bohemian (and often impoverished) existence and came to know life in the slums firsthand. These experiences inspired his first novel, Maggie, a Girl on the Streets, *which he published at his own expense under a pseudonym. While not widely read due to its realistic language, which was considered shocking at the time, the novel impressed members of New York's literary elite, setting the stage for the publication of his second novel,* The Red Badge of Courage *(1895). The story of a young man's initiation into the horrors of war, the book was hailed for its realism—all that more remarkable because Crane had never been in a battle—and catapulted Crane into literary prominence. Also in 1895, Crane published a book of short poems,* The Black Riders, and Other Line, *which would later prove influential but went largely unnoticed until after his death. For the rest of his short life, Crane continued working as a journalist while producing a series of masterful short stories, including "The Open Boat" (1898) and "The Blue Hotel" (1899), as well as four less-regarded novels and another collection of poetry,* War Is Kind *(1899). Plagued by ill-health and growing financial difficulties, Crane died of tuberculosis when he was only twenty-eight. "The Open Boat" is based on Crane's real-life experiences: in 1897, he was on assignment on a ship bound for Cuba that sank off the coast of Florida. Crane and four other men spent thirty hours in a dinghy before finally reaching the shore.*

THE OPEN BOAT

[1898]

A Tale Intended to be after the Fact, Being the Experience of Four Men from the Sunk Steamer COMMODORE

I

None of them knew the color of the sky. Their eyes glanced level, and were fastened upon the waves that swept toward them. These waves were of the hue of slate, save for the tops, which were of foaming white, and all of the men knew the colors of the sea. The horizon narrowed and widened, and dipped and rose, and at all times its edge was jagged with waves that seemed thrust up in points like rocks.

Many a man ought to have a bath-tub larger than the boat which here rode upon the sea. These waves were most wrongfully and barbarously abrupt and tall, and each froth-top was a problem in small-boat navigation.

The cook squatted in the bottom, and looked with both eyes at the six inches of gunwale which separated him from the ocean. His sleeves were rolled over his fat forearms, and the two flaps of his unbuttoned vest dangled as he bent to bail out the boat. Often he said, "Gawd! that was a narrow clip." As he remarked it he invariably gazed eastward over the broken sea.

The oiler, steering with one of the two oars in the boat sometimes raised himself suddenly to keep clear of water that swirled in over the stern. It was a thin little oar, and it seemed often ready to snap.

5 The correspondent, pulling at the other oar, watched the waves and wondered why he was there.

The injured captain, lying in the bow, was at this time buried in that profound dejection and indifference which comes, temporarily at least, to even the bravest and most enduring when, willy-nilly, the firm fails, the army loses, the ship goes down. The mind of the master of a vessel is rooted deep in the timbers of her, though he command for a day or a decade, and this captain had on him the stern impression of a scene in the grays of dawn of seven turned faces, and later a stump of a top-mast with a white ball on it that slashed to and fro at the waves, went low and lower, and down. Thereafter there was something strange in his voice. Although steady, it was deep with mourning, and of a quality beyond oration or tears.

"Keep 'er a little more south, Billie," said he.

"A little more south, sir," said the oiler in the stern.

A seat in this boat was not unlike a seat upon a bucking broncho, and, by the same token, a broncho is not much smaller. The craft pranced and reared, and plunged like an animal. As each wave came, and she rose for it, she seemed like a horse making at a fence outrageously high. The manner of her scramble over these walls of water is a mystic thing, and, moreover, at the top of them were ordinarily these problems in white water, the foam racing down from the summit of each wave, requiring a new leap, and a leap from the air. Then, after scornfully bumping a crest, she would slide, and race, and splash down a long incline and arrive bobbing and nodding in front of the next menace.

10 A singular disadvantage of the sea lies in the fact that after successfully surmounting one wave you discover that there is another behind it just as important and just as nervously anxious to do something effective in the way of swamping boats. In a ten-foot dinghy one can get an idea of the resources of the sea in the line of waves that is not probable to the average experience, which is never at sea in a dinghy. As each slaty wall of water approached, it shut all else from the view of the men in the boat, and it was not difficult to imagine that this particular wave was the final outburst of the ocean, the last effort of the grim water. There was a terrible

grace in the move of the waves, and they came in silence, save for the snarling of the crests.

In the wan light, the faces of the men must have been gray. Their eyes must have glinted in strange ways as they gazed steadily astern. Viewed from a balcony, the whole thing would doubtless have been weirdly picturesque. But the men in the boat had no time to see it, and if they had had leisure there were other things to occupy their minds. The sun swung steadily up the sky, and they knew it was broad day because the color of the sea changed from slate to emerald-green, streaked with amber lights, and the foam was like tumbling snow. The process of the breaking day was unknown to them. They were aware only of this effect upon the color of the waves that rolled toward them.

In disjointed sentences the cook and the correspondent argued as to the difference between a life-saving station and a house of refuge. The cook had said: "There's a house of refuge just north of the Mosquito Inlet Light, and as soon as they see us, they'll come off in their boat and pick us up."

"As soon as who see us?" said the correspondent.

"The crew," said the cook.

15 "Houses of refuge don't have crews," said the correspondent. "As I understand them, they are only places where clothes and grub are stored for the benefit of shipwrecked people. They don't carry crews."

"Oh, yes, they do," said the cook.

"No, they don't," said the correspondent.

"Well, we're not there yet, anyhow," said the oiler, in the stern.

"Well," said the cook, "perhaps it's not a house of refuge that I'm thinking of as being near Mosquito Inlet Light; perhaps it's a life-saving station."

20 "We're not there yet," said the oiler, in the stern.

II

As the boat bounced from the top of each wave, the wind tore through the hair of the hatless men, and as the craft plopped her stern down again the spray slashed past them. The crest of each of these waves was a hill, from the top of which the men surveyed, for a moment, a broad tumultuous expanse, shining and wind-driven. It was probably splendid. It was probably glorious, this play of the free sea, wild with lights of emerald and white and amber.

"Bully good thing it's an on-shore wind," said the cook. "If not where would we be? Wouldn't have a show."

"That's right," said the correspondent.

The busy oiler nodded his assent.

25 Then the captain, in the bow, chuckled in a way that expressed humor, contempt, tragedy, all in one. "Do you think we've got a show now, boys?" said he.

Whereupon the three were silent, save for a trifle of hemming and hawing. To express any particular optimism at this time they felt to be childish and stupid, but they all doubtless possessed this sense of the situation in their minds. A young man thinks doggedly at such times. On the other hand, the ethics of their condition was decidedly against any open suggestion of hopelessness. So they were silent.

"Oh, well," said the captain, soothing his children, "we'll get ashore all right."

But there was that in his tone which made them think, so the oiler quoth, "Yes! if this wind holds."

The cook was bailing. "Yes! if we don't catch hell in the surf."

Canton flannel gulls flew near and far. Sometimes they sat down on the sea, near patches of brown sea-weed that rolled over the waves with a movement like carpets on a line in a gale. The birds sat comfortably in groups, and they were envied by some in the dinghy, for the wrath of the sea was no more to them than it was to a covey of prairie chickens a thousand miles inland. Often they came very close and stared at the men with black bead-like eyes. At these times they were uncanny and sinister in their unblinking scrutiny, and the men hooted angrily at them, telling them to be gone. One came, and evidently decided to alight on the top of the captain's head. The bird flew parallel to the boat and did not circle, but made short sidelong jumps in the air in chicken-fashion. His black eyes were wistfully fixed upon the captain's head. "Ugly brute," said the oiler to the bird. "You look as if you were made with a jacknife." The cook and the correspondent swore darkly at the creature. The captain naturally wished to knock it away with the end of the heavy painter, but he did not dare do it, because anything resembling an emphatic gesture would have capsized this freighted boat, and so with his open hand, the captain gently and carefully waved the gull away. After it had been discouraged from the pursuit the captain breathed easier on account of his hair, and others breathed easier because the bird struck their minds at this time as being somehow gruesome and ominous.

In the meantime the oiler and the correspondent rowed. And also they rowed.

They sat together in the same seat, and each rowed an oar. Then the oiler took both oars; then the correspondent took both oars; then the oiler; then the correspondent. They rowed and they rowed. The very ticklish part of the business was when the time came for the reclining one in the stern to take his turn at the oars. By the very last star of truth, it is easier to steal eggs from under a hen than it was to change seats in the dinghy. First the man in the stern slid his hand along the thwart and moved with care, as if he were of Sèvres. Then the man in the rowing seat slid his hand along the other thwart. It was all done with the most extraordinary care. As the two sidled past each other, the whole party kept watchful eyes on the coming wave, and the captain cried: "Look out, now! Steady, there!"

The brown mats of sea-weed that appeared from time to time were like islands, bits of earth. They were traveling, apparently, neither one way nor the other. They were, to all intents, stationary. They informed the men in the boat that it was making progress slowly toward the land.

The captain, rearing cautiously in the bow, after the dinghy soared on a great swell, said that he had seen the light-house at Mosquito Inlet. Presently the cook remarked that he had seen it. The correspondent was at the oars, then, and for some reason he too wished to look at the light-house; but his back was toward the far shore and the waves were important, and for some time he could not seize an opportunity to turn his head. But at last there came a wave more gentle than the others, and when at the crest of it he swiftly scoured the western horizon.

"See it?" said the captain.

"No," said the correspondent, slowly; "I didn't see anything."

"Look again," said the captain. He pointed. "It's exactly in that direction."

At the top of another wave, the correspondent did as he was bid, and this time his eyes chanced on a small still thing on the edge of the swaying horizon. It was precisely like the point of a pin. It took an anxious eye to find a light-house so tiny.

"Think we'll make it, Captain?"

"If this wind holds and the boat don't swamp, we can't do much else," said the captain.

The little boat, lifted by each towering sea, and splashed viciously by the crests, made progress that in the absence of sea-weed was not apparent to those in her. She seemed just a wee thing wallowing, miraculously top up, at the mercy of five oceans. Occasionally a great spread of water, like white flames, swarmed into her.

"Bail her, cook," said the captain, serenely.

"All right, Captain," said the cheerful cook.

III

It would be difficult to describe the subtle brotherhood of men that was here established on the seas. No one said that it was so. No one mentioned it. But it dwelt in the boat, and each man felt it warm him. They were a captain, an oiler, a cook, and a correspondent, and they were friends, friends in a more curiously iron-bound degree than may be common. The hurt captain, lying against the water-jar in the bow, spoke always in a low voice and calmly, but he could never command a more ready and swiftly obedient crew than the motley three of the dinghy. It was more than a mere recognition of what was best for the common safety. There was surely in it a quality that was personal and heartfelt. And after this devotion to the commander of the boat there was this comradeship that the correspondent, for instance, who had been taught to be cynical of men, knew even at the time was the best experience of his life. But no one said that it was so. No one mentioned it.

"I wish we had a sail," remarked the captain. "We might try my overcoat on the end of an oar, and give you two boys a chance to rest." So the cook and the correspondent held the mast and spread wide the overcoat. The oiler steered, and the little boat made good way with her new rig. Sometimes the oiler had to scull sharply to keep a sea from breaking into the boat, but otherwise sailing was a success.

Meanwhile the light-house had been growing slowly larger. It had now almost assumed color, and appeared like a little gray shadow on the sky. The man at the oars could not be prevented from turning his head rather often to try for a glimpse of this little gray shadow.

At last, from the top of each wave, the men in the tossing boat could see land. Even as the light-house was an upright shadow on the sky, this land seemed but a long black shadow on the sea. It certainly was thinner than paper. "We must be about opposite New Smyrna," said the cook, who had coasted this shore often in schooners. "Captain, by the way, I believe they abandoned that life-saving station there about a year ago."

"Did they?" said the captain.

The wind slowly died away. The cook and the correspondent were not now obliged to slave in order to hold high the oar. But the waves continued their old impetuous swooping at the dinghy, and the little craft, no longer under way, struggled woundily over them. The oiler or the correspondent took the oars again.

Shipwrecks are *apropos* of nothing. If men could only train for them and have them occur when the men had reached pink condition, there would be less drowning at sea. Of the four in the dinghy none had slept any time worth mentioning for two days and two nights previous to embarking in the dinghy, and in the excitement of clambering about the deck of a foundering ship they had also forgotten to eat heartily.

For these reasons, and for others, neither the oiler nor the correspondent was fond of rowing at this time. The correspondent wondered ingenuously how in the name of all that was sane could there be people who thought it amusing to row a boat. It was not an amusement; it was a diabolical punishment, and even a genius of mental aberrations could never conclude that it was anything but a horror to the muscles and crime against the back. He mentioned to the boat in general how the amusement of rowing struck him, and the weary-faced oiler smiled in full sympathy. Previously to the foundering, by the way, the oiler had worked double-watch in the engine-room of the ship.

"Take her easy now, boys," said the captain. "Don't spend yourselves. If we have to run a surf you'll need all your strength, because we'll sure have to swim for it. Take your time."

Slowly the land arose from the sea. From a black line it became a line of black and a line of white—trees and sand. Finally, the captain said that he could make out a house on the shore. "That's the house of refuge, sure," said the cook. "They'll see us before long, and come out after us."

The distant light-house reared high. "The keeper ought to be able to make us out now, if he's looking through a glass," said the captain. "He'll notify the life-saving people."

"None of those other boats could have got ashore to give word of the wreck," said the oiler, in a low voice. "Else the life-boat would be out hunting us."

Slowly and beautifully the land loomed out of the sea. The wind came again. It had veered from the northeast to the southeast. Finally a new sound struck the ears of the men in the boat. It was the low thunder of the surf on the shore. "We'll never be able to make the light-house now," said the captain. "Swing her head a little more north, Billie."

"'A little more north,' sir," said the oiler.

Whereupon the little boat turned her nose once more down the wind, and all but the oarsman watched the shore grow. Under the influence of this expansion doubt and direful apprehension were leaving the minds of the men. The management of the boat was still most absorbing, but it could not prevent a quiet cheerfulness. In an hour, perhaps, they would be ashore.

Their backbones had become thoroughly used to balancing in the boat and they now rode this wild colt of a dinghy like circus men. The correspondent thought that he had been drenched to the skin, but happening to feel in the top pocket of his coat, he found therein eight cigars. Four of them were soaked with seawater; four were perfectly scatheless. After a search, somebody produced three dry matches, and thereupon the four waifs rode impudently in their little boat, and with an assurance of an impending rescue shining in their eyes, puffed at the big cigars, and judged well and ill of all men. Everybody took a drink of water.

IV

60 "Cook," remarked the captain, "there don't seem to be any signs of life about your house of refuge."

"No," replied the cook. "Funny they don't see us!"

A broad stretch of lowly coast lay before the eyes of the men. It was of low dunes topped with dark vegetation. The roar of the surf was plain, and sometimes they could see the white lip of a wave as it spun up the beach. A tiny house was blocked out black upon the sky. Southward, the slim light-house lifted its little gray length.

Tide, wind, and waves were swinging the dinghy northward. "Funny they don't see us," said the men.

The surf's roar was here dulled, but its tone was, nevertheless, thunderous and mighty. As the boat swam over the great rollers, the men sat listening to this roar. "We'll swamp sure," said everybody.

65 It is fair to say here that there was not a life-saving station within twenty miles in either direction, but the men did not know this fact and in consequence they made dark and opprobrious remarks concerning the eyesight of the nation's life-savers. Four scowling men sat in the dinghy and surpassed records in the invention of epithets.

"Funny they don't see us."

The light-heartedness of a former time had completely faded. To their sharpened minds it was easy to conjure pictures of all kinds of incompetency and blindness and, indeed, cowardice. There was the shore of the populous land, and it was bitter and bitter to them that from it came no sign.

"Well," said the captain, ultimately, "I suppose we'll have to make a try for ourselves. If we stay out here too long, we'll none of us have strength left to swim after the boat swamps."

And so the oiler, who was at the oars, turned the boat straight for the shore. There was a sudden tightening of muscles. There was some thinking.

70 "If we don't all get ashore—" said the captain. "If we don't all get ashore, I suppose you fellows know where to send news of my finish?"

They then briefly exchanged some addresses and admonitions. As for the reflections of the men, there was a great deal of rage in them. Perchance they might be formulated thus: "If I am going to be drowned—if I am going to be drowned—if I am going to be drowned, why, in the name of the seven made gods who rule the sea, was I allowed to come thus far and contemplate sand and trees? Was I brought here merely to have my nose dragged away as I was about to nibble the sacred cheese of life? It is preposterous. If this old ninny-woman, Fate, cannot do better than this, she should be deprived of the management of men's fortunes. She is an old hen who knows not her intention. If she has decided to drown me, why did she not do it in the beginning and save me all this trouble. The whole affair is absurd. . . . But, no, she cannot mean to drown me. She dare not drown me. She cannot drown me. Not after all this work." Afterward the man might have had an impulse to shake his fist at the clouds. "Just you drown me, now, and then hear what I call you!"

The billows that came at this time were more formidable. They seemed always just about to break and roll over the little boat in a turmoil of foam. There was a preparatory and long growl in the speech of them. No mind unused to the sea would have concluded that the dinghy could ascend these sheer heights in time. The shore was still afar. The oiler was a wily surfman. "Boys," he said swiftly, "she won't live three minutes more, and we're too far out to swim. Shall I take her to sea again, Captain?

"Yes! Go ahead!" said the captain.

This oiler, by a series of quick miracles, and fast and steady oarsmanship, turned the boat in the middle of the surf and took her safely to sea again.

There was a considerable silence as the boat bumped over the furrowed sea to deeper water. Then somebody in gloom spoke. "Well, anyhow, they must have seen us from the shore by now."

The gulls went in slanting flight up the wind toward the gray, desolate east. A squall, marked by dinghy clouds and clouds brick-red, like smoke from a burning building, appeared from the southeast.

"What do you think of those life-saving people? Ain't they peaches?"

"Funny they haven't seen us."

"Maybe they think we're out here for sport! Maybe they think we're fishin'. Maybe they think we're damned fools."

It was a long afternoon. A changed tide tried to force them southward, but wind and wave said northward. Far ahead, where coast-line, sea, and sky formed their mighty angle, there were little dots which seemed to indicate a city on the shore.

"St. Augustine?"

The captain shook his head. "Too near Mosquito Inlet."

And the oiler rowed, and then the correspondent rowed. Then the oiler rowed. It was a weary business. The human back can become the seat of more aches and pains than are registered in books for the composite anatomy of a regiment. It is a limited area, but it can become the theatre of innumerable muscular conflicts, tangles, wrenches, knots, and other comforts.

"Did you ever like to row, Billie?" asked the correspondent.

"No," said the oiler, "hang it!"

When one exchanged the rowing-seat for a place in the bottom of the boat, he suffered a bodily depression that caused him to be careless of everything save an obligation to wiggle one finger. There was cold sea-water swashing to and fro in the boat, and he lay in it. His head, pillowed on a thwart, was within an inch of the swirl of a wave crest, and sometimes a particularly obstreperous sea came in-board and drenched him once more. But these matters did not annoy him. It is almost certain that if the boat had capsized he would have tumbled comfortably out upon the ocean as if he felt sure that it was a great soft mattress.

"Look! There's a man on the shore!"

"Where?"

"There! See 'im? See 'im?"

"Yes, sure! He's walking along."

"Now he's stopped. Look! He's facing us!"

"He's waving at us!"

"So he is! By thunder!"

"Ah, now, we're all right! There'll be a boat out here for us in half an hour."

"He's going on. He's running. He's going up to that house there."

The remote beach seemed lower than the sea, and it required a searching glance to discern the little black figure. The captain saw a floating stick and they rowed to it. A bath-towel was by some weird chance in the boat, and, tying this on the stick, the captain waved it. The oarsman did not dare turn his head, so he was obliged to ask questions.

"What's he doing now?"

"He's standing still again. He's looking, I think. . . . There he goes again. Toward the house. . . . Now he's stopped again."

"Is he waving at us?"

"No, not now! He was, though."

"Look! There comes another man!"

"He's running."

"Look at him go, would you!"

"Why, he's on a bicycle. Now he's met the other man. They're both waving at us. Look!"

"There comes something up the beach."

"What the devil is that thing?"

"Why, it looks like a boat."

"Why, certainly, it's a boat."

"No; it's on wheels."

"Yes, so it is. Well, that must be the life-boat. They drag them along shore on a wagon."

"That's the life-boat, sure."

"No, by, it's—it's an omnibus."

"I tell you it's a life-boat."

"It is not! It's an omnibus. I can see it plain. See? One of the these big hotel omnibuses."

"By thunder, you're right. It's an omnibus, sure as fate. What do you suppose they are doing with an omnibus? Maybe they are going around collecting the life-crew, hey?"

"That's it, likely. Look! There's a fellow waving a little black flag. He's standing on the steps of the omnibus. There come those other two fellows. Now they're all talking together. Look at the fellow with the flag. Maybe he ain't waving it!"

"That ain't a flag, is it? That's his coat. Why, certainly, that's his coat."

"So it is. It's his coat. He's taken it off and is waving it around his head. But would you look at him swing it!"

"Oh, say, there isn't any life-saving station there. That's just a winter resort hotel omnibus that has brought over some of the boarders to see us drown."

"What's that idiot with the coat mean? What's he signaling, anyhow?"

"It looks as if he were trying to tell us to go north. There must be a life-saving station up there."

"No! He thinks we're fishing. Just giving us a merry hand. See? Ah, there, Willie!"

"Well, I wish I could make something out of those signals. What do you suppose he means?"

"He don't mean anything. He's just playing."

"Well, if he'd just signal us to try the surf again, or to go to sea and wait, or go north, or go south, or go to hell—there would be some reason in it. But look at him! He just stands there and keeps his coat revolving like a wheel. The ass!"

"There come more people."

"Now there's quite a mob. Look! Isn't that a boat?"

"Where? Oh, I see where you mean. No, that's no boat."

"That fellow is still waving his coat."

"He must think we like to see him do that. Why don't he quit it. It don't mean anything."

"I don't know. I think he is trying to make us go north. It must be that there's a life-saving station there somewhere."

"Say, he ain't tired yet. Look at 'im wave!"

"Wonder how long he can keep that up. He's been revolving his coat ever since he caught sight of us. He's an idiot. Why aren't they getting men to bring a boat out. A fishing boat—one of those big yawls—could come out here all right. Why don't he do something?"

"Oh, it's all right now."

"They'll have a boat out here for us in less than no time, now that they've seen us."

A faint yellow tone came into the sky over the low land. The shadows on the sea slowly deepened. The wind bore coldness with it, and the men began to shiver.

"Holy smoke!" said one, allowing his voice to express his impious mood, "If we keep on monkeying out here! If we've got to flounder out here all night!"

"Oh, we'll never have to stay here all night! Don't you worry. They've seen us now, and it won't be long before they'll come chasing out after us."

The shore grew dusky. The man waving a coat blended gradually into this gloom, and it swallowed in the same manner the omnibus and the group of people. The spray, when it dashed uproariously over the side, made the voyagers shrink and swear like men who were being branded.

"I'd like to catch the chump who waved the coat. I feel like soaking him one, just for luck."

"Why? What did he do?"

"Oh, nothing, but then he seemed so damned cheerful."

In the meantime the oiler rowed, and then the correspondent rowed, and then the oiler rowed. Gray-faced and bowed forward, they mechanically, turn by turn, plied the leaden oars. The form of the light-house had vanished from the southern horizon, but finally a pale star appeared, just lifting from the sea. The streaked saffron in the west passed before the all-merging darkness, and the sea to the east was black. The land had vanished, and was expressed only by the low and drear thunder of the surf.

"If I am going to be drowned—if I am going to be drowned—if I am going to be drowned, why, in the name of the seven gods who rule the sea, was I allowed to come thus far and contemplate sand and trees? Was I brought here merely to have my nose dragged away as I was about to nibble the sacred cheese of life?"

The patient captain, drooped over the water-jar, was sometimes obliged to speak to the oarsman.

"Keep her head up! Keep her head up!"

"'Keep her head up,' sir." The voices were weary and low.

This was surely a quiet evening. All save the oarsman lay heavily and listlessly in the boat's bottom. As for him, his eyes were just capable of noting the tall black waves that swept forward in a most sinister silence, save for an occasional subdued growl of a crest.

The cook's head was on a thwart, and he looked without interest at the water under this nose. He was deep in other scenes. Finally he spoke. "Billie," he murmured, dreamfully, "what kind of pie do you like best?"

V

"Pie!" said the oiler and the correspondent, agitatedly. "Don't talk about those things, blast you!"

"Well," said the cook, "I was just thinking about ham sandwiches, and—"

A night on the sea in an open boat is a long night. As darkness settled finally, the shine of the light, lifting from the sea in the south, changed to full gold. On the northern horizon a new light appeared, a small bluish gleam on the edge of the waters. These two lights were the furniture of the world. Otherwise there was nothing but waves.

Two men huddled in the stern, and distances were so magnificent in the dinghy that the rower was enabled to keep his feet partly warm by thrusting them under his companions. Their legs indeed extended far under the rowing-seat until they touched the feet of the captain forward. Sometimes, despite the efforts of the tired oarsman, a wave came piling into the boat, an icy wave of the night, and the chilling water soaked them anew. They would twist their bodies for a moment and groan, and sleep the dead sleep once more, while the water in the boat gurgled about them as the craft rocked.

The plan of the oiler and the correspondent was for one to row until he lost the ability, and then arouse the other from his sea-water couch in the bottom of the boat.

The oiler plied the oars until his head drooped forward, and the overpowering sleep blinded him. And he rowed yet afterward. Then he touched a man in the bottom of the boat, and called his name. "Will you spell me for a little while?" he said, meekly.

"Sure, Billie," said the correspondent, awaking and dragging himself to a sitting position. They exchanged places carefully, and the oiler, cuddling down in the sea-water at the cook's side, seemed to go to sleep instantly.

The particular violence of the sea had ceased. The waves came without snarling. The obligation of the man at the oars was to keep the boat headed so that the tilt of the rollers would not capsize her, and to preserve her from filling when the crests rushed past. The black waves were silent and hard to be seen in the darkness. Often one was almost upon the boat before the oarsman was aware.

In a low voice the correspondent addressed the captain. He was not sure that the captain was awake, although this iron man seemed to be always awake. "Captain, shall I keep her making for that light north, sir?"

The same steady voice answered him. "Yes. Keep it about two points off the port bow."

160 The cook had tied a life-belt around himself in order to get even the warmth which this clumsy cork contrivance could donate, and he seemed almost stove-like when a rower, whose teeth invariably chattered wildly as soon as he ceased his labor, dropped down to sleep.

The correspondent, as he rowed, looked down at the two men sleeping underfoot. The cook's arm was around the oiler's shoulders, and, with their fragmentary clothing and haggard faces, they were the babes of the sea, a grotesque rendering of the old babes in the wood.

Later he must have grown stupid at his work, for suddenly there was a growling of water, and a crest came with a roar and a swash into the boat, and it was a wonder that it did not set the cook afloat in his life-belt. The cook continued to sleep, but the oiler sat up, blinking his eyes and shaking with the new cold.

"Oh, I'm awful sorry, Billie," said the correspondent, contritely.

"That's all right, old boy," said the oiler, and lay down again and was asleep.

165 Presently it seemed that even the captain dozed, and the correspondent thought that he was the one man afloat on all the oceans. The wind had a voice as it came over the waves, and it was sadder than the end.

There was a long, loud swishing astern of the boat, and a gleaming trail of phosphorescence, like blue flame, was furrowed on the black waters. It might have been made by a monstrous knife.

Then there came a stillness, while the correspondent breathed with open mouth and looked at the sea.

Suddenly there was another swish and another long flash of bluish light, and this time it was alongside the boat, and might almost have been reached with an oar. The correspondent saw an enormous fin speed like a shadow through the water, hurling the crystalline spray and leaving the long glowing trail.

The correspondent looked over his shoulder at the captain. His face was hidden, and he seemed to be asleep. He looked at the babes of the sea. They certainly were asleep. So, being bereft of sympathy, he leaned a little way to one side and swore softly into the sea.

170 But the thing did not then leave the vicinity of the boat. Ahead or astern, on one side or the other, at intervals long or short, fled the long sparkling streak, and there was to be heard the whiroo of the dark fin. The speed and power of the thing was greatly to be admired. It cut the water like a gigantic and keen projectile.

The presence of this biding thing did not affect the man with the same horror that it would if he had been a picnicker. He simply looked at the sea dully and swore in an undertone.

Nevertheless, it is true that he did not wish to be alone with the thing. He wished one of his companions to awaken by chance and keep him company with it. But the captain hung motionless over the water-jar, and the oiler and the cook in the bottom of the boat were plunged in slumber.

VI

"If I am going to be drowned—if I am going to be drowned—if I am going to be drowned, why, in the name of the seven mad gods who rule the sea, was I allowed to come thus far and contemplate sand and trees?"

During this dismal night, it may be remarked that a man would conclude that it was really the intention of the seven mad gods to drown him, despite the abominable injustice of it. For it was certainly an abominable injustice to drown a man who had worked so hard, so hard. The man felt it would be a crime most unnatural. Other people had drowned at sea since galleys swarmed with painted sails, but still—

175 When it occurs to a man that nature does not regard him as important, and that she feels she would not maim the universe by disposing of him, he at first wishes to throw bricks at the temple, and he hates deeply the fact that there are no bricks and no temples. Any visible expression of nature would surely be pelleted with his jeers.

Then, if there be no tangible thing to hoot he feels, perhaps, the desire to confront a personification and indulge in pleas, bowed to one knee, and with hands supplicant, saying, "Yes, but I love myself."

A high cold star on a winter's night is the word he feels that she says to him. Thereafter he knows the pathos of his situation.

The men in the dinghy had not discussed these matters, but each had, no doubt, reflected upon them in silence and according to his mind. There was seldom any expression upon their faces save the general one of complete weariness. Speech was devoted to the business of the boat.

To chime the notes of his emotion, a verse mysteriously entered the correspondent's head. He had even forgotten that he had forgotten this verse, but it suddenly was in his mind.

180 In his childhood, the correspondent had been made acquainted with the fact that a soldier of the Legion lay dying in Algiers, but he had never regarded it as important. Myriads of his school-fellows had informed him of the soldier's plight, but the dinning had naturally ended by making him perfectly indifferent. He had never considered it his affair that a soldier of the Legion lay dying in Algiers, nor had it appeared to him as a matter for sorrow. It was less to him than the breaking of a pencil's point.

Now, however, it quaintly came to him as a human, living thing. It was no longer merely a picture of a few throes in the breast of a poet, meanwhile drinking tea and warming his feet at the grate; it was an actuality—stern, mournful, and fine.

The correspondent plainly saw the soldier. He lay on the sand with his feet out straight and still. While his pale left hand was upon his chest in an attempt to thwart the going of his life, the blood came between his fingers. In the far Algerian distance, a city of low square forms was set against a sky that was faint with the last sunset hues. The correspondent, plying the oars and dreaming of the slow and slower movements of the lips of the soldier, was moved by a profound and perfectly impersonal comprehension. He was sorry for the soldier of the Legion who lay dying in Algiers.

The thing which had followed the boat and waited had evidently grown bored at the delay. There was no longer to be heard the slash of the cutwater, and there was no longer the flame of the long trail. The light in the north still glimmered, but it was apparently no nearer to the boat. Sometimes the boom of the surf rang in the correspondent's ears, and he turned the craft seaward then and rowed harder. Southward, some one had evidently built a watch-fire on the beach. It was too low and too far to be seen, but it made a shimmering, roseate reflection upon the bluff in back of it, and this could be discerned from the boat. The wind came stronger, and sometimes a wave suddenly raged out like a mountain-cat, and there was to be seen the sheen and sparkle of a broken crest.

The captain, in the bow, moved on his water-jar and sat erect. "Pretty long night," he observed to the correspondent. He looked at the shore. "Those life-saving people take their time."

185 "Did you see that shark playing around?"

"Yes, I saw him. He was a big fellow, all right."

"Wish I had known you were awake."

Later the correspondent spoke into the bottom of the boat.

"Billie!" There was a slow and gradual disentanglement. "Billie, will you spell me?"

190 "Sure," said the oiler.

As soon as the correspondent touched the cold, comfortable sea-water in the bottom of the boat, and had huddled close to the cook's life-belt he was deep in sleep, despite the fact that his teeth played all the popular airs. This sleep was so good to him that it was but a moment before he heard a voice call his name in a tone that demonstrated the last stages of exhaustion. "Will you spell me?"

"Sure, Billie."

The light in the north had mysteriously vanished, but the correspondent took his course from the wide-awake captain.

Later in the night they took the boat farther out to sea, and the captain directed the cook to take one oar at the stern and keep the boat facing the seas. He was to call out if he should hear the thunder of the surf. This plan enabled the oiler and the correspondent to get respite together. "We'll give those boys a chance to get into shape again," said the captain. They curled down and, after a few preliminary chatterings and trembles, slept once more the dead sleep. Neither knew they had bequeathed to the cook the company of another shark, or perhaps the same shark.

195 As the boat caroused on the waves, spray occasionally bumped over the side and gave them a fresh soaking, but this had no power to break their repose. The ominous slash of the wind and the water affected them as it would have affected mummies.

"Boys," said the cook, with the notes of every reluctance in his voice, "she's drifted in pretty close. I guess one of you had better take her to sea again." The correspondent, aroused, heard the crash of the toppled crests.

As he was rowing, the captain gave him some whisky and water, and this steadied the chills out of him. "If I ever get ashore and anybody shows me even a photograph of an oar—"

At last there was a short conversation.

"Billie! . . Billie, will you spell me?"

"Sure," said the oiler.

VII

When the correspondent again opened his eyes, the sea and sky were each of the gray hue of the dawning. Later, carmine and gold was painted upon the waters. The morning appeared finally, in its splendor, with a sky of pure blue, and the sunlight flamed on the tips of the waves.

On the distant dunes were set many little black cottages, and a tall white windmill reared above them. No man, nor dog, nor bicycle appeared on the beach. The cottages might have formed a deserted village.

The voyagers scanned the shore. A conference was held in the boat. "Well," said the captain, "if no help is coming, we might better try a run through the surf right away. If we stay out here much longer we will be too weak to do anything for ourselves at all." The others silently acquiesced in this reasoning. The boat was headed for the beach. The correspondent wondered if none ever ascended the tall windtower, and if then they never looked seaward. This tower was a giant, standing with its back to the plight of the ants. It represented in a degree, to the correspondent, the serenity of nature amid the struggles of the individual—nature in the wind, and nature in the vision of men. She did not seem cruel to him then, nor beneficent, nor treacherous, nor wise. But she was indifferent, flatly indifferent. It is, perhaps, plausible that a man in this situation, impressed with the unconcern of the universe, should see the innumerable flaws of life and have them taste wickedly in his mind and wish for another chance. A distinction between right and wrong seems absurdly clear to him, then, in this new ignorance of the grave-edge, and he understands that if he were given another opportunity he would mend his conduct and his words, and be better and brighter during an introduction, or at a tea.

"Now, boys," said the captain, "she is going to swamp sure. All we can do is to work her in as far as possible, and then when she swamps, pile out and scramble for the beach. Keep cool now, and don't jump until she swamps sure."

The oiler took the oars. Over his shoulders he scanned the surf. "Captain," he said, "I think I'd better bring her about, and keep her head-on to the seas and back her in."

"All right, Billie," said the captain. "Back her in." The oiler swung the boat then, and, seated in the stern, the cook and the correspondent were obliged to look over their shoulders to contemplate the lonely and indifferent shore.

The monstrous inshore rollers heaved the boat high until the men were again enabled to see the white sheets of water scudding up the slanted beach. "We won't get in very close," said the captain. Each time a man could wrest his attention from the rollers, he turned his glance toward the shore, and in the expression of the eyes during this contemplation there was a singular quality. The correspondent, observing the others, knew that they were not afraid, but the full meaning of their glances was shrouded.

As for himself, he was too tired to grapple fundamentally with the fact. He tried to coerce his mind into thinking of it, but the mind was dominated at this time by the muscles, and the muscles said they did not care. It merely occurred to him that if he should drown it would be a shame.

There were no hurried words, no pallor, no plain agitation. The men simply looked at the shore. "Now, remember to get well clear of the boat when you jump," said the captain.

Seaward the crest of a roller suddenly fell with a thunderous crash, and the long white comber came roaring down upon the boat.

"Steady now," said the captain. The men were silent. They turned their eyes from the shore to the comber and waited. The boat slid up the incline, leaped at the furious top, bounced over it, and swung down the long back of the wave. Some water had been shipped and the cook bailed it out.

But the next crest crashed also. The tumbling boiling flood of white water caught the boat and whirled it almost perpendicular. Water swarmed in from all sides. The correspondent had his hands on the gunwale at this time, and when the water entered at that place he swiftly withdrew his fingers, as if he objected to wetting them.

The little boat, drunken with this weight of water, reeled and snuggled deeper into the sea.

"Bail her out, cook! Bail her out!" said the captain.

"All right, Captain," said the cook.

"Now, boys, the next one will do for us sure," said the oiler. "Mind to jump clear of the boat."

The third wave moved forward, huge, furious, implacable. It fairly swallowed the dinghy, and almost simultaneously the men tumbled into the sea. A piece of life-belt had lain in the bottom of the boat, and as the correspondent went overboard he held this to his chest with his left hand.

The January water was icy, and he reflected immediately that it was colder than he had expected to find it off the coast of Florida. This appeared to his dazed mind as a fact important enough to be noted at the time. The coldness of the water was sad; it was tragic. This fact was somehow mixed and confused with his opinion of his own situation that it seemed almost a proper reason for tears. The water was cold.

When he came to the surface he was conscious of little but the noisy water. Afterward he saw his companions in the sea. The oiler was ahead in the race. He was swimming strongly and rapidly. Off to the correspondent's left, the cook's great white and corked back bulged out of the water, and in the rear the captain was hanging with his one good hand to the keel of the overturned dinghy.

There is a certain immovable quality to a shore, and the correspondent wondered at it amid the confusion of the sea.

It seemed also very attractive, but the correspondent knew that it was a long journey, and he paddled leisurely. The piece of life-preserver lay under him, and sometimes he whirled down the incline of a wave as if he were on a hand-sled.

But finally he arrived at a place in the sea where travel was beset with difficulty. He did not pause swimming to inquire what manner of current had caught him, but there his progress ceased. The shore was set before him like a bit of scenery on a stage, and he looked at it and understood with his eyes each detail of it.

As the cook passed, much farther to the left, the captain was calling to him, "Turn over on your back, cook! Turn over on your back and use the oar."

"All right, sir." The cook turned on his back, and, paddling with an oar, went ahead as if he were a canoe.

Presently the boat also passed to the left of the correspondent with the captain clinging with one hand to the keel. He would have appeared like a man raising himself to look over a board fence, if it were not for the extraordinary gymnastics of the boat. The correspondent marveled that the captain could still hold to it.

They passed on nearer to shore—the oiler, the cook, the captain—and following them went the water-jar, bouncing gaily over the seas.

The correspondent remained in the grip of this strange new enemy—a current. The shore, with its white slope of sand and its green bluff, topped with little silent cottages, was spread like a picture before him. It was very near to him then, but he was impressed as one who in a gallery looks at a scene from Brittany or Holland.

He thought: "I am going to drown? Can it be possible? Can it be possible? Can it be possible?" Perhaps an individual must consider his own death to be the final phenomenon of nature.

But later a wave perhaps whirled him out of this small deadly current for he found suddenly that he could again make progress toward the shore. Later still, he was aware that the captain, clinging with one hand to the keel of the dinghy, had his face turned away from the shore and toward him, and was calling his name. "Come to the boat! Come to the boat!"

In his struggle to reach the captain and the boat, he reflected that when one gets properly wearied, drowning must really be a comfortable arrangement, a cessation of hostilities accompanied by a large degree of relief and he was glad of it, for the main thing in his mind for some moments had been horror of the temporary agony. He did not wish to be hurt.

Presently he saw a man running along the shore. He was undressing with most remarkable speed. Coat, trousers, shirt, everything flew magically off him.

"Come to the boat!" called the captain.

"All right, Captain." As the correspondent paddled, he saw the captain let himself down to bottom and leave the boat. Then the correspondent performed his one little marvel of the voyage. A large wave caught him and flung him with ease and supreme speed completely over the boat and far beyond it. It struck him even then as an event in gymnastics, and a true miracle of the sea. An overturned boat in the surf is not a plaything to a swimming man.

The correspondent arrived in water that reached only to his waist, but his condition did not enable him to stand for more than a moment. Each wave knocked him into a heap, and the under-tow pulled at him.

Then he saw the man who had been running and undressing, and undressing and running, come bounding into the water. He dragged ashore the cook, and then waded toward the captain, but the captain waved him away, and sent him to the correspondent. He was naked, naked as a tree in winter, but a halo was about his head, and he shone like a saint. He gave a strong pull, and a long drag, and a bully heave at the correspondent's hand. The correspondent, schooled in the minor formulae, said, "Thanks, old man." But suddenly the man cried, "What's that?" He pointed a swift finger. The correspondent said: "Go."

In the shallows, face downward, lay the oiler. His forehead touched sand that was periodically, between each wave, clear of the sea.

The correspondent did not know all that transpired afterward. When he achieved safe ground he fell, striking the sand with each particular part of his body. It was as if he had dropped from a roof, but the thud was grateful to him.

It seems that instantly the beach was populated with men with blankets, clothes, and flasks, and women with coffee-pots and all the remedies sacred to their minds. The welcome of the land to the men from the sea was warm and generous, but a still and dripping shape was carried slowly up the beach, and the land's welcome for it could only be the different and sinister hospitality of the grave.

When it came night, the white waves paced to and fro in the moonlight, and the wind brought the sound of the great sea's voice to the men on the shore, and they felt that they could then be interpreters.

➤ *QUESTIONS FOR READING AND WRITING*

1. How are you affected by the tone and description in the first paragraph? Have you ever experienced something like this? Explain.
2. This story is based on an actual event that Crane experienced and subsequently described as a reporter for a newspaper, *The New York World*. How do you suppose that news story differed from this work of fiction?
3. What is the relationship between the men and nature in this story? How does it compare to Crane's "A Man Said to the Universe" on page 1379?
4. Given the difficulty of their situation, why does the correspondent believe (in sec. 3, par. 1) that this "was the best experience of his life"?
5. Why does the correspondent wonder, "Was I brought here merely to have my nose dragged away as I was about to nibble the sacred cheese of life?"
6. The correspondent remembers a poem he learned as a schoolboy. Why does the poem about the soldier dying in Algiers have so much more meaning now? Have you ever had something you read long ago brought to life in a subsequent experience? Explain.
7. What do you think the last paragraph means? In what way are the survivors now able to be interpreters?

NATHANIEL HAWTHORNE (1804–1864)

Nathaniel Hawthorne was born in Salem, Massachusetts, to a once influential Puritan family. Two of his ancestors had served as judges: one in the persecution of Quakers, the other in the Salem witch trials. His father, a ship's captain, died when he was four, and his mother, after moving the family back to her parents' house, became a recluse, emerging from her room only for meals. Following an injury that left him lame, Hawthorne was

mostly educated at home. After attending Bowdoin College in Maine, he returned home to live with his sisters and mother, where he began writing and publishing stories. In 1828, he published a little-read novel about his college experiences, Fanshawe. *His next publication,* Twice-Told Tales *(1837) a collection of stories fared better. After his marriage in 1842 and the birth of a daughter, Hawthorne wrote less, working as a customs inspector at various times to support his young family. In 1849, following the death of his mother, Hawthorne moved back to Salem, where he wrote his masterpiece* The Scarlet Letter. *The book was an enormous critical and financial success, as was his next novel,* The House of the Seven Gables *(1851). Hawthorne was then financially able to devote himself fully to his writing. Later in his life, following the election of his college friend Franklin Pierce to the presidency, Hawthorne served as American consul at Liverpool from 1853 to 1857, and then remained in Europe until 1860, where he wrote his final novel,* The Marble Faun *(1860). He died in Concord, Massachusetts, in 1864.*

YOUNG GOODMAN BROWN [1828]

Young Goodman Brown came forth at sunset into the street at Salem village; but put his head back, after crossing the threshold, to exchange a parting kiss with his young wife. And Faith, as the wife was aptly named, thrust her own pretty head into the street, letting the wind play with the pink ribbons of her cap while she called to Goodman Brown.

"Dearest heart," whispered she, softly and rather sadly, when her lips were close to his ear, "prithee put off your journey until sunrise and sleep in your own bed tonight. A lone woman is troubled with such dreams and such thoughts that she's afeared of herself sometimes. Pray tarry with me this night, dear husband, of all nights in the year."

"My love and my Faith," replied young Goodman Brown, "of all nights in the year, this one night must I tarry away from thee. My journey, as thou callest it, forth and back again, must needs be done 'twixt now and sunrise. What, my sweet, pretty wife, dost thou doubt me already, and we but three months married?"

"Then God bless you!" said Faith, with the pink ribbons; "and may you find all well when you come back."

5 "Amen!" cried Goodman Brown. "Say thy prayers, dear Faith, and go to bed at dusk, and no harm will come to thee."

So they parted; and the young man pursued his way until, being about to turn the corner by the meeting-house, he looked back and saw the head of Faith still peeping after him with a melancholy air, in spite of her pink ribbons.

"Poor little Faith!" thought he, for his heart smote him. "What a wretch am I to leave her on such an errand! She talks of dreams, too. Methought as she spoke there was trouble in her face, as if a dream had warned her what work is to be done to-night. But no, no; 'twould kill her to think it. Well, she's a blessed angel on earth; and after this one night I'll cling to her skirts and follow her to heaven."

With this excellent resolve for the future, Goodman Brown felt himself justified in making more haste on his present evil purpose. He had taken a dreary road, darkened by all the gloomiest trees of the forest, which barely stood aside to let the narrow path creep through, and closed immediately behind. It was all as lonely as could be; and there is this peculiarity in such a solitude, that the traveler knows not who may be concealed by the innumerable trunks and the thick boughs overhead; so that with lonely footsteps he may yet be passing through an unseen multitude.

"There may be a devilish Indian behind every tree," said Goodman Brown to himself; and he glanced fearfully behind him as he added, "What if the devil himself should be at my very elbow!"

10 His head being turned back, he passed a crook of the road, and, looking forward again, beheld the figure of a man, in grave and decent attire, seated at the foot of an old tree. He arose at Goodman Brown's approach and walked onward side by side with him.

"You are late, Goodman Brown," said he. "The clock of the Old South was striking as I came through Boston, and that is full fifteen minutes agone."

"Faith kept me back a while," replied the young man, with a tremor in his voice, caused by the sudden appearance of his companion, though not wholly unexpected.

It was now deep dusk in the forest, and deepest in that part of it where these two were journeying. As nearly as could be discerned, the second traveller was about fifty years old, apparently in the same rank of life as Goodman Brown, and bearing a considerable resemblance to him, though perhaps more in expression than features. Still they might have been taken for father and son. And yet, though the elder person was as simply clad as the younger, and as simple in manner too, he had an indescribable air of one who knew the world, and who would not have felt abashed at the governor's dinner table or in King William's court, were it possible that his affairs should call him thither. But the only thing about him that could be fixed upon as remarkable was his staff, which bore the likeness of a great black snake, so curiously wrought that it might almost be seen to twist and wriggle itself like a living serpent. This, of course, must have been an ocular deception, assisted by the uncertain light.

"Come, Goodman Brown," cried his fellow-traveller, "this is a dull pace for the beginning of a journey. Take my staff, if you are so soon weary."

15 "Friend," said the other, exchanging his slow pace for a full stop, "Having kept covenant by meeting thee here, it is my purpose now to return whence I came. I have scruples touching the matter thou wot'st of."

"Sayest thou so?" replied he of the serpent, smiling apart. "Let us walk on, nevertheless, reasoning as we go; and if I convince thee not thou shalt turn back. We are but a little way in the forest yet."

"Too far! too far!" exclaimed the goodman, unconsciously resuming his walk. "My father never went into the woods on such an errand, nor his father before him. We have been a race of honest men and good Christians since the days of the martyrs; and shall I be the first of the name of Brown that ever took this path and kept"—

"Such company, thou wouldst say," observed the elder person, interpreting his pause. "Well said, Goodman Brown! I have been as well acquainted with your family as with ever a one among the Puritans; and that's no trifle to say. I helped your grandfather, the constable, when he lashed the Quaker woman so smartly through the streets of Salem: and it was I that brought your father a pitch-pine knot, kindled at my own hearth, to set fire to an Indian village, in King Philip's war. They were my good friends, both; and many a pleasant walk have we had along this path, and returned merrily after midnight. I would fain be friends with you for their sake."

"If it be as thou sayest," replied Goodman Brown, "I marvel they never spoke of these matters: or, verily, I marvel not, seeing that the least rumor of the sort would have driven them from New England. We are a people of prayer, and good works to boot, and abide no such wickedness."

20 "Wickedness or not," said the traveller with the twisted staff, "I have a very general acquaintance here in New England. The deacons of many a church have drunk the communion wine with me; the selectmen of divers towns make me their chairman; and a majority of the Great and General Court are firm supporters of my interest. The governor and I, too—But these are state secrets."

"Can this be so?" cried Goodman Brown, with a stare of amazement at his undisturbed companion. "Howbeit, I have nothing to do with the governor and council; they have their own ways, and are no rule for a simple husbandman like me. But, were I to go on with thee, how should I meet the eye of that good old man, our minister, at Salem village? Oh, his voice would make me tremble both Sabbath day and lecture day."

Thus far the elder traveller had listened with due gravity; but now burst into a fit of irrepressible mirth, shaking himself so violently that his snake-like staff actually seemed to wriggle in sympathy.

"Ha! ha! ha!" shouted he again and again; then composing himself, "Well, go on, Goodman Brown, go on; but, prithee, don't kill me with laughing."

"Well, then, to end the matter at once," said Goodman Brown, considerably nettled, "there is my wife, Faith. It would break her dear little heart; and I'd rather break my own."

25 "Nay, if that be the case," answered the other, "e'en go thy ways, Goodman Brown. I would not for twenty old women like the one hobbling before us that Faith should come to any harm."

As he spoke he pointed his staff at a female figure on the path, in whom Goodman Brown recognized a very pious and exemplary dame, who had taught him his catechism in youth, and was still his moral and spiritual adviser, jointly with the minister and Deacon Gookin.

"A marvel, truly, that Goody Cloyse should be so far in the wilderness at nightfall," said he. "But with your leave, friend, I shall take a cut through the woods until we have left this Christian woman behind. Being a stranger to you, she might ask whom I was consorting with and whither I was going."

"Be it so," said his fellow-traveller. "Betake you the woods, and let me keep the path."

Accordingly the young man turned aside, but took care to watch his companion, who advanced softly along the road until he had come within a staff's length of the old dame. She, meanwhile, was making the best of her way, with singular speed for so aged a woman, and mumbling some indistinct words—a prayer, doubtless—as she went. The traveller put forth his staff and touched her withered neck with what seemed the serpent's tail.

"The devil!" screamed the pious old lady.

"Then Goody Cloyse knows her old friend?" observed the traveller, confronting her and leaning on his writhing stick.

"Ah, forsooth, and is it your worship indeed?" cried the good dame. "Yea, truly is it, and in the very image of my old gossip, Goodman Brown, the grandfather of the silly fellow that now is. But—would your worship believe it?—my broomstick hath strangely disappeared, stolen, as I suspect, by that unhanged witch, Goody Cory, and that, too, when I was all anointed with the juice of smallage, and cinquefoil, and wolf's bane—"

"Mingled with fine wheat and the fat of a new-born babe," said the shape of old Goodman Brown.

"Ah, your worship knows the recipe," cried the old lady, cackling aloud. "So, as I was saying, being all ready for the meeting, and no horse to ride on, I made up my mind to foot it; for they tell me there is a nice young man to be taken into communion to-night. But now your good worship will lend me your arm, and we shall be there in a twinkling."

"That can hardly be," answered her friend. "I may not spare you my arm, Goody Cloyse; but here is my staff, if you will."

So saying, he threw it down at her feet, where, perhaps, it assumed life, being one of the rods which its owner had formerly lent to the Egyptian magi. Of this fact, however, Goodman Brown could not take cognizance. He had cast up his eyes in astonishment, and, looking down again, beheld neither Goody Cloyse nor the serpentine staff, but his fellow-traveller alone, who waited for him as calmly as if nothing had happened.

"That old woman taught me my catechism," said the young man; and there was a world of meaning in this simple comment.

They continued to walk onward, while the elder traveller exhorted his companion to make good speed and persevere in the path, discoursing so aptly that his arguments seemed rather to spring up in the bosom of his auditor than to be suggested by himself. As they went, he plucked a branch of maple to serve for a walking stick, and began to strip it of the twigs and the little boughs, which were wet with evening dew. The moment his fingers touched them they became strangely withered and dried up as with a week's sunshine. Thus the pair proceeded, at a good free pace, until suddenly, in a gloomy hollow of the road, Goodman Brown sat himself down on the stump of a tree and refused to go any farther.

"Friend," said he, stubbornly, "my mind is made up. Not another step will I budge on this errand. What if a wretched old woman do choose to go to the devil when I thought she was going to heaven: is that any reason why I should quit my dear Faith and go after her?"

40 "You will think better of this by and by," said his acquaintance, composedly. "Sit here and rest yourself a while; and when you feel like moving again, there is my staff to help you along."

Without more words, he threw his companion the maple stick, and was as speedily out of sight as if he had vanished into the deepening gloom. The young man sat a few moments by the roadside, applauding himself greatly, and thinking with how clear a conscience he should meet the minister in his morning walk, nor shrink from the eye of good old Deacon Gookin. And what calm sleep would be his that very night, which was to have been spent so wickedly, but so purely and sweetly now, in the arms of Faith! Amidst these pleasant and praiseworthy meditations, Goodman Brown heard the tramp of horses along the road, and deemed it advisable to conceal himself within the verge of the forest, conscious of the guilty purpose that had brought him thither, though now so happily turned from it.

On came the hoof tramps and the voices of the riders, two grave old voices, conversing soberly as they drew near. These mingled sounds appeared to pass along the road, within a few yards of the young man's hiding-place; but, owing doubtless to the depth of the gloom at that particular spot, neither the travellers nor their steeds were visible. Though their figures brushed the small boughs by the wayside, it could not be seen that they intercepted, even for a moment, the faint gleam from the strip of bright sky athwart which they must have passed. Goodman Brown alternately crouched and stood on tiptoe, pulling aside the branches and thrusting forth his head as far as he durst without discerning so much as a shadow. It vexed him the more, because he could have sworn, were such a thing possible, that he recognized the voices of the minister and Deacon Gookin, jogging along quietly, as they were wont to do, when bound to some ordination or ecclesiastical council. While yet within hearing, one of the riders stopped to pluck a switch.

"Of the two, reverend sir," said the voice like the deacon's, "I had rather miss an ordination dinner than to-night's meeting. They tell me that some of our community are to be here from Falmouth and beyond, and others from Connecticut and Rhode Island, besides several of the Indian powwows, who, after their fashion, know almost as much deviltry as the best of us. Moreover, there is a goodly young woman to be taken into communion."

"Mighty well, Deacon Gookin!" replied the solemn old tones of the minister. "Spur up, or we shall be late. Nothing can be done, you know, until I get on the ground."

45 The hoofs clattered again; and the voices, talking so strangely in the empty air, passed on through the forest, where no church had ever been gathered or solitary Christian prayed. Whither, then, could these holy men be journeying so deep into the heathen wilderness? Young Goodman Brown caught hold of a tree for support, being ready to sink down on the ground, faint and overburdened with the heavy sickness of his heart. He looked up to the sky, doubting whether there really was a heaven above him. Yet there was the blue arch, and the stars brightening in it.

"With heaven above and Faith below, I will yet stand firm against the devil!" cried Goodman Brown.

While he still gazed upward into the deep arch of the firmament and had lifted his hands to pray, a cloud, though no wind was stirring, hurried across the zenith and hid the brightening stars. The blue sky was still visible, except directly overhead, where this black mass of cloud was sweeping swiftly northward. Aloft in the air, as if from the depths of the cloud, came a confused and doubtful sound of voices. Once the listener fancied that he could distinguish the accents of townspeople of his own, men and women, both pious and ungodly, many of whom he had met at the communion table, and had seen others rioting at the tavern. The next moment, so indistinct were the sounds, he doubted whether he had heard aught but the murmur of the old forest, whispering without a wind. Then came a stronger swell of those familiar tones, heard daily in the sunshine at Salem village, but never until now from a cloud of night. There was one voice, of a young woman, uttering lamentations, yet with an uncertain sorrow, and entreating for some favor, which, perhaps, it would grieve her to obtain; and all the unseen multitude, both saints and sinners, seemed to encourage her onward.

"Faith!" shouted Goodman Brown, in a voice of agony and desperation; and the echoes of the forest mocked him, crying, "Faith! Faith!" as if bewildered wretches were seeking her all through the wilderness.

The cry of grief, rage, and terror was yet piercing the night, when the unhappy husband held his breath for a response. There was a scream, drowned immediately in a louder murmur of voices, fading into far-off laughter, as the dark cloud swept away, leaving the clear and silent sky above Goodman Brown. But something fluttered lightly down through the air and caught on the branch of a tree. The young man seized it, and beheld a pink ribbon.

"My Faith is gone!" cried he, after one stupefied moment. "There is no good on earth; and sin is but a name. Come, devil; for to thee is this world given."

And, maddened with despair, so that he laughed loud and long, did Goodman Brown grasp his staff and set forth again, at such a rate that he seemed to fly along the forest path rather than to walk or run. The road grew wilder and drearier and more faintly traced, and vanished at length, leaving him in the heart of the dark wilderness, still rushing onward with the instinct that guides mortal man to evil. The whole forest was peopled with frightful sounds—the creaking of the trees, the howling of wild beasts, and the yell of Indians; while sometimes the wind tolled like a distant church bell, and sometimes gave a broad roar around the traveller, as if all Nature were laughing him to scorn. But he was himself the chief horror of the scene, and shrank not from its other horrors.

"Ha! ha! ha!" roared Goodman Brown when the wind laughed at him. "Let us hear which will laugh loudest. Think not to frighten me with your deviltry. Come witch, come wizard, come Indian powwow, come devil himself, and here comes Goodman Brown. You may as well fear him as he fear you."

In truth, all through the haunted forest there could be nothing more frightful than the figure of Goodman Brown. On he flew among the black pines, brandishing his staff with frenzied gestures, now giving vent to an inspiration of horrid blasphemy, and now shouting forth such laughter as set all the echoes of the forest laughing like demons around him. The fiend in his own shape is less hideous than when he rages in the breast of man. Thus sped the demoniac on his course, until, quivering among the trees, he saw a red light before him, as when the felled trunks and branches of a clearing have been set on fire, and throw up their lurid blaze against the sky, at the hour of midnight. He paused, in a lull of the tempest that had driven him onward, and heard the swell of what seemed a hymn, rolling solemnly from a distance with the weight of many voices. He knew the tune; it was a familiar one in the choir of the village meeting-house. The verse died heavily away, and was lengthened by a chorus, not of human voices, but of all the sounds of the benighted wilderness pealing in awful harmony together. Goodman Brown cried out, and his cry was lost to his own ear by its unison with the cry of the desert.

In the interval of silence he stole forward until the light glared full upon his eyes. At one extremity of an open space, hemmed in by the dark wall of the forest, arose a rock, bearing some rude, natural resemblance either to an altar or a pulpit, and surrounded by four blazing pines, their tops aflame, their stems untouched, like candles at an evening meeting. The mass of foliage that had overgrown the summit of the rock was all on fire, blazing high into the night and fitfully illuminating the whole field. Each pendent twig and leafy festoon was in a blaze. As the red light arose and fell, a numerous congregation alternately shone forth, then disappeared in shadow, and again grew, as it were, out of the darkness, peopling the heart of the solitary woods at once.

55 "A grave and dark-clad company," quoth Goodman Brown.

In truth they were such. Among them, quivering to and fro between gloom and splendor, appeared faces that would be seen next day at the council board of the province, and others which, Sabbath after Sabbath, looked devoutly heavenward, and benignantly over the crowded pews, from the holiest pulpits in the land. Some affirm that the lady of the governor was there. At least there were high dames well known to her, and wives of honored husbands, and widows, a great multitude, and ancient maidens, all of excellent repute, and fair young girls, who trembled lest their mothers should espy them. Either the sudden gleams of light flashing over the obscure field bedazzled Goodman Brown, or he recognized a score of the church members of Salem village famous for their especial sanctity. Good old Deacon Gookin had arrived, and waited at the skirts of that venerable saint, his revered pastor. But, irreverently consorting with these grave, reputable, and pious people, these elders of the church, these chaste dames and dewy virgins, there were men of dissolute lives and women of spotted fame, wretches given over to all mean and filthy vice, and suspected even of horrid crimes. It was strange to see that the good shrank not from the wicked, nor were the sinners abashed by the saints. Scattered also among their pale-faced enemies were the Indian priests, or powwows, who had often scared their native forest with more hideous incantations than any known to English witchcraft.

"But where is Faith?" thought Goodman Brown; and, as hope came into his heart, he trembled.

Another verse of the hymn arose, a slow and mournful strain, such as the pious love, but joined to words which expressed all that our nature can conceive of sin, and darkly hinted at far more. Unfathomable to mere mortals is the lore of fiends. Verse after verse was sung; and still the chorus of the desert swelled between like the deepest tone of a mighty organ; and with the final peal of that dreadful anthem there came a sound, as if the roaring wind, the rushing streams, the howling beasts, and every other voice of the unconcerted wilderness were mingling and according with the voice of guilty man in homage to the prince of all. The four blazing pines threw up a loftier flame, and obscurely discovered shapes and visages of horror on the smoke wreaths above the impious assembly. At the same moment the fire on the rock shot redly forth and formed a glowing arch above its base, where now appeared a figure. With reverence be it spoken, the figure bore no slight similitude, both in garb and manner, to some grave divine of the New England churches.

"Bring forth the converts!" cried a voice that echoed through the field and rolled into the forest.

60 At the word, Goodman Brown stepped forth from the shadow of the trees and approached the congregation, with whom he felt a loathful brotherhood by the sympathy of all that was wicked in his heart. He could have well-nigh sworn that the shape of his own dead father beckoned him to advance, looking downward from a smoke wreath, while a woman, with dim features of despair, threw out her hand to warn him back. Was it his mother? But he had no power to retreat one step, nor to resist, even in thought, when the minister and good old Deacon Gookin seized his arms and led him to the blazing rock. Thither came also the slender form of a veiled female, led between Goody Cloyse, that pious teacher of the catechism, and Martha Carrier, who had received the devil's promise to be queen of hell. A rampant hag was she. And there stood the proselytes beneath the canopy of fire.

"Welcome, my children," said the dark figure, "to the communion of your race. Ye have found thus young your nature and your destiny. My children, look behind you!"

They turned; and flashing forth, as it were, in a sheet of flame, the fiend worshippers were seen; the smile of welcome gleamed darkly on every visage.

"There," resumed the sable form, "are all whom ye have reverenced from youth. Ye deemed them holier than yourselves and shrank from your own sin, contrasting it with their lives of righteousness and prayerful aspirations heavenward. Yet here are they all in my worshipping assembly. This night it shall be granted you to know their secret deeds: how hoary-bearded elders of the church have whispered wanton words to the young maids of their households; how many a woman, eager for widows' weeds, has given her husband a drink at bedtime and let him sleep his last sleep in her bosom; how beardless youths have made haste to inherit their fathers' wealth; and how fair damsels—blush not, sweet ones—have dug little graves in the garden, and bidden me, the sole guest, to an infant's funeral. By the sympathy of your human hearts for sin ye shall scent out all the places—whether in church, bedchamber, street, field, or forest—where crime has been committed, and shall exult to behold the whole earth one stain of guilt, one mighty blood spot. Far more than this. It shall be yours to penetrate, in every bosom, the deep mystery of sin, the fountain of all wicked arts, and which inexhaustibly supplies more evil impulses than human power—than my power at its utmost—can make manifest in deeds. And now, my children, look upon each other."

They did so; and, by the blaze of the hell-kindled torches, the wretched man beheld his Faith, and the wife her husband, trembling before that unhallowed altar.

65 "Lo, there ye stand, my children," said the figure, in a deep and solemn tone, almost sad with its despairing awfulness, as if his once angelic nature could yet mourn for our miserable race. "Depending upon one another's hearts, ye had still hoped that virtue were not all a dream. Now are ye undeceived. Evil is the nature of mankind. Evil must be your only happiness. Welcome again, my children, to the communion of your race."

"Welcome," repeated the fiend worshippers, in one cry of despair and triumph.

And there they stood, the only pair, as it seemed, who were yet hesitating on the verge of wickedness in this dark world. A basin was hollowed, naturally, in the rock. Did it contain water, reddened by the lurid light? or was it blood? or, perchance, a liquid flame? Herein did the shape of evil dip his hand and prepare to lay the mark of baptism upon their foreheads, that they might be partakers of the mystery of sin, more conscious of the secret guilt of others, both in deed and thought, than they could now be of their own. The husband cast one look at his pale wife, and Faith at him. What polluted wretches would the next glance show them to each other, shuddering alike at what they disclosed and what they saw!

"Faith! Faith!" cried the husband, "look up to heaven, and resist the wicked one."

Whether Faith obeyed he knew not. Hardly had he spoken when he found himself amid calm night and solitude, listening to a roar of the wind which died heavily away through the forest. He staggered against the rock, and felt it chill and damp; while a hanging twig, that had been all on fire, besprinkled his cheek with the coldest dew.

70 The next morning young Goodman Brown came slowly into the street of Salem village, staring around him like a bewildered man. The good old minister was taking a walk along the graveyard to get an appetite for breakfast and meditate his sermon, and bestowed a blessing, as he passed, on Goodman Brown. He shrank from the venerable saint as if to avoid an anathema. Old Deacon Gookin was at domestic worship, and the holy words of his prayer were heard through the open window. "What God doth the wizard pray to?" quoth Goodman Brown. Goody Cloyse, that excellent old Christian, stood in the early sunshine at her own lattice, catechizing a little girl who had brought her a pint of morning's milk. Goodman Brown snatched away the child as from the grasp of the fiend himself. Turning the corner by the meeting-house, he spied the head of Faith, with the pink ribbons, gazing anxiously forth, and bursting into such joy at sight of him that she skipped along the street and almost kissed her husband before the whole village. But Goodman Brown looked sternly and sadly into her face, and passed on without a greeting.

Had Goodman Brown fallen asleep in the forest and only dreamed a wild dream of a witch-meeting?

Be it so if you will; but alas! it was a dream of evil omen for young Goodman Brown. A stern, a sad, a darkly meditative, a distrustful, if not a desperate man did he become from the night of that fearful dream. On the Sabbath day, when the congregation were singing a holy psalm, he could not listen because an anthem of sin rushed loudly upon his ear and drowned all the blessed strain. When the minister spoke from the pulpit with power and fervid eloquence, and, with his hand on the open Bible, of the sacred truths of our religion, and of saint-like lives and triumphant deaths, and of future bliss or misery unutterable, then did Goodman Brown turn pale, dreading lest the roof should thunder down upon the gray blasphemer and his hearers. Often, awaking suddenly at midnight, he shrank from the bosom of Faith; and at morning or eventide, when the family knelt down at prayer, he scowled and muttered to himself, and gazed sternly at his wife, and turned away. And when he had lived long, and was borne to his grave a hoary corpse, followed by Faith, an aged woman, and children and grandchildren, a goodly procession, besides neighbors not a few, they carved no hopeful verse upon his tombstone, for his dying hour was gloom.

➤ *QUESTIONS FOR READING AND WRITING*

1. What is the significance of the names in this story? For example, is Faith aptly named? Explain.
2. In what way does the setting of this story, Puritan New England, influence your response?
3. Why do you suppose the stranger in the woods looks like Goodman Brown himself?
4. Do you think Brown's experience was real or a dream? Explain.
5. This is a story about good and evil. How are they defined here? In what way is this story about human nature? How would you interpret the story's theme?

LUKE (1st century A.D.)

The story of the prodigal son is taken from the fifteenth chapter of the Gospel According to St. Luke, the third book of the New testament. Little is known about the life of Luke, who was also the author of the Book of Acts. In one of his Epistles, Paul calls him "the beloved physician" (Col. 4:14), and tradition has it that he was also a painter. Today, he is considered the patron saint of doctors and painters.

THE PARABLE OF THE PRODIGAL SON [CA. 80 A.D.]

And he said, "A certain man had two sons: and the younger of them said to his father, 'Father, give me the portion of goods that falleth to me.' And he divided unto them his living. And not many days after, the younger son gathered all together, and took his journey into a far country, and there wasted his substance with riotous living.

"And when he had spent all, there arose a mighty famine in that land, and he began to be in want. And he went and joined himself to a citizen of that country, and he sent him into his fields to feed swine. And he would fain have filled his belly with the husks that the swine did eat: and no man gave unto him. And when he came to himself, he said, 'How many hired servants of my father's have bread enough and to spare, and I perish with hunger? I will arise and go to my father, and will say unto him, 'Father I have sinned against heaven, and before thee, and am no more worthy to be called thy son: make me as one of thy hired servants.'"

"And he arose, and came to his father. But when he was yet a great way off, his father saw him, and had compassion, and ran, and fell on his neck, and kissed him. And the son said unto him, 'Father I have sinned against heaven, and in thy sight, and am no more worthy to be called thy son.' But the father said to his servants, 'Bring forth the best robe, and put it on him, and put a ring on his hand, and shoes on his feet. And bring hither the fatted calf, and kill it, and let us eat, and be merry. For this my son was dead, and is alive again; he was lost, and is found.' And they began to be merry.

"Now his elder son was in the field, and as he came and drew nigh to the house, he heard music and dancing. And he called one of the servants, and asked what these things meant. And he said unto him, 'Thy brother is come, and thy father hath killed the fatted calf, because he hath received him safe and sound.' And he was angry, and would not go in: therefore came his father out, and entreated him. And he answering said to his father, 'Lo, these many years do I serve thee, neither transgressed I at any time thy commandment, and yet thou never gavest me a kid, that I might make merry with my friends: but as soon as this thy son was come, which hath devoured thy living with harlots, thou hast killed for him the fatted calf.' And he said unto him, 'Son thou art ever with me, and all that I have is thine. It was meet that we should make merry, and be glad: for this thy brother was dead, and is alive again; and was lost, and is found.'"

➤ *QUESTIONS FOR READING AND WRITING*

1. Why does the father give his prodigal son such a warm welcome back? Would you have been so forgiving and generous? Explain.
2. His oldest son is very upset, but the father says to him, "Son, thou art ever with me, and all that I have is thine." What does he mean? Would you be sufficiently comforted by this explanation?

JOYCE CAROL OATES (b. 1938)

Joyce Carol Oates was born into a blue-collar family in Lockport, New York, and even as a child, she was a prolific writer. Her best-known works include A Garden of Earthly Delights *(1967), the National Book Award-winning* Them *(1969) and* On Boxing *(1987). Oates currently lives in suburban New Jersey and is the director of the creative writing program at Princeton University. Many critics have complained about the graphic violence that is often present in her work. Oates has responded: "The more violent the murders in Macbeth, the more relief one can feel at not having to perform them. Great art is cathartic; it is always moral." "Where Are You Going, Where Have You Been," which first appeared in* The Wheel and Love and Other Stories *(1970),*

was the basis for the 1985 film Smooth Talk. *Her most recent novel is* Broken Heart Blues *published in 1999.*

Where Are You Going, Where Have You Been? [1970]

For Bob Dylan

Her name was Connie. She was fifteen and she had a quick nervous giggling habit of craning her neck to glance into mirrors, or checking other people's faces to make sure her own was all right. Her mother, who noticed everything and knew everything and who hadn't much reason any longer to look at her own face, always scolded Connie about it. "Stop gawking at yourself, who are you? You think you're so pretty?" she would say. Connie would raise her eyebrows at these familiar complaints and look right through her mother, into a shadowy vision of herself as she was right at that moment: she knew she was pretty and that was everything. Her mother had been pretty once too, if you could believe those old snapshots in the album, but now her looks were gone and that was why she was always after Connie.

"Why don't you keep your room clean like your sister? How've you got your hair fixed—what the hell stinks? Hair spray? You don't see your sister using that junk."

Her sister June was twenty-four and still lived at home. She was a secretary in the high school Connie attended, and if that wasn't bad enough—with her in the same building—she was so plain and chunky and steady that Connie had to hear her praised all the time by her mother and her mother's sisters. June did this, June did that, she saved money and helped clean the house and cooked and Connie couldn't do a thing, her mind was all filled with trashy daydreams. Their father was away at work most of the time and when he came home he wanted supper and he read the newspaper at supper and after supper he went to bed. He didn't bother talking much to them, but around his bent head Connie's mother kept picking at her until Connie wished her mother was dead and she herself was dead and it was all over. "She makes me want to throw up sometimes," she complained to her friends. She had a high, breathless, amused voice which made everything she said sound a little forced, whether it was sincere or not.

There was one good thing: June went places with girl friends of hers, girls who were just as plain and steady as she, and so when Connie wanted to do that her mother had no objections. The father of Connie's best girl friend drove the girls the three miles to town and left them off at a shopping plaza, so that they could walk through the stores or go to a movie, and when he came to pick them up again at eleven he never bothered to ask what they had done.

5 They must have been familiar sights, walking around that shopping plaza in their shorts and flat ballerina slippers that always scuffed the sidewalk, with charm bracelets jingling on their thin wrists; they would lean together to whisper and laugh secretly if someone passed by who amused or interested them. Connie had long dark blond hair that drew anyone's eye to it, and she wore part of it pulled up on her head and puffed out and the rest of it she let fall down her back. She wore a pull-over jersey blouse that looked one way when she was at home and another way

when she was away from home. Everything about her had two sides to it, one for home and one for anywhere that was not home: her walk that could be childlike and bobbing, or languid enough to make anyone think she was hearing music in her head, her mouth which was pale and smirking most of the time, but bright and pink on these evenings out, her laugh which was cynical and drawling at home—"Ha, ha, very funny"—but high-pitched and nervous anywhere else, like the jingling of the charms on her bracelet.

Sometimes they did go shopping or to a movie, but sometimes they went across the highway, ducking fast across the busy road, to a drive-in restaurant where older kids hung out. The restaurant was shaped like a big bottle, though squatter than a real bottle, and on its cap was a revolving figure of a grinning boy who held a hamburger aloft. One night in mid-summer they ran across, breathless with daring, and right away someone leaned out a car window and invited them over, but it was just a boy from high school they didn't like. It made them feel good to be able to ignore him. They went up through the maze of parked and cruising cars to the bright-lit, fly-infested restaurant, their faces pleased and expectant as if they were entering a sacred building that loomed out of the night to give them what haven and what blessing they yearned for. They sat at the counter and crossed their legs at the ankles, their thin shoulders rigid with excitement, and listened to the music that made everything so good: the music was always in the background like music at a church service, it was something to depend upon.

A boy named Eddie came in to talk with them. He sat backwards on his stool, turning himself jerkily around in semi-circles and then stopping and turning again, and after a while he asked Connie if she would like something to eat. She said she did and so she tapped her friend's arm on her way out—her friend pulled her face up into a brave droll look—and Connie said she would meet her at eleven, across the way. "I just hate to leave her like that," Connie said earnestly, but the boy said that she wouldn't be alone for long. So they went out to his car and on the way Connie couldn't help but let her eyes wander over the windshields and faces all around her, her face gleaming with a joy that had nothing to do with Eddie or even this place; it might have been the music. She drew her shoulders up and sucked in her breath with the pure pleasure of being alive, and just at that moment she happened to glance at a face just a few feet from hers. It was a boy with shaggy black hair, in a convertible jalopy painted gold. He stared at her and then his lips widened into a grin. Connie slit her eyes at him and turned away, but she couldn't help glancing back and there he was still watching her. He wagged a finger and laughed and said, "Gonna get you, baby," and Connie turned away again without Eddie noticing anything.

She spent three hours with him, at the restaurant where they ate hamburgers and drank Cokes in wax cups that were always sweating, and then down an alley a mile or so away, and when he left her off at five to eleven only the movie house was still open at the plaza. Her girl friend was there, talking with a boy. When Connie came up the two girls smiled at each other and Connie said, "How was the movie?" and the girl said, "*You* should know." They rode off with the girl's father, sleepy and pleased, and Connie couldn't help but look at the darkened shopping plaza with its big empty parking lot and its signs that were faded and ghostly now, and over at the drive-in restaurant where cars were still circling tirelessly. She couldn't hear the music at this distance.

Next morning June asked her how the movie was and Connie said, "So-so."

10 She and that girl and occasionally another girl went out several times a week that way, and the rest of the time Connie spent around the house—it was summer vacation—getting in her mother's way and thinking, dreaming, about the boys she met. But all the boys fell back and dissolved into a single face that was not even a face, but an idea, a feeling, mixed up with the urgent insistent pounding of the music and the humid night air of July. Connie's mother kept dragging her back to the daylight by finding things for her to do or saying, suddenly, "What's this about the Pettinger girl?"

And Connie would say nervously, "Oh, her. That dope." She always drew thick clear lines between herself and such girls, and her mother was simple and kindly enough to believe her. Her mother was so simple, Connie thought, that it was maybe cruel to fool her so much. Her mother went scuffling around the house in old bedroom slippers and complained over the telephone to one sister about the other, then the other called up and the two of them complained about the third one. If June's name was mentioned her mother's tone was approving, and if Connie's name was mentioned it was disapproving. This did not really mean she disliked Connie and actually Connie thought that her mother preferred her to June because she was prettier, but the two of them kept up a pretense of exasperation, a sense that they were tugging and struggling over something of little value to either of them. Sometimes, over coffee, they were almost friends, but something would come up—some vexation that was like a fly buzzing suddenly around their heads—and their faces went hard with contempt.

One Sunday Connie got up at eleven—none of them bothered with church—and washed her hair so that it could dry all day long, in the sun. Her parents and sister were going to a barbecue at an aunt's house and Connie said no, she wasn't interested, rolling her eyes to let her mother know just what she thought of it. "Stay home alone then," her mother said sharply. Connie sat out back in a lawn chair and watched them drive away, her father quiet and bald, hunched around so that he could back the car out, her mother with a look that was still angry and not at all softened through the windshield, and in the back seat poor old June all dressed up as if she didn't know what a barbecue was, with all the running yelling kids and the flies. Connie sat with her eyes closed in the sun, dreaming and dazed with the warmth about her as if this were a kind of love, the caresses of love, and her mind slipped over onto thoughts of the boy she had been with the night before and how nice he had been, how sweet it always was, not the way someone like June would suppose but sweet, gentle, the way it was in movies and promised in songs; and when she opened her eyes she hardly knew where she was, the back yard ran off into weeds and a fence-line of trees and behind it the sky was perfectly blue and still. The asbestos "ranch house" that was now three years old startled her—it looked small. She shook her head as if to get awake.

It was too hot. She went inside the house and turned on the radio to drown out the quiet. She sat on the edge of her bed, barefoot, and listened for an hour and a half to a program called XYZ Sunday Jamboree, record after record of hard, fast, shrieking songs she sang along with, interspersed by exclamations from "Bobby King": "An' look here you girls at Napoleon's—Son and Charley want you to pay real close attention to this song coming up!"

And Connie paid close attention herself, bathed in a glow of slow-pulsed joy that seemed to rise mysteriously out of the music itself and lay languidly about the airless little room, breathed in and breathed out with each gentle rise and fall of her chest.

After a while she heard a car coming up the drive. She sat up at once, startled, because it couldn't be her father so soon. The gravel kept crunching all the way in from the road—the driveway was long—and Connie ran to the window. It was a car she didn't know. It was an open jalopy, painted a bright gold that caught the sunlight opaquely. Her heart began to pound and her fingers snatched at her hair, checking it, and she whispered "Christ. Christ," wondering how bad she looked. The car came to a stop at the side door and the horn sounded four short taps as if this were a signal Connie knew.

She went into the kitchen and approached the door slowly, then hung out the screen door, her bare toes curling down off the step. There were two boys in the car and now she recognized the driver: he had shaggy, shabby black hair that looked crazy as a wig and he was grinning at her.

"I ain't late, am I?" he said.

"Who the hell do you think you are?" Connie said.

"Toldja I'd be out, didn't I?"

"I don't even know who you are."

She spoke sullenly, careful to show no interest or pleasure, and he spoke in a fast bright monotone. Connie looked past him to the other boy, taking her time. He had fair brown hair, with a lock that fell onto his forehead. His sideburns gave him a fierce, embarrassed look, but so far he hadn't even bothered to glance at her. Both boys wore sunglasses. The driver's glasses were metallic and mirrored everything in miniature.

"You wanta come for a ride?" he said.

Connie smirked and let her hair fall loose over one shoulder.

"Don'tcha like my car? New paint job," he said. "Hey."

"What?"

"You're cute."

She pretended to fidget, chasing flies away from the door.

"Don'tcha believe me, or what?" he said.

"Look, I don't even know who you are," Connie said in disgust.

"Hey, Ellie's got a radio, see. Mine's broke down." He lifted his friend's arm and showed her the little transistor the boy was holding, and now Connie began to hear the music. It was the same program that was playing inside the house.

"Bobby King?" she said.

"I listen to him all the time. I think he's great."

"He's kind of great," Connie said reluctantly.

"Listen, that guy's *great.* He knows where the action is."

Connie blushed a little, because the glasses made it impossible for her to see just what this boy was looking at. She couldn't decide if she liked him or if he was just a jerk, and so she dawdled in the doorway and wouldn't come down or go back inside. She said, "What's all that stuff painted on your car?"

"Can'tcha read it?" He opened the door very carefully, as if he was afraid it might fall off. He slid out just as carefully, planting his feet firmly on the ground, the tiny metallic world in his glasses slowing down like gelatin hardening and in the midst of it Connie's bright green blouse. "This here is my name, to begin with," he said. ARNOLD FRIEND was written in tarlike black letters on the side, with a drawing of a round grinning face that reminded Connie of a pumpkin, except it wore sunglasses. "I wanta introduce myself, I'm Arnold Friend and that's my real name and I'm gonna be your friend, honey, and inside the car's Ellie Oscar, he's kinda shy." Ellie brought his transistor radio up to his shoulder and balanced it there. "Now these numbers are a secret code, honey," Arnold Friend explained. He read off the numbers 33, 19, 17 and raised his eyebrows at her to see what she thought of that, but she didn't think much of it. The left rear fender had been smashed and around it was written, on the gleaming gold background: DONE BY CRAZY WOMAN DRIVER. Connie had to laugh at that. Arnold Friend was pleased at her laughter and looked up at her. "Around the other side's a lot more—you wanta come and see them?"

"No."

"Why not?"

"Why should I?"

"Don'tcha wanta see what's on the car? Don'tcha wanta go for a ride?"

"I don't know."

"Why not?"

"I got things to do."

"Like what?"

"Things."

He laughed as if she had said something funny. He slapped his thighs. He was standing in a strange way, leaning back against the car as if he were balancing himself. He wasn't tall, only an inch or so taller than she would be if she came down to him. Connie liked the way he was dressed, which was the way all of them dressed: tight faded jeans stuffed into black, scuffed boots, a belt that pulled his waist in and showed how lean he was, and a white pull-over shirt that was a little soiled and showed the hard small muscles of his arms and shoulders. He looked as if he probably did hard work, lifting and carrying things. Even his neck looked muscular. And his face was a familiar face, somehow: the jaw and chin and cheeks slightly darkened, because he hadn't shaved for a day or two, and the nose long and hawk-like, sniffing as if she were a treat he was going to gobble up and it was all a joke.

"Connie, you ain't telling the truth. This is your day set aside for a ride with me and you know it," he said, still laughing. The way he straightened and recovered from his fit of laughing showed that it had been all fake.

"How do you know what my name is?" she said suspiciously.

"It's Connie."

"Maybe and maybe not."

"I know my Connie," he said, wagging his finger. Now she remembered him even better, back at the restaurant, and her cheeks warmed at the thought of how she sucked in her breath just at the moment she passed him—how she must have looked to him. And he had remembered her. "Ellie and I come out here especially for you," he said. "Ellie can sit in back. How about it?"

"Where?"

"Where what?"

"Where're we going?"

55 He looked at her. He took off the sunglasses and she saw how pale the skin around his eyes was, like holes that were not in shadow but instead in light. His eyes were chips of broken glass that catch the light in an amiable way. He smiled. It was as if the idea of going for a ride somewhere, to some place, was a new idea to him.

"Just for a ride, Connie sweetheart."

"I never said my name was Connie," she said.

"But I know what it is. I know your name and all about you, lots of things," Arnold Friend said. He had not moved yet but stood still leaning back against the side of his jalopy. "I took a special interest in you, such a pretty girl, and found out all about you like I know your parents and sister are gone somewheres and I know where and how long they're going to be gone, and I know who you were with last night, and your best girl friend's name is Betty. Right?"

He spoke in a simple lilting voice, exactly as if he were reciting the words to a song. His smile assured her that everything was fine. In the car Ellie turned up the volume on his radio and did not bother to look around at them.

60 "Ellie can sit in the back seat," Arnold Friend said. He indicated his friend with a casual jerk of his chin, as if Ellie did not count and she should not bother with him.

"How'd you find out all that stuff?" Connie said.

"Listen: Betty Schultz and Tony Fitch and Jimmy Pettinger and Nancy Pettinger," he said, in a chant. "Raymond Stanley and Bob Hutter—"

"Do you know all those kids?"

"I know everybody."

65 "Look, you're kidding. You're not from around here."

"Sure."

"But—how come we never saw you before?"

"Sure you saw me before," he said. He looked down at his boots, as if he were a little offended. "You just don't remember."

"I guess I'd remember you," Connie said.

70 "Yeah?" He looked up at this, beaming. He was pleased. He began to mark time with the music from Ellie's radio, tapping his fists lightly together. Connie looked away from his smile to the car, which was painted so bright it almost hurt her eyes to look at it. She looked at that name, ARNOLD FRIEND. And up at the front fender was an expression that was familiar—MAN THE FLYING SAUCERS. It was an expression kids had used the year before, but didn't use this year. She looked at it for a while as if the words meant something to her that she did not yet know.

"What're you thinking about? Huh?" Arnold Friend demanded. "Not worried about your hair blowing around in the car, are you?"

"No."

"Think I maybe can't drive good?"

"How do I know?"

75 "You're a hard girl to handle. How come?" he said. "Don't you know I'm your friend? Didn't you see me put my sign in the air when you walked by?"

"What sign?"

"My sign." And he drew an X in the air, leaning out toward her. They were maybe ten feet apart. After his hand fell back to his side the X was still in the air, almost visible. Connie let the screen door close and stood perfectly still inside it, listening to the music from her radio and the boy's blend together. She stared at Arnold Friend. He stood there so stiffly relaxed, pretending to be relaxed, with one hand idly on the door handle as if he were keeping himself up that way and had no intention of ever moving again. She recognized most things about him, the tight jeans that showed his thighs and buttocks and the greasy leather boots and the tight shirt, and even that slippery friendly smile of his, that sleepy dreamy smile that all the boys used to get across ideas they didn't want to put into words. She recognized all this and also the singsong way he talked, slightly mocking, kidding, but serious and a little melancholy, and she recognized the way he tapped one fist against the other in homage to the perpetual music behind him. But all these things did not come together.

She said suddenly, "Hey, how old are you?"

His smile faded. She could see then that he wasn't a kid, he was much older—thirty, maybe more. At this knowledge her heart began to pound faster.

"That's a crazy thing to ask. Can'tcha see I'm your own age?"

"Like hell you are."

"Or maybe a coupla years older, I'm eighteen."

"Eighteen?" she said doubtfully.

He grinned to reassure her and lines appeared at the corners of his mouth. His teeth were big and white. He grinned so broadly his eyes became slits and she saw how thick the lashes were, thick and black as if painted with a black tarlike material. Then he seemed to become embarrassed, abruptly, and looked over his shoulder at Ellie. "*Him,* he's crazy," he said. "Ain't he a riot, he's a nut, a real character." Ellie was still listening to the music. His sunglasses told nothing about what he was thinking. He wore a bright orange shirt unbuttoned halfway to show his chest, which was a pale, bluish chest and not muscular like Arnold Friend's. His shirt collar was turned up all around and the very tips of the collar pointed out past his chin as if they were protecting him. He was pressing the transistor radio up against his ear and sat there in a kind of daze, right in the sun.

"He's kinda strange," Connie said.

"Hey, she says you're kinda strange! Kinda strange!" Arnold Friend cried. He pounded on the car to get Ellie's attention. Ellie turned for the first time and Connie saw with shock that he wasn't a kid either—he had a fair, hairless face, cheeks reddened slightly as if the veins grew too close to the surface of his skin, the face of a forty-year-old baby. Connie felt a wave of dizziness rise in her at this sight and she stared at him as if waiting for something to change the shock of the moment, make it all right again. Ellie's lips kept shaping words, mumbling along, with the words blasting in his ear.

"Maybe you two better go away," Connie said faintly.

"What? How come?" Arnold Friend cried. "We come out here to take you for a ride. It's Sunday." He had the voice of the man on the radio now. It was the same voice, Connie thought. "Don'tcha know it's Sunday all day and honey, no matter who you were with last night today you're with Arnold Friend and don't you forget it!—Maybe you better step out here," he said, and this last was in a different voice. It was a little flatter, as if the heat was finally getting to him.

"No. I got things to do."

90 "Hey."

"You two better leave."

"We ain't leaving until you come with us."

"Like hell I am—"

"Connie, don't fool around with me. I mean, I mean, don't fool *around*," he said, shaking his head. He laughed incredulously. He placed his sunglasses on top of his head, carefully, as if he were indeed wearing a wig, and brought the stems down behind his ears. Connie stared at him, another wave of dizziness and fear rising in her so that for a moment he wasn't even in focus but was just a blur, standing there against his gold car, and she had the idea that he had driven up the driveway all right but had come from nowhere before that and belonged nowhere and that everything about him and even about the music that was so familiar to her was only half real.

95 "If my father comes and sees you—"

"He ain't coming. He's at the barbecue."

"How do you know that?"

"Aunt Tillie's. Right now they're—uh—they're drinking. Sitting around," he said vaguely, squinting as if he were staring all the way to town and over to Aunt Tillie's backyard. Then the vision seemed to get clear and he nodded energetically. "Yeah. Sitting around. There's your sister in a blue dress, huh? And high heels, the poor sad bitch—nothing like you, sweetheart! And your mother's helping some fat woman with the corn, they're cleaning the corn—husking the corn—"

"What fat woman?" Connie cried.

100 "How do I know what fat woman. I don't know every goddam fat woman in the world!" Arnold Friend laughed.

"Oh, that's Mrs. Hornby. . . . Who invited her?" Connie said. She felt a little light-headed. Her breath was coming quickly.

"She's too fat. I don't like them fat. I like them the way you are, honey," he said, smiling sleepily at her. They stared at each other for a while, through the screen door. He said softly, "Now what you're going to do is this: you're going to come out that door. You're going to sit up front with me and Ellie's going to sit in the back, the hell with Ellie, right? This isn't Ellie's date. You're my date. I'm your lover, honey."

"What? You're crazy—"

"Yes, I'm your lover. You don't know what that is but you will," he said. "I know that too. I know all about you. But look: it's real nice and you couldn't ask for nobody better than me, or more polite. I always keep my word. I'll tell you how it is, I'm always nice at first, the first time. I'll hold you so tight you won't think you have to try to get away or pretend anything because you'll know you can't. And I'll come inside you where it's all secret and you'll give in to me and you'll love me—"

105 "Shut up! You're crazy!" Connie said. She backed away from the door. She put her hands against her ears as if she'd heard something terrible, something not meant for her. "People don't talk like that, you're crazy," she muttered. Her heart was almost too big now for her chest and its pumping made sweat break out all over her.

She looked out to see Arnold Friend pause and then take a step toward the porch lurching. He almost fell. But, like a clever drunken man, he managed to catch his balance. He wobbled in his high boots and grabbed hold of one of the porch posts.

"Honey?" he said. "You still listening?"

"Get the hell out of here!"

"Be nice, honey. Listen."

"I'm going to call the police—"

110 He wobbled again and out of the side of his mouth came a fast spat curse, an aside not meant for her to hear. But even this "Christ!" sounded forced. Then he began to smile again. She watched this smile come, awkward as if he were smiling from inside a mask. His whole face was a mask, she thought wildly, tanned down onto his throat but then running out as if he had plastered make-up on his face but had forgotten about his throat.

"Honey—? Listen, here's how it is. I always tell the truth and I promise you this: I ain't coming in that house after you."

"You better not! I'm going to call the police if you—if you don't—"

"Honey," he said, talking right through her voice, "honey, I'm not coming in there but you are coming out here. You know why?"

She was panting. The kitchen looked like a place she had never seen before, some room she had run inside but which wasn't good enough, wasn't going to help her. The kitchen window had never had a curtain, after three years, and there were dishes in the sink for her to do—probably—and if you ran your hand across the table you'd probably feel something sticky there.

115 "You listening, honey? Hey?"

"—going to call the police—"

"Soon as you touch the phone I don't need to keep my promise and can come inside. You won't want that."

She rushed forward and tried to lock the door. Her fingers were shaking. "But why lock it," Arnold Friend said gently, talking right into her face. "It's just a screen door. It's just nothing." One of his boots was at a strange angle, as if his foot wasn't in it. It pointed out to the left, bent at the ankle. "I mean, anybody can break through a screen door and glass and wood and iron or anything else if he needs to, anybody at all and specially Arnold Friend. If the place got lit up with a fire honey you'd come running out into my arms, right into my arms and safe at home—like you knew I was your lover and'd stopped fooling around. I don't mind a nice shy girl but I don't like no fooling around." Part of those words were spoken with a slight rhythmic lilt, and Connie somehow recognized them—the echo of a song from last year, about a girl rushing into her boy friend's arms and coming home again—

Connie stood barefoot on the linoleum floor, staring at him. "What do you want?" she whispered.

120 "I want you," he said.

"What?"

"Seen you that night and thought, that's the one, yes sir. I never needed to look any more."

"But my father's coming back. He's coming to get me. I had to wash my hair first—" She spoke in a dry, rapid voice, hardly raising it for him to hear.

"No, your daddy is not coming and yes, you had to wash your hair and you washed it for me. It's nice and shining and all for me, I thank you, sweetheart," he said, with a mock bow, but again he almost lost his balance. He had to bend and adjust his boots. Evidently his feet did not go all the way down; the boots must have been stuffed with something so that he would seem taller. Connie stared out at him and behind him Ellie in the car, who seemed to be looking off toward Connie's right, into nothing. This Ellie said, pulling the words out of the air one after another as if he were just discovering them, "You want me to pull out the phone?"

125 "Shut your mouth and keep it shut," Arnold Friend said, his face red from bending over or maybe from embarrassment because Connie had seen his boots. "This ain't none of your business."

"What—what are you doing? What do you want?" Connie said. "If I call the police they'll get you, they'll arrest you—"

"Promise was not to come in unless you touch that phone, and I'll keep that promise," he said. He resumed his erect position and tried to force his shoulders back. He sounded like a hero in a movie, declaring something important. He spoke too loudly and it was as if he were speaking to someone behind Connie. "I ain't made plans for coming in that house where I don't belong but just for you to come out to me, the way you should. Don't you know who I am?"

"You're crazy," she whispered. She backed away from the door but did not want to go into another part of the house, as if this would give him permission to come through the door. "What do you . . . You're crazy, you . . ."

"Huh? What're you saying, honey?"

130 Her eyes darted everywhere in the kitchen. She could not remember what it was, this room.

"This is how it is, honey: you come out and we'll drive away, have a nice ride. But if you don't come out we're gonna wait till your people come home and then they're all going to get it."

"You want that telephone pulled out?" Ellie said. He held the radio away from his ear and grimaced, as if without the radio the air was too much for him.

"I toldja shut up, Ellie," Arnold Friend said, "you're deaf, get a hearing aid, right? Fix yourself up. This little girl's no trouble and's gonna be nice to me, so Ellie keep to yourself, this ain't your date—right? Don't hem in on me. Don't hog. Don't crush. Don't bird dog. Don't trail me," he said in a rapid meaningless voice, as if he were running through all the expressions he'd learned but was no longer sure which one of them was in style, then rushing on to new ones, making them up with his eyes closed, "Don't crawl under my fence, don't squeeze in my chipmunk hole, don't sniff my glue, suck my popsicle, keep your own greasy fingers on yourself!" He shaded his eyes and peered in at Connie, who was backed against the kitchen table. "Don't mind him honey he's just a creep. He's a dope. Right? I'm the boy for you and like I said you come out here nice like a lady and give me your hand, and nobody else gets hurt, I mean, your nice old bald-headed daddy and your mummy and your sister in her high heels. Because listen: why bring them in this?"

"Leave me alone," Connie whispered.

135 "Hey, you know that old woman down the road, the one with the chickens and stuff—you know her?"

"She's dead!"

"Dead? What? You know her?" Arnold Friend said.

"She's dead—"

"Don't you like her?"

140 "She's dead—she's—she isn't here any more—"

"But don't you like her, I mean, you got something against her? Some grudge or something?" Then his voice dipped as if he were conscious of a rudeness. He touched the sunglasses perched on top of his head as if to make sure they were still there. "Now you be a good girl."

"What are you going to do?"

"Just two things, or maybe three," Arnold Friend said. "But I promise it won't last long and you'll like me that way you get to like people you're close to. You will. It's all over for you here, so come on out. You don't want your people in any trouble, do you?"

She turned and bumped against a chair or something, hurting her leg, but she ran into the back room and picked up the telephone. Something roared in her ear, a tiny roaring, and she was so sick with fear that she could do nothing but listen to it—the telephone was clammy and very heavy and her fingers groped down to the dial but were too weak to touch it. She began to scream into the phone, into the roaring. She cried out, she cried for her mother, she felt her breath start jerking back and forth in her lungs as if it were something Arnold Friend were stabbing her with again and again with no tenderness. A noisy sorrowful wailing rose all about her and she was locked inside it the way she was locked inside the house.

145 After a while she could hear again. She was sitting on the floor with her wet back against the wall.

Arnold Friend was saying from the door, "That's a good girl. Put the phone back."

She kicked the phone away from her.

"No, honey. Pick it up. Put it back right."

She picked it up and put it back. The dial tone stopped.

150 "That's a good girl. Now come outside."

She was hollow with what had been fear, but what was now just an emptiness. All that screaming had blasted it out of her. She sat, one leg cramped under her, and deep inside her brain was something like a pinpoint of light that kept going and would not let her relax. She thought, I'm not going to see my mother again. She thought, I'm not going to sleep in my bed again. Her bright green blouse was all wet.

Arnold Friend said, in a gentle-loud voice that was like a stage voice, "The place where you came from ain't there any more, and where you had in mind to go is cancelled out. This place you are now—inside your daddy's house—is nothing but a cardboard box I can knock down any time. You know that and always did know it. You hear me?"

She thought, I have got to think. I have to know what to do.

"We'll go out to a nice field, out in the country here where it smells so nice and it's sunny," Arnold Friend said. "I'll have my arms around you so you won't need to try to get away and I'll show you what love is like, what it does. The hell with this house! It looks solid all right," he said. He ran a fingernail down the screen and the noise did not make Connie shiver, as it would have the day before. "Now put your hand on your heart, honey. Feel that? That feels solid too but we know better, be nice to me, be sweet like you can because what else is there for a girl like you but to be sweet and pretty and give in?—and get away before her people come back?"

155 She felt her pounding heart. Her hand seemed to enclose it. She thought for the first time in her life that it was nothing that was hers, that belonged to her, but just a pounding, living thing inside this body that wasn't really hers either.

"You don't want them to get hurt," Arnold Friend went on. "Now get up, honey. Get up all by yourself."

She stood up.

"Now turn this way. That's right. Come over here to me—Ellie, put that away, didn't I tell you? You dope. You miserable creepy dope," Arnold Friend said. His words were not angry but only part of an incantation. The incantation was kindly. "Now come out through the kitchen to me honey and let's see a smile, try it, you're a brave sweet little girl and now they're eating corn and hotdogs cooked to bursting over an outdoor fire, and they don't know one thing about you and never did and honey you're better than them because not a one of them would have done this for you."

Connie felt the linoleum under her feet; it was cool. She brushed her hair back out of her eyes. Arnold Friend let go of the post tentatively and opened his arms for her, his elbows pointing in toward each other and his wrists limp, to show that this was an embarrassed embrace and a little mocking, he didn't want to make her self-conscious.

160 She put out her hand against the screen. She watched herself push the door slowly open as if she were safe back somewhere in the other doorway, watching this body and this head of long hair moving out into the sunlight where Arnold Friend waited.

"My sweet little blue-eyed girl," he said, in a half-sung sigh that had nothing to do with her brown eyes but was taken up just the same by the vast sunlit reaches of the land behind him and on all sides of him, so much land that Connie had never seen before and did not recognize except to know that she was going to it.

➤ *QUESTIONS FOR READING AND WRITING*

1. Describe Connie. Why is she so irked by her mother's criticism and comparisons to her older sister? What is her social life like?
2. Describe Arnold Friend. What is your reaction to him? If he called on you, would you go with him? Explain.
3. Why does Connie go with him? Did you find her "giving in" believable? What do you suppose will happen to her?
4. Arnold says, "What else is there for a girl like you but to be sweet and pretty and give in?" Do you think he's right? Explain.

TIM O'BRIEN (b. 1946)

Tim O'Brien was born in Austin, Minnesota. He was drafted immediately after he graduated from Macalester College in 1968, and served in the infantry for two years during the Vietnam War. He has since published four novels and a book of anecdotes, all based on his war experiences. He told an interviewer in Publishers Weekly *that for him writing "requires a sense of passion, and my passion as a human being and as a writer intersect in Vietnam, not in the physical stuff but in the issue of Vietnam—of courage, rectitude, enlightenment, holiness, trying to do the right thing in the world." The following story is taken from his collection* The Things They Carried *(1990), narrated by a character named "Tim O'Brien." His novel* In the Lake of the Woods *was named by* Time *magazine as the best novel of 1994. His most recent novel is* Tomcat in Love *(1998).*

THE THINGS THEY CARRIED [1990]

First Lieutenant Jimmy Cross carried letters from a girl named Martha, a junior at Mount Sebastian College in New Jersey. They were not love letters, but Lieutenant Cross was hoping, so he kept them folded in plastic at the bottom of his rucksack. In the late afternoon, after a day's march, he would dig his foxhole, wash his hands under a canteen, unwrap the letters, hold them with the tips of his fingers, and spend the last hour of light pretending. He would imagine romantic camping trips into the White Mountains in New Hampshire. He would sometimes taste the envelope flaps, knowing her tongue had been there. More than anything, he wanted Martha to love him as he loved her, but the letters were mostly chatty, elusive on the matter of love. She was a virgin, he was almost sure. She was an English major at Mount Sebastian, and she wrote beautifully about her professors and roommates and midterm exams, about her respect for Chaucer and her great affection for Virginia Woolf. She often quoted lines of poetry; she never mentioned the war, except to say, Jimmy, take care of yourself. The letters weighed ten ounces. They were signed "Love, Martha," but Lieutenant Cross understood that Love was only a way of signing and did not mean what he sometimes pretended it meant. At dusk, he would carefully return the letters to his rucksack. Slowly, a bit distracted, he would get up and move among his men, checking the perimeter, then at full dark he would return to his hold and watch the night and wonder if Martha was a virgin.

The things they carried were largely determined by necessity. Among the necessities or near-necessities were P-38 can openers, pocket knives, heat tabs, wristwatches, dog tags, mosquito repellent, chewing gum, candy, cigarettes, salt tablets, packets of Kool-Aid, lighters, matches, sewing kits, Military Payment Certificates, C rations, and two or three canteens of water. Together, these items weighed between fifteen and twenty pounds, depending upon a man's habits or rate of metabolism. Henry Dobbins, who was a big man, carried extra rations; he was especially fond of canned peaches in heavy syrup over pound cake. Dave Jensen, who practiced field hygiene, carried a toothbrush, dental floss, and several hotel-sized bars of soap he'd stolen on R&R[1] in Sydney, Australia. Ted Lavender, who was scared, carried tranquilizers until he was shot in the head outside the village of Than Khe in mid-April. By necessity, and because it was SOP,[2] they all carried steel helmets that weighed five pounds including the liner and camouflage cover. They carried the standard fatigue jackets and trousers. Very few carried underwear. On their feet they carried jungle boots—2.1 pounds—and Dave Jensen carried three pairs of socks and a can of Dr. Scholl's foot powder as a precaution against trench foot. Until he was shot, Ted Lavender carried six or seven ounces of premium dope, which for him was a necessity. Mitchell Sanders, the RTO, carried condoms. Norman Bowker carried a diary. Rat Kiley carried comic books. Kiowa, a devout Baptist, carried an illustrated New Testament that had been presented to him by his father, who taught Sunday school in Oklahoma City, Oklahoma. As a hedge against bad times, however, Kiowa also carried his grandmother's distrust of the white man, his grandfather's old hunting hatchet. Necessity dictated. Because the land was mined and booby-trapped, it was SOP for each man to carry a steel-centered, nylon-covered flak jacket, which weighed 6.7 pounds, but which on hot days seemed much heavier. Because you could die so quickly, each man carried at least one large compress bandage, usually in the helmet band for easy access. Because the nights were cold, and because the monsoons were wet, each carried a green plastic poncho that could be used as a raincoat or ground sheet or makeshift tent. With its quilted liner, the poncho weighed almost two pounds, but it was worth every ounce. In April, for instance, when Ted Lavender was shot, they used his poncho to wrap him up, then to carry him across the paddy, then to lift him into the chopper that took him away.

They were called legs or grunts.

To carry something was to "hump" it, as when Lieutenant Jimmy Cross humped his love for Martha up the hills and through the swamps. In its intransitive form, "to hump" meant "to walk," or "to march," but it implied burdens far beyond the intransitive.

5 Almost everyone humped photographs. In his wallet, Lieutenant Cross carried two photographs of Martha. The first was a Kodachrome snapshot signed "Love," though he knew better. She stood against a brick wall. Her eyes were gray and neutral, her lips slightly open as she stared straight-on at the camera. At night, sometimes, Lieutenant Cross wondered who had taken the picture, because he knew she had boyfriends, because he loved her so much, and because he could see the shadow of the picture taker spreading out against the brick wall. The second photograph had been clipped from the 1968 Mount Sebastian yearbook. It was an action shot—women's volleyball—and Martha was bent horizontal to the floor, reaching, the palms of her hands in sharp focus, the tongue taut, the expression frank and competitive. There was no visible sweat. She wore white gym shorts. Her legs, he thought, were almost certainly the legs of a virgin, dry and without hair, the left

[1] **R&R** rest and recreation [2] **SOP** standard operating procedure

knee cocked and carrying her entire weight, which was just over one hundred pounds. Lieutenant Cross remembered touching that left knee. A dark theater, he remembered, and the movie was *Bonnie and Clyde,* and Martha wore a tweed skirt, and during the final scene, when he touched her knee, she turned and looked at him in a sad, sober way that made him pull his hand back, but he would always remember the feel of the tweed skirt and from geology. He imagined bare feet. Martha was a poet, with the poet's sensibilities, and her feet would be brown and bare, the toenails unpainted, the eyes chilly and somber like the ocean in March, and though it was painful, he wondered who had been with her that afternoon. He imagined a pair of shadows moving along the strip of sand where things came together but also separated. It was phantom jealousy, he knew, but he couldn't help himself. He loved her so much. On the march, through the hot days of early April, he carried the pebble in his mouth, turning it with his tongue, tasting sea salt and moisture. His mind wandered. He had difficulty keeping his attention on the war. On occasion he would yell at his men to spread out the column, to keep their eyes open, but then he would slip away into daydreams, just pretending, walking barefoot along the Jersey shore, with Martha, carrying nothing. He would feel himself rising. Sun and waves and gentle winds, all love and lightness.

What they carried varied by mission.

When a mission took them to the mountains, they carried mosquito netting, machetes, canvas tarps, and extra bug juice.

If a mission seemed especially hazardous, or if it involved a place they knew to be bad, they carried everything they could. In certain heavily mined AOs, where the land was dense with Toe Poppers and Bouncing Betties, they took turns humping a twenty-eight pound mine detector. With its headphones and big sensing plate, the equipment was a stress on the lower back and shoulders, awkward to handle, often useless because of the shrapnel in the earth, but they carried it anyway, partly for safety, partly for the illusion of safety.

On ambush, or other night missions, they carried peculiar little odds and ends. Kiowa always took along his New Testament and a pair of moccasins for silence. Dave Jensen carried night-sight vitamins high in carotin. Lee Strunk carried his slingshot; ammo, he claimed, would never be a problem. Rat Kiley carried brandy and M&M's candy. Until he was shot, Ted Lavender carried the starlight scope, which weighed 6.3 pounds with its aluminum carrying case. Henry Dobbins carried his girlfriend's pantyhose wrapped around his neck as a comforter. They all carried ghosts. When dark came, they would move out single file across the meadows and paddies to their ambush coordinates, where they would quietly set up the Claymores and lie down and spend the night waiting.

10 Other missions were more complicated and required special equipment. In mid-April, it was their mission to search out and destroy the elaborate tunnel complexes in the Than Khe area south of Chu Lai. To blow the tunnels, they carried one-pound blocks of pentrite high explosives, four blocks to a man, sixty-eight pounds in all. They carried wiring, detonators, and battery-powered clackers. Dave Jensen carried earplugs. Most often, before blowing the tunnels, they were ordered by higher command to search them, which was considered bad news, but by and large they just shrugged and carried out orders. Because he was a big man, Henry

Dobbins was excused from tunnel duty. The others would draw numbers. Before Lavender died there were seventeen men in the platoon, and whoever drew the number seventeen would strip off his gear and crawl in head first with a flashlight and Lieutenant Cross's .45-caliber pistol. The rest of them would fan out as security. They would sit down or kneel, not facing the hole, listening to the ground beneath them, imagining cobwebs and ghosts, whatever was down there—the tunnel walls squeezing in—how the flashlight seemed impossibly heavy in the hand and how it was tunnel vision in the very strictest sense, compression in all ways, even time, and how you had to wiggle in—ass and elbows—a swallowed-up feeling—and how you found yourself worrying about odd things—will your flashlight go dead? Do rats carry rabies? If you screamed, how far would the sound carry? Would your buddies hear it? Would they have the courage to drag you out? In some respects, though not many, the waiting was worse than the tunnel itself. Imagination was a killer.

On April 16, when Lee Strunk drew the number seventeen, he laughed and muttered something and went down quickly. The morning was hot and very still. Not good, Kiowa said. He looked at the tunnel opening, then out across a dry paddy toward the village of Than Khe. Nothing moved. No clouds or birds or people. As they waited, the men smoked and drank Kool-Aid, not talking much, feeling sympathy for Lee Strunk but also feeling the luck of the draw. You win some, you lose some, said Mitchell Sanders, and sometimes you settle for a rain check. It was a tired line and no one laughed.

Henry Dobbins ate a tropical chocolate bar. Ted Lavender popped a tranquilizer and went off to pee.

After five minutes, Lieutenant Jimmy Cross moved to the tunnel, leaned down, and examined the darkness. Trouble, he thought—a cave-in maybe. And then suddenly, without willing it, he was thinking about Martha. The stresses and fractures, the quick collapse, the two of them buried alive under all that weight. Dense, crushing love. Kneeling, watching the hole, he tried to concentrate on Lee Strunk and the war, all the dangers, but his love was too much for him, he felt paralyzed, he wanted to sleep inside her lungs and breathe her blood and be smothered. He wanted her to be a virgin and not a virgin, all at once. He wanted to know her. Intimate secrets—why poetry? Why so sad? Why that grayness in her eyes? Why so alone? Not lonely, just alone—riding her bike across campus or sitting off by herself in the cafeteria. Even dancing, she danced alone—and it was the aloneness that filled him with love. He remembered telling her that one evening. How she nodded and looked away. And how, later, when he kissed her, she received the kiss without returning it, her eyes wide open, not afraid, not a virgin's eyes, just flat and uninvolved.

Lieutenant Cross gazed at the tunnel. But he was not there. He was buried with Martha under the white sand at the Jersey shore. They were pressed together, and the pebble in his mouth was her tongue. He was smiling. Vaguely, he was aware of how quiet the day was, the sullen paddies, yet he could not bring himself to worry about matters of security. He was beyond that. He was just a kid at war, in love. He was twenty-two years old. He couldn't help it.

A few moments later Lee Strunk crawled out of the tunnel. He came up grinning, filthy but alive. Lieutenant Cross nodded and closed his eyes while the others clapped Strunk on the back and made jokes about rising from the dead.

15 Worms, Rat Kiley said. Right out of the grave. Fuckin' zombie.

The men laughed. They all felt great relief.

Spook city, said Mitchell Sanders.

Lee Strunk made a funny ghost sound, a kind of moaning, yet very happy, and right then, when Strunk made that high happy moaning sound, when he went *Ahhooooo,* right then Ted Lavender was shot in the head on his way back from peeing. He lay with his mouth open. The teeth were broken. There was a swollen black bruise under his left eye. The cheekbone was gone. Oh shit, Rat Kiley said, the guy's dead. The guy's dead, he kept saying, which seemed profound—the guy's dead. I mean really.

The things they carried were determined to some extent by superstition. Lieutenant Cross carried his good-luck pebble. Dave Jensen carried a rabbit's foot. Norman Bowker, otherwise a very gentle person, carried a thumb that had been presented to him as a gift by Mitchell Sanders. The thumb was dark brown, rubbery to the touch, and weighed four ounces at most. It had been cut from a VC corpse, a boy of fifteen or sixteen. They'd found him at the bottom of an irrigation ditch, badly burned, flies in his mouth and eyes. The boy wore black shorts and sandals. At the time of his death he had been carrying a pouch of rice, a rifle, and three magazines of ammunition.

20 You want my opinion, Mitchell Sanders said, there's a definite moral here.

He put his hand on the dead boy's wrist. He was quiet for a time, as if counting a pulse, then he patted the stomach, almost affectionately, and used Kiowa's hunting hatchet to remove the thumb.

Henry Dobbins asked what the moral was.

Moral?

You know. Moral.

25 Sanders wrapped the thumb in toilet paper and handed it across to Norman Bowker. There was no blood. Smiling, he kicked the boy's head, watched the flies scatter, and said, It's like with that old TV show—Paladin. Have gun, will travel.

Henry Dobbins thought about it.

Yeah, well, he finally said. I don't see no moral.

There it *is,* man.

Fuck off.

30 They carried USO stationery and pencils and pens. They carried Sterno, safety pins, trip flares, signal flares, spools of wire, razor blades, chewing tobacco, liberated joss sticks and statuettes of the smiling Buddha, candles, grease pencils, *The Stars and Stripes,* fingernail clippers, Psy Ops leaflets, bush hats, bolos, and much more. Twice a week, when the resupply choppers came in, they carried hot chow in green Mermite cans and large canvas bags filled with iced beer and soda pop. They carried plastic water containers, each with a two-gallon capacity. Mitchell Sanders carried a set of starched tiger fatigues for special occasions. Henry Dobbins carried Black Flag insecticide. Dave Jensen carried empty sandbags that could be filled at night for added protection. Lee Strunk carried tanning lotion. Some things they carried in common. Taking turns, they carried the big PRC-77 scrambler radio, which weighed thirty pounds with its battery. They shared the weight of memory. They

took up what others could no longer bear. Often, they carried each other, the wounded or weak. They carried infections. They carried chess sets, basketballs, Vietnamese-English dictionaries, insignia of rank, Bronze Stars and Purple Hearts, plastic cards imprinted with the Code of Conduct. They carried diseases, among them malaria and dysentery. They carried lice and ringworm and leeches and paddy algae and various rots and molds. They carried the land itself—Vietnam, the place, the soil—a powdery orange-red dust that covered their boots and fatigues and faces. They carried the sky. The whole atmosphere, they carried it, the humidity, the monsoons, the stink of fungus and decay, all of it, they carried gravity. They moved like mules. By daylight they took sniper fire, at night they were mortared, but it was not battle, it was just the endless march, village to village, without purpose, nothing won or lost. They marched for the sake of the march. They plodded along slowly, dumbly, leaning forward against the heat, unthinking, all blood and bone, simple grunts, soldiering with their legs, toiling up the hills and down into the paddies and across the rivers and up again and down, just humping, one step and then the next and then another, but no volition, no will, because it was automatic, it was anatomy, and the war was entirely a matter of posture and carriage, the hump was everything, a kind of inertia, a kind of emptiness, a dullness of desire and intellect and conscience and hope and human sensibility. Their principles were in their feet. Their calculations were biological. They had no sense of strategy or mission. They searched the villages without knowing what to look for, not caring, kicking over jars of rice, frisking children and old men, blowing tunnels, sometimes setting fires and sometimes not, then forming up and moving on to the next village, then other villages, where it would always be the same. They carried their own lives. The pressures were enormous. In the heat of early afternoon, they would remove their helmets and flak jackets, walking bare, which was dangerous but which helped ease the strain. They would often discard things along the route of march. Purely for comfort, they would throw away rations, blow their Claymores and grenades, no matter, because by nightfall the resupply choppers would arrive with more of the same, then a day or two later still more, fresh watermelons and crates of ammunition and sunglasses and woolen sweaters—the resources were stunning—sparklers for the Fourth of July, colored eggs for Easter. It was the great American war chest—the fruits of science, the smokestacks, the canneries, the arsenals at Hartford, the Minnesota forests, the machine shops, the vast fields of corn and wheat—they carried like freight trains; they carried it on their backs and shoulders—and for all the ambiguities of Vietnam, all the mysteries and unknowns, there was at least the single abiding certainty that they would never be at a loss for things to carry.

After the chopper took Lavender away, Lieutenant Jimmy Cross led his men into the village of Than Khe. They burned everything. They shot chickens and dogs, they trashed the village well, they called in artillery and watched the wreckage, then they marched for several hours through the hot afternoon, and then at dusk, while Kiowa explained how Lavender died, Lieutenant Cross found himself trembling.

He tried not to cry. With his entrenching tool, which weighed five pounds, he began digging a hole in the earth.

He felt shame. He hated himself. He had loved Martha more than his men, and as a consequence Lavender was now dead, and this was something he would have to carry like a stone in his stomach for the rest of the war.

All he could do was dig. He used his entrenching tool like an ax, slashing, feeling both love and hate, and then later, when it was full dark, he sat at the bottom of his foxhole and wept. It went on for a long while. In part, he was grieving for Ted Lavender, but mostly it was for Martha, and for himself, because she belonged to another world, which was not quite real, and because she was a junior at Mount Sebastian College in New Jersey, a poet and a virgin and uninvolved, and because he realized she did not love him and never would.

Like cement, Kiowa whispered in the dark. I swear to God—boom-down. Not a word.

I've heard this, said Norman Bowker.

A pisser, you know? Still zipping himself up. Zapped while zipping.

All right, fine. That's enough.

Yeah, but you had to see it, the guy just—

I *heard,* man. Cement. So why not shut the fuck *up?*

Kiowa shook his head sadly and glanced over at the hole where Lieutenant Jimmy Cross sat watching the night. The air was thick and wet. A warm dense fog had settled over the paddies and there was the stillness that precedes rain.

After a time Kiowa sighed.

One thing for sure, he said. The lieutenant's in some deep hurt. I mean that crying jag—the way he was carrying on—it wasn't fake or anything, it was real heavy-duty hurt. The man cares.

Sure, Norman Bowker said.

Say what you want, the man does care.

We all got problems.

Not Lavender.

No, I guess not, Bowker said. Do me a favor, though.

Shut up?

That's a smart Indian. Shut up.

Shrugging, Kiowa pulled off his boots. He wanted to say more, just to lighten up his sleep, but instead he opened his New Testament and arranged it beneath his head as a pillow. The fog made things seem hollow and unattached. He tried not to think about Ted Lavender, but then he was thinking how fast it was, no drama, down and dead, and how it was hard to feel anything except surprise. It seemed un-Christian. He wished he could find some great sadness, or even anger, but the emotion wasn't there and he couldn't make it happen. Mostly he felt pleased to be alive. He liked the smell of the New Testament under his cheek, the leather and ink and paper and glue, whatever the chemicals were. He liked hearing the sounds of night. Even his fatigue, it felt fine, the stiff muscles and the prickly awareness of his own body, a floating feeling. He enjoyed not being dead. Lying there, Kiowa admired Lieutenant Jimmy Cross's capacity for grief. He wanted to share the man's pain, he wanted to care as Jimmy Cross cared. And yet when he closed his eyes, all he could think was Boom-down, and all he could feel was the pleasure of having his boots off and the fog curling in around him and the damp soil and the Bible smells and the plush comfort of night.

After a moment Norman Bowker sat up in the dark.

What the hell, he said. You want to talk, *talk.* Tell it to me.

Forget it.

55 No, man, go on. One thing I hate, it's a silent Indian.

For the most part they carried themselves with poise, a kind of dignity. Now and then, however, there were times of panic, when they squealed or wanted to squeal but couldn't, when they twitched and made moaning sounds and covered their heads and said Dear Jesus and flopped around on the earth and fired their weapons blindly and cringed and sobbed and begged for the noise to stop and went wild and made stupid promises to themselves and to God and to their mothers and fathers, hoping not to die. In different ways, it happened to all of them. Afterward, when the firing ended, they would blink and peek up. They would touch their bodies, feeling shame, then quickly hiding it. They would force themselves to stand. As if in slow motion, frame by frame, the world would take on the old logic—absolute silence, then the wind, then sunlight, then voices. It was the burden of being alive. Awkwardly, the men would reassemble themselves, first in private, then in groups, becoming soldiers again. They would repair the leaks in their eyes. They would check for casualties, call in dust-offs, light cigarettes, try to smile, clear their throats and spit and begin cleaning their weapons. After a time someone would shake his head and say, No lie, I almost shit my pants, and someone else would laugh, which meant it was bad, yes, but the guy had obviously not shit his pants, it wasn't that bad, and in any case nobody would ever do such a thing and then go ahead and talk about it. They would squint into the dense, oppressive sunlight. For a few moments, perhaps, they would fall silent, lighting a joint and tracking its passage from man to man, inhaling, holding in the humiliation. Scary stuff, one of them might say. But then someone else would grin or flick his eyebrows and say, Roger-dodger, almost cut me a new asshole, *almost.*

There were numerous such poses. Some carried themselves with a sort of wistful resignation, others with pride or stiff soldierly discipline or good humor or macho zeal. They were afraid of dying but they were even more afraid to show it.

They found jokes to tell.

They used a hard vocabulary to contain the terrible softness. *Greased* they'd say. *Offed, lit up, zapped while zipping.* It wasn't cruelty, just stage presence. They were actors and the war came at them in 3-D. When someone died, it wasn't quite dying, because in a curious way it seemed scripted, and because they had their lines mostly memorized, irony mixed with tragedy, and because they called it by other names, as if to encyst and destroy the reality of death itself. They kicked corpses. They cut off thumbs. They talked grunt lingo. They told stories about Ted Lavender's supply of tranquilizers, how the poor guy didn't feel a thing, how incredibly tranquil he was.

60 There's a moral here, said Mitchell Sanders.

They were waiting for Lavender's chopper, smoking the dead man's dope.

The moral's pretty obvious, Sanders said, and winked. Stay away from drugs. No joke, they'll ruin your day every time.

Cute, said Henry Dobbins.

Mind-blower, get it? Talk about wiggy—nothing left, just blood and brains.

They made themselves laugh.

There it is, they'd say, over and over, as if the repetition itself were an act of poise, a balance between crazy and almost crazy, knowing without going. There it is, which meant be cool, let it ride, because oh yeah, man, you can't change what can't be changed, there it is, there it absolutely and positively and fucking well *is*.

They were tough.

They carried all the emotional baggage of men who might die. Grief, terror, love, longing—these were intangibles, but the intangibles had their own mass and specific gravity, they had tangible weight. They carried shameful memories. They carried the common secret of cowardice barely restrained, the instinct to run or freeze or hide, and in many respects this was the heaviest burden of all, for it could never be put down, it required perfect balance and perfect posture. They carried their reputations. They carried the soldier's greatest fear, which was the fear of blushing. Men killed, and died, because they were embarrassed not to. It was what had brought them to the war in the first place, nothing positive, no dreams of glory or honor, just to avoid the blush of dishonor. They died so as not to die of embarrassment. They crawled into tunnels and walked point and advanced under fire. Each morning, despite the unknowns, they made their legs move. They endured. They kept humping. They did not submit to the obvious alternative, which was simply to close the eyes and fall. So easy, really. Go limp and tumble to the ground and let the muscles unwind and not speak and not budge until your buddies picked you up and lifted you into the chopper that would roar and dip its nose and carry you off to the world. A mere matter of falling, yet no one ever fell. It was not courage, exactly; the object was not valor. Rather, they were too frightened to be cowards.

By and large they carried these things inside, maintaining the masks of composure. They sneered at sick call. They spoke bitterly about guys who had found release by shooting off their own toes or fingers. Pussies, they'd say. Candyasses. It was fierce, mocking talk, with only a trace of envy or awe, but even so, the image played itself out behind their eyes.

They imagined the muzzle against flesh. They imagined the quick, sweet pain, then the evacuation to Japan, then a hospital with warm beds and cute geisha nurses.

They dreamed of freedom birds.

At night, on guard, staring into the dark, they were carried away by jumbo jets. They felt the rush of takeoff. *Gone!* they yelled. And then velocity, wings and engines, a smiling stewardess—but it was more than a plane, it was a real bird, a big sleek silver bird with feathers and talons and high screeching. They were flying. The weights fell off, there was nothing to bear. They laughed and held on tight, feeling the cold slap of wind and altitude, soaring, thinking *It's over, I'm gone!*—they were naked, they were light and free—it was all lightness, bright and fast and buoyant, light as light, a helium buzz in the brain, a giddy bubbling in the lungs as they were taken up over the clouds and the war, beyond duty, beyond gravity and mortification and global entanglements—*Sin loi!* they yelled, *I'm sorry, mother-fuckers, but I'm out of it, I'm goofed, I'm on a space cruise, I'm gone!*—and it was a restful, unencumbered sensation, just riding the light waves, sailing that big silver freedom bird over the mountains and oceans, over America, over the farms and great sleeping cities and cemeteries and highways and the golden arches of McDonald's. It was flight, a kind of fleeing, a kind of falling, falling higher and higher, spinning off the edge of the earth and beyond the sun and through the vast, silent vacuum where there were no burdens and where everything weighed exactly nothing. *Gone!* they screamed, *I'm sorry but I'm gone!* And so at night, not quite dreaming, they gave themselves over to lightness, they were carried, they were purely borne.

On the morning after Ted Lavender died, First Lieutenant Jimmy Cross crouched at the bottom of his foxhole and burned Martha's letters. Then he burned the two photographs. There was a steady rain falling, which made it difficult, but he used heat tabs and Sterno to build a small fire, screening it with his body, holding the photographs over the tight blue flame with the tips of his fingers.

He realized it was only a gesture. Stupid, he thought. Sentimental, too, but mostly just stupid.

Lavender was dead. You couldn't burn the blame.

Besides, the letters were in his head. And even now, without photographs, Lieutenant Cross could see Martha playing volleyball in her white gym shorts and yellow T-shirt. He could see her moving in the rain.

When the fire died out, Lieutenant Cross pulled his poncho over his shoulders and ate breakfast from a can.

There was no great mystery, he decided.

In those burned letters Martha had never mentioned the war, except to say, Jimmy, take care of yourself. She wasn't involved. She signed the letters "Love," but it wasn't love, and all the fine lines and technicalities did not matter.

The morning came up wet and blurry. Everything seemed part of everything else, the fog and Martha and the deepening rain.

It was a war, after all.

Half smiling, Lieutenant Jimmy Cross took out his maps. He shook his head hard, as if to clear it, then bent forward and began planning the day's march. In ten minutes, or maybe twenty, he would rouse the men and they would pack up and head west, where the maps showed the country to be green and inviting. They would do what they had always done. The rain might add some weight, but otherwise it would be one more day layered upon all the other days.

He was realistic about it. There was that new hardness in his stomach.

No more fantasies, he told himself.

Henceforth, when he thought about Martha, it would be only to think that she belonged elsewhere. He would shut down the daydreams. This was not Mount Sebastian, it was another world, where there were no pretty poems or midterm exams, a place where men died because of carelessness and gross stupidity. Kiowa was right. Boom down, and you were dead, never partly dead.

Briefly, in the rain, Lieutenant Cross saw Martha's gray eyes gazing back at him.

He understood.

It was very sad, he thought. The things men carried inside. The things men did or felt they had to do.

He almost nodded at her, but didn't.

Instead he went back to his maps. He was now determined to perform his duties firmly and without negligence. It wouldn't help Lavender, he knew that, but from this point on he would comport himself as a soldier. He would dispose of his good-luck pebble. Swallow it, maybe, or use Lee Strunk's slingshot, or just drop it along the trail. On the march he would impose strict field discipline. He would be careful to send out flank security, to prevent straggling or bunching up, to keep his troops moving at the proper pace and at the proper interval. He would insist on clean weapons. He would confiscate the remainder of Lavender's dope. Later in the day, perhaps, he would call the men together and speak to them plainly. He would accept the blame for what had happened to Ted Lavender. He would be a man about it. He would look them in the eyes, keeping his chin level, and he would issue the new SOPs in a calm, impersonal tone of voice, an officer's voice, leaving no room for argument or discussion. Commencing immediately, he'd tell them, they would no longer abandon equipment along the route of march. They would police up their acts. They would get their shit together, and keep it together, and maintain it neatly and in good working order.

He would not tolerate laxity. He would show strength, distancing himself.

Among the men there would be grumbling, of course, and maybe worse, because their days would seem longer and their loads heavier, but Lieutenant Jimmy Cross reminded himself that his obligation was not to be loved but to lead. He would dispense with love; it was not now a factor. And if anyone quarreled or complained, he would simply tighten his lips and arrange his shoulders in the correct command posture. He might give a curt little nod. Or he might not. He might just shrug and say, Carry on, then they would saddle up and form into a column and move out toward the villages of Than Khe.

➤ *QUESTIONS FOR READING AND WRITING*

1. Describe Jimmy Cross. What do you know about him? How does he change?
2. How are you affected by the setting? What brings the setting to life?
3. Kiowa believes that Cross is crying over Lavender's death. Do you agree? Is there any other reason he might be crying? Explain.
4. In addition to the physical things they carried, the narrator says, "They carried all the emotional baggage of men who might die." What do you think he means?
5. Why does he burn Martha's letters?
6. Why are things repeated so often in the story?

PHILIP ROTH (b. 1933)

Philip Roth was born in Newark, New Jersey. "The Conversion of the Jews" is taken from a novel, Goodbye Columbus, *for which he received the National Book Award in 1959. In much of his writing Roth focuses on aspects of contemporary Jewish life.* Portnoy's Complaint *(1969) and his later novels about a Jewish writer named Nathan Zuckerman—*My Life as a Man *(1974),* The Ghost Writer *(1979),* Zuckerman Unbound *(1981),* The Anatomy Lesson *(1983),* Zuckerman Bound *(1985) and* The Counterlife *(1986)—are typical of this focus. In 1998 he won the Pulitzer Prize for his novel* American Pastoral. *His most recent novel is* The Human Stain *(2000).*

THE CONVERSION OF THE JEWS [1959]

"You're a real one for opening your mouth in the first place," Itzie said. "What do you open your mouth all the time for?"

"I didn't bring it up, Itz, I didn't," Ozzie said.

"What do you care about Jesus Christ for anyway?"

"I didn't bring up Jesus Christ. He did. I didn't even know what he was talking about. Jesus is historical, he kept saying. Jesus is historical." Ozzie mimicked the monumental voice of Rabbi Binder.

5 "Jesus was a person that lived like you and me," Ozzie continued. "That's what Binder said—"

"Yeah? . . . So what! What do I give two cents whether he lived or not. And what do you gotta open your mouth!" Itzie Lieberman favored closed-mouthedness, especially when it came to Ozzie Freedman's questions. Mrs. Freedman had to see Rabbi Binder twice before about Ozzie's questions and this Wednesday at four-thirty would be the third time. Itzie preferred to keep *his* mother in the kitchen; he settled for behind-the-back subtleties such as gestures, faces, snarls and other less delicate barnyard noises.

"He was a real person, Jesus, but he wasn't like God, and we don't believe he is God." Slowly, Ozzie was explaining Rabbi Binder's position to Itzie, who had been absent from Hebrew School the previous afternoon.

"The Catholics," Itzie said helpfully, "they believe in Jesus Christ, that he's God." Itzie Lieberman used "the Catholics" in its broadest sense—to include the Protestants.

Ozzie received Itzie's remark with a tiny head bob, as though it were a footnote, and went on. "His mother was Mary, and his father probably was Joseph," Ozzie said. "But the New Testament says his real father was God."

10 "His *real* father?"

"Yeah," Ozzie said, "that's the big thing, his father's supposed to be God."

"Bull."

"That's what Rabbi Binder says, that it's impossible—"

"Sure it's impossible. That stuff's all bull. To have a baby you gotta get laid," Itzie theologized. "Mary hadda get laid."

"That's what Binder says: 'The only way a woman can have a baby is to have intercourse with a man.'"

"He said *that,* Ozz?" For a moment it appeared that Itzie had put the theological question aside. "He said that, intercourse?" A little curled smile shaped itself in the lower half of Itzie's face like a pink mustache. "What you guys do, Ozz, you laugh or something?"

"I raised my hand."

"Yeah? Whatja say?"

"That's when I asked the question."

Itzie's face lit up. "Whatja ask about—intercourse?"

"No, I asked the question about God, how if He could create the heaven and earth in six days, and make all the animals and the fish and the light in six days—the light especially, that's what always gets me, that He could make the light. Making fish and animals, that's pretty good—"

"That's damn good." Itzie's appreciation was honest but unimaginative: it was as though God had just pitched a one-hitter.

"But making light . . . I mean when you think about it, it's really something," Ozzie said. "Anyway, I asked Binder if He could make all that in six days, and He could *pick* the six days he wanted right out of nowhere, why couldn't He let a woman have a baby without having intercourse."

"You said intercourse, Ozz, to Binder?"

"Yeah."

"Right in class?"

"Yeah."

Itzie smacked the side of his head.

"I mean, no kidding around," Ozzie said, "that'd really be nothing. After all that other stuff, that'd practically be nothing."

Itzie considered a moment. "What'd Binder say?"

"He started all over again explaining how Jesus was historical and how he lived like you and me but he wasn't God. So I said I under*stood* that. What I wanted to know was different."

What Ozzie wanted to know was always different. The first time he had wanted to know how Rabbi Binder could call the Jews "The Chosen People" if the Declaration of Independence claimed all men to be created equal. Rabbi Binder tried to distinguish for him between political equality and spiritual legitimacy, but what Ozzie wanted to know, he insisted vehemently, was different. That was the first time his mother had to come.

Then there was the plane crash. Fifty-eight people had been killed in a plane crash at La Guardia. In studying a casualty list in the newspaper his mother had discovered among the list of those dead eight Jewish names (his grandmother had nine but she counted Miller as a Jewish name); because of the eight she said the plane crash was "a tragedy." During free-discussion time on Wednesday Ozzie had brought to Rabbi Binder's attention this matter of "some of his relations" always picking out the Jewish names. Rabbi Binder had begun to explain cultural unity and some other things when Ozzie stood up at his seat and said that what he wanted to know was different. Rabbi Binder insisted that he sit down and it was then that Ozzie shouted that he wished all fifty-eight were Jews. That was the second time his mother came.

"And he kept explaining about Jesus being historical, and so I kept asking him. No kidding, Itz, he was trying to make me look stupid."

"So what he finally do?"

"Finally he starts screaming that I was deliberately simple-minded and a wise guy, and that my mother had to come, and this was the last time. And that I'd never get bar-mitzvahed if he could help it. Then, Itz, then he starts talking in that voice like a statue, real slow and deep, and he says that I better think over what I said about the Lord. He told me to go to his office and think it over." Ozzie leaned his body towards Itzie. "Itz, I thought it over for a solid hour, and now I'm convinced God could do it."

Ozzie had planned to confess his latest transgression to his mother as soon as she came home from work. But it was a Friday night in November and already dark, and when Mrs. Freedman came through the door she tossed off her coat, kissed Ozzie quickly on the face, and went to the kitchen table to light the three yellow candles, two for the Sabbath and one for Ozzie's father.

When his mother lit the candles she would move her two arms slowly towards her, dragging them through the air, as though persuading people whose minds were half made up. And her eyes would get glassy with tears. Even when his father was alive Ozzie remembered that her eyes had gotten glassy, so it didn't have anything to do with his dying. It had something to do with lighting the candles.

As she touched the flaming match to the unlit wick of a Sabbath candle, the phone rang, and Ozzie, standing only a foot from it, plucked it off the receiver and held it muffled to his chest. When his mother lit candles Ozzie felt there should be no noise; even breathing if you could manage it, should be softened. Ozzie pressed the phone to his breast and watched his mother dragging whatever she was dragging, and he felt his own eyes get glassy. His mother was a round, tired, gray-haired penguin of a woman whose gray skin had begun to feel the tug of gravity and the weight of her own history. Even when she was dressed up she didn't look like a chosen person. But when she lit candles she looked like something better; like a woman who knew momentarily that God could do anything.

After a few mysterious minutes she was finished. Ozzie hung up the phone and walked to the kitchen table where she was beginning to lay the two places for the four-course Sabbath meal. He told her that she would have to see Rabbi Binder next Wednesday at four-thirty, and then he told her why. For the first time in their life together she hit Ozzie across the face with her hand.

All through the chopped liver and chicken soup part of the dinner Ozzie cried; he didn't have any appetite for the rest.

On Wednesday, in the largest of the three basement classrooms of the synagogue, Rabbi Marvin Binder, a tall, handsome, broad-shouldered man of thirty with thick strong-fibered black hair, removed his watch from his pocket and saw that it was four o'clock. At the rear of the room Yakov Blotnik, the seventy-one-year-old custodian, slowly polished the large window, mumbling to himself, unaware that it was four o'clock or six o'clock, Monday or Wednesday. To most of the students Yakov Blotnik's mumbling, along with his brown curly beard, scythe nose, and two heel-trailing black cats, made of him an object of wonder, a foreigner, a relic, towards whom they were alternately fearful and disrespectful. To Ozzie the mumbling had always seemed a monotonous, curious prayer; what made it curious was that old Blotnik had been mumbling so steadily for so many years, Ozzie suspected he had memorized the prayers and forgotten all about God.

"It is now free-discussion time," Rabbi Binder said. "Feel free to talk about any Jewish matter at all—religion, family, politics, sports—"

There was silence. It was a gusty, clouded November afternoon and it did not seem as though there ever was or could be a thing called baseball. So nobody this week said a word about that hero from the past, Hank Greenberg—which limited free discussion considerably.

And the soul-battering Ozzie Freedman had just received from Rabbi Binder had imposed its limitation. When it was Ozzie's turn to read aloud from the Hebrew book the rabbi had asked him petulantly why he didn't read more rapidly. He was showing no progress. Ozzie said he could read faster but that if he did he was sure not to understand what he was reading. Nevertheless, at the rabbi's repeated suggestion Ozzie tried, and showed a great talent, but in the midst of a long passage he stopped short and said he didn't understand a word he was reading, and started in again at a drag-footed pace. Then came the soul-battering.

Consequently when free-discussion time rolled around none of the students felt too free. The rabbi's invitation was answered only by the mumbling of feeble old Blotnik.

"Isn't there anything at all you would like to discuss?" Rabbi Binder asked again, looking at his watch. "No questions or comments?"

There was a small grumble from the third row. The rabbi requested that Ozzie rise and give the rest of the class the advantage of his thought.

Ozzie rose. "I forget it now," he said, and sat down in his place.

Rabbi Binder advanced a seat towards Ozzie and poised himself on the edge of the desk. It was Itzie's desk and the rabbi's frame only a dagger's-length away from his face snapped him to sitting attention.

"Stand up again, Oscar," Rabbi Binder said calmly, "and try to assemble your thoughts."

Ozzie stood up. All his classmates turned in their seats and watched as he gave an unconvincing scratch to his forehead.

"I can't assemble any," he announced, and plunked himself down.

"Stand up!" Rabbi Binder advanced from Itzie's desk to the one directly in front of Ozzie; when the rabbinical back was turned Itzie gave it five-fingers off the tip of his nose, causing a small titter in the room. Rabbi Binder was too absorbed in squelching Ozzie's nonsense once and for all to bother with titters. "Stand up, Oscar. What's your question about?"

Ozzie pulled a word out of the air. It was the handiest word. "Religion."

"Oh, now you remember?"

"Yes."

"What is it?"

Trapped, Ozzie blurted the first thing that came to him. "Why can't He make anything He wants to make!"

60 As Rabbi Binder prepared an answer, a final answer, Itzie, ten feet behind him, raised one finger on his left hand, gestured it meaningfully towards the rabbi's back, and brought the house down.

Binder twisted quickly to see what had happened and in the midst of the commotion Ozzie shouted into the rabbi's back what he couldn't have shouted to his face. It was a loud, toneless sound that had the timbre of something stored inside for about six days.

"You don't know! You don't know anything about God!"

The rabbi spun back towards Ozzie. "What?"

"You don't know—you don't—"

65 "Apologize, Oscar, apologize!" It was a threat.

"You don't—"

Rabbi Binder's hand flicked out at Ozzie's cheek. Perhaps it had only been meant to clamp the boy's mouth shut, but Ozzie ducked and the palm caught him squarely on the nose.

The blood came in a short, red spurt on to Ozzie's shirt front.

The next moment was all confusion. Ozzie screamed, "You bastard, you bastard!" and broke for the classroom door. Rabbi Binder lurched a step backwards, as though his own blood had started flowing violently in the opposite direction, then gave a clumsy lurch forward and bolted out the door after Ozzie. The class followed after the rabbi's huge blue-suited back, and before old Blotnik could turn from his window, the room was empty and everyone was headed full speed up the three flights leading to the roof.

70 If one should compare the light of day to the life of man: sunrise to birth; sunset—the dropping down over the edge—to death; then as Ozzie Freedman wiggled through the trapdoor of the synagogue roof, his feet kicking backwards bronco-style at Rabbi Binder's outstretched arms—at that moment the day was fifty years old. As a rule fifty or fifty-five reflects accurately the age of late afternoons in November, for it is in that month, during those hours, that one's awareness of light seems no longer a matter of seeing, but of hearing: light begins clicking away. In fact, as Ozzie locked shut the trapdoor in the rabbi's face, the sharp click of the bolt into the lock might momentarily have been mistaken for the sound of the heavier gray that had just throbbed through the sky.

With all his weight Ozzie kneeled on the locked door; any instant he was certain that Rabbi Binder's shoulder would fling it open, splintering the wood into shrapnel and catapulting his body into the sky. But the door did not move and below him he heard only the rumble of feet, first loud then dim, like thunder rolling away.

A question shot through his brain. "Can this be *me?*" For a thirteen-year-old who had just labeled his religious leader a bastard, twice, it was not an improper question. Louder and louder the question came to him—"Is it me? Is it me?"—until he discovered himself no longer kneeling, but racing crazily towards the edge of the roof, his eyes crying, his throat screaming, and his arms flying everywhichway as though not his own.

"Is it me? Is it me Me Me Me Me! It has to be me—but is it!"

It is the question a thief must ask himself the night he jimmies open his first window, and it is said to be the question with which bridegrooms quiz themselves before the altar.

75 In the few wild seconds it took Ozzie's body to propel him to the edge of the roof, his self-examination began to grow fuzzy. Gazing down at the street, he became confused as to the problem beneath the question: was it, is-it-me-who-called-Binder-a-bastard? or, is-it-me-prancing-around-on-the-roof? However, the scene below settled all, for there is an instant in any action when whether it is you or somebody else is academic. The thief crams the money in his pockets and scoots out the window. The bridegroom signs the hotel register for two. And the boy on the roof finds a streetful of people gaping at him, necks stretched backwards, faces up, as though he were the ceiling of the Hayden Planetarium. Suddenly you know it's you.

"Oscar! Oscar Freedman!" A voice rose from the center of the crowd, a voice that, could it have been seen, would have looked like the writing on a scroll. "Oscar Freedman, get down from there. Immediately!" Rabbi Binder was pointing one arm stiffly up at him; and at the end of that arm, one finger aimed menacingly. It was the attitude of a dictator, but one—the eyes confessed all—whose personal valet had spit neatly in his face.

Ozzie didn't answer. Only for a blink's length did he look towards Rabbi Binder. Instead his eyes began to fit together the world beneath him, to sort out people from places, friends from enemies, participants from spectators. In little jagged starlike clusters his friends stood around Rabbi Binder, who was still pointing. The topmost point on a star compounded not of angels but of five adolescent boys was Itzie. What a world it was, with those stars below, Rabbi Binder below . . . Ozzie, who a moment earlier hadn't been able to control his own body, started to feel the meaning of the word control: he felt Peace and he felt Power.

"Oscar Freedman, I'll give you three to come down."

Few dictators give their subjects three to do anything; but, as always, Rabbi Binder only looked dictatorial.

80 "Are you ready, Oscar?"

Ozzie nodded his head yes, although he had no intention in the world—the lower one or the celestial one he'd just entered—of coming down even if Rabbi Binder should give him a million.

"All right then," said Rabbi Binder. He ran a hand through his black Samson hair as though it were the gesture prescribed for uttering the first digit. Then, with his other hand cutting a circle out of the small piece of sky around him, he spoke. "One!"

There was no thunder. On the contrary, at that moment, as though "one" was the cue for which he had been waiting, the world's least thunderous person appeared on the synagogue steps. He did not so much come out the synagogue door as lean out, onto the darkening air. He clutched at the doorknob with one hand and looked up at the roof.

"Oy!"

85 Yakov Blotnik's old mind hobbled slowly, as if on crutches, and though he couldn't decide precisely what the boy was doing on the roof, he knew it wasn't good—that is, it wasn't-good-for-the-Jews. For Yakov Blotnik life had fractionated itself simply: things were either good-for-the-Jews or no-good-for-the-Jews.

He smacked his free hand to his in-sucked cheek, gently. "Oy. Gut!" And then quickly as he was able, he jacked down his head and surveyed the street. There was Rabbi Binder (like a man at an auction with only three dollars in his pocket, he had just delivered a shaky "Two!"); there were the students, and that was all. So far it-wasn't-so-bad-for-the-Jews. But the boy had to come down immediately, before anybody saw. The problem: how to get the boy off the roof?

Anybody who has ever had a cat on the roof knows how to get him down. You call the fire department. Or first you call the operator and you ask her for the fire department. And the next thing there is great jamming of brakes and clanging of bells and shouting of instructions. And then the cat is off the roof. You do the same thing to get a boy off the roof.

That is, you do the same thing if you are Yakov Blotnik and you once had a cat on the roof.

When the engines, all four of them, arrived, Rabbi Binder had four times given Ozzie the count of three. The big hook-and-ladder swung around the corner and one of the firemen leaped from it, plunging headlong towards the yellow fire hydrant in front of the synagogue. With a huge wrench he began to unscrew the top nozzle. Rabbi Binder raced over to him and pulled at his shoulder.

90 "There's no fire . . ."

The fireman mumbled back over his shoulder and, heatedly, continued working at the nozzle.

"But there's no fire, there's no fire . . ." Binder shouted. When the fireman mumbled again, the rabbi grasped his face with both his hands and pointed it up at the roof.

To Ozzie it looked as though Rabbi Binder was trying to tug the fireman's head out of his body, like a cork from a bottle. He had to giggle at the picture they made: it was a family portrait—rabbi in black skullcap, fireman in red fire hat, and the little yellow hydrant squatting beside like a kid brother, bareheaded. From the edge of the roof Ozzie waved at the portrait, a one-handed, flapping, mocking wave; in doing it his right foot slipped from under him. Rabbi Binder covered his eyes with his hands.

Firemen work fast. Before Ozzie had even regained his balance, a big, round, yellowed net was being held on the synagogue lawn. The firemen who held it looked up at Ozzie with stern, feelingless faces.

95 One of the firemen turned his head towards Rabbi Binder. "What, is the kid nuts or something?"

Rabbi Binder unpeeled his hands from his eyes, slowly, painfully, as if they were tape. Then he checked: nothing on the sidewalk, no dents in the net.

"Is he gonna jump, or what?" the fireman shouted.

In a voice not at all like a statue, Rabbi Binder finally answered. "Yes, yes, I think so . . . He's been threatening to . . . "

Threatening to? Why, the reason he was on the roof, Ozzie remembered, was to get away; he hadn't even thought about jumping. He had just run to get away, and the truth was that he hadn't really headed for the roof as much as he'd been chased there.

"What's his name, the kid?"

"Freedman," Rabbi Binder answered. "Oscar Freedman."

The fireman looked up at Ozzie. "What is it with you, Oscar? You gonna jump, or what?"

Ozzie did not answer. Frankly, the question had just arisen.

"Look, Oscar, if you're gonna jump, jump—and if you're not gonna jump, don't jump. But don't waste our time, willya?"

Ozzie looked at the fireman and then at Rabbi Binder. He wanted to see Rabbi Binder cover his eyes one more time.

"I'm going to jump."

And then he scampered around the edge of the roof to the corner, where there was no net below, and he flapped his arms at his sides, swishing the air and smacking his palms to his trousers on the downbeat. He began screaming like some kind of engine, "Wheeeee . . . wheeeeee," and leaning way out over the edge with the upper half of his body. The firemen whipped around to cover the ground with the net. Rabbi Binder mumbled a few words to Somebody and covered his eyes. Everything happened quickly, jerkily, as in a silent movie. The crowd, which had arrived with the fire engines, gave out a long, Fourth-of-July fireworks oooh-aahhh. In the excitement no one had paid the crowd much heed, except, of course, Yakov Blotnik, who swung from the doorknob counting heads. "Fier und tsvantsik . . . finf und tsvantsik . . . Oy, Gut!" It wasn't like this with the cat.

Rabbi Binder peeked through his fingers, checked the sidewalk and net. Empty. But there was Ozzie racing to the other corner. The firemen raced with him but were unable to keep up. Whenever Ozzie wanted to he might jump and splatter himself upon the sidewalk, and by the time the firemen scooted to the spot all they could do with their net would be to cover the mess.

"Wheeeee . . . wheeeee . . . "

"Hey, Oscar," the winded fireman yelled, "What the hell is this, a game or something?"

"Wheeeee . . . wheeeee . . . "

"Hey, Oscar—"

But he was off now to the other corner, flapping his wings fiercely. Rabbi Binder couldn't take it any longer—the fire engines from nowhere, the screaming suicidal boy, the net. He fell to his knees, exhausted, and with his hands curled together in front of his chest like a little dome, he pleaded, "Oscar, stop it, Oscar. Don't jump, Oscar. Please come down . . . Please don't jump."

And further back in the crowd a single voice, a single young voice, shouted a lone word to the boy on the roof.

"Jump!"

It was Itzie. Ozzie momentarily stopped flapping.

"Go ahead, Ozz—jump!" Itzie broke off his point of the star and courageously, with the inspiration not of a wise-guy but of a disciple, stood alone. "Jump, Ozz, jump!"

Still on his knees, his hands still curled, Rabbi Binder twisted his body back. He looked at Itzie, then, agonizingly, back to Ozzie.

"OSCAR, DON'T JUMP! PLEASE, DON'T JUMP . . . please please . . . "

120 "Jump!" This time it wasn't Itzie but another point of the star. By the time Mrs. Freedman arrived to keep her four-thirty appointment with Rabbi Binder, the whole little upside down heaven was shouting and pleading for Ozzie to jump, and Rabbi Binder no longer was pleading with him not to jump, but was crying into the dome of his hands.

Understandably Mrs. Freedman couldn't figure out what her son was doing on the roof. So she asked.

"Ozzie, my Ozzie, what are you doing? My Ozzie, what is it?"

Ozzie stopped wheeeeing and slowed his arms down to a cruising flap, the kind birds use in soft winds, but he did not answer. He stood against the low, clouded, darkening sky—light clicked down swiftly now, as on a small gear—flapping softly and gazing down at the small bundle of a woman who was his mother.

"What are you doing, Ozzie?" She turned towards the kneeling Rabbi Binder and rushed so close that only a paper-thickness of dusk lay between her stomach and his shoulders.

125 "What is my baby doing?"

Rabbi Binder gaped up at her but he too was mute. All that moved was the dome of his hands; it shook back and forth like a weak pulse.

"Rabbi, get him down! He'll kill himself. Get him down, my only baby . . . "

"I can't," Rabbi Binder said, "I can't . . . " and he turned his handsome head towards the crowd of boys behind him. "It's them. Listen to them."

And for the first time Mrs. Freedman saw the crowd of boys, and she heard what they were yelling.

130 "He's doing it for them. He won't listen to me. It's them." Rabbi Binder spoke like one in a trance.

"For them?"

"Yes."

"Why for them?"

"They want him to . . . "

135 Mrs. Freedman raised her two arms upward as though she were conducting the sky. "For them he's doing it!" And then in a gesture older than pyramids, older than prophets and floods, her arms came slapping down to her sides. "A martyr I have. Look!" She tilted her head to the roof. Ozzie was still flapping softly. "My martyr."

"Oscar, come down, *please,*" Rabbi Binder groaned.

In a startlingly even voice Mrs. Freedman called to the boy on the roof. "Ozzie, come down, Ozzie. Don't be a martyr, my baby."

As though it were a litany. Rabbi Binder repeated her words, "Don't be a martyr, my baby. Don't be a martyr."

"Gawhead, Ozz—*be* a Martin!" It was Itzie. "Be a Martin, be a Martin," and all the voices joined in singing for Martindom, whatever *it* was. "Be a Martin, be a Martin . . . "

140 Somehow when you're on a roof the darker it gets the less you can hear. All Ozzie knew was that two groups wanted two new things: his friends were spirited and musical about what they wanted; his mother and the rabbi were even-toned, chanting, about what they didn't want. The rabbi's voice was without tears now and so was his mother's.

The big net stared up at Ozzie like a sightless eye. The big, clouded sky pushed down. From beneath it looked like a gray corrugated board. Suddenly, looking up into that unsympathetic sky, Ozzie realized all the strangeness of what these people, his friends, were asking: they wanted him to jump, to kill himself; they were singing about it now—it made them that happy. And there was an even greater strangeness: Rabbi Binder was on his knees, trembling. If there was a question to be asked now it was not "Is it me?" but rather "Is it us? . . . Is it us?"

Being on the roof, it turned out, was a serious thing. If he jumped would the singing become dancing? Would it? What would jumping stop? Yearningly, Ozzie wished he could rip open the sky, plunge his hands through, and pull out the sun; and on the sun, like a coin, would be stamped JUMP or DON'T JUMP.

Ozzie's knees rocked and sagged a little under him as though they were setting him for a dive. His arms tightened, stiffened, froze, from shoulders to fingernails. He felt as if each part of his body were going to vote as to whether he should kill himself or not—and each part as though it were independent of *him.*

The light took an unexpected click down and the new darkness, like a gag, hushed the friends singing for this and the mother and rabbi chanting for that.

145 Ozzie stopped counting votes, and in a curiously high voice, like one who wasn't prepared for speech, he spoke.

"Mamma?"

"Yes, Oscar."

"Mamma, get down on your knees, like Rabbi Binder."

"Oscar—"

150 "Get down on your knees," he said, "or I'll jump."

Ozzie heard a whimper, then a quick rustling, and when he looked down where his mother had stood he saw the top of a head and beneath that a circle of dress. She was kneeling beside Rabbi Binder.

He spoke again. "Everybody kneel." There was the sound of everybody kneeling.

Ozzie looked around. With one hand he pointed towards the synagogue entrance. "Make *him* kneel."

There was a noise, not of kneeling, but of body-and-cloth stretching. Ozzie could hear Rabbi Binder saying in a gruff whisper, " . . . or he'll *kill* himself," and when next he looked there was Yakov Blotnik off the doorknob and for the first time in his life upon his knees in the Gentile posture of prayer.

155 As for the firemen—it is not as difficult as one might imagine to hold a net taut while you are kneeling.

Ozzie looked around again; and then he called to Rabbi Binder.

"Rabbi?"

"Yes, Oscar."

"Rabbi Binder, do you believe in God?"

"Yes."

"Do you believe God can do Anything?" Ozzie leaned his head out into the darkness. "Anything?"

"Oscar, I think—"

"Tell me you believe God can do Anything."

There was a second's hesitation. Then: "God can do Anything."

"Tell me you believe God can make a child without intercourse."

"He can."

"Tell me!"

"God," Rabbi Binder admitted, "can make a child without intercourse."

"Mamma, you tell me."

"God can make a child without intercourse," his mother said.

"Make *him* tell me." There was no doubt who *him* was.

In a few moments Ozzie heard an old comical voice say something to the increasing darkness about God.

Next, Ozzie made everybody say it. And then he made them all say they believed in Jesus Christ—first one at a time, then all together.

When the catechizing was through it was the beginning of evening. From the street it sounded as if the boy on the roof might have sighed.

"Ozzie?" A woman's voice dared to speak. "You'll come down now?"

There was no answer, but the woman waited, and when a voice finally did speak it was thin and crying, and exhausted as that of an old man who has just finished pulling the bells.

"Mamma, don't you see—you shouldn't hit me. He shouldn't hit me. You shouldn't hit me about God, Mamma. You should never hit anybody about God—"

"Ozzie, please come down now."

"Promise me, promise me you'll never hit anybody about God."

He had asked only his mother, but for some reason everyone kneeling in the street promised he would never hit anybody about God.

Once again there was silence.

"I can come down now, Mamma," the boy on the roof finally said. He turned his head both ways as though checking the traffic lights. "Now I can come down . . ."

And he did, right into the center of the yellow net that glowed in the evening's edge like an overgrown halo.

➤ *QUESTIONS FOR READING AND WRITING*

1. Describe and compare Itzie and Ozzie.
2. Do you think Ozzie is being deliberately "simple-minded"? Is he asking sincere questions? Explain.

3. Describe Rabbi Binder. Why is he so annoyed by Ozzie's questions? Imagine that the story is being told from his point of view. How would it change?
4. Do you think that Ozzie is really going to jump? Explain.
5. Do you think that the title of the story is appropriate? Is this a "conversion of the Jews"? Explain.
6. Do you agree with Ozzie, that "You should never hit anybody about God"? Explain.

JOHN STEINBECK (1902–1968)

John Steinbeck was born and grew up in Salinas, California, where he often witnessed the plight of the oppressed migrant farm workers he would later write about in novels like The Grapes of Wrath, *which won the Pulitzer Prize in 1940. Other of his best-known novels include* Of Mice and Men, Tortilla Flat, In Dubious Battle, East of Eden, *and* The Winter of Our Discontent. *One of the America's most acclaimed novelists, Steinbeck received the Nobel Prize for literature in 1962.*

THE CHRYSANTHEMUMS [1937]

The high gray-flannel fog of winter closed off the Salinas Valley from the sky and from all the rest of the world. On every side it sat like a lid on the mountains and made of the great valley a closed pot. On the broad, level land floor the gang plows bit deep and left the black earth shining like metal where the shares had cut. On the foothill ranches across the Salinas River, the yellow stubble fields seemed to be bathed in pale cold sunshine, but there was no sunshine in the valley now in December. The thick willow scrub along the river flamed with sharp and positive yellow leaves.

It was a time of quiet and of waiting. The air was cold and tender. A light wind blew up from the southwest so that the farmers were mildly hopeful of a good rain before long; but fog and rain do not go together.

Across the river, on Henry Allen's foothill ranch there was little work to be done, for the hay was cut and stored and the orchards were plowed up to receive the rain deeply when it should come. The cattle on the higher slopes were becoming shaggy and rough-coated.

Elisa Allen, working in her flower garden, looked down across the yard and saw Henry, her husband, talking to two men in business suits. The three of them stood by the tractor shed, each man with one foot on the side of the little Fordson. They smoked cigarettes and studied the machine as they talked.

5 Elisa watched them for a moment and then went back to her work. She was thirty-five. Her face was lean and strong and her eyes were as clear as water. Her figure looked blocked and heavy in her gardening costume, a man's black hat pulled down over her eyes, clod-hopper shoes, a figured print dress almost completely covered by a big corduroy apron with four big pockets to hold the snips, the trowel and scratcher, the seeds and the knife she worked with. She wore heavy leather gloves to protect her hands while she worked.

She was cutting down the old year's chrysanthemum stalks with a pair of short and powerful scissors. She looked down toward the men by the tractor shed now and then. Her face was eager and mature and handsome; even her work with the scissors was over-eager, over-powerful. The chrysanthemum stems seemed too small and easy for her energy.

She brushed a cloud of hair out of her eyes with the back of her glove, and left a smudge of earth on her cheek in doing it. Behind her stood the neat white farm house with red geraniums close-banked around it as high as the windows. It was a hard-swept looking little house with hard-polished windows, and a clean mud-mat on the front steps.

Elisa cast another glance toward the tractor shed. The strangers were getting into their Ford coupe. She took off a glove and put her strong fingers down into the forest of new green chrysanthemum sprouts that were growing around the old roots. She spread the leaves and looked down among the close-growing stems. No aphids were there, no sowbugs or snails or cutworms. Her terrier fingers destroyed such pests before they could get started.

Elisa started at the sound of her husband's voice. He had come near quietly, and he leaned over the wire fence that protected her flower garden from cattle and dogs and chickens.

10 "At it again," he said. "You've got a strong new crop coming."

Elisa straightened her back and pulled on the gardening glove again. "Yes. They'll be strong this coming year." In her tone and on her face there was a little smugness.

"You've got a gift with things," Henry observed. "Some of those yellow chrysanthemums you had this year were ten inches across. I wish you'd work out in the orchard and raise some apples that big."

Her eyes sharpened. "Maybe I could do it, too. I've a gift with things, all right. My mother had it. She could stick anything in the ground and make it grow. She said it was having planters' hands that knew how to do it."

"Well, it sure works with flowers," he said.

15 "Henry, who were those men you were talking to?"

"Why, sure, that's what I came to tell you. They were from the Western Meat Company. I sold those thirty head of three-year-old steers. Got nearly my own price, too."

"Good," she said. "Good for you."

"And I thought," he continued, "I thought how it's Saturday afternoon, and we might go into Salinas for dinner at a restaurant, and then to a picture show—to celebrate, you see."

"Good," she repeated. "Oh, yes. That will be good."

20 Henry put on his joking tone. "There's fights tonight. How'd you like to go to the fights?"

"Oh, no," she said breathlessly. "No, I wouldn't like fights."

"Just fooling, Elisa. We'll go to a movie. Let's see. It's two now. I'm going to take Scotty and bring down those steers from the hill. It'll take us maybe two hours. We'll go in town about five and have dinner at the Cominos Hotel. Like that?"

"Of course I'll like it. It's good to eat away from home."

"All right, then. I'll go get up a couple of horses."

25 She said, "I'll have plenty of time to transplant some of these sets, I guess."

She heard her husband calling Scotty down by the barn. And a little later she saw the two men ride up the pale yellow hillside in search of the steers.

There was a little square sandy bed kept for rooting the chrysanthemums. With her trowel she turned the soil over and over, and smoothed it and patted it firm. Then she dug ten parallel trenches to receive the sets. Back at the chrysanthemum bed she pulled out the little crisp shoots, trimmed off the leaves of each one with her scissors and laid it on a small orderly pile.

A squeak of wheels and plod of hoofs came from the road. Elisa looked up. The country road ran along the dense bank of willows and cottonwoods that bordered the river, and up this road came a curious vehicle, curiously drawn. It was an old spring-wagon, with a round canvas top on it like the cover of a prairie schooner. It was drawn by an old bay horse and a little grey-and-white burro. A big stubble-bearded man sat between the cover flaps and drove the crawling team. Underneath the wagon, between the hind wheels, a lean and rangy mongrel dog walked sedately. Words were painted on the canvas, in clumsy, crooked letters. "Pots, pans, knives, scissors, lawn mores, Fixed." Two rows of articles, and the triumphantly definitive "Fixed" below. The black paint had run down in little sharp points beneath each letter.

Elisa, squatting on the ground, watched to see the crazy, loose-jointed wagon pass by. But it didn't pass. It turned into the farm road in front of her house, crooked old wheels skirling and squeaking. The rangy dog darted from between the wheels and ran ahead. Instantly the two ranch shepherds flew out at him. Then all three stopped, and with stiff and quivering tails, with taut straight legs, with ambassadorial dignity, they slowly circled, sniffing daintily. The caravan pulled up to Elisa's wire fence and stopped. Now the newcomer dog, feeling out-numbered, lowered his tail and retired under the wagon with raised hackles and bared teeth.

30 The man on the wagon seat called out, "That's a bad dog in a fight when he gets started."

Elisa laughed. "I see he is. How soon does he generally get started?"

The man caught up her laughter and echoed it heartily. "Sometimes not for weeks and weeks," he said. He climbed stiffly down, over the wheel. The horse and the donkey drooped like unwatered flowers.

Elisa saw that he was a very big man. Although his hair and beard were greying, he did not look old. His worn black suit was wrinkled and spotted with grease. The laughter had disappeared from his face and eyes the moment his laughing voice ceased. His eyes were dark, and they were full of the brooding that gets in the eyes of teamsters and of sailors. The calloused hands he rested on the wire fence were cracked, and every crack was a black line. He took off his battered hat.

"I'm off my general road, ma'am," he said. "Does this dirt road cut over across the river to the Los Angeles highway?"

35 Elisa stood up and shoved the thick scissors in her apron pocket. "Well, yes, it does, but it winds around and then fords the river. I don't think your team could pull through the sand."

He replied with some asperity. "It might surprise you what them beasts can pull through."

"When they get started?" she asked.

He smiled for a second. "Yes. When they get started."

"Well," said Elisa, "I think you'll save time if you go back to the Salinas road and pick up the highway there."

40 He drew a big finger down the chicken wire and made it sing. "I ain't in any hurry, ma'am. I go from Seattle to San Diego and back every year. Takes all my time. About six months each way. I aim to follow nice weather."

Elisa took off her gloves and stuffed them in the apron pocket with the scissors. She touched the under edge of her man's hat, searching for fugitive hairs. "That sounds like a nice kind of a way to live," she said.

He leaned confidentially over the fence. "Maybe you noticed the writing on my wagon. I mend pots and sharpen knives and scissors. You got any of them things to do?"

"Oh, no," she said quickly. "Nothing like that." Her eyes hardened with resistance.

"Scissors is the worst thing," he explained. "Most people just ruin scissors trying to sharpen 'em, but I know how. I got a special tool. It's a little bobbit kind of thing, and patented. But it sure does the trick."

45 "No. My scissors are all sharp."

"All right, then. Take a pot," he continued earnestly, "a bent pot, or a pot with a hole. I can make it like new so you don't have to buy no new ones. That's a saving for you."

"No," she said shortly. "I tell you I have nothing like that for you to do."

His face fell to an exaggerated sadness. His voice took on a whining undertone. "I ain't had a thing to do today. Maybe I won't have no supper tonight. You see I'm off my regular road. I know folks on the highway clear from Seattle to San Diego. They save their things for me to sharpen up because they know I do it so good and save them money."

"I'm sorry," Elisa said irritably. "I haven't anything for you to do."

50 His eyes left her face and fell to searching the ground. They roamed about until they came to the chrysanthemum bed where she had been working. "What's them plants, ma'am?"

The irritation and resistance melted from Elisa's face. "Oh, those are chrysanthemums, giant whites and yellows. I raise them every year, bigger than anybody around here."

"Kind of a long-stemmed flower? Looks like a quick puff of colored smoke?" he asked.

"That's it. What a nice way to describe them."

"They smell kind of nasty till you get used to them," he said.

55 "It's a good bitter smell," she retorted, "not nasty at all."

He changed his tone quickly. "I like the smell myself."

"I had ten-inch blooms this year," she said.

The man leaned farther over the fence. "Look. I know a lady down the road a piece, has got the nicest garden you ever seen. Got nearly every kind of flower but no chrysanthemums. Last time I was mending a copper-bottom washtub for her (that's a hard job but I do it good), she said to me, 'If you ever run acrost some nice chrysanthemums I wish you'd try to get me a few seeds.' That's what she told me."

Elisa's eyes grew alert and eager. "She couldn't have known much about chrysanthemums. You *can* raise them from seed, but it's much easier to root the little sprouts you see there."

60 "Oh," he said. "I s'pose I can't take none to her, then."

"Why yes you can," Elisa cried. "I can put some in damp sand, and you can carry them right along with you. They'll take root in the pot if you keep them damp. And then she can transplant them."

"She'd sure like to have some, ma'am. You say they're nice ones?"

"Beautiful," she said. "Oh, beautiful." Her eyes shone. She tore off the battered hat and shook out her dark pretty hair. "I'll put them in a flower pot, and you can take them right with you. Come into the yard."

While the man came through the picket gate Elisa ran excitedly along the geranium-bordered path to the back of the house. And she returned carrying a big red flower pot. The gloves were forgotten now. She kneeled on the ground by the starting bed and dug up the sandy soil with her fingers and scooped it into the bright new flower pot. Then she picked up the little pile of shoots she had prepared. With her strong fingers she pressed them in the sand and tamped around them with her knuckles. The man stood over her. "I'll tell you what to do," she said. "You remember so you can tell the lady."

65 "Yes, I'll try to remember."

"Well, look. These will take root in about a month. Then she must set them out, about a foot apart in good rich earth like this, see?" She lifted a handful of dark soil for him to look at. "They'll grow fast and tall. Now remember this: In July tell her to cut them down, about eight inches from the ground."

"Before they bloom?" he asked.

"Yes, before they bloom." Her face was tight with eagerness. "They'll grow right up again. About the last of September the buds will start."

She stopped and seemed perplexed. "It's the budding that takes the most care," she said hesitantly. "I don't know how to tell you." She looked deep into his eyes, searchingly. Her mouth opened a little, and she seemed to be listening. "I'll try to tell you," she said. "Did you ever hear of planting hands?"

70 "Can't say I have, ma'am."

"Well, I can only tell you what it feels like. It's when you're picking off the buds you don't want. Everything goes right down into your fingertips. You watch your fingers work. They do it themselves. You can feel how it is. They pick and pick the buds. They never make a mistake. They're with the plant. Do you see? Your fingers and the plant. You can feel that, right up your arm. They know. They never make a mistake. You can feel it. When you're like that you can't do anything wrong. Do you see that? Can you understand that?"

She was kneeling on the ground looking up at him. Her breast swelled passionately.

The man's eyes narrowed. He looked away self-consciously. "Maybe I know," he said. "Sometimes in the night in the wagon there—"

Elisa's voice grew husky. She broke in on him, "I've never lived as you do, but I know what you mean. When the night is dark—why, the stars are sharp-pointed, and there's quiet. Why, you rise up and up! Every pointed star gets driven into your body. It's like that. Hot and sharp and—lovely."

75 Kneeling there, her hand went out toward his legs in the greasy black trousers. Her hesitant fingers almost touched the cloth. Then her hand dropped to the ground. She crouched low like a fawning dog.

He said, "It's nice, just like you say. Only when you don't have no dinner, it ain't."

She stood up then, very straight, and her face was ashamed. She held the flower pot out to him and placed it gently in his arms. "Here. Put it in your wagon, on the seat, where you can watch it. Maybe I can find something for you to do."

At the back of the house she dug in the can pile and found two old and battered aluminum saucepans. She carried them back and gave them to him. "Here, maybe you can fix these."

His manner changed. He became professional. "Good as new I can fix them." At the back of his wagon he set a little anvil, and out of an oily tool box dug a small machine hammer. Elisa came through the gate to watch him while he pounded out the dents in the kettles. His mouth grew sure and knowing. At a difficult part of the work he sucked his underlip.

80 "You sleep right in the wagon?" Elisa asked.

"Right in the wagon, ma'am. Rain or shine I'm dry as a cow in there."

"It must be nice," she said. "It must be very nice. I wish women could do such things."

"It ain't the right kind of a life for a woman."

Her upper lip raised a little, showing her teeth. "How do you know? How can you tell?" she said.

85 "I don't know, ma'am," he protested. "Of course I don't know. Now here's your kettles, done. You don't have to buy no new ones."

"How much?"

"Oh, fifty cents'll do. I keep my prices down and my work good. That's why I have all them satisfied customers up and down the highway."

Elisa brought him a fifty-cent piece from the house and dropped it in his hand. "You might be surprised to have a rival some time. I can sharpen scissors, too. And I can beat the dents out of little pots. I could show you what a woman might do."

He put his hammer back in the oily box and shoved the little anvil out of sight. "It would be a lonely life for a woman, ma'am, and a scary life, too, with animals creeping under the wagon all night." He climbed over the singletree, steadying himself with a hand on the burro's white rump. He settled himself in the seat, picked up the lines. "Thank you kindly, ma'am," he said. "I'll do like you told me; I'll go back and catch the Salinas road."

90 "Mind," she called, "if you're long in getting there, keep the sand damp."

"Sand, ma'am? . . . Sand? Oh, sure. You mean around the chrysanthemums. Sure I will." He clucked his tongue. The beasts leaned luxuriously into their collars. The mongrel dog took his place between the back wheels. The wagon turned and crawled out the entrance road and back the way it had come, along the river.

Elisa stood in front of her wire fence watching the slow progress of the caravan. Her shoulders were straight, her head thrown back, her eyes half-closed, so that the scene came vaguely into them. Her lips moved silently, forming the words "Good-bye—good-bye." Then she whispered, "That's a bright direction. There's a glowing there." The sound of her whisper startled her. She shook herself free and looked about to see whether anyone had been listening. Only the dogs had heard. They lifted their heads toward her from their sleeping in the dust, and then stretched out their chins and settled asleep again. Elisa turned and ran hurriedly into the house.

In the kitchen she reached behind the stove and felt the water tank. It was full of hot water from the noonday cooking. In the bathroom she tore off her soiled clothes and flung them into the corner. And then she scrubbed herself with a little block of pumice, legs and thighs, loins and chest and arms, until her skin was scratched and red. When she had dried herself she stood in front of a mirror in her bedroom and looked at her body. She tightened her stomach and threw out her chest. She turned and looked over her shoulder at her back.

After a while she began to dress, slowly. She put on her newest underclothing and her nicest stockings and the dress which was the symbol of her prettiness. She worked carefully on her hair, penciled her eyebrows and rouged her lips.

95 Before she was finished she heard the little thunder of hoofs and the shouts of Henry and his helper as they drove the red steers into the corral. She heard the gate bang shut and set herself for Henry's arrival.

His step sounded on the porch. He entered the house calling, "Elisa, where are you?"

"In my room, dressing. I'm not ready. There's hot water for your bath. Hurry up. It's getting late."

When she heard him splashing in the tub, Elisa laid his dark suit on the bed, and shirt and socks and tie beside it. She stood his polished shoes on the floor beside the bed. Then she went to the porch and sat primly and stiffly down. She looked toward the river road where the willow-line was still yellow with frosted leaves so that under the high grey fog they seemed a thin band of sunshine. This was the only color in the grey afternoon. She sat unmoving for a long time. Her eyes blinked rarely.

Henry came banging out of the door, shoving his tie inside his vest as he came. Elisa stiffened and her face grew tight. Henry stopped short and looked at her. "Why—why, Elisa. You look so nice!"

100 "Nice? You think I look nice? What do you mean by 'nice'?"

Henry blundered on. "I don't know. I mean you look different, strong and happy."

"I am strong? Yes, strong. What do you mean 'strong'?"

He looked bewildered. "You're playing some kind of a game," he said helplessly. "It's a kind of a play. You look strong enough to break a calf over your knee, happy enough to eat it like a watermelon."

For a second she lost her rigidity. "Henry! Don't talk like that. You didn't know what you said." She grew complete again. "I'm strong," she boasted. "I never knew before how strong."

Henry looked down toward the tractor shed, and when he brought his eyes back to her, they were his own again. "I'll get out the car. You can put on your coat while I'm starting."

Elisa went into the house. She heard him drive to the gate and idle down his motor, and then she took a long time to put on her hat. She pulled it here and pressed it there. When Henry turned the motor off she slipped into her coat and went out.

The little roadster bounced along on the dirt road by the river, raising the birds and driving the rabbits into the brush. Two cranes flapped heavily over the willow-line and dropped into the riverbed.

Far ahead on the road Elisa saw a dark speck. She knew.

She tried not to look as they passed it, but her eyes would not obey. She whispered to herself sadly, "He might have thrown them off the road. That wouldn't have been much trouble, not very much. But he kept the pot," she explained. "He had to keep the pot. That's why he couldn't get them off the road."

The roadster turned a bend and she saw the caravan ahead. She swung full around toward her husband so she could not see the little covered wagon and the mismatched team as the car passed them.

In a moment it was over. The thing was done. She did not look back.

She said loudly, to be heard above the motor, "It will be good, tonight, a good dinner."

"Now you're changed again," Henry complained. He took one hand from the wheel and patted her knee. "I ought to take you in to dinner oftener. It would be good for both of us. We get so heavy out on the ranch."

"Henry," she asked, "could we have wine at dinner?"

"Sure we could. Say! That will be fine."

She was silent for a while; then she said, "Henry, at those prize fights, do the men hurt each other very much?"

"Sometimes a little, not often. Why?"

"Well, I've read how they break noses, and blood runs down their chests. I've read how the fighting gloves get heavy and soggy with blood."

He looked around at her. "What's the matter, Elisa? I didn't know you read things like that." He brought the car to a stop, then turned to the right over the Salinas River bridge.

"Do any women ever go to the fights?" she asked.

"Oh, sure, some. What's the matter, Elisa? Do you want to go? I don't think you'd like it, but I'll take you if you really want to go."

She relaxed limply in the seat. "Oh, no. No. I don't want to go. I'm sure I don't." Her face was turned away from him. "It will be enough if we can have wine. It will be plenty." She turned up her coat collar so he could not see that she was crying weakly—like an old woman.

➤ QUESTIONS FOR READING AND WRITING

1. Have you ever been frustrated because you were not getting the attention you deserved? If you were placed in Elisa's position, would you feel the same way that she does? Explain.
2. Describe the setting of "The Chrysanthemums." What effect does the setting have on your response to the story? Which passages are most effective in conveying the setting to you?
3. Describe Elisa. Do you learn about her directly or indirectly? Explain.
4. How would you account for Elisa's sadness at the end of the story? Why do you think she is interested in the prize fights? Why does she ask, "do the men hurt each other very much?"
5. What is the primary conflict in the story? Is it external or internal? Explain.
6. What is the theme of this story? Why do you think it is called "The Chrysanthemums"?

◆ POETRY ◆

MATTHEW ARNOLD (1822–1888)

Poet and critic Matthew Arnold was born in Laleham, a tiny village along the Thames in England. His father, Dr. Thomas Arnold, was a famous headmaster of Rugby, one of England's most prominent schools for boys. Arnold attended Oxford University, where he spent as much time roaming the countryside and writing poems as he did on his formal studies. After working for a time for a member of parliament, Arnold secured a post as an inspector of schools in 1851, a position he held for most of his life. In addition, he served as a professor of poetry at Oxford for ten years, beginning in 1857. In his old age, Arnold embarked on two lecture tours of the United States (1883 and 1886). He died suddenly in 1888, shortly after returning from his second trip. A famous literary critic as well as a poet, Arnold strongly believed that the primary purpose of literature was a moral one—that it should "animate and ennoble" its readers. His first collection of poetry, The Strayed Reveler and Other Poems, *was published in 1849 and was followed by six others, including* Poems, Second Series *(1855), in which "Dover Beach" first appeared. His works of literary criticism include two volumes of* Essays in Criticism *(1865 and 1888),* Literature and Dogma *(1873), and* The Study of Poetry *(1880), in which he argued that "most of what now passes for religion and philosophy will be replaced by poetry."*

Dover Beach [1867]

The sea is calm tonight.
The tide is full, the moon lies fair
Upon the straits; on the French coast the light
Gleams and is gone; the cliffs of England stand,
Glimm'ering and vast, out in the tranquil bay.
Come to the window, sweet is the night-air!
Only, from the long line of spray
Where the sea meets the moon-blanched land,
Listen! you hear the grating roar
Of pebbles which the waves draw back, and fling,
At their return, up the high strand,
Begin, and cease, and then again begin,
With tremulous cadence slow, and bring
The eternal note of sadness in.

Sophocles long ago
Heard it on the Aegean, and it brought
Into his mind the turbid ebb and flow
Of human misery; we
Find also in the sound a thought,
Hearing it by this distant northern sea.

The Sea of Faith
Was once, too, at the full, and round earth's shore
Lay like the folds of a bright girdle furled.
But now I only hear
Its melancholy, long, withdrawing roar,
Retreating, to the breath
Of the night-wind, down the vast edges drear
And naked shingles' of the world.

Ah, love, let us be true
To one another! for the world, which seems
To lie before us like a land of dreams,
So various, so beautiful, so new,
Hath really neither joy, nor love, nor light,
Nor certitude, nor peace, nor help for pain-,
And we are here as on a darkling plain
Swept with confused alarms of struggle and flight,
Where ignorant armies clash by night.

➤ *QUESTIONS FOR READING AND WRITING*

1. Does this poem seem like a typical love poem to you? If so, how? If not, why not?
2. What is the speaker's attitude toward nature? Compare his attitude to that of the men in Stephen Crane's *The Open Boat*.

3. How do you think the speaker formed his impression of nature? To what extent is an answer suggested in the poem?
4. In the final image of the poem, the speaker says, "we are here as on a darkling plain / Swept with confused alarms of struggle and flight, / Where ignorant armies clash by night." What do you think he means?
5. According to the speaker, what is the importance of love in this world?

ELIZABETH BISHOP (1911–1979)

Elizabeth Bishop was born in Worcester, Massachusetts. Her father died when she was still an infant, and her mother suffered a serious mental breakdown and was institutionalized. Bishop was raised first by her mother's family in Nova Scotia, and then, when she was six, by her father's parents, who lived in Worcester. Sickly and shy, she spent most of her childhood immersed in books, before attending boarding school during her teens. While at Vassar College, her poetry attracted the attention of a librarian, who introduced Bishop to the poet Marianne Moore. Moore became Bishop's mentor, and her influence can be seen in Bishop's early work. Following graduation, Bishop lived in Key West for nine years, and then moved to Brazil, where she lived for almost twenty. Returning to the United States in 1966, she held positions at the University of Washington and the Massachusetts Institute of Technology before settling at Harvard University, where she was teaching when she died. Her collections of poetry include North and South *(1946),* A Cold Spring *(winner of the Pulitzer Prize in 1956), Complete Poems (winner of the National Book Award in 1970), and* Geography III *(1977). She was also a respected travel writer, publishing numerous volumes, including* Questions of Travel *(1965) and* Brazil *(1967). Often considered a "poet's poet," Bishop's poems are characterized by a spare style and a distinctive ironic voice.*

IN THE WAITING ROOM [1976]

In Worcester, Massachusetts,
I went with Aunt Consuelo
to keep her dentist's appointment
and sat and waited for her
in the dentist's waiting room.
It was winter. It got dark
early. The waiting room
was full of grown-up people,
arctics and overcoats,
lamps and magazines.
My aunt was inside

what seemed like a long time
and while I waited I read
the *National Geographic*
(I could read) and carefully
studied the photographs:
the inside of a volcano,
black, and full of ashes;
then it was spilling over
in rivulets of fire.
Osa and Martin Johnson
dressed in riding breeches,
laced boots, and pith helmets.
A dead man slung on a pole
—"Long Pig," the caption said.
Babies with pointed heads
wound round and round with string;
black, naked women with necks
wound round and round with wire
like the necks of light bulbs.
Their breasts were horrifying.
I read it right straight through.
I was too shy to stop.
And then I looked at the cover
the yellow margins, the date.
Suddenly, from inside,
came an *oh!* of pain
—Aunt Consuelo's voice—
not very loud or long.

I wasn't at all surprised;
even then I knew she was
a foolish, timid woman.
I might have been embarrassed,
but wasn't. What took me
completely by surprise
was that it was *me:*
my voice, in my mouth.
Without thinking at all
I was my foolish aunt,
I—we—were falling, falling,
our eyes glued to the cover
of the *National Geographic,*
February, 1918.

I said to myself: three days
and you'll be seven years old.
I was saying it to stop
the sensation of falling off

the round, turning world
into cold, blue-black space.
But I felt: you are an *I*,
you are an *Elizabeth*,
you are one of *them*.
Why should you be one, too?
I scarcely dared to look
to see what it was I was.
I gave a sidelong glance
—I couldn't look any higher—
at shadowy gray knees,
trousers and skirts and boots
and different pairs of hands
lying under the lamps.
I knew that nothing stranger
had ever happened, that nothing
stranger could ever happen.

Why should I be my aunt,
or me, or anyone?
What similarities—
boots, hands, the family voice
I felt in my throat, or even
the *National Geographic*
and those awful hanging breasts—
held us all together
or made us all just one?
How—I didn't know any
word for it—how "unlikely" . . .
How had I come to be here,
like them, and overhear
a cry of pain that could have
got loud and worse but hadn't?
The waiting room was bright
and too hot. It was sliding
beneath a big black wave,
another, and another.

Then I was back in it.
The War was on. Outside,
in Worcester, Massachusetts,
were night and slush and cold,
and it was still the fifth
of February, 1918.

➤ *QUESTIONS FOR READING AND WRITING*

1. Who is the speaker? How old is she? Does it matter? Explain.

2. What does the sound of Aunt Consuelo's voice reveal to her?
3. What do you think the speaker means by "But I felt: you are an *I,* / you are an *Elizabeth,* / you are one of *them*"?
4. In the last stanza, she says, "Then I was back in it." Where has she been? What is she "back in"?

STEPHEN CRANE (1871–1900)

(See biography on page 1302.)

A MAN SAID TO THE UNIVERSE [1899]

A man said to the universe:
"Sir, I exist!"
"However," replied the universe,
"The fact has not created in me
A sense of obligation."

➤ *QUESTIONS FOR READING AND WRITING*

1. What do you think the man expects from the universe? Why does he say, "I exist"? Are you surprised by the universe's response? Explain.
2. Compare this poem with Crane's story "The Open Boat" on page 1302.
3. Compare this poem to "Dover Beach" on page 1374.

EMILY DICKINSON (1830–1886)

Emily Dickinson was born in Amherst, Massachusetts, where her father, a one-time congressman, was the lawyer and treasurer of Amherst College. Dickinson spent an unhappy year at the New England Female Seminary (which would become Mount Holyoke College). Returning home, she gradually removed herself from outside responsibilities, eventually leading an almost solitary existence. She published only a tiny number of the nearly 2,000 exquisitely crafted and startlingly original poems she composed during her lifetime. Following her death, her family discovered her poems in a trunk in the attic. After making numerous changes, they published nine volumes of her work. Not until Thomas H. Johnson published his three-volume edition, Poems, *in 1955, did Dickinson's verses become available as she originally composed them. Her stature has continued to grow throughout the twentieth century, and today, together with Walt Whitman, she is considered one of the two great geniuses of nineteenth-century American poetry.*

Tell All the Truth but Tell It Slant [ca. 1868]

Tell all the Truth but tell it slant—
Success in Circuit lies
Too bright for our Infirm Delight
The Truth's superb surprise

As Lightning to the Children eased
With explanations kind
The Truth must dazzle gradually
Or every man be blind—

➤ *QUESTIONS FOR READING AND WRITING*

1. What advice is the speaker in this poem giving?
2. How does this poem compare with the popular saying, "Honesty is the best policy"? Do you think it's right to "tell it slant"?
3. Consider the words and images in this brief poem. Do you think they convey the message of the poem effectively?

After Great Pain, a Formal Feeling Comes [ca. 1862]

After great pain, a formal feeling comes—
The Nerves sit ceremonious, like Tombs—
The stiff Heart questions was it He, that bore,
And Yesterday, or Centuries before?

The Feet, mechanical, go round—
Of Ground, or Air, or Ought—
A Wooden way
Regardless grown,
A Quartz contentment, like a stone—

This is the Hour of Lead—
Remembered, if outlived,
As Freezing persons, recollect the Snow—
First—Chill—then Stupor—then the letting go—

➤ *QUESTIONS FOR READING AND WRITING*

1. What kind of "great pain" does the speaker make reference to?
2. To what extent is your response affected by your own experience? Do the images work for you? Explain.

Much Madness Is Divinest Sense [ca. 1862]

Much Madness is divinest Sense—
To a discerning Eye—
Much Sense—the starkest Madness—
'Tis the Majority
In this, as All, prevail—
Assent—and you are sane—

Demur—you're straightway dangerous—
And handled with a Chain—

➤ *QUESTIONS FOR READING AND WRITING*

1. What do you think the speaker means by "Much Madness"? By "Much Sense"?
2. Who is the "Majority" that prevail? Do you think they should? Explain.

THERE'S A CERTAIN SLANT OF LIGHT [CA. 1861]

There's a certain Slant of light,
Winter Afternoons—
That oppresses, like the Heft
Of Cathedral Tunes—

Heavenly Hurt, it gives us—
We can find no scar,
But internal difference,
Where the Meanings, are—

None may teach it—Any—
'Tis the Seal Despair—
An imperial affliction
Sent us of the Air—

When it comes, the Landscape listens—
Shadows—hold their breath—
When it goes, 'tis like the Distance
On the look of Death—

➤ *QUESTIONS FOR READING AND WRITING*

1. What is the setting for this poem? Why does the speaker call it "a slant of light" rather than a "light"?
2. What does she mean by "None may teach it"?

SHE SWEEPS WITH MANY-COLORED BROOMS [CA. 1861]

She sweeps with many-colored Brooms—
And leaves the Shreds behind—
Oh Housewife in the Evening West—
Come back, and dust the Pond!

You dropped a Purple Ravelling in—
You dropped an Amber thread—
And now you've littered all the East
With Duds of Emerald!

And still, she plies her spotted Brooms,
And still the Aprons fly,
Till Brooms fade softly into stars—
And then I come away—

➤ *QUESTIONS FOR READING AND WRITING*

1. Who is the "She" of the poem? What are her "many-colored Brooms" and what do they sweep?
2. In what way do the "Brooms fade softly into stars"?

ROBERT FROST (1874–1963)

(See biography on page 314.)

FIRE AND ICE [1923]

Some say the world will end in fire,
Some say in ice.
From what I've tasted of desire
I hold with those who favor fire.
But if I had to perish twice,
I think I know enough of hate
To say that for destruction ice
Is also great
And would suffice.

➤ *QUESTIONS FOR READING AND WRITING*

1. What do you think fire and ice symbolize in this poem?
2. How are you affected by the rhyme scheme? In what way does it serve as a vehicle for the poem's meaning?

"OUT, OUT . . ." [1916]

The buzz saw snarled and rattled in the yard
And made dust and dropped stove-length sticks of wood,
Sweet-scented stuff when the breeze drew across it.
And from there those that lifted eyes could count
Five mountain ranges one behind the other

Under the sunset far into Vermont.
And the saw snarled and rattled, snarled and rattled,
As it ran light, or had to bear a load.
And nothing happened: day was all but done.
Call it a day, I wish they might have said
To please the boy by giving him the half hour
That a boy counts so much when saved from work.
His sister stood beside them in her apron
To tell them "Supper." At the word, the saw,
As if to prove saws knew what supper meant,
Leaped out at the boy's hand, or seemed to leap—
He must have given the hand. However it was,
Neither refused the meeting. But the hand!

The boy's first outcry was a rueful laugh,
As he swung toward them holding up the hand,
Half in appeal, but half as if to keep
The life from spilling. Then the boy saw all—
Since he was old enough to know, big boy
Doing a man's work, though a child at heart—

He saw all spoiled. "Don't let him cut my hand off—
The doctor, when he comes. Don't let him, sister!"
So. But the hand was gone already.
The doctor put him in the dark of ether.
He lay and puffed his lips out with his breath.
And then—the watcher at his pulse took fright.
No one believed. They listened at his heart.
Little—less—nothing!—and that ended it.
No more to build on there. And they, since they
Were not the one dead, turned to their affairs.

➤ *QUESTIONS FOR READING AND WRITING*

1. To what extent does your own experience affect your response to this poem?
2. In what way does the setting of the poem emphasize what happens to the boy?
3. At the end of the poem, the speaker says, "And they, since they / Were not the one dead, turned to their affairs." Do you think "they" are being heartless? Why or why not?
4. The title of this poem is taken from Shakespeare's play *Macbeth.* When he receives the news that his young wife is dead, Macbeth begins a soliloquy that includes the line "Out, out, brief candle!" See if you can find the rest of this soliloquy (Macbeth, Act 5, Sc. 5) and compare it to this poem.

A. E. HOUSMAN (1859–1934)

(See biography on page 571.)

TO AN ATHLETE DYING YOUNG [1896]

The time you won your town the race
We chaired you through the market-place;
Man and boy stood cheering by,
And home we brought you shoulder-high.

To-day, the road all runners come,
Shoulder-high we bring you home,
And set you at your threshold down,
Townsman of a stiller town.

Smart lad, to slip betimes away
From fields where glory does not stay

And early though the laurel grows
It withers quicker than the rose.

Eyes the shady night has shut
Cannot see the record cut,
And silence sounds no worse than cheers
After earth has stopped the ears:

Now you will not swell the rout
Of lads that wore their honours out,
Runners whom renown outran
And the name died before the man.

So set, before its echoes fade,
The fleet foot on the sill of shade,
And hold to the low lintel up
The still-defended challenge-cup.

And round that early-laurelled head
Will flock to gaze the strengthless dead
And find unwithered on its curls
The garland briefer than a girl's.

➤ QUESTIONS FOR READING AND WRITING

1. Who is the "you" addressed by the speaker? Both the first and second stanzas make reference to carrying the subject "shoulder-high." What does the term mean in each stanza? In what way is it ironic?
2. Dying young is not a pleasant prospect. But what does the speaker mean by "Now you will not swell the rout / Of lads that wore their honours out." Is there a positive side to dying young? Explain.

GALWAY KINNELL (b. 1927)

Born and raised in Providence, Rhode Island, Galway Kinnell first became interested in poetry while attending Wilbraham Academy, a prep school in Massachusetts. He attended college at Princeton University (where his roommate was the poet W. S. Merwin) and later earned a master's degree from the University of Rochester. His first collection of poems, What a Kingdom It Was, *was published in 1960, and his latest,* Imperfect Thirst, *appeared in 1994. A dedicated teacher as well as a poet, Kinnell has taught at numerous universities and held writing workshops throughout the world. He currently divides his time between Vermont and New York*

City, where he is a professor at New York University. His intensely personal poetry often explores the darkest aspects of human consciousness. In a 1989 interview with Contemporary Authors, *Kinnell described the ideal reader: "As far as the person who buys and reads your poems is concerned, every living reader is an ideal reader. Anybody who recognizes the poem and puts something of his or her own experience into it is the ideal reader. The less than ideal reader is the one who reads without engagement: very often the critic."*

FROM THE DEAD SHALL BE RAISED INCORRUPTIBLE [1971]

In the Twentieth Century of my trespass on earth,
having exterminated one billion heathens,
heretics, Jews, Moslems, witches, mystical seekers,
black men, Asians, and Christian brothers,
every one of them for his own good,

a whole continent of red men for living in unnatural community
and at the same time having relations with the land,
one billion species of animals for being sub-human,
and ready to take on the bloodthirsty creatures from the other planets,
I, Christian man, groan out this testament of my last will.
I give my blood fifty parts polystyrene,
twenty-five parts benzene, twenty-five parts good old gasoline,
to the last bomber pilot aloft, that there shall be one acre
in the dull world where the kissing flower may bloom,
which kisses you so long your bones explode under its lips.

My tongue goes to the Secretary of the Dead
to tell the corpses, "I'm sorry, fellows,
the killing was just one of those things
difficult to pre-visualize—like a cow,
say, getting hit by lightning."

My stomach, which has digested
four hundred treaties giving the Indians
eternal right to their land, I give to the Indians,
I throw in my lungs which have spent four hundred years
sucking in good faith on peace pipes.

My soul I leave to the bee
that he may sting it and die, my brain
to the fly, his back the hysterical green color of slime,
that he may suck on it and die, my flesh to the advertising man,
the anti-prostitute, who loathes human flesh for money.

I assign my crooked backbone
to the dice maker, to chop up into dice,

for casting lots as to who shall see his own blood
on his shirt front and who his brother's,
for the race isn't to the swift but to the crooked.

To the last man surviving on earth
I give my eyelids worn out by fear, to wear
in his long nights of radiation and silence,
so that his eyes can't close, for regret
is like tears seeping through closed eyelids.

I give the emptiness my hand: the pinkie picks no more noses,
slag clings to the black stick of the ring finger,
a bit of flame jets from the tip of the fuck-you finger,
the first finger accuses the heart, which has vanished,
on the thumb stump wisps of smoke ask a ride into the emptiness.

In the Twentieth Century of my nightmare
on earth, I swear on my chromium testicles
to this testament
and last will
of my iron will, my fear of love, my itch for money, and my madness.

➤ *QUESTIONS FOR READING AND WRITING*

1. Who is the speaker in this poem? What is the poem's tone?
2. The first stanza begins "In the Twentieth Century of my trespass." The last stanza begins "In the Twentieth Century of my nightmare." What happens in between?
3. Compare this poem to "Dulce et Decorum Est" on page 1390 or "The Man He Killed" on page 1162.

YUSEF KOMUNYAKAA

Yusef Komunyakaa was born in Bogalusa, Louisiana, and served in the Vietnam War. His volumes of poetry include Copacetic *(1984),* I Apologize for the Eyes in My Head *(1986), and* Neon Vernacular, *which won the Pulitzer Prize in 1994. "Facing It," a poem about the Vietnam Memorial in Washington D.C., is taken from* Dien Cai Dau *(1988). He teaches at Indiana University.*

Facing It [1988]

My black face fades,
hiding inside the black granite.
I said I wouldn't,
dammit: No tears.
I'm stone. I'm flesh.
My clouded reflection eyes me
like a bird of prey, the profile of night
slanted against morning. I turn
this way—the stone lets me go.
I turn that way—I'm inside
the Vietnam Veterans Memorial
again, depending on the light
to make a difference.
I go down the 58,022 names,
half-expecting to find
my own in letters like smoke.
I touch the name Andrew Johnson;
I see the booby trap's white flash.
Names shimmer on a woman's blouse
but when she walks away
the names stay on the wall.
Brushstrokes flash, a red bird's
wings cutting across my stare.
The sky. A plane in the sky.
A white vet's image floats
closer to me, then his pale eyes
look through mine. I'm a window.
He's lost his right arm
inside the stone. In the black mirror
a woman's trying to erase names:
No, she's brushing a boy's hair.

➤ *QUESTIONS FOR READING AND WRITING*

1. Who is the speaker in this poem? What is the speaker's point of view?
2. Do you think "Facing It" is an appropriate title for this poem? Explain.
3. How many different things does he see reflected in the wall? In what way is it fitting that he mistakes the woman's brushing the boy's hair as trying to erase names?

Amy Lowell (1874–1925)

Amy Lowell was born into a distinguished New England family, where she spent much time browsing through her father's impressive library. She attended the Brooklyn

Institute of Arts and Sciences, Tufts College, Columbia University, and Baylor University. A 1902 visit to the theater, where she saw the famed actress Eleanora Duse, inspired her to become a poet, and she spent the next years perfecting her art, publishing her first volume of poems, A Dome of Many-Coloured Glass, *in 1912. About the same time she met Ada Dwyer Russell, the woman who would become her lifelong companion and editor. Greatly influenced by the imagist movement, which rejected sentimentality in favor of precision in images and language, Lowell traveled to Europe to befriend the movement's leading practitioners and returned to become its champion in the United States. Her books of poetry include* Sword Blades and Poppy Seed *(1914),* Men, Women and Ghosts *(1916), and the posthumously published* What's O'Clock, *which was awarded the Pulitzer Prize in 1926.*

Patterns [1915]

I walk down the garden-paths,
And all the daffodils
Are blowing, and the bright blue squills.
I walk down the patterned garden-paths
In my stiff, brocaded gown.
With my powdered hair and jewelled fan,
I too am a rare
Pattern. As I wander down
The garden paths.

My dress is richly figured,
And the train
Makes a pink and silver stain
On the gravel, and the thrift
Of the borders.
Just a plate of current fashion,
Tripping by in high-heeled, ribboned shoes.
Not a softness anywhere about me,
Only whalebone and brocade.
And I sink on a seat in the shade
Of a lime tree. For my passion
Wars against the stiff brocade.
The daffodils and squills
Flutter in the breeze
As they please.
And I weep;
For the lime-tree is in blossom

And one small flower has dropped upon my bosom.
And the plashing of waterdrops
In the marble fountain
Comes down the garden paths.
The dripping never stops.
Underneath my stiffened gown
Is the softness of a woman bathing in a marble basin,
A basin in the midst of hedges grown
So thick, she cannot see her lover hiding,
But she guesses he is near,
And the sliding of the water
Seems the stroking of a dear
Hand upon her.
What is Summer in a fine brocaded gown!
I should like to see it lying in a heap upon the ground.
All the pink and silver crumpled up on the ground.

I would be the pink and silver as I ran along the paths,
And he would stumble after,
Bewildered by my laughter.
I should see the sun flashing from his sword-hilt and the buckles on his shoes.
I would choose
To lead him in a maze along the patterned paths,
A bright and laughing maze for my heavy-booted lover.
Till he caught me in the shade,
And the buttons of his waistcoat bruised my body as he clasped me,
Aching, melting, unafraid.
With the shadows of the leaves and the sundrops,
And the plopping of the waterdrops,
All about us in the open afternoon—
I am very like to swoon
With the weight of this brocade,
For the sun sifts through the shade.

Underneath the fallen blossom
In my bosom
Is a letter I have hid.
It was brought to me this morning by a rider from the Duke.
'Madam, we regret to inform you that Lord Hartwell
Died in action Thursday se'ennight.'
As I read it in the white, morning sunlight,
The letters squirmed like snakes.
'Any answer, Madam,' said my footman.
'No,' I told him.
'See that the messenger takes some refreshment.
No, no answer.'
And I walked into the garden,
Up and down the patterned paths,

In my stiff, correct brocade.
The blue and yellow flowers stood up proudly in the sun,
Each one.
I stood upright too,
Held rigid to the pattern
By the stiffness of my gown;
Up and down I walked,
Up and down.

In a month he would have been my husband.
In a month, here, underneath this lime,
We would have broke the pattern;
He for me, and I for him,
He as Colonel, I as Lady,
On this shady seat.
He had a whim
That sunlight carried blessing.
And I answered, 'It shall be as you have said.'
Now he is dead.

In Summer and in Winter I shall walk
Up and down
The patterned garden paths
In my stiff, brocaded gown.
The squills and daffodils
Will give place to pillared roses, and to asters, and to snow.
I shall go
Up and down,
In my gown.
Gorgeously arrayed,
Boned and stayed.
And the softness of my body will be guarded from embrace
By each button, hook, and lace.
For the man who should loose me is dead,
Fighting with the Duke in Flanders,
In a pattern called a war.
Christ! What are patterns for?

➤ *QUESTIONS FOR READING AND WRITING*

1. Describe the setting of this poem. Do you think it's an appropriate setting for the news the speaker is told? Explain.
2. After receiving the news of her lover's death, the speaker says, "I stood upright too, / Held rigid to the pattern / By the stiffness of my gown;" What do you think she means?
3. She later says, "the softness of my body will be guarded from embrace / By each button, hook, and lace. / For the man who should loose me is dead." In what ways would he have "loosed" her?

4. How would you answer the question at the end of the poem? "What are patterns for?"
5. Compare this poem to Emily Dickinson's "After Great Pain, a Formal Feeling Comes" on page 1379.

WILFRED OWEN (1893–1918)

Born in the Shropshire region of England, Wilfred Owen spent two years studying to be a clergyman before becoming disillusioned with the Anglican church. In 1914, World War I broke out. Owen spent a year debating whether or not his Christian beliefs allowed him to fight. In 1915, he decided to enlist. He became a commander, and in 1916 was stationed with the Lancashire Fusiliers in the trenches in France. In 1917, Owen suffered a nervous breakdown and was sent to an army hospital in Scotland to recover. He spent fourteen months at the hospital, where, befriended by the poet Sigfried Sassoon, he turned to writing poetry. Shipped back to the front, he was killed in action at Sambre Canal, France, only one week before the end of the war. Only four of Owen's poems were published during his lifetime. The rest were collected and published by Sassoon in 1920. Sassoon said of Owen: "My trench sketches were like rockets, set up to illuminate the darkness. . . . It was Owen who revealed how, out of realistic horror and scorn, poetry might be made." The last two lines (and title) of "Dulce et Decorum Est" are taken from an ode by Horace, a great Roman Poet. It means: "It is sweet and fitting to die for one's country."

DULCE ET DECORUM EST

[1920]

Bent double, like old beggars under sacks,
Knock-kneed, coughing like hags, we cursed through sludge,
Till on the haunting flares we turned our backs
And towards our distant rest began to trudge.
Men marched asleep. Many had lost their boots
But limped on, blood-shod. All went lame; all blind;
Drunk with fatigue; deaf even to the hoots
Of tired, outstripped Five-Nines that dropped behind.

Gas! GAS! Quick, boys!—An ecstasy of fumbling,
Fitting the clumsy helmets just in time;
But someone still was yelling out and stumbling
And flound'ring like a man in fire or lime . . .
Dim, through the misty panes and thick green light,
As under a green sea, I saw him drowning.

In all my dreams, before my helpless sight,
He plunges at me, guttering, choking, drowning.

If in some smothering dreams you too could pace
Behind the wagon that we flung him in,
And watch the white eyes writhing in his face,
His hanging face, like a devil's sick of sin;
If you could hear, at every jolt, the blood
Come gargling from the froth-corrupted lungs,
Obscene as cancer, bitter as the cud
Of vile, incurable sores on innocent tongues,—
My friend, you would not tell with such high zest
To children ardent for some desperate glory.
The old Lie: *Dulce et decorum est*
Pro patria mori.

➤ QUESTIONS FOR READING AND WRITING

1. Who is the speaker in this poem? What is the setting?
2. He says at the beginning of the last stanza, "If in some smoldering dreams you too could pace . . . " "You" seems to refer to us—the readers. What does he assume about "us"? What does he assume would change our view?
3. Why does he call the Latin saying that is the title of this poem "The old Lie"?

CARL SANDBURG (1878–1967)

Born in Galesburg, Illinois, to Swedish-immigrant parents, Carl Sandburg quit school at thirteen and worked for a number of years at a series of low-paying jobs, even spending time as a hobo riding trains around the Midwest. Following his service in the army during the Spanish-American War (1898), Sandburg returned to Galesburg and worked his way through Lombard (now Knox) College. He left without a degree but with a sense that he wanted to be a poet, publishing his first (and largely forgotten) collection of poetry In Reckless Ecstasy *in 1904. For the next four years, Sandburg again worked at a number of odd jobs, until he married and eventually settled into a job as a reporter for the* Chicago Daily News. *In 1916, he published* Chicago Poems *and soon became one of the leading members of the Chicago Group, which included such famous writers as Theodore Dreiser, Ben Hecht, and Edgar Lee Masters. Beginning in the 1920s, Sandburg began touring the country with his guitar*

and giving readings of his poetry, a practice he continued until he died. In addition to his numerous volumes of free-verse poems, Sandburg published a monumental six-volume biography of Abraham Lincoln, one of his personal heroes, that won the Pulitzer Prize for history in 1940.

GRASS

[1918]

Pile the bodies high at Austerlitz and Waterloo.
Shovel them under and let me work—
I am the grass; I cover all.

And pile them high at Gettysburg
And pile them high at Ypres and Verdun.
Shovel them under and let me work.
Two years, ten years, and passengers ask the conductor:
What place is this?
Where are we now?

I am the grass.
Let me work.

➤ *QUESTIONS FOR READING AND WRITING*

1. What do "Austerlitz," "Waterloo," "Gettysburg," "Ypres," and "Verdun" refer to?
2. Why would the passengers ask the conductor, "What place is this?" Does it matter? Explain.

DYLAN THOMAS (1914–1953)

Dylan Thomas was born in Swansea, Wales, a region of England with its own linguistic and cultural heritage. Though he began publishing his work when he was only twenty, Thomas struggled throughout his life to make ends meet, first as a reporter in London, and later, when he was better established, by writing screenplays and short stories from his home in Wales. Beginning in the late 1940s, Thomas became internationally famous for his poetry readings both in person and on the radio, making numerous recordings and touring both in England and the United States. In 1953, Thomas, who was well-known for his drinking, died following a drinking binge in New York City. The influence of the Welsh language can be clearly felt throughout his works, particularly in his remarkable radio play Under Milk Wood *(1954), which depicts a day in the life of the inhabitants of a Welsh village.*

The Force That Through the Green Fuse Drives the Flower [1934]

The force that through the green fuse drives the flower
Drives my green age; that blasts the roots of trees
Is my destroyer.
And I am dumb to tell the crooked rose
My youth is bent by the same wintry fever.

The force that drives the water through the rocks
Drives my red blood; that dries the mouthing streams
Turns mine to wax.
And I am dumb to mouth unto my veins
How at the mountain spring the same mouth sucks.

The hand that whirls the water in the pool
Stirs the quicksand; that ropes the blowing wind
Hauls my shroud sail.
And I am dumb to tell the hanging man
How of my clay is made the hangman's lime.

The lips of time leech to the fountain head;
Love drips and gathers, but the fallen blood
Shall calm her sores.
And I am dumb to tell a weather's wind
How time has ticked a heaven round the stars.

And I am dumb to tell the lover's tomb
How at my sheet goes the same crooked worm.

➤ *QUESTIONS FOR READING AND WRITING*

1. Who is the speaker in this poem? To what is he comparing himself? What is "the force" that he is subject to?
2. What is he "dumb to tell the crooked rose"? Why is he "dumb" to communicate the "force" they share in common with so many aspects of nature?

Do Not Go Gentle into That Good Night [1952]

Do not go gentle into that good night,
Old age should burn and rave at close of day;
Rage, rage against the dying of the light.

Though wise men at their end know dark is right,
Because their words had forked no lightning they
Do not go gentle into that good night.

Good men, the last wave by, crying how bright
Their frail deeds might have danced in a green bay,
Rage, rage against the dying of the light.

Wild men who caught and sang the sun in flight,
And learn, too late, they grieved it on its way,
Do not go gentle into that good night.

Grave men, near death, who see with blinding sight
Blind eyes could blaze like meteors and be gay,
Rage, rage against the dying of the light.

And you, my father, there on the sad height,
Curse, bless, me now with your fierce tears, I pray.
Do not go gentle into that good night.
Rage, rage against the dying of the light.

➤ *QUESTIONS FOR READING AND WRITING*

1. Who is the speaker in this poem? To what extent do you think that influences his attitude toward this death?
2. Were you surprised by the advice of this poem? Why?
3. If "wise men know that dark is right" why do you think the speaker wants his father to rage against it?

JOHN UPDIKE (b. 1932)

(See biography on page 296.)

THE MOSQUITO

[1963]

On the fine wire of her whine she walked,
Unseen in the ominous bedroom dark.
A traitor to her camouflage, she talked
A thirsty blue streak distinct as a spark.

I was to her a fragrant lake of blood
From which she had to sip a drop or die.
A reservoir, a lavish field of food,
I lay awake, unconscious of my size.

We seemed fair-matched opponents. Soft she dropped
Down like an anchor on her thread of song.
Her nose sank thankfully in; then I slapped
At the sting on my arm, cunning and strong.

A cunning, strong Gargantua, I struck
This lover pinned in the feast of my flesh,
Lulled by my blood, relaxed, half-sated, stuck
Engrossed in the gross rivers of myself.

Success! Without a cry the creature died,
Became a fleck of fluff upon the sheet.
The small welt of remorse subsides as side
By side we, murderer and murdered, sleep.

➤ *QUESTIONS FOR READING AND WRITING*

1. To what extent can you connect this poem to your own experience? Do you think the images the speaker uses capture the experience? How many of your senses are evoked? Which images do you think work best?
2. What is the setting for this encounter? Who wins?
3. Compare this poem to John Donne's "The Flea" on page 568.

JAMES WRIGHT (1927–1980)

James Wright was born in Martins Ferry, Ohio. He earned a B.A. degree from Kenyon College and an M.A. and Ph.D. from the University of Washington. The poems collected in his first volume, The Green Wall *(1957), were formal in style and tone. He then embarked on a series of well-received translations, together with Robert Bly, of foreign poets (Cesar Valejo, Pablo Neruda, and George Trakl). The experience was transforming, and Wright, freed from the rigid formality that characterized his early work, published* The Branch Will Not Break *(1963) and* Shall We Gather at the River *(1968), collections that are generally considered to contain his best work. In 1971, he was awarded the Pulitzer Prize for his* Collected Poems. *In an interview published in the* Paris Review, *Wright said: "My chief enemy in poetry is glibness. My family background is partly Irish, and this means many things, but linguistically it means that it is too easy for me to talk sometimes . . . I have [to struggle] to strip my poems down."*

A BLESSING [1961]

Just off the highway to Rochester, Minnesota,
Twilight bounds softly forth on the grass.
And the eyes of those two Indian ponies
Darken with kindness.
They have come gladly out of the willows
To welcome my friend and me.
We step over the barbed wire into the pasture
Where they have been grazing all day, alone.
They ripple tensely, they can hardly contain their happiness

That we have come.
They bow shyly as wet swans. They love each other.
There is no loneliness like theirs.
At home once more,
They begin munching the young tufts of spring in the darkness.
I would like to hold the slenderer one in my arms,
For she has walked over to me
And nuzzled my left hand.
She is black and white,
Her mane falls wild on her forehead,
And the light breeze moves me to caress her long ear
That is delicate as the skin over a girl's wrist.
Suddenly I realize
That if I stepped out of my body I would break
Into blossom.

➤ *QUESTIONS FOR READING AND WRITING*

1. What is the setting of the poem? Where has the speaker just come from? What is gradually happening to him as the poem progresses?
2. What does he mean by "if I stepped out of my body I would break / Into blossom"? Why do you think the poem is called "A Blessing"?

PAUL ZIMMER (b. 1934)

(See biography on page 333.)

THE DAY ZIMMER LOST RELIGION

[1983]

The first Sunday I missed Mass on purpose
I waited all day for Christ to climb down
Like a wiry flyweight from the cross and
Club me on my irreverent teeth, to wade into
My blasphemous gut and drop me like a
Red hot thurible, the devil roaring in
Reserved seats until he got the hiccups.

It was a long cold way from the old days
When cassocked and surpliced I mumbled Latin
At the old priest and rang his obscure bell.
A long way from the dirty wind that blew
The soot like venial sins across the school yard
Where God reigned as a threatening,
One-eyed triangle high in the fleecy sky.

The first Sunday I missed Mass on purpose
I waited all day for Christ to climb down
Like the playground bully, the cuts and mice
Upon his face agleam, and pound me
Till my irreligious tongue hung out.
But of course He never came, knowing that
I was grown up and ready for Him now.

QUESTIONS FOR READING AND WRITING

1. Who is the speaker? What do you think about him? In the first stanza, why does he wait "all day for Christ to climb down"?
2. What has happened in the third stanza, when he says, "I was grown up and ready for Him now"?

◆ DRAMA ◆

DAVID MAMET (b. 1947)

David Mamet was born in Chicago and has become one of America's best-known playwrights for plays like American Buffalo, *which won the New York Drama Critics Circle Award, and* Glengarry Glen Ross, *for which he won the Pulitzer Prize in 1984. He has also written several successful screenplays including* The Verdict, *for which he received an Academy Award nomination, and a number of works of nonfiction. His latest play is* The Old Neighborhood *(1997).*

OLEANNA [1992]

to be in *Oleanna,*
That's where I would rather be.
Than be bound in Norway
And drag the chains of slavery."
—folk song

CHARACTERS

CAROL, a woman of twenty
JOHN, a man in his forties

SCENE The play takes place in JOHN's office.

ACT I

[JOHN is talking on the phone. CAROL is seated across the desk from him.]

JOHN: [*on phone*] And what about the land. [*Pause.*] The land. And what about the land? [*Pause.*] What about it? [*Pause.*] No. I don't understand. Well, yes, I'm I'm . . . no, I'm *sure* it's signif . . . I'm sure it's significant. [*Pause.*] Because it's significant to mmmmmm . . . did you call Jerry? [*Pause.*] Because . . . no, no, no, no, no. What did they say . . . ? Did you speak to the *real* estate . . . where *is* she . . . ? Well, well, all right. Where are her notes? Where are the notes we took with her? [*Pause.*] I thought you were? No. No, I'm sorry, I didn't mean that, I just thought that I saw you, when we were there . . . what . . . ? I thought I saw you with a *pencil.* WHY NOW? is what I'm say . . . well, that's why I say "call Jerry." Well, I can't right now, be . . . no, I *didn't* schedule any . . . Grace: I *didn't* . . . I'm well aware . . . Look: Look. Did you call Jerry? Will you call Jerry . . . ? Because I can't now. I'll be there, I'm sure I'll be there in fifteen, in twenty. I intend to. No, we aren't *going* to lose the, we aren't *going* to lose the house. Look: Look, I'm not minimizing it. The "easement." did she say "easement"? [*pause*] What did she *say*; *is* it a "term of art," are we *bound* by it . . . I'm sorry . . . [*Pause.*] are: we: yes. *Bound* by . . . Look: [*He checks his watch.*] before the other side *goes home,* all right? "a term of art." Because: that's right [*Pause.*] The yard for the boy. Well, that's the whole . . . Look: I'm going to meet you there . . . [*He checks his watch.*] Is the realtor there? All right, tell her to show you the basement again. Look at the *this* because . . . Bec . . . I'm leaving in, I'm leaving in ten or fifteen . . . Yes. No, no, I'll meet you at the new . . . That's a good. If he thinks it's necc . . . you tell Jerry to meet . . . All right? We *aren't* going to lose the deposit. All right? I'm sure it's going to be . . . [*Pause.*] I hope so. [*Pause.*] I love you, too. [*Pause.*] I love you, too. As soon as . . . I will. [*He hangs up. He bends over the desk and makes a note. He looks up. To CAROL.*] I'm sorry . . .

CAROL: [*Pause.*] What is a "term of art"?

JOHN: [*Pause.*] I'm sorry . . . ?

CAROL: [*Pause.*] What is a "term of art"?

JOHN: Is that what you want to talk about?

CAROL: . . . to talk about . . . ?

JOHN: Let's take the mysticism out of it, shall we? Carol? [*Pause.*] Don't you think? I'll tell you: when you have some "thing." Which must be broached. [*Pause.*] Don't you think . . . ? [*Pause.*]

CAROL: . . . don't I think . . . ?

JOHN: Mmm?

CAROL: . . . did I . . . ?

JOHN: . . . what?

CAROL: Did . . . did I say something wr . . .

JOHN: [*Pause.*] No. I'm sorry. No. You're right. I'm very sorry. I'm somewhat rushed. As you see. I'm sorry. You're right. [*Pause.*] What is a "term of art"? It seems to mean a *term,* which has come, through its use, to mean something *more specific* than the words would, to someone *not acquainted* with them . . . indicate. That, I believe, is what a "term of art" would mean. [*Pause.*]

CAROL: You don't know what it means . . . ?

JOHN: I'm not sure that I know what it means. It's one of those things, perhaps you've had them, that, you look them up, or have someone explain them to you, and you say "aha," and, you immediately *forget* what . . .

CAROL: You don't do that.

JOHN: . . . I . . . ?

CAROL: You don't do . . .

JOHN: . . . I don't, what . . . ?

CAROL: . . . for . . .

JOHN: . . . I don't for . . .

CAROL: . . . no . . .

JOHN: . . . forget things? Everybody does that.

CAROL: No they don't.

JOHN: They don't . . .

CAROL: No.

JOHN: [*Pause.*] No. Everybody does that.

CAROL: Why would they do that . . .?

JOHN: Because. I don't know. Because it doesn't interest them.

CAROL: No.

JOHN: I think so, though. [*Pause.*] I'm sorry that I was distracted.

CAROL: You don't have to say that to me.

JOHN: You paid me the compliment, or the "obeisance"—all right—of coming in here . . . All right. *Carol.* I find that I am at a *standstill.* I find that I . . .

CAROL: . . . what . . .

JOHN: . . . one moment. In regard to your . . . to your . . .

CAROL: Oh, oh. You're buying a new house!

JOHN: No, let's get on with it.

CAROL: "get on"? [*Pause.*]

JOHN: I know how . . . *believe* me. I know how . . . potentially *humiliating* these . . . I have no desire to . . . I have no desire other than to help you. But: [*He picks up some papers on his desk.*] I won't even say "but." I'll say that as I go back over the . . .

CAROL: I'm just, I'm just trying to . . .

JOHN: . . . no, it will not do.

CAROL: . . . what? What will . . . ?

JOHN: No. I see, I see what you, it . . . [*He gestures to the papers.*] but your work . . .

CAROL: I'm just: I sit in class I . . . [*She holds up her notebook.*] I take notes . . .

JOHN: [*simultaneously with "notes"*] Yes. I understand. What I am trying to tell you is that some, some basic . . .

CAROL: . . . I . . .

JOHN: . . . one moment: some basic missed communi . . .

CAROL: I'm doing what I'm told. I bought your book, I read your . . .

JOHN: No, I'm sure you . . .

CAROL: No, no, no. I'm doing what I'm told. It's *difficult* for me. It's *difficult* . . .

JOHN: . . . but . . .

CAROL: I don't . . . lots of the *language* . . .

JOHN: . . . please . . .

CAROL: The *language*, the "things" that you say . . .

JOHN: I'm sorry. No. I don't think that that's true.

CAROL: It is true. I . . .

JOHN: I think . . .

CAROL: It *is* true.

JOHN: . . . I . . .

CAROL: Why would I . . .?

JOHN: I'll tell you why: you're an incredibly bright girl.

CAROL: . . . I . . .

JOHN: You're an incredibly . . . you have no problem with the . . . Who's kidding who?

CAROL: . . . I . . .

JOHN: No. No. I'll tell you why. I'll tell . . . I think you're *angry*, I . . .

CAROL: . . . why would I . . .

JOHN: . . . wait one moment. I . . .

CAROL: It *is* true. I have *problems* . . .

JOHN: . . . every . . .

CAROL: . . . I come from a different *social* . . .

JOHN: . . . ev . . .

CAROL: a different economic . . .

JOHN: . . . Look.

CAROL: No. I: when I came to this school:

JOHN: Yes. Quite . . . [*Pause.*]

CAROL: . . . does that mean nothing . . . ?

JOHN: . . . but look: look . . .

CAROL: . . . I . . .

JOHN: [*Picks up paper.*] Here: Please: Sit down. [*Pause.*] Sit down. [*Reads from her paper*] "I think that the ideas contained in this work express the author's feelings in a way that he intended, based on his results." What can that mean? Do you see? What . . .

CAROL: I, the best that I . . .

JOHN: I'm saying, that perhaps this course . . .

CAROL: No, no, no, you can't, you can't . . . I have to . . .

JOHN: . . . how . . .

CAROL: . . . I have to pass it . . .

JOHN: Carol, I.

CAROL: I *have* to pass this course, I . . .

JOHN: Well.

CAROL: . . . don't you . . .

JOHN: Either the . . .

CAROL: . . . I . . .

JOHN: . . . either the, I . . . either the *criteria* for judging progress in the class are . . .

CAROL: No, no, no, no, I have to pass it.

JOHN: Now, look. I'm a human being, I . . .

CAROL: I did what you told me. I did, I did everything that, I read your *book,* you told me to buy your book and read it. Everything you *say* I . . . [*She gestures to her notebook. The phone rings.*] I do . . . Ev . . .

JOHN: . . . look:

CAROL: . . . everything I'm told . . .

JOHN: Look. Look. I'm not your *father.* [*Pause.*]

CAROL: What?

JOHN: I'm.

CAROL: Did I say you were my father?

JOHN: . . . no . . .

CAROL: Why did you say that . . .?

JOHN: I . . .

CAROL: . . . why . . .?

JOHN: . . . in class I . . .[*He picks up the phone. Into the phone.*] Hello. I can't talk now. Jerry? Yes? I underst . . . I can't talk now. I know . . . I know . . . Jerry. I can't *talk* now. Yes, I. Call me back in . . .Thank you. [*He hangs up. To CAROL.*] What do you want me to do? We are two people, all right? Both of whom have subscribed to . . .

CAROL: No, no . . .

JOHN: . . . certain arbitrary . . .

CAROL: No. You have to help me.

JOHN: Certain institutional . . . you tell me what you want me to do . . . You tell me what you want me to . . .

CAROL: How can I go back and tell them the *grades* that I . . .

JOHN: . . . what can I do . . . ?

CAROL: *Teach* me. *Teach* me.

JOHN: . . . I'm trying to teach you.

CAROL: I read your book. I read it. I don't under . . .

JOHN: . . . you don't understand it.

CAROL: No.

JOHN: Well, perhaps it's not well *written* . . .

CAROL: [*simultaneously with "written"*] No. No. No. I want to *understand* it.

JOHN: What don't you understand? [*Pause.*]

CAROL: *Any* of it. What you're trying to say. When you talk about . . .

JOHN: . . . yes . . .? [*She consults her notes.*]

CAROL: "Virtual warehousing of the young" . . .

JOHN: "Virtual warehousing of the young." If we artificially prolong adolescence . . .

CAROL: . . . and about "The Curse of Modern Education."

JOHN: . . . well . . .

CAROL: I don't . . .

JOHN: Look. It's just a *course,* it's just a *book,* it's just a . . .

CAROL: No. No. There are *people* out there. People who came *here.* To know something they didn't *know.* Who *came* here. To be *helped.* To be *helped.* So someone would *help* them. To *do* something. To *know* something. To get, what do they say? "To get on in the world." How can I do that if I don't, if I fail? But I don't *understand.* I don't *understand.* I don't understand what anything means . . . and I walk around. From morning 'til night: with this one thought in my head. I'm *stupid.*

JOHN: No one thinks you're stupid.

CAROL: No? What am I . . .?

JOHN: I . . .

CAROL: . . . what am I, then?

JOHN: I think you're angry. Many people are. I have a *telephone* call that I have to make. And an *appointment,* which is rather *pressing;* though I sympathize with your concerns, and though I wish I had the time, this was not a previously scheduled meeting and I . . .

CAROL: . . . you think I'm nothing . . .

JOHN: . . .have an appointment with a *realtor,* and with my wife and . . .

CAROL: You think that I'm stupid.

JOHN: No. I certainly don't.

CAROL: You said it.

JOHN: No. I did not.

CAROL: You did.

JOHN: When?

CAROL: . . . you . . .

JOHN: No. I never did, or never would say that to a student, and . . .

CAROL: You said, "What can that mean?" [*Pause.*] "What can that mean?" . . . [*Pause.*]

JOHN: . . . and what did that mean to you . . .?

CAROL: That meant I'm stupid. And I'll never learn. That's what that meant. And you're right.

JOHN: . . . I . . .

CAROL: But then. But then, what am I doing here . . . ?

JOHN: . . . if you thought that I . . .

CAROL: . . . when nobody wants me, and . . .

JOHN: . . . if you interpreted . . .

CAROL: . . . Nobody *tells* me anything. And I *sit* there . . . in the *corner.* In the *back.* And everybody's talking about "this" all the time. And "concepts," and "precepts" and, and, and, and, and, WHAT IN THE WORLD ARE YOU *TALKING* ABOUT? And I read your book. And they said, "Fine, go in that class." Because you talked about responsibility to the young. I DON'T KNOW WHAT IT MEANS AND I'M *FAILING* . . .

JOHN: May . . .

CAROL: No, you're right. "Oh, hell." I failed. Flunk me out of it. It's garbage. Everything I do. "The ideas contained in his work express the author's feelings." That's right. That's right. I know I'm stupid. I know what I am. [*Pause.*] I know what I am, Professor. You don't have to tell me. [*Pause.*] It's pathetic. Isn't it?

JOHN: . . . Aha . . . [*Pause.*] Sit down. Sit down. Please. [*Pause.*] Please sit down.

CAROL: Why?

JOHN: I want to talk to you.

CAROL: Why?

JOHN: Just sit down. [*Pause.*] Please. Sit down. Will you, please . . .? [*Pause. She does so.*] Thank you.

CAROL: What?

JOHN: I want to tell you something.

CAROL: [*Pause.*] What?

JOHN: Well, I know what you are talking about.

CAROL: No. You don't.

JOHN: I think I do. [*Pause.*]

CAROL: How can you?

JOHN: I'll tell you a story about myself. [*Pause.*] Do you mind? [*Pause.*] I was raised to think myself stupid. That's what I want to tell you. [*Pause.*]

CAROL: What do you mean?

JOHN: Just what I said. I was brought up, and my earliest, and most persistent memories are of being told that I was stupid. "You have such *intelligence.* Why must you behave so *stupidly?*" Or, "Can't you *understand?* Can't you *understand?*" And I could *not* understand. I could *not* understand.

CAROL: What?

JOHN: The simplest problem. Was beyond me. It was a mystery.

CAROL: What was a mystery?

JOHN: How people learn. How *I* could learn. Which is what I've been speaking of in class. And of *course* you can't hear it. Carol. Of *course* you can't. [*Pause.*] I used to speak of "real people," and wonder what the *real* people did. The *real* people. Who were they? *They* were the people other than myself. The *good* people. The *capable* people. The people who could do the things *I* could not do: learn, study, retain . . . all that *garbage*—which is what I have been talking of in class, and that's *exactly* what I have been talking of—If you are told . . . Listen to this. If the young child is told he cannot understand. Then he takes it as a *description* of himself. What am I? I am *that which can not understand.* And I saw you out there, when we were speaking of the concepts of . . .

CAROL: I can't understand any of them.

JOHN: Well, then, that's *my* fault. That's not your fault. And that is not verbiage. That's what I firmly hold to be the truth. And I am sorry, and I owe you an apology.

CAROL: Why?

JOHN: And I suppose that I have had some *things* on my mind . . .We're buying a *house,* and . . .

CAROL: People said that you were stupid . . .?

JOHN: Yes.

CAROL: When?

JOHN: I'll tell you when. Through my life. In my childhood; and, perhaps, they stopped. But I heard them continue.

CAROL: And what did they say?

JOHN: They said I was incompetent. Do you see? And when I'm tested, the, the, the *feelings* of my youth about the *very subject of learning* come up. And I . . . I become, I feel "unworthy," and "unprepared." . . .

CAROL: . . . yes.

JOHN: . . . eh?

CAROL: . . . yes.

JOHN: And I feel that I must fail. [*Pause.*]

CAROL: . . . but then you *do* fail. [*Pause.*] You have to. [*Pause.*] Don't you?

JOHN: A *pilot.* Flying a plane. The pilot is flying the plane. He thinks: Oh, my *God,* my mind's been drifting! Oh, my God! What kind of a cursed imbecile am I, that I, with this so precious cargo of *Life* in my charge, would allow my attention to wander? Why was I born? How deluded are those who put their trust in me, . . . et cetera, so on, and he crashes the plane.

CAROL: [*Pause.*] He could just . . .

JOHN: That's right.

CAROL: He could say.

JOHN: My attention *wandered* for a moment . . .

CAROL: . . . uh huh . . .

JOHN: I had a *thought* I did not like . . . but now.

CAROL: . . . but now it's . . .

JOHN: That's what I'm telling you. It's time to put my attention . . . see: it is not: this is what learned. It is Not Magic. Yes. Yes. *You.* You are going to be frightened.

When faced with what may or may not be but which you are going to perceive as a test. You will become frightened. And you will say: "I am incapable of . . . " and everything *in* you will think these two things. "I must. But I can't." And you will think: Why was I born to be the laughingstock of a world in which everyone is better than I? In which I am entitled to nothing. Where I can not learn.

[Pause.]

CAROL: Is that . . . [*Pause.*] Is that what I have . . .?

JOHN: Well. I don't know if I'd put it that way. Listen: I'm talking to you as I'd talk to my son. Because that's what I'd like him to have that I never had. I'm talking to you the way I wish that someone had talked to me. I don't know how to do it, other than to be *personal,* . . . but . . .

CAROL: Why would you want to be personal with me?

JOHN: Well, you see? That's what I'm saying. We can only interpret the behavior of others through the screen we . . . [*The phone rings.*] Through . . . [*To phone.*] Hello . . .? [*To CAROL.*] Through the screen we create. [*To phone.*] Hello. [*To CAROL.*] Excuse me a moment. [*To phone.*] Hello? No, I can't talk nnn . . . I know I did. In a few . . . I'm . . . is he coming to the . . .yes. I talked to him. We'll meet you at the No, because I'm with a *student.* It's going to be fff . . . this is important, too. I'm with a *student,* Jerry's going to . . . Listen: the sooner I get off, the sooner I'll be down, all right. I love you. Listen, listen, I said "I love you," it's going to work *out* with the, because I feel that it is, I'll be right down. All right? Well, then it's going to take as long as it takes. [*He hangs up. To CAROL.*] I'm sorry.

CAROL: What was that?

JOHN: There are some problems, as there usually are, about the final agreements for the new house.

CAROL: You're buying a new house.

JOHN: That's right.

CAROL: Because of your promotion.

JOHN: Well, I suppose that that's right.

CAROL: Why did you stay here with me?

JOHN: Stay here.

CAROL: Yes. When you should have gone.

JOHN: Because I like you.

CAROL: You like me.

JOHN: Yes.

CAROL: Why?

JOHN: Why? Well? Perhaps we're similar [*Pause.*] Yes. [*Pause.*]

CAROL: You said "everyone has problems."

JOHN: Everyone has problems.

CAROL: Do they?

JOHN: Certainly.

CAROL: You do?

JOHN: Yes.

CAROL: What are they?

JOHN: Well. [*Pause.*] Well, you're perfectly right. [*Pause.*] If we're going to take off the Artificial *Stricture,* of "Teacher," and "Student," why should *my* problems be any more a mystery than your own? Of *course* I have problems. As you saw.

CAROL: . . . with what?

JOHN: With my *wife* . . . with *work* . . .

CAROL: With work?

JOHN: Yes. And, and, perhaps my problems are, do you see? *Similar* to yours.

CAROL: Would you tell me?

JOHN: All right. [*Pause.*] I came *late* to teaching. And I found it Artificial. The notion of "I know and you do not"; and I saw an *exploitation* in the education process. I told you. I hated school, I hated teachers. I hated everyone who was in the position of a "boss" because I *knew*—I didn't *think,* mind you, I *knew* I was going to fail. Because I was a fuckup. I was just no goddamned good. When I . . . late in life . . . [*Pause.*] When I *got out from under* . . . when I worked my way out of the need to fail. When I . . .

CAROL: How do you do that? [*Pause.*]

JOHN: You have to look at what you are, and what you feel, and how you act. And finally, you have to look at how to act. And say: If that's what I *did,* that must be how I think of myself.

CAROL: I don't understand.

JOHN: If I fail all the time, it must be that I think of myself as a failure. If I do not want to think of myself as a failure, perhaps I should begin by *succeeding* now and again. Look: the tests, you see, which you encounter, in school, in college, in life, were designed, in the most part, for idiots. *By* idiots. There is no need to fail at them. They are not a test of your worth. They are a test of your ability to retain and spout back misinformation. Of *course* you fail them. They're *nonsense.* And I . . .

CAROL: . . . no . . .

JOHN: Yes. They're *garbage.* They're a *joke.* Look at me. Look at me. The Tenure Committee. The Tenure Committee. Come to judge me. The Bad Tenure Committee.

The "Test." Do you see? They put me to the test. Why, they had people voting on me I wouldn't employ to wax my car. And yet, I go before the Great Tenure Committee, and I have an urge, to *vomit,* to, to, to puke my *badness* on the table, to show them: "I'm no good. Why would you pick *me?*"

CAROL: They granted you tenure.

JOHN: Oh no, they announced it, but they haven't *signed.* Do you see? "At any moment . . ."

CAROL: . . .mmm . . .

JOHN: "They might not *sign*" . . . I might not . . . the *house* might not go through . . . Eh? Eh? They'll find out my "dark secret." [*Pause.*]

CAROL: . . . what is it . . . ?

JOHN: There *isn't* one. But *they* will find an index of my badness . . .

CAROL: Index?

JOHN: A " . . . pointer." A "Pointer." You see? Do you see? I *understand* you. I. Know. That. Feeling. Am I entitled to my job, and my nice *home,* and my *wife,* and my *family,* and so on. This is what I'm saying. That theory of education which, that *theory:*

CAROL: I . . . I . . . [*Pause.*]

JOHN: What?

CAROL: I . . .

JOHN: What?

CAROL: I want to know about my grade. [*Long pause.*]

JOHN: Of course you do.

CAROL: Is that bad?

JOHN: No.

CAROL: Is it bad that I asked you that?

JOHN: No.

CAROL: Did I upset you?

JOHN: No. And I apologize. Of *course* you want to know about your grade. And, of course, you can't concentrate on anyth . . . [*The telephone starts to ring.*] Wait a moment.

CAROL: I should go.

JOHN: I'll make you a deal.

CAROL: No, you have to . . .

JOHN: Let it ring. I'll make you a deal. You stay here. We'll start the whole course over. I'm going to say it was not you, it was I who was not paying attention. We'll start the whole course over. Your grade is an "A." Your final grade is an "A." [*The phone stops ringing.*]

CAROL: But the class is only half over . . .

JOHN: [*simultaneously with "over."*] Your grade for the whole term is an "A." If you will come back and meet with me. A few more times. Your grade's an "A." Forget about the paper. You didn't like it, you don't like writing it. It's not important. What's important is that I awake your interest, if I can, and that I answer your questions. Let's start over. [*Pause.*]

CAROL: Over. With what?

JOHN: Say this is the beginning.

CAROL: The beginning.

JOHN: Yes.

CAROL: Of what?

JOHN: Of the class.

CAROL: But we can't start over.

JOHN: I say we can. [*Pause.*] I say we can.

CAROL: But I don't believe it.

JOHN: Yes, I know that. But it's true. What is The Class but you and me? [*Pause.*]

CAROL: There are rules.

JOHN: Well. We'll break them.

CAROL: How can we?

JOHN: We won't tell anybody.

CAROL: Is that all right?

JOHN: I say that it's fine.

CAROL: Why would you do this for me?

JOHN: I like you. Is that so difficult for you to . . .

CAROL: Um . . .

JOHN: There's no one here but you and me. [*Pause.*]

CAROL: All right. I did not understand. When you referred . . .

JOHN: All right, yes?

CAROL: When you referred to hazing.

JOHN: Hazing.

CAROL: You wrote, in your book. About the comparative . . . the comparative . . . [*She checks her notes.*]

JOHN: Are you checking your notes . . . ?

CAROL: Yes.

JOHN: Tell me in your own . . .

CAROL: I want to make sure that I have it right.

JOHN: No. Of course. You want to be exact.

CAROL: I want to know everything that went on.

JOHN: . . . that's good.

CAROL: . . . so I . . .

JOHN: That's very good. But I was suggesting, many times, that that which we wish to retain is retained oftentimes, I think, *better* with less expenditure of effort.

CAROL: [*of notes*] Here it is: you wrote of *hazing.*

JOHN: . . . that's correct. Now: I said "hazing." It means ritualized annoyance. We shove this book at you, we say read it. Now, you say you've read it? I think that you're *lying.* I'll *grill* you, and when I find you've lied, you'll be disgraced, and your life will be ruined. It's a sick game. Why do we do it? Does it educate? In no sense. Well, then, what is higher education? Is it something-other-than-useful?

CAROL: What is "something-other-than-useful"?

JOHN: It has become a ritual, it has become an article of faith. That all must be subjected to, or to put it differently, that all are entitled to Higher Education. And my point . . .

CAROL: You disagree with that?

JOHN: Well, let's address that. What do you think?

CAROL: I don't know.

JOHN: What do you think, though? [*Pause.*]

CAROL: I don't know.

JOHN: I spoke of it in class. Do you remember my example?

CAROL: Justice.

JOHN: Yes. Can you repeat it to me? [*She looks down at her notebook.*] Without your notes? I ask you as a favor to me, so that I can see if my idea was interesting.

CAROL: You said "justice" . . .

JOHN: Yes?

CAROL: . . . that are all entitled . . . [*Pause.*] I . . . I . . . I . . .

JOHN: Yes. To a speedy trial. To a fair trial. But they needn't be given a trial *at all* unless they stand accused. Eh? Justice is their right, should they choose to avail themselves of it, they should have a fair trial. It does not follow, of necessity, a person's life is incomplete without a trial in it. Do you see?

My point is a confusion between equity and *utility* arose. So we confound the *usefulness* of higher education with our, granted, right to equal access to the same. We, in effect, create a *prejudice* toward it, completely independent of . . .

CAROL: . . . that it is prejudice that we should go to school?

JOHN: Exactly. [*Pause.*]

CAROL: How can you say that? How . . .

JOHN: Good. Good. *Good.* That's right! Speak up! What is a prejudice? An unreasoned belief. We are all subject to it. None of us is not. When it is threatened, or opposed, we feel anger, and feel, do we not? As you do now. Do you not? Good.

CAROL: . . . but how can you . . .

JOHN: . . . Let us examine. Good.

CAROL: How . . .

JOHN: Good. Good. When . . .

CAROL: I'M SPEAKING . . . [*Pause.*]

JOHN: I'm sorry.

CAROL: How can you . . .

JOHN: . . . I beg your pardon.

CAROL: That's all right.

JOHN: I beg your pardon.

CAROL: That's all right.

JOHN: . . . I'm sorry I interrupted you.

CAROL: That's all right.

JOHN: You were saying?

CAROL: I was saying . . . I was saying . . . [*She checks her notes.*] How can you say in a class. Say in a college class, that college education is prejudice?

JOHN: I said that our predilection for it . . .

CAROL: Predilection . . .

JOHN: . . . you know what that means.
CAROL: Does it mean "liking"?
JOHN: Yes.
CAROL: But how can you say that? That College . . .
JOHN: . . . that's my *job,* don't you know.
CAROL: What is?
JOHN: To provoke you.
CAROL: No.
JOHN: Oh. Yes, though.
CAROL: To provoke me?
JOHN: That's right.
CAROL: To make me mad?
JOHN: That's right. To force you . . .
CAROL: . . . to make me mad is your job?
JOHN: To force you to . . . listen. [*Pause.*] Ah. [*Pause.*] When I was young somebody told me, are you ready, the rich copulate less often than the poor. But when they do, they take more of their clothes off. Years. Years, mind you, I would compare experiences of my own to this dictum, saying, aha, this fits the norm, or ah, this is a variation from it. What did it mean? Nothing. It was some jerk thing, some school kid told me that took up room inside my head. [*Pause.*]

Somebody told *you,* and you hold it as an article of faith, that higher education is an unassailable good. This notion is so dear to you that when I question it you become angry. Good. Good, I say. Are not those the very things which we should question? I say college education, since the war, has become so a matter of course, and such a fashionable necessity, for those either of or aspiring *to* to the new vast middle class, that we *espouse* it, as a matter of right, and have ceased to ask, "What is it good for?" [*Pause.*]

What might be some reasons for pursuit of higher education?

One: A love of learning.

Two: The wish for mastery of a skill.

Three: For economic betterment.

[*Stops. Makes a note.*]
CAROL: I'm keeping you.
JOHN: One moment. I have make a note . . .
CAROL: It's something that I said?
JOHN: No, we're buying a house.
CAROL: You're buying a house.
JOHN: To go with the tenure. That's right. Nice *house,* close to the *private school* . . . [*He continues making his note.*] . . . We were talking of economic *betterment* [CAROL *writes in her notebook.*] . . . I was thinking of the School Tax. [*He continues writing. To himself.*] . . . *where is it written* that I have to send my child

to public school . . . Is it a law that I have to improve the City Schools at the expense of my own interest? And, is this not simply *The White Man's Burden?* Good. And [*Looks up to* CAROL.] . . . does this interest you?

CAROL: No. I'm taking notes . . .

JOHN: You don't have to take notes, you know, you can just listen.

CAROL: I want to make sure I remember it. [*Pause.*]

JOHN: I'm not lecturing you, I'm just trying to tell you some things I think.

CAROL: What do you think?

JOHN: Should all kids go to college? *Why* . . .

CAROL: [*Pause.*] To learn.

JOHN: But if he does not learn.

CAROL: If the child does not learn?

JOHN: Then why is he in college? Because he was told it was his "right"?

CAROL: Some might find college instructive.

JOHN: I would hope so.

CAROL: But how do they feel? Being told they are wasting their time?

JOHN: I don't think I'm telling them that.

CAROL: You said that education was "prolonged and systematic hazing."

JOHN: Yes. It can be so.

CAROL: . . . if education is so *bad,* why do you do it?

JOHN: I do it because I love it. [*Pause.*] Let's . . . I suggest you look at the demographics, wage-earning capacity, college- and non-college-educated men and women, 1855 to 1980, and let's see if we can wring some worth from the statistics. Eh? And . . .

CAROL: No.

JOHN: What?

CAROL: I can't understand them.

JOHN: . . . you . . . ?

CAROL: . . . the "charts." The *Concepts,* the . . .

JOHN: "Charts" are simply . . .

CAROL: When I leave here . . .

JOHN: Charts, do you see . . .

CAROL: No, I can't . . .

JOHN: You can, though.

CAROL: NO, NO—I DON'T UNDERSTAND. DO YOU SEE??? I DON'T *UNDERSTAND* . . .

JOHN: What?

CAROL: *Any* of it. *Any* of it. I'm *smiling* in class, I'm *smiling,* the whole time. What are you *talking* about? What is everyone *talking* about? I don't *understand.* I don't know what it *means.* I don't know what it means to *be* here . . . you tell me I'm intelligent, and then you tell me I should not be *here,* what do you *want* with me? What does it *mean?* Who should I *listen* to . . . I . . .

[He goes over to her and puts his arm around her shoulder.]

NO! [*She walks away from him.*]

JOHN: Sshhhh.

CAROL: No, I don't under . . .

JOHN: Sshhhhh.

CAROL: I don't know what you're *saying* . . .

JOHN: Sshhhhh. It's all right.

CAROL: . . . I have no . . .

JOHN: Sshhhhh. Sshhhhh. Let it go a moment. [*Pause.*] Sshhhhh . . . let it go. [*Pause.*] Just let it go. [*Pause.*] Just let it go. It's all right. [*Pause.*] Sshhhhh. [*Pause.*] I understand . . . [*Pause.*] What do you feel?

CAROL: I feel bad.

JOHN: I know. It's all right.

CAROL: I . . . [*Pause.*]

JOHN: What?

CAROL: I . . .

JOHN: What? Tell me.

CAROL: I don't understand you.

JOHN: I know. It's all right.

CAROL: I . . .

JOHN: What? [*Pause.*] What? *Tell* me.

CAROL: I can't tell you.

JOHN: No, you must.

CAROL: I can't.

JOHN: No. Tell me. [*Pause.*]

CAROL: I'm bad. [*Pause.*] Oh, God. [*Pause.*]

JOHN: It's all right.

CAROL: I'm . . .

JOHN: It's all right.

CAROL: I can't talk about this.

JOHN: It's all right. Tell me.

CAROL: Why do you want to know this?

JOHN: I don't want to know. I want to know whatever you . . .

CAROL: I always . . .

JOHN: . . . good . . .

CAROL: I always . . . all my life . . . I have never told anyone this . . .

JOHN: Yes. Go on. [*Pause.*] Go on.

CAROL: All of my life . . . [*The phone rings. Pause.* JOHN *goes to the phone and picks it up.*]

JOHN: [*Into the phone.*] I can't talk now. [*Pause.*] What? [*Pause.*] Hmm. [*Pause.*] All right, I . . . I. Can't. Talk. Now. No, no, no, I *Know* I did, but . . . .What? Hello. What? She *what?* She *can't,* she said the agreement is void? How, how is the agreement *void? That's Our House.*

I have the *paper;* when we come down, next week, with the payment, and the paper, that house is . . . wait, wait, wait, wait, wait, wait, wait: Did Jerry . . . is Jerry there? [*Pause.*] Is *she* there . . . ? Does she have a *lawyer* . . . ? How the *hell,* how the *Hell.* That is . . . it's a question, you said, of the *easement.* I don't underst . . . it's not the *whole agreement.* It's just the *easement,* why would she? Put, put, put, *Jerry* on. [*Pause.*] Jer, *Jerry:* What the *Hell* . . . that's my *house.* That's . . . Well, I'm no, no, no, I'm *not* coming ddd . . . List, *Listen, screw* her. You *tell* her. You, listen: I want you to take *Grace,* you take Grace, and get out of that house. You *leave* her there. Her and her lawyer, and you *tell* them, we'll see them in court next . . . no. No. Leave her there, leave her to *stew* in it: You tell her, we're *getting* that house, and we are going to . . . No. I'm *not* coming down. I'll be damned if I'll sit in the same rrr . . . the next, you tell her the next time I *see* her is in court . . . I . . . [*Pause.*] What? [*Pause.*] What? I don't understand. [*Pause.*] Well, what about the house? [*Pause.*] There isn't any problem with the hhh . . . [*Pause.*] No, no, no, that's all right. All ri . . . All right . . . [*Pause.*] Of course. Tha . . . Thank you. No, I will. Right away. [*He hangs up. Pause.*]

CAROL: What is it? [*Pause.*]

JOHN: It's a surprise party.

CAROL: It is.

JOHN: Yes.

CAROL: A party for you.

JOHN: Yes.

CAROL: Is it your birthday?

JOHN: No.

CAROL: What is it?

JOHN: The tenure announcement.

CAROL: The tenure announcement.

JOHN: They're throwing a party for us in our new house.

CAROL: Your new house.

JOHN: The house that we're buying.

CAROL: You have to go.

JOHN: It seems that I do.

CAROL: [*Pause.*] They're proud of you.

JOHN: Well, there are those who would say it's a form of aggression.

CAROL: What is?

JOHN: A surprise.

ACT II

[JOHN and CAROL seated across the desk from each other.]

JOHN: You see, [*Pause.*] I love to teach. And flatter myself I am *skilled* at it. And I love the, the aspect of *performance.* I think I must confess that.

When I found I loved to teach I swore that I would not become that cold, rigid automaton of an instructor which I had encountered as a child.

Now, I was not unconscious that it was given me to err upon the other side. And, so, I asked and *ask* myself if I engaged in heterodoxy, I will not say "gratuitously" for I do not care to posit orthodoxy as a given good—but, "to the detriment of, of my students." [*Pause.*]

As I said. When the possibility of tenure opened, and, of course, I'd long pursued it, I was, of course *happy,* and *covetous* of it.

I asked myself if I was wrong to covet it. And thought about it long, and, I hope, truthfully, and saw in myself several things in, I think, no particular order. [*Pause.*]

That I *would* pursue it. That I *desired* it, that I was not pure of longing for security, and that that, perhaps, was not reprehensible in me. That I had duties *beyond* the school, and that my duty to my home, for instance, was, or should be, if it were not, of an equal weight. That tenure, and security, and yes, and *comfort,* were not, of themselves, to be scorned; and were even worthy of honorable pursuit. And that it was given me. Here, in this place, which I enjoy, and in which I find comfort, to assure myself of—as far as it rests in the The Material—a continuation of that joy and comfort. In exchange for what? Teaching. Which I love.

What was the price of this security? To obtain *tenure.* Which tenure the committee is in the process of granting me. And on the basis of which I contracted to purchase a house. Now, as you don't have your own family, at this point, you may not know what that means. But to me it is important. A home. A Good Home. To raise my family. Now: The Tenure Committee will meet. This is the process, and a *good* process. Under which the school has functioned for quite a long time. They will meet, and hear your complaint—which you have the right to make; and they will dismiss it. They will *dismiss* your complaint; and, in the intervening period, I will lose my house. I will not be able to close on my house. I will lose my *deposit,* and the home I'd picked out for my wife and son will go by the boards. Now: I see I have angered you. I understand your anger at teachers. I was angry with mine. I felt hurt and humiliated by them. Which is one of the reasons that I went into education.

CAROL: What do you want of me?

JOHN: [*Pause.*] I was hurt. When I received the report. Of the tenure committee. I was shocked. And I was hurt. No, I don't mean to subject you to my weak sensibilities. All right. Finally, I didn't understand. Then I thought: is it not always at those points at which we reckon ourselves unassailable that we are most vulnerable and . . . [*Pause.*] Yes. All right. You find me pedantic. Yes. I am. By nature, by *birth,* by profession, I don't know . . . I'm always looking for a *paradigm* for . . .

CAROL: I don't know what a paradigm is.

JOHN: It's a model.

CAROL: Then why can't you use that word? [*Pause.*]

JOHN: If it is important to you. Yes, all right. I was looking for a model. To continue: I feel that one point . . .

CAROL: I . . .

JOHN: One second . . . upon which I am unassailable is my unflinching concern for my students' dignity. I asked you here to . . . in the spirit of *investigation,* to ask you . . . to ask . . . [*pause*] What have I done to you? [*pause*] And, and, I suppose, how I can make amends. Can we not settle this now? It's pointless, really, and I want to know.

CAROL: What you can do to force me to retract?

JOHN: That is not what I meant at all.

CAROL: To bribe me, to convince me . . .

JOHN: . . . No.

CAROL: To retract . . .

JOHN: That is not what I meant at all. I think that you know it is not.

CAROL: That is not what I know. I *wish* I . . .

JOHN: I do not want to . . . you wish what?

CAROL: No, you said what amends can you make. To force me to retract.

JOHN: That is not what I said.

CAROL: I have my notes.

JOHN: Look. Look. The Stoics say . . .

CAROL: The Stoics?

JOHN: The Stoical Philosophers say if you remove the phrase "I have been injured," you have removed the injury. Now: Think: I know that you're upset. Just tell me. Literally. Literally: what wrong have I done you?

CAROL: Whatever you have done to me—to the extent that you've done it to *me,* do you know, rather than to me as a *student,* and, so, to the student body, is contained in my report. To the tenure committee.

JOHN: Well, all right. [*Pause.*] Let's see. [*He reads.*] I find that I am sexist. That I am *elitist.* I'm not sure I know what that means, other than it's a derogatory word, meaning "bad." That I . . . That I insist on wasting the time, in nonprescribed, in self-aggrandizing and theatrical *diversions* from the prescribed *text* . . . that these have taken both sexist and pornographic forms . . . here we find listed . . . [*Pause.*] Here were find listed . . . instances " . . . closeted with a student" . . . "Told a rambling, sexually explicit story, in which the frequency and attitudes of fornication of the poor and rich are, it would seem, the central point . . . moved to *embrace* said student and . . . all part of a pattern . . ." [*Pause.*]

[*He reads.*] That I used the phrase "The White Man's Burden" . . . that told you how I'd asked you to my room because I quote like you. [*Pause.*]

[*He reads.*] "He said he 'liked' me. That he 'liked being with me.' He'd let me write my examination paper over, if I could come back oftener to see him in his office." [*Pause. To* CAROL.] It's *ludicrous.* Don't you know that? It's not *necessary.* It's going to *humiliate* you, and it's going to cost me my *house,* and . . .

CAROL: It's "*ludicrous* . . . "?

[JOHN picks up the report and reads again.]

JOHN: "He told me he had problems with his wife; and that he wanted to take off the artificial stricture of Teacher and Student. He put his arm around me . . . "

CAROL: Do you deny it? Can you deny it . . . ? Do you see? [*Pause.*] Don't you see? You don't see, do you?

JOHN: I don't see . . .

CAROL: You think, you think you can deny that these things happened, or, if they *did,* if they *did,* that they meant what you *said* they meant. Don't you see? You drag me in here, you drag us, to listen to you "go on"; and "go on" about this, or that, or we don't "express" ourselves very well. We don't say what we mean. Don't we? Don't we? We *do* say what we mean. And you say that "I don't understand you . . . ": Then *you* . . . [*Points.*]

JOHN: "Consult the Report"?

CAROL: . . . that's right.

JOHN: You see. You see. Can't you . . . You see what I'm saying? Can't you tell me in your own words?

CAROL: Those are my own words. [*Pause.*]

JOHN: [*He reads.*] "He told me that if I would stay alone with him in his office, he would change my grade to an A." [*To CAROL.*] What have I done to you? Oh. My God, are you so hurt?

CAROL: What I "feel" is irrelevant. [*Pause.*]

JOHN: Do you know that I tried to help you?

CAROL: What I know I have reported.

JOHN: I would like to help you now. I would. Before this escalates.

CAROL: [*Simultaneously with "escalates."*] You see. I don't think that I need your help. I don't think I need anything you have.

JOHN: I feel . . .

CAROL: I don't *care* what you feel. Do you see? DO YOU SEE? You can't *do* that anymore. You. Do. Not. Have. The. Power. Did you misuse it? *Someone* did. Are you part of that group? *Yes. Yes.* You Are. You've *done* these things. And to say, and to say "Oh. Let me help you with your problem . . . "

JOHN: Yes. I understand. I understand. You're *hurt.* You're *angry.* Yes. I think your *anger is betraying you.* Down a path which helps no one.

CAROL: I don't *care* what you think.

JOHN: You don't? [*Pause.*] But you talk of *rights.* Don't you see? *I* have rights too. Do you see? I have a *house* . . . part of the *real* world; and The Tenure Committee. Good Men and True . . .

CAROL: . . . Professor . . .

JOHN: . . . Please: *Also* part of that world: you understand? This is my *life.* I'm not a *bogeyman.* I don't "stand" for something, I . . .

CAROL: . . . Professor . . .

JOHN: . . . I . . .

CAROL: Professor. I came here as a *favor.* At your personal request. Perhaps I should not have done so. But I did. On my behalf, and on behalf of my group. And you speak of the tenure committee, one of whose members is a woman, as you know. And though you might call it Good Fun, or An Historical Phrase, or An Oversight, or, All of the Above, to refer to the committee as Good Men and True, it is a demeaning remark. It is a sexist remark, and to overlook it is to countenance of that method of thought. It's a remark . . .

JOHN: OH COME ONE. Come on. . . . Sufficient to deprive a family of . . .

CAROL: Sufficient? Sufficient? Sufficient? Yes. It is a *fact* . . . and that story, which I quote, is *vile* and *classist,* and *manipulative* and *pornographic.* It . . .

JOHN: . . . it's pornographic . . . ?

CAROL: What gives you the *right.* Yes. To speak to a *woman* in your private . . . Yes. Yes. I'm sorry. I'm sorry. You feel yourself empowered . . . you say so yourself. To *strut.* To *posture.* To "perform." To "Call me in here . . . " Eh? You say that higher education is a joke. And treat it as such, you *treat* it as such. And *confess* to a taste to play the *Patriarch* in our class. To grant *this.* To deny *that.* To embrace your students.

JOHN: How can you assert. How can you stand there and . . .

CAROL: How can you *deny* it. You did it to me. *Here.* You *did.* . . . You *confess.* You love the Power. To *deviate.* To *invent,* to transgress . . . to *transgress* whatever norms have been established for us. And you think it's charming to "question" in yourself this taste to mock and destroy. But you should question it, Professor. And you pick those things which you feel advance you: publication, *tenure,* and the steps to get them you call "harmless rituals." And you perform those steps. Although you say it is hypocrisy. But to the aspirations of your students. Of *hardworking students,* who come here, who *slave* to come here—you have no idea what it cost me to come to this school—you *mock* us. You call education "hazing," and from your so-protected, so-elitist seat you hold our confusion as a *joke,* and our hopes and efforts with it. Then you sit there and say "what have I done?" And ask me to understand that *you* have aspirations too. But I tell you. I tell you. That you are vile. And that you are exploitative. And if you possess one ounce of that inner honesty you describe in your book, you can look in yourself and see those things that I see. And you can find revulsion equal to my own. Good day. [*She prepares to leave the room.*]

JOHN: Wait a second, will you, just one moment. [*Pause.*] Nice day today.

CAROL: What?

JOHN: You said "Good day." I think that it is a nice day today.

CAROL: *Is* it?

JOHN: Yes, I think it is.

CAROL: And why is that important?

JOHN: Because it is the essence of all human communication. I say something conventional, you respond, and the information we exchange is not about the "weather," but that we both agree to converse. In effect, we agree that we are both human. [*Pause.*]

I'm not a . . . "exploiter," and you're not a . . . "deranged," what? *Revolutionary* . . . that we may, that we may have . . . positions, and that we may have . . . desires, which are in *conflict,* but that we're just human. [*Pause.*] That means that sometimes we're *imperfect.* [*Pause.*] Often we're in conflict . . . [*Pause.*] *Much* of what we do, you're right, in the name of "principles" is *self-serving* . . . much of what we do is *conventional.* [*Pause.*] You're right. [*Pause.*] You said you came in the class because you wanted to learn about *education.* I don't know that I can teach you about education. But I know that I can tell you what I *think* about education, and then *you* decide. And you don't have to fight with me. *I'm* not the subject. [*Pause.*] And where I'm *wrong* . . . perhaps it's not your job to "fix" me. I don't want to fix *you.* I would like to tell you what I *think,* because that *is* my job, conventional as it is, and flawed as I may be. And then, if you can show me some better *form,* then we can proceed from there. But, just like "nice day, isn't it . . . ?" I don't think we can proceed until we accept that each of us is human. [*Pause.*] And we still can have difficulties. We *will* have them . . . that's all right too. [*Pause.*] Now:

CAROL: . . . wait . . .

JOHN: Yes. I want to hear it.

CAROL: . . . the . . .

JOHN: Yes. Tell me frankly.

CAROL: . . . my position . . .

JOHN: I want to hear it. In your own words. What you want. And what you feel.

CAROL: . . . I . . .

JOHN: . . . yes . . .

CAROL: My Group.

JOHN: Your "Group" . . . ? [*Pause.*]

CAROL: The people I've been talking to . . .

JOHN: There's no shame in that. Everybody needs advisers. Everyone needs to expose themselves. To various points of view. It's not wrong. It's essential. Good. Good. Now: You and I . . . [*The phone rings.*]

You and I . . .

[*He hesitates for a moment, and then picks it up. Into phone.*] Hello. [*Pause.*] Um . . . no, I know they do. [*Pause.*] I know she does. Tell her that I . . . can I call you back? . . . Then tell her that I think it's going to be fine. [*Pause.*] Tell her just, just hold on, I'll . . . can I get back to you? . . . Well . . . no, no, no, we're *taking* the house . . . we're . . . no, no, nn . . . no, she will nnn, it's not a *question* of refunding the dep . . . no . . . it's not a *question* of the deposit . . . will you just call Jerry? Babe, baby, will you just call Jerry? Tell him, nnn . . . tell him they, well, they're to keep the deposit, because the deal, be . . . because the deal is going to go *through* . . . because I know . . . be . . . will you please? Just *trust* me. Be . . . well, I'm dealing with the complaint. Yes.

Right *Now.* Which is why I . . . yes, no, no, it's really, I can't *talk* about it now. Call Jerry, and I can't talk now. Ff . . . Fine, Gg . . . good-bye. [*Hangs up.*] [*Pause.*] I'm sorry we were interrupted.

CAROL: No . . .

JOHN: I . . . I was saying.

CAROL: You said that we should agree to talk about my complaint.

JOHN: That's correct.

CAROL: But we *are* talking about it.

JOHN: Well, that's correct too. You see? This is the *gist* of education.

CAROL: No, no. I mean, we're talking about it at the Tenure Committee Hearing. [*Pause.*]

JOHN: Yes, but I'm saying: we can talk about it *now,* as easily as . . .

CAROL: No, I think that we should stick to the process . . .

JOHN: . . . wait a . . .

CAROL: . . . the "conventional" process. As you said. [*She gets up.*] And you're right, I'm sorry if I was, um, if I was "discourteous" to you. You're right.

JOHN: Wait, wait a . . .

CAROL: I really should go.

JOHN: Now, look, granted. I have an interest. In the status quo. All right? Everyone does. But what I'm saying is that the *committee* . . .

CAROL: Professor, you're right. Just don't impinge on me. We'll take our differences, and . . .

JOHN: You're going to make a . . . look, look, look, you're going to . . .

CAROL: I shouldn't have come here. They told me . . .

JOHN: One moment. No. No. There are *norms,* here, and there's no reason. Look. I'm trying to *save* you . . .

CAROL: No one *asked* you to . . . you're trying to save *me?* Do me the courtesy to . . .

JOHN: I *am* doing you the courtesy. I'm talking *straight* to you. We can settle this *now.* And I want you to sit *down* and . . .

CAROL: You must excuse me . . . [*She starts to leave the room.*]

JOHN: Sit down, it seems we each have a . . . Wait one moment. Wait one moment . . . just do me the courtesy to . . .

[He restrains her from leaving.]

CAROL: LET ME GO.

JOHN: I have no desire to *hold* you, I just want to *talk* to you . . .

CAROL: LET ME GO. LET ME GO. WOULD SOMEBODY *HELP* ME? WOULD SOMEBODY *HELP* ME PLEASE . . . ?

ACT III

[At rise, CAROL and JOHN are seated.]

JOHN: I have asked you here. [*Pause.*] I have asked you here against, against my . . .

CAROL: I was most surprised you asked me.

JOHN: . . . against my better *judgment,* against . . .
CAROL: I was most surprised . . .
JOHN: . . . against the . . . yes. I'm sure.
CAROL: . . . If you would like me to leave, I'll leave. I'll go right now . . . [*She rises.*]
JOHN: Let us begin *correctly,* may we? I feel . . .
CAROL: That is what I wished to do. That's why I came here, but now . . .
JOHN: . . . I feel . . .
CAROL: But now perhaps you'd like me to leave . . .
JOHN: I don't want you to leave. I asked you to come . . .
CAROL: I didn't have to come here.
JOHN: No. [*Pause.*] Thank you.
CAROL: All right. [*Pause. She sits down.*]
JOHN: Although I feel that it *profits,* it would *profit* you something, to . . .
CAROL: . . . what I . . .
JOHN: If you would hear me out, if you would hear me out.
CAROL: I came here to, the court officers told me not to come.
JOHN: . . . the "court" officers . . . ?
CAROL: I was shocked that you asked.
JOHN: . . . wait . . .
CAROL: Yes. But I did *not* come here to hear what it "profits" me.
JOHN: The "court" officers . . .
CAROL: . . . no, no, perhaps I should leave . . . [*She gets up.*]
JOHN: Wait
CAROL: No. I shouldn't have . . .
JOHN: . . . wait. Wait. Wait a moment.
CAROL: Yes? What is it you want? [*Pause.*] What is it you want?
JOHN: I'd like you to stay.
CAROL: You want me to stay.
JOHN: Yes.
CAROL: You do.
JOHN: Yes. [*Pause.*] Yes. I would like to have you hear me out. If you would. [*Pause.*] Would you please? If you would do that I would be in your debt. [*Pause. She sits.*] Thank you. [*Pause.*]
CAROL: What is it you wish to tell me?
JOHN: All right. I cannot . . . [*Pause.*] I cannot help but feel you are owed an apology. [*Pause. Of papers in his hand.*] I have read. [*Pause.*] And reread these accusations.
CAROL: What "accusations"?
JOHN: The, the tenure comm . . . what other accusations . . . ?
CAROL: The tenure committee . . . ?
JOHN: Yes.
CAROL: Excuse me, but those are not accusations. They have been *proved.* They are facts.

JOHN: . . . I . . .

CAROL: No. Those are not "accusations."

JOHN: . . . those?

CAROL: . . . the committee [*The phone starts to ring.*] the committee has . . .

JOHN: . . . All right . . .

CAROL: . . . those are not accusations. The Tenure Committee.

JOHN: ALL RIGHT. ALL RIGHT. ALL RIGHT. [*He picks up the phone.*] Hello. Yes. No. I'm here. Tell Mister . . . No, I can't talk to him now . . . I'm sure he has, but I'm fff . . . I know . . . No, I have no time t . . . tell Mister . . . tell Mist . . . tell Jerry that I'm *fine* and that I'll call him right aw . . . [*Pause.*] My wife . . . Yes. I'm sure she has. Yes, thank you. Yes, I'll call her too. I cannot talk to you now. [*He hangs up. Pause.*] All right. It was good of you to come. Thank you. I have studied. I have spent some time studying the indictment.

CAROL: You will have to explain that word to me.

JOHN: An "indictment" . . .

CAROL: Yes.

JOHN: Is a "bill of particulars." A . . .

CAROL: All right. Yes.

JOHN: In which is alleged . . .

CAROL: No. I cannot allow that. I cannot allow that. Nothing is alleged. Everything is proved . . .

JOHN: Please, wait a sec . . .

CAROL: I cannot *come* to allow . . .

JOHN: If I may . . . If I may, from whatever you feel is "established" by . . .

CAROL: The issue here is not what I "feel." It is not my "feelings," but the feelings of women. And men. Your superiors, who've been "polled," do you see? To whom *evidence* has been presented, who have *ruled,* do you see? Who have weighed the testimony and the evidence, and have *ruled,* do you see? That you are *negligent.* That you are *guilty,* that you are found *wanting,* and in *error;* and are *not,* for the reasons sotold, to be given tenure. That you are to be disciplined. For facts. For *facts.* Not "alleged," what is the word? But *proved.* Do you see? *By your own actions.*

That is what the tenure committee has said. That is what my lawyer said. For what you did in class. For what you did *in this office.*

JOHN: They're going to discharge me.

CAROL: As full well they should. You don't understand? You're angry? What has *led* you to this place? Not your sex. Not your race. Not your class. YOUR OWN ACTIONS. And you're *angry.* You *ask* me here. What *do* you want? You want to "charm" me. You want to "convince" me. You want me to recant. I will *not* recant. Why should I . . . ? What I say is right. You tell me, you are going to tell me that you have a wife and child. You are going to say that you have a career and that you've worked for twenty years for this. Do you know what you've *worked* for? *Power.* For *power.* Do you understand? And you sit there, and you tell me *stories.* About your *house,* about all the private *schools,* and about *privilege,* and how you are entitled. To *buy,* to *spend,* to *mock,* to *summon.* All your stories. All your silly weak *guilt,* it's all about *privilege;* and you won't know it. Don't you see? You worked twenty years for the right to *insult* me. Any you feel entitled to be *paid* for it. Your Home. Your Wife . . . Your sweet "deposit" on you house . . .

JOHN: Don't you have feelings?

CAROL: That's my point. You see? Don't you have feelings? Your final argument. What is it that has no feelings. *Animals.* I don't take your side, you question if I'm Human.

JOHN: Don't you have feelings?

CAROL: I have a responsibility. I . . .

JOHN: . . . to . . . ?

CAROL: To? This institution. To the *students.* To my *group.*

JOHN: . . . your "group" . . .

CAROL: Because I speak, yes, not for myself. But for the group; for those who suffer what I suffer. On behalf of whom, even if I, were, inclined, to what, forgive? Forget? What? Overlook your . . .

JOHN: . . . my behavior?

CAROL: . . . it would be wrong.

JOHN: Even if you were inclined to "forgive" me.

CAROL: It would be wrong.

JOHN: And what would transpire.

CAROL: Transpire?

JOHN: Yes.

CAROL: "Happen?"

JOHN: Yes.

CAROL: Then *say* it. For Christ's sake. Who the *hell* do you think you are? You want a post. You want unlimited power. To do and to say what you want. As it pleases you—Testing, Questioning, Flirting . . .

JOHN: I never . . .

CAROL: Excuse me, one moment, will you?

[She reads from her notes.]

The twelfth. "Have a good day, dear."

The fifteenth. "Now, don't *you* look fetching . . ."

April seventeenth. "If you girls would come over here . . ." I saw you. I saw you, Professor. For two semesters sit there, stand there and exploit our, as you thought, "paternal prerogative," and what is that but rape; I swear to God. You asked me in here to explain something to me, as a child, that I did not understand. But I came to explain something to you. You Are Not God. You ask me why I came? I came here to instruct you.

[She produces the book.]

And your book? You think you're going to show me some "light"? You "*maverick.*" Outside of tradition. No, no. [*She reads from the book's liner notes.*] "of that fine tradition of *inquiry.* Of Polite *skepticism*" . . . and you say you believe in free intellectual discourse. YOU BELIEVE IN NOTHING. YOU BELIEVE IN NOTHING AT ALL.

JOHN: I believe in freedom of thought.

CAROL: Isn't that fine. *Do* you?

JOHN: Yes. I do.

CAROL: Then why do you question, for one moment, the committee's decision refusing your tenure? Why do you question your suspension? You believe in what *you call* freedom of thought. Then, fine. *You* believe in freedom-of-thought *and* a home, and, *and* prerogatives for your kid, *and* tenure. And I'm going to tell you. You believe *not* in "freedom of thought," but in an elitist, in, in a protected hierarchy which rewards you. And for whom you are the clown. And you mock and exploit the system which pays your rent. You're wrong. I'm not wrong. You're wrong. You think that I'm full of hatred. I know what you think I am.

JOHN: Do you?

CAROL: You think I'm a, of course I do. You think I am a frightened, repressed, confused, I don't know, abandoned young thing of some doubtful sexuality, who wants, power and revenge. [*Pause.*] *Don't* you? [*Pause.*]

JOHN: Yes. I do. [*Pause.*]

CAROL: Isn't that better? And I feel that that is the first moment which you've treated me with respect. For you told me the truth. [*Pause.*] I did not come here, as you are assured, to gloat. Why would I want to gloat? I've profited nothing from your, your, as you say, your "misfortune." I came here, as you did me the honor to *ask* me here, I came here to tell you something.

[*Pause.*] That I think . . . that I think you've been wrong. That I think you've been terribly wrong. Do you hate me now? [*Pause.*]

JOHN: Yes.

CAROL: Why do you hate me? Because you think me wrong? No. Because I have, you think, *power* over you. Listen to me. Listen to me, Professor. [*Pause.*] It is the power that you hate. So deeply that, that any atmosphere of free discussion is *impossible.* It's not "unlikely." It's *impossible.* Isn't it?

JOHN: Yes.

CAROL: *Isn't* it . . . ?

JOHN: Yes. I suppose.

CAROL: Now. The thing which you find so cruel is the selfsame process of selection I, and my group, go through *every day of our lives.* In admittance to school. In our tests, in our class rankings . . . Is it unfair? I can't tell you. But, if it is fair. Or even if it is "unfortunate but necessary" for us, then, by God, so must it be for you. [*Pause.*] You write of your "responsibility to the young." Treat us with respect, and that will *show* you your responsibility. You write that education is just hazing. [*Pause.*] But we worked to get to this school. [*Pause.*]

And some of us. [*Pause.*] Overcame prejudices. Economic, sexual, you cannot begin to imagine. And endured humiliations I *pray* that you and those you love never will encounter. [*Pause.*] To gain admittance here. To pursue that same dream of security *you* pursue. We, who, who are, at any moment, in danger of being deprived of it. By . . .

JOHN: . . . by . . . ?

CAROL: By the administration. By the teachers. By *you.* By, say, one low grade, that keeps us out of graduate school; by one, say one capricious or inventive answer on our parts, which, perhaps, you don't find amusing. Now you *know,* do you see? What it is to be subject to that power. [*Pause.*]

JOHN: I don't understand. [*Pause.*]

CAROL: My charges are not trivial. You see that in the haste, I think, with which they were accepted. A *joke* you have told, with a sexist tinge. The language you use, a verbal or physical caress, yes, yes, I know, you say that it is meaningless. I understand. I differ from you. To lay a hand on someone's shoulder.

JOHN: It was devoid of sexual content.

CAROL: I say it was not. I SAY IT WAS NOT. Don't you begin to *see* . . . ? Don't you begin to understand? IT'S NOT FOR YOU TO SAY.

JOHN: I take your point, and I see there is much good in what you refer to.

CAROL: . . . do you think so . . . ?

JOHN: . . . but, and this is not to say that I cannot change, in those things in which I am deficient . . . But, the . . .

CAROL: Do you hold yourself harmless from the charge of sexual exploitativeness . . . ? [*Pause.*]

JOHN: Well, I . . . I . . . I . . . You know I, as I said. I . . . think I am not too old to *learn,* and I *can* learn, I . . .

CAROL: Do you hold yourself innocent of the charge of . . .

JOHN: . . . wait, wait, wait . . . All right, let's go back to . . .

CAROL: YOU FOOL. Who do you think I am? To come here and be taken in by a *smile.* You little yapping fool. You think I want "revenge." I don't want revenge. I WANT UNDERSTANDING.

JOHN: . . . *do* you?

CAROL: I do. [*Pause.*]

JOHN: What's the use. It's over.

CAROL: Is it? What is?

JOHN: My job.

CAROL: Oh. Your job. That's what you want to talk about. [*Pause. She starts to leave the room. She stops and turns back to him.*] All right. [*Pause.*] What if it were possible that my Group withdraws its complaint. [*Pause.*]

JOHN: What?

CAROL: That's right. [*Pause.*]

JOHN: Why.

CAROL: Well, let's say as an act of friendship.

JOHN: An act of friendship.

CAROL: Yes. [*Pause.*]

JOHN: In exchange for what?

CAROL: Yes. But don't think, "exchange." Not "in exchange." For what do we derive from it? [*Pause.*]

JOHN: "Derive."

CAROL: Yes.

JOHN: [*Pause.*] Nothing. [*Pause.*]

CAROL: That's right. We derive nothing. [*Pause.*] Do you see that?

JOHN: Yes.

CAROL: That is a little word, Professor. "Yes." "I see that." But you will.

JOHN: And you might speak to the committee . . . ?

CAROL: To the committee?

JOHN: Yes.

CAROL: Well. Of course. That's on your mind. We might.

JOHN: "If" what?

CAROL: "Given" what. Perhaps. I think that that is more friendly.

JOHN: GIVEN WHAT?

CAROL: And, believe me, I understand your rage. It is not that I don't feel it. But I do not see that it is deserved, so I do not resent it . . . . All right. I have a list.

JOHN: . . . a list.

CAROL: Here is a list of books, which we . . .

JOHN: . . . a list of books . . . ?

CAROL: That's right. Which we find questionable.

JOHN: What?

CAROL: Is this so bizarre . . . ?

JOHN: I can't believe . . .

CAROL: It's not necessary you believe it.

JOHN: Academic freedom . . .

CAROL: Someone chooses the books. If you can choose them, others can. What are you, "God"?

JOHN: . . . no, no, the "dangerous." . . .

CAROL: You have an agenda, we have an agenda. I am not interested in your feelings or your motivation, but your actions. If you would like me to speak to the Tenure Committee, here is my list. You are a Free Person, you decide. [*Pause.*]

JOHN: Give me the list. [She does so. He reads.]

CAROL: I think you'll find . . .

JOHN: I'm capable of reading it. Thank you.

CAROL: We have a number of *texts* we need re . . .

JOHN: I see that.

CAROL: We're amenable to . . .

JOHN: Aha. Well, let me look over the . . . [*He reads.*]

CAROL: I think that . . .

JOHN: LOOK. I'm reading your demands. All right?! [*He reads. Pause.*] You want to ban my book?

CAROL: We do not . . .

JOHN: [*of list*] It says here . . .

CAROL: We want it removed from inclusion as a representative example of the university.

JOHN: Get out of here.

CAROL: If you put aside the issues of personalities.

JOHN: Get the fuck out of my office.

CAROL: No. I think I would reconsider.

JOHN: . . . you think you can.

CAROL: We can and we *will.* Do you want our support? That is the only quest . . .

JOHN: . . . to ban my *book* . . . ?

CAROL: . . . that is correct . . .

JOHN: . . . this . . . this is a *university* . . . we . . .

CAROL: . . . and we have a statement . . . which we need you to . . . [*She hands him a sheet of paper.*]

JOHN: No, no. It's out of the question. I'm sorry. I don't know what I was thinking of. I want to tell you something. I'm a teacher. I am a teacher. Eh? It's my *name* on the door, and *I* teach the class, and that's what I do. I've got a book with my name on it. And my son will *see* that *book* someday. And I have a respon . . . No, I'm sorry I have a *responsibility* . . . to *myself,* to my *son,* to my *profession.* . . . I haven't been *home* for two days, do you know that? Thinking this out.

CAROL: . . . you haven't?

JOHN: I've been, no. If it's of interest to you. I've been in a *hotel. Thinking.* [*The phone starts ringing.*] *Thinking* . . .

CAROL: . . . you haven't been home?

JOHN: . . . *thinking,* do you see.

CAROL: Oh.

JOHN: And, and, I owe you a debt, I see that now. [*Pause.*] You're *dangerous,* you're *wrong* and it's my *job* . . . to say no to you. That's my job. You are absolutely right. You want to ban my book? Go to *hell,* and they can do whatever they want to me.

CAROL: . . . you haven't been home in two days . . .

JOHN: I think I told you that.

CAROL: . . . you'd better get that phone. [*Pause.*] I think that you should pick up the phone. [*Pause.*]

[*JOHN picks up the phone.*]

JOHN: [*on phone*] Yes. [*Pause.*] Yes. Wh . . . I. I. I had to be away. All ri . . . did they wor . . . did they worry ab . . . No. I'm all right, now, Jerry. I'm f . . . I got a little turned *around,* but I'm *sitting* here and . . . I've got it figured out. I'm fine. I'm fine don't worry about me. I got a little bit mixed up. But I am not sure that it's not a blessing. It cost me my job? Fine. Then the job was not worth having. Tell Grace that I'm coming home and everything is fff . . . [*Pause.*] What? [*Pause.*] *What?* [*Pause.*] What do you *mean?* WHAT? Jerry . . . Jerry. They . . . Who, who, what can they do . . . ? [*Pause.*] NO. [*Pause.*] NO. They can't do th . . . What do you mean? [*Pause.*] But how . . . [*Pause.*] She's, she's she's *here* with me. To . . . Jerry. I don't underst . . . [*Pause. He hangs up.*] [*To* CAROL.] What does this mean?

CAROL: I thought you knew.

JOHN: What. [*Pause.*] What does this mean? [*Pause.*]

CAROL: You tried to rape me. [*Pause.*] According to the law. [*Pause.*]

JOHN: . . . what . . . ?

CAROL: You tried to rape me. I was leaving this office, you "pressed" yourself into me. You "pressed" your body into me.

JOHN: . . . I . . .

CAROL: My Group has told your lawyer that we may pursue criminal charges.

JOHN: . . . no . . .

CAROL: . . . under the statute. I am told. It was battery.

JOHN: . . . no . . .

CAROL: Yes. And attempted rape. That's right. [*Pause.*]

JOHN: I think you should go.

CAROL: Of course. I thought you knew.

JOHN: I have to talk to my lawyer.

CAROL: Yes. Perhaps you should.

[The phone rings again. Pause.]

JOHN: [*picks up the phone. Into phone.*] Hello? I . . . Hello . . .? I . . . Yes, he just called. No . . . I. I can't talk to you now, Baby. [*To* CAROL.] Get out.

CAROL: . . . your wife . . .?

JOHN: . . . who it is is no concern of yours. Get out. [*To phone.*] No, no, it's going to be all right. I. I can't talk now, Baby. [*To* CAROL.] Get out of here.

CAROL: I'm going.

JOHN: Good.

CAROL: [*exiting*] . . . and don't call your wife "baby."

JOHN: What?

CAROL: Don't call your wife baby. You heard what I said.

*[*CAROL *starts to leave the room. John grabs her and begins to beat her.]*

JOHN: You vicious little bitch. You think you can come in here with your political correctness and destroy my life?

[He knocks her to the floor.]

After how I treated you . . . ? You should be . . . *Rape you* . . .? Are you kidding me . . . ?

[He picks up a chair, raises it above his head, and advances on her.]

I wouldn't touch you with a ten-foot pole. You little *cunt* . . .

[She cowers on the floor below him. Pause. He looks down at her. He lowers the chair. He moves to his desk, and arranges the papers on it. Pause. He looks over at her.]

. . . well . . .

[Pause. She looks at him.]

CAROL: Yes. That's right.
[*She looks away from him, and lowers her head. To herself.*] . . . yes. That's right.

➤ *QUESTIONS FOR READING AND WRITING*

1. Describe John and Carol. Did you find yourself favoring one or the other as the play progresses? Explain.
2. The entire play is set in John's office. Why? In what way is this setting important to the play?
3. At the beginning of both Act 2 and Act 3, time has passed and we are presented with new and important information. Were you surprised or shocked by these revelations? Explain.
4. What is your reaction to the ending of the play? To the charge against John? To his physical attack of Carol?
5. Who do you think is right, John or Carol? Why?
6. What is the central idea expressed in this drama? What do you think the play means?

TERRENCE MCNALLY (b. 1939)

Terrence McNally was born in St. Petersburg, Florida, and raised in Corpus Christi, Texas. He attended Columbia University in New York City, receiving a B.A. degree in 1960. A prolific playwright, his plays include Bad Habits *(1971),* The Lisbon Traviata *(1986), and* Lips Together, Teeth Apart *(1992). He has adapted many of his plays for films, including The Ritz (1973),* Frankie and Johnny in the Claire de Lune *(which became 1991's* Frankie and Johnny*), and* Love! Valour! Compassion! *(1977). His latest play,* Master Class, *which is about legendary opera singer Maria Callas, won the 1996 Tony Award for Best Play.*

ANDRE'S MOTHER [1994]

CAL, a young man
ARTHUR, his father
PENNY, his sister
ANDRE'S *mother*

TIME: Now
PLACE: New York City, Central Park
[Four people–Cal, Arthur, Penny, and Andre's mother—enter. They are nicely dressed and each carries a white helium-filled balloon on a string.]

CAL: You know what's really terrible? I can't think of anything terrific to say. Good-bye. I love you. I'll miss you. And I'm supposed to be so great with words!

PENNY: What's that over there?

ARTHUR: Ask your brother.

CAL: It's a theatre. An outdoor theatre. They do plays there in the summer. Shakespeare's plays. [*To ANDRE'S MOTHER.*] God, how much he wanted to play Hamlet again. He would have gone to Timbuktu to have another go at that part. The summer he did it in Boston, he was so happy!

PENNY: Cal, I don't think she . . . ! It's not the time. Later.

ARTHUR: Your son was a . . . the Jews have a word for it . . .

PENNY [*quietly appalled*]: Oh my God!

ARTHUR: Mensch, I believe it is, and I think I'm using it right. It means warm, solid, the real thing. Correct me if I'm wrong.

PENNY: Fine, Dad, fine. Just quit while you're ahead.

ARTHUR: I won't say he was like a son to me. Even my son isn't always like a son to me. I mean . . . ! In my clumsy way, I'm trying to say how much I liked Andre. And how much he helped me to know my own boy. Cal was always two handsful but Andre and I could talk about anything under the sun. My wife was very fond of him, too.

PENNY: Cal, I don't understand about the balloons.

CAL: They represent the soul. When you let go, it means you're letting his soul ascend to Heaven. That you're willing to let go. Breaking the last earthly ties.

PENNY: Does the Pope know about this?

ARTHUR: Penny!

PENNY: Andre loved my sense of humor. Listen, you can hear him laughing. [*She lets go of her white balloon.*] So long, you glorious, wonderful, I-know-what-Cal-means-about-words . . . *man!* God forgive me for wishing you were straight every time I laid eyes on you. But if any man was going to have you, I'm glad it was my brother! Look how fast it went up. I bet that means something. Something terrific.

ARTHUR [*lets his balloon go*]: Good-bye. God speed.

PENNY: Cal?

CAL: I'm not ready yet.

PENNY: Okay. We'll be over there. Come on, Pop, you can buy your little girl a Good Humor.

ARTHUR: They still make Good Humor?

PENNY: Only now they're called Dove Bars and they cost twelve dollars.

[PENNY takes ARTHUR off. CAL and ANDRE'S MOTHER stand with their balloons.]

CAL: I wish I knew what you were thinking. I think it would help me. You know almost nothing about me and I only know what Andre told me about you. I'd always had it in my mind that one day we would be friends, you and me. But if you didn't know about Andre and me . . . If this hadn't happened, I wonder if he would have ever told you. When he was sick, if I asked him once I asked him a thousand times, tell her. She's your mother. She won't mind. But he was so afraid of hurting you and of your disapproval. I don't know which was worse. [*No response. He sighs.*] God, how many of us live in this city because we don't want to hurt our mothers and live in mortal terror of their disapproval. We lose ourselves here. Our lives aren't furtive, just our feelings toward people like you are! A city of fugitives from our parents' scorn or heartbreak. Sometimes he'd seem a little down and I'd say, "What's the matter, babe?" and this funny sweet, sad smile would cross his face and he'd say, "Just a little homesick, Cal, just a little bit." I always accused him of being a country boy just playing at being a hotshot, sophisticated New Yorker. [*He sighs.*]

It's bullshit. It's all bullshit. [*Still no response.*]

Do you remember the comic strip *Little Lulu?* Her mother had no name, she was so remote, so formidable to all the children. She was just Lulu's mother. "Hello, Lulu's Mother," Lulu's friends would say. She was almost anonymous in her remoteness. You remind me of her. Andre's mother. Let me answer the questions you can't ask and then I'll leave you alone and you won't ever have to see me again. Andre died of AIDS. I don't know how he got it. I tested negative. He died bravely. You would have been proud of him. The only thing that frightened him was you. I'll have everything that was his sent to you. I'll pay for it. There isn't much. You should have come up the summer he played Hamlet. He was magnificent. Yes, I'm bitter. I'm bitter I've lost him. I'm bitter what's happening. I'm bitter even now, after all this, I can't reach you. I'm beginning to feel your disapproval and it's making me ill. [*He looks at his balloon.*] Sorry, old friend. I blew it. [*He lets go of the balloon.*]

Good night, sweet prince, and flights of angels sing thee to thy rest!

[Beat.]

Goodbye, Andre's mother.

[He goes. ANDRE'S MOTHER stands alone holding her white balloon. Her lips tremble. She looks on the verge of breaking down. She is about to let go of the balloon when she pulls it down to her. She looks at it awhile before she gently kisses it. She lets go of

the balloon. She follows it with her eyes as it rises and rises. The lights are beginning to fade. ANDRE'S MOTHER*'s eyes are still on the balloon. The lights fade.]*

➤ *QUESTIONS FOR READING AND WRITING*

1. Describe the setting of this play. What has happened?
2. Andre's mother has no lines in this play. Why? What is her role?
3. Who is Cal? What is he trying to explain to Andre's mother? Do Cal's words tell us anything about the relationship Andre had with his mother? Explain.
4. At the end of the play, Andre's mother pulls the balloon down to her, kisses it, and lets it go. What do you think she means by this action?

◆ ESSAYS ◆

TWO READERS ~ TWO CHOICES

■ *EXPLORING "Sight into Insight"*

Making Connections Given the extraordinary journey she takes us on, it seems an oversimplification to reduce the theme of Annie Dillard's essay to her statement "It's all a matter of keeping my eyes open." But, in fact, that sentence neatly summarizes her essay. She has no need to transport us to some unfamiliar world to show us wondrous sights. Rather she describes what can happen if we take time to notice—really notice—the world already around us.

Reading her essay, however—like noticing the world around us—requires patience and imagination. But the payoff is substantial. To follow her advice is to *see* more completely, close up and far away—to be conscious of what we see and even more conscious of what we cannot see—not now, not yet, but maybe in a moment if we look carefully enough.

Your Experiences and Beliefs Before you read "Sight into Insight," it may be helpful to think about your own experiences and beliefs as they apply to some of the issues that emerge from this essay. Have you given much thought to *how and what* you experience when you see? To what extent do you take seeing for granted? To what extent do you notice what surrounds you?

ANNIE DILLARD (b. 1945)

Born in Pittsburgh, Pennsylvania, Annie Dillard attended Hollins College, earning a B.A. in 1967 and an M.A. in 1968. She won the Pulitzer Prize in 1975 for Pilgrim at

Tinker Creek—*only her second publication—a collection of essays recounting her experiences while living in secluded Tinker Creek in Virginia's Roanoke Valley. She has since published other volumes of nonfiction, including* Holy the Firm *(1978) and* The Writing Life *(1989), collections of poetry, and a novel,* The Living *(1992). She has long been associated with Wesleyan University, where she is currently writer-in-residence. Her work, which is deeply philosophical and often concerns itself with the natural world, is sometimes compared with that of Henry David Thoreau.*

Sight into Insight

[1974]

When I was six or seven years old, growing up in Pittsburgh, I used to take a precious penny of my own and hide it for someone else to find. It was a curious compulsion; sadly, I've never been seized by it since. For some reason I always "hid" the penny along the same stretch of sidewalk up the street. I would cradle it at the roots of a sycamore, say, or in a hole left by a chipped-off piece of sidewalk. Then I would take a piece of chalk, and, starting at either end of the block, draw huge arrows leading up to the penny from both directions. After I learned to write I labeled the arrows: SURPRISE AHEAD OR MONEY THIS WAY. I was greatly excited, during all this arrow-drawing, at the thought of the first lucky passer-by who would receive in this way, regardless of merit, a free gift from the universe. But I never lurked about. I would go straight home and not give the matter another thought, until, some months later, I would be gripped again by the impulse to hide another penny.

It is still the first week in January, and I've got great plans. I've been thinking about seeing. There are lots of things to see, unwrapped gifts and free surprises. The world is fairly studded and strewn with pennies cast broadside from a generous hand. But—and this is the point—who gets excited by a mere penny? If you follow one arrow, if you crouch motionless on a bank to watch a tremulous ripple thrill on the water and are rewarded by the sight of a muskrat kit paddling from its den, will you: count that sight a chip of copper only, and go your rueful way? It is dire poverty indeed when a man is so malnourished and fatigued that he won't stoop to pick up a penny. But if you cultivate a healthy poverty and simplicity, so that finding a penny will literally make your day, then, since the world is in fact planted in pennies, you have with your poverty bought a lifetime of days. It is that simple. What you see is what you get.

I used to be able to see flying insects in the air. I'd look ahead and see, not the row of hemlocks across the road, but the air in front of it. My eyes would focus along that column of air, picking out flying insects. But I lost interest, I guess, for I dropped the habit. Now I can see birds. Probably some people can look at the grass at their feet and discover all the crawling creatures. I would like to know grasses and sedges—and care. Then my last journey into the world would be a field trip, a series of happy recognitions. Thoreau, in an expansive mood, exulted, "What a rich book might be made about buds, including, perhaps, sprouts!" It would be nice to think so. I cherish mental images I have of three perfectly happy people. One collects stones. Another—an Englishman, say—watches clouds. The third lives on a coast and collects drops of seawater which he examines microscopically and mounts. But I don't see what the specialist sees, and so I cut myself off, not only from the total picture, but from the various forms of happiness.

Unfortunately, nature is very much a now-you-see-it, now-you-don't affair. A fish flashes, then dissolves in the water before my eyes like so much salt. Deer apparently ascend bodily into heaven; the brightest oriole fades into leaves. These disappearances stun me into stillness and concentration; they say of nature that it conceals with a grand nonchalance, and they say of vision that it is a deliberate gift, the revelation of a dancer who for my eyes only flings away her seven veils. For nature does reveal as well as conceal: now you-don't-see-it, now-you-do. For a week last September migrating red-winged blackbirds were feeding heavily down by the creek at the back of the house. One day I went out to investigate the racket; I walked up to a tree, an Osage orange, and a hundred birds flew away. They simply materialized out of the tree. I saw a tree, then a whisk of color, then a tree again. I walked closer and another hundred blackbirds took flight. Not a branch, not a twig budged: The birds were apparently weightless as well as invisible. Or, it was as if the leaves of the Osage orange had been freed from a spell in the form of red-winged blackbirds; they flew from the tree, caught my eye in the sky, and vanished. When I looked again at the tree the leaves had reassembled as if nothing had happened. Finally I walked directly to the trunk of the tree and a final hundred, the real diehards, appeared, spread, and vanished. How could so many hide in the tree without my seeing them? The Osage orange, unruffled, looked just as it had looked from the house, when three hundred red-winged blackbirds cried from its crown. I looked downstream where they flew, and they were gone. Searching, I couldn't spot one. I wandered downstream to force them to play their hand, but they'd crossed the creek and scattered. One show to a customer. These appearances catch at my throat; they are the free gifts, the bright coppers at the roots of trees.

5 It's all a matter of keeping my eyes open. Nature is like one of those line drawings of a tree that are puzzles for children: Can you find hidden in the leaves a duck, a house, a boy, a bucket, a zebra, and a boot? Specialists can find the most incredibly well-hidden things. A book I read when I was young recommended an easy way to find caterpillars to rear: You simply find some fresh caterpillar droppings, look up, and there's your caterpillar. More recently an author advised me to set my mind at ease about those piles of cut stems on the ground in grassy fields. Field mice make them, they cut the grass down by degrees to reach the seeds at the head. It seems that when the grass is tightly packed, as in a field of ripe grain, the blade won't topple at a single cut through the stem; instead, the cut stem simply drops vertically, held crush of grain. The mouse severs the bottom again and again, the stem keeps

dropping an inch at a time, and finally the head is low enough for the mouse to reach the seeds. Meanwhile, the mouse is positively littering the field with its little piles of cut stems into which, presumably, the author of the book is constantly stumbling.

If I can't see these minutiae, I still try to keep my eyes open. I'm always on the lookout for antlion traps in sandy soil, monarch pupae near milkweed, skipper larvae in locust leaves. These things are utterly common, and I've not seen one. I bang on hollow trees near water, but so far no flying squirrels have appeared. In flat country I watch every sunset in hopes of seeing the green ray. The green ray is a seldom-seen streak of light that rises from the sun like a spurting fountain at the moment of sunset; it throbs into the sky for two seconds and disappears. One more reason to keep my eyes open. A photography professor at the University of Florida just happened to see a bird die in midflight; it jerked, died, dropped, and smashed on the ground. I squint at the wind because I read Stewart Edward White: "I have always maintained that if you looked closely enough you could *see* the wind—the dim, hardly—madeout, fine debris fleeing high in the air." White was an excellent observer, and devoted an entire chapter of *The Mountains* to the subject of seeing deer: "As soon as you can forget the naturally obvious and construct an artificial obvious, then you too will see deer."

But the artificial obvious is hard to see. My eyes account for less than one percent of the weight of my head; I'm bony and dense; I see what I expect. I once spent a full three minutes looking at a bullfrog that was so unexpectedly large I couldn't see it even though a dozen enthusiastic campers were shouting directions. Finally I asked, "What color am I looking for?" and a fellow said, "Green." When at last I picked out the frog, I saw what painters are up against: The thing wasn't green at all, but the color of wet hickory bark.

The lover can see, and the knowledgeable. I visited an aunt and uncle at a quarter-horse ranch in Cody, Wyoming. I couldn't do much of anything useful, but I could, I thought, draw. So, as we all sat around the kitchen table after supper, I produced a sheet of paper and drew a horse. "That's one lame horse," my aunt volunteered. The rest of the family joined in: "Only place to saddle that one is his neck"; "Looks like we better shoot the poor thing, on account of those terrible growths." Meekly, I slid the pencil and paper down the table. Everyone in that family, including my three young cousins, could draw a Rome. Beautifully. When the paper came back it looked as though five shining, real quarter horses had been corraled by mistake with a papier-mache moose; the real horses seemed to gaze at the monster with a steady, puzzled air. I stay away from horses now, but I can do a creditable goldfish. The point is that I just don't know what the lover knows; I just can't see the artificial obvious that those in the know construct. The herpetologist asks the native, "Are there snakes in that ravine?" "No sir." And the herpetologist comes home with, yes sir, three bags full. Are there butterflies on that mountain? Are the bluets in bloom, are there arrowheads here, or fossil shells in the shale?

Peeping through my keyhole I see within the range of only about thirty percent of the light that comes from the sun; the rest is infrared and some little ultraviolet, perfectly apparent to many animals, but invisible to me. A nightmare network of ganglia, charged and firing without my knowledge, cuts and splices what I do see, editing it for my brain. Donald E. Carr points out that the sense impressions of one-celled animals are not edited for the brain: "This is philosophically interesting in a rather mournful way, since it means that only the simplest animals perceive the universe as it is."

A fog that won't burn away drifts flows across my field of vision. When you see fog move against a backdrop of deep pines, you don't see the fog itself, but streaks of clearness floating across the air in dark shreds. So I see only tatters of clearness through a pervading obscurity. I can't distinguish the fog from the overcast sky; I can't be sure if the light is direct or reflected. Everywhere darkness and the presence of the unseen appalls. We estimate now that only one atom dances alone in every cubic meter of intergalactic space. I blink and squint. What planet or power yanks Halley's Comet out of orbit? We haven't seen that force yet; it's a question of distance, density, and the pallor of reflected light. We rock, cradled in the swaddling band of darkness. Even the simple darkness of night whispers suggestions to the mind. Last summer, in August, I stayed at the creek too late.

Where Tinker Creek flows under the sycamore log bridge to the tear-shaped island, it is slow and shallow, fringed thinly in cattail marsh. At this spot an astonishing bloom of life supports vast breeding populations of insects, fish, reptiles, birds, and mammals. On windless summer evenings I stalk along the creek bank or straddle the sycamore log in absolute stillness, watching for muskrats. The night I stayed too late I was hunched on the log staring spellbound at spreading, reflected stains of lilac on the water. A cloud in the sky suddenly lighted as if turned on by a switch; its reflection just as suddenly materialized on the water upstream, flat and floating, so that I couldn't see the creek bottom, or life in the water under the cloud. Downstream, away from the cloud on the water, water turtles smooth as beans were gliding down with the current in a series of easy, weightless push-offs, as men bound on the moon. I didn't know whether to trace the progress of one turtle I was sure of, risking sticking my face in one of the bridge's spider webs made invisible by the gathering dark, or take a chance on seeing the carp, or scan the mudbank in hope of seeing a muskrat, or follow the last of the swallows who caught at my heart and trailed it after them like streamers as they appeared from directly below, under the log, flying upstream with the tails forked, so fast.

But shadows spread, and deepened, and stayed. After thousands of years we're still strangers to darkness, fearful aliens in an enemy camp with our arms crossed over our chests. I stirred. A land turtle on the bank, startled, hissed the air from its lungs and withdrew into its shell. An uneasy pink here, an unfathomable blue there, gave great suggestion of lurking beings. Things were going on. I couldn't see whether that mere rustle I heard was a distant rattlesnake, slit-eyed, or a nearby sparrow kicking in the dry flood debris slung at the foot of a willow. Tremendous action roiled the water everywhere I looked, big action, inexplicable. A tremor welled up beside a gaping muskrat burrow in the bank and I caught my breath, but no muskrat appeared. The ripples continued to fan upstream with a steady, powerful thrust. Night was knitting over my face an eyeless mask, and I still sat transfixed. A distant airplane, a delta wing out of nightmare, made a gliding shadow on the creek's bottom that looked to me a stingray cruising upstream. At once a black fin slit the pink cloud on the water, shearing it in two. The two halves merged together and seemed to dissolve before my eyes. Darkness pooled in the cleft of the creek and rose, as water collects in a well. Untamed, dreaming lights flickered over the sky. I saw hints of hulking underwater shadows, two pale splashes out of the water, and round ripples rolling close together from a blackened center.

At last I stared upstream where only the deepest violet remained of the cloud, a cloud so high its underbelly still glowed feeble color reflected from a hidden sky lighted in turn by a sun halfway to China. And out of that violet, a sudden enormous black body arced over the water. I saw only a cylindrical sleekness. Head and tail, if there was a head and tail, were both submerged in cloud. I saw only one ebony fling, a headlong dive to darkness; then the waters closed, and the lights went out.

I walked home in a shivering daze, up hill and down. Later I lay openmouthed in bed, my arms flung wide at my sides to steady the whirling darkness. At this latitude I'm spinning 836 miles an hour round the earth's axis; I often fancy I feel my sweeping fall as a breakneck arc like the dive of dolphins, and the hollow rushing of wind raises hair on my neck and the side of my face. In orbit around the sun I'm moving 64,800 miles an hour. The solar system as a whole, like a merry-go-round—unhinged, spins, bobs, and blinks at the speed of 43,200 miles an hour along a course set east of Hercules. Someone has piped, and we are dancing a tarantella until the sweat pours. I open my eyes and I see dark, muscled forms curl out of water, with flapping gills and flattened eyes. I close my eyes and I see stars, deep stars giving way to deeper stars, deeper stars bowing to deepest stars at the crown of an infinite cone.

15 "Still," wrote van Gogh in a letter, "a great deal of light falls on everything." If we are blinded by darkness, we are also blinded by light. When too much light falls on everything, a special terror results. Peter Freuchen describes the notorious kayak sickness to which Greenland Eskimos are prone. "The Greenland fjords are peculiar for the spells of completely quiet weather, when there is not enough wind to blow out a match and the water is like a sheet of glass. The kayak hunter must sit in his boat without stirring a finger so as not to scare the shy seals away. The sun, low in the sky, sends a glare into his eyes, and the landscape around moves into the realm of the unreal. The reflex from the mirror-like water hypnotizes him, he seems to be unable to move, and all of a sudden it is as if he were floating in a bottomless void, sinking, sinking, and sinking. . . . Horror-stricken, he tries to stir, to cry out, but he cannot, he is completely paralyzed, he just falls and falls." Some hunters are especially cursed with this panic, and bring ruin and sometimes starvation to their families.

Sometimes here in Virginia at sunset low clouds on the southern or northen horizon are completely invisible in the lighted sky. I only know one is there because I can see its reflection in still water. The first time I discovered this mystery I looked from cloud to no-cloud in bewilderment, checking my bearings over and over, thinking maybe the ark of the covenant was just passing by south of Dead Man Mountain. Only much later did I read the explanation: Polarized light from the sky is very much weakened by reflection; but the light in clouds isn't polarized. So invisible clouds pass among visible clouds, till all slide over the mountains; so a greater light extinguishes a lesser as though it didn't exist.

In the great meteor shower of August, the Perseid, I wail all day for the shooting stars I miss. They're out there showering down, committing hara-kiri in a flame of fatal attraction, and hissing perhaps at last into the ocean. But at dawn what looks like a blue dome clamps down over me like a lid on a pot. The stars and planets could smash and I'd never know. Only a piece of ashen moon occasionally climbs up or down the inside of the dome, and our local star without surcease explodes on our heads. We have really only that one light, one source for all power, and yet we must turn away from it by universal decree. Nobody here on the planet seems aware of this strange, powerful taboo, that we all walk about carefully averting our faces, this way and that, lest our eyes be blasted forever.

Darkness appalls and light dazzles; the scrap of visible light that doesn't hurt my eyes hurts my brain. What I see sets me swaying. Size and distance and the sudden swelling of meanings confuse me, bowl me over. I straddle the sycamore log bridge over Tinker Creek in the summer. I look at the lighted creek bottom: Snail tracks tunnel the mud in quavering curves. A crayfish jerks, but by the time I absorb what has happened, he's gone in a billowing smoke-screen of silt. I look at the water: minnows and shiners. If I'm thinking minnows, a carp will fill my brain till I scream. I look at the water's surface: skaters, bubbles, and leaves sliding down. Suddenly, my own face, reflected, startles me witless. Those snails have been tracking my face! Finally, with a shuddering wrench of the will, I see clouds, cirrus clouds. I'm dizzy, I fall in.

This looking business is risky. Once I stood on a humped rock on nearby Purgatory mountain, watching through binoculars the great autumn hawk migration below, until I discovered that I was in danger of joining the hawks on a vertical migration of my own. I was used to binoculars, but not, apparently, to balancing on humped rocks while looking through them. I staggered. Everything advanced and receded by turns; the world was full of unexplained foreshortenings and depths. A distant huge tan object, a hawk the size of an elephant, turned out to be the browned bough of a nearby loblolly pine. I followed a sharp-shinned hawk against a featureless sky, rotating my head unawares as it flew, and when I lowered the glass a glimpse of my own looming shoulder sent me staggering. What prevents the men on Palomar from falling, voiceless and blinded from their tiny, vaulted chairs?

20 I reel in confusion; I don't understand what I see. With the naked eye I can see two million light-years to the Andromeda galaxy. Often I slop some creek water in a jar and when I get home I dump it in a white china bowl. After the silt settles, I return and see tracings of minute snails on the bottom, a planarium or two winding round the rim of water, roundworms shimmying frantically, and finally, when my eyes have adjusted to these dimensions, amoebae. At first the amoebae look like muscae volitantes, those curled moving spots you seem to see in your eyes when you stare at a distant wall. Then I see the amoebae as drops of water congealed, blush, translucent, like chips of sky in the bowl. At length I choose one individual and give myself over to its idea of an evening. I see it dribble a grainy foot before it on its wet, unfathomable way. Do its unedited sense impressions include the fierce focus of my eyes? Shall I take it outside and show it Andromeda, and blow its little endoplasm? I stir the water with a finger, in case it's running out of oxygen. Maybe I should get a tropical aquarium with motorized bubblers and lights, and keep this one for a pet. Yes, it would tell its fissioned descendants, the universe is two feet by five, and if you listen closely you can hear the buzzing music of the spheres.

Oh, it's mysterious lamplit evenings, here in the galaxy, one after the other, it's one of those rights when I wander from window to window, looking for a sign. But I can't see Terror and a beauty insoluble are a ribband of blue woven into the fringes of garments of things both great and small. No culture explains, no bivouac offers real haven or rest. But it could be that we are not seeing something. Galileo thought comets were an optical illusion. This is fertile ground: Since we are certain that they're not, we can look at what our scientists have been saying with fresh hope. What if there are *really* gleaming, castellated cities hung upside-down over the desert sand? What limpid lakes and cool date palms have our caravans always passed untried? Until, by one, by the blindest of leaps, we light on the road to these places, we must stumble in darkness and hunger. I turn from the window. I'm blind as a bat, sensing only from every direction the echo of my own thin cries.

I chanced on a wonderful book by Marius von Senden, called *Space and Light.* When Western surgeons discovered how to perform safe cataract operations, they ranged across Europe and America operating on dozens of men and women of all ages who had been blinded by cataracts since birth. Von Senden collected accounts of such cases; the histories are fascinating. Many doctors had tested their patients' sense perceptions and ideas of space both before and after the operations. The vast majority of patients, of both sexes and all ages, had, in von Senden's opinion, no idea of space whatsoever. Form, distance, and size were so many meaningless syllables. A patient "had no idea of depth, confusing it with roundness." Before the operation a doctor would give a blind patient a cube and a sphere; the patient would tongue it or feel it with his hands, and name it correctly. After the operation the doctor would show the same objects to the patient without letting him touch them; now he had no clue whatsoever what he was seeing. One patient called lemonade "square" because it pricked on his tongue as a square shape pricked on the touch of his hands. Of another postoperative patient, the doctor writes, "I have found in her no notion of size, for example, not even within the narrow limits which she might have encompassed with the aid of touch. Thus when I asked her to show me how big her mother was, she did not stretch out her hands, but set her two index fingers a few inches apart." Other doctors reported their patients' own statements to similar effect. "The room he was in . . . he knew to be but part of the house, yet he could not conceive that the whole house could look bigger"; "Those who are blind from birth . . . have no real conception of height or distance. A house that is a mile away is thought of as nearby, but requiring the taking of a lot of steps. . . . The elevator that whizzes him up and down gives no more sense of vertical distance than does the train of horizontal."

For the newly sighted, vision is pure sensation unencumbered by meaning: "The girl went through the experience that we all go through and forget, the moment we are born. She saw, but it did not mean anything but a lot of different kinds of brightness." Again, "I asked the patient what he could see; he answered that he saw an extensive field of light, in which everything appeared dull, confused, and in motion. He could not distinguish objects." Another patient saw "nothing but a confusion of forms and colors." When a newly sighted girl saw photographs and paintings, she asked, "'Why do they put those dark marks all over them?' 'Those aren't dark marks,' her mother explained, 'those are shadows. That is one of the ways the eye knows that things have shape. If it were not for shadows many things would look flat.' 'Well, that's how things do look,' Joan answered. 'Everything looks flat with dark patches.'"

But it is the patients' concepts of space that are most revealing. One patient, according to his doctor, "practiced his vision in a strange fashion; thus he takes off one of his boots, throws it some way off in front of him, and then attempts to gauge the distance at which it lies; he takes a few steps toward the boot and tries to grasp it; on failing to reach it, he moves on a step or two and gropes for the boot until he finally gets hold of it." "But even at this stage, after three weeks' experience of seeing," von Senden goes on, " 'space,' as he conceives it, ends with visual space, i.e., with color-patches that happen to bound his view. He does not yet have the notion that a larger object (a chair) can mask a smaller one (a dog), or that the latter can still be present even though it is not directly seen."

In general the newly sighted see the world as a dazzle of color-patches. They are pleased by the sensation of color, and learn quickly to name the colors, but the rest of seeing is tormentingly difficult. Soon after his operation a patient "generally bumps into one of these color-patches and observes them to be substantial, since they resist him as tactual objects do. In walking about it also strikes him—or can if he pays attention—that he is continually passing in between the colors he sees, that he can go past a visual object, that a part of it then steadily disappears from view; and that in spite of this, however he twists and turns—whether entering the room from the door, for example, or returning back to it—he always has a visual space in front of him. Thus he gradually comes to realize that there is also a space behind him, which he does not see."

The mental effort involved in these reasonings proves overwhelming for many patients. It oppresses them to realize, if they ever do at all, the tremendous size of the world, which they had previously conceived of as something touchingly manageable. It oppresses them to realize that they have been visible to people all along, perhaps unattractively so, without their knowledge or consent. A disheartening number of them refuse to use their new vision, continuing to go over objects with their tongues, and lapsing into apathy and despair. "The child can see, but will not make use of his sight. Only when pressed can he with difficulty be brought to look at objects in his neighborhood; but more than a foot away it is impossible to bestir him to the necessary effort." Of a twenty-one-year-old girl, the doctor relates, "Her unfortunate father, who had hoped for so much from this operation, wrote that his daughter carefully shuts her eyes whenever she wishes to go about the house, especially when she comes to a staircase, and that she is never happier or more at ease than when, by closing her eyelids, she relapses into her former state of total blindness." A fifteen-year-old boy, who was also in love with a girl at the asylum for the blind, finally blurted out, "No, really, I can't stand it any more; I want to be sent back to the asylum again. If things aren't altered, I'll tear my eyes out."

Some do learn to see, especially the young ones. But it changes their lives. One doctor comments on "the rapid and complete loss of that striking and wonderful serenity which is characteristic only of those who have never yet seen." A blind man who learns to see is ashamed of his old habits. He dresses up, grooms himself, and tries to make a good impression. While he was blind he was indifferent to objects unless they were edible; now, "a sifting of values sets in . . . his thoughts and wishes are mightily stirred and some few of the patients are thereby led into dissimulation, envy, theft and fraud."

On the other hand, many newly sighted people speak well of the world, and teach us how dull our own vision is. To one patient, a human hand, unrecognized, is "something bright and then holes." Shown a bunch of grapes, a boy calls out, "it is dark, blue and shiny . . . it isn't smooth, it has bumps and hollows." A little girl visits a garden. "She is greatly astonished, and can scarcely be persuaded to answer, stands speechless in front of the tree, which she only names on taking hold of it, and then as 'the tree with the lights in it.'" Some delight in their sight and give themselves over to the visual world. Of a patient just after her bandages were removed, her doctor writes, "The first things to attract her attention were her own hands; she looked at them very closely, moved them repeatedly to and fro, bent and stretched the fingers, and seemed greatly astonished at the sight." One girl was eager to tell her blind friend that "men do not really look like trees at all," and astounded to discover that her every visitor had an utterly different face. Finally, a twenty-two-year old girl was dazzled by the world's brightness and kept her eyes shut for two weeks. When at the end of that time she opened her eyes again, she did not recognize any objects, but, "the more she now directed her gaze upon everything about her, the more it could be seen how an expression of gratification and astonishment overspread her features; she repeatedly exclaimed: 'Oh God! How beautiful!' "

I saw color-patches for weeks after I read this wonderful book. It was summer; the peaches were ripe in the valley orchards. When I woke in the morning, color-patches wrapped round my eyes, intricately, leaving not one unfilled spot. All day long I walked among shifting color-patches that parted before me like the Red Sea and closed again in silence, transfigured, wherever I looked back. Some patches swelled and loomed, while others vanished utterly, and dark marks flitted at random over the whole dazzling sweep. But I couldn't sustain the illusion of flatness. I've been around for too long. Form is condemned to an eternal danse macabre with meaning. I couldn't unpeach the peaches. Nor can I remember ever having seen without understanding; the color-patches of infancy are lost. My brain then must have been smooth as any balloon. I'm told I reached for the moon; many babies do. But the color-patches of infancy swelled as meaning filled them; they arrayed themselves in solemn ranks down distance which unrolled and stretched before me like a plain. The moon rocketed away. I live now in a world of shadows that shape and distance color, a world where space makes a kind of terrible sense. What gnosticism is this, and what physics? The fluttering patch I saw in my nursery window—silver and green and shape-shifting blue—is gone; a row of Lombardy poplars takes its place, mute, across the distant lawn. That humming oblong creature pale as light that stole along the walls of my room at night, stretching exhilaratingly around the corners, is gone, too, gone the night I ate of the bittersweet fruit, put two and two together and puckered forever my brain. Martin Buber tells this tale: "Rabbi Mendel once boasted to his teacher Rabbi Elimelekh that evenings he saw the angel who rolls away the light before the darkness, and mornings the angel who rolls away the darkness before the light. 'Yes,' said Rabbi Elimelekh, 'in my youth I saw that too. Later on you don't see these things any more.'"

30 Why didn't someone hand those newly sighted people paints and brushes from the start, when they still didn't know what anything was? Then maybe we all could see color-patches too, the world unraveled from reason, Eden before Adam gave names. The scales would drop from my eyes; I'd see trees like men walking; I'd run down the road against all orders, hallooing and leaping.

Seeing is of course very much a matter of verbalization. Unless I call my attention to what passes before my eyes, I simply won't see it. It is, as Ruskin says, "not merely unnoticed, but in the full, clear sense of the word, unseen." My eyes alone can't solve analogy tests using figures, the ones which show, with increasing elaborations, a big square, then a small square in a big square, then a big triangle, and expect me to find a small triangle in a big triangle. I have to say the words, describe what I'm seeing. If Tinker Mountain erupted, I'd be likely to notice. But if I want to notice the lesser cataclysms of valley life, I have to maintain in my head a running description of the present. It's not that I'm observant; it's just that I talk too much. Otherwise, especially in a strange place, I'll never know what's happening. Like a blind man at the ball game, I need a radio.

When I see this way I analyze and pry. I hurl over logs and roll away stones; I study the bank a square foot at a time, probing and tilting my head. Some days when a mist covers the mountains, when the muskrats won't show and the microscope's mirror shatters, I want to climb up the blank blue dome as a man would storm the inside of a circus tent, wildly, dangling, and with a steel knife claw a rent in the top, peep, and, if I must, fall.

But there is another kind of seeing that involves a letting go. When I see this way I sway transfixed and emptied. The difference between the two ways of seeing is the difference between walking with and without a camera. When I walk with a camera I walk from, shot to shot, reading the light on a calibrated meter. When I walk without a camera, my own shutter opens, and the moment's light prints on my own silver gut. When I see this second way I am above all an unscrupulous observer.

It was sunny one evening last summer at Tinker Creek; the sun was low in the sky, upstream. I was sitting on the sycamore log bridge with the sunset at my back, watching the shiners the size of minnows who were feeding over the muddy sand in skittery schools. Again and again, one fish, then another, turned for a split second across the current and flash! the sun shot out from its silver side. I couldn't watch for it. It was always just happening somewhere else, and it drew my vision just as it disappeared: flash, like a sudden dazzle of the thinnest blade, a sparking over a dun and olive ground at chance intervals from every direction. Then I noticed white specks, some sort of pale petals, small, floating from under my feet on the creek's surface, very slow and steady. So I blurred my eyes and gazed toward the brim of my hat and saw a new world. I saw the pale white circles roll up, roll up, like the world's turning, mute and perfect, and I saw the linear flashes, gleaming silver, like stars being born at random down a rolling scroll of time. Something broke and something opened. I filled up like a new wineskin. I breathed an air like light; I saw a light like water. I was the lip of a fountain the creek filled forever; I was ether, the leaf in the zephyr; I was flesh-flake, feather, bone.

When I see this way I see, truly. As Thoreau says, I return to my senses. I am the man who watches the baseball game in silence in an empty stadium. I see the game purely; I'm abstracted and dazed. When it's all over and the white-suited players lope off the green field to their shadowed dugouts, I leap to my feet; I cheer and cheer.

But I can't go out and try to see this way. I'll fail, I'll go mad. All I can do is try to gag the commentator, to hush the noise of useless interior babble that keeps me from seeing just as surely as a newspaper dangled before my eyes. The effort is really a discipline requiring a lifetime of dedicated struggle; it marks the literature of saints and monks of every order East and West, under every rule and no rule, discalced and shod. The world's spiritual geniuses seem to discover universally that the mind's muddy river, this ceaseless flow of trivia and trash, cannot be dammed, and that trying to dam it is a waste of effort that might lead to madness. Instead you must allow the muddy river to flow unheeded in the dim channels of consciousness; you raise your sights; you look along it, mildly, acknowledging its presence without interest and gazing beyond it into the realm of the real where subjects and objects act and rest purely, without utterance. "Launch into the deep," says Jacques Ellul, "and you shall see."

The secret of seeing is, then, the pearl of great price. If I thought he could teach me to find it and keep it forever I would stagger barefoot across a hundred deserts after any lunatic at all. But although the pearl may be found, it may not be sought. The literature of illumination reveals this above all: Although it comes to those who wait for it, it is always, even to the most practiced and adept, a gift and a total surprise. I return from one walk knowing where the killdeer nests in the field by the creek and the hour the laurel blooms. I return from the same walk a day later scarcely knowing my own name. Litanies hum in my ears; my tongue flaps in my mouth Ailinon, alleluia! I cannot cause light; the most I can do is try to put myself in the path of its beam. It is possible, in deep space, to sail on solar wind. Light, be it particle or wave, has force: you rig a giant sail and go. The secret of seeing is to sail on solar wind. Hone and spread your spirit till you yourself are a sail, whetted, translucent, broadside to the merest puff.

When her doctor took her bandages off and led her into the garden, the girl who was no longer blind saw "the tree with the lights in it." It was for this tree I searched through the peach orchards of summer, in the forests of fall and down winter and spring for years. Then one day I was walking along Tinker Creek thinking of nothing at all and I saw the tree with the lights in it. I saw the backyard cedar where the mourning doves roost charged and transfigured, each cell buzzing with flame. I stood on the grass with the lights in it, grass that was wholly fire, utterly focused and utterly dreamed. It was less like seeing than like being for the first time seen, knocked breathless by a powerful glance. The flood of fire abated, but I'm still spending the power. Gradually the lights went out in the cedar, the colors died, the cells unflamed and disappeared. I was still ringing. I had been my whole life a bell, and never knew it until at that moment I was lifted and struck. I have since only very rarely seen the tree with the lights in it. The vision comes and goes, mostly goes, but I live for it, for the moment when the mountains open and a new light roars in spate through the crack, and the mountains slam.

➤ *QUESTIONS FOR READING AND WRITING*

1. To what extent is your response to "Sight into Insight" influenced by your own experience?
2. Why do you think Annie Dillard writes about this topic? Is she writing to clarify things for herself or is she writing to share her discoveries with a wider audience? Do you think she is trying to persuade you to spend your time engaged in similar endeavors?
3. Does this essay teach a technique for appreciating nature? In other words, do you think you would be able to apply advice from the essay to your own appreciation of the natural world? Is there a sense in which the sort of communion with nature that Dillard describes defies description?
4. What does Dillard mean by the statement, "My eyes account for less than 1 percent of the weight of my head." Why is this a problem for her? Is this statistic meant to be appreciated literally or does it represent a more abstract problem? What other limitations interfere with Dillard's search to "see" things in nature?
5. Does this essay have relevance for urban dwellers? Do you think Dillard would spend her time similarly if she lived in a city? Why or why not?
6. What do you think of Dillard's quest? Is it worthwhile? Is it for you? Explain.

~ TWO STUDENT PAPERS

Depending on our experience of it, "Sight into Insight" is an essay about many different things. We may experience it as an essay about seeing for the first time, about imagination, about illusion or reality, or about paying attention to what really matters.

In the two critical essays that follow, Janice Bevilacqua and Jacquelyn Webster interpret "Sight Into Insight" by reexperiencing and articulating the moments of their reading—sharing with us and analyzing what impressed them so deeply about her writing. And while they take us on the same journey of perception and imagination, each student writer notices very different things along the way.

Janice Bevilacqua

Dr. Costanzo

English 102

April 10, 200X

Upon Reading "Sight into Insight"

There must have been some hidden energy that compelled Annie Dillard to write the essay "Sight Into Insight." The necessity to uncover mystery must have begun when she, at six or seven years old, satisfied her first "curious compulsions" by hiding pennies for a lucky passersby to discover. The urge to disrobe the universe of its many wonders did not release its grip on her. She continues to plant her pennies by way of words. Indeed, this particular essay may be thought of as one of those "free surprises." She offers us a chance to share her insight, to transcend ordinary human knowledge by taking her hand and allowing ourselves to be led into a rare state of awareness.

We should feel privileged when reading Dillard's text, for she grants us a new visual ability: to observe nature in its rawest form, to watch our surroundings in a way that enables us to understand what it is like to experience life fully if but for a moment. She encourages us to "see" in such a way that utilizes all of our senses so that when a "fish flashes," we are conscious of its little arch-stretch over the surface of water in addition to the sound of the water when it breaks, and the slap of the fish when it curves and dives back in. We must also be aware of these brief spectacles as extraordinary, since nature is "very much a now-you-see-it, now-you-don't affair" (1433).

There may be times when we try to catch a particular scene, such as a muskrat or a shooting star, and miss it. There may be times when vision is limited, like when night begins to knit an "eyeless mask" over our faces. However, even when we are bound and unable to see the obvious, we are at an advantage; when we are overcome by such blindness, we have no choice but to lengthen our self-boundaries and challenge ourselves to see differently. This perceptual expansion is thrilling. It provides us with the means to have a fresh look at the world and to attain knowledge that is often ignored in our culture. Lack of the knowledge that has somehow been filtered out of our consciousness has caused us to become unaccustomed to being receptive to all forms of life. If we would allow ourselves to be taught to open our eyes, to see through our "eyeless masks," we might be surprised at the wisdom we attain by learning about the hidden things.

Dillard reminds us that seeing truly is not a free process. It requires discipline, and a "lifetime of dedicated struggle" (1442). Thus, the art of perceiving clearly is a mystery in itself. It may be as sporadic as a shooting star, or as secretive as a pearl. In this respect, we may be considered an unlucky organism since, unlike many other simple living things, we are born with edited brains. Our capacity to see the actual universe is hindered at birth. Not only does every human being see differently, but each organism holds its own perception as well. This notion is frustrating. Although it is not evidence of impossibility, it is certainly an indication that we are slaves to our conceptions: we are required to perform laborious tasks in order to see exactly what lies before us.

Like nature, Dillard's essay must be considered at various slants. It must be looked at, looked over, and looked through to be of full value. It is like the fog across a field of vision, against a backdrop of deep pines: "you don't see the fog itself, but streaks of clearness floating across the air in dark shreds" (1435). Her writing is also marked by strips of clarity. The work is dappled with images that flare up into flames of truth and become a blaze of realization that no reader can miss. To go with her along the path by her creek is to go beyond familiar thoughts, into a haunting, yet authentic metaphor for the human condition. Dim trails in the woods become unchartered regions of the mind, and while we trek with her, we open our eyes to the world with her.

It is not often that we accept the challenge to look at our surroundings with a new vision. Dillard too understands that "this looking business is risky," (1437) and there inevitably exists a fear of being exposed by something we do not want to see, something that may knock us off our feet, cripple us crestfallen. Just as we are born with specific brains, so we are born into specific environments. We spend our entire lives settling into the comfort of what we know. We grow used to a particular way of life including culture, education, values, and attitudes. Thus, baring ourselves to rawness or knowledge that is stripped of its familiarity can be frightening. However, she tries to tell us that not taking this risk can be even more dangerous. Seeing outside of what is familiar provides us with the stimulation of having experienced something new and the urgency to cultivate those regions of the mind that remain untried.

Dillard speaks of the human condition in a promising manner. She says of nature that it "conceals with a grand nonchalance" (1433), then refers to vision as a "deliberate gift." Following these words of encouragement, she gives an example of being delightfully shocked by the ability to uncover the hidden marvels of nature by way of this "deliberate gift." While standing before what appeared to be a bare Osage orange tree, a hundred red-winged blackbirds suddenly took flight from its limbs, followed by another hundred, and another. The red-winged blackbirds might be likened to the pennies that the author hid as a child: each certainly a "surprise ahead." This example should serve as a reminder that humans and nature work hand in hand. We have been granted the ability to see as nature has been granted the ability to reveal.

To read Dillard's prose is to enter an alternative realm in which words give rise to images in a way that transports us to the space right by her side. Here, we may engage with her in the intimate act of passively experiencing the world and patiently awaiting its pleasures. There is a mysticism in her endeavor to open our eyes. She would like us to believe with her in the possibility of achieving ecstasy and comfort by welcoming mystery. There is an urgency behind her words. This blistering passion works to ignite the same hot fervor within us so that we too may one day come to rest upon a log, wide-eyed in an unknown dimension.

Work Cited

Dillard, Annie. "Sight into Insight." Exploring Literature. Ed. Frank Madden. New York: Longman, 2001, 1432-1443.

Jacquelyn Webster

Dr. Costanzo

English 102

April 15, 200X

Drifting and Gliding

There are few ways to describe Annie Dillard's writing better than, it drifts. She glides from idea to idea, gently, like a leaf on a soft current. In "Sight into Insight," she unfolds a world of powerful, illuminating descriptions enveloped in a Thoreau-like astonishment and reverence for the natural world. Dillard has traveled the path where the footprints of Emerson and Thoreau are fading, and has branched off into her own lush field of wildflowers and honeybees to dance with.

She began with a tale of her childhood, and I in my preset notion presumed that the rest of the pages would be filled with anecdotes and stories of her youth--a trip down memory lane. She did lead me into childhood. I don't mean back into my youth, but into a state of mind that can only be likened to that sustained simplicity known as childhood innocence. She used to hide pennies in the roots of trees as gifts to any passerby. "It was a curious compulsion; sadly, I've never been seized by it since" (1432). "Sadly," she says. What is inside that word? What is there to be sad for, I wonder, and before I finish asking myself that question, a soft wave of understanding floats over me with her help.

She gently slides her thoughts into the idea of a penny as a gift: "who gets excited by a mere penny?" (1432). What is such a meager offering worth, the adult mind questions. It is priceless, answers the child: "It is very dire poverty indeed for a man to be so malnourished and fatigued that he won't stoop to pick up a penny" (1432). Yes, I want to say to the author, somewhere I felt that. It's a malnourished soul that looks at a penny and judges it worthless. It is an aged and saddened heart that refuses the humbleness of the simple offering, and calculates that the energy needed for the endeavor is not worth the reward. I know that in a higher mood, in an air of simplistic gratitude, the shine of the copper, the allure of the out-of-place object, and the beauty of an unasked-for gift bestowed by someone unknown is precious. She writes, "There are lots of things to see, unwrapped gifts and free surprises. The world is fairly studded and strewn with pennies cast broadside from a generous hand" (1432). But in the world of knowledge and reason, I step on it, demean it, damn it for not being a quarter.

Finding a penny on the ground is a chance occurrence, and a gift. Much like the wild around us full of life and movement, this essay offers up any variety of sights at any moment. Dillard has cultivated an ability to appreciate the subtle ways of nature and the unpredictable encounters with wildlife: "Deer apparently ascend bodily into heaven, the brightest oriole fades into leaves. These occurrences stun me into stillness and concentration . . . they are the free gifts" (1433). Dillard carefully intertwines her wanderings through nature with discoveries of Divine sight, and spiritual union with all that surrounds her. She is engulfed by her world and beckons her own inner-light to shine, and feels its way through every moment. She leads us into the understanding of the value of experiencing every moment, "to hush the noise of useless interior babble that keeps me from seeing" (1442), and to keep the soul open to every instance of life by reevaluating the value of the sense of sight. She delves a great deal into perception: "The secret of seeing is to sail on a solar wind. Hone and spread your spirit till you yourself are a sail, whetted, translucent, broadside to the merest puff" (1442). The physical act of the eyes fall away, and the part of the human spirit that recognizes the unity of life billows open and perceives the world as an "unscrupulous observer" (1441).

Dillard tells of a book she read where patients, following a cataract surgery, were given sight for the first time. These people saw the world as shifting shapes and patches of color with no connection to depth, their entire reality was shifted. She tries to pull herself into that reality and walks through a day where she concentrates on the light and shadow side of everything, not on what she knew the object to be from her bank of knowledge, but how it shifted and blended with the shapes around her. She writes, "All day long I walked among shifting color patches that parted before me like the Red Sea and closed again in silence, transfigured wherever I looked back" (1440). My own thoughts on the world shift and spin when I read her words, and a sense of childlike wonder sweeps me to look out the window and see a tree not as a "tree" but as a mass of shapes and colors and shadows that branch off into the deep blue.

Throughout the essay there is a lingering notion of spirituality and union. Dillard consistently uses her senses to experience her world and invites us to join her with powerful images wrapped in simple words that seem to have never been put together before. She comes across as a teacher in the highest sense, in that she lends grand amounts of inspiration and intrigue simply by discussing her passion for the earth and her curiosity. She says, "Even the simple darkness of night whispers suggestions to the mind" (1435). She drifts along casually in her thoughts and seems to have chronicled them in a journallike style that lends us to pleasant and mystical illumination.

Never once does Dillard mention God, but it is a concept that rises every so often in her religiouslike discussions of perception. In a culture that is riddled with nontraditions and the breakdown of common religious connections, Dillard has embarked on a gradual road towards a paganlike appreciation of what she has seen in her own life. Her ideas and enlightened realities are closely related to the teachings of a wide variety of ancient, earth-based faiths. Taoist and Buddhist principles, which concentrate on calming the mind and slowing the flow of "interior babble," parallel the ideas and curiosities that Dillard takes us through gently and descriptively:

> "the literature of saints and monks of every order East and West . . . seem to discover universally that the mind's muddy river, this ceaseless flow of trivia and trash, cannot be dammed, and that trying to dam it . . . might lead to madness. Instead you must allow the muddy river to flow unheeded in the dim channels of consciousness . . . mildly acknowledging the presence without interest and gazing beyond . . . into the realm of the real where subjects and objects act and rest purely" (1442).

She has raised her writing to a level where it blends and coincides with "literature of illumination," and she herself can be read as a visionary of sorts.

Her essay doesn't conclude neatly and tightly, but instead shifts us into our own thoughts and curiosities. In her writing there is a careful progression of thoughts that do not read like an essay, but like a slow awakening from a comforting dream. She has combined an elated appreciation for the spiritual and natural with a careful eye and shifts the windows of perception for a moment, gently, deliberately, with great detail.

Work Cited

Dillard, Annie. "Sight into Insight." Exploring Literature. Ed. Frank Madden. New York: Longman, 2001, 1432–1443.

HENRY DAVID THOREAU (1817–1862)

Henry David Thoreau was born and raised in Concord, Massachusetts, to a hardworking but poor family. As a child, he worked at home in a so-called "family-circle" factory making pencils. Determined to get an education, he worked his way through Harvard, and afterward, held a series of posts as a teacher. Beginning in 1843, while working as a handyman at the house of the poet and philosopher Ralph Waldo Emerson, Thoreau became a part of the Transcendentalist movement—an influential circle of American writers and thinkers who that believed that the earth was a microcosm of the entire universe, and that the human soul was the same as that of the "Over-Soul." From 1845 to 1847, on land owned by Emerson, Thoreau lived in a cabin he built on Walden Pond in an effort to "front only the essential facts of life." He later edited the journal he kept during this period—Thoreau kept a journal his entire life—and published it as Walden: or, Life in the Woods *in 1854, which, though it attracted little notice during his lifetime, has become one of the most influential books in American literature. After Thoreau returned to the world, he worked for a time in his family's pencil business, and later traveled to Canada, Maine, Minnesota, Cape Cod, and New York. Politically active (as in his famous tract "Civil Disobedience," an explanation of his refusal to pay a poll tax while at Walden), he spoke publicly on many issues, most notably against the Fugitive Slave Law. He died in 1862 of tuberculosis, following a trip to Minnesota.*

FROM *JOURNALS*

Writing "with Gusto"

[September 2, 1951] We cannot write well or truly but what we write with gusto. The body, the senses, must conspire with the mind. Expression is the act of the whole

man, that our speech may be vascular. The intellect is powerless to express thought without the aid of the heart and liver and of every member. Often I feel that my head stands out too dry, when it should be immersed. A writer, a man writing, is the scribe of all nature: he is the corn and the grass and the atmosphere writing. It is always essential that we love to do what we are doing, do it with a heart. The maturity of the mind, however, may perchance consist with a certain dryness.

The Wisdom of Writing on Many Subjects

[September 4, 1851] It is wise to write on many subjects, to try many themes, that so you may find the right and inspiring one. Be greedy of occasions to express your thought. Improve the opportunity to draw analogies. There are innumerable avenues to a perception of the truth. Improve the suggestion of each object however humble, however slight and transient the provocation. What else is there to be improved? Who knows what opportunities he may neglect? It is not in vain that the mind turns aside this way or that: follow its leading: apply it whither it inclines to go. Probe the universe in a myriad points. Be avaricious of these impulses. You must try a thousand themes before you find the right one, as nature makes a thousand acorns to get one oak. He is a wise man and experienced who has taken many views; to whom stones and plants and animals and a myriad objects have each suggested something, contributed something.

Illegally Helping a Fugitive Slave

[October 1, 1851] 5 P.M.—Just put a fugitive slave, who has taken the name of Henry Williams, into the cars for Canada. He escaped from Stafford County, Virginia, to Boston last October; has been in Shadrach's place at the Cornhill Coffee-House, had been corresponding through an agent with his master, who is his father, about buying himself, his master asking $600, but he having been able to raise only $500. Heard that there were writs out for two Williamses, fugitives, and was informed by his fellow-servants and employer that Auger-hole Burns and others of the police had called for him when he was out. Accordingly fled to Concord last night on foot, bringing a letter to our family from Mr. Lovejoy of Cambridge and another which Garrison had formerly given him on another occasion. He lodged with us, and waited in the house till funds were collected with which to forward him. Intended to dispatch him at noon through to Burlington, but when I went to buy his ticket, saw one at the depot who looked and behaved so much like a Boston policeman that I did not venture that time. An intelligent and very well-behaved man, a mulatto.

There is art to be used, not only in selecting wood for a withe, but in using it. Birch withes are twisted, I suppose in order that the fibres may be less abruptly bent; or is it only by accident that they are twisted?

5 The slave said he could guide himself by many other stars than the north star, whose rising and setting he knew. They steered for the north star even when it had got round and appeared to them to be in the south. They frequently followed the telegraph when there was no railroad. The slaves bring many superstitions from Africa. The fugitives sometimes superstitiously carry a turf in their hats, thinking that their success depends on it.

These days when the trees have put on their autumnal tints are the gala days of the year, when the very foliage of trees is colored like a blossom. It is a proper time for a yearly festival, an agricultural show.

The Purpose of a Journal

[July 13, 1852] A journal, a book that shall contain a record of all your joy, your ecstasy.

Writers of Torpid Words

[July 14, 1852] A writer who does not speak out of a full experience uses torpid words, wooden or lifeless words, such words as "humanitary," which have a paralysis in their tails.

Living with 706 Copies of *A Week*

[October 28, 1853] For a year or two past, my *publisher,* falsely so called, has been writing from time to time to ask what disposition should be made of the copies of "A Week on the Concord and Merrimack Rivers" still on hand, and at last suggesting that they had use for the room they occupied in his cellar. So I had them all sent to me here, and they have arrived to-day by express, filling the man's wagon,—706 copies out of an edition of 1,000 which I bought of Munroe four years ago and have been ever since paying for, and have not quite paid for yet. The wares are sent to me at last, and I have an opportunity to examine my purchase. They are something more substantial than fame, as my back knows, which has borne them up two flights of stairs to a place similar to that to which they trace their origin. Of the remaining two hundred and ninety and odd, seventy-five were given away, the rest sold. I have now a library of nearly nine hundred volumes, over seven hundred of which I wrote myself. Is it not well that the author should behold the fruits of his labor? My works are piled up on one side of my chamber half as high as my head, my *opera omnia.* This is authorship; these are the work of my brain. There was just one piece of good luck in the venture. The unbound were tied up by the printer four years ago in stout paper wrappers, and inscribed,—

H. D. Thoreau's.
Concord River
50 cops.

So Munroe had only to cross out "River" and write "Mass.," and deliver them to the expressman at once. I can see now that I write for, the result of my labors.

10 Nevertheless, in spite of this result, sitting beside the inert mass of my works, I take up my pen to-night to record what thought or experience I may have had, with as much satisfaction as ever. Indeed, I believe that this result is more inspiring and better for me than if a thousand had bought my wares. It affects my privacy less and leaves me freer.

Up Railroad—Odors of Nature and Men

[June 16, 1854] 5 a.m.—Up railroad.

As the sun went down last night, round and red in a damp misty atmosphere, so now it rises in the same manner, though there is no dense fog. Poison-dogwood yesterday, or say day before, *i.e.*, 14th. *Rubus hispidus*, perhaps yesterday in the earliest place, over the sand. Mullein, perhaps yesterday.

Observed yesterday the erigeron with a purple tinge. I cannot tell whether this, which seems in other respects the same with the white, is the *strigosus* or *annuus*. The calla which I plucked yesterday sheds pollen to-day; say to-day, then. A *Hypericum perforatum* seen last night will probably open to-day. I see on the *Scirpus lacustris* and pontederia leaves black patches for some days, as if painted, of minute closely placed ova, above water. I suspect that what I took for milfoil is a sium. Is not that new mustard-like plant behind Loring's, and so on down the river, *Nasturtium hispidum;* or hairy cress? Probably the first the 19th. Heart-leaf. *Nymphœa odorata.* Again I scent a white water-lily, and a season I had waited for is arrived. How indispensable all these experiences to make up the summer! It is the emblem of purity, and its scent suggests it. Growing in stagnant and muddy [water], it bursts up so pure and fair to the eye and so sweet to the scent, as if to show us what purity and sweetness reside in, and can be extracted from, the slime and muck of earth. I think I have plucked the first one that has opened for a mile at least. What confirmation of our hopes is in the fragrance of the water-lily! I shall not soon despair of the world for it, notwithstanding slavery, and the cowardice and want of principle of the North. It suggests that the time may come when man's deeds will smell as sweet. Such, then, is the odor our planet emits. Who can doubt, then, that Nature is young and sound? If Nature can compound this fragrance still annually, I shall believe her still full of vigor, and that there is virtue in man, too, who perceives and loves it. It is as if all the pure and sweet and virtuous was extracted from the slime and decay of earth and presented thus in a flower. The resurrection of virtue! It reminds me that Nature has been partner to no Missouri compromise. I scent no compromise in the fragrance of the white water-lily. In it, the sweet, and pure, and innocent are wholly sundered from the obscene and baleful. I do not scent in this the time-serving irresolution of a Massachusetts Governor, nor of a Boston Mayor. All good actions have contributed to this fragrance. So behave that the odor of your actions may enhance the general sweetness of the atmosphere, that, when I behold or scent a flower, I may not be reminded how inconsistent are your actions with it; for all odor is but one form of advertisement of a moral quality. If fair actions had not been performed, the lily would not smell sweet. The foul slime stands for the sloth and vice of man; the fragrant flower that springs from it, for the purity and courage which springs from its midst. It is these sights and sounds and fragrances put together that convince us of our immortality. No man believes against all evidence. Our external senses consent with our internal. This fragrance assures me that, though all other men fall, one shall stand fast; though a pestilence sweep over the earth, it shall at least spare one man. The genius of Nature is unimpaired. Her flowers are as fair and as fragrant as ever.

➤ QUESTIONS FOR READING AND WRITING

1. Thoreau says, "We cannot write well or truly but that we write with gusto." Do you agree? Explain.

2. He also says, "It is wise to write on many subjects. "What different subjects does he write about in these excerpts? Does he write with "gusto"? Explain.
3. Compare Thoreau's journal entries with Annie Dillard's "Sight into Insight" on page 1432 or E. B. White's "Once More to the Lake" below.

E.B. White (1899–1985)

One of America's finest essayists, E. B. White was long associated with the New Yorker *magazine. In addition to his books of nonfiction,* One Man's Meat *(1944),* The Second Tree from the Corner *(1954), and* The Points of My Compass *(1962),he wrote three acclaimed children's books:* Stuart Little *(1945),* Charlotte's Web *(1952), and* The Trumpet of the Swan *(1970). In 1976, White published a collection of his best essays in* The Essays of E. B. White.

Once More to the Lake [1941]

One summer, along about 1904, my father rented a camp on a lake in Maine and took us all there for the month of August. We all got ringworm from some kittens and had to rub Pond's Extract on our arms and legs night and morning, and my father rolled over in a canoe with all his clothes on; but outside of that the vacation was a success and from then on none of us ever thought there was any place in the world like that lake in Maine. We returned summer after summer—always on August 1 for one month. I have since become a salt-water man, but sometimes in summer there are days when the restlessness of the tides and the fearful cold of the sea water and the incessant wind that blows across the afternoon and into the evening make me wish for the placidity of a lake in the woods. A few weeks ago this feeling got so strong I bought myself a couple of bass hooks and a spinner and returned to the lake where we used to go, for a week's fishing and to revisit old haunts.

I took along my son, who had never had any fresh water up his nose and who had seen lily pads only from train windows. On the journey over to the lake I began to wonder what it would be like. I wondered how time would have marred this unique, this holy spot—the coves and streams, the hills that the sun set behind, the camps and the paths behind the camps. I was sure that the tarred road would have found it out, and I wondered in what other ways it would be desolated. It is strange how much you can remember about places like that once you allow your mind to return into the grooves that lead back. You remember one thing, and that suddenly reminds you of another thing. I guess I remembered clearest of all the early mornings, when the lake was cool and motionless, remembered how the bedroom smelled of the lumber it was made of and of the wet woods whose scent entered through the screen. The partitions in the camp were thin and did not extend clear to the top of the rooms, and as I was always the first up I would dress softly so as not to wake the others, and sneak out into the sweet outdoors and start out in the canoe, keeping close along the shore in the long shadows of the pines. I remembered being very careful never to rub my paddle against the gunwale for fear of disturbing the stillness of the cathedral.

The lake had never been what you would call a wild lake. There were cottages sprinkled around the shores, and it was in farming country although the shores of the lake were quite heavily wooded. Some of the cottages were owned by nearby farmers, and you would live at the shore and eat your meals at the farmhouse. That's what our family did. But although it wasn't wild, it was a fairly large and undisturbed lake and there were places in it that, to a child at least, seemed infinitely remote and primeval.

I was right about the tar: it led to within half a mile of the shore. But when I got back there, with my boy, and we settled into a camp near a farmhouse and into the kind of summertime I had known, I could tell that it was going to be pretty much the same as it had been before—I knew it, lying in bed the first morning, smelling the bedroom and hearing the boy sneak quietly out and go off along the shore in a boat. I began to sustain the illusion that he was I, and therefore, by simple transposition, that I was my father. This sensation persisted, kept cropping up all the time we were there. It was not an entirely new feeling, but in this setting it grew much stronger. I seemed to be living a dual existence. I would be in the middle of some simple act, I would be picking up a bait box or laying down a table fork, or I would be saying something, and suddenly it would be not I but my father who was saying the words or making the gesture. It gave me a creepy sensation.

5 We went fishing the first morning. I felt the same damp moss covering the worms in the bait can, and saw the dragonfly alight on the tip of my rod as it hovered a few inches from the surface of the water. It was the arrival of this fly that convinced me beyond any doubt that everything was as it always had been, that the years were a mirage and that there had been no years. The small waves were the same, chucking the rowboat under the chin as we fished at anchor, and the boat was the same boat, the same color green and the ribs broken in the same places, and under the floor-boards the same fresh-water leavings and débris—the dead helgramite, the wisps of moss, the rusty discarded fishhook, the dried blood from yesterday's catch. We stared silently at the tips of our rods, at the dragonflies that came and went. I lowered the tip of mine into the water, tentatively, pensively dislodging the fly, which darted two feet away, poised, darted two feet back, and came to rest again a little farther up the rod. There had been no years between the ducking of this dragonfly and the other one—the one that was part of memory. I looked at the boy, who was silently watching his fly, and it was my hands that held his rod, my eyes watching. I felt dizzy and didn't know which rod I was at the end of.

We caught two bass, hauling them in briskly as though they were mackerel, pulling them over the side of the boat in a businesslike manner without any landing net, and stunning them with a blow on the back of the head. When we got back for a swim before lunch, the lake was exactly where we had left it, the same number of inches from the dock, and there was only the merest suggestion of a breeze. This seemed an utterly enchanted sea, this lake you could leave to its own devices for a few hours and come back to, and find that it had not stirred, this constant and trustworthy body of water. In the shallows, the dark, water-soaked sticks and twigs, smooth and old, were undulating in clusters on the bottom against the clean ribbed sand, and the track of the mussel was plain. A school of minnows swam by, each minnow with its small individual shadow, doubling the attendance, so clear and sharp in the sunlight. Some of the other campers were in swimming, along the shore, one of them with a cake of soap, and the water felt thin and clear and unsubstantial. Over the years there had been this person with the cake of soap, this cultist, and here he was. There had been no years.

Up to the farmhouse to dinner through the teeming, dusty field, the road under our sneakers was only a two-track road. The middle track was missing, the one with the marks of the hooves and the splotches of dried, flaky manure. There had always been three tracks to choose from in choosing which track to walk in; now the choice was narrowed down to two. For a moment I missed terribly the middle alternative. But the way led past the tennis court, and something about the way it lay there in the sun reassured me; the tape had loosened along the backline, the alleys were green with plantains and other weeds, and the net (installed in June and removed in September) sagged in the dry noon, and the whole place steamed with midday heat and hunger and emptiness. There was a choice of pie for dessert, and one was blueberry and one was apple, and the waitresses were the same country girls, there having been no passage of time, only the illusion of it as in a dropped curtain—the waitresses were still fifteen; their hair had been washed, that was the only difference—they had been to the movies and seen the pretty girls with the clean hair.

Summertime, oh, summertime, pattern of life indelible, the fadeproof lake, the woods unshatterable, the pasture with the sweetfern and the juniper forever and ever, summer without end; this was the background, and the life along the shore was the design, the cottagers with their innocent and tranquil design, their tiny docks with the flagpole and the American flag floating against the white clouds in the blue sky, the little paths over the roots of the trees leading from camp to camp and the paths leading back to the outhouses and the can of lime for sprinkling, and at the souvenir counters at the store the miniature birchbark canoes and the postcards that showed things looking a little better than they looked. This was the American family at play, escaping the city heat, wondering whether the newcomers in the camp at the head of the cove were "common" or "nice," wondering whether it was true that the people who drove up for Sunday dinner at the farmhouse were turned away because there wasn't enough chicken.

It seemed to me, as I kept remembering all this, that those times and those summers had been infinitely precious and worth saving. There had been jollity and peace and goodness. The arriving (at the beginning of August) had been so big a business in itself, at the railway station the farm wagon drawn up, the first smell of the pine-laden air, the first glimpse of the smiling farmer, and the great importance of the trunks and your father's enormous authority in such matters, and the feel of the wagon under you for the long ten-mile haul, and at the top of the last long hill catching the first view of the lake after eleven months of not seeing this cherished body of water. The shouts and cries of the other campers when they saw you, and the trunks to be unpacked, to give up their rich burden. (Arriving was less exciting nowadays, when you sneaked up in your car and parked it under a tree near the camp and took out the bags and in five minutes it was all over, no fuss, no loud wonderful fuss about trunks.)

Peace and goodness and jollity. The only thing that was wrong now, really, was the sound of the place, an unfamiliar nervous sound of the outboard motors. This was the note that jarred, the one thing that would sometimes break the illusion and set the years moving. In those other summertimes all motors were inboard; and when they were at a little distance, the noise they made was a sedative, an ingredient of summer sleep. They were one-cylinder and two-cylinder engines, and some were make-and-break and some were jump-spark, but they all made a sleepy sound across the lake. The one-lungers throbbed and fluttered, and the twin-cylinder ones purred and purred, and that was a quiet sound, too. But now the campers all had outboards. In the daytime, in the hot mornings, these motors made a petulant, irritable sound; at night, in the still evening when the afterglow lit the water, they whined about one's ears like mosquitoes. My boy loved our rented outboard, and his great desire was to achieve single-handed mastery over it, and authority, and he soon learned the trick of choking it a little (but not too much), and the adjustment of the needle valve. Watching him I would remember the things you could do with the old one-cylinder engine with the heavy flywheel, how you could have it eating out of your hand if you got really close to it spiritually. Motorboats in those days didn't have clutches, and you would make a landing by shutting off the motor at the proper time and coasting in with a dead rudder. But there was a way of reversing them, if you learned the trick, by cutting the switch and putting it on again exactly on the final dying revolution of the flywheel, so that it would kick back against compression and begin reversing. Approaching a dock in a strong following breeze, it was difficult to slow up sufficiently by the ordinary coasting method, and if a boy felt he had complete mastery over his motor, he was tempted to keep it running beyond its time and then reverse it a few feet from the dock. It took a cool nerve, because if you threw the switch a twentieth of a second too soon you would catch the flywheel when it still had speed enough to go up past center, and the boat would leap ahead, charging bull-fashion at the dock.

We had a good week at the camp. The bass were biting well and the sun shone endlessly, day after day. We would be tired at night and lie down in the accumulated heat of the little bedrooms after the long hot day and the breeze would stir almost imperceptibly outside and the smell of the swamp drift in through the rusty screens. Sleep would come easily and in the morning the red squirrel would be on the roof, tapping out his gay routine. I kept remembering everything, lying in bed in the mornings—the small steamboat that had a long rounded stern like the lip of a Ubangi, and how quietly she ran on the moonlight sails, when the older boys played their mandolins and the girls sang and we ate doughnuts dipped in sugar, and how sweet the music was on the water in the shining night, and what it had felt like to think about girls then. After breakfast we would go up to the store and the things were in the same place—the minnows in a bottle, the plugs and spinners disarranged and pawed over by the youngsters from the boys' camp, the Fig Newtons and the Beeman's gum. Outside, the road was tarred and cars stood in front of the store. Inside, all was just as it had always been, except there was more Coca-Cola and not so much Moxie and root beer and birch beer and sarsaparilla. We would walk out with the bottle of pop apiece and sometimes the pop would backfire up our noses and hurt. We explored the streams, quietly, where the turtles slid off the sunny logs and dug their way into the soft bottom; and we lay on the town wharf and fed worms to the tame bass. Everywhere we went I had trouble making out which was I, the one walking at my side, the one walking in my pants.

One afternoon while we were there at that lake a thunderstorm came up. It was like the revival of an old melodrama that I had seen long ago with childish awe. The second-act climax of the drama of the electrical disturbance over a lake in America had not changed in any important respect. This was the big scene, still the big scene. The whole thing was so familiar, the first feeling of oppression and heat and a general air around camp of not wanting to go very far away. In mid-afternoon (it was all the same) a curious darkening of the sky, and a lull in everything that had made life tick; and then the way the boats suddenly swung the other way at their moorings with the coming of a breeze out of the new quarter, and the premonitory rumble. Then the kettle drum, then the snare, then the bass drum and cymbals, then crackling light against the dark, and the gods grinning and licking their chops in the hills. Afterward the calm, the rain steadily rustling in the calm lake, the return of light and hope and spirits, and the campers running out in joy and relief to go swimming in the rain, their bright cries perpetuating the deathless joke about how they were getting simply drenched, and the children screaming with delight at the new sensation of bathing in the rain, and the joke about getting drenched linking the generations in a strong indestructible chain. And the comedian who waded in carrying an umbrella.

When the others went swimming, my son said he was going in, too. He pulled his dripping trunks from the line where they had hung all through the shower and wrung them out. Languidly, and with no thought of going in, I watched him, his hard little body, skinny and bare, saw him wince slightly as he pulled up around his vitals the small, soggy, icy garment. As he buckled the swollen belt, suddenly my groin felt the chill of death.

➤ *QUESTIONS FOR READING AND WRITING*

1. Who is the narrator and what is his relationship with the lake?
2. Are there places from your own past that carry so much meaning for you? Explain.
3. What is the significance of the narrator's "illusion that he [his son] was I, and therefore, by simple transposition, that I was my father"?
4. At the end of the essay, while watching his son buckle his bathing suit, the narrator writes, "suddenly my groin felt the chill of death." What do you think he means?

Case Studies in Composition

Thinking About Interpretation, Poetry, and Painting

Long before the advent of writing, people recorded their innermost feelings and impulses in images painted on cave walls. In fact, a number of cave paintings found recently in South Africa are nearly thirty thousand years old. Throughout history, artists have celebrated great writing by sculpting, painting, and drawing their responses to literature. The work of Homer, Shakespeare, Dickens, Joyce and many other writers has inspired sculpture, painting, and illustration. Art inspires art. Conversely then, it's not surprising that poems are inspired by great paintings.

In one way or another, the seven paintings that follow—and the poems written in response to them—have something to say about faith and doubt, a theme not limited to time and place. Like the brief quotations that open this thematic unit, these paintings and poems are a dialogue across history. W.H. Auden's modern poem, "Musee des Beaux Arts" responds to Brueghel's sixteenth century *Landscape with the Fall of Icarus,* itself a response to ancient Greek mythology. And Alan Devenish's "Icarus Again," is a 1999 poem written in response to the ancient myth, the paintings and poems it has inspired over the ages, and the tragedies of modern life. Native American N. Scott Momaday's modern poem, "Before an Old Painting of the Crucifixion" is inspired by *Crucifixion,* a work by sixteenth century Italian painter Tintoretto; Edward Hopper's painting *Nighthawk,* and the poems it prompts, David Ray's "A Midnight Diner" and Samuel Yellen's "Nighthawks" are all modern pieces; Van Gogh's nineteenth century *The Starry Night* evokes Anne Sexton's twentieth century "The Starry Night"; Jan Vermeer's *The Loveletter* speaks across 300 years to Sandra Nelson who answers with her poem "When a Woman Holds a Letter." The painter of *The Old Guitarist,* Pablo Picasso, is a contemporary of the poet, Wallace Stevens, who interprets his painting in "The Man with the Blue Guitar." Adrienne Rich had not been born when Edwin Romanzo Elmer painted his *Mourning Picture* in memory of his young daughter, Effie. Yet Rich's response to the painting, "Mourning Picture," brings Effie back to life as the mournful speaker of the poem.

Whatever they hold in common, each painting and poem is an individual work. So before you read the poems, look at each of the paintings separately and write your own response.

Before you read the accompanying poem, write your own response to each of the paintings.

- As you look at the painting, write down what strikes you first. How does it make you feel? What do you like most about it? Do you find anything disturbing?
- Do you sense a prevailing mood or tone? How do the colors affect you?

When you finish recording your responses to the painting, read the companion poem.

- Compare your response to the painting with the poet's response. How are they similar? How are they different?
- Has the poet mentioned anything that is not included in your response? Have you raised issues that the poet has not?

Compare the poem with the painting.

- Are the details of each the same? What details are contained in the poem that are not in the painting? What details are in the painting but not in the poem?
- Do the painting and the poem seem to be saying the same thing? If not, how do they differ? Which do you prefer?
- Has reading the poem revised your response to the painting? If so, how?

Poetry and Painting

Pieter Brueghel the Elder, (Dutch, 1520–1569). *Landscape with the Fall of Icarus.* Musées Royaux des Beaux-Arts, Brussels/Scala/Art Resource, NY.

W.H. AUDEN (1907–1973)

MUSÉE DES BEAUX ARTS [1940]

About suffering they were never wrong,
The Old Masters: how well they understood
Its human position; how it takes place
While someone else is eating or opening a window or just walking dully along;
How, when the aged are reverently, passionately waiting
For the miraculous birth, there always must be
Children who did not specially want it to happen, skating
On a pond at the edge of the wood:
They never forgot
That even the dreadful martyrdom must run its course
Anyhow in a corner, some untidy spot
Where the dogs go on with their doggy life and the torturer's horse
Scratches its innocent behind on a tree.

In Brueghel's *Icarus*, for instance: how everything turns away
Quite leisurely from the disaster; the ploughman may
Have heard the splash, the forsaken cry,
But for him it was not an important failure; the sun shone
As it had to on the white legs disappearing into the green
Water; and the expensive delicate ship that must have seen
Something amazing, a boy falling out of the sky,
Had somewhere to get to and sailed calmly on.

ALAN DEVENISH (b. 1948)

ICARUS AGAIN [1999]

You'd think we'd have enough of falling
since that sunny day high off the coast of Crete. Air disasters
appalling and impersonal. The bomber's hate
made potent with a bit of plastic and some altitude. Spacecrafts
with schoolteachers aboard—exploding over and over
again. The parents aghast at the pure Icarian sky of Florida
suddenly emptied of their child.

What is myth if not an early version of what's been happening
all along? (The arrogance of flight brought down
by faulty gaskets).

As Auden would have it: the way we plow through life
head bent to the furrow while tragedy falls from the sky.

Bruegel shows only the legs—flailing and white—scissoring
into a pitiless green sea.

Williams treats a distant casualty in his clinical
little sketch. (Did the astronauts feel their fall
or breathe instantly the killing fumes?)

Matisse plays it another way. It's color—Icarus' love
for color and who can blame him? His poor heart
waxing red as he falls through blue and what might be
a scatter of sunbursts or a vision of war—the enemy
aces sighting Icarus in their crosshairs over France.

In Ovid the line that never fails to move me is
And he saw the wings on the waves . . .
The way it comes to the father. His lofty design reduced to this
little detritus as he hovers in the left-hand corner of the myth
grieving wingbeats wrinkling the surface of the sea.

Even in bad prints of the Bruegel I can't help feeling sorry
for this kid. And dismay at our constant clumsiness. Our light
heart pulling us down. Love itself believing against all gravity
that what we say is what is bound to happen. How foolish to trust
our waxen wings and how foolish not to.

Jacopo Tintoretto (Italian, 1518–1594) *Crucifixion.* Scuola Grande di San Rocco, Venice, Italy/Erich Lessing/Art Resource, NY.

N. SCOTT MOMADAY (b. 1934)

BEFORE AN OLD PAINTING OF THE CRUCIFIXION

The Mission Carmel,
June, 1960

I ponder how He died, despairing once.
I've heard the cry subside in vacant skies,
In clearings where no other was. Despair,
Which, in the vibrant wake of utterance,
Resides in desolate calm, preoccupies,
Though it is still. There is no solace there.

That calm inhabits wilderness, the sea,
And where no peace inheres but solitude;
Near death it most impends. It was for Him,
Absurd and public in His agony,
Inscrutably itself, nor misconstrued,
Nor metaphrased in art or pseudonym:

A vague contagion. Old, the mural fades . . .
Reminded of the fainter sea I scanned,
I recollect: How mute in constancy!
I could not leave the wall of palisades
Till cormorants returned my eyes on land.
The mural but implies eternity:

Not death, but silence after death is change.
Judean hills, the endless afternoon,
The farther groves and arbors seasonless
But fix the mind within the moment's range.
Where evening would obscure our sorrow soon,
There shines too much a sterile loveliness.

No imprecision of commingled shade,
No shimmering deceptions of the sun,
Herein no semblances remark the cold
Unhindered swell of time, for time is stayed.
The Passion wanes into oblivion,
And time and timelessness confuse, I'm told.

These centuries removed from either fact
Have lain upon the critical expanse
And been of little consequence. The void
Is calendared in stone; the human act,
Outrageous, is in vain. The hours advance
Like flecks of foam borne landward and destroyed.

Edward Hopper (American, 1882–1967), *Nighthawks.* 1942. Oil on canvas, 84.1 x 152.4 cm. Friends of American Art Collection, 1942.51.

David Ray

A Midnight Diner by Edward Hopper [1970]

Your own greyhounds bark at your side.
It is you, dressed like a Siennese,
Galloping, ripping the gown as the fabled
White-skinned woman runs, seeking freedom.
Tiny points of birches rise from hills,
Spin like serrulate corkscrews toward the sky;
In other rooms it is your happiness
Flower petals fall for, your brocade
You rediscover, feel bloom upon your shoulder.

And freedom's what the gallery's for.
You roam in large rooms and choose your beauty.
Yet, Madman, it's your own life you turn back to:
In one postcard purchase you wipe out
Centuries of light and smiles, golden skin
And openness, forest babes and calves.
You forsake the sparkler breast
That makes the galaxies, you betray
The women who dance upon the water.

All for some bizarre hometown necessity!
Some ache still found within you!
Now it will go with you, this scene
By Edward Hopper and nothing else.
It will become your own tableau of sadness
Composed of blue and grey already there.

Over or not, this suffering will not say Hosanna.
Now a music will not come out of it.
Grey hat, blue suit, you are in a midnight
Diner painted by Edward Hopper.

Here is a man trapped at midnight underneath the El.
He sought the smoothest counter in the world
And found it here in the almost empty street,
Away from everything he has ever said.
Now he has the silence they've insisted on.
Not a squirrel, not an autumn birch,
Not a hound at his side, moves to help him now.
His grief is what he'll try to hold in check.
His thumb has found and held his coffee cup.

SAMUEL YELLEN (b. 1906)

NIGHTHAWKS [1951]

The place is the corner of Empty and Bleak,
The time is night's most desolate hour,
The scene is Al's Coffee Cup or the Hamburger Tower,
The persons in this drama do not speak.

We who peer through that curve of plate glass
Count three nighthawks seated there—patrons of life:
The counterman will be with you in a jiff,
The thick white mugs were never meant for demitasse.

The single man whose hunched back we see
Once put a gun to his head in Russian roulette,
Whirled the chamber, pulled the trigger, won the bet,
And now lives out his *x* years' guarantee.

And facing us, the two central characters
Have finished their coffee, and have lit
A contemplative cigarette;
His hand lies close, but not touching hers.

Not long ago together in a darkened room,
Mouth burned mouth, flesh beat and ground
On ravaged flesh, and yet they found
No local habitation and no name.

Oh, are we not lucky to be none of these!
We can look on with complacent eye:
Our satisfactions satisfy,
Our pleasures, our pleasures please.

Vincent van Gogh. (Dutch, 1853–1890.) *Starry Night.* 1889. Oil on canvas. 29 x 36 1/4" (73.7 x 92.1 cm). The Museum of Modern Art, New York. Acquired through the Lillie P. Bliss Bequest. Photograph © 2001 The Museum of Modern Art, New York.

ANNE SEXTON (1928–1975)

THE STARRY NIGHT [1961]

That does not keep me from having a terrible need of—shall I say the word—religion. Then I go out at night to paint the stars.

—Vincent van Gogh in a letter to his brother

The town does not exist
except where one black-haired tree slips
up like a drowned woman into the hot sky.
The town is silent. The night boils with eleven stars
Oh starry starry night! This is how
I want to die.

It moves. They are all alive.
Even the moon bulges in its orange irons
to push children, like a god, from its eye.
The old unseen serpent swallows up the stars.
Oh starry starry night! This is how
I want to die:

into that rushing beast of the night,
sucked up by that great dragon, to split
from my life with no flag,
no belly,
no cry.

Jan Vermeer (Dutch, 1632–1675) *The Loveletter*. c. 1670. Oil on canvas 44 x 38.5 cm. © Rijksmuseum Amsterdam.

Sandra Nelson (b. 1951)

When a Woman Holds a Letter [1993]

It is always from a man. Jan Vermeer
knows this as he paints the dark
note in Clarissa's right hand;
her left strangling the fretted neck coming
from the pear-shaped body of his
mandolin. Her upturned eyes may be tied
to a ferris wheel of sparrows' biting love.
Or she may feel the heavy curve of his instrument
against her stomach and her eyes
instinctively flip up to heaven to see
it anyone is watching. I am
probably wrong. There *is* another woman
behind her (a washer-woman whose head
is wrapped in a wimple to keep out the dirt).
Perhaps it is to her that Clarissa's eyes roll.

Pablo Picasso. (Spanish, 1881–1973), *The Old Guitarist.* 1903–04. Oil on panel. 122.9 x 82.6 cm. Helen Birch Bartlett Memorial Collection 1926.253. Courtesy The Art Institute of Chicago.

WALLACE STEVENS (1879–1955)

THE MAN WITH THE BLUE GUITAR [1937]

I

The man bent over his guitar,
A shearsman of sorts. The day was green.

They said, "You have a blue guitar,
You do not play things as they are."

The man replied, "Things as they are
Are changed upon the blue guitar."

And they said then, "But play, you must.
A tune beyond us, yet ourselves,

A tune upon the blue guitar
Of things exactly as they are."

II

I cannot bring a world quite round,
Although I patch it as I can.

I sing a hero's head, large eye
And bearded bronze, but not a man.

Although I patch him as I can
And reach through him almost to man.

If so serenade almost to man
Is to miss, by that, things as they are.

Say that it is the serenade
Of a man that plays a blue guitar.

III

Ah, but to play man number one,
To drive the dagger in his heart.

To lay his brain upon the board
And pick the acrid colors out,

To nail his thought across the door,
Its wings spread wide to rain and snow.

To strike his living hi and lo,
To tick it, tock it, turn it true.

To bang it from a savage blue,
Jangling the metal of the strings.

IV

So that's life, then: things as they are?
It picks its way on the blue guitar.

A million people on one string?
And all their manner in the thing,

And all their manner, right or wrong,
And all their manner, weak and strong?

The feelings crazily, craftily call.
Life a buzzing of flies in autumn air,

And that's life, then: things as they are,
This buzzing of the blue guitar.

Edwin Romanzo Elmer (1850–1923) *The Mourning Picture,* 1890. Oil on canvas, 28 x 36 in. (71.1 x 91.5 cm) Smith College Museum of Art, Northampton, Massachusetts. Purchased 1953.

Adrienne Rich (b. 1929)

Mourning Picture [1965]

The picture was painted by Edwin Romanzo Elmer (1850–1923) as a memorial to his daughter Effie. In the poem it is the dead girl who speaks.

They have carried the mahogany chair and the cane rocker
out under the lilac bush,
and my father and mother darkly sit there, in black clothes
Our clapboard house stands fast on its hill,
my doll lies in her wicker pram
gazing at western Massachusetts.
This was our world,
I could remake each shaft of grass
feeling its rasp on my fingers,
draw out the map of every lilac leaf
or the net of vines on my father's
grief tranced hand.

Out of my head, half-bursting,
still filling, the dream condenses—
shadows, crystals, ceilings, meadows, globes of dew.
Under the dull green of the lilacs, out in the light
carving each spoke of the pram, the turned porch-pillars,
under high early-summer clouds,
I am Effie, visible and invisible,
remembering and remembered.

They will move from the house,
give the toys and pets away.
Mute and rigid with loss my mother
will ride the train to Baptist Corner,
the silk-spool will run bare.
I tell you, the thread that bound us lies
faint as a web in the dew.
Should I make you, world, again,
could I give back the leaf its skeleton, the air
its early-summer cloud, the house
its noonday presence, shadowless,
and leave *this* out? I am Effie, you were my dream.

Expanding the Scope of Your Response

The poems accompanying these paintings are written specifically about them, so they provide an obvious comparison. But other works of literature contained under the theme of Faith and Doubt, or other themes, might also make a good source of comparison with one or more of these paintings.

- Do any of these paintings remind you of ideas expressed in other works you've read? If so, would this comparison provide a good source for an essay?

In Other Words and Images

Each image on the facing page of the opening of the theme sections in this book was chosen to convey an impression of that theme and the literature it contains.
- What does the oil-on-wood painting of the African American family on page 234 convey to you about the theme of Family and Friends? Does the painting seem to reflect any of the works that follow?
- How would you interpret the photograph of the women watching the man in the opening of Women and Men on page 497? Can you compare it or contrast it with literature in that section?
- In what way does the ninth century granite cross on page 811 speak to the theme of Heritage and Identity? Do any of the quotations or longer pieces of literature reflect something similar or contrary?
- What's your impression of the ballet dancers in the window on the facing page of Culture and Class on page 1103? Does it fit under that theme and with the literature in that section?
- How did you react when you saw the photo of the "winged man" on page 1286 of Faith and Doubt? Did you laugh? If so, what was funny? How does it express this theme?

Finding Connections with the Other Arts: Television, Film, Music, and Dance

It would be impossible to list all the TV shows, films, musical pieces, or dances that have been inspired by works of literature. The work of Shakespeare alone has been the inspiration for so many other arts. His plots and character types are a primary source for most TV sit-coms. Just in the past decade, numerous films of his plays have been produced including an academy award winning film, *Shakespeare in Love,* about Shakespeare himself. Verdi, Dvorak, Liszt, Debussy, Mendelssohn, Tchaikovsky, Strauss, and many other prominent composers have written operas and symphonies about many of Shakespeare's plays. And dancers have danced, among others, the ballet *Romeo and Juliet.*

- Consider your own interest in television, video, film, music, or dance. What connections can you draw between your experiences in those areas and the literature you've read?

A Student's Comparison and Contrast Essay: Process and Product

Barbara Pfister's Semantic Map in Response to van Gogh's painting *The Starry Night*

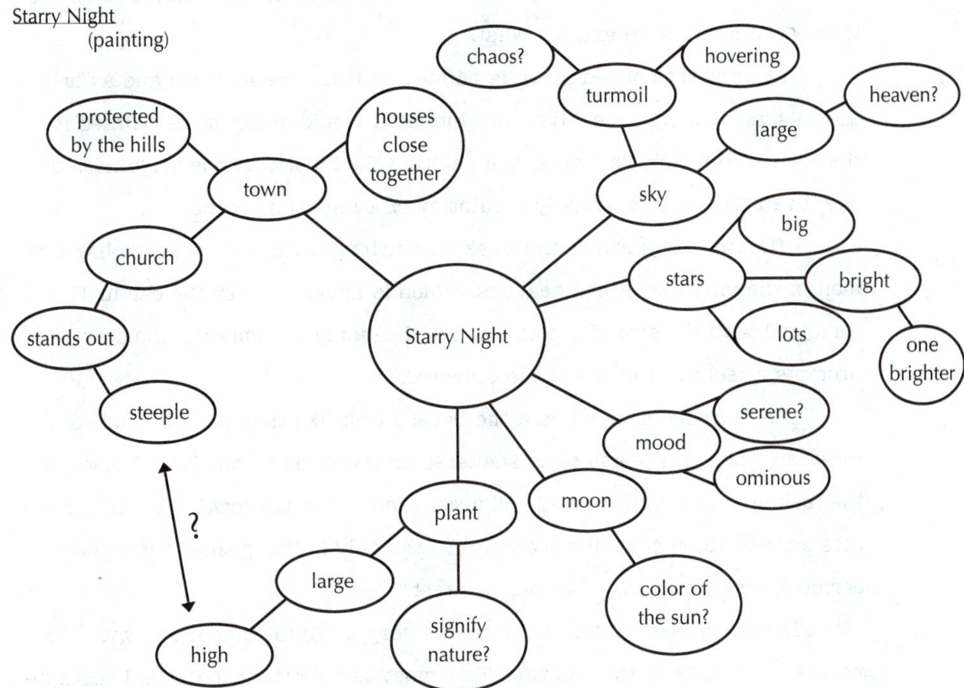

Barbara's Journal Response to van Gogh's painting *The Starry Night*

When I first looked at this painting, the overall impression I got was ominous and quiet, but not gloomy. The feeling was of both foreboding and powerful beauty at the same time.

I liked the short brushstrokes he used to paint this scene. They give the feeling of separate and distinct pieces that together make up the whole. The colors in the picture depict a night sky, but at the same time appear as vivid as day.

The sky takes up a major portion of the painting and it stands out quite vividly. I love the way van Gogh painted the stars. They appear to be very large and bright, not little pinpoints in the sky as we usually see them. Their size and brightness stress their importance in the picture. I think he is symbolizing the greatness of heaven or the universe. There is one star that is especially bright in the lower part of the sky and I feel this must mean something but I'm not sure exactly what.

The crescent shaped moon is painted as if it were as large and as bright as the sun. He didn't use silver or white, as I would depict it; he painted it the color of the sun. This gives the painting the illusion of the brightness of day, even though it is actually a painting of a nighttime scene.

I find the large swirls in the sky disturbing. I think they symbolize turmoil in the universe or the heavens, which is hovering over the earth. This combined with the size of the sky and its heavenly inhabitants, the stars, prompts a feeling of chaos in the universe.

The town seems small and the houses look like they are all huddled together. The town seems to be sheltered or protected by the hills. I also get the feeling of isolation. I see the church, centered in the lower part of the picture as very important. It appears to be the only building that is really discernible, and it stands out among the rest.

The plant seen in the foreground is very large in comparison with the rest of the objects in the painting. This must be important, because I think he could have easily painted the picture without it. I don't think it interferes with the painting though. I think its size, spanning almost the entire height of the painting, is stressing the importance of nature in the whole scheme of life.

After contemplating the importance or the meaning of the plant, I looked at the town and the church again. Maybe it is symbolic that the plant reaches all the way to the sky, signifying the relationship between nature and the heavens. The plant also seems to spear right through the swirling turmoil in the night. The steeple of the church, in comparison, barely reaches the horizon. I wonder if this is intentional and therefore, symbolic, or merely a coincidence.

I can summarize my feelings in a few different ways. The colors he used seem to imply that the heavens at night are as bright and clear as day, and perhaps that is how our understanding of the universe should be. With reference to the plant and the church, another idea is that people can only make a small attempt to understand the heavens or the universe, while nature is at one with the universe.

Barbara's Semantic Map in Response to Anne Sexton's poem "The Starry Night"

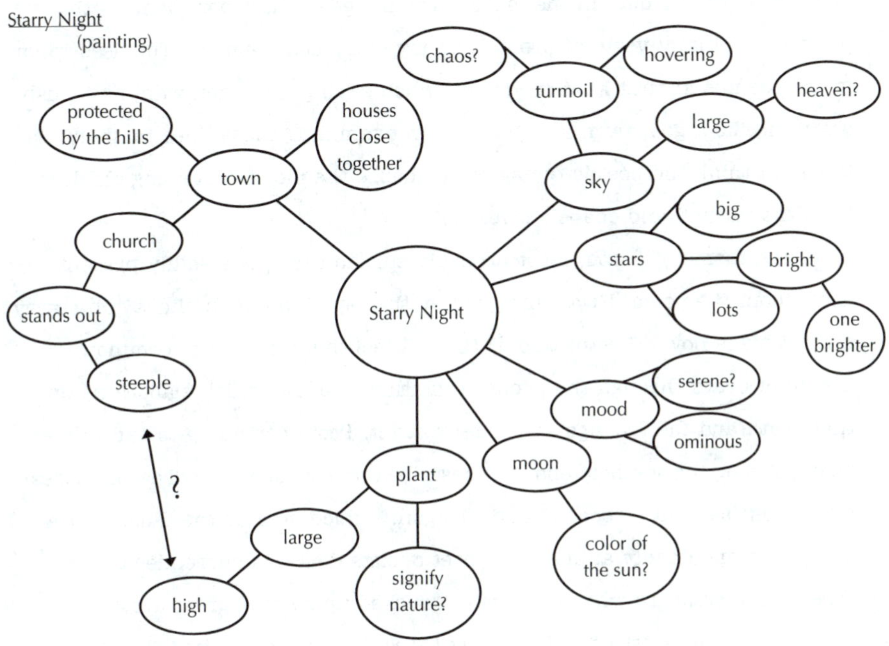

Barbara's Journal Response to Anne Sexton's poem "The Starry Night"

My initial reaction after reading this poem was one of despair and gloom. It projects an overall feeling of death or possibly suicide. The wording used through the poem is very vivid and somewhat violent in nature.

When the poet starts off the poem with the line "The town does not exist" (1), I got the impression of a dream, which led me to an initially pleasant feeling which would not last long as I read further. In examining the first three lines together, I feel the speaker is saying the town only exists in the eyes of death - the drowned woman. Is the poet questioning our view of reality? Maybe we can only see the truth of the universe in death.

I liked the description of the stars "boiling" in the sky. It created a very vivid picture in my mind. The way the poet gives the stars and the moon life is wonderful, saying the stars are alive and moving. Personalizing the moon was a bit confusing at first. I can remember as a child hearing the usual fairy tales of "the man in the moon." The image of the moon given in the poem was initially very different from my childhood memory. The description in the poem is at first kind of violent, when saying the moon wants "to push children, like a god, from its eye" (9). On examining these lines further though, I think the poet is trying to symbolize the moon protecting children from the turmoil and chaos above.

The theme of death, most probably suicide I feel, is steadily present throughout the poem. I was intrigued by the repetition of the lines "Oh starry night! This is how / I want to die" (5,6). I feel this carried the common thread of death through the poem to the third stanza, which elaborated on that death and the feelings associated with it. From beginning to end in the poem, the sky or the heavens, are described in a violent way. The poet uses the words "serpent," "beast," and "dragon," which creates the illusion of a dangerous and deadly animal. The poet depicts death as surrender to that threatening creature when she writes "sucked up by that great dragon..." (14). I find it interesting that the last three lines show no struggle against the menacing creature she described. This is what makes me think this poem is probably a view of suicide, describing someone lacking the will to live.

A Student Essay—Comparison and Contrast

Barbara Pfister

Dr. Madden

English 102

February 9, 200X

Quiet Contemplation or Silent Desperation?

Examining art in the written word or in a painting can be a very personal experience. We bring our own, sometimes very different, responses and interpretations to each work that we study or explore. As there seems to be no one correct interpretation, I find that keeping an open mind and looking at other's views may open up new avenues of thought.

I examined my responses to both Vincent van Gogh's "The Starry Night," and the poem "The Starry Night" written by Anne Sexton. I found a few similar ideas, and some very interesting differences. It is apparent that the poet had a very different response to the painting than I did.

When I first looked at the painting, the overall impression I got was ominous and quiet, but not gloomy. There was a feeling of both foreboding and powerful beauty at the same time. The short brushstrokes he used to paint the scene gave the feeling of separate and distinct pieces that together make up the whole. My initial reaction after reading the poem was one of despair and gloom. It projected an overall feeling of death or possibly suicide. The wording used through the poem is very vivid and seemed somewhat violent in nature.

The colors I see in the picture depict a night sky, but at the same time appear as vivid as day. The sky, taking up a major portion of the painting, stands out quite vividly. I love the way van Gogh painted the stars. They appear to be very large and bright, not little pinpoints in the sky as we usually see them. In the poem however, I found the description of the stars "boiling" in the sky captivating, but different from my reaction. It created a very vivid picture in my mind, and I liked the way the poet gave the stars life, saying they are alive and moving. Similar to the poet's description of the stars, I found the large swirls in the sky of the painting somewhat disturbing. I think they symbolize turmoil in the universe or the heavens, and that discord is hovering over the earth. This combined with the size of the sky and it's heavenly dwellers, the stars, prompts a feeling of chaos in the universe.

The crescent shaped moon in the painting is as large and as bright as the sun. Van Gogh didn't use silver or white, as I would portray it; he painted it the color of the sun. Anne Sexton's personalization of the moon was a bit confusing for me at first. I can remember as a child hearing the usual fairy tales of "the man in the moon." The image of the moon given in the poem was initially very different from my amiable childhood memory. The description in the poem is at first rather violent, when declaring the moon wants "to push children, like a god, from its eye" (9). On examining these lines further though, I think the poet is trying to symbolize the moon protecting children from the turmoil and chaos above.

The town, as it is portrayed in the painting, seems small and the houses look like they are all huddled together. The town seems to be sheltered or protected by the hills, but this also hints at an uneasy feeling of isolation. The church was not mentioned at all in the poem. I see the church, centered in the lower part of the picture, as being very symbolic. It appears to be the only building that is really discernible; it stands out among the rest.

When the poet started the poem with the line "The town does not exist" (1), I got the initially pleasant impression of a dream, which would not last long as I read further. The poet describes the plant shown in the painting as a "drowned woman." In examining the first three lines of the poem together, I feel the speaker is saying the town only exists in the eyes of death, the drowned woman. Is the poet questioning our view of reality? Perhaps we can only see the reality of the universe in the act of death.

I had a very different impression when contemplating the plant in the painting. It is very large in comparison with the rest of the objects pictured. This must be significant, because I think he could have easily painted the picture without it, if he felt it was in the way. I don't think it interferes with the painting though. I think its size, spanning almost the entire height of the painting, is stressing the importance of nature in the whole scheme of life. This is very different from the poet's interpretation of the meaning of the plant.

After contemplating the significance of the plant, I looked at the town and the church again. Maybe it is symbolic that the plant reaches all the way to the sky, signifying the relationship between nature and the heavens. The plant also seems to spear right through the swirling turmoil in the night. The steeple of the church, in comparison, barely reaches the horizon. I wonder if this is intentional and therefore, very symbolic, or merely a coincidence.

The theme of death, most probably suicide I feel, is steadily present throughout the poem. I was intrigued by the repetition of the lines "Oh starry night! This is how / I want to die" (5,6). I feel this carried the common thread of death through the poem to the third stanza, which elaborated on that death and the feelings associated with it. From beginning to end in the poem, the sky or the heavens, are described in a violent way, much different than the contemplative way I interpreted them. The poet uses the words "serpent," "beast," and "dragon," which creates the illusion of a dangerous and deadly animal. The poet depicts death as surrender to that threatening creature, when she writes, "sucked up by that great dragon..." (14). I found it interesting that the last three lines show no struggle against the menacing creature that she described. This apathy is what makes me think this poem is probably a view of suicide, describing someone lacking the will to live. There is a silent desperation in the poem. This is strikingly different when compared to the impression the painting left in my mind.

My overall feeling of the painting is more of a quiet contemplation about the relationship between mankind and the universe. The colors van Gogh used seem to imply that the heavens at night are as bright and clear as day, and perhaps that is how our understanding of the universe should be. When looking at the symbolism of the plant and the church, another notion is that people can only make a small attempt to understand the heavens or the universe, as symbolized by the church barely reaching the horizon. The plant, representing nature, is at one with the universe as it breaks through and spans the turmoil seen in the heavens.

If our understanding of the universe is as shallow as van Gogh has pictured it, perhaps that is the same desperation that Anne Sexton sees in the painting. This may explain the futility of life she described in her poem. From the broader perspective, these two different interpretations may actually be more similar than they seem.

Works Cited

Sexton, Anne. "The Starry Night." Exploring Literature, Ed. Frank Madden. New York: Longman, 2001, 1469.

van Gogh, Vincent. "The Starry Night" Exploring Literature, Ed. Frank Madden. New York: Longman, 2001, 1468.

Exploring the Literature of Faith and Doubt: Options for Writing and Research

Some Options for Writing About Faith and Doubt

1. Consider the ways your beliefs and values have affected your life. Do any of the stories, poems, plays, or essays in this section remind you of your own experiences or circumstances in your life? If so, choose one or more of these works and write a response essay that compares your experiences or circumstances with those in the literature.
2. Our own values, beliefs and/or doubts affect the way we see the world and can strongly influence our response to the literature in this section. We may agree or disagree with what an author says or what characters say or do. So too, this literature may influence us and the formation of our values and beliefs. Write an essay about the ways in which one or more works in this section either provoked a moral judgment on your part or helped you learn something.
3. In his 1788 work, *Critique of Practical Reason,* Immanuel Kant wrote: "Morality is not properly the doctrine of how we may make ourselves happy, but how we make ourselves worthy of happiness." Do you agree?

   Consider this quote, and write an essay about how an author or a character defines morality or his or her values in one or more works in this section.
4. In his poem, *In Memoriam,* Alfred Lord Tennyson expresses his view of faith and doubt in the following lines: There lives more faith in honest doubt, / Believe me, than in half the creeds." Do you agree?

   Write about this quote as it affects the way a character or an author sees the world in one or more works in this section.
5. Choose a quote (or quotes) in the introduction to this section on Faith and Doubt (p. 1287) and pair it (or them) with one of the longer pieces in this section that either supports it or argues against it. For example, Yamaga Soko's comment about the complete loyalty of the samurai warrior might be paired with Philip Roth's *The Conversion of the Jews,* which might be seen as an argument against it. If you choose R.D. Laing's comment about alienation, you might choose Matthew Arnold's poem *Dover Beach* to support it.

Write an essay that compares or contrasts a quote (or quotes) from the introduction with a story, poem, play, or essay that supports or argues against it.

A Research Option

Nathaniel Hawthorne's story *Young Goodman Brown,* Wilfred Owen's poem *Dulce et Decorum Est* and Terence McNally's *Andre's Mother* all have something important to say about the dilemma of faith and doubt. Each of these works, however, springs from a very different historical, social, or political context.

Expanding our exploration of literature to include the context in which these works were produced can be an enriching and enlightening experience. Choose one or more of these or other works in this section, and write a research essay which includes secondary source material about the historical, social, or political background of the literature.

Collaboration: Writing and Revising with Your Peers

In addition to applying your own values and standards to writing about the literature in this section, you may find it beneficial to share and discuss your work with classmates. Getting feedback from others can help you generate and clarify your ideas and revise and edit your writing more effectively.

Choose a work, a topic, or one of the options for writing about faith and doubt above, and work with a partner or in a small group. Exchange journal entries or response sheets, generate questions together, do a group semantic map (see p. 44), or simply share and respond to each other's ideas.

After you have written a rough draft of your essay, share it with a partner or your group. Respondents should function primarily as sensitive readers and give honest, constructive responses. They should try to be aware of each writer's purpose, discuss concerns particular to each writer, and comment on the effectiveness of the essay's organization, support, clarity, and voice (For a comprehensive checklist for revision, see p. 51).

In the final stage of your writing, editing and proofreading might be done in a similar fashion. A partner or group readers might help you check for correct grammar, spelling, punctuation, and typos (A comprehensive checklist for editing is on p. 52).

A Writing/Research Portfolio Option

A portfolio is a collection of your work, related materials and commentary about your work collected over time. Gathering materials in a portfolio will provide you with resources for research and development. You can use your portfolio to collect your writing about the literature in this section, to find a topic to write about, to revise or add to your work, or to keep multiple drafts and monitor the changes you make as you revise.

Among the resources you might include:

Your responses to the quotes and prompts about women and men at the beginning of this section, the questions you had right after you finished reading each piece of literature, your journal entries.

What your classmates, instructor or published critics had to say about the literature and how their comments may have influenced your interpretation.

Information you've gathered from the library and the Internet about the historical, social, political context of the work or its author.

APPENDIX

Critical Approaches to Literature

Earlier in the text you were briefly introduced to four different perspectives from which to interpret literature: reader-based, text-based, context-based, and author-based approaches. In this section we take a closer look at each of these critical perspectives.

Try to keep in mind that these approaches may easily overlap, and critics will often combine them in their analyses. A reader-based approach, though emphasizing personal response, may call on the text for detailed support or make reference to contextual issues. Text-based approaches, though emphasizing the text, may interpret the elements of the text through contextual knowledge. Context-based approaches may consider the attitudes of the reader and the author, and derive support from the text. Author-based criticism may consider the author's style and structure in the text and the influence of readers and contextual issues on the author.

The difference between one critical approach and another may be more a matter of emphasis than kind, and drawing upon several perspectives can yield a rich interpretation. What distinguishes one approach from another is the answer to a fundamental question: *Where is the meaning?* In the reader? In the text? In the world around the text? In the author? How we answer this question will determine the approach we take.

The explanations below will define each approach. To clarify their differences in practice, let's briefly apply each of them to two works of literature: the modern poem "Those Winter Sundays" (p. 12) and the ancient Greek drama *Antigonê* (p. 123). As you read these applications, it will be clear that some works of literature yield better results with some approaches than others.

Reader-Based Criticism

The basic premise of **reader-based** or **reader-response** critical theory is that literature does not exist separate from those who read it. The critical approach reflected in this book is reader-based. Readers are encouraged to respond personally to literature, to think about the ways their backgrounds influence their responses, and to support their responses with reference to the literature itself.

Throughout this book, readers have been encouraged to supplement this reader-based approach with other perspectives. Discussions of the elements of literature and close reading and textual analysis in Chapters 3 and 4 rely on text-based practices. So too, suggestions for secondary-source research in Chapter 5 encourage an exploration of literature typical of context-based and author-based approaches.

A reader-response approach to "Those Winter Sundays" might emphasize the reader's identification with the speaker in the poem. The student writer of the response essay at the end of Chapter 2, for example, compares her relationship with her father to that of the father-son relationship in the poem. She cites words and lines that remind her of her own situation and draws ample support from both her own life and the text of the poem to illustrate similarities and differences.

An example of a reader-response approach to *Antigonê* might include identification with or personal reactions to Antigonê, Ismenê, Creon, or Haimon. Readers might pass judgments on Creon or imagine how they would have behaved when faced with Antigonê's predicament. They might address which character is most like them, identify characters that remind them of people they know, and comment on how these personal connections affect their responses.

Further Reading on Reader-Based Criticism

Bleich, David. *Subjective Criticism.* Baltimore: Johns Hopkins University Press, 1978.

Iser, Wolfgang. *The Act of Reading.* Baltimore: Johns Hopkins University Press, 1978.

Rosenblatt, Louise. *The Reader, the Text, the Poem.* Carbondale, Ill.: Southern Illinois University Press, 1978.

Tompkins, Jane O. *Reader-Response Criticism: From Formalism to Post-Structuralism.* Baltimore: Johns Hopkins University Press, 1980.

Text-Based Criticism

Formalism

Formalism seeks to *objectify* the text—to examine it in isolation from its reader, its context, and its author. **New Criticism**, the most popular type of formalism, is not new. It was given its name more than half a century ago as a reaction to the older biographical and historical approaches that preceded it. Though its popularity has now declined, it was the most dominant form of literary criticism in the twentieth century. As the designation "formalism" suggests, this approach closely examines elements of form/structure and language such as genre, plot, characterization, narration, tone, irony, diction, imagery, metaphor, and symbol. A formalist critic constructs meaning by focusing exclusively on the elements of the text and the way they work together to form a unified, coherent whole.

Because the background, values, and feelings of the reader and the author cannot be objectively evaluated, formalism sees them as irrelevant or erroneous in the construction of a stable meaning. It classifies reliance on a reader's emotional response as an **affective fallacy** and reliance on knowledge of an author's life or intentions as an **intentional fallacy**.

A formalist response to "Those Winter Sundays," for example, would stick closely to the text of the poem. It might try to establish the meaning of the poem through analysis of the language, the images, symbols, speaker's tone, and how they work together to build and to support the speaker's concluding rhetorical question, "what did I know / of love's austere and lonely offices?" (13–14).

A similar approach to *Antigonê* might consider how well the play fulfills the definition of tragedy. It might examine the structure of the plot, details of characterization, function of the chorus, and way these elements form an organic unity—how the structure of the play naturally culminates in the final lines of Choragos as he sums up the meaning of the play.

Further Reading on Formalist Criticism

Brooks, Cleanth, and Robert Penn Warren. *Understanding Poetry.* New York: Holt, 1938.

Empson, William. *Seven Types of Ambiguity.* New York: Noonday Press, 1958.

Ransom, John Crowe. *The New Criticism.* New York: New Directions, 1941.

Richards, I. A. *Practical Criticism.* New York: Harcourt, 1928.

Deconstruction

Like formalism, **deconstruction** focuses exclusively on the text and requires close reading. Unlike formalism, however, which examines parts and relationships to construct a whole, the intention of deconstruction, as its name suggests, is to break down the whole—to deconstruct its meaning. While formalism emphasizes structure and the stability of interpreting the text in isolation, deconstruction insists on the instability and transitory nature of the text.

An early proponent of deconstruction was Jacques Derrida, who explained it through the French word *differance,* which means both "to differ" and "to defer." First, this view asserts that nothing can be known in isolation. We can only know the meaning of something by how it differs from something else to which it is related. All knowledge is based on difference, and all language is relational. We can only know "dark" in relation to "light," "up" to "down," "good" to "evil." Second, any stable or definitive meaning or interpretation must be deferred or put off perpetually because meaning, like the world, is always changing. What authors intend is different than what they write or what readers read. No text has a definitive meaning. So we cannot say one interpretation is right and another wrong.

Rather than attempting to construct an interpretation of its own, a deconstructionist approach to either "Those Winter Sundays" or *Antigonê* might try to reveal any number of alternative meanings for the poem or the play. It might question the credibility of the speaker in the poem and Choragos in the play and attempt to dismantle all other interpretations by demonstrating the instability of their meaning.

Further Reading on Deconstruction

Culler, Jonathan. *On Deconstruction: Theory and Criticism after Structuralism.* Ithaca, NY: Cornell University Press, 1981.

de Man, Paul. *Allegories of Reading*. New Haven: Yale University Press, 1979.
Derrida, Jacques. *Of Grammatology*. Trans. Gayatri Spivak. Baltimore: Johns Hopkins University Press, 1974.
Hartmann, Geoffrey H., et al. *Deconstruction and Criticism*. New York: Continuum, 1979.

Context-Based Criticism

Historical Criticism

The basic premise of **historical criticism** is that literature benefits from being read in its own historical context. Important to this perspective are the political, economic, and psychological influences of the era that produced the literature and its author. The audience for whom it was written and how its meaning and the connotations of its language may have changed over time are among the factors important to this type of interpretation.

A recent development in historical criticism, **New Historicism**, questions the validity of traditional historical criticism and argues that we can only view the past from the "informed" present. It insists that we see the past through our own values and view the "official" history of the ruling classes with skepticism, that the history of those defeated and oppressed must also be revealed.

A historical critic's view of "Those Winter Sundays" might identify the period in which the poem was set and examine the forces at work in that era. For example, the author was an African American born in 1913. Research into the economic conditions and racial attitudes prevalent during the period when the poet was growing up might help the reader understand the nature of the father's work and the cold and sparse setting of the poem.

A similar view of *Antigonê* might focus on the structure of Greek government and the tenets of Greek religion when the play was written. It might consider the burial of Polyneices and compare the audience's expectations of that era with those of a modern audience and explore the significance of those differences.

Further Reading on Historical Criticism

Auerbach, Erich. *Mimesis: The Representation of Reality in Western Literature*. Princeton, NJ: Princeton University Press, 1953.
Foucault, Michel. *Madness and Civilization*. Trans. Richard Howard. New York: Pantheon, 1965.
Greenblatt, Stephen. *Renaissance Self-fashioning: From More to Shakespeare*. Chicago, IL: University of Chicago Press, 1980.
Patterson, Annabel. "Historical Scholarship." *An Introduction to Scholarship in Modern Languages and Literatures*. ed. Joseph Gibaldi. 2nd ed. New York: 1992. 183–200.

Gender Criticism

Gender criticism examines how literature reflects sexual identity or orientation. It may address the ways in which an author's gender has influenced his or her work. It may examine the gender-based portrayal of literary characters and their behavior. It may explore the way in which literature supports or rejects societal norms that foster gender stereotypes. It may emphasize gay and lesbian issues.

Its most popular form is **Feminist Criticism** which has emerged as a powerful literary force during the last 50 years. Among the issues feminist critics address are literary depictions of women, assumptions about women generated by male writers, the recurring pattern in literature of male dominance, female passivity, and sexism in literature as it reflects the societies that fostered it.

A feminist response to "Those Winter Sundays" might consider the restrained nature of a father-son relationship that seems to suppress the communication of feelings. It might question why there is no mother in this household or why this male speaker took so long to realize his feelings for his father.

A similar approach to *Antigonê* might emphasize the overtly sexist nature of Creon's response to Antigonê and Ismenê—how his sexist words and attitude echoed an assumption about the inequality of the sexes tacitly supported by ancient Greek society. It might scrutinize the causes of Ismenê's passivity and the consequences of Antigonê's assertiveness.

Further Reading on Gender Criticism

Abel, Elizabeth, ed. *Writing and Sexual Difference.* Chicago, IL: University of Chicago Press, 1982.

Fetterly, Judith. *The Resisting Reader: A Feminist Approach to American Fiction.* Bloomington, IN: Indiana United Press, 1978.

Ruthven, K. K. *Feminists Literary Studies: An Introduction.* New York: Cambridge University Press, 1984.

Sedgwick, Eve. *Epistemology of the Closet.* Berkeley, CA: University of California Press, 1991.

Political-Economic Criticism

Political-economic criticism focuses on the influence and the consequences of the economic social order in literature. Its most popular form is **Marxist Criticism** which argues that literature reflects the class structure and class struggle that produced it. It emphasizes the social content of literature and scrutinizes the economic circumstances of literature for instances of exploitation. It also analyzes the ways in which text, author, and readers reveal class attitudes.

A Marxist view of "Those Winter Sundays" might emphasize the poor economic situation of this family—how their economic plight and its consequence, the unceasing labor of the father to make ends meet, has created circumstances that made it impossible for the father to have the time for meaningful communication with his son.

A similar view of *Antigonê* might expose the arrogance of Creon as typical of the ruling class—how he exploits and silences the proletariat/laboring class messengers and guards of Polyneices' body—and forces them to go against their own consciences.

Further Reading on Political-Economic Criticism

Eagleton, Terry. *Criticism and Ideology: A Study in Marxist Literary Theory*. London: New Left Books, 1976.

Lentricchia, Frank. *Criticism and Social Change*. Chicago, IL: University of Chicago Press, 1983.

Sartre, Jean-Paul. *What is Literature?* New York: Philosophical Library, 1949.

Williams, Raymond. *Marxism and Literature*. Oxford: Oxford University Press, 1977.

Psychoanalytic Criticism

Derived from the psychological theory of Sigmund Freud, **psychoanalytic criticism** emphasizes the underlying meaning in the narrative, actions, and dialogue of literature. Sexual symbols, dreams, and repressed feelings are central to a psychological analysis of the characters. The creative process and psychological makeup of the author may also be of special interest.

A psychoanalytic view of "Those Winter Sundays," for example, might focus on the repressed feelings of the speaker and question why his feelings of affection for his father have lain dormant for so many years. It might conjecture about the competition between father and son for the affection of the unnamed, unmentioned mother in this family.

Given the incestuous nature of the relationship between Antigonê's parents, Oedipus and Iocastê, a psychoanalytic critic might be overwhelmed with material for exploration here. For example, what psychological burden does Antigonê carry because of the bizarre relationship between her parents? Such a question might yield some very interesting ideas.

Further Reading on Psychoanalytic Criticism

Crews, Frederick C., ed. *Psychoanalysis and Literary Process*. Cambridge, MA: Winthrop, 1970.

Hartmann, Geoffrey. *Psychoanalysis and the Question of Text*. Baltimore, MD: Johns Hopkins University Press, 1979.

Kurzweil, Edith, and William Phillips, eds. *Literature and Psychoanalysis*. New York: Columbia University Press, 1983.

Trilling, Lionel. *Freud and the Crisis of Our Culture*. Boston, MA: Beacon, 1955.

Archetypal Criticism

Derived from the theories of psychologist Carl Jung, this approach assumes that we share a "collective unconscious" that has been shaped by the repeated experiences of our ancestors. It asserts that through this collective unconscious we indirectly share a knowledge of **archetypes**, universal images, patterns, and forms like the seasons, the sun, the moon, the wise old man or woman, fire, night, and blood. Of special interest to an archetypal critic are images, descriptive detail, plot patterns, and types of characters that appear frequently in literature and that seem to evoke nonrational but powerful responses from our unconscious memory.

An archetypal critic, for example, might approach "Those Winter Sundays" by identifying some of the more powerful images and symbols in the poem.

Both the speaker's and the reader's response to a father who "makes banked fires blaze," and "who had driven out the cold" as an archetypal image might prompt some rich exploration.

A similar view of *Antigonê* might explore the many haunting and powerful mythological images and references presented in the dialogue and choral odes throughout the play.

Further Reading on Archetypal Criticism

Bodkin, Maud. *Archetypal Patterns in Poetry*. New York: Vintage, 1958.

Campbell, Joseph. *The Hero with a Thousand Faces*. New York: Pantheon, 1949.

Frye, Northrop. *Anatomy of Criticism*. Princeton, NJ: Princeton University Press, 1957.

Lentricchia, Frank. *After the New Criticism*. Chicago, IL: University of Chicago Press, 1980.

Author-Based Criticism

Author-based or **biographical** criticism emphasizes the relationship between authors' lives and their works. Finding out about an author's life, of course, requires reading a **biography** or **autobiography** of the author. An effective literary biography brings the author's work and life together. And literary biographies can be highly controversial. A recent biography of poet Anne Sexton (see below), which published the private notes of her psychiatrist, prompted a strong reaction and raised serious questions about confidentiality.

Of special interest in biographical criticism is the way in which authors' lives have influenced their writing—how details and people in their own lives have entered their work. Exploring these connections may lead to a deeper understanding of a work's meaning.

A biographical critic's response to "Those Winter Sundays," for example, might include research on Robert Hayden's growing up and his relationship with his father. A biographical critic might seek connections between the events in Hayden's life and his psychological or emotional state when he wrote the poem.

A similar view of *Antigonê* might search for whatever details are available about the life and career of its author, Sophocles. With few biographical details available, a biographical critic might look for clues about Sophocles and his opinions in this and other plays and conjecture about his background based on knowledge of his contemporaries.

Further Reading and Examples of Biographical Criticism

Ackroyd, Peter. *Dickens*. New York: HarperCollins, 1990.

Edel, Leon. *Literary Biography*. New York: Harper and Row, 1957.

Ellmann, Richard. *James Joyce*. Oxford: Oxford University Press, 1983.

Jellinek, Estelle C., *Women's Autobiography: Essays in Criticism*, Boston, MA: Twayne, 1986.

Middlebrook, Diane Wood. *Anne Sexton; A Biography*. Boston, MA: Houghton Mifflin, 1991.

GLOSSARY

abstract language words which represent broad qualities or characteristics (e.g., interesting, good, fine, horrible, lovely)

allegory an extended metaphor

alliteration the repetition of initial consonant sounds in words close together (e.g. "**s**ad **S**unday **s**chool **s**uperintendent **s**tare")

allusion a reference to another literary / artistic/ historic, work, author, character, or event (frequently biblical or mythological)

amphitheater a semi-circular large, outdoor theater with seats rising in tiers from a central acting area

anecdote a brief personal story used to illustrate a point

archaic language language no longer in use

arena stage (or Theater in the Round) a theater with seats surrounding the stage

argumentative essay an essay that tries to prove a point by supporting it with evidence

aside a brief comment by an actor, heard by the audience, but not the other characters on stage

antagonist a character who seems to be the major force in opposition to the protagonist or main character

assonance the repetition of internal vowel sounds in words close together (t**i**me l**i**ne, fr**ee** and **ea**sy)

atmosphere the dominant mood or tone of setting

autobiography an account of the author's own life

ballad a narrative poem, usually sung or recited

blank verse unrhymed iambic pentameter

box set a stage set composed of "flats" or connected walls enclosing three sides of the stage, with an invisible "fourth wall" open to the audience

character a person in fiction, drama, or poetry

characterization the development of characters in fiction, drama, or poetry

catastrophe the reversal of the tragic hero's good fortune in Greek Tragedy

catharsis an emotional purging or cleansing experienced by an ancient Greek audience at the end of a tragedy

chorus A group of actors in Greek drama who comment on the action of the play. The role of the chorus came directly from drama as religious ritual and dates from a time when there were no individual actors. What the chorus says about the action reflects the traditional values of ancient Greek culture. Chorus members chanted their lines together and moved as a unit from side to side on the stage.

climax the turning point of plot in fiction or drama

comedy The traditional plot of comedy is the reverse of tragedy. The protagonist, usually an ordinary person, has a problem. The plot of the play is an extrication from the problem and improvement of circumstances. The reversal of fortune is from bad to good; the falling action becomes a rising action with a happy ending.

complication the building of the conflict in plot as part of the rising action

concrete language words which represent specific, particular, graphic qualities and characteristics

conflict the struggle of opposing external or internal forces. External conflict may be physical (characters against nature) or social (characters against each other or against society). Internal conflict is a struggle of opposing forces within a character.

connotation the personal definition or association triggered by a word

consonance repetition of final consonant sounds in words close together (sho**rt** and swee**t**, st**ruts** and f**rets**)

convention an accepted or traditional feature of a work (e.g., the Greek Chorus, the Shakespearian aside, blank verse)

couplet a pair of rhyming verse lines

crisis the turning point of plot (closely related to "climax" which seems to complete its action)

critical essay an essay which interprets and/or evaluates

denotation the literal, dictionary definition of a word

denouement the resolution of the plot in fiction or drama (an "untying" of the complications at the end of the story line)

dialogue conversation of characters in fiction or drama

didactic teaching a lesson or having a "moral"

documentation accounting for and giving credit to the origin of a source

dramatic monologue In a dramatic monologue, the poet, like an actor in a play, speaks through the voice and personality of another person.

dramatis personae the list of characters in a play

Elizabethan the era beginning with the reign of Elizabeth I, Queen of England from 1558 to 1603 and ending with the Puritan's closing of the theaters in 1642

ellipsis (. . .) indication of an omission of words in a quote

epic a long narrative poem, usually depicting the values of a culture through the adventures of a hero

explication a line by line explanation of a poem or other literary work

exposition the introduction of essential characters, setting, circumstances of a story or play

expository essay an essay which shares, explains, suggests, or explores information, emotion, and ideas

expressionism a movement in drama which emphasizes subjectivity of perception

falling action the action which follows the crisis and climax (*see also* catastrophe, denouement, resolution, catharsis)

figurative language language which expresses more than a literal meaning (e.g., metaphor, simile)

flat character a character not fully developed who seems to represent a "type" more than a real personality (*see also* stock character)

foot a combination of syllables which represent one measure of meter in a verse line

"fourth wall" the invisible wall open to the audience in a box set (*see also* box set)

free verse Poetry without standardized rhyme, meter, or structure. It is not formless, however, but relies on its own words and content to determine its best form.

genre a form or type of literature (e.g., fiction, poetry, drama, the essay)

groundlings Members of an Elizabethan audience who paid a very low entrance fee and stood in the open area below and around the stage. Because they stood on the ground unprotected from the weather—they were called "groundlings," a term meant to disparage their social standing as much as to describe their location in the theater.

hubris excessive pride which usually leads to the downfall of the tragic hero in Greek drama

hyperbole an exaggeration in figurative language

iambic an unstressed/stressed combination of syllables in a metrical foot

image / imagery descriptive language which helps us see, hear, smell, taste, or feel

inductive/deductive reasoning inductive reasoning moves from observation of specific circumstances and makes a general conclusion; **deductive** reasoning takes a general truth and applies it to specific circumstances

interpretation an analysis of a work to determine its meaning

limerick A five line poem. The first, second, and fifth lines rhyme (aaa - above) and so do the third and fourth (bb - above). The first, third, and fifth have the same verbal rhythm (**meter**) and length, and so do the second and fourth.

lyric poetry characterized by the expression of the poet's innermost feelings, thoughts, and imagination

melodrama plays with elaborate but oversimplified plots, flat characters, excessive sentiment, and happy endings

metaphor an implied comparison of two apparently dissimilar things

meter Describes rhythm in a poem. It refers to the pattern of stressed and unstressed syllables in a line of verse. The group of syllables making up one metrical unit is called a **foot**. The metrical feet most commonly used are **iambic** (unstressed - stressed), **trochaic** (stressed - unstressed), **anapestic** (two unstressed - one stressed), and **dactylic** (one stressed - two unstressed).

The number of feet in each line is described as **monometer** (one foot), **dimeter** (two feet), **trimeter** (three feet), **tetrameter** (four feet), **pentameter** (five feet), **hexameter** (six feet), **heptameter** (seven feet), and **octometer** (eight feet). The most common form of meter in poetry written in English is **iambic** (unstressed - stressed) **pentameter** (five feet)

microcosm a smaller version or "little world"

monologue a speech by a single character

mood the atmosphere or tone of a work

narrative essay An essay that tells a story. Most essays of this type spring from an event or experience in the writer's life.

narrative poem a poem that tells a story

narrator the voice of the speaker in a story

Neoclassicism a movement which dominated during the eighteenth century and was notable for its adherence to the "forms" of classical drama

ode a formal lyric poem recited for ceremonial occasions

onomatopoeia a word which sounds like what it represents (e.g., the "buzzing" of a bee)

orchestra the playing area in an ancient Greek theater

parados the ode chanted by the chorus as they enter in Greek tragedy

paraphrase to record someone else's words in the writer's own words

pentameter five feet of verse line

personal essay an essay which emphasizes a personal, subjective view

personification giving human qualities to things non-human

Petrarchan Sonnet The oldest form of the sonnet is the Italian or Petrarchan Sonnet (named for its greatest practitioner—Petrarch). Its rhyme scheme is usually an octave (eight lines) and a sestet (six lines). The octave usually follows a pattern of **abbaabba.** The concluding sestet may be **cdecde** or **cdcdcd** or **cdedce.**

plot The structure of the story. It's the pattern of twists and turns the story takes.

point of view The perspective from which the narrator speaks to us. Generally, the pronoun which dominates the narration will signal which point of view is represented. The terms most commonly used to identify point of view are **first person, third person, omniscient, objective,** and **shifting.**

primary / secondary sources A **primary source** is the original text or materials. A **secondary source** is commentary about that original material.

props objects or items used by the actors on the stage

proscenium arch a frame around the stage which separates the actors and the set from the audience

protagonist the main character in a story or drama

quatrain a four line stanza

Realism A movement in literature to represent life as it really is. It is often characterized by accurate depiction of ordinary people in their natural surroundings.

recognition the point near the end of a classic tragedy when the protagonist recognizes the causes and consequences of his reversal

resolution the final phase of the falling action in plot when things are returned to normal

reversal the change from good to bad fortune in classic tragedy; from bad to good fortune in classic comedy

rhyme when final vowel and consonant sounds in the last syllable of one word match those of another, usually at the end of lines

rhythm The pattern of sound in a poem. The most structured form of rhythm is meter, the pattern of stressed and unstressed syllables.

rising action that point in the plot when conflict and our emotional involvement intensifies

round character a fully developed character with the complexities of real person

satire ridiculing stupidity, vice, folly through exaggeration and humor

scansion analysis of the kind and number of metrical feet in a poem

script the printed text of a drama

sentimentality evoking a predictable emotional response with a clichéd prompt

set structures on the stage which represent the setting of the play

setting the environment in which the work takes place

Shakespearian Sonnet The most popular form in English is the English or Shakespearian Sonnet. It is a fourteen line poem of three quatrains (four line units) and a final couplet (a two line unit) in the rhyme scheme **abab cdcd efef gg**. It presents the content of the poem in predictable ways. The first two quatrains will often present a problem. The third quatrain is often pivotal and will begin a reversal. The final couplet most often suggests a solution.

simile is an announced comparison introduced with the words "like" or "as"

soliloquy Delivered by a character alone on the stage, **soliloquy** is a "thinking out loud" shared with the audience. They are usually statements of a philosophical, reflective nature, and they are highlights of Shakespeare's plays.

sonnet a fourteen line lyric poem usually in iambic pentameter

speaker the narrator of a story or poem

stage directions descriptions (in the text of the play) of the set, the props, voice and movements of the actors, and the lighting

stanza a unit of lines in a poem which usually share a metrical or thematic pattern

stock character a character not fully developed who seems to represent a "type" more than a real personality (*see also* flat character)

style the choice of words and sentence structure which makes each author's writing different

summary the material condensed to its main points

surrealistic drama seeks its truth in the irrationality of the unconscious mind

symbol an object or action that represents more than itself

symbolist drama seek its truth in symbols, myths, and dreams

syntax the ordering of words in a sentence

theme is the overall meaning we derive from the poem, story, play, essay

thesis the point of the essay

thrust stage a stage that extends into the audience

tone the attitude expressed by the writer toward the subject

tragedy classic tragedy follows the plight of a noble person who is flawed by a defect and whose actions cause him to break some moral law and suffer downfall and destruction

tragic flaw the tragic hero's flaw (often excessive pride or "hubris") which leads directly to a reversal of his good fortune (**catastrophe**)

tragic hero as defined by Aristotle, a man of noble stature who is admired by society but flawed

tragicomedy a play that combines the elements of tragedy and comedy

unities The unities of time, place, and action as principles of dramatic composition have been hotly debated since Aristotle's *Poetics.* In brief, **unity of time** suggests the action of the play occur in a 24 hour period; **unity of place** suggests the action occur in one place or location; and **unity of action** that all parts of the play should be related in a clear causal pattern.

unreliable narrator a narrator who tells the story from a biased, erroneous perspective

verse a line or the form of poetry

voice the personality or style of the writer or narrator that seems to come to life in the words

LITERARY AND PHOTO CREDITS

Literary Credits

Achebe, Chinua, "Marriage Is a Private Affair" from *Girls at War and Other Stories* by Chinua Achebe. © 1972, 1973 by Chinua Achebe. Used by permission of Doubleday, a division of Random House, Inc. and Harold Ober Associates, Inc.

Alexie, Sherman, "On the Amtrak from Boston to New York City" from *First Indian on the Moon.* © 1993 by Sherman Alexie. By permission of Hanging Loose Press.

Alvarez, Julia, "Dusting" from *Homecoming.* © 1984, 1996 by Julia Alvarez. Published by Plume, an imprint of Dutton Signet, a division of Penguin Books USA, Inc.; originally published by Grove Press. Reprinted by permission of Susan Bergholz Literary Services, New York. All rights reserved. "Snow" from *How the Garcia Girls Lost Their Accents.* © 1991 by Julia Alvarez. Published by Plume, an imprint of Dutton Signet, a division of Penguin USA, and originally in hardcover by Algonquin Books of Chapel Hill. Reprinted by permission of Susan Bergholz Literary Services, New York. All rights reserved.

Anderson, Michael, "'A Raisin in the Sun': A Landmark Lesson in Being Black" from *The New York Times*, 3/7/99. © 1999 by The New York Times Co. Reprinted by permission.

Angelou, Maya, from "Graduation" from *I Know Why the Caged Bird Sings.* © 1969 by Maya Angelou. Reprinted by permission of Random House, Inc. "Phenomenal Woman" from *And Still I Rise.* © 1978 by Maya Angelou. Reprinted by permission of Random House, Inc.

Anzaldúa, Gloria, "To Live in the Borderlands Means You" from *Borderlands/La Frontera: The New Mestiza.* © 1987 by Gloria Anzaldúa. Reprinted by permission of Aunt Lute Books.

Atwood, Margaret, "This is a Photograph of Me" from *The Circle Game.* © 1966 by Margaret Atwood. Reprinted by permission of House of Anansi Press, a division of Stoddart Publishing, 34 Lesmill Rd., North York, Ontario. "You Fit Into Me" from *Power Politics.* © 1971 by Margaret Atwood. Reprinted by permission of House of Anansi Press, a division of Stoddart Publishing, 34 Lesmill Rd., North York, Ontario.

Auden, W. H., "Musée des Beaux Arts" and "The Unknown Citizen" from *W. H. Auden: Collected Poems*, Edward Mendelson, ed. © 1940 and renewed 1968 by W. H. Auden. Reprinted by permission of Random House, Inc.

Baldwin, James, "Sonny's Blues," originally published in *Partisan Review.* Collected in Going To Meet the Man, © 1965 by James Baldwin. Copyright renewed. Published by Vintage Books. Reprinted by arrangement with the James Baldwin Estate. "Sweet Lorraine" from the Introduction to *To be Young, Gifted, and Black: Lorraine Hansberry in Her Own Words.* Originally published in Esquire (Nov. 1969). Collected in *The Price of the Ticket: Collected Non-Fiction, 1948–1985*, published by St. Martin's, 1985. Reprinted by arrangement with the James Baldwin Estate.

Bambara, Toni Cade, "The Lesson" from *Gorilla, My Love.* © 1972 by Toni Cade Bambara. Reprinted by permission of Random House, Inc.

Bettleheim, Bruno, from "Cinderella" from *The Uses of Enchantment.* © 1975, 1976 by Bruno Bettleheim. Reprinted by permission of Alfred A. Knopf, a division of Random House, Inc.

Bishop, Elizabeth, "In the Waiting Room" from *The Complete Poems 1927–1979* by Elizabeth Bishop. © 1979, 1983 by Alice Helen Methfessel. Reprinted by permission of Farrar, Straus & Giroux, Inc.

Brady, Judy, "I Want a Wife" as appeared in *Ms. Magazine*, December 31, 1971. © 1970 by Judy Brady. Reprinted by permission of the author.

Brooks, Gwendolyn, "We Real Cool" from *Blacks.* © 1991 by Gwendolyn Brooks. Published by Gwendolyn Brooks through Third World Press, Chicago, 1991. Reprinted by permission of the author.

Butler, Robert Olen, "Snow" from *A Good Scent from a Strange Mountain.* © 1992 by Robert Olen Butler. Reprinted by permission of Henry Holt and Company, LLC.

Carter, Steven R., "Hansberry's Artistic Misstep" from *Hansberry's Drama: Commitment Amid Complexity.* (Urbana, IL: University of Illinois Press, 1991).

Carver, Raymond, "Cathedral" from *Cathedral.* © 1981 by Raymond Carver. Reprinted by permission of Alfred A. Knopf, a division of Random House, Inc.

Chasin, Helen, "The Word *Plum*" from *Coming Close and Other Poems.* © 1986. Reprinted by permission of the publisher, Yale University Press.

Cheever, John, "The Enormous Radio" from *The Stories of John Cheever.* © 1947 by John Cheever. Reprinted by permission of Alfred A. Knopf, a division of Random House, Inc.

Chekhov, Anton, "The Lady with the Pet Dog" from *The Portable Chekhov* by Anton Chekhov, edited by Avrahm Yarmolinsky. © 1947, © 1968 by Viking Penguin, Inc. Renewed © 1975 by Avrahm Yarmolinsky. Used by permission of Viking Penguin, a division of Penguin Putnam Inc.

Cheney, Anne, from *Lorraine Hansberry.* © 1984 by GK Hall & Company. Reprinted by permission of The Gale Group.

Cisneros, Sandra, "Eleven" from *Woman Hollering Creek.* © 1991 by Sandra Cisneros. Published by Vintage Books, a division of Random House, Inc., and originally in hardcover by Random House, Inc. Reprinted by permission of Susan Bergholz Literary Services, New York. All rights reserved.

Cofer, Judith Ortiz, "My Father in the Navy: A Childhood Memory" from *Reaching for the Mainland & Selected New Poems.* © 1995 by Bilingual Press/Editorial Bilingüe at Arizona State University, Tempe, AZ. Reprinted by permission of the publisher.

Coleman, Wanda, "Sweet Mama Wanda Tells Fortunes for a Price." © 1979 by Wanda Coleman. Reprinted from *African Sleeping Sickness: Stories & Poems* with the permission of Black Sparrow Press.

Collins, Billy, "Victoria's Secret" from *Picnic, Lightning.* © 1998 University of Pittsburgh Press. Reprinted by permission of the University of Pittsburgh Press.

Cullen, Countee, "Incident." Reprinted by permission of GRM Associates, Inc., agents for the Estate of Ida M. Cullen, from the book *Color* by Countee Cullen. © 1925 by Harper & Brothers; copyright renewed 1953 by Ida M. Cullen.

cummings. e. e., "anyone lived in a pretty how town." © 1940, 1968, 1991 by the Trustees for the e. e. cummings Trust, from *Complete Poems: 1904–1962* by e. e. cummings, edited by George J. Firmage. Reprinted by permission of Liveright Publishing Corporation.

Davis, Natalie Zemon and Jill Ker Conway, "The Rest of the Story" as appeared in *The New York Times Magazine,* May 16, 1999. Reprinted by permission of the authors.

Devenish, Alan, "Icarus Again." © 1999 by Alan Devenish. Reprinted by permission of the author.

Dickinson, Emily, "Tell All the Truth but Tell it Slant," "After Great Pain, a Formal Feeling Comes," "She Sweeps with Many-Colored Brooms," "There is a Certain Slant of Light." Reprinted by permission of the publishers and the Trustees of Amherst College from *The Poems of Emily Dickinson,* Thomas H. Johnson, ed. Cambridge, Mass.: The Belknap Press of Harvard University Press. © 1951, 1955, 1979, 1983 by the President and Fellows of Harvard College. "Much Madness is Divinest Sense" from *The Complete Poems of Emily Dickinson,* edited by Thomas H. Johnson. © 1929, 1935 by Martha Dickinson Bianchi; © renewed 1957, 1963 by Mary L. Hampson. By permission of Little, Brown and Company Inc.

Didion, Joan, "Why I Write." © 1976 by Joan Didion. Originally published in *The New York Times Book Review,* Dec. 1976. Reprinted by permission of the author by arrangement with Janklow & Nesbit Associates.

Dillard, Annie, "Sight Into Insight" from *Pilgrim at Tinker Creek.* © 1974 by Annie Dillard. Reprinted by permission of the author and Blanche C. Gregory, Inc.

Doolittle, H. D., "Oread" from *Collected Poems, 1912–1944.* © 1982 by the Estate of Hilda Doolittle. Reprinted by permission of New Directions Publishing Corp.

Dylan, Bob, from "Blowin' in the Wind." Copyright © 1962 by Warner Bros. Music, copyright renewed 1990 by Special Rider Music. All rights reserved. International copyright secured. Reprinted by permission of Special Rider Music.

Ellison, Ralph, "Battle Royal" from *Invisible Man.* © 1984 by Ralph Ellison. Reprinted by permission of Random House, Inc.

Eliot, T. S., "The Love Song of J. Alfred Prufrock" from *Collected Poems 1909–1962.* Reprinted by permission of the publisher, Faber and Faber Ltd.

Erdrich, Louise, "The Red Convertible" from *Love Medicine.* © 1984, 1993 by Louise Erdrich. Reprinted by permission of Henry Holt and Company, LLC.

Espada, Martín, "Latin Night at the Pawnshop" by Martín Espada from *Rebellion is the Circle of a Lover's Hands.* (Curbstone Press, 1990). Reprinted with permission of Curbstone Press. Distributed by Consortium.

Faulkner, William, "A Rose for Emily" from *Collected Stories of William Faulkner.* © 1930 and renewed 1958 by William Faulkner. Reprinted by permission of Random House, Inc.

Ferlinghetti, Lawrence, "Constantly Risking Absurdity" from *A Coney Island of the Mind.* © 1958 by Lawrence Ferlinghetti. Reprinted by permission of New Directions Publishing Corp.

Francis, Robert, "The Pitcher" from *The Orb Weaver.* © 1960 by Robert Francis, Wesleyan University Press. By permission of University Press of New England.

Frost, Robert, "Fire and Ice" from *The Poetry of Robert Frost,* edited by Edward Connery Lathem. © 1951 by Robert Frost, © 1923, 1969 by Henry Holt and Co. Reprinted by permission of Henry Holt and Company, Inc.

Gaffney, Elizabeth, "Losses that Turn Up In Dreams" as appeared in *Wordsmith,* 1992. Reprinted by permission of the author.

Gallagher, Tess, "The Hug" from *Amplitude: New and Selected Poems.* © 1987 by Tess Gallagher. Reprinted by permission of International Creative Management, Inc.

Giovanni, Nikki, "Nikki-Rosa" from *Black Feeling, Black Talk, Black Judgment.* © 1968, 1970 by Nikki Giovanni. By permission of William Morrow & Company, Inc.

Gómez-Peña, Guillermo, "Documented/Undocumented," 1986. Reprinted by permission of Guillermo Gómez-Peña and Circuit Network.

Goodwin, Doris Kearns, "From Father, with Love." First published by Little, Brown & Co., MA. © 1986 by Doris Kearns Goodwin. Reprinted by permission of International Creative Management, Inc.

Grahn, Judy, "Ella, in a Square Apron, Along Highway 80" from "The Common Woman Poems." © 1969 by Judy Grahn. Reprinted by permission of the author.

Grimm, Jakob Ludwig Karl and Wilhelm Karl Grimm, "Cinderella" from *The Complete Grimm's Fairy Tales.* © 1944 by Pantheon Books, Inc. and renewed 1972 by Random House, Inc. Reprinted by permission of Pantheon Books, a division of Random House, Inc.

Hansberry, Lorraine, from *A Raisin in the Sun.* © 1958 by Robert Nemiroff, as an unpublished work. © 1959, 1966, 1984 by Robert Nemiroff. Reprinted by permission of Random House, Inc.

Hayden, Robert, "Those Winter Sundays." © 1966 by Robert Hayden, from *Angle of Ascent: New and Selected Poems.* Reprinted by permission of Liveright Publishing Corporation.

Heaney, Seamus, "Digging" and "Mid-Term Break" from *Death of a Naturalist in Poems 1965–1975.* © 1980 by Seamus Heaney. Reprinted by permission of Farrar, Straus & Giroux, Inc. and Faber and Faber Ltd.

Heker, Liliana, "The Stolen Party" from *Other Fires: Short Fiction by Latin American Women,* translated and edited by Alberto Manguel. "The Stolen Party" © 1982 by Liliana Heker. Translation © 1986 by Alberto Manguel. Reprinted by permission of Clarkson N. Potter, a division of Crown Publishers, Inc.

Hemingway, Ernest, "Hills Like White Elephants" reprinted with permission of Scribner, a division of Simon & Schuster, from *Men Without Women.* © 1927 Charles Scribner's Sons. renewed 1955 by Ernest Hemingway.

Hughes, Langston, "Dream Deferred," "I, Too," and "Theme for English B" from *Collected Poems.* © 1994 by the Estate of Langston Hughes. Reprinted by permission of Alfred A. Knopf, a division of Random House, Inc. "One Friday Morning" from *Short Stories.* © 1996 by Romona Bass and Arnold Rampersad. Reprinted by permission of Hill and Wang, a division of Farrar, Straus & Giroux, Inc. "Salvation" from *The Big Sea.* © 1940 by Langston Hughes. Copyright renewed © 1968 by Arna Bontemps and George Houston Bass. Reprinted by permission of Hill and Wang, a division of Farrar, Straus & Giroux, Inc.

Ibsen, Henrik, "A Doll's House." Reprinted from *Henrik Ibsen: Four Major Plays,* translated by James McFarlane and Jens Arup (Oxford World Classics, 1998). © James McFarlane 1961. By permission of Oxford University Press. Excerpt from "Notes for the Modern Tragedy" from "A Doll's House" from *Playwrights on Playwriting* by Henrik Ibsen, edited by Toby Cole. © 1960, renewed 1988 by Toby Cole. Reprinted by permission of Hill and Wang, a division of Farrar, Straus and Giroux, LLC. Excerpt from "Speech at the Banquet of the Norwegian League for Women's Rights" from *Ibsen: Letters and Speeches* by

Henrik Ibsen, edited by Evert Sprinchorn. © 1964, renewed 1992 by Evert Sprinchorn. Reprinted by permission of Hill and Wang, a division of Farrar, Straus and Giroux, LLC.

Joyce, James, "Araby" and "Eveline" from *Dubliners* by James Joyce. © 1916 by B. W. Heubsch. Definitive text © 1967 by the Estate of James Joyce. Used by permission of Viking Penguin, a division of Penguin Putnam Inc.

Kincaid, Jamaica, "Girl" from *At the Bottom of the River.* © 1983 by Jamaica Kincaid. Reprinted by permission of Farrar, Straus and Giroux, LLC.

King, Jr., Martin Luther, "I Have a Dream." Reprinted by arrangement with The Heirs to the Estate of Martin Luther King, Jr., c/o Writers House, Inc. as agent for the proprietor. © 1963 by Martin Luther King, Jr., copyright renewed 1991 by Coretta Scott King.

Kingston, Maxine Hong, "No Name Woman" from *The Woman Warrior.* © 1975, 1976 by Maxine Hong Kingston. Reprinted by permission of Alfred A Knopf, a division of Random House, Inc.

Kinnell, Galway, "The Dead Shall Be Raised Incorruptible" from *The Book of Nightmares.* © 1971 by Galway Kinnell. Reprinted by permission of Houghton Mifflin Co. All rights reserved.

Komunyakaa, Yusef, "Facing It" from *Dien Cai Dau.* © 1988 by Yusef Komunyakaa, Wesleyan University Press. By permission of University Press of New England.

Kumin, Maxine, "After Love" from *Selected Poems 1960–1990* by Maxine Kumin. © 1996 by Maxine Kumin. Reprinted by permission of W. W. Norton & Company, Inc.

Larkin, Philip, "This Be the Verse" from *Collected Poems.* © 1988, 1989 by the Estate of Philip Larkin. Reprinted by permission of Farrar, Straus and Giroux, LLC and Faber and Faber Ltd.

Lassell, Michael, "How to Watch Your Brother Die" from *Poems for Lost and Un-Lost Boys.* © 1990 by Michael Lassell. Reprinted by permission of the author.

Lee, Li-Young, "The Gift" © 1986 by Li-Young Lee. Reprinted from *Rose*, by Li-Young Lee, with the permission of BOA Editions, Ltd., Rochester, NY.

Lester, Julius, "The Heroic Dimension in *A Raisin in the Sun*," excerpt from the Introduction to *Les Blancs: The Collected Last Plays of Lorraine Hansberry*, edited by Robert Nemiroff , introd. by Julius Lester. (New York: Vintage Books, 1973). Introduction © 1972 by Julius Lester. Reprinted by permission of The Claudia Menza Literary Agency.

MacLeish, Archibald, "Ars Poetica" from *Collected Poems 1917–1982.* © 1985 by the Estate of Archibald MacLeish. Reprinted by permission of Houghton Mifflin Co.

Mamet, David, "Oleanna" from *Oleanna* by David Mamet. © 1992 by David Mamet. Reprinted by permission of Vintage Books, a division of Random House, Inc.

Mason, Bobbie Ann, "Shiloh" from *Shiloh and Other Stories.* "Shiloh" originally appeared in *The New Yorker Magazine.* © 1982 by Bobbie Ann Mason. Reprinted by permission of International Creative Management, Inc.

McNally, Terrence, "Andre's Mother." © 1994 by Terrence McNally. Reprinted by permission of William Morris Agency, Inc. on behalf of the Author. All rights reserved. CAUTION: Professionals and amateurs are hereby warned that *Andre's Mother* is subject to a royalty. It is fully protected by the International Copyright Union (including the Dominion of Canada and the rest of the British Commonwealth), the Berne Convention, the Pan-American Copyright Convention and the Universal Copyright Convention as well as all countries with which the United States has reciprocal copyright relations. All rights, including professional/amateur stage rights, motion picture, recitation, lecturing, public reading, radio broadcasting, television, video or sound recording, all other forms of mechanical or electronic reproduction, such as CD-ROM, CD-I, information storage and retrieval systems and photocopying, and the rights of translation into foreign languages, are strictly reserved. Particular emphasis is laid upon the matter of readings, permission for which must be secured from the Author's agent in writing. Inquiries concerning rights should be addressed to: William Morris Agency, Inc. 1325 Avenue of the Americas, New York, NY 10019. Attn: Gilbert Parker. "Andre's Mother" was originally produced by The Manhattan Theatre Company.

Meinke, Peter, "Advice to My Son" from *Trying to Surprise God.* © 1981. Reprinted by permission of the University of Pittsburgh Press.

Millay, Edna St. Vincent, "Lament" and "Sonnet XXX" of *Fatal Interview.* From *Collected Poems*, HarperCollins. © 1921, 1931, 1948, 1958 by Edna St. Vincent Millay and Norma Millay Ellis. All rights reserved. Reprinted by permission of Elizabeth Barnett, Literary Executor.

Miller, Neil, from *In Search of Gay America*, pp. 50–59. © 1989 by Neil Miller. Used by permission of Grove/Atlantic, Inc.

Mirikitani, Janice, "For My Father" reprinted from *Awake in the River*. © 1978 by Janice Mirikitani. By permission of the author.

Momaday, N. Scott, "Before an Old Painting of the Crucifixion" from *Before an Old Painting of the Crucifixion, Carmel Mission*, June 1960. (San Francisco: Valenti Angelo, 1975). Reprinted by permission of N. Scott Momaday. "Simile" from *Angle of Geese and Other Poems*. (Boston: D. R. Godine, 1974). © 1974 by N. Scott Momaday. Reprinted by permission of N. Scott Momaday.

Moore, Marianne, "Poetry" reprinted with the permission of Simon & Schuster from *Collected Poems of Marianne Moore*. © 1935 by Marianne Moore; copyright renewed © 1963 by Marianne Moore and T. S. Eliot.

Mora, Pat, "Immigrants" reprinted with permission from the publisher of *Borders*. (Houston: Arte Publico Press–University of Houston, 1986).

Morales, Rosario, "The Day it Happened" from *Callaloo* 15:4 (1992), 970–972. © Charles H. Rowell. Reprinted by permission of the Johns Hopkins University Press.

Munro, Alice, "Boys and Girls" from *Dance of the Happy Shades*. © 1968 by Alice Munro. Published by McGraw-Hill Ryerson Limited. Reprinted by arrangement with the Virginia Barber Literary Agency and McGraw-Hill Ryerson Limited. All rights reserved.

Nelson, Sandra, "When a Woman Holds a Letter" as appeared in *Ms. Magazine*, March/April 1993. © 1993 by Sandra Nelson. Reprinted by permission of the author.

Nemiroff, Robert, excerpts reprinted with the permission of Simon & Schuster from *To Be Young, Gifted, and Black: Lorraine Hansberry in Her Own Words*. © 1969 by Robert Nemiroff and Robert Nemiroff as Executor of the Estate of Lorraine Hansberry.

Oates, Joyce Carol, "Where Are You Going, Where Have You Been?" published in *The Wheel of Love and Other Stories*. © 1970 by Joyce Carol Oates. Reprinted by permission of John Hawkins & Associates, Inc.

O'Brien, Tim, "The Things They Carried" from *The Things They Carried*. © 1990 by Tim O'Brien. Reprinted by permission of Houghton Mifflin Co. All rights reserved.

O'Connor, Flannery, "Everything That Rises Must Converge" from *Everything That Rises Must Converge*. © 1962, 1965 by the Estate of Mary Flannery O'Connor and copyright renewed © 1993 by Regina O'Connor. Reprinted by permission of Farrar, Straus & Giroux, Inc.

O'Connor, Frank, "My Oedipus Complex" from *Collected Stories*. © 1931, 1950 by Frank O'Connor. Copyright last renewed 1981 by Harriet O'Donovan Sheehy, Executrix of the Estate of Frank O'Connor. Reprinted by permission of Alfred A. Knopf, Inc. and Harriet O'Donovan Sheehy, c/o Joan Daves Agency as agent for the proprietor.

Olds, Sharon, "35/10" and "Sex Without Love" from *The Dead and the Living*. © 1983 by Sharon Olds. Reprinted by permission of Alfred A. Knopf, a division of Random House, Inc.

Olsen, Tillie, "I Stand Here Ironing," © 1956, 1957, 1960, 1961 by Tillie Olsen, from *Tell Me a Riddle* by Tillie Olsen, Introduction by John Leonard. Used by permission of Dell Publishing, a division of Random House, Inc.

Owen, Wilfred, "Dulce et Decorum Est" from *The Collected Poems of Wilfred Owen*. © 1963 by Chatto & Windus, Ltd. Reprinted by permission of New Directions Publishing Corp.

Pastan, Linda, "Marks" from *The Five Stages of Grief* by Linda Pastan. © 1978 by Linda Pastan. Reprinted by permission of W. W. Norton & Company, Inc.

Piercy, Marge, "Barbie Doll" and "To Be of Use" from *Circles on the Water*. © 1982 by Marge Piercy. Reprinted by permission of Alfred A. Knopf, a division of Random House, Inc.

Plath, Sylvia, "Mirror" from *Crossing the Water*. © 1963 by Ted Hughes. Originally appeared in the *New Yorker*. Reprinted by permission of HarperCollins Publishers, Inc. and Faber and Faber Ltd.

Quindlen, Anna, "Mothers" from *Living Out Loud*. © 1987 by Anna Quindlen. Reprinted by permission of Random House, Inc.

Randall, Dudley, "Ballad of Birmingham" from *Poem Counterpoem*. (Detroit: Broadview Press, 1969). Permission to reprint granted by Broadview Press.

Ray, David, "A Midnight Diner by Edward Hopper." © 1998 by David Ray. First published in *Poetry*, 1970. Reprinted by permission of the author.

Rich, Adrienne, "Mourning Picture." © 1993 by Adrienne Rich. © 1966 by W. W. Norton & Company, Inc., from *Collected Early Poems: 1950–1970* by Adrienne Rich. Used by permission of W. W.

Norton & Company, Inc. "Rape" from *The Fact of a Doorframe: Poems Selected and New, 1950–1984* by Adrienne Rich. © 1984 by Adrienne Rich. © 1975, 1978 by W. W. Norton & Company, Inc. © 1981 by Adrienne Rich. Reprinted by permission of W. W. Norton & Company, Inc.

Rios, Alberto, "The Purpose of Altar Boys" from *Whispering to Fool the Wind Poems.* (NY: Sheep Meadow Press, 1982). © 1982 by Alberto Rios. Reprinted by permission of the author.

Robinson, Edwin Arlington, "Mr. Flood's Party" and "Richard Cory" reprinted with the permission of Simon & Schuster from *The Collected Poems of Edwin Arlington Robinson* (New York: Macmillan, 1973).

Rodriguez, Richard, from *Hunger of Memory.* Reprinted by permission of David R. Godine, Publisher, Inc. © 1982 by Richard Rodriguez.

Roethke, Theodore, "My Papa's Waltz," © 1942 by Hearst Magazines, Inc., from *Collected Poems of Theodore Roethke* by Theodore Roethke. Used by permission of Doubleday, a division of Random House, Inc.

Roth, Philip, "The Conversion of the Jews" from *Goodbye, Columbus.* © 1959, renewed 1987 by Philip Roth. Reprinted by permission of Houghton Mifflin Co. All rights reserved.

Sandburg, Carl, "Fog" from *Chicago Poems.* © 1916 by Holt, Rinehart and Winston and renewed 1944 by Carl Sandburg. Reprinted by permission of Harcourt, Inc. "Grass" from *Cornhuskers.* © 1918 by Holt, Rinehart and Winston and renewed 1946 by Carl Sandburg. Reprinted by permission of Harcourt, Inc.

Sarton, May, "The Rewards of Living a Solitary Life" from *The New York Times,* 4/18/74 (Op-Ed). © 1974 by The New York Times Co. Reprinted by permission.

Sexton, Anne, "Cinderella" from *Transformations.* © 1971 by Anne Sexton. Reprinted by permission of Houghton Mifflin Co. All rights reserved. "The Starry Night" from *All My Pretty Ones.* © 1962 by Anne Sexton, © renewed 1990 by Linda G. Sexton. Reprinted by permission of Houghton Mifflin Co. All rights reserved.

Shakespeare, William, "Othello" and "Hamlet" annotations from *The Complete Works of Shakespeare,* 4th Edition, edited by David Bevington. © 1997 by Addison-Wesley Educational Publishers, Inc. Reprinted by permission.

Shōnagan, Sei, "A Lover's Departure" from *The Pillow Book of Sei Shōnagan,* trans. Ivan Morris. © 1967 Columbia University Press. Reprinted by permission of the publisher.

Silko, Leslie Marmon, "The Man to Send Rain Clouds" from *The Man to Send Rain Clouds,* Kenneth Rosen, ed. (New York: Viking Press, 1974). © Leslie Marmon Silko. Reprinted with the permission of The Wylie Agency, Inc.

Sitton, Claude, "Birmingham Bomb Kills 4 Negro Girls in Church; Riots Flare; 2 Boys Slain," *New York Times,* September 15, 1963. © 1963 by The New York Times Co. Reprinted by permission.

Smith, Stevie, "Not Waving but Drowning" from *Collected Poems of Stevie Smith.* © 1972 by Stevie Smith. Reprinted by permission of New Directions Publishing Corp.

Song, Cathy, "The Youngest Daughter" from *Picture Bride.* © 1983 by Cathy Song. Reprinted by permission of the publisher, Yale University Press.

Sophocles, "Antigonê" from *Sophocles: The Oedipus Cycle, An English Version* by Dudley Fitts and Robert Fitzgerald. © 1939 by Harcourt, Inc. and renewed 1967 by Dudley Fitts and Robert Fitzgerald. Reprinted by permission of Harcourt, Inc. "Oedipus Rex" from *Sophocles: The Oedipus Cycle, An English Version* by Dudley Fitts and Robert Fitzgerald. © 1949 by Harcourt, Inc. and renewed 1977 by Cornelia Fitts and Robert Fitzgerald. Reprinted by permission of Harcourt, Inc. CAUTION: All rights, including professional, amateur, motion picture, recitation, lecturing, performance, public reading, radio broadcasting, and television are strictly reserved. Inquiries on all rights should be addressed to Harcourt, Inc., Permissions Department, Orlando, FL 32887-6777.

Soyinka, Wole, "Telephone Conversation." © 1962 by Wole Soyinka. Reprinted by permission of Melanie Jackson Agency, LLC.

Steinbeck, John, "Chrysanthemums." © 1937, renewed © 1965 by John Steinbeck, from *The Long Valley* by John Steinbeck. Used by permission of Viking Penguin, a division of Penguin Putnam Inc.

Stephens, James, "The Wind" from *Collected Poems.* Reprinted by permission of the Society of Authors as the literary representative of James Stephens.

Stevens, Wallace, "The Man with the Blue Guitar" from *Collected Poems* by Wallace Stevens. © 1936 by Wallace Stevens and renewed 1964 by Holly Stevens. Reprinted by permission of Alfred A. Knopf, a division of Random House, Inc.

Swenson, May, "Pigeon Woman" from *Nature.* © 1994 by the Literary Estate of May Swenson. Reprinted by permission of Houghton Mifflin Co. All rights reserved.

Thomas, Dylan, "Do Not Go Gentle Into That Good Night" and "The Force That Through the Green Fuse Drives the Flower" from *The Poems of Dylan Thomas.* © 1939 by New Directions Publishing Corp. Reprinted by permission of New Directions Publishing Corp. and David Higham Associates Limited.

Tan, Amy, "Mother Tongue." © 1990 by Amy Tan. First appeared in *The Threepenny Review*, Fall 1990. Reprinted by permission of the author and the Sandra Dijkstra Literary Agency. "Two Kinds" from *The Joy Luck Club.* © 1989 by Amy Tan. Used by permission of G. P. Putnam's Sons, a division of Penguin Putnam, Inc.

Toomer, Jean, "Reapers" from *Cane* by Jean Toomer. © 1923 by Boni & Liveright, renewed 1951 by Jean Toomer. Reprinted by permission of Liveright Publishing Corporation.

Trambley, Estela Portillo, "The Pilgrim" from *Trini.* © 1986 by Bilingual Press/Editorial Bilingüe at Arizona State University, Tempe, AZ. Reprinted by permission of the publisher.

Updike, John, "A & P" from *Pigeon Feathers and Other Stories.* © 1962 by John Updike. Reprinted by permission of Alfred A. Knopf, a division of Random House, Inc. "Ex-Basketball Player" from *The Carpentered Hen and Other Tame Creatures.* © 1957, 1982 by John Updike. Reprinted by permission of Alfred A. Knopf, a division of Random House, Inc. "The Mosquito" from *Telephone Poles and Other Poems.* © 1960 by John Updike. Reprinted by permission of Alfred A Knopf, a division of Random House, Inc.

Valdez, Luis, "Los Vendidos" reprinted with permission from the publisher of *Luis Valdez-Early Works.* (Houston: Arte Publico Press–University of Houston, 1971).

Walker, Alice, "Everyday Use" from *In Love & Trouble: Stories of Black Women.* © 1973 by Alice Walker. Reprinted by permission of Harcourt, Inc. "In Search of Our Mothers' Gardens" from *In Search of Our Mothers' Gardens, Womanist Prose.* © 1974 by Alice Walker. Reprinted by permission of Harcourt, Inc. "Women" from *Revolutionary Petunias and Other Poems.* © 1970 by Alice Walker. Reprinted by permission of Harcourt, Inc.

Wasserstein, Wendy, "The Man in a Case" from *Orchards: Seven Stories by Anton Chekhov and Seven Plays They Have Inspired*, published by Knopf. © 1986 by Wendy Wasserstein. No part of this material may be reproduced in whole or in part without the express written permission of the author or her agent. Reprinted by permission of Rosenstone/Wender.

Welty, Eudora, "A Worn Path" from *A Curtain of Green and Other Stories.* © 1941 and renewed 1969 by Eudora Welty. Reprinted by permission of Harcourt, Inc.

White, E. B., "Once More to the Lake" from *One Man's Meat.* Text © 1941 by E. B. White. Reprinted by permission of Tilbury House, Publishers, Gardiner, Maine.

Wilkerson, Margaret, excerpt from the Introduction to *Les Blancs: The Collected Last Plays of Lorraine Hansberry*, Robert Nemiroff, ed. (New York, Vintage Books Edition, 1994). Introduction © 1994 by Margaret B. Wilkerson. Reprinted by permission of Margaret Wilkerson.

Williams, Tennessee, from *The Glass Menagerie.* © 1945 by Tennessee Williams and Edwina D. Williams. Copyright renewed 1973 by Tennessee Williams. Reprinted by permission of Random House, Inc.

Williams, William Carlos, "At the Ball Game" from *Collected Poems: 1909–1939, Volume I.* © 1938 by New Directions Publishing Corp. Reprinted by permission of New Directions Publishing Corp.

Wilson, August, from *Joe Turner's Come and Gone.* © 1988 by August Wilson. Used by permission of Dutton Signet, a division of Penguin Putnam, Inc.

Woolf, Virginia, "Shakespeare's Sister" from *A Room of One's Own.* © 1929 by Harcourt, Inc. and renewed 1957 by Leonard Woolf. Reprinted by permission of Harcourt, Inc.

Wright, James, "A Blessing" from *The Branch Will Not Break.* © 1963 by James Wright, Wesleyan University Press. By permission of University Press of New England.

Yamada, Mitsuye, "The Question of Loyalty" from *Camp Notes and Other Poems.* © 1992 by Mitsuye Yamada. Reprinted by permission of the author and Kitchen Table: Women of Color Press, P.O. Box 40-4920, Brooklyn, NY 11240-4920.

Yeats, W. B., "The Lake Isle of Innisfree" reprinted with the permission of Simon & Schuster from *The Collected Works of W.B. Yeats, Volume I: The Poems*, revised and edited by Richard J. Finneran (New York: Macmillan, 1989).

Yellen, Samuel, "Nighthawks." First published in *Commentary*, 1951. Reprinted by permission of Marilyn Gaylin for the Estate of Samuel Yellen.

Zimmer, Paul, "The Day Zimmer Lost Religion" and "Zimmer in Grade School" from *Crossing to Sunlight*. © 1976 by Paul Zimmer. Reprinted by permission of the author.

Photo Credits

234: National Museum of American Art, Washington, DC/Art Resource, NY; 238: AP/Wide World Photos; 243: Mottke Weissman/Courtesy Dial Press; 266: Michael Dorris/Courtesy HarperCollins; 273: © Mur/Bettmann/Corbis; 286: AP/Wide World Photos; 292: AP/Wide World Photos; 296: Corbis; 306: AP/Wide World Photos; 312: Dorothy Alexander; 313: Rick O'Quinn; 314: Brown Brothers; 316: Courtesy Elizabeth Gaffney; 317: Nancy Crampton; 319: Nancy Crampton; 322: Gavin Geoffrey Dillard © 1996 Gavco/Courtesy Michael Lassell; 325: Dorothy Alexander; 326: AP/Wide World Photos; 327: Courtesy Glide Memorial Church; 329: Dorothy Alexander; 330: George Murphy/Courtesy W.W. Norton & Company; 331: AP/Wide World Photos; 332: John Eddy/Courtesy University of Pittsburgh Press; 333: Courtesy Paul Zimmer; 335: Bettmann/Corbis; 387: AP/Wide World Photos; 390: Nancy Crampton; 398: Culver Pictures; 402: Bettmann/Corbis; 497: © George S. Zimbel, 1954/2000. Courtesy Bonni Benrubi Gallery, NY; 501: Bettmann/Corbis; 513: Missouri Historical Society; 516: Bern Keating/Black Star; 523: Brown Brothers; 528 Bettmann/Corbis; 532: Bettmann/Corbis; 544: Berenice Abbott/Commerce Graphics, Ltd.; 549: Jerry Bauer; 560: Linda Haas/Courtesy Firebrand Books; 563: Nancy Crampton; 565: Laurance Acland/Courtesy Doubleday & Company; 568: National Portrait Gallery, London and the Marquess of Lothian; 570: © 1994 Jean Weisinger; 571: Hulton Getty/Liaison; 572: Dorothy Alexander; 573: Hulton Getty/Liaison; 574: Culver Pictures; 577: Gordon LaMeyer/Courtesy HarperCollins; 578: Hulton Getty/Liaison; 579: Stanford University News Service; 580: Dorothy Alexander; 582: Rollie McKenna/Courtesy Houghton Mifflin Company; 585: National Portrait Gallery, London; 700: AP/Wide World Photos; 706: Jerry Bauer; 711: Courtesy Judy Brady; 715: AP/Wide World Photos; 722: AP/Wide World Photos; 725: Bettmann/Corbis; 811: Photo Belzeaux-Zodiaque; 816: Willa Cather Pioneer Memorial Collection/Nebraska State Historical Society; 830: Nancy Crampton; 841: Sigrid Estrada; 843: Jerry Bauer; 853: Elliott Erwitt/Magnum Photos, Inc.; 862: Courtesy Putnam; 882: Marion Ettlinger; 884: Jean Weisinger/Courtesy Aunt Lute Books; 886: Bettmann/Corbis/UPI; 888: AP/Wide World Photos; 889: AP/Wide World Photos; 890: Culver Pictures; 891: Houghton Library, Harvard University, Cambridge, Massachusetts; 896 top: Dorothy Alexander; 896 bottom: Bettmann/Corbis; 898: Corbis; 899: Courtesy Arte Publico Press, University of Houston; 900: Bettmann/Corbis; 901: Courtesy Mitsuye Yamada; 902: Culver Pictures; 903: Bettmann/Corbis; 955: AP/Wide World Photos; 960: Bettmann/Corbis; 964: Bettmann/Corbis; 971: Nancy Crampton; 1093: Photofest; 1094: Donald Cooper/© Photostage; 1095: Photofest; 1096: Donald Cooper/© Photostage; 1103: Alfred Eisenstaedt/TimePix; 1107: Annie Valva; 1113: Philip Gould/Corbis; 1120: Bettmann/Corbis; 1128: Layle Silbert; 1132: AP/Wide World Photos; 1144: Achilles Studio, El Paso, Texas; 1150: Nancy Crampton; 1153: Berg Collection of English and American Literature, The New York Public Library. Astor, Lenox and Tilden Foundations; 1155: George Evans/Courtesy Black Sparrow Press; 1156: Joann Carney/Courtesy Billy Collins; 1160: © Roger Ressmeyer/Corbis; 1161: Courtesy University of Massachusetts Press; 1170: Nancy Crampton; 1172: Courtesy Scott Foresman and Company; 1173: AP/Wide World Photos; 1175: Bettmann/Corbis; 1177: Nati Harnik/AP/Wide World Photos; 1179: Bettmann/Corbis; 1180: John D. Schiff, Courtesy of New Directions Press; 1182: AP/Wide World Photos; 1193: AP/Wide World Photos; 1253: William Rubel/National Portrait Gallery/AP/Wide World Photos; 1258: Eugenio Castro, San Francisco; 1262: © Roger Ressmeyer/Corbis; 1266: Culver Pictures; 1276: Bettmann/Corbis; 1286: © Index Stock Imagery; 1289: Joseph Blackburn. Thomas Bulfinch, c. 1757 Oil on canvas, 30 x 26" (76.2 x 66 cm). Gift of Mr. and Mrs. J. Templeman Coolidge, 1945. Courtesy, Museum of Fine Arts, Boston. © 2000 Museum of Fine Arts, Boston. All Rights Reserved; 1291: Courtesy Scott Foresman and Company; 1302: Newark Public Library; 1320: Peabody Essex Museum, Salem; 1330: Jill Krementz; 1343: Jerry Bauer; 1354: Nancy Crampton; 1365: Courtesy Scott Foresman and Company; 1373: Hulton Getty/Liaison; 1375: Thomas Victor; 1378: Amherst College Library; 1383: Dorothy Alexander; 1385: Nancy Crampton; 1387: AP/Wide World Photos; 1390: Imperial War Museum, London; 1391: Bettmann/Corbis; 1392: Hulton Getty/Liaison; 1395: AP/Wide World Photos; 1397: Dorothy Alexander; 1428: AP/Wide World Photos; 1432: Nancy Crampton; 1450: Hulton Getty/Liaison; 1454: Hulton Getty/Liaison; 1462: Pieter Brueghel, the Elder. "Landscape with the Fall of Icarus." Musées Royaux des Beaux-Arts, Brussels/Scala/Art Resource, NY; 1464: Jacopo Tintoretto. "Crucifixion." Scuola Grande di San Rocco, Venice, Italy/Erich Lessing/Art Resource, NY;

1466: Edward Hopper. "Nighthawks" 1942. Oil on canvas, 84.1 x 152.4 cm. Friends of American Art Collection, 1942.51, © 2000 The Art Institute of Chicago. All Rights Reserved; 1468: Vincent van Gogh. "Starry Night," 1889. Oil on canvas, 29 x 36-1/4" (73.7 x 92.1 cm). The Museum of Modern Art, New York. Acquired through the Lillie P. Bliss Bequest. Photograph © 2001 The Museum of Modern Art, New York; 1470: Jan Vermeer. "The Loveletter," c.1670. Oil on canvas, 44 x 38.5 cm. © Rijksmuseum Amsterdam; 1472: Pablo Picasso. "The Old Guitarist," 1903-04. Oil on panel, 122.9 x 82.6 cm. Helen Birch Bartlett Memorial Collection, 1926.253, courtesy The Art Institute of Chicago. All Rights Reserved. © 2001 Estate of Pablo Picasso/Artists Rights Society (ARS), New York; 1474: Edwin Romanzo Elmer "The Mourning Picture," 1890. Oil on canvas, 28 x 36" (71.1 x 91.5 cm). Smith College Museum of Art, Northampton, Massachusetts. Purchased 1953.

INDEX OF AUTHORS, TITLES, AND FIRST LINES OF POEMS

INDEX OF TERMS

Dear Colleague:

Thank you for considering ***Exploring Literature***. This text is the result of several years of work, review and revision—and more than twenty five years experience teaching introductory composition and literature courses. Most of my students and most students taking literature courses at colleges and universities in this country are not English majors. If asked why they are taking a literature course, they are likely to respond "Because it's required." Or "It fit my schedule." It's not evident to them why literature is important. Other than completing the requirements for a course, they don't know why they are reading it. For these students, instruction in textual analysis and literary theory alone does not solve this problem. They need to have a stake in the process—a reason to care about literature. And they need the kind of support that will help them read differently and with more confidence. It is the intention of ***Exploring Literature*** to provide them with this support.

The narrative "voice" of the text is informal and conversational. It is written to be read by students—to be accessible, friendly and informative without being condescending. Its explanations, prompts, and literature may be used as needed, in or out of sequence, with maximum flexibility. For instructors who emphasize a reader-response approach, have their students keep journals, or write response essays about literature, Part 1 "Making Connections" provides a rich source of material. Those who would rather begin with a more text-based or contextual approach may move directly to Part II "Analysis, Argumentation, and Research," which emphasizes close reading, analysis of genre, interpretation, evaluation, and critical and research writing. Part III organizes the four genres of literature under five compelling themes: Family and Friends, Women and Men, Heritage and Identity, Culture and Class, and Faith and Doubt.

The literature in this book, a broad selection of both classic and contemporary literature, has been chosen for its quality, diversity, and appeal to students. The "Composition Casebooks" that follow the literature in each thematic unit are a rich and provocative resource for interpretation and biography; interpretation in cultural and historical context; interpretation and performance; interpretation, culture, and research; and interpretation—poetry and painting.

Exploring Literature is designed for instructors who believe, as I do, that an appreciation of literature depends as much upon the reader as the text, and who want to encourage the active, meaning making role of the student—not only to complete the requirements of a course—but as a prelude to a lifelong relationship with literature.

Sincerely,

Frank Madden

0321083970